History of Delaware County, Pennsylvania

ALLEN COUNTY PUBLIC LIBRARY
3 1833 01151 1232

HISTORY

OF

DELAWARE COUNTY,

PENNSYLVANIA.

BY

HENRY GRAHAM ASHMEAD.

ILLUSTRATED

PHILADELPHIA.
L. H. EVERTS & CO.
1884.

PRESS OF
J B LIPPINCOTT & CO,
PHILADELPHIA

TO

JOHN HOSKINS,

OF

PHILADELPHIA,

THIS WORK

IS RESPECTFULLY DEDICATED

BY HIS SINCERE FRIEND,

THE AUTHOR

PREFACE.

SINCE the publication of the admirable History of Delaware County, written by Dr. George Smith, nearly a quarter of a century ago, the interest awakened in the National Centennial resulted in directing general attention in almost every locality through the country to its early annals, and as a consequence in Delaware County, at least, much historical material was reclaimed from the past of which Dr. Smith could have had no information while preparing his work for the press. The present history has been written with the purpose of presenting, as far as could be done in a single volume, an authentic, exhaustive, and unbiased narrative of the events which have occurred in Delaware County from the period of the early settlements within its territory to the present time, and in so doing care has been taken to avoid any reference to incidents happening without its boundaries, excepting in those cases where it became necessary to give a brief account of the movements elsewhere in order to render the incidents related in the present work intelligible It will be noticed that very little attention has been given to the recital of political contests which have taken place in the county. The effervescent nature of such public incidents is such that after the reasons which have produced them have ceased to be potential, very little substance remains for the annalist to deal with in relating the story of the times that have passed

In that part of the work devoted to the histories of the several townships, the author has received the assistance of Mr. Austin N. Hungerford, a gentleman whose accuracy of research and comprehensive examination of documentary authorities has made his labors of the utmost value to the writer in the preparation of this history. To Mr. Hungerford's unwearying industry and quick appreciation of the data necessary to that end is largely due the full history given of the industrial establishments in the county. The pressure of time rendered it necessary that several of the township histories should be prepared by other writers. To Mr. Alfred Mathews was assigned Media borough, and Haverford and Radnor to Mr. John S. Schenck. Mr Mathews' narrative of the history of Media is very full and accurate, and must commend itself to the reader, not only for those features, but because of the graceful style in which the narrative is presented. The histories of Haverford and Radnor, written by Mr. Schenck, are also admirable presentations of the annals of those localities.

The author, in the preparation of this work, has been met with the utmost kindness by the residents of Delaware County, who responded promptly to his application for data and access to documents of a historical character. From William B. Broomall, Edward A Price, David M. Johnson, John B. Hinkson, George M. Booth, and others, he has received many favors. The introductory chapter of the General History was prepared by Dr. Ellwood Harvey, and that relating to the ten-hour movement was contributed by James Webb. These articles must commend themselves to the reader, as to style, comprehensiveness, and accuracy of statement. To the Historical Society of Pennsylvania the author desires to return his especial acknowledgments for favors shown, and also to Gilbert Cope, of West Chester, for like kindnesses. The atlas of Early Grants and Patents in Delaware County, prepared by Benjamin H. Smith, is the authority on which the author has based in most cases his references to the lands taken up by the early settlers.

The rupture of a blood-vessel in one of the eyes of the author rendered it impossible for him to read much of the proof of the General History, and possibly errors may occur therein which might have been avoided under other circumstances.

H. G. A.

CHESTER, Sept 9, 1884.

CONTENTS.

ILLUSTRATIONS.

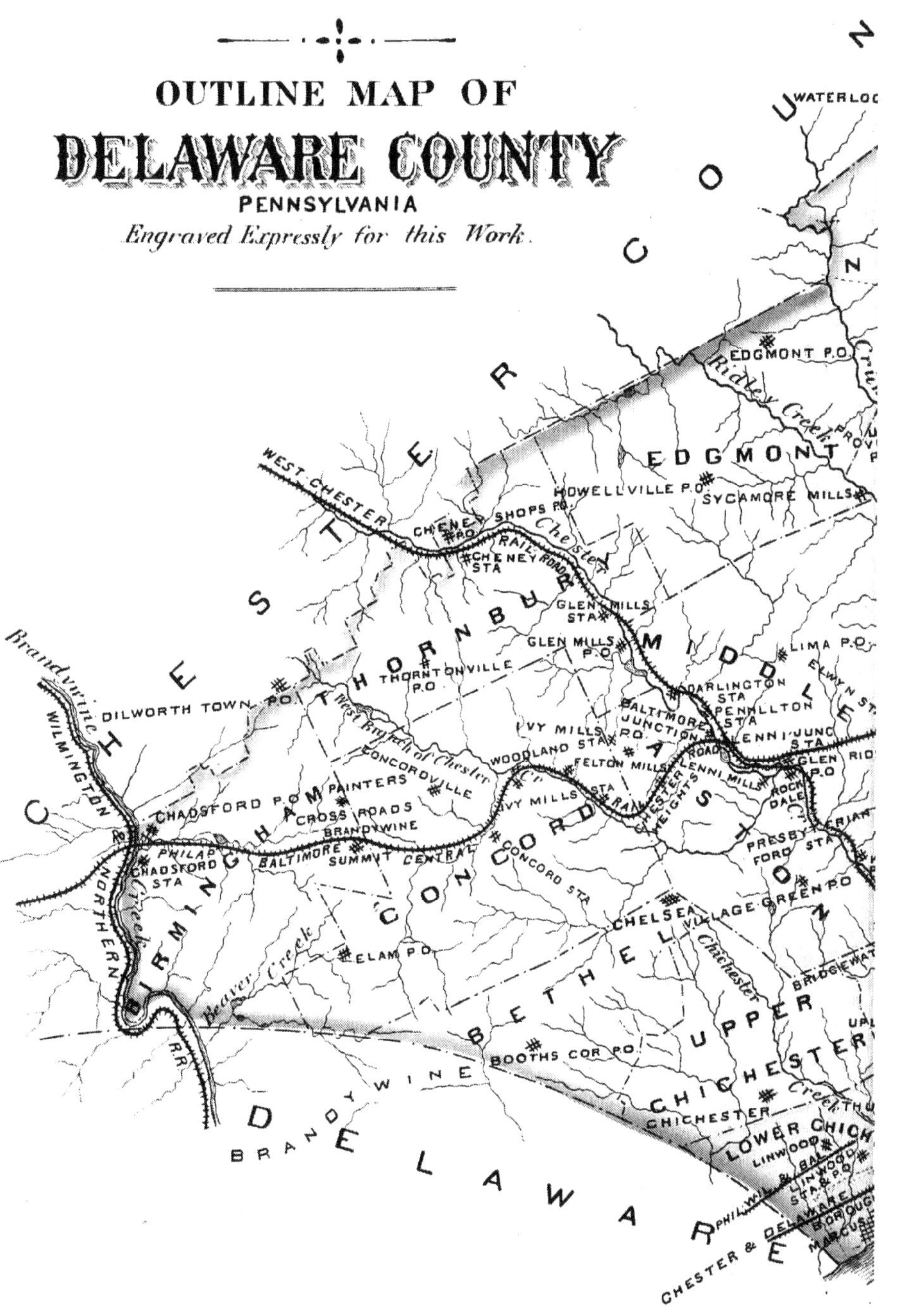
OUTLINE MAP OF
DELAWARE COUNTY
PENNSYLVANIA
Engraved Expressly for this Work.
C H E S T E R
C O U N
EDGMONT P.O.
Ridley Creek
EDGMONT
HOWELLVILLE P.O.
SYCAMORE MILLS
WEST CHESTER RAIL ROAD
CHENEY SHOPS P.O.
CHENEY STA
Chester Cr.
THORNBURY
GLEN MILLS STA
GLEN MILLS P.O.
THORNTONVILLE P.O.
MIDDLETOWN
LIMA P.O.
DARLINGTON STA
PENNELLTON STA
BALTIMORE JUNCTION
IVY MILLS P.O.
WOODLAND STA
FELTON MILLS
LENNI MILLS
CHESTER HEIGHTS
ROCKDALE
ASTON
Brandywine
WILMINGTON
DILWORTH TOWN P.O.
West Branch of Chester Cr.
CONCORDVILLE
PAINTERS CROSS ROADS
BRANDYWINE SUMMIT
CHADSFORD P.O.
CHADSFORD STA
PHILA & BALTIMORE CENTRAL
BIRMINGHAM
CONCORD
CONCORD STA
CHELSEA
VILLAGE GREEN P.O.
ELAM P.O.
Beaver Creek
NORTHERN R.R.
Creek
BETHEL
Chichester
UPPER CHICHESTER
BOOTHS COR P.O.
CHICHESTER
LOWER CHICHESTER
LINWOOD
LINWOOD STA & P.O.
CHESTER & DELAWARE
BRANDYWINE
D E L A W A R E

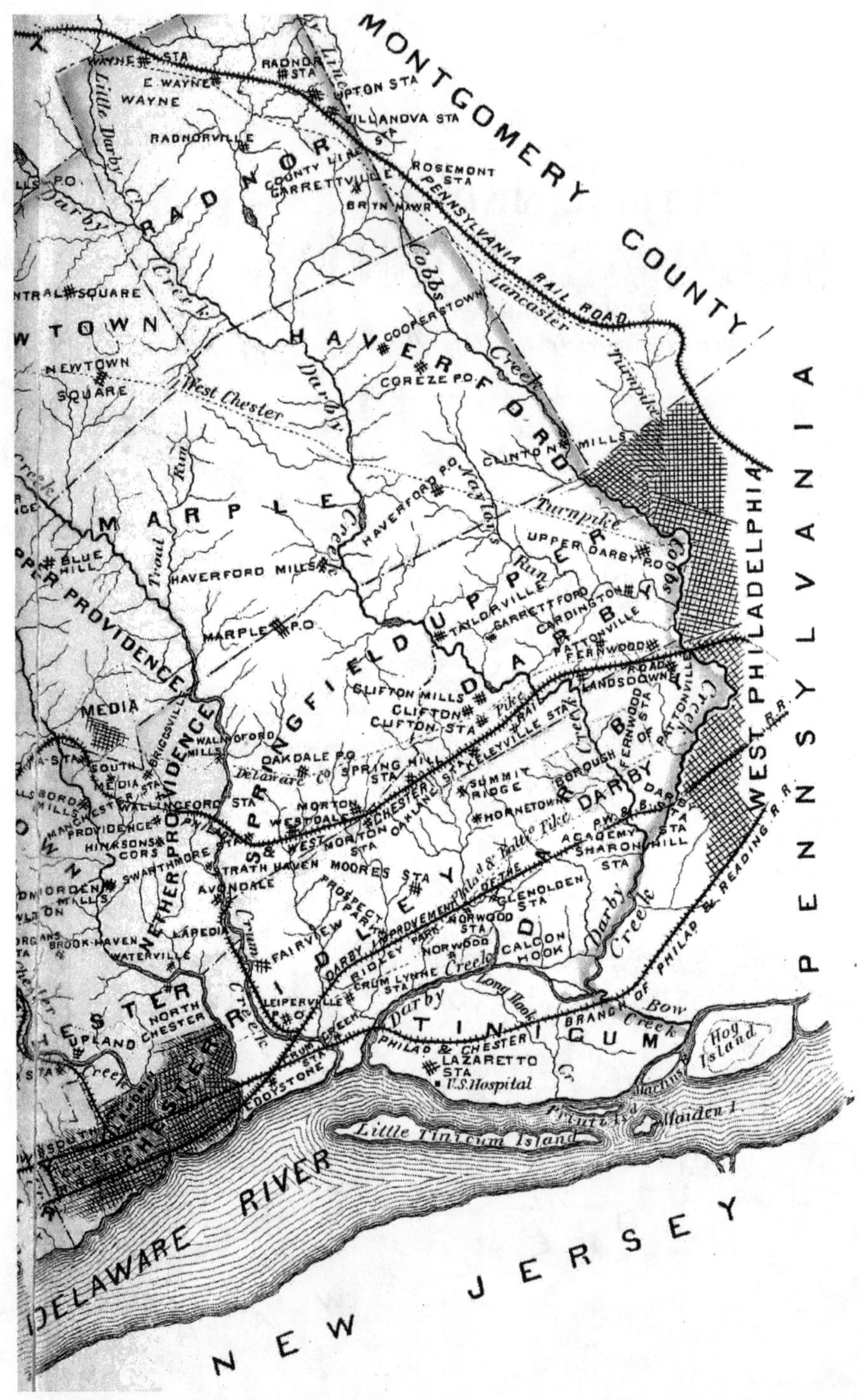
MONTGOMERY COUNTY
PENNSYLVANIA
NEW JERSEY
DELAWARE RIVER
WEST PHILADELPHIA
RADNOR
HAVERFORD
MARPLE
SPRINGFIELD
UPPER DARBY
DARBY
RIDLEY
TINICUM
NETHER PROVIDENCE
UPPER PROVIDENCE
NEWTOWN
CHESTER
MEDIA
PENNSYLVANIA RAIL ROAD
Little Tinicum Island
Hog Island
U.S. Hospital

HISTORY OF DELAWARE COUNTY.

CHAPTER I.

PHYSICAL GEOGRAPHY AND GEOLOGY OF DELAWARE COUNTY[1]

The surface of the county is hilly with very little exception in its western part, but somewhat level in its eastern portion. Its drainage is by several small streams, called creeks, that flow in a southerly direction and empty into the Delaware River. These and their tributary branches make Delaware a well-watered county. Almost every country house is supplied from a never-failing spring of pure, soft water, and nearly all the fields of every farm have running streams through them.

The flowing of these creeks down a surface inclined to the Delaware River, which is the southeastern boundary of the county, gives an abundance of water-power, which is used for various manufacturing purposes. The rapid flow of these streams and their numerous branches have cut deeply into the surface of the land, making it beautifully diversified by wood-crowned hills and fertile valleys and hill-sides. No one who has ever seen the charming scenery of this part of our State can exclude from the recollection of it the well-tilled farms, with their tastefully-planned homes, capacious barns, fields of waving grain, and the herds of cows that supply milk and butter of the very best quality to the Philadelphia market. Here grow luxuriantly all the fruits, grains, grasses, and vegetables of the temperate zone. The declension of the surface of the land toward the south brings it near to a right angle with the rays of the sun, which has an effect on its temperature that is equivalent to being a degree or more farther south. The lower altitude of lands touching tide-water also favors the mildness of the climate as compared with higher surfaces. Grass is ready for pasturing about ten days earlier in the spring than on the higher and more horizontal lands of similar quality a few miles farther north. The river has a considerable influence on the temperature of that part of the county bordering immediately on it. In winter the air may be for a long time at a freezing temperature before the river has ice on it, for the reason that the whole depth of water must be very near to the freezing-point before its surface can become ice, though the surface of the ground will be frozen by a single night of coldness.

Under such circumstances, and they occur every year, the two miles of width of water that is several degrees warmer than the general atmosphere has a very perceptible modifying influence. Fruits and flowers remain untouched by frost for several weeks after hard freezing has occurred in other parts of the county. In summer, evaporation keeps the river cooler than the surface of the land, which, becoming heated by the sun's rays, radiates the heat into the air above it. The air expanding by the heat becomes lighter, and rises, and is replaced by the heavier air from the river, which flows with refreshing coolness and moisture over the parched land. These river breezes are of daily occurrence whenever the surface of the land is warm and dry, and then visits are delightfully acceptable.

The geology of the county is somewhat peculiar. Our rocks belong to the earliest formation known to geologists. They were formed by the first process of hardening, which occurred when the surface of the great red-hot drop of molten matter which now constitutes the earth had cooled to the hardening-point. Having been formed by cooling from a melted condition, they are crystalline in structure. It appears that they have not been submerged in the water of seas or lakes, where, if they had been, deposits of mud, sand, and gravel might have been washed upon them, to afterwards be hardened into rocks, but that since rocks have existed on the earth these have been a part of the dry land. They contain no traces of the remains of organic beings, such as are found in the stratified rocks that are formed under water.

In many parts of the county great fissures have opened, in the remote past, into which the liquid rock of the earth's interior has been injected, forming what are known as dikes. Into these different kinds of rock have been forced, some being trap-rock and others serpentine. Coming from the earth's interior, this liquid matter was intensely hot, and heated the rocks on both sides the dikes so much as to change their texture by semi-liquefying them, and thereby favoring a recrystallization into different forms.

[1] Contributed by Ellwood Harvey, M.D., Chester.

Overlying the rocks of the country are deposits of gravel, sand, and clay. Some of these are results of the decomposition of the rocks themselves, but the greater part of them appear to have been brought from some other region, and the opinion is generally accepted that they were pushed from the country north of us by immense glaciers, that appear to have at one time covered all the northeastern parts of this country. The minerals of the county are very numerous. There are very few places in the whole country that offer such an extensive field for scientific research in this direction as the small county of Delaware.

CHAPTER II.

THE EARLY SETTLEMENT OF DELAWARE COUNTY TO THE GRANT OF THE PROVINCE TO WILLIAM PENN.

THE first vessel under the control of white men whose prow ever ruffled the bosom of the great sheet of water now known to the world as Delaware Bay was the "Half Moon" ("Halvemann"), of eighty tons burden, an exploring vessel belonging to the Dutch East India Company, commanded by Henry Hudson. The log-book of Robert Jewett, the mate, records that about noon of Friday, Aug. 28, 1609, a warm, clear day, "we found the land to tend away N. W. with a great bay and river." The lead line, however, disclosing many shoal places, the vessel, next morning, was put about and steered on a southeast course, the officers being convinced that "he that will thoroughly explore this great bay must have a small pinnace that must draw but four or five feet water, to sound before him."

The following year Sir Samuel Argall is said to have entered the bay; and in honor of Thomas West, Lord De La War, the then Governor of Virginia, he named it Delaware Bay. In 1610, Lord Delaware, it is stated, himself visited it, and again in 1618, when he died on his vessel when off the Capes. In 1614, Capt. Cornelius Jacobsz Mey, in the "Fortune," a vessel owned by the city of Hoorn, entered the bay, and in commemoration of his visit Cape Cornelius and Cape May between them still bear his name. Two years subsequent to Mey's voyage, Capt. Cornelius Hendrickson, in a small yacht, the "Restless," is positively asserted by some historians—and the statement is almost as positively denied by others—to have explored the Delaware as far as where the Schuylkill empties into the former river. If it be true that Capt. Hendrickson did actually sail up the stream to the place named, he was the first European of whom we have record that saw any part of the land now comprising the county of Delaware, for his vessel moved along the river the entire length of our southeastern boundary, and he must have noticed the localities where afterwards was planted that germ of civilization from which has evolved the great commonwealth of Pennsylvania.

The history of the various attempts of the Dutch and Swedish powers to establish permanent lodgment on the Delaware is a most interesting theme to the student of our colonial annals. Especially is this true since the indefatigable labors of the members of the Historical Societies of Pennsylvania, New York, and New Jersey have unearthed in recent years a number of authentic documents and historical papers whose very existence was unknown, which now shed much light on those early days of adventurous colonization. But the scope of this work forbids other than a brief narrative of these events excepting where, happening wholly within the territory now comprising Delaware County, they become part of the immediate story of this locality.

In 1621, in Holland, was incorporated the great West India Company, which while its object was a monopoly of the trade of the territory where it might locate posts simply for barter with the savages, the practical result of its efforts was the establishment of a permanent colony in New York and, in a measure, the settlement of the Delaware. Under the auspices of this company, in 1624, Capt. Mey located a garrison[1] near the mouth of Timber Creek, Gloucester Co., N. J., and built Fort Nassau, which post was abandoned the year following. Nevertheless the Dutch company did not relinquish its purpose of making a permanent lodgment on the Delaware, and with that end in view, Samuel Goodyn and Samuel Bloemmaert in 1631 purchased from three of the chiefs of the resident tribe of Indians a large tract of land, sixteen miles square, extending from Cape Henlopen northward towards the mouth of the river. To this purchase—although it was not made until after the arrival of the vessel in the winter of 1630–31, which was remarkably mild—Capt. Peter Heyes, in the ship "Walrus," conveyed a small colony, which he located on Lewes Creek, designing to establish a whale- and seal-fishery station there, as well as plantations for

---

[1] Dr. Smith ("History of Delaware County," page 9) states that from the deposition of Catelina Tricho, said to have been the first white woman at Albany, the colonists who located at and built Fort Nassau in 1624 were accompanied by females. The curious document (see "Documentary History of New York," vol. iii. page 49) is as follows:

"NEW YORK, February 14, 1684–5.

"The deposition of Catelina Tricho, aged fouer score yeares or thereabouts, taken before the right hono^ble^ Collo. Thomas, Leu^t^ and Governour under his Roy^ll^ high^ss^ James, Duke of York and Albany, etc., of N. York and its Dependencyes in America, who saith and declares in the pr'sens of God as followeth:

"That she came to this Province either in the year one thousand six hundred and twenty-three or twenty-fouer, to the best of her rememberance, an that fouer women came along with her in the same shipp, in which the Governor, Arien Jorissen, came also over, which fouer women were married at Sea, and that they and their husbands stayed about three weeks at this place, and then they with eight seamen more went in a vessel by ord^rs^ of the Dutch Governo^r^ to Delaware river and there settled. This I Certifie under my hand and ye Seale of this province.

"THO. DONGAN."

the cultivation of tobacco and grain The settlement was called Swanendale, or "Valley of Swans," because of the great number of those birds in the neighborhood After the erection of Fort Oplandt, and surrounding it with palisades, Capt Peter Heyes sailed for Holland, leaving Gillis Hossett, commissary of the ship, in command of the territory

Early in 1632 it was determined that David Pietersen De Vries, one of the patroons of the company and an experienced navigator, should repair to the colony on the Delaware with a number of emigrants, to join those already there, but before the expedition sailed from the Texel, May 24th of that year, the rumor was received that the little colony at Swanendale had been massacred by the Indians The truth of this intelligence was established when De Vries entered the Delaware, after a circuitous passage, on the 5th of December following, and a careful exploration was made in a boat the next day The fort was found a charred ruin, while the bones of the settlers and those of the horses and cows were discovered here and there bleaching in the sun The adroit De Vries, however, managed to secure the confidence of the Indians, and induced one of the natives to remain all night on his vessel, from whom he learned the circumstances connected with the massacre The particulars, as so related by the Indian, are thus recorded by De Vries [1]

"He then showed us the place where our people had set up a column to which was fastened a piece of tin, whereon the arms of Holland were painted One of their chiefs took this off, for the purpose of making tobacco-pipes, not knowing that he was doing amiss Those in command at the house made such an ado about it that the Indians, not knowing how it was, went away and slew the chief who had done it, and brought a token of the dead to the house to those in command, who told them that they wished that they had not done it, that they should have brought him to them, as they wished to have forbidden him not to do the like again They went away, and the friends of the murdered chief incited their friends, as they are a people like the Indians, who are very revengeful, to set about the work of vengeance Observing our people out of the house, each one at his work, that there was not more than one inside, who was lying sick, and a large mastiff, who was chained,—had he been loose they would not have dared to approach the house,—and the man who had command standing near the house, three of the stoutest Indians, who were to do the deed, bringing a lot of bear skins with them to exchange, sought to enter the house The man in charge went in with them to make the barter, which being done, he went to the loft where the stores lay, and in descending the stairs one of the Indians seized an axe and cleft his head so that he fell down dead They also relieved the sick man of life, and shot into the dog, who was chained fast, and whom they most feared, twenty five arrows before they could dispatch him They then proceeded towards the rest of the men, who were at work, and, going amongst them with pretensions of friendship, struck them down Thus was our young colony destroyed, causing us serious loss."

On Jan 1, 1633, De Vries, who by divers presents had so won the good opinion and friendship of the Indians that they concluded a treaty of peace with him, sailed up the river, and on the 5th of the same month reached the abandoned Fort Nassau, where he was met by a few Indians, who seeing him approaching, had gathered there to barter furs The Dutch captain told them he wanted beans, and that he had no goods to exchange for peltries, whereupon the savages told him to go to Timmerkill (now Cooper's Creek, opposite Philadelphia), where he could get corn An Indian woman to whom he had given a cloth dress secretly informed De Vries that if he went there he would be attacked, for the natives had murdered the crew of an English boat which was ascending the Count Earnest (Delaware) River Thus fully on his guard, the next day when De Vries went to Timmerkill he permitted the Indians to visit his vessel, at the same time informing the savages that their evil designs had been revealed to him by Manitou, the Indian god After making a treaty of permanent peace with them, being unable to obtain corn in any quantity on the Delaware, De Vries sailed to Virginia, where he purchased provisions and received from the Governor a present of six goats for Swanendale, to which he returned, and subsequently taking the colonists on his vessel, sailed to New York and thence to Europe Hence, in the summer of 1633 no settlement of Europeans was located at any point along the shores of Delaware Bay and River

In 1635 a party of Englishmen from the colony on the Connecticut River, consisting of George Holmes, his hired man, Thomas Hall, and ten or twelve others, attempted to make a lodgment on the Delaware, of which fact the Dutch authorities in New York seemed to have had information, and made preparation to thwart their design, for when the English squatters made an effort to capture Fort Nassau they found it garrisoned The English party were taken prisoners and sent to Manhattan, where they were permitted permanently to settle Thomas Hall, at the latter place, rose to some eminence, and was active in all the movements in the early days of New York while it was a Dutch province

In 1624, William Usselincx visited Sweden, and as as it was he who had drafted the first plan for the Dutch West India Company, he was invited by Gustavus Adolphus to remain in Sweden Although advanced in years, in 1626, Usselincx obtained from the king a charter for the Swedish West India Company, a commercial organization, whose project of forming a colony in "foreign parts" received the earnest support of Gustavus Adolphus and Axel Oxenstierna, the great chancellor of Sweden But nothing beyond the consent of Adolphus to the organization of the company seems to have been done, and even the official royal signature to the charter was never procured Hence after the death of the king the company was dissolved and the whole project apparently was abandoned, notwithstanding a publication of the privileges granted by charter, although unsigned by the late monarch, was made by Chancellor Oxenstierna This was the external appearance merely, for several persons were still earnest in the effort to establish the Swedish West India Company It is a peculiar circumstance that as late as the middle of the year 1635

[1] "Voyages of De Vries" New York Historical Society Collection (new series), vol iii page 23

the objective-point of the proposed expedition seemed to have been undetermined, the coast of Guinea and that of Brazil being under consideration, while the eastern coast of North America apparently offered no attractions whatever In the summer of 1635, Peter Minuit, who had some knowledge of the territory on the Delaware, entered into correspondence with the Swedish authorities, and early in 1637 he went to Sweden, where, after many difficulties, on Aug 9, 1637, the Admiralty issued a passport for the ships "Kalmar Nyckel" and "Gripen," the former a man-of-war, and the latter a sloop, or tender, which vessels comprised Minuit's fleet, the first Swedish expedition It is stated in a Dutch state paper that Minuit's colonists were "Swedes, the most of whom were banditti"[1] Unforeseen delays followed, until the winter was near at hand before the expedition finally made sail for the New World, after having put into the Dutch harbor of Medemblik for repairs It is stated by Professor Odhner,[2] of Sweden, that documentary evidence seems to establish the fact that the fleet arrived in the Delaware in March or early in April, 1638 Minuit about that time, it is known, purchased from the Indians a tract of land several days' journey in extent, located on the west bank of the river, whereon he set up the arms of Sweden, and with a salvo of artillery christened the fort he began building, near the present site of Wilmington, the "Kristina," in honor of the youthful queen whose flag he was the first to unfold on the American continent The river Christiana retains the name thus bestowed on the fort—for Minuit called that stream the Elbe—to this day Within the palisade were built two log houses, for the accommodation of the soldiers and for the storage of provisions After the little settlement had been provided with all necessaries to sustain life, and for barter with the Indians, Lieut Mans Kling was placed in command of the garrison, and Minuit, in July, 1638, sailed for Sweden, touching in his homeward voyage at the West Indies, where the sloop "Gripen" had preceded him At St Christopher he sold all the merchandise on the "Kalmar Nyckel," and in place of the cargo he had taken to the island loaded the vessel with tobacco When ready to sail Minuit and the captain of his vessel were invited to visit a Dutch ship, "The Flying Deer," and while on board of the latter a furious hurricane arose, compelling all the vessels in the roadstead to go to sea Several of the ships were dismasted, while others were lost, among the latter "The Flying Deer" She was never afterwards heard from The "Kalmar Nyckel" made search for the missing Swedish officers, but, learning no tidings of them, after several days sailed for Europe The sloop "Gripen" subsequently returned from the West Indies to the Delaware, where she was loaded with furs, and sailed for Sweden, reaching there in the latter part of May, 1639, having made the passage in five weeks

The same year Cornelius Van Vliet, a Dutch captain, was ordered to proceed in the "Kalmar Nyckel" to New Sweden, learn the condition of the colony, and make report of the country, no report having been made by Minuit, as it was the purpose of Queen Christina to people the land with Swedes To the latter end an effort was made to obtain willing emigrants, but failing in that, the government ordered the Governors of Elfsborg and Varmland "to lay hands on such marriaged soldiers as had either evaded service or committed some other offence, and transport them, with their wives and children, to New Sweden, with the promise to bring them back, if required, within two years, to do this, however, 'justly and discreetly,' that no riot might ensue"[3]

The "Kalmar Nyckel" on her second voyage to the colony sailed for Gottenburg, where she arrived in June, 1639 There she was detained more than three months, occasioned by the difficulty of procuring emigrants, cattle, horses, swine, implements for husbandry, and partly because of the negligence of the new commander of the second expedition Rev Reorus Torkillus, the first Swedish clergyman in New Sweden, is believed to have been one of the passengers on the vessel, which left Gottenburg in the early autumn of 1639 The ship was obliged to stop at Medemblik to be overhauled, she having sprung a leak, and, afterward, when having put to sea, she was twice compelled to return for repairs, until the crew stated they were not willing to sail in such a vessel and under such a captain Van Vliet was thereupon discharged, a new crew procured, and Capt. Pouwel Jansen, a Dutchman, given charge of the ship The "Kalmar Nyckel," after encountering a remarkable storm, that intercepted all navigation in the Zuider-Zee, finally, on Feb 7, 1640, sailed from the Texel for New Sweden Lieut Peter Hollandare, who had been appointed Governor of the province, accompanied the expedition, which, after a voyage of over two months, landed at Christiana on the 17th of April of the same year, where they found the colony planted by Minuit in good condition[4] The emigrants who accompanied the second expedition were of the most unpromising character, since Peter Hollandare records that "no more stupid, indifferent people are to be found in all Sweden than those who are now here," and the domestic animals transported in the ship were few and of poor quality On Nov 2, 1640,

1 Penna Archives, 2d series, vol v p 236

2 "The Founding of New Sweden" (*Penn Mag of History*, vol iii p 279) is a mine of interesting information on the early settlements of the Delaware River

3 "The Founding of New Sweden," by Professor C T Odhner Translated by Professor G B Keen, *Penn Mag of History*, vol iii p 396

4 This statement, which appears from Swedish documents, is in marked contrast to the assertion of Director Kieft, whose letter, dated in the latter part of May, 1640 ("New York Colonial Documents," vol i p 593), states, "The Swedes in the South River were resolved to move off and to come here" (New York) "A day before their departure a ship arrived with a reinforcement."

the ship "Friedenburg," under the command of Capt Jacob Powellson, having on board a number of Dutch colonists, with Jost Van Bogardt, who emigrated under the auspices of the Swedish crown, cattle, and "other things necessary for the cultivation of the country," arrived in New Sweden These emigrants occupied land three or four Swedish miles below Christiana Very little is known of the history of the colony from 1640 to 1643, saving that in 1642 a general sickness prevailed among the Swedish settlers on the Delaware[1]

The "Kalmar Nyckel" returned to Sweden in July, 1640. The home government, in its anxiety to obtain settlers for its American colony, had ordered the Governor of Orebro to prevail upon the unsettled Finns in that province to emigrate with their wives and children to New Sweden, while Mans Kling was instructed from the mining classes, and particularly from among the roaming Finns, who lived free of charge in the houses of the inhabitants of the Swedish forests, to procure settlers to be sent abroad The third expedition, in the "Kalmar Nyckel" and the "Charitas," sailed for New Sweden in 1641, and a number of the Finns came hither in those vessels Hence many of the early Swedish settlers were not of a class to be desired as founders of a new empire, for the archives of Sweden disclose the fact that quite a number of criminals and forest-destroying Finns were transported to the Delaware River settlements to rid the mother-country of their presence The Finns mentioned had, in violation of the mandates of the royal government, set fire to the forests in Varmland and Dal, that they might free the ground of trees to sow grain in the ashes, and for this act they were banished to the New World Professor Odhner directly asserts that in the province of Skaraborg, a trooper, who was condemned to death for having broken into the monastery gardens at Varnhem, was permitted to make his selection between being hanged or embarking for New Sweden, and as late as 1653[2] a criminal who had been convicted of killing an elk on the island D'Auland was sentenced to transportation hither

The fourth colony, and the one whose history most intimately connects itself with Delaware County, was that which left Gottenburg on Nov 1, 1642 This expedition, composed of the ships "Fama" and "Swan," was under the command of Lieut-Col John Printz, who had been commissioned Governor of New Sweden, Aug. 15, 1642, with an annual salary of one thousand two hundred dollars in silver and an allowance of four hundred rix-dollars for his expenses The journey was a long one, "the watery way to the West was not yet discovered, and therefore, for fear of the sand-banks off Newfoundland, the ships which went under the command of Governor Printz sailed along the coast of Africa until they found the eastern passage, then directly over to America, leaving the Canaries high up to the north"[3] They landed at Antigua, inhabited at "that time 'by Englishmen and negroes, with some Indians,' where they 'spent their Christmas holidays, and were well entertained,'" says Mr Holm, "'at the Governor's house' After quitting this seat of 'perpetual summer' (as the same gentleman depicts it) they encountered 'a severe storm,' accompanied at the last 'with snow,' which 'continued about fourteen days,' by which they 'lost three large anchors, a spritsail, and their mainmast, and the ship was run aground, but on the 15th of February, 1643, by God's grace, came up to Fort Christina, in New Sweden, Va,' in the precise phrases of the historian, 'at two o'clock in the afternoon' Here the first three Swedish expeditions had established their chief settlement, under Minuit and Hollandare, and here remained a short time also this fourth and greatest of the colonies, enjoying friendly intercourse with fellow-countrymen most glad to welcome them, and happily reposing from the distresses of their long and perilous voyage'"[4]

Under the instructions he had received from the home government, Printz, in the exercise of his discretion, located the seat of government at Tinicum Island, where he built a fort, which he called New Gottenburg, and resided for a time in the fortress, until he built his mansion-house, known in our annals as Printz Hall On this island the principal inhabitants then had their dwellings and plantations[5] With the fort at that place, Printz controlled the passage of the river above Tinicum, and when he, shortly afterward, built Fort Elsenburgh, at Salem Creek, placing therein four brass and iron twelve-pound cannon and one "pots-hooft,"[6] manned by twelve soldiers in command of a lieutenant, he rendered the Dutch fortress on the east side of the river above the mouth of the Schuylkill almost useless to the Holland colony, as was fully recognized by Hudde, who reported that Printz had closed "the enterance of the river"

We are told by Campanius that "In the beginning of Governor Printz's administration there came a great number of those criminals, who were sent over from Sweden When the European inhabitants perceived it they would not suffer them to set their foot on shore, but they were all obliged to return so that a great many of them perished on the voyage This was related to me, amongst other things, by an old, trustworthy man, named Nils Matsson Utter, who, after his return home, served in His Majesty's life-guards It was after this forbidden, under a penalty, to send any more criminals to America, lest Almighty God should let his ven-

[1] Winthrop, vol ii p 76

[2] 5 Penna Archives, 2d series, p 780, where is given Queen Christina's order of Aug 11, 1653, directing that Henry D'Oregrund, a malefactor under sentence of death, be sent to New Sweden

[3] Acrelius, "History of New Sweden," p 41

[4] Professor G B Keen's summary of Printz's voyage, in "Descendants of Joran Kyn," *Penna Mag of History*, vol ii p 326.

[5] Campanius, "History of New Sweden," p 79

[6] Hudde's Report, Penna Archives, 2d series, vol v p 104

geance fall on the ships and goods, and the virtuous people that were on board."[1]

This statement is in direct conflict with the report of Governor Printz in 1647, for therein he asked instruction from the home authorities "how long the criminals must serve for their crimes,"[2] and is told that nothing definite can be prescribed respecting that matter, that it is left to his discretion, but those who reform and perform their duty satisfactorily may be allowed the same wages as other free people. "But those who go on in the same wrong way as before and do not exhibit any improvement may have their punishment increased by you, Sir Governor, or may continue to serve without wages."[3]

The voluntary emigrants to New Sweden were of two classes, the freemen, those who were privileged to settle where they chose in the colony and to return to the mother-country at pleasure, and the company's servants, those who were employed at stipulated wages for a designated term. "There was a third, consisting of vagabonds and malefactors; these went to remain in slavery, and were employed in digging the earth, throwing up trenches, and erecting walls and other fortifications. The others had no intercourse with them, but a particular spot was appointed for them to reside upon.[4]

The first year under Printz's administration many of the settlers died, which the Governor states was due to hard work and the scarcity of food.[5] In four years thereafter (1647) we learn from the report furnished the home government that the total number of whites in the Swedish settlements on the Delaware was one hundred and eighty-three souls. Twenty-eight of the freemen had made settlements, and part of them were provided with oxen and cows. Tobacco seems to have been chiefly the crop grown, for in the return cargo of the "Golden Shark," in that year, was six thousand nine hundred and twenty pounds of tobacco, grown in New Sweden, the rest having been purchased from Virginia. To stimulate this project those persons who cultivated land were exempted by the home government for ten years from taxation. A grist-mill had been erected by Printz in 1643, about a quarter of a mile in the woods at "Kara Kung," otherwise called the Water-Mill stream, "a fine mill, which ground both fine and coarse flour, and was going early and late. It was the first that was seen in that country."[6] This mill was located on Crum Creek, and the holes sunk in the rocks to receive the posts supporting the frame-work are still to be seen, near the Blue Bell Tavern, on the Darby road.[7] Townsend Ward[8] tells us that in front of the old portion of the Blue Bell Tavern "is a carriage stepping-stone of considerable historical interest, for it is, perhaps, one of the first millstones used in what is now the territory of Pennsylvania, and was in use before Penn's arrival. The stone is circular in form, with a square hole through its centre. Not far from the inn, and in the bed of the creek, only a few feet west of the old King's (Queen's) road bridge, may be seen the holes, drilled in the rocks, in which were inserted the supports of the ancient mill wherein the stone was used. Mr. Aubrey H. Smith remembers finding, when a boy, a piece of lead weighing seventeen pounds, that had evidently been run, when melted, around an inserted post." Printz was much pleased with the mill, "which runs the whole year, to the great advantage of the country, particularly as the windmill, formerly here before I came, would never work, and was good for nothing."[9] Not only had he built this needed public improvement, but had caused some waterfalls to be examined as a site for saw-mills below the dam of the grist-mill, as well as three other places where oak-timber grew plentiful. But as he was without the saw-blades, and no person in the colony understood the management of such an establishment, Printz suggested to the home government that it would be worth considering, as a good trade in planking, pipe-staves, and timber could be made with the West Indies and other points, provided a proper vessel was kept in New Sweden to transport those articles to market.[10]

It is not my purpose to relate the history of the difficulties and trials which Printz had to contend with from the encroachments of the Dutch and English in their efforts to make a lodgment on the Delaware. That he was insolent in his manner to those whom he regarded as intruders on the Swedish territory cannot be questioned, if the statement of his enemies is to be credited. Hudde tells us that Printz replied to his

[1] Campanius, "New Sweden," p. 73.

[2] *Penna. Mag. of History*, vol. vii. p. 277.

[3] Count Oxenstierna's reply to Printz, *Penna. Mag. of History*, vol. vii. p. 283. In fact, we have reason to believe that during all our colonial history criminals were sent to the American plantations. In a series of articles on crimes and criminals, published in the *New Castle* (England) *Weekly Chronicle*, in 1883, the author says, "The statute of 39 Elizabeth was converted by James I. into an Act of Transportation to America, by a letter to the treasurer and council of Virginia, in the year 1619, commanding them 'to send 100 dissolute persons to Virginia, which the Knight Marshall would deliver to them for the purpose.' Transportation is not distinctly mentioned by any English statute prior to Charles II., which gives a power to the judges, at their discretion, 'either to execute or transport to America for life the mosstroopers of Cumberland.' This mode of punishment, however, was not commonly practiced until the reign of George I. The courts were then, by Act of Parliament, allowed a discretionary power to order felons to be transported to the American plantations. This lasted from 1718 to the declaration of American independence in 1776." The importation of criminals into this colony in the character of redemption servants, who were purchased from the officers in England, became such a public evil that on Feb. 14, 1729-30, the General Assembly by statute forbade masters of vessels, under heavy fines, landing such persons in the province, and extended the penalties to merchants who should import, sell, or dispose of such convicts in the province in violation of the act.

[4] Campanius, "New Sweden," p. 73.

[5] Printz's Report, *Penn. Mag. of Hist.*, vol. vii. p. 272.

[6] Campanius, p. 81. Of course the statement applies to the first mill run by water. We know, from Printz's report, that a windmill had preceded it.

[7] Record of Upland Court, p. 88.

[8] "A Walk to Darby," *Penn. Mag. of Hist.*, vol. iii. p. 262.

[9] Report for 1647, *Penn. Mag. of Hist.*, vol. vii. p. 274.

[10] *Penn. Mag. of Hist.*, vol. vii. p. 279.

suggestion that the Dutch were the earliest settlers on the Delaware, "that the devil was the oldest possessor of hell, but he sometimes admitted a younger one." That on another occasion, Printz treated contemptuously a letter he had sent him by a sergeant, in that he threw it towards one of his attendants who stood near him, saying, "There, take care of it," and that when the sergeant insisted on seeing the Governor, who left him to meet some Englishmen, he, the sergeant, was thrown out of doors, "the Governor taking a gun in his hand from the wall to shoot him, as he imagined, but was prevented from leaving his room," and that when the servants of the Dutch Company went to Tinicum, Printz unreasonably abused them, "so that they are often, on returning home, bloody and bruised," while John Thickpenny,[1] of the New England colony on the Delaware, deposed that, at Tinicum, Printz cursed and swore at the Englishmen, calling them renegades, and threw John Woollen, the Indian interpreter for the English settlers, into irons, which Printz himself fastened on his legs, and that he stamped with his feet in his rage. Despite all these statements, Printz was true to his sovereign's interest in the colony, even if he had failed in that respect in the Old World.[2]

On Feb. 20, 1647, when the ship "Golden Shark," which had arrived in New Sweden on the 1st of October of the preceding year, left the colony on the return voyage to Europe, Printz dispatched Lieut. John Pappegoya, as a special messenger to orally make a report of the growth and need of the settlement. Pappegoya had been one of the early Swedish settlers on the Delaware and had returned home, but desiring to revisit New Sweden, he came back in 1644, particularly recommended to the favorable consideration of Printz by the home government. It is believed at the time Pappegoya was sent to Sweden as bearer of dispatches he was then married to Armigart, Governor Printz's daughter, who figured prominently in our early annals. He returned to New Sweden in a short time (in those days of long voyages), for about in the middle of June, 1648, Hudde[3] mentions that the committee of the Dutch Council, after completing the purchase of land on the Schuylkill from the Indians, "with a becoming suite, sailed to Tinne Konck, and was received there by the commissay, Huygen and Lieut. Passegay (Pappegoya), who left them about half an hour in the open air and constaint rain," before they could obtain an interview with Governor Printz. When the latter, after administering the affairs of the colony on the Delaware for twelve years, sailed for Sweden in the latter part of the year 1653, he left the government in charge of his son-in-law, John Pappegoya.

May 21, 1654, the ship "Eagle" arrived at New Castle, having on board John Claudius Rising, who had been appointed commissary and Governor's assistant counsellor,—an office equivalent to Lieutenant-Governor; but Printz having sailed before Rising came, the full charge of the colony devolved upon him. His first official act was not only a violation of his instructions, but an error which was disastrous in its results to the colony. As the vessel came to at Fort Cassimir two guns were fired as a salute to the fortress, after which Rising demanded the surrender of the stronghold. The Dutch commander desired time to consider, but Rising ordered a force of thirty men to land and take the place by assault, refusing, as the Dutch alleged, "to give one hour's delay." Acrelius tells us, "A correct inventory was made of everything in the fort, and every one was allowed to carry off his property, whether belonging to the company or to private individuals;"[4] while Gerrit Becker, the Dutch commander, deposed, "I could scarcely induce him (Rising) by prayer not to be turned out naked, with his (my) wife and children, and all the property in this fort was confiscated by them."[5] The capture of this fortress having taken place about noon on Trinity Sunday, the Swedes called it the "Fort of the Holy Trinity;" and subsequently, under the supervision of Peter Lindstrom, the engineer, it was repaired, enlarged, and "as good as built anew."

On the 17th of June, 1654, Vice-Governor Rising held a council with the Indian sachems at Printz Hall, at Tinicum, and although the savages stated that the Swedish vessel had introduced among them diseases, of which many of their people died, the gifts which Rising laid before them were too tempting to be resisted, and a treaty of friendship was then "made between the Swedes and the Indians, which has ever since been faithfully observed on both sides."[6]

When the news of the capture of Fort Cassimir was received in Holland it excited much indignation among the directors, and although previous to that event the home government had not approved fully of Stuyvesant's action in erecting the fort at New Castle, all differences of opinion were swallowed up in the indignation and anger the seizure of the fortress aroused. Hence, Stuyvesant was ordered "to exert every nerve to revenge that injury, not only by restoring affairs to their former situation, but by driving the Swedes from every side of the river, as they did with us, provided that such among them as may be

---

1 Deposition of John Thickpenny, "New Haven Colonial Records," vol. i. pp. 97-99.

2 John Printz was well educated, and after he entered military life he rose rapidly during the Prussian and German war. In 1638 he was promoted lieutenant-colonel of West Götha Cavalry. In 1640 he shamefully and disgracefully surrendered the fortress of Chemnitz, and returned to Stockholm without the consent of the field-marshal. He was put under arrest, tried, and broken of his rank in the army. He was subsequently (Aug. 16, 1642) appointed Governor of New Sweden. On his return to the Old World he was made a general, and in 1658, Governor of the district of Jonkoping. He died in 1663, leaving no male issue to succeed to the title conferred on him in 1642.

3 Hudde's Report, Penna. Archives, 2d series, vol. v. p. 115.

4 Acrelius, "New Sweden," p. 63.

5 Penna. Archives, 2d series, vol. v. p. 253.

6 Campanius, p. 78.

disposed to settle under and submit to our government may be indulged in it."[1] In conformity with the spirit of these instructions, Stuyvesant silently but promptly made preparation for an aggressive movement against the Swedish settlement on the Delaware. To that end he gathered an armament and fleet, while the Swedes, unaware of the danger that lowered over them, made no unusual provision for defense. On Sunday, Sept. 4, 1655, the expedition under Stuyvesant, in seven vessels, with about six hundred men, set sail for the Delaware, and on the morning of the 9th of September anchored a short distance from Fort Cassimir, when Stuyvesant sent a lieutenant ashore to demand the restitution of the stronghold. Lieutenant Schute, the Swedish officer, desired time to communicate with his superior, which was refused. In the mean while the Dutch commander had landed a force which occupied all the approaches in rear of the fort, and, after some negotiation, the Swedish garrison capitulated on the morning of the 11th of September. After the reduction of Fort Cassimir the Dutch forces laid siege to Fort Christiana, and from Governor Rising's official report[2] we learn that the enemy made regular approaches until, having their guns in position in rear of the fort, Stuyvesant formally demanded the surrender of the post within twenty-four hours. The Swedish Governor, after a general consultation with the whole garrison, decided to accede to the demand he was powerless to resist. The articles of capitulation, among other matters, provided that the Swedish forces should march out of the fort with the honors of war,—drums and trumpet playing, flags flying, matches burning, and with hand and side arms. That they, as prisoners of war, were first to be conducted to Tinicum Island, and placed in the fort at that place until they could be taken to New Amsterdam.[3] Campanius asserts that "The Dutch then proceeded to destroy New Gottenburg, laying waste all the houses and plantations without the fort, killing the cattle, and plundering the inhabitants of everything that they could lay their hands on; so that after a siege of fourteen days, and many fruitless propositions to obtain more humane treatment, the Swedes were obliged to surrender that fortress for want of men and ammunition."[4]

From the fact that the articles of capitulation at Fort Christina stipulated for the detention of the Swedish prisoners of war at the fort at Tinicum, and that there is, so far as known, an absence of all documentary evidence to support the assertion made by Campanius, the conclusion seems irresistible that that author has confused his account of the doings at New Gottenburg with those occurring on the siege of Fort Christiana. Vice-Governor Rising, in his report,[5] already mentioned, when relating the pillaging of "the people without sconce of their property, and higher up the river they plundered many and stripped them to the skin," thus briefly narrated the outrages of the Dutch invaders at Tinicum. "At New Gottenberg they robbed Mr. Papegoija's wife of all she had, with many others who had collected their property there." Not a word has this man, who pictured the minutest incident of the siege of Fort Christiana, and the killing of Swedish "cattle, goats, swine, and poultry," to say about the investment of Fort Gottenburg, the resistance of its slender garrison for fourteen days, or the laying waste of all the houses and plantations without the forts. Certain it is, that the Swedish Church at Tinicum, Printz Hall, and other buildings stood uninjured long years after the Dutch power in North America had waned before the conquering standard of Great Britain. In 1680 "the remains of the large block-house, which served them (the Swedes) in place of a fortress," was on the island, together with "three or four houses built by the Swedes, a little Lutheran Church made of logs, and the ruins of some log huts."[6] In Rising's reply to Stuyvesant,[7] only thirty-four days after the capture of Fort Christiana, he does not mention the destruction of the post at New Gottenburg, but sets forth the following outrages committed by the Dutch in their conquest of New Sweden: "Your Honor's troops have behaved here as if they were in the country of their bitterest enemy, as the plundering of Tornaborg, Uplandt, Finland, Princedorp, and other places more clearly proves (not to speak of the deeds done about Fort Christiana), where the females have partly been dragged out of their houses by force; whole buildings torn down, even hauled away; oxen, cows, pigs, and other animals daily slaughtered in large numbers; even the horses were not spared, but shot wantonly, the plantations devastated, and everything thereabouts treated in such a way that our victuals have been mostly spoiled, carried away, or lost somehow." So, too, on Dec. 19, 1656,[8] the directors instruct Stuyvesant to occupy the

---

1 Hazard's Annals, p. 168.

2 Penna. Archives, 2d series, vol. v. p. 224.

3 Acrelius, "Hist. of New Sweden," p. 76.

4 Campanius, "New Sweden," pp. 85, 86. Smith, in his "History of New Jersey," page 34, says the Dutch "destroyed New Gottenburg, with such houses as are without the fort, plundering the inhabitants of what they had, and killing their cattle." From his account it also appears that the fort at Tinicum was defended fourteen days, and that the pillaging took place before the fort was surrendered. The statements of both Campanius and Smith were doubtless based on traditionary recitals, which, in descending from one generation to another, had confused two separate matters into one. Campanius' work was not published until 1702, nearly forty years after the circumstances narrated took place, while that of Smith was issued long subsequent to that date. To show how soon confusion may take place in matters connected with historical events it is only necessary to cite "An Account of the Seditious False Konigsmack in New Sweden" (*Penn. Mag. of Hist.*, vol. vii. p. 219), where is given, by an unknown writer, in 1683, an account of the attempted insurrection of the Long Fin, which occurred in 1669. The writer states, "These are the particulars which I received from the oldest Swedes," and yet he relates that the conspirators "went to Philadelphia and bought powder, balls, shot, lead, and so forth," nearly fourteen years before that city had an existence.

5 Penna. Archives, 2d series, vol. v. p. 227.

6 Journal of a Voyage to New York in 1679–80. Memoirs of the Long Island Hist. Soc., vol. i. p. 177.

7 Penna. Archives, 2d series, vol. vii. p. 487.

8 Ib., 496.

fort at New Gottenburg with eight or ten soldiers provisionally, "as well for the safety of the Swedes, now our subjects"

The Dutch had conquered, and the Swedish flag no longer floated over the disputed territory on the Delaware But the triumph was a costly one, the expenses of the expedition swelling so largely the debt of the Dutch West India Company that in the summer of 1656, to relieve itself from liability to the city of Amsterdam, the company ceded to the burgomasters of that municipality a portion of the Delaware River territory, extending from Bombay Hook to Christiana Creek, which subsequently was known as "the City's Colony," while the land north of that creek was termed "the Company's Colony"

Before intelligence of the conquest of New Sweden had reached the mother-country, on March 24, 1656, the Swedish ship "Mercury," with a hundred and thirty emigrants on board, entered the river John Paul Jacquit, the Dutch Governor, prohibited the captain of the vessel to land the crew or passengers, as well as refusing to permit him to ascend the river beyond Fort Cassimir John Pappegoya, who had not yet returned to Sweden, together with Capt Huygen, on March 30th wrote to the Council in New Amsterdam, requesting that these emigrants who came from Sweden should be permitted to settle in the colony, urging as reasons "the immense loss they would suffer, many good farmers would be ruined, parents separated from children, and even husbands from wife," but their appeals only made the Council hold more firmly to their resolution that the Swedes should settle at New Amsterdam, where their number could not be a constant menace to the authorities Much time was consumed in tedious negotiations, until at length the patience of the Swedish colonists was exhausted, and through the influence of Pappegoya with the savages, a number of the residents, Swedes and Indians, went aboard the vessel, when, in spite of the guns of the fort or the command of Governor Jacquit, the anchor was weighed, the "Mercury" sailed up the river, and landed her cargo and passengers at Christiana[1] The Dutch, fearing that some of the Indians on board might be injured, refrained from firing on the vessel in her passage by the fort

After the Dutch had acquired absolute sway on the Delaware the ancient Swedish capital at Tinicum seems to have been abandoned, possibly because of the grant of that island to Governor Printz, hence in the early records only occasionally, at this period, do we find allusion to any places lying within the boundary of the present county of Delaware Georan Van Dyck, who had been appointed sheriff of the company's colony, requested permission to establish the Swedish settlers in villages, and on June 12, 1657, the Council responded that he was "not only authorized and qualified, but also ordered and directed, to concentrate their houses and dwellings, but henceforth to erect them in shape of a village or villages, either at Upland, Passayonck, Finland, Kinghsessing, on the 'Verdrietige hoeck,' or at such places as by them may be considered suitable, under condition that previous notice be given to the Director-General and Council, in case they should chose some other places than those specified above"[2] This effort to gather the Swedish residents into villages failed, and it seems not to have been pressed earnestly until after William Beekman was appointed, Oct 28, 1658, vice-director of the company's colony on the Delaware, and even not then until the directors in Holland, under date of Oct 14, 1659,[3] recommend that the Swedes should be separated and scattered among the Dutch, since they, the directors, had reason to believe that the English may undertake "something against us there under the Swedish flag and name" In furtherance of this recommendation, Beekman, in March following, attempted to execute the order, but found that he could not get the Swedish settlers to choose a location for the village, every one asserting that he would keep his entire lot and fields[4] Miss Printz "objected to moving because the church was located at Tinicum, on her plantation, that her buildings were heavy, that she had offered her land rent free, but no one would live with her" Beekman also informed Stuyvesant that to enforce the edict then would result in great loss, as it would prevent the planting of spring crops, and he, therefore, had granted the Swedes five or six weeks longer before compelling compliance with the order Thus the matter rested, for the Dutch authorities could not convince the Swedes of the advantage of the proposed change, and they had not sufficient force at hand to compel obedience therewith[5] Beekman, however, constantly endeavored to prevail upon them to settle at Passayunk, but when the Swedes intimated that "they would rather go to Maryland than to remove to another place here and sponge upon the others," the project was finally abandoned by the authorities

The affair of the Delaware's having been so mismanaged that many complaints had been lodged with the authorities in New Amsterdam, Council on April 20, 1658, determining that these matters "as well as some necessary arrangements to be made among and regarding the Swedes, cannot well be attended to by a letter," ordered that Stuyvesant and Pieter Tonneman should personally visit the Delaware River settlements "for the special service and advantage of the company" On May 8th Stuyvesant was at Tinicum, for on that day Georan Van Dyck, Orloff Stille,

[1] Acrelius, "Hist of New Sweden," p 90 Vincent says (Hist. of State of Delaware, vol i p 276) that the passengers and cargo of the "Mercury" were landed at Marcus Hook On what authority that statement is based is not given

[2] Penna Archives, 2d series, vol vii p 511

[3] Ib, p 598

[4] Ib, p 628

[5] Acrelius, "Hist of New Sweden," p 96

Malthys Hanson, Peter Rambo, and Peter Kaik, the Swedish magistrates,[1] presented a petition to the General Director, asking for the appointment of a court messenger to serve summons, make arrests, and "the carrying out of sentences," and that they be allowed "free access to the commander at Fort Altona to get assistance from the soldiers in case of emergency" The third request was "that an order be made that nobody shall leave these boundaries without knowledge of the magistrates, much less, that the servants, man or woman of one, when they leave or run away without their masters' or mistress' permission, shall be concealed by the other"

From this petition, which was favorably received and acted on, we learn that Fort Gottenburg had at this time ceased to be a military post This was perhaps due to the fact that the Dutch officers were doubtful of the loyalty of the Swedes to the new administration, and thought it judicious to concentrate their forces at the most available and strongest fortification, that at Tinicum, being merely a block-house, was abandoned We also gather from the same document that the system of redemption servitude at that early stage of our history was recognized in this locality[2]

From the report of Jacob Alricks to the commissioners of the city's colony, Oct 10, 1658,[3] we ascertain that children from the almshouse at Amsterdam had been sent over to the Delaware River settlements and had been bound out among the residents there, the eldest for two, the major portion for three, and the youngest children for four, years He suggested that from time to time more of these young people should be dispatched hither, "but, if possible, none ought to come less than fifteen years of age and somewhat strong, as little profit is to be expected here without labor"

In a letter from Beekman to Stuyvesant, April 28, 1660,[4] the former states "that among the Fins at Opland there is a married couple who live very wretchedly together, and the wife is often fearfully beaten, and daily driven out of the house like a dog, which was continued through several years Nothing is heard of the wife, but he, on the contrary, has committed adultery Therefore the priest, the neighbors, the sheriff, and commissaries, and others besides, have appealed to me, at the request of the man and the woman, that they might be divorced, and the few animals and personal property be divided among them I answered that I would inform your Noble Worship of it and await orders" What was done finally in this case is unknown

On the night of Sept 20, 1661,[5] the wife of Rev Laurence Charles Laers, the Swedish priest at Upland, eloped with Joseph Jongh (Young), the fugitives leaving the settlement in a canoe Director Beekman, the next day, as soon as he was informed of the occurrence, dispatched an express to the Governor of Maryland and the magistrates at Sassafras River, requesting that should the parties come there they might be detained, and he notified of the fact Four days afterwards Beekman came to Upland to look after the property there of Jacob Jongh It appears that in his hasty flight Jongh had left his personal effects at Upland, and the next day the Rev. Mr Laers went to the house of Andreas Hendriexson, a Finn, where his wife's paramour had lived, and without notifying the authorities forced open the door of Jongh's room with an axe[6] The keys to the chest belonging to the fugitive being found in the apartment, the clergyman opened the luggage and appropriated some of the contents The Dutch authorities supposed, as they learned nothing from Maryland, that the runaways had gone to New England, whereas it is now almost conclusively established that this Jacob Jongh or Young made his way to Maryland, where he subsequently figured prominently in the early history of that colony[7] The abandoned husband, however, did not appear to be crushed by his wife's desertion, for in less than a month (October 15th) he asked Vice-Governor Beekman to be allowed the next day to make the first proclamation of the banns of his intended marriage with a girl of seventeen or eighteen years, which consent the former withheld until he could hear from Stuyvesant[8] The authorities in New Amsterdam apparently acted too slowly for the reverend lover, for November 8th[9] he again asked for advice "whether he may now marry again, as his household requires it" On December 15th[10] he was granted a provisional divorce, the decree being subject to Stuyvesant's approbation; but without tarrying until the latter signified his approval, the reverend gentleman, on Sunday, Jan 26, 1662, entered anew into the married relation, which act aroused the indignation of Beekman, and prejudiced him against "this fine priest" On April 14, 1662, the case against the Rev Mr. Laers was tried at Fort Altona He was prosecuted on behalf of the company for having broken into the room and making an inventory of the goods left by the absconding Joseph Jongh In the crude system of justice then in vogue on the Delaware, the court sentenced him to pay two hundred guilders, which had been advanced to Jongh to purchase grain for the company, forty florins in beavers which were due from Jongh to Director Beekman and Mr Decker, and was also fined forty guilders for usurping the authority of the court The unhappy defendant was in ad-

[1] Penna Archives, 2d series, vol vii p 631

[2] As to the latter statement, see Penna Archives, 2d series, vol vii p 716

[3] Ib, vol v p. 300

[4] Ib, vol vii p 634

[5] Ib., 5th series, vol vii p 668

[6] Ib, 669

[7] Johnson's "History of Cecil County, Md," pp 80–130

[8] Penna Archives, 2d series, vol vii p. 670

[9] Ib, 671

[10] Ib., 672

dition informed that "his new marriage was declared illegal."[1] The clergyman thereupon petitioned Governor Stuyvesant, setting forth that he broke the door open in the search for his wife, whom he imagined was concealed in that place; that he had found among Jongh's goods a few pairs of his (the petitioner's) wife's stockings; that he had no intention "to vilify the court;" that his acts were committed through ignorance, and that in his marriage "he did not suppose it should have been so unfavorably interpreted;" he therefore, to save his "reputation as a minister," prays that the Governor will disapprove of the sentence of the court, and "not inflict any further punishment" than that he has already undergone, since, independent of the fine of two hundred and eighty guilders, the desertion of his wife had cost him nearly two hundred guilders.[2] What was done with this petition does not appear.

From the report made by the commissioners and directors of the city's colony,[3] on Aug. 10, 1663, we learn that on the Delaware River it was found that "the Swedes, Fins, and other natives" had "made and erected there 110 good bouweries, stocked with about 2000 cows and oxen, 20 horses, 80 sheep, and several thousand swine." This was comparatively a good showing, and it induced the city of Amsterdam to accede to the proposition of the Dutch West India Company, that the former should, in discharge of the debt owed by the company, accept a deed for "all the country on the Delaware." In furtherance of this agreement a formal deed was executed Dec. 22, 1663, and the sway of the authorities at New Amsterdam ceased on the Delaware River. On the day after the date of this conveyance Beekman wrote to Stuyvesant that fifty farm laborers who had arrived in the ship "St. Jacob" during June of that year had been hired out to farmers, and that six or seven girls had been sent on the same vessel to cook and wash for the emigrants. He informed the director-general that "this is almost the same method as that of the English trade in servants."[4]

The authority of the city of Amsterdam over the entire Delaware River settlements was only of brief duration, and destined in a few months to be wholly overthrown. The crown of Great Britain had never acknowledged the right which the Dutch and Swedes maintained they had acquired by occupancy to the territory, and it was merely due to the intestine discord at home that the former nation had not earlier brought the mooted subject to the arbitrament of arms. Charles II., then firmly seated on the throne of England, on March 12, 1664, granted to his brother James, Duke of York and Albany, the territory now comprising the State of New York and New Jersey, and, by a subsequent grant, that of Delaware. With unusual promptness the duke fitted out an expedition, consisting of four vessels of war and four hundred and fifty men, including sailors and soldiers, which, under the command of Col. Richard Nicolls, sailed from Portsmouth, England, on May 25, 1664,[5] to reduce and occupy the Dutch possessions in North America. Sir Robert Carr, George Cartwright, and Samuel Maverick, Esquires, accompanied the expedition as commissioners appointed by the king, with power to hear and determine all military, civil, and criminal matters, and to proceed in all things for "settling the peace and security of the country," as also to adjust "boundaries between neighboring colonies and disputes between the Indians and the English."[6] The Governors of New England were instructed by the king "to join and assist them vigorously in recovering our right to those places now possessed by the Dutch, and reducing them to an entire obedience and submission to our government."[7] On the 25th of August the frigate "Guinea," the first vessel of the expedition to reach the point of destination, entered the lower bay of New Amsterdam, and a proclamation was issued guaranteeing protection to those persons who should submit to the English authority. The other vessel having arrived, after considerable negotiation, on the 9th of September, the Dutch authorities surrendered New Amsterdam to the English, the latter permitting the garrison to march out of the fort with all their arms, drums beating and colors flying. The English commissioners, when they had acquired possession of the settlement, changed the name of the place to New York, in honor of the duke. To secure control of the Delaware River territory, on the 3d (13th) of September, 1664, Sir Robert Carr was ordered to proceed thither with the frigates "Guinea" and "William" and "Nicholas" and "to reduce the same"[8] to an English province. The instructions given him, among other things, required that all planters were to retain their real and personal property unmolested by the conquerors, and Carr was particularly directed to conciliate the Swedes; that all persons were to be permitted liberty of conscience; the magistrates were to be continued in office for six months on subscribing to the oath of allegiance; the settlers were to be protected from violence in persons or estates; and the system of jurisprudence there is urged not to be disturbed for the present.[9] After a long and troublesome passage, the expedition arrived in the Delaware on the last day of September, and passed the fort at New Amstel without an exchange of shot, which was done, as Carr states, "the better to sattisfie the Sweede, who, notwithstanding the Dutches p^s-

[1] Penna. Archives, 2d series, vol. vii. p. 680.
[2] Hazard's Annals, p. 332.
[3] Penna. Archives, 2d series, vol. v. p. 470.
[4] Ib., vol. vii. p. 716.

[5] Old style; England at that time had not accepted the modern computation of time.
[6] Penna. Archives, 2d series, vol. v. pp. 507–512.
[7] Ib., 513.
[8] Hazard's Register, vol. i. p. 36; Penna. Archives, 2d series, vol. v. p. 536.
[9] Penna. Archives, 2d series, vol. v. pp. 536, 537.

wasions to yᵉ contrary, were soon our frinds." Carr then summoned the fort to surrender, and for three days negotiations were had between the opposing forces, which resulted in the magistracy of the place agreeing to surrender the town, a conclusion in which D'Hinoyossa and his soldiers declined to concur. "Whereupon," states Carr, in his official report,[1] "I landed my soldiers on Sunday morning following, & comanded ye shipps to fall downe before yᵉ Fort wiᵗʰn muskett shott, wᵗʰ directions to fire two broadesides apeace upon yᵗ Fort, then my soldiers to fall on. Which done, the soldiers neaver stoping untill they stormed yᵉ fort, and soe consequently to plundering; the seamen, noe less given to that sporte, were quickly wᵗʰin, & have gotten good store of booty; so that in such a noise and confusion noe worde of comand could be heard for sometyme; but for as many goods as I could preserve, I still Keepe intire. The loss on our part was none; the Dutch had tenn wounded and 3 killed. The fort is not tenable, although 14 gunns, and wᵗʰout a greate charge wᶜʰ unevitably must be expended, here wilbee noe staying, we not being able to keepe itt." We learn from Col. Nicolls' report to the Secretary of State[2] that the storming-party was commanded by Lieut. Carr and Ensign Hooke; and, notwithstanding the Dutch fired three volleys at them, not a man in their ranks was wounded in the assault. Sir Robert Carr, it seems, stayed aboard the "Guinea" until the fort was captured, when he landed and claimed that the property in the fort, having been won by the sword, was his and his troops. All the soldiers and many of the citizens of New Amstel were sold as slaves to Virginia by the English conquerors, and most of the negroes belonging to the Dutch settlers were distributed among the captors, as were also one hundred sheep, forty horses, sixty cows and oxen.[3] Lands and estates were confiscated, and granted by Sir Robert Carr to his officers, as well as the commanders of the vessels which took part in the expedition to the Delaware.

When the standard of Great Britain floated from the flag-staffs over the captured Dutch forts on the Hudson and the Delaware it marked the supremacy of the Anglo-Saxon race on the North American continent, and as authority was then exercised from Maine to Florida, on the Atlantic coast, by a homogeneous people, it made possible the great nation that was born to the world a century later. It was singularly fortunate, at this juncture, that the unbridled executive power in the new province was confided to so prudent and able a man as Col. Richard Nicolls proved to be, whose "administration was so wise and impartial that it enforced universal peace."[4] On the Delaware the Swedes, who had heretofore been held as a subjugated people, were in every respect benefited by the change, and even the Dutch settlers had reason to be glad that the tyrannical sway of Stuyvesant had ended. In May, 1667, Col. Francis Lovelace succeeded Col. Nicolls, and, as has been said by an able writer, "under Governor Lovelace the work of adjusting the government of the Delaware, so as to bring it slowly but steadily into conformity with English law, progressed systematically year by year, until it received an unexpected check in 1673 by the total, but temporary, suspension of English authority incident to the second conquest of the country by the Dutch."[5]

Late in the summer of 1671 the Indians had committed several atrocious murders, and it became necessary for Governor Lovelace to act cautiously but firmly to check further outrages, and to punish the culprits for the crimes already perpetrated. As preliminary to an Indian war he ordered that persons living in the outer settlements should thrash their grain and remove it and the cattle to a place of comparative safety; that no person, on pain of death, should sell powder, shot, or liquor to the savages, as also recommending the strengthening of garrisons and fortifications. Lovelace prudently had a conference with the Governor of New Jersey, to secure, if war should result, the co-operation of that province, since the murderers were said to be under that jurisdiction, and a meeting was held at New York, September 25th, and another at Elizabethtown, N. J., Nov. 7, 1671, when it was determined that it was injudicious at the then late season to begin an offensive movement against the savages, but that several companies of soldiers should be organized on the Delaware; that every man capable of bearing arms (between the ages of sixteen and sixty) should always be provided with powder and bullets fit for service, under a penalty; that block-houses should be erected at several places on the river; and also forbidding the shipment of grain unless a special license should be granted therefor. In the latter part of November the Indian sachems and William Tom, clerk of the court on the Delaware, held a council at Upland, at the house of Peter Rambo, at which the savages promised to bring the murderers to the whites within six days thereafter that they might be punished for their crimes, and if they could not bring them alive they agreed to deliver their dead bodies, as an earnest of their purpose to prevent a war between the races. It afterwards appeared that one of the guilty men escaped from his people, and could not be delivered as promised, but the other was captured. It is stated by Tom[6] that the smaller Indian, learning of the purpose of the sachems, went to the other and advised him to flee. The latter said he would go the next morning. Of the two Indians who had been dispatched to take the culprits one was a personal friend, and was loath to kill his captive, but when the latter learned that the sachems had determined he must

[1] Penna. Archives, 2d series, vol. v. p. 550. [2] Ib., 541.
[3] N. Y. Colonial Doc., vol. iii. p. 345; Vincent's Hist. of Del., p. 432.
[4] Gordon's "History of Pennsylvania," p. 30.
[5] Appendix B, Duke's Book of Laws, p. 447.
[6] Penna. Archives, 2d series, vol. v. p. 610.

die he placed his hands on his eyes and said, "Kill me" The other savage, not his friend, thereupon shot two bullets into his breast. The body was taken to Wiccaco and delivered to the whites, who transported it to New Castle, where it was hung in chains The other murderer escaped by flight The sachems faithfully notified the tribes that any of their people who should murder a white person would be similarly dealt with, and with this annunciation the cloud drifted by, greatly to the satisfaction of the magistrates on the Delaware, who were opposed to the war, because among other things they proposed to "make towns at Passayvncke, Tinnaconck, Upland, Verdrieties Hoocks, whereto the out plantacions" must retire in the event of a struggle [1]

The proscription on trade, which prevented vessels from ascending the Delaware River beyond the fort at New Castle, remained in force until the latter part of the year 1672, after which date no record remains, so far as known, of special licenses being given to trade above that point On Sept 29, 1671, Governor Lovelace authorized Capt Thomas Lewis, of the sloop "Royal Oak," "to trade and Trafic, as the said masters occasion shall require," on the Delaware above Newcastle, and no other vessel was permitted there to ship corn or provisions for exportation [2] But previous to this Capt Martin Crieger, who seems to have run a packet sloop regularly from New York to New Castle, had license to go to the latter point, and Mrs Susanna Garland was authorized to trade between those places [3] In about three weeks subsequent to the issuing of this license, permission was given the wife of Lawrence Holst to go in Capt Martin Crieger's sloop to New Castle, and "from thence to go up the River in some boat or Canoe to the Sweeds Plantations with shoes & such other of her Husband's Trade, & to return again without any maner of Lett, hinderence or molestation whatever" [4] March 20, 1672, John Schouten, in the sloop "Hope," was authorized to trade at New Castle and parts adjacent, while the same day John Garland, of New York, and Susanna, his wife, were licensed to "Traffick with the Indyans" on the river above New Castle [5] Mr Christoph Hoogland, Sept 28, 1672, was licensed to go on Criegers' sloop to New Castle, with the privilege to trade on the river Capt Crieger, who was a "Dutchman," seems to have run the packet between the places named for more than ten years, for in July, 1682, Deputy Governor Markham complained that Capt Crieger at New Castle had permitted Lord Baltimore the use of astronomical instruments, which were shipped by Markham at New York and intended only for him [6]

War having been declared in 1672 by England and France against the United Belgic Provinces, on the 30th of July, 1673, the colony of New York, with its dependencies on the Delaware River settlements, was recaptured by the Dutch fleet under Admiral Evertsen, and Capt. Anthony Colve was commissioned Governor-General of "New Netherlands with all its Appendencies" Peter Alricks was appointed commander on the Delaware, with instructions that the right of private property should not be disturbed, nor should that belonging to persons holding office under the Duke of York be confiscated where the party took the oath of allegiance to the Dutch government Freedom of conscience was assured to those who were followers of the true Christian religion according to the Synod of Dordrecht, but the new commander was instructed not to permit "any other sects attempting anything contrary thereto" [7] By the terms of the treaty of peace, Feb 9, 1674, the province reverted to the Duke of York, and English authority was re-established on Oct 1, 1674, when Maj Edmund Androsse, as governor, received possession of Fort James at New York, and appointed Capt Edmund Carr commander on the Delaware On Sept 25, 1676, the Duke of York's laws were promulgated as the rule of conduct on the Delaware River, and courts in conformity therewith were established, one of which was "above att Uplands," where quarterly sessions were directed to be held on the second Tuesday of the month

Early in the year 1675 the first member of the Society of Friends known to have resided within the boundaries of Delaware County purchased an estate at Upland Robert Wade, on March 21, 1675, bought the tract of ground known as Printzdorp from "Justina Armguard, alias vpo Papegay," for eighty pounds sterling,[8] whereon he subsequently erected the famous "Essex House"

---

[1] Penna. Archives, 2d series, vol vii p 756

[2] Ib., vol. v pp 605-607

[3] Ib., pp. 611, 612 [4] Ib., p 613 [5] Ib, 628

[6] *Penna. Mag of Hist.*, vol vi p 429

[7] Penna Archives 2d series, vol v p 636

[8] Recital in Deed from Jonathan Dickinson Sargeant and William Rotch Wister trustees under the will of Albanus C Logan, deceased, to John M Broomall, Deed Book L, No 2, page 673, etc., Recorder's office, Media, Pa The date of the conveyance to Wade is of record, 1673, but that there is a clerical error is evident from the following letter, which is published in 'A Further Account of New Jersey, in an Abstract of Letters written from thence by Several Inhabitants there Resident London, Printed in the year 1676," pages 6 and 7

"Dear and Loving Wife

"Having now an opportunty to let thee understand of my welfare, through the great mercy of God &c, and as to the other place it is as good or healthful place as man can desire to live in, and here is plenty enough of all provisions, and good English Wheat and Mault, plenty of Fish and Fowl, Indeed here is no want of anything, but honest people to Inhabit it, there is Land enough purchased of the Indians for ten times so many as we were and these Indians here are very quiet and Peacable Indians, In New England they are at Wars with the Indians, and the news is, they have cut off a great many of them, but in this place, the Lord is making way to exalt his name and truth, for it is said by those that live here abouts, that within these few years, here were five Indians for one now, and these that be are very willing to sell their land to the English, and had John Fenwick done wisely, we had not been disperst, but I hope it may all work for the best, And dear Wife, I hope thou will be well satisfied to come and live here, where we may live very quietly and Peacably, where we shall have no vexation, not tearing nor rending what we have from us, I have bought a plantation by the advice and consent of some Friends, upon which there is a very good house, a great deal of Out-housing, Orchards, and Gardens ready planted, and well fenced, I do intend (if God permit) after the

The Essex House[1] stood on the site of the present brick dwelling at the northwest corner of Second and Penn Streets, Chester. It was a story and a half in height, its southeast gable fronting the river, the rear or southwest side facing Concord Avenue, and its front, with a commodious porch, extended the entire length of the building to Chester Creek. Almost one hundred and ten feet southeastwardly from it stood the noted trees under which Penn landed, seven years after Wade became the owner of the estate. In the journal of the Labadists, Dankers and Sluyter, in 1679, particular mention is made of these trees. "We have nowhere seen," they record, "so many vines together as we saw here, which had been planted for the purpose of shading the walks on the river side in between the trees."[2] It seems that Wade, after the purchase of the estate from Mrs. Pappegoya, returned to Great Britain, whence, accompanied by his wife, Lydia, he sailed in the ship "Griffin," which arrived in the Delaware on the 23d of Ninth month (November), 1675. It was in that year, we are told, that William Edmundson, a public Friend from Ireland, made a second visit to America, and while he and his party journeyed, swimming their horses across the river at Trenton and the intermediate creeks, and camping out in the woods at night, when on the way to "Delaware Town, on the west side of the river Delaware," "there came up a Finland man, well-horsed, who spoke English. He soon perceived what they were, and gave them an account of several of their friends. His house was as far as they could ride that day, there he conducted them and lodged them kindly. The next morning being the first day of the week, they went to Upland (since named Chester), where a few Friends were met at Robert Wade's house. After meeting was over they took boat and went to Salem, where they met with John Fenwick and several families of Friends, who, with those at Chester, had come from England in that year with John Fenwick."[3] It is, however, nowise certain that the Essex House had been built when the first recorded meeting of Friends in Pennsylvania was held at Wade's dwelling at Upland, but that it had been erected before 1679, the statement of the Labadist ministers, already quoted as a note, conclusively establishes.

Governor Andross, on Sept. 25, 1676, promulgated the Duke of York's laws by proclamation, declaring that they "Bee likewise in force and practiced in this River and Precincts," excepting such ordinances as were peculiarly applicable to Long Island. At the same time he ordered courts to be held at three places on the river. That at Upland to be a Court of Quarter Sessions, and to begin on the second Tuesday of the month.[4]

The records of these early courts are historically interesting, for in them is found the story of the gradual growth of the English system of jurisprudence in the State, which will be related elsewhere in this work.

On March 4, 1681, Charles II. of England signed the great charter which conveyed to William Penn, in lieu of the sum of sixteen thousand pounds, which the king owed to Admiral William Penn, the enormous tract of land now known as Pennsylvania, and from that period our early annals become more interesting, for from that time we may date the actual founding of this great commonwealth. Almost immediately thereafter Penn sent his first cousin, William Markham, to the colony as his Deputy Governor. It is presumed that he came over in the ship "John and Sarah," from London, commanded by Henry Smith, which was the first to arrive here after the grant was made to Penn. Certain it is that Markham was in New York about June 15, 1681,[5] and previous to the 21st of that month he had presented his commission to the authorities at New York, for on that date the Governor and Council issued a proclamation announcing the royal grant and commanding all persons to recognize Markham as Governor of Pennsylvania. On August 3d following he was at Upland and had assumed the reins of power on the Delaware, for on the date last mentioned his Council took and subscribed to the oath of office. The members of the

Harvest is gotten in, to come to England for thee, and I hope thou wilt be willing to come, seeing here are several of thy Neighbours whom thou knowest well, as Richard Guy and his Wife and William Hancock and his Wife, and many others, and here is an honest Friend with me, that would have a fourth part of the Land &c., And so hoping these lines may find thee in good health, as through the great mercy and goodness of God I have never been better in health.

"My love to Richard Green, he desired me to send him some account of the Country, which to the best of my knowledge I will do, as to Buildings here is little until more People come over, for the Inhabitants that were here did generally Build their own houses, though after a mean manner, for they fell down Trees, and split them in Parts, and so make up a sorry House, &c. But here is Earth enough that will make very good Bricks, and Stone enough of severall sorts, as four that will stroke fire, which may make millstones, or what a man will put them to, they make their Lime of oyster shells, here is a good Land and a Healthful and Plentiful Country, here is no Tanner in all the River, but some Tann their Hides themselves, after their own manner. Here is good Oak enough, here is Hemp and Flax, good Water, and the Ground will bear anything that Groweth in England, and with less Pains and trouble, with my dear Love to thee I rest thy loving Husband

"ROBERT WADE.

"Delaware River, the place called
Upland, the 2d of the 2d month,
1675."

[1] In "A Journal of a Voyage to New York in 1679-80," Memoirs of Long Island Historical Society, vol. i. p. 183, it is recorded: "It was late before we left here and we therefore had time to look around a little and see the remains of the residence of Madame Popegay, who had her dwelling here when she left Tinicum." The diary the preceding day mentions that Robert Wade had brought the travelers to Upland after dark, and "we went to the house of the Quaker who had brought us down." So that there can be no doubt that the Essex House was never owned by Mrs. Pappegoya.

[2] "Journal of a Voyage to New York in 1679-80." Memoirs of Long Island Historical Society, vol. i. p. 183.

[3] Smith's "History of the Province of Pennsylvania." Hazard's Register, vol. vi. p. 182.

[4] Penna. Archives, 2d series, vol. iii. p. 783.

[5] A letter to William Penn from New York, dated June 25, 1681, says: "This is to acquaint thee that about ten daies since here arrived Francis Richardson with thy Deputy."—*Penn. Mag. of Hist.*, vol. vi. p. 175.

Governor's Council were Robert Wade, Morgan Drewt, William Woodmanse, William Warner, Thomas Fairman, James Sandilands, William Clayton, Otto Ernst Cock, and Lasse Cock, almost every one residents of the territory now Delaware County. "The proceedings of their first session were kept secret and little is known, except that the government of the new province was established with the capital at Upland, where we find Markham holding court on the 30th of November, 1681."[1] Markham made his residence at the Essex House,[2] and there the first summons from Penn, calling a General Assembly, were written and proclaimed, for, as is well known, the proprietary was Wade's guest on his first coming to the province in 1682.

CHAPTER III.

THE CIRCULAR BOUNDARY LINE BETWEEN DELAWARE COUNTY AND THE STATE OF DELAWARE.

THAT Lord Baltimore, long before the royal grant to Penn, during the Dutch ascendency on the Delaware, had made demand upon the Hollanders for all the land lying to the south of the fortieth degree north latitude is fully attested by the published records, but inasmuch as his representatives never, so far as we have knowledge, personally came to any locality in Pennsylvania, the story of that disputed territorial authority at that time is properly the subject-matter of the history of the State of Delaware, and does not come within the scope of this work.

The controversy respecting the proper adjustment of the boundary line between the territories of Lord Baltimore and William Penn was a long and bitter struggle, which, descending from father to son, covered nearly a century in tedious and expensive litigation before it was finally set at rest by the decree of Lord Chancellor Hardwick and the establishment of the noted Mason and Dixon line in conformity therewith. While the southern boundary of Delaware County presents a circular course extending the State of Delaware several miles at its northern limit beyond the straight line which elsewhere forms the southern boundary of Pennsylvania, that circle constitutes historically no part of the Mason and Dixon survey, which, during the Missouri Compromise debates in 1820, was made so familiar to the nation by John Randolph, who, in his remarks, constantly referred to it as the imaginary geographical line which marked the division between the free and slave States. Nearly four years previous to the grant of the territory to Penn, for the convenience of the then settlers on the Delaware, an amicable adjustment of the line dividing New Castle and Upland (afterward Chester County) was made. At a court held at Upland, Nov. 12, 1678, this proceeding is recorded as follows:[3]

"The Limits and Division between this and New Castle county, were this day agreed upon and settled By this Court and Mr. John Moll president of New Castle Court To be as followeth, vizt.

"This County of Upland to begin from ye north syde of oele franseus Creeke, otherwise Called Steenkill Lying in the boght above ye verdrietige hoeck, and from the said Creek over to ye singletree point on the East syde of the River."

This division, Edward Armstrong, in his valuable note to the "Record of Upland Court," has made intelligible to the modern reader. The creek, he tells us, at the time when the boundary line between the two counties was adjusted, known as Oele Francens, was at a late date called Streen or Stoney Creek, and is now recognized as Quarryville Creek, crossing the Philadelphia, Wilmington and Baltimore Railroad three and three-quarter miles below the mouth of Naaman's Creek, in Brandywine Hundred, New Castle Co., Del. "Verdrietige hoeck," or corner of land, was also called Trinity Hook, lying between Shellpot (a corruption of "Skelldpadde," the Swedish for "turtle") and Stoney Creeks. "Verdrietige" was a term derived from the Dutch "verdrietigh," signifying "grievous" or "tedious," owing to the character of the navigation in approaching that point, while "Singletree Point" is now "Old Man's Point," on the New Jersey shore, one mile below the mouth of "Old Man Creek."

The charter or patent of Charles II. to William Penn, bearing date the 4th day of March, 1681, as also in the proclamation of the king, April 2d of the same year, in defining the territorial boundaries of Penn's provinces, mentions the circular line as "on the South by a circle drawn at twelve miles distance from New Castle northwards and westwards into the beginning of the fortieth degree of northern latitude and then by a streight line westwards to the limits of longitude above mentioned."

After Penn had acquired jurisdiction of the territory by virtue of the royal grant, he dispatched his cousin, Capt. William Markham, as his Deputy Governor, to represent him in the province. The latter, in a letter to Penn, dated New York, June 25, 1681, says, "This is to acquaint thee that about ten daies since here arrived Francis Richardson with thy Deputy," and on the 3d day of August, 1681, Markham was in Upland, as stated in the preceding chapter.

In the latter part of August, 1681, Capt. William Markham, Deputy Governor of Pennsylvania, who had been intrusted by the king with a letter to Charles, Lord Baltimore, requesting the latter to "appoint with all convenient speed some person or persons who may in connection with the agent or agents of ye said William Penn make a true division & separation of ye said Province of Maryland and Pennsil-

[1] Duke of York's Book of Laws, p. 471.

[2] Sept. 23, 1682, Markham lived there, for he says, "Lord Baltimore was at my lodging at Robert Wade's."—*Penn. Mag. of Hist.*, vol. vi. p. 430.

[3] Record of Upland Court, page 119.

vania according to the bounds and degree of northern latitude expressed in our letters patent, &c," went to Maryland in order to settle as quickly as might be the controversy respecting the boundary line between the two provinces Markham also took with him a letter from William Penn to Lord Baltimore, urging the prompt adjustment of the vexatious dispute The lord proprietary of Maryland received Penn's representative with marked kindness, and as the latter was suffering from indisposition, induced by the intensely warm weather, Baltimore invited Markham to his house on the Patuxent River, where the latter became dangerously ill, and for nearly a month was incapable of being moved On his recovery he determined to return to Pennsylvania, but before his departure Baltimore and he arranged to meet at Upland on the 16th of October following, where observations should then be taken to ascertain precisely where the fortieth degree of northern latitude was, and thus adjust the disputed point of territorial boundaries Markham also promised to borrow from Col Lewis Morris, of New York, the necessary instruments for making the astronomical observations Unexpected, the passage of the vessel up Chesapeake Bay to its head was long and tedious, so that much of the time Markham had intended for his journey to New York was thereby consumed Hence, from the head of the bay, he addressed a letter to Lord Baltimore, Sept 25, 1681, requesting that the meeting should be deferred until the 26th of the same month When the Deputy Governor reached Upland he was again taken ill, and thereupon he wrote to Lord Baltimore, this time informing him that his physical condition was such that it would be impossible for him to attend to the adjustment of the boundary line until the following spring This letter was forwarded, but before it reached its destination Markham received a communication from Lord Baltimore, dated Oct 10, 1681, in which the latter stated that he could not come to Upland that year "for fear of the frost," which might intercept navigation, but inasmuch as the king's wishes in this matter have not been complied with, his lordship would place on Markham the responsibility of not meeting that year In the mean while both parties to the controversy maintained that his adversary was trespassing on his domain, and so convinced was William Penn that this was the case, that on Sept 16, 1681, he addressed letters to six of the most extensive land-owners in Maryland, whose possessions were located within the debatable territory, stating that he had no doubts that their estates were within his provinces, under his grant from the crown, and notified them to pay no taxes or assessments in obedience to any order of the lord proprietary or laws of Maryland This claim on the part of Penn caused many of the residents of the latter colony to resist the public levies, and so general was this sentiment in Baltimore and Cecil Counties that the military was ordered to assist the sheriffs in collecting the taxes Lord Baltimore, in his account of the difficulty respecting the boundaries, states that one of Penn's commissioners, William Haige, a Quaker, had taken astronomical observations at the head of the bay (Chesapeake), and that he was very much dissatisfied at the result he obtained Haige afterward went to Patuxent, where, in an interview with Baltimore, the latter charged him with having "taken some observations at Elk river, for his private satisfaction," which Haige acknowledged he had done, but said the instrument he had used was so small that nothing decisive could be arrived at.

The winter of 1681 passed without any definite action being had until May 14, 1682, when Lord Baltimore wrote to Markham, desiring to meet him at Augustine Herman's plantation[1] on June 10th, to adjust boundaries Markham, who was compelled to meet the Indians, to make payment for lands he had purchased from them, could not meet the Maryland commissioners at the time Baltimore had designated, since the Indians had deferred their annual hunt, nor was he ready, inasmuch that he was unable to procure the use of Col Morris' instrument until he had personally visited New York and entered security for its safe return For the latter purpose he went to New York on the 26th of May, 1682, and before he started he sent a message to Lord Baltimore, apprising him of his journey thither, and requested that the proposed meeting might be deferred until his return Baltimore, however, dispatched commissioners to represent him at the time fixed by him, and by them sent a letter to Markham, stating that they were fully qualified to act in his behalf, and trusting that they would be met by parties similarly commissioned on the part of Penn The Maryland commissioners, when they reached Herman's plantation, feigned to be surprised at not meeting Markham's representatives, and on the day designated by Baltimore (June 10, 1682) addressed a letter to Markham, which was delivered to the Deputy Governor, then in New York, by George Goforth In the communication the writers requested Markham to send the instrument he had promised to borrow from Col Morris, as also to dispatch duly qualified persons to meet with them The Maryland commissioners tarried several days at Herman's, ostensibly to await the coming of Markham's representatives, but in the mean while employed themselves in making astronomical observations[2]

---

[1] A tract of four thousand acres, still known as Bohemia Manor, Cecil Co, Md, on the east bank of Elk River, which was patented June 19, 1662, by Lord Baltimore to Augustine Herman, in consideration of the latter having undertaken to prepare a map of Maryland This chart was engraved and published by Faithorne, in London, in 1672, and is very accurate so far as it delineates the western shore of the Chesapeake and the peninsula lying between the Chesapeake and Delaware Bays (Johnston's "History of Cecil County, Md.," page 37)

[2] Extract of a letter to the Ld Baltimore from the commissioners appointed by his lordship to settle the bounds between Maryland and Pennsylvania, June 17, 1682 (published in *Pennsylvania Magazine of History and Biography*, vol vi p. 418, note)

"Wee have taken three severall observations & in all of them have not

The letter from the commissioners to Markham, as before stated, was delivered to him in New York, and he immediately procured the instrument, which he sent in a sloop to New Castle, and made his way homeward by land to Burlington, where he took a boat for the remaining distance. Pending these movements on the part of the Deputy Governor of Pennsylvania, the Maryland commissioners had gone to New Castle,—out of "a curiosity to see yt Towne," as they said,—and when they got there they learned that the sloop having Col. Morris' astronomical instrument was at the landing. They, aided by the entreaties of the Dutch inhabitants of the place, persuaded Capt. Criger, himself a Dutchman, to permit them to make use of the instrument. On Tuesday, June 27, 1682, it being a very clear day, the commissioners made several observations, and found that town was in thirty-nine degrees forty odd minutes north latitude. The next day Markham went to New Castle, where he learned that the Maryland commissioners had left the place the very night of the day they had used the instrument which the Governor of Pennsylvania had had so much trouble to procure. The following morning Markham sent William Haige to Herman's plantation, trusting that the Marylanders had gone thither, but before he got there they had renewed their journey southward. Markham thereupon wrote to Baltimore explaining his absence, and received in reply an intimation that in September he (Baltimore) proposed to send his commissioners again to meet him, and perhaps he might personally accompany them. On September 12th, Lord Baltimore sailed from Patuxent, reaching the Elk River on the 19th of the same month. There was no accommodation for his suite at Herman's, and after he had dispatched a message to Markham, who was then at Burlington, Lord Baltimore, with a number of persons, went to New Castle, from which place, on the evening of the 23d of September, he embarked in boats for Upland, reaching the latter hamlet that night. He lodged at the dwelling of Robert Wade, where Markham then dwelt. The following morning (Sunday) Markham (who had been informed that Baltimore was at New Castle, had hastened his return to meet him, and had reached home the same night that the Marylanders came to Upland) called on Lord Baltimore. The latter was accompanied by Col. Corsie, Maj. Seawell, Maj. Sawyer, four commissioners, and forty men "armed with carbines, pistols, and swords." The lord proprietary of Maryland, although Markham stated that it was the Sabbath, and not a day for the transaction of business, requested that his own as well as Col. Morris' instruments should be set up, so that it would be known how they agreed. Markham at length consented, it being understood that the degree of latitude should be ascertained the following day; but while the Pennsylvanians were absent one of Lord Baltimore's attendants took an observation, and reported that he found the latitude of Upland was thirty-nine degrees forty-five minutes. Next morning Baltimore desired to go farther up the river, as far as the fortieth degree, and, that ascertained, to follow that line westward as the boundary of the province. Markham, however, declined this proposition, stating that he (Baltimore) could have no claim on the river twelve miles northward of New Castle, because the king's grant to William Penn fully covered all the land on the Delaware above that point. Baltimore replied that he had nothing to do with the grant to Penn, but would be guided by the grant the king had made to him, many years before Penn's charter. The dispute thereupon waxed warm, during which Baltimore declared that he did not propose to bring the matter before the king and his Council, but designed to take his own wherever he found it; that if, as Markham asserted, New Castle was the centre of the circle, and a sweep therefrom must be had before the beginning of the direct line westward was established, "his Majesty must have long compasses." The interview terminated by Markham refusing to permit Lord Baltimore to ascend the river to make observations, and a demand from the latter that the Deputy Governor of Pennsylvania should furnish his reasons for his action in writing, a request which the latter immediately complied with.[1] The two Governors, however, agreed to meet at New Castle the next day, so that the point of forty degrees might be determined at the head of Chesapeake Bay.

In the afternoon of the 20th of September Lord Baltimore left Upland for New Castle, but before he stepped into the boat at the landing he spoke in a

differed two minutes & wee find Mr. Augustin Herman's house to lye in the latitude of 39d & 45m so that your Lordship has 15m. yet from hence due North which will go not farr short of Upland & this differs very little from their own observation lately taken as wee are credibly informed wee have used our endeavors in letting all here know of your Lordship's Desire to have the bounds determined & all seem much satisfied with your Lordship's proceedings much blaiming Mr. Markham that after so many flourishes he should bee thus backward; Wee question but ye Lines will fall to answer yor Lordship's expectacons & our true endeavors shall not be wanting to give your Lordship satisfaction."

[1] This letter is published in 6 *Penn. Mag. of History and Biography*, p. 432:

"*To His Excell'y My Lord Baltimore:*

"Whereas your lordship hath been pleased to Desire a reason of me under my Hand why I concurr not with your lordshipp in Laying out the bounds of this province Pennsilvania upon Delaware river: My Lord This is my reason that as I received all yt part of The river Delaware begiuning 12 Miles above New Castle Towne and so Upwards, ffrom The Government of New York which is according to The Express words of his Majesty's Letters Patent To our Proprietory Wm. Penn Esqr I most humbly Conceive That I am not to be accoumptable to any other person Than his Majesty or Royall Highness ffor any part of This Province laying upon Delaware River & soe bounded but if your Lordshipp be willing to lay out ye bounds betwixt This Province and your Lordshipp's Laying towards Chesapeake Bay and The rivers on That side I am ready and willing to wayte upon your Lordship for yt end & purpose.

"Upland in Pennsylvania 7ber 29th 1682.

"I am my Lord your Lordshipps most Humble Servt

"Wm. Markham."

loud voice to Markham, who was present, together with a number of the residents of the place "You are sensible, Capt Markham, that by an observation taken yesterday that this plantation is in thirty-nine degrees forty-seven minutes and some seconds, and must therefore be sensible that I am here about twelve miles to the southward of the degree of forty, which is my north bound as the same is Mr Penn's south bound Therefore, afore you and all the rest here present, I lay claim to this place and as far further as the degree of forty will reach" To this claim of Lord Baltimore, Markham made no response, but with courteous attention conducted the former to the boat, and thus they parted Baltimore, as he descended the river, halted at Marcus Hook, where he landed, and, going to each of the dwellings at that place, prohibited the residents from paying any more quit-rents to Penn, as the land did not come within his territory, but was part of Maryland, and that he, Baltimore, would return suddenly and take possession of his own This notification, particularly as the one who made it was attended with the pomp and circumstance of power, caused the utmost consternation among the settlers, who repaired to Upland the next day, just as Markham—the instrument being placed on board a boat—was about starting on horseback with his attendants for New Castle, and so great was the excitement consequent on Lord Baltimore's unexpected claim that Markham called his Council immediately together, and they decided that the Deputy Governor must remain at Upland "to quiet the disturbed people" Whereupon Markham wrote to Lord Baltimore that he could not meet him at New Castle under the circumstances [1]

Although the proprietaries of the two provinces could not adjust their dispute, for the expediency of the inhabitants the court at Chester, on March 14, 1683, declared that Naaman's Creek should be the boundary line between the two counties, and so generally was this recognized, that Thomas Holme, surveyor-general under Penn, in his "map of the improved part of the Province of Pennsylvania in America," observes this division

Nevertheless there was some confusion still existing, hence ten years later, in 1693, a petition was presented by some of the inhabitants of Chester County to the Governor and Council, stating that they were seriously inconvenienced because of there being no authoritatively recognized line between that county and New Castle The Council after discussing the topic, on the 9th of August, 1693,—

"*Resolved*, That for the present convenience of the government, and not for an absolute and final proprietarie division, but that the inhabitants on the borders of both counties may Know to which of the two to pay their levies, taxes, etc., and perform their other countie services, the bounds of New Castle county shall extend northward to the mouth of Naaman's creek and upwards along the southwest side of the Northmost branch (excluding the townships of Concord and Bethel) and not to extend backwards of the said northmost branch above the said two townships"

For eight years the boundary thus established seemed to meet in a measure the demands of the sparsely-settled country immediately effected thereby, although the constantly-growing disposition on the part of the inhabitants of the three lower counties (now the State of Delaware) to separate from the territory comprising the commonwealth of Pennsylvania was often manifested during the interval, and at length culminated in a petition from the Assembly to Penn, 20th of Seventh month, 1701, in which they urge "that the division line between the counties of New Castle and Chester be ascertained allowing the boundary according to the proprietary's letters patent from the King" Penn, then in Philadelphia, in response to this petition, replied, "It is my own inclination, and I desire the representatives of New Castle and Chester Counties forthwith, or before they leave town, to attend me about the time and manner of doing it" In conformity with the wish of Penn a conference was held, which resulted in a warrant being issued 28th of Eighth month, 1701, to Isaac Taylor, surveyor of Chester County, and Thomas Pierson, surveyor of New Castle County, requiring them to meet the magistrates of the two counties, or any three of them, and,—"In their presence to admeasure and survey from the town of New Castle the distance of twelve miles in a right line up ye said river and from ye said distance according to ye King's letters patent and deeds from the Duke and ye said circular line to be well-marked two-thirds parts of ye semi-circle"

The surveyor designated made report that, on the 4th day of Tenth month (December), 1701, in the presence of Cornelius Empson, Richard Halliwell, and John Richardson, justices of New Castle County, and Caleb Pusey, Philip Roman, and Robert Pyle, justices of Chester County, they ran the division lines, beginning at the point of the radial line, which was selected by the magistrates "at the end of the horse dyke next to the town of New Castle" Thence they measured due north twelve miles, the termination of that distance being "a white oak marked with twelve notches standing on the west side of Brandywine Creek, in the lands of Samuel Helm," thence, eastwardly, "circularly changing our course from the east southward one degree at the end of every sixty-seven perches, which is the chord of one degree to a twelve miles radius, and at the end of forty-three chords we came to the Delaware River, on the upper side of Nathaniel Lampley's old house at Chichester" The surveyors then returned to the marked white oak on Helm's land and ran a westwardly course, changing, as before, "our course one degree from the west-southward at the end of every sixty-seven perches, . . until we had extended seventy-seven chords, which, being added to the forty-three chords, make two-thirds part

[1] For fuller particulars of the interview between Baltimore and Markham, see 6 *Penn Mag of History and Biography*, p 412

of the semi-circle to a twelve-mile radius, all which said circular lines being well marked with three notches on each side of the trees to a marked hickory standing near the western branch of Christiana Creek."

The cost of the survey to the county of Chester is exhibited in the annexed interesting report of the Grand Jury:

"CHESTER the 24 of the 12 month 1701-2.

"We of the Grand Jury for the county having duly considered and carefully adjusted an account of charges contracted by running a circular line dividing this county from the county of New Castle and settling the boundaries and having duly and deliberately debated every article of the said account, do allow of the sum of twenty-six pounds nine shillings due to be paid by the county for said work.

"JAMES COWPER, *Foreman*."

Although there is a general impression that Mason and Dixon afterwards ran the circular line, that is a popular error; nor is it true, as stated in an excellent article published in a leading American periodical, that "in the difficulty of tracing this circle was the origin of the work of Mason and Dixon."[1] The survey of Isaac Taylor and Thomas Pierson, in 1701, before described, is the only one ever made of the circular boundary between Pennsylvania and Delaware. The act of May 28, 1715,[2] providing "for corroborating the circular line between the counties of Chester and New Castle," seems to have been a dead letter from its passage, and was repealed July 21, 1719.

It is an interesting fact, in view of the ease with which the justices, in 1701, arrived at the point in New Castle where the twelve-mile radius should begin,—"the end of the horse dyke next to the town of New Castle,"—to recall the manner in which the commissioners of Maryland, in 1750, attempted to reach a like starting-point. In the diary of John Watson,[3] one of the surveyors on behalf of Pennsylvania on that occasion, he mentions that the map of the Maryland officials had a puncture in it at a designated place within the limits of the town of New Castle from which they contended the radius of twelve miles should be measured. Watson subsequently learned that this point had been ascertained in this wise: "The commissioners of Maryland had constructed an exact plan of the town of New Castle upon a piece of paper, and then carefully pared away the edges of the draught until no more than the draught was left, when, sticking a pin through it, they suspended it thereby in different places until they found a place whereby it might be suspended horizontally, which point or place they accepted as the centre of gravity," hence the centre of the town.

As the notches made by Taylor and Pierson to mark the circular line in the lapse of time were obliterated, thereafter to be recalled only in vague and uncertain traditions, and as the story that on the re-examination, in 1768, by Mason and Dixon, of the line surveyed in 1751 by Emory, Jones, Parsons, Shankland, and Killen, that the "middle stone," planted by the latter surveyors at the southwestern boundary of the State of Delaware, was found overthrown by money-diggers, who believed because of its armorial bearing that it had been set up by Capt. Kidd to mark the spot where part of his ill-gotten treasures were secreted, had shifted its location many times, the impression became general that the stone planted by Mason and Dixon to mark the intersection of the three States had also been removed. Hence, in 1849, the Legislature of Pennsylvania authorized the Governor to appoint a commissioner to act in conjunction with similar commissioners representing the States of Delaware and Maryland to determine the points of intersection, and to place a mark or monument thereon to indicate its location. On behalf of Pennsylvania, Joshua P. Eyre, of Delaware County, was appointed commissioner. George Read Riddle represented Delaware, and H. G. S. Key, Maryland. The commissioners made application to the Secretary of War to detail Lieut.-Col. James R. Graham, of the corps of Topographical Engineers, who had acquired considerable prominence in adjusting the boundary of the United States and Mexico, to make the necessary surveys. On Oct. 30, 1849, the commissioners assembled at Annapolis, Md., where they had access to the notes of Mason and Dixon, as well as the agreement dated May 10, 1732, between Charles, Lord Baltimore, and the heirs and successors of William Penn, as also the subsequent agreement between Frederick, Lord Baltimore, and Thomas and Richard Penn, surviving heirs of William Penn, dated July 4, 1760, and the decree of Lord Chancellor Hardwick, May 15, 1750, which was the basis of the final settlement of the long controversy.

The commissioners, we are told by the accomplished historians of Chester County,[4] at the northeast corner of Maryland—the commencement of the Mason and Dixon east and west line—found that the stone planted in 1768 to designate the spot, in a deep ravine, on the margin of a small brook near its source, was missing. That several years before the commissioners visited the place it had fallen to the earth, and had been taken away and used as a chimney-piece by a resident in the neighborhood, who, with some slight propriety, had driven a stake into the ground to mark the spot where the stone once stood. The commissioners at that point erected a new stone with the letter P on the north and east sides, and M on the south and west sides. At the junction of the three States the commissioners set up a triangular prismatic post of cut granite, eighteen inches wide on each side and seven feet in length. It was inserted four and a half feet in the ground, and occupies the exact spot where the

[1] *Harper's Magazine*, vol. liii. p. 549.

[2] Dallas' "Laws of Pennsylvania," vol. i. p. 105.

[3] This diary in good preservation is owned by the Historical Society of Pennsylvania, to whom it was presented by the late William D. Gilpin, of Philadelphia. Gilpin stated that he found it among some old papers which had been sent to his mill as waste.

[4] Futhey and Cope's "History of Chester County, Pa.," p. 160.

old unmarked stone placed there by Mason and Dixon was found by Col Graham in 1849, who had the old boundary mark buried alongside of its more modern and pretentious fellow This new stone is marked with the letters M, P, and D, on the sides facing respectively towards the States of Maryland, Pennsylvania, and Delaware On the north side, below the letter P, are the names of the commissioners in deep-cut letters, with the date 1849

Col Graham, in his report, says,—

"At the meridian or middle point of the arc, corresponding to the length of the chord as we actually found it, and at the distance of one hundred and eighteen and four-tenths feet perpendicular from the middle point of said chord, a post of cut granite six feet long was inserted in the ground four and a half feet of its length This stone squares seventeen by fourteen inches It is rounded on the west side to indicate that it is on the curve, and on the east side the date 1849 is cut in deep figures

"The circular boundary between Pennsylvania and Delaware from the point of junction of the three States to river Delaware being yet unmarked, and a number of citizens residing near the common border being in doubt whether as to which State they belonged, the survey was conducted with such precision as to enable us to describe that boundary correctly, as will appear upon our map, for a distance of about three and three quarter miles northwestward from junction We have determined the distance by computation at which a due east line from northeast corner of Maryland will cut that circular boundary, and find it to be four thousand and thirty six feet, or seven sixty six of a mile We have also computed the angle with the meridian at the said northeast corner made by a line drawn from thence to the spire of the court-house at New Castle, and find it to be 70 degrees, 20 minutes, and 45 seconds east of south At the distance of 3786 feet, measured by the said line from the aforesaid northeast corner, this line will intersect the circular boundary "[1]

As stated before, no survey of the circular line between Delaware and Pennsylvania has ever been made since that run by Isaac Taylor and Thomas Pierson, in 1701, and it may be asserted without fear of contradiction that no person at this time knows exactly where the line dividing New Castle County, Del, and Delaware County, Pa, is, and where it enters the river

CHAPTER IV

WILLIAM PENN'S FIRST VOYAGE TO HIS PROVINCE IN 1682—THE CHANGE OF THE NAME UPLAND TO CHESTER, AND THE REASON IT WAS MADE

As stated in the preceding chapter, as soon as Penn had acquired title to the three lower counties,[2]—the present State of Delaware,—he made his arrangements to visit his colony, and so energetically did he act that in less than one week after the execution of the deeds by the duke on the 30th day of the Sixth month (August,—for the Friends of those days computed the year as beginning on the 1st of March), he sailed for Pennsylvania from Deal in the ship "Welcome," of three hundred tons burden, Robert Greenaway, commander, accompanied by about one hundred companions, mostly Friends, from Sussex, England The voyage was lengthy (smallpox having broken out on the vessel, of which disease thirty of the emigrants died on the passage), and on the 27th day of October, 1682, the "Welcome" stopped at New Castle, where Penn landed, and took possession of the three lower counties with all the pomp and circumstance usual at that time in the formal transfer of estates It is known he stayed at New Castle all night, and the next day the vessel stood up the river and cast anchor off the mouth of Chester Creek, opposite the house of Robert Wade, for, as is stated in the manuscript book of Evan Oliver, a passenger on the "Welcome," "We arrived at Upland in pensilvania in America, ye 28th of ye 8th month, '82 "[3]

Dr Smith, in referring to the landing of Penn, says, "He landed at Upland, but the place was to bear that familiar name no more forever Without reflection, Penn determined that the name of the place should be changed Turning round to his friend Pearson, one of his own society, who had accompanied him in the ship 'Welcome,' he said, 'Providence has brought us here safe Thou hast been the companion of my perils What wilt thou that I should call this place?' Pearson said, 'Chester,' in remembrance of the city from whence he came William Penn replied that it should be called Chester, and that when he divided the land into counties one of them should be called by the same name Thus for a mere whim the name of the oldest town, the name of the whole settled part of the province, the name that would have a place in the affections of a large majority of the inhabitants of the new province, was effaced to gratify the caprice or vanity of a friend All great men occasionally do little things '"[4]

Although Dr. Smith cites Clarkson's Life of Penn and Hazard's Annals in support of this statement, it will not bear investigation We know that Penn issued his proclamation three weeks after his arrival at Chester to the several sheriffs of the counties of Chester, Philadelphia, and Bucks, as well as the three lower counties, to hold an election for a General Assembly, to convene at "Upland " The original letter of Penn, now in the Historical Society of Pennsyl-

[1] Col Graham states that the want of a proper demarkation of boundaries between States is always a source of inconvenience and frequently of great trouble to parties residing therein, who are uncertain as to which State their taxes and personal services, jury duty and the like, are due He tells us that they found that William Smith, who had served as a member of the Legislature of Delaware, resided fully half a mile within Pennsylvania, measured on the shortest direction from his dwelling-house to the circular boundary

[2] Futhey and Cope, in a note to their History of Chester County, page 20, state, "Although the territory west of the Delaware had been governed by the Duke of York, he at the time held no valid title to any part of it King Charles II made a regular conveyance to him of the country comprised within the present territorial limits of the State of Delaware on the 22d of March, 1683, the deeds from the duke to Penn for the same country were executed on the 24th of August, 1682 See Hazard's Register, vol 1 p 429, 430, vol ii p 27 "

[3] Note in Martin's "History of Chester," p 62

[4] Smith's "History of Delaware County," p 139

vania, addressed to several gentlemen requesting them to meet him on the following "so-called Thursday, November 2, 1682," is dated "Upland, October 29, 1682," the day after his arrival, clearly indicating that he did not change the name of this city in the dramatic manner tradition has stated. There is no authentic list of the passengers on the "Welcome" extant, although Edward Armstrong has gathered the names of several of Penn's companions in the ship, which are generally accepted as well established by evidence, excepting that in that list the name of —— Pearson appears, to which is added, "supposed to be Robert," a statement that may well be questioned. As this mythical personage is represented to be an eminent member of the society of Friends, the records of meetings ought to disclose his Christian name, but it has never been found among the list of the early settlers. Hence we have reason to believe that the first person of the name of Pearson in this province was Thomas, and we know that neither of the Thomas Pearsons—for there were two of that name—came here until the following year, 1683.[1] The second of that cognomen in a diary memorandum written by himself, also in the Historical Society's collection, clearly states when he came. To quote his own words, after setting forth his various adventures, he says, "On ye 25th day of July, in ye year 1683, I set sail from Kingroad, in ye 'Comfort,' John Reed, Master, and arrived at Upland in Pennsylvania ye 28th of September 1683," almost a year after Penn's arrival. In the report of the vestry of St. Paul's Church, Chester, to the Society for the Propagation of the Gospel in Foreign Parts, in the year 1704, occurs this sentence: "The people of Chester County showed very early zeal to have the Church of England worship settled among them. This county is so called because most of the inhabitants of it came from Cheshire, in England. Chester, the chief town of the county, is finely situated on the river Delaware."

Bampfylde Moore Carew, the celebrated "King of the Mendicants," who, while escaping from banishment in Virginia, passed through Chester in 1739, in relating his adventures, records that he came "to Chester, so called because the people who first settled there came for the most part from Cheshire. . . . The place is also called Upland." Thirty years previous to Carew's coming, Oldmixon stated, in 1708, when mentioning the town of Chester, "This place is called Upland," and when he alludes to Chester County he gives the like and true reason for the name that Carew did: "so called because the people who first settled here came for the most part from Cheshire in England."[2] The Labadist missionaries, Danckers and Sluyter, record, nearly three years before Penn's coming, in describing their journey down the Delaware in 1679, that "It clearing up towards evening we took a canoe and came after dark to Upland. This is a small village of Swedes, although it is now overrun by English."[3]

In a letter from Penn, Nov. 1, 1682, the epistle is dated from Upland; but subsequently, Dec. 16, 1682, from West River, Md., Penn writes, "That an Assembly was held at Chester, *alias* Upland." These circumstances clearly establish that the official change of name had taken place previous to the last date and subsequent to the preceding one. In the letter of December 16th is the first time we have record of the name of Chester as applied to the old Swedish settlement at Upland.

The most rational conclusion is that Penn, when he changed the name of the town, doubtless within a few weeks after his arrival, and also designated the county of the like name when he divided the settled parts of Pennsylvania into three divisions, he did so in deference to the desire of the English settlers who had "overrun" the town, the major part of whom had come from that locality in England. As stated in the extracts quoted, the name of the shire-town soon became Chester, although its ancient name did not entirely disappear from familiar use until nearly three-quarters of a century had elapsed after William Penn's first visit to the province. The Pearson story for the first time appeared in our annals in Clarkson's "Life of Penn," a work which was not published until more than a century had elapsed after the incidents therein first recorded are said to have occurred. Until the publication of the work just alluded to, no writer makes any mention of the change of name having been suggested to Penn by "his friend Pearson."

The Swedes, we are told by Acrelius, received the English proprietary and his companions with great friendliness, carried up their goods and furniture from

[1] Martin's "History of Chester," page 499. See "Queries," *Penna. Mag. of History*, vol. iii. page 358, where the ubiquitous Mr. Pearson presents himself once more in a new light and demanding unexpected honors. The statement in the volume just cited is that in a recent life of Benjamin West it is said, "In the year 1677 or 1678, one Thomas Pearson, from England, settled in a cave on the west bank of the Delaware River, now below Philadelphia. He was a blacksmith by trade, and, it is said, wielded the first smith's hammer in Pennsylvania. About the first work done was to make small axes for his Indian neighbors, who in their short way termed him *Tom* or *Tommy*. In their language the word hawk signifies any tool used for cutting, hence the origin of the word *tomahawk*." That this was "the Pearson" is settled by the statement in the same book quoted from that he was the grandfather of Benjamin West. Here then is the man who, before Penn came, was the only blacksmith in Pennsylvania making "little hatchets" for the Indians, and from his Christian name and that of the article he produced caused the savages to coin the word "tomahawk." —— Pearson (supposed to be Robert) turns up in 1682 a passenger on the ship "Welcome," and the proprietary, especially for this —— Pearson's benefit, changes the name of "Upland" to "Chester" instantly and without reflection. In the future some enterprising historian may yet discover the man who swallowed the first oyster, and I have no doubt that Friend Pearson will have his claims present for that noteworthy act, and in all probability have that claim allowed.

[2] "The British Empire in America," etc., by J. Oldmixon, in Hazard's *Register*, vol. v. p. 180.

[3] "Journal of a Voyage to New York in 1679-80," by Peter Sluyter and Jasper Danckers; Memoirs of the Long Island Historical Society, vol. i. p. 183.

the ships, and entertained them in their houses without charge, "as many aged Quakers still relate with great pleasure"[1]

Penn, when he landed, resided temporarily at the dwelling-house of Robert Wade, and that fact has rendered the "Essex House" famous in our State annals Penn remained but a short time there as the guest of Wade, for after his return to Chester from New York, whither he had gone to "pay his duty" to the Duke of York by a visit to the latter's representative in that place, as well as from his visit to Maryland, he lodged, according to tradition, at the Boar's Head Inn, a noted public-house at Chester in the early days, which stood until March 20, 1848, when it was destroyed by an incendiary fire

---

CHAPTER V

THE FIRST ASSEMBLY OF PENNSYLVANIA, AND THE HOUSE WHEREIN IT MET

On the 18th day of November, 1682, three weeks after his arrival in the colony, William Penn issued his writs requiring the sheriffs of the several counties, in their respective bailiwicks, "to summon all the freeholders to meet on the 20th inst and elect out of themselves seven persons of the most note for wisdom, sobriety and integrity to serve as their deputies and representatives in General Assembly to be held at Upland, in Pennsylvania, December 6th (4th) next"

In pursuance of this proclamation the Assembly met at Chester on the day designated, Dec 4, 1682, and organized by the election of Nicholas Moore, of Philadelphia County, president of the "Free Society of Traders," as chairman of that body After the appointment of committees, four of the members were selected to apprise the Governor that the Assembly "humbly desired him to honor the House with a transmission of his constitutes"

It is an interesting historical fact that the very first record in the commonwealth regarding the meeting of a legislative body discloses that then, as now, "ways that are dark" were resorted to in the effort to secure the election of members in the interest of particular individuals On that occasion Edmund Cantwell, the sheriff of New Castle County, was charged with "undue electing a member to serve in Assembly from that county," in which effort he was ultimately thwarted, for the Committee on Elections and Privileges reported adversely to Abraham Mann, the sheriff's candidate, and in favor of John Moll, who was contesting his seat, in which conclusion the House concurred

The first two days of the session were consumed in hearing the case of contested election just mentioned, the adoption of rules governing the meeting, passing the act of union, which annexed "the three lower counties" (those comprising the present State of Delaware), and providing for the naturalization of the inhabitants thereof, as well as the Swedes, Finns, and Dutch settlers in Pennsylvania On the third day they received from William Penn the "Printed Laws" and the "Written Laws, or Constitutions" The "Printed Laws" were "the laws agreed upon in England," which had been prepared by learned counsel there, at Penn's desire, and printed in that country, and the "Written Laws, or Constitutions," were the ninety bills presented to the Assembly by the proprietary, out of which the meeting passed the sixty-one chapters of "the great body of the laws"[2] A strange fact is that not one of those enactments, as adopted, is now in force in this commonwealth As soon as the statutes had been acted on, the members from the lower counties particularly became anxious to return to their homes, and so intimated to the Assembly The Speaker considered this desire to adjourn as unbecoming in the members, and bordering on an insult to the Governor A committee of two of the deputies was appointed to wait upon Penn respecting it, and he consented "that the Assembly be adjourned for twenty-one days, which was accordingly ordered by the Speaker" The body failed to meet again at the time designated by adjournment, and at the next regular Assembly in Philadelphia it is recorded that the Speaker "reproves several members for neglecting to convene at the time appointed when the House last adjourned"

Nearly forty years ago an old structure stood on the western side of Edgmont Avenue, north of Second Street, which was commonly termed "The Old Assembly House," because of the popular belief that it was in this building that the first Assembly convened in Pennsylvania, Dec 4, 1682 Dr George Smith, in his valuable "History of Delaware County," conclusively established the fact that this building was the first meeting house of Friends in Chester, and was not erected until 1693, hence the first Assembly, which held its session more than ten years before that date, could not have met in that structure We know that on the 6th day of the First month, 1687, Joran Kyn, or Keen, made a deed conveying a lot in Chester, adjoining his "lot or garding," to certain persons in trust, "to use and behoof of the said Chester meeting of the people of God called Quakers, and their successors forever," and on this lot, now included in William P

[1] Acrelius, "History of New Swedon," p 111 That author returned to Sweden in 1756, and doubtless he might have talked to old persons who could recall the incidents connected with the arrival of the proprietary, as such an event would make a lasting impression on their young minds

[2] For a most interesting disquisition on the subject of the laws, the number enacted at the session of the Assembly, and other valuable information in relation thereto, see "Historical Notes, Part II, Appendix to the Duke's Book of Laws," pp 477–482.

Eyre's ground, on Edgmont Avenue, the ancient meeting-house was built

Dr Smith thereupon argues that the Assembly must have met in the court-house, or, as it was then known, "The House of Defense," which stood on the eastern side of Edgmont Avenue, above Second Street, and so projected into the roadway that, when Edgmont Avenue was regularly laid out as a street, it had to be removed The doctor rightly thinks, "It was the only public building in Upland, at the time, of which we have any knowledge." Martin, in his "History of Chester," accepts the doctor's conclusions as unquestionably accurate Nevertheless, both of these able historians are in error in this The thought escaped them that perhaps Penn saw that the "House of Defense" was too small for the purpose intended, and therefore a private dwelling was used for the meeting of the members [1]

Mrs Deborah Logan informs us in her notes to the "Penn and Logan Correspondence," [2] that the Assembly convened in the large, or, as then termed, "The Double House," by way of distinction, which James Sandilands, the elder, had erected for his own dwelling which stood near the creek, and subsequently, when the road to Philadelphia was laid out, near that highway On an old plan of the borough of Chester, made about 1765, now owned by William B Broomall, Esq, of that city, the lot on which "The Double House" stood is designated as beginning about one hundred and thirty feet southerly from the intersection of the present Edgmont Avenue and Third Street The lot itself was about one hundred and twenty feet front on the west side of Edgmont Avenue This house, which was spacious and pretentious for those times,—and would even now be regarded as an unusually large dwelling,—had unfortunately been built with mortar made of oyster-shell lime, which proved utterly valueless. In a few years the building showed signs of decay, then became a ruin, and as such continued until the beginning of the present century, when its foundations were removed In time its very existence was generally forgotten, so much so that, as is mentioned, some of our most accurate and painstaking historians were unacquainted with the fact that it had ever performed the important part it did in our early colonial annals

In considering the location of the house wherein the Assembly convened, it is unnecessary to refer to the first meeting-house of Friends The fact that it was not built previous to 1693 is proved conclusively from the original minutes of the Society, which takes it entirely out of the controversy After standing one hundred and fifty-two years it was torn down in April, 1845, by Joshua P and William Eyre, the then owners of the property

I believe that the Assembly met in the double house and not the House of Defense, and my reasons for this opinion are briefly these

The first record we have of the site of the Assembly building will be found in "The Traveller's Directory," [3] wherein it is stated in the notice of Chester that "The first Colonial Assembly for the province was convened in this place on the fourth day of December, 1682 '*A part of the old wall of the room still remains*'"

This wall could not have been part of the old House of Defense, for July 13, 1728, George McCall and Ann, his wife (Jasper Yeates' eldest daughter), and John Yeates conveyed to George Ashbridge the house now owned by the heirs of the late Sarah P Coombs, which dwelling, according to Armstrong, on the north side occupies about eleven feet of the south end of the site of the House of Defense On May 5, 1797, George Ashbridge, the grandson of the grantee just mentioned, sold the property to Dorothy Smith and Zedekiah Wyatt Graham as joint tenants In 1798, Mrs. Smith and Mr Graham, brother and sister, both died of the yellow fever, and the property passed to their nephew and four nieces in equal shares At that time the passage-way on the north side of the house was paved, and rose-bushes and other shrubbery grew in a bed alongside of the fence which divided the Smith and Graham property on the north from that of Henry Hale Graham No part of a wall was to be seen at the point designated several years before the beginning of this century, and it must have been there in 1802 had it been the site of the Assembly House

Official evidence, however, tells us that almost a hundred years before the "Traveller's Directory" was printed, the House of Defense was destroyed, for at the November court, 1703, the grand jury presented "the old Court hous, being a nuisance to the town in case of fire, and also the chimney of Henry

---

[1] The "House of Defense," we are told by Edward Armstrong, in his admirable notes to "The Record of Upland Court," p 202, "was rectangular in shape, its size was 14 by 15 feet, and, according to measurement, its S E corner stood about 84 feet from the N E corner of Front and Filbert The northern portion of the house of Mrs. Sarah P Combe occupies about eleven feet of the south end of the site of the House of Defense"

[2] Vol i p 46, "Descendants of Joran Kyn," the founder of Upland By Professor Gregory B Keen, *Penna Mag of History*, vol ii p 446

[3] "The Traveller's Directory or Pocket Companion By S S Moore and T W Jones, Philadelphia Published by Mathew Carey, 1802" An exceedingly rare volume, in library of Pennsylvania Historical Society Fifteen years subsequent to the publication of the Directory a correspondent of the West Chester *Federalist* visited Chester and records that, "On the bank of Chester Creek, which passes through the town, there is still shown an old wall, now making a part of a dwelling house, which formed one side of the first hall of justice in Pennsylvania—answering for the sessions of the Legislature and the Court of Justice, in both of which Wm Penn occasionally presided" (Martin's "History of Chester," p 122) The extract just quoted is of course full of historical misstatements, the narrative being based on perverted traditions related to the writer by the people of Chester of that day The old Assembly House is confused with the fourth court-house of Chester County, built by John Hoskins in 1695, and the wall mentioned still remains in the dwelling-house to this day (1884) It shows, however, that tradition at that time never located the site of Assembly House on the east side of Edgmont Avenue, where the House of Defense stood, —a species of negative proof

Hollingsworth, in Chester Town," and, thereupon, "The Court on deliberate consideracon orders the s[d] hous to be pulled down, and that Jasper Yeats, chief burges of ye borough of Chester, shall see ye order Pformed" Martin is of opinion that this order had reference to the House of Defense, and there seems to be no doubt but that the authorities were alarmed lest the great pile of logs, dry as they must be, would burn the small cluster of houses at Chester The site of the House of Defense subsequently became the property of Jasper Yeates, and he doubtless saw that the order of court was executed We certainly learn nothing further from the records of the old nuisance, hence the presumption is that it was abated

On the other hand, it is known that on the double-house lot the ruins of the dwellings remained for several years after the beginning of this century, and as it adjoined the lot to the south, where the Friends' meeting-house stood when the foundation of Sandeland's dwelling was removed to be used in other buildings, the tradition that the first Assembly had met there attached itself to the antiquated structure on the adjoining lot, and in time the fact that the double house had ever existed was generally forgotten So quickly did the tradition link itself to the meeting-house that John F Watson, in 1827 (only a quarter of a century after the "Traveller's Directory" had correctly located the place where the Assembly met), refers to it as the "old Assembly House," and Stephen Day, in 1843, in his "Historical Collections of Pennsylvania," follows with the same statement, until the error had made permanent lodgment in the popular mind, and is now difficult of eradication

---

CHAPTER VI

THE COLONIAL HISTORY TO THE WAR OF THE REVOLUTION

THE only hamlet in Pennsylvania which had received a distinctive name that was known to persons in England at the time Penn acquired title to the territory was Upland, and that that had done so was doubtless due to the fact that Robert Wade had already made it his home He being a Friend in communication with members of that religious sect in the mother-country, that circumstance directed the attention of the Quakers, "a society," says Acrelius, "that the realm could well spare," to the little cluster of rudely-fashioned dwellings on the banks of the Delaware Hence Friends (whom, fortunately for the United States, could be spared from Europe to plant on this continent those seeds of political truths and religious liberty which, germinating, have grown into a nation on the maintenance of which the future continuance of constitutional representative government on the earth largely depends), or Quakers, as popularly known, desiring to flee from persecution and ignominy at home, gladly availed themselves of the liberal conditions which Penn offered to persons anxious to leave England, and particularly did the latter meet the approval of those people whose poverty had been largely produced by reason of the heavy fines imposed on them simply because of the religious sentiments they maintained That Penn originally intended to locate his proposed capital city at Upland can hardly be questioned, for his instructions to his commissioners, Crispin, Bezer, and Allen, particularly directing them "that the creeks should be sounded on my side of the Delaware River, especially Upland, in order to settle a great toune," will bear no other legitimate construction That this was his purpose is evident from all the surrounding circumstances, and he only abandoned it when he learned that Lord Baltimore, by actual observation, had discovered that the site of the hamlet was in the debatable land as to ownership That the proprietary, after he had been informed of Lord Baltimore's persistent claims, had resolved to build a city farther up the river, before he first came to his province, will not admit of doubt, hence the result of the visit of William Penn to James Sandelands, mentioned as having taken place almost as soon as the former landed at Upland, when it was "talkt among the people that it was with Intent to have built a City" at that place, "but that he and Sanderlin could not agree,"[1] may perchance have interfered with some proposed improvement at the old Swedish settlement, but even had Sandelands assented to all that Penn may have required, it would not have eventuated in locating the contemplated "great town" at that point[2] Under the circumstances the risks, owing to the disputed ownership of that part of his territory, were too great for Penn to assume

Martin informs us on the authority of Mrs Sarah Shoemaker, aged ninety-two years, who died in Chester in 1825, and who had heard her grandfather, James Lownes, often speak of the times of which I am now writing, that during the winter of 1682–83, Upland presented a very animated appearance It was the only place then in the province, as stated, known to English ship-owners, and consequently, as the destination of all vessels was this port, most of the emigrants landed here, and several ships often rode at anchor at the same time off the hamlet It is said that the water was deep near the western shore, and vessels could approach so closely to land that the trees would often brush their upper rigging

The great influx of emigrants in the hamlet caused nearly every dwelling in it to be a house of entertainment, and as the people of that day, in the majority of instances, used beer instead of tea or coffee, that fact may account for the number of presentments by the

[1] The Brevinto, Penn vs Lord Baltimore, folio 105, Professor G B Keen's "Descendants of Joran Kyn," *Penna. Mag of Hist*, vol ii p 445

[2] Latrobe's "History of Mason and Dixon's Line"

grand juries of the residents along the Delaware "for selling beer, etc, without license, contrary to law" The proprietary himself is believed to have made his home at Chester during the greater part of the winter of 1682–83, and while here, it is said (on Nov 25, 1682), he divided the territory theretofore known as Upland into the three counties,—Chester, Philadelphia, and Bucks

William Penn, having called the city of Philadelphia into being,—he had named it before it had any actual existence as a town,—summoned the freemen throughout the province to hold an election on the 20th day of the Twelfth month, 1682 (February, 1683), to choose seventy two persons of most note for their wisdom, virtue, and ability to serve as members of a Provincial Council, to meet on "the 10th day of the First month next ensuing" (March, 1683), at the new capital From each county twelve men were returned under this order, but the several sheriffs also presented petitions from the people in their bailiwicks praying that only three of the twelve men returned as councilors be vested with the duplex character of councilors and assemblymen, and the remaining nine as simply assemblymen The petition presented by the people of Chester County was as follows [1]

"To WILLIAM PENN, *proprietary and governor of the province of Pennsylvania and territories thereof*

"The petition of the freeholders of the County of Chester respectfully showeth, That in obedience to the writ sent to our Sheriff we have chosen twelve persons for our delegates to serve in the provincial Council, but considering that the numbers of the people are yet small, and that we have few fit for or acquainted with such public business, and also that we are unable to support the charge of greater elections and Assemblies After our humble acknowledgments of the favor intended us therein, we take leave humbly to request that three of the twelve we have chosen may serve as provincial Councillors, and the other nine for the Assembly, which provincial Councillors are John Symcock (for three years), Ralph Withers (for two years), and William Clayton (for one year), leaving it to thee to increase the number, as occasion may serve, hereafter

[Signed] "JAMES BROWN & Co"

The assemblymen thus designated from Chester County were John Hoskins, Robert Wade, George Wood, John Blunston, Dennis Rochford, Thomas Bracy, John Bezer, John Harding, Joseph Phipps

These petitions, although in direct violation of the charter, were favorably acted on, but in the formation of Council Ralph Withers appeared as credited to Bucks County, while Christopher Taylor represented Chester It is not my purpose to make extended reference to the proceedings of the second Assembly further than to notice that the seal of Chester County at that session was established, bearing as its distinctive design a plow

The influx of immigrants into Pennsylvania for the few years immediately after Penn acquired ownership of the territory is unequaled in the history of the British colonial possessions in North America, and can only be likened in recent years to the marvelous growth of settlements in the oil region of this State, or localities west of the Mississippi, where precious metals are supposed to yield almost certain fortune to adventurers who locate there Within the limits of the present county of Delaware, before the close of the year 1683, the population began to preponderate largely of members of the Society of Friends, and at Chester, Marcus Hook, Darby, and Haverford permanent settlements of Quakers had been made, from which centres their influence extended outwards, giving tone and character to the whole people The few Swedes and Dutch who had preceded these Friends were soon absorbed in, and their individuality of thought and action was merged into that of the more intelligent majority, greatly to the benefit of the former The Welsh immigrants, who had secured a tract of forty thousand acres in a whole from Penn previous to leaving the Old World, found, on arriving in the colony, that they could not locate it within the city limits of Philadelphia, and were forced to push out into the then wilderness, and we find, in 1682, that their first lodgment with a few settlers was made in Merion and Haverford, from which they rapidly spread into Radnor, Newtown, Goshen, Tredyffrin, and Uwchlan

It was the fixed policy of William Penn, in order to avoid all causes of trouble with the Indians growing out of disputed rights to the soil, to purchase from the aborigines, and extinguish the title to the territory as rapidly as civilization pushed outward into "the backwoods" The ownership of the land within Delaware County was released to William Penn by the Indians in two deeds, both of which are interesting because of the consideration mentioned as having been paid to chiefs The first deed was executed over a year before William Penn returned to England, in 1684 The old document is as follows

"We, Secane & Icquoquehan, ——— Indian shackamakers, and right owners of ye Land Lying between Manaiunk, als Sculkill and Macopanackhan, als Chester Rivers, doe this 14th day of ye fift month, in ye year according to English account 1683, hereby graunt and Sell all our Right & Title in ye sd Lands Lying between ye sd River, begining on ye West side of Manaiunk, called Consohockhan, & from thence by a Westerly Line to ye sd River Malopanackhan, unto William Penn Propriet & Govern of ye Province of Pennsilvania &c, his heires & Assignes, for Ever, for and in Consideration of 150 fathom of Wampum, 14 Blanketts, 65 yds Duffills, 28 yds stroud watrs, 15 Gunns, 3 great Kettles, 15 small Kettles, 16 pr Stockins, 7 pr Shoes, 6 Capps, 12 Gimbletts, 6 Drawing Knives, 15 pr Sissors, 15 Combes, 5 Papers needles, 10 Tobacco boxes, 15 Tobacco Tongs, 32 Pound Powder, 3 papers Beads, 2 papers Red Lead, 15 Coats, 15 Shurts, 15 Axes, 15 knives, 30 barrs of Lead, 18 Glasses, 15 hoes, unto us in hand paid, the receipt whereof is hereby acknowledged have renounced all Claims & Demands for ye future from us or heires or Assignes, in or to ye premises In witness whereof we have hereunto sett or hands and seals ye day & year first above written

"The mark of × SECANE "The mark of × ICQUOQUEHAN

"Sealed and delivered in presence of
"PISEKICKEM
"The mark of × PETER RAMBO,
"The mark of × SWAN SWANSON,
"PHILIP TH LEHNMANN,
"JOS CURTEIS,
"CATEKUS, an Indian king" [2]

[1] Hazard's Annals, p 603

[2] Penna Archives, 1st series, vol i p. 65

The second deed was made after Penn had returned to England. The Provincial Council, on the 22d of the Seventh month (September), 1685, was notified by Capt. Lasse Cock that the Indians were anxious to dispose of their land between Upland and Appoquinomy. Council immediately appointed Thomas Holme, surveyor-general, John Simcock, and Col. William Markham, the then secretary of the body, to meet the Indians and purchase from them the territory named. The following deed, executed in ten days after the date given, shows how expeditiously the authorities acted in carrying out the original intention of Penn, the extinguishment of Indian titles; but the indefinite bounds, "so far as a man can ride in two days with a horse," clearly shows the superior bargaining abilities of the white man, and the success which attended this transaction might have prompted the noted "walking purchase" of a later date.

"THIS INDENTURE WITNESSETH That We Lare Packenah Tareekham Sickais Peltquessitt Tewis Essepenaick Petkhoy Kekelappan Feomus Mackalohr Melleonga Wissa Powey Indian Kings Sachemakers, Right Owners of all the Lands from Quing Quingus Called Duck Creek unto upland Called Chester Creek all along by the West Side of Delaware River and So between the Said Creeks Backwards *as far as a man can Ride in two days with a horse* for and in Consideration of these following good to Vs in hand paid and secured to be paid by Wm Penn Proprietary and Gouvnour of the Province of Pennsilvania and Territories Thereof, Viz Twenty Gunns Twenty fathom Matchcoat twenty Fathom Stroudwaters, twenty Blankets twenty Kettles twenty pounds Powder One hundred Barrs Lead forty Tomahawks One hundred Knives Fourty pare Stocking One Barrel of Beer twenty pound red Lead One hundred Fathom Wamphum thirty Glass Bottles thirty Pewter Spoons one hundred Awl Blades three hundred tobacco Pipes One hundred hands of Tobacco twenty Tobacco Tongs twenty Steels three hundred flints thirty pare Sissers thirty Combs Sixty looking Glasses two hundred Needles one Skiple Salt thirty pounds Shuger five gallons Mollassis twenty Tobacco Boxes One hundred Juise Harps twenty Hows, thirty Guimlets thirty Wooden Screw Borers & One hundred Strings Beeds Wee hereby Acknowledge in behalfe of Our Selves as Only Rright Owners of the aforesaid Tract of Land to Bargain and Sell And by these Presents doe fully Clearly and Absolutely Bargaine & Sell Unto the said Wm Penn his heirs and Assignes for Ever without any mollestation or hindrance from or by Us and from or by any other Indians whatsoever that Shall or may Claime any Right Title or Interest in or unto the Said Tract of Land or any Part thereof. In Witness Whereof Wee have hereunto Set our hands and Seals at New Castle the 2d day of the Eighth month 1685.

"Signed sealed and delivered unto Capt Thomas Holme Surveyr Genl of ye Province of Pennsylvania to & for ye use of William Penn Esqr Proprietary & Governr of ye aforesd Province & Territories thereunto belonging in the presence of us.

"PIETER ALRICKS	The Mark of
"LASSE COCK	OWEG HAM
"PHILIP TH LEHNMANN	The Mark of
"JAMES ATKINSON	OWEG ╳ HAM
"CHRISTOPHER GORR	The Mark of
"The Mark of	LIK ╳ HAMM
"JOHN ╳ WALKER	The Mark of
"EDWARD LARE	PATASKO ╳
"JOHN MANDY.	The Mark of
"The Mark of	MACK ╳ RASHUTE."[1]
"TAMMA ╳ GWARAN	

The general history of our county is very meagre of interesting incidents in the early days of the province other than the happenings which became matter for the intervention and adjudication of the courts; and as these subjects will be found collated and treated of in a distinctive chapter, no allusion will be made to them at this time.

The absence of William Penn from England afforded an opportunity to his enemies and for the friends of Lord Baltimore in the mother-country to press with earnestness objections to the former's title to the "three lower counties," now Delaware, as also to seriously menace his ownership of the greater part of the present county of Delaware (as well as others) in Pennsylvania. Hence it became imperatively essential that he should return to Great Britain; and preparatory to his departure he appointed Thomas Lloyd, James Harrison, and John Simcock—the former to be Deputy Governor, and, in the event of death, the others to succeed to that position in the order mentioned—to represent him in the province, and, in the contingency of his (Penn's) death before other officers were selected, empowered them to be "Commissioners & Guardians in Government to my dear Heir, Sprigett Penn." As the record shows that on Aug. 14, 1684, Penn presided for the last time in Council until he returned, nearly sixteen years subsequently, it is thought that he sailed not long after the date above mentioned.

At a Council held at Philadelphia, April 1, 1685, Thomas Lloyd presiding, the boundaries of the county of Chester were officially prescribed, as follows: "The county of Chester to begin at ye Mouth or Entrance of Bough Creek, upon Delaware River, being the upper end of Tinicum Island, and soe up that creek, dividing the said Island from ye Land of Andros Boone & Company; from thence along the several courses thereof to a Large Creek Called Mill Creek: from thence up the several courses of the said creek to a W.S.W. Line, which Line divided the Liberty Lands of Philadelphia from Several Tracts of Land belonging to the Welsh and other Inhabitants; and from thence E.N.E. by a line of Marked Trees 120 perches, more or less; from thence N.N.W. by the herford (Haverford) Township 1000 perches, more or less; from thence E.N.E. by ye Land belonging to Jno. Humphreys 110 perches, more or less; from thence N.N.W. by ye Land of John Eckley 880 perches, more or less; from thence continuing ye said Course to the Scoolkill River, wch sd Scoolkill River afterwards to be the natural bounds."[2]

Many complaints having been made respecting the manner in which Charles Ashcom, the deputy surveyor for Chester County, had encroached on the forty thousand acres which Penn had ordered set apart as the Welsh tract[3] (including Radnor and

---

[1] Penna. Archives, 1st series, vol. i. p. 95.

[2] Colonial Records, vol. i. p. 126. Dr. Smith ("History of Delaware County," p. 155), says, "This line continues to be the eastern boundary of Delaware County to the north line of Haverford. The resolution of the Council makes the next course run easterly instead of westerly, and is probably a mistake, as Radnor township never extended farther easterly than it now does."

[3] The survey of the Welsh tract was authorized by the following warrant from the proprietary:

"Whereas divers considerable persons among ye Welsh Friends have

REFERENCES TO THE SETTLEMENTS OF SEVERAL INHABITANTS IN THE COUNTY OF CHESTER

a	Phil. Roman.	6	Gibbons Hobbs.	33	Smith.	61	Tho. Taylor.
b	Wm. Hichcot.	7	J. Bluntston.	34	Jno. Batram.	62	Jno. Buckley.
c	Pet. Lounder.	8	Jos. Fern.	35	Edw. Gibbs.	63	Jos. Bushell.
d	Jno. Simcock.	9	Geo. Wood.	36	Amb. Boon.	64	Rob. Piles.
e	Rich. Far.	10	Wm. Wood.	37	Wm. Wood.	65	Jno. Gibbons.
f	Wm. Collet.	11	Pet. Ellet.	38	Rich. Tucker.	66	Rob. Southrey.
g	Jos. Philps.	12	Jno. Bluntston.	39	Har. Johnson.	67	Widdow.
h	Wm. Clayton.	13	Sam. Bradshaw.	40	Col. Hook.	69	Jam. Swarfar.
i	Jo. Beale.	14	Tho. Bradshaw.	41	Hansunin.	70	Jno. Houlson.
k	Mos. and Ben. Mendinhall.	15	Jam. Stanfield.	42	Mer. Morten.	71	Wm. Gregory.
l	Wm. Hichcot.	16	Ant. Sturgis.	43	Mountstoker.	72	Boweter.
m	Rob. Chamberlain.	17	Edw. Cartledge.	44	Jno. Henrickson.	73	Will. Edwards.
n	Wm. Brampton.	18	Jos. Pottor.	45	Tho. Nerbury.	74	Oswin Musgrave.
o	Tho. King.	19	Tho. Hood.	46	Jno. Simcock.	75	Churchman.
p	Tho. Moor.	20	Jos. Slayton.	47	Jno. Harding.	76	Free Schoole.
q	Nat. Park.	21	Pet. Lester.	48	Jno. Kingsman.	77	Dav. Ogdon.
r	Jno. Hannam.	22	Geo. Gleave.	49	Jno. Edg.	78	Jno. Hodskinson.
s	Godin Walter.	23	Geo. Mearis.	50	Rob. Cawdwell.	79	Jac. Chanler.
t	Tho. Hall.	24	Fra. Yornel.	51	Wal. Fosset.	80	Fra. Harrison.
u	Jno. Palmer.	25	Jac. Steedman.	52	Jno. Nixon.	81	Jno. Peusey.
v	Wm. Oubornn.	26	Jno. Steedman.	53	Jno. Simcock.	82	Jno. Prisner.
w	Jno. Brazor.	27	Jno. Steedman.	54	Sar. Baker.	83	Gil. Woolam.
1	Adam Roads.	28	Jno. Holwel.	55	Cha. Whitaker.	85	Jno. Prisnor.
2	Jno. Kerk.	29	Cha. Wheetaker.	56	Tho. Rawlins.	86	Wm. Woodmansee.
3	J. Bluntston.	30	Edm. Cartledg.	57	Fra. Cook.	87	Jno. Gibbons.
4	Cha. Lee.	31	Jos. Potter.	58	Tho. Ducket.	88	Fra. Harrison.
5	Sam. Sellers.	32	Tho. Hood.	60	Joel Baloy.		

Fac-simile of a part of Holme's Map, showing Settlers of Delawar

an original in the possession of Saml. L. Smedley, Phila., Pa.

Iaverford townships, in this county), in laying out ands for other purchesers, not recognized as distinctively Welsh settlers, in such a way as to interfere vith the continuity of "the Barony," and because the nhabitants of that territory were summoned to do ury and other public duties in both Philadelphia nd Chester Counties, in 1688 a lengthy petition was repared by them and forwarded by Col William Markham the same year to Penn in England It is ot known whether the letter was ever received by Penn; at least so far as the writer has information o notice was ever taken by the proprietary of the ommunication

The Welsh settlers in Radnor and Haverford, however, declined to recognize the division of the counies of Philadelphia and Chester, and silently refused o pay their proportion of the public taxes to the reasury of Chester County or to serve on juries The uthorities of the latter at length, having exhausted ll means at their command to compel recognition of heir jurisdiction, presented a petition from the jusices and inhabitants of Chester County to the Govrnor and Council, March 25, 1689, in which they epresented that the county was at first small, "not bove 9 miles square & but Thinly seated, whereby ye aid County is not able to Support the Charge hereoff," and that the Governor in "his Serious Conideration of our Weak Condition was pleased, out of Compassion to us, to grant an Enlargement of ye ame," which was subsequently done in the official oundaries before mentioned To support the allegaion that these limits had been approved by William Penn, John Blunstone testified "that a ffew days beore Gover Penn left this Province that upon ye bank y John Simcock's house I moved him to Deside this natter that had been so long Discoursed, who then, efore me and Others did Declare that ye bounds should thus runn from the mouth of Bow Creek to Mill Creek, wch should be ye bounds until it come to ye Land of Herford, and then to take in the Townds f Herford & Radnor, from thence to the Skoolkill, nd take in his mannour of Springtowne, then asked him if he would be pleased to give it under his hand, to avoyd ffurther Trouble, who answered he would, if any of us would Come the next day to Philadelphia, in order thereunto, one was sent, but what then obstructed I am not certaine, but yt ye Gover Departed about two days after" Randall Vernon testified that William Howell, of Harford, "Signified unto me" that he had "asked ye Gover to what County they should be joined or belong unto, & The Gover was pleased to answer him that they must belong to Chester County" Thomas Usher, sheriff of Chester County, testified that Penn said to him, "Thomas, I perceive that the Skoolkill Creek Comes or runs so upon the back of Philadelphia that it makes ye City almost an Island, so that a Robbery or the like may be there Committed, and ye offender gitt over ye Creek, and so Escape for want of due persute, &c, therefore I intend that ye bounds of Philadelphia County Shall Come about 3 or ffour miles on this side of the Skoolkill, and I would not have thee to take notice or to oppose that Sheriff on ye Execution of his office, about Kingses or the like, but I intend to enlarge this County downwards to Brandywine"[1] The Deputy Surveyor-General produced the official map, showing the county lines as before given, and stated that "it so is set out by order of the Governor and Provincial Council" Governor Blackwell and the Council intimated that as the bounds had been published in the map of Thomas Holme, which had been distributed in England, and as land had been sold and located according to that map, to change the boundaries now might result in much confusion to purchasers Besides, the Welsh settlers had refused to bear any part of the taxes or serve on juries in Philadelphia, as they had done in Chester County, claiming that they were a distinct "barony," and although the Governor and Council intimated that clearly the Welsh Tract was a part of Chester County, yet they refused to announce their final conclusion until the next morning, when, if the Welsh settlers chose to show cause why they should not be part of Chester County, they would be heard The next morning, Thomas Lloyd and John Eckley appeared on behalf of the Welsh, alleging that Penn had intimated to them that they would *form a county palatine*, but as they had no written evidence to substantiate that assertion, Council decided that the boundaries already shown to have been established must be confirmed Thereupon the strong arm of the law was extended to compel the reluctant Welshmen to yield obedience to the decree that had been made The Court of Chester County appointed John Jerman constable for Radnor, and John Lewis for Haverford, but these recipients of judicial favor failing to present themselves, the justices determined that the dignity of the bench should be maintained Hence we find that at court held "3d day of 1st week, 3d mo, 1689, ordered that Warrants of Con-

equested me yt all ye Lands Purchased of me by those of North Wales nd South Wales, together with ye adjacent counties to ym, as Haverordshire, Shropshire, and Cheshire, about fourty thousand acres, may e layd out contiguously as one *Barony*, alledging yt ye number allready ome and suddenly to come, are such as will be capable of planting ye ame much within ye proportion allowed by ye custom of ye country, & so ot lye in large and useless vacancies And because I am inclined and etermined to agree and favour ym wth any reasonable Conveniency & riviledge I do hereby charge thee & strictly require thee to lay out ye d tract of Land in as uniform a manner, as conveniently may be, upon e West side of Skoolkill river, running three miles upon ye same, & wo miles backward, & then extend ye parallell wth ye river six miles, nd to run westwardly so far as till ye sd quantity of land be Comleately surveyed unto ym Given at Pennsbury, ye 13th 1st mo 1684

"WILL PENN

"To THS HOLMES, Surveyor General"

In pursuance of this warrant the Surveyor General, on the 4th of the d month (April), 1684, issued an order to his deputy, David Powell, he irecting him to execute it The survey was probably made before the nd of 1684 See Smith's "History of Delaware County," pp 164-65

[1] Colonial Records, vol i pp. 263, 265

tempt be Directed to ye Sheriff to apprehend ye Bodyes of John Lewis and John Jerman for their Contempt of not entering into their respective offices of Constables (viz.) John Lewis for Harfort, and John Jerman for Radnor, when thereunto required by this Court."

At the same session, David Laurence, who had been returned as a grand juror from Haverford, failed to attend, and for his neglect or refusal to appear was presented by the grand inquest. The court fined Laurence ten shillings. The jury also presented "the want of the inhabitants of the townships of Radnor and Hartfort, and the inhabitants adjacent, they not being brought in to join with us in the Levies and other public services of this county." The movement to compel the Welsh to submit to the constituted authority did not cease, for at the following (June) court the commission of William Howell, of Haverford, was read, and he afterwards assumed the office and subscribed "to the solemn declaration" required. William Jenkins, of Haverford, at the same court, served as a juror. Haverford had yielded, but the court deemed it wise that public proclamation, as was then customary with all laws, should be made respecting this decree, hence we find this entry in the old record of the county: That at court, on Wednesday of the first week in June, 1689, "the Division Lyne between this County and Philadelphia was read, dated ye 1st of ye 2^d mo^th, 1685." At the December court following, John Jerman was qualified as constable of Radnor, and thereafter the two townships made no further objection to act with and pay taxes to the authorities of Chester County. In 1688 the inhabitants of the province were greatly alarmed by reason of a rumor diligently circulated that two Indian women from New Jersey had informed an old Dutch resident near Chester that the aborigines had determined, on a designated Thursday, to attack and massacre all the white settlers on the Delaware. To add to the general consternation, about ten o'clock at night of the evening fixed upon by the savages to begin the attack a messenger "out of the woods" came hurriedly into Chester with the report that three families, residing about nine miles distant, had been murdered by the Indians. The people of the town gathered to consider the startling intelligence, and at midnight a Quaker, resident at Chester, accompanied by two young men, went to the place named, where they found the three houses empty, but no signs of murder. The dwellers therein, alarmed by the rumor, had fled to the homes of their parents, about a mile distant on Ridley Creek. The further particulars of this alarm are thus given by Proud:[1]

"The master of one of these families being from home, had been informed five hundred Indians were actually collected at Naaman's Creek, in pursuit of their design to kill the English; and as he was hastening to his home, he thought he heard his boy crying out and saying, 'What shall I do, my dame is killed!' Upon which, instead of going home to know the certainty of the affair, he ran off to acquaint the government at Philadelphia, but being met by a person of more prudence than himself before he got to the city he was persuaded by him to return.

"The report, notwithstanding, soon arrived at the city, and was told with such alarming circumstances that a messenger was immediately dispatched to Marcus Hook, near the said Naaman's Creek, to enquire the truth of it. He quickly returned and confirmed the report, but with this variation, that it was at Brandywine Creek, at an Indian town, where the five hundred Indians were assembled, and that they, having a lame king, had carried him away, with all their women and children. These circumstances rendered the affair still more alarming, and with many amounted to a certainty.

"The Council were, at that time, sitting at Philadelphia on other affairs, when one of them, a Friend, supposed to be Caleb Pusey,[2] who lived in Chester County, voluntarily offered himself to go to the place, provided they would name five others to accompany him, without weapons; which, being soon agreed on, they rode to the place; but, instead of meeting with five hundred warriors, they found the old king quietly lying with his lame foot along on the ground, and his head at ease on a kind of pillow, the women at work in the fields, and the children playing together.

"When they had entered the wigwam the king presently asked them very mildly, 'What they all came for?' They told him the report which the Indian women had raised, and asked him whether the Indians had anything against the English. He appeared much displeased at the report, and said, 'The woman ought to be burnt to death, and that they had nothing against the English,' adding, ''Tis true there is about fifteen pounds yet behind of our pay for the land which William Penn bought, but as you are still on it and improving it to your own use, we are not in haste for our pay; but when the English come to settle it we expect to be paid.' This the messengers thinking very reasonable, told him they would undoubtedly be paid for their land.

"One of the company further expressed himself to the Indian King, in the following manner: 'That the great God, who made the world, and all things therein, consequently made all mankind, both Indians and English; and as he made all, so his love was extended to all; which, was plainly shown, by his causing the rain and dews to fall on the ground of both Indians and English alike; that it might generally produce what the Indians, as well as what the English sewed or planted in it, for the sustenance of life; and also by his making the sun to shine equally on all, both Indians and English, to nourish them all, extending his love thus to all, for they were naturally bound to love one another.'

"The King answered, 'What they had said was true; and as God has given you corn, I would advise you to get it in (it being harvest time); for we intend you no harm.' They parted amicably, and the messengers returning put an end to the people's fears."

The Revolution of 1688 in England was a serious obstacle to the rapid development of this province. William Penn was known to be a warm personal friend of the deposed king, from whose hand he had received many favors; hence, when the new monarchs were told that Penn was a Jesuit of St. Omers, a self-devoted slave to despotism, and even charged with conspiring for the restoration of James II., the royal ears hearkened attentively to the wildest rumors circulated by his enemies. Penn was twice examined before the Privy Council, and he was even held to bail for his appearance, but the Court of King's Bench discharged him, as no evidence was presented substantiating the charges lodged against him; there-

[1] Hist. of Pennsylvania, vol. i. page 336.

[2] Dr. Smith has correctly shown that Pusey was not a member of the Council that year. It is to be regretted that the name of this member of Council is not recorded, for his act was one of rare heroism. In all probability Proud has confused the incidents, in that he makes Pusey visit the Indians from Philadelphia, when doubtless—for he was of that stamp of noble men—the Quaker who at midnight rode from Chester, accompanied by two young men, to the scene of the alleged violence was Pusey.

upon he decided to return immediately to his colony, and to that end had gathered about five hundred persons to accompany him, the government had even ordered a convoy for the protection of the emigrants, when an infamous wretch accused him under oath of attempting to incite a treasonable outbreak in Lancashire, and Penn escaping arrest, was compelled to abandon his proposed colony, entailing on him serious loss Meanwhile in the province faction feelings and dissensions had been aroused until the three lower counties, now comprising the State of Delaware, actually separated from the three upper counties of Pennsylvania, their representatives refusing to act in conjunction with the authorities in Philadelphia At last Penn, in the hope of maintaining order, was compelled to appoint, in the beginning of 1692, Thomas Lloyd to be Governor of the province, and William Markham to be Governor of the territory (Delaware) The new order of things, however, failed to produce the harmony desired, so that reports of the confused condition of affairs in the province which went abroad supplied the crown of England with an excuse for suspending the proprietary rule, which was done by a commission from William and Mary, dated Oct 20, 1692, to Col Benjamin Fletcher to be Captain-General and Governor-in-Chief of Pennsylvania The commission to Fletcher set forth three reasons for the act of suspension, but the real incentive was the doubt of Penn's loyalty, which the latter's enemies had awakened in the royal breasts But whatever was the motive, the whole system of laws which had been enacted were revised, modified, and repealed by the throne in the authority vested in Fletcher There is little of interest, specially in reference to the radical changes thus made, connected with the annals of Delaware County, apart from that of the State at large, but among the seven members of the late Governor Lloyd's Council who protested so earnestly against any and all measures in contravention of Penn's charter this county was ably represented Governor Fletcher's understanding of the situation was made clear in his reply to a subsequent address by the Assembly, that "These Lawes and that model of government is desolved and at an end."

William Penn, than whom no more adroit politician (in the legitimate, not the conventional use of that word) appears on the pages of English history, waited for the royal distrust to subside in time, and by degrees the antagonistic feelings of the crown died away to such an extent that their Majesties themselves at last desired to restore Penn to the enjoyment of those rights of which they had arbitrarily deprived him. Hence, on Aug 20, 1694, the commission of Governor Fletcher was annulled, and letters patent granted to Penn fully restoring to him the Province of Pennsylvania and its territories The proprietary not having matters arranged that he could leave England at that time, commissioned William Markham Governor, which office the latter discharged until late in the spring of 1698, when he received a new commission as Lieutenant-Governor

In the fall of 1699 the yellow fever visited Philadelphia as a pestilence Many of the inhabitants died of the disease, and the utmost alarm prevailed throughout the province Although we have no direct record that the malady made its appearance at Chester, that such was the case may be inferentially concluded from the fact that the September court adjourned without transacting any business, an incident without a parallel in our county's history Later on, in November of that year, William Penn came for the second time to his colony, and before leaving England he announced that it was his intention to make his permanent residence in the province As the vessel sailed up the Delaware the proprietary caused it to be anchored off Chester, and, coming ashore, he for a second time became an honored guest at the Essex House Robert Wade, his friend, was dead, but Lydia, his widow, welcomed Penn, and here he met Thomas Story, who had recently returned from a religious journey to Virginia The next morning, as is related by Clarkson,[1] Penn was rowed across the creek in a boat to the eastern side, "and as he landed, some young men officiously, and contrary to express orders of some of the magistrates, fired two small sea pieces of cannon, and being ambitious to make three out of two, by firing one twice, one of them, darting in a cartridge of powder before the piece was sponged, had his left arm shot to pieces, upon which, a surgeon being sent for, an amputation took place" The young man, Bevan, thus injured died the following April, and the expenses attending the nursing and ultimate burial of the wounded lad were discharged by Penn

The proprietary was not destined to end his days in his colony William III, after the death of Mary, is believed to have regarded him in no friendly spirit, and when the proprietary learned that the ministry, with the intention of converting the provincial government into a regal one, had introduced a bill to that effect in Parliament, the consideration of which had been postponed until he could be present, the urgency of affairs compelled his prompt return to England He sailed from Philadelphia, Nov 1, 1701, never again to visit the commonwealth he had founded Before his departure he established a Council of State, and appointed Andrew Hamilton as Deputy Governor

The general history of our county, saving such incidents as relate to court proceedings, religious associations, organization of townships, and similar matters, which will be considered hereafter, is very meagre until the approaching struggle of the colonists with Great Britain threw the country into a commotion that tore asunder family ties, and strained the social and political fabric to its very foundation In a great measure previous to that period, year had followed

[1] Life of William Penn, vol ii p 163.

year without leaving any impression that has remained to our day. Even the absurd farce, on May 16, 1706, of the French invasion, in which Governor Evans played such a ridiculous part, seems to have made no lasting trace on our county's records, yet doubtless the messenger who rode with such hot haste to Philadelphia, and whose tidings caused such widespread consternation in the latter place[1] as he passed through Marcus Hook, Chester, and Darby, gave forth intimations that he was the bearer of momentous intelligence, for such a course would have been in full accord with the preconcerted scheme of the Governor to arouse general alarm in the province, and yet there seems not to be the faintest reference to this in our local annals.

On May 16, 1712, to the Provincial Council was presented "A Petition of a great number of the Inhabitants of the county of Chester, praying that yᵉ Burrough of the Town of Chester, in this Province, may be made a free Port, was read & Considered; And it is the opinion of the board that the matter may be presented to the Propry., that he may take proper methods Concerning the same & Consult the Courts of the Queen's Customs therein."[2] In all probability William Penn, whose energy was beginning to yield under the weight of years and constant pecuniary embarrassments, never gave this petition any serious consideration, his chief desire at that period appearing to be to rid himself of the trouble, vexation, and expense of the colony by its sale to Queen Ann for twelve thousand pounds. This transfer would doubtless have been effected had not a stroke of paralysis rendered Penn unable to formally execute the contract. During all the last century, as will be shown as we proceed in this narrative, Chester was a place where outward- and inward-bound vessels stopped for days together. On the 4th of Fifth month, 1730, at noon, James Logan dispatched a letter to his son, William, "on his voyage to Bristol, sent to him at Chester," and during the British occupation of Philadelphia almost all their transports and men-of-war lay off the former town. As just stated, William Penn's health became so impaired that he was unable to carry to an end his contemplated sale of the province to the crown, and from that time he never wholly rallied, his mind gradually becoming more and more feeble until his death, July 30, 1718.

The disputes respecting the northwestern boundary of the county of Chester, which had been, as supposed, officially determined in 1685, and after a protracted resistance had finally been accepted by the Welsh in 1689, in the early spring of 1720 again engaged the attention of Council, when at that time a petition of the inhabitants of the west side of Schuylkill was presented, setting forth that the commissioners of Chester County had compelled the payment by them of taxes levied by the assessors of that county, although they stated that ever since their first settlement they had paid their taxes to Philadelphia; that they had no trade with Chester, "seeing it is impossible for us to have any tolerably convenient road to Chester by reason of Rocks and Mountains," and also urged other arguments, all concluding with a prayer that the counties might be so divided as to place them within Philadelphia.[3] On Feb. 1, 1721, Council reported[4] that the General Assembly had acted on the matter, and that the secretary had made full examinations as to the official boundaries as theretofore established, but that he expressed his belief that the line then run "was done arbitrarily by the Surveyor-General, and that in his opinion it would have been more regular to carry the Division Line along the side of Radnor and the upper part of that called the Welch Line, laying all those Tracts called Manors to Philadelphia County." Council thereupon concluded that until the matter could "be more fully and effectually settled, the Commissioners and Assessors of Chester County should forebear to claim those Inhabitants . . . and that the said Inhabitants be permitted to pay their Taxes and do all other Duties to the county of Philadelphia as formerly." Chester County, however, declined to accept this decree without resistance, for on March 28, 1722,[5] David Lloyd (who at the time was chief justice of the province) and Nathaniel Newlin, in behalf of themselves, and the other commissioners appointed by the act of Assembly for Chester County, presented a petition to Council praying relief "from the unrighteous Attempts of the said persons to sever themselves from the said County of Chester." Council called the attention of David Lloyd to the fact that no regular division of the counties, so far as known, had been made, and the interdiction of the commissioners of Chester County from levying taxes only applied to cases where persons had been assessed in and had paid taxes to Philadelphia County, for it would be unreasonable to require on the same estate taxes in both counties, and, besides, those who had thus paid their assessments to Philadelphia County were only six in number, but they were of opinion that it was of great importance that the division-lines should be adjusted without delay. David Lloyd replied that there were persons yet living who remembered the running of the division-line, which was done, he believed, about the year 1688, under the administration of Governor Blackwell, but the commissioners of Chester County did not know where to apply for the record "or written proofs of it, except to the secretary, in whose custody all things of that kind should be kept." After an interesting statement relative to the custody of the papers of the former secretary, Patrick Robinson, Council instructed the

[1] Gordon's "History of Pennsylvania," p. 138.
[2] Colonial Records, vol. ii. p. 546.
[3] Ib., vol. iii. p. 111.
[4] Futhey and Cope's "History of Chester County," p. 41.
[5] Colonial Records, vol. iii. p. 158.

then secretary, James Logan, and Attorney-General Andrew Hamilton, without delay, to make search for the missing documents belonging to the records of Council, and the secretary was "ordered to make further search for the proofs that have been mentioned of the Division Line between the Counties of Philadelphia & Chester." With this announcement, so far as the minutes of Council are concerned, the whole matter dropped out of public notice, and adjusted itself in the manner suggested by Secretary Logan, by "laying all those Tracts called Mannors to Philadelphia County."

At a meeting of Council held Feb. 6, 1728–29, a petition was presented by the inhabitants of the upper part of Chester County, setting forth that "by Reason of their Great Distance from the County Town, where the Courts are held, Officers are Kept and Annual elections made," the inconvenience of attending court or obtaining writs and other legal process, being compelled to travel one hundred miles for such purposes, the want of a jail to imprison "Vagabonds and other dissolute People" who harbored among the frontier settlements where they believed themselves "safe from justice in so remote a Place," a division of the county should be made between the upper and lower parts, and that the upper portion should be erected into a county.[1] It is not within the scope of this work to follow the particulars of this movement, which finally resulted in the county of Lancaster being erected by the act of May 10, 1729.

We learn from the minutes of Council of Dec. 16, 1728,[2] that the propriety of again making Chester the seat of the Provincial Government was seriously considered. It seems that a resolution had been carried in the General Assembly which set forth, "that inasmuch as there has been of late several Indecencies used towards the Members of Assembly attending the Service of the Country in Philadelphia by rude and disorderly Persons unknown to this House," the Governor and Council were requested to select a place which they shall deem "more safe for the Members of Assembly and most convenient for the Dispatch of the Business of the Country." The Provincial Council, on their part, after considering the inconvenience of removal at that season of the year and setting out other difficulties, concluded that "if on further Experience the House shall continue in the same Sentiments that a Removal is necessary, the Board are of opinion that the same out [ought] to be adjourned to Chester, as the most convenient place for their meeting next to Philadelphia." The sober second thought of the indignant legislators, or the penitent petitions of the inhabitants of the Quaker city prevailed over the anger of the Assembly, and, on "further experience, the House" neglected to press the subject of removal, and thus Chester did not grasp the prize she was so willing to secure.

[1] Colonial Records, vol. iii. p. 343. [2] Ib., p. 340.

About 1730, the first mission of the Roman Catholic Church within the territory now comprising the present county of Delaware was located at the residence of Thomas Willcox at Ivy Mill, in Concord, to which fuller reference will be made in the history of that township. This religious sect did not progress very rapidly, for in 1757, in the census of Roman Catholics in Pennsylvania,[3] the following return shows that in Chester County there were

	Men.	Women.
"Under care of Robert Harding	18	22
" " Thomas Schneider	13	9
" " " " (Irish)	9	6
" " Ferdinane Farmer (Irish)	23	17
" " " " (German)	3	...

"These were all who took the sacrament above twelve years of age or thereabout."

On the afternoon of Aug. 11, 1732, Thomas Penn, the son of the proprietary, landed at Chester, and a messenger was dispatched to Philadelphia to apprise the Council and Assembly, then in session, of his arrival. The secretary of Council immediately came to Chester, with the congratulations of the authorities, and "to acquaint him—Penn—that to-morrow they would in person pay their respects to him." The following day the Governor and Council, accompanied by a large number of gentlemen, visited the borough, and "waited on the Honorable Proprietary and paid him their compliments. After dinner the Proprietary with his company, now grown very numerous, sett out for Philadelphia." On September 20th of the following year, John Penn arrived at Chester, from England, and was there met and welcomed by his younger brother, Thomas, who, with a large number of gentlemen, had come from Philadelphia to greet the eldest son of the founder. After passing the night at Chester, the next morning the party rode to the city, where they were received with manifestations of popular rejoicing.

In 1739, when England declared war against Spain, an expedition was proposed from the colonies to invade the West Indies, and the Governor, in a proclamation calling for recruits "to inlist in the important Expedition now on Foot for attacking and plundering the most valuable Part of the Spanish West Indies," notified the people of Chester and vicinity that those who proposed to recruit should call on James Mather in the borough, while Henry Hockley, Robert Finney, and Lazarus Finney were designated for like service in other localities throughout the then county of Chester. It seems that in this enterprise a number of redemption servants were enlisted, and notwithstanding the attention of Governor Thomas was drawn to that fact, he took no official action to prevent such recruiting, and the parties aggrieved were compelled to seek redress from the Assembly. That body promptly provided for the payment by the province of all losses sustained by masters whose servants had been accepted into the military forces, and accordingly, on June 3, 1741, to James Gibbons and

[3] Penna. Archives, 1st series, vol. iii. p. 144.

Samuel Levis was issued an order on the loan-office for £515 11s 9d, in payment for fifty-eight servants mustered by the officers in Chester County Other claims for damages suffered by similar enlistments were urged and paid, in one instance it was alleged that ten servants were taken from the iron-works at Coventry and Warwick, and those establishments were obliged to cease operation for a time, because their skilled labor had been marched away as recruits

On Dec 22, 1741, the Governor presented to Council a petition from the justices of the county of Chester, setting forth that great abuses had been "committed" in the county by the use of defective weights and measures, and that they, the justices, at the instance of some of "the substantial Inhabitants," as well as an address from the Grand Inquest, had "directed the purchasing of Standards of Brass for Weights & Measures, accordingly to his Majesty's Standard for the Exchequer" They therefore prayed that "the Governor would be pleased to appoint an Officer to keep the said Standards, and to Seal and Mark all Weights and Measures within the said County"[1] Isaac Taylor was the favored one who received the appointment, and the standards, we learn, cost the county £17 12s 11d[2]

On March 29, 1744, war was declared between Great Britain and France, and on the 11th of June of the same year Governor Thomas issued a proclamation[3] in which he not only announced the hostile position of the two nations, but strictly enjoined and required all persons in the province capable of bearing arms "forthwith to provide themselves with a Good Firelock, Bayonet, and Cartouch-Box, and a sufficient Quantity of Powder and Ball," that they might be prepared to attack the enemy or defend the province from invasion The Governor also urged the fitting out of privateers, not only as a war measure highly beneficial to the State, but "may bring great advantages to the Adventurers themselves" The Assembly, however, in which the Society of Friends largely predominated, took no step of a decided military character, but Franklin, by his pamphlet, "Plain Truth," aroused the public to a knowledge of the defenseless condition in which the province then stood A meeting of citizens was called, a regiment was formed in Philadelphia, and money was raised by a lottery to erect a battery below that city, on the river "These military preparations were necessary to intimidate a foreign enemy, and to curb the hostile disposition of the Indians, which had been awakened by several unpleasant rencontres with the whites"[4]

The crown having, on April 9, 1746, ordered that four hundred men should be raised in the province of Pennsylvania, to be part of the forces designed for the immediate reduction of the French Canadian colonies, Governor Thomas, on June 9th of the same year, issued his proclamation[5] to that effect, and under it four companies were recruited, commanded respectively by Capts Trent, Perry, Deimer, and Shannon The latter, John Shannon, of New Castle County, Del, was commissioned June 25, 1746, as captain, and authorized to enlist one hundred men[6] Professor Keen informs us that the company was to be recruited on the Delaware River[7]

That the men were collected in New Castle and Chester Counties the names on the roll fully establish, and aside from that inferential proof, we have positive evidence that the organization was quartered in the borough of Chester, for in January of the following year the petitions of James Mather, David Coupland, John Salkeld, and Aubrey Bevan, then tavern-keepers in that town, were presented to the Assembly, asking payment "for the diet of Captain Shannon's company of soldiers," while Dr Gandouit, a practicing physician in Chester at that time, also petitioned for payment for medicine furnished by him, as well as professional attendance on the sick soldiers[8] These companies were ordered to Albany, where they went into winter quarters From a letter from Capt Trent to Governor Thomas, written from Albany, Oct 21, 1746,[9] we learn that the troops were badly provided with blankets, and that the officers had been compelled to purchase a number for them, paying therefor in a draft on the Governor He stated that had they not supplied the troops with those articles the whole body would have deserted The weather was extremely cold, and as many as thirty men had already deserted from Capt. Shannon's company, giving as their reason the want of proper covering, and that they might as well take the chance of being killed in trying to make their escape as by remaining to surely die He related that one of Shannon's men, "when the snow was knee-deep, in attempting to make his escape, got frost-bit, and his companions, fearing to undergo the same fate, left him, when he miserably perished" The following month the captains of the four Pennsylvania companies united in an appeal to the Governor to supply the troops with necessaries, for "we have been making as near a calculation as possible of our provisions, & find, with the utmost frugality, we have not more meat than sufficient to serve till the 19th January, & as to our Bread & Rum, it falls far short of that time"[10] The troops, after being kept in cantonment until Oct 31, 1747, were discharged by proclamation of the Governor, wherein he declared the reason that "the late in-

[1] Colonial Records, vol iv p 507

[2] Futhey and Cope's "History of Chester County," p 49

[3] Colonial Records, vol iv p 696

[4] Gordon's "History of Pennsylvania," p 245

[5] Colonial Records, vol v p 39

[6] See his commission and instructions, Pennsylvania Archives, vol i p 688

[7] "Descendants of Joran Kyn," *Penna Mag of Hist.*, vol iv p. 108

[8] Futhey and Cope's "History of Chester County," p 49

[9] Penna Archives, 2d series, vol ii p 680

[10] Ib., p 681

tended expedition against Canada having been by his Majesty laid aside for the present."[1]

During the early summer of 1747 a French privateer entered Delaware Bay, and captured several inward- and outward-bound vessels.[2] The intelligence of these acts reaching Philadelphia on July 4th, pilots were forbidden by proclamation "to conduct, Pilot, or bring up any foreign Ship or Vessel carrying a Flag of Truce . . . to any Port or place within this Province above that Tract of Land lying in Chester county, commonly called and known by the name of Marcus Hook,"[3] unless special license was issued by the Governor. The following summer the Spanish and French privateers showed the utmost daring in cruising off the mouth of and in Delaware Bay.

On May 25, 1748, George Proctor, a prisoner of war, succeeded in escaping by swimming from the "St. Michael," a Spanish privateer, carrying twenty-two guns and a crew of one hundred and sixty men, which was at the time moored off Salem Creek. The deposition of the Proctor was taken, and an express sent immediately to Philadelphia with the intelligence, which threw the city into the utmost consternation, a condition of affairs which was in no wise allayed when on the following day the escaped sailor was himself sent to Philadelphia, the bearer of a letter from the authorities, stating that the Spanish vessel, about ten o'clock that morning, came up within gunshot of New Castle, and there anchored, with a spring on her cable. The tide, together with a calm, being against her, she was prevented getting nearer to that town, and as the people opened fire upon her, she weighed, and by her boats was towed "stern foremost, giving three Huzzas & one Gunn, hoisted Spanish Colours, & went down the River again." Council desired Capt. Ballet, commander of the sloop-of-war "Otter," to go down the bay and engage the privateer, but that officer stated that he had an encounter with a large French ship, in which his vessel had received such damage that required her to be hoved down for repairs.[4] The Spanish privateer, unmolested, remained in the bay for some time, during which she made prizes of a number of vessels. The result of the alarm, however, was to arouse the public to the necessity of organization; hence the bodies known as Associators, which had been called into existence during the previous December by the voluntary action of the people throughout the province, became firmly established, and the military education imparted thereby to the populace was of the utmost consequence to the patriot cause when, a quarter of a century later, the Revolutionary contest was forced upon the colonies. The following is the list of the officers of the two Associate Regiments of Chester County in 1747–48:[5]

Colonels, William Moore, Andrew McDowell.
Lieutenant-Colonels, Samuel Flower, John Frew.
Majors, John Mather, John Miller.

Captain David Parry. Lieutenant Isaac Davy. Ensign Nathaniel Davies.	Captain Job Rushton. Lieutenant Joseph Smith. Ensign James Dysart.
Captain Roger Hunt. Lieutenant Guyon Moore. Ensign William Littles.	Captain Andrew McDowell. Lieutenant John Cunningham. Ensign George McCullough.
Captain George Ashton. Lieutenant Robert Morrell. Ensign Edward Pearce.	Captain John McCall. Lieutenant John Culbertson. Ensign James Scott.
Captain William McKnight. Lieutenant Robert Anderson. Ensign Samuel Love.	Captain George Taylor. Lieutenant John Vaugn. Ensign Robert Awl.
Captain Moses Dickey. Lieutenant John Boyd. Ensign James Montgomery.	Captain James Graham. Lieutenant William Darlington. Ensign Francis Gardner.
Captain Richard Richardson. Lieutenant John Cuthbert. Ensign John Hambright.	Captain Robert Grace. Lieutenant John Kent. Ensign Jacob Free.
Captain John Williamson. Lieutenant James McMakin. Ensign John Johnson.	Captain Hugh Kilpatrick. Lieutenant William Buchanan. Ensign William Cumming.
Captain John Mathers. Lieutenant James Mathers. Ensign Joseph Talbert.	Captain William Bell. Lieutenant Robert McMullen. Ensign Rowland Parry.
Captain James Hunter. Lieutenant Charles Moore. Ensign Benjamin Weatherby.	Captain Joseph Wilson. Lieutenant James Cochran. Ensign Joseph Parke.
Captain John Miller. Lieutenant George Bently. Ensign Thomas Brown.	Captain Henry Glassford. Lieutenant Robert Allison. Ensign John Emmitt.
Captain William Clinton. Lieutenant Morris Thomas. Ensign William Carr.	Captain William Boyd. Lieutenant John Culbertson. Ensign John Donald.
Captain Thomas Hubert, Jr. Lieutenant John Rees. Ensign Anthony Richard.	Captain William Reed. Lieutenant Thomas Hope. Ensign Thomas Clarke.
Captain George Leggitt. Lieutenant Thomas Leggitt. Ensign Archibald Young.	Captain William Porter. Lieutenant Robert Mackey. Ensign John Smith.

In the autumn of the year 1748 a general sickness prevailed throughout the province. Kalm records that "the disease was so violent that when it attacked a person he seldom lived above two or three days, and of those who were taken ill with it very few recovered. It was a true pleurisy, but it had a peculiarity with it, for it commonly began with a difficulty of swallowing." . . . "The physicians did not know what to make of it, nor how to remedy it."[6]

In 1751 the act of Parliament,[7] which, as its title stated, was to regulate the commencement of the year and to correct the calendar then in use, was adopted. By its provisions Wednesday, the 2d day of September, 1751, was followed by Thursday, the 14th day of the same month, and as the act was intended to equalize the style in Great Britain, Ireland, and the colonies with that used in other countries in Europe, it was necessary that the Society of Friends should take action on so important a change. Hence the records of Chester Monthly Meeting respecting this alteration in style, as transcribed by Dr. Smith,[8] are here given entire:

[1] Colonial Records, vol. v. p. 127.
[2] Ib., p. 234.
[3] Penna. Archives, 2d series, vol. ii. p. 682.
[4] Colonial Records, vol. v. pp. 248, 252, 253, 256, 260, 261, 263, 264.
[5] Penna. Archives, 2d series, vol. ii. p. 506.

[6] Kalm's Travels, vol. i. pp. 376, 377.
[7] 24 Geo. II., c. 23, 1751.
[8] Hist. of Delaware Co., pp. 261, 262.

"Agreed that as by the late Act of Parliament for regulating the commencement of the year, that it is ordered that the first day of the Eleventh month next shall be deemed the first day of the year 1752, and that the month called January shall be successively called the first month of the year, and not the month called March, as heretofore hath been our method of computing

"That from and after the time above mentioned, the Eleventh month, called January, shall thenceforth be deemed and reckoned the First month in the year, be so styled in all the records and writings of Friends, instead of computing from the month called March, according to our present practice, and Friends are recommended to go on with the names of the following months, numerically, according to our practice from the beginning, so that the months may be called and written as follows That January be called and written the First month, and February called and written the Second month, and so on All other methods of computing and calling of the months unavoidably leads into contradiction

"And whereas, for the more regular computation of time, the same act directs that in the month now called September, which will be in the year 1752, after the second day of the said month, eleven numerical days shall be omitted, and that which would have been the third day shall be reckoned and esteemed the 14th day of the said month, and that which otherwise would have been the fourth day of the said month, must be deemed the 15th, and so on It appears likewise necessary Friends should conform themselves to this direction, and omit the nominal days accordingly"

In 1753 the French and Indian war was actually begun by a direct violation of good faith on the part of the French, and the struggle then inaugurated, although Great Britain did not declare war until 1755, finally terminated in the white standard of France giving place to the red-crossed banner of St George throughout that vast territory now known as British North America When, in the summer of 1755, Gen Braddock took up the line of march for Fort Du Quesne, there was but one impression in all the English provinces, and that was that victory was already assured to his arms We know that on May 28, 1755, the justices, sheriffs, and constables of the counties of Philadelphia, Chester, Berks, and Bucks were notified that sixty wagons were required for the use of Braddock's army, and that, if possible, they should be procured without harsh measures before the 8th day of June following, but if they were not willingly furnished they must be impressed It is, however, very doubtful whether any soldier from the then county of Chester was present at the fatal field of the Monongahela,[1] but when the news of the crushing defeat which made famous the rash, overbearing English general, who purchased with his life posthumous renown, came to astound the colonists as greatly as it amazed the English nation, many a young man from this locality enrolled himself in the hastily-recruited company which, commanded by Capt Isaac Wayne, was sent into Northampton County to guard the frontier inhabitants from threatened Indian attacks,[2] as also in that commanded by Capt George Aston[3] When, in the summer of 1758, Brig-Gen John Forbes took command of the troops collected to reduce Fort Du Quesne, in not a few instances the garb of the peaceful Society of Friends gave place to the dark-scarlet coat, faced with blue, the uniform of the Royal Americans, or the fringed hunting-shirt of the Pennsylvania Provincial Dr Smith[4] records that no less than eight young men in full membership with Radnor Meeting went into active military service in 1756, and were disowned by the society because of that open violation of its rules After Braddock's defeat, so intense was the feeling in Chester County[5] among the masses that on Nov 24, 1755, a letter was read in Council from Col William Moore, informing the Governor that two thousand of the inhabitants of that locality were prepared to march to Philadelphia to compel the Assembly to pass laws providing for the defense of the province As at the same meeting a letter from Mr Weiser, of Berks County, of a like import, was read, the Governor issued orders to the authorities in Philadelphia to take proper precautions to preserve the public peace Subsequently Moore's letter played a prominent part in the legislative and gubernatorial quarrels of that day, which, being more particularly the history of the State, requires no further mention in this work

In 1755 the English nation suffered a disgrace far greater than defeat to her arms, and that was the violent expatriation of the French Neutrals, or, as afterwards called, "Acadian exiles," from Nova Scotia These unfortunates were the descendants of French parentage, and by the treaty of Utrecht, in 1713, Great Britain had stipulated that these people should retain their lands on taking the oath of allegiance to the English king, and were not to be required to bear arms against the Indians or the French For nearly half a century both parties adhered to the terms of the treaty, but in 1755 the love of their ancient country animated a few of the Acadian young men to enlist under the standard of France, and at the capture of Beau Sejour three hundred were found in arms A number of these, however, were unwilling soldiers, forced into the ranks Governor Lawrence, of Nova Scotia, thereupon demanded of the whole population, amounting to over seven thousand souls, including

[1] Andrew Wallace (better known as Sergt Wallace, of Wayne's Bridge), in a sketch of his life published in Hazard's Register, vol xiii p 53, says, "About the 1st of May, 1754, I entered as a volunteer at Chester, and was appointed orderly sergeant in a company commanded by Capt John Hannum" (This was about the commencement of what was termed the French war) The company before referred to became a part of the regiment under the command of Col Charles Dack, of Virginia "We were afterwards marched from Chester to the Gum-Tree Tavern, in Chester County, and from thence to Carlisle, where we were placed under the command of Maj Samuel Hughs From the last-mentioned place we were marched to Fort Chambers, now Chambersburg, from thence to Fort Louden, to join the troops raised, and to be commanded by Gen Forbes, whose division was a part of the army commanded by Gen Braddock, in the year 1755, as no part of the immediate command of Gen Forbes was in that engagement." This statement was made by Wallace in 1833, when he was a petitioner for a pension, and he stated he was one hundred and four years old The aged veteran was possibly in error in his date He may have been in Forbes' expedition in 1758, but Forbes was not with Braddock in 1755 At the time Wallace places Hannum in command of a company the latter officer was not fourteen years of age

[2] Col Samuel Miles' Manuscript, Feb 4, 1802 Penna Archives, 2d series, vol ii p 517

[3] Futhey and Cope's "History of Chester County," p 51

[4] Smith's "History of Delaware County," p 264

[5] Colonial Records, vol vi p 729

those who had not been in arms, to take the oath of allegiance to the British monarchy unconditionally. This being refused, because it was a violation of the treaty, Lawrence expelled the Acadians from Nova Scotia, confiscated their property (excepting their money and household goods), burned their dwellings, and wasted their estates. In this wantonly cruel act husbands and wives, parents and children, were torn apart and transported to different parts of the British American colonies, while the vessels which carried them were so crowded that many died on the voyage. On Aug. 11, 1755, Governor Lawrence wrote to Governor Morris, of Pennsylvania, that he had shipped one hundred and sixty-eight men, women, and children to the latter province.[1] This letter, which was brought by the vessels on which the Acadians came, was received November 19th, and Council immediately commanded that a guard should be placed over the ship to prevent the landing of the exiles, but fresh provisions and necessaries were ordered to be delivered on board, and continued to be sent until Council determined what should be done with these people.[2] On the 25th of the same month Governor Morris, by message, informed the Assembly that he had the French Neutrals landed at Providence Island, as the doctor had reported that it would be dangerous to have them remain longer in the crowded vessel.[3] Early in December it was officially reported that in the ships "Hannah," "Three Friends," and "Swan" four hundred and fifty-four out of the five hundred French Neutrals assigned to Pennsylvania had been received at Providence Island. Governor Morris, touched at the wrongs these unhappy exiles had suffered, strove earnestly to reunite those families which had been separated in transportation.[4] On Feb. 20, 1756, the Assembly passed an act dispersing the Acadians in the several counties of Philadelphia, Bucks, Chester, and Lancaster, and making provision for their maintenance.[5] By the act three commissioners were appointed in each of the counties named to distribute the Acadians among the people, locating only one family in a township, and to have a supervisory care over them. Nathaniel Pennock, Nathaniel Grubb, and John Hannum were the commissioners named for Chester County. The Governor failing to approve the bill promptly, on March 3d a committee from the Assembly waited on him to know what "he had done" with it, and on the 5th he signed it. When the law was attempted to be enforced, the Neutrals claimed to be prisoners of war, but Governor Morris and Council, after considerable delay, decided, six months subsequent to the promulgation of the act, that under the treaty of Utrecht they were subjects of Great Britain.[6] Jan. 14, 1757, an additional act was approved, empowering the binding out and settling of the Acadians under age, and providing for the maintenance of their aged, sick, and maimed at the expense of the province. The unfortunate people, feeling the injustice that had been visited on them, having lost heart and refusing to work, were soon in the utmost want. One week subsequent to the passage of the law just mentioned, William Griffith informed Council that unless something was immediately done many of the French Neutrals would perish. Already death had been busy among them, for shortly after they landed more than one-half of them had died.[7] On March 21, 1757, Governor Denny caused the arrest of five of the Neutrals at the request of Lord Lowdoun, two in the city of Philadelphia, one in Frankford, "Paul Bujaud in Chester, and Jean Landy in Darby," because they were "suspicious and evil-minded persons, and have and each of them hath at divers Times uttered menacing speeches against his majesty and his liege subjects, and behaved in a very disorderly manner."[8] No wonder; for surely the poor men who were thrown in jail in Philadelphia had every reason to utter menacing speeches against the Hanoverian scoundrel who then sat on the throne of Great Britain. In Chester, before the act authorizing the overseers of the poor in the several townships to bind out the children of the Acadians, the former officials had in many cases refused to receive the exiles or minister to their wants, hence many of the latter had died with smallpox; but after the law of Jan. 14, 1757, became operative the condition of the Neutrals was considerably improved. The burden of their support, however, aroused the taxpayers of that day, and when four years later it was found that seven thousand pounds had been expended in the support of the exiles, a committee of the Assembly was appointed to inquire into the condition of these people, and to ascertain whether the cost of their maintenance could not be lessened. It was, after investigation, reported that the reason their children had not been bound out to service was mainly owing to the religious opinions of their parents, who feared that their offspring might be surrounded with objectional influences in the families of the English settlers or their descendants. The result of the report was finally the repeal of the law providing for the support of these exiles. The glamour of Longfellow's genius has made the wrongs of these Acadians more familiar to the popular mind than any of the many harsh and unjustifiable acts of ministerial minions in American colonial history, but to the student, the story of the banishment of these ignorant French people is a mere incident, the happening of which had little or no influence in shaping the direction of events. Even at that time among the Northern colonies the impression was being made on some thoughtful minds that at no distant day there would be an absolute separation from the mother-country.

[1] Colonial Records, vol. vi. p. 711.
[2] Ib., p. 713.
[3] Ib., p. 729.
[4] Ib., p. 45.
[5] Ib., vol. vii. pp. 14, 15.
[6] Ib., pp. 239, 240, 241.
[7] Gordon's "History of Pennsylvania," p. 500.
[8] Colonial Records, vol. vii. p. 446.

In the summer of 1758, Brig.-Gen John Forbes, as before stated, with three hundred and fifty Royal Americans, twelve hundred (thirteen companies) of Montgomery's Highlanders, twenty-six hundred Virginians, and twenty-seven hundred Pennsylvania Provincials, besides a thousand wagoners,[1] set out from Philadelphia intending the reduction of Fort Du Quesne Capt John Hasslet, of New Castle County, recruited a company on the Delaware River, and the roll shows that Chester County contributed at least the following persons to the ranks[2] of this organization

Peter Allen, enlisted May 7, born in Chester Co, aged 22, and by occupation a saddler
William Boggs, enlisted May 6, born in Chester Co, aged 40
James Breslin, enlisted May 12, born in Chester Co., aged 17
Edward Gallagher, enlisted May 12, born in Chester Co., aged 17
Thomas Harvey, enlisted May 12, born in Chester Co, aged 17
John McAfee, enlisted May 8, born in Chester Co, aged 21, and by occupation a laborer
James Thomas, enlisted May 8, born in Chester Co, aged 22, and by occupation a laborer
Samuel White, enlisted May 10, born in Chester Co., aged 26

In the same month and year Capt John Singleton enlisted a company of soldiers for Forbes' expedition The list of that organization shows that the following men were certainly from Chester County, and probably the number from this locality was greater than here represented [3]

William Henry, aged 22, resident of Chester, Pa, drummer
Samuel Armitage, aged 27, resident of Chester, Pa
William Bevard, aged 28, resident of Chester, Pa, weaver
Thomas Callican, aged 20, resident of Chester, Pa.
Thomas Connolly, aged 17, resident of Chester, Pa.
John Cross, aged 25, resident in Chester, Pa., cordwainer, "pock-pitt'd," "stout made"
John Cruthers, aged 16, resident of Chester, Pa
Hugh Davis, aged 20, resident of Chester, Pa., smith
William Foster, aged 25, resident of Chester, Pa
William Kennedy, aged 25, resident of Chester, Pa., weaver
John Long, aged 24, resident of Chester, Pa.
Edward McSorley, aged 22, resident of Chester, Pa
Terence Kealy, aged 35, residing in Chester, Pa., "pock-pitt d"
John Richeson, aged 27, residing in Chester, Pa, "cocke nose and smooth faced"
Patrick Roe, aged 22, residing in Chester, Pa, "bold looking"
John Shannon, aged 23, residing in Chester, Pa., chandler, "Irishman"
Edward Sheppard, aged 21, residing in Chester, Pa, "red hair and thin visaged"
David Way, aged 24, residing in Chester, Pa, tanner
Coupland David

Besides these organizations there was a company of Pennsylvania Rifles under Capt West, an elder brother of Benjamin West, the painter,[4] who was present with his command when, on Nov 25, 1758, the standard of Great Britain floated over the blackened and charred remains of the Fortress Du Quesne, and when the general, who had sworn the day previous to carry the works or leave his body beneath its walls, christened the heap of ruins Fort Pitt The army having retraced its steps, the government the following year determined to rebuild the dismantled fortification, or to erect a new one on its site Brig.-Gen. John Stanwick was placed in charge of this expedition, he having, on the death of Gen Forbes, succeeded to the command Troops were ordered to be enlisted, and on May 4, 1759, Gen Stanwick gave notice that a number of wagons would be required, and in order to avoid the impressment of horses or wagons, a certain rate of compensation had been fixed by the authorities, which would be paid to those persons who would willingly furnish teams From the county of Chester sixty-four wagons and four times as many horses were required[5] In the same locality a number of men enlisted, and doubtless the whole company recruited by Capt John Mather, Jr,[6] was credited to Chester County, because Mather himself was a resident of the borough of Chester, and the following men certainly resided in that neighborhood

John Gorsel, aged 16, of Chester, Pa, enlisted June 8, 1759, laborer
Evan Jones, aged 38, of Chester, Pa., enlisted May 27, 1759, laborer
Jacob Kirgan, aged 19, of Chester, Pa, enlisted May 27, 1759, weaver
Hugh Wallace, aged 17, of Chester, Pa, enlisted June 12, 1759, shoemaker

In Capt Robert Boyd's company appear the following persons who were undoubtedly residents of Chester County

James Campbell, aged 22, resides in Chester, Pa., enlisted June 13, laborer
James Darragh, aged 20, resides in Chester, Pa, enlisted May 11, laborer
Samuel Fillson, aged 18, resides in Chester, Pa., enlisted June 6, tailor
James Hamilton, aged 21, resides in Chester, Pa., enlisted May 21, laborer
George Matthews, aged 18, resides in Chester, Pa, enlisted June 2, laborer
Robert Saundford, aged 23, resides in Chester, Pa., enlisted May 25, laborer
John Small, aged 22, resides in Chester, Pa., enlisted May 1, laborer
John Travers, aged 20, resides in Chester, Pa., enlisted May 14, tailor
John Willson, aged 20, resides in Chester, Pa., enlisted May 7, tailor

In Capt James Armstrong's company from Chester County were

William Moore, aged 17, resides in Chester, Pa., enlisted May 9, hatter by trade
James Parr, aged 16, resides in Chester, Pa., enlisted May 9, laborer

In Capt. Jacob Richardson's company, Third Battalion provincial service, under command of Governor William Denny, appears the following

William Cassiday, aged 21, resides in Chester, Pa, enlisted Aug 20, carpenter

These are all the persons which can absolutely be designated as belonging to Chester County, but the

[1] *Penna Gazette*, 1758, No 1550 Winthrop Sargent, in his "History of Braddock's Expedition," page 270, make a difference in the number of men in Forbes' command He places the Virginia troops at sixteen hundred men

[2] Penna Archives, 2d series, vol ii p 551

[3] Ib, p 553

[4] Sargent's "History of Braddock's Expedition," p 274 Mr Sargent cites, in reference to the search of Sir Peter Halket for the remains of his father, slain in Braddock's defeat, a statement that the English nobleman was accompanied by Capt West Galt's "Life of West," p 65

[5] Penna Archives, 1st series, vol iii p 628

[6] Ib, 2d series, vol ii p 588

foregoing is but a very small part of the men who enlisted from this locality

The wagons required by Gen Stanwix, so far at least as Chester County was concerned, seem not to have been forthcoming, for on Aug 13, 1759, he wrote to the Governor from Bedford,[1] complaining that Lancaster County was the most backward, but that "Bucks and Chester have given us only Nominal Assistance, by sending us impressed Waggons, unfit for this Service, by the Weakness of the Horses and Carriages The Managers meet with more opposition in these two Counties than in any of the others, as the Magistrates seem unwilling to disoblige them, and unless they are spurred by the fear of incurring your Displeasure, I am afraid they will not exert their Authority in such a manner as will Answer the Purpose."

Notwithstanding the constant assertion of Gen Stanwix, the number of horses and wagons furnished by Chester County, according to the account-book of Roger Hunk,[2] was not inconsiderable, particularly when we consider that the expedition really was of little moment in the shaping of events, and was useful only in that it made permanent the settlement then first called Pittsburgh

The history of the province at this period is exceeding interesting, but, strange as it may appear, for almost a decade no event of sufficient importance to impress itself on the fleeting years seems to have occurred in our county The French war, which was most honorable to the colonial arms, was approaching its conclusion, and in 1761, after the subjugation of Canada was complete, the whole of the provincial forces raised by Pennsylvania were discharged, excepting one hundred and fifty men Considerable alarm was felt along the Delaware and at Philadelphia when the intelligence was received that about the beginning of the year (January 4th) 1762 Great Britain had declared war against Spain The defenseless condition of the city of Philadelphia, its wealth and importance, it was feared would attract the combined naval power of France and Spain to attempt its capture, therefore the Assembly, which had been hastily convened, appropriated twenty-three thousand five hundred pounds, the parliamentary allotment for 1759,[3] to the defense of the city, and also voted five thousand pounds to erect a fort mounting twenty guns on Mud Island, at the site of the present Fort Mifflin However, the province breathed more freely when, in January, 1763, news was received that on the 3d of November, 1762, peace had been proclaimed with both France and Spain

In 1765 we find that no less than three lotteries were authorized by the Legislature for the benefit of churches within the territory of the present county of Delaware, viz. St. Paul's, at Chester, St. John's, at Concord, and St. Martin's, at Marcus Hook 1768 "was a year of jubilee[4] for our good people, for the commissioners and assessors, after inspecting into the affairs of the county, "find no necessity for raising a tax this year"

The power and wealth exhibited by the colonies during the French war amazed the home government, hence Mr Grenville, in his desire to relieve the pressure of taxation at home,—the result of that war,—as well as to personally acquire reputation as a shrewd financier, proposed to raise a revenue from the colonies for the direct use of the British treasury The scheme was not devoid of arguments to commend it to a debt-ridden people, yet the history of the provinces ought to have clearly demonstrated that such a measure would be met with determined resistance The decided stand taken by the latter in 1754, when a plan for colonial taxation was suggested, should have fully indicated the temper of the people, who, whenever called on, had freely contributed pecuniary aid to the king by a vote of the Assembly, but who had always denied the right of the English Parliament to levy taxes on the provinces unless the latter had representation in the home legislative bodies And perhaps no more objectionable form could the duties be made to assume than that which levied a tax on colonial imports, which resulted in almost destroying the colonial trade with the Spanish and French West India islands It is unnecessary for me to discuss further this topic of colonial taxation, the resistance to which finally culminated in the Revolutionary war, and subsequently the formation of the United States as a nation

It seems that Chester was the outpost where the customs officer was stationed to board vessels and prevent violations of the revenue laws We learn that on Saturday afternoon, Nov 23, 1771, about four o'clock, Alban Davis, who was attached to the custom-house schooner then lying off Chester, noticed several vessels coming up the river, among the number a light brig and a pilot-boat Capt Thomas Muskett, of the revenue cutter, boarded the pilot-boat, and signaled the schooner to come alongside The crew on the pilot-boat then stated they wished to go down the river, which brought the inquiry from the officer what was their cargo, and the command to open the hatches or he would seize the vessel Those in charge of the craft being insolent, the officer "put the broad arrow on the boat's mast" Whereupon the captain of the latter said that, as he had no further business on the vessel, he would go ashore The revenue cutter and her prize, lashed together, had sailed up abreast of Red Bank, when the ebb-tide compelled them to anchor Shortly before ten o'clock that evening, a pilot boat coming down the river stood directly for the government schooner, when Capt Muskett

[1] Colonial Records, vol viii p 376

[2] Futhey and Cope's "History of Chester County," pp 54-58

[3] Gordon's "History of Pennsylvania," p 393

[4] Smith's "History of Delaware County," p 271

ordered them to keep off or he would fire at them, and was answered that he might fire and be damned, the river was as free to them as the cutter. Bearing down, the pilot-boat came alongside, when a man leveled a blunderbuss at Capt. Muskett, and gave him the choice to surrender or have his brains blown out. Even before the captain could make the selection about thirty men, armed with cutlasses and clubs, boarded the schooner, knocked down the captain and two of his men, and threw them into the hold, then fastened down the hatches. The captors ran the schooner ashore, cut her rigging and sails to pieces, and, unlashing the prize, sailed away with it. On December 5th Governor Richard Penn issued a proclamation, offering a free pardon to any one who should give information by whom the act was done.[1] But nothing was learned of the men who had thus boldly set the law at defiance.

The Navigation Act, which interdicted colonial trade with foreign nations, compelling the purchase of all goods from England directly, as before stated, aroused a storm of indignation, but the right of Parliament to regulate commerce was not questioned, hence the colonists could only retaliate by adopting the noted non-importation agreement. The Stamp Act and its subsequent repeal, in this locality as elsewhere, invoked popular resentment, and the line of demarkation between the ultra Whigs and the Loyalists became every month more distinct. In 1770 the act of 1767, imposing a duty on glass, paper, painters' colors, and tea imported into the colonies, was repealed, save the threepence per pound tax on tea. The colonists, strictly adhering to their determination to use no goods on which the detested duty was collected, modified the non-importation agreement so that it applied to tea only. In 1773 but little had been imported into America, and the East India Company which had then on hand nearly seventeen million pounds of tea, was permitted to export that commodity into any part of the world free of duty, hence, to the colonists, tea, even with the threepence tax, would be much cheaper than ever before, since the export duty of sixpence per pound was removed. The principle, however, of taxation without representation was still involved, and the colonists were violently excited, particularly when it was learned that the East India Company consented to ship cargoes to America only on the assurance of the British government that they should at least suffer no loss. The indignation consequent on this new attempt of Lord North to enforce the obnoxious duty was resisted at every port where tea-ships were consigned, and while in New England the destruction of the tea in the harbor of Boston on the night of Dec. 16, 1773, was more dramatic in its circumstances than the action taken by Philadelphia and the Whig populace along the Delaware River, the feeling of resistance was not more intense than at the latter place. In Philadelphia a public meeting of citizens was held in State-House yard on Oct. 16, 1773, when it was declared "that whoever shall directly or indirectly countenance this attempt (to send out the tea), or in any way aid or abet in unloading, receiving, or vending the tea sent while it remains subject to the payment of a duty here, is an enemy to the country," and strong measures were determined on to resist the landing of any tea in Philadelphia. On Nov. 29, 1773, Dunlap's *Pennsylvania Packet* announced,—

"The ship 'Polly,' Capt. Ayres, from London for this port, left Gravesend on the 27th of September with the *detested* TEA on board, and is hourly expected."

The excitement consequent on this brief news item was intense. On December 5th a committee was appointed to inquire the cause of the sudden and extraordinary rise in the price of tea, and the report made eight days after was not calculated to appease the popular indignation. The air was filled with rumors of the arrival of the "Polly," which proving premature, only added to the public anxiety and suspense. On Saturday (Christmas) the tea ship "Polly" arrived at Chester, she having followed another ship up

[1] Penna. Archives, 1st series, vol. iv. p. 445; Colonial Records, vol. x. pp. 8–14. *To show the unpopularity with which the custom-house officers were regarded, even among that class of the colonists whose feelings leaned towards the doctrine that the king could do no wrong, the following case is a good example.* On Wednesday afternoon, Feb. 8, 1775, Francis Welsh, in a boat with four men, boarded the schooner "Isabella" off Gloucester Point, and was told that the vessel was in ballast from Portsmouth, New England, whereupon the officer ordered the hatches to be removed. Capt. John Ritchey drew a pistol, declaring the first man who should attempt to search the schooner "he would blow to h—l." The pilot wanting to be put ashore, Officer Welsh remarked that no man should leave the vessel, but Ritchey ordered a boat manned, and the pilot was landed. Ritchey subsequently told Welsh that the schooner belonged to Capt. David Campbell, who was the sole owner, and every dollar he had in the world was in her and the cargo, which consisted of dry goods and other dutiable or contraband articles from Dunkirk, France. Welsh was permitted to look around the cabin, and saw, among other things subject to impost duties, thirty pounds of tea. That night, about nine o'clock, Capt. Campbell, the pilot, and two gentlemen came aboard, but the latter went away, and about an hour later three other gentlemen boarded the boat, who told the officer that he ought not to pursue Capt. Campbell, for it would ruin him. They offered Welsh twenty-five guineas, and promised him more if he would let the vessel go. About two o'clock at night Welsh formally seized the "Isabella" in the king's name, and ordered his men to take the helm. Upon this Campbell said the king never paid for her, and, drawing a pistol, put it to the pilot's head, swearing that if he did not run the vessel down the river without putting her ashore he would kill him. On the next ebb tide the schooner was abreast of Chester. Welsh and Campbell went ashore to get something to eat and while in the town the officer inquired for a justice of the peace. He went to Francis Richardson, but he was ill, and afterwards to Henry Hale Graham, whose sympathies leaned towards the crown, but he told Welsh that he had no authority to go on board any vessel. Welsh then called on Sheriff Vernon, the most pronounced loyalist in the county, and the latter stated he would go and summon some men to aid him, but he never came with the *posse comitatus*, and Welsh again boarded the boat, which, on the ebb, weighed anchor and got to New Castle before the tide changed. Here the officer tried to get assistance, but all the local authorities there begged to be excused. Welsh clung to the "Isabella" until she got within five miles of the Capes, when Capt. Ritchey ordered him and his men into their boat, and they were compelled at midnight to row for shore, which they reached after three hours' constant work. The collector of customs complained to the Governor and Council against the magistrates who had refused to aid his officer, but he was informed that the jurisdiction of any county in the province did not extend to the river, and magistrates therefore could not legally give any assistance in these cases. See Colonial Records, vol. x. p. 230.

the river, for no pilot would dare, in the heated condition of the people's mind, to bring that vessel to the city. The Whigs of Chester, as soon as they were convinced that the ship was lying off that town, dispatched a messenger post-haste to Philadelphia to announce the long-expected but unwelcome news. When he arrived, during the evening of that day, Gilbert Barclay, one of the consignees of the ship, who was a passenger in the vessel, had also gone to Philadelphia by post, and early the next morning he was waited on by a committee, who urged his renunciation of the commission so warmly that he deemed it the wisest plan to accede to their demands. This being accomplished, the committee appointed three of their number to go to Chester, and two others to Gloucester Point, to have an interview with Capt. Ayres, and acquaint him with the public feeling respecting his voyage and the cargo with which the vessel was ladened. The three gentlemen who had set out for Chester, when some distance below the city, were informed that the "Polly" at noon had weighed anchor, and was on her way to her port of destination. They, therefore, returned to the city. About two o'clock she appeared in sight at Gloucester Point, where, as the news had spread in all directions, a large crowd had gathered. When the vessel came sufficiently near she was hailed, and Capt. Ayres requested to come on shore. This he did, and, the people dividing so as to form a lane, he was conducted to the members of the committee, who represented to him the general feeling and the danger to him personally if he refused to comply with the popular demand. They also requested him to go with them to Philadelphia, where he could learn fully the temper and resolution of the masses. The next morning eight thousand people gathered in the State-House yard, when it was resolved that the tea should not be landed; that the vessel should not be reported or entered at the custom-house; that the tea must be taken back to England immediately; that a pilot must take charge of the "Polly," and on the next high-water take her to Reedy Island; that Capt. Ayres could stay a day in town to procure supplies for his return voyage; that he then should go to the vessel and put to sea immediately. On Tuesday, after being in the town forty-six hours, Capt. Ayres left the city where he had been so inhospitably received, and like a prudent man sailed for London, where he reported the unsatisfactory result of his voyage. On Feb. 5, 1774, Earl Dartmouth wrote to Governor Penn, that "the Insult that has been offered to this Kingdom by the Inhabitants of Philadelphia, in the Case of the 'Polly,' Capt. Ayres, is of a very serious nature, and leads to very important consequences." In conclusion, the earl demanded that "a Circumstance, which at present Appears so extraordinary, should be fully explained."[1] If it was, no record seems to have been preserved of that fact.

[1] Penna. Archives, 1st series, vol. iv. p. 480.

In 1774, when the news of the determined resistance made by the colonists to the landing of the tea was received in Europe, England was greatly excited at the intelligence, and Parliament hastily enacted several bills relating to colonial matters extremely offensive in their provisions. Because of the destruction of the tea in Boston harbor, the vengeance of the ministry was particularly directed against that town, hence the law which was known as the Boston Port Bill was passed, interdicting all vessels from landing and discharging, or of landing and shipping wares and merchandise at that port. As soon as these acts were promulgated in the colonies, a storm of denunciation and defiance swept across the land. Staid, dignified Philadelphia even yielded to the tempest, and on Saturday, June 18, 1774, at a large meeting of the leading citizens of that city, was passed a series of resolutions, among which was a call for the holding of a Continental Congress, and instructing the committee thus appointed to take steps necessary to have the province of Pennsylvania represented in the proposed assemblage. Rev. Dr. William Smith, Provost of the University of Pennsylvania, who addressed that gathering, in his calm, dispassionate remarks, with prophetic vision saw that the business they were then about meant "perhaps nothing less than whether the breach with the country from which we descended shall be irreparably widened." On June 28th, the committee sent a circular letter to every county in the province, particularly urging the appointment of a committee in the several counties to assemble in Philadelphia on Friday, the 15th of July, to meet the committee from the whole province. This letter was addressed to Francis Richardson, Elisha Price, and Henry Hayes, of Chester County, who by a peculiar coincidence issued the following call for a meeting of the people of the county on the day which two years afterwards was to become one of the most memorable in the world's history:

"*To the Freeholders and others, inhabitants of the County of Chester, qualified by law to vote for Representatives in General Assembly.*

"GENTLEMEN:

"The large and very respectable committee for the City and County of Philadelphia have wrote to us, the subscribers, requesting that a committee might be chosen for this county as soon as possible, to meet the committee from the other Counties of this province, at the city of Philadelphia on the 15th day of this instant, to deliberate on matters of the greatest weight and importance, not only to us, but to all America. And we are now assured, that on the account of the Indian disturbances his Honor—the Governor—has found it necessary to call the Assembly to meet, in their legislative capacity, on Monday the 28th of this instant; and we also find, that it is not only the opinion and request of the said committee for Philadelphia, but also the opinion and desire of a number of respectable persons of this county coinciding with our own opinions, as lovers of civil and religious liberty, that the committee of the several counties of this province should meet at Philadelphia, on the said 15th of this instant, in order to assist in framing instructions, and preparing such matters as may be proper to recommend to our representatives, at this meeting the Monday following.

"We have therefore thought proper on mature deliberation and by the advice of a number of gentlemen of this county, to appoint Wednesday, the 13th instant, at one o'clock in the afternoon, as a proper time for the inhabitants of this county to meet at the Court-House in Chester, to choose a number of our best and wisest men as a committee for this county, as shall be judged necessary to meet the other committees, at the time and place above mentioned, for the purpose aforesaid, and for such other purposes as may then be deemed useful and necessary And we sincerely hope that the good people of this county will give their attendance on that day, and calmly and heartily join with [us] in doing the business proposed, which we earnestly wish and desire may answer the good proposed, and the good purposes intended by it

"CHESTER, July 4, 1774"

The following is the record of the proceedings of the meeting

"At a meeting of a very respectable number of the freeholders and others, inhabitants of the county of Chester, at the court house, on Wednesday, the 13th of July, 1774, in consequence of public notice for that purpose given, Francis Richardson, Esq chairman,—

"This Assembly, taking into their serious consideration the present critical and alarming situation of American affairs and the unhappy differences now subsisting between Great Britain and her colonies, do agree and resolve, as follows, viz

"1 That the inhabitants of this county do owe and will pay all due faith and allegiance to our lawful and rightful sovereign lord, George the Third, king of Great Britain and the dominions thereunto belonging

"2 That it is an absolute right, inherent in every English subject, to have free use, enjoyment, and disposal of all his property, either by himself or representatives, and that no other power on earth can legally divest him of it

"3 That the act of Parliament lately passed for shutting up the port of Boston is unconstitutional, oppressive to the inhabitants of that town, in its consequences dangerous to the liberties of the British colonies, and that, therefore, we consider our brethren at Boston as suffering in the common cause of America

"4 That the protection of the liberties of America is an indispensable duty, which we owe to ourselves who enjoy them, to our ancestors who transmitted them down, and to our posterity who will claim them at our hands, as the best birthright and noblest inheritance of mankind

"5 We do agree with the Committee of the City and County of Philadelphia, that a Congress of Deputies from the said colonies is the most profitable and proper mode of procuring relief for our suffering brethren, obtaining redress, preserving our rights and liberties, and establishing peace and mutual confidence between our mother country and her colonies on a constitutional foundation

"6 The inhabitants of this county ought and will cheerfully adopt, adhere to, and assist in executing all and singular such peaceable and constitutional measures, which may hereafter be agreed upon and determined by the said general Congress

"7 It is our opinion that it would conduce greatly to the restoration of the liberties of America, should the colonies enter into a solemn agreement not to purchase any goods, wares, or merchandise imported from Great Britain, under such restrictions as be agreed upon by the Congress We, for our parts, sensible of the great advantages which must arise from promoting economy and manufacturing among ourselves, are determined to use as little of foreign manufactures, of what kind or quality soever, as our necessities will permit, until the several acts of the British Parliament, injurious to American liberty, be repealed

"8 That, as our brethren at Boston are now suffering in the cause of America, it is the duty of the inhabitants of this county, in common with the neighboring colonies, generously to contribute towards their support, and, therefore, the Committee hereafter appointed are requested immediately to open and set on foot a subscription for the said sufferers, and the money arising therefrom to be laid out and expended as the said committee, or a majority of them, shall judge best to answer the benevolent intention

"9 That the following persons, to wit Francis Richardson, Elisha Price, John Hart, Anthony Wayne, John Sellers, Hugh Lloyd, William Montgomery, Francis Johnston, William Parker, Richard Riley, Thomas Hockley, Robert Mendenhall, and John Fleming, or a majority of them, be and they are hereby appointed a committee for this county to meet and correspond with the committees of the several counties of this and the other colonies, and to join in such measures as to them shall appear necessary for the public good

"FRANCIS JOHNSTON, *Clk Com*"

The provincial meeting of deputies chosen by the several counties in Pennsylvania was held at Philadelphia, July 15, 1774, and Chester County was represented thereat by Francis Richardson, Elisha Price, John Hart, Anthony Wayne, Hugh Lloyd, John Sellers, Francis Johnston, and Richard Riley On the committee appointed to prepare and report a draught of instructions to be presented to the General Assembly asking that body to appoint delegates to the Continental Congress, then in session, Chester County was represented by Elisha Price. The Assembly unanimously concurred in the instructions and promptly appointed Joseph Galloway (their Speaker), Daniel Rhoads, Thomas Mifflin, John Morton, Charles Humphreys, George Ross, Edward Biddle, and (at a subsequent meeting) John Dickinson the delegates from Pennsylvania to the Continental Congress to be held at Philadelphia on the 5th day of September following Of these, two—Morton and Humphreys—were resident within the present county of Delaware

After agreeing to the Declaration of Rights Congress remained in session nearly eight weeks, having, on October 18th, adopted articles of confederation, signed two days thereafter, which date, Oct 20, 1775, the late distinguished orator, Henry Armitt Brown, maintained should be accepted as the commencement of the American Union, based upon freedom and equality On the 26th of October, after adopting an address to the people of Great Britain, a memorial to the inhabitants of British America,—the Canadian provinces,—and a loyal address to the king, the body adjourned to meet at Philadelphia, May 10, 1775 Before that Congress again assembled, in less than six months after it had adjourned, the April gales, as Patrick Henry had foreseen, sweeping from the North carried to the ears of the long-suffering colonists the clash of resounding arms, the last appeal had been made, and the Revolutionary struggle had actually begun

CHAPTER VII

THE REVOLUTIONARY STRUGGLE TO THE BATTLE OF BRANDYWINE

THE thoughtful men of that period who stopped in the midst of the popular clamor to consider the probable termination of the controversy between the mother-country and her colonies began to be alarmed at the excited temper of the public mind in both hemispheres, hence many of those persons who had been prominent in advising resistance to the arbitrary acts of Parliament, now when their reason taught them that the absolute overthrow of the power of Great Britain in the provinces, or the abject submission of the colonies, could alone set at rest the long dispute, hesitated, some retraced their steps, casting their lots with the established authority, others, shrinking from public view, ceased to be active on either side, while yet others, believing that man, mentally and socially, was but partially developed, picturing to themselves the possibilities of a free representative government, comprehending fully the lesson of the hour, braved the issue, and boldly advocated the adoption of a then untried Utopian scheme The great mass of the people—the majority uneducated—drifted with the day until events made them bitter partisans either for crown or Congress When sides became radical, as a general rule, the wealthy and cultured few, afraid of change, were loyalists, while the middle classes and the poor were Whigs

The direct result of the meeting of the Continental Congress of 1774 was to intensify the feeling of the masses in opposition to the ministerial powers, the address issued by that body being so calm and dispassionate, but so convincing, that it found ready response in popular approval Especially was this true of the resolution that all importations of English goods should be prohibited, and that no articles should be exported from the colonies to Great Britain after December, 1776, unless before that time Parliament had removed the obnoxious law against which the people in America complained In all parts of the colonies meetings were held to ratify and carry into execution the association recommended by Congress, and on Dec. 20, 1774, "a very respectable number of the inhabitants of the County of Chester convened at the Court-house in the Borough of Chester," at which the following persons were named as a committee to act for the county to that end, viz. Anthony Wayne, Francis Johnston, Richard Riley, Evan Evans, and James Moore, Esqs , Hugh Lloyd, Thomas Hockley, David Coupland, John Hart, Sketchley Morton, Samuel Fairlamb, David Coupland, John Crosby, Nicholas Diehl, Jesse Bonsall, Aaron Oakford, Benjamin Brannan, John Talbot, Joseph Brown, Samuel Price, John Crawford, John Taylor, Lewis Gronow, Edward Humphreys, Henry Lawrence, Richard Thomas, William Montgomery, Persifor Frazer, Thomas Taylor, John Foulke, Robert Mendenhall, Joseph Pennell, George Pierce, Nicholas Fairlamb, Samuel Trimble, Charles Dilworth, John Hannum, George Hoops, Joel Bailey, John Gilliland, Joseph Bishop, Jr , John Kerlin, Edward Jones, William Lewis, Patrick Anderson, Joshua Evans, Thomas Hartman, Dr Branson van Leer, William Evans, Joseph Cowan, Thomas Haslep, Patterson Bell, Dr Jonathan Morris, Andrew Mitchell, Thomas Buffington, James Bennett, Joseph Musgrave, William Miller, Richard Flower, Walter Finney, James Simpson, David Wherry, James Evans, Thomas Bishop, William Edwards, Jonathan Vernon, Jr , Lewis Davis, Sr , Joseph Gibbons, Jr , and Thomas Evans, which committee were "to be and continue from this time until one month after the rising of the next Continental Congress, with full power to transact such business, and enter into such associations as to them shall appear expedient "

Immediately after the committee had been selected that body organized by the appointment of Anthony Wayne, chairman, and Francis Johnston, secretary The following resolutions were then unanimously adopted

"1st That any twelve or more of the said Committee, meeting upon due notice, be empowered to enter upon and transact all such business as shall come under their consideration , *provided*, the majority agreeing shall not be less than twelve

"2d That the present unhappy situation of public affairs in general, and of this province in particular, renders it highly necessary that a Provincial Convention should be held as soon as possible, for which purpose twelve persons shall be appointed out of the said committee as delegates to attend the said Convention, at such time and place as shall be generally agreed on "

As there were no further matters requiring immediate attention, after the delegation of twelve to the Provincial Convention had been named, the committee adjourned to meet on Jan 9, 1775, at the house of David Coupland in the borough of Chester

In the mean while, in furtherance of the resolutions passed by the convention of the people of Chester County, held on July 15th, heretofore mentioned, as well as the similar resolution adopted by Congress, calling on the other colonies to aid with contributions the necessities of the inhabitants of Massachusetts, so long as the enforcement of the Boston Port Bill rendered such assistance needful, the people of Chester County made generous contributions to the fund Dr Smith shows that the purse strings of Friends were unloosened liberally to this end "Chester monthly meeting contributed £70 for the relief of Necessitous inhabitants of Massachusetts Bay and Provinces adjacent Darby meeting paid £33 14s for the relief of the poor and distressed in New England, while Haverford meeting responded to the request of the meeting for suffering, 'that Friends should contribute liberally for the relief of friends or others (in the New England Government), who are or may be reduced to indigent circumstances in this time of public calamity, and in a short time had the satisfaction to receive an affecting account of the state of the poor of these provinces, and of the distribution of the donations sent from hence ' "[1]

On Jan 23, 1775, the Provincial Convention assembled at Philadelphia, and continued in session for six days Chester County was represented in that body by Anthony Wayne, Hugh Lloyd, Richard Thomas, Francis Johnston, Samuel Fairlamb, Lewis Davis, William Montgomery, Joseph Musgrave, Joshua Evans, and Persifor Frazer Thomas Hockley and Thomas Taylor, who had been appointed delegates, failed to attend The proceedings of this body show that the men who composed it had carefully weighed the means necessary to build up and sustain a nation, while at the same time they comprehended that slavery, which then existed throughout the colonies,—largely due to the fact that Great Britain had always interdicted any restriction in the traffic,—was an ob-

[1] Dr Smith's "History of Delaware County," p 282

stacle which intruded itself in carrying out the idea of a free constitutional government, and should be done away with. Hence, to that end they resolved that the members of the General Assembly should be urged to pass a law prohibiting the future importation of slaves into the province.

On March 20th a meeting of the committee of Chester County was held at the house of Richard Cheyney, in East Calm, where Messrs. Hockley, Johnston, Gronow, Lloyd, Frazer, Moore, and Taylor were appointed a committee to draft a petition to the Assembly, "with regard to the manumission of slaves, especially relating to the freedom of infants hereafter born of black women within this Colony," and report at the following meeting, while each committeeman was instructed to "use his utmost diligence in collecting the several sums of money subscribed for the use of Boston, and pay the same" to Anthony Wayne, "treasurer," at the next meeting, after which the committee adjourned to meet on Wednesday, May 31st, at the house of David Coupland. But before that date had come, the reverberation of the musketry volleys at Lexington and Concord had stirred the blood of the Whigs throughout the colonies, and nothing was considered but how preparation should be made to meet the storm which had now broken on the country. Hence, in Chester County the committee met at an earlier day than that named when they adjourned in March, and published the following extract from the proceedings then had:

"IN COMMITTEE, CHESTER, May 22, 1775.

"WHEREAS, it appears very necessary in order to avert the evils and calamities which threaten our devoted country, to embody ourselves and make all the military preparation in our power; and it appears absolutely impossible to carry this laudable design into execution without observing the greatest order, harmony, and concord not only under the laws of civil government, but also while under arms and in actual duty, we therefore unanimously recommend the following Association, to be entered into by the good people of this County:

"We, the subscribers, do most solemnly resolve, promise, and engage under the sacred ties of honor, virtue, and love to our country, that we will use our utmost endeavors to learn the military exercise and promote harmony and unanimity in our respective companies; that we will strictly adhere to the rules of decency during duty; that we will pay a due regard to our officers; that we will, when called upon, support with our utmost abilities the civil magistrate in the execution of the laws for the good of our country, and that we will at all times be in readiness to defend the lives, liberties, and properties of ourselves and fellow-countrymen against all attempts to deprive us of them.

"Extract from the minutes.

"By order of the Committee,

"FRANCIS JOHNSTON, *Sec'y.*"

The enlistment of soldiers was at once begun, for on June 29, 1775, at a meeting of several officers of the militia of Chester County, it was determined that for the better regulation of the military in this district it was advisable that a meeting of all the officers in the companies should be held at the public-house of Richard Cheyney, in East Calm, on the 21st day of July next, the day immediately after the Continental Fair, at which meeting it was proposed to divide the county into the most proper and convenient military districts, to form several battalions, and to elect field-officers. The next day, June 30th, the Assembly by resolution recommended to the boards of commissioners in all the counties in the province, "as they regard the Freedom, Welfare, and safety of their County immediately to provide a proper number of good new Firelocks with Baynets fitted to them, Cartridge Boxes with Twenty-three Rounds of Cartridges in each box and Knapsacks," and in the apportionment five hundred of each of these equipments was the number the county of Chester was directed to procure.[1] By the same act the Assembly appointed a Committee of Safety, consisting of twenty-four members, those named from Chester County being Anthony Wayne, Benjamin Bartholomew, Francis Johnston, and Richard Riley, only the latter residing within the territory now comprising Delaware County. On July 10th, for the first time, was any of the committee from Chester County present at the meetings of the body, and on that occasion Francis Johnston and Anthony Wayne both took part in the proceedings.

In a letter dated at Philadelphia, July 10, 1775,[2] the writer says, "Travel through whatever part of this country you will, you see the inhabitants training, making fire-locks, casting mortars, shells, and shots, and making saltpetre, in order to keep the gunpowder-mills at work during the next autumn and summer. Nothing, indeed, is attended to but preparing to make a defence that will astonish the whole world."

On July 17th the Committee of Safety determined that eight good rifles should be assigned to each boat now building, a part of which were to be put into the hands of such men as Capt. Francis, of Philadelphia, and Col. Wayne, of Chester County, should engage to go as minute-men on the boats when required. At this time Wayne was colonel of militia only. The same day the committee requested "the good women" of the province to supply their family doctors "with as much scraped Lint & old Linen for bandages as they can conveniently furnish, that the same may be ready for the service of those that shall happen to be wounded in the defence of the country."

Considerable apprehension having been aroused among the members of the Society of Friends as to their position amid all this din and clash of approaching war, Congress, on July 18, 1775, by a resolution stated to those people "who from Religious Principles cannot bear Arms in any Cause, this Congress intends no Violence to their Conscience, but earnestly recommend it to them to Contribute Liberally in this time of universal calamity to the relief of their distressed brethren in the several colonies, and to do all other services to their oppressed country which they can consistently with their Religious principles."

The allusion to riflemen to be placed on the boats, who were to be men selected by Capt. Francis and Col.

[1] Colonial Records, vol. x. p. 279.

[2] Hazard's Register, vol. iii. p. 248.

Wayne, related to the defense of Philadelphia from a threatened attack by British vessels of war; hence a brief account of those defenses, so far as they refer to the history of Delaware County, should not be omitted from this work.

The obstructing of the Delaware River by *vaisseaux-de-frise* was the suggestion of Dr. Franklin, who also strongly urged the building of galleys,—vessels of considerable size, propelled by oars, and intended to be armed with heavy guns, besides carrying a number of marines,—as well as locating fortifications at certain places on the banks. The *chevaux-de-frise*, as the obstructions were popularly termed, consisted of large frames of timber, filled in with stones to cause them to sink, and from these frames huge beams shod with iron extended to the surface of the water. So energetically did Franklin labor, that although he had returned, May 5, 1775, after many years' absence in Europe, in four months he had three rows of these obstructions laid, the fort at Red Bank completed, and seven of the galleys afloat. One of the rows of *vaisseaux-de-frise* was sunk within the territory now of Delaware County, and extended across the main channel of the Delaware, opposite the upper end of Hog Island, and a mile and a quarter below Red Bank. Subsequently a row was laid to Billingsport, N. J. On Sept. 13, 1775, Richard Riley, from Marcus Hook, wrote to George Gray,[1] of the Committee of Safety, arguing that, as the provincial galleys would soon be finished, the entire fleet, in his opinion, should be stationed at the boundary of the province on the river, below the "shiver de fress's," and then, if they—the boats—"are any Protection, every Person above them will Receive a Benefit;" that as there was a large island opposite Marcus Hook, it would afford a harbor to the galleys; while if the fleet was stationed above the obstructions at the forts, "Chester and Marcushook may be reduced to ashes before any Relief can be obtained, which would be a Considerable Loss, as all the Records & other public papers of the county is their." This matter of the defenses at Marcus Hook seems to have been presented to Council; for on Nov. 16, 1775, it was resolved "that two tier of Chivaux de Frize be sunk, for the further Security of this province, in the Channel opposite or near to Marcus Hook."[2] That this resolution as to locating obstructions at Marcus Hook was never carried into effect is apparent, for the proceedings of the Committee of Safety show that on Jan. 18, 1776, Col. Wayne states to the committee that as large vessels must come within musket-shot of the shore at and near Marcus Hook, in his opinion "a Line or two of Chevaux de Frize placed there would be of considerable Service. The Shore near this narrow channel is nearly as high as Red Bank, and a battery of Cannon there would greatly annoy an Enemy."[3] On Feb. 15, 1776, Richard Riley again wrote to George Gray,[4] calling attention to the exposed condition of Marcus Hook, where, should the enemy come up the river, they would certainly land. He therefore urged erection of a battery on the shore, or the stationing of a floating one there, together with one or two companies of riflemen, to protect that part of the province, "now Intirely exposed, without the least defence or the least means for defence, being without Battery, arms, or ammunition, & of course, if left to continue, will be obliged to abandon their Habitations." In addition, as confirmatory proof that the obstructions did not extend below Chester, as late as July 24, 1777, Council ordered that before a master of a vessel could obtain an order for a "Chevax De Frize Pilot" he was compelled to swear that he would not permit such pilot to remain on the vessel from "the time she leaves the town of Chester."[5] The purpose of this order was to prevent any person knowing the unobstructed channel from getting access to British vessels, and for a reward imparting that knowledge to the enemy.

Early in the fall of the year the galleys were ready, as already stated, and, on Sept. 22, 1775, the Committee of Safety appointed Capt. John Moulder, of Marcus Hook, commander of the armed boat "Hancock;" but the latter, on the 10th of October following, notified the committee that he declined to act in that capacity.

The Committee of Chester County seems to have had no meetings during the summer, but in pursuance of a notice of the chairman, Wayne, they met on Monday morning, September 25th, at the Turk's Head Tavern,—now West Chester,—at which time the board of commissioners and assessors of the county were present. At this meeting the following disclaimer of all treasonable intentions on the part of the colonies was adopted and published in the Philadelphia newspapers of that day. The ignorance displayed in that resolution of the tendency of public affairs might be pardoned in Wayne, who was an admirable soldier but a wretched politician; but the committee certainly had among its members some men who could read the signs of the times better than to have issued such a document as that, particularly when it was known that statesmen like John Adams were openly advocating the independency of the colonies. The disclaimer was as follows:

"Whereas some persons, evidently inimical to the liberty of America, have industriously propagated a report, that the military associators of this County, in conjunction with the military associators in general, in-

[1] Pennsylvania Archives, 2d series, vol. i. p. 550.

[2] Colonial Records, vol. x. p. 404.

[3] Pennsylvania Archives, 2d series, vol. i. p. 471.

[4] Ib., p. 572.

[5] Ib., 501. Nearly two years before the order, Nov. 7, 1775, the Committee of Safety had ordered that five of the ten licensed pilots should be in readiness at Philadelphia to carry vessels down to Chester, and, having performed that service, were immediately to return by land or in skifts to the city. The other five were to be at Chester to bring vessels up the river, and are, immediately after piloting the vessel, to return to Chester by skift or land. In Chester the pilots were directed to be at the house of Mrs. Withy, to receive applications from owners or masters of vessels, every day from 10 to 1 o'clock, and none are to be absent except when on duty.—Colonial Records, vol. x. p. 390.

tend to overturn the Constitution, by declaring an Independency in the execution of which they are aided by this Committee and the board of Commissioners and Assessors with the arms now making for this County, and as such report could not originate but among the *worst* of men for the *worst* of purposes,—This Committee have therefore thought proper to *declare*, and they hereby do *declare*, their abhorrence even of an idea so pernicious in its nature, as they ardently wish for nothing more than a happy and speedy reconciliation, on constitutional principles, with that state from whom they derive their origin

"By order of the Committee

"ANTHONY WAYNE, *Chairman*"

The committee, after adopting the foregoing document providing for an election by the people in the several townships on the 11th day of October following, for persons to serve on the committee for Chester County for the ensuing year, then adjourned to meet in the borough of Chester on that date The next day, September 26th, the Council of Safety directed that an order for five hundred pounds should be drawn in favor of Chester County, the money to be expended in the purchase of arms and other munitions of war

The Assembly, Oct 19, 1775, reappointed the then Committee of Safety, and added new members thereto So far as Chester County was concerned, the representation remained unchanged, excepting that it was increased by the appointment of Nicholas Fairlamb,[1] the latter a resident of the present county of Delaware

The new committee of the county of Chester which had been selected on October 2d, by which some slight change was made in the *personnel* of that body, met shortly afterwards, and gave official publication to the following proceedings

"CHESTER, Oct 23rd, 1775

"Pursuant to public notice given, the Committee met at the house of David Coupland, in the borough of Chester On motion *ordered*, that each member of this Committee do immediately make return to the Chairman, of the quantity of Powder which he already has or may collect within his district, together with the price and the name of the owner thereof, that the same may be paid for

"On motion *resolved*, that Anthony Wayne, Francis Johnston, and Elisha Price Esqrs., Mr Richardson, Mr Knowles, Mr Lloyd, and Mr Brannan, be and they are hereby appointed a Committee of Correspondence for this County

"By order of the Committee

"FRANCIS JOHNSTON, *Sec'y*"

It may be doubted whether any of the muskets ordered for Chester County were delivered until this month, for on October 6th, Mr Dunwicke, a gunsmith, "now employed in making the Provincial Muskets for Chester County," asked Council for an order on the commissary for two pounds of powder, "to prove some of them now ready" Which request was granted, and the commissary ordered to be present when the firearms were tried [2]

The necessity for a more thorough organization in the several counties became so apparent that the Assembly, on Nov 25, 1775, adopted rules and regulations to that end, and at the meeting of the committee of Chester County, on December 26th, that body reorganized in conformity with the suggestions of the Legislature At the same meeting the committee

"*Resolved*, that Anthony Wayne, James Moore, Francis Johnston, Esq, Dr Samuel Kenedy, Caleb Davis, William Montgomery, Persifor Frazer, and Richard Thomas Gentlemen, or any five or more of them, be appointed, and they are hereby appointed to represent the county (if occasion be) in Provincial Convention for the ensuing year"

The provincial authorities were very active in pushing forward military organizations, for Washington was constantly drawing the attention of Congress to the fact that in a short time the term of service of many of the troops with him, besieging Boston, would expire, and the army must be filled with fresh men On Dec 9, 1775, Congress resolved that four battalions should be raised in Pennsylvania, and on the 15th provided that the Committee of Safety should be requested to recommend proper persons as field-officers, from which names Congress would select and commission the colonels, lieutenant-colonels, and majors Of all officers below the rank of major, the Committee of Safety were to make the appointments On Jan 2, 1776, the Committee reported the name of Anthony Wayne as colonel of the Fourth Battalion, which nomination was confirmed by Congress On the 3d of January the Committee nominated Francis Johnston as lieutenant-colonel, and on the 4th, Nicholas Haussegger as major of the same battalion, which nominations were promptly confirmed The next day the Committee of Safety appointed Persifor Frazer, Thomas Robinson, John Lacey, Caleb North, Thomas Church, Frederick Vernon, James Moore, and James Taylor captains of the several companies of the Fourth Battalion, and they were commissioned as of that date[3] The battalion rendezvoused at Chester on February 9th, and on the 17th, Col Wayne reported that five hundred and sixty officers and men were present at camp, and that ten commissioned officers were absent, with recruits, the number of which was sufficient, he believed, to make the battalion complete At that date he stated he "had only twelve rifles and twenty muskets," and was in want of every other article On January 22d, Congress ordered the companies, as fast as they were equipped, to march to New York Robinson's, Church's, and Lacey's companies, under the command of Maj Haussegger, reported at New York on the 28th The troops must have been housed even as far away from Chester as Darby, for on April 26th, Wayne arrived at New York, assumed command of his regiment there, and dispatched Maj Haussegger to Philadelphia to immediately bring on the other five companies, and we find that the next day he ordered Capt Lacey to return to Darby and settle for the board of his (Lacey's) men Capt Lacey always asserted that Wayne had promised to settle that account himself, and he sent him (Lacey) back simply to have an op-

[1] Colonial Records, vol x pp 373-74

[2] Ib., 356

[3] Penna Archives, 2d series, vol x p 119-136 Fourth Pennsylvania Battalion, Col Anthony Wayne

portunity "to give the command of his company to his 'pet,' Capt. Moore."

On Jan. 17, 1776, five days before Congress ordered Wayne's battalion to New York, the Committee of Safety resolved: "That Col. Wayne, Col. Johnston, Mr. Bartholomew, & Mr. Riley be a Committee to Examine the Fire-locks, Cartridge-Boxes, Knapsacks, &c., as ordered by Assembly to be provided for Chester County . . . and make return of the same to this Board."

The following day, January 18th, a member of the committee suggested that a thousand chosen riflemen should be recruited for the provincial service, which body should be stationed near Chester to harass the enemy in their march to Philadelphia, should they attempt the capture of that city.[1] At that time the general confidence in the efficacy of the obstructions in the river was such that the thought of an attack by water was rarely entertained. The suggestion was adopted, and in the spring of 1776, Col. Samuel Miles was appointed to the command of a regiment of one thousand riflemen, formed in two battalions. This body of men must have begun to assemble at Marcus Hook and Chester early in April, 1776, for on the 13th of that month the Committee of Safety had a report from Col. Miles that there was not sufficient "houses or other buildings" in or about the towns mentioned to quarter the troops then being raised, and Council authorized Col. Miles to purchase one hundred good tents on the most reasonable terms he could.[2] On April 17th, Caleb Davis made application to the committee for money to pay for fire-locks made in Chester County for the use of the province. He received fifteen hundred pounds for that purpose, to the order of the commissioners and assessors of the county, and also one hundred pounds for saltpetre, and two quarter-casks of gunpowder were ordered to be delivered to him.[3] On March 25, 1776, Henry Fisher, at Lewes, Del., by express, notified the Committee of Safety that a sloop-of-war was coming into Whorekill "Road with a Small Tender," and it being night, he could not state whether she was bound up the bay or not, but every effort would be made to prevent her procuring a pilot. The express was started at seven o'clock on Monday evening, and reached Chester by half-past two o'clock on Tuesday afternoon, where, after stopping forty minutes, Richard Kane, the messenger, left that place for Philadelphia. On the receipt of the dispatch, Council ordered Commodore Caldwell to send four well-manned and armed boats down the river to Reedy Island, which galleys were directed to act with Capt. Barry of the brig "Lexington," and endeavor to capture the English vessel. Caldwell subsequently returned, for Council on April 30th ordered the fleet to go down the river again, if Mr. Mease and Mr. Morris thought it necessary. It was ordered down, and in the mean time, as constant reports were being sent to the committee of the daily progress up the river of the British men-of-war, on May 7th, Robert Towers was directed to deliver to Col. Miles one thousand pounds of gunpowder and two thousand pounds of lead, "or as great a part thereof as is in store, and for the use of the Associators of Chester County, to be consigned there agreeably to Col. Miles' direction, 20,000 Cartridges for Muskets." At the date just mentioned the "Roebuck" of forty-eight, and the "Liverpool" of twenty-eight guns, were off New Castle, bound up the river, and the galley fleet was ordered to attack them, while at the same time Col. Miles, who was at the meeting of the Council, went at once to Marcus Hook with some powder and lead for his riflemen, and the next morning marched one hundred and fifty of his men—all of his troops for whom he had equipments—to Wilmington, which place he reached in time (two o'clock in the afternoon) to see the action between the galleys and the British ships. "I am convinced," he stated in his journal,[4] "that had the galleys been sufficiently supplied with ammunition in due time (although one-half of them appeared very shy, and never came within point-blank shot of the ships) that these vessels, at least the 'Roebuck,' would have fallen into our hands." Council, on June 12th, ordered Col. Miles to furnish from the provincial troops under his command guards over the powder-house, over the military stores deposited at the State-House, as well as the materials collected for fire-rafts at Philadelphia, stating the reason for this order was that the Continental troops had been withdrawn. Col. Atlee, on June 13th, from Chester, wrote to John Morton[5] that, under Col. Miles' order, he had detached four companies of "musquetrey," under Col. Parry, to Philadelphia, and would be pleased if the remainder of his battalion could be ordered there, "that they might jointly be properly Disciplined." On the 17th, Atlee was directed to move his whole battalion from Chester to be quartered in the barracks at Philadelphia. On July 3, 1776, Congress desired the Committee of Safety to send as many troops as they could spare immediately to Monmouth County, N. J., and the same day it is noted that "In Consequence of the following Resolve of Congress, a Letter was wrote to Colo. Miles, requesting he would give orders for the most Speedy March of the Rifle Battalione to this city."[6] From a letter written by Col. Miles to Richard Riley, dated July 10th, it appears that when the troops left Marcus Hook, in obedience to the foregoing order, a number of men inoculated for

1 Pennsylvania Archives, 2d series, vol. i. p. 471.

2 Colonial Records, vol. x. p. 540.

3 Ib., 545.

4 Pennsylvania Archives, 2d series, p. 519. (See Pennsylvania Archives, 1st series, vol. iv. p. 748, for Col. Miles' report. From some of the reports made by the commanders of the galleys and Pennsylvania vessels of war, it is evident that they had no great longing for the allotted task, that of capturing the British men-of-war.)

5 Ib., 1st series, vol. iv. p. 772.

6 Colonial Records, vol. x. p. 628.

the smallpox had been left there under charge of Dr Davis, who was afterwards ordered to join his company in the Jerseys, and the sick men "still remained at the Hook under the notice of Doct'r Chapman" Col Miles therefore desired Mr Riley to see that these sick men were served with every necessary provision[1]

As stated in the letter hereinbefore quoted, giving an account of the activity in military affairs in the provinces as early as July, 1775, the people were busy "in making saltpetre" Grave apprehensions were entertained early in the war that possibly that commodity could not be had in sufficient quantity to meet the demand in making gunpowder To prevent such a disaster the Committee of Safety made extraordinary efforts to instruct the people in the manner of preparing the necessary article Hence the following advertisement appeared in the *Pennsylvania Packet* in February, 1776

"To the Inhabitants of the County of Chester

"Pursuant to the recommendation of the Committee of Safety for the Province of Pennsylvania to the Committee for Inspection for the County of Chester, Benjamin Brannan, Walter Finney, and John Beaton were appointed to attend the saltpetre manufactory in the City of Philadelphia, in order to perfect themselves in said art, We having complied therewith, do hereby give notice to all those whose public virtue and patriotic spirit would excite them to such a valuable and necessary undertaking at this crisis of time, that attendance will be given at the house of Benjamin Brannan, in Darby,[2] on the 23d and 24th of February, at the house of Mr Cochran, in East Fallowfield, on the 27th and 28th, at the house of Mr Whitby (Withy), in the borough of Chester, on the 1st and second of March, at the house of Mr Hood, in Oxford, on the 4th and 5th, at the house of Mr Miller, in Birmingham, on the 6th and 7th, at the house of Mr Bell, in Kennet, on the 12th and 13th, and at the house of Walter Finney, in New London, on the 14th and 15th of said month, in order to teach and instruct all persons who may please to apply at the times and places above mentioned

"Benjamin Brannan,
"Walter Finney

"N B—The times and places in the North West district are not yet appointed"

The Council next turned its attention to the erection and operation of powder-mills On Feb 3, 1776, Dr Robert Harris proposed to the committee to build a mill on the Valley Stream, about twenty-five miles from the city, and stated that he would engage to be ready by the 1st of March to make one ton per week, on the same terms as the Committee of Safety would make with other parties[3] Dr Harris and the committee entered into the agreement, but he did not locate his powder-mill at the place where he first intended to have built it, for in John Ladd Howell's report to Owen Biddle, dated June 3, 1776,[4] he describes his works thus

"Doctr Robert Harris's, on Crum Creek, about three miles from Chester, begun to Work about the 23d ult The dimensions of the Mill House 30 ft by 20 ft, Head of Water about 2½ feet fall, about 6 ft Water Wheel 12 ft

"The Shafts that Worke (Eighty Stampers of 2¼ by 3¾ Inchs & eleven ft. Length) is thirty-two ft Long, five Mortars made of Two Inch Plank, about five foot each, one Stamper & Mortar for preparing Sulphur

"Drying House, 20 ft by 15 ft., neither floor'd nor plastered He has received one Ton of Salt Petre and five Hundred wht of Sulphur, or thereabouts, expected to deliver one Ton of Powder on the first Inst & the same Quantity Weekly

"The sides of the Mill House & Gable Ends of that & the Drying House being enclosed by Boards not sufficiently seasoned, are very open & must have a bad effect on the Powder, yet the Doctr is of a Different Opinion"

This mill was located in Springfield township at Strath-haven, on Crum Creek

In the same month, June, 1776, as the enlisted troops would be in all probability ordered away from Chester County, it was necessary to put the militia in such a condition that they could be called on in an emergency Hence we find that on June 1st Col William Montgomery was ordered to purchase a quantity of lead for the use of the Associators of Chester County,[5] and shortly after an estimate was made of the number of firearms in the county, and the following return was made[6]

1st Battalion, Col James Moore	380
2nd Battalion Col Thomas Hockley	400
3d Battalion Col Hugh Lloyd	300
4th Battalion, Col William Montgomery	450
5th Battalion, Col Richard Thomas	300
	1830

The dread that the enemy—whom it was known was preparing an expedition at Halifax—intended to make an attack on Philadelphia was so general that every means in the reach of the colony was employed to defend the city from the threatened assault. To that end, on June 19, 1776, Abraham Kinsey, the tenant of Samuel Galliway's estate on Hog Island, was notified that it might be necessary to "lay that island under Water on the near approach of the Enemy," but whatever injury he should sustain would be made good to him by the public On June 20, 1776, George Bryan, the naval officer, was also instructed that no application for a *cheveaux-de-frise* pilot should be allowed unless the captain on oath declared that he would not take the pilot farther down the river than Chester, except in cases where the vessels should go down the bay under convoy of Continental sloops of-war

On June 22d the committee ordered Robert Towers, commissary, to deliver to the colonels of the Battalions of Associators in Chester County the following quantities of ammunition

"To Colo James Moore

2300 Cartridges for Provincial Muskets
2070 do., sorted, for the other different Bores of Firelocks
1500 flints.

To Colo Thom's Hockly

2300 Cartridges for Provincial Muskets
2300 do., sorted, for the other different Bores of Firelocks
1600 flints

To Colo Hugh Lloyd

1840 do for Provincial Muskets
1610 do., sorted, for the other different Bores of Firelocks.
1200 flints

[1] Colonial Records, vol x p 783

[2] Dr Smith states (Hist. of Delaware County, p 288) that at that time Brannan lived in Upper Darby

[3] Penna Archives, 1st series, vol iv p 709

[4] Ib., p 765

[5] Colonial Records, vol x, p 592

[6] Penna Archives, 1st series, vol iv p 776

To Colo Wm Montgomery
2760 Cartridges for Provincial Muskets
2415 do., sorted, for the other different Bores of Firelocks
1800 flints

To Colo Rich'd Thomas
1840 Cartridges for Provincial Muskets
1610 do., sorted, for the other different Bores of Firelocks
1200 flints

"And to each of the said Colonels, the same proportion of loose powder and Lead, equal to the Quantity of Cartridges"[1]

By this time almost unconsciously the public mind in the colonies had been rapidly educated to an acceptance of the idea of absolute independence from the kingdom of Great Britain The stirring sentences of Paine's "Common Sense" had rung through the provinces like the blare of a trumpet, giving direction to the thoughts and ideas of the struggle, and "crystallized into fixed purpose the wishes and hopes for independence," until those persons who, as members of the committee of Chester County, had only a few months before declared "their abhorrence even of an idea so pernicious" now gave support freely to the movement for the establishment of a new nationality on the earth

Congress, on May 15, 1776, recommended "the respective Assemblies and Conventions of the United Colonies, where no government sufficient to the exigencies of their affairs has been hereunto established, to adopt such government as shall, in the opinion of the representatives of the people, best conduce to the happiness and safety of their constituents in particular, and America in general" In Pennsylvania, where the legislative power had (by popular consent or obedience) been transferred to the Committee of Safety, the people were unwilling to submit the matter to an Assembly which had become simply the empty form of authority Thereupon the Committee of Correspondence for Philadelphia communicated with all the county committees, appointing June 18th as a day for the meeting of a provincial conference to be held in Philadelphia On that day the body thus summoned assembled in Carpenters' Hall, and elected Col Thomas McKean president, Col Joseph Hart, vice-president, and Jonathan B Smith and Samuel C Morris, secretaries The county of Chester, in that body, was represented by Col Richard Thomas, Maj William Evans, Col Thomas Hockley, Maj Caleb Davis, Elisha Price, Samuel Fairlamb, Capt. Thomas Levis, Col William Montgomery, Col Hugh Lloyd, Richard Riley, Col Evan Evans, Col Lewis Gronow, and Maj Sketchley Morton The conference unanimously resolved that the then form of provincial government was "not competent to the exigencies of our affairs," and that it was necessary that a convention should be called for the purpose of forming "a new government in this Province on the authority of the people alone" Thereupon the conference made provision for representation of every county in the province, and for an election of members to the proposed Constitutional Convention On the 24th of June, 1776, the meeting adjourned, after each deputy had signed a declaration which stated their "willingness to concur in a vote of the Congress declaring the United Colonies free and independent States"

The momentous event which made the year 1776 one of the most noticeable in the history of the world was at hand For some time the fact that a separation was inevitable between the United Colonies and the mother-country was apparent, and the declaration of the deputies to the conference at Philadelphia, just mentioned, exhibits how popular the movement had already become Hence, when the committee of Congress appointed to draft a formal Declaration of Independence reported to that body on the 28th of June, it needed no prophet to foretell the fate of the measure when the question as to its adoption should be submitted to the members, and it occasioned no surprise when, after some alterations had been made in the document, on July 4, 1776, it was sanctioned by the vote of every colony Of the eight members from Pennsylvania on the day of its adoption, Robert Morris, John Dickinson, and Andrew Allen were absent, Benjamin Franklin, John Martin, and James Wilson voted in the affirmative, while Thomas Willing and Charles Humphreys recorded their voices against the Declaration Of these men deemed worthy to represent the then wealthiest province in the colonies in a Congress of the leading minds of the continent, it is a highly honorable record that there were two who were natives of the territory now Delaware County,—John Morton, of Ridley township, who voted in the affirmative, and Charles Humphreys, of Haverford township, who voted in the negative on the final question of the adoption of the Declaration

The convention which had been called to prepare a constitutional form of government for the republic of Pennsylvania met in Philadelphia July 15, 1776 Dr Benjamin Franklin presided over the assemblage The representatives from Chester County were Benjamin Bartholomew, John Jacobs, Thomas Strawbridge, Robert Smith, Samuel Cunningham, John Hart, John Mackey, and John Fleming This convention absolutely assumed the chief legislative and executive power in the province, appointed a Council of Safety, ratified the Declaration of Independence, and filled all the offices under the new order of things The body continued in session until Sept 28, 1776, when it adopted the constitution it had made, which went into effect immediately without being submitted to a vote of the people By its provisions the legislative power was reposed in a General Assembly acting as one House, the executive authority was vested in a president, who was to be chosen annually by the Assembly and Council in joint ballot the Council consisting of twelve persons who were elected in classes for a term of three years

[1] Colonial Records, vol x p 613

A council of censors was provided consisting of two persons from each city and county, the first members of which were to be chosen in 1783 and elected every seven years thereafter, whose province was to see that the legislative and executive branches had performed their duties properly, neither failing in nor exceeding their powers On Nov 13, 1783, the only council of censors ever chosen in pursuance of this constitution met at the State-House, Philadelphia, and continued its session until Sept. 25, 1784 Chester County was represented in that body by Anthony Wayne and John Evans The latter dying while a member of the council, James Moore was chosen in his stead, being present Dec 30, 1783, for the first time

After the Declaration of Independence, the men who had led the people forward to that step, now that the bonds that held them to the mother-country had been severed, put forth additional energy It was the days when the bullets used in the chase and in war, at least in America, were cast of lead, and generally by those who used them, hence the authorities were anxious to gather material which could at once be utilized for that purpose On July 8, 1776, the Committee of Safety ordered certain gentlemen to collect "all the Leaden Window-weights, clock-weights, and other Lead in Germantown and its Neighborhood, for which the Liberal price of six Pence per pound will be allowed" I do not find that the county of Chester was distinctly named so far as gathering lead is concerned, but on July 17, 1776, the Committee of Safety made a general demand as follows

"The Families who have leaden Window or Clock-Weights are earnestly requested to give them up immediately to the Persons appointed to Collect them Such Families may be assured that they will be supplied as soon as possible with Weights of Iron, and it is hoped the trifling Inconvenience of being for a few days without them will not be put in Competition with the Danger that may Arise to this Country from the want of a sufficient quantity of Lead for our Defence"[1]

Guard boats were stationed in Darby Creek,[2] for on July 26th, Capt Charles Lawrence, William Watkin, and Robert Tatnall represented to Council that the inconvenience of going to the fort for provisions was such that they desired Sketchley Morton might be appointed to furnish their supplies, which order was made[3] The uncertainty as to the destination of the English expedition still hung over all the provinces, and extraordinary efforts were made to meet the storm when it should burst On July 29th, Council ordered that fifty muskets should be delivered to Col James Moore, of Chester County, for the use of his battalion,[4] and on August 1st, Col Moore made application for "50 Bayonets or Tomhawks, 30 Hatchets, 100 screws, & 100 worms, for the use of his Battalion," and Commissary Towers was ordered to deliver these articles to the colonel[5] At this time there must have been an encampment of troops at Chester, for on August 5th, Council ordered £4 6*s* 3*d* to be paid James Pennell for wood delivered at that place "for the use of the Pennsylvania Musketry"[6] The report that the British fleet had rendezvoused off Sandy Hook on the 28th of June had allayed somewhat the dread of an attack on Philadelphia, but the long delay in disembarking the troops and the constantly receiving tidings that daily reinforcements were being made by transports and vessels of war to the armada that was to subjugate the colonies kept alive the apprehension that at any moment the fleet might weigh, and almost before the news could be carried to Philadelphia the guns of the hostile vessels would announce their presence in the Delaware Hence the alarming condition of the time demanded constant vigilance and preparation on the part of those men who, advocating independence, must do everything to resist the capture of the foremost city of the colony August 6th, one hundred stand of arms was delivered to Col Richard Thomas, of Chester County, for his battalion, and the following day thirty stand of arms was sent to Col Moore

The same day the muster-master, Davis Bevan, of the borough of Chester, was instructed "to Pass Col R'd Thomas's Battalion of Chester County with the Present number of Officers and Men," and the commissary was directed to supply the battalion with accoutrements, as also to immediately deliver to Col Thomas sixty stands of arms[7] The alarm increasing, as news of unusual activity in the British fleet was received by express, the militia was hastily armed and mustered into the service, hence we find that on August 8th the muster-master was ordered to pass Capt Thomas Heslep's company of the First Battalion of Chester County, commanded by Col Moore, with the number of officers and men then recruited There was intense anxiety in the county of Chester at that time and unusual activity, as is evidenced from the minutes of the Council of Safety. On August 12th, Col Richard Thomas received £196 3*s*, the price he had paid for eighty-one firelocks, bought of non-associators,[8] and on the 14th of the same month fourteen pounds was paid for cartridge-boxes and bayonet-belts for Col Thomas' command, while the same day £75 4*s* 6*d* was paid for like articles for the use of Col Moore's battalion[9] On the 20th of August the news, borne by express, reached Chester that the British fleet, under Sir Peter Parker, had been signally repulsed at Fort Moultrie, and a few days subsequently that the English army had disembarked on Long Island, and hence the "Flying Camp" was dispatched immediately to New York On August 23d, the day following that of the landing of Gen Howe's

[1] Colonial Records, vol x p 649

[2] In a letter from David Joy to Samuel Howell, Jan 16, 1776 (Penna Archives, 1st series, vol v p 700), the former suggested that a few fire rafts should "be kept in some creek below the Chevee de Frizes, in order to sett them on the Enemy on the flood Darby, Chester, or Racoon creeks will do."

[3] Colonial Records, vol x p 656

[4] Ib., p 659

[5] Ib., p 665

[6] Ib., p 670

[7] Ib, pp 672–73

[8] Ib., p 681

[9] Ib., p 685

army on Long Island, Maj. Caleb Davis was paid £202 10*s*. for necessaries for the Chester County quota of the Flying Camp, and the same day John Hart was paid £5 14*s*. 3*d*. mileage for his company of Col. Lloyd's Chester County battalion, and Capt. Pierce of the same organization received £6 8*s*. 7*d*. for mileage. The next day, August 24th, Capt. Andrew Boon of the Second Battalion received £6 2*s*. 6*d*. to purchase drums, fifes, etc., for his company. Many of these men who marched from Chester County with the Flying Camp never returned, but in the early gray light of the morning of the 27th of August, 1776, their ghastly faces stiffened in death, when the first pitched battle of the war was begun by an attack on the Pennsylvania "Flying Camp" on Long Island. How severely the troops from Chester County suffered on that disastrous day can be inferred from the letter of Capt. Patrick Anderson to Benjamin Franklin, dated from West Chester County, N. Y., Sept. 22, 1776,[1] and how bravely the women of Chester County acted at that time is shown by the following extract from the *New England Courant* of Sept. 5, 1776:[2]

"*Philadelphia, August* 27, 1776.—THE WOMEN OF CHESTER COUNTY, PENNA. Since the departure of the able-bodied men from the forks of the Brandywine, in Chester County, in the service of their country, the patriotic young women, to prevent the evil that would follow the neglect of putting in the fall crop in season, have joined the ploughs, and are preparing the fallows for seed; and should their fathers, brothers, and lovers be detained abroad in defense of the liberties of these States, they are determined to put in the crops themselves,—a very laudable example, and highly worthy of imitation."

The Council of Safety, on September 16th, resolved that the members of the Constitutional Convention, then in session, should recommend proper persons in their respective counties, to be appointed by Council, to purchase "blankets, coarse Woolens, Linens, & Stockings for the use of the Troops belonging" to Pennsylvania, and on the 4th of October, William Evans was desired "to purchase all the Coarse Cloths, Blankets, & Stockings in Chester County for the use of ye State, and draw on the Board for the Cost."[3]

The following summons from the Council of Safety to the justices of Chester County[4] explains itself so far as known, for there appears no further reference to the matter in the official records of Council:

"IN COUNCIL OF SAFETY,
"PHILADELPHIA, Oct'r. 9th, 1776.

"GENTLEMEN:

"You are hereby required to appear before this Council at Ten o'clock on Saturday morning, then and there to answer for your conduct in holding an Election on Tuesday of the first Instant, at the Borrough of Chester, apparently with a view of supporting the late Government of the King of Great Britain, in direct Violation of the resolves of Congress and of the late Convention of this State.

"By order of the Council.

"THOS. WHARTON, JUN., *Pres't.*"

On the 8th of November, 1776, Council order the sergeant-at-arms "to arrest Richard Swanwick, of Chester County," and bring him before that body, for what offense does not appear;[5] and the next day an order was made that Rev. Mr. Rodgers be "paid £70, being part of his wages as Chaplain to late Miles's and Atlee's Battalion." On the 8th, too, we learn that Council gave orders requiring "Provisions to be made at Chester for Troops to Rendevous there." That such an encampment was located at that place at that time is inferentially established by the fact that on November 14th, "Intelligence was rec'd by Express that several hundred Transports had sailed from New York & steered their Cource to the Southward, & expected to be intended for this City; whereupon the Council wrote a Circular Letter to the Commanding Officers of the Battalions of Militia, earnestly requesting them to march their respective Battalions to this city Immediately."[6]

The next day Col. Bayard was paid fifty-seven shillings for expenses going to Chester with Gen. Armstrong,[7] and on the 21st, George Weiss received £5 for riding express to Chester County to order the militia to be in readiness to march at short notice.[8] On the 23d, Council determined that the salt then in possession should be divided among the committees of the several counties, the proportion allotted to Chester being eighty bushels, which was to be sold to the people at the rate of fifteen shillings per bushel, and in no greater quantity than half a bushel to any one family. The salt was to be distributed equally according to the necessities of the people, "for which purpose they are to require a declaration of what quantity they are possessed of more than their just proportion of the necessary article at a time of such very great scarcity of it."[9] On the 28th, Council declared that the salt sent to the various counties, as mentioned, should be sold only to the militiamen who entered the service, or to their families[10] and reiterated the like order on November 30th.

On Nov. 27, 1776, Dr. Thomas Bond wrote from New Brunswick, stating that he had obtained permission to carry the sick American soldiers under his care, and stated that it would be well to consult Gen. Mifflin on the desirability of locating hospitals at Darby, Chester, Marcus Hook, Wilmington, and New Castle. "I think the Water Carriage from Trenton to these Places would save much Carting, & this plan much better than one propos'd, of sending the Sick to East Town, Bethlehem, Nazareth, Reading, etc."[11]

The times were unpropitious for the American colonists. The battle of Long Island had been fought and lost, New York had fallen, and Washington, apparently driven from post to post, was retreating across New Jersey, followed by the victorious foe. It was to

1 Penna. Archives, 1st series, vol. v. p. 26. See, in addition, Col. Atlee's journal, as well as that of Col. Miles, 1 Penna. Archives, 2d series, vol. i. pp. 512 to 522.

2 Futhey and Cope's "History of Chester County," p. 66.

3 Colonial Records, vol. x. p. 741.

4 Penna. Archives, 2d series, vol. i. p. 652.

5 Ib., p. 644.

6 Colonial Records, vol. xi. p. 3.

7 Ib., p. 5. 8 Ib., p. 11. 9 Ib., p. 13. 10 Ib., p. 20.

11 Penna. Archives, 1st serie, vol. v. p. 79.

prepare for the attack which threatened Philadelphia, alike by sea and land, that Council issued the order of Nov 14, 1776, for all owners of cattle along the Delaware River to make arrangements to remove their stock inland at least five miles, notifying the owners that if they failed to act promptly in carrying out the order when required, the board "may be under the disagreeable necessity of giving the most peremptory order for the removal and to see that the same be punctually and suddenly complied with"[1] At the same time the minutes of Council show that the utmost anxiety prevailed, and the activity displayed in collecting troops, for that time, was proportionally as great as when, ninety odd years later, the Confederate forces, under Lee, invaded Pennsylvania As Washington drew nearer to Philadelphia, retiring before the exulting enemy, his army dwindled to a mere handful of war-worn, ill-clad, ill-fed, ill-armed troops, fleeing across New Jersey, sorely pursued by Lord Cornwallis' overpowering force of twenty thousand men, the flower of the English soldiery, the nation's fate trembled on the verge of ruin On November 30th, Council resolved "that in the present alarming situation of affairs" no vessel should be permitted to leave the port of Philadelphia, and all shipping was interdicted passing through the *chevaux-de-frise* Money was immediately dispatched to the colonels of the militia organizations in the counties of Chester, Philadelphia, Bucks, Northampton, and the city of Philadelphia to furnish support to "the families of such associators as go into actual service and may stand in need of the same," which money was to be distributed among the families requiring supplies, "from time to time, according to their need, in the most discreet manner"[2] On December 1st dispatches were sent by expresses to Chester, Philadelphia, Bucks, and Northampton Counties to hasten the march of militia to reinforce Gen Washington in New Jersey On the 3d, Council desired the members of Assembly from the counties of Philadelphia, Chester, Bucks, and Lancaster to recommend immediately in the respective counties, proper persons to be appointed by the board to hire all the wagons in those counties[3] On the 4th, Dr Robert Harris was paid fifty-eight pounds for making powder at his mills, at Strath-haven, on Crum Creek, and the same day Mr Towers was ordered to deliver to Dr Harris a ton of saltpetre and sulphur, in proportion to make gunpowder[4] The same day John Morton was paid £3 6*s* for wharfage of the floating-battery "Arnold," in the preceding March This, doubtless, must relate to expenses incurred while the war-boats and galleys lay in Darby Creek

On the 8th of December the American army crossed the river from New Jersey to the west bank, and so eager were the pursuing enemy that they came in sight but a few moments after the rear-guard had passed over and destroyed the bridges. The English commander was so assured that the armed resistance of the colonies was virtually at an end, that leave was given Lord Cornwallis to return to England, and he had gone to New York with the intention of embarking for Europe The hopes of the colonists were over-clouded with doubts The Council, however, hurried forward the raw levies of militia to reinforce the wasted ranks of the Continental army On December 11th, Col Evan Evans, of Chester County, was paid £2 9*s* 4*d* for the transportation of the baggage of his company, as well as £2 0*s* 5*d* for flints and lead for his battalion. Col James Moore received one hundred pounds to advance a month's pay to his battalion,[5] and on the 14th, Col Evans received "1000 dollars to pay his Battalion of Militia a month's wages advance"[6]

On Dec 11, 1776, Capt Hammon, of the British vessel-of-war "Roebuck," landed Davis Bevan and Benjamin Canby at Lewes under parole, with instructions to proceed to Philadelphia and make arrangement for an exchange of prisoners of war It seems that the schooner "Nancy," of which vessel Davis Bevan was master, had been captured by the "Roebuck," and he, Canby, and other Americans, prisoners of war in the hands of the commander of the British vessel, were exchanged Dec 30, 1776

The cause of the united colonies seemed, previous to the holidays of 1776, almost beyond hope, only the most patriotic citizens could bear up against the constant reverses which attended the Continental arms, and it is not surprising that less than a week before the brilliant affair at Trenton Col Francis Johnston, in a letter dated from New London Cross-Road, December 21st, should present the following gloomy picture of the uncertainty that maintained among the inhabitants of Chester County respecting the outcoming of the struggle, and their hesitancy to part with any commodities in exchange for Continental currency He says,—

"I think it my Duty to inform you of the strange and perverse Change in Politicks which hath taken place through a great part of this County

"Even some *quondam associators*, as well as conscientiously scrupulous men, totally refuse to accept Congress money as payment for old Debts, And there are some so maliciously averse to our support of Liberty that they refuse to part with any commodity whatsoever, even the Necessaries of Life unless they can get hard money or the old Paper Currency of this Province Most of the Tavern Keepers who are friends on the Lancaster Road have pull'd down their Signs, & refuse the Soldiery Provisions or drink—they will assign you no reason for such conduct, the reason, however, is too evident, they are afraid to receive Congress Money"[7]

Col Johnston was not only incensed at the conduct of the people of Chester County, but on Jan 7, 1777, he gave Council to understand that the appointment of junior officers over his "head" was objectionable, particularly the case of Lieut-Col Penrose brought

[1] Colonial Records, vol xi p 4
[2] Ib., p. 23
[3] Ib, p 28.
[4] Ib., p 30
[5] Ib., p 44
[6] Ib., p 50.
[7] Penna Archives, 1st series, vol v p 100, see also 2d series, vol i. p 657 Ib., 1st series, vol v p 125

forth his indignation, but his wrath was mollified when, on Feb. 21, 1777, Congress promoted Col. Anthony Wayne to the rank of brigadier-general, and he (Johnston) was made the colonel of the Fifth Pennsylvania Regiment, Persifor Frazer its lieutenant-colonel, and Thomas Robinson its major. The term of the Fourth Pennsylvania Battalion had expired on Jan. 5, 1777, but it remained over until January 24th to allow other troops to be enlisted and forwarded to take its place. It is, however, not to be inferred from the foregoing remark that the Fourth Battalion marched away from the field in a body, for the fact is that the greater number of Wayne's men, being of Irish birth or descent, re-enlisted, under their old officers, in the Fifth Regiment of the Pennsylvania line.[1] Those who did not re-enter the service were ordered to Chester, where the battalion was mustered out Feb. 25, 1777. On the same day John Evans, of Chester County, was notified that he had been elected a member of the Council of Safety, the duties of which office he assumed shortly afterwards.

Although early in the year the storm of war, owing to Washington having assumed the offensive, had rolled away from Philadelphia, the Council did not lessen its efforts to place the Continental army in as efficient condition as possible, and to that end, on Jan. 13, 1777, it required the commissioners in the several counties in the State to furnish thirty-eight thousand bushels of horse feed, and of that total, four thousand bushels were required for Chester County. At this time the prevalent idea was that Gen. Howe proposed to make an attempt to capture Philadelphia by water, and this impression was confirmed when, on March 25th, James Molesworth, who bore a lieutenant's commission from Gen. Howe, was arrested in Philadelphia, charged with attempting to obtain a *chevaux-de-frise* and two bay pilots, to bring the British fleet up the Delaware. Not only did he attempt to corrupt pilots to that end, but he strove to have accomplices, whose duties it should be to spike the guns at Fort Island (Fort Mifflin), and to destroy the posts and ropes at the ferries. Molesworth was tried by court-martial, on the charge of being a spy, was found guilty, and hung March 31, 1777.[2] Previous to his execution he made a confession, and accused a number of persons as being implicated in the design to restore the royal authority in Philadelphia. Council hastened its preparation to meet the threatened invasion, and on April 3d a hundred wagons drawn by four horses was called for by the Board of War, to remove public stores from Philadelphia to the west side of the Schuylkill. Col. Caleb Davis, Maj. Evans, Col. William Dewees, and Isaac Webb were designated to hire such wagons in Chester County. On April 21st Council instructed the committees of the counties of Bucks, Philadelphia, and Chester "to take an Inventory of all the Flour, Wheat, Rye, and Indian Corn, Oats, Beef, Pork, Horses, Neat Cattle, Sheep, Hogs, &c., also Wagons, Carts, &c.," in each county, and make return as quickly as possible, so that in the event of sudden alarm the provender and live stock might be removed to a place of safety. This was the ostensible reason for this order, but in all probability the purpose was to ascertain how much and where located were the articles enumerated, so that, if necessary, they might be impressed for the use of the American army.

Robert Smith had been appointed lieutenant of Chester County on March 12, 1777, which office gave him the rank of colonel, and devolved on him the duties of raising, arming, and provisioning the military contingent in his district, and preparing the troops when called into service. They remained under his command until ordered to take the field. On April 12th, Col. Smith reported that Chester County then contained five thousand men capable of bearing arms, and he promised to use his utmost exertions to get his contingent in the greatest possible state of forwardness.[3] On April 24th, Congress requested that three thousand of the militia of Pennsylvania, exclusive of the militia of the city of Philadelphia, should be called, one-half of the "troops to rendezvous at Chester, on the Delaware." The following day Council ordered the lieutenants in the several counties to furnish men, although the number from Chester County was not designated. Each man was to be provided with a blanket, which was to be purchased; if that could not be done blankets were to be impressed, but in a way that should give the least offense to the public. The troops from the

[1] In Gen. Henry Lee's "Memoirs of the War in the Southern Department," vol. ii. p. 203, the *personnel* of the Pennsylvania Line is thus described: "Wayne had a constitutional attachment to the decision of the sword, and this cast of character had acquired strength from indulgence, as well as from the native temper of the troops he commanded. They were known by the designation of the Line of Pennsylvania, whereas they might have been with more propriety called the Line of Ireland. Bold and daring, they were impatient and refractory, and would always prefer an appeal to the bayonet to a toilsome march. Restless under the want of food and whiskey; adverse to absence from their baggage, and attached to the pleasures of the table. Wayne and his brigade were more encumbered with wagons than any equal portion of the army. The general and his soldiers were singularly fitted for close and stubborn action, hand to hand, in the centre of the army. Cornwallis, therefore, did not miscalculate when he presumed that the junction of Wayne would increase rather than diminish his chances of bringing his antagonist, Lafayette, to action."

[2] Penna. Archives, 1st series, vol. v. p. 282; Colonial Records, vol. xi. p. 197.

[3] *Penna. Mag. of Hist.*, vol. iv. p. 84: "The onerous duties of his office were discharged in an active, untiring, self-sacrificing spirit, and much of his property melted away during the war, partly from direct gifts to the army and to the needy families of the soldiers, and partly because his public duties gave him no time to attend to his private business. On one occasion when foragers were sent into Uwchlan to procure supplies for the famishing army at Valley Forge, Col. Smith assisting to load corn from his own stores into the wagon, was urged by his wife to keep enough to subsist his own family through the winter. He replied, saying that the soldiers' needs were greater than their own, and continued his work till the wagons were filled and his granary was almost empty. He spoke with feeling in his latter life of taking, on another occasion, unthreshed wheat to Valley Forge, and being met on his arrival at the edge of the encampment by numbers of hungry men, who seized the sheaves and mitigated the pangs of hunger by eating the grains, which they rubbed out with their hands." Ib., p. 85.

counties of Chester, Lancaster, and York were ordered to form a camp "at or near Chester"[1] Col Smith acted promptly, as did the other counties' lieutenants, for May 30th Council notified Congress that the militia called out by the recommendation of that body was encamped at the places named, part of the troops being already there and the remainder preparing to march, that as Council had but few arms fit for service, Congress was requested to furnish arms, tents, and camp equipage On June 11th, Benjamin Brannon, sub-lieutenant of the county of Chester, applied to Council for a cannon, that several companies of artillery had been formed in the county, hence he desired that the men might practice with the gun, and to that end also asked for a few pounds of powder On the 14th, Council ordered that the first class of militia should be immediately forwarded to camp, and the second class be ordered to march, and the third class be held in readiness to move on short notice The same day Col Robert Smith received one thousand pounds to equip the militia of Chester County, and he was also instructed to send to Philadelphia thirty wagons This activity was due to the intelligence Congress had received that Gen Howe proposed marching to and reducing Philadelphia When the British army, on June 13th, actually made an advance in two columns from Brunswick, the news was dispatched by Washington to Congress, and being received the next day, prompt measures were taken to meet the threatened attack On the 17th, Lewis Granow, sub-lieutenant of Chester County, received four thousand dollars to purchase substitutes, blankets, etc, and on the 20th four hundred stand of arms was delivered to Col Smith The next day he received a like number each of canteens, knapsacks, priming-wires, brushes, and cartouch-boxes John Beaton was appointed paymaster of the Chester County militia On the 21st two thousand dollars were appropriated for paying substitutes in Chester County, and on the 24th a like sum for the same purpose On July 12th Col Smith reported that notwithstanding repeated orders only three hundred and twenty men of the Chester County militia had arrived at Chester, and two hundred of these were substitutes Col John Hannum was then commanding officer at that station The alarm having passed away on the return of the British army to Brunswick on the 25th, Council, considering "the extreme inconveniency arising from the march of the militia in the time of Harvest," countermanded the order for the levies to go to camp, but instructed the lieutenants of the counties of Philadelphia and Chester that it was unnecessary to move the second class of militia, but that it should be held in readiness to march at the shortest notice On July 9th, Council requested the magistrates of the counties of Philadelphia, Chester, and Bucks to return the names of persons well qualified to take an account of all flour, wheat, grain, and other stores in the several counties, so that it might be removed "in case the Enemy's movements should make it necessary," and on the 29th Council appointed John Pearson, Nicholas Deihl, Isaac Hendrickson, Isaac Serrill, Harvey Lear, and Jacob Richards, to be added to a committee consisting of Samuel Levis, William Kerlin, and Sketchley Morton, which had been appointed to drive off the stock in the county of Chester on the approach of the British forces On July 20, 1777, Congress received information that a British fleet of one hundred and sixty sail was in the Narrows, on the way to Sandy Hook On the 22d, Washington, perplexed as to the destination of Howe, requested that trustworthy persons should be stationed at the Capes of the Delaware to give prompt notice if the fleet should appear in that quarter In the early morning of July 23d the expedition sailed, but owing to light winds and fog the fleet did not get in sight of the Capes until the 30th, when expresses from both Cape May and Lewes were sent to Council apprising that body that the fleet of two hundred and twenty-eight vessels was in sight Gen Mifflin was at the time in Chester, for he signed for and indorsed the time of departure from that place on the dispatch from Lewes Late on the 31st the hostile vessels bore away to the southward Gen Howe, in his narrative, states, "that finding it hazardous to sail up the Delaware, he agreed with the admiral to go to Chesapeake Bay, a plan which had been preconcerted in the event of a landing in the Delaware proving upon our arrival there ineligible"[2]

On July 9th, Gen Washington had requested Council to have a plan of the shore of the Delaware River made, and on the 18th that body notified the commander-in-chief that General Du Coudray had produced a plan of a fortification to be erected at Billingsport to prevent the enemy removing the *chevaux-de-frise* at that place, and the chart would be made of the shore of the river as soon as proper surveyors could be procured On the 24th the "proper surveyors" were procured, for four persons were directed to make "A Survey of the Shore of the River Delaware and of the land for about four miles to the Westward, taking in the Great Road leading to the Southward, when they may extend further than that distance from the river, and remarking the several places where an enemy may land and the kind of ground adjoining, whether marshy, hilly, open, or covered with woods, and when there are several heights near each other remark'g their altitudes and distances apart, remarking particularly the several Creeks and streams of water as high up, at least, as the tide flows, and the places where they may be

[1] Penna Archives, 1st series, vol v p. 321

[2] George H Moore, a gentleman whose assertion on any historical topic is always worthy of consideration, states in his work, "The Treason of Charles Lee," that this movement was made by Gen Howe, at the treasonable suggestion of Gen Lee, the English soldier who had received so many honors at the hands of the American Congress

forded or passed by bridges. Where there are Swamps near the river, or roads, not'g particularly their kinds & size nearly. Passes of difficulty to an army to be accurately surveyed and well described."

Nathan Sellers was directed to make the survey from the Schuylkill River to Christiana Creek, which included all the territory now Delaware County, in which duty he was enjoined to use secrecy and dispatch.

When the news of the arrival of the British fleet at the cape of the Delaware was received, Council prepared to meet the threatening attack, and as many of the militia were without guns, it was ordered that those persons who had not taken the oath of allegiance to the colonies should immediately be disarmed, "and their arms made use of by those who are willing to risk their lives to defend their liberties and property."[1] On August 1st the justices of Chester County returned the names of a number of citizens in the county who were, in their opinion, proper persons to take an account of the grain and other stores within twenty miles distant westward from the river Delaware, and also persons to provide for the poor who might be compelled to leave Philadelphia in the event of an attack on that city by the British forces. The major part, if not all, of the persons thus suggested resided without the present county of Delaware.

Washington was at this time in Philadelphia, and on August 1st, in company with Lafayette,—whom the commander-in-chief had met for the first time the day previous at a dinner-party,—he inspected the fortifications on the Delaware River,[2] and proceeded as far as Chester, from which place Washington, on the date just mentioned, addressed a letter to Gen. Putnam.[3]

On Aug. 14, 1777, Col. Galbraith wrote from Lancaster that he had dispatched nearly one thousand militia on foot for the camp at Chester, but they had neither arms, accoutrements, camp-kettles, etc.,—nothing except blankets.[4] Two days subsequently, John Evans, member of Council, wrote from Chester that about one thousand militia was assembled at that place from Berks County, part of two classes; from Cumberland one company, and part of two companies from Lancaster; the Chester County class "was about half completed, and when completed" would have arms sufficient for their own use, but several companies from other counties must be supplied. The quartermaster reports, he says, "that it will be difficult to find shelter for any more troops at this place, all the empty houses being now occupied.[5] The next day, Col. Jacob Morgan wrote from Reading that the greater part of the twelve companies from Berks County—two battalions under Cols. Daniel Hunter and Daniel Udree, comprising six hundred and fifty-six men—had marched for Chester, and by that time were doubtless at that place.[6] On the 18th, Col. Benjamin Galbraith notified Council that the third class of Lancaster County had marched to Chester, and requested that commissions for the officers of the three classes of militia from that county be sent there.[7]

In the mean while no further intelligence being received of the movements of the British fleet, the opinion became general that one of the Southern seaports was the point of destination, and as the expense of massing the militia bore heavily on the indigent commonwealth, on Aug. 20, 1777, Council called the attention of the Pennsylvania delegation in Congress to the fact that the militia called into service had encamped at Chester, and were still reporting there; that as it was the season for sowing winter wheat, on which the country largely depended, it would be a relief to industrious people if public affairs would permit the discharge of part of the militia at Chester, "particularly as they were deficient in arms and blankets and wholly unprovided with tents."[8]

The following day a dispatch was received in Philadelphia, stating that on the night of the 14th instant the British fleet had been seen standing in between the Capes of Chesapeake Bay. Washington, who was restless in his encampment on the Neshaminy, had that very day apprised Congress that he would move his army to the Delaware the next morning, proposing to march thence to the Hudson River, which proposition on his part, notwithstanding the reported news from the fleet, was approved by Congress. The commander-in-chief, however, determined to halt until further intelligence was received, which came the next day confirmatory of the enemy's presence in Chesapeake Bay. Washington at once ordered Gen. Nash, then at Trenton, N. J., to embark his brigade and Col. Proctor's corps of artillery, if vessels could be procured for the purpose, and proceed to Chester; or, if vessels could not be had, to hasten towards that place by land with all possible speed.[9] On the 23d the Continental army broke camp and moved for Philadelphia, through which city it passed early the next day, August 24th (Sunday), marching down Front Street to Chestnut, and up Chestnut to the Middle Ferry, Washington himself riding at the head of the column and Lafayette at his side. That evening the army encamped in and about Chester, and the next evening (the 25th) they reached Wilmington.[10] On the

1 Penna. Archives, 1st series, vol. v. p. 472.
2 Sparks' "Life of Washington," p. 232.
3 Sparks' "Correspondence of Washington," vol. v. p. 2.
4 Penna. Archives, 1st series, vol. v. p. 521.
5 Ib., p. 529.
6 Ib., p. 530.
7 Ib., p. 532.
8 Ib., p. 536.
9 *Penna. Mag. of Hist.*, vol. i. p. 282.
10 "Washington's Encampment on the Neshaminy," by William J. Buck; *Penna. Mag. of Hist.*, vol. i. p. 284. Irving says, in speaking of the 25th of August, "The divisions of Gens. Greene and Stephen were within a few miles of Wilmington; orders were sent for them to march thither immediately. The two other divisions, which had halted at Chester to refresh, were to hurry forward."—Irving's "Life of Washington," Riverside edition, vol. iii. p. 205. In Townsend Ward's most interesting "Walk to Darby" (*Penna. Mag. of Hist.*, vol. iii. p. 262) it is

morning of that day the British army landed at the head of Elk,[1] or, rather, some distance above the mouth of the Elk River[2]

The effect of the news of the approach of Gen Howe's expedition aroused Congress and Council to renewed exertion. The former, on August 22d, requested the State of Pennsylvania to keep four thousand militia in readiness to assist in repelling the threatened attack The following day Council ordered Col Henry, of the city and liberties of Philadelphia, to complete the third class of Philadelphia militia, which was ordered to march to Downingtown, while the artillery of the same locality was to assemble in numbers equal to three-eighths of the whole corps, which (with cannon) were ordered one-half to Chester and the other half to Downingtown, there to await the commands of Washington Maj-Gen John Armstrong, the veteran Indian fighter, was placed in command of the forces at Chester On the 26th Deputy Wagonmaster-Gen Thomas Hale applied to Council for wagons for Gen Nash's brigade, and the justices of Chester County were ordered to furnish seven wagons, which, if not immediately forthcoming, were to be impressed The following day the justices were required to send to Philadelphia twenty-five wagons

On August 29th Gen Armstrong wrote from Chester stating that matters there had "been that of a chaos, a situation more easy to conceive than describe" He had, however, forwarded at least eighteen hundred men, and also, in concert with Gen Potter, he had formed a rifle regiment of three hundred men, had given Col Dunlap, who was "not unacquainted with the business of a Partisan," command of it, and it would march to Marcus Hook the next day The three hundred men, as well as the one hundred and sixty which he would send to Wilmington that day, were not included in the number be had mentioned as already forwarded to Washington's army. He stated that the want of arms was the "great complaint at a crisis like this"[3] On August 31st Council authorized Gen Armstrong to buy blankets for the use of the troops, but if purchasing was impracticable to make as equal and moderate a levy of blankets as circumstances would permit upon the inhabitants of Chester County, "confining the same to persons who refuse to bear arms or take an active part in the defence of their bleeding country, now invaded by a cruel enemy" He was instructed to employ proper and discreet persons to make the levy, to appraise the blankets, certify the number and value of the articles, from whom taken, as well as the townships wherein the levies were made. The general was recommended to keep account of the blankets collected that they might be returned to the militia, so that the troops subsequently called into service could be supplied therewith[4]

The two days immediately succeeding the landing of the British at Elk were stormy, with lightning and thunder, which delayed the advance of their army. On the morning of October 27th, two divisions of light infantry, under Howe, moved forward, and the army of invasion thus began its march in the direction of the city of Philadelphia The lines of the royal troops, who had proceeded slowly and cautiously on Wednesday, the 3d day of September, extended from Aikentown (now Glasgow) to a point some distance northwest of the Baptist Church on Iron Hill, in Pencader Hundred, Del, when at the latter place their vanguard was encountered by Gen Maxwell's brigade, consisting of a detachment of Continental and the Maryland and Delaware militia. An English officer records, "The Rebels began to attack us about nine o'clock with a continued smart irregular fire for near two miles"[5] The American sharpshooters as usual did good service, but being inferior in number and without artillery, were pushed backward and finally compelled to retreat across White Clay Creek with a loss of forty killed and wounded The English claimed that their loss was three killed and twenty wounded,[6] but a woman who the following day had been in the British camp declared she saw nine wagon-loads of wounded brought in

On September 1st, Gen Armstrong had forwarded almost all the troops at Chester to Washington's command, and proposed following them himself the next day after he had adjusted some matters requiring his personal supervision

Three days later Council wrote to Gen. Armstrong stating that a part of the militia of Chester belonging to a class which had not been called into service had formed themselves into companies and had applied for ammunition and rations at headquarters, and had been refused Council was willing to encourage those people "at this juncture," and if they could be of use in the field, would "consider their two months service at this time as if they had served in future classes" These men were from the southern part of Chester County, and Col Smith the same day was directed to extend the like terms "to all other volunteers that may go forth in this common cause, they first accommodating their services to the ideas of Gen A."

On September 5th the American army was encamped

said, "It was here, along the higher ground on the left bank of the Kokari Konk (Cobb's Creek), that Washington, when moving towards the field of Brandywine was forced, by rains so heavy as to swell the stream almost beyond precedent, to remain three days inactive" Did not the incident thus described occur when the army was moving southward to meet Cornwallis in Virginia?

[1] 'Journal of Capt John Montressor," *Penna Mag of Hist*, vol v p 409 There is an error in the day of the week on which the landing was made, as recorded in the journal Capt Montressor notes Aug 25, 1777, as falling on Sunday, while the minutes of the Supreme Executive Council record Saturday as Aug 23, 1777

[2] Johnson's "History of Cecil County, Md," p 327

[3] Penna Archives, 1st series, vol v p 563

[4] Colonial Records, vol ix p 285

[5] Capt. Montressor's Journal, *Penna Mag of History*, vol v p 412

[6] Ib., p 413

n the east side of Red Clay Creek, and all the troops ı Wilmington were ordered to march to Newport, xcepting Gen. Irwin's brigade, which was to remain ı Wilmington, at work on the intrenchments at that lace. "The enemy," writes Gen. Armstrong, "as ır as we yet learn, appear to spread over some conīderable space of Country, but in a detached way from 'ouches Mills to some part of Nottingham."[1] The ame day the Navy Board recommended to Council ıat as there were reasons to believe that some vessels f the English fleet would attempt to approach the ity, a certain number of persons should be assigned › flood Hog Island, and that ninety or one hundred ıen should garrison the fort at Darby Creek. Council equested the Navy Board to see to the flooding of the sland, and ordered a company of artillery and a comany of "Musqueters," under the command of Col. ehu Eyre, to the works at Darby Creek.

Congress having recommended, on September 5th, call for five thousand militia of Pennsylvania, the ›llowing day Council directed the several lieutenants f the counties to order the militia to immediately ıarch to Darby, where they were "to rendezvous on ıe heights," and to "appear with what arms they ave, or can procure, and otherwise equipped in the est manner they may be able." These equipments, ıcluding blankets, Council assured the troops, would e paid for by the State in the event of their being taken by the enemy or otherwise unavoidably lost."[2] 'his call for militia only included those of the counties f Philadelphia, Chester, York, Cumberland, and Northumberland.[3] Why Lancaster was omitted does ot appear on the records of the Executive Council.

We also learn from the journal of Capt. Montressor, hief engineer of the British army, that three fugitives ame into Howe's camp on the 5th of September and eported that Gens. Mifflin and Cadwallader were, with what militia they have and can collect, at 'hester, with an intention to harass our rear."[4]

Deputy Quartermaster-General Mifflin, on Septemer 7th, wrote to Council from Newport, stating that ıe English army had disencumbered itself of all eavy baggage, and was then in light marching order. Vashington, thereupon, had directed all baggage, exepting blankets and "a few small clothes," to be sent way from the army, and for that purpose Quarterıaster Mifflin desired a hundred wagons be at once rdered to headquarters. These teams were "to be laced in the rear of the divisions, and immediately n an alarm the tents and small packs left with the ıen were to be sent over Brandywine." The followıg day Council directed one hundred wagons from 'erks, and a like number from Lancaster County, to eport to Mifflin.

Gen. Armstrong, on the 8th, stated that the night previous he had told Washington that in his opinion Howe's intention was to re-embark on the Delaware, cross to the New Jersey side, march up to the "Shevar de frize," clear the way for the fleet, and then bombard Philadelphia. He, therefore, was urgent for an attack on Howe in his camp.[5] The commander-in-chief, however, had strengthened his position, intending to offer battle on Red Clay Creek, but on the very day on which Gen. Armstrong wrote to Council, Howe advanced in two columns, one as if threatening an immediate attack, while the other, extending its left, halted at Milltown. At once Washington detected the intention of the British general, which was to march by his right, throw his army suddenly across the Brandywine, occupy the heights on the north of that creek, and thus cut the Continental arms absolutely off from communication with Philadelphia. Had Howe succeeded in that movement it is not probable that anything other than the total surrender of the American forces could have followed its consummation. That evening Washington held a council of war, at which it was decided at once to change position. At two o'clock in the morning the army was on the march, and had already crossed the Brandywine. On Tuesday afternoon, September 9th, in pursuance of the enemy's plan, Lieut.-Gen. Knyphausen, with the Third Division and two British brigades, marched for Kennett Square *via* New Garden. That afternoon, at half-past five o'clock, Gen. Howe ascertained that Washington had "evacuated Newport and Wilmington, and had taken post at Chad's Ford on the Brandywine Creek."[6] Washington having moved almost due north from Newport on the afternoon of the 9th, was intrenched on the high ground immediately north of the present Chad's Ford Hotel. During the night of the 10th, Maxwell's Light Infantry, which had the advanced posts, dug intrenchments on the west side, covering the approaches to the ford, and at this point Washington decided to deliver battle in defense of Philadelphia.

CHAPTER VIII.

THE BATTLE OF BRANDYWINE.

"THE Brandywine Creek, as it is called, commences with two branches called the East and West branches, which unite in one stream, flowing from West to East about twenty-two miles, and emptying itself into the Delaware about twenty-five miles below Philadelphia."[7] The union of these branches takes place over four miles above where the stream crosses the circular boundary-line dividing Delaware County

[1] Penna. Archives, 1st series, vol. v. p. 587.
[2] Ib., p. 592.
[3] Colonial Records, vol. xi. p. 293.
[4] *Penna. Mag. of Hist.*, vol. v. p. 414.
[5] Penna. Archives, 1st series, vol. v. p. 598.
[6] *Penna. Mag. of Hist.*, vol. v. p. 415.
[7] Irving's "Life of Washington," vol. iii. p. 213.

from the State of Delaware. The banks of the creek were steep, uneven, and covered with a heavy growth of forest trees at the period of which I am writing, and for the accommodation of public travel, roads had been cut and graded at convenient points to reach the fords of the Brandywine; that most generally used being on the direct road to Philadelphia and known as Chad's Ford. The topography of that section, in a military aspect, impressed the English chief of engineers as "an amazing strong country, being a succession of large hills, rather sudden with narrow vales, in short an entire defile."[1]

Washington, as before stated, at Chad's Ford, the centre of his position, where he anticipated the principal attack would be made, had stationed the main body of his army under command of Maj.-Gen. Greene, and comprising the brigades of Gens. Wayne, Weedon, Muhlenberg, and Maxwell's Light Infantry. Slight earthworks and a redoubt had been constructed, and Col. Proctor, with his Pennsylvania Artillerists, was in charge of the battery of six guns, which commanded the usual crossing of the stream at that place. Wayne's brigade, with Proctor's men, occupied the intrenchments, while Weedon's and Muhlenberg's brigades of Virginia troops were stationed some distance in the rear as a reserve. The Pennsylvania militia, under Gen. John Armstrong, constituted the left wing and extended through the rough ground—then known as Rocky Field—to Pyle's Ford, two miles below Chad's, and there Col. Jehu Eyre, with Capt. Massey's and McCullough's companies of the artillery militia of Philadelphia, had placed his cannons so as to prevent the crossing of the stream at that point by the enemy. The right wing of the American army was composed of six brigades, in three divisions, that of Gen. Sullivan's on the left, Gen. Lord Stirling on the right, and Gen. Stephens in the centre, reaching about two miles up the creek beyond Washington's headquarters, while the pickets were extended well up the stream, Maj. Spear being stationed at Buffington's Ford, now Brinton's, five miles beyond Chad's Ford.

On the evening of the 9th of September the two divisions of the British army under Lord Cornwallis and Maj.-Gen. Grant marched from Howe's headquarters, in Mill Creek Hundred, Del., to Hock Hossing Meeting-House, and the following morning moved to Kennett Square, reaching that place about noon, where Lieut.-Gen. Knyphausen's division was already encamped.

At daybreak next morning, the 11th of September, 1777, Gen. Howe marched his army in two columns against the American forces. The left wing, consisting of mounted and dismounted chasseurs, the first and second battalions of grenadiers, the guards, two squadrons of the Queen's Light Dragoons mounted, and two squadrons dismounted, and four brigades of infantry, comprising, according to English reports, seven thousand men, commanded by Lord Cornwallis and accompanied by Howe himself, who, on that occasion, we are told by Joseph Townsend, rode a "large English horse, much reduced in flesh," the result of the long voyage from New York and the scarcity of provender on shipboard. The American accounts, on the other hand, insist that this column amounted to thirteen thousand men. On that sultry autumn morning a thick fog hung like a curtain shutting out this movement from the eyes of the Continental scouts, and for miles the British troops, in light marching order, even their knapsacks laid aside, threaded their way along the road that ran northward almost parallel with the Brandywine for several miles without a whisper of their coming being borne to the ears of the American generals.

The column under Cornwallis having marched away, Knyphausen was not hurried in his movement, as his purpose was merely to amuse the Continental force in front of him until the left wing of the British army should have time to gain their right flank and rear. Hence it was about nine o'clock, four hours after Cornwallis had gone, that the Hessian general began to advance on the direct road to Chad's Ford. Early on the morning of the day of battle, Gen. Maxwell crossed at Chad's Ford, and with his riflemen had gone as far as Kennett Meeting-House to feel the British force, while small scouting-parties were extended even beyond that place. A graceful historical writer tells us that, as tradition has preserved the incident, a party of scouts had ventured to John Welsh's tavern, within the very clutches of Knyphausen, and there hitched their horses at the front of the inn, while they comfortably sampled the New England rum and apple whiskey in the barroom. The Hessians, who "wore their beards on their upper lip, which was a novelty in that part of the country," advancing, cut off the retreat of the American party by the front of the house, so that, abandoning their horses, they ran from the back door, turning, however, as they "fled, to discharge a spluttering volley that wounded one of their own horses left in the hands of the enemy."[2]

The riflemen began to harass the advancing troops, and, by resorting to trees, fences, and every available shelter, Maxwell thus maintained an efficient skirmish, sustaining himself well as he retired slowly before the heavy column moving against him. From behind the building and graveyard walls at Kennett Meeting-House a number of the sharpshooters inflicted much loss on the British troops, but were compelled to retreat before the overwhelming body arrayed against them. By ten o'clock Maxwell had by the pressure of superior numbers been forced back-

[1] Journal of Capt. John Montressor, *Penna. Mag. of History*, vol. v. p. 415.

[2] "Brandywine, 1777," by Howard M. Jenkins, in *Lippincott's Magazine* for September, 1877.

ward to the high ground on the west of the creek, and, after a bitter contest, to the ford itself Some troops being sent over to his assistance, he renewed the struggle, even regaining the heights Capt Porterfield and Waggoner, with their commands, crossed the ford, moved to the left of Maxwell, where they began a vigorous attack on Ferguson's Corps of Royal Riflemen, who at the time, together with a portion of the Twenty-eighth British Regiment, were engaged in throwing up light works, to put two guns in position on their right, to respond to Proctor's artillery, which had opened fire from the opposite bank The troops under Porterfield and Waggoner fought their way up a narrow, thickly-wooded valley, and forced a company of the enemy, supported by a hundred men from Gen Stern's Hessian brigade, to seek protection back of the stone house of William Harvey, the elder, who lived on the west side of the creek, until additional troops had hastened to their assistance Proctor, from the other side of the stream observing this, trained his guns on the advancing Britons, and the house came directly in the line of his fire William Harvey, then in his sixtieth year, had sent his family away from the dwelling, but, being a man of great personal courage, determined to remain to protect his property as far as he could from plunderers When the American guns opened, Harvey sat on his front porch, when a neighbor, Jacob Way, seeing him there, called out, "Come away, thee is in danger here! Thee will surely be killed!" The old gentleman merely shook his head, while his friend urged him in vain As they exchanged words a twelve-pound cannon ball from Proctor's battery passed through both walls of the kitchen, and plunged along the piazza floor, tearing up the boards and barely avoiding William's legs, until, a little farther on, it buried itself six feet deep in the earth It is recorded that William hesitated no longer, but sought a safer locality His house was thoroughly despoiled when the British came up"[1] He, however, lived nearly forty years after that trying ordeal

The pertinacity of the attack of Maxwell's brigade, as well as the audacious action of Porterfield and Waggoner, made it necessary for Knyphausen to send forward two brigades, supported by artillery, while at the same time a heavy column was marched toward Brinton's Ford, thus outflanking Maxwell, who was compelled to recross the Brandywine Simultaneously with these movements the Queen's Rangers, under Capt Weyms, of the Fortieth British Regiment, poured so hot a fire down the valley that Porterfield and Waggoner were also forced hastily to retire across the creek The high ground about half a mile back from the Brandywine, vacated by Maxwell, was immediately occupied in force by the enemy, and guns were placed in position by Knyphausen to command the ford From these occasionally a few shots were discharged, and responded to by Proctor's cannons, which desultory firing inflicted but little damage The casualties on the American side thus far had not exceeded sixty, while those of the British and Hessian troops were about one hundred and sixty Hence, at half past ten o'clock in the morning, when the enemy at Chad's Ford seemed disinclined to make any vigorous attack, Col Harrison, Washington's secretary, might be well excused for having dispatched a hurried note to Congress, stating that he had no doubt but that the enemy would be repulsed

Major Ferguson, the commander of the rifle corps in the English army, in a letter describing this battle, stated that while his men were lying concealed in a clump of woods, he noticed "a rebel officer in a hussar dress" pass in front of the American line, followed by another officer in dark green and blue, who was "mounted on a good gray horse, and wearing a remarkably high cocked hat" Ferguson ordered three of his men to creep towards and fire at them, but hardly had he done so when he recalled the command, for the Americans were so near that he felt to shoot at them would be little less than deliberate murder After the officers had passed some distance, they returned, and were again within easy reach of his sharpshooters The following day Ferguson, in conversation with a wounded American, learned "that Gen Washington was all the morning with the light troops, and attended only by a French officer in a hussar dress, he himself mounted and dressed in every respect as above described"

On the morning of the battle Gen Washington ascertained that Cornwallis had moved northward to some of the upper and unimportant fords, designing thus to turn the right flank of the American army. The commander-in-chief, fully aware that Maj Spear was posted at Buffington's Ford, whence he could dispatch intelligence of such a movement to Gen Sullivan, who would promptly communicate with him, had resolved to strike Knyphausen, while beyond the reach of the support of Cornwallis' division, and overwhelm him by numbers, and thus crush the British army in detail The Hessian general, it is known, did not begin his advance until nine o'clock in the morning, and it was rightly believed that Cornwallis would have to march twelve miles before he could cross the creek, even if he effected a passage at Buffington's Ford Between nine and ten o'clock Col Bland, with a few light-horsemen, crossed to the west side of the stream at Jones' Ford, three miles above Chad's, and, observing that Cornwallis' column was then approaching Trimble's Ford, on the west branch, he immediately dispatched a messenger with the tidings to Gen Sullivan Col Hazen also made a report of like import. The following dispatch, which Col Carrington[2] states is a model for clearness

[1] *Lippincott's Magazine* for September, 1877 "Brandywine, 1777," by Howard M Jenkins.

[2] Carrington's "Battles of the American Revolution"

in all details then needed, was sent by Lieut.-Col. Ross, of the Eighth Pennsylvania, to Gen. Sullivan, and by him in turn forwarded to Gen. Washington:

"GREAT VALLEY ROAD,
"11 o'clock A.M.

"DEAR GENERAL,—A large body of the enemy, from every account 5000, with 16 or 18 field-pieces marched along this road just now. The road leads to Taylor's Ferry & Jeffries' Ferry on the Brandywine, & to the Great Valley, at the Sign of the Ship, on Lancaster road to Philadelphia. There is also a road from the Brandywine to Chester, by Dilworthtown. We are close in their rear, with about 70 men. Capt. Simpson lay in ambush with 20 men & gave them 3 rounds within a small distance, in which two of his men were wounded; one mortally. I believe General Howe is with this party, as Joseph Galloway is here known by the inhabitants with whom he spoke, & told them that Gen. Howe was with them. Yours,

"JAMES ROSS, *Lieut.-Col.*"

Washington at once ordered Gen. Sullivan to cross the Brandywine and engage this division, to keep it employed, as it was the purpose of the commander-in-chief to attack the Hessian general immediately, shatter his command, and capture his baggage-train before the left wing, comprising the greater part of the British army, could retrace their steps and come to his relief. Gen. Greene was also directed to cross above Chad's Ford, in order to strike Knyphausen on the left flank. That officer, with the celerity of movement that was a conspicuous trait in his military character, promptly sent his advance guard across the stream at Brinton's Ford, where Sullivan's command lay, and was prepared to follow with his command. The commander-in-chief was to remain with Wayne, who was to cross the Brandywine at Chad's Ford in the face of the enemy. The fog which had clung to the earth in the early morning had vanished before the scorching sun, not yet midday high, and by noon this decisive movement would have been made, when the following note was delivered to Washington:

"BRENTON FORD,
"Sept. 11.

"DEAR GENERAL:—Since I sent you the message by Major Moore, I saw Major Spear of the militia, who came this morning from a tavern called Martin's, at the fork of the Brandywine. He came from thence to Welch's Tavern, & heard nothing of the enemy about the fork of the Brandywine, & is confident they are not in that quarter; so that Col. Hazen's information must be wrong. I have sent to that quarter to know whether there is any foundation for the report, & shall give your excellency the earliest information.

"I am, etc.,
"JOHN SULLIVAN."

The bearer of this dispatch was followed by Maj. Spear, who was sent by Gen. Sullivan to Washington to verbally make his report to the commander-in-chief, and this intelligence was speedily supplemented by a similar statement made by Sergeant Tucker, of the Light-Horse. These tidings were of the utmost consequence to the American general, for they argued that Cornwallis had merely moved off as a *ruse de guerre*, and that both wings of the British army were in supporting distance of each other. Hence the orders for crossing the creek were countermanded, Gen. Greene's advanced detachment was withdrawn, and the American army again resumed its former position. Washington, however, instructed Col. Bland to proceed to the extreme right and reconnoitre above the forks.

When the British invaded Chester County, Justice Thomas Cheyney, who was an outspoken Whig, was advised to absent himself from his dwelling in Thornbury, and to avoid personal danger he withdrew to the home of his relative, Col. John Hannum, at "Centre House," now the village of Marshallton, located between the East and West Branches of the Brandywine. Here Cheyney had passed the night of Sept. 10, 1777, and the next morning he, with Hannum, started to visit the American camp at Chad's Ford. As they rode along the highway near Trimble's Mill and Ford, on the West Branch, in descending the hill they saw a large body of soldiers, their scarlet uniforms designating them as British troops, descending the hills opposite. Halting, they watched the direction in which the column moved, and saw that it was making towards Jefferies' Ford, on the East Branch, their polished arms flashing and glittering in the sultry September sun. Having ascertained that fact, for a moment the two men consulted as to the course they should pursue, and finally it was decided that immediate intelligence of the presence of the British force at this point must be conveyed to Washington. Cheyney being mounted on a fleet hackney,—Dr. Harvey tells me it was a sorrel pacing mare,—started off in the direction of the American headquarters at a rapid pace, followed by Hannum, whose horse being less speedy was soon distanced, notwithstanding the squire turned the scales at two hundred pounds.[1]

Washington was seated under a cherry-tree which then stood—now blown down years ago—on the gentle declivity south of the road which leads to the crossing at Chad's Ford, when he saw a stout-built man without a hat, riding a sorrel horse, which jumped the fences that stood in the direction he was coming across the fields to where Washington was. It was Cheyney, who, having first reported to Sullivan his tidings, had been so discourteously received that he inquired and was told where Washington himself was to be found. The latter listened as the squire related what he had seen, and, as the chieftain seemed to hesitate, Cheyney exclaimed, "By h—ll, it is so!" and dismounting, he picked up a twig, drew a sketch on the ground of the upper roads, describing how the British passed the fords of the forks of the Brandywine, and where the enemy would probably be at that time. So accurately was this information imparted, that notwithstanding it was most unwelcome news, the general was reluctantly convinced of its truth. Some of his staff-officers, however, spoke sneeringly of the report made by the justice, and the excited man with an oath said to Washington, "If you doubt my word, sir, put me under guard till you ask Anthony

[1] Futhey and Cope's "History of Chester County," p. 586.

Wayne or Persie Frazer[1] if I am a man to believed," and then, turning to the smiling officers, his indignation found utterance. "I would have you to know that I have this day's work as much at heart as e'er a Blood of you!"[2]

The delays that had attended Squire Cheyney's attempt to apprise the Americans of the danger that threatened them had consumed considerable time, and hardly had Washington acknowledged the accuracy of the intelligence brought to him, when an orderly galloped hastily to the group and delivered a dispatch It read as follows

"TWO O'CLOCK P M

"DEAR GENERAL —Col Bland has this moment sent me word that the enemy are in the rear of my right and coming down They are, he says, about two brigades of them He also says he saw a dust, back in the country, for about an hour

"I am, &c,

"JOHN SULLIVAN"

Inclosed in this note was one addressed to Gen Sullivan, as follows

"A QUARTER PAST 1 O CLOCK

"SIR,—I have discovered a party of the enemy on the height, just on the right of the two widow Davis', who live close together on the road called the Forks road, about one half mile to the right of the meeting-house. There is a higher hill on their front.

"THEODORE BLAND"

By this time Washington knew that Gen Sullivan, a brave and patriotic officer, had permitted Howe once more to play with success the stratagem which had given him victory on Long Island, and for the like reason, Sullivan's neglect to make a proper reconnoissance It was a brilliant but dangerous movement of the English commander, separating his army into two divisions, seventeen miles asunder, and had not the second dispatch been sent by Sullivan, declaring on Maj Spear's assertion, that Cornwallis' division had not moved northward in the manner reported by Col Ross, the attack determined on by Washington could have been made on Knyphausen's division in overwhelming numbers, and in all likelihood would have been wholly successful Never in all his military career did Washington display greater capacity as a commander, than when he had decided to recross the Brandywine and engage the Hessian general No wonder was it then that the American chieftain ever after disliked to discuss the stragetic movements of that day

Gen Washington, knowing that his presence was necessary at the point menaced, was anxious to reach that part of the field as soon as possible, and desired to go thither by the shortest way To that end an elderly man of the neighborhood, Joseph Brown, who was well acquainted with the locality, was found and asked to act as guide The latter was loath to undertake this duty, and only consented to do so when the request assumed such a form that it could not with safety be refused One of the general's staff, who rode a fine horse, dismounted, Brown was lifted into the saddle, and the party started in the most direct route for Birmingham Meeting-House The mettlesome beast the guide rode cleared the fences as they dashed across the fields, the officers following at his heels So great was Washington's anxiety that he constantly kept repeating the command, "Push along, old man, push along, old man" Brown subsequently, in relating the incidents of this wild scamper across the country, stated that when they were about half a mile west of Dilworthtown, the bullets were flying so thickly that, as the noise of battle was now a sufficient guide to the American officers, and no notice was taken of him, he, unobserved, dismounted and stole away

Cornwallis, accompanied by the commander-in-chief, Sir William Howe, had marched his column from five o'clock in the morning through the woods that skirted almost his entire route on the west bank of the Brandywine During the first four hours a heavy fog clung to the earth, and a trying march it was that sultry day, with the dust rising in clouds under the feet of a moving army and the wheels of the parks of artillery and trains of baggage-wagons It was past the midday hour when the British column reached the west branch of the creek at Trimble's, and it was here, while making directly for Jefferies' Ford, that Cols Cheyney and Hannum watched it on the march, as heretofore related

On the west side of Jefferies' Ford Emmor Jefferies owned a fine farm, the home of his ancestors, and from his father's ownership of the real estate on both sides of the branch the crossing had received its name,—Jefferies' Ford When the British army first landed at Elk and moved in the direction of Wilmington, a number of the storekeepers, as well as other residents of that town, sent their goods to Chester County, near the forks of the Brandywine, whose peaceful quiet at that time it was supposed the march of armies never would disturb. In the house of Emmor Jefferies, who leaned somewhat to the royal side, it was thought goods could be safely kept But when the British soldiers learned that in his cellar a large quantity of liquors were stored, the thirsty, hungry men rolled out the barrels and casks, knocked in the heads, and drank freely, without asking the approval of the reputed owner Nor was that all Emmor Jefferies was himself pressed into service by Sir William Howe as a guide

It was not one o'clock when the vanguard of the British army passed the ford and pressed onward towards Osborne's Hill, near Sullivan's right Almost half a century ago Joseph Townsend (who, as a young man of twenty-one, was a witness of much appertaining to the battle) published his recollections of that day. He was attending that Thursday morning a mid-week meeting of Friends in the wheelwright-shop at Scon-

[1] Persifor Frazer was lieutenant-colonel of the Fifth Pennsylvania Line, recruited in Chester County He was born in Newtown township, and was a partner in the noted Sarum Iron-Works, in Thornbury

[2] Dr William Darlington's sketch of Thomas Cheyney in *Notæ Cestrienses* Newspaper clippings in Library of Historical Society of Pennsylvania

nelltown, for Gen. Washington had taken the Birmingham meeting-house as a hospital for his sick and wounded soldiers, even before he moved his army to Chad's Ford, and hearing a disturbance outside, the meeting was brought to a close. While endeavoring to quiet several of the women of the neighborhood, who were alarmed at the approach of the British troops, Townsend relates: "Our eyes were caught, on a sudden, by the appearance of the army coming out of the woods into the field belonging to Emmor Jefferies, on the west side of the creek, above the fording-place. In a few minutes the fields were literally covered over with them, and they were hastening towards us. Their arms and bayonets, being raised, shone bright as silver, there being a clear sky and the day exceedingly warm." This eye-witness records how "the space occupied by the main and flanking parties (of the British army) was near half a mile wide;" that Cornwallis "on horseback appeared very tall and sat very erect. His rich scarlet clothing, loaded with gold lace, epaulets, etc., occasioned him to make a brilliant and martial appearance, and that most of all the officers who conversed with us were men of the first rank, and were rather stout, portly men, well dressed, and of genteel appearance, and did not look as if they had ever been exposed to any hardship; their skins were as white and delicate as is customary for females brought up in large cities or towns."

The entire column of British troops had crossed Jefferies' Ford by two o'clock, its advance having reached the vicinity of Osborne's Hill, and in half an hour thereafter the whole body of men halted to refresh themselves, for they had not eaten since the early morning, and had marched about seventeen miles almost without a halt. Many of the soldiers on that weary tramp had fallen out of ranks, and exhausted remained along the road.[1]

When Washington first learned that the lost column of Cornwallis had been found, unfortunately for the Continentals in such a position that the inferior American force—in numbers, in discipline, and arms—would have to fight at great disadvantage, or, as Capt. Montressor states it, "were instantly obliged to divide their army, leaving part to oppose our right," Gen. Sullivan was ordered to bring his division to bear upon the British, and this compelled a forward movement of the whole right wing up the Brandywine. The American troops formed in a strong position above Birmingham meeting-house on a hill about a mile and a half removed from the British column, the ground falling gradually for more than half a mile in their immediate front "a natural glacis," and a thick woods covered their rear. As the divisions of Gens. Stirling and Stephens formed, Lord Cornwallis, on horseback,—Sir William Howe and his generals gathered about him,—sat watching the American officers arrange their line of battle, and as his glass showed him the disposition they were making, his eminent military abilities, never excelled in England's history during the last three hundred years, except by Marlborough, compelled him to pay this tribute to their merit, "The damned rebels form well!"

Cornwallis, under the immediate supervision of Sir William Howe, formed his battle array in three lines. The Guards were on the right of the advance, the First British Grenadiers to the left, the centre of the latter organization, supported by the Hessian Grenadiers, formed in a second line. "To the left of the Second Grenadiers, who held the centre, were two battalions of light infantry, with the Hessian and Anspach Chasseurs, supported by the fourth brigade, for a second line." The third brigade, consisting of the Fifteenth, Forty-fourth, and Seventeenth Regiments, was held in reserve, and was not called into action during the day. Both flanks of the British army were covered by very thick woods, and the artillery was advantageously disposed so that its fire might most seriously affect the American lines, and sustain the advance in its attack on the Continental troops.

Gen. Sullivan seems to have questioned his own judgment and hesitated to decide what was best to be done, when the true situation of the two armies was clearly presented to his mind. He had command of the entire right wing, hence the command of his immediate division devolved on Gen. DeBorre, his brigadier, a French officer of thirty-five years' experience in service, but a martinet, insisting on every little punctilio of military etiquette, even where such trifling matters might jeopardize the whole army. Hence when the latter marched his division to form, because it had laid along the Brandywine, fronting across, he insisted on moving his command on the right of Stephens and Stirling, which determination on his part made disorder in the division and occasioned an interval in the American line of over half a mile. It should be remembered that Stirling and Stephens as soon as they learned that the enemy were on their flank moved promptly, without waiting for orders from Sullivan, to the nearest good position from which they could resist the advancing British columns. Sullivan, thereupon leaving his old division in disorder, rode forward to where the other general officers were, and it was their unanimous opinion, he tells us in his report, "that his division should be brought on to join the other and the whole should incline further to the right to prevent our being out-flanked." Even the graphic account of the battle furnished by Gen. Sullivan shows that he lost that self-control which in Gens. Greene and Washington showed conspicuously during that afternoon of disaster to the American arms.

"At half-past two," he says, "I received orders to march with my division to join with and take com-

[1] "Journal of Capt. Montressor," *Penna. Mag. of History*, vol. v. p. 416.

mand of that and two others to oppose the enemy who were coming down on the right flank of our army I neither knew where the enemy were, or what route the other divisions were to take, and of course could not determine where I should form a junction with them I began my march in a few minutes after I received my orders, and had not marched a mile when I met Col Hazen with his regiment, which had been stationed at a ford three miles above me, who informed me that I might depend that the principal part of the British army was there, although I knew the report sent to headquarters made them but two brigades As I knew Col Hazen to be an old officer, and a good judge of numbers, I gave credence to his report in preference to the intelligence before received While I was conversing with Col Hazen and our troops still on the march, the enemy headed us in the road about forty rods from our advance guard I then found it necessary to turn off to the right to form, and so got nearer to the other divisions, which I at that moment discovered both in the rear and to the right of the place I was then at I ordered Col Hazen's regiment to pass a hollow way, file off to the right, and face to cover the artillery The enemy, seeing this, did not pass on, but gave me time to form my division on an advantageous height in a line with the other divisions, about almost a half mile to the left"

This gap of half a mile must be closed, and while this was being attempted at about half-past three o'clock,[1] the English commander hurled his well-disciplined soldiers full at the unformed Americans' right wing, and a half-hour previous to this assault the British guns had opened fire[2] The distance separating the combatants was about a mile and a half, the assaulting party being compelled to cross a valley and ascend a hill slope before they came to close quarters with their enemy

According to Joseph Townsend, an advance company of Hessians, when they reached "the street-road were fired upon by a company of the Americans who were stationed in the orchard north of Samuel Jones' brick dwelling-house," and the mercenaries scrambled up the bank of the road alongside the orchard, and resting their muskets on the upper rails, discharged them at the small body of Continentals This was merely an episode in the engagement, and was one of many similar incidents alluded to by Capt Montressor, in the remark, "Some skirmishing began in the valley in which the enemy was drove"[3] The American artillery Sullivan had placed in the centre of the line, where he had taken his position, and he ordered the guns discharged as quickly as possible to stop the progress of the British and to give the brigade under DeBorre time to form, for that body had been thrown "into the worst kind of confusion" before the assaulting party was upon them, and although Sullivan sent four of his aids, two of whom were killed in the effort to adjust the disorganized division, and had gone himself to rally the men who had fallen out of ranks, he succeeded only in partly forming there a line of battle

Conscious that the artillery on the centre commanded both the right and left of the line, he returned to that point, determining to hold the position as long as possible, knowing that if it was carried "it would bring on a total rout, and make a retreat very difficult" The right, however, was demoralized, and though some of the troops in that division were rallied and made a show of resistance, the greater portion could not "be brought to do anything but fly" In front of the American left was a plowed field, and the attack at this point was made by the Guards, the First British Grenadiers, and Hessian Grenadiers, and although it was claimed by Gen Howe that, notwithstanding a heavy fire of artillery and musketry, his troops pushed the rebels at once from the position they had taken, the fact is that for nearly an hour the struggle for the possession of the summit was continued, and although five times did the British soldiers drive the American troops from the hill, as often was it retaken The regiments of Drayton, Ogden, and Hazen's "Congress' Own" stood firm on the left, while the resistance of Stirling and Stephens was highly creditable, the main defense being made by the centre, where Sullivan exhibited great personal courage, and doubtless by his example animated his men in their contest with an overwhelming force At length the left wing broke and fled, pursued by the Guards and Grenadiers into a thick woods, whence the larger part of the American troops escaped, while the English were "entangled, and were no further engaged during the day" The centre still remained firm, and here Gen Conway, by the good conduct of his brigade, gained considerable reputation for himself (which he subsequently tarnished at Valley Forge), the Twelfth Pennsylvania, under his command, suffering very heavy loss Cornwallis now turned the whole fire of his artillery on the small body of men who still stood in line, and they were soon compelled to retire, a movement which was effected with some degree of steadiness and an occasional resumption of the offensive, since they took with them their artillery and baggage

The noise of heavy ordnance almost due north from Chad's Ford apprised Knyphausen that Gen Howe had succeeded in turning the right wing of Washington's army, and, although the musketry firing could be distinctly heard, it was not until an hour before the sun's setting that the Hessian commander made the attempt to cross at the ford[4] It is doubtful whether

[1] At half-past three the whole moved toward the enemy in three columns.—Journal of Capt Montressor, *Penna Mag of Hist*, vol v p 416

[2] Penna Archives, 2d series, vol x p 316

[3] *Penna Mag of History*, vol v p 416

[4] Penna Archives, 2d series, vol x p 316

Wayne had more than a thousand men who before that day had been under fire to resist the passage of the creek by the enemy. Knyphausen, taking advantage of the smoke from his own and the American cannon, for they had been firing for some time, marched his column, under the immediate command of Maj.-Gen. Grant, into the stream, and, notwithstanding Proctor's guns and the artillery with Wayne, plowed gaps in the advancing ranks, so that for days afterwards "the farmers were fishing dead bodies from the water,"[1] the crossing was made, and the redoubt captured. "Mad Anthony" knew that a retreat was inevitable, but his pugnacious nature, and that of the Pennsylvania line in his command, was loath to retire before an enemy, but the appearance of a large body of English troops from Cornwallis' division, on his right, compelled a hasty and disorderly retreat, in which he and Maxwell were compelled to abandon the greater part of their artillery and stores. The handsome black horse which Col. Proctor rode that day was shot from under him, but subsequently the State of Pennsylvania, in consideration of his bravery on that occasion, remunerated him for the loss he had sustained. The Pennsylvania militia, under Gen. Armstrong, which had taken no active part in the battle, fled with the rest of the American soldiers, and joined the demoralized body, which then almost choked the Concord road with a struggling mass of panic-stricken men hastening wildly in the direction of Chester.

Washington, when he received positive information that the British left wing had made its circuitous march from Kennett Square to Jefferies' Ford, the first part of the route under the guidance of Joseph Parker, whom Sir William Howe had compelled to point out the most direct road to Trimble's, and from Jefferies' Ford by Emmor Jefferies, and had already turned Sullivan's flank, started across the country for the scene of conflict, as already mentioned. He had immediately commanded Greene's division, consisting of Weedon's and Muhlenberg's brigade, to advance to the support of the right wing. With the promptitude ever noticeable in Greene's movements, the latter immediately put his division in motion. Weedon's brigade was on the advance, and at trail arms, the men, guided by the noise of battle, and knowing that Sullivan could have no line of retreat "but towards Dilworthtown, as the British right wing had outflanked it to the left, and intervened between it and Chad's Ford," double-quicked nearly to Dilworthtown, four miles in forty-five minutes, and then by a wheel to the left of a half-mile, he was enabled to occupy a position where, opening his ranks, he let the retreating, discomfited battalions pass through while he held the pursuing British in check and saved the American artillery.

Previous, however, to Greene's coming to their relief, a number of Americans were induced to make a stand, and rallied on a height to the north of Dilworthtown, where, under the personal command of Washington, who had reached the field, accompanied by Lafayette, the latter for the first time under fire in America, a stout resistance was made. It was here that the marquis was wounded. He stated that a part of the American line had broken, while the rest still held its ground; and to show the troops that he "had no better chance of flight" than they, he ordered his horse to the rear, and dismounted, he was endeavoring to rally the disorganized column, when he was struck in the left foot by a musket-ball, which "went through and through." The fact that Lafayette was wounded was immediately carried to Washington, "with the usual exaggerations in such cases." The surgeon endeavored to dress the injured foot on the battle-field, but the firing was so sharp that the attempt was abandoned, and the young Frenchman mounted his horse and galloped to Chester, where, becoming faint from loss of blood, he was "carried into a house and laid on a table, where my (his) wound received its first dressing."[2] Before he permitted his injuries to be cared for, Lafayette stationed a guard at the old decayed draw-bridge at Chester Creek (the site of the present Third Street bridge) to arrest stragglers and return them to their regiments. The Baron St. Ovary, who was aiding Lafayette in the endeavor to rally the American soldiers, was not so fortunate as the marquis, for he was captured by the English, and to be consigned to the tender mercies of that fiend, William Cunningham, provost-marshal of the royal army, was certainly less to be desired than a wound which healed kindly in two months.

The enemy meanwhile pressed the Americans backward until Weedon's brigade came in sight, and Sullivan joining him with some of his men, the battle continued until many of the fugitives had succeeded in effecting their retreat. At a place then called Dilworth's Path, now known as Sandy Hollow, the American army made its final stand. It is said by Irving that Washington, when riding in the neighborhood previous to the battle, had called Greene's attention to that locality, suggesting that if the army should be driven from Chad's Ford there was a point well calculated for a secondary position, and here Greene was overtaken by Col. Pinckney, an aid of the commander-in-chief, ordering him to occupy that place. Be that as it may, Greene formed there; Weedon's brigade, drawn up in the narrow defile, flanked on either side by woods, and commanding the road, while Greene, with Muhlenberg's—the fighting parson—brigade formed on the road on the right. The English troops, flushed with success, for it is idle to say they were not the victors of the day, came on, and were surprised at the unexpected resistance they

[1] Mr. Auge's statement, published in Futhey and Cope's "History of Chester County," p. 81.

[2] *Poulson's Advertiser*, Philadelphia, Feb. 25, 1825.

encountered here Charge after charge did they make, but were repeatedly driven back. Gen Howe states, "Just at dark the infantry, Second Grenadiers, and fourth brigade had a brief action beyond Dilworth, between the two roads which run from Dilworth to Chester" Capt Montressor tells us that here the heaviest fire during the battle for the time was poured on the British soldiers Indeed, he records, "Late in the evening, when the action was near concluded, a very heavy fire was received by our grenadiers from six thousand rebels, Washington's rear-guard, when Col Monckton requested me to ride through it to Brig-Gen Agnew's brigade and his (4) twelve-pounders, which I did in time enough to support them, and by my firing the (4) twelve-pounders routed the enemy"[1] The latter statement is not accurate, for Weedon, after holding his position until the demoralized troops had retreated down the Wilmington road to the Concord road, fell back in good order on Greene, and gradually the whole division drew off, showing their fangs to their enemy, who did not pursue the retiring Continentals It is even stated that many of the American officers were so enraged at the result of the conflict that they demanded to be led immediately against the enemy, but Washington shook his head, replying, "Our only recourse is to retreat" Greene, whose blood was up from the conflict and defeat, asked how far they must retreat? "Over every hill and across every river in America if I order you," was the stern reply[2]

The American troops, considering the circumstances, fought well Particularly was this true of the Twelfth Pennsylvania, commanded by Col Walter Stewart—said to have been the handsomest man in the Continental service—of Conway's brigade, of the Fifth Virginians, Woodford's brigade, commanded by Col. John Marshall, afterwards the great chief justice of the United States, and the Tenth Virginia, under Col Stevens, in Weedon's brigade The First, Third, and Sixth Maryland Regiments, and the First Delaware, under Gen Smallwood, acquitted themselves with marked bravery, while the Second, Fourth, and Seventh Delaware and German Regiments, four companies recruited in Pennsylvania, and the like number in Maryland, were the first to give way, and retired in disorder from the field This was largely due to the fact that Gen. DeBorre did not possess the confidence of his troops The Eighth Pennsylvania, Col Bayard, suffered greatly, and in the action Bayard was struck down by a cannon-ball, which broke the barrel of a rifle on the shoulder of Sergt Wyatt, as well as the sergeant's shoulder, and then struck Bayard on the head and shoulder, "turning him over on the ground for nearly two rods," when Lieut Patterson helped the colonel to his feet, who, the latter states, "was frantic" at his unceremonious treatment The Eleventh Pennsylvania lost so heavily that it was subsequently consolidated with the Tenth Capt Thomas Butler, of the Third Pennsylvania, for rallying a detachment of retreating troops, was on the field publicly thanked by Washington Capt Louis de Fleury conducted himself with such gallantry that Congress presented him with a horse to substitute his own, which was killed in the battle, and Gen Sullivan's horse, "the best in America," was shot under him in the engagement Count Casimir Pulaski, the Polish nobleman, highly distinguished himself that day, when, as a volunteer in the American Light-Horse, he rode within pistol-shot of the British lines to reconnoitre This action and his conspicuous bravery won him troops of friends, so that when he was appointed brigadier-general, with a command of cavalry, it met fully the approval of public opinion

The actual loss of the American forces can only be approximated, since Gen Washington never made a detailed report of this battle. The British claimed the loss was about a thousand killed and wounded and five hundred prisoners, together with nine "Branfield pieces, one more of a composition,[3] and one brass Howitzer, with several ammunition wagons"[4] Howe reported his own loss as only five hundred and seventy-eight killed and wounded, including officers, a statement that is not probably correct,[5] while Capt Mon-

[1] "Evelyns in America," by Gideon D Scull, Oxford, England, 1881 (privately printed), p 266

[2] Headley's "Life of Washington," p 256

[3] "We took ten pieces of cannon and a howitzer, eight were brass, the other two of iron of a new construction" Materials for History, by Frank Moore, quoted in *Penna Mag of History*, vol i page 294, note "In the war of the Revolution a singular cannon was made by a person who afterwards lived in the village (Mount Holly, N J) It was constructed of wrought iron staves, hooped like a barrel, with bands of the same material, excepting there were four layers of staves breaking joint, all of which were firmly bound together, and then bored and breached like other cannon William Denning (he died in the ninety fourth year of his age) was an artificer in the army of the Revolution He it was who, in the day of his country's need, made the only successful attempt ever made in the world to manufacture wrought-iron cannon, one of which he completed in Middlesex, Pa., and commenced another and larger one at Mount Holly, but could get no one to assist him who could stand the heat, which is said to have been so severe as to melt the lead buttons on his coat The unfinished piece is now (1844) in the Philadelphia Arsenal The one completed was taken by the British at the battle of Brandywine, and is now in the tower of London The British offered a stated annuity and a large sum to the person who would instruct them in the manufacture of that article, but the patriotic blacksmith preferred obscurity and poverty in his own beloved country, though the country for which he had done so much kept her purse closed from the veteran soldier until near the period of his decease" Barber and Howe's Historical Collections of New Jersey, pp 113-114

[4] *Penna Mag of History*, vol vi p 297

[5] In the *Penna Mag of Hist*, vol iv page 121, is given what purports to be a memorandum of the British forces at the battle of Brandywine, and the loss sustained by the several divisions The document was, it is stated, found in one of the British officers' marquet, at Germantown, Oct 4, 1777, which, after being in possession of Col Thomas Forrest, subsequently came to John F Watson, the annalist The total loss as given in the memorandum is nineteen hundred and seventy six In Headley's Life of Washington, page 258, is published a paper found among those belonging to Gen James Clinton, and in his handwriting, indorsed, "Taken from the enemy's Ledgers, which fell into the hands of General Washington's army at the action of Germantown" An examination of the two statements shows that the one is a copy of the other, although there is a difference of ten in the grand total, the latter being nineteen hundred and eighty-six This occurs in the loss of the First

tressor tells us that the British troops had sixty killed and three hundred wounded Certain it is that the English not continuing the pursuit is some evidence that they were in no condition to do so Thomas Paine declared that Brandywine, "excepting the enemy keeping the ground, may be deemed a drawn battle," and that as Washington had collected his army at Chester, "the enemy's not moving towards him next day must be attributed to the disability they sustained and the burthen of their wounded"[1] The dead of both armies, it should be remembered, were left on the field and had to be burned, while the number of wounded was so great, that on the Sunday following the battle (September 14th) Drs Rush, Leiper, Latimer, Way, and Coates, with Mr Willet, a mate in the hospital, with their attendants, who had been sent by Washington, arrived at headquarters of the British army, or, as Capt Montressor records the incident, came "to attend the wounded Rebels left scattered in the Houses about the field of Battle unattended by their Surgeons until now"

To return to the army, which was drifting down the road to Chester in a confused mass The artillery saved from the enemy's clutches jolted and surged along as rapidly as the tired horses could be made to go under the goading whip, while the baggage-wagons crowded to the front amid the oaths of the teamsters and the panic-stricken men who were forced to make room for the vehicles to pass Fortunately the early evening was still and clear, and the moon looked down on the defeated, demoralized men, who tiring at length of their senseless flight, the disorder in a measure ceased as the weary journeying came near an end, so that the guard at Chester bridge, placed there by Lafayette, succeeded in gathering the men into something like company and regimental order without much difficulty Greene's division, as well as many of the men from other commands, preserved a military organization, and they marched from the field in columns becoming the brave soldiers they had proved themselves to be on the heights of Brandywine

In Chester the noise of the distant cannonading could be distinctly heard, like far-away mutterings of thunder, and after the battle had been lost, the bearers of ill tidings traveled fast with their unwelcome intelligence Before dusk the first of the discomfited American forces began to straggle in, spreading all kind of rumors regarding the results of the contest, and the ancient borough was never so aroused In Philadelphia all was excitement Paine states that he was preparing dispatches for Franklin "when the report of cannon at Brandywine interrupted my (his) proceedings"[2]

Far into the night the American army kept marching into Chester, and it is related that after the moon had set Col Cropper, then a captain in the Ninth Virginia Infantry,—a part of Greene's command covering the retreat,—because of the darkness, and to prevent his men being crowded off the approaches to the bridge at the creek, fastened his handkerchief on a ramrod, and stood there holding it aloft as a signal until his command had filed by

Hon William Darlington has recorded the escape of Col Samuel Smith, of Maryland, from the field, as related to him by the old veteran, who subsequently defended Fort Mifflin so determinedly Having become separated from his command in the retreat, and, apprehensive of falling into the hands of the enemy, the colonel rode to the house of a Quaker farmer, whom he desired forthwith to conduct him by a safe route to Chester The latter protested against the undertaking, but Col Smith drew a pistol, stating that if he did not get his horse at once and do as he asked, he was a dead man The Quaker, in alarm, exclaiming, "What a dreadful man thou art!" did as he was told "Now," said Col Smith, "I have not entire confidence in your fidelity, but I tell you explicitly that if you do not conduct me clear of the enemy, the moment I discover your treachery I will blow your brains out" The terrified farmer thereupon exclaimed, "Why, thou art the most desperate man I ever did see" However, he brought the colonel safely to Chester and was rewarded for his services At midnight Washington addressed a letter to Congress, apprising that body of the loss of the battle. The missive is dated Chester, and traditionally in the Kerlin family, it is said, he wrote the letter at the Washington House, on Market Street It was published by the order of Congress, and is as follows

"CHESTER, September 11th 1777
"Twelve o'clock at night

"SIR —I am sorry to inform you that in this day's engagement, we have been obliged to leave the enemy masters of the field Unfortunately the intelligence received of the Enemy's advancing up the Brandywine and crossing at a ford about six miles above us, was uncertain and contradictory, notwithstanding all my plans to get the best This prevented my making a disposition adequate to the force with which the enemy attacked us on our right, in consequence of which, the troops first engaged were obliged to retire, before they could be reinforced In the midst of the attack on the right, that body of the enemy that remained on the other side of Chad's ford, crossed and attacked the division there under the command of General Wayne, and the light troop under General Maxwell, who after a severe conflict, also retired The militia under the command of General Armstrong, being posted at a ford about two miles below Chad's, had no opportunity of engaging

"But though we fought under many disadvantages, and were from the cause above mentioned obliged to retire, yet our loss of men is not, I am persuaded, very considerable, I believe much less than the enemy's We have also lost seven or eight pieces of cannon according to

Hessians at the Upper Ford, under Cornwallis,—the Forrest memorandum making it sixty, while that of Clinton's places it at seventy The two papers differ somewhat in designating the numerals of the British regiments The Clinton paper is probably the most accurate

[1] Paine's letter to Franklin, *Penna Mag of History*, vol ii p 283

[2] *Penna Mag of Hist*, vol ii p 283 Irving (Life of Washington, vol iii p 222) thus describes the excitement in Philadelphia "The scene of this battle, which decided the fate of Philadelphia, was within six and twenty miles of that city, and each discharge of cannon could be heard there The two parties of the inhabitants, Whig and Tory, were to be seen in groups in the squares and public places, awaiting the event in anxious silence At length a courier arrived His tidings spread consternation among the friends of liberty Many left their homes, entire families abandoned everything in terror and despair and took refuge in the mountains"

he best information I can at present obtain The baggage having been reviously moved off all is secure, saving the men's blankets, which at heir backs, many of them doubtless are lost

"I have directed all the troops to assemble behind Chester, where they re now arranging for the night Notwithstanding the misfortunes of hi day I am happy to find the troops in good spirits, and I hope another ime we shall compensate for the losses now sustained

"The Marquis La Fayette was wounded in the leg, and General Wool-ord in the hand Divers other officers were wounded and some slain, ut the numbers of either cannot be ascertained

"G WASHINGTON

"P S.—It has not been in my power to send you earlier intelligence, he present being the first leisure moment I have had since the engage nent"

The American army assembled to the east of Chester along the Queen's Highway, and Washington, after lispatching this letter, went to the present Leiperville, where, still standing on the north of the road, is the old stone dwelling, then the home of John McIlvain, n which the chief of that retreating army passed the night after the ill-starred battle of Brandywine

Gen Howe demonstrated in this battle his ability o command armies successfully, and the skill with which he manœuvred his troops in a country of hill and vale, wood and thicket, showed the accomplished, cientific soldier. The rapidity with which Washington brought order out of disorder was shown when the American troops marched through Darby to Philadelphia, on September 12th, in the soldierly bearing of that part of the army which the day before had led from the field a panic-stricken mob Taking all hings into consideration, never was Washington's wonderful command of men and extraordinary capacity to recover from disaster more exhibited than at this period of our nation's history, and that in this emergency the whole country turned to him as its foremost man is evidenced in that Congress, while the thunder of the cannons of Brandywine was yet heard n Philadelphia, clothed the commander-in-chief with almost dictatorial power for two months

CHAPTER IX

FROM THE DEFEAT AT BRANDYWINE TO THE CONCLUSION OF THE REVOLUTIONARY WAR

ON the afternoon of September 12th, the day succeeding the battle, Maj-Gen Grant, with the First and Second Brigades of the English army, marched rom Chad's Ford to Concord meeting-house, whence he sent out foraging-parties to bring in wagons, horses, provisions, and cattle from the surrounding neighborhood Early the following morning (Saturday, the 13th), Lord Cornwallis, with the Second Battalion of Light Infantry and Second Grenadiers, made a junction with Gen Grant and advanced to the Seven Stars, n Aston, within four miles of Chester The day was very cold, as the noticeable equinoctial gale of the following Tuesday was already threatening It may be that an advance party of the British troops that day went as far as Chester, for on Sept 13, 1777, James Dundas wrote from Billingsport that "the people employed here begin to be very uneasy, since we have heard that Chester is in possession of the enemy"[1] Notwithstanding this assertion, I doubt much whether the ancient borough was occupied by any of the commanding army officers at that time, for on September 15th Capt Montressor records in his journal[2] that "the Commander in Chief went with his Escort only of Dragoons to Lord Cornwallis' Post ¾ of a mile west of Chester," and under the same date he states, "This night at 8, the body with Lord Cornwallis moved from near Chester toward the Lancaster road"

The day following the battle of Brandywine, Council called for the militia in the several counties—the fourth class in Chester County—"to turn out on this alarming occasion," and to march to the Swede's Ford, on the Schuylkill, unless Washington should command them to rendezvous elsewhere On the 13th, Washington, whose army was resting at Germantown, instructed Col Penrose to overflow the ground upon Providence Island, which necessarily meant cutting the banks at Darby Creek, so as to prevent the English army, should it march immediately to Philadelphia, from erecting batteries in the rear of Fort Mifflin, or carrying it by a land force in that direction On September 15th, Washington broke camp at Germantown and marched his soldiers along the Lancaster road From the Buck Tavern, in Haverford township, he called the attention of Council to the pressing necessity for an immediate supply of blankets for the troops, stating that he had been "told there are considerable quantities in private hands, which should not be suffered to remain a moment longer than they can be conveyed away."[3] The American commander had fully determined to meet the British army again in battle before the city of Philadelphia should fall into the hands of the enemy For that purpose he had turned his column westward, and that evening Washington was encamped in East Whiteland township, Chester Co, in the vicinity of the Admiral Warren Tavern

Late in the afternoon of September 15th the report was received by Gen Howe that the American army, as he supposed, in flight, was "pursuing the road to Lancaster,"[4] and at eight o'clock that night, Lord Cornwallis moved from near Chester towards the Lancaster road, following the Chester and Great Valley road, "by way of the present village of Glen Riddle, Lima, and Howellville and by Rocky Hill and Goshen Friends' meeting-house"[5] The next morning Gen Howe, who had remained at Birmingham for five days

[1] Penna Archives, 1st series, vol v p 616

[2] *Penna Mag of Hist*, vol vi p 35

[3] Penna Archives, 1st series, vol v p 624

[4] *Penna. Mag of Hist*, vol vi p. 35

[5] Futhey and Cope's "History of Chester County," p 73

after the battle,[1] on the morning of the 16th, marched towards Lancaster by the way of the Turk's Head (now West Chester), Goshen meeting-house, and the Sign of the Boot, on the Downingtown road, and at eleven o'clock made a junction with Cornwallis' division, the latter column moving in advance until it had gone about a mile and a half north of Goshen meeting-house, where, about two o'clock, the two armies confronted each other, and Wayne attacked the British right flank with so much spirit that in a few moments the action would have become general, when, doubtless, owing to the discharge of musketry, the heavy, low-hanging, scudding clouds broke into a deluge of rain, accompanied by a tempest of wind, which resulted in separating the armies immediately So far as the American troops were concerned, they were in a few moments wet to the skin Their ammunition was ruined, owing to their cartouch-boxes and "tumbrels" being so defectively constructed that they were no protection from the rain About four o'clock, Washington retired to Yellow Springs, which place his army reached in the night, and the next morning the commander-in-chief retreated with the main army up the Schuylkill, crossing it at Parker's Ferry

While the English forces lay at Birmingham, Jacob James, a loyalist of that neighborhood, recruited in Chester County a troop of light-horsemen, and when the army marched away, he and his company followed the British standard "The Chester County dragoons, under Captain James, subsequently took part in the surprise of Col Lacey's Militia Brigade, lying at Crooked Billett," on April 30, 1778, and in March, 1780, Capt James was captured in North Carolina President Reed, on April 18th of the latter year, wrote to Governor Caswell stating that James had been "a distinguished Partizan here in the Winter 1777, & particularly active in Kidnapping the Persons in the Vicinity of the City who were remarkable for their Attachment to the Cause of their Country He was also extremely troublesome to the County by stealing & employing his Associates in stealing Horses for the British Army" President Reed therefore requested Governor Caswell "that he may not be exchanged as a common Prisoner of War, but retained in close Custody untill a favorable Opp'y shall present to bring him to this State for Tryal"[2] The regular British officers, however, were not over-scrupulous in this matter of appropriating horses to their use, for, on Sept 19, 1777, Lieut -Col Harcourt, with a party of dragoons and light infantry, came from Howe's encampment in Goshen, on the Philadelphia road, and from Newtown Square brought a hundred and fifty horses to the enemy[3]

The British not only had made these advances by land, but on September 17th Howe was notified that several of the English vessels of war had arrived in the river, "and three victuallers, one at anchor, in the Delaware off Chester"[4] The "Roebuck," Capt. Hammond, whose presence in the river, as heretofore noticed, had made that officer familiar with the navigation of the Delaware River, at least as far as Wilmington, was one of the advanced men-of-war Admiral Earl Howe, after the battle of Brandywine, hastened with his fleet into the river and anchored his vessels along the Delaware shore from Reedy Island to New Castle Washington, as well as Gen Howe, when the latter by "doubling on his tracks" had crossed the Schuylkill and captured Philadelphia, knew that the English commander must have uninterrupted water communication to maintain his army, and while the enemy were resolved to do everything they could to force the passage of the river, the American authorities were equally resolved to keep up, if possible, the obstruction "If these can be maintained," wrote Washington to Congress, "Gen Howe's situation will not be the most agreeable, for, if his supplies can be stopped by water, it may easily be done by land"[5] When the city fell, on September 25th, Gen Howe sent a messenger to notify the English fleet, then at Chester, that his had taken possession of Philadelphia That communication by the river must be had was well understood by the English officers, for, in a letter from Lieut -Col William Harcourt to Earl Harcourt, dated at Philadelphia, October 26th, he remarks that "it was absolutely necessary we should open a communication with our fleet,"[6] and in the letter he narrates the attempts, up to that time, made by the British commander to that end, the defeat of Col Dunop at Red Bank, the attack on Fort Mifflin, the repulse of the English forces there, and the destruction of the frigate "Augusta" and sloop of-war "Merlin," classifying them as "checks following so close upon the back of each other"

The enemy, however, had already made unwelcome visits to the section of country now Delaware County, for a resident of Philadelphia, under date of October 3d, records that "a foraging party went out last week towards Darby and brought in a great number of cattle to the great distress of the inhabitants"[7] We also learn that on October 5th (Sunday) a captain of the Royal Artillery, with thirty men, went to Chester to bring to Philadelphia two howitzers and a large number of mortars A battalion of Grenadiers and the Twenty-third or Welsh Fusileers accompanied them as an escort[8] On September 29th, Col Stirling, with two British regiments, crossed the river from Chester, and took possession of the fortifications at Billingsport, which was manned only by militia, who,

[1] See "A plan of the Operations of the British & Rebels Army in the Campaign, 1777," under Descriptive Letter F "The Evelyns in America," p 252

[2] Penna Archives, 1st series, vol iii p. 191

[3] *Penna Mag of History*, vol vi p 38

[4] Ib., p 37

[5] Sparks' "Correspondence of Washington," vol v p 71

[6] "The Evelyns in America," p 246

[7] "Diary of Robert Morton," *Penna Mag of Hist*, vol i p 12

[8] "Journal of Capt Montressor," *Penna Mag of Hist*, vol vi p. 42

after spiking the cannons and setting fire to the barrack, withdrew without firing a gun[1] The force under Stirling is stated by Col Bradford to have been Highlanders and marines from the man-of-war Capt Montressor says the troops were the Seventy-first Highlanders On October 4th the enemy retired, excepting three hundred men, after they had made some unsuccessful efforts to remove the obstructions sunk in the river there, and on October 6th the British set fire to all the works and house, and the men who had been left to garrison the fort were withdrawn The same evening Commodore Hazelwood of the Pennsylvania navy came down the river with the row-galleys, and attacked the British vessels of war between Fort Island and Chester The firing "was almost a constant cannonade," and resulted in the British vessels getting under way, retiring to Chester, where nine of his Majesty's war ships were then lying[2] The same evening the Forty-second and Tenth British Regiments, with two howitzers and two mortars, marched to Philadelphia to protect a large quantity of provisions landed at Chester for the use of the army, which were then being transported to the city. In the evening of October 11th, about three hundred American militia entered the town of Chester and captured the loyal sheriff of Sussex County, Del, who had sought shelter there under the British authorities The night after the battle of the Brandywine, Governor McKinley, of that State, was taken from his bed and made a prisoner In retaliation for that act the Governor offered a reward of three hundred dollars for the arrest of the sheriff, at whose instance it is said McKinley had been apprehended The day previous to this bold movement of the milita, Col Boyd, sub-lieutenant of Chester County, was instructed to call out the fifth class of the militia to defend the inhabitants from foraging parties, and that a troop of fifty horsemen should be organized for that purpose The ammunition required for these hastily-assembled forces was ordered to be placed at Col Boyd's immediate disposal On the 13th of October it was reported that Gen Proctor, with sixteen hundred men, was then in Newtown township, almost sixteen miles from Philadelphia[3] Potter had been ordered to keep a sharp lookout for parties of English foragers, and if possible prevent any provisions from being taken from the west side of the Schuylkill to Philadelphia for the use of the British troops Congress had also by resolution declared that any one who should furnish provisions or certain other designated supplies to the British forces, or who should be taken within thirty miles attempting to convey such interdicted articles to any place then occupied by his Majesty's soldiers, would be subject to martial law, and if found guilty of the offenses, should suffer death[4] Gen Armstrong, on the 14th, informed Council that his division had been separated, that Gen Potter with his brigade had been "sent to Chester County to annoy the Enemies' small parties, whether Horse or foot, that may be found on the Lancaster or Darby roads, prevent provisions going to the Enemy, &c I have heard," he continued, "of a fifth class of the militia of that County being ordered to remain for its own defence, which is very proper, the Commander of that Class ought to communicate with General Potter & occasionally take his instructions"[5] On the 15th the British fleet moved up the river and joined the "Roebuck" and "Vigilant," that then lay at anchor off Little Tinicum Island, the latter having the day before come up the Delaware sufficiently near to exchange shots with Fort Mifflin The Americans were still confidently relying on the strength of the *chevaux-de-frise*, being entirely unaware of the fact that Robert White, who had been employed to sink the obstructions, was a traitor, as his subsequent base conduct showed, and had designedly left the channel near the Pennsylvania side open[6] Yet even after the forts were in the hands of the British, the approach to the city of Philadelphia was regarded as so hazardous that most of the English vessels lay in the river below the Horse-Shoe, making the town of Chester the port where they discharged supplies for the army

Richard Peters, as secretary of the United States Board of War, on Oct 18, 1777, called President Wharton's attention to information received, that a great number of the inhabitants of Chester County had furnished intelligence to and supplied the enemy with provisions while they were in that county, without which assistance it was believed the British would not have succeeded in the capture of Philadelphia The authorities of the United States were determined to render such service impossible, and to that end urged upon the State that "the great principle of self Preservation requires that the most effectual means should be forthwith pursued to put it out of their Power to persist in their former Mal-Practices, by taking from them such Articles of Clothing & Provisions, & of the former particulary shoes, stockings & Blankets, as might serve for the comfort & subsistence of the Enemy's Army, & the Acquisition whereof is of absolute Necessity to the existence of our own" The War Department, therefore, urged on Council that "spirited and determined militia," commanded by discreet and active officers, should be immediately sent to Chester County to collect blankets, shoes, and stockings from all of the inhabitants that had not taken the oath or affirmation of allegiance to the State of Pennsylvania, and that all provisions and stock which might be useful to the enemy should be removed to a point beyond the latter's incursions

[1] Marshall's "Life of Washington," vol iii p 176

[2] Penna Archives, 1st series, vol v p 648.

[3] *Penna Mag of Hist*, vol i p 13

[4] Marshall's "Life of Washington," vol iii p 172

[5] Penna Archives, 1st series, vol v p 673

[6] *Penna Mag of Hist*, vol vi p 192, note

Gen. Washington, it was apprehended by Richard Peters, would order Gen. Potter to co-operate with the officers appointed for that purpose by Council.[1] On the 21st, which was possibly the day Council received the dispatch just mentioned, for it had been sent from York to Lancaster, Col. Evan Evans, Col. William Evans, Col. Thomas, Col. Gibbons, Col. Thomas Levis, Capt. William Brooks, and Capt. Jacob Rudolph were appointed to collect the articles enumerated from persons who had not publicly given in their adherence to the State of Pennsylvania, and were instructed to give certificates to owners whose goods were taken, allowing them three pounds for new single blankets. The articles thus taken were to be delivered to the clothier-general. Dr. Smith tells us that this order bore with unusual harshness on the Quakers, who were indeed a class peculiarly situated, their religious principles prevented them from taking the oath of allegiance and abjuration, for not only did they suffer from the inconvenience of parting with the necessaries for their family, but in addition, "their conscientious scruples would not permit them to receive the proffered compensation."[2]

At this time the British were making every effort to forward the siege they had begun of Fort Mifflin, where, under the supervision of Capt. Montressor, batteries had been erected on Providence Island in the rear of the fort and communication had also been established with the fleet by way of Bow Creek. On the 23d of October an unsuccessful attack was made on the fort, twenty vessels taking part therein, but in the action the frigate "Augustas," a new sixty-four gun ship, got aground, was set on fire, her magazine exploded and she was a total wreck, as was the "Merlin" sloop-of-war, which ran on the *chevaux-de-frise* and sunk. The day before the attempt to carry Red Bank by assault had resulted disastrously for the British arms. On the 25th, Col. Joseph Reed, then at Darby, wrote to Council that a deserter from the Hessian Losberg regiment stated that the British army "must retreat in a few Days to Wilmington if they cannot get up their Provisions. Great Distress for Provisions in Town." Hence, when the news of Burgoyne's surrender was received in Philadelphia on October 31st well might Capt. Montressor record: "We are just now an army without provisions, a Rum artillery for Beseiging, scarce any amunition, no clothing, nor any money. Somewhat dejected by Burgoyne's capitulation, and not elated with our late manœuvres as Dunop's repulse, and the 'Augustas' and 'Merlin' being burnt and to complete all, Blockaded."

Gen. Potter was active in his efforts to harass the enemy and cut off their means of supply, for we learn from a letter to President Wharton, written on October 27th, that when he first went to Chester County with his command the country people carried to the city all kinds of marketing, but that he had put an end to that trade, no one being suffered to go to Philadelphia without a pass. At the time he wrote, sixty ships of the enemy were lying at and below Chester. From the best information he could get he learned that provisions "is very scarce and deer in the city," and he also stated that he had moved all the beef cattle and the flour from that part of the county,—the territory now included within the present limits of Delaware County.

Two days after the date of this letter Gen. Washington (Oct. 31, 1777) wrote to Gen. Potter:

"As soon as the Schuylkill is fordable, I will send over a large body of militia to you, for the purpose of executing some particular matters. The principal one is to endeavor to break up the road by which the enemy have a communication with their shipping over the islands (by Bow Creek) if practicable; and to remove the *running-stones from the* mills in the neighborhood of Chester and Wilmington."

The commander-in-chief was very explicit in the orders to Gen. Potter, and the latter was instructed to execute them at once, and, if he had no teams or insufficient means of transporting the stones, he was directed to impress wagons. The grist-mills from which the stones were to be taken he designated thus:

"Lloyd's, about two miles on this side of Chester (afterward Lapadie, Leiper's Snuff-mills); Robinson's, on Naaman's Creek; Shaw's, about one mile back of Chester (now Upland), and the Brandywine mills. . . . The stones should be marked with tar and grease, or in some other manner, that it may be known to what mill they belong, that they may be returned and made use of in the future, and they should be moved to such distance that the enemy cannot easily recover them. If there is any flour in the mills it should be removed, if possible, after the stones are secured. I am informed that there is a considerable quantity in Shaw's mill, particularly, which there is reason to believe is intended for the enemy. It is very convenient to the navigation of Chester Creek, and should be first taken care of. I beg you may instantly set about this work for the reason above mentioned. That no previous alarm may be given, let a certain hour be fixed upon for the execution of the whole at one time, and even the officers who are to do the business should not know their destination till just before they set out, lest it should take wind."

In a postscript, Washington says, "I have desired Capt. Lee, of the Light-Horse, to give any assistance that you may want."[3]

That this order was carried into effect we learn from a letter dated Nov. 4, 1777, written by Maj. John Clark, Jr., to Washington, in which he informed the general that, "Near Hook fell in with Capt. Lee with a few dragoons and about sixty of foot, among whom were a few riflemen. . . . *The mills are dismantled*, and we drove off some fat cattle from the shore at Chester, which I believe were intended for the enemy."[4] I have been unable to find where the mill-stones were taken, or how long their owners were deprived of them. Certain is it that after the British evacuated Philadelphia, the mills mentioned were in full operation.

The service of light cavalry was indispensable in moving rapidly from place to place in order to intercept the enemy in their raids in the neighborhood of

[1] Penna. Archives, 1st series, vol. v. p. 680.

[2] Smith's "History of Delaware County," p. 319.

[3] Annals of Buffalo Valley, by John Blair Linn, p. 144.

[4] Bulletin of Penna. Hist. Society, vol. i. No. 10, March, 1847, p. 34.

the city and in rescuing booty from their foraging parties or in driving cattle beyond their reach So important was it deemed to have such bodies of men in Chester County that Council, October 31st, ordered Cols. Cheyney and Granow, without loss of time, to form three or four troops of light-horse, particularly in the southeastern parts of the county—now Delaware County—and in the formation of such mounted troops the advice and direction of Gen. Potter was to be taken. The militia officers designated immediately set about carrying out the orders they had received, for on November 8th, Gen. Potter, who then had his headquarters at Mr. Garret's, in Newtown, wrote to President Wharton that considering the close approach of winter, he doubted whether the men could be raised and equipped sufficiently early to be of any service in the then campaign, and that he then had volunteers who were acquainted with the country, and answered every purpose of dragoons. If it was necessary to have dragoons for an emergency, Washington would send any number that might be required. The reasons assigned by Gen. Potter seem to have fully satisfied Council, for nothing more appears in reference to the troops of light-horsemen from Chester County.

Meanwhile the British forces were making regular siege to Fort Mifflin, for the scarcity of provisions was such that already many articles of food had so advanced in price in Philadelphia that they had thereby been banished from the tables of all but the wealthier classes, and provender for animals was difficult to procure. Although the city had fallen, on the whole, considering the repulse of the fleet at Fort Mifflin and the defeat at Red Bank, together with the stirring tidings from the North that Burgoyne had been captured, the outlook for the enemy was in nowise promising. For a number of years before the war, the industrious residents of that part of Chester County bordering on the Delaware, at a considerable outlay of labor, time, and money, had constructed dikes or embankments of earth along the river bank, so that much of the low and swampy ground had been converted into rich meadow land. As a means of defense, Council had determined to cut these banks when necessary, and flood the meadows. Hence we find that on November 1st, Capt. Montressor, who was constructing the batteries on Carpenter's and Providence Islands, and who had effected communication with the fleet by the way of Bow Creek, records on that day that "two hundred of the Rebels employed in cutting up the road to Bow Creek, and breaking down the dam to overflow us." Previous to this, however, the meadows had been flooded, for in a letter to Gen. Potter, dated October 31st, Washington says, "I am glad to hear the flood had done so much damage to the meadows. Endeavor by all means to keep the breakers open." Still the engineers strengthened the batteries, the work of reducing the fort and opening the river continued.

The American army even then, before the winter at Valley Forge set in, was miserably deficient in clothing, and as the State authorities were highly indignant at the peaceable position assumed by the Society of Friends; on Nov. 8, 1777, Council appointed collectors in the several counties in the State to collect from those persons who had not taken the oath of allegiance,[1] or who had aided the enemy, arms, accoutrements, blankets, woolen and linsey-woolsey, cloth, linen, stockings, and shoes for the army. For Chester County, the following persons were named: Col. Evan Evans, Philip Scott, Esq., Elijah McClenaghan, Capt. John Ramsay, Patterson Bell, Esq., Thomas Boyd, Esq., Capt. Benjamin Wallace, William Gibbons, Col. George Pierce, Capt. McCay (Concord), Maj. Thomas Pierce, Capt. John Gardiner, Samuel Holliday, Col. William Evans, Capt. Israel Whellam, John Wilson, Capt. Samuel Vanlear, Thomas Levis, Esq., Capt. William Brookes, Capt. David Coupland, Col. Thomas Taylor, Capt. Allen Cunningham.

At this juncture John James, a loyalist, seems to have been especially objectionable to Council, hence on Nov. 13, 1777, all the officers of the commonwealth, both civil and military, were instructed to exert their utmost endeavors to apprehend him, so that he might be dealt with according to law; and the following day Col. Smith, lieutenant of Chester County, was notified that John James had been clandestinely sent out from Philadelphia by Gen. Howe into his territory, and the authorities were particularly desired to secure "that dangerous emissary and to bring him to condign punishment." To that end Col. Smith was instructed to watch the quarterly meetings of the Society of Friends, where, it was believed, he would endeavor to promote the views of the invaders. That he might be more readily detected, Council furnished a personal description of James, setting forth that he was then about thirty-five years of age, five feet ten inches in height, slenderly made, with a stoop in his walk, leans sidewise, and his shoulders falling greatly. His eyes were dark, and his hair, for he wore no wig, was of a dark hue. His apparel, it is stated, was generally a light drab, in "the strictest Quaker fashion, being lengthy in the skirts and without pockets," while his hat was very plain. He was, so the instructions stated, a native of Chester County, and would be better known to the people there personally than by any description Council could give of him. "For this man you have,

[1] No wonder is it that the Society of Friends, as a body, were not zealous in the interest of the Continental authorities, a sentiment that the men most active in the Revolutionary war were mainly responsible for. Washington, usually so just in all his acts and deeds, was eminently unjust to Friends. Even at the time was this patent to careful observers, for in a letter written from Philadelphia by a British officer, shortly after the capture of that city, he says, in speaking of those who remained when it fell, "Till we arrived I believed it was a very populous city, but at present it is very thinly inhabited, and that only by the *canaille* and the *Quakers* whose peaceable disposition has prevented their taking up arms, and consequently has engaged them in our interests, by drawing upon them the displeasure of their countrymen."

under cover of this letter," the order to Col Smith stated, "a warrant, tho' it is expected that all agents of the Enemy will be industriously sought after and apprehended by you and many other friends of their country without such formalities"[1] The arrest of John James and many other Friends had been specially ordered by Council in the month of August preceding the battle of Brandywine[2]

On Monday morning, Nov 10, 1777, the batteries opened on Fort Mifflin, which was bravely defended until the Saturday, when, about a half-hour before midnight, the garrison evacuated it, the enemy's fire having rendered it no longer tenable Before they retreated the Americans applied the torch, and when the royal troops took possession and hauled down the flag, which had been left flying at the staff-head, it was almost a ruin A noticeable incident of the siege, which shows the changes in the river, is thus mentioned in Howe's dispatch

"On the 15th, the wind proving fair, the 'Vigilant' armed ship, carrying 16 twenty four pounders, and a hulk with three 24 pounders, got up to the Fort through the Channel between Providence Island and Hog Island, those assisted by several ships of war in the Eastern channel, as well as by the batteries on shore, did such execution upon the Fort and collateral block-houses that the enemy, dreading our impending assault, evacuated the island in the night between the 15th and 16th and it was possessed on the 16th at daybreak by the grenadiers of the guards"

We are told by Marshall[3] that the water between Providence and Hog Islands had been deepened because the obstructions in the main channel had forced a strong current in that direction, which fact was entirely unknown to the garrison The sharpshooters from the round-top of the "Vigilant" kept the American guns silenced, for no sooner would a man show himself than he was fired at from the vessel with fatal effect The American galleys endeavored to drive the English man-of-war away, but without success, and the evacuation of the fort became absolutely necessary Lord Cornwallis, who was incensed at the stubborn resistance, and the loss its capture had occasioned to the British forces, with a round army oath denounced it as "a cursed little island"[4]

Fort Mercer, at Red Bank, still floated the rebel colors, and it was determined by the invaders to effect its reduction Hence, to that end, Gen Howe, on the evening of the 18th,[5] dispatched Cornwallis from Philadelphia with three thousand men, comprising the Fifth, Fifteenth, Seventeenth, Thirty-third, and Fifty-sixth Regiments, exclusive of the Hessians and Light Infantry, with twelve pieces of cannon and several howitzers,[6] together with a number of baggage-wagons, which body marched across the Middle Ferry on their way to Chester On the morning of that day a numerous fleet of British vessels sailed up to and anchored off Billingsport,[7] where was disembarked a large body of troops, estimated by the American scouts as nearly six thousand men They had "arrived a few days before from New York," under the command of Maj-Gen Sir Thomas Wilson, with whom were Brig-Gens Leslie and Patton[8]

As the division under Cornwallis was on the march to Chester they drove in the American pickets on the Darby road, who, retreating, sought shelter in the Blue Bell Tavern, on Crum Creek, and from the windows fired at the advancing English Two men of the Thirty-third Regiment were killed, one of the slain being the sergeant-major[9] The Grenadiers, enraged, broke ranks, rushed into the house, and there bayoneted five of the Americans who had taken refuge in the inn They would have killed all the militiamen had not the British officer interfered, and the whole picket, which had numbered thirty-three including the killed, were captured The column then resumed the march and encamped a few miles eastward of Chester, from which point marauding parties plundered the inhabitants The next day they reached Chester, where the whole of Cornwallis' command was embarked on transports by sunset, and it was conveyed across the Delaware to Billingsport, where he united his forces with those of Gen Sir Thomas Wilson

Washington, who had been apprised of this movement, ordered Gen Greene to repair to the support of Gen Varnum at Red Bank, and Gen Huntingdon was immediately detailed with a brigade to reinforce the garrison It is not within the scope of this work to narrate the circumstantial story of the unnecessary abandonment of Fort Mercer, which was vacated on the evening of the 19th, and the destruction, two days thereafter, of eight American armed vessels and two

---

[1] Penna Archives, 1st series, vol vi p 4

[2] Colonial Records, vol xi p 342

[3] Marshall's "Life of Washington," iii p 178

[4] Penna Archives, 1st series, vol vi p 23

[5] John Clarke, Jr, on Nov 20, 1777 (Penna Archives, 1st series, vol vi p 23), wrote to Paul Zantzinger, Esq, that at noon on the 17th, Cornwallis left Philadelphia for Chester with three thousand British and Hessian troops, but Gen Howe in his report unequivocally asserts that the soldiers began their march on the night of the 18th, in which statement he is supported by Robert Morton (*Penna Mag of Hist*, vol i p 28), and by Capt Montressor (*Penna Mag of Hist.*, vol vi p 193) Clark in a postscript to this letter says, "I dined at Chester yesterday, caught a person supplying the enemy at the wharf with provisions, the boat pushed off, and about thirty pounds of butter and an excellent cheese fell into my hands"

[6] Bulletin Pennsylvania Historical Society, No 10, March, 1847, p 15 Robert Morton (*Penna Mag of History*, vol i p 28) says the troops numbered three thousand five hundred Maj John Clark, Jr (Penna Archives, 1st series, vol vi p 23) in a letter to Paul Zantzinger places the command at three thousand, and in his letter to Washington in the Historical Society's Bulletin, the first citation of authority in this note, he makes the number five thousand Clark seems to have made a mistake of one day in the date he gives in the letters just quoted He reports Cornwallis as coming from Philadelphia on the 17th instead of the 18th, and his crossing to Billingsport on the 18th instead of the 19th

[7] Penna Archives, 1st series, vol vi p. 27

[8] Gen Howe's report, dated Nov 28, 1777 Hazard's Register, vol ii p 288

[9] John Clark, already quoted, says there was a captain, a sergeant-major, and three privates killed on the part of the English Morton says there were two grenadiers killed in the British forces, and Montressor put the enemy's loss a sergeant major I have followed Morton both as to the number of men under Cornwallis, and the number killed at the Blue Bell

floating batteries to prevent them from falling into the hands of the enemy. On the 20th, at mid-day, Cornwallis took possession of Fort Mercer, the force under his command amounting to six thousand men Thus the great water-way—the Delaware—was opened to the British fleet, and supplies could easily and without opposition be forwarded to the city in vessels of light draught Notwithstanding the river was cleared to the enemy their ships seemed not, in most instances, to have gone above Chester The day that Cornwallis crossed the river to Billingsport, Maj Clark, who was then at Mrs Withy's tavern, now the Columbia House, stated that "eighty sail lie opposite to Bridgeport" Capt. Montressor's journal shows that in most instances the British vessels ascended the Delaware no higher than Chester On Nov. 21, 1777, he records "This morning sailed from Chester, dispatches for New York" On April 8, 1778, he tells us "Arrived the 'Brune' frigate at Chester, having sprung her mainmast in the late Gale Arrived also the 'Isis,' ship of war, with 8 transports, part of 12 separated in ye gale" On the 22d "This day arrived at Chester a fleet of 35 sail from New York with forage, &c Also arrived the 'Eagle' (the flag-ship) with Lord Howe" On the 28th, "The 'Lord Hyde' Packet only sailed from Chester this morning," and on May 7, 1778, "The 'Porcupine' sloop of war arrived at Chester this evening from England, where she left 25th of March last" Joseph Bishop, an octogenarian resident of Delaware County, who died many years since, related that when a boy he stood on the porch of Lamoken Hall, now the Perkins mansion, in South Ward, and watched the fleet practicing, and on several occasions when receiving distinguished passengers, the yard-arms were manned and the vessels gayly dressed with many flags and streamers Even Gen Howe, when he sailed for Great Britain, was compelled to descend to the vessel by land, for on May 26, 1778, Montressor notes "Early this morning sailed from below Billingsport for England the 'Andromeda' frigate, Brine commander, in whom went General Sir William Howe" The day before Montressor had gone with Howe to Billingsport.

When it was determined that the Continental troops should go into winter quarters, the English general must have been speedily apprised of that movement, for on the 11th of December, the very day the army under Washington began its march from Whitemarsh to Valley Forge, and a portion of his troops had crossed the Schuylkill at Matson's Ford, Cornwallis was in force on the other side, where Gen Potter met him, we are told by Washington, "with a part of the Pennsylvania militia who behaved with great bravery, and gave them every possible opposition till he was obliged to retreat from their superior numbers" Cornwallis had in all probability made this movement as a reconnoissance, for portions of his command had been in the townships of Radnor, Haverford, and Darby On the 10th, the next day, from Matson's Ford he returned to Haverford, his command encamping for the night at the hillside on which Haverford meeting-house stands, and the next day he returned to Philadelphia The residents of those townships had cause to remember the merciless plunderings of the British troops during that raid

We learn that at this period some of the militia of Chester County had organized as a troop of horse, for on December 19th, Council ordered that in addition to their pay as infantry they should be allowed all the expenses of forage, when it could not be supplied by the commissary In the same month Lord Cornwallis had been sent to England by Gen Howe as bearer of dispatches, and subsequent thereto the English commander-in-chief, on December 22d, with seven thousand men marched out from Philadelphia, leaving Gen Knyphausen in command in that city, and encamped on the heights of Darby, his lines extending along the road from Gray's Ferry to the heights below the village, extending along the Springfield road to the dwelling then of Justice Parker, while their pickets in that direction were at the intersection of Providence and Springfield roads, near the house then of Mr Swain This movement of the British general was made for the purpose of protecting the transporting, by water, of a large quantity of forage, which the enemy had collected from the islands and in the neighborhood of Darby Gen Howe states that about a thousand tons were secured in this raid, sufficient, he estimated, for the winter consumption of the British army[1] On the 24th, Col John Bull notified President Wharton that "By Certain Intelligence Just Recd from Head Quarters the Enemy are in a Large Body in Chester County with Genl Howe at their head," and in consequence of that movement he had been ordered to march to Germantown or below, towards the enemy, with six regiments of militia Gen Potter, in a letter dated from Radnor, Dec 28, 1777,[2] wrote to President Wharton that to annoy Howe as much as possible, a detachment of Continentals with Morgan's riflemen had been sent from the American encampment to operate in connection with the militia under his command, and that they had kept close to the enemy's lines, that on Tuesday, the 23d, thirteen of the British light horses had been captured, and ten of their horsemen, while the next day two more of their horses and riders had been taken The activity of the Americans had prevented the enemy from plundering the inhabitants, as they usually did, but there had been little skirmishing, and but one of the American soldiers had been killed and two wounded, while upwards of twenty of the English had been captured, and a number of deserters had made their way to his lines On the other hand, Gen Howe reported that "the detachment returned on the 28th of

[1] Gen Howe's report, Jan 19, 1778 Hazard's Register, vol ii p 288

[2] Penna Archives, 1st series, vol vi p 141

December without any further attempt from the enemy to retard the progress of the foragers, than from small parties skulking, as is their custom, to seize upon the straggling soldiers One of these parties, consisting of two officers and thirty men, were decoyed by two dragoons of the Seventeenth Regiment into an ambuscade and made prisoners" Potter, it seems, agreed with Howe in the results of this raid, for he stated that the English had carried off large quantities of hay, and had provided themselves with winter fuel and forage, "and will bless themselves, and sit down in peace this winter in the city" Perhaps the militiamen captured by the British, mentioned by Howe, was the same party of whom Dr Smith records, that, under the command of Capt William Brooke, of Haverford, —who during the second war with England was a general of the Pennsylvania troops,—they were enjoying themselves in a house a mile below Darby, when the enemy suddenly surrounded the house Brooke jumped from a window and made his escape, but in getting over a fence found that in his leap he had partially dislocated his foot, to which he was subject "Putting his foot through the fence, and giving his leg a quick extension, the joint was brought into a proper condition," and he continued his flight until he reached a place of safety [1]

While the British forces held possession of the city and river, many acts of inhumanity are recorded of their foraging-parties The marine service was more objectionable in that respect than the army, and many cases are recorded of this brutality

Notwithstanding his advanced years, David Coupland, of Chester, was earnest in his advocacy of the cause of the colonies, and previous to the battle of Brandywine having entertained the Marquis de Lafayette at his home, he became very obnoxious to the Tories, hence, when the British authority was temporarily supreme, he was held under suspicion of communicating with the Continental authorities In the spring of 1778, when the "Vulture,"[2] a British man-of-war, lay off Chester, in the middle of the night, a boat's crew came ashore, and, going to David Coupland's dwelling, the present Stacey house, he was taken out of bed and conveyed to the vessel, where he was detained for many weeks a prisoner His age, as well as the anxiety consequent on his forced detention from home, his inability to learn aught of his family, the exposure and harsh treatment, induced a low, nervous fever At length, when the disease began to assume alarming symptoms, the commander of the "Vulture" had him conveyed ashore and returned to his home, but without avail He died previous to Aug 26, 1778, for his will was admitted to probate at that date About the same time Capt John Crosby, of the militia in the Continental service, was captured at his home and taken on board the vessel of war, sent to New York, and detained there in the old "Jersey" prison-ship for six months So extreme were the privations and hardships he had to undergo, that for the remainder of his life he suffered from their effects

The incidents happening during the Revolutionary struggle within the territory now comprising Delaware County were few, and generally comprise the adventures of a resident seeking to save his property from seizure, or an American soldier who, while on leave of absence, had had narrow escapes from being captured by the British troops Most of these events which have come to my knowledge will be related in the history of the townships wherein the incident happened Still, it should be remembered that while the army lay at Valley Forge the authorities were active in preparation to place the forces in as effective condition as their limited means would permit Hence, on Jan 9, 1778, Col Thomas Moore was appointed wagon-master of Chester County, and on the 30th of that month a requisition for sixty wagons was made on the county, and on February 17th, recruiting being enjoined to fill out the depleted regiments, Council, on Washington's recommendation, ordered Lieut James Armstrong, Lieut John Marshall, and Lieut William Henderson to Chester County in that service On March 11th, Robert Wilson was appointed one of the sub-lieutenants of Chester County instead of Col Thomas Strawbridge, and on the 23d of that month Col Andrew Boyd, holding the like office in the county, received two thousand musket cartridges for the use of the militia, in all probability for the use of the men instructed to prevent the farmers of the county carrying to Philadelphia and the enemy their produce, an act on their part which might call down upon them the severest punishment, since Council had authorized persons so violating their orders to be subject to military law, and if found guilty to pay the penalty with their lives

The collection of the militia fines was a frequent source of trouble in Chester County, and on several occasions we find that complaints were made to Council by the officers there that they were unable to execute the duties imposed by law upon them On May 22, 1778, Col Boyd, one of the sub-lieutenants, represented that in the townships in the south-easterly parts of the county,—necessarily part of the present county of Delaware,—many of the inhabitants were "disaffected," and "in a riotous & seditious manner commit Treason & felony, & oppose the execution of the Law" The lieutenant of the county, Col —— Smith, was thereupon instructed to select seventy-five men from the militia, with a captain, lieutenants, an ensign, and the proper number of non-commissioned officers, which company was to be employed in arresting all persons who should so resist the execution of the laws This specially detailed body was placed by Council in charge of Col Boyd,

[1] Smith's "History of Delaware County," p 325
[2] Martin's "History of Chester," p 175

who was expected to use the men only in making arrests, but "that nothing be done by them by way of Punishment," which was to be reserved until trial and sentence, for any other course would "be discreditable not only to Counsel but to the cause of Freedom" However, on June 4th, Cols Hannum and Cheyney informed the authorities that there was no occasion for the guard of men mentioned in order to collect the fines for non-service in the militia, that the ravages made by the enemy in their march through and raids in the county, as well as the great quantities of provisions, forage, and other supplies furnished to the American army were such that the residents there had great difficulties in raising money for substitutes and militia fines Council thereupon ordered the company of soldiers under Col Boyd to report to camp, and directed that in all cases where the parties to whom the certificates for articles furnished the government tendered those certificates in payment of their substitute money or for fine, they should be accepted by the officers, but this tender was not to include any who had obtained a certificate by assignment

On May 6, 1778, Council appointed William Evans, Thomas Cheyney, Thomas Levis, Patterson Bell, and John Hannum to act as commissioners for Chester County in enforcing the act of attainder, and on July 15th the Supreme Executive Council issued a proclamation calling on a large number of persons "who it is said have joined the Armies of the Enemy to render themselves & abide their legal trial for their Treasons, &c," and among the number were the following persons formerly residents of that part of Chester County which is now included within the present boundaries of Delaware County

"George Davis, Husbandman, now or late of the Township of Springfield, John Taylor, Tavern-keeper, John Moulder, Waterman, John Talbot, wheelwright, & Thomas Barton, Sawyer, all now or late of the Township of Chichester, Edward Grissil, Laborer, & John Wilson, Taylor, both now or late of the Township of Thornbury, William Milson, Taylor, Isaac Bullock, Laborer, Benjamin James, Cooper, & John Bennet, Jun'r, Laborer, all now or late of the Township of Concord, William Maddock, Tavern keeper, William Dunn, Laborer, Joseph Edwards, Mason, George Dunn, Taylor, James Malin, Laborer, & Gideon Vernon, Husbandman, all now or late of the Township of Providence, And Christopher Wilson, Husbandman, & John Taylor, Grazier, both now or late of the Township of Ridley Joshua Proctor, laborer, now or late of the Township of Newtown, Aaron Ashbridge, Waterman, Joseph Gill, Malster, Elias Wernon (" Vernon "), Taylor, all now or late of the Township of Chester, And David Rogers, Carpenter, now or late of the Township of Egmant, And John Supplee, William Caldwell & James Hart, Husbandmen, John Musgrove, Trader, and William Andrews, Fuller, all now or late of the Township of Darby, And William Smith of Tinicum Island, & William Anderson, Laborer, both now or late of the Township of Ridley, Henry Effinger, Junior, Hugh O'Cain, William Kennedy, Darby O'Cain & James McClarin, Laborer, & Isaiah Worrell, Miller, All now or late of the Township of Springfield, And Isaac Buck, Abraham Talkenton, Thomas Burns, William Clarke & George Good, laborers, and William Henry Taylor, all now or late of the Township of Providence And George Dunn & David Malin, Taylors, & William Bell, Laborer, all now or late of the Township of Newtown, and Robert Kissack, Weaver, James Brown, Wheelwright, James German & Enoch German, Cordwainers, & Michael Crickley, Laborer, all now or late of the Township of Haverford, all now or late of the County of Chester And Malin Dunn, Taylor, now or late of the Township of Providence, have severally adhered to & knowingly & willingly aided & assisted the Enemies of the State & of the United States of America, by having joined their Armies at Philadelphia in the County of Philadelphia, within this State We the Supreme Executive Council do hereby strictly charge and require the said George Davis &c to render themselves respectively to some or one of the Justices of the Supreme Court or of the Justices of the Peace on or before the third day of August next ensuing & also abide their legal trial for such their Treasons on pain that every of them the said George Davis &c not rendering himself as aforesaid & abiding the trial aforesaid, shall, from and after the said first day of August, stand & be attainted of High Treason, to all intents & purposes & shall suffer such pains and penalties & undergo all such forfeitures as persons attainted of High Treason ought to do And all the faithful subjects of this State are to take notice of this Proclamation & govern themselves accordingly "[1]

Gen Benedict Arnold, after the British army had evacuated Philadelphia, June 18, 1778, was placed in command of that city While there, as is well known, he used his official position to further his own personal ends, and one of his speculations finally re-

[1] Colonial Records, vol xi pp 513-18 Governor Guerard, of South Carolina, having applied for the name of all the persons who has been proclaimed as traitors in Pennsylvania, on Nov 28, 1783, John Morris prepared a certified list from which are taken the following names of persons from the present county of Delaware, and those who were then recorded as from Chester, without designating the townships where they resided Aaron Ashbridge, Chester, discharged, William Andrews, fuller, Darby, William Anderson, laborer, Ridley, Isaac Bullock, laborer, Concord, Isaac Buck, laborer, Providence, Thomas Burns, laborer, Providence, William Bell, laborer, Newtown, James Brown, wheelwright, Haverford, William Caldwell, husbandman, Darby, William Clark, laborer, Providence Michael Crickley, laborer, Haverford, George Davis, husbandman, Springfield, William Dunn, laborer, Providence, George Dunn, discharged, Malin Dunn, tailor, Providence, George Dunn, tailor, Providence, Henry Effinger, Jr, discharged, Abraham Falkenston, laborer, Providence, Samuel Fairlamb, yeoman, Chester, George Good, laborer, Providence, Joseph Gill, maltster, Chester, William Henry, tailor, Providence, Benjamin James, cooper, Concord, William Kennedy, laborer, Springfield, John Moulder, waterman, Chichester, John (William) Millson, tailor, Concord, William Maddock, tavern-keeper, Providence, John Musgrove, trader, Darby, David Maris, tailor, Newtown, Hugh O'Kain, laborer, Springfield, Darby O'Kain, laborer, Springfield, Joshua Proctor, laborer, Newtown, John Taylor, tavern-keeper, Chichester, John Talbot, wheelwright, Chichester, John Tayler, grazier, Ridley, Nathaniel Vernon, late sheriff, Nathaniel Vernon, Jr, laborer, Gideon Vernon, husbandman, Providence, Christopher Wilson, husbandman, Ridley, tried and convicted, Isaiah Worral, miller, Springfield Of Chester County—Thomas Bulla, husbandman, Timothy Hurst, gentleman, Henry Skyles, husbandman, John Swanwick, late of Custom house, Richard Swanwick, late of Custom house, Joseph Thomas, late sub sheriff A John Taylor, of Chester County, was pardoned May 30, 1783, on taking oath of allegiance and giving bonds for good behavior during the war By the time this list was made out it became a question which of the John Taylors herein mentioned had received the Executive clemency, and the master of the rolls himself acknowledges in a quere that he could not determine the controversy Penna Archives, 1st series, vol x pp 250-60 On June 3, 1783, John Briggs, who had been convicted of harboring Gideon Vernon, "an attainted traytor," was sentenced to a fine of fifty pounds and imprisonment to the 14th of October following, appealed to Council, who mitigated his punishment by remitting the imprisonment, on his entering security for payment of the fine, fees, and costs, and to be of good behavior for three years On Sept 13, 1783, President John Dickinson issued a proclamation offering a reward for the noted Doan brothers, and charging many others with being implicated in their crimes, among the number Gideon Vernon The proclamation stated that any one who should kill any of these persons fleeing from arrest, "he or they so killing shall be and hereby are justified, and in case of any prosecution shall be commenced against any person or persons for the same, he or they may thereto plead the general issue and give this act in evidence " Moreover, any person who should kill any of the persons named in the proclamation, on proof of that fact produced to the president of the State should receive a reward of three hundred pounds in good money Colonial Records, vol xiii pp 687-90

sulted in casting on his reputation and character, which seemed to have had only remarkable physical bravery as a redeeming trait, the suspicion that murder, as well as treason, was among the crimes of which he had been guilty The circumstances are briefly these Jesse Jordan, a deputy wagon-master of Chester County, on Sept 27, 1778, with a brigade of twelve wagons in his care, was ordered by Col Andrew Boyd, the wagon-master of the county, to Philadelphia, there to load with provisions, and thence to New Windsor Jordan was absent much longer than was expected On his return Col Boyd demanded the reason, and was told that when he reached Philadelphia, Deputy Quartermaster-General John Mitchell had ordered him, with his train of empty wagons, to Egg Harbor, N J, then a harbor for American privateers, where he was instructed to load with merchandise belonging to private persons This he did, and when he returned to the city the goods were delivered to stores kept by private individuals Col Boyd immediately laid the matter before Council, and on Jan 18, 1779, that body demanded an explanation of this transaction from Gen. Mitchell On the 23d the latter replied that he had sent the wagons to New Jersey by order of Gen Arnold, whereupon Council requested the general to inform them whether the goods transported were public or private, if the latter, to whom they belong, also desiring Arnold to refer them to the authority by which "public wagons of Pennsylvania were sent into another State to do business merely of a private nature" On January 30th, Jesse Jordan was fully examined respecting the circumstances of this trip While the matter was pending Arnold left the city, and Jordan and his teamsters being then "in great necessity," the Council considered that "the board ou't to relieve them, so far as to advance £450 until they can procure further redress" On the 25th of February, Deputy Quartermaster-General Mitchell appeared before Council, acknowledged that the blot in his memorandum book under date of Oct 30, 1778, was done by his orders to conceal an entry of his clerk "of the return of Mr Jordan's Brigade of waggons from Egg Harbor, & that the obliteration was made after the charge against Gen Arnold for having used the public waggons for his private business had come to his (Mitchell's) knowledge" He subsequently, on March 1, 1779, in a lengthy letter to President Reed, gave a circumstantial account of the matter, and on March 27th, Timothy Matlack, the secretary of Council, wrote to Jonathan Dickinson Sergeant, stating that Council had advanced Jordan four hundred and fifty pounds, to be repaid when he should recover compensation for the use of the wagons from Gen Arnold, and the body was anxious to learn whether legal proceedings had been instituted There appears no reference to the subject until October 10th, when Mr Sergeant informed Council that he had instituted suit for Jesse Jordan against Gen Arnold, but the action had at that time abated by the plaintiff's death, for "Jesse Jordan has been lately murdered in Chester County" That Arnold personally did that deed no one believed, but there was a general impression that of all men he had the greatest interest in the wagon-master's death, and after the former's treason many there were who thought that perhaps he knew more of the particulars of Jesse Jordan's "taking off" than he cared to tell

The privateer brig "Holker," named in honor of the French consul at Philadelphia, was owned by Robert Morris, and it is related that on one occasion the vessel, in lead ballast, reached the city very opportunely, for, at the time, the American troops were entirely out of bullets Her owner immediately turned her cargo over to the authorities for the use of the army On July 20, 1779, the "Holker" was lying at Chester, where a crew was being recruited for the privateer, and Maj George Harvy was instructed by Council to allow the then owner of the vessel, Mr McClanachan, to have ten tons of disabled cannons for ballast The price was not exactly stipulated, but the major, as some guide for him in adjusting that matter, was informed that when these disabled cannon were delivered at Chester the ironmaster would give one ton of bar iron in exchange for four tons of the old metal The brig, as before stated, was then lying at Chester, commanded by Capt Matthew Lawler, and at that place, from July 17th to August 2d, a crew was recruited for the vessel by Davis Bevan, captain of marines, who had before been mustering officer for the county of Chester The following list gives the names of the crew, as well as the sums paid each man at the time of enlisting [1]

	Received as Bounty				Received as Bounty		
	£	s	d		£	s	d
John Bayley	37	10	0	William Coulter	18	15	0
William Mackey	37	10	0	John Virdine	18	15	0
Christopher Battnel	37	10	0	John Hambright, Sr	18	15	0
George Trusk	37	10	0	John Cockshott	18	15	0
Joseph Marshall..	37	10	0	Nathaniel Carr	18	15	0
Nicholas Francis (1st)	37	10	0	Patt Cain	18	15	0
William Smith	37	10	0	John Whitehead	18	15	0
John Basset	37	10	0	Matthew Penell..	18	15	0
William Swanson	37	10	0	William Webb	18	15	0
Edward McDonagh	37	10	0	Roger Brown	18	15	0
William Johnson	37	10	0	James McAlester	18	15	0
John McGlocklin	37	10	0	George McCay	18	15	0
Joseph Claterbuck	37	10	0	George Wass	18	15	0
Frederick Waggoner	37	10	0	Allen Mongomery	18	15	0
David Kenedy	37	15	0	Thomas Burnel	18	15	0
Joseph Bowdin	37	10	0	John Plog	18	15	0
Eber Perry	37	10	0	David Bauskay	18	15	0
John Aruyz	37	10	0	David Harding	18	15	0
John Dunham	37	10	0	Patrick Shannon	18	15	0
George Geddey	37	10	0	John Slaughter	22	10	10
Nathaniel Heath	37	10	0	David Cahill	22	10	6
Charles Orsonall	37	10	0	Charles Griffith	18	15	0
Joseph Hulings	37	10	0	Matthew W Murray	18	15	0
Thomas Richards	37	10	0	George Parker	18	15	0
George Ennis	28	2	6	Andrew Rowar	18	15	0
William Thomson	28	2	6	Benedicteo Pida.	18	15	0
John Wallace	28	2	6	James Hambleton	18	15	0
Robert Longue (carpenter's mate)				Peter Abrams	18	15	0
	28	2	6	Jesse Hall	18	15	0
Peter Anderson	18	15	0	Richard Dickson	18	15	0
John Harkins	18	15	0	Patrick McCauld	18	15	0
David Coleman	18	15	0	John Crawford	18	15	0

[1] From the manuscript receipt book of David Bevans, captain of marines on the "Holker," now in the Delaware County Institute of Science, Media, Pa

	Received as Bounty.				Received as Bounty.		
	£	s.	d.		£	s.	d.
John Neagle	18	15	0	Anthony Elton	18	15	0
James Harper	18	15	0	Blenkine Cornaickle	18	15	0
Thomas Henry (a mulatto)	18	15	0	Samson Moore	18	15	0
William Smith (2d)	18	15	0	Daniel Binckar	18	15	0
Thomas Apkin	18	15	0	Joseph Seilings	18	15	0
Francis Brown	18	15	0	William Poke	18	15	0
Matthew McSherny	18	15	0	John Hoddy	18	15	0
John Fairland	18	15	0	James Robertson	18	15	0
James Hardin	18	15	0	Patrick McGinnis	18	15	0
George Shilstone	18	15	0	David Cahill	18	15	0
James Anderson	18	15	0	Richard Cockshott	18	15	0
Hugh Harris	18	15	0	Jeremiah Casey	18	15	0
Robert Cornish	18	15	0	Thomas Hornsby	18	15	0
Samuel Armitage	18	15	0	Cornelius Bookly	18	15	0
J. Bickham	18	15	0	Samuel Clayton	18	15	0
Dennis Lynch	18	15	0	Stephen Green	18	15	0
Richard Bickerton	18	15	0	Thomas Forrest	18	15	0
Ralph Horn	18	15	0	David Buchanan (a cabin boy)	7	10	0
Thomas Lee	18	15	0	Joel Jones			$100
Charles Rouff	18	15	0	Ekena Tessune			100
William McGlocklin	18	15	0	Porpino ——			100

July 28, 1779, Barney Cuningham receipted for £11 5s. for one band-vice for use of brig "Holker."

July 30, 1779, Thomas Fell receipted for thirty-six pounds for two muskets for use of brig "Holker."

Aug. 2, 1779, Thomas Lee receipted for fifteen pounds in part of prize money.

Aug. 2, 1779, George Geddey receipted for two hundred and four dollars by bounty paid David Forsyth and James McNeil, masters-at-arms.

The April preceding the "Holker" had captured a schooner of ten guns and forty men, and also two armed sloops early in the month of July, before she lay at Chester to refit and recruit her crew. In July, 1780, the "Holker" had an engagement off the coast of New Jersey with the loyal privateer "Lord Rodney," in which the cutter, after an action of an hour and a half, was captured, her commander, Samuel Moore,[1] and five of her crew killed, and twenty wounded. The "Holker" suffered severely in the engagement, her loss being six killed, including the first lieutenant, and fourteen wounded.[2]

The war-cloud had drifted away from Chester County, and never since that time have the good people of this section of the commonwealth been disturbed by the tread of hostile forces in martial array. But, although the husbandmen could resume their labors without the constant dread that inimical parties might gather the harvests and lay waste their fields, the State of Pennsylvania still made heavy demands on the public both for men and means to carry on the war.

In the fall of the year 1778, when Sir Henry Clinton, in accordance with instructions from the ministry, had detached five thousand men to the West Indies and three thousand to Florida, the destination of these troops being unknown, the mysterious preparations aroused widespread apprehension as to the objective point of the expedition. Naturally the public disquietude was increased when the attack on Little Egg Harbor and the butchery of the sleeping, unarmed infantry attached to Pulaski's brigade, was known. On October 19th, Council ordered that the militia in the counties of Philadelphia, Chester, Bucks, and Lancaster should be held in readiness to march at the shortest notice, but the minute-men were not further called out that year, nor were they in June, 1780, when Gen. Knyphausen crossed from New York and made an incursion into New Jersey. The purpose and extent of that movement being unknown, Council, on the 12th of that month, ordered the fourth class of the militia of the counties of Philadelphia, Bucks, and Chester to hold themselves in readiness to march to the support of the Continental army, should later intelligence indicate that such a movement was necessary. But orders to take the field were not issued. Not long afterwards, on July 28th, President Reed wrote a complaining letter to Col. Robert Smith, that Chester was lagging behind the other counties in forwarding volunteers, and urged him to exertion in furnishing the quota of militia, which must report, he said, according to Washington's command, at Trenton, by the 12th of August. In September of the following year (1781), after the army had gone southward, and Benedict Arnold was making preparations to undertake his infamous expedition, under the British flag, against New England, on September 25th, Col. Smith was again ordered to hold the militia of the county in readiness to march on a moment's notice to Newtown, Bucks Co., notwithstanding there was no recent tidings of the movements of the enemy at New York. The troops had assembled on the occasion, and had already begun to move as required, for, on October 10th, Col. Smith wrote Council that, as ordered, the fourth class of the militia of Chester County had twice marched, but as often the orders had been countermanded, and the men were on furlough till further commands were issued. The order to march had been countermanded before the troops left the county, and as but few of the enrolled men failed to appear, the fines on the delinquents would amount to a very small sum. The cost of supplying necessaries for the men was considerable, and hence, as the time was short, there was a general objection to assessing on the delinquents the "whole costs of the tour." No further particulars respecting the calling out of troops appear during the remainder of the war; although on Jan. 30, 1781, James Moore received five hundred pounds to enlist men into the Pennsylvania line from Chester County.

The incidents happening in the county now became of little general interest. On March 30, 1780, Col. Robert Smith was appointed lieutenant of the county, with Col. Thomas Cheyney, Lewis Gronow, Andrew Boyd, Thomas Levis, and Robert Wilson as sub-lieutenants. On June 8th the quartermaster-general stated that Col. Boyd had been instructed to send sixty wagons and teams from Chester County, but none had up to that time reported. Council, therefore, on the 21st, ordered a requisition on the several counties for wagons, fixing the quota of Chester at forty, which,

[1] *Penna. Mag. of Hist.*, vol. vi. p. 255.

[2] Penna. Archives, 2d series, vol. i. p. 370, in note C, it is said that the captain of the "Holker" was killed. The captain of the "Lord Rodney" was, but Matthew Lawler, captain of the "Holker," lived to be mayor of the city of Philadelphia from 1801 to 1804, both years inclusive.

if "cannot be procured in any other way, must be impressed" On July 25th, Council made requisition for supplies for the army, and Chester County was required to furnish eight hundred barrels of flour per month, two thousand bushels of forage per month, two hundred horses, forty wagons, and five hundred militia, and, on August 8th, David Denny for First, Owen Thomas, Second, Joseph Luckey, Third, David Wilson, Fourth, Thomas Strawbridge, Fifth, John Crosby, Sixth, George Price, Seventh, and Joseph Spear for Eighth Battalion, to collect quota of horses in Chester County, under direction of Col Andrew Boyd, wagon-master On August 10th, John Beatan was appointed paymaster of the militia, with instructions that Continental money was to be paid out at the rate of sixty dollars for one in that of State issues As an illustration of the depreciation of Continental money,—owing to the fact that Congress then could not levy a tax to provide for the redemption of these issues,—some of the payments made for cattle in 1780 are annexed

June 20, 1780 John Crozer received $6000 for 6 head of cattle
June 27, 1780, Gideon Gilpin £2400 for 6 cattle
June 27, 1780, Israel Gilpin £700 for 20 sheep
June 27, 1780, James Hannum £2000 for 5 cattle
June 27, 1780, Caleb Pyle £1240 for 5 cattle
July 12, 1780, Isaac Sewell £19 10s for 14 head of beef cattle

In the latter month, Commissary-Gen Ephraim Blaine gave notice that William Evans was his representative in Chester County to receive live stock, and that "the magazine" for such supplies was located in Philadelphia

Early in April, 1782,—for the vessel did not sail from Philadelphia until the 8th of that month,—occurred in Delaware Bay the remarkable engagement between the Pennsylvania vessel-of-war "Hyder Ali," commanded by Capt Joshua Barney, and the British ship "General Monk" The American vessel carried sixteen six-pound guns and a crew of one hundred and ten men, while that of the English had one hundred and thirty-six men and twenty nine-pounders The victory of the former was largely due to the fact that the understanding between Barney and his men was that every order should be executed as though an exactly opposite command had been given Thus, while the two vessels were approaching each other, Barney cried out, "Hard a-port your helm, do you want him to run aboard of us?" The Englishman heard the order and made preparations to counteract the movement, as the American captain hoped, so that when Barney's vessel answered the helm, which had been clapped hard a-starboard by the men at the wheel, the enemy's jib-boom caught in the fore-rigging of the "Hyder Ali," and there remained during the short engagement which followed, giving the latter a raking position The same confusion of orders mystified the British captain throughout the action, for, as understood, when Barney gave the command "Board!" his men were to fire, and when he shouted "Fire!" they were to board When the vessels ran together, as stated, Barney in a loud voice gave the order "Board!" and the stubborn Englishmen crowded forward to repel the enemy, when a broadside was discharged at close range, and so rapidly did the American gunners load, that in twenty-six minutes, the time the action lasted, the "Hyder Ali" had fired twenty broadsides The English vessel kept her colors flying until she had twenty killed and thirty-three wounded Among the former were the first lieutenant, purser, surgeon, boatswain, and gunner, among the latter Capt Rogers and every officer on board, except a midshipman The American loss was four killed and eleven wounded Captain Barney left the "Hyder Ali" at Chester, at which place he took Capt Rogers ashore to the house of a Quaker lady, who nursed him until he had entirely recovered from his wounds The victor proceeded to the city in his prize

In the latter part of 1782, Col Hannum, Col Frazier, and Dr Gardner, as representatives of the Council in Chester County, seized a quantity of British goods while passing through the county, designed for the prisoners of war at Lancaster The wagon-train was under a flag of protection granted by Washington. The seizure was made because of some alleged violation of the passport granted to those having the goods in charge Congress, immediately after receiving information of the fact, took action in the matter, and it was presented to the attention of Council in such a manner that the latter required the opinion of Attorney-General Bradford as to whether Council could summarily dispose of the case, and thus prevent a trial of the cause in Chester County Bradford was clearly of opinion that Council had no authority to interfere, asserting that if the goods seized were necessary for the prisoners of war and were covered by a passport issued by the commander-in-chief, they were not contraband or liable to condemnation, if the passports had been violated the offense was one against the law of nations, and punishable in our courts of judicature On Jan 17, 1783, Congress appointed a committee to confer with Council on the subject, and the following day President John Dickinson, in a special message, called the attention of the attorney-general to the matter On the 21st the committee of Congress, a committee from the General Assembly, and Council met in the chamber of the latter body, where the question was discussed, and the position of each fully understood, and adjourned to the 23d, when a representation of the case as agreed on was drafted, which, after being signed by Cols Hannum and Frazier and Dr Gardner, was referred to Congress, and thus the difficulty terminated, although on March 24, 1783, John Gardner, sheriff of Chester County, a brother of the doctor, was instructed by Council to proceed with the utmost diligence in securing such of the goods seized in the county which had not as yet been delivered to the person designated by the Secretary of War to receive the articles

The surrender of Cornwallis on the afternoon of Oct 19, 1781, was virtually the last great struggle of the Revolutionary war, although some sharp engagements followed that decisive event, and, as will be noticed in the preceding narrative subsequent to that date, the public records demonstrate the belief so general that the end was at hand, that matters other than the preparation and march of troops occupied almost exclusively the attention of the authorities On the 15th of April, 1783, Council issued a proclamation announcing a cessation of hostilities, but the treaty of peace was not concluded until November 30th The independence of the United States was announced by the king of Great Britain, in his speech on Dec 5, 1783

CHAPTER X

FROM THE REVOLUTIONARY WAR TO THE ERECTION OF DELAWARE COUNTY

WHEN the storm of war had subsided, Chester County, with the whole country, suffered severely in the process of adjustment from a warlike to a peaceful condition which naturally followed the recognition by the king of England of the independence of the confederate colonies The period between the cessation of hostilities until the establishment of the present form of Federal government was indeed dark and unpromising, when Washington himself could, expressing the regret he felt at the death of Gen Greene, pen these words, "I have accompanied it of late with a query whether he would not have preferred such an exit to the scene which it is more than probable many of his compatriots may live to bemoan" This locality had, it is true, recovered greatly from the effects of the pilferings and exactions it had sustained at the hands of the British troops when five years before the invading army overran the territory, but it nevertheless lost heavily in the fluctuation in values and general depression which followed the close of the war Added to this, the constant manifestations of weakness in the crude system of State and confederated government which had maintained from the period of the Declaration to the conclusion of the struggle, were in nowise calculated to allay public anxiety The war had for five years been carried on with Continental money, emanating from a body without authority to impose taxes, and absolutely dependent on the several State Legislatures for enactments regulating the lawful value of the currency they put forth, hence, as the confederation was held together by a wisp of straw, necessarily the Continental notes depreciated until, in September, 1779, the aggregate sum of these bills in circulation amounted to two hundred millions of dollars. The discount became so great, and so rapidly did the currency depreciate in value, that further issues of these notes were impracticable, and in the beginning of the year 1781 they ceased to circulate, becoming worthless,—dying as a medium of exchange in the hands of their possessors It was now absolutely essential that some new means should be provided to carry on the war In 1780, it will be remembered, the Bank of Pennsylvania was established, its purpose being to supply the army of the United States with provisions On May 17, 1781, Robert Morris proposed the plan for a bank to Congress, which scheme met the approval of that body, and it recommended that the several States should interdict any other banks or bankers from carrying on business within their territory during the war Congress, Dec 31, 1781, incorporated the Bank of North America with a capital of two million dollars, most of this being subscribed from abroad through the influence of Morris[1] The States of Massachusetts and Pennsylvania also granted charters of a similar character, and the first Bank of Pennsylvania having done its work was discontinued The immediate effects of the Bank of North America were highly advantageous, and aided materially in furnishing the means to carry on the war to a successful ending, but the exclusive privileges granted it, as well as the manner in which its business was conducted, created considerable dissatisfaction, until, in 1785, a petition, numerously signed by the citizens of Chester County, was presented to the Legislature, and so earnestly did the friends of the measure press the public complaints on that body that it revoked the charter granted by the State to the bank The institution, however, continued to act under Congressional authority, and in 1787 the Legislature rechartered the bank While the country was recovering from the extraordinary exertions consequent on the war, many estates changed owners, and the busiest man in the county was the sheriff, yet the pressure was beneficial, inasmuch as it compelled unusual exertion among the people, and the whole system of slovenly farming, which had theretofore been the rule, gave place to careful, intelligent husbandry, while enterprises were projected and carried on so that in a comparatively short time the public recovered from financial depression and made rapid strides in material improvements

Local matters now exercised in a large degree the attention of the people of the State in all sections In the county of Chester the project of removing the county-seat from the ancient town of Chester to a more central situation was revived, for the agitation of that question antedated the Revolutionary war, but during the latter struggle so much greater were the issues involved to the public at large, that the scheme was permitted to slumber by its most ardent friends Seated as the borough was on the ex-

[1] Judge Peters' account of Morris, published in Brotherhead's "Sketch of Robert Morris" in "Lives of Eminent Philadelphians now Deceased," p 708

treme southeastern edge of the county of Chester, it was doubtless a serious matter to those persons residing in such remote townships as Coventry, Honeybrook, or West Nottingham, when, as jurors, suitors, or witnesses, they were compelled to attend at court. It involved considerable labor to go and return in those days, and in winter time, when, in a warm spell, the roads would be wretched beyond expression, it was a journey such as no man of these modern times would contemplate calmly.

It is a theme for wonder now that previous to Jan. 28, 1766, no earnest effort was made to procure legislation looking to a proposed removal of the county-seat to a more central location. At the date mentioned a petition was presented to the Legislature, setting forth the grievances of a large number of people of the county because of the location of the court; they were so far removed from the public offices that that fact alone increased the fees charged for mileage by the officials. A class of cases of peculiar hardship they stated were, "that many poor widows are obliged to travel thirty or forty miles for letters of administration, and are put to much trouble in attending Orphans' Court at so great a distance." In consideration of these and other reasons, the petitioners urged the enactment of a law providing for the erection of a court-house, and the holding of court therein, as near the centre of the county as could possibly be done. This was supplemented on May 7th by nine other petitions of a like tenor, and on the following day the anti-removalists submitted twelve petitions, which, after calling the attention of the Legislature to the establishment of Chester as the shire-town during the first visit of William Penn to his province, in 1682,[1] as a further reason why the location of the county-seat should not be changed, they set forth "it is notorious" that those persons residing in the near neighborhood of the court attended its sessions three times as frequently as those living at a distance, while the deputy register, in the discharge of the duties of his office, had no connection with the courts of justice at all.

The war caused an absolute cessation of the movement until fourteen years had elapsed, when the inhabitants of the ancient shire-town stood aghast, in the face of an act of Assembly, passed March 20, 1780, which authorized William Clingan, Thomas Bull, John Kinhead, Roger Kirk, John Sellers, John Wilson, and Joseph Davis, or any four or more of them to build a new court-house and prison in the county of Chester, and when the proposed buildings should be ready for public use to sell the old court-house and prison in the borough of Chester. It is believed that the majority of the commissioners named were adverse to the proposed change,—hence the law remained a dead letter on the statute-book. But in 1784, the representatives in Assembly from Chester County being largely composed of removalists, a supplement to the former act was passed on March 22, 1784, which empowered John Hannum, Esq., Isaac Taylor, Esq., and John Jacobs, or any two of them, to put the law into execution. As all of the persons named were uncompromising removalists, they immediately set about enforcing its provisions. By the wording of the act they were restrained from erecting the new county buildings at a greater distance than one mile and a half from the Turk's Head Tavern in the township of Goshen. This location tradition asserts—a statement which Judge Futhey and Gilbert Cope say may reasonably be questioned—was inserted in this bill through the influence of Col. John Hannum, an adroit politician who, with an eye to his personal advantage, desired to bring a tract of land he owned within the site designated. In this, however, he made an error, for his premises subsequently proved to be more than two miles from the Turk's Head. The commissioners, notwithstanding Hannum's mistake, diligently began the erection of a court-house and prison adjacent, connected by a jail-yard. After the buildings had progressed until the walls were nearly completed, and while work was suspended thereon by reason of the severe winter and before the spring permitted its resumption, the people of old Chester succeeded, March 30, 1785, in having an act passed suspending the supplemental act under which the new structures were being erected.

To render themselves absolutely assured of retaining the county-seat in the ancient borough, a number of the anti-removalists gathered in Chester under command of Maj. John Harper, then landlord of the present City Hotel, and provided with arms, a field-piece, a barrel of whiskey, and other necessary munitions of war, took up the line of march for the Turk's Head, intent on razing the walls of the proposed court-house and jail to the earth. In the mean while Col. Hannum, learning of the hostile designs of the Chester people, dispatched couriers in all directions,

[1] "That in the first regulation of the said county, in the year One Thousand Six Hundred and Eighty-two, the Honorable William Penn, Esq., Proprietary and Governor of the Province of Pennsylvania, by virtue of the Royal Charter, did order that the Townsted or Village, then bearing the name of Upland, should be called Chester, and thereupon constituted it the Shire-Town of the County of Chester, and ordained and appointed all the Courts of Judicature for the Affairs of the County to be there held and kept, and the County Goal or prison to be and remain there forever; that the said William Penn, Esq., afterwards, to wit, on the Thirty-first day of October, One Thousand Seven Hundred and One, did grant, by charter, unto the Freeholders and Inhabitants of the said Borough, that the Sheriff and Clerk of the Courts of the said County for the time being, if not Residents in the said Borough should appoint and constitute sufficient Deputies, who should from Time to Time reside, or constantly attend, in the said Town of Chester, to perform the duties of their respective offices; which said Privileges (with respect to the holding of the Courts of Judicature at Chester), were afterwards established by John Evans, Esq., Lieutenant-Governor of the said Province, by an Ordinance issued by him, under the Great Seal, bearing Date the Twenty-second Day of February, One Thousand Seven Hundred and Seven and afterwards confirmed by an act of General Assembly, made perpetual, and passed in the Year One thousand Seven Hundred and Twenty-one." This interesting paper, so far as I have been able to ascertain, was first recovered from the dust of nearly a century by Messrs. Futhey and Cope, and published by them in their "History of Chester County," p. 116.

calling on the friends of removal to rally to the protection of the half-completed buildings, and Thomas Beaumont is said to have ridden all night from farmhouse to farmhouse in Goshen and Bradford townships, summoning the clan. The forces under command of Maj. Harper marched toward the Turk's Head, and at night were camped at the General Greene Tavern, a few miles east of West Chester, when Col. Hannum was first apprised of their approach. The latter collected his men within the building, the windows boarded on the out as well as the inside and the space between filled in with stones, loop-holes being arranged at convenient intervals through which the defenders could thrust their muskets, and each man had his place assigned him where, under designated officers, they remained awaiting the approach of the enemy. The next morning the Chester people came in sight of the fortification, when Maj. Harper planted his artillery on an eminence known as Quaker Hill, commanding the court-house. The absurdity of the matter dawning on the minds of some of the men in the ranks of Harper's troops, they contrived to bring about a cessation of hostilities, and the whole affair ended in a jollification, during which the cannon was repeatedly discharged in rejoicing over peace restored. The invaders were thereupon invited to inspect the unfinished structure. During the time the troops from old Chester were in the building, one of the latter, seeing the banner of the removalists floating from the flag-staff, struck it down, which so angered the defenders that it was with much difficulty their officers could restrain them from resenting the insult by immediately opening fire on their opponents.

Peace, however, was maintained. The armistice was based on the agreement of the removalists that they would desist from further work on the building until the Legislature should take action in the matter. Although the removalists suspended labor only until the anti-removalists were out of hearing,[1] they would not, had they preserved faith, been long delayed, for, at the next session, March 18, 1786, the following curiously-entitled act became a law: "An act to repeal an act entitled an act to suspend an act of the General Assembly of this Commonwealth, entitled an act to enable Wm. Clingan, etc.," and under its provisions the buildings at the new county-seat were finished. On the 25th of September, 1786, William Gibbon, the then sheriff of Chester County, by law was empowered to remove the "prisoners from the old jail in the town of Chester to the new jail in Goshen township, in the said county, and to indemnify him for the same."

[1] Dr. Smith's "History of Delaware County," p. 342, says, "It has come to the author traditionally that the attack of the Chester people was instigated by the removalists proceeding with the building after the passage of the Suspension Act. ... The fact that they were allowed to escape with impunity is rather corroborative of the idea that the attack was not altogether unprovoked, and rendered it probable that the cause for it assigned by tradition is the true one."

The old court-house and county buildings in Chester were sold on the 18th of March, 1788, to William Kerlin for four hundred and fifteen pounds.

A struggle which had arrayed in bitter feeling one section of the county of Chester against the other, and culminated in the erection of the eastern townships into the new county of Delaware, naturally drew forth many sarcastic articles on both sides of the controversy. The press of that day, however, did not furnish the same facilities for epistolary discussion as the present, hence the following address to the Legislature written by David Bevan,[2] an acrimonious anti-removalist, for the first time is given to the public:

"*To the Honor Representatives of the freemen of the Commonwealth of Pennsylvania.*

"Through the chanell of the press I make free to address your honor body, not choosing to petition in the usual mode, as I am too well acquainted with the manner pursued by some parts of Chester county, mustering scribes and getting poor-rate duplicates, and inserting names without asking consent. *You, gentlemen, will no doubt receive a number* of petitions from those who have already got every request they wanted from the Legislature, the removal of the seat of Justice or Court of Jurisprudence from the ancient borough of Chester to that elegant and notorious place called the Turk's Head (by some called West Chester), a place as unfit for the general convenience, and much more so, that any one spot that might be pointed out within ten miles square of the above-described place, except towards New Castle line.

"We have no doubt of petitions fabricated for this purpose, that Mr. T——s, the greatest advocate for this spot of any member of Chester county, might vociferate, as he often does, in the house, more for the display of his Talents than any universal good. Let us, therefore, beg, if we have sent one noisey member, that he may be heard, and, altho' he does stammer sometimes, perhaps, with the assistance of a few pebble stones, he may become a prodigee of the age, and (may he) exceed Demothenes to convince you of his superior abilities. I have a petition of his fabricating for the purpose of the Township of Edgmont, which shall be handed to the publick for their perusal as a pattern that any body politic corporate, &c., may have a form to fabricate petitions for such purposes, if ever any such may be needed."

On the other side the removalists were not deficient in scribes who presented the ludicrous aspect of the contest in rude derisive jests wherein their adversaries were burlesqued in sarcastic jingling verses, many of which in lapse of years have been entirely forgotten. One, however, has been preserved by Dr. William Darlington, in a sketch of West Chester prepared by him for the Directory of that borough, published in 1857. The author of the "Pasquinade" was Joseph Hickman, and, as we are told by Dr. Darlington, an old English wool-comber, Marmaduke Wyvil, about the beginning of this century "used to ramble about the country like an ancient Troubadour," and a glass of cider or whiskey "would at any time procure its recital with emphatic intonation and peculiar unction."

The ditty was known as "Chester's Mother," and designed to give expression to the woe of the prominent anti-removalists, who were dependent on the public for a livelihood at the county-seat, and their

[2] In the receipt book of David Bevan, in the Delaware County Institute of Science at Media, *will be found the draft of the above address*. If it ever, as a whole, was published before its insertion in this work, I fail to find it in the files of the newspapers of that period.

lamentation consequent on the prospective loss of "a nursing mother"

"LAMENT OVER CHESTER'S MOTHER

"Poor Chester's Mother's very sick,
Her breath is almost gone,
Her children throng around her thick,
And bitterly do moan

"Cries little 'Lisba[1] the first born—
'What will become of I,
A little orphan, held in scorn,
If Mama she should die?

"'Not only I will be opprest,—
I younger brothers have
Who cannot do without the breast
When Mama's in her grave'

"And then poor helpless Billy[2] cries—
'Oh! how shall I be fed?
What shall I do, if Mama dies?
I cannot work for bread

"'These little hands have never wrought
Oh! how I am opprest!
For I have never yet done aught
But hung on Mama's breast'

"Little Davis[3] he comes next
A puling, silly boy,
His countenance appeared perplex'd
And destitute of joy

"'How is our dear Mama?' he cried
'Think you we can her save?
How is the wound that's in her side
Which cursed Hannum[4] gave?'

"Says little Ned,[5]—'Upon my word,
Poor Mama will be slain,—
Though cursed Hannum lost his sword[6]
He's got it back again

"'What shall I do, if Mama dies?
What will become of Ned?'
The tears came trickling from his eyes
And straight he took his bed

"Then Caley,[7] he came next in view,—
His mouth was all awry,
Says he—'Oh! what will Caley do,
If dear Mama should die?

"'She might have liv'd for many a year,
And all her children fed,
If Hannum hadn't poisoned her—
Curse on his frizzled head!'

"Cries little John,[8] the youngest son,
Who just began to crawl—
'If Mama lives, I soon shall run,
If not, I soon shall fall

"'Oh! may Jack Hannum quickly die—
And die in grievous pain,—
Be sent into eternity
That Mama may remain

"'May all his projects fail, likewise—
That we may live again!'
Then, every one roll'd up his eyes
And cried aloud, 'Amen!'"

The ancient borough of Chester had been shorn of its chief glory, the little hamlet of sixty houses[9] was

[1] Elisha Price a nephew of Elisha Gatchell, who became so noted in the controversy between Penn and Lord Baltimore, was a lawyer of prominence in the last century, having been a student in the office of Joseph Parker He frequently represented Chester County in the Colonial Legislature, and in the troublous times preceding the active outbreak of hostilities in the war of Independence, he was an unflinching Whig When the merchants of Philadelphia and New York adopted their noted non-importation agreement and asked the support therein of the people in the outlying districts, he was one of three to whom was addressed the circular sent to Chester County, and was one of the committee selected by the Convention, July 15, 1774, held in this borough to consider the matter The following day he, with his associates, met similar committees from the other counties in Philadelphia In 1775 he was appointed one of the committeemen of correspondence from Chester County After the erection of Delaware County he was appointed an associate judge He was an earnest Episcopalian, and from 1767 to 1798 his name appears among the vestrymen and wardens of St Paul's Church His wife was descended from James Barton, a minister of Friends, and "an early settler," says Deborah Logan, "a gentleman and a person of excellent character" Elisha Price died in 1798, a victim of the yellow fever His two sons who survived him both lost their lives in the service of the government, Maj Price being one of the American invaders of Canada, during the war of 1812, and died there

[2] William Kerlin, then owner and landlord of the Washington House, Chester, a strong anti removalist

[3] Davis Bevan, captain of the schooner "Polly," captured by the "Roebuck" man of war, appointed mustering master of Chester County, was captain of marines on privateer "Holker," and afterwards a retail merchant in Chester He, of course, was a strong anti-removalist

[4] Col John Hannum, a militia officer of the Revolution He was a native of Concord township, but purchasing a large farm in East Bradford, he became an earnest removalist During the Revolutionary war he was one of the Committee of Seventy, appointed at the county meeting held at Chester Dec 20, 1774 Col Hannum was present with Wayne during the latter part of the day of Brandywine battle, and during the winter of 1777 was captured one night asleep in his bed by some British light-horse, who were conducted to his house by a loyalist neighbor He was taken to Philadelphia, where he was retained as a prisoner of war until the following spring, when he made his escape In 1778 he was appointed one of the five commissioners of Chester County under the act of attainder He was one of the justices of the peace, but resigned that office as well as commissioner of forfeited estates when, in 1781, he was elected to the General Assembly He was a member of that body until and including 1785, during which time he steadily fought the battle of removal to a successful conclusion He was very active in bringing about the repeal of the test law, and after the erection of the county of Delaware he filled many important offices in the county of Chester Col Hannum died Feb 7, 1799

[5] This reference the late Dr Darlington, of West Chester, stated, is either to Edward Vernon or to Edward Richards, but which is now uncertain

[6] This allusion is to the capture of Col Hannum, as heretofore mentioned

[7] Caleb Davis, who was prothonotary from 1777 to 1789, when Delaware County was erected, and was a strong opponent of removal

[8] Mayor John Harper was a stanch Whig and a brave soldier On Feb 9, 1776, he was appointed quartermaster of the Fourth Pennsylvania Battalion, commanded by Col Anthony Wayne, on Oct 12, 1776, he was commissioned ensign in Capt Taylor's company of the same battalion, Jan 1, 1777, he was appointed first lieutenant of the Fifth Pennsylvania Line, and was brigade major of Second Brigade at battle of Brandywine A few days subsequent to that engagement Maj Harper, in company with Lieut.-Col Persifor Frazer, was on a reconnoissance, when the whole party was captured by some of Gen Grant's command, and taken to Philadelphia Col Frazer succeeded in making his escape, but Harper, after the evacuation of the former city, was sent to the prison hulk at New York, where he was detained as a prisoner for over three years He was exchanged Nov 4, 1780 Towards the end or after the Revolution Maj Harper took the tavern now known as the City Hotel, and became mine host of the inn Of course he was opposed to removal On March 5, 1785, Harper, who was then coroner of the county, purchased the tavern property, doubtless well knowing that the Suspension Act of March 30, 1785, would be passed His action when the forces of old Chester moved against those at West Chester has been narrated in the text After the county-seat was removed to the latter place, Maj Harper, believing that the sun of Chester's prosperity had set never to rise again, emigrated to the new local capital, and became the landlord of the Turk's Head Inn there He died at Dilworthtown shortly after the beginning of this century, and was buried at the graveyard at Cheyney Shops, Thornbury

[9] Article "Chester, borough of," in Joseph Scott's "United States Gazetteer," first gazetteer published in the United States (Philadelphia) 1795

no longer the place where the weary suitor waited on the law's delays, or the culprit cringed in the dock; no longer did the court-house ring to the eloquent sentences of Wilson, Bradford, Chew, Levy, Sergeant, Reed, Rush, Laurence, and a score or more of noted lawyers, who, in that early day, rode circuit with the Supreme Justices, nor yet of Elisha Price and Henry Hale Graham, who made the old town their place of residence. The staffs of office had fallen from the tipstaves' clutch, the crier's often repeated admonition of "Silence in the court-room!" had become a verity; the jangling bell ceased to announce that the justices had taken their places on the bench, and the innkeepers would no longer mark with anxious longings the time for holding the quarterly courts, when their hospitalities should be taxed to the utmost, and money flow to their coffers. Now the vacant jail stared at the occasional passer-by with its barred windows, and the empty building returned a hollow echo to the blow of the reckless urchin who could summon courage to rap on its iron-bossed door. The very town seemed to stagnate, and the twinkle of triumph in the eyes of the Goshen and Western township people when in the spring of the year they journeyed hither to buy fish, was aggravating to the people of Chester beyond endurance. It was too much for the residents of the eclipsed county-seat to bear, hence they earnestly bestirred themselves in manufacturing public opinion looking to the erection of a new county, and so earnestly did they labor to that end that on Sept. 26, 1789, the following act was approved, authorizing a division of the county of Chester and the erection of a part thereof into a new county:

"WHEREAS, The inhabitants of the borough of Chester, and the southeastern part of the county of Chester, having by their petitions set forth to the General Assembly of the State, that they labor under many and great inconveniences from the seat of justice being removed to a great distance from them, and have prayed that they may be relieved from the said inconveniences by erecting the said borough and southeastern parts of the said county into a separate county; and as it appears but just and reasonable that they should be relieved in the premises,

"2. *Be it enacted, etc.*, That all that part of Chester County lying within the bounds and limits hereinafter described shall be, and the same is hereby erected into a separate county, that is to say, Beginning in the middle of Brandywine River, where the same crosses the circular line of New Castle County; thence up the middle of the said river to the line dividing the lands of Elizabeth Chads and Caleb Brinton, at or near the ford commonly known or called by the name of Chads' Ford; and from thence on a line, as nearly straight as may be, so as not to split or divide plantations, to the great road leading from Goshen to Chester, where the Westown line intersects or crosses the said road; and from thence along the line of Edgmont, Newtown, and Radnor, so as to include these townships, to the line of Montgomery County, and along the same to Philadelphia County line, and along the same to the river Delaware, and down the same to the circular line aforesaid, and along the same to the place of beginning, to be henceforth known and called by the name of 'Delaware County.'

"3. All that part of the township of Birmingham, which, by the line of division aforesaid, shall fall within the county of Chester, shall be one township, and retain the name of Birmingham; and all that part of the said township, which, by the division-line aforesaid, shall fall within the county of Delaware, shall be one township, and shall retain the name of Birmingham; and all such part of the township of Thornbury, which, by the division-line aforesaid, shall fall within the county of Chester, shall be one township, and shall retain the name of Thornbury, until the same shall be altered by the Courts of General Quarter Sessions of the said counties respectively.

"4. The inhabitants of the said county of Delaware shall, at all times hereafter, enjoy all and singular the jurisdictions, powers, rights, liberties, and privileges, whatsoever, which the inhabitants of any other county of this State do, may, or ought to enjoy by the constitution and laws of this State.

"5. The elections for the said county of Delaware shall be held at the old court-house, in the borough of Chester, where the Freemen of the said county shall elect, at the times and under the regulations directed by the constitution and laws of this State, a councillor, representatives to serve them in General Assembly, censors, sheriffs, coroners, and commissioners, which said officers, when duly elected and qualified, shall have and enjoy, all and singular, such powers, authorities, and privileges, with respect to their county, as such officers elected in and for any other county may, can, or ought to have, and the said elections shall be conducted in the same manner and form, and agreeably to the same rules and regulations as now are or hereafter may be in force in the other counties of this State.

"The justices of the Courts of Quarter Sessions and Common Pleas, now commissioned within the limits of the county of Delaware, and those that may hereafter be commissioned, or any three of them, shall and may hold Courts of General Quarter Sessions of the Peace and Gaol Delivery, and County Courts of Common Pleas, for the said county of Delaware, and shall have all and singular such powers, rights, jurisdictions, and authorities, to all intents and purposes, as other justices of the Courts of General Quarter Sessions and justices of the County Court of Common Pleas, in the other counties of this State, may, can, or ought to have in their respective counties.

"The sheriffs, coroners, treasurers, and collectors of excise hereafter to be appointed or elected in the said county of Delaware, before they, or any of them, shall enter upon the execution of their respective offices, shall give security for the faithful execution of their respective offices."

By the provisions of the act, John Sellers, Thomas Tucker, and Charles Dilworth were appointed commissioners "to run and mark the line dividing the counties of Chester and Delaware," and they scrupulously performed their duty. The act, probably hastily drawn, provided that the western boundary of Delaware County should begin in the middle of Brandywine River, where it crosses the circular line of New Castle County. Strictly following this direction, the result was a severing of a fraction of territory from the rest of the county of Chester. An examination of the map[1] shows that a short distance above Smith's bridge the circular line separating Pennsylvania from Delaware is crossed by the Brandywine, and that stream then makes a bend northward, and returning touches the circular line about half a mile northwest of the point where the river first enters the State. Delaware being erected out of Chester County, only that territory expressly coming within the designated lines of the new county could be included within it, hence this small tract of land lying between the circular line and the bend of the river remained a part of Chester County. The commissioners were directed to run the "line as nearly straight as may be, so as not to split or divide plantations," and while they fully carried out the latter

Israel Acrelius, however, in his "History of New Sweden," published in 1758, tells us that "Chester, the County-town on the Delaware, is sixteen miles below Philadelphia and has one hundred and twenty houses." Reynolds' Translation, p. 143.

[1] Dr. Joshua W. Ash's map of Delaware County, published in 1848, shows plainly this little part of Chester County which wedges itself into Birmingham, Delaware Co., and yet owes allegiance to and pays taxes in another jurisdiction.

instruction, the former seems to have been entirely overlooked, for a more crooked boundary-line could not have been surveyed had that been the intention of the persons making the division Certain it is more obliging commissioners would have been difficult of selection, if tradition be accepted, for the latter states that the owners of farms in the townships of Birmingham and Thornbury were permitted to choose in which of the two counties their plantations should be placed

From a draft in the possession of Dr Smith, which was probably prepared from the surveys made by the commissioners, that author was enabled to glean the following interesting particulars of the manner in which the line was finally adjusted, as well as some of the representations made to the Legislature when the act was pending before that body

"A straight line was run from the starting-point on the Brandywine to the intersection of the Goshen road by the western line, which is six miles three-quarters and fifty-four perches in length, whereas the crooked line between the same points, passing along the boundaries of the farm, cut by the straight line, and now forming the division-line between the two counties, has a length of eleven miles one quarter and nineteen perches On a line perpendicular to the above-mentioned straight line, the court-house at West Chester is only three miles three-quarters and fifty-eight perches distant The bearing of this perpendicular line is N 46° W It is charged in a note on the draft, that a member of the Legislature, while the act for a division of the county was under consideration, asserted that no part of the straight line run by the commissioners would come nearer West Chester than six miles The court-house at West Chester lies nearly due north from the commencement of the division-line on the Brandywine, and is a little over five miles distant from that point, whereas it was alleged at the session of Legislature at which the act was passed that the distance was nine miles From the intersection of the Goshen road and the county line to West Chester the distance in a direct line is four miles three-quarters and sixty perches, nearly, and the course N 85° W The shortest distance from the Street road to West Chester is nine hundred and thirty-five perches It also appears from the draft that another division-line had been proposed This commenced at the mouth of Davis' or Harvey's Run, on the Brandywine, and ran so as to include the whole of Thornbury township, in Chester County"[1]

That the people of the original township of Thornbury, who, by the division-line, were included within the limits of Delaware County, were dissatisfied therewith, we learn from the proceeding of the Legislature, for, on Nov 30, 1789, a petition was presented to that body from "the inhabitants and freeholders of the township of Thornbury, Delaware County, remonstrating against the act for erecting the said county, and praying they may be re-annexed to the county of Chester." The Legislature, it seems, had at last become weary of the constant wrangling growing out of the efforts for the removal to or retention of the seat of justice at designated localities in Chester County, which had extended over twenty years, and had now culminated in a division of the territory, they refused to further hearken to complaints, and the petition was therefore ordered to lie on the table

After the passage of the act of Sept 26, 1789, creating the county of Delaware, Kerlin sold the old court and jail building Nov 3, 1789, to the county for £693 3*s* 8*d*

The first election in the new county took place in October, 1789, all voters coming to Chester, where the poll for the entire territory was held On the 12th of October, President Mifflin and the Supreme Executive Council appointed John Pearson, Thomas Levis, Richard Hill Morris, and George Pearce to be justices of the peace, and on November 7th Henry Hale Graham was commissioned president judge of the courts of Delaware County Almost immediately thereafter it was discovered that this appointment was irregular, Graham at the time not having been commissioned as a justice of the peace, which was requisite to make him legally eligible to the position Thereupon President Mifflin desired Graham to return his commission, which he did, and on the 9th day of the same month he was appointed a justice of the peace, and the following day, president judge in and for the county of Delaware

The first constitution of Pennsylvania, framed by the convention which met early in July, 1776, aroused considerable opposition even at the time of its adoption, but when its crude and cumbersome provisions, after nearly fifteen years' trial, were found to bear unequally on the people, and legislative and executive authority was discovered to be sadly jumbled, the opinions became prevalent that the fraudulent law of the State required general revision When, on March 20, 1789, Representative Wynkoop offered a resolution in the General Assembly, providing for the calling of a Constitutional Convention, there was some opposition manifested, but the measure was finally adopted March 24, 1789, the six representatives from Chester County voting in the affirmative On September 15th the Assembly ordered the convention to assemble at Philadelphia on the fourth Tuesday of November following, and likewise directed at the next election that the several counties should select delegates thereto Two days subsequent to the adoption of these resolutions the county of Delaware was erected, hence, at the election in October, the people of the county selected John Sellers and Henry Hale Graham to represent them in the convention While attending the sessions of that body in Philadelphia, on Saturday, Jan 23, 1790, Henry Hale Graham died, and on Monday following the convention appointed

[1] Smith's "History of Delaware County," p 345

Messrs Roberts, Gray, Gibbons, Thomas Ross, and Sellers a committee to attend the funeral of Judge Graham the next morning, January 26th, at eleven o'clock On Wednesday, Mr Roberts reported "they had performed that service," and the same day the county of Delaware was directed to hold a special election on Wednesday, 3d of February to fill the vacancy occasioned by Graham's death On Friday Feb 5, 1790, the return of the special election was presented to the convention, and Nathaniel Newlin, who had been chosen a member of that body, was duly qualified and took his place therein

The last member of the Supreme Executive Council from Chester County was Col Richard Willing, of Haverford township When Delaware was erected Chester County discovered that the division had left the old territory without a member in Council, hence at the election in October, 1789, Dr Thomas Ruston was chosen to represent that county

Dr Ruston, on October 26th, addressed a petition to President Mifflin, claiming a seat in Council, because, as he argued, every county by law was entitled to one representative, and no councillor could represent more than one county, that by the erection of Delaware Col Willing virtually became its representative, for in that county his property and residence was located, and that Chester, believing a vacancy existed in Council, had, in accordance with law, filled the vacancies at the ensuing election The Supreme Executive Council, however, was unmoved by his reasoning, for on Oct 29, 1789, it was unanimously

"*Resolved*, That Dr Thomas Ruston cannot be admitted to take his seat as councillor for the county of Chester, that county being represented in Council by Col Richard Willing, who was elected on the fifteenth day of October, 1788"

With the adoption of the Constitution of 1790 the Supreme Executive Council ceased to be, and the last cause of contention between the two counties was laid at rest by the new and better order of things which was ushered into being when the republic of Pennsylvania gave place to the great commonwealth of the like name

---

CHAPTER XI

FROM THE ERECTION OF THE COUNTY OF DELAWARE TO THE SECOND WAR WITH GREAT BRITAIN

THE sparsely-peopled territory, which in the anger of defeat at the removal of the court-house from "Old Chester"—for so the ancient borough now began to be termed, to distinguish it from the newly-born West Chester—had formed a separate county government, now began bravely to organize its local administration, select its officers, and prepared to meet the obligations it had assumed So bitter had been the quarrel respecting the removal of the seat of justice in the old county of Chester, that in those townships which had been erected into Delaware County, regret for the step taken seldom found utterance, notwithstanding the cost of separate government soon began to be oppressive to the taxpayers The people unwillingly paid their taxes, scolded the rulers for want of economy in county matters, but rarely reflected that the additional cost had been the direct outcoming of their own action The burden of maintaining public highways and county bridges particularly bore heavily on the people The Queen's Highway from Darby to Chester, and the King's Highway from Chester to the State of Delaware, formed the direct line of communication to the Southern States, and travel was exceedingly heavy on these roads. The county was unable to keep those thoroughfares in good repair, their condition in winter time was so wretched that the press of that day, as well as travelers' letters, constantly referred to them in the most uncomplimentary terms The State, at length, in order that the county of Delaware might be relieved in a measure of the oppressive cost for the maintenance of these roads, which, in the major part, was incurred for the benefit of persons residing without her borders, authorized the county commissioners, by act of Assembly, April 11, 1799, to place toll-gates on the post-road for the term of five years, when the law expired by limitation, and to collect tolls from persons using that highway The county commissioners, in compliance with the law, placed a toll-gate at the bridge over Ridley Creek, and the following schedule of tolls was observed

Coach, light wagon, or other pleasurable carriage, with four wheels and four horses	25 cents
Coach, light wagon, or other pleasurable carriage, with two wheels and two horses	15 "
Chairs, sulkey, etc., with one horse	10 "
Sleigh, with two horses	6 "
Man and horse	2 "
Wagon, with four horses	12 "
Wagon, with two horses	8 "
Cart and horse	4 "
Every additional horse to carriages of pleasure	4 "
Every additional horse to carriages of burden	2 "

In 1793 the yellow fever raged as a dire pestilence in Philadelphia It is related that a party of boys in that year, at Chester, went in a boat to a vessel lying in the stream on which were several persons ill with the disease, and in that way it was communicated to some of the residents of the town and neighborhood, but it did not spread, nor was it as fatal as the same malady proved to be five years thereafter Ninety-four years before the period of which I am now writing, in 1699, when for the first time we have undoubted record of the yellow fever visiting the shores of the Delaware, Chester and the adjacent settlements suffered severely, but beyond that fact very meagre particulars respecting it have been preserved In 1793, however, the scourge in Philadelphia was so malignant that the city was almost depopulated, those of its inhabitants, as a rule, who had the means, fled for safety to the surrounding country districts The record of the noble deeds of a few men who remained in Philadelphia in that appalling time to minister to the sick and dying, as well as to give assistance and succor to the poor and needy, in true heroism far exceeds the achievements of the ordinary class of soldiers with whom history deals, who amid the din and smoke of battle sought the bubble reputation at the cannon's mouth, and for their courage have received the unstinted praises of poets and historians alike Nor is the cool, calm bravery of the men alluded to the only matter disclosed by the minutes of citizens which is worthy of commendation in other respects these records present a grand testimonial to the higher and better nature of mankind

I have just narrated the difficulties encountered by the inhabitants of this section in meeting the expenses of the county, but when the cry of distress went up from Philadelphia it awakened a responsive sympathy throughout our territory, and from people in all condition of circumstances contributions freely came It is an interesting fact that the first donation from Delaware County, which was received Oct 4, 1793, was from "Widow Grubb, of Chester," who presented "eighteen bundles of shirts and shifts for the use of the orphans under the care of the committee" On the 12th of the same month, John Pearson, of Darby, informed that body that a sum of money had been collected for the use of the orphans, and the same day Benjamin Brannan, of Upper Darby, gave notice that the people of Delaware County were raising money for the relief of the sick in the hospital and for persons in distress On the 15th the committee was notified that £161 6s 6d had been collected in Delaware County, that Nathaniel Newlin, of Darby, was ready to pay that sum to any person authorized to receive it The letter also stated that further contributions might be looked for Henry De Forest was instructed to go to Newlin's house, near Darby, and receive the money, which he did October 16th Mathew Carey and Caleb Lownes met Isaac Lloyd at Weed's Ferry, on the Schuylkill, from whom they received $1448 21, being part of the subscription made by citizens of Philadelphia residing in the neighborhood of Darby, to be applied to the use of the sick and poor of that city Two days thereafter, the 28th, Mathew Carey and Caleb Lownes by appointment visited Nathaniel Newlin's house, and received $641 91, a further donation from Delaware County, while the same day Thomas Levis, of Springfield, sent $13 for the like purpose On December 1st, John Pearson, of Darby, paid £12 10s, an additional sum raised by our people, and on Jan 18, 1794, the committee acknowledge $34 69 from citizens of Philadelphia residing in and near Darby The contribution from Delaware County amounted in all to $1291 57, a record of which this locality may justly be proud, when it is remembered that at that time the population was less than ten thousand persons all told The sum just stated was exclusive of the donations "from citizens of Philadelphia residing in and near Darby," which fund was contributed, among others, by Col Thomas Leiper, of Ridley, John Wall, a large real-estate owner in our county, Edward Tilghman, that distinguished lawyer, who refused the chief-justiceship of Pennsylvania, that it might be bestowed on his kinsman, William Tilghman, and whose country-seat was in Nether Providence, where Samuel C Lewis now resides, Raper Hoskins, who then owned the estate, and spent his summers at Greenbank, more recently the Porter House, at Chester, and others deserving prominent places in the history of Delaware County, as well as in that of the city of Philadelphia

In 1798 the yellow fever visited Philadelphia again, and once more the people fled, many carrying with them the seeds of the disease in their systems, to spread it at the places of refuge they sought Mrs Deborah Logan records that a woman from Philadelphia, dying of the fever in Chester, "exacted a promise from some of her friends that her body should be brought back to the city and buried in consecrated ground, and that in consequence of this bad vow the infection was first caught in the borough (Chester), where it spread with frightful rapidity, and depopulated whole families and streets"[1] On Edgmont Avenue, from Fourth Street to the river, there were then only seventeen houses within the space mentioned, more than thirty persons died, while in one of those dwellings[2] all the family excepting a boy of five years fell a victim to the plague Indeed, it is stated that almost one-fifth of the population of Chester was swept away before the fever had subsided At Chester Mills, now Upland, it was very virulent Richard Flower, the owner of the mills, was so severely attacked that he was believed to be dead, but when the burial party was about to place him in the coffin he spoke, and subsequently recovered, to live nearly half a century thereafter The cooper-shop at that place was made a hospital, and it is traditionally asserted that three dead bodies at one time were then awaiting interment Only thirty persons constituted the entire population In other localities near by the disease was equally fatal

The power of the Federal government to impose taxes, or in any wise to act within the limits of the several States, was during Washington's administration very imperfectly understood, and from that ignorance the difficulties in Western Pennsylvania, known in history as the Whiskey Insurrection, had their origin The settlers of that part of our commonwealth were largely Scotch-Irish, and naturally in traditions descended from fathers to sons recitals of the oppressive acts of the excisemen in the mother-country in discharging their official duties, which nar-

[1] Mrs Deborah Logan's manuscript "Reminiscences of Chester," contributed as notes to John F Watson's "Visit to Chester in 1827," in collection of the Historical Society of Pennsylvania

[2] The house adjoining on the north, the present residence of Jonathan Pennell

rations had so moulded the opinions of their descendants that, throughout all our colonial and early State history, any excise tax was regarded with open disapproval by a large class of citizens During the Revolutionary war the whole people submitted to the levying of duties on distilled liquors, yet at the conclusion of that contest those who were opposed to the measure combined and secured the repeal of the act of 1772 providing for the tax Hence when Congress, on March 3, 1791, at the suggestion of Secretary Hamilton, imposed a duty of four pence per gallon on distilled liquors, the law was openly defied in Fayette, Alleghany, Westmoreland, and Washington Counties of this State President Washington, on Sept 15, 1792, issued a proclamation requiring all persons to cease their resistance and submit to the law, which failed to have the desired effect On June 5, 1794, Congress amended the law, which action on its part, instead of satisfying those hostile to the tax, merely resulted in making them more clamorous for its absolute repeal. Deputy marshals and collectors, who had theretofore only been tarred and feathered, were now fired upon by large bodies of armed men and compelled to promise they would not attempt to exercise their authority The Federal government, however, determined to enforce the law, and instructions were issued to indict those distillers who refused to pay the duties These instructions on the part of the administration were productive of widespread disorder and organized open defiance President Washington, on Aug 9, 1794, published another proclamation, requiring all associations whose object was resistance to the excise law to disperse on or before the 1st of September following, at the same time directing a force of nearly thirteen thousand men to be immediately raised in Pennsylvania, New Jersey, Maryland, and Virginia to suppress the insurrectionary movement, which body of soldiers was required "to be held in readiness to march at a moment's warning"

On the same day Governor Mifflin called for the quota assigned to Pennsylvania, five thousand two hundred men, directing them to be armed and equipped as quickly as possible The number of troops required from Delaware County was twenty cavalrymen and sixteen artillerymen, which force was to compose part of the Second Brigade of the Third Division, under command of Brig-Gen Thomas Proctor[1] The call, however, was not responded to with alacrity, for Secretary Dallas, in his report to the Senate of Pennsylvania, says, "Returns from the County of Delaware. dated the 6th of September, 1794, stating a variety of difficulties that leave little hope of procuring by regular drafts the quota of this county," and he reiterated that assertion in his "report relative to the want of promptness of the militia,"[2] dated Jan 16, 1795 Indeed, from a letter written by Attorney-General Ingersoll to Governor Mifflin, May 25, 1795, it appears that in order to raise the quota in both Chester and Delaware Counties three thousand three hundred and ninety-six dollars had to be paid in bounties, Secretary Dallas pledging his personal credit to procure the amount expended[3] Why the quota of Delaware County was placed at only thirty-six men is difficult to understand, when we remember that in May of the same year, under the call of the President for ten thousand seven hundred and sixty-four militia in Pennsylvania to be held in readiness during the threatening difficulties on the frontier, our county was required to furnish two hundred and sixty-two men And it is equally incomprehensible why any difficulty was had in raising thirty-six men in the Whiskey Insurrection, when it is considered that in May, 1794, Governor Mifflin had ordered Adjt Gen Harmer to immediately organize and equip the militia of Philadelphia and the county of Delaware to be in readiness, if needed, to prevent any breaches of the neutrality laws by the cruisers of England or France within this State, or the equipment of any privateer at Philadelphia by either of the belligerent powers

However, Capt William Graham, a lawyer, of Chester, raised a company of cavalry, the greater part of the organization being recruited or drafted from the neighborhood of Chester, and the quota of Delaware County was filled When the troop was ready to march the ladies of Ridley township presented it with a white silk flag, trimmed with fringe of like material On it was painted a figure of Washington in full military costume, to whom an American eagle was descending bearing in its claws a sprig of laurel, while from its mouth was a ribbon with the motto, "Liberty or Death" The allegorical picture was surrounded by flags, drums, cannons, and other military emblems[4]

---

[1] In William Whitehead's "Historical Sketch of the Borough of Chester" (Directory of Chester, 1859-60) it is stated, "Chester sent a company of infantry to the scene of disturbance, under the command of Capt William Graham" Dr Smith merely says that Delaware County furnished a company under Capt Graham, and refers to the Directory of Chester as authority for the statement An article written in 1854 by William H Dillingham, and published in the *West Chester Republican* (quoted at large in Martin's "History of Chester," pp 169-170), entitled "Reminiscences of William Graham, Esq," says, "He commanded a troop of cavalry in the western expedition" Benjamin M Nead, Esq, of Harrisburg, in a sketch of the life of Brig Gen Thomas Proctor (*Penna Mag of History*, vol iv p 466), states that "on August 7, 1794, Gen Proctor was placed in command of the First Brigade, which marched with 1849 men, 96 of which were from Delaware county" The foregoing statement is the only one wherein the gross number of men is given, other than that which is presented in the text The latter I derived from various papers (in the fourth volume, second series, Pennsylvania Archives) relating to the Whiskey Insurrection Yet Mr Nead may be correct in the number mentioned, for he is a gentleman whose assertion on an historical point is always worthy of respect and consideration Unfortunately, I cannot find on record, at Media, the election returns for the year 1794 The troops called into service voted in the fields, and the duplicates for that year, if they could be found in the prothonotary's office, would give the names of every man from this county, and, of course, to obtain the number would be a simple matter of addition

[2] Penna Archives, 2d series, vol iv p 306

[3] Ib, p 532

[4] In 1840 this flag was in the possession of Dr Joseph Wilson It was carried in the great Whig procession, at Chester, on July 23d of that year by the delegation from Springfield

Governor Henry Lee, of Virginia, as chief commander of the army, took up the line of march for the scene of tumult, and an imposing body it was when we recall that Governor Thomas Mifflin led the Pennsylvania troops, Governor Richard Howell, of New Jersey, those from his State, Governor Thomas S Lee those from Maryland, and Gen Daniel Morgan those from Virginia President Washington, accompanied by Gen Knox, Secretary of War, Alexander Hamilton, Secretary of the Treasury, and Judge Richard Peters, followed the army In the mean time the more conservative part of the inhabitants of the offending counties, when they learned that the overwhelming force was coming against them, dispatched a committee to visit the President An interview was had, and the campaign finally ended without further bloodshed A few of the leaders in the insurrectionary outbreak were subsequently tried, and convicted of treason They were, however, pardoned by Washington, and the rebellion, which at one time promised to be difficult of suppression, melted away before the determined action of the Federal government

The general history of Delaware County, until the declaration of war between Great Britain and the United States, is very meagre of stirring incidents, and little took place excepting those matters which belong to the story of the several townships, or judicial narrative, which will be related under these headings, so that it is unnecessary to refer to those events in this summary of the county's annals Dr Smith has so admirably portrayed this placid period in our history that a reproduction of his statement will sufficiently represent the quiet but certain progress of that day "Owing to the European war that raged during this period," he says, "the commerce of our country was benefited, and there was an increased demand for its agricultural products Our county fully shared these advantages, and the result was an effort on the part of our farmers to improve their lands, and thereby to increase their products These lands in many places had become exhausted by a system of bad farming that is generally adopted in new countries, and it was not then uncommon to see large tracts abandoned for agricultural purposes and left uninclosed These exhausted tracts generally received the appellation of 'old fields' The use of gypsum and lime as manures now began to be introduced, the former at first worked almost miracles by the increased productiveness it imparted to the soil It was soon discovered, however, that its effects were greatly diminished by repeated application, and, as a consequence, it became less used, while lime, though slow in developing its benefits, soon became the general favorite with our farmers, and deservedly so, for it cannot be denied that it was owing to its extensive and continued application, combined with a better system of farming, that much of this county has been brought from an exhausted condition to its present state of fertility and productiveness"

CHAPTER XII

THE SECOND WAR WITH ENGLAND

In a work such as this it is not to be expected that space can be given to a discussion of the causes which led the Congress of the United States, on June 18, 1812, to a declaration of war against Great Britain, but it is sufficient to say that the act was looked upon as largely a political measure,—the Democratic party, which was then in power, declaring for a vigorous prosecution of the war, while the Federalists opposed the contest as unnecessary, injudicious, and destructive of our commercial prosperity In the city of Baltimore to such an extent was party spirit aroused that serious breaches of the peace and riotous attacks were manifested between the opposing political factions

In the county of Delaware, as elsewhere, there was a division of sentiment, but the preponderance of opinion was adverse to the war, and was outspoken in its disapproval On Aug 5, 1812, in the *Chester and Delaware Federalist* (now *Village Record*),[1] appeared the following advertisement

"COUNTY MEETING THE FEDERAL REPUBLICANS and all others friendly to PEACE and COMMERCE in Delaware county are requested to meet at the house of Isaac Cochran, in the township of Upper Providence, on Saturday, the 8th of August, at 2 o'clock P M, on business preparatory to the ensuing ELECTION in October and November next"

The county meeting thus called was largely attended Thomas Smith was appointed chairman, and Maskell Ewing secretary, and the following preamble and resolution were unanimously adopted

"The Congress of the United States having on the 18th of June last passed an act declaring war against Great Britain and her dependencies, which has thrown this heretofore happy and prosperous country into a hostile attitude, at a time, too, when we are unprepared by land or sea, our territory and citizens exposed to invasion and plunder, our commerce unprotected, a prey to an enemy whose ships have power to control the ocean,—

"*Resolved*, That we view the proceedings as hostile to the happiness and interest of this country, and consider the men who sanctioned it by their votes as unworthy of our confidence, that we will exercise every constitutional right to displace them and put those at the head of our affairs whom we deem capable of honestly representing us"

The resolution met with such general approval that a meeting of the young men of the county was called in the court-house at Chester, and on Aug 22, 1812, the building was crowded, many persons who attended being unable to enter the doors Samuel Edwards, Esq, then a rising young lawyer who had been admitted a few years previous, was called to preside, and Zedekiah W Flower was appointed secretary A lengthy address, evidently carefully prepared, was read, in which it was argued that no good reason, excepting the impressing of American seamen by English vessels, had been advanced by the advocates of the war, and even that cause should and could be removed by negotiation between the two nations The following resolutions were adopted

[1] No newspaper was then published in Delaware County

"*Resolved*, That we are determined to employ all our exertions to produce a speedy and honorable peace, and that we will obey all constitutional acts of our government

"*Resolved*, That, feeling confident that nothing but a change of men and measures will produce the blessings of peace and National prosperity, we consider it a solemn duty imposed on every citizen by true and genuine patriotism to use all honorable means in the exercise of the right of suffrage to procure an immediate change in the administration of the National Government, and thereby save us from the dreadful consequences of a protracted war

"*Resolved*, That at a time like the present, when one of our most flourishing and commercial cities has been subjected by an infuriated mob,[1] we consider it the duty of every citizen to aid and assist in suppressing all riots, tumults, and mobs, believing that they are tending to overthrow the only Republican government on earth

"*Resolved*, That although we do not apprehend any disturbance of the kind in this quarter, yet should any outrages be attempted we pledge ourselves to each other and to society to use our utmost exertions to support the laws and defend the lives and property of our fellow citizens against such proceedings"

Little of interest can be gleaned, at this late day, from our annals respecting the progress of the war That there were a number of soldiers enlisted from our county is fully ascertained, but the names of such persons have been forgotten in the lapse of time, and because they were recruited into organizations not strictly local We know that the two sons of Elisha Price, of Chester, both died in the service, one from diseases contracted, and the other killed in action on the Canadian frontier

An interesting scrap of local history is furnished in the following extract from the *Freeman's Journal*, published in Philadelphia, March 12, 1813, for it not only shows the means used to convey intelligence of important events in those days, but it indicates that the ancient borough of Chester was proud to have an opportunity to send forth to the public the news of the great victory achieved by the gallant captain who made that town his home

"Postscript Another Naval Victory —The following important note was endorsed on the way bill from Chester, Penna., received at the Post-office last night '"Essex" frigate captured the British frigate "Castor," and killed one hundred and fifty of her men' The report adds that the 'Essex,' Capt Porter, had arrived in the Delaware, March 10, 1813"

The safe arrival of the "Essex," thus reported, was only six days previous to the active blockade of the Delaware River and Bay by the British vessels of war "Poictiers," "Belvidere," and several smaller crafts under the command of Commodore Beresford On March 16th, when the former vessel lay off the village of Lewes, near Cape Henlopen, and threatened to open fire on the hamlet unless twenty-five bullocks and a proportionate quantity of vegetables should be contributed to the support of the English fleet, the news of the outrage was carried by couriers to arouse the people to resistance, and Delaware County promptly responded That organization was effected within our county previous to Admiral Cockburn's attack on and spoliation of Havre de Grace, and even before the latter's forces applied the torch to the village of Fredericktown, on May 6th, is evident from the official correspondence Under date of April 7, 1813, James Trimble, deputy secretary of the commonwealth, wrote to William Brooke, brigadier-general of the Third Division of militia, stating that on the application of Samuel Edwards and Thomas D Anderson, of Chester, Governor Snyder had consented to furnish sixty muskets with bayonets, and, if possible, as many cartridge-boxes, for the purpose of arming the Chester Company of Infantry, on condition that Messrs Edwards and Anderson, with two other gentlemen to be approved by Gen Brooke, should enter bonds to return the arms and accoutrements in good order in six months after they received them. On May 12, 1813, Secretary of State Boileau wrote to Thomas S Anderson that Governor Snyder was prepared to forward as early as practicable five or six hundred stands of arms and cartridge-boxes, and orders had been forwarded to Deputy Quartermaster-General Foering to furnish whatever ammunition might be required, but that there were no tents or other camp equipments belonging to the State, fit for use, that could be had He suggested that in the then season of the year, and in a country so thickly settled, the men in service might find shelter from any inclement weather in houses, barns, or temporary huts. He further stated that in 1793 Governor Mifflin had loaned one hundred and sixty tents to the Board of Health in Philadelphia, and Gen Foering would be instructed to ascertain their condition, and, if found fit for use, they would be delivered to Gen Brooke, the brigade inspector for the district including Delaware County. Under date of May 15, 1813, Secretary Boileau wrote to Joseph Engle that three hundred and fifty stands of arms, with other articles, had that day been forwarded to Chester, and as Gen. Brooke lived some distance from the latter place, the arms had been sent in Mr Engle's care, and he should receipt to the wagoner for them In a postscript he adds that after the muskets were loaded in the wagon it was found it would not carry more than three hundred boxes, and as it was thought the other articles were not as necessary as the guns, they had not been forwarded

The muskets mentioned in the letter to Anderson of May 12th, and those that were forwarded to Engle on May 15th, were doubtless intended to arm the emergency men, when the intelligence of the destruction of Fredericktown was received, together with the report that a large force of English troops, accompanied by Indians, who spared neither women nor children, had landed there, doubtless intending serious mischief The latter part of this rumor was without foundation

Nothing of interest appertaining to the war occurred in Delaware County for fifteen months, although the militia must have been held in readiness to move at short notice In the early part of March, 1814, Secretary Boileau wrote to Gen Brooke that a thousand muskets had been sent by the United States to the State arsenal in Philadelphia to arm the militia, and the quota of Delaware County would be de-

[1] Riots had occurred in Baltimore

livered when it became necessary. The cartridge-boxes which had been sent to Chester must have been sadly out of order, for in the same letter the Secretary says in respect to them, "Although not of the best quality, (they) will at least serve for a short campaign. Any man who receives a box can easily put a few more tacks to secure the belts." On the same day Secretary Boileau wrote to Deputy Quartermaster-General Foering, "That in case of a threatened invasion of the shores of the Delaware, and you should be called upon by Brig.-Gen. Brooke, of the Third Division, or Maj.-Gen. Steele, of the said division, for arms, equipments, and ammunition, that you furnish them with what may be deemed necessary."

The idea of gathering the militia into camps of instruction seems to have been the suggestion of President Monroe, for April 6, 1814, he wrote to Gen. Joseph Bloomfield, stating that the military organizations "ought to be assembled and a camp formed," suggesting that such cantonment should be on "some commanding, healthy ground between the Schuylkill and the heights of the Brandywine." The President urged the gathering of this force at once, as "we must keep together a nucleus at least of an army, with every necessary equipment, sufficiently strong to oppose the enemy on his landing until you can get the whole together to overwhelm him."[1]

In the early summer of 1814 the inhabitants of the Middle and Southern seaboard States were fully aware that England, now that peace in Europe had apparently released a large force of veteran soldiers from service there, and that they were under orders to America, meditated a decisive movement against the United States, and, being uncertain where the blow would be struck, made every effort to place all exposed situations on our coast in a position of defense. Hence when the city of Washington fell before the British army under Ross, on the 18th of August, when the incendiary Cockburn had applied the torch to the unfinished capitol, the library of Congress, the President's house, and other public buildings, and Baltimore was menaced, Governor Snyder promptly, on Aug. 27, 1814, issued a general order, setting forth that "the recent destruction of the capital of the United States, the threatened and probable conflagration of the metropolis of a sister State, and the general threatening aspect of affairs, warranted the opinion that an attack is meditated by the enemy on the shores of the Delaware." To repel the foe and to guard against surprise, he deemed it necessary to have a sufficient force "of freemen" ready for every emergency, and therefore required that the militia generally of the counties of Philadelphia, Bucks, Montgomery, Delaware, Chester, Lancaster, Dauphin, Lebanon, Berks, Schuylkill, Lehigh, Northampton, and Pike, in addition to those drafted for the service of the United States, under orders of July 22d, who were already subject to the orders of Gen. Bloomfield, "be held in readiness to march at a moment's warning."

The militia of Pennsylvania having been ordered to assemble at the town of York to the number of five thousand, on Sept. 8, 1814, Governor Snyder wrote to Gen. Bloomfield that he proposed asking the Secretary of War to transfer the troops to the shores of the Delaware for the defense of the city of Philadelphia and the country along the river. In his letter to President Monroe dated September 9th, the Governor advocated this movement, adding that the authorities "must at present rely upon the patriotic feeling which pervades Pennsylvania, rather than on coercing obedience to our militia laws, and before that feeling can have an effect, the enemy, by rapid movements, may have effected his depredatory incursions." He suggested a locality for the camp should be selected so that the troops would be marched in a few days either to the Delaware River or Chesapeake Bay. On the 10th, Governor Snyder wrote to the President that about six thousand volunteers had arrived in Philadelphia, and many others were on the march to that city; that Gen. Bloomfield thought a camp should be formed at Marcus Hook, where the volunteers should be organized under United States regulations, and Gen. Bloomfield would himself take command of the forces. The Governor was of the opinion that inasmuch as the militia had selected their own company officers, they would be unwilling to be consolidated into other bodies and have strange commanders placed over them. He, therefore, suggested that they should be organized in accordance with the laws of the State, in battalions and regiments, under which they would willingly serve the term of three months for which they had enlisted.

Immediately below Marcus Hook, to command the river, extensive earthworks were hastily constructed and mounted with cannon, while between Ridley and Crum Creeks earthworks were erected to control the Queen's Highway to Philadelphia. So intense was the alarm in the borough of Chester and county of Delaware that the records were packed ready to be transported, if necessary, at a moment's notice to the interior of the State.

On Sept. 18, 1814, Secretary Boileau wrote to Gen. Brooke that, during the alarm at Elkton the preceding summer, three hundred stands of arms had been sent to Chester for the use of the militia. These muskets Gen. Brooke was ordered to have delivered to him, and if any repairs to them were needed, to have them mended in the neighborhood, if possible, but if that could not be done, to send them to the State arsenal at Philadelphia for that purpose. He also required Gen. Brooke to inquire for and take into his possession the cartridge-boxes which had been forwarded to Chester at the same time the muskets were sent.

We learn, from a letter written by Secretary Boileau,

[1] Penna. Archives, 2d series, vol. vii. p. 735.

Sept 28, 1814, that the drafted men at that date, who were stationed at Marcus Hook, were destitute of tents and other camp equipments, while the volunteers had good quarters and were well supplied with all necessary camp furniture The cantonment was located just back of Marcus Hook cross-roads, was called Camp Gaines (subsequently Fort Snyder), and was under the command of Maj -Gen. Worrall Col William Duane, Adjt -Gen and Maj Hunter, both of the United States army, had the care of the camp and superintended its discipline

Dr Smith states, respecting the drafted troops from Delaware County, that "the first company was convened at the 'Three Tuns,' now the Lamb Tavern, in Springfield, on the 14th of October, and marched to Chester that day Its officers were Capt William Morgan, 1st Lieut Aaron Johnson, 2d Lieut Charles Carr, and Ensign Samuel Hayes This company remained at Chester two weeks waiting for camp equipage, before repairing to the encampment at Marcus Hook During this time the men occupied meeting-houses and other public buildings "[1]

From the manuscript Orderly Book of the Mifflin Guards of Delaware County, commanded by Capt Samuel Anderson, we learn that on Sept 15, 1814, that body of volunteer infantry was at Camp Bloomfield, Kennett Square, Chester Co That on the 17th of the same month they broke camp, and the troops marched to Gregg's Tavern, three and a half miles from Wilmington, while the following day they were in cantonment at Camp Brandywine, and on the 29th they were at Camp Dupont This cantonment was located in the neighborhood of Wilmington, Del , and was under the command of Brig -Gen Thomas Cadwalader Governor Snyder, on October 5th, visited the camp and was received with a Federal salute, fired under direction of Maj Provost, as soon as the head of the escort entered the main grounds, the troops presenting arms and "the drums giving the ruffles" Gen Bloomfield was superseded in control of the Fourth Military District, Oct 7, 1814, on which date Maj -Gen. Gaines assumed the command and reviewed the troops at Marcus Hook on the 12th of the same month

The discipline of the troops of course was very lax, and the desertions from camp numerous, therefore, October 19th, Gen Gaines issued a general order, in which he stated that he had received the finding of a court-martial, to which he had refused his approval, because the sentence imposed on certain soldiers found guilty of desertion, in his opinion, "has no adequate proportion to the offence committed by them Slight punishments for high military offences are worse than useless The infamous crime of desertion particularly calls aloud for the highest punishment Deserters must be shot"

A general order was issued on Oct. 14, 1814, dated at Marcus Hook, commanding that the Pennsylvania volunteers called into service under the order of Governor Snyder, Aug. 27, 1814, should be immediately organized under the act of Assembly of March 28, 1814 On Oct 29, 1814, the Delaware County Fencibles, Capt Serrill, was attached to the First Brigade Pennsylvania Volunteers till further orders

On Nov 15, 1814, Lieut -Col Raquet was ordered to march the next day with Capt Leonard's company of artillery, and Capts Mifflin's, Swift's, Brown's, Serrill's, and Murray's companies of infantry, and take a position to cover New Castle The artillery was to consist of two six-pounders and two howitzers On the same day, Gen Gaines issued an order approving the finding of the court-martial which sat at Fort Clemson, November 1st, for the trial of David Jefferies, a private in Capt Patterson's company, Thirty-second Regiment, United States Infantry, charged with desertion, who was found guilty, sentenced to be shot to death, and the execution ordered to take place the next day, November 16th, between twelve and four o'clock, at such place as Col Irwin, or the officer in command at Camp Clemson, near New Castle, should appoint

The dread of an immediate invasion or attack on the Middle Atlantic States having subsided, on Nov. 28, 1814, the artillery companies commanded by Capts Rodney and Reed, of Delaware Volunteers, were ordered to take post at New Castle for the defense of that town, and Gen Cadwalader was instructed to put the whole of the Advance Light Brigade in march for the city of Philadelphia, there to await further orders

That this was done appears from an affidavit of Abel Green, of Edgmont, on file in the prothonotary's office, Media, who, under date of April 7, 1855, states that he was a private in the company of Capt Benjamin Weatherby, which was drafted for the term of three months, and "was honorably discharged at Philadelphia on the 2d day of December, 1814" That the Mifflin Guards were ordered to Chester we know beyond dispute, because at the latter place, under date of Dec 10, 1814, Capt Samuel Anderson issued the following order

"The company will assemble for drill in Chester on every Wednesday and Saturday at ten o'clock until further orders The orderly or a sergeant acting as orderly will attend at my headquarters every morning at nine o'clock to receive and execute such orders as may be given All knapsacks, haversacks, and canteens in possession of the members will be delivered at my quarters on the next company day It is expected that the members will pay the same attention to the cleanliness of their arms as they did while in camp As a reward for industry, the four persons having the cleanest muskets on each day of parade will be excused from duty for one week The company will bear in remembrance that they are still in the service of the government, consequently that they are subjected to the penalties and punishments prescribed by the articles of war for the neglect of duty, disobedience of orders, or any other violation of the rules and regulations laid down for the government of the armies of the United States It is therefore expected that all orders from your commander will be respected and punctually obeyed Defaulters must and will be punished

[1] History of Delaware County, p 31 There is a slight error in the dates given by Dr Smith, since the official records at Harrisburg show that the company was in camp at Marcus Hook on Oct. 10, 1814.

"Those persons who formerly considered themselves as members of this company, but had not patriotism and fortitude sufficient to encounter the difficulties and endure the hardships and privations of the campaign, are ordered to deliver up their arms and accoutrements, being no longer considered members of the company."

On Dec. 21, 1814, Capt. Anderson issued this order:

"Company drills are dispensed with until further orders. For the conveniences of members the company will be divided into three classes. The first class will include all the members residing in Chester and its vicinity, to be under the immediate command of the captain. The second class will include those who reside in the neighborhood of Marcus Hook, and all others who may find it most convenient to meet at that place, to be commanded by Lieutenant Marshall. The third class will be under the command of Lieutenant Evans, to include all those who may find it most convenient to meet at the Black Horse Tavern in Middletown. The members of each class, respectively, will assemble at the quarters of the officer commanding on every Wednesday at 11 o'clock, A.M., with arms, except in wet weather. The officers commanding the second and third class will report to the Captain on every Thursday. The names of absentees to be inserted in their reports, also the names of those who neglect to keep their muskets in order. All such as neglect to comply with this order will be considered deserters and reported as such to the commanding General. Those who obtained leave of absence before the troops left camp, on account of sickness, and have not since reported themselves, will report forthwith, otherwise they will be reported as unfit for the service of the U. S. and discharged accordingly. The Quarter-Master will report to Philad. in order to procure the rations due to the company."

I have not learned when the volunteers were mustered out of the service of the United States. Martin says it was Dec. 6, 1814. The foregoing orders show that that date is inaccurate.

In 1863, when the bill was before Congress providing for pensions to the soldiers of the war of 1812, a meeting of the survivors of that struggle in Delaware County was called at the Columbia House, in Chester, on December 6th, and organized by the appointment of Hon. George G. Leiper chairman, and Capt. John Martin secretary. The object of the meeting being stated, it was

"*Resolved*, That we approve of the convention of soldiers of the war of 1812, which is to assemble at Philadelphia, on the Ninth of January next, and that the following persons are hereby appointed delegates to said convention from this county, viz.: James Serrill, George G. Leiper, Levi Reynolds, Henry Myers, David Hayes, George Litzenberg, and Aaron Johnson.

"*Resolved*, That the soldiers of the war of 1812, poorly clad, poorly fed, subjected to great exposure in defending the Coasts and a long line of Northern frontier, after a tardy delay, should not be stinted in the bestowment of Government bounty, and that any discrimination against the soldiers of 1812 is manifestly unjust.

"*Resolved*, That the above proceedings be published in the papers of this county, and that the Secretary be requested to forward a copy of them to Dr. J. B. Sutherland, of Philadelphia.

"GEORGE G. LEIPER, *Chairman*.

"JOHN MARTIN, *Secretary*."

The following is the roll of the soldiers of the volunteer and drafted companies from Delaware County:

ROLL OF MIFFLIN GUARDS, FIRST REGIMENT, PENNSYLVANIA VOLUNTEERS.

Commanded by Col. Clement C. Biddle.

Samuel Anderson, captain; Frederick Shull, first lieutenant; David A. Marshall, second lieutenant; William Biggart, ensign. (At an election held at Camp Dupont Oct. 21, 1814, John Caldwell was elected first lieutenant.)

Sergeants.—John Caldwell, Benjamin Haskins, William Evans, Henry Horne.

Corporals.—John Thomson, George Hawkins, John Marshall, Joseph Derrick, John Rowan.

Privates.—Samuel Edwards, Edward Minshall, Thomas Kille, John Garrett, John Lambert, John Lloyd, Joseph Hall, David Fisher, Joseph Martin, Jr., John Hawkins, Levi B. Martin, Thomas Parsons, Lazarus Martin, Daniel Broomall, Robert Beatty, Thomas Pedrick, James Burns, Jeremiah Brown, Samuel Palmer, Evan Bonsall, Thomas Merion, John Lutkin, Joseph Hooper, Jacob Duey, Robert Clark, Jonathan S. Bonsall, William Kinsey, William Helms, John McLain, Thomas Ash, Peter Long, Cornelius Macky, David Smart, Nathan Hayes, David Bonsall, Isaac Brooks, Daniel McGineley, John McGilton, Samuel Bunting, Philip Painter, George Myers, Davis Smith, Thomas P. Ash, Jonathan Quicksall, Thomas Fleming, Thomas Painter, William Beatty, James Evans, Thomas P. Smith, Charles Lear, John Stevenson, John Pyewell, William Geary, William H. Marshall, James Lock, Daniel Mitchell, John McKee, John Martin (Hook), Joseph Wilkinson, Leonard Cole, William Cummins, Thomas D. Barnard, Thomas Bowers, John Statton, John Hahn, George Ross, Thomas Williams, Moses Wells, Jr., Thomas McCullough, William Smith, Andrew Rively, John McCleaster, William Glover, Joshua Bonsall, Samuel Bonsall, Jr., Thomas Bonsall, Clement Smith, William Cox, John Shaw, George W. Johnson, William Jones, William Humphreys, John Frazier, John Meyers, John Wetherill.

ROLL OF DELAWARE COUNTY FENCIBLES, TWENTY-SECOND PENNSYLVANIA MILITIA.

Entered service Sept. 21, 1814. October 14th encamped at Marcus Hook.

James Serrill, captain; George G. Leiper, first lieutenant; James Serrill, Jr., second lieutenant; George Serrill, ensign; Moses Adams, sergeant-major.

Sergeants.—John B. Pearson, Richard R. Jones, David Rose, Jr., Joseph Oakford.

Corporals.—Henry Wood, Joseph Shallcross, Andrew Urian, John C. Farrell.

Musicians.—James Warner, Robert Holmes.

Privates.—John Stroop, Enoch Bonsall, Thomas J. Martin, Ellwood Ormsby, Mathew McNulty, Casper Trites, Jesse Z. Paschall, John Rively, Daniel Smith, John Dobbins, George Williamson, William Fines, Reuben Bonsall, Charles Justis, James Cleary, John Dunant, Richard G. Martin, Charles G. Snowden, Joseph Pyle, William Lindsay, George Caldwell, David Cummins, James Brattin, Aaron Martin, Joseph Hibbert, Lewis B. Stannard, Clement Hanse, Charles Bonsall, Charles Gibson, Charles Attmore, Miles McSweeny, Aaron Helms, Cadwalader M. Helms, Andrew Noblit, Andrew Enberg, Marshall Siddons, Thomas Bonsall, William McCormick, Samuel Bonsall, John Brown, John Hansell, Joseph T. Jones, William Torrance, John Dermont, William Grubb, John Bradford, John Martin (Chester), Townseud T. Johns, William Torrence, John McDermott.

ROLL OF CAPT. WILLIAM MORGAN'S COMPANY, FIRST COMPANY OF FIRST BRIGADE, THIRD DIVISION OF PENNSYLVANIA MILITIA.

Encamped at Marcus Hook Oct. 10, 1814.

Sergeants.—James Morgan, Caleb Smith, John Mather, Lewis Brook, Charles Crozer.

Corporals.—David Trainer, William Urain, George Davis, Isaac Smith.

Quartermaster-Sergeant.—Isaac Atmore.

Privates.—George Delainey, James Lee, William Gill, Samuel Brown, Vernon Lewis, Jeremiah Maul, William McClelin, Aaron Hibberd, Henry Handly, Adam Litzenburg, John Schringer, Benjamin Arment, William Fraim, Hezekiah Kamp, Isaac Jones, James Wright, Israel Jones, Philip Trites, William Wright, John Forsyth, Isaac Cox, William Armstrong, John Stewart, George Yoecome, Alexander Garey, Jacob Byers, William Stewart, John Tree, John Heppelfinger, John O'Harrah, Joseph Davis, Robert Low, John Smith, Isaac Burns, Jonathan Davis, William Mace, Robert Valentine, Jones Jone, William Eppright, Joseph Rhudolph (2), James Lindsay, Jr., John Latch, Enoch Ramsey, Evan Pennell, John Hoven, John Kerns, John Gare, Jr., Samuel Humphrey, William Orr, James Price, Hugh McDade, John Little, George Wells, John Hoff, Elias Worrell, Jonathan Vernon, Joshua Hardey, Joseph Green, Robert Lithgaw, James McDougal, Enoch Dickason, William Palmer, Thomas Taylor, Jonathan Morgan, George Dunn, Davis Smith, Joseph Rhudolph, John Gore, Samuel Wright, Thomas Rhudolph, Jacob Grim, David Smith, James Fraim, John Fraim, Samuel Lindsey, Lewis Williamson, John Crozer, William Trites, John Ewing, Michael Flahady, John Morton, John McDonnal, James Holdt, George Ely, John Cozens, Edward Waters, Septamus Flounders, John Green, Isaac Sharpless, John H. Worrell.

ROLL OF FIRST COMPANY, SIXTY-FIFTH REGIMENT PENNSYLVANIA MILITIA

Commanded by Lieut.-Col John L Pierson, of Ridley

Captain, John Hall, First Lieutenant, Matthew Dunbar, Second Lieutenant, William Scofield, Third Lieutenant, Thomas Olly, Ensign, Robert Dunn

Sergeants—Jacob Wise, John Bowers, Jr, Joseph Dunwoody, Jabez Lewis

Privates.—Joseph Bittle, Isaac Davis, Robert Corker, Moses Newlin, Joseph Fulton, Bennett Lewis, Thomas J Miles, Isaac Richards, John Daver, John Reyner, Joshua Lainhoff, Samuel Taylor, John Ormsby, Benjamin Scirril, John Mann, John Engle, John McGahey, John Cray, Peter King, Joseph Evens, Samuel Lynch, Abraham Miller, Philip Rap, Thomas Car, Armet Rossiter, William Phillips, Jacob Kulp, Ezekiel Shur, Jesse Shauer or Shawer, Jacob Root, Daniel Root, John Job, Frederick Hough, Isaac Zebai, John McKealher, George Hough, Daniel Rice, Thomas Scot, Jabez Nice, Samuel Lindsey, William Rudabaugh, Samuel Rudolph, James Blundat, William Field, Peter Burns, William Evens, Lewis Pennell, John Alexander, Edward McLary, Thomas C Pearce, Eli Roberts, Samuel Lindsey, John Standley, John Humphreys, Jacob Wiley, John Ferguson, John Hoofstickler, Benjamin Worrell, Thomas E Downs, James Everheart, Samuel Miller, S[ten], Samuel Miller, Wh[t], John Shaffener, John White, David Royer, Adam Poley Jacob Donahower, Samuel Walker, Peter Defrain, Conrad Baker, Jesse Boyer, David Shuteman, John Rap, Nathan Brook, Mittle Hause, Andrew Laird, Jacob Haven, Martain Sheater, John Walker, Alexander Clemans, Malen Rossiter, Miles Beaty, Francis Enos, William Fox, James McFagen, William McNeal, Marcus Boon, Charles Bugle, Mifflin Lewis, John Hoops, Jacob Jones, Able Lodge, Daniel Davis, Samuel Jenet, Philip Litzenburg, Benjamin Urian, John Hoiser, Denis Sheridan, George Brannan, James Hughs, Isaac Garrison, Mordecai Thomas, Philip Miller, Jacob Stonebeck, Henry Longacker, Abiza Rossiter, Able Williams, Jacob Smith, John Shinkle, Jacob King, Michael King, George Geger, Jacob Defrain, James Lundy, Jacob Longaker, James Adrikens, Henry Stophelbine, William Danafelser, Isaac Jones, Henry Sheet, John Possey, Daniel Young, George Litzenburg, John Saylor, Amos Griffith, Andrew Rively

ROLL OF FIFTH COMPANY, SIXTY-FIFTH REGIMENT PENNSYLVANIA MILITIA, CAPT JAMES LACKEY COMMANDING

Privates—Reuben Taylor George Roberts, Jacob Goodwin, James Degraut, Kenith McKinzy, John Smith, George Hersh, Hezekiah Jackson, Lawrence Wilson, Edward Salyards, Henry Garman Jacob Forwood, William Hoskins, Joseph Conway, Thompson Hunter, Samuel Sinquet, Jacob Howell, John McDonald, Levi Waldravin, Davis Morgan, David Rider, David Egee, William Town, John Framo, Joseph Rogers, John Cross, John Archer, Benjamin Torton, Samuel Eppright, William Thompson, William Sill, Matthew Scott, Thomas McKeown, Charles Rowland, John King, James Day, William White, William Bowers, Joseph H Lawrence, George Wells, Powell Clayton, Charles Griffith, John Burk, Benjamin Clare, Evan Griffith, John Walker, Richard Ford, William Bucknell, Hugh Love, David Williamson, Thomas Trimble, James Cummings, John Farrow, Samuel Griffith, John Galliuo, Francis Himes, John Funterwise, Thomas Hutcheson, Henry Pearson, Peter Pearson, Thomas Llewellyn, George L Davis, Joseph Farrow, Thomas Everson, Jonathan Crozier, James Brothers, Isaac White, John Kitts, William Martin, Jacob Essex, George Hannum, Benjamin Work, Edward May, Edward W Robeson, William Dempsey, Samuel Pennell, John Petterson, Timothy Pierce, William Hodge, Benjamin Thompson, William McCray, Abram Peck, John Gilmore, Thomas Kelly, Martin Bryan, Thomas Chaffin, John Nickles, William Sharp, Peter Young, Aaron Carter, Jeremiah Murry, Jesse Sharpless, Oswald Sill, John Bane, Isaac Eaches, John Beck, Bartholomew Shimer, Samuel Sullivan, John Haycock, Jacob Stanley, Thomas Cochran, Henry Carr, Atlee Porter, Samuel Cozens, Enmor Davis, Charles Rowland, George Farrow, John Wizer, Lazarus Weidner

ROLL OF SIXTH COMPANY, SIXTY FIFTH REGIMENT PENNSYLVANIA MILITIA, CAPT BENJAMIN WETHERBY

Entered United States service Sept. 20, 1814, encamped at Camp Snyder, Marcus Hook, Oct 17, 1814

Sergeants.—James McGuigan, John Taylor George Peters, Thomas Ash, Patrick McGuigan

Corporals—Samuel Roberts, Barney McGuigan, Benjamin Yarnall

Privates—Samuel Bittle, Eli Ratteu, James Mitchel, William Davis, James Huff, John Griffith, John Henthorn, John Gorby, Aaron Beale, Gilbert Burns, William McLaughlin, Sr, Jacob Stewart, John Varly, Thomas Marshall, Aaron Smith, John Davis, William Turner, John Kelly, Samuel Burnet, Jesse Green, James McCoy, Joseph Griffith, Henry Bean, Jesse McKinstry, Woodward Hampton, Nicholas Marrow, Daniel Likens, George McBride, Frederick Stimel, Alexander Torbert, Peter Harper, Richard Baker, Abel Green, Francis Harbinson, William Rauzel (or Raugel), David Cornog, Robert Valentine, William Graff, George Russell, Frederick Close, Curtis Barlow, Cornelius Wright, William Odenheimer, William Weare, John R Price, Archibald Dougherty, William Smith, Jacob Rizer, William Mace, Levan Bernard, Andrew Black, James Weare, Samuel Russell, Charles Smith, Thomas Mercer, Benjamin Allison, Isaac Tompkins, Richard Clayton, Aaron Lawrence, Jeremiah Dutton, John Smith, William McLaughlin David Torton, John H Craig, John Barlow, Vincent Jester, Charles McGarraty, John Alcot, John S Hannum, Robert Steel, Thomas Brown, James Hodge, George Hine, Peter Smith, John Burnet, Joseph Murphy, Jacob Young, Valentine Dick, David Jay, Abel Smedley, John S Travis, Richard Warnick, John Wheeling, James Taylor, John Hoops, Felix Fields, Henry Collins, Joseph Edworthy, Matthew Hopkins, James Weare, Jr, Alexander Parks, Baldwin Weaver, Thomas Jones, Anthony N Still, Andrew Hunter, Reuben Miles, John Hook, Jonathan Gibson, John King, Joel Scott, Nehemiah Baker, David Broomell, John Pyle

CHAPTER XIII

FROM THE SECOND WAR WITH ENGLAND TO 1850.

THE second war with England had almost wholly severed communication with the Old World, particularly with Great Britain, and the immediate result was an effort on the part of the people to meet the public demand for those commodities which previous to the beginning of hostilities were obtained entirely from Europe The numberless cruisers of England had swept the merchant marine of the Republic almost from the seas, until the only vessels bearing the American flag were men-of-war or letters-of-marque, hence the great demand from this cause stimulated the establishment of manufacturing enterprises, largely throughout the Eastern and in a measure in the Middle States

It should be remembered that during all our colonial history—not only our State but all the colonies—England had persistently, as in Ireland, forbidden the people to engage in manufacturing any articles which might come in competition with the industries of the home country Although writers during the middle of the last century in Great Britain argued that the American colonies would not for hundreds of years engage in manufacturing, basing their conclusion on the then known history of the world, that it was only "after there was such an overplus of inhabitants, beyond what is necessary for cultivating the soil, as is sufficient for forming large towns, where trade and manufacturing can be carried on to advantage," still there were others who rightly judged the geographical position of the American colonies might make them an exception to the rule as taught in the annals of the Old World The English Parliament early became alarmed at the development of the iron industry in the colonies, particularly in Pennsylvania, and the establishment of furnaces and rolling-mills, so that in 1749 an act was passed "to encourage the importation of pig- and bar-iron from His Majesty's colonies in America, and to prevent the erection of any mill or other engine for slitting or rolling of iron, or any plating Forge to work with a tilt-hammer or any furnace for making steel in any of the said colonies" At that time one forge we know was in operation in Thornbury township, at the present Glen Mills, and some years before that date was another on Crum Creek,—Peter Dick's Iron Works The numerous trades, such as carpenters and brick-makers, and the like, were early known on the Delaware, hence, from the references found in the Dutch records a quarter of a century before Penn came, I am confident that no bricks in any dwelling standing in Pennsylvania to day were made in Europe and brought here Indeed, the bricks which we know came from Governor Printz's mansion-house at Tinicum, present every appearance of having been hardened merely by the heat of the sun, and besides, the peculiar yellow clay of which they were made is still found on Tinicum Island Previous to 1698, we learn from Gabriel Thomas, who came to the colony before Penn, that "brickmakers have twenty shillings per thousand for their bricks at the kiln" Wool-combers, we are also told, "have for combing twelve pence per pound" It would seem from Thomas' account that even in that early day the people of the colony had turned their attention to producing articles of daily use, for he informs us that all sorts of very good paper was made at Germantown, and a fine German linen, 'such as no person of quality need be ashamed to wear, and in several places they make very good Druggets, crapes, camblets, and serges, besides other woolen clothes, the manufacture of all which daily improves" One of the first notices we have of the doings of the European settlers in Pennsylvania was that Governor Printz had built a yacht at Tinicum, and previous to 1758 we learn from Acrelius that Marcus Hook was noticeable for the building of ships, and in 1727 the first paper-mill in the old county of Chester was erected at the present Ivy Mills, in Concord In 1715, John Camm, a stocking-weaver, was located in Upper Providence, and in 1723 he warned the public against one Mathew Burne, who had been in his emplôy two years, part of the time at stocking-weaving, and that Burne was no longer connected with him, but "goes about selling stockings in John Camm's name" when the articles were not made by him Strange as it may seem, until William T Seal[1] had shown the contrary, this Mathew Burne was credited with having made the first stocking as a regular manufacturer in the United States But of more particular interest to our present purpose is Gabriel Thomas' reference to "the famous Darby river which comes down from Cumbry by Darby town, whereon are several mills, viz, fulling-mills, corn-mill, &c" Of course, these fulling-mills did not manufacture, but simply scoured the cloth made by the busy housewives of that day The wives and daughters of the early English settlers, as the Swedes who had preceded them, employed "themselves in spinning wool and flax, and many of them in weaving"[2]

During all the period before the Revolutionary war, the greater number of farmers in the colonies had looms for weaving in their dwellings, on which the women wove flax and tow-linen, cloth, and linsey-woolsey of coarse texture but strong and substantial Indeed, when power other than manual labor was first applied to any part of the process of preparing the raw material to manufacture linen, cotton, or woolen cloths, the mills were very small, containing only a few hundred spindles, where yarn simply was produced, which was afterwards woven by hand in the farm-houses From that fact the coarse fabrics of that day, in contra-distinction of the imported goods, were known as "domestic," a term which has been continued as the name of shirtings and sheetings even to this day, although the reason for the name had ceased a half-century ago So general was this individual manufacturing carried on in the colonies to the north of Maryland that David Dulany, the great lawyer of that colony, in 1765, wrote that "the poorest sort of people to the Northward make all their clothes"[3]

The unprecedented growth of the United States after the Revolution early directed the attention of thoughtful men to the subject of American manufactures, and foremost in advocacy of the establishment of such industries was Tench Coxe, of Philadelphia, —a member of our bar, and Assistant Secretary of the Treasury under Hamilton It is now generally conceded that the first manufactory of textile fabrics in the Union was established by Samuel Wetherell, in Philadelphia, previous to 1782, at which date he was making "Jeans, Fustins, Everlastings, Coatings, &c," suitable for every season of the year, as he informed the public by his advertisement in the *Pennsylvania Gazette* in April, 1782 Near the close of the year 1791, William Pollard, of Philadelphia, obtained a patent for cotton-spinning which was, we are told by Samuel Weller,[4] the first water-frame put in motion in Pennsylvania, but the enterprise failing, its want of success retarded the progress of cotton-spinning in that vicinity The time, however, was fast approaching when the spirit of enterprise, born of necessity, would stimulate the development of the manufacture of textile goods to an abnormal extent

[1] "History of Hosiery Industry in Philadelphia"—*Textile Journal*, March, 1883

[2] Campanius, p 90

[3] *Penna Mag of History*, vol iii p 148

[4] Manual of Power, pp 22-28

In the new era of industrial progress which was coming, the county of Delaware occupied no secondary position in the story of that time, but it marched abreast of the commonwealth in the movement which has resulted in placing Pennsylvania in the fore-front of manufacturing States As early as 1810, we are told by Dr. Smith,[1] an English family named Bottomly erected an addition to an old saw-mill on a small stream in Concord, and converted it into a woolen factory, to the great astonishment of the people in that neighborhood Dennis Kelley, the same author informs us, with the assistance of a Mr Wiest, about the beginning of the war, erected a small stone factory on Cobb's Creek, in Haverford, which enterprises, owing to the embargo and the demand for goods by the national government created by the war and the want of the people generally, the factory was compelled to run night and day up to its full capacity. The statement of Dr Smith, however, does not give our county its due credit in early manufacturing, for in Upper Darby, in 1798, Nathan and David Sellers had a cotton-mill, and, in Darby, Isaac Oakford had a fulling-mill and stamping-works At that date John Orna was employed there as a calico-stamper and Samuel Wetherington as a calico-printer Previous to May, 1812, Benjamin Smith and William Stedham had begun spinning and carding at William Siter's clover-mill, near the Spread Eagle Tavern, in Radnor, and advertised that they had placed a spinning-machine in their building "which will work for customers," and also setting forth the prices demanded by them for their labor

These factories were small, but the almost total prohibition of European goods had advanced the prices of American fabrics to such extravagant rates, and the profits realized to the manufacturers were so large, that it naturally stimulated men of means, desirous of rapidly making large fortunes, to embark in the business The result was that cotton- and woolen-mills sprang up in all parts of New England, and quite a number were located in the Middle States In the latter the majority were woolen-factories The war, as usually is the case, had inflated every article in prices,—flour had advanced to ten and fifteen dollars a barrel, a statement also true as respected other commodities, while real estate, during the time the nation was practically shut out from the world, had doubled and in many instances quadrupled in its supposed valuation No sooner was peace declared than the storehouses of the Old World opened, and the superior articles of European manufacture were thrown into the American market, and being offered at less prices than the actual cost of the coarsest domestic goods, found ready sale. The English mill-owners, pressed to meet their obligations at home, realized, even at a loss on their stock, in the vain hope of being able to withstand the pressure of a falling market, and succeeded in merely prolonging the period of their financial ruin But it finally came to them as it did to their American rivals

The public mind in this country, notwithstanding the present losses, had been aroused to the possibilities of manufacturing on a large scale, and the intervention of Congress was had in the tariff act of 1816, which imposed a duty of twenty-five per cent *ad valorem* on all cotton cloths for three years, the minimum valuation at the port of exportation being fixed at twenty-five cents per square yard, which was a specific duty of six and a quarter cents on every yard The tariff bill, however, was a sliding one, providing for a reduction of twenty per cent *ad valorem* at the end of three years, and the same rate was applicable to cotton twist, yarn, or thread, unbleached costing less than sixty cents per pound, and bleached or colored less than seventy-five cents per pound Delaware County had, as before stated, become largely interested in manufacturing, and then, as now, the people, irrespective of party, were ardent advocates of protection Public meetings were then held to give expression to this opinion The first gathering of citizens in this county friendly to "Domestic Industry," which I have met with, was held at the Rose Tree Tavern, then kept by Isaac Cochran, on July 3, 1819, of which meeting Maj William Anderson acted as president, and John Wilson secretary It was there

"*Resolved*, That George G Leiper, William Anderson, Benjamin Pearson, John Mattson, and John Willcox be a committee to draft articles for the formation of a society in Delaware County, and an address to the citizens to promote the important national object of fostering national industry"

The officers of the meeting were also instructed to publish the proceedings in the *Village Record*, *Downingtown Republican*, and Philadelphia papers, after which it adjourned to August 14th If there was any subsequent meeting at the time designated, I have failed to find reference to it in the newspapers of that day

In Delaware County the majority of cotton- and woolen-factories after the war, most of them hastily built or changed from ancient grist-mills and filled with crude machinery, were compelled to close, while the larger number were sold by the sheriff to meet the outstanding obligations of their owners Indeed, we are told by John P Crozer that about 1821 only one cotton-factory in Delaware County was in successful operation,—that of Wagstaff & Englehorn, and that that firm could continue was mainly due to the fact that the senior member of the firm was a practical cotton-spinner from England [2]

In considering that period of our history it should not be overlooked that all Europe as well as the

[1] History of Delaware County, p 353

[2] Life of John P Crozer, page 51 It is to be regretted that neither Mr Crozer nor Dennis Kelly, both actively engaged in manufacturing in Delaware County, and both familiar with the story of its early struggles, have left no extended historical account of that industry, presenting its birth, growth, and ultimate establishment as the leading industry in Delaware County

United States had just emerged from war, the long Napoleonic contest which had drained the resources of the Old World's governments to maintain armies in the field and navies on the sea. There, as here, on the cessation of hostilities business enterprises crumbled under the sudden withdrawal of the governments from the markets as purchasers, and failure followed failure as a rule. But in England, as on the Continent and in the United States, an impetus had been imparted to manufacturing industries which could merely be impeded, not arrested, and in the end its importance to mankind far outweighed the defeat of the great captain at Waterloo.

In the general depression of that period all suffered, and no class more severely than owners of real estate. In cases where farms and town-lots were encumbered, in the event of the foreclosure of the mortgages it rarely happened that properties when forced to sale brought more than the charge against them, and, although in Delaware County such sales were not so numerous as in other counties in this State, the rule stated maintained in almost every case.

In manufacturing, the protection offered by the tariff law aided largely in the ultimate success of these enterprises; but of greater importance was the introduction of power-looms, and to that fact more than the tariff should be ascribed the permanent establishment of cotton manufactories as a national industry. In 1826 we find that in Delaware County there were then fourteen woolen-mills, employing 228 hands; twelve cotton factories, employing 415 hands; and one power-loom mill, with 200 looms, employing 120 hands.

Six years afterwards, in 1832, there were eleven cotton-mills, employing 600 hands, and using a total of 19,500 spindles; three cotton-weaving mills, employing 480 hands and 400 power-looms; two cotton-spinning mills, employing 120 hands; and eight woolen-mills, with 350 hands; the entire yearly production being a total of $950,000. In the documents transmitted to Congress from Pennsylvania in that year, John P. Crozer stated that he had established his mill in 1825, that it was run by water-power, and that the capital invested was fifteen thousand dollars. From the year 1829 to 1830 the business had yielded him no profit, but since that time until he made the report it had been paying an average profit of eight per cent. on the capital invested, and that he annually expended two-fifths of that income in improvements. Woolen-mills, he stated, were doing better than that. At his mills the consumption of cotton was three hundred and eighty-three bales a year, and in the article he made there was no competition by foreign goods. At that time his mill gave employment to fifteen men, sixteen women, and twenty children, who worked twelve hours daily all the year round. The production of the mill was sold in Philadelphia to owners of looms on a credit of four months. If the tariff of twelve and a half cents, as provided in the bill pending before Congress at that time, should become a law, he stated he would be compelled to abandon the business; for although at the time no duties were necessary to protect him against foreign competition, yet the then tariff was not sufficient to absolutely protect him from European sacrifices. Finally, as a general conclusion, he declared that cotton-spinning was a "very uninviting" occupation.

It is unnecessary to continue the narrative of manufacturing in this county, as a whole, further at this time. The story of the rise, progress, success, and decay of the various industrial establishments will be given in the histories of the several townships and boroughs wherein such works have been or are located.

Free Public Education.—At the session of the Legislature in 1830–31, the first steps were taken towards a general free education of the children of the commonwealth by providing for the levying of a tax to create a school fund. At that time John Lindsay was the representative from Delaware County in the House, and John Kerlin in the Senate. It will be required here to retrace our steps. That Penn's intention before coming to his province was to provide for public instruction is evident from the twelfth article of his frame of government, which declared "that the Governor and Provincial Council shall erect and order all public schools," which declaration is twice repeated by the General Assembly, the last time in 1696. At the second General Assembly, held at Philadelphia March 10, 1683, when Penn personally presided, the general laws, chapter cxii., provided,—

"And to the End that Poor as well as Rich may be instructed in good and Commendable learning, Which is to be preferred before Wealth, Be it, &c., That all persons in this Province and Territories thereof, having Children, and all the Guardians or Trustees of Orphans, shall cause such to be instructed in Reading and writing; so that they may be able to read the Scriptures, and to write by that time they attain to twelve years of age. And that then they be taught some useful trade or skill, that the poor may work to live, and the rich, if they become poor, may not want. Of which every county court shall take care; And in case such parents, guardians, or overseers, shall be found deficient in this respect, every such parent, guardian, or overseer, shall pay for every such Child, five pounds, Except there should appear an incapacity in body or understanding to hinder it."

This law was abrogated by William and Mary in 1693, but in the laws "made and past" in the same year when Benjamin Fletcher as captain-general of Pennsylvania had superseded Penn's authority the law numbered twenty-five was enacted, entitled "The law about education of youth." It presents the foregoing provisions in the same language, except where it applies to guardians and trustees of orphan children, and in these cases those having the care of such minors were required to have them taught to read and write, provided the wards had "sufficient estate and ability so to do."[1] It nowhere appears in our colonial history, so far as I have learned, that public funds

[1] Duke of York's Laws, p. 238.

were set apart to pay the costs of educating the youth even in the slight acquirements then deemed essentials, but where such information was imparted, the costs of tuition must be discharged by the parent or guardian of the children so taught. By the middle of the last century it had become a practice generally in townships throughout the present county of Delaware, to provide schools for the instruction of youths to which the several residents of the neighborhood made voluntary contribution, but the sum so contributed was a contract that could be enforced by process of law. The idea, however, of free public instruction for the children of persons in indifferent circumstances is presented throughout all our State history. The section of the Constitution of 1776 which provided that "a school or schools shall be established in each county by the Legislature for the convenient instruction of youth, with such salaries to the teachers paid by the public as may enable them to instruct youth at low prices," did not bring into existence the free-school system of which we are now so proud, nor did the seventh article of the Constitution of 1790, which directed that "the Legislature shall, as soon as conveniently may be, provide by law for the establishment of schools throughout the State, in such manner that the poor may be taught gratis."

As far back in our county annals as 1794 we find Dr. William Martin, of the borough of Chester, in a lengthy article in the *Aurora* (a Philadelphia paper) for December 31st, urging the establishment of public seminaries of learning; but his views were far in advance of the times. On April 4, 1809, the Legislature enacted a law—the pauper law, as Thaddeus Stevens termed it—that the children of parents too poor to provide for the education of their offspring out of their own means, could have proper instruction given them at the public cost, and directing how the expenses thereby incurred should be defrayed. The act of April 3, 1831, provided that all money due the State by holders of patented lands, and all fees received by the land-office, should be invested until the interest annually would amount to one hundred thousand dollars, after which time the interest was to be applied to the support of common schools throughout the commonwealth. At the time of the passage of the act of April 1, 1834, about half a million dollars had been received from the sources named, and the opponents of the school law of 1834—for they were many and included a large number of the ablest and best men of the State—were clamorous in their denunciation of the Legislature for having, as they alleged, violated their plighted faith in providing for the support of the schools by direct taxation instead of waiting until the fund set apart in 1831 had accumulated to two millions of dollars, when the interest alone should be applied to the maintenance of the schools. The act of April 1, 1834, however, was submitted to the various townships in Delaware County, when the result showed that fourteen townships were favorable to the adoption of the law and seven against it. Dr. George Smith at that time was the senator from this district, and Samuel Anderson, representative, both of whom were warm friends of the measure, Dr. Smith being particularly active in advocacy of the bill. The opponents of the law in this county assembled Oct. 30, 1834, at the public-house of Isaac Hall, in Nether Providence, and the list of the committee then appointed indicates how strong and influential that opposition was. The meeting was presided over by Benjamin Pearson, and Jonas P. Yarnall was secretary. The following resolution was unanimously adopted:

"*Resolved*, That we disapprove of the law passed at the last session of the Legislature as a system of general education, believing that it is unjust and impolitic. That it was never intended by our Constitution that the education of those children whose parents are able to educate them should be educated at the public expense."

Dr. Joseph Wilson, Joseph Gibson, James S. Peters, George Lewis, and Benjamin Pearson were appointed a committee to draft a memorial to the General Assembly, which contained a statement that while not disapproving of the clause of the Constitution providing for the education of the poor gratis, yet the law of 1834 was oppressive inasmuch as it "imposed a disproportionate and unreasonable burden on the middle class of the community, who can partake but little of its benefits;" that the authority of the school directors under its provisions was unlimited, having power to tax the citizens to any extent, and being "responsible to nobody;" that the assessments for State and county purposes were sufficiently oppressive "without any addition to carry into operation an experiment of doubtful efficacy," and for these reasons they petitioned for the repeal of the law. Capt. James Serrill and Joseph Bunting were appointed a committee to have the memorial printed, and a committee of sixty-four persons was appointed to circulate printed copies for signatures, which papers were to be returned to the chairman by the first Monday of November following.

In the mean time the friends of the law were not less active, for on Nov. 4, 1834, the school delegates in the various townships, excepting those of Aston and Concord, together with the county commissioners, met in the court-house at Chester in accordance with the provisions of the act. George G. Leiper was chairman, and Homer Eachus secretary. The proceedings were not harmonious, but a resolution was adopted by a vote of thirteen to nine, providing that two thousand two hundred dollars should be appropriated for school purposes, and a meeting of the citizens at the usual places of election in each township was called to be held in the afternoon of November 20th to ratify or reject the action of the deputies. Those citizens who favored the act also assembled in convention at Hall's Tavern, in Nether Providence, on Nov. 13, 1834, when William Martin acted as president; J. Walker, Jr., and I. E.

Bonsall, vice-presidents, and J S White and A D Williamson as secretaries That meeting adopted the following resolution

"*Resolved*, That the tax levied by the Commissioners and Delegates ought to be extended to bonds, mortgages, stocks, etc, in the same proportion as on real estate, and that in order to raise an additional tax for the support of common schools, that the directors in the several districts shall meet as directed in the Seventh Section, and determine whether there shall be an additional tax, and if they decide in the affirmative, then the Clerk of the Board shall notify the directors, who shall determine the amount and be authorized to levy and collect such tax on bonds, mortgages and profitable occupations, as well as real estate, and the proper officers of the townships constitute a Court of Appeal in case any person may think himself aggrieved in the amount of tax so levied by said Directors"

The second resolution indorsed the course of Governor Wolf in the matter of popular education, as also that of the members of the General Assembly who had voted for the measure, and the third resolution appointed William Amies, Dr Jesse Young, Spencer McIlvain, Samuel T Walker, and William Martin to prepare a memorial to be presented to the Legislature This memorial stated that the signers were "deeply impressed with the importance of a proper system of education by common schools throughout the State They have examined the last act passed at the last session of the Legislature for that purpose, and are of opinion that the objects contemplated by the law would be greatly promoted by an alteration in the mode for raising the fund necessary to support public schools So far as the law bears equally on all, they cheerfully acquiesce in it, but some of its provisions they deem burdensome and unequal in their operations on a portion of their fellow-citizens The landed interest, as the law now exists, pays nearly the whole expense of the system, while many that are proper objects of taxation contribute but a very small proportion"

The memorial therefore suggested that bonds, mortgages, money at interest, and occupations should be taxed, as well as a fixed proportion to be paid by real estate, that such sums as may be necessary, beyond the State appropriation, should be levied by the school directors as a township tax, while the township officers should act as a Board of Redress The memorial concluded

"Your memorialists remonstrate against a repeal of the law, and are only desirous that the matter may have your deliberate consideration, sensible that such amendments will be adopted as you may deem most beneficial and just, tending to equalize the operations of the law, the effects of which will strengthen the system, disseminate knowledge among the people, the only sure means of perpetuating the principles of national Liberty"

Those opposed to the law presented thirty-three petitions to the Legislature, containing one thousand and twenty-four names, while those remonstrating against its repeal presented thirteen petitions, bearing eight hundred and seventy-three names It is creditable to Delaware County that the remonstrants against the repeal of the school law exceeded in numbers almost threefold that from any other county in the State

James W Baker, superintendent of the public schools of Delaware County, in his report for the year 1877, presented an interesting and valuable history of education in this county, in which he says, "On the 4th of November, 1834, of the twenty-one districts of the county, eleven accepted the law, viz, Birmingham, Chester, Haverford, Lower Chichester, Marple, Nether Providence, Radnor, Ridley, Upper Darby, and Upper Chichester In consequence of the obscurity of the law, and the difficulty of putting it in operation, only six accepted it the following year; but in 1836 all the districts but one accepted the new law enacted that year The last one joined the others in 1838"[1] On the other hand, in the report of James Findlay, secretary of the commonwealth, on the subject of common schools, submitted to the Legislature and dated March 2, 1835, it is stated that in Delaware County all the school districts had accepted the law, that the State appropriation was one thousand seventy dollars and ninety-three cents, and that two thousand two hundred dollars had been voted to be raised in that county by tax[2]

The narrative of the rise and progress of the beneficent public school system is from this time part of the story of the several townships, and will be therein related under the proper heading

On July 4, 1834, the equipped militia of Delaware County, as was usual with those organizations at that time, celebrated Independence Day with a parade, followed by a banquet On that occasion Gen Root presided, and at his right hand was a militia colonel, who was called on for a toast The latter, not having prepared himself, trusted to his genius and the occasion to creditably propose a sentiment when the time came, sat a moment in thought, and finally concluded his toast ought to be something of a military nature The guests called again upon the colonel before he had fully determined what he would say. In response, he arose and announced in a loud voice, "The military of our country—may they never want——" Here he hesitated,—"may they never want!" He came to a full stop, and looking imploringly at Gen Root, he whispered, "What the devil shall I say next?" "And never be wanted," whispered back the general "And never be wanted," roared the colonel The joke was too good to prevent it being related, and at length it found its way into the newspapers of the day, and now it is so popularly known in the country that long since its birthplace was generally forgotten

The military history of the county, other than that occurring in times of actual war, is brief and of a spasmodic character, usually the ground-swell after

[1] Report of Superintendent of Public Instruction for 1877, p 239
[2] Hazard's Register of Pennsylvania, vol xv p 194

the storm of battle had subsided In our early annals, the Swedish settlers and the Dutch were more or less under military organization, as were the English previous to the coming of Penn In the Duke of York's book of laws considerable space is devoted to ordinances relating to military service, and providing for the maintenance of bodies of soldiers As early as 1673 the Council at New York directed the enlistment of ten or twelve men from settlers on the Delaware, and ordered that every sixth man of the inhabitants should be summoned to build a fort for the defense of the river Previous to that date the presumption is that the troops were recruited abroad, and were brought hither in the character of soldiers James Sandelands, we are told by Dr Smith, came to the Delaware River settlement as a private under Capt Carr's command, and was discharged in 1669 In May, 1675, there was a company enlisted, for at a court held at Peter Rambo's in that month, James Sandelands, as a punishment for a "scandalous business" (he had thrown a drunken Indian out of his tavern at Upland, and injured him so that he died from the effect of his fall), was sentenced to pay a certain sum towards building a new church at "Weckahoe," a like sum to the sheriff, and was "put off from being Captain" Hans Junian, who had been lieutenant, was made captain, John Prince lieutenant, and Jonas Keen ensign The new captain and ensign were residents of the present Delaware County

On Sept 23, 1675, Capt John Collyer was by Governor Andross appointed commander of Delaware River, and he was particularly required to take care that the militia in the several places should be well armed, duly exercised, and kept in order We know that previous to that date, towards the end of the year 1671, it was ordered, "That every person that can bear arms, from 16 to 60 years of age, be always provided with a convenient proportion of powder and bullets, fit for service and their mutual defense, upon a penalty for their neglect herein to be imposed by the commission-officers in command, according to law That the quantity or proportion of powder and shot to be adjudged competent for each person to be at least one pound of powder and two of bullet"

All that I have learned respecting military organizations in the county previous to the Revolution has already been related, which is equally true of the war of Independence After peace was assured the militia of the State was regulated by law The *Pennsylvania Packet* states that at a meeting of the Chester County militia, commanded by Edward Vernon, on Oct 25, 1789, Rev. James Conarroe, of Marcus Hook, was appointed chaplain This notice was after the county of Delaware had been erected, but Edward Vernon and Mr Conarroe were residents of the new county, and in all probability the entire organization they represented was from the southeasterly part of the old county of Chester (the present Delaware County) The act of 1792, organizing the militia of the State, continued in operation for forty years without any definite action being taken by the people to correct its provisions Under the law of April 9, 1799, the militia of the commonwealth was arranged into regiments From it we learn that "in the county of Delaware the regiments commanded by Lieut.-Colonel Levis shall be No 65, and by Lieut-Colonel Wilcocks, No 110" Five years previous to the latter act, Jonah Lamplugh was convicted at the January session, 1794, of refusing to discharge the duties of the office of collector of militia fines, to which he had been appointed

It is unnecessary to recall the incidents of the whiskey insurrection and the war of 1812, related elsewhere During the latter struggle, the Delaware County Troop was organized, with Dr Joseph Wilson as captain, and it was commanded by Capt Pearson Smith when it took part in the ceremonies at the dedication of the Paoli Monument, Sept 20, 1817 The next year Dr Wilson again became its captain, and its lieutenants Baker and Cornog, and George Kirk quartermaster

In 1820, the Troop was reorganized, with John Hinkson, captain, Samuel M Leiper, first lieutenant; John Wells, second lieutenant, Evans Way, first sergeant, and George Kirk, color sergeant For some years it was part of the first squadron of Montgomery, Chester, and Delaware County cavalry In time interest in the organization began to flag, and it was believed that it might be revived in 1830, when an election was held, which resulted in the selection of Samuel M Leiper as captain, Edward H Engle as first lieutenant, John Wells as second lieutenant, Evans Way as first sergeant, and George Kirk as color sergeant The interest had gone, however, and after dragging along for six years the organization, in 1836, finally disbanded The Delaware County Blues was also an outgrowth of the war of 1812, and was commanded at first by Capt George Hawkins, and subsequently by Capt George Litzenberg It preserved its organization until 1836, when it also disbanded In 1817 the Delaware County Fencibles was commanded by Capt George G Leiper, and as such took part in the ceremonies at Paoli Judge Leiper was subsequently lieutenant-colonel of the Delaware County Battalion, and on Sept 4, 1823, announced his appointment of George Litzenberg as adjutant, Charles Bonsall quartermaster, and Dr Morris C Shallcross as surgeon Dr Wilson was major of the battalion, Capt George Hawkins had command of the Delaware County Blues, Capt Myers of the Delaware County Volunteers, and Capt. Weaver of the Pennsylvania Artillerists The latter company was organized about 1819, with John J. Richards as captain, and at his death, in 1822, Joseph Weaver, Jr, succeeded to the command, to give place in 1828 to Capt William Martin, and he subsequently to Samuel A Price The latter officer, in 1832, was colonel of the First Brigade, Third Division, and with Lieut John K Zeilin and J

M G Lescure, represented the county of Delaware at the military convention of the State, which assembled at Harrisburg January 2d of that year Col Price was one of the four vice-presidents of that convention He was succeeded in command of the Pennsylvania Artillerists by Capt John K Zeilin In 1817 the Union Troop, of Chester and Delaware Counties, was a military organization existing in the two counties, and at Paoli in 1817 had the right of the line under the command of Capt Harris This organization continued until 1838, when it was commanded by Capt William Haines, and John Lindsay was its first lieutenant In 1824 the Forty-ninth Regiment of militia of the county of Delaware was commanded by Col John Smith, Lieut-Col Benjamin F Johnson, and Maj Abner Barrett, while the Thirty-eighth Regiment, of the same county, was commanded by Col Benjamin Wetherby, Lieut-Col Benjamin Smith, and Maj Jonathan David

In 1857, the Delaware County Volunteers, organized about 1822, was disbanded, and from its fragments a new company—the Harmony Rangers—was formed, Capt Jesse L Green commanding, who was succeeded by Capt Simon Leany It was disbanded in 1842 In 1834, Lieut-Col Henry Myers was in command of the Delaware County Volunteer Battalion, succeeding Col George G Leiper in that office

Besides the foregoing military organizations, in 1824 there was a company of militia known as the Washington Artillerists, in 1833 the Union Guards, Capt George Kirk, and Jesse Sharpless orderly sergeant, and in 1840 the Delaware County Rangers, Capt Samuel Hall

On Friday, Oct 11, 1833, the City Troop of Philadelphia, commanded by Capt Hart, was met at Darby by the Delaware County Troop and escorted to Chester, where they remained until the Monday following, when they returned to Philadelphia, stopping to dine on that day at the tavern kept by J. R Lamplugh, in Darby

During the riots of 1844 in Philadelphia, a meeting was held at the court house in Chester, on July 15th, at which resolutions were adopted calling for the immediate organization of a corps of volunteers, "citizen soldiers," which body was directed to be equipped and armed, so that, if necessary, the authorities could call on it to preserve public order The next day, July 16, 1844, the Union Troop of Delaware and Chester Counties marched to Philadelphia, reaching that city in the evening, when they immediately relieved the Philadelphia Cavalry, which had been in service for some days, and were then worn out from loss of sleep

In August, 1844, the Delaware County Grays were organized by the election of John K Zeilin, captain, Charles W Raborg, first lieutenant, and Joseph Taylor second lieutenant. The following year the Forty-ninth Regiment of militia, in this county, was commanded by Col John K. Zeilin, and C W Raborg was adjutant, while the companies composing the organization were commanded by Capts Walter, Johnson, Crosby, Eyre, Ulrich, and Irwin The public feeling was then strongly adverse to military service On May 13, 1845, Maj Charles Peck, brigade inspector, visited Chester, reaching that place an hour before noon, when some of the older citizens waited on him, and apprised him that the boys in the town were armed with eggs, which they proposed to present to him in no quiet manner, and he hurried away without inspecting the undisciplined militia, which had assembled for that purpose, according to his published orders On Saturday, June 13, 1846, the Delaware County Grays were inspected by Maj Peck, Capt Zeilin having, through Governor Shunk, offered the services of the company to President Polk for the Mexican war The quota of Pennsylvania being filled, however, the offer was not accepted

The next year Maj Peck again visited Chester, when he was made the victim of a practical joke, which, as tradition ascribed, was suggested by John M Broomall Several of the practical jokers who then infested Chester induced the major to visit the prison, on the pretext that within its ancient precincts were several relics of the long ago worthy of the notice of a stranger The plan worked to a charm After the party had gained admission to the jail, the door was locked behind them, the keys were concealed, and all that day until evening the military gentleman and two of the roysters of Chester stood looking through a grated window in the second story, calling to the people below in the street to procure their release The keys could not be found until night had nearly come, but several times during the day the imprisoned men lowered strings to the crowd below and drew them up with provisions and other refreshments attached thereto After his release Maj Peck had several other jokes played upon him before he shook the dust of Chester from his feet, never to return to it again

Not only was the brigade inspector personally trifled with, but the commissioners of Delaware County failed to enforce the collection of the militia tax; hence Maj Peck instructed his counsel to bring suit against the county commissioners for their neglect in not issuing duplicates to the collectors for collection of the military fines The suit, however, never was pressed, the act being repealed by the Legislature in 1849

The following is the list of persons holding the office of brigade inspector for Delaware County, so far as I have been able to obtain their names

William Brooke, lieutenant of the county of Delaware	Aug 21, 1791
William Brooke, brigade inspector	April 11, 1793
John Crosby, brigade inspector	
John Crozer, brigade inspector	April 30, 1799
William Brooke, brigade inspector	April 25, 1800
Casper Snyder, brigade inspector	April, 1813
Col James Peck, brigade inspector	April, 1815
Nathaniel Brooke, brigade inspector	April, 1824
Thomas James brigade inspector	April, 1838
Maj Charles Peck, brigade inspector	April, 1842
Walter J Arnold, brigade inspector	April, 1861

Maj Arnold was appointed in 1859, but did not take out his commission until the attack on Sumter made it necessary to have such an officer to aid in forwarding troops in the early days of the civil war.

CHAPTER XIV

STORMS, FRESHETS, AND EARTHQUAKES

WE have little save tradition respecting storms, freshets, and earthquakes in the olden times It is only within the last half-century that any circumstantial records have been kept of such incidents in our annals On March 22, 1662,[1] William Beckman, in a letter, mentions the day before the tide in the Delaware was so high that a "galiot" was driven out of the Kil, but was recovered by the sailors of the ship "Di Purmerlander Kerck" The same night she was driven to the other (New Jersey) side of the river, and again the sailors rescued her from destruction

In 1683 we know that Chester mill and dam, which was located at the present site of Upland, "were soon carried away by the flood," and subsequent thereto a new dam, saw- and grist-mill was erected at that point, but the second dam, we are told in 1705, was "carried away by the flood"[2] In 1740, tradition states, an extraordinary and destructive freshet occurred in all the creeks in the county, but beyond that fact no particulars have been handed down to the present generation In the winter of 1795 a heavy, warm rain occasioned the melting of the snow on the hills and the ice in the runs and creeks of Delaware County, but as the streams were not, as in more recent years, blocked with dams, which backed up the water until the weight broke away the obstruction, the damage then sustained, although at the time it occurred regarded as great, was trifling when compared with that of 1843 In 1822 a noticeable freshet occurred in Delaware County consequent "on the rapid melting of the deep snow The mill-ponds were covered with a thick ice, which was broken up, and occasioned considerable damage in addition to that caused by the weight of the water in the creeks"[3] And again, in November, 1830, when the river rose so high that the piers at Chester were submerged and the embankments on the river were overflowed

On Friday night, Jan 24, 1839, rain began to fall, and continued without intermission until Saturday afternoon, when it ceased, the snow and ice, melting under the warm rains, filling the streams until they became more swollen than had happened for forty years before, and the ice, broken into masses and cakes, crashed and ground against each other as the rising water swept them outward to the river In many places the ice gorged the streams, damming the waters up until the pressure became so great that the temporary obstacle was torn away, and the arrested torrent burst in one great wave onward in its course, sweeping away mill-dams, bridges, and doing other damages as it sped seaward. The Westtown stage, as it crossed the hollow on the Providence side, near the bridge on Crum Creek, on the road from Springfield meeting-house to Rose Tree Tavern, was carried away by the irresistible velocity of the current, which rushed round the wing walls of the bridge at a distance of about eighty yards from that structure When the stage was borne away by the water it fortunately contained but two passengers, Joseph Waterman and a colored woman They, as well as the driver, succeeded in getting free from the vehicle, and, catching some bushes as they swept along, managed to support themselves until assistance came The driver finally swam to shore after being in the water three-quarters of an hour, while the passengers were extricated from their unhappy plight by means of ropes lowered to them by the residents in the neighborhood, who gathered to their assistance, but not until they had been in the icy water nearly three hours and were almost frozen One of the horses was drowned, and the other was not taken out until four hours had elapsed[4] On Saturday afternoon two sons of George Serrill, of Darby, made an attempt to save two horses on the marsh, a few miles below that village, but it was impossible to get to the animals, and turning to retrace their way the water had risen so much that the horses they rode became fractious, and plunged down a bank into the main creek The riders swam ashore, abandoning the animals, but the latter also landed safely The two horses on the meadow remained there until the Tuesday following before they could be reached and some hay taken to them They were found in almost three feet of water, and so completely surrounded by ice that it was impossible to extract them On Saturday evening a widow woman and her six children, living on Tinicum meadow, had to be taken off in a boat, the water at the time surrounding the house to the depth of seven

[1] N Y Historical Record, vol xii p 365

[2] Deed for Samuel Carpenter to Caleb Pussey, Dec 19, 1705

[3] Smith's "History of Delaware County," p 355

[4] John C Beatty states that George Dunn, seeing the woman in the water, ran half a mile and got a rope from the Rock House, and making it fast he sprang into the stream, swam to the woman, and by means of the rope she was drawn ashore When the news was brought to the axe factory six or eight men ran to the place and found Waterman standing on a post in a fence below the bridge It was learned he could not swim, and just after this fact was made known a cake of ice struck the post, throwing him into the current For twenty minutes he was not seen, and then he was discovered standing on another post, his face just out of the water A tree was felled so that it reached towards him, and George Dunn walked along it and cast a rope to Waterman, who caught it, and he was drawn ashore Next spring, after the ice had all washed away, Mr Beatty found the canvas mail-bag, but its contents were entirely ruined

feet. The inmates had sought safety in the second story, and were taken out through the window famishing and almost frozen. Severe as was the condition of that family, the situation of a man, his wife, and four children, residing on the bank of the Delaware, who had remained without food or fire for three days until relief came, was more distressing. One of the children was so benumbed with the cold that it was totally blind for nearly a day, while the other little ones were all more or less frost-bitten. The party who went to their assistance bore the children in their arms along the bank, between three and four miles, to a place of safety. A family residing on the meadow, between Darby Creek and the Schuylkill (not in Delaware County), seemed absolutely beyond relief, for around the dwelling for miles the ice and water had accumulated. But on Saturday afternoon a large boat was manned and pushed out across the meadow in the direction of the dwelling. The water froze on the oars, and the drifting ice-cakes seemed as if they would crush the boat, so heavily did they strike against its sides, but the crew held firmly to their purpose, and succeeded in rescuing the family, —a man, wife, and two children,—who without fire, food, and but scantily clothed, were in a perishing condition when help came to them. They were landed at William Davis' house on Darby Creek, who sheltered them. The woman was so completely exhausted that no sooner had she been received into Mr. Davis' dwelling than she fainted, and was with difficulty revived.

Many bridges were swept away and dam-breasts broken by the pressure of the flood; that at Penn's Grove and Rockdale was completely demolished. On Chester Creek, at Knowlton, John P. Crozer sustained damages amounting to five thousand dollars; William G. Flower, from Chester Mills, had fifty thousand feet of lumber floated away; William Eyre, Jr., of Chester, lost fifteen hundred feet of lumber; J. P. & William Eyre had fifty tons of coal swept off the wharf at the same place, and Samuel Bancroft had a boat loaded with coal to sink at the dock; Jabez Bunting, of Darby, lost three horses by the flood, and a break was made in the bank of Darby Creek, which caused the overflow of the Philadelphia, Wilmington and Baltimore Railroad, and interrupted travel for several days.

In four years after this freshet Delaware County was visited by a cloud-burst, which wrought wide-spread destruction along all the streams within its boundary that were of sufficient size to be termed water-powers. The circumstances connected with the noted "Lammas Flood" are briefly these:

On Saturday morning, Aug. 5, 1843, at daybreak, the sky indicated rain, and about seven o'clock a moderate fall set in, which, while it slackened, never entirely ceased until between the hours of two and six o'clock that afternoon, when the extraordinary opening of "the windows of heaven" took place which made such extended ruin and misery in a brief period of time. The rain, when falling most abundantly, came down in such showers that the fields in that part of the county removed several miles back from the river are said to have been flooded with water almost immediately, and where the road was lower than the surface of the ground on either side, the water poured into the highway in a constant stream of miniature cascades. The lightning played incessantly through the falling torrents, reflected from all sides in the watery mirrors in the fields producing a weird and spectral appearance, such that those who witnessed it could evermore recall. A peculiar feature of the storm was that Cobb's Creek, on the extreme eastern, and the Brandywine, on the western boundary of the county, were not swollen to any remarkable degree, clearly showing that the territory where the violence of the cloud-burst occurred was noticeably restricted to the feeders and bodies of Chester, Ridley, Crum, and Darby Creeks.

Dr. Smith states that "as a general rule, the heavy rain occurred later as we proceed from the source of the stream towards their mouths. The quantity of rain which fell decreases as we proceed in the same direction, particularly from the middle parts of the county downwards. In those sections of the county where its greatest violence was expended, the character of the stream more nearly accorded with that of a tropical hurricane than with anything which appertained to this region of country. The clouds wore an unusually dark and lowering appearance, of which the whole atmosphere seemed in some degree to partake, and this circumstance, no doubt, gave that peculiarly vivid appearance to the incessant flashes of lightning which was observed by every one. The peals of thunder were loud and almost continuous. The clouds appeared to approach from different directions, and to concentrate at a point not very distant from the zenith of the beholder. In many places there was but very little wind, the rain falling in nearly perpendicular streams; at other places it blew a stiff breeze, first from the east or northeast and suddenly shifting to the southwest, while at a few points it blew in sudden gusts with great violence, accompanied with whirlwinds, which twisted off and prostrated large trees, and swept everything before it."[1]

The hurricane which occurred in Bethel township during the storm is thus described:

"The wind blew from different points at different places in the same neighborhood, as is manifested from the position of uprooted trees, etc. A peach-orchard belonging to Mr. Clayton was blown down, the trees lying toward the northeast. An apple-orchard not very distant, lays prostrated towards the southeast. At John Larkins', two miles north of Clayton's, the gale appears to have been most violent.

[1] Dr. Smith's "History of Delaware County," p. 360.

The wind came from the southeast, and tore up a large quantity of heavy timber (said to be about two hundred cords) all in a narrow strip, not more than two hundred yards in width. A valley of woodland, bounded by pretty high hills, had nearly all of its timber blown down, and, what is very remarkable, the trees are not generally laid lengthwise of the valley but across it, with their tops towards the northeast, while on the adjacent hills but few trees were uprooted, one very large white-oak, however, which was deply and strongly rooted in a clay soil, was blown down."[1]

The almost instantaneous rise of the water in the creeks throughout the county is hardly paralleled in any flood on record, and the manner in which the current is related to have moved down the various streams to the Delaware would be incredible if it were not that the destruction it produced fully sustains the statements. In Cobb's Creek, as before mentioned, the water did not rise to a height beyond that usual in times of freshets, while Darby Creek, separated from Cobb's, in Upper Darby, by less than a mile of intervening land, was a wild, struggling torrent, swollen seventeen feet beyond its usual level, crushing even solid masonry before it as it rushed outward towards the river. Ithan Creek, a branch of Darby Creek, in Radnor, rose to such an unprecedented height that the arched stone bridge which spanned the stream on the old Lancaster road, near Radnor Friends' meeting-house, unable to vent the water, was undermined and fell, allowing the torrent to escape through its broken archway. On the west branch of Darby Creek, before that feeder enters Delaware County, considerable damage was done in broken dams, which, freeing the water therein restrained, resulted in augmenting largely the force of the freshet, which rushed in irresistible force to Hood's bridge, where the Goshen road crosses the creek, and the double arched stone structure there yielded before the mass of water that was hurled against it, attaining at that point a height of seven feet beyond the highest point ever before reached so far as records extend. In its mad career the torrent injured the mill-dam of Clarence and William P. Lawrence's grist-mill, and more than a hundred feet of the western wing wall of the stone bridge that spanned the creek on the West Chester road was swept away, the water reaching a point thirteen feet beyond its usual level. The stone bridge near where the Marple and Springfield line meets on Darby Creek had a large part of the guard wall demolished. At Heysville the lower story of the woolen-factory then occupied by Moses Hey was flooded and the machinery much injured, while the dam there was entirely swept away.

Farther down the stream the paper-mill of Palmer & Masker was badly damaged, thirty feet of the building was undermined and fell, a paper-machine ruined, while the race and dam were broken. Just below stood the paper-mill of Obern Levis, and there the water leveled the drying-house to its foundations, and, bursting through the doors and windows of the basement of the mill itself on one side, swept out at the other, doing great damage to the machinery and stock. A small cotton-factory at or near the site of the present Union Mills, above the Delaware County turnpike in Upper Darby, then occupied by John and Thomas Kent, was carried away by the flood, together with the machinery and stock, and an unoccupied dwelling was absolutely obliterated, nothing after the passage of the water remaining to mark the place whereon it stood. Three stone dwellings were partly carried away, and several private bridges were borne off by the current. At Kellyville the stone picker-house was washed away, together with the contents, and the basement story of the mill flooded. The next mill below, then owned by Asher Lobb's estate, on the Delaware County turnpike, and occupied by D. and C. Kelly, was flooded and the dam broken. It was here that a frame dwelling, near the bridge, occupied by Michael Nolan, his wife, five children, and a young woman, Susan Dowlan, was washed away. As the water swelled Nolan and his eldest son left the house to make arrangements to remove the family to a place of less danger, and not five minutes thereafter the wing wall of the bridge gave way, the loosened flood poured onward surrounding the house, and in half an hour bore the building from its foundations. The wife and four children were drowned. Susan Dowlan, when cast into the water, clutched as she was swept onward a branch of a tree, and thereby obtained a foothold on a knot which projected from its trunk in such a way that the trunk was interposed between her and the direction in which the floor was moving. Thus for nearly four hours she remained immersed to her waist in the water. When the freshet had subsided in a measure, Charles McClure, John Cunningham, and John Heller made an effort to rescue her. At great personal danger they ventured into the flood and obtained a position where the water was shoaling, but an angry torrent still rushed between them and the tree to which the woman clung. McClure, taking the end of a rope, swam to her, and fastening it around her she was drawn to a place of safety. When rescued she was so exhausted that she could not have held her footing much longer. The bodies of Mrs. Nolan and her four children were recovered the following day. The dam at Matthews' paper-mill, below Lobb's Run, was washed away to its foundation, and the water rushed violently through the floor of the mill, while farther on, at Bonsall's grist-mill, the dam and race were injured. The dam at Thomas Steel's mill, the last one on the creek at that time, was torn away completely, his cotton-house and stable removed by the flood, while the water, rising seventeen and a half feet at that point, inun-

[1] Report on the Great Storm and Flood, made to Delaware County Institute, Jan. 4, 1844, p. 11.

dated the lower floor of his factory When the large three-arched stone bridge at Darby, which had cost the county eleven thousand dollars, gave way and fell piece by piece until nothing but the abutments were left, Russell K Flounders and Josiah Bunting, Jr, the former twenty-one and the latter nineteen years of age, were standing on the bridge watching the angry waters, and were precipitated into the flood and perished The body of Flounders was found four days afterwards on the meadows two miles below, while Bunting's was not recovered for two weeks, when it was discovered wedged in among the broken arches of the bridge

In Crum Creek, immediately below the Chester County line, at Jonathan W Hatches' factory, a vacant dwelling-house was floated off, and the arch, one of the abutments, and part of each end of the wing walls of the stone bridge that spanned the creek on the West Chester road were washed away, while the stone arched bridge, known as Howard's bridge, on the road that intersected with the Newtown and Maple Line road, was almost destroyed Below this point and above Hunter's Run a sleeper bridge was bodily carried off its abutment At T Chalkley Palmer's flour-mills the torrent tore away a wide and strong embankment, swept into a ruin a stone wagon-house fifty feet in length, and caused other damages in the vicinity Trout Run, which empties into Crum Creek some distance below Palmer's mill, was so swollen that the dam at Willet Paxson's mill was broken down, and at the bridge that crosses the run on the road from Springfield meeting-house to the Rose Tree, the water forced a deep channel through the western abutment At Beatty's Hollow, where were located the edge-tool works, flour-, saw-, and plaster-mills owned by John C Beatty, the dam was broken All the buildings, except the flour-mill, together with the county bridge, which crosses the creek immediately below the works, were swept away Mr Beatty stated that in ten minutes the water rose seven or eight feet, that the bridge fell over as if there was no strength in it, the head gates burst, and "the edge-tool factory went with a tremendous crash, and in an instant there was nothing to be seen but water in the place where it stood"

The day of the flood Mr Beatty was putting in two new wheels and building a block for the head-block to rest on A neighbor seeing the work, said, "Mr Beatty, you are building a monument which will stand when you and your grandchildren are six feet under ground It can't get away" Yet at five o'clock that afternoon there was not a stone to be found in place Perciphor Baker, John Baker, and Mr Beatty went to the mill when they found the water rising, and at that time no water was within twenty-five feet of the door, yet five minutes afterwards Mr Beatty, chancing to look back, saw the water pouring in at the door they had just entered The three men got out of the window and ran across the race bridge not a moment too soon, for hardly had they reached a place of safety when the works and bridge were swept away before the wave of water, at least ten feet in height, which moved down the creek

At the paper-mill of John Lewis, now J Howard Lewis, part of the draw was swept away and the lower part of the mill flooded The wooden bridge which spanned the creek at the Philadelphia, New London and Baltimore turnpike road was carried off by the current, while the dam of George Lewis' cotton-mills —now Wallingford—was destroyed, as also a stone dye-house, and the lower story inundated, the water rising twenty feet above its usual level The dams at Strathaven and Avondale, the first located where Dick's Run enters the stream and the latter near where the Springfield roads cross Crum Creek (the factories at both places were then owned by William J Leiper and occupied by James Riddle), were partially swept away All the houses of the operatives at Avondale were submerged to the second stories, the county bridge had its guard wall destroyed, and a team of five horses was drowned, the water rising so rapidly that the animals could not be gotten out of the stable Farther down the creek George G Leiper's mill-dam was damaged and his canal broken, while a large tree coming down the stream root first was forced through one of the windows of the mill and got fastened in the machinery The stone bridge that crossed the Queen's Highway at Leiperville had a small portion of the western wing walls carried away, and thirty-six head of cattle belonging to John Holland, which had been borne down the stream, passed beneath the arch and succeeded in reaching the meadow below it uninjured

On Ridley Creek some slight damage occurred in Willistown, Chester Co, and the dam at the grist-mill of James Yarnall, near the county line, in Edgmont, on a stream that empties into Ridley Creek, sustained injury, while the county bridge that crosses the creek on the highway from Providence road to the school-house near Howellville, known as Russell's bridge, was injured to some extent At Amor Bishop's mill the dam was destroyed and the buildings considerably damaged Two houses, together with the furniture, were swept away Strangely, the bridge at this point remained intact, although the greater part of the abutments on the western side was overthrown by the water Edward Lewis' paper-mill below the Delaware County turnpike was demolished, as was also his saw-mill, and his flour-mill was nearly destroyed The county bridge above him was hurled from its place and went down with the flood Edward Lewis and his son, Edward, were in the third story of the grist-mill, when that structure began to yield and part of the walls fell, leaving them exposed in that perilous position They subsequently reached a place of safety by use of a rope The woolen-mill of Edward Taylor, then owned by Charles Sherman, was greatly injured, as well as the machinery and goods therein, the dam was destroyed and three houses carried away by the freshet. A double frame house, occupied by William Tombs and James Rigley and their families, floated down the stream, lodging against the factory, opposite a window in the picker-room. From the upper window of his house Rigley succeeded in passing his wife and child into the mill, and then rescued Tombs (who was ill at the time), his wife and two children from the garret of the house, to do which he was compelled to break a hole in the roof. How quickly he acted may be gathered from the fact that in six minutes from the time this house rested against the mill it was again whirling down the stream. Below the woolen-factory of Samuel Bancroft the water reached twenty feet above the usual level. A portion of the factory, fifty by thirty-six feet, was absolutely destroyed, a quantity of wool was washed away and lost, and four dwellings wrecked. The latter was a long stone building which had been altered into four houses. In one of the centre dwellings resided George Hargraves, his wife, five children, and his brother, William Hargraves, and in the adjoining one lived Thomas W. Brown, his wife and child. When the flood came they endeavored to secure the household goods in the basement; the water rose so rapidly that their escape was cut off, and they retreated to the second story. William Hargraves, finding the walls of the building yielding to the force of the flood, plunged into the water and was carried down the stream for more than half a mile until, catching in a standing tree, he succeeded in holding on until the flood subsided and he was saved. While there, his brother George and his four eldest children on a bed borne by the current, passed by, and a moment after William saw them hurled into the water and drowned. The bodies were found about nine miles farther down the stream, that of the youngest child firmly grasped in its father's arms. Jane Hargrave, the wife of George, when the water broke through the house, with her baby in her arms, was standing in a corner of the room, and strangely that part of the floor, only a few feet square, remained, and there the woman stood for five long hours until rescued by Thomas Holt. In the adjoining dwelling Thomas W. Brown, his wife, and child stood on a corresponding part of the floor where Mrs. Hargrave stood, only it was not more than half as large as that she occupied. All else of the two middle houses was carried away save that part of the wall which held up these broken pieces of the second-story flooring-boards.

On Vernon's Run, which empties into Ridley Creek, the dam of the flour-mill of Thomas Hutton was swept away. At Park Shee's paper-mill the breast of the dam and the buildings were much injured, and two small houses destroyed. Here the water rose to twenty feet. At Edward Taylor's lower factory,—now Bancroft's,—then owned by Charles Shermans, the dam was carried away, and the building used as a machine-shop and picker-house destroyed, together with the machinery therein. The basement story of the mill itself was submerged. The wooden county bridge on the road from Hinkson's to Sneath's Corner was swept away, and the abutments injured. Some damage was done to the rolling-mill of J. Gifford Johnson, while at the woolen- and flour-mills of Enos Sharpless, at Waterville, the water rose eighteen feet, flooding the basement story, doing considerable damage, and a counting-house, a bath-house, and a temporary bark-house floated off. The bridge was carried away, but lodged less than a mile down the creek, and was subsequently recovered. Three-fourths of the dam was destroyed. John M. Sharpless, at the same place, lost a cooper-shop and its contents, while at the stone bridge which spanned the creek on the Providence road the arches were swept away, and one of the abutments was almost entirely destroyed. At Pierce Crosby's mill—now Irving's—the water rose twenty-one feet above the usual level, the dam was carried away, one dwelling floated off, and the flour- and saw-mill much injured. The county bridge at Crosbyville was swept off its abutments and broken. Farther down the creek, at the Queen's Highway, the eastern abutment was washed out and the bridge whirled down the current, while the railroad bridge at the present Eddystone Station was greatly damaged and the tressel-work on the eastern side swept away.

On the east branch of Chester Creek the dam at the rolling and nail factory belonging to the estate of John Edwards, in Thornbury, was broken, and a like damage was done at the paper- and flour-mill of James M. Wilcox, where a protection wall at the end of his mill was torn away. The tilt-mill of Thomas Thatcher was absolutely destroyed, nothing remaining after the waters subsided but the tilt-hammer and grindstone. Grubb's bridge, on the State road, although not carried away, was badly injured. At Lenni the dam was destroyed and the county bridge rendered almost worthless, while about half a mile farther down the stream —at a large cotton factory belonging to the estate of Peter Hill, now Parkmount Mills, then unoccupied— the dam was broken and the mill injured.

It is necessary now to retrace our course up the east branch of Martin's or Rocky Run to David Green's cotton factory, located about half a mile south of Howellville. The dam here was washed away and the mill—the first story stone and the remainder frame—yielded to the torrents, and a large part of the stone work was removed, but sufficient remained to support the frame superstructure. The dam at the flour-mill of Humphrey Yearsley, in Middletown, about three-quarters of a mile south of the Edgmont line, gave way, as did also that at the saw-mill of Joseph Pennell, on Rocky Run, about three-quarters of a mile before the latter stream entered into the eastern branch of Chester Creek.

Ascending the west branch of the same stream, the first dam on Chester Creek was at Caleb Brinton's grist-, saw-, and clover-mill, in Thornbury, just above the Concord line, and here the dam gave way, as did also that of the flour-mill of Matthew Ash, in Concord, above Deborah's Run. The dam at the flour- and saw-mill of Casper W. Sharpless, about three-quarters of a mile lower down the stream, was broken, the water rising ten feet beyond its usual level. At the cotton-factory of Joseph M. Trimble, below the State road, the dam gave way, as did also that at the paper-mill of James M. Wilcox, at Ivy Mills. At this point the flood moved a store-house several feet, without destroying it. In Green Creek the water rose to an extraordinary height. At Samuel F. Peter's saw- and grist-mill, in Aston, just east of the Concord line and near the mouth of Green Creek, the dam was swept away and the saw-mill submerged to the roof. The freshet poured along the west branch and carried off the bridge where the Logtown road crosses that stream. At this place James Shelly Tyson's grist-mill was located, and here, as before, the dam broke and a dwelling-house was floated off. One mile below this point was the West Branch Mills of John P. Crozer, and less than a half-mile beyond, at Crozerville, was another cotton-factory belonging to the same gentleman. When the streams began to swell rapidly Mr. Crozer dispatched his son, Samuel A. Crozer, to the West Branch Mills, where he found the hands, as a precautionary measure, already engaged in removing goods from the lower to the upper story of the warehouse. Shortly after five o'clock the dam gave way, and soon after the warehouse, stone by stone, yielded to the flood, and fell with a crash, while at the same time the water-wheel, mill-gearing, dye-house and size-house floated away. Soon after, the northern wing of the three-story mill, forty-eight by thirty feet, began to give way, and, falling, carried with it eighty power-looms, much machinery, and goods. One of the corners of the centre building was also carried away, and the whole structure was momentarily expected to fall. But the flood had spent its fury, and the work of destruction ceased at this point. The lower story of the mill at Crozerville was flooded, and the cotton-house, containing a number of bales, was swept away, as was also the county bridge at this place, while the abutments were leveled to the foundation.

The two branches of Chester Creek meeting at Crozerville, the united flood ran madly down the stream, which was swollen nearly twenty-four feet above its ordinary level. A story and a half building, formerly used as a machine shop by John Garsed, who had just taken the tools out, was washed entirely away, and the machinery in Riddle's mills was much damaged. One of the two stone houses owned by George Peterson was washed away, and the other excessively damaged. The larger part of the furniture was floated out and borne off by the current. Near by John Rhoads, an aged man, owned four small houses, one of which was occupied by himself and family, and the others by tenants. The flood swept the buildings absolutely away, leaving no trace, when the waters subsided, that they had ever stood there.

At the time the torrent poured down upon them, John Rhoads, his daughters, Hannah and Jane, and his granddaughter, Mary Ann Collingsworth, were in the dwelling, and with it they were swept away. All of them were drowned. In one of the houses, Mary Jane McGuigan and her infant child was washed away and perished. Her body was found early in April, 1844, a short distance from where the house which she occupied at the time of the freshet stood. The body of John Rhoads was found two and a half miles down the creek, one of his daughters at Baldwin's Run, nearly five miles away, while the body of the other daughter was borne into the Delaware, and was found near Naaman's Creek, about six miles below the mouth of Chester Creek. The corpse of the grandchild was not found until nearly six months afterwards, when a heavy rain on Jan. 17, 1844, washed away some earth near where Rhoads' house had stood, and exposed the remains to view. The superstructure of the county bridge at Pennsgrove was carried away, and immediately below, at Rockdale, the two dams of Richard S. Smith's factories were destroyed, as well as a block of four stone houses, fortunately at the time unoccupied.

At Knowlton the water rose thirty-three feet above the ordinary level of the creek, but this was partly due to the fact that driftwood gathered against the bridge, choking up the archways and, acting as a dam, turned the body of the flood against the factories at that point. Mr. Crozer's "Knowlton Mill," a three-storied stone building, thirty-six by seventy-six feet, recently fitted with new machinery, was razed to its foundation, the roof floating off as a whole, and the bell in the cupola tolling as the mass undulated on the struggling torrent. It was well that the disaster occurred when it did, for the hands, over fifty persons, had all retired to their homes, hence not a life was there lost. At the same place a frame mill owned by Mr. Crozer, and occupied by James Dixon, was swept away. Every dollar's worth of property the latter had in the world was lost, besides he was left in debt nearly a thousand dollars; but Mr. Crozer, his creditor, although he had sustained a loss of over seventy-five thousand dollars, immediately released Dixon from the obligation. The resistless water, as it sped onward to the Delaware, carried away J. & I. P. Dutton's flour-mills, which had stood nearly a century, as well as the saw-mill, barn, and wagon-house at that point.

Even the mansion-house was invaded by the flood, and two rooms were stripped of their furniture. Jonathan Dutton barely escaped with his life. He was carrying some articles from the lower to an upper story of the mill, when the great mass of water came rushing down upon the building. He fled to the upper story, and, feeling that the structure was yielding to the torrents, he sprang out of a window, and fortunately succeeded in reaching a place of safety The county bridge was here destroyed

In the meadow just above Upland, Mary Jackson, a colored woman, was with her husband gathering drift-wood when the flood rushed down upon her, and hesitating for a moment in which direction to flee, he was overwhelmed by the water and drowned The Chester Flour- and Saw-Mills, then owned by Richard Flower, were much injured, and the bridge at that place was swept away and the abutment greatly damaged William G Flower, who was at the time lessee of his father's mill, was in the meadow when the waters rushed down upon him, and he was whirled along until he succeeded in catching a vine which was entwined around a large tree on the race bank, and by means of which he mounted into the branches, but the tree was torn up by the roots, and among drift-wood, timber, and trees he was carried down by the flood until he was lodged in a standing tree, to which he clung, although much exhausted, until the flood had in a measure abated, when Abner Wood bravely swam to him, carrying a rope, by means of which Mr Flower was safely brought to shore

At Chester the Philadelphia, Wilmington and Baltimore Railroad bridge was swept away, together with part of the western abutment, and the county bridge, at the present Third Street, was thrown from its place, but, as the superstructure was held by the chains on the eastern side, it did not prove a total loss The pattern-house, with its contents, at Jacob G Kitts' foundry, was floated away, as was the stone kitchen from William Kerlin's house, still standing on Third Street, near Penn, and the dwelling itself was much damaged, while a frame house and other outbuildings belonging to Mr Kerlin were destroyed The dwelling-house was occupied by William Benton, and all his household goods, his cart, dearborn, and other personal property were swept away A bureau, containing his and his children's clothing, his watch, and all the money he had, was found floating at Pennsgrove, N J, and was returned to Mr Benton by the finder It is reported that the water rose at Chester one foot a minute until it reached a point twenty-three feet higher than the ordinary high-water mark

As stated before, the volume of water on the Brandywine was not greatly increased, although some damage was done on that stream The branches of Beaver Creek, a feeder of the Brandywine, in Delaware County, being within the territory where the cloud-burst occurred, rose sufficiently to break the dam at the saw-mill of Reese Perkins, just above where the Delaware line, at the extreme southwestern line of Birmingham, joins Concord township. The loss, however, was not great Harvey's Run, which empties into the Brandywine a short distance below Chad's Ford, rose sufficient to break the dam of Thomas Brinton's grist-mill and that of Joseph P Harvey's saw-mill, but, so far as I have learned, very little damage other than that stated was sustained on that tributary

Thirty-two county bridges were destroyed or seriously injured by the flood, while the individual losses on Darby Creek and its tributaries amounted to twenty thousand dollars, on Crum Creek, twenty-four thousand dollars, on Ridley, thirty-nine thousand dollars, and Chester Creek, one hundred and five thousand dollars

On Saturday, July 8, 1853, a destructive hail-storm passed over the townships of Thornbury, Upper and Nether Providence, Springfield, Upper Darby, and Darby, leveling the crops to the earth, and producing other damage At Media over a hundred lights were broken in the court-house windows, a large number of those at the Charter House and in private houses, while at Crook's (Bancroft's) upper factory nearly every pane of glass on the west side of the building was broken

Thursday, Aug 11, 1870, the most violent storm and freshet to that time since the notable one of August, 1843, occurred, and the destruction it occasioned in Delaware County reached a quarter of a million dollars On Rocky Run, twenty-five feet of the breast of Humphrey Yearsley's flour-mill, in Middletown, was swept away, as was also that at James Pennell's mill, farther down the stream The flood, swollen by the contributions from these dams, rushed down upon the West Chester and Philadelphia Railroad bridge which spans the run above Wawa, and near Pennelton Station The five o'clock train from West Chester reached the bridge just when the water was the most turbulent, and the structure gave way beneath the weight of the train, together with the pressure of the flood The engine, baggage-car, and a passenger-car were thrown into the stream Fortunately, George W Evans, the engineer, noticing that the bridge seemed wavering, whistled "down brake," the headway of the train was in a measure arrested, and it so happened that the first passenger-car, which contained about thirty persons, lingered for a few moments on the edge of the stream, just sufficient to permit the escape of the passengers, and then it plunged into the water The fireman, who sprang from the engine when the whistle sounded, escaped without injury, but the engineer, brakeman, and baggage-master were much hurt

At Lenni the dam at the factory of Robert L Martin was broken, not less than a hundred feet of the dam-breast being torn away, and the loosened waters deluged the first story of the mill, damaging machinery, ruining goods, and making great havoc as it rushed by At Parkmount, near Lenni, a portion of the dam-breast at George Glodhill's mill also gave way Chester Creek was filled with floating rubbish, lumber, logs, pig-styes,—the squeaking animals still in the pens,—buckets, tables, stools, and hundreds of other articles were borne off by the rushing torrent At Samuel Bancroft's upper bank, on Ridley Creek, the water rose rapidly, flooding the lower floor of the mill, damaging machinery, and injuring goods The bridge over the race at this point was washed away At John Fox's Hillboro' Mills the dam was injured, the house over the water-wheel of the mill, and part of the dye-house, with articles of personal property, were carried off, causing a loss of ten thousand dollars The Rose Valley Mill of Antrim Osborn & Son was much injured, the dam breast broken, and the wool-sheds and other property were floated off, causing a damage of nearly six thousand dollars Two sloops belonging to Spencer McIlvain & Son were lifted over the bank at Ridley Creek and stranded thirty yards from that water-course, while the bridge over the Queen's Highway, although it was lifted a foot from its foundation, fortunately was not carried off its abutments At the paper-mill of J Howard Lewis, on Crum Creek, the damages sustained amounted to nearly five thousand dollars, and at the axe-works of John C. Beatty the loss of property was greater than at Lewis' mill

On Tuesday evening, July 11, 1871, violent rain fell in torrents for half an hour, accompanied by vivid lightning and heavy thunder The storm, which moved from the direction of New Castle and extended to Philadelphia, included only the river townships in its passage through this county In South Chester, the walls of several houses in course of erection were blown down and much other damage sustained In Chester part of the walls of the house of Humphrey Fairlamb, in North Ward, was destroyed, the roof of National Hall much injured, and in South Ward a frame building was bodily moved from its foundation In Ridley lightning struck a tree at J Morgan Baker's brick-yard, near Leiperville, shattering it to pieces, and Mrs John Dunlevy, while standing near the door of her house at Leiper's Landing, on Crum Creek, was struck by lightning When carried into the dwelling she showed no visible signs of life, and although respiration was resumed in a short time, she remained in a comatose state until noon of the next day At the dwelling of George Caldwell, on the Edgmont road, in Chester township, a large sycamore-tree was struck The lightning, it is said, like a great white ball, descended from the tree to the well-curb, where it exploded with a deafening noise Fences and trees were prostrated and uprooted, while the air was filled with broken branches during the violence of the storm

A furious gale, extending from Washington to the New England States, occurred on Wednesday, Feb 2, 1876 At Morton Station, in Springfield, an unfinished house was blown down, and at Aston a new barn being erected on the farm of George Drayton was also demolished The tin roofing of Patterson's mill, at Chester, was partly torn away, as was also that on the residence of Rev Henry Brown A portion of the roof of the Sunnyside Mill was blown off, as was also part of that of the barn at the Pennsylvania Military Academy In Chester township a house on the farm of Abram C Lukins was overturned, the roof of the picker-room of No 3 mill, at Upland, was carried bodily into the creek, and two brick houses near Kirkman's mill, in South Chester, had the roofs taken off by the gale The velocity of the wind is said to have exceeded forty miles an hour in this vicinity

On Sept 15, 1876, occurred a storm exceeding in violence any which had preceded it in thirty years Throughout the county the corn was blown flat to the earth and the blades stripped from the stalks by the wind, pears and apples shaken from the limbs and fences laid prostrate, while houses and outbuildings were unroofed and otherwise injured Tinicum Island and Morris' Ferry to the Lazaretto was almost entirely submerged Jacob Alburger's meadow of one hundred acres was overflowed, his corn crop almost destroyed, and many tons of hay floated off His loss was computed at several thousand dollars The banks of Darby Creek were breached in many places, and the damage sustained was great In Chester, all the cellars in the Middle Ward, near Chester Dock, were filled with water, and in some instances the dwellers in the houses in that locality were removed in boats to places of safety The floor of the chemical works, at the foot of Market Street was covered with water to the depth of two feet, and salt cake, valued at five hundred dollars, and other articles, were destroyed The tin roof of Irving & Leiper's mill was blown off, carrying with it many of the rafters, and a large quantity of coal was swept from the mill-wharf into the river, involving a loss of nearly seven hundred dollars The lower floor of Patterson's mill, near Chester Creek, was covered with water, causing much damage to the machinery, and the greater part of the coal for the mill was forced into the creek Morton, Black & Bro, at their lumber-yard, near the mouth of Ridley Creek, lost nearly five thousand dollars by the storm Along the line of the Philadelphia, Wilmington and Baltimore Railroad telegraph-poles were blown over the track, and in many cases the wires prevented the passage of the cars until removed The aggregate loss throughout the county was many thousands of dollars

Sunday, July 28, 1877, a rain storm of much violence visited our county, particularly the townships of Nether Providence, Middletown, Newtown, Edgmont, Marple, and Springfield The streams were gorged with the torrents of rain which had fallen, but noticeable was this the case with Crum Creek, which, about midnight, carried away the bridge at Paxon's Hollow, and another on the same road The culvert which crosses the road at George Allen's, unable to vent the water, blocked it there until it inundated the road for several hundred yards, making it impassable The highways through Upper Providence, Darby, Springfield, and other townships were much injured At Beatty's axe-factory the water rose ten feet, carried away the bridge at Holt's mill, and rushed forward towards the dam at Strathaven J Howard Lewis, hearing the noise of rushing waters, and fearing that a freshet might follow the rain, went to his paper-mill at midnight, and not long afterwards the waters of Crum Creek covered the lower floor of the building to the depth of three feet, but subsided without doing any serious injury save floating away several ricks of straw The dam at Strathaven banked the torrent for a time, but it only augmented the power of the flood, for when the obstruction finally gave way a roaring mass of water came with a rush down towards Avondale Neill Melloy, one of the operatives in John Greer & Co's mill at the latter place, had risen to smoke, and as the stars were shining brightly had walked to the hillside spring for a drink, when chancing to look up the creek he saw the flood approaching Without a moment's delay he ran from house to house waking the slumbering inmates Not a moment too soon, for the rushing water forced the foot-bridge away, uprooted trees, swept away the wool-house, poured into the mill and into the houses, from which the dwellers fled in their night clothing In several cases women sleeping in the upper stories were lifted through the windows by Neill Melloy (who preserved his presence of mind), and passed to parties without, who bore them to places of safety Over a dozen houses were flooded and greatly injured Daybreak disclosed the fearful damage that had been wrought, and everywhere were strewn broken articles of household furniture, while clearly defined in places along the banks and on the houses were marks showing that the water had risen to the height of fifteen feet

On the 9th of October following, the most violent rain-storm since 1843 swept over our county Early in the evening of that day the wind blew heavily, increasing to such an extent that the Philadelphia, Wilmington and Baltimore Railroad dispatched no trains from Philadelphia southward after nine o'clock, although the storm ceased an hour before midnight Chester Creek was swollen to a rushing torrent From a short distance above Rockdale down to its mouth great damage was done The dam at West Branch and Crozerville Mills broke, as did that at Glen Riddle, and much damage was done at J B Rhoads & Brother's mill at Llewellyn The hurrying water forced its way into the lower floors and engine-rooms of Crozer's mills at Upland, and a carpenter-shop at No 1 mill floated down the stream, accompanied with numerous articles of personal property which had been caught by the flood in its course At Chester boats and shallops torn from their moorings were carried out into the river, and the yacht "White Wing" drifted down the Delaware Along the line of the Chester Creek and Baltimore Central Railroad the damage was so great that for two days no trains passed over the road because of washouts and uprooted trees which lay upon the track At Bridgewater an engine and tender was thrown from the road by a break in the track there, and between Chad's Ford and Brandywine Summit the road had so sunk that it was dangerous A culvert east of the latter place was washed out, at Chad's Ford the railroad bridge was swept away, and a short distance below Concord Station a small bridge was carried off, while another near by had so sunk that it could not be crossed until repaired The lumber in the yard of Alexander Scott & Son at that place was strewn in every direction, while fences and trees were leveled to the earth Three acres of corn belonging to George S Cheyney was absolutely annihilated

At Darby, Griswold's mill was partially inundated, which, with the coal that was washed from the wharf, occasioned a loss of over ten thousand dollars A stable at the same place belonging to William D R Serrill was inundated, and two horses drowned Some damage was sustained by J Howard Lewis, at his paper-mill on Crum Creek, while at Morton a large unfinished stable belonging to Judge Morton was partly blown down, and much injury sustained at his brick-kilns, near by that station

A terrible tornado swept over this county on Wednesday morning, Oct 23, 1878, causing great destruction of property At Media trees, fences, and barns were leveled with the earth, and a dwelling-house on State Street, near Jackson, being erected by Ralph Buckley, was blown down, and Mr Buckley, who was in the building at the time, was buried in the ruins and seriously injured The sheds of the Methodist Church in Middletown were torn away, and the lumber so broken that it was useful only as kindling, while in all parts of the county great damages marked the tracks of the storm At Glen Riddle the wagon of James Howarth, the mail carrier, was thrown against a telegraph-pole just as he was entering the bridge over the West Chester Railroad, which prevented Howarth from being precipitated over an embankment nearly forty feet in height The wagon was demolished

In Chester the frame stable of the Hanley Hose Company was destroyed, so was also the drill-hall of the Pennsylvania Military Academy, and a row of eight unfinished houses on Second and Norris Streets were thrown down in a mass of ruins, as were some houses on Penn Street, above Sixth, then building The roofs of St Paul's, First and Second Presbyterian, Madison Street, and the Immaculate Heart of Mary Churches were injured, as were Patterson's, Ledward's, Gartside's, Barton's, and Irving & Leiper's mills, Sanville's spar-shed, Cox's sash-factory, the sugar-refinery, and the engine-house and mould-lofts at Roach's ship-yard were blown entirely or partially off In South Chester the front wall of a row of brick houses belonging to Mr Kirkman was forced in, and the Democratic wigwam at that borough torn to pieces Over fifty houses in Chester, North and South Chester, and Upland were unroofed The tide rose far above its usual height, so that the water covered the wharves, submerged the Front Street Railroad, flooded Roach's ship-yard, Lewis' Chester Dock Mills, and inundated the lower floor of the Steamboat Hotel Morton. Black & Brother's planing-mill and lumber-yard suffered damage amounting to three thousand dollars, while at Mendenhall & Johnson's, Dutton & Anderson's, and J & C D Pennell's lumber-yards the loss was large. Three canal-boats sunk at Weidner's wharf. As a storm simply it was the most furious one ever recorded as happening in this county.

Earthquakes.—The first earthquake which is recorded as having occurred in this vicinity was in October, 1727, and was so violent that in Philadelphia, New York, and Boston it "set the clocks to running down, and shook off china from the shelves,"[1] and in 1732 slight shocks were noticed in this part of the country. On Dec 7, 1738, a severe shock was felt at night, "accompanied by a remarkable rumbling noise, people waked in their beds, the doors flew open, bricks fell from the chimneys, the consternation was serious, but, happily, no great damage ensued."[2] On Nov 18, 1755, a severe shock was felt for eight hundred miles on the Atlantic coast, including this locality.[3] On the night of March 22, 1763, a smart shock was felt, and on Sunday, Oct 13, 1763, an earthquake, accompanied by a loud roaring noise, alarmed the good people of Philadelphia and surrounding country, and the congregations in churches and meeting-houses, fearing that the buildings would fall upon them, dismissed themselves without tarrying for the benediction. In an old volume on which is indorsed "Peter Mendenhall, his almanac for the year 1772," still in the ownership of his descendants in Chester County, under date of April 25, 1772, he records this interesting item: "At or near eight o'clock in the morning the roaring of an earthquake was heard, succeeded by a shake which made the house to tremble. A second ensued soon after the first had ceased, which was more violent." Peter Mendenhall then resided on a farm in Delaware County. On Jan 8, 1817, an earthquake occurred which tossed vessels about the river and raised the water one foot. On Sunday evening, June 17, 1871, about ten o'clock, the shock of an earthquake was distinctly felt in Delaware County, and on Monday morning, October 9th of the same year, at 8 40 o'clock, a severe shock was felt from Perryville, Md, to Philadelphia. The dwellings in the southern part of the county shook and trembled to their foundations, causing the inmates to run in alarm out of their houses. A rumbling sound as of the reverberation after the discharge of a cannon occurred during the shock. The quivering of the earth was more noticeable in the western part of this county and in Chester County. Bayard Taylor, who was at Cedarcroft, his residence, at Kennett Square, in a letter to the *New York Tribune* thus describes the shock in that locality:

"The first symptoms were a low, rumbling sound, which rapidly increased to a loud, jarring noise, as if a dozen iron safes were rolling over the floors. The house shook from top to bottom, and at the end of ten or fifteen seconds both the noise and vibration were so violent as to alarm all the inmates. I had frequently experienced heavy earthquake shocks in other countries, but in no instances were they accompanied with such a loud and long continued reverberation. For about fifteen seconds longer the shock gradually diminished, but the jarring noise was heard, seemingly in the distance, after the vibration ceased to be felt. The men at work in the field stated that the sound was first heard to the northward, that it apparently passed under their feet at the moment of greatest vibration, and then moved off southward. The birds all flew from their perches in the trees and hedges, and darted back and forth in evident terror. The morning had been very sultry and overcast, but the sky cleared and a fresh wind arose immediately afterwards. The wooden dwellings in the village were so shaken that the people all rushed into the streets. Some crockery was broken, I believe, but no damage was done to walls or chimneys. There was a light shock about midnight the following night. The first seemed to me to be nearly as violent as those succeeding the great earthquake which destroyed Corinth in 1858. It is thirty or forty years since any shock has been felt in this neighborhood."

On June 6, 1869, during a rainfall at Chester, occurred a shower of shells. Specimens of the shells were collected, and became the subject of consideration by the members of the Academy of Natural Sciences in Philadelphia.[4] The shells proved to be a new species of *Astarte*, a genus that is essentially marine and found in every sea. The delicate character of the specimens indicate a Southern habitat,—most probably the coast of Florida,—and as the storm came in that direction it is believed that they came from there, and possibly were lifted into the clouds by a water-spout. The specimens which were gathered by the late Hon Y S Walter, and presented to Mr John Ford, a member of the Academy of Natural Sciences, in remembrance of the peculiar circumstances in which they were discovered to the scientific world received the name *Astarte Nubigena*, or the cloud-born Astarte.

CHAPTER XV

THE TEN-HOUR MOVEMENT.[5]

ONE of the most important movements, and, in the results which have flowed from it, of great moment to the people of Delaware County, the State of Pennsylvania, and, more or less, to the country at large, was first put into practical effect in the eastern portion of this State, and mainly through the efforts of a comparatively few individuals in the county of Delaware.

Much has been said and much controversy elicited

1 Watson's Annals, vol ii p 413, Smith's "History of New Jersey," p 427

2 Smith's "History of New Jersey"

3 Martin's "History of Chester," p 163

4 *American Journal of Conchology* (new series), vol v p 118

5 Contributed by James Webb

as to the policy of attempting to regulate merely social or business questions by the aid or power of law. A great deal may be said on both sides, much of it probably to little or no good purpose. But the regulation of the time during which labor may be carried on in large manufacturing establishments has worked so well, and been productive of so vast an amount of unmixed good to at this time a full generation of factory operatives; the benefits and blessings derived from it by old and young, by both employer and employé during more than a third of a century, establish the beneficial effects of the policy beyond doubt or cavil. For many years in England after the introduction of labor-saving machinery and the consequent aggregation of large numbers of persons of all ages and of both sexes in manufacturing establishments, it became necessary for the successful prosecution of the business that some certain regulations be adopted to that end. Much of the machinery and many of the processes are of that character that can be operated with much greater success and far more advantageously by children and young persons than by adults. Indeed, if children were entirely banished from such establishments, it is a question whether many articles now made both for use and ornament would not have to be abandoned altogether, to the manifest disadvantage of the whole community. As time went on, and as manufacturing by machinery instead of mere manual labor became a success, it was altogether in human nature to endeavor to make as much out of it during a given time as possible; and as farming the soil and what is generally known as the mechanical trades were the chief employments of the people, and as each individual was his own "boss," it necessarily followed that every one was free to work as his necessities or his inclinations impelled him, or to lay off and rest when physical or other causes induced him to do so. Not so in the new system of combined labor in factories. The single individual must give way to the aggregate. Rules had to be made. The machinery must be started at a certain agreed-upon time, and must all stop together. There had to be order and uniformity, or the thing would not work. In this, the new system, precedent was followed. The old custom on the farm and in the shop was adhered to, to begin as soon in the morning and work as late at night as they could see. Of course, in the beginning, when the institutions were small and not yet fully organized or developed, there would be breaks from one cause or another, and the ill effects of the system would not be felt. It was only as it progressed, and the numbers engaged therein increased, and the necessity of all being employed at one time for the general good, that it became monotonous. Then was felt the depressing influence on the human mind and body of this then recognized custom. It has been described as worse than the British treadmill discipline, established for the punishment of crime, or the system of slavery as then existing in our own Southern States, the only difference being that the one was free to leave it and learn something new to enable him to live,—better if he could, or worse if he had to; the other had not that option. In England, where the system was first established, it made much slower progress than in the United States at a later period. But it was there that the depressing influence of the daily routine on the minds and bodies of those subject to it began to make itself heard in complaints both loud and deep. Unfortunately, at that time the masses of the people in England were without political power or influence. But a few humane and intelligent gentlemen of education, outside of their ranks, took up their cause, purely from motives of humanity. Notably among these was the late Richard Oastler, Esq., afterwards known among his humble adherents, from his zeal in their cause, as "the Old King." Some time after this their complaints reached the Houses of Parliament, when the late Lord Ashley took up the matter, and pressed it with such vigor and earnestness that it resulted in the passage of a law making eleven hours a day's work in all factories, and establishing Good Friday an additional legal holiday. A few years after this was followed by an amended law, reducing the time to be worked to ten hours a day, which remained in successful operation from that time to this. About the years 1846–47 the subject began to be earnestly discussed [1] in Pennsylvania. Philadelphia and Manayunk moved in the matter, and correspondence was had with Delaware County for organization there to obtain, if possible, the passage of a law establishing ten hours as a legal day's work in this State. The first general meeting of operatives appertaining to that end was held at the Seven Stars Hotel, now Village Green, in a hall generously loaned for that purpose by the late John Garrett.

At this meeting an organization was effected, and a committee of two from each mill in the county appointed as a central body. The committee met at the house of Mark Clegg, on the road leading from the Red Bridge to the Union Methodist Episcopal Church, opposite Crook's (now Bancroft's) lower mill, in Nether Providence, where they continued to meet weekly until the completion of their labors, which resulted in the passage of a law by the Legislature making ten hours a legal day's labor in all cotton, woolen, flax, paper, and glass manufactories in this commonwealth. Such is a brief epitome of this important work; its influence for good is, and has been, felt, not only in our own State, but measurably in every State where manufacturing exists, or is likely to

[1] Ten years before the date mentioned in the text, on Feb. 20, 1836, a meeting of operatives employed in cotton-mills on Chester Creek was held at the Seven Stars Tavern, of which meeting Lewis Coruog was president and John Haynes secretary. The object of the meeting was to oppose "the long-hour system enforced by employers on hands in cotton-mills against their will." In May, 1836, all the operatives on Chester Creek struck, demanding higher wages or less hours of labor.

exist, throughout our broad domain. But while this is a general history of this excellent and most highly important law, there are many incidents connected therewith, and the chief actors engaged in the work of bringing it about, that should not, in the interest of the present generation as well as those which shall succeed it, be lost entirely in oblivion. It is not to be expected that a measure, even of much less importance than this, entirely in the interests of labor, but at that time supposed to be in antagonism to capital, should be brought to completion in so short a time without opposition. The antagonism to it was persistent and strong. We impugn no man's motives. It was undertaken in the interests of humanity, and the result has proved the justice of the cause.

At the above meeting, in addition to the appointment of the committee alluded to and other routine business, a most inspiriting address, written by the late John Wilde, was adopted, and ordered to be printed. It was also inserted in the *Upland Union* and the *Delaware County Republican*, and signed by Thomas Ashworth as president, and Joseph Holt as secretary. The address was extensively circulated, and followed by a series of meetings at different points contiguous to the various mills and factories in the county. At these meetings speeches were made and other legitimate means used to concentrate public opinion to the importance of endeavoring to obtain a law to restrict this then great and growing evil.

In the *Delaware County Republican* of Nov. 19, 1847, appears the following editorial: "The press is taking hold of the ten-hour system now about being petitioned for by the factory operatives in good earnest. . . . Let those who oppose it just drop into a factory and work among the dirt and grease for fourteen hours each day for a twelvemonth, and tell us at the expiration of that time their opinion of the matter."

The next general public meeting of the operatives was at the old Providence Inn on Saturday evening, Nov. 20, 1847, when the following resolutions were unanimously adopted:

"*Resolved*, That the persons composing this meeting have been long and practically convinced of the injurious effect of the great number of hours now constituting a day's work in factories, upon the mental and physical powers of those subjected to such long-continued toil and confinement.

"*Resolved*, That this meeting hails with a lively satisfaction the increasing interest manifested by all the producing classes, and more particularly the expressed sympathy and support of the public press in aid of the present movement to ameliorate the condition of the factory operatives.

"*Resolved*, That we will continue our united exertions to procure by constitutional and legal means the passage of a law reducing the time of labor in factories to ten hours a day, or fifty-eight hours per week."

These resolutions were urged in stirring addresses by Messrs. Webb, Cotton, Ashworth, Walker, and Fawley.

A meeting of operatives and workingmen generally was held at Sneath's Corner on Saturday evening, Dec. 4, 1847. Dr. Jesse Young having suggested some doubts about the constitutionality of a law regulating the hours of labor for adults, a spirited debate arose between him and Messrs. Ashworth, Fawley, and Walker, which continued for more than an hour. Hon. Joseph Engle (one of the associate judges for Delaware County) being present was solicited for his opinion, and stated that he believed the Legislature had power to pass laws to promote the moral and physical well-being of the citizens of the State, and as the present object of the operatives appeared to him to be expressly designed for that highly commendable purpose, he had no doubt of either the right or justice of such legislation.

The following Saturday evening, Dec. 10, 1847, a meeting was held in the school-house at Hinkson's Corner, which was addressed by Messrs. Ashworth, Holt, F. Pearson, and Greenwood. The following resolutions were adopted:

"*Resolved*, That in the opinion of this meeting the present system is more particularly injurious to children employed in factories, depriving them in a majority of cases from ever acquiring the rudiments of a common education, so essentially necessary to enable them to perform the duties devolving on them as citizens of this Republic.

"*Resolved*, That we believe that the confinement of female operatives for twelve or fourteen hours in a day is highly injurious, depriving them of the opportunity of acquiring the necessary knowledge of domestic duties to enable them to fill their stations in well-regulated households, and deprives them of the means of acquiring a practical and useful education."

Similar meetings continued to be held, and petitions forwarded to the Legislature, and all other legitimate means used to obtain the passage of the much-desired law. On the 25th of March, 1847, the Senate passed the bill making ten hours a legal day's work in all factories in this State. It afterwards passed the House and became a law, to take effect on and after the 4th day of July, 1848.

As showing how the law was received at the time, we copy the two following editorials from newspapers contemporary with its passage:

"THE TEN HOURS' SYSTEM.—*The proprietors of Fairhill Factory, in* Philadelphia, have already extended the benefits of the ten-hour law to the operatives in their employ, and we understand that most, if not all, of the manufacturers of the city and county will comply with the requisitions of the law immediately after the fourth day of next month."[1]

Again,—

"We understand that a portion, if not all, of the manufacturers of cotton goods in this county (Delaware) have determined to close their factories for several weeks after the 4th of July next. It is said that most of them have a large stock of goods on hand, and failing to effect sales, they have concluded to await until the market becomes better."

Such were the differences of opinion among those who were supposed to be more pecuniarily interested in the future effects of the law. The actual effects of it I now proceed to show. The late John P. Crozer, who at that time was generally supposed to be the leading spirit in opposition to the new system, after a few years' trial when established, generously admitted the errors under which he had labored, and afterwards became one of its most friendly advocates.

[1] July, 1848.

Such was the state of feeling among the community at the time of which I write, 1848 Immediately anterior to the passage of the act many good men were divided in their opinions as to the policy of such a law A number contended that no power existed in a free government to determine how long a man should or should not work There was some plausibility in the point, for it had not then been ascertained that the government possessed a police power in just such cases But by public meetings, by private discussion, and particularly by the aid of the press, the popular mind was enlightened, and the proposed law began to be favorably looked on by the people While it had its persistent enemies, it had the most generous and warm friends Among the operatives themselves many opposed it The writer was present at a shop-meeting at one of our large establishments as a spectator merely, when one of the proprietors remarked that he did not think that a majority of their hands wanted shorter time Some of the operatives ventured to differ with him "Well, now," he says, "suppose we try?" A division was called, and while there appeared to be a majority for the shorter time, that majority was but very small This was not the case everywhere The representative in the Legislature from Delaware County in that year was Hon Sketchley Morton, and he advocated shorter time with earnestness and zeal, and did all he could to make it a success The same could not be said of our then senator. The committee sent petitions signed by nearly twelve hundred operatives to the senator and representative for the district The one to the House was duly presented by the representative, but the one to the Senate was never more heard from The committee wrote letters asking the reasons, but their fate was the same as that of the petition The name of Hon Samuel Marx, of Lehigh County, being suggested to the committee, they wrote to him, he consented, and did present the petition to the Senate, of which body he was then a member Of course this required the circulation anew of petitions for signatures

The friends and advocates of the cause had many other difficulties to contend against, prominent among which was to obtain a room wherein to hold their meetings for counsel and discussion No public hall existed in the county, so far as remembered, except Garrett Hall, above alluded to, and the court-house at Chester Sometimes a school-house could be obtained, and as the mills were long distances apart, the duties of the committee were difficult and fatiguing Saturday evening was the only night available for the purpose, and then a distance of from two to five miles had to be walked after stopping time (stopping time then being four and four and a half o'clock P M on Saturdays), and when much cleaning was required it would be five o'clock before leaving the mills Thus the operatives had only two or three hours for discussion, without infringing on the time absolutely required for natural rest Of course, this is only intended as historical reminiscences of those times as compared with the present experiences, and not as an argument *pro* or *con* Differences of opinion existed then as now as to the wisdom of the measure asked for It was then comparatively an untried experiment But the law, in its most essential features, has been fully justified by more than a third of a century's experience Still, like all things human, it has its imperfections The committee, at its first sessions, was not a unit as to the age at which a child should be allowed to commence work in a mill Full discussions were had, and it was generally agreed, in the interests of all parties, that ten years was a suitable limit, below which the law ought to intervene, but the number of hours per day that the mill should be run at all was the objective point to which attention was mainly directed It was contended that no power had a right to say how long or how little an adult person should be allowed to work, but that minors only were subject to the law's restrictions That portion of the act regulating the ages between ten and thirteen years has been practically a dead letter during all the time since its passage, until a few months ago,—1882–83 Some five or more years since attention was called to infractions of the spirit of the law,—some mills running until nine o'clock at night This evil kept growing, until Mr McGahee, an operative in one of the mills at Darby, in this county, called public attention to the manifest violations of the law in a letter addressed to a prominent newspaper, as also by posting copies of the act in public places in his neighborhood This caused very general adherence to the law as it stands, while it also showed its weak points, its advantages and imperfections. Probably the time may come, and it is to be hoped in the interests of humanity that it may come soon, when all concerned, both employers and employed, may come together on common ground and agree upon some age, taking all the circumstances into consideration, the business itself, the interests of employers and employed, the claims of widowed mothers, the duties of humanity and of the State at large, and so amend the law as to be just and satisfactory to all interested, and its beneficent features kept intact But this is a digression Our purpose is not to recommend, but to give a history of the movement itself

The law as passed by the Legislature in the session of 1847–48 provided that it should go into effect on and after the 4th day of July, 1848 That time came, the law became operative, and in Philadelphia, Manayunk, and other places was observed and worked harmoniously Such was not the case in Delaware County Strange to say that very shortly after the passage of the law it began to be foreseen that there was a probability that so far as this locality was concerned the act would be nullified Many of its most active and zealous friends withdrew and sought other means to secure a livelihood. A number of others remained at their homes, but went out on strike — one of the cases where such a course can be justified in that it was a strike in favor of, and against a violation of, law.

The following incident in connection with the strike in justice to all parties should not be omitted from this record. While the strike was pending the late Simeon Lord and William T. Crook, two of the manufacturers in this county, told their hands that they were willing to run their mills for ten hours if the rest would do so, that they would start on ten hours a day and try it for a month. If the rest did likewise they would continue so to run, but at the expiration of a month it was understood that they were free to do as the rest of the manufacturers did. This proposition was accepted and carried out in good faith on both sides during the term designated.

After a suspension for some time operations were resumed on the old system, and in violation of the law, notwithstanding the fact that by its provisions a penalty of fifty dollars was imposed on both the employer and parent of children under thirteen years of age, permitted to labor in factories. For five long years this state of things continued, when some of the more conscientious of the manufacturers not desiring to continue in this open violation of a plain law, proposed to the operatives that if they could induce the manufacturers of New England to join in the measure they would be willing to accede to their demands. Accordingly another movement was set on foot, meetings were again held, and a delegation consisting of the late John Wilde and Sandy M. Challenger was appointed. They at once attempted to discharge the duties of their mission, but were met at the outset by difficulties which were not unexpected. They were strangers (as it were) in a strange land. In an interview between the writer and Mr. Wilde after his return, the latter stated that they were somewhat at a loss how and where to commence their work. In this emergency he bethought himself of Benjamin F. Butler, Esq., then a prominent rising lawyer of Boston (now 1883 the Governor of the State of Massachusetts), who entered heartily into their plans, and gave them all the information in his power. Mr. Wilde stated that to him was to be attributed whatever of success they met with. After their return to Delaware County meetings were again called, at which the delegation gave an account of their stewardship. In the mean time the opposition to the law appeared to be dwindling away, and friends came to the aid of the workers. A general meeting was held at the court-house in Chester, at which the late Y. S. Walter, editor of the *Delaware County Republican*, presided, when it was agreed that a trial should be made of the effects of the new law. The late John P. Crozer was prominent in his endeavors to have the act put into practical operation, and after a few years' trial of the new, and as yet untried plan, was enthusiastic in its praise, the firm declaring that they got more work done per hour, or at a less rate of expense than ever before. Such is a brief outline of this little speck of nullification in the hitherto loyal county of Delaware. Although opposition existed, ofttimes in quarters where it was least expected, it was gratifying to find that the press of the county was uniformly on the side of the humble and weaker party. Y. S. Walter, of the *Delaware County Republican*, and Alexander McKeever, of the *Upland Union*, not only advocated the cause editorially, but threw open their columns for discussion on the merits of the question. Most of those who took an active part in the contest on this important measure have been called from the scenes of life, few only remain. But the work performed by their toils and labors continues as a blessing to posterity. A large portion of the privileges and opportunities now enjoyed by the working class, religious, social, and otherwise, were shut out from the factory operatives of a third of a century ago. Who among us would wish to go back to that period with all that that implies? Who can tell what effects would have been produced different from what has been, if we had continued to uphold a system of fourteen or fifteen hours' continuous monotonous labor out of the twenty-four, instead of the liberal and enlightened method now in operation?

CHAPTER XVI

THE REMOVAL OF THE COUNTY-SEAT TO MEDIA

IN considering the history of the removal of the county-seat from the ancient borough of Chester to Media, the present location, I must necessarily draw largely from the narrative of that event furnished by Dr. Smith, he having been an active advocate of the changes, although his recital takes coloring from his feeling somewhat in relating the incidents connected with that movement.

The first agitation of the measure occurred nearly thirty years before it was actually carried into effect, and is said originally to have been the outgrowth of political disappointment. Robert Frazer, a member of the bar of Delaware County, having been defeated in nomination for office by the delegates of Chester township and several of the districts lying in the immediate neighborhood of the county-seat, is said gave form and shape to the movement.

"Dissatisfaction had for some time existed among the people of the upper part of the county," says Dr. Smith, "on account of the seat of justice being situated on its southern margin. The people of the township of Radnor, residing much nearer to Norristown, the seat of justice of Montgomery County, than to Chester, petitioned for the annexation of their township to that county. The fact that the taxes of Montgomery were lower than those of Delaware is also said to have had an influence in promoting this movement. Be this as it may, the prospect of losing one of the best townships in the county was a matter of serious alarm, when its small dimensions were taken into consideration The discontented in the other remote townships seeing that the loss of Radnor would weaken their strongest ground of complaint, determined to test the question of a removal of the seat of justice of the county to a more central situation Accordingly a general meeting of the inhabitants of the county, 'both friendly and unfriendly' to the proposed removal, was convened on the 8th of June, 1820 The meeting was unusually large and very respectable, and after the subject of removal had been discussed very fully and rather freely, a vote was taken which resulted in favor of the removalists. Removal now became the leading topic of discussion throughout the county All party distinctions became merged in it, and the most ultra politicians of opposite parties united cordially on a removal or anti removal platform Meetings were held, and nominations were made accordingly The ballot-box showed the anti removalists in the majority George G Leiper, of Ridley, and Abner Lewis, of Radnor, both anti-removalists, were elected to the Assembly The anti-removalists, by the nomination of Mr Lewis, had secured nearly the whole vote of Radnor, under the belief that the election of the anti removal ticket afforded them the only chance of being annexed to Montgomery County The test was not regarded by the removalists as satisfactory, and they petitioned the Legislature for redress, but certainly with but small hopes of success In their memorial, which is very long, they set forth the fact of the effort of Radnor to be attached to Montgomery County, the dilapidated condition of the jail, the insalubrity of the air of Chester, the danger of the records from attack from an enemy, the badness of the water, etc And finally,' they say, 'to satisfy the Legislature that nothing is asked for by the petitioners which would throw any unreasonable expense on the county, assurances are given by one of the inhabitants—perfectly responsible and competent to the undertaking—that he will give an obligation to any one authorized to receive it, conditioned to erect the public buildings upon any reasonable and approved plan, for the sum of *fifteen thousand dollars*, to be paid in seven years, by installments, if the convenience of the county should require credit—and to take the present buildings and lots at Chester at a fair valuation as part pay' This petition was drawn, signed by nine hundred and nineteen citizens The number who signed the remonstrance is not known"

On March 21, 1821, Mr Evans, of Chester County, presented the petitions—there were nineteen of them—from the inhabitants of the county of Delaware to the House of Representatives, praying for the removal of the seat of justice, and on March 31st, Mr Lewis, of Delaware County, presented to the House twenty-five remonstrances from inhabitants of the county against such removal, and the petitions and remonstrances were laid on the table

"The people of Radnor," said Dr Smith, "appeared to relax their efforts to obtain legislation to authorize the township to be annexed to Montgomery County At the next election, John Lewis and William Cheyney, both removalists, were elected members of the Assembly, but from some cause they failed in obtaining the much-desired law authorizing the seat of justice to be removed to a more central situation The question after this effort appears to have been allowed to slumber for a time It was, however, occasionally discussed, and the removalists maintained a strict vigilance to prevent any extensive repairs being made to the public buildings at Chester"

The project slumbered for nearly a quarter of a century, but in the latter part of the year 1845 was revived with redoubled ardor The court-house at Chester was sadly out of repair, while the old jail was dilapidated and falling into ruins, and it became apparent that in the near future the county would be compelled to expend a considerable sum of money on the public buildings at the ancient seat of justice Hence the removalists on Nov 22, 1845, called a public meeting at the Black Horse Tavern, in Middletown, "to take into consideration the propriety of removing the seat of justice to a more central position" The result of this meeting was a call to the several townships on the 5th of December following "to elect two delegates in each, to meet on the 6th of December at the Black Horse Tavern, the delegates appointed to vote for the removal of the seat of justice, or otherwise, also to decide upon those (the sites) designated by this meeting, which of them shall be adopted" The following-named places were presented as suitable locations for the public buildings County property, in Providence, Black Horse, in Middletown, Chester, Rose Tree, in Upper Providence, and Beaumont's Corner, Newtown"

The roads on the 6th of December were in a wretched condition, so much so that the delegates representing several of the townships were unable to attend, while in others no meetings had been held On that day the following townships were represented Birmingham, Dr Ellwood Harvey, J D Gilpin, Chester, John K Zeilin, Y S Walter, Upper Chester, Robert R Dutton, Concord, M Stamp, E Yarnall, Edgmont, E B Green, George Baker, Marple, Abraham Platt, Dr J. M Moore, Middletown, Joseph Edwards, Abram Pennell, Newtown, Eli Lewis, Thomas H Speakman, Nether Providence, R T Worrall, Peter Worrall, Upper Providence, Emmor Bishop, Thomas Reese, Thornbury, Eli Baker, Daniel Green, Tinicum, Joseph Weaver, Jr

A vote being had on the proposed sites, the result showed eight votes in favor of the county property, six for the Black Horse, six for Chester, and two for the Rose Tree, but finally the county property received twelve votes, a majority of delegates present[1] The result obtained was not satisfactory to the anti-removalists, and a bitter wordy war was waged in the newspapers of that day An attempt was made to reconcile the conflicting elements by the committee appointed at the meeting of the 6th of December, and to that end a meeting was called at the hall of the Delaware County Institute of Science, on the 30th

[1] In Dr Harvey's copy of Smith's "History of Delaware County," is the following manuscript note in the doctor's handwriting "After voting with the minority against removal, I was urged by several other delegates to vote for a choice of locations, but refused to participate in that part of the proceedings, having no other choice than Chester"

Dr Henry further notes "I was a delegate in the first convention held to consider the matter, and opposed removal in accordance with my own convictions and the instructions of my constituents On further consideration of the subject, I changed positions, believing the majority should have a chance to settle the question, and also believing Chester would thrive more without it (the county seat) when her energies were better directed than towards living off the county offices and legal business of the county I thought Media would be a miserably poor place and Chester very prosperous Media has done better than I expected, and so has Chester"

Hon John M Broomall, in his "History of Delaware County for the Past Century" (a centennial historical sketch, published in 1876, page 9), says, in referring to the causes of removal, "For many years the popularity of Chester had been upon the wane Its people had given offense by endeavoring to rule the county, and only partially succeeded Jurors, parties, and witnesses believed themselves to be imposed upon by high charges, and they knew themselves to be sneered at and ridiculed by the tavern idlers, who constituted most of the *élite* of the town"

of that month The meeting was well attended, and an address to the people of the county formulated, as well as two different petitions to be circulated for signatures, desiring the Legislature to enact a law submitting the question to a popular vote At the time the Hon William Williamson, of Chester County, was senator for the district, and Hon John Larkin, Jr, was the member in the House from Delaware County, and, although both of these representatives were favorable to a law submitting the controversy to the vote of the people, yet neither favored an act in which the site of the proposed county-seat should be left as a future matter to be decided Hence, when the bill submitted in the House in that form was called up, Mr Larkin objected to it, for that reason, and it was defeated In 1846, Hon Sketchley Morton was elected to the Legislature, and at the session of 1847, when the act providing for the removal of the seat of justice, submitting the matter to the popular will whether the county-seat should be continued at Chester, or be removed to a point not more distant "than one-half of a mile from the farm attached to the house for the support and employment of the poor of Delaware County," nor more than a half mile from the State road leading from Philadelphia to Baltimore, Mr Morton, although adverse to the measure, voted in favor of the bill, and it was adopted As the time for the election drew nigh, the public excitement was fanned to fever heat, and the newspapers teemed with lengthy articles urging the peculiar views of the various writers on the question at issue, which in the lapse of years has become very uninteresting reading

The election was held on Oct 12, 1847, and resulted in a majority of seven hundred and fifty-two votes in favor of the proposed change in the location of the county-seat The opponents of the measure, inasmuch as the Supreme Court had decided that a law submitting to the vote of the people the power to determine whether spirituous liquors should or should not be sold in the respective townships when such a vote was had was unconstitutional, determined to test the validity of the law, which had been in like manner submitted to the people, respecting the change of the county-seat In the mean while the act of April 9, 1848, confirming the removal of the seat of justice was adopted, a proviso in that act, however, declaring it should not go into effect until the Supreme Court had decided the question as to the constitutionality of the law under which it had been voted on by the people At the December term of that year the case was argued, and at the following spring term the Supreme Court held the act to be constitutional In compliance with that decision the court records were removed from Chester to Media in the summer of 1851, on the completion of the public buildings at that borough

The incidents and happenings in the county from that date are so connected with the various townships wherein they occurred that practically the general history of the county terminates for the present. The glorious story of the civil war—for no locality in the loyal States exceeds in patriotism that of Delaware County in that trying period of our nation's annals—will be related in the succeeding chapter

Under the provisions of the Constitution of 1874 Delaware County became the thirty-second judicial district, the vacancy on the bench thereby created being filled early in that year by the appointment by Governor Hartranft of Hon John M Broomall, president judge At the ensuing election in November, Hon Thomas J Clayton was elected to the bench, and took his seat in January, 1875

CHAPTER XVII

THE CIVIL WAR

The war of sections, which had overhung the country for over forty years, burst upon the nation on Saturday, April 13, 1861, when the American flag was hauled down at Fort Sumter, under the assaults of Southern military men who, on the plains of Mexico, had proudly marched to victory under its folds Then the pent-up anger of the North broke all restraint, and a great people rose resistless in their might It was amazing with what rapidity the news sped from farm-house to farm-house that Fort Sumter would be evacuated by Maj Anderson on the morrow In Chester, Media, Darby, Rockdale, Kellyville, in all the towns, villages, and cross road hamlets in Delaware County, the people, abandoning their usual avocations, gathered in excited groups to discuss the engrossing intelligence, knowing not in what direction to give expression to their enthusiasm, save in demonstrations of patriotism Over the court-house at Media, at the town hall in Chester, and the public buildings throughout the county, over mills, workshops, stores, and private dwellings, before nightfall the stars and stripes floated to the winds, or where that was not done, the angry muttering of the populace soon compelled compliance with the popular will, and tri-colored badges were displayed on the breasts of almost every man, woman, and child, for the people were stirred as no living man then could recall the like in all our national history Sunday followed, and the anxiety to learn the latest news from the seat of war was intense, and in the absence of intelligence the suspense became oppressive On Monday morning, April 15, 1861, direction was given to the public excitement when President Lincoln issued his proclamation calling for seventy-five thousand troops to be enlisted for a period of three months, unless sooner discharged

In Media, on that Monday morning, the people crowded the court house, called thither by the ringing of the bell, when patriotic speeches were delivered, and finally it was determined to form a rifle-corps immediately After arrangements were made to obtain recruits, the meeting adjourned until Wednesday evening following, the 17th At Chester, on that same Monday evening, the old town hall, with its memories of the stirring days of '76, once more rang with patriotic calls to the people to arm in defense of liberty and human rights Nobly throughout the county was the response made, and the sound of the fife and drum was heard on all sides

On Wednesday night, at Media, the adjourned meeting reassembled in the court-house Edward Darlington was called to the chair, and Charles D Manley, Charles R. Williamson, James R Cummins, John R Roland, Robert Playford, and J Crosby Fairlamb acted as vice-presidents, and O F Bullard and Thomas V Cooper as secretaries. Speeches were made by John M Broomall, Joseph Addison Thomson, and Hugh Jones Brooke Among the thousand baseless rumors flashing along the wires that day was one which stated that Jefferson Davis, with ten thousand troops, was marching directly on Washington, determined on its immediate capture The intelligence, false as it was, served to rouse the patriotic indignation of the people, so that name followed name rapidly on the roll of those willing to be led at once against the enemy, and the ranks of the "Delaware County Union Rifles" were filled, while many men were anxious to be recruited even after the list had been closed So rapidly was the company organization effected that on Friday morning, April 19th, the men were assembled in front of the court-house, where, after a prayer by Rev Mr Gracey, they marched to the car, and were forwarded to Philadelphia There, at the Western Market-House, a collation was served, and the company addressed by Charles D Manley and H Jones Brooke The same afternoon they reached Harrisburg, where they encamped in the capitol grounds, and the next day, April 20th, were mustered into the service for three months

Company F, Fourth Regiment Pennsylvania Volunteers, mustered into service April 20, 1861, as follows

Captain, George Dunn, first lieutenant, T V Cooper, second lieutenant, A McMuron, sergeants, William Callum, Richard Stiles, Thomas J McMillan, J L Woodcock, corporals, Caleb Hooper, James Mulholland, John B Sully, William Durell, musicians, William Quail, Henry Carney

Privates—Henry J Baker, Thomas Broomall, John Baggs, Peter Brantz, William Baggs, John Britton, Matthew Blair, Robert Coppock, John Cottingham, John Clowney, Thomas Coulter, James Conner, John B Davis, Thomas Dyson, John M Davis, William Eckil, James Evans, Able Ford, Allen Ford, Lorenzo D Farra, William Farra, David Grubb, Thomas Griffin, James Gorman, John W Glen, Benjamin Graden, George W Glen, Henry Greenwood, Hamilton Gillon, Robert Henderson, John Hollingsworth, Patrick Hughes, Daniel Harigan, Robert Johnson, Stephen Johnson, Jeremiah Ketzler, Thomas Kelly, Thomas Laden, Benjamin H Magee, Michael Monahan Michael Martin, John McCuen, William McGinnis, Richard J Nuttle, John Palmer, John P Potts, Joseph Parker, William Roberts, Amos R. Rap, Franklin Redmond, Antrim Redmond, Ephraim Stirk, George Stikes, Samuel N Techton, William Townsend, John Yeehton, Baker C Wright, James W G Weaver, James Walters, James Wasson, James Worrell, John Williams, Lee L Yarnall

The Fourth Regiment, commanded by Col John F Hartranft, was the following day, April 21st, ordered to Philadelphia, where, under command of Col Dare, of the Twenty-third Regiment, acting brigadier, it was dispatched to Perryville, Md There it encamped that night, and the next day was ordered to embark on steamers for Annapolis, and thence moved to Washington, the riots in Baltimore having interrupted direct communication with the national capital The regiment had been so hastily sent forward that it was not then uniformed, although the soldiers were armed with muskets and carried ammunition in their pockets The Fourth remained at Annapolis until the 8th of May, when it was forwarded to Washington and quartered in the Assembly Buildings Sickness prevailing among the men, it was encamped about two miles from the city in the direction of Bladensburg On June 24th it was ordered to Alexandria, where on Sunday, June 30th, its pickets for the first time were engaged with a small party of the enemy The Fourth, in the organization of the army of McDowell, formed part of the First Brigade, Third Division Its hour of enlistment expired on Sunday, July 31, 1861, the day of Bull Run, when McDowell desired the regiment to remain until after the battle had been fought There being a difference of opinion among the men, it was finally marched to Washington, and thence by rail to Harrisburg, where it was mustered out of service McDowell, in his report after his crushing defeat, attempted to relieve himself from a part of the blame of that day's disaster by a slurring censure of the Fourth Pennsylvania, but the records of the War Department show that in the great majority of instances the men who composed that organization at Bull Run on subsequently bloody battle-fields manifested their valor and patriotism The Delaware County Union Rifles, however, had been discharged from the service the day before the battle, and any reflection Gen McDowell indulged in respecting the Fourth Regiment as a whole has no application to the Media company

In Chester, at the conclusion of the meeting of citizens held on Monday evening, April 15, 1861, steps were immediately taken for the enrollment of a company On Wednesday more than a sufficient number had been enlisted, and at the meeting of the company it was decided that the organization should be known as the "Union Blues" An election of officers was held, and Henry B Edwards was chosen captain Rev Mr Talbot, then rector of St Paul's parish, presented a sword he had worn when chaplain in the United States navy, to Capt. Edwards The Union Blues at once began drilling and equipping to respond at a moment's notice when ordered

On Saturday morning, April 20, 1861, the Union Blues were directed to proceed at once to Harrisburg, and at six o'clock that evening the company mustered in front of the Washington House, in Chester, where they were addressed by Frederick J Hinkson, who stated that the citizens of the borough pledged themselves that the wives and families of the soldiers depending on them for support should be protected and maintained during the absence of the men at the front. Addresses were also made by Rev. Mr. Talbot, rector of St. Paul's, and Mr. Sproull, of the Presbyterian Church. Rev. Father Haviland, of St. Michael's parish, personally contributed and solicited subscriptions to a fund to be used in equipping the men who had volunteered, and for the maintenance of the families of those who had gone in the service. As evening came the streets were crowded, and no one old enough to remember those early days of the war can forget the departure of the first troops who responded to the call of President Lincoln, or the ovation then extended throughout the North to the "boys in blue," before constant repetition in the years of battle which followed had imparted a sameness to the movements of soldiers. The crowd of people which gathered at the railway station, including cultured and refined women, was the largest the ancient borough had ever known until that time in all its history. And when the engine with the special train rolled from the station, the impression that war had indeed come upon the nation caused the populace to disperse in silence to their homes. The "Union Blues" reached Camp Curtin, at Harrisburg, the following day, and on Monday, April 22d, were mustered into the Ninth Regiment, Pennsylvania Volunteers, for a period of three months.' On May 4th the regiment was moved to West Chester, where it arrived at nine o'clock at night during a severe storm of sleet and snow, and as no arrangement had been made for their reception, they were quartered in the rooms attached to the old depot. The next day Col. Longnecker selected a location for cantonment, which was named Camp Wayne in honor of "Mad Anthony," of the Revolution. On May 26, 1861, the Ninth Regiment was ordered to Wilmington, Del., to prevent disloyal citizens in that State from forming military organizations for the Confederate service, and went into camp at Hare's Corner, between Wilmington and New Castle. The regiment, on June 6th, was ordered to Chambersburg to join Gen. Patterson's command, and was attached to the First Brigade, First Division, under Col. Miles. On Sunday, June 16th, Miles' Brigade crossed the Potomac, the Ninth having the right of the column, the troops wading the stream, the water reaching breast-high. Subsequently they were ordered to recross the river and take a position to cover the ford. On July 1st the brigade again passed over in the direction of Martinsburg, and on the 8th a forward movement of the whole army was ordered by Gen. Patterson in the direction of Winchester and Bunker Hill, but a council of war being held, it was decided to countermand the order. On the 17th of July, Longnecker's brigade marched towards Charlestown, where it encamped, remaining there until the 21st, when it marched to Harper's Ferry. On the 22d the Ninth Regiment was marched to Hagerstown, and thence forwarded to Harrisburg, when it was mustered out of service, the period of the enlistment having expired.

The following is the roll of Company I, Ninth Regiment, three months' Pennsylvania Volunteers:

Captain, Henry B. Edwards; first lieutenant, James G. Stacey; second lieutenant, William Blakeley; sergeants, William B. Stevenson, John Beck, James Williams, William Eves; corporals, Isaac Weaver, William R. Thatcher, Charles Storey, Jesse Cummings; musicians, Ezra Dransfield, Alexander King.

Privates.—John Booth, Joseph Barker, Joseph Brewster, Lewis Benner, John C. Barrowclough, Thomas Blythe, Isaac F. Badden, William H. Brown, David Burke, George Booth, Thomas W. Bruner, Edward Crowther, Edward Collison, Samuel Cross, Daniel Crowther, James Cliff, Allen Carr, Frederick Cutler, Frederick Crider, Simeon Davis, John Doyle, William Elliott, Theodore Ettienne, Robert Fogg, John Farraday, Joseph Grooves, William P. Huff, James Hewes, George Helms, William F. Jester, James P. Kelley, Edward Kay, Jonathan Kershaw, Edward Lilley, Edward Lyons, Thomas McNamee, William McNeil, John Marshal, William Marlor, Samuel McDaniel, George McAffee, John C. Morton, John Phillips, Daniel Pithie, Thomas F. Pierce, Anthony Quinn, Francis Rodrigos, Robert Reaney, Samuel Shephord, Francis Scott, Edgar Stevenson, William V. Shellinger, John Smith, Samuel Smith, Thomas Toy, Joseph Taylor, Jr., Richard Turner, George W. Wilson, Joshua L. Wilson, John Wagner, Robert Wright, Alfred Woodhead, George Weigan, Reed L. Weaver.

The two companies having gone to the front the citizens of the county did not relax their efforts, but in all directions home guards were formed and drilled in the manual of arms, such organizations being effected at Chester, Media, Rockdale, Darby, Linwood, Kellyville, Wildeville, Glen Mills, Village Green, Upland, and other localities. So rapidly did the organizations form that on July 4th, at Chester, a parade was made by the Wayne Guards, Capt. W. C. Gray; Home Guards, Capt. H. B. Taylor; Company A, Capt. George E. Darlington; Upland Guards, Capt. George K. Crozer, while on the same day, at the county-seat, the Village Green Guards, Capt. Barton; Glen Mills Guards, Capt. Willcox; Manchester Rifles, Capt. Ballentine; Upper Darby Home Guards, Capt. Buckley, joined with the Media Home Guards in a parade.

On Tuesday afternoon, April 23, 1861, an immense meeting of the people of the county was held in the court-house at Media. H. Jones Brooke was made president, and stirring addresses were delivered. Contributions amounting to two thousand five hundred dollars were made that day, and the county was divided into seven districts for the purpose of soliciting funds to equip troops and support the families of volunteers. Chester, Ridley, and Tinicum constituted the first district; the second comprised Media, Nether and Upper Providence, and all of Middletown east of Edgmont road; the third Marcus Hook, Linwood, Lower and Upper Chester, Bethel, and all of Aston south of Concord road; the fourth Concord, Birmingham, and Thornbury; the fifth Aston, east of Concord road, Middletown, west of Edgmont road, and Edgmont; the sixth Springfield, Darby, and Upper Darby; and the seventh Haverford, Marple, Newtown, and Radnor. The meeting, as taxpayers, called on the county commissioners at once to appropriate five thousand dollars, and twenty thousand dollars thereafter, to be used for the support of the families of those men who should join the army The activity did not cease here, for the subordinate committees in the several districts in two days after their appointment collected two thousand seven hundred dollars for the relief fund and in addition Samuel M Felton, president of the Philadelphia, Wilmington and Baltimore Railroad Company, sent a check for one thousand dollars to John P Crozer, as the contribution of the company Mr. Felton also notified the clerks in the employment of the road that those who should go to the front would receive their salaries while absent, and on their return from the war would be taken back into the railroad company's service. The women were as active as the men, and busy fingers found constant employment during all the four succeeding years of war in fabricating articles of clothing to minister to the comfort and healthfulness of the soldiers in the field

After the defeat at Bull Run had convinced the North that the revolting States were terribly in earnest, that they were brave men, ably commanded, and that a war which would dwarf all former wars in the world's history had begun, the popular excitement of the first three months of open hostilities settled into dogged determination that, cost what it might, the national authority should be maintained in every part of the land During the latter part of July, and in August, 1861, recruiting for new military organizations was brisk in the county Hereafter the local history of the time, so far as it relates to the several companies and regiments, will be presented in a connected account of such organizations

Twenty-sixth Regiment (Three-Years' Service) —Although the history of this regiment antedates the actual outbreak of hostilities, and, as will be recalled, under Col Small, it was attacked in Baltimore on April 19, 1861, when on its way to Washington to be equipped and armed, it is nowise distinctly connected with the annals of Delaware County until nearly a month subsequent to that event Under the call of the United States, May 3, 1861, for troops to serve a period of three years, William L Grubb began recruiting a company in Chester and the surrounding neighborhood This company was mustered in on May 31, 1861, as Company K, Twenty-sixth Regiment, and on Monday evening, June 16th, it went through Chester. The people in the ancient borough, knowing that the company was ordered to Washington, gathered at the station and along the railroad The boys in blue, as they caught sight of their friends and acquaintances, waved their hats from the car windows and platforms and cheered, which was taken up and answered by the people who had been watching their coming so anxiously The main body of the regiment was then at Washington guarding the quartermaster-general's stores, the arsenal, and the flying bridge at Georgetown The regiment was subsequently assigned to Gen Hooker's division, and early in April, 1862, was transported to the Peninsula, where it took part in the siege of Yorktown, and on May 5th, at the battle of Williamsburg in front of Fort Magruder, it drove the enemy out of the rifle-pits into the works, which position it held for eight hours until fresh troops came to its support, and the fort was taken It was engaged at Seven Pines, and in "the change of base," on June 19th, was in action at Savage Station On the 20th it was engaged in the battle of White Oak Swamp from noon to night, and just before dusk of that long summer day it made a brilliant bayonet charge, breaking the enemy's line, compelling them to retire, and the following day it took part in the battle of Malvern Hill On August 20th it was with Heintzelman's corps, dispatched to the support of Gen Pope In that campaign it was engaged at Bristoe Station on the 26th, and the next day opened communication for the army with its base of supplies On the 29th it marched through Centreville to Bull Run, going at once into the fight, where it suffered severely Capt Meekins, of Company K, was killed in this battle The next day the Twenty-sixth Regiment was held as support to three different batteries, which compelled it to march rapidly from point to point as occasion required At Burnside's defeat at Fredericksburg it was in the front line of battle, and was engaged with but slight intermission for thirty hours At Chancellorsville, on May 2, 1863, the regiment made a reconnoissance up the road in front of Hooker's headquarters to feel the enemy, and on the 3d it was held as a support to batteries after it had fallen back to the intrenchments, a movement made necessary after the Seventy-second New York had broken, leaving the flank of the Twenty-sixth uncovered and exposed to a heavy fire, by which it lost nearly a hundred men In the Gettysburg campaign it was with Gen Sickles, and reached the field on the evening of the 1st of July, 1863 The next day the regiment was on the extreme right of the division, and suffered severely Late in the day it sustained a charge of a Florida brigade, which it checked, and in turn charged the enemy, driving the latter in confusion, capturing many prisoners The loss of the Twenty-sixth Regiment in this battle was appalling It had gone into the fight with three hundred and sixty-four men, and its loss was two hundred and sixteen killed and wounded, this number including three color-bearers who were killed In Grant's campaign, on May 5, 1864, at the battle of the Wilderness, it was on the extreme left of the army and held its position, although repeatedly assailed On the 12th, at Spottsylvania Court-House, it took part in Hancock's grand charge with the Second Corps, and in the engagement the Twenty-sixth captured two Napoleon guns, which it turned with effect on the enemy It was actively engaged at the crossing of the North Anna River, and on the 27th of May crossed the Pamunkey River at

Nelson's Ford, where its term of service having expired it was ordered to Philadelphia, where, on June 18, 1864, in front of Independence Hall, it was mustered out

COMPANY C

Thomas V Cooper, private, served until after battle of Gettysburg, detached by order of War Department and placed in charge of government printing office at Camp Distribution, where he remained until close of war

COMPANY K

William L Grubb, capt, must in May 31, 1861, res Dec 30, 1861

John F Meekins, capt., must. in May 31, 1861, pro to 1st lieut. Feb 6, 1862, to capt. August, 1862, killed at Bull Run Aug 29, 1862

James L Seary, capt., must in May 13, 1861, pro to 1st lieut April 1, 1863, to capt April 13, 1864, must. out with company June 18, 1864

Peter P G Hall, 2d lieut, must in May 31, 1861, pro to adjt Aug 10, 1861

William H Phillips, sergt., must. in May 31, 1861, pro from corp to sergt., must out with company June 18, 1864

George W Rosevelt, sergt., must. in May 31, 1861, pro to sergt October, 1862, wounded, with loss of leg, at Gettysburg, disch on surg certif March 14, 1864

William Groundsell, sergt., must in May 31, 1861, trans to 99th Regt P V May 30, 1864, veteran

Samuel P Morris, sergt., must in May 31, 1861, died of wounds rec at Gettysburg July 2, 1863

Isaac Ford, corp., must in May 31, 1861, pro to corp, must out with company June 18, 1864

James Schofield, corp, must in May 31, 1861, pro to corp, must out with company June 18, 1864

Isaac Brown, corp, must in May 31, 1861, captured at Williamsburg, Va., May 5, 1862, disch on surg certif, date unknown

Nathan Larkin, corp., must in May 31, 1861, disch on surg certif March 19, 1863

James Ford, corp., must in May 31, 1861, trans to 99th Regt. P V May 30, 1864, veteran

Nathan R Van Horn, corp., must in May 31, 1861, killed at Gettysburg July 2, 1863

James L Gelsten, corp, must. in June 12, 1861, killed at Gettysburg July 2, 1863

Isaac Bird, corp., must in May 31, 1861 pro to corp Aug 15, 1863, died of wounds received at Spottsylvania Court House May 15, 1864, veteran

Alexander Graydon, musician, must in May 31, 1861, must out with company June 18, 1864, veteran

Privates.

Henry Abbott, must in May 31, 1861, disch Nov 4, 1862, for wounds received at Bull Run Aug 29, 1862

Lewis Bail, must in May 31, 1861, wounded at Spottsylvania May 15, 1864, absent at muster out

John Boylan, must in May 31, 1861, must out with company June 18, 1864

Thomas Brown, must in May 31, 1861, absent, sick, at muster out

Mark Bail, must in May 31, 1861, disch on surg certif July 21, 1861

George Braunon, must in May 31, 1861, disch Nov 4, 1862, for wounds received at Bull Run Aug 29, 1862

Thomas Blizzard, must in May 31, 1861, trans to 99th Regt P V May 30, 1864, veteran

William H Brown, must in Aug 29, 1861, trans to 99th Regt P V May 30, 1864, veteran

Lewis Bail, must in Aug 19 1863, drafted, trans to 99th Regt P V May 30, 1864, died June 19, 1864, at Andersonville grave 2180

William F Brant, must in April 14, 1864, trans to 99th Regt P V May 30, 1864

James T Bell, must in May 31, 1861, died of wounds received at Spottsylvania May 15, 1864

John Boyle, must in May 31, 1861

John Boyce, must in May 31, 1861

Jacob Cahn, must in May 31, 1861, reduced from sergt. Oct 1, 1862, disch on surg certif Oct 17, 1862

William H Clark, must in May 31, 1861, reduced from sergt March, 1863, trans to Co F, 26th Regt P V, April 1, 1863

James Cloud, must in May 31, 1861, trans to Vet Res. Corps, date unknown

William Cleniff, must in Aug 10, 1861, trans to 99th Regt P V May 30, 1864.

Edward Caves must in May 31, 1861

Joseph Dicks, must in June 4, 1861, must out with company June 18, 1864

William K Dobbins, must in Aug 29, 1861, trans to 99th Regt P V May 30, 1864

John Derlin, must in June 4, 1861, killed at Gettysburg July 2, 1863

Henry Dickinson, must in May 31, 1861

Jacob Evans, must. in May 31, 1861, absent sick, at muster out

William H Furgesen, must in May 31, 1861, must out with company June 18, 1864

Constantine Fuget, must in May 31, 1861, wounded at Gettysburg July 2, 1863, must out with company June 18, 1864

John Freeman, must in May 31, 1861, disch on surg certif Dec 5, 1862

Daniel C Ford, must in May 31, 1861, disch on surg certif Dec 2, 1863

Brinton Fryar, must. in Aug 29, 1861, wounded at Fair Oaks June 23, 1862, disch date unknown

William Fagan, must in Aug 19, 1863 trans to 99th Regt. P V May 30, 1864

Isaac Force, must. in May 31, 1861, not on muster-out roll

Henry Goodwin, must in May 31, 1861, must out with company June 18 1864

John Grubb, must in May 31, 1861, disch on surg certif July 21, 1861

James Grubb, must in May 31, 1861, pro from corp to sergt, reduced Oct 1, 1862, disch on surg certif Oct 17, 1862

James Gleason, must in Aug 19, 1861, drafted, died of wounds received at Spottsylvania Court House May 15, 1864

Joseph Grubb, must in May 31, 1861

William Hayes, must in May 31, 1861, wounded at Spottsylvania May 10, 1864, must out Aug 12, 1864

George Helms, must in May 31, 1861, disch on surg certif July 21, 1861

John S Hunter, must in May 31, 1861, disch on surg certif July 1, 1862

John Hammitt, must in Sept 20, 1862, trans to 99th Regt P V May 30, 1864

John K Hammitt, must in Sept 16, 1862 trans to 99th Regt P V May 30, 1864

Maxwell Hogarth, must in Sept 20, 1862, trans to 99th Regt P V May 30, 1864

Joseph Hogarth, must in Sept 20, 1862, trans to 99th Regt P V May 30, 1864

James Higgens, must in May 31, 1861, killed at Bull Run Aug 29, 1862

John Jordan, must in Sept 20, 1862, trans to 99th Regt P V May 30, 1864

Matthew Kersey, must in May 31, 1861, disch on surg certif July 21, 1861

Thursten Lowe, must in Aug 20, 1861, trans. to Vet Res Corps, date unknown

Samuel Latch, must in May 31, 1861, trans to 99th Regt. P V May 30, 1864, veteran

John O Long, must in May 31, 1861, trans to 99th Regt P V May 30, 1864, veteran

Norton Lindsay, must in May 31, 1861

George Miller, must in Jan 18, 1864, not on muster out roll

William H Miller, must in June 4, 1861, trans to Battery D, 4th N Y Art, May, 1862, must out March 18, 1865

William B Michael, must in May 31, 1861, disch on surg certif July 21, 1861

James Morris, must in May 31, 1861, trans to 99th Regt P V May 30, 1864, veteran

Francis Miller, must in Aug 19, 1863, drafted

Robert McGrath, must in May 31, 1861, must out with company

Archibald McNeil, must in June 6, 1861, trans to Vet Res Corps, date unknown

John McClem, must in June 12, 1861, died at Yorktown, Va., April 21, 1862

Robert McGathy, must in May 31, 1861

Samuel Pullen, must in May 31, 1861, wounded at Fredericksburg Dec 13, 1862, absent at muster out of company

William Phillips, must in May 31, 1861, wounded at Chancellorsville May 3, 1863, absent at muster out of company

William Paster, must. in May 31, 1861, disch on surg certif July 21, 1861

Andrew Phillips, must. in May 31, 1861, died of wounds received at Spottsylvania Court-House May 15, 1864, veteran
Benjamin Pine, must in May 31, 1861
William Rambo, must in May 31, 1861, wounded at Gettysburg July 2, 1863, absent at muster out of company
George W Robinson, must in April 14, 1864, trans to 99th Regt P V May 30, 1864
George Roan, must in Aug 10, 1861, killed at Gettysburg July 2, 1863
Samuel Radcliff, must in May 31, 1861
Stephen Rodgers, must in May 31, 1861
Samuel Rodgers, must in May 31, 1861
Andrew Sample, must. in May 31, 1861, trans to 99th Regt P V May 30, 1864, veteran
Godfrey Smith, must in Sept 16, 1862 trans to 99th Regt P V May 30, 1864, veteran
John Smith, must in Aug 20, 1863, drafted, trans to 99th Regt P V May 30, 1864
William S Swain, must in Aug 20, 1863, drafted, trans to 99th Regt P V May 30, 1864
Charles Shut, must in Aug 20, 1861, died at Washington, D C., May 23, 1862, buried in Military Asylum Cemetery
James Starr, must in May 31, 1861, must out with company June 18, 1864.
Benjamin F Sutch, must in May 31, 1861, wounded at Spottsylvania May 15, 1864, absent at muster out of company
Alvis Simpson, must in Aug 19, 1863, drafted, trans to U S navy April 18, 1864
Daniel Sowers, must in May 31, 1861
Edward Shields, must in May 31, 1861, disch on surg certif July 2, 1861
Francis Scott, must in Aug 29, 1861, wounded at Bull Run Aug 29, 1862, disch on surg certif October, 1862
Thomas Senior, must in June 13, 1861
William Studer, must in Aug 19, 1863, drafted
William Sailor, must in Aug 20, 1863, drafted
Henry Smith, must in Aug 20, 1863, drafted, died Aug 20, 1864, at Andersonville, grave 6289
George Toner, must in May 31, 1861, wounded at Mine Run Nov 27, 1863, must out with company June 13, 1864
William Wilson, must in Aug 5, 1861, trans to 99th Regt P V May 30, 1864, veteran
Malachi Walraven, must. in Sept. 5, 1861, trans to 99th Regt. P V May 30, 1864
George Wood, must. in Aug 20, 1861, killed at Gettysburg July 2, 1863
James Walsh, must. in May 31, 1861, died of wounds received at Chancellorsville May 3, 1863
Seth Yelt, must in May 31, 1861, disch on surg certif, date unknown

Thirtieth Regiment, First Reserves.—Early in May, 1861, Samuel A Dyer began recruiting men at Chester for a company of infantry then termed the "Keystone Guards" So rapidly had troops responded to the call of the President that the quota of Pennsylvania was filled, and for a time it seemed as though no men save those who had already been accepted would be mustered into service In this State Governor Curtin, with a better conception of the teaching of the times than any other man in official station in the north (excepting perhaps Simon Cameron), knowing that additional troops would shortly be required, determined to form several camps for military instruction in the State, and to collect there troops, who should be disciplined and equipped ready for the emergency which he saw must come This purpose Governor Curtin carried into effect, and the soldiers thus collected were subsequently known and will ever be recalled in the annals of the commonwealth in which they played no inconsiderable part, as "the Pennsylvania Reserves" The men who were recruited for the Keystone Guards, as stated, were quartered in the town hall, in Chester, for a week or ten days, maintained by the voluntary subscription of several citizens of the borough, and finally, the name being changed to "Slifer Phalanx," in honor of Hon Eli Slifer, then secretary of the commonwealth, the organization was ordered to report at the Girard House, Philadelphia, where it was mustered in May 31, 1861 While there a handsome flag was presented to the company by the ladies of Chester Hon Edward Darlington made the presentation address On June 4th the Slifer Phalanx left for Camp Wayne, at West Chester, where it became Company C, Thirtieth Regiment First Pennsylvania Reserves, for a term of three years' service

COMPANY A

Privates

Edward Blaine, must in June 4, 1861, wounded at Antietam Sept 17, 1862, must out with company June 13, 1864
William C Brogan, must in June 4, 1861, disch on surg certif Oct 12, 1862
Daniel Young, must in June 4, 1861, trans to 190th Regt. P V May 31, 1864, veteran

COMPANY C

Samuel A Dyer,[1] capt, must. in May 31, 1861, pro to lieut-col 175th Regt P V Nov 2, 1862
Joseph R T Coates, capt, must in May 31, 1861, pro from 1st lieut to capt March 1, 1863, to brev maj March 13, 1865, must out with company June 13, 1864
Edward Larkin, 1st lieut, must in May 31, 1861, pro from 1st sergt to 1st lieut March 1, 1863, to brev capt March 13, 1864, must out with company June 13, 1864
John H Taylor, 2d lieut., must in Sept 5, 1861, killed at South Mountain Sept 14, 1862
John M Thompson 2d lieut., must in May 31, 1861, pro from sergt to 2d lieut March 1, 1863, to brev 1st lieut March 13, 1865, must. out with company June 13, 1864
William O Ridgway, sergt., must in May 31, 1861, disch on surg certif June 25, 1863
Robert H Welsh, sergt., must in May 31, 1861, trans to 190th Regt. P V May 31, 1864, veteran
T McNamee, sergt., must in Feb. 28, 1864, trans to 190th Regt P V May 31, 1864.
J Ashbridge, corp., must in May 31, 1861 must out with company June 13, 1864.
John Jones, corp., must in July 10, 1861, must out with company June 13, 1864
David Lascom, corp, must in July 14, 1861, must out with company June 13, 1864
George McAffee, corp., must. in Aug 14, 1861 disch for wounds received at Bull Run Aug 30, 1862
Edward E. Flavill, corp., must in May 31, 1861, disch June, 1861
J H Williams, corp, must in May 31, 1861, disch on surg certif Dec 22, 1861
John McDonald, corp, must in May 31, 1861
Abram R Vansant, musician, must in May 31, 1861, trans to 190th Regt P V May 31, 1864, veteran

Privates

Samuel Ardis, must in May 31, 1861
Edward Butler, must in May 31, 1861
John Booth, must in July 10, 1861
John Brophy, must in May 31, 1861
William Rumford, must. in May 31, 1861
William Clineff, must in May 31, 1861, disch July 24, 1861
Aquilla Coates, must. in May 31, 1861, died Sept 26, 1861

[1] The One Hundred and Seventy fifth Regiment was composed of drafted men for nine months' service, and was part of Gen Spinola's brigade, was in service in North Carolina, and subsequently acted with the Army of the Potomac during Lee's advance into Pennsylvania It was mustered out of service at Philadelphia, April 7, 1863

William Curry, must. in May 31, 1861.
James Dougherty, must. in May 31, 1861; must. out with company June 13, 1864.
Charles Dougherty, must. in May 31, 1861; disch. July 24, 1861.
Daniel Donelson, must. in May 31, 1861; trans. to 190th Regt. P. V. May 31, 1864; veteran.
John Devlin, must. in May 31, 1861; trans. to Vet. Res. Corps Sept. 15, 1863; veteran.
George Edwards, must. in July 8, 1861; trans. to 190th Regt. P. V. May 31, 1864; veteran.
George Elliott, must. in July 8, 1861; trans. to 190th Regt. P. V. May 31, 1864; veteran.
Edward Elliott, must. in May 31, 1861; trans. to 190th Regt. P. V. May 31, 1864; veteran.
George Fields, must. in July 8, 1861; disch. by order of War Dept. Jan. 26, 1863.
George Farrend, must. in May 31, 1861.
Isaac Helms, must. in May 31, 1861; must. out with company June 13, 1864.
Edward Hickman, must. in May 31, 1861; disch., date unknown.
William Howard, must. in July 8, 1861; disch. July 12, 1861.
John Huff, must. in July 8, 1861; trans. to 190th Regt. P. V. May 31, 1864; veteran.
Luke Holsten, must. in April 1, 1864; trans. to 190th Regt. P. V. May 31, 1864.
Harry Hobaugh, must. in May 31, 1861; died Oct. 30, 1861.
John Hurst, must. in May 31, 1861.
Ralph Jones, must. in March 3, 1862; trans. to gen. hosp. July 18, 1862.
William Lammy, must. in March 3, 1862.
Peter Miller, must. in March 3, 1862; not must. into U. S. service.
John H. Murry, must. in Aug. 13, 1862; disch. on surg. certif. Dec. 30, 1862.
R. Mills, must. in September, 1861; died May 31, 1864, of wounds received in action.
Thomas Mills, must. in May 31, 1861.
Joseph Merton, must. in March 8, 1864; trans. to 190th Regt. P. V. May 31, 1864.
Frank McFate, must. in Aug. 13, 1861; must. out with company June 13, 1864.
Thomas McGarvey, must. in Aug. 13, 1864; died May 31, 1864, of wounds received in action; veteran.
Henry McClusky, must. in May 31, 1861.
William C. Paist, must. in May 31, 1861; must. out with company June 13, 1864.
James Pollock, must. in May 31, 1861; died Nov. 10, 1862, of wounds received in action.
William R. Ross, must. in May 31, 1861; must. out with company June 13, 1864.
John Roebuck, must. in May 31, 1861; not must. into U. S. service.
James Riley, must. in May 31, 1861.
Jesse Suplee, must. in May 31, 1861; not must. into U. S. service.
David Stevenson, must. in May 31, 1861; not must. into U. S. service.
William Stillwell, must. in May 31, 1861; not must. into U. S. service.
James Stewart, must. in May 31, 1861; not must. into U. S. service.
A. Shaw, must. in May 31, 1861; trans. to 190th Regt. P. V. May 31, 1864; veteran.
J. T. Schofield, must. in May 31, 1861; killed at Bethesda Church, May 30, 1864.
James Sanders, must. in May 31, 1861.
John Smith, must. in May 31, 1861.
William H. Taylor, must. in May 31, 1861; disch. Nov. 30, 1862, for wounds received at South Mountain, Sept. 14, 1862.
Joseph Turner, must. in May 31, 1861.
Thomas Vansant, must. in May 31, 1861; must. out with company June 13, 1864.
Samuel Williams, must. in May 31, 1861; must. out with company June 13, 1864.
George Worsley, must. in May 31, 1861; must. out with company June 13, 1864.
Collins Walker, must. in May 31, 1864; disch. Aug. 9, 1861.
Thomas Wilkinson, must. in May 31, 1861; not must. into U. S. service.
Thomas Wray, must. in July 13, 1861; not must. into U. S. service.
Patrick Waters, must. in July 9, 1861; not must. into U. S. service.
Robert Wray, must. in July 25, 1861; trans. to 190th Regt. P. V. May 31, 1864; veteran.
Alfred G. Webb, must. in May 31, 1861; killed at Fredericksburg, Dec. 13, 1862.
Solomon Wesler, must. in Feb. 10, 1862; killed at Spottsylvania Court-House Dec. 13, 1864.
George Welch, must. in May 31, 1861.

When the first intelligence reached Delaware County that Fort Sumter had been occupied by the Confederates, and the President had issued the call for troops, William Cooper Talley began recruiting at Crozerville and Rockdale an infantry company, then called the "Rockdale Rifle Guards." Subsequently the title was changed to the "Archy Dick Volunteers," so named in honor of Archibald T. Dick, a deceased eminent member of the bar of Delaware County. The quota of the State being full, Capt. Talley encountered the like difficulty in having the company accepted, as related respecting the "Slifer Phalanx." The action of Governor Curtin in forming the Pennsylvania Reserves, as heretofore stated, furnished the opportunity to this company to be accepted, and at Camp Wayne, on May 30, 1861, the organization was mustered into the Thirtieth Regiment, First Reserves, as Company F, for three years' service. The following is the roll of

COMPANY F.

William Cooper Talley, capt., must. in May 30, 1861; pro. to col. 30th Regt. P. V. March 1, 1863.
Joseph P. Drew, capt., must. in May 30, 1861; pro. to 1st lieut. March 1, 1863; to capt. Oct. 28, 1863; must. out with company June 13, 1864.
Henry Huddleson, capt., must. in May 30, 1861; res. August, 1863.
John F. Gorman, 1st lieut., must. in May 30, 1861; pro. from corp. to sergt. March 1, 1862; to 2d lieut. March 1, 1863; to 1st lieut. Oct. 28, 1863; must. out with company June 13, 1864.
James S. Peters, 2d lieut., must. in May 30, 1861; disch. June 23, 1863.
John McDaniels, 1st sergt., must. in May 30, 1861; com. 2d lieut. Oct. 1, 1863; not must.; missing in action at Bethesda Church May 30, 1864; trans. to 190th Regt. P. V. May 31, 1864; veteran.
Charles F. Sheaff, 1st sergt., must. in June 4, 1861; trans. from Co. A; pro. 1st sergt. January, 1862; died August, 1862.
James P. Dean, sergt., must in May 30, 1861; pro. to corp. Aug. 30, 1862; to sergt. March 1, 1863; must. out with company June 13, 1864.
Jacob C. Berstler, sergt., must. in May 30, 1861; disch. on surg. certif. July 26, 1861.
Samuel Batty, sergt., must. in May 30, 1861; disch. on surg. certif. Nov. 1, 1862.
John Blair, sergt., must. in July 10, 1861; pro. to corp. Aug. 30, 1862; to sergt. Jan. 1, 1864; trans. to 190th Regt. P. V. June 1, 1864; veteran.
John Blain, sergt., must. in July 10, 1861; pro. to corp. March 1, 1863; to sergt. March 1, 1864; trans. to 190th Regt. P. V. June 1, 1864; veteran.
G. W. Simmington, sergt., must. in May 30, 1861; pro. to corp. Aug. 30, 1862; to sergt. March 1, 1863; trans. to 190th Regt. P. V. June 1, 1864; veteran.
John Fitzgerald, sergt., must. in May 30, 1861; pro. to corp. July 21, 1861; to sergt. Aug. 30, 1862; died Dec. 22, 1863.
Pratt Baldwin, corp., must. in May 30, 1861; pro. to corp. Aug. 30, 1862; must. out with company June 13, 1864.
Joseph S. M. Houpt, corp., must. in May 30, 1861; pro. to corp. March 1, 1862; must. out with company June 13, 1864.
Joseph S. Wilson, corp., must. in July 10, 1861; disch. on surg. certif. Aug. 1, 1862.
Harrison Green, corp., must. in May 30, 1861; trans. to 190th Regt. P. V. June 1, 1864; veteran.
William Gray, corp., must. in May 30, 1861; trans. to 190th Regt. P. V. June 1, 1864; veteran.
John Hardy, corp., must. in May 30, 1861; trans. to gunboat service Feb. 2, 1862.
James Lewis, corp., must. in May 30, 1861; pro. to chief musician 30th Regt. P. V. March 1, 1864.

Hayes P. Griffith, musician, must. in July 10, 1861; disch. on surg. certif. Feb. 2, 1862.

William B. Drake, musician, must. in May 30, 1861; trans. to 190th Regt. P. V. June 1, 1864; veteran.

Privates.

John Alcott, must. in May 30, 1861; must out with company June 13, 1864.

Squire Booth, must. in May 30, 1861; must. out with company June 13, 1864.

Joseph Bradley, must. in May 30, 1861; must. out with company June 13, 1864.

Edmund Bradley, must. in May 30, 1861; must. out with company June 13, 1864.

William Burk, must. in May 30, 1861; must. out with company June 13, 1864.

Henry Briggs, must. in July 10, 1861; disch. May 1, 1863, for wounds received at Antietam Sept. 17, 1862.

John Brophy, must. in July 10, 1861; disch. on surg. certif. April 1, 1863.

John Butts, must. in Sept. 9, 1862; disch. on surg. certif. May 14, 1864.

William Bradley, must. in July 10, 1861; disch. on surg. certif. July 26, 1861.

John Baker, must. in May 30, 1861; disch. June 14, 1861.

Isaiah Budd, must. in May 30, 1861; died at Gettysburg, Pa., Aug. 1, 1863.

Henry Bailey, must. in May 30, 1861; killed at Mechanicsville, Va., June 26, 1862.

Washington Barr, must. in May 30, 1861.

John Cardwell, must. in May 30, 1861; must. out with company June 13, 1864.

Arthur Carroll, must. in May 30, 1861; must. out with company June 13, 1864.

Caldwell Carr, must. in May 30, 1861; trans. to Vet. Res. Corps October, 1863.

Edmund Coyle, must. in July 10, 1861; trans. to Vet. Res. Corps Sept. 27, 1863.

James Clark, must. in July 10, 1861; disch. January, 1863, for wounds received in action June 30, 1862.

James Cohen, must. in May 30, 1861; trans. to 190th Regt. P. V. June 1, 1864; veteran.

Leonard Carr, must. in May 30, 1861; trans. to 190th Regt. P. V. June 1, 1864; veteran.

Charles W. Cheetham, must. in July 10, 1861; killed at Charles City Cross-Roads June 30, 1862.

Wesley J. Cook, must. in May 30, 1861.

Patrick Doyle, must. in May 30, 1861; must out with company June 13, 1864.

William Dawson, must. in July 10, 1861; disch. on surg. certif. July 26, 1861.

Joseph Dougherty, must. in Nov. 9, 1862; trans. to 190th Regt. P. V. June 1, 1864.

John C. Ferguson, must. in May 30, 1861; must. out with company June 13, 1864.

John P. Fryer, must. in May 30, 1861; must. out with company June 13, 1864.

Edward Fitzgerald, must. in July 10, 1861; trans. to 190th Regt. P. V. June 1, 1864; veteran.

William Foulks, must. in May 30, 1861.

George Griffith, must. in May 30, 1861; must. out with company June 13, 1864.

Dennis Green, must. in May 30, 1861; must. out with company June 13, 1864.

Thomas Glass, must. in May 30, 1861; trans. to Vet. Res. Corps Sept. 27, 1863.

William T. Gatchell, must. in July 10, 1861; must. out with company June 13, 1864.

John Gamble, must. in May 30, 1861; disch. on surg. certif. October, 1862.

William Guilford, must. in May 30, 1861; disch. on surg. certif. August, 1861.

David Greenlee, must. in July 10, 1861; disch. on surg. certif. September, 1862.

John Goodwin, must. in July 10, 1861; disch. on surg. certif. July 26, 1861.

James Glass, must. in May 30, 1861; killed, accidentally, at Camp Pierpont, Va., November, 1861.

James Gorman, must. in Sept. 2, 1861; killed at Antietam Sept. 17, 1862.

Samuel Gray, must. in May 30, 1861.

Henry Gilkin, must. in May 30, 1861.

Thomas Galloway, must. in July 10, 1861; trans. to Vet. Res. Corps Jan. 15, 1864.

Isaac Healy, must. in May 30, 1861; disch. on surg. certif. July 26, 1861.

John Howard, must. in July 10, 1861; died of wounds received at Charles City Cross-Roads, Va., June 30, 1862.

Thomas Harner, must. in May 30, 1861.

George Humphrey, must. in July 10, 1861.

George M. Jones, must. in July 10, 1861; must. out with company June 13, 1864.

John W. Jones, must. in May 30, 1861; trans. to Western gunboat service Feb. 16, 1862.

Joshua Jeanes, must. in May 30, 1861; disch. on surg. certif. July 26, 1861.

Joseph C. Knox, must. in July 10, 1861; must. out with company June 13, 1864.

John Kilroy, must. in May 30, 1861; killed at Bull Run Aug. 30, 1862.

Haines J. Kernes, must. in July 10, 1861; died at Harrison's Landing, Va., Aug. 13, 1862.

Barney Kelly, must. in May 30, 1861; disch. May, 1862.

William Lees, must. in May 31, 1861; must. out with company June 13, 1864.

George Laird, must. in May 30, 1861; captured Feb. 14, 1864; must. out March 3, 1865.

Alexander C. Mathews, must. in May 30, 1861; trans. to Vet. Res. Corps October, 1863.

James Makeson, must. in May 30, 1861; trans. to Vet. Res. Corps Sept. 27, 1863.

Joseph S. Mott, must. in May 30, 1861; must. out with company June 13, 1864.

Thomas Mills, must. in May 30, 1861; disch. on surg. certif. Oct. 2, 1862.

Michael Maklem, must. in May 30, 1861; killed at Spottsylvania Court-House May 12, 1864.

Joseph Mills, must. in May 30, 1861; died at Baltimore, Md., July 10, 1864.

Wesley McBride, must. in May 30, 1861; must. out with company June 13, 1864.

Daniel W. McDade, must. in May 30, 1861; must. out with company June 13, 1864.

John McDade, must. in July 10, 1861; disch. March, 1863, for wounds received at South Mountain Sept. 14, 1862.

John McCracken, must. in May 30, 1861.

Michael Nolan, must. in May 30, 1861; disch. on surg. certif. July 26, 1861.

Jonathan R. Neal, must. in July 10, 1861; disch. on surg. certif. Feb. 11, 1864.

Edward O'Neal, must. in May 30, 1861; disch. on surg. certif. July 26, 1861.

James Oakes, must. in July 10, 1861; disch. March, 1863, for wounds received at Antietam Sept. 17, 1862.

James F. Pennypacker, must. in July 10, 1861; trans. to Vet. Res. Corps Nov. 25, 1863.

Adam Pilkington, must. in May 30, 1861; disch. on surg. certif. November, 1862.

George W. Parker, must. in May 30, 1861; disch. on surg. certif. March, 1863.

Samuel Parker, must. in May 30, 1861; disch. on surg. certif. July 26, 1861.

William Rowe, must. in May 30, 1861; disch. on surg. certif. July 26, 1861.

William Richardson, must. in May 30, 1861; trans. to 190th Regt. P. V. June 1, 1864; veteran.

John C. Roberts, must. in May 30, 1861; missing in action at Bethesda Church May 30, 1864; died in prison, date unknown.

Thomas Smith, must. in May 30, 1861; must. out with company June 13, 1864.

Moses Scott, must. in May 30, 1861; disch. on surg. certif. November, 1862.

William Stacy, must. in May 30, 1861; disch. on surg. certif. July 26, 1861.

John Stewart, must. in July 16, 1861; killed, accidentally, at Camp Pierpont, Va., November, 1861.

Edward Smith, must. in May 30, 1861; killed at Mechanicsville June 26, 1862.

James Shum, must. in Sept. 9, 1862; trans. to 190th Regt. P. V. June 1, 1864.

Edward Townsend, must. in May 30, 1861; must. out with company June 13, 1864.
George W. Timbler, must. in July 26, 1861; absent, in arrest, at muster out.
James W. Turner, must. in May 30, 1861; disch. on surg. certif. April, 1862.
Oliver Thomas, must. in July 10, 1861; died August, 1862.
John Wilde, must. in May 30, 1861; disch. on surg. certif. July 26, 1861.
James Willis, must. in May 30, 1861; disch. on surg. certif. July 26, 1861.
James Wyatt, must. in July 10, 1861; killed at Charles City Cross-Roads June 30, 1862.
Thomas Whiteman, must. in May 30, 1861.
James Wilson, must. in May 30, 1861.
Frazier Walter, must. in May 30, 1861.
Jacob Z. Webb, must. in July 10, 1861.
Joseph Whiteman, must. in May 30, 1861.
James Wilson, must. in July 10, 1861.

Although the Delaware County Companies C and F were mustered into the service of the State in the latter part of May, the organization of the regiment was not fully effected until June 9, 1861, when Biddle Roberts was chosen colonel; and in making his appointments he selected Lieut. Joseph R. T. Coates, of Company C, for quartermaster. On July 4th Governor Curtin reviewed the First and Seventh Reserves at West Chester. On the 21st the First Regiment was ordered to Washington, and at daylight the next day marched for Baltimore, reaching that place at nine o'clock the same evening. As Col. Roberts approached the city he was met by the police authorities, who advised him that, as the populace was much excited, it would be well not to attempt to pass through the streets. The colonel, however, ordered ammunition to be distributed to his men, and he marched through Baltimore without molestation. On July 26, at Camp Carroll, the regiment was mustered into the United States service, and immediately marched to Annapolis, where it was quartered in the naval school; remaining there until August 30th, it was moved to Tenallytown, Md., and assigned to the First Brigade under Gen. Reynolds, of McCall's division. In all the movements preceding the Peninsular advance it took part, and at Mechanicsville in that campaign it was on the extreme right of the Army of the Potomac, and under Fitz John Porter was in the battle of the 26th of June, 1862. There the First Regiment held the centre of the brigade, and in a struggle of three hours repulsed the enemy, sleeping on the ground it had held so valiantly. The next morning it was ordered to fall back, and the brigade retired in the direction of Gaines' Mills. On the 27th, the First and Eighth Reserves moved to the rear for ammunition. Fitz John Porter seeing this movement galloped to Col. Roberts and exclaimed, "Colonel, can't you form a line with the two regiments and stop those fleeing troops?" The answer was affirmative, if ammunition was furnished his men, and that being promised, the two regiments formed in line with a coolness and precision which received the warm approval of the general. On the 30th, at Newmarket, the First Reserves for five hours maintained its position, repulsing three distinct heavy charges of the enemy, and its gallantry on that occasion was specially mentioned in McCall's official report.

In Pope's campaign, on August 29th and the day following, it was constantly under fire, marching most of the time, and during the forty-eight hours was totally without food. On Sunday, the 14th of September, 1862, at South Mountain, the regiment charged the gorge and summit of the eminence held by a part of Hill's corps. The column rushed onward with a yell, driving the enemy before it, and gained the summit, where the First Reserve slept on their arms during the night, ready to resume the struggle in the morning, but the Confederates withdrew under cover of the darkness. The next morning Hooker personally came to the ground and thanked the regiment for its valor. In that terrific charge, Second Lieut. John H. Taylor, of Company C, son of Joseph Taylor, recently deceased, fell leading his command. On the 16th of September, the eve of Antietam, the First was skirmishing with the enemy during the night, and at daylight of the 17th it went in action and continued until nine o'clock, when it was relieved. Capt. Talley commanded the regiment in the greater part of that battle, Col. Roberts having been thrown in command of the First Brigade, and after Hooker was wounded, March 1, 1863, Capt. Talley was promoted to be colonel of the regiment.

At the battle of Fredericksburg, Dec. 13, 1862, the First Reserves charged across an open plain under a heavy enfilading artillery fire, and drove the enemy two hundred yards beyond his intrenchments, when finding that he was flanked on the right, the enemy strongly reinforced in front, and no supporting troops coming up in the rear, Col. Talley "was compelled to retire after having opened the way to victory." During Lee's invasion of Pennsylvania the regiments, on the 29th of June, 1863, marched with the main army for Gettysburg, and when the State line was crossed Col. Talley halted his men and announced that they were then on their own soil, where they must battle for their homes and families, and know no rest until Pennsylvania had been freed from every enemy in martial array.

On July 2d, arriving at Gettysburg, the regiment went immediately to the front, and on the right of Little Round Top charged the enemy with great gallantry, driving them back upon their reserve. On the 3d, in the brilliant charges made by the First Brigade, the First Regiment, commanded by Col. Talley, occupied the centre. The regiment took part in the battle of Bristoe Station and in the numerous movements of the Army of the Potomac during the latter part of 1863. In Grant's campaign, on the 5th of May, 1864, it was engaged in the battle of the Wilderness, and on May 8th, at the battle of Spottsylvania. Col. Talley was then in command of the brigade, and while charging for the third time through a thicket of pine, he was captured by soldiers of Ewell's corps, but the following day he, with several hundred prisoners, was rescued by Sheridan's cavalry The last day of service for the Pennsylvania Reserves was May 31, 1864, and on that day the First Regiment (Thirtieth of the line) took a conspicuous part in the battle of Bethesda Church. The next day, June 1, 1864, the Reserves were ordered home, and on June 13th were mustered out of service at Philadelphia On March 13, 1865, Col Talley received the rank of brigadier-general of volunteers, by brevet, for distinguished services in the field

Fifty-eighth Regiment (Three-Years' Service) — The county of Delaware, which furnished nearly fifty men to this regiment, in the official publications of the State receives no credit therefor, a statement that is equally true so far as it relates to other organizations, the general statement merely being made, "recruited in Philadelphia and vicinity." The fact is that nearly one-half of Company A was recruited in this county, while in Companies B, C, and K, men from this neighborhood were mustered into service among the first that enlisted in the ranks of the regiment. On March 8, 1862, the Fifty-eighth was ordered to Fortress Monroe, arriving at its destination the next day, Sunday, the 9th, while the action between the ironclad "Merrimac" and "Monitor" was in progress On May 10th it led the advance under Gen Wool, and after the surrender of the city of Norfolk on that day, the flag of the Fifty-eighth was unfurled over the custom-house, where it remained until the regiment was ordered to Beaufort, N C While at Norfolk, First Lieut Thomas I Leiper, of Company A, who, while the regiment was in Philadelphia before being ordered to the front, had been appointed adjutant, was assigned to the staff of Gen Thomas L Kane, under whom he was in service at the battles of Antietam and Gettysburg On Sept 9, 1863, Leiper was promoted captain of Company A, and he thereupon returned to his command

On June 27, 1862, the Fifty-eighth was ordered to garrison Washington, N C, at the head of navigation of the Pamlico River, and while there it was daily drilled in heavy artillery practice On the 16th of December, Capt Theodore Blakeley, of Company B, a gallant soldier from Chester, with a detachment of one hundred men, made a foray into the country fifteen miles southward, and captured a Confederate cavalry encampment, a captain, and sixty men, with all their horses and equipments, so absolutely surprising the enemy that they yielded without a gun being fired For this Capt. Blakeley was complimented in an order from department headquarters On May 1, 1864, the regiment joined the Army of the James, under Gen. Butler, in the operations against Richmond, and on the 9th the Fifty-eighth was in action near the Appomattox River, and the following day destroyed for a considerable distance the Petersburg and Richmond Railroad The regiment was subsequently transferred to the army under Grant, and at Cold Harbor, on the 3d of June, it charged the enemy's works, capturing the rifle pits, and, as related by a *New York Herald* correspondent,—"Here, however, the men found themselves close prisoners, for it was utterly impossible for a head or an arm to make its appearance without being riddled by bullets For two long hours the regiment held its position until it was reinforced" On the 15th, it having returned to the Army of the James, it was in the attack on the enemy's lines in front of Petersburg when the outer works were carried On June 24th the re-enlisted soldiers were ordered to Philadelphia on the regular furlough granted to all veterans re-entering the service, and because of the good conduct of the regiment twenty days beyond the usual time was granted to them Capt Leiper remained at the front in command of the men who had not re enlisted, and the recruits forwarded to the Fifty-eighth The furlough having expired, the regiment joined the army on the north of the James, and on September 28th the Fifty-eighth and One Hundred and Eighth Pennsylvania made the desperate assault on Fort Harrison in face of sixteen guns of heavy calibre, in which the colors of the Fifty-eighth were three times shot away, and out of the two hundred and twenty-eight men of that regiment who had made the charge, one hundred and twenty-eight were killed and wounded Among the former was the brave Capt. Theodore Blakeley, of Chester The fort, with its cannon, small-arms, battle-flags, and garrison, was captured in this intrepid charge. The same day the two regiments were ordered to assault the Star Fort, a mile to the left of Fort Harrison, and although the brave fellows scaled the works and spiked the guns, weakened by their previous feat and unsupported, they were obliged to fall back under the heavy fire played upon them by the enemy's gunboats

In the final campaign which resulted in the capture of Lee's army it bore an honored part, and after the enemy's force in the field was dispersed, it was assigned to duty in the lower counties of Virginia, and was mustered out at City Point, Va, Jan 24, 1866

COMPANY A

Thomas I Leiper, capt, must in Oct 19, 1861, pro to adjt May 1, 1862, assigned to staff of Gen Thomas L Kane from December, 1862, to September, 1863, pro to capt Sept 9, 1863, must. out Oct. 24, 1864, exp of term

William F Jester, sergt., must in Sept 16, 1861, pro to sergt Feb 27, 1863, must out with company Jan 24, 1866, veteran

John Brown, sergt., must in Dec 30, 1861, pro to corp May 3, 1863, to sergt Aug 17, 1865, must out with company Jan 24, 1866, veteran

Benjamin F Graden, sergt., must. in Sept 16, 1861, pro. to corp May 3, 1863, to sergt Aug 17, 1865, must out with company, veteran

Thomas Schofield, sergt, must. in Sept 16, 1861, pro to corp May 1, 1862, disch on surg certif March 1, 1863

Calvert Cardwell, sergt., must in Sept 12, 1861 pro to com-sergt Feb 21, 1863

Hamilton Gillon, sergt, must in Sept 16, 1861, pro to corp March 1, 1862, to sergt. March 3, 1863, veteran

Samuel Blythe, sergt, must in Sept 20, 1861, pro to sergt March 1, 1865, veteran

Oliver Jacob, corp., must in Oct. 15, 1861, pro to corp Sept 13, 1864, must. out with company Jan 24, 1866, veteran

James Stewart, corp., must in Nov 18, 1861, pro to corp Aug 17, 1865, must. out with company Jan 24, 1866, veteran

Edward Develin, corp, must in Sept 16, 1861, pro to corp June 3, 1863, must out Nov 1, 1864, exp of term

Samuel R Crooks, corp, must in Sept 16, 1861, pro to corp Aug 16, 1863, must out Sept. 13, 1864, exp of term

James Graden, musician, must in Sept 24, 1861, must out with company Jan 24, 1866, veteran

William W Stewart, musician, must in Aug 21, 1862, disch by G O June 12, 1865

Privates

William Bruton, must in Sept 17, 1861, disch on surg certif Oct 23, 1862

Robert Blakeley, must in Oct. 11, 1862, disch by G O June 12, 1865

Michael Burk, must in Aug 25, 1862, disch by G O June 12, 1865

Thomas Burk, must in Aug 28, 1862, captured at Chapin's Farm, Va, Sept 29, 1864, died at Richmond, Va., Feb 28, 1865

William Crossin, must in Sept 16, 1861, disch on surg certif May 29, 1863

John Cain, must in Sept 16, 1861, must out Oct 6, 1864, exp of term.

Richard Crowther, must in Aug 21, 1862, disch on surg certif May 29, 1863

Joseph Collison, must in Oct 7, 1861, must out Oct 6, 1864, exp of term

George Elliot, must in Sept. 16, 1861, must out Oct 6, 1864, exp of term

John Feeney, must in Aug 27, 1862, disch by G O June 12, 1865

William Gorman, must in Aug 26, 1862, disch by G O June 12, 1865

Richard Green, must in Nov 5, 1861, trans to Vet Res Corps Jan 15, 1865, veteran

Samuel Huston, must in Sept 17, 1861, disch on surg certif April 11, 1863

Charles Hardy, must in Sept 16, 1861, disch on surg certif Feb 25, 1864

Thomas Hardy, must. in Sept. 17, 1861, died at Washington, N C, March 5, 1864

Frank McGrath, must in Sept. 16, 1861, must out Sept 16, 1864, exp of term

John News, must in Sept 16, 1861, must out Sept. 11, 1864, exp of term

James Porter, must. in Sept 16, 1861, veteran

Bradford Reed, must in Sept 16, 1861, disch on surg certif March 27, 1862

William Schofield, must. in Sept 18, 1861, must out with company Jan 24, 1866 veteran

Benjamin Schofield, must. in Aug 27, 1862, disch by G O June 6, 1865

Robert Schofield, must in Aug 10, 1864, disch by G O June 28, 1865

William Vantine, must in Sept 16, 1861, killed in action April 29, 1863

Smith Williams, must in Oct. 21, 1862, absent, sick, at muster out

John P West, must in Aug 25, 1862, disch by G O June 12, 1865

John M Wood, must in Aug 2, 1862, disch by G O June 12, 1865

COMPANY B

Capt Theodore Blakeley, must. in Dec 10, 1861, pro from 2d to 1st lieut Jan 31, 1863, to capt July 1, 1863, killed at Fort Harrison, Va., Sept 29, 1864

COMPANY C

George C Healey, sergt, must in Nov 6, 1861, pro to corp Nov 26, 1863, to sergt. July 1, 1864, must out with company Jan 24, 1866, veteran

Privates

Edward Andrews, must in Nov 6, 1861, must out Sept 23, 1864, exp of term

Benjamin Quigley, must. in Nov 6, 1861, must out Sept. 10, 1864, exp of term

COMPANY K

James A Finney, sergt, must in Feb 20, 1862, pro to corp April 1, 1865, must out with company Jan 24, 1866, veteran

Sixtieth Regiment (Third Cavalry).—Early in July, 1861, Capt William L Laws recruited a company of cavalry in Delaware County, opening a station in Chester for that purpose The men were enlisted for three years, and as the regiment was the first of that arm of the service to organize for a lengthened period of duty, so it is believed that Capt. Law's men were the first in the State willing to enroll for three years Pennsylvania's quota being filled at the time, Col William H Young obtained permission to raise a regiment in any part of the country, which should be known as Young's Light Kentucky Cavalry Law's company, for some reason, was not accepted as a whole in this regiment, the greater number of the men being assigned to Company I, under Capt William K Grant, and the remainder distributed among the other companies Subsequently the regiment, which was entirely recruited in Pennsylvania, excepting Company D (from Washington City), was credited to this State, and then Governor Curtin requested Col Young's resignation

On Oct 31, 1861, he appointed William W Averill, an officer of the Fifth United States Cavalry, in Young's stead At first the new commander was very unpopular with the men because of the strict discipline to which he subjected the regiment, it under Young having been very loose, but its subsequent honorable story was largely the outgrowth of the stringent measures then adopted During the winter and spring of 1862 it was constantly in advance, and was the first Union force to enter the works at Manassas and ascertain that the enemy had abandoned the fortification there In the Peninsula campaign it was constantly in service, such as demanded from "the eyes of an army," and in the change of base, during that week of battles, the men were almost constantly in the saddle, covering the flanks of the columns At Antietam it rendered efficient service, and when the army, in October, crossed into Virginia it covered the right flank, which brought it constantly in collision with Stuart's and Hampton's command, and finally driving the latter into their hiding-places in the Blue Ridge On March 16th it encountered Fitz-Hugh Lee and Stuart's cavalry at Kelley's Ford, and there taught the enemy that the Northern cavalry, which they heretofore had ridiculed, was able to cope with the best horsemen of the Confederate army and defeat them Previous to the battle of Chancellorsville the Sixtieth Regiment rode in the noted raid which traversed the country in Lee's rear, and for a time severed his railroad communication with Richmond On the 19th of June, 1863, it took part in Buford's and Gregg's attack on Stuart, between Culpeper Court-House and Beverly Ford, in which the latter, after a five-hours' fight, was so signally defeated that for a time it compelled delay in the proposed invasion of Pennsylvania And two weeks later it was in the engagement at Aldie, which resulted in cutting off from Lee the whole of Stuart's command, so that the former was deprived of the greater part of his cavalry until after the battle of Gettysburg On the 2d of July, at that battle, the Sixtieth Regiment sustained the charge of Hampton's division in the latter's attempt to gain the rear of the Union army, and, although it was driven back by weight of numbers, when Custer came to its assistance it rallied and joined in the charge, in which the enemy was defeated with heavy loss It took part in the action at Old Antietam Forge, on the 10th of July, as well as that at Shepherdstown, on the 16th of the same month It led the brave charge near Culpeper Court-House, on September 13th, and was complimented in a general order for valor On October 14th it was engaged at Bristoe Station, and on the 15th, when the cavalry covered the army wagon-train of seventy miles, the Sixtieth was the rear-guard and sustained the attack of Gordon's division and repulsed it, holding its ground for over two hours before it was supported Once again, for this brave deed, Gen Buford issued an order commendatory of the skill and valor it displayed On the 26th, at New Hope Church, dismounting, it, with the First Massachusetts, sustained the charge of the Stonewall Brigade, maintaining its position for two hours, until Sykes' regulars had time to advance to its support During the Wilderness campaign with Grant it was constantly in service, and when Grant and Meade crossed the James on pontoon bridges, the Sixtieth acted as the escort. Its story in the engagements preceding the surrender of Lee is part of the history of those days of battle, and when, on the 3d of April, Grant and Meade entered Petersburg, it formed part of the escort to the generals When Lee surrendered, the Sixtieth Regiment was in the advance between the lines of battle of the two armies It was subsequently mustered out of service at Richmond on Aug 7, 1865

COMPANY A

James Phillips, private, must in Sept 15, 1862, captured, disch by G O May 28, 1865

COMPANY I

Matthias [illegible]oper, sergt., must in Aug 16, 1861, pro to corp Feb 1862, to sergt Aug 1863, must. out with company Aug 24, 1864

William H [illegible]field, sergt, must in Aug 17, 1861, pro from corp April, 1863, must out with company

George Phillips, sergt., must in Aug 17, 1861, pro to corp 1863, to sergt July, 1863, must. out with company

Edward Crowther, sergt., must in Aug 17, 1861, pro to corp 1863, to sergt July, 1863, must out with company

John Oaks, saddler, must in Aug 17, 1861, must out with company

Privates

James Aides, must. in Aug 17, 1861, wounded in action Oct 15, 1863, died, date unknown

William Blan[illegible], must in Aug 17, 1861, must out with company

John Byram, must in Aug 16, 1861, must out with company

William Brown, must in Aug 17, 1861

James W Carroll, must in Aug 16, 1861, absent, sick, at muster out

William Campbell, must in Aug 17, 1861, must out with company

Michael Curran, must in Aug 17, 1861, must. out with company

Joseph Cook, must in Aug 17, 1861, disch on surg certif May 30, 1862

Joseph Dalton, must in Aug 17, 1861, must out with company

Henry M Fuller, must in Aug 17, 1861, must out with company

Eli Hamilton, must in Aug 17, 1861, must out with company

William H Martin, must in Aug 16, 1861, must out with company

William Moore, must in March 23, 1864, trans to batt July 27, 1864 to 65th Regt P V June 6, 1865, veteran

James McGahey, must in Aug 17, 1861, must out with company

W McGinness, must in Jan 1, 1864, pro to corp battalion Sept 18, 1864, to sergt Co M, Dec 1, 1864, trans to batt July 27, 1864, to 65th Regt P V June 6, 1865, veteran

William Quinn, must in Aug 16, 1861, disch on surg certif July 23, 1863

John Ramsey, must in Aug 17, 1861, must out with company

Thomas Schofield, must in Aug 17, 1861, must out with company

Isaac E Wilde, must in Aug 17, 1861, disch Oct 9, 1862

William T West, must in Aug 17, 1861, captured Nov 27, 1863, must out June 21, 1865, exp of term

COMPANY C

Thomas Riley, private, must in Aug 1, 1861

COMPANY E

George W Rocas, bugler, must in Jan 1, 1864, trans to batt July 27, 1864, to 65th Regt. P V June 6, 1865, veteran

COMPANY F

Alexander King, sergt., must in Aug 16, 1861, pro to corp, to sergt Nov 1, 1863, must out with company

Oram Grigg, sergt, must in Aug 16, 1861, pro to corp, to sergt. March 25, 1864, must. out with company

James A Parcels, corp., must in Aug 16, 1861, pro to corp May 1, 1864, must out with company

James Rusk, bugler, must in Aug 16, 1861 must out with company

Privates

George Booth, must in Aug 16, 1861, must out with company

David A Brown, must in Aug 16, 1861, veteran

Charles Dwight, must in Jan 1, 1864, pro to corp batt May 1, 1865, trans to batt. July 27, 1864, to 65th Regt. P V June 6, 1865, veteran

William Mason, must in Aug 16, 1861, disch, date unknown

John O'Brien, must in Aug 16, 1861 died at Philadelphia Oct 25, 1863

Joseph L Pedrick, must in Aug 16, 1861, disch, date unknown

William Ramsey, must in Aug 16, 1861, must out with company

Samuel Shepherd, must in Aug 16, 1861, disch, date unknown

George Weigand, must in Aug 16, 1861, captured at Catlett's Station, Va. Oct 5, 1863* must. out Feb 14, 1865, exp of term

COMPANY K

John A Devers, 2d lieut., must in Aug 19, 1861, res Dec 5, 1861

Patrick Ford, sergt., must in Jan 1, 1864, pro to corp batt Sept 20, 1864, to sergt. Co M Dec 20, 1864, trans to batt July 27, 1864, to 65th Regt P V June 6, 1865, veteran

Privates.

John Armstrong, must in Aug 19, 1861

Thomas Dyson, must in Aug 19, 1861, must out with company

Allen Gartside, must in Aug 19, 1861, disch on surg certif

COMPANY M

Abel Wright, 1st lieut., must in Dec 10, 1861, trans from 2d lieut Co G to 1st lieut March 14, 1862, to adjt Sept 17, 1862

John W Ford, 2d lieut, must in Aug 16, 1861, trans from 1st sergt. Co E to 2d lieut. Sept 8, 1862, to 1st lieut Co I May 1, 1863

Michael Donohue, q m sergt., must in Aug 26, 1861, captured, must out with company Aug 24, 1864

Albert Bradbury, sergt., must in Aug 26, 1861, pro from corp to sergt, to 2d lieut Co D May 1, 1863

Benjamin McDonald, sergt., must in Aug 26, 1861, died Sept 12, 1861, of wounds received accidentally

Joseph A Ford, corp, must. in Aug 26, 1861, must out with company

Abel Ford, corp, must in Aug 26, 1861, captured, disch on surg certif Feb 12, 1863

Robert Coppock, farrier, must in Aug 26, 1861, disch, date unknown

Privates.

Thomas Broomall, must in Aug 26, 1861, trans to batt July 27, 1864

William Crozer, must in Aug 26, 1861, not on muster out roll

Nehemiah Ford, must in Aug 26, 1861, disch on surg certif Feb 1, 1862

Samuel Gray, must in Aug 26, 1861, disch on surg certif March 7, 1862

James McFadden, must in Aug 26, 1861, must out with company

William McDonald, must in Aug 26, 1861, disch on surg certif April 27, 1862

James Willis, must. in Aug. 26, 1861; captured; paroled; not on muster-out roll.
Thomas Donohue, must. in Aug. 26, 1861; captured; disch. June 12, 1862.
Patrick Shenan, must. in Aug. 26, 1861; disch. on surg. certif. Jan. 12, 1862.

Ninety-seventh Regiment.—In the latter part of July, 1861, Henry R. Guss, of West Chester, was authorized by the Secretary of War to raise a regiment for three years' service. Company D, the Concordville Rifles, Capt. William S. Mendenhall, was recruited in the western end of the county; Company G, the Broomall Guards (named in honor of Hon. J. M. Broomall), Capt. Jesse L. Cummins, was recruited mostly in Media and Chester and neighborhood; and Company I, Brooke Guards (so called in honor of Hon. Hugh Jones Brooke, post commissary of Pennsylvania, who contributed largely to the outfit and comforts of the men), Capt. George W. Hawkins, was recruited mostly from Springfield and Ridley townships. Many of the men had been in the three-months' service, and had some knowledge of military duties. The companies rendezvoused at Camp Wayne, near West Chester, where, on November 12th, the day it left for Washington, Governor Curtin presented the State colors to the regiment. It was shortly after ordered to Fortress Monroe, and subsequently to Port Royal, S. C., where it arrived off the harbor on the 11th of December, but heavy weather compelled the vessel to put to sea, and it was three days before the men could disembark. In January, 1862, it took part in the expedition to Warsaw Sound, Georgia, which resulted in the capture of Fort Pulaski, and on March 5th the Ninety-seventh was landed from the transport in the Florida expedition, and captured the town of Fernandina and Fort Church. In March, Gen. Hunter relieved Gen. Sherman, and the new commander ordered the evacuation of Florida. In a bold reconnoissance to Legarsville, S. C., in June, 1862, Company G (Broomall Guards) and Company H occupied Legarsville. On the 10th of June, in the Confederate attack at Secessionville, the Ninety-seventh stood the brunt of the fight until the gunboats could get into position and open fire with effect. In the fall of that year the regiment suffered severely with intermittent fever, five hundred men being at one time on the sick-list, and there were also many cases of yellow fever, a number of which proved fatal. In April, 1863, it was at Folly Island, Charleston Harbor, during the bombardment of Fort Sumter. At the storming of Fort Wagner the Fifty-fourth Massachusetts (colored) Regiment, leading the assaulting column, suffered dreadfully under the murderous fire from the fort, and when the attack failed, Companies C, D (Concordville Rifles), E, and I (Broomall Guards) stacked arms, and during the entire night were engaged in bearing off the wounded colored soldiers, Brig.-Gen. Stevenson urging them on in the merciful work with the oft-repeated expression, "You know how much harder they will fare at the hands of the enemy than white men." Never did troops expose themselves more than did these brave men, who in the darkness crawled on the ground to the very slope of the enemy's intrenchment, directed by the groans of the wounded, and dragged away the suffering black soldiers to where they would be taken and borne within the Union lines. Nowhere in all the scroll of history is recorded a nobler or braver deed than this. The regiment subsequently was active in the siege of Fort Wagner, which the enemy evacuated on the night of Sept. 6, 1863. The Ninety-seventh was ordered to Florida in October of that year, where it was engaged in reconnoissances and breaking up supply-stations of the enemy. In April, 1864, it was ordered to the Army of the James, under Gen. Butler, where it was attached to the First Brigade, Third Division. On May 9th it led the advance on Petersburg, detailed to destroy the railroad and telegraph wires, which work it accomplished, and the same day took part in the action of Swift Creek. When Beauregard, on the 18th, attacked the Army of the James, the pickets of the Eighth Maine were driven back, and the Ninety-seventh was ordered to retake the position, which was done in the face of a hot and destructive fire of musketry. On the evening of the 19th, when four of the companies had been driven back with fearful slaughter and the line broken, the remainder of the regiment, which included all the Delaware County companies, was ordered to advance and retake it. The command was obeyed with alacrity, and the line advanced, notwithstanding grape, canister, and musketry volleys tore frightful gaps in the ranks, until at last they were recalled, after having sustained a loss of nearly two hundred men killed and wounded. During all the campaign it was constantly in the advance, and on the 30th of June, Capt. Mendenhall, of Company D (Concordville Rifles), with three hundred from other regiments, was ordered to assault the enemy's works in front of the cemetery, an attack designed to direct the latter's attention from the real point of assault. The order was bravely obeyed, the works were captured and held until nightfall, although the real attack was not made. Over one-third of the force under Mendenhall was killed and wounded. On the 30th of July, when the mine was exploded, Capt. Hawkins (Brooke Guard), in command of five companies, successfully charged the enemy's rifle-pits. In this assault Capt. Mendenhall was wounded.

On the 15th of August the regiment took part in the action at Deep Bottom, and on the 16th at Strawberry Plains. On the 25th, at Bermuda Hundred, it was attacked by the enemy at the front while it was being relieved, and a part of its line was captured, which was afterwards retaken. It participated, on September 28th, in the capture of New Market Heights, and the same day took part in the unsuccessful assault on Fort Gilmore. On Oct. 27, 1864, the regiment had a short engagement with the enemy at Darbytown roads, in which Capt. George W. Hawkins was mortally wounded.

The story of the regiment, so far as it relates to the history of Delaware County in the main, closes about the end of October, 1864, when the period of service of the troops expired, for, although the numerical designation remained, the regiment after that time had little of its original elements, but was made up of drafted men and substitutes in nowise connected with our annals

COMPANY D (CONCORDVILLE RIFLES)

W S Mendenhall, capt., must in Sept 20, 1861, wounded at Bermuda Hundred, Va., May 20, and at Petersburg July 30, 1864, disch Oct 4, 1864, at exp of term

George W Williams, 1st lieut, must in Sept 9, 1861, disch on surg certif July 29, 1863

Isaac Fawkes, 1st lieut, must in Sept 20, 1861, pro from 2d lieut Sept 1, 1863, died May 20, 1864, of wounds received in action, buried in National Cemetery, City Point, Va, Section A, Division 1, grave 86

Henry Odiorne, 1st lieut, must in Sept 6, 1861, pro from 1st sergt to 2d lieut Nov 9, 1863, to 1st lieut July 10, 1864, com capt Dec 3, 1864, not mustered, died Jan 16th of wounds received at Fort Fisher, N C, Jan 15 1865

David W Odiorne, 1st lieut, must in Jan 1, 1864, wounded Sept 29, 1864, pro to 2d lieut Dec 5, 1864, to 1st lieut March 14, 1865, must out with company Aug 28, 1865, veteran

John W Brooks, 2d lieut, must in Jan 1, 1864, wounded May 18, 1864, pro from sergt April 6, 1865, must out with company Aug 28, 1865, veteran

Philip E Hannum, 1st sergt, must in Feb 29, 1864, wounded May 18, 1864, must out with company Aug 28, 1865, veteran

Charles H Hannum, 1st sergt, must in Sept 6, 1861, disch Sept 19, 1864, at exp of term

David Morrow, sergt., must in Jan 1, 1864, wounded at Bermuda Hundred, Va., May 20, 1864, pro from corp Oct 10, 1864, must out with company Aug 28, 1865, veteran

William McCarty, sergt., must in Jan 1, 1864, wounded Sept. 29, 1864, and at Fort Fisher, N C, Jan 15, 1865, must out with company Aug 28, 1865, veteran

Alfred Young, sergt, must in Jan 1, 1864, must out with company Aug 28, 1865, veteran

Samuel McBride, sergt., must in Sept. 6, 1861, wounded at Bermuda Hundred, Va., May 20, 1864, disch Sept 7, 1864, at exp of term

Isaac Sapp, sergt, must in Feb 29, 1864, wounded May 18, July 30, Aug 4 and 16, 1864, died March 12, 1865, buried in National Cemetery, City Point, Va, Section A, Division 3, grave 36, veteran

David H Freas, corp., must in Jan 1, 1864, died at Point Lookout, Md, May 23, of wounds received at Bermuda Hundred, Va, May 20, 1864, veteran

John Goodwin, corp., must in Feb 29, 1864, wounded at Bermuda Hundred, Va., May 20, 1864, must out with company Aug 28, 1865, veteran

Jacob H Hall, corp, must in Feb 29, 1864, wounded at Bermuda Hundred, Va., May 20, 1864, pro to corp April 1, 1865, disch by G O Aug 11, 1865, veteran

Thomas Kelly, corp., must in Jan 1, 1864, pro to corp April 22, 1865, must out with company Aug 28, 1865, veteran

Thomas Rutter, corp., must. in Jan 1, 1864, wounded Sept 29 1864, pro to corp April 23, 1865, must out with company Aug 28, 1865, veteran

John W Carter corp., must in Jan 1, 1864, wounded May 18, 1864, must out with company Aug 28, 1865, veteran

John Jorden, corp., must in Jan 1, 1864, wounded May 18 and Sept 29, 1864, pro to corp Aug 1, 1865, must out with company Aug 28, 1865, veteran

Wilbur F Flannery, corp., must in Sept 6, 1861, disch Sept 19, 1864, at exp of term

William H Snyder, corp, must in Sept 24, 1861, disch Sept 30, 1864, at exp of term

Robert Fairlamb, corp., must. in Sept 16, 1861, disch Sept 19, 1864, at exp of term

Isaac N Stout, corp, must in Jan 1, 1861, wounded at Bermuda Hundred, Va., May 20, 1864, disch on surg certif May 8, 1865, veteran

Hamilton Humes, corp., must in Jan 1, 1864, disch by G O June 24, 1865, veteran

Isaac B Hannum, musician, must in Feb 29, 1864, must out with company Aug 28, 1865, veteran

Harmen B Cloud, musician, must in Jan 1, 1864, wounded Sept 3, 1861, must out with company Aug 28, 1865, veteran

David M Claid, musician, must in Sept 6, 1861, disch Sept 19, 1864, at exp of term

James St John, musician, must in Nov 26, 1862, pro to principal musician May 1 1863

Samuel J Buckland, musician, must in Sept 16, 1861

Privates.

Charles Anderson, must in Nov 23, 1864, drafted, must out with company Aug 28, 1865

Charles B Aikins, must in March 4, 1865, substitute, must out with company Aug 28, 1865

Robert Burley, must in Feb 29, 1864, wounded at Petersburg, Va, June 30, 1864, absent, in hospital, at muster out, veteran

James Beaumont, must in Feb 29, 1864, wounded June 3 and Aug 16, 1864, must out with company Aug 28, 1865, veteran

William Beaumont, must in March 1, 1865, must out with company Aug 28, 1865

Edward Ballott, must in Sept 21, 1863, drafted, must out with company Aug 28, 1865

Charles Brown, must in Nov 21, 1864, substitute, disch by G O June 28, 1865

William Berry, must in Sept 6, 1861, disch on surg certif March 18, 1863

Robert Babe, must in Feb 29, 1864, disch August 20, for wounds, with loss of foot, received at Bermuda Hundred, Va., May 20, 1864, veteran

William W Bullock, must in Sept 6, 1861, wounded Aug 26, 1864, disch Sept 19, 1864, at exp of term

Daniel Burns, must in Sept 11, 1861, disch Sept 19, 1864, at exp of term

James Barr, must in Sept 16, 1861, wounded May 18, 1864, disch Sept 19, 1864, at exp of term

James S Bullock, must in Oct 26, 1861, wounded May 18, 1864, disch Oct 25, 1864, at exp of term

Abraham Barrone, must in Sept 30, 1864, drafted, disch by G O June 28, 1865

Charles H Blew, must in Sept 24, 1863, drafted, wounded May 18 and June 30, 1864, disch on surg certif June 12, 1865

Joseph Baker, must in Sept 24, 1861, died at Hilton Head, S C., July 25, 1862

Joseph Booth, must in Sept. 19, 1861, died at Morris Island, S C, Oct 3, 1863

James Brierly, must in Jan 1, 1864, died May 20, 1864, of wounds, with loss of leg, received in action, veteran

Richard Boyed, must in Oct 21, 1863, drafted

John Booth, must in Sept 23, 1861

William Cathcart, must in Feb 29, 1864, must. out with company Aug 28, 1865, veteran

John F Cloud, must in Sept. 6, 1861, disch on surg certif Dec 8, 1861

Lewis C Cloud, must. in Sept 6, 1861, disch on surg certif Dec 10, 1862

Henry A Cloud, must in Sept 6 1861, wounded at Deep Bottom, Va., Aug 16, 1864, disch Sept. 19, 1864, at exp of term

Charles S Cloud, must in Jan 1, 1864, died near Petersburg, Va., July 1, of wounds received June 30 1864, veteran

John Dowling, must in Feb 29, 1864, wounded at Petersburg, Va., July 30, 1864, must out with company Aug 28, 1865, veteran

Emanuel Derckman, must in Sept 24, 1863, drafted, wounded at Deep Bottom, Va., Aug 16, 1864, absent at muster out

John M Dewall, must in Sept 19, 1864, drafted, disch by G O June 28, 1865

John Dodson, must in Sept 21, 1864, drafted, disch by G O June 28, 1865

Benjamin Davis, must in Sept 20, 1861, died at Hilton Head, S C., Sept 10, 1862

Samuel Drake, must in Sept 6, 1861, died at Edisto Island, S C., June 8, 1862

Thomas Elliott, must in Jan 1, 1864, must out with company Aug 28, 1865, veteran

Joseph L Eyre, must in Sept. 16, 1861, killed on picket at Morris Island, S C., Aug 4, 1863

Robert J Furgeson, must in Feb 29, 1864, must. out with company Aug 28, 1865, veteran

Abner Frame, must. in Oct. 26, 1863; drafted; wounded May 18, 1864; disch. on surg. certif. April 4, 1865.
Francis Fairfield, must. in Oct. 26, 1863; drafted; must. out with company Aug. 28, 1865.
Abraham Fawkes, must. in Sept. 9, 1861; disch. Sept. 19, 1864, at exp. of term.
John D. Fair, must. in Sept. 19, 1864; drafted; disch. by G. O. May 23, 1865.
William H. Griffith, must. in Feb. 29, 1864; wounded Sept. 29, 1864; must. out with company Aug. 28, 1865; veteran.
Christopher Gribbin, must. in Sept. 24, 1863; drafted; absent, sick, at muster out.
James Geary, must. in Sept. 23, 1864; drafted; wounded at Darbytown road, Va., Oct. 27, 1864; disch. by G. O. June 8, 1865.
John M. Geigel, must. in Oct. 22, 1863; drafted; trans. to Vet. Res. Corps Sept. 39, 1864.
James Hamilton, must. in Jan. 1, 1864; wounded July 26, 1864; must. out with company Aug. 28, 1865; veteran.
Kennedy Humes, must. in April 15, 1864; must. out with company Aug. 28, 1865; veteran.
John Heller, must. in Oct. 19, 1863; drafted; must. out with company Aug. 28, 1865.
Henry Heck, must. in Nov. 16, 1864; drafted; must. out with company Aug. 28, 1865.
Benjamin Hughes, must. in Sept. 6, 1861; disch. on surg. certif. Sept. 27, 1863.
John C. Harmon, must. in Sept. 20, 1861; disch. Sept. 18, 1864, at exp. of term.
Richard S. Howarth, must. in Sept. 21, 1861; wounded June 16, 1864; disch. Sept. 10, 1864, at exp. of term.
Levi Hadfield, must. in Sept. 16, 1861; wounded June 16, 1864; disch. Sept. 10, 1864, at exp. of term.
Edward H. Hogg, must. in Oct. 23, 1863; drafted; wounded June 6, 1864; disch. on surg. certif. April 8, 1864.
Michael Hafner, must. in Nov. 12, 1864; drafted; disch. by G. O. June 16, 1865; burial record, died June 17, 1865; buried in Cypress Hill Cemetery, L. I.
Casper Heibel, must. in Sept. 24, 1864; drafted; disch. by G. O. June 28, 1865.
William Jones (1st), must. in Feb. 29, 1864; must. out with company Aug. 28, 1865; veteran.
William Jones (2d), must. in Oct. 19, 1863; drafted; absent, sick, at muster out.
William Jackson, must. in Sept. 25, 1863; drafted; must. out with company Aug. 28, 1865.
Smith Jones, must. in Sept. 24, 1863; drafted; wounded July 3, 1864; trans. to U. S. Army Aug. 6, 1864.
Michael Karney, must. in Feb. 29, 1864; must. out with company Aug. 28, 1865, veteran.
John C. Keyzer, must. in Sept. 16, 1861; disch. on surg. certif. Oct. 17, 1861.
John Kilroy, must. in Sept. 9, 1861; disch. on surg. certif. Oct. 24, 1861.
William H. Kelly, must. in Jan. 1, 1864; died Aug. 29, 1864, of wounds received near Petersburg, Va.; buried in National Cemetery, City Point, Section D, Division 1, grave 2.
John H. Louis, must. in Oct. 22, 1863; drafted; absent, sick, at muster out.
John Lechner, must. in Sept. 19, 1864; drafted; disch. by G. O. June 28, 1865.
Andrew D. Long, must. in Sept. 24, 1863; drafted; disch. on surg. certif. July 1, 1865.
Thomas M. Lancaster, must. in Sept. 11, 1861; died at St. Helena Island, S. C., Dec. 29, 1862.
Joshua Martin, must. in March 1, 1865; must. out with company Aug. 28, 1865.
Edward Maxwell, must. in Sept. 6, 1861; disch. on surg. certif. Dec. 10, 1861.
Ferdinand Martin, must. in Nov. 13, 1861; died at Hilton Head, S. C., April 15, 1863.
James Myers, must. in Oct. 19, 1863; drafted.
William W. McIntosh, must. in Jan. 1, 1864; wounded June 6, and at Fort Fisher, N. C., Jan. 15, 1865; must. out with company Aug. 28, 1865; veteran.
James McMannus, must. in Sept. 6, 1861; wounded May 18, 1864; disch. Jan. 10, 1865.
Patrick McGee, must. in Oct. 19, 1863; drafted; wounded June 30 and July 24, 1864; disch. by G. O. June 24, 1865.
James McClune, must. in Oct. 19, 1863; drafted.
Francis H. Pyle, must. in Jan. 1, 1864; must. out with company Aug. 28, 1865.
Walter Pyle, must. in Jan. 1, 1864; wounded June 18 and July 15, 1864; must. out with company Aug. 28, 1865.
Jacob Putell, must. in Oct. 19, 1863; drafted; wounded at Bermuda Hundred, Va., May 20, 1864; absent, in hospital, at muster out.
George K. Pierce, must. in Jan. 1, 1864; died July 26, 1864, of wounds received at Petersburg, Va.
Samuel Parker, must. in Jan. 1, 1864; wounded and captured at Deep Bottom, Va., Aug. 16, 1864; died at Salisbury, N. C., Dec. 16, 1864; veteran.
John Quinn, drafted; must. out with company Aug. 28, 1865.
James Rannels, must. in Sept. 24, 1863; drafted.
Solomon Shmach, must. in Feb. 28, 1865; substitute; must. out with company Aug. 28, 1865.
John Singer, must. in Feb. 24, 1865; substitute; must. out with company Aug. 28, 1865.
Francis W. Starkey, must. in Sept. 16, 1861; disch. Sept. 19, 1864, at expiration of term.
John Sheen, must. in Sept. 6, 1861; disch. on surg. certif. May 9, 1863.
John Smith, must. in Oct. 20, 1863; drafted; died at Hampton, Va., June 5th, of wounds received at Bermuda Hundred, Va., May 20, 1864.
John Thompson, must. in Feb. 29, 1864; wounded at Petersburg, Va., June 30, 1864; must. out with company Aug. 28, 1865; veteran.
Oliver Tennant, must. in Nov. 21, 1864; drafted; must. out with company Aug. 28, 1865.
Isaac Vanbuskirk, must. in Sept. 26, 1864; drafted; disch. by G. O. June 28, 1865.
William Watson, must. in Jan. 1, 1864; must. out with company Aug. 28, 1865; veteran.
Thomas White, must. in Sept. 23, 1863; drafted; must. out with company Aug. 28, 1865.
John Wright, must. in Sept. 21, 1863; drafted; must. out with company Aug. 28, 1865.
Anson Wheeler, must. in Nov. 11, 1864; drafted; disch. on surg. certif. May 29, 1865.
Caspar Wizling, must. in Nov. 12, 1864; drafted; disch. by G. O. July 29, 1864.
James Wright, must. in Sept. 9, 1861; died at Hilton Head, S. C., Oct. 23, 1862.
Joseph B. West, must. in April 15, 1864; died at Hampton, Va., May 26th, of wounds received May 18, 1864.
Jesse D. Walters, must. in Feb. 29, 1864; killed near Petersburg, Va., June 29, 1864; buried in National Cemetery, City Point, Section D, Division 4, grave 65; veteran.

COMPANY G (BROOMALL GUARDS).

Jesse L. Cummings, capt., must. in Oct. 15, 1861; res. May 1, 1862.
Caleb Hoopes, capt., must. in Oct. 15, 1861; pro. from 1st lieut. July 1, 1863; disch. Oct. 14, 1864, at exp. of term.
Washington W. James, capt., must. in Nov. 15, 1861; pro. from com.-sergt. May 26, 1865; must. out with company Aug. 28, 1865; veteran.
Gasway O. Yarnell, 1st sergt., must. in Sept. 26, 1861; pro. from sergt. May 27, 1863; wounded at Bermuda Hundred, Va., May 20, 1864; disch. Oct. 14, 1864, at exp. of term.
Joseph M. Burrell, 2d lieut., must. in Oct. 15, 1861; resigned Nov. 13, 1862.
William H. Eves, 2d lieut., must. in Oct. 3, 1861; pro. from 1st sergt. July 1, 1863; wounded at Petersburg, Va., July 10, 1864; disch. Oct. 22, 1864, at exp. of term.
Jeremiah Yost, 2d lieut., must. in Feb. 29, 1864; pro. from 1st sergt. May 26, 1865; must. out with company Aug. 28, 1865; veteran.
Franklin P. Clapp, 1st sergt., must. in March 16, 1864; wounded at Bermuda Hundred, Va., May 20, 1864; pro. to 1st sergt. July 19, 1865; absent on furlough at muster out; veteran.
William M. Collum, 1st sergt., must. in Sept. 16, 1861; disch. October, 1864, at exp. of term.
Reuben H. Smith, 1st sergt., must. in Sept. 30, 1861; pro. to hospital steward Sept. 14, 1862.
Charles E. Ottey, sergt., must. in March 16, 1864; pro. to sergt. July 19, 1865; must. out with company Aug. 28, 1865; veteran.
John L. Ray, sergt., must. in March 16, 1864; wounded at Petersburg, Va., June 30, 1864; pro. to sergt. July 19, 1865; must. out with company Aug. 28, 1865; veteran.
Charles Gray, sergt., must. in March 16, 1864; absent on furlough at muster out; veteran.

Thomas H. Dickel, sergt., must. in March 16, 1864; pro. to sergt. July 19, 1865; must. out with company Aug. 28, 1865; veteran.

Thomas J. McMullen, sergt., must. in March 16, 1864; disch. by G. O. May 26, 1865; veteran.

Thomas J. Wade, sergt., must. in Sept. 9, 1861; disch. October, 1864, at exp. of term.

Elias B. Grubb, sergt., must. in Oct. 10, 1861; disch. October, 1864, at exp. of term.

John C. Morton, sergt., must. in Oct. 10, 1861; trans. to Co. I Jan. 1, 1862.

David R. Cochran, sergt., must. in March 16, 1864; pro. to q.m.-sergt. July 19, 1865; veteran.

Simon Litzenburg, sergt., must. in Sept. 26, 1861; wounded May 18, 1864; killed at Petersburg, Va., July 30, 1864; buried in National Cemetery, City Point, Section D, Division 4, grave 174.

Reese L. Weaver, sergt., must. in Oct. 10, 1861; died at New York Oct. 12, 1863; buried in Cypress Hill Cemetery, L. I., grave 897.

Albin Edwards, sergt., must. in March 16, 1864; killed at Bermuda Hundred, Va., May 20, 1864; veteran.

Ezekiel T. Richie, corp., must. in March 16, 1864; wounded near Bermuda Hundred, Va., May 18, 1864; absent, sick, at muster out.

Francis Ebel, corp., must. in Nov. 2, 1863; drafted; must. out with company Aug. 28, 1865.

Joseph R. Parsons, corp., must. in March 16, 1864; must. out with company Aug. 28, 1865; veteran.

Henry Hards, corp., must in March 16, 1864; wounded at Bermuda Hundred, Va., May 20, 1864; must. out with company Aug. 20, 1865; veteran.

Matthias Kramer, corp., must. in Oct. 19, 1863; drafted; pro. to corp. July 19, 1865; must. out with company Aug. 28, 1865.

Patrick H. Harrigan, corp., must. in Jan. 9, 1863; pro. to corp. July 19, 1865; must. out with company Aug. 28, 1865.

William H. Cox, corp., must. in Sept. 9, 1861; disch. on surg. certif. May 27, 1863.

William N. Baker, corp., must. in Sept. 26, 1861; disch. on surg. certif. May 25, 1862.

Henry Hoofstitler, corp., must. in Sept. 30, 1861; disch. on surg. certif. March 3, 1863; burial record, died March 17, 1863.

John S. Culvert, corp., must. in Oct. 24, 1861; disch. October, 1864, at exp. of term.

Thomas Dunn, corp., must. in March 16, 1864; disch. by G. O. October 7th, to date Sept. 11, 1865; veteran.

Henry G. Yocum, corp., must. in Sept. 9, 1861; died at Fortress Monroe, Va., Dec. 21, 1865; veteran.

Israel Oat, corp., must. in Sept. 30, 1861; died at Hilton Head, S. C., Aug. 10, 1862.

Patrick Hughes, corp., must. in March 16, 1864; killed at Bermuda Hundred, Va., May 20, 1864; veteran.

John Doyle, corp., must. in Sept. 10, 1861; died at Hilton Head, S. C., Oct. 26, 1863.

John Edwards, corp., must. in Jan. 22, 1863; wounded at Petersburg, Va., July 30, 1864; died at Weldon, N. C., Aug. 21, 1865.

Jonathan S. Farra, musician, must. in March 16, 1864; must. out with company Aug. 28, 1865; veteran.

Privates.

William Anderson, must. in Aug. 21, 1863; drafted; must. out with company Aug. 28, 1865.

Lasher Asberry, must. in July 15, 1863; trans. to Department Southwest July 13, 1864.

John B. Brady, must. in Sept. 22, 1863; drafted; wounded at Petersburg, Va., June 30, 1864; absent in hospital at muster out.

Anthony Bish, must. in July 22, 1863; drafted; must. out with company Aug. 28, 1865.

Michael Banny, must. in Nov. 22, 1864; absent, sick, at muster out.

Joseph Barber, must. in Oct. 19, 1864; drafted; must. out with company Aug. 28, 1865.

William A. Brooks, must. in Feb. 28, 1863; wounded May 18, 1864; disch. by G. O. July 4, 1865.

Joseph H. Brensinger, must. in April 13, 1864; wounded May 18, 1864; disch. by G. O. July 5, 1865.

George P. Barr, must. in Sept. 23, 1861; discharged, date unknown.

Nehemiah Baker, must. in Sept. 27, 1861; died at Fernandina, Fla., Jan. 8, 1864.

Lewis Bentz, must. in Sept. 24, 1863; drafted; died at Point of Rocks, Md., Aug. 19, 1864.

John Barker, must. in July 22, 1863; drafted.

George Blanden, must. in Nov. 22, 1864.

William S. Coyle, must. in Oct. 3, 1861; disch. October, 1864, at exp. of term.

S. B. F. Chambers, must. in Oct. 3, 1861; disch. October, 1864, at exp. of term.

Charles Collum, must. in Nov. 22, 1864; disch. by G. O. June 18, 1865, at exp. of term.

Henry C. Carter, must. in Aug. 24, 1864; disch. by G. O. June 28, 1865, at exp. of term.

Phillip Caul, must. in Nov. 3, 1863; drafted.

Thomas Carr, must. in March 1, 1865.

John C. Chavanne, must. in Feb. 28, 1865.

John Dickson, must. in Oct. 7, 1861; died at Hilton Head, S. C., Oct. 21, 1863.

William Dawson, must. in Aug. 11, 1864; killed at Fort Fisher, N. C., Jan. 16, 1865.

William Efoux, must. in Sept. 24, 1863; drafted; killed at Petersburg, Va., June 30, 1864.

Samuel Fields, must. in April 13, 1864; must. out with company Aug. 28, 1865.

William B. Farra, must. in April 13, 1864; must. out with company Aug. 28, 1865.

John Frost, must. in Nov. 23, 1864; must. out with company Aug. 28, 1865.

Edward Fawkes, must. in Sept. 26, 1861; disch. on surg. certif. Dec. 9, 1863.

Stephen J. Fletcher, must. in Sept. 24, 1863; drafted; disch. by G. O. May 26, 1865.

Harry E. Foster, must. in Sept. 23, 1863; drafted; disch. by G. O. May 17, 1865.

Joseph Gardhurse, must. in Sept. 9, 1861; disch. October, 1864, at exp. of term.

George Green, must. in Sept. 17, 1861; died at Hilton Head, S. C., Sept. 20, 1862; burial record, Sept. 2, 1862.

William Henry, must. in March 16, 1864; must. out with company Aug. 28, 1865.

Ephraim Hutchinson, must. in Sept. 16, 1861; disch. on surg. certif. March 31, 1863.

Thomas L. Hinkson, must. in Sept. 23, 1861; disch., date unknown.

Charles Hatcher, must. in Sept. 26, 1864; disch. on surg. certif. Sept. 20, 1862.

Isaac A. Hoopes, must. in March 16, 1864; killed at Bermuda Hundred, Va., May 20, 1864; veteran.

Hend. L. Herkins, must. in March 16, 1864; wounded at Bermuda Hundred May 20, 1864; died at Wilmington, N. C., March 19, 1865; veteran.

Frederick Heitz, must. in Sept. 24, 1863; drafted; killed at Bermuda Hundred, Va., May 20, 1864; buried in National Cemetery, City Point, Section F, Division 1, grave 128.

John Hamin, must. in Nov. 25, 1864.

John H. Henderson, must. in Nov. 5, 1861.

Stephen Johnson, must. in Sept. 23, 1861; disch. on surg. certif., date unknown.

Joseph S. Johnson, must. in Oct. 11, 1861; disch. on surg. certif. Jan. 8, 1862.

Thomas T. Jones, must. in March 16, 1864; died at Fortress Monroe June 10th, of wounds received at Bermuda Hundred, Va., May 20, 1864; veteran.

Charles Kuhn, must. in July 22, 1863; drafted; wounded at Petersburg, Va., July 20, 1864; trans. to Vet. Res. Corps Jan. 7, 1865; disch. by G. O. Sept. 19, 1865.

Arthur Littell, must. in Aug. 15, 1863; drafted; must. out with company Aug. 28, 1865.

James C. Lane, must. in March 1, 1865; substitute; must. out with company Aug. 28, 1865.

John Lightner, must. in March 6, 1865; substitute; must. out with company Aug. 28, 1865.

Samuel Logsden, must. in March 4, 1865; drafted; must. out with company Aug. 28, 1865.

Samuel H. Lloyd, must. in March 16, 1864; wounded at Petersburg, Va., June 30, 1864; must. out with company Aug. 28, 1865.

John Laughlin, must. in Sept. 19, 1861; wounded at Bermuda Hundred, Va., May 20, 1864; disch. October, 1864, at exp. of term.

Thomas Leanord, must. in Oct. 26, 1861; disch. October, 1864, at exp. of term.

Thomas J. Lewis, must. in Sept. 30, 1861.

Alexander Miller, must. in Sept. 23, 1861; disch. on surg. certif. Feb. 25, 1863.

Herman Meiser, must. in July 29, 1863; drafted; wounded at Bermuda Hundred, Va., May 20, 1864; disch. by G. O., date unknown.

John Miller, must. in Aug. 27, 1864; disch. by G. O. July 28, 1865.

William Maloney, must. in Sept. 9, 1861; died at Fernandina, Fla., Dec. 1, 1863.

William D. Murray, must. in March 6, 1865; died at Raleigh, N. C., May 18, 1865.

George Miller, must. in Aug. 21, 1863; drafted.

Thomas McIntosh, must. in March 16, 1861; wounded June 16, 1862, Sept. 1, 1863, and May 20, 1864; absent, sick, at muster out; veteran.

Alfred McKnight, must. in March 4, 1865.

Bernard McKinney, must. in Jan. 13, 1865; not on muster-out roll.

John Nish, must. in Sept. 24, 1863; drafted; must. out with company Aug. 28, 1865.

Terrence O'Brien, must. in March 16, 1864; wounded at Bermuda Hundred, Va., May 20, 1864; killed at Strawberry Plains Aug. 17, 1864; veteran.

John O'Neil, must. in Nov. 22, 1863.

William Papjoy, must. in Sept. 23, 1861; wounded May 18, 1864; trans. to Vet. Res. Corps Jan. 1, 1865; veteran.

James Rogers, must. in Sept. 23, 1863; drafted; must. out with company Aug. 28, 1865.

Joseph Ray, must. in Sept. 9, 1861; wounded Sept. 1, 1863; disch. Oct. 1, 1864, at exp. of term.

Amos R. Rapp, must. in Sept. 16, 1861; disch. on surg. certif. Sept. 21, 1862.

Merritt C. Reeves, must. in Oct. 24, 1863; drafted; wounded at Bermuda Hundred, Va., May 20, 1864; disch. on surg. certif. April 25, 1865.

Philip Roothwig, must. in July 22, 1863; drafted; disch. on surg. certif. Feb. 14, 1865.

James Russell, must. in Sept. 29, 1861; died at New York Jan. 8, 1864; burial record, Jan. 30, 1864; buried in Cypress Hill Cemetery, L. I.

William Smith, must. in Oct. 15, 1863; drafted; disch. by G. O. May 29, 1865.

Robert Scott, must. in Aug. 30, 1864; must. out with company Aug. 28, 1865.

William T. Snyder, must. in March 16, 1864; wounded at Bermuda Hundred, Va., May 20, 1864; absent, in hospital, at muster out; veteran.

Edward Stein, must. in Sept. 23, 1863; drafted; must. out with company Aug. 28, 1865.

David Samuel, must. in Sept. 23, 1863; drafted; disch. by G. O. June 23, 1865.

Robert Smith, must. in Nov. 3, 1863; drafted; disch. by G. O. June 23, 1865.

Alexander Seaborn, must. in Nov. 4, 1861; wounded May 18, 1864; died at Alexandria, Va., October 10th, of wounds received at Petersburg July 30, 1864.

Theodore Solomon, must. in Sept. 23, 1863; drafted; wounded at Petersburg, Va., Aug. 24, 1864; died at Raleigh, N. C., May 26, 1865; burial record, buried in Cypress Hill Cemetery, L. I., grave 2887.

William Thomas, must. in Sept. 10, 1861; disch. October, 1864, at exp. of term.

A. McD. Talbot, must. in Oct. 30, 1861; wounded at Petersburg, Va., June 30, 1864; disch. October, 1864, at exp. of term.

Samuel R. Walton, must. in March 16, 1864; must. out with company Aug. 28, 1865; veteran.

Henry Walls, must. in March 16, 1864; must. out with company Aug. 28, 1865; veteran.

Philip Worrell, must. in March 11, 1864; must. out with company Aug. 28, 1865; veteran.

O. Rees Walker, must. in Sept. 23, 1863; drafted; wounded May 18, 1864; must. out with company Aug. 28, 1865.

William Wright, must. in Sept. 23, 1861; disch. Oct. 7, 1861; re-enl. Dec. 20, 1862; died at Fernandina, Fla., Nov. 28, 1863.

James Weaver, must. in Sept. 30, 1861; disch. on surg. certif. November, 1863.

George White, must. in Sept. 9, 1861; disch. October, 1864, at exp. of term.

Crosby D. Wilson, must. in Oct. 7, 1861; disch. October, 1864, at exp. of term.

Edward Worrell, must. in Oct. 7, 1861; disch. October, 1864, at exp. of term.

Patrick Waters, must. in March 16, 1864; wounded May 18, 1864; disch. on surg. certif. May 16, 1865; veteran.

James H. Worrell, must. in Oct. 23, 1861; disch. November, 1861.

Thomas P. Waddell, must. in Oct. 15, 1861; wounded May 20 and June 25, 1864; disch. October, 1864, at exp. of term.

James F. Warnock, must. in July 24, 1863; drafted; disch. by G. O. July 16, 1865.

James Wright, must. in Sept. 26, 1861; died at Fernandina, Fla., Nov. 20, 1863.

Edward E. Wade, must. in March 16, 1864; captured at Deep Bottom, Va., Aug. 16, 1864; died at Salisbury, N. C., Dec. 18, 1864; veteran.

John Worrell, must. in Sept. 9, 1861; died at Hilton Head, S. C., May 12, 1862.

Charles Young, must. in Oct. 7, 1861; disch. October, 1864, at exp. of term.

Frederick Young, must. in Oct. 24, 1861; disch. November, 1861.

COMPANY I (BROOKE GUARDS).

George Hawkins, capt., must. in Oct. 29, 1861; com. lieut.-col. Sept. 18, 1864; not mustered; died August 28th of wounds received at Darbytown road, Va., Oct. 27, 1864.

George W. Duffee, capt., must. in Feb. 29, 1864; pro. from 1st sergt. to 2d lieut. March 6, 1864; to 1st lieut. July 19, 1864; to capt. May 1, 1865; wounded at Fort Gilmore, Va., Sept. 23, 1864, and at Fort Fisher, N. C., Jan. 15, 1865; must. out with company Aug. 28, 1865; veteran.

Sketchley Morton, Jr., 1st lieut., must. in Oct. 19, 1861; died at Hilton Head, S. C., Nov. 12, 1862.

William H. H. Gibson, 1st lieut., must. in Feb. 29, 1864; wounded at Bermuda Hundred, Va., May 20, 1864; pro. from 1st sergt. to 2d lieut. July 28, 1864; to 1st lieut. May 1, 1865; must. out with company Aug. 28, 1865; veteran.

Annesley N. Morton, 2d lieut., must. in Nov. 16, 1861; res. April 16, 1862.

James Williams, 2d lieut., must. in Sept. 16, 1861; pro. from 1st sergt. April 16, 1862; res. Sept. 8, 1862.

John Knapp, 2d lieut., must. in Nov. 8, 1861; pro. from 1st sergt. Sept. 10, 1862; res. Feb. 13, 1864.

George M. Middleton, 2d lieut., must. in Jan. 1, 1864; wounded at Bermuda Hundred, Va., May 10, 1864, and at Fort Fisher, N. C., Jan. 15, 1865; pro. from 1st sergt. May 1, 1865; must. out with company Aug. 28, 1865.

William Ottewell, 1st sergt., must. in Feb. 29, 1864; wounded Aug. 26, 1865; must. out with company Aug. 28, 1865; veteran.

James E. Engle, 1st sergt., must. in Feb. 29, 1864; wounded, with loss of arm, at Bermuda Hundred, Va., May 20, 1864; pro. to 2d lieut. 16th Regt. Vet. Res. Corps Aug. 24, 1864; veteran.

William K. Wood, 1st sergt., must. in Nov. 10, 1861; wounded at Bermuda Hundred, Va., May 20, 1864; disch. Oct. 29, 1864, at exp. of term.

William P. Haymen, sergt., must. in Feb. 29, 1864; wounded at Bermuda Hundred, Va., May 20, 1864; must. out with company Aug. 28, 1865.

William H. Reese, sergt., must. in Oct. 19, 1861; wounded at Darbytown Road, Va., Oct. 27, 1864; disch. by G. O. Aug. 15, 1865; veteran.

Edward Horn, sergt., must. in Jan. 1, 1864; must. out with company Aug. 28, 1865.

Jacob Cline, sergt., must. in Feb. 29, 1864; must. out with company Aug. 28, 1865.

Thomas A. Watson, sergt., must. in Oct. 15, 1861; disch. on surg. certif. Sept. 20, 1862.

John C. Morton, sergt., must. in Oct. 11, 1861; disch. Oct. 21, 1864, at exp. of term.

Horatio A. Powell, sergt., must. in April 2, 1862; disch. April 2, 1865, at exp. of term.

Thomas Creigan, corp., must. in Feb. 29, 1864; wounded at Bermuda Hundred, Va., and at Fort Fisher, N. C., Jan. 15, 1865; must. out with company Aug. 28, 1865; veteran.

James B. Neville, corp., must. in Feb. 29, 1864; must. out with company Aug. 28, 1865; veteran.

George H. Barton, corp., must. in Feb. 29, 1864; must. out with company Aug. 28, 1865; veteran.

James Graff, corp., must. in Feb. 29, 1864; wounded Aug. 16, 1864; mustered out with company Aug. 28, 1864; veteran.

Charles Stewart, corp., must. in Jan. 1, 1864; wounded at Bermuda Hundred, Va., May 20, 1864; must. out with company Aug. 28, 1864; veteran.

Owen L. Smith, corp., must. in July 24, 1863; drafted; must. out with company Aug. 28, 1865.

Jabez Travis, corp, must in Feb 29, 1864, must out with company Aug 28, 1865, veteran

Francis Todd, corp., must. in Feb 29, 1864, wounded at Fort Fisher, N C., Jan 15, 1865, pro to corp July 24, 1865, must out with company Aug 28, 1865

Adolph Fry, corp., must in Oct 23, 1863, drafted, disch May 20, 1865, for wounds, with loss of arm, received at Fort Fisher, N C, Jan 15, 1865

William F Green, corp., must. in Feb 29, 1864, disch July 10, 1865, for wounds received at Bermuda Hundred, Va, May 20, 1864, veteran

John L Morton, corp, must in Sept 21, 1861, died at Fernandina, Fla., March 28, 1862

Robert Trowland, corp, must in Nov 15, 1861, died at Philadelphia, Pa., Nov 4, 1863

William T Thomson, musician, must. in Feb 29, 1864, must out with company Aug 28, 1865, veteran

John Parsons, Jr, musician, must in Feb 29, 1864, pro to principal musician March 1, 1864, veteran

Harry Hunter, musician, must in Oct 15, 1861, died at Hilton Head, S C., April 1, 1862

Privates

George Armstrong, must in Jan 19, 1865, drafted, must out with company Aug 28, 1865

John Abner, must in Feb 27, 1865, drafted

John H Brook, must in Oct 22, 1863, drafted, must out with company Aug 28, 1865

Morton Brontzman, must in Sept. 23, 1863, drafted, wounded at Bermuda Hundred, Va., May 20, 1864, absent, sick, at muster out

Charles Brown, must out Sept 24, 1863, drafted, disch by G O June 15, 1865

William H Baker, must in Sept 22 1863, drafted, died at Hilton Head, S C, Aug 2, 1864

Philip Clark, must in July 24, 1863, drafted, wounded July 16th and Aug 16, 1864, absent, sick, at muster out

Thomas Conn, must in July 24, 1863, drafted, absent, sick, at muster out

John Cole, must in Jan 18, 1865, drafted, must. out with company Aug 28, 1865

Sylvester Camp must in Feb 4, 1865, drafted, disch by G O June 15, 1865

Henry Carney, must in Oct 24, 1861, disch on surg certif Sept 27, 1863

Elias Cole, must in Sept 22, 1863, drafted, wounded at Bermuda Hundred, Va, May 20, 1864, disch by G O June 14, 1865

William W Chappin, must in Sept 28, 1864, drafted, disch by G O June 28, 1865

James Crosby, must in Sept 24, 1863, drafted

William Counelly, must in July 24, 1863, drafted

Daniel Crowley, must in Oct 23, 1863, drafted

William Davis, must in July 24, 1863, drafted, wounded at Bermuda Hundred, Va, May 20, 1864, must out with company Aug 28, 1865

William J Dunlap, must in Oct 9, 1861, wounded July 6, 1864, disch Oct 29, 1864, at exp of term

James Donovan, must. in Feb 29, 1864, disch June 9, 1865, for wounds received at Bermuda Hundred, Va, May 20, 1864, veteran

John Donovan, must in April 5, 1864, wounded July 15, 1864, trans to Vet Res Corps March 4, 1865, disch May 29, 1865

James Donnelly, must in Sept 23, 1863, drafted, killed at Bermuda Hundred, Va., May 20, 1864

William R Dicker, must in Oct. 16, 1861, died on steamer "Hero" June 18, 1864

Thomas Edwards, must. in Oct 9, 1861, disch on surg certif Oct 27, 1863

C O. Elbertson, must in Oct. 17, 1861, disch on surg certif May 9, 1863

Evan H Everman, must in Feb 29, 1864, died at Philadelphia, Pa, August 1st, of wounds received at Petersburg, Va, June 24, 1865, veteran

Patrick Finley, must in Dec 10, 1861, disch on surg certif Sept 3, 1864

George Frace, must in Nov 11, 1864, drafted, died at Raleigh, N C., May 13, 1865

Philander Foster, must in Jan 11, 1865, drafted, died at Raleigh, N C., July 5, 1865

John Gray, must in Feb 28, 1864, must out with company Aug 28, 1865, veteran

William T Gutterson, must in Jan 1, 1864, killed at Bermuda Hundred, Va, May 20, 1864, veteran

David W Gaul, must in Feb 29, 1864, killed at Bermuda Hundred, Va., May 20, 1864, veteran

Peter Goodrich, must in Sept 23, 1863 drafted

Isaac D Haines, must in July 24, 1863, drafted, must out with company Aug 28, 1865

Dennis Hawk, must in Nov 11, 1863, drafted, disch by G O June 10, 1865

Edward Helm, must in Feb 22, 1863, disch by G O June 6, 1865

Philip Heen, must in Sept 21, 1863, drafted, disch June 23, 1865, for wounds received at Bermuda Hundred, Va, May 20, 1864

Daniel Harrigan, must in Feb 29, 1864, wounded at Bermuda Hundred, Va., May 20, 1864 trans to Vet Res Corps May 15, 1865, veteran

Nathan T Harris, must in Nov 7, 1861, died at Hilton Head, S C., May 12, 1862

Caleb Horn, must in Oct. 31, 1861, died at New York June 27, 1864, burial record, Jan 30, 1864, buried in Cypress Hill Cemetery, Long Island, grave 1006

Charles L Harris, must in Oct 22, 1863, drafted

Sanford Irvin, must in Oct 24, 1861, disch on writ of *habeas corpus* Oct 28, 1861

Peter Johnson, must in July 28, 1863, drafted

Levi Kelly, must in Feb 23, 1865, drafted, disch by G O June 21, 1865

John Krissell, must in Sept 22, 1863, drafted, killed at Petersburg, Va, July 15, 1864

Christian Kneedler, must in Sept 25, 1863, drafted

Henry P Lindsay, must in Jan 1, 1864, must out with company Aug 28, 1865, veteran

James Lynch, must in Oct. 17, 1861, disch on surg certif Dec 22, 1863

James Lafferty, must in Oct 19, 1861, disch on surg certif April 5, 1864

Daniel W Lukens, must in Sept 21, 1861, wounded at Bermuda Hundred, Va, May 20, 1864, and at Darbytown Road, Va., Oct 27, 1864, disch Oct 29, 1864, at exp of term

Daniel Laurence, must in Sept 22, 1864, drafted, disch by G O June 23, 1865

Frederick W Leidtke, must in Feb 3 1862, pro to 2d lieut Co G, 11th Regt P V, Aug 28, 1862

James Lewis, must in Sept 23, 1863, drafted, wounded at Bermuda Hundred, Va, May 20, 1864

Michael W Mathias, must in Jan 1, 1864, must. out with company Aug 28, 1865, veteran

Peter Miller, must in Oct 23, 1863, drafted, must out with company Aug 28, 1865

Joseph E Myers must in July 22, 1863, drafted, must out with company Aug 28, 1865

Dennis Mahoney, must in July 30, 1863, drafted, must out with company Aug 28, 1865

James Mahoney, must in July 24, 1863, drafted, wounded at Darbytown Road, Va., Oct 27, 1864, must out with company Aug 28, 1865

Enos Marshall, must in Sept 21, 1861, disch on surg certif Sept 27, 1862

James F Maloney, must in Oct 27, 1861, disch on surg certif Oct 12, 1863

William Marrnyer, must in Sept 10, 1863, drafted

William R Morris, must in March 27, 1862, not on muster out roll

John McDermott, must in Feb 29, 1864, wounded at Fort Fisher, N C., Jan 15, 1865, absent, sick, at muster out

Alexander G McKeewen, must in July 24, 1863, drafted, wounded at Bermuda Hundred, Va., May 20, 1864, absent, in hospital, at muster out

Charles McMulligan, must in Nov 16, 1864, drafted, must out with company Aug 28, 1865

Robert McStraw, must in Nov 11, 1864, drafted, must out with company Aug 28, 1865

William McNeal, must in Sept 21, 1861, disch Oct 31, 1864, at exp of term

James McCabe, must in April 3, 1862, disch April 3, 1865, at exp of term

David T Nuttle, must in Feb 29, 1864, absent at muster out, veteran

Howard S Perlton, must in Sept 25, 1863, drafted

Adam S Pride, must in Nov 11, 1864, drafted, must out with company Aug 28, 1865

David Powell, must in July 23, 1864, drafted, wounded at Fort Fisher, N C, Jan 15, 1865, disch by G O June 10, 1865

William Pine, must in Dec 16, 1861, died at New York Oct 11, 1864, buried in Cypress Hill Cemetery, Long Island

Thomas Rodgers, must in Nov 16, 1864, drafted, must out with company Aug 28, 1865

John J Richardson, must in Sept 16, 1861, wounded at Petersburg, Va, July 15, 1864, disch Oct 29, 1864, at exp of term

Enoch H Rigby, must in Sept 16, 1861, disch Oct 29, 1864, at exp of term

Herbert Rodgers, must in Sept 21, 1861, disch May 4, 1865, for wounds received at Bermuda Hundred, Va, May 20, 1864 veteran

Michael Rhurr, must in Oct 22, 1863, drafted, trans to Reg U S A Aug 6, 1864

Joseph Sharp, must in Jan 1, 1864, must out with company Aug 28, 1865, veteran

David Simpson, must in Jan 1, 1864, must out with company Aug 28, 1865

Levi T Slutter, must in Sept 20, 1863, drafted, must out with company Aug 28, 1865

John Schraetzel, must in July 25, 1863, drafted, must out with company Aug 28, 1865

Jacob Sipe, must in Nov 16, 1864, drafted, must out with company Aug 28, 1865

Elijah Shaffer, must in Nov 11, 1864, drafted must out with company Aug 28, 1865

Henry Sage, must in Sept 26, 1864, drafted, disch by G O June 28, 1865

John W Shutt, must in Feb 29, 1864, died at Fortress Monroe July 14, of wounds received at Bermuda Hundred, May 20, 1864, veteran

Levers Sulverson, must. in July 20, 1863, drafted, died Aug 3, of wounds received at Petersburg, Va, July 30, 1864

Philip Schwartz, must in Nov 11, 1864, drafted, killed at Fort Fisher, N C, Jan 15, 1865

Henry Schlutt, must in July 13, 1863

Lemuel J Thompkins, must in Feb 29, 1864, wounded at Bermuda Hundred, Va., May 20, 1864, must out with company Aug 28, 1865, veteran

Evan Thomas, must in Oct 19, 1861, disch on writ of *habeas corpus* Oct 24, 1861

James B Thomas, must in Sept 27, 1864 drafted, disch by G O June 28, 1865

John Taylor, must in Sept 21, 1861, disch on surg certif June 27, 1863

Jonathan Todd, must in Jan 24, 1862, transf to Vet Res Corps Oct 31, 1863

George Watb, must in July 30, 1863, drafted, absent, sick, at muster out.

Franklin Vreiland, must in Sept. 21, 1863, drafted, trans to Vet Res Corps Oct 25, 1864

William H Ward, must in Feb 29, 1864, must out with company Aug 28, 1865, veteran

John Williams (1st), must in Oct 22, 1863, drafted, must out with company Aug 28, 1865

Richard Walraven, must in Sept 21, 1861, wounded at Bermuda Hundred Va, May 20, 1864, disch Oct 29, 1864, at expiration of term

John Williams (2d), must in Sept 23, 1863, drafted, disch by S O Oct 19, 1864

Robert Wangaman, must in Sept 21, 1864, drafted, disch by G O June 28, 1865

Spencer W Wilson, must in Nov 11, 1864, drafted, disch by G O Aug 18, 1865

Amos G Webb, must in Nov 19, 1861, died at Beaufort, S C, July 6, 1862

John Ward, must in Sept 21, 1861, died at Fort Schuyler, N Y, Oct 28, 1863

Isaac Wood, must in Oct. 7, 1861, killed at Petersburg, Va., July 29, 1864

Willard Waterman, must in Nov 11, 1864, drafted, died at Raleigh, N C, May 21, 1865, buried in National Cemetery, Section 20, grave 2

Jacob Wagoner, must in Nov 16, 1864, drafted, died at Portsmouth Grove, R I, July 20, 1865

George A Wesler, must in Nov 16, 1864, drafted

One Hundred and Sixth Regiment (Three-Years' Service)—The regiment was recruited in Philadelphia during the late summer and early fall of 1861, and was part of Baker's brigade, and at the battle of Ball's Bluff the One Hundred and Sixth was on the Maryland side, but for lack of transportation were unable to cross to the assistance of their comrades, who were being overpowered by the superior number of the enemy opposing them At the battle of Fair Oaks it supported Kirby's battery against Magruder's assault, the latter having sworn that as that battery was formerly in the United States army under his command, he was determined to capture it, but Magruder's repeated efforts to that end were unsuccessful At Savage Station, although exposed to a severe fire of artillery and musketry, it repelled for nearly three hours every charge made upon it, at one time during the engagement being engaged in a desperate hand-to-hand struggle At Antietam it suffered severely, in ten minutes, at a fence near Dunker Church, one-third of the entire regiment was stricken down At the battle of Fredericksburg, on the 13th, it charged, under a terrific artillery fire, to within seventy-five yards of the enemy's works, and from mid-day to darkness it held its ground, and on May 3, 1863, it advanced to the assistance of Sedgwick, commanding the Sixth Corps, at Salem Church, when the latter was fighting against overwhelming odds at that point

At Gettysburg the One Hundred and Sixth came on the field at midnight of July 1st and took position behind the low stone wall on the right centre of the line, in front of and to the left of Meade's headquarters On the afternoon of the 2d, when Sickles' line was broken the One Hundred and Sixth was part of Webb's brigade which marched to the gap in the line, and when it reached the crest the enemy, not sixty yards in front, were pressing on as to certain victory The brigade fired a close musketry volley at the advancing foe and then charged, striking the enemy on the left flank, hurling back his advancing column The One Hundred and Sixth and two companies of the Second New York pursued the retreating enemy as far as the Emmettsburg road The following day it was at Cemetery Hill, to support the Twelfth Corps, and stationed on the right of the Baltimore pike, near Rickets' Battery, it remained under the terrific cannonading of that day until the close of the battle During the Wilderness campaign it was almost constantly in action, and took part in Hancock's famous charge at Spottsylvania in the gray of the morning of May 12th It was engaged at the North Anna, and in the battle of Cold Harbor the brigade of which the One Hundred and Sixth was part attempted to drive the enemy from his intrenchment, but they were too strong, and the men, dropping on the ground, remained until night, when they threw up a breastwork, which they held Crossing the James, it took part in the action of June 14th before Petersburg, and the movement upon Jerusalem plank-road a week later The regiment was mustered out of service Sept 10, 1864

COMPANY I.

William A. Hughes, 2d lieut., must. in Aug. 24, 1861; pro. to 2d lieut. June 10, 1863; must. out with company Sept. 10, 1864.

James D. Witter, 1st sergt., must. in Aug. 24, 1861; pro. to 1st sergt. Oct. 1, 1862; must. out with company Sept. 10, 1864.

Samuel Hill, corp., must. in Aug. 24, 1861; must. out with company.

Jefferson Arthur, corp., must. in Aug. 26, 1861; captured at Petersburg, Va., June 22, 1864; trans. to Co. H, date unknown.

Jacob Pyewell, corp., must. in Aug. 28, 1861; trans. to Vet. Res. Corps Dec. 15, 1863.

Reuben Dansfield, corp., must. in Aug. 28, 1861; died Aug. 16, 1862.

Privates.

Isaac Campbell, must. in Aug. 28, 1861; disch. on surg. certif. November, 1862.

William Gamble, must. in Aug. 24, 1861; died Jan. 12, 1863.

Alfred J. Mudford, must. in Aug. 21, 1861; must. out with company Sept. 10, 1864.

Charles Roxborough, must. in Aug. 28, 1861; trans. to Vet. Res. Corps; died Aug. 28, 1864, at exp. of term.

John Stevenson, must. in Aug. 24, 1861; killed at Savage Station, Va., June 29, 1862.

John Knife. Howard Helms.

William McNeil.

COMPANY C.

Edward Lilley, private, must. in Sept. 21, 1861; disch. on surg. certif. March 22, 1863.

COMPANY E.

John McLaughlin, private, must. in Aug. 28, 1861; killed at Antietam, Md., Sept. 17, 1862.

One Hundred and Twelfth (Second Artillery) Regiment.—On the recommendation of Gen. McClellan, Charles Angeroth, of Philadelphia, in October, 1861, was authorized by the Secretary of War to recruit a battalion of heavy artillery,—afterwards enlarged to a regiment,—the Second Pennsylvania Heavy Artillery, the One Hundred and Twelfth of the line. On Feb. 25, 1862, seven companies were ordered to Washington. Remaining in the fortification there until the spring of 1864, the regiment had increased by enlistments to three thousand three hundred men, when it was divided into two regiments, the second body under the name of the Second Provisional Heavy Artillery. The new regiment was dispatched to the front, and, as infantry, assigned to duty in the Ninth Corps. It took part in all the battles of the Wilderness campaign, and suffered severely, June 17th, in the charge at Petersburg. In May, 1864, the original regiment was ordered to join the Army of the Potomac, and assigned to the Eighteenth Army Corps under Gen. Baldy Smith. The story of this organization—two in one—is that of the severe year of battle until the fall of Richmond and surrender of Lee. The Second Division, or Provisional Regiment, had hard service before Petersburg, losing in four months about one thousand men. It was part of the brigade which charged into the crater when the mine was exploded, and on the 29th of September, 1864, after Fort Harrison had been captured, the Second Pennsylvania Artillery and Eighty-ninth New York were ordered to charge on Battery Gilmore, but the movement not being supported it resulted disastrously, the Second Artillery losing in killed, wounded, and prisoners two hundred men. The history of the regiment is most honorable, but, being intrusted with the defenses of Washington for two years, it was deprived, until the last year of the war, of displaying on the blood-stained battle-fields, before Grant became commander of the Army of the Potomac, that valor which in a few months earned for the One Hundred and Twelfth merited distinction.

The following men were recruited from Delaware County:

BATTERY L.

Marion Litzenburg, 1st lieut., must. in Sept. 1, 1862; pro. to corp. Nov. 1, 1862; to sergt. June 1, 1863; to 1st sergt. November, 1864; to 2d lieut. Dec. 3, 1864; to 1st lieut. Dec 17, 1864; absent in detailed service in Freedmen's Bureau at muster out.

BATTERY E.

Lewis Moulder, private, must. in Nov. 23, 1863; captured; died at Salisbury, N. C., Jan. 14, 1865.

Charles Barges, private, must. in Nov. 23, 1863; killed at Petersburg, Va.

John H. Weaver, private, must. in Nov. 23, 1863; absent, sick, at muster out Jan. 29, 1866.

Samuel Long, 2d lieut., must. in Oct. 9, 1861; pro. to corp. Feb. 1, 1864; to sergt. Jan. 1, 1865; to 2d lieut. June 16, 1865; must. out with battery Jan. 29, 1866; veteran.

Thomas Chambers,[1] corp., must. in Dec. 21, 1863; captured at Chapin's Farm, Va., Sept. 29, 1864; pro. to corp. June 20, 1865; captured at Salisbury, N. C.; disch. by G. O. July 14, 1865.

John Dover, private, must. in Oct. 28, 1861; disch. Oct. 27, 1864, at exp. of term.

John Moulder, private, must. in Jan. 4, 1864; disch. by G. O. June 8, 1865.

William Neal, private, must. in Oct. 7, 1861; disch. Oct. 6, 1864, at exp. of term.

Alexander Phillips, q.m.-sergt., must. in Oct. 9, 1861; pro. to corp. April 22, 1864; to 1st sergt. Jan. 1, 1865; must. out with battery Jan. 29, 1866; veteran.

The One Hundred and Nineteenth Regiment (Three-Years' Service).—On Aug. 5, 1862, Peter C. Ellmaker, of Philadelphia, who had been authorized by Governor Curtin to enlist a regiment, began recruiting for the One Hundred and Nineteenth Pennsylvania. William C. Gray, of Chester, had raised a company in Delaware County known as the Delaware County Guards, which he tendered to the authorities here to be credited to this county, but was told that the quota was full and the commissioners did not feel justified in accepting them. Capt. Gray thereupon offered the company to Col. Ellmaker. The offer was accepted, and the organization was mustered in as Company E, of the One Hundred and Nineteenth Regiment, on Aug. 10, 1862. The demand for troops became so pressing that on August 31st, before the regiment was perfectly organized, it was ordered to Washington, the following day reported at the capital, and was assigned for the protection of the arsenal. About the middle of October it joined the Army of the Potomac, then in camp near Antietam, being assigned to the First Brigade, Second Division, Sixth Army Corps. "Though suddenly thrown among veterans of two campaigns," says Bates, "it

[1] In 1867, Thomas Chambers contributed to the *Delaware County Republican* a series of noticeably well-written papers, entitled "Memoirs of Life and Death in Rebel Prisons," in which the incidents happening therein, as he saw them, are graphically pictured.

was prepared by its thorough training to hold its place with credit." On Dec. 15, 1862, at Fredericksburg, the regiment was for the first time in action, and, although exposed to heavy artillery fire, maintained its ground like veterans. Subsequently, when the "Light Division" was organized, it was assigned to the Third Brigade, First Division, under Gen. Russell. On April 28, 1863, when Hooker advanced, under cover of night the brigade crossed the Rappahannock at Banks' Ford on pontoon-boats, drove in the Confederate pickets and held the position on the right bank of the river. The next morning it moved forward in line of battle and drove the ememy from the rifle-pits, which it held until May 3d, when the Confederates retreated and the corps was sent in pursuit, the One Hundred and Nineteenth and Ninety-fifth Pennsylvania Regiments detached and marched along the plank-road in the direction of Chancellorsville. At Salem Church the latter force coming upon the enemy posted in a woods, concealed from sight, an immediate engagement followed at close quarters. The One Hundred and Nineteenth, posted on the left of the road, were confronted by a largely superior force, but gallantly maintained its position, although it suffered severely, losing out of four hundred and thirty-two men twelve killed and one hundred and twelve wounded. The following day Sedgwick, learning that Hooker had been defeated and finding that the corps was outnumbered and would be overwhelmed, recrossed the river.

On July 1, 1863, the brigade was at Manchester, Md., when it was hastily summoned to Gettysburg, and at nine o'clock began its march, which, without intermission, was continued until four o'clock the next afternoon, when it reached the field of battle. On the morning of the 3d it moved to the extreme left of the line, in rear of Round Top, to meet any flank movement which might be made, but was not engaged, the enemy making no determined assault at that part of the field. On the 4th it was stationed at Little Round Top, and on the 5th was in advance in pursuit of the retreating enemy, with whom it had a slight engagement at Fairfield. Pursuit was then abandoned by Meade, but the One Hundred and Nineteenth, on the 13th of July, came upon the enemy at Hagerstown, and at once engaged the latter's skirmishers, but during the night the Confederates decamped.

On November 7th, at Rappahannock Station, the Confederates were in strong position, covering three pontoon bridges, when, at the earnest desire of Gen. Russell, he was ordered to storm the works, and, in the face of a murderous fire, the intrenchments were carried at the point of the bayonet, the whole of the enemy being captured. Gen. Meade, in his order, publicly thanked the storming party for their gallantry in the assault, in which four guns, two thousand small-arms, eight battle-flags, one bridge-train, and sixteen hundred prisoners were taken. In this short, fierce struggle the One Hundred and Nineteenth lost seven killed and forty-three wounded.

In the Wilderness campaign, on the 4th of May, 1864, the brigade crossed the Rapidan at Germania Ford, and at noon on the 5th became engaged, the One Hundred and Nineteenth holding the centre. The fighting continued until nightfall, and during it four color-bearers were killed or wounded. On the 10th the fighting was very severe, and in the terrible charge through the iron storm of death that afternoon the colors of the regiment were borne to the front and planted on the enemy's works, but being unsupported, it was finally forced to fall back, suffering fearfully as it retired. On the 12th it was in action from seven o'clock in the morning until nightfall, in the struggle known as the "Bloody Angle," or "Slaughter Pen," where it expended two hundred rounds of ammunition per man. From the 4th to the 12th of May, out of four hundred men fit for duty, the regiment lost two hundred and fifteen in killed and wounded. During all this series of severe engagements the One Hundred and Nineteenth was led by Capts. Gray and Landell, Col. Clark resuming command of the regiment on the 12th of that month.

On June 1st, at Cold Harbor, the brigade was ordered to feel the position of the enemy, and on the 12th it lay within one hundred and fifty yards of the Confederate line, under a constant fire. During all the fierce fighting which had occurred from the 1st to the 12th, Maj. Gray was in charge of the regiment, and afterwards continued to direct its movements at Bermuda Hundred and before Petersburg.

When Early was demonstrating in the valley of the Shenandoah, the Sixth Corps was dispatched to the support of the army there. On September 19th, at the battle of Winchester, the One Hundred and Nineteenth drove the entire rebel line for half a mile, until the latter, falling back on a strong position, its advance was temporarily checked. At four o'clock the Union line was strengthened, and Sheridan leading it forward, the enemy were driven before it in utter rout. On the 20th the brigade was detached for garrison duty in Winchester, where it remained until the following November.

During the last struggle of the war the One Hundred and Nineteenth was highly distinguished, for on April 2d the regiment, unaided, and under a fierce fire from front and flank, stormed and carried part of the enemy's intrenchments in front of Petersburg, capturing the opposing force, with all the artillery, small-arms, and colors. Col. Clark having been wounded early in the action, the command devolved on Lieut.-Col. Gray. The enemy in fleeing, on the 6th, was overtaken, strongly posted on Sailor's Creek. The brigade forded the stream, waist-deep in water, and charging on the demoralized Confederates captured them in mass. This was the last engagement in which the One Hundred and Nineteenth took part.

After the surrender of Johnston (the regiment had

marched to Danville, Va , to unite with Sherman's army) it returned to Washington, and on the 6th of June was mustered out at Philadelphia On May 13, 1864, Maj Gray was commissioned by Governor Curtin lieutenant-colonel, and on April 6, 1865, the President commissioned him lieutenant-colonel by brevet, for gallant and meritorious services before Petersburg and at the battle of Little Sailor's Creek, on March 10, 1865

The following is the roll of

COMPANY E

William C Gray, capt., must. in Aug 10, 1862, pro to maj June 29, 1864

James Cliff, capt , must in Aug 20, 1862, pro from sergt to 1st lieut May 31, 1864, to capt July 24, 1864, must out with company June 19, 1865

James Dutton, 1st lieut , must in Aug 20, 1862 pro from 1st sergt July 25, 1864, to capt April 6, 1865 , must out with company June 19, 1865

Jacob Bardsley, 1st sergt., must in Aug 11, 1862, pro to 1st sergt Nov 16, 1864 , com 2d lieut June 9, 1865, not must , must out with company June 19, 1865

Frederick Williams, sergt , must in Aug 11, 1862, wounded at Fort Steadman, Va , March 25, 1865, disch by G O July 5, 1865

George McClintock, sergt., must in Aug 20, 1862, pro to sergt Nov 16, 1864, must out with company June 19, 1865

Benjamin S Tindall, sergt., must in Aug 22, 1862, pro to sergt Jan 6, 1863 , prisoner from May 10, 1864, to April 19, 1865, must out with company June 19, 1865

Jeremiah O Leary, sergt., must in Aug 11, 1862, pro to sergt Dec 31, 1864, captured, ret March 17, 1865, must out with company June 19, 1865

Robert E Cuskaden, sergt., must in Aug 30, 1861, trans to Co F, 88th Regt P V., Dec 6, 1862

Nathan Heacock, sergt., must in Aug 22, 1862, died at Winchester Oct 4, of wounds received at Opequan, Va , Sept 19, 1864

James Elliott, corp., must in Aug 22, 1862, pro to corp Feb 24, 1863 , disch by G O , date unknown

Thomas M Seth, corp., must in Aug 25, 1862, pro to corp April 20, 1864, disch by G O June 8, 1865

Thomas Brunner, corp., must in Aug 20, 1862, absent, with leave, at muster out.

Privates

Henry Aull, must in Aug 19, 1862 , must out with company June 19, 1865

Samuel Braden, must in Aug 25, 1862, must out with company June 19, 1865

John Baker, must in Aug 29, 1862, trans to Vet Res Corps Dec 12, 1864, disch by G O July 10, 1865

James Burns, must in Aug 20, 1862, died at Charleston, S C., October, 1864

David P Congleton, must in Aug 22, 1862, must out with company June 14, 1865

Isaac Collesin, must. in Aug 25, 1862, prisoner from June 1, 1864, to May 14, 1865, must out with company June 19, 1865

Jonathan Culbert, must in Aug 20, 1862, died at Fredericksburg, Va , May 20, of wounds received at Spottsylvania Court House May 10, 1864

Samuel Clayton, must in Aug 30, 1862, not on muster-out roll

Joseph Denight, must. in Aug 27, 1862, must out with company June 19, 1865

William Ewing, must in Aug 20, 1862, wounded at Spottsylvania Court House, Va., May 10, 1864, absent, in hospital, at muster out

Robert Elliott, must in Aug 22, 1862, wounded in Wilderness, Va , May 5, 1864 , disch by G O., date unknown

Armstrong Elliott, must. in Aug 27, 1862 , disch on surg certif Dec 8, 1862.

Nathaniel Ewing, must in Aug 20, 1862, trans to Vet Res Corps Dec 12, 1864

Henry Hall, must in Aug 20, 1862, must out with company June 19, 1865

James C Hughes, must. in Sept 28, 1862 , must out with company June 19, 1865

Francis Hall, must in Aug 20, 1862

John Kincaid, must in Aug 30, 1862 , must. out with company June 19, 1865

Frederick Kyle, must in Aug 18, 1862, must out with company June 19, 1865

William Keers, must in Aug 19, 1862, disch by S O April 15, 1863

Matthew Liuten, must in Aug 19, 1862 , must out with company June 19, 1865

James Louther, must in Aug 19, 1862, wounded at Wilderness, Va , May 5, 1864, disch by G O June 5, 1865

Thomas G Lee, must in Aug 27, 1862, must out with company June 19, 1865

Adam Lord, must in Aug 22, 1862 , disch on surg certif Nov 9, 1864

William Logan, must in Aug 29, 1862 , not on muster-out roll

Newton H Morgan, must. in Aug 20, 1862, trans. to Vet Res Corps Jan 24, 1864

George Mills, must in Aug 25, 1862, not on muster out roll

William McCone, must in Aug 29, 1862, must out with company June 19, 1865

James McGee, must in Aug 25, 1862, wounded at Wilderness, Va., May 5 1864, disch by G O., date unknown

John A Peterman, must in Aug 20, 1862, captured, returned, disch. by G O , date unknown

Isaac Pike, must in Aug 20, 1862 , died at Washington, D C , Aug 15, 1864, of wounds received at Wilderness, Va , buried in National Cemetery, Arlington, Va.

W H Richardson, must in Aug 27, 1862, disch by G O May 26, 1865

Robert Beaney, must in Aug 20, 1862, com 2d lieut Aug 20, 1863, not mustered , killed at Rappahannock Station Va., Nov 7, 1863

William Roberts, must in Aug 28, 1862, died at Belle Plain, Va , Jan 21, 1863

William Rapine, must in Aug 25, 1862, died at Washington, D C , May 8, of wounds received at Salem Church, Va., May 3, 1863

John Scull, must in Aug 25, 1862, must out with company June 19, 1865

John C Steel, must in Aug 23, 1862, must out with company June 19, 1865

George S Smith, must in Sept 28, 1862, wounded at Fredericksburg, Va , Dec 13, 1862, disch by G O , date unknown

John Steel, must in Aug 20, 1862 , died at Annapolis, Md., Dec 8, 1863, burial record Oct 9, 1863, buried in Camp Parole Hospital Cemetery

William Stewart, must in Aug 19, 1862 , died at Washington, D C., of wounds received at Rappahannock Station, Va , Nov 7, 1863

David Sloan, must in Aug 19, 1862, killed at Spottsylvania Court-House, Va , May 12, 1864

Joseph Stevens, must. in Aug 22, 1862

John B Tetlow, must in Aug 20, 1862 , killed at Salem Church, Va., May 3, 1863.

William J Worton, must in Aug 25, 1862 , must out with company June 19, 1665

Ebenezer C Welser, must in Aug 20, 1862, disch by G O., date unknown

Robert Wright, must in Aug 25, 1862 , drafted, disch by S O March 24, 1864

Ebenezer Wilson, must. in Aug 20, 1862, not on muster-out roll

Martin Wolf, must in Aug 30, 1862, not on muster-out roll

Robert Walker, must in Aug 28, 1862, not on muster out roll

David Young, must in Aug 20, 1862, not on muster-out roll

One Hundred and Twenty-fourth Regiment (Nine-Months' Service) —Three companies of this regiment—Company B (the Delaware County Fusileers) Capt. Simon Litzenberg, Company D (Gideon's Band), Capt Norris L Yarnall, and Company H (Delaware County Volunteers), Capt James Barton, Jr —were recruited in Delaware County The regiment rendezvoused at Camp Curtin, but before an organization was effected the One Hundred and Twenty-fourth was ordered to Washington, and on Aug 12, 1862, was hurried forward At the national capital it was organized, with Joseph W Hawley, of West

Chester, as colonel; Simon Litzenberg, captain of the Delaware County Fusileers, lieutenant-colonel; and Isaac Lawrence Haldeman (Major Haldeman was previously on Gen. Dana's staff), first lieutenant of Gideon's Band, major. The One Hundred and Twenty-fourth was assigned to the First Brigade, First Division of the Eleventh Corps. On the evening of Sept. 16, 1862, having marched all day without rations, it reached Antietam Creek, and the hungry men had just received provisions, when an order came commanding it to move at double-quick to the support of Gen. Hooker, on the right wing. In the early dawn of the next morning, while the light was so indistinct that the several captains could hardly distinguish their companies, they were ordered to advance and became engaged with the enemy. Here they fought, being driven back and recapturing their position several times, holding their ground finally when the enemy's guns were silenced at three o'clock in the afternoon. The weary men, who had been engaged for eight hours, were then relieved and ordered to the rear, where Gen. Hancock held it in readiness to support the batteries on the right. That night it bivouacked on the field. In its first battle fifty men were killed and wounded, Col. Hawley being among the latter. The One Hundred and Twenty-fourth was subsequently assigned to the brigade commanded by Gen. Kane, and when it was transferred to the Twelfth Corps, Kane still continued its brigade commander in Geary's division. In the disastrous campaign culminating at Chancellorsville it took an active part. On May 1, 1863, it was on the right wing of the Twelfth Corps, and in the advance had pushed the enemy before it until it was in danger of being flanked, when it was ordered to retire to the position it held the evening previous. On May 2d it advanced along the Fredericksburg plank-road, and the brigade being unable to dislodge the enemy from their intrenchments, returned to their breastworks, and had hardly reached them when the demoralized Eleventh Corps came rushing in from the extreme right wing. Geary's division was immediately formed to check the pursuing enemy, and from ten in the morning until three o'clock in the afternoon it held its ground nobly until, outflanked, it was compelled to return to a second position, at which it readily repulsed every assault made upon it. On the 6th it recrossed the Rappahannock, and on the 9th of May, its period of service having expired, it was forwarded to Harrisburg, where it was discharged on the 16th of the month.

The following are the roll of the Delaware County companies:

COMPANY B.

Simon Litzenberg, capt., must. in Aug. 9, 1862; pro. to lieut.-col. Aug. 16, 1862.

John Woodcock, capt., must. in Aug. 9, 1862; pro. from 1st lieut. Aug. 16, 1862; must. out with company May 17, 1863.

Ralph Buckley, 1st lieut., must. in Aug. 9, 1862; pro. from 2d lieut. Aug. 16, 1862; must. out with company.

William H. Litzenberg, 2d lieut., must. in Aug. 9, 1862; pro. from 1st sergt. Aug. 16, 1862; must. out with company.

R. T. Williams, 1st sergt., must. in Aug. 9, 1862; pro. from sergt. Aug. 16, 1862; must. out with company.

Alex. E. Crozier, sergt., must. in Aug. 9, 1862; pro. from corp. Aug. 16, 1862; must. out with company.

James Carrick, sergt., must. in Aug. 9, 1862; must. out with company.

George Fields, sergt., must. in Aug. 9, 1862; pro. from private Oct. 10, 1862; wounded at Chancellorsville, Va., May 2, 1862; must. out with company.

John Shaw, sergt., must. in Aug. 9, 1862; must. out with company.

Daniel Crowder, corp., must. in Aug. 9, 1862; pro. to corp. Aug. 16, 1862; must. out with company.

John B. Silbey, corp., must. in Aug. 9, 1862; must. out with company.

William Major, corp., must. in Aug. 9, 1862; pro. to corp. Dec. 6, 1862; must. out with company.

Edwin Bouden, corp., must. in Aug. 9, 1862; must. out with company.

Lewis P. Watkins, corp., must. in Aug. 9, 1862; must. out with company.

John B. Trainor, corp., must. in Aug. 9, 1862; must. out with company.

Joseph McCoy, corp., must. in Aug. 9, 1862; pro. to corp. March 10, 1863; must. out with company.

John Ashworth, corp., must. in Aug. 9, 1862; pro. to corp. March 28, 1863; must. out with company May 17, 1863.

Thomas H. Kay, corp., must. in Aug. 9, 1862; disch. on surg. certif. March 28, 1863.

Israel L. Thomas, corp., must. in Aug. 9, 1852; disch. on surg. certif. March 10, 1863.

George Heath, musician, must. in Aug. 9, 1862; disch. on surg. certif. April 16, 1863.

Albert M. Neal, musician, must. in Aug. 9, 1862; disch. on surg. certif. Dec. 31, 1862.

Privates.

George W. Ayres, must. in Aug. 9, 1862; must. out with company May 17, 1863.

R. James Abernethy, must. in Aug. 9, 1862; must. out with company May 17, 1863.

John Baggs, must. in Aug. 9, 1862; must. out with company May 17, 1863.

Jacob Barlow, must. in Aug. 9, 1862; wounded at Antietam, Md., Sept. 17, 1862; absent, in hospital, at muster out.

Edwin Blakeley, must. in Aug. 9, 1862; must. out with company May 17, 1863.

Jerome Byre, must. in Aug. 9, 1862; wounded at Chancellorsville, Va., May 3, 1863; must out with company May 17, 1863.

Joseph H. Brensinger, must. in Aug. 9, 1862; must. out with company May 17, 1863.

Charles W. Broadbent, must. in Aug. 9, 1862; must. out with company May 17, 1863.

Peter Brands, must. in Aug. 9, 1862; must. out with company May 17, 1863.

William Brewster, must. in Aug. 9, 1862; must. out with company May 17, 1863.

Abraham Brewster, must. in Aug. 9, 1862; must. out with company May 17, 1863.

William Baggs, must. in Aug. 9, 1862; must. out with company May 17, 1863.

Joseph Barlow, must. in Aug. 9, 1862; killed at Antietam, Md., Sept. 17, 1862.

Edward Cooper, must. in Aug. 9, 1862; must. out with company May 17, 1863.

Thomas Chambers, must. in Aug. 9, 1862; must. out with company May 17, 1863.

Charles Creamer, must. in Aug. 9, 1862: absent, in hospital, at muster out.

William A. Dobbins, must. in Aug. 9, 1862; must. out with company May 17, 1863.

Thomas H. Dulton, must. in Aug. 9, 1862; must. out with company May 17, 1863.

William E. Daniels, must. in Aug. 9, 1862; must. out with company May 17, 1863.

John M. T. Doran, must. in Aug. 9, 1862; disch. on surg. certif. Feb. 28, 1863.

Elmer Edwards, must. in Aug. 9, 1862; must. out with company May 17, 1863.

Michael Fitzgerald, must. in Aug. 9, 1862; must. out with company May 17, 1863.

William B Farra, must in Aug 9, 1862, must out with company May 17, 1863
John Fields, must in Aug 9, 1862, disch on surg certif Jan 16, 1863
John Fryer, must in Aug 9, 1862
Samuel Greenwood, must in Aug 9, 1862, must out with company May 17, 1863
Morris Green, must in Aug 9, 1862
Thomas J Herron, must in Aug 9, 1862, must out with company May 17, 1863
Thomas Hill, must in Aug 9, 1862, must out with company May 17, 1863
William Henry, must in Aug 9, 1862, must out with company May 17, 1863
Hiram Hiyer, must in Aug 9, 1862, must out with Company May 17, 1863.
William H Hiyer, must in Aug 9, 1862, must out with company May 17, 1863
William H Henderson, must in Aug 9, 1862, must out with company May 17, 1863
John L Henderson, must in Aug 9, 1862, must out with company May 17, 1863
George Hormott, must in Aug 9, 1862, must out with company May 17, 1863
Abram Hunter, must in Aug 9, 1862, must out with company May 17, 1863
John Hoofstitler, must in Aug 9, 1862, absent, sick, at muster out
William H Haas, must in Aug 9 1862, must out with company May 17, 1863
Henry Hackman, must in Aug 9, 1862, absent, sick, at muster out.
Joseph S Johnson, must in Aug 9, 1862, must out with company May 17, 1863
William H Johnson, must in Aug 9, 1862, missing in action at Chancellorsville, Va., May 3, 1863
Andrew Kincade, must in Aug 9, 1862, must out with company May 17, 1863
Gardner Kelley, must in Aug 9, 1862, must out with company May 17, 1863
Crawford Kugler, must in Aug 9, 1862, must out with company May 17, 1863
Thomas W Kents, must in Aug 9, 1862, disch on surg certif Nov 5, 1862
Edward Kay, must in Aug 9, 1862, died at Washington, D C., Jan 20, 1863
Thomas Lomax, must in Aug 9, 1862, must out with company May 17, 1863
Matthew Lomax, must in Aug 9, 1862, must out with company May 17, 1863
James Logan, must in Aug 9, 1862, must out with company May 17, 1863
John A Leib, must in Aug 9, 1862, must out with company May 17, 1863
William Lary, must in Aug 9, 1862, died at Harper's Ferry, Va., Nov 24, 1862
Rufus K Lear, must in Aug 9, 1862
John Major, must in Aug 9, 1862, must out with company May 17, 1863
Chand Marshman, must in Aug 9, 1862, must out with company May 17, 1863
Minshall Martin, must in Aug 9, 1862, must out with company May 17, 1863
Jonas Mellor, must in Aug 9, 1862, must out with company May 17, 1863
James Makin, must in Aug 9, 1862, died at Washington, D C, March 1, 1863
Arthur McConville, must in Aug 9, 1862, must out with company May 17, 1863
William Nicholson, must in Aug 9, 1862, must out with company May 17, 1863
Jesse W Paist, must in Aug 9, 1862, must out with company May 17, 1863
John Patterson, must in Aug 9, 1862, must out with company May 17, 1863
Richard Pyott, must in Aug 9, 1862, must out with company May 17, 1863
Thomas Pilling, must in Aug 9, 1862, must out with company May 17, 1863
George Robinson, must in Aug 9, 1862, must out with company May 17, 1863
Alfred Roebuck, must in Aug 9, 1862, must out with company May 17, 1863
Edward D Sipler, must in Aug 9, 1862, must out with company May 17, 1863
George H Shillingford, must in Aug 9, 1862, must out with company May 17, 1863
John Schofield, must in Aug 9, 1862, must out with company May 17, 1863
Henry Shaw, must in Aug 9, 1862, must out with company May 17, 1863
Samuel Stork, must in Aug 9, 1862, must out with company May 17, 1863
Samuel Squibb, must in Aug 9, 1862, must out with company May 17, 1863
George Shermik, must in Aug 9, 1862, must out with company May 17, 1863
William Taylor, must in Aug 9, 1862, must out with company May 17, 1863
James Toomes, must in Aug 9, 1862, must out with company May 17, 1863.
Richard Toomes, must in Aug 9, 1862, must out with company May 17, 1863
James Trainor, must in Aug 9, 1862, must out with company May 17, 1863
John J Wilkinson, must in Aug 9, 1862, must out with company May 17, 1863
Benjamin Walraven, must in Aug 9, 1862, must out with company May 17 1863
Edward Worrell, must in Aug 9, 1862, must out with company May 17, 1863
Joseph Waddle, must in Aug 9, 1862, must out with company May 17, 1863
Frederick Young, must in Aug 9, 1862, must out with company May 17, 1863
Enos Yates, must in Aug 9, 1862, must out with company May 17, 1863

COMPANY D

Norris L. Yarnall, capt, must in Aug 13, 1862, must out with company May 15, 1863
I Lawrence Halderman, 1st lieut., must in Aug 11, 1862, pro to maj Aug 16, 1862
Joseph Pratt, 1st lieut, must in Aug 13, 1862, pro from 2d to 1st lieut Aug 16, 1862, must out with company
Joseph G Cummins, 2d lieut, must in Aug 9, 1862, pro from 1st sergt Aug 16, 1862, must out with company
C. D M Broomhall, 1st sergt, must in Aug 9, 1862, pro from sergt Aug 16, 1862, must out with company
John Frank Black, sergt., must in Aug 9, 1862, must out with company
William B Broomall, sergt., must in Aug 11, 1862, must out with company
Benjamin Brooke, sergt., must in Aug 9, 1862, must out with company
Benjamin T Green, sergt, must in Aug 9, 1862, pro from corp. Nov 1, 1863, must out with company
Frederick Eckfeldt, sergt, must in Aug 9, 1862, disch on surg certif Jan 19, 1863
Edward W Lewis, corp., must in Aug 9, 1862, pro to corp Aug 16, 1862, must out with company
W J MacPherson, corp, must in Aug 11, 1862, pro to corp Aug 16, 1862, must out with company
W Wayne Vogdes, corp., must in Aug 11, 1862, pro to corp Aug 16, 1862, must out with company
William H Beatty, corp., must in Aug 9, 1862, pro to corp Aug 16, 1862, must out with company
David W Eyre, corp., must in Aug 9, 1862, pro to corp Oct 2, 1862, must out with company
William T Innis, Jr, corp, must in Aug 9, 1862, pro to corp Oct. 2, 1862, wounded at Chancellorsville, Va., May 3, 1863, absent, in hospital, at muster out
John F Worrellen, corp., must in Aug 9, 1862, pro to corp Oct. 2, 1862, must out with company May 15, 1863
Joel Hollingsworth, corp., must in Aug 9, 1862, pro to corp Nov 1, 1862, must out with company May 15, 1863

Joseph J. Hall, corp., must. in Aug. 9, 1862; disch. on surg. certif. Jan. 15, 1863.

James Crozier, corp., must. in Aug. 9, 1862; died September 21st, of wounds received at Antietam, Md., Sept. 17, 1862.

William H. Howard, musician, must. in Aug. 11, 1862; must. out with company May 15, 1863.

H. H. Williamson, musician, must. in Aug. 11, 1862; died at Stafford Court-House, Va., Feb. 8, 1863.

Privates.

James B. Aitken, must. in Aug. 9, 1862; died at Bolivar Heights, Va., Oct. 27, 1863.

Hunter Brooke, must. in Aug. 9, 1862; must. out with company May 15, 1863.

Samuel Boker, must. in Aug. 9, 1862; must. out with company May 15, 1863.

Joseph A. Brinten, must. in Aug. 9, 1862; must. out with company May 15, 1863.

Stephen M. Blazier, must. in Aug. 9, 1862; must. out with company May 15, 1863.

Harry H. Black, must. in Aug. 9, 1862; must. out with company May 15, 1863.

William Batting, must. in Aug. 9, 1862; must. out with company May 15, 1863.

Cyrus Baker, must. in Aug. 9, 1862; must. out with company May 15, 1863.

William L. Bittle, must. in Aug. 11, 1862; wounded at Antietam, Md., Sept. 17, 1862; must. out with company May 15, 1863.

David Bradbury, must. in Aug. 9, 1862; disch. on surg. certif. Feb. 5, 1863.

Daniel B. Baker, must. in Aug. 11, 1862; disch. on surg. certif. May 21, 1863.

James Cheetham, must. in Aug. 9, 1862; must. out with company May 15, 1863.

Richard R. Cummins, must. in Aug. 11, 1862; must. out with company May 15, 1863.

George W. Cowan, must. in Aug. 9, 1862; must. out with company May 15, 1863.

John R. Cochran, must. in Aug. 11, 1862; must. out with company May 15, 1863.

Michael Crouse, must. in Aug. 9, 1862; must. out with company May 15, 1863.

Lorenzo F. Davis, must. in Aug. 9, 1862; must. out with company May 15, 1863.

Jesse Darlington, Jr., must. in Aug. 9, 1862; must. out with company May 15, 1863.

James Doughty, must. in Aug. 9, 1862; must. out with company May 15, 1863.

William G. Davidson, must. in Aug. 9, 1862; must. out with company May 15, 1863.

Harry R. Duey, must. in Aug. 9, 1862; must. out with company May 15, 1863.

Jesse Darlington, must. in Aug. 9, 1862; must. out with company May 15, 1863.

Elias Eckfeldt, must. in Aug. 9, 1862; must. out with company May 15, 1863.

William Y. Esben, must. in Aug. 9, 1862; must. out with company May 15, 1863.

Charles J. Esry, must. in Aug. 11, 1862; must. out with company May 15, 1863.

Salkeld L. Fairlamb, must. in Aug. 9, 1862; must. out with company May 15, 1863.

Jabez F. Fryer, must. in Aug. 9, 1862; must. out with company May 15, 1863.

Isaac N. Flounders, must. in Aug. 9, 1862; must. out with company May 15, 1863.

Milton Ford, must. in Aug. 9, 1862; must. out with company May 15, 1863.

Thomas Fields, must. in Aug. 9, 1862; must. out with company May 15, 1863.

Anderson Fielding, must. in Aug. 9, 1862; must. out with company May 15, 1863.

John L. Grimm, must. in Aug. 9, 1862; must. out with company May 15, 1863.

William Gamble, must. in Aug. 9, 1862; must. out with company May 15, 1863.

William H. Garrett, must. in Aug. 9, 1862; must. out with company May 15, 1863.

George W. Gardner, must. in Aug. 11, 1862; must. out with company May 15, 1863.

Edward B. Green, must. in Aug. 11, 1862; must. out with company May 15, 1863.

John H. Henderson, must. in Aug. 11, 1862; must. out with company May 15, 1863.

William G. Howarth, must. in Aug. 9, 1862; must. out with company May 15, 1863.

Brinton J. Heyburn, must. in Aug. 9, 1862; must. out with company May 15, 1863.

Andrew J. Haws, must. in Aug. 9, 1852; must. out with company May 15, 1863.

Alfred J. Hannum, must. in Aug. 9, 1862; must. out with company May 15, 1863.

John D. Howard, must. in Aug. 9, 1862; must. out with company May 15, 1863.

James H. Heacock, must. in Aug. 9, 1862; must. out with company May 15, 1863.

William H. Hoops, must. in Aug. 11, 1862; must. out with company May 15, 1863.

Thomas Hance, Jr., must. in Aug. 11, 1862; must. out with company May 15, 1863.

William Heyburn, must. in Aug. 9, 1862; died March 12, 1863.

Philip R. Johnson, must. in Aug. 9, 1862; wounded at Chancellorsville, Va., May 3, 1863; absent, in hospital, at muster out.

Edward Jackson, must. in Aug. 9, 1862; must. out with company May 15, 1863.

Rufus King, must. in Aug. 11, 1862; must. out with company May 15, 1863.

N. C. Longmire, must. in Aug. 9, 1862; must. out with company May 15, 1863.

James D. Linton, must. in Aug. 9, 1862; must. out with company May 15, 1863.

George D. Miller, must. in Aug. 9, 1862; must. out with company May 15, 1863.

Charles Moore, must. in Aug. 9, 1862; must. out with company May 15, 1863.

William L. Martin, must. in Aug. 9, 1862; must. out with company May 15, 1863.

James Moore, Jr., must. in Aug. 11, 1862; must. out with company May 15, 1863.

Millson L. Millson, must. in Aug. 11, 1862; must. out with company May 15, 1863.

James Newsom, must. in Aug. 9, 1862; must. out with company May 15, 1863.

Casper Pike, must. in Aug. 9, 1862; must. out with company May 15, 1863.

Richard A. Passmore, must. in Aug. 9, 1862; must. out with company May 15, 1863.

Caleb Y. Price, must. in Aug. 9, 1862; must. out with company May 15, 1863.

John Pugh, must. in Aug. 9, 1862; must. out with company May 15, 1863.

Samuel H. Palmer, must. in Aug. 9, 1862; must. out with company May 15, 1863.

Henry Paulding, must. in Aug. 9, 1862; must. out with company May 15, 1863.

John Palmer, must. in Aug. 9, 1862; must. out with company May 15, 1863.

John M. Pyle, must. in Aug. 11, 1862; must. out with company May 15, 1863.

Jacob B. Richards, must. in Aug. 9, 1862; must. out with company May 15, 1863.

Menanda Slack, must. in Aug. 9, 1862; must. out with company May 15, 1863.

Penel Stackhouse, must. in Aug. 9, 1862; must. out with company May 15, 1863.

George F. Springer, must. in Aug. 9, 1862; must. out with company May 15, 1863.

James C. Sorber, must. in Aug. 9, 1862; must. out with company May 15, 1863.

Stephen Smith, must. in Aug. 11, 1862; must. out with company May 15, 1863.

Mifflin W. Smith, must. in Aug. 9, 1862; must. out with company May 15, 1863.

Benjamin F Thomas, must in Aug 11, 1862, must out with company May 15, 1863
Walker Y Wells, must in Aug 9, 1862, must out with company May 15, 1863
James Waters, must In Aug 9, 1862, must out with company May 15, 1863
Joel E Watson, must in Aug 9, 1862, must out with company May 15, 1863
Charles W Watkins, must in Aug 9, 1862, must out with company May 15, 1863.
Henry Warburton, must. in Aug 11, 1862, must out with company May 15, 1863
Christian A Wall, must in Aug 9, 1862, must out with company May 15, 1863

COMPANY H

James Barton, Jr capt must in Aug 15, 1862, must out with company May 16, 1863
Frank M Nagles, 1st lieut, must in Aug 15, 1862, must out with company May 16, 1863
William H H Clayton, 2d lieut, must in Aug 15, 1862, must out with company May 16, 1863
John M Clayton, 1st sergt, must. in Aug 9, 1862, must out with company May 16, 1863
James McDade, sergt., must in Aug 9, 1862, must out with company May 16, 1863.
William G Knowles, sergt., must in Aug 9, 1862 wounded at Antietam, Md., Sept 17, 1862, absent, in hospital, at muster out
William T Shoemaker, sergt., must in Aug 9, 1862, pro from corp Jan 19, 1863, must out with company
Charles B. Roberts, sergt, must in Aug 9, 1862, pro from corp Jan 1, 1863, must out with company
William Pusey West, sergt., must in Aug 9, 1862, pro to com-sergt Sept 1, 1862
Thomas H Jackson, sergt., must in Aug 14, 1862, died at Washington, D C., Jan 19, 1863
Samuel K Crozier, corp., must in Aug 9, 1862, must out with company May 16, 1863
Lewis McGonegal, corp., must in Aug 9, 1862, must out with company May 16, 1863
John B McCay, Jr, corp., must in Aug 14, 1862, absent, in hospital, at muster out
Simon B West, corp., must in Aug 9, 1862, must. out with company May 16, 1863
C J Rhoeback, corp., must in Aug 9, 1862, must out with company May 16, 1863
Enos W Clair, corp., must in Aug 9, 1862, must out with company May 16, 1863
William Trainer, Jr, corp, must in Aug 12, 1862, pro to corp Jan 19, 1863, wounded at Chancellorsville May 2, 1863, must out with company May 16, 1863.
James C Hinkson, corp., must in Aug 9, 1862, pro to corp Jan 1, 1863, must out with company May 16, 1863
James P Evans, musician, must. in Aug 12, 1862, must out with company May 16, 1863
George B Hinkson, musician, must in Aug 12, 1862, must. out with company May 16, 1863

Privates

Joseph A Aiman, must in Aug 14, 1862, must out with company May 16, 1863
Joseph L Arment, must in Aug 12, 1862, must. out with company May 16, 1863.
George S Bensen, must in Aug 9, 1862, must out with company May 16, 1863
Charles Bonsall, Jr, must in Aug 9, 1862, must out with company May 16, 1863
William Burnes, must in Aug 9, 1862, must out with company May 16, 1863
Joseph H Bonsall, must in Aug 14, 1862, disch on surg certif Sept 27, 1862
Thomas Burk, must in Aug 9, 1862, died at Harper's Ferry, Va., Nov 3, 1862
Elias S Baker, must In Aug 9, 1862
John W Carr, must in Aug 9, 1862, must out with company May 16, 1862
Robert Casey, Jr, must in Aug 9, 1862, must out with company May 16, 1862
Joseph Cathcart, must in Aug 9, 1862, must out with company May 16, 1862
James P Chadwick, must in Aug 9, 1862, must out with company May 16, 1862
William H Clair, must in Aug 9, 1862, must. out with company May 16, 1862
William T Chandler, must in Aug 9, 1862, must out with company May 16, 1862
William T Clayton, must in Aug 9, 1862, must out with company May 16, 1862
John B Coughleton, must in Aug 12, 1862, must out with company May 16, 1862
William J Crowther, must in Aug 9, 1862, must out with company May 16, 1862
Thomas J Carmen, must in Aug 9, 1862, disch on surg certif Nov 17, 1862
George R Cross, must in Aug 9, 1862, disch on surg certif March 8, 1863
Frederick A Davis, must In Aug 9 1862, must. out with company May 16, 1863
Joseph Drake, must in Aug 9, 1862, must out with company May 16, 1863
John F Duffy, must. in Aug 12, 1862, must out with company May 16, 1863
Elias Eave, must in Aug 9, 1862, must out with company May 16, 1863
John Files, must in Aug 14, 1862, must out with company May 16, 1863
Ezekiel Ford, must in Aug 9, 1862, must out with company May 16, 1863
Alexander Gutterson, must in Aug 9, 1862 must out with company May 16, 1863.
Robert M Green, must in Aug 12, 1862, disch on surg certif Dec 30, 1862
Samuel F Heacock, must in Aug 9, 1862, must out with company May 16, 1863
Charles T Hanthem, must in Aug 9, 1862, must out with company May 16, 1863
Frederick Hartly, must in Aug 12, 1862, must. out with company May 16, 1863
Jonathan Heacock, must in Aug 9, 1862, must out with company May 16, 1863
Robert J Hanby, must in Aug 9, 1862, must out with company May 16, 1863
Edwin H Hickman, must in Aug 14, 1862, must out with company May 16, 1863
Benjamin F Hurst, must in Aug 14, 1862, must out with company May 16, 1863
William D Howard, must. in Aug 9, 1862, must out with company May 16, 1863
Charles Jackson, must in Aug 9, 1862, must out with company May 16, 1863
John Jackson, must in Aug 12, 1862, discharged, date unknown
David T Jones, must in Aug 14, 1862, must out with company May 16, 1863
J Ephraim Lobb, must in Aug 14, 1862, died at Stafford Court House, Va., March 8, 1863
J Wesley Miles, must in Aug 14, 1862, must. out with company May 16, 1863
George Mills, must in Aug 14, 1862, must out with company May 16, 1863
Jesse D Minshall, must in Aug 9, 1862, must out with company May 16, 1863
John Mott, must in Aug 9, 1862, must out with company May 16, 1863
Robert A McCall, must in Aug 9, 1862, must out with company May 16, 1863
Daniel McCue, must in Aug 12, 1862, must out with company May 16, 1863
Philip Nawn, must in Aug 9, 1862, must out with company May 16, 1863
Samuel W Neald, must in Aug 9, 1862, wounded at Chancellorsville, Va., May 3, 1863, must out with company May 16, 1863
Jesse Owen, must in Aug 9, 1862, must out with company May 16, 1863
John F Palmer, must. in Aug 9, 1862, must out with company May 16, 1863

John Peters, must in Aug 9, 1862, must out with company May 16, 1863

John W Philips, must in Aug 9, 1862, must out with company May 16, 1863

James Piard, Jr, must in Aug 9, 1862, wounded at Chancellorsville, Va, May 3, 1863, must out with company May 16, 1863

Harvey E Pierce, must in Aug 9, 1862, must out with company May 16, 1863

Horatio N Platt, must in Aug 9, 1862, wounded at Antietam, Md, Sept 17, 1862, must out with company May 16, 1863

George W Poole, must in Aug 9, 1862, must out with company May 16, 1863

Isaac E Price, must in Aug 9, 1862, must out with company May 16, 1863

Owen Z Pyle, must in Aug 12, 1862, must out with company May 16, 1863

Maurice Ragan, must in Aug 12, 1862 must out with company May 16, 1863

Jacob H Rice, must in Aug 5, 1862, must out with company May 16, 1863

Thomas Ryan, must in Aug 9, 1862, must out with company May 16, 1863

Albert Smith must in Aug 9, 1862, must out with company May 16 1863

Cheyney H Smith, must in Aug 9, 1862, must out with company May 16, 1863

John Standring, must in Aug 9, 1862 must out with company May 16, 1863

Joseph Taylor, must in Aug 12, 1862, must out with company May 16, 1863

John W Temple, must in Aug 14, 1862, must out with company May 16, 1863

Daniel Trainer, must in Aug 12, 1862, must out with company May 16, 1863

Livingston Tally, must in Aug 12, 1862

William S Vanhorn, must in Aug 12, 1862, must out with company May 16, 1863

Nehemiah Vansant, must in Aug 12, 1862, must out with company May 16, 1863

Ralph Welsh, must in Aug 12, 1862, must out with company May 16, 1863

John Whittington, must in Aug 12, 1862, must out with company May 16, 1863

Simon H White, must in Aug 12, 1862, must out with company May 16, 1863

Thomas Wildes, must in Aug 12, 1862, must out with company May 16, 1863

Moses Williams, must in Aug 12, 1862 must out with company May 16, 1863

Samuel R Zebley, must in Aug 9, 1862 killed at Antietam, Md, Sept 17, 1862

COMPANY G

Philip D Haines, 1st lieut, must in Aug 15, 1862, must out with company

William S Abel, 2d lieut, must in Aug 15, 1862, must out with company

The results of the disastrous campaign of Gen Pope in the summer of 1862, it was believed by the Confederate authorities had so depressed the North that a bold invasion of the latter territory might possibly cause a general popular movement to end the war even by the acknowledgment of the Southern Confederated States, or at least secure the recognition of the latter government by the English and French nations It was also thought that if there should be much accession to the Confederate ranks from Maryland it would be a strong argument to press on the European governments that a war of subjugation could never be successful, hence in the interest of humanity steps would be taken by these powers to terminate the hopeless struggle The result of the invasion, however, was just the reverse of these expectations In the mean while the United States, on Aug 4, 1862, ordered a draft for six hundred thousand men, three hundred thousand to be immediately called to the field On the 1st of September the authorities of the State announced that no county in the commonwealth had at that time sent as many soldiers to the army as Delaware County, according to population, that it then had 1474 men in the service, and its full quota was 1801 Upper Providence held the proud prominence of having contributed the greatest number of men, according to its inhabitants, of any locality in Pennsylvania, having sent one hundred and thirty-four soldiers to the field

On September 5th, Gen Lee with his entire command crossed the Potomac, and the whole North rose to resist the invasion, while, contrary to Confederate expectation, the desertions from the ranks of Lee's army were greater in numbers than the recruits which gathered under its standard in Maryland On Sept 4, 1862, Governor Curtin ordered the formation of military companies, and on the 11th called fifty thousand militia of the State to the field to protect the threatened commonwealth As a consequence the utmost excitement prevailed, all business was suspended, nothing occupying public attention but the organization of militia companies and forwarding them to the designated stations where State troops were ordered to report William Frick, at that time a leading business man of Chester, within a few hours after the call was issued, hastened to Harrisburg and tendered his services to the State in any capacity in which he was fitted to act Governor Curtin immediately appointed him colonel of the Third Regiment of militia, but he declined to accept the position, stating that his knowledge of military movements was too limited to have the command of such a body of men, but the Governor insisted that at least he should be major of that organization, and as such he was mustered into service

There was no Sunday in Delaware County on Sept 14, 1862, but all day long recruiting went on and men hastened their preparations to go to the front, while the busy hands of the women were actively employed in getting their fathers, husbands, and sons ready to march On Monday, September 15th, at Media, a company was fully recruited, of which Hon J M Broomall was chosen captain, which, fully equipped and mustered in, on the following day left for Harrisburg The same day the Chester Guards, commanded by Capt William R Thatcher, and the Mechanic Rifles of Chester, Capt Jonathan Kershaw, equipped partly by the Borough Council, which body appropriated fifteen hundred dollars, which soon was largely augmented by private subscriptions, was also dispatched for the State capital In Upper Darby the Darby Rangers, Capt Charles A. Litzenberg, a company from Thornbury and Edgmont, commanded by Capt James Wilcox, the Delaware County Guards of

Concord and Aston, Capt John H Barton, and the Upland Guards, Capt James Kirkman, were also dispatched to designated rendezvous The latter organization had taken so many men out of the mills at Upland that the factories there were compelled to close, as every able-bodied operator had joined the militia and gone for the front Samuel Bancroft, of Upper Providence, supplied the blankets for the militia, and declined to receive any compensation for the goods At that time it is creditable to the patriotism of Delaware County to record that out of a total male population of six thousand men subject to military duty nearly twenty-two hundred were under arms History nowhere records a more spontaneous uprising of a people than that displayed by the men of Delaware County in the face of this threatening danger to the State The troops from this section were, after their arrival in Harrisburg, assigned to various regiments and hastened to Chambersburg, where they were stationed at Camp McClure to await orders Just previous to the battle of Antietam it was seriously considered whether it was not necessary to cross the borders into Maryland as far as Hagerstown, that they might be in supporting distance of the Union army When the militia companies were informed of the contemplated movement the officers informed the men that it was voluntarily on their part whether they would go or not, that those who were willing to march beyond the State boundary, if so desired, should advance two paces to the front, and in response to this order not a dozen in all the Delaware County companies declined to volunteer However, the fierce battle of the 17th of September was fought and won, and when the defeated army of Lee in confusion retreated across the Potomac, the emergency having passed the militia were relieved from further service in the field The moral support these men rendered in promptly taking the field was of the utmost importance to the cause of the North at that juncture, and the spectacle it presented to the Old World was largely instrumental in preventing recognition by foreign nations of the Confederate State government

The following is the roll of the various militia companies from Delaware County

TENTH REGIMENT MILITIA

Organized Sept 10–16, 1862, and discharged Sept 25-27, 1862

COMPANY L —Captain, William B Thatcher, first lieutenant, Lewis M Larkin, second lieutenant, William G Price, first sergeant, Henry McIlvaine, sergeants, John M Omensetter, William G Evans, William C Dubree, Joseph H Hinkson, corporals, William N Pennell, James Morgan, Joel Lane, David M Johnson, George E Darlington, John W Otter, Richard F Flickwire, Francis R Shoemaker, musician, Charles Dickerson

Privates —Walter J Arnold, William Appleby, David Appleby, George Bottomly, James E Breckenridge, William Blakely, Joseph Blakely, Elwood Black, Benjamin F Bucha, Theodore Bell, Nathan Berry, Joseph Brewster, John Cunliff, J Engle Cochran, Allen Carr, George Cadmen, John Clark, Archibald Clark, Julius Dutton, Alfred O Deshong, James Dunkerly, Joshua P Eyer, Jr, Martin Faraday, Henry G Grubb, Henry Greenwood, James Glennan, Henry M Hinkson, Samuel Haigh, David E Holstein, Edwin Hewitt, Charles Hinkson, John Hinkson, Henry Hinkson, Amos Holt, Joseph Holt, John Holt, J Washington Irving, Benjamin Irving, Francis Harricks, John S Israel, R Morgan Johnson, Benjamin D Johnson, Theodore Lukens, Henry M Lukens, Mordecai Larkins, Jr, Samuel W Loveland, Benjamin Mason, Hamilton Morris, William Mackey, John F McFall, Daniel McCollum, John S. McFadden, William McConnell, James McClymont, Isaac Newton, Jr, William H Neur, David F Newlin, William J Oglesby, Samuel C Price, William Pattison, Charles D Pennell, John S Robinson, Charles A Story, Jr, John E Shaw, Arnold Shaw, Samuel Stevenson, George I St Leger, Henry B Taylor, William G Vernon, Preston E Wilson, Lewis D Wheaton, Hiram Williams

SIXTEENTH REGIMENT MILITIA

Organized Sept 17, 1862, disch Sept 25, 1862

FIELD AND STAFF —Colonel, Joseph Wilcox, major, Charles A Litzenberg, quartermaster, John J Rowland, quartermaster sergeant, Isaac Johnson

COMPANY B —Captain, Jonathan Kershaw, first lieutenant, Abram Lowery, second lieutenant, John W Bech, first sergeant, George W Wilson, sergeants, George Smith, Charles R Sweeney, Hugh Hatton, William D Pullen, corporals, Richard Turner, Thomas H Berry, Harry A Hopple, Thomas H Thompson, Nathaniel P Chadwick, Peter Goff, Charles Stringfellow, William Schofield, musicians, John Cullen, James G Hunter

Privates.—John Booth, Angelo D Bolga, Charles Barger, John Brauken, Edward Briley, Enos F Cloud, Edward E Cullen, George Clouser, John J Clark, William H Dickerson, John Dunkerley, Jesse Galligar, Jacob Greider, Jr, James Haws, William Latch, James Morris, Charles Martine, Theodore V Rosevelt, Joseph Rein, John Russell, William Smith, William Sweeney, Robert Smith, Jr, John Sykes, Richard T Turner, John W Warren

COMPANY C —Captain, John M Broomall, first lieutenant, William Ormsby, second lieutenant, John C Price, first sergeant, Terry Reilly, sergeants, Daniel McClintock, Fred Fairlamb, John Davis, Andrew T Walker, corporals, Ephraim Stark, Owen W Yarnall, Charles J Broomall, William James, Samuel P Rush, John L Moore, Jesse Hibberd, John Coburn

Privates —Philip Afflick, John H Anderson, Levi Baker, Alfred Baker, George W Bartle, J A Bend, Israel Briggs, George W Bishop, J H H Cline, John J Cloop, Emlen M Chalfant, Joseph R Campbell, Clement B Clingen, Jesse L Cummins, Walter C Curtis, James Davis, Joseph Doling, Robins P Dunn, Albert Dunn, George Edwards, Nathan Edwards, William Eves, Jr, Michael Fern, Thomas Forsythe, William G Goodley, Samuel F Gracey, Henry Green, Thomas P Grubbs, John G Haddock, John M Hall, W W Harvey, Samuel M Henderson, George W Hill, Jr, Henry Huddleson, Henry James, W S Johnson, Isaac Johnson (pro to q m - sergt), Isaac Kerlin, John Leland, Isaac C Litzenberg, John Lowe, Charles D Manley, Jr, Thomas E Malen, William Mitchell, William Moore, Waldron C McGuigan, William P H McCline, Benjamin F Niles, Henry Pennypacker, Pearson Pike, Charles C Porter, John W Pile, Davis Reese, Eber S Rigby, William A Seal, John Shipley, Joseph Shipley, James Taylor, David A Vernon, Nicholas F Walter, William H Walter, Jacob Wheateley, Isaac Worrall, Jr, Joseph Worrall, John E Worrall Thomas W Worrall, Henry C Worrall, Edwin C Worrall, John Y Worrall, John Wrigley, James R Worrall, George H Yarnall

COMPANY D —Captain, John H Barton, first lieutenant, William Walter, Second Lieutenant, Emmor S Leedom, first sergeant, Joseph Paschal, sergeants, Wesley Clayton, Mordecai Lewis, Edward Barton, Charles P Walters, corporals, Charles P Peters, William Hannum, William Chandler, John Baker, Jesse Scott, George Dutton, Zaddock Speakman, Charles McGinnis

Privates —Elijah Bussely, George Barnes, Samuel Barton, Jesse I Brozier, Edward E Bartleson, Osborn Booth, Alfred Broadbelt, James Braceland, Joseph Buckley, Henry Cheetham, William Congleton, Jared Darlington, James Finny, Shelley Ford, Robert Fulton, Patrick Gallager, Isaac Gilpin, Lewis Green, Joseph Griffith, William Girthwait, John Greenley, George W Hall, Joseph Hannum, Samuel Hannum, Samuel Hill, Jesse Jester, John Leamey, George W Lancaster, Samuel Lenderman, Jacob Miller, Thomas McCall, James McMullin, George McCracken, Joseph Osborn, Eli Pyle, William H Porter, William Palmer, Charles V Peters, William K Peters, Vernon Pyle, Michael Rail, William Rigby, John N Smith, Robert Smith, Aaron Swayne, Robert Taylor, George Turner, Aaron Tyson,

John L. Weedon, Henry Walter, John S. Wells, Joseph L. Wells, William Yarnall, Albert Darlington.

COMPANY E.—Captain, Amos Bonsall; first lieutenant, James Shillingford; second lieutenant, Levi Lukens; first sergeant, Thomas Kirk; sergeants, John Toppen, *William H. Garrett, Charles B. Lear*, Joseph Worrall; corporals, William Newton, Joseph B. Robinson, Jacob Wise, Henry Hancock, Lewis Bryan, Joseph P. Neath, Henry Sharkey, William Kirk; musicians, Morris Gilmore, John Welsh.

Privates.—Thomas J. C. Allen, Robert Anderson, Thomas Barr, William F. Carter, James Cocker, William Garrett, Thomas Hammel, Plinez Holstein, James Hill, John Leedom, Henry Myers, Thomas Pyott, William Pyott, Thomas Reman, John H. Robinson, William S. Rambo, George K. Smith, Charles Shillingsford, William Scott, Edmund Smith, John Allen, Henry Burhouse, Israel Cooper, Lewis D. Cook, John Donnell, Thomas Green, Benjamin F. Hannum, Reece C. Heacock, Richard Jones, Obern Lamey, Henry H. Major, Thomas W. Palmer, Isaac Robinson, James Robb, Thomas Robinson, John Smith, S. Charles Smith, John Schofield, *Thomas Sharp*, John Shillingford, Charles M. Worrall, Frank Alexander, Ellwood Baker, Cornelius Chadwick, Rolandis Cooper, William Geffing, James Gormley, Morris Hannum, John Holstein, George Long, Charles H. Lamar, John Noden, William Palmer, Frank B. Ridgeway, Daniel Rively, Michael Rambo, George W. Smith, Henry Shillingford, Robert Schofield, William Speak, James Wildes.

COMPANY F.—Captain, Joseph Wilcox (pro. to col. Sept. 17, 1862); first lieutenant, William H. Miller; second lieutenant, George W. Eachus; first sergeant, Robert Sill; sergeants, William Hall, William H. Huddleson, Edmund Green; corporals, Isaac Malin, Thomas Baker, Rufus Green, James Broomall, Davidson Baker, William Eachus, Abil Green, Smedley Green; musician, George Hall.

Privates.—Daniel Baker, John J. Baker, Walter A. Baker, L. Baker, Edwin M. Bittle, William Broomall, Davis Broomall, Mark Broomall, Robert M. Barnett, Charles M. Cheyney, George S. Cheyney, Hugh R. Cheyney, Timothy Donovan, Evans Eachus, Alfred B. Entriken, Oliver Farra, John W. Fryer, Ellwood B. Fryer, Robert Gamble, George S. Green, George L. Green, Pierce E. Hemphill, Thomas W. Hemphill, Edward Hickman, William Hines, Edward Howard, Passmore Howard, John T. Huddleson, Ellwood H. James, Bishop King, Helson Lamb, Henry Lodge, William H. Malen, Joseph R. Menough, John Menough, William Miles, Sr., William Miles, Jr., John S. Pyle, Charles P. Pyle, Humphrey Pyle, Ellwood Pyle, Richard T. Plummer, Joseph H. Regester, Friend W. Russell, John D. Roney, Smith Sharpless, Amos C. Sharpless, Enos P. Sharpless, Thomas J. Sharpless, Joseph M. Stackhouse, Meredith Stackhouse, Elhannan B. Stanley, John M. Steele, Joseph B. Taylor, John Yarnall, Albin Yarnall, Walker Yarnall.

COMPANY H.—Captains, Charles A. Litzenberg (pro. to major Sept. 17, 1862), J. Charles Andrews; first lieutenant, George S. Patchel; second lieutenant, Joseph L. Lewis; first sergeant, James D. Byerly; sergeants, John J. Hoopes, William H. Ferris, George Serrill, Richard Thatcher; corporals, Moses Bonsall, Charles Willis, Mordecai M. Shaw, Walker Hoopes, George Bonsall, John S. Hansell, Abel Lodge, Jr., Hamilton A. Burk.

Privates.—George Ash, Jr., Henry Bonsall, William C. Bonsall, B. Warner Bonsall, Reese Bonsall, Joseph C. Bonsall, Jesse Bonsall, William H. Bunting, Jacob S. Bunting, John Bunting, Joseph M. Bunting, Jr., Henry Burgoine, Edward Caine, James Carr, Samuel Carr, Andrew Coldy, G. Swayne Collier, Horatio P. Connell, George Davis, John Davis, Edward Earl, Samuel Edner, John Gartin, John A. Hall, Isaac H. Hibbert, J. Robert Howell, Henry Hoppin, George H. Laning, Henry M. Leech, Isaac R. Lincoln, William H. Morris, John P. Ottey, William Palmer, Henry Palmer, George Plumly, Josiah Preston, Henry H. Russell, Emmor E. Rudolph, Jacob S. Serrill, James P. Serrill, Jacob K. Simpers, Samuel W. Shaw, William H. Shiller, Valurius Sheller, James S. Swane, Albert G. Thatcher, Richard Thatcher, Edward Thatcher, John Verlenden, B. Frank Worrall.

TWENTY-FOURTH REGIMENT MILITIA.

COMPANY I (organized Sept. 13, 1862, and discharged Sept. 20–22, 1862).—Captain, James Kirkman; first lieutenant, Robert Britton; second lieutenant, Nathan Van Horn; first sergeant, George R. Vanzant; sergeants, Andrew Lampert, Thomas Clough, John Gilston; corporals, John W. Thompson, Patrick Carroll, John Ardes, William Blythe.

Privates.—John Armstrong, William Anderson, David Beaumont, Thomas Blakeley, Thomas Bradshaw, John Blythe, Ratcliffe Bridge, James Buckley, John Bail, Jonathan Cliff, Robert Cornog, Joseph Cook, Samuel Cottingham, Joseph Dickinson, William H. Dean, Robert Davis, Henry Foster, Luke Hepworth, Samuel Hopkins, James Hulme, Thomas Jolly, Joseph Kay, James Logan, George Marshman, William McIntyre, John McGovern, Charles McBride, James Orry, Henry Ogden, John Pretty, Samuel Pretty, David Pretty, Joseph Parkinson, Thomas Parkinson, Benjamin Perrin, James Ross, Edward Taylor, John Thompson, Samuel Talbot, John Taylor, William Vernon, John Wiser, James West, Joseph Wyatt, John Wyatt.

INDEPENDENT COMPANY MILITIA.

Organized Sept. 11, 1862. Discharged Sept. 25, 1862.

Captain, Charles G. Andrews; first lieutenant, Frank P. Wells; second lieutenant, Perry Ware; first sergeant, Charles Paul; sergeants, E. Pickett, James W. Wittermore, Henry Brown; corporals, Lathrop Farein, Laverin Pomroy, Loren B. Dewolf, Moses Brown.

Privates.—Obadiah Alderman, J. D. Abbey, Isaac Bowman, G. W. Batchelor, John Beaumont, Thomas Beaumont, John L. Brock, George Boroughs, R. A. Barnes, Liberty Carn, Calvin Carn, Myers H. Cole, J. N. Cook, John Campbell, W. A. Crane, Daniel Crouch, Loren Davenport, Martin Duboyce, Edwin Duboyce, Perry Eaton, E. F. Griffiths, S. J. Godfrey, G. J. Gorden, Albert Hartson, John Hilbert, Henry L. Hewit, Ira Hartwell, E. C. Hedding, C. H. Jackson, Abner N. Keep, William Kidder, Francis J. Kidder, Albert Keeler, O. R. Kirkland, R. J. Kennedy, Samuel Law, William Loomis, J. R. Morrison, D. C. Munger, Charles Newnhousen, Robert Okford, Samuel H. Paul, John H. Paul, Lester Paul, Isaiah Pelton, Seymour Patterson, Edward Richards, Henry Runnyan, John Runnyan, Earl Runnyan, Jacob Rubert, Benjamin N. Rogers, Wm. Spicer, F. M. Spaulding, C. E. Stitt, Sherman Stitt, J. L. Salisbury, T. J. Swap, C. L. Scott, Charles Selden, William Thornton, Thomas Thornton, Reuben Taylor, Augustus Weineeke, O. Wood, John Ware, John H. Wardwell, B. B. Wiser, H. J. Wright.

The story of Delaware County during those long years of war is almost a counterpart of every locality of the like character in the Northern States. The enormous drain upon the resources of the nation, the wholesale destruction of life and property stimulated an unusual activity in business to keep pace with the demand, and employed the surplus labor at high wages. The various industrial establishments ran day and night, and yet the market was often unable to furnish goods as rapidly as they were required. As the war advanced the Union armies were necessarily compelled to increase their numbers; every city, town or State, which was won by Northern troops required to be held by the bayonet, while long lines of communication, lengthening as the armies advanced, must be maintained uninterrupted. Hence it became absolutely essential that a great number of men should be called to the field, and as recruiting began to flag, the government was compelled to provide by law for compulsory military service. To that end, in the early summer of 1862, the President notified the various States that unless the required troops were furnished he would call for a conscription in accordance with the act of Congress. In Delaware County, as throughout the North, there was a popular feeling against the measure, and it was determined, if possible, to avoid the enforcement of the law, by offering bounties to men to enlist.

On July 26, 1862, a meeting of prominent citizens was held in the court-house at Media, at which John P. Crozer was chosen president, H. Jones Brooke and Edward Darlington, vice-presidents; Y. S. Walter, secretary; and addresses were made by ex-Judge

Haines and Joseph J Lewis It was finally determined to instruct the commissioners of the county to borrow fifteen thousand dollars, which sum was to be expended in bounties, additional to those paid by the general government, and for the protection of the commissioners, indemnifying bonds were to be given, in the event of the Legislature declining to enact a law legalizing the expenditure On Aug 4, 1852, the general government ordered a draft of six hundred thousand men, three hundred thousand of which number should be immediately called into service, the several States apportioning the quota of the different counties On September 1st, the authorities at Harrisburg announced that Delaware County had then more men in the field than any other in the commonwealth, according to population On August 10th, Samuel M Felton sent one thousand dollars to John P Crozer, a donation from the Philadelphia, Wilmington and Baltimore Railroad Company, to aid enlistments In the mean while Joshua P Eyre, who was appointed deputy marshal to enroll the male residents of this county, began the work intrusted to him, and so fully was it discharged that the list outnumbered the election returns almost a thousand names As the autumn came and recruiting had again fallen off, it was then found necessary to enforce the conscription, and on Wednesday, Oct 15, 1862, the names of two hundred and twenty men, required to fill the quota from Delaware County, were drawn under the supervision of Abel Lodge, of Nether Providence, draft commissioner, and the men so drafted were required to appear at Media on the following Wednesday, the 22d, for medical examination by Dr Joseph Rowland, of Upper Providence, examining surgeon On that day about one hundred presented themselves, when they were told that in the interval the quota had been filled At that time substitutes could be had for four hundred to five hundred dollars each

One Hundred and Fifty-second Regiment, Third Artillery (Three-Years' Service) —The Delaware County men recruited in this regiment were in the batteries ordered to the front to take part in the siege of Petersburg, being posted on the Bermuda front. Unfortunately, although the artillery regiments were as conspicuous as any other in the war, they never acted as a whole, and hence have not received the full credit due them

BATTERY G

James Elliott, private, must. in Jan 11, 1864, disch by G O June 15, 1865

Elias Eaves, private, must in Jan 18, 1864, must out with battery Nov 9, 1865, veteran

Arthur Marten, private, must in Jan 11, 1864, must out with battery

Artemus C Jenkins, private, must in Dec 30, 1863, must out with battery

BATTERY K

Charles B Roberts, private, must in Jan 15, 1864, must out with battery

Elias Baker

Charles Roberts

BATTERY M

Horatio Nelson Platt, 1st sergt., must in Feb 26, 1864, pro to corp Sept 1, 1864, to 1st sergt May 1, 1865, must out with battery Nov 9, 1865

William D Platt, corp., must. in Feb 25, 1864, pro to corp July 1, 1865, must out with battery

John S Fields, private, must in Feb 19, 1864, must out with battery, veteran

One Hundred and Sixtieth Regiment, Fifteenth (Anderson) Cavalry (Three-Years' Service) —In the early part of August, 1862, William J Palmer began recruiting a battalion of cavalry in Pennsylvania, which was subsequently increased to a full regiment When Lee crossed the Potomac and advanced into Maryland two hundred and fifty picket men were ordered to the front, while the remainder of the regiment was directed to remain in the Cumberland Valley The detachment mentioned in the Antietam campaign did effective duty in skirmishing and ascertaining the position of the enemy, and on the 15th of September, when the Confederate troops were retreating from Hagerstown, it charged through the village, capturing thirty stragglers On Nov 7, 1862, the regiment was transported to Louisville, Ky, and a month afterwards was ordered to join Rosecrans, at Nashville On December 26th, Rosecrans, then preparing to give Bragg battle, ordered the Fifteenth Cavalry to advance with Gen Stanley's division, but the greater part of the regiment stacked arms and refused to obey the command To the credit of Delaware County, among the three hundred who, deferring whatever grievances they might have to a future time for consideration, volunteered to go to the front, were the following Captain, Edward Sellers, Lieutenants, Joseph R Thomas, Edward C Smith, Annesley N Morton, Sergeants, Isaac Bartram, Simeon Lord, Jr, Marshall L Jones, George W Lukins, Geoffrey P Denis, John W Caldwell, Corporals, Hiram P Eves, Thomas A Jones, Henry W Pancost, Benjamin Bartram, Privates, Horatio D Snyder, Andrew J Buchanan, Richard Pancost, William Armstrong (the present sheriff), Edward W Jones, Augustus W Markley, Samuel Trimble, Charles P Sellers, Joseph S Bunting, and William P Powell The brave conduct of those three hundred volunteers from this regiment on that occasion was made the subject of a special commendatory order issued by Gen Rosecrans, and the historian Bates, in referring to this incident, declares that "the conduct of the men who followed the gallant Rosengarten and Ward, even under the most discouraging circumstances, and met death in the face of the foe, will never cease to be regarded with admiration and gratitude"

Stanley, covering with his command the right flank of the Union army, encountered the enemy on the 27th, whom he attacked, driving them nearly five miles, and on the 29th, at Wilkinson's Cross-Roads, in the engagement there, charged the largely superior force of the enemy, and, finally overpowered, was compelled to retire, not, however, until he again attempted to dislodge the Confederates by a desperate attack. During the four days of battle at Murfreesboro' the detachment was constantly on duty and suffered severely. On the 20th of January, 1863, Rosecrans made a proposition for the reorganization of the regiment, which was accepted, and the Fifteenth Cavalry was thereupon thoroughly organized and equipped. On the 4th of April, after a successful scouting expedition, on its return to camp Rosecrans reviewed the regiment, expressing himself pleased with its good conduct and soldierly bearing. Not only did he do this, but, to show his good feeling, in the Chickamauga campaign he detailed three companies of this regiment to act as his personal escort, while the remainder was instructed to scout and learn the topography of the country in advance of the army. This service brought it in frequent collisions with the enemy, in which its conduct was highly meritorious. So expert had the regiment become in scouting, that in January, 1865, it was especially ordered to watch the enemy and harass their foraging parties. By a bold dash it succeeded in capturing Gen. Vance, part of his staff, one hundred and fifty horses, and fifty men, besides recapturing twenty Union baggage-wagons and prisoners taken by the enemy, and within a week afterwards captured a train of eighteen wagons, ninety mules, and seventy-two men of the enemy. It was indeed the eyes of the army, and furnished important information to the general commanding. The story of its daring expeditions is full of interest, and its subsequent efficiency and valor amends for whatever error it committed in its early history, and several times, indeed, it gave occasion for complimentary orders from brigade and general commanders. Its pursuit of Hood's demoralized troops, after the battle of Nashville, was eminently successful and advantageous to the Union cause, and on May 8, 1865, when searching for Jefferson Davis, near the forks of the Appalachee and Oconee Rivers, it captured seven wagons, one containing one hundred and eighty-eight thousand dollars in coin, one with one million five hundred and eighty-eight thousand dollars in bank-notes and other securities, one containing four million dollars of Confederate money, besides considerable specie, plate, and valuables belonging to private parties in Macon. Two days afterwards Company G captured Gen. Bragg, his wife, and staff-officers. The war being at an end, the regiment went to Nashville, where, on the 21st day of May, 1865, it was mustered out of service.

COMPANY A.

Samuel C. Black, sergt., must. in Aug. 22, 1862; pro. to corp. March 1, 1863; to sergt. March 16, 1865; disch. June 1, 1865.

Hiram P. Eves, corp., must. in Aug. 22, 1862; pro. to corp. March 1, 1865; disch. June 21, 1865.

Harry G. Dennis, sergt., must. in Aug. 22, 1862; pro. from private March 1, 1863; disch. June 21, 1865.

COMPANY B.

Thomas A. Jones, corp., must. in Oct. 3, 1862; pro. to corp. Nov. 10, 1864; must. out with company June 21, 1865.

Privates.

Robert E. Hannum, Jr., must. in Aug. 22, 1862; must. out with company.

Harry C. Johnson, must. in Aug. 22, 1862; trans. to Co. C, date unknown.

William H. Johnson, must. in Aug. 22, 1862; disch. on surg. certif. Feb. 11, 1863.

Thomas Serrill, must. in Oct. 10, 1862; must. out with company.

COMPANY D.

Horatio D. Snyder, private, must. in Sept. 6, 1862; trans. to Co. M, date unknown.

COMPANY E.

Isaac Bartram, com.-sergt., must. in Oct. 3, 1862; pro. to corp Oct. 30, 1862; to com.-sergt. March 1, 1863; must. out with company.

COMPANY F.

Simeon Lord, Jr., sergt., must. in Aug. 22, 1862; pro. to corp. March 1, 1863; to sergt. May 12, 1863; must. out with company.

Henry W. Pancost, corp.

Privates.

William Armstrong, must. in Aug. 22, 1862; must. out with company.

James Buck, must. in Aug. 22, 1862; must. out with company.

Andrew J. Buchanan, must. in Aug. 22, 1862.

William Pancost.

COMPANY G.

H. McAllister, Jr., capt., must. in Oct. 3, 1862; pro. from 1st sergt. Co. L to 1st lieut. March 1, 1863; to capt. May 8, 1863; com. maj. June 1, 1865; not mustered; must. out with company.

E. Middleton, Jr., 1st sergt., must. in Oct. 3, 1862; pro. from private to sergt. March 1, 1863; to 1st sergt. May 8, 1863; com. 2d lieut. May 29, 1865; not mustered; must. out with company.

Geoffrey P. Lewis, sergt., must. in Aug. 30, 1862; disch. for promotion Feb. 18, 1864.

Marshall L. Jones, q.m.-sergt., must. in Oct. 3, 1862; pro. to corp. May 14, 1863; to q.m.-sergt. June 5, 1863; must. out with company.

George W. S. Allen, sergt., must. in Oct. 2, 1862; pro. from private May 15, 1863; died in Delaware County, Pa., Aug. 20, 1863.

Charles Pugh, corp., must. in Aug. 22, 1862; pro. to corp. March 16, 1865; must. out with company.

Privates.

Augustus W. Markley, must. in Aug. 22, 1862; trans. to Co. L, date unknown.

Edward W. Jones, must. in Oct. 3, 1862; trans. to Co. A, date unknown.

John R. Pugh, must. in Aug. 22, 1862; must. out with company.

E. G. Shortledge, must. in Sept. 3, 1864; disch. by G. O. July 7, 1865.

Samuel Trimble, must. in Aug. 30, 1862; must. out with company.

COMPANY H.

Edward Sellers, capt., must. in Aug. 22, 1862; pro. from sergt.-maj. May 8, 1863; res. March 6, 1865.

Theodore F. Ramsey, 1st lieut., must. in Aug. 22, 1862; pro. from q.m.-sergt. Co. M March 13, 1865; must. out with company.

Joseph R. Thomas, 1st lieut., must. in Aug. 22, 1862; pro. to sergt. March 1, 1863; to 1st sergt. March, 1863; to 2d lieut. Co. A, 180th Regt. P. V., Sept. 10, 1863.

John W. Caldwell, q.m.-sergt., must. in Aug. 22, 1862; pro. from private March 1, 1863; must. out with company.

George W. Lukins, com.-sergt., must. in Aug. 22, 1862; pro. from private March 1, 1863; must. out with company.

Charles P. Sellers, private, must. in Aug. 22, 1862; pro. to hosp. steward Nov. 1, 1862.

COMPANY I.

Edward C. Smith, 1st lieut., must. in Aug. 22, 1862; pro. from sergt. Co. F to 1st sergt. May 1, 1863; to 1st lieut. July 22, 1864; must. out with company.

COMPANY K.

Benjamin Bartram, corp., must. in Oct. 3, 1862; pro. to corp. Feb. 5, 1865; must. out with company.

COMPANY L.

Annerly N. Morton, 1st lieut., must. in Aug. 22, 1862; pro. to corp. Oct. 30, 1862; to 1st sergt. March 1, 1863; to 1st lieut. May 8, 1863; must. out with company.

Ellis L. Vandling, com.-sergt., must. in Aug. 22, 1862; pro. to corp. June 5, 1863; to com.-sergt. July 8, 1864; must. out with company.

John W. Zay, sergt., must. in Aug. 22, 1862; pro. to corp. March 10, 1864; to sergt. June 1, 1865; must. out with company.

Privates.

Joseph S. Bunting, must. in Oct. 10, 1862; disch. on surg. certif. Feb. 9, 1863.

Edward H. Engle, must. in Aug. 22, 1862; must. out with company.

William H. Powell, must. in Oct. 3, 1862; died at Nashville, Tenn., of wounds received at Stone River Dec. 29, 1862; buried in National Cemetery.

Terrill Ulrich, must. in Sept. 4, 1864; must. out with company.

The defeat of Hooker at Chancellorsville, in May, 1863, again aroused the hopes of the Confederate leaders that by a bold, rapid, and successful invasion of the North the war might be brought to a speedy termination. The unpopularity of the draft ordered in the Union States, it was believed by them, would be an important factor in bringing about the result they desired. The active, vigilant Executive of Pennsylvania saw the gathering storm, and began making preparations to meet it when it should come. Hence on June 12th he issued a proclamation asking the co-operation of the people of Pennsylvania in raising a home force for the protection of the State. Rumors of proposed Confederate invasions had been so often current that the plan suggested by Governor Curtin met with but slight public favor. The evidences that such a move was in contemplation, however, became so marked that on June 15, 1863, President Lincoln called for one hundred thousand militia from four States,—the quota of Pennsylvania being placed at fifty thousand men. Shortly before midnight on the 15th a Confederate force occupied Chambersburg, and the news was telegraphed all over the North.

On Monday, June 15th, the undoubted intelligence was received that Lee had invaded Pennsylvania, and the utmost excitement prevailed. In Chester a meeting was immediately held and a company recruited,—the Chester Guards and Linwood Guards consolidating,—while many of the citizens, aroused to the responsibility of the hour, hastened to Philadelphia, and united with military organizations there. In the Crozer United States Hospital, at Upland, eighty convalescent Union soldiers and a number of men from Bancroft's mill, in Nether Providence, formed a company, with Lieut. Frank Brown, of the Twelfth New Jersey, as commanding officer, and the next day left for Harrisburg; but on Wednesday they were ordered to return, transportation having been refused them at Philadelphia, as it was thought they were in no condition to undergo the fatigue of the campaign. At Media the excitement was, if anything, greater than at Chester. On Wednesday, the 17th, messages were sent in all directions to call the people together, and the court-house bell rang out a general alarm, so that at noon an immense assemblage gathered in the court-room, and steps were taken to enroll companies at once to go to the front. John M. Broomall had already collected a company, and on that evening started for Harrisburg. Dr. D. A. Vernon, and almost every man in the *Delaware County American* office, volunteered and went to the front. The next day the Delaware County companies of the One Hundred and Twenty-fourth Regiment, which had been mustered out only a month previously, again offered themselves to do battle for the nation, and the same evening Company B, Capt. Woodcock, and Company D, Capt. Yarnall, left for the State capital. The ranks being incomplete, Lieut. Buckley was ordered to remain at Media to collect the recruits, and on Monday, the 21st, he too followed the troops with a number of men. Capt. James Wilcox, with a company from Glenn Mills, and Capt. Benjamin Brooks, with a company from Radnor, left for Harrisburg on the 17th. John C. Beatty, of Springfield, suspended operations at his edge-tool works that his employés might enlist. At Darby, on Monday, when the news was received a strawberry festival was in progress, given by the Union League to the returned soldiers of the One Hundred and Twenty-fourth Regiment from that neighborhood, and a meeting was immediately organized, when in a short time a full company was recruited. While the enrollment was being made at one end of the porch, where the festival was held, at the other end contributions were being raised to provide for the families of those who would enlist. One aged gentleman subscribed a thousand dollars to the fund. The troops went to the front under command of Capt. Charles Andrews, on the Wednesday following. At Lenni, at short notice, thirty men enrolled who joined the Media company, and on Wednesday a meeting was held at the Black Horse, in Middletown, when a number of men were recruited. In Chester fifty or more colored men proposed to raise a company of their race, but the offer was not accepted.

The public was aroused to the true condition of affairs when, on the afternoon of June 26th, Gordon's brigade of Early's division of Lee's army occupied Gettysburg, and moved on toward Hanover and York. The same day Governor Curtin issued a proclamation calling sixty thousand militia to the field for forty days. The wildest rumors were in the air, and found ready credence. On Sunday, the 28th, at Media it was reported that a Confederate force was marching for Philadelphia, had already advanced as far as Oxford, and the excitement was intense. An old cannon was charged and repeatedly fired as an alarm-gun, while the bells in the town rang out a call for the people to assemble. H. Jones Brooke was chairman, and B. F. Baker secretary of the meeting. Before the people assembled Charles R. Williamson and Frederick Fairlamb collected two thousand three hundred dollars, which money was to be used in bounties, and when the people gathered the fund was largely increased, Mr. Fairlamb promising, if it was needed, to personally contribute one thousand dollars beyond the sum he had already given. The rumored advance of the Confederate soldiers spread over the county like a wave, occasioning the utmost consternation. Plate and valuables were packed ready to be transported to places of safety, while the money in the vaults of the bank at Chester was hastily gathered and carted away by the officers of that institution to Philadelphia, in order that it might be shipped to New York In Chester, on Monday, June 29th, a meeting of the citizens was held in the town hall, and Council, also assembling, appropriated ten thousand dollars for supplies for the families of volunteers A call for additional troops was then made, and in an hour eighty men enrolled under Capt William Frick In the case of George Baker, he and every man in his employment enlisted in the ranks, compelling the closing of his store during their absence The next day the company left for Harrisburg, the ranks now swollen to over a hundred men, many in the line whose gray hairs testified that patriotism, not the law's compulsion, had called them to the field At Upland, on Monday morning, the 29th, a spontaneous assemblage of the people took place, and as rapidly as the names could be taken man after man presented himself, until a company of seventy-two men was obtained George K Crozer was elected captain, and on Wednesday it went to Philadelphia, where it was attached to the Forty-fifth Regiment Pennsylvania Militia (First Union League Regiment), Col Frank Wheeler, and was encamped for a day or two at the Falls of Schuylkill, when the whole regiment was ordered to Shippensburg, soon after to Greencastle, near the Maryland line, and after the retreat of Lee it was stationed at Pottsville, returning to Upland Saturday, Aug 22, 1863, its term of service being extended beyond that of any Delaware County company of militia At Rockdale and Lenni, in addition to the men already sent forward, in ten hours a company of fifty was raised, and on Tuesday, July 2d, hastened to the State capital Of the number of militia required under President Lincoln's call on Pennsylvania of June 15th from Delaware County all excepting two hundred and fifty-five men had been forwarded by June 28th, and in two days thereafter twice the number necessary to fill the quota was in course of transportation to Harrisburg Over a thousand of the militia had responded

The Army of the Potomac in the mean while was advancing to meet the audacious enemy, and Lee learning from his scouts that he would be shortly confronted by that body of men, summoned his scattered forces to concentrate at Gettysburg So rapidly followed the movements of the armies that scarcely had the militia assembled at Harrisburg when, for three days, the opposing veterans of the North and South contended on the field of Gettysburg in the greatest battle ever fought by man of which we have authentic record, and at the conclusion of that struggle victory perched on the standard of the Union,—"the backbone of the rebellion" had indeed been broken

The militia companies were distributed as follows Company C (Capt Broomall), Company F (Capt Woodcock), Company G (Capt Bunting), Company A (Capt Andrews), and Company I (Capt Platt,—Capt Yarnall having been appointed lieutenant-colonel), were assigned to the Twenty-ninth Regiment, and were stationed for a time at Huntington, Company G (Capt Brooke) was assigned to the Twenty-eighth Regiment, Company A (Capt Frick) and Company F (Capt Huddleson) became part of the Thirty-seventh, and were at Harrisburg, Carlisle, Shippensburg, and on the Maryland line, while Company F (Capt Black) was assigned to the Forty-seventh, Col Wickersham, and was stationed at Williamsport, afterwards at Reading, and subsequently in the mining regions of Schuylkill County, where outbreaks were feared. All the companies from Delaware County returned between the 1st and 5th of August, excepting Capt Crozer's company, which was kept in service nearly three weeks longer than any of the other military organizations from this locality

TWENTIETH REGIMENT—EMERGENCY TROOPS OF 1863

COMPANY C

Mustered in June 17, 1863, discharged Aug 10, 1863

Second lieutenant, James Kirkman

Privates.—John Ardis, John Bail, David Beaumont, John Blythe, John Butler, Samuel Christy, Robert J Eagleson, John Gilmore, Artemus C Jenkins, Joseph Kay, John McLaughlin, John O'Hara, George Openshaw, Joseph Openshaw, John Pretty John W Thompson, Nathan Van Horn, William S Van Horn, John Ward, James West.

TWENTY EIGHTH REGIMENT,—EMERGENCY TROOPS OF 1863

Mustered in June 19-24, 1863, discharged July 27-28, 1863

COMPANY G

Captain, Benjamin N Brooke, first lieutenant, Frank Fennimore, second lieutenant, Samuel L Craig, first sergeant, Isaiah Matlack, sergeants, Joseph Baldwin, Emmor Childs, William H Potter, George W Blanchard, corporals, George Black, Charles H Hale, Fleming Park, Harrison C Lewis, John Frick, Nathan Brooke, John Henthorne, Randell C Norris, musicians, George Hampton, Nathaniel Lewis, Frank C Smith

Privates—Matthias P Anderson, Maris D Baldwin, John W Bolton, Hugh Blakeley, Charles V Bloom, Joseph P Bloom, Isaac W Davis, Ezr Davis, Henry Dewees, William C Duckett, Alfred W S Edwards Henry Eckert, James Eaveuson, Penrose Garrett, Orison Gleason, John Green, Samuel Gudshall, Jeremiah Griffith, Carver W Hall, James C Hayworth, Benjamin F Howard, William T Heins, William Hunter, Joseph Huffty, Jeremiah G Hughes, James B Jenkins, Lewis D Lafferty, Isaac Leamey, John C Lewis, Phineas Lewis, John P Litzenburg, Joseph Mann, John Mullen, William Mullen, Isaac McCoy, George T Phillips, Joseph T Phillips, Owen M Phillips, Hartman Prizer, Jacob Reinhard, Harrison Roberts, Isaac Roberts, Joseph Rowan, Marion Rossiter, Joseph Sharpless, Samuel Snyder, Francis Stewart, George Stewart, Gilbert H Todd, Isaac Walker, Henry C. Wells, George W White

COMPANY F

Captain, John Woodcock, first lieutenant, Ralph Bulkley, second lieutenant, Horatio G Hotchkiss, first sergeant, Roswell S Williams, sergeants, Alexander E Crozier, William Major, Edwin Bondin, Daniel Crowder, Lewis P Watkins, William B Faris, John A Lieb, Alfred Kenyon, Frederick A Davis, Hiram Hyzer, Thomas Lomax, Jonathan Henrock, musician, Ransaler McFarland

Privates—John T Adams, Enos Anson, Samuel T Allen, Charles W Broadbent James H Breuzinger, Ralph Crowther Nilson R Compfort, Enoch Chidester, Jerome A Chase, William Camp, William E Daniels, George F Drake, John Dunkerly, William Eastwood, Samuel Fields, John Ford, Edward Farrand, John Greenlee, David Greenlee, Cyrus Greenwood, George Henderson, Kennedy Humes, James R Kinsey, William H Litzenburg (promoted to sergeant-major June 23, 1863), Joseph Mulvaney, William Moore, Lyman Mayo, Charles D Manley, Dennis McLaughlin, George McClinn, Albert M Neil, Patrick Orin, Charles H Pedrick, George Robinson, Henry J Robinson, George Smith, John D Shutts, Lord W Scott, Aaron L Shew,

Pennell Stetser, William Shields, James O. Taylor, Joseph D. Tuckerman, Israel Thomas, Washington Thomas, Hezekiah P. Vanbariger, George Westfall, James Wilde, Bennett Wakeman, William P. Worrall, Calvin L. Walker.

TWENTY-NINTH REGIMENT, EMERGENCY TROOPS OF 1863.

Mustered in June 19, 1863; discharged Aug. 1, 1863; Lieut.-Col. Norris L. Yarnall.

COMPANY C.—Captain, John M. Broomall; first lieutenant, William Ormsby; second lieutenant, Thomas F. Beatty; first sergeant, Hays P. Griffith; sergeants, Orson F. Bullard, Davis N. Hannum, Isaac Johnson, Andrew T. Walker; corporals, John M. Hall, George Esrey, John Coburn, James Howard, Benjamin Crowther, Samuel Ottey, William P. Brooke, William W. Warner, Philip Afflick.

Privates.—James Albany, Edward Ashworth, William Black, Ezra Bailey, Michael Bradley, William Brannen, John Cathcart, Reuben Crowther, Ellwood Cornog, Albert Devers, John Doyle, Albert Dunn, William Duell, Joseph A. Doling, David Ellingsworth, David S. Edington, Michael Ferns, William F. France, John W. Fryer, William P. Frazer, William O. Fryer, Ellwood H. Gilbert, William S. Goodley, Robert N. Henderson, James Hill, Norris Hall, Joseph L. Heacock, Daniel Hurenstein, Israel Hartzell, Samuel Ingham, James H. Jacobs, Joseph Jones, Israel Jones, Jr., Henry Lowe, John Lowe, James F. Lowe, Walter Markley, James Mullowland, Hamilton P. Mason, Joseph B. Massy, Joseph P. Maris, David McAvoy, Daniel McAvoy, William McCartney, Alexander McFate, Patrick McGuigan, William Oaks, Mark Parker, James S. Pancost, Isaac S Parsons, Joseph Perkins, James Patten, Henry Pennypacker, Pearson Pike, George Riggs, Daniel Rively, Joseph Shipley, James Stamring, James Stewart, Samuel D. Stickler, William Taylor, James Taylor, Joseph Townsend, William H. Walter, William Waterson, Alfred N. Wier, —— Williams, Clayton Worrell, Mordecai Worrell.

COMPANY G.—Captain, Alfred Bunting; first lieutenant, William H. Thatcher; second lieutenant, Henry B. Taylor; first sergeant, William H. Churchman; sergeants, Joseph F. Brewster, James E. Giffin, Hamilton A. Burk, Charles W. Deors; corporals, Ezra Gray, William M. Black, John Richardson, Henry H. Taylor, Carman Richardson, James Hughes, John Clark, Jeremiah Zider, Richard M. Johnston; musicians, Shelly Sowers, John H. Weaver.

Privates.—Robert Anderson, George W. Appleby, George W. Arnold, William Bennett, Benjamin W. Blakeley, Robert Bell, John Bowers, John F. Barton, James Babcock, George Cadman, Archibald Clark, Isaac A. Campbell, John Culin, Jacob Crider, Elisha Crouch, John Q. Dartow, Charles Dougherty, Allison J. Dickerson, George Dyson, James Denight, Armstrong Elliott, William C. Field, James Feyer, John F. M. Forwood, James Fitzsimons, John H. Greenwood, Job Green, William P. Henderson, Joseph P. Howard, Joseph Howarth, Henry Hicken, Joseph G. Hampson, Edward Haraday, Samuel M. Hinds, David Harris, Henry Heacock, Wilmer Heacock, William Hinkson, Andrew Jackson, Daniel Kelley, John Lee, Samuel Mather, James R. McClelland, Thomas Nuttall, Jr., Peter Parson, Samuel C. Price, John Robinson, Francis R. Shoemaker, Benjamin Smith, Andrew Smith, John Taylor, Jacob Wagnor, Wright Wrigley, Levi Walcott, Robert H. Wood.

COMPANY H.—Captain, J. Charles Andrews; first lieutenant, George S. Patchel; second lieutenant, Joseph L. Lewis; first sergeant, James D. Byerly; sergeants, John J. Hoops, William K. Ferris, Richard Parson, Samuel Egner; corporals, John Field, Jacob K. Simpers, Henry H. Russell, William H. Bandfield, Charles Willis, John Cain, Joseph K. Printer, Frank B. Worrell; musicians, Annesley N. Kelthler, George S. Sipler.

Privates.—George Ash, Jr., Frederick Burkart, James Carr, Horatio P. Connell, John Davis, William Dougherty, James A. Flanagan, John Gorton, James Gormley, Thomas Green, Thomas W. Hawkins, Reece Heacock, John Howtant, Alonzo Heaps, Dennis Hinchey, Thomas J. M. Hoopes, William H. Johnston, Theodore Knight, Francis Kunsman, Charles A. Litzenburg, Rufus Lord, William H. Miller, Charles W. Moore, James Mulholland, Dennis McBride, William H. Norris, Samuel W. Ogden, Thomas J. Ottey, William Palmer, Joseph F. Poster, Frank B. Ridgway, Samuel W. Rudolph, Joseph S. Serrill, Valerius Sheller, Albert G. Thatcher, Edward C. Thatcher, Benjamin Thomas, Milton H. White, William Wilters, William P. West, Enos Yates.

COMPANY I.—Captain, Joseph Pratt; first lieutenant, C. D. M. Broomhall; second lieutenant, Benjamin Brooke; first sergeant, Edward W. Lewis; sergeants, William J. Macpherson, W. W. Vogdis, Hunter Brooke, Menander Slack; corporals, Lorenzo F. Davis, John Pugh, James H. Heacock, Richard R. Cummins, Stephen Smith, Stephen M. Blazier, George Eplic, Robert Edwards; musicians, John L. Grimm, William Williamson.

Privates.—Walter Bohanna, Alfred A. Bowen, Frank Brooke, James Cole, Harry Carr, George Cheyney, William Chidester, John Cunningham, Jesse L. Cummins, Charles L. Dubree, Gregory B. Elliott, Alfred B. Entrekin, Eli Flounders, Joseph Fell, William Farson, Andrew J. Groves, Joseph Hardcastle, Ralph M. Harvey, James T. Haddock, John G. Haddock, John A. Innes, Daniel W. Jeffries, Henry P. Johnson, Thomas J. Kitts, John W. Kay, John Lindsay, Joel Lodge, George Long, William Mackintosh, Joseph Millsen, Robert Masher, Edward Matlack, Lewis Moulder, Richard McKnight, Harry McKnight, Ambrose McDade, Joseph Y. Packer, Joseph Pratt, Rowland Pugh, Edwin Palmer, Robert C. Roberts, Thomas S. Ridgeway, Alexander Sherer, Jesse Scott, George M. Tyler, Nelson L. Talley, Aaron M. Tyson, Nicholas F. Walter, John Hunt, Robert Howarth.

THIRTY-SEVENTH REGIMENT MILITIA OF 1863.

Mustered in July 16, 1863; discharged Aug. 2, 3, 4, 1863.

COMPANY A.—Captain, William Frick; first lieutenant, Edward M. Lyons; second lieutenant, William G. Price; first sergeant, John E. Shaw; sergeants, Thomas Donechy, Charles D. Pennell, William C. Dubree, George Baker; corporals, Charles A. Story, John McFall, John Atkinson, David M. Johnson, Henry Hinkson, Robert M. Green, Charles Hinkson, Frederick Engle; musicians, Hamilton Sample, James Rawcliffe.

Privates.—Aaron Allen, David Appleby, James R. Abernethy, Abram Blakeley, Thomas Berry, Abram Birtwell, John Birtwell, Christopher Blakeley, William Blakeley, Thomas W. Baker, Jacob Boon, John Boon, Peter Boon, Henry Bradley, George F. Brinton, Thomas Chambers, James Cochran, George P. Dall, William P. Derr, Alfred O. Deshong, James Dunkerley, Julius A. Dutton, Joseph Eckersley, Peter H. Engle, Samuel Etchells, William Ewing, Edwin E. Flavill, J. Marshall Garrett, James Gartside, John Gartside, William H. Geary, Thomas Gibbs, Peter Goff, George Gorby, Robert C. Gorby, Jonathan Grant, Charles L. Grubb, James Hause, William Harrison, Joshua Hibberd, Jesse Hicken, Henry M. Hinkson, John Holt, Alfred Hooff, J. Washington Irving, John P. Jones, Jacob B. Kitts, Joseph Ladomus, Henry Larkin, Thomas Lees, Benjamin Mason, Jonas Miller, William Mills, Robert Mirt, William Moore, James Morgan, David W. Morrison, William P. Morrison, James Montgomery, Daniel McKinney, William J. Oglesby, William Patterson, Andrew Phillips, William R. Rice, George H. Ridgeway, William Schofield, Arnold Shaw, John Slawter, Robert Smith, Jr., Thomas O. Stephenson, Jacob B. Stewart, Henry Sutliff, Charles Sweeney, William H. H. Taylor, George Turner, Richard E. Turner, Richard T. Turner, Joseph Weaver, Thomas Wilkinson, Thomas Wood, Jacob B. Yates.

COMPANY F.—Captain, Harry Huddleson; first lieutenant, Joseph McCoy; second lieutenant, Samuel Bowker; first sergeant, Frederick Y. Young; sergeants, George Hastings, James Oakes, John McDade, Samuel C. Gray; corporals, David Jones, John C. Baker, John Keyser, James Dougherty, Edward Evans, William Shields, Monroe Graham, John Oakford; musician, John T. Husband.

Privates.—Isaac Anderson, Thomas Brobson, John Baggs, Joseph Cathcart, James Cleniff, George Cathcart, Nehemiah Ford, Joseph Ford, John Gambol, Job H. Graham, John Gray, John Gugory, Henry Gilken, Levi M. Houpt, Robert H. Hall, Bernard Hamill, Robert Howard, William Hickey, J. Rowland Lewis, John Lane, Thomas Lattimore, Terrence Landy, John Maloney, Enos Marshall, John McMurray, Alexander McBride, John McGilligan, Thomas B. Pedrick, David Roberts, Jacob Roberts, John Roebuck, Thomas Reed, John E. Smith, Samuel Scott, John Slater, John Silby, James Townsend, William Thornton, Peter Thornton, Edward Torbert, Reuben Taylor, Benjamin Wallraven, William Waters, John Wildes, Thomas Wildes, William Walters.

FORTY-FIFTH REGIMENT MILITIA OF 1863.

Mustered in July 16, 1863; discharged Aug. 29, 1863.

COMPANY B.—Captain, George K. Crozer; first lieutenant, John Graff; second lieutenant, Thomas Stewart; first sergeant, Robert S. Bentley; sergeants, George R. Vanzant, Richard Crowther, Ratcliffe Bridge, John Gilston; corporals, William Anderson, Ezra Danfield,

Thomas Clough, William H. Dean, John McGovern, Robert L. West, Agur Castle, Henry Greenwalt.

Privates.—Mark Allen, James Allen, William Burley, James Buckley, Mattison Bail, George Blakeley, Edwin Blakeley, James Breckenridge, Robert Cornog, John Cardwell, William Chalfant, James Cunliffe, James Canavan, Robert E. Cardwell, Sylvester Canavan, James Crowther, James R. Daniels, Richard Dawson, Isaac Dalton, William Dalton, William Dawson, John Deitrich, George Elliott, Robert Elliott, Andrew J. Fenton, Joseph Faulkner, John Faulkner, William Finley, Sr., William Finley, Jr., Charles Firth, Henry Foster, Allen Gartside, Robert Gartside, William Garthwaite, James Glennand, William Henderson, Luke Hepworth, Richard Hepworth, William Hill, Alexander Hopkins, Edward Howarth, Thomas Kay, James Lockwood, John Lavery, George W. Loveland, Andrew J. Lambert, William H. Makin, George Mousley, Arthur Martin, William Mackey, Samuel Montgomery, Davis Minster, Hamilton Morris, James Morgan, James Mills, Joseph McBride, William McClelland, William McNamee, Charles McBride, David G. Pretty, Samuel T. Pretty, James Ross, Samuel Saxon, Alexander Struthers, William Struthers, Joseph U. Scott, James Smith, Lewis Smith, Edward Taylor, George Turner, John Thompson, Nehemiah Vanzant, John Wyatt, William Ward, Casper Wilmer, William Whitaker, Joseph Wyatt, George Waters.

FORTY-SEVENTH REGIMENT EMERGENCY MEN OF 1863.

Mustered in July 9, 1863; discharged Aug. 14, 1863.

COMPANY E.—Captain, Harry H. Black; first lieutenant, Richard McClellan; second lieutenant, T. Grover Price; first sergeant, Audrew Beatty; sergeants, Joseph Morrell, Mordecai L. Lewis, J. Hunter Moore, James Wielde, Charles Moore (promoted to quartermaster-sergeant July 8, 1863); corporals, Cyrus H. Caley, Charles Smith, Joseph M. Dickinson, Clement Lawrence, Morris Hannum, William Scott.

Privates.—Joshua Beatty, William Buckley, John Bradon, William B. Braden, James Barrett, William Barrett, William Briggs, James Blythe, Charles Bovell, Frederick Christ, Charles Clark, John Dickinson, George W. Davis, Andrew Flinn, Hugh Fox, William Farra, William Garrett, William H. Gross, Richard Harrison, Isaac S. Jones, Alexander Johnson, Edward Knight, Mordecai Lawrence, William Lister, Samuel B. Moore, John L. Moore, George Myers, John Maitland, George McFarland, Mifford B. Note, Baldwin Pyle, John F. Ruse, William Smith, Caleb Smith, David E. Steele, Robert Schofield, George W. Sheaff, Henry Viceroy, Robert Viceroy, James H. Worrell, Ambrose Wood, Charles H. Worrall.

About the middle of the year 1863 conscription was actually enforced in some of the Northern States. In New York it brought on a riot the like of which was never known in that great city. In Delaware County extraordinary exertions had been made, and it was announced by those persons charged with the draft in this district that the quota had been filled; but the authorities at Washington stating that there was an error of one hundred and eleven men, a draft was immediately made (on Wednesday, June 17th). A public meeting was called at Media on Friday, the 19th, when it was resolved to pay three hundred dollars county bounty for recruits, and the quota was filled. The people breathed more freely, but on Oct. 17, 1863, when President Lincoln called for three hundred thousand men for three years or the war, and on Jan. 5, 1864, a draft should be made to fill the remaining quota assigned to every locality in the Northern States, again the people were aroused to the occasion. On Saturday, December 19th, a meeting was held at Media to encourage volunteering and avoid the draft, when it was urged that the commissioners should appropriate a sum to pay sufficient bounties to induce men to volunteer. On Wednesday, Dec. 30, 1863, a county meeting was held in the court-house at Media. John P. Crozer was chosen president and Samuel T. Walker vice-president, when it was decided to ask the commissioners to appropriate three hundred and fifty-two dollars bounty for every recruit, and petitions were prepared, which were given to committees of three in every township to obtain signatures of taxpayers obligating themselves to indemnify the commissioners in so doing, and also asking the Legislature to enact a law to legalize the expenditure. The draft was again avoided.

One Hundred and Eighty-eighth Regiment (Three-Years' Service).—This regiment was recruited out of the artillery early in 1864 as infantry, and assigned to the Eighteenth Corps, Third Division. It took part in the battle of Proctor's Creek on May 10, 1864, and on June 1st was engaged at Cold Harbor, where it suffered heavily. On the 16th of June it was in the battle before Petersburg, and on the 28th of July it was part of the force which charged on Fort Harrison, which it captured and turned the guns of the fort on the retreating enemy. The same day it attacked Fort Gilmore, but was repulsed, the killed amounting to nearly sixty, and the wounded to upwards of one hundred. It was mustered out of service Dec. 14, 1865.

COMPANY B.

William Pilger, corp., must. in Jan. 29, 1864; pro. to corp. Sept. 1, 1865; must. out with company Dec. 14, 1855.

COMPANY C.

John Davis, 1st lieut., must. in Nov. 3, 1862; pro. from corp. to sergt. May 18, 1864; to 1st sergt. June 6, 1865; to 1st lieut. Aug. 30, 1865; must. out with company.

Richard Renshaw, sergt., must. in Feb. 18, 1864; pro. to corp. Oct. 1, 1864; to sergt. Feb. 1, 1865; wounded Sept. 29, 1864; must. out with company Dec. 14, 1865.

COMPANY F.

William Henry Williams, sergt., must. in Nov. 30, 1863; pro. to corp. Dec. 1, 1864; must. out with company Dec. 14, 1865.

Privates.

Curnell Buckley, must. in Jan. 11, 1864; must. out with company.

Samuel D. Evans, must. in June 22, 1863.

Henry Donaldson, must. in Feb. 17, 1864; must. out with company.

Andrew Kestner, must. in Dec. 13, 1862; disch. May 24, 1865, for wounds received at Fort Harrison, Va., Sept. 29, 1864.

Edward Harity, must. in Feb. 25, 1864; must. out with company Dec. 14, 1865.

William Howard Shindle, must. in Feb. 24, 1864; disch. by G. O. May 26, 1865.

John Ward, must. in Jan. 18, 1864; disch. by G. O. Dec. 14, 1865.

Henry Williams, must. in June 22, 1863; must. out with company.

COMPANY E.

John Culin, corp., must. in Jan. 18, 1864; pro. to corp. Jan. 1, 1865; must. out with company.

Armor B. Gallagher, must. in March 21, 1864; must. out with company.

COMPANY H.

Isaac E. Wilde, 2d lieut., must. in Feb. 27, 1863; pro. to sergt., Battery I, 152d Regt., April 16, 1864; died at Broadway Landing, Va., July 26, 1864.

One Hundred and Ninety-seventh Regiment (Hundred-Days' Service).—This regiment was recruited under the auspices of the Coal Exchange Association of Philadelphia, and was known as the

Third Coal Exchange Regiment It was organized at Camp Cadwalader, July 22, 1864, with Capt John Woodcock, of Delaware County, major Shortly afterwards it was ordered to Mankin's Woods, near Baltimore, and instead of being sent to the front, as was hoped by the regiment (who were mostly veteran soldiers) would be done, it was ordered to Rock Island, Ill, where it was assigned to guarding camp for prisoners of war The number of prisoners—about nine thousand—was so great, and the duties required of the One Hundred and Ninety-seventh were so constant, that the service bore almost as heavily on the regiment as an active campaign, excepting casualties of battle Immediately after the arrival of the regiment at Rock Island, Capt Barton was appointed assistant provost marshal of the island, in which capacity he had immediate charge of the prisoners The prison covered about forty acres, surrounded by a board fence ten feet high, on the outside of which was a trench about twelve feet wide, filled with water The guard was mounted on an elevated platform on the outside of the fence, and within were barracks for the accommodation of the inmates The prisoners of war were provided with good food and comfortable clothing, and, notwithstanding, deaths were frequently arising from melancholiness or homesickness On Nov 11, 1864, the One Hundred and Ninety-seventh was mustered out at Philadelphia

COMPANY A

James Barton, Jr, capt., must in July 15, 1864, must out with company Nov 11, 1864

James C Hinkson, 1st lieut, must in July 15, 1864, must out with company Nov 11, 1864

Thomas H Berry, 2d lieut, must. in July 15, 1864, must out with company Nov 11, 1864

John M Clayton, 1st sergt., must in July 15, 1864, must out with company Nov 11, 1864

Ambrose McDade, sergt., must in July 15, 1864, must out with company Nov 11, 1864

Jesse D Minshall, sergt, must in July 15, 1864, must out with company Nov 11, 1864

William T Shoemaker, sergt, must in July 15, 1864, must out with company Nov 11, 1864

William Trainer, sergt., must in July 15, 1864, must out with company Nov 11, 1864

Cheyney H Smith, corp., must in July 15, 1864, must out with company Nov 11, 1864

Robert J Eagleson, corp., must in July 15, 1864, must out with company Nov 11, 1864

Joseph L Arment, corp, must in July 15, 1864, must out with company Nov 11, 1864

Henry Larkin, corp, must. in July 15, 1864, must out with company Nov 11, 1864.

Preston E Wilson, corp., must in July 15, 1864, must out with company Nov 11, 1864

Henry C. Hinkson, corp, must in July 15, 1864, must out with company Nov 11, 1864

Benjamin Crowther, corp, must in July 15, 1864, must. out with company Nov 11, 1864

George G Dutton, corp, must in July 15, 1864, must out with company Nov 11, 1864

George W Schopeid, musician, must in July 15, 1864, must out with company Nov 11, 1864

Privates

John B Allen, must in July 15, 1864, must out with company Nov 11, 1864

Theodore J Bell, must. in July 15, 1864, must out with company Nov 11, 1864

Samuel A Benson, must in July 15, 1864, must out with company Nov 11, 1864

James B Berry, must in July 15, 1864, must out with company Nov 11, 1864

Abram W Birtwell, must in July 15, 1864, must out with company Nov 11, 1864

John Birtwell, must in July 15, 1864, must out with company Nov 11, 1864

Frank Blagg, must in July 15, 1864, must out with company Nov 11, 1864

Peter Boon, must in July 15, 1864, must out with company Nov 11, 1864

Milton J Bowers, must. in July 15, 1864, must out with company Nov 11, 1864

James E Bracoland, must in July 15, 1864, must. out with company Nov 11, 1864

Mark Brewster, must in July 15, 1864, must. out with company Nov 11, 1864

Hamilton A Burke, must in July 15, 1864, must out with company Nov 11, 1864

John Cannavan, must in July 15, 1864, must. out with company Nov 11, 1864

Ed W Casey, must in July 15, 1864, must out with company Nov 11, 1864

Samuel K Chambers, must in July 15, 1864, must out with company Nov 11, 1864

Samuel Cook, must in July 15, 1864, must out with company Nov 11, 1864.

Samuel W Chadwick, must in July 15, 1864, trans Sept. 4, 1864, organization unknown

George H Derrick, must in July 15, 1864, must out with company Nov 11, 1864

James Dougherty, must in July 15, 1864, must out with company Nov 11, 1864

Albert Dutton, must in July 15, 1864, must out with company Nov 11, 1864

Alfred B Entrikon, must in July 15, 1864, must. out with company Nov 11, 1864

David Foster, must in July 15, 1864, must. out with company Nov 11, 1864

John Gallagher, must in July 15, 1864, must out with company Nov 11, 1864

Nelson G Green, must in July 15, 1864, must out with company Nov 11, 1864

Theodore J Gleason, must in July 15, 1864

Thomas Hance, must in July 15, 1864, must out with company Nov 11, 1864

C P Hannaway, must in July 15, 1864, must out with company Nov 11, 1864

L F Hendrickson, must in July 15, 1864, must out with company Nov 11, 1864

William Hopworth, must in July 15, 1864, must out with company Nov 11, 1864

Charles J Hewes, must in July 15, 1864, must out with company Nov 11, 1864

William Hill, must in July 15, 1864, must out with company Nov 11, 1864

Joseph P Hindeley, must in July 15, 1864, must out with company Nov 11, 1864

John M Hinkson, must in July 15, 1864, must out with company Nov 11, 1864.

George Horuing, must in July 15, 1864, must out with company Nov. 11, 1864

Spencer Howard, must in July 15, 1864, must out with company Nov 11, 1864

Harrison Hoffman, must in July 15, 1864, died at Rock Island, Ill, Oct 22, 1864

Isaac Jones, must in July 15, 1864, must out with company Nov 11, 1864

Martin Kelly, must in July 15, 1864, must out with company Nov 11, 1864

John H Kerlin, must in July 15, 1864, must. out with company Nov 11, 1864

James D Knight, must in July 15, 1864, must out with company Nov 11, 1864

John C Longbotham, must in July 15, 1864, must out with company Nov 11, 1864

Samuel W Loveland, must in July 15, 1864, must. out with company Nov 11, 1864
Benjamin H Mason, must in July 15, 1864, must out with company Nov 11, 1864
Fleming Maloney, must in July 15, 1864, must out with company Nov 11, 1864
John McDade, must in July 15, 1864, must. out with company Nov 11, 1874
Daniel McKinney, must in July 15, 1864, must out with company Nov 11, 1864
William McDonald, must in July 15, 1864, must. out with company Nov 11, 1864
Henry D McNeald, must in July 15, 1864, must out with company Nov 11, 1864
Vincent Nichols, must in July 15, 1864, must. out with company Nov 11, 1864
Samuel Nuttall, must in July 15, 1864, must out with company Nov 11, 1864
Joseph Osborne, must in July 15, 1864, must out with company Nov 11, 1864
Gibbons L Pharaoh, must in July 15, 1864, must out with company Nov 11, 1864
Emmor W Porter, must in July 15, 1864, must out with company Nov 11, 1864
Edwin L Powell, must in July 15, 1864, must out with company Nov 11, 1864
John H Pretty, must in July 15, 1864, must. out with company Nov 11, 1864
Samuel C Price, must in July 15, 1864, must out with company Nov 11, 1864
Silas L Sample, must in July 15, 1864, must out with company Nov 11, 1864
Joseph B Sample, must in July 15, 1864, must out with company Nov 11, 1864
Lewis J Smith, must in July 15, 1864, must out with company Nov 11, 1864
Nelson S Talley, must in July 15, 1864, must out with company Nov 11, 1864
William E Trainer, must in July 15, 1864, must out with company Nov 11, 1864
William Trainer, must in July 15, 1864, must out with company Nov 11, 1864
George W Turner, must in July 15, 1864, must out with company Nov 11, 1864
Terrill J Ulrich, must in July 15, 1864, trans Sept 4, 1864, organization unknown
Theodore A Vanzant, must. in July 15, 1864, must out with company Nov 11, 1864
John W Warren, must in July 15, 1864, must out with company Nov 11, 1864
William H Weir, must in July 15, 1864, must out with company Nov 11, 1864
William H Williams, must in July 15, 1864, trans Sept 8, 1864, organization unknown
William W Young, must in July 15, 1864, must. out with company Nov 11, 1864

COMPANY I

John Woodcock, capt, must in July 14, 1864, pro to maj July 22, 1864
Ralph Buckley, capt., must in July 14, 1864, pro from 1st lieut July 23, 1864, must out with company Nov 11, 1864
Roswell T Williams, 1st lieut., must in July 14, 1864, pro from 2d lieut July 23, 1864, must out with company.
James Carrick, 2d lieut., must in July 14, 1864, pro from 1st sergt July 23, 1864, must out with company
Edwin Bowden, 1st sergt., must in July 14, 1864, pro from sergt July 23, 1864, must out with company
Matthew Bennett, sergt., must in July 14, 1864, must out with company
Abel Ford, sergt., must. in July 14, 1864, must out with company
Daniel Crowther, sergt., must in July 14, 1864, must out with company
Samuel Greenwood, sergt, must in July 14, 1864, pro from corp. July 23, 1864, must out with company
Frederick A Davis, corp must in July 14, 1864, must out with company
Thomas Lomax, corp, must in July 14, 1864, must out with company
James Mulholland, corp, must in July 14, 1864, must out with company
Gardner Kelly, corp, must in July 14, 1864, must out with company
William Donnelly, corp, must in July 14, 1864, must out with company
John Scofield, corp, must in July 14, 1864, must out with company
Samuel Fields, corp, must in July 14, 1864, must out with company
Edward D Sippler, corp, must in July 14, 1864, pro to corp July 23, 1864, must out with company

Privates

Reuben Allen, must in July 14, 1864, must out with company
John Armstrong, must in July 14, 1864, must out with company
Ed Ashworth, must in July 14, 1864, must out with company
William Beaumont, must in July 14, 1864, must out with company
Henry Barber, must in July 14, 1864, must out with company
Uriah Beaumont, must in July 14, 1864, must out with company
William Buckley, must in July 14, 1864, must out with company
John Baggs, must in July 14, 1864, must. out with company
John Bargeley, must in July 14, 1864 must out with company
Charles E Bourne, must in July 14, 1864, pro to sergt-maj Aug 19, 1864
James Bonner, must in July 14, 1864
William Coppick, must in July 14, 1864, must out with company
Miles Dickerson, must in July 14, 1864, must out with company
Samuel Duncan, must in July 14, 1864, must out with company
Joseph Drake, must in July 14, 1864, must out with company
James Duffee, must in July 14, 1864, must out with company
William Douglass, must in July 14, 1864 must out with company
John Edwards, must in July 14, 1864, must out with company
Amor Eaches, must in July 14, 1864, must out with company
Joseph Faulkner, must in July 14, 1864, must out with company
John Faulkner, must in July 14, 1864, must. out with company
John Ford, must in July 14 1864, must out with company
Nehemiah Ford, must in July 14, 1864, must out with company
William France, must in July 14, 1864, must. out with company
Daniel Flynn, must in July 14, 1864, must out with company
Michael Fearns, must in July 14, 1864, must out with company
John Griggory, must in July 14, 1864, must out with company
John Gilkins, must in July 14, 1864, must out with company
John Hibbitt, must in July 14, 1864, must out with company
James Hibbitt, must in July 14, 1864, must out with company
David Hortenstine, must in July 14, 1864, must out with company
John Heartgreaves, must in July 14, 1864, must out with company
Edwin Hunter, must in July 14, 1864, must out with company
William Howith must in July 14, 1864, must out with company
John Holstein, must in July 14, 1864, absent, sick, at muster out
Jesse Haley, must in July 14, 1864, absent, sick, at muster out
Samuel Heacock, must in July 14, 1864, absent, sick, at muster out
James Hannum, must in July 14, 1864, must out with company
William Hickey, must in July 14, 1864, must out with company
John Heague, must in July 14, 1864
William Johnson, must in July 14, 1864, must out with company
Thomas Key, must in July 14, 1864, must. out with company
John Kieser, must in July 14, 1864, must out with company
Abram Lee, must in July 14, 1864, must. out with company
Roland Lewis, must in July 14, 1864, must out with company
Thomas Landimore, must in July 14, 1864, must out with company
Hugh Morrison, must in July 14, 1864, must out with company
William Milner, must in July 14, 1864, must out with company
William Mooney, must in July 14, 1864, must out with company
Wright Martin, must in July 14, 1864, must out with company
Edward Mullin, must in July 14, 1864, must out with company
Alfred H May, must in July 14, 1864, must out with company
John Moore, must in July 14, 1864, must out with company
Thomas Mageo, must in July 14, 1864, must out with company
Thurlow McMullen, must in July 14, 1864, must out with company
John McGill, must in July 14, 1864, must out with company
Dennis McLaughlin, must in July 14, 1864, must out with company
Daniel Newsome, must in July 14, 1864, must. out with company
John Otty, must in July 14, 1864, must. out with company
John Parker, must in July 14, 1864, must out with company
Richard Pyott, must in July 14, 1864, must out with company
Alvaen Quimby, must in July 14, 1864, must out with company
John Redman, must in July 14, 1864, must out with company
John Rigley, must in July 13, 1864, must. out with company
Samuel Standring, must in July 14, 1864, must out with company

William S. Sewell, must. in July 14, 1864; must. out with company.
William Scott, must. in July 14, 1864; must. out with company.
H. Shillingsburgh, must. in July 14, 1864; absent, sick, at muster out.
George W. Somers, must. in July 14, 1864; must. out with company.
John Scanlin, must. in July 14, 1864.
Samuel Thackery, must. in July 14, 1864; must. out with company.
John Thorp, must. in July 14, 1864; must. out with company.
Edwin Tolbert, must. in July 14, 1864; must. out with company.
John Thackery, must. in July 14, 1864; must. out with company.
James Taylor, must. in July 14, 1864; must. out with company.
Thomas C. Vernon, must. in July 14, 1864; must. out with company.
John Viccary, must. in July 14, 1864; must. out with company.
William Whittaker, must. in July 14, 1864; must. out with company.
Edward Worlall, must. in July 14, 1864; must. out with company.
John Worlall, must. in July 14, 1864; must. out with company.
Jacob Wheatley, must. in July 14, 1864; must. out with company.
Edward Wells, must. in July 14, 1864; must. out with company.
James Whilde, must. in July 14, 1864; must. out with company.

One Hundred and Ninety-eighth Regiment (One-Year's Service).—This regiment was recruited under the auspices of the Union League in Philadelphia in the summer of 1864, its ranks being filled in five weeks. On the morning of the 19th of September it was reviewed before the League House and presented by that association with regimental colors, and immediately proceeded to Petersburg, where it became part of the First Brigade, Fifth Division, of the First Corps of the Army of the Potomac. On the 30th of that month it took part in the battle of Peebles' Farm, and was scarcely formed in position when the enemy opened upon it a heavy artillery and musketry fire, but it held its ground, and finally, in the charge, drove the Confederates from their first line of works. On October 2d it held its lines under a fierce attack and severe firing from the enemy. On Feb. 5, 1865, at the battle of Hatcher's Run, at three o'clock, the Second Brigade was being hard pressed, when Gen. Sickles ordered the One Hundred and Ninety-eighth to its relief, and at the double-quick it charged across an open field and fell upon Mahone's "fighting brigade." The enemy was driven back, but during the night the Confederates succeeded, by massing their troops, in capturing a part of the Union line. At the first alarm the One Hundred and Ninety-eighth delivered a volley and charged with the bayonet. "The struggle for a time was hand to hand, muskets being clubbed and bayonets freely used." The enemy was finally driven back and the works regained. At the battle of Lewis' Farm, on March 29th, the One Hundred and Ninety-eighth encountered the enemy near the old saw-mill, and across a clear field of a thousand yards this regiment and the One Hundred and Eighty-fourth New York, led by Sickles, charged the enemy's works, reserving its fire until near the fortification, when it delivered a close and effectual volley, driving the foe. The regiment's loss was terrific, it afterwards being learned that three of the best Confederate brigades had confronted the Union troops in that engagement. On the 31st it was in action at White Oak Swamp and at Five Forks. On April 1st, after the Union assault had failed, Gen. Chamberlain, who was in command of the division, rode to Maj. Glenn, commanding the One Hundred and Ninety-eighth, and exclaimed, "Major, can you take those works and hold them?" The latter, turning to his troops, inquired, "Boys, will you follow me?" and he dashed forward, followed by his men. Twice the color-bearer was shot down, but the standard, caught up by another, was carried forward in the charge and planted on the enemy's works. Chamberlain promoted Glenn on the field for this deed, but later in the day the latter was fatally wounded. This was its last battle, the regiment being mustered out of service at Arlington Heights on June 3, 1865.

COMPANY K.

William R. Thatcher, 1st lieut., must. in Sept. 10, 1864; must. out with company June 4, 1865.
Benjamin Jones, corp., must. in Sept. 10, 1864; not accounted for.
Joseph F. Brewster, corp., must. in Sept. 10, 1864; prisoner from March 29 to April 5, 1865; disch. by G. O. June 21, 1865.
Charles Logan, corp., must. in Sept. 10, 1864; not accounted for.

Privates.

John H. Bartman, must. in Sept. 10, 1864; not accounted for.
Levi Booth, must. in Sept. 10, 1864; wounded at Hatcher's Run, Va., Feb. 7, 1865; not accounted for.
William H. Blizzard, must. in Sept. 10, 1864; not accounted for.
George E. Burk, must. in Sept. 10, 1864; not accounted for.
Michael Brennan, must. in Sept. 10, 1864; not accounted for.
Joseph F. Beeson, must. in Sept. 10, 1864; not accounted for.
William H. Costello, must. in Sept. 10, 1864; not accounted for.
David Chambers, must. in Sept. 10, 1864; disch. by G. O. May 31, 1865.
John B. Crook, must. in Sept. 10, 1864; not accounted for.
Edward Carson, must. in Sept. 10, 1864; not accounted for.
Armstrong Elliott, must. in Sept. 10, 1864; disch. by G. O. June 26, 1865.
James Fryer, must. in Sept. 10, 1864; not accounted for.
John E. Holt, must. in Sept. 10, 1864; not accounted for.
John Holt, must. in Sept. 10, 1864; wounded at Five Forks, Va., April 1, 1865; not accounted for.
Alfred T. Hart, must. in Sept. 10, 1864; not accounted for.
Henry Hickson, must. in Sept. 10, 1864; not accounted for.
Washington Hickson, must. in Sept. 10, 1864; wounded at Hatcher's Run, Va., Feb. 7, 1865; disch. by G. O. May 16, 1865.
Robert S. Johnson, must. in Sept. 10, 1864; disch. by G. O. June 2, 1865.
George W. Kaissinger, must. in Sept. 10, 1864; disch. by G. O. June 2, 1865.
George Latch, must. in Sept. 10, 1864; wounded at Lewis' Farm, Va., March 29, 1865; not accounted for.
Charles Logan, must. in Sept. 3, 1864; not accounted for.
Edward L. Morgan, must. in Sept. 10, 1864; not accounted for.
James Morgan, must. in Sept. 10, 1864; wounded at Lewis' Farm, Va., March 29, 1865; not accounted for.
Edward T. Mason, must. in Sept. 10, 1864; wounded at Five Forks, Va., April 1, 1865; disch. by G. O. June 9, 1865.
George Mills, must. in Sept. 10, 1864; not accounted for.
Chandler Marshman, must. in Sept. 5, 1864; not accounted for.
Samuel Pullen, must. in Sept. 5, 1864; not accounted for.
John O. Pike, must. in Sept. 5, 1864; not accounted for.
Jesse W. Paist, must. in Sept. 5, 1864; wounded at Lewis' Farm, Va., March 29, 1865; not accounted for.
Reuben Russell, must. in Sept. 5, 1864; not accounted for.
Charles G. Slawter, must. in Sept. 13, 1864; not accounted for.
James Schofield, must. in Sept. 13, 1864; not accounted for.
William Tomlinson, must. in Sept. 10, 1864; not accounted for.
Frederick P. Taylor, must. in Sept. 10, 1864; not accounted for.
Hiram Williams, must. in Sept. 10, 1864; wounded at Appomattox Court-House, Va., April 9, 1865; not accounted for.
Robert Weir, must. in Sept. 10, 1864; wounded at Lewis' Farm, Va., March 29, 1865; disch. by G. O. June 26, 1865.
George Wilson, must. in Sept. 10, 1864; not accounted for.
Jeff. W. Wetherill, must. in Sept. 10, 1864; wounded at Peebles' Farm, Va., Sept. 30, 1864, and at Five Forks, Va., April 1, 1865; disch. by G. O. July 17, 1865.
James Willis, must. in Sept. 5, 1864; not accounted for.

Two Hundred and Third Regiment (One-Year's Service).—This regiment was recruited as sharpshooters for Gen. Birney's division, but the general dying they were treated as ordinary infantry. The regiment was organized Sept. 10, 1864, and on the 27th of the same month they reached the army before Petersburg, and were assigned to the Second Brigade, Second Division, Tenth Corps, the same day. As the action at Chapin's Farm and New Market Road the Two Hundred and Third were employed in picketing Malvern Hill and escorting prisoners. On October 7th it took part in the battle on that day, and repulsed the assaults of the enemy, and was in action on the 27th on the Darlingtown road.

When the Army of the James was reorganized the Two Hundred and Third was part of the Second Brigade, Second Division, Twenty-fourth Corps. On Dec. 13, 1864, it embarked on transports at Fortress Monroe, and accompanied the naval expedition under Admiral Porter for the reduction of Fort Fisher, North Carolina. On Jan. 15, 1865, when the assault on the fort was made, the regiment was in Pennypacker's brigade, which drove the enemy from the palisadings. Here the Two Hundred and Third charged through an opening in the face of two guns, which it captured, and traverse after traverse was carried, and just as the fourth was charged Col. Moore, with his regiment's flag in one hand and his sword in the other, urging on the men, fell dead. From half-past three in the afternoon until late into the night the fight was stubbornly continued until the enemy finally yielded. In this memorable assault the colonel, lieutenant-colonel, one captain, and a lieutenant were killed, two captains and four lieutenants wounded; among the latter was Capt. Benjamin Brooke, of Company B.

Admiral Porter, in his report, states that Fort Fisher was "really stronger than the Malakoff Tower, which defied so long the combined powers of France and England, and yet it was captured by a handful of men under the fire of the guns of the fleet, and in seven hours after the attack commenced in earnest." On February 11th the regiment was in the advance on Wilmington, being thrown out as skirmishers, and succeeded in getting possession of the rifle-pits of the enemy in front of his works, but owing to the swampy nature of the ground and the dense undergrowth the line of battle could not advance. Hence the regiment in possession of the pits could not withdraw until night, when, stealthily, a few men at a time crawled away. The works were finally captured by a flank movement, which compelled the enemy to abandon his fortification.

The Two Hundred and Third was active in all the movements in North Carolina until April 26th, when Johnston surrendered, after which it was assigned to duty at Raleigh, where, on June 22, 1865, it was mustered out of service. Capt. Brooke, on June 22, 1865, was promoted lieutenant-colonel of the regiment.

COMPANY B.

Benjamin Brooks, capt., must. in Sept. 12, 1864; wounded at Fort Fisher, N. C., January 15th, and in action Feb. 11, 1865; pro. to lieut.-col. June 15, 1865.
George H. Eplee, 1st lieut., must. in Sept. 12, 1864; must. out with company June 22, 1865.
George R. Vanzant, 2d lieut., must. in Aug. 24, 1864; pro. from private Sept. 10, 1864; must. out with company.
Joseph M. Borrell, 1st sergt., must. in Sept. 12, 1864; absent with leave at muster out.
John B. Selvey, sergt., must. in Sept. 19, 1864; must. out with company.
William G. Davidson, sergt., must. in Sept. 30, 1864; absent on furlough at muster out.
Alfred J. Kent, sergt., must. in Sept. 24, 1864; must. out with company.
Ezra Drainsfield, sergt., must. in Sept. 24, 1864; pro. from corp. May 1, 1865; must. out with company.
John Lee, sergt., must. in Sept. 18, 1864; pro. to 1st sergt. Co. D Oct. 12, 1864.
John A. Morrow, corp., must. in Sept. 3, 1864; must. out with company.
John Famous, corp., must. in Aug. 26, 1864; must. out with company.
Samuel T. Allen, corp., must. in Sept. 2, 1864; must. out with company.
Richard Parsons, corp., must. in Aug. 24, 1864; must. out with company.
Charles T. Brooks, corp., must. in Sept. 5, 1864; wounded at Fort Fisher, N. C., Jan. 15, 1865; must. out with company.
John J. Vanzant, corp., must. in Aug. 31, 1864; must. out with company.
J. McGinly Wilhelm, corp., must. in Aug. 30, 1864; pro. to corp. May 1, 1865; must. out with company.
Miller Cox, corp., must. in Sept. 3, 1864; pro. to corp. May 16, 1865; must. out with company.
Andrew Lamport, corp., must. in Aug. 24, 1864; wounded at Fort Fisher, Va., Jan. 15, 1865; disch. by G. O. May 15, 1865.
Jacob Deffenderfer, musician, must. in Sept. 2, 1864; must. out with company.
Henry Nagle, musician, must. in Sept. 2, 1864; must. out with company.

Privates.

John Allen, must. in Aug. 26, 1864; must. out with company.
Mark W. Allen, must. in Aug. 26, 1864; disch. by G. O. June 10, 1865.
Thomas Armstrong, must. in Aug. 29, 1864; must. out with company.
John H. Anderson, must. in Sept. 3, 1864; must. out with company.
Watson Bail, must. in Aug. 24, 1864; must. out with company.
James Bowen, must. in Aug. 24, 1864; must. out with company.
John J. Boyer, must. in Sept. 8, 1864; must. out with company.
John Booth, must. in Aug. 31, 1864; must. out with company.
James P. Boon, must. in Sept. 15, 1864; must. out with company.
William Burley, must. in Aug. 19, 1864; must. out with company.
Jacob Boon, must. in Sept. 15, 1864; pro. to hospital steward Sept. 20, 1864.
August Baum, must. in Aug. 25, 1864; disch. by G. O. May 15, 1865.
Gillead Carter, must. in Aug. 24, 1864; must. out with company.
James Craggen, must. in Aug. 24, 1864; must. out with company.
William Chadwick, must. in Aug. 29, 1864; disch. by G. O. June 3, 1865.
Thomas Clowgh, must. in Aug. 24, 1864; must. out with company.
John J. Clar, must. in Aug. 24, 1864; died at Hampton, Va., January 23d, of wounds received at Fort Fisher, N. C., Jan. 15, 1865; buried in National Cemetery.
William H. Camp, must. in Aug. 18, 1864; died at New York, March 15th, of wounds received at Fort Fisher, N. C., Jan. 15, 1865; buried in Cypress Hill Cemetery, Long Island.
Henry Carmon, must. in Aug. 31, 1864.
John Conner, must. in Feb. 10, 1865; not on muster-out roll.
Joseph Carter, must. in March 3, 1865; not on muster-out roll.
Thomas Chubb, must. in March 3, 1865; not on muster-out roll.
Nathaniel Davis, must. in Sept. 2, 1864; must. out with company.
Theodore Drainsfield, must. in Aug. 24, 1864; must. out with company.
George Dilks, must. in Sept. 2, 1864; must. out with company.
Joseph Doyle, must. in Aug. 25, 1864; must. out with company.
John Duffee, must. in Sept. 5, 1864; wounded at Fort Fisher, N. C., Jan. 15, 1865; disch. by G. O. June 14, 1865.
Robert Entwistle, must. in Aug. 26, 1864; must. out with company.
Samuel Ewing, must. in Aug. 29, 1864; must. out with company.
Orange M. English, must. in Sept. 14, 1864; disch. by G. O. June 3, 1865.
Hiram Erisman, must. in Feb. 2, 1865; not on muster-out roll.
Abraham Favinger, must. in Aug. 26, 1864; must. out with company.
William E. Fetters, must. in Sept. 2, 1864; wounded at Fort Fisher, N. C., Jan. 15, 1865; must. out with company.

Elwood D Fryer, must in Sept 2, 1864, wounded near Wilmington, N. C, Oct 27, 1864, absent, on detached service, at muster out
John W Fryer, must in Sept 2, 1864, absent, sick, at muster out
William O Fryer must in Aug 31 1864, must out with company
William J Farra, must in Aug 29, 1864, died at Hampton, Va, Jan 23d, of wounds received at Fort Fisher, N C., Jan 15, 1865, buried in National Cemetery
John Grim, must in Sept 2, 1864, wounded near Wilmington, N C., Oct 27, 1864, disch by G O June 10, 1865
Elwood H Gilbert, must. in Aug 31, 1864, disch by G O June 15, 1865
Jesse Gore, must in Sept 3, 1864, must out with company
David Gordon, must. in Aug 27, 1864, absent, in hospital, at muster out.
Thomas Grant, must in Aug 18, 1864
Thomas J Harper, must in Aug 26, 1864, must out with company
Lewis Harper, must in Aug 26, 1864, must out with company
Charles Haas, must in Sept 1, 1864, must out with company
Edward Haycock, must in Sept 2, 1864, wounded at Fort Fisher, N C, Jan 15, 1865, absent, in hospital, at muster out
Luke Hepworth, must in Aug 26, 1864, must out with company
James Hulme, must in Aug 24, 1864, must out with company
Davis N Hahnem, must in Sept 3, 1864, disch by G O July 3, 1865
John M Hoffstitler, must in Sept 2, 1864, killed at Fort Fisher, N C, Jan 15, 1865
James Hogan must in Feb 9, 1865, not on muster out roll
L. Hays, must in Sept 16, 1864, not on muster out roll
David Hildebrand, must in Jan 28, 1865, not on muster-out roll
Perry Hipple, must in Feb 4, 1865, not on muster out roll
Joseph Jones, must in Aug 26, 1864, must out with company
Annesley N Keithler, must in Aug 31, 1864, disch by G O June 16, 1865
Edmond Kinch, must in Aug 26, 1864, wounded at Fort Fisher, N C, Jan 15, 1865, must out with company June 22, 1865
William M Kitts, must in Sept 5, 1864, died at Fortress Monroe, Va, Jan 8, 1865
Francis Lachlan, must in Aug 23, 1864, must out with company
Joshua Lodge, must. in Aug 29, 1864, must out with company
Joel B Lodge, must in Aug 19, 1864, must. out with company
John Lindsay, must in Aug 29, 1864 must out with company
Ebner Lewis, Jr, must in Sept 2, 1864 must out with company
A W Longnecker, must in Jan 30, 1865, not on muster out roll
Mitchell Martin, must in Aug 24, 1864, must out with company
George Mooney, must in Aug 29, 1864, must out with company
William A Mousely, must in Aug 31, 1864, must out with company
James Mills, must in Aug 19, 1864, must out with company
George Major, must in Aug 27, 1864, died at Philadelphia, Pa., Sept 11, 1864
Archer Myers, must in Feb 9, 1864, not on muster-out roll
Joseph Moyer, must in March 8, 1865, not on muster out roll
Daniel McClean, must in Aug 29, 1864, must out with company
John McGilty, must in Aug 29, 1864, must out with company
George McFadden, must in Jan 30, 1865, not on muster-out roll
John T McElroy, must in Jan 30, 1865, not on muster-out roll
Joseph Naylor, must in Sept 7, 1864, must out with company
Rufus W Noble, must in Aug 30, 1864, must out with company
Joseph H Ottey, must in Sept 3, 1864, must out with company
William Peoples, must in Aug 29, 1864, must out with company
Benjamin Pierce, must in Aug 31, 1864, must. out with company
William H Pool, must in Sept 2, 1864, must out with company
Samuel Playford, must in Aug 29, 1864, killed at Fort Fisher, N C., Jan 15, 1865
Emmor E Rudolph, must in Aug 29, 1864, disch by G O June 8, 1865
Robert Sample, must in Sept 2, 1864, must out with company
James Sample, must in Aug 24, 1864, wounded in action Feb 11, 1865, must. out with company
Joseph Smiley, must in Sept 2, 1864, must out with company
Theodore Smith, must in Aug 31, 1864, disch by G O June 25, 1865
Francis Stewart, must in Aug 29, 1864, must out with company
William H Swayne, must in Aug 29, 1864 wounded near Wilmington, N C., Oct 27, 1864, must out with company
Henry Stover, must in Aug 31, 1864
Lewis Smith, must in Aug 30, 1864
Myers Sergent, must in Jan 31 1865, not on muster-out roll
Frederick Sanders, must in Jan 30, 1865, not on muster out roll
Martin Sullivan, must in Oct 7, 1864, not on muster out roll
Evan L Thomas, must in Aug 29, 1864, absent, in hospital, at muster out
W M Vernon, must in Aug 24, 1864, died at Raleigh, N C., May 30, 1865
Thomas Waddecor, must in Aug 29, 1864, must. out with company
John C Wilhelm, must in Sept 2, 1864, pro to chaplain 45th Regt U S Colored Troops, May 8, 1865 must out Nov 4, 1865
George W Wolf, must in Aug 30, 1864, disch by G O June 3, 1865
Robert L West, must. in Aug 26, 1864, disch by G O July 25, 1865
James Wood, must in Aug 29, 1864, must out with company
Winfield S White, must in Sept 2, 1864, must out with company
Joseph Wyatt, must in Aug 19, 1864, must out with company
George F Washington, must in Aug 24, 1864, must out with company

Two Hundred and Thirteenth Regiment (One-Year's Men) —This regiment was recruited under the direction of the Union League Association of Philadelphia, and was organized March 2, 1865 Two days thereafter it was ordered to Annapolis, Md, where it was assigned to duty in guarding Camp Parole, and part of the regiment was ordered to Frederick City, to protect the lines of the Baltimore and Ohio Railroad In April it was concentrated at Washington, where it remained guarding the Northern defenses of the city until Nov 18, 1865, when it was mustered out of service

Daniel W Jeffries, asst surg, must in March 10, 1865, must out with regiment Nov 18, 1865

COMPANY G

James Carrick, 2d lieut., must in March 1, 1865, must out with company Nov 18, 1865
Jonathan Kershaw, 1st sergt., must in Feb 21, 1865, must out with company Nov 18, 1865
Abel Ford sergt., must in Feb 24, 1865, must out with company Nov 18, 1865
William Long, musician, must in Feb 18, 1865, must out with company Nov 18, 1865

Privates

Richard Alcutt, must. in Feb 17, 1865, must out with company Nov 18, 1865
John W Beggs, must in Feb 17, 1865, must out with company Nov 18, 1865
Michael Crouse, must in Feb. 21, 1865, must out with company Nov 18, 1865
Edward Deterer, must in Feb 16, 1865, must out with company Nov 18, 1865.
David Lynch, must in Feb 16, 1865, must out with company Nov 18, 1865
Franklin Mulford, must in Feb 18, 1865, absent, sick, at muster out
Daniel McBride, must in Feb 20, 1865, must out with company
Bernard McAtue, must in Feb 17, 1865, not on muster-out roll
William A Williams, must in Feb 24, 1865, must. out with company

Following are the names of residents of Delaware County who recruited in other regiments other than those already given

SURGEONS

Dr Joshua Owen, the first surgeon appointed in Pennsylvania, April 18, 1861, detailed to 54th Regt, must out Aug 1, 1861
Dr John M Allen, must in Oct 15, 1861, surg of 54th Pa, subsequently medical director of the Department of Western Virginia, and surgeon in chief of staff, his health failing he was honorably discharged Nov 4, 1864, after having been in hospital several months
Dr Charles Matthews, asst. surg., 54th Pa
Dr George B Hotchkin, surg of 44th Pa, must in Nov 12, 1862, and must out Sept 9, 1864
Dr S Chase King, asst-surg, 5th Cav, must in Dec 31, 1861, trans to 4th Cav March 20, 1865 resigned Aug 7, 1865
Dr Isaac T Coates, asst.-surg, 77th Regt, must in Sept 19, 1865, must. out Dec 6, 1865 Dr Coates had, previous to entering the army, been a surgeon in the navy
Dr Magee, asst-surg U S navy

Dr William H Forward, appointed asst -surg U S army June, 1861, pro to surg 6th U S Cav October, 1863, he was severely wounded in the breast, and after the ball was extracted little hopes were entertained of his recovery After a protracted illness he was enabled to rejoin his command, and is still in the army

Dr Passmore Middleton, of Darby, appointed surgeon in regular army, 1863

Dr Manley Emanuel, April, 1863, appointed asst -surg

43D PA REGT (1ST ARTILLERY, THREE YEARS)

Battery H, Martin Wolf, must in Sept 4, 1862, must out with battery June 27, 1865

64TH PA REGT (4TH CAVALRY)

Company C, H Hawkins

65TH PA REGT (5TH CALVARY, THREE YEARS)

Company C, John Booth, killed at Harrison's Landing, Va., Aug 1, 1862

Company D, Joshua E Dyer, 2d lieut, must in July 30, 1861, com 2d lieut Dec 3, 1864, not mustered captured at Stony Creek, Va., June 29, 1864, died in Confederate prison-pen in Florence, N C, Feb 16, 1865

Company H, Samuel Wallace, 1st lieut must in July 30, 1861, pro from sergt Co D to 2d lieut Jan 26, 1862, to 1st lieut January, 1863, killed near Williamsburg, Va, Jan 15, 1863

66TH PA REGT (THREE YEARS' SERVICE)

William Lewis, lieut col, must in Nov 1, 1862, disch April 29, 1864

Company C, Alisha Stetson, capt must in Jan 26, 1862, must out Oct 10, 1864

17TH PA REGT (6TH CAVALRY, RUSH'S LANCERS)

Charles L Leiper, col, must in 1861, pro to capt Co L, to maj Sept 1, 1864, to lieut -col Feb 1, 1865, to col March 20, 1865, to brig gen (brevet) March 13, 1865 trans to 2d Provisional Cavalry June 17, 1865

Company L, Lewis Miller, Jr, 1st lieut, must in Oct 5, 1861, pro to sergt Co L, captured May 10, 1864, pro from sergt June 22, 1864, com capt March 20, 1865, killed before being mustered as such

71ST PA VOL (CALIFORNIA, THREE YEARS' SERVICE)

Company A, John T Thatcher, sergt, must in May 21, 1861, disch on surg certif July, 1862

Company F, William Farrady, private, must in July 14, 1861, killed at Antietam Sept 17, 1862

Company I, George W Thatcher, corp, must in July 6, 1861, pro to corp Jan 1, 1864, must out with company July 2, 1864

72D PA REGT (THREE YEARS' SERVICE)

Company E, Phineas E Kelley, private, must in Aug 10, 1861, must out with company Aug 24, 1864

Company E Jesse A Gibson, private, must in Aug 10, 1861, died at Philadelphia March 10, 1864

77TH PA REGT (BAXTER'S ZOUAVES, THREE YEARS' SERVICE)

Company E, Joseph Groves, killed at Gettysburg

88TH PA REGT (THREE YEARS' SERVICE)

Company C, John McFeeters, sergt, must in Feb 29, 1864, pro to corp May 1, 1865, to sergt June 13, 1865, must out with company June 30, 1865

Company D, Robert Anderson, corp, must in Feb 26, 1864, wounded at Cold Harbor, Va, June 3, 1864, pro to corp May 1, 1865, in hospital at muster out

Company H, James M Thompson, sergt, must in Sept 11, 1861, pro from private, died Nov 16, 1862, of wounds received at Antietam, Md, Sept 17, 1862

89TH PA REGT (8TH CAVALRY, THREE YEARS' SERVICE)

Company L, Joseph Dyson, private, must in Sept 23, 1861, died near Washington in service Jan 25, 1862

95TH PA REGT (THREE YEARS' SERVICE)

Company A, John Macon, corp, must in Aug 21, 1861, killed at Williamsport, Va

Company F, Edward M Lyons, sergt, must in Sept 14, 1861, disch on surg certif Jan 30, 1863

Company F, Joshua M Wilson, private, must in Sept. 17, 1861, disch on surg certif Jan 6, 1864

Company H, J B W Aydelott, 1st lieut, must in Oct 1, 1861, pro to capt Sept 24, 1862, must out for promotion July 3, 1863

99TH PA REGT (THREE YEARS' SERVICE)

Company H, William H Groundsell, sergt, must in May 31, 1861, captured Sept 10, 1864, and died at Andersonville, Ga

113TH PA REGT (12TH CAVALRY, THREE YEARS' SERVICE)

Company H, Robert McCourt, 2d lieut, must in April 9, 1864, honorably discharged Dec 8, 1864

Company I, Albert G Bonsall, 2d lieut., must in April 21, 1862, disch Nov 5, 1862

118TH PA REGT (THREE YEARS' SERVICE)

Company F, Simeon Davis, died in service

Company E, Henry Lyons, must in Aug 20, 1862 absent, sick, at muster out

Company H, Edward T Brogan, died Dec 9, 1864

Company G, George Elliott, must in July 8, 1861, captured, killed at Salisbury, N C, while attempting to escape

161ST PA REGT (16TH CAVALRY, THREE YEARS' SERVICE)

Company I, Archer N Martin, 2d lieut., must in Sept 23, 1862, pro to 1st lieut. May 21, 1863, to capt June 4, 1863, brevet maj March 13, 1865, must out May 26, 1865, part of time on Gen Sheridan's staff

181ST PA REGT (20TH CAVALRY, THREE YEARS' SERVICE)

George W Eachus, q m, must in April 1, 1865, must out June 23, 1865

Company F, E E Bartleson, 2d lieut., must in April 1, 1865, pro to 1st lieut April 25, 1865, must out with 1st Provisional Cavalry, Co I, July 13, 1865

6TH NEW JERSEY VOLUNTEERS

Company I, James B Lilley, wounded in Wilderness May 5th, died May 15, 1864

48TH ILLINOIS VOLUNTEERS

George B Thatcher, adjutant, 1863

6TH CALIFORNIA REGIMENT

Henry M Black, col, graduate of West Point, 2d lieut 4th U S Infantry, detached to take command of regiment

UNITED STATES LIGHT ARTILLERY

John Lilley

As soon as the government of the United States announced that colored men would be recruited, a number of Delaware Countians entered the service The following is a partial list of those soldiers

THIRD U S REGIMENT

Company D (mustered 1863) —Edward Brown, Joseph Preston, William Summers, Samuel Brown

Company E (mustered 1863) —Samuel R Deny

Company F (mustered 1863) —William B Hall, George Anderson, Benjamin D Read

Company G (mustered 1863) —Perry Allen, George W Potts, Jr, Samuel Jones, Isaac Rothwell

SIXTH U S REGIMENT

Company A (mustered 1863) —Daniel Hopkins

Company D (mustered 1863) —Benjamin Harris

THIRTIETH U S REGIMENT

Company A (mustered 1865) —Corp Nesbert Hall

THIRTY SECOND U S REGIMENT

Company I (mustered 1864) —George Tospot

Company K (mustered 1864) —Reuben Tunway

FIFTY-FOURTH MASSACHUSETTS

Company C (mustered 1864) —John Ballard

ONE HUNDRED AND TWENTY SEVENTH U S REGIMENT

Company C (mustered 1864).—David Hall

Company F (mustered 1864) —Charles Johnson

REGULAR ARMY

Maj H Stacey, of Chester, appointed 1st lieut 12th U S Inf May 14, 1861, in 1862 took part in siege of Yorktown and battle of Gaines' Mill, Va., June 27, 1862, when he was wounded, was adjutant of 1st Battalion, 12th Inf, at second battle of Bull Run, Aug 30, 1862, and at Antietam, was in battle of Fredericksburg, Dec 11, 12, and 13, 1862, severely injured by an accident was detailed to light duty in Washington, D C, until February, 1863, and was on duty with company during draft riots in New York, in 1864 took part in Wilderness campaign, with his regiment. until June 8, 1864, when he was appointed acting aide-de camp to Brig Gen R B Ayres, commanding 2d Div, 5th Corps, pro capt Aug 17, 1864, was with Gen Ayres at explosion of mine in front of Petersburg, July 30, 1861, and took part at battle of Weldon Railroad, 18th, 19th, and 21st of August, 1864, appointed, September, 1864, commissary of musters of 2d Army Corps, Gen Hancock, commanding, and retained position until close of war and disbandment of corps, and while in the discharge of that office was in battle of Armstrong's Mills Hatcher's Run, and operations terminating in surrender of Gen Lee's army He was brevetted capt U S A for gallant services in the campaign, and brevetted lieut. col U S A for services at Weldon Railroad, since which time he has been in service at Washington, California, Nevada, and Arizona, where he was in several of the engagements with the Indians, in 1882-83 commandant at Plattsburg Barracks, N Y, at present on duty with his company

Delaware Countians in the Navy.—It is unnecessary under this head to refer to the remarkable race of naval captains,—the Porter family,—William David, David D, and Henry Ogden Porter, except to claim for our county these distinguished officers in our nation's history Even Farragut himself, when appointed, resided in Chester, and was educated here We have others, however, who "have done the State some service" in that branch of the national forces The following list of Delaware County's representatives in the navy during the civil war, I know, must be very incomplete, but that much is "at least secured"

Rear-Admiral Frederick Engle was born in Chester in 1799, and was fifteen years of age in 1814, when he entered the navy as a midshipman, sailing with Commodore Porter when he swept the seas of pirates, particularly the West Indies, and in many of the encounters with those enemies to mankind Midshipman Engle highly distinguished himself During the Mexican war, he had then become a captain, was in command of the steamship "Princeton," at that time the only steam vessel of war afloat in the navies of the world, and in the bombardment of Vera Cruz and the castle of San Juan d'Ulloa, March 22, 1847, a shot from his vessel made the first breach in the walls of the fortress During the war of the Crimea he was on duty in the Mediterranean and Black Seas, and visited the scene of battle In May, 1861, he was dispatched to the East India station to relieve Commodore Stribling, whose loyalty was suspected, of command of the flagship "Hartford" Engle journeyed overland from England to Hong Kong, where he took command of the vessel, which afterwards became famous in our national history under Farragut, and brought it safely home to Philadelphia, in December, 1861. He also brought with him the sloop "John Adams," twenty guns, and steam sloop "Dacota," six guns He was subsequently in command of the "Wabash" The forty-seven years of active service in the navy began to press heavily on him, and on Dec 11, 1861, he was placed on the retired list as captain On July 10, 1862, he was made commodore on the retired list, and in 1867 rear-admiral He died in Philadelphia, Feb 12, 1868, aged sixty-nine years

Commodore Pierce Crosby was born in Chester, Jan 16, 1824, entering the navy June 5, 1838, as midshipman, and in 1844 he became a passed midshipman, and in that rank served with distinction in the Mexican war He was promoted to lieutenant in 1853, and held that rank in 1861, when he was employed in Chesapeake Bay and in the Sounds of North Carolina, being complimented by Gen Butler for his conduct at the capture of Forts Hatteras and Clark In April, 1862, he was in command of the gunboat "Pinola," and during the night of the 23d that vessel and the "Itasca" led the fleet when Farragut determined to run by Forts Jackson and St Philip, and broke through the chain barrier stretched across the Mississippi at these forts He was present at the capture of New Orleans, April 25, 1862, and when Farragut and his fleet ran the batteries at Vicksburg, June 30th, and returned July 15th, in the same year, Crosby, in command of his vessel, shared in the glory of that daring act On Sept 13, 1862, he was promoted to captain, and during the year 1863-64 as fleet captain did effective service in command of the "Florida" and "Keystone State," North Atlantic Squadron Oct 3, 1864, he was promoted commodore, and in April, 1865, in command of the "Metacomet," he was active in the dangerous services preceding the capture of Mobile

Rear Admiral Thatcher in his dispatches of April 12th to the Navy Department, said, "I am much indebted to Commodore Crosby, who has been untiring in freeing the Blakeley River of torpedoes, having succeeded in removing one hundred and fifty,—a service demanding coolness, judgment, and perseverance" In the year 1872 he was in command of the frigate "Powhattan," and in 1877 was ordered to the navy-yard at League Island, retaining command there until 1881

Commander De Haven Manley, son of Charles D Manley, entered the United States navy Sept 25, 1856, and rose step by step until he reached the rank of commander, April 5, 1874

Capt Henry Clay Cochrane was appointed by President Lincoln second lieutenant in the Marine Corps, and passed the examination Aug 29, 1861, but his age precluded him from being commissioned as such immediately, hence he served as master's mate until March 10, 1863, when, having attained the required age, his appointment as lieutenant was confirmed by the United States Senate On Oct 20, 1865, he was promoted first lieutenant During the war he was in active service under Admirals Goldsborough, Dupont, Farragut, Porter, and Lee in the North and South

Atlantic, Gulf, and Mississippi Squadrons, and at the bombardment of Port Royal, S C, Nov 7, 1871, was a division officer on the gunboat "Pembina" In 1880, Lieutenant Cochrane was promoted captain, and is now on the flagship "Lancaster" on a three years' cruise in the Mediterranean and visiting European stations

THIRD ASSISTANT ENGINEERS U S NAVY

Robert S Taylor, com Aug 27, 1864, served on U S steamer "Primrose" dis July 5, 1865

Martin L Taylor, com Sept 6, 1864, served on U S steamer "Perriwinkle," monitor "Monadnock" and "Jacob Bell," dis Sept 22, 1865

William F Cutler, com 1864, served on U S steamer "Juniper"

Thomas H Thompson, com 1864, served on U S steamer "Verbena"

Thomas J Reaney, com Aug 22, 1864, served on U S steamer "Ironsides" and "Seneca," dis July 26, 1865

William G Vernon, com 1864 served on U S steamer "Wyandank" and "Commodore Read"

Thomas Lees, com Sept 8, 1864, served on U S steamer "Wyandank," "Dragon," and "Anticosta," dis. July 8, 1865

James Brannon, com 1864

Samuel Anderson, com 1864, assistant paymaster U S steamer "Jacob Bell"

William Smead, engineer

William Coverdill, engineer

John P Gartside, com 1864, engineer department, U S steamer "Ironsides"

Henry Pedlow, com 1864, engineer department, U S steamer "Ironsides"

J O Wilson, com 1864, engineer department

John Wolf, com 1864, engineer department

James Stevenson, carpenter, frigate "Wabash"

Samuel Oglesby, com April 27, 1864, served on "New Hampshire," and frigate "Wabash," took part in engagement at Fort Fisher, which resulted in its capture, trans to gunboat "Eutaw," and disch May 15, 1865

William Gelston, enl 1864

Thomas Gillespie Cochrane, captain's clerk, U S steamer "Alabama"

Herman Wolf, enl 1864, engineer's department

Robert C Rennio, quartermaster "Ironsides"

James Christie, quartermaster "Ironsides"

Edmund Pennell, messenger

James Phillips, yeoman

Drafts were made in several of the townships in Delaware County, and the last time the wheel was put in motion was April 7, 1865 The men who were drafted in Upper and Lower Chichester responded, and the greater part of them held for service On April 13th, Secretary Stanton ordered all enlistments and drafting to be discontinued in the United States, hence on Monday, April 25th, the drafted men in Delaware County were ordered to return to their homes

The war had terminated, and the North was in a tumult of exultation over the success that had at last crowned its efforts, the like of which history furnished no parallel Hence it was to be expected that the attention of the nation should be centred at noon of April 14, 1865, on those shattered, fire-marked ruins in Charleston harbor, where Maj Gen Anderson—in the presence of the survivors of his garrison, who on that day four years before had evacuated Fort Sumter—would with imposing ceremonies again unfurl over the broken masses of masonry the old flag, which had been hauled down without dishonor In Chester, on the afternoon of that day, the Invalid Corps and the soldiers in the United States hospital (now Crozer Theological Seminary), under command of Lieut Campion, and headed by the Union Brass Band, marched through the streets of the ancient borough, cheering and being cheered From the town hall, over factories, workshops, stores, and dwellings, the American flag was displayed, while almost every building was draped with the national colors Early in the evening the populace assembled in Market Square, where addresses were made by John M Broomall and Rev Messrs George and Meredith, at the conclusion of which Professor Jackson gave a beautiful exhibition of fire-works At nine o'clock a general illumination of the town took place, and the streets were crowded with people, on foot and in carriages, moving from point to point to view the display

While the inhabitants of many of the surrounding townships in Delaware County had come to Chester to rejoice over the long-hoped-for and glorious conclusion of the civil war, at half-past nine o'clock that night, at Ford's Theatre, in Washington, during a pause in the play of "Our American Cousin," the report of a pistol was heard, and a deed had been wrought which, in a few short hours, should change the national rejoicing into public mourning and misgivings Abraham Lincoln had been assassinated

The telegraphic operator in the town heard the alarming intelligence as it flashed over the wires to the press of the great cities, but the injunction of silence (of war time) kept him mute, and it was not until six o'clock the following morning (Saturday) that the news of the dreadful deed reached Chester All business ceased, the industrial establishments suspended operation, and no business place was opened save that of the news agents, which was filled with people, jostling each other in their anxiety to secure the morning papers giving the particulars of the tragedy By eight o'clock the death of the President was confirmed, and the proprietors of dry-goods stores were compelled to open their places of business that the people might replace the tricolored hanging of the preceding day with sombre black. By ten o'clock all the buildings were draped in mourning The like scene was enacted in every town and village in the county, for the people were stricken with grief for the great dead and with apprehension for the future On Wednesday, when the funeral of the murdered President was in progress at Washington, all business was suspended and every mill in the county closed on that day, while at the same hour in all the sanctuaries services were held, and the bells of the churches were tolled in every steeple At Chester the revenue cutter "William H Seward," lying off the town, fired minute-guns At Media the court room was crowded, and religious services were held therein The deep feeling of uncertainty and grief prevailing at that time will never be forgotten by those who were of sufficient age to recall that period in our history

After the surrender of the Confederate armies the troops were mustered out, and the soldiers of Delaware County returned to their homes to resume the peaceful routine of life This period had been looked forward to with apprehension, but the result showed one of the most remarkable features of that remarkable period,—the quiet absorption of a great army into the ranks of the people with hardly a ripple in the social realm

List of West Point Graduates —Since the establishment of West Point the following persons appointed from Delaware County have graduated from that institution

Francis Lee, Chester, admitted Sept 2, 1818, graduated second lieutenant, Twentieth Infantry, July 1, 1822

William H Price, Chester, admitted July 1, 1830, brevet second lieutenant, First Infantry, July, 1834

Henry M Black, graduated 1847, attached to Fourth Infantry, with rank of brevet second lieutenant

David Porter Heap, Chester, admitted July 1, 1860, first lieutenant, Corps of Engineers, June 13, 1864

Officers of United States Navy.—Delaware County has furnished a number of officers to the United States naval service besides those already mentioned, and the noted Porter family, to whom reference will be made elsewhere On Oct 28, 1844, Lieut Ferdinand Piper, United States navy, a native of Chester, was lost in the bay of Pensacola He had left the ship "Falmouth" that morning in a cutter, designing to bring supplies to the vessel When about midway to the landing a sudden flaw of wind struck the boat, and before sail could be shortened she was overturned All the men were encouraged by the good conduct and presence of mind of Lieut Piper, and were clinging to the overturned boat, when a heavy sea washed Piper, Professor William S Fox, and six of the seamen away and they were lost The schooner "Otter" rescued the survivors that evening

Midshipman James Anderson, son of Dr Samuel Anderson, a promising officer of the navy, died in 1840 while on a visit to his father, then residing at Rockdale

Lieut Samuel Edwards, United States Navy, who had charge of the battery which made the first breach in the walls at Vera Cruz in the Mexican war, died March 23, 1861 He was a nephew of Hon Samuel Edwards, of Chester, and his parents having died while he was a child he was reared by his uncle, who took just pride in the young man's rapid promotion He died just at the eve of the war of 1861

Edward Fayssoux Leiper, son of John C Leiper, appointed to the naval school at Annapolis since the war, is the only person from Delaware County who has graduated there since Commander Manley, twenty years ago He is now in temporary command of the "Arago" on South Atlantic coast survey service

---

CHAPTER XVIII

CRIMES AND PUNISHMENTS

WE have little or no information as to the criminal code which maintained among the early Swedish and Dutch settlers on the Delaware[1] The fragmentary

---

[1] The first trial recorded on the Delaware was the following "In the year 1645, November 25th, between ten and eleven o'clock, one Swen Wass, gunner, set Fort Gottenburg on fire In a short time all was lamentably burnt down, and not the least thing saved excepting the dairy The people escaped naked and destitute The winter immediately set in, bitterly cold, the river and all the creeks froze up, and nobody was able to get near us (because New Gottenburg is surrounded by water) The sharpness of the winter lasted until the middle of March, so that if some rye and corn had not been unthreshed I, myself, and all the people with me on the island would have starved to death But God maintained us with small quantities of provisions until the new harvest. By the sad accident the loss of the company, testified by the annexed roll, is four thousand *riksdaler* The above mentioned incendiary, Swen Wass, I have caused to be brought to court, and to be tried and sentenced, so I have sent him home in irons, with the vessel, accompanied by the whole record concerning him, submissively committing and referring the execution of the verdict to the pleasure of Her Royal Majesty and Right Honorable Company "—*Report of Governor Printz for* 1647, *Penna. Magazine of History*, vol vii p 273

Under the Dutch, the first instance of a criminal proceeding occurs in a letter from Alrichs, dated at New Amstel (New Castle), May 14, 1659, to Stuyvesant. He says, "In regard to the four men servants of Cornelis Herperts de Jager, who established in the county near here a brick kiln, and employed four persons at it, one of them, Peter —— by name, has come from Fort Orange as a brick-maker, and was married to a woman who came from Amsterdam, and with him owed a large sum to the city He has committed wicked crimes of theft of small cattle, as sheep, also of the city's weapons from the former ensign of the citizens, and has stolen several other things, for which he was publicly flogged and banished this town or place, but allowed to do his work outside in the country to earn his living and get out of his debts This one has been the leader, and he stirred up the others under this or that pretext They have together taken away four good muskets and other goods belonging to their master, and thus run away to the Manhatans" Alrichs desires Stuyvesant to arrest and return the men by "the first vessel" to New Amstel (Penna Archives, local series, vol vii p 561) William Beekman, April 28, 1660, writes to Stuyvesant that at "the last court day" Oele Stille and he had a difficulty in regard to a fine imposed on the Swedish priest. On the 19th of August, 1659, and on the 7th of April, 1660, court was held at Christiana, at which Peter Mayer, who was charged with an assault and battery, did not appear, was fined for his contempt ten guilders (*Ib*, 635) In 1661 there was a prison at Christiana (*Ib.*, 655)

Certain it is that the first record we have of a capital conviction and execution on the Delaware is related in a letter from William Beekman to Stuyvesant, dated Oct 24, 1662 (Penna Archives, second series, vol vii p 691) It appears from this and other authorities that Alexander D Hinojassa (who held that part of the river from New Castle to Cape Henlopen in opposition to the authority of Governor Stuyvesant, claiming that he had been appointed Governor over that territory to look after the company's interest, under the will of Jacob Alrichs) ordered the prisoner to be tried The circumstances are briefly these A vessel was wrecked on the coast, and a Turk on her succeeded in gaining the land, where he was taken by the Indians, who sold him to Peter Alricks, a resident of New Castle, who in turn sold him to an English planter in Maryland The Turk, with several other servants, made his escape to the Delaware, where he was pursued He was subsequently captured, and while being taken up the river in a boat, at Bombay Hook attempted and succeeded in making his escape In doing so he wounded two of the men seriously and the third slightly He was, however, again captured, taken to New Castle, and thrown into prison D'Hinojassa refused to deliver the man to his English master, who claimed him but ordered him to be tried before Van Sweeringham, who sat as judge The Turk was convicted of resisting and wounding his captors, and was sentenced to be hung On Sunday, Oct 19, 1662, the man was executed at Lewistown, his head afterwards "cut off and placed on a post or stake in the Horekill" (Penna. Archives, vol vii p 728, Duke

records which have been preserved incidentally in correspondence and official reports do not enlighten us as to the manner of trial or the authority exercised by those holding the courts at that early day. Hence the most important criminal case which presents itself in our annals, if the proceedings can be designated a trial, when the instructions given by Governor Lovelace and Council are considered, wherein the sentence is actually pronounced on the prisoner nearly two months before he was arraigned, is that of the "Long Finn." The circumstances of the case are briefly these. It was near the middle of the year 1669 that an adventurer, one Marcus Jacobson, *alias* John Brinckson, etc, but better known to the then inhabitants of the Delaware as the "Long Finn," because of his lofty stature, had succeeded in imposing himself on the Swedes as the son of Konnigsmark, a noted general of Sweden. Jacobson, it was alleged, was inciting the settlers of that nationality to rebellion against the English authority, with the design of re-establishing the Swedish power in the province. With him was associated a wealthy Finn, Henry Coleman, while Rev. Lawrence Lock, the former Swedish chaplain, was said to have "played the Trumpeter to the disorder," and Mrs Pappegoya, the daughter of Governor Printz, was charged with intermeddling "in so unworthy a design." Governor Lovelace, Aug 2, 1669, issued an order for the arrest of the Long Finn and his fellow-conspirators, accompanying the order with instructions as to the manner in which the trial should be conducted. In accordance therewith Capt Carry caused the arrest of the Long Finn, who was thrown into the fort at New Castle, in irons (in those days the irons were riveted on the limbs of a prisoner, and at West Chester, among the records in the commissioners' office, in the next century, are bills paid to blacksmiths for removing the fetters from culprits), while Henry Coleman, learning of his intended apprehension, abandoned his property, fled to the Indians, with whom he seemed to have had great influence, and is never more heard of. Dominie Lock and Mrs Pappegoya gave security for their appearance to answer the charges against them when required. The commissioners appointed by the Governor to try the case sat at New Castle, Dec 6, 1669, and, as was to be expected, the jury returned a verdict of guilty against Jacobson, who was thereupon sentenced in accordance with the punishment prescribed by Council, the 18th of October previous, which was, "that the Long Finn deserves to die for the same, yet in regard that many others concerned with him in that insurrection might be involved in the same Premunire, if the rigor of the law should be extended, and amongst them divers simple and ignorant people, it is thought fit and ordered that the said Long Finn shall be publicly and severely whipped and stigmatized or branded in the face with the letter R, with an inscription written in great letter and put upon his breast, that he receive that punishment for attempted rebellion, after which he be secured until he can be sent and sold to the Barbadoes, or some other of those remote plantations." On Jan 25, 1670, the Long Finn was placed on board the ship "Fort Albany," to be transported and sold to the Barbadoes, after which date nothing further respecting him is now known. His accomplices were sentenced to forfeit to the king one-half of their goods and chattels, while a small fine was imposed upon those of lesser note who had taken part in the rebellion. The case will always be an interesting one to the annalist, for therein is the first recorded trial under English procedure on the Delaware, in which a prisoner was formally indicted, arraigned, and a jury of twelve men impaneled, subject to challenge on the part of the prisoner, who are charged to render a verdict in accordance with the evidence.

of York's Book of Laws, p 459) The following account of the seditious false Konigsmark in New Sweden was translated by Professor G B Keen (the original manuscript, date 1683, is preserved in the Royal Library at Stockholm), and published in *Penn Mag of History*, vol vii p 219 "In Provost Acrelius's 'Beskrifning om de Swenska Forsamlingars Tilstand uti Nya Swerige,' p 1 3, is introduced what Pastor Rudman noted in the Wicaco Church book about the rioter among the Swedes, who called himself Konigsmark. These are the particulars which I received from the oldest Swedes. This impostor was by birth a Swede, but, for some crime committed by him in England, he was sent to Maryland, to serve there as a slave for a number of years. He ran away from there, however, and came to the Swedes in New Sweden, who were then subject to the English government. Here he made the Swedes believe he was descended from a great and highly-honorable family in Sweden, that his name was Konigsmark, that a Swedish fleet of war ships lay outside of the bay, and were, as soon as they entered, to take the land again from the English, and that he was sent to encourage the Swedes who lived here to shake off the foreign yoke, and to fall upon and slay the English as soon as they had heard that the Swedish fleet had arrived. A great many of the Swedes permitted themselves to be persuaded by this. They concealed the pretended Konigsmark for a long time, so that no one else knew anything of him, supplying him with the best meat and drink they had, by which means he fared very well. Moreover, they went to Philadelphia* and bought powder, balls, shot, lead, etc., to be ready at the first signal. Hereupon he caused the Swedes to be summoned to a supper, and after they had been drinking somewhat exhorted them to free themselves from the yoke, reminding them what they suffered from the English, and how the latter, partly by fraud and partly by force, had taken from them one large piece of land after another, and finally asked them whether they held allegiance to the king of Sweden or to the king of England. A part immediately declared themselves for the king of Sweden, but one of the most honorable of the Swedes, Peter Kock by name, said that as the country was English, and had been surrendered by the king of Sweden to the crown of England, he deemed it just to hold with the king of England. Thereupon Kock ran out and closed the door again, laying himself against it, that the so-called Konigsmark might not slip out, and called for help to make him prisoner. The impostor labored with all his might to open the door. Kock endeavored to prevent him by hurting him in the hand with a knife. Notwithstanding, he effected his escape, wherefore Kock immediately hastened to give information to the English, who then made search for him, and in a short time took him prisoner. The above named Peter Kock then said to him, 'You rascal, tell me what is your name, for we can see well enough that you are no honorable person?' The impostor then answered that his true name was Marcus Jacobson. He proved, besides, to be so ignorant that he could neither read nor write. Thereupon he was branded and sent to Barbadoes, where he was sold as a slave. The Swedes who permitted themselves to be imposed upon by him were punished by the confiscation of half their property, land, cattle, goods, clothes, etc"

* This, of course, is a mistake. In 1669 Philadelphia had not been located

The penal laws of the early English settlers partook in a large degree, so far as the punishment prescribed for their infraction was concerned, of the fierceness which characterized the criminal code of the mother-country at that period, while many of the legislative enactments were intended to correct, by severe penalties, those matters which are now regarded as subjects purely of personal concern and in no wise coming under public police regulation The rigor of the law was then so extended that servants tipling at inns or houses of public entertainment were punished by being put in the stocks for at least an hour, unruly children and servants, on complaint of their parents or masters, if the offender was sixteen years old, were whipped not exceeding ten stripes, while a servant who was convicted of assaulting his master, dame, or overseer, was to receive corporal punishment, in the discretion of the court, "saving life and member" The denial of God or his attributes was punishable with death, as was also the kidnapping of any person within the province He that bore false witness against his neighbor in a capital case was to be put to death, as was also the child that smote his natural parent The publisher of false news from the mother-country was subject to fines, and for the third offense was whipped not exceeding forty lashes No marriage could be solemnized unless both parties swore that they were single and legally qualified to enter into that relationship, while, in case of perjury, the party offending was ordered to "be bored through the tongue with a red-hot iron," besides incurring the penalties for adultery, which inflicted whipping, as well as fine and imprisonment Fornication between single persons was punishable by enforced marriage, or whipping, in the discretion of the court Laborers and servants were compelled to work the whole day, and "Sundays are not to be prophaned by Travellers, Laborers, or Vicious Persons"

The Duke of York's laws, however, announced full freedom of religious opinion to all Christian sects, as follows

"No congregation shall be disturbed in their private meetings in the time of prayer, preaching, or other divine services, nor shall any person be molested, fined, or imprisoned for differing in judgment in matters of religion who profess Christianity."

After Penn acquired the title to the province of Pennsylvania, and the great body of laws was enacted at the Assembly convened at Chester, Dec 4, 1682, much of the severity of the criminal code was done away with Profanity was made punishable by fine or five days' imprisonment, adultery subjected the party convicted to public whipping and one year's imprisonment, while for a second offense the term of incarceration was for life. Under the act of 1705 adultery was punished by whipping with twenty-one lashes and imprisonment for one year, or a fine of fifty pounds, a second conviction increased the imprisonment to seven years, and on the third conviction, in addition to the foregoing penalty, the culprit was directed to be branded on the forehead with the letter "A" For the crime of rape the convict forfeited half his estate to the party aggrieved, was publicly whipped, and underwent one year's imprisonment, while for the second offense he was incarcerated for life Drunkenness was punished by a fine, "or five days in the house of correction at hard labor, and being fed only with bread and water" A conviction of arson made the criminal liable to pay double damages, undergo incarceration for one year, and be subjected to such corporal punishment as the court thought proper to impose Bigamy made the party convicted liable to imprisonment for life, while burglary was punished by imprisonment at hard labor for three months, the prisoner was compelled to make fourfold satisfaction, and failing to do so, was imprisoned for seven years The child who should assault his parent was committed to the house of correction at hard labor during the pleasure of the parent Forgery was punished by three months' detention at hard labor If the crime was forging the seal of any county, the prisoner should undergo twelve months' imprisonment and be fined, while, if the offense was forging the seal of this province, he should suffer seven years' imprisonment and be fined at the discretion of the Governor and Provincial Council The theft of hogs or other cattle was punished, for the second offense, by a fine threefold the value of the articles taken and imprisonment for six months, while for a third offense the convict should be whipped with twenty-nine lashes and banished never to return again Persons convicted of premeditated murder, "according to the law of God, suffer death" This punishment did not work an entire forfeiture of his estate, but one-half of his possessions was "to be disposed of as the Governor shall see meet" The robbery of orchards, or the theft of any linen, woolen, or other articles left without doors, rendered the party convicted of any of these offenses liable to pay threefold the costs of the articles taken, or to be publicly whipped by the constable not exceeding twenty-one stripes, while the forcible robbery from any person of money or other articles was punishable by restoring fourfold the value of the goods stolen and being whipped not exceeding twenty-one stripes

The minor regulation interdicted all persons from taking part in stage plays, revels, masques, or offering of prizes, under a penalty of five shillings or ten days imprisonment, while card-playing, dicing, lottery, and evil sports and games were punishable by a like fine, or five days' detention in the workhouse at hard labor The drinking of healths was punishable by a fine of five shillings or five days' imprisonment, while railers and scolders were incarcerated at hard labor for three days, which, at the next General Assembly, was made punishable by gagging, and in that condition to stand one hour in a public place Subsequently horse-racing, shooting-matches, and such idle sports were interdicted, and if the offenders chanced to be servants, negro or Indian slaves, they were whipped with fifteen lashes and imprisoned six days, while for the second offense the whipping was increased to twenty-one lashes and the imprisonment to ten days.

The humane penal laws prepared by Penn and enacted at his suggestion, were summarily repealed by the act of May 31, 1718. William Bradford, who had been attorney-general and a judge of the Supreme Court of Pennsylvania, and died while discharging the office of Attorney-General of the United States, in an essay on the criminal law of this commonwealth, declares that the privilege which the act just alluded to conferred on Friends—that of testifying in court of justice on their solemn affirmations, instead of taking a corporal oath—was the inducement for adopting, in 1718, the sanguinary rigor of the English law, in violation of the humane policy which had previously influenced the Legislature of Pennsylvania on the subject of crimes and punishments. By the act mentioned high treason, petty treason, counterfeiting the currency, murder, robbery, burglary, rape, sodomy, manslaughter, witchcraft, and conjuration were punishable by death. Receiving stolen goods or concealing robbers, and murder where benefiting of clergy was craved, was punished by branding on the fleshy part of the left thumb the letter T for the first crime, and M for the latter, which branding was ordered to be done in open court by the jailer. By the act of Feb. 21, 1767, knowingly receiving stolen horses subjected the party convicted thereof to public whipping, not exceeding thirty-nine lashes, standing in the pillory one hour, and to be imprisoned at hard labor not exceeding three years, while by the same act counterfeiting gold and silver coins was punished by standing in the pillory one hour, to have both ears cut off and nailed to the pillory, to be publicly whipped not exceeding twenty-one lashes, and to forfeit a hundred pounds, which was divided equally between the government and the informer. The severity of the punishment, it seems, did not lessen the number of horses stolen. Therefore, March 10, 1780, the Legislature increased the penalty, providing that in the case of a second conviction, in addition to the foregoing punishment, the culprit should be branded on the forehead, "in a plain and visible manner, with the letters H T." That hardly over a century ago men were branded as a punishment we know, for at the special court for the trial of negroes, held at Chester, March 3, 1770, before William Parker and Richard Riley, justices, Negro Martin, the slave of Thomas Martin, was convicted of an attempted rape, and sentenced "to be whipped with thirty-nine lashes, well laid on his Bare Back, at the common whipping-post, between the Hours of one and three this afternoon, and be branded with the letter R on his forehead, and be exported out of this Province by his master within six months, never to return unto the same upon pain of death, and to be kept in Prison till exportation at his master's charge, and to pay the costs of Prosecution." And on Jan. 4, 1772, in the case of Negro Dick, the slave of mulatto Dinah, otherwise Dinah Jones, tried at a like special court, before John Morton and William Parker, Esqs., the defendant was convicted of a similar crime, and sentenced to a like punishment. On Sept. 15, 1786, the act was passed by the General Assembly which swept away many of the harsh features of our criminal code, substituting therefor in many cases a milder form of punishment.

In the early times public acknowledgment by the party accused of the wrong he had done, in many cases seemed to fill the measure of atonement demanded by the judges who dispensed justice among the first settlers of our county. Hence we find that at the court held at Chester, the 3d day of first week, Tenth month, 1689, Allen Robinett, Sr., who was arraigned "for writing scandalous and abusive papers against John Bristow, one of ye King's Justices and representatives in Council of ye People of this county, contrary to ye 29 law of this Province," having pleaded guilty, was sentenced that "he shall here in Publick acknowledge in particular his fault and crimes for which he stands Indicted, and pay all county charges," while at the same court Nicholas White and William Thomas, who were indicted for "Speaking words tending to sedition and breach of Peace, and persuading people (contrary to an order of court) not to pay ye Publicke Levies of this County, when thereunto lawfully required," who acknowledged the fact and prayed the mercy of "ye King and government," were acquitted, paying their fees. On the 14th day of the First month, 1693, Thomas Poe and Sarah Butler, convicted of fornication, were sentenced "to stand at the common whipping-post and for the offence to declare their offence to the People and also to pay a fine of twenty shillings and court charges." And at the same court John Clowes and Eleanor, then his wife, were also convicted of the like offense. They were sentenced to pay a fine of fifty shillings, and "Eleanor shall stand at the common whipping-post for one-quarter of an hour, with a paper upon her breast that I stand here for an example to all others for committing that most wicked and notorious sin of fornication." As late as February court, 1753, Owen Oberlacker, *alias* John Bradley, convicted "of speaking seditious words," was sentenced to stand in the pillory one hour, with the inscription, "I stand here for speaking seditious words against the best of Kings, wrote in a large hand, to be affixed to his back." Oberlacker was also subjected to the punishment of twenty-one lashes upon his bare back, well laid on.

This whipping of convicts, as is seen by the brief summary of the provincial criminal laws, heretofore given, was a favorite form of punishment in the early days, and continued to be inflicted until after the Revolutionary struggle had ended. One of the first cases I have found when this penalty was imposed is at the court held at Chester, 3d day, Twelfth month, 1684, when the record states that "John Martin being convicted of stealing money out of ye house of William Brown, was ordered twelve stripes on his bare back, well laid on, at the common whipping-post at Chichester, the 4th inst, between the ten and eleven hour in the morning" Samuel Jury, Aug. 29, 1704, for being the father of an illegitimate child, was sentenced "to be whipt with twenty-one lashes on his bare back, well laid on, and pay for the maintaining of said child as the law directs" This is the only instance, so far as I have learned, of a man being subjected to corporal punishment for this offense May 25, 1708, "Grace Phillips was sentenced to be whipt with twenty-one lashes, well laid on, at the common whipping-post in Chester" The last time when I find records of this corporal punishment being imposed is at the November court, 1788, when John Tully, convicted of horse-stealing, was sentenced to be whipped The case will be referred to hereafter

The punishment by whipping, to our modern ideas, was most cruel, and that it was extremely painful we have the authority of the editor of the *London Medical Times*, who a few years ago witnessed the flogging of a wife-beater at Newgate The degradation of the punishment and the effect the shame had upon persons of sensitive natures is well shown in a case recorded by Watson, wherein a negro, in 1743, who was brought to the whipping-post in Philadelphia to be scourged, took a knife from his pocket, and in the presence of the crowd, cut his throat, dying immediately of the self-inflicted injury

May 10, 1698, the Assembly passed a supplemental law respecting "robbing and stealing," whereby for the theft of any article amounting to five shillings or upwards, in addition to fourfold restoration of the value and public whipping, the punishment was increased, the culprit being "ordered by the court, upon penalty of banishment, to wear such a badge or mark of his or her thievery upon the outside of his or her outer garment in open view, upon the outer part of the Left Arme betwixt Elbow & Shoulder att all times when ever hee or shee shall travel or be seen from his or her habitation or plantation where hee or shee shall live on every day from Sun rising unto Sun setting, for the space of six months, which mark or badge of his or her thieving shall be thus, with a Roman T, not less than foure inches in length each way, and an inch in breadth, of a different colour from his or her said out garment either Red, Blew, or Yellow, as the Justices of the said court shall direct" This law, or rather the similar one of 1700, remained in force until superseded by the act of Feb 24, 1721 Under its provisions we find that at the court held at Chester, Third month 26, 1702, Benjamin Patterson being convicted of breaking into the house of Joseph Baker, of Upper Providence, and stealing ten pieces of eights, "the court gave judgment for two pounds eight shillings, to be paid to Joseph Baker, with lawful fees and" (Patterson) "to be whipt with eleven lashes on his bare back and wear a T according to law of yellow colour" Patterson was also sentenced to serve Joseph Baker, his master, one and a half years in consideration of the damages he had sustained. The graphic picture which Hawthorne, in the "Scarlet Letter," has drawn of Hester Prynne, who "on the breast of her gown, in fine red cloth, surrounded with an elaborate embroidery and fastastic flourishes of gold thread, appeared the letter A," will recur to almost every reader Although the persons who wore the insignia of their shame among their fellows in this county, in colonial days, may not have as romantic a story as that the novelist has elaborated, doubtless they felt keenly the degradation the hated letter entailed upon them It is unnecessary to refer to all the cases in which this punishment was imposed Sufficient is it to my purpose to state that the last instance which I find of this penalty being inflicted was at the court held Aug 28, 1716, when John Eburnethy, convicted on two indictments, was sentenced to receive twenty-one lashes on each judgment and to wear a Roman T, of a blue color, not less than four inches each way and one inch broad, for six months, and also to wear a Roman T, of a red color, of the like size, for six months

Standing in the pillory was one of the ordinary punishments of our colonial days The first case in which this penalty was imposed that I have found was at the court held at Chester the third day of the first week, 1689, when Thomas Lasy, an indentured servant of Richard Few, who was convicted on his own confession of counterfeiting pieces of eights, "and a bartering and exposing ye same for goods and other merchandize," was sentenced to stand "at ye Public Place of Correction att ye Town of Chester two Several Court days three hours each day with a Paper of his Crimes written in Capital letters afixed upon his Brest, and that he remaine in ye Sherifes Custody until he gives good Security to perform this Judgment and pay his fine" That this sentence was carried out we know, for John Simcock informed the next court that Robert Wade was passing the place where Thomas Lasy was "Suffering ye last Courts sentance," and that Wade said aloud, "What law has he broken? or what King's law hath he Broken?" The court, very sensibly, seems to have taken no notice of Wade's remarks, although in those days the dignity of the bench was sternly maintained, as the following instances disclose Abraham Buffinjall, at the court held the 3d day of Fourth month, 1685, being "lawfully convicted for abusing and menacing the magestracy of this county was ordered Twenty-one lashes at the public whipping-post on his bear back well laid on and fourteen days imprisonment at hard labour in the House of Correction," and at the court held at Chester the "3d day of 1st week of ye 8th month, 1687," Jeremy Collett, "for his Insolency and abuse of ye

Court and asserting laws which he could not Produce being thereunto required by the Court" was ordered to find security for his appearance at next court and to be of good behavior, "Butt upon refusal was Committed to ye Sherifes Custody" At the following court he was fined five pounds, which fine he petitioned might be remitted, and "the Court considering his Petition and that he putts himself upon ye King and Govern't milligates his former fine and admitts him to a fine of ten shillings to be levied upon his goods, &c, and all manner of Court charges to Sherife & Clerks, &c" Standing in the pillory for stealing or receiving stolen horses after the act of 1767 meant something more than merely being exposed to the gaze of the idle populace John Bartiff, at Chester, Aug 9, 1780, was found guilty of horse-stealing, and was sentenced by the court to receive "twenty-nine lashes on his bare back well laid on, to have both his ears cutt off and nailed to the pillory, to pay all costs of prosecution, to be imprisoned six months and to stand committed until this sentence be complied with" On Nov 28, 1780, Christian Gotlibb, convicted of the like offense of an aggravated nature, was sentenced "to pay a fine of one thousand pounds, to restore the stolen property or the value thereof, to stand one hour in the Pillory to-morrow morning between the hours of eight and ten o'clock, to be whipped on his bare back with twenty-nine lashes well laid on, to have his ears cut off and nailed to the Pillory, to pay all costs of prosecution and to be imprisoned six months and to stand committed after till fine and fee is paid"

It is rather a peculiar circumstance in our county annals, then including Chester County, that after the passage of the act of Sept 15, 1786, which specifically abolished the punishment of the pillory, whipping, branding, cutting off the ears of criminals and nailing them to the pillory for certain crimes, that on Nov 27, 1788, John Tully, who was convicted of horse-stealing, was sentenced "to stand one hour in the pillory between the hours of nine and twelve o'clock to-morrow morning, to be whipped with thirty-nine lashes on his bare back, well laid on, to have both ears cut off and nailed to the pillory and to be imprisoned six months," besides the payment of a fine and the costs

From the time of the promulgation of the "Duke of York's Book of Laws," in 1676, until the Constitution of 1790 gave power to the judges of the several counties to hold Courts of Oyer and Terminer, all cases of great crimes were under the duke tried by the Court of Assizes, under Penn, by the Provincial Council, until the law of March 10, 1685, made it the duty of the judges of the Provincial Supreme Court to hear and determine "heinous and enormous crimes in the respective county courts where the said crimes were committed" Although this act was repealed in 1690, the same rule prevailed until changed by the second Constitution of the State The first sitting of the Supreme Court in a criminal case in Chester which I find was on Oct 3, 1705 The suit is an interesting one, hence I give the proceedings somewhat at large

"Whereas James Gibbons, of the county of Chester, yeoman, being bound over to this court (county court held May 28, 1705) to answer such matters and things as on the Queen's behalf shall be laid to his charge by John Hoskins, High Sheriff of the said county, appeared, whereupon the Attorney-General gave the court to understand that the crime laid to the charge of the said Gibbons amounts to Burgulary, and for the court further satisfaction then he produceth the Sheriffs examination which being read as followeth

"Chester the 30th day of April 1704 the deposition of John Hoskins, High Sheriff of the County of Chester, aged about twenty seven years, being solemnly attested in the presence of God saith that last night about one o'clock James Gibbons, of the county, aforesaid, came with another person with him to this deponent unknown, and did break open the lock of his stable door and took out a sorril horse with a bald face which this deponent as Sheriff had taken on execution and when this deponent ran to him he with the other person with him made his escape thro' the lot and broke down the pails, whereupon this deponent seized on the horse with a halter on his head, which he supposes the said Gibbons brought with him, and also found a club in the stable, he presumes they brought with them and further saith not

"The circumstances of the fact being considered it is ordered that the said James Gibbons shall be and is hereby by the Justices committed into the jail of this County of Chester there to remain till he shall be delivered by due course of law"

The case being called at the Supreme Provincial Court, Oct 3, 1705, "the Sheriff was ordered to set the prisoner at the bar, which being done the indictment was read" (The indictment had been found by the grand jury at the county court) "David Lloyd moved that he may be admitted to speak of matters of Law unto the indictment before the prisoner plead, which is granted unto him, whereupon he desire it may be inspected by this Court whether or no the Justices session had power by their commission at that time of taking that indictment to enquire of that burgulary in the indictment mentioned" The court concluded to hold the matter under advisement until the afternoon session, when they decided that the justices had no jurisdiction, and on motion of David Lloyd the defendant was admitted to bail Gibbons appears, from the silence of the record, never to have been called on further to answer the charge

The first trial for homicide in this county, so far as has been ascertained, was that of Hugh Pugh, a millwright, and Lazarus Thomas, laborer, who were indicted for the murder of Jonathan Hayes, a resident of Marple and a justice of the county, in the year 1715 At the October court of that year the following reference to the trial will be found

"This Court request Henry Worley, Robert Carter and James Sandelands to see if they can procure some place yt may be more Convenient than the Court house for holding the Supreme Court for ye Tryall of those persons yt are holden in ye Gaol of ye County on Suspition of murder and to make such agreement as they may see needful for change and damages to be payd out of the County stock"

The records of the county at West Chester, from 1710 to 1720, are very meagre, and little or no information can be had by an inspection of the court paper of the circumstances surrounding the case We know, from the minutes of the Provincial Council, that the accused "had for several years appeared at the head of a lawless Gang of Loose fellows, common disturbers of the public peace," and that for some reason they had been admitted to bail The records of our county, however, are silent as reference thereto further than already given April 17, 1718, before David Lloyd, chief justice, and his associates, at Chester, the case was tried, resulting in a verdict of guilty Deputy Governor Sir William Keith was also present The prisoners were sentenced to be hanged on May 9, 1718[1] The following is a copy of the death-warrant

{ SEAL } "CHESTER, ss
"*To the Sheriff of the County of Chester*

"Whereas Hugh Pugh & Lazarus Thomas have this Day before us at a Court of Oyer & Terminer & Gaol Delivery held for the sd County been convicted of the murder of One Jonathan Hayes & have received Sentence to be Hanged by the neck until they be Dead

"These are therefore in his majesties name by virtue of the Power to us Granted by the Governours Commission Comand you that upon Fryday the Ninth day of May next betwixt the hours of Eight & Twelve in the forenoon of the same Day you Cause the sd Sentance to be put in Execucon, ffor which this shall be your Warrant Given under Our Hands & Seals at Chester afores'd the Seventeenth day of April In the ffourth year of the Reign of our Sovereign Lord George King of Great Britain &c Annoq Dom 1718

"DA'D LLOYD
"JASPER YEATES
"RICHALD HILL
"WILL'M TRENT"

The day previous to that fixed for their execution—May 8th—the condemned men petitioned the Governor for a reprieve until the pleasure of the king could be known, they having appealed to the crown, alleging that the following legal errors invalidated the whole proceedings

"1st. Because seventeen of the Grand Inquest who found the bill of Inditment against them and eight of the Petty Jury who found them guilty were Quakers or Reputed Quakers, and were Qualified no otherwise than by an affirmacon or Declaracon contrary to a statue made in the first year of your Mat'ies Reign

"2d Because the Act of Assembly of this Province by which Judges, Jury & Witnesses were pretended to be Qualified was made & past the Twenty eight Day of May, in the first year of your Majesties Reign,[2] which was after sd murder was supposed to be committed, and after another Act of Assembly of the same nature was repealed by her Late Majesty, Queen Anne

"3dly Because sd Act of Assembly is not consonant to Reason, but Repugnant & Contrary to the Laws, Statutes and Rights of your Majesties Kingdom "

The petition for a reprieve was rejected, and doubtless the culprits were executed at the time designated in the warrant Although the legal matter suggested in the prisoners' petition was never passed upon by a competent tribunal, for we have no record of any action of the supreme judges thereon, yet the points taken aroused such public alarm as to the legality of the proceeding, that in twenty-two days after the execution of Pugh and Thomas—May 31, 1718—the law was passed, which adopted the fierce criminal law of England in the province, simply in exchange for the right to use affirmations in place of "corporal oaths," the Assembly well knowing that the king would approve and confirm the act, which was done early in the following year[3]

At the Court of Oyer and Terminer, held at Chester, June 20, 1722, by David Lloyd, chief justice, and associates, the case of Rex *vs* William Hill and Mary Woolvin, was tried on an indictment for murder They were convicted, and as the sentence ran, "must be hanged by ye neck until they and each of them be dead " The case of these convicts, together with one William Batten, who was then in Chester jail under sentence of death, was considered by the Provincial Council, Aug 3, 1722, "and it was the advice of all the members present, to which the Governor was pleased to agree, that the said William Hill and Mary Woolvin be reprieved for the space of twelve months, in case no orders shall come from the Crown for the execution before the expiration of the said term, that the said William Batten, being convicted of divers horrid complicated crimes, be executed and hung in irons in the most public place at such times as the Governor shall appoint, and that the warrant for the execution be issued before the Governor set out for Albany "[4]

Aug 27, 1723, Edward Murphy was tried for murder and acquitted "Same day Elizabeth Murphy was indicted for murder and found guilty by ye Petty Jury and must be hanged by ye neck until she is dead And ye Sherif is ordered to Execute her accordingly on ye 13th of 7 month 1724 "[5] Sept 1, 1724, the bill of costs in the above cases, amounting to £2 6*s* 6*d* each, signed by Robert Assheton, was allowed by the commissioners and assessors[6]

At a Court of Oyer and Terminer, held May 21, 1727, "John Hendricks who was indicted for shooting by misfortune one Albert Hendricks, late of the county

[1] See for full particulars of the matter before Provincial Council, Colonial Records, vol iii pp 40, 41

[2] 1715 The act designated was "for the case of such as conscientiously sought to take the solemn affirmation formerly allowed in Great Britain " It was repealed July 21, 1719

[3] See also in confirmation of this statement "the humble address and representation of the Governor and General Assembly," the — day of May, 1718 (Proud's "History of Pennsylvania," vol ii p 101), wherein the address to the king sets forth, "That for this end we have laboured, more generally of late, to regulate the proceedings in our Courts of judicature, as near as possibly could be done, to the constitution and practice of the laws of England

"That, from many years experience, we are not only convinced that the *solemn affirmation* allowed in Great Britain to the people called Quakers, doth, in all respects, and in every case, here answer the legal and essential purpose of an oath "

[4] The last case wherein I find that a man was gibbeted in Pennsylvania was that of Thomas Wilkinson, who had been found guilty of piracy April 23, 1781, and sentenced to be hanged The Supreme Executive Council, May 17, 1781, directed the execution to take place Wednesday, May 25, 1781, between 10 A M and 2 o'clock P M that day, on Windmill Island, in Delaware River, and that "the body of the said Thomas Wilkinson be taken down to Mud Island, in the said river, and hanged in chains on the north end of the said island " (Colonial Records, vol xii p 730) Some doubt arising as to the legality of the prisoner's conviction, on May 22d Council reprieved Wilkinson for twenty-one days (*Ib.*, 732), after which the record is silent as to his fate, except on Oct 6, 1781 (*Ib.*, xiii p 76), David Henderson was paid £17 10*s* 0*d* specie, "amount of his account for making a gibbet for Thomas Wilkinson "

[5] Supreme Court Docket, Prothonotary's office, Media, Pa

[6] Futhey and Cope's "History of Chester County," p 407

of Chester, Labourer and found guilty by his own confession, whereby ye Goods and Chattles of the said John Hendricks become forfeited to our Sovereign Lord, ye King. Upon which he puts himself on the mercy of our sd Lord the King and produces in court his pardon from ye Governour of this Provence, under ye Great Seal of the said Provence and prays ye same may be allowed and ye same is allowed per cur."[1] At the same court Rachel Lindley and Robert Box, indicted for murder, were acquitted.

In April, 1728, a few Indians belonging to the Twetchtweys, a tribe without the borders of the province, made their appearance near the Warwick Iron Work, on French Creek, and, being well armed, created wide-spread alarm among the settlers. The air was filled with rumors of Indian outrages and murder. John and Walter Winter, two brothers, respectable farmers, it is thought under the apprehension of the savages, and believing that they were doing the State a service, fell upon a party of Indians at Cassea, when Walter Winter shot and killed an aged man named Toka Collie, who was friendly to the whites. John Winter, at the same time, shot one of the Indian women, and then ran and knocked out the brains of an old squaw, "Quilee," otherwise "Hannah." The Winter brothers, with Morgan Herbert, bore the corpses of the two Indian women from the road where they had fallen, and covered them with leaves. The two former men carried two Indian girls (one a cripple) before one of the county officers, demanding a reward for what they had done. Samuel Nutt, the iron-master at the forge, dispatched John Petty to the Governor with a letter informing him of the occurrence. The latter had warrants issued for the arrest of the men, and, on a "hue and cry," the two Winters, together with Morgan Herbert, their neighbor, were taken into custody and lodged in the jail at Chester, in all probability the old prison on Edgmont Street. John and Walter Winter were tried before David Lloyd, Richard Hill, and Jeremiah Langhorne, for the murder of the Indian woman, Quilee, June 19, 1728, and the jury found the defendants "Guilty of ye murder afd and must be hanged by the necks until they and each of them be dead."[2]

Governor Gordon issued the warrant, fixing Wednesday, July 3, 1728, as the date of the execution. Morgan Herbert was convicted at the same court as an accessory to the murder, but he was recommended in a petition numerously signed by citizens, as well as by the judges who tried the case, setting forth that "though in strictness of law Herbert's offence may be adjudged murder, yet it appeared to them that he was not active in perpetrating thereof, but unhappily fell into ye company of those that committed it." The Governor granted a reprieve to Herbert, who was finally pardoned. The Winters seem to have done the deed under the impression that the Indians were at war with the whites, "and they felt justified in killing any of the natives with whom they met." A reason which, considering the times in which they lived, takes from the act that wicked animus which constitutes morally the crime of murder.

At the Oyer and Terminer, held at Chester, "27, 7 ber, 1728," William Davis was indicted for murdering his master, William Cloud. The jury returned a verdict of guilty, "And ye sd William Davis being asked what he had or could say why sentence of Death should not pass against him says no more than what he has sayd before.

"Therefor it is considered by ye Court here that h be taken back to prison from whence he came an from thence to ye place of execution and there l hanged by ye neck untill he be Dead and his body ye Disposal of ye Governor."[3]

On Saturday, Aug. 1, 1752, at the house of Elea Davis, in Tredyffrin, a brutal murder was commi by Bryan Doran, James Rice, *alias* Dillon, and Tho Kelley. It seems that Rice and Kelley were told Doran that Eleanor Davis, an old woman, J n Thomas, an aged man, and Rachel Jones, a yo g woman, lived together in the house; that they pt good cider, and "that the old woman had a grea al of money, he believed three or four hundred po ds, in the house." It was thereupon arranged that Doran should go to the dwelling and ask a night's lodging. At bedtime he was to come to the door and cough once, which was the signal to the men outside that no persons save the usual inmates were there. Rice and Kelley, who had disguised themselves by r ng black earth on their faces, loitered about the p ses until the signal was given, when they, with illon, entered the house. The latter, armed with short broad-bladed sword, then called "a hanger," clared that he was going to England, and demanded all the money the old people had. Receiving no answer, he began to strike and stab the parties who had given him shelter. Rice and Kelley, who were armed with sticks, joined in the base assault. The inmates succeeded in escaping at the doors, were followed by the assassins and knocked down, but the old lady continued to scream, which so alarmed the robbers that they fled without plundering the house, making their escape on two horses which they appropria to their use. Eleanor Davis and John Thomas were killed, and Rachel Jones was dangerously wounded. The Provincial authorities offered a reward of one hundred and fifty pounds, and the friends of the slain man and woman forty pounds, for the apprehension of the murderers. Rice and Kelley were shortly afterwards arrested, and tried at Chester, November 27th of the same year, the latter pleading guilty to the indictment, while Rice was found guilty by the jury. James

[1] Supreme Court Docket, Media, Pa.

[2] Ib.

[3] Ib.

Rice was executed Dec 9, 1752, and Kelley (who had been respited to identify Bryan Doran, as a person of that name had been arrested in Maryland, but subsequently shown not to be the assassin) was hung Dec 16, 1752

At a Court of Oyer and Terminer, held at Chester, Aug 25, 1760, John Lewis was convicted of the murder of his wife, Ann The Provincial Council, Sept 8, 1760, issued a warrant directing his execution

In 1705 an act creating a special court for the trial of negroes was passed by the colonial authorities, and, although a Supreme Court for the trial of negroes was created and judges commissioned by Lieutenant-Governor John Evans, in February, 1706-7, our records show nothing respecting any tribunal under that enactment until May 28, 1762, at which time a "Special Court" was held at Chester, "before John Hannum and John Morton, Esqs, two of his Majestys Justices of the Peace within the County aforsd particularly Commissioned," with the assistance of six of the most substantial freeholders of the neighborhood, who were "lawfully & legally summoned, returned, Sworn & affirmed well and truly to give their assistance and judgment on the tryal of such Negro or Negroes as shall be charged or accused before them of committing any Murder, Manslaughter, Buggery, Burglary, Rapes, attempts of Rapes or any High or Heinous offence committed acted or done within the sd county" The first case was that of Negro Abraham Johnson, a slave of Humphrey Marshall, who was arraigned on an information exhibited by Benjamin Chew, attorney-general, charging the defendant with "murdering a certain negro man named Glascow, the slave of Alexander Boyd" The court assigned Joseph Galloway, Esq to defend the accused "The court find defendant not guilty of murder, but that he is guilty of homicide *se defends*," and thereupon discharged the prisoner from arrest on the charge, but held him for payment of costs

At a like special court held March 2, 1764, Phœbe, the slave of Joseph Richardson, was tried for "Feloniously & Burglarily breaking and entering the Mansion house of Thomas Barnard, and stealing thereout divers Goods and Chattles, the property of the said Thomas Barnard" . "And now on hearing proof in this Case It is considered and adjudged by this Court that the said defendant Negro Phœbe is Guilty of the Felony & Burglary aforesaid in Manner and form &c And thereupon it is further considered and adjudged by this Court that the said defendant Negro Phœbe be led to the prison from whence she came and from thence to the place of Execution and there be Hanged by the Neck till she be dead" By the act of March 5, 1725-26, negro slaves convicted of capital offenses were to be valued, and such valuation was to be paid to their masters out of the colonial treasury In this case Phœbe was valued at fifty-five pounds, which it seems was paid to her master, Joseph Richardson

On Nov 30, 1754, Chief Justice William Allen and Alexander Steadman, the latter commissioned that year one of the puisne judges of the Supreme Court, presided at the Oyer and Terminer, at Chester, at which Jane Ewing was tried and found guilty of the murder of her bastard male child, on April 3d of the previous year, and was sentenced to death "It being reported to the Governor by the Justices of the Supreme Court that they discovered on her trial no kind of remorse," and that the evidence showed that her crime was an aggravated one, a warrant for her execution on Saturday, Jan 29, 1765, was issued

Aug 15, 1768, John Dowdle and Thomas Vaughan were tried for having, March 31, 1768, murdered Thomas Sharp The prisoners were convicted and sentenced to be hung The Provincial Council ordered that they be executed in the county jail on Saturday, September 17th, of the same year

At the Court of Oyer and Terminer, held by the justices of the Supreme Court at Chester, June 11, 1770, Matthew McMahon was tried and convicted of the murder of John McClester, laborer, of Middletown A warrant directing his execution on Saturday, June 30, 1770, was issued

At a similar court held at Chester, March 23, 1772, Patrick Kennedy, Thomas Fryer, Neal McCarther, and James Dever were tried on a charge of rape, committed on Jane Walker, of Thornbury, in November of the year previous They were all convicted and sentenced to death Patrick Kennedy was ordered to be executed on Saturday, May 2, 1772, but the others were reprieved during the pleasure of the Lieutenant-Governor, Richard Penn

On Saturday, Dec 26, 1772, Henry Philips, a laborer, who had been convicted of the murder of Richard Kelley, was executed at Chester by order of the Provincial Council

John Jones, Aug 23, 1773, was convicted of burglary and sentenced to death, but Lieutenant-Governor Richard Penn commuted his sentence to transportation, conditioned that he should "never return unto the Province"

In the summer of 1775, James Willis was convicted of the murder of Daniel Culin, and Governor John Penn ordered his execution to take place Saturday, Sept 30, 1775

During the gloomy days of the Revolution several murders appear to have been committed, the perpetrators of which, so far as the records show, were never discovered, or at least not brought to justice On Sept 16, 1775, John Faughnai, a peddler, was brutally murdered and robbed on the highway, near the Red Lion Inn, in Uwchlan township, in the county of Chester Suspicion pointed to Fleming Elliott, who could not be found, and the Governor offered a reward of fifty pounds for his arrest, apparently without success Early in 1778, Benjamin Harmon was murdered under aggravating circumstances in Chester County, and Henry Skyles was charged with being the principal in the crime, while Thomas Boyd, James Wilson, John Hastings, and Charles Caldwell, all of Lancaster County, were said to be accessories thereto They all escaped arrest, although Thomas Wharton, Jr, president of the Executive Council, on March 24th of that year, offered a reward of one thousand pounds for the apprehension and delivery to justice of the men named, or two hundred pounds for any one of them In the fall of the year 1779, Jesse Jordan, who had brought suit in Philadelphia against Gen Benedict Arnold several weeks before, was found murdered in Chester County, the place of his residence, and again the perpetrators of the act escaped "unwhipped of justice"

James Fitzpatrick.—The character of "Sandy Flash," in Bayard Taylor's "Story of Kennett," is founded on the adventures and the deeds of a sturdy freebooter, who for more than a twelvemonth kept the good people of the county of Chester in constant alarm and dread by his audacious and frequent crimes The name of James Fitzpatrick in Chester and Delaware Counties is still surrounded with that peculiar glamour of crime which is so often associated with the acts of bold, bad men, and to this day his deeds are recalled by the representatives of the old families of this section with no little local pride, for the subject of their theme was, at least, no ordinary desperado

James Fitzpatrick was born in Chester County, and when quite a lad was indentured by his father, an Irish emigrant in indigent circumstances, to John Passmore, of Doe Run, as an apprentice to the trade of blacksmithing His early life was distinguished by no unusual incidents He worked faithfully at the anvil until he attained his majority and acquired some local prominence as a shoer, and was known the neighborhood round as an excellent judge of horses His bodily strength is said to have been enormous, his physical endurance noticeable, and he conspicuously excelled all the young men of the locality where he resided in athletic sports Personally he was handsome, above the average height in stature, he was erect and graceful in carriage, his complexion florid, his features well formed, his eyes a clear bright blue in color, and his hair sandy and luxuriant On several occasions he had exhibited extraordinary personal courage, circumstances which, subsequently remembered, increased the alarm of the Whigs when Fitzpatrick became an active, unscrupulous partisan of the cause of the king

After serving the full term of his apprenticeship with Mr Passmore, he worked as a journeyman at several forges in the county until the outbreak of the Revolutionary war, when he enlisted in the military service of the province Subsequently, in the shaping of events, he became attached to the Flying Camp, and accompanied that organization to the city of New York There, for some slight breach of military discipline, he was punished by flogging The penalty imposed for his dereliction was more than he would bear, and deserting in the night-time, he swam the Hudson River, and made his way across New Jersey to Philadelphia, intending to proceed to his home in Chester County In the latter city he was recognized, apprehended, and being absent without leave of his commanding officers, was lodged in the old Walnut Street prison, whence he was released on consenting to re-enter the Continental army, for at that time men were eagerly sought for to bear arms The imprisonment was resented by Fitzpatrick as a wrong that had been done him, therefore, at the first opportunity which presented itself, he again deserted and returned to his home in Chester County, where, for a time, he worked honestly at his trade and in odd jobs at harvesting for the farmers in the neighborhood

During the summer of 1777, Fitzpatrick, with several other men, was mowing in the field of his late master, John Passmore, in West Marlborough township, when he was taken into custody as a deserter by two Continental soldiers, who had been sent from Wilmington to arrest him Fitzpatrick having been captured by surprise, was compelled to resort to subterfuge to recover his liberty By a plausible story respecting clothing that he would require, and a request to be permitted to bid good-by to his aged mother, he prevailed upon the soldiers (who were instructed to bring their captive to Wilmington) to accompany him to his mother's residence, a tenant-house on Mr Passmore's land When they reached the dwelling, Fitzpatrick opened the door and quickly grasped his rifle from behind it, where he was accustomed to keep that firearm, leveled it at the soldiers, and swore that he would kill them if they did not leave immediately They had learned sufficiently of the determination of character of their prisoner to believe that he would not hesitate an instant to make his threat good, hence, acting upon the better part of valor, they hastily retreated Fitzpatrick, as soon as the men had fled, returned to the meadow where he had been at work, and renewed his labor as coolly as if no unusual incident had occurred to disturb the placidity of his every day life

The implacable hatred to the patriot cause which was engendered in the mind of Fitzpatrick as the result of corporal punishment inflicted on him while with the Continental army in New York soon had the opportunity to vent itself upon the Whigs of Chester County, whom he believed had betrayed his whereabouts to the colonial military authorities On the 25th of August, 1777, the British forces, eighteen thousand men, under Gen Howe, landed at the head of the Elk, in the movement against Philadelphia which resulted in the capture of that city Fitzpatrick promptly repaired to the camp of the British army, was subsequently present at the battle of Brandywine, and accompanied the victorious enemy to Philadelphia, from which city he made many petty plundering excursions into Chester County, in which predatory expeditions he was accompanied by Mordecai Dougherty, a Tory from the same neighborhood whence Fitzpatrick came. The latter had been reared in the family of Nathan Hayes, residing near Doe Run, and, as supposed, the two worthies had known each other in their youth. After Fitzpatrick joined the English forces, he always spoke of himself as captain, and dubbed Dougherty with the title of lieutenant; but whether either of them were ever commissioned as such by Sir William Howe is very doubtful.

In June, 1778, while Fitzpatrick and his associate were engaged in one of these predatory raids, the British army evacuated Philadelphia, and the two men determined to remain in Chester County and carry on the war as an independent, irregular body. To that end they made their headquarters at a point known as Hand's Pass, near the present town of Coatesville, and had also secluded hiding-places along the Brandywine in Newland and West Bradford townships, one of which, J. Smith Futhey says, "was on the high hill on the west side of the creek, near the present Marshall's Station, on the Wilmington and Reading Railroad." From these retired places of concealment Fitzpatrick and Dougherty issued to make desperate expeditions, or to undertake daring adventures, which, in a short time, rendered their names a terror to the Whigs of that neighborhood, for, as to the Tories, they regarded them as their friends, and never molested them. The collectors of the public revenue, however, were their especial prey, and oftentimes unfortunate tax-gatherers who fell in their way were made the victims of the utmost brutality. Frequently, after stripping them of all their money, they would tie the unhappy officials to convenient trees and flog them unmercifully. On one occasion, one of these men was not only robbed of a large sum of money by Fitzpatrick and his companion, but he was taken to one of their hidden lurking-places in the woods, where he was detained for two weeks, to the consternation of his family, who could only account for his absence by the supposition that he had been murdered.

At another time two tax-collectors, armed with muskets, met a man walking alone whom they did not know, and entered into conversation with him. During the interview one of the officials inquired of the stranger whether he had seen Fitzpatrick, or if he could give him any information as to the whereabouts of that individual, remarking at the same time that he rather preferred that he should encounter that person, for if he did, he, Fitzpatrick, should not escape from him so easily as he had done from other collectors who had fallen in with him. The stranger continued the conversation a few minutes longer, when, turning suddenly upon the men, he disarmed them both, then quietly informed them that he was Capt. Fitzpatrick, and that he would be obliged to them for their money. From the boastful Capt. McGowan, one of the collectors, he took his watch, but as the latter said it was a family relic, doubly valuable to him on that account, he returned it promptly. Capt. McGowan wore his hair in a neat queue, of which he was very vain, and as a particular indignity Fitzpatrick cut it off close to his head. He also despoiled the unfortunate military officer of his sword and pistols, and then tied him to a tree and administered a sound flagellation. At its conclusion Fitzpatrick informed the crestfallen man that he had heard him, McGowan, boasting while at an inn a few miles distant, what he would do with him should he encounter him, and he had therefore given him the opportunity to make his boast good. A local writer of rude verse of the period in commemorating Fitzpatrick's exploits alludes thus to this incident:

> "Some he did rob, then let them go free,
> Bold Capt. McGowan he tied to a tree.
> Some he did whip and some he did spare,
> He caught Capt. McGowan and cut off his hair."

Subsequently, when the outlaw was in chains in his cell in the jail at Chester, Capt. McGowan visited Fitzpatrick to inquire what he had done with the sword and pistols he had taken from him. The prisoner asked him if he remembered the tavern where he had expressed his wish to meet him, and the tree to which he was tied to be flogged by the man he was looking for. These questions were answered in the affirmative. Thereupon Fitzpatrick told him that about three hundred yards to the southwest of that tree he would find his sword and pistols, concealed between the bark and wood of a decayed oak log. It is stated that the arms were found at the place thus designated.

The audacious courage of the man frequently manifested itself in the most reckless acts of bravado on his part. On one occasion fifty or more persons, all well armed, gathered together with the avowed purpose of taking Fitzpatrick, dead or alive, but being unsuccessful in their search they repaired to an inn, where, seated upon the porch, they discussed the recent exploits of the outlaw and the liquors of the tavern at the same time, until the crowd became excited, and many of the men expressed a desire to meet Fitzpatrick, who was well known to almost every one present. Suddenly, during the heat of the conversation, the outlaw, with his rifle in his hands, presented himself before them, called for a glass of liquor, drank it, and after paying for it withdrew as quietly as he had come, excepting, as he backed off, he announced that he would shoot the first man who stirred to molest him. Then walking backward, holding his rifle menacingly toward the body of men, he moved away until he had attained, as he regarded, a sufficient distance from his enemies, when he turned and fled into the woods.

Several weeks before the British army evacuated Philadelphia, Fitzpatrick and Dougherty, in one of their expeditions from that city, repaired to the houses of Joseph Luckey and Peter Burgardine, where they committed acts of the most flagrant lawlessness The whole neighborhood was aroused by the outrages, and Col Andrew Boyd, the then lieutenant of the county, wrote to the Executive Council of Pennsylvania that he had caused diligent search to be made for the culprits, but unsuccessfully, as the loyalists of Newlin and adjoining townships aided and secreted the malefactors Council thereupon declared the two men outlaws, and offered a reward of a thousand dollars for their arrest, or a like sum for that of Fitzpatrick alone The Whigs of Chester County thereupon made cause against the men, and repeatedly large bands assembled to capture the outlaws, and numerous plans were resorted to to effect that object Nevertheless the best-laid schemes looking to that end miscarried, the proscribed men eluded every ambushment, and by fresh outrages, in other sections of the county, added to the consternation which their deeds had created among the patriots It is related that on one occasion a meeting of the Whigs was called at a tavern on the West Chester road to devise plans for the capture of Fitzpatrick and his companion With amazing effrontery Fitzpatrick presented himself in disguise at the assembly A militia captain present rendered himself peculiarly conspicuous by his repeated declarations that he wanted to see Fitzpatrick, whom he had never met, and volunteered to capture him and bring him to justice The outlaw, who had heard these boasts, unperceived took a candlestick from the mantel-shelf, secreted it in his pocket, and then approaching the noisy captain, told him if he would withdraw with him into another room he would inform him how, when, and where he could see the brigand, and have an opportunity to capture him The latter consented to go with him Fitzpatrick, after they had entered the room designated, shut and locked the door, then leveled the candlestick at the captain's head, saying as he did so,—

"Young man, you want to see Captain Fritz I am that person I'll trouble you for your watch and the money you may have about you"

The entrapped hero hastily complied with the request, whereupon Fitzpatrick tied his hands behind him with his own handkerchief

"Now, sir," he said, as he unlocked the door, "you may go back to your friends and tell them that you wanted to see Captain Fritz and you have seen him"

The prominence given to Fitzpatrick by the Executive Committee in proscribing him and offering a large reward for his capture was accepted by the latter as a flattering recognition of his abilities, and the alarm with which his deeds were regarded by the Whigs He was repeatedly shot at by concealed marksmen, but always escaped unscathed, until the notion became prevalent that his was a charmed life, his shrewdness in avoiding snares to entrap him, his ability, courage, and readiness in eluding pursuit, together with his apparent recklessness in thrusting himself almost within the clutches of his enemies merely to disappoint them afresh, served to deepen the general impression heretofore mentioned A short time after a price was set upon his life, to manifest his contempt of the proclamation and his mean opinion of the bravery of his foemen, in broad daylight, armed only with a pair of pistols and a dagger, he entered the hamlet of Kennett Square, deliberately walked through its streets, the people whom he met making way for him to pass, and repaired to the "Unicorn," the ancient and most noted hostelry in the village, destroyed by fire in January, 1875

He unhesitatingly entered the bar-room, in which a crowd of twoscore men were assembled, talking of the outlaw—for he was the constant topic of conversation—and making copious draughts upon the good cheer of "mine host," the jolly, jovial Maj John Bell, until they had become boisterously intoxicated In that condition many of the men—as seems to have been customary on those occasions—expressed the desire to meet Fitzpatrick, whose personal peculiarities were well known to almost every one present The reckless man, apparently as if an accustomed frequenter of the inn, called for a glass of liquor, drank it, and quietly walked away, without the least molestation by word or sign from any one The insolent intrepidity of the act so utterly astonished the crowd that they did not recover their amazement until Fitzpatrick was out of range of their firearms

His robberies were bold, and to the sheer effrontery of many of his deeds was he indebted for his immunity from arrest On one occasion, when a number of men were harvesting in a field on the farm of James Shields, Fitzpatrick and Dougherty presented themselves, and the former informed Mr Shields that he had called at his house and borrowed his watch, his silver shoe-buckles, and his shoes Shields said, promptly,—

"You must return them"

"That will depend altogether upon your behavior towards us," was the reply of the outlaw, with a laugh

Archibald Hambleton, a young man who was reaping in the field at the time, was taken into custody by Fitzpatrick and his companion, who compelled him to go with them to his parents' home There the outlaws appropriated to their own use a rifle, powder-horn, and shot-pouch, and Fitzpatrick forced Hambleton to swear on a Bible that he would not follow, betray, disturb, or molest any of his (Hambleton's) neighbors, many of whom were Tories, in retaliation for the theft He also told Hambleton if he violated his oath in any respect he and Dougherty would return there and burn not only his parents' house, but the houses of every rebel in the neighborhood

The brutal punishment of flogging,—then a part of the military law of every nation,—which had caused Fitzpatrick to desert the cause of the colonies and sustain that of the loyalists, seemed, after his personal experience in the Continental army, to have become his favorite mode of punishment. On all occasions he employed castigation as a remedy for every wrong, suppositious or actual, which he had sustained. It is related that on one occasion a man from Nottingham township, when in pursuit of Fitzpatrick, went to the house of the latter's mother, where he behaved in an insolent manner, hoping thereby to compel her to tell him the whereabouts of her son. Among other things, to show his authority when dealing with a proscribed outlaw, he broke her spinning-wheel. Fitzpatrick, when informed of the indignities which had been shown his parent, vowed that he would be revenged, and contrived to have a message delivered to the offender, in which he apprised him that he might expect a visit from him shortly, and could, if so disposed, make whatever arrangements he deemed necessary to receive his guest in a proper form. The man laughed at the threat, said he would be glad to see Fitzpatrick (they all said that), and if he came he would not, in all probabilities, have occasion to ask the hospitality of any other person after he had gotten through with him. Nevertheless, Fitzpatrick kept his promise. One morning he suddenly confronted the man who had ill-treated his mother at the door of his own house, and commanded him, in a peremptory manner, to immediately follow him to the woods. He who had been so prolific in defiances when the danger was remote had not the courage to resist when Fitzpatrick presented himself in person, but cowardly obeyed his orders. The outlaw tied him to a tree and administered a castigation, which was laid on with a strong arm, and, perhaps, with more good will on the part of the whipper than in any case when Fitzpatrick punished his enemy by flagellation.

Despite his many crimes, there was a rough chivalry in the character of the man which exhibited itself in his marked gallantry towards women, in his open, generous disposition to aid them on when ill fortune bore heavily; indeed, he was never known to rob a poor man or ill-treat a female. Many are the instances related when he bestowed upon the destitute that which he had taken from those in good circumstances, and the weak or defenseless never suffered at his hands. On one occasion an old woman, who made a meagre living by peddling from house to house odds and ends of female apparel, encountered Fitzpatrick in the neighborhood of Caln Friends' meeting-house. She was at the time on her way to Philadelphia to buy goods, and all the money she possessed was on her person. She had never seen Capt. Fitzpatrick, and she informed the tall, handsome stranger that she was told that the outlaw had made some demonstrations in that neighborhood a short time before, and she was afraid that she might fall in with him and be robbed of all her money. Fitzpatrick, by a few questions, drew from her the particulars of her business, and her difficulty in winning an honest livelihood. He then good-naturedly told her she need be under no apprehension, Fitzpatrick never warred upon the weak or defenseless, that she was talking to that personage; and taking a purse from his pocket containing several gold pieces, he gave it to her to aid her in increasing her scanty stock of goods. Then, wishing her a safe journey, he turned into the woods and disappeared.

The short but eventful career of the outlaw was rapidly drawing to an end. On Saturday afternoon, the 22d day of August, 1778, shortly after five o'clock, Fitzpatrick went to the house of William McAffee, a well-to-do farmer, who resided in Edgmont township, in the present county of Delaware, near Castle Rock, a cluster of peculiar rocks, bowlder upon bowlder in picturesque confusion, a place often visited by tourists as a natural curiosity, not far from Crum Creek, where that stream is crossed by the West Chester road, and about ten miles from old Chester, on the Delaware. The house stood on a plantation known as the Castle Rock Farm, now owned by Mr. William Taylor, whose present dwelling stands on the site where McAffee's house was then located. It seems that Fitzpatrick had visited the family, who were ardent Whigs, on a former occasion, and had taken from them some articles of value. On the afternoon above mentioned, Mr. and Mrs. McAffee and their son, Robert, a captain of a military company, were at tea, when the latter glancing out of the door saw a man armed with a rifle, a pair of pistols in his belt, and a sword at his side approaching on horseback. As he came from the direction of the American camp, the captain supposed the horseman was a soldier in the Continental service. The latter rode to the door, dismounted, and asked whether William McAffee lived there. An affirmative response was made to this interrogatory, whereupon the stranger entered the room and inquired,—

"Are you Capt. Robert McAffee?"

"I am Robert McAffee," was the rejoinder of the son.

"And I am Capt. Fitzpatrick."

"If that be so," quietly said the young man, "sit down and take a cup of tea with us; you are welcome to it."

But Fitzpatrick, who seemed to have entertained personal enmity against the McAffees, rudely refused the invitation, declaring, with an oath, that he would neither eat nor drink, nor would he leave the house until he had stripped its inmates of all the money they had; that he was levying contributions from the rebels, and that he had fixed upon one hundred and fifty pounds as the sum to be paid him by the McAffees. Thereupon presenting his pistol at Capt. McAffee, he ordered the members of the family to deliver to him all articles of jewelry and money they had upon their persons. A pair of well-made low shoes, or pumps, with silver buckles, worn by the son, particularly pleased Fitzpatrick's fancy, and, kicking off those he wore, he immediately appropriated those articles to his own use. The shoes, however, were rather small for the outlaw, and when he put them on his heels pressed the counters down. During a moment when Fitzpatrick's attention was drawn elsewhere, Capt. McAffee threw the keys of his chest, together with some Continental bills which he had had in his pockets, behind the door. His mother obtaining possession of the keys went up-stairs, and unlocking the chest in which a large sum of money was, secreted it under a quantity of wheat which was stored in the garret. Fitzpatrick, as soon as he became aware that Mrs. McAffee had left the room, threatened to kill her son if he did not immediately cause her to descend. In response to the call the mother promptly appeared, accompanied by Rachel Walker, the hired woman. Fitzpatrick having ransacked every place in the lower rooms where he supposed money or plate could be secreted, ordered all the inmates of the dwelling to ascend to the upper apartments. In the passage the outlaw observed Capt. McAffee's rifle, which he discharged and threw out of the door, remarking that it could lie there until it was wanted. At the foot of the stairs William McAffee endeavored to dissuade Fitzpatrick from ascending, promising him immunity from punishment for what he had already done to them; but the latter, believing that there was a large sum of money in the house, adhered to his purpose, and drawing his sword, placed the point of it at the breast of the old man, threatening to run him through if he did not immediately proceed.

When in the upper rooms, Fitzpatrick commanded Capt. McAffee to unlock his chest and produce the one hundred and fifty pounds already demanded. The latter, in a tone of well-assumed astonishment, exclaimed,—

"How can you expect that so young a man as I am would have so large a sum of money in my possession?"

However, he promptly opened the chest, the keys of which his mother had returned to him, and told Fitzpatrick to search it. The outlaw complied with this invitation, but not finding the money, which, it is supposed, he had learned was in the possession of Robert McAffee, his disappointment was great, and, turning to the captain, said that in lieu of the money he would compel him, as he was his prisoner, to take part in his next campaign, and to that end he must provide himself with a horse and clothing, for it would be a long and severe expedition. The threat was not to be misunderstood, and Capt. McAffee was convinced that his only hope for liberty, possibly life itself, was in the capture of the outlaw.

Fitzpatrick ordered Capt. McAffee, his father and mother, in the order given, to stand in a row on his right hand, while Rachel Walker stood a short distance from and in front of him. The pumps which the outlaw had appropriated to his own use, being down at the heels, seemed to have annoyed him. He laid his arms, except a pistol which he kept in his hand, on the bed, and placing one of his feet on the side of the bedstead, he strove to force, with both hands, the shoe on his foot. Capt. McAffee, who was a large and muscular man, saw that the opportunity to put his resolution into effect was now presented, and, springing suddenly, he seized Fitzpatrick from behind in such a way as to prevent the latter the full use of his arms, and then, after some struggling, managed to throw him to the floor. The outlaw strove desperately to free his hand in which he still clutched the pistol. Rachel Walker thereupon caught the weapon, and, although in the scuffle her hand was badly hurt by the lock, she stoutly maintained her hold until she wrested the firearm from his grasp. As the men were still struggling, Rachel threw a double woolen coverlid over the head and face of Fitzpatrick, holding it in that position, which partially smothered him, and gave McAffee complete mastery over the prostrated man.

David Cunningham, a hired man on the farm, who had entered the house, hearing the noise of the scuffling, came up-stairs. He was immediately ordered by Capt. McAfee to get a rope and secure Fitzpatrick. While Mrs. McAfee was striving to bind his feet, he kicked her so violently in the side that she fell against the partition at the other end of the room. After the unhappy man was firmly bound, he begged earnestly of his captor that he would blow out his brains and make an end of his misery. Capt. McAffee told him that he would deliver him to the proper authorities, and to that end he sent David Cunningham to inform the nearest Whig neighbors of the capture, with a request that they would aid in guarding the prisoner from any attempted rescue. This being done, Cunningham was instructed to proceed to the American camp, and ask that a guard be sent to take Fitzpatrick to a place of safety.

Rachel Walker, after the capture had been made, armed with the pistol she had wrested from the outlaw, stood sentinel at the door of the apartment, but when David Cunningham rode away on his errand, she remembered that Dougherty and other companions of the outlaw might be lurking in the neighborhood, and she immediately started to bring Miss Jane McAffee home from the house of a friend near by before night came on. As the two women were returning they met a young man and woman walking together. The news the former had was too momentous to be kept, and they therefore imparted to the latter the fact that Fitzpatrick had been taken and was then a prisoner at McAffee's. This information aroused the latter's curiosity, and together the four repaired to the house. When they came into the room the young woman seated herself on the bed on which Fitzpatrick was lying, and apparently deeply moved with pity at the sight of the handsome man pinioned, her womanly sympathies exhibited themselves in an effort to comfort him. She smoothed his hair with her hand, and when he complained of being chilly, she threw a covering over him.

The immediate neighbors of the McAffees were loyalists, and the nearest Whigs were about two miles distant, hence it was between eight and nine o'clock before any assistance was had to prevent a rescue. Capt. McAffee then, exhausted by the struggle and the excitement which he had been under, repaired to an adjoining apartment to rest himself. Some time after he had retired it was discovered that Fitzpatrick, whose body was covered by the quilt, had freed his arm from the rope, and it was suspected that the young woman had been mainly instrumental in loosing the bonds. He was speedily rebound, and the rope was drawn so tightly that he complained that it hurt him. No attention was paid by the men present to the remonstrance of the prisoner, and he appealed to Miss Jane McAffee, who called her brother. The latter declared that Fitzpatrick should not be ill used, and although he must be bound, the ropes should not be drawn unnecessarily tight to cause him pain. About eleven o'clock one of the men who were guarding Fitzpatrick sat near the window, when he was immediately fired at, the ball lodging in the weather-boarding of the house beneath the sill. A number of the men present made search for the assailant, whom they believed to have been Dougherty, but failed to apprehend him. They merely found a sword, which was recognized as one that Fitzpatrick had taken from a patriot officer. Two hours after midnight the guard dispatched from the American camp to escort Fitzpatrick to a place of safe detention arrived, and taking him in charge, conveyed him to Old Chester, where he was lodged in jail early the following morning. Dougherty, after the capture of his superior, passed entirely out of public notice, and nothing is known of his subsequent career. He may have taken part in the series of annoyances to which Capt. McAffee and family were subjected after the capture of Fitzpatrick. Two stacks of oats were burned, the spring-house opened, all the milk-pans therein ruined, and the manes and tails of the horses on their farm cut off, and other outrages perpetrated.

On the 15th of September Fitzpatrick was tried and convicted of burglary and robbery, and sentenced to be hanged. The Executive Council of the State approved the sentence, and designated the 26th day of the same month as the time when the execution should take place. While confined in the old jail in Chester, after conviction, Fitzpatrick made an effort to escape. He filed his chains and would have succeeded in his attempt had it not been that iron bars, imbedded in the masonry of the flue of the chimney, prevented his egress in that way, and the noise made in striving to break them out aroused his keepers. He was, therefore, removed by order of Council to the then recently-erected prison on Walnut Street, Philadelphia, as a place of greater security. There he twice broke his handcuffs off in one night, but was prevented from effecting his escape by the vigilance of the guards. The day previous to his execution he was conveyed to Chester.

On the morning of the 26th day of September, 1778, at the intersection of Providence and Edgmont Avenues, in North Ward, Chester, James Fitzpatrick met his fate. Tradition hath it that after the rope was adjusted about his neck and the cart drawn from beneath the gallows he fell to the earth on his feet, and that by standing on his toes the strain on his neck was removed. This the hangman saw, and springing upon the shoulders of the doomed man, the increased weight forced the body down until James Fitzpatrick was actually strangled to death.

Joseph Bates, who had been convicted of burglary, was ordered by the Executive Council to be hung May 20, 1780, at two o'clock P.M., "at the usual place of execution[1] in Chester."

In May, 1780, William Boyd, a collector of the public taxes in Chester County, while in the discharge of his duties, was murdered by John and Robert Smith, who, after the commission of the act, fled. President Joseph Reed, with the approval of the Executive Council, offered a reward of twenty thousand dollars for the arrest of the murderers. They were making their way across New Jersey to join the British army, in New York, when they were apprehended by Sheriff Furman, of Monmouth County. They were brought to Chester, where, June 26, 1780, they were tried, convicted, and ordered to be hung, at the usual place of execution, on Saturday, July 1st, four full days alone intervening between their condemnation and death.

On Oct. 26, 1784, the Executive Council directed a warrant to the sheriff of Chester County requiring the execution of Joseph Clark, John McDonnell, and John Varnum, *alias* Benson, who were then under sentence of death for burglary, on Tuesday, Nov. 2, 1784.

Elizabeth Wilson.—The unhappy life-history of Elizabeth Wilson is one of the most popular traditions of Delaware and Chester Counties, and for nearly a century has been told and retold by the old residents of Delaware and Chester Counties and by their descendants, until many of the details, as so related, have gathered about the true narrative much that is unreliable if not absolutely false. Although I have striven to substantiate every item by careful investigation, perchance some of the imaginary particulars which have clustered around the sad, true history of Elizabeth Wilson may yet cling to the story in the present narration.

Elizabeth Wilson was the daughter of a farmer residing in East Bradford township, Chester Co., who in the conflict of political opinions preceding and during the Revolutionary war was earnest and honest in the advocacy of the crown. His means

[1] The intersection of Edgmont and Providence Avenues.

barely raised him above poverty, but he was esteemed and respected by the community in which he lived. His daughter, a bright, sprightly lass at the age of sixteen, was noted for her personal beauty, which as she matured was more and more conspicuous. At that time she became much interested in the religious exercises conducted by Elder Fleeson, an itinerant Baptist clergyman, who was earnest in his efforts to establish permanently the peculiar tenets of his faith in Chester County, wherein several congregations of that religious belief had existed from an early date.

The strong Tory sympathies of her parents caused him to regard the capture of Philadelphia, in 1777, as the harbinger of the good time approaching when the king should come to his own again, and Elizabeth, during the occupancy of the British army of that city, visited it, and remained for several weeks at the Indian Queen Inn, on Fourth Street, which at that time was kept by a distant relative of her parents. While there her loveliness attracted the attention of a young man, an incident which years afterwards brought her to an unnatural death,—that of a convicted felon.

After the war had ceased Elizabeth Wilson again visited Philadelphia, for the attractions of the metropolis of the commonwealth, the glare and glitter of the city, had made such an impression on her mind that the quiet stillness of the country became distasteful to her, while the drudgery of rural life, much greater than in our day, she endeavored to avoid by seeking employment at the Indian Queen Inn, where as a relative, by rendering some service in the household affairs, she was received as one of the family. The young man heretofore mentioned resided at the inn as a boarder, and Elizabeth, then in the full maturity of her beauty, became warmly, devotedly attached to him. His attentions were so marked that no doubt was entertained by her relatives in the city that a marriage between the young couple would ultimately result. They, like Elizabeth, did not suspect the traitorous heart of the young man, who, during the war, had acquitted himself as a bold, dashing officer. Sufficient it is to my purpose to state that the poor girl, unmarried, when on the eve of becoming a mother, was informed by the parties with whom she was living in Philadelphia that she must withdraw herself from their dwelling.

Whither to go she knew not, but at length she determined to seek the shelter of her father's house, and learning that a farmer living in the same neighborhood with her parents was in the city, she asked the privilege of riding thither in his market-wagon. It was late in the night, in those days of early hours, that she alighted from the vehicle at the gate of her childhood's home, and, in great agony of mind and body, she wearily made her way to the door of the house, which stood some little distance from the highway, and when there she was so exhausted that she could not rap for admission, but sank on the steps. Her moanings, however, aroused her father, who raised the window and inquired, "Who's there?" "A poor sick woman," was the faint response to his question. The old man's feeling of humanity was touched, and he and his wife—Elizabeth Wilson's step-mother—hurried to the door, and raising the poor girl, bore her to a settee, without recognizing her as their child. And then before morning Elizabeth gave birth to two male children.

As soon as the mother had again strength she rode to Philadelphia to find the father of her sons, who had, a little while before their birth, absented himself from the Indian Queen, giving out that he had gone away on business and would be absent some time. On her arrival in the city she found him. He received her apparently with pleasure, and after they had been together several hours she remounted the horse and returned to Chester County.

The Sunday following, while her parents were absent at worship, she dressed herself, and taking her babes with her left the house, stating that she was going to meet their father and be married. She walked in the direction of Newtown Square, and for a week (excepting a neighbor going along the road conveyed her a short distance in his wagon, from which she alighted on the King's Highway leading to Philadelphia, and seating herself on a rock on the roadside, near the farm of Mr. Cope, in East Bradford, where he last saw her nursing her infants) nothing more was heard respecting her for a week or more; although it afterwards appeared that about dusk the same day she came to the Indian Queen Inn, in Philadelphia, haggard, and exhibiting all the indications of an unsound mind. Her children were not with her.

A week or so after the disappearance of Elizabeth Wilson, while some gunners were traversing the woods on the east side of the Edgmont road, above Street road, their dogs discovered the bodies of two murdered babies hidden beneath a felled tree, a little earth and twigs having been thrown upon the corpses to conceal them from sight. The remains were immediately taken to her father's house,—for she was at once under suspicion,—where they were fully identified by the clothing as her children. A coroner's jury was impaneled, and a verdict rendered charging the crime of murder on the absent mother. She was shortly thereafter arrested and lodged in the old jail in Chester. When taken into custody she remained silent, refusing to make any statement as to the deed, and a sluggish apathy marked her demeanor, saving at times when she would weep passionately and appeal to heaven for mercy.

When the Court of Oyer and Terminer for Chester County was held, the grand jury indicted her for murder and she was arraigned for trial, but to the clerk's inquiry, "How say you, prisoner at the bar, are you guilty or not guilty?" she made no response save weeping violently. Judge Atlee (William Augustus Atlee, one of the puisne judges of the

Supreme Court, appointed Aug 17, 1777), kindly turning to the unfortunate girl, asked her whether she had counsel, and receiving a shake of the head in reply, he ordered that the plea of "not guilty" be taken, assigning also counsel to defend her The latter asked that the trial might be delayed until the following day, so that he would be afforded an opportunity to consult with his client and make preparation for her defense, a request which was immediately granted

The next morning when court assembled the prisoner's counsel announced that he did not know, under the circumstances, what to do, that he had failed, despite his utmost efforts, to obtain a single word in answer to his questions from Elizabeth Wilson, that he was impressed that there was something in this case so exceptionally out of the ordinary course of crime, that the ends of justice might be reached and an endeavor made to fathom the mystery he asked the bench to defer the trial to the next court Judge Atlee, knowing that to proceed meant conviction for the prisoner, in the goodness of his heart ordered that the trial should go over to the following term

During the interval an effort was made to solve the mystery which shrouded the murder in obscurity, while, notwithstanding the terrible consequences that would ensue to her if she still remained obstinately silent was made plain to Elizabeth Wilson, not a word could she be induced to say respecting the crime, but every interview with her terminated in an outburst of tears, which would continue for hours When her case finally came up for trial, although the sympathies of the court and lookers-on were decidedly with the prisoner, the evidence produced all led to the conclusion that she was guilty of the crime for which she had been indicted Attorney-General Bradford, at the conclusion of the address of the prisoner's counsel, refused to marshal the evidence for the government, and when Judge Atlee came to charge the jury he turned to the accused and asked her, even at that late moment, to make some declaration, to say something in the terrible condition in which she then stood, but she merely shook her head, muttering, "I cannot! Jesus, have mercy on me!" Atlee, in his remarks, was brief, and simply defined the law of murder, without in any wise intimating to the jury his conclusions on the facts in the case The latter, although no testimony had been offered for the defense, as an evidence of the general sympathy existing in the community, were several hours deliberating on the verdict, and it is related that as the foreman returned their finding, "Guilty," his voice was scarcely audible to those nearest him, notwithstanding the stillness in the court-room was intense The judge immediately, as was then the custom, pronounced the sentence of the law, fixing the date of execution for Wednesday, the 7th of December, 1785

While the friendless girl—for her parents, who had not forsaken her in her misfortune, now turned from her when she was charged with murder, and had remained obstinately silent as to the accusation—was on trial, her only brother, William Wilson, was employed on a farm in a retired part of Lancaster County, and, as news traveled slowly in those days, he was absolutely ignorant of the great danger in which his sister was then placed But one morning, less than a week before the time fixed for her execution, William, while engaged in his ordinary labor, suddenly stated to those with whom he was at work that he must immediately go to Chester, for he was wanted there When he repaired to the house and informed his employer (Dr Fahnestock's grandfather, and the doctor narrated this incident), the latter strove to persuade him to remain, and desired to know why he was so anxious to go at that time William merely responded, "I do not know, but I must go and find out what it is" And he immediately set out for Chester, stopping as he journeyed thither at his father's house, where he learned for the first time of the children's birth, their death, and that Elizabeth had been indicted, tried, and in a few days would be hanged for their murder Without further delay he hastened to Chester, reaching here on the afternoon of Monday, the 3d of December, hardly forty-eight hours before the time designated for her execution The imprisoned girl had been daily visited, after her sentence, by Elder Fleeson and the rector of St Paul's Church, and the former stated to Dr Fahnestock that her constant prayer for several days before her brother actually came was that the Lord would direct William to her in her great extremity As soon as the latter had access to the prison, although he had partly promised his father that he would make no effort to have an interview with the woman who had brought such deep sorrow to her aged parent, and after the excitement consequent on his visit had in a measure subsided, Elizabeth stated that she had something to communicate to him in private He, however, replied that if it was purely a personal matter, he would consent, but if it was aught relating to the crime, he would not hear her unless two other witnesses besides the clergymen who were with her were present It was court-week, and her brother requested Judge Atlee, Attorney-General Bradford, Sheriff Gibbons, and the prisoner's counsel to come to the cell, and in their presence, at the repeated solicitation of William Wilson, the condemned woman made a full confession, the substance of which was as follows

That when she visited Philadelphia after the birth of her children, at the interview she had with her "undoer," he promised to meet her at Newtown Square on the Sunday following, at which time they would be married, and he would provide for the mother and her offsprings On the day designated he met her, but it was several miles beyond the place appointed, where the road led through a dense woods He received her with warmth of manner, and requested her to walk some distance aside, where they would be removed from the observation of persons who might be passing along the highway. The weary woman seated herself on the trunk of a felled tree, having both the children in her arms. After some conversation the man asked Elizabeth to permit him to take one of the children, that he might see whether it resembled him. He held the baby in his arms for a moment, then, after a pause, he laid it on the ground, and, snatching the other from its mother's embrace, deposited it alongside of its brother. The inhuman father thereupon demanded that Elizabeth should destroy her infants. She unhesitatingly refused to injure them, but in turn besought him to spare their lives, promising that if he did she would never more trouble him, but would work willingly, or even beg her and their daily bread, for the children were dearer to her than her life. He, however, brutally replied that he could have no mercy for a fallen woman or her sinful offspring, and thereupon drawing a pistol, he pointed it at her, while at the same time he placed his feet on the infants' breasts, and, before she could prevent him, he crushed them to death. The murderer then compelled the unhappy woman, on peril of her life, to swear by her soul's everlasting welfare that she would never reveal the dreadful deed nor the name of the chief actor in the crime, but that she would tell all persons who might inquire for the children that they had been taken to New Jersey to nurse and be reared. In conclusion, Elizabeth Wilson declared, "To the truth of this statement I appeal to the Searcher of all hearts, before whose dread tribunal I am to appear next day after to-morrow."

The declaration of the prisoner was reduced to writing, and she swore to its truth, while the signatures of all present were attached to the document, attesting that the confession had been made in their hearing. Armed with this paper, William Wilson, night as it was, with all speed hastened to Philadelphia to obtain a respite from the Executive Council, with what success the following extract from the Pennsylvania Colonial Record (vol xiv p 591) exhibits:

"The petition of William Wilson, brother to Elizabeth Wilson, now confined in jail of Chester under sentence of death, accompanied by a confession of the said Elizabeth, was read, and, in consideration of the circumstances stated therein, it was Ordered,—That the warrant issued by the Board for the Execution of Elizabeth Wilson on Wednesday, the Seventh instant, be revoked, and that another issue, directory of her execution on the third day of January, 1788."

William Wilson, immediately after he had given proper notice to the authorities of Chester County of the action of the Supreme Executive Council, set off for West Jersey, where his sister's betrayer was said then to be living. He found him, and when confronted by Wilson, he declared that he did not know his sister, and had not been in Philadelphia for two years. Wilson thereupon returned to Chester, had an interview with Elizabeth, and succeeded in finding a witness who would testify that the man whom she accused had not only been in Philadelphia and lodged at the same house with her, but he had procured other important testimony to substantiate her charge, when he was taken severely ill. The time granted by Council had nearly expired, and sick as he was, William Wilson made his way to Chester, intending to go thence to Philadelphia for a further respite. When he reached this place in the afternoon he was astonished to learn that the stay of execution would expire the next day, whereas he had thought it was not out until the day following. Immediately on learning of this error he hastened to Philadelphia through a heavy rainfall, and, according to a statement of one of the members of Council,[1] "unfortunately he went to the President's (Dr Franklin), where, notwithstanding all his entreaties, it was some time before he could get to see him, and when he did he stayed, endeavoring to persuade the doctor to give him a line to the sheriff, which the former, thinking it improper, refused, and directed him to me. I was just leaving the Council-chamber when he came, all the other members but one having gone. I immediately wrote, 'Do not execute Wilson till you hear further from the Council,' and directed it to the sheriff. I well knew the board intended to grant a further respite."

Wilson started immediately on his return, the rain in the mean while having increased until it now descended in heavy torrents, and the road in places was submerged in the water which the wayside ditches could not carry away as fast as it fell. On reaching the Middle Ferry over the Schuylkill—there was no bridge at that time—he found it was impossible to get conveyance over the river on such a night as it was and in the pelting storm. At daylight the next morning William was at the ferry, but the river, swollen by the preceding day's rain, was so threatening that the ferryman refused to attempt the passage of the stream, and, although Wilson told him that a human life hung on his movement, it was all in vain, he declined to endanger his own existence on any consideration. The hours were passing, and at last, fully assured that nothing would induce the ferryman to cross the river with the boat, William Wilson fastened the respite in the lining of his cap, which he placed on his head, then spreading a handkerchief over all, he tied the ends securely under his chin, and with great difficulty forced the horse he rode into the water. Right nobly did the animal breast the swiftly-flowing current which washed down the wide channel with terrific force, and in all probabilities it might have made the way safely to the other side had his course not been frequently impeded by drift-ice, and even heavy pieces of timber came driven onward by the flood, which, striking the beast, turned him repeatedly aside. At length, just when the edge of the current

1 Martin's "History of Chester," p 185

on the western side of the river had been passed, and the most difficult part of the crossing had been overcome, the horse, completely exhausted, sank, leaving William Wilson to battle with the wildly-rushing waters. By this time a number of persons, despite the storm that was raging, had gathered at the ferry-house, and the utmost anxiety prevailed among them as they watched the bold swimmer struggling with the stream, which ran like a sluiceway to the Delaware. The remarkable muscular strength of the man served him well, and although, physically, he was greatly exhausted when he landed on the opposite shore, two miles below the point where he entered the river on the Philadelphia side, he immediately set about procuring another horse, and, after considerable delay, he started for Chester under spur and whip. The highway by this time was mid-leg deep with pasty mud.

About mid-day at the latter place the storm abated, and as no reprieve had come, Sheriff Gibbons ordered the preliminary arrangements to be made for the execution. Nevertheless, he determined to delay carrying out the sentence of the law to the last moment possible under his warrant, and even after the prisoner had been placed in the cart and the procession, followed by a large number of persons, was on its way to the usual place of execution, he stationed duly qualified deputies at some distance on the road to Philadelphia to notify him by white flags of the approach of William Wilson with the papers he believed he would bring staying the work of death. The solemn cortege had reached the place designated,—a wild cherry-tree on "Hangman's Lot," at the intersection of Edgmont and Providence Avenues, one of the branches extending some distance at right angles to the trunk, and whereon a little over seven years previously James Fitzpatrick had met his fate,—and the last moment designated for the execution was at hand. The unfortunate culprit was ordered to stand up in the cart, and the fatal noose was placed about her neck. There, in the presence of death, she reiterated that her former statement was true in every particular, then, after a few moments were spent in prayer, the last moment for carrying out the mandate of the law had come, and the cart in which she stood was drawn from beneath her feet. Elizabeth Wilson had been landed into eternity, but so engrossed were the spectators with anxiety for the coming of her brother that but few in the assembly knew when she was swung off, so intently were they watching the line of white flags leading to the Queen's Highway.

A deep silence followed, hardly a word was spoken for more than a quarter of an hour save in whispers, when in the far distance a tiny white flag was observed to be waved to and fro, to be caught up and repeated by the other flagmen, and a few moments thereafter a haggard, travel-stained man, bespattered with mud, bestriding a horse struggling from weakness, that put forth renewed effort under the goading whip and spur, came into sight, holding in his hand at full arm's length a paper. The sheriff immediately cut the rope. The hoarse voice of the man shouting "A reprieve! a reprieve!" was now audible, and a few moments thereafter William Wilson's horse fell, throwing the rider senseless, almost under the bough where his sister's body had lately been suspended. He came twenty-three minutes too late. The neck of the unhappy girl had been dislocated, and she had died without a struggle.

When resuscitated, to the surprise of all beholders the man's face was stamped with lines of age and the dark locks of youth had turned to snowy whiteness. Agony in a few moments had done the work of years.

The *Pennsylvania Packet* for Jan. 12, 1786, refers to the execution as follows:

"On Tuesday, the 3d inst., the woman who was tried and convicted at Chester, of murdering her two bastard children, ten weeks after their birth, was hanged at that place pursuant to her sentence, the respite given by the Honourable Council having expired."

The sequel to this extraordinary case is peculiarly marked with dramatic features. When William Wilson was restored to health, for he lingered for some time after his sister's execution with a low fever, in which he, in delirious dreams, re-enacted his remarkable efforts to save Elizabeth's life, he withdrew himself from the haunts of men, and taking up his abode in the Hummelstown cave in the Swatara Mountains, Dauphin County, led a solitary life, employing himself at his trade in making grindstones, which he sold to Mr. Wolfersberger, of Campbellstown. His cave was furnished with a table, a stove, a bed of straw, and a few cooking utensils. He was cleanly in his habits, and (a noticeable thing in these days) never shaved his face, but let his long, snowy beard sweep his breast, and he employed all his time when not at work with reading diligently his Bible and religious books. He was popularly known as the "Pennsylvania Hermit."

In the *Harrisburg Intelligencer* of Oct. 13, 1821, I find the following notice of his death:

"Died lately at his lonely hovel among the hills, twelve miles southeast from Harrisburg, Pa., —— Wilson, who for many years endeavored to be a solitary recluse from the society of men, excepting as far as was necessary for his support. His retirement was principally occasioned by the melancholy manner of the death of his sister, by which his reason was partially affected. She had been condemned to die near Philadelphia for murder, in the hope of concealing her shame from the world, and the day of execution was appointed. In the mean time her brother used his utmost means to obtain her pardon from the Governor. He had succeeded, and his horse foamed and bled as he spurred him homeward. But an unpropitious rain had swollen the stream, he was compelled to pace the bank with bursting brain and gaze upon the rushing waters that threatened to blast his only hope. At the earliest moment that a ford was practicable he dashed through, and arrived at the place of execution just in time to see the last struggle of his sister. This was the fatal blow. He retired to the hills of Dauphin County, where he employed himself in making grindstones for a livelihood. He was very exact in his accounts, but was observed frequently to be estranged, and one morning was found dead by a few of his neighbors, who had left him the evening previously in good health."

Long years ago the residents of Chester would frequently relate the occasional appearance of a spectral white horse and rider which on stormy nights could be seen and heard clattering along Fourth Street at a headlong pace to the prison door, and that reached, the noise ceased and the apparition faded into the darkness. Many of the superstitious people of that day firmly believed that the phantom steed bore the unhappy William Wilson, whose fruitless ride to Philadelphia to obtain a respite for his sister that I have narrated still lingers in the traditions of our county.

Jan. 21, 1786, Robert Wilson, or Elliott (for the "Colonial Record" uses both names in referring to this prisoner), was under sentence of death in the old jail at Chester, but the Executive Council saw fit to defer the execution until February 11th of the same year. Before that date came the Council pardoned him, on condition that "he transport himself beyond the seas, not to return to the United States."

On June 5, 1786, from the proceedings of the Executive Council we learn that at that date John McDonough and Richard Shirtliffe were in jail at Chester, under sentence of death for rape, and that the sheriff of the county was ordered to execute them on Saturday, June 17, 1786. Subsequently, with a refinement of cruelty hardly to be looked for from the men at the head of the State government, Council ordered that Richard Shirtliffe should be reprieved until further orders, directing, however, that the welcome intelligence should not be imparted to him until he had been taken under the gallows. What became of him subsequently I have not learned, but in less than four months there was a general jail delivery from the old jail at Chester, when, under the act of Sept. 25, 1786, Sheriff Gibbons removed all the prisoners to the new jail in Goshen township (now West Chester), and the "black stage, the cross-beam, the rope, and all the hideous apparatus of death" was removed, not to be erected again in this locality for the third of a century.

Although no capital conviction was had in Delaware County for twenty-nine years after its creation in 1789, it must not be supposed that no trials for murder occurred during that interval, for such would be a serious error. At the Court of Oyer and Terminer held April 25, 1797, Jacob Rudolph, of Darby township, was tried for killing John Barr by striking him on the head with an iron rake. The defendant was convicted of involuntary manslaughter, and sentenced to six months' imprisonment and costs. At a like court held in April, 1801, Samuel Black, Catharine Black, and Sarah Campbell, of Marple, were tried for having beaten a negro girl named Patt with sticks so severely that she died from the injuries sustained. The jury returned a verdict of not guilty as to all the defendants. Patrick Gallahoe, laborer, was tried Oct. 28, 1802, for the murder of Alexander McKettuck by striking him with a stick. The jury found the prisoner guilty of murder in the second degree, and he was sentenced to sixteen years' imprisonment, four of which was to be solitary confinement and the remainder of the term at hard labor. On Jan. 30, 1806, Samuel Howard, a laborer, was tried for the murder of Abraham Stevenson. The accused had thrown the deceased into the river, where he was drowned. Howard was convicted of manslaughter, and sentenced to five years' imprisonment in the penitentiary at Philadelphia.

At the October sessions, 1806, Francis Patterson was indicted and convicted of challenging Curtis Lownes, of Ridley, to fight a duel. The accused was sentenced to pay costs of prosecution, a fine of five hundred dollars, and to undergo an imprisonment in the county jail at hard labor for one year. In addition he was deprived of all rights of citizenship within the commonwealth for the term of seven years.

On April 14, 1818, John H. Craig was tried for the murder of Squire Hunter, of Newtown, an account of which crime will be found in the history of that township.

At the January Oyer and Terminer, 1819, Charles Norton was convicted of rape, attended with aggravated circumstances. Judge Ross sentenced him to be confined "in the goal and penitentiary-house of Philadelphia for a period of twenty-one years from this day, and to be confined and kept at hard labour, fed and clothed, as the Act of Assembly directs, and be placed during one-fourth of the said term in the solitary cells, that he pay the costs of prosecution, and be committed till the whole sentence is complied with." Thomas Prevard, who was convicted at the same court of a similar offense, received a like sentence. Henry Duffey, at the January Oyer and Terminer, 1820, was convicted of rape, and sentenced to imprisonment for fifteen years.

At the April court, 1820, Benjamin Bevan was tried for the manslaughter of Ebenezer Cook by a blow on the head with a stick, causing death in three days thereafter. The jury by their verdict acquitted the accused.

At the October Court of Oyer and Terminer, 1824, Michael Munroe, *alias* James Wellington, was convicted of the murder of William Bonsall, and Washington Labbe of murder in the second degree. An account of this case will be found in the history of Upper Darby township.

On Jan. 16, 1827, James Fleming was tried for the

murder of Patrick Gill The prisoner had a knife in his hand when he was attacked by Gill, and in the quarrel Fleming struck the deceased with the weapon in the left side near the groin, causing the latter's death the same day The defense was that the act was done in self-protection, and the jury acquitted Fleming

On Oct 23, 1829, Thomas Brooke was arraigned for the murder of William Brook, a Revolutionary soldier, the indictment setting forth that the accused had struck the deceased on the head with a stick, which killed him instantly. Hon Edward Darlington, the then deputy attorney-general, abandoned the case after a few witnesses had been examined for the commonwealth, stating that "there was not a shadow of proof to support the accusation" The jury, without leaving the box, acquitted the defendant

Charles Williams, a colored man, who had been convicted of burglary, on Oct 24, 1829, was taken by Sheriff Broomhall, of Delaware County, to undergo a term of imprisonment at Cherry Hill It is stated that Williams was the first prisoner from any part of the State ever confined in the present Eastern Penitentiary

At November court, 1836, Richard Milner Martin, a colored man, was tried for killing William Patton by striking him on the head with a stick of wood He was acquitted On Nov 29, 1838, Thomas McLaughlin was tried for the murder of William Pierce The defendant, November 16th of the same year, struck the deceased on the head with a handspike, and from the injury death ensued the same day The jury convicted the accused of manslaughter, accompanying their finding with a recommendation of the prisoner "to the most extended leniency of the court" McLaughlin was sentenced to two years' imprisonment in the penitentiary

May 28, 1841, Thomas Cropper was convicted of the murder of Martin Hollis, and executed Aug 6, 1841, in the jail-yard at Chester This was the last capital conviction in Delaware County A full account of this case will be given in the history of Birmingham

On Nov 23, 1841, Thomas Vanderslice, known to the detectives as "Old Tom Vanderslice," was tried for passing counterfeit money He refused to employ or have counsel assigned to conduct his defense, but managed his own case, and made a speech to the court (Judge Bell was on the bench) which was remarkable for its boldness and impudence He was convicted, and sentenced to three years' incarceration in the penitentiary After his discharge, on March 24, 1848, he fell into the river at Dock Street wharf, Philadelphia, and was drowned

On May 27, 1845, Alexander Harris, *alias* Dobson, was tried for the murder of Ruth Harris, an infant The accused was a colored man, and the child was the fruits of his criminal intimacy with a white woman The body of the infant was found at "Deep Hole," in Darby Creek, at Calcoon Hook, in a bag, in which was a heavy stone to sink it in the water The jury, after three hours' deliberation, found the prisoner not guilty

Nov. 27, 1846, Isaiah Spencer, indicted for shooting William Davis in the left breast, from which wound the latter died instantly, was arraigned Spencer plead guilty to manslaughter, and was sentenced to two years in the penitentiary

May 28, 1862, Martha J Long, of Chester, was tried for the murder of her bastard child The prosecution strove to show how she had strangled it, but the jury acquitted her of murder, but found her guilty of concealing the death of a bastard child The court sentenced her to three months' imprisonment

On Feb 23, 1864, George Wilkinson was indicted for the murder of Ellen Jones and John Blair, in Middletown The particulars of this crime are narrated in the history of that township

On Feb 26, 1866, John Ward, charged with engaging in a prize-fight with Farrell, near Linwood, which brutal exhibition took place on February 3d of the same year, was tried and convicted The court sentenced him to two years' imprisonment in the Eastern Penitentiary

Jan 6, 1869, James Weir, a lad thirteen years of age, living in Chester, was tried for the murder of John Thomas, a youth of sixteen The boys were employed in Patterson Mill, had quarreled, and in the scuffle Weir, with his pocket-knife, stabbed Thomas, who died almost immediately The jury convicted the prisoner of manslaughter, and he was sentenced to one year's imprisonment On November 25th of the same year Thomas Bryson, a shoemaker, of Marple, was tried for the murder of William Stinson The deceased and the accused had a difficulty on September 22d, during which Bryson struck Stinson on the head with a stone, inflicting an injury from which death ensued the following day The jury found a verdict of manslaughter, with a recommendation to the mercy of the court Bryson was sentenced to two years' imprisonment

Aug 22, 1870, Sarah Seaburn, a widow, was tried for the murder of her father, Geo. Clay, of Upper Darby She had struck him with a hatchet on the head, producing almost instant death The jury acquitted her on the ground of insanity, and she was committed to the county-house

Nov 25, 1872, Joseph Worrall, Jr, was tried for the murder, in August preceding, of David Neidig The deceased, with a number of ladies and gentlemen, were walking near Lima, when all of the party, excepting the deceased, went into the yard of Mr Stork's dwelling for a drink of water One of the party in the yard cast a stone, striking the house, and Worrall, who was in the house, came out and threw a stone violently at the crowd, who were then in the road, which struck Neidig on the head He died three days afterwards The jury found the accused guilty of involuntary manslaughter, and he was sentenced to one year and nine months' imprisonment.

On Sept. 22, 1875, Charles McDevitt, a peddler, sixty years of age, living in Upper Darby, was tried for the murder of James Fletcher, of Haverford. On May 21st McDevitt was ordered away from Fletcher's house, was put out of the gate, and his bundle was tossed over in the road to him. "Throw my stick over, too," he said to Fletcher. From this a quarrel resulted, and during the scuffle the peddler stabbed Fletcher near the heart, killing him almost immediately. The jury convicted McDevitt of manslaughter, and he was sentenced to imprisonment for one year.

James Sheridan, a hired man on the farm of Samuel H. Hibberd, of Haverford, was killed Dec. 6, 1875, under the following circumstances: Six young men, accompanied with dogs, were gunning on Mr. Hibberd's farm, where persons were interdicted from trespassing. The owner of the place took a double-barreled gun, and, going to where the parties were, shot one of the dogs. This brought on a serious difficulty between the trespassers, Mr. Hibberd, and his hired men. In the struggle Sheridan grappled with John Baird, and the prosecution strove to show that Thomas Cromie, who had a gun, fired the shot killing Sheridan, or that Frederick Troup had deliberately shot him from a lot adjoining. The case was tried March 10, 1876, the jury retired on Saturday night, and on Monday afternoon returned a verdict of voluntary manslaughter. The court sentenced Frederick Troup, John Baird, and Thomas Cromie each to three years' imprisonment in the county jail.

On March 8, 1876, Josiah Porter, a colored man, was tried for the murder of Joseph Murray. The supervisors of Ridley were repairing the Lazaretto road, just above the Queen's Highway, and Porter, Murray, and a number of other men were there working. Some difficulty occurred between the two men respecting a shovel, which Murray took from Porter and then threw it back. The latter seized the shovel, and as Murray turned to walk away struck him over the head with it. Murray died several hours after receiving the blow. The jury found the prisoner guilty of murder in the second degree, and he was sentenced to ten years' imprisonment in the county jail.

On the night of July 29, 1876, Lewis Kershaw, a police officer of Chester, arrested three young men in South Ward, and while he was taking them to the lock-up several persons interfered, and James McGinley broke away and ran, pursued by the officer. The latter overtook his prisoner, a scuffle followed, during which the officer's pistol was discharged, the ball lodging in McGinley's side, wounding him so severely that he died before morning. The grand jury at the September court ignored the bills of indictment against Kershaw which were laid before them by the district attorney.

John Duffey, charged with the murder of Thomas Conner, at Rockdale, on the night of Aug. —, 1880, was tried Sept. 27, 1880. The commonwealth sought to show that Duffey and William Frame had had a dispute, and a short time afterwards, when at the Rockdale depot, where there were a number of persons, Duffey fired at Frame, the ball striking Conner, a young man in no wise party to the difficulty, killing him instantly. The defense alleged that in drawing his pistol it was accidentally discharged, and there was no intention on Duffey's part to injure any one. The jury convicted him of involuntary manslaughter, and he was sentenced to nine months' imprisonment in the county jail.

On Sept. 23, 1881, Patrick Kilcorse was tried for the murder of his wife on the 4th of July previous. The prisoner had quarreled with his wife the night before, and she had sought shelter in an outhouse, where she remained all night. In the morning the neighbors heard a heavy blow, and going in found Mrs. Kilcorse lying on the floor, blood trickling from her head. It was proposed to send for a doctor, but the prisoner said, "No, d——n her, let her die." The jury convicted Kilcorse of murder in the second degree, and he was sentenced to twelve years' imprisonment in the penitentiary.

On June 7, 1883, Dennis Green, a colored man of Chester, was tried for the murder of James Clark. The defendant struck the deceased on the head with a blackjack, on the night of the 23d of February. Clark, after receiving the blow, went home, and was found dead in his bed the following morning. The jury convicted Green of murder in the second degree, but recommended him to the mercy of the court. He was sentenced to ten years' solitary confinement in the penitentiary.

William H. Collins, on Sept. 26, 1883, was arraigned for the murder of his wife, near Lee's Dam, at Leiperville. The prosecution sought to show that on June 5th the accused, an intemperate man, had beaten his wife, also of intemperate habits, and had stamped on her with his feet, inflicting such injuries that she died the same night. Collins was convicted of murder in the second degree, and sentenced to twelve years' imprisonment in the penitentiary.

CHAPTER XIX.

MANNERS AND CUSTOMS—HOW INHABITANTS OF DELAWARE COUNTY LIVED IN FORMER YEARS.

Houses.—The progress of a nation is traced not in the life of an individual, who, from some personal or fortunate circumstance, was elevated for the time being above his fellows, but is found in the narrative of the daily lives of the people, whereby we learn how they were sheltered, fed, and clothed, and the manners and customs which marked them as a whole. Hence, believing as I do that civilization means nothing more than advanced cultivation, which brings as its results comforts and luxuries before unknown, as well as the general diffusion of knowledge in the arts and sciences, constituted the true annals of a people, I purpose, as briefly as I can, to present a sketch of how the inhabitants of Delaware County lived from the early settlement until within recent years.

We have little record of the Swedish settlers along the Delaware previous to the coming of Penn in 1682, but from these meagre accounts we learn that the houses of the early Swedish settlers were built of logs, and the doors were so low that a person of ordinary stature was compelled to stoop in entering or leaving the buildings, while the apartments within had low ceilings, hardly over six feet in the clear, and the roughly-hewed rafters supporting the roof were devoid of laths and plaster. The windows were small, mere frames set in the logs, and although the families who indulged in more costly luxuries than their neighbors had the openings glazed with isinglass, in general only a rough board slide shut out the cold on extreme winter days, and was usually closed during the night. The chimneys, with huge fireplaces, were occasionally built of gray sandstone, but often the stacks were erected of turf on the outside of the houses. In many of the early dwellings small rooms just large enough to spread a bed were partitioned off from the main lower apartments, and the floors were laid in stone, or, oftener, simply clay, which by constant use became very hard.

With the English settlers came many of the improvements which the progressive age between 1640 and 1680 had introduced into general use, but so rapid was the influx of immigrants, mostly Friends, fleeing from the religious oppression they had been subjected to in the mother-country, that habitations could not be erected quickly enough to supply the demand, even where the simple form of building suggested by Penn[1] was constructed, and many families sought shelter in great trees, while others of the new-comers were compelled, in many instances, to dig caves in the ground, near the river-bank and those of the creeks, wherein they took up their abode until they could construct permanent habitations. These caves were mere excavations or cellars in the bank, and were about three feet in depth, while over these openings brush was placed so as to form an arched roof about six feet in the clear, which was covered with sods. In such a cave as this Emanuel Grubb was born, near Upland, in 1682. The sufferings of these settlers were great, for it should be remembered that most of them were "not people of low circumstances, but substantial livers," and in the work of constructing these rude habitations women who had been used to all the refinements and comforts of English life at that day were compelled to take part, and aided their husbands and fathers therein, for hired labor was scarce and could hardly be had at any price.

The log cabins of the early settlers were generally built on low ground for a twofold purpose, to be near a spring of water and for protection from the bleak and piercing winds of winter. In the construction of these habitations the logs were notched together at the corners, which after being raised were hewn down both inside and outside, while the spaces between the logs were filled in or "chinked" with stones or wood, and then plastered over with mortar or clay. The roofs were covered with oak shingles. Locks in ordinary use were unknown; the doors were opened by strings, which on being pulled from the outside raised heavy wooden latches within, to which they were made fast, and intrusion was prevented when the inmates pulled the latch-strings in at the outer doors. From this common practice originated the ancient saying descriptive of generous hospitality, "The latch-string is always out." The chimneys of the English settlers, as well as those of the Swedish houses, were of immense size, frequently capable of receiving a cord-wood stick, in those days when wood was abundant and the cold intense. Frequently, too, benches would be placed at each side of the chimney so that persons could seat themselves near to and enjoy the blaze, particularly when the heat therefrom to a large percentage was drawn up the stack and discharged into the atmosphere outside.

As heretofore stated, a number of the English settlers were in good circumstances, and before many years brick and stone dwellings were erected. In the towns this was noticeably the case, and as bricks were made at Chester[2] as early as 1684, and previous to

[1] "To build there an House of thirty foot long and eighteen foot broad, with a partition neer the middle, and an other to divide one end of the House into two small Rooms, there must be eight Tree of about sixteen Inches square, and cut off to Posts of about fifteen foot long, which the House must stand upon, and four pieces, two of thirty foot long and two of eighteen foot long, for Plates, which must lie upon the top of these Posts, the whole length and breadth of the House for the Gists to rest upon. There must be ten Gists of twenty foot long to bear the Lofts and two false Plates of thirty foot long, to lie upon the ends of the Gists for the Rafters to be fixed upon, twelve pair of Rafters of about twenty foot, to bear the Roof of the House, with several other small pieces, as Wind-beams, Braces, Studs, etc., which are made out of the Waste Timber. For covering the House, Ends and Sides, and for the Loft, we use Clabboard which is Rived feather-edged of five foot and a half long, that well Drawn, lyes close and smooth. The Lodging Room may be lined with the same and filld up between, which is very Warm. These houses usually endure ten years without Repair.

	£	s.	d.
For the carpenter's work for such a House, I and my servants assisting him, together with his Diet	7	00	
For a Barn of the same Building and Dimensions	5	00	
For Nails and other things to finish Both	3	10	

"The lower floor is the Ground, the upper Clabboard. This may seem a mean way of Building, but 'tis sufficient and safest for ordinary beginners." (Direction to such persons as are inclined to America, 1682, *Penn. Mag. of Hist.*, vol. iv. p. 334.)

[2] Vice-Director Alrichs, under date of Sept. 1, 1657, wrote to Stuyvesant from New Castle, and among other things states, "Since Sr Cornelius Hogeboom, a brick-maker, has arrived here, and his son and brother's son are living at Fort Orange (Albany) or on the road to Mrs-

that date at Burlington and Philadelphia, the wealthier classes employed that material for building purposes The houses then erected were generally large and roomy, giving the inmates almost all the comforts, so far as the buildings were concerned, then known to the mother country The old Porter house in Chester, built by David Lloyd thirty-nine years after Penn first landed in Pennsylvania, was an imposing structure even to the hour of the explosion which destroyed it, and affords to the present generation the opportunity to learn with what stability the buildings were constructed in the early time

Early Schools—The settlers were not unmindful of intellectual training, and in the act of March 10, 1683, which set forth that "to the end that the Poor, as well as the Rich, may be instructed in good and commendable learning, which is to be preferred above wealth," is given the first outline of the public-school system which promises to be in the future, as it has been in the past, the anchor of safety to the nation in times of public peril It is difficult to determine when the first school was established in our county, but certain it is that at the middle of the last century there were quite a number scattered throughout the territory now included within our boundaries These structures were generally of logs, and the urchins sat on frames fashioned in every case from the side slabs from the saw-mills, while books were scarce Townsend Ward[1] describes the manner of teaching practiced towards the end of the last century by no less a person than Alexander Wilson "His scholars were instructed in the mode of those days, which has become so obsolete now that the very first steps in it are a puzzle to the adult The alphabet in the form of a cross was called the Christ Cross Row Each vowel had to be sounded 'by itself,' when it was reached, and the word 'by itself' repeated The rapidity of pronunciation, however, soon turned 'by itself' into 'bisself,' so the anxious urchin rushed through his alphabet in this way, 'A, bisself a, B, C, D, E bisselfe, F, G, H, I bisselfi, etc He ended with a z as now, but called it izard, and the flourish at the end, Ampersand, he called Ann pussy Ann"

In a letter[2] dated Chester township, Tenth month, 1725, from Richard Park to his sister, Mary Valentine, then in Ireland, the writer states that "Uncle Nicholas Kooper lives very well, he rents a Plantation & teaches School and his man doe his Plantation work," which is the first mention of a pedagogue by name since Evans Petterson, in 1672 The schoolmaster of that day was a local despot, the children were under his absolute sway from the time they left their homes until they returned thereto again in the afternoon His sceptre was the birch, and often would he wield his emblem of power to the discomfiture of the unhappy lad who had aroused his wrath

Household Duties of the Women.—At home the matron and her growing daughter had their daily routine of labor, which, beginning oftentimes long before daybreak, extended into the night until the old saw,

> "A man's work is from sun to sun,
> But a woman's work is never done,"

was often proved a truth Her household duties were severe and varied, demanding some knowledge of medicine sufficient to open a vein in a case of emergency, or the preparation of certain infallible remedies to cure intermitting, remitting, and bilious fevers and children's disorders, composed of the most nauseating herbs, simmered to a sickening decoction, which was doled out to the unfortunate patients in generous potation With the exception of her husband's Sunday coat, which was the one, carefully preserved, that he had worn at his wedding, the mother had to make all the garments worn by the father and boys from the flax and wool, all the bedding and household linen had to be made at home, as well as the beds, which required that a goodly flock of geese be kept to supply the feathers, which had to be steamed and cured for that purpose, the poultry came under the supervision of the women, as did also the care of the young calves, cheese and butter had to be made for the market, frequently, too, the gardening for the family table was left to the care of the females of the household, and the gathering and drying of herbs always was a part of their duty In the butchering season pork and salt meat must be cured sufficiently for the whole year, sausage and lard made for the winter These were extra matters just thrown in to fill out the odds and ends of the matron's time, for the duties mentioned did not include the every-day work of cooking, milking, carrying water, scrubbing, darning, and for the first twenty odd years of her married life to still the crying babe or nurse it, and often then, as she hushed the sobbing child asleep, her busy fingers plied the knitting-needles, so that not a moment of her time should be idled away, and the weekly washing and ironing, nor yet the day set apart for dipping candles, which entered into the domestic economy with the regularity of the annual county taxes It was an interesting and intellectual occupation on candle day, when several huge kettles filled with melted tallow were suspended from the crane over the blazing logs, while at the opposite side of the kitchen two or more long poles, about two feet apart, stretched their full length from one chair seat to another, the abutments on which the ends of the rods rested Across these poles were pendent strands of tow at designated distances, for at the time of which I now write candle-wick had not been invented

Hutters therefore he goes there to visit the same and to speak (with them), also to see if he can persuade them to come with him" Alrichs urges Stuyvesant to use his influence to have Hogeboom locate on the Delaware (Penna Archives, 2d series, vol vii p 516.) May 14, 1659, Alrichs states that Cornelis Herperts de Jagor had "established in the country near here a brick kiln and employed 4 persons at it" (*Ib*, p 561)

1 "A Walk to Darby," *Penna Mag of History*, vol iii p 258

2 *Penna Mag of History*, vol v p 351

Near these poles were great kettles containing melted tallow, which floated on the top of hot water, and into the kettles the women would dip the strands of tow and hang them, each in its place, on the stick to dry. Before the proper amount of tallow was deposited by this slow process on the wick—for the thicker the candle the more brilliant the light—the weary dipper would walk many a mile before her work was finished. After the candles were made they had to be carried on the poles to a dry, sunny spot in the garret, where they could harden and become thoroughly dry. The good wife, however, had to see that the best room was sprinkled with clean white sand, and it was a matter of pride to draw various figures thereupon with the broom. The high-backed walnut, and (after the introduction of the wood as appropriate for furniture during Queen Anne's reign) mahogany chair and tables were waxed and polished till they reflected like a mirror. In every house there were the warming-pans of brass, which must be kept scoured and hung in easy reach, so that they could be used to take the chill off the sheets in bedrooms that were as cold "as Greenland's icy mountains." And when flax was prepared for spinning the matron sat early and late, particularly during the long winter evenings the humming noise of the big wheel was constantly heard.

To be sure, the lads and lasses of that day had their merry-making, although their sports to us seem somewhat like hard work. Flax-pulling, when the boys and girls pulled along together and bound it into small sheaves, was regarded as fun, while the "husking" parties at night were looked forward to with great expectations and much preparations, quilting and carpet-ball sociables—the latter after the Revolution, when people discovered that from rags a strong, serviceable covering for floors could be made—were much in vogue, and were concluded usually with dancing and boisterous games.

Evening Amusements.—Usually at night, when the winter evening meal was ended and the room had been put to rights, the family would assemble round the open-mouthed fireplace in the kitchen, where on the hearth the massive andirons sustained a crackling mass of hickory-wood, lapped by the flaming tongues as the blaze "went roaring up the chimney wide." Along the heavy, unplastered joists of the floor above, darkened with age and smoke, from iron hooks were suspended a goodly number of portly hams, dried beef, long ropes of onions, and dried apples. On the deal table, without a cover, a tallow candle shed a dim, uncertain light around the apartment, and often the black and crisped wick required to be snuffed, while not unfrequently a thief would get in the candle, and the tallow on one side would run to the base of the stick in a rivulet of melted grease. In one of the angles of the room a large corner cupboard afforded through its glass doors glimpses of an array of blue china which at this day would have been the idol of the collection craze, and an eight-day clock in a tall mahogany case ticked in the chilly hall, while the moon moving along the opening in the dial, represented usually by a cherub's face, plump and florid-cheeked, told the farmer when and when not to plant his crops. Around the cheery fire the family, seated on hard, uncushioned chairs, gathered, the females spinning, or perchance Miss-in-her-teens, who had paid a visit to her relatives in the city, would be busily employed working in crewel geometrical figures of a dog, sheep, or other fabulous animal or plant, the like of which never existed "in the heavens above, the earth below, or the waters under the earth." The hunting- or watch-dog, curled close to the fire, dozed as his owner smoked, talked of the weather, the crops, the state of the market, his or others' stock, or laid out the next day's work.

Perchance, when a neighbor dropped in, the conversation would relate to the social happenings of the vicinity, or at intervals of that great world, the city, but it usually drifted into recollections of the old people, narrations of hunting adventures, and marvelous tales of witches, goblins, and haunted places. The old people would relate traditionary stories of Margaret Mattson, the witch of Ridley Creek, and her divers ill-doings, they would tell how it was recorded by Hesselius, the Swedish priest, that in the early time of the settlement rain fell on a particular black oak for fifteen days, while not a drop of moisture touched the other trees in the neighborhood, and how a captain of a certain ship, noted for his profanity and crimes, while sailing up the Delaware, was seized bodily by the devil, who hurled him into the river, where he was drowned, in full sight of many lookers-on.[1] But, strange as it may seem, no stories of men suddenly and mysteriously changed into wolves, the were-wolf of Swedish folk-lore, seem ever to have taken root in this soil. There would be, however, narration of the terrible and supernatural. It would be told how Blackbeard, the pirate, used to anchor his vessel off Marcus Hook, where, at the house of a Swedish woman whose name, Margaret, he transformed into Marcus, because of the locality of her dwelling, he and his crew held mad revels there, and the expression "Discord Lane" became so connected with the town's story that it has ever since been preserved as the title of one of its streets. So, too, would they describe the Bloody Tree, near Chester, on the King's Highway, whose leaves were spotted with gore, and from whose branches, if a twig was cut or broken off, oozed a sap-like blood,[2]—the indelible mark of a brutal, un-

[1] Acrelius, "History of New Sweden," pp 279-80

[2] This story is really of Maryland origin, and was transplanted here as such narratives are usually transitory in character. The legend of the "Bloody Holly Bush" is as follows: "There is also a legend current among the old citizens of Elk Neck, which may properly be called the legend of the 'Bloody Holly-Bush,' which originated from a murder committed on the Ferry farm while it was occupied by Hans Rudolph, the proprietor of the ferry. Rudolph had a negro slave, who for some reason was confined in jail at the point, and who made his escape and

atoned murder that nature would not permit to be effaced Sometimes a swaggering braggart would declare that as he rode along the White Horse level, on the Queen's Highway, through Ridley, he had encountered the ghost of Luke Nethermarke, who, about the middle of the last century, in galloping his horse at night amid the storm and the darkness as he hastened homeward, rode into a tree which had been blown down by the gale and was killed, while others would tell the story of the phantom sentinel, who, when an English vessel of war was lying off Tinicum during the British occupation of Philadelphia, was stationed to walk post over one of the boats sent ashore with a foraging party, was shot and killed by the Whigs in the neighborhood, and whose spectre annually reappears on the anniversary of the night on which he was slain Sometimes the tradition was of Moggey,[1] who refused to rest quietly in her grave, of the phantom white steed and rider, who dashed semi-occasionally on dark and stormy nights through the streets of Chester, of the murdered peddler at Munday's Run, who showed the ragged cut in his brawny throat, or the slain woman who made the archway of the old granary at Chester a spot to be avoided after dusk, while the mere school-lads in the vicinity of Chester would tell of the evil spirit, a caco-demon,[2] who inhabited the cellar of the old school house at Welsh and Fifth Streets

Sometimes the stories would relate to money buried along the shores of the Delaware and its tributary streams by pirates, who had slain a comrade or a captive that the murdered man should guard the blood-stained treasure ever from all save the hands of those who had sold themselves to perdition for the accursed gold I can remember as a lad how some of the old people told me as a truth the adventures of three men from the neighborhood of Chester, who strove to obtain a hidden treasure buried on the river-shore on Laws' or Jeffery's farm (I do not remember the exact location), how they dug in silence until the top of a large iron box thickly covered with bosses was uncovered, how one of the men in the exuberance of his joy spoke, and the box sank out of sight, amid heavy thunder, which growled and muttered overhead, and strange lights which flashed and danced through the darkness as the disappointed men hastened away. This was only one of the number of narratives of treasure-diggers in various locations, while along Chester and Ship Creek, Darby and Marcus Hook Creeks, many places were designated where treasures had been buried The belief in witchcraft had not died out absolutely thirty years ago, for a case occurred in this county wherein charms were used to thwart the evil eye of an old woman, whom it was believed had cast a spell over the cattle of a person of the same township, and the myth of the divining rod was accepted as true by many persons Samuel Breck, as late as 1820, states that Alexander Wilson, a Quaker preacher, was noted as possessing "the gift of finding water with a divining rod"[3]

Snake stories then as now were much relished by the rustic populace, and awakened general interest William Moraley[4] relates that "In a Wood near a Place called Ophoginomy (Appoquinimink, New Castle Co, Del), I espied a Snake lying in a Pathway, endeavoring to shun it by going out of the Road, I accidentally trod upon another, which immediately twined itself about my Right Leg and squeezed it so hard that I was afraid it would have broken After I had stood sometime, expecting to be bit, the snake dropped upon the Ground and I came off unhurt I viewed it and found I had tread upon the Head, which prevented its Biting I look'd upon this as a Mercy, and return'd Thanks to the Author of Good for my Deliverance It was a Horn Snake, Six Foot Long"

The latter statement, of course, brings Moraley's adventure within the line of snake stories, for most persons of the present day would believe he saw a unicorn, if he said so, as readily as they do that he saw a horn (?) snake But Capt Heinrichs, of the Yager Corps, in 1778,[5] writing from Philadelphia to friends in Germany, records a snake story that fills the measure to overflowing He says, "There is nothing more terrible than the big rattlesnake, which is from twelve to sixteen feet long, and which, as it is believed here, kills at its glance A countryman in my quarters lost a relative of his in this way some years ago He had gone hunting, and seeing a bear standing still, aimed at and shot it, scarcely had he reached the bear when he too was obliged to stand motionless, remaining thus awhile, fell and died, all this was caused by a rattlesnake, which was perched in a high tree"

Marriages—Governor Printz recognizes the Biblical injunction in his report for 1647[6] to the West India Company, wherein he set forth the wants in the infant colony of certain skilled labor, adding, "All these are of great necessity here, and, above all, a

swam across the river, and procured a gun and hid himself beside a log about a mile from the old ferry-house His master, while hunting for him, approached his place of concealment and shot him, his blood bespattering the green leaves of a holly bush near where he stood The *leaves of a holly bush still growing there are flecked with crimson spots,* as is alleged, from some supernatural cause There is no doubt of the red spots being on the leaves of the holly bush, but they are caused by some peculiarity of the soil in which it grows"—*Johnson's History of Cecil County, Md.*, p 200

[1] "The site of Knowlton, up to the year 1800, was a perfect wilderness Near the head gates of the mill there was formerly the mark of a grave the occupant of which tradition named Moggey, and from that circumstance the crossing of the creek was named Moggey's Ford As Moggey had the reputation of making her appearance occasionally, it required no little courage in the traveler in early times to cross the ford at night"—*Dr Smith's History of Delaware County*, p 399

[2] Sketches of Public Schools of Chester, by W B Broomall, *Delaware County Republican*

[3] Breck's "Recollections," p 303

[4] "The Voyages and Adventures of William Moraley," written by himself Newcastle (England), 1743

[5] *Penna Mag of Hist*, vol i p 43

[6] Ib, vol vii p 276

good number of unmarried women for our unmarried freemen and others," but whether this request was complied with by the home authorities does not appear, so far as I have ascertained After the territory had passed into the ownership of the English crown, and subsequently under Penn's, we learn that spinsters were one of the rarities of the province, for quaint old Gabriel Thomas informs us that "old maids were not to be met with, for all commonly marry before they are twenty years of age"

The state of marriages soon became the subject of legal enactment, which, under the Duke of York laws, was not to be entered into unless the bans had been asked in the church three several days, or a special license had been procured, and the marriage must be registered If there was no church or meeting-house in the locality where the parties lived, notice must be given by posting the names on the door of the constable's house, and on those of two of the overseers of the poor The legal age for females was as now,—twenty-one years,—excepting in cases when the parents were dead, when it was eighteen years

Among the laws agreed upon in England by Penn before he came to the province were the following regulating marriages

"That all marriages (not forbidden by the law of God, as to the nearness of blood and affinity by marriage) shall be encouraged, but the parents or guardians shall be first consulted, and the marriage shall be published before it be solemnized, and it shall be solemnized by taking one another as husband and wife before credible witnesses, and a certificate of the whole, under the hands of parties and witnesses, shall be brought to the proper Register of the county, and shall be registered in his office '

To prevent clandestine marriages, the person performing the ceremony in violation of law, by the act of March 10, 1683, was fined twenty pounds, while the parties married were fined ten pounds Under the administration of Governor Fletcher the notice of an intended marriage must be posted on the meeting- or court-house door one full month before the ceremony was performed, and when solemnized it must be in the presence of at least twelve persons By the act of 1693 a justice of the peace was required to be present at every marriage, and the certificate must be signed by twelve persons who were present on the occasion This requirement was, however, not applicable to parties who were married according to the form of the Church of England The act of 1700 imposed a fine of five pounds on all persons present at a clandestine marriage, and they were also liable to pay to the party aggrieved all damages that they may have sustained by reason of such marriage Under this law a servant who married without the consent of his or her master being first had thereto was compelled to serve one year after the expiration of his or her indentured term, and if a free man married a bonded servant woman, he was required to pay whatever damages the master could prove he had suffered by the act, and where a free woman married a bonded servant man, she was subject to make payment to her husband's master for the damage her marriage had occasioned the latter, the sum to be assessed by the justices

Robert Wade, a good man and true, who lived up to the law, and so far as was in his power insisted that others should do so, at the court held first and second days of first week, Tenth month, 1684, presented Joseph Cookson "for taking a wife contrary to the good and wholesome Laws of this Province," and the court ordered that Cookson should find security for ten pounds

At the court held 3d day of Tenth month, 1685, a case was tried that showed that practical jokes were played in early times which, as now, resulted to the disadvantage of some person The circumstances in the instance mentioned were briefly these Matthew Risley was at the public-house of Henry Hollingsworth, on Edgmont Avenue, Second Street, Chester, when a company "came from Maryland to the inn Some of the latter knew Risley, and the conversation turned on marriage, when one of the Marylanders asked Risley whether he could marry a couple now?" to which interrogation he replied, "Yes, for twenty pounds," but afterwards said that he would do it for two pieces of eight The former then stated "she was an heiress" Risley, however, declared that for a pot of beer he would clear them even if she was an heiress Thereupon the Marylanders called for two pots of beer and gave them to Risley, who told the woman she must get up very early in the morning and mount the horse first, and then take the man she desired for her husband up behind her on the horse If she did this he promises "to clear them all" The arrangement, however, seemed not to meet their approval, but they earnestly insisted on being married that night Whereupon Risley "went and got a Bible, and so proceeded as far as they thought they could well let him, and then one of the company untied a morning gown, as the man had on, and so he discovered him to be a man and not a woman that he was marrying" This circumstance coming to the ears of the grand jury, that body presented Risley, who, at the next court, on being arraigned, acknowledged the facts as herein stated, whereupon the court sentenced him to receive thirteen lashes, pay the costs and be for the term discharged The clerk records (the only instance I find where such an entry is made), "which said number of lashes were laid on his bare back" Under what law this corporal punishment was inflicted I have failed to learn

At the December court in the previous year the grand jury presented "Edward Beyer and Jeane Collett for being unlawfully married about the 13 of the 7th month last 1697." The defendant, Edward Beyer, "came into Court and proffered a petition and declared it was thro' ignorance, and the Court, considering of the same, moved that he pay the charges of the Court and to make his address to the Governor."

The court records afford several instances of the violation by and punishment of indentured servants under the act of 1700 for marrying without the consent of the masters having been had thereto; but I will refer only to one interesting case, which was heard Feb. 26, 1633-34. Job Harvey, by petition, informed the court that Joseph Fisher, his servant, had married Mary Jones, a free woman, without his consent, and asked that the offenders may be dealt with according to law. "Therefore it is considered by the Court whereby adjudged that the said Joseph Fisher for his said Offence Serve his sd Master or his Assigns one year after the Expiration of his former Servitude and that the sd Mary Jones (or by what other name she may be now called) pay the sd Job Harvey for her said offence the sum of Six pounds or serve the said Job Harvey or assigned one year in Lieu thereof."

Dr. Smith states[1] that at a meeting of Friends at Haverford, in 1699, it was ordered, in respect to courtship in the future, "that all young men among Friends make known their intentions to their parents or guardians before they acquaint the young woman's relations, and to make it known to the woman's parents or guardians, before they speak to them, and if they do otherwise, that they shall condemn the same before they proceed any further." This restriction, at this time, was general in the society. The records of Friends' meeting in those early days is largely composed of matters appertaining to marriages among the members, and in faded ink is noted these matters which, to the then living, was the most momentous step in life. In the minutes of Chester Meeting, under date of Sixth month 27, 1705, is recorded the wise act of a young woman, who learned before, not after the ceremony was performed, that there was wanting on her part that true affection without which marriage life is utterly miserable. In the case alluded to, Thomas Martin and Jane Hent had passed meeting, but for some reason the ceremony had not followed this approval, and the woman's meeting, where matters of that kind would more likely be talked about, briefly informs us "the above sd marriage not being accomplished, two women Friends, viz.: Alice Simcock and Rebecca Faucett spoak to Jane Hent to know the Reason thereof and her answer was that shee could not Love him well enough to bee her Husband. She also said that shee was very sorry that shee had proceeded so far with him."

In the early part of the last century the wedding-day was held as a festival, and William Moraley informs us that, about 1735, among the Pennsylvania colonists, "Their marriages are very chargeable, many times Wife's Fortunes being expended at the Celebration of the Nuptials." At that time the bride going to church, or after the ceremony to her future home, wore a long black hood over her head instead of a bonnet. Two yards of rich paduasoy, Watson tells us, was required to make this hood, and it was the custom to loan this article of apparel, so that one hood covered the heads of many brides before it was discarded as too shabby for further use. Towards the middle of the last century marriages were usually celebrated about noon, and generally at the house of the bride's parents. The utmost good feeling prevailed, and the cheer made up in its abundance whatever it might lack, according to our modern notions, in variety or display of the confectioner's skill. About the beginning of this century it may be questioned whether any person then residing within this county of Delaware had ever tasted ice cream, but the wedding dinner was something to gladden the eyes of a hungry man, while punch was dealt out in profusion. In addition to the feast at home, it was the custom to send out cakes, meats, and punch to everybody in the neighborhood, rich or poor alike, whether visitor or not of the family. In the evening usually the bride and groom were escorted to their home by a long procession of old-fashioned chairs or gigs containing their friends or relatives, and, if the family permitted such vanities as dancing, after the supper had been cleared away an old negro, who played by ear on a sharp, rasping violin, would strike up the music of some contra (country) dance or jig, keeping time to the air with his feet, the beat of which on the bare floor could be heard above the squeaking sounds of his fiddle. When the company formed in two long rows and the smiling musician played "Sir Roger de Coverley," or, as we of this generation term it, the "Virginia Reel," each couple at the head of the line knew it was their turn to begin by a signal from the dusky Orpheus, which consisted of a profound bow, accompanying the motion by an emphatic stamp on the floor. The gentlemen, in their pumps, would then exhibit some extraordinary figures, interspersing the merriment with the double-shuffle or cutting the pigeon-wing, while the smiling girls would bounce about on the tips of their toes very much as they do in this year of grace, 1884. Sometimes, when a few of the more ambitious young people, who had visited the city, desired to astonish the natives, they would go through the mazy movement of the minuet to the astonishment of the rustics. Many games of forfeit filled in the hours, while the elders would have a rubber at whist with something depending on the result to add zest to play, or try their fortune at high-low-Jack and the game. About nine o'clock, or ten at the latest, the bride would be spirited away by her maids, and shortly after the groomsmen would conduct the newly-made husband to his wife. At a later hour the company would ascend to the bridal chamber, taking with them refreshments to the married couple, generally in the form of liquor. Then one of the bride's stockings would be thrown across the bed

[1] History of Delaware County, p. 198.

among the guests, and the person that it struck, it was believed, would be the next one of the company to be married. After good wishes for the future welfare of the wedded pair, and a kiss to the bride by every man present, the assembly would depart to their respective homes.

Burials.—Death is surer even than taxes, hence it is to be expected that early in our county annals we should learn of provisions being made to inter the dead. As far back as 1746, Campanius records that at the Swedish graveyard at Tinicum "the first corpse that was buried was Andrew Hansan's daughter, Catherine, and she was buried on the 28th of October, which was Simon's and Jude's day."

In the Duke of York's laws it is stated that the private burial of servants and others had occasioned much scandal, that by such a custom it could not be ascertained if death had resulted from natural causes or violence, "for remedy whereof, and for the greater decency of burials," it was provided that a public burial-place should be set apart and fenced in each parish, and before any corpse should be buried three or four of the neighbors should be called in, one of whom must be an overseer of the poor, whose duty it was to view the body, and if there were not suspicious circumstances, "yet according to the decent custom of Christendom they may accompany it to the grave." The burial of a free person or an indentured slave in any localities other than the public graveyard was interdicted by law, unless in their lifetime the deceased had signified their desire of being interred elsewhere.

Funerals in the early days were as extravagantly costly, the circumstances of the people considered, as at the present day; not in the undertaker's bill or carriages used, for the corpse was borne to the place of interment, we are told by William Worrall, during the greater part of the last century on men's shoulders, the coffin being swung on poles, so that the funeral procession, generally walking, might wind along the pathways with more ease, for they often followed the footpaths over the fields to the place of sepulture, but in the feasts given to those who attended the ceremonies. The poles spoken of by Mr. Worrall must have been the primitive bier, which are alluded to in the records of Chester meeting, under date of Seventh month 30, 1706, in which "it is agreed at this meeting that a decent bear bee Keept att every Grave Yard, and that every preparative (meeting) within the limits of this meeting do get one made speedily."

As soon as a death occurred in a family the neighbors came in and made arrangements for the funeral, scouring the brass-work until it shone like new coin, for the old furniture was decorated with many brass ornaments, scrubbing the uncarpeted floors, dusting, baking, and cooking, until the house of mourning was fairly put to rights and the repast prepared for the funeral day. Warners were started out on horseback to ask persons to be present at the burial services, who on riding to the door of the dwelling would announce in monotonous tones, "Thyself and family are respectfully invited to attend the funeral of Thomas Smith, Fourth day next at two o'clock," while others would make frequent visits to the cross-road store to lay in groceries and other necessary articles needed for the table. Others of the neighbors would take their place as watchers over the body, which, stretched on a cooling board with a sheet over it, was never left alone. At night lighted candles were placed in the room, and refreshments provided for those who were sitting up with the corpse. The pictures and looking-glasses in the room where the body lay were covered with white muslin, so that the dead figure would not be reflected therein.

After the body was interred, in the case of the death of a man of means, all the company would return to the house and the will would be read. The disposition of his estate by the deceased would afford a topic of conversation in the neighborhood for a week at least.

The following is a bill for funeral services of one John Middleton, of Delaware County, Pa., in 1719. The original copy is in the possession of Taylor Thompson, undertaker in New Garden township, Chester Co. It is as follows, *verbatim:*

"An account of John Middleton's funerell charge is Cr. 10 1719

to 6½ gallons of wine at 6*s*-6*d* per gal	£02	02*s*.	3*d*.
to 3 galons of rum at 4*s* 6*d* per galon	00	13	6
to quar. of a hundred suger an spice	00	15	0
to flowar	00	12	0
to a barroll sider	00	12	0
to butter and ches	00	16	0
to a holand sheet	01	00	6
to the cofing and diging the grafe	00	19	6
	7	10	9

"5 mo 1 1719 paid to the doctor gandr wit for £00 16 6."

The custom then was, and it was continued until the beginning of this century, when a young unmarried woman died, the body was borne to the graveyard by young girls, doubtless introduced by the early Irish settlers, and a like custom prevailed at the funeral of a child. Miss Sarah Eve,[1] in her journal, under date of July 12, 1773, records: "In the evening, B. Rush, P. Dunn, K. Vaughan, and myself carried Mr. Ash's child to be buried; foolish custom for Girls to prance it through the streets without hats or bonnets." The custom of young girls acting as pall-bearers at the funeral of their female companions and young children seems to have continued in Philadelphia during the second decade of this century, for in the diary of Miss Hannah M. Wharton, under date of Dec. 19, 1813, it is recorded: "We have had a melancholy occurrence in the circle of our acquaintance since I last wrote, in the death of the accomplished and amiable Fanny Durdin. Six young ladies of her intimate acquaintance, of which I was one, were asked to be the pall-bearers. We were all dressed in white, with long white veils." Mrs. Catharine Ulrich informs me that she can remember, about 1825, when

[1] *Penna. Mag. of Hist.*, vol. v. p. 194.

the grandchild of the tenant, then occupying the old Brobson house, at the northeast corner of Third and Penn Streets, Chester, died, that four young girls, dressed in white, bore the corpse on a bier to the graveyard

Food and Dress—The Swedes on the Delaware River, we are told, in a letter addressed by one of themselves, in the year 1693, to John Thelin, of Gottenberg,[1] "were almost all husbandmen, and our meat and drink is after the old Swedish custom The country is very rich and fruitful, and we send out yearly to our neighbors on this continent and the neighboring islands bread, grain, flour, and oil We have here, thank God, all kinds of venison, birds, and fishes Our wives and daughters spin wool and flax, and many of them weave" The Swedish clergyman, Rev Eric Biork, a few years afterwards, states that there were "no poor in the country, but all provide for themselves, without any cases of want"

The first English settlers give us an interesting account of the sturdy race of the North which had preceded them in subduing the wilderness of the Western World Thomas Parker, under date of Feb 10, 1683,[2] writes,—

"There are Swedes and Finns who have lived here forty years, and lived an easy life through the abundance of commodities, but their clothes were very mean before the coming of the English, from whom they bought good ones, and they begin to show themselves a little proud They are an industrious people They employ in their buildings little or no iron They will build for you a house without any other implement than an axe With the same implement they will cut down a tree and have it in pieces in less time than two other men would spend in sawing it, and with this implement and some wooden wedges they split it and make boards of it or anything else they please with much skill The most of them speak English, Swedish, Finnish, or Dutch They plant a little tobacco and a little Indian corn The women are good housekeepers The most of the linen they wear they spin the flax and make themselves"

In the early part of the last century among the English settlers, under ordinary circumstances, bread and milk and pie formed the breakfast meal, or often only pop-robbin, a combination of eggs and flour made to a batter and boiled in milk, appeased their wants For dinner a bountiful dish of pork or bacon with a wheat-flour pudding or dumplings, with butter or molasses, was the bill of fare, while mush or hominy, with milk and butter and honey, sufficed for the evening repast On important occasions, when venison and other wild game was in season, chocolate, which was sweetened with maple-sugar, formed the basis of the entertainment William Worrall, of Ridley, stated that he never saw tea or coffee until about 1750, when his father brought some tea from Philadelphia, and his aunt, who then lived with them, and had charge of the house, did not know how to use it until she had received the proper information from one of her neighbors who had been instructed in the art of tea-drawing in the city The prudent conduct of Worrall's aunt was not imitated by one of her friends, residing in the vicinity, who, when she first had tea introduced into her house, boiled the leaves and served them with butter It was at this time such a rarity that even in the houses of the wealthy the hostess would measure with scales the amount of leaf necessary to draw tea for the company, or as in modern days we put it, "count the noses" of her guests Later on in the rural districts, before and after the Revolution, the daily fare consisted of salt pork or beef,—fresh meat was an occasional dainty,—rye bread, potatoes, cabbage, hominy, and turnips, while in summer-time beans and peas made their appearance on the table The latter were eaten with the knife, no one having the patience to chase peas over a dinner plate with the wide-spreading, two-tined forks, with massive buck handles, which were then in general use

During the latter part of the last century silver plate was in every household, and each article had its history, as it was handed down from parents to child as heirlooms, and was often made the subject of disposition by will But for ordinary use pewter platters, porringers, and tankards were employed, and were kept so bright that they shone like a mirror, while pewter pots filled the place of our modern glass tumblers and goblets In many instances it was customary for the family, including the domestics and hired men, to gather around the same board, the slaves at the bottom of the table If perchance some acquaintance came to tea, which was a popular custom among the women of the wealthier class in town and country just previous to the Revolution, the party always dispersed so that the company might get home before it was time for candle-lighting, and to put their children to bed

In 1745, Dr Franklin invented the open stove, which he called the Alter Idem, but which is still known by his name, and it won its way almost immediately to popular favor At one time all the old houses in this section of the country, whose owners were in easy circumstances, had in the parlor a Franklin stove In the ancient stone dwelling standing on the left hand side of the Queen's Highway, about five hundred feet above where the mill, race, and quarry railway crosses the road at Leiperville, is still to be seen one of these stoves

On the night of the battle of Brandywine, after writing a letter from Chester to Congress, apprising that body of the defeat of the American army, Washington joined his troops, that had gathered "back of Chester," between Leiperville and Darby Tradition states that the general sat for some time in the old house, before the stove, silently watching the fire that

1 Watson's Annals, vol ii p 233

2 *Penna Mag of Hist.*, vol vi p 324

burned brightly on the iron hearth, for the night was chilly and the autumnal equinox was then threatening which broke so violently five days thereafter as to compel a suspension of hostilities in the pitched battle which Washington tendered to Gen Howe near Goshen meeting-house Perhaps that night in Ridley, in the firelight, the whole plan of the proposed but interrupted battle was digested and arranged in the mind of the commander-in-chief, whose mental balance no disaster could disturb

Less than seventy years ago the usual cooking utensils in a well-regulated kitchen consisted of a large iron stewing pot, a tea-kettle, Dutch oven, a frying-pan, skillet, a gridiron, and earthen dishes for baking bread and pies, while on the window-sill or on the floor was the mark which told by the sunlight the hour of noon

The usual dress of the Swedish people on the Delaware in early days was strongly but rudely fashioned of skins of animals, and their heads were covered with caps of the same material, the hair clinging to the hide Their shoes, very similar in form to the Indian moccasins, were made from the skins of animals slain in the chase The women were all compelled to employ the same material in making their jackets and petticoats, and the beds were covered with deer-, wolf-, and bear-skins Many of the heads of families had the apparel they had worn at home in Europe safely packed away, which, on occasions of public festivals, were ceremoniously brought forth and donned by the owner, to the admiration of the young folks born in the colony

The dress of the great body of the people previous to the Revolution,—those, I mean, who had their daily labor to do,—was very simple, many of the descendants of the first settlers clinging tenaciously to the buckskin of the early days of the province, out of which material their breeches and jackets were made. In 1725, from the letter written from Chester township, by Robert Park to Mary Valentine, already mentioned, we find the writer stating that "In Summer they wear nothing but a skirt and linnen drawers Trowses, which are breeches and stockings, all in one made of Linnen, they are fine Cool wear in Summer." Underclothing such as we now require was at that time seldom worn Oznaburg, a cheap, heavy shirting, made of hemp-tow, was the material of which boys' shirts, and often those worn by men, were made, and a coarse tow-cloth was used for trousers. Shoes, which were seldom worn in summer-time, were generally, in the country, made of neat leather, fastened by large brass buckles on each instep, unless that was more costly than the wearer could afford, when shoe-strings answered instead The men and boys from the rural districts were easily recognized on the streets in Philadelphia, because, in winter and on unusual occasions, they wore leather breeches and apron Almost all mechanics before the Revolution—carpenters, masons, coopers, painters, and similar tradesmen—wore, when at work, great leather aprons, which covered the most of their breast and reached down below their knees, such as blacksmiths now use at the forge, and their ordinary apparel was yellow buckskin breeches, check shirts, and red flannel jackets All of them wore real beaver hats, an article that then formed a part of their freedom outfit Hired women dressed in linsey-woolsey or worsted petticoats, and wore coarse leather shoes, of which they were particularly careful It is often related of those "good old days," when people deemed it a mark of effeminacy to ride to church, that it was not uncommon to see both men and women trudging along the highway barefooted, their shoes and stockings in their hands, and when they came near to their place of destination they would seat themselves by the road, put on their shoes and stockings, and adjust their apparel into proper trim to enter the church, meeting, or dwelling-house

As previously stated, about the middle of the last century wealth began to manifest itself among the inhabitants of the cities, towns, and in the country immediately under the influence of the centres of trade The education of the people, of course, largely reflected the aristocratic tone of the mother-country, hence special privileges and offices of honor and profit came to be monopolized by a few families, who soon learned to regard themselves as better than the general public. This class dressed in a style which peculiarly marked them as of the higher order of society Wigs, which were in use in Penn's time, continued to be worn until the disaster at Braddock's field, when the British and colonial officers, in fleeing from that fatal place, cast aside in their flight their wigs as incumbrances, and afterwards appearing in public with their natural hair, the fashion soon changed to the queue In the days of big wigs it was no infrequent incident at the dinner-table for the large buttons on the sleeve of the servant's livery to catch in the mass of horse-hair, leaving the bare pate of the guest exposed, while the wig dangled from the servant's arm The dress of gentlemen at that period was of varied colors. It was no uncommon sight to see a scion of the aristocratic families attend in a black velvet coat, green waistcoat embroidered with silver figures, yellow velvet breeches fastened at the knee with diamond buckles, and the legs incased in blue stockings The calf-skin shoes were clasped with large silver buckles, studded with imitation or, in some cases, real diamonds Fine lace neckerchief and wristbands, with a cocked hat, completed the costume, saving when a dress sword hung at the left side, the scabbard protruding between the stiffened skirts of the coat After and during the Revolution white coats, embroidered with gold, were fashionable, but the prevailing color among all classes was indigo blue, and, as the dyer's art was indifferently understood, it is said that in a hasty shower the color would often wash out or be transferred to the skin of the wearer, and, in addition, when the rain caused the powder in the hair to trickle down the back in a pasty mass, the plight of the individual must have been extremely disagreeable. Those persons whose duty required them to be abroad in all kinds of weather used oil-cloth cloaks, and a like covering protected their hats from the wet.

The dress of society women in the olden times was as much the subject of fashion's capricious whims as it is to-day. I here propose briefly to mention a few articles of apparel worn during the last century, and notice some of the demands the mode made upon its votaries. When elaborate hair-dressing (requiring several hours to be consumed in curling, crisping, and arranging one's head) was in vogue it was no unusual circumstance for a lady to have her hair dressed forty-eight hours before a ball, and to sit dozing in a chair during the intervening nights, for it would have utterly destroyed her toilet had she lain down. Hoops were enormous during the greater part of the last century, until shortly before the Revolution; not the light elastic skirt worn recently, but heavy clumsy affairs which had to be tilted to one side in passing through a narrow doorway. When they began to subside, callimanco padded with wool, made into petticoats, took their places, while over the latter were worn finely-quilted Marseilles, silk, or satin petticoats, the gown open and without a front, so that it might be displayed. Caps were generally used, and the style which is now known as "The Martha Washington" was at that day called "The Queen's Night-cap." Stays were worn by the wealthy, as a rule; costly affairs they were, finished in quilted silk or satin. Worsted dresses, with a plain white apron reaching almost to the ground, were used for ordinary every-day life, and matrons and maids had long, large pockets strapped around their waist beneath their gowns (Lydia Locket, we remember, lost her pocket), and a round pin-cushion, inclosed in a silver rim, and a pair of scissors were pendent from the girdles with silver chains. Large cloaks of red cloth were very fashionable, and for many years no bonnets for ladies were made of any other material than black silk or satin. During the early part of this century beaver bonnets were much worn, and when that addition was made to a lady's toilet, like a camel's-hair shawl of to-day, she was expected never again as long as she lived to need another best hat for winter. All women in moderate circumstances wore pattens in 1772, and as they stamped over the streets the racket of these unwieldy affairs could be noticed a long way off, and going late to church the delectable clatter they made drew eyes on the tardy comers and aroused the sleeping Christians. Women in middle life in the last century wore worsted dresses and check aprons to church, and very few females, unless the wife or daughter of a lawyer, doctor, or clergyman, or merchants in large business, thought of wearing silks, satin, or velvet. The servants wore short gowns and petticoats of coarse domestic goods, and their dress indicated at once their station in life. They stood in awe of their employer, and called him usually master and his wife mistress.

Use of Liquors.—The custom of drinking, so far as we have information, was generally indulged in by all classes throughout Christendom (Mohammed forbade the use of intoxicating liquors among his followers as a religious obligation) until within a comparatively recent period, for, as is well known, in the first quarter of this century it was a reproach to a man among the upper class if he could not drink his three bottles of sherry after dinner without falling beneath the table, while "the four-bottle man" was looked up to as a social hero. Hence it is not surprising that we find in our earliest annals that among the Swedes who settled on the Delaware both men and women were addicted to an over-indulgence in intoxicating beverages. We are told by Peterson DeVries that Governor Printz "weighed upwards of four hundred pounds, and drank three drinks at every meal," and the same writer describes the Swedes "as not very sober, as they bought from the captain of the vessel a good quantity of wine and sweetmeats, and that neither here nor in Virginia was intoxication punished by whipping." Of Dominie Laurence Lock, the Swedish chaplain, we learn his "great infirmity seems to have been an overfondness for intoxicating drinks," but he certainly must have gotten over this weakness, for Campanius records "that he died in the Lord in 1688."

After the coming of Penn, from the court records it appears that drunkenness was of frequent occurrence. At the court held 3d day of 1st week, Tenth month, 1686, "Haunce Urian was fined five Shillings for being drunk upon Tinicum Island," while at the court held at Chester, 3d day of 1st week, Seventh month, 1687, many cases of drunkenness were tried. I give extracts from the records of that session as a few instances of the manner in which infractions of the law against intemperance were punished in these early days:

"Robert Stephens was presented by ye Grand Inquest for being Drunk at Chester since ye last Court for which he was fined by Ye Court 5s. James Sandelains was fined 5s. for suffering Robert Stephens to be Drunk in his House."

"John Chard was Presented by Ye Grand Inquest for being Drunke about ye beginning of July last, for which he was fined by Ye Court 5s."

"John Edge being convicted before John Blunstone and George Maris for being Drunke was fined by Ye Court 5s."

"Neales Quist paid 5s. for being Drunk at Chester."

The two following cases, which I cite at large from the old court records (tried at the session just mentioned), will present a general idea of the importance given to the breaches of the law against intemperance:

"Thomas Bowles being summoned to appear att this Court to answer ye Complaint of our Sovereign Lord ye King and Chiefe Proprietary for suffering the King's Leidge People to be drunk att his house was upon the same Indicted. The Grand Inquest find the Bill, Whereupon he is Called to ye Barr and Pleads not Guilty and refers himself to God and ye Country.

"John Taylor being attested declareth that Thomas Bowles told him that he lett Lasie Coleman have soe much rum till he was soe drunk that he was forct to be carried to his canow. Albertus Henrickson being attested declareth that he did see Harmon Johnson soe drunk att Thomas Bowles' that . . . Thomas Usher being attested declareth that Samuel Weight did call for tife[1] att Thomas Bowles' house and he heard Thomas Bowles say why might he not have it since he doe pay for it. Andrew Friend being attested declareth that Thomas Bowles sold him and William Cob two bowles of Punch and att another time he sold ye Trumpeter's soune (son) a Canu of Tife.

"The jury's verdickt know this that we doe finde Thomas Bowles Guilty according to ye Indicktment. Hereupon Judgment is granted that he pay 10s. and costs of suit."

At the same court Thomas Bowles was also "Presented by ye Grand Inquest for selling rum by small measures without lysence. Remitted upon condition that he doe soe no more and that he pay his fees."

The second case is as follows:

"Richd. Crosby being sumoned to appear at this Court to answer the Complaint of our Sovereign Lord the King and the Chiefe Proprietary for being Drunke and committing other misdemeanors, was for ye same Indicted. The Grand Inquest find the bill. The testimony of Anne Sanderlaine declareth that upon ye 29th day of ye 4th month last, Richard Crosby was in Drink att Chester and very unruly. Philip Denning declareth that ye same day Richard Crosby was very much disordered by drinke and that he was very abusive. William Goford declareth that Richard Crosby being much in Drink Challenged ye Sweads or English or any other man att Cudgells, Wrasling or any other such violent exercise and further more did strike him upon ye head and did trip up his heels twice and yt he heard him say ye Sweads were rogues and did take part with ye Indians. John Clue declareth ye same. Johannes ffriend declareth that he heard Richard Crosby call ye Sweads Rogues and that they did take part with ye Indians against ye English.

"Before ye Petty Jury went out upon ye cause, he submitting himselfe unto ye Court, was fined 5s. and ordered to pay Court charges, and soe to be acquitted."

Crosby was not simply an arrant braggart in his liquor, for the court records show that he kept the settlers in fear by his prowess, and was not choice of his words in expressing his opinion of the justices before whom he was frequently required to appear. But Crosby was not the only person who was belligerent in his cups in that early day, for at the court held at Chester on 3d day of 2d week, Seventh month, 1688, "Thomas Robins and Thomas Woodmans being convickted before John Bristow for Drunkeness, breach of Peace, breaking ye great Cabin doore and ye head of Samuel Harrison, mate on board of ye ship Tryall, was for ye same called to ye Barr. But upon their submission to ye Court was ordered to pay 5s. with all Court charges."

Dr. John Watson strives to account for the immoderate use of liquor among the early settlers by arguing that rum and tobacco were regarded as preventives of dumb agues, fever and ague, and similar disorders, and that the people, imagining the air and water of "this hot climate" to be unwholesome, employed the luxuries named as antidotes. From the immediate ill effects of drinking cold water when overheated with labor in the summer-time, and the fevers and agues which attacked them in the fall of the year, the populace became confirmed in the opinion that liquor, at least, was essential for their well being, and as they had no conveniences to make beer that would keep in hot weather, they adopted the practice of the laboring people in the West Indies and drank rum. Hence he ascribes the general and continued use of intoxicating liquors to this opinion, which having "once so far gained ground as to influence general habits and customs on an erroneous principle, it requires much labor and a long time to wear them (the customs) out."[2] The true reason was that each of the settlers brought with him the manners and customs of his native land, and, as stated before, all Christian people at that period used liquor to excess.

To the Society of Friends the first protest against the immoderate use of liquor can be traced, and to them is justly due the credit of curtailing much that was certainly injurious in the custom during the last century.

At taverns in the colonial days it was not the rule as now to hand the bottle to the guest to help himself according to his capacity, but the landlord filled small glasses, known as "jiggers," and if the party was not satisfied therewith, he was compelled to pay for his second drink. At that time, 1730, we are told by William Moraley that "Cyder is the most plentiful here of all Liquors, besides which they have Mead, Methlegin, Perry, and Peach Drink. The Beer not good. Madeira Wine is the only Wine used. Rum is sold for Three pence the Half Pint, or Ten pence a Quart. Half a Pint of Rum being mixed with three Half Pints of Water or Small Beer, makes Bombo, but mixed with Cyder, makes Sampson, an Intoxicating Liquor."

In the early part of the last century nothing, it seems, could be done without liquor. At the birth of an infant the women of the neighborhood collected at the house, and wine or cordial waters was distributed to the guests, while rum, either buttered or made into hot tiff, was given to the mother, as it was then deemed to be essentially necessary for her speedy recovery.

At the raising of houses and barns liquor was an important element, and the cedar branch on the top of the building announced that good cheer would supplement the work. No crop, it was thought, could be garnered without a liberal use of stimulants, and in 1700 at funerals it was then the custom for a servant (usually a negro) to carry around among those assembled sugar cakes, hot liquor, and wine, of which all present, both young and old, partook. It was given to every person, those as well standing in the street or sitting at the door. It was then not an unusual thing for a person fond of his glass to take a position so that he might be served among the first, and then to take another station so that he would receive, like Benjamin, a double portion. The abuse of

[1] "Tiff, or tipp, is made of small beer, rum, and sugar, with a slice of bread toasted and buttered."—Acrelius' *History of New Sweden*, p. 162.

[2] Watson's Annals, vol. ii. p. 521.

this hospitality became so marked that Chester's Monthly Meeting (Twelfth month 22, 1724-25) took definite action thereon, as follows:

"At our Quarterly Meeting it was desired ye friends take care at Burralls not to make great provision as to provide strong Liquors & hand it about; but lett Every one take yt is free to take it as they have ocation and not more than will doe them Good."

Notwithstanding this testimony against the absurd custom, it continued to be practiced almost to the beginning of this century, and often families, to furnish "the funeral baked meats," cramped themselves to such an extent that in many households where death had intruded the most rigid economy was entailed on the survivors for months to discharge the costly hospitality of the funeral day.

For years at public sales it was the practice to hand bottles of liquor and hot rum round among the crowd, until it had grown such an evil that in 1750 the General Assembly took notice of it, and gave the reason for the then enactment, that "inasmuch as a pernicious custom has prevailed in many places of giving rum and other strong liquors to excite such as bid at vendues to advance the price, which, besides the injustice of the artifice, leads to great intemperance and disorder." Hence it was declared a penal offense for any person in the future to give or sell liquor on such occasions, subjecting the party convicted thereof to a fine of four pounds for the first, and five pounds for every subsequent, violation of the law.

Justice, too, it seems, must needs invoke the use of liquor to rightly adjust the scales. At the Court of Oyer and Terminer, held at Chester, November, 1752, James Rice, *alias* Dillon, and Thomas Kelly were tried and convicted for the murder of Eleanor Davis and John Thomas. The following bill paid the commissioners for "the Justices' Expenses at the Court of Oyer and Terminer, November, 1752," gives an idea of the entertainment required by the judges of the Supreme Provincial Court while making their circuit:

	£	s.	d.
"Punch	0	1	6
Sling	0	0	6
Three dinners	0	4	6
8 half-peck of Oats	0	4	0
Bowel of punch	0	1	6
Bowel of punch	0	1	6
Oats	0	0	6
Bowel of punch	0	1	6
Bowel of punch	0	1	6
Wine	0	2	6
Suppers	0	6	0
Punch	0	1	6
Liquor	0	0	6
8 half peck Oats	0	4	0
Bitters	0	0	3
Cordiall	0	1	3
Punch	0	0	3
Punch	0	0	3
Wine & bitters	0	1	6
8 breakfasts	0	8	0
Quart wine & bitters	0	3	0
Punch	0	3	0
7 dinners	0	10	6
Punch	0	3	0
8 half-peck of Oats	0	4	0
6 suppers	0	6	0
Cordiall	0	1	0
To wine	0	1	0
Two nights' pay for 8 horses	0	16	0
	5	2	0

No public business, it seems, could be properly done without the use of liquor. It was customary to allow jurors in capital cases the use of liquor when deliberating on their verdict. In the commissioners' office, at West Chester, the following bill, dated 1745, is on file paid by the county:

"For commissioners, assessors, justices, and grand jury:

	£	s.	d.
Wine	0	2	8
Punch	0	3	0
Mare Wine	0	5	4
Punch	0	3	0
Nimbo	0	2	8
One bole bruke	0	2	0
Total	0	18	8"

The Origin and Brief Notice of the Temperance Movement in Delaware County.—As stated before, Friends, as early as February, 1725, gave testimony at Chester Meeting against the inordinate use of liquor at funerals, and from time to time thereafter they moved in the endeavor to check the widespread habit of drinking to excess, until by degrees their influence extended beyond their own society, and gradually a general sentiment was aroused, until much of the evil was done away by the force of public opinion. There was at that time no effort looking to a prohibition of the manufacture or sale of liquors, and it is doubtful whether the latter movement extends backward in our national history half a century. In this county, so far as I have knowledge, the first society organized for temperance work was known as "The Darby Association for Discouraging the Unnecessary Use of Spirituous Liquors;" and from the address issued by that body on the 17th of Sixth month, 1819, I find they protested against the fashionable custom of treating, and called upon farmers to discard liquor from the harvest-fields and meadows, which, if done, they say in a few years workingmen would cease to expect it as a privilege or claim it as a right. The association advised the formation of similar associations throughout the land.

A Delaware County temperance society was organized in 1835, and strongly urged the formation of auxiliary societies in each township. So rapidly did the movement develop, that on Monday, Oct. 5, 1835, a temperance harvest home was held at Zion meeting-house, Darby, while at the county meeting of the organization, in the Methodist Church, Chester, March 22, 1837, there were delegates from Waterville, Leiperville, Marple, Lima, Chester, Wesleyan, Haverford, Haddington, and the Union Society of Shoemakerville present. Lodges in Lower Chichester, Darby, and other townships were also established.

The movement had so spread in 1842 that many merchants throughout the county announced that they kept "temperance grocery-stores;" and in August, 1844, John Hawkins, in Upper Darby, on the West Chester road, opened a temperance hotel,—the Howard House, on which occasion the temperance people of the county assembled in large numbers, and appropriate services were held, while in the same year the

Washington Hotel, in Chester, ceased to be a license house When it was opened as a temperance tavern flags were suspended across Market Street, a great concourse of people gathered, a brass band furnished music, and speeches were made by prominent tee-totalers

The question of license soon became a political issue, and so concentrated was the pressure brought upon the Legislature that that body passed a bill, which was approved by Governor Porter April 7, 1846, authorizing a vote by the people of the State, by which the electors of cities, boroughs, and townships could determine whether liquor should legally be sold therein On March 19, 1847, the following vote was cast for and against license in the localities named

	For	Against
Aston	89	100
Bethel	31	22
Birmingham	20	54
Chester borough	88	103
Chester township	40	90
Concord	60	15
Upper Chichester	18	27
Lower Chichester	56	60
Darby	70	62
Upper Darby	3	119
Edgmont	51	46
Haverford	36	85
Marple	45	82
Middletown	113	77
Newtown	40	65
Upper Providence	50	59
Northern Providence	41	88
Radnor	86	107
Ridley	79	79
Springfield	31	77
Thornbury	40	21
Tinicum	7	11
	1094	1471

As will be seen in Bethel, where there had never been license granted, so far as I have ascertained, and where the only application ever made to the court of Delaware County, in 1802, was rejected, the majority was for license, and in Ridley the vote was a tie In the western part of the State a case was made and carried to the Supreme Court to test the law, and at the September term, 1847, Judge Bell delivered an opinion holding the act unconstitutional, inasmuch as it delegated to the people part of the functions of the Legislature, which the fundamental law had reposed solely in the latter body This decision absolutely paralyzed the "Sons of Temperance," their organizations disbanded, and for some years only a desultory contest against license was continued by a few individuals, noticeable in Upper Darby, until finally even their protest ceased

After the war of the Rebellion terminated an organization known as Good Templars was formed in Delaware County, and grew rapidly, until in August, 1869, a mass meeting was held at Media The court-room was crowded by members from the various lodges in the county So formidable had the roll become in numbers that they demanded and procured the passage by the Legislature of the special act for Delaware County of March 9, 1872, better known as the "Holiday Law," which was followed by a movement throughout the State, on the part of the temperance associations, resulting in the act of March 27, 1872, providing that every three years thereafter, at the cities, boroughs, and township elections, the electors therein should vote whether liquor should or should not be sold in such cities and counties, which act is better known as the "Local Option Law" The following is the vote in this county in the spring of 1873, when the question was submitted to the people

	For	Against
Aston	110	77
Bethel	23	36
Birmingham	31	49
Chester township	38	110
South Chester	80	112
Concord	56	96
Upper Chichester	15	35
Lower Chichester	52	99
Darby borough	86	69
Darby township	45	29
Upper Darby	82	109
Edgmont	45	39
Haverford	85	78
Media	70	154
Marple	43	89
Middletown	158	104
Newtown	63	39
Upper Providence	71	59
Lower Providence	23	78
Radnor	92	93
Ridley	51	82
Springfield	49	81
Thornbury	49	40
Tinicum	15	6
Upland	30	117
	1462	1880

Majority against license, 418, exclusive of Chester City

CHESTER CITY

	For	Against
North Ward	253	242
Middle Ward	302	125
South Ward	261	246
Majority for license	203	

Subsequently the Legislature by the act approved by Governor Hartranft, April 12, 1875, repealed the Local Option Law of 1872, and the special law for Delaware County, of March 9, 1872, was repealed by the act of April 18, 1878

In concluding this chapter I have written to little purpose if I have failed to show that the present age is much better than "the good old times of Adam and of Eve" It is only by throwing in bold contrast the past with the present that we mark the great progress of mankind I unhesitatingly state my belief that in morals, in education, in general health, the people of to-day are as much improved over those who lived and acted during our Revolutionary struggles as the latter were superior in that respect to the early settlers If we could place the old manners of life side by side with those of the present generation, we would be easily convinced that the comforts which now surround the families of moderate means far exceed that maintained among the comparatively wealthy classes of our land a century ago When we remember that in Penn's time not a floor in the province was covered with a carpet, that tooth-brushes were unknown, and, in fact, that it was regarded as a mark of effeminacy for many years after his day to clean the teeth at all, that personal cleanliness was not considered essential either to comfort or health, that less than a hundred and fifty years ago, among the aristocratic ladies, their enormous head-dresses when once fixed were not disturbed or altered for a month, until they became as intolerable to the wearer as they had long been offensive to all who drew near; when women wore scratch-backs suspended at their girdles (a pretty picture it must have been to watch these big head-dresses bobbing about as the wearer twisted and pulled one of the scratch-backs up and down, to allay the intolerable itching on that part of the body); when pewter plates were used in place of china or delft, a miserable tallow candle, or at best a wax taper, at night alone shed a flickering uncertain light; when only the wealthy could buy books, and when the young high-born lady pored over the pages of "Tom Jones," "Joseph Andrews," or "Roderick Random," unrestrained, and the farmer, if he could read, was restricted to the almanacs, which, stitched together as the years passed by, hung suspended on a nail near the chimney-place; when the pious church-goers sat bolt upright in an uncushioned pew, and for two or three hours in midwinter remained shivering in the church without a fire, while the tedious clergyman hurled weighty sermons on doctrinal points, which he himself did not comprehend, at his unfortunate audience; when on cold mornings the fire was out, the dismal housewife gouged great pieces of flesh out of her fingers in trying to procure a spark from the flint and tinder, while men among us now of middle age can recall when they as boys sat in an out-house breaking great lumps of coal with a hammer to make it fit the stove, until they cursed the day that gave them birth.

Notwithstanding our comforts, those who follow us in a hundred years will be thankful that they have not to endure the hardships of the present age, and that they enjoy many things conducive to man's happiness which are now unknown.

CHAPTER XX.

TRAVELING AND TRANSPORTATION, WITH AN ACCOUNT OF THE RAILROADS IN THE COUNTY.

In these days of rapid transit, when inside of eighty days a man can "put a girdle round about the earth," it is a difficult matter to comprehend the slow journeys of the olden time, or that hardly three hundred years ago travelers had no choice but to ride on horseback or walk. Nor was that all they had to contend with, at least in this colony, for as early as Sept. 22, 1676,[1] it was a law, "That if hereafter any Stranger or person unknown shall come to or Travill through any Towne or place within this Government without a Passport or Certificate from whence hee came and wither hee is bound, shall bee lyable to bee Seized upon by any Officer of the Towne or Place unto which hee comes, or through which he shall travill, there too bee Licenced untill hee can Cleare himselfe to bee a free Man, and shall defray the Charges of his Detention there, by his worke of Labour (if not otherwise able to give Satesfaction) in the best way and Manner hee shall bee found capable."

Indeed, previous to the year 1700, strangers were by law forbidden to travel from place to place, and so strict was the regulation that ferrymen were compelled to enter into bond not to carry any person unknown to them, unless he could produce a traveling pass signed by a magistrate; and innkeepers were required to notify the officers of the law when strangers sought lodgings at their houses, so that the authorities might inquire into the antecedents of their guests.

Under William Penn it became almost as difficult to get away from the colony as to travel in it. For the fifty-fifth law provided "that Every person intending to depart or leave the Province & Territories thereof, Shall publish his or her intention in writing, affixed to the door of the County Court, where hee or shee inhabits thirty days before his or her Departure, and Shall have a pass under the County Seal." All captains of vessels were forbidden to carry a person away unless he or she was provided with such a pass, and the violation of that injunction rendered the captain responsible for all damages any one might suffer by reason of the passenger having absconded. Similar laws were enacted in 1700 and 1705.

The first mention of a pass being granted occurs at the court held in Chester, 6th of Eighth month, 1685, where it is recorded that "Robert Cloud had a pass granted him to depart the Province, dated ye 26th day of ye 9th month, 1685, his brother William Cloud, of Concord, being his security to Safe ye Country Harmless."

All men then traveled by land on horseback. Ladies at that time rode on pillions (a pad or cushion attached to the hinder part of the saddle and fixed on the horse), behind some relative or servant-man, unless, like Queen Christina, of Sweden, they preferred to ride astride the animal, as men did. In the latter part of the year 1678 it is recorded in the journal of Peter Sluyter and Jasper Danekers, the Labadist missionaries, that Ephraim Herman, who accompanied the travelers from New York to New Castle, had his wife with him, and she rode all the way, excepting that part which was made in boats, on a pillion behind her husband. In the first quarter of the last century it is told of John Salkeld, the noted public Friend (who, about 1708, built the house which now stands partly in the roadway on Norris Street, above Third, South Ward, Chester), that on one occasion, during a religious visit to New Jersey, he was accompanied by his daughter, Agnes, riding on a pillion behind her father; that after meeting he rode

[1] Duke of York's Laws, p. 72.

away, leaving his daughter at the house of worship, and that he did not notice that she was not with him until he had gone several miles The late William Worrall, of Ridley, who was born in Marple in 1730, used to relate that in his youthful days, at marriages, the bride rode to meeting behind her father or next best friend, seated on a pillion, that after the ceremony was over and the wedded couple were ready to return, the pillion was then placed behind the saddle of the husband, and his wife would in that manner be conveyed to her new home At that time, and until a very recent period, all houses, in the country at least, had high horse blocks for women to use in mounting behind the men who rode the animals These blocks were usually three stone steps, and were also located near by all the old churches and meeting-houses In more modern days they were used to mount into side-saddles

In the early times all merchandise and freight was transported on pack-horses Grain was thus carried to market in large sacks, holding between two and three bushels, which were placed on pack-saddles, and a lad mounted on one animal would lead three or four in a line behind the one he rode Mr Worrall also stated that in his youth "there were no carts, much less carriages They hauled their grain on sleds to the stacks. He assisted his father to carry on horseback one hundred bushels of wheat to Charles Humphrey's mill, in Haverford township, which he sold for two shillings a bushel" In this statement he was partly correct We know that by means of pack-horses the most unwieldy articles were then transported,—bars of iron, barrels of whiskey, and other necessaries

Mr Worrall was not, however, accurate in declaring that there were no carriages in the province in his early manhood, for in 1725 there were eight gentlemen of means, including the Governor, each of whom was reported to own a four-wheeled carriage drawn by two horses, and at that time one of the number was kept in the present county of Delaware by Chief Justice David Lloyd, who lived in the old Porter house, as it was known to the present generation, at the foot of Welsh Street That they were clumsy vehicles cannot be doubted, for even the chair or old-fashioned sulky, that many of the older people can yet recall, was nothing but a common arm-chair on leather braces, suspended over a pair of wheels The latter conveyance was exceedingly light in weight, which was only proper at that time, when between the highwaymen, who perchance would bid you "stand and deliver" at any moment, and the miry road, almost hub-deep in winter, which might stall you for half a day, no prudent man was justified in traveling a hundred miles without first making his will and so far as he could winding up his affairs, for he had no assurance that he would ever return alive, hence the lighter the vehicle he rode in the greater would be his chance of getting safely home again

The roads in early times were simply narrow passes for horsemen, and the bridges, as shown by the court records, were built for the passage over the streams of persons traveling in that manner On Nov 24, 1708, the justices ordered James Hendrickson to repair the bridge over Chester Creek, and also the same day the court "further agreed that the said James Hendrickson shall build a bridge over Marcus Hook creek in the Queen's Road, where the old bridge now is, and erect it 10 foot broad and so long as is sufficient and necessary for the same to extend, and to build it all of white oak timber completely finished" The roads, too, previous to 1700, were impassable for horsemen, and travel by water was even intercepted in these times At a court held in Chester, Seventh month 14, 1692, a case was called, and neither party to the suit appearing, the records show this entry, "The Court considering that the weather was so bad that it was impossible for anyone to get down the River they thought fitt to continue the action until the next Court"

The people residing near the navigable streams, certainly before the beginning of the eighteenth century, traveled from place to place by water It was not until about 1720 that any carriages, save that of Penn's family, were used in the province, and they were then so rare that in passing along the road they excited as much attention from the rustics as a circus does at this time About the middle of the century they had come into fashion among the grandees of our colonial days We are informed that Col Harrison, of Virginia, in 1755, passed through Chester in his chaise[1] on his way southward, having Mrs Belchior, of Maryland, under his protection We know that Gen Washington rode through the country with a coach and four, with two postilions and an outrider in showy livery Frequently he passed through Chester in this style, or rather his family would be in the carriage, while he, mounted on a handsome horse, which he rode remarkably well, would follow, the wonder and admiration of the dwellers in the ancient borough, who would gather along the streets to see him pass He generally stopped at the Washington House, and when his imposing equipage would halt before the door of the old tavern, the entire business of the town would cease, and the people would loiter around until the great man and his coach had rumbled away in the distance

In 1732 a line of stages ran from Burlington to Amboy, across New Jersey, connecting at each end of the route with sail-boats These fast stage-coaches, for such they were called, showed at that period remarkable progress in means of passenger transportation A journey then was no unimportant event, when by the clumsy stage a man could travel about forty miles a day, that is, if the roads were in good condition, while even to do this, if the highway was

1 "Maryland Gossip in 1755," *Penna Mag of Hist.*, vol iii p 146

heavy, he must rise at three or four o'clock in the morning and prolong the ride far into the night. In the winter, if the road was much traveled, it soon became a quagmire, into which the horses would frequently sink to their knees in the adhesive mud. Then all hands would have to get out and help pry the great lumbering vehicle, which was hub-deep, out of the trouble. As recent as Jan. 10, 1834, the Queen's Highway between Chester and Darby was so bad that the mail-coach from Washington stuck fast in the mud below Darby, and had to be drawn to that village by oxen; while on Jan. 9, 1836, a heavy lumber box on runners, used as an omnibus between Darby and Philadelphia, stuck fast in a snow-drift near the former place, and it was two days before it could be moved.

I have not definitely ascertained when the first stage-line was established between Philadelphia and Baltimore, but Martin[1] gives the abstract of a long advertisement which appears in the *Independent Gazetteer, or the Chronicle of Freedom*, published in Philadelphia, Jan. 2, 1788. Greeshorn, Johnson & Co., of "the Philadelphia, Baltimore and Eastern Shore Line of Post Coach Carriages," state that carriages will set out on Fourth Street, nearly opposite the old Indian Queen Tavern, during the winter on Mondays and Thursdays of every week, at ten o'clock in the forenoon, and arrive in Baltimore on Wednesdays and Saturdays in good season for dining. The passengers on their way from Philadelphia will dine at the "Queen of France Inn," kept by Mr. John Jarvis, twenty-two miles from the city. In the issue of the same paper, July 12, 1788, the notice is somewhat changed, and the rates of fare are given thus:

	Miles.	£	s.	d.
"From Phila. to Chester	15	0	5	0
" Chester to Qu. of France	7	0	2	8
" Q. of F. to Wilmington	6	0	2	6
" Wil. to Christiana Br	10	0	3	4
" Christiana Br. to Elk	12	0	4	2
" Elk to Susquehanna	16	0	7	6
" Phila. to Susque. Br	66	1	5	6
" Susque. to Baltimore	37	Gratis		

"The passengers sleep the first night at Christiana bridge."

In the same journal, issue of Feb. 11, 1788, the following note is given: "The proprietors of the Old Line of Stages, having united with the lines from New York to Philadelphia, and thence to Baltimore, will begin to run on Monday, the 18th inst. The stages will leave the New York and Baltimore Stage Office on 4th Street, two doors from the Indian Queen, Kept by Mr. James Thompson, at 6 o'clock on the mornings of Mondays, Wednesdays, and Fridays, and will return again on Tuesdays, Thursdays, and Saturdays each week during the Winter Season."

At the time mentioned there must have been rival lines running to Baltimore, that of Greeshorn, Johnson & Co., and G. P. Vanhorne, Kerlin & Co. The following advertisement appears in the *Pennsylvania Packet*, March 11, 1790:

"PUBLIC STAGES.

"The well-established Mail Stages between the City of Philadelphia and Baltimore continue their regular Tours respectively from each place by the way of the Susquehannah, on Mondays, Wednesdays, and Fridays. Returning on Tuesdays, Thursdays, and Saturdays. To facilitate the dispatch and arrival of the Public Mails is an obligation indispensable, and every exertion to accommodate engages the duty and interests of the proprietors. The passengers are therefore requested to be early in their preparations for the Stages starting, as the most assiduous efforts are requisite and will be practiced, to render general and complete satisfaction.

"G. P. Vanhorne, Kerlin & Co.

"N.B.—Regulations to be seen in the Stage office at the George Inn."

William Kerlin and Matthias Kerlin, Jr., were both interested in stage coach companies, by which occupation they became wealthy; Matthias Kerlin retiring from business about 1792 with an ample fortune, returned to Delaware County, his native place, to reside.

The *American Annual Register* for 1796, published Jan. 19, 1797, presents the unattractive picture of the post-road through the county at that period, and the unpleasant experiences that then awaited the traveler. It says, "The roads from Philadelphia to Baltimore exhibit for the greater part of the way an aspect of savage desolation. Chasms to the depths of six, eight, or ten feet occur at numerous intervals. A stage-coach which left Philadelphia on the 5th of February, 1796, took five days to go to Baltimore. The weather for the first four days was good. The roads are in a fearful condition. Coaches are overturned, passengers killed, and horses destroyed by the overwork put upon them. In winter, sometimes, no stage sets out for two weeks." Isaac Wild, Jr., of Dublin, in 1796 visited this country, and describing his journey by stage from Philadelphia to Baltimore, he records, "The driver had frequently to call to the passengers in the stage to lean out of the carriage, first on one side, then at the other, to prevent it from oversetting in the deep ruts with which the road abounded. 'Now, gentlemen, to the right,' upon which all the passengers in the stage stretched their bodies half out of the carriage to balance it on that side; 'Now, gentlemen, to the left,' and so on. These performances took place about every half-mile. If the road was contiguous to a wood, they just cut down a few trees to open a new passage, an operation which they called making a road."

During the first thirty odd years of the present century there were several lines of stages running between the points named,—Reeside, Stockton & Stokes, Murdock & Nasp, and Janviers' rival lines of coaches. They changed their horses and stopped for meals at designated places, and made certain inns their headquarters. The large stable-yards around the old Washington Hotel (Reeside's line stopped at that house), the Columbia House, and the City Hotel (then known as the Eagle and afterwards as the National), in Chester, were necessary for the change of horses and coach stopping-places. It was a busy scene in those times when the lumbering stage, with

[1] History of Chester, p. 194.

its coachman, in the winter-time, wrapped in a great coat of many capes, expertly throwing a whip with a long lash that sounded in the frosty air like the crack of a pistol, the horses at a full gallop, came into sight, the coach-body surging on its heavy leather springs, rumbling over the hard-frozen, lumpy road, and at last turning into the spacious inn-yard The ear-splitting blast from the guard's horn, which was always blown in coming into the town, brought every one to the windows of the houses, for it was something to be regretted, for twenty-four hours at least, in those days if the stage chanced to go by unobserved Often, too, the guard, out of very wantonness, would "toot his horn" just to see the horses in the field, who came trotting to the roadside fences to look at the passing wonder, scamper at the noise, and sometimes to alarm the farmers jogging along in the road before the stage About the beginning of this century, at the run which crosses the King's Highway just below Thurlow Station, the guard once blew a blast to quicken up a lady's horse that was ambling along in a sleepy manner, and did it so effectually that the rider was thrown to the earth and into the run, receiving such injuries that she died within a few minutes

After the commissioners appointed by Governor Snyder had laid out the street or State road, in 1815, which was afterwards known as the Baltimore, Philadelphia and New London turnpike, lines of stages were placed on that highway, and John Way, the then landlord of the Concordville Hotel, stated, in his petition in 1830, that his house was located "on the road leading from Philadelphia to New London cross-road, at which the stage teams are now daily changed on their tours between Philadelphia and Baltimore"

Albert Gallatin, in 1807, then Secretary of the Treasury, in a report to the Senate of the United States, states that "the Lancaster road, the first extensive turnpike that was completed in the United States, is the first link of the great western communication from Philadelphia" The road passes through the extreme northeastern verge of Haverford and diagonally through Radnor, and at an early date lines of stage-coaches ran along this noted highway

Shortly after the Revolution Chester seems to have been a place of considerable attraction as a Sunday resort, and that the public, desirous of visiting the ancient borough, might not lack transportation a Sunday line of stages was run to supply that demand, as we learn from the following advertisement in the *Philadelphia Gazetteer* for July 3, 1789

"The Subscriber intends to run a Carriage from this city to Chester every Sunday and means to carry passengers at a lower rate than the regular stage, and in order that they may arrive in Chester in time for the Sermon, the Coach will leave the INDIAN QUEEN, on Fourth Street at half-past 5 o'clock in the morning At Chester a fresh set of able-bodied Horses will be provided to return, so that the company may start thence in time for an agreeable refreshment at Messrs Grays, and arrive in Philadelphia as early as they wish

"MATTHIAS KERLIN, JR"

The general local travel from the neighborhood of Chester to Philadelphia was sadly cared for in the beginning of this century Persons living on the King's Highway, below Chester, and the Queen's Highway, above that town, would have their trunks brought to the front gates of their houses and wait for the Baltimore or Wilmington stage to come, and, if there chanced to be a vacant place, they were taken in and carried to their destination, but frequently the coachman shook his head and drove by without stopping To meet this want, about 1830, Chester rose to the dignity of having a line of stages to Philadelphia I copy the following advertisement from the *Weekly Visitor* of Dec 9, 1831

"PHILADELPHIA AND CHESTER COACHES

"John Pucians respectfully informs the inhabitants of Chester and vicinity that he has commenced running a line of stages between Philadelphia and Chester, leaving Philadelphia every morning at 8 o'clock, starting from the Sign of the Camel on North Second street and stopping for passengers at the Sign of the Cross Keys, corner Second and Lombard streets, and leaving Chester every afternoon at three o'clock, starting from the hotel of Samuel R Lamplugh"

Lamplugh at that time kept the Columbia House, but the steamboats were then furnishing comparatively excellent transportation, and the enterprise languished, and finally the coaches were discontinued

In alluding to the difficulties that beset the traveler by the public roads, mention was made of highwaymen Perhaps it would have been better had the term foot pads been used, for in no instance that I have found did the thief present himself handsomely appareled, mounted on a dashing steed, with a black silk mask covering the upper part of his face, but, in truth, he had usually a hang-dog appearance, without any of the mythological accessories that are always present in the highwaymen of the novelists

In the fall of 1798 Richard Flower, of Chester Mills, was stopped on the Queen's Highway near the run that crosses the road below Thurlow Station by a man who demanded his money Mr Flower apparently was complying with the unwelcome request when, seeing his opportunity, he struck the thief a blow on the head with his heavy riding-whip, which felled him to the ground, and then urging his horse into a run he made his way safely home

In the *Post Boy* for May 25, 1824, is the following account of a highway robbery committed in this county on the night of the 21st of May of that year

"ROBBERY—On Friday evening last Mr Samuel Black, of this county, being in his market cart, on his way home from Philadelphia, was attacked on the West Chester road by five robbers, armed with clubs, an axe, etc., who led the horse and cart into the woods, bound Mr Black in the cart, and after beating him, took what money they could find in his pockets, and left him in a mangled and insensible condition On their first appearance Mr Black succeeded in concealing his watch and pocket-book (which contained the principal part of his money and some papers) where they were not discovered One of the robbers, who was very much intoxicated, threatened to take the life of Mr Black, and there is no doubt he would have put his threat in execution had he succeeded in getting into the cart, which he attempted to do After they had left him some time, Mr Black recovered sufficiently to unbind himself, and succeeded in getting to the nearest house It would be well for persons who travel in the night to be prepared for the reception of such villains."

The last case I shall mention occurred about ten o'clock on the night of Feb. 8, 1838, when Warren Gibbon, returning from market, was stopped on the highway, a short distance west of Darby, by three men, who caught his horse by the head. Two of the men then held Gibbon, while the third presented a pistol at his breast with one hand and robbed him with the other. They took from him seventy-five dollars, his watch, and some of his clothing.

There was, of course, during all the time of which I write, the natural highway, the Delaware, and the early emigrant made constant use of it in going from settlement to settlement. Among the first mention respecting transportation the canoe is prominent, and we know that after Governor Markham's coming there appears to have been constant communication by water between the settlements from Burlington to the Capes of the Delaware. Gabriel Thomas, in his "History of Pennsylvania," published in 1698, states that "Chester, the German town, New Castle, and Lewistown" are the four great market towns, and "between these towns the watermen constantly ply their wherries." In October, 1698, Joseph Holt and Isaac Warner were drowned in the river, near Tinicum, by the upsetting of the ferry-boat going from New Castle to Philadelphia, and on the 23d of the preceding month John Barnskill was a passenger from Chester to Philadelphia in a ferry-boat, when it was overturned by a sudden gust of wind and he was drowned. Shallops constantly plied between the villages of Marcus Hook and Chester to Philadelphia in the last century, and during the months of June, July, August, and September, 1790, John Fitch ran a steamboat, the "Perseverance," as a passenger- and freight-boat on the Delaware, between Philadelphia, Trenton, Burlington, Chester, Wilmington, and Gray's Ferry, advertising her trips regularly in the newspapers of that day. During that summer his steamboat ran over three thousand miles in these trips. This was seventeen years before Robert Fulton made his noted journey in the "Clermont," in September, 1807, from New York to Albany. Fitch was a watchmaker, and during the Revolution repaired old muskets. One day, it is stated, he was walking along the stage-road near Newtown, N. J., suffering with rheumatism in his feet, and was so much annoyed by passing wagons that he declared, "I will make steam carry me." He did so, but the machinery of the "Perseverance" was so defectively constructed that it was constantly breaking down, and ultimately ruined its inventor.

In the last decade of the last century and in the early part of this the "Chester Planter," a shallop, built by Richard Flower to carry flour from the Chester Mills (the present site of Upland) to Philadelphia, would frequently take passengers to and from the places named, but in time the vessel became so old and decayed that it was run on the bank at Mount Mellick, on the opposite side of the creek from Upland, where its frame remained many years, until it entirely rotted down.

Previous to 1819, Capt. John D. Hart ran the sloop "John Wall" as a passenger- and freight-boat between Chester and Philadelphia, leaving the former place on Mondays and Thursdays, and returning every Wednesday and Saturday. The "Wall" continued on the line until and including the year 1828. In 1824, John Ashmead Eyre owned the sloop "Mary and Louisa," commanded by Capt. James Eyre, which he ran as an opposition packet from Chester, and in 1830 the sloop "Hunter," Capt. Harrison, made regular trips. In 1827, Peter Deshong ran the sloop "Mary and Louisa" as a regular packet between Chester and Philadelphia, leaving the former place every Tuesday and Friday, and returning Thursdays and Saturdays. Joshua P. and William Eyre built the sloop "Jonas Preston," which for many years, commanded by Capt. H. J. Gibson, was the noted packet between Chester and Philadelphia. She subsequently became the property of John Larkin, Jr., and William Booth, who were engaged in freighting between the points mentioned for several years, running a daily line of packets. In 1849 the firm had the sloops "John G. Johnson," Capt. Green, and the "John M. Broomall," Capt. Huston, on the line, and in 1851 the "Jonas Preston" was added, so that one vessel would leave and another arrive at Chester the same day. The "Jonas Preston" ultimately became the property of J. & J. Baker, and on April 6, 1868, when off the light-house near Fort Mifflin, heavily laden with coke, she was struck by the swell from the "Eliza Hancock," which caused her to capsize and sink. In 1850, Pancoast Levis ran the packet "Mary J." between the points named, and the same year William T. Crook established a line of packet schooners, making weekly trips between Chester and New York, employing therein the schooners "William," Capt. Collins, and the "Rebecca," Capt. Russell.

In 1865 the steam freight-boat "Chester" was built by P. Baker & Co., and ran between Philadelphia and Chester, and in the following year the propeller "Lamokin" was placed on the same route by J. & C. D. Pennell, as an opposition boat. In 1871 the lines were consolidated, and in 1872 the Delaware River Transportation Company (a new organization) was formed. The latter company built the "City of Chester," and subsequently became the owners of the Union lines. They have now on the route the freight steamboats "Eddystone," "Mars," and the "Mary Morgan," a large and commodious passenger steamer. The officers of the company are: President, J. Frank Black; Treasurer, J. Howard Roop; Secretary, Capt. Frank S. Baker.

In April, 1870, the Electric Line between Wilmington and New York, *via* the Delaware and Raritan Canals, in connection with their lines, established direct tri-weekly communication from Chester to New

York, placing additional steamers on the route for the purpose. The facility thus afforded to dispatch and receive goods without transshipment was recognized by the manufacturers and business men in the southwesterly part of the county, and the enterprise proved a success from the beginning.

In the fall of 1883 a new organization, the Chester Steamboat Company, was formed, and the steamboat "Artisan" placed on the route, running as a freight-boat between Chester and Philadelphia.

In 1882 the steam barge "Sarah," of which Capt. Deakyne was manager, began running daily between Chester and Philadelphia, but after a few months' service withdrew.

In the spring of 1883, R. W. Ramsden, who was proprietor of the Pioneer Stage Line from Chester to Upland, started a freight line from Chester to Philadelphia, running the steam barge "M. Massey." He continued in this enterprise until the fall of that year, when his boat was burned at the foot of Edgmont Avenue.

Railroads.—That part of the Pennsylvania Railroad which passes through a small part of Haverford, and diagonally through Radnor township, was originally the Columbia Railroad, built by the State. That part of it nearest to Philadelphia was not completed and opened to trade and travel until 1834. The cars at first were propelled by horse-power, the distance between Columbia and Philadelphia, eighty-two miles, requiring nine hours for the trip, the horses being changed every twelve miles. The cars were built after the form of the old stage-coaches, only larger, the entrance door at the side, and the driver seated on an elevated box in front.

The first locomotive put on the road was the "Black Hawk," which had been built in England. As the eastern end of the railroad for steam purposes was not completed, the engine was drawn to Lancaster over the turnpike road. When the wonderful curiosity was to perform the trial-trip between Lancaster and Columbia, Governor Wolf and most of the State officials were present to witness the novel sight. The "Black Hawk," however, disappointed the audience, who had been informed by an Irishman employed by the road to keep the track clear of the crowd. "Get out of the track!" he shouted; "when she starts, she'll go like a bird, and ye'll all be kilt!" But when the moment came, and the engineer applied the lever, the locomotive would not move, and did not until by pushing the train was started.

The eastern end of the road having been completed, on Wednesday, Feb. 28, 1834, the first train of cars from Lancaster to Philadelphia passed over the road, drawn by "Black Hawk," the distance between Lancaster and the head of the Inclined Plane having been traversed in eight and a half hours. Levi G. James, of Chester, who then resided in Radnor, can recall the excitement along the railroad on that day, the people flocking for miles around to witness the novel spectacle, and how the crowd cheered when the laboring engine, groaning, passed along with the train. The experiment had been successful, and so superior to horses did the locomotive demonstrate itself, that in 1837 there were forty engines in use on the road, and the horses, as a power, ceased to be used.

The extension from the Pennsylvania Railroad to West Chester, which was opened Dec. 25, 1833, aroused a rivalry in Old Chester, and a number of citizens of Delaware County procured the passage of the law of April 11, 1835, incorporating the Delaware County Branch Railroad Company, authorizing the construction of a railway from Chester, along the creek of the same name, to intersect at West Chester with the extension road there. The movement first received shape in November, 1833, when a meeting was held at the Black Horse Hotel to ascertain the probable cost of the proposed road; and as there were then nine cotton-mills, eight grist-mills, two paper-mills, three iron-works, and eleven saw-mills along the proposed route, it was believed the freight from these industries would pay a handsome profit on the costs. The capital invested in manufacturing was then a million of dollars, while the estimated cost of the road—eighteen miles—was twenty thousand dollars per mile, or three hundred and sixty thousand dollars for the road laid.

After the passage of the act, on June 18, 1835, subscription-books were opened at the Coffee-House, kept by John Bessonett, Jr., No. 86 South Second Street, Philadelphia, and no person was permitted to subscribe for more than ten shares on any one day. The books were to remain open for three days. A survey was made and stakes driven, but beyond that the project languished.

It was revived in the spring of 1848, and a survey was again made. The stakes driven at that time by the engineers were much the same course as those of twelve years previous, and those which followed twenty years afterwards, when the Chester Creek Railroad was built. The flicker of hope of 1848 was only a forerunner of the time when such a work must, in the necessity of public accommodation, be constructed. The latter was built under the provisions of the acts of Assembly of April 16, 1866, and April 17, 1867, and by the aid and assistance given to the enterprise by Samuel M. Felton, the public believed it must be pushed forward to completion. And it was.

The first time the whistle of a locomotive was heard on that road was Nov. 4, 1868, when the engine attached to the construction train passed some distance along the line, and the horses and cattle in the neighborhood, unused to such screeching, scampered from the roadside in alarm. In the spring of 1869 the road was completed and opened to public travel.

On April 2, 1831, the Legislature of Pennsylvania incorporated the Philadelphia and Delaware County Railroad Company. The charter lay dormant until

1835, when an organization was effected, and a board of directors elected. On Jan. 18, 1832, the Legislature of Delaware chartered the Wilmington and Susquehanna Railroad Company, with power to build a railroad from the Pennsylvania State line through Wilmington to the Maryland State line, towards the Susquehanna River; and on March 5, 1832, the Legislature of Maryland incorporated the Baltimore and Port Deposit Railway Company, with power to construct a road from the points named, and nine days subsequent the same authority incorporated the Delaware and Maryland Railroad to build a road from a point to be selected by the company at the Maryland and Delaware State line to Port Deposit, or any other terminus on the Susquehanna River. All of these companies had organized previous to 1836, when in January of that year the Philadelphia and Delaware County Railroad applied to the Legislature for power to increase its capital, which was granted, and at the same time the title of the company was changed to the Philadelphia, Wilmington and Baltimore Railroad. Negotiations were entered into by the latter company with the Delaware and Maryland Railroad, which finally resulted in the latter granting the former the right of way from the Delaware State line to Wilmington. And on Dec. 20, 1837, the road was completed from Wilmington to Chester, so that an engine and train of cars came from the former to the latter place, but did not cross the bridge over Chester Creek, the rails not having been laid over that stream. On January 15th the road was opened for public travel from Philadelphia to Wilmington.

The railway from Wilmington to Perryville had also been opened on the 4th of July, 1837, and the road from Baltimore to Havre de Grace on the 6th of July on the same year. At this time, although there was but one road, it was owned by three corporations, but on Feb. 5, 1838, they consolidated with a capital of two million two hundred and fifty thousand dollars, Matthew Newkirk being elected the first president.

"Although the road was now in condition for use, it was, as compared with modern roads, very incomplete. The track was constructed of iron bars nailed upon wooden string-pieces, called mud-sills, which rested on the ground, and consequently were continually getting out of position. It was not until after the lapse of some years that this defect was remedied by the introduction of wooden ties."[1]

It is doubtful whether the foregoing statement applies to the road so far as the Pennsylvania Division was concerned. Martin tells us that "the track of the railroad was originally laid with flat bars, called strap-rail, weighing about fifteen pounds per yard, fastened upon a continuous stringer with cross-ties and mud-sills, and with a gauge of four feet eight and a half inches."

[1] Johnson's "History of Cecil County, Maryland," p. 430.

The road was surveyed, so far as its construction through Delaware County is concerned, by William Strickland and Samuel H. Kneass, and in their report to the president and directors of the Philadelphia and Delaware County Railroad in 1835, they state that the whole length of the line of survey from Broad and Prime Streets, Philadelphia, to the Delaware State line was sixteen and three-fourths miles, and they, not without apparent glee, felt "justified in estimating the amount of passengers from data which their investigation afforded" at about one hundred and fifty persons per day. They also express the belief that if the proposed route to Baltimore be adopted (as was done), the distance being thereby reduced to ninety-three miles, the time of passage "may be readily performed in five hours."[2]

The contract for grading the roadway through Delaware County was awarded to John Cochran, William Eves, and John J. Thurlow, the latter having purchased Spencer McIlvain's interest in the original contract. The road was laid the greater part of the distance on the low, level meadow-land between Gray's Ferry and Chester, the earth for grading being supplied from the excavation of the ditches on each side of the track. While the men were working on the road, six laborers, in May, 1837, attempted to cross from one side of Darby Creek to the other in an old boat which lay on the shore, but it leaked so that when in the middle of the stream it sunk, and two of the men were drowned.

The annoyance to the railroad of being compelled to maintain a draw-bridge at Darby Creek was excessive, and after a year or so trial, the company petitioned the Legislature, in 1839, for right to build a permanent bridge across that stream. The proposition met with general opposition from the people of this county, and John K. Zeilin, then representative, obtained a report adverse to the bill. The railroad made no further effort looking to the removal of the draw-bridge at that point.

It is said that the plan of connecting a rope to the bell of an engine drawing a train of cars, so that the conductor might communicate with the engineer, was an idea of John Wolf, a noted conductor in the early days of the Philadelphia, Wilmington and Baltimore Railroad history. It seems that he had a cord running through the cars and made fast to a log of wood in the cab of the locomotive, which gave notice to the engineer when to stop or go ahead. On one occasion the former and Wolf had a disagreement, and at that time in railroad management the train was supposed to be in charge of the engineer while in motion, the conductor being but a secondary figure. Wolf had pulled the rope once or twice to indicate that he wanted the train to stop at the Blue Bell, but the engineer paid no attention, and rushed past the station without even slacking speed. The conductor

[2] Hazard's Register, vol. xvi. p. 245.

in anger clambered over the tender, and demanded why his signal to stop had not been obeyed "I'm in charge of this train, and will stop when I think best at any point not a regular station," replied the engineer This put Wolf to his mettle, and it resulted finally in the train being stopped, and, in the presence of the passengers, the conductor and engineer fought until the latter was completely conquered Never after that time was Wolf's signal disregarded, and the connecting cord was found to work so advantageously that it was adopted on all the railroads in the United States

After the completion of the road, the consolidated companies, now the Philadelphia, Wilmington and Baltimore Railroad Company, found that while their capital was two and a quarter millions, the cost of the road and equipping it had amounted to nearly four and a half millions of dollars The original subscribers to the stock, which promised such a golden harvest, soon found that the day when a dividend would be paid was uncertain, while creditors were clamorous for payment, and to liquidate these pressing claims two mortgages, amounting to three millions, had to be given The sturdy farmers who had placed a few hundred dollars in the stock of the company began to grow uneasy of waiting for dividends which never came, and by degrees their holdings passed into the market, where they were purchased as investments by wealthy capitalists of the Eastern cities In 1851, Samuel M Felton was elected president of the road, and during his administration the track, rolling stock, and landed estate of the company, which had deteriorated in the endeavor to relieve the road of its heavy debt, was relaid, increased, and improved The Philadelphia, Wilmington and Baltimore Railroad was put into a position to meet the great demand which came upon it ten years later in forwarding troops to the national capital So admirable was Mr Felton's management that the stock paid heavy dividends, and as a consequence it was rarely seen in the market, and if so, it was quickly purchased at a premium In 1865, Mr Felton resigned the presidency of the road, and as a testimonial of the great service he had rendered to the company a present of one hundred thousand dollars was made to him on his retiring from the position he had so admirably filled

Isaac Hinkley was elected to fill the place made vacant by Mr Felton's retiracy, and during the latter's presidency the improved line of railway was laid from Gray's Ferry through Darby, Sharon Hill, Prospect Park, Norwood, Ridley Park, Crum Lynne, and other stations which have been located on the line of the new road, now dotted along almost its entire length by handsome villas and country residences Ground was broken on Nov 11, 1870, and the first train passed over the Darby improvement, as it was popularly known, early in 1873 In the late spring of 1881 the Philadelphia, Wilmington and Baltimore Railroad passed into the hands of the Pennsylvania Central Railroad, H F Kenney, the superintendent of the former road, having been retained in charge of the Delaware and Southern Division of the Pennsylvania Railroad, which includes the old Philadelphia, Wilmington and Baltimore, the Chester Creek, the Baltimore Central, and the Philadelphia and West Chester Railroads, besides other roads in the State of Delaware

The West Chester and Philadelphia Railroad was incorporated April 11, 1848, and on Jan 17, 1852, the contract for building the road, except laying the rails, entered into with Gonder, Clark & Co, who were to receive three hundred thousand dollars in cash and two hundred thousand dollars in stock of the road for the work On Monday, July 16, 1855, the middle span of the railroad bridge, then being constructed over Ridley Creek, gave way, precipitating five men to the earth, one hundred and nine feet below, and three were instantly killed In the autumn of that year the road had been completed, and trains were running to Media, at the close of 1856 the road had extended from Rockdale to Lenni, and by Jan 1, 1857, to Grubb's bridge, the present Wawa The road was an expensive one to build, due to the deep valleys and many streams it crossed, so that at one time its stock had fallen to almost nominal value In the latter half of the year 1858 the road was pushed onward with remarkable rapidity, the rails being laid from Wawa to West Chester, so that the first train of cars from Philadelphia by the direct road reached West Chester on Tuesday, Nov 11, 1858, and on the following Thursday a celebration was held in the borough in honor of the event In May, 1880, the Philadelphia, Wilmington and Baltimore Railroad Company purchased the West Chester and Philadelphia Railroad, and on the subsequent transfer of the former road to the Pennsylvania Central, the West Chester road was included

The Philadelphia and Baltimore Central Railroad was incorporated March 17, 1853, and by act of April 6, 1854, was authorized to form a union with a corporation chartered by the State of Maryland On Jan 3, 1855, ground was broken for the road on the farm of Darwin Painter, in Birmingham, Delaware Co, Dr. Frank Taylor, the president of the road, turning the first sod between Chad's Ford and Grubb's bridge On Monday, June 1, 1857, the laying of the track from Grubb's bridge was begun, but it was not completed to Chad's Ford for public travel until some time in the year 1858, when trains ran as far as that point *The road, which became the property of the* Philadelphia, Wilmington and Baltimore Railroad Company, passed with the transfer made by the latter corporation to the Pennsylvania Central Railroad, already mentioned

The Chester and Delaware River Railroad Company was incorporated in 1872 by letters patent under the free railroad law of Pennsylvania Its terminal points were from Thurlow to Ridley Creek, a distance of about four miles. The incorporators were John M. Broomall, William Ward, William A. Todd, Samuel Archibald, Amos Gartside, James A. Williamson, James Kirkman, William H. Green, and Samuel H. Stephenson. Previous to the date of incorporation, Messrs. Broomall and Ward had constructed a spur track from a point below Thurlow Station of the Philadelphia, Wilmington and Baltimore Railroad to the bridge works in South Chester, for the accommodation of those works. The Philadelphia, Wilmington and Baltimore Railroad Company furnished the rails and cross-ties at an annual rental. The demand of other manufacturing establishments along the river soon became urgent for similar accommodations, and the owners of those industries joining with the original projectors, and the authorities of South Chester borough acting in unison with reference to granting privileges on Front Street, the railroad was extended up to the city limits. When the boundary was reached the same demand arose from establishments in Chester, and the city authorities, following the example of the Borough Council, gave a hearty support to the enterprise, and the result was the extension of the road to Penn Street. At this period, (1872) the Philadelphia and Reading Railroad Company became the lessee of the old bed of the Philadelphia, Wilmington and Baltimore Railroad from Gray's Ferry to Ridley Creek. The Reading company being owners of a large tract of land on the river near Marcus Hook, assumed control of the railroad on Front Street, finished its extension across Chester Creek, and connected it with its branch purchased from the Philadelphia, Wilmington and Baltimore Railroad Company. The Chester and Delaware River Railroad Company still preserves its separate corporate existence, the present officers being those of the Reading company, excepting William Ward, who is one of the directors. The completion and operation of this railroad has been followed by the most marked results. Many manufacturing establishments of the largest capacity have been erected on the line, owing to facilities afforded for transportation of heavy freights.

CHAPTER XXI.

REDEMPTIONERS AND SLAVERY IN DELAWARE COUNTY.

When the system of redemptive servitude first appeared in our history I fail to ascertain, but certain it is that it related in the first instance to English emigrants solely, and did not show itself until after the territory had been subjugated by the arms of Great Britain. I am aware that Professor Keen states that the only person, so far as known, who came to New Sweden on the "Griffin," on the first expedition in 1637, and remained in the colony, was Anthony, a bought slave, who served Governor Printz at Tinicum in 1644, making hay for the cattle, and accompanying the Governor on his pleasure yacht, and was still living there on March 1, 1648. But he was a slave (the first on our shore), and was not a redemptioner, who, to reimburse the owners and master of a ship for his passage and provender on the voyage, agreed that his services might be sold for a stipulated period. In the Duke of York's Laws occurs the first notice of the system, which, while it had many harsh and objectionable features, gave to the colonies great numbers of energetic and thrifty settlers, who, by reason of their poverty, never could have come to the New World had it not been for the redemptive system. The law mentioned provided that "no Christian shall be kept in Bondslavery, villenage, or Captivity, Except Such who shall be Judged thereunto by Authority or such as willingly have sould or shall sell themselves."[1]

The first record of the transfer of a redemption or indentured servant previous to the grant to Penn was at a court held at Upland, June 13, 1677, and is set forth in the quaint phraseology of that period:

> "Mr. John Test brought In Court a certaine man-servant named William Still, being a taylor by traede, whome hee the sd Test did acknowledge to have sold unto Capt'n Edmond Cantwell for the space and tearme of foure years, beginning from the first of Aprill Last past; The sd William Still declared in Court to bee willing to serve the said Capt'n Cantwell the aboved tearms of foure yeares."[2]

After Penn came to the province, in 1682, the subject of indentured servants received the immediate attention of the Governor, and among the laws enacted by the first and succeeding General Assemblies were those requiring a registration of persons so held to servitude; forbidding the assignment of servants to persons residing without the province; exempting them from being levied on in executions against their masters; forbidding the harboring of a servant for a longer period than twenty-four hours without giving notice to a justice of the peace of the whereabouts of such servant; interdicting bartering with a servant for goods belonging to his master, and limiting the period of servitude for all unindentured servants of seventeen years of age at five years, and those under that age until they should attain the age of twenty-one years. Masters were also required to bring such servants before the court within three months after their arrival in the province, that the term of service might be determined by the justices. The early records contain many cases growing out of this species of servitude, which for a century and a half maintained in this State, and gave to it many of its most respected families.

At the court held the 3d day of 1st week, Seventh month, 1686, Thomas Usher, the then sheriff, complained that William Collett was holding Thomas

[1] Book of Laws, p. 12.

[2] Record of Upland Court, p. 51.

Cooper "in his service by an unlawful contract, upon which it was Ordered that William Collett doe forthwith Sett the said Thomas Cooper att Liberty, and allow him the Customs & Law of the Country in that case Provided for Servants."

This is the first case I have found in which the custom of the country is alluded to, although it is frequently mentioned thereafter. The act of March 10, 1683, provided that at the expiration of the term of servitude a bonded servant was entitled to receive "One new Sute of Apparell, ten bushels of Wheat or fourteen bushels of Indian corn, one Ax two howes, one broad and another narrow, and a Discharge from their Services." By the act of 1693 the custom was declared to be "two suits of apparell," together with the other articles named in the law of 1683, and by the act of 1700 the servant was to have "two compleat suits of apparel, whereof one shall be new, and shall also be furnished with one new axe, one grubbing hoe, and one weeding hoe, at the charge of their master or mistress." This continued to be the law until the act of March 9, 1771, repealed so much of the act of 1700 as related to the furnishing of a new axe, a grubbing- and a weeding hoe.

The great body of mechanics in the early colonial days originally came to the province as redemptioners, and the cases are frequent showing that this was the rule. The first instance, save that of William Still, heretofore mentioned, and the only one I shall cite, as to this statement, occurred at the court held 1st 3d day of First month, 1689-90, when "James Hayes Petitioned this Court to have his Toles [tools] from Jemmy Collett wch according was Ordered that the said Toles was to be delivered Imediately into the hands of James Sandelands for the use of the said Hayes. The said Hayes paying to Jeremy Collett what he Justly Owes him. The said James Hayes Promised Here in open Court to searve James Sandelands his Heirs, Exs., Adms. or Assigns the Residue of the Tyme of his Indenture Excepting Two Months and fifteen days wch James Sandelands gave him."

The freeman who was unfortunate to contract debts in those days, when the body could be taken in execution in a civil suit, to save himself constant trouble, frequently sold himself to liquidate the claims against him. The case of George Chandler at the court held first 3d day of 1st week, First month, 1689/90, shows how debts were discharged by personal service. Thomas Rawlins complained that Chandler was indebted to him in 34*s.* 8½*d.*, and the creditor was clamorous for payment. The court thereupon liquidated all Chandler's obligations in this wise:

"Ordered that the said George Chandler by his Consent doo sell himself a servant for Two years and five Months wth Edward Beazer, the said Edward Beazer paying to the said Rawlins the said sum of 34*s.* 8½*d.* and the Remainder wch would make up the Sume of Ten pounds wch was £8 5*s.* 3½*d.* to be paid to his ffather in Law, William Hawkes."

In the court held Feb. 6, 1739/40, James Reynolds informed the justices, "by his petition that being indebted to sevll psons, as by a list pduced appears To the sum of Eight pounds, thirteen shill. and five pence with Costs and having no other way to satesfy these Debts prays to be Admitted to pay by Servitude which is allowed, And ordered to Serve his Creditors Two Years in full satisfaction for ye said Debts and Costs." Indeed, in satisfaction of court charges, sale of the defendant's services has been ordered.

The court records often show that when a question of more than ordinary importance was to be presented to the justices, the latter would call into their counsel those persons whose position seemingly gave them peculiar opportunities for information on the matter under consideration. Hence we find at an Orphans' Court held at Chester, Nov. 29, 1705, Peter Evans, register-general of the province, was present, occupying a place on the bench, when Richard Adams presented a petition "Concerning the estate of Thomas Clayton, dec'd," as followeth, in these words:

"Chester.—To the Worshipful Commissioners & Register General now sitting in the Orphan's Court held for the County of Chester, the humble petition of Richard Adams, of Edgmont, of this County, Carpenter, shewest,—

"'That whereas Thomas Clayton, a bond servant unto your petitioner, about 6 years ago, on his voyage from England unto this province, died at sea, leaving behind him Elinor, a child of about the age of seven years, and a boy of about 5 years of age, named Richard, for which children's passage your petitioner paid in England, & hath ever since maintained them with meat, drink, and apparill.

"'May it, therefore, please your Worship to consider the premises, and to make such order thereupon as to your Worship may seem most convenient, and your petitioner shall ever pray, etc.

'Richard Adams.

"'Nov. 2, 1705.'

"Upon reading of which petition the Court orders the said Richard Adams to bring an inventory of the estate of the said Thomas Clayton, which he was sworn to do and return to next Orphans' Court, and the Court appointed Thomas Barnsley and William Pickle to appraise the said goods, and make return to the said court.

"The Court having considered Richard Adam's charge against the two orphans, Richard & Elinor Clayton, does allow 26 pounds to Richard Adams, Pennsylvania money, for their passage & diet in England, and diet on board ship, diet in Maryland, and bringing them up in Pennsylvania.

"Ordered that Elinor Clayton, an orphan, of the age of 14 years shall serve Daniel Hoopes for the term of 7 years from this day, on condition that the said Daniel teach her to read, knit, and sowe, and pay 12 pounds according to the order of this Court. Richard Clayton, an Orphan, being brought to this Court, is ordered by said Court to serve Edward Dauger, of Chester, Cooper, for a term of 9 years from this day, on consideration that the said Edward teach, or cause to be taught, the said Richard the trade of a cooper, and find and allow sufficient meat, drink, lodging, and apparill during the said term, and also to teach him to read & write, & pay 14 pounds 5 shillings to the order of this Court."[1]

As the provinces increased in population and wealth the trading in redemptioners became a business. A

[1] Of this Richard Clayton nothing now seems to be known. The Claytons of Delaware County are descended from William Clayton, a passenger with his family on the ship "Kent," who purchased an estate at Marcus Hook, the deed to which was acknowledged at the Court held March 13, 1678/9. Gilbert Cope states that he died in 1689, while Thompson Westcott says his death occurred in 1682. If Westcott is right, there were five William Claytons in unbroken succession. If Cope is correct there were four William Claytons, the eldest son in each generation, including the first settler of the name, in the list.

few men speculated in these emigrants as they would cattle. They would purchase the redemptioners from the master of the vessel, or the merchants to whom they were consigned, at wholesale, and then drive them through the country to be sold at retail at an enormous profit. The men engaged in this trade were known as soul-drivers. But finally the business became precarious, so many of the redemptioners escaping from their owners while traveling through the country to find a market, that about the year 1785 the trade was absolutely discontinued. One of these dealers, named McCullough, became noted in the trade in Chester County, and prospered so that he would go to Europe and gather a drove of redemptioners, which he would sell at a greater profit than he could make by buying of the intermediate dealer. The late Joseph J. Lewis has recorded an amusing incident of the trade, in which McCullough, instead of selling, was sold by one of his herd, as follows:

"The fellow, by a little management, contrived to be the last of the flock that remained unsold, and traveled about with his master without companions. One night they lodged at a tavern, and in the morning the young fellow, who was an Irishman, rose early and sold his master to the landlord, pocketed the money, and marched off. Previously, however, to his going he used the precaution to tell the purchaser that his servant, although tolerably clever in other respects, was rather saucy and a *little* given to lying—that he had even presumption enough at times to endeavor to pass for master, and that he might possibly represent himself as such to *him*. By the time mine host was undeceived the son of Erin had gained such a start as rendered pursuit hopeless."[1]

The last reference to the sale of redemptioners in Delaware County is related in a sketch of Abraham Peters, of Lancaster County, written by the late Col. John W. Forney, which was published in *Progress* in 1879. The colonel stated that in 1811 Peters was hauling grain from Lancaster County to the mills on the Brandywine, and was requested by his sister to buy a small German girl from a vessel for her.

"The vessels stopped at Chester. So, after he had disposed of his grain, he mounted one of his horses and rode to Chester. He went on board an emigrant vessel, and as he spoke German, he was soon surrounded by a crowd, each one requesting to be bought, as they preferred to get into families where German was spoken. He called the captain and made known his errand. The captain told him he had two small orphan girls on board, their mother having died on the voyage. He asked forty dollars for the two, but as Mr. Peters only wanted one, and could take but one on horseback with him, the captain said he would charge him twenty-five dollars for one, and if he sent him a purchaser for the other, he would give her for fifteen dollars. Before parting the girls were going to divide their dead mother's effects, but Mr. Peters would not allow this, as he assured them that Katy, the girl he was taking with him, would find plenty, and therefore insisted on the other keeping all except the clothes that Katy was wearing. Again assuring the captain that he would try and find another purchaser, he started for Wilmington, and was soon on his way home. Katy was a bright and lovely girl, and soon forgot her sorrow as she stood at the front of the wagon looking at and admiring the horses. He had proceeded but a short distance from Wilmington when he met a fine old Quaker gentleman and his wife driving to town. The lady saw the little girl, and admiring her, stopped and wanted to buy her. But Mr. Peters told her that he had bought the girl for his sister, and therefore could not sell her, but told her of the little sister that was left behind on the vessel, and requested them to go to Chester and buy her. He gave a few lines to the captain, and reminded him of the fifteen dollars he had agreed to take.

"The Quaker promised to go and buy the sister. They gave each other their addresses, and promised to write and keep the girls in communication with each other. Katy was installed in her new home, and under the kind, motherly treatment of Mrs. Bausman grew up to be a fine woman. Her sister also found a good home with the Quaker family. Correspondence was kept up between the families, and yearly visits were made alternately with the girls, and very friendly relations sprung up between the families, which were kept up long after the girls were free. When Katy had served out her time and arrived at a proper age, she was married to a worthy German baker in Philadelphia. She esteemed it a great pleasure to visit her former mistress, to whom she was ever thankful for the good, religious training she received from her."

Slaves.—When slavery of the negro and Indian races first showed itself in the annals of Pennsylvania is difficult of ascertainment, for it is well known that previous to the grant of the province to William Penn the Swedes and Dutch settlers had the pernicious system of servile labor implanted in the territory. In 1677, James Sandelands was the only person on the Delaware River from Upland northward who owned a slave. The wrong, however, did not go long unchallenged after the English power had acquired ownership of the soil, for as early as 1688 the Friend settlers at Germantown issued their now famous protest against the holding of their fellow-men in bondage. Although the movement was purely addressed to the conscience of the public, and did not prevent the importation of negroes to the colony, it was the corner-stone on which the principles of emancipation of slaves in every Christianized nation of the earth were subsequently erected. In 1696 the Yearly Meeting of Quakers put themselves broadly on record as follows: "Friends are advised not to encourage the bringing in any more negroes." From these small beginnings the sentiment adverse to slavery extended, and when Penn made his second visit to this province in 1700, he was instrumental in incorporating in the discipline of the society provisions regulating the

[1] "Sketches of the History of Chester County," published in the *Village Record*, West Chester, 1824.

treatment of slaves among those members of that religious order who, at that time, did not regard the holding of bondsmen as a moral wrong. Not only did the proprietary take that step, but he proposed to the Assembly two bills, one regulating marriage among negroes and the other establishing trials of slaves before magistrates, instead of leaving them as theretofore entirely under the control of their masters. The latter bill only became the subject of legislative enactment.

The Quarterly Meeting held at Chester for the county of Chester, Sixth month 1, 1700, prohibited the members of the meeting from purchasing Indians as slaves, and in 1711 the same meeting declared that it was "dissatisfied with Friends buying and encouraging the bringing in of negroes." Four years after Chester Monthly Meeting again brought this matter prominently before the society, and determined to press it at the Yearly Meeting. That this was done is evidenced by a letter of Isaac Norris in 1715, quoted by Watson, wherein the writer says, "Our business would have been very well were it not for the warm pushing by some Friends of Chester, chiefly in the business of negroes. The aim was to obtain a minute that none should buy them for the future."

The agitation of the subject had so attracted public attention to the evil of slavery that the Assembly as early as 1705 levied an impost duty on slaves brought within the province, and in 1710 again enacted a similar law. In 1711 an act was passed absolutely forbidding the importation of slaves, but the English ship-owners, at that time largely interested in the traffic in negroes, influenced the crown to declare the colonial law nugatory. The Assembly in the following year imposed a duty of twenty pounds a head on every slave brought into Pennsylvania, and again Queen Anne crushed the provincial statute at the instance of those who were growing wealthy in the trade.

The opponents of the system of slavery were not dismayed into silence by the royal mandate, but in 1716, 1728, and 1730 Chester Quarterly Meeting, with no uncertain sound, pressed the matter on the attention of the Society of Friends, and in 1761, Dr. Smith tells us a member of Chester meeting was dealt with by that body for having bought and sold a negro, but having made a proper acknowledgment he was not disowned.

That slaves were generally owned and kept by persons of wealth and by farmers in Chester County at an early date is fully established by an examination of the records, which show in settling estates frequent mention of negro slaves. The first case in this county where slaves were manumitted that I have found is in the will of Lydia Wade, widow of Robert Wade, dated the 30th day of Fourth month, 1701. Lydia Wade, in all probability, died in July, and her will, probated Aug. 8, 1801, before Register-General Moore, at Philadelphia, has the following clauses respecting her slaves:

"16ly. My will is that my negroes John and Jane his wife shall be sett free one month after my decease.

"17ly. My will is that my negro child called Jane shall be sett free after it have lived with my negro John twelve years and after that with my kinsman John Wade five years."

As the spirit of liberty spread abroad among the people during the colonial difficulties with Europe, the impression that it was unjust to keep mankind in bondage became so general that it caused many persons in the colony, whose principles were more dear to them than money, to manumit their slaves. In the year 1776 a number of slaves were so made free. William Peters, of Aston, in that year manumitted four bond-servants,—a man, woman, and two children. The document relating to the two last I copy in full:

"To all people to whom these presents shall come: I, William Peters, of Ashtown, in the County of Chester and Province of Pennsylvania, having a certain malattoe boy named Jack, aged about foure years under my care and in my service and also a Mulatto Gerl named Grace aged about two years Likewise under my care. Now Know Ye, that for and in Consideration that all mankind have an Equal, Natural and Just Right to Liberty I do by these Presents promise and Declair that the said Jack and Grace, he when he shall arive at the age of twenty-one that is to say on the first day of the Eighth month in the year of our Lord one thousand Seven Hundred and Ninety-three and She when she shall arrive at the age of Eighteen, that is to say on the first Day of the Eighth month in the year one thousand Seven Hundred and Ninety-two, they shall be and is hereby Declared, Discharged, Manumitted and at full Liberty and for myself, my Heirs, Executors, Administrators and Assigns and all other persons Claiming under me or any of them do quit all Claim after that time to the said Jack and Grace which by the Laws or Customs of this province or any other Government might have subjected them to Slavery or Deprived them of the full Enjoyment of Liberty. In witness whereof I have hereunto set my hand and seal the Seventh Day of the Eighth month in the year of our Lord one thousand Seven Hundred and Seventy-Six,

"WM. PETERS. [L. S.]

"*Signed and sealed in the presence of*
"BENJAMIN HOUGH,
"SAMUEL TRIMBLE."

In 1777 the public sentiment among Friends against slavery had become so general that the ownership of a bondsman for life was regarded as a sufficient cause in itself for the meeting to disown members thus offending. As stated before, the conviction of the wrong and evil of slavery made permanent lodgment in the opinion of the people, when the struggle between the colonists and England began, increasing as the spirit of liberty increased until, March 1, 1780, the Assembly enacted a law providing for the gradual abolition of the entire system of servile labor in the commonwealth. Its provisions required a registration of all slaves to be made prior to the 1st day of November following in the office of the clerk of the Court of Quarter Sessions in the several counties, and declared that all persons born after that date in Pennsylvania should be free, excepting the children of registered slaves, who should be servants to their parents' masters until they had attained twenty-eight years, after which age they also became freemen. Under this law a registry of the slaves of Chester County, giving the name, age, sex, and time of service of each person held as a slave, as also the name of the owners and the township where they resided, was carefully made. The record shows the following slaves, the number owned by each master, as well as the residences of the latter in the territory now comprising Delaware County:

Robert Magorgan, of Haverford township, farmer, registers a mulatto child then aged 6 months, a servant until he shall attain the age of 31 years.

Hugh Goveen, of Haverford, farmer, registered a negro woman, Phillis, aged 21; a negro boy, Peter, aged 7 years, slave for life; and a mulatto girl, Poll, aged 16, a servant until she is 31 years.

Samuel Johnson, of Haverford, farmer, registered a negro woman, Dinah, 45; a negro girl, Sall, 14; a mulatto boy, Jem, 8; a mulatto boy, Joe, 5½ years; and a mulatto boy, Peter, 2 years old, all slaves for life.

Hester Hortright, of Haverford, gentlewoman, records a negro boy named Joe, aged 15, a slave for life.

Richard Willing, of Haverford, farmer, records a negro man, Dick, 40; a negro man, Ishmael, 28; a negro man, 21; and a negro woman, Molly, aged 42, all slaves for life.

John Lindsay, Haverford, farmer, records a negro girl 7 years old, a slave for life.

Edward Hughes, of Haverford, carpenter, records a negro boy, Will, aged 1 year and 8 months, a slave for life.

Charles Humphreys, of Haverford, miller: his sister, Elizabeth Humphreys, and the estate of Rebecca Humphreys, deceased, record a negro woman, Nancy, 70; a negro man, Cezar, 36; a negro man, Tone, 34; a negro woman, Nancy, 44; a mulatto woman, Judy, 25; a mulatto girl, Alice, 10; a mulatto boy, Tommey, 8; and a mulatto female child, Fanny, 13 months, all slaves for life.

Jacob Richards, of Aston, yeoman, records a negro man, Dick, 64; a negro man, Jym, 30; a negro girl, Flora, 12; a mulatto boy, Peet, 5; a negro girl, Rose, 3; a female child, Sylvia, 16 months, all slaves for life, and a negro servant woman then 22, until she attains the age of 25 years.

The heirs of Philip Evans, of Aston, deceased, register a negro woman, Dinah, 27; a negro boy, Adam, 6; a negro girl, Abby, 4; and a negro girl, Sylvia, aged 2 years, all slaves for life.

William Twaddle, of Aston, forgemaster, registered a negro man, Sam, 35; a mulatto boy, Tom, 6; a negro wench, Seal, 19, all slaves for life.

Isaac Maris, of Marple, yeoman, registered a negro wench, Bet, aged 17, a slave for life.

Dr. Bernard Vanleer, of Marple, registered a negro boy, George, aged 15, a slave for life.

Archibald Dick, of Lower Chichester, registered a negro man, Cuff, 40; a negro woman, Nance, 20; a negro boy, Statia, 14; a negro girl, Flora, 7; and a mulatto boy, Benn, aged 2 years, all slaves for life.

Joseph Walker, of Lower Chichester, yeoman, registered a negro boy, Jack, aged 10, a slave for life.

Samuel Price, of Lower Chichester, farmer, registered a negro man, James, 26; a negro man, Oliver, 24, slaves for life; and a mulatto boy, Joe, aged 4 years, a servant till he attains the age of 31 years.

George Craig, of Marcus Hook, clerk, registered a negro woman, Phebe, 32; a negro boy, Phil, 7; a mulatto boy, Jack, 3 years and a half; and a mulatto girl, Amy, aged 1 year and 9 months. At a later time, for the date is not given, George Craig records a negro man, Thomas, aged 50 years. All of these slaves for life.

Richard Baker, of Middletown, yeoman, records a negro girl, Kassee, 13 years, a slave for life, and a mulatto servant-boy, Phineas, 17 years old, until he attains the age of thirty-one years.

Mary Ann Doyle, of Middletown, seamstress, records a negro girl, Ruth, aged 10 years, a slave for life.

William Doyle, of Middletown, records a negro girl, aged 5 years, a slave for life.

Joseph Gibbons, of Springfield, inn-holder, records a negro girl, Phebe, aged 8 years, a slave for life.

Thomas Levis, Esq., of Springfield, records a negro boy named Scipio, aged 16 years, a slave for life.

James Crozer, of Springfield, farmer, records a mulatto servant-man, Anthony Walsh, aged 22, until he attains 31 years; and a negro woman-servant, Amelia, aged 19, until she attains the age of 21 years.

Lewis Davis, of Springfield, yeoman, records a mulatto servant, Rebecca, aged 21, until she attains the age of 31.

Caleb Davis, Esq., of Springfield, records a negro boy, Frank, aged 15, a slave for life.

Samuel Levis, of Springfield, paper-maker, records a negro boy, James Knox, 18, and a negro girl, Flora Knox, aged 10 years. Both slaves for life.

John Levis, Sr., of Springfield, yeoman, records a negro boy, Essex, aged 12; a negro boy, Frank, 10; a negro boy, Harry, 6; and a negro boy, Milford, aged 4, all slaves for life.

George Lownes, of Springfield, cutler, records a negro man, Tom, aged 26, and a negro woman, Hannah, aged 19, servants until they attain the age of 31.

John Ogden, of Springfield, yeoman, a mulatto girl, Poll, aged 15, a slave for life.

Nicholas Diehl, of Tinicum, grazier, records a negro man, Lonnon, aged 26; a negro man, Cojo, 24; a negro girl, Dinah, 7; and a negro boy, Cæsar, aged 5, all slaves for life.

Benjamin Rue, of Tinicum Island, grazier, records a negro girl, Jude, aged 13, a slave for life.

John Taylor, of Tinicum Island, grazier, records a negro girl, Jude, aged 6, a slave for life.

William Smith, of Tinicum, yeoman, records a negro girl, Nance, aged 5 years, a slave for life, and a negro servant girl, Eamy, 12 years old, till she attains the age of 31 years.

John Miller, of Tinicum, yeoman, records a negro boy, Jesse, aged 13, a slave for life.

John Odenheimer, of the borough of Chester, farmer, records a negro man, Anthony Welsh, aged 45, a slave for life.

Mary Withey, of the borough of Chester, gentlewoman, records a negro woman, Phillis, 58, and a negro woman, Sophia, aged 32 years. Both slaves for life.

Capt. Edward Vernon, of the borough of Chester, inn-holder, records a mulatto woman, Kate, 20; a mulatto boy, 16; a negro man, Jym, 65; a negro woman, Jinn, 21; and a negro child, Dann, aged 9 months, all slaves for life. He also records a mulatto servant-boy, aged 12 years, until he attains the age of 24 years.

Rachael Weaver, of the borough of Chester, inn-holder, administratrix of the estate of Valentine Weaver, deceased, records a negro man, Joe, 60; a negro woman, Dinah, 60; a negro boy, Jack, 15; a negro boy, Peter, 13 years; and a negro girl, Violet, aged 11. All slaves for life.

Elisha Price, Esq., of the borough of Chester, records a negro man, Peter, aged 24 years, a slave for life.

Samuel Shaw, of the borough of Chester, miller, records a negro man, Peter, 36, and a negro man, Buff, age 23. Both slaves for life.

Boaz Matthews, of Upper Darby, blacksmith, records a negro man named Cæsar, aged 37, a slave for life.

Sarah Harman, of Upper Darby, seamstress, records a negro woman, Clarissa, aged 19, a slave for life.

Samuel Smith, of Darby township, yeoman, records a negro man, Milford, 58, and a negro man, Tom, 23. Both slaves for life.

John Crosby, Jr., of Ridley, yeoman, records a negro girl, Fann, aged 10 years, a slave for life.

Sketchley Morton, of Ridley, grazier, records a negro boy, Jeffrey, aged 14, a slave for life.

John Morton, of Ridley, farmer, records a negro man, George, 52; a negro woman, Dinah, 47; a negro girl, Hannah, 7; and a female negro child, 1 year old, all slaves for life.

Thomas Smith, of Ridley, farmer, records a negro man, Jim, 20; a negro boy, Cato, 10; a negro girl, Phebe, 14; and a negro girl, Hannah, aged 9, all slaves for life.

John Quandril, of Ridley, weaver, records a negro man, Jack, aged 60, a slave for life.

John Crozer, executor of the estate of John Knowles, late of the township of Ridley, deceased, records a negro man, Scipio, 24; a negro woman, Pathena, 41; a negro girl, Fanny, aged about 14; a negro girl, Tabitha, 11; and a negro girl, Jane, aged 8, all slaves for life.

Isaac Hendrickson, of Ridley, farmer, records a negro man, Tone, 40; a negro woman, Nance, 36; a negro boy, Frank, 12; a negro girl, Bett, 10; a negro boy, Tone, 7; a negro boy, Joe, 5; a negro girl, Pol, 3; and a negro girl, Dine, aged 6 months, all slaves for life.

Morton Morton, of Ridley, yeoman, records a negro man, Cæsar, 28; a negro woman, Liz, 30; a negro boy, Annias, 8 years and 7 months; and a negro boy, Samuel, aged 8 years and 7 months; a mulatto boy, John, aged 6 years and 4 months; and a mulatto boy, Jacob, aged 6 years and 4 months (Mr. Morton may possibly have had a pair of twins in his household); a mulatto girl, Sarah, 3 years and 3 months; and a mulatto boy, Peter, 1 year and 10 months, all slaves for life.

Lewis Trimble, of Ridley, yeoman, records a mulatto woman, Peg, 23; and a negro girl, Liz, 13, all slaves for life.

John Worrall, of Ridley, yeoman, records a mulatto servant boy, Philip Brown, aged 3 years and 9 months, until he shall attain the age of 31 years.

Harvey Lewis, of Ridley, yeoman, records a negro servant-man, James,

21, and a negro servant-woman, Hannah, 16, until they shall have attained the age of 31 years

Thomas Cheyney, Esq, of Thornbury, records a negro girl, Lizey, 9, and a negro boy, Isaac, aged 6 years slaves for life

Joshua Way, of Thornbury, yeoman, reports a negro woman, Phillis, 21 years, a slave for life

Mark Wilcox, of Concord, paper-maker, records a negro man, Prince, 55, a negro man, Cæsar, 25, a negro woman, Pegg, 30, a negro boy, Luke, 8, a negro boy, Tim, 8, and a negro girl, Suck, aged 3, all slaves for life

Mark Wilcox, of Concord, executor of the estate of Thomas Wilcox, late of the same township, deceased, records a negro girl, Luce, aged 14 years, a slave for life

John Jerman, of Newtown, yeoman, records a negro woman, Venus, aged 32, a slave for life

Jonathan Hunter, of Edgmont, yeoman, records a negro woman, Phillis, 30, a negro lad, Paddy, 10, a negro boy, Samson, a negro girl, Prude, 6, and a negro girl, Phillis, aged 3 years, all slaves for life

In addition to the foregoing list the following persons made returns of slaves, but the residences of the owners are not given, hence I cannot designate how many, if any, were residents in the territory now comprising Delaware County

Thomas May, four slaves, John Cuthbert, one, James Boyd, two, John Vanlasey, four, James McCainent, two, George Boyd, one, Capt Thomas Wiley, one, Catherine Kelso, one, Robert Carry, one, Thomas Scott, one, William Steel, two

Under the provisions of the foregoing act, after the creation of Delaware County, the following births of negro children of slaves belonging to the persons whose names are given are recorded

Jan 28, 1794, Adam Deihl, of Tinicum, grazier, negro female child, Nancy Norris, born Sept 24, 1794

April 29, 1794, William Burns, of Marcus Hook, inn-keeper, two negro children,—first, female named Flora, born 14th day of February, 1794, second, male named Cuff, born 16th day of March, 1794

Jan 6, 1795, Israel Elliott, Esq, of Tinicum, grazier, female negro child named Phebe, daughter of Dinah McCormick, born 10th day of September, 1794

Nov 12, 1796, Israel Elliott, Esq, of Tinicum, grazier, female negro child named Elizabeth, daughter of Dinah McCormick

In 1799, Elizabeth Evans, of Aston, was assessed for one woman slave valued at two hundred and fifty dollars

The act of Assembly, March 29, 1798, provided for the registration of all children born of slaves within six months after their birth, declaring that only children thus registered could legally be held as slaves until the age of twenty-eight years Under its provisions the following births are recorded

Feb 27, 1799, Mark Wilcox, Esq, of Concord, negro male child named Charles Gibson, son of Susanna Gibson, born 2d day of September, 1798

July 2, 1806, William Anderson, of Chester, male mulatto bastard child named Francis, born 17th day of February last

Sept. 22, 1809, Mary Calhoun, female negro child named Margaret Reddon, born 5th day of April last

The foregoing is the last record of the birth of a slave-child in Delaware County

Among the records of the county will be found a paper executed by the heirs of Isaac Levis, of Middletown, under date of Aug 4, 1801, setting forth that the decedents owned "a negro boy named John, now about twenty-three years of age, and it being apprehended that the heirs may have some claim on the said negro," they release all rights they may have to his person or services

In the same year, August 1st, Israel Elliott, Esq, of Tinicum, being the owner of "negro Primus Neid," a slave for life,—then in his twenty-eighth year,—"in consideration of his Integrity, honesty and uprightness during his servitude" manumitted "Primus," requiring all "the Lieged people of the United States of America" to recognize his late slave as a free man

The return of deaf and dumb and slaves in each township in the State in 1829 shows one slave in Delaware County, held in Chester[1] The census of 1790 showed fifty slaves in Delaware County; that of 1800, seven, while in 1810 not one was returned In 1820 there was one, and in 1830 the number had swollen to two

The last notice of the effete system of slavery, so far as the official records of the county are concerned, will be found on file in the office of the prothonotary, at Media, whereby Elizabeth H Price, of Cecil County, Md, under date of Nov 15, 1830, in consideration of one hundred and ten dollars, "released from slavery, manumitted and set free, Rasin Garnett, being under forty-five years of age, of a healthy constitution, sound in mind and body, and capable by labor to procure to him sufficient food and raiment, with other requisite necessaries of life"

The old colonial law which authorized the apprehension and imprisonment of negro or white persons suspected of being runaway slaves or servants was continued in practice until the beginning of this century

The record of the Court of Quarter Sessions shows that on Jan 27, 1795, "Negro Jacob committed on suspicion of being a runaway, there appearing no claimant, he was, on motion, discharged from his confinement," while on "Jan 27, 1801 Lewis Thoston, a prisoner charged with being a runaway servant," was discharged by proclamation

I have not learned who was the last slave owned in the county of Delaware, but I know that in 1828 "Aunt Sallie" died at Lamokin Hall, in the borough of Chester She had been the slave of John Flower, formerly of Marcus Hook and Chester, who moved to Philadelphia during the Revolutionary war, where he became a prominent and wealthy merchant He had manumitted Sallie many years before his death (which occurred in 1824), but she refused to leave her owner's house, where she tyrannized over the servants and regulated his diet, telling him what he could and could not have for dinner Her supreme contempt was bestowed on "the poor niggers of no family" By the will of her master the interest of several thousand dollars was to be used for her support for the remainder of her life She declared that she was the daughter of a negro king, and had been purchased by the captain of a slaver from the tribe

[1] Hazard's Register, vol iv p 376

that had captured her in war After her master's death she refused to live with any of her race, but came to Chester, to the house of Richard Flower, the brother of her late owner, where she insisted on remaining, because, as she declared, she "was one of de family"

John Hill Martin says, "John Crosby (the judge) owned the last two negro slaves in Delaware County, 'Old Aunt Rose' and her husband, 'Sampson' After they were freed by law, this ancient couple lived in an old log cabin on the left-hand side of the road running from the old Queen's road, northwest from near Jacob Hewes' residence, below Leiperville, then called Ridley, to 'Crosby's mill' They died at an extreme old age"[1]

After the war of 1812, when the system of servile labor, which previous to that struggle had grown into almost general disfavor in the Southern States, was found to be a source of enormous wealth in raising cotton, the acreage devoted to the cultivation of that staple increased rapidly, so that slaves more than doubled in price, while the demand exceeded largely the supply To meet this want arose a class of desperate, lawless men who made the kidnapping of free negroes in the Northern States and spiriting them away to the sunny South a regular trade, having designated stations, hiding-places, and accomplices in the nefarious business Although Delaware County was on the border, very few attempts, so far as I have learned, were made to kidnap negroes within our territory The first case I find occurred on Sunday, Jan 7, 1835 John Paschall, a farmer, residing on the highway leading from the West Chester road to Darby, in the evening of that day was foddering his cattle in the barn, assisted by a black boy about twelve years old When Paschall returned to the house he missed the lad, and diligent search was immediately made for the boy, which was continued during the greater part of the night without success Shortly before noon the day following the boy returned, and related that two men, one of them a negro, had seized and tied him in the barn, after which they put him in a wagon and carried him to a house in Chester, where his captors and the people in the house drank until they became grossly intoxicated While they were in that condition the lad managed to get a knife from his pocket, and with his teeth opened it. Then cutting the cords which bound his hands and feet, he escaped from the window, fled to the woods, where he remained all night, and made his way to his master's house the next day

On Sunday, Aug 12, 1844, the quiet of Chester was broken by a hue and cry in pursuit of four colored men who had, it was said, murdered George Sharp, of Wilmington, Del, at the "Practical Farmer," about seven miles distant. A number of horsemen and footmen joined in the chase Within a mile of Darby three of the fugitives were overtaken, and brought to the jail at Chester The truth appeared the next day No murder was committed, but in attempting to arrest one of the colored men as a fugitive slave a struggle took place, and the man broke from the grasp of Sharp, who fell to earth The latter had died of heart-disease The three men were, however, held in custody, but on Wednesday, the 28th, when the owner of the slave came to claim him, it was found that they all had escaped The incarcerated men had taken the pump-handle and spear, and had tied them together, and with their blankets had made a rope, with which they scaled the prison-yard walls, and decamped They were never recaptured

In August, 1852, a colored camp-meeting was held at Cartertown, where it was noticed that a negro from Delaware, in company with two worthless white men, had been acting in such a way as to excite suspicion that his intention was to kidnap some of the colored persons present A committee was appointed to watch his movements, and, being convinced that his purpose was as mentioned, he was taken into the woods, where he was strapped to a tree and "beaten with many stripes" When released he fled hastily away, never to show himself again in the neighborhood

On the evening of the 25th of January, 1853, Richard Neal, a colored man in shackles, was brought in a carriage to Chester, and the intelligence that he was so detained spread, creating unusual excitement in the ancient borough It soon became known that the man was charged by one Capt Mayo, of Anne Arundle County, Md, with having excited his wife and children, slaves of Capt Mayo, to run away Neal was a freeman, but had been arrested on a requisition from the Governor of Maryland, and Capt. Mayo proposed to take the prisoner to that State in the midnight train While awaiting the cars here a *habeas corpus* was served on the officers, which the Marylanders at first were disposed to resist, drawing their pistols and swearing they would not recognize the writ Townsend Sharpless, conspicuous by his height and a light-colored overcoat he wore, coolly held the writ, and defied the angry men to disobey the order of the court Neal was finally placed in the lock-up, where he remained all night The following morning several hundred persons, residents of Chester and the neighborhood, assembled at the depot, determined that the law should be carried out When the south-bound train stopped, an officer got off and read a warrant commanding the appearance of Col Mayo and his party in Philadelphia to answer the writ The whistle sounded, and the train at length started on its way to Baltimore, amid the shouts of the populace The officers then removed the shackles from the prisoner, and he was taken to Philadelphia It was subsequently learned that Neal had formerly been a slave, had been manumitted, and had married a slave of Col Mayo He afterwards came to Philadelphia, where he was employed by

[1] History of Chester, p 213

Townsend Sharpless as a coachman. During the interval he strove to raise money to purchase the freedom of his family, but his wife, before he had succeeded in gathering the sum required, ran away, got to Baltimore, where she was captured and sold to a planter—

"Way down South, in the land of cotton."

The story of the unfortunate negro became known, several parties were warmly interested in his behalf, and three thousand dollars was raised, his family purchased, and brought to Philadelphia, where they were living when he was arrested. As soon as the true facts were made known to Governor Bigler, he recalled his approval of the requisition.

CHAPTER XXII

AGRICULTURE, WITH A BRIEF MENTION OF OUR DOMESTIC ANIMALS

GABRIEL THOMAS, the first historian of our State, in his quaint volume published in 1698, in describing the productions, says, "Their sorts of grain are wheat, rye, peas, barley, buckwheat, rice, Indian corn, and beans, with great quantities of hemp and flax, as also several sorts of eating roots, such as turnips, potatoes,[1] carrots, parsnips, etc., all of which are produced yearly in greater quanties than in England, those roots being much larger and altogether as sweet, if not more delicious. Cucumbers, coshaws, artichokes, with many others, most sorts of saladings, besides what grows naturally wild in the country, and that in great plenty, also as mustard, rue, sage, mint, tansy, worm-wood, penny-royal, and most of the herbs and roots found in the gardens of England."

The corn (wheat) harvest, the same author tells us, was ended before the middle of July, and in most years the yield was twenty and thirty bushels of wheat for every one sown. While another writer, in 1684, records that "the corn of this province, which the Indians use, increases four hundred for one. It is good for the health, put in milk or to make bread." Gabriel Thomas states that there were several farmers, who at that time (prior to 1698) sowed yearly between seventy and eighty acres of wheat each, besides barley, oats, rye, peas, beans, and other crops, and that it was common to have two harvests in the year,—"the first of English wheat and the second of buck or French wheat."

The labor of the men on the farm in early times was much more arduous than at the beginning of this century, and absolutely appalling when contrasted with that of the present day. Thomas Cheyney, of Thornbury, in July, 1796,[2] in describing the laborious manner of life at that time states that "every one that is able to do anything are as busy as nailers. I know many men that are worth thousands of pounds that will mow, make hay, reap, and draw hay and grain into their barnes as steady as hirelings, and those that are able, if they do not work, are looked upon with kind of contempt. Here in the country they are slighted and are not company for anybody."

The plow which was in use during the colonial period resembled in almost every respect those represented in the sculpture on the ruined temples of ancient Egypt, and like those, in most cases, were drawn by oxen. The entire implement was of wood, the mould-board a heavy block of the same material, which was sometimes covered with pieces of iron or the skin of a gar-fish to assist it in shedding the earth. As a whole it was clumsy and defective, hence it is not to be wondered that many of the farms in Delaware County, about the middle of the last century, after the same crop from the same land had been raised for years without rotation, and without manure, were deemed so poor and exhausted that their owners sold them to any one who would buy, almost at any price, so that they might emigrate to Lancaster County and "the back woods," where the unbroken mould was so rich that "it tickled with a hoe it yielded an abundant harvest." One of the plows in common use towards the end of the last century is now owned in West Chester, Pa. The wooden mould-board, nearly three feet in length, shod with iron, is very heavy, but shallow, the beam is so low that in use it frequently became choked with grass, stubble, or manure, hence a boy had often to walk by its side all day long and clear it of the rubbish thus gathered.[3] The English historians claim, and perhaps justly, that James Small, of Berwickshire, Scotland, in 1785, was the first to introduce the plow with a cast-iron mould-board and a wrought-iron share. That he so introduced these improvements may be true, but Townsend Ward and John F. Watson both state that previous to the date given "William Ashmead, of Germantown, made for himself a plow with a wrought-iron mould instead of the customary board. This great improvement was much admired by Gen. Lafayette, who purchased four of these plows for his estate,—La Grange. The improve-

[1] Watson records that potatoes "were very slow of reception among us. It was first introduced from Ireland in 1719 by a colony of Presbyterians settled at Londonderry, in New Hampshire." (Annals of Philadelphia, vol. ii. p. 420.) The quotation from Thomas' "History of Pennsylvania," published in London, twenty-one years before the date, according to Watson, when potatoes were first introduced into the English American colonies, shows that the latter assertion is not correct. The latter statement of Watson (same volume, page 486–87), that potatoes during his mother's childhood were little esteemed as food, may be literally true, as also the record he made of the remark of Col. A. J. Morris, that in the early days that vegetable was called Spanish potatoes, "and were very sharp and pungent to the throat and smell." He (Col. Morris) said Tench Francis first imported our improved stock, which by frequent cultivation he much improved.

[2] Futhey and Cope's "History of Chester County," p. 337.

[3] Ib., p. 339.

ment was soon adopted by another person, who made the mould-board of cast iron."[1] It was fortunate for Ashmead that he did not attempt to introduce his plow into general use, for many years afterwards Charles Newbold, of New Jersey, in the effort to have the agriculturists adopt a cast-iron plow he claimed to have invented, expended thirty thousand dollars in the attempt, and was at length compelled to abandon it, because the farmers were of the opinion that the cast iron poisoned the ground.

The harrow was early introduced, since Gabriel Thomas, in 1698, refers to that implement. "Their ground," he states, "is harrowed with wooden tyned harrows, twice over in a place is sufficient." And in colonial days, as was practiced until about the beginning of this century, the harvests were reaped by the sickle, all hands—men, women, and children—laboring in the fields from sunrise to sunset, with a short interval at noon for rest. The wages then, as contrasted with those at present paid for such work, were very low, but a pint flask of whiskey was always given each hand in the morning. It was severe toil, the position in reaping requiring the bending over of the body, the right arm swinging the sickle, and the left gathering the bunches of grain, which were thrown into heaps and bound into sheaves. The custom previous to the Revolutionary war was for the reaper to take two corn rows, cutting through always in one direction, and then, with his sickle on his shoulder, binding the sheaves as he came back. Twenty-five or thirty dozen was an ordinary day's work, but sometimes a rapid hand would reach forty dozen.

It is not surprising that redemption servants, many of whom had been reared in the cities of the old world, frequently ran away from their masters before the period of their indenture had expired, to avoid the incessant labor which farming then entailed upon them. Scythes were, of course, in use in our earliest annals, but it was not until the beginning of the present century that the cradle, with its many fingers, began to take the place of the sickle and the reaping-hook, and although there were men who predicted that it would never be brought into general use, as was the case in more recent times with the reaping-machine, it soon won its way to popular favor. Every man of middle age can recall, when the harvest was ready for reaping, how all the able-bodied men on the farm, together with several additional hands hired for the occasion, would take their stations, the man at the extreme right starting ahead of the one to his left, and the latter following in order until, with a swinging motion, all at the same time would cut a swath from five to six feet in width from one side of the field to the other, while frequent pauses would be made to sharpen the scythe, the stone for the purpose being carried in a leather girdle around the waist of the reaper. The sound made by the stone on the steel blade would be heard at considerable distance.

In early times, when the bundles were ready to be taken to the barn or stack they were loaded on sleds, and in that manner transported thither. Bishop[2] informs us that in 1750 only the best farmers had carts on their farms, while the most of them used sleds both in summer and winter, a statement corroborated by William Worrall, of Ridley, who, speaking of the older manners about the middle of the last century, says "there were no carts, much less pleasure carriages. They hauled their grain on sleds to the stacks, where a temporary threshing floor was erected." On these floors the grain was thrashed out by horses, which were driven in a circle, and after the heads were deemed to have been well cleared of the seed the straw was thrown to one side with forks and the grain swept up, ready for another lot of bundles to be unbound and submitted to a like process. In the barns, however, the thrashing was usually done with the flail, and on a still day the sound of the heavy thump of the oaken breaker on the floor, which acted like a drum, could be heard a long way off. In 1770, John Clayton, doubtless of this county, who had invented a machine for thrashing wheat, received from the colonial government the exclusive privilege of making and selling this machine within this province.[3] This was sixteen years before the thrasher invented for the same purpose by Andrew Meikler, of Scotland, and the one still used in England, was patented. We have no description of Clayton's invention nor of the manner in which it was received by the farmers, who at that time were loath to take hold of new ideas, believing that agriculture was so thoroughly understood that nothing, let it promise never so much in saving of time or labor, was worth investigation.

I have been unable to ascertain when the fan was first used to winnow cereals, but in the early days, in all probability, the grain was held in the hand, which was shaken as the contents were permitted to fall through the fingers, so that the breeze might blow the chaff away from the heavy seeds, which fell directly to the ground, in the same manner that many of the aborigines now employ to separate the grain from the chaff. It is known that previous to the Revolution fans were in use in Chester County, although the work was not performed as thoroughly as is now done by the modern machines.

In the old colonial days the woodland was brought into condition for tillage by girdling the trees, and two men could thus destroy the forest on twenty or thirty acres in one year. There was little underbrush, owing to the custom among the Indians, annually in the fall, of setting fire to the grass and leaves in the woods, so that "a cart or wain," we are told by Gabriel Thomas,

[1] "Germantown Road and its Associations," *Penna. Mag. of Hist.*, vol. vi. p. 139; Watson's Annals of Philadelphia, vol. ii. p. 66.

[2] Bishop's "History of American Manufactures."

[3] Colonial Records, vol. ix. p. 698.

"may go through the middle of the woods between the trees without getting any damage." The rich soil, exposed to the sun through the leafless branches of the dead trees, was prolific, and, as we learn from a writer in 1684, if an emigrant arrived in Pennsylvania in September, two men could easily prepare that fall land for corn sufficient to return "in the following harvest twenty quarters, which are a hundred and sixty bushels English measure, and this should not cause astonishment when it is considered that a bushel of wheat sown produces forty bushels at harvest." Wheat, until after the Revolution, was seeded between the rows of corn at its last plowing in August, and the seed was chopped in around the hills with a hoe. During the war of independence the Hessian fly, which is said to have been brought to this country in the provender transported hither for the use of the mercenary soldiers, multiplied so rapidly that they destroyed the early sown wheat, and this circumstance changed the season of planting. Rye was grown largely, for it not only made a favorite whiskey and sold readily, but it supplied almost all the coffee used in the rural districts, and until manufactured goods did away with home spinning every farmer had a patch of flax sown on his place. Many old persons can remember how pretty the sight was when the blue blossom was on the flax and "the bloom was on the rye." The apple- and peach-orchards in early days were always planted near the house, from the fruit of which the family distilled cider, apple-jack, and peach brandy, as well as kept barrels of the former fruit, while large quantities of apples and peaches were always dried for winter use.

When Governor Printz first came to this country, it is reported that the grass even in the woods grew to the height of two feet, but as that statement was made by an aged Swede, whose father came over with the Swedish Governor, to Professor Kalm, in 1748, it may be accepted with some grains of allowance. It has also been claimed that Col. Thomas Leiper, one of the most public-spirited men the State has ever had, introduced clover to the colony, a statement that will not bear investigation, for in 1709, Jonathan Dickinson, in a letter, speaks of buying red clover-seed, remarking that "the white clover already tinges the woods as a natural production."[1] The old system of husbanding, in vogue until threatened starvation compelled the farmers to change the ruinous plan, is set forth in a letter from Squire Thomas Cheyney, of Thornbury, written in 1796 to relatives in England.[2] He says,—

"Our land is mostly good, but we have dropt our old method of farming. We used to break up our fields in May, cross or stir them in August, and sow them with wheat and rye in September. This was done once in three or four years in rotation: in the intermediate spaces between them were pastured. The land would produce from twelve to twenty bushels per acre. This way was followed until the land run out, as we call it. We planted corn, sowed barley, oats, and flax, likewise buckwheat, in small portions of land allotted for that purpose, which took the greatest part of our dung to manure it; our meadows got some, and we had very little left for our Winter grain. We followed this old way until we could scarcely raise our bread and seed."

Dr. Smith records that as early as 1734 silk was made in the colony, the insects being fed on the native mulberry leaves. In 1770 an effort was made to arouse general interest in the culture, and to that end premiums were given to the person sending the greatest weight of cocoons to "a public filature established in Philadelphia." In 1771 Chester County sent three hundred and thirty-five pounds, the following being the names of the contributors:

	Pounds.	Ounces.
Grace Beale	4	11
Mary Parker (Chester)	10	0
Mary Pearson (Darby)	51	11
Abigail Davis (Chester)	3	3
Sarah Fordham (Darby)	6	0
Ann Cochran (Darby)	25	12
Rachel Hayes (Darby)	13	12
James Millhouse	52	0
Ann Davis	2	15
Elizabeth Bonsall	7	0
Mary Davis	2	4
Sarah Dicks	47	10
Catharine Evans	14	44
Mary Jones	19	12
Jane Davis (Chester)	28	12
Jacob Worrall	2	0
Margaret Riley	11	10
John Hoopes (Chester)	23	10
Henry Thomas (Chester)	8	6
	335	0

Mary Newlin, of Concord, died in 1790, in her one hundred and second year. She was born in Thornbury in 1688, and it is stated that she "remembered when her father and others deaded the timber and burned the leaves, and hoed in their wheat by hand, their being few horses and scarce a plow in the settlement."[3]

Goats we know were early sent to the Delaware River settlement, and we have reason to believe that other domestic animals were transported to New Sweden with the colonists. Horses are spoken of long before the coming of Penn. In 1679 the journal of Sluyter and Danckers mentions them as used for riding, and many other references to these animals occur in our early annals. Penn, when he came in 1682, brought with him "three blooded mares, a fine white horse, not full blooded, and other inferior animals, not for breeding, but for labor," while in 1699, when he returned the second time, intending to remain in the province, he brought with him Tamerlane, a colt by Godolphi Barb, to whom the best horses in England trace their pedigree. But previous to Penn's last coming we have the statement of Gabriel Thomas, that the "horses in Pennsylvania

[1] Watson's Annals, vol. ii. p. 485.

[2] Futhey and Cope's "History of Chester County," p. 339.

[3] Ib.

are very hardy, insomuch that being very hot with riding or otherwise, they are turned out into the woods at the same instant and yet receive no harm" Robert Rodney, in a letter written in 1690,[1] in speaking of the trade of the colony and the articles shipped to the West Indies, mentions horses, "of which we have very good," and also states that "a good breeding mare" is sold for five pounds, in the currency of the province In 1683 the Assembly had forbidden the exportation of horses or mares without permission, under a fine of ten pounds Under the Duke's law (1676) the owner of horses which were running at large, as was then the custom, was compelled to have a private brand or mark, and the town(ship) was required to have its brand to be burned on the horses owned by persons living within its boundary, while an officer was designated to register the age, color, and natural and artificial marks of the animal A person buying or selling an unmarked horse was subject to a fine of ten pounds In 1683 horses in the woods had so multiplied that an act was passed providing that no stallion under thirteen and a half hands should run at large, under a penalty of five pounds, and by act of May 10, 1699, the height was made thirteen hands, and a horse under that size could be taken up and impounded by any freeholder or ranger While by the act of May 9, 1724, no stallion, unless thirteen hands high from the ground to the withers, reckoning four inches standard measure to one hand, and of a comely proportion, "was permitted to run at large in the woods" During all our colonial history an officer, termed ranger, was appointed by the court to enforce the laws respecting domestic animals, and to impound those found roaming at large unmarked The office continued until the beginning of this century, for at the January Court of Quarter Sessions, 1804, Joseph Neide, of the borough and township of Chester, was appointed ranger for the county of Delaware In a letter written by Robert Park, from Chester township, Tenth month, 1725, to Mary Valentine, in Ireland, he desired that a saddle and bridle may be brought to him by his sister, who was about emigrating, and states, "Lett the tree be well Plated & Indifferent Narrow, for the horses here are Large as in Ireland, but the best racers and finest pacers in the World" Horses were not shod until about the middle of the last century

Rev Israel Acrelius, in 1758, mentioned the fleet horses owned by the descendants of the Swedish settlers on the Delaware The horses were then broken to pace, that being the favorite gait It was a pacer which bore Squire Cheyney to Gen Washington on the morning of Sept 11, 1777, with the intelligence that the bulk of the British army had crossed the Brandywine at the upper ford, and it was a pacer which Jefferson made fast to the railing of the capitol at Washington while he went in and took the oath as President of the United States In June, 1879, the residents of Chester and vicinity had an opportunity of seeing the pair of dappled-gray Arabian stallions which were presented to Gen Grant by the Sultan of Turkey By the personal request of Gen Beale the animals were sent to this city, and the horses, whose pedigree could be traced more than a thousand years, were viewed while here by a large number of people

In early days, and in fact until the first decade of this century, cattle, as before stated, ran wild in the woods Capt Heinricks, of the British army, in 1778, stated that "perhaps the reason why the domestic animals are not half so good as ours is because they are left out winter and summer in the open air" Gabriel Thomas informs us in the infancy of the province some farmers had "forty, some sixty, and from that number to one or three hundred head of cattle, their oxen usually weigh two hundred pounds a quarter They are commonly fatter of flesh and yield more tallow (by feeding only on grass) than the cattle in England"

William Worrall stated that before the Revolution the natural meadows and woods were the only pasture for the cattle of Delaware County, "and the butchers from Philadelphia could come out and buy one, two, or three head of cattle from such of the graziers as could spare them, for the supply of the market" To distinguish the cattle of one owner from those belonging to others, the early laws required every person to brand his cattle with his individual mark Under the Duke of York all horned cattle were to be branded on their horns After Penn acquired possession of the province the act of 1683 compelled owners to brand their cattle when six months old In 1685 the time was extended to one year, and in 1690 the age of the stock when it must be branded, or deemed strays, was extended to eighteen months These brands and marks were regularly entered on record on the docket of the Quarter Sessions At a court held at Chester, Fifth month 1, 1684, we find "George Maris's cattle mark A slit on the tip of the near ear, his brand mark G M" On Sixth month 5, 1684, the record sets forth, "The ear mark of John Blunstone, of Darby, a crop in the near ear and a hole in the farr ear, his brand mark I B" On 3d day of 1st week, Fourth month, 1686, "John Hannum's ear mark, a crop under slit of both ears, his brand I H on the near buttock" While at court 3d day of 1st week, Seventh month, 1686, the record is made of "John Harding's ear mark, a crop on the inside of ye far ear, his brand mark I H on the farr buttock" That the cattle did not increase as rapidly as was desired at an early period we inferentially learn from the act of First month, 1683, which interdicted the killing of a cow, calf, or ewe lamb for three years under a fine of five pounds, one half of which was to go to the informer.

In 1876 the *Delaware County American* published the recollections of William Sheldon, of Upper Provi-

[1] *Penna Mag of Hist.*, vol vi p 312

dence, respecting the price at which cows sold for forty years preceding that date From it we learn that previous to and including 1835 good cows could be bought from $18 to $24, in 1836 for $20, in 1837 and 1838 for $23 In 1839 and 1840 the price advanced to $39, while the following year (1841) they fell to $19, and continued at those figures for 1841 and 1842 In 1845 the price was $23, in 1846, $25, and fluctuated between $22 and $25 during the next two years In 1849-53 the average price was $26 In 1854 the price advanced two dollars, and in 1855 and 1856 it had advanced to $30 In 1857, $34, but in 1858 and 1859 it fell to $28 In 1861-62 the price was $35, and during the next three years $65 was the average, and since then the market has been high

Sheep were early introduced, and we learn from Gabriel Thomas, that previous to 1698 of these useful animals there were "considerable numbers, which are generally free from these infectious diseases which are incident to these creatures in England, as the rot, scab, or maggots They commonly bring forth two lambs at once, some twice in one year, and the wool is very fine and thick and is also very white" Capt. Heinricks in 1778 records that "there are plenty of sheep, but as the farmer drives them into the woods he loses the wool, however, he sells the skin for 8s York money."

In the early times hogs were a very important part of the stock of the planters, for in most cases salted swine-flesh comprised the daily animal food consumed during the winter months Hence it is not surprising that attention was early had to laws protecting the owner in his property, particularly when the hogs were turned out in the woods to shift for themselves They must have found abundant food, for we learn that hogs about a year old when killed weighed about two hundred pounds and the flesh was remarkably sweet, which, it was believed, was the result of the animals feeding on fruit which then abounded in a wild state

Capt Heinricks, a German officer, who saw almost nothing to praise in Pennsylvania, at least had a good word to say for the swine "Hogs," he writes, "are quite as good here as the best in Holstein, for there is a good mast for them in the woods, and they feed there the whole year" Under the Duke of York's laws, hogs were required to be branded, and the "theft of swine or other cattle" was punished for the first offense with a fine and the cropping of one ear Under Penn, by the act of March 10, 1683, the party convicted of this offense was compelled to pay threefold the value of the hog stolen, for a second offense a like punishment and six months' imprisonment, and for the third conviction a fine of twenty-nine lashes and banishment, never to return to the colony, under such penalty as the County Court saw proper to impose in its discretion. At the December court, 1687, the grand jury presented Ann Neales, widow, of Ridley, for keeping a dog which worried and killed her neighbors' hogs, and also harboring an Indian boy named Ohato, who was detected in urging the dog to kill the hog. The widow declared that the dog belonged to Peter Cox, but when the case was called she submitted to the court and "Putts herself upon ye mercy of ye King and Governor," whereupon she was fined ten shillings and costs The Indian boy was held in twenty pounds to be of good behavior, and Andrew Friend became his surety

When the meadow-land in Chester borough began to be improved, swine running at large was found to be very objectionable, especially to those who were "Improving the Marshes and Ditches and Drains," and to remedy the evil the Assembly in 1699 forbade unringed and unyoked hogs and goats from being at large in that town, and all such animals so taken up were forfeited to the county of Chester, while all damage done by hogs or goats owned by parties living outside the boundaries prescribed were to be made good to the party injured by the owner of the animal The act designated the limits of Chester,—to be southward by the Delaware River, westward by Chester Creek, northward by the King's road, and eastward by Ridley Creek The act of 1705 declared that no swine without rings or yokes should be permitted to run at large within fourteen miles of the navigable parts of the Delaware River, and that in the towns of Philadelphia, Chester, or Bristol they should not be allowed to run at large "whether yoked or ringed or not" The fine imposed was to be equally divided between the government and the informer

The ordinary domestic fowls seem to have been abundant in the province in the early time Gabriel Thomas tells us that "chickens, hens, geese, ducks, turkeys, &c, are large and very plentiful all over the country," and eighty years after this statement was made Capt Heinricks records, "There are plenty of Guinea fowls, but not so many as in the Jerseys and Long Island Turkeys belong to the wild animals, and are in the woods in flocks like partridges Ducks and geese are common and as good as ours, but no better"

CHAPTER XXIII

WILD ANIMALS, FISH, ETC, OF DELAWARE COUNTY

WHEN the first European settlers located in Delaware County the territory abounded with wild game, and for more than a hundred years thereafter large animals in a state of nature were common Gabriel Thomas informs us in his "History of Pennsylvania," that when he lived in the province, previous to 1698, "there are in the woods abundance of red deer—vulgarly called stags—for I have bought of the Indians a whole buck—both skin and carcass—for two gills of gunpowder Excellent food—most delicious, far exceeding that in Europe, in the opinion of most that are nice and curious people," while Mahlon Stacey, writing to a friend in England, says, "We have brought home to our houses by the Indians seven or eight fat bucks in a day, and sometimes put by as many, having no occasion for them"[1]

Deer seem to have been abundant until after the middle of the last century in the more remote townships, for in 1824, William Mode, then living on the west branch of the Brandywine, East Fallowfield township, Chester County, in his eighty-second year, related that as a boy he remembered when deer were so plentiful that their tracks in the wheat-fields in time of snow were as if a flock of sheep had been driven over them, and on one occasion his father returned home, having the carcasses of two, which he had shot, on his sled Samuel Jefferis who died at West Chester, Feb 28, 1823, aged eighty-seven, stated that deer were common in his neighborhood in his early manhood, while Watson records that in 1730 a woman in Chester County (then including Delaware County) "going to mill spied a deer fast asleep near the road She hit it on the head with a stone and killed it"

Black bears were frequently slain in the early days, and they generally met their fate because of their partiality for swine-flesh The animal in search of this dainty morsel would approach near the settlement, and when he had selected a hog to his taste, he would spring suddenly upon his victim, grasp it in his fore legs, and, erecting himself on his hind ones, would walk away with the porker squeaking at his unhappy situation The cry of the hog usually brought the owner to the rescue of his property; but if he failed in overtaking the bear, he would in all probability capture the animal before many hours, for after eating sufficient to satisfy his appetite, he would return to devour the remainder of the carcass at his leisure The settlers knowing this weakness, would set a heavy smooth-jawed steel trap, attached to which was a long drag chain ending with iron claws The bear once caught in the trap, would drag the chain along the ground, and the claws catching upon the bushes would compel him to such exertion in freeing himself that he would become exhausted, and when overtaken, as his track would be readily followed, he fell a comparatively easy prey to the huntsman

In 1721 a bear was killed near Darby, and yet ten or fifteen years later, when Nathaniel Newlin, of Concord, married Esther Midkiff, of Darby, her parents objected to the marriage, not because they had any disinclination to the suitor, but for the fact that he lived in the backwoods of Concord, and there were bears there, while of Mary Palmer, wife of John Palmer, of Concord, one of the first settlers of that township, it is recorded that she drove a bear away from a chestnut-tree with a fire-poker or poking-stick[2]

[1] Proud's "History of Pennsylvania," vol i p 152

[2] Genealogical Record of Palmer and Trimble Families, by Lewis Palmer, p 27

But bears sometimes came closer to the settlement than "the backwoods of Concord" In the winter of 1740–41, so memorable for its extreme cold weather, it is related by Mrs Deborah Logan that one night an old man, servant of Joseph Parker (then owning and living in the old Logan house, still standing on the north side of Second Street, above Edgmont Avenue, Chester), rose from his bed, and, as he was a constant smoker, he descended to the kitchen to light his pipe The watch-dog was growling fiercely, and he went to the window to ascertain the cause. The moon was up, but partly obscured by clouds, and by that light the old man saw an animal which he took for "a big black calf" in the yard He thereupon drove the creature out of the inclosure, when it turned, looked at him, and he then saw it was a black bear The beast, it is supposed, had been in some way aroused from its winter torpor and had sought shelter from the cold, which may account for its apparent docility The next morning it was killed in the woods about a half-mile distant from the house William Worrall stated that when a lad in Marple a large bear made an inroad into the neighborhood and escaped with impunity, although great exertions were made to secure it

The early settlers were much annoyed by the wolves, who preyed on their flocks and herds In the Duke of York's laws, promulgated on the Delaware, Sept 22, 1676, it was provided that if any person, "Christian or Indian," brought the head of a wolf to the constable he was to be paid, "out of the publicque charge, to the value of an Indian coat," and the constable was required to nail the head over the door of his house, previous to which he must cut off both the ears, "in token that the head is bought and paid for" In 1672 the amount paid for wolves' heads was found to be burdensome, and it was ordered that the sum of twenty-five shillings per head should be reduced to twenty shillings, and the several towns were obliged to maintain wolf-pits This was the law respecting the killing of wolves in force in the province from the date of the promulgation of the Duke's "Book of Laws," until the coming of Penn in the latter part of the year 1682 The eighty-sixth law, enacted by the first Assembly at Chester, provided that if any person, excepting an Indian should slay a he wolf he should receive ten shillings, and for a she wolf fifteen shillings, out of the public fund The wolf's head must be brought to a justice, who should cause the ears and tongue to be cut out If an Indian killed a wolf he was paid five shillings "and the skin for his pains," which latter clause was stricken out of the law May 10, 1690, by the Assembly which met at New Castle, and Indians were placed on a like footing with the whites, receiving the same reward

The law was more easily enacted than the money could be raised to pay the wolf-head bounty. The court previous to 1700 seemed constantly compelled to take action looking to the collection of taxes sufficient to discharge these pressing demands At the court held at Chester, the 3d day of 1st week, Tenth month, 1687, it was "Ordered that Warrants be Directed to ye respective Constables of each Township in this county for raising of a levy to be used towards ye destroying Wolves and other Hurtful Vermin, as follows, viz For all lands taken up and inhabited one shilling for every hundred acres, for all Lands taken up by non-residents and so remaining unoccupied eighteen pence for every hundred acres, All freemen from sixteen years of age to sixty, one shilling, All servants, soe qualified, six pence" This order did not secure the sum necessary to keep the county and the wolf-hunters square in their accounts, so that on the 6th day of 1st week, Tenth month, 1688, "The Grand Inquest doe alsoe allow of ye Tax for ye wolves' heads and that Power be forthwith Issued forth to Compel those to pay that are behind in their arrears, And that receipts and disbursements thereof be made to ye grand Inquest at ye next County Court" But this action of the grand jury did not result as desired, so that Oct 2, 1695, the grand inquest reported that the county was in debt, not only on account of the prison, which was not completed, but that "there were several wolves' heads to pay for," and they therefore levied a tax of one pence per pound on personal and real estate and three pence poll-tax The jury also gave the rule by which the valuation should be made thus "All cleared land under tillage to be assessed at 20 shillings per acre, rough lands near river £10 per hundred acres, land in woods" (that is, uncultivated land on which no settlement had been made), "£5 per hundred acres, horses and mares at £3, cows and oxen at 50 shillings, sheep 6s, negro male slaves from sixteen to sixty years of age at £25, and females at £20 Chester Mills (at Upland) £100; Joseph Cochran's mill (where Dutton's now is), £50, Darby Mill, £100, Haverford Mills (on Cobb's Creek), £20, Concord Mills (now Leedom's), £50," and all tavern-keepers were assessed at twenty pounds This is the last mention I find of wolves as forming the subject of a grand jury's action in our county annals, but many bills are on file in the commissioner's office, in West Chester, for the wolf bounty

In 1705 the constantly-increasing flocks of sheep caused the wolves to venture nearer the settlement to prey on those domestic animals; hence, in 1705, the law was changed, so that if any person would undertake as an occupation to kill wolves, devoting three days at least in each week to that pursuit, and entering into recognizance at the County Courts to that effect, such person was entitled to receive twenty-five shillings for every head he brought in This was not extravagant when we remember that at Germantown as late as 1724 wolves were reported as often heard howling at nights, while in 1707 they approached so closely to the settled parts of Philadelphia as to render the raising of sheep a precarious business.

By the act of March 20 1724/5, the Assembly provides the following rewards for killing wolves and red foxes For every grown dog or bitch wolf, 15s, for every wolf puppy or whelp, 7s 6d, for every old red fox, 2s, and for every young red fox or whelp, 1s I do not know whether the reward for killing foxes was ever repealed, for the accounts in the commissioner's office at Media show that on Second month 12, 1791, James Jones was paid 13s 6d for fox scalps These animals were very numerous in the last century, for William Mode, heretofore mentioned, stated that in his early days foxes carried off their poultry, and "on one occasion a man threshing espied one in the evening coming towards the barn, lay in ambush with a club, with which he knocked it over and killed it"[1] The smaller animals, such as squirrels, raccoons, and "that strange animal the 'possum,'" as Gabriel Thomas calls them, "she having a false belly to swallow her young ones, by which means she preserves them from danger when anything comes to disturb them," were numerous In the year 1749, we are told by Kalm, six hundred and forty thousand black and gray squirrels were shot, the bounty paid in the several counties that year amounting to eight thousand pounds at three pence a head The drain was so great on the county treasuries that the premium was reduced one-half Great numbers of pheasants and partridges were found in all sections of the county, while wild turkeys in winter were often seen in flocks in the corn and buckwheat-fields feeding, and Mr Worrall could well remember when there were great quantities of wild turkeys The latter related that he once saw a flight of pigeons which lasted two days "They flew in such immense flocks as to obscure for a considerable time the rays of the sun. Thomas Coburn, Caleb Harrison, and Peter Heston went out at night in Martin's Bottom, and they told him (Worrall) that when they were in the woods where the pigeons roosted the noise was so great that they could not hear each other speak On viewing the place the next morning, they found large limbs of the trees broken off from the immense weight and pressure of the lodgers" About the time of Penn's coming the wild pigeons flew in such masses "that the air was sometimes darkened," and, flying low, great numbers were knocked down with sticks by those persons who had no firearms The birds not immediately used were salted down for future consumption

The act of 1700, offering a reward for killing blackbirds and crows, states in its preamble that "by the innumerable quantities of blackbirds and crows that continually haunt in this province and territories, to the great prejudice, hurt, and annoyance of the inhabitants thereof, being very destructive to all sorts of corn and grain that is raised therein, so that people's labor is much destroyed thereby," a reward of three

[1] Statement of William Mode in 1824, *Village Record*, West Chester, Pa

pence per dozen for blackbirds and three pence for every crow killed was offered out of the public fund, the party killing the birds being required to produce their heads before the proper officer in each county, and by the act of March 20, 1724/5, the person claiming the reward for killing crows was required to bring not less than six at one time to the nearest justice, who should "see their bill cut off," after which the magistrate was authorized to give an order for the reward on the county treasurer.

In 1748, Peter Kalm, the Swedish naturalist, records that the old residents stated that the number of birds was then diminishing; that in the days of the early settlers the water was covered by all kinds of water-fowl, and that about 1688 it was no unusual thing for a single person to kill seventy or eighty ducks of a morning, while an old Swede, then ninety years old, told Kalm that he had killed thirty-three ducks at one shot. Capt. Heinricks, of the Hessian troops, however, who could see nothing agreeable in our country, says that "like the products of the earth, animals too are only half developed. A hare, a partridge, a peacock, etc., is only half grown. Wild game tastes like ordinary meat."

In early times swans were said to abound on the Delaware, but it is a circumstance to which William Whitehead, in his interesting sketch of Chester, directed general attention, that at that time "we do not hear of the more modern rail- and reed-birds, which now afford profit and pleasure to the sportsman in the fall season." It has always been a question among ornithologists as to the locality where the rail-bird breeds, but in 1876 James Pierce picked up an unfledged rail-bird on Chester Island whose feathers were not sufficiently grown to enable it to fly, which incident furnished strong evidence that the birds breed on the marshes and meadows along the Delaware, a proposition which had been stoutly maintained by some well-informed persons and as earnestly denied by others.

It is worthy of record that a gentleman in Chester in 1851 caught a white blue-bird, an albino, its plumage being of snowy whiteness.

Of our fishes, William Penn, in his "Further Account of the Province of Pennsylvania," published in 1685, refers to the fact that "mighty whales roll upon the coast near the mouth of the Bay of Delaware." A century and a quarter after he wrote this, in 1809, a clever-sized whale was caught in the Delaware, near Chester. Watson informs us that it "became a subject of good speculation," and was exhibited at Philadelphia and elsewhere. "Thomas Pryor, who purchased it, made money by it, and in reference to his gains was called 'Whale Pryor.' The jaws were so distended as to receive therein an arm-chair, in which the visitors sat." In April, 1833, near Chester, three seals were seen, and one of them was caught in a shad-seine, and kept on exhibition. Previous to this, on Jan. 21, 1824, a seal was shot in the Delaware, near Repaupo, by Jonas Steelman, a resident of New Jersey, and occasionally sharks of the man-eating species have been seen or caught in the river above Chester. On Aug. 4, 1851, William Haines, Henry Post, and George Ennis caught a shark in a seine while fishing for catfish near the Lazaretto. It measured nine feet in length and five feet across the fins. In August, 1876, Captain Smith, while fishing for herring, saw a shark in the river just above Chester.

William Penn, in the pamphlet mentioned, states that "sturgeons play continually in our rivers in summer," and it is said could be counted by dozens at a time, leaping into the air and endangering the boats, while of shad, which he tells us are called "allocs" in France, by the Jews "allice," and by "our ignorant shad,"[1] "are excellent fish, and of the bigness of our largest carp. They are so plentiful that Capt. Smyth's overseer at the Skulkil drew 600 and odd at one draught; 300 is no wonder, 100 familiarly. They are excellent Pickeled or smok'd as well as boyld fresh. They are caught by nets only." He also informs us that six shad or rock were sold for twelve pence, and salt fish at three farthings a pound. The rock-fish Penn stated were somewhat larger and rounder than the shad, while he mentioned a whiter fish, little inferior in relish to the English mullet, which were plentiful, and the herring, he tells us, "swarm in such shoals that it is hardly creditable. In little creeks they almost shovel them up in their tubs." There is among the lesser fry "the catfish or flathead, lamprey eale, trout, perch, black and white smelt, sunfish, etc." The eels in former time must have been monstrously large, for, as late as 1830, one measuring nearly six feet in length and of proportionate girth was reported as having been caught off the mouth of Chester Creek, which was a giant as compared with that captured by Capt. Peter Boon, in June, 1869, which was over three feet in length and weighed ten pounds.

Locusts were known in early days, and in 1749, Kalm alludes to them as returning every seventeen years, showing that even then the peculiar interval of time between their coming in great numbers had been noted. The first mentioned, however, of locusts, so far as I have seen, is recorded in Clay's "Swedish Annals," as follows:

"In May, 1715, a multitude of locusts came out of the ground everywhere, even on the solid roads. They were wholly covered with a shell, and it seemed very wonderful that they could with this penetrate the hard earth. Having come out of the earth, they crept out of the shells, flew away, sat down on the trees, and made a peculiar noise until evening. Being spread over the country in such numbers, the noise they made was so loud that the cow-bells could scarcely be heard in the woods. They pierced the bark on the branches of the trees, and deposited their eggs in the openings. Many apprehended that the trees

[1] It is stated that the timid nature of these fish gave it the name of shad. The early settlers noticed that the overhanging of trees on the river or streams frequented by this fish, casting a shade upon the water, frightened them, and hence from this peculiarity they were called shadow-fish, or the fish that is frightened at a shadow, and in time the first part of the word alone came to be used as the name of the fish.

would wither in consequence of this, but no symptoms of it was observed next year. Hogs and poultry fed on them. Even the Indians did eat them, especially when they first came, boiling them a little. This made it probable that they were of the same kind with those eaten by John the Baptist. They did not continue long, but died in the month of June."

In the early days flies were more abundant than in our times, and during the occupation of Philadelphia the flies were very annoying to the residents of that city. "You cannot conceive," wrote Capt. John Heinricks, in 1778, "of the superabundant swarms of flies."[1] If flies attracted attention, certain it is that the early settlers, as well as all subsequent European visitors, were much surprised and interested in our phosphorescent beetles, or, as more commonly called, fire-flies. Thomas Moore has used these insects with effect in one of his most admired ballads. The origin of our common bees has long been a mooted question, because the Indians always declared that they were unknown in this country until the advent of Europeans, and termed them "the white man's fly." "Bees," writes Gabriel Thomas, in 1698, "thrive and multiply exceedingly in these parts. The Swedes often get great stores of them in the woods, where they are free for anybody. Honey (and choice, too) is sold in the Capital City for five pence per pound. Wax is also plentiful, cheap, and considerable commerce." That nocturnal pest, the mosquito, was general in the early time, and, within the recollection of the writer, in the vicinity of Chester they were more numerous thirty years ago than at the present day. They were certainly abundant in the early days of Swedish sway on the Delaware, for we learn that shortly after Governor Printz built Fort Elsinborg, near the mouth of Salem Creek, Campanius records "At last within a few years it was demolished by the Swedes themselves, who could not live there on account of the great numbers of moschetoes. After they left it they used to call it *Myggenborg*,—that is to say, Moscheto Fort."

CHAPTER XXIV.

DELAWARE COUNTY CLIMATE, TOGETHER WITH NOTICES OF REMARKABLE WEATHER.

In 1633 it is recorded that De Vries was frozen up in Wyngaert's Kill from January 17th to February 3d, and that he did not return to Swansdale until the 20th of February. The Dutch colonists "did not imagine that we had been frozen up in the river, as no pilot or astrologer could conceive that in the latitude from the thirty-eighth and a half to the thirty-ninth such rapid running rivers could freeze." Governor Printz states in the early days of the colony, that the "winter is sometimes as sharp that I have never felt it more severe in the Northern parts of Sweden."[2]

The winter of 1657 is the first record of intensely cold weather we find in the annals of this colony, for the Delaware River was frozen in one night so that a deer could run over it, which, the Indians stated, had not occurred within the memory of their oldest living person, nor was there any tradition of it ever happening before that time. On Jan. 14, 1660, William Beekman wrote, "We are bravely blockaded by frost, but we are not affraid of it, as we are, on the contrary, well provisioned." And on the 25th of the same month he records, "Two days ago the ice broke up, so that we shall shortly have free water."[3] The winter of 1681 was also remarkable for its severity, for on the 11th of December the river was closed in one night so that all navigation was interrupted, while the succeeding winter, that of 1682, was very mild, scarcely any ice forming, to be followed the next year with intense cold. In that year William Penn, in a letter to Lord North, says, "The weather often changeth without notice, and is constant almost in its inconstancy!" while a writer in 1684 says,[4] "The air is generally clear and agreeable. The summer is longer and warmer, and the winter shorter and sometimes colder than in England." The latter statement was certainly true of the winter of 1697–98, when the river was frozen so solidly that wagon-loads of hay were repeatedly dragged across the Delaware at Christiana.

The summer of 1699 was extremely warm, and the winter of 1704 was so cold that snow fell over a yard in depth, the deepest on record, and birds, deer, and other animals perished, unable to find sustenance. The winter of 1700 was very mild, while in February, 1714, flowers were seen in the woods near Philadelphia. The summer of 1724 was known as "the hot summer," which certainly must have been true of 1730, when eight persons dropped dead in the streets of Philadelphia in one day; while the winter of that year was bitterly cold, and the summer of 1734 was so warm that many men in the harvest-fields died, and great numbers of birds were found dead, owing to the heat. In the winter of 1739–40, when the cold was so intense in Europe, snow fell to a depth of three feet; the tops of the fences were covered, and sleds passed over them in every direction on the hard crust. The Delaware was frozen over until the 15th of March.

The suffering among the exposed settlers in Lancaster County, then on the borders of civilization, was extreme, the *Pennsylvania Gazette* recording that they were compelled to subsist on the deer which had died, and it was no unusual event to find ten or twelve of those creatures lying within a comparatively short distance of a spring, while great numbers of squirrels

[1] *Penna. Mag. of Hist.*, vol. i. p. 41.

[2] Report for 1647, *Penna. Mag. of Hist.*, vol. vii. p. 272.

[3] Penna. Archives, 2d series, vol. vii. pp. 619, 628.

[4] *Penna. Mag. of Hist.*, vol. vi. p. 312.

and birds were frozen to death The horses, cows, and other domestic animals exposed in the woods without shelter perished In many instances the stags and does fed at the hay-ricks with the cattle and became domesticated

On the 17th of March, 1760, the *Gazette* informs us, occurred "the greatest fall of snow ever known since the settlement" The roads in every direction were closed The majority of the members of the Assembly were unable to get to Philadelphia, the snow, it is recorded, being in some places seven feet deep Dec 31, 1764, the river was frozen over in a night, and in 1770 the river closed on December 18th, and remained so until Jan 18, 1771

Capt John Heinricks, of the Hessian Yager Corps, in his letter from Philadelphia in the early part of the year 1778, states, in reference to our climate and seasons, "The cold in winter and the heat in summer is quite moderate, but the thunder-storms in summer and the damp reeking air in spring and autumn are unendurable In summer mists fall and wet everything, and then in the afternoon there is a thunderstorm And in winter, when the trees are frosted in the morning it rains in the afternoon Such phenomena are common here"[1]

This officer of one of the crack regiments of the mercenary troops, in his comfortable quarters on the Schuylkill, might thus complacently write of the moderate cold of that winter, but the ill clad and ill fed Continental troops at Valley Forge, as they clustered about the camp-fires, record a different impression of the weather, although Capt John Moutressor, of the British army, states in his diary, under date of March 14, 1778, "Weather very warm for the season, Layloche and Gooseberry leaves starting," while on the 17th of the same month he mentions, "Fine weather, frogs croaking in swamps, indicating spring"[2]

The summer of 1778 was intensely warm, while the winter of 1779-80 was bitterly cold, the Delaware remaining for three months closed At Philadelphia an ox was roasted on the river, and the ground was frozen to the depth of five feet

The strength of the ice can be imagined when we remember that that winter the British army crossed from New York to Paulus Hook, drawing their cannon and wagons as on the solid earth The winter of 1784 was very cold, and on Feb 6, 1788, the thermometer registered three degrees below zero The midsummer of 1789 was very warm, but in August the weather was so cool that fires had to be lighted in houses for the comfort of the inmates Jan 2, 1790, the air and water were so warm that boys bathed in the river, while in the following winter the thermometer was five degrees below zero

The winter of 1801-2 was milder than any which had preceded it since 1700, which it very much resembled, and Watson records that shad were in market on the 17th of February, 1802, while the early winter of 1805 was so mild that farmers plowed their land until within a few days of Christmas, but the new year ushered in intensely cold weather, while February of 1807 was extremely cold, extending even to the Southern Gulf States On the 19th of February, 1810, the mercury at eight o'clock in the morning registered seven degrees below zero The year 1816 is known as "the year without a summer," and it was equally remarkable in that respect in Europe as on this continent Frost and snow were common in every month of the year June was the coldest ever known in this latitude Snow fell in Vermont to the depth of ten inches, in Maine, seven, in Massachusetts and Central New York, three inches Fruit and vegetation was scarce and did not fully mature

On the 20th of July, 1824, a noticeable storm of rain and hail is recorded as having occurred at Chester Jan 19, 1827, the Delaware was frozen over at Chester, and up to that date that winter no snow had fallen, nor did it snow until some time after the river had closed The winter of 1824 was so mild that on the 9th of February a shad was caught at Bombay Hook

On Friday evening, Jan 12, 1831, one of the most severe snow-falls on record in this vicinity occurred The storm continued all of the next day The result was that the mail and stages were much impeded for three days on the roads from Philadelphia to Wilmington, but the cross-roads leading westward from the river were blocked with snow nearly to the tops of the fences, and in that condition was almost every road in the county On Monday, Jan 15, 1831, court began in Chester, and the juries and witnesses found their way across the fields, a few on horseback, but mostly on foot The president judge did not arrive, and on Wednesday the associate judges, who transacted some business, adjourned the court[3] During the winter of 1833-34 the river was closed, and Theodoric and Hamilton Porter drove a pair of horses in a sleigh from Chester to the navy-yard, Philadelphia, on the ice, and returned in the same manner On May 7, 1846, the snow fell for two days, blocking up the roads so that access to Chester by the highways was interrupted for several days Trains on the Philadelphia, Wilmington and Baltimore Railroad could not run for two days because of the great drifts, and during that time no mail passed north or south over that road

The year 1838, Dr Smith records, "was remarkable on account of a great drought that prevailed throughout a large extent of country, embracing Delaware County From about the 1st of July till nearly the 1st of October, no rain fell except a few very slight showers The earth became parched and vegetation dried up All the later crops failed, and, what added greatly to the injurious effects of the drought, myriads of grasshoppers made their appearance and vora-

[1] *Penna Mag of Hist.*, vol i p 41

[2] Ib, vol vi p 197

[3] Hazard's Register, vol vii p 248

ciously devoured nearly every green blade of grass that had survived to the period of their advent Even the blades and ears of Indian corn were greatly injured in many places Cattle suffered much for want of pasture, and many persons were obliged to feed them on hay during the months of August and September, or upon corn cut from the field "[1]

The winter of 1855 was remarkable Up to March 16th the weather was comparatively mild, but on that date the cold was so intense that the Delaware was closed, and many persons living in this neighborhood crossed over the river on foot and in sleighs On the night of March 6, 1858, the Delaware was frozen solidly in one night, the preceding winter months having been so mild that no ice had formed until the middle of February The steamer "Keystone State," from Savannah, on the evening of March 5th, had to lay to at the pier at Chester, where she was compelled to discharge her cargo and transport it the remainder of the distance by rail

On Sunday, Jan 7, 1866, a cold wave visited Chester, increasing until by Monday morning the thermometer was ten degrees below zero, and nothing to compare to it had been known for thirty odd years. Even now it is recalled as the "cold Monday"

On the 20th and 21st of March, 1868, the most violent snow-storm known in the neighborhood for a quarter of a century occurred The trains on the railroad were delayed several hours, no mail reaching Chester on Saturday, March 21st, until after mid-day, while the roads throughout the county were impassable by reason of the drifts

The winter of 1872-73 was cold, while that of 1873-74 was mild But the following year, 1874-75, was intensely cold On February 10th the river was solidly frozen, and many persons walked from Chester piers to the bar on the ice, and the day previous the thermometer stood at two degrees below zero The winter of 1876-77 was mild, while that of 1880 was cold, and, taking the mean temperature, it is said to have been the coldest winter since 1856 The streams leading into the Delaware were frozen six inches in thickness, and the depth of snow estimated at one foot to sixteen inches on a level

---

CHAPTER XXV

THE COURT, BENCH, AND BAR OF DELAWARE COUNTY

BEYOND the possibility of refutation, it can be asserted that at Tinicum, in the present county of Delaware, justice was first dispensed within the limits of the State of Pennsylvania, and in all probabilities this remark will hold good as to the entire Delaware River territory Crude and capricious doubtless was the code of laws administered by Governor Printz, who was required, in obedience to the instructions given him, to "decide all controversies according to the laws, customs, and usages of Sweden," and in these matters he was expected to "adopt and follow all the laudable manners, customs, and usages of the Kingdom of Sweden"[2] This was certainly a task more difficult to perform than to require, for the codification of all the Swedish statutes, manners, and customs had then but recently been made,[3] hence it is no wonder that his Excellency the Governor of New Sweden, who, in 1647, reported "the whole number of men, women, boys and girls and children now living here is 138 souls,"[4] occasionally, even in the sparsely-settled colony, found himself face to face with nice points of law which his military education furnished him no precedents to meet, and particularly was his position embarrassing because he was expected to maintain a sharp outlook for the interest of the company, which would necessarily compel him to act in the dual capacity of plaintiff and judge in the same case Under the circumstances we can understand why he says, "Again, I have several times solicited a learned and able man to administer justice and attend to the law business, sometimes very intricate cases occurring, in which it is difficult, and never ought to be tnat one and the same person appear in the court as plaintiff as well as judge"[5] The Governor was clothed with civil and criminal jurisdiction, he was especially directed to enforce obedience and order, and could punish great offenders not only with imprisonment but even with death, "according to the crime," in the latter cases, however, execution could only be done "according to the ordinances and legal forms, and after having sufficiently considered and examined the affair with the most noted persons, such as the most prudent assessors of justice that he can find and consult in this country"[6]

Beyond the foregoing brief mention of the administration of justice on the Delaware under Swedish rule, I have been unable to find any further reference thereto Truly is it, as a recent accomplished writer remarks, "A mere trace, fitful at best, and rendered more faint by the shadows of time"[7] The Dutch records, unfortunately, are hardly more explicit than the Swedish on the subject of legal tribunals among the early settlers on the Delaware before the conquest of the territory by the English Jean Paul Jacquet, who was appointed vice-director Nov 29, 1655, was instructed to "administer law and justice to citizens as well as soldiers," while Andrew Hudde, the sec-

---

[1] History of Delaware County, p 359

[2] Penna Archives, 2d series, vol v p 773

[3] Record of Upland Court, p 30

[4] *Penna Mag of Hist.*, vol vii p 273

[5] Ib, p 278

[6] Instructions to Governor Printz, Penna Archives, 2d series, vol v p 773

[7] Dukes Book of Laws, Historical Notes of Benjamin M Nead, p. 427

retary, was "to book all matters complaints, defaults, arrests, with the reasons thereof, also all judgments, sentences, and decisions," while the vice-director was enjoined to "strictly observe and have observed the placards and ordinances made and published heretofore against the sale of brandy or strong drinks to the savages, regarding the robbing of gardens or plantations, the running about the country, drinking on the Sabbath, and profanation of the same" The court where breaches of these ordinances were to be tried was a meeting of Council, which was to be called only by the order of the vice-director, and all matters pending before that body were to be decided by "a majority of votes," and in case of a tie the vice-director was "to have a double vote" In cases of military or concerning the company's property, the vice-director, beside the members of Council, was instructed to add two sergeants, who were to sit as part of the court, but where the matter was purely a civil one, "between freemen and servants of the company, two suitable freemen were to be substituted instead of the sergeants"[1]

This tribunal seems to have exercised legislative as well as judicial powers, for it is recorded that on Feb 13, 1656, all persons at New Castle were required to inclose their lots before the 15th of March following, and, failing to do so, were punishable by a fine of six guilders The owners of goats were also instructed to provide keepers for these animals On May 22d Council directed that the swine at that place should be yoked within twenty-four hours, under the penalty of having the creatures killed by the soldiers[2] At the February court, before mentioned, Thomas Broen, who was charged with having beaten a servant so that he was rendered unable to labor, was ordered to provide for the latter until he was restored to health The defendant, for having spoken disrespectfully of Vice-Director Jacquet, possibly because of the sentence, was placed under arrest In July a Swede and Finn, charged with violating the law respecting the sale of liquor to Indians, in extenuation of their act pleaded ignorance of the law, which seems to have been regarded as a valid excuse, for they were discharged

Early in 1657, Jacob Alrichs was appointed vice-director of the city's colony on the Delaware (part of the Delaware territory, for Christiana River to Bombay Hook had been transferred to the city of Amsterdam by the Dutch West India Company for moneys advanced), and in the latter part of April he arrived at New Castle That there then was a court held on the river is established from the prayer of the Swedish inhabitants that a court-messenger and provost might be appointed for them Sheriff Van Dyck proposed "one Jurgen, the Fin on the Crooked Kil," for the office, which suggestion received, June 12, 1657, the approval of Governor Stuyvesant From this, however, the inference naturally is that the court was held at New Castle or Christiana, and was lacking in every essential the received ideas of a judicial tribunal, inasmuch that Alrichs, on March 30, 1658, in a letter to Stuyvesant, says, "I found the government here to consist and be attended to by the Vice-Director or Commander, sitting over military delinquents with military persons, and over citizens with citizens, as ordered by your Honor, to whom I, upon my arrival, represented and showed the charges which were to be taken in consideration afterwards"[3] From the foregoing remark, Mr Nead maintains that a regular set of laws or ordinances had been promulgated for the general government of the Delaware River settlement shortly after the conquest by the Dutch, and that Alrichs' instructions clearly contemplated the continuance and enforcement of these ordinances,[4] a conclusion which is doubtless correct Certain it is that an attorney practiced before the court, for March 30, 1658, Alrichs writes, "I have also to pay the attorney, Schelluyn, for salary earned by him in the suit against Dirck Cornelissen Heunich, skipper of the ship 'Prins Maurits,' but it seems that the expenses ought to be paid out of the deposited sum, the proceeds of the sale of the goods, unless your Honor understood that we should not consider this"[5] This is the first recorded appearance of an attorney in our annals On Oct 10, 1658, Alrichs informed the authorities at Amsterdam that he had "received the police and law books which were sent out, consisting of 2 parts and a duplicate of each, and we shall make use of them , but (not) the by-laws of the city, at the end of which the customs of Antwerp are annexed and printed," whereof mention is frequently made in the dispatch[6]

On May 8, 1658, the Swedish magistrates at Tinicum presented a petition to Governor Stuyvesant, who was then visiting the settlements on the Delaware, requesting that they might be properly instructed respecting the discharge of their duties, and that a court messenger or officer should be appointed to serve summons, make arrests, and enforce the sentences of the courts[7] The meagre information we have seems to indicate that the Holland conquerors deemed it wise policy to continue the old Swedish magistrates in office, the latter nationality being largely that of the majority of the inhabitants, obedience would be more easily rendered to their former rulers than to new men, with whose language and person the people were generally unacquainted The sitting of the court was at Fort Altena, for the company's colony, which included all this locality, and they were held "three or four times during the year

---

1 Penna. Archives, 2d series, vol vii pp 490–491

2 Acrelius, "New Sweden," p 92

3 Penna. Archives 2d series, vol vii p 520

4 Duke's Book of Laws, p 435

5 Penna. Archives, 2d series, vol vii p 528

6 Ib, vol v p 304.

7 Ib, vol vii p 531

according to demand or circumstances" The letter wherein the foregoing facts appear was written by William Beekman, vice-director, to Stuyvesant, April 28, 1660,[1] and is particularly interesting to the annalist, for it furnishes a more comprehensive insight as to the manner in which judicial affairs were conducted, together with the scope of inquiry and the jurisdiction of the courts under the Dutch ascending on the Delaware, than any other paper of that time From it we learn that Peter Rambo, a Swede, and one of the commissioners, had already grown weary of public cares and desired to resign the office, that at the court held the 19th of August in the preceding year twelve or fifteen of the "Swedish or Finnish Nation," who had been summoned to appear by Jager, the court messenger, failed to attend the session, and that thereupon Beekman made a rule that hereafter for any similar default "committed wantonly and intentionally, without the hindrance of sickness or God's weather and wind," the party so offending should be fined ten guilders, the reason for the rule being "that no one should be delayed in his claim" because of the voluntary absence of those persons who should be in attendance It was difficult, however, to compel the rude settlers to recognize the law's power to correct wrong or the province of the court to meddle in personal affairs In the same letter Beekman relates that Mr Learsen, the Swedish priest at Upland, having been violently assaulted and "fearfully beaten" by Peter Mayer, complained to him, and that he had ordered both parties to the quarrel to be summoned, but before the day fixed for the hearing "the affair was settled between them, thus asserting that the judge had nothing to say about it" Peter Mayer, who it seemed was inclined to indulge in assaults and batteries, paid his fine for non-attendance The judges, then as now, did not always agree in their conclusion as to the law or the jurisdiction of the court Beekman complained that Oele Stille, one of the Swedish magistrates, had "made strong opposition to him" at the last court-day, because the former had suspected Stille of permitting the Swedish priest to perform a marriage in his presence without proclamation having been first made in church, and against the will of the parents of the contracting parties Beekman, as president judge, imposed on the clergyman a fine of fifty guilders, to which decision Stille dissented, stating that the court had no jurisdiction to correct such affairs, that it was a matter for the Consistory of Sweden alone to inquire into The priest seemed to be governed by the dissenting opinion, for when summoned to appear he informed the officer that he had nothing to do with the court of Christiana, and did not attend Proceedings in divorce, it would appear, were not within the province of the tribunal, for the letter states that there was then "among the Fins at Opland" a married couple "who live very wretchedly together, and the wife is often fearfully beaten, and daily driven out of the house like a dog," which condition of matrimonial infelicity had continued for several years The trouble was so generally known that at length a Swedish priest at Upland, the neighbors, the sheriff, and the commissioners, at the request of the man and wife, applied to Vice-Director Beekman, desiring that they might be divorced, and the few animals and personal property they owned be divided between them The whole matter was referred to Stuyvesant, but whether the divorce was ever granted does not appear in any record now published Dr Smith was of the opinion that the parties to this unhappy marriage resided near Marcus Hook, the territory in that neighborhood then being known as Finland

The matters thus set forth from Beekman's letters peculiarly relate to our history, and are exceedingly interesting, since all the persons mentioned resided within the limits of the present county of Delaware, and because it is conclusive of the fact that at that time no court existed within the territory belonging to the present State of Pennsylvania

Notwithstanding the differences in opinion between Vice-Director Beekman and Stille, the latter still continued as one of the magistrates, for on the trial of Evert Hendrickson for a dastardly assault on Joran Kyn, at Upland, on the 6th and 16th of April, 1663, the court at Fort Altena, where the case was heard, consisted of Vice-Director Beekman, Oele Stille, Mats Hanson, and Peter Cock, commissioners

The plaintiff in this proceeding had been worried by the defendant's hog running on his land, and he had pointed his gun at the animal, when the defendant assaulted him with a stick, endeavoring to break his head The plaintiff in warding off the blows received a stroke on the elbow which disabled his arm for a month Hendrickson not satisfied with this, went home and brought his gun, saying at the same time to Kyn, "I would like right well to shoot you down now, you scoundrel" The evidence established that the preceding autumn the defendant had threatened the life of the plaintiff, at which time he put a knife to the plaintiff's throat, stating he had a mind to cut his head off The first assault had been overlooked by Kyn, on condition that he would give him no further trouble The witnesses united in the opinion that Hendrickson was a desperado "who troubled the place at Upland's Kil"[2] The defendant was banished for his ill doings, and removed to the neighborhood of New Castle

In the early fall of the following year Sir Robert Carr, in command of the English forces, subjugated the Dutch provinces on the Delaware, but in the articles of capitulation, dated Oct 1, 1664, it was stipulated that "the Scout, the Burgomaster, Sheriffe,

[1] Penna Archives, 2d series, vol vii p 635

[2] Documents Relating to the Colonial History of New York, vol xii, pp 424-26

and other inferior magistrates shall use and exercise their customary Power in Admins'on of Justice within their precincts, for six months or until his Ma'ties pleasure is further known "[1]

Under the terms of this agreement the Dutch magistrates continued in office until April 21, 1668, when Governor Lovelace commissioned Sir Robert Carre, scout, and Hans Block, Israel Helme, Peter Rambo, Peter Cock, Peter Alricks, or any two of them, as councilors, "to advise, hear, and determine by the major vote what is just, equitable, and necessary in the case or cases in question "[2] Steadily but slowly Governor Lovelace from that time began bringing the judicial system of England into use, retiring that of the Dutch, which had prevailed, as speedily as circumstances permitted, but so gradually that the radical change would be made, and at the same time do no violence to the colony by unsettling at one swoop the whole body of ordinances, manners, and customs with which the people had grown familiar by long usage The attempted rebellion of the Long Finn, in the summer of 1669, afforded the Governor an opportunity to make some sweeping innovations in the criminal procedure, and that case will ever be memorable in our annals, inasmuch that for the first time we have undoubted record of a trial on the Delaware, wherein the defendant was formally indicted and a jury of twelve men impaneled, who were subject to challenge on the part of the prisoner, and charged, after the testimony was concluded, by the commissioners to find "the matter of fact according to the evidence "[3]

Governor Lovelace, knowing well the power which appearances lend in controlling the ignorant classes, early in our history, under English rule, hedged the bench about with all the pomp and circumstance necessary to impress the citizens of that day with the importance and dignity of the judicial office In 1671, Governor Lovelace instructed Capt Carr, on the Delaware, to set up the king's arms in the court-house, and to have the same insignia of majesty borne on the staffs carried by the officers in attendance[4]

At that date in all probability there were inferior courts held on the Delaware at several designated places by the justices to determine controversies in trifling cases and petty infractions of criminal law, although the records do not absolutely establish the fact other than that on May 17, 1672, a town court was directed to be held at New Castle, to be presided over by the bailiff and six assistants, with jurisdiction to try all cases of debt or damage to the value of ten pounds, from whose decision there was no appeal, it inferentially appears that about that date a court was already established at Upland On Aug 8, 1672, on petition of Jan Cornelis, Mattys Mattyson, and Martin Martinson, of Calcoone Hooke, in the present township of Darby, which set forth that Iszael Holmes had obtained a patent to land "upon the island" (subsequently known as Smith's Island) "over against Calcoone Hooke," without ever having had possession or pretence thereunto before," Governor Lovelace, on the date given, made an order "to Authorize & Empower the Court at Upland with the Assistance of one or two of the High Court to examine unto the matter and make report of the Truth thereof," that he might make "some Order thereupon according to Equity and Good Conscience"[5] Certain it is that when, on July 30, 1673, the English standard was supplanted by that of their High Mightinesses the Lord States-General, and the flag of the Netherlands again floated over this territory, the Dutch Council at New York, Sept. 12, 1673, established "one court of Justice for the inhabitents of Upland, to which provisionally shall resort the inhabitents both on the east and west banks of Kristina Kill and upwards unto the head of the river" At the same time Council instructed the inhabitants of the Delaware River territory, "for the maintenance of good order, police, and so forth," to nominate eight persons in each of the judicial districts as magistrates, and from the names thus submitted Council would select and appoint those officers[6] These courts were of very limited jurisdiction, for on the 26th of the same month Council issued instructions for the government of the Delaware River settlement, in which it was distinctly announced that all criminal offenders should be referred to the Governor-General and Council, the sheriff in those cases was directed to arrest, detain, and forward the prisoner, "under proper safeguard, to the Chief Magistrate, together with good and correct information for or against the offenders Smaller offences, such as quarrels, abusive words, threats, fisticuffs, and such like, are left to the jurisdiction of the magistrates of each particular village" In civil cases where the amount in dispute was sixty florins (Beaver)[7] or under, the decisions of the magistrates were final, and where the sum was over sixty, and amounting to two hundred and forty florins, the party aggrieved could appeal to the sheriff and councilors,—one person to fill the latter office being annually appointed from each judicial district,—whose decisions should be final The courts also possessed restricted legislative powers, such as enacting laws providing for the laying out of highways, erecting churches, school-houses, or similar public works, observances of the Sabbath, and the manner of "setting off lands and gardens," and other matters appertaining to agriculture They could also make ordinances against fighting, wrestling, and "such petty offenses," provided such regulations were as far as possible conformable to the laws of the "Fatherland and

1 Penna Archives, 2d series, vol v p 545

2 Ib., vol vii p 722

3 Ib, p 728

4 Ib., p 757

5 Ib., vol v p 621, Hazard's Annals, p 398

6 Penna Archives, 2d series, vol v. p 631

7 Then the standard of value

the statutes of that (this) Province," but all such enactments "of any importance" were required to be presented to the Governor for his approval before being promulgated. In the same document will be found instructions as to the manner of electing persons to fill the higher offices, a system which was adopted by the English authorities when the territory again passed into their possession, and maintained in a measure for many years after the State of Pennsylvania had in turn cast off the British yoke. It was that "towards the time of election the Sheriff and Schepens (magistrates) shall nominate as Schepens a double number of the best qualified, the honestest, most intelligent and wealthiest inhabitants . . . to be presented to the Governor, who shall make his selection therefrom." His Excellency, however, reserved the right to reappoint any of the old justices he might desire to continue in office.[1] There was no stated time for holding these courts, but they were called in session as occasion required.

The Dutch authority, however, by the terms of the treaty between Great Britain and Holland, ceased on Feb. 9, 1674; but as Major Edmund Andross, the representative of the Duke of York, to whom the king had reconfirmed the province after it became an English dependency, did not take formal possession until the 31st of October following, it is to be presumed that judicial matters up to that date were conducted according to the Dutch form of procedure. Two days thereafter the Governor ordered that the old magistrates on the Delaware, excepting Peter Alricks, who were in office when the Dutch captured the province in July, 1673, should be "established for the space of six months or further orders."[2] On November 4th Capt. Edward Cantwell, who had been the former sheriff under the English rule, was reappointed to the same office. The magistrates thus reappointed were Peter Cock, Peter Rambo, Israel Helme, Lars Adrecksen, Woolle Swain; and William Tom was appointed clerk.

The jurisdiction of the courts on the Delaware River seems not to have been extended so as to give them cognizance of high grades of criminal offenses. Hence we find that on Feb. 21, 1675, Governor Andross issued a commission for holding a Court of Oyer and Terminer at New Castle, for the trial of several prisoners charged with rape, which commission was addressed to five justices of New Castle Court, and Justices Cock, Rambo, Holme, Andriesen, and Swain, of Upland Court, requiring any seven or more of them, as soon as conveniently may be, "to sitt one or more Times during the space of one whole week, if Occasions require, for the hearing, trying, giving Jugdement, & causing the same to be put in Execution, according to Law."[3]

Early in the same year it was generally reported that James Sandelands, of Upland, in ejecting a drunken Indian from his house, had so roughly treated the latter that he had died from the injuries received. On April 23d of that year Governor Androsse wrote to Capt. Cantwell, that "as to James Sandyland (if you are not sure of him being criminally guilty) you ought to have had a court, that he might have a Legall Tryall and so either be justly detained, punished, or releast."[4] In pursuance of these instructions, a special court was held at New Castle on May 13, 1675, Governor Sir Edmund Andross presiding in person, assisted by three commissioners, one from New Castle, from Upland, and Whore Kill. "The bench," old documents tell us, was "called over and placed on the Governor's left hand. Governor Philip Carteret of New Jersey, on the right with Mr. Samuel Edsall, Mr. Thomas Wandall, Mr. Joseph Smith, Mr. John Jackson, Mr. William Osburne." The jury, as provided by the Duke of York's laws, which, however, had not been extended to the Delaware River settlements, consisted of seven freemen. The court being in session, James Sandelands was "brought to answer a presentment by the Sheriff for suspicion of being the cause of the death of an Indyan." The presentment was read, and the defendant "pleads to it not guilty." Sandelands thereupon related "the whole story of the Indyan being at his house and him putting him out of doors." The aboriginal witnesses did not relate a consistent story; one stated the deceased had died in five days after his fall, while others made the interval of life after being ejected from the tavern six and eight weeks. It should, however, be remembered that while the Indians were giving their testimony, Sandelands, by leave of the court, went to them "and had a talk with them." The jury, after being charged, withdrew to deliberate, and finally rendered a verdict: "They find the prisoner not to be Guilty, Hee is ordered to be cleared by Proclamacon."

On Sept. 22, 1676, Governor Andross promulgated an ordinance introducing the Duke of York's laws, and establishing courts of justice on the Delaware in conformity therewith. One of the tribunals was located at Upland, and was to consist of justices of the peace, three of whom would constitute a quorum, the oldest justice presiding, having the powers of a Court of Sessions, with jurisdiction over all matters under twenty pounds in civil causes and in criminal cases, excepting those where the punishment extended to life imprisonment or banishment, when appeals were to be allowed to the Court of Assizes. In proceedings in equity and suits where the claims were less than five pounds, judgment could be given by the court without a jury, unless the latter was claimed by the parties litigant. The sessions were to be held quarterly, beginning on the second Tuesday of the mouth, and rules governing practice, unless repugnant to the laws of the government, could be made

[1] Penna. Archives, 2d series, vol. v. pp. 637, 638.
[2] Ib., p. 649.
[3] Ib., p. 667.
[4] Ib., vol. vii. p. 737.

by the court, and were to continue for one year. A record of all proceedings was to be kept in the English language, to which every person should have free access "at due or seasonable times," and for that purpose a clerk was to be appointed by the Governor, on the recommendation of the court.[1]

In pursuance of this ordinance, on Nov. 14, 1676, the first court under the new code of laws convened at Upland, when Capt. John Colier and Capt. Edmund Cantwell, specially authorized by Governor Andross, administered the oath of office to the newly-commissioned justices,—Peter Cock, Peter Rambo, Israel Helme, Lace Andriesen, Woole Sweinsen, and Otto Ernest Cook.[2] Ephraim Herman[3] was appointed clerk. The first order made by the court was "that Mr. William Tom, the former clarke, should deliver unto the present clark, Eph. Herman, the Records and other publicq bookes and wrytings belonging to the court,"[4] while the first case called was that of Thomas Spry against the estate of Hendrick Johnson, deceased, and the plaintiff not appearing in person or by attorney, the court ordered a non-suit, with costs.[5] Executions were also ordered against all the persons who had refused to pay William Tom, the former clerk, the costs of court, and the clerk was likewise directed to write to the Governor respecting compensation claimed by Justice Helme for services rendered as interpreter with the Indians. Jan Jansen and Morten Mortensen were appointed guardians for the heirs of Hendrick Johnson, deceased, it being represented to the court that the estate of the minors was being wasted. This is the first instance of record in this State of such appointment, and while the guardians were instructed to prepare an inventory of the estate, they do not seem to have been required to give bond for the faithful performance of the trust.

Ephraim Herman appears to have kept a full record of all matters coming before the tribunal, for he not only gives a brief statement of the evidence in many of the cases, but he spread in full on the minutes the commissions of the justices and his own, as well as the correspondence he was instructed by the court to have with the Governor. He particularly invites the latter's attention to "how the Charges of this Court when they sitt may bee found, Concidering that wee all Live att a Great distance from our Court place and the Amercem[ts] (by Reason of the small number of actions) amounting to Little."

The court, when it adjourned until the second Tuesday in March next, was emphatic, for it adds, "and no sooner by Reason of the Ceason, and so it is to Continue and be kept quarterly," an order which, so far as it related to the Quarter Sessions, continued in practice for about a quarter of a century.

The next court convened on the 13th of March, 1676/7, when the tendency to the continuance of a cause, when called, exhibited itself as decidedly as it does now, after the lapse of two centuries. In one case where Morton Mortensen, of Ridley, sued Mouns Staecke for the value of an ox, which the defendant and his servant had killed, the plaintiff's witnesses "being supened," but failed to appear, the case was continued, the court stating that if the witnesses did not appear at the next term "they to be fined." At this session we find the first mention in our annals of a deed being acknowledged in open court, a practice which still prevails respecting sheriffs' deeds.

The next Quarter Sessions was held June 13, 1677, and the proceeding shows us that at that time redemptive servitude was a recognized system, for at this court John Test, in the presence of the bench, made acknowledgment that he had sold William Sill, a tailor by trade, to Capt. Edmond Cantwell, for nearly four years, the unexpired term of his servitude. Many suits were pressed to judgment at this session against John Ashman, who, appearing to have purchased a number of articles on credit, and then left the province and his creditors, the latter, then as now, scrambled for the insolvent's estates, and no less than five judgments were entered and two attachments allowed that day. The court appointed Lace Cock and Mathias Holsteyn to appraise the goods and chattels of John Ashman, and they were sworn to the performance of the trust. It also appeared that there was a dispute respecting "the fly (meadow) of those of Carkoen's Hock"[6] and Lace Dalbo, "the court taking into consideration the fact that before the next court "itt will bee too Late to mow the Hay, doe order that hans Peterse and the Reste of Carkoens hoeck doe mow the hay of the sd fly for the present and untill their case bee heard." An interesting fact in this term was that the first rules of court respect-

[1] Penna. Archives, 2d series, vol. vii. pp. 783, 784.

[2] From this date to the second Tuesday of September, 1681, the original records of the Upland court are in possession of the Historical Society of Pennsylvania. In 1860 these valuable documents were published by the society with copious notes and an introduction by Edward Armstrong. The original records were found by Deborah Logan in an old book-case, which had formerly belonged to her grandfather, Joseph Parker, deputy register for Chester County, which had stood for years in the Logan house, in Chester. The existence of the document was unknown almost for a century, until accidentally discovered in a secret drawer in this old book-case.

[3] Ephraim Herman resided in New Castle, and held the appointment for the same office in the court at that place.

[4] This order was obeyed, for on Aug. 14, 1677, Governor Andross wrote to justices in New Castle: "I have also by Mr. Ephraim Herman returned you the old Records, the Confusedness or ill Order of which I can no other wayes remedy, butt thatt Mr. Tom, the then Clerke, do forthwith putt ye same in Order, and write or cause them to bee fairly coppyed in a fitt booke, and attested by him and answer for any defects." (Penna. Archives, 2d series, vol. vii. p. 789.) This appears never to have been done, for, under date of Feb. 25, 1677-78, it is related that Tom, who had been thrown in prison for debt, had died therein. (Documents relating to the Colonial History of New York, vol. xii.)

[5] For the next five years, until nearly the end of the year 1681, the references being to "The Records of Upland Court," it is unnecessary to furnish the citation of the authority relied on for statements made in the text.

[6] Mr. Armstrong states that this was the point formed by the junction of Cobb's Creek with Darby Creek, and had for its western boundary Darby, and for its northern Cobb's Creek. (Records of Upland Court, p. 58, note.)

ing pleadings and attorneys we have record of were announced. "That all declarations must be Entered at Least the day before the cort at which the clarke is to attend att Upplands," and "That no persons bee admitted to plead for any other person as an attorney In Cort without hee first have his admittance of the Cort or have a warrynt of Attorney for his so doing from his Clyant" It was hardly necessary for the court to have made any rule in relation to attorneys, for on the 19th of May the Governor and Council adopted an ordinance "that pleading attorneys bee no Longer allowed to practize in ye government, but for ye depending cases" At the November session we find record that this ordinance was for the second term "openly Read in full Cort"

The most important case tried at this session was an action for assault and battery committed on Justice Helme by Oele Oelsen The justice in his evidence stated that the defendant "first with Evil words abused" and afterwards beat him "and his shirt all torne In peeces by the sd deft," and as he, the plaintiff, was one of the members of the court, he desired that "bee may bee so maintained" The defendant testified that he was first struck by the plaintiff, but Sheriff Cantwell "desires that the court will take the Case in Consiederacon and not suffer that a Justice of the Peace shall be so abused" After other witnesses had been examined by the court "and heard the debates of both parties," the defendant was fined two hundred and ten guilders, sixty to the poor or church, the remainder to the sheriff, and "doe further order yt the sd Oele Oelsen doe humbly aske forgiveness of Justice Israell helm and the Cort for his sd offence" The defendant having publicly asked pardon for his act, "The Cort and High Sherife Conciedering that the Sd oele was a poore man with great Charge of Childeren, uppon his humble submission did Remit and foregive him the one hundred and fifty Gilders fyne"

At the subsequent court, Sept 11, 1677, the difficulty respecting the meadow-land at Calcon's Hook was heard, and it was ordered that the plaintiffs should select "indifferent men," who should view the land and ascertain whether they had not their quantity, after which, if the parties could not agree, the case was referred to the Governor for adjudication Many applications were presented at the court by parties desiring to have certain lands surveyed and set apart to them, while the clerk was allowed two hundred guilders for his "last year's service, trouble and expenses," to be paid out of the tax to be laid

In the olden times, as now, litigation arising from absurd disputes was occasionally brought before the court, hence at the November session of 1677, Neeles Laersen, the innkeeper, brought an action against John Test, in which he complained that the defendant had "been troublesome to his son about a knyf" (knife), and he "desires to know the Reason of the same The Court haveing heard the debates of both parties, and finding the businesse and difference of noe vallue, did order the partees to be friends and forgive one the other, to which the parties agreed Neeles Laersen Ingaging to pay the Clercq and sherrefs fees"

On April 3, 1678, the first meeting of the justices of Upland in private session, as such assemblages afterwards were called, is noted as being held at the house of Justice Peter Cook, "in ye Schuylkill," where the public accounts were audited and approved

At the court held on the second Tuesday of June, 1678, for the first time is mentioned proceedings for the foreclosure of a mortgage In that case Christopher Barnes had mortgaged his plantation and crops of corn and tobacco for fourteen hundred and ninety-four guilders and six styvers The court appointed James Sanderlands, Albert Hendricks, and Oele Franssen to appraise the farm and crops of wheat and tobacco, and the mortgageor, then in court, "Ingaged to make a good Tytle of ye Land & plantation to ye Plt if not fully paid otherwise" So also at the same session is presented the first application of an indentured servant to be discharged (freed) at the expiration of the term of servitude, where the master illegally held him beyond the period specified in the agreement The court ordered Oele Swensen, at the next court, to produce the indenture of Benjamin Goodman, his servant, or bring "witnesses that can Testify about ye business" This Swensen failing to do at the November term, Goodman was discharged At the same term an application was made to the court by Jan Conelisson, of Amesland, for the protection and maintenance of his son, Erik, who was "bereft of his natural Sences, and is turned quyt madd," the father pleading that his poverty prevented him supporting his son The unfortunate maniac must have been dangerous to be at large, for the court ordered "that three or 4 persons be hired to build a little Blockhouse at Amesland for to put in the sd madman, and att the next Court, order will bee taken yt a small Levy bee Laid for to pay for the building of ye house" Dr Smith believed that this "little blockhouse," built under this order, may properly be regarded as the first lunatic asylum in Pennsylvania.[1]

To provide for the maintenance of the tribunal, at this term was ordered a "Levy or small Tacx of fyve gilders pr head on every Tydable person for defraying of the Courts setting Charges, as heretofore, the Levy to bee paid by Every prson upon (at) Trimeconck (Tinicum) Island between this & the 6th of October next Ensuing"

There seems to have been corporal punishment in a case at this court, of which no record appears other than that James Sandelands was ordered to be paid one hundred and one guilder "for payment of the

[1] Provision was made under the Duke of York's laws (pages 58-64) for the manner in which the charge for the support of "distracted persons" was to be levied.

Indians that whip, &c.," which sum Sandelands seems to have advanced out of his private purse; and at the same session, in a cross-action between William Orian and Jan Jansen, each alleging that the other threatened his life, the court ordered both parties to be bound "to their good behavior & order Each to pay halfe Costs."

The most important order made at this court was that which required that "Every person should within the spaces of twoo months, as far as his Land Reaches make good and passable ways, from neighbour to neighbour, with bridges when itt needs, To the End that neighbours on occasion may come together. Those neglecting to forfeit 25 gilders." This is the first record of any action respecting highways made by a court acting in the territory now Pennsylvania, although nearly four years previous to this date, at a special court held at New Castle, on the 13th and 14th of May, 1666, Governor Andross presiding, it was "ordered that Highways shall be cleared from place to place within the precincts of this government." [1]

At the court held on the 12th of March, 1678–79, James Sandelands, as attorney of Marmaduke Randall, presented a claim against the estate of Walter Wharton, deceased, for eighty guilders, which was for rent due for a house in Upland, and prayed that he might be ordered payment out of the estate, with costs, as also a personal claim of Sandelands against the estate for four hundred and twenty-eight guilders. In both cases judgment was awarded. Wharton was the surveyor for the Delaware River settlement. From a letter from Justice Moll, of New Castle Court, to Secretary Nicolls, of New York, under date of Jan. 20, 1680, we learn that Ralph Hudgjson had buried Wharton, and had charged about twelve hundred (guilders) for the funeral expenses, and that the court had promised to grant an order on Capt. Cantwell at the next session for that sum. The amount was so exorbitant that Justice Moll hesitated, for he says, "Others have been buried as handsome for one-third of ye money. . . . The Chancellor of Maryland, I know, allows all administrators alyke for funeral charges. If they will be astravigand they must doo itt upon their owne meanes not upon ye creditor's account." [2]

Edmund Draufton brought suit against Dunck Williams, demanding two hundred guilders as compensation for services rendered in "teaching the deft. Children to Read one Year." Richard Ducket, a witness for the plaintiff, testified "that hee was present at ye makeing of ye bargaine, & did hear that ye agreem't was that Edmund draufton should Teach Dunkes Children to Read in ye bybell, & if hee could doe itt in a yeare or a halfe yeare or a quart then hee was to have 200 gilders." The court awarded "Judgment in favor of the plaintiff for the amount claims and costs of suit." This is the first record in our annals of children being in anywise educated, other than the clause in the Duke's Book of Laws admonishing the people to care for the instruction of children and servants in matters of religion and the laws of the country, while at the same time parents and masters were strictly enjoined "to bring up their Children and Apprintices in some honest Lawfull Calling, Labor or Employment,"—one of the few regulations of the olden times which the present age might readopt with advantage to the State.

At the November court was heard a matter which it seems strange to our modern ideas could have occupied the attention of the most potent, grave, and reverend judges whose duty it was to hold aloft the balance of justice in our early colonial days. The church-wardens of Tinicum and Wicaco Churches brought to the notice of the bench "that the fences about ye Church Yards and other Church buildings are much out of Repair, and that some of the People members of ye sd churches are neglective to make the same up." The court, after due consideration, determined "to order authorize & Impower the Respective church wardens of ye sd Twoo Churches . . . do order & summons the Repective members of ye sd churches from tyme to tyme and att all tymes when it shall be found necessary, to build make good and Keepe in Repair the sd Churchyard fences as also, the Church and all other the appurtenances thereof and if any of the sd members upon warning doe prove neglective In the doing of their Proportion to the same, They and Each of them to forfeit fifty gilders for Each such neglect to be Levyed out of their goods and Chattles Lands and Tennements."

This intermeddling of the court in purely church matters was in accordance with the spirit of the Duke of York's laws, wherein much attention was devoted to ecclesiastical topics. The church-wardens were, under its provisions, required twice in each year, on the second day of the June and December sessions, in open court, to deliver a written "true presentment" of all misdemeanors, such as swearing, profane Sabbath-breaking, drunkenness, fornication, and adultery, "and all such abominable sinnes," which to their knowledge had been committed and the guilty parties remain unpunished. Their powers were so extended that they could compel the attendance of any person whom they believed had knowledge of such misdemeanors to testify respecting such charges, and if the latter failed to attend they were liable to be fined by the court.

At the same court Francis Steevens sued Claes Jansen on balance of an account for goods sold and delivered. The defendant pleaded in defense that "hee proffered & paid ye Plf. in pompkiens according to agreement." The plaintiff in rebuttal called Thomas

[1] Dr. Smith's "History of Delaware County," pp. 101, 102. That author, who had inspected this record, states that the manner of making the roads was left to the respective inferior courts. That order, of course, was binding in this jurisdiction.

[2] Documents relating to the Colonial History of New York, vol. xii. p. 643.

Stroud, who testified that "hee being sent by frank Stevens to fetch ye pompkiens did demand them, but Claes Jansen did refuse to bring them down to ye water syde" After a summing up of the evidence on both sides the court ordered "that ye deft, Claes Jansen, pay unto ye plt Twenty gilders in wheat and Twenty-six in pumpkiens, after ye rate of sixteen gilders pr hundred Together with costs of suite"

Sometimes then, as now, the patience of the court gave way, but in one case the majority of the bench managed to thrust the tedious matter upon one of their fellow-justices Hans Petersen had sued Henry Colman for an account of forty-three guilders, and when the case was called the defendant was absent Thereupon the court said "the matter in dispute being so Inconsiderable that itt is not worth ye Longer Continuance The Court therefore Impowered Justice Otto Earnest Cook to hear & Examine the act & Case and to make a Final End & determination thereof as he shal find Just and Equitable"

Courts cannot be maintained without expense to the public, particularly to suitors, a view of political economy which soon dawned on the understanding of the justices Early in the record, Nov 13, 1677, the court made an order that 'the Levy or Pole money for defraying the publicq charges" amounted to twenty-six guilders for every taxable person, and that payments would be received in the following species wheat at five, rye and barley at four, and Indian corn at three guilders per bushel, tobacco at eight stivers per pound, pork at eight, and bacon at sixteen stivers per pound Skins were to be received at current prices, as was also wampum Sheriff Cantwell was instructed to collect the tax, and if necessary to levy on the delinquent's goods, which he was to have appraised by two of the neighbors of the party whose articles were seized For collecting the tax, the sheriff was to receive at the rate of five shillings to the pound

The litigants soon began to learn that lawsuits were luxuries which must be paid for, for at the March term, 1679-80, the bench took action on the matter of unpaid costs, and entered the following order on the quaint old record

"Whereas the Law allowes to ye cort for Every Judgment Given by the cort 2s 6d, and the same being hitherto not Collected or paid, and the cort being in great want of some meanes to pay and defray their necessary Charges of meat & drinke, etc It is therefore this day Resolved and the undersheriffe William Warner, is hereby Impowred to Collect & Receive from ye following persons for Each action, that is to say Judgment accord to ye annexed List the sume of 2s 6d., and that heo bee accountable & give a Just and Exact account of his Receipt to ye Court att next Court day"

Then followed a list of forty suits, criminal and civil, wherein the costs were still unpaid Possibly the justices soon learned, as lawyers do, that of all hard collections the hardest is to gather in the cost of a lawsuit where the party to pay

"Expects a reversion and gets a reverse"

Hence it occasioned no surprise to find at the next term, on June 8th, the judges striving to meet the courtal expenses of the tribunal by the following modes

"Itt was this day by the Cort taken Into Consideracon & ordered that for ye defraying of ye charges of this Cort's sitting Each person shall pay Yearly one scipple of wheat or 5 gilders according to former order & Practice, and also That all the arrier of ye former Jears bee delivered & brought into Justice Otto Earnest (Cock) att Tinorigceng Island, such as prove neglective to be fetched by ye Constable by way of restraynt"

Even this order did not altogether satisfy the court, "being in want of monneyes for ye defraying of ye publicq Charges of their sitting," but just before the adjournment the justices ordered the clerk to prepare a list of those persons who were in arrears, and particularly a fine of two hundred guilders, which list was directed should be delivered to "ye high sheriffe, whoe is hereby ordered to collect ye same and to be accompatible att ye next Court, with further power that In case any should refuse ye payment of ye sd Just Cort fees that in such a Case hee should use ye uttmost extreamity by ye Lawe allowed"

On the 8th of June, 1680, the commissions of the new justices appointed by Governor Androsse "was Read publicqly att Upland" The newly-commissioned magistrates, however, did not fully comprehend the responsibilities connected with the office, for the court at the June term, 1680, finding that Upland Creek, where the court hitherto had held its sessions, was at the lower end of the county, for the benefit of the majority of the people "thought fitt for ye future to sitt & meet att ye towne of Kingsesse on ye Schuylkill,"[1] and at the June sessions of 1681, Justices Henry Browne and George Brown failing to be present, they "were boath fyned for not attending ye Court to supply their places Each ten pounds according to ye Law books" These fines, however, were in all probability never collected, for, before the next court assembled, the territory had been transferred by the king's charter to William Penn, and under the new power a thorough reorganization of the provincial authority was made

It is necessary, however, to retrace our narrative in order of time, so as to notice a few important cases which were tried before that event took place

At the October sessions, 1680, Claves Craw sued Hans Peters for slander The defendant had called the plaintiff a thief, and on the trial, the defendant not being able to prove the truth of his assertion, the court ordered that "ye deft openly declared him selfe a Lyar, & that he shall further declare ye Plt to bee an honest man & pay 20 gilders to ye Plt for his Losse of tyme, together with Costs of suite" At the same court a case was continued on the application of the

[1] The site of the town of Kingsesse Dr Smith has fully established was located below the old Philadelphia, Wilmington and Baltimore Railroad (now Reading Railroad extension to Chester), and east of the Island road, in late township of Kingsessing, county of Philadelphia (Smith's "History of Delaware County," p 123, note.) Armstrong, in a note to "Record of Upland Court' (p 171), had located it in the immediate vicinity of the Swedish mill erected by Governor Printz near the Blue Bell Tavern on the Darby road

plaintiff, who alleged that four of the material witnesses had been subpœnaed but did not attend. This session was prolific of suits for defamation. Justice Otto Earnest Cock brought an action against Moens Peterson Staecket for having called his honor a hog-thief, and the justice indignantly demanded that the defendant, "if he or any other can, will prove ye same or otherwise that hee may bee punisht according to Lawe." The defendant protested that he had no recollection of ever having made such an assertion, and if he had, "that itt must have been in his drink." The court, however, after the witnesses were examined, that the high character of a judge should not be lightly assailed, ordered the defendant to pay one thousand guilders, and to acknowledge that he had "wrongfully, falsly & malisiously slandered & blamed" the plaintiff. The defendant, in order to escape the dire wrath of the bench, "did willingly in open court declare as above & humbly desires forgiveness & prayes that ye fyne may bee remitted. Upon ye Intercession of Justice Otto Earnest the cort did remit ye fyne abovesd."

During the whole period covered by the record of Upland Court, there are but two cases in which juries were impaneled to try questions of fact, and that this was so was doubtless owing to the provision in the Duke's laws that where a plaintiff desired the issue tried by a jury he was required to give bonds, when he entered suit, that he would pay "One Day's Cost of a jury."[1] The first case wherein a trial by jury is set out on the record was Nov. 12, 1678, and was had in an action brought by William Orian against Joh. D'Haes on a disputed account. The plaintiff had craved a jury, and twelve men were impaneled, who returned a verdict for the plaintiff for an amount somewhat less than his demand. "The court thought fitt to suspend the verdict of the Jury and the determinacon of this case till next court day, att wch tyme both plt and deft are to bring their bookes In court." That is the reason given in the record for setting aside the verdict, but it is very likely that this was an easy way the bench took of getting out of acknowledging that they had made a mistake. Perhaps a suggestion was received at side bar that the law explicitly directed that "no jury shall exceed the number of seven, nor be under six, unless in special causes upon Life and death the justices shall thinke fitt to appoint twelve."[2]

Two years thereafter, on Oct. 13, 1680, the next jury trial took place. The jury in this case, as in the former one, consisted of twelve men, and their finding was sustained, for we are informed "the court doe allow of ye jury's verdict & passe judgment accordingly." Doubtless the finding was just, yet as the jury numbered twelve, and it being a civil suit, it was a body clearly unknown to the law, and on appeal, if pressed, the verdict must have been set aside. But in those early times, the magistrates being unlearned in legal matters, firmly believed and acted on the doctrine announced in latter years in Philadelphia by a well-known lay judge, that "natural equity abhors sharp points of law." As we progress in our narrative an instance will be cited in our judicial history sustaining this declaration. It is, however, not uninteresting to note that at the last session of court, before the province passed into the ownership of Penn, a technical point was raised by Jonas Neatson, who had been apprehended on the suit of Andries Peters, Esq. The defendant appeared, alleging that he was not timely "arrested." This was a knotty point the judges desired to think over, for the record informs us that "the Case is referred til next court." The term fixed upon at the adjournment for holding the next session was Sept. 13, 1681, but although a court did convene on that date, it was with new justices and at the ancient town of Upland, where Deputy Governor William Markham had located the capital of the province of Pennsylvania. The new justices were William Clayton, William Warner, Robert Wade, Otto Earnest Cock, Lassey Cock. All of the foregoing were also members of the Governor's Council, while William Byles, Robert Lucas, Swan Swanson, and Andrew Bankson were not in such intimate relationship with his Excellency. All the bench were new to that office, save two Swedes, who were formerly justices, but the English element now outnumbered the former nationality. The first act of moment at this session was the proclamation by Markham that the duke's laws were abrogated, and all legal proceedings thereafter were ordered to be conducted "according to the good laws of England." A most admirable change if there had been any one in commission on the bench having any extensive knowledge of these laws, but as there was not, criminal actions were entertained by the court and tried by petit juries without the intervention of a grand inquest.[3]

Every controversy of fact was now submitted to the conclusion of a petit jury's verdict, but the old manner of computing values by the Dutch guilders could not be so quickly set aside, for the last verdict at that session was for sixty-two guilders. If the court records are of any value in showing how quickly

1 Duke of York's Book of Laws, p. 67. 2 Ib., p. 33.

3 Dr. Smith says ("History of Delaware County," p. 136), "The first Grand Jury that ever sat in Pennsylvania, of which there is record, was summoned to attend at this Court" (that of Sept. 12, 1682, a year subsequent to the time mentioned in the text). "Their names, as given in the minutes of the Court, are William Clayton, Thomas Brassey, John Symcock, Tho. Sary, Robert Wade, Laurence Cock, John Hart, Nath'll Allen, William Woodmanson, Thos. Coebourne, John Otter, and Joshua Hastings, being one-half the usual number. These jurors were summoned in the case of Lassey *alias* Laurence Dalboe, and are called his 'Grand Jury.'" It was merely a petit jury, as we now understand the term, the word "grand" doubtless being used by the clerk without comprehending the import of that term, for the record shows that the jury passed upon the fact of the person's guilt, and did not present him for another jury to finally acquit or convict him of the charge. However, the first grand jury did sit in Chester at the June term, 1683.

the new system of computation was adopted, it demonstrates that the people of that day more speedily accepted the new order of things than did our Revolutionary sires in discarding the pounds, shillings, and pence to substitute in their stead the American standard of money.

On Nov 30, 1681, the next session of the court began It was presided over by Markham, and at that term we learn in the olden days, as at the present, the calendar sometimes melted away, for only four cases were tried, one was withdrawn, and one continued. At the next court, March 14, 1682, Markham also presided, and before the bar Henry Reynolds was arraigned for "selling strong drinks by small measure in his house contrary to the Governor's and Council's order" The defendant pled guilty to the charge, but on his submission to this court was discharged The indiscriminate sale of liquors early demanded the attention of the authorities, the Dutch records frequently mention the desire of the government to prevent abuses in that respect, while, under the Duke of York, the sale was hedged about with many restrictions Not only were these provisions spread on the statute-book, but Governor Androsse, under date of Aug 14, 1677, in his letter to the magistrates respecting the administration of justice, directed the special attention of the courts to these enactments "Pray take care and fitting Orders for Ordinaryes," he says, "that they bee fitt persons duly Lycenced, and well provided according to Lawe, and that none else be admitted to retaile "[1]

The clear, good sense which was conspicuously exhibited by William Penn on many occasions was perhaps never better illustrated than when in coming to his province in 1682, he determined to continue the courts already established therein, with whose manner of administering justice the people had grown familiar Certain it is that he advocated radical changes in the civil and criminal code, removing much of the severity of the latter, while he enlarged the responsibilities of individuals to the community, but these innovations were made by legislative bodies, drawn from the people, and the means he employed to effect the end in view was conducive to the public weal, the discussion of measures of government resulting in enlarging the intelligence of the masses The law enacted Dec 7, 1682, requiring all persons who were not by birth subjects of Great Britain within three months thereafter to make declarations of their intentions to become "freemen," resulted in retiring, for the time being, all the Swedish justices Hence, at the February session, 1682-83, John Simcock, a newly-appointed justice, acted as president of the tribunal, which then consisted only of five magistrates But Otto Earnest Cock must have declared his intentions soon afterwards, for at the June term, 1683, when Penn personally presided, the familiar figure of Justice Cock once more appeared on the bench

To this court, held June 27, 1683, the first grand jury of record in Pennsylvania was summoned[2] That grand inquest consisted of seventeen persons,—James Kennerly, James Sandelands, George Foreman, Neal Lawson, John Corneleus, Richard Buffington, Thomas Minshall, John Harding, Mans Stankitt, Oele Rawson, George Wood, Albert Hendrickson, Herman Johnson, Nathaniel Evans, Robert Robinson, William Woodmanson, Richard Few The jury, as the old docket emphatically records the lesser body, was composed of twelve persons, and it seems at that time the traverse jury was sworn at the beginning of the court, to "justly try & deliver in your verdict in all cases depending that shall be brought before you during this session of court "[3]

One of these cases was brought by John Day against Henry Reynolds for £4 9s 2d, the balance of an account which the defendant was to discharge by delivery of a cow and calf at a designated time This the latter failed to do, hence the litigation The jury rendered the following curious verdict "The jury find for ye Plaint'd give him a cow & calf, ye same to be deliv'd with in 7 dayes, or £4, 19s, 2d, at ye choyce of ye Plaint, or ye value thereof in Porke, Beefe or corne in ye 8 mo next, & 40s down and costs of Suite "

The first clause of the duke's laws imposed a fine of ten pounds on justices and high constables for each and every day's absence from the sessions of the court Twenty years thereafter, on May 20, 1685, the General Assembly enacted a law making a justice who should not attend court finable in any sum not exceeding thirty shillings The custom of acknowledging deeds openly in court, so that a record might be spread on the minutes, which had prevailed under the duke, continued in practice, as did the registration of the brand-marks of the owners of cattle running at large in the woods

The court exercised the power of laying out roads, excepting the King's Highway, which was the duty of Council, of protecting indentured servants from their masters' exactions or abuse, settling disputes as to term of servitude, and compelling the bondsmen to perform their duties by corporal punishment, or when they attempted to escape, adding on their detection,

[1] Penna Archives, 2d series, vol vii p 790

[2] Proud states ("History of Pennsylvania," vol i p 240) that "the first Grand Jury in Pennsylvania was summoned on the 2d of Third month of the year (1683) upon some persons accused of using counterfeit silver money They convicted a person whose name was Pickering and two others, his accomplices " On the 25th of Eighth month, 1683 (October), Council ordered, "That an Indictment be Drawne against Cha Pickering & Samll Buckley, grounded upon evidence taken before that board " In the afternoon, "A Grand Inquest were Impaneled and Attested whose names are as follows " (Here is given the names of twenty four men, and Council adjourned until the next morning, October 26th, when the following record was made "The Grand Jury being called Over went forth to find the Bill against Charles Pickering and returned and found ye Bill as being a Heynous and Grevious Crime A Petty Jury were Impannelled and Attested," which consisted of twelve men (See Colonial Records, vol i pp 86 to 88)

[3] Forms of attestation for juries adopted by Penn Records at New Castle, quoted in Futhey and Cope's "History of Chester County," p 25

as the law directed, additional time to serve, where the latter by their misdeeds occasioned a loss to their owners Some of the peculiar duties then devolving on the court were contracting for county building, bridges, levying the taxes and similar matters now discharged by the county commissioners, as also auditing the public accounts,—a work now incumbent on the county auditors,—and many other matters became the subject of the court's consideration It had jurisdiction of all breaches of the peace, misdemeanors and other offenses, excepting in cases of heinous or enormous crimes In this the scope of inquiry had been enlarged after Penn's coming, but burglary and arson, which were punishable with death on a third conviction, under the duke's law, now made the party liable to imprisonment, and in the latter crime, whipping The jurisdiction of the county courts was restricted so far as the high grade of crimes were concerned, until the Constitution of 1790 gave the judges of the Court of Common Pleas in each county the right to act as justice of oyer and terminer and general jail delivery for the trial of capital and other offenses

A peculiar adjunct of the county courts provided by the act of March 10, 1683, were the peacemakers, three persons in every precinct chosen yearly,[1] to whom the parties litigant could refer their difficulties by agreement in writing, and the decision of these peacemakers was as conclusive as that of the court, and the judgment so rendered was registered as "other judgments are[2] One of the awards made by the peacemakers at Chester, at the court held 3d day 1st week Eighth month, 1687, in a suit for assault and battery brought by Samuel Baker against Samuel Rowland, is worthy of notice It was that "Samuel Rowland shall pay the lawful charges of this court and give the said Samuel Baker a Hatt, and so Discharge each other of all manner of Differences from the Begining of the world to this Present day" Although the Assembly on May 11, 1692, declared that the law relative to peacemakers was inoperative, the remnants of that system linger still in our practice, in arbitration, the modern form of the ancient peacemakers

The provisions for summoning jurors, under the Duke of York's laws, instructed the constables "to warn so many of the overseers to attend as juryman" as the pending causes might seem to require, and in the event of the panel being exhausted, the jury could be supplied "with so many able and discreet men as shall attend the court, or shall happen to be inhabitants of the Towne where the court shall be held"[3] In cases where the law was obscure, "as the jury cannot be satisfied therein," they could return an alternative verdict, viz, "If the law be so on such a point we find for the plaintiff, but if the law be otherwise we find for the defendant," in which case the court must determine, as a matter of law, in whose behalf the verdict was to be recorded A majority of the jury could find a verdict By the law of March 10, 1683, under Penn's government, it was provided that a grand inquest should attend in every county court, and bring in their presentments[4] twice a year, when, on that presentment, an indictment was regularly framed and the prisoner admitted to bail to the next court, so as to give him an oppo[illegible]nity to make a proper defense The traverse jury w[illegible]rawn in the following manner "The names of the [illegible] shall be writ in small pieces of paper and p[illegible] hat and shaken, forty-eight of whom shall [illegible]rawn by a child, and those so drawn shall stand for the Sheriff's return And the first twelve, not reasonably excepted against shall stand and serve for the tryal"[5]

A remarkable jury was summoned at Chester on the 27th of Sixth month, 1689, which for nearly two hundred years was the only instance on record in the United States until 1878, when a similar jury was impaneled at Cheyenne, Wyoming Territory At the date first given, a servant girl pleaded guilty to the charge of fornication, and being sentenced to be whipped, she alleged that she was *enceinte* and could not undergo corporal punishment The man had also pled guilty to the charge The record states, "Upon which they were both called to the bar, where they made their appearance, and upon her further confession and submission a jury of women, whose names are underwritten, ordered to inspect the said Mary Taberfield's condition" The jury consisted of Lydia Wade, Sarah Usher, Hester Rawlence, Mary Carter, Jane Hawkes, Mary Hoskins, Elizabeth Musgrove, Mary Bayless, Elizabeth Hastings, Mary Little, Jane Moulder, and Ann Sanderlands "They make return that they cannot find that she is 'enceinte,' neither be they sure she is not" At the court held 3d day 1st week Eighth month, 1689, the female defendant was called to the bar and further examined, when she declared that, notwithstanding her testimony "she doe now freely declare to ye contrary and submitts to ye mercy of ye King and Governor" Whereupon she was sentenced to "receive 10 strips upon her bear backe well laid on at ye Common Whipping Pos[illegible] att Chester" John Eldridge was discharged on p[illegible]g a fine of three pounds and all the court charges

This, however, is not the first record of corporal punishment being inflicted, for at the June court, four years previous thereto, Abraham Effingall [illegible] convicted of "abusing and menacing the majestracy of this county," and was sentenced to receive "twenty-one lashes att the Publicke Whipping-Post on his bear

1 Lawrence Lewis, Jr, in his learned sketch of "Courts of Pennsylvania in the Seventeenth Century" (*Penna Mag of Hist*, vol v p 153), says, "These peacemakers were not elected by the people, but appointed annually by the county courts," citing as his authority the address of Hon James T Mitchell on adjournment of District Court of Philadelphia, 1875, pp 4 and 5

2 Duke of York's Book of Laws, p 128

3 Ib., p 33

4 Ib., p 129

5 Ib, p 129

Backe, well laid on and 14 dayes Imprisonment at hard labour in ye House of Correction"

By the provisions of the act of March 10, 1683, the justices of each county court were directed to sit twice in every year "to inspect and take care of the estates, usage and employment of orphans, which shall be called the Orphans' Court," which was to be held the first 3d day of the week in the First and Eighth months annually, the reason of the law being stated "that care may be taken of those that are not able to take care of themselves"[1] The records of the county of Chester show that the first court, under the title "Orphans' Court," was held on the "3d day in ye 1st week of ye 8th m[illegible]th, 1687" Under the act of May 10, 1688, the [illegible]iction of the court was extended to the con-an[illegible]decedents' estate, with power to order sales of the [illegible]perty for the payment of debt, or the maintenance [illegible]r education of children, the support of the widow, or the disposition of a part of the land, to raise funds to improve the remainder. These powers, however, were exercisable only "with the approbation of the Governor or Council"[2] Although this law distinctly stated it was, to be in force for one year and "no longer," the Orphans' Court had come to stay, and although it subsequently was the object of many statutes defining its powers and proceedings, it became so entirely a part of the machinery of government that it could not be done away with

Previous to the act of May 10, 1684, there was no high Appellants' Court in the province other than the Governor and Council, but at the time designated a Provincial Court consisting of five judges was created, which was to sit twice a year in Philadelphia, and two members of the court at least, every fall and spring annually, were directed to "goe their circuits into everie respective county in the Province," to hold a court of appeals, as well as to try all criminal causes of a high grade, questions of title to land and other cases[3] of which the county courts had no jurisdiction

The following year the inconvenience of this court only having cognizance of cases involving the title of real estate, was the subject of much complaint, and the Assembly abolished that part of its jurisdiction, while at the same time it defined more explicitly its appellant's powers and the criminal cases, which were to be in the first instance the subject-matter of its [illegible]quiry The number of judges was to be reduced to three, but subsequently they were restored to five

Under the colonial government and under that of the commonwealth until a change was made by the Constitution of 1790, all criminal cases punishable with death were tried before the judges of the Provincial or Supreme Court, and for that reason a search among the old county court records to find mention of criminal cases of a high grade is always attended with little or no success That much of the records of the Provincial Court must be lost beyond hope of recovery is evident from the reply of David Lloyd to Governor Blackwell, for on the 25th of Twelfth month, 1688–89, when ordered to produce the records of the courts, he stated that "they were not recorded otherwise than on a quire of paper"[4]

A little over a year after Penn first came to his province—no Provincial Court had been then established—he was called upon to preside in a case of more than ordinary interest, it being nothing less than the trial of an alleged witch This proceeding was had eight years before the stupid excitement at Salem, Mass, ran its course At that period, in all the British American colonies the statute of England passed in 1603 was in force, which punished the impossible crime of witchcraft in some of the provinces with death Indeed, in the commission and instructions to the justices of Chester County from Governor Keith, dated Nov 24, 1719, they were directed to inquire of all "Witchcrafts, Inchantments, sorceries, Magic Arts, &c"[5] and this absurd law continued in force in Pennsylvania until the act of Sept. 23, 1794, by which it was repealed[6] The case mentioned was that of Margaret Mattson and Yetho Hendrickson,—the former the wife of Neels Mattson, a Swedish settler who owned and resided on a plantation on the river on the west side of Crum Creek, in Ridley township, while the latter was the spouse of Jacob Hendrickson, who, it is believed, also resided in that neighborhood

On Feb 7, 1683/4, they were brought before Penn and the Council at Philadelphia, and "examined and about to be proved witches," when it was ordered that Mattson and Hendrickson should enter bonds in fifty pounds each for the appearance of their wives to answer the charge on the 27th of the same month At the time designated the trial was had, Attorney-General John White being present Penn charged the grand jury, and that body found a true bill against Margaret Mattson The defendant being unable to speak English, Lasse Cock was qualified as interpreter The traverse jury was impaneled, on which appeared Robert Wade, John Gibbons, Jeremiah Collet, Walter Martin, and others, from this county The first witness produced was Henry Drystreet, who testified that for twenty years he had heard that the prisoner was a witch, and had cast spells on several cows James Sandelands' mother had told him that Mrs Mattson had bewitched one of her cows, but that Mrs Sandelands had afterwards said that she had been mistaken, it was not her cow, but that of another persons which would die Charles Ashcom testified that the defendant's daughter-in-law, her son Anthony's wife, had told him that she had sold her cows because her mother-in-law had bewitched them, and that afterwards, having taken the spell off of Hendrick-

[1] Duke of York's Book of Laws, p 131
[2] Ib, p 180
[3] Ib., p 168
[4] Colonial Records, vol i p 245
[5] Duke of York's Book of Laws, p 383
[6] Dallas' "Laws of Pennsylvania," vol iii p 119, sect 4

son's cattle, she had put it on their oxen. He also stated that the defendant's daughter-in-law one night had called him up hastily, and when he came to her she told him that she had seen a great light and that the old woman, with a knife in her hand, stood at the foot of her bed crying out, desiring "John Symcock to take away his calves, or else she would send them to hell." Annakey Coolin stated that her husband took the heart of a calf which had died, as they thought, by witchcraft, and boiled it, whereupon the prisoner came into their house and inquired what they were doing? They answered they were boiling the flesh, when she replied that it would have been better had they "boiled the bones," with several other unseemly expressions. Margaret Mattson, in her defense, asserted that she did not care anything for the evidence given by Drystreet, but had "Sandelands mother come, she would have answered her;" as for Charles Ashcom's testimony on "her soul" she denied it, and demanded where was her daughter? "Let her come and say so."

As to Annakey Coolin's attestation concerning the geese, she denied it. The notes of evidence do not show what this assertion was. She declared she was at the time never out of her canoe, and as respected the calf's heart, she denied ever having said anything concerning it. The prisoner at its conclusion again denied everything, declaring that the witnesses had all spoken "by hearsay." Penn thereupon charged the jury, who retired, and brought in a verdict of "guilty of having the common fame of a witch, but not guilty in manner and form as she stands indicted." Neal Mattson and Anthony Neelson gave bonds in fifty pounds each for her good behavior for six months, as did also Jacob Hendrickson for Yethro Henderson, and the prisoners were discharged.[1]

The foregoing, however, is not the only instance of the hidden art in our annals. In 1695, John Roman and his two sons, residing in Chichester, were reported to be students of astrology and other forbidden mysteries. The public tongue had so discussed the matter that on the 9th of Tenth month, 1695, Concord Monthly Meeting gravely announced that "the study of these sciences bring a vaile over the understanding and a death upon the life." John Kingsman and William Hughes were ordered to speak to the parties, and have them attend at next monthly meeting. The offenders were seen, and stated that if it could be shown wherein it was wrong, they would desist from further investigation in those arts. For several months the matter was before Concord Meeting, without resulting in suppressing the dreaded evil, and early in 1695, Chester Quarterly Meeting had the case of the Romans before that body for having practiced Rhabdomancy, or consulting with a staff, and such like things. In other words, the Romans had faith in the efficacy of the divining-rod, a belief which has not entirely died away. The grand jury, however, learning of the matter, presented Robert Roman for the dire offense, and, in order to eradicate the wickedness, they presented the following books: "Hidons Temple of Wisdom, which teaches Geomancy, and Scot's discovery of Witchcraft, and Cornelias Agrippas teach Necromancy." Whereupon the justices ordered "as many of these book as can be found," should be brought to the court. We have no information whether the books were brought, but Robert Rowan was, when, on submission to the court, he was fined five pounds and costs, promising that he would never more practice the art, but behave himself well for the future. He was discharged. Since which time our records show no further allusion to witchcraft.

In the case of David Lloyd *vs.* James Sandelands, called at the court held 3d day of Fourth month, 1690, John White appeared as attorney for plaintiff, and doubtless at the suggestion of Lloyd, who was a well-read and shrewd lawyer, the former interposed a technical challenge to the array of the jury, or as the quaint record states it, "alleged that ye jury was not Lawfully summoned soe would not com to tryall." The defendant, who appeared in person, therefore craved a nonsuit on the refusal of the plaintiff to proceed with the case. The justices, as previously stated, abhorring sharp points of law, summarily disposed of the legal difficulty, for it "being referred to ye court ye court granted the same." This decision may have been just; but surely there was no occasion for the justice at the court held on the 10th day of Tenth month, 1700, when complaint had been lodged before that tribunal, stating that liquor was sold by a particular individual without having received the approval of the session, to have tantalizingly told George Oldfield, when called before the bar to produce his license, "but he having none, the court ordered him to get one if he can forthwith."

The reasons assigned by William and Mary, when, on Oct. 20, 1693, they superseded Penn's authority by appointing Col. Benjamin Fletcher Governor of Pennsylvania, were doubtless not the true motives prompting the act, but certain it is, that in the end their Majesties' bad faith resulted beneficially for the people. The difficulties which had occurred between the legislative body and the executives of Penn's selecting, showed that the popular mind was determined to adhere to constitutional rights and forms under the charter, but the natural feeling of respect for the proprietary personally softened the bitterness of the struggle. When, however, a stranger, a usurper in a measure, and an overbearing man with whom the people were not in sympathy, was placed in authority, nothing but the naked possession of power remained to hold the public in obedience. But when that man undisguisedly informed the General Assembly that the laws and model of the government were disallowed and at an end, and threatened the province

[1] Colonial Records, vol. i. pp. 94–96; Hazard's Register, vol. i. p. 108.

with annexation to New York or Maryland, it awakened the open resistance of David Lloyd, the master-mind in the colony, whose courage was of that unflinching kind which never hesitates in the defense of honest opinion, and whose address in debate and knowledge of law peculiarly fitted him to lead at that juncture the party advocating the rights of the people. To this day the citizens of Pennsylvania and the Union are reaping the benefits resulting from the sturdy battle made by that brave Quaker lawyer for popular liberty nearly two centuries ago, for be it understood, David Lloyd dared even to stand between Penn and the accomplishment of the purposes of the latter when he believed that the object could only be obtained by interfering with the general welfare of the province. David Lloyd was the first lawyer we have knowledge of residing within the county. His first appearance in the Assembly was as a Representative from Chester County in 1693. The following year he was Speaker of that body, and in that capacity bore the full blunt of Governor Fletcher's wrath. He was the father of the bar of Pennsylvania, and to him, above all others, is due the credit of assimilating the crude legislation of that early period into a system of jurisprudence, while the acts which moulded our tribunals of justice into form, and invested them with clearly-defined powers and jurisdiction, were in the majority of instances either drafted in whole or revised by that eminent lawyer, whose learning and integrity lent lustre to the Supreme Court, wherein for fourteen years he presided as the chief justice of the province. David Lloyd should ever be held in grateful remembrance by the people of the State, for whose lasting welfare he did so much.

By the act of Oct. 27, 1701, county courts were required to be held at the town of Chester on the third day of the last week in February, May, August, and November. Three justices constituted a quorum, and they were empowered to deliver the gaols, award process, and hold all manner of pleas of the crown, exempting felonies punishable with death. The civil jurisdiction covered all classes of actions, and the practice was to conform as nearly as possible to that of the Common Pleas of England, while in declaration and pleas brevity, plainness, and verity were required, and "all fictions and color in pleadings" to be avoided. They had equity powers, and all matters of maritime disputes not cognizable in the Court of Admiralty were to be heard and determined at the county courts. Appeals were allowed from the final judgment of these tribunals, the party appellant entering security as at present.

The judges of the Supreme Provincial Court were to go on circuit twice in each year, the act requiring such court to be held in Chester on the 2d day of Eighth month and on the 18th day of Second month, for the trial of all felonies and to hear appeals in civil cases. By the act of Feb. 10, 1710, the Supreme justices were not required to go semi-annual circuits in the counties outside of Philadelphia unless cases were pending there for trial, and commissions of oyer and terminer were issued by the Governor. The act of 1710 was in 1713 repealed by Queen Anne, and on the 20th of July, 1714, Lieutenant-Governor Gookins, following the precedent of Governor Evans, published an ordinance of like tenor establishing the several courts in the province. One of the three Supreme justices could hold circuit court under the act of May 22, 1722, but by the act of May 20, 1767, although the Supreme bench was increased to four members, it would seem that all the judges were required to ride circuit twice a year if occasion demanded, and the expenses of the judges and clerk of the Supreme Court, with their servants, in the event of there being court held in any of the counties, were to be paid by that county during the session therein. The judges and their attendants were to be conveyed over any ferry in the province "without paying any ferriage, fee, or reward for the same."

The Courts of Common Pleas in the several counties continued to exercise in main the jurisdiction conferred on the county courts by the act of Oct. 27, 1701. During our colonial history all the courts were frequently subject-matter of legislative enactments. When Governor Evans and the Assembly could not agree on a law relative to the courts, for the act of Oct. 27, 1701, had been repealed by the order of Queen Anne's Council, Feb. 7, 1705, and his Excellency had on two several occasions ordered all the courts in the province to adjourn because of her majesty's action, on the Eleventh month 2, 1707, the Governor published an ordinance establishing courts of justice. This authority he claimed he could exercise under the charter to Penn when the welfare of the province required it. The particulars of the protracted struggle between the Assembly and Governor Evans belong to the history of the State as a whole, hence do not come within the scope of this work. In this ordinance, however, the Governor provided for special sessions of the County Court of Common Pleas every six weeks, which should be held by two justices for the return of process. It also provided that a special Court of Common Pleas could be held in cases where the defendants were about to remove out of the province, such defendant or defendants making request for such court to sit. In these extraordinary courts the costs were double those at ordinary sessions. The Courts of Quarter Sessions, as distinctive from the County Court, first appear in Governor Evans' ordinance in 1707, and were directed to be held in Chester on the last Tuesdays of February, May, August, and November, the Common Pleas beginning on Wednesday following. By act of Feb. 28, 1710, the Court of Quarter Sessions could not be held in Chester "above the space of two day," which provision was incorporated into the act of 1715 and May, 1722. On Aug. 26, 1727, the term of the sessions was extended to three days. By the act of May 28, 1715, the justices of the Court of Quarter Sessions were directed "to set such reasonable price on all Liquors Retailed in publick houses and provender for horses in publick stables, from time to time, as they shall see fit, under the like penalties as in such cases are enacted by the laws and statutes of Great Britain" The records show that this act, and a subsequent one providing for regulating the sale of these articles, was not a dead letter on the statute-book

By the act of 1710, already mentioned, the judges of the county courts were authorized, in case of disputed accounts between copartners and joint tenants, to appoint an auditor or auditors, who "for their pains in awarding such accounts to be paid by the party on whose side the balance appears" This provision was taken from the English statute passed two years before the colonial act was approved, and is the first appearance in our jurisprudence of the appointment of auditors by the court In the act of Feb 28, 1710, we find the title prothonotary used for the first time in reference to the county courts, and on May 28, 1715, those officers were directed, after issue joined to prepare a trial list, "which sd Lists shall be publickly set up in the court house during the sitting of the court"

By the act of Sept 29, 1759, the justices of the Court of Quarter Session were interdicted from being commissioned justices of the Common Pleas The salary of the justices of the County Courts in colonial days was twenty shillings each for every day so employed Notwithstanding the meagre pay, the justices held their office in high esteem, and were quick to resent anything which appeared to be contempt of the person or process of the court The early records furnish many instances in support of this assertion On 26th of Sixth month, 1702, "John Worrelow, being one of the petty jury for contempt of court by departing from his fellow-jurors and going into another province before they gave in their verdict is fined fifty shillings," and on the "1st day of the 7th mo, 1702," Edward Prichett "for his contempt of court in spitting in the face of Walter Faucett in open court is fined twenty shillings"

JUSTICES PREVIOUS TO THE ERECTION OF DELAWARE COUNTY

1657 —*Magistrates for the South River* Oloff Stille, Mathys Hanson, Peter Rambo, Peter Cock

November, 1674 —*Justices for Upland* Peter Cock, Peter Rambo, Israel Helm, Lace Andries, Oelle Swenson

Oct 3, 1676 —Peter Cock, Peter Rambo, Israel Helm, Lace Andries, Oelle Swenson Otto Ernest Cock

May 28, 1680 —*Commissioned by Sir Edmund Andros* Otto Ernest Cock, Israel Helm, Lasse Cock Henry James, George Browne

1681 —*Commissioned by Governor Markham* William Clayton, William Warner, Robert Wade, William Byler, Robert Lucus, Hendrias Bankson, Thomas Fairman, James Sandelands, Swen Swenson, Andries Bankson, Otto Ernest Cock, Lassey Cock

1682 —*Commissioned by Penn* John Simcock, Thomas Brassey, William Clayton, Robert Wade, John Bezer Otto Ernest Cock, Ralph Withers

1682 —Christopher Taylor, William Wood, Robert Wade, John Blunston, Nicholas Newlin, George Maris, James Saunderlaue, John Harding, Thomas Usher

April 6, 1685 —John Simcock William Wood, Nicholas Newlin Robert Wade, George Maris, Thomas Usher, Robert Piles John Blunston

1686 —Bartholomew Coppock, Samuel Levis, Francis Harrison

1687 —John Bristow, Edward Bezer

March 19, 1689 —John Simcock, John Bristow, Bartholomew Coppock, Jr, John Blunston, George Maris, Francis Harrison, and Nicholas Newlin

May 4, 1689 —William Howell

Jan 2, 1689-90 —John Bristow, John Bevan, John Blunston, Nicholas Newlin, Francis Harrison, Samuel Levis, James Sandelands, William Howell, Joshua Fearne

Seventh, 6, 1690 —John Simcock

Tenth, 8, 1691 —William Jenkins, present at court

May 13, 1693 —George Foreman, Jeremiah Collet, Thomas Smith, Thomas Withers

Sept 11, 1694 —*At Court* Jasper Yeates

1698.—Caleb Pusey, Philip Roman

1700 —Ralph Fishbourne

Sept 25, 1703.—*Commissioned* John Gwest, Jasper Yeates, Caleb Pusey, Philip Roman, Jonathan Hayes Ralph Fishbourne, Jeremiah Collett, Walter Martin, Nathaniel Newlin

1704.—*Commissioned by Governor Evans before May 30th* Jasper Yeates, Caleb Pusey, Jeremiah Collett, Philip Roman, Jonathan Hayes

1709 —Thomas Powell, Nicholas Pyle, Henry Pierce

Nov 24, 1711 —Jasper Yeates, Robert Pyle, Caleb Pusey, Nicholas Pile, Jonathan Hayes, William Hayes, William Davis, Henry Nayle, Richard Webb

May 13, 1713 —Caleb Pusey, Nicholas Pile, William Davis, Henry Nayle, Richard Webb, Nicholas Fairlamb, John Blunston Jr, Thomas Edwards

May 30 and June 11, 1715 —Caleb Pusey, Nicholas Pyle, Richard Webb, Henry Pierce, Henry Nayle, Nicholas Fairlamb, John Blunston, Jr, Richard Hayes

Aug 26, 1717 —Jasper Yeates, Caleb Pusey, Richard Webb, Henry Nayle, Richard Hayes, Henry Pierce, John Wright, John Wood, David Harry, John Worrall, Joseph Coeburn, Henry Hayes, Joseph Pennock

July 4, 1718.—John Wright (to be next to Jasper Yeates, Nicholas Newlin, Andrew Job, Elisha Gatchell, John Cartledge, Francis Worley

Aug 19, 1718 —Same commission, with Andrew Hamilton

Nov 24, 1718.—Jasper Yeates, John Wright, Caleb Pusey, Richard Webb, Henry Nayle, Richard Hayes, Henry Pierce, Nathaniel Newlin, John Wood, Joseph Coebourne, Henry Hayes, James Gibbons, Andrew Job, Elisha Gatchell, John Cartledge, Francis Worley

Nov 24, 1719 —Isaac Taylor

May 22, 1722.—John Wright, Caleb Pusey Henry Nayle Richard Hayes, Henry Pierce, Nathaniel Newlin, John Wood, Joseph Coebourn, Henry Hayes, James Gibbons, Andrew Job, Elisha Gatchell, Francis Worley, Isaac Taylor, James Mitchell

November 22d.—Same justices (except Andrew Job), and James Smith, Thomas Reid

Feb 18, 1723 —John Wright, Caleb Pusey, Henry Nayle, Richard Hayes, Henry Pierce, Nathaniel Newlin, John Wood, Henry Hayes, James Gibbons, Elisha Gatchell, Francis Worley, Isaac Taylor, James Mitchell, John Crosby, Thomas Reid, Abraham Emmit, Jr, James Roddy

1724.—John Wood, Samuel Nutt, John Crosby, Abraham Emmit, Jr, Thomas Reid, George Aston, Tobias Hendricks, Andrew Cornish, Mercer Brown, Evan Lewis, William Pyle

May 12, 1725 —John Wright, Henry Nayle, Henry Pierce, Nathaniel Newlin, John Wood, Henry Hayes, Isaac Taylor, Samuel Nutt, John Crosby, Thomas Reid, George Aston, James Roddy, Tobias Hendricks, George Stewart, Andrew Cornish, Mercer Brown

Aug 25, 1726 —John Wright, Richard Hayes, Henry Pierce, Nathaniel Newlin, John Wood, Henry Hayes, Isaac Taylor, Elisha Gatchell, Samuel Nutt, John Crosby, Abraham Emmitt, Jr, Thomas Reid, George Aston, Tobias Hendricks, Andrew Cornish, Mercer Brown, Evan Lewis, William Pyle

Oct 10, 1727 —James James

Aug 25, 1729 —Richard Hayes, John Wood, Henry Hayes, Elisha Gatchell, Samuel Nutt, John Crosby, Abm Emmet, Jr, George Aston, Mercer Brown, Evan Lewis, William Pyle, James James, John Parry, James Gibbons

Feb 19, 1729-30 —Richard Hayes, Henry Pierce, Henry Hayes, Elisha Gatchell, John Crosby, Abraham Emmit, Jr, Mercer Brown, James James, John Perry, James Gibbons, Joseph Pennock, Samuel Hol-

lingsworth, Joseph Brinton, Nicholas Pyle, and the chief burgess of the borough of Bristol (Chester)
Dec 1, 1733.—All acting justices recommissioned, and Caleb Cowpland
May 25, 1734 —Joseph Haines
Dec 2, 1737 —John Evans
Nov 22, 1738 —Caleb Cowpland, Joseph Haines, John Evans, Richard Hayes, Henry Pierce, Henry Hayes Elisha Gatchell, John Crosby, Caleb Cowpland, Abraham Emmit, James James, John Parry, Joseph Pennock, Samuel Hollingsworth, Joseph Brinton, Joseph Haines, William Pim, Joseph Bonsall, the chief burgess of the town for the time being, Joseph Parker
April 4, 1741 —Henry Pierce, Henry Hayes, Elisha Gatchell, John Crosby, Caleb Cowpland, William Moore, Abraham Emmit, Joseph Pennock, Joseph Brinton, William Pim, Joseph Bonsall, Joseph Parker, William Webb, John Mather, Ralph Pyle, John Taylor, Job Ruston, Charles Grant, the chief burgess of Chester for the time being
Dec 17, 1745.—John Crosby, Elisha Gatchell, Caleb Cowpland, William Moore, Abraham Emmit, Joseph Pennock, Joseph Brinton, William Pim, Joseph Bonsall, William Webb, John Mather, Job Ruston, Charles Grant, Samuel Flower, Thomas Cummings, John Parry, Andrew McDowell, the chief burgess of Chester for the time being, Joseph Parker
May 19, 1749 —Caleb Cowpland, Elisha Gatchell, William Moore, Joseph Pennock, Joseph Brinton, William Pim, Joseph Bonsall, John Mather, Charles Grant, Samuel Flower, Thomas Cummings, Thomas Worth Aaron Ashbridge, John Churchman, John Miller, Richard Richison, Isaac Davis, John Scott, William Read, the chief burgess of Chester for the time being
Aug 21, 1751 —Joshua Pusey and Samuel Lightfoot.
May 25, 1752 —William Moore, Elisha Gatchell, Joseph Bonsall, John Mather, Charles Grant, Samuel Flower, Thomas Cummings, Thomas Worth, Aaron Ashbridge, John Churchman, John Miller, Isaac Davis, John Scott, Joshua Pusey, Samuel Lightfoot, Edward Brinton, Mordecai Moore, Mordecai James, the chief burgess of Chester for the time being
Feb 22, 1757 —William Moore, John Mather, Samuel Flower, Thomas Worth, Aaron Ashbridge, John Miller, Isaac Davis, John Scott, Samuel Lightfoot, Edward Brinton, Mordecai Moore, the chief burgess of Chester, Alexander Johnston, John Morton, John Culbertson, William Clingan, John Paschall, William Parker, Timothy Kirk
Feb 23, 1761.—Thomas Worth, Samuel Flower, John Miller, Isaac Davis, Edward Brinton, the chief burgess of Chester, Alexander Johnston, John Morton, John Culbertson, William Clingan, William Parker, Timothy Kirk, John Hannum, John Price, Roger Hunt, John Fairlamb, George Currie, Henry Hale Graham

The Governor issued a *supersedeas* to Samuel Lightfoot, Edward Brinton, Thomas Worth, and John Morton, forbidding them to act as judges of the Common Pleas, the law under which they had been appointed having been abrogated by the king

Nov 19, 1764.—*Members of Council* William Moore, Thomas Worth, Samuel Flower, John Miller, Isaac Davis, Edward Brinton, Alexander Johnston, John Culbertson, William Clingan, William Parker, John Hannum, John Price, Henry Hale Graham, Richard Riley, Charles Cruikshanks, Richard Baker, James Gibbons, James Moore, William Swaffer, Evan Evans, Thomas Hockley, Joseph Pyle, Thomas Temple, Warwick Miller
At court, May, 1771, and after —Joshua Cowpland
At court, May 28, 1776 —Nicholas Fairlamb (No court was held in Chester County from this date until Aug 26, 1777)
April 4, 1777 —Isaac Davis, Evan Evans, James Moore, Benjamin Bartholomew, John Mackey, William Gibbons, Joshua Evans, Isaac Pearson, Daniel Griffith, Patterson Bell, John Hannum, Robert Smith, Philip Scott, Thomas Taylor, Thomas Cheyney
July 25, 1777 —Thomas Levis, Thomas Boyd, Robert Ralston, John Hart, and Richard Reiley, who had been elected, were commissioned
Aug 22 1777 —Caleb Davis, Esq, qualified as one of the justices of the Court of Common Pleas, he being the prothonotary of Chester County at that date
July 30, 1778.—William Evans appointed one of the justices of the peace for the county of Chester

The following is a list of the justices of Chester County from the Revolution to May 28, 1779, as gathered from a letter of Caleb Davis to Council [1]

Isaac Davis, Evan Evans James Moore, Benjamin Bartholomew, Daniel Griffith Patterson Bell, John Hannum, Robert Smith, Philip Scott, Thomas Taylor, Thomas Cheyney Thomas Levis, Thomas Boyd, William Evans, William Clingan

From the same letter we learn that at that date there were no justices in the First District,—Chester, Upper and Lower Chichester, Aston, Bethel, and Middletown, and in the Second District,—Darby, Radnor, and Haverford, or in the Third,—Newtown, East Town, Willistown, and Goshen Hence almost the whole territory now comprising Delaware County was unrepresented in the bench of justices

June 4, 1779, Alexander Johnston, Sept. 15, 1779, David Mackey, *vice* Johnson, declined, March 21, 1780, John Pearson, Nov 18, 1780, William Clingan appointed presiding justice of the court, Dec 7, 1781, William Haslet, March 9, 1782, David Mackey, June 26, 1782, James Beaton, Common Pleas and Orphans' Court, July 31 1783, John Bartholomew, June 5, 1784, George Pierce, Daniel Griffith, Common Pleas, Sept 24, 1784, Thomas Levis, Common Pleas, Oct 1, 1784, John Ralston, Oct 9, 1784, Thomas Cheyney, Oct 13, 1784, Cheyney commissioned justice of Common Pleas. Jan 21, 1785, Philip Scott, Common Pleas, June 16, 1786, Persifor Frazer, Common Pleas, June 22, 1786, William Clingan, president Court of Common Pleas, Quarter Sessions, and Orphans' Court, Oct. 9, 1786, Adam Grubb, Richard Hill Morris, Common Pleas, Dec 22, 1787, John Pearson, Common Pleas, Sept 16, 1788, Charles Dilworth, John Hannum, Common Pleas, Feb 16, 1789, William Haslet, Common Pleas, April 11, 1789, John Worth, Common Pleas, June 5, 1789, David Mackey, Common Pleas, June 16, 1789, Walter Finney

The last court held at the borough of Chester before the division of Chester County was on Aug 29, 1786, and continued by adjournment from day to day to August 31st, when the session ended

The first court held after the erection of Delaware County was on the 9th of November, 1789, when it was discovered that the commission of Henry Hale Graham, as president judge of the Court of Common Pleas, was irregular, inasmuch that he was not a justice of the peace at the time of his appointment However, the justices held the court, Justice John Pearson presiding There being no bar, William Tilghman, who, seventeen years thereafter, was appointed by Governor McKean chief justice of Pennsylvania, addressed the court and finally moved his own admission After Mr Tilghman had been sworn, he moved the admission of William L Blair and other lawyers That day eight gentlemen were qualified as members of the bar of Delaware County

Henry Hale Graham, the first president judge, was born in London, July 1, 1731. His father, William Graham, emigrated to the colony of Pennsylvania in 1733, first settling in Philadelphia, subsequently at Darby, and, finally, at Chester His son entered the office of Joseph Parker, then deputy register of Pennsylvania for the county of Chester, and on the former's death, in 1766, was appointed to the vacant position, which included that of prothonotary, register, and re-

[1] Penna. Archives, vol vii p 444

corder. He had been commissioned one of the justices of the county in 1761, and again in 1775. When the Revolutionary struggle was at hand Graham's feelings leaned toward the support of the mother-country, his wife teaching him to yield obedience to constituted authorities. Hence, in March, 1777, Thomas Taylor was appointed to succeed him, and seems to have entered into the discharge of the duties of the office, for Taylor's name appears on some of the documents on file in the Orphans' Court at West Chester. For some reason now unknown, on April of the same year Benjamin Jacobs was appointed, but refused to serve, when Caleb Davis was appointed in his place. The latter accepted, but it appears from the proceedings of the Supreme Executive Council, under date of July 28, 1777, "that Henry Hale Graham, Esq., late Prothonotary, had, under divers pretences, neglected to deliver up to him, the said Davis, the Books, Records, Papers & Seals belonging to the said office," whereupon Council issued a warrant directing Davis "to enter in the day time, with proper assistants, the dwelling House & Out Houses of the said Henry Hale Graham, Esq., & search for and take possession of & secure in some safe place the Books, Records, Papers & Seals belonging to the said Office."[1]

After the Revolution, November, 1783, Henry Hale Graham was a practicing attorney in the courts of Chester County. On Nov. 7, 1789, he was appointed by Governor Mifflin president judge of the courts of Delaware County; but it appearing that, not being a justice of the peace at the time, he could not act as president of the Quarter Sessions and Orphans' Court, on Nov. 9, 1789, Governor Mifflin requested the return of the former commission, and the same day Graham was commissioned a justice of the peace.[2] On the next day, November 10th, he was appointed president judge of the court. At the fall election in that year Henry Hale Graham was chosen one of the delegates to the Constitutional Convention of 1789–90, and while attending the meeting of that body in Philadelphia he died, Jan. 23, 1790. John Pearson, the first named in the commission to the associate justice, became the president judge of the courts, *ad interim*.

Under the judicial districting, on the adoption of the Constitution of 1790, the First Judicial District comprised the counties of Philadelphia, Bucks, Montgomery, and Delaware, and in pursuance of that division James Biddle, who was commissioned by Governor Mifflin, Sept. 13, 1791, president judge of the Common Pleas of Philadelphia, became president judge of the First Judicial District, and continued in the discharge of that office until June 19, 1797, when John D. Coxe was commissioned president judge. I have little or no information respecting either of these judges, but on July 31, 1805, Governor McKean appointed William Tilghman president justice. The latter, a conspicuous figure in a line of distinguished jurists, was a native of Talbot County, Md., and early in 1772, when sixteen years of age, began reading law under the direction of Benjamin Chew, of Philadelphia. In 1783, after eleven years' study of law, Tilghman was admitted to the bar of his native State. Before 1789 he removed to Philadelphia, where he rose rapidly to the front rank of the profession. In 1801 he was appointed chief judge of the Circuit Court of the United States. The organization of this court was stoutly opposed, and from the fact that the appointments were made on March 3, 1801, and that night sent to the Senate and confirmed before President Adams vacated to make room for Thomas Jefferson, the judges were facetiously termed "the midnight judges." The act creating this court was repealed at the next session of Congress, April 29, 1802, and Tilghman resumed the practice of the profession. However, as previously stated, he was appointed president judge of the Court of Common Pleas of the First District in 1805, a position he held less than seven months, for the death of Chief Justice Shippen making a vacancy, on Feb. 25, 1806, Tilghman was appointed chief justice of Pennsylvania. He died in 1827.

On Feb. 24, 1806, the State was redistricted, the counties of Chester, Delaware, Montgomery, and Bucks becoming the Seventh District, and in April, 1806, Governor McKean appointed Bird Wilson president judge. The new judge was then in his thirtieth year, having been born early in 1777. He was the son of Hon. James Wilson, a signer of the Declaration of Independence, who, it will be remembered, successfully defended some Tories charged with treason in Philadelphia, which so enraged the populace of that city, that a riot resulted on the 4th of October, 1779.[3] Bird Wilson, at fifteen years of age, graduated from the University of Pennsylvania, whereupon he began reading law with Joseph Thomas, of Philadelphia, and after being admitted was employed in the office of the commissioner of bankruptcy. For eleven years he presided over the courts of this county, sitting for the last time at the October sessions, 1817, when he resigned to become a clergyman of the Episcopal Church. In 1821 he was appointed a professor in the Theological Seminary of that denomination in New York, retaining the chair for almost three decades. Out of respect to his distinguished worth, he was appointed, June 25, 1850, emeritus professor in his department. Judge Wilson edited an edition of Bacon's "Abridgment of the Law," in seven volumes, afterwards enlarged by Bouvier to ten. Bird Wilson died April 14, 1859,

[1] Colonial Records, vol. xi. p. 254.

[2] Penna. Archives, 1st series, vol. xi. p. 638.

[3] In Frederick D. Stone's "Philadelphia Society One Hundred Years Ago," *Penna. Mag. of Hist.*, vol. iii. pp. 389–392, will be found a graphic account of this riot. Col. Thomas Leiper, of Ridley, was among the number of prominent men who voluntarily entered Wilson's house and defended it and him from the fury of the mob.

at New York He reached the advanced age of eighty-two.

Governor Findlay, on Jan 28, 1818, appointed John Ross, of Easton, to the vacant judgeship of the Seventh District At the time of his appointment Mr Ross was a member of Congress from the district comprising Northampton, Bucks, Lehigh, Wayne, and Pike Counties, having served in that body in the Eleventh, Fourteenth, and Fifteenth Congresses, resigning during the latter term to accept the appointment of judge He presided in our courts for the first time on April 13, 1818, at which term Craig was tried and convicted of murder By the act of March 12, 1821, the Fifteenth Judicial District was erected, comprising the counties of Delaware and Chester, and Ross remained judge of the Seventh District,—Bucks and Montgomery. Hon John Ross, in April, 1830, was appointed an associate judge of the Supreme Court, to the seat made vacant by the death of Judge Todd On May 22, 1821, Governor Heister appointed Isaac Darlington, of the borough of West Chester, president judge of the Fifteenth District, and the latter sat as such for the first time at the old court-house in Chester, Oct 23, 1821

Isaac Darlington was in his fortieth year when appointed to the bench, his birth having occurred Dec 13, 1781 He was by trade a blacksmith, having worked at the forge with his father, but disliking that occupation, he taught school a short time, and finally, when in his eighteenth year, entered the office of Joseph Hemphill, at West Chester At the November term, 1801, he was admitted to the bar, although lacking two or three weeks being of age, his examiners remarking that a few days more or less was of little consequence when the student had passed an examination so creditable to him He rose rapidly at the bar, and having served a term in the Legislature in 1807–8, declined further election, believing that it was a hindrance in his profession During the latter part of the war of 1812 he served with the militia of Pennsylvania, encamped at Marcus Hook for the defense of Philadelphia In 1816 he was elected a member of the Fifteenth Congress, again declining renomination At the time of his appointment as judge he was deputy attorney-general of Chester County By the Constitution of 1838, his term of office would have expired on Feb 27, 1839, and to avoid the operation of that clause the bar suggested that the judge should resign before the provisions of the Constitution went into effect, it being the unanimous desire of the profession that he should continue on the bench In accordance with this request he tendered his resignation, it was accepted, and shortly thereafter he was reappointed judge of the district by Governor Ritner On Jan 15, 1839, Governor Porter was inaugurated, and, he knowing that the object was to give Judge Darlington a further term of ten years, instructed Attorney-General Douglass to sue out a *quo warranto* On Monday, April 29, 1839, the matter was to have been heard by the Supreme Court, but the Saturday previous Judge Isaac Darlington died at his home in West Chester of gout, to which he had been subject for years When his death was announced in the Supreme Court, Chief Justice Gibson dismissed the proceedings, at the same time paying a high tribute to the character and learning of the dead justice

The judges of the Supreme Court in their circuits occasionally held sessions in the old court-room at Chester On Thursday, Aug 1, 1828, Chief Justice Gibson presided at the trial of a feigned issue upon an appeal from the Orphans' Court, in a suit by the executor of the estate of John Crosby, the late judge, against John F Hill The case occupied three days, and was ably tried, Benjamin Tilghman and Samuel Edwards representing the plaintiff, and Joseph R Ingersoll and Archibald T Dick the defendant The jury retired on Saturday evening, and returned a verdict for the plaintiff on Monday morning The *Weekly Visitor*, published at Chester, for Aug 8, 1828, stated

"To show the unwearied industry and perseverance of Judge Gibson in his official duties, it is worthy of remark that, on Monday morning at six o'clock, he left Philadelphia for this place, where he arrived at about eight, received the verdict of the jury, and at nine was on board the boat returning to the city"

On May 16, 1839, Governor Porter appointed Thomas S Bell to the judgeship made vacant by Darlington's death He was a Philadelphian by birth, and, like his predecessor, was admitted to the bar six months before he attained his majority In May, 1821, he located at West Chester, and in two years thereafter was deputy attorney-general of Chester County, continuing in that office for six years He was a member of the Constitutional Convention of 1837, and was returned as elected to the State Senate in 1838, and took a prominent part in the difficulties characterizing the beginning of the legislative proceedings in January following, known as the "Buckshot War" His seat in that body was contested by and awarded to his competitor Judge Bell was in his fortieth year when he was appointed to the bench, which he certainly adorned by his learning and his courteous bearing to the bar and public alike, although, on one occasion, in Delaware County, he aroused considerable feeling in sentencing a child ten years of age to a protracted term of imprisonment for stealing a small sum of money

On Dec 18, 1846, Governor Shunk appointed him one of the puisne judges of the Supreme Court, a position he filled until Dec 1, 1851, when the office became elective Judge Bell died June 6, 1861, in his sixty-first year, a cancer with which he had long been troubled finally terminating his life

The vacancy occasioned in this district by the removal of Judge Bell to the Supreme bench was attempted to be filled by Governor Shunk, who, in December, 1846, appointed John M Forster, of Harrisburg, to the office. His bearing on the bench was excessively polite, but he did not create a favorable impression; and, although his appointment, when first presented in the Senate, had been confirmed, the objection from the district was so unanimous that it was reconsidered and finally rejected. Governor Shunk thereupon appointed James Nill, of Chambersburg, early in February, 1847, to the vacant seat on the bench. Judge Nill had a fair knowledge of law, but the feeling that the appointment was not one which should have been made was strong enough to secure Judge Nill's rejection by a tie vote in the Senate when the name was presented to that body for confirmation.

The courts of Delaware County being without a president at the March term, 1848, the session was held by Associate Judges Engle and Leiper, the former charging the grand jury. Although the criminal side of the court had been conducted as well as usual, the civil cases (many of them involving questions of nice distinctions of law) were continued, and the bar of Delaware as well as Chester County was anxious that the vacant place on the bench should be filled. To that end the lawyers in the district united in the request to Governor Shunk that he would appoint his son-in-law, Henry Chapman, of Doylestown, president judge. The Governor assented to the petition, but he was named too late to take part at the March term in Delaware County, as just stated. Perhaps a more acceptable selection could not have been made, for in all respects Judge Chapman filled the measure demanded by the bar and people.

It was during his incumbency that the county-seat was removed to Media, the last court being held in the old building at Chester May 26, 1851, and when it adjourned, on Friday, the 30th, the ancient structure was dismantled of its furniture.

Under the provisions of the amendments to the Constitution changing the judicial office from an appointive to an elective one, the term of Judge Chapman, as also those of the associate judges (Leiper and Engle), expired by limitation at the close of the year 1851. So acceptably had the former presided in the district that both parties signalized their willingness to continue him on the bench if he would allow his name to be presented to the people, but as the Constitution positively required the judges should be residents of the district during the period in which they served, which he could not do without serious inconvenience, he was compelled to decline the nomination. On Monday, Nov. 24, 1851, for the last time Judges Chapman, Leiper, and Engle held court, the session continuing until Wednesday, the 26th of that month. All business having been disposed of, the court was about to adjourn, when Hon. Edward Darlington rose and with a brief and appropriate address presented the following resolutions:

"At a meeting of the bar of Delaware County, held at the Charter House, in the borough of Media, Monday, Nov. 24, 1851, on motion, Edward Darlington, Esq., was appointed chairman, and Joseph R. Morris, secretary.

"The object of the meeting was stated by the chair, whereupon John M. Broomall, Esq., offered the following resolutions, which being seconded by Robert McCay, Jr., Esq., were unanimously adopted:

"*Resolved*, That we look with profound regret upon the approaching period which will terminate the judicial career of the Hon. Henry Chapman as president judge of the court of this county.

"*Resolved*, That his well-tried legal abilities and his strict integrity and impartiality have entitled him to the respect and confidence, as well of ourselves as of the people of the county, who have not willingly parted with his services.

"*Resolved*, That the judges of the court carry with them in their voluntary retirement from the bench our best wishes for their future happiness and prosperity, and we tender to them our sincere thanks for the uniform kindness and courtesy which has always characterized their intercourse with the bar.

"On motion of Charles D. Manly, Esq., the chair was instructed to present a copy of the foregoing resolutions to the bench in open court."

The judges were entirely unprepared for this testimonial of good feeling from the bar, but Judge Chapman rose, thanked the bar and the people of the county for the forbearance they had ever shown toward his failings, and the uniform kindness and respect which had been extended him while on the bench. Remarks of a similar tenor then followed from Judges Leiper and Engle. The proceeding was not an empty form or ceremony, but was prompted on the part of the bar and responded to by the bench by the mutual esteem entertained by the one for the other.

Judge Chapman having declined nomination, at the election held in October, 1851, Townsend Haines, of West Chester, was chosen president judge of the courts. Judge Haines, when elevated to the bench, was sixty years of age, his birth occurring Jan. 7, 1792. His early life was passed on his father's farm, but during the intervals of labor he applied himself diligently in acquiring information which was useful to him in after-years. In 1815, in his twenty-third year,—previous to which time he had taught school,—he entered the office of Isaac Darlington (afterwards judge), and was called to the bar in 1818. His practice the first year was very meagre; indeed, it never was extensive, although he was very able in criminal cases, but in heavy civil litigation he was rarely engaged. His brilliant powers of advocacy were recognized, and when a jury was the tribunal to decide a controversy, Mr. Haines was often employed to make the address to that body; but when questions involving great principles of law were being discussed he never appeared to advantage. He was an adroit cross-examiner, but he relied on his natural talent in debate, and was averse to the laborious study which always characterizes a great lawyer. Mr. Haines drifted naturally into politics. In 1826–27 he was a member of the Legislature, and the following year was nominated for Congress, but was unexpectedly defeated, the popularity of Andrew Jackson carrying the Democratic ticket in a strong Federal district onward to victory. On the resignation and death of Governor Shunk, William F. Johnson, the Whig Speaker of the Senate, by virtue of that office, assumed the gubernatorial office under the Constitution, and in July, 1848, he appointed Mr Haines Secretary of the Commonwealth, which position he retained under Johnson, who was re-elected in the fall of the year 1848 After serving the full term as secretary, in February, 1850, Mr Haines was appointed treasurer of the United States by President Taylor While discharging the duties of that office he was nominated to the judgeship of the Fifteenth Judicial District, to which position he was elected, defeating Judge Thomas S Bell, whose term on the Supreme bench under the Constitution ended in December of that year Haines thereupon resigned the treasurership of the United States and returned to West Chester He was commissioned by Governor Johnson Nov 6, 1881

On the bench he was respected as a lawyer, and his social qualities ever rendered him a favorite with the bar and public He was a noted conversationalist, and it is said no man could relate an anecdote better than he While holding court at Media the judge, on one occasion, desired to consult the Digest, and asked Reuben Litzenberg, then a newly-appointed tipstaff, to bring "Purdon" to him The name was new to Litzenberg but off he started to hunt the man, whom he supposed he was directed to straightway carry before the court He searched through the building without success, and at length returning, he went to the judge at side bar, and stated in a low voice, "Judge, I guess the man's gone, I can't find him anywhere" "Man! man!" wrathfully exclaimed the judge, "you're a stupid ass I don't want any man I sent you for a book" It is also told of the judge that on one occasion, as he was entering the court-house, a hardened offender, who at almost every Quarter Session was present, charged with selling liquor without license, and who had recently undergone a sentence for that misdemeanor, accosted him "Well, judge," he said, "I'm out now" "Yes, yes, I see," was the reply, "but it's no fault of mine I gave you all I had in my pocket that I could give you"

Judge Haines presided for the last term at November court, 1861, and on the 28th of that month the bar of Delaware County presented resolutions of esteem to him on retiring from the bench

At the expiration of his term of office Judge Haines declined to be a candidate for re-election, but returned to practice in West Chester, continuing therein until his death in October, 1865, in his seventy-fourth year He possessed rare talent for versification, his ballad of "Bob Fletcher" being a rustic picture which still deservedly maintains its popularity

At the October election, in 1861, Hon William Butler was chosen to succeed to the judicial office vacated by Judge Haines Mr Butler had at the time of his election been sixteen years in practice at the Chester County bar, having been admitted in 1843 In the fall of 1856 he was elected district attorney of Chester County, continuing in that office until the fall of 1859 Judge Butler was commissioned by Governor Curtin Nov 20, 1861, entering upon the duties of the office in the following December, presiding for the first time in Delaware County at the February court, 1862 He soon rose to high rank among the judges of the State. His mind was analytical, and with such rapidity in the trial of a case he grasped and understood the point at issue, that the lawyers engaged often stood amazed in finding how soon the case, under his judicial sifting, was divested of all redundant circumstances or immaterial pleading As a *nisi prius* judge he had few equals and never a superior He presided at the trial of Udderzook for the murder of Gross at the Oyer and Terminer of Chester County, October, 1873 The case was one which attracted much attention throughout the country, and the charge of Judge Butler was a model for its clearness and comprehensiveness On Feb 12, 1879, he was appointed to the United States district judgeship made vacant by the death of Judge Cadwalader, an office which he still fills

The vacancy on the bench occasioned by the erection of the Thirty second Judicial District was filled in April, 1874, by Governor Hartranft, who appointed Hon John M Broomall president judge The latter was born in Upper Chichester township, and his family had taken a prominent part in the history of Delaware County for nearly two centuries In early life, while still a student at Friends' Academy, at Wilmington, he taught in that institution with much success In 1837 he began reading law under Judge Bouvier, of Philadelphia, and on Aug 24, 1840, was admitted to the bar of Delaware County At first he was inclined to devote himself to agricultural pursuits on the homestead farm in Chichester, but by degrees, and apparently without effort on his part, it began to be noised about that he was a bright, smart fellow, and knew as much law as any of the attorneys So, imperceptibly, he drifted into practice, and soon found pleasure in the clash of argument and excitement of a sharply-contested trial Politics and law usually go hand-in-hand, hence in 1851 and 1852, very naturally, Mr Broomall was a representative of Delaware County in the Legislature, and in 1854 a member of the State Revenue Board He was a member of the Thirty-eighth, Thirty-ninth, and Fortieth Congresses, being first elected thereto in 1862

In the fall of 1862, when Washington City was threatened, as also the invasion of Pennsylvania, by Lee's army, John M Broomall commanded Company C, Sixteenth Regiment Pennsylvania militia In the summer of 1863, previous to the battle of Gettysburg, Mr. Broomall was mustered in as captain of Company C, Twenty-ninth Regiment, emergency men, being in service from June 19th to August 1st of that year

Twice Mr Broomall has been a member of the Electoral College of Pennsylvania, first, in 1860, at Abraham Lincoln's first election, and in 1872, when

Gen. Grant was chosen President for the second term. In 1873 he was a delegate to the Constitutional Convention, and on the floor of that assemblage his remarks were always listened to with attention and consideration, and he was recognized as among the leaders in thought in that body. When that Constitution was adopted, under its provisions the county of Delaware became the Thirty-second Judicial District, and as before stated, in April, 1874, Mr. Broomall was appointed the first president judge, and was qualified on May 2d. At the Republican County Convention of the same year Judge Broomall was nominated for the office for the term of ten years, but at the ensuing election he was not successful.

Judge Broomall has been a busy man throughout his whole career. Far-sighted, and possessed of comprehensive views and remarkable executive abilities, shortly after being called to the bar he became impressed with the belief that Chester was peculiarly advantageously located for a manufacturing centre, and with that purpose in view he and several others labored to give the ancient hamlet a direction to that end, and how well that object was obtained the thriving city of Chester and its growing suburban districts fully attests. As an orator Judge Broomall will be recalled by his "Remarks on the Life and Character of Thaddeus Stevens," delivered in the House of Representatives, at Washington, Dec. 17, 1868, and his oration at the Bi-Centenary of the Landing of William Penn at Chester, Oct. 23, 1882. Judge Broomall, notwithstanding his active, useful life, had kept abreast with modern thought in science and literature. As a writer he is vigorous and comprehensive, remembering Lord Coke's reference to "apt words." In 1876, on the appointment of the Delaware County Institute of Science, he wrote the "History of Delaware County for the Past Century," an admirable *résumé* of the happenings in this locality during the first hundred years of the nation's life, and in 1872 wrote a highly creditable "History of Chester" for Moran's "Delaware River and West Jersey Railroad Commercial Directory."

Judge Broomall was succeeded on the bench by the present incumbent, Judge Clayton, who, on Jan. 4, 1875, assumed the duties of the office. Thomas J. Clayton was also to the manor born, his ancestry having settled at Marcus Hook previous to the royal charter to Penn.

The future judge was born in Bethel township, Jan. 20, 1826, and in early life proposed studying medicine, but changing his intentions he read law in Wilmington, and was admitted to the bar of Delaware County, Nov. 24, 1851, this being the second time court was held at Media, and the last time Judge Chapman presided in the district. Mr. Clayton removed to Philadelphia in 1852, where he entered the ranks of the profession and rapidly acquired a large and remunerative practice, in jury cases his forensic powers soon bringing him into prominence. In 1856, Governor Pollock appointed him on his staff with the rank of colonel, the only office he ever held of a political character outside the line of his profession. In 1868 he made a tour of Europe, and while abroad contributed a series of letters to the *Delaware County Republican* descriptive of his travels, which were subsequently published in book form. In 1873 he again passed the summer vacation in the Old World, and, as on his former visit, he furnished from time to time an account of his journeying to the county press. In the fall of 1874 he was nominated by the Independent Republicans for the office of president judge of this district, the Democrats making no nomination, and at the election on October 3d of the same year he was chosen to that office, the duties of which he is still discharging. Judge Clayton is social in his disposition, an agreeable conversationalist, and speaks French with fluency. As a lawyer he stands well with the profession throughout the State, many of his opinions, as published in the *Delaware County Reporter*, being frequently cited in other districts with approval. In January, 1880, the bar of Chester County tendered a complimentary banquet to Judge Clayton at West Chester, he having been called to preside in the courts there in cases with which Judge Futhey had been connected as counsel previous to the latter's being raised to the bench. The printed bill of fare on that occasion was a rare specimen of legal wit, which the bar of Chester County may well recall as creditable to those who prepared it.

The act of Sept. 26, 1789, creating the county of Delaware provided that "the justices of the Courts of Quarter Session and Common Pleas now commissioned within the limits of the county of Delaware and those that may hereafter be commissioned or any three of them, shall and may hold courts," and the act conferred on those justices all the powers, rights, jurisdiction, and authorities of justices of the county courts of other counties.[1] Some doubts having been suggested as to the validity of this clause in the act, the Supreme Executive Council on Oct. 9, 1789, determined to be advised on the constitutionality of that section, hence it was

"*Resolved*, That the opinion of the attorney-general be taken upon the following question, viz., 'Whether justices of the peace and pleas who have been commissioned for a certain county, and a part of that county erected into a separate county, can continue to exercise the powers of the peace and pleas in that part erected into a new county and separated from the old one?'"

The same day Attorney-General Bradford wrote his opinion, which was submitted to Council the following morning. He states,—

"I have considered the clause in the act of Assembly for erecting Delaware County. . . . As the Constitution vests the appointment of all judges in the Supreme Executive Council, and a new court is here erected, I am of the opinion that no act of the Legislature can appoint the judges of that court, or give any persons authority to act as such without being commissioned for that purpose by the President and Council;

[1] 2 Smith's "Laws of Pennsylvania," p. 490; Bliss' "Delaware County Digest," pp. 2 and 39.

that part of the act, therefore, must be merely void. As to justices of the peace, they having been already elected by the people and residing in their proper districts, I am of opinion that such authority may be continued by an act of the Legislature, and that such an act would not infringe upon the Constitution."[1]

The Supreme Executive Council, acting on this opinion, appointed the judges of the courts two days thereafter, excepting in the case of William Richardson Atlee, whose commission being subsequently to the act of Sept. 26, 1786, was valid. Following is a list of all the associate justices and judges of the courts of Delaware County from its erection until the Constitution of 1874 abolished the office:

	Commissioned.
William Richardson Atlee	Sept. 28, 1789
Richard Hill Morris	Oct. 12, 1789
Thomas Levis	Oct. 12, 1789
John Pearson	Oct. 12, 1789
George Pearce	Oct. 12, 1789
Elisha Price	March 16, 1790
Joel Willis	July 15, 1790
Under Constitution of 1790:	
John Sellers	Sept. 17, 1791
Richard Riley	Sept. 17, 1791
Mark Willcox	Sept. 17, 1791
Hugh Lloyd	April 24, 1792
Benjamin Brannon	June 5, 1794
John Crosby	April 26, 1799
John Pierce	Jan. 5, 1823
William Anderson	Jan. 5, 1826
Joseph Engle[2]	Jan. 5, 1827
Henry Myer	Dec. 27, 1833
George Smith	Dec. 28, 1836
Under Constitution of 1838:	
Joseph Engle	Jan. 26, 1842
Joseph Engle	March 11, 1847
George G. Leiper	Feb. 25, 1843
George G. Leiper	Feb. 16, 1848
James Andrews	Nov. 10, 1851
Sketchley Morton	Nov. 10, 1851
Frederick J. Hinkson	Nov. 12, 1856
James Andrews	Nov. 12, 1856
Charles R. Williamson	Jan. 10, 1860
George Smith	Nov. 23, 1861
James Andrews	Nov. 23, 1861
Thomas Reese	Nov. 8, 1866
Bartine Smith	Nov. 8, 1866
Thomas Reese	Nov. 17, 1871
Bartine Smith	Nov. 17, 1871

William Richardson Atlee was commissioned one of the justices of the Court of Common Pleas of Delaware County Sept. 28, 1789, two days after the act erecting the county of Delaware became a law. The bounty of the Supreme Executive Council did not stop at this, but they showered on Atlee that day the offices of prothonotary, clerk of the Quarter Sessions and Orphans' Court. Under the resolution of Council, June 11, 1777, prothonotaries sat as judges of the Court of Common Pleas. In November, 1790, he was married to Margaret, only daughter of Gen. Wayne, settled at Chester,[3] and on May 9, 1791, purchased a greater part of the triangular lot between Market Street and Edgmont Avenue, and from Fifth Street to the railroad. There he lived in a stone dwelling, which was torn down to make place for the house of the late Mrs. Gray. On Sept. 4, 1791, he was reappointed by Governor Mifflin to the offices of prothonotary, etc., and again on March 16, 1792. At the next court following, April term, 1792, the grand jury made this presentment:

"*To the Honorable Court of Quarter Sessions now sitting:*—The Grand Inquest for the Court of Delaware, Present William Richardson Atlee, Prothonotary and Register for the Probate of Wills, &c., for said county for extortion in the following instances, viz.:

"For charging of his fees on the several writs of Partition hereinafter mentioned, three pounds, viz.: First, For issuing a writ for the division of the estate of Jacob Richards. Second, For issuing a writ for the division of the estate of Margaret Smith and the heirs of Rebecca Garrett. Third, For issuing a writ for the division of the estate of John McIlvain. Fourth, For issuing a writ for the division of the estate of David Gibson. Fifth, For issuing a writ for the division of the estate of William and Reese Peters.

"For charging John Travis his fees on an action brought against him and ended the first court, thirteen shillings and sixpence. For charging Peter Defield, on an action brought against Charles Lindsay ended before the court, fourteen shillings and sixpence. For charging Joseph Lewis fourteen shillings and sixpence, ended in like manner.

"As Register for charging and receiving from the executors of the estate of John Hunt two pounds, eleven shillings and sixpence for probate and granting Letters of Administration.

"Also for charging and receiving from the executors of the estate of Joseph Davis, two pounds, eleven shillings and sixpence for Probate and Granting Letters of Administration and also for charging and receiving a fee of one pound, two shillings and sixpence for answering the simple question whether a bond was real or personal estate, which we are of the opinion is illegal, he not been an attorney or counsellor of record in this county.

"Also for charging and receiving of Alice Spear, a poor woman, one pound, five shillings and sixpence for two guardianship orders, altho' she has paid Miles McCarty three shillings for drawing petitions to present to the Court to obtain the same.

"By order of the Grand Jury,

"David Bevan, *Foreman.*"

At the July session the grand jury found true bills of indictment against Atlee on all the charges; the cases were called on trial at the October term, and on all the prosecutions the defendant was acquitted. Atlee understood the fee bill, and notwithstanding the assaults thus made upon him, held his office with a tenacious grasp, until, desiring to enter the list of attorneys, he yielded the place to Davis Bevan April 6, 1796, and on the 26th of July following was admitted to practice in the courts of Delaware County, after which date he passed out of our annals so far as I have information.

On Oct. 12, 1789, Richard Hill Morris was commissioned by President Mifflin justice of the Court of Common Pleas. He was appointed a justice of the Court of Quarter Sessions of Chester County in 1786, but beyond that fact I have no knowledge of Judge Morris. The same day George Pearce, of Aston, was commissioned Justice of the Common Pleas. He was a justice of Chester County in 1784, and during the Revolutionary war was lieutenant-colonel of the Third Battalion of militia. Other than these facts, I know nothing of Judge Pearce's career. John Pearson was also commissioned the same day. He was a resident of Darby and a Revolutionary soldier. He was first lieutenant in the Eleventh Pennsylvania Line, and was promoted captain Sept. 7, 1777. The regiment suffered so severely at Brandywine that on July 1, 1778, it was consolidated with the Tenth Regiment, in which organization Capt. Pearson was still retained

[1] Colonial Records, vol. xvi. pp. 186-88.

[2] Judge Engle was appointed in 1827, but the date of the commission I have not learned. Either it is not of record or I have overlooked it in my researches.

[3] Martin's "History of Chester," p. 252.

in command of a company. On Jan. 17, 1781, he was transferred to the Second Pennsylvania, and on Jan. 1, 1783, held a commission on the 3d, but appears to have resigned about that time. In October, 1778, he was on recruiting service in Philadelphia, and on the 6th of that month addressed a letter to the Supreme Executive Council, complaining that Timothy Matlack, secretary of that body, had spoken discouragingly to him respecting the money required to pay recruits, and he had then on his personal credit borrowed one hundred pounds to pay "five fine fellows," and could not "get a farthing of it." At the January sessions, 1793, while he was on the bench, an indictment was sent before the grand jury, in which he was charged with having written a libelous article against Nathaniel Newlin, which appeared in Bradford's *Pennsylvania Journal* in October, 1792, but the bill was ignored. In the fall of 1793, Judge Pearson was active in soliciting funds in Delaware County, to be applied to the relief of the sufferers in Philadelphia during the yellow fever scourge in that city, after which date I have no further information respecting him.

On Oct. 12, 1789, Thomas Levis was appointed one of the justices of the Court of Common Pleas of Delaware County. My impression is that he resided in Springfield. The first record I find of Judge Levis is in 1770, when he appears as one of the assessors of Chester County,—a board of six persons performed the duty at that time in the entire county,—and continued in the office until 1773, when he became one of the county commissioners. At the election held in Chester County, July 8, 1776, to choose delegates to the Constitutional Convention of 1776, he was one of the judges at Chester borough. During the war he was a captain of a militia company, and Oct. 1, 1777, was directed, with six other militia officers, to seize arms, blankets, shoes and stockings, etc., in that district for the use of the Continental army, the levy to be made on persons believed to entertain feelings not in accord with American independence. On May 6, 1778, he was appointed one of the commissioners of confiscated estates, and in a letter dated July 18th of that year, he complained that the printer had made a mistake by misplacing a letter so that a Whig was transposed by the proclamation into a Tory, and he was not pleased with the change. He was one of the sub-lieutenants of Chester County, and Sept. 24, 1784, was commissioned one of the justices of the Common Pleas for Ridley, Springfield, Marple, Upper and Nether Providence, a position which was not new to him, for he was appointed to the like office in July 25, 1777. He was county treasurer in 1778, and probably in 1782–84. No record appears at West Chester for those years, which is the only break for a number of years, and we learn from the minutes of the Supreme Executive Council that on Feb. 21, 1788, a certificate was filed from Edward Burd, "that Thomas Levis, Esquire, hath entered sufficient security to prosecute with effect an appeal from the settlement of his accounts as late Treasurer of the county of Chester by the Comptroller General was read, and the said appeal allowed." He was appointed a justice of the Court of Common Pleas in 1789. In 1799 he was lieutenant-colonel of the Sixty-fifth Regiment Pennsylvania militia, after which date I lose all record of Col. Levis.

Elisha Price was commissioned justice of the Court of Common Pleas and Quarter Sessions, March 16, 1790, but as I have given the main particulars of his life in a note to the ballad "Lament over Chester's Mother," it is unnecessary to reproduce it here; and of Joel Willis, who was commissioned justice of the Common Pleas July 15, 1790, I know nothing other than that fact.

On Sept. 17, 1791, Governor Mifflin appointed John Sellers one of the associate judges of the courts of Delaware County. A sketch of Judge Sellers will be found in the history of the township of Darby.

Sept. 17, 1791, Governor Mifflin appointed Richard Riley an associate judge of Delaware County, in which office he continued to serve until 1808, sitting for the last time at the October court of that year. He was of English parentage, and was born at Marcus Hook, Dec. 14, 1735. At twenty-nine years of age, in 1764, he was one of the county assessors, and the same year he was appointed one of the justices of the county, whose commission then required that they should hold court. In 1770 he was one of the justices commissioned to hold a special court in Chester County for the trial of negroes; and on the 3d day of March, in that year, he, with William Parker, held such a court in Chester, at which was tried "Negro Martin," the slave of Thomas Smith, of Tinicum, on a charge of rape. Riley was an earnest Whig during the Revolution, and was one of the thirteen members of the Committee of Correspondence of Chester County appointed at the meeting held at Chester, July 13, 1774, and was one of the eight delegates to the Provincial Conference at Philadelphia, July 15th, of that year, which took decided action advocating resistance to the encroachments of Great Britain on the rights of the colony, and requesting the Assembly to appoint delegates to the Continental Congress, which met in Philadelphia, September 3d following. He was one of the delegates to the second Provincial Convention, which met in Philadelphia, Jan. 23, 1775, when he advocated instructing the delegates from Pennsylvania, appointed by that convention to Congress, which assembled May 10, 1775, to vote for independence. On June 30th of that year he was appointed by the Assembly one of the Committee of Safety, representing Chester County; and on Jan. 17, 1776, was, with Cols. Wayne and Johnson and Mr. Bartholomew, appointed an inspector of arms provided by the Committee of Safety for Chester County. That he was earnest in his efforts to render an attack on Philadelphia almost impossible, by extending the fortifications below Marcus Hook, is shown in his letter of Feb 15, 1776, to the committee In 1777, Riley was again commissioned a justice of the county After the erection of Delaware County, he was elected a member of the Legislature for the year 1790-91, and, as before mentioned, in 1792 was commissioned associate judge It is related that he was a nervous man and easily irritated One cold night, in the early part of this century, an Irishman, knowing this peculiarity, knocked at the door of his residence in Marcus Hook, after the judge was in bed His honor, putting his head out of the window, inquired who it was, and what was wanted The stranger replied that he had an important matter, respecting which he wanted his opinion The judge hastily dressed and came down "What is it, my man, you want to see me about?" "I was awanting to know, your honor, which side of the river this is" "This side, you infernal fool!" roared the judge, as he slammed the door to with a bang Judge Riley died Aug 27, 1820, in his eighty-fifth year

On Sept 17, 1791, Governor Mifflin commissioned Mark Wilcox one of the associate judges of Delaware County, an office he retained until about 1822 Mark Wilcox was the son of Thomas Wilcox, who settled in Concord in 1727, on the west branch of Chester Creek, where about that date he built the second paper-mill in the United States, now known as Ivy Mills The settler died in 1779, leaving the business to his son, Mark, who was born on the estate in 1743 During the Revolutionary war much of the paper used in printing the Continental money, as well as the official blanks required by Congress and the State authorities, was made at the old mill on Chester Creek He was judge of the election held to select delegates to the Constitutional Convention of 1776 In 1777 the Executive Council impressed forty-eight reams of writing-paper at his mills for the use of that body, and it was not paid for until March 19, 1783, when an order for sixty-eight pounds in specie was given to Mark Wilcox in settlement of the claim In 1777 he was one of the county assessors, and in 1780, under the law requiring registration of slaves, he reported six slaves for life as his property On April 3, 1788, the Supreme Executive Council appointed five commissioners, under the act of March 28th, of that year, to open certain roads in the counties of Northampton and Luzerne, in which commission Mark Wilcox was included The work confided to the committee was performed satisfactorily, for on April 28th, of the same year, Council decided that one thousand pounds should be paid to the committee for their trouble In 1788, Mark Wilcox was a member of the General Assembly from Chester County, in 1799 he was lieutenant-colonel of the One Hundred and Tenth Regiment, and, after the erection of Delaware, was for nearly thirty years one of the associate judges He died in 1827, aged eighty-four years

Governor Mifflin, April 24, 1792, commissioned Hugh Lloyd, of Darby, one of the associate judges of the courts of Delaware County, and he continued on the bench a third of a century, the longest term in our judicial history He was born in 1742, and when the difficulties preceding the Revolutionary war were dividing the populace, he took active sides with the colonists He was one of the committee of thirteen appointed at the county convention, held at Chester, July 13, 1774, as delegates to the convention of similar committees from the other counties in the province, which assembled in Philadelphia July 15th, of that year, and from whose action the Continental Congress, which met in the same city on the 5th of September following, had its origin He was one of the committee appointed at the county convention, Dec 20, 1774, to carry into execution the association of the late Continental Congress, and he was also one of the ten delegates from Chester County to the Provincial Convention which met in Philadelphia, Jan 23, 1775 Just previous to the Declaration of Independence he was one of the thirteen delegates from the county to the Convention in Philadelphia on June 18, 1776, which declared that all authority of Great Britain should be suppressed in the province, and called a convention to meet on the 15th of July following to frame a constitutional government Strange as it now seems, he was one of the judges of election in the borough of Chester on July 8th, when delegates to that convention—he being a candidate—were voted for Early in the war he was appointed colonel of the Third Battalion of Chester County militia, and his command was frequently called into service during the latter part of 1777 and the first six months of the year following After peace was declared Col Lloyd pursued the even tenor of his way, but when Delaware County was erected, in 1789, he was one of the representatives in the General Assembly, and was re-elected to the same office in 1791 In 1792 he was appointed one of the associate judges of the county of Delaware in the place of Joel Willis, serving faithfully on the bench until finding the weight of years pressing upon him he tendered his resignation to Governor Shulze as follows

"I, the within named Associate Judge of Delaware County, aged 83 years 10 months and 9 days, by attending every court for 33 years—one Orphans' Court only excepted—having performed the duties of the within commission to the best of my judgment and ability, do by these presents resign and surrender up my said commission to his Excellency, the Governor, with the hope that a successor may be appointed to the satisfaction of the majority of said county In testimony whereof I have hereunto set my hand this 31st day of December, A D 1825 With sentiment of regard, &c.,

"HUGH LLOYD"

Tradition relates that Judge Lloyd, who, on one occasion, being asked if the duties devolving on an associate judge were not onerous, replied, "Yes, very I sat five years on the same bench in the old court-house at Chester without opening my mouth One day, however, towards night, after listening to the details of a long and tedious trial, the president leaning over towards me and putting his arms across my shoulders, asked me a question 'Judge,' said he, 'don't you think this bench is infernally hard?' To this important question I replied, 'I thought it were' And that's the only opinion I ever gave during my long judicial career "[1]

At the advanced age of ninety-three, Judge Lloyd died of paralysis "The old machine had broken down and can't be repaired," he remarked to those who, hearing him fall to the floor, ran to his assistance Two days thereafter he died

Benjamin Brannon was appointed by Governor Mifflin, June 5, 1794, one of the judges of the courts of Delaware County I have gathered very little information respecting Judge Brannon He resided in Upper Darby, was an earnest Whig, and during the year 1776 was appointed to instruct the people of Chester County in the mode of making saltpetre for the State powder-mills In 1777 he was one of the sub-lieutenants of the county, and on June 11th of that year applied for cannon to arm several artillery companies formed in his jurisdiction, and on July 29th five hundred pounds was given him to pay bounty to substitutes He was county commissioner in 1779, and in 1782 he was a representative in the Assembly from Chester County Other than the facts stated I have no record of Judge Brannon

John Crosby, of Ridley, was appointed by Governor Mifflin, April 26, 1799, one of the associate judges of Delaware County He, like his fellow-associate, Hugh Lloyd, was a descendant of the early English settlers who emigrated to Pennsylvania when Penn acquired title to the province He was born at the family homestead, on Ridley Creek, March 11, 1747/8 In 1776, in his twenty-ninth year, he entered the service as first lieutenant in a company of the First Battalion of Pennsylvania militia, attached to the Flying Camp, which had been recruited by his brother-in-law, Capt Culin It is related that on the day the organization was mustered in at the White Horse Tavern, one of the privates, enraged at something said by Capt Culin, shot that officer, inflicting a wound of which he died Crosby thereupon succeeded to the command, and as such marched the company to the encampment at Perth Amboy After the capture of Philadelphia by the British, in the fall of 1777, Crosby (a militia officer and not in the Pennsylvania troops enlisted for the war) was with Governor Porter, intercepting the foraging parties of the enemy

One night in the winter of 1777-78 he was at his home in Ridley when a boat's crew from a British man-of-war, lying off Chester, ascended the creek and took him prisoner Crosby was in the act of washing his face at the pump, near the house, when he was captured He was taken to New York and confined on the British ship "Falmouth" During his imprisonment, which lasted six months, his hair turned white, consequent on the harsh treatment received and insufficient food then furnished to the American prisoners of war He was finally released on parole, his wife going to New York, at great personal risk, to intercede with the English authorities in his behalf John Crosby, as stated, was commissioned, in 1799, associate judge of Delaware County, and continued on the bench until 1826 He died about the date given as the conclusion of his judicial career

On Jan 5, 1823, John Peirce was appointed associate judge of the Court of Common Pleas He died in Nether Providence in December, 1833, aged seventy-nine years, but beyond his appointment and death I have no further information respecting Judge Pierce Henry Myers was appointed to the place on the bench made vacant by his death

William Anderson was born in Virginia[2] in 1762, and although only fifteen years of age, joined the Continental army, serving therein five years, and was present at the siege of Yorktown and the surrender of Lord Cornwallis After the war he settled in Chester, and became the landlord of the Columbia House, which hostelry he purchased in 1796 In 1803 he erected the Anderson mansion, at Fifth and Welsh Streets, Chester He was a member of the Eleventh and Twelfth Congresses of the United States, and served for a third term in the Fifteenth In 1824 he was chairman of the committee of Delaware County[3] on the reception of Lafayette When the committees from Delaware, Chester, and Montgomery Counties, together with a committee from the immediate vicinity of Valley Forge, met the marquis at the State-House, in Philadelphia, September 29th of that year, Maj Anderson, being a Revolutionary soldier, was selected to make the address, on behalf of all the committees, to the "Nation's Guest," and when the latter came to the borough of Chester he accepted the major's hospitality On Jan 5, 1826, Governor Shulze appointed Maj Anderson one of the judges of the county courts, which position he resigned to accept an office in the custom-house in Philadelphia. His daughter, Evelina, became the wife of Commodore David Porter Maj Anderson died Dec 16, 1829, aged sixty-seven years

Joseph Engle, of Nether Providence, was born Jan 10, 1770 He was thirty-six years of age before he attained any office of prominence in the county, being elected in 1806 one of the commissioners, and on May 24, 1809, was commissioned prothonotary, recorder, register, and clerk of the courts, to which office he was recommissioned on Jan 14, 1812, and again on Dec 20, 1814 In 1824 he was one of the committee

---

1 Martin's "History of Chester," p. 196

2 Lanman's "Dictionary of Congress" asserts that Maj Anderson was born in Chester County, a statement which conflicts with family traditions, and, besides, his name does not appear among the Revolutionary officers from Pennsylvania

3 The committee from Delaware County consisted of the following gentlemen William Anderson, Dr Samuel Anderson, Joseph Engle, George G Leiper, Samuel Edwards, Esq, Archibald T Dick, Esq, William Martin, and Henry Myers

of five appointed by Delaware County to receive Lafayette, and in the fall of that year he was again elected one of the commissioners. In 1826-27 he was a member of the Legislature, and in the latter year was appointed by Governor Shulze to the associate judgeship made vacant by the resignation of Maj. Anderson. His long association with the courts as clerk gave him considerable knowledge of the manner in which legal matters were therein conducted, and frequently during Judge Darlington's term as president judge—the latter was subject to severe attacks of gout—Associate Judge Engle was compelled to preside, charging the grand jury and trying the cases. Jan. 26, 1842, he was recommissioned, although on that occasion his nomination had been sent to the Senate over a year before the date given, and was not confirmed, owing to the fact that at the December court, 1840, Judge Engle had been presented by the grand inquest for an alleged disturbance at the preceding Presidential election at Chester, the complaint being made by William Eves, Sr., Isaac Lloyd, and James McClarum. The proceedings failed in court at the February sessions, but the quarrel was carried to Harrisburg, and prevented for a time the confirmation by the Senate of the appointment of Judge Engle. In 1851, his term having expired, and being advanced in years, he retired from public life. Judge Engle died Oct. 18, 1857, aged eighty-seven years and nine months.

Henry Myers was prothonotary, recorder, register of wills, and clerk of the courts of Delaware County for three terms, being commissioned Jan. 17, 1824, Dec. 21, 1826, and Jan. 18, 1830. In 1824 he was one of the committee from Delaware County appointed to receive Gen. Lafayette. On Dec. 27, 1833, he was commissioned one of the associate judges, and while discharging the duties of that office was elected, in 1836, senator from this district, then comprising Delaware, Chester, and Lancaster Counties, serving in that capacity for four years. At the expiration of the term he retired from public life. On Feb. 23, 1855, Judge Myers died. He left his home, in Upper Darby, on the morning of that day, and when night came, not having returned, his family immediately instituted a search for him, but without success until the following day, when his body was discovered near Cobb's Creek. The intense cold had benumbed him so that he sank to the earth and perished.

Dr. George Smith was appointed by Governor Ritner, Dec. 8, 1836, one of the associate judges, and subsequently elected by the people to the same position in 1861. I present a sketch of the useful life-work of this eminent native of Delaware County in the article on physicians, and it is unnecessary to repeat it here.

On Feb. 25, 1843, George Gray Leiper was appointed by Governor Porter an associate judge of the courts of Delaware County. He was a son of Col. Thomas Leiper, of Ridley, and was born in Philadelphia, Feb. 3, 1786. He graduated from the University of Pennsylvania in 1803, when in his seventeenth year, and after his marriage made his home permanent on the Leiper estates, in Ridley township. Here in 1811 he established the first Sunday-school in the annals of the county. During the war of 1812 he was first lieutenant in Capt. James Serrill's company, the Delaware County Fencibles, which organization was mustered into service Sept. 21, 1814, and December 6th, of the same year, was discharged. In 1818 he built, at his own cost, the Ridley (Leiper) Presbyterian Church. In 1822-23 he was a Representative in the Legislature, and while there he so strongly and successfully urged State appropriation for the maintenance of the Deaf and Dumb Asylum, in Philadelphia, that in recognition of his services he was chosen a director of that institution, and continued until his death. In the fall of 1824 he was one of the committee from Delaware County appointed to receive Gen. Lafayette. In 1828 he was elected a member of the Twenty-first Congress, and although strongly pressed to be a candidate for re-election, refused, even when President Jackson, a warm personal friend of Mr. Leiper, personally requested him to allow his name to go before the people for a second term. In 1843, as above stated, Governor Porter appointed Mr. Leiper one of the associate judges, to which position he was reappointed by Governor Shunk, Feb. 16, 1848, and continued on the bench until the office was made elective. Judge Leiper retired from active public life, devoting his attention to the care of his large estate. He died at Lapidea, his residence on Crum Creek, Nov. 18, 1868, in his eighty-third year.

At the October election of 1851, James Andrew, of Darby, was chosen to the office of associate judge, and was commissioned Nov. 10, 1851. He and Sketchley Morton were the first associate judges elected by the votes of the people. James Andrew held no other county office than that of judge, but so acceptably did he discharge the duties of the position that he was re-elected in 1856, his commission being dated November 12th of that year, and in 1861 he was again called to a seat on the bench. At the expiration of his term, having attained threescore and ten, he retired from public service.

Sketchley Morton was born in Springfield, Oct. 12, 1810, his father's (John S. Morton) farm constituting much of the present village of Morton, on the West Chester and Philadelphia Railroad. From his early manhood he devoted himself mainly to merchandising and other business enterprises in which he was engaged, declining to take any very active part in political movements. He was, however, elected a member of the Legislature, serving during the session of 1847-48, at a time when the question of removing the seat of justice had divided the people of the county into removalists and anti-removalists, and although he was adverse to the change, his action in the House in pressing a bill to carry out that purpose, after the question had been submitted to a popular vote, was highly commendatory In the fall of 1851 he was elected one of the associate judges of the courts, his commission dating Nov 10, 1851, and he served one term on the bench In 1852 he was chosen president of the Delaware County Mutual Insurance Company, and was continued in that position until October, 1878, when he resigned Sketchley Morton died Feb 9, 1878, aged sixty-seven years

Frederick J Hinkson, Sr, was elected one of the associate judges of Delaware County courts in 1856 An account of Judge Hinkson will be found elsewhere in this volume

Only two of all the persons who have been associate judges of the county of Delaware are living The oldest, in point of commission, is Charles R Williamson, he having been commissioned by Governor Packer, Jan 10, 1860, to fill the position on the bench made vacant by Judge Hinkson's resignation The other is Judge Thomas Reese In the succeeding October, Dr George Smith was elected to the office Mr Williamson had also been county treasurer. He resides in the borough of Media

Bartine Smith was chosen one of the associate judges of the courts of Delaware County at the October election in 1866, his commission bearing date November 8th of that year He was born in 1803, and was for many years a merchant in Haverford On April 14, 1840, he was appointed a justice of the peace, was reappointed April 15, 1845, and elected to the same position in the spring of 1862 In 1861 he was clerk to the county commissioners, continuing as such until he was elected to the bench In 1871 he was re-elected to the judicial office, and continued therein until the expiration of his term, when the provisions of the Constitution abolishing the office became operative Judge Smith died Dec 12, 1877, aged seventy-four years

Judge Thomas Reece was born in Middletown township, Delaware County He was elected associate judge in 1866, and served a continuous period of ten years A further sketch of Judge Reece will be found in the history of Media

On Nov 23, 1876, just previous to the termination of the official career of Associate Judges Smith and Reece by the limitation of the Constitution of 1874, a banquet was given at Media to the retiring judges by the members of the bar and county officers Highly complimentary resolutions were adopted, handsomely engrossed, and presented to Judges Smith and Reece, and speeches appropriate to the occasion were made On Dec 1, 1876, the associate judges retired from the bench and the time-honored office ceased to be, and henceforth became simply a part of the annals of the county

As a rule it may be accepted that from the establishment of the colonial government until 1790, criminal cases, excepting those of trivial character, were prosecuted on the part of the government by the attorney-general in person This statement, however, is not without exception, for at the court held at Chester on the 3d day of 1st week Tenth month, 1684, on the trial of Edward Hulbert Taylor, who was indicted for larceny, the records state that Charles Pickering "pleads as attorney to ye King," which is the first case in which it is directly asserted that counsel appeared on behalf of the government, although it is evident that Attorney-General John White was present in that capacity at the trial of Magaret Mattson, at Philadelphia, before Penn and the Council, 27th of the Twelfth month, 1683 In Taylor's case, as in that of Mattson, the appearance of an attorney for the prosecution was of slight effect, for the prisoner was acquitted by the jury At the Court of Quarter Sessions at Chester, May 25, 1708, Thomas Clark, who was commissioned attorney-general on the 8th of that month, "appeared in open court and was qualified attorney-general for the county of Chester, according to law" The county records on the subject furnish us with but meagre information, and that not of much general interest By the act of Feb 28, 1710, the justices of the county courts, and the mayor and recorder of Philadelphia, respectively were empowered to admit attorneys to plead in these courts, and on misbehavior could suspend or prohibit attorneys from practicing before their tribunal The act of May 31, 1748, provided that "in trials of all capital crimes, learned counsel shall be assigned the prisoner" On May 22, 1722, the Assembly passed a law providing for the admission of attorneys in any of the county courts, "which said attornies so admitted may practice in all the courts of this province without any further or other license or admittance" A note in 1st Dallas "Laws of Pennsylvania," on this section of the act of 1722,[1] conveys the impression there were no other statutory enactments respecting attorneys until that of Sept 23, 1786, but such impression is erroneous, the act of Aug 26, 1727, provided "that there may be a competent number of persons, of an honest disposition and learned in the law, admitted by the justices of the said respective courts to practice as attornies there, who shall behave themselves justly and faithfully in their practice" That this act was generally observed is evident from the fact that the oath administered to attorneys at the present day is almost identical with that set forth in the enactment It was "And before they are so admitted shall take the following qualification, viz, 'Thou shalt behave thyself in the office of Attorney within the Court according to the best of thy learning and ability, and with all good Fidelity as well to the Court as to the Client, thou shalt use no Falsehood, nor Delay any Persons Caused for Lucre or Malice"[2] The admission in any of the county courts was as before an admission to all in this province, and attorneys in all civil cases were compelled to file

[1] 1st Dallas, p 185

[2] Duke of York's Book of Laws, p. 403

their warrant of attorney, or failing to do so no statutory fee could be taxed in the bill of costs to the party so in default. The act of Sept. 25, 1786, gave to the courts in the several counties power to make rules governing their own practice, after which date the admission of attorneys appear constantly on the minutes of our courts, although previous to that time on the record a number of lawyers were required to be regularly qualified before they were permitted to practice.

The following is a complete list of deputy attorneys-general and district attorneys from the erection of the county to the present time:

February session, 1790.—William Bradford, Jr., attorney-general in person.
July session, 1790.—Thomas Ross, under William Bradford, Jr.
August session, 1790.—Joseph Thomas, under William Bradford, Jr.
October session, 1791.—Joseph Thomas, under Jared Ingersoll.
October session, 1795.—William Sergeant, under Jared Ingersoll.
January session, 1796.—Thomas Ross, under Jared Ingersoll.
October session, 1797.—William Sergeant, under Jared Ingersoll.
January session, 1799.—Thomas Ross, under Jared Ingersoll.
April session, 1809.—Richard Bache, Jr., under Walter Franklin.
January session, 1811—John Edwards, under Joseph Reed.
January session, 1812.—Edward Ingersoll, under Jared Ingersoll.
January session, 1813.—Benjamin Tilghman, under Jared Ingersoll.
April session, 1813.—Edward Ingersoll, under Jared Ingersoll.
January session, 1814.—John Edwards, under Jared Ingersoll.
April session, 1814—Edward Ingersoll, under Jared Ingersoll.
January session, 1815.—Robert H. Smith, under Jared Ingersoll.
April session, 1815.—William H. Dillingham, under Jared Ingersoll.
January session, 1817.—Henry G. Freeman, under Amos Ellmaker.
October session, 1818.—Samuel Rush, under Thomas Sergeant.
January session, 1821.—Archibald T. Dick, under Thomas Elder.
April session, 1824.—Edward Darlington, under Frederick Smith.
April session, 1830.—John Zeilin, under Samuel Douglass.
August session, 1833.—Robert E. Hannum, under Ellis Lewis.
March session, 1836.—John P. Griffith, under William B. Reed.
February session, 1839.—P. Frazer Smith, under Ovid F. Johnston.
February session, 1845.—Robert Frazer, under John K. Kane.
November session, 1845.—Joseph J. Lewis, under John K. Kane.
November session, 1848.—John M. Broomall,[1] under James Cooper.
February session, 1850.—Charles D. Manley, by appointment of court.
May session, 1850.—Thomas H. Speakman, under Cornelius Darragh.

By act of Assembly May 1, 1850, the office of deputy attorney-general in the several counties was abolished, and district attorneys were directed to be elected, of persons learned in the law, at the ensuing election in October, to serve for a period of three years.

At the October election in 1850, Thomas H. Speakman was chosen by the popular vote, and at the November court he presented his certificate asking to be qualified. A petition was also presented to the court, signed by a number of citizens (sworn to by Charles D. Manley and Joseph Weaver, Jr.), stating that Speakman was not a resident of Delaware County, and not eligible for that reason to the office. It also set forth that Robert McCay, Jr., was elected, inasmuch as the votes cast for Speakman were illegal. The matter was continued under advisement, and at the May court, 1851, it was decided that "in consequence of the inability of Thomas H. Speakman, Esq., to serve the office of District Attorney, Robert McCay, Jr., Esq., be appointed to discharge the duties of the office for the remainder of the year."

1851.—Robert McCay.
Nov. 24, 1851.—Edward Darlington.
1854.—Jesse Bishop.[2]
1857.—Edward A. Price.
1860.—John Hibbard.
1863.—Francis M. Brooke.[3]
1866.—Charles D. M. Broomhall.
1869.—George E. Darlington.
1872.—David M. Johnson.
1876.—Vincent Gilpin Robinson.
1879.—Vincent Gilpin Robinson.
1882.—Jesse M. Baker.

The early records are confused respecting attorneys, for in many cases where that word is used it refers to attorneys-in-fact and not attorneys-at-law, while in many of the cases persons not learned in the law appeared on behalf of the parties litigant. As early as 1683, John White and Abraham Mann, known to be attorneys-at-law, appeared on the court records. At the court held first Third day of first week, Seventh month, 1690, in the case of Thomas Holmes *vs.* Charles Aston, Charles Pickering and Patrick Robinson appeared as attorneys for plaintiff, and John White and Caleb Pusey for the defendant. The jury finding in favor of the defendant, the attorneys for the plaintiff "craved an appeal to ye next Provinciall Court in law," and his attorneys, Charles Pickering and Robert Longshore, became surety in one hundred pounds that the plaintiff would prosecute "ye appeal now Granted to ye next provinciall Court in Law against a judgment now obtained & to pay all costs and damage if ye appellant be again cast." All the persons herein mentioned as attorneys were laymen, excepting John White.

In 1698, John Moore and David Lloyd were practicing attorneys.

That there were but four lawyers in the province as late as 1709 we learn from two petitions presented to the Provincial Council. The first was that of James Heaton, read April 2, 1708, in which he set forth that he had been sued in an action of trover and conversion, in Bucks County, by Joseph Growden, and that he had obtained a writ of error to the Supreme Provincial Court, that in the mean while the plaintiff had arrested him on the same cause of action by process of the court in Philadelphia; that the cases were likely to be heard nearly at the same time, and that the plaintiff was a judge of the Provincial Court, "and further, that he has retained all the lawyers in the county (that have leave to plead) against him." The petitioner then asked that an impartial judge should be appointed to hear the case, assign him counsel, or "set the day for trial," so that, "if he be at

[1] John M. Broomall resigned.

[2] Jesse Bishop resigned, and on Nov. 24, 1856, Edward A. Price was appointed by the court in his place. Mr. Price was the youngest man ever holding the office, having been admitted the preceding March of that year.

[3] Francis M. Brooke resigned, and the court appointed C. D. M. Broomhall to fill the unexpired term, and the latter was elected at the ensuing election.

the charge of procuring some from New York he may not be disappointed." Growden was present, and verbally replied that the actions were not for the like cause, and that he had only employed one attorney, John Moore, but that he was not able to attend, and therefore had a brother lawyer to appear for him, "by which means, without any design of his (Growden's), two became Concerned in it." Counsel decided that the petitioner "himself be left to procure his own Counsel," and directed Jasper Yeates, the second judge of the province, "without fail to attend the Provincial Court at Bucks to prevent any Disappointment."[1] On March 1, 1708/9, Francis Daniel Pastorius presented his petition to Council in respect to a suit in ejectment, brought by one Sprogel, against the Frankford Company, in the courts of Philadelphia, in which he stated that the plaintiff had "fee'd or retained the four known Lawyers of the Province," to prevent the defendant from obtaining any advice in law, "wch sufficiently argues his cause to be none of the best."[2]

The following persons, known to be attorneys learned in the law, appear on the record in the courts of Chester County at the dates given:

1726.—Ralph Assheton, John Kinsey, Peter Evans, Francis Sherrard, Joseph Growden, Jr.

1730.—Alexander Keith (admitted February 23d).

1734.—William Rawle.

1735.—John Ross (admitted August 27th), James Hamilton, John Robinson, Thomas Hopkinson.

1736.—Alexander Piercey (admitted December 1st), James Keating, Andrew Hamilton.

1738.—William Assheton (admitted November 28th).

1739.—William Peters.

1740.—John Webb.

1741.—Trench Francis, Edmund Acworth (February 23d), Neil Harris.

1742.—Robert Hartshorne, Richard Peters, John Mather, James Read (admitted September 1st).

1743.—John Moland, Townsend White.

1744.—David Edwards.

1745.—Benjamin Price.

1747.—John Lawrence.

1748.—Edward Shippen, Jr.

1749.—Joseph Galloway, John Evans.

The foregoing list is doubtless far from being perfect, but it is all that was found by Judge Futhey and Gilbert Cope, and in my researches I have not discovered any names omitted by them.

In the early days of the province it was the custom for students-at-law to make application for admission by petition, and the following one, on file at West Chester, presented by John Ross, was generally the form used:

"*To the Worshipful, the Justices of the County Court of Common Pleas at Chester:*

"The humble Petition of John Ross. Gent. showeth:—

"That Your Petitr. has served as an apprentice to an attorney at law in the province of Pennsylvania for the space of five years last past. Therefore Your petitr. prays to be admitted as an attorney of this Court.

"John Ross.

"Chester, Aug. 27th, 1735."

The following is a list of attorneys admitted previous to July 4, 1776:

	Admitted.
David Finney	February, 1752.
Thomas Otway	May, 1753.
John Price	August, 1753.
William Morris, Jr	August, 1753.
Benjamin Chew	November, 1754.
Samuel Johnson	February, 1755.
Thomas McKean	May, 1755.
David Henderson	August, 1755.
William Whitebred	November, 1755.
George Ross	November, 1756.
John Armond	November, 1756.
John Morris	August, 1760.
Nicholas Waln	February, 1763.
James Tilghman	August, 1763.
Hugh Hughs	February, 1764.
John Currie	May, 1764.
Elisha Price	May, 1764.
Lindsay Coates	November, 1764.
Andrew Allen	February, 1765.
Alexander Porter	May, 1765.
Nicholas Vandyke	May, 1765.
Alexander Wilcocks	May, 1765.
Joshua Yeates	August, 1765.
Stephen Porter	August, 1765.
Richard Peters, Jr	August, 1765.
James Biddle	August, 1765.
James Allen	August, 1765.
Henry Elwes	August, 1765.
James Loyre	November, 1765.
Isaac Hunt	August, 1766.
David Thomson	August, 1766.
James Vandyke	August, 1766.
William Hicks	November, 1767.
James Wilson.	November, 1767.
Jacob Rush	February, 1769.
Miers Fisher	August, 1769.
Daniel Clymer	August, 1769.
John Ruley	August, 1769.
Stephen Watts	November, 1769.
Abel Evans	May, 1770.
James Lukens	August, 1770.
Thomas Good	August, 1770.
Joseph Read	August, 1771.
George Noarth	August, 1771.
Jacob Bankson	August, 1771.
Francis Johnson	August, 1771.
Asheton Humphreys	August, 1771.
Richard Tilghman	February, 1772.
John Lawrence	August, 1772.
Peter Zachary Lloyd	August, 1772.
Christian Hook	February, 1773.
William L. Blair	May, 1773.
Phineas Bond	May, 1773.
John Stedman	August, 1773.
John McPherson	August, 1773.
William Lewis	November, 1773.
Edward Tilghman	May, 1774.
Gunning Bedford	November, 1774.
Andrew Robson	February, 1775
John Vannost	May, 1775.
William Prince Gibbs	February, 1776.
Collinson Read	May, 1776.

Admitted after July 4, 1776:

John Morris	August, 1777.
Andrew Robeson	August, 1777.
William Lewis	August, 1777.
William L. Blair	August, 1777.
John Kaley	August, 1777.
George Ross	August, 1778.
Jonathan D. Sergeant	August, 1778.
Jacob Rush	August, 1778.
Elisha Price	August, 1778.
Alexander Wilcocks	August, 1778.
Gunning Bedford	August, 1778.
John Pancost	August, 1778.
Edward Burd	February, 1779.
Francis Johnston	February, 1779.
Henry Osborne	May, 1779.
George Campbell	August, 1779.
Jacob Bankson	August, 1779.
Jared Ingersoll	November, 1779.
William Bradford, Jr	November, 1779.
Moses Levy	November, 1780.
Nicholas Vandyke	February, 1791.
John Coxe	February, 1791.
William Moore Smith	August, 1781.
John Lawrence	August, 1781.
Nathaniel Potts	November, 1781.
Joseph Reed	February, 1782.
John F. Mifflin	May, 1782.
Daniel Clymer	August, 1782.
John Vining	August, 1782.
John Wilkes Kitter	May, 1783.
Henry Hale Graham	November, 1783.
William Rawle	November, 1783.
Samuel Sitgrave	Feb. 24, 1784.
William Ewing	November, 1784.
Peter Zachary Lloyd	May, 1785.
Jacob R. Howell	May, 1785.

[1] Colonial Records, vol. ii. p. 407.

[2] Ib., p. 430.

	Admitted
Thomas Ross	May, 1785
Joseph B McKean	August, 1785
John Todd	November, 1785
Robert Hodson	May, 1786
Charles Smith	May, 1786
John Young	May, 1786
Benjamin Chew, Jr	August, 1786
B R Morgan, Jr	August, 1786
Richard Wharton	August, 1786
Thomas Memminger	August, 1786
James Hanna	Aug 13, 1786
David Smith	February, 1787
James Wade	February, 1787
John Joseph Henry	February, 1787
William Richardson Atlee	February, 1787
William Montgomery	August, 1787
Sampson Levy	August, 1787
James Hopkins	August, 1787
Samuel Roberts	August, 1787
Samuel Bayard	November 1787
Matthias Baldwin	November, 1787
James A Bayard	November, 1787
Thomas Armstrong	February, 1788
Peter S Duponceau	May, 1788
Jasper Yeates	August, 1788
Peter Hoofnagle	August, 1788
Joseph Hubley	August, 1788
William Graham	November 1788
John Hallowell	February, 1789
Joseph Thomas	May, 1789
Robert Porter	May, 1789
Charles Healty	May, 1789
Anthony Morris	May, 1789
John Craig Wells	August, 1789
John Cadwallader	August, 1789
John Moore	August, 1789

As heretofore stated, when the county of Delaware was erected, as a matter of course, there was no attorney of record The difficulty was met by William Tilghman, who addressed the court, and finally in his own behalf moved his admission to the bar of Delaware County, which motion received the approval of the bench The record, therefore, shows·

	Admitted
William Tilghman	Nov 9, 1789
William L Blair (on Tilghman's motion)	" 1789
Joseph Thomas	" 1789
Thomas Ross	" 1789
William Graham	" 1789

William Graham, the only son of Judge Graham, was born in Chester in 1767, and, studying law, was admitted to the bar at the date given During the Whiskey Insurrection in Western Pennsylvania, in 1794, at which time he was chief burgess of Chester, he commanded a troop of cavalry from Delaware County, and while in that command the exposure brought on a disease of the throat, which affected his voice at times so that he could not speak above a whisper. This vocal difficulty became permanent a few years afterwards, owing to the fact that in company with several gentlemen, he went gunning to Chester Island, and became separated from his companions When darkness came he could not be found, and his friends returned to Chester, determining at early dawn to resume their search for him All that night he remained on the bar, and as he was short in stature, the tide rose until his head and shoulders were alone out of the water When rescued next morning his voice was entirely gone, and he never again recovered it so as to be able to speak in public, and even in conversation he was often almost inaudible He died Dec. 19, 1821

	Admitted
Benjamin Morgan	Nov 9, 1789
Anthony Morris	—— — 1789
John Todd	—— — 1789
Alexander Wilcox	Feb 9, 1790
William Bradford, Jr	Feb 9, 1790
Jacob Bankson	Feb 9, 1790
Elisha Price	Feb 9, 1790
Robert Porter	Feb 9, 1790
Thomas B Dick	Feb 9, 1790

Thomas B Dick was born near Marcus Hook, March 12, 1766, read law with Thomas Ross, Esq , and admitted to the bar of Delaware County at the date mentioned In 1794 he removed to Eastern Pennsylvania, but returned to Chester in 1798, where he acquired a large practice, owing to his reputation as an able advocate He was commissioned prothonotary, recorder, register, and clerk of the courts of Delaware County, Feb 22, 1806, retaining that office until Jan 2, 1809 On April 21, 1811, he was gunning in a row-boat on the Delaware, and a severe snow-storm coming on, he was drowned How the accident occurred is not known, he being alone at the time His body was not recovered until eight days thereafter

	Admitted
Moses Levy	Feb 9, 1790
William Rawle	Feb 9, 1790
Benjamin Morgan	Feb 9, 1790
Anthony Morris	Feb 9, 1790
Sampson Levy	May 11, 1790
Matthias Baldwin	May 11, 1790.
Jonathan D Sergeant	Nov 9, 1790
George Campbell	Nov 9, 1790
John Thompson	Nov 9, 1790
Nicholas Diehl	May 10, 1791
Robert H Dunkin	May 10, 1791
John C. Willis	May 10, 1791
Isaac Telfall	Aug 10 1791
Seth Chapman	Nov 7, 1791
Thomas Armstrong.	Dec 2, 1791
Robert Frazer	July 30 1792

Robert Frazer was, we are told by Dr Smith, a resident of the upper part of the county, and he it was who drew the petition to the Legislature in 1820 for the removal of the county-seat from Chester to a more central location Martin relates the following anecdote of Mr Frazer "A client, a well-known close-fisted old miller, called on him one day for some advice in reference to a difficulty about his mill-dam and water-power privileges He found Mr. Frazer in his office, legs in comfortable position higher than his head, taking his ease and smoking. The miller, taking a seat, proceeded to relate his grievance at length, and then asked what he should do Frazer, still leaning back and puffing his cigar, paid no attention to the question At last the impatient client burst out with 'D——n it, Mr Frazer! Did you hear what I said?' With a humorous twinkle of his eye, Frazer replied 'Oh, yes, but do you expect a mill to run without water?'"[1]

	Admitted
John Ross	July 31, 1792
Thomas W Tallman	Jan 29, 1793
John D Cox	April 30, 1793
Joseph Hemphill	October, 1793
John Horn[2]	Jan 29, 1795
Caleb Pierce[2]	Jan 29 1795
William Sergeant	April 27, 1795
James Hunter	October, 1795
David Moore	Jan 23, 1796
William Martin	April, 1796

[1] History of Chester, p 475

[2] Admission moved by Samuel Price, Esq , whose admission I do not find on record

A sketch of Dr. Martin appears in the chapter on physicians of Delaware County, for in that calling—he was a member of both professions—he was most prominent.

	Admitted.
William Richardson Atlee	July 26, 1796.
Michael Kepple	July 28, 1796.
Alex. James Dallas	Nov. 1, 1796.
Bird Wilson	April 7, 1797.
William Ewing	Oct. 30, 1797.
Wash. Lee Hannum	April, 1798.
Joseph Reed	May 2, 1798.
Jonathan T. Haight	Jan. 28, 1799.
Charles Chauncey	Jan. 28, 1799.
John Sergeant	July 30, 1799.
John Taylor	April, 1800.
William Hemphill	July, 1800.
Nicholas G. Williamson	January, 1801.
Jona. W. Condey[1]	April, 1801.
Rich. Peters, Jr[1]	April, 1801.
Richard Rush[1]	April, 1801.
John Ewing, Jr	July 20, 1801.
William Robinson, Jr	Jan. 25, 1802.
Isaac Darlington	Jan. 25, 1802.
Thomas Bradford	July 29, 1803.
James Day Barnard	April 30, 1804.
Peter Arrell Brown	May 3, 1804.
Charles Fisher Frazer	Oct. 30, 1804.
Charles Kisselman	Oct. 30, 1804.
Richard Bache, Jr	May 8, 1805.
Samuel Edwards	April 30, 1806.

Samuel Edwards was born in Chester township March 12, 1785. He was a descendant of William Edwards, who, coming from Wales early in 1682, settled in Middletown. He read law with William Graham, and was admitted to the bar April 30, 1806. He was at that time a Federalist, and as such, with his party, was opposed to the second war with Great Britain. Hence we find him acting as chairman of the meeting of the young men of that political faith held in the court-house at Chester Aug. 22, 1812. But the war actually begun, he threw aside all fealty to party, and when Admiral Cockburn was threatening the borders of Pennsylvania and had applied the torch to all the property he could not steal at the head of the Chesapeake, Samuel Edwards was one of the first to advocate arming the militia and marching against the invaders. In April, 1813, he and Thomas D. Anderson made application to the State for muskets to arm the Chester company of infantry, giving their personal bonds to the commonwealth for the arms, and that body marched to Elkton to resist the British forces at that place. In the fall of the year 1814 he was in active service as a private in the Mifflin Guards, commanded by Capt. Samuel Anderson. This organization was a company of the First Regiment, Pennsylvania Volunteers, under Col. Clement C. Biddle. Mr. Edwards acted as secretary of the company, and the orderly book, the greater part in his writing, is like copper-plate in beauty of chirography. While in the military service he was elected a member of the Legislature, and during the session of 1814-15 he represented Delaware County in that body, and was re-elected to the session of 1815-16. In 1819, Mr. Edwards, then a Democrat, was elected to the Sixteenth, and again in 1825 to the Nineteenth Congress, serving therein as a colleague of James Buchanan, towards whom he was during the remainder of his life a warm personal friend. Although Mr. Edwards served no other term in Congress, yet during Jackson's and Van Buren's administration, it was charged throughout the country that five persons—Samuel Edwards, George G. and Samuel M. Leiper, Levi Reynolds, and James Buchanan—were the powers behind the throne. In 1824, Mr. Edwards was one of the committee appointed by Delaware County to receive Gen. Lafayette. In 1832 he was chief burgess of Chester, and from 1838 to 1842 was inspector of customs at that port. For many years he was a leader of the bar, and he and Benjamin Tilghman were counsel for John H. Craig, convicted of the murder of Squire Hunter, in 1818. Never was a case better tried on the part of the defense than this was. For many years he was a director of the Delaware County Bank and Delaware Mutual Insurance Company. He was also counsel for the Philadelphia, Wilmington and Baltimore Railroad.

Mr. Edwards died at Chester Nov. 25, 1850, aged sixty-five years. A meeting of the bar was held on the 26th, at which Judge Chapman presided, and J. R. Morris acted as secretary. Associate Judge Leiper announced the death of Mr. Edwards, and an address was made by Judge Thomas S. Bell, then on the Supreme bench, who came to Chester that he might take part in the memorial services of his deceased friend. Speeches were also made by Hon. Edward Darlington and Hon. Joseph J. Lewis.

	Admitted.
Joseph Barnes	Oct. 23, 1806.
Benjamin Shober	Jan. 21, 1807.
John Edwards, Jr.	Oct. 19, 1807.

He was the great-grandson of William Edwards, the Welsh settler at Middletown, and was born July 15, 1786, at the Black Horse Tavern, in that township, his father, Nathan Edwards, being then the landlord and owner of the inn. John Edwards studied law, and was admitted to the bar of Delaware County at the date stated. In 1811 he was deputy attorney-general for Delaware County, and in 1824 was one of the counsel for the defense in the trial of Wellington for murder of Bonsall. After that date he seems to have devoted his attention to the iron business at the rolling-mills, near Glen Mills, which he owned, and to politics, a pursuit in which he was unusually successful. In the fall of 1838 he was elected a member of Congress from the Fourth District, then comprising the counties of Delaware, Chester, and Lancaster, serving in the Twenty-fifth and Twenty-sixth Congresses, for he was re-elected a second term. He died in October, 1845, aged fifty-nine years, and was buried at Middletown meeting-house.

	Admitted.
Bayse Newcomb, Jr	Oct. 19, 1807.
William H. Todd	April 17, 1809.
Thomas R. Ross	April 17, 1809.
Ziba Pyle	July 17, 1809.
Samuel H. Jacobs	Jan. 21, 1811.
Jonathan Dunker	July 24, 1811.
Edward Ingersoll	Jan. 20, 1812.
Randall Hutchinson	Jan. 20, 1812.
Thomas D. Anderson	Jan. 23, 1812.

[1] Admission moved by Thomas B. Adams, Esq., whose admission I do not find on record.

H Edwards

Thomas Dixon Anderson, the only son of Maj William Anderson, was born in Virginia, in 1790, just previous to the removal of his father to Chester He was admitted to the bar at the above date When the British fleet under Admiral Cockburn had taken Frenchtown, in April, 1813, and destroyed it, the alarm was extreme in Southern Pennsylvania and Delaware Mr Anderson and Samuel Edwards, Esq, made immediate application to the State authorities for arms to equip an infantry company at Chester, and sixty muskets and equipments were forwarded to that place in compliance with this demand

In the official rolls of the militia called into service in the fall of the year 1814, I do not find Thomas D Anderson's name Perhaps he had removed to Tennessee, of which State he was attorney-general He was subsequently appointed United States consul at Tunis and Tripoli, where he continued a number of years As he advanced in life his eyesight became so much impaired that he retired from public life and returned to Chester, residing in the old Anderson house at Fifth and Welsh Streets, where he died

	Admitted
Clymer Ross	April 13, 1812
Charles Harland	April 13, 1812
James Madison Porter	July 26, 1813
Michael W Ash	July 26, 1813
Charles J Cox	July 26, 1813
Charles Catlin	Jan 17, 1814
William Bowen	April 12, 1814
William A Dillingham	April 12, 1814
Thomas F Pessants	April 12, 1814
James Henderson	July 28, 1814
Jonathan Hampden	July 28, 1814
John Kerlin	July 28, 1814

John Kerlin was prominent in politics and business in the county He was the fourth president of the Bank of Delaware County In 1824 he served four years in the State Senate from the Sixth District, then including Chester County, and in 1828 was re-elected to the same office for a like period He died in Philadelphia, May 21, 1847, aged fifty-four years

	Admitted
Robert H Smith	Jan 16, 1815
Benjamin Chew	April 10, 1815
Isaac D Barnard	Jan 16 1816

Isaac D Barnard was born in Aston township, March 22, 1791 When thirteen years old he was placed as a clerk in the prothonotary's office at Chester, then held by Thomas B Dick, and subsequently for two years was in the prothonotary's office at Philadelphia In 1811 he began reading law with William Graham, and was admitted to the Delaware County bar at the date given, and on May 17th of the same year was admitted to the bar of Chester County During the war with England he was commissioned captain of the Fourteenth United States Infantry, and took part in the battle at Fort George, where his signal bravery and ability earned for him promotion to the rank of major He served faithfully in the campaign of the Northeastern border, and at the battle of Plattsburg, owing to the death and disability of his superior officers, the command of the corps devolved on him He also so distinguished himself at the battle of Lyon's Creek that he was honorably mentioned in the official reports of the generals commanding At the close of the war the government desired Barnard to remain in the army permanently, but he declined, and located in West Chester, where he soon attained a large practice, and a year after his admission was appointed deputy attorney-general for Chester County In 1820 he was elected from the district comprising Chester and Delaware Counties State senator, and in 1824 he was tendered the president judgeship of Lancaster and Dauphin Counties, which he declined In 1826 he was appointed by Governor Shulze, Secretary of the Commonwealth, and the same year was elected by the Legislature senator of the United States, a position he acceptably filled until 1831, when he resigned on account of failing health He died Feb 18, 1834

	Admitted
Archibald T Dick	Jan 16, 1816

He was born Dec 21, 1794, in all probability at Eaton, at which place his father, Thomas B Dick, then resided He studied law at Chester, and was called to the bar at the date stated During the fall of 1814 he was one of the emergency men at Fort Du Pont He had considerable practice for those days, was an active politician, and in 1834 was the Democratic candidate for Congress He died Aug 13, 1837

	Admitted
Samuel I Withy	April 8, 1816
Matthias Richards Sayres	July 22, 1816
Henry C Byrne	Aug 26, 1816
Edward D Cox	Oct 22, 1816
Thomas Kittera	Jan 20, 1817
Henry G Freeman	Jan 20, 1817
Matthew Morris	April 14, 1817
John Kentzing Kane	April 14, 1817
James C Biddle	April 14, 1817
Samuel Rush	Oct 19, 1818
Charles Sidney Cox	Oct 19, 1818
John J Richards	Jan 19, 1819
Joseph P Norburry	July 16, 1819
Nathan R Potts	July 16, 1819
David Paul Brown	July 16, 1819
William Milnor, Jr	July 16, 1819
John Duer	Aug 18, 1819
Arthur Middleton	Aug 18, 1819
Richard C Wood	Aug 18, 1819
Robert R Beale	Oct 17, 1820
William Williamson	Jan 17, 1821
Edward Darlington	April 9, 1821
William Martin	July 27, 1821
Townsend Haines	Jan 21, 1822
Aquilla A Brown	Jan 21, 1822
John P Owens	April 8, 1822
John M Reed	June 19, 1822
William S Haines	July 22, 1822
Thomas S Bell	April 14 1823
Thomas F Gordon	April 14, 1823
Bond Valentine	April 14, 1823
Edward Richards	July 28, 1823
Thomas A Budd	July 28 1823
Abraham Marshall, Jr	July 28, 1823
Thomas Dunlap	Oct 23, 1823
Francis E Brewster	Oct 28, 1823
Nathaniel Vernon	April 13, 1824
William Kimber	April 11, 1825
John P Griffiths	April 13, 1825
Mordecai Taylor	July 27, 1825
Daniel Buckwalter	Jan 26, 1826
John S Newbold	Jan 26, 1826
William Darlington	July 24, 1826
Samuel Chew	July 24, 1826
Henry H Van Amringe	July 24, 1826
William T Smith	July 24, 1826
Lewis G Pierce	Oct 16, 1826
John Cadwalader	Jan 16, 1827
Joseph J Lewis	April 9, 1827
Joseph S Cohen	April 9, 1827
John K Zeilin	Aug 10, 1827

John K. Zeilin was born in Philadelphia in 1803. On attaining his majority he came to Chester and was appointed Oct. 25, 1824, deputy prothonotary and clerk of the courts under Henry Myers. While so employed he read law with Hon. Edward Darlington, and was admitted to practice at the time stated. A pleasing, ready speaker, he was prominent in political and military movements of the day. In 1830, Attorney-General Douglass appointed him deputy attorney-general for Delaware County, and he prosecuted for the State until Dec. 20, 1832, when he was commissioned by Governor Wolf prothonotary, etc., for the county, retaining the office until Aug. 20, 1834, when John Hinkson superseded him. Under John Richards he was appointed deputy register of wills. In 1837–38 he was a member of the Legislature, and was re-elected to the session of 1839. In 1842, Judge Randall, of the United States District Court, appointed Mr. Zeilin commissioner of bankruptcy in Delaware County. At the Whig Convention, Sept. 18, 1846, he received the nomination to Congress, it being understood that the term was to be conceded to Delaware County. The convention in Montgomery County had named John Freedley, and the *confrères* from the two counties had twice met without adjusting the ticket, each county demanding the representative. In the mean while the Democrats had nominated Samuel M. Leiper, whose popularity was such that it was generally believed he would defeat Zeilin at the polls. This impression was so strong that at length Zeilin was induced to withdraw, yielding the nomination to Freedley, who was elected. Col. Zeilin was active in all military affairs in the county during his residence therein. On May 15, 1833, he was elected captain of the Pennsylvania Artillery, and colonel of the Forty-seventh Regiment on Aug. 3, 1835, a position he held until 1849. During the riots in Philadelphia in 1844 he had charge of the Delaware County militia companies on duty in that city, and at the outbreak of the Mexican war tendered the Delaware County military companies to the President, but the quota of Pennsylvania was full, hence the offer was not accepted. In 1852 he removed to Philadelphia, where he died Aug. 6, 1876, in his seventy-third year.

	Admitted.
Owen Stoever	Oct. 15, 1816.
Davis H. Hoopes	Oct. 16, 1816.
Frederick A. Reybold	Jan. 22, 1828.
John Wayne Ashmead	April 14, 1828.
John H. Bradley	Oct. 20, 1828.
William C. Brown	Oct. 20, 1828.
David J. Desmond	Jan. 22, 1859.
James A. Donath	April 15, 1829.
Levi Hollingsworth	April 15, 1829.
Robert E. Hannum	July 27, 1829.
P. Frazer Smith	Nov. 23, 1829.
John C. Daniel	Jan. 18, 1830.
Peter Hill Engle	April 13, 1830.

Peter Hill Engle was a son of Judge Joseph Engle. In 1836 he removed to Wisconsin Territory, where he filled several offices of distinction, being at one time Secretary of State. He afterwards returned to his native county, and resumed practice. He died Feb. 17, 1844.

	Admitted.
Andrew T. Smith	April 14, 1830.
John C. Nippes	March 2, 1831.
George L. Ashmead	April 11, 1831.
Charles C. Rawn	April 11, 1831.
John Rutter	Nov. 28, 1831.
Thomas W. Morris	Nov. 30, 1831.
Robert B. Dodson	Nov. 30, 1831.
Thomas R. Newbold	Aug. 27, 1832.
John Swift	April 22, 1833.
David H. Mulvany	Feb. 25, 1834.
Joseph Hemphill, Jr	May 30, 1834.
Horatio Hubbell	Aug. 23, 1835.
Samuel F. Reed	Nov. 24, 1835.
Daniel McLaughlin	Aug. 22, 1836.
Joseph Williams	Aug. 27, 1836.
Horatio G. Worrall	Feb. 27, 1837.
William M. Tilghman	Feb. 28, 1837.
James Hanna	May 22, 1837.
William H. Keating	Aug. 28, 1837.
William M. Meredith	Aug. 28, 1837.
Henry J. Williams	Aug. 28, 1837.
John Freedley	Aug. 30, 1837.
Thomas M. Jolly	Aug. 30, 1837.
John B. Sterigere	June 4, 1838.
William E. Whitman	June 7, 1838.
John D. Pierce	Nov. 27, 1838.
Saunder Lewis	Nov. 27, 1838.
Frederick E. Hayes	May 25, 1840.
Elihu D. Farr	May 26, 1840.
John M. Broomall	Aug. 24, 1840.
Uriah V. Pennypacker	Aug. 26, 1840.
Christopher Fallon	Nov. 24, 1840.
B. Franklin Pyle	Aug. 23, 1841.
Charles B. Heacock	Aug. 24, 1841.
Isaac S. Serrill	Aug. 25, 1841.
Addison May	Aug. 26, 1841.
Garrick Mallery	Nov. 25, 1841.
Paul Beck Carter	May 23, 1842.
William D. Kelley	May 23, 1842.
James Mason	Aug. 23, 1842.
Lewis Allain Scott	Nov. 30, 1842.
Mortimer R. Talbot	Nov. 30, 1842.
William P. Foulke	May 22, 1843.
John M. Simmes	May 22, 1843.
Benjamin C. Tilghman	May 21, 1843.
Henry Chester	May 27, 1843.
William R. Dickerson	Aug. 28, 1843.
Matthew A. Sanley	Nov. 27, 1843.
John Smith Futhey	Nov. 27, 1843.
Edward Hopper	Nov. 30, 1843.
Samuel Hood	March 1, 1844.
Thomas H. Speakman	Aug. 26, 1844.
Jesse M. Griffith	Nov. 5, 1845.
Ashbel Green	Feb. 24, 1845.
Constant Guillou	Feb. 24, 1845.
Robert Frazer	Feb. 24, 1845.
William Wheeler Hubbell	May 6, 1845.
R. Rundel Smith	Aug. 25, 1845.
James B. Everhart	Aug. 25, 1845.
Joseph P. Wilson	Nov. 24, 1845.
Samuel B. Thomas	Feb. 26, 1846.

Samuel Baldwin Thomas was born in Chester County, and was admitted to that bar June 18, 1844, and on the date given in the list became a member of that of Delaware County. On Nov. 28, 1848, he was commissioned prothonotary of Chester County, and in 1851 was secretary of the West Chester and Philadelphia Railroad. In 1854 he went to Philadelphia, where he practiced his profession. In August, 1857, he removed to Media, and opened an office in the court-house. In 1860 he "stumped" the State in the interest of Andrew G. Curtin, and after the latter was inaugurated Governor he commissioned Mr. Thomas, Jan. 16, 1861, Deputy Secretary of the Commonwealth. In 1863, Col. Thomas was placed at the head of the military department of the State. At the expiration of his term of service he returned to Media, and was appointed a commissioner of the Revenue Board, and subsequently commissioner of bankruptcy. Samuel B. Thomas died Dec. 2, 1872.

Galaxy Pub Co Philadelphia

John Hibberd

[illegible]

Joseph R. Morris was a promising member of the bar, and although but thirty-five years of age had acquired an excellent practice. On [illegible], Dec. [illegible], 18[illegible], while talking to a friend in [illegible], he dropped dead.

[illegible]

Ezra Levis was thirty years in full practice at the bar of Delaware County when he died, Jan. 28, 1879. During his career he never sought office, but in the line of his profession was earnest, conscientious, and well read. He was an abolitionist from conviction, when to entertain those sentiments was certainly destructive of all political aspirations; but Ezra Levis gave expression to his opinion then as at all times during his life when he believed he was in the right.

[illegible]

John Hibberd was born near where Media now stands, in Delaware County, Pa., May [illegible], 18[illegible]. He is the only son of Thomas and Margaret Hibberd, whose only daughter, Hannah, died in Chester, Oct. [illegible], 1870. His ancestors were members of the society of Friends, and his earlier ancestry was Saxon, Norman, and Welsh. His mother, born in 17[illegible], the daughter of John and Amelia Powell, was a woman of remarkable qualities. His paternal grandfather, Jacob Hibberd, died in 18[illegible]. Mr. Hibberd was mathematically educated, his last instructor having been the late Enoch Lewis, a well-known scholar and scientist, then residing in Chester County, Pa. After leaving school, he was engaged for some time in teaching, and in April, 18[illegible], removed with his parents to Belmont County, Ohio, where he devoted himself assiduously to the study of the law, and in October, 18[illegible], was admitted to practice at the bar of Belmont County. His most interesting and notable case there was one in which a bill in equity had been filed, praying for a perpetual injunction against process on a judgment. It was a case of long standing, resolutely contested; the greatest vigilance was employed in the securing of testimony, with strong efforts to impeach and sustain witnesses. The ability and patience with which the [illegible] facts were brought out excited much comment, and the case afforded an excellent opportunity for the exercise of the power of logical argument.

He formed the acquaintance of literary, scientific, and distinguished professional men, and from 18[illegible] to near the end of 18[illegible] took an active and prominent part in the political contests of his adopted State. As he became a champion of the Free-soil and anti-slavery movement when the cause was unpopular in that part of the State and there were few to defend its principles, much labor devolved upon him in those early conflicts. He was a member of the Republican party from its organization, and has ever taken a decided interest in the leading political questions of the times. He was a firm supporter of President Lincoln, and in a speech delivered in Philadelphia, in October, 18[illegible], pronounced a "glowing eulogium" on the character of that [illegible] man and wise ruler. While a citizen of Ohio, in 18[illegible], he began to lecture on temperance, and he has since been identified with that cause; many years ago he occasionally lectured on the subject of education. After the decease of his parents, he located permanently in his native county, and since the beginning of 18[illegible] has been engaged in [illegible] legal business in Chester, and has continued [illegible] in that growing city, or in its vicinity. He was elected district attorney of Delaware County by a large majority in the fall of 18[illegible], and, during his term of three years, exercised the functions of that office with marked ability and acceptance. Having declined a re-election in 18[illegible], he has since, in addition to his professional duties, devoted much time to a fuller investigation of equity, constitutional and international law, as well as other branches of jurisprudence. He has ever recommended an honorable course in the profession, and condemned the practice of defeating the ends of justice by vexatious litigation; he has continued to cultivate the languages which contribute to successful legal research and confer a more extended general culture, continuing also a diligent student of the English classics, history, biography, oratory, and political economy.

John Hibbard

	Admitted
John A Gilmore	Feb 26 1846
Nathaniel B Brown	May 25, 1846
Richard C McMurtrie	May 25, 1846
William F Boon	May 25, 1846
Robert M Lea	Aug 24 1846
Nathaniel B Holland	Aug 24, 1846
Marshall Sprogell	Aug 24, 1846
Samuel A Black	Nov 23, 1846
Robert McCay	Feb 22, 1847
George Palmer	Feb 22, 1847
Washington Townsend	Aug 23, 1847
James H Hackleton	Aug 23, 1847
Henry B Edwards	Nov 22, 1847
George W Ormsby	Feb 22, 1848.
John Banks	May 22 1848
Joseph R Morris	Aug 28, 1848

Joseph R Morris was a promising member of the bar, and although but thirty-five years of age, had acquired an excellent practice On Sunday, Dec 4, 1859, while talking to a friend in Media he dropped dead

	Admitted
William Butler	Aug 28, 1848
Gilbert R Fox	Aug 28, 1848
Henry Freedley	Aug 28, 1848,
Enoch Taylor	Aug 28, 1848
Harlan Ingram	Nov 27, 1848
Thomas H Maddock	Nov 27, 1848
Charles D Manley	Feb 26, 1849
Ezra Levis	May 28, 1849

Ezra Levis was thirty years in full practice at the bar of Delaware County when he died, Jan 23, 1879 During his career he never sought office, but in the line of his profession was earnest, conscientious, and well read He was an abolitionist from conviction, when to entertain those sentiments was certainly destructive of all political aspirations, but Ezra Levis gave expression to his opinion then as at all times during his life when he believed he was in the right

	Admitted
Paschall Woodward	May 28, 1849
William Hollingshead	May 28, 1849
John Markland	Aug 27, 1849
Robert Alsop	Feb 25, 1850
John Fairlamb Roberts	Feb 25, 1850
Thomas Greenback	May 27, 1850
Jesse Bishop	May 27, 1850
John H Robb	May 27, 1850
John Titus	Aug 26, 1850
Joseph R Dickinson	Nov 25, 1850
Thomas Leiper	May 26, 1851
George Norton	May 28, 1851
Thomas J Clayton	Nov 24 1851
Francis Darlington	Feb 23, 1852
James M Goodman	Feb 26, 1852
William B Waddell.	May 24, 1852
Benjamin A Mitchel	Aug 23, 1852
Abraham L Smith	Nov 28, 1853
Edward Olmstead	March 6, 1854
J Williams Biddle	March 6, 1854.
William Vogdes	May 22, 1854
Robert S Paschall	May 22, 1854
Edward A Price	March 17, 1856
William Nicholson	June 6, 1856
Robert D Chalfant	June 6, 1856
John W Stokes	Nov 24, 1856.
James Otterson	Aug 24, 1857
Andrew Zane	Feb 22, 1857
Peter Wychoff	May 24, 1857
John Hibberd	—— — 1857

John Hibberd was born near where Media now stands, in Delaware County, Pa, May 31, 1821 He is the only son of Thomas and Margaret Hibberd, whose only daughter, Hannah, died in Chester, Oct 19, 1870 His ancestors were members of the society of Friends, and his earlier ancestry was Saxon, Norman, and Welsh. His mother, born in 1790, the daughter of John and Amelia Powell, was a woman of remarkable qualities His paternal grandfather, Jacob Hibberd, died in 1827 Mr Hibberd was mathematically educated, his last instructor having been the late Enoch Lewis, a well-known scholar and scientist, then residing in Chester County, Pa After leaving school, he was engaged for some time in teaching, and in April, 1845, removed with his parents to Belmont County, Ohio, where he devoted himself assiduously to the study of the law, and in October, 1847, was admitted to practice at the bar of Belmont County His most interesting and notable case there was one in which a bill in equity had been filed, praying for a perpetual injunction against process on a judgment It was a case of long standing, resolutely contested, the greatest vigilance was employed in the securing of testimony, with strong efforts to impeach and sustain witnesses The ability and patience with which the numerous facts were brought out excited much comment, and the case afforded an excellent opportunity for the exercise of the power of logical argument

He formed the acquaintance of literary, scientific, and distinguished professional men, and from 1848 to near the end of 1852 took an active and prominent part in the political contests of his adopted State. As he became a champion of the free-soil and anti-slavery movement when the cause was unpopular in that part of the State and there were few to defend its principles, much labor devolved upon him in those early conflicts He was a member of the Republican party from its organization, and has ever taken a decided interest in the leading political questions of the times He was a firm supporter of President Lincoln, and in a speech delivered in Philadelphia, in October, 1864, pronounced a "glowing eulogium" on the character of that eminent man and wise ruler. While a citizen of Ohio, in 1849, he began to lecture on temperance, and he has since been identified with that cause, many years ago he occasionally lectured on the subject of education After the decease of his parents, he located permanently in his native county, and since the beginning of 1857 has been engaged in desirable legal business in Chester, and has continued to reside in that growing city, or in its vicinity He was elected district attorney of Delaware County by a large majority in the fall of 1860, and, during his term of three years, exercised the functions of that office with marked ability and acceptance Having declined a re-election in 1863, he has since, in addition to his professional duties, devoted much time to a fuller investigation of equity, constitutional and international law, as well as other branches of jurisprudence He has ever recommended an honorable course in the profession, and condemned the practice of defeating the ends of justice by vexatious litigation, he has continued to cultivate the languages which contribute to successful legal research and confer a more extended general culture, continuing also a diligent student of the English classics, history, biography, oratory, and political economy

In 1878, deprecating the continuance of sectional strife, being convinced that the Republican party had become very corrupt, believing that the system of currency and finance, which was sustained by such men as Sherman and Garfield, was affecting and would continue most seriously to injure the real interests of the American people, prompted by a philanthropic feeling on behalf of the toiling masses, he took an active part in the national greenback labor movement. In his addresses before the people he labored to show them that the law alone must determine what is money; that the leading elements of society, the moral and spiritual, the social and political, depend in great measure on the proper solution of the monetary questions, which were and would continue to be of immense importance. As a man of strong convictions he still has an earnest sympathy for those principles, which of late years have been so much discussed and ably defended by a body of patriotic men, who have made great sacrifices for the welfare of their common country in opposing the misrepresentations and arrogant demands of a despotic money-power. He regards the legal-tender decision lately rendered by the Supreme Court of the United States as being of more actual value than anything ever before enunciated by any legal tribunal, either of ancient or modern times, and as reflecting the highest credit on those learned jurists, who agreed almost unanimously, after long and careful examination, in reaching a wise, constitutional, and just conclusion, which virtually settles the matter forever. He contends, too, that the decision has come opportunely, as vast multitudes are in a condition of enforced idleness, many of whom may be profitably employed in constructing defenses along our extensive line of sea-coast,—liable as we are at any time to be annoyed by the smallest naval power,—and in making internal public improvements of great extent and utility; the expense of such undertakings to be defrayed by fiat paper money, to be issued by the general government, and made a full, absolute, legal tender for all purposes, public and private; thus tending in every way toward enlarging, building up, and rendering perpetual the republic of North America with a grand industrial civilization; at the same time doing much by the light of our example to promote liberty and establish republics in other parts of the world. Mr. Hibberd has thus become liberally educated, and has participated in most of the great progressive movements of his age and country. In relation to all the principal offices, he advocates a large reduction of salaries, and is the steadfast opponent of currency, telegraph, railroad, land, and other great monopolies.

	Admitted.
Samuel Simpson	May 24, 1857.
M. J. Mitcheson	Aug. 28, 1857.
Francis C. Hooton	Nov. 23, 1857.
Aaron Thomson	May 23, 1859.
John K. Valentine	May 23, 1859.
Jacob F. Byrnes	May 23, 1859.
John P. O'Neal	May 23, 1859.
William Ward	Aug. 22, 1859.
Joseph R. T. Coates	Aug. 22, 1859.
O. Flagg Bullard	Aug. 22, 1859.
Frank M. Brooke	Oct. 17, 1859.
H. Ryland Warriner	Dec. 29, 1859.
John S. Newlin	June 4, 1860.
Richard P. White	Aug. 25, 1860.
Nathan S. Sharpless	Sept. 3, 1860.
John Charles Laycock	Oct. 15, 1860.
J. Alexander Simpson	Nov. 26, 1860.
John H. Brinton	Nov. 27, 1860.
John Eyre Shaw	Jan. 25, 1861.
A. V. Parsons	Sept. 23, 1861.
T. Passmore Handbest	Sept. 23, 1861.
William T. Haines	March 30, 1862.
David M. Johnson	June 23, 1862.
M. J. Micheson	Aug. 27, 1862.
William O'Neil	Nov. 26, 1862.
James Doyle	Nov. 26, 1862.
Wayne McVeagh	May 26, 1863.
John B. Hinkson	Aug. 24, 1863.
James Barton, Jr.	Nov. 23, 1863.
James H. Lyttle	Dec. 28, 1863.
William Booth Broomall	Dec. 28, 1863.
John Dolman	July 11, 1864.
John O'Byrne	Nov. 28, 1864.
William Henry Sutton	Feb. 27, 1865.
George F. Smith	Aug. 30, 1865.
Eldridge McKonkey	Nov. 27, 1865.
Theodore H. Oehleschlager	May 28, 1866.
William F. Johnson	May 28, 1866.
William M. Bull	May 28, 1866.
Jesse Cox, Jr.	Aug. 27, 1866.
William H. Yerkes	Aug. 27, 1866.
J. Howard Gendell	March 2, 1867.
George Easty	March 2, 1867.
William F. Judson	May 27, 1867.
Wencel Hartman	Feb. 25, 1868.
George M. Pardoe	March 24, 1868.
Albert S. Letchworth	Sept 28, 1868.
James Parsons	Sept. 28, 1868.
A. P. Reid	Sept. 28, 1868.
John C. Bullitt	Sept. 28, 1868.
Alexander Reed	Sept. 28, 1868.
Orlando Harvey	Nov. 25, 1868.
William H. Dickinson	Nov. 28, 1868.

Mr. Dickinson was one of the most promising members of the bar. In 1878 he was elected the first recorder of the city of Chester. By reason of ill health he was compelled to resign the office, and finally to relinquish practice entirely. He died March 24, 1883.

	Admitted.
James Ross Snowden	Feb. 22, 1869.
George H. Armstrong	Feb. 22, 1869.
Thomas J. Diehl	Feb. 22, 1869.
William J. Harvey	Sept. 27, 1869.
Henry C. Howard	Nov. 23, 1869.
Perry M. Washabaugh	Nov. 23, 1869.
Charles Eyre	Nov. 24, 1869.
Christian Kneass	Feb. 28, 1870.
Samuel Emlen	Nov. 28, 1870.
W. W. Montgomery	March 2, 1870.
W. W. Wistar	March 2, 1870.
William McGeorge, Jr.	Feb. 27, 1871.
Edward C. Diehl	May 25, 1871.
J. L. Farrien	Feb. 29, 1872.
Rees Davis	March 4, 1772.
Morton P. Henry	March 26, 1872.
Carroll S. Tyson	March 26, 1872.
V. Gilpin Robinson	Aug. 29, 1872.
James O. Bowman	Aug. 29, 1872.
James Vincent McGinn	Sept. 23, 1872.
Wesley Talbot	Nov. 25, 1872.
Abram H. Jones	Nov. 25, 1872.
John B. Thayer	Nov. 25, 1872.
John R. Reed	Nov. 25, 1872.
George M. Rupert	Dec. 23, 1872.
Paul M. Elsasser	Dec. 23, 1872.
John V. McGeoghegan	June 23, 1873.
I. Newton Brown	Aug. 24, 1873.
Edward H. Hall	Nov. 24, 1873.
David F. Rose	Nov. 24, 1873.
George M. Booth	Feb. 23, 1874.
H. A. L. Pyle	June —, 1874.
Hutchinson Sprogel	Aug. 27, 1874.
Charles W. Beresford	Sept. 28, 1874.
Thomas H. Foreman	Oct. 26, 1874.
William H. Caley	Nov. 24, 1874.
H. G. Ashmead	Feb. 23, 1875.
George B. Lindsay	Feb. 23, 1875.
Wilber F. Calloway	Feb. 23, 1875.
Theodore F. Jenkins	March 22, 1875.
S. Davis Page	March 22, 1775.
William McMichael	May 22, 1875.
R. Jones Monaghan	May 22, 1875.
Joseph F. Purdue	June 29, 1875.
George W. Bliss	Sept. 20, 1875.

	Admitted
John F Reynolds	Sept 22, 1875
Walter S Pearce	Nov 1, 1875
John V Rice	Dec 14, 1875
Alfred Driver	Dec 13, 1875
Alfred Tyson	Jan 3, 1876
Henry M Fussell	Jan 17, 1876
James McKinlay	June 8, 1876
A S Biddle	June 13, 1876
A C Fulton	Sept 19, 1876
D Smith Talbot	Sept 19, 1876
Joseph W Barnard	Oct 9, 1876
John F Young	Oct 9, 1876
Weldon B Heyburn	Nov 6, 1876
William M Thompson	Nov 6, 1876
Harry L Kingston	Dec 7 1876
Henry Pleasant Jr	Jan 8, 1877
Henry C Townsend	Jan 8, 1877
William B Huston	Feb 5, 1877
John B Hannum	Feb 5, 1877
William S Windle	March 5, 1877
Benjamin F Fisher	March 12 1877
Albert T Goldbeck	March 12, 1877
Frederick C Cleemann	April 2, 1877
J B Dickinson	June 4 1877
John M Broomall Jr	Sept 17, 1877
Benjamin L Temple	Sept 20, 1877
Edmund Jones	Dec 3, 1877
Townsend E Levis	March 4, 1878
Patrick Bradley	April 7, 1878
William S Sykes	April 7, 1878
J Newton Shanafelt	March 6, 1878
S Grafton David	June 3, 1878
John A Groff	June 6, 1878
Truxton Beale	Sept 16, 1878
Rowland Evans	Sept 29 1878
Charles A Logan	Oct 14, 1878
David Garrett	Dec. 2, 1878

David Garrett, in March, 1881, was elected recorder of the city of Chester He died the following August

	Admitted
Oliver B Dickinson	Dec 3, 1878
Ward R Bliss	Dec 3, 1878
George T Bispham	Feb 3 1879
Oliver C McClure	March 5 1879
Curtis H Hannum	March 14 1879
William E Littleton	June 3, 1879
Edward C Quinn	June 9, 1879
Horace P Green	June 9 1879
Garrett Pendleton	July 7, 1879
W Ross Brown	July 7, 1879
Edward H Weil	Sept 22, 1879
Abraham Wanger	Nov 3, 1879
N H Strong	Dec 3, 1879
Joseph M Pile	Dec 4, 1879
H F Fairlamb	June 16, 1880
James S Cummins	Sept 20, 1880
Jesse M Baker	Sept 22, 1880
William A Porter	Sept 25, 1880
Henry J McCarthy	Sept 2, 1880
Ellwood Wilson, Jr	Sept 27, 1880
Edward W Magill	Sept 27, 1880
John B Booth	Dec 6, 1880
Samuel S Cornog	Dec 6, 1880
Benjamin N Lehman	Dec 6, 1880
David W Sellers	Dec 21, 1880
John B Robinson	March 7, 1881
William Herbert	March 14, 1881
R Gordon Bromley	March 14, 1881
Garrett E Smedley	Sept 22, 1881
George Caldwell Johnson	Dec 5 1881
Edward S Campbell	Dec 20, 1881
Henry L Broomall	Feb 6 1882
Harwell A Cloud	Feb 6, 1882
Isaac Chism	Feb 16, 1882
Joseph L Caven	March 4, 1882
Alfred Frank Curtis	June 5, 1882
John W Shortlidge	Nov 6, 1882
Wilmer W Lamborn	Dec. 19 1882
Joseph T Bunting	April 2, 1883
William B Thomas	Sept 24, 1883
Isaac Johnson	Dec 17 1883
William A Manderson	March 17, 1884
Edmund Randall	April 7, 1884
Damon Y Kilgore	April 7, 1884
Mrs Carrie Burnham Kilgore	June 2, 1884
Samuel Lyons	June 9, 1884

Criers—As far as I have ascertained the following persons have been appointed criers of the court Aug 28, 1843, William Thompson, May 24, 1852, William Beeby, Nov 22, 1858, Samuel Otty

On Dec 4, 1871, the Law Library Association of the members of the Delaware County bar was formed, and Hon John M Broomall was elected the first president and Charles D Manley secretary The association was incorporated by the court May 30, 1872

CHAPTER XXVI

PHYSICIANS AND MEDICAL SOCIETIES

It is very likely that the Swedish home authorities in preparing for the colonization of the Delaware, fully aware of the necessity which might arise for the services of a physician, took the precaution to include among the earliest settlers some person skilled in the art of medicine as then practiced, and capable of performing ordinary surgical operations Of this, however, no positive evidence has thus far been discovered Governor Printz, in his expedition, which reached its destination Feb 16, 1643, was accompanied by a surgeon (then called a barber), but history has failed, as far as known, to record the name of the first disciple of Esculapius who thus located on our shores The report of Governor Printz for 1647[1] informs us that "the reason so many people died in the year 1643 was that in the commencement of the settlements they had hard work and but little to eat" Previous to this, in 1641–42, sickness prevailed on the Delaware to such an extent that it scattered the English colony at Salem, and it is alleged that the Swedes also suffered severely from it In 1647 the influenza visited the colony as a scourge, and it is recorded that "such as bled or used cooling drinks died, such as used cordials or more strengthening things recovered for the most part" The summer and fall of 1658 the Delaware River settlements were visited by severe illness We are told by Alrichs,[2] in a letter dated June 26th of that year, that "sickness and hot fevers (are) prevailing here have kept us back badly and made many pining" On August 9th he writes, 'A general fever-like disease has raged here again for some time and it is prevailing much among the inhabitants. The Lord pleased to take us into his merciful protection and relieve many weak people from it" October 7th, he states, "A burning and violent fever rages badly but few old ones have died, but rather many young children who could not endure it" Alrich also wrote respecting this epidemic, "our situation, which is certainly very disheartening by an ardent prevailing fever and other diseases, by which the large majority of the inhabitants are oppressed and broken down, besides that our barber (surgeon) died, and another, well acquainted with his profession, is sick"[3]

---

[1] *Penna. Mag of Hist.*, vol vii p 262

[2] Penna. Archives, 2d series, vol vii p 539

[3] Note to "Contribution to Medical History," by Dr Casper Morris, "Pennsylvania Historical Society Memoir," vol i

We know that Dr Timon Stiddem accompanied the expedition which brought Governor Rising to our shore, landing at Fort Casimir, May 21, 1654,[1] and that he took the oath of allegiance to Peter Stuyvesant in September, 1655, after the Dutch conquest of the colony Certain it is that Dr Stiddem resided for some time at Upland, for on the trial of Evert Hendrixson[2] for an outrageous assault on Joran Kyn, he was one of the most important witnesses for the prosecution, stating in his testimony that the Finn, at different times, and without cause, came before his (the doctor's) door, where he made a great noise and trouble with his axe, that on one occasion, when he was going in his canoe to bleed Jacob Swenson, Evert stoned him on leaving Upland Kill (Chester Creek), so that he was in fear of having his boat sunk or being himself wounded, that he finally got out of the creek, but he was drenched by the splashing of the stones in the water, and finally "he was compelled to leave Upland's kil" because of this ruffian

On Dec 18, 1663, he was appointed by Dr Jacop, who, it appears, held the appointment of the Dutch Company on the Delaware, as his successor, but D'Hinolossa objected to Dr Stiddem, whom he regarded as Beekman's friend,[3] as previous to that date he had been appointed surgeon for the colony under Beekman's jurisdiction The doctor settled at Wilmington, and Governor Lovelace, May 23, 1671, patented to him a tract of land on which a great part of that city was subsequently built He died previous to April 24, 1686, for his will was admitted to probate on that date Professor Keen[4] states that one of the descendants of the doctor now has the metal case, with his name and title engraved upon it, in which he carried his surgical instruments when visiting patients in the Swedish colony

The next physician in point of time is mentioned by name in a letter from Alricks, May 25, 1657,[5] in which he states that Mr Jan Oostiug, the surgeon, has given a memorandum of necessary medicines, and the following year, Oct 10, 1658, he writes,[6] "William Van Rosenberg, who came over as surgeon, put forth sundry claims against the people whom he attended on the passage in as much as his wages did not run at the time on the voyage, and he used his own provisions There were on board the ship considerable sickness, accidents, and hardships, in consequence of a tedious voyage One hundred souls required at least a hogshead or two of French wine and one of brandy, and a tub of prunes had also to be furnished for refreshments and comfort to the sick of scurvy and suffering from other troubles through the protracted voyage, for from want thereof the people became so low that death followed, which is a pretty serious matter Here, on shore, I see clearly that the poor, weak, sick and indigent sometimes have need necessarily of this and that to support them one cannot easily or well refuse, though it be sometimes but a spoonful, frequently repeated it amounts to more than is supposed" Dr Van Rosenberg, it is believed, was to supersede Dr Oostiug, for Alrichs states that "the barber (surgeon) also speaks of a house which Master Jan occupied being too small for him, he hath a wife, servant and child or children also" Westcott[7] states that the doctor who died in the year 1658, as before mentioned, was Dr Oostiug, and the one who was sick was Dr Van Rosenberg, certain it is the latter was living in 1662

Quite early in our annals statutory provision was made respecting the professions, for in the Duke of York's Book of Laws it was declared, so far as this colony was concerned, in 1676,—

> "That no Person or Persons whatsoever Employed about the Bed of Men, women or Children, at any time for preservation of Life or health as Chirurgions, Medicines Physicians or others, presume to Exercise or put forth any Arte Contrary to the known approved Rules of Art in such mistery or Occupation, or Exercise any force, violence or Cruelty upon, or to the Bodice of any whether Young or old, without the advice and Counsell of the such as are skillfull in the same Art (if such may be had) or at least of some of the wisest and gravest then present and Consent of the patient or patients, if they be Mentis Compotes, much less Contrary to such Advice and Consent upon such severe punishment as the nature Of the fault may deserve, which Law nevertheless, is not intended to discourage any from all Lawful use of their skill but rather to encourage and direct them in the right use thereof, and to inhabit and restrain the presumptious arogancy of such as through Confidence of their own skill, or any sinister Respect dare bouldly attempt to Exercise any violence upon or toward the body of young or old, one or other, to the prejudice or hazard of the Life or Limb of man, woman or child"[8]

In 1678/9 Dr Thomas Spry was a witness in a case tried at Upland on March 12th of that year

In the Journal of Sluyters and Dankers,[9] who visited Tinicum in 1679, it is stated that they met at that island Otto Earnest Cock, a Swede, whom they speak of as "late medicus," indicating that he had been, but was not then, a practicing physician Before that date, however, we find that at the court held at Upland, Aug 24, 1672, a petition was presented from certain residents of Amasland, which clearly indicates that the midwife who gave to that

[1] It may be questioned whether the date given as of Dr Stiddem's arrival is not erroneous In the deposition of John Thickpenny (New Haven Colonial Record, vol i p 106) it is stated that while George Lamberton and the English settlers, who had been expelled from New Jersey by Governor Printz in 1643, were at Tinicum, Printz's wife and Timothy, the barber (surgeon), strove to get John Woollen drunk by furnishing him a quantity of wine and strong beer, with the intention, while he was intoxicated, of making him say that George Lamberton "had hired the Indians to cut off the Swedes" If the doctor who came with Printz was "Timothy" Stiddem, then he was in New Sweden ten years before the date given in the text, which is the time mentioned by Professor Keen as the probable date of the doctor's arrival on the Delaware ("Descendants of Joran Kyn," *Penna Mag of Hist.*, vol iii p 337)

[2] "Documents relating to the History of the Dutch and Swedish Settlements on Delaware River," vol xii p 424

[3] Penna Archives, 2d series, vol vii p 697

[4] "Descendants of Joran Kyn," by Professor G B Keen, *Penna Mag. of Hist.*, vol iii p 339 (note)

[5] "Documentary History of New York," Penna Archives, 2d series, vol v p 288

[6] Penna Archives, 2d series, vol v p. 305

[7] History of Philadelphia, chap iii (*Sunday Dispatch*)

[8] Duke of York's Book of Laws, p. 20

[9] Journal of Voyage to New York in 1679-80, Memoirs of the Long Island Historical Society, vol i p 177

place the name it still has was located in Ridley previous to that year [1] Hence from the number of physicians, or "practioners of physick," already shown to be present in the colony previous to the year 1698, the remark of Gabriel Thomas was hardly true even at that time, that "of lawyers and physicians I shall say nothing, because this country is very peaceable and healthy Long may it so continue, and never have occasion for the tongue of one nor the pen of the other, both equally destructive to men's estate and lives, besides, forsooth, they hang-men like have a license to murder and make mischief."

Dr John Goodsonn was a physician in Chester in 1681 [2] He was termed "Chirurgeon to the Society of Free Traders," came from London, and settled in Upland for a short time previous to the first visit of William Penn He subsequently removed to Philadelphia Dr Smith states he "was probably the first practicing physician in Pennsylvania" [3] In this remark, however, the author quoted is incorrect In 1694, Dr Goodsonn was appointed Deputy Governor under William Markham, his commission being signed by William Penn He resided in Philadelphia in 1690, for his letter to William Penn is dated from that city, 20th of Sixth month of that year [4] Prior to 1700, Joseph Richards is mentioned as a physician at Chester, where he owned real estate [5]

The records of the physicians who practiced in this county during the last century can only be gathered from old letters or accounts filed in estate in the Orphans' Court, where sometimes the physician's name is given among the claims paid

Isaac Taylor, who had been formerly sheriff of Bucks County in 1693, and was a noted surveyor in primitive days, "at the time of his death was a resident of Tinicum Island, practising the art of surgery" The statement of Professor Keen, just quoted, is directly opposed by that of Gilbert Cope,[6] who tells us Dr Taylor died in Thornbury in 1728 Dr Isaac Taylor's son John we know was a surveyor and physician, as his father had been, but in 1740 he embarked in the iron business, erected the noted Sarum Forge, at the present Glen Mills, on Chester Creek

We learn from a petition on file in West Chester that in November, 1736, Alexander Gandonett was located in Chester, and he describes himself as a "Practioner in Physyck" He asked the court to grant him a license for the sale of liquor. He states

"Your Petitioner, by way of his Practice, is Obliged to Distill several sorts of Cordiall writers and it being often Requested by several of the inhabitants of this County to sell the same by small measure your Petitioner Conceiving that the same be of absolute necessity by way of his Practice yet that it may be Considered to be within the Act of Assembly for selling liquor by small prays your honours for the premises"

His application was recommended by Joseph Parker (the clerk of the court), John Salkeld, Thomas Cummings, Joseph Hoskins, John Wharton, and thirteen others, most of whom resided in Chester, or close in the vicinity of the borough, and were all prominent citizens The court, however, did not immediately take action on the petition, for it is indorsed, "Referred to further Consideration" After this we learn nothing further of the fate of his "Cordiall waters" The doctor we know was in practice in Chester in January, 1747, for at that time he asked payment from the province for medicine and attendance on the sick soldiers of Capt Shannon's company quartered there

John Paschall, who is said to have been born in Darby, about 1706, was never regularly educated for the profession, but he acquired considerable medical and chemical knowledge, which made him conspicuous in his day He practiced medicine in the county, residing at Darby, and prepared a nostrum called "The Golden Elixer," which was widely advertised as "Paschall's Golden Drops" He died at Darby in 1779, aged about seventy-three years

Dr Jonathan Morris was born in Marple, May 17, 1729 He studied under Dr Bard, of Philadelphia, and after he had graduated located in Marple, where he practiced until near the close of his life, which was extended until within one month of his ninetieth year

In St Paul's churchyard, in the city of Chester, is a slab of marble lying lengthwise, which bears this inscription

"Here lies
PAUL JACKSON, A M
He was the first who received a Degree
In the College of Philadelphia
A man of virtue, worth and knowledge
DIED 1767, AGED 36 YEARS"

Paul Jackson, whose remains repose in the vault covered by this slab, was not only prominent as a physician, soldier, linguist, and chief burgess of Chester at a time when that office was one of great honor, but in his short life had become distinguished as one of the most accomplished scholars in the colony He was of Scotch-Irish parentage, and became Professor of Languages in the College of Philadelphia (now the University of Pennsylvania) "His Latin compositions, which were published, secured for him a reputation for correct taste and accurate scholarship" [7]

His studious application impaired his health, and when Gen Forbes led the expedition against Fort Du Quesne he was appointed, May 11, 1758, captain of the Third Battalion of the Pennsylvania Regiment (Governor William Denny, colonel) [8] His active life as a

[1] "Amasland was first called Amman's land A midwife formerly lived at the place where Archer's farm now is, hence that place, and subsequently the whole tract around it, received the name of Amman's Land, now Amas Land."—*Acrelius' History of New Sweden*, p 204, *Record of Upland Court*, p 65

[2] Colonial Records, vol i p 429

[3] Smith's "History of Delaware County," p 465

[4] *Penna Mag of Hist.*, vol iv p 192

[5] Martin's "History of Chester," p 495

[6] History of Chester County, p 738.

[7] *Penna Mag of Hist*, vol ii p 59 (note)

[8] Penna Archives, 2d series, vol ii p 564

soldier restoring him to health, he concluded to study medicine After he received his degree he came to Chester, where he married Jane, daughter of John Mather, and practiced his profession with marked success He was, as stated before, chief burgess of Chester His widow, in three years after his death, married Dr David Jackson, a brother of her first husband The latter, during the Revolutionary war, was surgeon-general of the Pennsylvania troops, appointed Sept 30, 1780 He graduated at the first medical commencement of the University of Pennsylvania, June 21, 1768, and was recorded as of Chester County [1]

The late Dr Charles J Morton[2] wrote, at the request of the Delaware County Medical Society, an interesting biographical notice of the centenarian physician, Bernhard Van Leer, which Dr Smith has most admirably abridged for insertion in his "History of Delaware County" In the following account of the venerable physician I have largely used the exact words of Dr Smith's sketch

Bernhard Van Leer, the son of John George Van Leer, was born near Isenberg, in the electorate of Hesse, in 1686, and emigrated to the province of Pennsylvania when eleven years of age The family located in Marple, and Bernhard, or Bernhardus, as he was then called, remained a few years with his father, and then returned to Germany for the purpose of studying medicine in his native land It is said that he was accompanied by a neighboring youth, John Worrell, who had the same object in view Young Van Leer remained in Europe seven years, and not only studied medicine but also the classics and French Some time after his return to this country, and shortly after he commenced the practice of his profession, he was married to Mary Branson, the daughter of a wealthy merchant of Philadelphia, who died many years before her husband, after having given birth to five children, two of whom, Branson and Benjamin, became physicians Dr Bernhard Van Leer married again, and by the latter marriage there were nine children, one of whom was Dr Bernard Van Leer, of Marple The elder Dr Van Leer was a man of great physical vigor In his one hundredth year he rode on horseback from Marple to his Chester County farm, a distance of thirty miles, in one day In his one hundred and second year he was cruelly maltreated by burglars who entered his house because he refused to disclose his hidden treasure He did not fully recover from his injuries then received He died on the 26th of January, 1790, aged one hundred and four years

His practice was chiefly conducted in his office It is said that in the diagnosis of disease he relied very much upon the appearance of some of the secretions that were brought to him for inspection His remedies for the most part were from the vegetable kingdom, and generally of the mildest form

This system was certainly not adhered to by his son, Branson, who seems to have located in the borough of Chester, where he acted as the county physician, for the following bill shows that at least one of his patients had her full share of medication

Chester County to Dr Branson Van Leer, *Dr*

1769			£	s	d
Jan	25	Bleeding Ann Gregory	0	2	6
"	25	A vomit	0	0	6
"	26	Pleuritec drop	0	4	2
"	26	Six pectoral powders	0	3	0
"	26	A cordial julep	0	4	6
"	27	A cordial julep	0	4	6
"	27	Six pectoral powders	0	3	0
"	27	A pectoral linctus	0	3	0
"	27	Pleuritic drops	0	4	2
"	28	Six pectoral powders	0	3	0
"	28	Two blistering plasters	0	5	0
"	28	Plaister	0	1	6
"	29	Six pleuritic drops	0	3	0
"	29	A purging Bolus	0	1	6
"	29	A cordial julep	0	4	6
"	30	Purging ingredients	0	2	0
"	30	Plaister	0	1	6
"	30	Six pectoral powders	0	3	0
"	31	A cordial julep	0	4	6
Feb	1	Six pectoral powders	0	3	0
"	1	Pleuritec drops	0	4	0
"	1	A pectoral linctus	0	3	0
"	1	A cordial julep	0	3	0
"	2	Six pictoral powders	0	3	0
"	2	A cordial julep	0	4	6
"	4	A febrifuge julep	0	4	6
"	4	A pectoral linctus	0	3	0
"	4	Plaistor	0	1	6
"	4	Purging bolus	0	1	6
"	4	A pectoral linctus	0	3	0
"	8	A pectoral linctus	0	3	0
"	8	A cordial julep	0	4	6
"	10	A pectoral linctus	0	3	0
			£5	8	6

Of Dr Richard Van Leer I have learned nothing other than that he was a physician, while of Dr Bernard Van Leer, he practiced in this county, living on the old homestead in Marple, where he died in February, 1814

Dr Benjamin Van Leer settled in New Castle County, Del, for in 1762, in the advertisement of the lottery for St Paul's Church, Chester, it is stated that tickets can be had of him and several other gentlemen in that locality [3]

John Worrall, the lad who accompanied Bernhard Van Leer to Europe, is said to have been a son of Peter Worrall, of Marple, and that he graduated in Germany as a physician, returned to Delaware County, and settled in Upper Providence In 1724 he married Hannah Taylor, and died while still a young man His son, Dr Thomas Worrall, was born in Upper Providence in 1732, and married Lydia Vernon, an aunt of Maj Frederick and Capt Job Vernon, who rendered good service to the American arms in the Revolution, and a sister of Gideon Vernon, who was conspicuous during that struggle for his loyalty to the English crown, and whose estates were confiscated by the authorities of Pennsylvania because of his warm espousal of the British cause Dr Thomas Worrall in his practice made use largely of our native herbs, as did many of the physicians in

[1] History of University of Pennsylvania, Memoirs of Penna Hist Soc., vol iii p 197

[2] *The Medical Reporter*, No vii., April, 1856

[3] *Pennsylvania Journal*, Jan 14, 1762

those days He died in 1818, aged eighty-six years Hon William Worrall, of Ridley, has one of the medical works he frequently consulted in his practice, and in his handwriting on the fly-leaf, in faded ink, can easily be read

> "Thomas Worrall's doctor book,
> God give him grace to in it look"

Some of the remedies in vogue in the time of the Revolution would not be accepted by the profession, and hardly meet the approval of the general public of this day I copy from the manuscript receipt-book of Capt Davis Bevan,[1] used during July and the early part of August, 1779, when enlisting at Chester a crew for the privateer brigantine "Holker," of which vessel Bevan was captain of marines, the following remedy

> "A RECEIPT FOR A SORE MOUTH.—To a gill of vinegar add a spoonful of honey and ten or twelve sage leaves, set these on a few coals in a clean earthen cup and let it boil a little, then burn the inner soal of an old shoe that has been lately worn, which when burnt to a coal, rub to a fine powder, take out the sage leaves and add a thimble full of the powder, with half as much allum powdered Stop it close in a bottle and wash your mouth twice a day, after breakfast and after supper It seldom fails to cure in a few days, and will fasten teeth loosened by the scurvey"

Dr John Cochran, of Chester County, director-general of the military hospitals during the Revolution, does not seem to have practiced in the territory now comprising Delaware County, and the same remark is true of Dr Samuel Kennedy, who was surgeon of the Fourth Battalion of the Pennsylvania troops and senior surgeon in the military hospital

Dr William Currie,[2] a native of Chester County, in his youth intended to study theology, but he abandoned that purpose, read medicine, and graduated at the college at Philadelphia On the breaking out of the Revolutionary war, his father, the rector of St David's Church, Radnor, and a loyalist, opposed his desire to enter the Continental service, but he persisted, and served as a surgeon in 1776, attached to the hospital on Long Island and subsequently at Amboy On the conclusion of the struggle, Dr Currie, then in his twenty-ninth year, located in the borough of Chester, where he practiced medicine, and married a daughter of John Morton, the signer of the Declaration of Independence Previous to 1792 he removed to Philadelphia, and published his "Historical Account of the Climate and Diseases of the United States" In 1811 he issued "Views of the Diseases most prevalent in the United States, with an account of the most improved methods of treating them," and in 1815 his last work, "General View of the Principal Theories or Doctrines which have prevailed at different periods to the present time" He died in Philadelphia in 1829

Dr John Morton, the third son of John Morton, the signer of the Declaration, was a surgeon in the Continental service, was taken prisoner, and while so detained he died on the British prison ship "Falmouth," in New York harbor "The late John S Morton, of Springfield, had for some time a letter in his possession, written by Dr Morton to his father while he was a prisoner, in which he said they were almost starved, and could eat brick-bats if they could get them"[3]

During and after the Revolution, Dr John Smith was a practicing physician located in Lower Chichester In 1783 he married Dorothea, sister of Henry Hale Graham She died in 1798 of yellow fever, and it is said her husband had died several years before this time

Dr Peter Yarnall, who, between the years 1780 and 1791, resided in Concord, practicing his profession, in which he was highly successful, had a very eventful career He was by birthright a Friend, but in 1772, when eighteen years of age, he quarreled with his master, for at that day all young men had to serve an apprenticeship, ran away, and enlisted The influence of his family succeeded in getting him released from the service Immediately on attaining his majority he began reading medicine, but when the colonies appealed to arms he enlisted in the American army, acting as surgeon's mate in the field and in several hospitals His health, however, failing, in 1778 he asked for and received his discharge Thereupon he applied himself diligently to the study of his profession, and in 1779 he graduated from the College of Medicine of Philadelphia, and returned to the service as surgeon's mate, sailing on the privateer "Delaware," but again he resigned, and practiced in the Pennsylvania Hospital In 1780 he reunited with the Quakers, became a public Friend, located in Concord, and married, in 1732, Hannah Sharpless, of Middletown In 1791 he removed to Montgomery County, where, his wife having died, he for the second time married He died in 1798, the year the yellow fever was so fatal to the profession

Dr Elisha Cullen Dick, who was called upon, together with Dr Brown as consulting physician, by Dr Craik, the medical attendant of Washington during the fatal illness of the latter in December, 1799, was a native of Delaware County, having been born near Marcus Hook Cross-road in 1762 He seems never to have practiced here, but married, October, 1783, Hannah Harman, of Darby He settled at Alexandria, Va, where he soon gathered a large practice It is said that Dr Dick, when all hopes of the recovery of Washington "with less extreme remedies had been abandoned, proposed an operation which he ever afterwards thought might have proved effective in saving the general's life, but it did not meet with the approval of the family physician"[4]

[1] The book is now in possession of the Delaware County Institute of Science, to whom it was presented by Dr Allen, of Chester

[2] Biographical notice of Dr William Currie, Hazard's Register, vol vi p 204

[3] Martin's "History of Chester," p 145

[4] The fullest sketch of Dr Dick yet published will be found in Thomas Maxwell Potts' "Centenary Memorial of Jeremiah Carter," p 75

At the beginning of the year 1799 the following physicians were practicing in Delaware County, residing in the townships mentioned:

William Pennell, Aston; Nicholas Newlin, Caleb S. Sayres, Lower Chichester; Joseph Shallcross, William Gardiner, Darby; Jonathan Morris, Bernard Van Leer, Marple; John Knight, Middletown; Jonas Preston, Newtown; John Cheyney, Thornbury.

The same year Jane Davis kept "an apothecary-shop" in Chester, the first person who ever kept a store of that kind in the county, although it seems that about that time Dr. Sayres had a shop attached to his dwelling at Marcus Hook.

Dr. William Martin, the grandfather of John Hill Martin, the author of the "History of Chester and its Vicinity," was born in Philadelphia in 1765, and was a man of much prominence in the annals of Delaware County. He was a physician as well as a lawyer, a justice of the peace, and chief burgess of Chester, and, in April, 1789, when Washington passed through Chester on his way to Philadelphia, Dr. Martin made the address of congratulation to the President on behalf of the town. In the year 1798 the yellow fever visited Chester as a fearful scourge. Dr. Martin was much alarmed, and seemed to have a presentiment that he would die of the pestilence. It is said that he frequently rode to the windows of the houses where persons were sick with the fever, would learn the condition of the patient, and prescribe and furnish the medicine without entering the dwelling. In September of that year, however, a British vessel was lying off Chester with all hands ill with the fever. Dr. Martin was sent for; he attended, and, as he had feared, he contracted the disease from which he died, Sept. 28, 1798.

It is recorded of him that he would never attend the funerals of any of his patients, and being pressed for a reason why he declined to be present replied, "No, sir; it looks too much like a carpenter taking his own work home."

Dr. Caleb Smith Sayers, who settled at Marcus Hook about 1789, was a descendant of Richard Sears, —the New England branch of the family still adhere to that manner of spelling the name,—who located at Plymouth, Mass., in 1630. Dr. Sayers was born in Elizabeth, N. J., his immediate ancestor being among the first settlers of that place. His residence at Marcus Hook still stands on Church Street, fronting the Delaware, a porch running along the entire front of the building. During the yellow fever in 1798, so constant and laborious was his practice consequent on the epidemic, that his physical strength failed under the excessive strain, and he died in 1799 at the early age of thirty-one years. He was at that time surgeon of the Eighth Battalion of Militia of the county of Delaware, commanded by Lieut.-Col. Edward Vernon. His son, Edward S. Sayers, who was consul for Brazil and vice-consul for Portugal, died in Philadelphia in March, 1877, aged seventy-seven years.

Dr. Jonas Preston was born in Chester, Jan. 25, 1764. He read medicine with Dr. Bond, of Philadelphia, attended lectures at the Pennsylvania Hospital, and after the usual course of medical instruction attainable at that time in the United States he went to Europe, graduating at the University of Edinburgh in 1785, and subsequently attended lectures at Paris. On his return to this country he located at Wilmington, Del., for a short time, thence removed to Georgia, but returning to Delaware County, he entered energetically into the duties of his profession, and soon acquired an extensive practice in Chester and Delaware Counties, confining himself almost entirely to obstetric cases, in which special department he soon established a reputation extending beyond the limits of the territory mentioned. During the Whiskey Insurrection in 1794 he volunteered as surgeon in the army. This caused him to be expelled from meeting, but he frequently said Friends might disown him, but he would not disown them. He represented Delaware County for eight terms in the Legislature, from 1794 to 1802, and in 1808 he was elected State senator, and was distinguished for his liberal views and sagacious foresight. About 1817 he removed from Marple to Philadelphia, but previously had been elected president of the Bank of Delaware County, succeeding John Newbold. While here he was an ardent advocate of all measures having for their object agricultural improvements. After his removal to Philadelphia he enjoyed a large and remunerative practice, and notwithstanding his busy life he had time to take an active part in many benevolent objects. He was a constant visitor at the Pennsylvania Hospital, and also Friends' Asylum at Frankford. He was a director of the Pennsylvania Bank, Schuylkill Navigation Company, and other corporations. During his long professional career he had so frequently seen distress among the honest poor classes that when he died, April 4, 1836, he left by will four hundred thousand dollars "towards founding an institution for the relief of indigent married women of good character, distinct and unconnected with any hospital, where they may be received and provided with proper obstetric aid for their delivery, with suitable attendance and comforts during their period of weakness and susceptibility which ensues." Under this provision in his will was established the Preston Retreat, in Philadelphia, one of the noblest institutions of enlarged charity within the commonwealth of Pennsylvania. Dr. Preston was buried in Friends' graveyard, on Edgmont Avenue, in Chester, but his remains have been removed therefrom in recent years.

Dr. William Gardiner. I have thus far learned nothing beyond the facts set out in the list mentioned. I presume he was the son of Dr. Joseph Gardiner, who, in 1779, was a member of the Supreme Executive Council from Chester County. We do know that Dr. William Gardiner had a son, Dr. Richard Gardiner, who was born in Darby in 1793, who was a graduate of the University of Pennsylvania, and practiced in Darby, afterwards in Newtown, until 1835, when he removed to Philadelphia In the latter place he studied homœopathy, and graduated, in 1848, from the Homœopathic College He subsequently acquired a large and lucrative practice in Philadelphia Dr Gardiner died in 1877, in his eighty-fifth year

Dr Isaac Davis, son of Gen John Davis, was born in Chester County, July 27, 1787, and in 1806 became a student of medicine under Dr Joseph Shalcross, of Darby, graduated in 1810, when he began practice in Edgmont, but on the breaking out of the war of 1812 was appointed surgeon of the Sixth United States Infantry He died at Fort Jackson, Miss, July 21, 1814

Dr Jacob Tobin seems to have practiced in Chester about the beginning of this century, as did Dr Richard Tidmarsh Dr —— Brown had a number of patients in the same locality, but I have been unable to learn his first name or the place of his residence I do not know anything more of Drs Tobin and Tidmarsh than their names Dr George W. Bartram was a practicing physician, residing in Chester, where he kept a drug-store in the house which formerly stood on the site of Brown's Hotel He was a justice of the peace, chief burgess of the borough for a number of years, and customs officer at the Lazaretto Previous to 1818, Dr Edward Woodward was in practice in this county, and resided in Middletown In 1808 Dr Nathan Hayes was a practicing physician in Edgmont

Dr Job H Terrill came to Chester early in this century, and in October, 1809, purchased the house on Market Street where Maurice Beaver lately had his tin-store, the grounds extending to Fourth Street The doctor was a man of fine conversational powers, possessing a ready vocabulary, and was rapid in his utterances. He was a noted lover of horses, and always kept one of the best, if not the best, in Chester He would have his negro man, Ike, train his horses on Welsh Street, and would stand and watch them speeding along from Edgmont road to the Porter house and back. He always rode in a sulky, and in getting in one day his horse started, threw him against the vehicle, and injured his thigh so severely that it brought on a disease which ultimately proved fatal He died Jan. 20, 1844, aged fifty-nine years

Dr. Samuel Anderson was not a native of this county, but his career therein was one of much honor and public usefulness. In early life he entered the United States navy as assistant surgeon, but after holding the commission a few years he resigned the service and located in Chester, when he began the practice of his profession, securing in a short time a prominent position During the war of 1812 he raised a company of volunteers,—the Mifflin Guards, —became its captain, and served with his command in the fall of 1814 at Camp Du Pont for three months In 1815–18 he represented Delaware County in the Legislature, and was elected sheriff in 1819 In 1823 he was again appointed assistant surgeon in the United States navy, and assigned to the West India station, then commanded by Commodore Porter, but he was compelled to resign therefrom on account of his health Returning to Delaware County, he was elected, 1823, 1824, and 1825, to the Legislature, and the following year represented the district composing Delaware, Chester, and Lancaster Counties in Congress In 1829–33 he was a member of the Legislature, and the last year the Speaker of the House In 1834–35 he was again the representative from this county, and made the report of the joint committee of the two houses relative to the alleged abuses in the Eastern Penitentiary, at that time one of the most important questions before the people of the State Dr Anderson then resided in Providence, on the farm now owned by Samuel Lewis He subsequently removed to Rockdale, where he practiced his profession until 1841, when he was appointed inspector of customs at the Lazaretto In 1846 he was elected justice of the peace in Chester, an office he held at the time of his death, Jan 17, 1850, in his seventy-seventh year Dr Anderson was a tall, slender, conspicuous personage, of fine mind, an agreeable speaker, and a ready, fluent debater For many years he was president of the Delaware County Bible Society He married Sarah Moore (she was then a widow), daughter of Jacob Richards, and her sister, Susan, was the wife of Dr Caleb S Sayers, of Marcus Hook Mrs Anderson survived the doctor nearly twenty-one years, dying Nov 4, 1870, in the ninety-fifth year of her age

Among the physicians who practiced in Delaware County from 1800 to 1850 (at which latter date the Delaware County Medical Society was organized, and a list of the doctors then practicing was made and has ever since been regularly kept) I find notice of the following

Ellis C Harlan was in practice and resided at Sneath's Corner, Chester township, early in this century He, with Dr William Gray and several other physicians, on Friday night, Dec 17, 1824, made an autopsy of Wellington's body (he had been hung about noon of that day) in the old pole well-house, as it was then known, which, modernized, still stands on the north side of Third Street, below Franklin Street, Chester. Dr Jesse Young succeeded Dr Harlan about 1825, and continued at Sneath's Corner until his death, Aug 29, 1852 Dr Young, however, a short time previous to his decease, had associated with him Dr James Serrell Hill, at any rate, the office of the latter being at Dr. Young's residence Dr David Rose succeeded Dr Young at Sneath's Corner, and still resides there practicing his profession

Dr Benjamin Rush Erwin practiced in Upper Providence until the fall of 1829, when he removed to Philadelphia, and Dr Joseph Leedom succeeded him, to be in turn succeeded, in 1843, by Dr James Boyd, of Montgomery County, whose residence and office was at the Rose Tree Tavern Dr James Wilson was in practice in Nether Providence many years before 1840, while in 1838, Dr William L Cowan, a Thomsonian physician, had his office near Friends' meeting-house, in that township

Dr Gideon Humphreys was a practicing physician in Aston in 1820 Of the latter it is related that, on one occasion when he desired to prepare a skeleton from the corpse of a colored man drowned in Chester Creek, he borrowed a very large iron kettle from a neighbor In the night, while he was at work in the spring-house, a huge fire under the pot, some one passing near saw the light, went to the spring-house, and reported next day that the "Doctor had boiled a darkey's head in the pot" This coming to the ears of the owner of the article, she, when it was sent home, returned it, saying, "Tell the doctor to keep that pot to boil another nigger in I won't have the nasty thing in my house" Dr George R Morton was located at Village Green in 1827 He seems to have removed from Marlborough, Montgomery Co, for on July 10, 1826, he contributed to the *American Medical Review* an interesting account of a horned woman residing in that locality[1] Dr —— Byington was in practice in Aston about 1833 Dr Samuel A Barton was there previous to 1840, and Dr Richard Gregg, then residing at Wrangletown, had a number of patients in that locality He subsequently removed to Lima, where he died in July, 1872 Dr Joseph Wilson was a practicing physician in Springfield in 1812, and was captain of the Delaware County troop of horse and prominent in the political movements of the day In 1837, Dr James Jenkins was located in Radnor, as was also Dr Joseph Blackfan, and the same year Dr J F Huddleson was in Thornbury In 1833, Dr M C Shallcross resided in Darby, and was in full practice, about 1840 he removed to Philadelphia, locating near Haddington, where he associated himself with Dr J P Stakes, and for some time continued from that place to practice in Delaware County Dr Shallcross died in Philadelphia, Nov 30, 1871, aged eighty-one years About 1823, Dr Joshua W Ash began practice in Upper Darby, where he continued until his death, in March, 1874, in the seventy-seventh year of his age He was a member of Friends' meeting, warmly interested in the Delaware County Institute of Science, and prominently connected with the Training-School for Feeble-Minded Children The first map of Delaware County, drawn from actual surveys, was published in 1848 by the doctor In 1833, Dr Caleb Ash was in Darby, his office located opposite Friends' meeting-house Prior to 1848, Dr George Thomas was in full practice at the same place, but in 1845 he seemed to have located in Newtown or Edgmont, and about 1833, Dr William Gray Knowles was in Darby; he subsequently removed to Baltimore, and is now a resident of Upland In 1852, Dr P J Hoopes was a physician in that village, and in the same year Dr James Aitkins was in practice in Edgmont, as in 1842 was Dr H Bent, a botanic Thomsonian physician In 1840, Dr Phineas Price was located in Bethel, and was conspicuous in a noted controversy he had with Levis Pyle At August court, 1849, Dr Price was indicted and convicted of an assault on Pyle The parties had met in the Methodist Church to adjust some church business, a dispute arose between them respecting characters, when Dr Price forcibly ejected Pyle, hence the prosecution In 1844, Dr Price had been tried by the church, if my informant is correct in his statement, because of some religious opinions which were regarded as unsound Andrew Hance and the doctor subsequently got into a newspaper controversy, and finally each of them published pamphlets For some statement made in that issued by Dr Price he was sued for libel, whether criminal or civil proceedings were instituted I do not know In 1844, Dr. J H Marsh practiced in Concord, as did Dr George Martin in 1852

[1] Hazard's Register, vol ii p 11

Dr William Gray, a member of the well-known family of Gray, of Gray's Ferry, was for many years one of the most noted men of the county He was born in 1795, and in early life he had gone to his uncle, Thomas Steel, a miller in Darby, to learn that business, but finding the occupation uncongenial, he abandoned it, and studied medicine under his relation, Dr Warfield, of Maryland After he graduated he settled in Chester, where for many years he had a large and lucrative practice He died May 12, 1864

Dr John M Allen, in 1844, practiced in Chester, his office then being in Charles W Raborg's drug-store, where Charles A Story, Sr, now has his cigar-store In the spring of 1845, Dr Allen leased Dr. Terrill's house and altered the front part of the building into a drug-store, where he soon secured a large and profitable business In 1851, Dr Allen purchased the property where Mortimer H Bickley's large building now stands, and continued there until the breaking out of the war, in 1861, when he was appointed surgeon of the Fifty-fourth Pennsylvania Volunteers, and subsequently medical director of the Department of West Virginia, and surgeon-in-chief of staff, in which position he served until late in the year of 1864, when his health broke down, and he was honorably discharged from the service after having been in the hospital several months He is now alderman of the Middle Ward, an office he fills most creditably

During the forties, and until about 1855, Dr James Porter practiced in Chester, residing at that time in the old Porter house Dr R K Smith, a physician at Chichester Cross-roads, in 1841 sold his practice to Dr Manley Emanuel, who succeeded him there, although Dr Smith still continued to practice in

Delaware County Dr Emanuel, subsequently to 1870, removed to Philadelphia, where he died July 18, 1880, aged eighty-three years His son, Dr Lewis M Emanuel, who was born in London, and was a lad of seven years when his father settled in Upper Chichester, after he graduated began practicing at Linwood, but during the war of the Rebellion he became an assistant surgeon in the field The exposure consequent thereon induced consumption, which terminated in his death in 1868

Dr Jesse Kersey Bonsall was by birth a Delaware countian, studied medicine and graduated at the University of Pennsylvania, and for a time located in Schuylkill County, but an opportunity offering, he went to Manila, the capital of the Philippine Islands, where he practiced successfully for several years In 1842 he returned to Delaware County, having accumulated while abroad what at that time was regarded as an ample fortune Here he pursued his professional calling, residing in Chester until his death, Nov 7, 1858, aged sixty-one years

Professor Charles D Meigs, M D, who, however, never practiced in our county, was for many years at the head of the Jefferson Medical College, in Philadelphia, at one time connected with the Obstetrical Department of the University of Pennsylvania, and whose work on the diseases of women gave him a world-wide reputation in the profession, died suddenly, at his residence in Aston, June 23, 1869 He was in his seventy-eighth year at the time of his death On the morning of Nov 21, 1872, Dr Tracey E Waller, a practicing physician at Marcus Hook, where he had been located for several years, was found dead in his bed He had retired the night before apparently in good health Dr Chittick Verner—said to be a descendant of Lord John Lammey, a Huguenot, who, with his brother James, fled from France to escape persecution and became a British subject—died in Chester, April 4, 1877 Dr Verner was educated for the ministry, but abandoned it when the court at Castle Derg, Ireland, appointed him syndic for the town of Ardistraw, a position he held for several years. In 1847 he emigrated to America, and became surgeon-steward at the Naval Asylum, Philadelphia While there he studied medicine, graduating at Jefferson College, and during the Rebellion he was in service in the field as a surgeon At the close of the war he practiced medicine in Philadelphia, but the death of his brother, to whom he was devotedly attached, so preyed on him as to unsettle his mind From that time to his death he was insane He never practiced in this county

On Feb 10, 1880, Dr Joshua Owens died of paralysis in Chester, aged sixty-five years Dr Owens was a native of Elizabethport, N. J, and a graduate of Jefferson College, Philadelphia He first located at Elkton, Md, but a few years subsequently removed to Chester. During the war of the Rebellion he was senior surgeon of Pennsylvania, and was the first volunteer physician to reach Washington after the attack on Fort Sumter He was one of the first medical directors of divisions, and was assigned to duty with the Army of the Potomac In 1863 he was commissioned surgeon-general of New Mexico, a position he resigned in 1865 Dr Owens and his two sons made a tour of Europe on foot, and the graphic descriptions of his travel and noted places he saw, which appeared in the *Delaware County Republican*, were highly interesting The doctor was a strong and vigorous writer

Dr Mordecai Laurence, a venerable physician, died in Haverford, Feb 21, 1880, in the seventy-seventh year of his age

Dr George Smith was born in Haverford, Feb 4, 1804 He graduated at the University of Pennsylvania, April 7, 1820, and practiced in Darby and its vicinity for five years, when, coming into possession of a large estate, he retired from the active duties of the profession, superintending his farm, and devoting his leisure moments to literary and scientific studies From 1832 to 1836 he was State senator, the district then comprising Delaware and Chester Counties, and while a member of that body, as chairman of the Senate Committee on Education, he drafted the bill in reference to public schools, which, warmly supported by Thaddeus Stevens and George Wolf, passed substantially as reported by Dr Smith, and thus the first practical enactment respecting free public education in the State was secured On Dec 8, 1836, Governor Ritner appointed Dr Smith an associate judge of Delaware County, and in 1840 he was elected to the same position for a second term So earnest was Dr Smith in his advocacy of popular education that, at considerable personal inconvenience, he consented to act as superintendent of the common schools in the county for several years, as well as president of the school board for Upper Darby district In September, 1833, he, with four other public-spirited men, founded the Delaware County Institute of Science, and was president of the organization for nearly half a century In 1844, Dr Smith, John P Crozer, and Minshall Painter were appointed by the Delaware County Institute a committee to prepare an account of the extraordinary rain-storm and flood of August 5th of that year in this county, and the greater part of the preparation of that work, an octavo pamphlet of fifty-two pages, printed in solid small pica type, was done by Dr Smith In 1862 he published his "History of Delaware County," a volume which will stand as an enduring monument to the learning, accuracy, and thoroughness of its author, and, so long as American history continues to be a theme of investigation and study, will be quoted and referred to as authority On the morning of Feb 24, 1884, full of years and honor, Dr George Smith passed into eternity, leaving the world the better in that he had lived

Dr Isaac Taylor Coates, a native of Chester County,

was born March 17, 1834 Determining to study medicine, his means being limited, he taught school in Delaware County to obtain the required sum necessary not only for his own support, but to complete his professional education In 1858 he graduated from the University of Pennsylvania, and within a short time sailed for England as surgeon of the packet-ship "Great Western" He shared, in common with his cousin, Bayard Taylor, a desire to visit foreign lands, and for several voyages he remained attached to the ship, and, while in port at Liverpool, he made short journeys to various points in Europe He subsequently settled in Louisiana, but on the breaking out of the Rebellion came north, tendered his services to the government, and was appointed surgeon on the steamship "Bienville," on the South Atlantic Blockading Squadron In 1864 he was transferred to the frigate "St Lawrence," and later to the gunboat "Peosta" In 1867 he was surgeon of the Seventh United States Cavalry, under Custer, and made the arduous tour of the Southwest, returning home *via* Arizona and California In 1872 he visited Peru, and was appointed medical director of the Chimbote and Huazaz Railroad, that wonderful tramway through the clouds, then being made over the mountains by Henry Meigs While at Arequipa, in 1873, Dr Coates made the first ascent of the Mistic volcano, eighteen thousand five hundred and thirty-eight feet high, and in doing so he was compelled to abandon his guide, who was completely exhausted in the attempt In 1876 he returned to the United States by crossing the Andes to the navigable head-waters of the Amazon, and descending that river to Para, whence he sailed for home In 1878, after practicing in Chester during the interval, Dr Coates returned to Brazil as surgeon of the Collins expedition, which was designed to construct a railroad around the rapids of the Madeira River

The sad fate of that expedition is fresh in the recollections of our people, for among those who went were many persons from Delaware County, some of whom fell victims of the cruel hardships they were compelled to undergo in a strange land, while others never again regained their shattered health,—Dr Coates was among the latter Hence he spent several years in traveling in Colorado, California, and New Mexico, and while returning to Delaware County to place his son, who accompanied him, at Swarthmore College, he was taken ill, and died at Socorro, N M, June 23, 1883 Dr Coates was an accomplished writer and eloquent speaker In 1876 he delivered the Centennial oration in Chester, on Oct 22, 1882, he was the orator at the Penn Bi-Centennial at Los Angeles, Cal In 1877 he delivered an admirable lecture at Chester, entitled "Land of the Incas," and on the "Archæology of Peru" before the Academy of Natural Sciences in Philadelphia Dr Coates was a member of the American Geographical Society, the Pennsylvania Historical Society, the Academy of Natural Sciences of Philadelphia, and other scientific and learned bodies

Dr Alfred M Owens, son of Dr Joshua Owens, a surgeon in the United States navy, a native of Delaware County, died at Pensacola (Florida) Navy-Yard, Aug 22, 1883, of yellow fever, then an epidemic at that station His wife, who was with her husband, died on the 27th of the same month with the like disease

Dr Jonathan Larkin Forwood was born in West Chester, Chester Co, Pa, Oct 17, 1834 His father, Robert Forwood, a native of Delaware, was a farmer, and was the descendant of a prominent English family, the first of the name in this county having settled in that State about 1700, from whom the Forwoods of Pennsylvania, Virginia, and Alabama trace descent His mother, Rachel Forwood, was a daughter of William and Sarah Larkin, a descendant of John Larkin, who settled in Maryland, becoming the purchaser of a large tract of land in Cecil County, Md, in 1682, before the coming of Penn, and from whom all the Larkins of Delaware County are descended Young Forwood was without means, hence his early education was necessarily restricted to that which could be obtained in the public schools, and in the State of Delaware, where his parents had removed a few years after his birth, common schools were the exception, not the rule, and he was unable to obtain tuition there excepting during three months in the winter, and that for only three years prior to attaining his fifteenth year Having determined to secure an education, his devotion to books, his studious and strictly moral habits, his self-reliance and determination, all combined to aid him in that endeavor Working during the day at whatever he could get to do to earn a livelihood, and pursuing his studies in the evening and far into the night at a cost of youthful pleasures, at the early age of eighteen he had qualified himself to pass an examination as a teacher

In his nineteenth year a newspaper by the merest chance fell in his way In it he saw an advertisement for teachers in a school in Montgomery County of this State Without informing any one of his intention, he left home, went to Eagleville, was examined, and accepted by the directors This was announced to young Forwood after dark on a September day in 1851 He must return home until the beginning of the session, but how to do this with but twenty-five cents in his pocket was a serious question Knowing that to confess poverty is to be placed at a disadvantage, he kept the secret to himself, and bravely walked from Eagleville to Philadelphia, a distance of twenty-three miles, during which journey he had nothing to eat, and was compelled to take his boots off and walk in his bare feet, for the rubbing of the leather had covered his feet with blisters He arrived at daybreak on Sunday in Philadelphia, where he took the stage for Darby, paying his last penny for that short ride From Darby he walked to

was born March 17, 1834. Determining to study medicine, his means being limited, he taught school in Delaware County to obtain the required sum necessary not only for his own support, but to complete his professional education. In 1858 he graduated from the University of Pennsylvania, and within a short time sailed for England as surgeon of the packet-ship "Great Western." He shared, in common with his cousin, Bayard Taylor, a desire to visit foreign lands, and for several voyages he remained attached to the ship, and, while in port at Liverpool, he made short journeys to various points in Europe. He subsequently settled in Louisiana, but on the breaking out of the Rebellion came north, tendered his services to the government, and was appointed surgeon on the steamship "Bienville," on the South Atlantic Blockading Squadron. In 1864 he was transferred to the frigate "St. Lawrence," and later to the gunboat "Peosta." In 1867 he was surgeon of the Seventh United States Cavalry, under Custer, and made the arduous tour of the Southwest, returning home via Arizona and California. In 1872 he visited Peru, and was appointed medical director of the Chimbote and Huaraz Railroad, that wonderful tramway through the clouds, then being made over the mountains by Henry Meigs. While at Arequipa, in 1873, Dr. Coates made the first ascent of the Mistic volcano, eighteen thousand five hundred and thirty-eight feet high, and in doing so he was compelled to abandon his guide, who was completely exhausted in the attempt. In 1876 he returned to the United States by crossing the Andes to the navigable head-waters of the Amazon, and descending that river to Pará, whence he sailed for home. In 1878, after practicing in Chester during the interval, Dr. Coates returned to Brazil as surgeon of the Collins expedition, which was designed to construct a railroad around the rapids of the Madeira River.

The sad fate of that expedition is fresh in the recollections of our people, for among those who went were many persons from Delaware County, some of whom fell victims to the cruel hardships they were compelled to undergo in a strange land, while others never again regained their shattered health,—Dr. Coates was among the latter. Hence he spent several years in traveling in Colorado, California, and New Mexico, and while returning to Delaware County to place his son, who accompanied him, at Swarthmore College, he was taken ill, and died at Socorro, N. M., June 24, 1883. Dr. Coates was an accomplished writer and eloquent speaker. In 1876 he delivered the Centennial oration in Chester; on Oct. 22, 1882, he was the orator at the Penn Bi-Centennial at Los Angeles, Cal. In 1877 he delivered an admirable lecture at Chester, entitled "Land of the Incas," and on the "Archæology of Peru" before the Academy of Natural Sciences in Philadelphia. Dr. Coates was a member of the American Geographical Society, the Pennsylvania Historical Society, the Academy of Natural Sciences of Philadelphia, and other scientific and learned bodies.

Dr. Alfred M. Owens, son of Dr. Joshua Owens, a surgeon in the United States navy, a native of Delaware County, died at Pensacola (Florida) Navy-Yard, Aug. 22, 1883, of yellow fever, then an epidemic at that station. His wife, who was with her husband, died on the 27th of the same month with the like disease.

Dr. Jonathan Larkin Forwood was born in West Chester, Chester Co., Pa., Oct. 17, 1834. His father, Robert Forwood, a native of Delaware, was a farmer, and was the descendant of a prominent English family, the first of the name in this county having settled in that State about 1700, from whom the Forwoods of Pennsylvania, Virginia, and Alabama trace descent. His mother, Rachel Forwood, was a daughter of William and Sarah Larkin, a descendant of John Larkin, who settled in Maryland, becoming the purchaser of a large tract of land in Cecil County, Md., in 1682, before the coming of Penn, and from whom all the Larkins of Delaware County are descended. Young Forwood was without means, hence his early education was necessarily restricted to that which could be obtained in the public schools, and in the State of Delaware, where his parents had removed a few years after his birth, common schools were the exception, not the rule, and he was unable to obtain tuition there excepting during three months in the winter, and that for only three years prior to attaining his fifteenth year. Having determined to secure an education, his devotion to books, his studious and strictly moral habits, his self-reliance and determination, all combined to aid him in that endeavor. Working during the day at whatever he could get to do to earn a livelihood, and pursuing his studies in the evening and far into the night at a cost of youthful pleasures, at the early age of eighteen he had qualified himself to pass an examination as a teacher.

In his nineteenth year a newspaper by the merest chance fell in his way. In it he saw an advertisement for teachers in a school in Montgomery County of this State. Without informing any one of his intention he left home, went to Eagleville, was examined, and accepted by the directors. This was announced to young Forwood after dark on a September day in 1853. He must return home until the beginning of the session, but how to do this with but twenty-five cents in his pocket was a serious question. Knowing that to confess poverty is to be placed at a disadvantage, he kept the secret to himself, and bravely walked from Eagleville to Philadelphia, a distance of twenty-three miles, during which journey he had nothing to eat, and was compelled to take his boots off and walk in his bare feet, for the rubbing of the leather had covered his feet with blisters. He arrived at daybreak on Sunday in Philadelphia, where he took the stage for Darby, paying his last penny for that short ride. From Darby he walked to

[illegible]-Pub Co Philadelphia.

J. L. Forwood

Chichester, in this county, where his parents then lived He found his mother filled with anxiety his mysterious absence occasioned, and received a reprimand for his conduct. He told his mother that on the following day he would leave home forever, that the world was his theatre, and he was going to act his part creditably She did not, however, realize this until she saw the young man gathering together his clothing, when she presented him with enough money to carry him to Eagleville, where he began his independent career, and continued to teach until the following spring at a salary of twenty-five dollars a month At this time young Forwood took the money which he had been enabled to save out of his salary and entered himself as a student at Freeland College until the spring of 1852, when he gave all the money he had saved and taught a class in geometry as part payment for his tuition He left there at the end of that session, in 1854, and applied for a school in Springfield, Delaware Co, and was accepted

Dr Charles J Morton was then one of the directors The doctor one day asked young Forwood what was his object in life, and whether he proposed teaching school for a small pittance for the remainder of his days? He replied that he intended to enter one of the professions. Dr. Morton offered the young man the free use of his medical library and any instructions he might require Forwood accepted this kind offer, and here was the great turning-point of his life The following spring, at the close of the session of 1855, the schoolmaster was made the recipient of a silver cup, with an appropriate inscription, which he still has in his possession In the fall of the same year Forwood was entered in the University of Pennsylvania, having saved sufficient money to defray the tuition of one term It was suggested to the young man that there were other and cheaper medical colleges, but knowing that his profession would be his only capital in life, he determined to procure the best medical education His money failing him, about the close of 1855 he was compelled to teach school again, and procured a situation once more at Middletown

In the summer of 1856, finding that he had not been able to gather enough money to go on with his medical studies, he submitted to an examination, and received a scholarship in the University In the spring of 1857 he graduated with honors in all the seven branches of medicine He was compelled, however, to borrow forty dollars from his uncle, Jonathan C Larkin, for whom he had been named, to pay for his diploma Dr Forwood came at once to Chester, where he settled, having completed one of the epochs in his life's history Here, in his practice, he paid particular attention to surgery, a branch which had not been followed by any physician in Chester for a long time. In 1858, Dr Forwood performed the first amputation of a leg that had been done in this city for fifty years. His operations in surgery have covered almost all important cases since then He has operated four times successfully lithotomy, a work seldom attempted, except in medical colleges and by professors of surgery

In 1864, when the municipal hospital of Philadelphia was burned, the board of health located it at the Lazaretto, and Dr Forwood was requested to take charge of it, and did so for four years, until the new buildings were completed After the battle of Gettysburg, when the wounded Confederate soldiers were sent here, the doctor was called upon to take a department in the hospital, and while there performed several splendid operations, among others that of amputation at the shoulder joint On leaving this public institution the doctor received the highest testimonials from the officers in charge In 1867 he started the *Delaware County Democrat*, and although the county committee of the party had declared that no Democratic paper could be supported, he by his untiring energy made it not only a financial success, but one of the most unflinching Democratic organs of the State Its editorials were outspoken and fearless In the same year he was elected to Council from the Middle Ward, and took a leading part in that body He was, upon taking his seat, made a member of the Street Committee, and for more than three years the chairman

In the spring of 1872 he was elected mayor of Chester in the most exciting political contest the municipality had known to that time His election was contested, Gen William McCandless and William H Dickinson appearing as counsel for Forwood, and William Ward and J M Johnson for the contestant Three terms he was elected mayor in succession, and in 1884, after an intermission of three years, was again elected to the office, although the Republican majority is usually nearly five hundred He has been frequently a delegate to the Democratic County and State Conventions, and member of the State Executive Committee In 1874 he was the Democratic candidate for Congress, and in 1876 an elector on the Presidential ticket during the noted candidacy of Tilden and Hendricks In 1880 he was a delegate to the National Democratic Convention which nominated Gen Hancock for President, and in 1884, when Governor Cleveland was named for the same office As a public speaker Dr Forwood ranks high, and as a political manager few men excel him

Successful as has been his political career, his chosen profession is the field of his ambitious desires, and to-day, although he has secured a large and remunerative practice, he is devoted to the study of medicine and surgery, paying particular attention, at the present, to gynæcology, in which special branch he is attaining an extended reputation in nowise confined to this locality, but patients from many of the great cities visit him for medical treatment Several operations performed by him were so noticeable that full account thereof was published in medical works for the information of the public.

Half a century ago the Thomsonian practice of medicine had many warm advocates throughout the country, and Delaware County had several doctors adhering to the rules of treatment under the theory. In 1838 so numerous had the adherents to the system grown that a society known as the Thomsonian Friendly Botanic Society of Delaware County was organized, and on June 2d of that year held a meeting at Providence Friends' meeting-house. This first assemblage was also the last, or, if it was not, I am unable to find anything further respecting it.

The Delaware County Medical Society owes its origin to the chance conversation of two physicians, Dr. Ellwood Harvey, then of Birmingham, and Dr. George Martin, of Concord, which resulted in the conclusion that they would make an attempt to organize a county society, which should be connected with that of the State. The first meeting of physicians to that end was held in Chester, Thursday, May 2, 1850, at the law-office of Hon. John M. Broomall, when, on motion of Dr. Harvey, a temporary organization was effected by calling Dr. Joshua Owen to the chair and the appointment of Dr. Martin secretary. The following resolutions were then offered by Dr. Martin:

"WHEREAS, Experience has fully shown that the progress of any Art or Science is promoted by the frequent reunion and full interchange of the personal observation of those whose profession is connected with it; and,

"WHEREAS, The organization of County Medical Societies throughout the State is calculated to produce such results; and,

"WHEREAS, It is of the highest importance to introduce throughout every county of our State an elevated Code of Ethics for the government of our profession by which the members of it will be held under recognized censorial head, which may tend to increase its respectability on the one hand and unite it against the encroachments of Charlatanism on the other; Therefore, we the physicians of Delaware county here assembled do hereby

"*Resolve*, That it is expedient to form ourselves into a medical association, which shall bear the name of the 'Delaware County Medical Society.'

"*Resolved*, That the Society shall be considered as a branch of the Medical Society of the State of Pennsylvania."

A committee of three was appointed to draft a constitution, and the physicians of the county were invited to meet in Penn Buildings, Chester, on May 30, 1850, to effect a permanent organization of the society. At the time designated the constitution of the association was adopted. By its provisions any person of respectable standing in the profession, of good moral character, who was a graduate of any medical school recognized by the Pennsylvania State Society, or who had been for fifteen years in practice in the county as a regular physician, was eligible to membership, provided such physician did not prescribe any remedy the compounds of which he was unacquainted with, or who was interested in any way in patent medicines or in collusion with any apothecary to procure patronage or profit, or who claimed superior qualifications in the treatment of any disease. The members were interdicted from rendering any medical service gratuitously to any clergyman or physician whose name was attached to any certificate in favor of patent medicines, or who permitted reference in favor of such nostrums to be made to him.

Dr. Jesse Young was chosen the first president; Dr. Joshua Owens, vice-president; Dr. Robert Smith, secretary; and Dr. Ellwood Harvey, treasurer. A committee was also appointed to ascertain and report the names of all practitioners of medicine in the county, whether regular or irregular. For several years the society met promptly at designated times at the houses of the members, and much interesting information was imparted, highly beneficial to the profession. Among the most important work under the auspices of the society was the geological survey of the county, which was made in 1851 by Drs. Harvey and Martin, associated by Dr. Samuel Trimble, of Concord township, an expert micrologist. The chart and the report made by these gentlemen was published in the transactions of the State Society, and it is the basis of all subsequent geographical publications in reference to our county. In the fall of 1852 the Delaware County Medical Society, in connection with that of Chester County, effected an arrangement for the publication of a quarterly journal, *The Medical Reporter*, the first number of which was issued July, 1853. This periodical was conducted by five editors,—Drs. J. F. Huddleson and George Martin, of Delaware County, and Drs. W. Worthington, Isaac Thomas, and Jacob Price, of Chester County. It contained the proceedings of the doctors in the counties, with papers read, addresses delivered before, and reports of cases made to either of the two organizations, together with editorial and other items of interest. It was published for three years, when it was discontinued. The society, so far as our county was concerned, about 1856, "languished and languishing did live," until at the meeting on Feb. 24, 1857, Dr. Maris presented the following resolution, which was adopted:

"*Resolved*, That all books and other property belonging to the society be placed in the hands of Dr. R. H. Smith, to become the property of any medical society organized in Delaware County, provided such society is a branch of the Pennsylvania State Medical Society, and formed within one year; otherwise to be delivered into the hands of the treasurer of the State Medical Society."

This testamentary disposition of the effects of the society having been duly made, a resolution which had been laid over from a former meeting, which set forth "that it is expedient that the Delaware County Medical Society be, and it is hereby dissolved," was adopted by a unanimous vote.

On March 16, 1857, a meeting of the physicians of Delaware County was called at the Washington House, Chester, to reorganize the Medical Society, and on the 30th of the same month an adjourned meeting was held at the Charter House, Media, when an organization was effected by the election of Dr. Hillborn Darlington, president; Dr. Manly Emanuel, vice-president; Dr. George B. Hotchkin, secretary; and Dr. Charles H. Budd, treasurer. Further action was deferred until the next meeting, which was held at Media, May 26, 1857, but the attendance was so small that it was deemed proper to defer all matters to the next meeting appointed to be held at the Washington House, Chester, Aug. 25, 1857. At the latter date hardly any persons attended and the project was abandoned for the time being.

On April 19, 1861, by invitation of Dr. Joseph Parrish, superintendent of the Pennsylvania Training School for Feeble-Minded Children, near Media, a number of physicians from various parts of Delaware County met to witness an exhibition of the pupils of that institution. It was stated that invitations had been sent to every physician in the county whose name was known to Dr. Parrish, but in consequence of a heavy storm then prevailing, and the national excitement consequent on the bombardment of Fort Sumter, many failed to attend. The meeting was so profitable and agreeable that the physicians present resolved that the Delaware County Medical Society should be revived. A temporary organization was made by calling Dr. Parrish to the chair and appointing Dr. J. L. Forwood secretary, and on May 10, 1861, the society was permanently re-established by the election of Dr. Manly Emanuel, president; Dr. Joseph Parrish, vice-president; Dr. George B. Hotchkin, secretary; and Dr. Joseph Rowland, treasurer. The rebellion then upon the country demanded the services of so many physicians—and Delaware County furnished its full quota—that those doctors who remained were so busy that they rarely attended the meetings of the society, which were held occasionally, but no record of the proceedings was kept. At the conclusion of the war, on May 16, 1865, an adjourned annual meeting was held at the office of Dr. J. L. Forwood, in Chester, and on his motion it was resolved that "In consequence of the long interruption to the meetings occasioned by the general unsettlement of the country, etc., that the constitution of this society be formally readopted; the signatures of those present be affixed as active members, and that gentlemen hereafter received be regularly balloted for as required by our Constitution." An election was then held, which resulted in the election of Dr. Manley Emanuel, president; Dr. J. L. Forwood, vice-president; Dr. Isaac N. Neilson, secretary; and Dr. Charles J. Morton, treasurer. This was merely a spasmodic movement, for nothing further seems to have been done until March 16, 1869, when a meeting was held at Dr. Parrish's sanitarium, at Media, which was addressed by Dr. Emanuel, who appealed to the medical men of the county to awaken from their lethargy and co-operate for the common good through the valuable means presented by an energetic and well-organized medical society. The following officers were then elected: Dr. Manley Emanuel, president; Dr. J. L. Forwood, vice-president; Dr. Isaac N. Kerlin, secretary; and Dr. Theodore S. Christ, treasurer. The meetings of the society from that time to the present have been well attended, and the interchange of opinions and discussions on topics relating to the science and practice of medicine at these gatherings has resulted in much benefit to the profession. On May 21, 1879, the State Medical Society met in Holly Tree Hall, Chester, on which occasion over two hundred and fifty persons assembled. The session continued Wednesday afternoon and evening and during Thursday. The following Friday the society visited the Training School for Feeble-Minded Children at Media, where the ceremonial installation of officers of the State Society for the succeeding years was performed.

The officers of the Delaware County Medical Society in 1883 were Dr. William B. Ulrich, president; Dr. R. H. N. Milner, vice-president; Dr. Linnæus Fussell, secretary; and Dr. John B. Weston, treasurer.

The following-named physicians of the county have been and are members of the society:

George Martin........Concordville.
Manley Emanuel........Linwood.
Ellwood Harvey........Chester.
Charles S. Heysham........Newtown Square.
Robert K. Smith........Darby.
Joshua Owen........Chester.
Charles J. Morton........ "
Caleb Ash........Darby.
Joseph Wilson.
Samuel A. Barton........Village Green.
Thomas Turner.
Reuben H. Smith........Media.
J. C. Hutton........Chelsea.
Joseph Rowland........Media.
A. W. Mathew........Aston.
George Smith........Upper Darby.
J. Howard Taylor........Concordville.
Jesse W. Griffith........Ridleyville.
J. P. McIlvain........Media.
J. T. Huddleson........Thornbury.
J. Morris Moore........Newtown.
Hillborn Darlington........Concordville.
James S. Hill........Chester township.
J. Siter Parke........Radnor.
Edward Young........Chester.
John A. Thomson........ "
George B. Hotchkin........Media.
James W. Hoey........Lenni.
John M. Allen........Chester.
Jonathan L. Forwood........ "
Joseph Parrish........Media.
Isaac N. Kerlin........ "
James J. McGee........United States Navy.[1]
William H. Forwood........Chester.
Charles D. Meigs........Thornbury.
Henry Pleasants........Radnor.
Charles W. Pennock........Howellville.
Henry M. Kirk........Upper Darby.
William T. W. Dickeson........Media.
Isaac T. Coates........Chester.
T. L. Leavitt.
F. Ridgely Graham........Chester.
Theodore S. Christ........ "
J. Pyle Worrall........Media.
Lewis M. Emanuel........Linwood.
C. C. V. Crawford........Village Green.
Orrin Cooley.
Francis E. Heenan........Chester.
Samuel P. Bartleson........Clifton Heights.
William B. Ulrich........Chester.
James E. Garretson........Darby.
M. Fisher Longstreth........ "
William C. Bacon........Upper Darby.
John T. M. Forwood........Chester.
David Rose........Sneath's Corner.
Edward Maris........Howellville.
Charles H. Bubb........Darby.
Henry M. Lyons........Media.
John G. Thomas........Newtown Square.
Jacob Boon........Darby.
Samuel Trimble........Lima.
D. Francis Condie.

---

[1] Dr. McGee was in charge of Military Hospital, Chester, during the illness of Dr. Leconte, 1862.

Henry M. Corse.
Edwin Fussell.............................Media.
Linnæus Fussell........................... "
Edward T. Gammage.........................Chester.
John W. Eckfeldt..........................Haverford.
Dillwyn Greene............................Marcus Hook.
Francis F. Rowland........................Media.
Rebecca L. Fussell........................ "
Daniel W. Jefferis........................Chester.
John B. Mitchell.......................... "
Joshua Ash................................Clifton Heights.
D. G. Brinton.............................Media.
George R. Vernon..........................Clifton Heights.
Joseph H. Horner..........................Thornton.
Robert A. Given...........................Clifton Heights.
Conrad J. Partridge.......................Ridley Park.
David K. Shoemaker........................Chester.
Eugene K. Mott............................ "
John Wesley Johnson....................... "
William S. Ridgely........................ "
Philip C. O'Reiley........................ "
Mrs. Frances W. Baker.....................Media.
T. P. Ball................................Chester.
John B. Weston............................South Chester Borough.
A. Edgar Osborne..........................Media.
—— Pennypacker............................Media.
Robert H. Milner..........................Chester.
F. Marion Murray..........................Lenni.
Horace H. Darlington......................Concordville.
Henry B. Knowles..........................Clifton Heights.
William B. Fish...........................Media.
Henry C. Bartleson........................Fernwood.
Thomas C. Stellwagon......................Media.
J. Willoughby Phillips....................Clifton Heights.
William Bird..............................Chester.
Fletcher C. Lawyer........................Howellville.
Clarence W. DeLannoy......................Chester.
Joseph Crawford Egbert....................Radnor.
Lawrence M. Bullock.......................Upland.
Charles Carter............................Wallingford.
William S. Little.........................Media.
Henry Seidell.............................South Chester Borough.
Mrs. Hannah J. Price...................... " " "
Henry C. Harris...........................Landsdown.
George M. Fisher..........................South Chester Borough.

Dr. John T. M. Cardesa and his son, Dr. John D. M. Cardesa, well-known physicians, residing at Claymont, Del., have a large practice in Delaware County. Dr. Anna M. Broomall, daughter of Hon. John M. Broomall, of this county, is a graduate of the Woman's Medical College, Philadelphia, located in that city, and has a large and growing practice. All of these last-named doctors are adherents of the allopathic school.

Dr. Cyrus S. Poley kept a drug-store in Chester in 1870, and removed therefrom after 1876, for in that year Governor Hartranft appointed him surgeon of the Eleventh Regiment Pennsylvania Militia, comprising the troops in this military district.

A Brief History of Homœopathy in Delaware County.[1]—Delaware County has the honor of being the birthplace of those veteran homœopathic practitioners, Drs. Walter Williamson, Richard Gardiner, and Gideon Humphreys, all espousing the cause at nearly the same time, and last, but not least, of being the residence of Dr. A. E. Small, at the time of his conversion to homœopathy.

Dr. Walter Williamson introduced homœopathy into the county in the year 1836. He graduated at the University of Pennsylvania in 1833, and immediately settled in Marple. He moved to Newtown in 1835, and in the spring of 1836 his attention was directed to the new system of medical practice. At the earliest opportunity he obtained all the books and pamphlets then published in the English language which had any bearing upon the subject, commenced the study of its doctrines, and began to practice it in the vicinity, where not even the name itself had ever been heard, except by one family, John Thomas, of Upper Providence. He rapidly gained a large practice, but in 1839 he moved to Philadelphia, owing to seriously-impaired health. He was one of the founders of the Homœopathic College of Pennsylvania, the first institution in the country to teach this system of practice, and from 1848 until his death in 1879 he filled one of the professorships in the college. Dr. Williamson was born in Delaware County, July 4, 1811.

The second practitioner to unfurl the standard of homœopathy in Delaware County was Dr. M. B. Roche. He settled near Darby in 1839, and continued the practice there for three years. In 1842 he was succeeded by Dr. Alvan E. Small, a native of the State of Maine, and a graduate of the Medical Department of Pennsylvania College. He practiced in Upper Darby as an allopathic physician in 1840, and became a homœopathic in 1842. Dr. Small continued to practice in the county until he moved to Philadelphia, in 1845.

Dr. James E. Gross, a native of New England, graduated at the Homœopathic Medical College of Pennsylvania in 1850, and soon afterwards settled in Darby to practice, but remained there only a few months, and then moved to Lowell, Mass.

Dr. Stacy Jones, student of H. N. Gurnsey, M.D., graduated at the Homœopathic Medical College of Pennsylvania in March, 1853, and settled in Upper Darby. He remained in his first location for three years, and then moved into the borough of Darby, where he continues to practice.

Dr. Charles V. Dare, a native of New Jersey, graduated at the Homœopathic Medical College of Pennsylvania in March, 1854, and very soon afterwards settled in the borough of Chester. Dr. Dare was the first homœopathic physician in Chester. He continued to practice there until he sold his practice to Dr. Coates Preston, in March, 1858.

Dr. Coates Preston, a native of Pennsylvania, graduated at the Homœopathic Medical College of Pennsylvania in March, 1853, and first settled at Sculltown, N. J. In the spring of 1824 he moved to Woodstown, N. J., where he continued to practice until he moved to Chester, succeeding Dr. Dare. In the course of a few years he built up quite a large practice in Chester and the surrounding neighborhood. On account of a serious illness in the winter of 1865, and the consequent feebleness of health which continued through the following spring months, Dr. Preston was induced to take into partnership Dr. H. W. Farrington, but after a few months' trial of the new relationship the connection was dissolved. Dr. Preston continued his practice, and Dr. Farrington took an office at another place in Chester, but

[1] From MS. prepared by Walter Williamson, M.D., in possession of his family. (See "Transactions of the World's Homœopathic Convention," Philadelphia, 1876.)

after a few months moved to Beverly, N J, and since to California Dr Preston outlived much of the prejudice and opposition against the new practice which existed among the people in his locality when he first settled in Chester, and firmly established homœopathy in the respect and confidence of the community on a broad and firm foundation He removed to Wilmington, Del, in the spring of 1881, and died there on the 9th of August in the same year

Dr Davis R Pratt, a native of Newtown, graduated at the Homœopathic Medical College of Pennsylvania in March, 1816, and practiced in his native place In 1863 he moved to Philadelphia, and subsequently to Trenton, N J, where he remained until compelled by ill health to relinquish the duties of the profession He died of bronchitis on Jan 28, 1868

About 1863, Dr E D Miles practiced medicine in Media Dr John F Rose, after serving in the army, at the close of the war of the Rebellion settled in Media, July 1, 1865 Immediately after the death of Dr. Henry Duffield, of Chester County, Dr Rose moved to that borough in February, 1866

Dr. Robert P Mercer graduated at the Homœopathic Medical College of Pennsylvania in March, 1861, and in the following month located at Marshalton, Chester Co, Pa In January, 1863, he was appointed to the entire charge of the medical department of the Chester County almshouse After discharging the duties of that office on strictly homœopathic principles for two years, he resigned in 1865, and removed to Wilmington, Del

In November of the same year (1865), at the solicitation of Dr Preston, Dr Mercer moved to Chester, where he is still in successful practice

Dr Henry Minton Lewis graduated at the Hahnemann Medical College of Philadelphia in March, 1869, and settled in Chester soon after, where he remained for three or four years, when he moved to Brooklyn, N Y. Dr Trimble Pratt graduated at the Hahnemann Medical College of Philadelphia in March, 1870, and settled in Media the following June

In addition to the above, there are in Chester in successful practice at the present time Drs Charles W Perkins, Samuel Starr, William T Urie, Frederick Preston, and Franklin Powell, and at Upland, Dr Isaac Crowthers

The Homœopathic Medical Society of Chester and Delaware Counties was organized in October, 1858, by the meeting together of Drs Duffield, of New London, Hawley, of Phœnixville Hindman, of Cochranville, Johnson, of Kennett Square, Wood and Jones, of West Chester It has been in a prosperous condition ever since, having four meetings annually, which are held in January, April, July, and October Dr Duffield was its first president Its present membership is thirty-four

In addition the following physicians, who have not connected themselves with either the Allopathic or Homœopathic Medical Societies, are in practice in this county Charles A Kish, William F Campbell, George W Roncy, Samuel C Burland, Chester, William Calver, Booth's Corner, Henderson Hayward, Birmingham, Benjamin S Anderson, Marple, William P Painter, Darby, Franklin Soper, Ridley Park, William S S Gray, Village Green, Lawrence M Bullock, Upland, Andrew Lindsay, Radnor, John G Thomas, Newtown, Henry L Smedley, Media, James Edwards, Springfield Eliza C Taylor practices in Marcus Hook, Chester, and Thornbury

---

CHAPTER XXVII

CIVIL LISTS

PROTHONOTARY, CLERKS OF COURT, RECORDER OF DEEDS, AND REGISTER OF WILLS

Thomas Revell, Sept 13, 1681, to Aug 22, 1683, Robert Eyre, Oct 17, 1683, to December, 1689, Joshua Fearne, September, 1690, to April 18, 1693, John Childe, June 13, 1693, to March, 1690-1700, Henry Hollingsworth, June 11, 1700, to Feb 22, 1708-9, John Simcock, May 24, 1709, to 1716, Joseph Parker, 1724 to 1766 Henry Hale Graham, 1766 to 1777, Benjamin Jacob, March 22, 1777, to April 4, 1777, Caleb Davis, July 1, 1777

REGISTER OF WILLS

John Simcock, 1714 to May, 1716, Joseph Parker, Aug 14, 1716, to Jan 12, 1759, Henry Hale Graham March 5, 1757, to Feb. 13, 1777, Thomas Taylor, March 25, 1777, John Breaton, April 6, 1782, Persifor Frazer, April 8, 1786

RECORDER OF DEEDS

John Bristow in office March 10, 1688, Joshua Fearne, March 25, 1691, Robert Eyre, March 26, 1693, John Childe, Jan 3, 1695, Henry Hollingsworth, Dec 10, 1700, Peter Evans, April 17, 1706, John Simcock, Jan 28, 1707, after which date three offices, prothonotary, recorder, and register, were held by one person

Delaware County was erected in 1789, since which time the following persons have filled the office of prothonotary, recorder of deeds, register of wills, and clerks of court

William Richardson Atlee, Sept 28, 1789, Davis Bevan, April 6, 1796, James Barnard, May 11, 1800, Thomas Brinton Dick, Feb 22, 1806, Joseph Engle, May 24, 1809, Benjamin Pearson, March 11, 1818, Thomas Robinson, March 8, 1821, Henry Myers, Jan 17, 1824, John K Zeilen, Dec 20, 1832, John Hinkson, Aug 28, 1834, John Richards, Jan 9, 1836, Samuel Weaver, Jr, Dec 7, 1838, James Houston, Nov 12, 1841, Joseph Taylor, Nov 22, 1844, James Sill, Jr, Nov 11, 1847, Nicholas F Walter, Nov 25, 1851, Nicholas F Walter, Nov 21, 1853, Thomas Forsythe, Nov 25, 1859, Benjamin F Baker (unexpired term of Forsythe), Nov 12, 1862, George Esrey, Nov 26, 1862, Orson Flagg Bullard, Nov 23, 1865, Isaac Johnson, Dec 29, 1874

Mr Johnson filled the office of prothonotary until January, 1884, when Morris P Hannum, the present incumbent, was qualified

By act of Assembly, Feb 19, 1860, the office of prothonotary and that of recorder of deeds was directed to be filled by different persons

RECORDER OF DEEDS

Frederick Fairlamb, Nov 26, 1862, Frederick R Cutler, Nov 21, 1871, Canby S Smith (unexpired term of Cutler), May 24, 1873, Charles P Walter, Jan 18, 1875, Edward Blaine, Dec 20, 1880

Edward Blaine is the present incumbent, having been re-elected November, 1883

By act of March 20, 1873, the office of register of wills and clerk of Orphans' Court was made a separate office Thomas Lees, the first register under this act, commissioned Dec 13, 1874, is the present incumbent, he having been elected four terms in succession, the last time in November, 1883

Coroner —The first reference we find to the office of coroner is at a court held 6th day of Fifth month, 1684, when the sheriff and clerk of court complained that court fees had not been paid them, execution was issued to collect the amount claimed, and on the 8th day of Seventh month, 1684, "James Kenela, Coroner," made the return to the writs To show the manner of making the return of inquest in the early days, and "Ay, marry, is't crowner's-quest law," I append two of these returns

"The 5th of 5th mo 1699, We whose names are here subscribed being summoned & attested by the Coroner to View the Corpse of Ann Cruett do find by the best evidence that can find by two witness & several others big in place that nothing did procure her death but the heat of the weather and it been please God to visit her sudden death As witness our names

Jno Humphrey	Benj Humphrey
Jno Roberts	Rowland Powell
Philip Prisse	Evan William
Ellis Ellis	Thos Pennell
Humphrey Ellis	Thos Reice
Daniel Humphrey	Danl Laurence"

"Edgemond the 6 of the 5 mont 1699 We whose names are under written summoned and attested by the coroner to view the body of Sarah Baker having made strict enquiry & also have what evidence could be found attested to what they know & we find no other but that it pleased Almighty God to visit her with death by the force of thunder and to this we all unanimously agreed Subscribe with our names the day and year above writteu

Thos Worrellow	Ephraim Jackson
Robt Pennell	David Ogden
Jno Worrall	Thomas Bowater
Joseph Baker	William Gregory
Wm Corburne	Charles Whitaker
Peter Treggo	Jno Turner
"Approved by me	JACOB SIMCOCKE, *Coroner*"

The following list embraces the persons who have been commissioned coroners of Chester County until the erection of the county of Delaware, in 1789, and from that date those who have held the office in the latter county

James Kennerly, in office 1684, Jacob Simcock, 1696 Henry Hollingsworth, 1707, Henry Worley, 1710, Jonas Sandelands, Oct 3, 1717-20, Robert Barber, Oct 4, 1721, John Mendenhall, Oct 4 1726-27, Robert Parke, Oct 3, 1728, Abraham Darlington, Oct 4, 1729, John Wharton, Oct 3, 1730-31, Anthony Shaw, Oct 3, 1732-33, John Wharton, Oct 4, 1734-36, Stephen Hoskins, Oct 4, 1737, Aubrey Bevan, Oct 4, 1738-42, Thomas Morgan, Oct 4, 1743-45, Isaac Lea, Oct 4, 1746-50, Joshua Thomson, Oct 3, 1751, John Kerlin, Oct 4, 1752, Joshua Thomson, Oct 3, 1753-60, Philip Ford (*vice* Thomson, deceased) May 22, 1761-62, Davis Bevan, Oct. 4, 1763-64, Abel Janney, Oct 4, 1765, John Trapnall (*vice* Janney, resigned), May 27, 1766, Joseph Gibbons, Jr, Oct 4, 1768-70, John Crosby, Jr, Oct 6, 1771-72, John Bryan, Oct 4, 1773-75, Harvey Lewis, Oct 2, 1775, David Denny, Nov 24, 1778, Allen Cunningham, Oct 19, 1780, Benjamin Rue, Oct 12, 1782, John Harper, Oct 20, 1783, Isaac Thomas, Oct 4, 1785, John Harper, Oct 3, 1786, John Underwood, Oct 15, 1787

After Erection of County of Delaware

Jonathan Vernon, Oct 16, 1789, Caleb Bennett, Oct 21, 1791, William Price, Jan 25, 1793 John Odenheimer, Jr, Oct 17, 1795, James Birchall Oct 12, 1798, Oct 21, 1801, Oct 16, 1804, Oct 23, 1807, Oct 26, 1810, Nov 8, 1816, Dec 6, 1819, Dec 4, 1822, Abraham Kerlin, Nov 13, 1829, Daniel Thomson, Nov 2, 1830, Joel Lane, Oct 25, 1833, Dec 22, 1836, John Lloyd, Dec 4, 1839, Moses Reed, April 14, 1840, John Lloyd, Dec 3, 1842, Stephen Horne, Dec 1, 1845, Seth C Thomas, Dec 23, 1848, Dec 1, 1851, Reuben H Smith, Nov 6, 1854, Isaac Johnson,[1] Nov 28, 1857, William A Minshall,[2] April 24, 1858, Samuel Long, Sr, Dec 7, 1858, Washington B Levis, Nov 27, 1861, Jan 9 1865, George H Rigby,[3] Nov 23, 1865, Dec 8, 1868, William Anderson Minshall, Dec 29, 1871, Jan 19, 1875, Horace W Fairlamb, Dec 18, 1877, Abram J Quimby, Dec 20, 1880, Horace W Fairlamb, Dec 27, 1883

Sheriffs —Under the Dutch authority on the Delaware an officer, entitled a schout, performed duties such as are now required from the sheriffs, but the jurisdiction was more varied, and had legislative as well as executive powers reposed in that officer Under the Duke of York, on May 17, 1672, Governor Lovelace and Council decided that "the office of Schout to be converted into a Sheriff for the Corporation and River, and that he be annually Chosen" The electors in that early day named two persons for the office, and from those two the Governor made his selection, a system which was adopted by Penn in the "Charter of Privileges," granted in 1701, and prevailed under the State Constitutions of 1776 and 1790 Until the Constitution of 1838 gave the people the right, by their votes, to elect one person to the office, the absurd provisions of the Constitution of 1776 prevailed, which was to elect two persons from whom the Governor made his selection, and to whom he issued the commission

The following list of persons who have filled the office of sheriff is believed to be as accurate as it is now possible to make it

Capt. Edmund Cantwell, 1676-81, John Test, September, 1681-82, Thomas Usher, November, 1682-83, Thomas Withers, December, 1683-84, Jeremy Collett, January, 1684-85, Thomas Usher, June, 1686, to April, 1687, Joshua Fearne, June, 1687, to June, 1689, George Foreman, August, 1689, to March, 1691-92, Caleb Pusey, June, 1692, to April, 1693, Joseph Wood, April 28, 1693-97, Andrew Job, December, 1697-1701, John Hoskins, June, 1701-8, John Simcock, 1708, John Hoskins, 1709, Henry Worley, 1715, Nicholas Fairlamb, Oct 3, 1717-19, John Crosby, Oct. 4, 1720, John Taylor, Oct 4, 1721-28, John Owen, Oct 4, 1729-31, John Parry, Oct 3, 1732-34 John Owen, Oct 3, 1735-37, John Parry, Oct 4, 1738-39, Benjamin Davis, Oct 3, 1740-42, John Owen, Oct 4, 1743-45, Benjamin Davis, Oct 4, 1746-48, John Owen, Oct 8, 1749-51, Isaac Pearson, Oct 4, 1752-54, John Fairlamb Oct 4, 1755-58, Benjamin Davis Oct. 4, 1759-61, John Fairlamb, Oct 4, 1762-63, Philip Ford, Oct 4, 1764-66, John Morton (*vice* Ford, deceased), Oct 28, 1766-68, Jesse Maris, Oct 5, 1769-71, Henry Hayes, Oct 5, 1772-73, Nathaniel Vernon, Oct 5, 1774-75, Robert Smith, March 29, 1777, Charles Dilworth, Oct 17, 1778, Robert Smith, Nov 21, 1778, David Mackey, Oct 16, 1779, John Gardner, Oct 19, 1780, William Gibbons, Birmingham, Oct 20, 1783, Ezekiel Leonard, West Bradford, Oct 13, 1786

Since Erection of Delaware County

Nicholas Fairlamb, Oct 16, 1789, same, Oct 21, 1790, James Barnard, Oct 18, 1792, Abraham Dicks, Nov 12, 1795, date of commission for

---

[1] Died in office

[2] For Johnson's unexpired term, George Rosevelt, who had been elected, refusing to serve

[3] For unexpired term of W B Levis

second term, John Odenheimer, Oct 12, 1798, Matthias Kerlin, Jr, Oct 21, 1801, John Odenheimer, Oct 16, 1804, Richard P Floyd, Oct. 23, 1807, Isaac Cochran, Oct 25, 1810, Daniel Thomson, Oct. 19, 1813, Robert Fairlamb, Oct 16, 1816, Samuel Anderson, Oct 23 1819, Joseph Weaver, Jr, Oct 21, 1822 John Hinkson, Oct 17, 1825, Jehu Broomball, Oct 22, 1828, William Baldwin,[1] Oct 28, 1831, Charles Baldwin, March 5, 1834, Samuel A Price, Oct 22, 1834, Evans S Way, Oct 25, 1837, John Larkin, Jr, Oct 27, 1840, Samuel Hibberd, Oct 27, 1843, Robert R Dutton, Nov 16, 1846, Jonathan Esrey,[2] Oct 22, 1849, Henry T Esrey, May 20, 1851, Aaron James, Nov 17, 1851, John M Hall, Nov 2, 1854, Jonathan Vernon, Nov 10, 1857, Morris L. Yarnall, Nov 15, 1860, Abraham Vauzant, Nov 16, 1863, Caleb Hoopes, April 11, 1866, Evan C Bartleson Nov 23, 1869 Charles W Matthew, Dec 29, 1875, John J Rowland, Dec 21, 1878, William Armstrong, Dec. 22, 1881

County Commissioners—The office of county commissioner, we are told by Judge Futhey, was created not long prior to 1820, the duties discharged by them being first performed by the justices and grand jury conjointly, and afterwards by the grand jury and assessors The first commissioners of the county were elected to serve one year, and the board at that time comprising four members, is inferred from a petition presented from Chester County to the Assembly at the session of 1721-22, asking "that three commissioners may be elected yearly" Petitions of like tenor being presented from other counties, on May 12, 1722, the act to that effect was passed, excepting that it provided that one commissioner should be elected annually, thus extending the period of service of the commissioners to three years

The following is a list of commissioners since 1721, and the date of their appointment or election

1721, David Lloyd, Nathaniel Newlin, Henry Miller (in office), 1722, Robert Pyle, 1723, Nathaniel Newlin, 1724, Samuel Hollingsworth, 1725, Robert Pyle, 1726, Isaac Taylor, 1727, William Webb, 1728, Henry Miller, Evans Lewis, elected by commissioners and assessors in August, *vice* Isaac Taylor, deceased, 1729, Samuel Nutt, 1730, Evan Lewis, 1731, Jacob Howell, 1732, Samuel Lewis, 1733, George Aston, 1734, John Davis, 1735, Richard Jones, 1736, Samuel Lightfoot, 1737, John Parry, Jr, 1738, William Jeffries, 1739, John Davis, 1740, John Parry, Jr, 1741, John Yarnall, 1742, John Davis, 1743, Jacob Howell, 1744, Joseph Mendenhall, 1745, John Davis, 1746, Thomas Pennell, 1747, Joshua Thompson, 1748, Isaac Davis, 1749, Thomas Pennell, 1750, Edward Brinton, Samuel Bunting, *vice* Thomas Pennell, deceased, 1751, William Lewis, 1752, John Fairlamb, 1753, Robert Miller, 1754, Thomas Pearson, 1755, Joseph Ashbridge, 1756, Joseph Davis, 1757, Joseph James, 1758, John Hannum, 1759, Jonas Preston, 1760, Joseph Pennock, 1761, John Griffith, 1762, Lewis Davis, 1763, John Price, 1764, Benjamin Bartholomew, 1765, Richard Baker, 1766, John Davis, 1767, Robert Pennell, 1768, John Webster, 1769, John Evans, 1770, Jesse Bonsall, 1771, Robert Mendenhall, 1772, John Fleming, 1773, Thomas Levis, 1774, Thomas Taylor, 1775, William Evans, 1776, Sketchley Morton, 1777, David Cloyd, 1778, Andrew Boyd, 1779, Benjamin Brannan, 1780, John Bartholomew, 1781, Joseph Strawbridge, 1782, Caleb James, 1783, John Davis, 1784, Joseph McClellan, 1785, Caleb James, 1786, Caleb North, 1787, John Worth, 1788, Joseph Gibbons

After the erection of Delaware County, in 1789, at the general election in that year the following commissioners were elected and served

1790, Edward Hunter, Gideon Gilpin, James Barnard, in 1791, John Jones was elected in place of Hunter, and Gilpin, Barnard, and Jones served for that and the year 1792, when all record is lost until 1797, when David Platt and Richard Lloyd were commissioners, in 1798, Isaac G Gilpin was elected, 1799, Thomas Bishop, 1800, Thomas Vernon, 1801, Jonas Eyre,[3] 1802, John Hunter, Josiah Lewis, 1803, John Odenheimer died, and Pierce Corsly was appointed to fill vacancy, 1804, Pierce Corsly, 1805, Joseph Gibbons, and Josiah Lewis having died or resigned, Nehemiah Baker was appointed to fill vacancy, and was also elected that year, 1807, Joseph Engle, 1808, William Mendenhall, 1809, George B Lownes, 1810, Thomas Bishop, 1811, Preston Eyre 1812, Thomas Hemphill, 1813, Maris Worrell, 1814, John Brooke, 1815, Robert Fairlamb, 1816, John Willcox, William Levis, Jr,[4] 1817, Joseph Davis, 1818, William Hill, 1819, John Lindsay, Jr, 1820, Joseph Henderson, 1821, George Green, 1822, Joseph Engle, 1823, Edward Hunter, 1824, William Johnson, 1825, James Sill, 1826, Samuel H Eves, 1827, James Maddock, 1828, Joseph Bishop, 1829, Oliver Levis, 1830, Evan Evans, 1831, David Siter, 1832, David Trainer, John Aitkins, 1835, James Serrill, 1836, James S Peters, 1837, Isaac Fawkes, 1838, Spencer McIlvain, 1839, Edward Lewis, Jr 1840, Davis Beaumont, 1841, Thomas Williamson, 1842, Thomas Steele, Jr, 1843, Isaac Yarnall, 1844, George Harvey, 1845, David Worrell, 1846, Samuel Palmer, 1847, Edmund Pennell,[5] 1848, Mark Bartleson, 1849, Caleb J Hoopes, 1850, John D Gilpin, 1851, Anneseley Newlin, 1852, James Barton, 1853, William H Grubb, 1854, Robert Plumstead, 1855, Thomas Pratt, 1856, Peicipher Baker, 1857, Samuel Leedom, 1858, James Clowd, 1859, Elwood Tyson, 1860, Van lear Eachus, 1861, Thomas Reece, 1862, Nathaniel Pratt, 1863, Joseph Lewis, 1864, Daniel James, 1865, George Drayton, 1866, William D H Serrill, 1867, Charles Johnson, 1868, T Baker Jones, 1869, Jacob M Campbell, 1870, William Russell, 1871, John B Heyburn, 1872, John B Holland, 1873, James McDade, 1874, Elias Baker

The same commissioners remained in office until the first Monday of January, 1876

Before the expiration of the period of service of the old board of commissioners, before the provisions of the Constitution of 1874 went into effect respecting that office, James McDade, one of the commissioners, absconded When the county statement was published, the people stood aghast at the exhibit made, and on March 17, 1876,—

"The grand jury reported that the commissioners for the year 1875 have exceeded their authority in borrowing money on promissory notes, which sums amounted to $206,227 57, and the discounts to $3043.90, while tax-collectors were permitted to remain in arrears on collections, with discounts allowed to them to the amount of $40,952.18.

"In the opinion of the grand jury this is highly improper, and should be fully investigated, and measures taken to collect said tax That by the said report (that of the county treasurer) it appears that the expenditures for repairing bridges and for new bridges has cost the county for the same year the sum of $58,375.66 That in the financial condition of the county the grand jury deems this an extravagant expendi-

---

[1] Sheriff Baldwin died Feb 14, 1834 His son was appointed to fill vacancy

[2] Sheriff Esrey dying in office, his son was appointed to fill the vacancy

[3] On his resigning, on April 29, 1802, the county minutes show "Upon the resignation of Jonas Eyre, one of the commissioners of the county of Delaware, the following person was appointed by the court and commissioners, viz., John Odenheimer, Esq, to serve in place of said Jonas Eyre"

[4] On Oct 21, 1816, "the court and John Willcox and William Levis, Jr, remaining commissioners, being assembled together, do appoint Richard Flower county commissioner until the next general election, in place of Robert Fairlamb, who has been elected and commissioned sheriff of the said county, and has declined serving in the office of commissioner"

[5] "Feb 25, 1847, the petition of Samuel Palmer and Edmund Pennell was presented, showing that a vacancy had occurred in the board of Commissioners of Delaware County by the death of David Worrell. Whereupon the court, together with the two remaining commissioners of said county, have appointed Thomas Steele, Jr, of the township of Marple, in said county, a commissioner to fill said vacancy until the next general election"

ture that the commissioners were not warranted in making, and that they have reason to believe that irregularities have occurred in awarding contracts for the same, which should be investigated. That by the same report, printing and stationery for the same year has cost the county $3095.58; this is in addition to the amount paid by the commissioners, but not allowed by the auditors. This appears to the grand jury to be an extravagant expenditure for that purpose. By the same report there has been paid D. Corson for the storage of the turn-table from the Front Street bridge, $115. With such continued expenditures, this turn-table will prove a serious burden, and the grand jury recommend its early disposal.

"The grand jury also report that bonds of the company which have been paid or exchanged have not been properly cancelled, merely an erasure of the commissioners' names, and that some of these partially-cancelled bonds have in some manner disappeared from the commissioners' office, and have been wrongfully used, and that the coupons on those bonds have been presented and paid out of the county treasury since the cancellation of the bonds. The grand jury consider that these matters should be more fully and thoroughly investigated, and urge upon this department of the public trust a more careful and economical administration. The treasurer further reports that for 1875 there has been paid out of the treasury for road damages the sum of $4608, and the grand jury deem it proper to say that it is questionable whether such expenditure is warranted in the condition of the county finances, as perhaps many of the roads laid out must benefit, with the number already improved, but few of the citizens."

This action of the grand jury directed public attention directly to the gross mismanagement of public affairs, but as it subsequently proved the greater part of the objectionable transactions were done by the absconding commissioner, without the knowledge of his fellow-member of the board, the authorities were powerless to punish the offender.

Under the Constitution of 1874 the following commissioners were elected for the period of three years, the term of service beginning in the year set opposite to their names: 1876, Owen W. Yarnall, Abram C. Lukens, Edward H. Engle; 1879, Owen W. Yarnall, Abram C. Lukens, Jesse Brooke.

In that year Jesse Brooke, the regular Democratic candidate, was elected over Edward H. Engle, Independent Democrat, by two votes, and proceedings were instituted to test the validity of Brooke's election by the friends of Engle. The matter was referred to an examiner, but pending the hearing the contest was abandoned.

1882, Owen W. Yarnall, Benjamin F. Pretty, Jesse Brooke.

County Treasurer.—In the early time the office of county treasurer appears to have been a gift at the disposal of the commissioners and assessors, and it must have been remunerative other than the salary or commissions attached to the office, for John Taylor, in 1741, offers to perform the duties of the office "without bringing any charge against the county," and the same year two other patriots, Joseph Brinton and Joshua Thomas, also offered to serve the public gratis. Brinton, who was the incumbent, succeeded in retaining the position. In 1790, when the board of assessors ceased to be, the commissioners adopted the plan of appointing the outgoing commissioner county treasurer, or, as it was then called, the commissioner's treasurer, and continued generally to observe that rule until 1838, when under the Constitution of 1837, the office was made elective.

The following is the list of county treasurers of the old county of Chester:

1695, Jeremiah Collett; 1697–1702, Walter Martin; 1704, Caleb Pusey; 1706–9, Walter Martin; 1720–23, Henry Pierce; 1724–26, Philip Taylor; 1740–46, Joseph Brinton; 1756–60, Robert Miller; 1761–64, Humphrey Marshall; 1765, Jesse Maris, Jr.; 1766–69, Lewis Davis; 1770–76, James Gibbons; 1770–72, Richard Thomas; 1775, Philip Taylor; 1775–77, John Brinton; 1778, Thomas Levis; 1779, William Evans; 1780, Persifor Frazer (March 22d); 1781, David Cloyd; 1785, Andrew Boyd and David Cloyd; 1786–87, William Evans; 1788, Andrew Boyd.

TREASURERS OF THE COUNTY OF DELAWARE.

1790, Edward Richards; 1799, Seth Thomas; 1806, Joshua Lewis; 1809, John Thompson; 1812, Robert Fairlamb; 1815, John Thompson; 1822, Robert Fairlamb; 1825, John Russell; 1827, Homer Eachus; 1830, William Eyre; 1833, Oborn Levis; 1835, Samuel T. Walker; 1838, William Eyre; 1839, Davis Beaumont; 1840, William Eyre; 1840, William Eyre, Jr. (unexpired term of William Eyre); 1841, John Miller; 1844, Richard F. Worrell; 1846, Benjamin F. Johnson; 1848, Marshall Eachus; 1850, Edmund Taylor; 1852, Samuel Dutton; 1854, Joseph H. Hinkson; 1856, Jackson Lyons; 1858, Charles R. Williamson; 1860, Charles Johnson; 1862, David R. Ralston; 1864, William Hinkson; 1866, William H. Eves; 1868, William F. Mathews; 1870, John J. Hoopes; 1872, John D. Howard; 1874, Alvin Baldwin; 1876, Henry B. Taylor; 1879, William P. Yarnall; 1882, Stephen Clowd, Jr.

Directors of the Poor.—The early settlers were not unmindful of their duty in providing for the sick, infirm, and destitute, who could not care for themselves. At a court held on the sixth day of Eleventh month, 1684, it was

"Ordered that y[e] Inhabitance of Concord, Bethel and Chichester meet on the 3rd day of the next weeke att Henry Renolds to conferre together how to Provide a maintainance for Miriam Thomson and her child."

The court, on March 25th of each year, appointed for the several townships two persons, who were to act as overseers of the poor in the township where they resided, and such persons were usually selected from the wealthiest men in the locality. The court records are filled with cases respecting the settlement of paupers, hence to avoid much of that contention the act of May 31, 1718, was passed, to define the law governing residence of those persons needing relief from the public. This act required that all persons who should be receiving public assistance, including the wives and children of such pauper, if residing with him, "Shall upon the Shoulder of the right Sleeve of the upper Garment of every such Person in an open and visible manner, wear such a Badge or Mark as is hereinafter mentioned and expressed, That is to say, a large Roman (P) together with the first Letter of the Name of the County, City or Place whereof such Person is an Inhabitant, cut either in red or blue Cloth, as the Overseers of the Poor it shall be directed or appointed."

The failure of "any such poor person" to comply with this provision rendered him or her liable to be taken before a justice of the peace, when, in the discretion of the magistrate, the public allowance could "be abridged, suspended, or withdrawn," or the offender committed to the House of Correction, "there to be whipped and kept at hard Labour for any Number of Days not exceeding Twenty-one, as to the said Justices should seem meet."

On Feb. 13, 1804, the act of Assembly was approved providing for the election in Delaware County, at the following general election, of three reputable citizens to be directors of the poor, who were instructed to meet, and by lot to divide themselves into three classes, "the place of the first to be vacated at the expiration of the first year, of the second at the expiration of the second year, and of the third at the expiration of the third year; so that those who may be chosen, after the first election, may serve for three years; and one-third be chosen annually,"[1] which manner of electing the directors and the period of service remained in use until changed by the second section of Article xiv. of the Constitution of 1874.

In the report of the committee of the Legislature on the operation of the poor law, made Jan. 29, 1825, the statement from Delaware County was, "The establishment of a house of employment in this county has increased the number, or from some other cause, there is more than when maintained in the different townships; but we have no hesitation in saying that the effect has been such as to make their situation more comfortable, the morals and health better preserved."

In 1855 the directors of the poor, having been authorized by the act of May 8, 1854, to sell the old county-house and farm at Media, sold the estate in the fall of that year for a sum over fifty thousand dollars, and purchased the farm of Abraham Pennell, one of the directors, containing about one hundred and one acres, for sixteen thousand dollars, and contracted with John Eves & Co., of Nether Providence, to erect the building for twenty thousand three hundred dollars. The proceedings of the board aroused considerable feeling in the county, and a public meeting was held on the 29th of December, 1855, "to investigate the action of the Directors of the Poor in changing the location of the public property;" and an adjourned meeting was held on Jan. 18, 1856, when a bitter debate was had, after which the whole matter drifted by, and in a short time had ceased to attract any further public attention.

The following is the list of directors of the poor, giving the year when each director became a member of the board:

1805, William Anderson, Jonathan Heacock, John Smith (resigned and John Thomson appointed); 1806, Thomas Pennell, Philip Moore; 1807, John McIlvain; 1808, Benjamin W. Oakford; 1809, David Pratt; 1810, George W. Oakford (died in office, John McIlvain appointed), William Peters, Jr., John Worrall; 1811, Thomas Garrett; 1812, George Miller; 1813, Francis Wesley; 1814, John Powell; 1815, George B. Lownes; 1816, Joseph Hoskins; 1817, William Trimble; 1818, William Mendenhall (in place of William Trimble), Enos Sharpless; 1819, Samuel Garrett; 1820, Jesse Darlington; 1821, Joseph James; 1822, James Craig; 1823, Enos Williamson; 1824, Micajah Speakman; 18 5, Isaac Yarnall (in place of Speakman, resigned), John Larkin; 1826, Oborn Levis; 1827, Joseph Henderson; 1828, Thomas Dutton; 1829, Isaiah Fawk; 1830, John Kerns; 1831, John Hinkson; 1832, David Lyons; 1833, Robert N. Gamble; 1834, James Ogden; 1835, Edward Lewis; 1836, Samuel Hale; 1837, Jesse Walter; 1838, George Martin; 1839, Capt. James Serrill; 1840, James Barton; 1841, Moses D. Palmer; 1842, George Lewis; 1843, Caleb J. Hoopes; 1844, Moses D. Palmer (he resigned and George F. Gilpins appointed); 1845, James J. Lewis; 1846, Marshall Painter; 1847, John Clayton; 1848, Joel Evans; 1849, John Miller; 1850, Thomas Williamson; 1851, J. Edward Garrett; 1852, Abraham Pennell; 1853, William Trainer; 1854, Joseph B. Leedom; 1855, Jacob Byers; 1856, Samuel A. Barton; 1857, Francis Leedom; 1858, Samuel Johnson; 1859, E. B. Loveland; 1860, William H. Grubb; 1861, Judge Tyson; 1862, Samuel B. Leedom; 1863, Peter W. Green; 1864, Joseph Powell; 1865, Baldwin Howard; 1866, Fredrick J. Hinkson; 1867–68, Powell, Howard, and Hinkson; 1869–71, Powell, Howard, and William Trainer; 1872, James Shelley Tyson, Joel Sharpless; 1873, Edgar T. Miller; 1874, Jesse Hibberd; 1875, Chalkley Harvey; 1876–77–79–80, Chalkley Harvey, Jesse Hibberd, John H. Kerlin; 1880–81, Chalkley Harvey, John H. Kerlin, Milton Edwards; 1882, Chalkley Harvey, Milton Edwards, Henry L. Donaldson; 1883, Henry L. Donaldson, John B. McCay, Jr., Joseph Leedom.

[1] Bliss' "Delaware County Digest," p. 48.

County Auditors.—During all the period while Delaware County was a part of Chester County the accounts of the public officers were audited by the court, which was found to be injurious, inasmuch as they were often given hurried examination, the justices growing weary of the dry column of figures submitted to their inspection and approval. The evil became so noticeable that the Legislature sought to rectify it, hence we find that on

"August 11, 1791 The Court appoints John Talbot, Mark Wilcox and William Pennock, as auditors to settle &c., the accounts of the Treasurer and Commissioners of the County, in conformity to the act of Assembly of March 30, 1791. Read three times in Court."

Subsequent appointments by the court were as follows:

1792, John Pearson, Abraham Pennell, and Richard Flower; 1793, Benjamin Brannon, Thomas Newlin, Abraham Sharpless; 1795, Samuel Price, Esq., John Hurn, and Caleb Pierce; 1796, John Crosby, Esq., Elisha Price, Esq., and William Martin; 1797, John Crosby, Esq., William Martin, Esq., Thomas Newlin, Esq.; Nov. 26, 1798, "The Court nominate John Crosby Esq. and Thomas Newlin, Esq. be continued and adds Richard Flower in the room of William Martin, the other Auditor, deceased;" 1799, Edward Hunter, Esq., William Trimble, and Nicholas Newlin; 1800, Abraham Pennell, Joseph Shallcross, John Talbot; 1801–2, Nathaniel Newlin, Esq., Joseph Pennell, Jacob Gibbons; 1803, Benjamin W. Oakford, Moses Palmer, Pierce Crosby; 1804, William Anderson, Thomas Smith, Frederick Fairlamb; 1805, Abraham Sharpless, Richard P. Lloyd, John Thomson; 1806, Moses Palmer, Benjamin W. Oakford, Dr. Jonas Preston; 1807, Dr. Jonas Preston, Moses Palmer, Pierce Crosby; 1808, William Pennock, Moses Palmer, Pierce Crosby; 1809, Moses Palmer, Edward Hunter, Maskill Ewing; 1819, Moses Palmer.

In 1821 the office became elective.

1823, William Bishop, Enoch Abraham, Samuel Hewes; 1824, Cyrus Mendenhall; 1825, Joseph Gibbons; 1826, Enos Sharpless; 1827, Henry Moore; 1828, Abner Lewis; 1829, Daniel Abraham; 1830, Benjamin Serrill; 1831, John D. White; 1832, James McMullin; 1833, Alexander McKeever; 1834, Joseph Gibson, William S. Flower (in room of James McMullin); 1835, William Eyre; 1836, H. Jones Brooks; 1837, Caleb J. Hoopes; 1838, Casper W. Sharpless; 1839, George Smedley; 1840, Joel Evans; 1841, William J. Wilcox; 1842, Minshall Painter; 1843, Jesse Brooke, Jr.; 1844, Robert E. Hannum; 1845, Jonathan Miller; 1846, John Sellers, Jr.; 1847, Frederick Fairlamb; 1848, Jacob Parry; 1849, Randle Bishop; 1850, William Eyre; 1851, Lewis Miller; 1852, Randle Bishop, William Eyre, Lewis Miller; 1853, William Ogden; 1854, Abraham P. Morgan; 1855, Walter Y. Hoopes; 1856, J. Lewis Garrett; 1857, William D. Pennell; 1858, —— ——; 1859–60, Robert E. Hannum, John D. White, Jacob Smedley; 1861, James H. Ogden; 1862, J. H. Omensetter; 1863,

James Clowd; 1864, Walter Y. Hoopes; 1865, Samuel Dutton; 1866, Joseph Walter; 1867, same auditor; 1868, I. Hunter Moore; 1869, Curtis Cheyney; 1870, George Broomall; 1871, Eber Lewis, Jr.; 1872, Daniel James; 1873, Charles P. Walter; 1874, Pearson Pike; 1875, Charles H. Cheyney; 1876 (under Constitution of 1874), William J. Smith, Jared Darlington, Jacob Boon; 1879, Jared Darlington, Thomas Coulter, Joseph Pratt; 1882, Jared Darlington, William S. Sykes, J. Lewis Garrett.

Members of Congress.—In 1789 the members of Congress from Pennsylvania were elected on a general ticket, which ran throughout the commonwealth. The Apportionment Act of 1791 first gave Congressional districts, and by it Philadelphia and Delaware County became the First District, and was entitled to one member. In that year Thomas Fitzsimmons, of Philadelphia, was elected, and served until 1793. In the mean time, dissatisfaction had been created because of the manner in which the State had been districted, and the law was repealed, and again, in 1793, the members from our State were elected on a general ticket. In 1795 an Apportionment Act was passed which met general approval, and John Richards, of Philadelphia, represented our people, and in 1797 and 1801, Richard Thomas, of the same place, was the member of the House of Representatives from this district. In 1801, Joseph Hemphill, from Delaware County, was Congressman.

By the Apportionment Act of 1802 the city and county of Philadelphia and the county of Delaware became the First Congressional District, and was entitled to three representatives, of which number Delaware County furnished: Jacob Richards, 1803–9; William Anderson, 1809–15.

The Apportionment Act of 1812 constituted the same territory as the First District, with four representatives. As will be noticed, Maj. Anderson was continued for one term under this act: Thomas Smith, 1815–17; William Anderson, 1817–19; Samuel Edwards, 1819–27.

By the Apportionment Act of 1822, Chester, Delaware, and Lancaster Counties were made the Fourth Congressional District, entitled to three members, and twice under its provision Mr. Edwards was our representative: Dr. Samuel Anderson, 1827–29; George Grey Leiper, 1829–31.

In 1830, during the Anti-Masonic excitement, seven candidates were named by the opposing factions and presented to the people. Three Delaware County gentlemen were nominated,—Archibald J. Dick, Edward Darlington, and John Edwards,—and all of them defeated. The district during the years 1831 to 1833 was represented by Joshua Evans and David Potts, Jr., of Chester, and William Heister, of Lancaster County. By the Apportionment Act of 1832 the same territory comprised the Fourth Congressional District, and was entitled to the same number of members: Edward Darlington, 1833–39; John Edwards, 1839–43.

By the act of 1843, Delaware and Montgomery Counties comprised the Fifth Congressional District, and was entitled to one member: Francis James, of Montgomery, 1843–45; Jacob S. Yost, 1845–47; John Friedley, 1848–51.

In 1848 Montgomery County conceded the representative to Delaware County, and John K. Zeilin was nominated by the convention in the latter county. The Democrats had nominated Samuel M. Leiper, whose election over Zeilin was not doubted; hence a convention of the Whigs was called at the Black Horse, and Zeilin was requested and unwillingly compelled to resign the nomination in favor of Friedley: John McNair, Montgomery, 1851–53.

The Apportionment Act of 1852 made Delaware and Chester Counties the Sixth Congressional District, with one member: William Everhart, Chester County, 1853–55; John Hickman, Chester County, 1855–63.

The apportionment of 1862 made the same territory the Seventh District: J. M. Broomall, Delaware County, 1863–69; W. Townsend, Chester County, 1869–77.

The act of 1873 made the same counties the Sixth District: William Ward, Delaware County, 1877–84; J. B. Everhart, Chester County, 1883.

The dates given herein are the times of service, and not the dates of election.

MEMBERS OF THE GENERAL ASSEMBLY FROM CHESTER COUNTY.

1682.—John Simcock, Thomas Brasey, Ralph Withers, Thomas Usher.

1683.—John Hoskins, Robert Wade, George Wood, John Blunsten, Dennis Rockford, Thomas Bracy, John Bezar, John Harding, Joseph Phipps.

1684.—Joshua Hastings, Robert Wade, John Blunsten, George Maris, Thomas Usher, Henry Maddock.

1685.—John Blunsten, George Maris, John Harding, Thomas Usher, Francis Stanfield, Joshua Fearne.

1686.—Robert Wade, John Blunsten, George Maris, Bartholomew Coppock, Caleb Pusey, Samuel Levis.

1687.—John Blunsten, George Maris, Bartholomew Coppock, Caleb Pusey, Edward Bezar, Randal Vernon.

1688.—John Blunsten, James Sandelands, George Maris, Robert Pile, Edward Carter, Thomas Cobourn.

1689.—James Sandelands, Samuel Levis, John Bartram, Robert Pile, Jonathan Hayes.

1690.—John Briston, William Jenkins, Robert Pile, Joshua Fearne, George Maris, Caleb Pusey.

1691.—Record wanting.

1692.—Philip Roman, George Maris, Bartholomew Coppock, Robert Pile, Caleb Pusey, Thomas Withers.

1693.—John Simcock, George Maris, David Lloyd.

1694.—David Lloyd (Speaker), Caleb Pusey, Samuel Levis.

1695.—John Blunsten, Bartholomew Coppock, William Jenkins, Robert Pile, Walter Fawcet, Philip Roman.

1696.—John Simcock (Speaker), John Blunsten, Caleb Pusey.

1697.—John Blunsten (Speaker), Bartholomew Coppock, Thomas Worth, Jonathan Hayes.

1698.—Caleb Pusey, Samuel Levis, Nathaniel Newlin, Robert Carter.

1699.—John Blunsten (Speaker), Robert Pile, John Worrilow, Robert Carter.

1700.—John Blunsten (Speaker), Robert Pile, Richard Ormes, John Hood, Samuel Levis, Henry Levis.

1701.—Joseph Baker, Samuel Levis, Nathaniel Newlin, Nicholas Pile.

1702.—John Blunsten, Robert Pile, Nathaniel Newlin, Andrew Job.

1703.—Nicholas Pile, John Bennet, Andrew Job, David Lewis, Nathaniel Newlin, Joseph Baker, Robert Carter, Joseph Wood.

1704.—Nicholas Pile, John Bennet, Nicholas Fairlamb, Joseph Cobourn, John Hood, Richard Hayes, Joseph Wood, Isaac Taylor.

1705 —Nicholas Pile, John Bennet, John Hood, Joseph Wood, Isaac Taylor

1706 —Samuel Levis, Richard Hayes, Francis Chadds, Joseph Baker, Evan Lewis, John Hood, George Pearce, William Garrett

1707.—Francis Chadds William Smith, Samuel Levis, Richard Hayes, John Hood, William Garrett, John Bethel

1708.—Daniel Williamson, Samuel Levis, Richard Hayes, John Hood, Thomas Pearson, William Bartram, Daniel Hoops

1709.—Samuel Levis, John Maris, John Hood, Henry Lewis, Daniel Williamson, Daniel Hoops, Richard Hayes, William Smith

1710 —Nicholas Pile, Joseph Baker, William Lewis. John Wood, Nathaniel Newlin, Ephraim Jackson, Caleb Pusey, Isaac Taylor

1711 —Francis Yarnall, John Bezer, Caleb Pusey, Nicholas Pile, Nathaniel Newlin, Joseph Baker, Nicholas Fairlamb, David Llewellyn

1712.—Caleb Pusey, David Lloyd, William Davis, Nicholas Fairlamb, Joseph Wood, George Harlan, Isaac Taylor, John Maris

1713 —David Lloyd, William Davis, Joseph Baker, Nathaniel Newlin, Nicholas Fairlamb, Richard Hayes, William Brinton, John Blunston

1714 —David Lloyd, Nathaniel Newlin, Nicholas Pile, Evan Lewis, John Miller, Benjamin Meudenhall, Samuel Garrett, Richard Maris

1715 —David Lloyd, Henry Hayes, Samuel Garrett, Henry Lewis, William Pile, Edward Beazer, Philip Taylor, David Lewis

1716.—David Lloyd, John Blunston, Henry Hayes, Joseph Pennock, David Harry, John Maris, John Worrell Henry Oburn

1717.—David Lloyd, Nathaniel Newlin, Richard Hayes, Samuel Garrett, James Gibbons, John Wood, George Maris, Henry Miller

1718 —David Lloyd, Richard Hayes, Nathaniel Newlin, John Wright, James Gibbons, Henry Lewis, Henry Oburn

1719.—Isaac Taylor, Joseph Pennock, Moses Key, John Bezer, Nathaniel Newlin, John Maris, James Gibbons, Evan Lewis.

1720 —Joseph Pennock, Samuel Levis, Israel Taylor, John Maris, Ralph Pile, Daniel Williamson, David Lewis

1721.—Samuel Levis, Jr, William Pile, Daniel Williamson, Isaac Taylor, David Lewis, Henry Oburn, Nathaniel Newlin, Israel Taylor

1722 —Samuel Levis, Jr, Joseph Pennock, David Levis, William Pile, Daniel Williamson, Israel Taylor, Nathaniel Newlin, Isaac Taylor

1723 —Moses Key, Joseph Pennock, William Webb, Thomas Chandler, David Lloyd (Speaker), John Crosby, Samuel Lewis, Jr, Samuel Nutt

1724.—Moses Key, Joseph Pennock, William Pile, Thomas Chandler, Elisha Gatchell, John Parry, John Crosby

1725.—Thomas Chandler, David Lloyd (Speaker), William Webb, John Wright, Samuel Hollingsworth William Pusey, George Ascheton, William Paschall

1726 —David Lloyd (Speaker), Samuel Nutt, Samuel Hollingsworth, John Wright, Richard Hayes, Joseph Pennock, Thomas Chandler, William Pusey

1727 —John Parry, Samuel Hollingsworth, David Lloyd, Thomas Chandler, John Carter, Daniel Williamson, Simon Meredith, William Webb

1728 —Thomas Chandler, David Lloyd, Samuel Hollingsworth, John Parry, William Webb, Philip Taylor, John Carter, Henry Hayes

1729 —Caleb Cowpland, Richard Hayes, Joseph Brinton, Thomas Chandler, Samuel Gilpin, James James, Joseph Pennock

1730.—Henry Pierce, John Taylor, Samuel Levis, John Parry, Thomas Chandler, Samuel Gilpin, William Webb, Henry Hayes

1731 —Joseph Harvey, John Parry, Samuel Levis, Caleb Cowpland, John Taylor, Joseph Brinton, Henry Pierce, Evan Lewis

1732 —Caleb Cowpland, Joseph Harvey, Joseph Brinton, Thomas Thomas, William Webb, Joseph Pennock, John Davis, William Hewes

1733 —Caleb Cowpland, Joseph Harvey, Joseph Pennock, Joseph Brinton, John Davis, Thomas Thomas, John Owen, William Moore

1734 —Joseph Harvey, Joseph Brinton, Caleb Cowpland, John Evans, William Webb, William Moore, John Owen, Joseph Pennock

1735 —Joseph Harvey, William Moore, Joseph Pennock, Caleb Cowpland, John Evans, John Parry, Joseph Brinton, Thomas Cummings.

1736 —Joseph Harvey, Thomas Cummings, John Evans, Caleb Cowpland, William Webb, William Moore, Thomas Chandler, John Parry

1737 —Thomas Chandler, John Harvey, John Evans, Thomas Cummings, William Moore, James Gibbons, William Hughs, Richard Hayes

1738.—William Moore, James Gibbons, Thomas Chandler, Joseph Harvey, John Owen, Thomas Tatnall, William Hughs, Jeremiah Starr

1739 —James Gibbons, Thomas Chandler, Joseph Harvey, William Hughs, Jeremiah Starr, William Moore, Samuel Levis, John Owen

1740 —Thomas Chandler, Joseph Harvey, James Gibbons, William Hughs, Samuel Levis, John Owen, Jeremiah Starr, Thomas Tatnall

1741 —Same as 1740

1742 —Same as 1740.

1743.—Jeremiah Starr, James Gibbons, Thomas Chandler, Joseph Harvey, Joseph Pennock, Samuel Levis, George Ashbridge, Jr, Francis Yarnall

1744.—George Ashbridge, Francis Yarnall, Joseph Pennock, Samuel Levis, James Gibbons, Joseph Harvey, Thomas Cummings, Thomas Chandler

1745 —Joseph Pennock, Thomas Cummings, George Ashbridge, Francis Yarnall, Robert Lewis, Joseph Harvey, Samuel Levis, Thomas Chandler

1746 —Francis Yarnall, George Ashbridge, Robert Lewis, Thomas Worth, Samuel Levis, Peter Dicks, Thomas Chandler John Owen

1747.—Samuel Levis, Francis Yarnall, George Ashbridge, Thomas Worth, Peter Dicks, John Owen, John Davis, Thomas Chandler

1748 —Thomas Worth, George Ashbridge, Francis Yarnall, John Davis, John Owen, Joseph James, Thomas Chandler, Joseph Gibbons

1749 —Joseph Gibbons, George Ashbridge, Henry Hockley, Thomas Chandler, Nathaniel Grubb, Nathaniel Pennock, Roger Hunt, Thomas Cummings

1750 —Same members as 1749

1751 —Joseph Gibbons, Thomas Cummings, George Ashbridge, Nathaniel Grubb, Peter Dicks, Nathaniel Pennock, Henry Hockley, Thomas Chandler

1752 —Joseph Gibbons, Thomas Cummings, Nathaniel Grubb, William Peters, Jacob Howell

1753.—Thomas Cummings, Nathaniel Pennock, George Ashbridge, Joseph Gibbens, Nathaniel Grubb, Peter Dicks, William Peters, Joseph Jones

1754 —Members of 1753 re-elected

1755 —Same members re-elected

1756.—Joseph Gibbons, Peter Dicks, John Morten, Roger Hunt, George Ashbridge, Hugh Trimble, Nathaniel Pennock, Nathaniel Grubb

1757 —Joseph Gibbons George Ashbridge, John Morton, Roger Hunt, Isaac Wayne, Nathaniel Grubb, Hugh Trimble, Joshua Ash

1758 —The members of 1757 re elected

1759 —John Morton, George Ashbridge, Joshua Ash Joseph Gibbons, Hugh Trimble, Roger Hunt, Peter Dicks Isaac Wayne

1760 —George Ashbridge, John Morton, Roger Hunt, Joshua Ash, Joseph Gibbons, Nathaniel Pennock, Isaac Wayne, William Boyd

1761 —George Ashbridge, Joseph Gibbons, Nathaniel Pennock, Joshua Ash, Isaac Pearson, John Morton, Isaac Wayne, Roger Hunt

1762 —George Ashbridge, Nathaniel Pennock, Joshua Ash, Isaac Pearson, John Morton Isaac Wayne, Joseph Gibbons, John Jacobs.

1763 —George Ashbridge, Joshua Ash, Isaac Pearson, John Morton, Isaac Wayne, Joseph Gibbons John Jacobs

1764 —George Ashbridge, John Morton, Nathaniel Pennock, Joshua Ash, Isaac Pearson Charles Humphreys, John Jacobs, John Fairlamb

1765 —Same members re-elected

1766.—John Morton, George Ashbridge, Nathaniel Pennock, John Jacobs, Charles Humphreys, Isaac Pearson, Joshua Ash, John Minshall

1767.—Isaac Pearson, Charles Humphreys, John Sellers, George Ashbridge, John Minshall, Jonas Preston, John Jacobs, John Sellers, Nathaniel Pennock

1768 —John Jacobs, Nathaniel Pennock, George Ashbridge, Charles Humphreys, John Sellers, John Minshall, Isaac Pearson, John Crosby

1769 —George Ashbridge, Charles Humphreys, Isaac Pearson, John Sellers, John Jacobs, John Minshall, John Crosby, John Morton

1770 —Same members re elected

1771.—Same members re-elected

1772.—Charles Humphreys, Isaac Pearson, John Morton, John Jacobs, John Minshall, James Hockley, George Ashbridge, Benjamin Bartholomew

1773.—Isaac Pearson, Benjamin Bartholomew, John Jacobs, Charles Humphreys, John Morton, James Gibbons, John Minshall, Joseph Pennock

1774.—Benjamin Bartholomew, John Jacobs, Charles Humphreys, John Morton, James Gibbons, Joseph Pennock, Isaac Pearson, Anthony Wayne

1775.—Same members, except Joseph Pyle was elected in the place of Anthony Wayne.
1776.—John Jacobs, Caleb Davis, Joseph Gardiner, John Fulton, Samuel Cunningham, John Sellers.
1777.—Joseph Gardiner, John Fulton, Samuel Cunningham, John Culbertson, Stephen Cochran, Lewis Gronow.
1778.—John Fulton, Joseph Gardiner, Patrick Anderson, John Culbertson, Stephen Cochran, John Fleming.
1779.—David Thomas, Henry Hayes, John Fulton, James Boyd, Patrick Anderson, Joseph Parke, William Harris, Sketchley Morton.
1780.—David Thomas, Henry Hayes, William Harris, Joseph Parke, James Boyd, Patrick Anderson, John Culbertson, Evan Evans.
1781.—Persifor Frazer, John Culbertson, Thomas Maffat, Evan Evans, John Hannum, James Moore, Patrick Anderson, John Lindsay.
1782.—Persifor Frazer, Thomas Strawbridge, David Thomas, Benjamin Brannan, John Lindsay, Thomas Maffat, James Boyd, Evan Evans.
1783.—David Thomas, Evan Evans, John Hannum, Joseph Parke, Richard Willing, Thomas Potts, Thomas Bull, Edward Jones.
1784.—Richard Willing, Anthony Wayne, Edward Jones, Robert Ralston, James Moore, Joseph Strawbridge, Persifor Frazer, Thomas Potts, Charles Humphreys.
1785.—Anthony Wayne, Robert Ralston, James Moore, Thomas Bull, John Hannum, Robert Smith, Samuel Evans, Jonathan Morris.
1786.—James Moore, Richard Willing, Robert Ralston, Samuel Evans, Richard Thomas, Townsend Wheelen.
1787.—Same members re-elected.
1788.—Richard Thomas, James Moore, Mark Willcox, John McDowell, Caleb James, Richard Downing, Jr.

MEMBERS OF THE SENATE OF PENNSYLVANIA FROM DELAWARE COUNTY.

In a District with Philadelphia (for four years).

1790.—John Sellers.
1794–99.—Nathaniel Newlin.
1800.—John Pearson.
1804.—William Pennell.

In a District with Chester County (for four years).

1808.—Jonas Preston.
1812.—John Newbold.
1816.—Maskell Ewing.
1824–28.—John Kerlin.
1832.—Dr. George Smith.

In a District with Chester and Montgomery Counties.

1836.—Henry Myers (for four years).
1839.—John T. Huddleson (for three years).

In a District with Chester County (for three years).

1848.—H. Jonas Brooke.
1854.—James J. Lewis.
1860.—Jacob S. Serrill.

From Chester and Delaware Counties.

1865.—Dr. Wilmer Worthington (from Chester County).
1869.—H. Jonas Brooke.
1873.—William B. Waddell (from Chester County).
1874–84.—Thomas V. Cooper.

MEMBERS OF THE HOUSE OF REPRESENTATIVES FROM DELAWARE COUNTY.

1790–91.—Hugh Lloyd, Richard Riley.
1791–92.—Nathaniel Newlin, Hugh Lloyd.
1792–93.—Joseph Gibbons, William West.
1793–94.—Nathaniel Newlin, William West.
1794–97.—Jonas Preston, William West.
1797–1801.—Jonas Preston, Moses Palmer.
1801–2.—Benjamin H. Smith, Jonas Preston.
1802–3.—Benjamin H. Smith, Isaac G. Gilpin.
1803–4.—William Pennell, Benjamin H. Smith.
1804–8.—William Pennell, William Trimble.
1808–9.—Thomas Smith, William Trimble.
1809–12.—Thomas Smith, William Pennock.
1812–14.—William Cheyney, John Thompson.
1814–15.—Samuel Edwards, William Cheyney.
1815–16.—Samuel Anderson, Samuel Edwards.
1816–18.—Samuel Anderson, William Cheyney.
1818–19.—William Cheyney, John Kerlin.
1819–20.—John Kerlin, Thomas Robinson.
1820–21.—George G. Leiper, Abner Lewis.
1821–22.—John Lewis, William Cheyney.
1822–23.—Samuel Anderson.
1823–25.—Abner Lewis.
1825–26.—Samuel Anderson.
1826–27.—Joseph Engle.
1827–28.—William Martin.
1828–29.—Edward Siter.
1829–30.—Samuel Anderson.
1830–31.—John Lindsay.
1831–35.—Samuel Anderson.
1835–36.—William Mendenhall.
1836–37.—John Hinkson.
1837–39.—John K. Zeilin.
1840–42.—Joshua P. Eyre.
1842–44.—H. Jonas Brooke.
1844–46.—John Larkin, Jr.
1846–48.—Sketchley Morton.
1848–50.—James J. Lewis.
1850–52.—John M. Broomall.
1852–54.—Jonathan P. Abraham.
1854.—Thomas H. Maddock.
1855.—Charles D. Manley.
1856.—Hiram Cleaver.
1857.—Thomas D. Powell.
1858–59.—William D. Pennell.
1860.—Chalkley Harvey.
1861–62.—William Gamble.
1863.—Chalkley Harvey.
1864.—Edward A. Price.
1865–66.—Elwood Tyson.
1867.—John H. Barton.
1868–69.—Augustus B. Leedom.
1870.—Thomas V. Cooper.
1871.—Tryon Lewis.
1872.—Thomas V. Cooper.
1873.—Orson Flagg Bullard.
1874–76.—William Cooper Talley.
1875–76.—William Worrall.
1877–78.—O. F. Bullard.
1877–80.—Y. S. Walter.
1879–81.—Nathan Garrett (elected to fill Bullard's unexpired term).[1]
1881–84.—Robert Chadwick.
1882–84.—William G. Powell.

CHAPTER XXVIII.

THE TOWNSHIP OF TINICUM.

THE island of Tinicum, now comprising the township of the same name, is located in the Delaware River, about two miles from the eastern limit of the city of Chester. At the southwestern end of the island is the mouth of Darby Creek, and, proceeding towards the source of that stream eastwardly two miles and a half, a sinuous estuary, termed Bow Creek, unites with Darby Creek, when from the place of this union the latter changes its course in a northwardly direction, while Bow Creek flowing eastwardly enters the Delaware about three and a half miles from the mouth of Darby Creek; thus forming the island of Big Tinicum, as it is frequently called to distinguish it from the

[1] Nathan Garrett died in office, and Isaac P. Garrett elected to fill unexpired term.

low, narrow, marshy strip of land lying nearly in the middle of the river, extending almost the entire length of Tinicum Island proper, which is known as Little Tinicum Island. At its broadest part Tinicum is about a mile and a half in width, and its circumference is in the neighborhood of nine miles. It contains two thousand seven hundred and fifty acres, two thousand of which are marsh or meadow land, the average level of the ground being four feet below high water-mark. Originally Big Tinicum Island consisted of but five hundred acres, the remainder of the land having been reclaimed from the water by the construction of banks or dikes.

From a description of Tinicum in 1679–80 we learn that then it was about two miles long, or a "little more than a mile and a half wide. . . . The southwest point, which only has been and is still cultivated, is barren, scraggy, and sandy, growing plenty of wild onions, a weed not easily eradicated. On this point three or four houses are standing, built by the Swedes, a little Lutheran Church made of logs, and the remains of the large block-house, which served them in place of a fortress, and the ruins of some log huts. This is the whole of the manor. The best and pleasantest quality it has is the prospect, which is very agreeable."[1] The Indian name of this island was Tanakon, Tutacaenung, and Teniko, which, after the Swedes settled there, was changed to Nya Gotheberg,[2] and subsequently termed by the Dutch the Island of Kattenberg,[3] while the English changed the Indian name Tennakong, as it is more usually written, to Tinicum.

The first settlement of Europeans in Pennsylvania of which authentic records exist was made on the island of Tinicum by the Swedish Governor, John Printz, subsequent to Feb. 15, 1643, in exercising the discretion reposed in him by the home government as to the site of his residence. "The convenient situation of the place," we are told by Acrelius, "suggested its selection."[4] Professor Keen declares that "the encroachments of the neighboring Dutch, and the recent repairs of their little Fort Nassau, determined the new Governor to remove to the more commanding post of Tutæaenugh, or Tinicum."[5] Certain it is, that shortly after Printz reached the province he changed the location of the capital, removing to Tinicum, where he erected a "new fort provided with considerable armament," which he named Nya Gotheborg, and also caused to be built a mansion for his own residence, surrounded by "a fine orchard, a pleasant house, and other conveniences," to which he gave the name of Printzhof.[6] At the same place also "the principal inhabitants had their dwellings and plantations," but at the conclusion of the year 1645 the settlement in that vicinity was small, and the dwellings few, for Hudde reports that "there are some plantations which are continued nearly a mile, but few houses only at considerable distance one from the other, the farthest is not far from Tinnekonk, which is an island, and is toward the river side secured by creeks and underwood."[7] The fort was simply a block-house, for Andrias Hudde describing it states "that it is a pretty strong fort, constructed by laying very heavy hemlock (greenen) logs the one on the other."[8] In less than two years after it was erected it was totally destroyed by fire. On Nov. 25, 1645, Swan Wass, a gunner, between ten and eleven o'clock, set the fort on fire, and in a short time all was burned, nothing being saved except the dairy.[9] Vincent says "that the conflagration was occasioned by the neglect of Swen Wass, who had fallen asleep, and a candle which he had left burning set fire to the structure."[10] Printz, however, treated the act as a criminal one. Hence in his report he spoke of Swen Wass as "the above-mentioned incendiary," and informed the home government that he had caused the man to be tried, that he had been convicted and sentenced, and he had sent him to Sweden, in irons, that the sentence might be executed." The destruction of the fort was a severe ordeal for the colonists, for winter had set in bitterly cold, the river and creeks were frozen, and, as New Gottenberg was on an island, no one could get to it; and as Printz reports, "the sharpness of winter lasted until the middle of March; so that, if some rye and corn had not been unthreshed, I myself, and the people with me on the island, would have starved to death. But God maintained us with that small quantity of provisions until the new harvest." Here also Printz had "a commodious church built," a small log structure, which the Governor reported he had adorned and decorated "according to our Swedish fashion, so far as our limited resources and means would allow," which sanctuary was appropriately consecrated "for divine services" by Rev. John Campanius, on the 4th of September, 1646. A burial-place was also laid out, and Campanius records that "the first corpse that was buried there was that of Catherine, the daughter of Andrew Hanson. She was buried on the 28th of October, in the said year, being the feast of St. Simon and St. Jude."[11]

As with all European colonists, the impression prevailed among the Swedes that precious metals would be found in the New World. Hence, in his report for 1647, Governor Printz says, "Mines of silver and gold may possibly be discovered, but nobody here

1 Journal of a Voyage to New York in 1679–80; Memoirs of the Long Island Historical Society, vol. i. p. 177.

2 Acrelius, "History of New Sweden," p. 69.

3 Penna. Archives, 2d series, vol. vii. p. 496.

4 History of New Sweden, p. 42.

5 *Penna. Mag. of Hist.*, vol. ii. p. 327.

6 Campanius, p. 79.

7 Penna. Archives, 2d series, vol. v. p. 104.

8 Ib.

9 Report of Governor Printz for 1647, *Mag. of Hist.*, vol. vii. p. 273.

10 History of Delaware, p. 196; Hazard's Annals, p. 84; Massachusetts Historical Collections, vol. vi. (N. S.) p. 434; Winthrop, vol. ii. p. 254.

11 Campanius' "New Sweden," pp. 79, 80.

has any knowledge about such things."[1] The report was however current that gold existed in large quantities on the eastern shores of the Delaware in the neighborhood of Trenton. Peter Lindstrom, the Swedish engineer, records that an Indian coming to Tinicum, seeing a gold ring on the hand of Governor Printz's wife, "inquired of her why she wore such a trifle upon her finger?" The Governor hearing this asked the American whether he could procure such stuff for him? If he could, he would give him a great deal that was good in return. Whereupon the American answered, "I know where there is a mountain full of this!" On this the Governor took an armful of red and blue cloth, also lead, powder, looking-glasses, needles, etc., and showing them to him, said, "See here what I will give you if you will bring me a piece of that in proof of what you have said; but I will send two of my people along with you." To this he would not agree. He said, "I will first go and bring you the proof; if that satisfies you, then there is time enough for you to send some one with me." Promising the proof, he thereupon received some pay. A few days thereafter he returned with a piece as large as two fists, which the aforesaid Governor tested, and found that it abounded in good gold, and obtained a considerable quantity from it, from which he afterwards had gold rings and bracelets made. He therefore promised the American a much greater reward if he would show our people, whom he would send with him, where that mountain was situated, which he also promised to do; but said that he had not leisure for it at that time, but would come back again after some days, and then he again received some presents. After the American came to his countrymen and began to boast before them, they compelled him to tell for what he had received his gifts; and when they came to know it they put him to death so that that place might not become known to us, supposing that it might bring some mischief upon them."[2] Acrelius believed that this statement was absolutely fictitious, and the representation was made "to bring to the light unknown regions for the purpose of enticing people over the great sea, and to secure settlers."[3]

Arnold De Lagrange, as late as 1680, reported that there was an iron-mine on Tinicum, but a visitor there at that date says "that as to there being a mine of iron ore upon it I have not seen any upon that island or elsewhere and if it were so, it is of no great importance for such mines are so common in this country that little account is made of them."[4]

At Tinicum the first vessel constructed by Europeans within the present State of Pennsylvania was built, and in his report for 1647, Governor Printz says, "I have caused the barge to be fully constructed, so that the hull is ready and floating on the water; but the completion of the work must be postponed until the arrival of a more skilled carpenter, the young men here declaring they do not know enough to finish it."[5] That this vessel was completed we learn from an order issued by Stuyvesant after the capture of New Sweden by the Dutch, dated March 26, 1657, in which he states, respecting the pleasure-boat of the late Governor Printz, which "he is informed" is decaying and nearly rotten where she then laid, that if Peter Meyer would satisfy the attorneys of the late Governor Printz, and discharge Stuyvesant from responsibility under the terms of the Swedish capitulation, he (Meyer) might be permitted to make use of the boat for transporting letters.[6]

In the little log sanctuary at Tinicum, until May, 1648, officiated Rev. John Campanius, who earnestly strove to instruct the Indians in the tenets of his church. To aid him in the endeavor to Christianize the savages he applied himself to the study of their language, and mastered it sufficiently to translate the Lutheran Catechism into the dialect of the Lenni Lenape family of the great Algonquin tribe. He was the first person to translate a book into the Indian tongue, and although his work was not published until 1696, when it was printed by the royal command at Stockholm, still he antedated a few years Eliot's labors to impart instruction to the Indians by translating the Bible into the Mohegan dialect, although the latter's work was put to press thirty years before that of Campanius. The reverend pastor was relieved at the date mentioned by Rev. Lears Carlsson Lock, who appears to have had, after 1656, the exclusive care for twenty-two years of religious affairs in the colony. The Swedes in those early days, we are told by the late Joseph J. Lewis, in his "History of Chester County,"[7] used to attend church at Tinicum, "to which they came in canoes from New Castle and other places along the Delaware, both above and below the island."

On the return of Governor Printz to Sweden, his daughter, Armegat, yet remained at and occupied Printzhof at Tinicum, and after the conquest by the Dutch of New Sweden, notwithstanding the recommendation of Stuyvesant to the directors, in 1656, to occupy the fort at that place and garrison it, it seems not to have been done, for in 1680 it was a ruin, and at that date is mentioned as "the remains of the large block house."[8] Armegat Printz, for she seems to have clung to her maiden name, was very haughty in her bearing and oppressive toward the poor in her pride of station. Inasmuch as the estate on which the little

[1] *Penna. Mag. of Hist.*, vol. vii. p. 272.

[2] Acrelius, "History of New Sweden," p. 66 (note); Gordon's "History of Pennsylvania," pp. 596–97 (note D); Lindstrom's "Manuscript Journal," in possession of American Philosophical Society, Philadelphia.

[3] Acrelius, p. 66.

[4] Memoirs of Long Island Historical Society, vol. i. p. 177.

[5] Hazard's Annals, p. 231.

[6] *Penna. Mag. of History*, vol. vii. p. 276.

[7] Published in 1824 in the *Village Record*, at West Chester.

[8] Memoirs of Long Island Historical Society, vol. i. p. 178.

church was built belonged to her father, whose attorney she was, she claimed that structure as part of her possessions But the edifice was, nevertheless, used for religious services, and although she sold the church to La Grange, with the island, the Swedes still worshiped therein On May 24, 1673, to show her contempt for the Swedes, she sold the bell after she was put into possession of the estate in the execution in the ejectment suit, to which reference will be made The receipt given by her on that occasion is interesting, since it relates to the first church-bell we have record of in our country's history, although long years before that date mention is made of a bell used by the courts at New Castle to summon the people together The following is the receipt given by her [1]

(Copy) "LAUS DEO, MAY 24, 1673

"I, the undersigned, Armegat Printz, acknowledges to have transferred to the congregation of the adherents of the Augsburg Confession in this place, the bell that has been on Tennakong, that they may do therewith what pleases them, and promise to keep them free from all claims that are made Before the undersigned witnesses given as above

"ARMEGAT PRINTZ

"His mark,
P K
"PETER KOCK
"His mark,
X
"JONAS NELSSON"

The Swedish congregation at Tinicum, Acrelius tells us, purchased the bell back again before Armegat left the Delaware finally for Europe, paying therefor two days' labor in harvest-time The date of her departure is unknown, but she was at Upland, Chester, on March 3, 1676,[2] nearly three years after the bell was sold We also know that at a court held at New Castle by Governor Andross, May 13 and 14, 1675, it was ordered "That church at Tinicon Island Do serve for Upland & pts adjacent"[3] In this little log church, for many years, Pastor Lock preached to the Swedish settlers, and when the English conquered the territory, bringing with them their contempt for the clergy,[4] it was evident the change of rulers was not to his benefit To be sure, as measured by the standard of this day, the reverend gentleman seems to have worn the cloth with little credit to his profession, but the times were rude, the sports were rude, and if, as stated, his "great infirmity seems to have been an over fondness for intoxicating drinks," it was the general weakness of that age Finally, as years crept apace, the old dominie grew infirm, became so lame that he could not help himself, and was compelled to suspend active labor in the ministry Rev Jacob Fabritius, of the Wiccaco Church, could be of little use to Tinicum congregation, for while the latter's flock grew, Lock's did not, and as Pastor Fabritius was blind, and had to be led when he walked about, the little church on Tinicum languished until, about the beginning of the eighteenth century, it ceased to be used for religious services In time it fell into ruins, and long before the beginning of the present century had entirely disappeared

The graveyard mentioned by Campanius has been eaten away by the washing of the tide It is related by Aubrey H Smith, late United States district attorney, of Philadelphia, that his father and the latter's sister, when children, while walking along the river-shore at Tinicum, at the site of the burial-ground, saw coffins projecting from the banks where the earth had been worn away by the water Printzhof, that noted mansion of the Swedish Governor, stood until the summer of 1822 on the high ground of the island, and "the interior bore evident marks of great antiquity in its structure," but at the date stated the greater part of the ancient building was destroyed by fire[5] Dr Smith records that "the dilapidated remains of what was said to be the chimney of this mansion were standing within the recollection of the author, and up to this time one of the small foreign-made bricks, of a pale yellow color, of which it was partly constructed, may be occasionally picked up in this vicinity Its site was a short distance above the present Tinicum Hotel, and on the opposite side of the road[6]

The administration of the affairs of the province under Printz must have been exceedingly gratifying to the crown of Sweden, for in less than nine months after Governor Printz landed on the Delaware, Queen Christina, on Nov 6, 1642, made a grant, "On account of the long and excellent services which the lieutenant-colonel and Governor of New Sweden, our very dear and beloved John Printz, has rendered to us and to the Crown of Sweden, and also on account of those which he is daily rendering to us in the government of the country and which he is engaged to render us as long as he shall live the place called Tenekoor New Gottenberg, in New Sweden, to enjoy it, him and his lawful heirs, as a perpetual possession"[7] Governor Printz, when he came to the colony, was accompanied by his wife and daughter, Armgart, the latter was subsequently married to Lieutenant John Pappegoya, who, on Printz's return to Sweden, near the close of the year 1653, was left in charge of the government of the colony, and after the coming of John Rysinge, who superseded him in authority, the latter remained, for in Rysinge's letter to the ministers of Sweden, July 11, 1654, he recommended Pappegoya as a proper person to be appointed schute or sheriff on the Delaware[8] At that time the presumption is Governor Rysinge resided at Tinicum, for on June

[1] Acrelius, "History of New Sweden," p 86

[2] *Penna. Mag of History*, vol ii p 467

[3] N Y Colonial Documents, vol xii. p 526, Hazard's Annals, p 417

[4] Macauley's "History of England" (Am Book Exchange ed), vol i pp 210, 212

[5] "Topographical and Medical Sketch of Tinicum Island," by George F Lehman, M D, published in *Journal of Medical and Physical Science*, Philadelphia, 1833

[6] History of Delaware County, p 31

[7] Penna Archives, 2d series, vol v p 776

[8] Hazard's Annals, p 155

17th of that year a council was held by him with the Indian sachems, at Printz Hall, on which occasion some of the Indians complained that the Swedes had brought much evil upon them, for many of the savages had died since the former came to this country. Naaman, one of the chiefs, made a speech, in which he declared the Swedes were a very good people. "Look," said he, pointing to the presents, "see what they have brought us, for which they desire our friendship." So saying, he stroked himself three times down the arm, which among the Indians is a token of friendship. Afterwards he thanked the Swedes on behalf of his people for the presents they had received, and said that friendship should be observed more strictly between them than it had been before; that the Swedes and Indians had been in Governor Printz's time as one body and one heart (striking his breast as he spoke) and thenceforward they should be as one head, in token of which he took hold of his head with both his hands, and made a motion as if he was tying a strong knot, and then he made this comparison, that as the calabash was round without any crack, so they would be a compact body without any fissure, and that if any one should attempt to do any harm to the Indians, the Swedes should immediately inform them of it; and, on the other hand, the Indians would give immediate notice to the Christians of any plot against them, even if it were in the middle of the night." Several savages, after they had been presented with brandy and wine, followed with similar remarks, and advised the Swedes to settle at Passyunk, where the Indians were numerous, and where, if any of the latter attempted to do the Swedes mischief, they could be punished. Finally, they desired to confirm the title to the land which the Swedes had already purchased from them. This being done, "there were set upon the floor in the great hall, two large kettles and many other vessels filled with *sappaun*, which is a kind of hasty pudding, made of maize and Indian corn. The sachems sat by themselves; the other Indians all fed heartily and were satisfied. . . . The treaty of friendship which was then made between the Swedes and the Indians has ever since been faithfully observed on both sides."[1]

Lieut. John Pappegoya is generally believed to have returned to Sweden shortly after the arrival of Rysinge, an impression evidently founded on the statement of Acrelius, that "the Vice-Governor, John Pappegoya, had determined to take his departure from the country, and the government was therefore handed over to the said commissary, John Risinge."[2] The latter reached New Sweden, May 23, 1654, and yet on March 30, 1656, John Pappegoya was still in New Sweden, for on the date given he announced to Governor Stuyvesant the arrival there of a Swedish ship, the "Mercury," and that the Dutch authorities on the Delaware had refused permission to the crew and passengers to land.[3] This is the last mentioned of John Pappegoya, and inasmuch as it proves that he did not return directly to Sweden after the arrival of Rysinge, as is stated by Acrelius, it is very likely that he never did return to Europe, but died in the province.

After New Sweden had been conquered by the arms of Stuyvesant, in September, 1655, Governor Rysinge states that the Dutch forces "at New Gottenberg robbed Mr. Pappegoya's wife of all she had, with many others, who had collected their property together there."[4] About twelve months after the conquest of the province, "Armgard Papigaay," as the Dutch record the name (the document, however, is signed "Armgard Prints"), petitioned that letters patent should be issued to her for her father's land at Printzdorp (Chester) and at "Tinnakunk" (Tinicum Island). Stuyvesant and his Council, in response, accorded her permission, pursuant to the terms of capitulation, "to take possession and cultivate the lands of her Lord and Father at Printzdorp."[5] Nothing was said as to Tinicum, but Armgart Pappegoya continued to occupy the lands there, and we learn, from a letter from Vice-Director William Beekman, dated May 12, 1660, that "Miss Printz requests that she may deliver here, for her taxes, a fat ox, fat pigs, and bread corn." Doubtless when Governor Stuyvesant was at Tinicum, on May 8, 1658, where he had a conference with the Swedish magistrates, he lodged at Printz Hall, for we know that at that time the block-house there was no longer occupied by the armed forces of the government. In the summer of 1657 the Dutch authorities sought to prevail upon the Swedish inhabitants on the river to gather themselves together in villages, and in 1660 the matter was pressed earnestly by the vice-director, under instructions from Stuyvesant, but we learn from Beekman's official correspondence that the resolute daughter of the former Swedish Governor resisted the order, stating that she could not remove "on account of her heavy buildings, also because the church stands there," and stating, as an additional reason, that although she had offered her lands "rent free, but nobody as yet shows inclination to live with her."[6]

If, as it appears, no one was inclined to live with her, there was one person at least who desired to become the owner of her possession at Tinicum Island. Joost De La Grange, on May 29, 1662, purchased from her as the agent of her father, John Printz, then in Sweden, the estate, "together with the houseing and stock thereupon, for the sum of six thousand guilders, Holland money," one-half to be paid in cash, two thousand when she reached Holland, and the remaining thousand in one year thereafter.

De La Grange immediately entered into possession

1 Campanius, pp. 76–78.

2 History of New Sweden, p. 63.

3 Hazard's Annals, p. 212.

4 Penna. Archives, 2d series, vol. v. p. 227.

5 Ib., vol. vii. p. 494.

6 Ib., p. 628.

of the estate, and Mrs Pappegoya sailed for Europe, arriving at Holland on the 31st of July of that year[1] The bill of exchange being presented and payment refused, it was protested, and the energetic woman must have taken passage for the colony in the first vessel sailing thence for the New World, since, in November following, she had obtained judgment against La Grange, from which final decree the defendant entered an appeal On November 21st Beekman wrote that he had gone "to Tinneconk at request of Huygens and used every exertion to settle differences respecting the protested bill of exchange, but did not succeed"[2] Governor John Printz had died in 1663, and a fresh difficulty was thrown in the way of Armgart Pappegoya's collecting the money, for her three sisters in Sweden objected to the payment of the three thousand guilders still due from the purchaser until a new power of attorney had been executed by them Armgart, in the mean while, erected a house at Printzdorp (the estate at Upland afterwards sold to Robert Wade), "who had her dwelling here when she left Tinekonk,"[3] and it seems that she was in very indigent circumstances, for on Aug 13, 1672, in her petition to Governor Lovelace, she stated she lived alone and had only one servant-man, who she asked might be excused from "Traynings in the Company in wch he is Inlisted, & also give her Lycence to Distill in her own Distilling Kettle some small Quantitys of Liquors for her own use & her servts & laborers as before mencon'd"[4] To add to her discomfiture in prosecuting her suit, Joost De La Grange, several years before, went to Holland to collect the money due him there, so that he might discharge the remainder of the purchase-money, but on the voyage he became ill and died,[5] leaving a widow, Margaret, and a minor son surviving him The widow remained in possession of the premises for several years In the mean while the English had conquered the territory, and accompanying their forces to the Delaware was Andrew Carr, who subsequently married the widow La Grange Apparently to forestall any action Mrs. Pappegoya might take to secure possession, on Oct 1, 1669, Governor Lovelace was induced to issue a patent to "Andrew Carr & Margaret his wife, formerly the wife of Joost De La Grange, deceased, to confirm to them a certain Island in Delaware river called by the name of Matiniconck, containing by estimation three hundred acres more or less, the said Island lying about 6 Dutch miles up the river from the town of Newcastle, bounded on the Northwest with the Mill Kill, on the South by the river & on the North, East or North & East with Bow Kill"[6]

[1] Penna Archives, 2d series, vol vii p 799
[2] Hazard's Annals, p. 342
[3] Memoirs of Long Island Historical Society, vol i p 183
[4] Hazard's Annals, p 399, Penna Archives, 2d series, vol vii p 623.
[5] Memoirs of Long Island Historical Society, vol i p 179
[6] Smith's "History of Delaware County," Appendix C, p 520.

After this patent was granted Andrew Carr and his wife resided at Tinicum for some time without any proceeding being instituted against them, when Margaret Carr, having fallen heir to an estate in Holland, Andrew, his wife, and her young son by the former marriage went to Europe to look after the inheritance, leaving Capt John Carr, as their attorney, in charge of the Tinicum property Within a short time after the departure of Andrew Carr's family Armgart Pappegoya brought suit for the recovery of the island, summoned Capt John Carr before a special court held at New Castle by Governor Lovelace, and there by consent, it was removed to the General Court of Assizes, held at New York, in October, 1671 The case began on Wednesday afternoon, the 12th, and continued until Friday afternoon, the 14th, when, on the verdict of the jury, judgment was entered for the plaintiff, with costs and charges[7] On Jan 27, 1672, the Governor and Council, after having consulted with the bench as to the amount "of interest and forbearance of the principal Debt" (three thousand guilders), allowed fifty-five pounds for such interest, leaving the other charges to be determined by law, and appointed Peter Alricks, Capt Edmund Cantwell, William Tom, and Capt. Walter Wharton to appraise and value the island of Tinicum, and the goods, chattels, or estates of the defendants On Feb 20, 1672, an execution was issued to Sheriff Cantwell, directing him "to put the said Jeuffro Prince into possession of the said Island and the Stock thereupon wch if it shall not prove sufficient to satisfy the said Debt you are to Secure and Levy the rest in the hands of whom you can find any of the Estate of the said Andrew Carr & Priscilla his wife whether in the hands of Capt John Carr their attorney or any other, and if any part of the said Estate hath been disposed of since the beginning of this Process the parties who have done the same are to make it good out of their own estate"[8]

The execution seems to have been carried only partially into effect The following year the Dutch again acquired possession of the province, and during the latter's rule over the colony the proceedings were held in abeyance However, after the English authority was again restored, Governor Andross, on Jan 12, 1675, issued a warrant to Sheriff Cantwell, setting forth that inasmuch as the former execution had not been "fully effected Att the request of the said Jeuffre Armigart Prince als Pappeay, That the former Execution may be renewed," he was directed to proceed according to the judgment[9] The second execution was fully enforced, and the same year, on March 22d, Jeffro Armgart Printz, *alias* Pappegoya, sold the island to Otto Earnest Cock "for fifteen hundred guilders in *zeewant*, as it (the estate) was

[7] Hazard's Annals, pp 400-1
[8] Penna Archives, 2d series, vol vi pp 626-28
[9] Ib, p. 666

very much decayed and worn out,"[1] the deed "reserving ye churchyard as it now stands fenced in with ye said church, with free liberty to the inhabitants in general to repair thither to their devotions or burials"[2] Armgart also gave a power of attorney to the purchaser to receive possession of the estate from the sheriff

In 1678, Arnold De La Grange, the son and heir, who had gone abroad, being now of age, came to the province, and went to Tinicum Island, claiming its possession Otto Earnest Cock replied that he knew nothing of the matter, and if he, De La Grange, had any lawful claim, he ought to apply to the court, not to him, for his title was founded on its judgment, but if he wished to purchase it, he could have it for three hundred pounds sterling, or at an agreed-upon price The young man thereupon became angry, and threatened to appeal to London "That you can do," said Cock, "if you have money enough All this affects me not since I have bought and paid for it and have been put in possession of it by the Court"[3] In the same year, 1678, Arnold De La Grange, in a lengthy petition to Governor Andross, set out the story of the sale to his father, the suit which was instituted against John Carr during his stepfather's absence beyond the seas, pleading the misnomer of Percilla for Margaret in the title of the suit, and that the judgment was defective because it was rendered against a man beyond seas, against a *femme covert*, and affected the vested right of a minor who was not represented in the suit in any wise Concluding, he asked that the Governor and Council "will please to direct some way for his relief," either by a hearing in equity or an order requiring Cock to refund the sum paid by his father[4] Nothing seems to have been done with this petition, but De La Grange, just before the territory passed into the possession of Penn, began an action against Otto Earnest Cock at the Upland Court on June 14, 1681, but the quaint record states "This action referred till next Court that there's noe Court without Justice otto whoe is a party"[5]

The following is *verbatim* the record of the case, copied from the docket of the

"Court held at Chester 22d 6 mo 1683

"Arnoldus Delagrange, Plaintiff, Otto Ernest Cock, Defendant The plaintiff sues and declares as heir to Tynnacu Island and premises It is acknowledged by Jno White (ye defendt attorney) that ye plaint's father was legally possessed of Tinicum Island & premises in ye declaration mentioned by virtue of his purchase from Armgard Prince, but sayth (in regard pte [part] of the purchase money was only paid) that ye said Lady Armgard Prince had Tryall & execution thereupon & was put into possession of ye same premises and sold ye same premises to ye defendt

"The plaint (by Abraham Man his attorney) setts forth that hee ye sayd Plaint (who was Heire to ye sd Island) at ye tyme of se sayd Tryall & Execucon was then und age & in Holland, & therefore could make noe defence, & further yt the said Heire (the Plaint was not menconed in ye said Tryall, the Accon being comenced against one Andrew Carre & Prisilla his wife, mistaken in ye execucon for ye mother of ye Plaint, whose mother's name was Margaretta

"The Testimony of Nicholas More, Secretary in writing and his hand produced on behalf of ye plaint

"Shackamackson, ye 20th of ye 5th month
al July, 1683

"I do solemnly declare that about ye moneth of May last past of this present yeare, Mr Otto Ornst Cock of Tynnacu Island came to mee at Shackamackson (having before spoken to me of a Tryall yt was to bee at Upland, Between Mr Lagrange & himselfe, about ye Island of Tynnacu, and told mee among many other things that hee wished hee had never sold mee ye said Island, and said hee Hee wished he had lost 50£ rather than to have put his hand to eyther my Conveyance or Mr Lagrange Agreemt, saying that hee was undone 'Why?' said I 'Because,' said hee, 'I have wronged Lagrange children from their Rights' 'Well,' said I, 'Mr Otto, if you beleeve in yor concience that ye Island is his let him have it I will not take any advantage of it, either against him or you' 'Yes,' said hee, 'it is his, and if you will doe soe & part with it, I shall give you thanks and repay you your charges' 'Well,' said I, 'you shall have it, and I will endeavr to make Mr Lagrange & you ffriends without any wrong' This was in ye presence of Major Fenwick, Thomas Fairman & Michael Neelson, all which I attest under my hand

"N More, Secretary

"Israell Helme's Deposition

'Israell Helme being required to declare what hee knowes, concerning ye Bargaine between ye sayd Armgard Prince, & ye Plaints ffather for Tynnacu Island & premisses, deposeth That Lagranges ffather was to give ye sayd Armgard for ye same Six Thousand Dutch Guilders, and yt hee knows there was three Hundred Dutch Guilders thereof pd, but knows of ye paymt of noe more, And further sayth that ye Three Thousand Guilders (which is Three Hundred pounds) was to bee paid in this Countrey by agreemt between Jacob Swanson & ye ffather of ye Plaint & further sayth that when the Plaints ffather dyed, hee ye said Plaint was a little child, and further sayth not

"ffop Johnson's deposition

"ffop Johnson being required to declare where hee knowes in ye premisses, Deposeth That hee ye said ffop & ye above mentioned Israell was desired by Mrs Armgard Prince ats Popinjay, to demand ye remainder of ye sayd Six Thusand Guildes which was Three Hundred pounds of Mrs Delagrange (ye Plaints mother) And yt shee ye said Mrs Delagrange (upon ye same demand) sayd shee could not pay it, and further sayth not

"To which ye sayd Plaint replyes (by his aforesd attorney) That if the Deft can make it appeare ye sayd money is unpayd, and can show their Right to receive it, hee is ready to discharge what can be made appeare to remayne due of ye sd Purchace, But denyes yt ye Deft hath any legall right to demand ye same

"The Juryes Verdict The Jury finde for ye Plaint and alsoe give him his costs of suite and fforty Shillings damage. the Plaint paying to ye Deft Thirty & Seaven pounds & Tenne Shillings, according to an agreemt betweene ye Plaint and Deft produced & Read in this Cort & alsoe delivering ye Block house & pticulers in ye same agreemt mentioned

"Judgmt is thereupon Awarded"

Execution was issued on this judgment, for at the October court, 1683, "The Sheriff made returne of two executions, one against Henry Reynolds the other against Otto Earnest Cocke att ye suite of Arnoldus Delegrange for ye Island of Tinicum" The plaintiff having acquired possession of the estate, in less than a year sold the island, for at the September court, 1684, "Christopher Taylor, President (Judge) in Open Court deliver over a Penall Bond of Performance for four hundred pounds unto Arnoldus Delegrange & bearing Date ye 2d day of September, 1684, being for the payment of two hundred pounds att or upon ye 1st day of November, 1685" Christo-

[1] Memoirs of Long Island Historical Society, vol i p 189

[2] Book of Patents, Harrisburg, cited in Smith's "Atlas of Delaware County," p 11

[3] Memoirs of Long Island Historical Society, vol i p 179

[4] Penna. Archives, 2d series, vol vii pp 799-81

[5] Records of Upland Court, p 189

pher Taylor also in open court "delivered up Arnoldus Delegrange receipt to Robert Turner for one hundred pounds old England money as alsoe the said Christopher Taylor did promise to Save the said Arnoldus Delegrange harmlesse from all Damages that may Accrue thereby" The same day "Arnoldus Delegrange Past over a deed in open court unto Christopher Taylor for ye Island Commonly known by the name of Mattinnaconcke, bearing Date the 2d of the 12th moneth 1684"

This Christopher Taylor had been a teacher of a classical school in England, in which country he was imprisoned for his religious opinions,—adherence to the society of Friends In 1682 he emigrated to Pennsylvania, first settling in Bucks County, which he represented in the Assembly held at Chester, Dec 4, 1682, acting in that body as chairman of the Committee on Election and Privileges, and was also one of the "Committee of Foresight" for preparation of provincial bills[1] In July, 1684, he was one of the justices of Chester County, and doubtless had then settled at Tinicum, which, after he had acquired title, he termed "College Island," because, as it is believed, he there had a school in the higher branches of education The fact that he surrendered to De La Grange a receipt given by the latter to Robert Turner, leads to the impression that the latter had entered into an agreement with De La Grange for the purchase of Tinicum, and that Turner had made the contract for Taylor, or had transferred to him his interest in the agreement of sale Turner appears to have been an intimate friend of Christopher Taylor, for the latter, dying in 1686, made him his executor of his will It appears that Taylor in his lifetime had sold the island to Ralph Fretwell, and after his death Turner brought suit as executor against Fretwell for £590 17*s* 9*d* At the sheriff's sale the property was purchased by Turner Isaac Taylor, who was not satisfied with the disposition the testator had made of his property, "putt in Cavett against ye Probate of his father's will," but subsequently withdrew it[1] As executor, on the 9th of First month, 1697-98, Turner by deed conveyed to Israel and Joseph Taylor, the sons of the decedent, and to John and Marie Busly—the latter a daughter of the testator—the island of Tinicum At the same court, Joseph Taylor, John and Marie Busly, conveyed their two-thirds interests in the island to their brother, Israel, who was formerly sheriff of Bucks County, and, as it appears, to pay them for their part of the estate, he was compelled to borrow the money on mortgage from Turner

As one of the most noted civil cases in the judicial annals of our State, that of Paul B Carter *vs* The Tinicum Fishing Company, which was continued in litigation for over thirty years, grew out of the title thus acquired by Israel Taylor to the island, it is proper in this connection to hastily present the historical side of that noted case Israel Taylor, who was a physician and practiced his profession at Tinicum, died subsequent to 1709, for, in the address of the General Assembly to Governor Goodkin, in alluding to the injurious effect of the issuing of special marriage licenses by the Governor, the document gives as an instance the case of "Israel Taylor, whose Daughter had liked to have been stolen by Coulour of a Lycense lately granted to one James Barber, of Chester County"[2] Israel Taylor died leaving, so far as I have information, four sons and six daughters, as follows Christopher, Thomas, Benjamin, and Samuel Taylor, Mary (who married Jonas Sandelands), Dianah Cartman, Hannah Lloyd, Eleanor Molloy, Sarah Bailey, and the wife of Enoch Elliott Christopher, the grandson of the first Christopher Taylor, was married, but his wife dying before him, apparently without leaving children, he made a will Dec 8, 1748, and died shortly after, for the testament was admitted to probate on the 24th day of the same month The will contained a clause as follows

"I give and devise unto the said David Sanderlin my fishing place to him and his heirs forever and likewise it is my will that he shall have the help and use of my negroes Milford and Harry, one month in each year in fishing time, till they respectively attain to thirty years of age I give and bequeath to David Sanderlin aforesaid my negro boy Tinuecum till he attain to thirty years of age and then to be set free"

David Sandelands died intestate within four months after the death of his uncle, Christopher Taylor, and letters of administration on his estate were granted to his sisters, Rebecca Smith and Mary Claxton, with their husbands Mrs Claxton died in 1750, but in October, 1752, the jury appointed to partition the lands and tenements of David Sandelands awarded the fishery to the heirs and legal representatives of Mary Claxton, "dividing the said fishery into five equal parts" The court, in 1754, approved the petition made by the jury

Between the years 1796 and 1805, Joseph Carter purchased by three deeds the five shares of this fishery allotted to the heirs of Mary Claxton, and in the last deed, that of 1805, the fishery was described as "Beginning at the mouth of Darby creek and extending up the river Delaware as far as necessity may require for the benefit of fishing or that ever was made use of" Joseph Carter died Feb 2, 1830, and by his will, dated July 16, 1828, he devised his fishing-place at the Lazaretto to his two sons, Joseph and Cloud, as tenants in common[3] In 1832, William Carter purchased Cloud Carter's interest in the fishery The following year Joseph Carter died without children, and letters of administration were granted to his brother, William Carter, who, already owner of one-half of the fishery by purchase, began proceedings in partition, and in those proceedings the sheriff, Jan 12, 1834, advertised the estate to be partitioned as "the right and privilege of fishing in the river Delaware from

[1] Colonial Records, vol i p 195

[2] Ib, vol ii p 455.

[3] Thomas Maxwell Potts's "History of the Carter Family," p 66

the point where the road called River road joins said river to the mouth of Darby Creek in township of Tinicum and right and privilege of hauling and drying seines and nets upon shore of said river from line of garden formerly of Capt Roe to mouth of Darby Creek with privilege of occupying with nets, seines, boats, and cabin, and space of ground as is necessary in fishery"

For some cause the proceedings seem not to have been pressed to sale, perhaps by reason of the pendency of the suit of Mary Hart against Jacob Hill,[1] in which the question was raised as to what had passed to David Sandelands under Christopher Taylor's will, whether it was a fee simple to the river-bank or merely an easement The Supreme Court in 1835 held it was the latter The matter thereupon rested, so far as title to the fishery was concerned, until proceedings in partition were pressed, and on Aug 24, 1847, Sheriff Robert R Dutton sold eight-fourteenths of the fishery to Paul B Carter, and by several deeds thereafter the latter acquired title until, Sept 19, 1852, he was the owner, in fee, of twelve-fourteenths of the fishery In 1865, Paul B Carter began proceedings in partition, the jury appointed returning a report to the February term, 1866, that the fishery could not be devised, and valued it at seven thousand five hundred dollars Sheriff Vanzant, on March 26, 1866, conveyed the whole title to Paul B Carter, he having become the purchaser of the easement in partition From that date until within a few years past the case was in constant litigation[2] The question in dispute grew out of an alleged erection of a stone sea-wall and pier by the Tinicum Fishing Company, which resulted in rendering the old Taylor fishery valueless The company had purchased, in 1856, at sheriff's sale, a tract of about twenty acres, and subsequently they erected a large and commodious house, which was furnished especially for the use of a social club, but the long and tedious lawsuits finally caused the members to lose all interest in the association, the real and personal estates in November, 1879, passing under the sheriff's hammer, and the Tinicum Fishing Company became thereafter merely a topic for the annalist

At a court held 3d day 1st week Tenth month, 1687, the grand jury "Presented Thomas Boules of ye Island of Tenecum for killing and converting to his own use divers Hogs and Piggs of Thomas Smith with others belonging to ye King's Leidge People" This is the first reference I find to Thomas Smith, who was then settled in Darby, but subsequently his descendants became large owners of real estate on the island; that portion of Tinicum which connected the present with the story of the past being still owned by Aubrey H Smith, his direct descendant In the will of Christopher Taylor, dated Dec 8, 1748, he mentions William Smith, leaving him "one shilling sterling" This William Smith I presume was the father of the late Thomas Smith, member of Congress from Delaware County At any rate, the old Taylor mansion-house on the island subsequently became the property of Thomas Smith It was built of stone, and it is said that while it was building the family resided in an old log hut made of white cedar logs, "cut no doubt in the marshes hard by, though not a tree of that species is now known to grow in Pennsylvania It was thoroughly repaired some years ago by Aubrey H Smith, Esq, and bids fair to stand for another century or more"[3]

It is stated that about the beginning of this century Tinicum Island "was so unhealthy that farmers were compelled to get their work done before September, as by that period the ague and remittent fever left no body able to work, but by banking and draining the water off the meadows the health of the place gradually improved, and from 1821 it has been considered very salubrious"[4] Ferris records that in Printz's time and later, vessels drawing four or five feet of water could sail from Fort Gottenberg across the meadows to the mouth of the Schuylkill[5] About the middle of the last century companies were incorporated by the provincial government and empowered to bank the meadows, while independently of these companies private parties had reclaimed much of the submerged land

Previous to the Revolution, Little Tinicum Island, heretofore mentioned, was partly reclaimed, twelve acres being banked in and inhabited When the English fleet ascended the river in 1777, the British naval officers were apprehensive that this tract of land might be utilized by the Continental authorities as a site for defensive works to interrupt their retreat, and to prevent such a use being made of it they cut the banks in many places and overflowed them, since which time the banks have never been restored In heavy tides it is nearly overflowed, but usually presents a large uncovered surface[6] Dr Smith states one of the earthworks on the Delaware River "was near the mouth of Darby Creek, doubtless on the island of Tinicum"[7] Perhaps it was Little Tinicum Island, which may have caused the English to flood that place

In the early part of this century the island of Tinicum proper was nearly submerged, consequent on the freshets occasioned by sudden thaws of ice and snow in the spring, or breaks in the banks In 1819 the banks broke, and the water rushed in overflowing the island road for four miles, and on Feb 22, 1822, the lowlands were almost inundated, boats sailing within

1 Wheaton's (Pa Sup. Ct.) Reports, vol i p 124

2 See case reported in 11 Smith (Pa State) Reports, p 34, 27th Smith, p 310, and 9 Norris (Pa. State) Reports, p 86

3 Martin's "History of Chester," p 154

4 Topographical Sketch of Tinicum Island, already quoted

5 Ferris' "Original Settlements on the Delaware," p 70

6 Ib., p 71

7 History of Delaware County, p 299

four hundred yards of the Lazaretto to Penrose's Ferry, over the meadows and fences a distance of four miles[1] On Sept 1, 1850, a heavy rain fell which covered with water the meadows of Tinicum to the depth of six feet, and inundated the railroad from a short distance below Gray's Ferry nearly to the Lazaretto, in some places undermining the cross-ties and in others sweeping them entirely away, so that travel by rail was suspended for more than a week

Previous to the Revolution, Joseph Galloway, a noted lawyer of Philadelphia, who, when the struggle finally came cast his fortune on the side of the English crown, owned a tract of two hundred and twelve acres of the easterly end of the island, all of it being reclaimed land The commonwealth of Pennsylvania instituted proceedings against him, and his estates were forfeited His land on Tinicum was sold by the commissioner of forfeited estates in Chester County, in September, 1779, and on Feb 19, 1780, the State made a deed for one hundred and eighty-seven and a half acres to James Budden, John Dunlap, Jacob Morgan, John Mease, Thomas Leiper, Joseph Carson, and John Chaloner, but it seemed that Abraham Kentruzer was in possession of the premises as Galloway's tenant and refused to yield the premises to the purchasers, and on April 28, 1780, the Supreme Council instructed the sheriff to put the latter in possession of the estate At a later date, May 17, 1780, William Kerlin purchased the remaining part of the tract, containing something over twenty acres[2]

The following is the list of the justices of the peace for Tinicum township

Benjamin Brannon	Aug 19, 1791
Israel Elliott	Oct 28, 1791
Benjamin W Oakford	Feb 14, 1794
Caleb S Sayers	Aug 6, 1799
Benjamin Hays Smith	April 3, 1804
Samuel Davis	Feb 20, 1810
Thomas Smith	July 3, 1821
Joseph G Malcolm	July 30, 1831
Thomas Maddock	Jan 8, 1834
Charles Sellers	June 20, 1836
William Hunter	April 10, 1849

Quarantine Station—In the last decade of the eighteenth century the city of Philadelphia was scourged with yellow fever, and so great was the alarm at the proximity of the Lazaretto, then located just back of Fort Mifflin, on Providence Island, that it was determined to change the site of that station, hence on Aug 7, 1799, the Board of Health of Philadelphia purchased from Morris Smith and Reuben Smith ten acres of land on the island of Tinicum, and immediately began the erection of the buildings there which were completed in 1800, and quarantine was established there for the first time in 1801 The old two-story building, the steward's quarters, was modeled after the Pennsylvania Hospital, at Eighth and Pine Streets, Philadelphia, and although it is now not occupied as a hospital, in early times the wings were used for that purpose The building is flanked on the right by the physician's residence and on the left by that of the quarantine master The present hospital building stands about one hundred yards to the rear of the steward's quarters There is also an ancient brick building known as the old custom-house, three stories high, which we learn from a letter written on Jan 5, 1847, by Joseph Weaver, Jr, United States custom officer, had not been occupied for many years previous to that time for any purpose, and then suffering much from neglect Hon R J Walker, Secretary of the Treasury, authorized Mr Weaver to rent it to a person who would take good care of it, the United States reserving the right to store goods therein, if necessary The building was leased to John Pedrick, a ship-carpenter, at a rental of thirty dollars per annum

Shortly after the quarantine station was located at Tinicum, at the October session, 1804, the Board of Health endeavored to have John Ferguson, master of the schooner "Monongahela Farmer," which had come from New Orleans bound to Philadelphia, indicted for a breach of quarantine, the charge being that after the vessel had come to an anchor and was undergoing quarantine, he permitted thirty-two passengers "to go ashore" from his vessel before they had submitted to the required examination The grand jury, however, ignored the bill

In June, 1824, a man was landed from an oyster boat at Chester, dangerously ill with smallpox A meeting of the borough Council was immediately held, but they having no power to act, several of the citizens sent the man in a market wagon to the Lazaretto, and while waiting at that place to be admitted, he asked for a drink of water, which being given him he drank, and immediately fell back in the conveyance dead The *Philadelphia Gazette* of that day attacked the borough authorities and citizens for this act, and for a time a sturdy war of words was carried on in the *Post Boy* at Chester, and the Philadelphia journals

No serious objection was made to the location of the quarantine until recent years In the latter part of June, 1870, the brig "Home," from Jamaica, came to off the Lazaretto When visiting her the health officers learned that the captain of the vessel had died and was buried at sea four days after the brig had sailed from Black River, Jamaica She was loaded with logwood, and although at the time there appeared to be no sickness on the vessel, she was in such a filthy condition that she was ordered to be taken to the United States government wharf, adjoining the quarantine grounds After twenty days, during which she was fumigated, the brig was pronounced clean, and permission given to proceed to her destination In the interim canal boats were sent from Philadelphia to remove the logwood, and on one of these boats a woman and boy sickened and died On Friday, July 15th, a large quantity of filthy rags on the "Home" were taken ashore and

[1] Smith's "History of Delaware County," p 299

[2] Colonial Records, vol vii pp 256, 331, 352, Penna Archives, 1st series, vol viii p 208

burned, the wind blowing strongly from the south. The next day, Saturday, Mrs. Ann Enos and Ann Sharp, at the hotel then kept by Jacob Pepper, were taken sick, and on the following Friday they both died. On Tuesday, July 26th, Mrs. Eva Kugler, wife of the steward of the quarantine, was taken ill, and died on Saturday. Dr. Cardeza, who was in attendance of Mr. Pepper's family, declared the fever was "a stranger" in this locality, and suggested that unusual care should be taken to prevent contagion. The inference was plain, and when Dr. William B. Ulrich unhesitatingly pronounced it yellow fever the public in the neighborhood, in Chester, and even in Philadelphia, became greatly alarmed lest it might spread. Dr. William S. Thompson, the Lazaretto physician, and Mrs. Gartsell, a nurse who had been attached to the station for fifteen years, were attacked with the disorder. Dr. John F. M. Forwood, of Chester, who twice before had the fever in the Southern States, was summoned to act at the Lazaretto, being appointed temporary physician there. Dr. Thompson and Mrs. Gartsell died on the 11th of August, and on the 13th, Robert Gartside, the quarantine master, fell a victim to the disease. Notwithstanding the fact that Dr. Forwood had had the disease before, he was stricken with the fever, and Dr. Ulrich was called to attend on all the cases there. By the 18th of August the fever had subsided, no new cases having appeared for several days, and all who were then sick of the disorder recovered. About twenty cases of yellow fever occurred. Of these Jacob Pepper, Ann Eliza Enos, Ann Sharp, Dr. Thompson, Robert Gartside, Eva Kugler, Mrs. Gartsell, William H. Dillmore, and the woman and her son on the canal-boat died.

The alarm had subsided, but at the following session of the Legislature a bill was introduced, which was favorably reported, providing for the sale of the quarantine station on Big Tinicum Island, the purchase of Little Tinicum Island, and the erection of buildings there for the Lazaretto. The project was sustained by a petition of a thousand residents of Delaware County, but the bill finally died on the calendar. At the session of 1872 the scheme for removal of the Lazaretto was again presented, the site to which it should be changed being left undetermined in the bill. The Board of Health in Philadelphia at that time memorialized the Senate in opposition to the proposed act, alleging, among other reasons, that the United States in 1871 had rebuilt the long wharf (two hundred and eighty feet), and had completely repaired the large stone government warehouse used for storage of cargoes from infected vessels detained at quarantine. They also declared that Tinicum had but one hundred and twenty-five inhabitants all told, and had remained almost stationary in population for seventy years, while during that time only three dwellings had been erected in the township. The memorial concluded by asserting that the present site was highly eligible and unobjectionable as regards the surrounding neighborhood. The removalists were again defeated.

The following is a list of the physicians and quarantine masters at the Lazaretto since the station was established in 1801 :

LAZARETTO PHYSICIANS.

Name.	Commissioned.
Dr. Michael Leib	Sept. 19, 1800.
" Nathan Dorsey	1806.
" George Buchanan	July 4, 1806.
" Edward Lowber	1808.
" Isaac Heister	1809.
" Thomas D. Mitchell	May 27, 1813.
" Joel B. Sutherland	May 1, 1816.
" George F. Lehman	March 4, 1817.
" Joshua W. Ash	March 29, 1836.
" Wilmer Worthington	Feb. 9, 1839.
" Jesse W. Griffiths	April 5, 1842.
" Joshua T. Jones	March 5, 1845.
" James S. Rich	Dec. 14, 1848.
" T. J. P. Stokes	1852.
" Henry Pleasants	Feb. 16, 1855.
" J. Howard Taylor	May 31, 1856.
" L. S. Filbert	March 13, 1858.
" D. K. Shoemaker	Jan. 30, 1861.
" Thomas Stewardson	May 21, 1864.
" George A. Fairlamb	May 3, 1865.
" William S. Thompson	Jan. 21, 1867.
" J. Howard Taylor	Aug. 11, 1870.
" D. K. Shoemaker	Nov. 4, 1873.
" W. T. Robinson	1878.
" Samuel Walker	1884.

QUARANTINE MASTERS.

Thomas Egger	—— —, 1799.
Capt. William Lake	April —, 1809.
Christopher O'Conner	May 1, 1816.
Capt. Thomas Moore	May 19, 1818.
Henry Kenyon	Aug. 16, 1819.
Joseph M. G. Lescure	March 31, 1831.
Stephen Horne	" 19, 1836.
Benjamin Martin	Feb. 9, 1839.
Alexander McKeever	April 6, 1842.
Capt. John H. Cheyney	March 13, 1848.
Jared Ketcham, of Chester County, was appointed, but after a few months' service resigned.	
William V. McKean[1]	Feb. 12, 1852.
Matthew Van Dusen, Jr.	—— —, 1853.
Jacob Pepper	Feb. 16, 1855.
Lewis R. Denan	March 9, 1858.
Robert Gartside	Jan. 20, 1861.
Nathan Shaw	April 15, 1864.
Thomas O. Stevenson	" 20, 1867.
Robert Gartside	Feb. 28, 1870.
Dr. John H. Gihon	Aug. 11, 1870.
" A. W. Matthews	—— —, 1873.
" C. C. V. Crawford	—— —, 1879.
Horace R. Manley	—— —, 1883.

On July 8, 1872, Governor Geary visited the Lazaretto, the only time, so far as I have knowledge, that the quarantine station was ever visited by the executive officer of the State.

The old fox-hunters of a past generation used to relate a notable chase on Tinicum, which occurred as long ago as Saturday, Feb. 1, 1824. On that morning, about eleven o'clock, John Irwin and James Burns (Chester), George Litzenberg, Philip Rudolph, and others (of Providence), started a fox on the island, and after a warm run the dogs were within fifty yards of him, when he sprang on the roof of an oven, then to a shed adjoining the house of Mr. Horne, jumped in at the second-story window, and neither huntsmen nor hounds had noticed it. A boy looking on told where the fox had gone, and one of the hunters, ascending the shed, entered the room and pushed down the sash. Just as he did this a girl of the fam-

[1] Mr. McKean resigned in May, 1853.

ily came in the room and shut the door The fox, finding exit from the apartment by the door closed, ran to the chimney, which he ascended From its top he sprang to the roof of the house and thence to the ground He was not captured until near sundown, when he holed at the root of a hollow tree, which he ascended to the forks, whence he was dislodged by a stick being thrust at him, and descending to the roots, he was taken in the usual way and bagged

Tinicum has been a choice locality for startling sensations from the earliest date As far back as the 8th of Third month, 1698, Joseph Holt and Isaac Warner were drowned by the ferry-boat from New Castle to Philadelphia being overset in a gust of wind The evidence showed that Robert White, who was at Isaac Taylor's house, went to the river to bathe and saw a corpse, whereupon he called Isaac Blawn, and the latter said, "Let us go forward and we shall find more," and he went, and they did see another, and they called Isaac Taylor and all his household and went down together When the bodies were recovered Taylor told Isaac Blawn to search them On Holt they found a piece of eight and some small money, a silver seal, some keys, and four gold rings on his finger On Warner they found a carpenter's rule, fourteen pieces of eight and a half, and some other money Warner had gone aboard the boat at New Castle, much intoxicated, carrying a speckled bag of money The whole tenor of the evidence taken would seem to indicate that a rumor had gone abroad that the dead men had a considerable sum of money with them, and that those who had found the bodies at Tinicum had appropriated part of it to their own use Taylor, it appears, had the matter fully investigated and the testimony of a number of witnesses taken at large The case is an interesting one, inasmuch as it goes into the details of the clothing and other matters of value to the students of history in arriving at a just conception of the customs and habits of the early settlers

Almost a hundred and fifty years after this event, on Sunday, Jan 1, 1843, the good people of Tinicum were astonished to find the dead body of a man hanging from the limb of an apple-tree on the estate of Richard Welling On examining the clothing of the deceased a carpenter's rule and a memorandum-book, containing the name of Daniel Barber, was found No further particulars were ever learned respecting the dead man

On Sunday, May 12, 1861, the body of a young girl, about fourteen years of age, was found in a ditch on the farm of Jacob Allberger, and, from the appearance of the body, and the fact that tufts of grass had been pulled up by the roots, it was believed that murder had been done in the hope of concealing an infamous outrage The night previous to the supposed murder a colored man, who lived in the neighborhood, stated that he had heard voices as if some persons were talking, but his dogs were barking at the time so that he could not distinguish what was said The body was brought to Chester The next morning the Philadelphia papers contained an advertisement asking information respecting Elizabeth Cox, of Germantown, and the personal description answered to that of the body found at Tinicum The parents of the missing girl came to Chester, and recognized the corpse as that of their daughter, who was of unsound mind The case aroused such public indignation that on May 24th the county commissioners offered a reward of two hundred dollars for the arrest and conviction of the person or persons who had committed the murder Mayor Henry, of Philadelphia, also appointed two detective officers to investigate the facts, and on May 31st they reported that the evidence seemed to establish that the girl, in partial derangement, had wandered from home, was overtaken by night, and had fallen into the ditch, that the banks of the ditch showed that she had struggled to get out, but, as one foot and leg almost to the knee had become fastened in the adhesive mud, she could not extricate herself, but, finally exhausted, had fallen into the water and drowned The result of the post-mortem examination strongly corroborated this theory. At all events the case ceased at that point and if murder had been committed, those who did the deed escaped "unwhipped of justice"

On Friday, March 30, 1877, the body of a man, which subsequently proved to be that of Oliver Saxton, of Philadelphia, was found on the meadow, near the tenant-house on the estate of Aubrey H Smith, then occupied by James Reid The circumstances of his death were soon learned It appeared the deceased, a few days before, had gone to Little Tinicum Island duck-shooting, and when returning in the evening, owing to a heavy storm of rain and snow, was unable to reach his place of destination, and was taken on the yacht of Joseph Woods The yacht, owing to the storm, was driven ashore on Tinicum, and in the endeavor to get her off the men on her lost their boots in the mud, and finally were compelled to abandon her and seek the fast land in their bare feet It was night, and the men separated to find shelter Saxton went to the cabin of Henry Roan, near the bank, but was denied admittance Woods, who reached the same cabin shortly after Saxton had been there and gone away, was also denied shelter, but on the payment of several dollars was permitted to pass the night there Saxton attempted to reach Reid's house, but, being overcome with the cold, he fell to the ground and died When found the skin was worn from his feet, and his legs were torn by the briers through which he had forced his way

For almost a century Tinicum was a part of Ridley township, but at the May court, 1780, a petition, signed by twenty-three "inhabitants, owners, and occupiers of land in the Island of Tinicum," was presented, which set forth "that the inhabitants of the Island aforesaid, as a part of the township of Ridley, have heretofore paid a great part of the tax for the support of the roads in said township, and also maintained and supported the roads on the Island at their own cost and charge, without the least assistance from the other part of the township And whereas the dams on said Island, made for the purpose of preventing the tides from overflowing the meadows belonging to your petitioners, were in the year 1777 cut and destroyed, with a view of retarding the progress of the enemy, at that time invading this State, whereby the roads on said Island were greatly damaged, to the very great prejudice of your petitioners, and as it is not in our power to derive any assistance from the inhabitants of the other part of the township, we conceive it to be a hardship to be obliged to support their road"

The petition concluded with a prayer that the court will, for these reasons, proceed "to divide the Island of Tinicum from the township of Ridley and to make a distinct township of it," with the like powers exercised by the other townships in the county

On Aug 31, 1780, the court allowed the prayer of the petitioners, and from thenceforth the township of Tinicum became a separate district, having all the rights and obligations of other townships Indeed more, for while the general act of March 20, 1810,[1] provided that "no person should be compelled to serve as constable more than once in every fifteen years," in the same law the township of Tinicum was exempt from the operation of the law, because there was not a sufficient number of persons residing on the island eligible to hold that office, unless within fifteen years a person could be compelled to act in that capacity for more than one year

Several references in our early Swedish annals lead to the conclusion that a school was established on the island of Tinicum in the primitive days of European settlement there, and that the clergyman of the parish acted in a dual capacity, that of the pedagogue being connected with his ministerial duties As before mentioned, it is generally maintained by historians that Christopher Taylor had there a school in the higher branches of education previous to 1685 The foregoing statement, however, is inferentially arrived at from collateral evidence purely, and is in no wise the subject of direct proof Indeed, we have no positive knowledge of a school being kept on Tinicum previous to 1843, about which date Elizabeth Griffiths, a daughter of the then physician in charge at the Lazaretto, had a school in the Dutch house,—the first building on the grounds of the Board of Health, on the left-hand side of the road as you approach the river from Morris' Ferry The title Dutch house was given to the building because of its being used to quarantine the crew and passengers of a Dutch vessel in the early days of the Lazaretto Miss Griffiths was followed by a male teacher, one Culin, but he remained there only for a brief season, when the school was abandoned About 1847 another school was established in a small frame house, on the site of the primitive Swedish Church, the land now owned by George McLaughlin, but the teacher, whose name was Wilson, became dissatisfied, and he relinquished its care It also was abandoned, and in time the building itself was removed In 1854 the first public school on the island, a small brick structure, was erected, the neighbors gratuitously laboring in its building, so that it cost not more than two hundred dollars in actual money expended For many years it served its purpose, but in time it became dilapidated, the walls spreading, the plaster fallen from the laths in place, and the floors decayed It was thoroughly inspected, pronounced hopeless of repair, and the directors decided to remove it, and in its place to put up another —the present school-house—on the site, which was done in 1868, at a cost of about four thousand dollars The schools maintained there are now in good condition, with the average attendance of pupils

The following persons have been directors of the schools of Tinicum District On Nov 28, 1834, the court, under provision of act of 1834, appointed George W Bartram and Jabez Bunting inspectors of schools for the township

1840, Dr Samuel Anderson, Edward B Smith, 1842, Thomas Jarman, Minshall Eachus, Jacob Roan 1843, John Elkins, D J W Griffith, 1844, William Hunter, Thomas M Smith, 1845, James Howell, William Johnson, 1846, William Johnson, 1847, Stephen Smith, J Weaver, 1848, John Goff, John Pedrick, 1849, John Goff, William Ward, William Johnson, Stephen Smith, William Hunter, 1850, John G Dyer, Alexander H Smith, 1851, William Ward, Humphrey Drooke, 1852, B E Carpenter, George Horne, 1853, no report, 1854, William Ward, Amos Johnson, 1855, John Hart, William Hunter, 1856, William Ward, 1857, Amos Johnson, John Holland, Alexander McKeever, 1858, John Hart, Alexander McKeever, 1859, William Ward, Alexander McKeever, 1860, Amos Johnson, Alexander T Carr, 1861, John Hart, William West, 1862, William Ward, 1863, Joseph P Horne, D A Middleton, 1864, John Hart, 1865, Charles D Johnson, John Stewart 1866, William Glenn, B F Miller, 1867, Edward B Ward, Charles D Johnson, 1868, no report 1869, Thomas E Howard, Thomas O Stevens 1870, Edmund B Ward, Benjamin F Miller, 1871, J W Ward, F J Carey, 1872, William Wood, Daniel Dills, 1873, Edward B Ward, W H Wood, 1874, B F Miller, James Reed, 1875, William Hiller, Charles H Horne, 1876, Amos Johnson, Charles D Johnson, 1877, Richard Wood, Lewis Kugler, 1878, Theodore Lukens, Adam Miller, 1879, Theodore Lukens, J Miller, 1880, B. Dillmore, Joseph B Miller, 1881, Charles Horne, Richard P Ward, William Miller, 1882, B F Miller, Charles H Horne, 1883, George G Miller, Peter Goff, 1884, William Boyd, William McCall

The Islands —During all our colonial administration the government never claimed authority over the river, the crown holding that it had exclusive jurisdiction therein So fully was this acquiesced in that as late as January, 1775, the Supreme Council declared that the river Delaware, not being included within the body of any county of the province, the jurisdiction of the courts of Chester County did not extend into the river, and respecting it no legal process was valid issued from such courts This as-

[1] Bliss' "Delaware County Digest," p 17

sertion covered all the islands on the Delaware excepting Big Tinicum Island. Hence, after the termination of the Revolutionary war, it became necessary for the States of Pennsylvania and New Jersey to determine to which of these States the islands should be assigned. In that adjustment Hog Island, Martin's Bar, Printz's Island, Maiden Island, and Little Tinicum Island were allotted to Pennsylvania, while Monas' Island, Chester Island, Chester Island Bar, Tonkin's Island, and Marcus Hook Bar became part of New Jersey. I have, of course, considered the partition of the islands so far only as relates to those lying in front of the present county of Delaware. The Legislature of Pennsylvania, by act of Sept. 25, 1786, annexed the islands named as allotted to this commonwealth to Chester County, particularly specifying that "the whole of Hog Island, which lies opposite to the said boundary of Philadelphia and Chester, and of the marshes surrounding the said island, is hereby annexed to and shall be deemed to be part of the said county of Chester and of the nearest township of the said county."[1]

Under the provisions of this act Hog Island became part of Tinicum township, as, in fact, did all the islands facing Delaware County, the title to which Pennsylvania had acquired by the terms of its treaty with New Jersey. Very early in our history we find mention of Hog Island, for at the last court held under the authority of the Duke of York, June 14, 1681, it appears that "Justice Otto Earnest Cock acquaints the Court that hee has bought and paid of ye Indian proprietors a certain swampy or marshy Island, called by ye Indians Quistconck, Lying att the upper End of Tinnachkonck Island in ye river opposite Andrews Boones Creeke, and desires ye Corts approbation. The Cort, haveing well informed themselves about ye premisses, doe allow thereof."[2] Armstrong tells us that this swampy island, now known as Hog Island, on Lindstrom's manuscript map appears under the high-sounding title of "Keyser Eyland, Ile des Empereurs."[3]

This island has played no insignificant part in the story of our county. Previous to the Revolution it had become the property of Joseph Galloway, to whom allusion has already been made. On July 29, 1775, when the Council of Safety was laying the obstructions in the Delaware River, it was decided to sink the frames opposite the upper end of Hog Island in preference to Billingsport,[4] and on June 19, 1776, when an attack by the British fleet on Philadelphia seemed imminent, Abraham Kinsey, the tenant under Galloway on Hog Island, was notified that the committee deemed it necessary to overflow the island with water on the near approach of the enemy, and all injuries he would sustain by that act should be made good to him by the public.[5] There is no evidence, however, to show that the land was then intentionally submerged. In 1780 the real estate of Joseph Galloway had been confiscated to the State, and on December 15th of that year, complaint having been made to the Supreme Council that Benjamin Rue, Francis Proctor, Joseph Ogden, William Eckhart, and Mark McCall "had taken forcible possession of Hog Island," the parties were brought before Council and compelled to enter bonds for their appearnce at the next Court of General Sessions for the county of Chester, to answer the trespass.[6] The defendants, appearing to have taken possession under color of title adverse to that acquired by the State under the confiscation laws, maintained their position during a bitter and constant litigation extending over nearly ten years, and were several times after the instance mentioned arrested and held in recognizance to answer at court, but the threatened criminal proceedings were never pressed. In December, 1780, the island was sold as confiscated estate to James Mease, Hugh Shiell, and Samuel Caldwell, of Philadelphia, and on the 4th of January following Council instructed the sheriff of Chester County to put the purchasers in possession, "they paying the incidental expenses;" and in the mean while, Abraham Kintzing was required to retain possession of the island in behalf of the State, and the sheriffs of Philadelphia and Chester Counties were directed, if necessary, to "assist him in holding possession against all intruders." At the same time the attorney-general was instructed "to support the claim of the State against sundry persons who have lately attempted to take possession under some pretended rights, and take proper steps to cause the persons who are witnesses to the late forcible entry to attend at the next Chester court, in order to lay the complaint therein before the grand jury."[7]

On Feb. 16, 1781, Council ordered the island to be surveyed, and the following day a committee, consisting of Dr. Gardner, Gen. Potter, and William Van Campen, was appointed to confer with a similar committee, which the Assembly was requested to name, "touching a valuable island in the Delaware called Hog Island, seized by the agents for confiscated estates in the county of Philadelphia, on the property of Joseph Galloway, an attainted traytor, and which Col. Proctor and others are attempting to take into their possession."[8] The committees seem to have conferred, and it was decided to retain Jonathan D. Sergeant to appear in behalf of the commonwealth, a retaining fee of fifteen pounds to appear "in a cause depending respecting Hog Island."[9] The controversy continued, and on July 14, 1781, another sale of land on the island was made by the agents of the State in Chester County, in which some special order of the

[1] Bliss' "Delaware County Digest," pp. 38, 39.
[2] Record of Upland Court, p. 190.
[3] Ib., p. 191.
[4] Colonial Records, vol. x. p. 294.
[5] Ib., p. 607.
[6] Ib., vol. xii. p. 570.
[7] Ib., p. 592.
[8] Ib., p. 631.
[9] Ib., p. 634.

Council was violated; hence the agents were directed to receive no part of the purchase money, but were commanded to attend the meeting of Council to "account for their proceedings."[1] The State, on May 9, 1782, acknowledged a deed to Samuel Caldwell (the other purchaser seems to have abandoned all claim to the estate) for one hundred and five acres of banked meadow at Hog Island, the consideration being one hundred and seventy-five thousand pounds Continental money and a yearly rent of seven bushels and a half of "good merchantable wheat, payable to the Trustees of the University of Pennsylvania."[2] However, Council seemed unable to put the purchaser in possession of the estate, notwithstanding repeated orders to the sheriff of Philadelphia to assist Caldwell with whatever force was necessary to effect that end. The litigation was continued, for on June 3, 1782, Jared Ingersoll received nine pounds in specie, and on the 7th of the same month Mr. Sergeant received a like sum as fees in the case. During the summer of 1783 the remaining part of the island not already purchased by Caldwell was sold to several officers of the Pennsylvania line, the agents of the State receiving the certificates of money due to those soldiers in payment, but on August 30th of that year Council ordered the certificates to be returned to the officers, and that the island should remain the property of the State until otherwise disposed of.[3] Caldwell, however, seemed not disposed to reconvey his land to the State, whereupon, on Jan. 8, 1784, the attorney-general was instructed to institute suit against him for the recovery of the estate. Late in the year 1786 the commonwealth was still in litigation, for it retained William Bradford, Jr., Jonathan Dickinson Sergeant, and Edward Tilghman in the suit brought against it by Thomas Proctor, "respecting the right to Hog Island."[4] The case seems to have continued until May 5, 1789, when it was tried, for on the 2d of that month, Mr. Kennedy, the secretary of the land-office, was directed to deliver certain papers in his possession to Caldwell, they being "necessary on the tryall of Hogg Island."[5] The commonwealth was finally beaten in the suit, the title of Thomas Proctor and his associate owners being recognized as valid. In the *Pennsylvania Packet* for March 6, 1790, appears the following advertisement:

"HOG ISLAND.—To let on a lease for years, situate on the River Delaware, ten miles from the city of Philadelphia and seven miles by land, containing 200 acres of the richest maddow and may be immediately entered upon. For terms apply to the subscribers.

"THOMAS PROCTOR.
"JOSEPH OGDEN.
"WILLIAM ECHART.

"PHILADELPHIA, *May 3d.*"

The island subsequently became the property of Samuel Murdock, Isaac Reeves, and John Black, who, in 1840, petitioned the court of Delaware County to connect the island to the main land by a bridge, and were authorized themselves to erect "a free bridge on posts or abutments, provided that an aperture of not less than 25 feet wide and of height not less than 8 feet above high-water mark, should be left, which aperture should at all times be kept free from obstruction, so as to admit of passage of shallops." The bridge was erected, but the connection with the main land was made in Philadelphia County, and the petition to the court of Delaware County was simply, it would appear, to prevent any trouble with the county authorities for interrupting the public (water) highway. The island, owned by Edgar N. and John Black, is now a marvel of fertility, and so complete is the manner of banking and diking that breaks in the embankments are now as uncommon as they were common years ago. The last serious break occurred during the storm of Nov. 1, 1861, when the island was submerged, and the loss of property was great, three hundred head of sheep drowned being only one item in the list of damages. On Jan. 20, 1882, in an unused barn on the island, the body of a man was found. He had hung himself, and as the remains were not discovered for several weeks after the act, the rats had mutilated the arms and legs. The remains were identified as those of Charles J. Deacon, an insurance agent, of Philadelphia.

Martin's Bar, which formerly lay between Hog Island and Big Tinicum Island, and by the banking and diking of the river front has within recent years almost disappeared as a separate piece of earth, remained in the ownership of the State until within a comparatively recent period, although, in December, 1789, John Lockart petitioned "for the right of pre-emption of a small island in the river Delaware, between Tinicum and Hogg Island containing about ten or fifteen acres;" but on the second reading of his petition, December 12th, Council decided "the request of the said John Lockart cannot be complied with."[6] The bar had considerably increased in thirty years, for in the patent granted to Thomas K. Wallace by the State, March 28, 1821, Martin's Bar was found to contain sixty-seven acres and forty perches.[7]

On Jan. 3, 1881, the court of Delaware County confirmed the port warden's line, above Little Tinicum Island. Towards the eastern end of Little Tinicum Island lie the two small islands known as Printz and Maiden Islands. The former was patented to Thomas H. and Aubrey H. Smith, Feb. 13, 1841, and contained fourteen acres and eighty-one perches. It is now owned by Aubrey H. Smith. Maiden Island—said to have derived its name from a young girl who was overset in a boat managing to get to this place, where for two days she remained before rescued—is owned by a company of Philadelphians, who propose to erect coal-oil works there and on Little Tinicum Island.

1 Colonial Records, vol. xiii. p. 11.
2 Ib., p. 279.
3 Ib., p. 280.
4 Ib., vol. xv. p. 117.
5 Ib., p. 472.
6 Ib., vol. xvi. p. 230.
7 Smith's "Atlas of Early Land Grants in Delaware County," map 16.

Licensed Houses.—In Tinicum, although it is the oldest settlement in our county, and probably in the State, license to keep a house of public entertainment does not appear until after the yellow fever epidemic of 1798, when the authorities of Philadelphia had determined to locate the Lazaretto, or quarantine, thereon.

On July 27, 1799, Thomas Smith filed his petition, setting forth "that a Public Lazaretto is about to be established upon the Island of Tinicum, that will cause considerable intercourse between the city of Philadelphia, and the said Lazaretto, that a house of entertainment will be necessary at or near the same That your petitioner is about to erect suitable buildings to accommodate the public on the road near to said Lazaretto, which he will have ready on or before the 1st day of October next," and requested license for the same The signers of his petition certify that they are well acquainted with the situation, as also with Charles Lloyd, the person to occupy the house, and recommend him as a person suitable "to run a hotel"

Shortly afterwards the health authorities took action in Smith's behalf, as will be seen by the following communication sent to the court and filed with the petition

"HEALTH OFFICE, 7th Mo 22, 1799

"*To the Judges of the Court of Quarter Sessions for the County of Delaware*

"The Board of Health considering the propriety of establishing a well-regulated inn in the vicinity of the intended Lazaretto, now building on Tinicum Island, are of the judgment the place fixed on by Thomas Smith as the most suitable, in their view, and do recommend the said Thomas Smith to the court to obtain a license for his house near the said Lazaretto

"By order of the Board of Health
"EDWARD GARRIGUES, *President.*
"PAXHALL HOLLINGSWORTH, *Secretary*
"JAMES HALL, *Resident Physician of Port*
"THOMAS EGGOR, *Quarantine Master*
"HEART NORBERRY, *Steward of the Lazaretto*"

The court granted license to Charles Lloyd for the year 1800

At the same time that Thomas Smith's petition was presented, Benjamin Rue desired to be permitted to keep a public-house in the dwelling he then occupied He sets forth that "as the Board of Health of the City of Philadelphia are about to erect buildings there for the reception of imported goods, to prevent, if possible, a return of the dreadful calamity which has so frequently desolated Philadelphia, the concourse of people necessarily attending on a business of such importance, your petitioner conceives will make an Inn indispensably necessary"

The court seemed to think very much in the same way, for instead of one inn they permitted two to be established, and Rue's application was favorably considered for the year 1800 His expectation of "the concourse of people" who would visit Tinicum seems not to have been realized, for after license was awarded him, in 1802, his name disappears from the records, so far as licenses in this neighborhood are concerned.

Charles Lloyd seems to have moved to Benjamin Rue's house, where he had licenses until 1807, when Elizabeth Harrison was granted license for the house formerly kept by Lloyd, and continued there until 1811, when Esther Taylor became the landlady for that year Who kept it during 1812 can only be gathered from the petition of John Hart, in 1813, in which he desires license for the house "lately Mary Taylor's" This John Hart was the great grandson of Edward Hart, who (with Tobias Preak, both being officers in the town of Flushing, on Long Island) for refusal to carry out Governor Stuyvesant's cruel orders against Quakers, was thrown into prison John Hart, like Rue, it seems, was disappointed in the amount of business for a public-house at Tinicum, for the next year he made no application for license, and in John Ward's petition, in 1815, he alludes to the place as "house lately occupied by John Shreen," who owned the property In 1817, however, he appears once more as "Mine Host" of the Tinicum Tavern, and continued thereat until 1829, when his widow, Mary Hart, followed him, the hotel having been left by John Shreen to his daughter, Mary Hart, until 1834, at which time the license was granted to John L Fryberg

In 1838, George Bastian, Jr, was the proprietor, to be followed the next year by William Nugent Samuel L Ferman succeeded Nugent in 1843, to give place, in 1844, to R M Rutter, and he in turn, in 1845, to John Hall In 1848, John Goff procured the license, and remained there until 1850, when, having rented the Steamboat Hotel, in Chester (which he purchased the following year), the Lazaretto Hotel was again kept by R M Rutter, who, in 1853, was succeeded by Henry Pepper John Hart, the younger, in 1855 followed Pepper, and continued to receive the court's approval until 1863, when his petition was rejected because it was filed too late However, he was on time the following year, as well as in 1855, after which Amos Johnson, Jr, had license granted him, which the same year he transferred to Henry Goff, who remained there until 1869, when Jacob Pepper made application for hotel license, which was denied him, but he was authorized to keep an eating-house In 1870, Pepper again made application, his petition being warmly indorsed by John Hickman and Sketchley Morton in personal letters to the judges Judge Morton in his letter states that in consequence of the old hotel (Rue's building) being abandoned as a public-house for two years, Tinicum was without a tavern, and it was necessary to have a public-house there He recommended Pepper warmly, and stated that he (Pepper) "had just erected a large house containing twenty-two apartments, sixteen of which were sleeping-rooms" Pepper at last succeeded in procuring a restaurant license, but in the fall of that year the yellow fever as an epidemic prevailed at the Lazaretto, he was stricken with the disease and died His widow, Annie E Pepper, kept the house the following year, and John T Huddell in 1872 In 1873 and 1874 license was prohibited outside of Chester, but on the repeal of the local option law, David Wells was licensed in 1875 and 1876

In 1876, William Miller made application for a hotel license at the Riverview Hotel, the new house Pepper built, which was granted him, and annually thereafter until the present time at the same house

In 1877, David Wells obtained license for that year at the old Tinicum Hotel, and in 1878 he was succeeded by C H Newhall, and he in turn, in 1879, by Daniel Birmingham William H Reed kept the old tavern in 1880–81, to give place to James E Ford in 1882 Ford kept the house one year, and in 1883, Peter Goff, the present landlord of the old Tinicum Tavern, succeeded to the business

CHAPTER XXIX

ASTON TOWNSHIP

DR SMITH states that "this township probably derived its name from Aston, a village of Berkshire, England In 1686, Edward Carter, then a resident in what is now Aston, was appointed constable for Northley "[1] The opinions of all our local historians agree in that the name of Northley was applied to Aston previous to 1687 to designate that locality from other municipal districts in the county Edward Carter doubtless gave the name to the township, as was customary in those early days, in remembrance of his old home beyond the sea, for he came from Aston, in the parish of Bampton, Oxfordshire, England, emigrating to the province in 1682[2] He first located in Chichester, but subsequently removed to his tract of two hundred and fifty acres in Aston, and was appointed the first constable of that township, which assumed its present name the following year (1688), when John Neal (Nields) was appointed to the like office for the township of Aston, which is the first mention of that name in our record, and is properly accepted as the date at which the municipal district was established Carter was a prominent man in the early days of the province, having served as member of the Assembly in 1688, as trustee of Chester Meeting the year previous, and Chichester and Concord Monthly Meeting was regularly held at his house until 1703, about which time he is believed to have died[3] Carter was not the first settler in Aston, for on Oct 8, 1682, Charles Ashcom, the surveyor, returned five hundred acres of land laid out for John Dutton, on the west of Upland Creek, beginning at "Nathaniel Evans' corner tree," and so "unto the woods," and tradition says that John Dutton settled on the land and built a house in the meadow, near the creek, but, being disturbed by floods, he removed a few rods farther back, and erected his dwelling on a large rock near a small rivulet A portion of this rock may still be seen near the road from Rockdale to Village Green, the remainder having been removed for building purposes some years ago "[4] It is also stated that the family of John Dutton followed an Indian path when they moved from Chester to the back settlement[5]

Even before Dutton William Woodmansey took up a hundred acres at the southeastern end of the township, on Chester Creek—the present Bridgewater—in 1680, naming his home in the forest "Harold," and there the society of Friends frequently held their meetings He was one of Governor Markham's Council, having been several years in the colony before the charter to Penn, coming a passenger in the ship "Kent" in 1677 Joseph Richards, who never lived in the township, in August, 1682, had surveyed to him three hundred acres in the southern part of the township, including the site of Village Green After his death it was divided among his children, and on a portion of this tract of land, after it passed into the possession of the Barnard family, Gen Isaac D Barnard, the only Delaware countian who has been United States senator from Pennsylvania, was born in 1791 An intervening strip of land, between Richard's tract and Chichester and Chester townships' lines, containing one hundred and twenty-five acres, was surveyed to Anthony Weaver in February, 1681, and to this estate he gave the name Northley, by which Aston was first known Dr Smith relates that Anthony, being convinced that he wanted a wife, and as the women were generally Quakeresses, he whispered his convictions to Ann Richards, of Chichester, which resulted in the couple coming to meeting where the matter was discussed, and, although Anthony honestly "owned himself to be none of us," the marriage was permitted to proceed[6] As usual in such cases, the wife's religious predilections soon became those of her husband

Among the early settlers of Aston was Thomas Mercer, who took up a hundred acres of land on Chester Creek, near Dutton's mills, and Nathaniel Evans, in October, 1682, had surveyed to him a tract of three hundred acres, oddly shaped so as to have the largest part extend along the creek from Elwood Tyson's land to within a short distance of the Presbyterian Ford, and yet stretching west across the entire township Above the Dutton tract, John Neild, in 1682, had surveyed to him two hundred and fifty acres, which included the site of the present village of Rockdale, and following the creek to West Branch continued along the latter stream until at Llewellyn

[1] History of Delaware County, p 400

[2] Thomas Maxwell Potts' "History of Carter Family," p 9

[3] Ib, p 11

[4] Cope's "Genealogy of the Dutton Family," p 32

[5] Ib, p 37

[6] History of Delaware County, p 510

it intersected with an easterly line drawn at right angles, thence to Chester Creek. The Crozer estate is almost entirely included in this patent. In 1695, John Neild was married to the widow of John Dutton, the settler, and the latter, having married a man not in membership with Friends, found that her action occasioned considerable concern to the good people of that sect.

The upper end of the present township of Aston, a tract of one thousand acres, was surveyed to Thomas Brassey in 1684, which subsequently was divided previous to 1710 into smaller farms. A tract of one hundred and nineteen acres bordering on Concord township was surveyed to Thomas Martin, and at this day part of that land is still in the ownership of his descendant,—Thomas Martin. John Pennell also acquired over two hundred acres of the Brassey land, but the farm above the State road, where Mark Pennell now lives, was not a part of the original farm purchased by John Pennell in 1700. Among the original owners of land in Aston, above where the West Branch crosses the township, among the earliest purchasers was Gilbert Woolman, two hundred and fifty acres which property extended northwest from Llewellyn, including J. B. Rhodes, C. W. Mathues, Thomas Swaine, and the Lewis estate to the east of Logtown road; while William McCracken's and Caleb Heyburn's farms are located on the two hundred and fifty acres, which were surveyed to Mary Moore, May 10, 1684. J. W. Thatcher's estate on Chester Creek above Pennellton Station is part of the twenty-one acres surveyed to Caleb Pusey in 1707–8.

The taxables in Aston in 1715 were as follows: Robert Carter, John Pennell, Moses Key, John Dutton, Thomas Dutton, Thomas Woodward, John Neild, James Widdows, William Rattew, Samuel Jones, Thomas Barnard, Abraham Darlington, John Hurford, Jonathan Monroe, Thomas Gale.

Freemen,—Thomas Dunbabin, Isaac Williams, Joseph Darlington, Edward Richards, Samuel Stroud.

At a court held the third day of the first week Tenth month, 1688, the grand jury laid out the highway from Chichester to Aston, as follows:

"Ffrom Delaware by James Browns along ye old Road Betwixt Jeremy Colletts and James Hulbert soe along ye same Road to a marked White Oake, thence along on ye West sid of a marked Poplar tree near ye Meeting House, from thence by a lyne of marked trees to ye West Corner of Joseph Richardson's fence, from thence by a lyne of marked trees to a marked Black Oake standing by Astone Road."

On the same day the grand jury laid out the road from Aston to Edgmont:

"Beginning att a Spanish Oake about Edward Carter's and soe along ye Cutt Road and down ye Vallie which Joseph Richardson had fenced in, from thence through John Beales Pasture along by William Woodmansees along ye old Road over Chester Creek's soe along ye Old Road."

Previous to this date the road from Aston to Chester had been granted by the grand jury, "The Inhabitance of ye Township of Aston Petioned for one Road way to ye Town of Chester, and another to ye town of Chichester." It is, however, unnecessary to further quote the exact line as presented in the report of that body to courts, the foregoing being deemed sufficient to indicate the manner in which such returns were made.

The following is a list of the justices of the peace for Aston township:

Thomas Newlin....................Aug. 19, 1791.
Matthias Kerlin....................July 4, 1808.
Thomas Pierce....................Feb. 8, 1814.
James Bratton....................Feb. 3, 1820.
Joseph Fox....................Dec. 4, 1823.
John Mattson....................Dec. 13, 1823.
Joseph Bowen....................Nov. 10, 1824.
Joseph Trimble....................April 21, 1827.
Robert Frame....................Jan. 15, 1829.
Robert Hall....................Feb. 8, 1831.
William Mendenhall....................Dec. 6, 1836.
Robert Hall....................April 14, 1840.
James McMullin....................April 12, 1842.
John Taylor....................April 13, 1847.
Isaac C. Denick...April 15, 1851, May 26, 1856, April 9, 1861.
John Blackburn....................April 11, 1867.
John T. Aikley....................March 23, 1877.
Charles W. Haycock....................April 9, 1881.
John T. Aikley....................April 10, 1882.

The second day following the battle of Brandywine, Lord Cornwallis, "with the 2d Battalion Light Infantry and 2d of Grenadiers, marched at half past six in the morning, to join the body under Major General Grant and to move on towards Chester. . . . At 5 o'clock this afternoon the troops with Lord Cornwallis reached Ashtown, within 4 miles of Chester."[1] Here Gen. Cornwallis established his headquarters, the encampment extending from Mount Hope to the lower part of Village Green, where in an old brick house, still standing, that officer made his temporary residence. From here he dispatched parties in every direction to secure supplies for the British army, seizing for that purpose the flour in all the mills within reach of his troops. The soldiers who were sent out on these expeditions frequently despoiled the inhabitants of everything they could carry away, although the orders from Howe and Cornwallis expressly forbade such unlicensed plundering. On the night of Sunday, Sept. 14, 1777, three British soldiers—Dr. Smith says they were Hessians—crossed Chester Creek, above Dutton's mill, to the dwelling of Jonathan Martin, now the property of George Dutton, and plundered the family of many things, among them some articles belonging to Mary Martin, a daughter, then eighteen, who indignantly reproved them for their unmanly conduct. One of the soldiers, in anger at her reprimand, slightly wounded Miss Martin with a bayonet. The men, still on plunder bent, proceeded about three-quarters of a mile in a southeasterly direction to the house of Mr. Coxe, in Chester township, near Sneath's Corner, now the property of Robert McCall, where they stole a number of articles, among which was a silver watch. Mr. Coxe had a

[1] Journal of Capt. John Montressor, *Penna. Mag. of History*, vol. vi. p. 39.

daughter about the same age as Miss Martin. The next morning the two girls went to the headquarters of Lord Cornwallis, where complaint was made personally to that officer or Gen. Howe, who, with an escort of dragoons, had that day visited Cornwallis' extreme outpost, three-quarters of a mile west of Chester, in the neighborhood of the present Cartertown. Dr. Smith, who heard the incident related by Thomas Dutton and Joseph Mencil, stated that Gen. Howe "promised that if they could point out the men, they should be punished. The troops were at once formed into line, when the girls passed along and pointed out the robbers, after which they retired to some distance. The officers then put the troops through various evolutions, leaving the men in different positions. The same men were again pointed out by the girls as the guilty parties. The operation was again repeated with a like result. The men were then searched, when some of the stolen property was found upon them. They were tried by a court-martial and all convicted. Two of them were sentenced to be hung, and the third to perform the office of executioner. Upon whom the extreme penalty should be inflicted, the question was decided by casting lots. The two men were hung on the limb of an apple-tree on the property owned by George L. Nield, in Aston, and what is remarkable, they were allowed to remain hanging after the army moved away."[1] The two men, we learn from Capt. Montressor's journal, were executed on the 15th of September, and that one was a grenadier and the other a light infantryman.[2] That night at eight o'clock Cornwallis moved his whole command toward the Lancaster road, and at eleven o'clock the next day Gen. Howe made a junction with the troop of the former, the commander-in-chief having marched with the bulk of the army from near Dilworthtown by the Turk's Head (West Chester), Goshen meeting-house, and the hotel, the sign of the Boot.

Damages sustained by the inhabitants of Aston township from the British army in September, 1777:

	£	s.	d.
Taken from John McClaskey by the British under Cornwallis, September 13th and 14th	95	7	6
Taken from John Noblit by the British under Cornwallis, September 16th	4	0	0
Taken from James Pennell by the British under Cornwallis, September 16th	186	7	9
Taken from George Pierce, Esq., September 13th, 14th, and 15th	771	15	0
Taken from George Witherow	165	0	0
" Robert Rankin, September 13th and 14th	22	12	6
	£1245	2s.	9d.

Thomas Dutton, the centenarian, used to relate that on the evening of the 13th of September, when the British troops, under Cornwallis, encamped at Village Green, extending in a crescent form westwardly to Mount Hope, he was afraid the soldiers would kill his mother's cows, which were then pasturing in close proximity to the troops, so, lad as he was, not ten years of age, he marched boldly to the camp and drove the cattle home. An officer noticed the boy's action, and doubtless thinking that where those cows belonged good cheer could be had, ordered four soldiers to follow while he walked with young Dutton to his home. The latter, child-like, answered every question put to him by the officer, and when the house was reached the soldiers waited without to guard against the capture of their commander, who had entered the dwelling. The widow Dutton was much alarmed, but the officer assured her that the soldiers did not come to rob the people, but advised her as long as the troops lay in the neighborhood to bolt and bar every door and window, for the camp-followers, under a pretence of lighting a pipe, a drink of water, or other trifling matter, would strive to get access to the house and plunder it. The brave fellow who had lost one of his hands in Flanders paid for his meals, and the timely warning in all probability saved the widow from loss.[3] This lad, born in Aston, Feb. 2, 1769, died Sept. 12, 1869, in the same township, his span of life having been extended to one hundred years, seven months, and eleven days. When twenty-one years of age, he having learned the tanning business, obtained permission from his grandfather to build a tan-yard on the former's estate in Aston, and Thomas Dutton erected a dwelling partly of stone and partly of logs, and a tan-house, into the wall of which is built a stone bearing the initials T. D., and the date 1790. The young man, who had married, appears to have devoted himself to his trade, and not only did he establish a reputation in business, but his industrious habits so favorably impressed his grandfather that Richard Dutton conveyed "in consideration of the natural love and affection he bore" his grandson, the two acres on which the dwelling and tan-yard were located. Subsequently by his grandfather's will he received a large tract of land surrounding these two acres. Here he continued until 1808, when he removed to New York State, but in 1817 resumed his trade as tanner at the old location, using a steam-engine at the work purchased of William Parrish, a manufacturer of Philadelphia, the first, it is said, ever set up in Delaware County. The good people of that day shook their head doubtingly at the ultimate success of his "new-fangled notions." Here he continued until 1848, at which time, being nearly eighty years of age, he ceased to take an active part in business. He could distinctly remember hearing the cannon which were fired in Philadelphia in commemoration of the adoption of the Declaration of Independence, and was of sufficient age to vote for Washington at his second election, and excepting the first term of Monroe, had voted at every Presidential election, casting his ballot for the last time for Gen. Grant, in November, 1868.[4]

[1] Smith's "History of Delaware County," p. 314.

[2] *Penna. Mag. of Hist.*, vol. vi. p. 38.

[3] Genealogy of the Dutton Family, by Gilbert Cope, p. 51.

[4] Ib., pp. 57, 58.

"MARDON."

RESIDENCE OF DR. ELLWOOD WILSON,

ASTON TOWNSHIP, DELAWARE CO., PA.

On Feb. 2, 1869, when Thomas Dutton completed his century of life, his family connection and friends, amounting to nearly one thousand persons, assembled at his house in Aston, on which occasion interesting ceremonies appropriate to the unusual event were had. The venerable man lived until the following autumn, and only three instances are recorded in Delaware County of persons who lived to a more advanced age than that reached by Thomas Dutton.

In 1850, Nathan P. Dutton, his mother, Rachel (Pennell) Dutton, and Richard P. Slawter died in Aston, the cause of their death being exceedingly remarkable. On Saturday afternoon, August 8th of that year, a public sale of household goods was being held in a house near Village Green, when a storm accompanied by lightning occurred. The house where the vendue was in progress was struck, the fluid entering the peak of the roof, passing down between the weather-boarding and plastering until it reached the first story, "when it divided, one portion passing in at a hook driven in the wall, from which a looking-glass was suspended, and striking Nathan P. Dutton, who was standing under the glass, upon the top of the head, leaving but a slight mark. The fluid passed to his left arm above the elbow, thence down his body, burning the skin in its passage. He lived about five minutes, and was sensible of his approaching dissolution. The fluid passed from him to John McClay, who was standing near, struck him in the back, and ran down both his legs, burning the skin and clothes from his body, tearing his shoes to fragments, and leaving a small hole in the toe of one of them, as if perforated by a bullet. The other branch of the fluid struck Richard P. Slawter, who was standing outside of the house, and felled him to the ground. He was taken up, but expired in about fifteen minutes. Rachel Dutton, the mother of Nathan, was in an adjoining room, and, on being told of the fate of her son, she came out and immediately commenced to render every assistance in her power to restore him to animation. After laboring with great anxiety for nearly half an hour she gradually fainted away, and, continuing to lose respiration, she expired in about three-quarters of an hour after the death of her son."[1]

The foregoing is not the only freak of lightning worthy of record as having happened in Aston. On Monday evening, June 19, 1848, during a heavy storm, the dwelling of John Hall, in that township, was struck by lightning, and a lady sitting in the house was so severely stunned that she was unconscious for several hours.

As late as 1770, Dr. Smith tells us, a family of Indians had a wigwam on the Aston side of Chester Creek, on or in the vicinity of the present farm of George Drayton, but they did not remain there constantly. Their names were Andrew, Isaac, his son, and two women, sisters, Nanny and Betty, one of whom was the wife of Andrew. The latter died about the year 1780, and was buried in the graveyard of Middletown Friends' meeting-house.[2]

On the evening of Sept. 11, 1777, a number of the stragglers from the defeated American army, hungry, demoralized, and exhausted in their flight from the field at Brandywine, collected in the neighborhood of Logtown, where they passed the night, sleeping in the outbuildings and open fields. The next morning most of them rejoined their commands.

Several acres of land lying in the sharp angle formed by the union of the Marcus Hook and Concord roads at Village Green early in this century were the property of John Hoskins, and there occurred in the olden times an accident which is still recalled to the minds of many of the aged residents of the county. On Jan. 5, 1819, a six-year-old son of John and Mary Hoskins, in the absence of his parents, caught up an old firelock standing in the room back of a door, which had been charged about the preceding Christmas, and which the owner had several times attempted to discharge without success. The child pointed the gun at his sister, four years older than himself, saying, "I'm going to shoot," pulling the trigger as he spoke. The gun, unfortunately, was discharged, and the shot lodged in the bowels of the girl, causing instant death.

In February, 1836, a strike occurred at Crozer's West Branch Mills, occasioned by the discharge of William Shaw, one of the hands, and in May of the same year the operatives employed in the cotton-factories along Chester Creek struck for higher wages. In April, 1842, wages having been reduced, a general strike followed. Meetings were held, and on May 16, 1842, eight of the operatives were arrested on a charge of inciting the others to riot. On May 24th the trial began, and continued one week. It was alleged that the strikers caused Burt & Kerlin's mill to stop work by shutting down the head-gate, and one Broadbent, an operator who would not join the strikers, was overtaken going to work and kicked, cuffed, dragged to creek, and ducked. It was alleged that a party, consisting of two or three hundred men, gathered at Rockdale, when a committee was appointed to go to John Garsed and John D. Pierce, at Pennsgrove Mills, and compel the hands to cease work there, and that a procession of about fifty men, of Rockdale, armed with clubs, canes, and a few with pistols, went to Kelly's factory, in Upper Darby, to compel the operatives there to join in the strike. Mark Wild, Hiram McConnell, and Maj. Rowe were convicted of conspiracy. Wild and Rowe were fined twenty dollars each. McConnell was ordered to pay thirty-five dollars fine. The jury acquitted all the eight men indicted for riot, but ordered McConnell to pay the costs of prosecution.

[1] *Delaware County Republican*, Aug. 9, 1850.

[2] Smith's "History of Delaware County," p. 400.

A fatal accident occurred at Rockdale on Saturday, Dec. 17, 1859. A violent storm rendered the night unusually dark. Maris Waddle, of Middletown, was driving down the steep hill at James Brown's (now Atwood B. Hoskins') store, when his horses took fright, backed the wagon over the side of the road at that point, and the vehicle, in falling a distance of ten feet to the wall below, turned, crushing the driver beneath it. When the wagon was removed Waddle's lifeless body was found lying under the broken vehicle.

The original township of Aston, which at the upper end conformed to the straight east and west line dividing that township, Concord, and Middletown from Thornbury, and Edgmont remained undisturbed until 1842, when, on July 20th of that year, the Assembly enacted a law changing the line of Aston, so that that part of the old township lying above Stony Bank School-house—a direct line drawn thence eastward from Concord township-line to Chester Creek—was annexed to Thornbury township.[1] Again, in 1870, an effort was made by the citizens of the upper end of Aston to divide the present township, the difficulty growing out of the alleged disproportion of the number of schools and the unequal division of the taxes for road purposes. A petition was presented to the court, but at the election held, under order of court, October 18th of that year, the project was defeated at the polls.

Peters' Grist- and Saw-Mills.—On Green Creek, a feeder of the West Branch of Chester Creek, near Concord township-line, the Peters' grist- and saw-mills are located. The date when the tract on which the mills are erected was first taken up does not appear of record, but on June 10, 1703, one hundred acres were resurveyed to Isaac Taylor, to whom a patent for this land was issued Jan. 12, 1704. It subsequently became the property of William Peters, who, in 1750, erected the brick dwelling-house now standing, the date-stone in its walls bearing his initials, "W. P," and the numerals of the year just stated.

Previous to 1790 a stone fulling-mill had been built, and between that date and 1799 a saw-mill had also been erected, for the assessment-roll of Aston township, in the latter year, shows that at that time a fulling-mill and a saw-mill were then on the estate. This saw-mill, in several ancient documents, is called "a slitting-mill," it being employed in slitting logs to be used in building ships. In 1826 the fulling-mill was in disuse and a grist-mill and saw-mill were in operation; in the former from six to ten thousand bushels of grain was ground, and in the latter about fifty thousand feet of lumber sawed per annum. On June 4, 1842, Samuel F. Peters, a grandson of William Peters, purchased the property, retaining title thereto until Feb. 8, 1872, when Samuel F. Peters sold it to Charles J. Johnson, who is now operating the mills as the "Forest Queen Mills."

Tyson (now Llewellyn) Mills.—Previous to the Revolution, Robert Hall and Abraham Sharpless owned and operated a grist-mill on the West Branch of Chester Creek. The traces of the old race which fed those works and the remains of the ancient dam can be discerned to this day. The old race on the other side of the creek from the present mills evidently was in use for a mill, probably that of 1772, of which mention is made in the road-docket of a road as being laid out at that time from Daniel Sharpless' smithshop (Logtown) to Hall & Sharpless' mill. Hall subsequently acquired title to the entire property, and on April 5, 1798, he sold thirty-four acres, on which was then erected a stone house, a grist- and saw-mill, to Thomas Jones, and became a store-keeper in Aston, while Jones operated the mill, certainly unsuccessfully, for he became insolvent, and on July 20, 1800, John Odenheimer, sheriff of the county, conveyed twenty-eight and three-quarter acres of land, with the buildings, to Capt. John Richards. The latter retained title to the estate two years, when on Oct. 23, 1802, he sold the premises to James Tyson. The purchaser, then a young man of thirty-three, continued to operate the mills (having, in connection with the grist-, erected an oil-mill) for more than half a century until his death, March 15, 1858, aged eighty-six years. During the flood of 1843 much property was destroyed at these mills, the race and dam being almost obliterated. On March 25, 1864, Elwood Tyson, executor of his father's estate, sold the premises, excepting three-quarters of an acre, to John B. and Samuel Rhodes, who changed the old mill into a cotton- and woolen-factory, and in 1868 erected the present main building, a structure one hundred and ten by fifty-seven feet, two stories in height. In 1872 an addition of one hundred and thirty-five feet was made to the mill, the whole, including the building put up in 1868, being enlarged by the erection of a third story, and in 1879 another addition of one hundred and twelve feet and three stories was built, making the whole length of the main mill three hundred and fifty-five feet, in which are nearly four hundred looms. The industry, as it developed, necessarily built up a village, which now contains about one hundred tenement houses. For the convenience of the operatives a store was established at Llewellyn in the summer of 1877, and in 1880 it was made a postal station, John B. Rhodes being appointed postmaster. In addition to these mills the firm are now running the Knowlton Mills under a lease, and have purchased the West Branch Mills, which they are also operating.

John B. Rhodes, the senior member of the firm, is the grandson of John Rhodes, who emigrated from Yorkshire, England, in 1827, and settled in Aston township, where his death by drowning—together with that of two daughters—occurred during the great freshet

[1] Bliss' "Delaware County Digest," p. 98.

John B. Rhoades

A [illegible] accident occurred [illegible] on Saturday, Dec. [illegible] [illegible] unt[illegible] [illegible] was dri[illegible] the [illegible] hill at [illegible] At[illegible] [illegible] fri[illegible] the [illegible] side of the road at th[illegible] and the vehicle [illegible] a distance of te[illegible] the wall [illegible] the driver be[illegible]. When the wagon was removed [illegible] dl[illegible] lying under the broken ve[illegible].

The original [illegible] of Aston, which at the upper e[illegible] line d[illegible] Concord, and Middletown f[illegible] remained undisturbed u[illegible] of that year the As[illegible] [illegible] the line of Aston, so [illegible] part of the old township lying above [illegible] [illegible] line drawn thence [illegible] [illegible] township-line to Chester Creek— [illegible] township. Again, in [illegible], an effort was made by the citizens of the upper end of Aston to divide the present township, the [illegible] [illegible] out of the [illegible] disproportion of [illegible] and the unequal division of [illegible] for road purposes. A petition was presented [illegible] at the election held [illegible] of that year, the project was defeated [illegible].

Peters' Grist- and Saw-Mills.—On Green Creek, [illegible] of the West Branch of Chester Creek, [illegible] the Peters' grist- and saw-mills are located. The date when the tract on which the mills are erected was first taken up does not appear of record, but on June 10, 1703, one hundred acres were [illegible] to Isaac Taylor, to whom a patent for this land was issued Jan. 12, 1764. It subsequently became the property of William Peters, who, in 17[illegible], erected the [illegible] dwelling-house now standing, [illegible] bearing his [illegible] and the [illegible] of the year just stated.

Previous to 17[illegible] [illegible] had been built, and [illegible] had also been erected [illegible] of Aston township, [illegible] at that time a full[illegible]

[illegible]

Charles [illegible], who is now operating the mills as the "[illegible] Mills."

Tyson and Llewellyn Mills.—Previous to the Revolution, Robert Hall and Abraham Sharpless owned and operated a grist-mill on the West Branch of Chester Creek. The traces of the old race which fed those works and the remains of the ancient dam can be discerned to this day. The old race on the other side of the creek from the present mills evidently was in use for a mill, probably that of 1772, of which mention is made in the road-dockets of a road as being laid out at that time from Daniel Sharpless' smithshop (Logtown) to Hall & Sharpless' mill. Hall subsequently acquired title to the entire property, and on April [illegible], 17[illegible], he sold thirty-four acres, on which was then erected a stone-house, a grist- and saw-mill, to Thomas Jones, and [illegible] store-keeper in Aston, while Jones operated the mill, certainly unsuccessfully, for he became insolvent, and on July [illegible], 18[illegible], John [illegible], sheriff of the county, conveyed twenty-eight and three-quarter acres of land, with the buildings, to Capt. John Richards. The latter retained title to the estate two years, when on [illegible], 18[illegible], he sold the premises to James Tyson. The purchaser, then a young man of thirty-three, continued to operate the mills (having, in connection with [illegible], erected an oil-mill) for more than half a century until his death, March 16, 18[illegible], aged [illegible] years. During the flood of 1843 much property was destroyed at these mills, the race and dam being almost obliterated. On March [illegible], 18[illegible], [illegible] Tyson, executor of his father's estate, sold the premises, excepting three-quarters of an acre, to John B. and Samuel Rhodes, who changed the old mill into a cotton- and woolen-factory, and in 18[illegible] erected the present main building, a structure one hundred and ten by fifty-seven feet, [illegible] in height. In 18[illegible] an addition of [illegible] was made to the mill, the [illegible] [illegible]

[illegible]

Eng. by A.H.Ritchie

John B Rhodes

RESIDENCE OF JOHN B. RHODES,
ASTON TOWNSHIP, DELAWARE CO., PA.

of August, 1843. His son, William, followed him to America the year after, and also located in Aston township, where he was employed in a factory devoted to the manufacture of cotton fabrics. He married, prior to his emigration, Hannah Kay, and had children,—John B., William, Samuel, Thomas (deceased), Ann, and Susanna,—all of whom were born in the United States. John B., the eldest, whose birth occurred Jan. 27, 1829, in Aston township, at the early age of six years entered a cotton-factory with a view to becoming proficient in that branch of industry. He was employed in the different departments of a weaving-mill, and ultimately acquired a practical knowledge of all branches of the business. His education was meanwhile gained at the sessions of a night-school (the public-school system not yet being introduced in this part of the State), and confined principally to the rudiments, habits of thought and observation having been of great service to him during his youth as in later life. He remained an employé of the factory until his majority was attained, and was then married by Bishop Alfred Lee, of Delaware, to Annie L., daughter of William Warren, of Middletown township, who was of English parentage. Their children are William K. (deceased), Charles B., Alfred L., John, Jr., Richard Somers, Ann L., and Jennie C. (deceased). On his marriage, Mr. Rhodes embarked in the business of store-keeping at Crozerville, Delaware Co., where he remained prosecuting a successful trade until 1864. He then purchased from Elwood Tyson, Esq., what is known as the Aston Mills property, and has since been engaged in the manufacture of doeskins, jeans, and dress-goods. His marked success prompted him, in 1866, to rent the Knowlton Mills, at Knowlton, in Middletown township, which are still controlled by him. To this already extensive manufacturing venture was added, in 1882, the purchase of the West Branch Mills, in Aston township, which are running to their full capacity. In the management of these extensive interests his energy and business tact have been exceptional, contributing essentially to the success of every enterprise in which he has engaged. From humble beginnings Mr. Rhodes has risen by inherent force and strong purpose to be an influential factor in the industries of the county. He is in politics a Democrat. He was a delegate to the St. Louis Convention which in 1876 nominated Tilden and Hendricks for the first offices in the gift of the people. He is a prominent Odd-Fellow, member of Benevolent Lodge, No. 40, of Aston, and has represented it in the Grand Councils for a number of years, his father having been in 1831 one of its charter members and organizers. He is a regular attendant upon the services of the Methodist Episcopal Church, though educated in the tenets of the Protestant Episcopal faith.

The Old Forge at Rockdale.—The first mention of a forge at this place, so far as we have yet ascertained, occurs in a deed dated Nov. 16, 1785, whereby Abraham Pennell conveyed to his brother, Dell Pennell, a tract of ground "whereon is erected an iron forge." That this forge was built subsequent to 1750 is evident from the return of John Owens, sheriff of Chester County, who, on the 24th of June in that year, made report to the Governor in relation to the iron-works in this county. In 1780 the forge was assessed to Dell Pennell, and doubtless operated by him until 1802, when it was conducted by William Speer and Joseph Churchman. The land whereon it stood was part of a large tract to which the father of Abraham and Dell Pennell for many years had title. The deed to Dell Pennell conveyed to him two hundred acres in Middletown and one hundred acres in Aston townships, "whereon is erected an iron forge, with the full and free liberty and privilege of raising the water of the forge dam within four inches of the top of the figures 1785, and an auger hole in a rock on the northwest side of the dam." Dell Pennell, on May 21, 1802, conveyed to Nathan Sharpless the right to use the waters of Chester Creek for the use of Sharpless' "grist-mill dam, where it now stands, and has long stood across the creek above our Forge dam." On the same day Nathan Sharpless and Rachel, his wife, granted to Dell Pennell the "right of an abutment on our land where the old forge dam now stands and has long stood across Chester Creek, and to repair and rebuild from time to time, and at all times, said dam so as to raise the water therein as high as is expressed in the deed from Abraham Pennell and Hannah, his wife, to the said Dell Pennell," which refers to the figures 1785 and the auger-hole in the rock. The day after these grants were made, May 22, 1802, Dell Pennell sold to George Chandler the iron-works and eight acres of land. The latter seems not to have operated the forge, but Abraham Sharpless and Francis Wisley conducted the business there, at least they did in 1807, and on July 21, 1808, when Chandler sold to Thomas Odiorne, a merchant of Malden, Middlesex Co., Mass.,—a relative of the Wilcox family,—that certain messuage, iron-works, etc., and eight acres of ground. In 1809 the nail-mill was built. After the sale to Thomas Odiorne, Capt. Henry Moore, of Portsmouth, N. H., took charge of the works, and continued there until after the death of Thomas Odiorne, the elder, and in the settlement of the estate Thomas Odiorne, the younger, on Aug. 28, 1815, conveyed his interest in the property to George Odiorne, of Boston, for five thousand six hundred dollars, and the same day George Odiorne sold to his brother-in-law, Capt. Henry Moore,—the latter had married Ann Odiorne,—in consideration of fifteen thousand dollars, all his right in the real estate, consisting of eight acres fifteen perches, "with the messuages, iron- and nail-works, and other buildings thereon erected," and the right of water and to build dams, together with his interest in twenty and three-fourth acres of land. To these mills Capt. Moore gave the name "Old Sable Works." In 1830, when William McCracken began work there, Capt. Moore's establishments consisted of a nail-slitting and rolling-mill, as also a grist- and cotton-mill. The nail-mill was located on the island where the unoccupied stone mill now stands, and was in Middletown. The grist-mill was in Aston, adjoining the rolling- and slitting-mill, and had been built by Capt. Moore about 1827. The iron ore and coal used in smelting was hauled to the mills from Chester and Marcus Hook, to which places those articles were brought in shallops. Richard S. Smith, of Philadelphia, who acted as Moore's agent for the sale of nails manufactured by him, had advanced large sums of money to Moore, and on May 23, 1832, the latter conveyed the estate to Smith to secure him for the advances, with the understanding that the property would be reconveyed on payment of the sums due. In 1833, Moore failed, and the estate passed absolutely to Smith. Capt. Moore, previous to 1826, had built on the site of the forge a stone cotton-mill, four stories and an attic in height. —— Lewis and John S. Phillips operated the cotton-weaving factory from the time it was erected until some years after the property was purchased by Smith. They gave place to Henry Burt and —— Kerlin, who operated it until the spring of 1843, when they became embarrassed and made an assignment. The grist-mill was in that year occupied by Henry Gorman. The mills lay idle nearly a year, when they were rented to Barnard McCready, who purchased them in 1845, and the following year he was an exhibitor at the National Fair, at Washington, and received special mention for the printed cotton goods he made. He erected a spinning-mill adjoining the old factory (now changed into dwelling-houses), and continued to conduct the business until his death, when he was succeeded by his son, Thomas, and his son-in-law, Robert Ewing. It was subsequently leased for ten years to John G. Steen & Samuel Riddle, and at the expiration of that term was purchased by Alexander Balfour, and operated by him for a short period, when it was sold to Samuel Riddle. The cotton-mill which stood on the site of the old forge was entirely consumed by fire on May 20, 1873. It was then operated by Whittaker & Lewis in the manufacture of cotton yarn.

The old forge-dam stood about twenty feet above the bridge at Glen Riddle, and was removed by Samuel Riddle in 1875. Two thousand feet above the forge-dam was that of the Sharpless Mill. The present dam at Rockdale was built in 1845.

The other works of Barnard McCready were located in Middletown, and their story will be told in the history of that township.

Thatcher's Tilt-Mill.—Previous to 1811 there was a tilt-mill situated on Chester Creek above Grubb's Bridge, and near Wawa Station, the junction of the West Chester and Philadelphia Railroad and the Baltimore Central Railroad, which was owned and operated by Joseph Thatcher. The land whereon it was located had been selected, doubtless, with an eye to its admirable water-power by Caleb Pusey, the noted miller of early colonial days. In 1812, Enos Thatcher had control of the works, and in 1815 the firm became Thomas & Enos Thatcher. The stimulating effect of the war with England caused an extension of the business, but with the return of peace it, as with all manufacturing industries, became precarious, hence it is with no astonishment we find it recorded in 1826 that the "tilt- and blade-mill," owned and occupied by Thomas Thatcher, had not been "much used in times past." Nevertheless, the last named, through good and bad times, retained the ownership of the mill until his death, in 1840. Indeed, at that time there was a stone tilt-mill, forty by forty-one feet, with four fires, two of which were blown by water-power, a new wheel having been built for that purpose, to which a lathe could be attached, as well as grindstones and polishing-wheels. Near by the mill was also a coachmaker's shop, twenty-five by thirty-seven feet, and two stories in height. In 1841, Joseph and Isaac Thatcher were engaged in making at that mill "scycloidal" self-sharpening plows. In the flood of 1843 this tilt-mill, belonging to the heirs of Thomas Thatcher, was swept away by the water, nothing being found after the rushing current had subsided but the tilt-hammer and the grindstone. In 1852, John W. Thatcher carried on blacksmithing and coach-building near by for several years. The property is still in the ownership of the family, John Thatcher being the present proprietor.

Lenni Mills.—Thomas Griffith, on Jan. 2, 1797, conveyed to John Lungren, paper manufacturer of Upper Providence, a tract of land containing one hundred and sixty-seven acres, on which was "a messuage and mill-seat." This land was described as situated in Aston, along Chester Creek, adjoining lands of John Rattew, Levi Mattson, and other lands of Thomas Griffith. It was stipulated in the deed that Lungren was to have the right to "use the water of a small run, which at present empties itself into the race belonging to the saw-mill formerly existing upon the premises," which right was especially granted for "the mill in contemplation to be shortly erected by the said John Lungren for the manufacture of paper upon a part of the premises hereby intended to be granted." The same day, Jan. 2, 1797, Jonathan Pennell, blacksmith, conveyed to John Lungren "all rights to adjoin or abut the dam which will belong to the mill called a Paper-Mill, intended shortly to be built by the said John Lungren." The lands of Jonathan Pennell were on the opposite or east side of Chester Creek, in Middletown township. The paper-mill was erected in 1798, and was assessed in Aston township in 1799. The dam built at the time the mill was put up had become so decayed in 1815 that a new dam was constructed to take the place of the first. John Lungren continued to operate this mill until his death, about 1816, when the property descended to his sons, Charles and William Lungren. The latter rented the premises for several years, and in 1825 sold the estate to Peter Hill, who built a cotton-mill thereon thirty-five by fifty-five feet, three stories in height, and the same year conveyed the estate to William Martin and Joseph W. Smith. It was the new proprietor who gave to the locality the name it now bears,—Lenni,—for William Martin, who operated the factory, called it Lenni Mills. At that time the paper-mill—two vats—was operated by John B. Duckett, who manufactured weekly sixty reams of quarto-post paper and thirty-three reams of printing-paper. Martin indorsed heavily for a friend. The latter carried Martin with him in his bankruptcy, and on Aug. 25, 1827, the premises were sold by the sheriff, Mrs. Ann Sellers, the mother-in-law of Peter Hill, becoming the purchaser, as trustee of Hannah S. Hill, her daughter. David Lamotte & Sons thereupon rented the mill. It appears that a new factory was erected on the property, for on Dec. 30, 1845, a stone mill and drying-house at Lenni took fire, and was entirely consumed. The mill had been used as a store-house and machine-shop, and at the time of its destruction did not contain a large stock of goods. The following year, May, 1846, Lamotte exhibited "Ashland tickings," made by him at the Lenni Mills, at the National Fair, Washington, D. C., which article received special mention. In 1850, Peter Hill died, and Lamotte removed from Lenni to Wilmington, Del., where he died, Sept. 20, 1877, aged ninety-six years. The mills were then rented to Gen. Robert Patterson, and the stone mansion-house erected by John Lungren was occupied by Robert L. Martin, Patterson's agent. In 1873, Joseph Kenworthy became the superintendent of the Lenni Mills, and continued there until 1882, when they were closed. They are now idle. The road leading from Lenni Mills to Lenni is still called the Lungren road.

Crozerville Mills.—The land on which the Crozerville mill now stands was owned in 1810 by John Rattew, having been in the possession of his ancestors for three generations. On December 24th of that year he entered into an article of agreement with Isaac Bottomley, a clothier of Concord, granting on certain conditions ten acres of land on Chester Creek, "touching both branches so as to take in a mill-seat." On this tract Isaac Bottomley erected a woolen-mill, and on July 1, 1811, John and Thomas Bottomley, also clothiers of Concord, purchased from Isaac Bottomley an interest in the business and the agreement with Rattew. On Jan. 25, 1812, John Rattew conveyed the title of the property to Isaac, John, and Thomas Bottomley. During the second war with England the factory made considerable money for its owners, but with the return of peace the shrinkage in values embarrassed the Bottomley Brothers, and the difficulties were increased by the death of John and Thomas at different times. By various proceedings in court the title to the property was finally vested in the survivor, Isaac Bottomley. Innumerable troubles crossed his path until he could stem the tide no longer, and on April 2, 1824, Sheriff Joseph Weaver, Jr., sold the personal property in the factory. The machines thus disposed of consisted of "one carding machine, one spinning Billy of forty spindles, two spinning Jennys, one of eighty and the other of forty spindles, one Picker, three weaving Looms, with reeds and gears, and other articles not enumerated." This factory was noted in its days, hence we publish the list of machinery contained therein that it may be seen how vast is the change sixty years has wrought in manufacturing in our county. On the 2d of April, 1826, Isaac Bottomley sold the real estate to John B. Duckett, which sale included the mill and fourteen acres of land. Duckett at the time he purchased the property was operating a small paper-mill on the Lenni estate (already mentioned), then owned by William Martin and Joseph W. Smith. Shortly after the purchase Duckett built a paper-mill, thirty by eighty-six feet, three stories in height, on this site, taking the power to drive the machinery from the West Branch. In 1837, he having failed, the mill property was transferred to the Bank of Delaware County, at which time there was on the estate, besides the mill, a mansion-house, nine tenements, and a store building. In 1838 that institution conveyed the property to John P. Crozer, who in the following year erected the present stone mill, fifty-three by one hundred and fifty-six feet, and three stories in height. Mr. Crozer operated this mill until his death, in 1866, when it was conducted by Samuel A. Crozer for one year, at the expiration of which time he associated Samuel C. Lewis in the business under the firm-name of Crozer & Lewis. In 1875, Mr. Lewis withdrew from the firm, and Crozer conducted it till 1881, when he rented the mill to his son-in-law, the present proprietor, William H. H. Robinson. The difference of the two periods in the development of our manufacturing interest is noticeable when we contrast the number of spindles used by Isaac Bottomley, one hundred and sixty, and find that the present mill to-day requires five thousand in the manufacture of cotton yarns exclusively.

West Branch Cotton Mills.—Between 1790 and 1795, Aaron Mattson built a stone mill, on the west branch of Chester Creek, which he operated as a paper-mill until 1824, when, becoming involved, the premises were taken in execution, and on Dec. 6, 1824, was sold by the sheriff to John P. Crozer. The latter, in speaking of this estate, says, "I bought the little mill-seat with an old rickety building and over one hundred and eighty acres of land, for seven thousand three hundred and thirty dollars. My kind brother, J. Lewis, again aided me in raising the money. I mortgaged to Thomas Woodward for four thousand dollars and borrowed the balance as best I could, with J. Lewis' security. This was in the autumn of 1824, and I was to have possession in the spring of 1825, at which time I removed."[1] Mr. Crozer changed the paper-mill into a cotton-factory, and in 1826 had there ten carding engines of twenty-four inches, thirteen hundred and thirty-eight spindles, on which he spun eleven hundred pounds of cotton-yarn per week. At that time there were dwelling houses on the estate for nine families. In the noted flood of 1843 the eastern end of the factory was carried away, with the size-house, water-wheel, many looms, and the dry-house, containing yarns and goods valued at several thousand dollars. In 1846, John P. Crozer exhibited ticking at the National Fair, Washington, and the goods received special mention. At West Branch, Mr. Crozer continued to reside until May, 1847, when, having completed his dwelling at Upland, he removed thither. The West Branch Mill, however, remained in the ownership of the Crozer family until 1882, when it was sold to John B. Rhodes, who now owns and operates it.

Pennellton (Bridgewater) Mills.—In 1826 the site of these mills was known only as a mill-seat, and it was not until 1845 that Isaac Morgan built a stone cotton-factory forty by forty-five feet, and four stories in height, to which he gave the name "Pennellton," in honor of Hannah Pennell, his wife. The first occupant of the Pennellton Mill was Edward Leigh, who carried on cotton-spinning and weaving therein from 1846 to 1850, when he was succeeded in the same business by Charles and Joseph Kenworthy, from 1851 to 1855. They in turn gave place to —— Lewis, and he to John Campbell, of Philadelphia. The latter relinquished the mill to Patrick Kelley, who manufactured a grade of goods known as "Powhattan," which became noted in the market, and in a few years made him comparatively wealthy; so much so that, desiring to retire in December, 1863, he sold his entire interest in the business and machinery to Hugh Shaw and David Reese Esrey, who remained at the Pennellton Mills until the summer of 1866, when, having built Powhattan Mill, No. 1, in North Chester, the old factory on Chester Creek was purchased from Isaac Morgan by Joseph Willcox & Co., who changed it to a paper-mill, and gave it the present name, "Bridgewater." In January, 1872, Samuel Haigh & Co., of Philadelphia, purchased the estate and changed it to a woolen-factory, and have operated it from that date. The mill contains five sets of sixty-inch cards, four sell-factory mules, three thousand one hundred and nine spindles, and other necessary machinery. The original mill has been enlarged by an addition to the western end. The mills are now known as the Gladstone Mills, but the locality is still called Bridgewater.

Schools.—The history of schools in Aston is interesting, and can be traced in our annals certainly to the year 1777, for Thomas Dutton used to relate that the day of the battle of Brandywine—he was then nine years of age—the pupils had assembled at the school as usual, but when the booming of the cannon at Chad's Ford, but a few miles distant, was heard, the aged master, James Rigby, dismissed the scholars, saying, "Go home, children; I can't keep school to-day." After the English troops had withdrawn from the neighborhood of Village Green, doubtless the school resumed its sessions; but of that fact we have no positive evidence. The presumption is, however, that at the beginning of this century no building especially designed for school purposes had been erected in that township. This fact seems to be established from the deed dated May 11, 1802, by which Samuel Hewes, of Aston, conveyed to William Pennell and Thomas Dutton, of the same township, "for the use of a school, a house thereon to be built," a lot of land comprising an acre, which was part of a tract of fifty-nine acres which Thomas Goodwin had sold, Nov. 1, 1799, to Hewes. This lot was to be held "in trust and for the use of a school, a house to be built thereon for the use, benefit, and behoof of the subscribers towards building said house." The names of such subscribers were annexed in a schedule to the original deed,—that part of it is not on record in the recorder's office,—which trust was to continue for the heirs and assigns of the parties therein named, and in case it should at any time be deemed proper to sell the lot and school-house, it was provided that the trustees for the time being could convey a fee-simple title to the purchaser, after such sale had been authorized by the majority vote of the subscriber, the purchase money to be divided in proportion to the amount contributed by each subscriber. The building thus erected was known as the octagon school-house, at Village Green, and therein, about 1820, James McMullen was the pedagogue. In 1836, after the Public School Act had gone into effect and the board of directors for Aston township was organized, the old school-house passed into the possession of the township, and on Sept. 30, 1836, a school was opened there, Nicholas F. Walter being employed as teacher in the lower room at a salary of twenty-five dollars per month, and Mrs. Moore was appointed teacher in the upper room.

At first the school law was not looked upon with favor by the residents of Aston, for at the election held at the Seven Stars in 1834, at which the question was submitted of raising a school fund, the vote stood forty-one against twelve in the affirmative. At a meeting of the school board, held on May 6, 1836, after the act of that year had become a law, Richard S. Smith, who had been appointed a delegate to the convention, held at Chester, on the 2d of the same month, reported that a tax of seven thousand five hundred dollars had been levied in the county by the school directors, and a meeting of the people was ordered to be held in the several townships on the 17th of May,

[1] Biographical Sketch of John P. Crozer, written by himself, p. 66.

"WAWA."

to make such township appropriations as would secure the State and county appropriation for school purposes It was decided at this meeting of the board to add a sum of two-thirds of a county rate, which amounted to five hundred dollars, and on May 17th the question as to the sum was submitted to a popular vote, which resulted in the measure being adopted, fifty-eight votes for to nine against the measure

On June 10, 1836, a proposition was made to secure the building known as Martin's school-house, and the owners agreed to rent it at two dollars per month The directors, on June 16th, consented to accept the offer, on condition that a list of the contributors should be furnished the board, so that the proportional share of the rent could be paid to each of the contributors It was also determined that an effort should be made to obtain possession of the school-house then being erected by John P Crozer at West Branch, as well as the house expected to be built at Rockdale, for the school term The proposition looking to the occupancy of the Stony Bank school-house was accepted, and on Sept 3, 1836, it was ordered by the board that John Sharpless should be asked to deliver the key of that building This school-house was built on a lot containing two acres and four-tenths of a perch of land, which Thomas Pennell, on March 9, 1796, had conveyed for nine hundred and ninety-nine years, to Daniel Sharpless, of Middletown, Abraham Sharpless, Emmor Williamson, and Jacob Pyle, of Aston, on the payment of twenty pounds Pennsylvania money, and a "yearly rent of one American cent, if demanded," the grantees promising to erect "a good & sufficient stone school-house of the dimensions and form as shall be agreed on by such persons as shall subscribe for that purpose" It was opened for tuition by the directors of the public school on Oct 31, 1836, for a period of six months Previous thereto the directors finding the building was much out of repair, twenty dollars was appropriated to put it in condition for public use The school board also by resolution agreed to accept the children of contributors of the old Village Green and Stony Bank schools, on the payment of two hundred and twenty-five dollars per quarter to the board of directors for the township

Martin's school-house was subsequently known as the Logtown school, and the latter name in 1880 was changed to Chester Heights school, its present title. A school being required at Rockdale, the board directed that a suitable building should be obtained there for that purpose, if possible, and Richard S Smith, a director, offered to give the use of a house there rent free, "provided it is left in as good condition as the Board finds it" This offer was accepted, and the dwelling standing back of the present "Mountain House" became the first public school at that point, L White Williams being the first teacher This building had been used as a school during Henry Moore's ownership of the land In 1853 the Aston public school, the present building, was erected at Rockdale, in 1880 the school house at Llewellyn was built Messrs Haigh & Co, in the fall of the year 1875, offered to give an acre of ground at Bridgewater as the site for a school-house, but for some reason these gentlemen and the directors did not come to a definite understanding until June, 1879, when the offer was accepted, and a brick building erected on the ground thus donated

The following is a list of the school directors of Aston township

1840, Samuel A Barton, John Garsed, 1842, Mark Pennell, Stephen Hall, 1843, Mahlon Monsell, George Thompson, 1844, James McMullen, Stephen Hall, 1845, John W Thatcher, Thomas Martin, 1846, George Thompson, Edwin Hannum, 1847, Thomas Williamson, Andrew W Mathues, 1848, Thomas Martin, John Dutton 1849, Edward Hannum, James W McCracken, 1850, Samuel B Hall, Nicholas F Walter, 1851, Samuel R Hall, Thomas Martin, 1852, James McCracken, Edwin Hannum, 1853, Nicholas F Walter, William Hannum, 1854, George Thompson, James Bleyler, 1855, George Thompson, Edwin Hannum, 1856, Elwood Tyson, William Burns, 1857, James W McCracken, Phineas Dickson, 1858, Andrew W Mathews, J Hervey Barton, 1859, John B Rhodes, Robert L Martin, 1860, George Yarnall, Robert L Martin, 1861, Edwin Hannum, James W McCracken, 1862 William Brown, James Bleyler, 1863, Charles Hart, William Brown, 1864, William McCracken, Benjamin Crowther, 1865, Edwin Hannum, Thomas Swayne, 1866, Thomas Pancoast, Elwood Tyson, 1867, Thomas Pancoast, Lewis Martin, 1868, William G Davidson, William F Mathews, 1869, C. C V Crawford, William Carson, 1870, Judge Tyson, John Neal, 1871, John B Rhodes, Samuel A Crozer, 1872, Charles W Mathues, James W McCracken, 1873, C C V Crawford, C R Hayburn, 1874, John D Kiser, Samuel K Crozer, 1875, S A Fields C W Mathues, 1876, C C V Crawford, Caleb R. Heyburn, 1877, Samuel A Field, James W McCracken, 1878, Samuel H Hall, John B Neal, 1879, S M Challenger, C R Heyburn, 1880, Elwood Tyson, Joseph N Scott, 1881, Samuel Rhodes, Samuel K Crozer, 1882, E P Hannum, Samuel Challenger, 1883, W. S S Gay, Robert Taylor, 1884, Caleb R Heyburn, James C McGraw

The private schools in Aston, other than the old-time contribution schools, have not been numerous, but their story, so far as I have yet learned, is full of interest During the second war with England, Joseph Neef, a Frenchman, who attempted to establish the system of study then employed at the noted Pestallozzi, in Switzerland, removed from Philadelphia to Village Green, where he remained for several years David Glascoe Farragut, who, almost half a century afterwards, became the great naval hero of the nineteenth century, while residing at Commodore Porter's home at Chester, became a pupil of Mr Neef The latter had as a tutor in his school Phiquepal D'Arusmont, a Frenchman, who subsequently became prominent because of his marriage to Fanny Wright, —the strong-minded lecturer of half a century ago,— who drew upon herself public denunciation simply because her views and opinions were noticeably in advance of the age in which she lived She was possessed of large means, and the marriage, on the part of D'Arusmont, was mercenary, and eventuated in a few years in a separation between the ill-mated couple Previous to 1820, Joseph Neef closed his school at Village Green and removed therefrom

About 1845, Rev Benjamin S Huntington, an Episcopal clergyman, established a seminary for young ladies at Aston Ridge, which soon acquired popularity, the scholars being drawn largely from the Southern States. The principal, however, was constantly enlarging the building until finally he became bankrupt.

An interesting incident occurred in June, 1851, when, in removing an old house adjoining the seminary building to make room for proposed improvements, a beam was found on which was distinctly marked the date, "February 26, 1704," and in the cellar wall was discovered a leaden medal of unknown date, but evidently of great age. This house, which was built of hewed logs of yellow poplar, was erected by Thomas Dutton (born in England in 1679) at the date mentioned, and was located on part of the original Dutton tract of five hundred and ninety acres. On Jan. 14, 1859, Benjamin S. Huntington sold the estate to William Moronoy, and the latter conveyed it, on May 4th of the same year, to "The Philadelphia Theological Seminary of St. Charles Borromeo," where, while the new seminary was building at Overbrooke, the educational work of this institution of learning was conducted, Rev. Jeremiah F. Shanahan, the present bishop of Harrisburg, occupying the presidential chair in the college while it remained in Aston. When the new building was completed in the summer of 1871, the estate near Village Green, comprising twenty-eight and a half acres, was offered for sale. On September 7th of that year the property was sold to "The Sisters of St. Francis" of Philadelphia. For a time the old seminary building was used for the novitiate of the community, but it soon became too small to meet the demands of the order, and by permission of Archbishop James F. Wood a new convent was erected, the corner-stone of which was laid May 29, 1873, Archbishop Wood officiating. On May 29, 1879, the corner-stone of the new chapel was laid, and on Oct. 4, 1881, the chapel of "Our Lady of Angels" was dedicated by the Very Rev. John White, of St. Peter's Church, Philadelphia, he being authorized thereto by Archbishop Wood. The convent is under the supervision of Mother Mary Agnes, general superior, and here those wishing to join the community are received and trained for their future calling to minister at the bedside of the sick in hospitals or in private houses, or teaching children in parochial schools. There are upwards of two hundred and fifty sisters in the community, all of whom come every year to this novitiate to make their annual retreat. The present beautiful edifice, "The Convent of Our Lady of the Angels," is a conspicuous object in the charming rural picture which strikes the eye as you approach it from any direction.

About 1857, J. Harvey Barton established a seminary at Aston Ridge in a large brick building still on the Rockdale road, near by the Baptist Church. It was an institute in which both sexes were received and educated, and deservedly ranked high, many of its pupils having risen in the battle of life to prominent positions. For several years Hon. James Barton, Jr., Stephen C. Hall, and other well-known citizens of the county were employed as instructors at the seminary. In 1866, J. Harvey Barton discontinued the school, since which time the building has been occupied as a dwelling.

Churches—Mount Hope Methodist Church.—This sanctuary is situated on the Concord road, just above Village Green, on the noted "Aston Ridge," and its story begins three-quarters of a century ago, in 1807, when the original building was erected on a lot of land given for that purpose by Aaron Mattson, a noted paper-manufacturer in the township in those early days, and within that quiet "God's Acre" the body of the generous donor, at an advanced age, was laid to rest many years ago. The deed from Mattson to Powell Clayton, Edward Carter, Daniel Carter, Robert Johnson, John Little, George Sneath, and Peter Longacre recites that the lot shall be held "forever in trust, that they shall erect and build . . . thereon a house or place of worship for the use of the members of the Methodist Episcopal Church in the United States of America, only those preachers appointed by the General Conference, and none others, to preach and expound God's holy word therein." The church was of stone, in size thirty by forty feet, and, as was the case with all the early churches, particularly those built by the Methodist society, was plainly finished and furnished, wanting in almost all the accessories of comfort now deemed so essential to a place of worship. For years the church was dependent on the services of the circuit preacher, and when his duties called him to other places the local minister led the congregation in religious exercises. During its early struggles Rev. James Caughey, a noted revivalist from England, visited the United States, and during his journeyings preached in the remote Mount Hope Church, and for miles around the people gathered there to hear his sermon. The result of his preaching was a noticeable increase in the membership of Mount Hope, and the building soon became too small to accommodate the congregation. In 1838 an addition of twenty feet was made to the edifice, the building entirely remodeled, and six acres of ground purchased, in addition to that already comprised in the churchyard. In May, 1847, Rev. John Mills, who was then the pastor in charge, died, and was buried in the graveyard at Corner Ketch. Mr. Mills was by birth an Englishman, and had served fifteen years as a soldier in the British army, but being converted to the gospel teachings, had devoted the remainder of his life to the ministry of the Methodist Church.

Sept. 3, 1860, Mount Hope Methodist Church was incorporated, and in 1877 the commodious parsonage was erected near the sanctuary, the sum expended being partly the purchase-money received from the sale of the old parsonage lot at Marcus Hook to the Wilmington Circuit by Lewis Massay, which is more fully alluded to in the account of St. George's Church, Lower Chichester.

In the churchyard at Mount Hope several generations of the old families of Aston are interred. Conspicuous among that number was George McCracken, who died only a few months before he had attained his hundredth year of life. George McCracken died on his estate on West Branch of Chester Creek in 1873. He was born in Ireland in 1773, and shortly after he came to this country (early in the century) settled in Aston, and continued to reside there until his death. Although his career was not marked with remarkable incidents outside of the usual happenings of rural life, he was a good citizen, who left an unblemished name to his numerous descendants. Four years before his death, on May 1, 1869, while a number of the family and friends had assembled at Mr. McCracken's house to attend a funeral there, the upper floor or the porch, on which about thirty persons were standing at the time, gave way, and fortunately, although several persons were hurt, no serious injury was sustained by any one. In 1851 the church was part of Mount Hope Station, and in 1852 it became Village Green Circuit; from that date the pastors have been as follows: 1851, Rev. John B. Maddox; 1852–53, Rev. Ignatius T. Cooper, D.D.; 1854–55, Henry G. King; 1856–57, Henry Sutton; 1858, Ignatius T. Cooper, D.D.; 1859–60, Henry H. Bodine; 1861–62, Rev. James Flannery; 1863–64, Rev. James L. Houston; 1865–66, Rev. Henry Mauger; 1867–68, Rev. William C. Johnson; 1869–71, Rev. John A. Watson; 1872–74, Rev. Edward Townsend; 1875–77, Rev. William McGee; 1878–80, Benjamin T. Spring; 1881–83, George T. Hurlock; 1884, William Rink. In March, 1878, Mount Hope Church was set off as a special station.

Crozerville Methodist Episcopal Church.—In the autumn of 1851 a number of the members of Mount Hope Circuit residing in the immediate neighborhood of Rockdale, believing that the cause of Methodism could be advanced by the erection of a church edifice at that place, gathered at the house of Rev. John B. Maddox, near Village Green, which meeting resulted in the organization of a board of trustees and the appointment of a building committee. The trustees were Norris L. Yarnall, Archibald McDowell, John Blackburn, Robert Moss, Robert McCartney, John Thompson, William McBride, Amos Cummings, and David Burnite, and the building committee, Dr. Barton, Rev. Henry G. King, and Archibal McDowell. The first meeting of the trustees was held in Parkmount school-house on Nov. 18, 1851, when, to aid the movement, John P. Crozer donated a lot of ground for the church building, and also subscribed generously to the building fund. In the spring of 1852, although the structure had not been erected, a petition was presented to the Philadelphia Conference urging that the Rockdale Church, as it was then known, should be separated from Mount Hope and constituted a regular station. The request was favorably considered and Rev. George W. McLaughlin appointed the first pastor. At that time services were held in the Temperance Hall at Taylortown, now known as Lenni. The first Quarterly Conference was held on June 13th, and continued the following day, at which Rev. T. J. Thompson, presiding elder, was chairman. The church edifice in the mean while had been pushed forward, and was completed in the summer of 1852, the audience-room being formally dedicated on June 27th of that year, Rev. Dr. William Ryan, of Philadelphia, preaching the dedicatory sermon. On that day nearly seven hundred and fifty dollars was contributed. At the Quarterly Conference held Feb. 19, 1853, as a recognition of the generous favors extended to the society by Mr. Crozer, a resolution was adopted to change the name of the church from Rockdale to Crozerville, which order was made, and by that title the congregation was incorporated December, 1860. The basement of the church was completed in September, 1852. The attendance increased rapidly, and by degrees the indebtedness which had rested on the church was liquidated until, in 1866, it was absolutely freed from debt. Ten years subsequent to the last date the parsonage was erected and carriage-sheds built at the church, the cost of these improvements amounting to two thousand two hundred dollars. During twenty years' service the original edifice became dilapidated, and in the summer of 1882 the congregation renovated and thoroughly renewed the structure, which was formally reopened Oct. 22, 1882, Dr. A. J. Kynitt preaching the sermon.

The following pastors have been in charge of the Crozerville Church since its founding: Revs. George N. McLaughlin, 1852; Dr. Ignatius T. Cooper, 1854; John O'Niel, 1856; Joseph Dare, 1858; Alfred G. Scott, 1860; John Frame, 1862; Francis W. Harvey, 1864; Edward P. Aldred, 1865; Welmer Coffman, 1867; Stephen Townsend, 1869; Henry White, 1870; A. L. Welon, 1872; H. U. Tebring, 1874; Abel Howard, 1875; James C. Wood, 1877; T. W. McClary, 1879; Alex. M. Wiggins, 1881; Ravil Smith, 1882.

Chester Heights Camp-Meeting Association.—In 1872 an association of Methodists purchased a farm in Aston, on the line of the Baltimore Central Railroad, and was incorporated under the title Chester Heights Camp-Meeting Association. The tract contains about one hundred and sixty-two acres, of which about sixty was woodland, which is inclosed with a close fence seven feet high, having gates located at convenient points for the admission of those attending the meetings. The improvements consist of a large excursion-house, seventy by one hundred and twenty feet; a portion of this building is two stories in height, which is used as lodging-rooms, while in the rear building is one story open at the sides, and can be used in rainy weather for holding religious services. In front are three or four hundred settees, capable of seating between three and four thousand persons, so arranged that all in attendance can have an uninterrupted view of the speakers The grounds are supplied with water from a neighboring stream, which is forced to a reservoir by a steam pump A number of handsome permanent frame dwellings have been built in the grove, which add greatly to the attractive appearance of the grounds The hour of each meeting is announced by the ringing of a bell, which can be heard at considerable distance By the provisions of the act incorporating the association the grove can be used only for purposes not in conflict with the discipline of the Methodist Church, and no excursion where dancing is permitted can be allowed access to the grounds A post-office, known as Chester Heights, has been established by the United States at this station on the road, and during the continuance of the camp the mail distributed here is large The association furnishes free railroad tickets to ministers to the Heights and lodging while there The cost of lighting, water, police, and other regulations designed for the general comfort and safety of the guest is paid by the association The location of the camp at this point has been advantageous to the neighborhood, and affords a market for many articles of produce raised by the farmers near by

Crozer Chapel at West Branch—In 1836, John P Crozer erected a stone school-house sixty feet in length by about forty feet in breadth, which, inasmuch as it was occasionally occupied for divine service, was generally known as the Chapel The building was two stories in height, the second floor being used for school purposes and the lower room for a Sunday-school, and, whenever opportunity offered, preaching by any clergyman of a recognized religious sect was had therein, the chapel not being in any wise a denominational church After the establishment of the free public school this building was used by the directors of Aston for many years for school purposes It has now ceased to be so used, but, still standing, has been changed into dwelling-houses, and is now the property of John B Rhodes

"The Blue Church"—About 1818 the church which was known by this name was erected, almost entirely at the cost of James Lindsay, on the west side of the Logtown road, a short distance above where the highway leading from Lima intersects with the former road On March 1, 1822, James Lindsay, of Aston, conveyed to William Glenn, James McMullen, Samuel Hunter, and their successors, trustees of the First Branch of the United Presbyterian Congregation of Aston, Providence, and Springfield, "for and in consideration of the love of God and promotion of Religion, and also in consideration of the sum of one dollar," for the use of the congregation mentioned, "a small lot of land with a meeting-house built thereon" Rev John Smith, an Irishman, was the first and only pastor of Mount Gilead, for such he designated the church, having assumed the charge in 1819, and he will be recalled as the first advocate of the cause of temperance outside of the society of Friends in Delaware County; and until his death, on May 10, 1839, he never permitted an opportunity to pass unimproved to urge his views thereon After his death, which resulted from his horse treading on him as he led the animal to water, the church languished John P Crozer records, under date of Monday, October 4, 1842, in his diary, "I was yesterday at the 'Blue' meeting-house A stranger was there, sent by the Presbytery of Philadelphia to this and the Middletown meeting-house to make some attempt to infuse life into these decaying churches" The attempt, however, so far as the Blue Church was concerned, was fruitless It finally ceased to be used as a place of worship, until to-day the building has disappeared, and the ancient God's acre, wherein the "forefathers of the hamlet sleep," is indistinguishable from the field which surrounds it

The Baptist Church at Village Green.—Early in 1860 a Methodist Church was erected at Village Green, which was dedicated May 17th of that year, and was retained by that religious denomination until 1865, when dissension spread in the congregation, which resulted finally in the lot and building being sold by the sheriff, Richard S Smith becoming the purchaser For several years it was conducted as a Church of England mission, but finally, as the weight of years pressed heavily on Mr Smith, who was its main support, it languished until 1871, when it was sold to Mrs Sallie K Crozer, and for ten years was conducted as a mission, under the direction of the Crozer Theological Seminary, the students in that institution supplying the pulpit In 1881 it was made a separate church, and Rev Miller Jones was called to the charge At that time a parsonage was purchased and ground adjoining the church, on which sheds for the shelter of vehicles and horses were erected The church is now in a flourishing condition

The Baptist Chapel at Bridgewater.—The brick chapel at Bridgewater was built in 1874 on a lot purchased from Samuel Haigh & Co in that year It is a missionary station under the control of the Upland Baptist Church, and its supplies are furnished from the students of Crozer Theological Seminary

Calvary Episcopal Church.—In 1833, Richard S. Smith, an active Episcopalian, who had recently removed from Philadelphia to Rockdale, established a Sunday-school in a vacant room in the upper story of his nail mill at that place, his wife, Mrs. Elizabeth Beach Smith, and his daughters teaching the scholars, while he discharged the duties of superintendent The nearest Episcopal Church at that time was five miles distant, hence the residents in the neighborhood of Rockdale of that denomination were compelled to worship at Mount Hope Methodist Church or the Presbyterian Church at Middletown The success attending the Sunday-school was so marked that it was resolved to form a congregation of Episcopalians at that locality, and to that end

Bishop Onderdonk authorized Kingston Goddard, a student of divinity, to officiate at Rockdale as lay-reader. The field was so promising that, under the auspices of the Advancement Society, Rev. Marmaduke Hurst was detailed as missionary, the bishop designating the feeble congregation as Calvary Church and admitting the parish to representation in the Convention. The number of worshipers which gathered in the mill-room grew so rapidly that it was determined, if possible, to raise sufficient funds to erect a church edifice, and so untiring were the efforts of Mr. Smith and those associated with him in the movement, that, notwithstanding many rebuffs, at length the subscriptions obtained aggregated a sum to justify the outlay. On Aug. 18, 1836, Bishop Onderdonk laid the corner-stone. The building was hastened forward, the roof raised, the floor of the church laid, the basement designed for the Sunday-school plastered, and in the latter apartment, on Christmas-eve, 1836, the first services were held, Rev. Richard D. Hall, rector of St. Paul's Church, Chester, officiating on that occasion. In October, 1838, Rev. Mr. Hurst tendered his resignation, and Rev. Alfred Lee was appointed rector at a small salary, it being understood that a dwelling should be provided for his family; but as no parsonage could be procured the rector was invited to make his home at Mr. Smith's house, which he did, and he continued there while he was in charge of the parish. During his ministry the congregation raised means sufficient to finish the church and furnish it. The ability displayed by the rector in this remote rural church was such that it attracted general attention in Eastern Pennsylvania and Delaware, and when, in 1841, the Diocese of Delaware elected the first bishop of that State, Rev. Mr. Lee was the unanimous selection of that body. He thereupon resigned his charge at Rockdale to assume the exalted station to which he had been called. In 1845, Mr. Smith, who in that year sold his real estate at Rockdale, presented to the church an acre of ground adjoining the sanctuary, which tract he had reserved in the sale of his property. The present main stone structure, with its lofty spire, for many years was a conspicuous object outlined against the sky, but it was devoid of a clock. In 1859, John B. Rhodes and Thomas Blackburn, both young in years, and at that time employed in the mills in the neighborhood, resolved that Calvary Church steeple should be lacking in that respect no longer, but when they broached the subject they were ridiculed by the older persons in the congregation. They had, however, determined that a clock should be had, and as they were without means they resolved themselves to make the time-piece. Learning that the works of an old clock, which had been discarded by one of the churches in Philadelphia as worn out, could be purchased for a small sum, the young men bought it, and every spare moment they devoted to repair it, until they were satisfied that it was in thorough order, when it was placed in the steeple to the astonishment of the residents of the village. For several months the hands marked the time to a charm, and the bell proclaimed the passing hours with commendable exactness. One Sunday, just as the rector had announced his text, the clock began to strike, and it kept on striking until it had scored a hundred hours, and was hammering industriously away, as if determined to reach a thousand before it would cease its reckless announcements. John B. Rhodes, who was present, could bear it no longer, but hastening up to where the untruthful time-piece ticked and struck, he removed it from its exalted position, and although since then Calvary Church has had another and more trustworthy clock, the marvelous performance of the one I am relating still lingers in the recollections of the good people of that locality.

In 1868 the congregation determined, "as a thank-offering for the blessings of peace," to enlarge and beautify the church, and to that end erected wings to the edifice, so that the structure was in the form of a cross, the two new transepts representing the arms, and the shorter limb being the new chancel addition. The new walls were of brick pebble-dashed, and the old walls were studded, lathed, and plastered, and finished in the natural color of the mortar. The first story is used as Sunday-school rooms. The ceiling of the church is of yellow pine oiled, with walnut ribs and mouldings. The windows are enameled glass, excepting that in the chancel, which is a stained-glass memorial window to the first wife of the late Robert L. Martin. On Feb. 14, 1869, worship was resumed in the church, Bishop Lee, of Delaware, officiating in the consecrating services. The cost of these improvements was about five thousand dollars. Since that time a lot of three acres was purchased at Rockdale by Bishop Potter, William Martin, and Richard S. Smith, and presented to the church for a parsonage, and thereon a handsome stone double house has been erected, at a cost of seven thousand dollars. The rectors of Calvary Church have been as follows:

Rev. Marmaduke Hirst, 1835–38; Rt. Rev. Alfred Lee, D.D., 1838–41; Rev. Benjamin S. Huntingdon, 1841–47; Rev. Charles W. Thomson, 1847–48; Rev. Charles Brick, D.D., 1848–53; Rev. John K. Murphy, 1853–68; Rev. William Ely, 1868–74; Rev. James Walker, 1874.

On Sunday, June 24, 1883, the semi-centennial anniversary of Calvary Church was observed, with appropriate ceremonies, the venerable Richard S. Smith making an historical address on that occasion. Since that time Mr. Smith has passed away, but on the inner walls of the church the congregation, with excellent taste, have erected a tablet to the memory of the man who founded, and in its infancy sustained, the struggling parish by his energy and means.

St. Thomas' Church, Ivy Mills.—The Catholic residents of Aston for many years attended worship in St. Mary's Church, the noted chapel in the mansion of the Willcox family at Ivy Mills, in Concord township, but in time the congregation grew so numerous that it became necessary to erect a sanctuary at a more convenient location for those living in Rockdale and its neighborhood Hence to that end a tract of land was purchased from Nicholas F Walter on Aug 26, 1852, the deed being made to the Rt. Rev J N Newman, bishop of the diocese of Philadelphia, which lot was to be held in trust for the congregation of Ivy Mills On Sunday, Aug 29, 1852, the corner-stone of the church of "St Thomas the Apostle" was laid, Rev Mr. Sourin, of Philadelphia, conducting the ceremonies The imposing church edifice was finished in 1856, and on Oct 20, 1856, Rev Charles Joseph Maugin was appointed the first pastor In 1858 he was succeeded by Rev Nicholas Walsh, and in the latter part of that year a frame parsonage was erected, at a cost of two thousand four hundred and forty-four dollars In 1860, Rev Thomas Kyle was in charge, and in 1862, Rev Henry Wright He was succeeded by Rev John Wall in 1864, and in 1866, Rev James J McElroy became the pastor of St Thomas' Church The latter, in 1868, gave place to Rev James F Kelley, and he in turn, in 1870, to Rev John Cox In 1872, Rev Michael Lawlor was its pastor On Tuesday night, Feb 4, 1873, the parsonage was totally destroyed by fire, originating in a defective flue The contents of the building were saved, and by the utmost exertions the church edifice, which stood in close proximity, was rescued from the flames, which threatened its destruction The following October Rev John J Wood was in charge, and during his pastorate a substantial brick parsonage was erected He was followed, in 1875, by Rev Andrew J Gallagher, and on Oct 14, 1877, the present pastor, William F Cook, was installed The congregation now numbers about fourteen hundred persons, and a mission chapel is attached to this church, located near Elam

Licensed Houses —The granting of licenses to any resident of Aston does not appear of record until 1762, but as early as August court, 1740, Thomas Vernon, of Aston, presented a petition for leave to keep a house of entertainment, alleging that there is no tavern on either road for twelve or fourteen miles where his house is located, or, as he expressed it, "seated on the Great road side Leading from severall parts of Bradford, Burmingham, Thornbury, West Town and Concord to Chester, allso on the road Leading from Chad's foard to Philadelphia through Providence," but he was unable to move by his representation the judicial mind in his favor This description would seem to locate him in the northwestern end of the township

As stated above, in 1762, James Johnston was licensed to keep a public-house, and I believe that it was located at Village Green In 1764, William Pennell succeeded him in the business, and continued until 1770, when George Pierce in turn followed him However, in 1765, James Cole had license, and in 1768, Abraham Aston was shown favor by the court, while Pennell held the license at this house In 1776, George Pierce's name appeared for the last time In 1778, James Pennell had the privilege accorded him, and in 1780 Joshua Vaughan was licensed to keep the tavern known as the "Seven Stars," and was so licensed until 1787 In the following year Peter Wade received the court's approval, and James Pennell in 1789, when Chester County court ceased to distribute its indulgences in the township

The "Seven Stars" was kept by Thomas Marshall in 1790, when the new county of Delaware was created, and he continued there until 1793, when Samuel Hewes was granted license, and yearly received the approval of the court until his death, in 1820, when the business was carried on by his widow, Sarah, until 1824 In that year Samuel F Hughes became the proprietor, to be superseded in that capacity, in 1826, by Jemima Massey, who yearly thereafter, until 1834, was granted license for the old public-house, which, if I am rightly informed, was the headquarters of Lord Cornwallis when the British army was encamped for several days near Village Green in the fall of 1777 John Garrett, in 1835, became the host of the "Stars" During the agitation of the ten-hour movement, in 1847, John Garrett took active part with the operatives in their organization, and so obnoxious did he make himself to the opponents of that measure that he deemed it unwise in that year to petition for license, hence J Lewis Garrett made the application John Garrett, however, held his position, and permitted the workingmen to assemble in his hall in public meetings without charge to them for the rooms In the following year John Garrett petitioned again for the right to keep a public-house at the "Seven Stars," as also in 1849, which was granted to him In 1850, J Lewis Garrett made the application, and annually thereafter (excepting in 1856, '57, '58, '59 and 1860, when John Garrett applied, and during 1873-74, the years of local option), his petition being favorably acted on On March 20, 1862, while J Lewis Garrett was standing in the bar of the hotel, a bullet, shattering a window-glass, struck him on the neck, under the right jaw, passed through the larynx, and lodged in the left side of the neck, just beneath the skin, inflicting a dangerous wound Some boys were shooting at a mark in a field near by This bullet, before it struck Mr Garrett, had passed through a two-inch pine board and the side of a carriage At the old tavern is a copy of the first edition of "Purdon's Digest," on the fly-leaf of which is engrossed, in the handwriting of James McMullen, an old school-teacher

"The property of the inhabitants of the township of Aston Not to be taken from the Seven Stars Tavern while the elections are held there

"March 31, 1820"

In 1862, James Schofield received license for an

eating-house at Rockdale, and in 1864 full license for the "Mountain House." Schofield dying in 1865, his widow, Hannah, made the application that year, which was favorably considered, to be the next rejected. In 1870, William Carson obtained license for the Mountain House, but failed in 1871 to receive the approval of the court. In 1875, Carson again was authorized to keep a public inn at the "Mountain House," a privilege which annually thereafter has been extended to him.

Associations and Secret Societies.—The People's Literary Association, which was incorporated by the court of Delaware County, Aug. 25, 1870, had erected a commodious building, in the second story of which is a large hall used for entertainments, lectures, and public meetings. The ground on which the building is located, containing half an acre, was given by John P. Crozer, on May 24, 1860, under certain conditions, to the association. The corner-stone of the building was laid July 4, 1860, but nothing was done to complete the hall. The gift from Mr. Crozer was to become operative when three-fourths of the estimated cost of erecting a suitable edifice for the purposes contemplated in the charter of the association had been collected. The association, having failed at the time of the latter's death to carry out this provision, this lot, under his will, was devised to Samuel A. Crozer for life, with remainder to his grandson, John P. Crozer, Jr. An application being made to court to have the executors of the will convey the land to the association, under the terms of the original gift, the Crozer family willingly acquiesced in the application, and on June 21, 1871, the court ordered the executors to "make a binding deed to the People's Literary Association of Rockdale." The organization is now in a flourishing condition. A provision in the charter declares,—

"Should the association at any time terminate its existence by giving up its charter, or in any other way that may be determined upon for that purpose, all the property of the association, in whatever form, must revert to the public school fund of the townships of Middletown and Aston, to be divided equally between them."

In the fall of the year 1872 the members of the Rockdale Base-Ball Club formed the Rockdale Cornet Band, which was incorporated by the court of Delaware County, Feb. 26, 1874. The organization purchased a lot of ground in the village, on which, in the spring of 1882, was erected a handsome building, twenty-five by thirty-five. The band is under the leadership of George Blair, and the members are all residents of the immediate neighborhood.

There are several secret societies in Aston, the eldest in time being Benevolent Lodge, No. 40, Independent Order of Odd-Fellows. The lodge was chartered Sept. 2, 1831. On July 4, 1848, its hall, at Village Green, was dedicated. The procession of the order on that occasion, up to that time, was the largest ever had in the county, being nearly a mile in length, the officers of the Grand Lodge and Grand Encampment being present. The lodge has now one hundred and forty-two members. Noble Grand, James C. Megraw, and Samuel K. Crozer, Secretary.

The next society in age is the Rockdale Lodge, No. 50, American Protestant Association, which was organized Feb. 28, 1854, and has now forty-five members. Samuel Hopkins is the present Worshipful Master.

On Feb. 22, 1869, Energy Lodge, No. 9, Junior American Protestant Association, was chartered, and has sixty-five members. Smith Yarnall is Worshipful Master, and James A. Bates, Secretary.

July 22, 1869, Lenni Tribe, No. 86, Independent Order of Red Men, was chartered, and has now eighty-five members. William Frame is Sachem, and Charles R. Yarnall, Chief of Records.

Charles Dickens Lodge, No. 41, Sons of St. George, was chartered March 24, 1879. It has about fifty-five members. John Lee is the present President, and Samuel Harmer, Secretary.

CHAPTER XXX.

BETHEL TOWNSHIP.

THIS municipal district, which was the smallest township in the original county of Chester, is about three miles in length and a mile and a half in breadth at the widest part, the whole area being scarcely five miles square, is mentioned as early as 1683,[1] and again at the court held on the Eleventh month 6, 1684, the inhabitants of "Concord, Bethell, and Chichester, were ordered to meet on the third day of the next weeke," at the tavern of Henry Reynolds, in Chichester, and confer as to the maintenance of a poor woman and her child. This township is on the summit between the Delaware and the noted Brandywine Creek. The soil, which is lighter than that nearer the river, and in some places stony, is very productive, yielding abundant harvests of wheat and corn. Clay, used for making fire-bricks, and kaolin abound in the western part of the township bordering on Concord. Dr. Smith states that "the name of this township, for anything that is known to the contrary, was imported directly from Palestine. This word is said to signify 'House of God,' *Beth* being the name of the second Hebrew letter, which is made after the fashion of a Hebrew house. Bethel hamlet had an existence at a very early date, and was probably composed of the first rudely-constructed dwellings of the early emigrants, who built them near together for safety."[2] At the September court, 1686, Edward "Beasar" was appointed constable "ffor Bethell Lyberty." In 1683, Edward Bezer and Edward Brown had five hundred

[1] Futhey and Cope's "History of Chester County," p. 162.

[2] History of Delaware County, p. 382.

acres surveyed to them in the northeasterly end of the township On this estate Bethel hamlet, afterwards known as Corner Catch or "Ketch"—the name having, it is said, originated from the fact that so many roads centred there that five corners are the result, and a traveler could easily be confused as to the proper highway he should take,—and at present the village of Chelsea is located Southeast of this tract, in the same year, Francis Smith had three hundred acres set apart to him by the provincial surveyor Adjoining Bezer's and Brown's land to the west, on the line of Concord township, was a plot of one hundred and fifty acres which had been surveyed in 1683 for John Gibbons, and south of that tract was an estate of the like size, part of five hundred acres purchased from Penn by Gibbons, which in the year mentioned he transferred to Robert Southey, to whom it was surveyed West of these last-mentioned estates, and divided from them by the road leading from Concord to Booth's Corner, was an oddly-shaped tract of two hundred acres, which was patented to Francis Harrison in 1686 South of the Wilmington road, from Booth's Corner to the circular line of Delaware State, was a tract of a hundred and odd acres, which was part of a large holding of four hundred acres, the greater part in Delaware, which had been surveyed to Isaac Warner in 1683, while on the middle branch of Naaman's Creek, and crossing over the line into Upper Chichester, was a tract of about one hundred acres, being about half the tract of two hundred acres surveyed to Robert Cloud in 1685, and by him transferred to William Cloud the year following

At a court held the third day of the first week, Fourth month, 1686, the grand jury reported that they had laid out the road from Bethel to Chichester (Marcus Hook) The ancient return is exceedingly interesting, and is as follows

"The Grand Inquest made returne of a Highway from Bethell to Chichester of sixty foote broad as followes (viz) Beginning at the Side of Concord towards the River on the street or Highway of Concord first through the land of John Gibbons his House on the Right Side then through the land of Robert Southey late Deceased his house on the left Side thence through Robert Piles Land his house on the right hand then through Joseph Bushells land his House on the Left hand, thence through ffrancis Smith's land thence through Thomas Garretts Land, his house on ye Right hand thence through ffrancis Harrison and Jacob Chandlers Land downe the Point to a small branch of Namans creek thence up ye Hill to the first Inclosed of ffrancis Harrisons, the field on ye left hand Then through James Brownes land thence downe to another Branch of Namau's Creeke through Walter Martens land up the Point his House on ye right hand thence through Jeremy Colletts land Bearing towards the left hand his house Standing on ye left hand from thence to the lands of Chichester beginning att the head of a small swamp on the left hand thence downe Cross the Kings road or Highway towards ye foote of ye Hill to a lyne tree marked with 5 notches thence downe to ye Rivers Side the line between James Browne and William Clayton Junior Whereunto wee the Present grand Jury of ye County of Chester have sett our Hands

"JOSEPH RICHARDS, *foreman*,

"Tho Worth	"Joseph Bushell
"Jno Gibbons	"Michaell Blunstone
"Tho. Coleborne	"Randall Vernon
"Joseph Baker	"John Bartrome
"Edward Beasar	"Wm Brainton
"Walter Marten	"Saull Levis"

The action of the grand jury seemed to have met the approval of the public, for at the court on the "3d day of 1st week of ye 7 mo 1686 The Inhabitance of Bethell and Concord Presented a Paper to the Court Signifying their good liking of the Road lately laid out by the Grand Jury to Chichester."

From this report, following the road from the Concord line to that of Upper Chichester, we can form an idea of the location of the early settlers' houses in the western end of the township at that date We learn that John Gibbons' dwelling was on the right side of the road, and that Robert Southey had died, but his late dwelling stood on the left-hand side of the highway, near a little feeder of Green's Creek, that Robert Pyle had his house on the right side of the road, and above the present highway leading from Booth's Corner to Chelsea (At the dwelling of Robert Pyle and Edward Bezer, the monthly assemblings of Chichester Friends' Meeting were frequently held.) Joseph Bushel at that time owned a tract of one hundred and forty acres south of Robert Pyle's plantation, and his dwelling stood on the right side of the road At this time Thomas Garrett had taken up on rent two hundred acres of land, now part of the farms of Charles M Cheyney and William Goodey, and had built a house thereon to the right of the road as a person moved in a southerly course Thus it seems at that date there were five settlements made along the road thus laid out, which crossed the township in a northwesterly direction

Notwithstanding the unusual demonstration of pleasure by which the people of Bethel and Concord expressed their satisfaction with the road, they certainly did not improve their opportunities, for at the court held 3d day, 1st week, First month, 1688, it appears that "Wee of ye Grand Inquest doe psent ye Townships of Bethell and Chichester for neglecting ye clearing of a Road in ye respective Libertyes between Concord and Chester," and further, that "Wee alsoe psent ye Road lying between ye Townships of Bethell and Chichester for not being Cleared and made passable" This presentment was due to the fact that a change had been made in the course of the road, for on the 3d day of 1st week, Tenth month, 1688, the grand jury altered the line of the highway decided on in 1686, as follows

"Beginning at Concord street end and so along ye Road formerly laid out to a marked White Oake below Walter Martens by a lyne of marked trees on ye South West Side of ye Old Road to a marked great White oake from thence along ye road formerly laid out to Delaware by or near James Brown's House"

Although the change in the highway to Marcus Hook was made in the township of Upper Chichester, doubtless to please Walter Martin, it aroused such public opposition in the townships bordering on the circular line between New Castle and Chester County that, at the June court, 1689, "The Inhabitances of Concord, Bethell and Chichester Petitioned against y[e] Highway lately laid out from Concord and Bethell to y[e] River for that between Walter Martens and Jeremy Colletts the way is not soe good and Passable as the former Road. Ordered that the former way be there Continued."

John Gibbons, who settled on the tract of one hundred and fifty acres in Bethel, lying south of the boundary line of Concord township, in 1683, was the founder of one of the largest and most respectable families of the old county of Chester. He was a man of superior education to that of most of his neighbors, and as his wife had had similar advantages in England, the couple were regarded as leaders of thought in this section of Chester County. He was one of the jury on the trial of Margaret Mattson for witchcraft, already mentioned, and the family tradition asserts that he it was who framed the compromise verdict which prevented a disagreement of the jury, and secured her from the ordeal of a second trial. Notwithstanding the high repute in which John and Margery Gibbons were held by the early settlers, the adherence which they gave to George Keith's religious teaching caused them to be disowned by Friends. In 1700 the Bethel homestead was conveyed to John Gibbons by his parents. The latter was equally as outspoken in his views as his parents, and as his mother was in nowise chary in giving expression to her convictions, her son was often compelled to advocate and defend her opinions. In 1702 he was disowned for accepting his mother's views, as well as at the close of meeting standing up and declaring that John Lea was no gospel minister. Among his other transgressions which induced the society to disown him was because he "declined to take off his hat in time of prayer." The stubborn offender died in 1706, his mother subsequent to that year; and John Gibbons, the elder, lived on the Bethel plantation until his death, about 1721.

At the house of Robert Pyle, hereinbefore mentioned, the Friends of Concord, Bethel, Chichester, and Birmingham frequently held their Monthly Meeting, and it was there, on the 12th of the First month (March), 1688, that the first movement in the county by the society of Friends designed to prevent the sale of liquors to the Indians was made. Chester Meeting does not appear to have acted as promptly, for it was not until "y[e] 2d of ye 5 month (July), 1688," at the meeting held at the house of Walter Faucits, that a similar entry is found on its minutes. The record of the proceedings of this meeting at Pyle's dwelling, so far as it relates to the sale of strong drink to the Indians, is interesting, and as the testimony was signed by those Friends who were present, the names of many of the first settlers in the southwestern section of Delaware County were attached thereto. It read:

"From our Yearly Meeting held at Philadelphia the 7th of the 7th month, 1687, it being recommended to us by the Quarterly Meeting of Philadelphia, the great evil and bad effect that hath appeared by selling Indians Rum and other strong Liquors, and a paper being by them presented, which was read amongst us, relating thereto, which upon due consideration was approved of, and in concurrence therewith we give forth this Following Testimony, being deeply sensible and heartly grieved with a business of this nature, which is too frequently up and down amongst us, Especially in that as some go under the profession of Truth, whom it was expected should have been better examples, whom we fear are not wholly clear of it, and therefore we give forth this as our Testimony. As our sense that the practice of selling Rum and other strong Liquors to the Indians directly or indirectly, or exchanging rum or other strong liquors for any goods or merchandise with them, considering the abuse they make of it, is a thing contrary to the Lord and a great grief and burthen to his people, and a great reflection and dishonor to the truth, so far as any professing it are concerned; and for the more effective preventing of this evil practice we advise as aforesaid that our testimony may be entered in every monthly meeting book, and every Friend belonging to their monthly meeting to subscribe the same.

"Signed in the behalf of the meeting

"ANTHONY MORRIS"

"Wee the members of this monthly meeting having united wth the above Testimony do subscribe our names to it as followeth:

"William Clayton, Sr.	Thomas King
"Nicholas Newlin	George Pierce
"John Kingsman	William Brinton
"Edward Bezer	John Harding
"Hugh Durburrow	Robert Pyle
"James Brown	Jacob Chandler
"Nathaniel Lamplugh	William Cloud, Sr.,
"Joseph Bushall	Philip Roman."
"John Bennett	

The list of taxables of Bethel township for 1693 shows that the following persons had settled there or, in the case of two persons on the list, owned real estate on which they did not reside:

	£	s.	d.
John Gibbons	0	8	4
Ralph Pile	0	8	4
John Bushell	0	6	0
Nicholas Pile	0	4	2
Edward Beazer	0	8	4
Robert Eyre	0	4	2
Thomas Garrett	0	2	6
Edward Beazer for John Howard	0	6	0
Robert Eyre for Thomas Copper	0	6	0
	2	13	10

In the next quarter of a century the number of settlers had doubled, for the taxables of Bethel in 1715 are thus given: Robert Pyle, John Grist, Robert Booth, Edward Beazer, John Cannady, Benjamin Moulder, Joseph Pyle, John Hickman, Edward Dutton, Edward Pennock, William Griffith, John Hopton, John Gibbons, Thomas Durnell.

In 1759, when Gen. John Forbes made demand on Chester and the other counties in the province for teams to be used in transporting the baggage of the army about to march under his command to the site of Fort Du Quesne, Edward Whitaker paid "a bounty" of ten pounds "in behalf of the township" of Bethel, John Cooper was credited with a wagon entered in the service, and John Wilson with the cartage of oats and flour from Carlisle to Loudon.[1]

A short distance below the Concord line, on part of the old Gibbons tract, is the estate of Albin Baldwin, deceased (at one time county treasurer). The old house still standing on this property, on the right side of the Bethel and Chichester road, is one of the earliest brick buildings in that section of the county. As is usual, tradition tells us the bricks were imported

[1] Futhey and Cope's "History of Chester County," p. 55.

from Europe, which it is proper to state is one of those deeply-seated and widely-diffused popular errors the historian encounters in all old settlements in the Middle and Eastern States The fact is that the clay was dug and the bricks burned near where the house stands, a general custom in the last century The original structure was a story and a half in height, the bricks being laid in headers and stretchers, in the style known as "Flemish bond," the black-glazed ends of the headers alternating with the red stretchers laid lengthwise for the purpose of ornamentation, as was frequent in early days The old building has been raised in height and added to in recent years

During the few days the British were encamped in Birmingham and Aston, after the battle of Brandywine, the good people of Bethel were annoyed and plundered by the foraging parties of the enemy The latter appropriated the personal property which the Continentals had forgotten to impress, for many of the Revolutionary soldiers swore and stole equally to any troopers under the sun After both armies had marched away it was a lucky household that could boast of a pair of blankets, while poultry and pork, silverware and silver money, whiskey (essential as bread in those days) and watches had almost wholly disappeared That section of country was swept comparatively clear of horses and neat cattle, while in a number of cases the residents were left entirely destitute of food This loss occasioned by the presence of armed forces was large in Bethel, but the value of the articles taken by the British plundering parties cannot now be ascertained, for no returns were made, so far as has been learned, in that township, in conformity with the act of Assembly providing for the filing of sworn statements of the damages sustained by the people in those sections of the State through which the invading army made its way

In June, 1872, a reunion of the descendants of John Larkin, Sr , and Martha, his wife, took place at the old homestead in Bethel There were eighty persons present, among whom were three brothers and four sisters, the eldest being seventy-seven and the youngest sixty-three years old John Larkin, the first of the family in Delaware County, was born in Lower Chichester early in the eighteenth century, and after his marriage with Esther Shelley, of Chichester, in 1731, he removed to Bethel In 1799 his two sons, Isaac and ——, were living in the township, the first owning a farm of two hundred and seven acres, and the latter one hundred and twenty-one acres Ex-Mayor Larkin, of Chester, as well as all the Larkins in Delaware County, are descended from John, who settled in Bethel about 1750 I have failed to learn when the first of the family came to the American colonies, but it was certainly before the coming of Penn That this is so the records of Cecil County establish In a deed made by Ephraim Augustus Hermen to Thomas Larkin of eight hundred and eighty-three acres of land in 1715, the indenture recites that previous to Aug 14, 1682, John Larkin, father of Thomas, had patented that number of acres, which tract was afterwards, including many more acres, patented to Augustine Hermen In the deed made in 1715 it is stated, "and that the said Thomas Larkin had made his right to the said land appear to be prior to the right of the Hermens, for these reasons, and for divers other good and valuable considerations, Hermen, who was then lord of Bohemia Manor, and his wife, conveyed their interest in the land to Larkin "[1]

Bethel has two villages and one Corner Chelsea, which is in the north part of the township, was formerly known as Corner Ketch (Catch) In 1833, Reece Pyle sold the land at the Corner to Robert McCall, who, in that year, built the stone dwelling he now occupies, and in the following year built the frame store Previous to the purchase by McCall, in the last century, Caleb Perkins had a store and shoemaker's shop at the Corner, and about 1820 a small store was located, then kept by Norris Hannum, but he had discontinued business before 1833 At the latter date Mrs Sturgis was conducting a little shop in a building occupying the lot now owned by Samuel Jester Robert McCall continued in business there for many years, and was succeeded by John Hoffman, who in time gave place to Daniel Dutton, he to George Adams, he to James C Armstrong, and the latter to Samuel H. Pierce, who is now conducting it, as well as discharging the office of postmaster of the village About 1858 Chelsea was accorded the dignity of a postal station, and John Hoffman appointed its first postmaster

Booth's Corner is located in the western part of the township, almost midway between Concord and Upper Chichester townships In 1831, William Mousley had a log blacksmith-shop on the corner where the store of Isaac Booth is now located In that year Wesley Clark purchased the opposite corner, and erected a wheelwright- and blacksmith-shop In 1835, Isaac Booth purchased the ground whereon Mousley's shop stood, erected the store building, and from that time the corner took its present name

Zebley's Corner is at the extreme southern part of the township, bordering on the Delaware State line, and boasts a store and a few dwelling-houses

The following is a list of justices of the peace for Bethel township

Samuel Price	Aug 30, 1791	Joseph Trimble.	April 21, 1827
Joseph Marshall	May 20, 1800	Robert Frame	Jan 15, 1829
Matthias Kerlin	July 4, 1808	Robert Hall	Feb 8, 1831
Thomas Pierce	Feb 5 1814	Wm Mendenhall	Dec 6, 1836
James Bratton	" 3, 1820	Johns P Eyre	April 14, 1840
Joseph Fox	Dec 4, 1823	Samuel Register	June 4, 1858
John Mattson	" 13, 1823	Albin Baldwin	April 22, 1868
Joseph Bowen	Nov 10, 1824		

Siloam Methodist Church is a branch of the Bethel Church of Delaware, the former having been organized in 1852, at which time about fifty persons

[1] Johnston's "History of Cecil County, Md.," p 103

formed the membership of Siloam. A lot of ground, comprising an acre and a half, was given to the congregation by Samuel Hanby and Samuel Hance, each contributing three-quarters of an acre. The handsome stone sanctuary, forty-two by sixty feet, was hastened forward, and in the latter part of 1852 the building had so far progressed that the basement-story was dedicated, and services regularly held therein. On Sept. 24, 1854, the church, then completed, was dedicated, Revs. Mr. Hurey and Andrew Manship, of Philadelphia, conducting the services on that occasion. The building was erected at a cost of four thousand five hundred dollars, of which sum one-half had been contributed from time to time while it was in process of construction, and the remainder was collected on the dedication day. The church was embraced in the Mount Lebanon Circuit, and was under the pastoral charge of Rev. William H. Burrell. He has been followed by the following pastors: James Hand, Thomas Newman, Francis B. Harvey, Isaac Merrill, —— Smith, John France, John Dyson, Joseph S. Lane, William W. McMichael, Edward F. Kenney, George W. Lybrand, William T. Magee, and Maris Graves, the present incumbent. During Mr. Kenney's pastorate serious charges of gross immoral conduct were made against him, and the long investigation and subsequent trial before the ecclesiastical court aroused great interest in the immediate neighborhood and surrounding districts. His acquittal on all the charges by the Annual Conference, in 1876, was particularly gratifying to Siloam Church, and when the announcement was made of the result of the trial, the congregation expressed their sympathy in applause, an unusual occurrence in a religious meeting. The present membership of the Siloam is one hundred and fifty, and the Sunday-school connected with the church has one hundred pupils. James C. Hinkson is the present superintendent. The church was incorporated by the court of Delaware County, Nov. 23, 1868.

In 1871 a mission of Siloam Church was established at Chelsea, in a chapel which had been built by Dr. Phineas Price, on the Chester and Concord road, east of the village, many years before. The building was purchased by the congregation of Siloam Church, and was formally dedicated July 22, 1871, Rev. Mr. Lane conducting the services on that occasion.

Schools.—About the beginning of this century Cæsar Paschal, a colored servant of Mark Wilcox, owned a tract of ground in the angle formed by the intersection of the Chester and Concord road with the Chichester and Concord road at Corner Catch (Chelsea). He sold an acre of land to a committee for the purpose of erecting thereon a school building. A log house was located in the middle of this lot, so as to afford ample play-ground for the children. How long this building was occupied for school purposes is unknown, but it certainly was not used as such for any considerable length of time, but was sold to Robert R. Hall, who moved the log structure to the roadside and converted it into a dwelling. The premises are now owned by Samuel Regester.

Previous to 1780 a subscription stone school-house was built on the corner of Kirk road, where Thomas Booth's shops now are. John Foulk, Powell Clayton, and another resident of the township whose name is forgotten, were the trustees. At one time Nathaniel Cloud was the teacher, and the mother of Wesley Poole was a pupil under his instruction. The floor of the building was laid in bricks, and was cold and cheerless in the winter days, the roaring wood-fire being insufficient to warm it thoroughly. Powell Clayton, who was the surviving trustee, sold the lot to Isaac Booth, who tore the building down in 1825, but for several years before that date schools had ceased to be held there. In 1824 a school was opened in a stone building erected on a lot purchased from John Larkin, on the Bethel road, east of Booth's Corner, afterwards known as number one public school. It was likewise a subscription school, Nathaniel Larkin, Thomas Booth, and John Larkin being the trustees. Charles Willis was the first teacher there,—and subsequently by George Walters and Adam Mendenhall. In this school-house one United States senator and Governor of Arkansas (Gen. Powell Clayton) and two judges (William Clayton, of the Ninth District Court of Arkansas, and Thomas J. Clayton, president judge of Delaware County) were educated, as were many of the present residents of Bethel. The old building remained until 1868, when it was torn down and the present structure, twenty-eight by thirty-five feet, was erected at a cost of sixteen hundred and sixty-one dollars. Osborn Booth was the builder.

On Sept. 9, 1839, a lot containing fifty-five perches was purchased from Foulk Cloud, at Booth's Corner, for $27.50. (The latter, it will be recalled, while trimming peach-trees at his residence, at Booth's Corner, on the afternoon of Dec. 15, 1870, was stricken with paralysis, and died in a few hours.) On this lot a one-story octagon house was erected and used as a public school for several years, when it was burned. The directors rebuilt it, using the old wall, and it continued in use until 1870, when it was torn down, the present structure, known as school number two, being erected on its site at a cost of seventeen hundred and eighty-nine dollars. Nelson G. Green was the contractor.

On May 22, 1860, a lot containing eighty-four square perches was purchased from Curtis Barlow, on the Bethel road, a short distance west of Chelsea, and the present school-house, known as number three, erected.

Under the act of 1834 the court appointed in that year Robert McCall and John Larkin inspectors. Following is a list of the school directors of Bethel since 1840:

1840, Nathaniel Pratt, Nathaniel Cloud, 1842, Foulk Cloud, Nelson Clayton, 1843, Moses Pyle, Thomas Zebley, 1844, Samuel Register, Nelson Clayton, 1845, John Clayton, Jonas Eyre, 1846, Moses Pyle, Albin Baldwin, 1847, Nelson Clayton, Nathaniel Williams, 1848, Wesley Poole, John Clayton, 1849, Albin Baldwin, Thomas Booth, 1850, Foulk Cloud, Wesley Poole, 1851, Wesley Clark, Benjamin Larkin, 1852, Samuel F Larkin, Albin Baldwin, 1853, Thomas Booth, Sharpless Green, 1854, Benjamin Larkin, Thomas S Philips, 1855, Albin Baldwin, Owen Zebley, 1856, Robert W Barton John H Cheyney, 1857, Nathan L Eyre, Reese Baldwin, 1858, no report, 1859, Samuel Goodley, Robert Logan, 1860, J W Hance, Robert H Barlow, 1861, Albin Baldwin, Sharpless Green, 1862, Robert Logan, Wesley Poole, 1863, Robert H Barlow, Benjamin Worrilow, 1864, Clarkson Way, J J Shields, 1865, Charles M Cheyney, Samuel Dalton, 1866, James S Peters, Robert H Barlow, 1867, Albin Baldwin, Benjamin Worrilow, 1868, William S Goodley, Joseph Larkin, 1869, Charles W Poole, Reece Baldwin, 1870, Charles M Cheyney, Sharpless Green, 1871, William S Goodley, Joseph Larkin, 1872, C. W Poole, R Baldwin, 1873, Nathan Cloud, Wesley Poole, 1874, William S. Goodley, Joseph Larkin, 1875, Thomas Talley, James Booth, 1876, Thomas Booth, George Ebright, 1877, Charles M Cheyney, Charles Young, 1878, C. W Poole, A Pierce, 1879, Thomas Hinkson, Charles Young, 1880, Charles M Cheyney, Charles Young, 1881, C W Poole, Alban Pierce, 1882, Thomas Hinkson, Clark W Baldwin, 1883, Charles M Cheyney, William Mathews, 1884, C W Poole, Alban Pierce.

Nearly a mile west of Chelsea, on the Bethel road, is the "Lancaster" farm, where are now the noted garnet-mines About 1873, Charles Williams, who then owned the estate, directed considerable attention to the garnet sand found on the farm, but his object was more to have the larger pebbles set in gold as personal ornaments than for any use in industrial pursuits John H Smedley, of Middletown, a noted geologist and mineralogist, believing that the large deposits of garnets in Bethel could be utilized in all trades in which emery was used for grinding, shaping, and burnishing of metal goods, early in the following year urged upon several firms in Philadelphia the development of the mines to that end, but without success Five years after this discouraging attempt to utilize the deposits of garnets in Bethel, an agent of a New York firm, largely engaged in the manufacture of sand-paper and emery, visited Mr Smedley to consult with him respecting the corundum of Delaware County and its use in their business Smedley informed him that he believed the garnet sand would be of much greater value to them than corundum. The result was a visit to the "Lancaster" farm, and its ultimate purchase by Herman, Behr & Co, of New York, of the forty-seven-acre tract, at a cost of one hundred dollars an acre In the fall of the year 1879 the work of digging was begun, and has been prosecuted with success The value of the garnet-sand varies from thirty to one hundred dollars a ton The first quality is used in making emery-wheels, the second in sand-paper, and the third is sold to stone-cutters for polishing marble

Bethel Lodge, No 191, Knights of Pythias, is located at Booth's Corner

---

BIOGRAPHICAL SKETCHES.

ROBERT McCALL

Mr McCall is of Scotch lineage, and the grandson of Thomas McCall, who resided in Concord township. The children of the latter were seven in number, of whom George, the youngest, married Margaret McKay, daughter of Robert McKay, and had children,—William, Joseph, Rebecca, Robert, Mary, Thomas, and Margaret Robert, the third son, was born on the 14th of July, 1802, in Concord township, and during the period of his early life resided in the county of his birth He improved the slight advantages of education offered, and on attaining his majority developed the exceptional business capacity which has since made his career a successful one Opening a general store at Thornton, Delaware Co, he remained six years in that locality, and then removed to another location in Thornbury, where he also became the proprietor of a similar store, and founded an extensive trade In 1834 he came to Chelsea, Bethel township, erected a store, and conducted a thriving business until 1862, when he retired from mercantile ventures, and purchased a farm to which for a brief period he devoted his energies He, however, continues to occupy the residence in Chelsea he erected fifty years ago, having relinquished the cares of business Mr McCall during his extended life has maintained a reputation for integrity and scrupulous honesty, while his judgment and keen perceptions have aided greatly in the success which has attended his mercantile pursuits He married, March 13, 1834, Mrs Anna M, widow of Dr Jesse Hamer, of Thornbury, and daughter of Dr John H Cheyney, of Delaware County She died in April, 1875, and he was again married to Mrs Lydia P, widow of Thomas P Powel, of Concord Mr McCall was formerly a Democrat in his political predilections, but later espoused the principles of the Republican party He has not been the recipient of any distinguished political honors from the fact of his indifference to such marks of deference. He is a member and rector's warden of St. John's Protestant Episcopal Church of Concord

CHARLES M. CHEYNEY

Charles M Cheyney, the grandfather of the subject of this sketch, was born in Delaware County in 1781, and married Prudence Dutton, the birth of whose only child (a son), David R, occurred June 1, 1809 He early engaged in teaching and subsequently entered the counting-house of a Philadelphia firm, for whom he was book-keeper He was not active as a politician, and the incumbent of no official positions other than those connected with the township. He was married to Elleneanor B Kenney, whose birth occurred in the State of Delaware in 1804, and had

Robert McCall

Charles M. Cheyney

Charles M. Cheyney

Thomas Booth Sr

children,—Anna, Robert (who died in youth), John H (who entered the service during the late war, and after an active military career of two years and nine months was fatally wounded at the battle of Mine Run), and Charles M The last named was born in Thornbury township, Delaware Co, Oct. 26, 1835, and received his education at the public schools of the vicinity, with the additional advantage of a brief period at a private school in Media He then engaged in the labor incident to farm-life, and was thus employed at the time of his enlistment in Company F, Twentieth Pennsylvania Cavalry, under Col John E Wynekoop, for a period of seven months' service before the close of the late war Mr Cheyney was married in 1861 to Sallie J Hall (born in 1838), whose great-grandparents came from their native land with William Penn, and purchased land of him in Concord township, Delaware Co, where they settled George Hall, her grandfather, married Jane James, whose son, Mifflin Hall, father of Mrs Cheyney, was born in 1808, and married Lydia McCullough in 1835 Mr and Mrs Cheyney have had nine children,—John H, Arthur B, David M, Lucius L, William T, Charles R, James S, Harrie B, and Albert B Mr Cheyney is a Republican in his political views and has filled various township offices, having served for eighteen years as a member of the school board In religion he is a supporter, though not a member, of the Methodist Episcopal Church He has since his marriage been engaged in farming in Delaware County

---

THOMAS BOOTH, Sr

Two brothers of the Booth family emigrated from England, if tradition be correct, about two centuries ago, one of them, whose name was Robert, having married, and had among his children a son, Robert, who settled in Bethel township His son, Thomas, the grandfather of the subject of this biography, married Phœbe Cloud, and had children,—James, Joseph, Robert, Nathaniel, Jemima, John, and Isaac The last-named son is the only survivor of this number James Booth was born in 1790, on the homestead in Bethel, which he occupied, and the land of which he cultivated until his marriage He then removed to land purchased by his father, and now owned by the subject of this sketch. He married Lydia Forwood, and had children,—Thomas, Mary, Ann, Phœbe, and one who died in infancy. Thomas Booth was born in 1817, in Bethel township, and spent his childhood upon the farm of his father Having lost that parent when seven years of age, he became an inmate of the home of his uncle, John Booth. After receiving limited advantages of education he entered upon a career of labor, and at twenty-one became owner of the homestead, having inherited his share and purchased the remaining interest He married, in 1844, Susanna Marshall, daughter of John Marshall, who was of English descent, and has children,—Sarah Ann (Mrs John M Hinkson, of Concord), Thomas, Samuel (deceased), and Lydia Emma (deceased)

Thomas married Leah Talley, of Delaware, and has children,—Laura and Thomas About 1854, Mr Booth became a merchant at Booth's Corner, and continued thus employed for some years, after which he returned to the farm, and again resumed the duties of a farmer He is in politics a stanch Republican, and has held various township offices, as also the appointment for many years of postmaster at Booth's Corner Having now abandoned active labor, he still resides in the township, and by his advice and experience aids his son, who cultivates the farm

---

CHAPTER XXXI

BIRMINGHAM TOWNSHIP

At the extreme southwestern end of Delaware County is Birmingham township, which in early days was pronounced as though written Brummagen The Brandywine Creek constitutes the entire western boundary of the township This stream was called by the Swedes Fiskekill, and the present name, by tradition, is asserted to have been given to the creek from the fact that after the conquest of New Sweden by the Dutch, in the fall of the year 1655, a Dutch vessel, ladened with brandy, termed by the Dutch "brandwein," wintered in the stream, and, being cut through by the ice in the following spring, sank The wreck of this vessel is said to have remained until the middle of the last century on the northern side of the stream, several hundred yards above the juncture of the Brandywine with the Christiana River[1] The name of the township, Birmingham, it is generally supposed was given to the territory by William Brinton, the first white settler known to have located in that neighborhood, in remembrance of the town of the like name in England, near which he resided previous to his emigration (in 1684) to the New World At that time he was a man beyond the noonday of life, and accompanied by his wife, Ann, his junior by five years, a son (William) and two daughters (Elizabeth and Esther), he pushed out beyond the extreme limit of civilization, where he erected a log cabin, as was then the custom, near a spring, among a heavy growth of hardwood trees, preferring to undergo the privations which must necessarily attend his residence there than to submit to the persecutions which, for conscience' sake, he had been forced to endure in his native land. He had purchased from Joseph Allibone and William Morgan four hundred acres, and his patent was so located that a century later, when the county of Delaware was erected out of Chester,

[1] Ferris' "Original Settlements on the Delaware," p 196 Vincent's "History of Delaware," vol i p 262.

the line of demarkation cut his original tract into almost equal parts, giving a like portion to both of the counties. The first winter the emigrants passed in the "backwoods," that of 1685–86, was unusually rigorous, bringing in its train severe privations. To such extremity was the household reduced, owing to their remote situation, that the family tradition records they would all have perished by starvation had not the Indians supplied them with game and grain. His settlement, or the tract patented to him, had on it at the time an Indian town. The savages never disturbed him, but, on the other hand, always seemed glad to be of service or minister, so far as they could, to his or his family's necessities.

Slowly the land in that locality was settled, but the residents for several miles, who were mostly of the society of Friends, would occasionally hold religious meetings at his dwelling, which was familiarly termed "the cabin." When George Keith sowed dissension in the society, William Brinton leaned to the precepts of the former, but he ultimately became reconciled, and died in 1700, at threescore years and ten, in full membership with Friends. His wife had died the preceding year, and both were buried on the homestead farm, the place of their interment being on the right-hand side of the road leading from Dilworthtown to Painter's Cross-road. William Brinton had acquired considerable real estate subsequent to the patent mentioned, and at his death was considered as possessed of large means.

William Brinton, the younger, who was a stripling of seventeen when his father settled in Birmingham, at the age of twenty-three married Jane, a daughter of Richard Thatcher, of Thornbury. After his father's death, he built, in 1704, a stone house a short distance south of Dilworthtown, which, still standing, remained for over a hundred and seventy-five years almost as it was when he erected it. It is only in the last few years that it has undergone any alteration. He was an enterprising man, being one of the projectors and owners of a company grist-mill in Concord, the first located in that section, and was largely instrumental in the erection of Concord Friends' meeting-house, to which he contributed liberally. His wife, when fifty-four years of age, in 1724, accompanied Elizabeth Webb, a ministering Friend, in a religious visit to New England, the entire journey being made on horseback. From a letter written by her from Long Island, it appears that she was particularly pleased with a horse she saw there "with a white star in his face." In 1695 he was constable of Birmingham, and in 1713 was a member of the Legislature from Chester County. He died in 1751, aged eighty-four years. The offspring of this couple—from whom all the Brintons derive descent—was numerous. Edward Brinton, their third son, died in 1799, aged ninety-four years. From the birth of his grandfather, William Brinton, Sr., the immigrant, in 1630, to the date of his own death, is an interval of one hundred and sixty-nine years,—a remarkable period of time to be covered by three generations in one family.

William Brinton's, Sr., daughter, Ann, about or shortly after her father left England for the province, had intermarried with John Bennett, a blacksmith, who, with his wife immigrated the next year and settled on lands of his father-in-law. In 1686, John Bennett was appointed constable for Birmingham, which is the first official record of that municipal district in our county's annals.

The next settler in Birmingham, after Brinton and his son-in-law, Bennett, were Peter and Sarah Dix, which name in the lapse of years was changed to Dicks. The land patented to him was the first tract taken up extending to Brandywine Creek, and thereon he built his cabin in the thick forest, with no neighbor nearer than about two miles away. This tract was not located within the limits of the present county of Delaware, but the dividing line runs along the southern and part of the eastern boundary of his estate. His son, Peter Dicks, however, played a prominent part in our colonial history in his efforts to foster manufacturing, and will be referred to elsewhere.

Joseph Gilpin and Hannah, his wife, are believed to have settled in Birmingham in 1695, certainly not later than that date. They were people of position in England, being descended from Richard de Guylpin, to whom in 1206 the baron of Kendal gave the manor of Kentmere, as a reward for having slain a ferocious wild boar that infested the forest of Westmoreland and Cumberland. Under the will of William Lamboll, of the city of Reading, England, Joseph Gilpin received a part of the large tract of land which had been surveyed and located in Birmingham in 1683, to Lamboll. Gilpin, as did all the Quaker settlers of the day, knew the power of religious oppression, and gladly came to the province to take possession of his inheritance. When he settled on the estate he dug a cave at the side of a large rock, on the present farm of Albin Harvey, wherein he resided for a number of years, and where thirteen of his family of fifteen children were born.[1] It was on this property that two valuable varieties of apple originated,—the Gilpin, also called carthouse and winter red-streak, and the house-apple, also called gray house-apple. They were two of several hundred of new varieties produced from seeds brought from England by the first settlers. Only these two were worthy of perpetuation by grafting.

The farm in Birmingham, where the first Gilpin settled, remained in the ownership of their descendants until recent years. Joseph Gilpin, some years after he made his settlement, built a frame house, and removed from his cave to that dwelling. In 1745, adjoining the frame, a brick house was erected. On the evening of Thursday, Sept. 11, 1777, the house then

[1] Johnson's "History of Cecil County, Md.," p. 511.

owned by George Gilpin was occupied by Gen. Howe as his headquarters, and there the commander-in-chief remained until the following Tuesday, when the British army moved to the Boot Tavern, in Goshen township. The farm, with the old dwelling standing thereon, is now owned by Elias Baker, and the latter every now and then in plowing turns up British pieces of coin, dropped by the invaders of a century ago.

Francis Chadsey, or Chads, as the name afterwards came to be written,—now frequently and improperly spelled Chadd,—emigrated from Wiltshire, England, early in 1689, with his wife, and resided at or near Chichester until about 1696, when his name appears on the list of taxables for Birmingham. It is presumed that he located on the five hundred acres surveyed to Henry Bernard, or Barnet, early in March, 1684, and conveyed to Daniel Smith, March 28, 29, 1686, which tract included all the present village of Chad's Ford. Francis Chads did not, however, acquire title to the estate until Nov. 24, 1702, and on May 4th of the following year he purchased one hundred and eleven acres adjoining his estate to the southeast, from Edmund Butcher. Chads served as a member of the Assembly from Chester County for the years 1706 and 1707, and about that time, it is believed by Gilbert Cope, he erected his corn-mill, the first in Pennsylvania, on the Brandywine, for dying in 1713 he devised to one of his sons "a half share in my corn-mill." This mill, which is supposed to have been a log building, was permitted to go to decay, until in time its very site was forgotten; indeed, that it had ever existed passed out of the memory of man, until in 1860, in making the excavations for the foundations of the brick mill erected by Caleb Brinton, a short distance west of the station of the Baltimore Central Railroad, at Chad's Ford, a log with an old wrought-iron spike was found, with other evidences establishing the location of Chads' mill. That this was the first mill on the Brandywine, as is frequently asserted, cannot be successfully maintained, for as early as May 17, 1689, a petition of "ye Inhabitants of Brandywine River or Creek against ye dam made upon ye creek, wch hinders ye fish passing up to ye great damage of ye inhabitants,"[1] shows conclusively that a mill of some kind had then been erected. We know that twenty years before Chads' mill was built, on April 2, 1667, "Cornelius Empson's petition Concerning a Bridg Road and Water mill on Brandywine Creek was Read."[2] This mill, however, was in Delaware.

John Chads, who received the larger part of his father's estate, after his marriage to Elizabeth Richardson, in 1729, is believed to have built the old stone house close to the spring, still standing, the most northern one in the village of Chad's Ford, which was opposite the then ford of the Brandywine. In 1829, when the bridge was erected, the petition for its construction being presented to court July 17, 1828, the road crossing the stream was carried to the south, its present course.

The tradition in the neighborhood is that the log cabin of Francis Chads had stood near by where the present stone building now stands. As the tide of emigration moved westward public travel necessarily increased, and as the Brandywine in rainy weather and in spring-time was so swollen that it was almost impossible to cross it, John Chads was solicited to establish a ferry at that place, and to aid him in that public work the county loaned him thirty pounds to meet the expense he was put to in building a "flatt or schowe." He seems to have been ready to enter into the duties required in 1737, for on August 30th of that year the following records appear in the proceedings of the Court of Quarter Sessions:

"John Chads having petitioned the court setting forth that by the concurrence of the Justices and by order of the Commissioners and Assessors, a ferry being erected over Brandywine creek on the road leading from Philadelphia to Nottingham, and no rates for the same established, prays that such rates be set for the same, as to the court may seem reasonable: Whereupon the court taking the same into consideration, have adjudged the rates hereafter mentioned may be demanded and taken by the said John Chads, or his assigns or successors in the said ferry:

"For
- Every horse and rider, four pence.
- Every single person on foot, three pence; if more, two pence each.
- Every ox, cow, or heifer, four pence each.
- Every sheep, one pence.
- Every hog, three half-pence.
- Every coach, wagon, or cart, one shilling and six pence.
- Every empty wagon or cart, nine pence.
- Every steed, four pence.

"To the aforesaid rates the justices have subscribed their names:

"Richard Hayes,
"John Crosby,
"Henry Hayes,
"Samuel Hollingsworth,
"John Parry,
"Abraham Emmitt,
"Caleb Cowpland,
"Elisha Gatchell,
"Joseph Brinton."

The story of the ford is so intimately connected with the tavern at that point that all further reference to it will be found in the narrative of the license houses of Birmingham, excepting the fact that in 1760, the year of John Chads' death, it appears that the old flat was worn out, and for "rebuilding the Flatt" he charged the county £44 3*s.* 6*d.*, one of the items in the bill rendered being "To five weeks diet to boat-builder at six shillings per week £1 10*s.*" The post planted on the west side of the Brandywine to fasten the ferry rope to, was still standing in 1827, but the rope, windlass, and boat had disappeared. About the date given Hetty Brown, a colored woman, who kept a small store at the ford, where she sold cakes and beer, for a small sum would ferry passengers across the creek in a boat, which she shoved with a pole. John Chads' widow was living at the ford on the day of the battle of Brandywine, in the stone house already mentioned. Dr. Darlington related that Amos House, a

[1] Colonial Records, vol. i. p. 292.

[2] Ib., p. 199.

nephew of Elizabeth Chads, who was then a widower, had come to reside with his aunt, and superintend the farm. On the morning of the battle, Washington and a few officers rode to the field just above Chads' house, and were busy with their field-glasses, when Amos House and several others, out of sheer curiosity, approached the group of officers. The British artillery from the opposite bank fired several cannon-balls into the field near by, whereupon Gen. Washington remarked to the unbidden company, "Gentlemen, you perceive that we are attracting the notice of the enemy; I think you had better retire." A hint which was promptly taken.[1] Amos House, a descendant of this Amos House, still a resident of Chad's Ford, at the American Centennial, in 1876, had the control of the dairy established by the Dairymen's Association on those grounds, which will be recalled by all who visited the Exhibition.

In 1707, Samuel Painter, a son of Painter or Pariour (for the name is sometimes spelled in that way), became a resident of Birmingham, having purchased something over five hundred acres of contiguous land from several parties in the neighborhood of the present Painter's Cross-roads. He was a tailor by trade, and appears to have thriven in his occupation, for at the time of his death he was the owner of more than a thousand acres in Birmingham, lying nearly equally divided between the present Delaware and Chester Counties. This large estate was not contiguous, that in Chester County being widely separated from his possessions in Delaware County.

In 1688, as heretofore mentioned, it was reported that the Indians on a certain day had determined to massacre the whites, and, as rumor asserted that five hundred warriors of the savages had assembled at an Indian town on the Brandywine, "and that they having a lame King, had carried him away with all their women and children," this alarming intelligence was hastily borne to Philadelphia, reaching there while the Provincial Council was in session. A member of that body, a Friend, voluntarily proposed to go to the place with five other persons, unarmed, and the offer being accepted, they rode to the Indian town on the Brandywine, where, instead of meeting savages in war-paint, they found the old chief "quietly lying with his lame foot along on the ground, and his head at ease on a kind of pillow, the women at work in the field, and the children playing together."[2] The delegation was assured that the rumor was false, and the woman who had raised the report ought to be burned to death. The site of the Indian town was in the neck of land above the present Smith's bridge, on which afterwards the iron-works of Twaddle were erected, known in more recent times as the old paper-mill.

On June 24, 1729, the Indian chief Checochinican addressed a letter to the Governor and Council, alleging that when they sold their interest in the lands watered by the Brandywine to Penn, he had granted them "a wrighting for the creek of Brandywine up to the Head thereof, which said wrighting, by some Accident, was Lost with all land a mile wide of ye Creek on each side, which afterwards we Disposed of so far up as to a Certain known rock in ye said creek."[3] As this disputed title does not touch any portion of the land in Delaware County, but relates to that located in Newlin township, in the present county of Chester, extended consideration of the topic does not come within the scope of this work. The Indians, however, so long as any of them remained, insisted that a strip of land a mile wide on both sides of the stream had been reserved to them in their sale to Penn. Andrew and Hannah, the last Indians in the neighborhood of Birmingham, who lived in a hut or wigwam on the high ground on the east side of the creek, above where the Baltimore Central Railroad bridge crosses the stream, always made claim to this land. I am informed by Amos C. Brinton, of Wilmington, a native of Birmingham, and a gentleman well informed as to the olden times of that locality, that the old Indians did not attempt to till the ground, but went from house to house demanding their meals, and if it chanced that the meal was over, they would scold violently because it had not been delayed for them. Hannah made baskets and gathered herbs to the last. She died about 1800, having survived her husband several years. Andrew was buried on the original tract patented to William Brinton, Sr., his grave being located on Dix Run, about half a mile south of Dilworthtown. Indian Hannah, the last of her tribe, died in the Chester County almshouse. She expressed a wish to be buried in a certain Indian burying-ground which she designated, but was buried with other paupers on the almshouse grounds.

It has been published that the British forces at Chad's Ford, on Sept. 11, 1777, crossed below the ford. This, however, is incorrect. The enemy waded across the stream above the ford. The road taken by the American Reserves to Birmingham meeting-house was up the ravine from William Harvey's house, past the barn, over the hill to and across Dix's Run, up the next hill to and across the road from Dilworthtown to the Brandywine, at a point between the James Brinton and Darlington residences; thence nearly northeast across the Bennett land to the Sandy Hollow road which led to Birmingham meeting-house, the scene of that part of the battle of Brandywine. One wing of Greene's command was shown the way by George Hannum, who piloted them across the Gilpin lands from the Philadelphia and Chad's Ford road to the south of Dilworthtown.

The old Benjamin Ring Tavern, where Washington had his headquarters, was on the north side of the

[1] Futhey and Cope's "History of Chester County," p. 80.
[2] Proud's "History of Pennsylvania," vol. i. p. 337.
[3] Penna. Archives, vol. i., 1st series, p. 239.

great road which leads to the ford, about a mile east of the Brandywine It was of stone, two stories in height, with a hipped roof, and became the property of Eli Harvey in 1807, after the death of Benjamin Ring Eli Harvey was the great-grandson of William Harvey, the immigrant, who, at the age of thirty-four, in 1712, came to Pennsylvania, and settled on a tract of three hundred acres in "the woods of Kennett," on the west side of the Brandywine and above the ford William, the immigrant, was succeeded on the home farm by his son, William, he by his son, Amos, he by his sons, Marshall and Eli, Jr Eli Harvey, of Chad's Ford, was the father of Hannah (who married Robert Peirce), Joseph P, Amos, Chalkley, Edith (who married Isaac Watkin), Evelina (married Thomas Brinton Darlington), Ellwood, Lewis P, Philena (married Mordecai Lewis), and Mary (who married Watson P Magill)

William Harvey, the grandson of the immigrant, resided on the east bank of the Brandywine, this land extending from below the Delaware line above and beyond Chad's Ford Below the Delaware line the crossing of the stream is still known as Harvey's Ford, and the day of the battle his house at Chad's Ford was in the line of the American cannon, and was damaged by a shot from Proctor's gun The ball, which buried itself in the ground after passing through William Harvey's house, is still in the possession of his relatives, as is also an oak chair which was brought to the colony by the immigrant

William Harvey, another grandson of the immigrant, lived on the ground occupied in part by the American army at the Chad's Ford battle, and being a Friend, commonly called a Quaker, and a non-combatant, took no part on either side, but remained about his work as if nothing unusual was going on When the British passed by his house in pursuit of the retreating Americans, they made him a prisoner, and marched him near the front of the army As they went up the hill east of his house, on the brow of which was a fence covered with bushes, he saw the Americans pointing their guns towards him and the British through the bushes, and was almost stunned by the fearful flash and roar of their simultaneous discharge He was astonished to find himself alive, and still more on observing that not a man was killed or wounded The Americans had fired over their heads The British, or, more correctly, their Hessian allies, then rushed up to the fence and fired at the retreating Americans with deadly effect When the British reached Dilworthtown, William Harvey, with a few other prisoners, were confined in the cellar under the tavern, from which they made their escape by wrenching out the window-frame On his way home through a woods, he saw a pair of laced boots protruding from a hollow log, and upon closer investigation discovered his colored girl hidden there He remained a Quaker, but on account of the active interest he manifested in the cause of the revolting colonies, after the battle of Brandywine, he was called by the title of major to the end of his life

The inhabitants of Birmingham suffered greatly from the British foraging parties The following is a list of damages sustained

	£	s	d
From William Dilworth by the British army, under Sir William Howe (and damages), while encamped at Dilworthtown after the battle of Brandywine, September 11th to 16th	48	2	0
From Charles Dilworth "property taken, damages, waste, spoil, and destruction done and committed by the army of the King of Great Britain and their adherents under the immediate command of Sir William Howe,"[1] September 11th to 16th	820	15	3
From Joseph Dilworth, ditto	522	12	2½
From Charles Porter, "a very poor man," ditto..	8	7	6
From William Chapman, ditto.	16	3	3
From John Martin, September 12th to 16th	242	4	6
From William Harvey, Jr, "taken and destroyed the 11th day of September (and thereabout) by the army of his Britanic Majesty, commanded by Sir William Howe, K B, Supporter of Tyranny, Falsifier of his word, and plunderer of private property"	562	16	6
From John Bennett, September 11th to 16th	401	1	4
From George Brinton, ditto	[illegible]44	11	8
From Rachel Hannings ditto	47	12	6
From Caleb Brinton,[2] ditto	[illegible]92	18	8
From Israel Gilpin, ditto	607	12	6
From Thomas Hannum, September 11th	42	2	0
From John Henderson, September 11th to 16th	536	6	11
From John Chamberlain, September 13th to 16th	57	0	3
From Gideon Gilpin, September 11th	502	6	0
From Jesse Graves September 11th to 16th	212	14	8
From Thomas Davis, ditto	24	5	7
From James Dilworth, ditto.	13	0	0
From Charles McCrea, September 11th to 17th	41	13	4
	5844	6	7½

The lands of Lewis P Harvey, "the National Kaolin Company," was formerly part of the manor of Rockland —the manor located in the county of New Castle, but crossing the Brandywine into Birmingham,—and part of the land of the kaolin-works was included in the warrant for two hundred and fifty acres given to Robert Chalfant in 1701, he having settled there two years before that date From him it is believed the Chalfant family have descended

Churches—Presbyterian.—In the bend of the road leading down to Corner Ford, on the property of William H Seal, the Lower Brandywine Presbyterian Church formerly stood, and some of the old gravestones in the little burial-ground can still be seen there The Presbyterians early in the last century had churches in this vicinity,—in log buildings,—one located at Marlborough, known as the Upper Brandywine, and the one on the Seal farm, called the Lower Brandywine Church It was established here in 1720, and for a long period of years services would occasionally be held in this unpretentious structure, but finally, after the Revolution, it was abandoned, the congregation assembling for worship at the "old log meeting" at Centreville, Del Rev Mr Reed was the pastor in charge of this little wayside sanctuary during the war of independence, and tradition states that it was this clergyman who, in the darkness of the morning of Sept. 9, 1777, guided Washington when the American army moved from Stanton, Del, to Chad's Ford,

[1] Among the items charged is "the time of a Servant Lad, Patrick Kelly, about 14 months to stay, went off with the army, £10"

[2] Including "two books,—'Barclay's Apology,' and 'Young Man's Best Companion'"

crossing the Brandywine at Harvey's Ford, below Smith's bridge. For nearly a century the Presbyterians of Birmingham were without a church building, but on Monday, June 3, 1878, a church of that denomination was dedicated at Dilworthtown. The building is of serpentine stone, and is lighted with stained glass memorial windows. The church was the direct outgrowth of the labor of Miss Cassy Brinton, a daughter of Hill Brinton, of Thornbury, who, about 1860, started a Sunday-school at Dilworthtown. For years that hamlet had been termed "the Devil's Half-Acre," and many of the old people declared that it was known the country round as furnishing more drunken men, more fights and disturbances, than any locality of the like size in twenty miles. That unpleasant reputation has long since passed away from Dilworthtown, and now better manners, if not better whiskey, will be found in the village.

Baptist.—The Baptist Church in Birmingham, the third of that denomination in Pennsylvania, was instituted May 14, 1715, the membership comprising fifteen persons, but nearly a quarter of a century previous to that date religious services by Baptists are said to have been held on the same ground where the church was afterwards erected. At first the meetings for worship were held at private houses, but in a few years the congregation determined to build a church, which was done in 1718, a log structure being erected on a lot of land which had belonged to Edward Butcher, doubtless given by him for that purpose. The first permanent pastor was William Butcher, a native of Birmingham, in 1719. He was twenty years of age when intrusted with the charge of the church. In 1721 he received a call to New Jersey, and died in that province in his twenty-sixth year. The struggling congregation continued to worship in the primitive building until 1770, when it was demolished, and a stone structure erected on its site. For forty years it had been without a regular pastor, until 1761, when Rev. Abel Griffith was installed. Here he remained until 1767, when he resigned, but in 1775 he returned to the charge of the church, continuing there until 1790. In 1791, Rev. Joshua Vaughan was installed. He was by birth a Chester countian, by trade a blacksmith, and during the Revolution, when David Mackey was sheriff, he was the jailer at the prison in Chester. While in that employment he was baptized by the Rev. Philip Hughes, a Baptist clergyman, who frequently preached at the county-seat. It is related that, when the minister and he were walking to the stream to be baptized, some one in jest asked who they were. "We are Philip and his jailer," retorted Vaughan. He continued in the pastorate until the summer of 1808, when he died. His remains lie in the burial-ground alongside the church.

The fourth pastor was Rev. Charles Moore. He was an Episcopalian, residing in Concord, and as the church of that denomination in that township was without a rector he frequently conducted the services there as a lay preacher. In 1802 he became a Baptist, being immersed in the Brandywine at Chad's Ford. In 1812 he was licensed to preach, and in the fall of the year 1813 he was ordained pastor of the church, and continued in charge of the congregation until 1848. It is remembered that Rev. Mr. Moore, as he grew older and saw the wonderful growth of the United States (he died in 1847), he would frequently relate how, as a child of six years, he was taken to the State-House yard, Philadelphia, when the old liberty bell with its brazen tongue proclaimed the birth of the new nation.

Rev. Joseph Walker, who succeeded Mr. Moore, was a native of Delaware County, having been born in Lower Chichester in 1787. In 1822 he was licensed to preach, and in 1824 became the pastor of the church at Marcus Hook, continuing there twenty-four years, during which period he frequently preached at Birmingham. In 1848 he became the pastor of the latter church, and continued there until 1863, when he resigned, his seventy-six years having brought with them the infirmities of age. On Feb. 10, 1870, the present and third church, on the same site, was dedicated, and not quite three weeks thereafter the aged pastor, Mr. Walker, having completed, excepting two weeks, his eighty-third year of life, died in Alleghany City.

The sixth pastor was Rev. Jesse B. Williams, who was ordained in 1866, and remained in charge of the Brandywine Church until 1869, when he was succeeded by the seventh pastor, Rev. Isaac M. Haldeman. The latter was a native of Concordville, Delaware Co., and was twenty-six years old in 1871, when installed pastor of the Brandywine Church. Just previous to his taking charge of the congregation the old stone building was torn down and the present edifice erected. It was dedicated Thursday, Feb. 10, 1870, and on that occasion, it appearing that two thousand dollars was still due for work and materials, Samuel A. Crozer offered to discharge five hundred dollars of it, if the remaining fifteen hundred dollars could be collected. This was done and the church freed from debt. Mr. Haldeman's pastorate was eminently successful, and the church thrived under his care as it had never done before. In April, 1875, he resigned to accept a charge in Wilmington, Del., and was followed by Rev. John Reader, who continued there from May, 1877, until the following April, when he resigned. In May, 1878, Rev. Alexander MacAuthor, a graduate of Crozer Theological Seminary in that year, was ordained, but resigning in the following February, the present and tenth pastor, Rev. J. Wesley Sullivan, also a graduate of Crozer Theological Seminary, was installed in June, 1880, and is now in the fourth year of a successful pastorate. Before dismissing the account of the Brandywine Baptist Church, it is proper to recall Robert Frame, who, dying Feb. 20, 1871, in the seventy-eight years of life which had been allotted to him, could remember the three sanctuaries, the old log, the first stone, and subsequently the present, third and imposing, structure, and, perhaps, to no man is the Brandywine Baptist Church more indebted than to Robert Frame, who through life labored to advance its interest and well-being

The adherents to the forms and rituals of the Church of England, until within a year, had no house of worship in Birmingham, but it must not be supposed that there were no earnest Episcopalians in that township Ralph Pyle was an ardent churchman, and by his will, dated Jan 1, 1739, provision was made for three sermons to be preached on three certain days in each year at Concord parish, by a minister of the Church of England

St. Luke's Protestant Episcopal Church.—Services according to the ritual of the Episcopal Church were had at Chad's Ford from time to time, the first consecutive services having been held by Rev J Coupland, rector of St John's Church, Concord, which were continued during the rectorship of Rev H. B Dean The congregation assembled in the school-house and at private houses St John's parish being without a rector, until the election of the present incumbent, Rev J J Sleeper, services were necessarily discontinued, but on the latter being installed rector, a determined movement was made to locate a permanent church organization at Chad's Ford J M Baker entered earnestly into the movement, and the result was that funds were collected justifying the erection of a church edifice A lot was secured from John Arment, and on June 11, 1883, the corner-stone was laid by Rev W H Graff, of Philadelphia, assisted by Rev. John Bolton, of West Chester, and Rev J J Sleeper, rector of St John's parish On May 1, 1884, St Luke's Church was opened for divine service, the rector of St John's parish officiating, assisted by Rev Messrs Henry Brum, William H Graff, William M Jefferis, John Bolton, Richardson Graham, H Greenfield Schow, and George C Moore At the conclusion of the services, as a testimonial to Rev J J Sleeper for his untiring efforts to establish the church at Chad's Ford, a costly gold watch was presented to him On May 12, 1884, the church was organized by Rev Joseph J Sleeper, rector of St John's parish, the first vestrymen being Frank Graff, Frank Tempest, Dr H Hayward, L S Williamson, W William Ring, J T Brittingham, and George K Barney Mr Williamson was elected accounting warden After the board of vestrymen organized, Rev Joseph J Sleeper was elected rector, and J M Baker treasurer of the building fund Frank Graff was appointed rector's warden by Mr Sleeper The church is an ornate frame structure, located a short distance northwest from the railroad station at Chad's Ford.

Friends' Meeting-House.—In the old township of Birmingham, before its dismemberment at the time Delaware County was erected, stood the ancient historic Birmingham Friends' meeting-house The old battle-scarred building, in the division of the township, fell to the lot of Chester County However, as Friends in Lower Birmingham for over a hundred and fifty years have assembled in the structure to commune together in religious exercises, I will briefly touch on its history The first house, which was of cedar logs, was erected in 1722, on grounds given by Elizabeth Webb for that purpose, and the burial-lot was inclosed with a post-and-rail fence About 1763 the oldest part of the present stone meeting-house was built, and the old log house used as a stable Subsequently an addition was made to the stone building on the east end Tradition states that the stone walls surrounding the burial-ground, in the battle of Brandywine, were used by the American riflemen, and the dark spots on the oaken floor are said to have been made by the blood of wounded soldiers, the building having been used as a hospital for nearly a week, or until the British army marched to the Boot Tavern In the old "God's Acre" surrounding the building for many years, in digging fresh graves, relics of the slain in that battle were disinterred As late as 1828 a writer,[1] in describing a visit to the old meeting-house and battle-field, says,—

"You may be shown a gold coin of the olden time which some Hessian private had concealed, with several of its fellows, in the cue of his hair, and which may have recently been disinterred with his mouldering remains, or you may visit the Birmingham graveyard, and as you see the sexton turning up, some two feet below the surface, the bones of a British soldier, with fragments of his red coat still retaining its color, his stock buckle, pocket glass, flints, and buttons (stamped with the number of his regiment), contrast the peaceful scenes which now surround you and the peaceful tenets of the religious society worshiping in the humble tabernacle near with that terrible day when mighty armies here met in conflict, this spot echoed back the tempest of war, shook with the thunder of artillery, and was literally drenched with the blood of the slain "

Tradition asserts that a young man named Percy, supposed to be a relative of the Duke of Northumberland, was killed near the meeting-house "When he had arrived with the regiment he accompanied, in sight of the Americans ranged in order of battle upon the heights near Birmingham meeting-house, he surveyed the field around him for a moment, and then turning to his servant, handed him his purse and his gold watch to take charge of, remarking, 'This place I saw in a dream before I left England, and I know I shall fall here' The coincident was striking and remarkable, the event verified the prediction His name is not mentioned in the British official account of the battle, because he held no commission in the army He was merely a volunteer" Gideon D Scull, writing from Rugby, England, Feb 5, 1880, says, respecting this alleged incident of the battle,—

"To the Editor of the Delaware County Republican

"The recent revival in some of your papers of the old popular belief that Earl Percy, or some near relative of that name, was killed at the Battle of Brandywine, has no foundation whatever in fact Lossing also asserts that he never was present even in that engagement

[1] Hazard's "Register of Pennsylvania," vol I p 365

"Earl Percy succeeded his father in 1786, but was summoned to Parliament in 1777, as Baron Percy. He married, in 1764, Lady Anne Stuart, 3d daughter of the Earl of Bute, by whom he had no issue, and from whom he was divorced by act of Parliament in 1779.

"In the register of Westminster Abbey the following entry duly attests his burial there:

"'1817. July 19. The most noble Hugh Percy, Duke and Earl of Northumberland, Earl and Baron Percy, Baron Lucy, &c., &c., (died) at Northumberland House, Strand, July 10th, aged 75. (Buried) in the Northumberland vault in St. Nicholas Chapel.'

"Earl Percy's father was Hugh Smithson, 2d son of Sir Hugh, who was 3d Baronet of Stanwick, county of York. Hugh Smithson succeeded to his father's title and estates in 1749–50, and married Lady Elizabeth Seymour, whose father was Charles Seymour, 7th Duke of Somerset (known as the proud Duke of Somerset), and who was, in 1749, created Earl of Northumberland, he having married Lady Elizabeth Percy, only daughter of Joseline, 11th Earl of Percy, who died in 1670, at the age of twenty-six, without male issue. Sir Hugh Smithson assumed the name of Percy, and was created, in 1766, Earl Percy and Duke of Northumberland. He was succeeded by his 2d son in 1786, who died in 1817, and was buried, as before mentioned, in Westminster Abbey.

"A glance at the Percy pedigree in Burke's 'Peerage' is sufficient to convince any one that Earl Percy (of 1777) could not possibly have had any male relatives of his name who could have been present at the battle of Brandywine in 1777. There were, however, several children of the Duke's (Earl Percy's father) who were recognized as his illegitimate offspring by different mothers, two of whom were buried in Westminster Abbey, in the South Cross. They were named Philadelphia and Dorothy Percy. The former died in 1791 and the latter in 1794.

"They had a half brother James Macie, who some years after assumed his father's name of Smithson, and who died in Genoa, Italy, in 1826, and is the same person who left his fortune, which was large, to found the Smithsonian Institution at Washington, D. C. He commences his will thus, 'I, James Smithson, son of Hugh, first Duke of Northumberland, and Elizabeth, heiress of the Hungerfords of Audley, and niece of Charles, the Proud Duke of Somerset.' So that this James Smithson was well born both on his father's and on his mother's side.

"The Proud Duke of Somerset received this sobriquet on account of his intolerable pride. After his wife's death he again married, and it is recorded that on one occasion his new spouse, who was also of high birth, placed her hand upon his shoulder. Thereupon he drew himself up in a haughty manner and said, 'Madam! my first wife was a Percy, and she never dared to take that liberty.' He was also fond of remarking that he really pitied Adam, 'for he had no ancestors.'

"After reading Judge Futhey's communication, one feels inclined to think that there must have been some foundation for the various statements and traditions current in the neighborhood of the battle-field, coming down, as they have done, from the life of such respected and truth-telling old Friends as he cites, and it is not at all improbable than an illegitimate son of the Duke of Northumberland was wounded and died and was buried on the battle-ground. But supposing there was such a one, his name need not necessarily be looked for amongst the British list of dead, under the name either of Percy or Smithson, for many of different names claimed paternity of Earl Percy's father."

Mills.—The story of the Brandywine in reference to the industrial establishments located along that creek, as well as those on its tributary streams in Delaware County, is interesting. In attempting to relate it, I propose to begin at the Delaware State line, and follow the creek up to where the line dividing Chester and Delaware Counties intersects with that stream. Beaver Creek empties into the Brandywine just south of the circular line, and there, partly located in Delaware County and partly in the State of Delaware, is the grist-mill of Marshall Brinton. "The Beaver Valley Mills" at one time were owned by Thomas Gibson, a practical millwright, who, in 1808, sold them to John Farra, who repaired or rebuilt the mills. At the latter's death the estate was sold to Lewis Smith, and he subsequently conveyed the mills to Marshall Brinton, who enlarged the building by addition of an upper story and put in improved machinery. The mills are now owned by Joseph Brinton. Following Beaver Creek, near the highway leading to Smith's bridge, was a woolen-factory, built in 1817 by John Farra, who leased it to La Forrest brothers, but in 1824 it was burned, and remained as the flames had left it until 1830, when it was rebuilt on part of the old walls as a paper-mill. As such it was occupied by William and John Gilmore for a year, when Farra took possession, and manufactured paper therein until his death, in June, 1832. He was succeeded by his son, Daniel. On May 15, 1851, the paper-mill in its turn was destroyed by fire. The property then passed into the ownership of Frank Tempest, who rebuilt the mill and added to the machinery an engine, so that either water or steam-power could be used. Still following the east branch of Beaver Creek, on the same highway, near Tempest's mill, in 1809, Peter Hatton built a fulling-mill, and in 1817 he erected a woolen-factory, wherein were manufactured flannels, satinets, cloth, etc. The fulling-mill has gone to decay, but the factory is still standing, now idle for the purpose it was built, the water which formerly furnished it power being now used to assist in driving the machinery in Tempest's paper-mill, both mills now being owned by the Tempest family. In 1826 the two mills were supplied with water by the same race. The machinery consists of one pair of stocker and two carding engines. The business was carried on by his sons, Samuel and Gideon Hatton. In 1843 the Hatton mill was owned by Philip Hizer, and the dam there was washed away in the flood of that year. In the bend of Beaver Creek, just beyond the circular line, in the State of Delaware, was the woolen-factory built in 1825 by Charles Dupont, and operated by Lewis Sacriste, but the structure was washed entirely away in the flood of Aug. 5, 1843. Farther along its east branch, in close proximity to the line of Concord township, is located the old Green saw-mill. It was built shortly after the beginning of this century, and subsequently became the property of Reece Perkins, who owned it in 1843 at the time of the flood; afterwards it was owned by Daniel Farra, Jr., then by Samuel Talley, and now by William Hinkson. On the west branch of Beaver Creek, according to the map of Dr. Joshua Ash, in 1848, there was an axe-mill,—edge-tool works,—owned by William Morrison. I have no information respecting this establishment.

Returning to the Brandywine, just below the Delaware State line is Smith's bridge, which was built on piers in 1816, and in 1822 was swept away in a freshet. It was rebuilt, to be again carried off by the water in 1839. At the side of where the single-arched bridge now stands is a ford, which is occasionally used to this day. Following the creek above Smith's bridge, in the bend of the stream, is Willis' or Corner Ford. On the day of the battle of Brandywine, Gen. Armstrong's lines extended to that point for the purpose of preventing the English troops from crossing there.

As we proceeded in the abrupt bend of the creek to the south, near where Twaddell's old paper-mill stands, at the beginning of this century was a saw-mill, which has long ago disappeared Previous to 1777, William Twaddell became the owner of the estate, comprising all the neck of land, and here he erected iron-works in connection with the saw-mill In 1780 he was in Aston, and in that year called himself a "forge-master," and registered three slaves as his property At that time he doubtless was working the old forge at Rockdale It is by tradition asserted that when the American army lay encamped at Chad's Ford, Twaddell bargained with a number of deserting militiamen to dig a race for him, extending from above Pyle's Ford to his saw-mill, situated nearly three-quarters of a mile below When the race was about finished, Twaddell, in apparent alarm, came running to where the men were working, shouting out, "The British! the British!" whereupon the deserters hastily decamped without waiting to be paid for the job The iron-works were erected subsequent to 1780 The distance which Twaddell had to cart the ore before and the iron after smelting induced him to change the works into powder-mills in 1807, which were known as the "Cannon Powder-Mills," and as such they continued until 1831, at which time he had two powder-mills and four drying-houses, when they were again changed into paper-mills

It is alleged that on several occasions there were explosions at the mills while powder was made there, but in no instance was any person injured Just above Twaddell's dam, which crossed the Brandywine obliquely, Thomas Gibson had a saw-mill on the west side of the creek, the dam of the latter being at right angles to the stream Even now, when the water is low and clear, the race can be traced down to where Gibson's saw-mill stood Long years ago the mill was struck by lightning, the building destroyed, and the sawyer killed Half a mile above Pyle's Ford is the Twin or Barney bridge, at John B Barney's farm, from which circumstance the bridge is frequently called by his name The term Twin was applied to it because while one span crosses the creek the other spans the meadow at Barney's, which was done by the commissioners on the score of economy, believing the bridge over the land would cost less than to fill the eastern approach with earth

An interesting event happened in April, 1880, at John B Barney's residence, when his son, accompanied by his bride from New York, visited the old homestead It was the ninetieth anniversary of the birth of Mrs Barney, and on that occasion a bottle of wine that had been recovered from the wreck of the British sloop-of-war "Mercury,"[1] which was sunk in the North River, seven miles above New York, in 1777, was opened When taken from the wreck the bottle was full of wine and almost imbedded in oysters In 1822 it was opened when John B Barney was named, and had been sealed anew to be again opened nearly sixty years thereafter

The bridge of the Baltimore Central Railroad, below Chad's Ford, was built in 1859 In forming the embankment for this bridge, in September, 1859, the skeleton of a soldier was found, together with the brass belt-buckle and leather buttons of his uniform, the latter indicating that it was the remains of an English soldier A bullet—the one which had deprived him of life—was found among his rib bones At the east of the bridge stood Chads' mill, heretofore mentioned, the remains of which were discovered in 1860, when Caleb Brinton, Jr, built the present merchant-mill at that point Previous to that time Brinton had built a large frame building for a merchant-, flour-, and saw-mill on Dix's Run, above the Delaware County line There he conducted business for some time, but the water-power being insufficient, he moved the machinery to the larger building he erected on the site of Chads' old mill Following the creek a short distance below the county bridge at Chad's Ford is the mouth of Harvey's Run The first mills on this stream were those erected by Benjamin Ring some years previous to the Revolution, and comprised grist-, fulling-, and saw-mills The mills subsequently became the property of Eli Harvey, and in time that of his son, Joseph P. Harvey, and are now part of the estate owned by Joseph Turner The old mills have disappeared—were torn down by Turner to erect in their place a large grist and merchant-mill Still following the east branch of Harvey's Run, about a mile east of Chad's Ford, was a saw-mill, said to have been erected by one of the Butcher family about the beginning of this century In March, 1819, it is recorded that Benjamin Hampton, the sawyer at this mill, while running through a large poplar log, heard the saw strike against an unusually hard substance, which he found to be a forty-four-pound cannon-ball, completely imbedded in the wood so as to leave no external mark It was a relic of the battle, the tree having been cut just back of the grove, on the west side of the creek, where the British artillery was stationed The old solid shot, however, absolutely destroyed the teeth of the saw This mill disappeared sixty years ago, but the property was purchased in 1842 by Job Pyle, who set up a saw mill there to cut the timber felled on the farm Pyle sold the estate to Thomas Brinton, who repaired the mill, and also put in buhrs to grind feed

Retracing our steps to the west branch of Harvey's Run, immediately opposite and some distance up the road, where Chalkley Harvey's house stood, was in the olden times a corn-mill, while some distance farther up the road was an oil-mill for grinding linseed The place where the mill stood can still be traced by the indentations in the bank on the north side of the road

[1] Is not there some error in the name? Was not the vessel the "Hussar," and did she not sink in the East, not the North, River?

JUSTICES OF THE PEACE FOR BIRMINGHAM.

Thomas Newlin	Aug.	19, 1791
Joseph Brinton[1]	May	20, 1800
Matthias Kerlin	July	4, 1808
Thomas Pierce	Feb.	5, 1814
Joseph Brinton, reappointed	Feb.	3, 1820
Joseph Fox	Dec.	4, 1823
John Mattson	Dec.	13, 1823
Joseph Bowen	Nov.	10, 1824
Joseph Trimble	April	21, 1827
Robert Frame	Jan.	15, 1829
Robert Hall	Feb.	8, 1831
William Mendenhall	Dec.	6, 1836
Robert Frame	April	14, 1840
John D. Gilpin	April	14, 1840
Robert Frame	April	15, 1845
Robert Frame	April	9, 1850
Robert Frame	April	10, 1855
Robert Frame	April	10, 1860
Robert Frame	April	28, 1865
Darwin Painter	April	28, 1865
Joseph C. Turner	April	10, 1869
Franklin Worrelow	April	15, 1873
Miles Frame	March	15, 1876
P. Miles Frame	April	9, 1881

[1] Brinton seems to have conducted himself in his office in such a manner that complaint was made to the Senate and House of Representatives. In the journal of the latter body for Jan. 11, 1816, from the report of the committee it appears that Brinton had been charged with demanding and receiving illegal fees, altering his docket by interlining without the knowledge of one of the parties to the suit, to the injury of the latter; refusing to furnish transcript of his docket when demanded and legal fee tendered for such transcript, fining persons for the violation of laws unknown to the people of the commonwealth, demanding and receiving the coat from a man's back to satisfy costs, and on one occasion it seems he commanded a person brought before him on a writ to go down on his knees and ask his (the justice's) pardon, which the man did. The House and Senate, on Jan. 16, 1816, adopted the following address:

"To SIMON SNYDER, *Governor of the Commonwealth of Pennsylvania.*

"The Senate and House of Representatives of the said Commonwealth represent:

"That it has been proved to our satisfaction that Joseph Brinton, a Justice of the Peace, residing in the County of Delaware, ought not to be continued as such. Therefore we request that Joseph Brinton be removed from said office."

The address having been forwarded to the Governor, the latter, on March 19, 1816, sent the following message to both Houses of the Legislature:

"A supersedeas under the great seal of the State has issued, predicated upon, and carrying into effect the address of the Legislature for the removal of Joseph Brinton, Esq., late Justice of the Peace in and for the County of Delaware.

"SIMON SNYDER."

The following is the supersedeas and the sheriff's return, as appears of record in the recorder's office, at Media:

"PENNSYLVANIA, *ss.* Simon Snyder. Seal. } "In the name & by the Authority of the Commonwealth of Penn., Simon Snyder, Governor of the said Commonwealth, To Joseph Brinton, of the County of Delaware, sends greeting.

"Whereas by a commission under the hand of my predecessor, the late Governor McKean, and the great seal of the state, dated at Lancaster the 20th day of May, in the year One thousand Eight hundred, you, the said *Joseph Brinton*, were appointed a justice of the peace in and for the district numbered two, composed of the township of Concord, Aston, Birmingham, Upper Chichester, Thornbury, & Bethel, in the County of Del. And, whereas, by an address to me from both houses of the Legislature for the reasons therein contained, it is recommended and requested that you may be removed from the said office.

"Now know you that in compliance with the recommendation & request contained in the afsaid address from the General Assembly, and by virtue of the authority of same in such case given in and by the Constitution of this Commonwealth, I do hereby revoke and annul the afsaid Commission of Justice of the peace, & all and every the powers rights & duties incident thereto. Given under my hand And the Great seal of the State at Harrisburg, the thirtieth day of January, in the year of our Lord One thousand eight hundred and sixteen and of the Commonwealth the fortieth.

"By the Governor. "N. B. BOILEAU, *Secy.*

"Del. Co.

"Penn. SS. Before me, Jno. Caldwell, Esq., one of the Justices of the Peace in & for *Del. Co., afsd, personally* appeared Daniel Thomson, Esq., High Sheriff of said County, & on his solemn affirmation by me duly administered did declare & say that on the 6th inst. he delivered to the wife of Joseph Brinton, at the said Joseph's dwelling-house in said County, a supersedeas, signed by his Excellency, Simon Snyder Esquire, Governor of the Commonwealth of Pennsylvania & issued under the great seal of the state, at Harrisburg, the thirtieth day of January, 1816, removing the said Joseph Brinton from the office of Justice of the Peace for the second district in the Coty of Del., afsd. And that on the same day and immediately after he, this affirmant, left the said dwelling he met the sd Joseph Brinton and informed him of his having left the said Supersedeas at his house.

"Aff. & Sub. Feb. 8, 1816, "DAN'L THOMSON,
"before me. JNO. CALDWELL." *Sheriff.*"

Schools.—The first school-house in Birmingham township, in this county, was located on a lot conveyed by John Burgess, April 30, 1806, to Jesse Green, Peter Hatton, James Smith, John Chandler, and John Hecklen, in trust, for "the use of a school, but for no other purpose whatever." In the deed Burgess reserved the timber growing on this lot. A stone school-house was built there by the contributions of the neighboring residents. It was located in the southeastern part of the township, and for many years was known as Mount Racket, the name being derived from the noise made by the children in play. Brinton Dick was the teacher here at one time. In 1825, Eli Harvey gave the use of an old hipped-roof house, which had been built before the Revolution by Chads, it is said, for school purposes, and, in addition to the house, furnished the firewood gratis. This building was used as a school until the public school system was adopted. About 1826, Joseph Russell lived at the Baptist Church, and taught school in a shed adjoining his dwelling. He also taught in the hipped-roof house already mentioned and in Chads' spring-house, then owned by Haddock, at the village, which was used before and after the school law went into effect. Milcena Gilpin taught a subscription school in the dwelling-house that stands near the old Butcher Mill, the property being then owned by her father, Isaac G. Gilpin. This was about the years 1828 to 1830. Near Dilworthtown, on Thomas Williamson's property, was a frame school-house, the lot being an acre of ground, which Williamson sold for one dollar. This school was discontinued in 1841, when the directors purchased a tract containing sixty-one square perches from John D. Gilpin, and the old school building and lot thereon reverted to Gideon Williamson. The school law having been accepted, the following named school-houses were built by the school directors.

In addition to these places where "the young ideas were taught to shoot," there was an octagon building erected near Squire Robert Frame, known as the Frame School-House; another, near the property of Robert Bullock, and therefore known as the Bullock School. After the public-school system was adopted these old buildings ceased to be used or became the property of the township. On May 23, 1837, forty-four square perches of land was purchased from John Heyburn, on the highway leading from the Wilmington road to Smith's bridge. On Nov. 16, 1838, Robert Bullock sold to the directors eighty-one square perches, almost in the centre of the township. On Jan. 18, 1841, John D. Gilpin conveyed to the officials the school southwest of Dilworthtown. Isaac Smith, of New Castle County, Del., conveyed to the township, Oct. 11, 1849, fifty-six square perches of land, near Smith's bridge, at Beaver Mills, on which was subsequently erected a school-house. The latter building rendered the old Burgess School unnecessary, and on Oct. 31, 1861, Chalkley Harvey, who was instructed by the court to sell that property, conveyed it to Samuel Painter for ninety-seven dollars, which sale was duly confirmed. The schools of Birmingham at this time are well regulated, and attended by a large number of scholars.

The following is a list of the school directors of Birmingham township:

1840, Ziba Dilworth, David Martin; 1842, John D. Gilpin, Ziba Darlington; 1843, Emma Garrett, Milton Stamp; 1844, Augustus Cornog, George Hannum; 1845, William Shields, Nathaniel Speakman; 1846, John D. Gilpin, John Heyburn; 1847, George Hannum, John F. Engle; 1848, Malachi Barton, Aaron James; 1849, Lewis Smith, Thomas Brinton; 1850, Nathaniel Speakman, William H. Wilson; 1851, Daniel Farra, Ziba Dilworth; 1852, Clarkson Way, Hiram Kipe; 1853, Gideon Williamson, Elwood Michener; 1854, William H. Willson, William W. Twaddell; 1855, Jacob G. Kitts, Hiram Kipe, Clarkson Way; 1856, Samuel Gamble, Gideon Williamson; 1857, Clarkson Way, Paul Jeffries; 1858, John Esrey, Emmor Garrett; 1859, John D. Gilpin, Gideon Williamson; 1860, John B. Heyburn, Lewis H. Bullock; 1861, William W. Twaddell, David W. Eyre; 1862, John B. Barney, William Russell; 1863, Robert Frame, Lewis Smith; 1864, Albin Baldwin, Sharpless Green; 1865, Samuel Speakman, Edmund R. Gilpen; 1866, J. B. Heyburn, Lewis Smith; 1867, Franklin Whirlow, Charles B. Sprogall; 1868, Gideon Williamson, Lewis H. Bullock; 1869, Fred. Brinton, P. M. Frame; 1870, Emmor C. Jeffries, John Esrey; 1871, Crosby Fairlamb, Jacob G. Kitts; 1872, Amos W. House, Robert G. Smith; 1873, T. Speakman, J. C. Turner; 1874, Cresley Fairlamb, Alban Harvey; 1875, Lewis H. Bullock, Caleb R. Watkins; 1876, J. C. Turner, Townsend Speakman; 1877, R. C. Fairlamb, Alban Harvey; 1878, J. E. Heyburn, John Arment; 1879, G. Rawlings, G. E. Heyburn; 1880, Alban Harvey, R. C. Fairlamb; 1881, P. Miles Frame, John Arment; 1882, George E. Heyburn, Lewis Bullock; 1883, Alban Harvey, R. C. Fairlamb; 1884, Dr. H. Hayward, P. Miles Frame.

Gen. Lafayette's Visit in 1825.—The circumstances respecting the visit of Gen. Lafayette and his son, George Washington Lafayette, to the battle-field at Brandywine on Tuesday, July 26, 1825, and his reception there by the committees of Delaware and Chester Counties, are thus admirably related in a recent volume:[1]

"Early in the morning the general was waited upon at Messrs. Dupont, with whom he had lodged, by John W. Cuningham, Esq., one of the committee of arrangements, attended by Samson Babb and William Williamson, two of the marshals of the day, by whom he was conducted to Chad's Ford. The general was accompanied by his son, M. La Vasseur, his secretary, M. Baudouis, a distinguished lawyer from Paris, the Messrs. Dupont, Messrs. Louis McLane and N. G. Williamson, committee from Wilmington, and Messrs. Joseph S. Lewis, Tilghman, and Biddle, committee of Councils from Philadelphia. They reached Chad's Ford about ten o'clock A.M., where the veteran was received by the committees of Chester and Delaware Counties, headed by their respective chairmen, Col. Joseph McClellan and Capt. William Anderson. At this place, also, Maj.-Gen. Isaac D. Barnard and his aids, Col. Leiper and Daniel Buckwalter, Esq., attended by Brig.-Gens. Evans and Stanley, and their aids, in full uniform, also the Chester County troop of cavalry, commanded by Lieut. Jones, and the Delaware County troop of cavalry, commanded by Capt. Vanleer, the whole under the command of Maj. Wilson, were in waiting to escort the general over the battle-ground. Jesse Sharp, Esq., chief marshal, with his aids, Thomas H. B. Jacobs and Jesse Conard, Esq., and assistant marshals Samson Babb, William Williamson, Joshua Hunt, Thomas H. Brinton, Joshua McMinn, Isaac Trimble, David Potts, Jr., Richard Walker, Jonathan Jones, Joseph P. McClellan, also attended to regulate the movements of the great concourse of citizens, in carriages, on horseback, and on foot, who had gathered at this point, eager to see and welcome the nation's guest.

"The general received the greetings of the people, and viewed the interesting heights around Chad's Ford, and the field where the armies encamped the night before the battle, and pointed out the positions of Gen. Wayne and Maxwell's brigades. He inquired if any one could point out where the bridge of rails was across the Brandywine, but no one was able to give the information. He then resumed his seat in his barouche, with his companion-in-arms, Col. McClellan, by his side, and the procession, which had been formed, advanced towards Painter's Cross-roads. About a mile from the ford the general stopped and alighted from his carriage to see Gideon Gilpin, a very aged man, confined to bed, at whose house he had made his headquarters before the battle. The sick man was gratified at the sight of the veteran, who pressed his hand cordially and wished him every blessing. The procession then proceeded by way of Painter's Cross-roads to Dilworthtown. After a brief halt it turned to the left, and proceeded to the main battle-ground. When they came in sight of the Birmingham meeting-house, Lafayette arose in his carriage and addressed himself in French to his son and companions, spoke animatedly for some time, pointing out to them the different positions of the armies. All the surroundings were familiar to him. He pointed out the spot, in a field of Jacob Bennett, a short distance east and south of where the road from the meeting-house comes in at right angles with the east-and-west road, as the place where he was wounded. He then proceeded to the meeting-house, where another concourse had assembled to greet him. After viewing the ground here he alighted, with his companions and friends, at the mansion of Samuel Jones, a short distance north of the meeting-house, to which he had been previously invited, and partook

[1] Futhey and Cope's "History of Chester County," pp. 130, 131.

of refreshments provided for the occasion. A large collection of balls and other relics of the memorable conflict, which had been found at different periods on the battle-ground, were exhibited, and excited much interest."

The Murder of Martin Hollis by Thomas Cropper.—The peaceful, law-abiding people of Birmingham, early in the year 1841, were shocked by the report that a murder had been committed in the neighborhood of Dilworthtown, and the mere fact that the parties to the tragedy were in humble station did not lessen the public horror at the act, for both the slayer and the slain were known to many of the residents of the township. The particulars of the murder and the vindication of the law, as I have learned them, are as follows:

Thomas Cropper, then in the employment of John Leonard, a miller in Pennsbury township, Chester Co., was a tall, active colored man of prepossessing appearance, who had received sufficient education to enable him to read and write with ease. In Birmingham township, on the property of Ziba Darlington near Dilworthtown, lived Martin Hollis, a colored man, and his wife Elizabeth, the latter a half-sister to Cropper, to whom she was much attached. Hollis and his wife did not dwell happily together, and they separated, a rumor prevailing that the affection existing between Elizabeth and her half-brother exceeded the bounds of propriety. The husband's mind seemed to have been firmly settled in that opinion; hence he was bitter in his denunciations of Cropper. On Saturday, Feb. 28, 1841, about midday, the two men met, when Cropper asked Hollis how Elizabeth was. The latter angrily exclaimed, "How dare you ask me anything about Elizabeth? I'll let you know better." Cropper replied, "I think I have a right to ask for her." Still angry, Hollis passionately retorted, "I'll show you something pretty quick," dismounting from his horse as he spoke, and catching up a large stone from the highway in each hand, continued, "I'll split your brains out." Cropper had also armed himself with a heavy stone, which he held in his right hand, while Perry Hall, the father of Elizabeth Hollis and the putative father of Cropper, and John Leonard, who were present, attempted to prevent Hollis from getting within striking distance of Cropper. At length Hollis, becoming calmer, remounted his horse and rode away. In less than an hour after this chance meeting Cropper went to the house of Perry Hall, where his sister lived, and spoke of the conduct of Hollis at the mill, quietly remarking, "He was trying to show himself." Dressing in his best suit, Cropper, taking his gun, left the house, stating he was going to a tailor's to be measured for a coat.

About a half-hour thereafter he and Martin Hollis were together at the house of William Wright, a colored man, where Elizabeth Hollis was then living, keeping house in rooms in the second story. The husband called his wife to come down, and then asked her what articles she had there owned by Thomas Cropper. She said nothing but an umbrella which laid on the table, and the husband told her to get it, which she did, and together the husband and wife went out at the door, shutting it behind them, to where Cropper stood, his gun in his hand. "Thomas, take this umbrella," said Hollis, "go away, and never speak to her again, not even if you meet her on the road." Cropper replied, "Not after this time." The husband thereupon said something further, when the gun was discharged, and Hollis fell backwards against the house, dead, the ball having entered the back of his neck and passed out at his waist. Mary Wright, who was in the house at the time, ran to the door just as Elizabeth Hollis opened it and hurriedly ran in. Mrs. Wright slammed the door to and locked it. Cropper, rattling the latch and knocking several times against the door, finally called out, "Elizabeth, come down here, for you are the occasion of this, and I'll give you the next load!" The murderer moved a few steps from the house, stopped, and gazed intently, as if desirous of executing his threat. Then he walked from the scene of the tragedy in the direction of Wilmington. At a late hour that night Cropper returned to the house of Perry Hall, carrying with him the gun he had taken from there at noonday. He was scraping his feet at the door when Mrs. Hall opened it, and he said, pleasantly, "Well, mother." The latter, however, forbade him to enter the house, stating that he was a murderer, and the constable, accompanied by a number of men, had been there seeking him. Cropper thereupon asked if Hollis was dead. Receiving an answer in the affirmative, he expressed regrets for the act, and hastily walked away.

The authorities made every effort to discover the whereabouts of the culprit, who it was believed would endeavor to get to New York. On Friday, March 5th, the step-father of Cropper, who was employed at the farm of Carver Worthington, near West Chester, was observed to help himself largely to provisions at meals, and after supper he was noticed taking some of the remaining food to the barn. This, with the fact that the old man had appeared to be unusually depressed, aroused suspicion that Cropper was lurking near by. Information was sent to West Chester, and Constable McCartney was instructed to search the barn, where it was believed the murderer was concealed. The officer and several other persons searched the building, and in the mow they gently thrust pitchforks into places where the fugitive might be hidden, and into the surface of the hay. At length one of the party found that his fork came in contact with an unyielding body, and thrusting against it, a voice said, "Don't stick me." The hay being thrown aside, Cropper was discovered. When arrested he denied that he was Cropper, stating that his name was John Carter; that he had only that evening come from New York, and was a total stranger in this section of the country. Despite his protests he was taken before Squire Flemming, who committed him to await the action of the authorities of Delaware County. It chanced that Mr. Irwin, the then superintendent of the Chester County jail, and who had formerly been sheriff, had frequently seen, and recognized the prisoner as Thomas Cropper. At a subsequent hearing the accused acknowledged that he was Cropper, but declared that he had shot Hollis purely in self-defense. His identity having been established, Thursday, March 29, 1841, Hon. John Larkin, then sheriff of Delaware County, brought Cropper to the jail at Chester, as well as Elizabeth Hollis, the latter being detained as a witness.

On Friday, May 28, 1841, the case was called for trial, Judge Thomas S. Bell presiding, the commonwealth being represented by Deputy Attorney-General P. Frazer Smith, and the prisoner by Hon. Edward Darlington and Townsend Haines, Esq. The evidence was not voluminous; the jury retired at seven o'clock in the evening, and at half-past ten returned a verdict of guilty of murder in the first degree. On Monday, June 1st, the sentence of the law was pronounced, the court-room being crowded, even the windows blocked up with men who could not gain admission to the room.

After his sentence the prisoner seemed almost unconscious of his unhappy situation, but, with apparent indifference to the manner of his death, made full preparations for his funeral, ordering his coffin and winding-sheet, and requested that as soon as they were made they should be deposited in his cell until required for use. His request was complied with, but when they were brought to the jail he shuddered at the sight, and desired that they might be taken away. As the day fixed for his execution drew near, he made several attempts to escape, and in doing so filed some of the bars in the chimney in his cell apart. His hair was crisp and abundant, and he had concealed a watch-spring file therein so adroitly that for a long time the authorities could not discover the tool with which he accomplished his work. The jail at Chester, old and decayed, was so insecure that to insure his detention it became absolutely necessary to place him in heavy irons, which were chained to the floor.

The Governor had ordered the sentence to be executed on Friday, Aug. 6, 1841, and as Cropper was much concerned as to the final disposition of his body after death, being extremely fearful that it would be given to the physicians for dissection, he requested that he should be hung not later than eleven o'clock, in order to allow time to carry the remains to the African burial-ground, at Kennett Square.

About ten o'clock on the day designated his manacles were removed and Cropper attired in a white robe; the procession was formed, and moved to the place of execution in the jail-yard. The condemned man ascended the scaffold with a firm step, and listened attentively while the death warrant was read. He was attended by two colored ministers, who prayed and sang with him. At the conclusion of the religious exercises, Cropper desired a few minutes longer for prayer, followed by a short speech to those present. His feet were then bound with heavy cords, and when the trap was sprung the cords binding his feet became loosened, and a moment after his arms also broke from their fastenings, and he threw up his hands and grasped at the rope above his head. Jeremiah Stevenson, one of Sheriff Larkin's deputies on that occasion, pinioned Cropper's arms again,—a merciful act, for the half-hanged man clutched wildly with his hands at the rope by which he was suspended, and his suffering was rendered more intense because of that effort.

After the body had hung half an hour it was cut down, the physicians having pronounced life extinct, and the corpse was placed in the coffin he had ordered. Being a Mason, he requested that the insignia of the order should be placed thereon, which was done. The executed man ordered that the expenses of his funeral should be paid out of the means he had accumulated, and the remainder of his estate he bequeathed to Elizabeth Hollis.

Hotels in Birmingham.—Respecting the houses of entertainment in Birmingham, under license from the courts of Chester County, it is very difficult to designate those which at the present would be in their locations confined to that part of the township now included within the county of Delaware.

The first record of license there is to John Wyth, Birmingham (generally), was allowed June 20, 1715, and is confined to a brief note of the fact that it was so granted.

The first petition of record was presented to the court Aug. 28, 1722, by John Bentley, wherein he represents that "Having Taken a house In the Township of Birmingham And Intending, with your Honours permission to sett up an Ordinary for the Vending of Beer and Syder for the Succor and Support of Travailers, his house being By the Great Road Leading to Nottingham and Maryland, And he being likewise very much Induced thereunto by severall of the neighbors Importunity," etc. He was recommended to the favorable consideration of the justices by William Brinton, Joseph Brinton, Samuel Painter, Joseph Gilpin, John Chalfant, James Houstowne, Providence Scot, Pattrick Scott, John Bickingham, and Daniel Moore. What was done with his petition that year does not appear, but in 1723 he had license allowed him, as also in the year following. I conclude that it was approved, especially since in his application, dated Aug. 31, 1725, he declares that he has "kept a publick House in the township of Birmingham for some years past." He seems to have lost his privilege, however, for Nov. 30, 1731, he states in his petition "that for some years past he had license to keep a house of entertainment in Birmingham, but through some misrepresentations had been obstructed in a continuance." His application was in that year indorsed by Thomas Chandler and thirty-eight other persons, and was approved.

Aug. 26, 1727, James Townsends, a resident of Birmingham, narrates in his petition his reasons for desiring the court's kindly consideration in the following words: "Whereas your petitioner Lyeth under very great hard ships Liveing on ye great Road Side and very much oppressed by Travailers wich is too much for me to Bear, therefore your peticioner prays you will Grant me a License to keep a house of Entertainment, and your peticioner will in Bounden duty ever pray." His application seems to have melted the stern hearts of the justices, for the license was allowed, and seems to have been continued until 1731, for on the clerk's list of that year his name appeared among those whose petitions had been approved.

August court, 1732, Thomas Bullock's petition shows that "having obtained license at last November to sell beer & Sider now wishes to have full licence," which was awarded him. His name appears on the clerk's list of approved licenses for the year 1734, after which it is not found.

At the court held Feb. 26 (last Tuesday in February), 1733/4, Joseph Webb, living on the road from Concord to "Forks of Brandywine," applied for license, which was refused to him, while on Aug. 27, 1734, Robert Hannum states in his petition that he "hath taken to ffarm ye Plantation and appertinances in the township of Birmingham where Mary Stevens lately dwelt known by the name of the hoop and Tun Tavern." His application is recommended by Joseph Gilpin, Samuel Painter, William and Edward Brinton, Calvin Cooper, John Chads, and nineteen others. He was successful, and license was granted him, continuing from year to year until 1738, after which date his name is not on the clerk's list of licenses approved.

John Chads, Sept. 1, 1736, calls the attention of the court to the fact that he "has undertaken to keep a ferry and wishes to keep a public Inn on road from Phila. to Nottingham, in Birmingham." To which petition the court accedes and granted license to Chads. From year to year he is regularly recommended to the Governor for license. But something must have gone astray in his manner of conducting the business of innkeeping, as will be seen by his petition, Aug. 31, 1742, which sets forth that "by the Favour of the Honorable Court had for this Considerable time past A Recommendation granted him annually in order to obtain Lycense to keep a publick House or House of Entertainment in Birmingham, aforesaid: And your Petitioner not being Conscious he hath Forfeited his right to the said Favour by any abuse thereof." This petition is indorsed "not allowed."

Under like date "a representation" from William Webster, John Baily, Joseph Pennock, John Strode, and thirty other signers, was presented which states that "having heard yt John Chads, Jr., to bee Soprest or put down from Publick house keeping . . . that Itt Is a house that Lies most Convenient to the ford or ferry Boat on Brandywine and Ceeps the best Entertainment for man and horse on the upper Road from Maryland to philadelphia and Likewise Keeps a very orderly house, not allowing of Either drunkeness or Swaring." This representation is indorsed "not Regarded."

Chads was determined that his license should be renewed, for very shortly after the refusal of the court to continue his as a house of public entertainment, he presented a petition, signed by himself and a considerable number of inhabitants of Chester County to the Commissioners and assessors, setting forth that "pursuant to an agreement made with their predecessors in the year 1737, he built a boat and suitable appurtenances for the conveying of people and carriages over Brandywine Creek, with the money that he borrowed of the County for that purpose, the sum of which was 30 pounds, and it being evident as ye petitioner conceives, that the profits of the said ferry, will not without some consideration compensate for the charge thereof, and that the Honorable Justices, hath at last August Court, thought proper to deprive him the sd John Chads from keeping a house of entertainment, near the sd ferry, which he had done heretofore. They therefore request that the said John Chads may be acquitted & discharged from the payment of the sum of money above mentioned, and also from the care and management of sd. boat and appurtenances, and some other person appointed to act therein in his stead."

This shrewd movement on the enemy by the flank was not the only effort of Chads, but he charged the bench in column when, under date of Nov. 30, 1742, a petition "of sundry inhabitants of Kennett and places adjacent" in favor of John Chads, as one of "sundry inhabitants and freeholders of the said County on the west side of brandyWine," and still another from "sundry Inhabitants of Concord and other adjacent Places," and even yet another from "inhabitants of Nottingham and places adjacent" is presented. These petitions, which are signed in the aggregate by one hundred and seventy-one persons, are couched in the same language, and state to the court that "being sensible that we may be Liable to great Disappointments as well on account of Entertainment, as also ye attendance of ye boat over ye said Creek wch has been greatly servicable to our Inhabitants & more especially to Strangers unacquainted with ye sd. Creek," they ask for these reasons that license may be granted to Chads.

The same day the personal petition of John Chads was presented, in which he says "that whereas many of the Inhabitants of the Townships on the West side of Brandywine and others of my neibourhood have aqwainted me with their Intention To Petion the Court for their Recommendation to the Governor for his Lycense to keep a publick house as heretofore have don, and Desired me to signifie to the Court my Inclination to Gratifie them in there desire and to shew myself willing to serve my frends in Genrall, as well as soport of myself, if the Court thought fitt to Grant it mee, and these are to Request of theis honourable Court to Grant my frenns the prayer of their petion and also to Take into their Prudent Consideration what measures to Take abought the Boate to Render it as servicable to Travelors as heretofore have been."

The number of petitions and the sly reference of Chads, that there might be some difficulty at the ford if his license was not granted, was too much for the justices, and the above-mentioned application of Chads bears this indorsement: "Allowed according to ye Prayer of ye Petition." In 1743 the license was renewed and so continued to him until 1746, when he was succeeded in business by James House, who rented the premises to whom the license was extended,—he giving security to perform all things relating to the ferry over "Brandewine" according to agreement with the commissioners and assessors. It was continued to House until 1752, when he in turn gave place to Amos Harvey, who became the landlord of the inn. To the latter license was annually allowed until the year 1756, when his name disappeared from the records. Henry Hays was granted license in 1757, but whether it was for this tavern I cannot as yet determine; but in 1767, William Kerlin received license for the "Chad's ford" Tavern, and annually thereafter was on the list until 1772, when Joseph Davis petitioned and stated in his application that it was for the premises "formerly John Chads' where a tavern has been for thirty years." Davis was the landlord of the hostelry at the time of the battle of Brandywine, although the county records for that year are missing respecting licenses, for in 1778 Gideon Gilpin is granted license for the tavern, and the petition sets forth that he succeeds Joseph Davis in business. To Gilpin license is annually allowed by the court of Chester County until the date of the creation of Delaware County, his last application being presented in the year 1789. At that time Gilpin was the landlord of the house now known as Gen. Lafayette's headquarters, in which no license has been had for nearly a century.

I lose all trace of the old tavern at the ford until 1806, when Benjamin Davis, in his petition, states that "Brandywine Creek is in the township, and from the present way of crossing said creek, when the waters are high, travellers are often detained, which for that, as well as many other causes, renders a house of public entertainment necessary at that locality,"—a course of reasoning that resulted in a decision such as he desired from the court. I know that in 1800 Benjamin Ring had license for an inn in Birmingham,—the old Washington headquarters; that he was refused license in 1802, when a remonstrance from the "inhabitants in and near Concord" against his house was presented to court. In the following year, 1803, Joshua Ring obtained leave to keep a public-house after a previous petition in the same year had been rejected, and in 1805, in his application, Ring gives the name of the tavern as the "United States Arms, on the road from Chester to Lancaster." In addition, in 1807, Thomas Monks petitioned for license for a house in Birmingham, which had been formerly kept by Benjamin Ring & Son. His application was met with a remonstrance from Isaac G. Gilpin, who stated that he was a resident of the township, that he knew Monks and the house he kept, that "the entertainment for travellers and others at said house is not good, and by no means such as the public ought to expect on so public a road." Petition was rejected, although the preceding year the court had recommended Thomas Monks to the Governor as a proper person to have license, and thereafter the "United States Arms" disappeared as an inn in Birmingham. The house and farm became the property of Eli Harvey, as before mentioned.

John Way, in 1807, prayed that license might be granted him at the old Chad's Ford Inn (this tavern was the hipped-roof house at Eli Harvey's), and as an additional reason for the location of a public-house at that point, urged that "Brandywine creek by the present way of crossing is often impassable from the frequent great freshets therein." The court gave approval to his petition, and Way remained there until 1810, during which time he built the present tavern house, when Thomas Burnett succeeded to the business until 1817, when he gave place to Jacob Smith, Jr. The latter remained at the tavern only one year, for in 1818 Thomas H. Bullock had license for the house, which he states is commonly known as the "Rising Sun." In 1823, John Norrett was landlord for one year, but in 1824 Thomas H. Bullock returned to his former station, and in 1828 the latter was succeeded by Nathan S. Burnett. In 1830, Ezra Lamborn, who called the house the "Chad's Ford Inn," was landlord, and continued such until 1834, when Jones Eavenson rented the premises, still retaining the old name. The following year Eavenson associated Joseph D. Valentine in the business, and the firm received the license in 1835 for the "sign of the Bridge." In 1836, John Entreken was authorized to keep the public-house at Chad's Ford, and in 1838 Milton Stamp was landlord of the "Bridge Inn, near the Eastern end of Bridge." Stamp, however, did not secure the grace of the court without a struggle, for a remonstrance signed by George Brinton, Jr., William Painter, Samuel Painter, Harlan Webb, Eli Harvey, Chalkley Harvey, Joseph P. Harvey, and Robert Frame was presented, alleging that the inn was unnecessary, as the locality was well supplied with public-houses at reasonable distances from each other, and stating that they believed "the mode and manner of keeping said public-house has not been in accordance with moral and religious propriety, and that it was injurious to the best interests of the neighborhood, hence we (the remonstrants) respectfully ask the court to remove the evil." Edward Brinton also presented his individual remonstrance, in which he stated that he had for thirty-five years been engaged in "public business," the last fifteen within about a mile and a half of Chad's Ford Tavern; that he had "experienced great inconvenience and loss in business by the encouragement held out to his apprentices and hired men to meet there on various occasions to their great moral injury while in the company of the dissipated and profane, which common report says, and I believe truly, do too often assemble there, that there were more taverns than public convenience requires, which was particularly the case with the Chad's Ford Tavern, that must look principally to neighboring custom for support." This remonstrance concludes: "It has been observed by some writer that no person nor associations are at liberty to indulge in any acts or practices in the face of the community which by their necessary operations are calculated to corrupt and debauch the youthful or the unwary, to incite to licentiousness or crime."

The court, however, deemed the house a public necessity and granted the license to Milton Stamp, continuing so to do annually until 1843, when in the fall of that year John M. Dusham had the license transferred to him. The latter, in 1845, gave place to Edward B. Hoskins, who in his petition states that the tavern was known as the "Chad's Ford Inn." In 1847 it received license, as did most of the public-houses in Delaware County, as a temperance inn, but the next year, when the local-option law of that day was declared unconstitutional by the Supreme Court, the Chad's Ford Tavern received full license, and it was extended to Hoskins until 1854, when John Evans had the control of the ancient hostelry. The following year the court refused their consent, and so annually kept the house under the ban of their displeasure for three years, although there were not wanting applicants for the position of "mine host." In 1858, Philip Mullin presented his petition to court, which was supplemented by a petition from James Twaddell, of Philadelphia, who represented to the judges that he had resided in the latter city for fifty years, and was a reputable citizen; that he was owner of the Chad's Ford Tavern, which had been kept as a public-house for the last fifty years or more; that he had held the property for three years, and his tenants had been refused license, although well recommended. The reason for this denial Mr. Twaddell could not understand, nor could the neighbors in Birmingham, he stated, since the house was in much better order than when he purchased it, as he had expended over a thousand dollars, and proposed to make further improvements if circumstances should warrant it. The applicant who had rented the property was well recommended, and would no doubt keep a reputable public-house if the court would only give him an opportunity to do so. But the bench turned a deaf ear to his pleadings. The following year Isaac C. Lindsay leased the hotel, and the owner smiled once more when the judge announced that the new applicant had received the judicial approval. Annually thereafter the house remained as a tavern,—in 1862, under the control of Benjamin French and Horatio J. Sheppard, and the following year under French alone. In 1864, Charles Mendenhall had license, as well as in 1865. In 1866 the house remained without a tenant, and in 1867, Charles Twaddell was granted privilege to keep a public inn there. William Seal, Jr., in 1869 was the landlord, and remained so until 1871, when he gave place to Charles Davis, who in turn was followed by Jackson McFarland in 1876. In 1880, John D. Makiever had become the landlord, and continues as such to the present time.

Kaolin Pits.—Over fifty years ago Amos C. Brinton says white clay lay on top of the ground in James Russel's meadow, and small quantities were used by the fullers in fulling-mills. It is also stated that potters from up the Great Valley came down occasionally and carried some of it to their works, and that one man used the white clay for adulterating white lead and soap. It was not, however, until 1863 that any particular effort was made to bring the white clay in this section into use. At that time the property that in 1848 belonged to Thomas H. Bullock was in possession of Caleb Hayburn, who had purchased it of William McKay, a son-in-law of Bullock. Brinton J. Hayburn, a butcher, came one day with his butcher's cart from Caleb Hayburn's place to Concordville. Some of the clay was on the wheels of his cart. When Mrs. George Rush was buying some beef, the white clay attracted her attention, and Brinton told her that it would take grease out of cloth. She took some of it and tried it on a carpet, and accomplished the result. He also told her it was potters' clay. George Rush became interested, and went over to the farm, procured some of the clay, and wrote to E. B. Shee, a paper manufacturer of Philadelphia, and also interested in mining in South Carolina. Mr. Shee in the course of a short time came to Concordville, and visited the farm with Mr. Rush. More samples were obtained, which Shee took to Philadelphia, where it was shown to Bartles Shee and Christian Spengler, on Minor Street. Mr. Spengler also came to the place and examined it.

In 1864, Edward Shee purchased sixty acres of land of Caleb Hayburn for ten thousand dollars, in the interest of Edward B. Shee, Bartles Shee, George Rush, Christian Spengler, and Henry Shillingford. Pits were sunk on the farm, and samples of the clay were sent to different parties. Negotiations had been in progress with several persons in New York, who formed the "Union Woolen Company of New York," with Edward Peckham, president. To this company the land was sold for thirty thousand dollars, and the deed from Hayburn made to the company. Work was at once begun, under the charge of George Rush, and clay shipped to potteries in Trenton, N. J., and other places. In 1865 the property was sold to William Wharton, of Philadelphia, who worked the pits about a year, and sold to Lewis P. Harvey, of Chad's Ford. The National Woolen Company was then organized, of which Lewis P. Harvey was principal owner and manager. Hansom H. Johns was one of the partners, and together they conducted the works many years, furnishing to potteries in Trenton, Pittsburgh, Cincinnati, Liverpool, and elsewhere, clay at the rate of one hundred tons per month. Later, Mr. Johns retired from the company; Tilghman Johnson became a partner, and this firm are now operating the works.

Brandywine Summit Kaolin Works.—In 1880, John Griffin, of Phœnixville, bought of Isaac Bullock sixty-three acres, and in that year work was begun. Buildings were erected in 1881. Clay is supplied to whiteware-makers in Liverpool, Ohio, and Trenton. William S. Manley has been in charge of the works from the first.

In 1882, Hamilton Graham began work on property adjoining the above. It was abandoned in 1853, and in September of that year was purchased by the Brandywine Kaolin Works.

CHAPTER XXXII.

THE CITY OF CHESTER.

In 1644 the present site of Chester, east of the creek of that name, was a tobacco plantation, occupied by farm servants in the employment of the Swedish company. About that time many of the colonists began to seek grants of the broad acres on the main land, and the ground between Ridley and Chester Creeks was selected by Jöran Keen, and to him the Swedish government granted a patent for a tract of land one and a half miles inland, following the right bank of Chester Creek above its mouth, and reaching along the Delaware eastward as far as Ridley Creek. The plot at its northwestern limit, at the present Crozer Theological Seminary, was a half-mile in breadth, and a diagonal line ran thence eastwardly to Ridley Creek. Jöran Keen, or Kyn (as his name was written by the Swedes, and also from his peculiar complexion known as "snohuitt" or "snow white"), was one of the earliest European residents upon the Delaware River within the boundaries of the present State of Pennsylvania, and for more than a quarter of a century was the chief proprietor of lands at Upland, afterwards Chester. He was born in Sweden about 1620, and came to America, in company with Governor Printz, in the ship "Fama," and resided at Tinicum. He was a soldier, whose duty was to attend daily upon the Governor, and travel with that dignitary wherever he might go, as one of his Excellency's body-guard. As before stated, Keen received the grant of a royal tract of ground, and it is believed that when Printz left the colony to return to Sweden, Keen resigned his military position and gave his undivided attention to agriculture.[1]

The land on the west bank of Chester Creek, extending along the river as far as Marcus Hook, Queen Christina, of Sweden, granted to Capt. John Ammundson Besk, "his wife and heirs," by patent dated Aug. 20, 1653, in consideration of faithful services he had rendered to the State. Besk, who is believed to have been a man of large means, never entered into possession of this vast tract of ground, and it seems to have been held and claimed by Armgart Pappegoya, the daughter of the first Swedish Governor, Printz. In a letter from the Dutch vice-director, Beekman, under date of Sept. 14, 1662, he writes, "I inquired into the situation of a certain lot of land on the Southwest side of Upland Kill, and was informed by the Swedish Commissaries and other ancient inhabitants of said nation, that the aforesaid is called Printz's village, which has always been in possession during 16 years of the Swedish Governor, John Printz, and his daughter who owns it."

Chester, in 1645, was a place of such insignificance that Andreas Hudde, an agent of the Dutch, who had been sent by Governor Kieft to learn the number, condition, armament, and military force of the Swedes, made no mention of it in his report. It is even doubtful whether at that time Jöran Keen had erected a house on his land, inasmuch as in the "Rulla," dated by Printz at "Kihrstina" (Christiana), June 20, 1644, the statement appears that Upland was a tobacco plantation, as already mentioned. Between the years 1646 and 1648 a considerable settlement must have been made at this point, for in Hudde's interview with the Passyunk Indians, in that year, they spoke of Upland, among other places, in the possession of the Swedes, and charge the latter with having stolen the land from them, while in Campanius' account of New Sweden, "Mecoponacka," or Upland, is mentioned in the year 1648 (the date of the elder Campanius' return to Sweden) "as an unfortified place, but some houses were built there. It was situated between Fort Christina (near Wilmington) and New Gottenburg (Tinicum), but nearer the latter. There was a fort built there some time after its settlement. It is good even land along the river shore."[2]

The Indian name of the site of the present city of Chester was Mecoponacka; the Swedish, Upland; the Dutch, Oplandt; and the English, Chester and Upland indifferently until the former entirely absorbed

---

[1] *Penna. Mag. of Hist.*, vol. ii. p. 325.

[2] Campanius, p. 79.

the latter in designating the borough about the middle of the last century. The proper Indian name of Chester Creek was Meechoppenackhan, according to Heckewelder, in his "Indian Names," which signifies "the large potato stream," or "the stream along which large potatoes grow." This was corrupted into Macopanachan, Macopanackhan, and finally into Mecopanacka. The Indian tribe which owned the land whereon Chester stands, according to John Hill Martin, was the Okehockings, and were subsequently removed by the order of William Penn, in 1702, to "the tract in Chester county, formerly laid out to Griffy Jones, but now vacant."

The story of Penn coming to Upland, the change of the name of the hamlet and the county to Chester, the meeting of the first Assembly, the courts held therein have already been narrated in the general history, and it is unnecessary to recapitulate those incidents here. During the winter of 1682–83, Penn resided in the Boar Head Inn, an ancient building which stood until March 21, 1850, when it was destroyed by fire. The noted hostelry stood on the line of the present street, on the footway approaching it having ascent to the building. It was one story and a half high, with peaked roof, the gable end standing toward Third Street, and from it, just below the eaves, projected the crane from which the old sign of a boar's head was suspended. The house was constructed of heavy frame timber, filled in with brick, and outside as well as inside the laths, which were interlaced in a kind of basket pattern, were covered with plaster made of oyster-shell lime and mud, while, in place of hair, swamp-grass was employed to hold the composition together. The doors were peculiar in the manner in which they were hung; a peg or projection from the door above and below fitted into holes made in the frames, and on these they swung instead of hinges. The windows, with the exception of the one in the kitchen, were small; the glasses, four by three in size, were set in lead. The roof was of split-shingles, the kitchen floor was laid in flagging, some of which were as large as six by eight feet, and under these was a body of eighteen inches of sand on which they rested. In the kitchen, on the side opening to the west, was a large double door, through which a cart-load of wood could be drawn if desired. The chimney was an enormous affair, nearly sixteen feet in width, and the wide-mouthed old fireplace was spacious enough to hold entire cord-wood sticks on great iron dogs, while on either side in the fireplace were benches, where, on excessively cold days, the chilled inmates of the house could rest themselves while enjoying the blazing fire on the hearth. The cellar was of dressed stone, the joints true, every stone set square, and as carefully laid as the masonry of the City Hall.

Penn, shortly after his arrival at Chester, sent for James Sandelands, the elder, to confer with him, for it was "talkt among the people" of that day "that it was Intent to have built a City (at Upland), but that he and Sanderlin could not agree." The conclusion of this interview was that Penn had to look elsewhere for a site for the future metropolis of Pennsylvania, if it be true that Penn at that time proposed building a "great town" there. The refusal of the chief owner of land, at Chester, to accede to Penn's desires was disastrous in its results, and was discovered when too late to avoid its consequences, although an attempt was made to correct it, in a measure, on Nov. 19, 1700, when the petition of James Sandelands, the younger, was presented to Governor William Penn, on his second visit to the colonies, and his Council, in session at New Castle, setting forth that the royal patent to the proprietary gave him "absolute power to . . . erect and incorporate Towns, Hundreds and Counties and to incorporate Towns in Boroughs, & Boroughs into Cities & to make & constitute Fairs & Markets herein, with all other convenient privileges & Immunities according to the merits of the Inhabitants & fitness of ye places. . . . And whereas ye Petitioner is possessed of a certain spot of land lying in sd Countie of Chester, verie fitt & naturally commodious for a Town & to that end lately caused ye sd. spot of Land to be divided & Laid out into Lotts, Streets & Market place, a Draft & Model whereof (the generallie desired & Leiked of by ye sd Inhabitants of sd Countie) is notwithstanding herewith presented & submitted to your honors for your approbation and consent." The same day it was ordered, after the heirs of James Sandelands, the elder, had appeared before Council, that "the Proprietary & Governor & Council having approved of the within Petition & of the design thereof & Looking upon the place within proposed to be fitt for a Town did not onlie approve of ye within & annexed model, but also did erect & do hereby erect the said spot of Land so modelled & Laid outt Into a Town provided the same do not encroach upon other men's Land without their express consent under their Hands and Seals, and saving to the Proprietor & Governor & everie one their right."[1]

The first street laid out by authority was ordered by the grand jury, Eighth month 2, 1686, which body reports that they "doe lay out a street and a landing upon the creek to the corner lot far as over against the north west corner of the Court House fifty foote in breadth and from thence up the said Chester town for a street 30 foote in breadthe." This highway was at first called Chester Street, then Front Street, that runs along the creek, and now Edgmont Street or Avenue. In 1689 the grand jury continued the street from the present Second Street to low-water mark on the Delaware River, and from the northwestern corner of the then court-house, to low-water mark on the creek. This latter short street seems to have been closed at a later date, perhaps before the year 1690, for David Lloyd had the Governor and Council about that time to lay out a street thirty-eight feet wide on

[1] Martin's "History of Chester," p. 80.

the line of the present Second Street, from Chester Creek to the plantation he had purchased from Neeles Laerson's heirs in 1689. The plot of the town approved by Penn, Nov. 19, 1700, as shown by many ancient deeds, is almost exactly the plan of the old parts of this city as now laid out on the official map. In November, 1699, William Penn came a second time to his colony, and during that visit to the province he chartered the borough of Chester. The document is of interest, and we therefore give it entire, since many have no knowledge whatever of this old charter:

"Preamble: William Penn, true and absolute Proprietary and Governor-in-Chief of the Province of Pennsylvania and Territories thereunto belonging: To all to whom these shall come, Sends Greeting. Whereas in my first Regulation and Division of the Counties of this Province I thought fit to order. That the Townsted or Village then having the Name of Upland should be called Chester, which I thereupon constituted the Shire-town of the County of Chester and ordered and appointed all my courts of judicature, for the Affairs of that county to be there held and kept and the County goal or Prison to be and remain there for ever. AND whereas about the same Time, or soon after, for the Encouragement of the said Town, I was pleased to grant unto my ancient Friend John Simcock in Behalf of himself and others the Inhabitants of the said Place the Privilege of a Market to be there weekly held and kept. After which the said Inhabitants of the said Place, the Privilege of a Market to be thus weekly held and kept. After which the said Inhabitants, upon their special Instance, did also obtain from my late Lieutenant Governor and Council a Grant for two Fairs to be held in the said Town yearly. All which the inhabitants of the said Town, and of the adjacent Parts of the said County of Chester, having humbly besought me to confirm unto them, together with such additional Privileges an Francises as I might think fit or requisite for the better Encouragement of the Settlers, and Regulation of Trade therein.

"Now Know Ye, That I, favouring the just and reasonable Request of said Inhabitants, have of my own free Will erected, and do, by these Presents for me, my Heirs, and successors, erect the said Town into a Borough, which Town and Borough shall extend from the River Delaware two miles backwards into the Woods, and shall be bounded Eastward with the west side of Ridley Creek, and westward with the East side of Chester Creek to the said extent of two miles backwards from the River and shall ever hereafter be called Chester. And I further will that the Streets, Landings and Market-place in the said Town shall for ever hereafter be, continue and remain, as they are already and have lately been laid out and modelled and approved of by me and my council, then setting at New Castle. And I do hereby name and constitute Jasper Yeates, Ralph Fishbourn, Paul Saunders and Robert Barber, to be present Burgesses and James Lounes, High-Constables of the said Borough, who shall so continue until the tenth Day of the first Month next. On that Day, as also as the same day in the same month yearly afterwards for ever, it shall and may be lawful to and for the Freeholders and Housekeepers of the said Town and Borough publickly to meet in some convenient Place within the said Town, to be by them appointed for that Purpose, and then and there nominate, elect and chose by the Ballot of the inhabitants of the said Town, fit and able men to be Burgesses and High constables, with such other Officers as by the Burgesses and Freemen shall be judged needful for assisting and serving the Burgesses in managing the affairs of the said Borough, and Keeping of the Peace therein from time to time, And the Burgess first chosen in the said Election shall be called the Chief Burgess of the said Town.

"And I will and ordain. That all the said Burgesses for the Time being shall be, and are hereby impowered and authorized to be Conservators of the Peace within the said Borough; and shall have Power by themselves and upon their own view, without any Law proceedings, to remove all Nuisances and Incroachments out of the said Streets as they shall see Occasion: With Power also to arrest, imprison, and punish Rioters and Breakers of the Peace, and to bind them and all other offenders and Persons of evil Fame to the Peace or good Behaviour, as fully and effectually as any of the Justices of the Peace in the said County can do, and return or bring the Recognizances by them to be taken to the Court of Qwarter-Sessions for the said County. And that the said Chief Burgess from time to time shall, by Virtue of these Presents, without any further or other commission, be one of the Justices of the Peace, and one of the Justices of the County-Court and Qwarter Sessions, Oyer and Terminer and Goal-delivery, in and for the said County of Chester. And shall have full Power and Authority with the rest of the said County Justices, or a Qworum of them or by himself, where the laws of this Province, &c., direct one Justice to award Process and hold Pleas cognizable, by and before the Justices of the said County of Chester from time to time.

"And I do hereby grant and appoint. That the Sheriff and Clerk of the Courts of the said County of Chester for the Time being, if not Residents in the said Borough shall appoint and constitute sufficient Deputies, who shall from time to time reside or constantly attend in the said Town of Chester, to perform the Duties of their respective offices. But before any of the said Burgesses, Constables, or other Officer, shall take upon them the execution of their respective Offices they shall subscribe the Declaration and Profession of their Christian Belief, according to the late Act of Parliament, made in the first Year of the Reign of King William, and the late Queen Mary, intitled 'An act for exempting their Majesties' Protestant Subjects, dissenting from the Church of England, from the Penalties of Certain Laws.' And they that are to be newly elected for Burgesses, Constables and other Officers from time to time shall be attested for the due Execution of their respective Offices and shall subscribe the said Declarations and Profession of Belief before the old Burgesses, or such of them as go off and are not again chosen in the New Elections: But in case the old Burgesses are all chosen by the new Elections, then they shall have Power, and are hereby impowered and qualified to act upon their former Attests and Qualifications. And I do further grant and ordain, that the High-Constables of the said Borough for the Time being shall be Clerk of the Market, who shall and may have Assize of Bread, Wine, Beer, Wood and other Things; and to do, execute and perform, all Things belonging to the Office of Clerk of the Market within the said Town and Borough of Chester.

"And I do for me, my Heirs and Assigns, grant unto the said Burgesses and their Successors, That if any of the Inhabitants of the said Town and Borough shall be hereafter elected to the Office of Burgess or Constable as aforesaid, and, having notice of his or their Election, shall refuse to undertake and execute their Office to which he is chosen, it shall be lawful for the Burgess or Burgesses then acting to impose moderate Fines upon the Refusers, so as the Burgess's Fine exceed not Ten Pound, and the Constable's Five Pounds; to be levied by Distress and Sale, by Warrant under the Hand & Seal of one or more of the Burgesses, or by other lawful Ways, to the Use of the said Town being to summon and assemble Town-meetings, from time to time, as often as they shall find Occasion: At which Meetings they may make such Ordinances and Rules (not repugnant to or inconsistent with the Laws of this Province) as to the greater Part of the Town-meeting shall seem necessary and convenient for the good Government of the said Town. And the same Rules and Ordinances to put in Execution, and the same to revoke, alter and make anew, as Occasion shall require. And also impose such Mulcts and Amerciaments upon Breakers of the said Ordinances as to the Makers thereof shall be thought reasonable; to be levied as is directed in Case of Fines, to the Use of the Town, without rendering any Account thereof to me, my Heirs or Assigns: With Power also to the said Meetings to mitigate or release the said Fines and Mulcts, upon the submission of the Parties.

"And I do further grant to the said Burgesses and Inhabitants of the aforesaid Town and Borough of Chester, That they and their successors shall and may, for ever hereafter, hold and keep within the said Town in every Week of the Year one market on the fifth Day of the Week called Thursday: And also two Fairs there in every Year, the first of them to begin the fifth Day of the third Month, called May, and to continue that Day and two Days after; and the other of the said Fairs to begin the fifth Day of October and to continue till the seventh Day of the same Month in such Place and Places in the said Town as the Burgesses from time to time shall order and appoint.

"And I do further grant, That neither I, nor my Heirs or Assigns, shall or will seize any of the Liberties or Franchizes hereby granted, nor take any Advantage against the said Borough for the non-using or waving the present Execution of any of the Powers or Privileges hereby granted.

"In Witness whereof I have hereunto set my Hand and caused my Great Seal to be affixed. Dated the One-and-thirtieth Day of October, in the Year of our Lord One Thousand Seven Hundred and One, 1701.

"WILLIAM PENN."

"*Recorded Pat. Book Vol. 2, p. 138.*"[1]

[1] Hazard's Register, vol. iii. p. 264.

The borough grew slowly, for Oldmixon refers to it in 1708 as containing "one hundred houses." Bampfylde Moore Carew, in 1739, stated that it "contains about a hundred houses, and a very good road for shipping." In 1758, Acrelius said, "it had 120 houses, which gives endorsement to the assertion of Lewis Evans, in a letter written in 1753,[1] that "Chester, Bristol, and Newtown have been long at a stand." Peter Kalm, the Swedish naturalist, in the fall of 1748, journeying from Wilmington to Philadelphia, mentions in his journal "Chester, a little market town which lies on the Delaware. The houses stand dispersed. Most of them are built of stone and two or three stories high; some are, however, made of wood." The *Delaware County Republican* of July 1, 1836, states, Chester "has about 140 dwellings."

In 1713 the inhabitants of Chester County petitioned Governor Goodkin and Council "that ye Borough of the Town of Chester, in this Province, may be made a free Port." The petition was referred to William Penn, who took no action in the matter. Over a century thereafter, in March, 1838, the inhabitants of the borough of Chester petitioned the Councils of Philadelphia to have Chester made a port of entry, promising, if that was done, to build a railway from the piers to intersect with the Philadelphia, Wilmington and Baltimore Railroad. The project was so flattering to the hopes of the people of the place that, on March 7, 1840, an act of Assembly was obtained empowering the authorities to lay such track in the streets, but nothing ever came of the scheme.

In 1739 the noted clergyman, George Whitefield, preached in Chester, and so great was his fame and the excitement throughout the colony, occasioned by his eloquence, that about seven thousand persons gathered here to listen to his sermon. It is said that a cavalcade of one hundred and fifty horsemen accompanied the noted divine hither. It was during this year that Bampfylde Moore Carew, heretofore mentioned, passed through Chester, and he relates how the people for many miles around flocked to the places where Whitefield was to preach. Carew came here on Sunday, "stayed all night, and the next morning he inquired of one Mrs. Turner, a Quakeress, who formerly lived at Embercomb, by Minehead, in Somersetshire. From her he got a bill (money) and a recommendation to some Quakers at Darby, about five miles further." This Mrs. Turner lived at the northeast corner of Third Street and Concord Avenue, the property of the late Mrs. Shaw.

The story of Chester in its stationary condition is so interwoven with that of the county that it cannot be separated the one from the other. And it is unnecessary to refer to it here, since it is told in the general history heretofore given. On several occasions enterprising men have endeavored to give business impetus to the old borough. Jasper Yeates, in 1698, erected extensive granaries on the creek, and established a large bakery. It was located at Second and Edgmont Streets. The eastern abutment of the bridge there is built partly on the site of the old granary. The second story of the building was used for the storage of grain, while the lower was the biscuit-bakery. The enterprise failed to satisfy, for in a letter from James Logan to Penn 5th First month, 1708/9, it is set forth:

"The Country people of this Province having of late generally fallen upon the practice of bolting their own wheat and selling or shipping the flour, Jasper Yeates, a man of a working brain for his own interest, found his trade at Chester to fall under a very discouraging decay. Upon this he has frequently discoursed of removing to New Castle, where he is possessed of a large tract of land close to the town."

The old granary was substantially built of stone and brick, the walls being nearly three feet wide. The lime and mortar had so cemented the materials together that when it was demolished in April, 1853, by Mr. Pusey, of Chester County, to erect on its site a large flouring-mill, it almost defied the efforts of the workmen to pull it down. During the Revolution Joseph Ashbridge baked much of the "hard tack" for the American army, and in 1812 it was used for a like purpose for the United States. The archway of the building, which led from Edgmont Street to the creek, was a place of dread to the children in the olden times, for it was stated a woman had been murdered there and her uneasy spirit lingered about the place of her untimely "taking off."

Between 1761 and 1770, Francis Richardson, to whom Grace Lloyd devised the greater part of her large estate, built extensive warehouses and two piers, known as Richardson's Upper and Lower Wharf (in 1816 conveyed to the State, and in 1823 conveyed by the commonwealth to the United States), believing that Chester could be made a rival of Philadelphia as a shipping-point for grain and produce, but the difficulties with the mother-country totally ruined him. In 1732, Joseph Howell was a tanner in Chester, and continued in that occupation at the old tan-yard (now Frederick J. Hinkson's) on Edgmont Street, near Third, until 1764, when Isaac Eyre purchased the property and carried on the business. In 1799, John Birchall had the tannery there, and William Brobson followed him until 1863. The latter dying, the business was continued by Hon. Frederick J. Hinkson and J. S. Bell; later by I. J. & C. Hinkson, sons of Judge Hinkson, and more recently by the Chester Morocco Company.

In 1782, Jonathan Pennell, a blacksmith, had a shop on Edgmont Avenue, near Front, and William Spear in the same trade, in 1799, where Ladomus' block now stands. John Baggs was employed in one of these shops or with Jonathan Morris, who had a shop at that time on the southwest corner of Fifth and Welsh Streets. William Hawken was then the

[1] Martin's "History of Chester," p. 62.

village wheelwright. About 1800, William Ford was a shipwright at Chester. I do not know how long he had been in business as such, but we do know that on July 1, 1778, Col Jehu Eyre was placed in charge of the department for building boats for the State, having four separate sets of ship-carpenters at work at different locations, with one at Chester, under charge of Capt William Bowers[1] Samuel Lytle sawed ship-plank for their vessels It is stated a gunboat was built in the woods upon the creek since known as "Ship Creek," so that it might be hidden from the view of any English man-of-war ascending the river, and after it was launched it was discovered that it was a foot or so wider than the passageway between the abutments at Third Street bridge, and could not make its way to the Delaware The stream still retains the name, but the circumstance from which it derived that title has generally been forgotten

The first description of Chester after the Revolution which I have found describes the town thus [2]

"Chester, borough of, a post-town of Pennsylvania, and capital of Chester County [Delaware County] It is situated on the northwest side of Delaware River, between Ridgely [Ridley] and Chester Creek, fifteen miles southwest of Philadelphia It contains about sixty dwellings, built on a regular plan, a court-house, and jail Courts of Common Pleas and General Quarter Sessions of the peace are held here the third Monday in February, May, August, and November This town is remarkable for being the place where the first Colonial Assembly was convened, which was on the 4th of December, 1682 As it affords an agreeable morning's ride, and having genteel accommodations, it is the resort of much company from Philadelphia in the summer season It was incorporated by an act of Assembly December [March], 1795, and is governed by two burgesses, one high constable, one town clerk, and three assistants. The powers of the corporation are much limited, they are wholly confined to the preservation of peace and order among the inhabitants of the borough"

Almost all the inhabitants of the venerable borough believed that the removal of the county-seat to Media would be a fatal blow to the prosperity of the town, that it would rapidly sink in population and as a business point Few persons comprehended that the hour for its advancement had come The purchase by John P. Crozer of the old Chester mill-site to the northwest of the borough, the erection at that place of a cotton-mill, and the location of James Campbell at Leiperville, to the northeast, where he built up a large business in manufacturing cotton goods, had directed the attention of a few thoughtful men to the possibilities and advantages of Chester as a manufacturing centre

To properly appreciate the condition of Chester at that time, it is necessary to present a brief picture of the borough, which, after the Revolution, was incorporated with all the rights and privileges of a shire-town by act of Assembly of March 5, 1795. It had, however, remained almost stationary in respect to population and business enterprises In 1840 the population of the borough was seven hundred and forty persons of all ages and sexes The town occupied, in a scattered manner, the space extending from the Philadelphia, Wilmington and Baltimore Railroad to the river, and from Welsh Street to Chester Creek But a small part was built upon, and in the area given, most of the houses, many of them dilapidated, had been erected in the preceding century, and the place showed all the features of a finished town The change which has since that time so developed the little fishing village, for Chester was scarcely more than that, first began to show itself about 1842 A few properties then changed owners at fair prices

The great difficulty in the way of Chester was that it was surrounded by large farms held by persons in easy circumstances, who would not sell a foot of ground at any price, and who looked upon those who proposed to build a city here as visionary men, who would run themselves in debt and ultimately fail Time, however, brought these farms into the market Death and debt have no respect for conservatism, and by degrees these agencies worked in behalf of the change that was dawning The first of these tracts of land which came into the hands of the progressive spirits who were guiding the new order of things was that of William Kerlin, a fifty acre plot, the Essex House tract, lying between the post-road and the river, on the west bank of Chester Creek

John M Broomall, then residing in Upper Chichester, supposed that he had bought the farm in 1846, at one hundred and fifty dollars an acre, but the agent, Charles D Manley, though authorized to sell at that price, was, to his great mortification, unable to get his principal to execute the deed and the sale fell through In the early part of 1849, Mr Broomall, who had in the mean while removed to Chester, purchased the farm again of Mr Kerlin himself after considerable negotiation, at two hundred dollars an acre A time was fixed for executing the contract of sale, but before the day came, Mr Kerlin again changed his mind In December following, John Edward Clyde, who was quite anxious that a sale should be effected, meeting Mr Kerlin on the street, agreed to purchase the farm, and insisted that the former should go at once to the office of Mr Broomall The latter declined to enter into a negotiation except upon the condition that the deed should be forthwith executed and the sale consummated, if a price could be agreed upon The condition was accepted, Hon Edward Darlington was sent for as counsel for Mr Kerlin, and in half an hour the deed was executed, the price paid being two hundred and fifty dollars an acre During the negotiations, in the early part of 1849, Mr Broomall had offered to John P Crozer and John Larkin, Jr, each an equal interest with himself in the farm he then believed he had purchased from Mr Kerlin. The attention of both of these gentlemen had been attracted to Chester as the site of a future city if it could only get room to grow, and they had been looking at the Kerlin farm as a possible outlet Before the actual purchase took place, Mr Larkin bought a large part of the farm of John

[1] *Penna. Mag of Hist*, vol iii p. 423

[2] Joseph Scott's "U S Gazetteer" (Philadelphia, 1795, first "Gazetteer" of the United States published), title "Borough of Chester"

Cochran to the north of the town, now forming a considerable portion of the North Ward. He declined to accept Mr. Broomall's proposal, and the Kerlin farm was bought by Mr. Crozer and Mr. Broomall in equal shares.

On Jan. 5, 1850, John Larkin, Jr., purchased eighty-three acres of land, which had formerly been a race-course, from John Cochran. This tract had been included in the estate of David Lloyd, and the greater part of it was embraced in the purchase, May 1, 1741, made by Joseph Hoskins from Grace Lloyd, and which he devised to his nephew, John Hoskins, of Burlington, N. J. The latter sold the property to his son, Raper Hoskins, March 22, 1791, and he dying seized of the property, his widow, Eleanor, administered to the estate, and sold it, April 27, 1799, to Thomas Laycock. The latter dying, and his heirs making default in payment, the property was sold by John Odenheimer, sheriff, Oct. 26, 1806, to Anthony Morris, who in turn sold it to Maj. William Anderson, and the latter conveyed it to John Cochran, May 26, 1823, who dying intestate, the estate was conveyed by the heirs to John Cochran, the younger, who sold it to John Larkin, Jr., at the time already stated. The entire tract was in one inclosure; the only improvement, so far as buildings were concerned, was the small stone house, still standing, with its gable end to Edgmont Avenue, below Twelfth Street, and a frame stable. The land, after it ceased to be a race-course, had been used as a grazing lot for cattle.

Both tracts were laid out in streets and squares, and almost immediately signs of improvement began to manifest themselves in the present North and South Wards. Many of the old residents looked on in amazement, and often the quiet remark went round, "These men will lose every dollar they have in this business." The enterprising men, however, paid little attention to these prognostications of misfortune. Dwelling-houses were erected, streets laid out and graded, and capital was invited to locate in this vicinity. Early in the year 1850, James Campbell, of Ridley, purchased the lot and bowling-alley formerly belonging to the Delaware County Hotel, which lot was located on the north side of Fourth Street, where part of the market-house now stands. This building he altered to receive looms, and in March, 1850, within three months of the purchase of the Kerlin and Cochran farms, for the first time the noise of the shuttle was heard in the borough. When the public buildings were sold, Mr. Campbell bought the prison and work-house, and at much expense he changed the ancient structure into a cotton-mill, thus making the first permanent establishment in which textile fabrics were woven within the bounds of the present city of Chester.

In 1856, John P. Crozer conveyed his interest in the joint property to Mr. Broomall, for the cost and legal interest thereon, reserving only the half-square of ground on Penn and Second Streets, where the Baptist Church now stands. This was Mr. Crozer's own proposition, and on being reminded that more than enough land had been sold to pay the entire costs, leaving four-fifths of it as clear profit, he replied that he had gone into the enterprise not to make money, but to aid in the development of Chester, and he was quite content that the profits should go to Mr. Broomall, who had done the chief part of the work; that his assistance was no longer necessary, but that he would let his capital remain, to be repaid by Mr. Broomall, with interest, at his own time and convenience. Of course this offer was gratefully accepted.

In the present North Ward, Mr. Larkin, in spite of great opposition, carried out his designs fully. It is related that although he laid out the streets in that part of the town, and dedicated them to the public, the borough authorities refused to keep the highways in repair, and at his own expense he maintained a force of men at work upon them. On one occasion, when a member of the Town Council complained that the streets in the old part of the borough were neglected, contrasting them with those of Larkin-town, which were neat and well kept, and declaring that the public moneys should not all be expended in one locality, another member informed the speaker that Chester had never contributed a dollar for that purpose, and that Mr. Larkin had personally paid for all the highways made, as well as maintaining them in repair. Not only did he do this, but he constantly built houses, stores, foundries, shops, and mills, in conformity with a rule he had adopted at the beginning of his enterprise that every dollar he received from the sale of lands or buildings should be expended in further improvements, and hence, for any person desiring to start in business, he would erect the required structure, and lease it to him or them, with the privilege of purchasing the property at its cost price within ten years. Mr. Larkin has built over five hundred houses and places of business, several being large cotton-mills. In 1881 he sold the last vacant building-lot remaining out of the original eighty-three acres he had bought as an unimproved tract, thirty-one years before. More than thirty years Mr. Larkin spent industriously and earnestly in making the North Ward what it is, and only during the last ten years did he receive much assistance, from the labor of others to the same end, in dotting it all over with dwellings and industrial establishments.

To return to the river front: Mr. Broomall, in conjunction with William Ward, in 1862, purchased the farms of Edward Pennell and James Laws, which were brought into the market, and were soon dotted over with houses and manufacturing establishments.

On March 5, 1795, the borough of Chester,[1] which

[1] In "Gordon's Gazetteer," published in 1832, is presented the following description of the old borough a half-century ago:

"Chester, Post-town, Borough and seat of justice of Delaware County, 121 miles N. of Washington City, and 96 miles S.E. of Harrisburg, on

had been governed under the charter granted by Penn in 1701, was incorporated by an act of Assembly, and from time to time thereafter powers and privileges were procured from the State authorities. On April 6, 1850, a new charter was granted by the General Assembly. In 1866 the ancient borough had so grown in population and industries that the act of Feb. 14, 1866, was obtained, by which Chester was incorporated as a city, since which date, until the Constitution of 1874 interdicted special legislation, several supplemental and amendatory acts were had explanatory of the statute of 1866.[1] The story of the progress of the city, its industries, historical buildings, institutions of learning, and other topics which demand consideration in a work such as this will be presented under appropriate headings.

The following is a list of chief burgesses and the civil officers of the city of Chester:

1703. Jasper Yeates.
1730. Nicholas Pyle.
1731. Thomas Cummings.
1733. Caleb Cowpland.
1738. Joseph Parker.
1741. Charles Grantham.
1745. Joseph Parker.
1749. William Read.
1751. Mordecai James.
1752. Samuel Howell.
1753. Thomas Morgan.
1757. Joseph Hoskins.
1759. Jonathan Cowpland.
1762. Edward Brinton.
1763. Dr. Paul Jackson.
1779. David Cowpland.
1789. Dr. William Martin.
1794. William Graham.
1798. Isaac Eyre.
1832. Samuel Edwards.
1833. William Martin.
1835. George W. Bartram.
1847. Robert R. Dutton.
1848. William Brobson.
1849. Charles D. Manley.
1851. George W. Bartram.
1852. Alexander McKeever.
1853. Henry L. Powell.
1854. Job Rulon.
1855. Samuel Starr.
1856–57. John Edward Clyde.
1858. Stephen Cloud, Jr.
1859. Robert Gartside.
1860. George Baker.
1861. N. Walter Fairlamb.
1862. George Baker.
1863. Jeremiah W. Flickwir.
1864–65. George Baker.

MAYORS OF THE CITY OF CHESTER.

1866. John Larkin, Jr.[2]
1872. Dr. Jonathan Larkin Forwood.[3]
1881. James Barton, Jr.
1884. Dr. J. L. Forwood.

the river Delaware, 15 miles S.W. of Philadelphia. This is the most ancient town of Pennsylvania. There were several dwellings and a Quaker meeting here before the grant to William Penn of 1681. It was then known as 'Upland,' but the name of Chester was substituted by the Proprietary, at and before the granting of the Borough charter, on the 31st of Oct., 1701. The first adventurers, under Penn, landed here on the 11th of Dec., 1681, and were compelled to remain the winter, the river having been frozen over the night of their arrival. On the 4th of Dec., 1682, the first Provincial Assembly was holden here, memorable for having enacted, in a session of three days, seventy laws, comprising an efficient code for the government of a political society. There are still standing in this ancient town some old houses, among which is the church. Perhaps few places in the country have improved less. There is a water-power near it, but it is not great, and the business of the surrounding country lies in Philadelphia. It may contain at present about 134 dwellings, chiefly of stone and brick. A substantial and neat Court-House of stone, surmounted by a cupola and bell, brick offices, and a stone prison, 5 taverns, 4 stores, an Athenæum, the Delaware County Bank, a Church, and Quaker meeting-house. A manufactory of straw paper has lately been established near the town. For the accommodation of the trade of the Delaware there are some piers sunk in the river opposite the town, which have been lately repaired by the U. S. Population in 1830, only 848. There are here six practicing Attorneys and two Physicians."

[1] Bliss' "Digest of Delaware County," title, "Municipal Corporations—Chester," p. 375.

[2] Re-elected in 1869.

[3] Re-elected in 1875 and also in 1878.

CITY RECORDERS.

William H. Dickinson, March 21, 1878.
David Garrett, March 10, 1881; died in office Aug. 16, 1881.
I. Newton Shanafeldt, March 10, 1882, re-elected and commissioned April 5, 1883.

CITY SOLICITORS.

1866. William Ward, who was elected annually thereafter until October, 1872, when he resigned, and same month Orlando Harvey was elected annually thereafter until 1881, when the term was increased to three years, and in April, 1884, he was re-elected for three years.

PRESIDENTS OF CITY COUNCIL.

1866. William Ward.
1869. William A. Todd.
1873. Y. S. Walter.
1875. Amos Gartside.
1877. Dr. Theodore S. Christ.
1878. Robert Anderson.
1879. John A. Wallace.
1880. Robert Anderson.
1881. Henry B. Black (present incumbent).

CLERKS OF COUNCIL.

1866. Henry L. Donaldson.
1868. Dr. John M. Allen.
1873. Charles H. Allen.
1875. Mordecai Lewis (the present clerk).

MEMBERS OF THE CITY COUNCIL.

1866.—*North Ward*, James Stephens, Charles F. Kenworthy, John Hinkson, N. Walter Fairlamb, Charles A. Weidner; *Middle Ward*, Samuel A. Dyer, Ellis Smedley, George Flood, Crosby P. Morton, Stephen Cloud, Jr.; *South Ward*, William Ward, William B. Reaney, William A. Todd, James Scott, Amos Gartside.

1867.—*North Ward*, J. Wesley Ottey; *Middle Ward*, Dr. J. L. Forwood, William C. Gray; *South Ward*, William G. Price.

1868.—*North Ward*, I. Engle Hinkson, John O. Deshong, Jr.; *Middle Ward*, Y. S. Walter;[4] *South Ward*, George Derbyshire.

1869.—*North Ward*, Percipher Baker, Edmund Esrey; *Middle Ward*, William Appleby, David S. Bunting, David W. Morrison; *South Ward*, William Ward, William A. Todd, Amos Gartside.

1870.—*North Ward*, James Ledward; *South Ward*, William G. Price.[5]

1871.—*North Ward*, N. Walter Fairlamb; *Middle Ward*, Dr. J. L. Forwood, J. Frank Black; *South Ward*, Joseph R. T. Coates, James A. Williamson.

1872.—*North Ward*, Jonathan Kershaw, James Ledward, John O. Deshong, Jr.; *Middle Ward*, Henry Hinkson, George Goeltz, William Appleby; *South Ward*, George Robinson, George Derbyshire.[6]

1873.—*North Ward*, James Ledward; *Middle Ward*, Jonathan Pennell, Y. S. Walter; *South Ward*, James Barton, Jr., Thomas I. Leiper, George Weigand.

1874.—*North Ward*, J. Humphrey Fairlamb, William Armstrong; *Middle Ward*, William Hinkson; *South Ward*, Frederick J. Hinkson, Jr.

1875.—*North Ward*, Daniel Robinson, John O. Deshong, Jr.; *Middle Ward*, George Goeltz, Dr. Theodore S. Christ; *South Ward*, Amos Gartside, George Weigand.

1876.—*North Ward*, Samuel Danfield; *Middle Ward*, John B. Hinkson, Henry Hinkson; *South Ward*, Robert Anderson, Daniel Brown.[7]

1877.—*North Ward*, Samuel Greenwood, Thomas Clough; *Middle Ward*, Frank S. Baker; *South Ward*, John A. Wallace, Robert Chadwick.

1878.—*North Ward*, John Young, Samuel R. Palmer; *Middle Ward*, Henry B. Black, Paul Klotz; *South Ward*, William F. Cutter.[8]

[4] Mr. Walter was elected by Council to fill the place made vacant by the death of George Flood.

[5] David W. Morrison resigned, and July 18, 1870, Ellis Smedley elected by Council to take his place; I. Engle Hinkson died October, 1870, and Council elected John Hinkson in his stead.

[6] James A. Williamson resigned, and George Robinson elected in his stead. William G. Price resigned, and Gideon Speakman elected by Council. Jonathan Kershaw resigned, and James Stephens elected by Council. George Derbyshire died June, 1872, and Thomas I. Leiper elected by Council. William A. Todd resigned, and William B. Broomall elected by Council to fill vacancy.

[7] On May 1, 1876, Frederick J. Hinkson, Jr., resigned, and Thomas I. Leiper was elected by Council to fill the unexpired term until the ensuing charter election.

[8] Daniel Brown resigned Dec. 2, 1878, and Dr. Robert P. Mercer was elected by Council in his stead. February, 1879, Samuel R. Palmer died, and February, 1879, George M. Booth elected by Council in his stead.

1879.—*North Ward*, Frank S. Baker; *Middle Ward*, George McCall; *South Ward*, William Fennell.[1]

1880.—*North Ward*, Abraham Blakeley, Samuel Oglesby; *Middle Ward*, Isaiah H. Mirkil; *South Ward*, John A. Wallace.[2]

1881.—*North Ward*, Thomas Clough, Richard Miller; *Middle Ward*, Henry B. Black; *South Ward*, Henry Palmer, David M. Johnson, George G. Jones.[3]

1882.—*North Ward*, Frank S. Baker; *Middle Ward*, Perry M. Washabaugh, William J. Oglesby; *South Ward*, William B. Broomall, Joseph McAlden.[4]

1883.—*North Ward*, Samuel Black, John B. Hannum; *Middle Ward*, Robert Smith, Jr., J. Frank Black; *South Ward*, Thomas J. Houston.[5]

1884.—*North Ward*, Richard Miller, Samuel Oglesby; *Middle Ward*, J. Frank Black, Henry B. Black; *South Ward*, Dr. Robert P. Mercer.[6]

CITY SURVEYORS.

Joseph Taylor, Alfred Owens, William H. Flaville, Edward Roberts.

LIST OF JUSTICES, INCLUDING THE TOWNSHIP AND BOROUGH OF CHESTER.

John Crosby, Joel Willis, April 30, 1791; Davis Bevan, Aug. 19, 1794; Miles Macarty, April 13, 1796; Elisha Price, April 15, 1796; William Martin, Aug. 9, 1797; Isaac Eyre, Oct. 12, 1798; Nicholas Fairlamb, Dec. 6, 1798; Aaron Morton, May 3, 1799; Joseph Marshall, Thomas Hinkson, May 20, 1800; John Pearson, June 21, 1802; James Wuthey, July 4, 1806; Jacob Edwards, Jan. 1, 1807; John Caldwell, Nov. 15, 1814; Joseph Walker, Feb. 3, 1820; Samuel Smith, March 12, 1822; David Marshall, Dec. 3, 1824; George W. Bartram, June 3, 1824; Benjamin F. Johnson, Oct. 25, 1825; Abraham Kerlin, June 7, 1830; Samuel T. Walker, Nov. 11, 1831; John Afflick, June 6, 1834; Samuel Shaw, Nov. 18, 1835; William Martin, June 10, 1836; William Eyre, Dec. 21, 1838; George W. Bartram, Sept. 23, 1839.

JUSTICES OF THE BOROUGH AND CITY OF CHESTER.

George W. Bartram, Abraham Kerlin, April 14, 1840; Samuel Anderson, April 14, 1846; John Larkin, Jr., Frederick Fairlamb, April 9, 1850; Henry J. Powell, April 13, 1852; Frederick Fairlamb, April 10, 1855.

South Ward.—Samuel Ulrich, June 4, 1856, June 25, 1861, May 8, 1866, and May 8, 1871; Joseph Entwisle, May 1, 1872; Benjamin F. Welser, March 15, 1876; Samuel L. Armour, March 15, 1880, April 9, 1881.

Middle Ward.—Robert Gartside, April 10, 1860; John H. Baker, April 15, 1861; Jeremiah W. Fleckner, April 28, 1865, and April 30, 1866; Henry M. Hinkson, April 25, 1867; I. Edward Clyde, May 1, 1872; John M. Allen, March 28, 1878, and May 7, 1883.

North Ward.—Joseph Holt, April 10, 1860, May 17, 1865, May 8, 1871, May 8, 1876; Daniel B. Thomson, Aug. 25, 1881, and May 8, 1882.

Places of Worship—Friends' Meeting-House.—The first recorded meeting of the society of Friends in the province of Pennsylvania was that mentioned as being held at the house of Robert Wade, at Upland, in 1675, when William Edmundson, an eminent minister, then on a religious visit to the American colonies, was present. Previous to the coming of Penn, at a monthly meeting held 11th of Seventh month (September), 1681, it was agreed "Yt a meeting shall be held for ye service and worship of God every First Day at ye Court House at Upland." On the 6th of the First month, 1687, Jöran Kyn sold a lot of land, sixty feet in front and width, between parallel lines to the creek, adjoining his garden, on the west side of the present Edgmont Street, above Second, to John Simcock, Thomas Brasey, John Bristow, Caleb Pusey, Randal Vernon, Thomas Vernon, Joshua Hastings, Mordecai Maddock, Thomas Martin, Richard Few, Walter Fawset, and Edward Carter, "to the use and behoof of the said Chester—the people of God Called Quakers and their successors forever." Although the land was purchased it was several years before the building was erected, the evidence apparent establishing that six years elapsed before the meeting-house was finished.

The first direct notice of such a movement was at the meeting at Walter Faucet's "ye 6th of ye 4th month, 1687," when it was "Agreed that Bartholomew Copock and James Kinerly Randall Vernon and Caleb Pusey do agree and Contract wth such workman or men as they shall se meet to build a meeting house att Chester 24 foot Sqwar and 10 ft. high in the Walls & that the above s^d persons do Come themselves and the workman or men if they do agree & Give accompt thereof to the next Mo: meeting." The project languished, so far as the records show, until the "13th of ye 8th mo. 1690," when Chester meeting appointed a committee "to take the subscriptions of Middletown, Edgmont, Springfield, Upper & Nether providence and Marple of what these friends are free to Give towards the building a meeting house in Chester. Viz^t for Upper providence Randall Malin, for Middletown John Worrall, David Ogden, for Edgmont, Thomas Worrelle, James Swaffer, for Springfield, George Morris, Junr, & Mordica Maddock, for Marple Thomas Person and Josiah Taylor."

The committee appear to have worked diligently, for on the minutes of Chester meeting, but without date, appears the following:

"SUBSCRIPTIONS BUILDING OF A MEETING HOUSE IN THE TOWNE CHESTER.

	£	s.	d.
"Thomas Powell	2	0	0
Thomas Brassey	3	10	0
Randall Vernon	3	00	00
Thomas Vernon	1	00	00
John Sharpless	1	10	00
Walter ffaucet	1	10	00
John Hoghkins (Hoskins)	1	10	00
Caleb Pusey	1	00	00
Robert Barber	1	00	00
Joshua Hastings	1	00	00
John Baldwin	0	05	00
John Broomall	0	05	00
John Bristow	5	00	00
John Simcocke	5	00	00
William Woodmansee	0	07	00
Jacob Simcock	0	10	00
James Sharpless	0	5	00
Andrew Job	01	00	00
James Whittacree	00	05	00
Mord. Maddock	03	00	00
John Simcock, juner	00	10	00
Robert Taylor	00	06	00
Edward Walter	10	06	00
Edward Carter	2	00	00
John Beall	00	06	00
Charles Brookes	00	06	00
William Browne	00	10	00
Thomas Vernon, young?	01	00	00
Francis Worly	00	10	00
Willm Caborne	01	00	00
Joseph Caborne	01	00	00
John Edge	01	00	00
John Crosby	01	00	00

1 John Young died February, 1880, and Samuel Greenwood elected by Council in his stead.

2 Robert Chadwick resigned Nov. 15, 1880, and William G. Price elected by Council in his place. March 7, 1881, Robert Anderson resigned, and Henry Palmer elected by Council in his stead.

3 John A. Wallace resigned Jan. 3, 1882, William B. Broomall elected by Council in his stead.

4 Oct. 16, 1882, Perry M. Washabaugh resigned, and B. F. Baker elected by Council in his stead.

5 Henry Palmer resigned May 16, 1883, Dr. Robert P. Mercer was elected by Council in his stead.

6 William B. Broomall resigned, and James Fryer was elected by Council in his place.

	£	s.	d.
John Parker	00	10	00
John Martin	01	00	00
Tho Martin	01	00	00
Nat. Evans	01	00	00
John Churchman	00	00	00
Henry Churchman	00	10	00
Thomas Calbourne	3	00	00
John Worall	01	00	00
Randall Maillen	00	10	00
robert Vernon	01	00	00
tho Minshall	1	00	00
peter tailler	00	06	00
Joseph Vernon & Jacob Vernon	01	00	00
John hoskins Jonut	10	10	00
James Swaford	00	04	00
William Swaford	00	06	00
henry Worley	00	10	00
John Powell	01	00	00
thomas Joans	00	06	00
Laraunce rooth	00	10	00
	11	12	00
George Churchman	11	00	00"

It does not, as stated, appear when this subscription was collected, but we know that nothing was done towards erecting the meeting until the 6th of "ye 2^d^ mo., 1691," when, at the house of Walter Faucit, we find that "Its agreed by this meeting that John Bristow & Caleb Pusey do forthwith agree wth and Inploy workmen in the Building the meeting house ats Chester (wth stone) on the place that was formerly bought for that purpose the situateing of wch as also the manner of Building the sayme is Left to their Discretion and that this meeting do Defray the Charges of the saime so that it exceed not above one Hundred pounds and that there bee one Convenient Chimney att Least and that the s^d^ John Bristow and Caleb Pusey do Give account of what they have done at ye next month meeting." On the 12th of Eighth month, 1691, the meeting appointed Walter Faucit and Randall Vernon to "Goe to those y^t^ subscribed to the Building the meeting house that they forthwith bring their pay unto Calebs Mill and make report at ye next month meeting." Some of the subscribers seem to have regretted their liberality, for on 11th of Second month, 1692, it was ordered that "Randall Vernon and Randall Malin Goe to Thomas Powell and Return him the two pounds tenn shillings that hee saith hee lent toward building the meeting house and paying for the Ground it Stands on att Chester and make Returne of their proceeding to the next mo. meeting." There was doubtless some dispute respecting the payment of these moneys to Powell, for on the 1st of the Eleventh month, 1693, "a memorandum" was entered of record in which Randall Malin, Robert Vernon, and Peter Taylor certify that they were at Powell's house and the money had been paid to him in their presence. On the 5th of First month, 1693/4, John Simcock, Randall Vernon, Walter Faucit, Robert Baker, and Robert Carter were directed to meet John Bristow and Caleb Pusey "in order to make up the accompts wth them concerning the meeting house att Chester and also to Receve the Deed of the Land the s^d^ house stands upon." At a meeting held at Robert Vernon's, 2d of Second month, 1694, John Bristow brought the deed and the account of disbursement in erecting the building. The deed was given to John Simcock for safe keeping, and Walter Faucit, Caleb Pusey, and Robert Barber were directed to "Inspect into and Cast up the s^d^ accompts wth him" (Bristow).

The impression which so long held undisputed sway that the first Assembly in the province sat in this old meeting-house has ceased to be a disputed topic among historians, but the question which part of the ancient building was first erected was long in dispute. The records of Chester Meeting, which are explicit, leave even that no longer a debatable point. The building being of stone, that part of it which faced on Edgmont Street was the original structure, and the brick addition towards the creek was placed there after Friends had worship in there for several years. As late as 1848, when the building was inspected by a critical observer, these facts were established by the house itself. Whitehead tells us, "The brick part bore evidence of having been subsequently added as a kitchen, having an oven built within and forming part of the original wall. The timbers, too, were in a better state of preservation." Indeed, it may be asserted without fear of contradiction that the latter part was not erected until after 1701, for Lydia Wade bequeathed thirty pounds—a large sum in those days—to Chester Meeting, twenty of which were "towards the Inlarging and finishing the meeting-house of Friends in the towne of Chester," the remaining ten pounds were to be expended by the women's meeting, to be "disposed of as they shall think fitt for the servis of Truth." This sum was received from the executor of Lydia Wade's will, for on the 24th of Ninth month, 1701, Caleb Pusey paid that amount to the meeting, which payment is acknowledged by the records.

When the meeting-house was first built, it seems some of the neighbors had encroached on the lot, for on Eighth month 4, 1797, "John Simcock's on behalf of the meeting required Henry Hollingsworth to remove his shop from off the land belonging to the Meeting House, who promised so to do."

In the old structure Penn frequently spoke, and many pleasant memories clustered about this first meeting of Friends, and therein services were held for forty-three years, until, in 1736, the society found it necessary to erect a larger building to accommodate its increasing membership, and the house on Edgmont Street was sold to Edward Russell, who added a garret-story to the front building, and possibly erected the back part. In recent years the house was used by Samuel Long as a cooper-shop, and was sold in 1844 to Joshua and William P. Eyre, when partition was made of Long's estate.

On April 18, 1736, Caleb Coupland conveyed the southern part of the lot on Market Street, south of Third Street, on which the meeting-house now stands, to Jacob Howell, Thomas Cummings, John Owen, Samuel Lightfoot, John Salkeld, Jr., and John Sharpless, and the latter the same day executed a declaration in trust setting forth that they held the land as trustees and for the use of the members of Chester Meeting. As the society waxed stronger they required more land, the meeting-house having been located toward the northern line of the lot, hence, April 29, 1762, they purchased from Jesse Maris, who had acquired the property by descent from his father, George Maris, subject to a yearly rent of six pounds to the heirs of James Sandelands. The trustees, Jonas Preston, John Fairlamb, Caleb Hanison, and James Barton, to whom it was conveyed by Jesse Maris, May 1, 1762, executed a declaration of trust to Chester Meeting.

The discussion which had prevailed in the society of Friends during the early part of this century respecting certain doctrinal points, culminated in an open rupture in 1827, when a division of Friends took place, those members who sustained Elias Hicks in his opinions retaining their connection with Chester Meeting being in the majority, the structure on Market Street became the house of worship of the Hicksite branch of the society. In 1883 the building was thoroughly repaired and modernized internally.

The Friends' graveyard on the west side of Edgmont Avenue, I had thought, was the first burial-place of the society in Chester, but recent examination has caused me to change that opinion. The first reference to a Friends' graveyard at that town was at a meeting on 1st of Fourth month, 1682, when it was agreed that "Thomas Cobourn, Randal Vernon, & William Clayton do view or see that pece of Ground w[ch] is ordered for a Buriall place also to see about the fencing of itt wth a Lasting fence and if there bee stones neare and convenient." The site selected seems not to have met the approval of the whole meeting. Indeed the location of the lot was not then definitely fixed upon, for on the 5th of Twelfth month, 1682/3, John Hastings, Robert Wade, Richard Few, and Thomas Cobourn were instructed to "view the Buriall place to Consider what Quantity may be meet also what Way or how it may be Best fenced about." A report from this committee appears never to have been made. Therefore on the 11th of Fourth month, 1683, the same persons, excepting that Thomas Brasey was substituted for Richard Few, were directed to "View and Look out a piece of Land for a Buriall place and bring in their Accompt thereof to the next monthly meeting." A burial-place was accepted, for on the 5th of Ninth month, 1683, John Hastings and Thomas Vernon were directed to "fence the burial grounds as soon as may bee." Where this graveyard was is not absolutely known, but I believe that it was on the east side of Edgmont Avenue, south of Seventh Street, the present steam grist-mill of L. L. Luken & Co. being located partly thereon. In April, 1880, when excavations were made for the foundations of the mill, a number of human bones were unearthed, which had been deposited in a row. At that time no person seemed to be aware that Friends had ever but two graveyards, one at the present location, and the other on Edgmont Avenue above Twelfth Street, a burial-place for the negroes, owned by members of Chester Meeting; but the evidence is now conclusive that there was a graveyard previous to the one now walled in with heavy masonry adjoining the Beal house-lot on the north. On the 31st of the Sixth month, 1702, at a meeting held at Chichester, it appears that "Chester meeting proposeth theer intentions of purchasing a burying place in the town, which this meeting approves of, provided they preserve and keep in Good order the Old Burying Place." The graveyard purchased about this date was not inclosed with a stone wall as we now see it many years previous to the Revolution. Grace Lloyd, by her will, 6th of Fourth month, 1760, directed her executors to "pay £10 towards walling in the front part of the graveyard belonging to the people called Quakers in Chester with brick or stone." And nearly ten years later, 31st of Twelfth month, 1769, Joseph Hoskins, by will, bequeathed £10 "for the use of enclosing or fencing the burying ground belonging to the Friends of Chester meetings in such manner as their Preparative Meeting of Chester shall direct and appoint." The extracts from these wills clearly prove that as late as the first of the year 1770 no wall had been erected around the grounds wherein the bodies of many of the noted personages of the ancient borough lie. David Lloyd and Grace, his wife, Caleb and David Coupland, Henry Hale Graham, Davis Bevan, John Salkeld, John Mather, and others of the early settlers and leading men of the last century in the province are interred in that God's acre, now in the heart of a busy city, while the remains of a number of persons who fled to this province to escape persecution in Europe lie there forgotten because the prohibition by the society of stones to mark the graves of those who slumber within the burial-grounds belonging to their meetings.

The graveyard for negroes above mentioned was on Edgmont road, above Twelfth, and was used for the interment of slaves by the sufferance of the then owner of the land. The latter, Grace Lloyd, in her will, dated 6th of Fourth month, 1760, made the following bequest:

"And it is my mind and will, and I do hereby order and direct that the *piece of burying ground*, being forty feet, fronting Edgmont Road, in said borough, thence seventy feet back and forty feet in breadth, shall at all times hereafter, forever, *be used for and as a burying place for negroes*, that is to say, for such as shall have belonged to my late husband or myself, and such as do or hereafter may belong to Friends of Chester Meeting, and such as in their life-time desire to be buried there, but not for any that are executed, or lay violent hands upon themselves, and that none be buried there without the consent of the Overseers of Friends' Meeting at Chester."

The lot thus set apart was surrounded by a tall, thick-set hedge, but after the execution of several persons at the intersection of Edgmont and Providence roads (the colonial law then requiring the burial of the body of the culprit near the gallows) rendered the locality a place of dread, and the superstitious negroes soon began to regard it as a spot to be avoided when living and shunned as a place of interment. In time even that the lot had been ever used as a graveyard was forgotten until the clause in Lydia Wade's will directed attention to it. In 1868, John and James C. Shedwick erected the row of houses on the east side of Edgmont Avenue, above Twelfth, and while the excavations for the cellars were being made a number of human bones were exposed. At that time they were thought to be the remains of Indians, the fact that it was the site of an old graveyard being unknown to the public.

St. Paul's Church and Burial-Ground.—A tract of ground was donated to the Swedish Church by Armgard Pappegoya for glebe or church land in Upland early in the history of the settlement. The plot of land on the south side of Third Street, east of Market Square, where the old burial-ground now is, and where the first St. Paul's Church building was erected, was, previous to that structure being placed there, a burying-place for the dead of the Swedish colonists at Upland. This fact is established by the report of Mr. Ross to the Society for the Propagation of the Gospel in Foreign Parts in 1714, wherein he distinctly makes this declaration. He also states, they (the Swedes) "had likewise a Church endowed with a valuable Glebe not far from the place of burial, but of this building there remains no sign at this day." John Hill Martin thinks this reference is to the block-house, or House of Defense, which was torn down by order of the court in 1703, an opinion which is doubtless correct. Acrelius tells us that the Swedes held religious services usually in the forts and houses of defense. The fact is satisfactorily established that the Swedes were obliged to have sentinels regularly posted during public worship to apprise the congregation within of any attempted attack by the Indians, of which the early settlers seemed to be constantly apprehensive. Every student of our early annals is aware that after the cargo of the "Black Cat," which had been ladened with articles of merchandise for the Indians, became exhausted, and the Swedish settlers' capacity for making presents had ceased, the savages seriously considered in council whether the Europeans should be exterminated or permitted to remain. An old Indian succeeded in preventing a breach between the two races by assuring the young braves that courageous and vigilant men, armed with swords and muskets, would be difficult to subdue. The clergymen were particularly obnoxious to the savages, because the latter believed that during divine services the minister—he alone speaking and all the rest remaining silent—was exhorting the congregation against the Indians. Acrelius also tells us that a block-house answered the purpose very well (as a church):

"The Indians were not always to be depended upon that they would not make an incursion, fall upon the Christians, and capture their whole flock. It was, therefore, necessary for them to have the religious houses as a place of defense for the body as well as the soul. The churches were so built that after a suitable elevation, like any other house, a projection was made some courses higher, out of which they could shoot; so that if the heathen fell upon them, which could not be done without their coming up to the house, the Swedes could shoot down upon them continually, and the heathen, who used only bows and arrows, could do them but little injury."[1]

In 1700, Rev. Mr. Evans was sent to Pennsylvania by the Society for the Propagation of the Gospel in Foreign Parts, and located in Philadelphia. He is frequently mentioned in the history of the society as going to Chester, Chichester, Concord, and Radnor, each about twenty miles distant from Philadelphia, and while constant allusion is made to a church edifice existing in that city, no intimation is given of any such building in either of the other places designated. I am aware that in taking down the old St. Paul's Church building, in July, 1850, after it had stood one hundred and forty-eight years, two bricks, burned exceedingly hard and considerably larger in size than those in use at the present day, closely cemented together, and with the figures 1642 cut upon them, were found. These numerals must have been made upon them many years subsequent to that date, for in 1644 there was not a house standing in the present limits of Chester. Independently of that fact, we have documentary record of the exact date of the building, so circumstantially set forth that there is no room remaining for doubt.

In an account of the building of St. Paul's Church, Chester, furnished to the Society for the Propagation of the Gospel in Foreign Parts, Mr. Ross, the then missionary of the society, in his report, June 25, 1714, says,—

> "In the Swedish Dormitory—the old Swedish burial ground—James Sandelands, of Chester, (or as it was first called, Upland,) Merchant, a man of good reputation in the country, was on account of affinity interred to keep up the memory of this founder of a growing family; twas agreed amongst his relations that his grave, as also that of his kindred and family, who were or might be buried there should be distinguished & set apart from the rest of the burying ground by an enclosure or wall of stone. This design was no sooner formed & noised abroad, but it was happily suggested by a projecting fellow in Town, that, if it seemed good to Mr. Sandelands' relations, the intended stone wall about the place of the interment might be with somewhat more changes carried up and formed into a small chapel or church. This new motion was well liked by ye sd relations and encouraged by everybody in the neighborhood that wished well to the church of England, but they who put life into this proposal & prosperously brought it to pass were Joseph Yeates, merchant in Chester, and James Sandelands, son to the above named Mr. Sandelands, the latter of which two gentlemen, besides other gifts, gave some land to enlarge the church yard, but the former, to wit: Mr. Yeates, a zealous asserter of our constitution in church and State, must be allowed to have been the main promoter of the founding of St. Paul's upon Delaware."

The report further alludes to other persons "parishers, who were chief helpers to carry on the work,"—

[1] History of New Sweden, p. 176.

Jeremy Collett, John Hannum, Henry Pierce, Ralph Pyle, and Thomas Barnsly, but especially does he commend Thomas Powell for the gift of a valuable piece of land "for a minister's house, garden, and other conveniences." He also applauds Hon. Col. Francis Nicholson, of whom he says, "We may safely say no man parted more freely with his money to promote the interest of the church in these parts, nor contributed so universally towards ye erection of Christian synagogues in different and distant plantations in America."

The small but compact fabric of brick thus erected, and said to be one of the neatest on this continent, was forty-nine feet in length by twenty-six feet in breadth, and was well and substantially finished inside. The main entrance, which was wide and spacious, closed by double doors, was at the north side of the church, and the access to the building was from Market Street, through the yard.

The old church must have had a sun dial, perhaps over its main door, such as is still to be seen at the court-house of Somerset County, Md., for, in 1704, the wardens claim credit for "cash pd ye ferymen for Bringing Down ye Dyal, 1*s.* 8*d.*; ac of nayles for setting up ye Dyall, 1*s.* 2*d.*; money spent and pd ye men for setting It up, 4*s.*"

The inside of the church was divided into four parts by two aisles, one extending from the double doors, and the other from the pulpit to the extreme western part of the church. The roof was oak, and the rafters white-oak, hewed with a broad axe. The chancel was spacious and paved with brick, as were also the aisles. In the west end of the church, and directly opposite the pulpit, built into the wall, was the well-known slab of gray sandstone, six feet in length by three in breadth, now in the Sunday-school room of the new church edifice, erected to the memory of James Sandelands, the elder. Along the borders of the old slab, in large capital letters, are the words:

"Here lies interred the bodie of
James Sandelands, Merchant
in Upland, in Pensilvania,
who departed this mortal life
Aprile te 12, 1692, aged 56 years,
and his wife,
Ann Sandelands."

Its face is divided into two parts, the upper bearing in cipher the initials "J. S." and "A. S.," the arms of the Sandelands family—argent, a band azure. On the border, dividing the upper from the lower part, are the words, "Vive Memor Lethi FFugit Hora." The lower half contains many emblems of mortality,—the tolling bell, the passing bell, the skull and cross-bones, the hour-glass, an upright coffin bearing on its side the words, "Memento Mori," "Time Deum," and in either corner, crossed, a sceptre and mattock, and a mattock and spade.

Queen Anne, whom Horace Walpole dubbed "the wet-nurse of the church," presented to the parish a handsome pulpit, a communion-table "well rail'd in and set out with a rich cloth, and a neat chalice;" the two former articles were located at the east end of the edifice. This chalice and salver, the queen's gift, as well as a similar chalice, presented to the congregation by Sir Jefferey Jeffries, are still in possession of the church wardens, and employed in the sacrament of the Lord's Supper to the present time; but the pulpit and communion-table have long since been removed. The chalices and their salvers are of hammered and very pure silver. The one presented by the queen has engraved upon it the words "Annæ Reginæ." The gift from Sir Jefferey Jeffries was made in March, 1715, and consisted of a small bell, "a rich cloth, and a neat chalice." In time the bell was replaced by a larger one.

At a meeting of the vestry, March 30, 1741, twenty-three members of the congregation subscribed funds to "& for in consideration of purchasing a bell for said church," and at a meeting of the same body, April 15, 1745, a bell-tower or turret, to hang the bell, was ordered "to be built of stone in the foundation from out to out, Twelve by Fourteen foot." The belfry, built according to these directions, was to the west of and entirely detached from the church. The bell, which was made in England, and had cast on it the words "Roger Rice, Chester, 1743," was paid for in advance, in 1742, by a bill of exchange for thirty pounds, and, as the sum obtained by subscription amounted to only half that amount, John Mather donated the remaining fifteen pounds.

The stone-work, twenty-five feet in height, was surmounted by a frame structure in which the bell hung. The tower, including the wooden addition, was over fifty feet. The belfry was entered by a door on the south side. The frame superstructure was square until it reached the plate on which the rafters rested, and the roof faced four ways, receding to a point, which was ornamented with a weather-vane. In each side of the frame-work was a slatted window, so that the sound of the bell would not be obstructed any more than necessary. Within the interior was a rough ladder, which the sexton had to climb when he tolled the bell, although for church services it was rung by a long rope, which descended to within a few feet of the ground floor.

The foundation of the ancient structure was laid July, 1702, and on Sunday, Jan. 24, 1703 (new style), St. Paul's day, the edifice was opened to public worship, Rev. John Talbot preaching the first sermon in the church. The general impression is that Rev. George Keith was the first clergyman to hold divine services in St. Paul's, but in that gentleman's "Journal and Travels," published in London, 1706, occurs this passage: "Sunday, Jan. 24, 1702," (1703 N. S.) "I preached at Philadelphia, on Matthew v. 17, both in the forenoon and afternoon, Mr. Evans, the minister, having that day been at Chester, in Pennsylvania, to accompany Mr. Talbot, who was to preach the first

MURAL TABLET

James Collins, John Hannum, Henry Pierce, Ralph Pyle, and Thomas Barnsly, but especially does he commend Thomas Powell for the gift of a valuable piece of land "for a minister's house, garden, and other conveniences." He also applauds Hon. Col. Francis Nicholson, of whom he says, "We may safely say no man parted more freely with his money to promote the interest of the church in these parts, nor contributed so universally towards ye erection of Christian synagogues in different and distant plantations in America."

The small but compact fabric of brick thus erected, and said to be one of the neatest on this continent, was forty-one feet in length by twenty-six feet in breadth, and was well and substantially finished inside. The main entrance, which was wide and spacious, closed by double doors, was at the north side of the church, and the access to the building was from Market Street, through the yard.

The old church must have had a sun dial, perhaps over its main door, such as is still to be seen at the court-house of Somerset County, Md., for, in 1704, the wardens claim credit for "cash pd ye ferymen for bringing Down ye Dyal, 1s. 8d.; ac of nayles for setting up ye Dyall, 1s. 2d.; money spent and pd ye men for setting It up, &c."

The inside of the church was divided into four parts by two aisles, one extending from the double doors, and the other from the pulpit to the extreme western part of the church. The roof was oak, and the rafters white-oak, hewed with a broad axe. The chancel was spacious and paved with brick, as were also the aisles. In the west end of the church, and directly opposite the pulpit, built into the wall, was the well-known slab of gray sandstone, six feet in length by three in breadth, now in the Sunday-school room of the new church edifice, erected to the memory of James Sandelands, the elder. Along the borders of the old slab, in large capital letters, are the words:

"Here lies interred the body of
James Sandelands, Merchant
in Upland, in Pensilvania,
who departed this mortal life
April ye 12, 1692, aged 56 years,
[illegible] his wife,
[illegible] Sandelands."

The face is divided into two parts, the upper bearing in cipher the initials "J. S." and "A. S.," the arms of the Sandeland's family,—argent, a bend azure. On the border, dividing the upper from the lower part, are the words, "Vive Memor Lethi Fugit Hora." The lower half contains many emblems of mortality,—the tolling bell, the passing bell, the skull and cross-bones, the hour-glass, an upright coffin bearing on its side the words, "Memento Mori," "Time Drum," and in either corner, crossed, a sceptre and mattock, and a mattock and spade.

Queen Anne, whom Horace Walpole dubbed "the wet-nurse of the church," presented to the parish a handsome pulpit, a communion-table "well rail'd in and set out with a fine cloth, and a surf-chalice;" the two former articles were located at the east end of the edifice. This chalice and salver, the queen's gift, as well as a similar chalice, presented to the congregation by Sir Jeffrey Jeffries, are still in possession of the church wardens, and employed in the sacrament of the Lord's Supper to the present time; but the pulpit and communion-table have long since been removed. The chalices and their salvers are of hammered and very pure silver. The one presented by the queen has engraved upon it the words "Annæ Reginæ." The gift from Sir Jeffrey Jeffries was made in March, 1718, and consisted of a small bell, "a rich cloth, and a neat chalice." In time the bell was replaced by a larger one.

At a meeting of the vestry, March 30, 1741, twenty-three members of the congregation subscribed funds to "& for in consideration of purchasing a bell for said church," and at a meeting of the same body, April 15, 1745, a bell-tower or turret, to hang the bell, was ordered "to be built of stone in the foundation from out to out, Twelve by Fourteen feet." The belfry, built according to these directions, was to the west of and entirely detached from the church. The bell, which was made in England, and had cast on it the words "Roger Kice, Chester, 1743," was paid for in advance, in 1742, by a bill of exchange for thirty pounds, and, as the sum obtained by subscription amounted to only half that amount, John Mather donated the remaining fifteen pounds.

The stone-work, twenty-five feet in height, was surmounted by a frame structure in which the bell hung. The tower, including the wooden addition, was over fifty feet. The belfry was entered by a door on the south side. The frame superstructure was square until it reached the plate on which the rafters rested, and the roof faced four ways, ascending to a point, which was ornamented with a weather-vane. In each side of the frame-work was a slatted window, so that the sound of the bell would not be obstructed any more than necessary. Within the interior was a rough ladder, which the sexton had to climb when he tolled the bell, although for church services it was rung by a long rope, which descended to within a few feet of the ground floor.

The foundation of the ancient structure was laid July, 1702, and on Sunday, Jan. 24, 1703 (new style), St. Paul's day, the edifice was opened to public worship, Rev. John Talbot preaching the first sermon in the church. The general impression is that Rev. George Keith was the first clergyman to hold divine services in St. Paul's, but in that gentleman's "Journal and Travels," published in London, 1706, occurs this passage: "Sunday, Jan. 24, 1702" (1703 N. S.) "I preached at Philadelphia, on Matthew v. 17, both in the forenoon and afternoon, Mr. Evans, the minister, having that day been at Chester, in Pennsylvania, to accompany Mr. Talbot, who was to preach the first

Drawn by Paul Weber.

MURAL TABLET.

In St. Paul's Church, Chester, Penn[a]

sermon in the church after it was built" Mr Keith did preach here on February 7th and August 3d of that year, and records · 'We were kindly entertained at the house of Jasper Yeats there," and on "Sunday, April 9, 1704, I preached at Chester, on John iv 24, being my last sermon there." In 1704, Rev Henry Nichols was appointed missionary to St Paul's parish, by the Society for the Propagation of the Gospel in Foreign Parts, and reported that the people were well inclined to the Church of England, although they had previous to that time no "fixed minister till now," and that the congregation had made a subscription of sixty pounds a year towards the support of their rector.

In 1718, Rev John Humphrey, who was in charge of the parish, reported to the society that he could not get a house in Chester to live in, and therefore had to buy a plantation of a thousand acres, about three miles distant. He was not altogether acceptable to parishioners, and, on April 5, 1717, they petitioned the society to appoint another person, which was done, and Samuel Hesselius was substituted in his stead

· Thirty-four years after Mr. Humphreys had complained of the absence of a parsonage, in 1752, the Rev. Thomas Thompson writes to the society · "I found no church wardens or vestry, no house for the minister to live in, nay, not a fit house to hire." Mr Thompson, it seems, formed no better opinion of the people than the people did of the rector, for in "Rev Dr Perry's papers relating to the history of the church in Pennsylvania, 1780 to 1778," Rev Thomas Thompson is referred to as a man of bad character

The congregation, however, failed to provide for the missionaries as the rules of the society required, and in 1762 a notice was given them, that if they did not procure better accommodations for their clergyman, and "maintain a glebe, a dwelling-house, and their church and burying-grounds in decent order and repair," the society would withdraw its mission from them To accomplish these ends the congregation issued a scheme in January of that year to raise £562 10s by a lottery The advertisement, after setting forth these facts, states "They," the congregation, "find themselves under the disagreeable necessity to apply to the publick by way of a Lottery, not doubting that it will meet with all suitable encouragement from the well-disposed of every denomination, as it is intended for the Glory of God, and consequently for the good of the Province" There were 1733 prizes and 3267 blanks, making 5000 tickets in all. The drawing was to take place either in Chester or Philadelphia, on March 1, 1762, and continue until all the tickets were drawn The managers add this addenda to their advertisement.

"N B.—As the above sum will fall vastly short of completing everything as could be wished, it is hoped that if any are scrupulous as to the method of raising money, yet wish well to the Design, and are willing to promote the same, if such Persons will deliver their Liberality into the hands of Mr Charles Thomson, Merchant in Philadelphia, or to any of the Managers aforesaid, it will be gratefully acknowledged and carefully applied accordingly"

There is little of interest connected with the church for more than twenty years following the lottery.

In 1835, the old church proving too small for the accommodation of the congregation, extensive repairs were made to the ancient edifice The old pews were increased in number, each of the large square ones were made into two small ones, the high backs lowered, the double doors walled up, a gallery built across the western end, and under it the main entrance to the church was made The old pulpit with the sounding-board was not removed, and the great oriel window to the east, in the rear of the clergyman's desk, was not disturbed These changes made it necessary to remove the old Sandelands tablet It was placed in the wall on the outside of the building, and during the spring, when the stonework was being whitewashed, it was repeatedly treated to a coat of that abominable compound by the sexton's wife, who did all chores of that character about the church The ancient bell-tower was torn down, and a small belfry built in the roof at the western end of the building The bell, which with such difficulty had been procured from England more than a century before, had become damaged by long service, and it was determined to have it recast George W Piper and J Gifford Johnson took the bell in a wagon to Philadelphia, to Wiltbank's foundry, for that purpose Before this bell was recast the foundry was destroyed by fire, and the heat was so great that tons of metal were fused into a mass Wiltbank, however, furnished a bell, but it is more than probable that not an ounce of the material in the old one cast by Roger Rice entered into the composition of the one which hangs in the belfry of the present church No doubt but that the good people of that day believed they were doing a wise act in disturbing the antiquated appearance of the ancient structure and decking it out in modern toggery, just as their successors fifteen years afterwards were actuated by the same idea when they razed the entire building to the ground, and that, too, without getting enough stones from the ruins to lay a third of the basement of the new edifice. Matters drifted on with the parish until 1850, when the change in the current set in, and Chester, after slumbering a century and a half, started into activity. St Paul's Church awakened with the rest, and began to make provisions for the new order of things. But the error of that day, and it was a serious one, consisted in destroying absolutely the old sanctuary.

The new church structure, which was erected on the north side of Third Street, was built after a plan prepared by T U Walter, architect, of Philadelphia, and the cost, it was believed, would not exceed five thousand dollars, although it ultimately cost nearly double that sum The corner-stone was laid July 25, 1859 Rt Rev. Alfred Lee, D D, Bishop of Delaware, and Rev. Charles W Quick delivered addresses The building, forty-four by forty six, was of pointed stone, in the Gothic style, the spire one hundred and twenty-four feet from the ground. The main door was approached by a flight of stone steps, one of which was the slab which had formerly covered the remains of Robert French, one of the descendants of Jöran Kyn, the founder of Chester, and to-day is one of the flagging in the sidewalk to the Sunday-school, on the east side of the church.

The church was opened Sunday, May 4, 1851, Rev. Mr. Balch officiating. But it appears not to have been consecrated by Bishop Potter until Tuesday, Dec. 23, 1851. Bishop Lee preached the consecration sermon. Drs. Suddards and Balch, and Revs. Messrs. Bean, Ridgely, Huntington, Micheson, Hawes, and Hand were present and officiated on that occasion. The constant growth of our busy city, and the increase in the number of the worshipers, soon began to tax the seating capacity of the new structure, and for several years after the close of the war it became evident that additional room must be provided to meet this want. In 1872 the demand was so imperative that the congregation determined that the church building must be remodeled, and steps were taken promptly to carry out that end. On Sunday, June 14, 1872, services were held in the sanctuary for the last time previous to the changes being made, and for ten months the edifice was closed during the alterations. The south end of the church was demolished, and a new addition, considerably increasing the seating capacity, a handsome Gothic front of Ridley granite, sepentine, and Cleveland stone combined, which approaches closely to the sidewalk, and a towering steeple and belfry erected. On Sunday, April 13, 1873, the congregation renewed religious services in St. Paul's, and Rev. Henry Brown, the rector, preached a historical sermon.

During a heavy thunder-storm, on Sunday, June 3, 1877, the lightning struck the rod on the steeple, and in its descent the electric fluid unloosened the water-pipe where it was attached to the wall, below the eaves, and making a round hole through the mortar of the solid masonry, it entered the church, ran along the gas-pipe, tore a hole in the plaster, and again forced its way between the joints of the stone wall, to the outside of the building, and thence to the ground.

In 1883 the church was thoroughly repaired, handsomely frescoed and decorated. On Sunday afternoon, March 9, 1884, it caught fire from a defective flue. The damage on that occasion exceeded two thousand dollars.

John Hill Martin, in his "History of Chester," gives the following list of ministers of St. Paul's from 1702 to the present time: Revs. Evan Evans, 1702–4; Henry Nichols, 1704–8; George Ross, 1708–14; John Humphreys, 1714–26; Samuel Hesselius, 1726–28; Richard Backhouse, 1728–49; Thomas Thompson, 1751; Israel Acrelius, 1756; George Craig, 1758–81; James Conner, 1788–91; Joseph Turner, 1791–93; Levi Heath, 1796–98; Joshua Reece, 1803–5; William Pryce, 1815–18; Jacob Morgan Douglass, 1818–22; Richard Umstead Morgan, 1822–31; John Baker Clemson, D.D., 1831–35; Richard D. Hall, 1735–37; Mortimer Richmond Talbot, 1837–41; Greenberry W. Ridgely, 1842–43; Anson B. Hard (associate rector), 1844–48; Charles W. Quick, 1849–50; Lewis P. W. Balch, D.D., 1850–53 (resigned, and removed to Virginia); Nicholas Sayre Harris, 1852–55 (Mr. Harris was a graduate of West Point); Daniel Kendig, 1855–59; M. Richard Talbot, 1859–61; J. Pinckney Hammond, 1861–63; Henry Brown, 1863.

In the wall of the Bible-class room, in the basement of the church, is the Sandelands tablet. The stone is disintegrating, and in a few years will crumble away.

James Sandelands, the elder, was a Scotchman, and there is some reason to believe that his father was Capt. Jacob Everson Sandelyn (the name perhaps incorrectly spelled by the early annalists), who, as master of the ship "Scotch Dutchman," visited the Swedish settlements on the Delaware in the year 1646, and sold to the Governor "duffel-cloth and other goods" to the value of two thousand five hundred guilders. His mother, we know, lived here in February, 1683, for she is mentioned in the trial of Margaret Mattson, of Ridley, for witchcraft. The first allusion to James Sandelands is in the patent of Aug. 6, 1665, "for two lots of land in Upland at Delaware, upon the North side of the creek or kill." On June 13, 1670, patents were granted to him for two other lots similarly situated, adjoining the property of his father-in-law, Jöran Keen.

In a deed in 1680 he is designated as "merchant," but there is no evidence to show what particular goods he dealt in, excepting a record that having purchased tobacco in Maryland, which was not delivered according to agreement, "a Certayne great Boate or Siallop," belonging to the delinquent consignor, was attached and "publicqly sould." The records of the early courts show that he frequently appeared as attorney for the suitors before that tribunal. In 1677 he is mentioned as the only person on the Delaware River, from Upland northwardly, who owned a slave, and is recorded as one of the "responsible housekeepers" at this place. He was appointed by Col. William Markham one of the Deputy Governor's Council in 1681, and was constituted one of the justices of the newly-organized Upland court. From 1688 to 1690 he was a member of the General Assembly of the province of Pennsylvania. James Sandelands died April 12, 1692, aged fifty-six years. I have given a brief notice of this early colonist because St. Paul's was a memorial church, erected to keep him in the recollection of the inhabitants of Chester, wherein he had passed a busy and enterprising life.

His wife, Ann, after a brief widowhood, married Peter Baynton, who subsequently abandoned her and returned to England, leaving her in such destitute circumstances that the Provincial Council, May 19, 1698, ordered the residue of his property in Chester should be appropriated to her support. He returned subsequently, and apparently was repentant for his misdeeds. Ann died, and Oct. 5, 1704, was buried by the side of her first husband, James Sandelands. As her name appears on the old tablet in St. Paul's Church, it proves that the stone was not set up by the descendants of Sandelands until after that date.

In a closet in the Sunday-school, some time ago, was deposited, for safe keeping, the noted tombstone which for many years attracted the attention of all strangers visiting the old churchyard, because of its antiquity, the manner in which the sculptor had performed his work, and the singularity of the inscription. The stone was cracked and in bad condition. The inscription reads,—

"FOR
THE MEMORY OF
FRANCIS BROOKS,
who died August
the 19, 1704
Aged 50 years.

In Barbarian bondage
And cruel tyranny
For ten years together
I served in Slavery
After this Mercy brought me
To my country fair
And last I drowned was
In River Delaware."

Martin states that Francis Brooks was a negro. The inscription would seem to indicate that Brooks was a native of the American colonies, and as his age at death precludes the idea of his birth in Upland, the chances are that he was a New Englander or Virginian.

The most noted monument in St. Paul's ground, at least within recent years,—for, strange as it may appear, neither Trego, in his "Geography and Historical Accounts of Pennsylvania," nor Burrowes, in his "State Book of Pennsylvania," both published within the last forty years, make any mention of John Morton,—is that of the signer of the Declaration of Independence, whose remains lie beneath a plain Egyptian obelisk of marble, eleven feet in height, its four sides forming precisely the four cardinal points of the compass. The inscription on the west side of the monolith is as follows:

"Dedicated to the memory of
John Morton,
A member of the First American Congress from the State of Pennsylvania, Assembled in New York in 1765, and of the next Congress, assembled in Philadelphia in 1774.
Born A.D., 1724—Died April 1777."

On the east side of the shaft is as follows:

"In voting by States upon the question of the Independence of the American Colonies, there was a tie until the vote of Pennsylvania was given, two members of which voted in the affirmative, and two in the negative. The tie continued until the vote of the last member, John Morton, decided the promulgation of the Glorious Diploma of American Freedom."

On the south side of the stone is cut the statement:

"In 1775, while speaker of the Assembly of Pennsylvania, John Morton was elected a Member of Congress, and in the ever memorable session of 1776, he attended that august body for the last time, establishing his name in the grateful remembrance of the American People by signing the Declaration of Independence."

On the north side of the shaft is inscribed the following sentence:

"John Morton being censured by his friends for his boldness in giving his casting vote for the Declaration of Independence, his prophetic spirit dictated from his death bed the following message to them: "Tell them they shall live to see the hour when they shall acknowledge it to have been the most glorious service I ever rendered to my country."

This monument to John Morton was erected Oct. 9, 1845, sixty-eight years after his death. A regard for the truth of history compels me to state that there is not a particle of evidence to establish the assertion engraved on the stone that John Morton gave the casting vote for the adoption of the Declaration of Independence. Indeed, the little information we have bearing on that point absolutely negatives the inscription on the monument in St. Paul's graveyard.

St. Luke's Protestant Episcopal Church.—The church organization was effected on Nov. 28, 1868, when the court of Delaware County incorporated the rector, church wardens, and vestrymen of St. Paul's Protestant Episcopal Church. The corner-stone of the neat little Gothic stone sanctuary at the southeast corner of Third and Broomall Streets, South Ward, was laid on Monday morning, Feb. 1, 1869, Right Rev. William Bacon Stevens, Bishop of Pennsylvania, officiating, assisted by Revs. Messrs. Brown, of Chester, Reed, of Linwood, Clemson and Potcken, of Delaware, Morrell, of New York, Stone, of Montgomery County, and Long, of Scranton. In order that Bishop Stevens should be in Philadelphia as early as possible on important business, Superintendent Kenney ordered the New York express train to stop at Lamokin and receive the distinguished divine. St. Luke's was then included in St. Paul's parish, and Rev. Henry Brown, the rector, had charge of the chapel, for such in the beginning it was designed to be during its erection. The funds of the building committee having become exhausted before the church was completed, the congregation for a time worshiped in the edifice, which was then without pews, settees being used in their places, and the unplastered walls presenting a rough and uninviting appearance. After Sunday, May 8, 1870, services were held there in the morning and evening, Thomas R. List, a student at the Divinity School of Philadelphia, being employed as lay reader, which duties he discharged until June 19, 1873, when he became rector of the parish. The church, now firmly established, was due largely to the efforts of John Burrows McKeever, William Ward, Samuel Archbold, Samuel Eccles, Jr., William H. Green, William A. Todd, Maj. Joseph R. T. Coates, and their wives and other ladies of St. Paul's Church, South Ward, and South Chester. Edward A. Price and wife presented the parish with a handsome communion service—silver tankard, paten, chalices, and plates for alms, while F. Stanhope Hill and Mrs. Hannah Depue gave the pulpit Bible. On May 19, 1874, St. Luke's Church was admitted into the Diocesan Convention, Samuel Archbold and William Ward being the first lay deputies. In 1874, John Burrows McKeever, who was an ardent friend of the new parish, died, and through the efforts of Rev. Mr. List a memorial font was placed in the church in whose behalf he labored so zealously. In September, 1875, Rev. Mr. List, having received a call to a church in Philadelphia, resigned the rectorship. In October of the same year, Rev. George Clifford Moore, the present rector, was called, and almost immediately after his installation he began the advocacy of the abolition of pew-rents, substituting therefor voluntary contributions. In 1876, Charles Kenworthy bequeathed three hundred and fifty dollars to the parish, which sum was applied towards liquidating the mortgage, and the following year, Elizabeth Kerlin, by will, gave one hundred and fifty dollars, which was used in like manner until, in 1880, the entire debt was extinguished. The parish, at present, is in a flourishing condition.

St. Michael the Archangel.—The imposing Catholic Church of St. Michael's is the second sanctuary erected on the site, the first having been razed, in 1874, to make room for the present edifice. The church organization extends backward in the history of our city over forty years. In 1842 a number of Catholics employed in this neighborhood—the nearest church being located nine miles distant—determined to establish one of that denomination in the borough. Application was made to Rt. Rev. Francis Patrick Kendrick, Bishop of Philadelphia, for permission to organize a congregation and erect a church in Chester. In response to the request the bishop assigned Rev. Philip Sheridan to the parish, and earnestly did he labor to accomplish the end in view. July 12, 1842, a lot was purchased on Edgmont road, and Thursday, September 29th, of the same year the corner-stone was laid by Bishop Kendrick. June 25th of the year following the church was dedicated to Almighty God under the patronage of St. Michael the Archangel, the Rt. Rev. Dr. Moriarty preaching the dedicatory sermon. Rev. Messrs. Sourin and Sheridan, accompanied by a large number of ladies and gentlemen, came from Philadelphia on the steamer "Bolivar," Capt. Whilldin. The first church building was of stone, in Gothic architecture, seventy-five by forty-two feet, the tower in front rising one hundred and five feet above the level of the street. For many years St. Michael's Church was the most noticeable building in Chester, and so conspicuous was it that the gilded cross, surmounting the lofty spire, could be seen glittering many miles away as the town was approached in any direction. On Sunday, Aug. 9, 1846, a violent storm of rain and wind occurred, which loosened some of the masonry, and a stone hurled by the fury of the blast, falling on the roof, crushed through it into the aisle below, breaking the pews and the floor of the main apartment. For nearly seven years no regular pastor was assigned to the parish. Occasional visits were made by Fathers Sheridan, Lane, Sourin, Walsh, Amat, and Dr. O'Hara until July 12, 1850, when Rev. Arthur P. Haviland, who had been ordained a priest in Philadelphia, June 29th of the same year, was appointed to the charge of St. Michael's parish. So faithfully did he labor that in a short time the building became too small to accommodate the worshipers, and for many years the parish struggled under that difficulty.

In 1854 the parsonage adjoining the sanctuary was built, and the same year Father Haviland was assigned an assistant, Rev. Patrick McEnroe. On Sept. 20, 1858, a bell, the present one, weighing one thousand pounds, was raised to its designated place in the tower, and for almost a quarter of a century its well-known tones have daily been heard in the thriving city of Chester. On the occasion of raising the bell to its allotted place a large concourse of people was present, the services being conducted by Archbishop Wood. In 1867, Father Haviland went to Europe, and during his absence the parish was in charge of his assistant, Rev. Edward McKee, Father McEnroe having been removed to Mauch Chunk. On the return of Father Haviland, Father McKee was assigned to Catasauqua, and Rev. Father Shankey became his assistant for a brief period, to be followed in succession by Revs. Fathers William F. Cook, Thomas McGlynn, Hugh McGlynn, James Timmins, and Patrick J. Mackin.

Early in 1873, notwithstanding the parish had been divided, and the Church of the Immaculate Heart erected in the South Ward, it became evident that the old edifice was insufficient to accommodate the congregation, and it was resolved to erect a new sanctuary. Before the plans to this end could be fully matured the financial disturbances in the fall of that year so paralyzed business that it was deemed inexpedient to begin the demolition of the old and the erection of the new edifice until the industrial dejection had in a measure abated. In the summer of the following year permission was granted by the Rt. Rev. Bishop Wood to demolish the old structure and rear in its stead a larger and more attractive building. To that end, on July 29, 1874, the pews were taken out of the church, and the parochial school-house, which had been erected in 1866, was prepared for use as a temporary chapel. August 11th following the excavations for the foundation of the new edifice were made, and on the 31st of the same month the old building was leveled to the earth. The corner-stone of the new church was laid Sunday, Nov. 1, 1874, by the Rt. Rev. Bishop Wood. The new structure is one hundred and seventy-eight feet in length, and the façade forty-two feet. Its height from the pavement to the eaves is sixty-eight feet, while from the centre of the façade rises a tower of ninety-two feet in height The cost of the sanctuary approximated one hundred thousand dollars.

The structure is built of Leiperville granite, with polished granite trimmings and columns from Maine Externally and internally the edifice is artistically and handsomely finished The ceiling of the central aisle rises to the altitude of fifty-five feet above the floor, supported by graceful columns, while the altar (thirty-eight feet in height, with side altars for the Virgin and St Joseph) and furniture are elaborate and beautiful, making as a whole the most imposing building in the county Two large frescos, one a copy of Murillo's Conception, the other a St Joseph, the latter an original by Baraldi, are admirable specimens of art Sunday, Nov 5, 1882, the church was dedicated with appropriate ceremonies by Rt Rev Bishop Shanahan, of Harrisburg On Sunday, Oct 3, 1880, the ceremony of blessing the cross which surmounts the centre tower of the church was performed by Archbishop Wood, over two thousand persons being present on the occasion

Church of the Immaculate Heart of Mary— In the spring of 1873, the parish of St Michael's having become densely populated, and the congregation attending the old sanctuary having grown so large, it was deemed expedient to institute a new Catholic Church in South Ward, and a committee waited on Rt Rev Bishop Wood to that end After several interviews with the committee the bishop consented to the division, and July, 1873, he appointed Rev John B Kelley pastor in charge of the parish, which was named the Immaculate Heart of Mary Two days after his appointment Father Kelley was drowned while bathing at Atlantic City, and Rev Thomas J. McGlynn was assigned to the pastorate The parishioners immediately erected a frame chapel on Second Street near Broomall, and the congregation was organized therein Prompt steps were taken towards the building of a permanent church edifice, and the following fall, Sept. 23, 1874, the corner-stone of the brick Gothic church of the Immaculate Heart of Mary, at the northwest corner of Second and Norris Streets, was laid by the Rt Rev Bishop Wood. On Wednesday, Feb 23, 1876, the frame chapel was totally destroyed by fire, and so rapidly did the flames spread that only a few benches were saved, the organ, church furniture, and vestments of Father McGlynn being consumed, involving a loss of four thousand dollars.

The work on the new church edifice was pressed earnestly forward, and it was dedicated on Rosary Sunday, Oct 1, 1876 The ceremonies were conducted by the Most Rev James F Wood, D.D, Archbishop of Philadelphia, assisted by Rev A J McConomy, chancellor of the archdiocese, and attended by Revs E F Pendercese, Francis P O'Neill, A J Gallagher, T J Barry, James Timmins, and Thomas J McGlynn.

The church is of brick It is lighted by fourteen stained-glass windows on either side, and the rear of the sanctuary is adorned by a large painting of the Transfiguration The altar is chaste and ecclesiastical in aspect

In 1883 the parish began the erection of a three-story brick parochial school-house, conforming in its exterior architecture with that of the church edifice, which was completed in 1883

Rev Father McGlynn has been in charge of the parish ever since it was organized, and under his immediate supervision all the permanent improvements have been made

First Baptist Church—The Kerlin farm was purchased in 1850 by John M Broomall and the late John P Crozer in equal shares, and after a large part of the real estate had been sold so as to repay the original outlay, Mr Crozer, in 1856, conveyed his interest in all the land remaining to Mr Broomall, reserving, however, the absolute title in the half-square of ground on Penn and Second Streets Mr Crozer stated at the time of the conveyance that he designed that locality as a site for a Baptist Church This intention was doubtless due to the fact that previous to the autumn of 1854 occasional religious exercises by Baptist clergymen had been held in Chester, but it was not until the fall of the year mentioned that any regularly stated services were had, when Rev William Wilder, of the Upland Baptist Church, established worship in the court-house, and it was continued under Mr Wilder's supervision for four years In the spring of 1858, Mr Crozer donated the ground at the northwest corner of Second and Penn Streets, seventy feet on the first and one hundred and twenty-seven on the latter, for a church During the summer of the same year Benjamin Gartside, at his personal cost, built a chapel twenty-three by forty feet, which building, now standing in the rear of the church, was completed during the month of August, and worship was held there every Sunday afternoon Rev Miller Jones, then stationed at Marcus Hook, and Rev William Wilder conducted the services In the spring of 1863 an effort was made to erect a building and to have the congregation recognized as a church, but the public excitement consequent on the battle of Gettysburg postponed definite action until Sept 24, 1863, when the chapel, built by Mr Gartside, was dedicated as the First Baptist Church of Chester, and Rev Levi G Beck was, May 24, 1864, ordained its first pastor

The same year a sufficient sum was pledged to the building fund to justify the building of a sanctuary. The corner-stone was laid July 2, 1864, and in the fall the edifice was so far advanced that the lecture-room could be used for religious services The work on the church was continued, and in the fall of the following year all had been completed, but as it had been decided that the main apartment should not be used until the debt of the building committee, amounting in all to sixteen thousand dollars, had been discharged, it required several weeks to gather the fund This was done, and Dec 28, 1865, the church was dedicated, Rev J Wheaton Smith, D D, officiating on that occasion After two years' pastorate, Rev Mr Beck was elected secretary of the Baptist General Association of Pennsylvania, which office he accepted, and resigned his charge of the church in April, 1866 On Feb 22, 1866, the First Baptist Church of Chester was incorporated by the court of Delaware County For several months after Mr Beck's resignation went into effect the congregation was without a regular minister, until November, 1866, when Rev Andrew Fuller Shanafelt was called, and assumed the duties of the pastorate in December of the same year During his ministry James Irving presented the lot on Second Street, immediately adjoining the church, for a parsonage, and Benjamin Gartside erected the present building at his personal cost In 1874, Mr Shanafelt's health was so much impaired that he was granted a vacation to travel in Europe and the Holy Land He returned in the fall apparently much improved, but his application to duty brought on a return of his physical weakness, causing his death March, 1875 The following July Rev Z T Dowen became the pastor, and for two years remained in charge, when he resigned August, 1877, and returned to England In November of the same year Rev A G Thomas, the present pastor, was called, and began his ministerial work in the following December

Madison Street Methodist Episcopal Church — The name "Chester" appears in the minutes of the Philadelphia Conference in the list of appointments of preachers as early as the year 1774, when Daniel Ruff and J Yearby were assigned to that circuit Subsequent to that date the following appointments were made by Conference to that circuit

1775, Richard Webster, 1776, preacher's name omitted, 1777, Robert Lindsay, 1779, James Cromwell, 1780, name omitted, 1783, R Ellis, J Hagerty, Thomas Haskins, 1788, R Cann, J Milburn, 1789, William Dougherty, James Campbell, 1790, Sylvester Dougherty, J Cooper, 1791, J McClaskey, J Robinson, S Miller, 1792, James Lovell, J Wheelwright, 1793, Robert Cloud, William Hunter, 1794, William Early, James Smith, 1795, J Jarrell, T F Sargeant, J Robinson, 1796, Thomas Bell, Samuel Welsh, 1797, William Colbert, 1798, William P Chandler, Daniel Higby, 1799, W Colbert, J Herron, E Larkin, R Bouhan, 1800, R Sneath, S Tenison, T Jones, 1801, William Hunter, S Timmons, R McCoy, 1802, William Hunter, John Bechtel, 1803, Anning Owen, William Brandon, 1804, William Hunter, J Osborn, J Stephens, 1805, William Hunter, D James, J Moore, 1806, John Walker, William Early, 1807, Daniel Ireland, Peter Beaver, 1809, appointment not recorded, 1810, Richard Sneath, John Fox, 1811, Richard Sneath, James Laws, 1812, Thomas Dunn, William S Fisher, 1813, W S Fisher, J Fernon, Joseph Samson, 1814, George Sheets, Thomas Miller, S P. Levis, 1815, Asa Smith, Joseph Samson, 1816, William Torbert, Charles Reed, 1817, William Hunter, William Torbert

Notwithstanding these appointments, it is very doubtful whether, at those times, there were any Methodists in the ancient borough of Chester, the name being given to a circuit extending in territory from the river Delaware nearly to the Susquehanna, and from Philadelphia County to the Maryland line.

The first absolute knowledge we have of a meeting of that denomination is in 1818, when John Kelley and his wife, Esther, moved to this place Mr Kelley had been a local preacher in St George's Church, Philadelphia, and shortly after locating in Chester held services in his own house, where he organized a class The circuit preacher soon afterwards established a regular appointment for preaching, and on Sundays religious services were held in the court-house for many years In that structure the noted Bishop Asbury, it is said, preached on several occasions The denomination grew gradually, and several attempts were made to raise funds sufficient to build a house to meet in, but all efforts failed to that end, until in 1830, sufficient means had been obtained to justify the congregation in erecting, not without considerable difficulty, a stone church on Second Street, at the corner of Bevan's Court, which building was greatly due to the energy and efforts of the late David Abbott, and was named in honor of the bishop, "Asbury Chapel" The society was still largely dependent on the circuit minister, although more frequently the services were conducted entirely by the local preachers The congregation attending the church had grown so large in 1845 that Chester was made a station, and Rev Isaac R Merrill was appointed pastor in that year

Although the following clergymen appear by the records of Conference to have been appointed to Chester Circuit, many names therein were at no time, so far as can be ascertained, stationed in Chester, yet the list is worthy of preservation, and is therefore inserted in this work 1818, John Goforth, Samuel Budd; 1819, John Robertson, Phineas Price, 1820, William Leonard, Thomas Davis, 1821, David Bartine, Thomas Davis, 1822, David Bartine, John Tally, 1823, Thomas Miller, William Allen, 1824, Henry Boehm, John Woolson, 1825 Henry Boehm, Levin Prettyman, 1826, Jacob Gruber, S Grace, J Tally, 1827, Jacob Gruber, 1828, T Miller, E Reed, 1831, William Ryder, N Chew, J Tally, 1832, William Ryder, J B Ayres, J Tally, 1833, J B Ayres, J Edwards, R E Morrison, J Tally, 1834, William Ryder, R Anderson, 1835, William Ryder, R Anson, J Tally, 1836, R E Kemp, J Tally, 1838, William Torbert, G Orem, J Tally, 1839, J. Edwards, G Orem, J Talley, 1840, I T Cooper, J Edwards, J Tally, 1842, D Daily, Thomas Sumption,

J. Tally; 1843, D Daily, H. G King, J. Tally; 1844, H G King, J. B Ayres, J. Tally, 1845, J. B. Ayres, J W. Arthur, 1846, J. Humphries, J Henries, I. R. Merrill; 1847, S Townsend, J Henry, L Storks, J Tally, 1848, S Townsend, W. K Goentner, J Shields, J. Tally

During Mr Merrill's pastorate, at May term of court, 1846, the church was incorporated, and thereupon the congregation immediately began the erection of the second stone meeting-house on Fifth Street below Market Street, the corner-stone being laid Aug 11, 1846 Rev Dr Hodgson, of Philadelphia, and Rev Dr Kennedy, of Wilmington, were present and assisted the pastor, Rev Isaac R Merrill, in the services on that occasion In 1850, the church edifice being insufficient, an addition of twenty feet was made to the building, a gallery erected, and the outside of the structure rough-casted

In 1847, Mr Merrill was succeeded by Rev Levi Storks,*[1] who, in 1848, was followed by Rev John Shields In 1849, Rev Newton Heston* was appointed, and continued until 1851 In 1850, the year when Chester began to develop rapidly, the church had three hundred and two members Rev Samuel G Hare* was appointed in 1851, and was followed the succeeding year by Rev John B Maddux,* who continued pastor until 1854, when Rev William Mullin was appointed in his stead, and in 1856 was followed by Rev John W Arthur* Rev Allen Johns* was appointed pastor in 1858, and the following year was succeeded by Rev John Ruth* During the latter's pastorate, in 1860, the membership had grown to three hundred and twenty-two Rev William Urie* was assigned to the charge of the church in 1861, and was succeeded in 1863 by Rev. James E Meredith,* who, after he ceased to be its pastor, became a clergyman of the Episcopal Church, and at the time of his death was in Texas as rector of a parish of that denomination Mr Meredith was followed, in 1866, by Rev Henry E Gilroy, and in 1869, Rev James Cunningham was appointed to succeed him The old meeting-house on Fifth Street was now unable to accommodate the number of worshipers, and it was determined to erect a new edifice. To that end a lot on the northeast corner of Seventh and Madison Streets was purchased, and the corner-stone of the new church building laid Wednesday, July 17, 1872, Rev Henry Brown, rector of St Paul's, and Rev. A. W. Sproull, pastor of the First Presbyterian Church, assisting Rev James Cunningham in the ceremonial and religious services on that occasion The new church, which is built of green serpentine stone, with granite trimmings and corner blocks, and finished very tastefully and at much expense, was dedicated May 3, 1874 The old church building on Fifth Street, in 1873, was sold to Tuscarora Tribe of Red Men, No 29, who changed it into a hall for public amusements The enterprise, however, failed of success, and the property was sold to Robert H Crozer, who, in March, 1879, in consideration of six thousand dollars, conveyed it to the German Lutheran congregation of St Paul's Church, and is at the present time devoted to the purposes for which it was originally built,—a house of worship During the greater part of the time the building of the edifice was being carried on Rev John B Maddux* was the minister, having succeeded Mr Cunningham in the fall of 1872. In 1875, Rev Joseph Welsh was appointed pastor, and was succeeded in 1878 by Rev William C Robinson In 1881, Rev Dr William J Paxson was appointed, and was succeeded in 1884 by the present pastor, Rev Theodore Stevens The church is in a most flourishing condition, its membership in 1880 being six hundred and twenty-six, and it has largely increased in that respect since that time

Trinity Methodist Episcopal Church.—In 1865 the membership and congregation of the Fifth Street Methodist Church had so increased that it was deemed proper by the Quarterly Conference to effect a church organization in South Ward, and to that end thirty members held regular religious worship in the Crozer Academy, on Second Street, west of Franklin

On June 26, 1865, Trinity Methodist Episcopal Church of Chester was incorporated by the court of Delaware County, and on August 25th of the same year an amended charter was granted by the same authority In the summer of the same year the congregation began the building at the corner of Third and Parker Streets, known as Trinity Church, Rev Mr Twiggs, now of Wilmington Conference, being then pastor in charge The edifice had been roofed in, when, in October, 1865, a terrific northeast storm utterly demolished the building, heaping it into the cellar a mass of ruins There the *debris* remained until 1866, when the congregation, under the direction of Rev William McCombs as pastor, erected a frame chapel on the ground to the west, now used by D H. Burns as a marble yard, and the same year built what is now the Sunday-school The main structure during the same year was recommenced and pushed forward until it was roofed in The debt of the congregation amounted to twenty thousand dollars In the fall of the year the chapel was completed and dedicated, on which occasion a sum of five thousand dollars was raised, and to that amount the debt was extinguished In the spring of 1867, Rev Isaac Mast was appointed, and continued in charge for two years, during which period five thousand dollars additional of the debt was paid off, the floors of the main church laid, and the membership largely increased In 1869, Rev George W F Graff became the pastor, and continued in that relationship three years During his ministry the church proper was completed, and dedicated by Bishop Simpson It had cost six thousand dollars additional, but of that sum five thousand dollars was

[1] Those marked with an asterisk (*) are deceased

subscribed on dedication day. The congregation during that period built what is now known as the South Chester Methodist Episcopal Church, then styled the mission chapel. Independent of the sums mentioned, the congregation raised ten thousand dollars and applied it towards liquidating the indebtedness of the church. In the spring of 1872, Rev. Samuel Pancoast was assigned to the pastorate, and during his term of three years the entire debt was discharged. In 1875, Rev. Samuel W. Kurts was appointed, and was followed, in 1878, by Rev. John F. Crouch, during whose pastorate many important improvements were made to the church. In 1880, Rev. Noble Frame was assigned to the church, and in the spring of 1882, Rev. Thomas Kelley, the present pastor, was appointed.

Union African Methodist Episcopal Church.—Early in the century Robert Morris, who was then a slave in the lower part of the State of Delaware and a favorite with his master, was told by the latter that a judgment had been obtained against him, and the sheriff was about to make a levy on his property. He was anxious that Morris should not be seized to satisfy the debt, and told him to make his way to Chester, and, if possible, to get some one there to buy him. The slave acted as his master suggested, made his way safely to Delaware County, and finally succeeded in inducing Charles Lloyd, the then landlord of the "Blue Bell" Tavern on Cobb's Creek, in Kingsessing, to purchase him from his master for three hundred dollars,—a stipulation in the bill of sale that the slave should be free when he attained the age of thirty years. Morris faithfully served his new master, who ever regarded the money he had paid as simply a loan which the colored man could discharge by his labor. After Morris was free he came to Chester, and, being ardently religious, he organized a church of his race in that borough. At first only four persons could be induced to attend the meetings, which were held in a house then occupied by a colored man named Williams, on Third Street, west of Concord Avenue; by degrees the movement spread until, about 1831, sufficient means had been collected to purchase a lot on West Street, south of Third Street, from Matthew J. Bevan, on which a frame church was erected, which is still standing (now altered into a dwelling). In 1832, Rev. Samuel Smith was appointed local preacher, and continued in charge of the church until 1837; but his pastorate was financially unsuccessful, the expenses of the organization finally resulting in creating a burdensome debt, and Robert Morris again came to Chester to the assistance of the congregation. Rev. Benjamin Jefferson was assigned to the pastorate of the church, in which capacity he continued until 1874, nearly forty years' continuous service. The latter strove energetically to liquidate the encumbrance, and succeeded in clearing the church of debt. In 1860 the frame building had been removed and a stone structure erected, the fund being collected and applied to the building so as not to again plunge the congregation into financial troubles. In 1875, Rev. Lorenzo D. Blackston became the pastor, and the following year he was succeeded by Rev. Henry Modo. Again, in 1877, Rev. Benjamin Jefferson was assigned to the charge of the church. It was during his second pastorate, which continued until 1880, that the sanctuary was rebuilt as it is at the present time. In 1880, Rev. Lewis J. Jones was in charge of the church; in 1881, Rev. Francis H. Norton; and in 1883, Rev. Lewis J. Jones.

Union Church has established a mission church in Media, which is now a flourishing body, while the membership of the parent church has largely increased.

Asbury African Methodist Episcopal Church.—This religious body was organized by Rev. Stephen Smith, of Philadelphia, Oct. 26, 1845. The same year the congregation purchased the church property on Second Street, east of Market, for seven hundred dollars, at which location they have continued to worship for nearly forty years. At first, as with all Methodist churches in this city, the body was supplied at times by circuit preachers, but generally the services were conducted by local clergymen. In 1849, Rev. Henry Davis was appointed the first regular pastor, and was succeeded, in 1850, by Rev. H. G. Young, who, in turn, was followed, in 1853, by Rev. J. G. Bulah. In May, 1854, Rev. James Holland was assigned to the church, and was succeeded, in 1856, by Rev. Adam Driver, who was followed, in 1858, by Rev. J. G. Bulah. In 1860, Rev. J. G. Garrish was appointed, and in 1861, Rev. G. W. Johnson became pastor. The next year Rev. W. D. N. Schureman was assigned to the church, and in 1863, Rev. Jeremiah Young was appointed pastor, and during his ministry the church was rebuilt. On Nov. 25, 1867, the Asbury African Methodist Episcopal Church was incorporated by the court of Delaware County. He was followed, in 1869, by Rev. G. Boyer, and in 1871, Rev. G. T. Waters became pastor. He was followed, in 1874, by Rev. L. C. Chambers, and in 1877, Rev. T. Gould succeeded him. In 1879, Rev. J. S. Thompson was assigned to the church, and in 1881 the present pastor, Rev. C. C. Felts, was appointed, and during his ministry the congregation purchased a parsonage on Madison Street, above Sixth. The church has also sent out its mission body in the William Murphy Church, on Eagle Street, below Second, in South Chester. In 1883, Rev. M. F. Slubey was pastor, and in 1884, Rev. Leonard Patterson was assigned to the charge of the church.

First Presbyterian Church.—The Presbyterian residents of Chester, previous to 1850, often attended divine services at Leiper's Church, in Ridley, but more frequently the Episcopal or Methodist Churches, both of which denominations had "a local habitation and a name" in the ancient borough. In the fall of the year stated the late Rev. James W. Dale, every Sunday afternoon, conducted religious exercises in the court-house according to the Presbyterian formula, and continued to preach therein for more than a year. In 1851, I. E. Cochran, Sr., gave the lot, part of the land taken by him in partition of his father's (John Cochran, the elder) estate, at the southeast corner of Fourth and Welsh Streets, on which they built a Presbyterian Church, and he, together with the late Joseph H. Hinkson, contributed largely of their means towards the erection of the present edifice. On Sunday, July 18, 1851, the dedicatory service was preached by Rev. Joseph H. Jones, of Philadelphia. Nearly a thousand dollars were collected during the day in aid of the church. The congregation was organized with seventeen communicants. Mrs. Henrietta Mifflin Clyde, who died Sept. 28, 1874, aged eighty-two years, was the last survivor of that number. Robert Benedict was ordained as the first ruling elder. In the sanctuary, since it was renovated, enlarged, and adorned about eight years ago, the handsome stained-glass memorial windows then placed in the church in most cases bear the names of persons who were among its original founders. After it was organized, for two years Rev. James O. Stedman supplied the pulpit every Sunday, conducting services for the first time on Oct. 31, 1852. He was followed, in 1854, by Rev. George Van Wyck until 1856, when Rev. Alexander W. Sproull was called, and installed as the first regular pastor there. On Dec. 11, 1873, the present pastor, Rev. Philip H. Mowry, was called, and installed December 11th of that year.

Chester City Presbyterian Church.—The influx of population west of the Third Street bridge was particularly noticeable after the establishment of Reaney's ship-yard just previous to the breaking out of the rebellion, and efforts were made by several gentlemen to organize a Sunday-school for religious instruction of the many children in that neighborhood. To that end a school was begun Dec. 14, 1862, in the Academy building, now the Second Street Grammar-School, with John L. Entwisle, superintendent; Joseph Hinkson, assistant; and Abram R. Perkins, treasurer. The school thus founded grew speedily, and those instrumental in its beginning soon determined to establish the Chester City Presbyterian Church, to be located in the South Ward. The great difficulty was in obtaining a suitable building, which impediment was overcome by the gift of a lot at the southeast corner of Third and Ulrich Streets, by Reaney, Son & Archbold, upon which Thomas Reaney, who was warmly interested in the undertaking, built the present edifice at his personal cost. The church was begun in the summer of 1865, and completed the following year. The furnishing and upholstering of the sanctuary was principally done at the joint expense of Mr. Perkins and Mr. Reaney. While the congregation was worshiping in the lecture-room, the church proper being unfinished, an application was made to the Presbytery of Philadelphia for organization, and on Feb. 15, 1866, the congregation elected John X. Miller and Peter G. Rambo elders, who were thereupon ordained in those offices by a committee appointed by Presbytery. Feb. 25, 1866, the congregation called Rev. Martin P. Jones as pastor, at a salary of one thousand dollars, and the committee was empowered, at their discretion, to advance the sum to twelve hundred dollars a year. He accepted the call, and was ordained April 12, 1866. He remained in charge of the church until Jan. 1, 1869, he having tendered his resignation several months before. The church was without a minister from that date until June 22d of the same year, when Rev. Augustus T. Dobson, who had been called the 25th of the previous March, at a salary of fifteen hundred dollars, was installed. The subsequent failure of the firm of Reaney, Son & Archbold crippled the church greatly, but the earnest efforts of the congregation, in conjunction with the pastor, relieved it from its embarrassment. John Henry Askin contributed five hundred dollars, and Abraham R. Perkins one hundred and fifty dollars. The congregation notified the pastor that, under the circumstances, his salary must be reduced to one thousand dollars a year, and at that sum it continued until he resigned, in October, 1881. Rev. Thomas J. Aikin, the present pastor, was called Dec. 6, 1881, and installed April 12, 1882.

Third Presbyterian Church.—This memorial church—it was built to commemorate the reunion of the Old and New School Churches—is located at the southwest corner of Twelfth and Upland Streets. The lot was purchased in 1871, and the building, which is of brick, with pilasters, Gothic windows, and high, pitched roof, was erected as a mission Sunday-school by the First Presbyterian Church, but when the division in that congregation took place, those who withdrew accepted the Sunday-school building in unfinished condition, determining to constitute therein a Third Presbyterian Church, which was fully consummated Oct. 16, 1872, with forty-two persons enrolled as members. The congregation, after it was organized, worshiped in the chapel until July of the following year, when the western end of the building was removed, twenty-five feet added to its length, and a recess pulpit constructed. The lot and building cost nearly fifteen thousand dollars. The church was reopened and dedicated Oct. 5, 1873. After the organization of the church, Rev. Dr. Edwin W. Bower, of Lincoln University, officiated as temporary minister until Feb. 13, 1873, when Rev. Charles F. Thomas was unanimously elected to the pastorate. He was installed April 16, 1873, at a salary of sixteen hundred dollars, which was subsequently increased to eighteen hundred dollars, but his health failing, he resigned Feb. 20, 1878. Rev. Dr. Bower was called April 3, 1878, but he declined, and the congregation, May 31st of the same year, called Rev. Thomas McCauley, the present pastor, at the same salary received by Mr. Thomas. Mr. McCauley accepted Oct. 1, 1878, and was installed the 10th of the same month.

St. Paul's German Lutheran Church.—In August, 1878, a church organization was effected with twelve members, under the charge of Rev. J. T. Boyer, and on Feb. 3, 1879, the society was chartered. In May, 1879, the meeting-house formerly used by the Methodists, on Fifth Street, was purchased for six thousand dollars from George H. Crozer. On Sunday, May 18, 1879, the church was consecrated, Revs. Dr. C. Shæffer, president of the Lutheran Ministerium of Pennsylvania, A. T. Geissenheiner, of Philadelphia, and J. Lewberger, of New Jersey, conducting the services. The building internally was remodeled, and on July 10, 1879, was dedicated by the pastor, Rev. J. T. Boyer. The latter remained in charge of the church until the last of September, 1880, when he was succeeded, October 3d of the same year, by Rev. E. H. Gerhart, who served as the pastor until September, 1882, when he resigned, since which time the pulpit was supplied by students from the Lutheran Seminary in Philadelphia, until June, 1884, when the Rev. E. H. Pohle, pastor of a church in Philadelphia, assumed charge of St. Paul's at Chester. The church has a membership of twelve, and a Sunday-school connected with it of forty pupils. The services are wholly conducted in the German language.

Public Schools.—The information which has descended to the present time respecting the primitive schools in colonial days is more inferential than positive. From the constant reference to the schooling of children in the early records, the conclusion is reached that considerable attention was given to the education of the young among the English settlers after Penn had obtained possession of the colony. The instruction of youths in reading and writing was part of the duties enjoined on the clergymen in charge of the Church of England parishes maintained under the auspices of the Society for the Propagation of the Gospel in Foreign Parts, and I seriously question whether, until the school-house of 1770 was built, any other teachers were employed in Chester to instruct children. I am aware it is asserted that in 1741 a petition was presented to the Bishop of London, emanating from St. Paul's Episcopal Church of Chester, complaining of Friends who, as is stated, when asked to contribute to the support of the parish schoolmaster, "did what none but Quakers dare do in a country under the government of a Protestant king; that is, they engaged a rigid, virulent Papist to set up school in the Town of Chester." Of this school under the auspices of St. Paul's Church Charles Fortescue is said to have been the master.[1]

[1] "History of Colonial American Catholic Church," p. 220. No reference can be found in the records of St. Paul's Church respecting this statement; but it should be added that those records were abominably kept at that date; nor yet can anything be found on the minutes of Chester Friends' Meeting, which, on the other hand, are exhaustive records, the most trivial matters being noted. In fact, Friends' records negative, by the absence of any reference to the matter, the idea that at any time a school was maintained by the society in Chester.

On Aug. 6, 1731, Aubry Bevan, John Salkeld, Jacob Howell, Thomas Cummings, and Thomas Morgan made a declaration of trust respecting a lot at the southeast corner of Fourth and Edgmont Streets, which had been conveyed to them "with the intent that a school-house should be erected and built upon the said lott . . . with all convenient speed, at the public charge of the people called Quakers, who shall cause a fair well-built school-house to be erected upon the said lott . . . which shall be for the use and service of the people called Quakers in Chester, and others in the said township forever. . . . The nomination of a schoolmaster, from time to time, and at all times hereafter, is to be in the Members of the Preparative Meeting at Chester, and that no other person presume to teach in said school-house without such nomination and appointment." We know beyond question that no school building was ever erected on that lot, and that no person other than the Episcopal clergyman taught in Chester, seems incidentally established from the fact that John Baldwin, who did not die until after Nov. 11, 1731, by his will directs that his two grandsons, John and Joshua Baldwin, "shall be kept to school till they be fitt to go to trades, and then to be put to good trades." In the account filed by Peter Dick, one of the executors, he is allowed credit for the schooling of Joshua for "2 quarters," and that "Richard Backhouse was paid 19 shillings" for his tuition. Backhouse was the clergyman in charge of St. Paul's Church, and continued as the rector until his death, in November, 1749. Indeed, we know that the first movement among Friends looking to the establishment of schools was at the Yearly Meeting in 1746, when that body advised the several Monthly Meetings "to encourage and to assist one another in the settlement and support of schools."

It may be assumed, at least so far as we have evidence, that no school other than that connected with St. Paul's parish was maintained in the borough of Chester previous to 1770. Joseph Hoskins, in his will bearing date the 31st day of the Twelfth month, 1769, made this important public devise:

"Item. I give and devise unto my friends Henry Hale Graham and William Swaffer, a certain lot of ground situate in the Borough of Chester, beginning at the intersection of Welsh or Back street and the King's road, and to extend along the said King's road one hundred feet, and from thence parallel with the said Welsh or Back street one hundred feet, and from thence parallel with the said King's road one hundred feet to the said Welsh or Back Street, and thence by the same street one hundred feet to the place of beginning. To hold to them the said Henry Hale Graham and William Swaffer and their heirs forever upon special trust and confidence nevertheless and to and for the uses, intents and purposes hereinafter mentioned, expressed and declared, and none other; that is to say, for the use, benefit and behoof of all and every the inhabitants of the said Borough and township of Chester for the building and erecting a school house or school houses or other edifices for the teaching and instructing and educating of youths therein, and my will is that the Trustees aforesaid enter into and be in quiet and peaceable possession of the said lot of ground immodiately after some part of the materials are got ready for erecting a school house thereon."

Joseph Hoskins did not die until 1773, and his will was not probated until the 21st of July of that year, but so unbounded was the confidence of his neighbors in his integrity, that in 1770 they built a school-house on the lot thus by will subsequent vested in the trustees, although their then title was simply the statement of Hoskins, that he had made such testamentary disposition of his real estate. We have every assurance to believe that he gave liberally of his income towards the building itself. Not only did he give this land, but in his will he also directed thirty pounds (a large sum in those days) to be paid by his executors to John Eyre and James Barton, to be applied "for the schooling and educating of such poor children belonging to the inhabitants of the Borough and township of Chester as the said Preparative Meeting for the time being shall think fit to order and direct."

This school-house was built of brick laid in headers and stretchers, the ends of the headers being burnt black, a mark of architectural beauty in that day. It was two stories in height, and the bricks were said to have been imported from England,—which, of course, is the merest fancy,—and in the south gable the large numerals 1770 were inserted in the wall, being formed by the black ends of the headers. Small as the building was, it was more than sufficient for the use to which it was dedicated. As the structure was erected near the east end of the lot, Hoskins permitted more land to be taken than he actually gave by his will, so that ample space for a playground could be had. This was the starting-point of our present system of free public instruction, and it was a most praiseworthy act in the board of school directors of the city of Chester that, in the year 1882, when putting up a new building at Fifth and Welsh Streets for the use of the superintendent, with school-rooms on the second floor, they recognized the noble act of Joseph Hoskins, who, almost forgotten, had slumbered for more than a century in Friends' graveyard, by designating the new structure "Joseph Hoskins' School."

Among the rules prescribed by the trustees on Jan. 9, 1796, the following appears:

"8th. It shall be the duty of the Trustees to see y[t] no book containing the tenets or doctrines of any sect in religion be taught in the school, or any that may convey improper political principles to the children of Republicans, since no others ought to be admitted but such as teach the pure principles of religion, as contained in the Holy Writings of the Prophets and Evangelists—of morality and love of virtue; such as teach us the love of liberty and our country—obedience to her laws—detestation of tyranny and oppression, and hatred of anarchy and licentiousness."

In the lapse of years the names of the first pedagogues who swayed the birch—the emblem of authority—have been forgotten; but from 1806 to 1818, Samuel Lytle, an Irishman, was the teacher there, and among the pupils that came under his care was the future Admiral Farragut, then living in the family of Commodore Porter. Here the great seaman received the rudiments of his education. From 1824 to 1830, William Neal was in charge of the school, at which time it was known as the Chester Academy.

The first private school (for that at Fifth and Welsh Streets was classified under the head Charity School, after the passage of the law of 1802) of which we have knowledge was established on Third Street, west of the bridge, about 1822, by Mrs. Irvin, and was restricted to primary pupils. The following years Miss Eliza Finch kept a school in the old Logan house on Second Street near Edgmont. Among her pupils was the present Admiral David D. Porter, and his brothers, William, Theodore, and Hamilton, and under her tuition they received their elementary education. She continued here until 1830, when she abandoned its cares and opened a store in its stead. About the time Miss Finch retired Caleb Pierce assumed the duties of instructing the youths of Chester whose parents would not permit them to attend the old school at Fifth and Welsh Streets, establishing his select school in a summer-house, which had been built by Major Anderson nearly forty years before that date, in the rear of the Columbia House. In 1834, James Campbell, a graduate of Union College, New York, taught the Chester Academy, succeeding Mr. Neal, and the same year a Mr. Jones was principal of "the Chester High School," which was established in "a commodious building," the site of which I cannot locate. In 1840 the public-school system having been generally accepted, Caleb Pierce discontinued his select school and accepted the position of teacher at the old school-house on Welsh Street, but in 1843, when the building was enlarged by an addition at the north end almost as large as the original structure, James Riddle was chosen principal, and four lady assistants appointed. In the same year Mrs. Frances Biddle established a day-school for young ladies in the Sunday-school room—a frame building—attached to St. Paul's Church. In 1845, James Dawson had a select school in one of the rooms of the school building, the public demand not requiring the use of all the apartments there. In 1850, when Chester began to enlarge its population, the school-room was so taxed that in 1853 the directors purchased a lot on Franklin Street, South Ward, and erected the building known as the Franklin Street school, and the growth of North Ward compelled the erection of the Eleventh Street school in 1858. Notwithstanding the increase of school-houses, the population so outran the accommodation afforded that in 1864 schools were established in the Crozer Academy, on Second Street, and in 1867 primary schools were opened in the Baptist Chapel, on Penn Street, and in the basement of the African Methodist Church, on Second Street, the latter for the accommodation of colored children. At that date a colored school for advanced pupils was also maintained by the directors in a frame house on Welsh Street. The demand still keeping in advance of the buildings, in 1867 the present high school was erected, although it was not completed ready for occupancy until the following summer In 1870 it was necessary to afford better facilities in North Ward, and in that year the Morton Avenue building was erected, and in 1871 the Patterson Street school house was built and set apart as a colored school In 1874 the Eleventh Street school was enlarged and remodeled In 1875 the old school building on Welsh Street was taken down and a large brick school-house built, and in 1878 the Howell Street school-house was erected In 1882 the Joseph Hoskins school building was built, and in 1883 the lot at Eleventh and Madison, formerly occupied by the Larkintown Sunday-school, was purchased by the directors, and will be built upon in 1885

The corps of teachers are excellent, the examination of applicants for position as instructors is very thorough, and a general average of education imparted to the pupil will compare favorably with that of any city in the country The graduates of the Chester High School are as carefully taught as in most academies in the land, the universities excepted, and the system of opening the higher branches of education to both the sexes has resulted most advantageously The present faculty of the high school is, Principal, Emma J Hahn, Assistants, Jennie McLaren and Frederica E Gladwin The superintendents of the public schools of Chester, since that office was established by the Legislature when the city was separated from the county of Delaware, and authorized to maintain and govern the schools in the municipal district without reference to those in the county, have been as follows 1868, A A Meader, 1875, A Robinett, 1878, Charles F Foster, the present incumbent

The following list presents the names of the directors of the public schools for the borough and present city of Chester, so far as the same remain of record Under the act of 1834, the court in that year appointed as school inspectors Archibald T Dick and Jesse J Maris

1840, John H Denning, Samuel Weaver, 1841, Samuel Little, Edward Darlington, John H Denning, Samuel Weaver, Humphrey Johnson, and Jacob G Kitts composed the full board of school directors, 1842, John Hinkson, Alexander McKeever, 1843, Jeremiah W Flickner, 1844, Joseph H Hinkson, Isaac S Williams, 1845, Joseph Taylor, Frederick J Hinkson, 1846, Edward Darlington, Spencer McIlvain, 1847, William Weaver, Abram Cobourn, 1848, Peter W Green, Isaac S Williams, 1849, John Larkin, Jr, Charles D Manley, 1850, Samuel Crozer, Jesse Young, 1851, Rev Anson B Hard, William Trout, George W Bartram, John McClimate, Alexander McKeever, Robert R Dutton, 1852, Robert E. Hannum, George W Moore, 1853, James Campbell, Davis B Stacey, Isaac Engle Cochran, 1854, Alexander M Wright, Lewis Thatcher, 1855, E S Hewes, Frederick S Hinkson, 1856, James J Porter, William L Grubb, 1857 Alexander M Wright, Samuel Shaw, 1858, Dr Charles J Morton, William Hinkson, 1859, Frederick J Hinkson, Stephen Clowd, 1860 (North Ward), ——, (Middle Ward), ——, (South Ward), Benjamin Gartside, 1861 (North), William McDevitt, (Middle), William Hinkson, (South), ——, 1862 (North), John M Larkin, (Middle), Edward R Minshall, (South), ——, 1863 (North), Alexander M Wright, (Middle), ——, (South), Benjamin Gartside, 1864 (North), John O Deshong, Jr, (Middle), Dr Ellwood Harvey, (South), Charles W Deans, 1865 (North), ——, (Middle), Caleb Emlin, (South), Abram R Perkins, 1866 (North), Henry L Donaldson, (Middle), ——, (South), Samuel Eccles, Jr, 1867 (North), ——, (Middle), Stephen C Hall, (South) Alfred Taylor, resigned, and William B Burmace elected to vacant seat, 1868 (North), ——, (Middle), Thomas Appleby, (South), John H Barton, 1869 (North), Joseph Kenworthy, Simeon Cotton, (Middle), ——, ——, (South), John C Price, ——, 1870 (North), Henry L Donaldson, (Middle), Samuel H Leeds, (South), Dr Ellwood Harvey, 1871 (North), Simeon Cotton, (Middle), Henry B Taylor, (South), John Fountain, 1872 (North), Dr F Ridgley Graham, (Middle), Samuel H Leeds, (South), Jonathan Grant, 1873 (North), Dr William B Ulrich, (Middle), ——, (South), ——, 1874 (North), William J Harvey, (Middle), Mrs S M Springer, (South), John Fountain, 1875 (North), William H Dickinson, (Middle), Stephen C Hall, (South), Jonathan Grant, 1876 (North), Dr F Redgley Graham, (Middle), Charles Roberts, (South), John C Price, 1877 (North) H L Donaldson, (Middle), William Hinkson, (South), J Harry Thompson, 1878 (North), Jonathan Johnson, (Middle), Samuel H Leeds, (South), Jonathan Grant, 1879 (North), Daniel Robinson, (Middle), William Hinkson, (South), John C. Price 1880 (North), H L Donaldson, (Middle), Levi G James, (South), J H Thompson, 1881 (North), Jonathan R Johnson, (Middle), Stephen Clowd, Jr, (South), Jonathan Grant, 1882 (North), Daniel Robinson, (Middle), Samuel H Leeds, (South), John C Price, 1883 (North), H L Donaldson, (Middle), Dr Samuel Starr, (South), Josiah C Ross, 1884 (North), Jonathan R Johnson, (Middle), Samuel Clowd, Jr, (South), Jonathan Grant.

The Pennsylvania Military Academy—By act of Assembly, April 8, 1862, the Pennsylvania Military Academy was incorporated as a university under the title Chester County Military Academy This title the Court of Common Pleas of Chester County, on application for the board of trustees, changed immediately to its present name It was then organized and located at West Chester, with Col Theodore Wyatt as its president, where it soon became noted as an institution of learning Founded during the Rebellion, it made a special feature of military instruction, and to the forces of the United States in the civil war it contributed many officers from its roll of students When Lee's army invaded the State the battery of the academy, manned by cadets of the institution and citizens of West Chester, was in service for two months, and was commanded by the authorities. After the close of the war the Crozer Normal School building, at Chester, Delaware Co, which had been used by the government as a hospital, was vacated by the United States, and, as it furnished accommodations superior to those the school then had, these premises were leased, and the institution was moved here in December, 1865 The Pennsylvania Military Academy at its new location grew rapidly in public favor, and so large did the number of students become that it was decided to secure its present site and erect and equip buildings adapted to its wants In 1867 the institution conferred its first degrees on its graduates, and in September, 1868, the building having been completed in the mean while, the academy occupied its new quarters, to the northeast of the the city,—a landmark presenting a prominent appearance when viewed from the north or east in approaching Chester, and especially from the Delaware River In its new building the academy, in September, 1868, accommodated one hundred and fifty cadets and officers

On the afternoon of Feb 16, 1882, the main edifice was entirely destroyed by fire, the origin of which is unknown, although the flames were first discovered in the laboratory, then located in the upper story

After the destruction of the academy, in twenty days subsequently the term was resumed temporarily at Ridley Park As soon as the losses were adjusted by the insurance companies, the erection of a new building upon an improved and enlarged plan was commenced The main structure is two hundred and seventeen feet long, fifty feet in depth, four stories in height, surmounted with a dome, which towers many feet above all, presenting a view therefrom unequaled in the county. The building, which was completed, ready for occupancy, Sept. 13, 1882, is divided by fire-walls, and is believed to be as nearly fireproof as it is possible to render it, while in a sanitary point, as well as in respect to the accommodation to secure the comfort and convenience of its inmates, the new academy structure is most admirably planned A laboratory, at some distance from the main edifice, is an ornate and well-arranged building, sufficiently removed to render it improbable that any fire which might occur therein could seriously endanger the Military Academy proper The drill-hall and gymnasium, one hundred and thirty and sixty feet respectively, are admirably adapted to the uses for which they were designed

The present academic staff is composed as follows Col Theodore Hyatt, president and professor of Greek; Capt Charles E Hyatt, vice-president, professor of Rhetoric and Elocution, Capt R Kelso Carter, professor of Mathematics and Civil Engineering, Lieut William W. Galbraith, United States army, professor of Military Science and Mathematics, Lieut Emile L Feffer, professor of French, German, Spanish, Latin, and Greek, Capt Benjamin F Morley, professor of Chemistry, Physics, and Tactics, Dr Joseph S Burns, professor of Latin, Greek, and English Literature, Dr John R. Sweney, professor of Music, Charles S Fahnestock, professor of Penmanship, Drawing, and English Branches, William B Ulrich, M D, lecturer on Hygiene, Frederick E Powell, adjunct professor of Mathematics and English Branches, Edgar P. Hershey, adjunct professor of Rhetoric, Silas P Comfort, instructor in Mathematics and Technical Drawing

Chester Academy—This institution of learning, located at the southwest corner of Broad and Potter Streets, was founded, in 1862, by Charles W Deans, who had just previous to that date been superintendent of the public schools of Delaware County It was then known as the Chester Academy and Normal School In 1865, Professor George Gilbert, then of Philadelphia, purchased Mr Deans' interest in the academy, including the school furniture, and at once reorganized the institution, enlarged the accommodations, thoroughly revised and advanced the course of study, and employed additional teachers The reputation of the academy steadily advanced, and in 1871, six years after he became principal of the institution, Professor Gilbert purchased both the school building and the residence to the east The school-rooms have all been recently enlarged to nearly double their original capacity and thoroughly refitted The aim of the school is to afford facilities for students preparing for college, for teaching, or for general business, and to direct them in the course of study necessary to successfully qualify them for the occupations in life which they may select The present faculty of the academy comprises George Gilbert, principal, instructor in Latin, Greek, and the Higher Mathematics, M Louisa Clancy, Music, French, and Literature, Mrs T M Gilbert, Writing, Drawing, and History, H Jennie Cornell, Primary Department, Addie H Pyle, Hannah R Lenderman, and Jennie McCoy, English Branches The pupilage is about one hundred and twenty

Piers at Chester—The present public wharves at Chester, one a short distance east of the foot of Market Street, and the other at the foot of Edgmont Avenue, are comparatively of recent construction Between the years 1760 and 1770, Francis Richardson, to whom the land on which these piers abut had been devised by his aunt, Grace Lloyd, erected a pier at end of Edgmont Avenue, and another to the eastward of the present Market Street pier, the latter remained until after 1826, but they were of crude construction, lacking the stability of those now in use During the war of 1812 it became apparent that some protection was absolutely demanded at this point for vessels navigating the river in winter, for when the Delaware at the Horseshoe was frozen, it prevented all communication by water with Philadelphia. The commerce of the latter city at that time greatly exceeded that of any port in the United States, and so frequent was the loss of vessels by drifting ice that on March 11, 1816, an appropriation of $10,935 32 was made by the General Assembly, "to be employed for the erection of piers for the river Delaware at the Borough of Chester" David Porter, Joseph Engle, and William Graham being appointed commissioners, who should "cause to be erected, placed, and sunk in the said river Delaware at the Borough of Chester, two or more good and sufficient piers, for the security of vessels navigating the said river, and shall also cause to be built and constructed good and sufficient wharves, to be so connected with the said piers as to afford a safe and easy landing for vessels coming to at the same, and for this purpose they shall have power to employ suitable workmen, and obtain cessions to the Commonwealth of ground within the said Borough of Chester, necessary for the erection and construction of such wharves and piers, *Provided*, That the said cessions be obtained without any consideration from the Commonwealth." The act also provided that while the commissioners were to give bonds for the faithful performance of their duties, they were not to receive any compensation for their labor The work was also required to be begun within one year, and completed within five years from the date of the passage of the act.

By the act of March 24, 1817, an additional sum of eight thousand dollars was appropriated, one-half of which amount was to be paid to the commissioners when work was resumed on the wharves at Chester, and the remainder on the 1st of June, 1818, "or so soon thereafter as the said work shall be completed," and by the same act William Anderson was substituted for Commodore David Porter. The work was to be proceeded with within one year, and completed within three years after the passage of the act.

Previous to the date of the law the owners of the land on which the piers abutted ceded their interest in the wharves to the State. The deed conveying the upper pier is as follows:

"THIS INDENTURE, made the 20th day of June, 1816, between Davis Bevan, of the Borough of Chester, in the county of Delaware, and the Commonwealth of Pennsylvania, gentlemen, of the one part, and the said Commonwealth of Pennsylvania of the other part Whereas, by an Act making an appropriation for the erection of piers in the river Delaware, at the Borough of Chester, in Delaware County, David Porter, Joseph Engle and William Graham, Esq., are authorized to obtain cessions to the Commonwealth of ground within the said Borough of Chester, necessary for the erection and construction of the wharves and piers provided the said cessions be obtained without any consideration from this commonwealth, and whereas the wharf lying on the North east side of High Street, in the said Borough of Chester, commonly called 'Richardson's wharf,' has by good and sufficient assurances in the law became vested in fee simple in the said Davis Bevan, who is desirous to aid the public interest by ceding his title thereto to the Commonwealth, for the purpose aforesaid: Now this indenture witnesseth, that the said Davis Bevan in consideration of the premises and also in consideration of the local advantages which will arise from the contemplated work, hath granted, bargained, sold, ceded, surrendered and confirmed, and by these presents doth grant, bargain, sell, cede, surrender and confirm unto the said Commonwealth of Pennsylvania, all that the above mentioned wharf, situated, lying and being in the said Borough of Chester, on the North east side of High Street and extending from low water mark on the river Delaware to the fast land, being in breadth from low water mark to a button wood tree Standing on the North east side of said wharf about twenty-one feet, and thence to the fast land opposite the north end of a stone stable of the breadth of twenty feet, measuring from the South-west side of said wharf, as the foundations now exist. Together with all and singular the logs and bolts, stone and other material belonging to and connected with said wharf, to have and to hold the same for the purposes aforesaid with the appurtenances to the said Commonwealth of Pennsylvania forever; provided always nevertheless, that unless the said Commonwealth shall proceed to carry on the contemplated work within the period mentioned in the aforesaid recited law, then this Indenture and the estate hereby granted and ceded shall cease and become void. And the said Davis Bevan doth reserve to himself and to his heirs the right liberty and privilege to pass to, upon and from the said wharf, with free ingress egress and regress, to and for him and his heirs and his and their servants and workmen, with horses, carts and carriages at all times and seasons for the loading and hauling of goods and merchandise or other property, and for shipping and sending away the same."

The lower pier, at the foot of Edgmont Avenue, was sold by the sheriff of Chester County after Richardson's failure to William O'Neal, and he, on Nov. 4, 1797, conveyed it with other real estate to Ephraim Pearson. The latter ceded that wharf to the State of Pennsylvania by the following instrument, dated May 6, 1816:

"*To all people to whom these Presents shall Come.* I Ephraim Pearson of Chester, Delaware County, send greeting and whereas by an Act making an appropriation for the erection of piers in the river Delaware, at the Borough of Chester in Delaware County, David Porter, Joseph Engle and William Graham, Esq., are authorized to obtain cessions to the Commonwealth of ground within the said Borough of Chester, necessary for the erection and construction of the Wharves and piers provided the said cessions be obtained without any consideration from this Commonwealth. Now know ye that I, the said Ephraim Pearson, do hereby grant, transfer and cede to the Commonwealth of Pennsylvania all that piece of ground known by the name of 'Richardson's Lower Wharf,' lying on the river Delaware, between the mouth of Chester creek and Front Street continued and extended from high water mark to low water mark, being in the Borough of Chester, aforesaid. To have and to hold the same, to the said Commonwelth forever, for the purpose of erecting and constructing wharves and piers, and for no other purpose; provided that if the said Commissioners shall not make use thereof for the purpose aforesaid, within the time limited by the above recited Act for finishing their work, then the cession to be void."

The State of Pennsylvania completed the piers at Chester, but constant repairs had to be made to them, until the commonwealth sorely repented accepting the wharves, which, even after the State had reconstructed them, were indifferent structures. Chester being the residence of Commodore Porter, and many of the noted men of the navy being often there, the town acquired reputation in that branch of the public service, hence government vessels frequently wintered in the space between the piers, riding at anchor where now is solid ground. The State, desirous of being relieved from the charge of this white elephant, intimated that if the government of the United States would stipulate to keep the piers at Chester in good condition and repair, the commonwealth would cede to the former their title to the piers. The influence of navy officers was used. The United States accepted the proposition, and on April 11, 1825, the commonwealth of Pennsylvania formally ceded the piers at Chester to the national government.

The Logan House (Second Street, near Edgmont Avenue).—This dwelling was built by Jasper Yeates in the year 1700, on ground purchased from David Lloyd, Dec. 11, 1699, and formerly a stone on which was cut the initials "J. & C. Y.," with the date 1700 underneath, similar in appearance to the date-stone of the old Porter house, was set in one of the gables. These initials stood for the names Jasper and Catharine Yeates. It was two stories in height, with a tent-like roof forming an attic within, with steep sides. Over the first-story windows was a pent-roof, similar to that remaining on the old City Hall, and a porch at the front door, with seats at each side of the door, at right angles to the building. A wide door-way gave access to the spacious hall, many small diamond-shaped panes of glass set in lead, in the large window-sashes, gave light to the several apartments, and casements at the head of the stair landing furnished the same to the wainscoted hall-way. All the rooms were wainscoted also, and the panels were painted or stained in imitation of mahogany. Large closets were on each side of the wide chimney-places, lighted by windows in the outer walls. Under the high wooden mantel-pieces in the parlor and the room opposite, across the hall, the fireplaces were lined with illuminated tiles, delineating incidents of Scriptural history. Large buttresses were built against the gables for strength, and smaller ones to guard the brick walls on each side of the main building. These buttresses were subsequently removed.

Jasper Yeates, of Philadelphia, a native of Yorkshire, England, married Catharine, daughter of James Sandelands, the elder, and in 1697 purchased mills and a tract of ground at the mouth of Naaman's Creek. The next year he built a goodly-sized structure between Chester Creek and Edgmont Avenue for a granary or store-house for grain on the second floor, and established a bakery in the lower room. It should be recollected that two hundred years ago Chester Creek, at that point, was considerably to the westward of the present stream.* He was a prominent man of his day. He was appointed by Penn, when the proprietary created the borough of Chester, Oct. 13, 1701, one of its four burgesses. In 1703 he was chosen chief burgess of the borough, and is believed to have been the first person holding that office. He was one of the justices of Chester County, afterwards one of the justices of the Supreme Court of the province; a member of the Provincial Council, and a member of the General Assembly. He and his brother-in-law, James Sandelands, the younger, were the principal promoters of the building of St. Paul's Church. He died previously to May 2, 1720, for his will was probated at New Castle, Del., at the date last given. He left six children surviving him,—four sons and two daughters.

John Yeates, the third son of Jasper and Catharine Yeates, was born at Chester, March 1, 1705. He inherited from his father the "dwelling house" at Chester, with the "boulting" wharf, gardens and lots near the same town, "bought of Jonas Sandelands and Edward Henneston." He was a shipping merchant, and resided for a time in the island of Barbadoes, and afterwards in Philadelphia, where he acquired considerable real estate. Later in life he sustained large pecuniary losses in business ventures, and through the influence of friends, in 1764, was appointed comptroller of customs at Pocomoke, Md. He died there the following year. Under date of Sept. 4, 1733, John Yeates and Elizabeth (Sidbotham), his wife, conveyed the mansion-house and lot, of which I am speaking, to Joseph Parker, as well as other lands in Chester.

Joseph Parker was a nephew of the noted and eccentric Quaker preacher, John Salkeld. He was a native of Cumberland, England, and in 1714, at the age of twenty-five, came to the province and settled at Chester to be near his uncle. He entered the office of David Lloyd, and after Lloyd's death he succeeded him as register and recorder of Chester County. In 1724 he was prothonotary of the courts, and in 1738 he was commissioned a justice of the peace, a position of much dignity in colonial days. In 1730 he married Mary, daughter of James Ladd, of Gloucester County, N. J. His wife died the following year, leaving one child, a daughter, Mary. Joseph Parker died May 21, 1766.

Mary Parker, born April 21, 1731, at Chester, to whom the Logan house descended, was married to Charles Norris, of Philadelphia, in the old Quaker meeting-house, Sixth month 21, 1759. Her husband died Jan. 15, 1766, and she returned to Chester and resided in the parental mansion until her death, Dec. 4, 1799. She was the mother of three sons and one daughter, Deborah, to whom by will she devised the Logan house.

Deborah Norris was born in Philadelphia, Oct. 19, 1761, and was a small child when her widowed mother returned to Chester. She was married to Dr. George Logan, a grandson of James Logan, Sept. 6, 1781, and removed to the Logan family seat, Stenton, where she resided until her death, Feb. 2, 1839. Deborah Logan was a woman of much literary ability, and a historian of great attainments. Indeed, her remarkable store of antiquarian information justly entitled her to the appellation of "The Female Historian of the Colonial Times." She had mingled freely with the leading spirits of the Revolutionary period, and her cousin, Charles Thomson, the first and long confidential secretary of the Continental Congress, was through life an intimate visitor at her house, and from him she learned much of the inner history of those times. In 1814, Mrs. Logan believing the correspondence of William Penn and James Logan contained much valuable information respecting the early history of the commonwealth, she began the task of collating, deciphering, and copying the manuscripts in her possession, many of the documents being much decayed and difficult to read; but she industriously worked, rising in the winter-time before sunrise and at daylight in the summer, for a period of several years. Her manuscripts made eleven large quarto volumes, and formed two clever-sized octavo volumes when published by the Historical Society of Pennsylvania. John F. Watson, the annalist, obtained many of the interesting items in his popular work from Mrs. Logan. The old dwelling is now owned by Mrs. Rebecca Ross.

The Old Hoskins (Graham) House (Edgmont Avenue below Third Street).—John Simcock, of Ridley, received a patent from the Duke of York for sixteen yards, fronting upon Chester Creek and running back into the land of Neeles Laerson, bounded on the north by lands of Jöran Keen, and on the south by land of Neeles Laerson. On the 5th day of Sixth month, 1684, Simcock sold to John Hoskins (then spelled Hodgkins) the tract of land, and the latter, in the year 1688, built the house now standing at the south-east corner of Edgmont Avenue and Graham Street.

The house thus erected was used by him as an inn, and was a substantial structure, as is evidenced even in its present declination by an inspection of the building. It is two stories in height, with attics; the steps and porch, which were located before the street-line was definitely fixed, extend a goodly distance into the sidewalk. A hall-way runs through the centre of the building; a wide, easily-ascended staircase rises from the rear of the entry at the south side to the apartments above. The balustrade is fashioned of hard wood and is very massive, while the steps of ash in many places show marks of worms, who have eaten deep grooves in the solid planking. The windows in the lower rooms are deeply recessed within the apartments, and old-time seats constructed therein. The heavy beams supporting the upper floors stand prominently out from the ceiling. In the rooms on the first and second floors on the north side of the house the high, old-fashioned wooden mantels over the large

HOSKINS (GRAHAM) HOUSE, BUILT IN 1688.

fireplaces are flanked by enormous closets, which are lighted by small windows in the outer walls; those in the southern end have been walled up. The floors are laid in hard wood, and the flooring-boards are wide,—almost the entire width of the trees from which they were cut. The ceilings are lofty for the time when the building was erected, and the house is divided into numerous sleeping apartments intended to accommodate many guests. The steep roof externally would indicate that the attics were so low that they would be uncomfortable to the inmates, whereas the contrary is the fact. The kitchen, which is built in an L on the northeastern end of the house, is large; the fireplace comprising almost the entire eastern end, —now inclosed as a closet,—is of that ample size, usual among our ancestors, that the benumbed wayfarers could seat themselves at either side of the chimney, on benches provided for that purpose, and enjoy the warmth of the roaring fire of huge logs, formerly the only way employed to heat that part of the building. In the days of its ancient grandeur there was a portico or veranda in the rear of the main building extending ten or twelve feet outward, which was inclosed with lattice-work, where, in the summer-time, the hospitable table was spread. An old oven, long since torn down, was attached to the house on the north side of the kitchen, and a well of good water, now abandoned, was located in the rear and at some distance from the portico.

John Hoskins and Mary, his wife, were natives of Cheshire, England, and came to this country in the year 1682. In August, 1684, he purchased from John Simcock the property whereon he afterwards built the house; and he had purchased Ninth month 21, 1681, from Penn, before leaving England, two hundred and fifty acres of land, which was laid out to him in Middletown township, between the lands of Richard Crosby and David Ogden, Fourth month 27, 1684. He was a member of the General Assembly which sat March 12, 1683. His will, dated Eleventh month 2, 1694/5, and probated Aug. 15, 1698, in Philadelphia, is signed John Hodgskins, but the renunciation of the executors named therein, dated 12th of Sixth month, 1698, speaks of him as John Hoskins. He left two children, John and Hannah, and his widow, who although aged, married in 1700, George Woodier, of Chester. His daughter, Hannah, married, in 1698, Charles Whitaker. His estate was a large one for those times, the appraisement amounting to £450 12*s.* 2*d.*, and the different articles set forth therein, as contained in the various rooms of the house wherein he died, answer to the number in the present Graham house.

His son, John Hoskins, married in 1698, Ruth Atkinson, and in 1700, when only twenty-three years of age, was elected sheriff of the county, an office the duties of which he discharged so successfully that for fifteen years in succession, excepting during the year 1708, he was continued in that office. To him the old homestead descended, and here he lived until his death, Oct. 26, 1716. He was the father of four sons and one daughter, Mary, who married John Mather. One of the sons, I suppose, died before their mother, for in the will of Ruth Hoskins, dated July 3, 1739, she mentions only her sons Stephen and Joseph Hoskins,—although John was still living,—and devised to her son-in-law, Mather, a house and lot. Stephen Hoskins was born in Chester, Twelfth month 18, 1701/2, and Joseph was born in the same place, Fourth month 30, 1705.

Stephen Hoskins married, in 1727, Sarah Warner, of Maryland, and moved into that province, but returned to Chester, 1730, and was elected coroner of Chester County. About 1743 he removed to Philadelphia, and it was to his son, John, of Burlington, that Joseph Hoskins, of the Porter house, devised the real estate of which he died seized. This Joseph Hoskins, to whom more particular reference will be made in account of the Porter house, purchased the homestead from his brother, John, to whom it was awarded in partition of John Hoskins', the elder, estate, and on June 4, 1762, Joseph sold the house and lot to Henry Hale Graham. A brief notice of Judge Graham has been given herein, as also an account of William Graham, his son, to whom the property descended. The house and lot was sold by the heirs of William Graham to John G. Dyer in 1857, by whose estate it is now owned.

The Old Porter (Lloyd) House.—It is doubtful whether any building in the United States, whose history extends over more than a century and a half, has had connected in the title to the property so many distinguished owners as will be found in that of the old Porter house in this city, whose record was closed in that appalling tragedy, in 1882, which enshrouded our city in mourning for a season.

By patent dated April 9, 1669, Francis Lovelace, Governor-General under the Duke of York, granted unto Neeles Laerson, *alias* Friend, a large tract of ground comprising one hundred and fifty acres, but which by subsequent survey proved to include in the boundary lines one hundred and eighty-three acres. The patent reserved a yearly rent of one and a half bushels of winter wheat, payable to the king. Laerson entered into possession of the land thus allotted him, built upon and improved the premises. By will, dated Dec. 17, 1686 (he died the following year), Laerson gave authority to his wife to sell the real estate in her discretion. In exercise of this power, Ann Friend (the family had by this time assumed the English *alias* as their family name, and had abandoned the Swedish patronymic absolutely), the widow, Andrew Friend, son and heir of Laerson and Johannes Friend, the second son, by deed dated May 27, 1689, conveyed the estate to David Lloyd. Lloyd, however, after he built the house whose history I am writing, seemed to have had some doubts of the sufficiency of the title, and therefore, thirty-four years subsequently, July 13, 1723, he had Ann Friend (then one hundred and five years old), and Gabriel Friend and Laurence Friend, the younger sons of Neeles Laerson and Ann, his wife, execute a deed conveying the premises he had purchased in 1686. Parts of the estate thus acquired were sold by Lloyd to Joseph Richardson, and to Rodger Jackson, but he subsequently repurchased the land thus conveyed, and in addition acquired from Jonas Sandelands a considerable tract, until the estate had increased to about five hundred acres.

David Lloyd, a sketch of whose eventful, useful life is given in the chapter on the bench and bar, was twice married. His second wife was Grace Growden, whom he married after the year 1703, for several deeds of that year are executed by him alone, indicating that at that time he was a widower. By his first marriage he was childless; by his second, he was the father of one son, who, at an early age, was killed by an accident. He died "6th day of ye 2d month" (May), 1731, aged seventy-eight years, for such is the inscription on his tombstone in Friends' graveyard here. If it be a fact that he was seventy-eight years old when he died, David Lloyd could not have been born in 1656, and yet all the authorities agree in giving the latter date as that of his birth. By his will, dated March 24, 1724, after a few bequests, the remainder of his estate is devised to his wife, Grace, who was twenty-seven years younger than her husband.

The old mansion was built in 1721, and the slab on which was engraved the letters "L. L. D. & G., 1721," which was formerly in the western gable of the dwelling. The house was of stone, massively built, and was one of the best specimens of colonial grandeur which had descended to our time. It received many additions to it after it passed into the possession of Commodore Porter, such as the building of the cupola on the roof, the walling up of the open corner chimney-place and substituting therefor the grates and marble mantels which were seen there when the ruins were visited by thousands of people after the explosion. Lloyd lived sumptuously in the old mansion, then, as before stated, one of the most imposing dwellings in the New World, entertaining largely and keeping a retinue of servants. He was one of the eight gentlemen of means in the province, including the Governor, who, in the year 1725, are recorded as owning four-wheeled carriages drawn by two horses.

Grace Lloyd, in her widowhood, was attended faithfully by her friend, Jane Fenn, a noted minister of Friends, until the latter married, and in turn became the mistress of the old dwelling. Jane Fenn was born in 1698, in London, and when very young was strongly impressed with the belief that it was her duty to go to Pennsylvania, and after several years had elapsed, in which she struggled against the impression, she sailed in 1712, in company with a Welshman, Robert Davis, who with his family were emigrating to Pennsylvania. Davis had paid her passage, and she had obligated herself to return the outlay out of the first money she could earn; but when he insisted that she should bind herself as a servant for four years to repay him the money, she resisted, as she had not come as a redemptioner. Davis had her arrested for debt. She was thrown into prison, but was relieved therefrom by some Friends, who paid the claim and employed her in their families as a teacher of their children. At this time she was not a Quaker, but the kindness of these people attracted her towards them, and finally she united with the society and became ultimately one of its most efficient ministers. It is recorded that at a meeting at Haverford, David and Grace Lloyd came in, and immediately Jane Fenn, who was present, was impressed with the conviction that "these were the people with whom she must go and settle," while David and Grace Lloyd were in their turn impressed with Jane, "and it was fixed in their minds to take her for the Lord's service." She lived with them until 1727, when she visited England and Ireland on a religious mission, and returned to Chester in 1730, a short time previous to David Lloyd's death. She remained with his widow until her (Jane Fenn's) marriage to Joseph Hoskins, Eighth month 26, 1738, at Chester Meeting.

On May 1, 1741, Grace Lloyd conveyed the mansion and most of the real estate she acquired under her husband's will to Joseph Hoskins, reserving two acres of ground, and "also the room in the southwest corner of the mansion-house, called the dining-room, the room on the northeast corner of said house, called the parlor, with a closet and milk-house adjoining, the chamber over the said dining-room, the chamber over the said parlor, one-half part of the garret, the front part of the cellar, the old kitchen and chamber over it, the chaise-house, the use of the pump, cider-mill and cider-press to make her own cider, and part of the garden, with free liberty of ingress, egress and regress into and out of all and every the premises for the term of her natural life without impeachment of waste." Grace Lloyd died in 1760.

THE PORTER (LLOYD) HOUSE, BUILT IN 1721, DESTROYED BY EXPLOSION FEB. 17, 1882.
[From photograph owned by W. W. Amos.]

Joseph Hoskins was one of the most useful citizens Chester has ever numbered among its residents. He was an enterprising, public-spirited man, doing good and asking no mere gratification of his personal vanity by coupling his gift with conditions that the donor's name should be made conspicuous and held in remembrance because of these works by which others should be benefited. He gave because his heart prompted the act in the love he bore his fellows. Joseph Hoskins was born in Chester, June 30, 1705, and seems to have been an active man of business. When twenty-six years of age he made a voyage to the island of Barbadoes, but returned after a short absence, and in 1739, after his marriage, he went to Boston on business. In the early days of our country a journey such as this was a remarkable event in a man's life, and at this time more persons can be found in Chester, in proportion to its population, who have visited Japan than, at the period I am alluding to, who had made a voyage to Boston. He was made chief burgess of Chester and one of his majesty's justices of the peace in 1758. By his will, dated Twelfth month, 1769, he devised certain lands in the borough of Chester for school purposes, more fully mentioned under that heading, and also gave ten pounds towards inclosing Friends' graveyard, on Edgmont Avenue, with a brick or stone wall. Being childless, the residue of his estate, after a few bequests to relatives and friends, he devised to his nephew, John Hoskins, of Burlington, N. J. This John Hoskins, in 1750, had married Mary, a daughter of Joshua and Sarah Raper, of Burlington, and their son, Raper Hoskins, who came to Chester in charge of his father's property there, on May 2, 1781, married Eleanor, daughter of Henry Hale Graham, while Joseph Hoskins, Raper Hoskins' brother, married, June 12, 1793, Mary, a younger daughter of Henry Hale Graham. John Hoskins, to whom the estate descended under Joseph Hoskins' will, after holding the title to the premises for eighteen years, on March 22, 1791, made a deed conveying a large tract of land, comprising that whereon the old mansion-house stood, to Raper Hoskins. The latter having died in the fall of the year 1798, a victim of the yellow-fever scourge in Chester, his widow, Eleanor Hoskins, was granted letters on his estate, and in discharge of her duties sold the property, April 28, 1799, to Thomas Laycock The estate subsequently was purchased by Maj William Anderson Evelina Anderson, the daughter of the major, having intermarried with David Porter, in that year the newly-wedded couple made their home at the old mansion, excepting during the times when Porter was located at naval stations in charge of the government yards Feb 24, 1816, William Anderson and Elizabeth, his wife, "in consideration of the natural love and affection which they have and bear for their son-in-law, the said David Porter, as well for and in consideration of one dollar," conveyed to David Porter, in fee, the house, improvements, and a trifle over three acres and a half of land

David Porter was born in Boston, Feb 1, 1780, and was appointed midshipman April 3, 1793 He was a lieutenant on board the "Constellation" when that frigate captured the French vessel of war, "L'Insurgent," in February, 1799, and was promoted for his bravery on that occasion In 1800 he was wounded in an engagement with pirates off Santo Domingo, and was promoted to the command of the "Enterprise" While commanding that vessel he captured a Tripolitan corsair He had charge of the expedition which destroyed several feluccas, ladened with wheat, under the batteries at Tripoli, in which engagement he was again wounded In 1803 he was captured in the frigate "Philadelphia," when that vessel grounded in the harbor of Tripoli, was taken prisoner, and for eighteen months was held as a slave In 1806 he commanded the "Enterprise," and fought and severely handled twelve Spanish gunboats near Gibraltar In 1812 he was commissioned captain, and placed in command of the "Essex," which vessel he rendered famous in our country's annals, although he finally lost the ship in one of the most noted naval combats of history with two British vessels of war off Valparaiso In 1815 to 1816 he was one of the naval commissioners, and in the latter year made a successful cruise against the pirates that then infested the Gulf of Mexico In consequence of some infraction of naval law he was suspended for six months, in 1826 he resigned his commission and entered the Mexican navy as its commander-in-chief, an office which he soon resigned In 1829 he was appointed United States consul at Algiers, and when that country was conquered by the French he was made United States charge d'affairs at Constantinople, and while discharging the duties of that office he negotiated several important treaties with that government He died at Pera, near Constantinople, March 3, 1843, and his remains were brought to this country and interred in Woodland Cemetery, Philadelphia Mrs Evelina Porter survived her husband twenty-eight years, dying Oct 1, 1871, in her eightieth year

David Porter left five sons and two daughters The eldest daughter, Evelina, married Capt Harris Heap, and the youngest, Imogene, married Mr. Harris

William David Porter, the eldest son, born in New Orleans in 1810, entered the navy in his eighteenth year During the early part of the Rebellion his loyalty was unjustly suspected when he was in command of the sloop-of-war "St. Mary," on the Pacific station He was, however, assigned to duty on the Mississippi River, where he fitted out the gunboat fleet, and was placed in command of the "Essex," which took part in the attack on Forts Henry and Donelson, in which latter engagement a ball from the fort plunged through the boiler of his vessel, and the escaping steam so severely scalded Porter that he ultimately died from its effects, May 1, 1864 Notwithstanding his feeble health, he ran the batteries between Cairo and New Orleans, took part in the attack on Vicksburg, destroyed the rebel ram "Arkansas" near Baton Rouge, and assisted in the attack on Port Hudson He had by this time become so ill that he was ordered to New York to recruit his shattered health, and died there at the date stated.

David D Porter, the present admiral, is said to have been born in Philadelphia in 1813, although in his letter to the Hanley Hose Company respecting the date-stone of the Porter house he speaks of Chester as his native place When a mere lad at school in this city, one Saturday afternoon he and the late George W Piper provided themselves with several pounds of powder, and made what the boys call a squib The match seeming to have gone out, David Porter and his companion got down on their knees and blew the flame The squib exploded, and Porter and Piper were blown over the fence, near the old mansion The hair on their heads was burned off, as well as their eyebrows, and the skin of their faces and hands was blistered badly This was the future admiral's "baptism of fire" He entered the navy as midshipman in 1829, and from 1836 to 1840 was attached to the coast survey He took part in the Mexican war, and in 1861 joined the Gulf Squadron, in command of the "Powhatan" He was in command of the mortar-boats in the attack on the forts below New Orleans, in 1862, and did important duties on the Mississippi and Red Rivers in 1863-64 He was conspicuous in the siege of Vicksburg, for which he was made rear-admiral In 1864 he was in command of the North Atlantic Blockading Squadron, and rendered efficient services in the capture of Fort Fisher, in January, 1865 In 1866 he was made vice-admiral, and in 1876 admiral of the United States He is the present owner of the old Porter property in this city

Theodoric Porter, the third son, entered the regular army in 1838 as lieutenant in the Seventh United States Infantry, and was killed in a skirmish with the Mexicans, April 18, 1846, during Gen Taylor's advance previous to the battle of Palo Alto It is stated by army officers that he stayed out of camp the night before the battle, and his body was found the next morning with several dead Mexicans lying around his corpse

Fifty-two years ago, when David D. Porter and his younger brother, Theodoric, were living at the old mansion, the winter was very severe and the river Delaware was frozen over. The two venturesome men announced their determination to sleigh to Philadelphia. Many of the residents of Chester tried to dissuade them from the attempt, but at nine o'clock in the morning they started from the foot of Welsh Street, David driving. The mouths of the creeks were piled with ice several feet in height, and they were compelled to take the inside channel. A goodly part of their journey was performed on enormous cakes of ice which were entirely loose from the shore. At noon they reached the navy-yard, and, returning, left that place at three o'clock. The cold had become so intense that the two men were compelled to stop and build a fire on the ice to warm themselves. Resuming their journey, they reached Chester at nine o'clock at night. They had traveled thirty miles on the frozen surface of the river, a feat never attempted before, or, if it had been, no record thereof has been made.

Henry Ogden Porter (or "Budd," as he was familiarly called), the fourth son, named for his uncle, Capt. Henry Ogden, was in the navy, and afterwards in the revenue service. During the Rebellion he was an acting lieutenant in the navy, and fought his vessel—the gunboat "Hatteras"—off Mobile, in an engagement with the "Alabama," until she sunk, her flag still flying proudly as she disappeared beneath the water. He died, about seventeen years ago, near Washington.

Hamilton Porter, the next brother, was a lieutenant in the navy (on the "Flirt"), and while in the service died of yellow fever, Aug. 10, 1844.

The old house, after Commodore Porter's family ceased to use it as a residence, was leased to a number of tenants, until at last the location of the gas-works in that neighborhood rendered it no longer a desirable dwelling, and it was leased, in 1862, to Professor Jackson, of Philadelphia, for a pyrotechnic manufactory. On Friday morning, Feb. 17, 1882, shortly after seven o'clock, fire was discovered in the kitchen of the old structure, and the alarm was responded to promptly by the fire department, although the entire force had been out late the preceding night battling with the flames which had laid the Pennsylvania Military Academy in ruins. The crowd which had gathered about the Porter house kept back because of the report which had been spread among them that gunpowder was stored in the establishment, but when they saw the chief of the fire department and the members of the various fire companies approaching near to the structure, they drew closer to the scene. Flames at this time were observed coming out of the windows on the west side, and in half an hour after the firemen had arrived and had gone into service a slight explosion occurred, which occasioned no injury. The men who had fled in alarm when this explosion took place, being assured that all danger was past, returned to the work of saving the building from absolute destruction. Hardly had the firemen again mounted the ladders and resumed their labors, when a second explosion took place, which leveled the walls of the old kitchen to the ground and tore huge gaps in the northern and southern walls of the main building. The air was filled with stones, which were hurled to great distances, killing in all eighteen persons and wounding fifty-seven, many of the latter still bearing upon their persons the disfiguring marks of their narrow escape from death. The houses in the neighborhood were in many instances damaged, and window-glasses were shattered at considerable distances from the scene of the explosion. Never before in our city's history was there such wide-spread horror and dismay as on that fatal morning.

Business was entirely suspended, and each person sought to learn if any of their family, friends, or acquaintances were among those who had been killed or injured. Every effort was immediately made to alleviate the sufferings of the wounded, and for the relief of those families wherein death from explosion had occurred. To that end a fund amounting to about ten thousand dollars was subscribed within a few weeks and distributed by a committee appointed for that purpose. The occurrence of this frightful calamity is too recent to require more than this brief mention now, but it will pass into our history as one of the most appalling events which has ever happened in Chester, and for many years to come will be narrated by those who witnessed it to succeeding generations in all the vivid details that memory always lends to such an incident.

The Huertine House.—The brick building on the south side of Third Street, more than midway in the block toward Edgmont Avenue, which is now occupied by Browning & Co. as a clothing-house, was built by William Huertine subsequent to 1712; for August 12th of that year John Musgrove and Mary, his wife, sold to William Huertine the ground on which the house was afterwards erected, subject to a yearly quit-rent of two shillings to the heirs of James Sandelands, the younger, and the same day Jonas Sandelands and Mary, his wife, confirmed the grant, reserving to the heirs of the grantor a yearly quit-rent of two silver shillings. William Huertine, who was a silversmith, erected the house, but subsequently removed to New York, where he died. His widow, Elizabeth, and his children and heirs, March 2, 1724, conveyed the house and grounds—a larger tract of land—to Ruth Hoskins, who in her will, dated July 3, 1739, devised the house and lots to her son-in-law, John Mather, he paying fifty pounds to John, Ruth, and Mary Hoskins, the grandchildren of the testators, and children of her son, Stephen Hoskins.

It was generally believed by our local historian that John Mather was the landlord of the present City

Hotel, which after the Revolution was known as the "Ship George Washington" A full investigation of the records establishes the fact that Mather never was a publican, but a practicing attorney of the courts of Chester County He resided in this house, and by his will, June 28, 1768, devised it to his grandson, John Mather Jackson, who, on March 26, 1783, sold the premises to Edward Vernon The latter had rented the dwelling in 1780, and had obtained license for the house, which he purchased at the date mentioned In 1784, Vernon sold the property to Frederick Engle, who devised it to his daughter, Sarah, wife of Thomas Killie, and in 1804 the latter sold it to Preston Eyre In the fall of the year 1814 the Bank of Delaware County was established in this dwelling,—the home of the cashier, Preston Eyre In 1844 the latter conveyed the premises to his son-in-law, Hon Edward Darlington, who resided there until 1858, when he in turn sold it to Mrs Jane Flavill On March 25, 1863, Thomas Moore purchased the house and lot, and carried on therein a hardware-store with success Mr Moore retired from active business several years ago, since which time he has devoted himself to scientific studies, and to him more than all others the city is indebted for the establishment of the Chester Institute of Science and Mechanic Arts

The Old Lloyd House (Second and Edgmont Avenue) —David Lloyd obtained title for the green, or the church land lying between the creek and Welsh Street, and south of Neeles Laerson's tract of ground to the river Delaware, Dec. 28, 1693, by deed from the church wardens to the Swedish congregation "at Wiccocœ," which act on his part is criticised severely by Rev Mr Ross in his letter, June 21, 1714, to the Society for the Propagation of the Gospel in Foreign Parts. "Ye Glebe lands," he said, alluding to this tract, "was irreligiously sold by some Swedes under ye name of church-wardens, to a powerful Quaker, who now plows and sows it, and disposes of it at his pleasure, but 'tis hoped his precarious title will be one day inquired into, and the Church restored to her rights again" This tract, which had been given to the Swedes' church by Armgard Pappegoya, could not be wrenched out of the strong grasp of David Lloyd, and notwithstanding the determined opposition of Jasper Yeates, he succeeded in having the land confirmed to him by the proprietary government

That the house at the southeast corner of Edgmont Avenue and Second Street was built by David Lloyd seems absolutely certain, since in his deed to William Pickles, May 4, 1703, it is specifically set out in the indenture that the house was at that time erected. Its appearance supports the statement, for its architecture marks it as contemporaneous with the Logan and Hoskins houses The executors of the estate of William Pickles sold the premises to John Baldwin, and the estate passing to Baldwin's grandchildren, John Baldwin and John Pierce, they sold the house to Jonas Preston The latter built a wharf on the creek, part of the stone placed there for that purpose being removed when the present Second Street bridge was erected. Adjoining the wharf by the creek-side he erected a stone store-house, which stood until after the middle of this century, when it had degenerated into a place to keep swine. After the death of Jonas Preston the premises were purchased by John Wall, a merchant of Philadelphia, who had married Hannah Grubb, widow of Richard Flower, of Chichester The purchaser never lived in the house, but after May 16, 1777, John Flower (Wall's step-son), on his marriage to Elizabeth Beethom, at the Chester Meeting, resided in the old building It is traditionally stated that Elizabeth Flower was so alarmed when the battle of Brandywine was fought—the noise of the distant cannonading could be heard in Chester—that she was taken ill, and so serious were the effects of her fright that she lingered a long time on the eve of dissolution, and died in October of the following year In 1782, John Wall sold the property to William Siddons, who kept a tavern there in 1778–79

A short time prior to the Revolutionary war Siddons was charged with the murder of a peddler of jewelry, who was found with his throat cut near Munday's Run, and the body robbed of all the money the dead man was supposed to have about him at the time of the homicide When the crime was perpetrated, and Siddons was under suspicion, a rhymster of rude verse of that day composed a ballad, beginning,—

"At Munday's Run, near Chester town,
Old Siddons knocked the peddler down,
And robbed him of his golden store,
And left him weltering in his gore"

Siddons was arrested, indicted, and tried, but on the hearing of the case he was enabled to prove a complete and uncontradicted *alibi*, while the prosecution was predicated purely on circumstantial evidence, which failed to connect the accused in any direct way with the commission of the crime The fact that he was charged by some of his neighbors with a felony of such hideous character embittered his entire after-life. William Siddons died June 22, 1820

The dwelling subsequently was purchased by Lewis Ladomus, and in 1869 was occupied by John Hanley, a well-known citizen of Chester, from whom the Hanley Fire Company derived its name "Jack" Hanley, in the latter ten years of his life, was totally blind He died in 1874 The old Lloyd house is now owned by Jonathan Pennell.

The Barber House.—David Lloyd, under date of June 14, 1699, conveyed a lot on the northeast corner of Second Street and Edgmont Avenue to Robert Barber, and he it was who erected the dwelling adjoining the present Edgmont House to the east. The house was an imposing one in its day. The pent-roof over the second-story window still remains, although the porch, which formerly projected out some distance on the sidewalk, has been removed. It has two doors: the eastern one leading into the parlor, and the western door into the hall-way, a room of the same size as the one on the opposite side, and in this apartment the staircase ascended to the rooms above. Back of this was the sitting-room, while in the rear of the parlor was a dining-room. The fireplaces and hearths in the hall-room and the parlor were laid in blue tiles, presenting scenes from scriptural history, and in the chambers above, on each side of the fireplaces, were large closets, similar to those in most dwellings built at that period.

John C. Beatty, of this city, states that in this house, in the northwest room on the first floor, the wound of Gen. Lafayette, after the battle of Brandywine, was dressed by Mrs. Mary (Gorman) Lyons.[1] In support of this statement he narrates the following incident, which he recalls as having occurred when Lafayette was in Chester in 1824. Mr. Beatty's grandfather, John Caldwell, who did good service for the Continental cause, took him (Beatty) to see the "national guest," and when his grandfather had shaken hands with Lafayette he said, "You don't remember me, general?" "Yes, I do," replied the Frenchman; "you're John Caldwell; I remember you very well; you stood by me when my wounded foot was dressed." That day Caldwell walked with his grandson to this house, and the former showed him (Beatty) where the table stood in the room on which Lafayette laid while his injuries were cared for. During the Revolution, Elisha Price owned and lived in this house. The house is now owned by Isaiah H. Mirkil.

The *Delaware County Republican* for Jan. 10, 1845, says that the citizens of Delaware County "tended upon and dressed the wounds of the beloved Lafayette, when he lay wounded in the Friends' Quaker meeting-house at Chester." John Hill Martin states,[2] "Gen. Lafayette rode on horseback to Chester from the battle-field at Brandywine, where he was wounded, but remained there only one night, in the old 'Ladomus House,' at the southeast corner of Third Street and Edgmont, now occupied by Bawer's clothing-store." At present a public-house—the Lafayette Hotel—is kept there.

The Morgan (Terrill) House (Market below Fourth Street).—The old building standing on the east side of Market Street, the second structure south of Fourth Street, was built by Evan Morgan. The land was part of the twenty acres patented May 31, 1686, to James Sandelands, the elder, and was conveyed by John Crosby and wife, Jan. 20, 1723, to Thomas Griffing, subject to a yearly quit-rent of one shilling. This John Crosby was a son of Richard, the first of that name who came to Pennsylvania after Penn acquired title to the province. Griffing sold the house and lot to Evan Morgan in 1725, and his son, John Morgan, in 1783, conveyed the premises to Jemima Dasey, widow of the Baptist clergyman at Marcus Hook, and her sister, Mary Linard. Mrs. Dasey and her maiden sister carried on a dry-goods and trimming-store there until October, 1809, when the house and lot was sold to Dr. Job H. Terrill. Some of the old people of Chester can recall Mary Linard as an elderly woman, lame, and hobbling along, leaning on a cane when walking. The property is now owned by Mrs. Emeline Deshong, to whom it descended from her father, Dr. Terrill.

The Caldwell Mansion.—The handsome dwelling on the west side of Edgmont Avenue, north of Twelfth Street, since it was modernized by Col. Samuel A. Dyer during his ownership of the property, is nevertheless an ancient building. The ground upon which it stands is part of a tract of one hundred and twenty acres which was patented April 2, 1688, to Eusta Anderson. June 21st of the same year Anderson conveyed it to Charles Pickering, who, on Oct. 13, 1688, conveyed the property to David Lloyd, and he in turn sold twenty acres of it, subject to a yearly rent of one silver shilling, to John Hoskins, the elder, who, dying seized of the estate, it passed by descent to his son, John Hoskins, the younger. The latter dying intestate, his widow, Ruth, and his son, Stephen Hoskins, and his daughter, Mary Hoskins, and her husband, John Mather, in 1733, released their interest in the premises to Joseph Hoskins, another son of John Hoskins, the younger, and he in turn, April 9, 1741, conveyed the land to Stephen Cole. This latter deed, in 1744, and under a power of sale in his will, his executors, April 17–18, 1746, conveyed the premises to John Caldwell, who, shortly after he acquired possession of the estate, built the mansion-house still standing. He was a native of Dublin, and is said to have been the son of an Irish nobleman. He came to this country early in the last century, and seems to have acquired considerable property. He died subsequent to June 5, 1772, and in his will, which bears that date, he devised his real estate to his two sons,—two shares to the eldest, and the other share to the youngest. After the death of their father John purchased the one-third interest of his brother, George, in the homestead. John, known to the last

[1] A letter written by Joseph Weaver, Jr., in 1843, alludes to the house where Lafayette's wound was dressed. The letter is as follows:

"CHESTER, DELAWARE COUNTY, April 3, 1843.

"HON. CALVIN BLYTHE.

"*Dear Sir*:—I take the freedom of recommending to your attention Mr. Crossman Lyons, of this place, as a suitable person for the situation of Collector of Customs at Marcus Hook. From a long acquaintance with Mr. Lyons I feel warranted in representing him as a man that will well and efficiently execute his duties.

"It may not be improper to add that Mr. Lyons is a son of a Revolutionary character who served his country during the whole of that War, in sustaining our Independence, and his mother was the lady who waited upon and dressed the wounds of Lafayette, at Mrs. Withey's Tavern (now the Columbia House) in Chester, after the battle of Brandywine.

"I am very respectfully yours truly,

"JOSEPH WEAVER, JR."

[2] History of Chester, p. 254.

generation as Squire Caldwell, was a carpenter and builder by trade, and was born and died in the old dwelling. He is said to have been a private in the Continental army during the Revolutionary war, and the musket he carried—one captured from the Hessians at Trenton—is now owned by James Black He is also said to have been a lieutenant in the American service, and fought against the Indians on the frontier, who were waging war on the colonists in the interest of the crown When the royal forces were in possession of Philadelphia, and the English squadron lay off Chester, the squire was much troubled with foraging parties from the fleet John Caldwell stood it for a time, but every fresh visit from the enemy aroused his indignation until he could remain quiet no longer, and in a small boat he rowed out to the flag-ship, demanding an interview with the admiral, Earl Richard Howe He was kindly received, and in the conference he informed the English commander that his men had taken from him all his pork, provisions, milk, and butter until his family had been left in want of the necessaries of life The admiral listened attentively, said that he would prevent any more depredations on the squire's property, and asked the latter to make out a bill for articles already taken, which was done, and the paymaster was ordered to discharge his claim immediately John Caldwell returned to his home, the unaccustomed clinking of broad gold pieces in his pocket making his heart lighter and mitigating his angry feelings until he almost wished the foraging parties would visit his farm once more, that a like cure for his injuries could be again prescribed by the British officer

Squire Caldwell acquired considerable estate He purchased and added to the homestead plot the triangular lot at the intersection of Edgmont and Providence Avenues, which was known in early times as "Hangman's Lot," because public executions had there formerly taken place The culprits were suspended from a wild cherry-tree, on one of the lower branches, which extended some distance almost at right angles to the trunk, and it is traditionally related in the Caldwell family that on one occasion from the windows of the mansion across the street the inmates of the old dwelling saw pendent from that fatal branch a man who was executed for stealing a lady's work-box, which stood temporarily on the sill of an open window, so that he could filch it without difficulty John Caldwell died Nov 24, 1834, intestate, and on Feb 23, 1835, Thomas Caldwell, his eldest son, elected to take the homestead at the valuation placed on it in proceedings in partition The latter was owner of the old house only for a brief season, for he died Aug 20, 1835, and the estate was held in common by his heirs until May 22, 1864, when it was purchased by Henry B Edwards In the spring of 1870, Col Samuel A Dyer became the owner of the property, and the ancient dwelling was modernized. In November, 1872, Col Dyer sold the property to A L Bonaffon It is now owned by Godfrey Keebler, of Philadelphia, and occupied by Rev Thomas McCauley, pastor of the Third Presbyterian Church

The Ashbridge House—The ancient dwelling standing on the east side of Edgmont Avenue, between Second and Graham Streets, is partly built on the site of the House of Defense The ground on which it stands was part of the estate of Jasper Yeates, who devised it to certain of his heirs, for July 13, 1728, George McCall and Ann, his wife (Jasper's eldest daughter), and John Yeates, by release, granted this house and other lots to George Ashbridge The latter was a Friend who as early as 1688 emigrated, as a young man, to Pennsylvania and settled near Chester Who it was built the house I fail to learn, but in all probability George McCall or John Yeates did, for the title to the ground was in these parties fully eight years after the death of Jasper Yeates, before they parted with the premises Ashbridge, by his will, March 1, 1747/8, devised the estate to his second son, George, who seems to have been an adroit politician, for, elected to the General Assembly in 1743, he managed to maintain the confidence of Friends (he being one of the society) until 1773 How for thirty consecutive years he contrived to avoid committing himself on many of the votes taken during the long French war, which appropriated men and money to carry on that struggle, is incomprehensible, but in the latter year the society "report they have taken an oppty with one of the representatives in Assembly and that he do not apprehend culpable" That he was active in the Assembly, and must have been a man of more than the general average out of which representatives are made, is evidenced by the perusal of the journal of Samuel Foulke[1] On the death of the second George Ashbridge the premises passed to his eldest son, George Ashbridge, the third of that name in the chain of title, who sold it, May 5, 1797, to Dorothy Smith and Zedekiah Wyatt Graham, sister and brother of Henry Hale Graham, as joint tenants Dorothy, who had married John Smith, of Lower Chichester, Twelfth month 4, 1783, was a widow at this time Zedekiah Graham was a wealthy bachelor, and the brother and sister lived together in this house Of the brother, Deborah Logan writes "He was a man of such integrity and worth that I have heard him characterized as an Israelite, indeed, in whom there was no guile" The affection between them was so marked that in his will he gave to her the income of his whole estate during life, while she devised to her brother one-third of her property absolutely Zedekiah Graham died of yellow fever in 1798, and his sister, who nursed him in his illness, was attacked by the scourge, and sent for her nephew, William Graham, who had abandoned his home and fled to the country

[1] *Penna Mag of Hist.*, vol v pp 64, 65, 68, 71

to escape the pestilence. It is related that the latter sat on his horse in the street while the nurse from the second-story window informed him as to the disposition his aunt wished to make of her estate; thus the will was written, attached to a string, and drawn up to the chamber of the dying woman, who refused to permit any of her kin to visit her, and thereby encounter the risk of infection. By her will, Nov. 17, 1798 (the whole title to the house having vested in her by survivorship), she devised it to her nephew and four nieces in equal parts. Three of the nieces and the nephew conveyed their interests to Catharine G., the fourth niece, and wife of Capt. Thomas Robinson, in October, 1812.

Thomas Robinson was a captain in the merchant service, but during the Tripolitan war a lieutenant under Commodore Preble when that officer, in command of the American squadron, bombarded Tripoli, June 21, 1804. Robinson was in charge of one of the bombards—vessels carrying mortars—on that occasion; the shrouds of his vessel were shot away, and her hull so shattered that it was with the utmost difficulty she could be kept above water. During the war of 1812 he was a volunteer lieutenant in the navy, and was on board the frigate "President" when the latter vessel was captured. As will be remembered, Commodore Decatur, in command of the "President," went to sea from New York, Jan. 14, 1815, and at daylight the following morning the American officer discovered that the English squadron, comprising the seventy-gun ship "Majestic," the fifty-gun frigates "Endymion," "Pomona," and "Tenedos," were in chase of the vessel. By noon Decatur found that he was outsailing all of the enemy's ships except the "Endymion," which vessel had steadily gained on him, until, at five o'clock in the evening, that frigate had obtained a position on his starboard quarter, and opened a destructive fire on the sails and rigging of his vessel. Decatur was compelled to bear up and engage the enemy, in the hope of disabling her before the remaining vessels could arrive to her assistance. A warm action of two hours and a half followed, which resulted in the British frigate dropping astern, her guns silenced, and her masts gone by the board. During the latter part of the battle with the "Endymion" Robinson had charge of the trumpet. It is stated that the first, fourth, and fifth lieutenants on the "President" were killed or wounded, and Decatur called for Lieut. Gallagher to take the trumpet, but Robinson, "hearing the hail, came up from the gun-deck," whereupon Decatur said, "Take the trumpet, sir;" and Robinson took command of the deck. The American frigate made sail and attempted to escape, but the English squadron had come within gunshot of the "President" while that vessel was engaged in the encounter with the "Endymion," and being crippled by the heavy fire she had sustained, Decatur was compelled to strike his flag to the British frigates "Tenedos" and "Pomona."

Capt. Robinson, after his discharge as a prisoner of war (for the naval action was fought after the treaty of peace had been signed), returned to the merchant service, but the news of the loss of the American packet-ship "Albion" on the coast of Ireland, April 21, 1822, as well as the explosion of the steamboat "Etna," in New York harbor, May 15, 1824, under his command, and the frightful loss of life on those occasions, so impressed Robinson with the responsibility appertaining to the office of captain of a vessel that he refused ever again to take command of a ship.

Catharine G. Robinson, his wife, died Jan. 24, 1836, and by her will, Feb. 27, 1834, devised the house to her daughter, Sarah P. Coombe. The latter lived in the old house for many years, and vacating it, she rented the Coombe property. At her death, March 5, 1865, the estate became vested in her heirs, who still retain the ancient dwelling.

Lamokin Hall.—The original Salkeld house, built about 1708 by John Salkeld, Sr., as it now stands in the way of Norris Street, between Third Street and the Philadelphia, Wilmington and Baltimore Railroad, must shortly be removed to make room for improvements on that thoroughfare. During the last half-century it was used as the tenant-house on the Kenilworth estate after John W. Ashmead built the large mansion in 1838 (since torn down), and also by Dr. William Young, who purchased the estate in 1849. The Perkins house, or, as it was known to a past generation, "Lamokin Hall," was erected many years afterwards by John Salkeld, a son of the noted original emigrant of that name.

John Bristow, to whom a large tract of land was granted by patent from the proprietary, died seized of the estate, and his son, John, an edge-tool maker, Feb. 25, 1702/3, conveyed to Henry Wooley a goodly number of these acres. The latter in turn, Jan. 27, 1706/7, conveyed the premises to John Salkeld, a man of means and education, whose ready wit and quickness in repartee made him noted in his generation, and many of his telling rejoinders are recounted even to this day. Salkeld visited this country in 1700, before he settled permanently here, and on the 9th of Seventh month, 1705, he and his wife, Agnes (Powley), sailed for Philadelphia. In the following year he purchased the property mentioned and came to this vicinity to reside. He was an effective preacher, and made many religious visits to neighboring meetings in Pennsylvania, New Jersey, and Delaware, and several times to New England, Long Island, and on one occasion to Great Britain and the West Indies. He, as I have already stated, was a natural humorist, and a few of the stories which have descended to our own time will repay narrating.

One day Salkeld was wearing a new hat that had a button and loop, then quite fashionable, and he was remonstrated with by a Friend for adhering to the usages and customs of the world. John tore off the offending part of his apparel, remarking, "If my friend's religion consists of a button and a loop I would not give a button and a loop for it." On another occasion, when at a meeting of Friends, the speaker who was addressing the audience being so tedious that many in the assembly were almost asleep, Salkeld sprang to his feet, exclaiming, "Fire! fire!" Every one was awake immediately, and many put the query, "Where?" "In hell!" responded John, "to burn up the drowsy and unconverted." After he returned from a religious journey to New Jersey, he said, "I have breakfasted with the Ladds, dined with the Lords, and slept with the Hoggs," the names of the families that entertained him. One time as he walked from his corn-field, a Friend by the name of Cloud passing by, said, "John, thee will have a good crop of corn." Salkeld afterwards relating the circumstance, stated that he heard a voice coming out of a Cloud, saying, "John, thee will have a good crop of corn." He rode at one time a horse with a blaze in its face, and a neighbor who thought to be merry with him, said, "John, thy horse looks pale in the face." "Yes, he does," he replied; "and if thee had looked as long through a halter as he has, thee would look pale in the face too."

He was personally about medium size, but his wife, Agnes, was very tall and muscular, hence her descendants, who are all noticeably tall, inherit this characteristic from her. John Salkeld died Sept. 20, 1739, and by will devised the farm of one hundred acres, on which the house stood, to his son, David Salkeld, and left the plot of ground whereon Lamokin Hall was subsequently built to his wife, Agnes, and she, by will Seventh month 11, 1748, devised the estate to John Salkeld, the younger. The latter, in 1731, had married Elizabeth Worrall, who became the mother of thirteen children. John Salkeld, the younger, by will Dec. 13, 1776, devised his real estate to his eight children (the others had died in childhood) in equal parts, his whole estate, however, being charged with his wife's support. In the distribution of the property the land under consideration was allotted to his son, Peter, who built the western end of Lamokin Hall. Dec. 7, 1789, he sold the property to Jacob Peterson. The latter conveyed it to James Withey, who made the addition to the eastern end of the old house about 1796.

James Withey having become insolvent the property was sold by Sheriff Fairlamb, April 12, 1819, to Charles Justice and William Graham. The purchasers interchanged deeds, dated Feb. 27, 1821, by which Charles Justice acquired absolute title to the land south of the Post road, and William Graham that north of the same highway. The latter having trust-money belonging to his sisters in his hands at the time of his death, Lamokin Hall was in the distribution of his estate transferred to his sister, Henrietta, who had married Richard Flower.

John W. Ashmead, who had built the house on the farm adjoining, after the death of his father-in-law, Mr. Flower, purchased the estate June 3, 1844, from the Hon. Edward Darlington, trustee to sell the property, for the purpose solely of adding a trifle over an acre to the lawn of his dwelling, so that his house should be located in the centre of the lawn. After thoroughly repairing Lamokin Hall he sold it Sept. 5, 1846, to Abram R. Perkins for six thousand dollars. The latter had been a successful merchant in Philadelphia, but his purchase of the property at that price, thirty-six years ago, was, perhaps, in the shaping of events, one of the most fortunate transactions in his business career, for the premises in that period have so increased in value that it alone has made his estate worth thirty times what it originally cost him.

Charles Justice, on his portion of the old Withey estate, which extended from about the present Ulrich Street on the east to Lamokin Run on the west, and from the Post road to the river, built (in 1828) the large brick dwelling, still standing, on Second Street east of Pennell Street, the brick used being made on the farm, and burned in a damp kiln. The property was subsequently purchased by Edmund Pennell, and the dwelling is still called the Pennell house.

The Thomas Barton House.—John Wade, of Essex House, on July 27–28, 1736, conveyed to Thomas Barton a tract of land, which, from the peculiar bend in Chester Creek, its eastern boundary was known as the "Horseshoe." The plot contained a trifle over seventy-one acres, and was sold subject to the payment of ten shillings annually forever towards the support of a free school in Philadelphia. In September of the same year John Wade conveyed twenty-one and a half acres to Thomas Barton, in addition to those already purchased, subject to two shillings yearly forever, for the like purpose, which charge on the land had been created by the will of Robert Wade. Subsequently the trustees of the school in Philadelphia accepted a ground-rent on Arch Street in that city, and discharged the Wade estate from the payment of the annual rent mentioned.

Thomas Barton, who was an Irishman, is said to have been a sea captain, and, retiring from that avocation, he settled in Chester, where he married, and became the ancestor of the Barton family of Delaware County. He had, however, between the date of the purchase of this land and the conveyance of the estate to Jonas Preston, been engaged in coach-making, for in the deed to the latter, Feb. 19, 1759, the grantors are described as "*Thomas Barton, coach-maker, and Susanna, his wife*," and in referring to the Wade deeds, it is stated "the said Thomas Barton has since [1736] erected a brick messuage or tenement thereon." This house is still standing in the rear of Joshua P. Eyre's mansion on Seventh Street.

The Sandelands House.—The ancient dwelling standing on the west side of Edgmont Avenue, interposing itself directly in the way of the extension of Fourth Street to Chester Creek, was built by Jonas Sandelands, the second son of James Sandelands, the elder, previous to Aug 21, 1732, for at that date Arthur Shields and Mary, his wife, as the administrators of Sandelands' estate (his widow, Mary, having married Shields) conveyed the premises as a messuage and lot to Jacob Howell, a tanner by occupation, who, on May 1, 1733, conveyed the messuage and a portion of the land to John Wharton, a saddler, of Chester, who subsequently removed to Philadelphia, having first sold, July 20, 1749, the premises to William Pennell The latter, by will, Twelfth month 20, 1756, devised the property to his three sons,—James, Robert, and William Robert and William Pennell, Dec 20, 1762, transferred their interests to their brother, James The latter, by will, Dec 22, 1763, devised it to his son, Thomas, who died unmarried and without issue, and his title vested in his four brothers,—William, James, Nathan, and Jonathan The three first named, April 9, 1782, conveyed their interests to Jonathan Pennell, the grandfather of the present owner

Jonathan Pennell was a blacksmith, and at the time he purchased his brothers' interest did not reside in the house, which had been used as a hospital and barracks by the American troops during the Revolutionary war, and was then in a dilapidated condition

It is related that when he first proposed to locate here and purchase from the other heirs the entire interest in the property, he called on Henry Hale Graham, and desired his opinion as to his prospects of success in his avocation at Chester The latter, in response, stated that he could not answer with any degree of certainty, he simply knew that all blacksmiths in the town, theretofore, had grown so desperately poor by crooking their little fingers that in a short time they could not keep iron cold In other words, that intemperance had so reduced them that they could keep no stock in their shops, but were compelled to part with it to satisfy the cravings of their appetites However, Pennell must have impressed Graham favorably, for he loaned him two hundred and fifty pounds, and stipulated that he would receive the principal at any time in sums of ten pounds So industriously and energetically did Pennell labor that he succeeded far beyond his expectations He soon began making payments as designated, and so often did he present himself with the stipulated amount of ten pounds in liquidation of the gross sum that one day, when he came on that errand, Graham, after he receipted for the money, said, "Good gracious, man, where do you get all this money?" "I hammer it out of cold iron," was the reply of Pennell, who had not forgotten his first interview with the judge He ultimately acquired considerable means, and became the owner of much real estate Jonathan Pennell devised the house and lot to his son, Edmund, and the latter, Feb 3, 1877, conveyed it to his son, Jonathan Pennell, who resides therein

Licensed Houses in Chester—The Boar's Head Inn, heretofore mentioned as the noted public-house where Penn spent the winter of 1682–83, was early in the eighteenth century kept by Jonathan Ogden, until 1727, when James Trego made application for the license, and David Lloyd, chief justice of the province, recommended him in a letter to the justice by a remonstrance against another applicant "It is my opinion," he says, "that one will be sufficient on that side of the Creek to answer the true end of Inn-keeping, And If we had less on this side [the east] the Creek It would be much better" On Aug 30, 1732, William Robinson had the license, but at the August court, 1734, it was denied to him because he then "Stands Indicted at New Castle for an Assault" On the 28th of the same month he boldly states that "being informed the justices would not allow him a recommendation as usual understand he is accused of some misdemeanor, but wishes to be heard face to face by his accuser," but without success William Weaver, on May 27, 1735, informed the court that he "hath Taken to ffarm the house, with the appurtenances, Commonly Called and known by the name of the Spread Eagle Tavern, where William Robinson lately Dwelt, in the Township of Chester," which indicates that the old house had changed its name In 1738, Abraham Taylor was the landlord, and in 1741–42 the petition of William Hays states that for some years past he had license at the "Spread Eagle," after which date the old inn passes out of the public records

The Black Bear Inn—The hipped-roof house at the northeast corner of Third and Penn Streets was erected early in the last century, for in the will of John Salkeld, Sr, Feb 17, 1733/4, five years before his death, he devised the premises to his son, Thomas, and designated it as "the house and lot wherein my son-in-law, Anthony Shaw, now dwells" How long Shaw lived there after the date mentioned I have not learned, but John Salkeld, Jr, on Aug 30, 1737, on ' Westerly side of Chester Creek, on great road to New Castle," presented his petition to court stating that he wished to keep "a publick house," and being a maltster by trade, desired license to sell "Beer and Syder" In 1746 it was kept as a public-house by John Salkeld, the younger, for in that year he, among other innkeepers, presented a petition to the Legislature, asking compensation for the "diet of Capt. Shannon's company of soldiers," quartered here during the early part of the French war At this time he was a tenant of his brother, Thomas, for the latter in his will, June 21, 1749, after making specific devises of other lands, gave the residue of his estate to his brother, John Salkeld The latter by his will, Dec 14, 1775, gave an eighth part of his estate, which was large, to his daughter Sarah He died early in 1776, for his will was probated January 29th of the same year In the distribution of her father's estate, the Black Bear Inn became her portion Sarah

Salkeld had married George Gill, an Englishman, several years before her father's death, for in the latter's will he leaves ten pounds to his grandson, John Gill, and in all probability she was then landlady. George Gill was an outspoken Tory in the Revolutionary struggle, and so ardent was he in the defense of the English army and ministry that after the battle of Brandywine, at the time the residents of Chester were smarting under the outrages perpetrated on them by the royal troops, he was compelled to leave this neighborhood when the enemy abandoned Philadelphia, and was proclaimed a traitor to the colonies. When the British forces evacuated New York, at the close of the war, Gill followed them to Halifax. Subsequently he returned to Chester, was arrested, and thrown into prison, but was discharged therefrom by the act of Assembly, which, under certain conditions, allowed free pardon to proclaimed traitors to the united colonies. The public-house was kept from 1785 to 1789 by William Hazelwood, and known as "The Ship in Distress." The dwelling subsequently became the property of Hon. Frederick J. Hinkson, and is now owned by his sons,—Henry and Frederick J. Hinkson, Jr.

The Blue Ball Inn.—The old dwelling at the northeast corner of Second and Market Streets was erected by Francis Richardson between the years 1765 and 1770. The land whereon it stands was devised to him in 1760 by Grace Lloyd. At the time he began the erection of this house Richardson believed he was on the high road to great business prosperity, but before he had finished it he became financially embarrassed, owing to mistaken efforts to advance Chester to the front rank as a commercial rival of Philadelphia. There were holes still in the brick walls until 1883, when the dwelling was repaired and modernized, where, when the house was building, the timbers were inserted on which rested the boards of the scaffolding. It is said by Martin that in the days before the Mechanics' Lien law, when masons were not paid for their work, these holes were always left in the wall to indicate to their fellow-craftsmen that default had been made in that respect, and no mason would fill them in until the builders' claims had been discharged.

When the house was first built it was a noted inn, and from its peculiar sign—a blue ball suspended from the end of a pole or staff, which projected from a hole in the wall, in the gable-end on Market Street—it was known as "The Blue Ball Inn." Its then landlord was Samuel Fairlamb, who had married Hannah, the daughter of Francis Richardson. It was one of the dwellings struck by the balls from the English vessel of war which opened fire on the town in 1777, as narrated elsewhere, and the shot is said to have passed directly through one of the rooms in the second story.

The City Hotel.—On the 10th of December, 1700, James Sandelands, the younger, conveyed the land on the northwest corner of Third Street and Edgmont Avenue, on which this building was afterwards erected, to David Roberts, and on May 26, 1714, Jonas Sandelands, the brother of James, and Mary, his wife, confirmed the tract of ground to Roberts, reserving, however, a yearly ground-rent of three shillings to his heirs. I believe the building was erected by David Roberts shortly after his purchase from James Sandelands. He received license there in 1717. In 1728, David Roberts sold the property to Ruth Hoskins, widow of Sheriff John Hoskins. On March 5-6, 1738, Ruth Hoskins conveyed the property to her son-in-law, John Mather. He was a prominent citizen, an attorney with a large practice, and a justice of the peace, an important dignitary in those days. John Mather leased the premises to James Mather, perhaps his brother, since John Mather named his only son, James, probably for the person mentioned. That James Mather kept the tavern here in 1746 we know, for he was one of the number of innkeepers who petitioned the Legislature for payment of certain claims, more fully referred to in the account of the Black Bear Inn, and in the journal of William Black, who was the notary of the commissioners appointed by Governor Gooch, of Virginia, to unite with those from the colonies of Pennsylvania and Maryland to treat with the Iroquois or Six Nations of Indians in reference to the land west of the Alleghany Mountains. In describing the journey of the commissioners from Virginia and Maryland to Philadelphia, under date of Saturday, May 25, 1744, he records,—

> "Nine miles from Wilmington, and at the line dividing New Castle and Chester counties, were waiting the High Sheriff, Coroner and under Sheriff of Chester county, who conducted us to Chester Town, six miles further, where we arrived a few minutes before nine at night, and put up at Mr. James Mathew, (Mather) the most considerable house in the town; most of the company being very much fatigued with the day's ride being very warm, they inclin'd for beds soon after they alighted, and tho' for my part I was not very much tir'd, yet I agreed to hug the pillow with the rest."

The next entry in his journal, doubtless after refreshing slumber, is headed "Chester in Pennsylvania, Sunday, the 26," and he records his doings in, and impression of, Chester, of that day, thus:

> "This morning, by the time the sun return'd to Enlighten My Bed Chamber, I got up with a Design to take a view of the town. It is not so large as Wilmington; neither are the Buildings so large in General, the Town stands on a Mouth of a Creek of the same name, running out the Delaware and has a very large wooden Bridge over it, in the middle of the Town, the Delaware is reckon'd three miles over at this place, and is a very good Road for Shipping; the Court House and Prison is two tolerable large Buildings of Stone, there are in the Town a Church dedicated to St. Paul, the Congregation are after the manner of the Church of England; A Quaker Meeting and a Sweed's '(?)' Church; about 10 of the Clock, forenoon, Comm'rs and us of their Leeve went to St. Paul's; where we heard a Sermon Preach'd by the Reverend Mr. Backhouse, on the 16th Chapt. of St. Luke, 30 & 31st Verses, from this some of us paid a Visit to the Friends' who were then in Meeting, but as it happened to be a Silent One, after we had sat about 15 min., they Shook hands and we parted, from this Return'd to our Inn, where we had a very good Dinner, and about 4 in the Evening Set out for Philadelphia, Accompanied by the Shffs, Coroner, and several Gentlemen of the Town, past thro' Darby a Town 7 miles from Chester, Standing on a creek of the same name and at a Stone Bridge about half a mile fur-

ther, was met by the Sheriff, Coroner, and Sub Sheriff of Philadelphia County Here the Company from Chester took their leave of Us and return'd "[1]

James Mather subsequently purchased the lot on which National Hall was erected, and there in an old stone house for many years kept a public-house It is so described in the deed from Mary Morris to Jonas Eyre

Mary Hoskins, who had married John Mather, was a most admirable wife and mother Her careful training of her daughters is evidenced by the fact that both of them became the wives of distinguished men, and are alluded to by writers of acknowledged position on several occasions for their personal excellence and womanly worth Ruth Mather, to whom the property was devised by her grandmother, married Charles Thomson, one of the most noted men in our national annals He was a native of Ireland, and during all the difficulties with the mother-country was an ardent Whig He was the first secretary of the Continental Congress of 1774, and continued in that office during the long struggle of the Revolution In recognition of the faithful discharge of his duties, he was chosen to bear to Washington the intelligence of the latter's nomination to the Presidency of the United States Of him John Adams, in his diary, writes, "Charles Thomson is the Sam Adams of Philadelphia, the life of the cause of liberty" He retired from public office, and during his latter days translated the Septuagint which was published in four volumes in 1808 He died in Lower Merion, Montgomery Co, in 1824, in his ninety-fifth year

Ruth Thomson died without children surviving her John Mather, by his will, dated May 26, 1768, devised the premises to his daughter, Ruth, and his son-in-law, Charles Thomson, and in the event of the death of Ruth without children, then to his granddaughter, Mary Jackson Jane Jackson and Ruth Thomson were named as executors Jane alone took out letters testamentary Charles Thomson, after the death of Ruth, his wife, without children, March 5, 1785, released to Mary Jackson all his right and title in the premises

A description of the old tavern is furnished in the following advertisement, which was published in the *Pennsylvania Gazette* in the early part of that year

"TO BE SOLD—A COMMODIOUS TAVERN IN THE BOROUGH of Chester, now in the tenure of Mr Peter Salkend,—the house is three stories high, has four rooms on each floor,—large kitchen adjoining, and a well of excellent water at the kitchen door, the stabling is good, can contain upwards of forty horses, and has room above for six tons of hay, there are a large yard and garden belonging to the house, also five acres of highly improved pastures This house has been a well accustomed Inn for upwards of forty years past For terms apply to the subscriber in Philadelphia

"DAVID JACKSON

"January 19, 1785

"N B.—Depreciation certificates of the officers and soldiers of the Pennsylvania line, as also final settlements of the said line, at their current value, will be taken in part payment for the above premises"

[1] *Penna Mag of Hist.*, vol i p 240 I have stated in "Historical Sketch of Chester" that James Mather was landlord of the Lafayette House This, I find, from examination of authorities of which I had then no knowledge, is an error.

On March 5, 1785, Mary Jackson conveyed the hotel to Maj John Harper, who gave it the name of "The Ship George Washington" Harper was the landlord of this tavern when the removal of the county-seat to West Chester was the important topic of consideration in Chester County, and the part he took in that struggle has already been mentioned in this work Harper having removed to West Chester, he made default in the payment of the interest on the mortgage Suit was brought by the executor of Mary Jackson, deceased, and on Aug 1, 1788, Ezekiel Leonard, sheriff, deeded the tavern and lot to her executor, Dr David Jackson, of Philadelphia, and the latter conveyed it, Jan 14, 1793, to Matthias Kerlin, Jr, of Trenton, N J, who was the brother of William Kerlin, the owner and host of Washington House, and subsequently returned to Delaware County to reside

On March 30th of the same year, Kerlin sold the tavern to William Pierce, of Lower Chichester, who devised the estate to his widow, Mary She married David Coates, of Philadelphia, and the latter and his wife conveyed the property, Feb 27, 1802, to Abraham Lee, of Saint George's Hundred, Del, and he, in turn, March 22, 1803, sold the property to Edward Engle, who kept the hotel until he died (about 1810), and his widow, Mary Engle, continued the business until 1833, when she retired and leased the premises to John J Thurlow The ancient hostelry under Mrs. Engle's supervision was the fashionable and popular hotel of the borough In 1824, when Gen Lafayette was the guest of Chester, the First City Troop of Philadelphia was quartered at her house, then known as the Eagle Tavern, for in a description of a journey from old Ireland to Chester, written in verse by Philip Sexton, then living at Squire Eyre's, on Edgmont Avenue, during the early part of this century, he referred to this hotel thus

"If you stand on the bridge
And look to the east,
You'll there see an eagle,
As big as a beast

"Call at this tavern
Without any dread,
You'll there get chicken,
Good mutton, and bread"

Mrs Engle was the mother of the late Rear Admiral Frederick Engle, who died in 1866, and of Capt. Isaac E Engle, of the merchant service, who died in 1844 Her daughter, Mary, married the late Hon Samuel Edwards, a member of the bar and representative in Congress from this district from 1819–21, and again from 1825–27, who died, leaving surviving him his son, Henry B Edwards, Esq, a member of the bar, a leading citizen of Chester, and a daughter, Mary Engle Edwards, who intermarried with Edward Fitzgerald Beale, at that time lieutenant in the navy, and noted for his celebrated ride across Mexico with dispatches from Commodore Stockton during our war with that country, subsequently prominent as superintendent of

Indian affairs and in exploring expeditions, constructing public highways, and in surveys for projected railroads In 1860 he was appointed surveyor-general of California, and under Gen Grant's second administration was United States Minister to Austria Gen Beale is one of the largest land-owners in the world, his estate in California comprising two hundred thousand acres of land

Mary Engle's daughter, Abby, married John Kerlin, Esq , a member of the Delaware County bar, and for many years president of the Bank of Delaware County Her son, Frederick E Kerlin, died in California more than twenty years ago, and the other son, Capt Charles Kerlin, a well-known merchant captain, now retired from service, lives in New Jersey The latter in May, 1853, brought to Chester the first Chinese ever known to have been in that town His strange dress, and "tail" three feet in length, drew a large crowd of boys together, who followed him whenever he appeared in the streets

Mrs Engle was succeeded in business by John J Thurlow, about 1828 I quote from John Hill Martin the following graphic description of the old hotel in its palmiest days as a stopping-place for one of the lines of stages which then passed through Chester for Baltimore, Washington, and the South He says,—

"How well I remember 'Thurlow's,' in the days of its busy greatness' well I remember how, when I was a boy, I lingered near its hospitable doors to see the handsome horses of the Reeside, Stockton & Stokes, Murdeck & Sharp, and Janvier's rival lines of stage coaches changed , the smoking steeds detached by active hostlers, and the new relay of well groomed horses substituted, and saw the 'Stage driver,' an important man in those days, with his great coat of many capes and long whip , the well dressed travelers sauntering about talking and smoking after their meal, waiting for the stage Oft I have peeped into the small, clean bar-room, in the centre of which stood a large coal stove (in winter) in a large sand box, that served as a huge spittoon In one corner of the room stood a semi-circular bar, with its red railings reaching to the ceiling, into whose diminutive precincts the jolly landlady could scarcely get her buxom person, while her husband with his velveteen shooting coat, with its large buttons and its many pockets, excited my intense admiration At his heels there were always two or three handsome setter dogs, of the finest breed and well trained Sometimes I got a glimpse of the south-west room This was the parlor, back of it was a room where travelers wrote their letters, and back of the bar was a cozy little room, mine hostess' sanctum, into which only special friends were admitted All these are now one large American bar-room

"In reading accounts of the old English inns of coaching days, my mind involuntarily reverts to 'Thurlow's,' for there on the walls were hanging the quaint old coaching and hunting prints imported from England, and around the house was 'Boots,' and the 'Hostler,' and 'the pretty waiting-maid with rosy cheeks,' all from old England The horses are all hitched, the passengers are 'all aboard,' the driver has taken his seat (the guard is blowing his horn having taken one inside), is gathering up his many reins , now he feels for his whip, flourishes it over his four-in-hand, making a graceful curve with its lash, taking care not to touch his horses, but does it with a report like a rifle shot, the hostlers jump aside, and with a bound and a rush, the coach is off for Washington or Philadelphia, carrying perchance within it Clay, Webster, or Calhoun And of a winter's evening when I have stolen out from home, I have passed the 'Tavern,' and seen seated around its cheerful fire the magnates of the town, telling stories of other days (as I now could tell their names) And sometimes peeping through the green blinds, I have seen a quiet game of whist going on , perchance it was 'all fours,' or else a game of checkers or dominoes "[1]

Mr. Thurlow retired from business about 1840, and was succeeded by Maurice W Deshong, who kept the house for a few years, and was followed by Maj Samuel A. Price, who continued the business until 1853, when the late George Wilson became the host After a few years Mr Wilson retired, and was in turn succeeded by Lewis A Sweetwood The death of Mrs Mary Engle, in 1870, at the advanced age of ninety-four years, compelled a sale of the hotel and other property, by order of Orphans' Court, to settle her estate, and in that year William Ward, as trustee to make the sale, conveyed the hotel property to Jonathan Pennell, who, in turn, the same year, sold the premises to Paul Klotz, the present owner The latter has made important additions and improvements to the eastern end of the ancient building

The Washington House.—This ancient hostelry was erected on a part of the twenty acres which by patent dated May 31, 1686, the commissioner for William Penn conveyed to James Sandelands. In 1720, Sandelands sold the land to John Wright, he in turn conveyed it to William Pennell, he to James Trego, who died the owner of the ground In 1746, Aubrey Bevan purchased the lot, which had been used to pasture cattle, from the widow and son of Trego In the following year Aubrey Bevan erected the present hotel building and gave it the title "Pennsylvania Arms," as will be seen by an inspection of his will He was an active and leading citizen of Chester, and the structure, considering the time when it was built, evidences fully the progressive spirit which controlled his efforts Aubrey Bevan died in 1761, and by will devised this property to his daughter, Mary , she, together with her husband, William Forbes, by deed dated April 1, 1772, conveyed the estate to William Kerlin, a wealthy man, as wealth was then regarded, and a fervent Whig during the Revolutionary struggle

After the evacuation of Philadelphia by the British army, Kerlin named his hostelry "The Washington House," a name it has been continuously known by to this day Gen Washington often, in passing through Chester on his way to and from Mount Vernon to the seat of government in New York and Philadelphia, stopped at this hotel, and on those occasions a certain room, the best in the house, was assigned to his use The ancient mahogany chairs which stood in the room occupied by the first President during these visits are still preserved among the descendants of William Kerlin He took an active part in the discussion from 1780 to 1786 respecting the proposed removal of the county-seat to West Chester, and after the county-seat had been finally removed from Chester he labored energetically to bring about the formation of the present county of Delaware Kerlin did not remain mine host of the Washington House until his death, for by his will, proved April 29, 1805, he alluded, in his devise to his

[1] History of Chester, p. 262

daughter, Sarah Piper, to "the tavern house" being at that time "in the tenure of Isaac Tucker."

Maj. Joseph Piper, who held a position in the Philadelphia custom-house, under Gen. Steele, the then collector, after the death of his father-in-law resigned his office, removed to Chester, and kept the Washington House, owned by his wife, until his death, in 1827. It is related that Maj. Piper, being in Chester, saw Sarah Odenheimer,—formerly Sarah Kerlin, —a well-formed, blooming widow, on horseback, and was so impressed with her appearance that he wooed, won, and wedded her for his wife. After his death his widow continued the business at the hotel for several years, but ultimately becoming weary of it, she leased the premises to Evan S. Way, who had formerly kept a tavern in Nether Providence. He was a conspicuous man in the military affairs of the county a half-century ago, an officer in the Delaware County troop, and kept the hotel until he was elected sheriff, in 1837. The house was then rented to Maj. Samuel A. Price. He was a genial gentleman, who is yet remembered by many of our old residents, an earnest politician, and in 1834 was elected sheriff of the county. In early life he was noted for his manly beauty. An interesting item respecting the old hostelry during Maj. Price's occupancy was related in *The Delaware County Advocate* several years ago. The article stated that Gen. Harrison, in 1840, after he had received the Whig nomination for the Presidency, was returning from Washington, accompanied by a number of gentlemen from New York, stopped for dinner at the Washington House, and while there received the congratulations of the citizens of Chester. After dinner had been served the cloth was drawn, wine, as usual on such occasions, was placed on the table, and several toasts were drunk. It was observed that Harrison drank water, and being thereupon pressed to take wine, he rose and said, "Gentlemen, I have refused twice to partake of the wine cup; that should have been sufficient; though you press the cup to my lips, not a drop shall pass their portals. I made a resolve when I started in life that I would avoid strong drink, and I have never broken it. I am one of a class of seventeen young men who graduated, and the other sixteen fill drunkards' graves, all through the habit of social wine-drinking. I owe all my health, happiness, and prosperity to that resolution. Will you urge me now?"

The circumstance and remarks made by Harrison were related by one of the gentlemen present nearly forty years afterwards, hence the language used on that occasion may not be accurately reported, although the substance is doubtless correctly rendered.

Sarah Piper, by her will, proved Sept. 13, 1841, directed that "the tavern-house and thereto belonging, be sold within one year after my decease." In compliance with that request, although there was a longer interval than one year, her executors sold, April 2, 1844, the premises to Henry L. Powell, who in turn, October 11th of the same year, conveyed it to Edward E. Flavill. Mr. Flavill conducted the hotel as a temperance house, and Samuel West, an earnest temperance advocate, employed Edward Hicks, a Quaker artist, to paint a swinging sign,—one side presenting a delineation of Penn's landing at Chester, and the other Penn's treaty (?) with the Indians,—which he presented to the landlord. This old sign, still in good preservation, is owned by the present proprietor of the Washington House, Henry Abbott. The business proving unremunerative, Flavill sold the property, Jan. 1, 1849, to Thomas Clyde. Mr. Clyde had formerly kept an extensive country store at the northeast corner of Market Square, the building now owned and occupied by John C. Williams, and the eating-house of Mr. Dixon, adjoining, having been erected by him for his dwelling and store. He was also largely interested in quarries on Ridley Creek. Mr. Clyde continued the hotel as a temperance house with indifferent success for over nine years, when he conveyed the property, April 12, 1856, to John G. Dyer. Mr. Dyer had formerly been a clerk in the store of the late Joshua P. Eyre, and subsequently had carried on the dry-goods and grocery business in Philadelphia, Chester, and Rockdale, was customs-officer at the Lazaretto, and was connected with the late James Campbell in the manufacture of cotton goods at Leiperville. He was a man of fine conversational powers, possessing a ready, copious vocabulary and pleasing address, which particularly fitted him for the business of keeping a hotel. He died Oct. 26, 1881. In 1868, John G. Dyer conveyed the estate to Samuel A. Dyer, and he, June 1, 1871, sold it to Henry Abbott, who still owns the property, and is the popular host of the Washington House at this time. In 1883, Henry Abbott, Jr., at an outlay of many thousand dollars modernized the old structure internally, and made extensive additions in the rear of the building, preserving, however, its time-honored appearance on Market Street.

The Columbia House.—The land on which this ancient building stands was included in the patent dated May 31, 1686, whereby the commissioners of William Penn conveyed to James Sandelands, the elder, in fee, twenty acres of ground in Chester. The land descended to Jonas Sandelands in the distribution of his father's estate. Jonas Sandelands died subsequent to 1721, for at that time he held the office of coroner of Chester County, and his widow, Mary, married before 1731, Arthur Shields. Aug. 31, 1732, Arthur Shields and Mary, his wife, the administrators of Jonas Sandelands' estate, conveyed a tract of land containing over two acres to William Trehorn, subject to a yearly ground-rent of five shillings, to be paid to the heirs of Jonas Sandelands. Trehorn and Catharine, his wife, sold the land Nov. 14, 1733, to Richard Barry, who built the present building previous to Dec. 7, 1736, and lived therein, for at the last-mentioned date he mortgaged the premises, and it is stated in that instrument that he had "erected a new brick messuage upon the lot." "Barry made Considerable preparation to follow the Employment of a Distiller of Liquors." In February, 1738–39, he asked the court for a license at this house, but he failed to obtain the assent of the justices. In 1746, John Hanly, who had purchased the estate, procured the judges' favor, and continued annually to receive it until 1770, when he died, although after the year 1764 he had removed to the house he owned at the northwest corner of Market and Fifth Streets, which then stood on part of the ground where Dr. Grey's residence was in recent years. The Columbia House (in 1764) was rented by John Withy, a retired English army officer, and he having died in 1765, the following year his widow, Mary, procured the license. Mrs. Withy was a pensioner of the British government for sixty pounds per annum. On July 18, 1771, she purchased the property, and during the time she was hostess the inn was reported to be the best-kept tavern in America, and as such is frequently referred to in publications of that day. This reputation brought to her house numbers of prominent personages when journeying between the seat of government and points south of Chester. Mrs. Withy subsequent to the Revolution retired from the business and removed to Lamokin farm. Her son, Samuel, maintained the most aristocratic notions, and became very unpopular with the mechanics and workmen by declaring that people in their condition should be restricted from dressing in the same fabrics as used by their more pecuniarily fortunate neighbors, so that the wealthy and the laboring citizens could be designated by their apparel.

In this hotel tradition asserts the wounds of Lafayette were dressed by Mary (Gorman) Lyons, but that incident is claimed as having happened at three other houses in the town of Chester. On Sept. 1, 1796, Mary Withy sold the premises to Maj. William Anderson, who at the date of his purchase had been landlord of the hotel for two years, for it is stated that he had built a frame summer house and an ice house while the property was in his possession as tenant. Maj. Anderson was a member of Congress and associate judge of the courts of Delaware County. A brief sketch of his life is given in the chapter relating to the bench and bar, hence there is no reason to repeat it now. In 1803 he built the Anderson mansion, still standing at the northwest corner of Welsh and Fifth Streets, and after that time until he relinquished the hotel, his family resided in that dwelling. On March 2, 1814, Maj. Anderson sold the hotel to Nimrod Maxwell, of Huntingdon, who carried on the business there for several years, when he leased the house to John J. Thurlow, who remained until 1828, when he removed to the National Hotel, at Edgmont Avenue and Third Street, and James Paist, Jr., kept the Columbia House. Maxwell having died insolvent, suit was brought against his executors, and April 12, 1830, Jehu Broomhall, sheriff, sold the estate to the Delaware County Bank, which corporation held the title for several years, during which time Samuel Lamplugh was landlord. March 13, 1833, the bank conveyed the property to Thomas Ewing and Eliza, his wife. During the latter ownership, the hotel was kept by John Richards, the late prothonotary, and he was succeeded by Frank Lloyd, who, still living near Darby, loves to recount the pranks and sports of the olden time, when woe awaited a stranger at the hands of the madcap roysterers of the ancient borough. Thomas Ewing and wife conveyed the estate, Jan. 17, 1839, to Capt. Elisha S. Howes. He was a veritable "salt," who had earned his title as master of merchant ships, and he kept it for several years, until he relinquished it to embark in the grocery business, and March 27, 1848, sold it to James Campbell, who, after making extensive repairs to the building, conveyed it, March 13, 1854, to John Harrison Hill, who had kept the tavern at Leiperville. The property being sold by the sheriff, was purchased May 27, 1856, by Mark B. Hannum, who conveyed it, April 1, 1857, to Mrs. Elizabeth Appleby, who now owns it. Under the able management of the present landlord, Thomas Appleby, the old hostelry has become almost as noted as it was a century ago.

The Blue Anchor Tavern and the Stacey House.—The story of the old building at the southwest corner of Market and Fount Streets begins on Aug. 29, 1732, when James Trego presented his petition, stating "that your Petitioner (has) Built a new House on the Green, near the Court-House, for that purpose," and desires a license "at ye said house as usually he had in the said Town heretofore," which was allowed him. On May 29, 1733, John West, the father of Benjamin West, "Humbly showeth that your Petitioner has taken to ffarm the house, with the Appurtenances, where James Trego Lately Dwelt on the Green, near the Court-House," and was accorded the desired license. David Coupland, on Feb. 23, 1741/2, had leased the house where John Hanly dwelt in Chester,—"the Blue Anchor,"—received license, and Hanly removed to the Columbia House. Coupland kept the house in 1746, for in that year he, with other innkeepers of Chester, petitioned the Legislature for payment of the "diet furnished to Captain Shannon's company," which troop was part of the forces enlisted during the old French war.

David Coupland was born in Yorkshire, England, and came to the colony with his parents in 1723, his brother Caleb having preceded him nearly nine years. In 1730 he married Isabella Bell, and from that time seems to have taken an active part in the movements of the day. Although by birthright a Friend, we find that in 1758, when Brig.-Gen. John Forbes commanded the expedition which resulted in the capture of Fort Du Quesne (now Pittsburgh), David Coupland enlisted as a private in the company of Capt John Singleton, and during that campaign, he, with Benjamin Davis and John Hanby (Hanly), agreed to pay Hugh Wilson, of Lancaster County, five pounds as a bounty, for entering one wagon in the expedition, to be credited to the borough of Chester

When the misunderstanding between the colonies and England began David Coupland immediately took sides with the former, and was earnest in his efforts to sustain the cause of the Whigs At the assembling of the people of Chester County in the old court-house in this city, Dec 20, 1774, for the purpose of choosing a committee "to carry into execution the Association of the late Continental Congress," David Coupland was one of the committee chosen, and when the body adjourned it was agreed that it should meet on Jan 9, 1775, at the house of David Coupland, and from time to time it held its sessions at his tavern He was taken prisoner in 1778, in the night-time, by a boat's crew from a British man-of-war lying in the river off Chester, as heretofore related, and, as he was an aged man, he died in consequence of the harsh treatment to which he had been subjected Who immediately succeeded Coupland I have not learned, but in 1790 Enoch Green was the landlord, in 1796, Rebecca Serrell In 1801, Jesse Maddux received the license It is related that he had a number of ducks of rare species, which, with pardonable pride, he would frequently show his guests On one occasion a prisoner in the jail opposite threaded a strong cord through a number of grains of corn, and dropped the bait into the street, the other end being fastened to one of the iron bars in his cell-window A plump drake, seeing the tempting morsel, bolted it, and the man began to draw in his catch The squeaking of the duck apprised mine hostess that something out of the usual way had happened, and she hastened to the door When she beheld the extraordinary rise in poultry, she exclaimed, "You rascal, you! that duck's mine!" "That," replied the prisoner, coolly, "depends on whether this string breaks or not"

In 1806 the license was granted to Rose Maddux, and the following year to Jesse Agnew, who appears to have named the tavern the "Hope Anchor" In 1817, Susan Dutton was the landlady of the Fountain Inn, and in 1818, Elizabeth Pennell had license for the "Hope Anchor" The following year John Irwin leased the tavern In 1824, having purchased the inn building, he changed the name to the "Swan," and removed the old sign, and replaced it with one representing a white swan swimming in blue water, which creaked on gusty days as it swung in the frame at the top of a heavy pole planted near the curbstone at the intersection of the streets Old Chester Lodge, No 69, Ancient Free and Accepted Masons, met in the third story of the building until it surrendered its charter, in 1836, and after that date the lodge-room was used by the Odd-Fellows. In 1854, Irwin died, and his widow continued the business until 1844, when Maurice W Deshong leased it and changed the name to the Delaware County House In 1852, John Cochran purchased the property, and converted the ancient inn into two stores and dwellings The corner store is now owned by the heirs of Edward R Minshall, and in 1879 was licensed as a hotel, at present kept by Edward Kelly The adjoining store and dwelling is now the property of Joseph Ladomus, in which he carries on the jewelry business

The Stacey House, immediately adjoining the hotel to the south, which was never used as an inn, was devised by David Coupland to his daughter, Sarah, who, in 1783, married Benjamin Bartholomew The latter was a member of the Assembly from Chester County, and when that body, June 30, 1775, appointed a Committee of Safety, consisting of twenty-five members, Bartholomew was one named from this district He was very active and efficient in discharging the duties of the position He died in 1784, and his wife, who survived her husband many years, resided in the house until near her death, and by will devised the premises to her niece, Tacey Ann (Bevan), who had married George Stacey The house is now owned by the heirs of Sarah Van Dyke Stacey, wife of David B Stacey, a well-known, highly-respected, and accomplished gentleman, whose memory is still cherished by those who were so fortunate as to have numbered him among their acquaintances

The Steamboat Hotel—Grace Lloyd, by her will, dated the 6th day of Fourth month, 1760, devised unto her cousin, Francis Richardson, of Philadelphia, after certain specific devises of lands and bequests of personal property to other parties named therein, "all the rest, residue, and remainder of my lands, plantations, lots of ground, rents, tenements, hereditaments, and real estate whatsoever and wheresoever" This Francis Richardson entered into possession of the real estate thus devised to him, and began very extensive improvements He erected between the years 1761 and 1770, the substantial building at the northeast corner of Market and Front Streets, now the Steamboat Hotel, as a dwelling for his family, built extensive warehouses and a wharf at the site of the present upper government pier, which wharf stood until the year 1816, and was known as "Richardson's wharf," and prepared for a large business as a shipper of grain While he was making these improvements he was remonstrated with by many of his friends for his outlay of money in the undertaking, and he was much incensed at their short-sightedness Unfortunately for his enterprise, the brewing troubles with the mother-country worked disastrously for his speculations, and resulted in entirely ruining him His daughter, Deborah, was married at Chester, June 10 1773, to Joseph Mifflin, and the same year Deborah, Hannah, and John, together with their father, became members of Chester Friends' Meeting Hannah married Samuel Fairlamb, Grace married Isaac Potts, and Frances married Clement Biddle The four daughters of Francis Richardson were much admired for their beauty, and the exquisite transparency of their complexion was so remarkable that the gallants of those days reported that, when they drank a glass of wine, "it might be seen trickling down their fair throats" An elder son, who was born in Philadelphia, and named after his father, Francis, we are told by the annalist, Watson, "was a person of great personal beauty," a statement Mrs. Deborah Logan fully corroborates About 1770 this son went to London, having formed a passionate longing for military life from associating with the British officers in Philadelphia, and secured a commission in the King's Life Guard, of which crack regiment he subsequently became colonel [1] His brother John, who was a Friend when the Revolutionary war broke out, was quite active in military movements, and for that cause was disowned by Chester Meeting in 1775 Francis Richardson died subsequently to the year 1779, for in April of that year he was the lessee of a frame store-house on the east side of Market, south of Fourth Street, which afterwards became the property of Dr Job Terrill, and now of Mrs John O Deshong He died insolvent, and his real estate, dwelling, and warehouses were sold after his death by Ezekiel Leonard, high sheriff, July 2, 1787, to Robert Eaglesfield Griffith, a lawyer of Philadelphia, who, on May 4, 1789, conveyed the estate to Davis Bevan

This Davis Bevan was of Welsh descent, and was one of the most conspicuous characters in our city's annals He was married to Agnes Coupland, daughter of David Coupland, and was thirty-seven years of age when the battles of Lexington and Concord were fought He is stated to have been an officer in the Continental army, and Martin[2] relates the following incident in his career as a soldier

"He was with Washington at the battle of Brandywine, in 1777, and after the defeat of the American forces he carried dispatches from General Washington to the President of the Continental Congress, then sitting in Philadelphia, announcing the result of the engagement A gentleman by the name of Sharp accompanied Capt Bevan Proceeding some distance from the army they observed they were pursued by a party of British light horse Mr Sharp was not so well mounted as Captain Bevan, who had a thoroughbred mare of great action and endurance Finding that the light horse were gaining on them constantly, and that Mr Sharp would persist in urging his nag up the hills in spite of his advice to the contrary, Capt Bevan said, 'Sharp, if we keep together our capture is certain, therefore I think you had better take the next cross-road that we come to, and I will continue on They will follow me, but I am confident they cannot capture me' This proposal was agreed to, and as soon as Mr Sharp had turned off, Capt Bevan gave the rein to his mare, and his pursuers soon finding themselves distanced gave up the chase When Capt. Bevan reached the Schuylkill during the night, he found, owing to a heavy freshet, the ferry boat was either unable to run, or had been carried down the river A boatman, however, rowed him over while his mare swam by the side of the boat He landed safely on the Philadelphia shore, and replacing his saddle, he hastened to deliver his dispatches This officer had various adventures, and often ran great risks while the American army was at Valley Forge On one occasion he went to visit his wife at the house of a Mr Vernon, where she had come from Philadelphia, for the purpose of seeing him Mr Vernon's house was but a short distance from the British lines, and it was therefore necessary that considerable caution should be exercised to prevent capture by the numerous parties of British foragers scouring the country Mr Vernon's sons were posted around the house at convenient points for observation to give warning of the approach of enemies, and Capt Bevan went to bed About the middle of the night one of the boys came to his room, and informed him that a mounted party were approaching the house and he had better prepare to take his departure Being rather an obstinate man he did not seem to believe the report, but presently another picket came in and told him that he would certainly be captured if he remained any longer He sprang out of bed, hurried on his regimentals, and reached the back door just as the British party knocked at the front He got to the stable, where he found his mare already saddled, and leading her out, and mounting, he leaped the farm yard inclosure, and, being perfectly familiar with the country, he had no difficulty in evading his enemies"

During the Revolutionary war the house, whose southern gable-end, as we know, stood near the river, which at that time was a bold, gravelly shore, was a conspicuous mark, and when the British frigate "Augusta," in 1777, sailed up the Delaware to be sunk afterwards in the attack on Fort Mifflin, her commander, in sheer wantonness, opened fire on the defenseless town One of the shot shattered the wall in the gable-end towards the river, and the owner repaired the breach by placing a circular window in the opening thus made It still remains there.

The house for many years was unproductive, various tenants occupied it, but because of the tradition that shortly after the Revolution a negro named

[1] It is related that Sir William Draper made a tour of the American colonies a short time after his newspaper encounter with "Junius" "During his stay in Philadelphia no one was so assiduous in his attentions to him as Mr Richardson, better known at that time by the name of Frank Richardson, then from Europe, on a visit to his friends This gentleman was one of the most singular and successful of American adventurers The son of one of our plainest Quakers, he gave early indications of that cast of character which raised him to his present station, that of a colonel in the British guards At a time when such attainments formed no part of education in Pennsylvania, he sedulously employed himself in acquiring skill in the use of the small sword and the pistol, as if to shine as a duelist had been the first object of his ambition Either from a contempt for the dull pursuits of the 'home keeping youth' of this day, or from the singularity of his propensities repelling association, he was solitary and rarely with companions Fair and delicate to effeminancy, he paid great attention to his person, which he had the courage to invest in scarlet, in defiance of the society to which he belonged, in whose mind's eye, perhaps, as to that of the blind man of Luke, this color from their marked aversion to it, resembles the sound of a trumpet, and no less in defiance of the plain manners of the city, in which, except on the back of a soldier, a red coat was a phenomenon, and always indicated a Creole, or Carolinian, or a dancing master With these qualifications, and these alone, perhaps, Mr Richardson at an early age shipped himself for England, where soon having the good fortune to establish a reputation for the theatre, he was received into the best company, and thence laid the foundation of his preferment. Such, at least, was the generally received account of his rise But whether accurate or not, his intimate footing with Sir William is an evidence of the style of his company whilst abroad, as well as the propriety of his conclusion that his native land was not his sphere As the story went, on Mr Richardson's first going to England, he happened to be in the same lodgings with Foote, the comedian, with whom he became intimate One day upon his coming out of his chamber, 'Richardson,' said Foote to him, 'a person has just been asking for you, who expressed a strong desire to see you, and pretended to be an old Philadelphia acquaintance But I knew better, for he was a d——d ill-looking fellow, and I have no doubt the rascal was a bailiff, so I told him you were not at home' But here either Foote's sagacity had been at fault, or he had been playing off a stroke of his humor, the visitor having really been no other than Mr ——, a respectable merchant of Philadelphia, though not a figure the most debonair to be sure"—"Reminiscences," Hazard's Register, vol vi p 167.

[2] History of Chester, pp 42, 43

Laban had been killed in the dwelling, being struck on the head with an axe, whose blood was said to have made an indelible stain behind the door where he fell, and whose spirit wandered around the place of his untimely death, they were of a class that could not afford to pay remunerative rent for the premises.

After the death of David Bevan, his son, Matthew Lawler Bevan, sold the property to John Ford, who petitioned, in 1827, for license for "the Steamboat Hotel" stating that having lately purchased that certain large brick messuage, situated on Market Street, at the upper pier, he is "desirous to keep the same as a public house of entertainment for the accommodation of watermen passing up and down the river Delaware, and also of travelers." This petition was accompanied by a recommendation from the masters, pilots, etc., of vessels of the port of Philadelphia, in which they "certify that if license was granted to keep a public house, situate at the Upper Pier in Chester, it would be a great convenience and accommodation to watermen passing up and down the river Delaware, more especially in the winter season, during the time of ice, etc." The business seems not to have been successful, for in June, 1831, Jehu Broomhall sold the property to Samuel Smith, who leased it to Henry T. Reese, who was succeeded the next year by Welcome D. Niles, for at the August court, 1833, the court directed that a rule should be entered against Niles, to appear on the first day of the November Court of Quarter Sessions to show cause "why the license hereinbefore granted to him should not be forfeited, on account of his suffering disorderly riots and improper conduct" in the house. In 1835, Nelson Wade was the landlord. He was followed by Crossman Lyons, a well-known citizen of Chester, the son of a Revolutionary soldier, who, when a young man, had joined Washington's army in its retreat through New Jersey, had followed the fortunes of the Continental troops through the war until its close, when he settled in Chester, and married Mary Gorman, a woman of extraordinary nerve, whose busy hands dressed many of those wounded at the battle of Brandywine, who were brought to this city for attention. She it was who waited on and dressed the wounds of Marquis de Lafayette, on the evening of that disastrous day. Crossman Lyons, Oct. 12, 1844, purchased the property, and a few years subsequent he leased it to Howard Roberts, who, after keeping the hotel for about three years, declined to continue the business longer, and Mr. Lyons resumed the post of "mine host" until Nov. 12, 1851, when John Goff, who had been the landlord the year previous, purchased the property. After his death, in 1857, his widow continued the hotel, and she having died in 1883, the old hostelry is presided over by her son, John Goff.

The Lafayette House.—The house at the southwest corner of Third Street and Edgmont Avenue is one of the oldest buildings in our city, and in a deed from James Sandelands, the younger, Sept. 10, 1700, to Stephen Jackson, the property is described as a house and lot, thus showing that the structure antedates that instrument. Stephen Jackson, on June 17th of the following year, transferred the property to John Worrilow, and he in turn conveyed it, Aug. 29, 1704, to Philip Yarnall. The latter, after retaining title to the estate for twenty-nine years, sold the dwelling and lot to John Mather, Sept. 26, 1733, who in his will, May 28, 1768, devised it to his daughter, Jane. She first married Dr. Paul Jackson, who dying in 1767, the following year she married Dr. David Jackson. The latter and his wife, Feb. 27, 1775, conveyed the property to James Sparks, a merchant of Philadelphia. The probabilities are that Dr. David Jackson had lived in this dwelling, for in 1769 he was a resident of Chester. In 1784, William Kerlin owned and resided there until his death, in 1804, when the property descended to his son, John, subject to his mother's life estate. John dying in 1817, his executors sold the house to James Chadwick, who devised it to his son, John. The latter, while owning the property, purchased two frame buildings at Marcus Hook, and placing them on scows, had them floated up to Chester, where he erected them on the eastern end of his property on Third Street. Both of these houses are now owned by the estate of Henry Abbott, Sr., deceased. This was considered a marvelous feat in those days.

The dwelling, in 1830, became the property of Charles Alexander Ledomus, whose heirs still own it. In 1875 it was leased to Caleb P. Clayton, who obtained license for the old house and gave it the name Lafayette House, tradition having credited the dressing of the wounds of the French general in that building.

Schanlan's Tavern.—In the historical introduction to William Whitehead's "Directory of the Borough of Chester," for the years 1859–60, it is stated, "In the second house from the corner of Work Street [now Fourth] on the east side of Market, was a hotel kept by John Scantling, an Irishman, and the resort of all the sons of the Emerald Isle." That the house in which John Brooke now carries on the manufacture of harness was at one time an inn, the records of the old county of Chester before the erection of Delaware County fully establish. At that time only the dwelling, afterwards the residence of Dr. Terrill, was on the same square to the north of John Brooke's store. It was in the store-building Schanlan—for that was his name, not Scantling—kept public-house. It was erected by Thomas Morgan previous to 1756, for the building was there when it was sold in that year to William Eyre, of Bethel. The latter rented the premises to Davis Bevan, who kept tavern there from 1765 to 1771, when he was succeeded by John Schanlan. At first the court turned away from Schanlan, but he obtained the judicial favor and continued to receive it until 1783, when Dennis McCartney had the license there. The following year (1784) Davis Bevan purchased it, and therein engaged in a general store, as mentioned elsewhere. The business was continued in this house by Isabella Bevan after the death of her father. It was subsequently occupied as a hat store and factory by Maj. Samuel A. Price, and while it was owned by Henry L. Powell, he had a boot and shoe store there. In 1846, Joseph Entwisle owned the property, and thereon he had the first bakery established in Chester for custom business, the old granary of Jasper Yeates being restricted to the manufacture of "hard tack" for ships' stores. When Entwisle built a bleaching-mill in South Ward, in 1851, he sold the house and lot to John Brooke, who has continued in one occupation and in one locality for a greater number of years than any person at present in Chester, and has gathered during that period a large business and a competency.

The Goeltz House (Edgmont Avenue above Third Street).—The frame structure on the east side of Edgmont Avenue, south of Fourth Street, is not an ancient building. In all probability it was built about seventy years ago. It was formerly a stable, attached to the house which was subsequently erected on the lands donated previous to 1704, by Thomas Powell, to the parish of St. Paul, for the gift is mentioned in Rev. Mr. Nichol's letter to the London Society for Propagating the Gospel in Foreign Parts, and in 1718, Rev. John Humphreys, under date of October 24th, alludes to it as containing the foundation of a parsonage (the front on Third Street) which the congregation started to build, "but were not able to accomplish in & it remains as it has been these 3 years, just about 4 feet above the ground as a reproach to them and an infamous mark of their Poverty." The parish did erect a building on the premises many years afterwards, certainly subsequently to 1762, which they leased previous to 1830, to William Kelley, as well as the stable on Edgmont Avenue. Kelley resided in the house on Third Street, wherein he kept a restaurant, and in the stable he had a bottling establishment, the first business of that kind ever in Chester. The church wardens, however, were instructed to sell the premises on ground-rent, and in compliance with that order George B. Lownes and Pierce Crosby, May 5, 1831, conveyed the premises to William McCafferty, subject to a ground-rent of ninety-seven dollars yearly. The latter, in 1839, sold the lot on Edgmont Avenue, on which was the stable, to Ehrenreich Goeltz. Goeltz changed the stable into a house, and on the rear of the lot erected a soap factory and chandlery, which business he carried on until his death. In the distribution of the latter's estate, the house and factory became the property of his son, George Goeltz, the present owner.

A peculiar circumstance connected with this building is that, several years ago when the alterations were being made in the cellar, in excavating, at the depth of three feet below the then bottom, a perfect rubble pavement, similar to those in the roadway of many of our streets, was found, respecting which no person had the slightest information as to the reason why it was there, when it was laid, or by whom.

The Old Johnson Tavern (on the west side of Edgmont Avenue).—Adjoining the lumber and coal-yard of Jonathan Pennell, to the north, is an ancient building which is believed to have been built by Jacob Howell, subsequent to 1732, when he acquired title to a tract of land, on part of which the dwelling was erected previous to Dec. 10, 1748, at which date Isaac Howell, a son of Jacob, conveyed the lot and "messuage" to William Pennell. In 1784, Samuel Johnson purchased the property and kept it as a public-house, but becoming involved, it was sold by Sheriff Ezekiel Leonard, July 5, 1787, to Robert Pennell. A brother of the then owner, James Pennell, kept it as an inn; and as an attraction for the public had a tame tiger, which he had taught to perform a number of tricks. Pennell, when he removed to the Black Horse Hotel, in Middletown, took the animal thither, and one day, when angry, it attacked and killed its master. The building, after it ceased to be a public-house, had several owners, and is now part of the estate of Frederick J. Hinkson, Sr., deceased.

The Brown Hotel.—In 1875, Benjamin Morris, who had been landlord of a popular public-house—now Genther's Hotel—on Market Street above Third, purchased the old Cole House on Third Street below Market Square, where, about the beginning of this century, Jane Davis had an apothecary-shop, the first in Chester, and in more recent years the residence of Dr. J. L. Forwood. Morris removed the old structure, and erected in its stead the present spacious hotel building. The property having been purchased by George W. Weaver, deceased, whose estate still owns it, Morris leased the Beale House, the old Samuel Edward mansion, at Sixth and Market Streets, and removed thither. After several tenants had occupied the Morris House, Maj. Daniel Brown leased it, and is the present landlord of the hotel, now known by his name.

Banks and Bankers.—The Delaware County National Bank was chartered under the act of March 21, 1814, then popularly known as the "Omnibus Bank Act," which was passed by the Legislature over the veto of Governor Simon Snyder, and with the exception of but one other similar institution incorporated by the same law, has been the most successful bank created by that act, for although a number of corporations started under its provisions, the great majority of them failed within a few years. On Aug. 27, 1614, the meeting of the first board of directors was held, that body consisting of Jonas Eyre, Pierce Crosby, Joseph Engle, Preston Eyre, George G. Leiper, Peter Deshong, Samuel Anderson, Enos Sharpless, Charles Rogers, John G. Hoskins, and Jonas Preston. Thomas Robinson and John Newbold, who were members, did not attend. At this meeting John Newbold was elected president *pro tempore*, and a committee, consisting of Engle, Hoskins, and Sharpless was appointed to ascertain what would be necessary, and the probable cost "of making Jonas Sharpless' house fit for the use of the bank and for the family of the cashier," and Hoskins and Eyre were appointed on behalf of the bank to enter into a contract for the purchase of Sharpless' house at a price not exceeding three thousand dollars This house was located on one of the corners of Market Square On Sept 5, 1814, Preston Eyre, who at the time owned the house and kept a general country store in the building now the property of Thomas Moore, on Third Street, at present occupied by Browning & Co as a clothing store, was elected cashier *pro tempore* The committee appointed to purchase Sharpless' house on October 3d reported that a defect had been discovered in the title of that property, and they were instructed to ascertain whether such blur could be removed, but on the 31st of the same mouth they reported that "the defect in title cannot be remedied" Hence, on November 7th, it was ascertained that a dwelling and lot near the market-house, belonging to Elizabeth Pedrick, could be bought for eighteen hundred dollars, and a committee was appointed to coutract for the purchase of the property and to have the title examined

This house occupied the site of the present bank building It was a frame structure, which stood on an eminence, steps leading up to the porch, and where the Chester National Bank stands a large gate opened to the lot, through which cattle were driven to pasture in the field surrounding the house At that time the dwelling was occupied by two aged spinsters, named Springer, who kept a cake- and candy-shop there In the mean while Preston Eyre, who had been elected, on November 28th, permanent cashier, at a salary of six hundred dollars per annum, agreed to allow the use of the front room of his house on Third Street to the bank, he being paid one hundred and fifty dollars a year as rent for that apartment and a small frame building adjoining it The contract, however, stipulated that Eyre should find the fuel and candles for the bank without further compensation and "with liberty given to the directors to leave the contract when they see proper" Joseph Engle and Peter Deshong were at the same meeting instructed to make such alterations to the house of the cashier "as will accommodate this bank for a temporary purpose"

On Nov 28, 1814, the first regular board of directors was elected, consisting of John Newbold, Jonas Eyre, Samuel Anderson, Peter Deshong, John G Hoskins, Thomas Robinson, George G Leiper, Jonas Preston, Charles Rogers, Joseph Engle, Pierce Crosby, John Cowgill, and Nimrod Maxwell The same day John Newbold was chosen president of the bank On the 26th of December the agreement to purchase the lot of Elizabeth Pedrick was entered into, and the bank not having perfected its plans for a building, determined, as a precautionary measure, to rent the property for the time being, and it was rented by Capt Robinson On March 10, 1815, the committee to prepare plans submitted their report, in which they stated that the banking-house, which would be of brick, ought to be located in that part of the lot which fronted on Market Street and the public square. The suggestions were accepted, and Pierce Crosby, Joseph Engle, Jonas Eyre, John G Hoskins, and George G Leiper appointed the building committee On March 16, 1815, they were instructed, if they could get possession of the property rented to Robinson,—who in the mean while had resigned from the board,—to take the house down and use the materials in it to the best advantage

At this time the position of president was purely one of honor, no salary being attached to the office, but the board of directors at the conclusion of the year would appropriate such sum as they thought the services were worth, and liberality was certainly not strikingly displayed in the amount tendered On May 1, 1815, at the close of the first six months, a dividend of five per cent was declared, and on November 6th of the same year a similar amount was payable to the stockholders,—that being the showing of the first year of business During that year John Cowgill and John Newbold resigned as directors, and Jonathan Pennell and John McIlvain took their places in the board In the mean while the bank building had progressed so that on Nov 20, 1815, business was for the first time conducted in that structure, and on the 27th of the same month the dwelling was ready for occupancy by the cashier On that day the latter's salary was increased to nine hundred dollars, he was also instructed to occupy the dwelling part of the bank rent free, and was, in addition, allowed forty dollars per annum "for supplying hickory wood for the bank" The building, torn down in 1882, appears to have cost, inclusive of the land, $10,354 34 Early in that year William Graham had been elected solicitor of the bank at an annual salary of fifty dollars

The business of the institution had so increased that on Feb 19, 1816, Peter Hill was appointed bookkeeper, "it having become necessary for an officer to be appointed to keep the books of the bank and in other respects to assist the cashier in performing the ordinary duties of banking," at an annual salary of seven hundred dollars It seems that in the early part of this century the banks were obliged to keep open on holidays, for on Monday, Dec 25, 1820, it was recorded, "Being Christmas, no business was done in the bank," and during the terrible depression of 1821 the general uncertainty of business is shown by the following statement, under date of September 21st: "No notes discounted this day nor money loaned" On Feb 17, 1823, the first watchman, John Kelley, was employed at the rate of one hundred dollars per annum, "to commence on 1st day of March next"

So successful had the institution proved that other parties at the session of 1832-33 made an effort to obtain a charter for another bank, and the act incorporating "The Farmers' and Manufacturers' Bank of Delaware County" passed both Houses, but was vetoed by Governor George Wolf In the fall of 1834 it was ascertained that a large amount of redeemed notes of the bank had gotten into circulation, and would have to be again paid It is traditionally asserted that quite a number of these notes had been thrown into the open fireplace, and the draught was so strong that many of them, borne upward in the chimney, were scattered in the street, were gathered by parties unknown, who circulated them in Philadelphia, and they were again presented to the bank for payment Be that as it may, the dividend was passed several times between 1834 and 1837, and the earnings of the bank were appropriated to make up the deficiency found to exist in the capital of the institution

The bank soon recuperated, and for years conducted a steadily-increasing and profitable business, ranking in credit second to no other in the State of a like character. When the civil war came, and all was excitement, even the staid directors seem to have imbibed something of the war spirit, for on April 22, 1861, the president was instructed to subscribe two hundred dollars towards the purchase of "two hundred muskets to be kept by the town to be used for the defense of the people and property of the place" On May 5, 1864, the bank made a donation of five hundred dollars to the Great Central Fair, held in Philadelphia for the United States Sanitary Commission

During the invasion of the State by the rebel army under Gen Lee, in June, 1863, on the 29th of that month, the directors instructed the president and cashier to make arrangements for the safe depository of the money and other valuables of the bank, if in their discretion such removal was deemed necessary. On Wednesday, July 1st of that year, Caleb Emlen and Jonathan R Johnson were dispatched in a wagon to Philadelphia with the money and valuables, starting from Chester at a very early hour in the morning The sum intrusted to these messengers —clerks in the bank—was several hundred thousand dollars, and although they were well armed, their responsibility was so great—fearing lest they might be attacked by parties who had learned of the proposed transfer—that when they placed the specie and other valuables in the custody of the Bank of North America, Philadelphia, to be forwarded to New York with that of the latter bank, should occasion demand it, they breathed freely once more under the sense of relief it brought them

On March 14, 1864, the old Delaware County Bank ceased as an active State institution, but it had merely changed front, and was chartered by the United States as the Delaware County National Bank During the transition state the board of directors seem to have acted in settling the affairs of the old institution until Nov 11, 1864, when the following board was elected (the last under the old State charter) Edmund Pennell, Joshua P Eyre, William W Maddock, William Hannum, Edwin Hannum, Jacob Smedley, Joseph Engle, Frederick Fairlamb, William Booth, David Trainer, James Irving, Samuel Starr, and John H Baker On March 6, 1865, after the amount of money necessary was deposited in the United States Treasury to secure the charter, the surplus funds of the old bank were divided among the stockholders, paying a dividend of seven dollars per share, and on Dec 28, 1868, a further dividend of two dollars and fifty cents was declared, which finally settled all the outstanding business of the old bank

The institution under the national charter throve and prospered, the remarkable financial abilities of the late John O Deshong being conspicuous in the conduct of its affairs. It was everywhere known as a strong and well-managed institution, usually carrying large sums of money in its vaults Hence it is not to be wondered that efforts were made to rob it On the night of Jan 12, 1872, such an attempt was made, the burglars striving to effect an entrance by boring six holes with an auger through a back window-shutter, which, however, failed to penetrate the iron lining. The watchman heard the noise and gave the alarm, but the robbers fled before pursuit could be made

In 1882 the old structure, built in 1815, was demolished, the business being removed into an adjoining building on Third Street, and the present fine banking-house erected in its stead In all its appointments it is a model building, and reflects credit on the institution and on the architect, P Welsh, and besides is an ornament to our city It seems hardly credible that a structure such as it is could have been erected for fifty thousand dollars, and yet the building proper cost thirty-five thousand dollars, while the vault and fixtures aggregated fifteen thousand dollars additional This was certainly a necessary and judicious expenditure The new building was opened for business Jan 29, 1884

Following is a list of the presidents of the Delaware County Bank John Newbold, Nov 28, 1814, to March 23, 1815, Dr Jonas Preston, March 30, 1815, to Nov 20, 1815, Pierce Crosby, Nov 27, 1816, to Nov 15, 1834, John Kerlin, Nov. 15, 1834, to November, 1841, Jesse J Maris, Nov 22, 1841, to December, 1860, Frederick J Hinkson, Dec. 12, 1860, to Feb 8, 1864, Edmund Pennell, Feb 15, 1864, to Dec 25, 1868.

Presidents of the Delaware County National Bank Samuel A Crozer, March 14, 1864, to Jan 16, 1865; Edmund Pennell, Jan 16, 1865, to Jan 19, 1874, David Trainer, Jan. 26, 1874, to Jan 25, 1875, Robert H Crozer, Jan 25, 1875, to March 5, 1877, Ellwood Tyson, March 12, 1877, present incumbent

Cashiers of the Delaware County Bank: Preston Eyre,[1] Nov. 28, 1814, to Dec. 11, 1834; Charles S. Folwell, December, 1832, to March 3, 1836;[2] Frederick J. Hinkson, March 10, 1836, to July 25, 1853; James G. McCollin, Aug. 10, 1853, to Aug. 13, 1860; William Taylor, Sept. 6, 1860, to March 17, 1864; Caleb Emlen, March 24, 1864, to Nov. 11, 1864.

Cashiers of the Delaware County National Bank: Caleb Emlen, May 14, 1864, to February, 1874; J. Howard Roop, Feb. 19, 1874, present incumbent.

Present board of directors: Ellwood Tyson, Joshua P. Eyre, David Trainer, Robert McCall, D. Reese Esrey, William S. Blakeley, Thomas Appleby, Thomas Scattergood, John O. Deshong, Jr.

Every successful business enterprise is largely the result of the individual efforts of those men who have controlled, directed, and shaped its course. Naturally it is the exponent of the tact and forethought of those persons on whom the responsibility of its management has been cast. John O. Deshong, Frederick J. Hinkson, and Edmund Pennell were conspicuous in their connection with the Delaware County National Bank. Hence it is eminently proper that their biographical sketches should accompany this history of the bank they did so much to place in the high position it now holds in business circles.

John Odenheimer Deshong was born in Delaware County, Pa., Sept. 6, 1807, his parents being Peter Deshong and Mary Odenheimer Deshong. He was the eldest of three children, the others being Maurice W. and S. Louisa. His education was received in private schools in Chester, Pa., and immediately upon attaining manhood he engaged in general merchandising at the corner of Fourth and Market Streets, Chester, in which he was quite successful. In 1843 he engaged in the lumber business in Chester, and being prosperous was able to retire from active business in 1849. He soon after turned his attention to financial affairs, using his capital as a dealer in commercial paper, in which he became a large and successful operator, and continued it until his death. He avoided all financial speculations of uncertain success, and his pecuniary losses were surprisingly small in comparison with the large amount of capital used in his business.

From 1845 until his decease he was almost continuously a director of the Bank of Delaware County, of which institution his father was one of the original directors. He was also for many years a director of the Chester Gas Company, and on his decease the board of directors passed unanimously, and recorded among the minutes, a series of resolutions, a part of which is here quoted as an expression of the opinion and feelings of those who knew him intimately: "That his intercourse with his colleagues was marked by uniform kindness and courtesy, and his counsels were always for justice and fair dealing as well to the community as to the stockholders." The directors of the Delaware County National Bank, into which the Bank of Delaware County had been merged, also recorded resolutions expressive of the great loss that had been sustained: "In the decease of one whose well-known business qualifications, sterling integrity, and excellent judgment entitled him to the respect and grateful remembrance of stockholders and directors."

Mr. Deshong was a Republican in politics, but would never for a moment seriously consider any proposition to become a candidate for any office, though he wielded a large influence on local public affairs by unobtrusive advice and timely suggestions. His counsel to friends with reference to their own affairs was always valuable, and frequently given to those in whom he felt an interest. He was decided, prompt, and self-reliant, with strong and lasting affection for those he loved. A reader of standard works, with a retentive memory, his mind was well stored with useful knowledge, but conspicuous above all other intellectual traits was his clear insight into the motives and capacities of others. His foresight in business matters was marvelous, his grasp of comprehension embracing not only his own, but the affairs of others to an extent that was often astonishing.

In social intercourse Mr. Deshong was genial and sprightly, fond of pleasantries and friendly jokes, always meeting his friends with a cheerful smile and a pleasant word.

On Dec. 6, 1826, he was married to Emmeline L., daughter of Dr. J. H. Terrill, of Chester, by which union were seven children, of whom Alfred O., John O., Jr., Louise (wife of J. E. Woodbridge), and Clarence survive. Mr. Deshong died on May 28, 1881, in his seventy-fourth year.

The Hinkson family came from the county of Cavan, in the North of Ireland. The oldest members of the family there say that three brothers emigrated in the seventeenth century from Hanover, in the North of Germany, to Ireland.

In the burial-ground of the family, in Belturbet churchyard, many of the Hinksons are buried. The Hinksons of this country are descended from John Hinkson and Jane, his wife, who, with one son, came to this country from Ireland, and settled in Upper Providence township, Delaware Co. They had eight children, four sons and four daughters, viz.: John (who married Abigail Engle), George (who married Catharine Fairlamb), Thomas (who married Mary Worrilow), James (who married Elizabeth Crossley), Jane (who married Thomas D. Weaver), Mary (who was unmarried), Sarah (who married William Hawkins), and Nancy (who married Joseph Dickerson). The descendants live in Pennsylvania, Ohio, Illinois, and Maryland. The parents of Frederick James Hinkson were John Hinkson, Jr., of Lower Provi-

[1] Preston Eyre died in Dubuque, Iowa, April 18, 1859, aged eighty-seven years.

[2] Resigned to accept a position in the Bank of the United States, and died in Germantown, Dec. 28, 1875, aged eighty years.

[illegible] of the Delaware County Bank: Presley [illegible], 1864, to Dec. 13, 1824; Charles B. [illegible] 1852, to March 3, 1856; Frederick J. Hinkson, March 20, 1856, to July 25, 1856; [illegible] Aug. 29, 1859, to Aug. 13, 1860; [illegible] Sept. [illegible] 1860, to March 17, 1864; [illegible] March 24, 1864, to Nov. 11, 1864.

[illegible] of the Delaware County National Bank: [illegible] May 14, 1864, to February, 1871; J. [illegible] Feb. [illegible] 1871, present incumbent.

Present board of directors: Edward Tyson, Joshua P. Eyre, David Trainer, Robert McCall, D. Reese Esrey, [illegible], Thomas Appleby, Thomas [illegible], John O. Deshong, Jr.

Every successful business enterprise is largely the result of the individual efforts of those men who have controlled, directed, and shaped its course. Naturally it is the exponent of the tact and forethought of those persons on whom the responsibility of its management has been cast. John O. Deshong, Frederick J. Hinkson, and Edmund Pennell were conspicuous in their connection with the Delaware County National Bank. Hence it is eminently proper that their biographical sketches should accompany this history of the bank they did so much to place in the high position it now holds in business circles.

John Odenheimer Deshong was born in Delaware County, Pa., Sept. 6, 1807, his parents being Peter Deshong and Mary Odenheimer Deshong. He was the eldest of three children, the others being Maurice W. and S. Louisa. His education was received in private schools in Chester, Pa., and immediately upon attaining manhood he engaged in general merchandising at the corner of Fourth and Market Streets, Chester, in which he was quite successful. In 1840 he engaged in the lumber business in Chester, and being prosperous was able to retire from active business in 1850. He soon after turned his attention to financial affairs, using his capital as a dealer in commercial paper, in which he became a large and successful operator, and continued it until his death. His [illegible] of financial operations, of [illegible] [illegible], and his [illegible] [illegible] [illegible] [illegible] [illegible] [illegible] [illegible] [illegible] in his business.

From 1840 until his decease [illegible] was [illegible] a director of the Bank of Delaware County, of which institution his father was [illegible] directors. He was also for [illegible] years a director of the Chester Gas Company, and on [illegible] the board of directors passed [illegible] among the minutes, a series of [illegible], a part of which is here quoted as an expression of the opinion and feelings of those who knew him intimately:

"That his intercourse with his colleagues was [illegible] by uniform kindness and courtesy, and his counsels were always for justice and fair dealing as well to the community as to the stockholders." The directors of the Delaware County National Bank, into which the Bank of Delaware County had been merged, also recorded resolutions expressive of the great loss they had been sustained: "In the decease of one whose [illegible] business qualifications, [illegible], and excellent judgment entitled him to the [illegible] and grateful remembrance of [illegible]."

Mr. Deshong was a Republican in politics, but would never for a moment seriously consider any proposition to become a candidate for any office, though he wielded a large influence in local public affairs by unobtrusive advice and timely suggestions. His counsel to friends with reference to their own affairs was always valuable, and frequently given to those in whom he felt an interest. He was decided, prompt, and self-reliant, with strong and lasting affection for those beloved. A reader of standard works, with a retentive memory, his mind was well stored with useful knowledge, but conspicuous above all other intellectual traits was his clear insight into the motives and capacities of others. His foresight in business matters was marvelous, his grasp of comprehension embracing not only his own, but the affairs of others to an extent that was often astonishing.

In social [illegible] Mr. Deshong was genial and sprightly, fond of pleasantries and friendly jokes, always meeting his friends with a cheerful smile and a pleasant word.

On Dec. 6, 1836, he was married to Emmeline L., daughter of Dr. J. H. Terrill, of Chester, by which union were seven children, of whom Alfred O., John O., Jr., Louisa (wife of J. E. Woodbridge), and Clarence survive. Mr. Deshong died on May 28, 1881, in his seventy-fourth year.

The Hinkson family came from the county of Cavan, in the North of Ireland. The oldest members of the family there say that three brothers emigrated in the seventeenth century from Hanover, in the North of Germany, to Ireland.

In the [illegible] of the family, in Belturbet churchyard, many of the Hinksons are buried. The Hinksons of this country are descended from John Hinkson and Jane his wife, who, with one son, came to this country from Ireland, and settled in Upper Providence township, Delaware Co. They had eight children, five sons and three daughters, viz.: John (who married [illegible]), George (who married Catharine [illegible]), Thomas (who married Mary [illegible]), John (who married Elizabeth Crossley), Jane (who married [illegible] B. [illegible]), Mary (who was unmarried), Sarah (who married William Hawkins), and Naomi (who married Joseph Dickinson). The descendants live in Pennsylvania, Ohio, Illinois, and Maryland. The parents of Frederick James Hinkson were John Hinkson, Jr., of Lower Provi-

[illegible] Kent [illegible] Delaware, [illegible] 1826, [illegible]

[illegible] in the Bank of the United States [illegible] Dec. 19, 1832, aged eighty years.

Eng^d by A H Ritchie

J. A. Dishon

F. J. Hinkson

[illegible] township, and Abigail, a daughter of Frederick [illegible], formerly of the borough of Chester. They were married in 1784. Their children (besides F. J. Hinkson) who reached maturity were: Jane (who married Ambrose Smedley, a farmer of Middletown township; she died in 1873, in her eighty-ninth year), [illegible] (who married David Baker, of Middletown township,—he was a carpenter and builder), John (whose business was that of a farmer. His first wife was [illegible], a daughter of Joseph Worrall, of Upper Providence; his second, who is now living in Chester, is Orpha, a daughter of Joseph Naide, of Chester township. John held the position of steward of the House of Employment of this county, was sheriff, a member of the State Legislature, and a recorder of deeds and register of wills), Mary (who married Abraham Hamor, formerly of Middletown, and afterwards of Marshallton, in Chester County), Joseph (who was a carpenter and builder. He married Ann, a daughter of Samuel Black, of Marple), Orpha (who married [illegible] Evans, of Upper Providence, afterwards of Chester township), and Edward Engle Hinkson (who married Sarah, a daughter of Samuel Shuster, of Chester township. He was a carpenter and builder. He was the first building inspector of the city of Chester, held the office for several years, and until his death). All of the children of John Hinkson, Jr., are deceased.

Frederick J. Hinkson was born Nov. 8, 1803, in the township of Upper Providence. When he was quite young his parents moved into Middletown township. Soon after his father's decease (which happened when he was fifteen years old) he entered the store of Abraham Hamor, of that township. Mr. Hamor, in connection with his store, carried on tailoring. Mr. Hinkson having learned his trade, that of a tailor, went to school. He subsequently taught school at Upper Providence meeting-house, at Village Green, then at Columbia, in Lancaster Co., and again at Village Green. While teaching at the last-named place he was elected a clerk in the Bank of Delaware County, at Chester, in which institution, in the capacity of clerk, cashier, and president, he remained for over thirty years. He entered the bank in 1828, and resigned in 1864, for the benefit of his health.

For many years the Bank of Delaware County (now "The Delaware County National Bank") was the only one in the county. Mr. Hinkson drove occasionally from Chester to the Black Horse Tavern (a noted cattle market), in Middletown township, and sat there to cash checks, and to do other banking business with the drovers. Although he at times took with him and brought back large sums of money, he was never molested. Before leaving the bank he engaged in the tanning business at the old yard, on Edgmont Avenue, in Chester, which his father-in-law, William Brobson, had carried on for many years. During a part of the time he had as a partner James S. Bell. He (Mr. Hinkson) sold out, in 1865, to his sons, Charles and F. J. Hinkson, Jr., who continued the same business until the decease of Charles in 1872, when the tanning business was discontinued. Since then F. J. Hinkson, Jr., has kept a store at the old stand for the sale of leather and findings. The old tannery, after more than a century of continued usefulness in tanning and finishing leather, such as slaughter, tall, loom, harness, bridle, skirting, welt, wax-upper, and calf-skins, which helped to drive the machinery of industrial establishments, to harness the horses and to shoe the people, is a thing of the past.

Mr. Hinkson was for twenty years treasurer of the borough of Chester. He was also the treasurer of the first building association started in Chester. It was called the Chester Building Association. John M. Broomall was the first president. F. J. Hinkson filled the same position subsequently. It was organized in January, 1850. There have been many associations since, which have rendered great help in building up Chester.

In 1856, Mr. Hinkson was elected one of the associate judges of the county. He resigned before his time expired. He was also elected a director of the poor and a jury commissioner, and was a treasurer of the Farmers' Market Company of Chester. He served often as an executor and guardian, and performed his duty with conscientious fidelity.

The firing on Fort Sumter, April 12, 1861, aroused the loyal North to intense excitement. The people of Delaware County felt the patriotic impulse, and immediately took action to stand by the government. The *Delaware County Republican*, in its issue of April 26, 1861, said, "Capt. Edward's company, the Union Blues, received marching orders on Saturday morning last, at nine o'clock. At six o'clock the volunteers were mustered in front of the Washington House, where they were addressed from the piazza by Judge Hinkson, who informed them that the citizens of the borough had pledged themselves that the wives and children of the soldiers should be properly cared for in their absence. The speaker paid a high compliment to the men who were about to enter the service of their country. The Rev. Mr. Talbot, of St. Paul's Episcopal, and the Rev. Mr. Sproull, of the First Presbyterian Church, also made patriotic speeches. The company left that night for Harrisburg. Measures were soon taken to form relief committees, to raise money to maintain the families of those who might be in the service of their country. A county meeting was held at Media, April 23, 1861 (of which Hon. H. Jones Brooke was chairman), which divided the county into seven districts, each district to have a committee of three, with power to increase to twelve. Each district was to have a treasurer, and collecting and distributing committees. The district treasurer was to return the funds collected to the county treasurer appointed by the meeting. The money was to be distributed pro rata among the districts, the amount given to each family to be regulated by the [illegible] made by the

dence township, and Abigail, a daughter of Frederick Engle, formerly of the borough of Chester. They were married in 1784. Their children (besides F. J. Hinkson) who reached maturity were: Jane (who married Ambrose Smedley, a farmer of Middletown township; she died in 1873, in her eighty-ninth year), Ann (who married David Baker, of Middletown township,—he was a carpenter and builder), John (whose business was that of a farmer. His first wife was Jemima, a daughter of Joseph Worrall, of Upper Providence; his second, who is now living in Chester, is Orpha, a daughter of Joseph Naide, of Chester township. John held the position of steward of the House of Employment of this county, was sheriff, a member of the State Legislature, and a recorder of deeds and register of wills), Mary (who married Abraham Hamor, formerly of Middletown, and afterwards of Hamorton, in Chester County), Joseph (who was a carpenter and builder. He married Ann, a daughter of Samuel Black, of Marple), Orpha (who married Jacob Evans, of Upper Providence, afterwards of Chester township), and Edward Engle Hinkson (who married Sarah, a daughter of Samuel Slanter, of Chester township. He was a carpenter and builder. He was the first building inspector of the city of Chester; held the office for several years, and until his death). All of the children of John Hinkson, Jr., are deceased.

Frederick J. Hinkson was born Nov. 8, 1803, in the township of Upper Providence. When he was quite young his parents moved into Middletown township. Soon after his father's decease (which happened when he was fifteen years old) he entered the store of Abraham Hamor, of that township. Mr. Hamor, in connection with his store, carried on tailoring. Mr. Hinkson having learned his trade, that of a tailor, went to school. He subsequently taught school at Upper Providence meeting-house, at Village Green, then at Columbia, in Lancaster Co., and again at Village Green. While teaching at the last-named place he was elected a clerk in the Bank of Delaware County, at Chester, in which institution, in the capacity of clerk, cashier, and president, he remained for over thirty years. He entered the bank in 1828, and resigned in 1864, for the benefit of his health.

For many years the Bank of Delaware County (now "The Delaware County National Bank") was the only one in the county. Mr. Hinkson drove occasionally from Chester to the Black Horse Tavern (a noted cattle market), in Middletown township, and sat there to cash checks, and to do other banking business with the drovers. Although he at times took with him and brought back large sums of money, he was never molested. Before leaving the bank he engaged in the tanning business at the old yard, on Edgmont Avenue, in Chester, which his father-in-law, William Brobson, had carried on for many years. During a part of the time he had as a partner James S. Bell. He (Mr.

F. J. Hinkson, Jr., who continued the same business until the decease of Charles, in 1872, when the tanning business was discontinued. Since then F. J. Hinkson, Jr., has kept a store at the old stand for the sale of leather and findings. The old tannery, after more than a century of continued usefulness in tanning and finishing leather, such as slaughter, belt, loom, harness, bridle, skirting, welt, wax-upper, and calf-skins, which helped to drive the machinery of industrial establishments, to harness the horses and to shoe the people, is a thing of the past.

Mr. Hinkson was for twenty years treasurer of the borough of Chester. He was also the treasurer of the first building association started in Chester. It was called the Chester Building Association. John M. Broomall was the first president. F. J. Hinkson filled the same position subsequently. It was organized in January, 1850. There have been many associations since, which have rendered great help in building up Chester.

In 1856, Mr. Hinkson was elected one of the associate judges of the county. He resigned before his time expired. He was also elected a director of the poor and a jury commissioner, and was a treasurer of the Farmers' Market Company of Chester. He served often as an executor and guardian, and performed his duty with conscientious fidelity.

The firing on Fort Sumter, April 12, 1861, aroused the loyal North to intense excitement. The people of Delaware County felt the patriotic impulse, and immediately took action to stand by the government. The *Delaware County Republican*, in its issue of April 26, 1861, said, "Capt. Edward's company, the Union Blues, received marching orders on Saturday morning last, at nine o'clock. At six o'clock the volunteers were mustered in front of the Washington House, where they were addressed from the piazza by Judge Hinkson, who informed them that the citizens of the borough had pledged themselves that the wives and children of the soldiers should be properly cared for in their absence. The speaker paid a high compliment to the men who were about to enter the service of their country. The Rev. Mr. Talbot, of St. Paul's Episcopal, and the Rev. Mr. Sproull, of the First Presbyterian Church, also made patriotic speeches. The company left that night for Harrisburg. Measures were soon taken to form relief committees, to raise money to maintain the families of those who might be in the service of their country. A county meeting was held at Media, April 23, 1861 (of which Hon. H. Jones Brooke was chairman), which divided the county into seven districts, each district to have a committee of three, with power to increase to twelve. Each district was to have a treasurer, and collecting and distributing committees. The district treasurer was to return the funds collected to the county treasurer appointed by the meeting. The money was to be distributed *pro rata* among the districts, the amount given to each soldier while at home. The first district consisted of the borough of Chester and of the townships of Chester, Ridley, and Tinicum. The members of the committee were F. J. Hinkson, Samuel A. Crozer, and Thomas A. Gesner.

The county committees appointed by the county meeting of April 23, 1861, met at Media, April 29th. F. J. Hinkson was chosen president; Jackson Lyons, of Haverford, vice-president; Henry Green, of Edgmont, corresponding secretary; Dr. G. B. Hotchkin, of Media, recording secretary. Auditors, Thomas Pratt, of Middletown; James Cloud, of Concord; and Washington James, of Nether Providence; Hon. Charles R. Williamson, of Media, was appointed treasurer for the county. These committees, and others that were formed, did a noble and patriotic work, second only in value to that of the brave men from Delaware County who on land and water upheld the cause of the imperiled Union.

In September, 1862, the Governor made a call for fifty thousand men to defend the State. On Tuesday, September 16th, Capt. Thatcher had a full company. On the 17th Capt. Kershaw's company was organized. The Town Council made an appropriation of fifteen hundred dollars, which was judiciously expended by John Larkin, Jr., Benjamin Gartside, and F. J. Hinkson.

In 1874, F. J. Hinkson was a candidate for the State Legislature by a popular call, and so great was the vote cast for him that, although there were three tickets in the field (he being named as an Independent), he was only defeated by a trifling plurality. He was not a member of any religious denomination. He believed in the principles of the society of Friends, and attended meeting. The only time when he deviated from the peaceable teachings of that society was during the late war, when he actively and outspokenly stood by the government.

In 1837 he married Hannah H., the only daughter of William and Rebecca Brobson. She was born June 9, 1814, and died Jan. 9, 1844. F. J. Hinkson died Sept. 10, 1879. They are buried in the Friends' burying-ground in Chester. Their children were William B., born Nov. 22, 1838; he died in 1871, unmarried; Henry, born April 14, 1840; he married Lucy, a daughter of David F. Craig, of Wilmington, Del.; Charles, born Nov. 21, 1841; he married Arabella, a daughter of R. R. Dutton, of Chester; he died in 1872, and is buried in the Chester Rural Cemetery; and F. J. Hinkson, Jr., born Oct. 4, 1843.

Henry was for years a member of the late firm of Hinkson & Smedley, who were engaged in the dry-goods and grocery business in Chester. Henry and F. J. Hinkson, Jr., are both ex-members of the Council of Chester.

On the 4th of July, 1876, F. J. Hinkson, Jr., delivered the Centennial address at the celebration at Upland. Samuel A. Crozer read the Declaration of Independence.

The ancestors of Edmund Pennell were members of the Penn colony, and settled in Rockdale, Aston township, where they were owners of one thousand acres of valuable land. His grandfather was probably William, whose children were William, James, Nathan, Thomas, Jonathan, and several daughters. The last-named son was born in Edgmont township, and in early life apprenticed to his brother-in-law as a blacksmith. He, in 1786, removed to Chester, and there followed his trade for many years. He married Sarah Hibberd, of Upper Darby township, whose children were two sons,—James and Henry Hale. By a second marriage to Ann Delaney, of Chester, were born children,—Edmund, and Jonathan who died in 1798, Sarah Ann, Edmund (2d), Sydney, Jonathan (2d), Nathan, and several who died in early life. Edmund, the subject of this biography, was born April 22, 1802, in Chester, which has been his lifetime residence. After receiving such advantages of education as the schools of the day afforded he entered the shop of his father as an assistant, though not with a view to perfecting himself in the trade. Much of his attention was also given to the cultivation of a farm in the suburbs of the borough. During the year 1835 he purchased a tract of land now embraced within the limits of the South Ward of Chester, and was for many years actively engaged as a farmer. On selling this land, in 1863, he made the city his permanent residence. Mr. Pennell was, in December, 1830, married to Miss Elizabeth J., daughter of John and Elizabeth Price. Their children are Jonathan, Anna Elizabeth (Mrs. Charles C. Larkin), Charles D., Martha S. (Mrs. Joshua P. Eyre), William, Mary C., and Edmund and Sally deceased. Mr. Pennell has been a leading spirit in the business development of Chester, as also in its growth and improvement. His father, who was an early director of the Delaware County Bank, was, at his death, succeeded by his son, Edmund, who, on the adoption of the national system, became its first president, and filled the office of director for more than thirty years. He was early in his political career a Whig, and subsequently a Republican, having been, in 1846, elected county commissioner. During his official term of three years the county-seat was removed to Media, which was surveyed and plotted under his auspices. He has also served as a member of the borough council. Both Mr. and Mrs. Pennell are Orthodox Friends in their religious faith. In the winter of 1880 this venerable couple celebrated their golden wedding, which was the occasion of congratulations from a numerous assemblage of children, grandchildren, and friends.

The First National Bank.—After the national banking law went into effect, and as one of the sections of the act required that all funds received by revenue officers and other collecting agents of the United States should be deposited in the First National Bank in the towns, cities, and districts wherein

Edm^d Pennell

soldier while at home. The [illegible] consisted of the borough of Chester and of the townships of Chester, Ridley, and Tinicum. The members of the committee were F. J. Hinkson, Samuel A. Crozer, and Thomas A. [illegible].

The [illegible] the county meeting of [illegible] at Media, April 20th. F. J. Hinkson [illegible] Jackson Lewis, of Haverford [illegible] Green, of Edgmont [illegible], Dr. [illegible] of Media [illegible] Thomas Pease, of [illegible] Charles R. Williamson, of Media [illegible] Chester [illegible] that were [illegible] work [illegible] from Delaware County [illegible] held the rank of [illegible].

In September, 1862, [illegible] fifty thousand men [illegible] September [illegible] the [illegible] Hinkson's company was organized. The Town [illegible] an appropriation of fifteen hundred dollars, which was [illegible] expended by John Larkin, Jr., Benjamin Gartside, and [illegible] son.

In 1874 [illegible] Hinkson was a candidate of the State Legislature [illegible] popular [illegible] the votes cast for him [illegible] although there were three tickets in the field [illegible] an independent, he was only defeated by [illegible] plurality. He was not a member of any religious denomination. He believed in the principles of the Society of Friends, and attended meeting. The only time when he deviated from [illegible] meetings of that society was during the war [illegible] outspokenly [illegible] the government.

In 18[illegible] the only daughter of [illegible] She was born [illegible] J. Hinkson [illegible] Friends [illegible] Their children were [illegible] he died in 1871, [illegible] he married [illegible] daughter of [illegible], of Washington, [illegible] 1841; he married Ann [illegible] H. Dutton, of Chester [illegible] Cemetery [illegible] Hinkson, Jr., [illegible] a member of the [illegible] Hinkson [illegible] were engaged in the [illegible] in Chester [illegible]

[illegible] F. J. Hinkson, Jr., [illegible] at the celebration at [illegible] read the Declaration of [illegible]

The ancestors of Edmund Pennell were members of the Penn colony, and settled in Rockdale, Aston township, where they were owners of one thousand acres of valuable land. His grandfather was probably William, whose children were William, James, Nathan, Thomas, Jonathan, and several daughters. The last-named son was born in Edgmont township, and in early life apprenticed to his brother-in-law as a blacksmith. He, in 1780[?], removed to Chester, and there followed the trade for many years. He married Sarah Hibbard[?], of Upper Darby township, whose children were two sons,—James and Henry Hale. By a second marriage to Ann Delaney, of Chester, were born children,—Edmund, and Jonathan who died in 1798, Sarah Ann, Edmund (2d), Sydney, Jonathan (2d), Nathan, and several who died in early life. Edmund, the subject of this biography, was born [illegible] 1808[?], in Chester, which has been his lifelong residence. After receiving such advantages of education as the schools of the day afforded he entered the shop of his father as an assistant, though [illegible] in perfecting himself in the trade. Much of his attention was also given to the cultivation of land in the suburbs of the borough. During the year 1838 he purchased a tract of land now embraced within the limits of the South Ward of Chester, and was for many years actively engaged as a farmer in tilling this land. In 1868, he made the city his permanent residence. Mr. Pennell was, in [illegible], married to Miss Elizabeth J., daughter of [illegible] and Elizabeth Price. Their children are [illegible], Anna Elizabeth (Mrs. Charles C. Larkin), [illegible], Martha S. (Mrs. Joshua P. Eyre), William, Mary C., and Edmund and Sally deceased. Mr. Pennell has been a leading spirit in the business development of Chester, as also in its growth and improvement. His father, who was an early director of the Delaware County Bank, was, at his death, succeeded by his son, Edmund, who, on the adoption of the national system, became its first president, and filled the office of director for more than thirty years. He was early in his political career a Whig, and subsequently a Republican. He has been, in 1846, elected county commissioner. During his official term of three years the county-seat was removed to Media, which was surveyed and [illegible] under his auspices. He has also served as a member of the borough council. Both Mr. and Mrs. Pennell are Orthodox Friends in their religious faith. In the winter of 1889[?] this venerable couple celebrated their golden wedding, which was the occasion of congratulations from a numerous group of children, grandchildren, and friends.

The First National Bank.—When the national banking law went into effect, one of the sections of the act required that all funds received by revenue officers and other disbursing agents of the United States should be deposited at the First National Bank in the towns, cities, and districts wherein

Edmd Pennell

John Larkin Jr.

that officers were authorized to act, it became an important matter to secure the first charter for a national bank in Chester, where, by reason of its manufacturing interests, the United States revenue tax amounted to many thousands of dollars. Hence, on Feb. 26, 1864, Samuel M. Felton, Thomas Reaney, Samuel Archbold, Benjamin Gartside, Amos Gartside, Abraham R. Perkins, J. T. Rutter, Samuel Eccles, Jr., Jacob Simes, John Gartside, and William Ward signed articles of association for a national bank to be located in Chester, and William Ward was dispatched to Washington to secure the charter. The bank was not regularly organized until May 16, 1864, when Abraham R. Perkins was elected president, William Taylor cashier, and a board of directors chosen, consisting of Abraham R. Perkins, Samuel M. Felton, Thomas Reaney, Benjamin Gartside, Samuel Archbold, Samuel Eccles, Jr., and William Ward. The seal of the bank had been agreed upon at a previous informal meeting, when it was decided it should represent a steam-engine and power-loom, the distinctive industries of the city. On March 24, 1864, the bank purchased a house and lot at the southwest corner of Second and Penn Streets for thirty-four hundred dollars, and there, at the date already given, the First National Bank opened its doors to receive deposits and to conduct a general banking business. The location of the building was on a side street, away from the centre of trade, hence it was determined to remove to another and better situation when opportunity should offer. To that end, on Oct. 10, 1870, the present banking-house, immediately south of the town hall, on Market Street, was purchased from George Baker, the front removed, a serpentine-stone front substituted, and internally the structure was arranged to meet the requirements of a banking institution. On Jan. 18, 1871, the First National Bank began business at its new location, and the following day, January 19th, Abraham R. Perkins, having removed from Chester, and because of failing health resigned the presidency, to which position John Larkin, Jr., was elected on the 23d of the same month. The old banking-house on Penn Street was purchased by George Baker, and later sold to Orlando Harvey, who converted it into a dwelling-house. On May 30, 1881, Frank B. Palmer was elected cashier, William Taylor having resigned that office, which he had held since the incorporation of the bank. The present board of directors is as follows: John Larkin, Jr., Benjamin Gartside, John Gartside, Mortimer H. Bickley, James Irving, William E. Broomall, and William Hausman.

John Larkin, Jr., the president of the First National Bank, is one of four men to whom Chester is indebted for much of its present prosperity, the other three being John P. Crozer, James Campbell, and John M. Broomall.

John Larkin, the great-grandfather of the subject of this biographical sketch, emigrated from England, and was one of the earliest settlers in Delaware County. He had among his children a son, Joseph, whose son, John, married Martha Thomas, whose ancestors were of Welsh descent. Their son, John, was born Oct. 2, 1804, in Concord township, Delaware Co., and after limited advantages of the country schools, was employed until twenty-one years of age upon his father's farm. He engaged in mercantile pursuits for one year at Chichester, and later for three years at Marcus Hook. He in 1832 purchased a freight-vessel and established a packet-line between Marcus Hook and Philadelphia, which was continued until 1839, when he sold the vessel, wharf, and business interest. He was elected sheriff of Delaware County in 1840, and on the expiration of his term removed to a farm of one hundred and fifty-five acres in Lower Chichester, upon which he had erected new and commodious buildings. During the years 1845 and 1846, he represented his district in the State Legislature. Mr. Larkin, in 1848, made Chester his home, and the same year built two vessels and established a daily line of packets between that city and Philadelphia, the boats having previously run but twice a week. He in 1849 formed a copartnership with William Booth, under the firm-name of Booth & Larkin, for the purpose of running packets daily from Chester to Philadelphia in the interest of the coal and lumber business. The firm enjoyed a prosperous career until 1852, when the partnership was dissolved, and Mr. Larkin's attention was directed to real-estate operations consequent upon the exchange, in 1850, of his farm for eighty-three acres in the North Ward of Chester, formerly used as a race-course. This property was at once laid out in streets and the lots sold for building purposes. In 1851 he entered into a contract to erect for Abram Blakeley a cotton-mill of any dimensions, which contract was completed before the specified time and adequately illustrates the energy and business capacity of the subject of this sketch. He also erected the same year, twenty-two dwellings, and by the large sale of lots was enabled to carry out to the fullest extent the various beneficent enterprises he had projected. This movement, which gave a decided impetus to Chester and its manufacturing interests, was followed by the erection of a total of one hundred and forty-six dwellings and thirteen manufacturing establishments of various kinds. Mr. Larkin, in 1871, sold the last unimproved building-lot, and thus disposed of the eighty-three acres he originally acquired. In 1870 he purchased a tract of land at Marcus Hook, containing twenty-three acres, which was at once laid out in streets and building-lots. On this he erected sixty dwellings, two machine-shops, two foundries, and a large hosiery-mill. He has been actively identified with the municipal interests of Chester, was for eleven years a member of the Borough Council and for six years president of that body. On its incorporation as a city in 1866 he was chosen its first mayor,

such officers were authorized to act, it became an important matter to secure the first charter for a national bank in Chester, where, by reason of its manufacturing interests, the United States revenue tax amounted to many thousands of dollars. Hence, on Feb. 25, 1863, Samuel M. Felton, Thomas Reaney, Samuel Archbold, Benjamin Gartside, Amos Gartside, Abraham R. Perkins, L. T. Rutter, Samuel Eccles, Jr., Jacob Sinex, John Gartside, and William Ward signed articles of association for a national bank, to be located in Chester, and William Ward was dispatched to Washington to secure the charter. The bank was not regularly organized until May 15, 1864, when Abraham R. Perkins was elected president, William Taylor cashier, and a board of directors chosen, consisting of Abraham R. Perkins, Samuel M. Felton, Thomas Reaney, Benjamin Gartside, Samuel Archbold, Samuel Eccles, Jr., and William Ward. The seal of the bank had been agreed upon at a previous informal meeting, when it was decided it should represent a steam-engine and power-loom, the distinctive industries of the city. On March 24, 1864, the bank purchased a house and lot at the southwest corner of Second and Penn Streets for thirty-four hundred dollars, and there, at the date already given, the First National Bank opened its doors to receive deposits and to conduct a general banking business. The location of the building was on a side street, away from the centre of trade, hence it was determined to remove to another and better situation when opportunity should offer. To that end, on Oct. 10, 1870, the present banking-house, immediately south of the town hall, on Market Street, was purchased from George Baker, the front removed, a serpentine-stone front substituted, and internally the structure was arranged to meet the requirements of a banking institution. On Jan. 18, 1871, the First National Bank began business at its new location, and the following day, January 19th, Abraham R. Perkins, having removed from Chester, and because of failing health resigned the presidency, to which position John Larkin, Jr., was elected on the 23d of the same month. The old banking-house on Penn Street was purchased by George Baker, and later sold to Orlando Harvey, who converted it into a dwelling-house. On May 26, 1884, Frank R. Palmer was elected cashier, William Taylor having resigned that office, which he had held since the incorporation of the bank. The present board of directors is as follows: John Larkin, Jr., Benjamin Gartside, John Gartside, Mortimer H. Bickley, James Irving, William B. Broomall, and William Hannum.

John Larkin, Jr., the president of the First National Bank, is one of four men to whom Chester is indebted for much of its present prosperity, the other three being John P. Crozer, James Campbell, and John M. Broomall.

John Larkin, the great-grandfather of the subject of this biographical sketch, emigrated from England, and was one of the earliest settlers in Delaware County. He had among his children a son, Joseph, whose son, John, married Martha Thomas, whose ancestors were of Welsh descent. Their son, John, was born Oct. 3, 1804, in Concord township, Delaware Co., and after limited advantages of the country schools, was employed until twenty-one years of age upon his father's farm. He engaged in mercantile pursuits for one year at Chichester, and later for three years at Marcus Hook. He in 1832 purchased a freight-vessel and established a packet-line between Marcus Hook and Philadelphia, which was continued until 1839, when he sold the vessel, wharf, and business interest. He was elected sheriff of Delaware County in 1840, and on the expiration of his term removed to a farm of one hundred and fifty-five acres in Lower Chichester, upon which he had erected new and commodious buildings. During the years 1845 and 1846, he represented his district in the State Legislature. Mr. Larkin, in 1848, made Chester his home, and the same year built two vessels and established a daily line of packets between that city and Philadelphia, the boats having previously run but twice a week. He in 1849 formed a copartnership with William Booth, under the firm-name of Booth & Larkin, for the purpose of running packets daily from Chester to Philadelphia in the interest of the coal and lumber business. The firm enjoyed a prosperous career until 1852, when the partnership was dissolved, and Mr. Larkin's attention was directed to real-estate operations consequent upon the exchange, in 1850, of his farm for eighty-three acres in the North Ward of Chester, formerly used as a race-course. This property was at once laid out in streets and the lots sold for building purposes. In 1854 he entered into a contract to erect for Abram Blakeley a cotton-mill of any dimensions, which contract was completed before the specified time, and adequately illustrates the energy and business capacity of the subject of this sketch. He also erected, the same year, twenty-two dwellings, and by the large sale of lots was enabled to carry out to the fullest extent the various beneficent enterprises he had projected. This movement, which gave a decided impetus to Chester and its manufacturing interests, was followed by the erection of a total of one hundred and forty-six dwellings and thirteen manufacturing establishments of various kinds. Mr. Larkin, in 1881, sold the last unimproved building-lot, and thus disposed of the eighty-three acres he originally acquired. In 1870 he purchased a tract of land at Marcus Hook, containing twenty-three acres, which was at once laid out in streets and building-lots. On this he erected sixty dwellings, two machine-shops, two foundries, and a large hosiery-mill. He has been actively identified with the municipal interests of Chester, was for eleven years a member of the Borough Council, and for six years president of that body. On its incorporation as a city, in 1866, he was chosen its first mayor, and held the office for six consecutive years, refusing to receive a salary for his services. He was one of the originators of the Chester Rural Cemetery, and for years president of the association. He was also one of the founders of the Chester Mutual Insurance Company, and has been its president since the beginning of its business operations. He has also been, since 1871, president of the First National Bank of Chester. Mr. Larkin was in 1827 married to Miss Charlotte, daughter of Capt. Erasmus Morton, to whom were born children, Charles C., Caroline (Mrs. John M. Broomall), John M. (deceased), Lewis M., Nathan, Francis, Henry, Mary (Mrs. Thomas Gilbert). Mrs. Larkin died in 1847, and he was again married to Miss Mary A., daughter of William Baggs, whose children are Clarence and Ella (Mrs. Richard Wetherill). Mrs. Larkin's death occurred in 1877.

The Chester National Bank.—This institution, under the above title, was chartered as a national bank March 1, 1884, and began business as such on the 1st day of April thereafter. Samuel A. Dyer was chosen president; Samuel H. Leeds, cashier; and a board of directors elected, consisting of J. Frank Black, Robert Wetherill, Hugh Shaw, Charles B. Houston, William Appleby, George B. Lindsay, Jonathan Pennell, H. B. Black, and Samuel A. Dyer. Its career has been one of marked success, its business being largely in excess of that which its founders anticipated. The banking-house is located on West Third Street near Market Square, a handsome granite building, which was erected in 1873 by Samuel A. Dyer and William Appleby for a private banking office, to which afterwards large additions and improvements were made. In 1875, William Appleby retired from the firm, and the business was continued by Col. Dyer until it was finally merged into the Chester National Bank.

The Chester Library.—By the record of the old Library Company of Chester, it appears, "a number of the most considerable inhabitants of the borough having from time to time had in consideration the good consequences that would result from the erection of a public library in the said borough for the promotion of useful knowledge, did at length proceed to enter into articles for the forming themselves into a company for that purpose, agreeable to which articles they met on the tenth day of May, Anno Domini, 1769, in order to pay in the sum of money proposed to be advanced by each member, and to elect and chuse proper officers for the more effectual carrying their design into execution. At which time were chose: Directors—Henry Hale Graham, Elisha Price, David Jackson, Nicholas Fairlamb, Thomas Moore; Treasurer, Thomas Sharpless; Secretary, Peter Steele."

Previous to this meeting preliminary affairs had been adjusted, for on the 14th day of February, 1769, an explicit agreement, entitled "Articles of the Library Company of Chester," had been adopted, signed and sealed, the latter marks with a scrawl of a pen, but the first sixteen names had attached to each a veritable wax seal, stamped with the armorial bearings of Henry Hale Graham, "That for distinction sake," the old agreement declares, "the subscribers in company, now and hereafter at all Times, are and shall be called the Library Company of Chester." The subscribers obligated themselves each to pay thirty shillings to raise a fund for the purchase of books. At no time should the number of subscribers exceed one hundred, and no one could be a shareholder unless he had subscribed to the articles of association. Each and every subscriber was required yearly to pay seven shillings and sixpence, a neglect to do so being punishable with a fine, and at the end of two years, if such shareholder was still in default, he should "therefrom forever after be excluded from the said partnership," and his share forfeited. The association was to continue "for and during the space of one hundred years," and the books and effects of the company should remain "the indistinguishable property of all the members."

The books in the library were loaned to subscribers for designated periods, according to the size of the volume, and a note was required to be given conditioned for the payment of twice the value of the book in case of its loss. On the 6th of September, 1769, the directors and officers of the company met "at Joseph Ogden's, in Philadelphia, to purchase books," which was done. The library was kept in Francis Ruth's house, and he was directed "to make a press of dimensions at least sufficient to contain the said books," for which he was to be paid forty shillings. On Aug. 10, 1770, it was ordered after "the next purchase of books a set of compleat catalogues shall be printed at the expense of the Company, and each member shall be entitled to one for his own use." On Nov. 10, 1770, Henry Hale Graham, Elisha Price, and Hugh Lloyd were instructed to buy books "with what money is in bank." At that date Ruth had not furnished the "press," and he was fined for his neglect, and informed that if it was not done in three weeks he would be fined seven shillings and sixpence. He finished it, and on May 25, 1771, complained that the price for which he had agreed to make it was too low, whereupon the directors allowed him three pounds, out of which, however, they deducted his fines, and the cost of a book, "The Husband," which he could not account for. The treasurer paid him one pound thirteen shillings and ten pence. Prior to May 15, 1775, the library was removed to the old schoolhouse at Fifth and Welsh Streets, and a board partition separated the place where the books were kept from the other part of the room. During the Revolution there appear to have been but few business meetings of the company, the last one held May 20, 1775, and the next occurring May 10, 1780. Interest had been lost in the association, and on Aug. 1, 1789, it was discussed whether the company should not disband and the books and other property be distributed among the members, but it was decided that no such action could be had without an act of the Legislature. The company dragged thereafter. On Aug. 22, 1835, the books had been removed to the town hall, a frame structure covering half of the market-house, which stood in Market Square, comprising one room about twenty feet square. The old frame town hall is now owned by J. Edward Clyde, having been removed to Fifth Street east of Market when the market-house was torn down, in 1857, and is now a Chinese laundry. When the building was demolished the library was temporarily placed in a room in the old court-house, remaining there until 1866, when it was removed to the office of Joseph Taylor, in National Hall. In 1840 the title of the association was changed to "The Chester Library Company" by act of Assembly, but the ancient "partnership" had become so enfeebled by its weight of years that it could not be recuperated, so that when in January, 1871, it was removed to a room in the second story of the Farmers' Market, on Fourth Street, it was laid away to accumulate dust on its unused volumes, and that such an association exists in this city has been almost forgotten.

Holly Tree Hall, on the north side of Seventh Street west of Edgmont Avenue, is a brick building containing on the upper floor a large audience-room capable of seating over six hundred persons, handsomely fitted and arranged for lectures and public entertainments, while on the lower floor is a commodious library and reading-room, and a large apartment specially furnished for the use of Miss Laura J. Hard's Bible-class. In the front there are two rooms leased for store purposes. Holly Tree Hall is the outgrowth of an attempt of Miss Hard to provide a resort where workingmen and females might assemble in the evening for conversation and reading. To this end she labored diligently, succeeding in enlisting the public in the enterprise. Money and books were donated, and in January, 1873, three rooms were leased over H. B. Taylor's hardware store, on Third Street near Market Square, and the "Mechanics' Reading-Room" opened to the public. The apartments soon became too small to meet the demand made upon them, and it was determined to erect a building adapted to the purposes intended. A charter was obtained from the court, stock was issued, and in May, 1877, the present building was built. There are nearly two thousand volumes on the shelves of the institution, the books being free to all who may visit the library, but can only be taken therefrom by stockholders, and the reading-room is well supplied with daily newspapers of Philadelphia, the local press, and current standard American periodicals. The officers of the association are Hugh Shaw, president; George B. Lindsay, secretary; and Miss Laura Hard, treasurer.

Chester Institute of Science.—A call for a meeting of citizens to consider the advisability of forming an Institute of Science was issued on Feb. 26, 1882, by Thomas Moore, Adam C. Eckfeldt, and Dr. F. R. Graham. Mr. Moore had long been interested in the matter, and it was through his efforts that the first steps towards a formal organization were taken. On Thursday, March 2, 1882, the following gentlemen assembled at the office of D. M. Johnson, Esq.: Thomas Moore, Adam C. Eckfeldt, Dr. F. R. Graham, George Gilbert, Felix de Lannoy, Ward R. Bliss, Henry B. Taylor, Dr. R. H. Milner, D. M. Johnson, Dr. C. W. Perkins, Henry Palmer, Dr. C. W. de Lannoy, and B. F. Morley. Adam C. Eckfeldt was called to the chair, and Dr. De Lannoy was made secretary. Great interest was shown in the matter, and, after some general discussion of the subject, a committee, consisting of Ward R. Bliss, Thomas Moore, and Dr. De Lannoy, was appointed to draft a constitution and bylaws.

A second meeting was held at the Armory, on Friday, March 10th. George Gilbert was called to the chair, and Capt. B. F. Morley appointed secretary. A constitution was adopted, and under it an election was held, April 14th, and the following permanent officers were chosen: President, George Gilbert; Vice-Presidents, Adam C. Eckfeldt, Professor F. de Lannoy; Secretary, Thomas W. Scott; Treasurer, Thomas Moore; Librarian, Henry B. Taylor; Managers, Dr. Ellwood Harvey, Henry Greenwood, M. Louise Clancy, Dr. R. H. Milner, and Dr. C. W. de Lannoy.

Thomas W. Scott, secretary, resigned November 10th, and John Miller was elected in his stead. Upon the removal of the latter from the State, Charles St. J. McKee was made secretary on Feb. 9, 1883. Owing to business engagements Mr. McKee resigned, and Frank R. Gilbert became secretary on the 9th of November.

At the first stated meeting, on April 14, 1882, D. M. Johnson, Esq., Hon. Y. S. Walter, and Thomas Lees were appointed a committee to procure a charter; and on June 5th the society was incorporated by the Court under the title of the "Chester Institute of Science and Mechanic Arts." The members named as corporators in the charter are as follows:

George Gilbert, Ellwood Harvey, Y. S. Walter, Thomas Moore, F. de Lannoy, H. B. Taylor, Thomas Lees, D. M. Johnson, Thomas W. Scott, Charles F. Foster, Thomas B. Robinson, Benjamin D. Johnson, Reuben Yarnall, J. L. Forwood, J. T. DeSilver, Clarence Larkin, Benjamin F. Baker, M. L. Clancy, Ward R. Bliss, and H. G. Ashmead.

The objects of the society are "to promote the diffusion of general and scientific knowledge among the members and the community at large, and the establishment and maintenance of a Library, Historical Record, and a Museum."

A library of two or three hundred volumes is already collected. The museum, of several thousand specimens, has already reached such proportions as to command much attention from visitors. The departments of mineralogy, antiquities, entomology, numismatics, etc., are well represented, and rapidly increasing in interest.

Early in the fall of 1882 it was deemed best to supplement the work of the monthly meetings by a series of weekly lectures and discussions. Under this arrangement there have been given before the institute, since its organization, over one hundred lectures and addresses by distinguished gentlemen from abroad or by its own members. Great interest has been shown in the meetings, and the constant donations and continued applications for membership show that the society has a strong hold upon the people.

The regular meetings of the institute are held at Fourth and Market Streets on the second Friday of each month, except July and August, but through the fall, winter, and early spring meetings are held on every Friday evening. All meetings are open to the public.

It is, perhaps, worthy of record that the first successful course of lectures in Chester was held under the direction of the institute during 1883–84. Sixteen lectures were given, all of a high order of merit, by some of the most distinguished talent in the country.

The institute is only two years old, but it has a membership of over one hundred and fifty. It is in a sound financial condition, and its most active promoters include the ablest scientific and literary people of Chester. The society is a necessity, and it will therefore live and flourish.

Jefferson Library Association.—A number of persons living near the ship-yards of John Roach being desirous of having a library and reading-room in that section of the city, gathered together about the 1st of January, 1881, and organized an association with the above name. Arrangements were made to fit up the present room on Third Street below Kerlin, in the block belonging to the Fennel estate. About the 1st of March in that year, John Roach, Jr., donated to the association a number of very valuable books and several valuable pictures. Other donations followed, and as funds accumulated purchases of books, and at present the library has about five hundred volumes. The tables are also supplied with the papers and magazines of the day.

The rooms are opened every evening, and the membership is eighty-five.

The present officers are John B. Saunders, president; James Barroclough, secretary; James Salter, librarian; James P. Barr, treasurer.

The Post-Boy and Upland Union.—The history of the press in this city is a notable one, and perhaps no town in Pennsylvania of the same population has been the birthplace of as many newspaper enterprises as Chester. Its earliest publication was the *Post-Boy*, a weekly folio, fifteen and a half by nine and a half inches, owned and edited by Steuben Butler and Eliphalet B. Worthington, the editorial rooms and printing-office being located in the Colbourn house, on Third Street, directly opposite Brown's Hotel, which is now being removed to erect on its site a large drug-store and dwelling. The first number was issued Monday, Nov. 8, 1817, and bore the motto, "Intelligence is the life of liberty." The paper was edited, printed, and distributed through the county by post-riders; which was done by Worthington and William W. Doyle, then a small lad, who had entered the office as an apprentice. The second issue of the paper was changed to Friday. Little attention was paid to passing events, and save only a few advertisements of local interest it might have been published in Boston or New York. During the first months a solitary local item presented itself to the readers of the *Post-Boy*, and, as it is the first local incident recorded in a newspaper distinctively published in Delaware County, we reproduce it:

"A Live Eel.—An eel was caught in Chester Creek a few days since by Messrs. Sutton and Burk, which weighed six pounds, and was upwards of two feet and six inches in length."

In the latter part of the year 1824, Butler sold his interest to Worthington, who continued to issue it until 1826, when he sold it to Joseph M. C. Lescure, who changed the name to the *Upland Union*, and increased the size of the paper. Lescure had his office on Market Street, nearly opposite to the court-house, and in addition sold "blank-books, stationery, spelling- and copy-books, slates, dictionaries, Testaments, etc.," which branch of business he seems to have discontinued after he removed his printing-office to the north side of Fifth Street below Market. Mr. Lescure continued the *Upland Union* with indifferent success until 1838, when he sold the paper to Joseph Williams and Charles F. Coates. Of the latter we have no information other than given. Williams we know was a lawyer of attainments, a good political speaker, who could "sing a wine-song or a hymn, preach a sermon or deliver a temperance lecture, besides being a clever amateur performer on several musical instruments."[1] He was one of the assistant secretaries of the convention which amended the Constitution of Pennsylvania in 1837. The newspaper was edited by Mr. Williams only for a short time, when it was sold to Alexander Nesbit. Williams was appointed by President Polk a judge in Iowa. During the Mexican war a volunteer company paraded in front of the hotel where the judge was lodging, and the captain told the former he had marching orders. Judge Williams offered himself as a volunteer. "The company is full," was the reply. "Perhaps you want a musician?" said the judge. "We want a fifer," responded the captain. "I'm your man!" exclaimed the judge, and he at once donned the uniform and marched away, playing "Yankee Doodle" like a regular. The quota being filled, the company was not forwarded to the front.

1 *Philadelphia Spirit of the Times*, 1846.

Y. S. Walter

After the Territory became a State, Mr Williams was made chief justice

Alexander Nesbit in turn sold the *Upland Union* to Alexander McKeever, an active Democrat, who continued its publication until March 30, 1852, when he discontinued it

Samuel Anderson McKeever, a son of the editor of the *Upland Union*, born in Chester, died in March, 1880, at Pilatka, Fla The young man had been connected with the press of the city of New York, and in 1874, in connection with James B Mix, published "The New York Tombs," an interesting, but in several instances inaccurate, story of that noted prison and the conspicuous prisoners who had been confined therein In 1858 an attempt was made to revive the *Upland Union*, and it "languished, and, languishing, did live," under the editorial control of Mr Brimner, who at the same time edited the *Pennsylvanian* in Philadelphia, and William Cooper Talley, of Delaware County, but it finally suspended Feb 19, 1861, the last-named person having removed to Norristown.

During the Presidential contest of 1828, William Russell began the publication of the *Weekly Visitor*, and Strange N Palmer was employed to edit it in the interest of the opponents of the Democratic party, to which political organization the *Upland Union* gave earnest support. The owner and editor of the new organ disagreed in their views, which difficulty terminated by a sale of the establishment to thirty gentlemen, warm advocates of John Quincy Adams, Palmer being still retained to edit the paper The fact being noised abroad, the *Upland Union* dubbed its opponent "The Son of Many Fathers," and predicted its early demise In that prognostication it was right, for at the close of the campaign it was sold to Thomas Eastman, who continued it, and it languished until 1832, when it died. Palmer, after he severed his connection with the *Visitor*, removed to Schuylkill County, where he subsequently became a judge

The Delaware County Republican—In the summer of 1833 the material and press of the *Weekly Visitor* were purchased by Y S Walter, who removed them to the village of Darby, and published the first number of the *Delaware County Republican*, on August 31st of that year The *Upland Union*, shortly after the *Republican* made its appearance in the county, stated that "the first person who Walter consulted was an old Tory of the Revolution, a partisan of King George, who conducted Lord Howe into Philadelphia, and escaped hanging for treason only by burying himself for several weeks in the neighboring woods of Darby" The allusion has lost its point in lapse of years, but the whole story is doubtless false, editorial unpleasantness in those days being carried on, and statements made without regard to fairness or truth On Oct 25, 1841, Walter removed his printing-office to Chester, locating on the northeast corner of Market Square, thence, in March, 1845, to the brick building on Third Street, now occupied by William Lamb as a hat-store In 1851 the paper was again removed to Penn Buildings, and in 1876 to the new and commodious office erected by Walter at Market and Graham Streets During the fifty years the *Republican* was edited by Walter it grew steadily in size until, at the time of his death, it was four times as large a sheet as when first issued at Chester On Sept 1, 1882, the *Delaware County Republican* was purchased by Ward R Bliss, under whose able management the oldest paper in the county has been compelled to enlarge its size to accommodate the increasing advertising demands on its columns

Young S Walter was born in Philadelphia, Feb 14, 1812 His father, Capt Peter P Walter, was of Scotch descent, and owner of a line of vessels trading to the West Indies He died when his son was quite young, leaving him in charge of his grandfather at Bedford, Pa, where he was educated in the common district schools He left school in 1826, and was apprenticed to the printing business with Thomas R Gettys, of the same place, remaining with him until 1829, when he began life on his own account as a journeyman in Philadelphia and New York, continuing that occupation until 1833 He then removed to Darby, and on August 4th, of the same year, established the *Delaware County Republican*, which he continued to publish in that place until November, 1841 In that year he removed to Chester, where he still published the paper on Whig and Republican principles One of the most noteworthy features of his journal was the strong and emphatic opposition he made to slavery, being one of the earliest advocates of its entire abolition in this country, and the articles which frequently appeared on this subject had so much weight, and were so ably and forcibly written, that they materially increased the sale of his paper, which had a larger circulation than any in the county He sent forth from his office many apprentices who obtained eminent positions in the country, among whom may be mentioned William Ward, the first lawyer in Chester, John W Forney, Jr, of the *Philadelphia Press*, Henry T Crosby, chief clerk of the War Department at Washington, D C, and many others Mr Walter was inspector of customs at Marcus Hook from 1842 to 1844, and postmaster at Chester during President Lincoln's first term of administration He was also at different times member of the Council of the borough and city of Chester, as also president of that body He was prominent as an originator of the Farmers' Market of Philadelphia, and of the corresponding one at Chester He was also president of the Chester Library Company, organized in 1769, and influentially connected with many other enterprises and institutions of a local and general character Mr Walter was married, in 1833, to Lætitia, daughter of Jesse Warne, of Philadelphia Throughout his long course of editorial and journalistic life he uniformly maintained a high character for ability and integrity, and contributed largely by his personal influence and by his pen towards the spread of that high tone of morality which ever marked his own career. The death of Mr. Walter occurred May 22, 1882, in his seventy-first year.

Delaware County Democrat.—In 1835, Caleb Pierce established a weekly newspaper under the above title in advocacy of Henry A. Muhlenberg's candidacy as Governor, but it was short-lived. In October, 1856, John G. Michelon began the publication of a weekly, called the *Upland Union and Delaware County Democrat*, and its life was also but a span. Oct. 5, 1867, the *Delaware County Democrat* was established by D. B. Overholt, whose interest was shortly afterwards purchased by Dr. J. L. Forwood, who continued the publication of the paper until the fall of 1871, when he sold it to Col. William Cooper Talley. Early in 1876 John B. McCay purchased it, but shortly afterwards sold it to William Orr, who at the time was publishing the *Democratic Pilot*, a paper which had been started in 1872, and had died and been resurrected several times. The two papers were merged into one, and were sold by the sheriff, on an execution against Orr, to Dr. Forwood, in 1877, who, in turn, sold it to William A. Gwynne. The latter, in August, 1879, disposed of his interest to Edw. J. Frysinger, whose father, H. Frysinger, then became publisher, and issued the first paper under his editorial charge, Sept. 4, 1879. At the time Mr. Frysinger purchased the *Democrat* it had less than one hundred and seventy-five *bona-fide* subscribers, and only a nominal advertising patronage. It was purchased for the estimated value of the printing materials belonging to the office, the good will being considered valueless. The energy, enterprise, and talent which Mr. Frysinger devoted to his paper has made it a remunerative and valuable property, and its circulation has very largely increased. Being the only Democratic newspaper in the county, the field for extending its circulation is yet both broad and inviting.

On the 11th of February, 1884, H. & Ed. J. Frysinger issued the first number of the *Daily Herald*, as an independent journal with "Democratic tendencies." This newspaper venture was designed originally merely for the spring election, and more especially the mayoralty campaign; but before the first issue appeared it had been determined to establish it permanently.

The Delaware County Advocate.—John Spencer, who had a printing-office in the second story of the old City Hall building, and Richard Miller, on June 6, 1868, issued the *Chester Advocate*, a weekly newspaper; size, fifteen by twenty inches, four columns to the page. It was distributed gratuitously at first. The paper was so well conducted and its reading matter so well selected that it soon met with public favor. The proprietorship continued as above until May, 1869, when Mr. Miller withdrew, and Mr. Spencer took sole charge. The paper was enlarged from time to time, and soon a subscription of fifty cents per year was charged. The popularity of the *Advocate* spread beyond the limits of Chester City, and in September, 1874, Mr. Spencer changed its title to *The Delaware County Advocate*, and raised its subscription price to one dollar per year. It is now a nine-column folio, thirty-one by forty-four inches, has an extensive circulation throughout the county, and is regarded as one of the most valuable newspaper properties in the neighborhood of Philadelphia.

Chester Evening News.—Saturday, June 1, 1872, the first number of the *Evening News* was issued by F. Stanhope Hill, as editor and proprietor. It was a folio sheet, eighteen by twenty-five. The title of the paper was changed June 17th of the same year to *Chester Evening News*. The first month of its publication the venture was regarded by the inhabitants of the city in no kindly spirit, and many were the prognostications of ultimate failure, but by degrees it won its way to public favor. Mr. Hill, Oct. 1, 1872, sold his interest to William A. Todd, and the latter continued its publication until his death, Aug. 18, 1879, when it was purchased by William H. Bowen, Oliver Troth, and Charles D. Williamson. During Mr. Todd's ownership the circulation had so increased that he was compelled to twice enlarge the presses to meet the growing popular demand. The new owners assumed the conduct of the paper September 29th of the same year, and immediately after enlarged it by an addition of two inches to the columns. Mr. Williamson did not take an active part in editing the paper until nearly a year subsequent to its purchase, and in less than twelve months after he began work in the office as city editor he died, and his interest was purchased by the surviving partners. Nov. 4, 1880, the *News* was again enlarged by an addition of another column to each page, and to meet its steadily-increasing circulation its proprietors have twice been compelled to add new presses of increased capacity and speed. In 1883, for the third time the size of the paper was enlarged. The *Chester Evening News*, although strongly Republican in tone, is never offensive in its presentation of its political preferences.

Chester Daily Times.—Maj. John Hodgson, who had established the *Jeffersonian* in West Chester, having sold that paper to the present proprietor, came to Chester in the summer of 1876, and in September of that year issued the first number of the *Chester Daily Times*, the second daily afternoon paper published in Chester. Mr. Hodgson continued as its editor until his failing health compelled him to dispose of it, March 7, 1877, to J. Craig, Jr., who had been on the editorial staff since its first issue. He managed it quite successfully, displaying considerable ability and enterprise in its conduct. On October 20th, of the same year, Mr. Craig sold the *Times* to John Spencer, the proprietor of *The Delaware County Advocate*. The owner enlarged the paper from five to six columns and otherwise improved it. He continued its publication until April 15, 1882, when he sold it to the Times Publishing Company, its present owner The latter had purchased *The Delaware County Gazette*, which, under the title of *The Delaware County Paper*, had been established, in 1876, by Col William C Gray, and subsequently passed into the ownership of John McFeeters, then Maj D. R B Nevin, who changed its name to the *Gazette*, and finally of A Donath The *Times*, under its new management, has shown great energy, and to keep pace with the increase of circulation and advertising patronage has been enlarged three times, until now it is one of the largest daily papers published in the State, excepting those in Philadelphia and Pittsburgh It is ultra Republican in tone and well edited

The Weekly Reporter, an octavo publication, advertising legal notices, and reporting in full the opinions of the courts of Delaware County, was established March 31, 1881, by Ward R. Bliss, Esq Mr Bliss has continued *The Weekly Reporter* with marked ability Recently the opinions which have appeared in the *Reporter* have been published in a handsome volume, entitled "Delaware County Reports"

In 1882, *The Chester Business Mirror*, a monthly advertising paper, was published by Edward Frysinger, and is now well established

In August, 1842, Edward E Flavill and Mr Jackson published *The Chariot*, an advocate of the cause of temperance The paper was printed in Philadelphia, but after a few numbers had been issued it was discontinued

Occasionally, in 1848, a small folio, *The Owl*, was published in Chester and circulated at night It was very personal in its articles, and although many of its gibes and hits are pointless now, at the time of its publication it caused much excitement in the ancient town

In April, 1850, S E Cohen, a new agent in the borough, began the publication of the *Chester Herald*, issuing it monthly, subsequently changing it to a weekly sheet, and finally discontinued it at the end of twelve months.

In 1857, *The Evening Star*, a literary paper, made its appearance under the auspices of the Washington Literary Association, being at that time edited by Edward A Price and Miss Kate Taylor, but, as with many similar publications, interest in it abated, and it was abandoned

On Oct 27, 1866, the *Chester Advertiser*, a weekly advertising sheet for gratuitous circulation, was issued by John Spencer and Dr. William Taylor April, 1867, Mr Spencer ceased to be a partner in the enterprise, and Dr Taylor continued its publication until the following October, when it suspended

In 1869, H. Y Arnold and Wilmer W. James began the publication of a weekly advertising sheet, —*The Independent.* Arnold soon after withdrew, and James associated J. J. Shields with him in the enterprise, until 1871, when the latter retired, and James continued the paper until 1874, when it was discontinued

The Delaware County Mail was established Nov 27, 1872, by Joseph T. DeSilver & Co Nov 27, 1876, it was sold to the proprietors of *The Delaware County Paper*, and merged into the latter publication.

The *Public Press* was issued May 3, 1876, by Thomas Higgins and Robert Simpson, but its publication was suspended during the same year

The Commercial Advertiser, a Democratic paper, was published by J M Stowe & Co in February, 1878, but after a few issues the publishers abandoned the enterprise.

In 1877, during a revival of the temperance movement, Andrew J Bowen began the publication of *The Temperance World*, and after several issues changed the title to *The Chester World* In a few months interest in the paper ceased, and it finally was discontinued

In October, 1883, the first number of *The Brotherhood*, a monthly journal devoted to the interests of the Brotherhood of the Union (H F), was issued by the Brotherhood Publication Company, Charles K Melville, editor The paper is printed by Melville & Hass, and is the official organ of the order in Pennsylvania, New Jersey, and Delaware

The County Bridges.—The first bridge erected over Chester Creek, where the King's road (the present Third Street) crosses that stream, was a draw-bridge In 1686 the court ordered the building of a horse-bridge over the creek, near Chester, as the King's road at that time did not pass through the borough, but to the north of the town, through the present borough of Upland, where a horse-bridge had been erected shortly after Penn's arrival, for at court held 6th day of First month, 1687, "Nathin' Evins, Supervisor of y[e] King's wayes for Chester, presented Caleb Pusey & Jno Hodskins [Hoskins] for not laying y[e] planks on y[e] bridge over Chester creek." There is no evidence that the order of the court as respected that bridge was ever carried into effect, indeed, the contrary seems to be negatively established, for at the December court, 1699, Ralph Fishbourne presented a petition "for a convenient road from the west side of Chester creek, where the ferry is kept for to lead to the now King's road" The court thereupon appointed six viewers to lay out "the said roadway in the most convenient place they can for the convenience of the inhabitants"

In 1700, the inconvenience arising from the roundabout way became such an annoyance to the traveling public and the inhabitants of the borough of Chester that a determined and successful effort was made to change the route of the King's highway, so that it should pass through the town and nearer the river To avoid interrupting the free navigation of the stream, it was determined that the creek be spanned by a draw-bridge Accordingly, in that year, an act of the Colonial Assembly was procured which authorized the erection of a bridge over the creek at Chester, and ordered the justices of the County Court "to lay out a road from the King's Road that leads to New Castle and Maryland to the intended place for a bridge over Chester creek" The act required that the bridge should have a draw to it, provided for the employment of a man to attend to it, and specified what his duties were,—to draw it up when necessary to let sloops and shallops pass to and from the mills situated on the creek, and also designated that a space of twenty feet should be left clear between the timbers or stonework for "the conveniency" of rafts and logs passing to said mills

As early as the 4th day of the Fourth month, 1690, a public highway had been laid out from Chester Creek to Chichester Creek, but it was along the bank in front of the Essex House, as the report filed shows

"Wee of the Grand Jury doe Lay out A foot way of Six foot Wid att the Lest, beginning att Chester Creek over against the Comon Landing place, from thence upon a Strait Line over the Swamp of Robert Wades to the Corner of Robert Wades' pales, and so a long by the said pales and feuce to a popeler and White Wallnot Standing by the said Robert Wades fence, and so to Remain a Longe the Syde way Accordingly, as it is already Marked and Cutt out unto Chichester"

The Queen's highway, which runs from Darby to Chester bridge, at Third Street, was not laid out until 1706, and it is stated that the bend in the road from the Lincoln Mills to Fifth Street, and then continued the highway direct along Market Street to Third, was due to the influence of Jasper Yeates, the course chosen bringing the road along part of his property and that belonging to the estate of his father-in-law, James Sandelands The people of that day declared that "God and Nature intended the road to cross directly across the creek, but the Devil and Jasper Yeates took it where it was located"

The bridge was in course of construction late in the fall of 1708, for at the court held November 24th of that year, it was ordered "that 24 foot of Chester bridge at the east end and 42 foot at the west end be filled with wood and earth with all expedition" The county treasurer was directed to supply Henry Worley and Henry Hollingsworth with money "out of the county stock" to pay for the work "And it is further ordered, that James Hendrickson is to perform and finish all the carpenter work relating to taking up the planks and new railing the whole Bridge, and laying the planks where it wants as soon as the work is fit for it, for which he is to have five shillings per day, and his man, Rich[d] Weaver, four shillings per day, finding themselves"

The bridge thus made must have been indifferently constructed, for on Jan 7, 1709, the following agreement was made and spread at large on the record of the court

"It is agreed on by the justices and Jasper Yeates aforesaid, in manner following, viz That the bridge over Chester Creek, in the Town of Chester, be sufficiently and completely repaired in manner following, to wit that the planks at the westerly end of said bridge be taken up 24 feet in length and the place be filled with earth, and those of the planks that are sound and fit to be used to be to repair some other parts of the said bridge, and what new planks may be wanting for repairing said bridge be procured two inches and a half thick, and good oak posts and rails and braces affixed on each side of said bridge, only making use of so many of the old rails that are good, which used to be placed at one end of the said bridge, and that it be so repaired as aforesaid, or what more the men hereafter appointed overseers of the said work may think necessary to be done, be wholly completed and finished before the 15th day of April next

"And the justices and Grand Jury aforesaid have and hereby do order and appoint Robt. Hodgson and Jos Coburn to be overseers of the said work, and for to agree with some workmen to do the same within the time limited for which said work, when finished, do also for the said Robt Hodgson and Jos Cobourn's trouble in the premises, they are to be paid out of the county stock, and that the dangerous places in the said bridge, by reason of the holes and rotten planks, &c, be forthwith repaired for the present security"

At the court held Oct 3, 1710, the following further reference to this bridge appears of record

"Jasper Yeates, to prevent further debate with the county, allows the county two ditches on each side the causeway, on the Westerly side of Chester Creek to enlarge the Road in breadth, making it 40, with which the Justices, Grand Jury, and Assessors, are satisfied and that is to determine all further dispute

"It is further agreed on by the Justice, Grand Jury, and Assessors that Jos Coburn do forthwith, as speedily as may be, repair the bridge and causeway at Chester creek, and remove the causeway on the East side of the creek straight with the street called James Street (now Third) and frame it and make it wharf-like at the end of the bridge near low water-mark, and twenty feet wide and thirty feet along the street, and make the causeway from the said wharf as far further as will make it good and easy passing and repassing for carts, etc., and he is to make the wharf and causeway of wood and fill in with good sound wood, and lay it over the top with gravel and earth, and that he keep an account of how many cords of wood he makes use of, all other charges which he may be at about the said work, and bring in his account when he has done his work in order to be left to the judgmt of two men mutually chosen between the said Jos Coburn, and the Justices, and so much money as the said two men so as aforesaid chosen shall allow him for the work that be his price, and also that he repair the causeway on the Westerly side the said Creek, and bring in his account to be allowed as aforesaid"

In the preamble to the act of Assembly, approved Aug 14, 1725, which was intended to prevent the obstruction of the navigation of Chester Creek, it is set forth that the draw-bridge which had been erected "is now gone to decay, and requires it to be rebuilt or repaired," and the act "direct the County Commissioners to repair the bridge within a period of twelve months"

In a letter from Maj John Clark, written at Mr Davis' house in Darby, Nov 17, 1777,[1] to Gen Washington, the writer says, "The bridge at Chester, on the west side the creek, has caved in, it may be made passable for a few foot, individuals now cross it"

In the act of Sept 3, 1778, it is stated that the drawbridge, which had been built in 1700[2] and repaired in 1725, "is decayed and ruined, and that public necessity, as well as the convenieuce of travellers on the highroad, requires that a good, safe bridge over Chester Creek should always be maintained and

[1] Bulletin Hist Soc of Penna., vol v (March, 1847) p 11

[2] Clearly an error in date, the petition for the highway through Chester being first presented to the Provincial Council March 19, 1705 6, and the survey was not made until 1706 Besides, the extracts from the court records show that no bridge was built at Chester previous to the fall of 1708, and that the bridge was not then finished

kept in repair, that the draw or engine to raise and lower the same is of no public utility and is attended with extraordinary expense and inconvenience to the public" In view of these facts the act declares "that the commissioners and assessors, with the concurrence of the magistrates of the county of Chester, shall, as soon as may be, cause a new bridge to be built at the place where the old bridge formerly stood, leaving at least twenty feet clear between the timber or stone-work, and not less than eighteen feet in breadth, and eight feet headway at high water, for the easy passage for rafts, floats, shallops, and other crafts, and the said bridge be made fast and close continued from one side of the creek to the other, without any draw or opening for a mast."

The bridge erected in obedience to this act was a wooden structure, which was supported by heavy wrought-iron chains passing over iron columns located on either abutment. Each link of the chain, Martin says, was about two feet in length, and at either side of the bridge was a large plank cut to resemble an arch Over each arch was a sign, the body color white, and bearing the following notification in black letters

"Walk your horses and drive not more than fifteen head of cattle over this bridge, under a penalty of no less than $30"[1]

This structure was carried off its abutments by the water during the noted flood of Aug. 5, 1843, and swept by the torrent against Eyre's wharf, where it remained, held fast by one of the chains which did not part, on the eastward side of the creek Isaiah H Mirkil and Jerry Stevenson for more than two months ferried horses, cattle, wagons, carriages, and pedestrians across the creek in a scow The county commissioners raised the old superstructure to its former position, in the fall of 1843, at a cost of two thousand one hundred and fifty dollars One of the links or staples to which the chain was attached is still to be seen standing in the roadway, at the north-east side of the present bridge, in front of the store now occupied by F C Torpey, in Ladomus' block

In 1850 Chester began rapid strides in material improvements The old bridge being deemed insufficient to meet the public demand, early in 1853 John Edward Clyde prepared a petition for a new structure, and Isaiah H Mirkil circulated the paper for signatures. The petition was met with a remonstrance by several citizens of the town, who desired that the structure should be a draw-bridge, if a new one was built, and so energetically was the matter pushed on each side that the good people of Chester were soon divided into new bridge and anti-new bridge advocates It was a contest which in that day agitated the newly-awakened borough from centre to circumference The struggle eventuated in the erection of the present iron structure in 1853. On the southeast end of the bridge, on the main stanchion (cast in the iron), is a shield, which informs the reader that the superstructure was built by F Quickley, of Wilmington, Del, in the year above stated, and that the county commissioners during whose term in office the work was completed were A. Newlin, J Barton, and W. H Grubb The bridge originally was without sidewalks, which were added, in 1868, to accommodate the public, who up to that time had been compelled to walk in the present roadway of the bridge in passing from one ward to another In 1872 the county commissioners made some repairs to the bridge, —relaid the planking, which was worn and decayed in many places,—but so enormous is the demand now made on this bridge by the public that no repairs can for any length of time keep it in good condition

The Seventh Street bridge, over Chester Creek, was built in 1870, being opened for public travel December 27th of that year The superstructure is of iron, but the traveling public have ever regarded this bridge with doubts as to its stability, hence it is seldom used by vehicles carrying heavy freight

The Ninth Street bridge, over Ridley Creek, is a substantial structure, which was erected in 1880–81, being opened to public use on June 27, 1881

At the December court, 1880, a lengthy petition, signed by almost all the manufacturers and owners of industrial works in the South and Middle Wards, was presented to court asking for the appointment of a jury of view for a bridge at Second Street, which was done, and almost a year subsequently to that date (Dec 12, 1881) the Court of Quarter Sessions confirmed the action of the jury of view, which previously had been approved of by two grand juries The bridge which was built across Second Street during the year 1883 is the most substantial structure erected by the public in the county of Delaware

The untiring perseverance of Isaiah H. Mirkil, after many years, culminated in securing a patient hearing, and resulted in the erection of the Second Street bridge In recognition of his public service, on the eastern abutment, on the southerly side of the bridge, William B Broomall had the words, "Isaiah H Mirkil, Pontifex Maximus," in large letters, cut deep in the solid granite coping

Ship-Building—During the colonial days a number of small coasting vessels were built at Chester, and after the English army evacuated Philadelphia, in 1778, a regular station for building gunboats for the commonwealth of Pennsylvania was established at that place Samuel Lyttle, whose descendants are still residents of the neighborhood, was employed by the State authorities in sawing planks for vessels, and received his pay in Continental money, which depreciated greatly before he could dispose of it

In 1844, Archibald McArthur was a shipwright in Chester, and built in that year the schooner "Richard Powell," which,—framed of Delaware County oak, —when inspected thirty years afterwards, was found to be as solid and sound as when launched In

[1] History of Chester, p. 58

May, 1849, Jacob Sinex, who had been a shipwright in Marcus Hook, removed to Chester, and in connection with Mr. Hargis, established a boat-yard in the ancient borough. On Dec. 8, 1852, this firm launched the schooner "Mary Pickup," of two hundred and sixty tons, the largest vessel ever built up to that date at Chester. In 1856, William B. Fortner had located as a ship-builder at Chester. The first steamboat shaft ever forged in the borough was made for the steamboat "Young America," in June, 1859, at the foundry of Chester A. Weidner & Co.

Roach's Ship-Yard.—In 1859, Thomas Reaney, who had been a member of the firm of Reaney & Neafie, in Philadelphia, removed to Chester, he having purchased the lot of ground on the Delaware River, where the Pennsylvania Oil-Works had been located in 1855, and had been destroyed by fire several years subsequent to that date. There he established an extensive ship-yard in connection with William B. Reaney and Samuel Archbold, the firm being Reaney, Son & Archbold, the industry itself being known as the Pennsylvania Iron-Works. Here a large business was done, which required the erection of costly buildings, wharfing, and filling in of the river-front, together with an outlay of many thousands of dollars in the purchase of machinery. At these works during the civil war the United States war vessels, the double-enders "Wateree," "Suwanee," and "Shamokin" were built, hull and engines complete, ready to go to sea, as were also the monitors "Sagamon" and "Lehigh," and the light-draught monitor "Tunxis;" two powerful tug-boats for the United States, the "Pinta" and "Nina," were constructed at these works. Among the list of other vessels built by Reaney, Son & Archbold, was the fleet river-steamer "Samuel M. Felton." In 1871 the firm made an assignment, and the yard and machinery was purchased by John Roach, who established "The Delaware River Iron Ship-Building and Engine Company" thereat, which since that time has become so familiar to the people of the United States. In the year 1873–74, at these works, were built for the Pacific Mail Steamship Company the "City of Peking" and the "City of Tokio," each being four hundred and twenty-three feet in length, with a capacity of five thousand and seventy-nine tons,—the largest vessels built in this country. The "City of Para" was launched April 6, 1878, in the presence of the President of the United States, and hundreds of distinguished guests from all parts of the country and thousands of spectators. The following-named vessels have been built since for the same company: "City of San Francisco," "City of New York," and "City of Sydney," each three thousand and twenty tons; "San José," "San Juan," and "San Blas," each two thousand and eighty tons; the "City of Panama" and the "City of Guatemala," each fourteen hundred and ninety tons.

In the year 1873 the iron-clad sloops-of-war "Alert" and "Alliance" were built for the United States government. The name of the latter was later changed to "Huron." It was wrecked and lost off the coast of Virginia.

In 1875 the United States monitor "Miantonomah," iron-clad, double-turret, was built, and is now at Hampton Roads. There are at present in process of construction for the government the "Boston," "Atlanta," and "Chicago" (still on the stocks), the "Puritan," a monitor, double-turret, with a capacity of two thousand eight hundred and ninety-eight tons, and the dispatch-boat "Dolphin," the last two lying at the docks.

The following United States monitors have been refitted at the yards: "Wyandotte," "Nahant," "Jason," "Passaic," "Nausett," "Niobe," "Cohoes," "Modoc," and "Napa."

In 1875 the "Graciosa" was built as a dispatch boat for the Spanish government.

On Tuesday morning, May 22, 1877, the steamship "Saratoga," which was on the ways, after it had been blocked up to be launched on the high tide, was observed to be pulling, and the order was passed down along the side of the ways to "stand clear." A number of men under the vessel ran from beneath it, and after a few moments, no others appearing, the order was given to cut the shoes which held the vessel, for it was straining hard to tear itself loose. As the ship started swiftly to the river, those who witnessed it greeted her movements with cheers, which in a moment after were hushed, when a cry of terror went up from those nearest the ways that a number of the workmen, who had not gotten from under the "Saratoga" when the shoes were cut, had been caught in the packing, which had been carried down with the vessel (a mass of timbers and block at the point where the ways are nearest the ground on the margin of the river), and had been killed or were so injured that death must ensue. The news spread with marvelous rapidity. The workmen in the yard were from all sections in the city and South Chester, and the anxiety to learn whether among the killed and wounded were relatives and friends caused a general suspension of business. The streets leading to the ship-yard were soon thronged with people hastening thither, and a crowd of men, women, and children besieged the outer gates clamorous for admission. The physicians—for every medical man in the city had been summoned to the works—had directed that to avoid confusion and excitement the public should not be admitted to the office where the dead and dying had been carried. All that medical skill could do was done, but with the exception of three men who were slightly injured, all those who were under the "Saratoga" at the time the vessel was launched were killed or died in a few hours thereafter. The following is a list of the dead: Edward Burke, Charles Wright, Sr., Edward Fawley, John J. Crewe, John Neilson, George Woof, and Bernard Cannon.

In the year 1877 there was built at the yards for the United States government a sectional dry-dock in four sections, having a total length of one hundred and sixty-eight feet and one hundred and eighteen feet in width. After completion it was shipped to Pensacola, Fla., where it was placed.

Vessels have been built for the Oregon Steamship Company of San Francisco, Old Dominion Steamship Company of New York, Ocean Steamship Company of Savannah, Brazilian Mail Steamship Company, Cromwell Line of New York, C. H. Mallory & Co. of New York, J. E. Ward & Co. of New York. Since 1871 ninety vessels have been built at these yards.

There is used annually at these works about sixteen million pounds of iron, and about fifteen hundred men are employed. The yards embrace about thirty-two acres, with a frontage on the river of twelve hundred feet. The buildings include a brick three-story structure forty-three by forty-four feet, occupied as offices and draughting-rooms; foundry, one hundred and eleven by one hundred feet, blacksmith-shops, boiler-shops, machine-shops, and many other buildings. Fifty comfortable dwellings are adjacent to the yards for the use of employés.

John Roach, Sr., proprietor of the celebrated iron ship-yard at Chester, and of the Morgan Iron-Works in New York City, is one of the most remarkable self-made men of the country. Few life-stories can equal his in incident and interest. None can furnish more striking illustration of what may be accomplished by purpose, perseverance, and pluck, backed by a will which no difficulties could daunt, and by a heroism of moral character which no test or trouble could overcome.

Mr. Roach was born in County Cork, Ireland, Dec. 25, 1816. In his veins flows that Irish blood which has produced so many eminent names in Parliamentary and military history, of the purest and sturdiest to be found in Great Britain's isles. His family were highly respectable and well-to-do trades-people. Until he was thirteen he had such schooling as his native neighborhood afforded, this, however, consisting rather more in the application of birch than of useful instruction on the teacher's part, and in devotion to sport rather than to study on the part of the scholars. The school-days, such as they were, were cut short by money embarrassments at home, Mr. Roach's father having become involved by indorsements to such extent as to cause his financial ruin, and finally his death from grief.

Inspired with the indomitable resolution which has been the marked characteristic of his career, the boy determined to seek his fortunes in America. The previous emigration of an uncle was one inducement to this step, and, in the expectation of finding this uncle in New York, at the age of sixteen he crossed the ocean, and landed a stranger, alone and almost penniless, in the metropolis. There he learned, to his dismay, that his uncle was in Texas. Left thus to face the fact that he had no one to whom he could turn for help, and that his small supply of money must soon be gone, he resolved to work at anything he could find to do to earn his passage back to Ireland. Bethinking himself of a man who had once worked for his father, and who was now settled in New Jersey, he made inquiries, and at length found him in Monmouth (now Ocean) County, N. J. Here he received a welcome, but aid was beyond the poor man's ability. Near by was a brick-yard, however, and he got work as a hand with the wheelbarrow. That was the beginning of a self-earned fortune. But the toil was very severe for one so young, and he was treated more like a slave and brute than a human being. A month at this brought him seven dollars. Then he went to the place where Mr. James P. Allaire, of New York, was building the Howell Iron-Works, and applied for work. As he could get nothing better, he hired out as attendant on the masons. He worked till he had saved fifty dollars. When it is recalled how low the wages were for such labor, it will be seen with what perseverance these hard-earned dollars were made and laid aside. Always before him was the purpose to rise to something higher. In this spirit he boldly went to the foreman of the department where iron hollow-ware was made, and offered his fifty dollars as meeting the requirement for apprenticeship to the trade. The foreman laughed at his pretensions, and refused to receive him. Not to be put down thus, he applied to Mr. Allaire himself, and by his intelligent remarks, bright face, and worthy ambition so impressed the proprietor that he gave orders to have the young man admitted to the foundry. Here he had many obstacles to contend with, but made steady progress notwithstanding. His associates were ignorant, rough men, with no idea of bettering their condition. A barrel of whiskey was kept for general use, contributions for this purpose being exacted from each person. Young Roach contributed, but refused to partake of the liquor. At the end of the first year he had five hundred dollars due him, and at the end of the second one thousand dollars more. The conditions on which the fifty dollars were paid to learn this trade were that a certain class of articles moulded and cast from the melted iron should be paid for by the piece. The more and faster the person worked the more he made, and while many with the same chance as himself made nothing, by his skill and his indefatigable industry, working over-hours, and wasting none of his energies, he succeeded in saving this handsome sum. It was from the start his firm conviction that no man could rise in the world who could not lay by something in whatever position he might be.

By this time he had married. Planning for the welfare of his family, he concluded to go into the new West and buy land with a view to settlement on a farm. Drawing five hundred dollars of his money, and traveling west by canal and stage and other slow methods of those days, he at length reached what is now the site of Peoria, Ill., and bought three hundred acres of land in the neighborhood, paying his five hundred dollars as security. It seemed settled that John Roach was to become an Illinois farmer. But there was a different course of life mapped out for him, with more telling work for his country. By one of those providences which some wrongly consider to be chance, just at this time Mr. Allaire failed. That ended the Illinois farming. Mr. Roach, not being able to get his thousand dollars, could not make the further payments, forfeited what he had already paid, and found himself far from home, without money enough to get back, and in a land where a day's wages was not money, but as much corn as a man could carry on his back. That would not pay fare, since there was no market where it could be turned into cash.

But there was no such idea as "give up" in his head. Within twenty-four hours after learning of his loss, he was working his way homeward on the canals; and in some four months after his departure from New York, with high hopes of success in the great West, he was back again, richer in experience, but poorer in pocket, with nothing to do but begin over. He had, however, the capital of a thoroughly-mastered trade, a powerful constitution, and an indomitable will.

Mr. Allaire, who had resumed business, was glad to regain so skillful a workman. Mr. Roach, however, was not satisfied with his old trade, and learned that of making castings for machinery. Here again a foreman opposed him, but Mr. Allaire knew his valuable qualities, and insisted that he should be taken into the foundry. He rose rapidly, and subsequently was offered the place of the very foreman who had opposed him, but refused to take it from him. He worked himself ill by his over-hours and his intense application, and for a long time it was thought he would die of consumption; but the strong constitution stood him in good stead, and he recovered.

When he got two hundred dollars ahead again,—and it was slower work saving now with a family to support,—he determined that he must be something more than a workman in a foundry if his children were to be properly cared for and educated. He finally hit upon the scheme of starting out for himself by buying a small foundry in Goerck Street, New York City,—the Etna Iron-Works,—then in the hands of a receiver, and for sale. The property consisted of only two lots of ground, forty by one hundred feet; but before he left for yet larger works it was enlarged, so as to cover fifty city lots. Nothing ever grew smaller under his hands. Finding three other mechanics, each having two hundred dollars, who were willing to join in the enterprise, the property was bought for four thousand seven hundred dollars, with a small cash payment, which left an equally small cash capital with which to begin business. The firm became Roach & Johnson, and the subsequently famous Etna Iron-Works sought public patronage,—that is, Mr. Roach sought it. The responsibility of the purchase was taken by him, and his partners left the management of everything to him. Where he was bound to succeed, they were doubtful; where he was resolute, they were holding back; where he was enterprising, they were timid. Those days showed the man. He scoured the city for work. He was unknown, without cash capital, credit, or influential friends; but his pluck shone in his face and inspired confidence. The first work he got, after long search, was to make some grate-bars for a Brooklyn distillery. When this was done there was not a dollar left of the cash capital, and he himself took the bars to the distillery, and asked for immediate payment, frankly stating that money with him was scarce, and he would willingly make a reduction for cash. His struggles for success in this foundry were such as few men go through. The partners early became discouraged, and he promptly bought their interest, giving them his note for three hundred dollars and a mortgage as collateral, and keeping them in his employ. Not one of them rose afterwards to a proprietor's place. He made frank statements to the iron merchants of his condition and prospects. His work was always satisfactory, both in price and character; his contracts were always kept to the letter; and his known probity of character gradually obtained for him a limited credit. Often during this period he had to obtain credit in order to support his family, because it took all the money he had to pay his workmen on Saturday night. During all his more than forty years of proprietorship and employment of thousands of workmen, never once did his men fail to receive their weekly wages when they were due.

Mr. Roach's first decided rise was when he was fortunate enough to get a contract for an iron building, and made eight thousand dollars in six months. This work was so satisfactory that his business and credit were increased largely. He took contracts which were beyond the capacity of his works, but tore down the old buildings, and in forty days had new and adequate works in operation, and carried out the contracts. That was characteristic of the man. Any work he could get to do he was sure he could provide the necessary capacity to do.

Business was now fairly prosperous with him when, in 1846, by the explosion of the boiler, his works were mostly destroyed by fire, and what was far more grievous, with accompanying loss of life. No insurance was recovered, and again he found himself nearly ruined. But he had an enlarged experience, an established business, and a sound though not large credit, being so much the richer by his hard toiling years. To go on with his contracts without loss of time he laid pipes and carried steam from a boiler in a factory over two hundred feet away to his own engine, which in the general wreck had singularly escaped destruction. By so doing, in forty-eight hours

Eng^d by A.H. Ritchie

John Roach

work was resumed. By extraordinary exertions he overcame the most distressing discouragements and re-established the foundry. There came out once more the indomitable spirit of the man. Business men generally recognized the fact that nothing could crush John Roach, and from that time his credit was good anywhere, and his word was as good as his bond. Pluck and patience and persistency will powerfully tell. All men honor the man who makes himself the master of misfortunes.

With the profits of the business in eight years Mr. Roach built an establishment having facilities to construct larger marine-engines than any yet built in this country. He was bound that nothing in his line should be done anywhere in the world that he could not do. He sent an agent to Europe to examine the greatest establishments there, and thus was able to avail himself of all the advantages in selection and arrangement of machinery. Some of the tools introduced were the largest in the country. Where other works were unimproved he was constantly making advance in facilities. He stimulated the inventive genius of his workmen, and was quick to adopt a good thing when he found it. Having gone through every branch of his business, and understanding every detail, his eye was swift to see and his judgment was rarely at fault. Nothing escaped his personal attention. His capacity for work was wonderful. His pay-lists enrolled from nine hundred to fifteen hundred men. Two immense engines were built by him in these works for the iron-clad "Dunderberg," and the engines for the double-end gunboat "Winooski," the steam frigate "Neshaming," the great sound steamers "Bristol" and "Providence," and other large vessels. No work was too great or too difficult for him to do, and do at its best, and no unsatisfactory work went out of his establishment. His superior facilities enabled him to do work in shortest time and at lowest price. In 1858 he took into partnership one of his sons, and the firm became, as at present, John Roach & Son.

But Mr. Roach's ambition was not yet satisfied. The Etna Works, large and complete as they were, lay distant from the river-front and lacked other advantages. In 1867 he bought the Morgan Iron-Works, an immense establishment at the foot of Ninth Street, on the East River. These works were built in 1838 by T. F. Secor & Co., and in 1850 were bought by George W. Quintard, who conducted them until 1867. The engines for a large number of first-class merchant and war vessels were constructed in them. They consist of various buildings,—foundries and shops,—occupying six city blocks, giving a water-front of three hundred feet. Great alterations were made and the establishment was brought to the highest point of capacity and perfection. For the construction of marine-engines of the old style there was no superior plant in the world.

But when the works were brought to this condition another discouraging train of circumstances came on which threatened to make establishment and experience useless and the property of little value, except as real estate.

During the civil war our shipping was driven from the sea, and England embraced the opportunity to get possession of the carrying trade formerly ours. For years a revolution had been going on in ship-building, in the change not only from wood to iron, from sail to steam, but from the wooden side-wheeler to the iron propeller, and from the ordinary to the compound engine. No compound engine had at that time been built in this country. Our iron interest had not been developed. And at this time, when England was in possession of the carrying trade, and when everything that entered into the construction of a ship was taxed, the free-ship cry was raised in Congress. This utterly discouraged capital invested in the iron business, and nearly all the great iron-works in New York, Philadelphia, and Boston were closed up. Mr. Roach held on. He looked over the whole subject,—saw the need of this great country for ships and its danger without the power to build them,—and had faith to believe that the people would demand a revival of the American carrying trade. He proved his faith by investing all he had in the ship-yard and engine-works at Chester, an establishment which covers some twenty-five acres and thirty branches of skilled labor, and has in many respects no equal in the world, and where a finished ship, from the ore up, can be produced. Over three thousand men are in his employ, and nowhere are to be found superior facilities or superior ships. Nearly one hundred splendid iron steamships have been launched by him, and no unsatisfactory work has he ever done. It is a remarkable fact that in his business career of over forty years Mr. Roach has never been sued, nor has he ever brought suit against any man with whom he has had dealings. His ability to manage men is as marked as his executive powers. Strikes have been markedly absent from his work-shops, and his men have ever been treated with kindness and consideration. He is a model employer.

By his persistency in advocating an American policy of protection not only for American ships, but for all American industries, Mr. Roach has done more than any other one man to stem the tide of foreign influence in favor of free trade, which means the pauperization of American labor in favor of foreign labor. By his powerful arguments before Congressional committees, arguments which proved unanswerable, he has, year after year, fought and defeated the bills for free ships and free trade introduced into Congress; his opponents have conceded that they owe defeat to him alone. This will secure him high honor at the hands of the American people when our history shall be written, and when, free from prejudice, men shall be able to see how much the country and its industries owe to the firm stand taken and maintained with consummate ability by Mr. Roach.

He is a man of genial disposition, a fluent and persuasive speaker, overflowing with broad and sound ideas on all subjects. He has aided many a young man and influenced him to make something of himself. The rules which he has followed and which he would recommend to all are these:

1. Keep your promises and appointments.
2. Never let a customer go away dissatisfied, if you can possibly help it.
3. Never lend a friend your note, rather loan him the money, if you can spare it. Never indorse another man's note as an accommodation.
4. Do no business with a man who is troublesome, and whom you know you cannot satisfy.
5. Pay your bills and workmen promptly when pay is due.
6. Be honest and honorable in all things, and kind to all men.

The rules are characteristic of a man whose life cannot be studied by young men without advantage, and who is worthy of the honors that have been conferred upon him by those who know his worth.

Sauville Spar-Yard.—In 1865 John Sauville established a spar-yard at the foot of Parker Street. The masts and spars used at Roach's ship-yard are here hewn from the large timbers which are brought from Clearfield City, in this State, and the spruce logs are brought from Maine.

The Frick's Boat-Yard.—In 1860, William Frick and William Wilson, formerly of the firm of Frick, Slifer & Co., of Louisburg, Pa., came to Chester and purchased a large tract of land on the river, adjoining the yard of Reaney, Son & Archbold. Here they erected piers, which extended nearly seven hundred feet from the fast land into the water, and expended thousands of dollars in filling in the low and marshy ground so that it might be utilized for the purposes of a boat-yard. The firm made a specialty of building canal-boats, and had established a large business, giving employment to nearly a hundred hands, when the civil war unsettled value and so advanced the costs of materials that it was very precarious to enter into heavy contracts to be carried out in the future. Frick & Co. had undertaken to build a large number of canal-boats at a designated price, which at the period the contract was entered into, and the cost of material at that time, promised to yield a large profit to the builder, but the inflation came, lumber and iron advanced threefold in value. The parties for whom the boats were to be built demanded that the firm should carry out its contract, although to do so would entail the loss of many thousands of dollars. Finding that the strict letter of the agreement would be required, Frick & Co. strove to carry out their obligation in good faith, but the losses entailed embarrassed them, and culminated ultimately in financial failure. The boats were delivered, but the builders were ruined, and that in a contract which when made promised a large margin of profit.

Besides the yards already mentioned, Charles A. Weidner, at the Chester Iron-Works, on Second Street, between Edgmont and Market Streets, built several river steamboats and other vessels. In 1873 the United States revenue marine steamer "Manhattan" was built at this establishment, and at the time was pronounced by the government inspectors the best vessel ever constructed for that service in the country. In 1876 Nathan Pennell and George Robinson had a ship-yard in South Ward, near Essex Street, and that year the tug "Mary Ann" was built at this yard. The depression of 1877 caused the proprietors to abandon and retire from the business, which was at that time very unpromising.

Court-Houses and Prisons.—At the session of Upland Court, Nov. 14, 1676, an order was made providing that Neeles Laerson be paid "for his charges for keeping the Court last year." Neeles Laerson was a tavern-keeper, and his inn is believed to have been on Edgmont Avenue, north of the present Second Street. He was the owner of one hundred and eighty-one acres of land in Chester, covering a large part of the present thickly built-up portion of the city to which I am now referring. Neeles Laerson was a quarrelsome neighbor, as will be seen by an examination of the records. In 1678, James Sandelands, on behalf of the inhabitants of Upland, called the attention of the court to the fact that Laerson had built a fence closing the old and usual way to the meadow, which obstruction the court ordered the latter to remove. On the same day the church wardens complained that in taking possession of two lots in Chester, which he had bought from Dominie Lasse Carolus, he had included some of the church or glebe lands. The court ordered that he should be allowed that which he had bought, but if it was found that he had taken more than was by right his, it should be annexed to the church lots.

The first court of which we have information was, as shown, held at Learson's inn, but the justice ordered, Nov. 13, 1677, that Capt. Hans Jargin, who had been occupying the building as a barracks for his company, should "fit up" the House of Defense, or block house, and furnish it "fitt for the Court to sitt in against ye next Court." Although there is no positive record showing that the House of Defense was used by the court for its sessions, it is now generally conceded that the evidence fully establishes the fact that it was so occupied. This building, which was constructed of logs, stood on the east side of Edgmont Avenue, about eighty-four feet from the present Second Street, was rectangular in shape, and was fourteen by fifteen feet in dimensions. It was erected at an angle to Second Street, and extended into the roadway of Edgmont Avenue. Neeles Laerson, March 13, 1678, was ordered by the court "to make or leave a lane or street from Upland creek to ye House of Defence or County House" between that time and the next court, and in default to be fined at the discretion of the judges. As the early settlers traveled almost wholly by water, it was very essential that there should be free access from the creek to the public buildings, and this means of communication the pugnacious Laerson seems to have interrupted until the strong arm of the law dealt summarily with him. It appears that the court-house was then a place where articles were exposed by the public for sale. The court, on 3d day of First month, 1684, determined that a revenue might be derived from this source; hence the old record shows this strange entry:

"Ordered that all people that shall make use of the Court House for sellerage of any goods shall for every Tonne pay after ye rate of three Shillings fourpence a Tonne for any time not exceeding a week, And for what time it shall continue afterwards half so much."

How long the House of Defense was used as the public buildings of the county is not known, but in 1703, after two other buildings in succession had been occupied by the court, the grand jury presented the old block-house "as being a nuisance, and dangerous of taking fire, and so would endanger the town." "The Court,"—so runs the old entry on the docket,—"in deliberate consideration, ordered the said house to be pulled down, and that Jasper Yeates, Chief Burgess of the Borough of Chester, shall see the order performed." Previous to 1683—there seems to have been no place for the detention of prisoners in Chester for two years before that date—"John Ward for sundry Felons, committed to the custody of the Sheriff, and made his escape with irons upon him."

The third court-house, or the third building wherein court was held, was built in 1684–85. Dr. Smith says, "A jail was erected at the same time, but there is reason to believe that it was built near the creek, and that there was a street laid out between the two buildings." Henry Hollingsworth, who was a Friend, "for cutting the eaves of the new prison," was dealt with by meeting the same year. This court-house Dr. Smith located on the east side of Edgmont Street, which John Hill Martin thinks is an error, and that it was on the west side of that highway, an opinion which meets the approval of the present writers. The student of our ancient annals will find more confusion in the authorities respecting the sites of the several court-houses than in any other details of the early days of the colony. This last building, after it was no longer used for county purposes, was ordered by the court, at the March session, 1701, "to be set on sale the 6th day of the Third month next, papers to be set up to give notice that it is to be sold at Vandew."

Whether the sale was had according to this order does not appear, but the property must have passed to Ralph Fishbourn, of Chester, gentleman, for in the latter part of the year 1705 the Legislature passed an act "to assure, grant, and convey unto Ralph Fishbourn one messuage, cottage-house, or tenement, and lot of ground thereunto belonging, situated in Chester, in the county of Chester, formerly known by the name of the 'Old Court-House.'"

The fourth court-house, so far as its foundation is concerned, is still standing on the west side of Edgmont Avenue nearly opposite the House of Defense, its precise location being two hundred and fifty-six feet six inches from the southwest corner of Edgmont Avenue and Third Street. It was built by John Hoskins in 1695, and he conveyed the lot to the county the same year. The old building, now owned by Jonathan Pennell, has a part of the wall of this court-house standing in the northern gable of the present structure, between the two end windows, and extending up nearly to the second story. The old part of the wall, and that which was added after it ceased to be the county building, is still easily discernible. The jail was in the cellar, and the iron rods which formerly barred the prisoners' escape from confinement, while admitting fresh air to the cells, still remain in the weather-stained frames in the foundation walls. The court-rooms and jury-rooms were in the first and second stories.

At the same court, March, 1701, at which the sale of the old court-house erected in 1684 was ordered, the prison being found inadequate to retain the culprits, Jasper Yeates, Ralph Fishbourn, Joseph Cobourn, and Andrew Jobe were appointed supervisors to build a new prison on the grounds of James Sandelands, the younger, and were instructed that the erection should be twenty-five feet in length by eighteen feet in width in the clear. This structure, so far as the prison was concerned, was built, for the old draft of Chester, now owned by William B. Broomall, Esq., locates this building as south of the court-house built by Hoskins in 1695, and Sandelands, by his attorney, David Lloyd, in open court, delivered a deed for the land to the commissioners of the county.

We have serious doubt whether the court-house alluded to in the report of the grand jury of the 24th of February, 1701, was ever built. The grand inquest on that occasion called the attention of the court to "the necessity of a Court Hous and prison hous," but stated also that "there is little money in the bank, and that many have not paid their moiety ½ rate of the last assessment, desire that such may be forced." They also recommended the speedy gathering of the county tax remaining unpaid, and requested the justices to issue warrants therefor, and end their report with the declaration that in their opinion "Law and Justice cannot have its perfect courc without such housis for their distribution as aforesaid." We know that at the December court, 1701, the justices ordered repairs to be made "to the court and prison hous," and appointed Walter Martin, John Hoskins, and Henry Worley to be supervisors and oversee the work, with power to provide materials, employ workmen, and to finish the repairs as speedily as possible. The supervisors were also instructed to provide a pair of stocks and a whipping-post. Whether the expense of the building of the new court-house, as desired by the grand jury, in 1701-2, was greater than the county could undertake, cannot now be determined, but there is no documentary evidence to show that such a structure was ever erected, and we indorse the opinion of Dr. Smith and John Hill Martin that the next court-house in chronological order was the old building on Market Street, known to us of the present day as the City Hall.

COURT-HOUSE AND JAIL.

The fifth court-house, including the tavern of Neeles Laerson in the number, was the massive stone structure still standing on the west side of Market Street, which was built in 1724, the date-stone being in the south wall, but covered with the dull brownish preparation which still defaces the ancient edifice, and hides the numerals from sight. The building has the pent-roof projections over the first-story windows, as was the style of architecture of that day, and as originally constructed was surmounted with a small belfry rising from the centre of the roof, in which formerly hung a bell, with the words "Chester, 1729" cast in the metal. The bay or semi-circular projection at the north side, in the rear of the judges' bench, was added at a later date. The jury-rooms were in the second story of the building. Dr. Smith tells us that tradition has handed down an incident "as having happened during the building of the court-house, or some other public building in Chester," which he relates as follows:

"During the progress of the work a young lady was observed to pass and repass the building daily, dressed in very gay attire. After the promenade had been continued for some time, one of the workmen, less mannerly than his associates, upon the appearance of the lady, called out,—

"'In silk and scarlet walks many a harlot.'

"The young lady, feeling indignant at the insult, promptly replied,—

"'By line and rule works many a fool.'"

Unfortunately for the tradition connecting this incident with Chester, the same story is told respecting the erection of an edifice in York, England, which building antedates the discovery of America by the Genoese mariner, and the anecdote is related of several localities in Great Britain years before we have knowledge that any European had settled at Upland.

When the new court-house was finished an act of Assembly was procured "to enable the trustee to sell the old Court House and prison belonging to the borough and county of Chester," and in 1725 the building mentioned, the one built in 1695, and part of the wall of which stands in the house now owned by Jonathan Pennell, on Edgmont Avenue, was sold to William Preston, of Philadelphia, mariner, for twenty-seven pounds.

The presumption is that the old jail, which stood at the northwest corner of Fourth and Market Streets, was built previous to the date of the erection of the court-house on the same street. The act of Feb. 22, 1718, required "that within the space of three years after the 25th day of March, 1718, a house of correction, or work-house, shall be built . . . in Chester, at the charge of the county of Chester." The old work-house stood directly in the rear of the prison, and the fact that it was located on the thoroughfare leading from Market Street to Edgmont gave the name of Work Street to the highway for more than a century. The prothonotary's office, which still stands back from the present building-line of Market Street, and now owned by James Hampson, was not erected in that year, for at "the private session" of the court, held at the house of John Hannum, in Concord, Dec. 15, 1724, Joseph Parker petitioned the court, "setting forth ye great danger ye records of ye county lay in, as well as by casualties of fire, as other accidents;" the court "allows ye petition to be reasonable, and orders ye clerk to present ye same before ye commissioners and assessors of ye same county, in order that they may fit a room in ye new Court House for keeping ye said records in; and when prepared order ye old clerk to transmit all ye said records to ye place so appropriated accordingly, and not to be removed without ye Court's direction." Twelve years after this order Joseph Paken, in his petition dated Jan. 24, 1737, gives a woeful description of the then condition of the court-house. He says,—

"Which said Court house was at the Public Expense Furnished with Tables, Chairs, fire shovels, Tongs, D ggs, fenders, as many as Reasonably adjudged Necessary But whoever the Person charge the same was Committed to It is Apparent to Every Person that will make use of his Eyes that the Doors are most Commonly Left Open for Horses and Cattle to go in and out at Pleasure, the Furniture broke and Exceedingly Deminished, and the place made a Common Stage whereby Rude people break the windows, Treads down Ceiling and Commits many Disorders, which, if not timely Prevented must end in the Ruin thereof, As the great Danger which proceed by the person Intrusted by you with the Care thereof In making the same a Dwelling house and Keeping Fires therein for some months Together"

The court-house appears to have been much out of order, for on March 1, 1737/8, the commissioners and assessors agreed with John Owens to repair it as follows:

"The Lower floor and the Bar and to provide Convenient Seats for the Petty Jury to sitt on when in Court and to repair the windows and shutters below stairs and above the Chimney case in the Grand Jury room and to repair the Three Tables belonging to the several rooms above stairs, and the Benches and to fix a Turn'd Column or Pillar to support the Ceiling where the Bell rope comes thro' and to cause the Ceiling to be Repaired, and to Provide as many Boards as may lay a floor over the s[d] Ceiling and to make & put up shutters for the Belfry (or place where the Bell hangs) and Likewise to make a window in the Gable End in the Garret or Upper Room and glaze the same, and to Endeavor to procure (with the help of Joseph Parker) the chairs that is wanted belonging to the Court House as also the Tongs and fire Shovels"

These repairs were made, for some of the improvements designated, particularly the setting up of a turned column to support the upper floor, was in the apartment and removed after the building had passed into the ownership of the city of Chester, when the upper apartments were altered into the present Council chamber

As stated, the date of the erection of the prothonotary's office is well known, and I doubt whether the building antedates the Revolution, for, on July 28, 1777, the records of the county were in the possession of the late prothonotary, and at his residence, for on that date the Executive Council authorized Caleb Davis,—Benjamin Jacobs not having qualified,—who was appointed in Jacobs' stead, to "enter the dwelling and out-houses of H. H. Graham, take possession of the books and papers of the county, and remove them to a place of safety" Joseph Parker had kept the records in an office alongside his dwelling-house,—the old Logan house on Second Street,—and Henry Hale Graham had after that deposited the records in his office, the one story building on Edgmont Avenue, north of Graham Street, now belonging to the estate of Henry Abbott, deceased It seems that in the growth of the business before the County Court, the rooms in the second story of the court-house were necessary for the use of the grand and petit juries, and hence the order of the court of Dec 15, 1774, had to be disregarded. The prothonotary's office, I am of opinion, must necessarily have been erected subsequent to the battle of Brandywine, for it was the dread of the threatened British attack on Philadelphia which occasioned the alarm of Council as to the safety of the county records, and called forth the order to Caleb Davis.

The old county prison and work-house, as before stated, were built previous to or about the same time as the court-house The jail was two stories high, built of square cut stone, and extended westwardly along Fourth Street In the front part of the building was the sheriff's house This was a structure two stories and an attic in height, presenting in the front to the street the general style of the court-house Back of the prison, and extending along Fourth Street, was the work-house, also of stone In 1741 the court-house and jail were repaired and painted, and a well dug in the court-house yard The old pump, with a heavy iron handle, stood within the memory of many of our older residents a nuisance in winter, because of the drippings therefrom forming ice and rendering its locality a dangerous one to pedestrians. Many years ago the trunk was taken out and the well filled in Part of the old brickwork of the well is under the front foundation of the store No 404 Market Street During the year just mentioned the commissioners paid Nathan Worley £10 for planks used in flooring the two dungeons on the east side of the prison, and Thomas Morgan was paid £5 11*s.* 6*d* for one hundred and fifty pounds of spikes used in laying the dungeon floors In front of the gaol and extending to the court-house doors was a double row of Lombardy poplars which afforded a pleasant shady walk in the summer, and frequently during periods of political excitement here the orator of the day held forth and saved the nation by his noisy mouthings The old trees at length grew so unsightly, many of their branches having died, that over half a century ago the poplars were cut down and a double row of lindens were planted to replace the ancient trees under whose towering branches our Revolutionary sires discussed the Boston Port Bill and other measures preceding the actual outbreak of hostilities between the colonies and the mother-country, and within the venerable structure proceedings were had to raise the quota of the Continental troops required from Chester County, as in after-years similar meetings were held to provide soldiers during the rebellion

On the removal of the county-seat to West Chester, the old court-house and public buildings in Chester were sold, on the 18th of March, 1788, to William Kerlin, for £415 After the passage of the act of Sept 26, 1789, creating the county of Delaware, Kerlin sold the property Nov. 3, 1789, to the county for £693 3*s.* 8*d* As long as Chester remained the seat of justice of Delaware County courts continued to be held in the old building, and at times it must have been exceeding unpleasant to those who were compelled to attend, particularly in rainy weather, when, as is stated by a county newspaper in 1843, the mud on the floor was nearly an inch in depth. It was certainly not in this condition on Tuesday, Oct 5, 1824, when Gen Lafayette was the guest of Chester He was accompanied by Governor Shulze and staff, Gen Cadwalader and staff, and many of the dignitaries of

Philadelphia. The steamboat did not reach the landing until eleven o'clock at night, but a line of boys, each bearing a lighted candle, was formed, extending, it is said, from the wharf to the Washington House. Most of the houses in the town were brilliantly lighted, and the windows decorated with transparencies and designs. At one o'clock in the morning the general and friends were "regaled with a sumptuous entertainment" at the court-house, which had been prepared by the ladies of Chester. Lafayette remained in the ancient borough during Wednesday, when he reviewed the volunteers of Delaware and Chester Counties, and on Thursday, at seven o'clock in the morning, he started in a coach and four for Wilmington, accompanied by a suitable escort.

The old jail, during the last ten years it was used as a place for the detention of prisoners, was "a miserable old rattle-trap, nearly all the bars of the windows rusted off and the ceilings and windows anything but secure." This is the description given of the jail building in 1841 by the editor of the *Delaware County Republican*. In truth it could only retain those inmates who were too indolent to make an effort to escape.

In 1824, when Joseph Weaver was sheriff, a convict named Tom Low succeeded in making his escape from confinement. He had been in the jail-yard, as was usual, at a certain time of the day, and, being forgotten, he managed to get possession of a spade, with which he burrowed under the yard-wall, coming out about fifteen feet from the court-house. He was never recaptured. In the latter part of May, 1844, Henry Johnson escaped from the jail by scaling the wall. His sentence would have expired the next day, but, learning that a commitment had been lodged against him in Philadelphia, and that he would be taken there for trial for another offense as soon as discharged, he declined to serve out the full term of his imprisonment. Indeed, the old jail had no terrors for the professional cracksman, for on the night of Jan. 20, 1844, the dwelling in the front, then occupied by Sheriff Hibberd, was entered by burglars, who decamped with the wearing apparel of the family and other articles of value. On Sept. 6, 1847, two prisoners attempted to escape by making ropes of their blankets, but a passer-by, noticing the head of one of the men just above the wall, gave the alarm, and they were prevented from making a general jail delivery. George Harris, a colored man, by the same means escaped on July 9, 1847, and was not recaptured, while another of his race (Brown), who had four times before left the jail without the consent of the county authorities, on July 4, 1848, took the privileges of the day and regained his freedom, shaking off the dust of the old prison for the fifth time. After the county buildings at Media were being constructed Arthur Goodwin, a prisoner in the jail at Chester, on Sunday, Dec. 1, 1850, dug through the walls. But as the convict returned to his own house the sheriff had little difficulty in recapturing him. This is the last prisoner who defied the bolts and bars of the old jail, for on Dec. 9, 1850, the property in the borough was offered at public sale by the county commissioners. The court-house and two lots were sold to the borough authorities for two thousand six hundred and one dollars, the prothonotary's office and lot, adjoining it on the north, to James Hampson for fifteen hundred and twenty-five dollars, and the jail and lots adjoining to James Campbell for three thousand five hundred and twenty dollars.

A large frame building which stood in the rear of the jail and work-house was bought by Campbell previous to his purchase of the old prison, and here he began alterations for the reception of looms. In the *Delaware County Republican* of Feb. 1, 1850, the following reference is made to the change then being made,—the dawning of Chester's prosperity:

"Improvements in Chester.—Appearances indicate that in the spring our borough will take a start in the march of improvement. Our friend, James Campbell, of Leiperville, has made arrangements for manufacturing of cotton goods in the building back of the jail. He will start with fifty power looms, driven by a ten horse-power steam engine, and will soon increase the number to one hundred. In this mill will be the first looms ever set in motion on the spot first occupied as the capital of Pennsylvania, and Mr. Campbell will be the Columbus in manufacturing in Chester."

In the issue of the same journal for April 5, 1850, appeared the following local:

"PIONEER FACTORY.—The new manufacturing establishment projected in the borough by Mr. James Campbell, of Ridley, was put in partial operation last week, and the puffing of the steam-engine and the music of the shuttle are daily heard in our midst, causing us increased wonder why a town possessing so many and rare advantages as our own was not years ago converted into a great manufacturing mart. Mr. Campbell is about to extend his buildings, and in a short time will have one hundred looms in active operation. The machinery used is handsomely finished and of a superior kind. We have examined a specimen of the goods made by it, and predict that they will find a ready sale in whatever market they may be offered."

As before stated, the factory mentioned in the *Republican* was the old bowling-alley, which stood on the north side of Fourth Street, where part of the market-house is now located. The *Republican* failed to record an incident which happened when the first loom was started in the Pioneer Mills by the late James Ledward, then in Campbell's employ. A number of citizens of Chester were present when the machinery first began to move, and as they saw it in motion, all present broke into a cheer, and afterwards they one and all sang "Hail Columbia." Many who were then employed in the first manufacture of textile goods in Chester will recall this incident to memory. After Mr. Campbell purchased the jail and work-house, he tore down the northern wall of the old structure and built out in that direction, so that his mills, retaining the name "Pioneer Mills," extended over to and included the prison-yard walls. In the new addition he kept the Jacquard looms, and thereon were woven quilts and fabrics of a like character. The great difficulty he had to contend with was the scarcity of water, and to meet this want he expended thousands of dollars in sinking wells in the yard. The new enterprise, which had required a large outlay of means, was getting well established when the panic of 1857 came upon the country, spreading ruin in all directions, and crushing down industrial establishments by the thousands. Mr. Campbell at that time became financially embarrassed, and in 1858 the "Pioneer Mills" passed into the ownership of the late Gen. Robert E. Patterson.

After Campbell had erected the Pioneer Mills, the heirs of William Kerlin brought an action in ejectment against him, alleging that the land and buildings which Kerlin had conveyed to the county of Delaware in 1789 was conditioned on the use of the premises as a court-house and jail, and that inasmuch as the buildings had ceased to be used for the purposes intended, the title reverted to the heirs-at-law of Kerlin. The court below decided that the deed from Kerlin to the county was absolute and for a valuable consideration, with power of alienation in the county; and an appeal being taken to the Supreme Court, this opinion was sustained.

James Campbell

James Campbell, to whom Chester owes so much for its present manufacturing prominence, was born in Stockport, England, on Aug. 12, 1805, where at an early age he entered a mill, learning thoroughly the trade of cotton-weaving. Energetic and self-reliant, he came to this country in his early manhood, determining to make his way in this world. He sought employment at the factory of Mr. Philips, at Rockdale, and subsequently became the manager of the mills at Pennsgrove, then owned by James Houghton, now by Samuel Riddle, continuing there until 1837, when his employer removed to Groveville, N. J., to which place James Campbell declined to go, although he was urged to do so by Houghton, who was loath to part with him. At that time John Garsed, whose eldest daughter (Angelina) Campbell had married, had a machine-shop at Pennsgrove, and he offered to his son-in-law six cotton-looms, which he had made for parties who had failed in business and could not take the machines. Campbell accepted the offer, and placed the looms in a vacant building at Pennsgrove, and began his career as a manufacturer. Industrious and progressive, he soon established a reputation in business, and in the following year Hon. George G. Leiper proposed to erect an additional story to the bark-mill, at Leiperville, so as to afford sufficient room for the machinery required in a cotton-factory, if Campbell would agree to lease the property after the change was made. The offer was accepted, and in that locality Campbell was very successful, accumulating considerable capital, which he subsequently lost in his effort to develop the borough of Chester into a manufacturing town. His object was attained, hundreds have profited by his endeavors, but in the panic of 1857, when many of the commission-houses with whom he dealt suspended, it embarrassed him, and finally caused his failure. So great had been his struggles to prevent this result that his health broke under the strain, and after several years of almost unintermitting illness, during which his indomitable energy never forsook him, he died, May 14, 1862.

The mill, after Campbell's failure, was occupied by James Stevens until about 1863, when Messrs. Roberts, Wilson & Willey carried on the manufacturing business therein. In 1865, Gen. Patterson sold the

Market Street front to James Chadwick, who, in 1866, tore down the old building and erected Lincoln Hall While taking down the tall flag-pole which stood on the sidewalk at Fourth and Market Streets, where it had been erected during the excitement occasioned by the news of the bombardment of Fort Sumter, the halyards were drawn through the block, and Charles Martine clambered up to make a rope fast so that the pole, lower and topmast, might be pulled over into the street After he had reached some distance the pole, which had rotted where it entered the ground, broke off level with the sidewalk and fell, fatally crushing Martine beneath it The rear part of the old prison passed into the ownership of John Cochran, and on part of the lot the market-house now stands Chadwick sold the property to Messrs Gartside & Sons, and they in turn conveyed it to Chester Lodge, No 236, F A M, who now own it

When the present mayor's office was being built, in 1866, in digging the cellar, the southeast end wall of the old prothonotary's office fell, and a three-months' old infant of Michael Biggans, the then occupant of the dwelling, who was asleep in a bed against the wall in the second story, was thrown into the cellar among the *débris*, a distance of twenty feet, without sustaining any harm, while a child a few years older, sleeping in the same room, was buried in the broken bricks and plaster without receiving any serious injuries

After the borough authorities acquired title to the old court-house they made many changes, provided a commodious hall in the second story for the use of the Council, which is to-day used by their successors, the Council of the city of Chester, they also removed the old belfry and built a steeple, in which was placed a four-dialed clock and a new bell The old one, which had called together judges, lawyers, jurors, and suitors for nearly a century and a quarter, was removed to the ancient school-house at Fifth and Welsh Streets

Broad Street Mills.—The buildings at Broad and Crosby Streets, owned by James Stevens, and used for the manufacture of bed-ticking, warps, and cops, were originally built for a sash-factory and machine-shop, the first on Broad Street, the second on Crosby Street In 1856 they were used by James Campbell for the manufacture of cotton goods, and at his death, in 1862, passed into the hands of Gen Patterson, under the charge of James Stevens They were purchased by Mr. Stevens in March, 1882 Since Mr Campbell's time the buildings have been much enlarged and improved, and the old machinery replaced with new The main mill on Broad Street is two hundred and six by twenty-eight feet, three stories high, and on Crosby Street two hundred and twenty-two by thirty-six feet The latter is two stories high, with the exception of sixty feet, which is one story In this part is the dye- and finishing-house, sixty by sixty feet, provided with a small engine, and a pump for forcing water over the building in case of fire The machinery consists of eighty-five looms, nine thousand and forty-eight spindles, and sixteen cards, driven by two engines, with two sets of boilers

The Keokuk Mills were established in 1852, by Benjamin Gartside Land was purchased at the foot of Fulton Street, and the original structure, ninety by thirty-eight feet, four stories, was built On the 11th of August, 1852, a bricklayer employed in building the chimney of the engine-house of the factory fell from the scaffold to the ground, a distance of sixty feet, he was severely but not seriously injured In 1858-59 land adjoining to the north was bought, and additional buildings erected On the 1st of January, 1857, James and Amos Gartside, sons of Benjamin, were admitted as partners, the firm-name becoming B Gartside & Sons, and has continued as such to this time The works occupy over two acres of ground, comprising the square between Front Street and the Delaware River and Parker and Fulton Streets The mill is supplied with four sets of cards, eighty looms, and the necessary machinery for the manufacture of woolen jeans The power is supplied by a seventy horse-power engine Three thousand pounds of raw material are used per week, and fourteen thousand yards of goods are manufactured per month Seventy hands are employed

Benjamin Gartside was born in Rochdale, Lancashire, England, May 26, 1794 After a limited education in his native country he learned the trade of hand-loom weaving, and continued it until his emigration to the United States in 1831 Coming at once to Philadelphia, he found employment at the Blockley Mills, and remained until 1833, when Manayunk became his home and Joseph Ripka his employer In 1838 he engaged in business on his own account, first using but one hand-loom, but as business increased, introducing four power-looms In 1840 he rented a mill on the Wissahickon Creek, fitted it with appropriate machinery and power-looms, and conducted the business until 1843, when he removed to Cardington, Delaware Co, and there leased a mill for nine years Here he introduced a new and complete set of machinery, making it in every way suitable to the business he proposed conducting He was very successful during his residence at the latter place, which he left on removing to Chester to continue the business in a factory which he built in 1852 This was at the time one of the most complete establishments in the country, and was subsequently increased in dimensions by the purchase of additional lands and the erection of other buildings A full description of the business and its various ramifications having been given elsewhere, renders repetition here unnecessary Mr Gartside, by a technical knowledge of the business, together with great industry and strict integrity, has enjoyed a career of remarkable prosperity On the 1st of January, 1857, he admitted his sons, Amos and James, into partnership, the firm becoming Benjamin Gartside & Sons. Since his resi-

Keokuk Mills. B. Gartside & Sons, Chester Penn

B. Gartside

B. Gartside

Amos. Gartside

James Gartiot

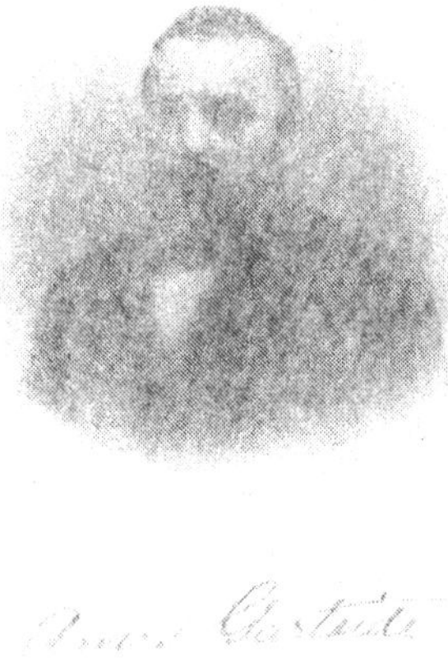

James Gartside

dence in Chester, Mr. Gartside has been actively identified with its growth and prosperity. He was in politics early an Old-Line Whig, and later became a Republican. He was for many years a councilman of the borough, and filled various other positions of trust. He was the originator of the First National Bank of Chester, and has also been director of the Chester Mutual Insurance Company. He was also prominent in the projection of the Chester Rural Cemetery, and has, by his public spirit and liberality, ever been a promoter of all measures tending to the development of the city of his adoption. In religion he is a Baptist, and one of the oldest deacons in period of service in the church of which he is a member. Mr. Gartside was married in 1815 to Miss Elizabeth Kershaw, of Rochdale, England. Their children are Enoch, Robert, Mary (Mrs. John Kershaw), John, James, Ann (Mrs. Jonathan Grant), Amos, and Joseph.

Amos Gartside, son of Benjamin and Elizabeth Kershaw Gartside, was born in Rochdale, Lancashire, England, Oct. 23, 1829, and with his parents became a resident of the United States in 1831. His primary education was chiefly obtained at the common schools, though supplemented by a course at the Germantown Academy. Having finished his studies, at the age of eighteen he entered his father's factory for the purpose of becoming proficient in the art of woolen-weaving. Here he became thoroughly acquainted with the business in all its details. When his father left Cardington, Delaware Co., and established mills at Chester, his son accompanied him and remained in his employment until 1857, at which time he was, together with his brother, James, admitted to a partnership. He was the same year married to Miss Emma, daughter of James Pierce, of Chester, whose children are Elizabeth (Mrs. H. G. Pennell), Mary Ann, and Amy Alberta, who survive; and John, Georgie, and Katie, deceased. Mr. Gartside has manifested an active interest in public affairs, and done much to advance the growth of the city of Chester. He was for sixteen years a member of the City Council, and president of that body. He was formerly a Whig in politics, and more recently became a Republican. He has been active in advocating the principles of his party, and represented the Sixth Pennsylvania District as a delegate to the National Convention, held in Chicago in 1880. He has been for eight years a member of the Board of Port Wardens. Mr. Gartside has also been largely identified with business enterprises as director of the Steel Casting Company, of the Eureka Steel Casting Company, and of the Chester Mutual Insurance Company. He is the originator of many public works in the city of Chester, and has filled the office of president of the Chester Water-Works since its organization. He was also a director of the Chester Improvement Company, and of the McCaffry Direct Street Carting Company. He is furthermore a director of the Delaware River Railroad, and was largely instrumental in securing the terminus of the Chester Railroad at Chester. His business qualities are characterized by a remarkable degree of judgment and general ability, which gives him an influential position in the commercial world.

James Gartside, son of Benjamin and Elizabeth K. Gartside, was born in Rochdale, England, on the 20th of October, 1823, and emigrated with his father to America in 1831. He enjoyed but limited advantages of education, and at the early age of eight years entered the mill of his uncle, James Kershaw, where he acquired the trade of a spinner upon throstles. He subsequently removed to Manayunk, and found employment with Joseph Ripley. His father having started a milling interest at Blockley, his son continued with him at that point, as also at Roxbury and elsewhere. The mills established by Benjamin Gartside at Chester, in 1852, were successful; his son having been admitted to the firm in 1857, which partnership is still retained by him. He was on the 17th of August, 1851, married to Elizabeth, daughter of Joseph T. and Susannah Smith, of Blockley (now the Twenty-fourth Ward of Philadelphia). Mr. Gartside joined the emergency recruits during the late war, in defense of Gettysburg, and on the expiration of his period of service resumed his business. In politics he is a Republican, but not active as a politician. In religion he is a supporter of the Baptist Church.

Arasapha Mills.—Abraham Blakeley, the senior partner of the firm of A. Blakeley & Sons, began manufacturing cotton goods at Knowlton, Jan. 1, 1847, with Phineas Lownes. In the fall of 1853, Blakeley disposed of his interest to J. William Lewis, and removed to Chester, where, in September, 1854, he commenced the manufacture of tickings, denims, and stripes in the three-story brick building, one hundred by forty-five feet, erected by John Larkin in that year, at Eleventh and Walnut Streets. On the 1st of January, 1860, his son, Benjamin W. Blakeley, became associated in the business, under the firm-name of A. Blakeley & Son. In 1873 the firm erected a three-story building, one hundred and two by fifty-five feet, a finishing-room, forty by thirty feet, offices, and other buildings. On the 1st of January, 1874, the present firm was constituted by the admission of William S. Blakeley, another son of Abraham Blakeley. The mills, in 1873, were refitted with new and improved machinery. Additions were made to the buildings in 1874 and in 1877. The main building is at present two hundred and seventy-six by fifty feet; dye-house, one hundred by forty feet, with storage-sheds for six hundred bales of cotton.

The mills contain 276 looms, 35 setts of cards, and 8500 spindles. The power is supplied by a Corliss engine, with three sets of boilers; 33 bales of cotton are used, and 80,000 yards are manufactured per week; 200 persons are employed.

Abraham Blakeley, who is of English descent, and

the son of Abraham and Nanny Turner Blakeley, was born July 5, 1806, in Dewsbury, Yorkshire, England, where he remained until twenty years of age After very limited advantages of education he became an employé of a cotton-factory at Staley Bridge, Lancashire, and remained thus occupied until 1828, when, having determined to emigrate to the United States, he sailed in April of the same year, and on the 29th of the following month landed in Philadelphia During the succeeding eighteen months he was engaged as a weaver of woolen goods by Messrs Bullock & Davis, of Germantown In the fall of 1829 he removed to Pottsville, and made it his residence until 1833, when he entered the factory of John P Crozer, of Delaware County, as foreman of the weaving department At the close of the year 1846 he formed a copartnership with Phineas Lownes, as Lownes & Blakeley, and the firm embarked in manufacturing at Knowlton in 1847. Disposing of his interest in the autumn of 1853 he removed to Chester, and embarked in his present extensive enterprise, the manufacture of cotton goods

Having purchased the interest of a special partner in 1857, he operated the factory alone until the admission of his son, Benjamin W, who now assumes as partner its active management, Mr Blakeley still remaining the financial head of the firm He was married in 1836 to Miss Betsey Walker, a lady of Irish extraction, to whom was born one son, Benjamin W Mrs Blakeley died in January, 1837, and he was again married Aug 2, 1838, to Miss Maria A, daughter of James P and Sarah Miles Their children are Sarah (deceased), Eliza (Mrs Henry E Gilroy), Sophia (Mrs John N Wilson), Sarah E, Mary E (Mrs John P Graham), Anna M (deceased, Mrs William Lister), William S, Alice M (deceased), and Henry G Mr Blakeley has since his residence in Chester been among its most enterprising and public-spirited citizens, and has contributed largely to the building up of its trade and its importance as a manufacturing centre He was formerly an Old-Line Whig, and later became a Republican He is not active as a politician, but has served as member of both branches of the Borough and City Councils He is a member of the Madison Street Methodist Episcopal Church, in which he is both trustee and steward, and has been one of its most active workers

Phœnix Cotton- and Woolen-Mills—These mills were built by Spencer McIlvaine at the corner of Ninth and McIlvaine Streets, and operated by John Green as the Continental Mills In May, 1871, they were sold to J Blazedell, Jr, of Chicopee, Mass The same year they came into possession of John Maxon, by whom they were operated till 1882, when they were sold to Ashforth & Downey, of Philadelphia, who now own and operate them under the management of John Maxon The mills contain one hundred looms, twenty-one hundred and sixty spindles, and four sets of cards The mills were partially destroyed by fire in January, 1878, and again in November, 1879

Mohawk Mills—The building now occupied by this mill was originally built by John M Broomall for T Bickum Price as a machine-shop, and for a short time that business was conducted there by Price & Mulford In 1856, Samuel Eccles, Jr, purchased the building and changed it into a cotton-mill In 1868 he removed to Baltimore, and the mill passed through several hands till May 13, 1871, when the property was purchased by Robert Hall, who, on the 1st of January, 1872, admitted his son as a partner in the business The original building was twenty-five by fifty feet, and two and a half stories in height, and later a building fifty by thirty-seven feet, and two stories high, was erected Mr Hall, in 1872, increased the capacity of the works by the erection of a two-story building twenty-five by thirty-seven feet, two stories in height The mill contains two sets of cards forty-eight inches, two self-acting mules, three hundred and thirty spindles each, and forty-four looms Forty-four hands are employed, to whom three hundred and twenty-five dollars per week are paid Twenty-seven hundred pounds of raw cotton and wool are used, and ten thousand two hundred yards of goods are manufactured weekly

Irving and Leiper Manufacturing Company—James Irving erected, in the year 1853, a mill one hundred and twenty by forty-six feet, three stories in height, between Front Street and the Delaware River, at the corner of Franklin Street It was not put into operation till 1859, when a partnership was formed between James and David Irving and Thomas I. Leiper under the firm-name of Irving & Leiper The death of David Irving occurred in 1862, and the business was continued by James Irving and Thomas I. Leiper until 1878, when the Irving & Leiper Manufacturing Company was incorporated, with James Irving, president, Thomas I Leiper, treasurer, and Charles H Worthington, secretary The main building at present is two hundred and thirty by fifty feet, three stories in height Engine-room forty feet square, picker-room forty by sixty feet, warehouse thirty by seventy feet There are seventy-six sets of cards and twelve thousand spindles, driven by a four hundred horse-power engine Three thousand bales of cotton are used in a year, from which are produced weekly twenty-two thousand pounds of yarn A force of one hundred and seven hands is employed

Victoria Mill—This mill was established by John Gartside, who in 1860 erected a building four stories in height, sixty-five by thirty-three feet, and in 1873 erected an addition fifty by thirty-three feet At present there are two buildings, one, one hundred and twenty by forty, the other one hundred and twenty by thirty. There are four sets of cards, twenty-four broad looms, two thousand one hundred spindles, and all the machinery requisite to manufacture the best qualities of woolen cassimere and cloakings Three thousand

Abraham Blakeley

the son of Abraham and Nancy Turner Blakeley, was born July 5, 1806, in Dewsbury, Yorkshire, England, where he remained until twenty years of age. After very limited advantages of education he became an employé of a cotton-factory at Staley Bridge, Lancashire, and remained there occupied until 1828, when, having determined to emigrate to the United States, he sailed in April of the same year, and on the 9th of the following month landed in Philadelphia. During the succeeding eighteen months he was engaged as a weaver of woolen goods by Messrs. Bullock & Lewis, of Germantown. In the fall of 1829 he removed to Pottsville, and made it his residence until 1836, when he entered the factory of John P. Crozer, of Delaware County, as foreman of the weaving department. At the close of the year 1846 he formed a copartnership with Phineas Lownes, as Lownes & Blakeley, and the firm embarked in manufacturing at Knowlton in 1847. Disposing of his interest in the autumn of 1852 he removed to Chester, and embarked in his present extensive enterprise, the manufacture of cotton goods.

Having purchased the interest of a special partner in 1857, he operated the factory alone until the admission of his son, Benjamin W., who now assumes as partner its active management, Mr. Blakeley still remaining the financial head of the firm. He was married in 1832 to Miss Sarah Walker, a lady of Irish extraction, to whom was born one son, Benjamin W. Mrs. Blakeley died in January, 1837, and he was again married Aug. 6, 1838, to Miss Maria A., daughter of James L. and Sarah [illegible]. Their children are Sarah (deceased), Eliza (Mrs. Henry E. [illegible]), Sophia (Mrs. John N. Wilson), Sarah E., Mary E. (Mrs. John [illegible] Graham), Anna M. (deceased), [illegible] (Mrs. William Lister), William E., Alice N. (deceased), and Henry G. Mr. Blakeley has since his residence in Chester been among its most enterprising and public-spirited citizens, and has contributed largely to the building up of its trade and its importance as a manufacturing centre. He was formerly an Old Line Whig and later became a Republican. He is not active as a politician, but has served as member of both branches of the Borough and City Councils. He is a member of the Madison Street Methodist Episcopal Church, in which he is both trustee and steward, and has been one of its most active workers.

Phœnix Cotton- and Woolen-Mills.—These mills were built by Spencer McIlvaine at the corner of Ninth and McIlvaine Streets, and operated by John Roach as the Continental Mills. In May, 1871, they were sold to J. [illegible], Jr., of Chicopee, Mass. The same year they came into possession of John [illegible], by whom they were operated till 1882, when they were sold to [illegible] & Downey, of Philadelphia, who have operated them under the [illegible] of John [illegible]. The mills contain [illegible] looms, twenty-one hundred and sixty [illegible] four sets of cards. The mills were partially destroyed by fire in January, 1878, and again in November, 1879.

Mohawk Mills.—The building now occupied by this mill was originally built by John M. Broomall for T. Bickum Price as a machine-shop, and for a short time that business was conducted there by Price & Mifford. In 1856, Samuel Eccles, Jr., purchased the building and changed it into a cotton-mill. In 1858 he removed to Baltimore, and the mill passed through several hands till May 18, 1871, when the property was purchased by Robert Hall, who, on the 1st of January, 1872, admitted his son as a partner in the business. The original building was twenty-five by fifty feet, and two and a half stories in height, and later a building fifty by thirty-seven feet, and two stories high, was erected. Mr. Hall, in 1872, increased the capacity of the works by the erection of a two-story building twenty-five by thirty-seven feet, two stories in height. The mill contains two sets of cards forty-eight inches, two self-acting mules, three hundred and thirty spindles each, and forty-four looms. Forty-four hands are employed, to whom three hundred and twenty-five dollars per week are paid. Twenty-seven hundred pounds of raw cotton and wool are used, and ten thousand two hundred yards of goods are manufactured weekly.

Irving and Leiper Manufacturing Company.—James Irving erected, in the year 1858, a mill one hundred and twenty by forty-six feet, three stories in height, between Front Street and the Delaware River, at the corner of Franklin Street. It was not put into operation till 1859, when a partnership was formed between James and David Irving and Thomas I. Leiper under the firm-name of Irving & Leiper. The death of David Irving occurred in 1862, and the business was continued by James Irving and Thomas I. Leiper until 1878, when the Irving & Leiper Manufacturing Company was incorporated, with James Irving, president; Thomas I. Leiper, treasurer; and Charles H. Worthington, secretary. The main building at present is two hundred and thirty by fifty feet, three stories in height. Engine-room forty feet square, picker-room forty by sixty feet, warehouse thirty by seventy feet. There are seventy-six sets of cards and twelve thousand spindles, driven by a four hundred horse-power engine. Three thousand bales of cotton are used in a year, from which are produced weekly twenty-two thousand pounds of yarn. A force of one hundred and seven hands is employed.

Victoria Mill.—This mill was established by John Garside, who in 1869 erected a building four stories in height, sixty-five by thirty-three feet, and in 1873 erected an addition fifty by thirty-three feet. At present there are two buildings, one one hundred and twenty by forty, the other one hundred and twenty by thirty. There are four sets of cards, twenty-four broad looms, two thousand one hundred spindles, and all the machinery requisite to manufacture the best qualities of woolen cassimeres and cloakings. Three thousand

Eng.d by A.H. Ritchie.

Abraham Blakeley

Galaxy Pub Co Philadelphia

John Gartside.

Four hundred pounds of wool is used per week, from which is manufactured eighteen hundred yards of double-width goods. Fifty-four hands are employed.

John Garside, son of Benjamin and Elizabeth Kershaw Garside, was born on the 29th of October, 1821, in Rochdale, Lancashire, England. After a brief period at school he became an apprentice to the "piecing" business, and in 1830 removed to the United States with his parents. Finding employment ... in the Blockley Mills, Philadelphia, he remained until 1835, and then accompanied his father to Manayunk, and when the latter embarked in manufacturing in 1838, became an employé of his ... He continued thus employed until 1849, when on his removal to Chester he formed a copartnership with Samuel Gill, under the firm-name of Gill & Garside, and conducted a spinning business until 1850, [illegible] father having erected the Kershaw [illegible] rented a room in the building for [illegible] his business [illegible]. During [illegible] [illegible] of the [illegible] [illegible] [illegible] the [illegible] [illegible] mill in the city of Chester. [illegible] [illegible] of the First National Bank [illegible] and identified with the active business interests of the city. Mr. Garside was married in 1848 to Miss Margaret, daughter of Joseph Smith, of Blockley. Their children are Enoch (deceased), Benjamin, Eliza (deceased), Laura, and Joseph.

Chester Dock Mills.—The business of this firm was established, in 1853, by Phineas Lawson and J. William Lewis at [illegible], Middletown township, where they continued until 1865, when the [illegible] stone building two hundred [illegible] feet by [illegible] three feet, and other necessary buildings were erected at Third and Garfield Streets, Chester, and the business was removed to the new location. The members of the firm at present are J. William Lewis and Albert A. Roop. Employment is given to one hundred and fifty persons, to whom six thousand eight hundred and fifty dollars is paid monthly. Nine hundred and fifty thousand pounds of cotton is used yearly in the manufacture of plaids, Osnaburgs, ginghams, checks, and stripes. Ninety thousand yards of cloth and fifteen thousand pounds of yarn are produced weekly. Thomas Clough, Sr., is superintendent.

Patterson Mills.—The main building, three hundred and thirty-five feet long, eighty feet wide, and two and three stories in height, was erected by Gen. Robert Patterson in 1866, fitted with machinery and put into operation in August, 1867. It is situated on a four-acre tract of land, between Fifth Street and Baltimore Railroad, and between [illegible] and Chester Creek. The machinery consists of three hundred looms, sixty-five sets of cards, and about fourteen thousand spindles, which are operated by a Corliss engine with eight boilers. Twenty thousand pounds of cotton are used, from which is manufactured sixty-seven thousand yards of cotton goods per week. Two hundred and ten hands are employed, whose wages are five thousand dollars monthly. The mills are now owned by the estate of Gen. Robert Patterson, and are in charge of James D. Davis.

Sunnyside Mills.—The buildings at the corner of Morton Avenue and Ledward Street, fifty by one hundred feet, and two stories in height, were erected in 1865, by Henry McIlvaine and John Hinkson, who leased the property to Lamy & Buck for a tannery. They were not put in operation, but on the 24th of July, 1866, James Ledward, who had been foreman in the mills of John P. Crozer & Son from 1847 to 1851, purchased the property and fitted the mills with improved machinery, and commenced the manufacture of [illegible], [illegible], [illegible], etc., [illegible] of fifty hands. [illegible] [illegible] [illegible] July 1, 1871, John [illegible] [illegible] [illegible] was admitted [illegible] [illegible] January, 187[illegible], the [illegible] [illegible] and in the March follow[illegible] [illegible] [illegible] [illegible]. The buildings were [illegible] and [illegible], and on the [illegible] January, 1874, they were [illegible] one hundred and four looms, seventy-[illegible], four sets of cards, two self-acting mules of [illegible] hundred spindles each, and other necessary machinery.

They were operated by John Ledward until [illegible], when they were totally destroyed by fire and never rebuilt. [illegible] 1st of January, 18[illegible], the buildings [illegible] to the Joseph [illegible] [illegible] [illegible] of Kent, [illegible] [illegible] [illegible] [illegible] [illegible] [illegible] [illegible] [illegible] operated [illegible] [illegible] [illegible] the business [illegible] [illegible] [illegible] have remained vacant.

[illegible] Mills.—On the 1st of January, 18[illegible], James Barton, Jr., and Simeon Cotton associated together for the purpose of manufacturing tickings, stripes, and denims. They purchased of Henry McIlvaine and John Hinkson, who were building a mill one hundred by fifty feet, three stories high, with a two-story addition sixty-six by thirty feet, and fitted the mill with ninety looms and five thousand spindles. The power was supplied by an eighty horse-power Corliss engine. Simeon Cotton sold his interest to James Barton, Jr., in the spring of 1876. Barton continued the business for several years, and discontinued it in 1881, since which time the mills have been closed.

Yeadon Mills.—The buildings were erected in 18[illegible] by McGees & Co., of Philadelphia, for the manufacture of denims and tickings, and were known as the Fulton Mills. They were operated by John Brewster. Early in May, 1870, the mills were entirely destroyed by fire. The grounds were purchased, the mills rebuilt by William Bullock, and the

John Garside.

four hundred pounds of wool is used per week, from which is manufactured eighteen hundred yards of double-width goods Fifty-four hands are employed

John Gartside, son of Benjamin and Elizabeth Kershaw Gartside, was born on the 25th of October, 1821, in Rochdale, Lancashire, England After a brief period at school he became an apprentice to the "piecing" business, and in 1831 removed to the United States with his parents Finding employment at once in the Blockley Mills, Philadelphia, he remained until 1835, and then accompanied his father to Manayunk, and when the latter embarked in manufacturing, in 1838, became an employé of his mills He continued thus employed until 1850, when on his removal to Chester he formed a copartnership with Samuel Cliff, under the firm-name of Cliff & Gartside, and conducted a dyeing business until 1852 His father having erected the Keokuk Mills, he then rented a room in the building for the prosecution of his legitimate trade During the rebellion he served as one of the emergency recruits during the Gettysburg campaign, resuming business on his return He is now the exclusive proprietor of an extensive woolen mill in the city of Chester He has been for many years a director of the First National Bank of Chester, and identified with the active business interests of the city. Mr Gartside was married in 1846 to Miss Margaret, daughter of Joseph Smith, of Blockley Their children are Enoch (deceased), Benjamin, Eliza (deceased), Laura, and Joseph

Chester Dock Mills—The business of this firm was established, in 1853, by Phineas Lownes and J William Lewis at Knowlton, Middletown township, where they remained until 1864, when the three-story stone building two hundred and fifty-one feet by fifty-three feet, and other necessary buildings, were erected at Third and Garfield Streets, Chester, and the business was removed to the new location The members of the firm at present are J William Lewis and Albert A Roop Employment is given to two hundred and fifty persons, to whom six thousand eight hundred and fifty dollars is paid monthly Nine hundred and fifty thousand pounds of cotton is used yearly in the manufacture of plaids, Osnaburgs, ginghams, checks, and stripes Ninety thousand yards of cloth and fifteen thousand pounds of yarn are produced weekly Thomas Clough, Sr, is superintendent

Patterson Mills.—The main building, three hundred and thirty-five feet long, eighty feet wide, and two and three stories in height, was erected by Gen Robert Patterson in 1866, fitted with machinery and put into operation in August, 1867 It is situated on a four-acre tract of land, between Fifth Street and Baltimore Railroad, and between Penn Street and Chester Creek The machinery consists of three hundred looms, sixty-five sets of cards, and about fourteen thousand spindles, which are operated by a Corliss engine with eight boilers. Twenty thousand pounds of cotton are used, from which is manufactured sixty-seven thousand yards of cotton goods per week Two hundred and ten hands are employed, whose wages are five thousand dollars monthly The mills are now owned by the estate of Gen. Robert Patterson, and are in charge of James D Davis

Sunnyside Mills—The buildings at the corner of Morton Avenue and Ledward Street, fifty by one hundred feet, and two stories in height, were erected, in 1865, by Henry McIlvaine and John Hinkson, who leased the property to Lenny & Burk for a factory They were not put in operation, but on the 26th of July, 1866, James Ledward, who had been foreman in the mills of John P Crozer & Son from 1847 to 1851, purchased the property and fitted the mills with improved machinery, and commenced the manufacture of cottonades, cassimeres, doeskins, etc., with a force of fifty hands Additions were made to the buildings from time to time. July 1, 1871, John I Ledward, a son of the proprietor, was admitted to partnership On the 4th of January, 1873, the warehouse was destroyed by fire, and in the March following the picker-house, warping- and weaving-rooms were also destroyed The buildings were rebuilt and enlarged, and on the 1st of January, 1874, they were running with one hundred and four hands, seventy-two looms, four sets of cards, two self-acting mules of six hundred spindles each, and other necessary machinery.

They were operated by John Ledward until 1882, when they were totally destroyed by fire, and again rebuilt. On the 1st of January, 1884, the buildings were rented to the Joseph Turner & Son Manufacturing Company, of Kent, Portage Co, Ohio, who put in the necessary machinery for manufacturing worsteds, and operated them for five months, when they removed the business to Ohio, since which time the buildings have remained vacant.

Algodon Mills—On the 1st of January, 1866, James Barton, Jr, and Simeon Cotton associated together for the purpose of manufacturing tickings, stripes, and denims They purchased of Henry McIlvaine and John Hinkson, who were builders, a mill, one hundred by fifty feet, three stories high, with a two-story addition sixty-six by thirty feet, and fitted the mill with ninety looms and five thousand spindles The power was supplied by an eighty horse-power Corliss engine Simeon Cotton sold his interest to James Barton, Jr, in the spring of 1876 Barton continued the business for several years, and discontinued it in 1881, since which time the mills have been closed

Yeadon Mills.—The buildings were erected in 1867 by McCrea & Co, of Philadelphia, for the manufacture of denims and tickings, and were known as the Fulton Mills They were operated by John Brewster Early in May, 1870, the mills were entirely destroyed by fire The grounds were purchased, the mills rebuilt by William Bullock, and the name changed to Yeadon Mills In 1866, Denis, Anderson & Co established a business in Conshohocken for the manufacture of fancy cassimeres, and in 1870, G P Denis removed to Chester, purchased these mills, and operated them In 1880 additions were made to the buildings and machinery At present the main building—stone and brick—is one hundred and thirty feet in width by two hundred feet in length The mills contain thirty-eight broad Knowles & Crompton looms, two thousand two hundred and eighty spindles, four sets Engle sixty-inch cards, and other machinery, which is driven by a one hundred and twenty horse-power Corliss engine About one hundred and twenty hands are employed, twenty-six thousand pounds of raw material are used weekly in the manufacture of three thousand two hundred and fifty yards of fancy cassimeres

Lilley & Son's Manufacturing Company—On the 1st of August, 1873, John Lilley & Son established the business of manufacturing cotton and woolen cloth and cotton yarn A mill was erected on Front Street, one hundred by fifty-four feet, and in the rear a building one hundred and twenty-two by forty feet, these buildings were connected by one eighty by thirty-six feet The machinery consists of one hundred and eleven looms, three thousand two hundred and fifty-two spindles, twenty-five cards, one hundred persons are employed, twelve thousand pounds of raw material are used weekly, from which is produced twenty-five thousand yards of cloth On the 3d of January, 1880, the company was incorporated under the name of Lilley Manufacturing Company John Lilley, Jr, is superintendent

Chester City Mills—These mills were established in 1877 by Branagan & Lamb, who erected a building forty by forty feet, with the necessary structures adjacent, at the corner of Front and Parker Streets, for the purpose of manufacturing woolen yarns and woolen and cotton jeans The mills were supplied with ninety looms, seventeen hundred spindles, five sets of cards, which are driven by a sixty horse-power engine Four thousand pounds of raw material are used per week, from which is produced seventeen thousand yards of goods Seventy hands are employed, forty of whom are women

S A Crozer & Son's Chester Mills—In 1837, Jacob G Kitts established the first foundry in Delaware County, on the lot where Crozer's new cotton-mill partly stands, on Edgmont Avenue, above the present post-office In his advertisement in the *Delaware County Republican*, Sept 29, 1837, he states,—

"The subscriber, having established an iron-foundry at Chester, is now ready and prepared to receive orders for iron castings of all kinds and descriptions, such as mill gearing and machinery for flour- and paper-mills, horse-power for thrashing-machines, wheels for railroad cars, axles, etc All of which will be made and fitted up to order"

In 1837, Kitts & Kerlin carried on the business, and erected the first stationary-engine and steam-boiler ever started in Chester, "and its advent produced," wrote John M Broomall, "more sensation among the simple villagers than did the fall of the French monarchy" In 1840 the firm made the second engine and boiler used in Chester, for the tannery of William Brobson In 1841 "brass- and bell-foundry" was added to the title of the works In 1844, Kitts, who had resumed entire control of the "Chester Iron-Foundry and Machine-Shops," failed, and was succeeded the same year by Charles Cornog, Cadwallader Evans, and Ferdinand Cornog, which firm carried on an extensive business in 1845, building a twenty-five horse-power engine for David Trainer, and casting a pinion-wheel, weighing two thousand four hundred pounds, for William T Crook's factory. In 1851 they built a boiler for Samuel Riddle's mill, forty feet in length, thirty-six inches diameter, and weighing eight thousand pounds In those early days of Chester manufacturing establishments, this was regarded as remarkable work In the year 1880, S A Crozer & Son erected near Chester Creek, north of the post-office, on Edgmont Avenue, a brick building, two stories in height, one hundred and forty by sixty feet, with picker-room twenty-four by sixty feet Six thousand three hundred and thirty-six spindles and forty-eight sets of cards were placed in the mill The power is supplied from a Corliss engine with three boilers Work was commenced in June, 1881 Fifteen men, forty-five women and girls, and twenty boys are employed, whose monthly wages are nineteen hundred dollars Fifty thousand pounds of cotton per month is used, from which is produced weekly twelve thousand pounds of warp-yarn The mills are under the charge of William D Howard

Lincoln Manufacturing Company—In 1881 a stock company was organized in Chester, with a capital of one hundred thousand dollars, for the purpose of manufacturing cotton yarns Land was purchased on Morton Avenue, and a brick structure, seventy feet in width by one hundred and ninety feet in length, two stories high, was erected, and fitted with modern machinery An engine- and boiler-house, fifty by sixty feet, was built, supplied with a two hundred horse-power engine The machinery consists of six thousand eight hundred and forty spindles and thirty-four Foss-Pevey cards Thirty-three bales of cotton are used weekly, from which twelve thousand pounds of yarn are produced About sixty-five hands are employed

The directors are S Emlen Meigs, of Philadelphia, president, Chalmers Dale, of New York, A Blakeley, Richard Wetherill, and W S Blakeley, of Chester, treasurer

The Stotesbury Mill.—The building on the corner of Fourteenth Street and Edgmont Avenue was erected in 1874 by J Lewis Crozer, and in that year the manufacture of cotton yarn was then established by James M Stotesbury The building is of stone,

one hundred and sixty feet by sixty-two feet, and one story in height. The machinery consists of twelve sets of cards and three thousand five hundred and twenty spindles. Twenty-eight thousand pounds of yarn was spun monthly, using thirty-two thousand pounds of raw cotton. The works were operated by Mr. Sugenheim till 1883, when they were closed, and have not since been operated.

Bower's Mill.—In 1872, James Bower & Son began business in Waterville, in the old Sharpless cotton-mill, as a manufacturer of shoddy. At the corner of Sixth and Madison Streets a building had been erected about 1860 by Hinkson & McIlvaine, as a planing-mill, sash-and blind-factory. It later passed to Fairlamb Brothers, who continued the business till 1877, when Bower & Son came into possession, and removed their machinery from Waterville to this place. Improvements had been made from time to time, and in the spring of 1884 a new building of brick and stone was erected [illegible] which they now occupy. The material used is [illegible] waste, which is manufactured into [illegible].

Morton & Black's Saw-Mill and Sash-Factory.—The business was established in 1865, at the foot of Morton Avenue, by Crosby P. Morton and J. Frank Black. In the next year Henry B. Black became a member of the firm, and continued till 1879, when he retired. The main building is one hundred and fifty feet long, forty feet wide, and two stories high, with a fire-proof engine-house thirty by sixty feet, and offices adjacent. Three hundred thousand feet of lumber per month are used in the construction of doors, sash, blinds, and all kinds of wood-work necessary for the construction of buildings. [illegible] men are employed, whose wages are [illegible] hundred dollars per month. The works are under the charge of William Hinkson, Jr. A lumber yard is connected with the factory, and all the lumber used at the mill is from the yard.

Cocoa Mat and Matting-Works.—This building, occupied by the works, was erected in 1861, by Joseph Entwistle and Henry L. Powell, who commenced therein the bleaching and finishing of cotton goods. Later, Mr. Powell sold his interest to Entwistle, who continued till 1866, when John Hall became associated with him, and in 1866 John Longbottom became a partner. At this time the firm commenced the manufacture of shoddy. About 1868, Mr. Entwistle retired from the firm, which continued in business for a short time, when the mill was burned. The building was rebuilt. In 1871, Charles Roberts leased it and therein began the spinning of cotton yarn, and continued there till 1878, when John Thompson & Son purchased the business. The latter continued to operate the mill until 1882, when the building was leased by Edward S. Worrell for the manufacture of cocoa mat and mattings. Prior to 1880, J. Frank Black established the business in a building which stood on the corner of Second Street and Edgmont Avenue. Mr. Worrell soon afterwards became associated with Mr. Black, who later sold his interest to Mr. Worrell. The latter continued the business until May, 1882, when part of the ground on which the building stood was required in the construction of the Second Street bridge. The present building occupied by the water-works was rented, and in September, 1882, the building was ready for occupancy, having been thoroughly fitted with improved machinery. There are sixteen hand-looms and two power-looms, which are operated by thirty-five employés. Two thousand five hundred dozen of mats and one thousand rolls of matting are made per annum.

Chester Edge-Tool Works.—John C. Beatty, son of William Beatty, who established the business over seventy-five years ago, removed his works from Springfield to the city of Chester in the year 1871. He erected a brick building two stories in height, and one hundred and seventy feet in length. These works were operated by Beatty until April, 1878, when they were purchased by [illegible] Black, his son-in-law, who made additions to the works. Early in April, 1880, the main building was destroyed by fire, and rebuilt the same year. The works comprise the mills, grinding- and polishing-mills, forge-shops, and other buildings necessary to carry on the business successfully. The goods marked "Beatty" are known in every market for the excellence of the material used and the superior quality of the articles made.

Samuel Black, the grandfather of Henry B. Black, was of Scotch-Irish ancestry, and an early resident of Marple township, in Delaware County. He was united in marriage to Miss Catherine Van [illegible], and had children,—Jacob, Samuel, William V., Lewis, Catharine V., and John. William V. was born in Marple township, Aug. 27, 1790, and died Nov. 3, 1880, in his eighty-eighth year, having been during his active life both a farmer and a merchant. He married Miss Mary, daughter of Isaac [illegible], of Delaware County, and had children,—Catharine (Mrs. A. C. Lindsey), Isaac C., Samuel G., Elizabeth Jane, William, Hannah Maria, Susannah, Henry B., and J. Frank, four of whom survive. Henry B. was born May 8, 1827, in Upper Darby township, Delaware Co., from whence, on attaining his eighth year, he removed with his parents to Haverford township. His education was principally derived from public schools, with the advantage of one year's instruction under more favorable circumstances. On completing his studies, he became interested as a clerk with his father in Media, and managed the business until 1850, when he was admitted to a partnership in a general country store. Here he remained until 1865, meanwhile becoming a partner with his brother in the same business, when in the spring of the latter year he sought a more extended field in Chester, and became a member of the firm of Morton, Black & Bro., who were engaged in lumber and coal trade, steam saw- and planing-mills, sash and blind manufacturing,

one hundred and sixty-five by sixty-two feet, and one story in height The machinery consists of twelve sets of cards, and three thousand five hundred and twenty spindles Twenty-eight thousand pounds of yarn was spun monthly, using thirty-two thousand pounds of raw cotton The works were operated by Mr Stotesbury till 1883, when they were closed, and have not since been operated

Bower's Mill—In 1873, James Bower & Son began business in Waterville, in the old Sharpless cotton-mill, as a manufacturer of shoddy At the corner of Sixth and Madison Streets a building had been erected about 1860 by Hinkson & McIlvaine, as a planing-mill, sash- and blind-factory It later passed to Fairlamb Brothers, who continued the business till 1877, when Bower & Son came into possession, and removed their machinery from Waterville to this place Improvements had been made from time to time, and in the spring of 1884 a new building of brick and stone was erected on the lot which they now occupy The material used is assorted waste, which is manufactured into wool

Morton & Black's Saw-Mill and Sash-Factory.—The business was established in 1865, at the foot of Morton Avenue, by Crosby P Morton and J Frank Black In the next year Henry B Black became a member of the firm, and continued till 1879, when he retired The main building is one hundred and fifty feet long, forty feet wide, and two stories high, with a fire-proof engine-house thirty by sixty feet, and offices adjacent. Three hundred thousand feet of lumber per month are used in the construction of doors, sash, blinds, and all kinds of wood-work necessary for the construction of buildings Fifty men are employed, whose wages are fifteen hundred dollars per month The works are under the charge of William Hinkson, Jr. A lumber yard is connected with the factory, and all the lumber used at the mill is from the yard

Cocoa Mat and Matting-Works—This building, occupied by the works, was erected in 1851, by Joseph Entwistle and Henry L Powell, who commenced therein the bleaching and finishing of cotton goods Later, Mr. Powell sold his interest to Entwistle, who continued till 1860, when John Hall became associated with him, and in 1865, John Longbottom became a partner At this time the firm commenced the manufacture of shoddy About 1868, Mr. Entwistle retired from the firm, which continued in business for a short time, when the mill was burned. The building was rebuilt In 1871, Charles Roberts leased it, and therein began the spinning of cotton yarn, and continued there till 1875, when John Thompson & Son purchased the business The latter continued to operate the mill until 1882, when the building was leased by Edward S Worrell, for the manufacture of cocoa mat and mattings Prior to 1878, J Frank Black established the business in a building which stood on the corner of Second Street and Edgmont Avenue Mr Worrel soon afterwards became associated with Mr Black, who later sold his interest to Mr Worrel The latter continued the business until May, 1882, when part of the ground on which the building stood was required in the construction of the Second Street bridge The present building owned by the water-works was rented, and in September, 1882, the building was ready for occupancy, having been thoroughly fitted with improved machinery There are sixteen hand-looms and two power looms, which are operated by thirty-five employés Two thousand five hundred dozen of mats and one thousand rolls of matting are made per annum

Chester Edge-Tool Works—John C Beatty, son of William Beatty, who established the business over seventy-five years ago, removed his works from Springfield to the city of Chester in the year 1871 He erected a frame building, two stories in height, and two hundred and seventy feet in length. These works were operated by Beatty until April, 1875, when they were purchased by H B Black, his son-in-law, who made additions to the works Early in April, 1880, the main building was destroyed by fire, and rebuilt the same year The works comprise tool-mills, grinding- and polishing-mills, forge-shops, and other buildings necessary to carry on the business successfully The goods marked "Beatty" are known in every market for the excellency of the material used and the superior quality of the articles made

Samuel Black, the grandfather of Henry B Black, was of Scotch-Irish ancestry, and an early resident of Marple township, in Delaware County He was united in marriage to Miss Catherine Van Leer, and had children,—Joseph, Samuel, William V, Ann, Catherine V, and John William V was born in Marple township, Aug 22, 1796, and died Nov 24, 1883, in his eighty-eighth year, having been during his active life both a farmer and a merchant He married Miss Maria, daughter of Isaac Cochran, of Delaware County, and had children,—Catherine (Mrs J C Lindsey), Isaac C, Samuel G, Elizabeth Jane, William, Hannah Maria, Susannah, Henry B, and J Frank, four of whom survive Henry B was born May 9, 1837, in Upper Darby township, Delaware Co, from whence, on attaining his eighth year, he removed with his parents to Haverford township His education was principally derived from public schools, with the advantage of one year's instruction under more favorable circumstances On completing his studies, he became interested as a clerk with his father in Media, and managed the business until 1859, when he was admitted to a partnership in a general country store Here he remained until 1867 (meanwhile becoming a partner with his brother in the same business), when in the spring of the latter year he sought a more extended field in Chester, and became a member of the firm of Morton, Black & Bro, who were engaged in lumber and coal traffic, steam saw- and planing-mills, sash and blind manufacturing, and controlled the Chester dock He retained his connection with this firm until 1879, having in 1875 purchased the Chester Edge-Tool Works of John C Beatty, to which since the latter year he has devoted his exclusive attention Mr Black was married on the 24th of October, 1860, to Miss Lydia Ann, daughter of John C Beatty, of Media, and has children,—John B, William V (deceased), Lillian M (deceased), Ada J, Bessie S, and Maria C Mr. Black is in politics an active Republican, has been for three successive terms a member of the City Council, and its president during a large portion of the time He is identified with the Chester National Bank as one of its directors He is in religion a Presbyterian, an elder of the Third Presbyterian Church of Chester, and has been for some years superintendent of its Sabbath-school He is also active in the cause of temperance, as also in all Christian and philanthropic enterprises

The Riverside Dye-Wood Mills—In 1835 a business was established at Waterville, by Smith & Hartshorne, that later developed into the present Riverside Dye-Wood Mills Later the works came into possession of John M Sharpless, by whom they were conducted till his death, in 1875 In 1878 the firm of John M Sharpless & Co purchased the old site of Frick, Wilson & Co's boat-yard, west of Roach's yard, embracing twelve acres, having a frontage of two hundred and twelve feet on the Delaware River On the 1st of April, 1879, the foundations of buildings were laid, and buildings erected during that year The dimensions of the main building are one hundred and thirteen feet front by sixty feet deep, the redwood-mill forty-seven by fifty-four feet, and the extract buildings fifty-two by fifty feet, in front of which is about one hundred and eighty feet of wharfage, where there is a depth of fifteen feet of water at low tide The main and extract buildings are four stories in height, and the adjoining mill two and a half stories About sixty hands are employed The firm-name, John M Sharpless & Co, is retained The present members are Thomas Scattergood, Richard Chambers, and John W Pepper

Combination Steel and Iron Company—The main building, two hundred and eighty by eighty feet, with wing eighty by seventy feet, was erected in 1880, and operations commenced March 1, 1881 John Roach is president, George E Weed, secretary and treasurer, and C A Weed, general manager The works contain eight heating furnaces, a rail-mill with a capacity of producing thirty thousand tons of iron per annum, a twelve-inch bar-mill with capacity of producing six thousand tons per annum, and a twenty-inch mill for angle-iron of ten thousand tons' capacity per annum One hundred and seventy-five men are employed

Eureka Cast-Steel Company.—The works of this company are located on the corner of Broomall and Sixth Streets, South Ward, and were erected in 1877, and commenced operations in September of that year. The area of the works is embraced in the limits of two hundred and two feet on Broomall Street, and two hundred and eighty-five feet on the line of the railroad The building is of L shape, has a frontage on Broomall Street of one hundred and thirty-two feet, and to the same extent is parallel with the Philadelphia, Wilmington and Baltimore Railroad, and in the narrowest part fifty feet wide As it is divided, we may specify the main building as one-storied, forty-one feet over all in height, the machine shop, eighty feet long and twenty-five feet wide, comprising the pattern-shop and pattern-safe. In the main building there are five furnaces,—four for annealing purposes and one for heating These are, on an average, eleven by eleven feet in dimensions The cupola, where the metal is heated, is forty-three feet in height, five feet in diameter, with a melting capacity of sixteen tons of iron The planing-machine, used in the finishing of the casts, is the best adapted to the purpose yet invented The vertical engine that supplies the power needed was built by Jacob Naylor, of Philadelphia, is of twenty-five horse-power, and is perfect and noiseless in its operations It supplies the blast-works, the planing-machine, drill-press, rumblers, emery-wheels, grindstones, elevator, etc The smoke-stack, connected with the annealing and heating furnaces, is eighty-five feet in height, five feet in diameter, and on the north side of the building Steel castings are manufactured solely. One hundred and twenty tons of raw material are used per month, and one hundred persons are employed The officers of the company are John A Emrick, president, W H Dickson, secretary and treasurer, Frederick Baldt, superintendent

Robert Wetherill & Co—This firm originated in a copartnership of Robert and Richard Wetherill, Jan 1, 1872 The property bounded by Sixth, Upland, and Seventh Streets, two hundred and seventy by one hundred feet, was purchased and large buildings were erected The machine-shop is two stories in height and forty by eighty feet, with foundry attached one hundred by fifty feet, a boiler-shop one hundred by forty feet, with pattern loft one hundred by fifty feet They have at present seven large buildings, covering a square of ground One hundred and fifty tons of pig-iron, seventy-five tons of plate, and twenty tons of wrought iron are monthly used in the manufacture of Corliss engines, boilers, shafting, and gearing Two hundred and fifty men are employed, and monthly receive ten thousand dollars in wages The works comprise machine-shops, smith-shop, foundry, boiler-shop, casting-house, pattern-shop, pattern store-house, store-rooms, and offices

Chester Steel Casting Company.—This company was organized in 1870, and in 1871 erected at Sixth and Norris Streets a foundry two hundred feet in length by fifty feet in width, and other buildings covering an area of two hundred and fifty square feet.

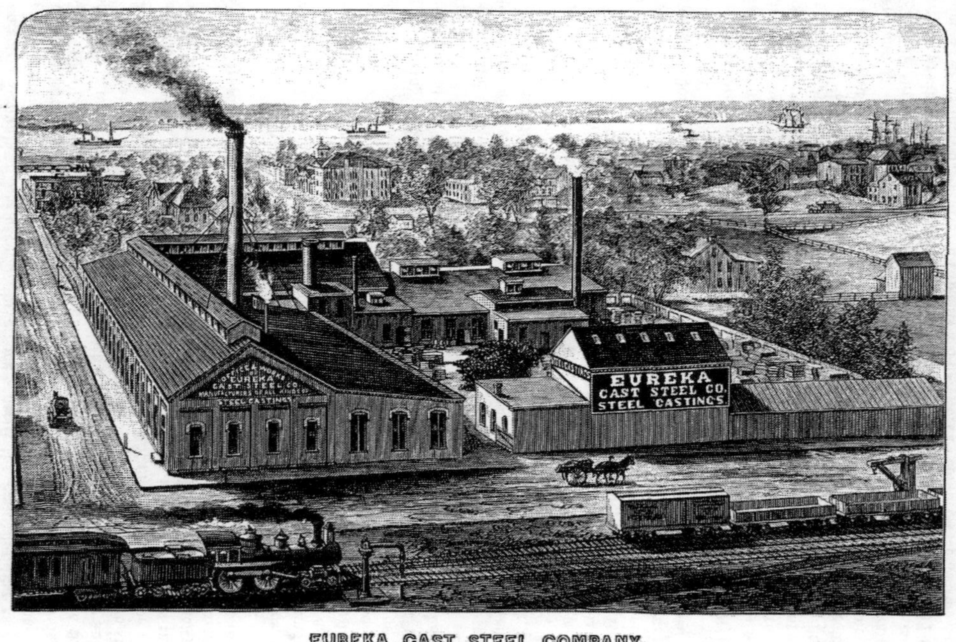

EUREKA CAST STEEL COMPANY,
MANUFACTURERS OF STEEL CASTINGS,
CHESTER, PA.

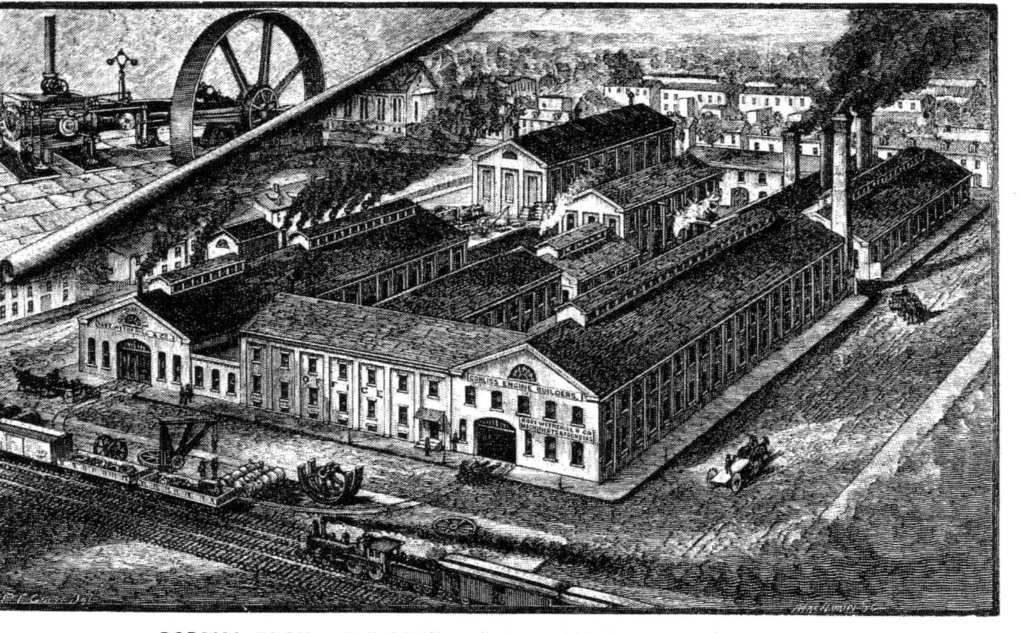

CORLISS ENGINE BUILDERS, BOILERS, SHAFTING, AND GEARING.
ROBERT WETHERILL & CO.,
CHESTER, PA.,

The machinery consists of two engines with three boilers, a heating-furnace, and seven annealing furnaces The works were at first under the charge of Samuel Archbold, president of the company, assisted by Mr McHaffy, a native of Glasgow, who was the patentee of a process of making steel, which this company are using At present one hundred hands are employed under the charge of John J Deemer

The Phœnix Iron Works were established by James Massey, in 1867, at the corner of Seventh and Potter Streets The main building is one hundred by fifty feet, two stories high, the foundry one hundred and ten by thirty feet The goods manufactured are finishing machinery, fulling-mills, washing machines, tentering machines, stock-dryers, dyeing and sizing machines, broad looms, and gigs The works are now owned by Thomas S Hall

The Chester Sugar-House —In 1867, James Baker & Co purchased five acres of land at the foot of Market Street, owned by Thomas I. Leiper, on which there were no buildings Much of the land was a marsh, overgrown with reeds, which it was necessary to fill up a distance of twelve feet before it could be made practically useful.

Prior to the erection of the large building, piles had to be driven to secure a solid foundation for the structure This was followed by the building of an extensive pier, and the dredging of the river to allow vessels of heavy draft to approach the wharf to unload their cargoes. After the erection of the first building additions were made thereto, all kinds of the best and most approved machinery were purchased, and the refinery was in every respect well equipped, the outlay, exclusive of the cost of the real estate, being over four hundred thousand dollars In the summer of 1872 the firm suspended, and the refinery passed into other hands John H Barton and Stephen C Hall leased the works, and for a time manufactured low-grade sugars, but ultimately abandoned the enterprise The real estate is now owned by Mr Folsom, of Philadelphia, and has been idle for several years

Color-Works.—The Delaware County Iron-Works were established in 1850 by William Trout & Co Land was purchased on Second Street below Market, by John M. Sharpless, and large buildings were erected in which the firm mentioned carried on a foundry and machine-shop for a time, when the property passed to other hands On the 1st of February, 1881, it came into possession of H. C Eyre & Co, who conducted the same business till the spring of 1884, when the works were leased to parties in Philadelphia, who are now refitting the buildings for the preparation and manufacture of pigment colors, printing varnishes, and refined oils

The Chester Chemical Works were established about 1860 by Mr McIntyre, and are now owned by George S Coyne Large buildings were erected at the foot of Market Street for the manufacture of muriatic, nitric, and pyroligneous acids, ammonia, oxymuriate of antimony, muriate and oxymuriate of tin, and muriate of iron The stills for muriatic acid have a capacity of five thousand pounds per week, for nitric acid of one thousand pounds per week, for ammonia of two hundred pounds per day Seven hundred barrels of Glauber salts are made annually from the residue left in the muriatic acid stills Robert Lidstone is superintendent.

Taylor's Carriage-Works —The business was established by Enos Taylor, grandfather of the present partners, early in this century At that time chaises, gigs, riding-chairs, and 'sulkies' were the principal manufacture. About 1830, Enos Taylor built a sulky for a naval officer, who took it to South America as a present to a person there to whom he was under obligations The vehicle was so highly esteemed among the wealthy residents of Valparaiso that Taylor received orders for a number of similar carriages, which were shipped thither Joseph Taylor, his son, succeeded him in 1832, continuing the business many years, and was succeeded by his sons, William and Edward C Taylor, who still conduct it It was first located at Fifth and Welsh Streets, later at Sixth and Pine Streets, and in 1874 removed to the corner of Twelfth and Edgmont Avenue, where they still are located

Stark's Carriage-Works.—In 1871, I P Branin, who established carriage-works in Philadelphia in 1854, removed his business to Chester, at shops on the corner of Fifth and Welsh Streets, and in May, 1876, removed to Sixth and Pine Streets, where buildings, eighty by eighty-four feet, with an addition of forty by eighty feet, were built Mr. Branin remained in business at this place till April, 1883, when he returned to Philadelphia

In May, 1879, Davis & Stark established a carriage-factory at the corner of Fifth and Welsh On the 1st of October in that year, Mr Davis withdrew from the firm, and Mr Stark continued the business at the same place until April 1, 1883, when he removed to the shops of I. P Branin, corner of Sixth and Pine Streets, where he now is.

Ocheltree's Carriage-Works —The works of Mr. Ocheltree were established on Edgmont Avenue below its present site in 1877. The increase of business demanded greater facilities, and land was purchased in 1879, and the present building, one hundred and twenty by forty feet, two stories in height, erected on Edgmont Avenue above the post-office, and supplied with the best machinery for the manufacture of fine carriages

Lukens' Grist-Mill —L L Lukens & Co began business on Sixth Street in 1877, and in June, 1879, removed to Seventh Street, below Edgmont Avenue The mill is operated by a thirty horse-power engine An elevator for unloading grain is in use The mill has a capacity of thirty thousand bushels per annum

Stroud & Co.'s Planing-Mill.—In 1871, John H. Stroud and Robert Booth established the sash-factory on the south side of Front Street and Concord Avenue. The machinery consists of one engine and boiler. Fourteen men and two boys are employed at a monthly pay of six hundred dollars. Two hundred thousand feet of lumber is used per year. In 1876 the mill was destroyed by fire, and the firm then moved to their present location, corner Front and Concord Avenue. The main building is of brick, forty-five by forty feet, three stories, with a two-story engine-room, twenty-five by twenty feet, and a commodious office. The mill contains all the latest improved machinery.

Penn Street Planing-Mill.—In 1875, Henry M. Hinkson erected on Fourth and Penn Streets a two-story brick building, one hundred by forty feet, as a planing-mill and sash- and blind-factory, and rented it to Miller Cox, who began business Sept. 1, 1876, continuing it until May, 1881, when Mr. Hinkson established the present business at this mill. Eleven hands are employed, and one hundred thousand feet of lumber is used annually in the manufacture of sash, blinds, doors, and other building material.

Miller Cox's Sash-Mill.—The business was established by Miller Cox, Sept. 1, 1876, at the Penn Street Planing-Mill, and in April, 1881, he removed to the new mill at Seventh and Penn Streets. Fifteen men are employed, and one hundred and fifty thousand feet of lumber is used annually in the construction of sash, doors, blinds, and other building material.

Hamilton's Box Factory.—A brick building, thirty by sixty, at the corner of Front and Franklin Streets was fitted with machinery for the manufacture of boxes, and supplied with power from the Lilley Manufacturing Company adjoining. About fifty thousand feet of lumber is used per month. The factory is occupied by John Hamilton.

Price's Brick-Yard.—In 1854, John C. and William G. Price established a brick-yard on the site of the Yeadon Mills at the corner of Tenth and Upland Streets. About 1864, seven acres of land at Fifth and Parker Streets were purchased of William and Joshua P. Eyre. In 1879, while the firm were having clay dug on the lot at the northeast corner of Concord Avenue and Sixth Street, they uncovered the bottom of an old kiln, respecting which the oldest resident could give no information. The idea which prevails among many of our people that bricks in old dwellings in this city were of English make is entirely erroneous, for not two years after Penn's first coming, in a lease made by Robert Wade, of the Essex House, to Robert Goforth, dated March 12, 1684, part of the property leased is described as abutting on an old brick kiln, near Chester Creek. A careful examination of the locality shows that the old kiln unearthed was the one mentioned in the lease, and without doubt the Hoskin-Graham house, Logan house, and others here, were built of brick from this yard. At the Price yard, at the present time, are manufactured thirty thousand machine-made bricks per day. Three kilns are in use, and twenty men are employed.

The Delaware County Insurance Company.—In the winter of 1834–35, four gentlemen were accustomed to meet in a small frame store kept by Jonathan P. Newlin, on the west side of Ridley Creek, north of the Queen's highway, on the lands owned by Spencer McIlvain. William Martin, Spencer McIlvain, John L. Crosby, and Jonathan P. Newlin were the four men who discussed at this meeting the need of a local insurance company, and finally they by the act of April 10, 1858, with others, were named commissioners to receive subscriptions for a company, which by the charter thus granted was termed "The Delaware County Insurance Company." Subscription-books were opened at the public-house of Isaac Hall in Nether Providence, and so eager were the substantial citizens of the county to invest in the enterprise that on the day the subscriptions were received the crowd was so large that many persons "absolutely fought their way into the commissioner's rooms in their anxiety to obtain the stock."[1]

On July 27, 1835, the first board of directors, consisting of John P. Crozer, Joshua P. Eyre, John L. Crosby, Archibald T. Dick, Samuel M. Leiper, Charles Kelly, David Trainer, George Serrill, and John Bancroft, met and elected George Serrill president and William Martin secretary. In the fall of this year the company began business, its office being in the double house at the northeast corner of Market Square, Chester, where it continued until 1837, when it was removed to the present "Stacey Mansion," on Market Street, south of Fourth. Here it continued until 1843, when it was determined to enlarge the business of the company and to remove its office to Philadelphia. To that end the act of Assembly, March 17, 1843, was procured, changing the title of the corporation to "The Delaware Mutual Safety Insurance Company," under which name, in Philadelphia, it became one of the most successful insurance institutions in the United States. The list of the presiding officers of the company indicates that residents of the county of Delaware have always held a prominent place in its management. George Serrill, the first president, was elected July 27, 1835; William Eyre, Jr., Sept. 5, 1842; William Martin, Jan. 3, 1844; Thomas C. Hand, Oct. 30, 1862. The latter is the only one in the list who was not from Delaware County. In the present board of directors, Hon. Edward Darlington, who was elected Sept. 5, 1842, still retains that office, and Spencer McIlvain, the only one of the four gentlemen who organized the movement in the country store in Ridley a half-century ago, is now living; has been a director since Jan. 5, 1846.

The grandfather of Spencer McIlvain, who was of Scotch descent, resided in Ridley township, where he was an extensive and successful farmer. He

[1] Martin's "History of Chester," p. 359.

Eng'd by A H Ritchie.

Spencer McIlvain

married Lydia Bernard, of Chester County, and had children,—John, Jeremiah, Richard, Hugh, James, Lydia, Judith, and Margaret. Jeremiah, the father of the subject of this biographical sketch, was born in Ridley township, on the 28th of June, [illegible], and married Elizabeth Spencer, of Bucks County, whose birth occurred Sept. 30, 1770. Their children were Lydia (Mrs. Edward H. Bonsall), Elizabeth (Mrs. Joseph Hewes), Spencer, John S., Jeremiah, Ann (Mrs. Lewis Miller), Samuel, and several who died in childhood. Spencer, of this number, was born March 27, [illegible], on the homestead in Ridley township. After such advantages of education as the vicinity afforded, he became a pupil of a school at Burlington, N. J., and on his return engaged with his father in various business enterprises. The saw-mill, the farm, and the tannery each received a share of his attention, though the former interest absorbed much of his time. In 1828, the year succeeding the death of his father, Mr. McIlvain married Miss Sarah Crosby, daughter of John and Sarah Crosby, of Ridley township. Their children are Henry, who married Miss Sallie U. Hanna, of Philadelphia, and has two sons,—Edwin and Henry,—and Ann S. (Mrs. Edward T. Diehl), of Philadelphia, whose children are Sallie M. D., Ella F., and Mary. Mr. McIlvain has spent much of his active life cultivating his farm, fattening cattle for the Philadelphia market, and working his stone-quarries. On the sale of his landed property, in 1872, he removed to his present residence in Chester, which has since been his home. Here he has been identified with various business interests, as director of the Delaware County National Bank and the Delaware Mutual Insurance Company, and in the erection of various mills and dwellings, giving an impetus to the growth of the city. Mr. McIlvain was in early life a Whig, and on the organization of the Republican party joined its ranks. He has not sought office at its hands, though for a term was commissioner of the county. He was educated in the religious faith of the Society of Friends.

The Chester Mutual Insurance Company was incorporated by the court of Delaware County, Feb. 28, 1874. The organization of an insurance company in Chester had been considered prior to this date, and as early as February, 1869, the charter for a stock company had been obtained, but became void by reason of non-user before Jan. 1, 1874. After that date the projectors of the stock company, together with other persons desiring the organization of an underwriting association on the mutual plan, formed the Chester Mutual Insurance Company, the original subscribers being John M. Broomall, William Booth, John Larkin, Jr., William Ward, John O. Deshong, George Broomall, David Trainer & Sons, Samuel Montgomery, Mortimer H. Bickley, George Baker, William B. Broomall, Benjamin F. Baker, Perciphor Baker, Lewis & Parker, Lewis M. Larkin, B. Gartside & Sons, David S. Bunting, James Irving, Jonathan and Charles D. Pennell, George M. Booth, Henry L. Donaldson, George M. Pardoe, Abraham Blakeley, and Morton & Black. The first meeting of the subscribers was held March 9, 1874, when a board of directors was elected, consisting of John Larkin, Jr., George Broomall, William Ward, J. Newlin Trainer, Mortimer H. Bickley, William Booth, Perciphor Baker, William B. Broomall, James Irving, George M. Pardoe, Benjamin Gartside, and William D. H. Serrill. John Larkin, Jr., was elected president, Mortimer H. Bickley vice-president, and George M. Booth secretary and treasurer. The board of directors from that date to the present has been changed as follows: In 1877, John Sharpless was substituted in place of William Booth, who declined re-election; in 1878, Frederick J. Hinkson in place of William Ward, who desired to retire from the board, and in the same year Jonathan Pennell succeeded to the place formerly held by George M. Pardoe; 1880, Benjamin F. Baker was chosen to the seat made vacant by the death of Judge Hinkson; 1882, Samuel A. Dyer was elected in the room of Perciphor Baker, deceased; in 1883, John Larkin, Jr., declined re-election, and Henry L. Donaldson was chosen in his stead, and the same year, Amos Gartside was elected in place of Benjamin Gartside, resigned. On Jan. 1, 1884, John Larkin, Jr., declined to continue to act as president, a position he had held since the organization of the company, and Jonathan Pennell was elected to that office. At the first regular meeting of the directors, in 1874, it was decided that the company should effect insurance to the amount of one hundred and forty-six thousand dollars, and on April 1, 1874, the first policy was issued. A singular circumstance was that the first policy issued by the Chester Mutual Insurance Company was to John M. Broomall, Jr., on stock in the building at the northwest corner of Market Square, Chester, and the building was insured by his father, George Broomall, in the Delaware County Mutual Insurance Company, the policy being the first issued by the latter corporation in 1835. The business of the Chester Mutual has been almost exclusively confined to Delaware County, the risks judiciously distributed, and the amounts limited, desiring to transact a safe rather than a large business. This policy gave the company credit in the beginning, and not only enabled it to accumulate a surplus fund sufficient to meet any ordinary demand, but placed the Chester Mutual in good standing with the best similar insurance companies in the State. When the company was organized it occupied a part of the law-office of Ward & Broomall, but in October, 1875, it leased the back part of the building at the southeast corner of Market Square, where it continued until June, 1881, when it was removed to more spacious rooms in the front of the same building.

Chester Gas Company.—The project of lighting the city with gas had been agitated early in the year 1855, but for some reason the scheme failed to enlist

Spencer M'Ilvain

married Lydia Bernard, of Chester County, and had children,—John, Jeremiah, Richard, Hugh, James, Lydia, Judith, and Margaret. Jeremiah, the father of the subject of this biographical sketch, was born in Ridley township, on the 29th of June, 1767, and married Elizabeth Spencer, of Bucks County, whose birth occurred Sept. 30, 1770. Their children were Lydia (Mrs. Edward H. Bonsell), Elizabeth (Mrs. Jacob Hewes), Spencer, John S., Jeremiah, Ann (Mrs. Levis Miller), Samuel, and several who died in childhood. Spencer, of this number, was born March 27, 1803, on the homestead in Ridley township. After such advantages of education as the vicinity afforded, he became a pupil of a school at Burlington, N. J., and on his return engaged with his father in various business enterprises. The saw-mill, the farm, and the tannery each received a share of his attention, though the former interest absorbed much of his time. In 1828, the year succeeding the death of his father, Mr. McIlvain married Miss Sarah Crosby, daughter of John and Sarah Crosby, of Ridley township. Their children are Henry, who married Miss Sally C. Pierson, of Philadelphia, and has two sons,—Edwin and Henry,—and Ann E. (Mrs. Edward C. Diehl), of Philadelphia, whose children are Sallie M. D., Ella F., and Mary. Mr. McIlvain has spent much of his active life cultivating his farm, fattening cattle for the Philadelphia market, and working his stone-quarries. On the sale of his landed property, in 1872, he removed to his present residence in Chester, which has since been his home. Here he has been identified with various business interests, as director of the Delaware County National Bank, and the Delaware Mutual Insurance Company, and in the erection of various mills and dwellings, giving an impetus to the growth of the city. Mr. McIlvain was in early life a Whig, and on the organization of the Republican party joined its ranks. He has not sought office at its hands, though for a term was commissioner of the county. He was educated in the religious faith of the society of Friends.

The Chester Mutual Insurance Company was incorporated by the court of Delaware County, Feb. 26, 1874. The organization of an insurance company in Chester had been considered prior to this date, and as early as February, 1869, the charter for a stock company had been obtained, but became void by reason of non-user before Jan. 1, 1874. After that date the projectors of the stock company, together with other persons desiring the organization of an underwriting association on the mutual plan, formed the Chester Mutual Insurance Company, the original subscribers being John M. Broomall, William Booth, John Larkin, Jr., William Ward, John O. Deshong, George Broomall, David Trainer & Sons, Samuel Montgomery, Mortimer H. Bickley, George Baker, William B. Broomall, Benjamin F. Baker, Perciphor Baker, Lewis & Parker, Lewis M. Larkin, B. Gartside & Sons, David S. Bunting, James Irving, Jonathan and Charles D. Pennell, George M. Booth, Henry L. Donaldson, George M. Pardoe, Abraham Blakeley, and Morton & Black. The first meeting of the subscribers was held March 5, 1874, when a board of directors was elected, consisting of John Larkin, Jr., George Broomall, William Ward, J. Newlin Trainer, Mortimer H. Bickley, William Booth, Perciphor Baker, William B. Broomall, James Irving, George M. Pardoe, Benjamin Gartside, and William D. H. Serrill. John Larkin, Jr., was elected president, Mortimer H. Bickley, vice-president, and George M. Booth secretary and treasurer. The board of directors from that date to the present has been changed as follows: In 1877, John Sharpless was substituted in room of William Booth, who declined re-election; in 1878, Frederick J. Hinkson in place of William Ward, who desired to retire from the board, and in the same year Jonathan Pennell succeeded to the place formerly held by George M. Pardoe; 1880, Benjamin F. Baker was chosen to the seat made vacant by the death of Judge Hinkson; 1881, Samuel A. Dyer was elected in the room of Perciphor Baker, deceased; in 1884, John Larkin, Jr., declined re-election, and Henry L. Donaldson was chosen in his stead, and the same year, Amos Gartside was elected in place of Benjamin Gartside, resigned. On Jan. 1, 1884, John Larkin, Jr., declined to continue to act as president, a position he had held since the organization of the company, and Jonathan Pennell was elected to that office. At the first regular meeting of the directors, in 1874, it was decided that the company should effect insurance to the amount of one hundred and forty-six thousand dollars, and on April 1, 1874, the first policy was issued. A singular circumstance was that the first policy issued by the Chester Mutual Insurance Company was to John M. Broomall, Jr., on stock in the building at the northwest corner of Market Square, Chester, and the building was insured by his father, George Broomall, in the Delaware County Mutual Insurance Company, the policy being the first issued by the latter corporation in 1835. The business of the Chester Mutual has been almost exclusively confined to Delaware County, the risks judiciously distributed, and the amounts limited, desiring to transact a safe rather than a large business. This policy gave the company credit in the beginning, and not only enabled it to accumulate a surplus fund sufficient to meet any ordinary demand but placed the Chester Mutual in good standing with the best similar insurance companies in the State. When the company was organized it occupied a part of the law-office of Ward & Broomall, but in October, 1875, it leased the back part of the building at the southeast corner of Market Square, where it continued until June, 1881, when it was removed to more spacious rooms in the front of the same building.

Chester Gas Company.—The project of lighting the city with gas had been agitated early in the year 1855, but for some reason the scheme failed to enlist the approval of capitalists at its inception The constant references in the newspapers to the advantages which must follow the use of a better means than oil-lamps for furnishing light to the large manufacturing establishments which were then located in the borough, directed public opinion so favorably to the scheme that on April 4, 1856, the Chester Gas Company was incorporated, and William Bucknell, of Philadelphia, assumed the responsibility of erecting the works on the east side of Welsh Street, and laying the pipes in the streets So rapidly was the enterprise carried forward that on Sept 19, 1856, for the first time gas was used in the town of Chester This statement, however, applied to that furnished by a company for general consumption, for several years before that date John M Broomall had used private gas-works to light his dwelling on Penn and Second Streets The officers of the company from the date of incorporation have been as follows

Presidents—1856, John M Broomall, 1858, John Larkin, Jr , 1859, Frederick Fairlamb, 1870, Jonathan R Johnson

Secretaries—1856, Frederick Fairlamb, until 1859, when the offices of secretary and treasurer were consolidated, one person being elected to discharge their duties

Treasurers—1856, William Eyre, Jr , 1857, John Larkin, Jr , 1858-59, John H Baker, 1865, John O Deshong, Jr, who resigned on June 5, 1882, and J Howard Roop was elected treasurer and secretary

Within recent years the works have been largely increased by the erection of additional gasometers, and many miles of service-pipe have been laid The mills, many dwellings, and stores in Upland are supplied with gas from these works

Farmers' Market Company.—About the middle of the last century—for in 1745 an ancient deed mentions "the proposed market-place"—the old market-house in the square at the intersection of Market and Third Streets was built It stood on a brick platform about fifty feet in length, extending along Market Street, and thirty in breadth, surrounded by curb-stones The roof was supported by seven brick pillars on each side, and between the third and fourth columns, on the east and west side, were small arches, while the ceiling was arched, plastered, and covered with a shingle roof About 1830 a frame structure was erected over the market-house, which was used as a town hall, and was reached by a wooden stairway on the east side of the building In the spring of 1857 the old building was taken down, and in May of the same year Joshua P and William Eyre, Jr, built a market-house back of National Hall, on Edgmont Avenue As the city grew the demand for a commodious market-place became so pressing that in the spring of 1868 an association was formed under the title of "Farmers' Market Company of Chester" A lot extending from Fourth to Fifth Street, in the rear of the old prison and court-house, was purchased from John Cochran, stock to the amount of eighteen thousand dollars subscribed for, and the present market building erected, which was opened for the sale of provisions on Dec 11, 1868 The cost of the lot and building amounted to twenty-six thousand dollars The first officers of the company were John G Dyer, president, Benjamin F Baker, secretary, and Frederick J. Hinkson, Sr, treasurer The present officers are as follows President, Lewis Palmer, Secretary and Treasurer, Edmund Jones, Superintendent, Edward Jones, Directors, Lewis Palmer, George Trimble, H L Paschall, William Sharpless, Samuel H Wells

The Water-Works.—Very early in the history of the awakening of Chester from its lethargy of a century and a half the need of an abundant water-supply in the town became apparent James Campbell, in his efforts to develop the ancient borough into a manufacturing centre, encountered the greatest difficulties in securing sufficient water to supply the boilers of his mills with steam, and in the effort to avoid the cost and labor of carting water from Chester Creek he spent thousands of dollars in sinking wells in the yards of the Pioneer factory and the Henry Clay Mills, on Broad and Mechanic Streets To overcome the difficulty an effort was made, in 1853, to establish a private water company in Chester, but the project failed, several persons only would subscribe for the stock, and the amount pledged reached but a few thousand dollars The necessity for the introduction of water became constantly more pressing as the town improved,—the safety of property, the demands of large business enterprises, the public craving for a better water than generally found in the wells in Chester (which was distasteful to many persons by reason of its peculiar flavor), the delayed wash-days (when the cisterns and rain-barrels were empty), all combined to awaken public demand for the erection of water-works Particularly was this the case in the South Ward, where many of the mills were erected at points removed from the creek In April, 1866, an act of Assembly was obtained empowering the city of Chester to build water-works, should a majority of the property-holders vote in favor of ratifying the provisions of the act An election was held which resulted in the Middle and North Wards refusing to ratify the act, while the South Ward adopted it But the want still existed; and as the city extended, and became more compactly built, the danger from fire increased and rendered it imperative that some action should be taken at once

The act of March 2, 1867, authorizing the councilmen of the South Ward of the city of Chester, their successors, etc, to erect water-works, was accepted April 15th of that year, and the board of directors formed, consisting of Amos Gartside, William Ward, William A. Todd, William B Reaney, and William G Price Amos Gartside was elected president, William Ward, treasurer, William A. Todd, secretary

It was decided to use the water of the river Delaware as the surest source from which to draw the supplies for the city. Isaac S. Cassin, who had been chief engineer of Philadelphia, was selected to prepare plans and specifications and to supervise the construction of the works. Joseph R. T. Coates and Robert Gartside received the contract for the building of the works, and water was pumped into the basin of the reservoir for the first time on the evening of July 1, 1868. The contract was completed in the month of October following, and the works, after a professional inspection by Chief Engineer Graeff, accepted by the board.

The original capacity of the pumps was eight hundred thousand gallons per day. In 1878 additional compound pumping-machinery was placed in the works, at the foot of Franklin Street, with a capacity of two million five hundred thousand gallons every twenty-four hours. In the fall of 1882 a thirty-inch flexible-joint pipe was extended into the channel of the Delaware River six hundred feet from shore and three hundred and ten feet from end of pier. Previous to that time the water was taken from near the shore, and was frequently muddy, an objection which is now removed. There are sixty-five fire-hydrants in the city, and water is supplied to twelve hundred consumers. Robert Anderson is superintendent of the works.

The Chester Street Railway Company.—In 1870 the recognized need of a public means of passenger transportation from one section of the city to the other was attempted to be filled by the establishment of an omnibus line, the route extending from the Pennsylvania Military Academy, in North Ward, to Third Street and Highland Avenue, in the borough of South Chester. The project failed after a few months' trial, and those who purchased stock in the enterprise derived considerable experience from the investment, even if the assets of the company were insufficient to discharge its outstanding obligations. In the spring of 1882 the question of street-railways began to be discussed among a number of the capitalists of Chester and South Chester, the only public means of communication between the remote limits of these places, several miles apart, being a line of rickety, uncomfortable stages. Upland, a mile and a half beyond the city line to the northwest, was then considered impracticable of access by reason of the steep hills on the road. Several attempts to establish a street railway in Chester had, prior to this time, been made by capitalists in Philadelphia and elsewhere, but all of them had failed before work of laying the road had commenced.

The capital required to build and equip the road was subscribed almost exclusively by citizens of Chester and South Chester, and the stock was distributed among a large number of holders. On June 27, 1882, the first meeting of the subscribers was held at the office of George B. Lindsay, Esq., in Chester, when the name "The Chester Street Railway Company" was adopted, and officers elected. Richard Peters, Jr., was chosen president; Hugh Shaw, vice-president; William Appleby, treasurer; George B. Lindsay, secretary and solicitor. The board of directors was as follows: Richard Peters, Jr., Hugh Shaw, William Appleby, George B. Lindsay, J. Frank Black, Samuel H. Dyer, F. Washington Thomas, William S. Blakeley, Thomas J. Houston, J. Newlin Trainer, and Robert Wetherill. The capital stock of the company was fixed at fifty thousand dollars, to be divided into one thousand shares of the par value of fifty dollars each, which sum was required to be paid in full on every share taken. A charter was obtained from the commonwealth and ordinances adopted by the city of Chester and borough of South Chester, that of the city being approved by the mayor July 26, 1882. On Oct. 17, 1882, the building of the road was begun, and completed the middle of January following. The route of the road extends from Clayton Street, the southern limits of South Chester, along Third Street to Market Square, in the city of Chester; thence up Market Street to Edgmont Avenue to Thirteenth Street, where the stables, car-house, and office are located, the length of the road being about three miles. On Feb. 1, 1883, the company began regularly to operate the road, with forty horses and five cars. The schedule of time was every half-hour from an early hour in the morning to a late hour at night, and the fare established at five cents. The amount of travel from the first day exceeded all expectations, and a few weeks later additional cars and horses were put on the road, and the time of the starting of the cars changed to every fifteen minutes. E. Mitchell Cornell, formerly secretary and treasurer of the Second and Third Streets Railway of Philadelphia, was appointed superintendent, and elected secretary of the company. In compliance with a general desire, the company determined to extend the road to Upland, on condition that the borough authorities should reduce the grades on the hills. This was done, and on July 14, 1883, the road was completed to that borough, thus increasing the length of the road to four miles. Cars began running on that date from Upland to Market Square every half hour. The working stock has been increased to sixty-seven horses and mules and twelve cars. Each car, which is in charge of the driver, is drawn by two horses. No conductors are employed, the fares being deposited by the passengers in Slawson patent boxes. The traffic on the road averages two thousand passengers per day. The enterprise is in a prosperous condition, has no debt, and has paid from the beginning a small semi-annual dividend.

The Union League.—On March 23, 1863, a meeting of prominent citizens of the borough and immediate neighborhood of Chester assembled in National Hall for the purpose of forming a Union League, and organized by electing Henry B. Edwards president, John Larkin, Jr, William H Flavill, John H Baker, James Cochran, John Gartside, Samuel Eccles, Jr, James Irving, Samuel A Crozer, David Trainer, and Thomas H Maddock, vice-presidents, Frederick J Hinkson, treasurer, Walter J Arnold and William Hinkson, recording secretaries, William Ward, corresponding secretary, the Executive Committee, Abraham R Perkins, Amos Gartside, William B Reaney, Joseph Entwisle, Alexander M Wright, William Sharpless, Thomas Appleby, Stephen Cloud, Jr, Joseph H Hinkson, George Wilson, Thomas Moore, John E Shaw, William A Menshall, Thomas H Mirkil, Frederick Fairlamb, Perciphor Baker, Abraham Blakeley, William Frick, Dr F Ridgley Graham, Frank Field, Eliakim T Robb, Charles J Kenworthy, Henry L Donaldson, Thomas Clough, James Kirkman, John J Thurlow, Jacob Perry, Abraham T Patterson The membership consisted of persons entertaining all shades of political opinions, the constitution of the organization requiring that every person who should become a member of the League should sign the roll, which sets forth

"We the undersigned citizens of the United States, hereby pledge our earnest endeavors to put down the existing rebellion against the rights and liberties of the people, and to spare no efforts to suppress all sentiments and acts calculated to oppose or bring our government into disrepute"

The League leased the large double frame house at the southwest corner of Fourth and Welsh Streets, which was handsomely furnished, and rooms set apart for entertainment of guests, as well as apartments for chess and other amusements Here the League continued until 1865, when it removed to National Hall On June 15, 1865, the members of the organization decided to dissolve the League At that date the following persons were its officers President, Henry B Edward, Vice-presidents, William Frick, Samuel Archbold, Treasurer, Thomas Appleby, Secretary, L T Rutter, Executive Committee, Joshua P Eyre, William H Morton, Thomas H Mirkil, George Wilson, Y S Walter

Chester Republican League—In the beginning of the political campaign which resulted in the election of President Garfield in November, 1880, an organization called the "Veteran Republican Club" was formed by some of the older citizens of the party, for the purpose of frequent consultations upon the political interests of the city, the dissemination of campaign documents, procuring speakers, holding public meetings, and perfecting the details of securing a full vote at the election The officers of the club were George B Lindsay, president, James M Peoples, secretary, Stephen C Hall, treasurer The club held its meetings in Edgmont Hall, and did valuable service for the Republican ticket The efficiency of the club was recognized after the election was over by an increased membership and a general desire that it should be re-established in a permanent form, with literary and social, as well as political purposes Accordingly a charter was obtained, and the club was erected into a corporation under the name of "Chester Republican League" The officers were G P Denis, president, Amos Gartside and J P Crozer, vice-presidents, Ward R Bliss, secretary, George B Lindsay, treasurer, and a board of directors consisting of Ward R Bliss, George B Lindsay, W. B. Broomall, John J Ledward, Thomas H Mirkil, Jonathan Pennell, F W Thomas, John Maxson, Jr, and Edward J Worrell. Rooms in the Cochrane building, on Market Street below the railroad, were temporarily occupied Steps were at once taken to secure a permanent location, and resulted in the purchase, in June, 1881, of the Joshua P Eyre property at Fifth and Edgmont Streets, Chester, by a syndicate composed of members of the club The cost of the property was sixteen thousand dollars The house and grounds were at once improved to suit the needs of the club A portion of the upper stories was devoted to apartments for the use of such members as desired to make their home there, and the remainder of the premises was fitted up for parlors, reading-rooms, chess- and other game-rooms A large apartment in the basement was fitted and furnished as a billiard-room No liquors whatever are furnished on the premises The care of the house and grounds, subject to a house committee, was given to a janitor and his wife, who reside in the building The club has been remarkably successful Its membership numbers about two hundred, and includes a large number of the prominent Republican politicians and business men of the city and county Its initiation fee is ten dollars, and its annual assessment is the same The club gives an annual reception at Christmas, which is participated in by the members and their friends

Young Men's Christian Association.—The first Young Men's Association formed in Chester was organized in 1860, with Samuel A Crozer as president Meetings were held in Penn building on Market Square The breaking out of the civil war the next year distracted the attention of the young men, and the association lingered until 1863, when it suspended No attempt was made to revive it until 1870, when a second organization took place, having for its president George K Crozer. This association also met for a time in Penn building, and afterwards removed to the City Hall, where in 1874 it again suspended Mr George Derbyshire and Charles C Larkin had acted as president of the association

In November of 1875, an association was again formed, mainly through the exertions of Dr W. S. Ridgely, who became its first president The officers were chosen from the different church organizations of the city. Rooms were fitted up in the Ward building near the railroad depot The aim and end of the association was to bring young men under religious influence

After continuing for some time in the Ward building, arrangements were made to remove to a room in Holly Tree Hall, which was done, and the association remained till 1880, when rooms were obtained over the post-office, and a reading-room opened For some reason this was not successful, and the association returned to Holly Tree Hall, where they remained till March, 1884 The association was not accomplishing much good work by the methods employed, and it was determined to reorganize and adopt the plans and methods now used by other associations In accordance with this decision the association was suspended, Nov 14 1883, and a new board of managers elected, who held their first meeting on the 5th of December Ward Bliss was chosen president, T W Stone, vice-president, B Frank Beatty, secretary, B F Hall, treasurer At the meeting in November, the Rev S A Taggert, secretary of the State Association, explained new methods of working now in use At that meeting a committee was appointed to select a room suitable for the association This committee reported, Jan 4, 1884, that rooms could be had in Samuel Black's building on Market Street On the 15th of January they were authorized to secure the rooms and fit them for use The room on the first floor in front is an office, where are directories, time-tables, and the office of the general secretary In the rear is a reading-room, which is supplied with the magazines, papers, secular and religious The second story is fitted as a conversation-room, connected by folding doors, with a well-furnished parlor These rooms can be thrown into one, and are used for public talks, lectures, and religious meetings The building was dedicated March 2, 1884, with appropriate services Addresses were delivered by the Rev Thomas McCauley, Rev Henry Brown, Rev Dr P H Mowry, and Dr John F Van Leer

The association is controlled by a board of managers composed of fifteen persons, who form the executive, finance, and lecture committees

The other work of the association is delegated to seven committees, chosen from the members, as follows Membership, Reception, Christian Work, Employment and Boarding-house, Work for Boys, Visiting, and Invitation.

The membership at the last annual report was sixty-seven

The present officers are Ward R Bliss, president, T W Stone, vice-president, B Frank Beatty, secretary, Theodore Hampson, general secretary; B F Hall, treasurer.

The presidents who served the association from its organization, in 1875, to November, 1883, were Dr W S. Ridgely, Thomas W Stone, Charles C Larkin, Col Theodore Hyatt, Charles C Larkin, and Dr John F. Van Leer.

Building Associations —Chester is eminently a city which has been benefited largely by the establishment of loan associations, by which means men of limited incomes were enabled to build or purchase homes It is not extravagant to say that one-fourth of the present improvements in Chester have been made by the opportunity offered to industrious toiling mechanics by these associations In 1850 the Chester Building Association, the first incorporated in the borough, was formed, John M Broomall being the president and Joseph Taylor the secretary It continued ten years and ten months, during which time it loaned sixty-two thousand dollars to its members In 1852 the Penn Building Association was formed, William Hinkson being the secretary In eleven years it ran its course, during which time it had loaned many thousands of dollars to its stockholders In 1853 the South Ward Association was organized, and in August, 1854, the Washington Building Association was founded, and both of these organizations settled their affairs and were disbanded The Second Chester was instituted Nov 24, 1860, and the William Penn on April 1, 1865 In November of the same year the North Ward Building Association was founded, H L Donaldson secretary On March 9, 1867, the City Association was instituted, and in July, 1869, the Delaware County was founded, and has issued a new series every year thereafter, the first series expired in 1879 The present officers are William Dolton, president, D M Johnson, treasurer, Orlando Harvey, secretary and solicitor The Mechanics Building Association was established in 1873,—President, Benjamin F Baker, Solicitor, John B Hannum, Treasurer, Charles Roberts, Secretary, H L Donaldson In October, 1873, the Chester and Upland Association was founded, with Daniel V Hoffman, president, David Garrett, secretary, Amos Gartside, treasurer, and D M Johnson, solicitor In May, 1874, the Third Chester Building Association was organized, with Benjamin F Baker, president, Jonathan Jennell, treasurer, Edmund Jones, solicitor, and George M Booth, secretary The Excelsior Building and Loan Association was instituted in 1876, of which D M Johnson is president, P M Washabaugh, secretary, Jonathan R Johnson, treasurer, and Orlando Harvey, solicitor On June 12, 1879, the Fidelity Association was established,—Jonathan Pennell, president, H L Donaldson, secretary, Jonathan R Johnson, treasurer, and John B Hannum, solicitor, and in November, 1879, the Iron-Workers Building Association was organized, with David Houston, president, and George B Lindsay solicitor The Home Building and Loan Association was organized in February, 1881, with Jonathan Pennell, president, P Bradley, secretary, J Howard Roop, treasurer, Ward R Bliss, solicitor The Keystone Building Association was organized May, 1882,—President, John Spencer, Secretary, O B Dickinson, Treasurer, Thomas Lees, Solicitor, D M Johnson The People's Building and Loan Association was formed May, 1883,—President, Amos Gartside, Treasurer, D M Johnson, Secretary, H L Donaldson, Solicitor, John B Hannum The Provident Building and Loan Association was organized October, 1883,—President, Joseph F Brewster, Secretary, Garrett Pendleton, Treasurer, Oliver Troth, Solicitor, Patrick Bradley The Industrial Building and Loan Association was established June, 1884,—President, Josiah C Ross, Treasurer, D M Johnson, Secretary, Oliver Troth, Solicitor, Edmund Jones

The Military.—Since the conclusion of the civil war there have been several military organizations in Chester under State regulations, but owing to the defective feature of the law, the companies, until the recent revision of the statutes governing those bodies, were usually short-lived The present effective management of the National Guard of Pennsylvania gives promise of more thoroughness in the militia, and hence it may reasonably be expected that Company B, of the Sixth Regiment, will have a longer existence than any organization which has preceded it.

The first company of soldiers in Chester, after the time mentioned, was the Chester City Safeguards, a colored company of militia, organized in 1870, and commanded in succession by Andrew Johnson, Isaac B Colwell, and Isaac Emory, until the fall of 1872, when it was disbanded

On Sept 12, 1872, Company A, of the Gartside Rifle Battalion, was organized, with Capt Daniel Brown commanding Capt Brown subsequently was appointed major, and George F Springer was elected captain of Company A in his stead Company B, of the same regiment, was organized March 19, 1873, Capt David S Gwynn commanding, but he resigned, and the company elected William A Todd as captain The organization finally disbanded In July, 1875, the Morton Rifles, so called in honor of John Morton, the signer of the Declaration of Independence, was organized, with James Barton, Jr, as captain, and in August, 1875, was mustered into the Eleventh Regiment, National Guard of Pennsylvania Capt Barton was subsequently promoted aid to Gen Dobson, and Charles A Story, Jr, was elected to the captaincy Subsequently Capt Story resigned, and John M. Householder was chosen to succeed him During the riots of July, 1877, the company was ordered to Pittsburgh, where it did good service, but was the next year mustered out The Hartranft Rifles were organized January, 1876, by Capt Perry M Washabaugh, and April 20, 1876, were mustered into service as Company B, Eleventh Regiment, and subsequently, after the appointment of Capt Washabaugh to the staff of the brigadier-general commanding the division, he was succeeded by Robert H Wood, and followed by William H Williams This company was also called into active duty during the Pittsburgh riots, and was finally mustered out of service

Company A, Eleventh Regiment, National Guard of Pennsylvania, was mustered into service March 30, 1881, with B F. Morley, captain, Frank G Sweeney, first lieutenant, and John J Hare, second lieutenant The company soon showed such efficiency in drill that, when the State authorities consolidated the military force of the commonwealth,—although the youngest company in the State,—by general order No 11, July 8, 1881, the title of the company was changed to B, Sixth Regiment, First Brigade, National Guard of Pennsylvania In the summer of the same year a scheme was broached by Lieut-Col Washabaugh towards erecting an armory, and to that end a charter was obtained, stock was taken by several prominent citizens, a lot, sixty feet in front by one hundred and twenty feet in depth, was purchased, and an armory, after a design by P A Welsh, was built. The structure, begun Aug 4, 1881, costing, including land, about fifteen thousand dollars, is too recent to require fuller description here Sufficient it is to say that it is the home of one of the best, if not the best-drilled company in the service of the State, and is an ornament and a credit to our city The building, located on the south side of Fifth Street, east of Crosby Street, was opened on Tuesday, Dec 7, 1881, with a fair which lasted ten days, and yielded several thousand dollars towards the liquidation of the debt of the armory company

The roll of Company B at the present time is as follows

Capt Frank G Sweeney was a military instructor at Pennsylvania Military Academy from September, 1877, to June, 1879 elected 1st lieut Co A, 11th Regt., March 30, 1881 (changed to Co B, 6th Regt., July 8, 1881), elected capt Co B, 6th Regt., Dec 4, 1882

First Lieutenant James A Campbell enl as a private in Co A, 11th Regt, March 30, 1881, app 2d sergt June 6, 1881 (changed to Co B, 6th Regt, July 8, 1881), pro to 1st sergt July 29 1881, elected 1st lieut Jan 8, 1883

Second Lieutenant George C de Lannoy enl as a private in Co A, 11th Regt., March 30, 1881, app 4th sergt June 6, 1881 (changed to Co B, 6th Regt., July 8, 1881), pro to 3d sergt July 29, 1881, pro to 2d sergt Oct 19, 1882, pro to 1st sergt Nov 17, 1882, elected 2d lieut Feb 5, 1883

Sergeants, T Edward Clyde, J Frank Fairlamb, Horace F Larkin, Harwell A Cloud, J Engle Baker

Corporals, William J Morgan, Charles B Rose, J Alexander Cochrane, Milton M Allen, Robinson McCurdy, George C Worrell, Samuel A Price, Frank L Brown

Privates, James H Birtwell, Theodore Blakeley, Charles B Cathing, Radcliffe Chadwick, William G Clyde, William R Carson, William H Derbyshire, Dean J Deakyne, Edward Dougherty, Jackson B Fields, Arthur Grant, U S Grant, N Clarence Grove, Emil O Haas, Alfred Hinkson, Lewis E Hinkson, John A Ladomus, Edward Miles, Frank B Eddy, George C Johnson, R Bruce Mowry, Alvin G Mills, Theodore Mooney, Charlton McCurdy, Edwin P McIlvain, Harry S McIlvain, Edward A Price, Arthur G Rose, Matthew F Ross, R Wilson Roberts, D Elmer Reasin, William S Ranier, Hilyard B Sweeney, Charles R Sweeney, Garrett G Slawter, George B Smedley, William N Sparks, Horace F Temple, David M Unangst, J M B Ward, S Ulrich Ward, Robert P Wilson

The Fire Department—As early in our history as October, 1696, an act was passed by the Colonial Assembly designed "for preventing of accidents that may happen by fire in the towns of Philadelphia and New Castle," and as the provisions of this law were made in 1700 operative in Chester also, it is interesting to learn the safeguards which by legal enactments our ancestors attempted to establish in the infant settlements to avoid destructive fires The act prescribed that ten days after the publication of the law any person "who should set on fire their chimneys to cleanse them, or shall suffer them to be foul, that they shall take fire so as to flame out at the top," on conviction, should be fined *forty shillings* By the same enactment, within twenty days after its promulgation, "every owner of every dwelling-house within the towns aforesaid, shall provide and keep in or by his or her house a swab twelve or fourteen foot long, and a Bucket or pail, to be always ready agt such accidents of fire." The act of Aug 26, 1721, repealed that part of the old law which required swabs and buckets to be kept in every house under a penalty, but the advantage of having such articles was so apparent that it became the rule to have leather fire-buckets in every house in the village, which were suspended from the ceilings in the hallway, so that in the event of an alarm they were easily obtained by opening the front door At a fire it was the recognized duty of every able-bodied man to fall into the line, which extended from the burning building to the most available point where water could be had, and along this line full buckets would be passed to those persons who had taken post near the flames, to throw the water upon them, and the empty buckets would be returned the same way to be refilled Persons who refused to fall into line and pass buckets were usually doused with water as a punishment by their indignant neighbors After the fire had been subdued, or it had ceased because it had totally destroyed the building, it was rare sport for the boys to gather the leather fire-buckets and return them to their several owners, for every man's name was painted on his bucket

I do not know when the first fire company was established in Chester, but seven months ago I found among a quantity of old paper in a waste store a torn leaf from a book which was the record of a fire company. From the scrap which has fallen into my possession, it seems evident that the organization was similar in character to that of Darby borough On July 8, 1808, is given a list of members as follows William Graham, John Caldwell, James Withy, John Odenheimer, James Birchall, William Anderson, Jonathan Morris, Ephraim Pearson, Isaac Eyre, Jonathan Pennell, Joseph Engle, Daniel Broomall, William Siddons, Jonas Eyre, Samuel Anderson, Joseph Piper, and Jonas Sharpless From the report of the various committees appointed, we learn that in that time the buckets and ladders are up and in good order, but that "the engine and hose want oiling" Whitehead, in his historical introduction to the "Directory of Chester for 1850–60," says, "A beer-house, called the Globe, was once kept upon James Street, below Market, by a man named Scott, but abandoned as a public-house for nearly fifty years It was burned down in 1830, and the site is now occupied by the Upland buildings owned by Samuel A Price" This building was brick, with a curb-roof It had been a tavern in 1796, kept by William Harrison, and was known as "The Indian Queen" Harrison's widow, Elizabeth, followed her husband in the business until 1805, when Samuel Price had the house, when it was known as "The Ship" After that date it ceased to be an inn, but became an eating-house, the first ever established in Chester Martin[1] says Scott sold catables and table-beer, and that the fire occurred in 1835 or 1836, not in 1830, as stated by Whitehead

The doggerel lines, which bring back the names of residents of Chester about 1790, are said to have been written shortly after a fire which consumed an old shed on the property of John O Deshong, in North Ward The lines, so far as they remain to this day, are as follows

"Fire! Fire! cried Anthony Guyer,
Where? where? said Squire Eyre,
It's up street, said Parson Heath
It's down town, said Dr Brown
It's here! it's here! cried Charlie Lear
It's in Anderson's Hall, said Capt Paul
You are all wrong! cried Peter Deshong
It's up in the shed, said Morris' Deb[2]
You lie! you lie! cried Kerlin's Sie[2]
I'll go to it, said Mrs Hewitt
You sha'n't! you sha'n't! said John Denant
It's time you're startin'! said Dr Martin
You'd better be quick, said Thomas Dick
I'll be there in an hour, said Richard Flower
Here's my bucket, said Jonathan Duckett
Put on the water, said Martin Carter
They're all too lazy, said Mrs Daisy
The roof is rotten, said Johnny Shotten
Keep off my toes, said Odenheimer's Rose[2]
I'll make them whiz, said Odenheimer's Liz"[2]

The fire-engine was known as the "Liberty," and was housed in a one-story frame building, still standing, between the City Hall and the First National Bank, now used as a coal-house and a place of deposit for all the trash which accumulates in the mayor's and other offices in the hall Samuel Edwards was president of the company in 1832 Some time after 1844 a new hand-engine was purchased, the "Friendship," which was more generally known as the "Pickle Tub," from the fact that in 1850, at the fire at Market Square, some of the active firemen of that day emptied the contents of a tub, in which a lady had been greening pickles, into the engine, and it began squirting pickles at the fire, until an unusually large one got fastened in the nozzle, and effectually stopped the flow After the introduction of water into the city, the old fire-engine became useless, and steps were taken to organize an efficient fire department

The Franklin Fire Company was instituted Nov. 30, 1867, and incorporated Feb 22, 1869 During that year the lot on Concord Avenue was bought, and a two-story brick hose-house, fifty by twenty-two feet, was erected For over ten years this house served the purpose for which it had been built, although, after

[1] History of Chester, p 277

[2] Slaves of the families whose names are given

the company had purchased, in 1874, the steam fire-engine "Franklin," at a cost of four thousand dollars, the organization was much cramped for room. At first the handsome Silsby steamer was drawn by hand, but the company purchased a pair of horses, and it became necessary to enlarge the building. This was done in 1882; the old structure was removed, and a new building, three stories in height, erected, on which was located a look-out station, and a large bell suspended therein. The cost of this improvement was three thousand dollars. In October, 1882, the building was dedicated. On the roll of the Franklin Fire Company at this date (July, 1884) are seventy-eight active members. Samuel Phillips is president; Benjamin D. Ayers, Jr., secretary; and Thomas Brooks, chief engineer.

The Hanley Hose Company derives its name from John Hanley, "Old Blind Jack," as he was called, who, though sightless, was earnest and active in effecting the organization of the company. The Hanley Hose Company, No. 1, of Chester, was instituted Jan. 12, 1869, and was incorporated by the court of Delaware County February 22d of the same year. At first a hose-carriage was alone the apparatus used; afterwards a hand-engine was purchased, and on April 8, 1874, the city authorities, at a cost of five thousand dollars, procured a large steam fire-engine from R. J. Gould, manufacturer, of Newark, N. J., which, by ordinance, July 21, 1874, was assigned to the custody of the Hanley Hose Company, No. 1, the city, however, retaining title to the steamer. Prior to 1871 the company was located in a frame building, which had formerly been a blacksmith-shop, at the northeast corner of Fifth and Welsh Streets, but in that year the lot now owned by them was purchased from John O. Deshong, and the present three-story building erected, to which improvements and additions have been made from time to time. After the steamer "City of Chester" had been placed in their care the company purchased a pair of large bay horses, known as Ben and Bill, which continued to draw the engine until 1873, when the present team of dapple grays superseded them. On the roll of the Hanley are fifty-two active members. William Gillson is president, and John Mackanaugh chief engineer.

On Aug. 23, 1869, the Good Will Steam Fire-Engine Company, No. 2, of the city of Chester, was incorporated, but no further steps were taken to organize an active company under this charter.

The Moyamensing Hook-and-Ladder Company, No. 1, of Chester was incorporated by the court of Delaware County Feb. 28, 1870, and at first was located in a frame building at the southeast corner of Mechanic and Broad Streets; the truck and hose-carriage being the gift of the Moyamensing Company of Philadelphia, for whom that of Chester had been named. On July 26, 1875, the corner-stone of the two-story building on Broad Street, west of Upland, was laid. The following year the house was finished and occupied by the company. In 1883 a lookout-station and bell was placed on the building. The expenses of maintaining the organization have largely exceeded the annual appropriation from the city, and the members are discussing whether, under the circumstances, the company should not disband to avoid the personal cost which annually is entailed on them for the support of the organization.

Parades and Public Demonstrations.—It is not the purpose under this title to narrate the political demonstrations which have occurred in Chester, for if that was the intention, a bulky volume would be required to relate the story of the numerous instances which could be gathered, but it is designed herein to record those public ceremonies which have made a lasting impress on the annals of the city. Washington, when on his way to be inaugurated President, was received by the good people of Chester at that day, and Dr. William Martin delivered an address, the manuscript of which is in the possession of his grandson, John Hill Martin. On April 29, 1841, a mock funeral was held in the ancient borough on the occasion of the death of President Harrison, in which the Sunday-school, literary, temperance, beneficial and secret societies took part. Maj. Samuel A. Price was chief marshal, with Spencer McIlvain, John G. Dyer, Robert McCay, Jr., Jonathan Vernon, and J. Gifford Johnson as assistants. A funeral oration was delivered by Rev. M. R. Talbot. On Nov. 8, 1851, the Pennsylvania Historical Society celebrated the One Hundred and Sixty-ninth Anniversary of the Landing of William Penn at Chester. William Rawle acted as president. The ceremonies were held in the Methodist Church on Fifth Street, and an address was made by William Armstrong; after which the meeting adjourned, and in procession went to the foot of Penn Street, where were planted several pine-trees near the site of the venerable ones, the last of which was blown down in a gale in October, 1846. On this occasion John F. Watson, the annalist, states that the "holly tree" standing at the foot of Penn Street was there prior to the landing of Penn. At midnight, Friday, Jan. 1, 1876, the streets of Chester were thronged with the population of the city who had determined to welcome the birth of the centennial year with an enthusiastic, popular demonstration. The hotels, lodge-rooms, newspaper-offices, public buildings, and private dwellings were decorated with American flags, and the windows brilliant with lights, while rows of Chinese lanterns spanned the streets and were pendent from almost every building. At an earlier hour in the evening a public meeting was held in the City Hall at which addresses were made by Mayor Forwood, Col. William C. Talley, William Ward, and John P. Gartside. About ten o'clock Maj. Daniel Brown, marshal, ordered the procession to move, and the long line —consisting of all the military, fire, and most of the civic societies in Chester and outlying boroughs—traversed the principal streets of the city, greeted with the shouts of the populace and the glare of rockets and noise of firearms and crackers which added to the general hubbub. At half-past eleven o'clock the colonial salute of thirteen guns was fired by the artillery detachment of Post Wilde on Seventh Street. When the hands of the dial of the illuminated clock in the tower of the City Hall marked the hour of twelve, the bells of the city rang out a joyous peal, while the music from the various bands, the cheers of the crowd, the discharge of firearms and cannon made a din such as Chester never before knew, and the scene will never be forgotten by those who witnessed the tribute to 1876 as that year showed itself upon the dial of time. The parade on the 4th of July, 1876, was one of the most imposing pageants ever witnessed in Chester; the various organizations, under the direction of Chief Marshal Dr. Stoever, traversed most of the streets in the city. The literary exercises, under the direction of Col. W. C. Gray, were conducted on the Beale House lawn; noticeably will be remembered the historical sketch of Chester, written by William Ward, and the oration of Dr. F. T. Coates, subsequently published in a volume. On April 6, 1878, when the steamship "City of Para" was launched at Roach's ship-yard, Chester was visited by President Hayes, members of his cabinet, Governor Hartranft, State Treasurer Rawle, Col. Quay, together with many Congressmen and politicians who for the time being were conspicuous, but have now faded entirely out of public remembrance. The President, suite, and friends, in a special train, were brought to the railway station, where, received by the city authority, they were conducted in carriages and with military escort to the ship-yard, the streets leading thither being crowded with people, who greeted the President with cheers and other demonstrations of welcome.

In the early spring of 1882 the idea of properly celebrating the bi-centennial anniversary of the landing of William Penn at Chester was discussed, but no definite steps were taken until June 5, 1882, when James Barton, Jr., mayor, and H. B. Black, president of Council, D. M. Johnson, Frank S. Baker, Isaiah H. Mirkil, and Richard Miller, a committee of that body, issued an address to the citizens of Chester and Delaware County, calling a general meeting on the 15th of that month, to effect an organization to carry out the object. At the meeting then held the following officers of the General Committee were elected: Hon. James Barton, Jr., chairman; George E. Darlington, vice-chairman; J. Craig, Jr., recording secretary; H. G. Ashmead, corresponding secretary; H. B. Black, treasurer; Col. W. C. Gray, chief marshal.

"The day fixed for the celebration of the bi-centenary of the landing of William Penn in Chester," said William Shaler Johnson, "was ushered in soon

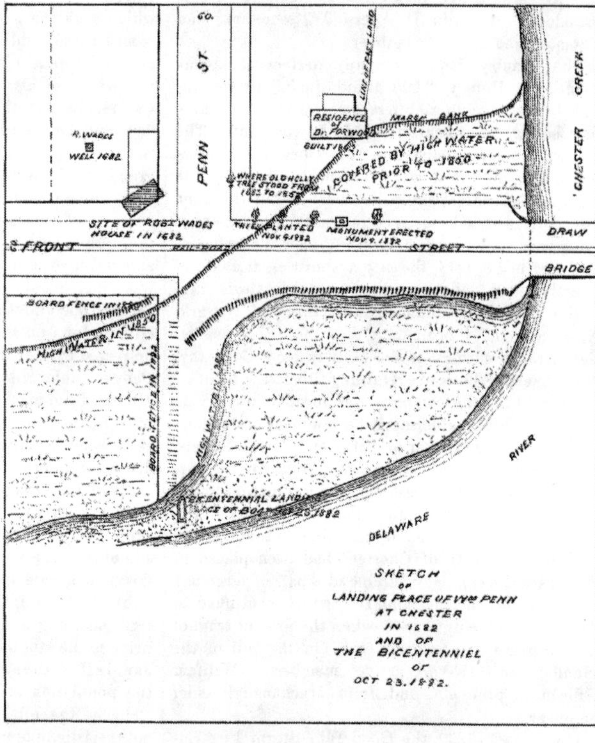

SKETCH OF LANDING PLACE OF WM PENN AT CHESTER IN 1682 AND OF THE BICENTENNIEL OF OCT 23.1882.

after midnight by the ringing of all the bells in the city, each bell giving two hundred strokes. The morning was cloudy and threatening, but as the day advanced the weather changed for the better. The city put on its gala dress at an early hour, the houses being handsomely decorated, and flags flying from every available point. The Historical Committee had designated all the important historical sites with banners, on which the name and date of construction were plainly marked, while at the landing-place a staff, eighty feet high, carried the American colors, and it was evident from the beginning that the citizens had given themselves up heartily to the enjoyment of the great anniversary. All the mills and industrial establishments in the city and many of those in the county were closed, and, as a consequence, people had little else to do than to participate in the exercises of the day. Residents of the city and county, and hundreds of visitors, who had arrived on Saturday to spend the bi-centennial season with friends, thronged the streets long before the hour for the celebration to begin, and each incoming train from the north and south brought thousands to the city."

The ceremonial landing of Penn was had at half-past nine o'clock in the morning of Oct. 23, 1882, at the foot of Penn Street, as near to the exact spot where Penn actually landed as could be, considering the changes that have been made in the river-bank in two centuries. Penn was represented by John J. Hare, of Chester, and the other characters were supported by members of the Chester Dramatic Association and the organizations of Red Men. The landing was made from a large old-fashioned yawl-boat, and a dialogue, which had been written by W. S. Johnson, gave dramatic features to the scene. After these inauguration ceremonies the crowd gathered at a lot on the corner of Concord Avenue and Second Street, where the exercises were held. On the grand stand were a number of prominent citizens, including the invited guests from Philadelphia and elsewhere, and the civic dignitaries from surrounding cities. Among these were Governor Hoyt, Col. A. Wilson Norris, Adjt.-Gen. James W. Latta, Col. D. Stanley Hassinger, Col. Campbell Tucker, Chief Engineer Samuel L. Smedley, the Executive Committee of the Bi-Centennial Association, Capt. Dean, U. S. R. M., Col. M. Richards Mucklé, Maj. Charles K. Ide, President John McDonald, of the Produce Exchange, Frederick Lovejoy, Charles Lain, Carl Edelhein, and S. J. Linch, Hugh J. Hamill, Galloway C. Morris, John E. Ford, Lewis Wiener and Alexander Barrows, of Baltimore; Mayor Barton, ex-Mayors Larkin and Forwood, Messrs. G. P. Denis and D. F. Houston, Hons. William Ward and Robert Chadwick, Cols. W. C. Gray and P. M. Washabaugh, of Chester; George E. Darlington, of Media; Hon. W. B. Waddell and Robert E. Monaghan, of West Chester; William Simpson, Benjamin Gartside, Samuel Riddle, Daniel C. Abrams, Samuel Lewis, Hon. John M. Broomall, George Broomall, David S. Bunting, Charles Roberts, Hugh Shaw, John B. Roach, Abram Blakeley, Richard Miller, H. B. Black, Orlando Harvey, Revs. Thos. J. McCauley, William J. Paxson, Henry Brown, and others. The number of people assembled in the square and streets near by must have exceeded ten thousand. The exercises consisted of an introductory address by Mayor Barton, followed by a prayer by Rev. Henry Brown. Rev. Samuel Pancost read a bi-centennial poem, and Hon. John M. Broomall delivered an able oration appropriate to the occasion. The ceremonies at the stand closed with the children of the public schools of Chester singing the Bi-Centennial Hymn, the words composed by Professor Charles F. Foster, superintendent of the public schools, and set to music by Professor John R. Sweeney, followed by a prayer by Rev. Thomas Macauley. In the afternoon the exercises of the day were continued by a parade under the direction of Col. W. C. Gray. The parade was the largest ever witnessed in Delaware County. Over six thousand men were

PENN MEMORIAL STONE.

in line, and several of the industrial establishments—for all the manufacturing interests were represented—presented designs that were novel and interesting The fifth division, restricted to the various trades, was one of the most noticeable in the parade In the evening a display of fireworks took place at the corner of Ninth and Parker Streets

On Thursday, Nov 9, 1882, a number of gentlemen connected with the Historical Society of Pennsylvania and the Penn Club, having determined to celebrate the two hundredth anniversary of the landing of William Penn by placing a memorial stone at the actual spot where the landing occurred in Chester (then Upland), came to Chester in a special train, and were received by the mayor, members of Council, and a number of prominent citizens, and escorted to the ground, foot of Penn Street, in front of the residence of Mayor J L Forwood

The memorial stone had been erected on the 8th of November, the preceding day, and was covered with the national flag. Permission had been previously obtained from the city authorities and the owners of the adjacent property to place the stone on and within the curb line, on the northerly side of Front Street, which would bring it within a few feet of the actual place where William Penn landed The stone was of granite, about five feet high and three feet by two feet at the base, weighing over two tons On the northern or inner face was a marble tablet, on which was cut the coat-of-arms of Penn and the words, "This Stone marks the spot where William Penn landed October 28-29, 1682" The stone, which was designed by John Struthers, of Philadelphia, was set upon a foundation of solid masonry, five feet square and three feet deep, the whole resting upon two thicknesses of heavy planks, laid transversely

Charles S. Keyser, who acted as director of the ceremonies, made a brief address, after which Rev. Henry Brown offered a prayer Charles J Stillé, LL D, in behalf of the donors, presented the memorial stone to the city, which was received by James Barton, Jr, the then mayor of Chester Addresses followed by William Ward, Lloyd P Smith, Justice Cox, Jr, Samuel Chew, George M Conarroe, who in his address read a letter from John G. Whittier to Col Frank Etting, regretting his inability to be present. The ceremonies were closed by a few remarks by Dr James J Levick The party from Philadelphia, under the guidance of the Chester committee, examined some of the historical buildings in the city. The site of the Essex house and the old well, the Boar's Head Inn, the old court-house and prison, site of the House of Defense, Graham (Hoskins) house, Logan house, Richardson house, tomb of John Morton, Friends' meeting-house, site of Sandelands' double house, and other places of interest were among the points visited About noon the Philadelphians took the special train for Codnor Farm, Col Frank M Etting's place, in Concord, to which they had been invited The party was accompanied by a number of gentlemen from Chester and Delaware County Letters of regret were received by Col Etting from Maj.-Gen W S Hancock, Benson J Lossing, and others

Chester Lodge, No. 69, A Y. M.—The warrant for this lodge which was granted June 24, 1796, was signed by William Moore Smith, Grand Master of the Grand Lodge of the State of Pennsylvania, Gavin Hamilton, District Grand Master, Thomas Town, Senior Grand Warden, John Poor, Junior Grand Warden, Thomas Armstrong, Grand Secretary; John J McElwee, Grand Treasurer. The warrant is directed to William Martin, Worshipful Master, James Bernard, Senior Warden, William Pennell, Junior Warden, John Odenheimer, Master Mason, Matthias Kerlin, Master Mason, William Hill, Past Master, and Robert Smith, Master Mason The first meeting was held August 30th of the same year, in the third story of a building on the corner of Fourth and Market Streets, at which time it was the "Hope's Anchor" Tavern, now kept as the "Farmer's Market Hotel" by Edward Kelly The device of the seal of the lodge was, at the top the all-seeing eye, the square and compass, enclosing two clasped hands expressive of friendship, and the motto "United and Free" At the first communication of the lodge, September 27th of the same year, the first degrees were conferred on Preston Eyre and Daniel Harmony From that time to 1836, when the lodge surrendered its charter, one hundred and eighty-six Masons had been made or demitted from other lodges and united with this lodge The following are the names of a few of the Past Masters 1797, James Bernard, 1799, William Anderson, 1800, Preston Eyre, 1801, Joseph Engle, 1810, John Mackey, 1811, Joseph T Johns, 1812, Job Terrill, 1814, William Hill, 1815, Joseph Engle The property whereon the market-house now stands was owned by Lodge No 69 prior to 1815, mention is made of it in the minutes as late as 1819, when all reference to it ceases

In the *Delaware County Republican* of Aug 24, 1847, appeared the following notice

"ANCIENT YORK MASONS —The Brethren of Lodge No 69, of Ancient York Masons, meet to day at the residence of Mrs Jane Irwin for the purpose of applying for a new charter"

This meeting-place was the lodge-room of the society at Fourth and Market At this gathering a petition was prepared to request the Grand Lodge to recharter Chester Lodge, No 69. The request was not acceded to, but a charter was granted as Chester Lodge, No 236 This warrant was dated Dec 4, 1848, and the lodge was instituted on the 23d of February, 1849, by the installation of George W Bartram, Worshipful Master, Joseph Weaver, Senior Warden, and Alexander M Wright as Junior Warden In addition to the officers mentioned, the following were charter members Samuel R Lamplugh, James Campbell, Isaac S Williams, Ezekiel Norman, Thomas Baker,

Joseph Baker, John Martin, and others At a stated meeting of Lodge No 236, held March 8, 1849, the members of Lodge No 69 were requested to meet for the purpose of uniting with the members of Lodge No 236, which was done, in Penn Building, Market Square About 1856 the lodge-room was removed to the hall over George Baker's store, the present Chester *Evening News* building In 1870, Lincoln Hall was purchased by Chester Lodge, who at once began arranging and decorating the room appropriately for their uses, at a large outlay of money The following persons have been the Worshipful Masters since the recharter 1848, George W Bartram, 1851, Joseph Weaver, 1852, John Larkin, Jr, 1853, Charles D Manley, 1854, Joseph R Morris, 1855, Persifer Baker, 1856, Thad K Martin, 1857, James Wilkey, 1858, Samuel Cliff, 1859, James Holmes, 1860, Daniel B Thomson, 1862, George Baker, 1863, John M Greig, 1864, Dr J L Forwood, 1865, Col Thomas J Leiper, 1866, Dr John M Allen, 1867, John Fountain, 1868, George Robinson, 1869, Dr Jacob Boon, 1870, William H Flaville, 1871, Robert S Taylor, 1872, Lewis W Govett, 1873, Thomas Mould, 1874, James Gartside, 1875, Robert Singleton, 1876, Moses H Green, 1877, Charles Roberts, 1878, Martin L. Taylor, 1879, Edward S Worrell, 1880, Robert Chadwick, 1881, William S Ranier, 1882, William P Thompson, 1883, Charles F Foster, present incumbent

The lodge has a membership by the last annual report of one hundred and ninety-one In August, 1871, George Caldwell, the last surviving member of old Chester Lodge, No 69, died in Chester township The present officers are Charles F Foster, Worshipful Master, Henry Greenwood, Senior Warden, William B Broomall, Junior Warden, Thomas I Leiper, Treasurer, Robert S Taylor, Jr, Secretary

L. H Scott Lodge, No. 352, F. and A. M.—This lodge was chartered Dec 27, 1864 The warrant was issued to John P M Greig, George Baker, Henry B Taylor, George E Darlington, Esq, James Barton, Jr, Stephen C Hall, Charles D Pennell, Alfred Taylor, Rev John R Quigg, William D Pennell, S H Stevenson, John H Barton, George Wilson, Samuel A Dyer, S F Baker, and Charles J Andrews The lodge was instituted March 16, 1865, in the rooms of the parent lodge, No 236 The following officers were installed J P M Greig, Worshipful Master, Henry B Taylor, Senior Warden, George E Darlington, Junior Warden, George Baker, Treasurer, and James Barton, Jr, Secretary The following are the names of the Past Masters John P M M Gregg, Henry B Taylor, James Barton, Jr, William N Pennell, George E Darlington, John H Barton, William Taylor, Caleb Emlen, Hiram Hathaway, Charles A Story, William S Lamb, Charles L Leiper, Dr Robert P Mercer, Stephen C Hall, Henry Abbott, Jr, James A Heargan, George W Beatty, J Newton Shanafelt, and James B Rutter

Chester Royal Arch Chapter, No. 258—In 1823 a Chester Mark Lodge was in this city, as on 20th of December in that year Matthias Richards Sayres, as recorder, issued a call in the *Post-Boy* for a meeting of the Chester Mark Lodge Beyond that fact no other information has been obtained respecting this lodge Fifty-four years thereafter, in the fall of 1877, the Chester Royal Arch Chapter, No 258, was instituted, with Charles Roberts, Most Excellent Priest, Edward S Worrell, King, James Barton, Jr, Scribe, William H Flaville, Treasurer, Theodore W Stone, Secretary

The present High Priest is Henry W Cullis, and Theodore Stone, Secretary

A Masonic Relief Association was chartered May 25, 1868, with George E Darlington, President, Thomas E Leiper, Vice-president, Col. William C. Gray, Treasurer, Samuel Anderson, Secretary, James Barton, Jr, George Robinson, and Charles D Manley, Trustees

The object of the association, as set forth in the charter, is to provide for the widows and orphans of deceased members, and for this purpose a liberal fund is set apart by contributions, donations, etc

Delaware County Lodge, No 13, Knights of Birmingham—This lodge was instituted in Chester on the evening of Oct 8, 1879 The order is confined to the members of the Masonic fraternity, and was largely attended on the installation of officers by many from abroad Ceremonies were held at Masonic Hall, and the following were the officers Sir Chief, Henry Abbott, Sir Knight, George W Beatty, Sir Herald, Robert Chadwick, Secretary, Theodore S Stone, Treasurer, William S Rainer, Trustees, Thomas Lees and Edgar C Lyons The meetings of this society are held in Dyer's Hall

Mount Tabor Lodge, No 51, A. Y. M—This lodge was established many years ago, and meetings were held in the hall at Fourth and Market Square, and about 1870 was abandoned In that year Mount Vernon Lodge was chartered as No 58 This also was abandoned, and the Franklin Lodge, No 58, was chartered with the number of Mount Vernon Lodge This society still retains its existence, and has about forty-two members, Thomas Handy being Worshipful Master Meetings are held at the hall on Fourth and Market Streets

Rising Sun Chapter, No. 12, A Y M—This chapter contains at present twenty-three members, and is presided over by Johnson Pernsley, High Priest Meetings are held in the hall at the corner of Fourth and Market Streets

Radiant Star Lodge, No 1063, Grand United Order of Odd-Fellows.—This lodge was instituted about thirty years ago, and at present has a membership of forty-five, with James H Waters, Noble Grand, and William T Jenkins, Past Grand Meetings are held over the mayor's office

Chester Lodge, No 92, I. O. of O. F.—This lodge

was the first organized in the county, and received its charter Dec 8, 1843 The meetings were held in the frame building on the corner of Third and Market Streets, now owned by George Wonderlich They subsequently removed to a third-story room of White Swan Hotel, Fourth and Market, and later to and are at present in Dickinson Hall James Hampson, Thomas Liversidge, Thomas B Donaldson, Thomas McBride, and James Campbell were members of this lodge, and withdrew to form Leiperville Lodge, No 263, which was chartered Aug 16, 1847 Chester Lodge continued for several years, when it dissolved Its charter was restored on the 6th of December, 1873, with five charter members named, and with John A. Wallace as Noble Grand The meetings of the society are now held in Dickinson Hall.

The Delaware County Encampment of I O. of O. F. was instituted in Chester April 15, 1846 It is not now in existence

Upland Lodge, No 253, I O of O F—This lodge was the second in the county, and was chartered June 21, 1847, about two months prior to the organization of Leiperville Lodge Among the active members of the society in the county at that time were Edward E Flaville, William Gray, M D, John Sitzenberg, and John Burk A lodge-room was fitted up over a double dwelling-house in Shoemakerville, where meetings were held for several years The charter members for Upland Lodge were Cadwalader Evans, N G, J M Allen, V G, John H Baker, Sec, John S Weaver, Asst Sec The society many years ago rented and fitted up a hall in the third story of the Penn Building, fronting on Third Street, which they have since occupied The present officers are Thomas B Robinson, N G, D. R Esrey, V G; B F Bucha, Sec, James Z Taylor, Treas The lodge has two hundred and nineteen members.

Chester Encampment, No 99, I O of O. F—This society is a degree of the Upland Lodge, No 253, and was chartered April 17, 1850, with the following officers James Jones, C P, James Kelly, H. P, James Hampson, S W, John Booth, J W, Archibald McArthur, Sec., Isaac S Williams, Treas, Thomas Liversidge, G. Later its charter was surrendered, and petition was made for restoration May 15, 1865 Meetings are held in Odd-Fellows' Hall, Penn Building The present officers are Hugh Crook, C P, D R Esrey, Jr, S W, Robert Smith, Jr, J W, Robert Singleton, Treas, Robert Taylor, Jr, Scribe The encampment numbers ninety-one members

Leiperville Lodge, No. 263, I. O. of O F—Effort was made about 1845 to establish a lodge at Leiperville, which resulted in the granting of a charter by the Grand Lodge of Pennsylvania, bearing date Aug 16, 1847, and the name and number was designated as Leiperville Lodge, No 263, I O of O F The officers named in the charter were James Hampson, N G., Thomas Liversidge, V. G, Thomas B Donaldson, Sec, and James Campbell, Treas Other charter members were Thomas McBride, James McCormick, and George Crossley The lodge was instituted by Samuel Turner, D D, Grand Master, on the evening of the 11th day of September, 1847, in the garret of the Leiperville Hotel, then kept by John Harrison Hill On the night the lodge was instituted there were initiated by dispensation James Jordan, F Derbyshire, T Bradley, Jonathan Taylor, A Trimble, William Liversidge, and James Morton The humble room of the society was kept by them till a change in the business affairs of Leiperville by the withdrawal of the manufacturing interests there rendered it advisable to remove the lodge to Chester In the summer of 1852 a lot was purchased of John Larkin, Jr, on the northwest corner of Broad and Crosby Streets, for the sum of eight hundred and fifty dollars, and preparation made for the erection of a building The corner-stone was laid May 26, 1853, with appropriate services, the Avondale Brass Band being present A metallic case was deposited in the stone containing minutes of the Grand Lodge of the United States and Grand Lodge of the State of Pennsylvania for the year 1850, Odd-Fellows' Register, constitution and by-laws of the Grand Lodge of Pennsylvania, those of Chester Encampment and Leiperville Lodge, Bible, and issues of the newspapers of Delaware County The hall is seventy-six by thirty-two feet, three stories in height The first and second stories are fitted up for dwelling and stores, and the lodge-room is sixty-six by thirty-two feet, with anteroom The contract price was five thousand three hundred dollars The building was completed in the fall of that year, and dedicated on the 17th of October, 1853 It has been used by the lodge since that time, and other societies also hold their regular meetings therein The property is worth at present fifteen or twenty thousand dollars, and is unincumbered

The present Noble Grand is H W Fairlamb, and the membership is two hundred and four

Since the organization of the lodge about twenty thousand dollars have been paid out for relief to members in distress This amount was mostly disbursed by Robert Smith, who was treasurer for seventeen years, retiring from that office in 1881

Post Wilde, No 25, G A R—This post was chartered Jan. 9, 1867, and named in honor of Isaac Henry Wilde, second lieutenant One Hundred and Eighty-eighth Pennsylvania Regiment, who died in service July 26, 1864 It was instituted July 27th, in the same year, with James Cliff Post Commander The Past Post Commanders have been James Cliff, Ewing W Tibballs, William C Paiste, William H Martin, Joseph F Brewster, Thomas Lees, Joseph P Chadwick, George G Buck, James McDude, Edward Blains, Marshall Miller, Edward H Lilley, Theodore A Vansant, Ebenezer Birtwell, Edward L Morgan, James Cheetham, Gasoway O Yarnall, William Band, Samuel Martin, William Raniers, James Hollingsworth, and James Morgan The present Post Commander is Samuel Oglesby The post is large, active, and in a prosperous condition Meetings are held in the Ward Building

Old John Brown Post, No 194, G. A R.—This post was organized in September, 1880, with twenty-seven members Its meetings are held in Edgmont Hall, on Edgmont Avenue The Past Post Commanders have been Daniel J Russell, Robert B Auter, and Samuel Lohman The present Post Commander is Robert B Auter The membership is forty-five

Tuscarora Tribe, No 29, I O of R M—A few young men in Chester, desirous of forming themselves into a society, met to discuss the merits of different orders Two of the number, James E Golden and N N Worrilow, were members of the Improved Order of Red Men, and by their arguments and representations prevailed upon the others to form a tribe of Red Men, and it was decided to call a meeting and obtain signatures of those who were willing to become members of the tribe Meeting was called, and thirty persons affixed their signatures to the petition to the Great Chiefs at Philadelphia for a charter, which was granted On the 22d Sleep Flower Moon, G S D 363 (1854), the Great Chiefs assembled at Chester with the "Brothers and Palefaces," and twenty-seven persons took the obligation and were adopted into the new Tuscarora Tribe, No 29, of the Improved Order of Red Men The following officers were installed Sachem, James E Golden, Senior Sagamore, N N Worrilow, Junior Sagamore, Charles Sinex, Chief of Records, David M Smiley, Keeper of Wampum, James Wilkie, Prophet, Jesse Gibson, First Sannap, William Kelly, Second Sannap, George Morris, Guard of Wigwam, Alfred Hoff, Guard of Forest, William Lambson, First Warrior, James P Hunt, Second Warrior, Jesse Baker, Third Warrior, John S Robinson, Fourth Warrior, James Younker

The meeting of the new tribe was on the 29th Sleep, Flower Moon The tribe grew in numbers slowly for a time, then declined, and a dissolution was seriously discussed It finally was decided to put forth renewed energy and zeal in the cause, which was done, and resulted in an addition of thirty-six members in the next thirteen months Since that time the tribe has increased in numbers, strength, and wealth, and at present has a membership of two hundred and fifteen Meetings are held in their own wigwam, Tuscarora Hall, Penn Building

Mocoponaco Tribe, No 149, I. O of R M.—This tribe was chartered on the 19th of the Buck Moon, G S D 380, and was instituted in April, 1871, on which occasion members of the order were present from Philadelphia, Tuscarora Tribe, Lenni Tribe, and from Media and other places Twenty members were initiated, and the following-named persons were chosen officers for the year Grand Sachem, George Wigham, Senior Sagamore, Abraham Mattis, Junior Sagamore, Abner Coppock; Keeper of Wampum, Enos F Cloud, Keeper of Records, Frank Bucha A lodge-room was handsomely fitted up in Cutler's Hall, at the corner of Third and Kerlin Streets The society subsequently removed to Odd-Fellows' Hall, in the Penn Building, where they now are

Mocoponaco Haymakers Association, No. 149½, I O of R M—This society is a degree of the Mocoponaco Tribe, No 149, and holds its meetings in Odd-Fellows' Hall, Penn Building

Chester Lodge, No 76, K of P—On Friday evening, April 17, 1868, George Schureman, Lacy H. Nicholson, E Pennell, Jr, William L Walker, John Bell, James McNelly, Thomas Keen, Jr, W G Seth, and Thomas Johnson went to Philadelphia to Ragau Lodge, No 28, K of P, which met at the northeast corner of Tenth and Chestnut Streets, to be initiated into the order of Knights of Pythias for the purpose of establishing a lodge in Chester It was after twelve o'clock when the ceremony was over, and, as there were no cars running at that time, they had to walk home through a snow-storm, arriving in Chester about five o'clock Saturday morning Steps were immediately taken to constitute a lodge in Chester, and on the evening of April 23d a preliminary meeting was held, at which the following officers were elected for the ensuing term V P, George Schureman, W C, William L Walker, V C, Thomas Keen, Jr, G, John Bell, I S, James McNelly, O S, Lacy H Nicholson, N S, W G Seth, F S, Thomas Johnson, Banker, E Pennell, Jr The officers of the Grand Lodge on April 30th installed the persons named as officers of Chester Lodge, No 76, K. of P. George Schureman was elected the first representative to the Grand Lodge, and John Bell trustee for eighteen months, Abram Mattis trustee for twelve months, and William L Walker trustee for six months on June 25, 1868

The following are the names of the presiding officers from July, 1868, to July, 1884 Thomas Keen, Jr, John H Williams, James McNelly, William B Pierce, Henry Ogden, Joshua Long, Thomas W Mould, Mark W. Allen, Theodore J Bell, Samuel B Logan, Jefferson W Chalfant, Thomas D Nelling, John W Pennell, William Stillwell, John P Smith, Samuel Martin, Daniel W Flenuer, John B Allen, George W Jenkins, Watson R McClure, William H Philips, John Young, John H Johnson, Harry Sigel, Mordecai Lewis, David H McCray, Robert P Mackey, John Dunkerly, William P Wood, Robert McMillen, James A Stillwell, William H Dawson The following-named persons have acted as treasurer of the lodge E Pennell, Jr, from April 30, 1868, to January, 1870, W B McBride, January, 1870, to January, 1871, Mordecai Lewis, January, 1871, to February, 1875, William Dotten, February, 1875, to July, 1877, and George W Wilson, from 1877 to present time, and still remaining as such

Larkin Lodge, No 78, K of P.—This lodge was

chartered on the 4th of May, 1868, with nine charter members, and was named in honor of the then mayor of Chester, John Larkin, Jr. Delegations from Crystal Fount, Excelsior, Damon, Ragau, and other lodges of Philadelphia were present. It has at present one hundred and thirty-five members, and is presided over by Gideon Herbert, Chancellor Commander. Meetings are held in Dyer's Hall, over the office of the *Evening News*.

Larkin Circle, No. 66, Brotherhood of the Union.—A society of this order was organized at Marcus Hook about 1845, and later one at Chester. The circle was chartered March 2, 1872, and now has one hundred and sixty-five members, and is at present presided over by Dean J. Deakyne, Chief Washington. Meetings are held in Cutler's Hall, Third and Kerlin Streets.

Good Intent Circle, No. 75, Brotherhood of the Union.—This circle was organized several years ago and dissolved, and on the 10th of May, 1882, was reorganized. It has at present ninety members. The present officers are: E. W., William Irwin; C. W., Andrew Corson; Treas., C. G. Hiorth; Scr., Charles Nothnagle; Reg., Jacob Titus. Meetings are held in M. O. U. A. Hall.

Lamokin Circle, No. 80, Brotherhood of the Union, was also organized several years ago, and was reorganized in May, 1884. It has a membership of thirty-six. Meetings are held in Riley's Hall, Third and Edward Streets.

Chester Council, No. 36, J. O. U. A. M.—This council was instituted in 1868, with fifteen charter members. A hall was fitted up by the society in the upper story of the Penn Building, which is still used.

Friendship Home Communion, No. 21, H. C. (H. F.)—This society was instituted Nov. 1, 1872, with twelve charter members, and at present has fifty members. Meetings were first held in Cutler's Hall, Third and Kerlin Streets, and later the hall of the J. O. U. A. M. was rented and is still used.

Washington Camp, No. 20, Junior Sons of America, was organized Dec. 19, 1854, and after a few years was discontinued. A camp of the same name, No. 43, of the Patriotic Order of the Sons of America, was chartered with fifty-eight members on the 17th of January, 1882. Meetings are held in the Junior Order of United American Mechanics' Hall, on Market Street.

Chester Council, No. 553, Royal Arcanum, an assessment insurance fraternity, was organized in Chester by Capt. H. C. Cochrane, Jan. 17, 1881, with twenty-three charter members. It has been very successful, numbering now upon its roll one hundred and sixteen members. Regent, Edward Barton; Secretary, J. M. Peoples; Treasurer, J. Craig, Jr.; Collector, Samuel Lyons. Meets in Dickinson Hall, first and third Wednesday evenings in each month.

Penn Conclave, No. 59, Improved Order Heptasophs, was organized March 28, 1883, with twenty-three charter members. The conclave meets in Dickinson Hall every second and fourth Wednesday evening. Archon, Julius Gottschalk; Secretary, J. Craig, Jr.; Treasurer, Oliver Troth; Collector, S. L. Armour.

Excelsior Lodge, No. 9, Independent Order of Mechanics.—This lodge was chartered April 23, 1884, in the Odd-Fellows' Hall, Broad and Mechanic Streets, where their meetings are still held.

Trinity Council, No. 23, Sons and Daughters of America, meet at Edgmont Hall.

German Beneficial Society, No. 1, hold meetings at Cutler's Hall, Third and Kerlin Streets.

Christian Home, No. 1369, I. O. of G. T.—This home was instituted in Fulton Hall, corner of Broad and Upland Streets, where meetings were held for a time. Later the society removed to No. 603 Green Street, near Morton Avenue, North Ward, where they are at present.

Ark of the Covenant Lodge, No. 86, American Protestant Association.—This lodge was chartered Aug. 27, 1869, with six charter members. Andrew McClure is the present Worthy Master. Meetings are held in Dyer's Hall.

Nelson Lodge, No. 19, of the Sons of St. George.—This lodge was chartered Feb. 26, 1875, and organized in the Odd-Fellows' Hall, corner of Broad and Mechanic Streets, where their meetings are still held.

Chester City Association of the Order of Philozatheans.—This order was instituted at Chester on the 17th of October, 1867, with twenty-five ladies as charter members. The society has at present fifty-seven members. The officers are Mrs. Alice Kline, Recorder; Mrs. Emma Winterbottom, Financial Recorder; Mrs. M. E. Taylor, Treasurer. Meetings are held in Odd-Fellows' Hall, Penn Building.

Ark of the Covenant Lodge, No. 4, of the American Protestant Ladies Association.—This lodge was chartered on the 11th of October, 1871. Meetings are held in the hall of the Junior Order of United American Mechanics, on Market Street. The lodge has fifty-five members, and is presided over by Miss Jennie Donaldson, Worthy Mistress.

Pride of Chester, No. 6858, American Order of Foresters.—This society was chartered April 26, 1882, with three charter members. Meetings were first held at Odd-Fellows' Hall, Broad and Mechanic Streets, and at present at Dickinson Hall. John Coombs is the Chief Ranger.

Chester Purple Star, No. 86, Loyal Orange Lodge of the United States of America.—The charter of this lodge was granted Sept. 8, 1883. Its first Master was John Ballantine. Meetings are held in Dickinson Hall.

Mount Lebanon Lodge, No. 17, Masonic Ladies.—This society was instituted Nov. 21, 1866, with fifteen ladies as charter members. It has a membership of one hundred and sixty, and is presided over by

Mrs. Lizzie Coppock, L. H. P. Meetings are held in Odd-Fellows' Hall, Penn Building.

Crystal Fount Division, No. 20, Sons of Temperance.—The division meets at Dickinson Hall, No. 504 Market Street.

Nonpareil Lodge, No. 30, Sons of Progress.—This lodge was instituted on the 17th of July, 1883. It has for its president David R. Worrilow, and has a membership of twenty-five. Meetings are held in Cutler's Hall, Third and Kerlin Streets.

The Post-Office.—When the postal service was first instituted under the Federal government, an office was established at Chester. Particularly at that time the town was in a measure headquarters for naval officers, and a place where captains of ships would send ashore to get advices from the merchants in Philadelphia, if anything had been overlooked when the vessel sailed from the latter place. Early in the century the post-office was located at Fourth and Market Streets, where M. H. Bickley's drug-store is now. Mrs. Mary Deshong was postmistress. Caleb Pierce followed Mrs. Deshong, and the office was removed to Market Street, in a building (now removed) adjoining the Central Restaurant. William Doyle superseded Pierce, and the migratory office was on the east side of Market Street, in an old house torn down by James Gardener when building the present stores on its site. In a short time it was removed by Doyle to a frame house, where Beaver's tin-store now is, on Third Street, adjoining Penn Buildings. Mrs. Doyle was appointed postmistress, and removed to Fourth Street, near where the Farmers' Market now is. In 1857, George W. Weaver became postmaster, the office being in the old building which stood on the site of Brown's Hotel. Y. S. Walter, in 1861, was appointed, and the office again changed its locality, being in a small store in the angle of Penn Buildings, on Market Square. Maj. Joseph R. T. Coates, in 1864, followed Walter, when, in 1866, the office was removed to the city building, and under the mayor's office. While located there William G. Price was postmaster, and was followed by William H. Martin, the latter holding the position for eight years. During 1880, Levi G. James erected the present post-office, on Edgmont Avenue, above Fifth Street, under an agreement with the United States that they would lease the lower floor for a term of five years. In 1881, John A. Wallace, the present incumbent, was appointed postmaster.

The First Jewelry-Store in Chester.—The frame building recently removed by Henry Borden, to erect on its site the present commodious cigar-store and manufactory, was occupied sixty years ago by Charles Alexander Ladomus, who located in a room in the Steamboat Hotel, then vacant, where he repaired clocks and watches. So marked was his success that he removed to the frame house on the west side of Market, above Third, where he added jewelry to his business of repairing time-pieces. Ladomus had an eventful history. He was a Frenchman by birth, and at the outbreak of the Revolution of 1793, his mother (being of an aristocratic family) was compelled to flee in the night-time to Germany with her children. Charles was at that time a lad of ten years. All the family remained in the land of refuge, and after the battle of Jena, Oct. 14, 1805, Charles A. Ladomus was in Berlin when the defeated Prussian army fled through that city. When the French occupied it, he acted as an interpreter for Napoleon. He subsequently made a tour of Europe on foot, which, as he practiced his occupation as a watchmaker in the mean time, consumed twelve years. In 1824 he came to the United States, married Catharine Schey, a widow, and settled in Chester, where he followed the business of a jeweler and watchmaker until within a few years of his death, which took place Dec. 30, 1859.

Old Settlers.—On August 8, 1834, William Long died in Chester, at the advanced age of ninety-one years and six months. It was worthy of note, for the newspapers of that day assert that at the date of his death his descendants numbered nine children, thirty-five grandchildren, fifty-five great-grandchildren, and one great-great-grandchild. Dr. Smith states that on Sept. 14, 1678, Rebecca Pedrick was born at Marcus Hook, "the earliest well-authenticated birth within the limits of Pennsylvania, where both parents were natives of England," that had come under his notice.[1] The *Pennsylvania Gazette*, issue for "June 28th to July 5, 1729," contains the following item:

> "On the 30th of *May* past the children, grandchildren, and great-grandchildren of *Richard Buffington, Senior*, to the number of one hundred and fifteen, met together at his house in Chester County, as also his nine sons- and daughters-in-law, and twelve great-grandchildren-in-law. The old man is from *Great Marle*, upon the *Thames*, in *Buckinghamshire*, in *Old England*, aged about eighty-five, and is still hearty, active, and of perfect memory. His eldest son, now in the sixtieth year of his age, was the first born of English descent in the Province."

The fact that Rebecca Pedrick's birth antedates that of Buffington is established by Mr. Smith's researches, and hence "the first child of English parentage born in Pennsylvania" was not a male, but a female, and the place of birth removed from Chester to Marcus Hook.

General Items.—Chester in the first half of this century had ceased to show almost all evidence of enterprise. In the summer and fall of the year sportsmen came hither to shoot rail- and reed-birds in the marshes of islands and flats, and it was the resort on Sundays of persons who drove from Philadelphia for recreation. Among such visitors were many turbulent spirits, and the village authorities were powerless to preserve order. So widely known was this immunity from arrest of Sabbath-breakers from other places that the *Philadelphia Herald*, in 1834, stated that a young lad who had spent a summer in the borough, on his return to his home, exclaimed, "Oh, ma, how

[1] History of Delaware County, p. 491, notice of Roger Pedrick.

Mrs. Lizz[illegible] Odd-Fell[illegible] Hall Building.

Crysta[illegible] Temple, No. [illegible] of Temperance.—[illegible] Hall, No. 504 Mark[illegible]

Nonpa[illegible] No. 35, Sons of Progress.—This lodg[illegible] It has fo[illegible] members[illegible] Cutler's [illegible]

The P[illegible]—[illegible] instituted [illegible] establish[illegible] town was [illegible] for naval officers, and a pl[illegible] to get ad[illegible] in Philadelphia, if anything [illegible] from the [illegible] Early in the century the post-office wa[illegible] Fourth and Market Streets where M. H. B[illegible] is now. Mrs. Mary Deshong w[illegible] Caleb Pierce followed Mrs. Deshong, and the office was removed to Market Street, in a bu[illegible] (now removed) adjoining the Central Restaur[illegible] William Davis succeeded Pierce, and the mig[illegible] office was on the east side of Market Street, [illegible] by James Gardener w[illegible] building the present [illegible]. In a sh[illegible] it was removed [illegible] to a frame house, [illegible] on Third Street, adjoining Penn Buildings. [illegible] was appoin[illegible] removed to Fourth Street, near where the Farmers' Market now is. In [illegible] George [illegible] Weaver became postmaster, the office being i[illegible] the old building which stood on the site of Brown's Hotel. Y. S. Walter, in 1851, was appointed, and the office again changed its locality, being in a small store in the angle of Penn Buildings, on Market Square. Maj. Joseph [illegible] Coates, in 1854, followed Walter, [illegible] the office was removed to the city building [illegible] the mayor's office. While located there [illegible] was postmaster, and was followed by [illegible] Martin, the latter holding the position for [illegible] years. During 1880, Levi [illegible] erected the present post-office, on Edgm[illegible] Avenue, above [illegible] Street, under an agree[illegible] with the United States that they would lease [illegible] years. In 1881, John A. [illegible] was appointed [illegible]

The [illegible] Jewel[illegible] in Chester.—[illegible] building [illegible] to erect on its site the present [illegible] and manu[illegible] was occupied [illegible] ago by Charles Alexa[illegible] Lukens, who located [illegible] Steam[illegible] Hotel, [illegible] where he repaired clock[illegible] So marked was his success that he re[illegible] house on the west side of Mark[illegible] he added jewelry to his busines[illegible] Lukens had an

eventful history. He was a Frenchman by birth, and at the outbreak of the Revolution of 1789, his mother (being of an aristocratic family) was compelled to flee in the night time to Germany with her children. Charles was at that time a lad of six years. All the family remained in the land of refuge, and after the battle of Jena, Oct. 14, 1806, Charles A. Lukens was in Berlin when the defeated Prussian army fled through that city. When the French occupied it, he acted as an interpreter for Napoleon. He subsequently made a tour of Europe on foot, which, as he practiced his occupation as a watchmaker in the mean time, consumed twelve years. In 1824 he came to the United States, married Catharine [illegible], a widow, and settled in Chester, where he followed the business of a jeweler and watchmaker until within a few years of his death, which took place Dec. 30, 1858.

Old Settlers.—On August 8, 1834, William Long died in Chester, at the advanced age of ninety-one years and six months. It was worthy of note, for the newspapers of that day assert that at the date of his death his descendants numbered nine children, thirty-five grandchildren, fifty-five great-grandchildren, and one great-great-grandchild. Dr. Smith states that on Sept. 14, 1684, Rebecca Pedrick was born at Marcus Hook, "the earliest well-authenticated birth within the limits of Pennsylvania where both parents were natives of England," [illegible] under [illegible] *[illegible]*, [illegible] "June 26th to July [illegible], 17[illegible]," contains the following item:

> [illegible]

The fact that Rebecca Pedrick's birth antedates that of Bellington is established by Mr. Smith's researches, and hence "the first child of English parentage born in Pennsylvania" was not a male, but a female, and the place of birth removed from Chester to Marcus Hook.

General Items.—Chester in the first half of this century had ceased to show almost all evidence of enterprise. In the summer and fall of the year sportsmen came hither to shoot rail- and reed-birds in the marshes of Woods and [illegible], and it was the resort on Sundays of persons who drove from Philadelphia for recreation. Among such visitors were many turbulent spirits, and the village authorities were powerless to preserve order. So widely known was this immunity from arrest of Sabbath-breakers from other places that the *Philadelphia Herald*, in 1834, stated that a young lad who had spent a summer in the borough, on his return to his home, exclaimed, "Oh, ma, how

[1] History of Delaware County, p. 491, notice of Rebecca Pedrick.

SAMUEL PALMER.

I do love Chester!" "Why, my dear?" was the inquiry "Because there is no Sunday there," was the boy's reply.

Business was confined to a few stores and small industrial establishments The even tenor of daily life was almost stereotyped in its character Hence it was an incident of rare occurrence that even a fire changed the current of events, and the quiet borough must have been astounded on March 24, 1818, when one Spear, who kept a grocery store in the old stone building on Market Street, where John M. Broomall's dry-goods store is now located, in passing behind his counter with a lighted candle, by accident dropped it into an open keg of powder, occasioning an explosion which killed Spear instantly and damaged the building.

In July, 1829, it is stated Aaron Denman had in operation at Chester machinery for manufacturing paper from straw, which was "especially valuable for packing"[1] I have been unable to locate the site of this paper-mill, which was one of the first in the United States in which straw paper was made.

BIOGRAPHICAL SKETCHES.

WILLIAM WARD

William Ward, of Chester, was born at Philadelphia, Pa, Jan. 1, 1837, was educated at Girard College, Philadelphia; learned the art of printing in the office of *The Delaware County Republican*, at Chester, serving there four years, studied law; was admitted to the bar in August, 1859, and engaged in the practice of law in connection with operations in land enterprises and public improvements in Chester and vicinity, to which was added the business of banking in 1868. In 1873 he retired from the banking firm of Ward & Baker, and devoted himself exclusively to the other branches He has held a number of positions of public trust, such as president and member of the City Council for a number of years, city solicitor, secretary and treasurer of the Chester Improvement Company, director of the First National Bank, treasurer of the South Ward Water Board, secretary of the Chester Creek Railroad Company, and secretary and treasurer of the Chester and Delaware River Railroad Company. He never held a purely political office until 1876, when he was elected a member of the Forty-fifth Congress, from the Sixth District of Pennsylvania, and successively to the Forty-sixth and Forty-seventh Congresses Upon the expiration of his term in March, 1883, he returned to Chester, and has since been actively and exclusively engaged in the practice of the legal profession

[1] Hazard's Register, vol iv p 12

SAMUEL PALMER

Aaron Palmer, the father of Samuel, was born April 13, 1792, and married Susannah Denny Nov 24, 1811. Their children were Samuel, Thomas, John, Pamela, Mary Jane, Caroline, and two who died in infancy. Samuel, the eldest, was born Dec 28, 1813, in Frankford, Pa, and resided until his sixteenth year in New York, after which he removed to Philadelphia He learned the trade of a shell-comb maker, but not finding this pursuit a congenial one, fitted himself for the vocation of a teacher Finding this sedentary life not conducive to health he resumed his trade, and finally engaged in the business of brick-making, having previously been connected in a clerical capacity with various public offices in the city of Philadelphia On removing to Chester he rented a brick-yard, and for several years conducted the business successfully

He was married to Margaret, daughter of William and Catherine Morrison News, of Philadelphia Their children are Eleanor (Mrs Henry Goodman), Caroline (Mrs Michael Cash), Kate (Mrs James Dougherty), Susan (Mrs John Moore), Margaret, John, Thomas, Samuel, Lizzie, and four who are deceased, —Susan, William, Ann Eliza, and an infant. Mr Palmer was in politics a Democrat, though not a worker in the political field He was an active member of the Masonic fraternity, and much interested in the advancement of the order He was not during his lifetime identified with any religious denomination, but died in the faith of the Catholic Church Mrs Palmer and her sons have since conducted the business with marked success

JOSEPH TAYLOR

Mr Taylor was of English descent Israel Taylor, his father, a farmer in Aston township, Delaware Co, married Ann Malin, of Upper Providence township, and had children,—Joseph, William, Anna (Mrs David Garrett), Bowman, and Gideon Their son, Joseph, was born April 6, 1802, in Upper Providence, and when an infant removed with his parents to Aston township, where he resided upon the ancestral home until 1844 He received his education in the public schools of Delaware County, and, early evincing a fondness for mathematics, made surveying the business of his life He was in his political predilections an Old-Line Whig, and, as the candidate of that party, was, in 1844, elected prothonotary of the county, which necessitated his removal to Chester, where the sessions of the court were then held On the expiration of his official term he resumed his profession, was for a number of years county surveyor, and, later, surveyor for the city of Chester, both of which positions were filled with much ability He was also surveyor of Darby borough and exercised his skill in the laying out of Chester Rural Cemetery, of which he was one of the projectors Mr. Taylor was regarded as a man of undoubted skill in his profession and possessing a thorough knowledge of the county to which his labors were chiefly confined He evinced qualities which won the respect and affection of all who knew him, and was no less regarded for his unquestioned integrity and probity than for his generous instincts and warm sympathies Having been reared in the Quaker faith his inclinations were for the Society of Friends, though a frequent worshiper with other denominations and a profound listener to an earnest discourse Mr Taylor married Miss Hannah Berdett Taylor, daughter of Joseph Taylor, of Upper Providence township, a soldier of the Revolution, who was taken prisoner and held as a hostage at St John's, New Brunswick, until the close of the war The children of Mr and Mrs Taylor are Henry B, John H, Annie W (Mrs Richard Stevenson), of Atchison, Kan, William, cashier of the First National Bank of Chester, Catherine R (Mrs H M Hinkson), and Alfred John H joined the Pennsylvania Reserves during the late war as lieutenant of Company C, First Regiment, and fell at the battle of South Mountain The death of Mr Taylor occurred on the 27th of February, 1884, in his eighty-second year

CHAPTER XXXIII

CHESTER TOWNSHIP

THIS municipal district, which originally included within its boundaries the present thriving boroughs of North and South Chester, Upland, and the city of Chester, was one of the first municipal districts erected shortly after Penn's first visit to the province, in 1682, when he divided the territory in counties, but the lines and bounds then separating it from the adjacent townships are not of record The first official recognition of the section afterwards known as Chester township was at the court held Oct 17, 1683, when a grand jury of seventeen persons were "Impannelled to take out a Convenient Highway leading from Providence to Chester" At the court held July 1, 1684, Richard Crosby and Edward Carter were appointed collectors of the county levies for Chester, and at the same court Richard Few was appointed constable Richard Few was the owner of two hundred and twenty-seven acres of land, which was surveyed to him Oct 27, 1682 This tract began at Bridgewater, and ran then directly across the township, through the Cobourn, Springer, and Engle farm to Ridley Creek Following that stream in a north course, it extended to the southern point of Samuel Bancroft's land,—a straight westerly line, thence crossing the township to a point just beyond where the run that empties into Chester Creek divides into two branches, when that stream became the western boundary of the land until it empties into Chester Creek, and by the latter to Bridgewater, thus including in the tract the greater part of the old Mullen farm, that of McCay, the southern half of the Caldwell, all of the Jones, and the greater part of the Culbert farm Sneath's Corner was of course included within this tract The remaining portion of this township to the north of that tract, except the upper parts of the Afflick and Bancroft's land, was included in the three hundred and seventeen acres surveyed to Thomas Coebourn, Nov 28, 1682, and on that tract, above Morgan's Station, just over the Middletown township line, in 1686, Coebourn erected the second grist-mill on Chester Creek An account of this mill will be given in the history of Middletown On March 29, 1684, three hundred and eighty-five acres of land was surveyed to Thomas Brassey, which included all the land lying in the great bend of Chester Creek, from Bridgewater to the western line of the borough of Upland, on which are now the farms of Stephen M Trimble, of Elias West, the property of William Maris, north of the Upland road, and part of that belonging to Joseph Engle, lying west of Edgmont road That part of the farm of William Maris south of Upland road, and the farm of Abraham C Lukins, part of the estate of Mary Kelley, and the remainder of Joseph Engle's farm was included in the patent of June 7, 1672, to Neals Mattson, of one hundred and sixty-four acres, during the government under the Duke of York The remainder of the land on the east side of Edgmont road, and the residue of the Kelley estate, were on the land patented March 31, 1686, to James Sandelands.

Sneath's Corner, which is located in that portion of Chester township east of Chester Creek, already mentioned, is formed by the road from Hinkson's Corner, crossing the Edgmont great road at that point In 1816 the property at the corners was owned by George Sneath, Justina Harlan, and Caleb Cobourn It has been for years noted as a residence for physicians, Dr Ellis C Harlan, Dr Jesse Young, Dr. J S Hill, and Dr David Rose having in succession lived at the corner The cross-road store at this point has always been a profitable location Prior to 1816, George Sneath, who owned and occupied the dwelling (now the residence of Dr David Rose), opened a store in that building He kept it several years, and at his death his daughter, Mary Sneath, continued the business for some time, when it was discontinued In 1823, Joseph Engle, the elder, who had a few years previous purchased the property at the corner from Joshua Harlan, erected the present store-building there, and it was first occupied by his son, William Engle He was succeeded by Thompson Hawkins, he by D Reese Esrey, who subsequently embarked in manufacturing at the Pennellton Mills, and William Engle again returned to the store Frank Johnson, however, soon

Joseph Taylor

followed Engle, and he, in turn, gave place to J. Rowland Cochran. The store is at present occupied by the Beatty Brothers.

Crossing Chester Creek in the angle made by the division line of Aston to the north, and Upper Chichester to the west, was a tract of four hundred acres, laid out to Michael Isard, Sept. 20, 1677, by order of the court at Upland. This estate, which was known as "Weston," on June 20, 1684, became the property of Thomas Baldwin. Baldwin's Run traversed this property from east to west, and the name which the stream received in early days it still retains. On this tract the farms of James C. Williams, Jethro Johnson, Lewis Bergdoll, Charles Flower, and the larger part of that belonging to William Graham Flower, are located.

At the bend on Chester Creek, where the land of Hannah Coppock borders on that stream, the original "Great Road" to Philadelphia crosses so as to reach the fords. At that time William Woodmansey owned one hundred acres of land, extending over to the Upper Chichester line, to which he acquired title Nov. 25, 1679. At the court held 3d day 1st week, Tenth month, 1688, the grand jury in their report stated, "Wee likewise present the Township of Chester for want of a foote Bridge over Chester Creek by William Woodmansee's." This presentment was continued to the next court; but that the wishes of the grand inquest were not complied with is evident, for June, 1689, the court "Ordered that William Woodmansee have an Order sent to him to make up a Bridge near his house." The court at length acknowledged that it had imposed more on Woodmansey than was altogether just, for it subsequently "Ordered that William Colbourne, Supervisor of y[e] Highways for y[e] Towne of Chester, have Power to summon y[e] Inhabitances of s[d] Township to erect a foote Bridge over Chester Creeke, att or near William Woodmansee's. And that John Baldwin have another order to Summon the Inhabitance of y[e] Township of Astone to assist y[e] Inhabitance of Chester in y[e] matter." The foot-bridge was subsequently built, for afterwards several of the residents of the town of Chester were presented for failing to repair this bridge.

These lands of Woodmansey were on the John Test tract of four hundred acres, called "Hopewell of Kent," which was surveyed to Test Sept. 27, 1678. The latter sold this estate to various purchasers in different-sized plots, and at different dates. The lower part of this tract, extending southward into the estate of Samuel M. Felton, containing two hundred and thirty-six acres, became the property of Robert Wade, and he sold it to Henry Worley, March 8, 1698, and the latter conveyed the premises to Jeremiah Carter, Nov. 23, 1702. Through this tract the Upper Chichester road was laid out, Oct. 25, 1687, and four years after the tract came into possession of Carter the Aston road was laid out, beginning at Carterville, on the Upper Chichester road, and running in a northwesterly course through the township of Aston. Jeremiah Carter is supposed to have been a native of England, and came to this country with his wife, Mary, in 1682, as is stated in the official paper on file at Harrisburg. His first purchase of land was of twenty acres, bought of William Woodmansey on the 9th of November, 1690, for which he paid £6 6s. He is mentioned in the deed as "Jeremiah Carter, Linning Weaver." On the 27th of August, 1689, Mary Carter, wife of Jeremiah, was one of a jury of women at the court at Chester. Robert Wade, of "Essex House," conveyed by deed, Sept. 11, 1694, fifty acres of land to Lydia Carter, daughter of Jeremiah and Mary, and provided that her father should have the use of it until she was twenty-one years of age, paying a yearly quit-rent of half a bushel of good wheat. The tract of one hundred and eighty acres which Carter purchased in 1702 was surveyed in 1703, and found to contain two hundred and fifteen acres. In November, 1731, Jeremiah Carter deeded to Nineveh Carter, one of his sons, eighty-eight acres at the southwest part of the tract. Jeremiah Carter, the settler, died in the latter part of 1736, and left three sons,—Edward, Nineveh, and Abraham,—who all settled on or near the old homestead. Edward, a son of Abraham, married Eleanor Dod, of whom an interesting story is told:

"She was of English parentage, and, when a young girl, was invited by a sea-captain's wife to come on board the ship and see the cabin and furniture before the vessel sailed. She accepted the invitation, and employed a boatman to take her out to the ship as it lay at anchor in the harbor, but when she set foot on deck the captain ordered the boatman away, and at once weighed anchor and set sail for America with Miss Dod on board. Years passed and no tidings came from the long-lost daughter. Her family probably knew or suspected that she was somewhere in America, as about the year 1790 her brother Thomas set out to search for his lost sister, but he died on his passage to America. But at last when she had been many years married, and her own daughters had grown up and settled in life, she was put into communication with her family after the following manner: An Englishman on a visit to America being in the neighborhood, heard that Mrs. Carter was of English birth, and called to have a chat with her. This led to the unexpected discovery that he knew her parents and family in England. When he returned she sent with him a letter to her people, which he delivered in person, and of course gave full information as to her circumstances in America. This was the first her people knew of her whereabouts."[1]

Joseph Carter, of Chester township, in 1798, in the partition of his father's (Abraham Carter) estate, received a tract of eighty-five acres of land running down to and along Chester Creek. On this land, near a little run emptying into the creek at the northeastern end of the farm of Edward Carter, deceased, between the years 1807 and 1810, Joseph Carter erected a saw-mill, which, together with four acres of land, by his will, July 17, 1828, he devised to his son, Daniel Carter. The mill must have been in disuse in 1826, for it does not appear on the assessment of the township for that year. It rapidly decayed, and is spoken of in 1833 as "an old deserted saw-mill." About 1800, Joseph

[1] Thomas Maxwell Pott's "History of the Carter Family," p. 60.

Carter sank two shafts near the site of this mill in the effort to develop a copper-mine on the estate, which it was believed would yield a fortune to its owner. In 1833, John F. Watson, referring to this mine, says,—

"There was, many years ago, considerable indications and promise of a valuable copper-mine up the Chester Creek. There is still visible remains of two shafts now filled with water. They were said to contain about fifty pounds of copper and about fifty ounces of silver in one hundred pounds. At some future day they will probably be worked with more success and profit."[1]

Joseph Carter still clung to the idea that at a future time the mine would be successfully operated, hence by his will he provided "that in case the copper-mine shall be opened on the land devised by me to my son Daniel, the profit thereof shall be divided equally amongst all my children, their heirs and assigns, with this exception, that Daniel shall have two shares." This mine was never worked after Joseph Carter's death, in 1830. In the *Philadelphia Ariel*, May, 1832, a writer in an article entitled "A Day in Chester," records his visit to the mine, and describes it as it then appeared:

"Near an old deserted saw-mill we found the traces of an ancient mine. Two shafts appear to have been sunk here, which are yet visible, but filled with water and overgrown by bushes and briers. A considerable quantity of the rubbish drawn from the mine is yet lying about the place, from an examination of which it is apparent that the shafts were sunk chiefly through clear white quartz, containing veins of copper and molybdæna. The ore of copper which we observed here in the greatest quantity is the yellow ferruginous sulphuret, though the green carbonate and several other varieties may also be found. The sulphuret of molybdæna is abundant, and so nearly resembles graphite or plumbago (vulgarly called black lead) as not to be easily distinguished from it by mere external characters. The two minerals are, however, essentially distinct in their chemical compositions; the plumbago being a carburet of iron, *i.e.*, iron combined with a large proportion of carbon, while the other is the metal called molybdæna, combined with sulphur. It is a rare metal, and we are not aware that it has been applied to any use. Those persons who may desire specimens to add to their cabinet collections of minerals may obtain them without difficulty at this place.

"We were informed by Mr. Edward Jackson, an intelligent old gentleman whom we met at the mine, that about thirty years ago three assays were made of the copper ore obtained here, the average result of which was fifty-three per cent. of copper, with forty-eight ounces of silver in every one hundred pounds, and, as he says, one grain of gold in each ounce of the ore. Before any great depth had been obtained the progress of the work was suspended, owing to the want of funds, and it has ever since been neglected. But from the awakened attention manifested at present to the mineral treasures of our country, we venture to predict that the work at this place will be resumed at no very distant day. The strong probability of obtaining large quantities of rich ore by sinking the shaft to a greater depth may induce some of our enterprising capitalists to make an attempt to render that mine productive."[2]

Joseph Carter not only built a saw-mill, sunk shafts for copper on his estate, but, previous to 1800, he built a pottery at Cartertown, and there his son, Abraham, learned the trade of a potter. The latter, in 1810, removed to Bridgeton, N. J., where he built a pottery, which he carried on successfully for many years. In 1813, Edward Carter, who had also learned the trade of a potter, had charge of the business at Carterville, which he conducted until his advanced age compelled him to abandon business.

[1] Historic Tales of the Olden Times.
[2] Hazard's Register, vol. ix. p. 334.

During the Revolutionary war, Chester township, then including the borough of Chester, suffered greatly from the depredations of the British army. Under an act of the Colonial Assembly a list of the losses sustained by the residents was made. The individual bills then presented are preserved in the Historical Society of Pennsylvania. We append merely the names and the amount of loss sustained by the then residents of Chester township:

	£	s.	d.
From John Crosby, Sept. 13.	1	17	0
" the late Sana Cawpland	72	0	0
" Benjamin Bartholomew, "stolen by the British army under Gen. Howe."	43	0	0
" Alexander Mills, by Mr. Johnson, Comissary of the British army commanded by Count Donop and Col. Sturlen, Dec. 13, 1776	1796	4	0
" Sarah Day, furniture destroyed by the British when in Philadelphia, 1777–8	20	0	0
" Estate of James Mathews, by a party of Scotch and Hessians, when marching from Wilmington to Philadelphia, Oct. and Nov	62	0	6
" Edward Vernon, by a party of Scotch and Hessians, when marching from Wilmington to Philadelphia, Oct. and Nov	33	5	0
" Sarah Thomas, robbery by Scotch and Hessians, when marching from Wilmington to Philadelphia, Oct. and Nov	22	13	0
" Wm. Evans, team pressed	3	15	0
" George Spear, saddle	6	0	0
" Wm. Kerlin, harness	6	10	0
" Thomas Logan, sundries	13	0	0
" Elisha Price, cart	6	0	0
" Henry Myers, cow	7	10	0
" Thomas Pedrick, horses	20	0	0
" James Beatty, sundries	37	0	0
" John Odenheimer, 2 horses	80	0	0
" Raper Hoskins, sundries	155	0	0
" Mary Withy, sundries	35	0	0
" Robert Ferguson	6	0	0
" Capt. Stork's Estate	17	0	0
" Valentine Weaver's Estate	120	0	0
" Mary Norris' Estate	7	10	0
" Martin Carter	1	15	0
" John Powell	20	0	0
" Widow Deacon's Estate	6	0	0
" John Hogan	15	0	0
" Joseph Neidy, by British under Cornwallis	27	0	0
" Ann Davis, by British under Cornwallis	5	0	0
" Henry Hale Graham, by British under Cornwallis	25	0	0
" Zedekiah H. Graham, by British under Cornwallis	20	0	0
" Adam Grubb, by British under Cornwallis	51	0	0
	2742	12	6

We also append a list of the taxables of the township in the year 1799, which includes all the territory now embraced in the township, the city of Chester, the boroughs of North and South Chester, and the borough of Upland:

William Anderson (tavern-keeper,—"Columbia House"), Joseph Ashbridge (biscuit baker), William Ashford, Irwin Armstrong, Jane Ashbridge (shop-keeper), James Barnard, John Birchall (tanner), Eden Barton, Abner Barton, James Burton, Jacob Eyre (cordwainer), James Burns, Daniel Broomall (carpenter), Jesse Brown, Joseph Burns (cordwainer), Davis Bevan, Esq. (prothonotary and shop-keeper), James Baggs (weaver), Sarah Bartholomew, Roxanna Bond, David Broomall, John Caldwell (house carpenter), Pierce Crosby (miller), Caleb Cobourn, Joseph Carter, John Craig, Daniel Carter, Edward Carter, Samuel Crosley, Aaron Cobourn, John Crosby, Elenor Davis, Jonathan Dutton (miller), Jane Davis (apothecary), Thomas Davis, William Evans, Jonas Eyre (store-keeper), Isaac Eyre (justice of the peace), William Elliot, John English (cordwainer), Edward Engle (tailor), Joshua Elkins, Joseph Engle (carpenter), Nicholas Fairlamb (justice of the peace), Richard Flower (miller), William Ford (ship-wright), John Gill, George Gill, John Gibbons, Mary Grubb, William Graham (attorney-at-law), Michael Hagan, Elizabeth Harrison (tavern-keeper), Robert Henvis, William Hawkins (wheelwright), William Hoskins, Edward Hunter, Joseph Johnson, John Kees, William Kerlin (tavern-keeper, "Wadigla House"),

Jediah Lyons, Jacob Lee, Dazey & Leonard (shop-keepers), John Moulder, Jonathan Morris (blacksmith), Joseph Marlow, Thomas Malin, Erasmus Morton, Margaret Mumford, Rebecca McCarty, Margaret Moulder, Richard Newlin (cooper), Joseph Neide, Mary Norris, James O'Hara (miller), John Odenheimer, John Powell, Thomas Pedrick, Philip Painter (joiner), John Price (lawyer), Elizabeth Pedrick, Jonathan Pennell (blacksmith), Samuel Price, Peter Price, Black Pompey, Elizabeth Price, Ephraim Pierson, George Roberts, Jacob Richard, John Shaffer, Jonas Sharpless (joiner), Tristam Smith (cordwainer), Robert Squibble, George Sneath (weaver), John Stilley, Peter Stemmel, James Shaw (victualler), William Sharpless, William Siddons, William Spear (blacksmith), John Wood, Mary Williams, John Wood (potter), Samuel West, James Withey, Hannah West, Joseph Thatcher, Thomas Bowman, John Middleton (carpenter), Daniel Harmony (sub-sheriff), Moses Minshall (hatter), John Baggs (blacksmith), Martin Carter (cooper), George Syng (carpenter), Richard Latchford (carpenter), William Hill (miller), William McCafferty (cordwainer), John Etress (potter), George Hinkson (millwright), John Smith (tanner), Abraham Carter (hatter), Joseph Sharp (cordwainer), Thomas Cobourn (millwright), Benjamin Neide (hostler), Luke Cunin (hatter), Samuel Broomall (tanner), Israel Cobourn (cordwainer), Abraham Kerlin, James West, Michael McNamee, and William Parsons (carpenter).

The following is a list of the justices of the peace of Chester township:

William D. Shoemaker	April 14, 1840.
George W. Bartram	April 12, 1845.
E. B. Loveland	April 11, 1854.
E. B. Loveland	May 3, 1859.
Thomas R. Nichol	April 9, 1881.

Schools.—There is some evidence to support the assertion that as early as 1787 a frame school-house was erected at Cartertown, but documentary evidence, the deed of partition in the Carter estate, positively asserts, in 1793, that this building was then standing. It was known as the Mud Wasp, and stood on the site of the present ice-house on the estate of Samuel M. Felton. It was built by Collins McLaughlin, a Scotchman, who taught therein until he was compelled to abandon the occupation because of his deafness. Henry L. Powell was a pupil there in 1821, and Paul B. Carter later. In this school-house the early Methodists in that section of the county held occasional meetings. In 1828 a church and school-house was built in the Carter burial-ground, which was known as the "Ebenezer" Methodist Church. The funds necessary to erect this unpretentious meeting-house were contributed by John Lloyd, Gilead Carter, and others. Here a school was taught for many years, but finally it was taken down by Abraham Carter, and its site inclosed in the graveyard lot. The present school-house, known as "Franklin Public School," near the residence of Samuel M. Felton, was built in 1871.

Prior to 1800, Caleb Cobourn donated a lot of ground at Sneath's Corner, and a log school-house, thirty feet square and one story in height, was thereon erected. Between the years 1819 and 1823 the following pedagogues taught there: Silas Hoff, John Caldwell, George Powell, and Isaac Powell. The log house was used until 1824, when it was replaced by the present stone building, which originally was thirty feet square; it has been remodeled as occasion demanded.

The following is the list of directors of Chester township, which at first included Chester borough, all of Chester township, and Upland. In 1859 Chester borough was set off as a school district from the rest of the township, and the several boroughs as they were erected were also made separate districts:

1840, John H. Denning, Samuel Weaver; 1842, John Hinkson, Alexander McKeen; 1843, J. W. Hickman, Alexander McKeen; 1844, Joseph H. Hinkson, Isaac S. Williams; 1845, Joseph Taylor, Frederick J. Hinkson; 1846, Edward Darlington, Spencer McIlvain; 1847, William Weaver, Abram Cobourn; 1848, Peter W. Green, Isaac S. Williams; 1849, John Larkin, Charles D. Manley; 1850, Samuel Crozer, Jesse Young; 1851, Peter W. Green, F. J. Hinkson; 1852, Edmund K. Edwards, David S. Bunting; 1853, no report; 1854, David Irving, Samuel A. Crozer; 1855, D. S. Bunting, E. B. Loveland; 1856, Jeremiah Flickner, E. M. Edwards; 1857, Samuel A. Crozer, William L. Gregg; 1858, Peter W. Green, E. B. Loveland; 1859, E. R. Edwards, James Irving; 1860, S. A. Crozer, A. Castle; 1861, William L. Gregg, John Beatty; 1862, John Harvey, E. B. Loveland; 1863, James Kirkman, S. A. Crozer; 1864, David Rose, William L. Gregg; 1865, Israel Mattock, J. William Lewis; 1866, J. W. Lewis; 1867, David Rose, William Roebuck; 1868, Joseph A. Kite, Thomas J. Leiper; 1869, W. L. Gregg, George Grubb; 1870, David Rose, Reece Esrey; 1871, E. R. Edwards, John Eves; 1872, Joseph L. Carter, C. L. Pierce; 1873, Joseph Engle, John Beatty; 1874, Thomas B. Mace, W. Graham Flower; 1875, Jacob Ebright, C. L. Pierce; 1876, John Beatty, Joseph Engle; 1877, G. W. Flowers, Thomas Mace; 1878, Caleb L. Pierce, Jacob Ebright; 1879, David F. Rose, Joseph Engle; 1880, Thomas Mace, William G. Flower; 1881, Jacob Ebright, Caleb L. Pierce; 1882, Joseph Engle, David F. Rose; 1883, Thomas B. Mace, William G. Flower; 1884, Caleb L. Pierce, Jacob Ebright.

CHAPTER XXXIV.

THE BOROUGH OF UPLAND.

ALTHOUGH the site of the first mills erected in the province of Pennsylvania after the territory passed into the ownership of Penn were located within this municipal district, it nevertheless remained a part of the township of Chester until May 24, 1869, when the borough of Upland was incorporated by the Court of Common Pleas of Delaware County. The boundaries of the municipality were described in the order as follows:

"Beginning at a point on the north side of the Upland road where it crosses a stream of water called 'Ship Creek;' thence down the said Ship Creek, the several courses thereof, about eighty perches, to the east side of Chester Creek, at low-water mark; thence up the said creek at low-water mark, and on a line of the city of Chester, five hundred and eighty perches, to a stone on the east bank of the said Chester Creek, a corner of William West's land; thence by said West's land north nineteen and one-half degrees, east seventy-four perches and seventy-three one-hundredth of a perch to a stone; thence north eighteen and a half degrees, east ninety-six perches and three-tenths of a perch to a stone by William Maris' land; thence south seventy-three and a half perches, east ninety-seven perches, to a stone a corner of Abraham Lukens' land; thence by the said Lukens' land north twenty and three-fourth degrees, east forty-eight perches and seven-tenths of a perch to a stone a corner of Richard Wetherill's land; thence by the same south seventy-two degrees, east thirty perches and twenty-eight one-hundredths of a perch to another corner of said Wetherill's land; thence by the same north twenty-three degrees, east thirty-six perches and fifty-two one-hundredths of a perch to a stone another corner of the said Wetherill's land; thence by and through the same and through lands of J. Lewis Crozer south sixty-four degrees, east ninety-two perches to a stake in the west line of Chester Rural Cemetery; thence by the said cemetery south twenty-six and a half degrees, west forty perches and eight-tenths of a perch to a post on the north side of the Chester and Upland road; thence along the north side of the said Upland road south seventy-two and a half degrees, east eighty perches, and north seventy-one and three-fourth degrees, east seventeen perches, and thirty-four one-hundredths of a perch, to the place of beginning, containing three hundred and thirty-five acres of land."

Ten years subsequent to the erection of the borough, on Sept. 18, 1879, the court made an order adding to the incorporated area of the borough of Upland as follows:

"Beginning at a stone a corner of Abraham C. Lukens' land, and a corner of the said borough of Upland; thence partly by the said borough of Upland, and partly by the borough of North Chester, north twenty and one-half degrees, east ninety-four perches and fifteen one-hundredths of a perch to a stone, a corner of the said Abraham C. Lukens' land; thence partly by the same and partly by lands of the heirs of Jesse J. Maris, deceased, north seventy-seven degrees, west one-hundred and thirty perches and three-tenths of a perch to a stone; thence by lands of the said Jesse J. Maris, deceased, south five and one-fourth degrees, west eighty-five perches to a corner, a stone by Samuel A. Crozer's land, in a line of the said Upland borough; thence south seventy-three degrees, east ninety-seven perches, to the place of beginning, containing sixty-five acres two roods thirteen perches, thirty-nine acres two roods and two perches thereof being lands of the heirs of Jesse J. Maris, deceased, and twenty-six acres and eleven perches being lands of the said Abraham C. Lukens."

Prior to the dates given the act of April 21, 1851, dividing the township and the borough of Chester, was obtained, and by its provisions the elections for the township were directed to be held at the schoolhouse in Upland.

Forty years ago the site of the thriving borough of Upland was occupied only by the mansion-house of the then owner of the land, six tenement-houses for the mill-hands, a cooper-shop, a four-story stone grist-mill, and a frame saw-mill, with the usual out houses on ordinary farms. To-day it is one of the neatest manufacturing villages in the United States, containing a population approximating three thousand persons. On the hill-crests to the north of the village are located the palatial residences of the Crozer family, the well-kept grounds adding largely to the attractiveness of the place. The Chester Street Railway Company has extended its road to Upland, which affords easy access to the city and the mills, and many of the private residences and stores are supplied with gas by the Chester Gas Company. In 1854 the Bank of Delaware County issued notes of the denomination of twenty dollars, on which were engraved a view of Upland as a vignette. At the present time the same engraving is used as a head-piece on certificates of stock issued by that corporation.

By virtue of the charter incorporating Upland as a borough its local affairs have been controlled by a chief burgess and Council. Following is a list of these officials:

CHIEF BURGESSES OF UPLAND.

1869, Samuel A. Crozer; 1874, George K. Crozer; 1876, Robert H. Crozer; 1878, J. William Lewis; 1880, Robert H. Crozer; 1881, J. Lewis Crozer; 1882, George K. Crozer; 1883, J. Lewis Crozer; 1884, John P. Crozer.

MEMBERS OF BOROUGH COUNCIL.

1869, William Band, F. B. Jarman, J. Lewis Crozer, Benjamin Crowther, Robert H. Crozer, J. William Lewis; 1870, J. Lewis Crozer, Robert H. Crozer, William Band, Michael Leech, James Sample, J. William Lewis; 1872, Robert H. Crozer, Morris P. Hannum, George K. Crozer, F. B. Jarman, J. William Lewis, M. E. Parker; 1873, Morris P. Hannum, George K. Crozer, F. B. Jarman, J. William Lewis, Augur Castle, Robert H. Crozer; 1874, George W. Knowles, Samuel A. Crozer, F. B. Jarman, Morris P. Hannum, J. William Lewis, Robert H. Crozer; 1875, J. Lewis Crozer, Samuel A. Crozer, Benjamin F. Pretty, J. William Lewis, Robert H. Crozer, George W. Knowles; 1876, Samuel A. Crozer, George K. Crozer, William D. Howard, Benjamin F. Pretty, Morris P. Hannum, F. B. Jarman; 1877, George K. Crozer, Samuel A. Crozer, F. B. Jarman, J. William Lewis, George W. Knowles, William Robuck; 1878, Samuel A. Crozer, George W. Knowles, George K. Crozer, F. B. Jarman, H. Marshall, Joseph Dransfield, Jr.; 1879, Benjamin F. Pretty, George W. Knowles, William Howard, William Band, Samuel A. Crozer, William Grimrod; 1880, Samuel A. Crozer, George K. Crozer, J. William Lewis, Calvert Cardwell, William Newton, William Roebuck, William Grimrod; 1881, Samuel A. Crozer, George K. Crozer, John P. Crozer, William Grimrod, William Newton, Calvert Cardwell; 1882, Samuel A. Crozer, J. William Lewis, Calvert Cardwell, J. Perry Lukens, William Newton, Jacob Mills; 1883, Samuel A. Crozer, William Grimrod, William Maris, James W. Barker, Augur Castle, John P. Crozer; 1884, Samuel A. Crozer, George K. Crozer, William Maris, J. William Lewis, Dr. L. M. Bullock, Benjamin F. Compton.

JUSTICE OF THE PEACE.

Daniel G. Crompton, commissioned July 20, 1869, March 24, 1874, June 27, 1879, March 30, 1880.

The Pusey House.—The oldest building in the State of Pennsylvania is the Pusey house, at Upland, which is preserved by the Crozer family as a sacred relic connecting the olden times of the province with the active progressive present. The structure standing to-day, almost as it was when built by Caleb Pusey, is on the north side of the mill-race, to the west of the road leading to the bridge spanning Chester Creek, facing to the south, and is about thirty feet in length, fifteen feet in breadth, and one story in height, crowned with a hipped roof, which gives to it the appearance of being a story and a half building. The walls, which are noticeable in their thickness, are of stone and brick, while the floor is of broad solid oak planking. The brick part of the old wall was evidently put there to take the place of stones which became loose and fell out of position, a fact strongly supported by an inspection of the inner side, which shows no bricks at all. The bricks in the eastern gable were placed there, it is said, after Chester Mills had become the property of Samuel Shaw, when he repaired the structure. The house has two doors and two windows in the front, while a dormer-window is in the roof, and the roof itself has been several times renewed. A dwarfed door-way gives admission to the room, with low ceilings and the heavy beams supporting the floor above, still disclosing the marks of the broad axe which, two centuries ago, hewed the felled timber into form, and to the left of the room is a step-ladder, inclosed in a rude gangway, giving access to the apartments overhead. There is the old wide-mouthed fireplace (now inclosed), before whose hearth—whereon the ruddy flames flared and flickered two centuries ago—the founder of a great commonwealth and his trusty friend and agent, Pusey, sat discussing the prospects of their business enterprise, or laying plans for the future welfare of the colony.

If it be correct that Caleb Pusey made the noted visit, in 1688, to the Indian town on the Brandywine, where the iron-works of William Twaddell were subsequently erected, when the province was started from its propriety by the rumor that the aborigines were about to begin hostilities and massacre the whites, then, indeed, it is true that "Caleb Pusey, going out unarmed into the forest to meet a threatened attack of the savages, is a more heroic figure than blustering Miles Standish, girt with the sword he fought with in Flanders" To the left of the fireplace, within easy reach, still remains the deep square hole in the wall which the early settlers frequently made in their dwellings, as a sort of tobacco-pouch, so that the consolation which comes with smoke should be always close at hand and accessible to their guests and to themselves

Caleb Pusey was one of the most active men of the early settlers in Pennsylvania, honest, sagacious, and absolutely fearless Notwithstanding his ignorance of "school learning,"[1] he has left an impress on our State history which will ever remain He was a last-maker by trade, and emigrated in 1682, accompanied with his wife, Ann, settling at the present site of Upland His name is inseparable from that of Chester Mills, although long before his death he had parted with all interest in the land and business carried on there He died in February, 1726/7, leaving no male descendant bearing his name

It is hardly necessary, at this day, to correct the impression conveyed by Richard Townsend, in the extract published by Proud,[2] or the direct statement of Stephen Day, in his "Historical Collections of Pennsylvania," that Richard Townsend "erected the dwelling for the accommodation of his family while he was tending the first mill erected in the province" That statement has been corrected so often that it may be accepted, if any historical fact has been established, as no longer a subject for refutation The land on which the house stood was a tract of one hundred acres patented to Pusey, Fourth month 10, 1684, and was known by the name "Landing Ford," the King's road crossing Chester just above his plantation

The Chester Mills.—The first mill in the province of Pennsylvania was the Swedish water-mill, built by Governor Printz, on the east side of Cobb's Creek, near the noted Blue Bell Tavern, at Paschalville, in the county of Philadelphia But at the time Penn obtained possession of the province that structure had fallen into disuse and had been abandoned to decay, it necessarily having been rudely constructed The first mills in the county of Chester were brought to the province in the "Welcome," with Penn, having been framed and fitted so that they might be put together with expedition when the land of promise had been reached Previous to the departure of William Penn from England, in 1682, he entered into a verbal copartnership with Philip Ford, John Bellars, Daniel Worley, Daniel Quare, John Barker, Richard Townsend, John Bickley, Thomas Burberry, and Caleb Pusey, all at that time in England, and it was agreed among them to erect one or more water-mills, to the cost of which they were to contribute in proportionate shares, for the agreement among themselves partook of the nature of a stock company, and each party received the interest in the venture in proportion to the amount contributed Caleb Pusey was appointed agent and manager of the "said joint concern" The tract on which the mill was erected was patented to Pusey, "for the use of the mill," Second month 5, 1690 Many of the partners in the enterprise never came to the province William Penn, we are told by Hon Joseph J Lewis, in his sketches of Chester County, was present when the first dam was made It is documentary evidence, in an old deed, dated Dec 19, 1705, now owned by the Crozer family, that in 1683, Caleb Pusey, "with the advice of the sd Proprietary and such others of the said partners as there were in the Province," erected a "corn mill on Chester creek, near his new dwelling house," which mill, with the dam belonging to it, were soon carried away by the flood Caleb Pusey afterwards, by advice of Penn and "ye other partner that was here" (doubtless Richard Townsend), erected a little above where the first mill stood another grist- and saw-mill upon part of the twenty acres patented for the use of the mill at the cost of the firm The second dam was in turn swept away by flood, and he erected a third dam, at the distance of a mile beyond where the others were located, and constructed a race to convey the water to the mill. The expenses attending these constant repairs were so great that the outlay far exceeded the earnings of the mill, and Pusey borrowed money from time to time from Robert Turner, a merchant of Philadelphia, in order to pay for the improvements

In settlement of these advances Pusey, on June 21, 1688, drew a bill of exchange on Daniel Worley & Co (the court record gives the name Whearley), merchants, of London, partners in the mills, for one hundred and eighty-seven pounds, payable at forty days' sight to Robert Turner or order On Oct 15, 1688, the original bill was presented to the drawee, who said "that he would not accept the s[d] bill for that the others Concerned in the same would not allow their proportionable shares," and the bill was protested At the following March court, 1689/90, Turner sued Pusey, who came into court and acknowledged judgment for £293 10*s* 4*d* Considerable delay was had in issuing execution, apparently with the intention of having the matter adjusted, but the partners still refusing, with the exception of Penn and Pusey—Richard Townsend had sold his interest to Pusey several years before—the mills were finally taken on execution, June 14, 1692, and the coroner Jacob Simcock,

[1] Smith's "History of Pennsylvania," Hazard's Register, vol vii p 83

[2] History of Pennsylvania, vol i p. 229

—Pusey was sheriff of the county at the time,—was required to sell the estate in payment of the debt. The property was assessed at five hundred and fifty pounds. It was offered at public sale, but found no buyers, and on Sept. 13, 1692, the coroner sold the interest of the delinquent parties to Robert Turner at the appraisement, and the latter sold his interest to Samuel Carpenter, who, for thirteen years, until Dec. 19, 1705, was a partner with Penn and Pusey in the milling business. Doubtless when repairs were made to the mill, in 1699, the rude iron vane bearing the initials W. P. (William Penn), S. C. (Samuel Carpenter), C. P. (Caleb Pusey), and the date, 1699, was placed on the building. When Richard Flower owned the property the old vane surmounted the dwelling-house of the owner, but on gusty nights, turning in the wind, it squeaked and groaned so noisily that it was taken down. In 1870, Reese W. Flower presented it to the Historical Society of Pennsylvania, and it now points the wind on that building, although so added to and gilded that those who remember it as it was in Upland would hardly recognize it now.

In 1705, Carpenter sold his interest to Pusey, and on March 15, 1706, Pusey sold his interest in "all those three water corn-mills and saw-mills, commonly called and known by the name of Chester Mills," to William Penn, and the property subsequently had several owners. About 1745, the old mill having been almost destroyed by an accidental fire, a new stone mill was built by Joseph Pennell, the then owner of the property, and the grandfather of John P. Crozer, who was a builder, worked on the structure, which stood, I think, until 1858, when it in turn was destroyed by fire. The dam-breast was built in 1752 by Samuel Shaw while he was owner of the property.

In 1764, Shaw was returned as constable of Chester township, an office which in colonial days was selected only from owners of real estate. Shaw was not anxious to serve the public in that capacity, and to avoid the honor thus thrust upon him presented the following petition to the court:

"*To the Honourable Justices of the Court of Private Sessions, held at Chester on the 26th day of March*, 1764:

"The petition of Samuel Shaw, of Chester Township, Miller, Humbly Showeth—

"That your Petitioner understands that he is on the return for the office of Constable of the said Township for the ensuing year: That your Petitioner has formerly served that office, and there are several others places that have never served, and it being a custom that all places in the s[d] Township should serve in their turns before any should be obliged to serve again, your Petitioner apprehends it will not fall to his turn to serve for several years yet to come; and your Petitioner has annexed a list of some persons' names who are Inhabitants of the said Township, and have never yet served, as your Petitioner stands instructed.

"That your Petitioner has lived but a few years in the said Township, and now hath a very large family, and is also involved in such a multiplicity of business at present that he cannot serve the said office at this time without greatly prejudicing his own private affairs. That when your Petitioner dwelt in the county of Philadelphia he was commissioned by the Go[r] as a Major and Captain of a Company, and being an old regular soldier did discipline several other Companies as well as his own without any reward from the Government, which proved a Considerable Expense to him, as well as a hinderance to his own private concerns.

"Your Petitioner therefore most humbly Prays that your Honors will be pleased to take the premises into consideration and excuse him at present from the said Office of Constable, and appoint some other person to that office in his stead.

"And your Petitioner shall ever pray, etc.

"SAMUEL SHAW."

Attached to the above quaint document is the following: "List of Persons who have not served as Constables: Jacob Howell, Jr., John Eyre, George Spear, David Jackson, Henry Platt, Thomas Sharpless, Thomas Roman, Philip Roman, Jacob Ridgeway, Valentine Weaver, John Salkeld (part of a year formerly)."

On Oct. 31, 1777, Gen. Washington ordered Gen. Potter to remove the millstones at Chester Mills so that no flour could be ground there for the British army, and we know that these orders were obeyed, but where the stones were removed to is not known. Subsequent to the Revolution, in the shrinkage in the value of real estate, the Chester Mills passed out of the ownership of Samuel Shaw, and were purchased by Henry Hale Graham, who subsequently sold them to his son-in-law, Richard Flower. In 1793, Richard Flower purchased from Oliver Evans the right to use the latter's patent "for elevating grain and meal from the lower to the upper stories, and conveying the same from one part of the mill to another, and for cooling the meal and attending the Bolting Hoppers." The motive-power, we learn from this old document, then consisted "of two Water wheels situate on Chester Creek . . . called Chester Mills." The same year Richard Flower made entry under the act of Assembly at the county court of the brands exclusively used by him at these mills, which were "Chester Superfine," "Chester," "Chester Middlings, No. 2–96," "No. 4–98." While he was still engaged in milling, Richard Flower made several successful ventures in shipping flour to Europe. When the misunderstanding existed between France and the United States, previous to 1800, he, in connection with his brother, John, his half-brother, Reece Wall, and his brother-in-law, Capt. John McKeever, loaded three vessels with flour and cleared them for Liverpool. All three of the ships were captured by French cruisers and condemned in French prize courts, although one of the vessels was within sixty miles of the Delaware Bay when taken. The loss he sustained by French spoliation was so great that he never again attempted to seek a foreign market for his breadstuff. During the war of 1812 the American troops were instructed to impress all the flour at Chester Mills for the army, but the government paid full value for all that was taken. In 1824 he was succeeded at Chester Mills by his son, William G. Flower, who continued to operate them until the death of Richard Flower, in 1843. The Chester Mills were sold to John W. Ashmead, under proceedings in the Orphans'

John P. Crozer

—Pusey was sheriff of the county at the time,—was required to sell the mills in payment of the debt. The property was assessed at five hundred and fifty pounds. It was offered at public sale, but found no buyers, and on Sept. 10, 1692, the coroner sold the interest of the delinquent parties to Robert Turner at the appraisement, and the latter sold his interest to Samuel Carpenter, who, for thirteen years, until Dec. 19, 1705, was a partner with Penn and Pusey in the milling business. Doubtless when repairs were made to the mill, in 1699, the vane-iron bearing the initials W. P. (William Penn), S. C. (Samuel Carpenter), C. P. (Caleb Pusey), and the date 1699, was placed on the building. When Richard Flower owned the property the old vane surmounted the dwelling-house of the owner, but on gusty nights, turning in the wind, it squeaked and groaned so noisily that it was taken down. In 1870 Reese W. Flower presented it to the Historical Society of Pennsylvania, and it now points the wind on that building, although so oiled it and gilded that those who remember it as it was in Upland would hardly recognize it now.

In 1705, Carpenter sold his interest to Pusey, and on March 16, 1706, Pusey sold his interest in "all those three water corn mills and one mill, commonly called and known by the name of Chester Mills," to William Penn, and the property subsequently had several owners. About 1740, the old mill having been almost destroyed by an accidental fire, a new stone mill was built by Joseph Pennell, the then owner of the property, and the grandfather of John P. Crozer, who was a builder, worked on the structure, which stood, I think, until 1855, when it in turn was destroyed by fire. The dam-breast was built in 1753 by Samuel Shaw while he was owner of the property.

In 1764, Shaw was returned as constable of Chester township, an office which in colonial days was selected only from owners of real estate. Shaw was not anxious to serve the public in that capacity, and to avoid the honor thus thrust upon him presented the following petition to the court:

"*To the Honourable* [illegible] *ber on the 26th day of* [illegible]

"The petition of Samuel Shaw, [illegible] Miller, Humbly Showeth—

"That your Petitioner [illegible] office of Constable [illegible] your Petitioner [illegible] others places the [illegible] places in the s^d Township [illegible] be obliged to serve [illegible] his turn to serve [illegible] annexed a list of [illegible] Township, and [illegible] structed.

"That your Petitioner [illegible] ship, and now hath [illegible] multiplicity of business [illegible] at this time with [illegible] when your Petitioner [illegible] missioned by the [illegible] an old regular sol[illegible] has been without any [illegible] considerable [illegible] business.

"Your Petitioner therefore most humbly Prays that your Honours will be pleased to take the premises into consideration and excuse him at present from the said Office of Constable, and appoint some other person to that office in his stead.

"And your Petitioner shall ever pray, etc.

"SAMUEL SHAW."

Attached to the above quaint document is the following: "List of Persons who have not served as Constables: Jacob Howell, Jr., John Eyre, George Spear, David Jackson, Henry Platt, Thomas Sharpless, Thomas Roman, Philip Roman, Jacob Ridgeway, Valentine Weaver, John Salkeld (part of a year formerly)."

On Oct. 31, 1777, Gen. Washington ordered Gen. Potter to remove the millstones at Chester Mills so that no flour could be ground there for the British army, and we know that these orders were obeyed, but where the stones were removed to is not known. Subsequent to the Revolution, in the shrinkage in the value of real estate, the Chester Mills passed out of the ownership of Samuel Shaw, and were purchased by Henry Hale Graham, who subsequently sold them to his son-in-law, Richard Flower. In 1793, Richard Flower purchased from Oliver Evans the right to use the latter's patent "for elevating grain and meal from the lower to the upper stories, and conveying the same from one part of the mill to another, and for cooling the meal and attending the Bolting Hoppers." The motive-power, we learn from this old document, then consisted "of two Water wheels situate on Chester Creek . . . called Chester Mills." The same year Richard Flower made entry under the act of Assembly at the county court of the brands exclusively used by him at these mills, which were "Chester Superfine," "Chester," "Chester Middlings, No. 2—96," "No. 4-96." While he was still engaged in milling, Richard Flower made several successful ventures in shipping flour to Europe. When the misunderstanding existed between France and the United States, previous to 1800, he, in connection with his brother, John, his half-brother, Reese Wall, and his brother-in-law, Capt. John McKeever, loaded three vessels with flour and cleared them for Liverpool. All three of the ships were captured by French cruisers and condemned in French prize courts, although one of the vessels was within sixty miles of the Delaware Bay when taken. The loss he sustained by French spoliation was so great that he never again attempted to seek a foreign market for his breadstuff. During the war of 1812 the American troops were instructed to impress all the flour at Chester Mills for the army, but the government paid full value for all that was taken. In 1825 he was succeeded at Chester Mills by his son, William G. Flower, who continued to operate them until the death of Richard Flower, in 1843. The Chester Mills were sold to John W. Ashmead, under proceedings in the Orphans'

John P. Crozer

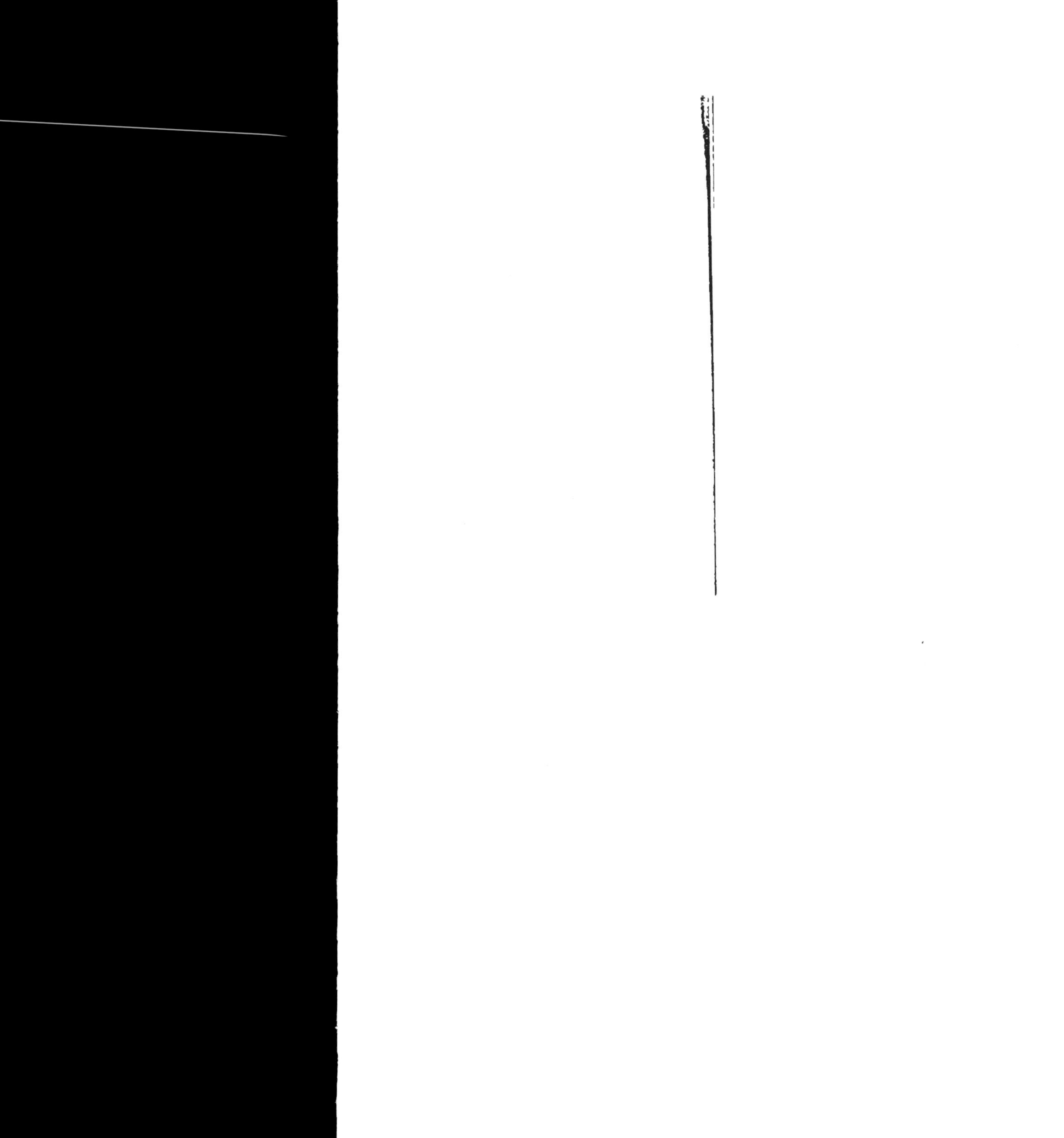

Court, and in 1845 the latter conveyed them, together with a tract of land of something over sixty acres, to John P. Crozer

In 1845, after the purchase from John W. Ashmead of the Chester Mills, John P Crozer immediately made preparation for erecting a cotton-factory at that place. The following year he built the mill known as No 1, a five-story stone structure, one hundred and thirty-eight feet in length by fifty in width, and also erected a number of stone dwelling-houses for the operatives In June, 1847, there were forty-six tenements on the property, and an eighty horse-power engine had been attached to the factory, so that in the event of the water in the creek at any time proving insufficient to operate the machinery the mill might not be compelled to suspend for that cause At that date there were one hundred and fifty power-looms, eleven self-acting mules, with three thousand eight hundred and sixty-four spindles, while the whole number of spindles amounted to six thousand This mill has been much enlarged, and at present contains eight thousand nine hundred and eighty-eight throstle-spindles, two thousand nine hundred and ninety-two mule-spindles, and two hundred and ninety-eight looms In 1852, John P Crozer built mill No 2, one hundred and fifty-eight feet in length by fifty-two feet in width, four stories and an attic in height, and containing seven thousand spindles and one hundred and fifty looms This mill, after it passed to Samuel A. Crozer, was enlarged, and now contains seven thousand four hundred and fifty-six throstle-spindles, four thousand four hundred mule-spindles, and nine cards In 1863, to meet the demand for the goods he then manufactured, John P Crozer erected mill No 3, fifty-two feet by two hundred and twenty-two feet, four stories in height, in which were used six thousand spindles and one hundred and fifty looms This mill contains seven thousand one hundred and forty throstle-spindles, two thousand one hundred and twelve mule-spindles, and two hundred and fifty-six looms Mills No 1 and No 3 have capacity to consume ninety bales of cotton weekly, and produce eighty-two cases of goods per week William I Woodward is manager of the mills of John P Crozer's Sons After the death of Mr. Crozer, in 1866, the mills were divided among his sons, Samuel A Crozer taking No 2 mill, and Nos 1 and 3 being operated by J Lewis, George K and Robert H Crozer, under the firm-name of J P Crozer & Sons

In the township of Springfield, Delaware Co, at a place called for a time West Dale, now Swarthmore, and near the college of that name (which stands on a part of the property), in the same house, were born two persons destined to be celebrated in their respective spheres of action Benjamin West, one of America's most celebrated painters and a president of the British Royal Academy, and John P. Crozer, a manufacturer, and especially noted for his philanthropic and benevolent actions

John Price Crozer was born Jan 13, 1793, and was the son of John and Sarah Price Crozer

The first ancestor of John P Crozer in America was James Crozer, who, with his four brothers,—Samuel, John, Robert, and Andrew,—emigrated from Ireland in the early part of the eighteenth century Soon after arriving in this country James Crozer was married to a lady of English descent named Gleave, whose parents resided in Springfield

John Crozer, the father of John P, married Sarah Price, daughter of John Price, of English descent He was a carpenter, and pursued his occupation in Philadelphia till after his marriage After residing for a short time on a farm owned by the estate of John Knowles, of which he was executor, he purchased the farm at Springfield, now owned by the trustees of Swarthmore College, and upon which John P. was born Though following the humble trade of a carpenter he possessed an education far superior to his calling, and was a good Latin scholar and well versed in the classics His religious views were in sympathy with the society of Friends, though he was not a member of any denomination

Sarah Price Crozer was a woman of strong religious convictions, gentle and charitable towards all She had been educated as an Episcopalian, and was a sincere and earnest friend to all real Christianity, without regard to creed She endeavored to instill by her life and teaching the principles of godliness and true grace in the minds of her children, and to teach them the ways that lead to true greatness

The children of John and Sarah P Crozer were Elizabeth (who became the wife of John Lewis), James, Sarah (who became Mrs Samuel Y Campbell), John Price, and Samuel

The educational advantages of John P Crozer were very limited He began attending school at the age of six years at the little stone school-house about three-quarters of a mile from his home, and here all the days of his school-life were spent excepting a short term of three months at a school about two miles away The amount of knowledge that could be acquired at these schools was very meagre, and was mostly comprised in the three "r's,"—"readin', ritin', and 'rithmetic" His studies were, however, prosecuted vigorously, and supplemented by the small but well-selected library of his father he acquired a much better education than was usually attained at that day

At the early age of fourteen he became a member of the First Baptist Church of Philadelphia, having been converted under the ministrations of the Rev Dr Staughton

From his early childhood he had been accustomed to the hard labor of the farm, and from his seventeenth year had rested upon his young shoulders almost its entire management Upon attaining his majority, in consideration of this fact his father had given him a one-third interest in its profits In

1816 his father died, and his mother's death occurred the next year.

He was very desirous of purchasing the farm, and preventing its falling into the hands of strangers, but upon carefully considering the matter in all its lights he became convinced that it was not practicable.

In 1820, after leasing the farm pending its sale, he made an extended trip through Pennsylvania, Ohio, Kentucky, and the then sparsely-settled country in Indiana and Illinois. The trip was made almost entirely upon horseback, and covered a distance of twenty-seven hundred miles, extending from April to December. Upon his return the farm had been sold, and his share of the property was about two thousand four hundred dollars. This, together with a little more than one thousand dollars additional, was his sole capital, and with it he began his business career.

His first enterprise was in connection with Mr. G. G. Leiper, who had bought the home-farm, and was that of conducting a saw- and merchant grist-mill. The capital was to be furnished equally, and the rent of the mill owned by Mr. Leiper was to offset Mr. Crozer's personal services. After prosecuting the business vigorously, and accumulating a large stock of lumber, the depression in business prevented a ready or profitable sale, and to prevent a failure, which he foresaw, he retired from the business with the consent of his partner. After looking around for a new field, he decided to engage in cotton manufacturing, and to this end rented Mr. G. G. Leiper's mill on Crum Creek. His entire capital was about three thousand seven hundred dollars; this, with two thousand dollars put into the business by Mr. John Lewis, was the entire capital at commencement.

The business was at first small, and many were the difficulties to be overcome, but by unceasing personal effort and patient, tireless economy he was at last upon the high road to success. In 1825 he bought the property known as Mattson's paper-mill, on the west branch of Chester Creek, and after altering it as seemed necessary, he moved his machinery here in the autumn of that year. From this time onward his business interests grew larger and larger, and continued to increase as long as he remained in business. In 1845 he purchased the Flower estate, about two miles from Chester, and gave it the name of Upland. Here he erected an elegant and spacious mansion, and to it he removed from West Branch on April 19, 1847. From this time to the date of his death he made his home at Upland, and dispensed that generous hospitality for which the place is noted. Though a man of great business cares and ventures to engross his time, his enlarged and advanced views of the duties of a Christian, and of the responsibilities of the enjoyment of property, made him an active and incessant worker in benevolent projects.

Mr. Crozer died at his home at Upland, on Sunday morning, March 11, 1866. Among the many good works he accomplished, and to which he was a liberal contributor, were the building of the First Baptist Church at Upland, the endowment of a Professorship in the University at Lewisburg, the founding of the Normal School at Upland, after his death endowed by his family and now the Crozer Theological Seminary. He was president of the Pennsylvania Colonization Society; president of the board of directors of the American Baptist Publication Society; president of the Pennsylvania Training-School for Feeble-Minded Children, at Media; president of Home for Friendless Children at Twelfth and Fitzwater Streets, Philadelphia; president of Women's Hospital at Philadelphia; president of Pennsylvania Baptist Education Society. He was one of the founders of the Christian Commission, and, together with George H. Stuart, represented the city of Philadelphia at the meeting in the city of New York, on Nov. 14, 1861, at which the Commission originated. During the war of the Rebellion he gave the use of his school at Upland for a hospital. It would be almost impossible to enumerate the services of this benefactor of human kind, so numerous are they, and his benefactions seem to have been guided by an intelligence more than human. He passed away in the seventy-fourth year of his age, in the full possession of his strength of mind, still planning future acts of benevolence.

Mr. Crozer was married on the 12th of March, 1825, to Miss Sallie L. Knowles, the daughter of a near neighbor of his youth. She was a lady of intelligence and education, and an active participant in all of his plans for good. In addition to grace of mind she had that grace of the heart which springs from pure goodness and innate, true Christianity. To them were born in the fullness of time nine children, —Samuel A., Margaret, Elizabeth, J. Lewis, Sallie K., James, George K., Robert H., and Emma. Of these James died Oct. 25, 1838, Sallie in August, 1852, and Margaret in March, 1870. His widow died August 3, 1882, aged eighty-two years.

The Schools of Upland.—Prior to the year 1849 the children residing at Upland were compelled to attend school at Sneath's Corner, or at the "Old Mud Wasp" at Cartertown. The distance from Upland to these schools was a serious difficulty to the residents of the village, for in the winter season and early spring the roads would often for weeks together be almost impassable, the clay soil having softened to a thick adhesive mud. Female children frequently could not go to school for days together. John P. Crozer, in the year mentioned, proposed to the school directors of Chester township that if they would establish a school at Upland he, at his personal expense, would erect a building which could be used exclusively for school purposes without cost to the board. This offer was accepted, a house was built on Rose Street, not far from the Pusey house, a school was established, and Mrs. Warren Dixon was employed to teach the pupils. For nine years this building was used by the directors, but in 1858 the number of children applying for admission to the public school compelled the erection of a new building A lot was purchased at the corner of Sixth and Upland Streets, and the brick school-house known as No. 1 was built In 1880 it was enlarged, and has now accommodations for four schools Upland had increased so much in population that in 1868 the Hill school-house, a stone building known as No 2, was erected, and two schools established therein In the six schools at the present time about three hundred and twenty-five pupils are in attendance

When the borough of Upland was incorporated, in 1869, it was made an independent school district In 1880, John W Parsons was appointed principal of the schools, a position which he still retains

The directors of the public school of Upland borough have been as follows

1869, Rev J W Pendleton, Benjamin F Pretty, Rev Dr George D B Pepper, George H Crozer, James Blight. 1870 James Sample, Augur Castle, 1872, George Vansant, William Band, 1873, Rev Dr George D B Pepper, Daniel G Compton, 1874, John Gilston, Morris P Hannum, 1875, Benjamin F Pretty, Calvert Cardwell, 1876, Joseph Dalton, Jr, Daniel G Compton, Timothy Keeley, 1877, William Baud, William Give, 1878, Mark W Allen, John Gilston, Morris P Hannum, 1879, James West, Augur Castle, 1880, J Parry Lukins, Joseph H Carroll, Benjamin Crowther, James H Moore, 1881, Benjamin Crowther, Garrett Pendleton, 1882, John McMurray, John Greenaway, 1883, Lewis J Smith, George T Watson, Joseph H Carroll, 1884, Dr Isaac Crowther, James A Forsyth

The Upland Baptist Church—In the spring of 1851 John P. Crozer began the erection of a church edifice, previous to which date religious services conducted by Baptist clergymen were held in a room in the factory In March of the following year the structure was so far advanced that it was dedicated, and on Nov 17, 1852, when fully completed, was publicly recognized as a house of worship, prominent Baptist clergymen taking part in the ceremonies on that occasion Rev John Duncan was the first pastor, but he resigned in 1854, and Rev William Wilder was called and accepted the pastorate of the church, continuing in the discharge of the duties appertaining thereto until July, 1865 In November of that year Rev James M Pendleton was installed as the minister, a relationship which was continued eighteen years, until the latter part of October, 1883, when he resigned One night in the early spring of the year 1871 the reverend gentleman had a remarkable adventure with several burglars He was awakened by a light in his study, which adjoined his sleeping-room, and, believing that by neglect the gas had been allowed to burn at that late hour, arose As he approached the room the light was extinguished, and a determined voice ordered the clergyman to return to his bed and lie quiet This command was obeyed, and the owner of the articles which were then undergoing inspection in another room by strangers overheard one of the intruders remark to the other, "If he don't lie still put a bullet through him" The doctor remained quiet until daylight came, when he arose to find the burglars had gone, as also a gold watch, a pair of gold spectacles, and thirty dollars in money During Dr. Pendleton's pastorate the church prospered, and in 1873 the edifice was for the second time enlarged, the improvements made in that year costing fourteen thousand dollars, the first addition to the original building having been made in 1860 Not only did the membership of the Upland Church increase threefold during the pastorate of Rev Dr Pendleton, but a mission chapel was established at Leiperville, and another at Bridgewater, while the Baptist Church at Village Green and in South Chester were originally offshoots from the parent sanctuary at Upland The church in the borough since Dr Pendleton's resignation has been without a regular pastor, the services being conducted by Prof E H. Johnson, of the Crozer Theological Seminary, with marked success, for during the brief period in which he preached there one hundred and thirty persons were added to the roll of members Rev C L Williams, a recent graduate of the Crozer Seminary, is at present in charge of the church The brick parsonage was built by John P Crozer in 1855, and is a roomy, comfortable dwelling

Crozer Theological Seminary—Just beyond the incorporated limits of the city of Chester, to the northwest and within the borough of Upland, is located the institution of learning which was established by the Crozer family, in 1868, as a memorial of their father, the late John P Crozer In 1857, Mr Crozer had begun the erection of the present main building, at a cost of forty-five thousand dollars, with the intention of locating there a normal school, and in September of the following year it was formally opened as an academy of the higher grades of intellectual training, and as such was continued for several years

The war-storm having burst with fury on the country, early in June, 1862, Mr Crozer tendered, without charge, to the United States the building as a hospital, conditioned only that it should be returned to him, after it was no longer required, in as good condition as when he placed it at the disposal of the government The offer was accepted, the necessary changes in the building made, and on June 18, 1862, Dr. George K Wood, formerly an assistant surgeon in the regular army, was appointed surgeon-in-charge of the hospital As soon as it was ascertained that a hospital would be established there, on the date last mentioned a number of ladies organized a society known as "The Soldiers' Relief Association," of which Mrs Samuel A Crozer was first directress, Mrs Abby Kerlin, assistant directress, Mrs Samuel Arthur, secretary, Mrs J. Lewis Crozer, assistant secretary, Mrs John P Crozer, treasurer, with a directress in every township in the county For some time the sick, disabled, and dying soldiers in this hospital were supplied with all the delicacies and luxuries so necessary to tempt the appetite and assuage the anguish of the inmates of that house of bodily suffering The first patient was admitted July 17, 1862, and on the 29th of the same month the steamer "State of Maine" arrived at Chester with two hundred and twenty-three sick and wounded Union soldiers on board, who had been captured in the Seven Days' Fight before Richmond, and had just been exchanged The building contained nearly a thousand beds, but so great was the demand made upon the hospital that thirteen hundred persons, including patients, surgeons, attendants, and guards, were gathered within its walls Until the 14th of July, 1863, the hospital was used almost exclusively for wounded Union soldiers, but after the battle of Gettysburg the Confederate wounded, left on the field by Gen Lee in his retreat, were so many that the government was compelled to designate a certain hospital for the reception of the rebels, and the one at Chester was selected for that purpose

In July, 1862, Rev John Pinckney Hammond, a brother of Surgeon-General Hammond, and at the time rector of St Paul's Church, Chester, was appointed chaplain of the hospital This selection proved unsatisfactory to a large number of the most active friends of the institution, whose desire was to minister to the wants of the unfortunate men who were sent thither, unrestrained by cumbersome and unnecessary rules, the enforcement of which caused much difficulty in the working of the auxiliary bodies connected with the institution Dr J L Le Conte, the noted entomologist, on July 14, 1862, was appointed to succeed Dr Wood He adhered firmly to the rules already promulgated respecting visitations to the hospital, which largely obstructed the unselfish and earnest work of the ladies of "The Soldiers' Relief Association," while returning nothing in exchange for the hindrance offered The dispute between the hospital authorities and the people culminated in petitions for the removal of these officers being presented to the appointing power, and at last they were removed in the fall of 1862, but not until Hon John M Broomall, the then member of Congress, had repeatedly demanded such action Dr Eben Smith succeeded Dr Le Conte

After the hospital was set apart for the reception of Confederate wounded, a picket-fence, twelve feet in height, was built, surrounding the grounds, and guards were stationed to prevent the escape of convalescent prisoners of war Notwithstanding the vigilance of the authorities, one dark stormy night in August, 1863, Capt Edward Shay, of the Sixteenth Mississippi Regiment, and Lieut Davis, of Gen Trimble's staff, evaded the guard and escaped

The hospital furnished accommodation for more than six thousand wounded soldiers, and many men to-day, North and South, remember with grateful hearts the kindness they received while inmates of the hospital at Chester While located here, Dr Ellwood Harvey was assistant surgeon from July, 1862, to September of the same year, Dr F Ridgely Graham, from October, 1862, to June, 1863, and Dr J L Forwood from July 21, 1863 Dr. Charles J. Morton was also assistant surgeon.

At the conclusion of the war, in 1865, the building was returned to its owner, and in December of the same year Col Theodore Hyatt leased the property until the summer vacation of 1868. John P Crozer having died March 11, 1866, as soon as the Pennsylvania Military Academy had vacated the building the Crozer family, as a memorial of their father, as before stated, determined to set it apart as a Baptist Theological Seminary, and it was formally dedicated to that object on Friday, Oct 2, 1868

The seminary has, beside the land and buildings, an endowment fund of two hundred and fifty thousand dollars, so judiciously invested that the interest therefrom meets fully the ordinary expenses of the institution. There is also a lecture fund of ten thousand dollars, the interest of which is applied to defraying the cost of lectures on subjects not directly appertaining to the educational course The Crozer family in 1882 gave fifty thousand dollars to endow a professorship as a memorial of their mother, the late Mrs Sallie K Crozer Connected with the seminary and erected on the campus is "Pearl Hall," founded by William Bucknell, in memory of his late wife, Margaret, daughter of John P Crozer, and the name it bears —Pearl—is the signification of Margaret in the Latin tongue Mr Bucknell's gift, including the sum expended in the structure and books, amounted to fifty thousand dollars Pearl Hall was formally opened on June 14, 1871, one of the conditions of the trust being that the library shall be free to the young men of Delaware County The building, a Greek cross, is of serpentine stone, the floor of the main apartment laid in tiles, and is admirably arranged for the purposes of the library, which comprises about ten thousand volumes, a large number being works of reference, but in the collection are many early-printed and scarce books In a few instances the only known copies of several theological treatises extant are to be found in this library In 1881, Mr Bucknell gave an additional sum of ten thousand dollars, the interest of which is to be applied yearly to the purchase of books for the library One of the conditions is as follows

"If at any time the inhabitants of Delaware County should be debarred by any action of the Trustees or Faculty from the privilege of consulting the Library, or should the Library ever cease to bear the 'Bucknell' name, I wish this ten thousand dollars to be taken as the foundation of a Public Library for Delaware County, that being my native county, by any corporate body of Christian men who will secure with this fund only pure, moral, and religious literature, and who will protect the Library by charter from any possibility of indebtedness"

The seminary building is of brick stuccoed, two hundred feet in length, forty in width, and three stories in height, with basement From the rear of the building is an addition, forty feet wide and fifty feet in length, at right angles to the main structure. The present faculty consist of Rev Henry G Weston, D D, president and professor of Preaching and Pastoral Duties; Rev. George R. Bliss, D.D., LL.D., professor of Biblical Interpretation; Rev. John C. Long, D.D., professor of Church History; Rev. Elias H. Johnson, D.D., professor of Christian Theology; Rev. James M. Stiffler, D.D., professor of New Testament Exegesis; and Rev. Barnard C. Taylor, A.M., assistant professor of Biblical Interpretation.

Upland Lodge, No. 428, K. of P.—This lodge was instituted May 21, 1874, with twenty charter members, and at present contains one hundred and twenty-four members. The Past Chancellors are here given: George Booth, Mark W. Allen, Jefferson W. Chalfant, James West, James Holme, John Gilston, B. F. Pretty, Samuel J. Lee, Lewis J. Smith, John W. Allen, George Phillips, John O. June, Thomas O. Bryan, William Hardman, William Miller, William Burns, Alexander McEwen, John Hepworth, John Nichols, Albert Chowish, George E. Forsythe, Henry O. Bryan, A. F. Alexander, Robert S. Bentley, G. A. McDaniel, and Bristol R. Lord. The present secretary is Lewis J. Smith.

CHAPTER XXXV.

SOUTH CHESTER BOROUGH.

THE whole of the territory now included within the municipal boundaries of South Chester was part of the enormous tract granted by Queen Christina, of Sweden, on Aug. 20, 1653, to Capt. Hans Ammundson Besk, which extended from Marcus Hook Creek to Chester Creek. Besk, it seems, never entered into possession of this land, and after the British power acquired title to the province, and previous to Nov. 25, 1679, Albert Hendricks had received a patent from the English Governor for a tract containing five hundred acres, lying between Lamokin Run and Haeryck Kill (Hendricks' Run, and now known as Harwick Run). The land thus patented to Hendricks was known as "Lamoco," or, as now written, Lamokin. On this tract were located the farms of James Laws and John Jeffrey, along the river, while that part of the farm of John W. Ashmead west of Lamokin Run, all of Jeremiah W. Fleckwir, Jennie Carr, Crossman Lyons, the Taylor lands, and that part of the farm of Daniel Robinson lying east of his house on a line running northwest to intersect with Highland Avenue, a short distance above the Frick mansion, were also included therein. The remainder of the territory was part of a patent of five hundred and fifty acres surveyed July 30, 1675, to John Johnston, James Justason, and Peter Hendrickson, "adjoining to the said River side between two creeks, the one called Marrity's Creek dividing this from yᵉ land of Marityes Hook, and the other called Harwick's Creek, which at the mouth thereof divideth this from the land Called Lamokey."[1] Within this tract on the river were the farms of John J. Thurlow, Dr. Hayes, and Erasmus Morton, and above the post road was the Daniel Robinson farm, other lands of John J. Thurlow, and Erasmus Morton.

The eastern boundary of the present borough of South Chester, as it had been the western boundary of the old borough of Chester since the act of incorporation, March 5, 1795, and is still that of the city of Chester, was Lamokin Run.

At the court held at Upland, on Tuesday, Nov. 25 and 26, 1679, occurs the first mention of record of the name Lamokin. Before the justices at the time stated:

"Albert Hendrix of Lamoco Apearing in Court, declared to Transport and make ouer unto John Test of Upland all his Right Tytle and Interest to a Certayne small parcell of Land, Lying and being at yᵉ head of Upland Creeke beginning att Robberd Waedes markt beetch tree standing att yᵉ syde of the Creeke, and soe up along the Creek syde to a small gut or Run, and soe up along the sᵈ run to a markt whyte oake tree and soe stricking downwards againe wᵗʰ a Lyne of markt Trees to the place of beginning, itt being a narrow slipe alongst the run or Creeke syde and Contaynes about fourthy acres of Land; This Land being part of a greater quantity Granted unto him yᵉ sᵈ Albert by Pattent from yᵉ Governoʳ and Called Lamoco; and hee yᵉ sᵈ albert declared to have Received full satisfaction for the same.

"John Test of Upland, declared in Coʳᵗ to Transport and make ouer unto Richard Boveington and John Grub all and singular the slip of Land here abovementioned, made ouer unto him the sᵈ John Test by albert Hendrix of Lamoco and declares to have Received full satisfaction of them yᵉ sᵈ Richard and John for ye same."[2]

Although the land thus conveyed is in Chester township, being part of the Green and Carter farms lying along Chester Creek, the record is interesting, as therein occurs, as before stated, the first reference to Lamokin, which is traditionally asserted to be an Indian word signifying "the Kiss of the Waters." The accuracy of this derivation we have no means of ascertaining.

The country lying between Chester and Marcus Hook was, early in the last century, very thinly settled, and the public duty of maintaining the King's highway through that section pressed so heavily upon the people that at court held Aug. 28, 1707, was presented an "application of the overseers and Inhabitants of the West side of Chester Creek, that the road there are very burdensom and chargable to them in regard to their small number, and requesting the Court would appoint the inhabitants on the East side of the sᵈ creek to aid and assist them in mending and repairing the Bottoms and low grounds in the Road to Chichester, so far as their township goes, promising them to maintain and hereafter to keep all the sᵈ road.

"Its Ordered by the Court that Jno. Hoskins, supervisor, do summon the inhabitants of his precinct to meet Guyan Stephenson, with the inhabitants on the West side, and repair the bottoms & low ground aforesaid, & that afterwards the inhabitants of the West side do always repair & support the sᵈ Road."

---

1 Smith's "History of Delaware County," Appendix, Note C, p. 521.

2 Record of Upland Court, pp. 149 and 150.

At the upper end of the present borough, on Lamokin Run, between the King's highway and the river, was the James Laws farm; the old mansion, owned by Samuel Eccles, Jr., is still standing at the foot of Edwards Street, surrounded by towering trees. The red-cedar pillars of the porch still remain, as they were when the dwelling was noted for the hospitable reception which awaited a guest under its roof-trees. Farther along on the sandy beach in front of this farm was a valuable shad and herring fishery, which was leased annually in the spring for a goodly rental, until the improvement along the river rendered it valueless. In the olden time, tradition relates, a pirate buried his treasure on this shore, and many were the stories told of the unsuccessful attempts made by daring money-diggers to recover the corsair's hoard. Above the post-road was the narrow strip of land following Lamokin Run, on the Ashmead farm, where, on the north of the railroad, was the grove first used for a picnic-ground in 1844, when the Sunday-school of the First Presbyterian Church of Philadelphia visited the ground. In after-years, under the name of Young's Grove, it became quite a resort for pleasure parties. Alongside of this property was the "Fairview farm," belonging to Jeremiah W. Flickwir. Tradition states that in the last century, when wagers at play were the rule, the then owner of the land being seated so that the cards he held could be seen in a mirror, his antagonist succeeded in winning this farm, because of the advantage the looking-glass gave him. Just below the Fairview farm was a tract of two or three acres, owned by Jennie Carr, who resided in a log house, with a pole-well near the door, located on the post-road, near where Morton Street is now. Flickwir purchased the land, tore down the old log building and the dividing fences, making the few acres an addition to a large field below the railroad and west of the lane now Flower Street. To the west of the Carr lot was a small property owned by Crossman Lyons, alongside of which was another small plot, owned by Taylor. To the west of the latter was the Daniel Robinson tract, noted forty years ago for an orchard of luscious peaches which grew thereon. Below this estate was part of the Thurlow farm, while to the west of the last-named property was part of the Erasmus Morton estate, which extended to the Lower Chichester line. South of the post-road, to the west of the Laws farm, was the John Jeffreys property, the owner of which was a noted sportsman in his day, who was so expert a shot that often, with the fowling-piece reversed, the trigger instead of the hammer being uppermost, he would, for a small wager, shoot at pennies thrown into the air, and rarely did he fail to strike the coin before it fell to the earth. To the west of Jeffreys was the farm of John J. Thurlow, who, when he retired from hotel-keeping, purchased the estate at the present Thurlow Station, on the Philadelphia, Wilmington and Baltimore Railroad, whereon he built a commodious house, taken down about ten years ago, to which he gave the name of "Sporting Hall," and here for many years the annual "Harvest Homes" in the southwestern part of the county were held, on which occasions the people for miles around would gather, and on the thrashing-floor the beaux and belles passed away the afternoon and evening in dancing, while the old folks enjoyed the hours in conversation and quiet pleasures. When the railroad company established a station in the immediate neighborhood of "Sporting Hall" the depot was named "Thurlow," in honor of the then owner of the real estate near by.

Mr. Thurlow is of English parentage, and the son of Thomas and Mary Thurlow. He was born in the county of Essex, England, on the 1st of February, 1795, and during his youth enjoyed but limited advantages of education. He was, however, as a lad, industrious and quick of perception, which qualities rendered his services valuable at the early age of fifteen to Thomas Barston, of Yorkshire, who made him general manager of his business, which included the charge of his real estate, together with the purchase and sale of property. Desiring a wider field than was offered at home to a young man of ambition, he sailed at the age of twenty-four for America, landing in the city of Philadelphia on the 12th of June, 1819. Mr. Thurlow at once repaired to Newport, Delaware Co., and after purchasing a farm opened a public-house. In 1823 he removed to Chester, and became the landlord of a hotel called "The Sign of the Ship," over which he presided for seven years, and in connection with it established a line of stages running from Philadelphia to Baltimore. At the expiration of the fourth year he sold this property and became the landlord of the "City Hotel," which he kept for ten years. Much of the responsibility in connection with the management of this hotel Mr. Thurlow left to the care of his efficient wife, while he engaged in the construction of various public works. He aided in the building of the Pennsylvania Canal, having the contract for the completion of a section, and subsequently constructed the Spruce Street tunnel for the Pennsylvania Railroad. He also built a tunnel on the North Pennsylvania Railroad, and eleven and a half miles of the Philadelphia, Wilmington and Baltimore Railroad. After an active business career Mr. Thurlow determined to enjoy the more quiet and congenial pursuits of the farm, and located upon land two miles from the city of Chester, where he has since been exclusively devoted to the employment of an agriculturist. He was first married in England, in 1819, to Miss Mary, daughter of Richard Shepherdson, of Yorkshire, whose two children are Thomas, a resident of Washington, D. C., and Emeline (Mrs. George McMullen), of San Francisco, who was lost on the ill-fated steamer "Golden Gate" when *en route* to her father's home. Mrs. Thurlow's death occurred in 1863, and he was again married on the 15th of June, 1867, to Miss Rachel Brewton, daughter of Capt. Wil-

J J Thurlow

Wm. H. Green

liam Brewton, of Charleston, S C, and granddaughter of Capt. Daniel Brewton, of the merchant service.

He has been identified with the public interests of Chester, and for years a director of the National Bank of Chester Mr Thurlow was formerly in politics an Old-Line Whig, and subsequently became a Republican, but has taken no active part in the political campaigns of the day He was educated in the tenets of the Protestant Episcopal Church, and is a worshiper at St Paul's Episcopal Church, of Chester Mr Thurlow is in his ninetieth year, and still enjoys exceptional health and mental vigor

Six years before public attention was directed to the availability of South Chester as a manufacturing locality, William H Green saw the opportunities which that section of Chester township presented as a business point Hence in 1864 he purchased lands on Delaware Avenue and Reaney Street, and erected the Vulcan Works To him above all other men is to be ascribed the credit of first giving direction to that locality, so far as an industrial centre is concerned It was not the effort of combined capital, strong by incorporation and association, but the individual energy of one man, who fully comprehended the advantages which South Chester presented for manufacturing At first the Vulcan Works were conducted in a building forty by one hundred and twenty feet, but so earnestly and understandingly did the proprietor labor, that success came because it was merited, not merely the result of large capital and concentration of other interests to maintain and support the enterprise The Vulcan Works have been enlarged by a handsome brick structure, one hundred and forty-four by one hundied and twenty feet, with other necessary buildings thirty feet square The latter are used as a cupola-house and oven, and as a casting-, cleaning-, and boiler-house The articles manufactured are of steel, iron, and brass A specialty is made of brass and steel valves and cocks of all kinds, while a large amount of general machine-work is also done In 1883 several valves were made at these works for the water department of Philadelphia, each of which weighed six tons, and were the largest valves ever made in the world A practical mechanic, William H Green has earned his success by dint of hard work, unfaltering energy, and shrewd business judgment As the pioneer of industrial works in South Chester, he has done much to bring about that marvelous growth which has in a few years developed that borough from a rural suburb to a prosperous, busy town, now numbering its inhabitants by many thousands of active, industrious people

George Green, the grandfather of William H Green, resided in Stockport, county of Cheshire, England, where he was a professor of music Among his twelve children was Moses, a native of Stockport, born in 1805, who married Miss Jane Campbell, daughter of Joseph and Mary Campbell, of the same town, and had children,—William H, Sarah, John, James, Jane, Mary, Sarah, and Moses Mr Green emigrated to America in 1847, and engaged in the calling of an engineer until his death, which occurred in October, 1879 His son, William H, was born in Stockport, Aug 3, 1831, and on completing an ordinary school education was apprenticed to the trade of a machinist and engineer On attaining his sixteenth year he removed to Manchester, and in 1850 emigrated to America His first location was Philadelphia, where for three years he pursued his trade, and then removed to Richmond, Va, which city became his residence until September, 1857, while acting as superintendent of the machine and engineer department of the Tredegar Iron-Works In 1857, Mr Green married Miss Elizabeth Chalmers McKenzie, of Richmond Their children are William H, Margaret, Jane, Mary (deceased), Laura (deceased), Alfred Tennyson, Lillie Christina, and George Thomas Reed List During the year of his marriage Mr Green's skill was made available by the Bureau of Steam Engineering, at Washington, when he was assigned to the navy-yard in Boston, and acted as superintendent of the construction and repairing of the steam machinery of all vessels fitting out at that port In 1861 he received from the government a commission as chief engineer, and in 1863 resigned to assume the direction of the Globe Works in Boston, then doing much of the general machine-work for the government Here he remained until his removal to Chester in 1864, where he established in June of the same year the Vulcan Works, new buildings having been erected for the purpose, and an extensive and successful business in brass and iron instituted In politics Mr Green is a conservative Democrat, always seeking men of ability and character for office irrespective of party He was elected the first burgess of the borough of South Chester, has been a member of the Council, and also member and president of the Board of School Directors He is active in the Masonic fraternity, having attained the rank of a Knight Templar He is a member and one of the wardens of St Luke's Protestant Episcopal Church of Chester

In 1868, Norris L Yarnall located in Chester township, at the foot of Flower Street, and erected the Auvergne Mills, the second manufacturing enterprise in the territory which was subsequently made South Chester. An account of this mill will be found hereafter

In 1863, John M Broomall and William Ward purchased the farms of James Laws and John Jeffrey, and in 1863, Broomall & Ward, together with Seybert & McManus, of Reading, the farms of George Wilson, John J Thurlow, and William Johnson These lands were surveyed and laid out in building-lots and sold on advantageous terms, which resulted in the erection of a number of houses and giving direction to the march of improvement tending westward along the river front

On April 15, 1869, the Legislature constituted the

territory between the following described boundaries, the district of Lamokin: "Beginning at a point on the Delaware River where the line dividing the townships of Chester and Lower Chichester meets the same; thence a northwardly course, partly on the said line and partly on the line dividing the said township of Chester and Upper Chichester, to the north side of Chichester road; thence along the north side of the said Chichester road an eastwardly course to a point opposite Highland Avenue; thence crossing the said Chichester road at right angles to a point on the south side of the same; thence along the south side of the said Chichester road an eastwardly course to the corner of land belonging to the heirs of William G. Flower, deceased; thence on the line dividing the lands of the said heirs of William G. Flower, deceased, Israel Maddock, heirs of Sydney Baker, deceased, and Stephen C. Hall, on one side, and lands of Samuel M. Felton, Daniel Robinson, lands late of Robert Taylor, and land late of James Garland, and land late of Dr. William Young, on the other side, to a point in the southern line of the said Flower's land and in Lamokin Run, where the northern line of the city of Chester meets the same; thence down the said run a northwardly course to the said Delaware River; thence down the same a westwardly course to the place of beginning shall be and the same is hereby established, erected, and incorporated into a separate and independent district from the remainder of the said township for road purposes, and shall be known by the name of the District of Lamokin."

The act of March 12, 1870, provided, "That the District of Lamokin, in the County of Delaware, together with two certain tracts of land, each containing about twenty acres, lying adjacent to the said district, and now or formerly owned respectively by Stephen C. Hall and the heirs of Sidney F. Baker, deceased, be and the same is hereby constituted a Borough, under and subject to the general Borough laws of this Commonwealth, except as hereby changed, with the name, style, and title of the Borough of South Chester, in the County of Delaware."

The same act declared, "That the said Borough constitute a separate school and election district, and that the place for holding the first and all subsequent elections shall be at the brick public school-house in the said district."

Prior to the passage of the act changing the title from District of Lamokin to South Chester the act of March 3, 1870, had provided that the Court of Common Pleas of Delaware County should adjust the indebtedness of Chester township and the District of Lamokin, while the act of Feb. 20, 1872, authorized the same court to make a division of the school-funds and property between Chester township and South Chester.

The officers of the borough of South Chester since its incorporation are as follows:

BURGESSES.

April, 1870, Thomas J. Clayton; October, 1870, William H. Green; October, 1871, to 1873, Thomas J. Clayton; February, 1874, Thomas J. Clayton; February, 1875, John P. Gartside; April, 1875, John P. Gartside (reorganization under Constitution of 1874); April, 1876, John P. Gartside; April, 1877, to 1882, David F. Houston; April, 1883, to 1884, Norris L. Yarnall.

CLERKS OF COUNCIL.

April, 1870, Christopher Blakeley; October, 1870, Solomon W. May; 1875, Z. T. Bartleson; 1877, Gasway O. Yarnall.

MEMBERS OF COUNCIL.

Chosen at first election, April, 1870.—Thomas I. Leiper, Samuel M. Felton, William H. Morton, Solomon W. May, David Brown.[1]

October, 1870.—Samuel M. Felton, David Brown, Thomas I. Leiper, John W. Martin, Solomon W. May.

October, 1871.—John J. Thurlow, Norris L. Yarnall, Isaac Major, Marmaduke Gray, Joseph Byram, John P. Gartside.

October, 1872.—James E. Holt, John W. Martin, Edward O'Donnell.

October, 1873.—James Hutchinson, Norris L. Yarnall, John R. Nowland, Edward Y. Seiders, John W. Martin, Caleb C. Clayton.

February, 1874.—James Hutchinson, Norris L. Yarnall, Edward Y. Seiders.[2]

February, 1875.—Marmaduke Gray, John R. Nowland.

April, 1876 (Reorganized).—Norris L. Yarnall, Marmaduke Gray, James Hutchinson, John R. Nowland, William H. Green, Joseph Byram, John Law.

April, 1877.—Michael Honan, John Law.

April, 1878.—John R. Nowland, Thomas Doyle.

April, 1879.—Patrick Reily, William H. Green.

July, 1879.—Michael Honan resigned, Joseph Byram elected to fill vacancy.

April, 1880.—Norris L. Yarnall.

April, 1881.—John R. Nowland, T. A. McDowell, Simeon H. Cotton.

April, 1882.—John Law, Edward Ferry.

April, 1883.—William J. Brown, Casper H. Snyder.

April, 1884.—John R. Nowland, T. A. McDowell.

JUSTICES OF THE PEACE.

David H. Hill	May 17, 1870.
James M. Gray	Jan. 14, 1874.
A. P. Fields	March 13, 1875.
John Deveney	March 25, 1878.
Ambrose Wood	April 14, 1880.
A. P. Fields	March 3, 1880.
Joseph Brown	April 9, 1881.
John Freshley	April 9, 1881.
A. P. Fields	March 27, 1882.
William H. Wallace	May 7, 1883.

The first vote by a colored man in Pennsylvania was at the first election in the borough of South Chester, April 14, 1870, which ballot was cast by William Henry Cooper.

In 1879 the borough authorities erected a spacious town hall, with a Council chamber in the second story, and the cellar arranged as a lock-up and place of detention for persons under arrest. The building was dedicated Oct. 27, 1879.

Schools.—Before South Chester became a borough, and while the territory was part of Chester township, the school-house that now stands unused on the public ground was built, and under the provisions of the act of Feb. 20, 1872, the court of Delaware County assigned the building and lot to the directors of the borough, and it was used as a school until after the completion of the present buildings on the same ground. Immediately after the organization of the borough pre-

[1] Elected but declared not eligible, and Council appointed Norris L. Yarnall in his stead.

[2] Resigned October, 1874, and Council elected Marmaduke Gray to fill vacancy, November, same year.

parations were made to build a new school-house, and in the next year (1871) the large and commodious brick edifice was erected on the public grounds, on Third Street, at a cost of seven thousand dollars. On the same grounds, in 1883, the directors erected, at a cost of eight thousand dollars, the high school building, which is of brick and two stories in height. In 1874 a brick school-house for colored children was erected on Townsend Street, between Front and Second Streets, at a cost of four thousand dollars. It is now used for public-school purposes, irrespective of color. In 1879–80 a brick school-house, two stories in height, at a cost of five thousand dollars, was erected on what is known as the forty-acre lot, in the northeastern end of the borough. In 1881 a two-story brick house was built, at a cost of four thousand dollars, on the corner of Second and Thurlow Streets.

The first school board was organized April 30, 1870, with the following members: Thomas J. Leiper, James Kirkman, William H. Green, Owen Lynch, James Bowen, James Elliott. Aug. 9, 1870, James Elliott resigned; Samuel H. Stevenson filled the vacancy by appointment of board.

Members of the school board since that time have been as follows:

June 6, 1871, James Kirkman, James Bowen, Owen Lynch, D. C. Thompson, James Coonan, S. H. Stevenson: June 4, 1872, James Kirkman, James Coonan, D. C. Thompson, T. J. Clayton, William Fow, John McDowell; Oct. 11, 1872, James Kirkman resigned, J. R. Nowland. appointed; Dec. 6, 1872, Solomon W. May appointed to vacancy caused by death of William Fow; June 11, 1873, T. J. Clayton, Solomon W. May, D. C. Thompson, J. R. Nowland, John McDowell, James Kirkman; April 3, 1874, Rev. W. R. McNeil and Rev. S. W. Gehrett appointed in place of James Coonan and D. C. Thompson resigned; Nov. 11, 1874, T. J. Clayton resigned, W. H. Green appointed; March 5, 1875, S. W. Gehrett resigned, Z. T. Bartleson appointed; June 7, 1875, W. R. McNeil, John McDowell, James Kirkman, J. R. Nowland, Z. T. Bartleson, J. A. Watts; April 7, 1876, W. R. McNeil resigned, G. O. Yarnall appointed; June 5, 1876, G. O. Yarnall, Z. T. Bartleson, John McDowell, Casper Culp, J. A. Watts, Jacob Sears; June 5, 1877, G. O. Yarnall, John McDowell, Jacob Sears, J. A. Watts, Z. T. Bartleson, James Bradley; June 3, 1878, G. O. Yarnall, John McDowell, Jacob Sears, James Bradley, Z. T. Bartleson, J. A. Watts; June 4, 1879, Jacob Sears, James Bradley, John McDowell, J. A. Watts, B. H. Smith, Thomas Belmont; June 10, 1880, Jacob Sears, John McDowell, Wm. Belmont, B. H. Smith, J. A. Watts, Z. T. Bartleson; June 6, 1881, Jacob Sears, John McDowell, Wm. Belmont, B. H. Smith, Z. T. Bartleson, Casper Culp; June 7, 1882, Jacob Sears, B. H. Smith, John McDowell, C. G. Neal, Casper Culp, and Z. T. Bartleson; Oct. 11, 1882, Jacob Sears resigned, G. O. Yarnall appointed; June 13, 1883, B. H. Smith, Z. T. Bartleson, Casper Culp, C. G. Neal, O. T. Pancoast, John McDowell; June 7, 1884, B. H. Smith, John McDowell, C. G. Neal, Z. T. Bartleson, O. T. Pancoast, Dr. J. B. Weston.

The Felton Fire Company.—The company was organized early in 1882, and in the same year erected, at a cost of three thousand dollars, a brick building on Third Street, between Morton and Jeffrey. The association, which at present has seventy-four members on its roll, have a hose-carriage, but are contemplating the purchase of a steamer. R. Peters, Jr., is president of the company.

South Chester News.—This paper was established by W. Warren Webb, March 23, 1883, as an advertising medium, and conducted as such for about six months, when it was changed to a four-column weekly newspaper, and later enlarged to six columns. The office is at No. 1726 West Third Street, South Chester. It is Republican in politics.

Plain Speaker.—This paper was established by Olin T. Pancoast, in an office at 2105 West Third Street. The first number was issued Aug. 1, 1883, and contained four columns, later was enlarged to five columns. On the 5th of July, 1884, the office was removed to No. 1929 West Third Street. It is Republican in politics.

South Chester Methodist Episcopal Church.—This society was organized in 1870, under the care of the Rev. S. W. Gehrett. In the next year a lot, one hundred and forty by one hundred feet, was purchased of John M. Broomall, at the corner of Third and Jeffrey Streets. Upon this lot the society erected on Jeffrey Street, in 1870, a brick edifice, thirty-six by sixty-three feet, which is used as a chapel. This church was built as a mission chapel of Trinity Methodist Episcopal Church of Chester, and was dedicated in November, 1871. The Rev. Mr. Urie, of Wilmington, preached the dedicatory sermon. The society intend in the near future to erect a church on the corner of Third and Jeffrey.

The society now numbers one hundred and forty members. A Sunday-school containing two hundred and eight pupils, under the superintendency of John Neal, is in connection with the church. A parsonage, on the corner of Second and Jeffrey, is owned by the society. The names of the pastors who have served the church from its organization are here given: Revs. S. W. Gehrett, David McKee, Dr. Matthew Sorin, John B. Maddux, David M. Gordon, Abel Howard, Eli Pickersgill, Matthias Barnhill, and Israel M. Gable, the present pastor.

Baptist Chapel.—The First Baptist Church of South Chester was organized in 1871. A lot was purchased by Samuel A. Crozer, on the corner of Third and Jeffrey Streets, and a chapel built thereon by Mr. Crozer.

The pastors who have served the church have been the Revs. William R. McNeal, Reece W. Perkins, Alexander McArthur, and Henry B. Harper, the present pastor. The church has two hundred members, and a Sunday-school of three hundred and fifty pupils, under the charge of the pastor.

St. Daniel's Methodist Episcopal Church.—This church was organized in 1871, and erected at a cost of about four thousand dollars. The brick church is on Edwards Street, between Third Street and the railroad. The pastors who have served the church are Revs. —— Henson, —— Broden, George Washington, —— Jolly, —— Webb, J. Hugh Peirce, N. Morris, Dr. Butler, and J. J. Campbell, the present pastor. The church has about one hundred and seventy-five members.

First Baptist Church.—This church was organized in the spring of 1879, and through the liberality of Samuel A Crozer, a brick structure, fifty feet in length and thirty-three feet in width, was erected on Second Street, below Lamokin It was dedicated in August, 1879 The Rev Dr Griffith, of Upland, preached the dedicatory sermon The church has about seventy members, and the Rev Samuel Christian is pastor

African Methodist Episcopal Bethel Church.—This society was organized in the old school-house on the public grounds in May, 1871 A lot on Engle Street, between Second and Front Streets, was purchased of John M Broomall, the consideration being one dollar By the exertions of William Murphy two thousand dollars were subscribed and used for the erection of a brick edifice twenty-five by thirty-eight feet It was dedicated June 6, 1872 The first pastor was the Rev G T Waters He was succeeded by the Rev W H Davis, Henderson Davis, John M Davis, John W Norris, and Thomas H Moore, the present pastor. The church has at present one hundred members

Bethany Mission—The First, Second, and Third Presbyterian Churches of Chester united in establishing a mission called Bethany in South Chester The corner-stone of a brick chapel, thirty-five by sixty, was laid by John Wanamaker, of Philadelphia, on the 25th of June, 1884 The box deposited in the stone contained a Bible, copies of the papers in Chester and South Chester, a paper containing the names of the ministers of the Presbyterian Churches, names of the former and present Sunday-school officers, and the names of the teachers On the day when the corner-stone was laid Mr Wanamaker addressed the audience, and concluded by subscribing one hundred dollars towards the building fund Subscriptions followed rapidly, and over a thousand dollars were contributed in a short time

Auvergne Mills.—Norris L Yarnall erected a stone mill two and a half stories in height for the manufacture of Kentucky jeans, at the foot of Flower Street, in 1868, which was in operation till Oct 3, 1873, when it was destroyed by fire It was rebuilt in the fall and winter of that year, and manufacturing resumed there in April, 1874 Additions have been made from time to time to the mills The present main structure is fifty feet in width by one hundred and twenty in length, an engine-house twenty by twenty feet, a picker-house thirty-two feet square, a dye-house sixty-five by seventy feet connected therewith The machinery consists of eighty-eight looms, four sets of woolen cards forty-two by forty-eight inches, and two self-acting mules with six hundred and seventy-six spindles each About six thousand pounds of cotton and wool are used weekly in the manufacture of twenty thousand yards of cloth

River Mills—These mills, located at the foot of Jeffrey Street, were built, in 1872, by Capt James Jerome, and were operated by him for the manufacture of cotton warp until 1875, at which date they were rented by Charles Roberts In 1871, Mr Roberts began the manufacture of cotton yarn in the building belonging to the water-works, now used as the Cocoa Matting Works by Edward S Worrell In 1875, Mr Roberts removed to the River Mills One of the buildings is sixty-six feet in width by one hundred and fifty feet in length, two stories in height. The necessary out-buildings comprise the engine- and boiler-rooms, dye-house, picker- and finishing-room. The other mill is fifty feet in width by one hundred feet in length, two stories in height, and has in connection therewith an engine- and boiler-room, dye-house, and dry-room The machinery consists of one hundred and fifty looms, five thousand five hundred cotton spindles and eighteen cotton-cards, one thousand woolen spindles, and two sets of woolen-cards The power used to drive the machinery is supplied by three engines, one of ninety horse-power, one of forty horse-power, one of twelve, and five tubular boilers One hundred and sixty hands are employed Eight thousand pounds of raw material are used weekly, from which is produced thirty-six thousand yards of tickings, cheviots, and Kentucky jeans

Trainer's Mill.—The Chester Improvement Company awarded a contract in May, 1872, to Samuel Montgomery to erect on their land a building for a cotton-factory sixty feet in width by two hundred and thirty-eight feet in length, two stories in height. The contract price was fifty thousand dollars, and the buildings to be completed by Nov 1, 1872 The property was occupied by D Trainer & Sons, who placed therein eleven thousand spindles, fifty-four spinning-frames, forty-six cards, and nine speeders for the manufacture of fine yarns The engine that drives the machinery is a two hundred horse-power Corliss engine The mill has a capacity of spinning three thousand pounds of yarn weekly

Wyoming Mill—The mill building was erected in 1873, fitted with machinery by Samuel Montgomery, and operated by his sons for several years, when it was purchased by John Roberts and Abner Coppock, by whom it was operated about two years and a half It then remained idle several years, and on the 10th of October, 1882, it was again put in operation by Joseph Byram, who is the present occupant The mill has fifty-eight looms, one thousand spindles, and two cards, driven by a sixty horse-power engine Three thousand pounds of cotton are weekly made into cotton yarn, and thirteen thousand yards of cotton cloth are made weekly Fifty hands are employed

Centennial Mill—This mill was established by Simeon Cotton, in May, 1876, at which time he had completed the main building, one hundred by fifty feet, at the foot of Second and Clayton Streets, and manufacturing was commenced therein May 11, 1876 Three thousand six hundred spindles and thirteen cards are used, and sixteen bales of cotton are manufactured weekly into seven thousand pounds of cotton warp

Garfield Mill.—The Garfield Mill, a two-story brick building, one hundred by fifty feet, was erected at the corner of Morton Street and the Philadelphia, Wilmington and Baltimore Railroad, by Messrs. Law & Devenney, in the year 1881, and fitted with machinery for the manufacture of cotton yarn. Subsequently its capacity was doubled, and it now contains three thousand and twenty-four spindles and fourteen cards, which are driven by an eighty horse-power engine. Twenty loom-hands are employed, and five thousand three hundred pounds of cotton yarn is produced weekly.

Oil-Cloth Works.—About eighteen years ago Eli D. Pierce erected on his farm in Nether Providence a building for the tanning of sheep-skins. The business increased so rapidly that he purchased land at the foot of Tilghman Street, where he erected frame buildings, and removed thereto. Here he began largely the tanning of goat-skins, and continued till the spring of 1882, when, by reason of the failure of business men in Boston, to whom he sold largely, he was compelled to make an assignment. In the summer of that year the buildings were rented by Edward S. Worrell, who fitted them with the most improved machinery for the manufacture of oil-cloth. Six thousand yards of oil-cloth are made weekly. George P. Worrell is superintendent.

Chester Rolling-Mills.—The Chester Rolling-Mills were incorporated March 10, 1875, with John Roach, John Q. Denny, C. B. Houston, John B. Roach, D. F. Houston, and Garret Roach, as corporators. John Roach was chosen president, C. B. Houston secretary and treasurer. The original capital of the company was three hundred thousand dollars, which was increased to five hundred thousand dollars in 1880, and in 1882 to six hundred thousand dollars. The real estate of the old bridge and steel-works was purchased, at the foot of Wilson and Hayes Streets, between Townsend and Highland Avenue, and from Front Street to Delaware River. In that year (1875) the company commenced the erection of main rolling-mill building, one hundred and sixty by one hundred and eighty-five feet; in 1879 it was doubled, and is now three hundred and twenty by one hundred and eighty-five feet, the capacity of the works being increased in proportion. Above the rolling-mill, in 1880, the blast-furnace was erected, covering about one and a quarter acres with its different buildings, and was put in blast Nov. 1, 1881. The machinery is of the latest and most improved kinds.

The steel-works, erected in 1881, are ninety by one hundred and forty feet. The first blast was made April 1, 1882. Five hundred hands are employed, and the wages amount weekly to six thousand dollars. The capacity of production of these works is three hundred tons of plate, seven hundred tons of pig-iron, and three hundred tons of steel ingots weekly. Fourteen hundred tons of ore, six hundred tons of limestone, and one thousand tons of coal are used weekly. Much of the ore is imported direct from Spain and Africa. The present officers of the company are John Roach, president; Charles B. Houston, treasurer; Richard Peters, Jr., secretary; and Thomas J. Houston, general manager.

The Chester Pipe and Tube Company was incorporated in 1877, with a capital of three hundred thousand dollars. Seventeen acres of ground at the intersection of Front and West Streets was purchased, and two large brick buildings and other smaller ones erected. Twenty thousand tons of skelp iron are used, from which is manufactured eighteen thousand tons of wrought-iron pipes annually. Two hundred hands are employed.

Standard Steel Casting Company.—This company was incorporated June 22, 1883, with Pedro G. Salom, president; William E. Trainer, vice-president; Richard Wetherell, treasurer; John B. Booth, secretary. Ten acres of ground were purchased at Thurlow Station, on the line of the Philadelphia, Wilmington and Baltimore Railroad, and a building, one hundred and fourteen feet in width by one hundred and sixty feet in length, was erected. Work was commenced on the 1st of March, 1884, with seventy hands. The mill has a capacity of producing three thousand tons of steel per annum.

Chester Oil-Works.—In September, 1880, the Chester Oil Company was organized. A large tract of land along the river front and on the southwestern limit of South Chester borough was purchased, and the large buildings, which cover an area of twelve acres, were built. On the 23d of March following the refining of oil was commenced, and twenty thousand barrels of crude oil is used per week. Twelve large stills with a charging capacity of ten thousand barrels, two agitators, six bleachers, and six large boilers for engine and pumping purposes, with much other machinery, are used in turning out two thousand barrels of refined oil per day, and naphtha, tar, and other products. The company have a storage capacity for one hundred and forty-six thousand barrels of crude oil tankage and six thousand barrels of other tankage. Three of the largest pumps have each a capacity of three thousand barrels per hour. They carry fourteen-inch suction-lines and twelve-inch supply-lines. Beneath the surface of the entire ground is a network of pipes, all of which are accurately drawn on a plan of the works, so that at any time an engineer with compass and chain can not only find any pipe desired, but every joint and stop-cock can be designated and its size and use told. There is not a tank or a building anywhere in the works that is not well protected in case of fire, as both steam and water can be turned on in all of them in such quantity as to extinguish the flames. Four artesian wells have been sunk to obtain cold water for condensing purposes. One of these is four hundred and fifty feet deep and furnishes seventy barrels per hour. The ordinary supply of water is obtained from the river

There is wharfage for thirteen vessels, with a depth of twenty to twenty-four feet at low water, and for the protection of the shipping in winter ice piers have been erected, which are the only private ones on the Atlantic coast. Seventeen different kinds of oil are made and shipped to all parts of the world. Besides barrels, five-gallon tin cans are used for this purpose, works for the manufacture of the latter having just been completed and fitted with intricate and expensive machinery. Little, if any, of this work is done by hand. The tin is cut, squared, bent into proper shape, stamped, and soldered by machinery. The last operation is performed by an ingenious invention of Frank W. Edward, superintendent of the works, and the machine can turn out ten thousand perfectly soldered cans in ten hours. Before shipment these cans are packed, two being placed in a wooden box, which is also made entirely by machinery. Three hundred and seventy-five hands are employed.

The Seaboard Oil Company, composed of Crew, Levick & Co., was organized in 1881, and purchased a tract of land on Front Street, between Trainer and Booth Streets. Eight buildings were erected, which cover about three acres. Eight engines, three boilers, and fifteen stills are used in the manufacture of lubricating oils, paraffine oils and wax, refined burning oils, gasoline, and naphtha. Thirteen hundred barrels of crude oil are consumed daily. Thirty-three men are employed. Charles T. Miller is superintendent.

Delaware Oil-Refining Works.—The Delaware Oil-Refining Company was established by W. F. Young, in August, 1881, at its present location, between Second and Front and Johnson and Price Streets, South Chester. It was incorporated Oct. 15, 1881, as the Delaware Oil-Refining Company. The works comprise eight good-sized buildings of brick and frame, covering about half an acre. The articles manufactured are paraffine oil and wax. The engines are sixty-five horse-power, and there are six stills, the weekly capacity of which is four hundred barrels. Eighteen hands are employed. Five hundred and fifty barrels of residuum of petroleum oil are used per week, and the weekly capacity of the works is three hundred and fifty barrels of oil and fifty of wax.

Law & Devenney's Brick-Yard.—This firm established a brick-yard on an eight-acre tract of land situated on Morton Street and the line of the Philadelphia, Wilmington and Baltimore Railroad. They have three large kilns, and produce daily twenty-three thousand bricks, which requires the labor of forty-five men.

Robinson Brick-Yard.—Adjoining the yard mentioned above and situated on Sixth and Eagle Streets is a brick-yard that was established by James Caven. The business was later conducted by Charles Fairlamb, Fairlamb & Robinson, and since 1876 has been carried on by D. Robinson. Forty men are employed, and seventeen thousand bricks are made daily.

Palmer Brick-Yard.—The brick-yard situated on Third Street north of West Street was established in 1865 by Mrs. M. Palmer, who still conducts it. Twelve men are employed, and about seven thousand bricks are turned out daily. Thomas Palmer is in charge.

South Chester Ship-Yard.—Joseph K. Clouser established, November, 1881, a ship repair-yard at the foot of Lamokin Street. Fifteen men are employed. It is the only yard nearer than Marcus Hook where repairing of wooden vessels is made a specialty.

CHAPTER XXXVI.

NORTH CHESTER BOROUGH.

THE territory now comprising the recently-erected municipal district of North Chester borough, was in the distribution of land surveyed and patented to four of the early settlers of the province. The upper part of the borough was part of the one hundred and eighty-four and a half acres surveyed to James Sandelands Dec. 2, 1685, and adjoining this tract to the southeast was the land surveyed the same day to Thomas Brassey, containing the same number of acres as were in the Sandelands plot. On the last-mentioned estate the villages of Shoemakerville and Irvington are located. At the southwestern end of the borough, on Dec. 18, 1685, one hundred and ninety-seven acres was surveyed to Eusta Anderson, the greater part of which is not included in North Chester; that part which is within the borough is popularly known as Powhattan, because of the mills of that name being thereon erected. The remaining land at the southeast of the borough was part of the three hundred and seventy acres patented to Israel Helms, June 18, 1668.

By act of March 14, 1873, that part of Chester township hereinafter described was incorporated as the borough of North Chester.

"Beginning at a point in the middle of the public road leading from the borough of Upland to Edgmont Road, being at the intersection of the boundary lines of the city of Chester, the borough of Upland, and the township of Chester; thence along the northeastern boundary of the said borough of Upland to the line dividing the properties of A. C. Lukens and John Wetherill; thence along the said line to the southern side of Edgmont Road; thence along the said southern side to a point opposite the line dividing the properties of Mary Kelly and Isaac Engel Cochran; thence crossing the said road and along the said line to Ridley Creek; thence down the said creek to the northern boundary of the said city of Chester; and thence following the said boundary to the place of beginning; said limits including the town or villages of Paultown, Powhattan, Waterville, and Shoemakerville."

The borough elections were directed to be held the third Friday in March of each year at the Oak Grove school-house. The act also created North Chester a separate school and election district. At the time of the erection of the borough the Powhattan Mills and Irvington Mills were located within the municipal district, and were then in successful operation. The Chester Rural Cemetery was within its limits, and the little hamlets that had in former years gathered around the early mills were stationary or had lost the vitality to increase. What was known as Shoemakerville was laid out about 1830 by William D. and R. Shoemaker, and in 1833 there were at the place a store, blacksmith- and wheelwright-shop, several stone and frame dwellings. Hopes were entertained that it might grow to be a town of some importance, but it did not thrive, and is now but little larger than it was three years after it was begun. In 1842, Robert E. Evans kept store in Shoemakerville, and in 1850, John C. Murray had a coach-factory at that place.

On Aug. 23, 1847, at Burk & Powell's quarry, a ledge of rock weighing about eighty-six tons which had been displaced by a sand-blast fell. Burk was under it at the time, and hearing a noise above him attempted to escape, but his foot was caught by the falling rock and literally crushed into a mass. He was taken to his home in Shoemakerville, but bled to death before a physician could be summoned. The blood-stains on the floor of his then dwelling are visible to this day, and for many years the owner of the house had difficulty in obtaining tenants who would remain over a day or two in the building.

The first election for burgess and Council was held on the 29th of March, 1873. John M. Sharpless was elected burgess, but declined to serve, and at the organization of Council, on the 7th of April, 1873, Henry L. Powell, of the Council, was chosen to act as chief burgess, since which time the burgesses elected have been as follows:

1874, Stephen Parson; 1875, Hugh Shaw; 1876, Adam C. Eckfeldt; 1877, Thomas Coulter; 1878–79, Henry Greenwood; 1880, Anthony McMunn; 1881–84, John W. Martin.

MEMBERS OF BOROUGH COUNCIL.

1873.—Joseph G. Fell, Henry L. Powell, Hugh Shaw, John Wetherell, James Irving, Daniel McCurdy.

1874.—Joseph G. Fell, Henry Greenwood, Hugh Shaw, Edward S. Worrell, John Walker, John Wetherell.

1875.—John Farmer, Henry Greenwood, James Tongue, John Walker, Edward S. Worrell, John Wetherell.

1876.—Nathan Berry, Henry Greenwood, J. Harlan Miller, Hugh Shaw, John Wetherell, James Tongue.

1877.—Nathan Berry, Henry Greenwood, James Morgan, Abram Taylor, Hugh Shaw, John Wetherell.

1878.—Samuel L. Wood, Isaac Parson, James Wall, Edward S. Worrell, William H. Brangan, Theodore Dransfield.

1879.—Hugh Shaw, John W. Martin, Isaac Parson, John H. Evans, William Neale, William Hunter.

1880.—Hugh Shaw, John W. Martin, James Elder, Edward S. Worrell, Cornelius Allison, Capt. Randle.

1881.—Hugh Shaw, Henry Beaumont (three years), Edward S. Worrell, Alexander McFate (two years), W. W. McNutt, Thomas Cook (one year).

1882.—W. W. McNutt, Theodore Dransfield (three years), John Robinson (one year).

1883.—Edward Buckley, C. S. Esrey (three years).

1884.—Henry Beaumont, John Robinson (three years).

TREASURERS.

D. R. Esrey, from 1873 to 1879; C. W. Andrews, from 1879 to 1885.

CLERKS.

Charles Worthington, 1873–74; C. W. Andrews, 1875–77; David Aarons, 1878–84; Wright Sutcliffe, 1884.

JUSTICE OF THE PEACE.

Robert E. Hannum, March 13, 1875; March 30, 1880.

Friends' Meeting-House at Shoemakerville was built by the members of the Orthodox branch of the society in 1828, on land donated for that purpose by Enos Sharpless. It is a stone building, forty by sixty feet, and stands on a large plot of ground well shaded by forest trees, and adjoins the Oak Grove school-house. The prominent members of the society were Enos, John, Henry, Isaac, George, Daniel, and John M. Sharpless, Jesse J. Maris, Stephen M. Trimble, Richard Wetherell, and Gideon Smith, the last a ministering Friend. The present membership of the society attending this meeting is about fifty persons.

The North Chester Baptist Church was founded April 26, 1873. At that date a few persons favorable to the establishment of a congregation, and the erection of a place of worship for the Baptist denomination in the borough, met at the residence of James Irving, where, after some informal agreement and understanding, the congregation was organized by the appointment of James Irving chairman, and E. Mills clerk. At this meeting it was decided to erect a church edifice in North Chester borough, ten members of regular Baptist churches registering their names as an earnest of their purpose. Invitations were sent to the Union Baptist Church at Media, the First Baptist Church at Chester, the Baptist Church of South Chester, as also that of Ridley, and Mantua Baptist Church, Philadelphia, to meet in council with the organization in North Chester borough. On May 9, 1873, this council met and organized by the appointment of Rev. Dr. J. M. Pendleton, of Upland, to preside, and William R. McNeil, of South Chester, secretary. The visiting brethren were requested to take part in the exercises. The recognition services being concluded, Rev. Edward Wells was called to the pastorate of the church. In the eleven years which have intervened since its organization the church has had three pastors: Rev. P. S. Vreeland, who assumed pastoral charge Oct. 1, 1876; in January, 1879, Mr. Vreeland resigned, and on Aug. 31, 1879, the present pastor, Rev. John Brooks, was called, being ordained Oct. 2, 1879. The congregation has grown rapidly, largely composed of the operatives in the mills,—the present membership being about sixty. Pecuniarily the church has been sustained largely by the liberality of James Irving, who built the present sanctuary, and donated it and the lot on which it stands to trustees for the use and benefit of the congregation. The date stone has the figures 1872 cut upon it, which is clearly an error. No organization was effected looking to a church congregation there until April, 1873. It was recognized in May, and the church dedicated in June of that year, 1873.

Schools.—The first school-house erected in what is now North Chester was on a lot which was sold by Daniel Sharpless, March 18, 1813, to William Davis, Pierce Crosby, and Enos Sharpless, who were chosen trustees by the inhabitants in that part of Chester township. The lot had twenty-three square perches, and thereon a one-story stone school-house was soon erected. This building was used for school purposes until the erection of the present Oak Grove school-house, in 1860. In 1836 the Sharpless school-house passed into the control of the directors of Chester township, and in 1873 was transferred by authority of the act erecting the borough to the directors of that municipal district.

In 1830, two years after the building of Friends' meeting-house, that society built a small frame structure below the meeting-house, on the road to the Waterville Mills, wherein Miss Ann McGill (afterwards Mrs. Richard Wetherell) and Miss Amy Griffith were early teachers. The pupils in that school had a small plot of ground on which they vied with each other as to who could raise the best roses, violets, and other flowers, as also beets, parsnips, and various kinds of vegetables. This piece of land was fenced and guarded with jealous care, being carefully locked when school was not in session. School has been kept in this house from 1830 to the present time, but not with any degree of regularity. After the erection of North Chester borough, the two-story brick school-house on Twenty-second Street was erected, and is now used for that purpose. The first directors of the borough were elected in March, 1873, and were Josiah Berry, H. Greenwood, Nathan Berry, H. L. Powell, D. R. Esrey, and Daniel McCurdy.

The directors since that time have been as follows:

1874, Hugh C. Sample, Jonas Tongue, E. Wells; 1875, John Shaw, Edmund Wells, Henry L. Powell; 1876, D. R. Esrey, Henry Beaumont; 1877, Robert Campbell, James Moss; 1878, George W. Gilton, A. P. Garfield; 1879, D. R. Esrey; 1880, John Wetherell, Adam C. Eckfeldt; 1881, Rev. John Brooks, James Moss; 1883, D. R. Esrey; 1884, William H. Floville, H. L. Powell.

Chester Rural Cemetery.—This association was organized in 1863, and incorporated by act of Assembly March 18, 1863. The preamble of the act set forth:

"WHEREAS, The following named citizens of the Borough and Township of Chester, in the county of Delaware, have agreed to subscribe the sum of one thousand dollars each, for the purpose of providing a public cemetery, to be located within the limits of said borough or township, therefore,

"Sec. 1. *Be it enacted*, &c., by the Senate and House of Representatives of the Commonwealth of Pennsylvania in General Assembly met, and it is hereby enacted by the authority of the same, That Benjamin Gartside, Frederick Fairlamb, Joshua P. Eyre, Abraham Blakely, John Larkin, Jr., Raney, Son and Archbold, John H. Baker, George Wilson, Joseph Taylor, Samuel M. Felton, Samuel A. Crozer, Mortimer H. Bickley, John P. Crozer, and such other persons as may hereafter subscribe and contribute each a like sum, and their successors, be and they are hereby created and declared a body politic and corporate, for establishing a public cemetery to be located in either the borough or township of Chester, by the name, style, and title of the Chester Rural Cemetery Association."

The stockholders at their first meeting, March 21, 1863, elected Joshua P. Eyre president, and John H. Baker secretary of the company. A tract of forty acres, belonging to I. Engle Hinkson, a short distance north of the limits of the borough of Chester, the land extending from Edgmont to Upland road, was purchased, the price paid being two hundred and fifty dollars per acre. The plot was immediately laid out for the purposes of a cemetery, the first interments within its lines being the Confederate soldiers who died at the United States Hospital (now the Crozer Theological Seminary). Over one hundred and fifty of these men were buried within the grounds. The first lot was purchased by Bennett Dobbs, Sept. 26, 1863, and his wife, Nancy, was buried therein two days afterwards, September 28th. No deed was given for this lot until two months had elapsed, the first conveyance bearing date Dec. 7, 1863. Nearly in the centre of the cemetery an artificial lake was made, the water being supplied by a run which passed in a northwesterly course through the grounds. On Dec. 10, 1869, a sad accident occurred at this lake, on which Herman L. Cochran, son of John Cochran, and Mattie H. Irving, daughter of James Irving, both about sixteen years, were skating when the ice broke and they were drowned. "The Soldiers' Monument," a tribute to the soldiers of the civil war enlisted from Delaware County, stands on the highest point of land in this cemetery. Although this testimonial was erected in the name of the citizens of the county, the funds necessary to procure and put it in place were contributed by a few persons. Much credit was due to Mrs. Mary B. Leiper, who was untiring in her efforts to procure the means required. The Soldiers' Monument, a bronze figure by Martin Millmore, representing a private soldier standing at rest, and elevated on a massive granite pedestal, was dedicated Sept. 17, 1873, with appropriate ceremonies. Col. W. C. Gray read a history of the Soldiers' Monument Association, Col. John W. Forney delivered an address, and after the procession returned to Chester the very creditable work of the artist was committed to the seclusion of a burial-ground, whence only the corroding hand of time is likely to remove it.

Irvington Mills.—The site of these mills is on the tract surveyed to Thomas Brassey in 1685, and of which one hundred and seventy-six acres, on Aug. 20, 1705, became the property of Caleb Pusey. It has been generally accepted that the report of the road laid out in 1713 "from Providence Lower road by Richard Crosby's mill to Edgmont road" had reference to the mill erected at Crosbyville, and that it had been built prior to that date. In reading the report of the jury carefully it seems clearly to point to the Jarvis or Crosby mills farther up the creek, where now is located the Media water-works. When the mills at the present Irvington were erected we have failed to learn, but prior to 1767 grist- and saw-mills were located there which previous to 1790 came into the ownership of the Crosby family. In 1799 the saw-mill had fallen into disuse. The stone grist-mill must have been an expensive building, for in the year last mentioned the mill was assessed at four thousand dollars, while the same year the Flickwir house, on Third Street, now being removed, was rated at two hundred

and thereon a one-story stone school-house was soon erected. This building was used for school purposes until the erection of the present Oak Grove school-house, in 1860. In 1866 the Sharpless school-house passed into the control of the directors of Chester township, and in 1873 was transferred by authority of the act erecting the borough to the directors of that municipal district.

In [illegible], shortly after the building of Friends' meeting-house, that society built a small frame structure below the meeting-house, on the road to the Waterville Mills, wherein Miss Ann McGill (afterwards Mrs. Richard Wetherell) and Miss Amy Griffith were early teachers. The pupils in that school had a small plot of ground on which they vied with each other as to who could raise the best roses, violets, and other flowers, as also beets, parsnips, and various kinds of vegetables. This piece of land was fenced and guarded with jealous care, being carefully locked when school was not in session. School has been kept in this house from 1850 to the present time, but not with any degree of regularity. After the erection of North Chester borough, the two-story brick school-house on Twenty-second Street was erected, and is now used for that purpose. The first directors of the borough were elected in March, 1873, and were Josiah Berry, H. Greenwood, Nathan Berry, R. L. Powell, D. R. Esrey, and Daniel McCurdy.

The directors since that time have been as follows:

1874, [illegible] Wells; 1875, John Shaw, Edmund Watts, Henry L. Powell; 1876, D. R. Esrey, Henry [illegible]; 1877, Robert Campbell, James Moss; 1878, George W. Gibbons, A. F. Lambert; 1879, D. R. Esrey; 1880, John Wetherell, Adam C. Eckfeldt; 1881, Rev. John Rooke, James Moss; 1882, D. R. Esrey; 1883, William M. Neville, R. L. Powell.

Chester Rural Cemetery.—This association was organized in 1863, and incorporated by act of Assembly March 14, 1865. The preamble of the act set forth:*

The stockholders at their first meeting, March 21, 1863, elected Joshua P. Eyre president, and John H. Barton secretary of the company. A tract of forty acres belonging to [illegible], a short distance north of the limits of the borough of Chester, the land extending from Edgmont to Upland road, was purchased, the price paid being two hundred and fifty dollars per acre. The plot was immediately laid out for the purposes of a cemetery, the first interments within its lines being the Confederate soldiers who died at the United States Hospital (now the Crozer Theological Seminary). Over one hundred and fifty of those men were buried within the grounds. The first lot was purchased by Bennett Dobbs, Sept. 26, 1863, and his wife, Nancy, was buried therein two days afterwards, September 28th. No deed was given for this lot until two months had elapsed, the first conveyance bearing date Dec. 7, 1863. Nearly in the centre of the cemetery an artificial lake was made, the water being supplied by a run which passed in a northwesterly course through the grounds. On Dec. 16, 1869, a sad accident occurred at this lake, on which Herman L. Cochran, son of John Cochran, and Mattie H. Irving, daughter of James Irving, both about sixteen years, were skating when the ice broke and they were drowned. "The Soldiers' Monument," a tribute to the soldiers of the civil war enlisted from Delaware County, stands on the highest point of land in this cemetery. Although this testimonial was erected in the name of the citizens of the county, the funds necessary to procure and put it in place were contributed by a few persons. Much credit was due to Mrs. Mary B. Leiper, who was untiring in her efforts to procure the means required. The Soldiers' Monument, a bronze figure by Martin Millmore, representing a private soldier standing at rest, and elevated on a massive granite pedestal, was dedicated Sept. 17, 1873, with appropriate ceremonies. Col. W. C. Gray read a history of the Soldiers' Monument Association, Col. John W. Forney delivered an address, and after the procession returned to Chester the very creditable work of the artist was committed to the seclusion of a burial-ground, whence only the corroding hand of time is likely to remove it.

Irvingtan Mills.—The site of these mills is on the tract surveyed to Thomas Brassey in 1686, and of which one hundred and seventy-six acres, on Aug. 20, 1705, became the property of Caleb Pusey. It has been generally accepted that the report of the road laid out in 1712 "from Providence Lower road by Richard Crosby's mill to Edgmont road" had reference to the mill erected at Crosbyville, and that it had been built prior to that date. In reading the report of the jury carefully it seems clearly to point to the Jarvis or Crosby mills farther up the creek, where now is located the Media water-works. When the mills at the present Irvington were erected we have failed to learn, but prior to 1767 grist- and saw-mills were located there which previous to 1790 came into the ownership of the Crosby family. In 1790 the saw-mill had fallen into disuse. The stone grist-mill must have been an expensive building, for in the year last mentioned the mill was assessed at four thousand dollars, while the same year the Flickwi house, on Third Street, now being removed, was rated at two hundred

* Whereas, The following named persons of the borough and township of Chester, in the county of Delaware, have agreed to subscribe [illegible] for the purpose of providing a public cemetery, to be located within the limits of said borough or township; therefore,

Be it enacted by the Senate and House of Representatives of the Commonwealth of Pennsylvania in General Assembly met, and it is hereby enacted by the authority of the same, That Benjamin Gartside, [illegible]

Engd by A.H. Ritchie

James Irving

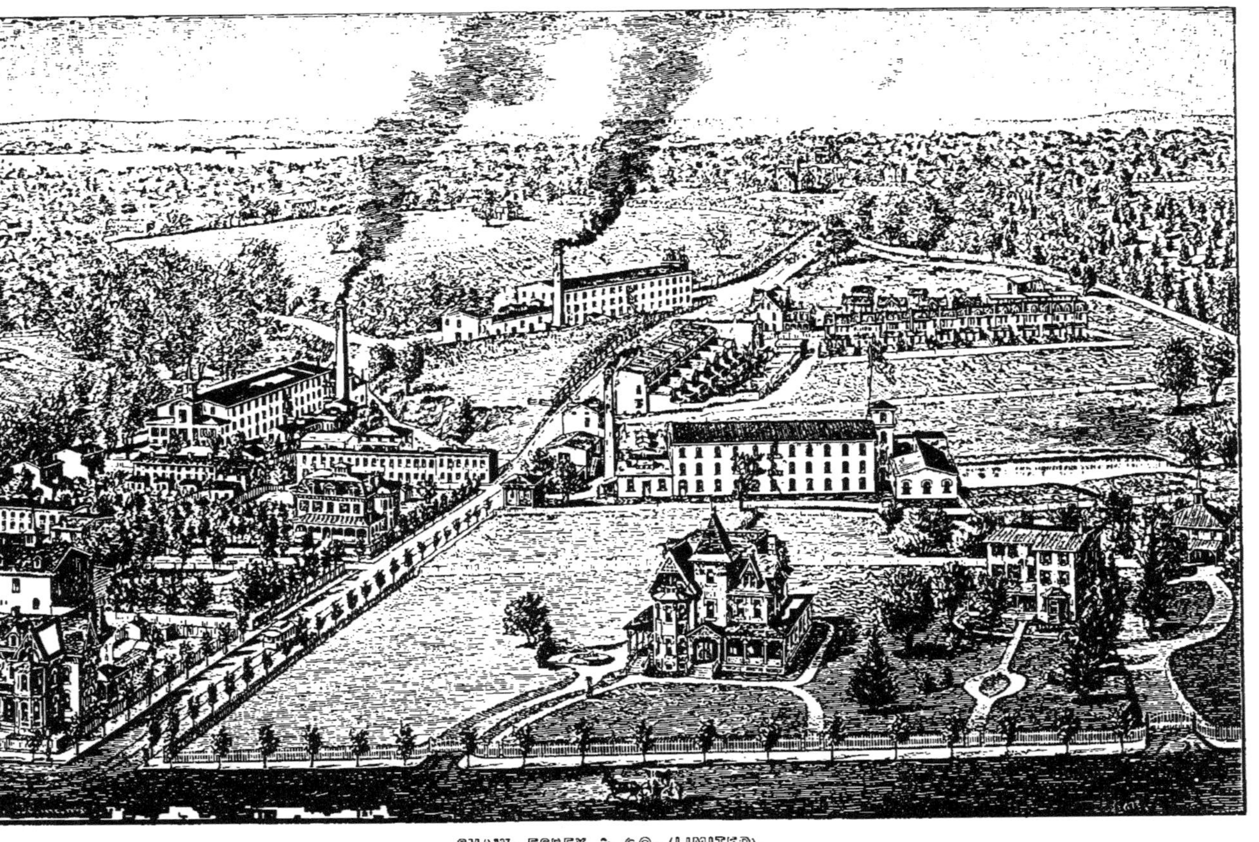

SHAW, ESHEY & CO. (LIMITED),
COTTON AND WOOLEN MANUFACTURERS,

and fifty dollars, by which we can form an opinion as to the value of the mill property at that day. In 1826, Pierce Crosby had not only the grist-mill, which was making thirty to fifty barrels of flour a day, but there was a saw-mill on the estate which cut between two and three hundred thousand feet of lumber per annum. In 1843, Crosby leased the mills to James Riddle and Henry Lawrence, who changed them to a woolen factory, which they continued to operate until 1845. In that year James and David Irving, who had established the Irvington Mills in Philadelphia in 1842, leased the Crosbyville Mills and removed their business to that location, where they remained as tenants of the Crosbys until 1857, when they purchased the property. The business had so increased that in 1860 the firm erected Mill No. 2, a building one hundred feet in length by forty feet in width. In 1862, David Irving died, and his interest in the business was purchased by James Irving, who continues manufacturing at Irvington, the old mill seat being now known by that name. On Jan. 1, 1866, Washington Irving was given an interest in the business, the firm being James Irving & Son. The son, however, died the following September, but the firm remained unchanged in title, and in 1879, James Irving's son, William A. Irving, was admitted to an interest in the mills. In 1873 the old grist-mill building was removed, and a four-story stone structure one hundred and seventy-two by fifty feet erected on its site by James Irving, and Mill No. 3, a stone factory forty by fifty feet, two stories in height, was built in 1880 by James Irving. The machinery in these mills consists of one hundred and six looms, two thousand one hundred spindles, and six sets of cards, the goods manufactured being woolen doeskins and tweeds.

James Irving, the subject of this biographical sketch, was born in 1817 in New York, where his parents, John and Jeannie B. Irving, emigrated from Glasgow, Scotland, and settled in the year 1811. The family subsequently removed to Montgomery County, Pa., where the two sons, James and David, were apprenticed to Bethel Moore, then one of the largest woolen manufacturers in the State, and with him learned the trade of which he was master. In 1842 they began business in Philadelphia County, and remained until 1846 in that locality.

James Irving the year previous removed to Delaware County and established woolen-mills at Irvington, under the firm-name of J. & D. Irving, which continued until the death of David Irving, in 1862, when James Irving & Son succeeded to the business. James and David Irving and Thomas I. Leiper also established in Chester, Pa., a mill for the manufacture of cotton yarns, under the firm-name of Irvings & Leiper, now the Irving & Leiper Manufacturing Company.

James Irving, in May, 1839, was married to Christiann, daughter of John Berry, of Chester County, Pa. Their children are Jeannie M. (wife of Hugh Lloyd, of Darby, Pa.), E. Matilda (wife of William H. Starbuck, of New York), William A., and D. Edwin. Both the sons are interested with their father in business. Mr. Irving was in politics formerly a Henry Clay Whig, and actively participated in the political issues of the day. He later became a conservative Republican, and indorses the platform of the party in general. He is a director of the First National Bank of Chester, and has been for a long time one of the active trustees of the University of Lewisburg, Union County, Pa., one of the best educational institutions of the State. He is in his religious views a Baptist, and member of the North Chester Baptist Church of Chester, Pa.

Powhattan Mills.—In the fall of 1863, Hugh Shaw and D. Reese Esrey entered into partnership as Shaw & Esrey, and purchasing from Patrick Kelly the machinery and personal property in the Pennellton Mills, at Bridgewater, together with his interest in the brand of goods known as Powhattan jeans, began the manufacture of cotton and woolen jeans and all-wool jeans at those mills, employing sixty hands and producing four hundred thousand yards of goods annually. In 1865 the firm bought a plot of ground on Green Street, Chester, from Spence McIlvain, designing to erect a mill thereon; but early in the spring of 1866, D. R. Esrey purchased from John Cochran six acres of ground and the mansion on the Engle property at Powhattan, near Chester, and the firm concluded to buy other lands adjoining, consisting of three acres. On this plot they immediately erected the building now known as Powhattan Mill, No. 1, removing from the Pennellton Mills the machinery purchased from Kelly and adding a new set of woolen machinery. In September, 1866, operations were begun at the new location. To the machinery in this mill a set of woolen machinery was added in 1867, and another set in 1872. Besides the mill building the firm erected four tenement houses. At first the basement of Mill No. 1 was rented to Joseph G. Fell, who, in one part, was engaged in weaving cotton cloths, and the remainder of the basement to Joseph Monroe for the manufacture of warps. In 1871 the business of Shaw & Esrey had so increased that, to keep pace with the demand for their goods, another lot of ground was purchased and Mill No. 2 was erected. In this building, in the fall of the year, four sets of woolen machinery were placed, in 1872 two other sets were added, and again in 1874, making a total in both mills of fourteen sets and two hundred and twenty-eight roller and clipper-looms. The power in each mill is furnished by an eighty horse-power Corliss engine, receiving steam from six boilers, of one hundred and fifty horse-power. Mill No. 1 is one hundred and seventy-eight feet in length by fifty-five feet in width, and three stories in height. To it is attached a two-story dye-house thirty-two by fifty-five feet, and a one-story dye-house twenty-five by fifty-five feet. There is also attached to this mill a boiler-house thirty-two by sixteen feet, and all necessary buildings. Mill No. 2 is one hundred and fifteen feet in length by fifty-eight feet in width, three stories in height. To it are attached an engine-, boiler-, dry- and dye-houses, forming a wing one hundred and fifty by thirty-three feet, and directly at the other end of the main building is a weave-shed, one hundred and sixteen by forty feet, one story in height. There is also detached a spreader and a mixing-room, seventy by thirty feet, two stories in height, and other necessary buildings. Connected with these mills are thirty-five comfortable dwelling-houses, two- and three-storied buildings, erected by the firm for the convenience of the operatives. The grounds connected with the Powhattan Mills comprise twenty acres. The goods manufactured in these mills are known in the market as Powhattans, Covingtons, Provident, and all-wool jeans.

In the spring of 1877, Shaw & Esrey decided to erect a third mill, to be used exclusively for the manufacture of a finer class of goods. This building is one hundred and thirty-eight by fifty-five feet, three stories in height, with engine-, boiler-, dry-, dye-, and store-houses attached. In January, 1878, the firm began operations in this mill with four large sets of the best and latest-improved machinery, and in 1880 added two more sets of the same kind of machinery. In January, 1878, the firm of Shaw & Esrey was changed under the act of Assembly to a limited company. At that time the property owned by the company consisted of three mills, out-building, and machinery, fourteen dwelling-houses, and a tract of land, in all, with a capital of three hundred thousand dollars. The company consisted of Hugh Shaw, D. Reese Esrey, John Shaw, H. C. Esrey, and William H. Shaw. In 1879 the stock of H. C. Esrey, deceased, was transferred to C. S. Esrey, and he was admitted to the company. In 1878 the firm having occasion to use the basement of No. 1 mill, required Joseph G. Fell and Joseph Monroe to vacate it, and fulling and finishing machinery for finishing the wool doeskins, cashmeretts, and cassimeres made at No. 3 mill was placed therein. An admirable system prevails in these mills. Everything that can contribute to the progress of the business or the welfare of the employés is secured, without regard to the trouble or expense it may occasion. Many of the dwelling-houses are owned by the operatives, the firm having always striven to aid their hands to that end. The arrangements for extinguishing fires are unsurpassed, water and steam being introduced into each room by an automatic process, and an automatic alarm is also attached to give warning should any fire occur in the buildings. Each mill is provided with a steam pump in constant readiness, and each and all pumps are connected, so that should a fire occur in one mill, where by any accident the pump could not be worked, either of the other pumps could be used in its stead. Detached from each mill is a large building for storage of wool, cotton, and other materials. The Powhattan Mills at the present time contain twenty sets of cards, seven thousand one hundred and thirty-four spindles, and three hundred and thirty looms. The yearly production is about two million five hundred thousand yards, and three hundred hands are employed in the mills.

Hugh Shaw is of English parentage, his paternal grandfather having resided at Grotten Head, Yorkshire, England, where he was a successful weaver. His children were James, Alice, Betty, and Ann. James was born in the year 1800, in Saddleworth, Yorkshire, England, and learned the trade of a spinner, which he followed for many years. He married Betty, daughter of Daniel Andrew, of Shelderslow, Saddleworth, Yorkshire, and had children,—Samuel (deceased), Hugh, William, John, Andrew (deceased), James, and Elizabeth. His son, Hugh, was born Dec. 2, 1823, in Lees, near Oldham, Lancashire, England. Having entered the mills at an early age, he enjoyed but limited advantages of education, obtaining instruction principally in night-schools, from contact with others, close observation and research. He continued as a spinner until 1843, when on emigrating to the United States he entered the mills of W. T. Crook, at Crooksville, Delaware Co., Pa. Here he subsequently became foreman, and continued so until 1854, when he engaged in farming in Chester township. He remained thus employed until 1863, when forming a copartnership with D. R. Esrey, the interest in the mills of Patrick Kelly, of Aston township, was purchased, and the firm embarked in the manufacture of Powhattan jeans. In 1866 a mill was erected near Chester; in 1871 the increase of business warranted the building of another mill, and in 1877 a third was erected, doeskins and cassimeres having been meanwhile added to their productions.

The firm named was in 1878 changed to a limited company, with Hugh Shaw, D. R. Esrey, John Shaw, H. C. Esrey, and W. H. Shaw as members, the interest of H. C. Esrey, deceased, being in 1879 transferred to C. S. Esrey. Mr. Shaw married as his first wife Miss Anna Whittaker, of Lancashire, England. There were born to this marriage several children, the only survivor of whom is Elizabeth (Mrs. Samuel Crowther). By a second marriage, in 1853, to Miss Ann, daughter of Samuel Boaz, of Worcester, England, are children,—William H., Mary B., and Hannah C. Mr. Shaw is in his political predilections a Republican. He is identified with the Chester National Bank as one of its directors, and is also a stockholder in the Glenmore Worsted Mills of Philadelphia. In religion he is a worshiper with the congregation of the Third Presbyterian Church of Chester. He is an active member of the Masonic fraternity, in which he has risen to the rank of a Knight Templar.

Joseph Esrey, the grandfather of David Reese Esrey, who was of English descent, resided in Radnor township, Delaware Co. He married Miss Hannah Haley, of Chester County, and had children,—John,

Eng^d by A.H. Ritchie

Hugh Shaw

Hugh Shaw

Eng.d by A.H.Ritchie.

D. R. Esrey

Adam C. Eckfeldt

William, Joseph, Jonathan, Richard, Margaret, Elizabeth, Mary, Ann, and Sydney. Jonathan, of this number, was born, in 1791, in Delaware County, which was his life-long residence. His death occurred in 1851, while serving a term as sheriff of the county. He married Miss Margaret Newlin, and had one child, a son, Edmund. By a second marriage, to Miss Jane, daughter of William and Sarah Hawkins, his children were Sarah, Eliza Ann, George W., David R., Lydia, Henry F., Mary E., William, Jonathan, Jane, and Sydney. David Reese was born Dec. 4, 1825, in Ridley township, and at an early age removed to Wallingford, Nether Providence, where his youth was occupied in various industrious pursuits or in attendance upon the limited advantages offered by the country school. In 1844, at the age of eighteen, he left the paternal roof to enter a store at Brook Haven, Chester township. Continuing here for a number of years, he in 1850 purchased the stock of the owner, and remained disbursing goods to his various country patrons until 1866. Discerning, after an exceptionally successful career as a merchant, a profitable field in the business of a manufacturer, he in December, 1863, in connection with Hugh Shaw, purchased of Patrick Kelly, of Aston township, his interest in the Pennellton Mills, with the right to manufacture Powhattan jeans. In 1866 they erected a mill in the suburbs of the city of Chester, which was occupied immediately on its completion. In 1871 another mill, known as Mill No. 2, was erected, and in 1877, Mill No. 3,—meanwhile including doeskins and cassimeres among their products. The firm-name was in 1878 changed, and John Shaw, H. C. Esrey, and William H. Shaw admitted to a limited partnership. At the death of H. C. Esrey, in 1879, Charles S. Esrey was made a member of the firm. Mr. Esrey was, on the 25th of April, 1850, married to Margaret, daughter of Jonathan M. Marker, of Upper Darby. Their children are Jonathan M. (deceased), Henry C. (deceased), Charles S., William H., and Mary Ella (who died in infancy). Mr. Esrey was formerly in politics an Old-Line Whig, and later became a Republican. Though decided in his political views he has not aspired to public office, other than those immediately connected with the township. He is a director of the Delaware County National Bank. Mr. Esrey is a member of Madison Street Methodist Episcopal Church of Chester, and president of its board of trustees.

The North Chester Brick-yard was established by Samuel J. Rose in 1869, he having been engaged in the same business at Upland Street near Tenth, in the city of Chester. The present yard, under the management of S. J. Rose & Son, comprises fifteen acres of land on Providence Road and Twenty-first Street. Brick of all description used in ordinary building are here manufactured. Three kilns are required in the business, which gives employment to forty men and boys. Twenty-two thousand is the daily average of brick made in this yard.

BIOGRAPHICAL SKETCH.

ADAM C. ECKFELDT.

Jacob Eckfeldt, the grandfather of Adam C., was a soldier in the war of the Revolution, and manufactured bayonets for the army. He emigrated with his wife from Mecklenburg, Germany, and settled in Philadelphia. Among his sons was Adam, born in the latter city, who learned the trade of a blacksmith and machinist, which craft he followed in the city of his birth. He established a factory for the manufacture of wrought-iron nails, and by the excellence of his work obtained large contracts from the United States government for the construction of machinery for the United States Mint. He married Miss Margaret Baush, of Philadelphia, whose children were Sarah, Jacob R., Anna Mary M., Elias B., Susannah, Adam C., and Margaretta. Adam C. was born Aug. 26, 1812, in Philadelphia, where his youth was devoted to study, supplemented by a course at an excellent school at Doylestown, Pa. After a brief career in the commission business in his native city, he removed to Haverford township, Delaware Co., and in connection with his brother devoted his energies to the cultivation of a farm. In 1838, by the decease of this brother, he came into possession of the farm, which he continued to cultivate until 1865. Mr. Eckfeldt made his calling a matter of scientific study, and introduced all the modern appliances which serve to modify the labor of the husbandman. He returned again to Philadelphia for a brief period, and in 1868 purchased his present home in North Chester, where he has since resided. Mr. Eckfeldt was married in 1839 to Miss Rebecca, daughter of Jacob Sulger, of Philadelphia, whose children are Elias B., Anna S., and Margaretta. The first of these children enlisted during the late war in Company D, One Hundred and Twenty-fourth Regiment Pennsylvania Volunteers, for a service of nine months, and fell at the battle of Antietam. Mr. Eckfeldt was a second time married on the 21st of May, 1851, to Miss Martha Ann, daughter of John Campbell. They have one daughter, Sarah E., wife of Dr. Charles Perkins. In his political predilections Mr. Eckfeldt is a Republican, having formerly affiliated with the Old-Line Whig party. He has refused various proffers of office, but served for ten years with acceptance as justice of the peace for Haverford township. He is an elder in the Third Presbyterian Church of Chester, and active in church and Christian work.

CHAPTER XXXVII

UPPER CHICHESTER TOWNSHIP

The records of Chester County are silent respecting the time at which the original townships in that part of the territory now Delaware County were erected, nor is there any description of the lines dividing one township from the other In the early days of the province the term Chichester generally was used to indicate that section of the county now comprising Upper and Lower Chichester We know that previous to 1686 Chichester had been surveyed, that some difficulty was had respecting the survey, and at the October court of that year the justices "Ordered that the township of Chichester extend its bounds as formerly laid out by Charles Ashcom, until further order" The peculiar western line which separates the upper township from Bethel was run to conform to the lines of the tracts surveyed to the early settlers, and doubtless the authority which adjusted the boundary of the several municipal districts at that time permitted freedom of choice among the land-owners as to the township in which their real estate should be located Certain it is, a more irregular line than the western boundary of Upper Chichester it would be difficult to lay out

Among the earliest settlers of the township was Walter Martin, the founder of St Martin's Church, the tract of five hundred acres surveyed to him being at this time parts of the farms of John B McCay, George Broomall, and Samuel Vernon Adjoining Martin's land to the east were two hundred and fifty acres surveyed to Jeremiah Collett, June 16, 1682, being lands sold in England by Penn to Joan May, in September, 1681, which right to locate that number of acres in the province May transferred to Collett The latter was an earnest churchman, and by will devised a certain sum of money to be applied to the support of the rector of St Martin's Church, and providing for services according to the Episcopal ritual to be held in that church on certain days in each year thereafter Andrew Osborn, David Boyd, John Stevenson, P Birnbaum, and Thomas Beeson's farms are located on the Collett tract. Above Walter Martin's, or rather part of his plantation, on the road from Concord to Chichester, was a plot of sixty acres, which, on Oct 6, 1684, became the property of James Brown This James Brown came from Bedfordshire, England, and settled on the tract mentioned, located on the east branch of Naaman's Creek, and gave the name of "Middleton" to his new home, possibly from the location of the land near the centre of the township, although previous to that date he had received a patent for one hundred and fifteen acres known as "Podington," lying north of Jeremiah Collett's tract, and bounded on the east by Chichester Creek In December, 1685, he purchased one hundred acres lying between the two divisions of the east branch of Naaman's Creek from Thomas Garrett, to whom the land was laid out in April of that year. The plantation known as "Middleton" is now part of the farm of John B Okie "Podington" is now the property of Andrew Armstrong, while the one hundred acres lying between the dividing streams of the east branch of Naaman's Creek, above mentioned, is now part of the farms of John B McCay, Mrs E M Halsey, and John B Okie It is stated by George Churchman, in his "Reminiscences of Nottingham," written in 1822,[1] that James Brown and William Brown were brothers, that the former came to Pennsylvania in 1693, and the latter in 1696, a statement which partakes of the two-brother theory so frequently presented in family history, whereby, as a rule, the second generation is confused with the first

William Brown subsequently became the owner of the Podington estate, but it was not until June 21, 1705, at which date no person named James Brown owned land in Upper Chichester It is probable that William Brown and James Brown, who subsequent to 1696 purchased nine hundred acres in Nottingham, were sons of James Brown, the immigrant On the east side of Chichester Creek, at the line dividing Upper and Lower Chichester, and extending to Chester township, was a tract of five hundred acres, which was purchased by William Withers, and on Jan 22, 1682, was conveyed to Thomas Withers On this tract was included the real estate of Jeremiah L Brown, Daniel N Larkin, Matthew Boyd, Robert McClintock, E and T Worrilow, Susan Harvey, John H Williams, W F Patterson, John G Smeet, Mary and Susan Magin, Edward Johnson, Donaldson, and part of T Roberts and the Norris estates Above Withers' land was a plot of one hundred acres surveyed to Thomas Clifton, June 24, 1684 This estate passed to James Brown in 1685, and it was on this purchase that he gave the ground on which Chichester Friends' meeting-house was built The tract bought from Clifton extended from the Chichester Creek to Chester township, and on it parts of the farm of Jeremiah C Brown, T Roberts, and the Norris estates are located Above this last mentioned tract to the north, on Sept 4, 1682, four hundred acres were surveyed to Henry Hastings and Richard Buffington, which includes the upper part of the farm of Jeremiah Brown and T Roberts, all of that belonging to Joseph R Johnson, that of Charles Posotta, the most of James M Craig's, as well as those of W Henry Dutton and Thomas Dutton Above this four-hundred-acre tract was a plot of three hundred and fifty acres, which, on Nov 16, 1683, was surveyed to John Kingsman This tract began at a point where Baldwin's Run crosses the line between Chester and Upper Chichester townships, extending directly westward to the junction of Greer's and Bezer's Runs, when the course of the latter

[1] Published in *Oxford* (Chester County) *Press*, July 16, 1876

was followed in a northeasterly direction to the point where the Upper Chichester road crosses the last-named run, and then a straight line to the upper corner of Thomas V. Dutton's farm. The road from Chichester to Aston traversing the township almost due north, running through the tract of Jeremiah Collett, William Withers, Thomas Clifton, Henry Hastings, and Richard Buffington, and John Kingsman, was laid out 1688, while the Upper Chichester road was laid out on Oct. 25, 1687. On this tract part of Charles Dutton's farm is located, as are also those of Thomas W. Henry and David M. Dalton. David Morrow's land is entirely within the boundary of the Kingsman patent, as is that of Benjamin Elliott, a part of Samuel Wells, and a very small part of Thomas V. Dutton's plantation. Due west of Kingsman's land was the five hundred acres surveyed to John Bezer, June 19, 1682. The run which traversed the entire length of his estate received its name from that fact. The greater part of the William Booth farm, all of Mrs. Reynolds, A. Jester and E. Jester properties, and all of Salkeld Larkin's land lying east of the road from Concord to Chichester, which was laid out Jan. 19, 1716/7, are included within the original Bezer tract. The farms of T. B. Jones and Simon H. White are entirely a part of the one hundred and eighty-four acres patented to Walter Martin, Jr., June 10, 1703, which was at the northwest extremity of Upper Chichester. In the oddly-shaped line dividing Bethel from the township under consideration the farms of Thomas Marshall, Joseph Newlin, George Hammond, H. Barnes, Joseph Pyle, Mrs. Nathan Pennell, and parts of the farms of Salkeld Larkin and Mrs. E. M. Halsey, are located on the tract of two hundred and fifty acres surveyed to Francis Harrison April 3, 1683, known in early days as "Jacob's Well," that name having been given to it because of a noted spring of water on the lands. West of the Concord road, including all the land between the road and the easternmost feeders of Naaman's Creek, extending from Larkin's school-house lot through the lands of Salkeld Larkin, southward to and embracing that of J. Todd as also the northern end of John B. Okie's farm, was included in the fifty acres surveyed to William Thomas, June 2, 1682. On the west side of the east branch of Naaman's Creek the entire remaining territory in the township was included in four tracts. At the northwest and along the creek into Bethel, William Clowd had two hundred acres surveyed to him Sept. 28, 1685, one hundred of which was in Bethel and a like number in Upper Chichester, which included the properties of William S. Goodley, Thomas Painter, John C. Ogden, and the upper part of the farm of John B. McCay. The next tract to the south, containing two hundred acres, extending from the middle branch of Naaman's Creek, touching at its southern end the circular line, was patented Nov. 12, 1683, to Henry Reynolds, and included the farms of Charles W. Hance, the greater part of that of John B. Smith, as also much of that of John B. McCay. Intruding itself between the west line of Reynolds' tract of two hundred acres, already mentioned, and the circular line was a triangular piece of land, part of a tract of five hundred acres surveyed April 23, 1684, to William Cloud,—the Prince property. At the southwestern limit of the territory was a tract of two hundred and fifty acres, which was located Sept. 5/6, 1681, to George Anderson, and by him transferred, Dec. 15, 1683, to Henry Reynolds. The circular boundary line of the State of Delaware traverses this tract. That part of it which became part of Upper Chichester is now the property of George Broomall, J. S. Beeson, and parts of the farms of John H. Smeet and John B. McCay.

The list of taxables for the year 1715 shows the following persons as the then residents of Upper Chichester: Enoch Flower, William Chandler, Walter Marten, Henry Reynolds, Francis Reynolds, Ruth Chandler, George Leonard, Francis Routh, Matthew Wood, John Bezer, John Kingsman, Humphrey Scarlet, James Whitaker, Shadrick Scarlet, Thomas Linvill, Thomas Withers, Jeremiah Collett, John Chambers, Richard Weaver, Jeremiah Cloud; Freeman, Richard Mashell (Marshall).

We give the following list of the taxables in the township in the year 1799:

Joseph Arkew, Daniel Brown, Nathaniel Brown, John Booth, John Burns (cordwainer), Peter Brown, James Craig, Mordecai Cloud, Pierce Crosby, Jonathan Dutton, Jacob Denibarker, Charles Dinger (saddler), Rachel Dutton, Caleb Eyre (grazier), Isaac Engle, William Ford, Rebecca Huston, Ann Huston, Matthias Kerlin, Joseph Larkin, Bezer Lamplugh, Josiah Lamplugh, George Martin, Joseph Martin (blacksmith), John Oliver, Adam Peirce, Susanna Pennell, Isaac Pennell (cordwainer), Phebe Reynolds, James Rowen, Jacob Richards, Thomas Ryerson, Susanna Robeson, Sarah Moore, John Smith (blacksmith), James Shelley, John Sholtz, John Talbot (miller), Caleb S. Sayers, Joseph Talbot (saw-mill), Thomas Wilson, Joseph Walker, James Withey, John Dutton (tailor), James Henderson (weaver), Thomas Young (weaver), Jeremiah Dutton (cordwainer), Elijah Farr (blacksmith), Aaron Huston (hatter), Joseph Pennell (cordwainer), Edward Pennell (cordwainer), Samuel Pearson (miller), George Wood (carpenter).

The division of Chester into Upper and Lower Chichester was made early in 1700 by the people of that section to facilitate public business. About the middle of the last century an effort was made to have the division which had been thus made officially recognized, and to that end the following petition was presented to the court:

"*To the Honourable Justices of the Court of General Quarter Sessions held at Chester on the 27th of February*, 1753.

"The Petition of divers of the Inhabitants of the Township of Upper Chichester in the said County in behalf of themselves and others of the said Township

"Humbly Sheweth

"That the limits of the Township of Upper Chichester aforesaid are not fully determined by proper Authority but remain uncertain.

"That your Petetioners labour under very great hardships and Inconveniencies for want of the true lines thereof being Settled, especially the line dividing the township of Lower Chichester from the said township of Upper Chichester.

"Your Petitioners therefore Pray that your Honours would be Pleased to appoint a Set of men to run-out, Survey, mark, and fix the Boundries of ye said township of upper Chichester, but more especially to run-out, mark and fix the line dividing the townshs of upper & lower Chichester afores[d] or such other Way as you in your Wisdoms shall see meet

"And your Petitioners as in duty Bound Shall Pray

"Kingsman Dutton	Francis Routh
"Joseph Askew	Benj[a] Reynolds
"William Askew	W[m] Clayton
"Harry Reynolds	Jesse Platt
"Jacob Dingee	John Dutton
"Mary Clayton	Francis Routh, Jun[r]
"Benj[a] Weldon	Nicholas Newlin
"Joseph Wood	Daniel Brown"

The movement was, however, met by sturdy opposition from the leading citizens and land-owners of Lower Chichester, which was presented to the court at the same session as that at which the people of Upper Chichester preferred their request The following was the counter-statement made by the remonstrants

"*To the Honourable Justices of the Court of General Quarter Sessions of the Peace to be held at Chester on the 27th day of February*, 1753

"The Petition of Several of the Inhabitants of the Township of Lower Chichester in the said County on behalf of themselves & the rest of the Inhabitants of s[d] Township Humbly Showeth

"That Your Petitioners Apprehend that the Inhabitants of the Township of Upper Chichester Intend to Petition your honours for men to be Appointed to Run out Survey Mark and Fix the Boundaries of the said Townp of Upper Chichester, but more Especially the Line dividing the Township of Upper Chichester from the Township of Lower Chichester afsd But as the said Townships are as they now Stand, Convenient enough, they Apprehend there is no Need of any Separation, And as Your Petitioners, have of late laboured under many hardships by Reason of Mending the highways in the said Township of Lower Chichester, they being very bad, and also by reason of having Several Poor to Provide for, for which reasons and for none Else Your Petitioners Conceives the Inhabitants of the said Township of Upper Chichester Intends to Petition Your honours

"Your Petitioners, therefore Pray that your honours Would be Pleased to Reject the said Petition of the Inhabitants of Upper Chichester And Your Petitioners as in duty bound Shall Ever Pray &c

"Jno Marshall	Benj[a] Moulder
"George Chapman	Adam Clayton
"Rich[d] ffower	Rich[d] Mostly"
"Joseph Coborn	

The knotty question thus submitted to the justices for adjudication the grave magistrates seemed loath to determine, but in some way not apparent permitted the matter to drag along for six years, during which time the reasons for the official recognition became apparent to the remonstrants Hence at the August court the following petition was presented, bearing the signatures of almost every freeholder in Upper and Lower Chichester, which was approved by court

"*To the Honourable Justices of the Court of General Quarter Sessions of ye Peace to be held at Chester for the County of Chester, the 28th day of August, Anno Dom* 1759

"The Petition of the Inhabitants of the township of Upper Chichester and of the Inhabitants of the township of Lower Chichester in the said county

"Honestly Sheweth

"That on or about the year of our Lord 1718 the then Inhabitants of the township of Chichester did (among themselves) divide the said township into two townships and did call the upper part thereof Upper Chichester and the lower part thereof Lower Chichester, that through some Neglect or omission at that time the division was not (as your petitioners can find) ever presented to or approved of by the Court, that Notwithstanding the said Omission the township of Chichester has ever since been deemed and reputed two distinct & seperate townships in all respects save that of maintaining the Poor, that it does appear by the records of this Court that they are called two Townships, that some uneasiness and Contention have lately arisen & may hereafter arise occasioned by the division aforesaid not being recorded among the records of the Court to prevent which for the Future Your Petitioners humbly pray that the township heretofore called Chichester may now be divided and that the division line may Begin at the corner of the land of Francis Johnston & in the line of the land of Joseph Parker, Esq., and extending thence West by South along the Head of the Hook lotts untill it intersects the line dividing the Counties of Chester and New Castle and that the township of Upper Chichester may in all respects hereafter be deemed, & taken to be a distinct & seperate township from that of lower Chichester & Your Petitioners Shall Pray

"W[m] Lamplugh	William Askew
John Dutton	ffrancis Booth
Moses Vernon	Franc Routh, Jun[r]
Dav[d] Weatherly	Hugh Linn
Mordecai Clowd	William Eyre
Thomas Dutton	William Huston
Benj[a] Weldon	Samuel Hewes
Saml[l] Minshall	William Linsey,
Tho[s] Vernon	John Brown
Joseph Askew	Edward Inskep
Nicholas Newlin	Tho[s] Maris
Jeremiah Collett	Sam[l] Kain
Henry Reynolds	Jno Marshall
John Sharpless	Zach Pedrick
Daniel Sharpless	Jno Riley
Isaac Weaver	Richard Clark
Thomas Swayne	Tho[s] Phillips.
Jacob Deriger	Daniel Brown
David Jackson	Moses Moore
George White	

"The freeholders of Nether Providence In Concurrence with the above Petitioners have subscribed their names

"W[m] Lindsay	John McMuhill
James Sharpless	Joseph Vernon

"Allowed"

The following is the list of the justices of the peace for Upper Chichester

Samuel Price	Aug 30, 1791
John Edwards	Jan 24, 1797
Joseph Marshall	May 20, 1800
Matthias Kerlin	July 4, 1808
Thomas Pierce..	Feb 5, 1814
James Bratton	Feb 3, 1820
Joseph Fox	Dec 4, 1823
John Mattson	Dec 13, 1823
Joseph Bowen	Nov 10, 1824
Joseph Trimble	April 21, 1827
Robert Frame	Jan 15, 1829
Robert Hall	Feb 8, 1831
William Mendinhall	Dec 6, 1836
James Huston	April 14, 1840
James Huston	April 15, 1845
James Huston	April 15, 1851
John B Ohle..	Aug 20, 1881
William Hannum	April 10, 1882

Chichester Friends' Meeting —The present Friends' meeting-house is the second building erected by that society on the lot of two acres lying east of Chichester Creek, in the sharp angle of the road leading from Chichester Cross-roads to the highway from Aston to Marcus Hook Chichester Meeting, for record and business, was held for the first time on the 17th of First month, 1684, although religious services had been had in that section of the county as early as 1682 The meeting originally comprised Aston, Bethel, Birmingham, Concord, Thornbury, and Westtown, and beyond the limits of these townships, west and north, indefinitely At this time the religious meetings were held at private houses, and after the organization of Monthly Meetings, Friends would assemble at designated dwellings

In the record of Chichester Meeting we find that a

subscription was taken among Friends at the Quarterly Meeting held in Fourth month, 1687, to "enable a poor man to build a house." This practical charity was so noticeably the rule in the society that William Moraley, in 1752, records:

"The Quakers have a Custom of raising Money at their several Meetings, as I observ'd before, with which they do many Charitable Offices to the Poor and Indigent. I have myself experienced the Effects of their Benevolence. If any Person, though a Stranger continues to do well, by preserving a good Character, and they have a good Opinion of them, they will enquire into his Circumstances, and if it appears he is Distressed in his Business for Want of Stock, or necessary Implements to carry on his Trade, they will set him up out of this Money, without demanding any Security either by Bond or Promissory Note; and if he repays them, will relieve other Persons in the like Circumstances. If he never repays them, they will never give him any Trouble."

The want of a proper meeting-house for the society soon made itself felt, and hence we learn that an effort was being made to erect a building for that purpose. The minutes state:

"At a monthly meeting held at Chichester the 11th of Eleventh month, 1688, it was proposed and agreed to build a meeting-house upon a parcel of land granted by James Brown, as by deed may further appear, and some time afterward it was agreed by Friends to fence in a burial-ground upon the said land joining to the meeting-house. The subscriptions thereunto are as follows, viz.:

	£	s.	d.
"James Brown	3	2	0
John Kingsman	2	5	0
John Harding	3	6	0
Thomas Withers	0	16	6
Edward Bezer	2	8	6
Joseph Bushell	1	8	0
Jacob Chandler	2	10	0
Philip Roman	1	15	0
Francis Harrison	1	12	0
William Hughes	1	0	0
Susanna Beezer	2	0	6
Nathaniel Lamplugh	2	4	0
William Brown	0	16	0
John Ayres	0	1	0
Francis Chadsey	1	10	0
Robert Pyle	2	8	0
William Clayton, Sr.	3	2	0
John Beales	0	10	0
William Clowd, Sr.	1	4	0
Elizabeth Lockley	0	10	0
Edward Carter	0	6	0
Widow Johnson	0	2	0
Edward Walter	0	6	0
Nicholas Pyle	0	10	0
Roger Smith	0	5	0
William Clayton, Jr.	0	6	0
Total	36	4	0"

The deed from John Brown, dated fourth day of Tenth month, 1688, in consideration of one shilling and sixpence, conveyed the two acres heretofore mentioned to William Clayton, Sr., Philip Roman, Robert Pyle, Jacob Chandler, Joseph Bushell, and John Kingsman, in behalf of and for "the only use of the people of God called Quakers. . . . Provided always and at all times, that if any one or more of the above said purchasers, or any one or more than shall be lawfully chosen to succeed hereafter, shall fall from the belief of the Truth as held forth by the people of God called Quakers, as aforesaid, either in a profane and scandalous life, or in doctrines, and continue therein, it shall and may be lawful in such case, for the aforesaid people of the town and county aforesaid, by their order and consent in their monthly meeting, always and at all times to remove and put out any such one or more of the said purchasers, or any other that shall succeed. And always and at all times hereafter to nominate and chose and put in one or more in his or their room, as they shall see fit."

It is presumed that the meeting-house was erected shortly after these proceedings were had, but the exact date is not recorded. In the ground surrounding the building many generations of Friends belonging to Chichester Meeting have been buried, but the testimony of the society in early times being opposed to the erection of tombstones, the resting-place of many of the first settlers in that quiet graveyard cannot now be designated with any degree of certainty. On Dec. 4, 1768, the old meeting-house was totally destroyed by an accidental fire. The following year the present meeting-house was erected, and tradition records that the greater part of the fund raised for that purpose was contributed by Richard Dutton, and Friends, in recognition of his generous aid, caused a stone bearing, in rude figures, the date "1769" and the initials "R. D.," the latter divided by a small star, to be built into the gable of the house.

While Cornwallis' command lay at Aston, from the 13th to the night of the 15th of September, 1777, British foraging-parties went out from Village Green in all directions, and one of these marauding expeditions halted at the meeting-house, and in mere wantonness shot repeatedly at the closed doors, the marks of the bullet-holes being readily seen in the front door to this day. Nehemiah Broomall, for many years sexton of the meeting-house, used to relate how the British army, on its way from the Brandywine to Philadelphia, encamped near the old meeting-house, and on that occasion the soldiers were permitted to discharge their muskets at the doors as a pastime. The British army never moved in that direction; the closest the division under Cornwallis approached Chichester meeting-house was about two and a half miles away, as that commander marched down the Concord road towards Chester. In the last half-century the attendance on religious worship in the venerable meeting-house has been growing less and less; still, it is said Jonathan Larkin often would be the only person who would attend regularly Fifth-day meeting, and the hour allotted to worship would be passed by the one person present in silent communion with his God.

Upper Chichester Meeting.—In the fall of 1829, after the division in the society, those Friends belonging to Chichester Meeting who adhered to the teachings of Elias Hicks retained ownership of the old meeting-house, while those known as Orthodox, in connection with Friends of Concord, determined to erect a new place of worship in Upper Chichester, near the residence of Salkeld Larkin. A lot was donated for that purpose on the Marcus Hook and Concord road, and Joseph Talbot, Thomas Griffith, Isaac Morgan, George Martin, Nathan Larkin, Salkeld

Larkin, Joseph Pennell, Isaac Hughes, and Hester Hughes were organized in accordance with the rules of the society to act as a preparative meeting. On the lot given for the purpose a stone meeting-house, thirty-two by forty feet, was erected in 1831. In the same year a school was organized, and for two years John Reeves taught the pupils in the meeting-house. In 1834 a stone school-house twenty-five by thirty feet was built, and was under charge of the Monthly Meeting. Joseph Bennett and his daughter, Louisa Bennett, were teachers, as were also John Cardwell and Thomas Speakman. After the public-school law was adopted, and until the directors erected a school-house, the building just mentioned was rented and used for school purposes. During the lifetime of Salkeld Larkin he was the head of the meeting, and at his death, April, 1870, aged ninety years, Nathan Pennell succeeded, to be followed in turn by Caleb Eyre. In 1883, Upper Chichester Meeting was "laid down," and Friends in that section united with Concord Meeting.

Schools.—In 1793 the society of Friends established a school in Upper Chichester, which was maintained and continued under the auspices of that religious organization until the public-school system was accepted and introduced in the township, when its further continuance was unnecessary. Besides the school under the supervision of Friends, previous to 1825, was a subscription school kept in a brick house erected for that purpose on the site of the present No. 1 public-school building, a short distance north of Chichester Cross-road, McCaysville, and Chichester, for the cluster of buildings—wheelwright- and blacksmith-shops, and a few dwelling-houses—at the intersection of the Chichester and Concord road have been known by all three of these names. On Dec. 31, 1819, a meeting of the citizens of Delaware County was held in this school-house to form a society for the suppression of vice and immorality. Thomas Ryerson was appointed chairman, and John Kerlin secretary. George Martin, Jr., Dr. R. M. Huston, Thomas Ryerson, Joseph Walker, Jr., Thomas Dutton, and James Brattock were appointed to draft a constitution and by-laws, which they were instructed to report at a meeting to be called at a future time to be determined. As they seem never to have reported, and as the names are all those of Upper and Lower Chichester residents, the other sections of Delaware County appear to have taken no interest in the movement. Hence the projectors of the society failed to effect an organization. After the adoption of the school law of 1836 the building was placed in charge of the school directors, and was continued to be used until 1867, when the old structure was taken down, and the present two-story brick building erected. The lower story was built by the school directors, at a cost of two thousand five hundred dollars, and the second story was erected and completed at a like cost by the voluntary contributions of the citizens of the township, who were desirous of providing a room for Sunday-schools, and where public meetings could be held. After the question of continuing the public schools in the township had been decided in the affirmative by a popular vote, in 1837, on January 4th of the following year John Talbot was appointed teacher at the brick school-house, near Chichester Cross-roads, but he seemed totally unable to control the pupils, and on February 15th the school was discontinued until the directors could obtain the services of a more efficient teacher. After a few weeks Joseph Henderson was employed for the remainder of the term, and the school was opened. The children attended, but no complaint appears of record of the new pedagogue's inability to command obedience from the scholars.

The Dutton school-house, at the intersection of the Upper Chichester road with the highway leading from Aston to Marcus Hook, was built many years before the free public-school system was established in the commonwealth, and because of the material employed in the construction of its walls and the abundant use of lime, was also known as the stone or white school-house. The lot and house being located on lands formerly of Richard Dutton, it is very probable that this was the site of the early Friends' school, and that Dutton, who did not die until 1795, had, two or three years before that date, given the lot and contributed to the erection of the building for educational purposes. Let that be as it may, after public schools were established in Upper Chichester the Dutton building passed into the control of the directors, and continued to be used for such purposes, an addition, in 1838, having been made to the house. On May 22, 1837, Elizabeth Harvey began teaching at this school, but on December 18th of the same year John Lloyd was the master there. In 1870 the directors purchased additional land adjoining the school lot from William H. Dutton, the ancient stone house was removed, and the present school-building erected, at a cost of nineteen hundred dollars, the contractors being Mifflin Wright and Benjamin F. Green.

The two schools mentioned had become so crowded that on Dec. 9, 1842, an additional school was opened in a house of Salkeld Larkin, on the Chichester and Concord road, of which Larkin Pennell was the first teacher. This was known as No. 3 school, and continued to be kept in Larkin's house until 1859. On the 26th of May of that year an acre of land was purchased from Enos Thatcher, near Salkeld Larkin's, and a stone house, twenty-four and a half by twenty-nine feet, was erected. This was known as Larkin's school-house. In 1874 the directors discontinued instruction in this building. The following year school was resumed there, to be discontinued in June, 1876, since which time it has not been used for educational purposes.

After the passage of the act of 1834, under its provisions the court appointed Joseph Henderson and William Booth inspectors of the public schools for

Upper Chichester. The township, however, did not adopt the law, but under that of 1836 organized public schools. The following is a list of those persons who have discharged the duties of school directors therein:

1837, George Martin, Salkeld Larkin, Abraham Johnson, Jeremiah C. Brown, John B. McCay, William H. Grubb; 1838, George Martin, William Smith, Jonathan Dutton; 1839, William Booth, Robert R. Dutton, Andrew Hance, Robert B. Craig; 1840, Joseph Henderson, Joseph Pennell; 1842, Jonathan Dutton, Andrew Home; 1843, John Stevenson, George Harvey; 1844, John M. Broomall, Jonathan C. Larkin; 1845, Jonathan Dutton, George Broomall; 1846, Harry B. Grubb, Stephen Madgin; 1847, John B. McCay, Jonathan C. Larkin; 1848, George Broomall, William Grubb; 1849, Robert McClintock, Joseph Casey; 1850, Andrew Hance, Jonathan C. Larkin; 1851, Robert M. Brown, Larkin R. Broomall; 1852, Samuel Wells, William H. Grubb; 1853, William Cloud, William H. Grubb; 1854, William H. Grubb, Larkin R. Broomall; 1855, Caleb E. Thomas, David Boyd; 1856, Harry B. Grubb, Jeremiah C. Brown; 1857, William H. Grubb, David Boyd; 1858, John E. Warne, Thomas Roberts; 1859, George Broomall, Jeremiah C. Brown; 1860, George Broomall, David Boyd; 1861, James Larkin, David N. Larkin; 1862, Abram Ward, Robert M. Brown; 1863, Clark W. Hance, James Craig; 1864, James Larkin, Thomas B. Jones; 1865, Davis O. Barlow, Joseph R. Johnson; 1866, Clark H. Hance, Lloyd Norris; 1867, James Larkin, Nathan Pennell; 1868, David H. Dalton, Andrew Osborne; 1869, Melchior Ebright, John Todd; 1870, Nathan Pennell, Alvanza W. Jester; 1871, Thomas Harvey, C. W. Hance; 1872, Thomas Harvey, William McCay; 1873, Joseph Newlin, John B. McCay; 1874, Samuel Vernon, Mrs. D. H. Dutton; 1875, Clark W. Hance, Pennell Eyre; 1876, James McClintock, Joseph Newlin; 1877, Charles W. Todd, William G. McCafferty; 1878, David Dutton, John B. McCay; 1879, Joseph Newlin, E. B. Jester; 1880, Andrew Osborne, William G. McCafferty; 1881, David H. Dutton, John B. McCay; 1882, E. B. Jester, Lewis Fraim; 1883, Lewis Fraim, Andrew Osborne; 1884, John B. McCay, Sr., William O'Donnell.

James Annesley, Earl of Anglesey.—Of all notable cases which have been presented to judicial tribunals for adjudication it is doubtful whether any can be found in the records of civilized nations which presents more romantic incidents than those set forth in the trial of fact between James Annesley *vs.* the Earl of Anglesey, in the Irish Exchequer Court, in 1743. The circumstances of this cause have not been overlooked by the novelist, and on them Smollett founded "Roderick Random," Sir Walter Scott "Guy Mannering," and, in more recent times, Charles Reade "The Wandering Heir." The case is reported in Howell's "State Trials," Burk's "Celebrated Trials connected with the Aristocracy," and in other authoritative works. It has been alleged that the incidents in the case, so far as this territory is concerned, are disproved, because the records of Chester County are silent as to James Annesley's imprisonment in the jail at Chester or the trial of the fugitives with whom he was captured. The objection, however, is untenable. The crime was one punishable with death, and the county courts were prohibited from trying such issues, hence no mention of the case would appear on the records of our county, such entry being made only on the docket of the Supreme Provincial Court, and the minutes of that tribunal have not been preserved (so far as known), excepting in a book, covering about ten years prior to 1728, of trials held in Chester County by the supreme judges. The volume is in the office of the prothonotary of Delaware County, at Media. Annesley, for a period of his term of service as a redemptioner, was a resident of Chichester, hence we present a brief account of his extraordinary adventures as found in a recent publication:[1]

"Arthur Annesley, Viscount Valencia, who founded the families both of Anglesea and Altham, was one of the stanchest adherents of Charles II., and had a considerable hand in bringing about his restoration to the throne. Immediately after that event his efforts were rewarded by an English peerage, his title being Baron Annesley, of Newport-Pagnel, in the County of Buckingham, and Earl of Anglesea. Besides this honour he obtained the more substantial gift of large tracts of land in Ireland. The first peer had five sons. James Annesley, the eldest son, having married the daughter of the Earl of Rutland, and having been constituted heir of all his father's English real property and a great part of his Irish estates, the old earl became desirous of establishing a second noble family in the sister kingdom, and succeeded in procuring the elevation of his second son, Altham, to the Irish peerage as Baron Altham of Altham, with remainder, on failure of male issue, to Richard, his third son.

"Altham, Lord Altham, died without issue, and the title and estates accordingly devolved upon Richard, who, dying in 1701, left two sons, named respectively Arthur and Richard. The new peer, in 1706, espoused Mary Sheffield, a natural daughter of the Duke of Buckingham, against the wishes of his relatives. He lived with his wife in England for two or three years, but was at last obliged to flee to Ireland from his creditors, leaving Lady Altham behind him in the care of his mother and sisters. These ladies, who evidently hated her, set about ruining her reputation, and soon induced her weak and dissipated husband to sue for a divorce, but, as proof was not forthcoming, the case was dismissed. Thereupon his lordship showed a disposition to become reconciled to his wife, and she accordingly went over to Dublin in October, 1713, and through the good offices of a friend a reconciliation was effected, and the reunited couple, after a temporary residence in Dublin, went to live at Lord Altham's country-seat of Dunmain, in the County of Wexford. Here, in April or May, 1715, Lady Altham bore a son, which was given to a peasant woman, named Joan Landy, to nurse. At first the young heir was suckled by this woman at the mansion, and afterwards at the cabin of her father, less than a mile from Dunmain. In order to make this residence a little more suitable for the child it was considerably improved externally and internally, and a coach-road was constructed between it and Dunmain House, so that Lady Altham might be able frequently to visit her son.

"Soon after the birth of the child Lord Altham's dissipation and his debts increased, and he proposed to the Duke of Buckingham that he should settle a jointure on Lady Altham, and for this purpose the pair visited Dublin. The effort was unsuccessful, as the estate was found to be covered by prior securities; and Lord Altham, in a fury, ordered his wife back to Dunmain, while he remained behind in the Irish capital. On his return his spite against her seemed to have revived, and not only did he insult her in his drunken debauches, but contrived an abominable plot to damage her reputation. Some time in February, 1717, a loutish fellow named Palliser, who was intimate at the house, was called up to Lady Altham's apartment, on the pretence that she wished to speak with him. Lord Altham and his servants immediately followed; my lord stormed and swore, and dragged the supposed seducer into the dining-room, when he cut off part of one of his ears, and immediately afterwards kicked him out of the house. A separation ensued, and on the same day Lady Altham went to live at New Ross.

"Before leaving her own home she had begged hard to be allowed to take her child with her, but was sternly refused, and at the same time the servants were instructed not to carry him near her. The boy therefore remained at Dunmain under the care of a dry-nurse, but, notwithstanding his father's injunctions, was frequently taken to his mother by some of the domestics, who pitied his forlorn condition. When he came to an age to go to school, he was sent to several well-known seminaries, and was attended by a servant both on his way to them and from them; 'was clothed in scarlet, with a laced hat and feather,' and was universally recognized as the legitimate son and heir of Lord Altham.

"Towards the end of 1722, Lord Altham—who had by this time picked up a mistress named Miss Gregory—removed to Dublin, and sent for

[1] Celebrated Claimants. London, 1873.

his son to join him. He seemed very fond of the boy, and the woman Gregory for a time pretended to share in this affection, until she conceived the idea of supplanting him. She easily persuaded her weak-minded lover to go through the form of marriage with her, under the pretence that his wife was dead, took the title of Lady Altham, and fancied that some of her own possible brood might succeed to the title, for the estates were by this time wellnigh gone. With this purpose in her mind she used her influence against the boy, and at last got him turned out of the house and sent to a poor school; but it is, at least, so far creditable to his father to say, that he did not quite forget him, that he gave instructions that he should be well treated, and that he sometimes went to see him.

"Lord Altham's creditors, as has been stated, were very clamorous, and his brother Richard was practically a beggar: they were both sadly in want of money, and only one way remained to procure it. If the boy were out of the way considerable sums might be raised by his lordship by the sale of reversions, in conjunction with the remainder-man in tail, who would in that case have been Lord Altham's needy brother Richard. Consequently the real heir was removed to the house of one Kavanagh, where he was kept for several months closely confined, and in the mean time it was industriously given out that he was dead. The boy, however, found means to escape from his confinement, and, prowling up and down the streets, made the acquaintance of the idle boys of Dublin. Any odd work which came in this way he readily performed, and although he was a butt for the gamins and an object of pity to the townspeople, few thought of denying his identity or disputing his legitimacy. Far from being unknown, he became a conspicuous character in Dublin; and although from his roaming proclivities it was impossible to do much to help him, the citizens in the neighborhood of the college were kindly disposed towards him, supplied him with food and a little money, and vented their abuse in unmeasured terms against his father.

"In 1727, Lord Altham died in such poverty that it is recorded that he was buried at the public expense. After his death his brother Richard seized all his papers, and usurped the title. The real heir then seems to have been stirred out of his slavish life, and declaimed loudly against this usurpation of his rights, but his complaints were unavailing, and, although they provoked a certain clamor, did little to restore him to his honors. However, they reached his uncle, who resolved to put him out of the way. The first attempt to seize him proved a failure, although personally superintended by the uncle himself; but young Annesley was so frightened by it that he concealed himself from public observation, and thus gave grounds for a rumor, which was industriously circulated, that he was dead. Notwithstanding his caution, however, he was seized in March, 1727, and conveyed on board a ship bound for New-castle, in America, and on his arrival there was sold as a slave to a planter named Drummond.

"The story of his American adventures was originally published in the *Gentleman's Magazine*, and has since been rehearsed by modern writers. It seems that Drummond, who was a tyrannical fellow, set his new slave to fell timber, and, finding his strength unequal to the work, punished him severely. The unaccustomed toil and the brutality of his master told upon his health, and he began to sink under his misfortunes, when he found a comforter in an old female slave, who had herself been kidnapped, and who, being a person of some education, not only endeavored to console him, but also to instruct him. She sometimes wrote short pieces of instructive history on bits of paper, and these she left with him in the field. In order to read them he often neglected his work, and, as a consequence, incurred Drummond's increased displeasure and aggravated his own position. His old friend died after four years, and after her death he resolved to run away. He was then seventeen years of age and strong and nimble, and, having armed himself with a hedging-bill, he set out. For three days he wandered in the woods until he came to a river, and espied a town on its banks. Although faint from want of food, he was afraid to venture into it until nightfall, and lay down under a tree to await the course of events. At dusk he perceived two horsemen approaching, the one having a woman behind him on a pillion, while the other bore a well-filled portmanteau. Just as they reached his hiding-place, the former, who was evidently the second man's master, said to the lady that the place where they were was an excellent one for taking some refreshment; and bread and meat and wine having been produced from the saddle-bags, the three sat down on the ground to enjoy their repast. Annesley, who was famished, approached closer and closer, until he was discovered by the servant, who, exclaiming to his master that they were betrayed, rushed at the new-comer with his drawn sword. Annesley, however, succeeded in convincing them of his innocence, and they not only supplied him with food, but told him that they were going to Apoquenimink to embark for Holland, and that, out of pity for his misfortunes, they would procure him a passage in the same vessel. His hopes were destined to be very short-lived. The trio remounted, and Annesley had followed them for a short distance painfully on foot, when suddenly horsemen appeared behind them in chase. There was no time for deliberation. The lady jumped off and hid herself among the trees. The gentleman and his servant drew their swords, and Annesley ranged himself beside them, armed with his hedge-bill, determined to help those who had generously assisted him. The contest was unequal, the fugitives were soon surrounded, and, with the lady, were bound and carried to Chester gaol.

"It appeared that the young lady was the daughter of a rich merchant, and had been compelled to marry a man who was disagreeable to her; and that, after robbing her husband, she had eloped with a previous lover who held a social position inferior to her own. All the vindictiveness of the husband had been aroused; and when the trial took place, the lady, her lover, and the servant were condemned to death for the robbery. James Annesley contrived to prove that he was not connected with the party, and escaped their fate; but he was remanded to prison, with orders that he should be exposed to public view every day in the market-place; and that if it could be proved by any of the frequenters that he had ever been seen in Chester before, he should be deemed accessory to the robbery and should suffer death.

"He remained in suspense for five weeks, until Drummond chanced to come to Chester on business, and recognizing the runaway, claimed him as his property. The consequence was that the two years which remained of his period of servitude were doubled; and when he arrived at New Castle, Drummond's severity and violence greatly increased. A complaint of his master's ill-usage was made to the justice, and that worthy was at last obliged to sell him to another; but Annesley gained little by the change. For three years he continued with his new owner in quiet toleration of his lot; but having fallen into conversation with some sailors bound for Europe, the old desire to see Ireland once more came upon him, and he ventured a second escape. He was recaptured before he gained the ship, and under the order of the court, the solitary year of his bondage which remained was increased into five. Under this new blow he sank into a settled state of melancholy, and seemed so likely to die that his new master had pity upon his condition, began to treat him with less austerity, and recommended him to the care of his wife, who often took him into the house and recommended her daughter, Maria, to use him with all kindness. The damsel exceeded her mother's instructions, and straightway fell in love with the good-looking young slave, often showing her affection in a manner which could not be mistaken. Nor was she the only one on whom his appearance made an impression. A young Iroquois Indian girl, who shared his servitude, made no secret of her attachment to him, exhibiting her love by assisting him in his work, while she assured him that if he would marry her when his time of bondage was past she would work so hard as to save him the expense of two slaves. In vain Annesley rejected her advances and tried to explain to her the hopelessness of her desires. She persistently dogged his footsteps, and was never happy but in his sight. Her rival, Maria, no less eager to secure his affections, used to stray to the remote fields in which she knew he worked, and on one occasion encountered the Indian girl, who was also bent upon visiting him. The hot-blooded Indian then lost her self-control, and having violently assaulted her young mistress, sprang into the river close by and thus ended her love and life together.

"Maria, who had been seriously abused, was carried home and put to bed, and her father naturally demanded some explanation of the extraordinary quarrel which had cost him a slave and very nearly a daughter. The other slaves had no hesitation in recounting what they had seen, or of saying what they thought, and the truth came out. Annesley's master was, however, resolved to be certain, and sent him into her room, while he and his wife listened to what passed at the interview. Their stratagem had the desired success. They heard their daughter express the most violent passion, which was in no way returned by their slave. As they could not but acknowledge his honorable feeling and action, they resolved to take no notice of what passed, but for their daughter's sake to give him his liberty. Next day his master accompanied him to Dover, but instead of releasing him, as he had promised his wife, sold him to a planter near Chichester for the remainder of his term.

"After various ups and downs, he was transferred to a planter in New-castle County, whose house was almost within sight of Drummond's plantation. While in this employ he discovered that he was tracked by the brothers of the Indian girl, who had sworn to avenge her untimely fate, and nearly fell a victim to their rage, having been wounded by one of them who lay in wait for him. By another accident while he was resting under a hedge which divided his master's ground from a neighbouring plantation he fell asleep, and did not awake until it was perfectly dark. He was aroused by the sound of voices, and, on listening, found that his mistress and Stephano, a slave on another farm, were plotting to rob his master and to flee to Europe. Repressing his desire to reveal the whole scheme to his master, he took the first opportunity of informing his mistress that her infamy was discovered, and that if she persevered in her design he would be compelled to reveal all that he had overheard. The woman at first pretended the utmost repentance, and not only earnestly promised that she would never repeat her conduct, but by many excessive acts of kindness led him to believe that her unlawful passion had changed its object. Finding, however, that she could not prevail upon him either to wink at her misdeeds nor gratify her desires, she endeavored to get rid of him by poison; and an attempt having been made upon his life, Annesley resolved once more to risk an escape, although the time of his servitude had almost expired.

"On this occasion he was successful; and having made his way in a trading ship to Jamaica, got on board the 'Falmouth,' one of his majesty's ships, and declared himself an Irish nobleman. His arrival, of course, created a great stir in the fleet, and the affair came to the ears of Admiral Vernon, who, having satisfied himself that his pretensions were at least reasonable, ordered him to be well treated, wrote to the Duke of Newcastle about him, and sent him home to England. He arrived in October, 1741. His uncle Richard had in the mean time succeeded, through default of issue, to the honors of Anglesea, as well as those of Altham, and became seriously alarmed at the presence of this pretender on English soil. At first he asserted that the claimant, although undoubtedly the son of his deceased brother, was the bastard child of a kitchen wench. He next tried to effect a compromise with him, and subsequently endeavored to procure his conviction on a charge of murder. It is also said that assassins were hired to kill him. But it is certainly true that Annesley having accidentally shot a man near Staines, the Earl of Anglesea spared neither pains nor money to have him convicted. He was tried at the Old Bailey, and being acquitted by the jury, proceeded to Ireland to prosecute his claim to the Altham estates. On his arrival at Dunmain and New Ross, he was very warmly received by many of the peasantry. His first attempt to secure redress was by an action at law. An action for ejectment was brought in the Court of Exchequer in Ireland for a small estate in the county of Meath, and a bill was at the same time filed in the Court of Chancery of Great Britain for the recovery of the English estates.

"In Trinity term, 1743, when everything was ready for a trial at the next ensuing assizes, a trial at bar was appointed on the application of the agents of the Earl of Anglesea. The case began on the 11th of November, 1743, at the bar of the Court of Exchequer in Dublin, being, as is noted in Howell's 'State Trials,' the longest trial ever known, lasting fifteen days, and the jury (most of them) gentlemen of the greatest property in Ireland, and almost all members of parliament. A verdict was found for the claimant, with *6d.* damages and *6d.* costs. A writ of error was at once lodged on the other side, but on appeal the judgment of the Court below was affirmed. Immediately after the trial and verdict, the claimant petitioned his Majesty for his seat in the Houses of Peers of both Kingdoms; but delay after delay took place, and he finally became so impoverished that he could no longer prosecute his claims.

"James Annesley was twice married; but although he had a son by each marriage, neither of them grew to manhood. He died on the 5th of January, 1760."

The Talbot Mill.—In 1767, John Talbot built a stone grist-mill on the east branch of Naaman's Creek, which for many years was noted in that section of the county commanding a large and remunerative trade. The mill, shortly after 1820, passed into possession of Nathan Pennell. In 1826 it was owned by his heirs and rented to Mordecai Larkin, and subsequently to others. It was finally purchased by William McCay, and subsequently became the property of his son, John B. McCay. In 1884 the ancient mill was entirely consumed by fire.

Dutton's Saw-Mill.—On a branch of Green Creek, and on the tract of land surveyed to John Kingsman in 1682, a saw-mill was built shortly after the middle of the last century by Kingsman Dutton, the grandson of the settler, Kingsman's daughter Elizabeth having married John Dutton. The date stone on the east gable of the two-story brick house standing near the east branch of Aston township, erected by Kingsman Dutton, bears that date, and it is supposed that he built the saw-mill about that time. He died leaving his estate much involved, and the premises were sold by the sheriff in 1768. Joseph Talbot became the owner of the mill and plantation, and the estate descended to his grandson, Benjamin Elliott, who removed the old saw-mill building in 1860; it having been long discarded, became dilapidated and an unsightly ruin.

Evening Star Lodge.—The only secret society in Upper Chichester, Evening Star Lodge, No. 13, of the Daughters and Sons of St. Luke, was chartered in June, 1879. The members of this lodge, an organization of colored men and women, reside mostly in Lower Chichester, although the meetings are held at Upper Chichester Cross-roads. The society was instituted with thirty charter members, but the number has largely increased since that time.

The quiet stillness which pervades the township of Upper Chichester, wherein license to keep public-house has not been granted for almost a century, was rudely shaken on Wednesday, Jan. 20, 1869, when the body of a female was found in the middle branch of Naaman's Creek, on the farm of George Broomall, which is located in the southwestern end of the township on the circular line. The utmost excitement prevailed. The dead girl was a stranger, and although the circumstances strongly suggested that she had committed suicide, inasmuch as her hat and veil were found on the bank near by, and her under-skirt had been removed and wrapped around her head in a way that indicated that she had placed it in that position, yet there was much anxiety to learn the cause prompting the act. It was subsequently ascertained that the deceased was Ellen Haggerty, and that her mind had become diseased, the result of religious excitement. The body had lain in the water four days before it was discovered.

CHAPTER XXXVIII.

LOWER CHICHESTER TOWNSHIP.

A FEW years before the Dutch wrested the authority from the Swedes on the Delaware, Queen Christiana, of Sweden, was graciously pleased to grant a large tract of land in the colony to Capt. John Ammundson Besk, his wife, and heirs, in consideration of services he had rendered the State and was expected to render to the government in the affairs of New

Sweden. The following translation of this royal gift is reputed to be the most accurate extant:[1]

"We Christiana, by the Grace of God, Queen of Sweden, Gothen and Wenden, Grand Princess of Finland, Duchess of Eastland, &c.:

"Be it known that of our favor, and because of the true and trusty service which is done unto us and the Crown, by our true and trusty servant, Captain Hans Ammundson Besk, for which service he hath done, and further is obliged to do so long as he yet shall live; so have we granted and given unto him freely as the virtue of this open letter is and doth show and specify, that is, we have given and freely granted to him, his wife and heirs, that is heirs after heirs, One Certain piece and tract of land, being and lying in New Sweden, Marcus Hook by name, which does reach up to and Upwards of Upland Creek, and that with all the privileges, appurtenances and conveniences thereunto belonging, both wet and dry, whatsoever name or names excepted of them, that is which belonged to this aforesaid tract of land, of age, and also by law and judgment may be claimed unto it and he and his heirs to have and to hold it unmolested forever for their lawful possession and inheritance. So that all which will unlawfully lay claim thereunto, they may regulate themselves hereafter. Now for the true confirmation hereof have we this with our own hand underwritten, and also manifested with our seal, in Stockholm, the 20th of August, in the year of our Lord, 1653.

"NEILS TUNGELL, Secretary.

"CHRISTIANA [L. S.]."

Only that portion of Lower Chichester lying east of Marcus Hook Creek was included in this patent, as has been very conclusively shown by the late Edward Armstrong, and it is unnecessary for me to further allude to his argument.[2] The land west of that creek, comprising all the remaining territory now known as Lower Chichester, was patented by Governor Andros, March 28, 1679,[3] to Charles Jansen, Olle Rawson, Olle Nielson, Hans Hopman, John Hendrickson, and Hans Olleson, containing one thousand acres. Dr. Smith says, in the survey, it is mentioned that this land "was formerly granted unto the said persons in the time of the Dutch Government."[4] The quit-rent reserved in the patent by the Duke of York was ten bushels of winter wheat. At Upland Court, March 13, 1678/9, Rodger Pedrick appeared and acknowledged that he had sold to William Hughes, in fee, half of his land at Marcus Hook, which land he, Pedrick, had purchased of John Hendrickson; and at the same court, Hans Ollsen (Olleson) acknowledged a deed to William Clayton for all his land, "right & interest of & to his houses and appurtances Lying and being att Marretties hooke."[5]

The ancient name of Marcus Hook was sought to be changed by the residents of that locality early under Penn's administration, for at the court at Upland, June 13, 1682, the old records show that "the grant formerly made from Governor Markham to the inhabitants of Marcus Hook, at their request for the the calling of said Chichester, which said Grant bears date the Twentieth day of April, Anno 1682, and was read and published in the Court held at Upland June the Sixteenth, Anno 1682, according to order as a record thereof."

Although in legal documents for many years thereafter the settlement at Chichester is thus designated, the popular name was so fixed in the public mind that it would not accept the more modern title, and to this day, despite legislation and executive power, the village still retains its time-honored nomenclature.

In September, 1682, as before mentioned, Marcus Hook was visited by Lord Baltimore when the latter was on his way to New Castle, after his unsatisfactory interview with Markham at Upland, and by his assertion of title to that place and all the territory north of the degree of forty, occasioned the utmost consternation among the settlers there. The first appearance in our records of Chichester township was at the court held 27th of Fourth month (June), 1683, when Willard Hughes was appointed constable for "Chichester liberty." What territory was included in that term liberty is now purely conjectural, but Dr. Smith is doubtless correct in declaring that it was probably the township of Chichester, as it had been laid out by Charles Ashcome. That there was some dispute respecting the bounds of that municipal district is evident from the decree of court made the 6th day of Eighth month, 1685, whereby it was "Ordered that the township of Chichester extends its bounds as formerly laid out by Charles Ashcome until further ordered."

After the coming of Penn, in 1682, Marcus Hook grew apace, and for a time it was a formidable rival to Chester. In 1708 the two places were of almost equal size, for a writer at that time, describing them, states that both of these settlements "consist of almost 100 houses."[6]

In the early judicial records of Chester County, Chichester, being an important locality, furnished perhaps more than its due proportion of business for the courts of those days, which, no doubt, was largely owing to the fact that during the Swedish administration the Fins, who were mostly of the convict class of the mother-country, had collected to the east of that hamlet. The cases were generally of that character of misdemeanors prevalent among the lower order of society,—particularly where ignorance is the rule. I do not propose to draw largely from the records or to present extended extracts from the proceedings in those cases, but I cannot refrain from calling attention to two trials, the particulars of which, even in the lapse of two centuries, will be of interest to the modern reader. The first case was tried at

1 Martin's "History of Chester," p. 7.

2 Record of Upland Court, p. 135. See note 2.

3 Benjamin H. Smith's historical introduction to atlas of early grants and patents of Delaware County, page xii. "This tract was called 'common,' and comprised all the land between Naaman's Creek and Chichester Creek, extending from the river to the present line dividing Upper and Lower Chichester. There appears to have been a partition of the tract among the owners, but owing to the vagueness of the descriptions as recorded, it is now a matter of great difficulty to locate the original property. Many deeds from the patentees remain on record."

4 History of Delaware County, p. 521.

5 Record of Upland Court, p. 135.

6 "Pennsylvania in 1708," by J. Oldmixon; Hazard's Register, vol. v. p. 180.

Chester on the 7th day of Second month, 1685, and at that time aroused intense public feeling, due, largely, to the prominent social position of the parties litigant, as also the serious matter involved As the case terminated, it would have been better for the plaintiff if he had never instituted the action Henry Renolds, of Marcus Hook, who became a resident there early in 1680, was a publican, keeping a tavern in the village (at which he sold liquor with license when he could get the court's approval, but whether he obtained that permission or not he persisted in vending ardent spirits), seems to have been a man of quick temper, which would often cause him to do that which was of the utmost disadvantage to him At the court held at the date stated, Renolds sued Justa Anderson for scandalous and defamatory words, in that he had reported that Renolds had beaten his servant girl and the next day she died The plaintiff showed by James Sandelands, James Brown, William Hawkes that Justa Anderson had asserted that he saw Henry Renolds "beat and kicke his maide and that he saw her alive no more" The defendant was able to show by Thomas Pearson that when he was at Renolds' house he saw the latter lift "up the tongs" and threaten to strike his maid-servant "for not eating such things as was provided for her," while Wooly Rosen, who lived just below Naaman's Creek, in New Castle County, testified that while he was at Renold's the girl asked him for some milk, which angered her master,—she was an indentured servant,—and he struck her "one Blow with a broome Staffe, asking her whether there was not vituals enough in the house?" William Cornell declared that he saw Renolds "Beate his maide with a Broome staffe and afterwards kicked her as she was by ye fire" While Robert Moulder related a marvelous story that the night the girl died "he see the maide sleeping by ye fireside, and sometimes afterward shee went to bed, after which a 'revelation' came to him that the maide would dye that night" Prudence Clayton, Renolds' mother-in-law, who, after the girl died, had been sent for "to lay her out, did not remember that shee did see any manner of hurt about her" The jury found, however, for the defendant, and the case had aroused such public attention that James Kenneily, the first coroner of whom we have record in Chester County, intervened in the matter This we learn from the order of the court, held 1st 3d day of Seventh month, 1685, that "Execution be granted against Henry Renolds for ye Crowner's fees, charges of Inquest & taking up ye said Renolds' maide, with all other charges whatsoever thereunto belonging" The sheriff in this execution levied on an ox, and Renolds at the next court had to pay £4 10*s*, when "the court ordered him his Oxe againe"

The other case was heard at a court held at Chester on the 1st day of 3d week, Fourth month, 1690, when John Martin, a weaver, was tried for having stolen from the house of Thomas Brown fourteen dressed deer-skins, of the value of thirty shillings Thomas Brown, the plaintiff, testified that the accused had acknowledged the theft, but the interesting feature of the case was presented in the manner in which the crime was traced to the prisoner It appeared from the evidence of Francis Chads, who, before his removal to Birmingham, was a shoemaker in Chichester, that he had mended the shoes worn by Martin, and that he had done so "with 2 nails & 2 plates towards ye towes of his shoes" William Clayton stated that he and Thomas Brown, Jr, while the prisoner and Thomas Brown, Sr, were talking, had gone to the house of Thomas Brown, Sr, where Martin lived, "and there we saw the print of a shoe, and we followed it, and we perceived it to be print with nails & a pleat with nails, & we followed it to the swamp & there in a hollow tree we found the skins, and afterwards we took the measure & went to James Brownes & compared the measure with the prisoners It seemed to be the very same" George Foreman, a justice, testified that on the morning of the theft Brown told him of his loss, that his house had been broken open, and asked for a search-warrant, which he issued He also states, after the search had been made, that he told Brown to "go to his house & see if there were no tracks of anybody He went & returned shortly after, saying there was a print of a foot Then I went to his house myself & saw the window open, & upon the ground the print of a shoe with nails & clamps of iron We followed the tracts down to the side of the fence, & then along the swamp until we came upon Wm Clayton's new cleared field, and there in a swamp, in a hollow tree, we found fourteen drest skins Then we went to James Brown's house & took along with us the measure of the print of the shoe & measured John Martin's, and it seemed to us to be the very same Martin seemed to be startled at my taking his shoes off" The jury convicted the prisoner, and he was sentenced to be sold for eight years to another province, to make good all damages to the party aggrieved, and his master's charges,—he was an indentured servant,—amounting in all to £17 7*s* 9½*d*, and to "receive 39 lashes well Laid on his Bare Back at ye Cart's Tayl"

If tradition be accepted as authority, at the conclusion of the seventeenth and the first and second decades of the eighteenth century the pirates which then infested the Atlantic coast from New England to Georgia would frequently stop at Marcus Hook, where they would revel, and when deep in their cups would indulge in noisy disputation and broils, until one of the streets in that ancient borough from that fact was known as Discord Lane, which name the same thoroughfare has retained for nearly two centuries Blackbeard, who for many years kept the coast in alarm, with his crew it is said often visited Marcus Hook, where at the house of a Swedish woman there, to whom he gave the title of Marcus, although her name was really Margaret, he was accustomed to indulge in the wildest disorder and drunken debauches[1]

At the meeting of the Provincial Council in Philadelphia, Aug 11, 1716, Governor William Keith called the attention of Council to ' the great losses which this colony has already sustained beyond any of its neighbors by our Trade's being blocked up and infested with pirates at the Capes of this river and bay," and further informed them "that one Trench, a noted pirate, who has done the greatest mischief of any to this place has been lurking for some days in and about this town"[2] We know that on Friday, Sept 1, 1698, a pirate ship and tender landed fifty armed men and plundered Lewistown[3] In May, 1701, a French pirate appeared above Bombay Hook,[4] and for many years thereafter the colonial records show the constant alarms the province was subjected to by fears of piratical demonstration on the settlements on the river

In 1698, when Gabriel Thomas wrote his quaint "History of Pennsylvania," he specified, among the four great market towns, Chester as enjoying that privilege, and "likewise all those towns have fairs kept in them" It seems that Marcus Hook, shortly after this statement was made, desired to invest itself with the dignity of a market and fair, for at the Council at Philadelphia, May 16, 1699, at which Governor Markham presided, the minutes show[5]

"Upon reading the petition of some of the Inhabitants of Chichester, in the Countie of Chester, Requesting a weeklie markett & two fairs in the year, After a full debate yrupon, the Leivt Gov & Council granted ym a weeklie market on friday's to be keept in broad street as is desired"

On Feb 14, 1700, Penn having returned, and personally presiding over the deliberations of Council, on the minutes of that body under the date given is the further reference to Marcus Hook as a market town[6]

"The petition of the ffreeholders in and about the Town of Chichester was read, setting forth that Lieut Gov Markham & Council, had granted to the said Town of Chichester, the Privilege of a fair and Market, and therefore humbly requests that what was then imperfectly done, the Gov would be pleased fully to Compleat and perfect"

"*Resolved*, That they shall have a Charter for a ffair & Market, with this proviso That because some Complaints have been made agst fairs in General, their fairs should, notwithstanding anything Contain'd in the said Charter, be put down whenever it should be thought fitt that the other fairs of the Government should be also suppressed"

It was not, however, until seven months after Penn had consented to grant a charter to Marcus Hook that he actually gave the ambitious borough the charter, with all the rights and privileges, defined in an official document The following is a copy of that charter, and it is very interesting, inasmuch as it locates the habitations of the prominent men of that day residents there, and presents other historical data

"William Penn, True & Abzolute Propr & Governor in Chiefe of the Province of Pensilvania & Terri'es thereunto belonging

"To all to whom these p'sents shall come SENDETH GREETING

"Whereas, the ffreeholders & Inhabitants of the lower parts of the County of Chester, on the river Delaware in the sd Province, through a laudable desire & inclination of improving the sd parts, by setling more close together, & enlarging of commerce, have humbly besought mee that I would erect into a market town a certain comodious place, well situated for that purpose, aforetime commonly called MARCUS HOOK, with the privilidges of a FAIR & WEEKLY MARKET to be held therein

"KNOW YE, THEREFORE, That I, favoring the just & reasonable request of the sd ffreeholders & Inhabitants, by virtue of the powers by the King's Letters Patent to me & my heirs given & granted, have erected, & do, for me, my heirs & successors, by the tenour of these p'sents, erect into a Market Town the sd place, aforetimes called MARCUS HOOK, or such part thereof as is hereinbefore described, under the bounds & limits hereinafter mention'd That is to say, all that tract or space of ground lying & being situate on the river Delaware BEGINNING at the upper point of the land of Jonas Sandilands upon the river & extending along the sd river to the lower point of the land of Nathaniel Lamplugh, about two hundred & fifty perches, be it more or less, and from the river Dellaware extending backwards about one thousand feet, by lines at right angles with the river, from the sd two points to the sixty foot road leading to Chester, which town, as above bounded, I will shall be called CHICHESTER, as of late it has usually been called, and I doo hereby grant unto the inhabitants of the sd town free ingress and egress, by land & water, to & from the sd town, through

[1] Trench, or Drummond, let his family name be what it may, was as grotesquely conspicuous a villain as can be found in the annals of crime Blackbeard, for that was his piratical name, in person tall, of swarthy complexion, and with an exuberant black beard of extraordinary length covering his whole face, from which his sobriquet was derived, and which he used to twist into numberless small tails, the ends tied with bows of brightly colored ribbons, was a picture sufficiently repulsive, one would think, without calling in, as additional decoration when in battle, three braces of huge pistols dangling across his shoulders, and lighted matches protruding from beneath his hat to illuminate his dusky face and savage eyes with a supernatural glare His was, indeed, when prepared for action, a figure to be gazed upon with fear and apprehension Socially he was a sensual polygamist, whose harem of fourteen wives was the scene of brutalities such as even his hardened crew could not witness unmoved with pity, and yet which no one dared to reprove To render his power over his lawless men absolute, he announced that he had entered into a compact with hell, and once, when at sea, a mysterious personage appeared on the ship, sometimes aloft, sometimes on deck, sometimes below, who spoke to no one but Blackbeard, and who disappeared as secretly as he had come among them The crew firmly believed that this was the veritable devil himself, and that this was but one of many dark communications their chieftain held with the powers of evil At another time when afloat, it is recorded he said, maddened with drink, "Come, let us make a hell of our own, and try how long we can bear it." Going below with some of his crew, he caused the hatches to be closed, and had several large tubs filled with sulphur and other combustible articles, to which he set fire, then while the thick choking vapors rolled in dense columns throughout the ship, he danced and filled the sickening air with his profanity, until those above released the half suffocated and fainting men from their perilous situation which, apparently, gave the piratical chieftain no respiratory uneasiness His convivial pleasantries were also of a similar hideous character, for once when drunk, seated at the head of his cabin table, he blew out the candles, cocked his pistols, and crossing his hands fired on each side at his associates, one of whom was wounded so desperately that he never recovered This incident Blackbeard often himself related in gleeful moments, stating in conclusion, "If I did not now and then kill one of my men, they would forget who I am" In the fall of the year 1718 the Governor of Virginia sent Lieut. Maynard with two vessels to cruise for Trench, and on the 21st of November he encountered the pirate, who, fortunately, then had but a small crew on board his ship A bloody fight resulted,—Maynard and Blackbeard contested hand to hand,—and it is related that the corsair received over twenty wounds with swords, and almost as many bullets struck him, before he was slain Maynard cut off the dreaded pirate's head and affixed it to the bowsprit of his vessel, and thus he entered Hampton Roads with the ghastly, grinning token of his success exposed to public view

[2] Colonial Records, vol iii p 64

[3] Ib, vol i p 539

[4] Ib, vol ii p 21

[5] Ib, vol i p 558

[6] Ib., vol ii p 12

all parts of this Province & Terr'ies As also to lay out all such streets, highways, lanes, alleys & passages in the sd town, as to them shall seem meet & convenient to lay out for the accommodation thereof, & more especially, that there shall be one street called ffront street, leading from the upper to the lower part of the sd town The whole length of the sd town, bounded to the north north west, with a line paralell to the river, at the distance therefrom that Wm Clayton's dwelling house now stands, and in breadth fifty foot Also, one other street called Broad street beginning at the sd ffront street, on the east north east of the sd House of Wm Clayton, running in a direct line north north west, one thousand ffeet or thereabouts, to the sd sixty foot road leading to Chester, & in breadth the same distance that now is between the sd Wm Clayton's House & the house now of Roger Jackson, for the length of two hundred and fourteen feet, & at the extent of the sd two hundred and fourteen feet there shall be a Publick Market Place, in breadth one hundred and forty feet, & in length along the Broad street two hundred and thirty feet & from the sd market place to the sixty foot road afores^d, the sd Broad Street shall be in breadth one hundred feet Also, one other street called New street, in breadth twenty five foot, beginning at the sd ffront street at the distance of ffour hundred & twenty foot to the east north-east of Broad Street & running in a direct line north north-west, to the sd sixty foot road Also one lane, called Market Lane, in breadth thirty foot, beginning at the sd New street ffour hundred & fourteen feet from the ffrout street & running parralell to the sd ffront street, three hundred eighty three feet into the Market Place Also, one other lane called Discord Lane, in breadth thirty foot, beginning at the south corner of the Market Place & running west southwest, paralell to the sd Front Street, to the outhermost bounds of the town, which sd street, Market Place, & Lanes, I do hereby grant & confirm for the sd publick uses forever, together with all other such streets, squares, alleys or passages as now are or hereafter shall be laid out as aforesd, reserving always to all persons whatsoever all the rights & inheritances which they now have or hereafter may have or lawfully claim in or to any lands or lotts within the bounds or limits aforesd, the publick streets, ways, lanes, alloys & Market Place only excepted And I doe further, for me, my heirs & successors, grant to the sd inhabitants and ffreeholders, to have, hold & keep a free market in the sd Market Place, on the sixth day of every week, forever, with ffree leave and liberty, to & for the sd inhabitants & all others who shall resort thither to buy & sell on the sd sixth day of every week at the said place, all manner of provisions & other necessaries for life, with the right, privlidges & immunities whatsoever that to a free market, according to the comon customs & usages of England do belong For the better regulation of which Market, I do hereby constitute & appoint Walter Marten clark thereof, to be succeeded, in case of death, removal from the sd place or other incapacity by such person & persons in the sd office forever, as two justices of the Peace for the County of Chester, dwelling in or nearest to the sd town, together with six of the chiefe inhabitants thereof, to be chosen in the Market Place by the ffreeholders of the town & township of Chichester, shall appoint, with full power to the sd Walter Marten & his successr, to be appointed as aforesd, to discharge all the parts & duties of the sd office of Clark of the market as ffully & amply, to all intents & purposes, as any other Clark of the Market within this Government may or can And, for the greater incouragement of trade to the sd town, by the resort of persons from remoter parts, I doe further grant to the sd inhabitants, ffreeholders & others, ffull power & liberty to Have, Hold & Keep a Publick Fair, to be held on the nine & twentieth day of September, & on ye two days ffollowing, in every year, for all lawful wares & merchandizes in the sd Market Place, and for horses & cattle in the upper part of Broad street, adjoyning the sd Market Place Provided, That there shall be no unlawful sports, plays, gaming, revelling, drunkenness or debauchery, nor any other disorder, nor loose & idle practises, tolerated in the sd ffair, in any part or place thereof, or in the sd town, by reason of the sd fair, at any time whatsoever, nor any ale, wine, rume or other strong liquors, sold in the sd fair, but in the usuall dwelling houses of the sd town And for the better regulation of the sd fairs and preservation of good order therein, I doe hereby constitute & appoint Walter Marten & Philip Roman, Wardens of the sd ffair, to be, in case of death, removall from the sd place, or other incapacity, succeeded by such two persons in the sd office, forever, as two Justices of the Peace of the county of Chester, dwelling in or nearest to the sd town, with twelve of the chiefe freeholders of the town & township of Chichester, (to be chosen as aforesd) shall think fitt to appoint, and upon the decease, removall or other incapacity of any of the sd Wardens to act any further in the sd office, no fair shall be held in the sd town till a successor or successr to the sd Warden or Wardens be duly chosen, according to the tenor of these p'sents, anything herein contain'd to the contrary notwithstanding, And I doe hereby grant to the sd Wardens & to their successors to be elected as aforesd full power forever to exercise within the sd fairs every year, during the time they shall be kept, all necessary jurisdiction & authority for suppressing of vice, maintaining good order, & regulating all other things whatsoever within the sd town, to the sd fairs immediately relating

"In Witness Whereof, I have caused these, my Letters to be made Patent, Witness myself, at Philadelphia, the twelfth day of September, in the thirteenth year of the reign of William the Third, over England, Scotland, Ffrance, and Ireland, King, &c, & the one & twentieth of my Govermt over this Province of Pennsilvania, Annoq d'm 1701

"Wm Penn

"Recorded ye 17th, 7br, 1701

"By comand of the Propry
& Governr

"James Logan, *Secry*"

On one occasion, at least, the good people of Marcus Hook attempted to give vitality to this charter, hence sixty years after it was granted a meeting of the residents was held April 29, 1760, whereat John Wall and John Crawford were chosen successors of Walter Martin and Philip Roman and John Flower, clerks of the market, after which date the old charter has lain accumulating the dust of a century undisturbed The powers of the people in their collective characters in those days certainly was much overestimated, for in Lower Chichester,

"At a town meeting held this 17th March, 1770, it is unanimously agreed by us present that every freeholder not attending at the two annual elections & not showing a sufficient reason shall be subject to pay into the Overseers of the Poor the sum of one shilling to be applyed as will be thought most proper & any of the officers not attending shall be subject to the payment of two shillings to be employed as aforesaid And farther it is agreed that the publick expenuses at Town Meeting shall be regulated & fixed for the whole year to any sum not exceeding Ten Shillings in Regard to the Poor by the Overseers by them to be allowed in their accounts

"*Present*—Jacob Worril, Richard Riloy, Samuel Lampiugh, John Crawford, Wm Dockeity, Arch'd Dick, Adam C Clayton, Isaac Lawrence, Jno Flower, Joseph Marshall, Rich'd Clayton, Benj Miller, Joseph Clayton, Samuel Armor"

In the last century Marcus Hook was noted for the number of vessels built there Acrelius, in 1755, made particular mention of this industry, while in 1748, Peter Kalm, the Swedish naturalist, who remained for a brief season at Chichester, records that "they build here every year a number of small ships for sale, and from an iron work which lies higher up in the country they carry iron bars to this place and ship them" The furnace mentioned was the famed Sarum Forge, on Chester Creek, near the present Glenn Mill In 1753, William Howell, of Marcus Hook, was a leading shipwright at that place, and in that year sold a lot of ground to Charles Norris, on the southeast side of Discord Lane, extending to high-water mark on the Delaware[1] In 1800, Samuel Trimble was also a ship-builder there

The ancient town continued to remain prominent as a ship-building locality until the tonnage of vessels in recent years had increased so greatly that its lack of large yards, capital, and other facilities restricted the industry to small coasting crafts As late

[1] Deed of partition of estate of Charles Norris, May 24, 1788, Deed-Book D, No 23, p 303, etc Recorder's office, Philadelphia

as the middle of this century Samuel T. Walker carried on quite an extensive trade in the building of schooners and sloops, the work being done by Woodward & Farray, who seem to have been sub-contractors under him. In May, 1849, Jacob Sinex, who had been for several years engaged in ship-building at Marcus Hook, removed to Chester, where he carried on the same business. At the present time Samuel J. Burton has a ship-yard at the Hook, and in March, 1884, a large-sized schooner was launched from his yard.

William Cranston, who died in 1811, aged seventy-seven, in Delaware, was a native of Marcus Hook, and in early life was a noted ship-builder in that borough (was assessed as such in 1800), as was Simon Sherlock, with whom Cranston had served his apprenticeship. Simon Cranston, born at Marcus Hook in 1768, and died near Stanton, Del., in 1856, aged eighty-eight years, was named by his father in honor of his old master. He frequently related that he could remember, as a lad of eight years, when the British fleet coming up the river opened fire on the town. His recital of that incident is as follows:

"The fleet lay opposite the town, and the Continental Light-Horse were stationed back of the village. My parents' dwelling lay between the two forces. The fleet fired on the troops, and the British sent a boat ashore, and an officer told my mother to take her children into the cellar; in her fright she took them outside of the house and down into the cellar, in that way exposed to the flying balls." [1]

In the fall of the year 1784, we learn from a letter written by Judge Francis Hopkinson, that a vessel had been built at Marcus Hook; was attached by a tradesman, on a claim for work and materials furnished in construction of the craft. When she was launched the attachment was laid, but the owners forcibly ejected the officers and moved the vessel to Wilmington. The judge was anxious that the State government should take "the most speedy measures for bringing the offender to answer for the Indignity they have thrown on a Court of Justice of this Commonwealth." [2]

Peter Kalm, to whom reference has just been made, in the fall of the year 1748 tarried a brief season in Marcus Hook, and spoke of it by its legal name, Chichester, as "a borough on the Delaware, where travelers pass the river in a ferry." How long this regular mode of conveyance to New Jersey was maintained does not appear. But about the beginning of this century an attempt was made to sustain such a means of communication with the eastern shore of the river, but after a brief trial it was abandoned for want of patronage. Kalm made particular reference to the fact that in the town and neighborhood were "many gardens, which are full of apple-trees sinking under the weight of innumerable apples." In 1828 the newspapers of that day called attention to a remarkable cabbage-tree, then growing in the garden of John S. Van Neman, at Marcus Hook, which was five feet high, eleven and a half feet in circumference, and had twenty limbs, on which were more than fifty small heads of cabbages.

At the beginning of this century Marcus Hook was the residence of one of the early noted painters of the United States. I copy the account of him given by Thompson Westcott: [3]

"Adolph Ulrick Westmuller, a native of Sweden, after having painted in Europe, came to America, at the age of forty-four years, in 1794, and settled at Philadelphia. He brought with him some of his paintings, which were greatly admired. President Washington sat to him. He recopied, it is said, for James Hamilton, the portraits of the Hamilton family, and then Hamilton destroyed the originals. Westmuller went back to Europe in 1796, where he lost money by the failure of a great house in Stockholm. He came back to Philadelphia in 1800, and brought with him his celebrated picture of Danæ, which, being a nude figure, was exhibited only to such as might apply to view it; and from the exhibitions Westmuller received a handsome income. He remained in Philadelphia some years, married a lady of Swedish descent, and finally removed to Marcus Hook, Delaware Co., where he lived until his death, in 1812. His pictures were sold at auction shortly after his death, and brought good prices. For a copy of his Danæ five hundred dollars were paid."

St. Martin's Episcopal Church.—Walter Martin, of Upper Chichester, a Quaker, tradition relates, who being "dealt with" by that society, became embittered against Friends, on Dec. 18, 1699, "for divers good causes and considerations him thereunto moving," conveyed to the town and inhabitants of Chichester—Marcus Hook—an acre and one perch of ground for a church and free burial-place for the inhabitants, "Quakers and reputed Quakers only excepted." This ancient deed is explicit as to the doctrine to be taught by the persons who should avail themselves of the donor's bounty to erect a church or meeting-house there. "The inhabitants of said town and township, which are to have free liberty to build a church, chapel, or meeting-house, are intended to be such as own the two ordinances of the sacraments of baptism and the Lord's Supper of bread and wine; and such as own the resurrection of the bodies of the dead, and own the ordinance of singing of psalms in the praise of God in the congregation, or in their families, and such as own the taking of an oath on the Bible, according to the laws of England, if lawfully called thereto for the confirmation of the truth; and it is to be a free burying-place to such as will bear part of the cost of keeping up the fences, or concern them-

[1] Martin's "History of Chester," page 109.

[2] Penna. Archives, 1st Series, vol. x. page 355.

[3] History of Philadelphia, chap. cxvi., *Sunday Dispatch* of Philadelphia.

selves with building a church, chapel, or meeting-house thereon."

This lot, the donor strictly declared, was to be kept for the purposes expressed in the deed, "and for no other, whatever," and explained his exception against Friends, "because the Quakers have a meeting house of their own in the said township" William Thomas, the quaint document provided, should be the "first sexton or grave digger for the town of Chichester, during his life, or so long as he is able to perform duties appertaining to the office of sexton or grave digger," with power to those "concerned" in keeping the burying-place to name a successor when Thomas should cease to act in that capacity

The adherents of the Church of England in that neighborhood availed themselves of Walter Martin's gift, "feeling little or no satisfaction in their own minds, without having a sacred place set apart for holding public worship according to the ritual of that church," but "being few in number and of less ability to build a place of worship," in the year 1702 they purchased from John and Tobias Hendrickson a rude frame building, which had been used as a blacksmith-shop, for which they paid about five pounds, and all the male residents aided in moving the structure to its new location, where it was subjected to a bountiful coat of whitewash within and without, rude benches constructed, and the nameless church, other than that which it derived from its location, was established In connection with St Paul's, at Chester, and the church at Concord, it became a missionary station, under the protection and support of the Society for Propagating the Gospel in Foreign Parts Rev Evan Evans, in a letter written in 1707, states that in 1700 he was sent over as missionary to Philadelphia, but the churches of that denomination increased so rapidly that he was frequently compelled to make long and weary journeys to preach to the scattered congregations, "for this reason," he states, "I went frequently to Chichester,"[1] until, in 1704, Rev Henry Nichols was placed in charge of St. Paul's parish, then including the churches at Chester, Marcus Hook, and Concord Walter Martin died in 1719, and was buried in a lot in the churchyard which he had reserved as a place of interment for himself and friends The place where his remains lie is marked with a head- and foot-stone, which, a half-century ago, by order of the wardens and vestry, was redressed and the letters re-cut The ancient monument presents, near the top, the carved representation of an hour-glass and cross-bones, and bears the following inscription

> "In the memory of Walter Martin,
> buried June 26, 1719, aged 68 years
>
> "The just man lives in good men's love,
> And when he dies, he's bless'd above"

In 1714, Rev John Humphreys was in charge of the parish, and continued as the rector until 1725, when he went to Baltimore (?), and refused to return unless the churches at Marcus Hook and Chester would raise his salary to forty pounds per annum This the parish appears not to have done, for from a paper dated April 5, 1727, signed by Ralph Pile, of Birmingham, Philip Ottey, and others, it is stated that, in 1726, "a great mortality reigned amongst us, we were obliged to desire the Rev Mr Hesselius, the Swedish minister at Christiana, who, out of his pious and Christian disposition, came to bury our dead, and seeing the disconsolate condition of our churches, offered to assist us once a month at our churches, which he still continues to do"[2] In the summer of 1728, Rev Richard Backhouse was appointed missionary to St Paul's parish by the society The letter apprising Governor Gordon of the appointment of Mr Backhouse is dated at London, August 3d of that year[3] Rev Israel Acrelius, who came from Sweden in 1749, arriving at Christiana on July 20th of that year, states that so constant were the demands made upon him to hold divine services in the Episcopal Churches at Concord and Marcus Hook, besides his direct charge at Christiana, and as each church desired him to preach there on Sundays, it became impossible to satisfy the congregations, for "there were not as many Sundays in the months as there were congregations to serve The good old Swedes now began to murmur, partly at the minister, that they never got to hear him on Sunday in their own church, and partly at the English, who wished to have him with them, and never once paid his expenses of travel"[4] The parish of St Paul's was then without a rector, Rev Richard Backhouse having died at his home in Chester, Nov 19, 1749 He had been succeeded by Rev Thomas Thompson, who abandoned his charge, apparently, shortly after he assumed the responsibilities of the position

In the will of Jeremy Collett, in 1725, a legacy of fifty pounds was bequeathed for the "better support of the Episcopal minister officiating in the chapel" at Marcus Hook, doubtless a welcomed addition to the slender means of that congregation Twenty years after that date, in 1745, the old frame structure becoming insufficient to meet the need of the neighborhood, an effort was successfully made to provide a better house of worship A fund was raised sufficient to erect a small brick church, about twelve by sixteen feet, which was surmounted by a belfry and an iron vane, in which the figures 1745 were cut. Three years subsequent to the erection of this new edifice, the old frame structure being still standing was used from time to time as a school-house, under the auspices of

[1] Hazard's Register of Pennsylvania, vol iii p 358, Dr Perry's "Papers Relating to the Churches in Pennsylvania," p 33

[2] The above statement appears in a note to Martin's "History of Chester," p 97 The statement is slightly erroneous The town of Baltimore was not laid out until 1730 The sesqui centennial of that city was held in the fall of 1880 Mr Humphreys could hardly have gone there in 1725 He doubtless went to Whetstone Point, now within the city limits, for, as we know, Whetstone Point was incorporated as early as 1706

[3] Penna Archives, 1st Series, vol i p 226

[4] Acrelius, p 305

the church organization. A new difficulty arose, for in a letter written by Mr. Backhouse, June 26, 1748, a year before his death, he says, "The Moravians have hired a house to keep their meetings in twice a month at Marcus Hook, to which place my congregation resort, but I hope (and believe) more through curiosity than anything else, because they show me the same respect they ever did, and carefully attend the church as formerly, when it is my turn to be there."[1]

In 1759, Rev. George Craig become the rector, having been sent from London as a missionary by the Society for Propagating the Gospel in Foreign Parts, and continued in charge of the church during almost the entire war of the Revolution, until 1783. He died a few years subsequent to this date, and his remains were deposited in the aisle of the church. It was during his rectorship, in 1760, that the nameless sanctuary received the title it now bears, St. Martin's, and it was accepted by the vestry at the suggestion of Emanuel Grubb, as commemorative of Walter Martin, its founder. The annalist Watson states that Emanuel Grubb was the first child of English parents born after the grant to Penn of the province, 1681, and that his birth occurred in a cave in the bank of the river, near Chester. The statement, however, as regards the date of birth is contradicted by the tombstone in St. Martin's churchyard, the inscription being,—

"Emanuel Grubb,
Died August 9, 1757,
Aged 85 years and 10 days."

which makes the date of his birth to have been July 30, 1682.

In 1765 the Episcopal Churches at Chichester and Concord were going to decay, and to raise money to repair these buildings and to aid other churches in other localities, in January of that year the Assembly passed an act authorizing a lottery to secure the sum of £3003 15*s*., and although the Governor returned the bill for some amendments,[2] we know that such an act was finally approved, for in 1769 the provincial treasurer paid to St. Martin's Church £66 13*s*. 4*d*., the share it was entitled to as the proceeds of that lottery.

In 1845 the old church, built one hundred years before, became so dilapidated, and besides was insufficient to meet the requirements of the congregation, that it was determined to build a new edifice, which was promptly done, and the present building, the third, was erected. In 1822 St. Martin's Church, which, previous to that date, had been a part of the parish of St. Paul's, of Chester, became a separate organization, and from that time has been in charge of the following rectors: Rev. Benjamin S. Huntington, 1852–53; Rev. John Baker Clemson, 1853–58; Rev. Henry Hall Hickman,[3] April 8, 1860; Rev. Joseph A. Stone, 1860–68; Rev. J. Sturgis Pearce, 1863–71; Rev. Gustavus Cleggett Bird, 1871.

In 1860 the old brick school-house, which had been built in the hitching-yard belonging to the church in 1801, was taken down by William Trainer, who gave one hundred dollars for the material, and with the bricks obtained from the old building Mr. Trainer erected the wall on the north side of the hitching-yard. The sheds belonging to the church cover the site of the old school-house, and on Sunday, Oct. 15, 1870, a pair of horses belonging to Thomas W. Wookward, of Linwood, being back from the shed, broke through and fell into the well which was formerly used, but having been covered with a few boards and some earth, in time was forgotten, until the incident narrated brought its existence to memory. One of the horses broke its neck in the fall, and the other was found severely injured when extricated. In 1871 the congregation erected a parsonage adjoining the Odd-Fellows' Hall, the church in all its preceding history never before having a residence for its rector. The land was donated for that purpose, and the cost of the building subscribed by several of the wealthier members of the congregation. In 1879, John Larkin, Jr., presented a tract of ground comprising about two acres adjoining the churchyard to St. Martin's Church, thus adding space to the burial-lot, which in almost two centuries had grown crowded with the dead of many generations.

St. George's Methodist Church.—The Methodists had no church organization in Lower Chichester until 1835. In that year Rev. Brooke Eyre visited Marcus Hook, where at that time only three persons resided who were members of that denomination. Mr. Eyre was invited to preach in a shoemaker's shop; and so earnestly and effectively did he address his audience that an interest was immediately aroused. While the excitement was at its height one of the three Methodists in the town chanced to enter the store of William Trainer, and in conversation said if they, the Methodists, had a church in Marcus Hook it would be of great benefit to the village and neighborhood. "Build one," said Mr. Trainer; and, taking down a pass-book, he wrote the formula of a subscription, and headed the list with a promise to pay twenty dollars towards building a Methodist Church. With that beginning the paper was circulated, John Larkin, Jr., contributing the like sum. That afternoon between two and three hundred dollars was pledged to the object, and in less than three weeks a sufficient amount was obtained to justify the erection of a plain wooden structure on Discord Lane, where the Methodist burying-ground is now located, the land for that purpose being sold by William McLaughlin at a trivial price. The building was supplied with rude uncushioned benches, and a raised platform at one end, where an unornamented board desk served as a pulpit. The congregation was poor, and hence it had to rely on the circuit preachers to conduct its regular

[1] Perry's "Papers Relating to the Churches in Pennsylvania," p. 251.

[2] Colonial Records, vol. ix. p. 243.

[3] On Wednesday evening, May 2, 1860, Mr. Hickman was walking from the cross-roads to Marcus Hook, when he fell dead.

services, but the body increased steadily in membership. On Feb. 20, 1839, Lewis Massey and wife made a deed of trust of a house and a lot of land in Marcus Hook as a parsonage for the minister of the Chester Circuit, which lot of ground was located on Broad Street, where the present church edifice now stands, and it continued to be held by the Wilmington Conference until St. George's Church became a station, in 1870. At that date the board of trustees decided to petition the Court of Common Pleas to be empowered to convey to the trustees of Marcus Hook Methodist Church one hundred feet on Broad Street, and extending in depth the whole length of the lot, to be used for the erection of a church thereon, and to sell the remaining part of the lot to John A. Stevenson for two thousand five hundred dollars, which sum was proposed to be used in the purchase of another parsonage, the house in Marcus Hook, then dilapidated, being six miles distant from the place where the clergyman of Chester Circuit was appointed to preach. The court authorized the trustees, in November, 1873, to make the deed to Stevenson in fee-simple, free, and discharged from all the trusts mentioned in the deed of trust.

The old frame church, in the thirty-five years of constant use, had grown too small for the congregation, and besides was fast falling to decay; hence it was resolved to build a new sanctuary. The corner-stone was laid on Saturday, July 8, 1871. Edward S. Farsons, although not a member of the church, took warm interest in the building, and it was through his influence in a large degree that the present ornate church edifice was erected, which is one of the most imposing structures in the ancient borough.

Previous to 1868 the Methodist Episcopal Church of Marcus Hook was one of the five appointments which constituted the Chester Circuit. In 1868 the territory embraced in the Philadelphia Annual Conference was divided into two Annual Conferences. The part lying between the Susquehanna and the Delaware Rivers, and north of the Delaware State line, was made the Philadelphia, while the State of Delaware and the Eastern Shore of Maryland constituted the Wilmington Conference. After this division Marcus Hook was the only appointment of the old Chester Circuit which remained in the Philadelphia Conference, the other appointments becoming part of the Wilmington Conference. The following year (1869) the Marcus Hook Church was made a station, and Rev. E. H. Hoffman was appointed pastor. On Nov. 22, 1869, a charter was secured, in which the church was named Cokesbury, in honor of the first bishops of the Methodist Episcopal Church, Thomas Coke and Francis Asbury, and that still remains as the charter-name of the church, although at the present it is popularly known as St. George's Church. At the close of the year 1869 the church had seventy-nine members in good standing, and the property belonging to the station was valued at four hundred dollars. In March, 1870, Rev. J. H. Wood was appointed pastor, and was succeeded the following year by Rev. George A. Wolfe, who continued there for two years. It was during his pastorate the present church edifice was built, at a cost of nine thousand dollars; and when the building was dedicated there was an incumbrance of three thousand dollars upon it.

The following is a list of the pastors of St. George's Church from that time: 1873–74, Rev. William M. Gilbert; 1875, Rev. T. W. Maclary; 1876, Rev. M. Lorin; 1877–78, Rev. A. M. Wiggins; 1879–81, Rev. R. Smith; 1882–84, Rev. William K. Macneal.

The debt which remained on the church at the time of its dedication was discharged in full during the pastorates of Rev. T. W. Maclary and Rev. R. Smith. At the present time there are one hundred and fifty-one members of the church in good standing, and the property is valued at nine thousand dollars, and is free of debt.

Baptist Church.—The Baptist Church of Marcus Hook was organized May 3, 1789, the members forming the association being Rev. Eliphaz Dazey, who died about 1796, Judge Richard Riley, Richard Moore, Thomas Perkins, George Price, John Walker, who subsequently became a Baptist clergyman, George White, William Perkins, Mary Riley, the judge's wife, Jemima Dazey, who after her husband's death kept a store in Chester, on Market Street, in the second house from the southeast corner of Fourth Street, Sarah Cannell, Christiana Dick, Hannah Moore, Elizabeth Parsons, Mary Perkins, Elizabeth Walker, and Sarah Price. The later was the wife of Samuel Price, who owned a large part of the real estate where the villages of Linwood and Trainer's are now located. The church was built by subscription, and erected in 1789,[1] the cost of the structure being £164 16*s.* 6½*d.* It was built of bricks, which were made from clay dug near by, and burned in a clamp-kiln. The dimensions were twenty-two by twenty-five feet, one story in height. The gallery was located at the south end of the auditorium, and the congregation sat on plain benches having backs to them. At the north end was a raised platform set off from the remainder of the apartments by a baluster and a seat for the minister. The wood-work was in its natural state, excepting the windows and doors, which were painted white. In 1814 the congregation had increased so much in number that an addition of fifteen feet was made to the length of the church, and pews with doors took the place of the old benches. The church as an organization was admitted into the Philadelphia Baptist Association Oct. 6, 1789. For many years Bristow was the sexton of the church, and it is related that on the evening of May 17, 1853, while the old man was driving his cow homeward, he fell to the earth dead.

The corner-stone of the present handsome church

[1] Smith's "History of Delaware County," p. 302.

edifice was laid Sept 10, 1853, and the same night the box deposited in the stone was robbed of its contents The church was completed the following year, and on Oct 21, 1854, the first services were held therein In March, 1862, Mary Moulder, the daughter of Joseph and Margaret (Flower) Moulder, died at Marcus Hook, aged one hundred and five years, and was buried in the Baptist burial-ground at that place She had been an earnest member of the church nearly three-quarters of a century

The list of pastors of Marcus Hook Baptist Church is as follows Rev Elephaz Dazey, May 3, 1789, to April 2, 1796, Rev John Walker, Sept 5, 1818, to March 10, 1821, Rev Joseph Walker, Aug 7, 1824, to —— 1842, Rev D L McGear, Aug 9, 1845, to June 13, 1846, Rev Theophilus Jones, May 20, 1848, to Feb 7, 1849, Rev Isaac Gray, May 1, 1853, to Jan 4, 1855, Rev Miller Jones, 1858 to 1861, Rev E W Dickinson, D D, August, 1862, to Dec 8, 1875, Rev H B Harper, May 6, 1876, to April 17, 1878, Rev C C W Bishop, Sept 23, 1879

Hebron African Methodist Church —This religious society was organized about 1837 The first meetings were held in a log house which stood on the road from Dutton's Cross-roads to Upper Chichester Cross-roads In 1844 a lot was purchased from John Mustin, and the present frame church erected during the pastorate of Rev Abraham C Crippin The pastors from the organization of the church have been as follows Rev Israel Geott, Rev Jeremiah Downer, Rev John Cornish, Rev Henry J Young, Rev Abrahem C Crippin, Rev Isaac B Parker, Rev John L Armstrong, Rev Adam Drener, Rev Jeremiah Buley, Rev William W Schureman, Rev Sheppherd Holcomb, Rev Jeremiah Young, Rev Peter Gardiner, Rev Caleb Woodward, Rev Jacob Watson, Rev George W Johnson, Rev William H Davis, Rev Henderson Davis, Rev John W Davis, Rev John W Norris, and Rev Thomas H Moore, the present pastor The church has a membership of thirty, and the trustees are Samuel Anderson, William D Laws, and Peter Lunn

The Schools —The first school of which we have any information in Chichester was conducted under the auspices of the Society for the Propagation of the Gospel in Foreign Parts, and was held in the old frame house of worship on St Martin's lot, after the first brick sanctuary was erected, in 1745, and continued for nearly sixty years In 1801 a new brick school-house was erected on the church lot, the fund for that purpose being raised by contributions among the members of the parish Here, too, all the public meetings of the township appear to have been held, certainly after 1805 The old school-house was torn down in 1860 by William Trainer, as mentioned in the account of St Martin's Church About 1854 the school-house known as Cedar Grove was erected near the Baptist graveyard, and the building on the St Martin's lot ceased to be used for school purposes

After the passage of the school act of 1834, the directors of Lower Chichester were active in the advocacy of the system, and the following year erected a school-house near the present Linwood Station, on lands given by John D White, one of the directors, for that purpose The building was defectively constructed, the walls cracked, and being pronounced unsafe, it was pulled down, and another house built in 1844 at Rocky Hill The old site being near the railroad, was believed to be dangerous to the children On Dec 7, 1876, the court, on the petition of Samuel Hickman, ordered his farm on the east and west branches of Naaman's Creek to be attached to Upper Chichester school district In 1880 an ornate school-house was built on the great Southern Post road, near Trainer's Station.

In 1860, and for some time thereafter, the Misses Emanuel kept the Linwood Seminary in Lower Chichester

The full list of school directors of Lower Chichester township is as follows

1834, Joseph Walker, Jr, John D White, 1840, Samuel F Walker, Joseph Marshall, 1842, David Trainer, William Eyre, 1843, Peter N Gamble, Charles P Bunting, 1844, William McGlaughlin, William Trainer, 1845, Joseph P Pyle, 1846, William Eyre, William B Roberts, 1847, John Stewart, John F Broomall, 1848, John Larkin, David Trainer, 1849, no report, 1850, Benjamin F Johnson, John Stewart, 1851, David Trainer, James Price, 1852, Charles P Bunting, William H Rigby, John Stevenson, 1853, Edward McDade, Townsend Rowand, John F Broomall, 1854, John R Casey, John Stevenson, 1855, Peter N Gamble, Charles F Wishman, 1856 Manuel Emanuel, Peter N Gamble, George C Healy, 1857, Thomas Taylor, Alfred Bunting, 1858, Isaac Eyre, Jacob English, 1859, Manuel Emanuel Isaac Hendrickson, 1860, Alfred Bunting, Daniel C Green, 1861, Samuel Spansey, Jacob English, 1862, Isaac Hendrickson, William Trainer, 1863, J R Casey, Benjamin Johnson, 1864, Daniel C Green, William Appleby, 1865, Samuel Spansey, Benjamin D Johnson, 1866, William H Rigby, Isaac Heacock, 1867, Frank Gray, George Barton, 1868, William Barto, Dr Manley Emanuel, 1869, Nathan Pennell, Alfred Bunting, 1870, Frank Gray, Charles Weston, 1871, William L Derrickson, Tracy E Walker, 1872, Isaac Eyre, John Roberts, 1873, Stephen Hall, E W Casey, 1874, Frank Gray, Edwin Lisler, 1875, J Eyre, John Lamplough, 1876, J E Green, Clifford Loughead, William M Black, 1877, no report, 1878, John D Goff, Clifford Loughead, 1879, Clarence Larkin, John Lamplough 1880, J E Green, S J Burton, 1881, B D Johnson, A D Hastings, 1882, John Roberts, Clarence Larkin, 1883, James Philips, Henry Heacock, 1884, John D Goff, William Trainer

Licensed Houses, Lower Chichester —One of the first cases which occurs in our county annals wherein license is alluded to was heard "November 30, 1661, before William Markham, Esq, and Justices," the defendant being a resident of Lower Chichester. The case, as it appears of record, is set forth in the quaint phraseology of that period

"Henry Reynold having appeared at this court to answer for his selling strong liquor by small measure in his house contrary to the Governors and Council's order, upon his submission to the court, was discharged"

Six years subsequently to this proceeding, at December court, 1687, another of the early settlers at Marcus Hook figured in connection with a violation of the license law, as follows

"Robert Moulder being yt last Court Indichted for suffering Thomas Clifton and Samuel Baker to be Drunk att his house was upon ye same called to ye Barr Butt nothing being Proved ordered to keep an ordinary provided he keep Horse meat & man's meate"

Moulder must have been indicted under that clause in the "Duke's Booke of Law" which, promulgated Sept. 22, 1676, enacted that "no Licenced Person shall suffer any to Drink excessively or at unseasonable hours after nine of the Clock in or about any of their houses upon penalty of two shillings, six pence for every Offence if Complaint and proof be made thereof" Hence it would seem that the defendant was at the time keeping a licensed house of entertainment, for Law 10, enacted by the first General Assembly in December, 1682, at Chester, "against such as Suffer Drunkenness in their houses, and about Ordinances," clearly could have been intended to punish those only who, having special privileges confided to them, exercised the same to the injury and disadvantage of the public The penalty prescribed for this offense was that they "who suffer such excess of Drinking in their house, shall be lyable to the punishment with the Drunkard," which was, for the first offense a fine of five shillings or five days' detention at hard labor in the House of Correction, and to be "fed only with bread and water," while for the second and all subsequent convictions, "ten shillings or ten days' labor, as aforesaid"

The case of Peter Stewart, who was tried in October, 1688, for feloniously breaking open the chest of John Wickham, who was then stopping at the house of William Clayton, seems to indicate, from the sentence, that at that date Clayton was keeping a public-house at Marcus Hook The record shows that he was not licensed in 1704, for at the conclusion of that year he was presented "for keeping an Ordinary without license," but petitioning the court for such license it was granted to him.

The first instance I have found of license being granted in Lower Chichester, other than to Clayton and Moulder, occurs under date of May 25, 1714, when Richard Edwards presented his petition to keep a public-house at Chichester, which was allowed. In 1720, Edward Smout had license granted him for a house of entertainment, with leave "to sell all sorts of liquor," at Chichester, and continued there until Feb 26, 1724, when his petition states that he "had obtained license for a publick house at Chichester, but now removed to Chester and desires license there," which was approved by the court Feb 23, 1725, Andrew Rawson informed the justices that he had taken the house late of Edward Smout, in Chichester, which house he asked might be continued as a license house, which was granted

Elizabeth Clayton, wife of William Clayton, Jr, Sixth month 28, 1717, petitioned for a renewal of license in Chichester, possibly at the house kept by her father-in-law, William Clayton, Sr, in 1688, as mentioned above On Ninth month 23, 1719, William Clayton asked to be permitted "to keep a common ale house in the house where he dwells" On Aug 20, 1720, he was given full license for a public inn, and Aug 25, 1724, he petitioned for renewal of this privilege The following year Elizabeth Clayton states that, "having for several years past obtained ye Honours Recomendacon," ask that it be continued, which was approved for that as well as the following year, as also in 1727

In 1728, Thomas Clayton obtained the grace of the courts, which was extended to him during the year following In 1730 the license was granted to William Weldon, who had rented the premises Aug 27, 1734, Thomas Clayton again presented his petition to the court, in which he says, that "having some years ago leased the house where he formerly Dwell at Chichester & kept a house of entertaint there to one William Weldon, who ever since kept a publick house and the terms of the said leace being near expired, your petitioner Inclined to return their again," but the justices were not so inclined at that session, yet, on Nov 26, 1734, when Clayton again petitioned for the license, setting forth that "your Petitioner's father having kept a house of entertainment for several years in Chichester until his Decease and your Petitioner some time after his said ffather's Decease, until his affairs Called him abroad," etc, had followed the same occupation, the court yielded to his importunity, and annually thereafter his name appears on the list of approved licenses, until 1756, when Hannah, his widow, kept the house, and remained there until 1770 In that year John Flower purchased the property and continued the business until 1787, when license was granted to him for the last time at "The Ship" Caleb Pierce followed the next year, when Sarah Flower, a maiden daughter of John Flower, took charge of the house in 1789 In 1803 she received license from the court of Delaware County, after which I fail to trace the license until 1808, when John Marshall had the house, and remained there until 1809, when Jonas Fairlamb followed him

Benjamin Collam kept the Ship in 1810, and in 1811, Mary Goodwin was granted license there In 1813, Thomas Noblet petitioned leave to keep a house of entertainment at the "noted old stand formerly kept by Mr and Miss Flower, and lately by John Marshall, who has removed to another place in Marcus Hook," which was accorded him. The next year the house ceased to be an inn and being then much dilapidated, it was taken by Rev John Walker, who taught school therein for several years with success The ancient hostelry subsequently was used as a store, and was such on the evening of May 16, 1872, when it was totally destroyed by fire At the date mentioned Charles P Bunting occupied it, and the accidental overturning of a vessel containing an inflammable liquid, which took fire from a lamp in Mr Bunting's hands, resulted in a few moments in enveloping the building in flames Even the records of the school board, in Mr Bunting's custody, were destroyed, and he narrowly escaped being burned to death The loss was over twelve thousand dollars The broken walls of the ancient structure as the fire left them are still to be seen at the southwest corner of Front and Broad Street, Marcus Hook

On Front Street, "facing the lower pier," in the early part of this century, David Marshall, who had been a lieutenant in Wayne's regiment, kept the tavern known as the "sign of George Washington" In his petition for the year 1799, he states the place "has been a noted stand for the space of forty years A great number of shipping lying for the space of three months and upwards opposite your petitioner's tavern, and his house is constantly crowded with persons from vessels" Over half a century before he filed this petition, John Kerlin, in 1748, had license for many years at this place, and after being kept as an inn by several parties, William Pierce seems to have become the landlord, until it was taken by Marshall, who continued to receive the court's approval until 1824, when it in turn ceased to be a public-house

In 1771, Reece Peters obtained license for a house on Front Street, and in his petition states that it was the house formerly occupied by William Hughes In 1787 John Taylor was granted license there, after which it ceased to be an inn until 1804, when Joseph Merrihew, in his petition for the old house of Reece Peters, urged the court as an inducement for their bounty that "if granted license, intends to keep ferry boats in order to transport horses, cattle, and heavy articles to New Jersey, as for want of such conveyance the public very frequently suffer great inconveyance, there being no ferry on either side of the Delaware from New Castle to Gloucester Point" The court granted his application, but as he did not petition at the next court, he doubtless found that the business was not remunerative In 1814, Isaac Dutton, who had been refused license at the old Blue Ball, obtained the court's favor for this stand, which he dubbed the Fountain Inn, and under that title William Warden kept it in 1816, but the following year changed the name to the Eagle, and John Perrine, who succeeded him in 1818, added to the sign the word "Golden" Eagle In 1821, Richard Barry followed as the landlord, but the next year he was denied license In 1828, Margaret Marshall kept the house, and in 1830, James Marshall followed her, and continued as landlord of the Farmers and Mechanics' Inn until 1841, when John Larkin Jr, kept it for three years, after which time it disappeared finally from the list of public-houses in Lower Chichester

At the cross-road, below where the Union Hotel stands, in former years was a tavern, the record of which I cannot trace farther back than 1812, when it was kept by Thomas Noblet, who took with him the name he had formerly used at the Union Hotel, "the United States Arms," and gave it to this house It subsequently was kept by Fanny Irving, and she was followed by Susan Dutton Objection being made to the continuance of the license, she removed to Wilmington, and the house ceased to be a public inn

The Old Blue Ball Tavern.—Nathaniel Lampleu (Lamplugh), Oct 10, 1727, stated to the court that he "had been at considerable charge in building a house for public house on King's Road to Newcastle" and asked license for the same, which was allowed, and annually continued to him until Aug 31, 1731, when Samuel Gray presented his petition to court, alleging that he had "taken to farm ye House with the appurtenances Commonly called & known by ye name of the Blew Ball Tavern, where a house of Entertainment hath been for some considerable time & now is kept" Gray remained at the noted inn, which was about a half-mile above the Delaware State line, until 1736, for on August 31st of that year Thomas Howell states that "having taken the house when Samuel Gray lately Dwell on the Great Road from Chester to New Castle, in the township of Chichester," he desired license, and it was granted to him annually thereafter until 1753, when he having died, the tavern was kept by his son until 1765, when Jonathan Pugh was the landlord He was succeeded in 1765 by William McCoy, who seems to have died, for the next year Rachel McCoy had licensed, and in 1767, who gave place to John McCoy, and the latter in 1770 to Archibald Dick, who in his petition states that he succeeds McCoy in business, and that the building and farm are his property Here Archibald Dick continued yearly to receive license until and including 1776, when, so far as the records show, his last application was in 1776, which was approved Dick is said by Martin to have lived like a nabob at the Blue Ball, or rather as that author erroneously, I think, located his dwelling as being the large frame house standing at the southwest corner of the Chichester (Hook) Cross-roads, which at that period was an imposing structure He says that when Dick visited Philadelphia, he drove thither "in a barouch with four splendid horses, with his negro driver and servant," and that he was the owner of fine stock [1]

May 4, 1772, Mr Dick announced in the *Pennsylvania Packet* that he has purchased the "noted horse Dove, imported from England by Dr Hamilton," and in the same paper, May 17, 1773, he advertises that he has "at Marcus Hook the horse Pennsylvania Farmer, without exception the greatest beauty in America, under care of David Miller" During the Revolutionary war he was active in behalf of the colonies, and held in 1779 the office of assistant quartermaster-general, and in 1780 was assistant forage-master for

[1] History of Chester, p. 305

Chester County He must have resided in Chester in 1779, for in the *Pennsylvania Packet* of July 1st of that year is published a letter from Archibald Dick, dated "Liberty Hall, Chester, June 28, 1779" He died March 9, 1782 His distinguished son, Dr Elisha Cullen Dick, who was born near Marcus Hook, March 15, 1762, was one of the consulting physicians called in by Dr Craik, the family physician, to visit Gen Washington in his last illness "When all hope of recovery from less extreme remedies had been abandoned, Dr Dick proposed an operation which he ever afterwards thought might have proved effectual in saving the general's life, but it did not meet the approval of the family physician"[1] Archibald Dick was succeeded in business as host of the Blue Ball by Zebidee Hollingsworth, who remained there until 1783, in which year Dr Dick sold his undivided half-interest in his father's real estate, April 29, 1783, to Isaac Dutton, for nine hundred and eighty-five pounds Thomas B Dick made partition of the estate, and the Blue Ball was taken by Isaac Dutton, who continued there until his death in 1793, and from 1794 to 1808 the inn was kept by Elizabeth Dutton, his widow. In 1809, Benjamin Collum had the tavern, and also in 1810 The following year, and that of 1812, the court refused to license the Blue Ball In 1814, Cornelius Pratt stated in his petition that he had purchased the property with the express view of occupying it as a tavern, that the house and stables were the most commodious for an inn "of any on the road between Chester and the State line," having been constructed and prepared long since for such use, that since the unfortunate obstruction to the navigation of the Delaware and Chesapeake, the road aforesaid has been so much used by travelers and wagoners as to have made it difficult sometimes to find convenient and uncrowded accommodation, "your petitioner, suffering under an oppressive restraint by the want of a license, and loosing that just and reasonable advantage of applying his property to end most profitable and beneficial to his family" He seems, however, to have purchased it subject to the condition of obtaining the license In 1817, William Worden petitioned, but the court rejected the application, as also in the year 1818, when Susanna Dutton petitioned "to keep a public house at the old Blue Ball Tavern, about five miles below Chester," but was refused The continued denial of license at last compelled a sale of the property, and John M Smith, having purchased it in 1821, after considerable pressure being brought to influence the court, succeeded in obtaining the approval of the judges. In 1822, Ashbill Taylor became landlord, and continued there until 1828, when John Bowlen, Jr, succeeded him In 1830 and 1831 James Marshall, 1832, John Bowlen, Jr, in 1832, William Holston until 1834, when the Blue Ball was a temperance house In 1835, Priscilla Thompson was the landlady, in 1837, James Plunket was mine host, and in 1838 he was succeeded by Sarah Bullock From that date the old Blue Ball inn disappeared from the list of public-houses, even the ancient building itself being demolished In 1843, John Larkin, Jr, built in close proximity to the site of the noted tavern the large square house which he sold to John Cochran in 1850

The site of the old Blue Ball subsequently became the property of Thomas W Woodward, an extensive wholesale tobacco merchant of Philadelphia On Feb 19, 1873, while Mr Woodward was conversing with his family, he suddenly expired, dying in the chair in which he was then seated

The Union Hotel—John Flower, who had kept tavern at another location in Lower Chichester from 1729 to 1734, and perhaps before the first date, in 1736, presented his petition, setting forth that "having lived long in this county, and now unable to labour for maintenance of wife and family, hath taken an House lately erected on the main Road from Chichester into the back parts of Chester county, where the same Crosses the Road leading from Philadelphia to New Castle," and desired to keep a public-house thereat, but the court refused to grant him the license, although in the following year they gave him the privilege He died in 1738, and that year his widow, Mary, was granted the right to continue the business, and that the court extended its indulgence to her the following year we learn from the remonstrance of residents of Lower Chichester, dated Aug 29, 1739, against the petition of Elizabeth Bond for hotel license The latter, on Aug 30, 1738, the year previous, had presented a petition, in which she informed the court that she "is Left a widdo with a Considerable Charge of small Children, and having no way to maintain them but by my hard Labour," asks that she be permitted "to sell Beer and sider" Her application being indorsed by a number of the most substantial citizens, the justices acted favorably on her request The following year, however, when she presented herself, with the statement that "having three small children to maintain, wishes to sell rum and other liquors, by small measure," a remonstrance was filed by the inhabitants of Lower Chichester, representing that "there are already four public-houses—Thomas Clayton, Mary Flower, William Weldon, and Thomas Howell—in the township," and that no necessity exists for another, whereupon her application was rejected

In 1741, Humphrey Scarlet, who had married the widow Flower, was licensed at the cross roads until 1746, when he dying also, the widow again succeeded to the business in 1747, and in 1749, she having married her third husband, John Rain, became the landlord Rain was no exception to the rule, and he dying in 1756, Mary again became the landlady. In 1759, Richard Flower, her son by her first husband,

[1] Thomas Maxwell Pott's "History of Carter Family," p 79

had license for the inn. He died in 1763, and his widow, Hannah, continued the business until 1768, when she married John Wall, who seems to have had license for a public-house in the township from 1759 to 1764. The following year, 1769, Wall was succeeded by Joseph Gribble, and the latter, in 1773, gave place to John Dunlap, who, in his petition, stated that the inn was then known as the "Ship Princess Amelia." In 1774, David Ford followed Dunlap, and in 1776 John Taylor became the landlord, the title of the tavern having been changed to the King of Prussia. In 1778, Jacob Cobourn followed as mine host of the inn, after which date I lose record of it until 1791, when Henry Odenheimer had license for the tavern, including 1793. In 1795–96, John Walker was the host, while in 1798–99, Henry C. Barker was the landlord. He was succeeded, in 1800, by John Selah, at which time the inn was known as "the Sign of the Leopard."

In 1803, Charles Afflick became mine host of the Leopard, and was followed by Henry C. Barker, in 1804. For six years Jacob D. Barker was the landlord, to be succeeded, in 1810, by Edward Salliard, and he in turn, in 1811, by Thomas Noblett, who called the house "the United States Coat of Arms," and, in 1813, Jacob D. Barker again returned to the cross-road inn. The petition of Barker, in 1820, states the house is known as "The Union Inn." In 1824, George Hoskins followed Barker, and continued there until 1839, when John Harper, Jr., had the license. In 1841, William Appleby became the landlord, and remained there as such until 1850, when he having died, the license was continued to his widow, and she in turn was followed by her son, William Appleby, in 1861. The latter remained as landlord of the ancient hostelry until 1866, when William Wilson had license until 1873,—the year of local option. In 1876 the house was again licensed to his widow, Hannah H. Wilson, and she continued annually to receive the court's approval until 1884, when the license was withheld from all houses in Lower Chichester.

At this road-side inn the great men of the last generation have stopped, that their horses might be watered and themselves refreshed. William Trainer informs me that he can distinctly remember seeing John Quincy Adams riding along the road to and from Washington, with four horses to his coach, and with out-riders. The sturdy farmers of that day gazed with a kind of awe as "the leaders of the political parties" passed by with their followers without deigning, in many cases, to return the profound bows of the rustic freemen.

The Spread Eagle.—In 1782, William Burns obtained license for the tavern facing the upper pier, the name of the house being set forth as the "Tun and Punch Bowl," but in 1791 the name was changed to the Spread Eagle, which title it retains to this day. In 1815, Burns having died, the tavern was kept by his widow, Hannah, but the following year Henry Houghton was the landlord, who was succeeded, in 1817, by John Marshall, and in 1819, Benjamin Fitman succeeded the former. Ann Lane kept the tavern in 1820, and John Barton in 1821, who gave place to John Manderson in 1823. Margaret Marshall followed the former in 1827, and the next year William McLaughlin, who had purchased the property, kept the tavern there. In 1842, Charles P. Morris was the landlord, and the next year Jesse M. Justice, who was followed by Lydia A. Justice. George C. Healey had the house in 1850, and in 1853, Charles P. Swing. Edward Chandler had license in 1855, and Humphrey P. Gibson in 1856. In 1850, Mary A. Gibson was the landlady of the Spread Eagle, and two years thereafter William Wilson became the landlord. In 1864, Lewis Wolcott had license granted him, but the same year he transferred it to Robert K. Jacquett, and in 1868, John J. Thurlow secured the court's favor, but he soon afterwards transferred it to Henry Wilkins. After the local option law was repealed William H. Gibson had the hotel until 1878, when John H. Kerlin became the landlord, to give place, in 1880, to Caleb C. Perkins, who is the present host of the ancient public-house, to which license was refused by the court in 1884.

The population of Lower Chichester was small in 1715, if we form our opinion from the following names returned by the assessors as the male taxables of that township: Philip Roman, Jonah Roman, Robert Roman, John Rawson, Richard Bezer, Philip Pedrick, Anthony Baldwin, William Flowers, Mordecai Howell, John Royley, Richard Edwards, William Clayton, William Hewes, William Hewes, Jr., John Hopton, Richard Crosby, John Ross; Freemen, John Flower, Thomas Clayton, and Thomas Howell. That the above list is far from complete is evident. The name of Lamplugh does not appear, and yet we know from the county records, other than the assessors' returns, that the family did reside then in that locality. Indeed, the records of the old borough and township, as with Chester, are sadly deficient, while the traditions are very inaccurate.

In 1799 the following names appear on the assessment-roll for the year:

Samuel Amor, Charles Affleck, William Burns, Sr. (innkeeper), William Burns, Jr. (waterman), John Burns (cordwainer), Jacob Burns, Henry C. Baker (innkeeper), Nathaniel Brown, Curtis Clayton, Joseph Clayton (pumpmaker), Richard Cockshott (carpenter), William Connell (shop-keeper), William Cranson (shipwright), Benjamin Cloud, Thomas Connarroe, Elizabeth Dutton (innkeeper), Zachariah Derrick (wheelwright), William Fordson, John Harding (tanner), William Howell (cordwainer), David Johnson, Benjamin Johnson, Melchior Looen (shop-keeper), David Marshall (shop-keeper and tavern-keeper), Joseph Marshall (shop-keeper), John Marshall (innkeeper), Hester Mitchell, Joseph Merrihew, Hannah Moore, George Martin (tailor), Nicholas Newlin (physician), Samuel Rice (justice of the peace), John Prince, Sarah Perkins, Richard Riley (judge), Joel Scott (pilot), Caleb Sayers (physician), Samuel Trimble (shipwright), Joseph Walker, Thomas Wallace (tailor), Thomas Wilson, Thomas Biggert (weaver), Nehemiah Broomall, Joseph Cobourn, Jr. (cordwainer), George Derrick (wheelwright), John Ellis, Thomas Eanix (carpenter), John Goodwin (wheelwright), William Max-

RESIDENCE OF J. N. TRAINER,

well (weaver), James Marshall (weaver), John Richards (millwright), Heber Thomas (joiner), James Thomas, James Burns (carpenter), Benjamin Talley (cordwainer), Ellis Wright (carpenter), Thomas York (merchant).

It will be noticed that the above list of taxables presents almost without exception the names of English settlers, so rapidly did the latter race supplant their Swedish predecessors.

The time when the old market-house, removed in 1870, which stood in Broad Street, was erected in Marcus Hook I have been unable to ascertain, but as it was a counterpart of the similar building which stood in Market Square, Chester, I do not believe it antedates the middle of the last century, that in Chester having been erected subsequent to 1744. I learn that about 1838 a town hall, or large room, was built on the top of the market-house, running the entire length of the building, and here public meetings, singing-schools, and the like were held. Nothing seems now to be known regarding the mill which stood on Front Street, almost at the extreme south-westerly limit of the borough, as shown in a plan of the town of Chichester, said to have been made by Isaac Taylor, the surveyor of Chester County, about 1701, which date I much question, since the plan shows a road in early times, called the road to Chester, extending from New Street, obliquely, to the King's Highway, a short distance west of the bridge over Chichester Creek, and we know that short road was not laid out until 1704.

King's Highway and Chichester Creek Bridge.—The present Southern post-road was not laid out until June, 1704, as appears from the following report:

"By virtue of a law made at New Castle the 27th day of the 9th mo., 1700, Confirmed at Philadelphia the 5th day of the 10 mo., 1701, ordering and appointing the Justices of the County Court for this county to lay out a road from the King's Road that leads to New Castle and Maryland near as may be to Ralph Fishborn the intended place for a bridge over Chester Creek. We the present Justices did accordingly this day view and lay out the said road but in regard some of the inhabitants of the township of Chichester did declare that they would never cut nor clear the same. We order and appoint the inhabitants of the township of Chester with such others as are willing to assist them at their own proper charge for the more effectual answering the said law and speedy accommodation of all travellers to cut and clear the road as we have now laid it out & make return to us of their so doing the next Court of Quarter Sessions to be held at Chester, aforesaid. Given under our hands the 10th day of June in the year 1704.

"Caleb Pusey,
"Jonathan Hayes,
"John Guest,
"Jasper Yeates,
"*Justices.*

"We the inhabitants of the Township of Chester in pursuance to the within order of Court Do certify to the Court that according as the Justices was pleased to make the within mentioned road we have at our own charge cut and cleared the same requesting it may be recorded and confirmed according to law. Witness our hands.

"Edward Danger.	George Simson.
James Townes.	Joseph Edge.
Robert Barber.	James Sandiland.
Charles Whitaker.	John Hoskins.
Paul Sanders.	John Wade.
Samuel Tomlinson.	William Pickles.

"Allowed in open court the 29 day of August, 1704, and ordered to be Entered on Record."

A bridge over Chichester Creek on this road was erected prior to 1708, for on Nov. 24, 1708, the justices, commissioners, and assessors of Chester County, in open court, entered into an agreement for building or repairing the bridge at Chester Creek, and the record states,—

"It is further agreed that the said James Hendrickson shall build a bridge over Marcus Hook Creek in the Queen's Road, where the old bridge now is, and erect it ten feet broad and so long as is sufficient and necessary for the same to extend, and to build it all of white oak timber completely finished with and the said bridge to be finished at or before the 1st day of April next, in consideration the said James shall be paid £14.

"Further ordered that the causeway at the end of the bridge shall be repaired and made a sufficient road and it is also ordered that Philip Roman shall be Supervisor of the same to agree with workman and see it completely finished."

The Linwood Mills, at Trainer's Station, on Chichester Creek, occupy the site of a grist-mill erected on that stream, about the middle of the last century, by John Price, the then owner of the land. In 1790, Samuel Price, his son, owned the mill, which was operated by George Pearson. In 1806, Samuel Price having died previous to 1802, David Trainer, the father of the present owner, purchased the grist-mill, and in 1811 a John R. Pine built a saw-mill near by on his late father's estate; but subsequent to 1813, David Trainer, Sr., in connection with Gideon Jacques, purchased the saw-mill and carried on the grist- and saw-mill at that place. The former was driven by an overshot wheel, while the saw-mill was fed by a separate race, the waters being discharged into that which turned the grist-mill. In the fall of the year 1814, when the militia of Pennsylvania summoned to the field by the President of the United States to repel the threatened invasion by the British army were assembled in encampment near Marcus Hook, the troops, numbering over five thousand men, were located on this and adjoining estates, and close by, at Widow Price's, Maj.-Gen. Gaines, of the regular army, in command of the department, had his headquarters, and in the neighborhood of the mills reviewed the entire force on Oct. 12, 1814.[1] The logs used at the saw-mill were generally floated by water to a point very near the building, and it was necessary that the water-way should be preserved; hence to that end the General Assembly, on March 24, 1817, declared Lower Chichester Creek, "from the mouth thereof up the same to the mill of David Trainer and Gideon Jacques, be and the same is declared a public highway for the passage of rafts, boats, and other vessels, and it shall be lawful for the inhabitants and others desirous of using the navigation of said creek to remove all natural and artificial obstructions which may be within the same."[2] The

[1] I have seen it stated that Gen. Anthony Wayne was the commanding officer who reviewed the troops on that occasion. Of course that is a mistake. "Mad Anthony" died at the present site of Erie, Dec. 15, 1796, and had been dead almost eighteen years when the review took place.

[2] Bliss' "Digest of Delaware County," p. 19.

act itself declared that under no construction were its provisions to be held as authorizing the removal, injuring, or impairing of the bridge spanning the great post road.

In 1837 the old grist-mill was changed into a cotton-factory, and an addition, eighty by forty feet, two stories in height, erected, which was operated by David Trainer, Jr., and John Hastings, Jr., until 1842, when, the firm having lost heavily in that year through the failure of the commission house with whom they dealt, the partnership was dissolved, and under discouraging prospects David Trainer continued the business there. At the National Fair, at Washington, D. C., in May, 1846, the goods made at Trainer's mill received special notice. Success attended his efforts, and he had already accumulated considerable means, when at his father's death, in 1849, the estate became his by inheritance. Two years thereafter Mr. Trainer met with a serious loss in the destruction of his mill by fire.

On Monday morning, Oct. 13, 1851, between one and two o'clock, as the night-train from Baltimore came in sight, the conductor and engineer noticed a bright flickering light in the mill, and as no one in the neighborhood seemed to be stirring, the train was stopped and the alarm given. The fire was supposed to be the work of an incendiary, as the flames had broken out in a cotton-shed where fire was never used. The loss amounted to fifty thousand dollars, of which only eighteen thousand dollars was covered by insurance. While the walls of the burned factory were being demolished a tremendous mass fell, burying a mason named Armstrong to his waist in the rubbish, and to the surprise of all who saw the accident, when extracted he was found to have sustained no serious injuries. The work of rebuilding was pushed rapidly, and on Aug. 1, 1852, the old structure having been replaced by a new mill three and a half stories high, one hundred and ten by fifty feet, fully stocked with new machinery, operations were resumed. In 1865 an addition of ninety feet was added to the mill, thus making the main building two hundred by fifty feet, to which were attached spacious buildings used as cloth- and picker-rooms, a dye- and finishing-house and an engine-room. In 1865 the firm became David Trainer & Son, J. Newlin Trainer having been taken into partnership, and again, in 1868, it became D. Trainer & Sons, William E. and Edward Trainer having been admitted into the firm. In 1869 mill No. 2 was erected. It is a two-story building, sixty by five hundred and two feet, with the necessary outbuildings for boilers, engines, etc., and in the spring of the following year, having been fitted with the best and improved machinery, the firm began manufacturing in this mill. In the fall of that year the neat iron bridge spanning Hook Creek, near the mill, which had been made at the Chester Bridge-Works, was put into its place. An industry such as this, giving employment to a large number of persons, necessarily resulted in building up in its immediate vicinity a village of dwellings for the operatives. In 1873 the Chester Improvement Company erected a large factory in South Chester, which was purchased by D. Trainer & Sons, and is now known as Mill No. 3. A brief account of this mill will be found in the historical account of South Chester borough. In 1878, at the Paris Exposition, David Trainer & Sons were awarded a bronze medal for superior tickings manufactured at their mills.

David Trainer was born in Delaware County, Pa., on the 9th of July, 1814, and reared on the farm where his birth occurred, and where he still resides. Here he enjoyed such advantages as the subscription schools of the period afforded. His father, David Trainer, had purchased, in 1806, the property, consisting of a farm and flouring-mill erected before 1753 by John Price, and the lad was employed on the farm and about the saw-mill, which had been erected by his father in 1812. In 1837 an addition was made to the old flouring-mill, and the whole having been fitted with machinery, was put in operation for the manufacture of cotton goods by the son and John Hastings, Jr. The firm become deeply involved by the failure of their commission merchant in 1842, and having dissolved the partnership, David Trainer resolved to retrieve his fortunes single-handed. Upon the death of his father, March 1, 1849, he fell heir to the estate, consisting of the mills and some fifty acres of land. A disastrous fire destroyed the old mill Oct. 8, 1851, but nothing daunted he took immediate steps for rebuilding, and by Aug. 1, 1852, the old flouring-mill had been replaced by a new structure and equipped with new and improved machinery. In 1865 he enlarged this mill, and in 1869 erected Mill No. 2, which was followed in 1873 by the erection of Mill No. 3. These structures are models of comfort and convenience. In addition he has erected three mansion-houses and eighty-five dwellings for the accommodation of his operatives, in whose welfare he manifests a deep interest. Having thoroughly educated his sons, and acquainted them with the practical details of cotton manufacture, he gave to each an interest as he attained his majority, the firm now being D. Trainer & Sons. Mr. Trainer became connected with the Bank of Delaware County in 1833, and upon its reorganization as the Delaware County National Bank he was chosen a director, and in 1873 elected its president, serving a term of two years, when he was re-elected, but declined the honor. He is in politics a stanch Republican, having formerly voted the Whig ticket. He is in his religious associations an Episcopalian and member of St. Martin's Church, of Marcus Hook, of which he is senior warden. Mr. Trainer is public-spirited and enterprising, courteous to all, and a vigorous supporter of every public improvement.

Diamond Mills.—On the east branch of Naaman's Creek, near the northwest boundary of the township, is the saw- and grist-mill of Samuel Hockman, which is one of the old mill-seats and landmarks of the

section, declared that under no construction were its provisions to be held as authorizing the removal, injuring, or impairing of the bridge spanning the great post road.

In 1837 the old grist-mill was changed into a cotton-factory, and an addition, eighty by forty feet, two stories in height, erected, which was operated by David Trainer, Jr., and John Hastings, Jr., until 1842, when, the firm having lost heavily in that year through the failure of the commission house with whom they dealt, the partnership was dissolved, and under discouraging prospects David Trainer continued the business there. At the National Fair, at Washington, D. C., in May, 1846, the goods made at Trainer's mill received special notice. Success attended his efforts, and he had already accumulated considerable means, when at his father's death, in 1849, the estate became his by inheritance. Two years thereafter Mr. Trainer met with a serious loss in the destruction of his mill by fire.

On Monday morning, Oct. 13, 1851, between one and two o'clock, as the night-train from Baltimore came in sight, the conductor and engineer noticed a bright flickering light in the mill, and as no one in the neighborhood seemed to be stirring, the train was stopped and the alarm given. The fire was supposed to be the work of an incendiary, as the flames had broken out in a portion of the mill where fire was never used. The loss amounted to fifty thousand dollars, of which only eighteen thousand dollars was covered by insurance. While the walls of the burned factory were being demolished a tremendous mass fell, burying a mason named Armstrong to his waist in the rubbish, and to the surprise of all who saw the accident, when extracted he was found to have sustained no serious injuries. The work of rebuilding was pushed rapidly, and on Aug. 1, 1852, the old structure having been replaced by a new mill three and a half stories high, one hundred and ten by fifty feet, fully stocked with new machinery, operations were resumed. In 1865 an addition of [illegible] feet was added to the mill, thus making the main building two hundred by fifty feet, to which were attached various buildings used as cloth- and picker-[illegible] and finishing house and an engine-room. [illegible] the firm became David Trainer & Son, J. Newlin Trainer having been taken into partnership, and [illegible] 1868, it became D. Trainer & Sons, William [illegible] Trainer having been admitted into the firm [illegible] mill No. 2 was erected. It is a two-story [illegible] by five hundred and two feet, with the necessary outbuildings for boilers, [illegible], etc., and in the spring of the following year, having been fitted with the best and improved machinery, the firm began manufacturing in this mill. [illegible] the iron bridge spanning [illegible], which had been made at [illegible] Bridge Works, was put into its place. An [illegible] with this, giving employment to a large [illegible] factories resulted in building up in its immediate vicinity a village of dwellings for the operatives. In 1873 the Chester Improvement Company erected a large factory in South Chester, which was purchased by D. Trainer & Sons, and is now known as Mill No. 3. A brief account of this mill will be found in the historical account of South Chester borough. In 1878, at the Paris Exposition, David Trainer & Sons were awarded a bronze medal for superior tickings manufactured at their mills.

David Trainer was born in Delaware County, Pa., on the 9th of July, 1814, and reared on the farm where his birth occurred, and where he still resides. Here he enjoyed such advantages as the subscription schools of the period afforded. His father, David Trainer, had purchased, in 1806, the property, consisting of a farm and flouring-mill erected before 1750 by John Price, and the lad was employed on the farm and about the saw-mill, which had been erected by his father in 1812. In 1837 an addition was made to the old flouring-mill, and the whole having been filled with machinery, was put in operation for the manufacture of cotton goods by the son and John Hastings, Jr. The firm became deeply involved by the failure of their commission merchant in 1842, and having dissolved the partnership, David Trainer resolved to retrieve his fortunes single-handed. Upon the death of his father, March 1, 1849, he fell heir to the realty, consisting of the mills and some fifty acres of land. A disastrous fire destroyed the old mill Oct. 13, 1851, but nothing daunted he took immediate steps for rebuilding, and by Aug. 1, 1852, the old flouring-mill had been replaced by a new structure and equipped with new and improved machinery. In 1865 he enlarged this mill, and in 1869 erected Mill No. 2, which was followed in 1873 by the erection of Mill No. 3. These structures are models of comfort and convenience. In addition he has erected three mansion-houses and eighty-five dwellings for the accommodation of his operatives, in whose welfare he manifests a deep interest. Having thoroughly educated his sons, and acquainted them with the practical details of cotton manufacture, he gave to each an interest as he attained his majority, the firm now being D. Trainer & Sons. Mr. Trainer became connected with the Bank of Delaware County in 1858, and upon its reorganization as the Delaware County National Bank he was chosen a director, and in 1878 elected its president, serving a term of two years, when he was re-elected, but declined the honor. He is in politics a staunch Republican, having formerly voted the Whig ticket. He is in his religious associations an Episcopalian and member of St. Martin's Church, of Marcus Hook, of which he is senior warden. Mr. Trainer is public-spirited and enterprising, courteous to all, and a vigorous supporter of every public improvement.

Diamond Mills.—On the east branch of Naaman's Creek, near the northwest boundary of the township, is the saw- and grist-mill of Samuel Hickman, which is one of the old mill-seats and landmarks of the

Galaxy Pub Co Philada.

David Haines

county Towards the end of the last century it was the property of Nathan Pennell, but he having died about 1800, it was leased to Andrew Steel, and in 1802, Nehemiah Broomall became its owner In 1826 the mill is recorded as grinding between three and five thousand bushels of grain per annum, while the saw-mill was run only occasionally, and was not rated as a first-class mill On Oct 19, 1829, Nehemiah Broomall sold the property to Benjamin Hickman for three thousand dollars

A strange incident connected with the mill occurred on Saturday night, Aug 23, 1849 Benjamin Hickman that night was aroused shortly before midnight by the barking of his dog, and going out to the mill saw no one Before he entered the house the dog barked furiously, and then Hickman noticed a light in the woodshed He called several times to know who was there, but receiving no answer he discharged his gun, and the report was followed by an exclamation, "You have shot me!" Hickman went to the place, and found a haggard, withered old woman lying on the ground, the shot having taken effect in different parts of her body. She had collected a large amount of combustible materials in a mass, apparently with the intention of setting fire to them A physician was sent for, and the next day the woman, who would not tell her name, was lodged in jail She was subsequently sent to the county house After Benjamin Hickman's death the widow, Ann, conducted the business The mill is now owned by Samuel Hickman, who has erected a new merchants' mill on the old site, and at this time the brand of "Diamond Mills" is accepted by the trade as the equal of any flour in the market

In 1870, John H Barton and Jarius Baker erected a sugar-refinery on a tract of land to the east of the upper pier at Marcus Hook It was a large brick building, forty-five by fifty-six feet, and towering upwards to the height of sixty feet A new wharf was built adjoining the upper pier, and a canal or way was dug to enable vessels of large size to come close to the building to receive or discharge cargoes In April, 1871, sugar was first made in the refinery. Early on Sunday morning, Feb 25, 1872, fire was discovered in the char room, and in two hours thereafter nothing remained of the building but the fire-marked walls The loss was one hundred and twenty-five thousand dollars, which was not entirely covered by insurance Subsequently, James Baker, using the standing wall, erected a large flour-mill on the site of the refinery, but four years after the first fire the new structure was in its turn totally consumed, the fire being, it is supposed, an incendiary one

In 1878, John Larkin, Jr, purchased the site of the burned flour-mill, and using part of the walls, erected a machine-shop and foundry, which was occupied by Keesey & Hubbell for a few months, when they abandoned the enterprise In 1880 the Pioneer Iron-Works, a limited company, became the lessees of the establishment, but after building seven iron vessels it failed, and the premises were rented by Charles C Glover, who manufactured steam-fittings therein, which business also proved to be unsuccessful The building is now leased to Joseph Kidd, who is engaged in manufacturing iron conductors for the Union Line cable-roads in Philadelphia, and has at the present time an iron vessel on the stocks, building for parties in New York

In 1871, Mr Larkin erected a large brick building, three stories in height, intended for a shoe-factory. It was occupied by Morton Bowker for a few months, but was subsequently changed into the Riverside Hosiery-Mill, and on Sept 1, 1877, Clarence Larkin and John G Campbell began manufacturing hosiery therein In October of the same year Mr Campbell withdrew, and the business has been conducted by Clarence Larkin from that date About 1875, John Larkin, Jr, built a machine-shop and foundry on Market Street It was occupied by William Pearson for some time in building hosiery machinery, but more recently it was rented by the Titanic Steel-Casting Company It is now unoccupied Within the last few years Mr Larkin has built sixty houses in Marcus Hook In all the history of the town for a century and a half preceding Mr Larkin's improvement, the number of houses erected in that period did not equal those built by Mr Larkin in the time mentioned

Kaolin has been found in Upper Chichester, for in 1839, when William Trainer was digging in the side of a hill near his dwelling, a body of clay was exposed, which was submitted to Professor Hare, William J S Warner, and Professor Rogers, the State geologist, for examination, and the last-named person pronounced it the purest porcelain clay he had ever seen No effort seems to have been made to put this article in the market Although kaolin has been found in several townships in Delaware County, only in Birmingham has the industry ever been established or maintained

During all its history Marcus Hook was prominent as a fishing station In a description of the village in 1802, published in the "Traveller's Directory" for the year, it is mentioned as "a place engaged in shad and herring fisheries" Inhabitants of the deep other than the fishes mentioned have occasionally been captured off Marcus Hook In July, 1869, William Blizzard caught off that place a shovel-nosed shark, which measured over five feet in length and weighed a trifle over two hundred pounds On May 16, 1879, a sea-lion was taken in a seine near Marcus Hook Its captors being under the impression that it would injure their net, killed it It was thought it had escaped from the Zoological Garden in Fairmount Park several weeks previous to the time it was caught

On Saturday evening, Jan 26, 1879, a remarkable accident occurred near Linwood as the southward-bound express-train was approaching that station

The wind was blowing furiously, when two students of Princeton College, named Vaughan and Larkin, attempted to pass from one car to another. Vaughan was swept from the platform by the strength of the gale, and his skull fractured by the fall. Larkin's life was saved simply by his coat catching on the knob of the car-door, which held him on the platform until the conductor and brakesman came to his assistance.

Societies.—In 1845 a band was located at Linwood, which furnished the music on several occasions for public meetings and military displays. I have no further information of the organization than is here given. On June 14, 1869, the Linwood Building Association was organized, with George Broomall, president; William H. Dickinson, secretary and solicitor; and David Trainer, treasurer. The association has settled its business and disbanded.

Farmers' and Mechanics' Lodge, No. 185, I. O. of O. F., was instituted July 11, 1846, with the following charter members: Richard Leach, Robert Black, James Stott, William Appleby, Sr., James Phillips, Stewart Smith, John Stevenson, Sr., George Williams, Townsend Rowand, and Edward Waggoner. On the night of institution nine candidates were initiated, making a total membership of nineteen. During the year twenty-five persons were initiated, making a membership of thirty-five at the beginning of the year 1847. Since that time the lodge has been in active operation, never suspending benefits, paying promptly all lawful claims on the treasury. On July 4, 1849, the corner-stone of the present Farmers' and Mechanics' Odd-Fellows' Hall was laid, C. C. Burr, of Philadelphia, delivering the address on that occasion. John Larkin, Jr., was largely instrumental in suggesting and carrying forward the building to completion. The total number of members of Lodge No. 185 since its institution is two hundred and thirty-four, of which number thirty-two have been buried. At present the membership is seventy-two. The lodge since it was instituted has paid over ten thousand dollars in benefits, mostly distributed in Upper and Lower Chichester, and, besides, has about four thousand dollars safely invested. Four of the charter members still survive.

Wawasett Tribe, No. 172, I. O. of R. M.—This tribe was instituted eighth sun, flower moon, G. Y. D. 381 (8th day of May, 1872), with twenty-one charter members. The tribe now numbers eighty-one members. The appointed chiefs are: 1st S., R. H. Dutton; 2d S., L. K. Bane; G. of F., Wilmer Heacock; G. of W., Frank H. Wooley; 1st W., George B. Rowand; 2d W., Amos Pennell; 3d W., James P. Yeager; 4th W., Levin C. Barton; 1st B., Ellis Maxwell; 2d B., Isaac McKinley; 3d B., Daniel Congleton; 4th B., George W. Vernon, Jr. The elective officers are: S., Andrew Mahla; S. S., Charles Green; J. S., George W. Morton; P., Samuel Congleton; C. of R., F. S. Vernon; K. of W., I. F. Hendrickson.

Golden Star Council, No. 319, O. U. A. M.—This council was chartered July 9, 1873, with twenty-two members, and Isaac J. Brown, Councilor. The first meeting was held in the second story of the machine-shop on the southwest corner of Fourth and Market Streets, Marcus Hook. After that council met until November of the same year at the Spread Eagle Hotel. At that date the society rented the hall attached to the hosiery-mills, and used it as a council-chamber until the room was required for mill purposes. By dispensation from the State Council granted Dec. 1, 1880, council was authorized to remove to Linwood Station, where they leased Odd-Fellows' Hall one night in a week. The present Councilor is Edward Truitt, and the number of members is fifty-three.

Linwood Lodge, No. 499, K. of P.—This lodge was instituted May 12, 1884, by District Deputy Daniel W. Flenner, of Chester. Meetings are held in the Odd-Fellows' Hall. John D. Goff is C. C. The present number of members is fifty-six.

Old Residents and their Homes.—Dr. Caleb Smith Sayers settled at Marcus Hook, where he practiced his profession until his death, in 1799, at the early age of thirty-two years. He was a victim of yellow fever, with which he was attacked after visiting a man on a vessel who was lying ill, the captain being ignorant of the serious nature of the disease. The house where the doctor lived, almost as it was in his day, facing the river, still stands. At the time of his death he owned sixty-three acres of land in Upper Chichester, and a brick house and lot and half an acre of ground in Marcus Hook. His son, Hon. Edward S. Sayers, who was consul for Brazil and vice-consul for Portugal, at Philadelphia, died March 29, 1877, was born at Marcus Hook shortly after his father's death. Subsequently thereto the family removed to Philadelphia, where Edward S. Sayers became a prominent merchant. When the Emperor Dom Pedro visited the Centennial Exposition, he was always attended by Mr. Sayers, the latter in early life having personally become acquainted with the royal family in Brazil. In early times Marcus Hook appears to have been a favorite locality for physicians, and success seems to have attended their efforts there. In 1799, Dr. Nicholas Newlin not only had his own residence and one hundred and ninety-eight acres of land, but he owned several houses which he rented to families,—a very unusual thing at that period.

During the second war with England, Marcus Hook in the fall of the year (1814) was the designated encampment of Pennsylvania militia called to the field, as well as a few regiments from Delaware, and the United States regular army, the force gathered there amounting to eight or ten thousand men. During the time of the threatened attack on the city of Philadelphia by Admiral Cockburn, the armed gunboats patroled the river to a point near New Castle, and it was no unusual thing for the residents of Marcus Hook to see three or four of these gunboats sailing by the town in a day. They were flat sloop-rigged crafts, of forty or fifty tons, carrying one large gun, and commanded by an officer and ten or twelve men, the latter armed with muskets, cutlasses, and pikes.

The old houses standing east of the creek, Morton, Johnson, Pennell, and several others, were all erected before or about the middle of the last century, the clay being dug and the bricks made and burned near where the houses were built. On those farms to this day the excavations made in digging the clay can be pointed out. The Pennell house was built in two parts, the kitchen in 1744, by William Hendrickson, who then owned the property. The figures given have been pressed in the bricks in several places. He sold the estate to John Smith, who built the main part of the present house. Smith was an Irish Quaker, who settled near Kingsessing, and married a Bunting, of Darby. It is stated by tradition that, when looking for a farm, he was told that this was one of the best in the county, and purchased it. He subsequently acquired much real estate in the neighborhood. The Trainer family, in the maternal line, are descended from John Smith. Elizabeth Smith, the centenarian, who died in 1802, aged one hundred and three years, and is buried in St. Martin's graveyard, is said to have been a sister of John Smith, but was always a stanch member of the Church of England, and a liberal contributor to the struggling parish of St. Paul. The inscription on the gravestone in St. Martin's Church-yard where she lies is simply—"Elizabeth Smith. Born August, 1699. Died October, 1802,"—thus proving that she had lived in three centuries. The Johnson house, on the west side of the great post-road, near Stony Run, was built about the same period mentioned as the date of the Pennell building, and with the exception of about twenty years, as long as our records run, the estate has been in the ownership of the family. Benjamin F. Johnson, the old squire, as he was termed, then an octogenarian, on Nov. 9, 1871, died suddenly while seated at his supper-table. A man of studious habits for years, he had maintained the reputation of being one of the best-informed men in the county, and in his lengthened lifetime had been county treasurer, a justice of the peace for nearly half a century, and for sixty successive years a vestryman of St. Martin's Church,—the longest period of continuous service, in any capacity, so far as I have knowledge, ever performed by a resident of this county.

The Eyre mansion, just west of the line of the borough of South Chester, is of more recent date, having been built by William Eyre about the beginning of this century. Forty years ago, Jan. 2, 1845, Martin Sullivan, a lad on this farm, fell through the funnel in the barn on that estate and was instantly killed.

The village of Linwood is a direct outgrowth of the Philadelphia, Wilmington and Baltimore Railroad, and its history does not extend backward in our annals a half-century. The incidents connected with the story of Lower Chichester I have already given, so far as I have information.

In 1878, John Lenkins, a printer, began the publication of a newspaper in Lower Chichester, called *The Linwood Times*. After one issue the paper was suspended.

The following is a list of justices of the peace:

Names.	Date of Commission.
Samuel Price	Aug. 30, 1791.
Joseph Marshall	May 20, 1800.
James Withey	July 4, 1806.
Jacob Edwards	Jan. 1, 1807.
John Caldwell	Nov. 15, 1814.
Joseph Walker	Feb. 3, 1820.
Samuel Smith	March 12, 1822.
David Marshall	March 3, 1824.
George W. Bartram	June 3, 1824.
Benjamin F. Johnson	Oct. 25, 1825.
Abraham Kerlin	June 7, 1830.
Samuel T. Walker	Nov. 11, 1831.
John Afflick	June 6, 1834.
Samuel Shaw	Nov. 18, 1835.
William Martin	June 10, 1836.
William Eyre	Dec. 21, 1838.
George W. Bartram	Sept. 23, 1839.
Jordan D. Bitting (borough of Marcus Hook)	April 14, 1840.
Benjamin F. Johnson	April 14, 1840.
William Eyre	April 14, 1840.
John Larkin, Jr. (borough of Marcus Hook)	April 9, 1844.
Benjamin F. Johnson	April 15, 1845.
William Eyre	April 15, 1845.
Edward Waggoner (borough of Marcus Hook)	April 14, 1846.
Benjamin F. Johnson	April 9, 1850.
William Eyre	April 9, 1850.
Samuel T. Walker (borough of Marcus Hook)	April 11, 1854.
Benjamin F. Johnson	Oct. 23, 1855.
William Eyre	Oct. 23, 1855.
Benjamin F. Johnson	April 10, 1860.
Alfred Bunting (borough of Marcus Hook)	April 10, 1860.
Manley Emanuel	April 15, 1861.
Benjamin F. Johnson	April 28, 1865.
Robert A. Loughead	April 16, 1867.
Samuel T. Walker	April 14, 1867.
I. Henry Walker (borough of Marcus Hook)	April 13, 1869.
Robert A. Loughead	April 19, 1872.
Henry Larkin	April 15, 1873.
Daniel Fergerson	March 25, 1876.
Robert A. Loughead	July 2, 1877.
John A. Green	March 25, 1878.
Robert A. Loughead	April 10, 1882.
John A. Green	April 6, 1883.

The Marcus Hook Piers.—The wooden piers at Marcus Hook were erected by the State of Pennsylvania subsequent to the Revolutionary war. Previous to that date there were wharves at that place,—one in front of lands belonging to William Burns and the other that of Robert Moulder (the latter generally known as Moulder's wharf). They, of course, were indifferent structures, mere landing-places, affording no protection to vessels during the heavy spring freshets and ice-drifts. In January, 1785, it appears a committee of merchants in Philadelphia memorialized the State government,[1] setting forth the necessity for the construction of new piers along the Delaware River at designated localities, and the advantage to be gained by such an outlay in maintaining the commercial supremacy of the city by affording protection to vessels in the winter season and during the ice-runs in the spring, for at that period it was no rare incident for crafts at anchor to be cut through by the heavy ice and sunk. The ship "John" was lost in that way, and the shoal still known by the name of that vessel was formed by the deposits settling around

[1] Penna. Archives, 1st series, vol. x. p. 406.

the sunken hulk. The State government regarded the project with approval and submitted the memorial to the port wardens, and on May 13th the latter body made a favorable report, on which the Supreme Executive Council ordered the wardens to enter into contracts with the owners of lands at Marcus Hook, abutting on the river, so that any "improper extension" of wharves into the Delaware at that place would be prevented thereafter.[1] Drawings of the proposed improvements had also been prepared, for on May 19th Council delivered the plans for the piers at Marcus Hook to the port wardens, with the understanding that they were to be returned "when called for."[2] Previous to that date (on May 7, 1785) Thomas Davis submitted a bid for the construction of the piers, four in number, in which, for the sum of four thousand one hundred pounds in specie, he agreed to have the piers "so far carried on & made this spring as to be sufficient for receiving & protecting the shipping next winter and the whole work to be completed on or before the first Day of September, 1786."[3]

Thomas Davis, however, appears not to have received the contract, but on the 1st of June, 1785, the owners of land on the river at Marcus Hook executed the following contract, which, as it is an important document, the full text is given:[4]

"Articles of agreement, made the first day of June, in the year of our Lord one thousand seven hundred and eighty-five between the Supreme Executive Council of the Commonwealth of Pennsylvania, in behalf of the said Commonwealth, of the one part and sundry persons whose names are hereunto subscribed and seals affixed of the other part:

"Whereas, The said Supreme Executive Council have contracted and agreed with a certain ——— for sinking and building of sundry piers at Marcus Hook, in the county of Chester, in the State of Pennsylvania, for the accommodation of vessels entering into and going out of the Port of Philadelphia. And

"Whereas, The said said several persons whose names are hereunto subscribed and seals affixed, are seized of sundry lots or pieces of ground situate on the river Delaware, at Marcus Hook aforesaid, and lying near or between the piers so intended to be sunk as aforesaid: Now, it is hereby agreed by the said Supreme Executive Council in behalf of the said Commonwealth, with the said several persons whose names are hereunto subscribed and seals affixed, their heirs, executors, administrators and assigns, that they, their heirs, executors, administrators and assigns, may have and enjoy the liberty and privilege of sinking, building and carrying out from the ends of their respective lots, any piers, wharves or other erections whatever, provided the same be not carried out further than the extent of the wharf or pier now called Moulder's Pier, lying to the southward of the said lots of ground and of the wharf or pier intended to be sunk by William Burns, opposite the wharf or pier called Bunn's Pier, lying to the northward of the said lots of ground. And the said several persons whose names are hereunto subscribed and seals affixed, do hereby, for themselves, their heirs, executors, administrators and assigns, several covenant promise, and grant, and agree to and with the said Commonwealth of Pennsylvania, not to build, sink, or carry out any piers, wharfs or other erections whatsoever, from the ends of their respective lots, further than the extent aforesaid, and permit or suffer all persons whatsoever to pass and repass across and along their respective wharves, and to permit and suffer all vessels lying at the public piers to load and discharge their cargoes without any let, hindrance or molestation by or from them, or any or either of them, or their, or any of or either of their heirs, executors, administrators or assigns.

"In witness whereof, the President of the said Supreme Executive Council hath set his hand hereunto, and caused the seal of the said Commonwealth to be hereunto affixed, and the said several persons have hereunto subscribed their names and affixed their seals, the day and year first above written.

"Joseph Few. [L. S.]	John Dickinson. [L. S.]
"John Crawford. [L. S.]	John Flower. [L. S.]
"Rich'd Riley. [L. S.]	William Burns. [L. S.]
"Robt. Moulder. [L. S.]	John Price. [L. S.]
	Thomas Moore. [L. S.]

"Sealed and delivered by John Crawford, Richard Riley, Robert Moulder, John Flower, William Burns, John Price, and Thomas Moore, in presence of

"Nath'l Falconer,
"Jos. Bullock.

"Sealed and delivered by Joseph Few, in presence of us.

"George Ord,
"John Hazelwood."

On Wednesday, June 8th, two of the port wardens appeared at the session of the Supreme Council, and delivered the foregoing agreement, and submitted several proposals made by Joshua Humphreys and Thomas Conarroe for building the piers at Marcus Hook. On the 15th the contract was awarded to Thomas Conarroe, of the Northern Liberties of Philadelphia, wharf-builder, and Council ordered that the wardens of the port should be furnished with a copy of the agreement "for the building and sinking four piers, etc., etc., at Marcus Hook, on the river Delaware," with authority to the wardens to make payments as they severally became due.[5] The manner of the work or the price agreed upon, so far as Conarroe was concerned, does not appear, but we learn something from the proposals presented by Joshua Humphreys. The four piers were not four separate and distinct piers, each leading directly to the land, but an inner and an outer pier, forming one landing-place, the sluice-way between Moulder's wharf and the first pier being forty feet, while between the inner and the outer pier there was a sluice-way of thirty feet, both of these sluices being spanned by heavy sleepers and floored with two-and-a-half-inch oak planks, the pier over all two hundred feet, the outer pier thirty feet wide. The other pier at William Bunn's wharf was to be in all respects similar to the lower pier (Moulder's) already described.[6]

Conarroe seems to have prolonged the work at the piers, if the bid of Thomas Davis, already mentioned, is any indication of the time deemed necessary by other contractors for building them.

The piers were in an unfinished condition in December, 1786, for on the 15th of that month Thomas Moore, of Marcus Hook, wrote to the port wardens that the Spanish frigate "Loretto" was then lying about ten or fifteen feet without the pier, and "her mooring made fast to the Ties of the same (still in an unfinished state)," and, as the ice on the river was unusually heavy, and "forcing itself against the stern of the frigate," the contractor Conarroe and residents of the place were apprehensive that great injury might be done to the pier.[7] The same day the war-

[1] Colonial Records, vol. xiv. p. 460.
[2] Ib., p. 464.
[3] Penna. Archives, 1st Series, vol. x. p. 713.
[4] Colonial Records, vol. xiv. p. 474.
[5] Ib.
[6] Penna. Archives, 1st Series, vol. x. p. 471.
[7] Ib., vol. xi. p. 99.

dens called the immediate attention of the Supreme Council to the danger, and the following day John Hazelwood and Nathaniel Falconer, members of the Board of Port Wardens, were dispatched to Marcus Hook, bearing a letter from President Benjamin Franklin to Capt De Ugarte y Lianes, of the ' Loretto." The gentlemen were instructed by Franklin in writing as to their course of action, which was to deliver the letter, view the situation of the ship and pier This being done they were directed to offer the Spanish officer their opinion as to the best means to secure her from damage by driving ice, which advice was to be put in writing If the commander refused to follow their advice, and they deemed his action would be injurious to the pier, that they should apprise him that the matter would be made the subject of a demand on his government for all damages sustained They were also especially instructed to inquire into the rumors "of Injuries done by his People to the Inhabitants," and if it appeared that the reports were well founded, to request the captain to prevent such injuries for the future On Dec 17, 1786, Hazelwood and Falconer were at Marcus Hook, and by letter informed the commander that they had come there to aid and assist him in placing the vessel in a place of safety, "as the Winter setting in sooner than common, with a very severe Frost, which filled the Rivers suddenly with Ice, and fearing, as you are Strangers, & unacquainted with the dangerous situation that ships are thrown into by the violence of the Ice in this River, therefore it is our Opinion & Necessary there should be an Anchor & Cable got out from the Bows of the Ship to the Shore, in Order to Support the Post & Fasts that are now out to keep the Ship from going off the Bank, and that we also recommend that some of the Guns may be run over, in Order to list the Ship in towards the wharf, and that there be some Spars got ready pointed & drove down, on the Starboard Quarter, Then, we are of Opinion the ship will remain perfectly safe" That this advice was followed we learn from the Spanish commander's letter of thanks to President Franklin, which he dates from the "Frigate N S De Loretto, at Anchor in the Delaware, now secured in one of the Moles at Marcus Hook"[1] The ship wintered at that place Two large cannons, said to have been put ashore from this Spanish vessel of war, remained on the pier at Marcus Hook for at least a third of a century

Conarroe seems to have lost money on the contract, and he petitioned Council to make him whole On June 21, 1787, the port wardens attended the session of Council, and were instructed to inquire into the loss, if any, sustained by the contractor, growing out of "difficulties he has met with in the said business," to report to Council, together with their opinion[2] On the 26th the port wardens reported, stating that two hundred and fifty pounds would be "but a very moderate compensation for the services rendered by him in erecting and completing the piers at Marcus Hook," on which report Council ordered the treasurer of the commonwealth to pay Thomas Conarroe that sum[3]

In the description of Marcus Hook which appears in an exceedingly rare book, the "Travellers' Directory," published in Philadelphia, 1802, it is stated that the creek of that name is eighteen miles and three-quarters from Philadelphia by the post road, and adds, "at the confluence of this creek with the Delaware is a small town called Marcus Hook, where vessels are defended from the ice in winter by long wharves or piers made for that purpose"

Marcus Hook has ever been a dangerous place for unprotected shipping As late as Dec 24, 1842, the brig "Henrietta," owned by John De Costa, of Philadelphia, was caught in a severe storm and blown ashore a short distance below Marcus Hook The drifting ice was so heavy that the ship was cut through and sunk in nine feet of water The wreck was afterwards moved to Naaman's Creek, but proved a total loss On Feb 4, 1871, the ship "Research," bound for Antwerp, with the largest cargo of coal oil ever to that time shipped from Philadelphia, struck on the Hook rocks, a short distance above Marcus Hook, where she sank in twelve feet of water The cargo was lightered and the vessel raised

The Hunter-Miller Duel.—On Sunday, March 21, 1830, William Miller, Jr, of Philadelphia, a young lawyer of much prominence, was killed in a duel with Midshipman Charles G Hunter, of the United States navy The meeting took place a short distance below the Delaware State line, near Claymont, and created much excitement in Delaware County, where for many years afterwards it was a favorite theme for narration in stores and public places where people assembled in the evening Strange as it may seem, the two men who stood facing each other on that Sabbath morning, at the inception of the misunderstanding were not parties to the quarrel which resulted so tragically, but were drawn into it in the endeavor to bring about a settlement of the difficulty The circumstances connected with the fatal encounter are briefly these

In Philadelphia, on Friday afternoon, Feb 17, 1830, Henry Wharton Griffith meeting R Dillon Drake at the house of a friend, accompanied by several gentlemen, the parties being well acquainted went to a billiard-room at Third and Chestnut Streets, where Griffith, while playing, was asked by Drake whether he would try a game with him Griffith was a noted billiard-player, and, as he stated, knowing his superiority to Drake in that respect, he merely smiled and made no reply The latter, apparently enraged at this trifling circumstance, struck Griffith in the face,

[1] Penna. Archives, 1st Series, vol xi pp 100–102

[2] Colonial Records, vol xv p 228

[3] Ib, p 233

following the assault with several other blows That evening Griffith sent a message to New York to Midshipman Charles H Duryee, of the United States navy, requesting him to come to Philadelphia, and at the same time addressed a note to Drake apprising him that a friend would wait on him to demand satisfaction for the insult This letter Drake returned by the bearer On Tuesday night, the 21st, Midshipman Duryee reached Philadelphia, and the next morning waited on Drake as the friend of Griffith Drake refused to entertain any message, alleging that Griffith's reputation was not above reproach, and for that reason he could not accord to him the satisfaction of a gentleman Capt Vorhees, of the navy, when the result of the interview was repeated, wrote a certificate stating that under similar circumstances in his own case, he would not hesitate to meet Griffith Armed with this certificate Duryee returned to Drake, when the latter referred him to William H Carmac Then it was asserted that Griffith in having addressed a letter to a lady to whom Dr Drake, a brother of R Dillon Drake, was to be married on the very day the assault took place,—which letter was derogatory of Dr Drake,—had by that act put himself beyond gentlemanly recognition At the meeting William Miller was introduced by Drake to Duryee Pending these proceedings eight days had elapsed

On February 26th, Duryee, who declared that he would post Drake as a coward, was challenged by the latter, William Miller being the bearer of this note The next day Lieut Hampton Westcott, United States navy, on behalf of Duryee, replied that the latter could not accept the challenge until Drake had given Griffith satisfaction To this Drake stated that he must decline "the degradation of placing himself on a level with that degraded individual" The matter did not rest here, for on March 7th several gentlemen of New Brunswick, N J, friends of Duryee, whom it appears in now accepting the challenge was placed in questionable position among his brother officers, wrote to William Miller, asking that the whole matter be referred to a committee appointed by both sides, to which proposition Miller (on the 9th) replied that both Drake and he looked upon the difficulty as finally and satisfactorily settled

On March 10th, Midshipman Charles G Hunter, then barely twenty-one years of age, came to Philadelphia as Duryee's friend, and wrote to Miller demanding the immediate delivery of the letter written from New Brunswick, giving the latter one hour to reply The result was an interview between Hunter and Miller, at which Hunter stated Miller had destroyed a letter which, he said, was the one in controversy A few days after this interview the New Brunswick letter was printed

Hunter thereupon announced that Miller's base and ungentlemanly conduct in suffering a letter to be published after he declared it had been destroyed was such that he demanded immediate satisfaction, and on March 17th dispatched Lieut Westcott with a cartel to Miller The latter in writing denied being in any wise connected with the publication, and being entirely ignorant of it, declined to receive the challenge from Hunter During the interview, R Dillon Drake entered the office and handed to Miller a manuscript copy of the New Brunswick letter, stating that it had been in the possession of his brother, Dr Drake Miller, turning to Westcott, said, "You see, sir, that I fulfill my promise to Mr Hunter, and will destroy the copy in your presence" "I do not care about seeing it destroyed," replied Westcott, "as there are printed copies of it in circulation"

On Saturday, March 20, Hunter posted Miller, and concluding the document by stating that he held Miller in the utmost contempt as a coward, and knew him to be guilty of base falsehood, "yet I am, and always will be, ready to meet him whenever he may think proper to accept" Previous to this publication, on March 17th, Midshipman Duryee sent Hunter to Drake, accepting his challenge of February 26th, but Drake declined the meeting at that late day

After Hunter's statement was posted, Lieut Edward Byrne, as the friend of Miller, waited on Hunter with a written acceptance of his challenge, and was referred to Westcott, who would arrange with him for the meeting It was agreed that the duel should take place the next morning at the nearest boundary of the State of Delaware, and that besides the seconds on both sides one gentleman should be present For some reason it was not until noon of the next day—Sunday—that the combatants left Philadelphia in separate carriages for Chester One party, consisting of Miller, Byrne, Craig, and a surgeon, left the dwelling on Chestnut Street which formerly occupied the site of the present *German Democrat* building, while the other, consisting of Hunter, Westcott, Duryee, and another gentleman, left the United States Hotel, which stood on the north side of Chestnut Street, opposite the custom-house At Chester the suspicions of the residents of that quiet village were aroused, for it was rightly conjectured that a duel was the object of this Sabbath journey, and the people in the ancient borough were greatly excited over the mysterious silence preserved by the party as to their destination When Naaman's Creek was crossed arrangements were immediately made for the interchange of shots It was subsequently alleged by Hunter's friends that, after the first fire, if Miller should act as a brave man, Hunter had determined to withdraw the charge of cowardice, and upon Mr. Miller's friend declaring on his honor that he believed Miller innocent of the publication of the letter, the parties should be reconciled The paces being measured off, and each end of that distance marked with a stone, the preliminaries were gone through with and the men stationed Not a word passed on the grounds between the principals in the duel, and so far as remembered all that either said was the assenting answer to the question, "Gentlemen, are you ready?" At the word both fired in accordance with the agreement, so nearly together that the separate reports of the pistols could hardly be distinguished Instantly Miller wheeled, and, uttering an exclamation, fell to the earth Hunter, advancing towards the fallen man, said in a loud voice, "Gentlemen, I assure you that I had no enmity against that man, his blood must rest upon the heads of others who have dragged him into their quarrels" Miller died almost immediately, the bullet having perforated his lungs As soon as the fatal result of the encounter was ascertained, the gentlemen who had accompanied the dead man to the field urged Hunter, Westcott, and Duryee to leave the State before the determination of the duel could be known, and acting on that advice they hired conveyances, were driven to New Castle, where they boarded an out-bound vessel and finally reached New York

The dead man was placed in a sitting posture on the back seat of one of the carriages, a cap, fashionable at that time, drawn down over his forehead so as to shade his eyes to prevent them being seen by any one glancing into the vehicle To hold the body upright one of the men sat by its side and two on the front seat, and they managed to preserve the semblance of life (in what was really a corpse) to a casual observer passing by This carriage started on the journey to Philadelphia, the second being occupied by the surgeon and the gentleman who accompanied Hunter, and had not fled to New Castle In the mean while several young men of the neighborhood of Chester who had been riding in the vicinity of Claymont learned that a duel had taken place, and as they preceded the carriages, the fact became known abroad, and it was determined, if possible, to arrest the principals at the bridge over Chester Creek A number of the citizens of Chester assembled there for that purpose By this time night's shadows had settled down, and as the first carriage came in sight of the bridge, the driver, noticing that a body of men seemed gathering there, and knowing his coach bore an unusual passenger, whipped his horses almost to a run, crossed the bridge in a gallop, and passed on unmolested The second carriage, however, came along at an easy trot, and was without difficulty brought to a full stop, when it was found that only the surgeon and a looker-on had been detained Shortly after they were permitted to resume their journey to Philadelphia

The first carriage, after it had dashed through the village, continued on the way to its destination, and it was about nine o'clock that night when it halted with its ghastly passenger at the house on Chestnut Street from which that noonday it had taken away the dead—then a living man Rumor relates how all that night the men kept the corpse in a room, while those present drank deeply, due largely to the extreme excitement under which they labored The next day the father of the dead man was informed of his son's fate, and shortly after six o'clock the following morning the remains were interred without waiting for the form of a coroner's inquest.

The duel caused the utmost excitement throughout the country, and on Saturday following, March 27th, Mr Moore, of Beaver County, in the House of Representatives, at Harrisburg, offered a resolution that the President of the United States be respectfully requested to strike the said Lieut Charles G Hunter from the roll of the navy, and also requesting the Governor of Pennsylvania to forward a copy of the resolution to the President On Monday, the 29th, the resolution was adopted and forwarded immediately

On the following day the Secretary of the Navy wrote to the President

"NAVY DEPARTMENT,
"March 30, 1830

"SIR It has been proved to my satisfaction that Lieuts Edward Byrne and Hampton Westcott, Passed Midshipman Charles H Duryee, and Midshipman Charles G Hunter, of the navy of the United States, were recently concerned in a duel which took place between the last-named officer and William Miller, Jr, of Philadelphia, which resulted fatally to the latter I respectfully recommend to you that the names of the said officers, Edward Byrne, Hampton Westcott, Charles H Duryee, and Charles G Hunter, be erased from the list of officers of the navy of the United States

"I am very respectfully,
"JOHN BRANCH"

On the back of the letter the Executive indorsed

"Let the above named officers of the navy be stricken from the roll
"ANDREW JACKSON
"31st March, 1830"

Shortly after this was done a number of influential persons declared that the proceeding was arbitrary, that the men had been dismissed without a hearing, and petitions were circulated for signatures, asking that they might be reinstated and an inquiry could be had as to the circumstances attending the duel William Miller, Sr, the father of the slain man, personally petitioned the President that Hunter might be reinstated, that he did not regard him as guilty of his son's death, but that his life had been sacrificed to the absurd code of honor which then maintained in the naval service of the government Hunter was reinstated, and during the Mexican war was court-martialed and dismissed from the squadron because he had captured the town of Alvarado and the Mexican forts in that vicinity without having been ordered by the commodore to do so Ever after he was known as Alvarado Hunter

The writer can recall Hunter just previous to his death in St Joseph's Hospital, New York, when poor, dissipated, and broken in health, it was a gleam of sunlight on his darkened life journey when those who knew him in better times nodded their recognitions or shook his trembling hand His life had been embittered and full of troubles, all dating from that quiet Sunday, near the Delaware, when a man he had never met but twice in his life lay dead before the unerring aim of the best pistol-shot in the American navy. James Gordon Bennett, Sr., at his own cost, placed a tombstone over the grave of an accomplished, brave gentleman, who had dare to capture an enemy's town and fortress without orders, and was suspended because he was victorious.

The Webb and Marshall Duel.—Forty years ago Thomas F. Marshall was one of the most conspicuous men in public life. As an orator he was the foremost Kentuckian of any period, and ranked superior to Clay, Crittenden, Barry, Pope, Rowan, Bledsoe, Menefee, the Breckinridges, and the galaxy of brilliant men who carried the name of their State to the front in the spoken literature of the nation. So potential was his eloquence that in 1841, when he offered himself a candidate for Congress from the Ashland district, no antagonist could be found to contest with him on the hustings the issues of the hour, and without opposition he was elected a member of the Twenty-seventh Congress. On the floor of the House he was an earnest advocate of the repeal of the bankruptcy bill of 1841, while Col. James Watson Webb, editor of the *Courier and Enquirer*, a daily paper of large influence, published in New York City, was as earnestly enlisted on the other side, and took occasion in his editorials to criticise severely those opposed to his views. Marshall's prominence in advocacy of the measure made him a distinguished figure, and the shafts of Col. Webb's sarcasm and vituperation were frequently directed at the tall Kentuckian, so especially that their purpose was not to be misunderstood.

Early in 1842, Col. Monroe Edwards had been arrested in Philadelphia, charged with forging drafts amounting to sixty thousand dollars on Brown Brothers, the bankers, and other well-known business men of New York. He was taken into custody on a requisition from the Governor of New York. The trial ranks as one of the American *causes célèbres*. The colonel had played no trivial part in the pomp and fashion of the day; he was a man of conspicuous presence, of fine address, and a cultivated conversationalist, who had mingled familiarly, abroad and in the United States, in the best society. The case attracted additional attention because of the magnificent array of counsel employed. The defense was represented by Hon. John J. Crittenden, of Kentucky; Hon. Thomas F. Marshall, of the same State; Messrs. William M. Evarts, J. Prescott Hall, and Robert Emmett, of New York. The commonwealth was represented by Hon. James R. Whiting, district attorney (familiarly known as "Little Bitters," because of his sarcasm), assisted by Hon. Ogden Hoffman, United States district attorney for the Eastern District of New York, then the most brilliant forensic orator of the United States, whose address in behalf of Richard P. Robinson, when tried for the murder of Helen Jewett, has ever been regarded as a masterpiece of legal advocacy.

The trial began on the 7th of June, 1842, before Judge William Kent, and the *Courier and Enquirer* of that date published editorially the following paragraph:

"We learn from the *Tribune* that the Hon. T. F. Marshall, after wandering about the country for some thirty days lecturing on temperance and giving his experience as a devotee of the bottle, has returned to this city to defend the notorious Monroe Edwards. When he gets back to Washington he will have been absent about forty days, for which he will doubtless draw from the treasury, with the sanction of his brother members, three hundred and twenty dollars! Now, while the editor of the *Tribune* was advocating the reduction of the army and navy, why did he not gently hint to Congress the necessity of reducing their own pay, and of not paying themselves anything from the public purse while making mountebanks of themselves or devoting their time to advocating the cause of notorious swindlers."

Mr. Marshall, when he came to make his address to the jury at the close of the evidence, alluded to this attack on him, and said,—

"Now, I would venture to assert that under all the circumstances of the case, so far as the public are acquainted with them, that the parallel of that paragraph cannot be found in the whole history of the press of this country. But to the attack itself, gentlemen, let me explain the nature and cause of it. It is, let me tell you, a mere personal matter. It is intended for me alone, and for the sole gratification of wreaking private revenge in certainly the most dignified manner and under the most humane circumstances. In short, I did not believe that human revenge on one individual could be conceived in so lofty, so exalted a manner, but I do believe that I was alone the motive, the sole victim sought. But so elevated were the feelings of this writer, so intent was he of gratifying his revenge on me, that he entirely forgot the cruel and unmanly manner in which he was wreaking it upon the unfortunate prisoner, who had never done him the slightest injury or ill will. I regret exceedingly that this thing is so, and I regret that it occurred, and that this explanation is necessary. I feel the awkwardness of it, and I am aware if the counsel on the opposite side choose to make an ungenerous use of it, it may be made a subject of attack on me. But I felt compelled to make this statement, and it has happened to be my misfortune, my most unpleasant situation, to have had to notice this same disreputable source of attack twice recently, and both times in discharge of my public duties, and I will explain to you the circumstances that drew forth this *noble* mode of revenge, the precious morsel against myself. Last winter this same writer made a charge against Congress—I state the substance of the charge—that a quantity of British coin had been brought to this country for the purpose of bribing the members of Congress, of which I was one, and that they had been bought to the tune of one hundred thousand dollars apiece! I, in my place in Congress, instantly repelled the charge, and in very mild language for so gross an attack. This brought a letter from the writer of the article asking me to retract what I said. Well, I reviewed the ground, and I didn't retract it, and haven't retracted it, and I never would retract it on the face of the earth till I die! This brought a second letter, but no retraction followed, and there stuck the correspondence and here is the revenge. Well, I don't know that I am exactly the thing represented in this corrupt paper, but I believe that I can lay some claim to the character of a gentleman, that I am a tolerably good judge of what pertains to the character of a gentleman,—at least as well as the man who wrote that article, and who pretends to be a gentleman. But I will simply remark that in Congress, at the bar, before the people, in all those various characters,—all of which I consider are merged in the character of a gentleman,—that I stand ready at any time and at all times for whatever I am responsible, and for anything that may have occurred in this so perfectly filthy a quarrel. Under any circumstances, I pledge my honor that I shall plead no privilege that pertains to my position as a member of Congress, and I do hope that such gentlemen as have any personal revenge to gratify against me will seek some other mode and place, if they can, and not by means of the public prints gratify their malice against me by attacking my client,—such time and place as gentlemen can seek, and they will always find me ready to meet them."

Although Marshall had thus publicly intimated that he not only expected, but would accept, a challenge from Col. Webb, no such message came. The conviction of Monroe Edwards, and the remarks the prisoner made to the court, complaining that he had been hounded by the press, doubtless deepened the impression on the mind of Marshall that he had been most grossly insulted and ill-used. He, therefore, at the termination of the trial, addressed a note to Col. Webb, demanding satisfaction, and gave it to Lieut. Duke to present to the colonel. When the epistle was delivered to the latter, he, through Mr. Charles Livingstone, informed Lieut. Duke that in the city of New York Col. Webb could not receive such a message, but that he would be in Wilmington, Del., with his friend, Maj. Morell, on Friday, the 24th day of June, at two o'clock in the afternoon, and he would then receive any communication Mr. Marshall might desire to send him.

At the time designated the parties met at Wilmington, I believe at the Indian Queen Hotel, on Market Street. In this, however, I may be in error. Here the challenge was again proffered by Marshall, and was accepted by Webb, who, it was understood, went there to be challenged. Marshall was accompanied by Dr. Carr, of Baltimore, in the capacity of second, and Dr. Gibson, of the same city, a son of Professor Gibson, of Philadelphia, as surgeon, Mr. Hunt, of Kentucky, and his (Marshall's) brother being present as friends. Col. Webb was attended by Maj. Morell, proprietor of the New York *Courier*, as second, Dr. Tucker, formerly of Virginia, then of Philadelphia, as surgeon. Josiah Randall, Esq., father of ex-Speaker Samuel J. Randall, of Philadelphia, and George Bryer, Esq., were present as his friends. After the preliminaries were arranged, and articles written providing for the manner in which the duel was to be conducted, both the principals, accompanied by their friends, left Wilmington, intending that the encounter should take place the same evening. The presence of Marshall and Webb in that city quickly became known, and as the intelligence of the bitter blood between the gentlemen had preceded them, the purpose of their visit was surmised, and the authorities were immediately on the alert. The duelists drove in their carriages to Marcus Hook, or rather the present Linwood, but as a number of persons, said to have been nearly one hundred, were following them, they stopped at the Union Hotel, at Hook Cross-roads, then kept by William Appleby. Here Col. Webb (for the purpose of quieting the suspicions of the authorities of Delaware County, for he learned that Hon. John Larkin, Jr., then sheriff, was in the neighborhood, and would use every means at his disposal to prevent the proposed breach of the public peace) left his carriage, went to Marcus Hook, embarked in a boat, and was rowed across the river to the Jersey shore. The impression then became general that Marshall would shortly follow Webb, and that the duel would be fought in New Jersey during the following day.

The crowd that had gathered stood on the pier watching the movements of the boat, which was rowed slowly along the opposite shore, without indicating any disposition on the part of the inmates to disembark on that side of the river. Several persons followed the course of the boat by the use of telescopes, until evening coming on, darkness screened the movements of the little craft from further observation. Then the assembled crowd reluctantly dispersed.

Col. Webb, taking advantage of the darkness, lingered on the river in the boat until late at night, when he returned quietly to Appleby's, about eleven o'clock, and passed the remainder of the night in his carriage. Marshall and his friends were comfortably housed in the Union Hotel. An hour before daybreak all the parties interested in the duel assembled, and a few minutes before four o'clock the carriages, closely following each other, left the hotel and started for the place designated for the encounter to take place,—an open field on Samuel T. Walker's farm, a few yards to the south of the King's Highway, and just within the Delaware State line. Two gentlemen from Philadelphia, who had not been invited, were present, as well as between thirty and forty persons who resided in the neighborhood.

When the seconds had measured the ground—ten paces—they marked the extremities of the line with stones, one at each end, where the principals were to be stationed. By this time it was daybreak. Maj. Morell tossed a coin to determine the choice of positions, and the silver fell in the grass, a fact which gave rise to some controversy between Dr. Carr and Maj. Morell, the seconds, as to which of the parties had won, both gentlemen resolutely declining to yield. Marshall hearing the dispute, cried in an impatient tone of voice to Dr. Carr,—

"Give it to them, doctor, give it to them. I came here to have a shot at him, and I do not mean to be baffled by trifles."

"We ask you to give nothing," proudly and angrily replied Maj. Morell. "We ask but what is our right."

Marshall's second, however, having yielded the point as instructed by his principal, he, Dr. Carr, tossed a coin to determine whose second should give the word. In this fortune again favored Col. Webb.

The principals took their places when told to do so with alacrity, and with the utmost coolness. Neither had attired himself in apparel best calculated to fight a duel in with the least danger to the wearer. Marshall's tall form, six feet two inches in height, erect, symmetrical, and lithe, was clad in a blue cloak, dark coat and pantaloons, and a light vest. Col. Webb, above the average height in stature, was dressed in a dark coat, vest, and light-brown pair of pantaloons. Each of these two men, as they stood at the places assigned them, placed his left foot against the stone, before mentioned, so as to stand firmly, the right leg advanced slightly towards his antagonist, the weight of the body being supported mainly by the left leg The pistols—ordinary dueling-pistols—having been loaded, Dr Carr, Marshall's second, then desired that the articles of agreement which were to govern the encounter should be read by Maj Morell One of the clauses stipulated that the friends of the duelists on the ground should be searched Col Webb's second and friends insisted that under the terms of the agreement Marshall should himself be searched Thereupon Dr Carr walked over to where Col Webb stood, and received from him his watch, which was worn on the left side of his vest, in a fob-pocket, with a slight gold chain extending across the right breast Col Webb, as he took these trinkets from his person, did not move from the position in which he had been placed by his friends Maj Morell remained standing at the place when he had read the agreement, and Marshall, noticing this, approached him, and requested the major to search him This the latter persistingly declined to do, whereupon Marshall produced a small pocket-comb and several other trifling articles, stating that they were all he had in his pockets He then returned to his place

Maj Morell, in a clear, distinct voice, inquired, "Gentlemen, are you ready?"

"I am," responded Col Webb

"No, I am not," replied Mr Marshall And for a moment he paused, while every person gazed earnestly and wonderingly at him He looked fixedly and searchingly at Col Webb for a minute or two, then unfastening his cloak, and slowly lifting his hat from his head, he tossed both articles of apparel from him without having apparently altered his position in the least

"Now, sir," he said, "I am ready"

During this peculiar proceeding on the part of his antagonist Col Webb preserved the utmost coolness and self-possession

Maj Morell glanced hastily at the combatants, and then in full, audible tones exclaimed, "Fire! One—two—three!"

Just before the word "one" the pistols were discharged, and so simultaneous were the reports that for a moment it was believed that Col Webb had not fired his weapon at all The ball from his pistol, however, had fallen in a direct line, and entered the ground almost at the feet of Marshall, while the latter's ball struck the earth ten feet in front, and about three feet to the right of where Col Webb stood

Marshall then raising his pistol in the air above his head, cried, "Another shot"

A parley was thereupon had between the seconds, who consulted with their principals, and it was determined that another fire should be exchanged The pistols were accordingly loaded once more and placed in the hands of the two men who stood facing each other, without having changed position from that in which the first fire had been had

Again the word was given, and again the pistols were discharged

At the word "Fire!" both men brought their weapons to a level, and before the word "two" was spoken, as at the first discharge, the reports mingled together The ball from Col Webb's pistol passed in close proximity to the person of Marshall, but he escaped without a scratch Col Webb for a moment after the firing kept his position, apparently unhurt, then he faltered on the left foot Maj Morell, his second, believing that his principal was unharmed, was looking in the direction of Marshall, when Dr Carr suddenly exclaimed,—

"Sir, your friend is falling Why don't you catch him?"

Dr Carr, as soon as he noticed that Col Webb was staggering, had called thus to Maj Morell, but without waiting for a response he sprang towards and caught Col Webb in his arms and gently laid him on the grass, supporting his shoulders Dr Tucker, the wounded man's surgeon, came forward and examined the injury The ball had entered the left leg just below the knee, on the back part of the inside, and had passed out on the outside of the leg After the wound had been examined Dr Carr returned to Marshall, when the latter inquired where Col Webb had been hit The doctor stated that he was wounded below the knee

"What!" exclaimed Marshall, "hit in the knee! It is the damnedest lowest act of my life! We must exchange another shot That man has injured me more than any other being on earth If he can stand I expect and demand that we shall exchange another fire"

Dr Carr immediately walked over to Maj Morell and told him that Marshall desired a third shot The major quickly responded that it would depend upon Col Webb's condition, and Dr Tucker would decide as to that The wound by this time was bleeding profusely Maj Morell, addressing himself to Dr Tucker, said,—

"Dr. Carr informs me that Mr Marshall insists on a third shot if Col Webb can possibly stand The demand strikes me as unwarrantable, as Col Webb's wound, it seems to me, will put him at most serious disadvantage, but I desire that you, doctor, shall decide this matter"

Quite a number of the bystanders by this time had gathered around the seconds, and listened anxiously to the conversation

"Col Webb's wound might, of course, have been more dangerous," replied Dr Tucker "As it is, it may be serious, for my examination has not yet been sufficiently thorough to determine whether any of the nerves or muscles have been permanently injured. It fortunately now appears to be only a flesh wound Under any circumstances, however, it is impossible

William Trainer

for Col Webb to continue the matter at present I will not listen to it, sir."

Marshall's brother, who had withdrawn some distance from the ground where the duelists stood during the firing, now joined the group, and said, with much warmth of manner,—

"It is absurd to talk about another shot This matter has already gone far enough. Tom has no right to ask it of Col Webb, but he should rather thank God that things are not more serious than they are"

The bystanders now joined in and declared that they would not permit the duel to be continued, that both the gentlemen ought to be satisfied, at least for the time being Col Webb, who was lying on the ground, supported in the arms of Maj Morell (who, after he had told Dr Tucker the import of Marshall's demand, had returned to the side of his principal), inquired what was the subject-matter of discussion Maj Morell stated that Marshall was not satisfied, and had demanded another exchange of shots

"I have entertained no unkind feelings towards Mr Marshall at any time," replied Webb, "nor do I now feel unkindly towards him I do not know why he should bear such uncompromising malice against me"

When it was announced to Marshall that the second and surgeon of Col Webb, and even the bystanders, would not consent to the continuation of the duel at the present time, he shrugged his shoulders, remarking,—

"We've no further business here, we may as well return to the hotel" And almost immediately Marshall and his friends left the grounds, both parties apparently entertaining the same hated feeling towards each other as when they met In a few moments after Marshall left, Col Webb was assisted to his feet by his friends, and partly lifted over the fence and placed in his carriage, which drove off to Appleby's

Marshall and his party went to Marcus Hook, intending to get aboard the steamboat, but finding that they could not do so, they returned to the Union Hotel for breakfast Marshall meeting Mr Randall on the porch, inquired how Webb was, trusted that his wound would not be a serious one, and expressed regrets that he had insisted upon the third shot His excitement and anger, seemingly, had entirely abated Marshall and his party, later in the day, went directly to Baltimore and Washington

At the Union Hotel, Col Webb had his wound dressed anew, and while the surgeon was probing he is said to have watched the movements of the doctor with interest, but without exhibiting the least fear or indicating in anywise that he was suffering pain At an early hour Col. Webb's party drove to Philadelphia, reaching that city at half-past nine o'clock in the forenoon, and stopped at the United States Hotel, where the wound was again examined, and some apprehension expressed that it might be necessary to amputate the leg This anticipation was not realized Col Webb in a few days became much better, and his flow of spirits never deserted him On one occasion when a friend asked him if he was not tired of being confined to his bed, he, with a good-natured laugh replied, "I can't help it, I am under Marshall law"

On the return of Col Webb and Maj Morell to New York, they were arrested for violating the statutes of that commonwealth, which made it penal to leave the State to accept, fight, or be anywise connected with a duel The grand jury found a true bill against Webb, he was tried, and the jury rendered a verdict of guilty The case excited general public attention, and Webb was for a season one of the noted sensations His friends brought enormous pressure on Hon Silas Wright, then Governor, who made him the object of executive clemency

On June 9, 1845, Washington Keith and Morris Meredith, both of Philadelphia, fought a duel on the old field,—where, it was said, the stones marking the spaces where Hunter and Miller stood remained undisturbed, and every spring were whitewashed to make them conspicuous By a stupid blunder of the seconds, at the word only one of the principals (Keith) fired, his ball lodging in Meredith's thigh The wounded man, too badly injured to return the fire of the man who had shot without being shot at, was brought to Chester, where Dr McClellan, who had attended as one of the surgeons, extracted the ball, and after many weeks the wound healed kindly There was, however, no further effort made to give Meredith a chance to rectify the error He had escaped with his life, and honor's demands had been fully met

BIOGRAPHICAL SKETCH.

WILLIAM TRAINER

David Trainer, the grandfather of William, emigrated from Ireland when nine years of age, and entering the service of George Hinkson, of Nether Providence, Delaware Co, remained until he attained his majority He married Martha, daughter of Bethel Robert Booth, to whom were born children,—Jane, Lydia, Mary, Martha, Margaret, Prudence, and David He married, a second time, Margaret Morton, whose children were Daniel, Edith, George, and James. Mr Trainer for a while cultivated a farm, after which he engaged extensively in the quarrying of stone, in Ridley township, in connection with his former occupation His son, David, was born Feb 19, 1777, in Darby township, and during his active life was both a farmer and a miller. He was an influential citizen, public-spirited and progressive, in politics a pronounced Federalist, and for one or more terms commissioner of the county He married Mrs Sarah Newlan, of Lower Chichester township, whose birth occurred March 27, 1771. Their children were Sarah (Mrs. James H. Walker), William, Josiah, Mary (wife of Capt. Frank Smith), and David. Mr. Trainer died Feb. 29, 1846, in his seventieth year, and his wife, July 29, 1849, in her seventy-ninth year. Their son, William, the subject of this sketch, was born Dec. 10, 1806, in Lower Chichester township, where his life has been spent. After such advantages of education as were obtainable in the neighborhood were enjoyed, he became for six months a pupil of Benjamin Tucker, a celebrated Quaker instructor resident in Philadelphia. Returning to his home, the labor of the farm engaged his attention until twenty-one years of age, after which a year was spent in travel in the West. Another year was employed as superintendent of the work connected with the Delaware breakwater, after which he embarked in the business of store-keeping at Marcus Hook, and in 1838 resumed the labors of a farmer. He was married, in 1832, to Miss Mary P., daughter of Israel Heacock, of Darby township, whose children are Emma (wife of Joseph McElrey), Henry Clay, David E., and William,—all married and residing in Philadelphia. The death of Mrs. Trainer occurred, after a most useful and exemplary life, on the 12th of September, 1883. Mr. Trainer, after his marriage, inherited the farm which is his present home, and continued its cultivation until 1883, when he abandoned active labor. In politics he was early a Federalist, after which he became an earnest supporter of the Whig principles of which Henry Clay was the able exponent, and now votes the Republican ticket. He was formerly active in local politics, and for many years director of the poor of the county. Under his supervision the old almshouse property at Media was sold, and land purchased at advantageous figures in Middletown township, on which the present spacious buildings are located. Mr. Trainer was educated in the Quaker faith, but, with his wife, in 1837 became a member of the Protestant Episcopal Church of Marcus Hook, though at present one of the congregation of the Methodist Episcopal Church of that place.

CHAPTER XXXIX.

CONCORD TOWNSHIP.

Concord Township, the largest municipal division in the county of Delaware, is first mentioned at the court "held at Chester, for the County of Chester, on the 27th of the 4th month, called june, 1683," at which session John Mendenhall was appointed constable for "Concord liberty." The name it bears is believed to have been bestowed because of the harmonious feelings which in early times prevailed among the settlers there. The township was laid out originally in a rectangular form, and a road exactly in the centre (called Concord Street) ran from Bethel, on the south, to Thornbury, on the north, dividing it in halves. This street, laid out in 1682, appears never to have been opened to public travel. The southwestern end of Concord, which intrudes into Birmingham, rendering the boundary-lines of that township the most irregular in the county, resulted from the fact that the lines of the manor of Rockland, in New Castle County, ran along the western boundary of Concord, and, after the division of Pennsylvania and Delaware, the Rockland manor lands were patented to settlers who, doubtless, selected and were annexed to the township in which they wished their lands located. This idea is inferentially established by the fact that no land, either in Concord or Birmingham townships, within the manor was patented previous to 1701, in which year Penn authorized the division between Pennsylvania and the three lower counties—the present State of Delaware—to be made. That part of the Rockland manor which is now in Concord was patented by four persons. George Lee, Dec. 23, 1701, had surveyed to him two hundred acres bordering on Bethel to the Concord line. Nathaniel Newlin received two patents, June 2, 1702, for six hundred acres,—one of two hundred and the other of four hundred acres,—beginning at the eastern boundary of the original township and extending to the present western line of Concord. His patents were located on the north of Lee's tract, and included almost all the lands between parallel lines, except one hundred and thirty and a half acres, which were surveyed to Francis Chads, April 9, 1702. This tract began a short distance west of Elam, and ran eastward to the original township-line. The irregular piece of land, which juts to a point almost northwest into Birmingham, was patented to John Chevers, as two hundred acres, Oct. 28, 1708.

Early in the history of the township the savages, whose custom was to roam undisturbed wheresoever they pleased, hunting for game and killing the swine, became an annoyance to the settlers in the "back woods" of Concord. This disposition on the part of the red men created much trouble, and soon became so detrimental to the residents that on Nov. 16, 1685, they presented a petition to the Provincial Council respecting it, which is of record as follows:

"The Complaint of ye friends, Inhabitants of Concord and Hertford" (Haverford),—widely separated townships,—"against the Indians, for ye Rapine and Destructions of their hoggs, was Read.

"Ordered that ye Respective Indian Kings be sent for to ye Councill with all speed, to Answer their Complaint.

"The Inhabitants of the Welsh Tract Complains of the same, by an Endorsement on ye aforementioned Complaint."[1]

What ultimately resulted from this action of the Concord settlers does not appear of record, nor has tradition preserved anything respecting it.

At the southwestern end of the original township of Concord was a tract of three hundred acres, which

[1] Colonial Records, vol. i. p. 162.

Zouche, Baron of Codnor, No. 161, in the foreground.

"CODNOR FARM."

RESIDENCE OF COL. FRANK M. ETTING,

was surveyed to William Beazer March 29, 1683, and which shortly afterwards passed into the ownership of William Cloud, who, although an aged man, accompanied by his family, came to the colony among the earliest settlers and moved "into the woods" at Concord. He was a native of Calne, county of Wiltshire, and from him the Cloud family of Delaware County claim descent. Just above his tract John Beal, who had married Mary Cloud, took up two hundred acres on rent in 1683, but he subsequently removed. Nearly midway of the township, extending from the western limits of Concord as originally surveyed to Concord Street, which ran north and south, dividing the district into halves, was a tract of five hundred acres, which was surveyed Oct. 12, 1683, to John Haselgrove. This estate, after passing through several owners, none of whom were residents, in 1710 was acquired by Henry Peirce, who settled on this land and was taxed therefor in 1715. Above Concordville, John Lee, on Dec. 3, 1701, received a patent for one hundred and fifty-two acres. He was a woolcomber by trade, and came from Wiltshire, England, in 1700, and settled in Concord. He lived until 1726, and was a noted public Friend in the early days of the province. Above Lee's tract John Mendenhall purchased three hundred acres of land, which was patented to him June 27, 1684. On this property Concord Friends' meeting-house was located, the land being given by Mendenhall for that purpose. He is believed to have come from Mildenhall, county of Sussex, England, and was one of the original projectors and owners of the Concord Mills. Above the Mendenhall tract William Byers had two hundred acres surveyed to him Jan. 17, 1683/4, which, in 1693, passed into the ownership of Nicholas Pyle. He settled in Concord, in 1686, at which time he may have already occupied the estate. In the company's mills he took an active part as one of the owners. He was a member of Assembly, serving as such for six years, and was an active, enterprising man, whose energy did much to tame and subdue the wilderness. In 1701 he purchased the western half of the five hundred acres taken up by William Hitchcock, which extended from the east to the west boundary across the township, for on that part of the estate bought by him the Society Mills were located. The tract of two hundred and fifty acres lying above Pyle's land was surveyed to Philip Roman, February, 1682/3, but it is not probable that he ever resided thereon. On the eastern side of Concord Street, extending from that road to the eastern line of the township, and immediately south of Thornbury, John Harding, at the same date as Roman, acquired title to two hundred and fifty-five acres of land, but he, as with Roman, never resided on the property. Just south of this tract was the William Hitchcock land, already mentioned, which was subsequently purchased by Benjamin Mendenhall, who resided thereon in 1715, and probably followed his occupation of wheelwright. In 1714 he was a member of the Assembly, and, retaining the good opinion of the public, he lived to an advanced age, dying in 1740. Below this tract Nicholas Newlin, on Sept. 24, 1683, received five hundred acres. He was reputed as very wealthy, a nobleman by descent, being one of the De Newlandes, who had come over with the Conqueror. Although of English family, he emigrated, with his wife and children, from County Tyrone, Ireland. He was appointed a member of the Provincial Council and a justice of the courts. His son, Nicholas, was about twenty-four years old when he accompanied his father to Pennsylvania, a man of education and means. In 1698 he was a member of Assembly, and served as such at several different periods. He was also appointed one of the proprietaries' commissioners of property, and a justice of the courts. In 1722 he was one of the trustees of the loan-office, a position he continued to fill until his death. On the Newlin lands, Codnor farm, owned by Col. Frank M. Etting, the author, is located.

Below the present Markham Station, on the Baltimore Central Railroad, was a tract of two hundred acres, patented to Thomas King, July 22, 1684, and thereon he resided until his death, in 1706. On the south of King's land was one hundred acres surveyed to Thomas Moore in 1684, while immediately below him were two hundred acres, patented July 15, 1684, to Nathaniel Park. Jeremiah Collett on March 1, 1682/3, took up two hundred acres on tract immediately south of Park's plantation. On March 1, 1686, this property passed to John Hannum, who gave the ground at the northwest corner of the tract on which St. John's Church was built. He was the grandfather of Col. John Hannum, of the Revolution, who was the controlling mind which caused the removal of the county-seat to West Chester, an act which eventually resulted in the erection of Delaware County. Col. Hannum, it is said, was born on this plantation. South of the Hannum property were three hundred acres, which on July 12, 13, 1682, were surveyed to George Strode, of Southampton County, England, a grocer by trade, but beyond that fact very little is now known respecting him. Directly south of Strode's tract were one hundred acres entered on rent Sept. 24, 1683, by William Hawkes, which on March 26, 1688, were patented to John Palmer. The latter, tradition says, was enticed away from his widowed mother's home, in England, and came as a redemptioner to the colony. He married Mary Suddery, a woman of great courage, for it is related that on one occasion she drove a bear away from a chestnut-tree on this plantation with a fire-poker, or poking-stick. Two hundred acres south of the Palmer tract was surveyed to William Oborne July 3, 1688, and a similar tract to the south of Oborne's land was patented to John Beazer, Aug. 4, 1684, but he did not reside on the estate. Dennis Rochford, Feb. 10, 1682, had surveyed to him five hundred acres, to the south of the Bezer land. Rochford was an Irishman, from Emstorfey,

County of Wexford, and accompanied William Penn in the "Welcome" His wife, Mary, died on the passage in that plague-smitten vessel, as did also two of his daughters He settled on the estate in Concord, and in 1683 was a representative from Chester County in the Assembly On Oct 6, 1691, Thomas Green purchased four hundred acres of the Rochford lands He, with his wife, Margaret, and two sons, Thomas and John, settled in Concord in 1686, possibly on the tract he subsequently bought From him the Green family of Delaware County trace descent The remaining one hundred acres bordering on the Bethel line was sold to William Clayton, Jr, Feb 14, 1684/5, but he never resided on the land in Concord

Concord Friends' Meeting-House —The land for a Friends' meeting and graveyard at Concord, the sixth in the county, was conveyed or rather leased to trustees, by John Mendenhall, in 1697, they paying "one peppercorn yearly forever" In that year a sum was obtained by subscription for fencing in a burial-ground at Concord, and at a monthly meeting held at the house of George Pearce, on the 10th day of Fourth month, 1697, the following paper was read

"WHEREAS, the has been some differences by some that have separated from Friends in their subscriptions towards their building of meeting-houses, &c, for the service of Truth, We, whose names are hereunder subscribed, do promise and oblige ourselves hereby, that if we, or any one or more of us should separate ourselves from the Society and Communion of these Friends of Concord, Birmingham, and Thornbury, that now we walk in fellowship with, either in doctrine, life or conversation, we will make no trouble amongst these people by reason of any right we, or any one of us think we have because of this, or any other subscription that was, or may be, towards building a meeting-house or making a burial place for the youse of the said people of God called Quakers And we further promise to relinquish and lay aside all pretence of right or claim whereby any disquiet may arise among the aforesaid people of God called Quakers, of Concord, Birmingham, and Thornbury According to the purport, true meaning and intent of the written as above said, we subscribe as follows

	£	s	d		£	s	d
"Nath'l Newlin	7	10	0	Peter Dix	5	15	0
Benj Mendenhall.	5	10	0	George Pearce	5	6	0
Elizabeth Hickman	1	5	0	Isaac Taylor	2	8	0
Thomas Ring	3	5	0	Wm Brinton, Sr	3	10	0
Nicholas Pyle	3	6	0	Wm Brinton, Jr	2	16	0
William Cloud	3	6	0	John Mendenhall	2	16	0
William Collett	2	0	0	Benj Woodward	1	18	0
Edward Jones	1	16	0	John Bennett	4	5	0
Nicholas Newlin	6	15	0	John Hertchim	1	2	6
Robert Way	1	6	0	Joseph Edwards.	0	15	0
Edward Bennett	1	6	0	Joseph Gilpin	0	10	0
Thomas Radley	1	0	0	Samuel Scott	0	10	0
Richard Thatcher	1	15	0	John Sanger	0	6	0
Francis Chadsey	1	6	0	Goodwin Walter	0	5	0
Jonathan Thatcher	1	10	0	Daniel Davis	0	5	0
John Newlin	5	10	0				
Henry Osburn	2	5	0		56	0	3"

Although this sum was subscribed for the building of a meeting house in Concord, it seems not to have been completely ready for use until 1710, and was then a frame or log structure, which, in 1728, gave place to a brick edifice In the early times the meeting-houses had no stoves in them, but were partially warmed by charcoal fires, which were built on large stones in the centre of the building, which were allowed to die out before the hour set for meeting, or were warmed by open wood-fires in wide chimney-places Concord meeting-house was warmed by these latter means, large wood-fires being built in the attic at each end of the building, to which members would resort previous to assembling in the apartment below Concord meeting-house having become too limited in its dimensions to meet the wants of Friends of that neighborhood, a movement was made looking to its enlargement or the building of an entirely new edifice In the winter of 1788, while Friends had assembled to consider that question, the house caught fire from the soot in one of the chimneys, and despite the efforts of those present was burned, leaving only the brick walls Immediate steps were taken to rebuild the house, the expense being borne jointly by Concord Monthly and Quarterly Meetings, the former agreeing to pay six hundred pounds, one-third of the estimated costs, and the six Monthly Meetings in Chester County obligating themselves to discharge the remaining two-thirds The present Concord meeting-house was built under these circumstances, the old walls being used, an addition being made thereto The cost of the structure exceeded largely the estimate, and a call was made for three hundred and seventy-five pounds additional to complete the meeting-house In this old building for seventy years the question of human slavery was discussed, and by degrees the feeling grew that it was unjust, until on 20th day Second month, 1800, at Concord Quarterly Meeting for the first time appeared on its record this announcement "Clear of importing, disposing of, or holding mankind as slaves" At two o'clock on Friday, Sept 12, 1777, Maj-Gen Grant, with the First and Second Brigades of the British army, marched from Chad's Ford to Concord, and some of his men were quartered in the old meeting-house, while foraging parties scoured the "country and woods" near by, picking "up Waggons, Horses, Ammunition, Provision and cattle, and several Rebels that had secreted themselves"[1] Tradition records that the meeting-house was made a hospital by the English for their wounded, but the inference is more probable that disabled American soldiers, in striving to escape, were found in the woods by the English scouting parties, were brought there, and on Sunday following, when Dr Rush with three surgeons came to "attend the wounded Rebels left scattered in the Houses about the field of Battle, unattended by their Surgeons till now," he visited that building on his errand of mercy Gen Grant, tradition also asserts, occupied as his headquarters, while he tarried at Concord, a house built in 1755, near St John's Church, which in recent years has been removed to make room for needed improvements The English officer, when he advanced to unite with Lord Cornwallis at Village Green, left a guard at the meeting house for the short time intervening before the whole British army marched away from that neighborhood never to return The venerable Friends' meeting-house had

1 Journal of Capt John Montressor, *Penna Mag of Hist.*, vol vii p 34

been the scene of many incidents connected with the family history of the old families of Concord and surrounding townships which will ever render it a place of interest and considerate care

St. John's Episcopal Church—The first mention of an Episcopalian Church at Concord occurs in the letter of Rev Evan Evans, dated London, Sept 18, 1707, on "the state of the church in Pennsylvania, most humbly offered to the venerable Society for the Propagation of the Gospel in Foreign Parts" Rev Mr Evans, in 1700, was sent to Philadelphia by Bishop Compton, the then Bishop of London, to aid by his ministry and teachings the infant Christ Church, the congregation of which, in 1696, had erected a place of worship in the "Great town" in the colony This missionary gave glowing accounts of the growth of the doctrines of the Church of England among the people of the province, and in order to show how deeply the seed he had sown had taken root, records, "And the true religion (by the frequent resort of persons from remote parts to Philadelphia) did so spread, and the number of converts did so increase that I was obliged to divide myself among them as often and as equally as I could, till they were formed into proper districts, and had ministers sent over to them by the venerable society For this reason I went frequently to Chichester, which is twenty-five miles, Chester or Upland, twenty, Maidenhead, forty (where I baptized 19 children at one time), Concord, twenty, Evesham, in West Jersey, fifteen, Montgomery, twenty, and Radnor, fifteen miles distant from Philadelphia All which, though equally fatiguing and expensive, I frequently went to and preached, being by all means determined to lose none of those I have gained, but rather add to them till the society otherwise provided for them"

In the same letter Mr Evans states, "Our winters, being severe in these parts, detain many from church whose plantations lie at a distance, and for that reason Mr Nicholas preached sometimes at Concord in the week-days"[1]

The first St. Paul's Church at Chester was built in 1702, and on Sunday, Jan. 24, 1703 (new style), it was opened for public worship In 1704, Rev Henry Nichols was assigned by the Society for the Propagation of the Gospel in Foreign Parts as missionary in charge of St Paul's parish, then including Marcus Hook and Concord, hence the week day services mentioned by Mr Evans must have been held in that year, certainly prior to 1707 On March 17, 1682/3, Jeremiah (or, as he is usually termed in the early records, "Jeremy") Collet, an earnest Episcopalian, entered on rent two hundred acres of land in Concord, and on March 1, 1686, conveyed the property to John Hannum (who settled in Concord about that time, certainly within two years thereafter), an ardent churchman, who is alluded to by Rev Mr Ross in his report to the society, June 25, 1714, in which he furnished "an account of the Building of St Paul's at Chester," as among the "Parishers who were chief helpers to carry on the work" In 1702, John Hannum gave a lot of ground at the northwest corner of his tract on which to erect a church, and doubtless a log building was located thereon about that year A tradition prevails that long previous to this date the Swedes were accustomed to hold divine service in Concord A similar tradition maintained until within recent years that the early Swedish settlers had a church at Chester on the site of the old St Paul's, but careful investigation has so fully demonstrated the error of this statement that it is no longer an open question Indeed, previous to Penn coming it is extremely doubtful whether a Swedish person ever saw the territory now Concord township The tradition originated in the fact that often for months together no clergyman of the Church of England could be procured to preach in these remote settlements And as late as 1751, Rev Israel Acrelius records that the Swedish pastor in charge of the Lutheran Church at Christina was frequently requested to preach in the Episcopal Churches, "as otherwise their (the parishioners') children would become unchristened heathens or Quakers, their churches would be changed into stables alongside of Quaker meeting-houses They praised Mr Tranberg as a warm-hearted man, who had always assisted them The Provost, therefore, took some time to see whether it was possible to please everybody He preached once a month in all these places He was at Christina every Sunday, but on week-days and saints' days in the others That became the rule, and at first was all right, but afterwards each congregation wanted preaching on a Sunday So there were also added the churches at Concord and Marcus Hook, which presented the same request, and then there were not as many Sundays in the month as there were congregations to serve, and so Christina would always have been vacant The good old Swedes now began to murmur, partly at the minister, and partly at the English, who wished to have him with them and never once paid his expenses of travel"[2] Hence, while the names of several Swedish ministers appear among the list of pastors of St Paul's, St Martin's, and St John's Churches, they were there merely to fill a vacancy, and were never regularly ordained rectors of St Paul's parish, which included until 1835 St John's Church in Concord

Ralph Pyle, of Concord, who was a liberal contributor to the first church of St Paul's, at Chester, in his will, dated Jan 1, 1739, and proved Sept 1, 1741, provided

"*Item* I give twenty pounds, that is to say, the Interest of the said money, for the use of a minister of the Church of England, to preach three Sermons yearly in the Township of Concord, that is to say, the

1 "Episcopal Church in Pennsylvania," Hazard's Register, vol iii pp. 338, 339

2 Acrelius' "History of New Sweden," p 305

Sunday before Christmas Day, the Sunday before Easter, and the Sunday before Whitsunday, that is the lawful interest of the said twenty pounds shall be carefully paid unto such minister yearly who shall preach the sermons at the times as above mentioned, whilst there is a Church remain in Concord aforesaid."

Although this bequest was not made a specific charge on the real estate of Ralph Pyle, yet William Pyle, his son, by will Jan. 8, 1745/6, proved four days thereafter, devised to his son, John Pyle, a plantation of two hundred and fifty-six acres in Birmingham, subject to the annual payment of this and other "demands which his grandfather, Ralph Pyle, ordered to be paid by his last will and testament." The peculiar feature of this devise was that the land on which the grandfather's bounty was made a charge by William Pyle in his devise to his son, was conveyed to him by his father, Ralph, twenty years before the latter made his will, in which the above bequest was made.

Six years prior to the death of John Hannum—he died in 1730—Isaac Taylor, the noted surveyor of Chester County, on Sept. 25, 1724, surveyed the plot of ground given to the church twenty-two years prior to that date. The log church erected in 1702 was located on the present cemetery, just below the Foucitt lot, and the old church records "the graves of Rev. Richard and Mary Saunderlands were at the church-door." I have been unable to designate who Rev. Richard Saunderlands was. His name does not appear in Professor Keen's carefully-prepared and exhaustive history of the descendants of James Sandelands, of Chester. The first books of the church have been lost, and no record remains prior to 1727. That the congregation of St. John's Church was organized and recognized many years previous to that date is accepted as historically established the reference made to it by Rev. Mr. Evans, heretofore mentioned, can leave no doubts existing, and the fact that Queen Anne presented, in 1707/8, a silver communion set to St. John's Church, at Concord, is confirmatory of this statement. The frame structure was the only house of worship for the Episcopalians of Concord for many years. In February, 1765, the Provincial Assembly passed an act authorizing the raising of £3003 15s. by a lottery, the proceeds to be divided among the congregations of St. Peter's Church, in Philadelphia, St. Paul's, in Chester and in Carlisle, to be used in furnishing those churches, to build a church at Reading, to repair the church at Molltown, in Berks County, and Huntingdon township, York County, "and for repairing the Episcopal churches in Chichester and Concord, and purchasing a glebe for the church at Chester, in the county of Chester." In 1769 the treasurer of the Province paid to the congregation at Concord its proportion of the funds netted by this lottery. With this sum in 1773 a western end, laid with brick, was added to the frame church, and in 1790 an eastern end, laid with stone, took the place of the early rude structure in which the congregation for nearly a century had worshiped. The new building, however, did not cover the site of the first church. In 1837 another addition was made, but as the edifice had been erected at various dates, and was insufficient to meet the requirements of the congregation, it was determined to build a new church. On June 15, 1844, the corner-stone of the present building was laid, and the work was so hastened to completion that on Oct. 27, 1844, the new church was consecrated by Bishop Lee, "acting with the permission and at the request of Bishop Henry W. Onderdonk, Bishop of Pennsylvania." With the exception of such repairs as from time to time became necessary, the present building is the one erected in 1844. A large chancel window was placed in the church as a memorial of the late Bishop Onderdonk, and several other smaller memorial windows have also been erected. New furniture since the building was completed has taken the place of that of ancient days. St. John's Church has an endowment of one thousand dollars, a bequest of the late Mrs. Elizabeth Sharpless. During the years 1883–84 a new church was erected in the parish,—St. Luke's, at Chad's Ford,—which is in charge of Rev. J. J. Sleeper, rector of St. John's.

The pastors of St. John's parish have been as follows:

Revs. Evan Evans, Henry Nichols, George Ross, John Humphreys, John Backhouse, Thomas Thompson, George Craig, John Wade, James Connor, James Turner, Levi Heath, Joshua Reece, M. Chander, William Pryce, Jacob M. Douglass, Samuel C. Brinckle, Jacob Douglass, George Kirke, John Baker Clemson, M. D. Hirst, E. Wilson Wiltbank, Alfred Lee, Samuel C. Stratton, Benjamin S. Huntington, R. B. Claxton, W. H. Trapnell, Charles Buck, John R. Murphy, Richardson Graham, John B. Clemsen, M. Christian, J. J. Craigh, Joshua Coupland, H. Baldwin Dean, Joseph J. Sleeper, the present rector.

It is unnecessary to refer to the Roman Catholic Church establishment in Concord, that being presented in the account of Ivy Mills and the Willcox family.

The Taxables in 1715 and 1799.—The following taxables appear on the assessment-list for 1715, of taxables in Concord:

Nath. Newlin, Jur, Nicholas Pyle for ye mill, James Clamston, Nath. Newlin, Senr, Joseph Cloud, Henry Oburn, John Palmer, John Palmer, Jur, Godwin Walter, George Robinson, Jacob Pyle, Ralph Pyle, Henry Peirce, Matthias Carlo, Ralph Evenson, James Heavrd, William Amme, Thomas Smith, John Lee, Robert Chamberlin, Robert Chamberlin, Junr, Thomas West, William Hill, Morgan Jones, Thomas Durnall, George Lee, Daniel Evans, Joseph Nicklin, John Hannum, Benjm Mendenhall, John Mendenhall, John Newlin, Joseph Edwards, Thomas Broom, William fforde, ffrancis Pulin, John Penneck, James Chiffers, John Hackney, Christopher Penock.

ffreemen, Caleb Pearkins, Richard ffar, Peter Poulston, John Pennock, John Engram, Henry Jones, Thomas Ealthan.

In the assessment for the year 1799, the following persons appear as taxables in the township:

William Alleson, taylor; Moses Bullock, mason; John Ball, weaver; Joseph Cloud, carpenter; Joseph Hutton, mill-house, currying-shop, and tan-yard, tanner; James Jefferies, tavern-keeper and store-keeper; Thomas Marshall, one stone mill and currying-shop, tanner; Thomas Newlin, Esq., justice of peace; Nathaniel Newlin, saw-mill; Thomas Newlin, blacksmith; John Newlin, stone grist-mill, miller; Moses Palmer, assemblyman and hatter; John Palmer, saddler; John Perkins, shoemaker; Micajah Speakman, blacksmith; Thomas Speakman, joiner; Jacob Thomas, store-keeper; William Trimble, one saw-mill, one large paper-mill; Ann Vernon, tavern-keeper; William Vernon,

J R Scott

"SCOTLAND FARM."

RESIDENCE OF ALEXANDER SCOTT.

St Andrew 3d, Herd Register No 251

saw-mill; William Willis, taylor; William Walter, miller, one stone grist-mill; William Howard, millwright.

Inmates.—Abeshai Mellon, weaver; Wheleback Paulin, tanner; Robert Selah, paper-maker; William Clughson, paper-maker; George Moore, paper-maker; William Hull, mason; Thomas Willcox, paper-maker; Jesse Plankinghorn, wheelwright; Thomas Melleon, weaver; Thomas Hance, weaver; Joseph Finch, miller; James Cloud, millwright; Thomas Cheney, hatter; John Masson, shoemaker; Daniel Doaks, wheelwright; James Hall, mason; Pridey Kimber, carpenter; John Hatton, carpenter; James Mendenhall, wheelwright; Moses Perkins, shoemaker; John Selah, paper-maker.

LIST OF THE JUSTICES FOR CONCORD TOWNSHIP.

Names.	Date of Commission.
Thomas Newlin	Aug. 19, 1791.
Thomas Pierce	Feb. 5, 1814.
Matthias Kerlin	July 4, 1808.
James Bratton	Feb. 3, 1820.
Joseph Fox	Dec. 4, 1823.
John Mattson	Dec, 13, 1823.
Joseph Bowen	Nov. 10, 1824.
Joseph Trimble	April 21, 1827.
Robert Frame	Jan. 15, 1829.
Robert Hall	Feb. 8, 1831.
William Mendenhall	Dec. 6, 1836, April 14, 1840.
Casper W. Sharpless	April 15, 1845, April 9, 1850, April 28, 1857, April 24, 1862.
Edward J. Willcox	April 11, 1867.
Darwin Painter	April 11, 1867, April 15, 1872, March 23, 1877, April 10, 1882.

Roads.—On Oct. 25, 1687, the grand jury, or those members of that body who attached their names, laid out a thirty-feet wide road from Dilworthtown, following the course of the present road to a point a short distance south of the present Concord Station, and above St. John's Church, on Concord road, at which point the road widened to forty feet, as will be noticed by following the description in the report submitted to court:

"Laid out a High way from Burmingham to Concord, being a thirty-foote way, by vertue of an order of Court bearing date ye 4th of October, 1687, laid out by us, Walter Marten, John Mendenhall, John Kingsman, William Cloud, Rich. Thatcher, being one-third part of ye present grand Jury of ye county of Chester, as followes, viz.:

"Beginning att a white oake standing on a Small Branch att William Branton's, marked with five knotches; thence along a lyne of marked trees between Alice Brunson and land lat Edward Turner to Concord corner tree; thence doune Concord lyne Between ye said Alice Brunson and Philip Roman to a white Oake marked with five knotches; then crosse ye Corner of said Philip Roman's land; then crosse William Hitchcock's land; thence crosse land that was William Biases; thence crosse John Mendenhall's land; thence crosse land that was Peter Lounders'; thence crosse part of John Symcock's land to ye foote-Bridge of Thomas Moore; then crosse part of ye said Thomas Moore's land to a White Oake marked with five knotches.

"Laid out by vertue of ye aforesaid Order, a fourty-foote Road from Concord to ye King's Highway in Chester, as followeth, by us, whose hands are under written, ye 25th of October, 1687.

"Beginning at a white oake with five knotches, standing att ye corner of Nathaniell Park's land, next Thomas Moore's land; thence through ye land of ye said Nathaniell; thence cross John Hannum's land; thence crosse George Strond's land; thence crosse John Palmer's land; thence crosse land late William Oburne's; thence crosse land late John Beasar's; thence crosse Dennis Rochford's Land; thence crosse William Clayton, Junr's land to ye Hamlett of Bethell.

"Thence crosse Edward Beason's land; thence cross ffrancis Smith's land; thence crosse Robert Eyre's land to Chichester; thence crosse Walter Martin's land; thence crosse land late John Beasars'; thence crosse John Kingsman's land; thence crosse Henry Hastings' and Richard Buffington's land; thence cross James Brown's land; thence Thomas Wither's land to Chester.

"Thence crosse part of Robert Wall's land to a small blacke oake marked with 5 knotches, standing att the King's Highway.

"WALTER MARTEN, JOHN KINGSMAN,
"JOHN MENDENHALL, WILLIAM CLOUD."
"RICHARD THATCHER,

At the court held on "3rd day, 2d week, 7th month, 1688, George Strode, Nathaniel Parker, John Palmer, John Hannum, Thomas Moore, John Sanger, Robert Pyle, Petitioned against ye Road lately laid out through the town of Concord. Ordered that ye Grand Inquest doe Inspect ye Road, and make report to ye next Court under ye hands of noe less than twelve."

All these petitioners owned land on the present Concord road, south of the present Concord Station, on the Baltimore Central road. The jury, however, confirmed that highway, but the road leading from Concord to Birmingham at Dilworthtown appears not to have been immediately opened, but remained until May 21, 1707, when, after twenty years, the route as laid out by the jury in 1687 was finally accepted.

The losses sustained by the residents of Concord, occasioned by the pillaging of the British army in 1777, was severe, and the extent of the damages inflicted in that township will never be ascertained. The greater part of the inhabitants were Friends, whose religious principles precluded them from demanding pay for articles destroyed in war. Under the act providing for a registration of claims for damages on account of the British spoliations, the following demands were filed:

	£	s.	d.
From Alexander Vincent, Sept. 13	90	17	6
" William Hannum	329	10	0
" James Hatton	6	0	0
" Amos Mendenhall	10	0	0
" Alexander Lockhart	183	0	0
" Thomas McCall	3	7	0
" Samuel Mendenhall	4	0	0
" Same person, Concord	61	14	0
" James Taylor (by Knyphausen's party)	34	10	0
" William Pierce, September	75	15	0
" William McCoy, Sept. 13	16	0	0
" Patrick Gamble, " 15	146	15	0
	961	5	6

Isaac Arment, who died in Concord, Nov. 23, 1848, aged ninety years, could recall the fact that he was living at Chad's Ford on the day the battle of Brandywine was fought, and from the heights on the east side of the creek, which afforded a commanding view of the scene, he witnessed the engagement, of which, as years rolled by, he delighted to relate to those who would listen to his recollection of those stirring days.

Schools.—The first reference in anywise in Concord township to the subject of education occurs in the will of Ralph Pyle, dated Jan. 1, 1739. The clause is as follows:

"*Item*, I give twenty pounds the Interest thereof to the use hereafter mentioned viz: to support the Schooling of a poor mans child who shall then reside either in Concord or in the Township of Birmingham in the County of Chester, So if the Parents of the said child shall be Established Church of England, to be paid by my Heir and him and his Heirs successively and shall have the liberty to put such child out to school and shall change the child once in three years, if any arrears by book for the children."

This bequest was subsequently made a charge on land in Birmingham by William Pyle, of that township, the son of Ralph, who in his devise of a plantation to his son, John, charged the estate with the payment of bequests contained in Ralph Pyle's will. Nothing has come to our knowledge respecting this schooling of a poor man's child other than stated.

The first schools known to have been established in the township were conducted under the charge of the society of Friends. One such school is believed to have been located in Friends' meeting-house about 1779, and in 1793 a dwelling was built close by for the accommodation of the teacher. In 1827 a school-house had been erected, a two-storied building, and, it is alleged by County Superintendent Baker, in his report for 1877, was partially graded. In the following year the division in the society of Friends occurred, and from that date the Orthodox and Hicksite branches educated their children in separate schools. Under the act of 1804 school directors in Delaware County had been elected prior to the law of 1834. On March 18, 1825, Concord elected trustees of schools for three years. Ralph C. Marsh, William Mendenhall, and James M. Willcox were returned to court as elected. At that time school was held at Mattson's, and preparations were made to accept other houses in the township. In 1834, when the school law was passed, the court appointed James M. Willcox and W. H. Palmer to act as inspectors of schools until directors had been elected. On Nov. 4, 1834, a county convention was held at the court-house at Chester, to which delegates, chosen by the several townships, were requested to be present. Concord neglected or refused to elect delegates, and the township was not represented at the meeting. The opposition there was so general that it was not until the act of 1836 was passed that Concord accepted the provisions of the law. That is the received opinion, and yet, in 1835, $165.90 was received by the township as county and State appropriations.

The first board of directors elected under the act of 1836 consisted of William Mendenhall, James M. Willcox, Joseph Cloud, Joseph Palmer, Robert N. Palmer, and Reece Pyle, and on August 27th of that year the first meeting was held at the public-house of James Hannum. It was resolved that Neal Duffee should be employed as teacher for Lower School, No. 2 (Mattson's); Jesse Green, for Union School, No. 3 (near Elam); and Alexander McKeever, for the Upper School (Concord Hill), at twenty-five dollars per month of twenty-four days.

The following notice was soon after posted in the township:

"NOTICE.—At a meeting Concord, Sept. 2, 1836. To all concerned. The Directors of the district of Concord have resolved to open three schools in said District, viz.: At Millers or Lower School and Union School, near Newlins store and Upper School, Concord Hill, on second day the 12th inst. for the reception of all children over four years old for tuition and instruction.

"By order of the Board,

"REECE PYLE, *Secretary*."

On the 8th of October, 1836, Alexander McKeever was notified by the board that his pay would cease at the expiration of two months, but on the 13th of May, 1837, he was again chosen with Neal Duffee and Jesse Green to teach the schools. June 7, 1838, the directors employed Moses M. Lincoln teacher for school No. 1, Amos H. Wickersham No. 2, Jesse Green No. 3. Wickersham resigned January 14th, and Feb. 11, 1839, James G. Hannum was appointed in his place. The question of continuing the public schools in Concord seems to have been undecided as late as 1840 when in May of that year an election was held, and it was voted to continue them. In the year 1853 the school-houses in the township were known as follows: No. 1, Hatton's; No. 2, Mattson's; No. 3, Gamble's; and No. 4, Sharpless'.

The first school-house erected in the township, except that of the Friends at Concord Hill, was upon a lot of land which by deed dated Dec. 10, 1796, Levi Mattson gave in trust for that purpose. The people of that section, to the number of eighteen, appointed Moses Palmer, Stephen Hall, William Hannum, Nathaniel Walter, and Thomas Hatton, trustees to accept the real estate. It consisted of half an acre of land situated on the north side of the great road from Concord to Chester. A one-story stone school-house was erected by contribution from the neighbors upon this lot and used for school purposes. The building was under direction of trustees until the school law was accepted. The old contribution school passed to the control of the directors, and in the notice of Sept. 2, 1836, it is mentioned as Miller's or Lower school. John Larkin, Jr., of Chester, and Mrs. George Sharpless, of Springfield, were pupils here from 1812 to 1815; John McClugen was a teacher at that time. His Saturday night libations at the Cross-Keys Tavern often incapacitated him from appearing Monday morning in proper condition to teach. William Neal, Nicholas Newlin, and Thomas Haines were also teachers. In 1859, when the directors were about erecting a new house on this lot, the deed from Mattson could not be found, and much doubt was expressed as to the title, but subsequently the deed was procured and recorded. The title being perfected, the directors contracted with Robert Barleu to erect a stone school-house at a cost of nine hundred and forty-four dollars, which was completed Sept. 15, 1859. It has been used for school purposes. On the 13th December, 1826, Robert N. Gamble sold to Joseph Larkin, William McCall, and Samuel Hance (who were trustees of schools of the township in that year) a half-acre of land on the road leading from Naaman's Creek road to Concord road, in consideration of having a school-house erected thereon. A school-house was built and used under the charge of trustees until 1836, at which time it was placed in care of the directors of the public schools, when it was known as School No. 3. It was maintained by them until 1856, when a new house was erected at Johnson's Corners which is still in use. The Gamble lot was sold to William H. Slawter, and the sale confirmed by the court Feb. 27, 1860. The land is now owned by Mrs. Mary Collins, who resides there. The lot at Johnson's Corners was purchased by the directors from Thomas Harlan, July 28, 1856, for one hundred and ninety-eight dollars and twenty-five cents, and Emmor Taylor contracted for the erection of a frame school-house at a cost of nine hundred and sixty-three dollars, to be completed Nov. 15, 1856, when it took the place of Union School, No. 3, mentioned above.

On April 15, 1837, the directors appointed a committee to ascertain whether a suitable lot could be obtained for the erection of a public school-house. This action was rendered necessary by the refusal of Friends to allow the school-house at their meeting-house to be longer under the charge of the directors. No mention is made of a report of this committee, and on the 14th of May, 1838, the board of directors resolved to rent a house in the vicinity of Concord meeting-house for the purpose of a free school. James S. Peters and Samuel Trimble were appointed to rent and furnish a room. On May 24th, they reported that they had rented a house of Matthew Ash, in which school was opened and kept for a long time. The first agitation to build a school-house in Concordville was made in 1860, and April 26th, in that year, a meeting was called to consult on the subject. Nothing, however, was accomplished until 1873-74, when the present commodious two-story brick house was built, at a cost of four thousand dollars. It is located on the State road at the western end of the village.

On the 15th of June, 1847, the school directors purchased ninety-six square perches of land of Casper Sharpless. A stone school-house was erected, and school opened May 15, 1848, with Sarah C. Walton as the first teacher. This house was used till 1870, when the lot was exchanged with Fairman Rogers, and the present brick house, forty by forty feet, was erected. It is located in close proximity to Markham Station.

On May 3, 1851, the board of directors resolved to build a school-house to supply the place of No. 1, and on the 9th of September, 1852, purchased ninety-six perches of land of Hannah Hatton and Deborah Peters. A contract was made with Robert Barlow to erect the building for five hundred and fifteen dollars. This house was built, and was known as the Spring Valley House. It was used until 1874, when it was abandoned, and the district was absorbed in the present No. 1 District, at Concordville, and McCartney District, No. 5.

The McCartney school-house lot was purchased of Samuel Myers about 1878, and the present house erected. This is known as No. 5, and is situated in the south part of the township below Smith's Cross-road.

The following is a list of the school directors since 1840, as obtained from the election records of Media:

1840, Joseph Hannum, Robert Mendenhall; 1841, ——; 1842, John H. Marsh, Peter W. Mattson; 1843, Marshall Cloud, Moses D. Palmer; 1844, Samuel Hanes, William W. Palmer; 1845, John H. Marsh, Evan P. Hannum; 1846, Robert Gamble, Thomas Marshall; 1847, Samuel Hance, William W. Palmer; 1848, Thomas Marshall, Peter W. Mattson; 1849, Edward Green, Matthew Wood; 1850, Joel Swayne, Thomas P. Powell; 1851, Joseph Walter, Isaac Tussey; 1852, Nathaniel Pratt, Andrew Hudson; 1853, Davis Richard, Samuel Myers; 1854, Robert H. Palmer, John Sharpless; 1855, Andrew Pratt, David L. Manley; 1856, John Miller, Thomas Hinkson; 1857, Davis Richards, John Hill; 1858, William Gamble, R. H. Hannum, Joseph Johnston; 1859, David S. Manley, Job Hoopes; 1860, John Shaw, George Rush; 1861, George Drayton, Henry L. Paschall; 1862, John H. Newlin, Robert H. Hannum; 1863, Emmor S. Leedom, Thomas W. Johnson; 1864, Henry L. Paschall, Penrose Miller; 1865, R. H. Hannum, John H. Newlin; 1866, Samuel Bennington, T. W. Johnson; 1867, H. L. Paschall, Penrose Miller; 1868, R. H. Hannum, T. I. Peirce; 1869, Samuel Bennington, T. W. Johnson; 1870, Lewis Palmer, Peter Ingram; 1871, R. H. Hannum, Milon S. Heyburn; 1872, no report; 1873, Lewis Palmer, D. Darlington; 1874, Henry Bishop, George Rush; 1875, Samuel Bennington, Thomas W. Johnson; 1876, R. H. Hannum, William Gamble; 1877, Ralph M. Harvey, Harry Bishop; 1878, Thomas W. Johnson, Samuel Bennington; 1879, William Gamble, R. H. Hannum; 1880, Henry C. Bishop, Samuel N. Hill; 1881, Thomas W. Johnson, W. G. Powell; 1882, Isaiah H. Miller, R. Henry Hannum; 1883, John L. Tucker, Joseph Trimble; 1884, Elwood Hannum, Daniel Fields.

Maplewood Institute.—A large tract of land, near Friends' meeting-house, at Concordville, was purchased by Professor Joseph Shortledge, who erected thereon a building fifty by eighty feet, three stories in height, especially designed for a seminary of learning. In the fall of 1862 he established a school, which was conducted successfully, both sexes being admitted as pupils. The academy was well patronized, and soon won its way in public favor. On April 6, 1870, it was chartered by an Act of Assembly, as the "Maplewood Institute," with collegiate privileges. Shortly after this date the building was enlarged by the addition of a wing to the rear, forty by eighty feet, affording facilities which were much needed. The institute at the present time has accommodations for eighty pupils, a well-selected library, and is also well supplied with chemical and philosophical apparatus.

Ward Academy.—In 1882, Benjamin F. Leggett erected on the road from Concord Station to Concordville a commodious building for educational purposes, and therein established the Ward Academy. Although an institution of recent date, it has been well attended, and gives promise of extended usefulness. It has grown rapidly in public approval, and is firmly established.

Leedom's Mills.—At the court held Oct. 2, 1695, occurs the first mention of Concord Mills, now Leedom's. The grand jury, following the recommendation of a previous grand inquest "to lay an assessment" to pay the judges' fees, to meet the county expenses, and provide funds for the erection of the prison then building, assessed Concord Mills at ten pounds. According to Smith's map of early grants and patents, accepting the above date as the year of the erection of Concord Mills, in 1695, the company's enterprise was located on the west branch of Chester Creek, and on the tract of five hundred acres which was entered by William Hitchcock, Sept. 8, 9, 1681, secured to him Feb 18, 1682, and a patent was issued therefor June 27, 1684 This tract was a long and narrow strip, extending the entire width of the township, near its northern boundary On Feb 7, 1701, Hitchcock sold two hundred and fifty acres of this land on the west of Concord Street road, laid out in 1682, — the road has ceased to be, excepting the upper part known as Thornbury Street,—to Nicholas Pyle, and the same day the remaining two hundred acres east of the road was conveyed to Benjamin Mendenhall Concord Mills is on the extreme eastern and lower end of the Pyle tract, the race beginning a long distance above the mill, on the west branch of the creek The mill was built by a company of which William Brinton, the younger, of Birmingham, was one of the owners and the chief projector of the enterprise In those days the mill was of great importance to the neighborhood, for prior to its erection there was none within several miles, and hauling was difficult excepting in the winter, when sleds moved easily over the frozen snow The assessment in 1695, which gave the appraised value of this mill as ten pounds, clearly indicates that it was a frame structure, which subsequently, at a date not ascertained, gave place to a stone building In 1715, Nicholas Pyle had charge of the mill, for he appears on the assessment-roll for that year "for ye mill" When Concord meeting-house was burned, in 1788, the mill was used as a temporary place for Friends to gather until the present meeting-house was rebuilt At that time it was owned by Thomas Newlin, who had acquired title to the mill prior to 1780 From 1790 to 1810, John Newlin rented and operated it, and in 1817 he became the owner A short distance below this mill, in 1696, Nicholas Newlin built a saw-mill, which in 1790 was owned by Nathaniel Newlin, in 1802 by Thomas Newlin, and in 1817 by Benjamin Newlin The grist-mill, from 1810 to 1820, was rented and operated by Mendenhall and Pennell, and after the latter date by John Newlin He continued there many years The grist- and saw-mill subsequently became the property of Casper W Sharpless, and finally was owned by George Drayton The latter, in 1859, sold thirty-eight acres and the upper mill to Samuel Leedom, by whose son, Emmor S Leedom, both the saw- and grist-mill are now held as trust estate

Hill's Mill —On Sept 24, 1683, five hundred acres of land was surveyed to Nicholas Newlin, which, lying to the south of the Hitchcock tract, extended from the eastern township line westward to Concord Street road, which ran north and south, dividing the township in the centre Within this estate, which was patented to Newlin May 1, 1685, a part of the head-waters of the west branch of Chester Creek were embraced, and through the lower part of Newlin's land, running east and west, Providence and Concord road was laid out Aug 15, 1715 Twenty-two years prior to this highway being approved, Aug. 21, 1693, a road still in use, beginning east of the present school-house on that road, and running thence northward to the Thornbury line, was laid out by the grand jury On April 2, 1703, the tract was resurveyed to Nathaniel Newlin, the son of Nicholas, and was found to contain five hundred and fifty-two acres of land The following year (1704) Nathaniel Newlin built a stone grist-mill on the west branch of Chester Creek, now owned by Samuel Hill In the walls of this old mill is a date-stone marked "Nathan and Ann Newlin, 1704" This mill passed from Nathaniel or Nathan Newlin to his son Thomas, and in 1817 was sold to William Trimble as twenty seven acres, and the "Lower Mill" Thomas Newlin having for many years previous to that date been the owner of the "Upper Mill," or Society Mill, as it was known in early days, and now as Leedom's The terms Upper and Lower Mills being used to designate the one from the other, after they had both become the property of Newlin The Lower Mill later came into possession of Abraham Sharpless, who operated it several years, and after his death it was sold by Casper W Sharpless, executor of his father, Abraham Sharpless, in April, 1861, to John Hill & Son The junior member of the firm, Samuel, operated it until the death of his father, John Hill, when the latter's interest was acquired by his son, Samuel Hill, who is the present owner of the mill

Trimble, or Felton Mills —In 1734, William Trimble appeared at Friends' Meeting at Concord with Ann Palmers, and there they declared their intention of marriage Soon after their marriage, William Trimble bought one hundred acres of land, the half of the two hundred acres patented to Thomas King, July 22, 1684 The part purchased adjoined the Nicholas Newlin Mill land, to the south of the latter In 1742, William and Ann Trimble built a stone house, which is still standing, and now owned by Dr Joseph Trimble William Trimble, the younger, had on this estate a saw-mill in 1782, and prior to 1799 had erected a paper-mill, which was operated as such by him until 1813, when it was changed to a cotton-factory at the instance of John D Carter, an Englishman, who had just previous to that time immigrated to Pennsylvania This factory was four stories in height, sixty by thirty-four feet, and was conducted by Carter until 1826, when he purchased the Knowlton Mills and removed there The Trimble cotton-factory at that time contained four carding-engines, ten hundred and sixty-eight spindles, and spun seven hundred and fifty pounds of cotton yarn weekly The mills, after Carter's removal, were leased by Jacob Taylor, and later by Joseph Trimble, Charles Cheelham, Callaghan Brothers, and others In March, 1873, the mills were destroyed by fire, and the property was sold to Gen Robert Patterson The executors of the Patterson estate, on July 1, 1884, sold the site of these mills to George Rush, Jr , who is rebuilding the burned mills, wherein he proposes to manufacture the Rush roller skates, of which article he is the patentee Early in this century, Samuel Trimble conducted the saw-mill in the immediate neighborhood of the Trimble paper-mill, and continued there many years

Marshall's Tannery—In the year 1785, Thomas Marshall had a tannery and stone bark-mill on the west bank of Chester Creek, below the present Marshall Mill It was still owned and operated by him in 1826, and later fell into disuse The property is now owned by Ellis P Marshall

In 1770, Robert Mendenhall was operating a saw-mill on the Mendenhall tract, which he conducted till 1788, when it was in charge of Stephen Mendenhall, and later went out of use In 1788, Thomas Hatton owned and operated a saw mill until 1799, when John Hatton succeeded him in the business, and also conducted a currying-shop and tan-yard In 1802, Joseph Hatton appears to have control of the business, and he conducted it subsequent to 1830 In 1770, John Newlin was operating a grist-mill, and in 1774, Cyrus Newlin and Daniel Trimble were also engaged in that occupation In 1782, Abraham Sharpless and Hugh Judge were each running a grist-mill About 1800, William Walter built a grist-mill, which was operated by him many years A grist- and saw-mill is now on the site of the mill, which is owned by his descendants In 1788, William Hannum was operating a saw-mill on Green Creek, where in 1811 the business was conducted by William Hannum, Jr., who in the same year had a tan-yard connected with the mill In 1818, Aaron Hannum built a grist-mill, which, prior to 1826, had been changed by John Hannum to a fulling-mill and woolen-factory, which was operated by John Jones At that date the machinery consisted of two carding-engines, one belly of thirty-six spindles, one jenny of fifty spindles Subsequent to 1848 the business was abandoned and the building no longer used as a factory

In 1811, Matthias Corliss had a carding- and spinning-machine in Concord, which he operated for a short time In 1779, Henry Myers owned a saw-mill on Concord Creek, which, in 1811, was owned and operated by John Myers, and in 1848 by Jesse Myers It is not in use at the present time Prior to the last century William Vernon had a saw-mill on Green Creek, near the Bethel line, which was discontinued many years ago

Johnson's Corners—The locality known by the above name was the site of the old Three Tun Tavern, established by Nathaniel Newlin in 1748, which was kept as a public-house until 1814 The property in 1848 was owned by John H Newlin and William Johnson A school-house was erected there in 1856, which is still used A store was at the Corners in 1875, but is discontinued The land on the west side of the road is now owned by Thomas Johnson The grounds of the Brandywine Summit Camp-Meeting Association are located on the farm of Thomas Johnson Camp-meetings have been held at the place for twelve or fifteen years, but without organization In the summer of 1884 an association was formed, and a charter was granted by the court of Delaware County The association obtained a lease of twenty acres of land, and meetings are held there in the month of July or August The Brandywine Summit Camp-Meeting is under the charge of the Wilmington Conference

Elam.—The tract of land on which the hamlet is situated was first granted to Francis Chads, and contained one hundred and thirty and a half acres of land It was resurveyed April 9, 1702 and April 19, 1708, it was sold to John Willis The road that runs northerly through it was laid out in February, 1705 At the place now called Elam, formerly known as Pleasant Hill, James Smith lived, and in 1819 he petitioned court for a license, which was not granted him till 1823 A full account of his troubles will be found in the account of the licensed houses Subsequent to 1832, the property was sold as the estate of James Smith to Edward Hoskins It passed from Hoskins to Joseph Cheyney, and later to William May, whose heirs are now in possession of the land In 1848 there was at the place a store, post-office, and tavern The store was built by Marshall P Wilkinson, and later was sold to Miller & Yarnall Mrs Mary A Yarnall now conducts the store and post-office, having been postmistress since 1865

The Elam Methodist Episcopal Church, situated a short distance from Elam, was established as a branch of the Siloam Methodist Episcopal Church, of Bethel, in 1882 A lot was purchased of Daniel Husband and Jehu Tolley, and a neat stone chapel, thirty by forty-five feet, was erected The pastors of Siloam Church, Bethel, have this in charge

Concordville—Except the few dwellings clustered about the Friends' meeting-house at this point there was no conspicuous settlement until 1831, when John Way was licensed to keep a public-house there, and in the next year a mail station was established, and known as the Concordville Post-office A line of stages from this time ran through the village on the New London, Philadelphia and Brandywine Turnpike John Way acted as postmaster until 1844, when he was succeeded by George Rush, who in June, 1869, was followed by Mrs Sheoff The latter held the office for only a short time, and was succeeded by George Rush, the present incumbent, who established a store at Concordville in 1844

Ivy Mills and the Willcox Family—For many reasons a historical sketch of the Willcox family is interesting, identified as it has been with Delaware County since an early period Their business, established in this county as far back as 1729, has continued in the family for more than a hundred and fifty years, descending from father to son through five successive generations This is the oldest business house now standing in the United States It has had intimate relations not only with Franklin, Carey, and all the principal printing-houses of the last century, but also with the authorities of all of the old Colonies that issued paper money in the colonial days for forty years preceding the Revolution, with the Continental authorities of the Revolutionary period, and with the United States authorities ever since that period, all in the line of its regular business as manufacturers of printing, currency, and security papers. On three different occasions, far apart, the services it was able to render the government, in times of war and discredit, were so important that it may be said they were services of necessity. After more than a century and a half of continuous business the principal place of manufacturing is still within two miles of the original location, and the mercantile house still remains in Minor Street, Philadelphia, where it has always been.

The Willcox family in Pennsylvania dates back to 1718, in which year Thomas Willcox and his wife Elizabeth (*née* Cole), settled in Delaware County, selecting their future home on the west branch of Chester Creek, in Concord township. Their property has passed by inheritance four times from father to son, and is now owned by their direct descendant of the fifth generation of the same name as the founder, Thomas Willcox.

The name Willcox (Wild Chough) is undoubtedly of Saxon times and origin, as the family crest (a Cornish chough upon a pile of rocks) indicates. The chough is a red-legged raven of the southwest of England, and the first Willcox was so called, doubtlessly, because he bore a wild chough (pronounced gutturally) upon a shield or pole in the many battles fought in those rude days.

Thomas Willcox, originally from Devonshire, England, came over young, as he and his wife lived together in Concord from 1718 until his death, in 1779, his wife dying in the following year. They were of the Roman Catholic faith, as are all their descendants of the name in Pennsylvania to-day, and the family is believed to be the oldest Catholic family in the State. At their house was established one of the earliest missions in Pennsylvania, but at what precise date cannot now be determined, as the early records of some of the Jesuit missions (of which this was one) were destroyed by a fire at St. Thomas, Md., where they were kept, but it is supposed to be about 1732. A room devoted to chapel purposes has always been reserved in the mansion-house of all the successive proprietors up to this time, and the Catholics of the neighborhood have ever been invited and accustomed to attend the religious services conducted there. Many articles of the old chapel furniture, such as chalice, missal, vestments, etc., that have been in use there from the beginning, are still preserved and prized by the family. In 1852, chiefly at the cost of James M. Willcox, the then proprietor of Ivy Mills, the church of St. Thomas was built near Ivy Mills, since which time the private chapel has been maintained for occasional services and private devotion.

Thomas and Elizabeth Willcox had nine children, —John, Anne, James, Elizabeth, Mary, Deborah, Thomas, Mark, and Margaret. The eldest son, John, and Mary (married to John Montgomery) removed to North Carolina in early life, settling near Fayetteville, and their descendants of several generations are numerously scattered throughout the Southern States. The counties of Willcox in Georgia and Alabama, respectively, have taken name from some of these, and the old family Christian names of Thomas and Mark are carefully handed down among the Southern branches of the family. The eldest daughter, Anne, married James White, and a distinguished Governor of Louisiana of that name was her grandson. Her grave and tombstone are in old St. Mary's churchyard on Fourth Street, in Philadelphia, the lettering nearly obliterated by time. John's and Mary's descendants embrace many of the best-known names in nearly all the cotton States, and are particularly numerous along the Ocmulgee River in Georgia, and in the Carolinas. The original home in Concord, including the large farm and Ivy Mill, descended to the youngest son, Mark, born in Concord in 1743.

Mark Willcox, better known in the community as Judge Willcox for the last thirty years of his life, after an early study of law entered into business with his father for a time, and then removed to Philadelphia, where he became a prominent merchant of that city. The firm (Flahavan & Willcox) consisted of his brother-in-law Thomas Flahavan and himself, and their books, some of which are still preserved, show that they owned several vessels, and traded principally with Wilmington and Newberne, N. C., and with London, Dublin, Rotterdam, and Amsterdam. Some of the letters of their letter-book, covering the period of 1783 to 1787, are interesting, and contain valuable materials connected with the history of the time, regarding not only Philadelphia and vicinity but a number of other places. In one, for instance, of date Philadelphia, March 20, 1786 (per ship "Adolph," Capt. Clarkson, *via* Amsterdam), they write to their correspondents Messrs. Roquett F. A. Elsires and Brothers Roquett, of Rotterdam, requesting the latter to sell in Europe all or part of six thousand acres of land belonging to the firm, lying above Mount Vernon on the Potomac, and, subsequently, in letter of date April 21, 1786, they thus enter into a fuller explanation of the location and value of the lands.

"Should you not be able to sell, you'll keep the Papers in your hands belonging to us until you hear from us. We have the pleasing news from a Gentleman who has Lands in the same Neighborhood, & has moved lately 28 Families on them, that the County is settling faster than any other in the States, & he says he makes little doubt of those Lands being soon settled as thick as within 20 Miles of Philadelphia. There is another advantage which they have, that we neglected to mention to you in our former Letters, that is, that General Washington's Lands are in the vicinity of our's, that Virginia has undertaken to clear the Potowmack River, and that the General has the Direction of it, & no doubt as well for his Country's Interest as his own, will forward the

"Upper Glen Mills," erected 1836. "Ivy Mills," erected 1729. "Lower Glen Mills," erected 1845.

WILLCOX'S PAPER MILLS.

work as fast as possible. Also that a Town is to be built within 5 Miles of the Lands by Order and Permission of Government. You may therefore Insure them as prime Lands and of the First Quality. There is very little doubt but in a little time this will be the first Country in the World. There may be some Objections Respecting the Savages, but this you may clear up by informing to a Certainty that there are no Savages within a hundred Miles of them, &c., &c.

"With great esteem,

"FLAHAVAN & WILLCOX."

The future "town to be built by order of Government" is the present city of Washington, rapidly becoming one of the most beautiful capitals of the world. The "savages" are now far enough away.

They were very extensive owners of land, as will appear from the following extract of a letter to the same correspondents, in Rotterdam, dated June 4, 1787:

"Since then we have Accts. from France to Gentlemen here, who had letters from their Correspondents in Europe, of their contracting with the Farmer General for 200,000 acres in the neighbourhood of our Lands, for 200,000 French Crowns, & that the Government was sending out Settlers. If so no doubt it will add to the value of our Lands. If you could not sell on advantageous terms you had better find out the Gentleman that sold those Lands and send him the papers. Perhaps he may have it in his power to sell ours along with his Own. Or, if you could sell a larger tract, say twenty thousand acres more, that is, if Speculators in Land would rather have a larger Tract, we would have you engage 20 or 30 Thousand Acres more, and shall send you out all the papers, or deliver them to your Order. We have also Accts. from England of Mr. Vancouver's selling 100 Thousand Acres to English settlers who are coming out next Spring, so that that Place will be as thick as any Place in the States. If these Schemes should fail send back the papers as Quick as Possible. You will soon hear if this news of sale to Farmer General is true and you will be able to judge whether a tryal in France will answer." It is also well known that Mark Willcox, following the example of many prominent men of means in Philadelphia at that time and long after, committed the mistake of investing in lands in many of the interior counties of Pennsylvania, instead of at their very doors. The rapid growth of the city was not foreseen, nor the overleaping by emigration of the mountainous districts of Pennsylvania, where they purchased, for the rich and vast valley of the Ohio and Mississippi. The whole tenor of this venerable letter-book shows plainly the great and lasting depression in all business that followed the Revolution. Its foreign correspondence contains many references to public matters transpiring at the time, one of which to the great Convention of '87 shows the feeling of the intelligent portion of the community in regard to it. This letter is of date July 18, 1787: "We have nothing new to Relate you except that Our Grand Convention, being deputed from the different States, is now sitting here. They have sett for upwards of six Weeks, and are as Respectable a Body as one ever had to meet on Public Business, as well for their Understanding & Fortunes as for the unbounded Confidence being placed in them by their Constituents. The purport of this Meeting is to see into the Situation of the Foederal Union, mend Defects, and Strengthen it upon such solid Basis as will give power to Congress as well as many Resources, so that they'll be reputable abroad as well as at Home. In the mean time to guard against the Infringing upon the Liberty of the Subject. This, no doubt, they will be able to Accomplish, as the People are Tired of the Loose Manner in which they have been Governed for Some time."

The last reference to the convention appears in a letter dated Sept. 25, 1787, as follows: "The Convention has broken up, & has recommended us a Code of laws which, if adopted, will make us Happy at Home and Respected abroad, and we have little doubt of their being adopted, as the People are Generally for it. Nor is there any doubt of General Washington being Universally appointed President General, &c."

There are many precious bits of history and historical reference in this old book which should not be lost, and which will become more valuable as time passes and the still fresh tints of recent history fade away.

Mark Willcox's first wife was his partner's sister, Ellen Flahavan; another sister became the wife of Mathew Carey and the mother of the late Henry C. Carey, of Philadelphia, whose writings on social science and political economy have given him a world-wide reputation. Among the brothers-in-law an intimate friendship always existed, ending only at the death of Mark Willcox, in 1827. The only child of this first marriage, Ellen Willcox, was educated at the only boarding-school in Pennsylvania at that time, the Moravian School at Bethlehem. She married William Jenkins, of Baltimore, Md., and their descendants, quite numerous, are among the best-known and most-esteemed citizens of that city. His second wife was Mary Kauffman, daughter of Dr. Theophilus Kauffman, of Strasburg, Germany, who came to Philadelphia long before the Revolution, and who died some years afterwards in Montgomery County, whither he removed away from the "rebels," who had captured the city, and with whose Revolutionary ideas he had no sympathy.

When his father died, in 1779, Mark Willcox continued to live in Philadelphia, and carried on the manufacturing of paper at the Ivy Mill. At what date he removed from the city is not precisely known, but one of the letters in the letter-book spoken of mentions the fact of his living in the country in 1789. The old Ivy Mill had then been running sixty years, and was the second paper-mill built on the American continent, the Rittenhouse mill, on the Wissahickon, being the only one before it. Following its lead, a number of paper-mills were built in Delaware County, commencing on Chester Creek, and as late as the beginning of the nineteenth century more paper was made in Delaware County, Pa (then shorn to its present dimensions), than in all the rest of the whole United States This was the pioneer county in that particular industry, and long it held its pre eminence The old Ivy Mill, after standing over a hundred years, was torn down fifty-four years ago, or rather the greater part of it, and rebuilt by James M Willcox Two men of two generations, father and son, had conducted it ninety-eight years The ponderous machinery, however, of modern mills silenced it long ago, but it still stands, a silent relic of its early time Its wheel has long since decayed, its stone gable is thickly covered with the venerable ivy-vine whose root came over the ocean (in 1718) from near the old Ivy Bridge, in Devonshire, and the day is drawing near when it will begin its last change into a picturesque ruin as ancient as we have them in this New World The old mill has a history deeply interesting from its connection with the printing-presses of historic men, and perhaps more so from its relations to the old colonial governments that preceded the formation of the United States, and the general government subsequently The Colonies were wont to issue each its own particular currency, and up to the time of the Revolution the paper for all the money of all the Colonies, from Massachusetts to the Carolinas, was manufactured by Thomas Willcox at his Ivy Mill, after which followed, out of the same mill, the paper for the Continental currency, and after that the paper for the government issues made necessary by the war of 1812

After Mark Willcox removed to the country (about 1789) he never afterwards returned to the city to live He was a man of erudition, and a genial but dignified gentleman, and up to the time of his death (in 1827) it was his habit and pleasure to receive frequent visits from his many friends in town, who would drive their twenty miles to pass some days, in the old-fashioned way, at his pleasant country home

Many years before his death Judge Willcox had associated his sons, John and Joseph, in business with him, but retired early, as the books show that in 1811 the firm consisted of John and Joseph Willcox Joseph died young and unmarried, and John again united with his father, the product of the mill being always principally bank-note, bond, and similar papers John died in 1826, leaving two daughters, and his widow married, some years afterwards, Lieut John Marston, Jr, U S N, who has survived her He now (1884), as Rear-Admiral Marston, resides in Philadelphia, enjoying good health at eighty-nine years of age

On the death of John Willcox his youngest brother, James M, assumed charge of the hereditary mill, and threw more vigor and activity into the business than it had ever known His father dying the following year, James became the sole proprietor Three years afterwards he tore down the mill that had run for a century, and built upon the site a new one of double capacity, with improved machinery Bank-note paper still continued to be the specialty For a long period not only were the banks of the United States supplied with their paper from the Ivy Mill, but its lofts were at times piled with peculiar-looking papers of various tints, bearing the ingrained water marks of most of the governments and banks of South America Nearly the whole Western Continent drew its supplies from there, such was the reputation of the establishment, and Eastward its paper went as far as Italy and Greece But an end had to come to this The sagacity of James M Willcox foresaw the impending changes that were to revolutionize the paper manufacture, and he began early to prepare for them, at first by improving and enlarging facilities, and then by adopting at once the revolutionary processes according to their best features, for which he had not long to wait He was very early to appreciate the full merits of the Fourdrinier machine, and one of the first enterprising enough to adopt it In 1835 he purchased from the heirs of Abraham Sharples the elder, on the main branch of Chester Creek, and about two and a half miles from Ivy Mills, an extensive water-power, and the property on which the Sharples iron-works, consisting of rolling- and slitting mills, had been situated Here he built the first of the mills known as the Glen Mills, in which was placed one of the new Fourdrinier paper-machines of the largest class then known He took his sons, Mark and William, into partnership, and for many years conducted a large and successful business, dividing his attention among his various interests,—his farm, the Ivy Mill, the Glen Mill, and his mercantile house in the city In 1846 he built the second of the Glen Mills Soon after his health became precarious, and, although he suffered much, he remained actively engaged in the details of all his many engagements as long as he lived On March 3, 1852, he completed his long-contemplated arrangements and retired from business, leaving it to his three sons, Mark, James, and Joseph, and died unexpectedly before the following morning He was a man of unusual intelligence, strength and earnestness of character, and fervent religious convictions that governed all his intercourse with other men No man was better known or more respected in the entire community His charities accorded with his means His influence was great, and always for good, and his death was a public loss Born in 1791, and dying in 1852, he was not sixty-two years of age His remains repose in the old family burying-ground upon the Ivy Mills property, where those of his father and grandfather were laid before him, and in the same ground lie the remains of many colored people, formerly slaves of his ancestors when slavery existed in Pennsylvania, and a number of their descendants for several generations

Without change of title, Mark, James M, and

manufacturing on Chester Creek, and as late as the beginning of the nineteenth century more paper was made in Delaware County, Pa. (then known by its present designation), than in all the rest of the whole United States. This was the pioneer county in that important industry, and long it held its pre-eminence. The old Ivy Mill, after standing over a hundred years, was torn down fifty-four years ago, or rather the greater part of it, and rebuilt by James M. Willcox. The lives of two generations, father and son, had extended to ninety-eight years. The ponderous machinery, however, of modern mills silenced it long ago, but it still stands, a silent relic of its early times. Its wheel has long since decayed; its stone gable is thickly covered with the venerable ivy whose root came over the ocean (in 1718) from near the old Ivy Bridge, in Devonshire; and the day is drawing near when it will begin its last change into a picturesque ruin as ancient as we have them in this New World. The old mill has a history deeply interesting from its connection with the printing-presses of historic men, and perhaps more so from its relations to the old colonial governments that preceded the formation of the United States and the general government subsequently. The Colonies were wont to issue each its own particular currency, and up to the time of the Revolution the paper for all the money of all the Colonies, from Massachusetts to the Carolinas, was manufactured by Thomas Willcox at the Ivy Mills; after which followed, out of the same mill, the paper for the Continental currency, and after that the paper for the government issue made necessary by the war of 1812.

After Mark Willcox [illegible] (1793) he [illegible] afterwards [illegible] to the city, to live. He was a man of erudition, and a genial and [illegible] gentleman, and up to the time of his death (in 1827) it was his habit and pleasure to receive frequent visits from his many friends in town, who would drive their twenty miles to pass some days, in the old-fashioned way, at his pleasant country home.

Many years before his death Judge Willcox had [illegible] in business with him [illegible] books show that in 1811 the firm consisted of John and Joseph Willcox. [illegible] and John again [illegible] with his father, the product of the mill being [illegible] principally bank-note and [illegible] papers. John died in 1836, leaving two daughters and his widow [illegible] some years afterwards, [illegible] John [illegible], Jr., [illegible] (1868), [illegible] Philadelphia, [illegible] eighty-four years of age.

[illegible] John Willcox his younger brother, James M. [illegible] the business [illegible] the sole proprietor. Three years afterwards he tore down the mill that had run for a century, and built upon the site a new one of double capacity, with improved machinery. Bank-note paper still continued to be the specialty. For a long period not only were the banks of the United States supplied with their paper from the Ivy Mill, but its lofts were at times piled with peculiar-looking papers of various tints, bearing the ingrained water-marks of most of the governments and banks of South America. Nearly the whole Western Continent drew its supplies from there, such was the reputation of the establishment; and Eastward its paper went as far as Italy and Greece. But an end had to come to this. The sagacity of James M. Willcox foresaw the impending changes that were to revolutionize the paper manufacture, and he began early to prepare for them; at first by improving and enlarging facilities, and then by adopting at once the revolutionary processes according to their best features, for which he had not long to wait. He was very early to appreciate the full merits of the Fourdrinier machine, and one of the first enterprising enough to adopt it. In 1835 he purchased from the heirs of Abraham Sharpless the elder, on the main branch of Chester Creek, and about two and a half miles from Ivy Mills, an extensive water-power and the property on which the Sharpless iron-works, consisting of rolling- and slitting-mills, had been situated. Here he built the first of the mills known as the Glen Mills, in which was placed one of the new Fourdrinier paper-machines of the largest size then known. He took his sons, Mark and William, into partnership, and for many years conducted a large and successful business, dividing his attention among his various interests,—his farm, the Ivy Mills, the Glen Mill, and his mercantile house in the city. In 1846 he built the second of the Glen Mills. Soon after his health became precarious, and, [illegible] he suffered much, he remained actively engaged in the details of all his many engagements as long as he lived. On March 8, 1852, he completed his long-contemplated arrangements and retired from business, leaving it to his three sons, Mark, James, and Joseph, and died unexpectedly before the following morning. He was a man of unusual intelligence, strength and earnestness of character, and fervent religious convictions that governed all his intercourse with other men. No man was better known or more respected in the entire community. His charities [illegible] with his means. His influence was great, and always for good, and his death was a public loss. Born in 1791, and dying in 1852, he was not sixty-two years of age. His remains repose in the old family burying-ground upon the Ivy Mills property, where those of his father and grandfather were laid before him; and in the same ground lie the remains of many colored people, formerly slaves of his ancestors when slavery existed in Pennsylvania, and a number of their descendants for several generations.

Without change of title, Mark, James M., and

James M Millroy

Joseph, the three oldest sons of James M Willcox, succeeded to the Ivy Mills and Glen Mills business in 1852 In 1866, Joseph retired from business, after disposing of his interests to his elder brothers, since when he has devoted his time to scientific pursuits, chiefly in the departments of geology and mineralogy In the mean time the civil war had broken out, and the government was again forced to the issue of paper money, this time on a scale unprecedented in the history of the world For the third time, under the pressing necessities of war and broken credit, it had recourse to the Willcox House to supply its needs Fortunately this had kept in advance of the times, and the brothers had, but a few years before, succeeded in changing the manufacture of bank-note paper by bringing it also upon the Fourdrinier machine, thus enabling themselves to produce more in a day than the old practice, by hand process, could produce in a month When, therefore, the emergency came they were able to meet it, first with one large mill, and soon after with a second The supply was maintained, and always up to the requirements of the government All the bank-note paper-mills of Europe, save one, are still hand-mills, and it is not too much to say that, at that time, all of them united could not have supplied the paper needed for our government's issues of paper money

In 1864 the United States Treasury Department, prompted by the desire to prevent the counterfeiting of its issues, undertook the task of manufacturing a currency paper for its own use, and imparting to it some peculiarity of character by which counterfeiting could be detected A costly mill with Fourdrinier machine was built on the lower floor of the Department building, and experiments at great cost were conducted there for four years There was no outcome of any value, the attempts were all failures, and the Treasury mill ended where it had begun, with an inferior quality of simple white paper It was then torn out, and the Willcox Brothers were invited to undertake a task that the Department, with all the scientific aid it could command, had failed in, and that had never yet been successfully performed anywhere This they were prepared to do by means of a peculiar paper invented by them, and patented three years before The "localized-fibre" paper, manufactured for many years after this at the Glen Mills for the notes and bonds of the government, attained not merely a national, but a world-wide, reputation, for it accomplished the object desired So jealously was it guarded by the government that for ten years the mills and premises were occupied by a government officer with a numerous police and detective force, and some forty employés of the Treasury Department, to insure that no sheet or bit of paper should be abstracted for unlawful purpose, and that every sheet should be counted and registered as made, and tracked through the various stages towards completion, until it should be delivered over to the express company to be taken away for use During that period not a sheet, out of hundreds of millions made, was lost or missed, not a counterfeit seen on any treasury note or bond of the issue or series that began with that paper, and at the end, when Secretary John Sherman, in 1878, removed the manufacture of government paper from Pennsylvania, the paper account at Glen Mills balanced, a clear quittance was given, and the Treasury issue of paper money with which he began his administration was free from counterfeits

In 1880, Mark Willcox purchased his brother James' interest in the Glen Mills property, the Philadelphia business, and the Sarum farm adjoining Glen Mills, of which they had been joint owners Some years before he had purchased from his younger brothers, Edward and Henry, the old Ivy Mills estate, so that at his death, in April, 1883, he had acquired possession of nearly all the properties of the family in Delaware County that had historical interest His two sons, James Mark and William, the present owners of the Glen Mills property, have recently enlarged the principal mill and are actively engaged in the old business, the mercantile department of which is still conducted by them at No 509 Minor Street, Philadelphia These two young men constitute the oldest business house of any description in the United States, one that has continued from father to son, in one locality, a hundred and fifty-five years The Ivy Mills property, the original home, now belongs to the youngest brother, Thomas, of the same name as the founder of the family in America

James M Willcox the younger, whose portrait is herein presented, was born at Ivy Mills, in the same house in which his father and grandfather were born, Nov 20, 1821 He is the fourth son of James M Willcox, and the second son of a second marriage contracted in 1819 His mother was Mary eldest daughter of Capt James Brackett, of Quincy, Mass, in which State the Bracketts have resided for ten generations The first of them, also Capt James Brackett, was born in Scotland, in 1611, and came over with the early Puritans This ancestor figures in Hawthorne's "Scarlet Letter," as captain of the soldiery and custodian of the jail in which Hester Prynne was confined Her mother, Elizabeth Odiorne, descended from the ancestor of that name who came over with the Church of England colony that founded Portsmouth, N H The old Odiorne mansion is still standing, and is one of the most interesting antiquities of that place James M Willcox's early school years were passed at Anthony Bolmar's boarding-school, at West Chester, Pa, and thence he passed to Georgetown College, D C, whose reputation for superior classical and literary training has always been recognized After leaving college he commenced the study of medicine, but before completing the course changed his intentions and went to Italy, where he spent three years, mostly in Rome and its vicinity, in the study of ancient and modern languages, the higher mathematics, and philosophy There existed nowhere better or higher schools of languages and philosophy than the Roman Propaganda and Sapienza In them the Latin, instead of being an object of study, was the text of the class-books, the medium of communication, the spoken and written language of the schools In it Greek, Hebrew, the sciences, and philosophy were learned and expounded by the professors The rare advantages within his grasp the young American student employed to the best advantage, and brought home a full share of the honors competed for, becoming an accomplished linguist, speaking several languages, and attaining in the end to the Doctorship in Philosophy This degree is lightly given in the United States, frequently without any course of philosophy at all, but in the universities of Continental Europe it is conferred on but few, on account of the very severe course and examination required in logic, metaphysics, and ethics, as well as in physics and mathematics At this time Mr Willcox enjoyed the privilege of the acquaintance and conversation of men whose names are now historical in the literary world, the recollection of which he now cherishes as among the most pleasant of his life Not the least among these friends was the greatest of all linguists, ancient or modern, Cardinal Mezzofanti, who was master of forty languages, and with whom he made a study of ancient Anglo-Saxon In 1847 he received from Pope Pius IX his degree in philosophy, the diploma issuing, not from the faculty, but, as a special favor, directly from the Pontiff, as thus set forth in its text "Pius Papa Nonus, volens eum speciali gratia cumulare, eum Doctorem in Philosophia creavit, cum omnibus honoribus et oneribus quæ Philosophiæ Doctoribus propria sunt" This diploma, it is unnecessary to say, is much valued and preserved with great care After spending some months in visiting many parts of Europe Mr Willcox returned home in the fall of 1847, with health somewhat impaired, and some years afterwards entered into business with his father and brother at Glen Mills Transferring the same industry and ambition into practical business that he had carried into his scholastic career, he gradually introduced features into it so radical as to entirely change its character

The advantages of superior education are not lost in any career in life, for the discipline and enlargement of the mind attained can be advantageously applied almost anywhere One of Mr Willcox's first aims was to raise the paper manufacture to a higher level, out of the routine into which it seemed to have settled, and to this end he conducted a series of experimental researches, producing, in the course of a few years, as he relates, a greater variety of papers than had ever before been made by any one person Taking as his department of the business the practical manufacture, he turned special attention towards the plan of making bank-note paper by machinery, and with complete success Then, impressed with the importance of checking, and perhaps preventing, the counterfeiting of money, so commonly and easily done at that time, he conceived the task of accomplishing with paper what the bank-note companies, with their arts of fine and geometrical engraving, could not accomplish, the result being the invention of the "localized-fibre" paper, so long and so efficiently used by the United States government for its notes and bonds For many years, as was said before, this distinctive paper was manufactured at Glen Mills, under the government's supervision and protection Its success at home brought it to the favorable consideration of the governments of Europe, and in 1878, under agreement with the Imperial Government of Germany, Mr Willcox sent out an agent to Berlin, near which city was put in successful operation a bank-note paper-mill with the special machinery required, as at Glen Mills, for the manufacture of the German currency paper So pleased were the authorities with the product of the new mill that he received from them a testimonial stating that the contract had been more than carried out, to their great satisfaction, and the localized-fibre paper became the currency paper of the Empire An exhibit of this protective paper was subsequently made at the great Paris Exhibition, and there received the highest possible award of "Diplôme d'Honneur"

The chemical paper long used by the United States Treasury Department for the stamps and checks of the department, and called "Chameleon" paper on account of its sensitive changes when tampered with, was also Mr Willcox's invention, and put an end to the counterfeiting and re-using of Internal Revenue stamps, by which the government had long been extensively robbed of its revenue Thus in many parts of his business he found fields for the employment of knowledge acquired outside of its ordinary sphere, and so succeeded in vastly enlarging its proportions and lifting it to the highest plane of usefulness During this long period of active life and heavy cares his earlier tastes for literature were not neglected, and the hours unoccupied by business were generally devoted to scientific study He has been an occasional contributor to *The American Catholic Quarterly Review*, always upon subjects of metaphysical philosophy, and a few years ago he published the conclusions from a long course of abstract reading and reflection in an octavo volume of[1] logico-metaphysics, taking strong ground throughout, from the stand-point of rational analysis, against the growing materialistic atheism of the times, impelled thereto, as set forth in the dedication, by the desire to contribute his part in a good work He has in progress, he states, two other works of somewhat kindred character, upon which he labors alternately, which will require several years to complete

[1] Elementary Philosophy, Parts I and II By James M Willcox, Ph D Porter & Coates, No 822 Chestnut Street, Philadelphia

When the scheme for a Centennial Exhibition was projected Mr Willcox was among the first to earnestly advocate that it should be international, and to do all in his power to advance it He was appointed a member of the first Board of Finance created by act of Congress, and at a later day was requested by the Centennial Commission to act as one of the Judges of the Exhibition, of whom there were one hundred American and one hundred foreign selected At the first meeting of the committees he was chosen President of Group XIII, and after six months' active duty in that capacity he wrote, by request, a critical compendium of the entire work of his committee for publication. His services were recognized in a letter of thanks, with a special medal, by the Commission In 1852 he married Mary Keating, of Philadelphia, daughter of Jerome Keating, who, in partnership with John J Borie, was one of the early manufacturers of Manayunk, and granddaughter of John Keating, a distinguished officer of the French army in the last century, who, for having captured the island of St Eustache from the British, was decorated by Louis XVI, and made Chevalier of the Order of Saint Louis Of this marriage there are five children living, of whom two are married, one residing at Colorado Springs and the other in Philadelphia His present wife is Katharine, daughter of the late Abraham W Sharples, of Thornbury township, and granddaughter, on her mother's side, of Right Rev Henry U. Onderdonk, formerly the Episcopalian Bishop of Philadelphia. Of this marriage there are two children, both living The family have lived in Spruce Street, Philadelphia, for many years, but still retain possession of a farm in Thornbury, near Cheyney's Station

Since his retirement from regular business in 1880, Mr Willcox has been in the habit of spending the winter months in Florida He early foresaw the phenomenal development of South Florida, little known six years ago, but now rapidly distancing the northern part, and made extensive purchases of property in Orange County and on Indian River that are now very valuable With the care of these and his material interests at home, the responsibilities of directorship in some large corporations, the continued pursuit of scientific study, and the labor upon his works in hand, he indulges in little leisure, and, to judge from the past and present, is not likely to find the pleasures of idleness as long as he lives

Licensed Houses—The first record that appears of license being granted in Concord is at the August court, 1722, when the petition of Mathias Karle (Kerlin) was presented, asking that he be permitted to keep a public-house in that township, and to sell rum and other liquors therein, which application was approved by the justices At the same court John Hannum desired the privilege of keeping a house of entertainment to sell "Beer and Sider," which was also granted Kerlin's name annually thereafter, to and including the year 1726, appears of record, after which it is omitted from the clerk's list, as is also that of Hannum from the list of 1731 Hannum's house, I learn from the application of his son, John Hannum, in 1747, was on the road from Chester to Nottingham,—the Concord road,—and the latter's name appears annually thereafter up to 1760 In 1761, Robert Hall succeeded Hannum, and in 1771, John Palmer followed Hall in business, and continued there until 1776 In 1782, Frederick Steen seems to have kept this house, then called the "Buck," and the following year John Gest succeeded him Robert Burnett obtained license for 1784, and William Hannum from 1785 to 1787, when William Lockart took his place until 1788, at which date the inn disappears as a public-house

To return to Kerlin's inn On Nov 24, 1730, Matthias Kerlin presented his petition, in which he states that he "had license for several years and no complaint made, but on account of other affairs had declined making application for a considerable time, now wishes to renew," which application was granted

Michael Atkinson, Aug 31, 1731, presented his petition, wherein he sets forth that for some time past "he had a recommendation to keep a public-house in West Town, and being desirous to remove into Concord, found a suitable place, but hearing that Matthias Kyrlin had an inclination to get into that business, he went to him and received a denial of the report" Atkinson then agreed with the landlord for a term of years at eight pounds per annum, and obtained license to remove into Concord "The license now being expired," he wished it renewed It appears that, notwithstanding Kerlin's declaration that he did not propose to apply for license, he did present his application to the court, which was supplemented by the following petition emanating from the "Inhabitants of Concord," bearing date Aug 31, 1731, "That whereas our Township have been through some misfortune in some measure oppressed by so many publick houses allowed in our town, & by some this last year without our knowledge or good liking Let us have but one of that Calling, and if you think fit to grant recommendation to Mathias Kyrlen we shall, &c," be pleased if the court act on these suggestions The remonstrance was signed by Benjamin Mendenhall, Thomas Downing, and nine others

The foregoing remonstrance is indorsed "Allowed," while the petition of Atkinson is marked "Not Allowed" Kerlin's name appears regularly on the clerk's list from that date to 1738, when I lose sight of him until 1745, when he regularly is allowed to entertain the public until Feb 26, 1750, when his petition states that he has kept tavern twenty-eight years, that his family is small, as his children are provided for, but he is unable to work at his trade of shoemaking As an additional reason why he should be allowed license, he urges that he and his wife are descendants of the "first adventurers who came into this province when money would not purchase

Bread." The court, however, declined to grant him the privilege desired.

In 1785, William Underwood was licensed to keep public-house in Concord. In 1786, Samuel Johnson, Alexander Lockart, and Caleb Taylor received the court's approval. The latter, in 1788, had the privilege continued to him.

In 1748, Nathaniel Newlin was granted license for his house "near several great roads," and it was continued to him until 1776, excepting during the years 1757–59, when William Smith seems to have been the landlord, and in 1760 no names appear of record. License may have been, but probably was not, denied to Newlin during that period. This house was on the Wilmington and Great Valley road, near where the Naaman's Creek road crosses the former highway, now Johnson's Corners. From 1776 to 1782 there is no record respecting license in Concord; in fact, the tracing of successive landlords for public-houses in that township is more difficult than in any other in our county, Ridley and Lower Chichester not excepted. In 1782, Amos Mendenhall had license; in 1774, John Burnett; and from 1758 to 1788, Thomas Maddock, when I lose trace of this house. In 1791, however, John Fred appears to have been landlord of Newlin's Tavern, and in 1800, James Jeffries kept the house, to yield it, in 1806, to John Hickman. In 1810, Charles Hughes had license for The Three Tuns (a favorite name for inns at that day), and Nathaniel Newlin superseded Hughes in 1814, and continued as "mine host" there only one year, when, in 1814, Thomas Smith took his place for a season as the landlord of the old house. After that year the owner declined to have it longer licensed as a tavern.

Moses Bullock, Jr., in his application for the year 1815, says that the noted tavern, The Three Tuns, the property of Nathaniel Newlin, is about "to Drop, and your petitioner has lately erected a convenient House for Business on the same road leading from the Borough of Wilmington to Great Valley, about half a mile from the former stand, and a tavern will be badly wanted in said neighborhood." Bullock's Tavern,—for his application was allowed,—we learn from the remonstrance against James Smith, was located on the Wilmington road, about a quarter of a mile above Elam. It was known as the Buck, and he was licensed annually thereafter until 1832, when as a public inn it disappears from the records.

In 1783, Joshua Vernon had leave to keep a tavern known as The Blue Ball, at which house he was superseded, in 1787, by James Oliver, who had license only for that year, while Joshua Vernon received the privilege to keep an inn at a house located on the Concord road a short distance beyond Chelsea. The ancient hostelry, well known as the Cross-Keys, no longer as a public-house, is now owned by Michael McGinnis. In 1789, the last year the justices of Chester County granted license for the territory now comprising Delaware County, Joshua Vernon was the only person in Concord to whom the judges show partiality. Under the new order of things, at the first court held at Chester, after the division, he received license, and was continued yearly to be favored until 1796, when James Jeffries succeeded him at the Cross-Keys. The latter was the landlord until 1799, when Ann Vernon had the license, and in 1800, George Mattson followed her. Thomas Ring had the house in 1802; Samuel Chapman was there in 1805, and the next year he gave place to Jonathan Paul, Jr., who, in 1807, was succeeded by Amos Waddell. In 1809, Curtis Jeffries was "mine host," but he surrendered the honors to Amos Waddell the next year, and the latter, in 1811, to Peter Harper. In 1812, James Marshall took the responsibility of the Cross-Keys on himself, and sustained them during the second disagreement with England, and for three years after the cruel war was over, when, in 1818, David Howes succeeded him, to be superseded the next year by William Baldwin. The latter remained there for eight years, until 1828, when Reece Pyle had license for the inn, and in 1833, Nathaniel Stevens became the last landlord of the Cross-Keys of Concord, for after 1836 it disappears from the list.

In 1817, Joseph Hannum petitioned court for license to keep a public house of entertainment on the West Chester and Concord road, although it would have been more accurate had he said on Concord road, for the White Horse Inn was located on the latter highway, a short mile above Chelsea. The old building, partly of logs and partly of stone, recently the property of Robert M. Smith and now owned by J. & J. Darlington, still stands. He was successful in his application, and he received the court's favor annually thereafter until 1837, when it ceased to be a tavern. During all the time it was a licensed house, the electors of Concord, Birmingham, Bethel, and that part of Thornbury lying west of a public road, from Street road by the shops and continuing by the house of Jacob Parks, to the road dividing the townships of Concord and Thornbury (in 1823), all voted at this inn, while in 1830 the second election district of Delaware County, comprising Concord, Birmingham, Bethel, and Thornbury, had their polling-place at the White Horse, and continued annually to be held there until and including 1837, when a tavern at that place was discontinued.

On Jan. 15, 1819, James Smith, the owner and occupier of the premises at the intersection of the roads leading from Wilmington to West Chester, and from Brandywine to New London Turnpike road, states in his petition that he is desirous of keeping a public-house at that location, and to that end has improved his property and provided himself with buildings and other things necessary and convenient for that business. On Jan. 18, 1819, a remonstrance from the inhabitants of Concord and Birmingham sets forth that the signers "have heard with much consurn that James Smith has petitioned your honours to grant him a Licence to keep a house of public entertainment on the Wilmington road, in the neighborhood of the public houses on the same road, one of them but one-quarter of a mile above and the other one mile and a half below, which is sufficient to accommodate the public Besides it is feared that if the number of public houses should be encreased that some of them will have to resort to neighboring custom for support" The court rejected the petition, as also a similar one dated October 18th of the same year, which was indorsed by seventy-nine signatures The remonstrance filed against the latter application states that the petitioner wanted "to locate a tavern at the intersection of the road from Chandlers bridge to the Philadelphia and New London Turnpike road with the road from West Chester to Wilmington, which we consider wholly useless and apprehensive, and would be injurious for many reasons On the West Chester and Wilmington road there is a tavern, about one quarter of a mile above the aforementioned intersection, and below it there is one in New Castle County, a small distance more than a mile, so that travelers from West Chester to Wilmington can need no opportunity for refreshments more than is already afforded The other road from Chandler's bridge is but lately laid out and your remonstrants confidently state that few (if any) loaded travelling waggons have been seen on that road, besides the said road crosses the Concord road not more than a quarter of a mile from Hannum's Tavern, so that those who have really occasion to pass along the said cross road can have no difficulty in obtaining refreshments in passing at either of the intersections" The remonstrants continue, "Although they acknowledge the names of many inhabitants of Delaware County very respectable, are signed to the petition of James Smith, yet it is a matter of certainty that a large proportion of the signers are inhabitants of the State of Delaware, inhabitants of Chester County, and other places distant from James Smith's, who probably can have no opportunity of knowing the facts set forth in his petition nor any occasion of passing by the said cross road" The remonstrance had sixty names attached thereto

Jan 27, 1820, James Smith again petitioned for a license for the house, his application being signed by one hundred and twenty-four persons He also filed an additional paper with seventy-six names attached, in which the signers state "that, learning that a large number of respectable citizens stating" (to the petition already filed) "their belief that a Tavern is much wanted at the stand where the said James Smith lives and that he is a suitable character to keep such house of entertainment We under the influence of a similar opinion and from a conviction that the public convenience would be promoted by such an establishment, which is needed both for the accommodation of travellers and drovers using the road with cattle, unite in requesting that license be granted to Smith" The court, however, shook their judicial heads, and again the petitioner was turned unsatisfied away The next year he remained dormant, but March 22, 1822, he appears again The judges held his petition under advisement and finally refused it, but at the April court, 1823, James Smith came off with flying colors, and after four and a quarter years of bitter struggles the Drove Tavern, at present in Elam, was established In 1826, James Smith changed the name of the house to the Drovers' and Travelers' Inn, and it was so kept by William Smith in 1827 In 1831 the tavern was licensed to Jane Smith, in 1835, to James, and in 1837 to William Smith, who remained there until 1844 In the latter year Milton Stamp became the landlord of the old hostelry, changing its name again to the Drove, and the following year he gave it a new title, that of Pleasant Hill In 1849, Isaac B Gilpin succeeded to the business, to be followed in 1854 by Edward B Hoskin, and in 1856 Joseph Cheyney became the "mine host" of the inn John Reven had license the following year, and in 1858 Charles Cheyney received the court's favor In 1859, William S Cheyney was the landlord, and continued as such until 1860, when Joseph Cheyney had license granted him, but he died before taking it out, and the privilege was extended to his widow, Mary Cheyney In 1864, William E May became the proprietor of The Farmers' and Drovers' Inn, to be succeeded, in 1868, by Richard T Plummer, who restored the more modern title, Pleasant Hill, to the tavern In 1869, Joseph Chandler was the landlord, to be followed, in 1870, by Plummer, who owned the property The house was not licensed from 1871 to 1875, when Zadock T Speakman had license granted him, to be succeeded, in 1878, by Benjamin French In 1879, William F May was landlord, and, in 1881, was followed by Jackson McFarlan In 1883, when the general remonstrance against granting any license in Concord was presented, the court denied to McFarlan the privilege for the sale of liquor at Elam, exactly sixty years after James Smith was first granted the right to keep a public-house there

The Concordville Inn was established as a public-house in 1830, in which year John Way was granted license there, and being centrally located in the township, after Joseph Hannum retired from tavern-keeping, the election polls were ordered to be held at that point In 1858, John Way declined to apply, and the privilege for that year was granted to David M Hannum, but he failing to take out the license, George W Taylor was permitted to enjoy it in his stead The latter continued annually to petition successfully until 1861, when he was followed by Zadock T Speakman, who, in 1869, gave place to James Cloud The latter called the house the Concordville Hotel, and in 1871 he was the only person in the township who received the approval of the court In 1872, Frank H Cloud had the license, after which time it does not appear to have had the indorsement of the Quarter Sessions until 1876, when the present owner and landlord, James Neeld, secured that favor. Annually thereafter he was among the licensed houses until April, 1883, when two lengthy petitions, one signed by one hundred and twenty-eight men, and the other by one hundred and fifty women, were presented to court protesting "against granting of any hotel license in the said township, and especially against granting license for the sale of intoxicating liquors to James Neeld, of Concordville, or Jackson McFarlan, of Elam, . . . believing that such license and sale is fraught with results disastrous to the comfort, prosperity, and morality of a portion of our people and the disturbance of our peace, that their petitions are very generally signed by those who bear but a small share of taxation, and who are intoxicated to their own injury. We are fully persuaded that such licenses are not necessary for the accommodation of the public, and that our neighborhood will be better without them." After a lengthy hearing, Judge Clayton refused to grant the license. At the January court, 1884, the license was restored to the Concordville Hotel.

BIOGRAPHICAL SKETCHES.

CHARLES W. MATHUES.

The Mathues family are of Irish lineage, Andrew, the grandfather of Charles W., having emigrated after the war of the Revolution, and settled in Baltimore County, Md. He was united in marriage to a Mrs. Smith, widow, and had a son, William, born Dec. 16, 1796, in the above county, where his early life was spent. When about twenty-one years of age he came to Chester County, Pa., and followed the trade of a paper-maker. He married Susan McHenry, whose children were Andrew W., John McHenry, William F., Moses R., Charles W., David S., Alexander C., and Susan E. (Mrs. Daniel Hart). Charles W. was born March 15, 1830, in Chester County, and when thirteen years of age became a resident of Delaware County, at which early period of his life he began a self-supporting career by entering the cotton-mill of John P. Crozer. After two years spent at that point he became an employé of other mills in the vicinity, and at the age of twenty entered the professional field as a student of dentistry. Concluding, however, not to practice, he became a clerk for N. L. Yarnall, at Lenni, and subsequently purchased and ran a stage line for a period of two years. He, in 1851, married Amanda, daughter of Milcah Richardson, and has children,—Andrew W., William M., Mary E., Susan M., Charles G., Samuel W., Amanda E., and Ida May. Having determined to become a farmer, Mr. Mathues, in 1857, rented land in Aston township, and subsequently in other localities, finally purchasing a farm in the above township, which his son now cultivates. In 1879 he located in Concord, and has since that time filled a position of prominence as an agriculturist in that township. He is in politics a pronounced Republican, and as a representative of that party was elected in 1875 sheriff of Delaware County, which office he held for the term of three years, as also various township offices. He has since that time been devoted to the cultivation of his farm. Mr. Mathues is a member of the Independent Order of Odd-Fellows, as also of the Improved Order of Red Men, the Knights of Pythias, and the American Protestant Association. He is active as a leader in the temperance cause, and has carefully shunned the use of strong drink and tobacco during his lifetime. These correct principles, together with habits of industry and self-reliance, have rendered him independent. In religion he worships with the Methodist Episcopal Church.

THOMAS P. POWEL.

Davis Powel, the father of the subject of this biographical sketch, was born in Chester County, and married Miss Catharine, daughter of Thomas Pennell. Their children were Thomas P., Charles Rogers, Davis, Benjamin Rush, Hannah A. (Mrs. William Baldwin, of Harford County, Md.), and G. Washington. Mr. Powel eventually removed to Maryland, where he purchased an extensive landed property, and remained until his death. His son, Thomas P., was born on the 7th of April, 1811, in Philadelphia, and in early life repaired with his father to Maryland, where he enjoyed superior advantages of education. Circumstances influenced his removal in youth to Concord township, Delaware Co., where he engaged in the cultivation of the estate of his maternal relatives. In 1861, having inherited the farm, he made it his residence, and during the remainder of his life followed the business of a farmer. He married, on the 3d of February, 1852, Miss Lydia, daughter of William Garrigues, of Philadelphia, and granddaughter of Samuel Garrigues, of Haverford township. Their only son, William G., now occupies the Pennell homestead, which, in the direct line of descent, is the property of Mrs. Powel and her son. The latter is actively identified with the public measures of the county, was for years secretary and treasurer of the Republican Executive Committee of the county, as also its chairman in 1880, and in 1882 was elected to the State Legislature. Thomas P. Powel made his influence felt in the social and political life of the county. He was in politics a Democrat of the Jeffersonian school, and an ardent supporter of the principles of his party. During the sessions of 1857–58 he was its representative in the State Legislature, and served on the Committees on Agriculture, Railroads, etc. He also filled various less important offices in connection with the township. Though a Friend by virtue of his antecedents, he worshiped with the congregation of St. John's Protestant Epis-

...ia.

...since that time filled a
...r agriculturist in that
...s a prominent Repub-
...of that party was elected
...County, which office he
...s, as also various town-
...er time been devoted to
... Mr. Mathews is a mem-
...der of Odd-Fellows, the
...f Red Men, the Knights
...e Protestant Association.
...e temperance cause, and
...e of strong drink and to-
...hese correct principles,
...y and self-reliance, have
... In religion he worships
... Church.

...owel.

... the subject of this ske-
...in Chester County, and
...ughter of Thomas Bey-
...e Thomas P., Charles
...Bush, Hannah A. (Mrs.
...el County, Md.), and G.
...ntually removed to Mary-
...r extensive landed pro-
...death. His son, Thomas
...April, 1811, in Philadel-
...ained with his father to
...d, superior advantages of
...induced his removal in
..., Delaware Co., where he
... the estate of his maternal
...inherited the items he made
...the remainder of his life
...farmer. He married, on
...Miss Lydia, daughter of
...Philadelphia, and grand-
...gross, of Haverford town-
...liam G., now occupies the
...in the direct line of de-
...Mrs. Powel and her son.
...ified with the public inter-
...years secretary and trea-
...ecutive Committee of the
...n in 1860, and in 1865 was
...istors. Thomas P. Powel
...the social and political life
...politics a Democrat of the
...n ardent supporter of the
...during the session of 1857-
...s in the State Legislature,
...ittee on Agriculture, Rail-
...d various less important
...the township. Though a
...convictions he worshiped
...St. John's Protestant Epis-

owner and landlord, James [illegible] Not long subsequently thereafter he was among the [illegible] until April, 1880, when two lengthy petitions, one signed by one hundred and twenty-eight men, and the other by one hundred and fifty women, were presented to court, protesting against the granting of any hotel license in the said township, and especially against granting license for the sale of intoxicating liquors to [illegible] of [illegible], or Jackson [illegible], of Elam, [illegible] that such license [illegible] fraught with [illegible] dangerous to the comfort, prosperity and [illegible] of a portion of our people [illegible] disturbance of our peace, that such petitions [illegible] and by those who bear but [illegible] who are intoxicated to [illegible] fully persuaded that such [illegible] for the accommodation of the public [illegible] neighborhood will be better without them. [illegible] hearing, Judge Clayton refused to grant the license. At the January court, [illegible] license was removed to the Concordville [illegible]

[illegible]APHICAL SKETCHES.

[illegible] W. MATHUES.

[illegible] Andrew, [illegible] of Chester Co., having emigrated [illegible] of the Revolution, and settled in [illegible] county, Md. He was united in marriage to a [illegible], and had a son, William, born [illegible], in the above county, where his early [illegible] twenty-one years of age [illegible] county, Pa., and followed the [illegible] He married Susan Mc[illegible] Andrew W., John Mc[illegible] Charles W., David S., [illegible] Chester [illegible] a [illegible] early period [illegible] After two [illegible] Having determined [illegible] Mary E., Susan M., Charles [illegible] and Ida May. Having determined [illegible] Mr. Mathues, in 1857, rented [illegible] township, and subsequently in other localities, finally purchasing a farm in the above township, which his son now cultivates. In 1879 he located in Concord, and has since that time filled a position of prominence as an agriculturist in that township. He is in politics a pronounced Republican, and as a representative of that party was elected in 1875 sheriff of Delaware County, which office he held for the term of three years, as also various township offices. He has since that time been devoted to the cultivation of his farm. Mr. Mathues is a member of the Independent Order of Odd-Fellows, as also of the Improved Order of Red Men, the Knights of Pythias, and the American Protestant Association. He is active as a leader in the temperance cause, and has carefully shunned the use of strong drink and tobacco during his lifetime. These correct principles, together with habits of industry and self-reliance, have rendered him independent. In religion he worships with the Methodist Episcopal Church.

THOMAS P. POWEL.

Davis Powel, the father of the subject of this biographical sketch, was born in Chester County, and married Miss Catharine, daughter of Thomas Pennell. Their children were Thomas P., Charles Rogers, Davis, Benjamin Rush, Hannah A. (Mrs. William Baldwin, of Harford County, Md.), and G. Washington. Mr. Powel eventually removed to Maryland, where he purchased an extensive landed property, and remained until his death. His son, Thomas P., was born on the 7th of April, 1811, in Philadelphia, and in early life repaired with his father to Maryland, where he enjoyed superior advantages of education. Circumstances influenced his removal in [illegible] to Concord township, Delaware Co., where he engaged in the cultivation of the estate of his maternal relatives. In 1843, having inherited the farm, he made it his residence, and during the remainder of his life followed the business of a farmer. He married, on the 3d of February, 1852, Miss Lydia, daughter of William Garrigues, of Philadelphia, and granddaughter of Samuel Garrigues, of Haverford township. Their only son, William G., now occupies the Pennell homestead, which, in the direct line of descent, is the property of Mrs. Powel and her son. The latter is actively identified with the public measures of the county, was for years secretary and treasurer of the Republican Executive Committee of the county, as also its chairman in 1880, and in 1882 was elected to the State Legislature. Thomas P. Powel made his influence felt in the social and political life of the county. He was in politics a Democrat of the Jeffersonian school, and an ardent supporter of the principles of his party. During the sessions of 1857–58 he was its representative in the State Legislature, and served on the Committees on Agriculture, Railroads, etc. He also filled various less important offices in connection with the township. Though a Friend by virtue of his antecedents, he worshiped with the congregation of St. John's Protestant Epis-

C. W. Mathews

Thos P Powel

Charles Palmer

Charles Palmer

Lewis Palmer

copal Church of Concord, and was a member of the vestry of that church. Mr. Powel was frequently called upon to act as trustee of estates and guardian, while his unbiased judgment made his services especially valuable in cases requiring arbitration. In public life he was a man of sterling integrity, the strictest justice, and great decision of character. In his social relations he was distinguished by an eminently sympathetic, kind, and benevolent nature. His death occurred Jan. 7, 1872, in his sixty-first year.

CHARLES PALMER.

John Palmer, the progenitor of the family in Delaware County, in 1688 purchased one hundred acres of land in Concord township, the greater part of which has remained in the possession of his descendants to the present time. He married Mary Southery, and had among his children a son, John, who married Martha Yearsley, whose son, Moses, inherited two-thirds of the homestead. He married Abigail Newlin, whose only son, John, born in 1745, married Hannah, daughter of Abram Martin, of Aston, and had children, ten in number, of whom John, born in 1788, in conjunction with the occupation of a farmer, learned the trade of a saddler. He married Beulah, daughter of William Walter, of Centreville, Del., and had children,—Lewis, William W., John, Rachel, Charles, Hannah, Lydia, and Beulah. By a second marriage to Elizabeth Hall were born no children. Charles Palmer, whose birth occurred Sept. 16, 1811, in Concord township, spent his youth at the home of his parents. At the age of sixteen he removed to Wilmington, Del., and served as a merchant's clerk. He later repaired to Chester, Pa., and acted in the same capacity for J. P. & William Eyre, remaining with them until his marriage, in 1833, to Deborah, daughter of Benjamin and Mary Pitman, of Monmouth County, N. J. Their children are Mary F. (Mrs. Edward Darlington), Lewis, James (deceased), Edwin H. (deceased, who served in the late war), and Hannah Ann (deceased). Mrs. Palmer died Nov. 1, 1870. She was a woman of marked character, and much respected in her neighborhood for works of charity and love. He was again married in 1874 to Joanna Stoll, of Concord, who survives. After his marriage Mr. Palmer engaged in mercantile pursuits at Beaver Valley, Del.; but finding that no trade could there be successfully conducted without the sale of liquor, he abandoned mercantile ventures and became a farmer. In 1842 he was appointed steward of the County House, and filled the office with entire satisfaction for a period of twelve years. On the expiration of this term he purchased the Hall homestead, in Concord township, and during the remainder of his life engaged in the cultivation of its broad acres. He was, as an early Whig and later as a Republican, actively interested in public men and measures. As supervisor for a term of years he did much to improve the roads of his township. He held the offices of director of the First National Bank of Media for several years, and of the Delaware County Mutual Insurance Company from its organization. He was in religion a member of the society of Friends, and attended the Concordville Friends' Meeting. His death occurred April 12, 1876, in his sixty-fourth year. The following resolution of the Delaware County Mutual Insurance Company on the occasion of his decease bears witness to his character:

"*Resolved*, That in the death of Charles Palmer the company has lost one of its most faithful and efficient officers and society a useful member. Active and energetic in the discharge of his duties, moderate and conscientious in his counsels, prompt and constant in his attendance at our meetings, and pleasant in his intercourse with his fellow-members, his absence will be noted and his loss felt. His helping hand was ever ready for those who were needy, and his death will be mourned by many to whom his unostentatious kindness has been extended when struggling in the toils of adversity."

The First National Bank of Media, also, in a similar series of resolutions, expressed the fact

"That in his death the board and society have lost one of their most useful members, one who by his attention and integrity contributed in a considerable degree to the success of the institution. Pleasant and considerate to all with whom he had intercourse, his loss will be greatly deplored."

LEWIS PALMER.

Lewis Palmer, the son of Charles and Deborah Pitman Palmer, was born Oct. 2, 1837, in Concord township, and in early youth removed to the present site of the borough of Media, where he remained until sixteen years of age. His education was principally received at the school of S. M. Janney, of Loudoun County, Va., and in Chester County, Pa. On completing his studies he returned to the farm and cultivated the land on shares for his father. He was married in 1862 to Hannah H., daughter of Joseph and Susan Pancoast, of Salem County, N. J., and has children,—Charles, Joseph P., Mary D., Anna T. (deceased), Edwin L., and Samuel C. Charles, of this number, graduated with honor at Swarthmore College, and is now engaged in teaching. Mr. Palmer, on the death of his father, inherited the paternal estate upon which he now resides. He devotes his attention principally to the manufacture of butter for the Chester market. He has also given some thought to genealogical research, and prepared with much labor and care a record of the various branches of the Palmer and Trimble families. He is in politics a Republican; has served for six years as school director, and been a leading spirit in the erection of commodious school buildings in Concord township. He has also been one of the most earnest advocates of the temperance cause in the township. Mr. Palmer is a member of the Delaware County Institute of Science, and corresponding member of the Historical Society of the State of Delaware. He is also president and director of the Farmers' Market of Chester. In religion he is a Friend, and an acknowledged minister of the Concord meeting. His views on religious subjects are, however, of a liberal character.

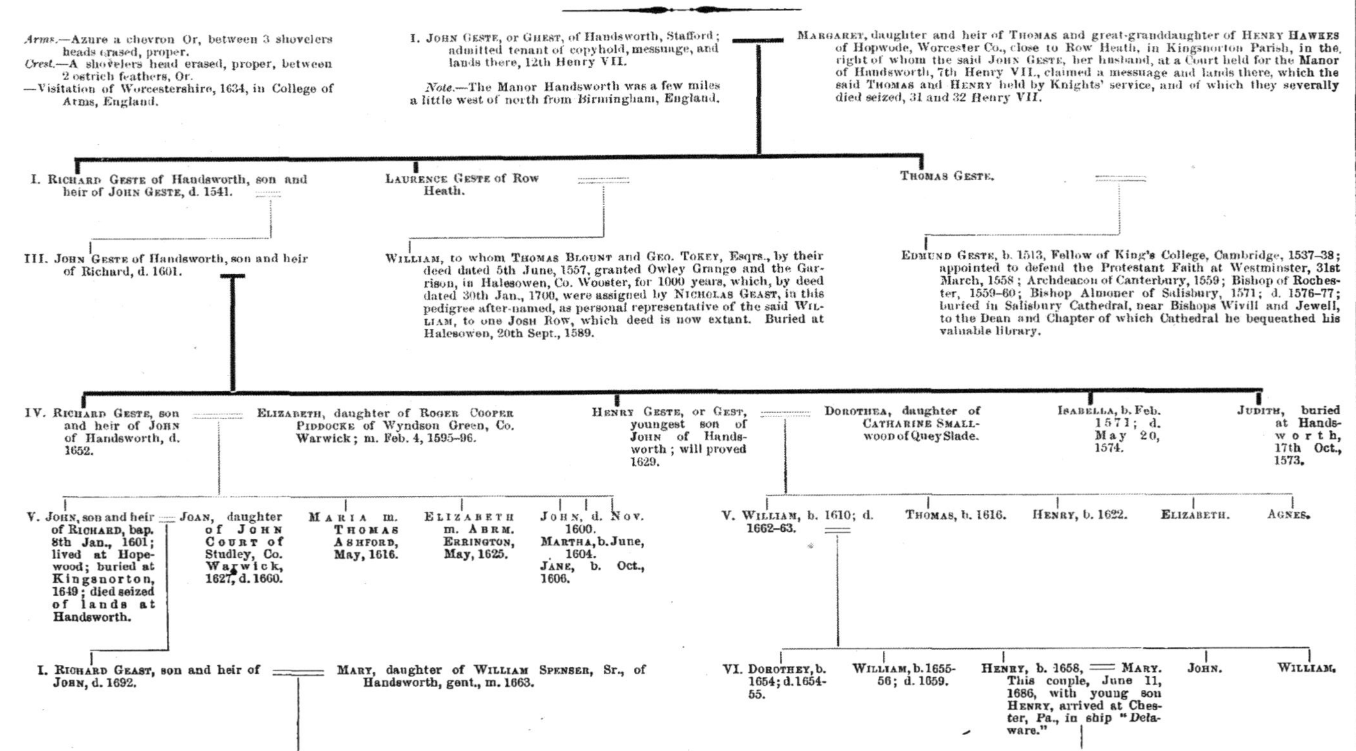

PEDIGREE OF THE GEST, GESTE, GHEST, GEAST FAMILY

(OFTEN BUT ERRONEOUSLY IN LAST TWO CENTURIES GUEST).

Deduced from the Court Rolls of Handsworth, the Ministers Registers of that place, Shustoke, and other Parishes, including those of St. Martin's, Birmingham. From Title Deeds and other Authorities in both England and the United States of North America.

Arms.—Azure a chevron Or, between 3 shovelers heads erased, proper.
Crest.—A shovelers head erased, proper, between 2 ostrich feathers, Or.
—Visitation of Worcestershire, 1634, in College of Arms, England.

I. JOHN GESTE, or GHEST, of Handsworth, Stafford; admitted tenant of copyhold, messuage, and lands there, 12th Henry VII.

Note.—The Manor Handsworth was a few miles a little west of north from Birmingham, England.

MARGARET, daughter and heir of THOMAS and great-granddaughter of HENRY HAWKES of Hopwode, Worcester Co., close to Row Heath, in Kingsnorton Parish, in the right of whom the said JOHN GESTE, her husband, at a Court held for the Manor of Handsworth, 7th Henry VII., claimed a messuage and lands there, which the said THOMAS and HENRY held by Knights' service, and of which they severally died seized, 31 and 32 Henry VII.

I. RICHARD GESTE of Handsworth, son and heir of JOHN GESTE, d. 1541.

LAURENCE GESTE of Row Heath.

THOMAS GESTE.

III. JOHN GESTE of Handsworth, son and heir of Richard, d. 1601.

WILLIAM, to whom THOMAS BLOUNT and GEO. TOKEY, Esqrs., by their deed dated 5th June, 1557, granted Owley Grange and the Garrison, in Halesowen, Co. Wooster, for 1000 years, which, by deed dated 30th Jan., 1700, were assigned by NICHOLAS GEAST, in this pedigree after-named, as personal representative of the said WILLIAM, to one JOSH ROW, which deed is now extant. Buried at Halesowen, 20th Sept., 1589.

EDMUND GESTE, b. 1513, Fellow of King's College, Cambridge, 1537–38; appointed to defend the Protestant Faith at Westminster, 31st March, 1558; Archdeacon of Canterbury, 1559; Bishop of Rochester, 1559–60; Bishop Almoner of Salisbury, 1571; d. 1576–77; buried in Salisbury Cathedral, near Bishops Wivill and Jewell, to the Dean and Chapter of which Cathedral he bequeathed his valuable library.

IV. RICHARD GESTE, son and heir of JOHN of Handsworth, d. 1652. = ELIZABETH, daughter of ROGER COOPER PIDDOCKE of Wyndson Green, Co. Warwick; m. Feb. 4, 1595–96.

HENRY GESTE, or GEST, youngest son of JOHN of Handsworth; will proved 1629. = DOROTHEA, daughter of CATHARINE SMALLWOOD of Quey Slade.

ISABELLA, b. Feb. 1571; d. May 20, 1574.

JUDITH, buried at Handsworth, 17th Oct., 1573.

V. JOHN, son and heir of RICHARD, bap. 8th Jan., 1601; lived at Hopewood; buried at Kingsnorton, 1649; died seized of lands at Handsworth. = JOAN, daughter of JOHN COURT of Studley, Co. Warwick, 1627, d. 1660.

MARIA m. THOMAS ASHFORD, May, 1616.

ELIZABETH m. ABRM. ERRINGTON, May, 1625.

JOHN, d. Nov. 1600.

MARTHA, b. June, 1604.

JANE, b. Oct., 1606.

V. WILLIAM, b. 1610; d. 1662–63. =

THOMAS, b. 1616.

HENRY, b. 1622.

ELIZABETH.

AGNES.

I. RICHARD GEAST, son and heir of JOHN, d. 1692. = MARY, daughter of WILLIAM SPENSER, Sr., of Handsworth, gent., m. 1663.

VI. DOROTHEY, b. 1654; d. 1654–55.

WILLIAM, b. 1655–56; d. 1659.

HENRY, b. 1658, = MARY. This couple, June 11, 1686, with young son HENRY, arrived at Chester, Pa., in ship "Delaware."

JOHN.

WILLIAM.

JOSEPH GEST.

REBEKAH GEST.

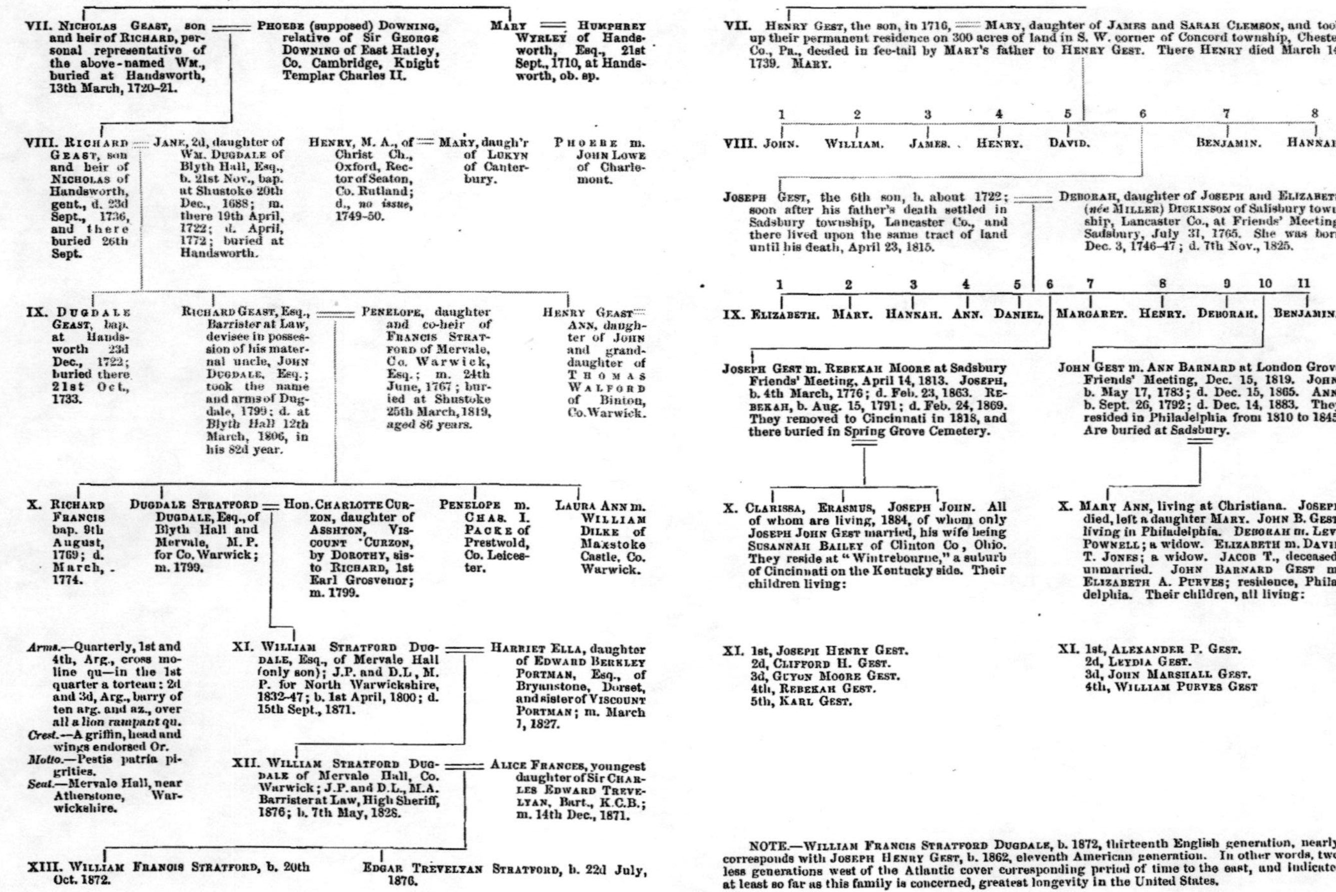

VII. NICHOLAS GEAST, son and heir of RICHARD, personal representative of the above-named WM., buried at Handsworth, 13th March, 1720–21. = PHOEBE (supposed) DOWNING, relative of Sir GEORGE DOWNING of East Hatley, Co. Cambridge, Knight Templar Charles II.

MARY = HUMPHREY WYRLEY of Handsworth, Esq., 21st Sept., 1710, at Handsworth, ob. sp.

VIII. RICHARD GEAST, son and heir of NICHOLAS of Handsworth, gent., d. 23d Sept., 1736, and there buried 26th Sept. = JANE, 2d, daughter of WM. DUGDALE of Blyth Hall, Esq., b. 21st Nov., bap. at Shustoke 20th Dec., 1688; m. there 19th April, 1722; d. April, 1772; buried at Handsworth.

HENRY, M. A., of Christ Ch., Oxford, Rector of Seaton, Co. Rutland; d., *no issue*, 1749–50. = MARY, daugh'r of LUKYN of Canterbury.

PHOEBE m. JOHN LOWE of Charlemont.

IX. DUGDALE GEAST, bap. at Handsworth 23d Dec., 1722; buried there 21st Oct., 1733.

RICHARD GEAST, Esq., Barrister at Law, devisee in possession of his maternal uncle, JOHN DUGDALE, Esq.; took the name and arms of Dugdale, 1799; d. at Blyth Hall 12th March, 1806, in his 82d year. = PENELOPE, daughter and co-heir of FRANCIS STRATFORD of Mervale, Co. Warwick, Esq.; m. 24th June, 1767; buried at Shustoke 25th March, 1819, *aged 86 years.*

HENRY GEAST = ANN, daughter of JOHN and granddaughter of THOMAS WALFORD of Binton, Co. Warwick.

X. RICHARD FRANCIS bap. 9th August, 1769; d. March, 1774.

DUGDALE STRATFORD DUGDALE, Esq., of Blyth Hall and Mervale, M. P. for Co. Warwick; m. 1799. = Hon. CHARLOTTE CURZON, daughter of ASSHTON, VISCOUNT CURZON, by DOROTHY, sister to RICHARD, 1st Earl Grosvenor; m. 1799.

PENELOPE m. CHAS. I. PACKE of Prestwold, Co. Leicester.

LAURA ANN m. WILLIAM DILKE of Maxstoke Castle, Co. Warwick.

Arms.—Quarterly, 1st and 4th, Arg., cross moline qu—in the 1st quarter a torteau: 2d and 3d, Arg., barry of ten arg. and az., over all *a lion rampant qu.*
Crest.—A griffin, head and wings endorsed Or.
Motto.—Pestis patria pigrities.
Seat.—Mervale Hall, near Atherstone, Warwickshire.

XI. WILLIAM STRATFORD DUGDALE, Esq., of Mervale Hall (only son); J.P. and D.L., M. P. for North Warwickshire, 1832–47; b. 1st April, 1800; d. 15th Sept., 1871. = HARRIET ELLA, daughter of EDWARD BERKLEY PORTMAN, Esq., of Bryanstone, Dorset, and sister of VISCOUNT PORTMAN; m. March 1, 1827.

XII. WILLIAM STRATFORD DUGDALE of Mervale Hall, Co. Warwick; J.P. and D.L., M.A. Barrister at Law, High Sheriff, 1876; b. 7th May, 1828. = ALICE FRANCES, youngest daughter of Sir CHARLES EDWARD TREVELYAN, Bart., K.C.B.; m. 14th Dec., 1871.

XIII. WILLIAM FRANCIS STRATFORD, b. 20th Oct. 1872.

EDGAR TREVELYAN STRATFORD, b. 22d July, 1876.

VII. HENRY GEST, the son, in 1716, = MARY, daughter of JAMES and SARAH CLEMSON, and took up their permanent residence on 300 acres of land in S. W. corner of Concord township, Chester Co., Pa., deeded in fee-tail by MARY'S father to HENRY GEST. There HENRY died March 14, 1739. MARY.

VIII. 1 JOHN. 2 WILLIAM. 3 JAMES. 4 HENRY. 5 DAVID. 6 7 BENJAMIN. 8 HANNAH.

JOSEPH GEST, the 6th son, b. about 1722; soon after his father's death settled in Sadsbury township, Lancaster Co., and there lived upon the same tract of land until his death, April 23, 1815. = DEBORAH, daughter of JOSEPH and ELIZABETH (*née* MILLER) DICKINSON of Salisbury township, Lancaster Co., at Friends' Meeting, Sadsbury, July 31, 1765. She was born Dec. 3, 1746–47; d. 7th Nov., 1825.

IX. 1 ELIZABETH. 2 MARY. 3 HANNAH. 4 ANN. 5 DANIEL. 6 7 MARGARET. 8 HENRY. 9 DEBORAH. 10 11 BENJAMIN.

JOSEPH GEST m. REBEKAH MOORE at Sadsbury Friends' Meeting, April 14, 1813. JOSEPH, b. 4th March, 1776; d. Feb. 23, 1863. REBEKAH, b. Aug. 15, 1791; d. Feb. 24, 1869. They removed to Cincinnati in 1818, and there buried in Spring Grove Cemetery.

JOHN GEST m. ANN BARNARD at London Grove Friends' Meeting, Dec. 15, 1819. JOHN, b. May 17, 1783; d. Dec. 15, 1865. ANN, b. Sept. 26, 1792; d. Dec. 14, 1883. They resided in Philadelphia from 1810 to 1845. Are buried at Sadsbury.

X. CLARISSA, ERASMUS, JOSEPH JOHN. All of whom are living, 1884, of whom only JOSEPH JOHN GEST married, his wife being SUSANNAH BAILEY of Clinton Co, Ohio. They reside at "Wintrebourne," a suburb of Cincinnati on the Kentucky side. Their children living:

X. MARY ANN, living at Christiana. JOSEPH died, left a daughter MARY. JOHN B. GEST, living in Philadelphia. DEBORAH m. LEVI POWNELL; a widow. ELIZABETH m. DAVID T. JONES; a widow. JACOB T., deceased, unmarried. JOHN BARNARD GEST m. ELIZABETH A. PURVES; residence, Philadelphia. Their children, all living:

XI. 1st, JOSEPH HENRY GEST.
2d, CLIFFORD H. GEST.
3d, GUYON MOORE GEST.
4th, REBEKAH GEST.
5th, KARL GEST.

XI. 1st, ALEXANDER P. GEST.
2d, LEYDIA GEST.
3d, JOHN MARSHALL GEST.
4th, WILLIAM PURVES GEST

NOTE.—WILLIAM FRANCIS STRATFORD DUGDALE, b. 1872, thirteenth English generation, nearly corresponds with JOSEPH HENRY GEST, b. 1862, eleventh American generation. In other words, two less generations west of the Atlantic cover corresponding period of time to the east, and indicate, at least so far as this family is concerned, greatest longevity in the United States.

ANCESTORS OF { MARY CLEMSON, wife of HENRY GEST; DEBORAH DICKINSON, wife of JOSEPH GEST, Sr ; REBEKAH MOORE, wife of JOSEPH GEST; ANN BARNARD, wife of JOHN GEST; and ISAAC HAINES, husband of HANNAH, sister of JOSEPH and JOHN GEST. }

CAPT STARR, of the Parliament Army, after the war, settled in Ireland

BENJAMIN and MARY CANBY resided at Thorn, Yorkshire, England, 1668

JACOB CLEMSON, Acrelius mentions as one of the early Swedes on the Delaware

MATHEW and JANE DICKINSON of Cumberland Co., England, had son, DANIEL DICKINSON, who maintained 10,000 sheep, was K B C He settled his son, DANIEL DICKINSON, near Londonderry, Ireland, in 1696 This Daniel's son went to America, 1725

JAMES MOORE and family resided in Co Antram, Ireland

JOHN and MARY STARR of Cort-hill, Cavan after of Meath Co., Ireland

THOMAS CANBY arrived at Philadelphia, July, 1684, settled in Bucks Co, m SARAH JERVIS, Oct 2, 1693

GUYON MILLER and wife, MARGARET (HENDERSON), left Co Armagh, Ireland, 1702 Settled in Kennot township

ANDREW MOORE and wife, MARGARET, daughter of GUYON and MARGARET MILLER, with son JAMES, came (1723) to Sadsbury, Lancaster Co

JAMES and SARAH CLEMSON, a family of means at Chichester, 1699, Chester Co

JEREMIAH STARR and REBECCA (JACKSON) m Nov 10, 1716 Settled in London Grove, Chester Co., 1717

THOMAS CANBY, b Aug 12, 1702

MARY CLEMSON m 1716, HENRY GEST, settled on 300 acres of land in S W corner Concord township, Chester Co

JOSEPH DICKINSON m ELIZABETH MILLER, Aug 25, 1732, at Chester and New Castle Monthly Meeting Settled in Piqua Valley Salisbury township, Lancaster Co JOSEPH left the home in Ireland, given him by his father, came to Chester Co., 1725

JAMES MOORE (b 1716) m Feb 16, 1741, ANN STARR (b Nov 1, 1717), at New Garden Monthly Meeting, by whom he had children,—ANDREW, JEREMIAH, JOHN, JAMES, REBEKAH, and ANN

BENJAMIN CANBY (b June 29, 1726) m MARTHA WHITSON, Oct 5, 1752

JOSEPH GEST (b about 1722) m DEBORAH DICKINSON (b Twelfth month 3, 1746), at Sadsbury Monthly Meeting, Seventh month 11, 1765, and resided upon the 200 acre tract previously acquired by JOSEPH in that township, Lancaster Co JOSEPH d April 25, 1815, DEBORAH Nov 7, 1825 They had eleven children, of whom MARY, ANN, DAVID d young, HENRY, DEBORAH'S twin-brother, also died young, DEBORAH d in Sadsbury, First month 13, 1872, aged 92 years, never married ELIZABETH m JOHN MOORE, HANNAH m ISAAC HAINES, JOSEPH m REBEKAH MOORE, MARGARET m JOHN WILLIAMS, JOHN m ANN BARNARD, BENJAMIN m MARY CANBY

JAMES MOORE (b Aug 8 1761), Miller, Farmer, and Physician, m 2d JANE CANBY (b Jan 4, 1772) of Bucks Co JAMES d April 3, 1842, and JANE Sept 21, 1839 Their children,—BENJAMIN, REBEKAH, JAMES C., ANN, SARAH, JANE, CANBY, LEWIS, JOHN B., ELLIS P., and HENRY

JOSEPH GEST (b March 4, 1776, at Sadsbury) m April 14, 1813, REBEKAH MOORE (b July 15, 1791), at Sadsbury Monthly Meeting In which township, Lancaster Co, they resided until 1817, when they removed, with their daughter, CLARISSA (a child) to Cincinnati, Ohio, their after home JOSEPH d Feb 23, 1863, REBEKAH, Feb 24, 1869, buried in Spring Grove Cemetery Their surviving children (1884), CLARISSA, ERASMUS, JOSEPH JOHN, reside in Cincinnati, O

JOHN HAINES (son of RICHARD) was settled, 1683, in a cave, where now is Lamberton, New Jersey, m Oct. 10, 1684, ESTHER BOSTON

ABIAH TAYLOR of Didcot, Berkshire Co, England

WILLIAM PASSMORE of Ruscomb Parish, Berks Co, England, m Jan 6, 1654, MARGERY BALL

GEORGE STRODE of Millbrook, Southampton, England, purchased of Penn, 1682, 500 acres, Concord township

ELIZABETH, daughter of EVAN PROTHERO of Wales, m Nov 4, 1694, MORGAN JAMES She d 1737

ISAAC HAINES m CATHERINE DAVID, 1714 In 1717 settled on 254 acres N E side West Chester, Chester Co

RICHARD BARNARD, b 1611, d 1698, from Sheffield, England, 1682, to Middletown, Chester Co First wife DEBORAH, second, FRANCES

ABIAH TAYLOR m DEBORAH, daughter of JOHN GEARING, at Farrington Meeting, Feb 18, 1694 Moved from Berkshire, England, and settled on the Brandywine, 1702 He d 1747

JOHN PASSMORE m MARY, daughter of HUMPHRY BUXCEY, in England Nov 3, 1701 Settled in Kennot, 1714, after in West Moreland township He d about 1746

JOHN STRODE m MAGDALENE JAMES of Newtown, Chester (now Delaware) Co, Pennsylvania

ISAAC HAINES, JR (b Aug 10, 1718) m MARY COX, Aug 5, 1744

RICHARD BARNARD m Dec 7, 1715, ANN TAYLOR, b 1695 He was b Chester Co., 1684, d 1767 Land in Hill Town

GEORGE PASSMORE m MARGARET STRODE Sept 10, 1742 Both b in West Marlborough, Chester Co, he Feb 23, 1719, she

ISAAC HAINES (b) m LYDIA DAVIS, 1772

JEREMIAH BARNARD m June 6, 1787, at London Grove Meeting, MARY PASSMORE, b Dec 18, 1753, in West Marlborough, Chester Co., and there d Jan 13, 1830 JEREMIAH was b in same township, Jan 1, 1717, d Aug 28, 1799 To their marriage certificate both signed "BERNARD"

ISAAC HAINES m HANNAH GEST, Tenth month 27, 1790 ISAAC d Second month 11, 1840, HANNAH d Eighth month 9, 1847

JOHN GEST m ANN BARNARD, at London Grove Monthly Meeting, Dec 15, 1819 ANN, b West Marlborough Chester Co, Sept 26, 1792, d in Christiana township, Lancaster Co, Dec 14, 1883 JOHN GEST b Sadsbury township, Lancaster Co, May 17, 1783, and there d Dec 15, 1865 This family resided in Philadelphia from 1810 to 1845, after at Sadsbury Their surviving children (1884) —MARY ANN, resides at Christiana, Lancaster Co, Pa, JOHN BARNARD GEST, at Philadelphia, DEBORAH, widow of LEVI POWNELL, in Sadsbury township, Lancaster Co, ELIZABETH, widow of DAVID T JONES, at Christiana, Pa, JOSEPH and JACOB T, both deceased JOSEPH left one daughter, MARY L, living in N J, unmarried

CHAPTER XL

DARBY TOWNSHIP

In alluding to the name of the municipal district which in early times included Upper and Lower Darby as one township, Dr Smith says, "Perhaps the opinion is universal that our ancestors, who came from the county of Derby, in England, corrupted the spelling of the name in their former place of residence when they, in kind remembrance, adopted it for their home in America The corruption, if it be one, was effected in England before our ancestors migrated to America In the 'New World of Words,' published in 1671, *Darby* and *Darbyshire* are given, but not Derby or Derbyshire, and in the certificates brought over by early Friends, it is almost uniformly spelled with *a* instead of *e* The author of the work referred to makes the name of the English town a contraction of the word Derwentty, 'because it standeth on the river Derwent' This would make the proper spelling of the name *Derby*, but it is clear that our ancestors brought the name with them as it was generally written when they migrated to America, and so it has remained, notwithstanding some fastidious persons have made efforts from time to time to change it "[1]

Darby was settled almost immediately after the coming of Penn, and in 1683 was recognized as one of the localities where a permanent lodgment had been made, but, despite that fact, the population must have been sparse for more than a quarter of a century, for Mrs Ann Davis, who was born at Darby—she was the daughter of John Bethel, the miller—informed Dr William Martin, in 1790, "that she was born in the place where Darby now is, and remembered playing with the Indian children in the neighboring wigwams "[2] In 1684 Darby Friends' Meeting had been established, the members meeting at the dwelling of John Blunston, which was located nearly in front of the present meeting-house, and near the mill-race which was "digged" through Blunston's meadow In the same year the first official record of Darby occurs in the list of collectors "to gather the assessment for the building of the court-house " Thomas Worth and Joshua Fearne were appointed to those offices for Darby, and Mons Stacker and William Cobb "for Amosland & Calcoone Hook." The latter was recognized as a distinct municipal district until 1686, when Calcoone Hook was made a part of Darby township, and Amosland was annexed to Ridley

Calcon or Calkoen's Hook comprised all the territory between Cobb's Creek on the east, and the Mokorampates Kill or Muckinipattas Creek on the west, and derives its name from the Swedish word *Kalkon*, "a turkey," *Wulda Kalkoen*, "wild turkeys," having "very much abound in that vicinity "[3] Later the territory known by that name became restricted to that part lying south of the Philadelphia, Wilmington and Baltimore Railroad, while its eastern boundary was Morhorhootink, as shown in the atlas of the early grants in Delaware County The historical map of Pennsylvania terms the stream *Tenakong Kolen*, and Acrelius says that "Nyecks Kihl" was the Indian name of Darby Creek, which it will be difficult to convince the public ought to be accepted as a term known to the Indian tongue, even on the authority of the usually accurate historian of New Sweden On June 18, 1668, Governor Lovelace issued a patent to Israel Helme, Hendrick Jacobson, Ole Kock, and Jan Minsterman for that "portion of land on West side of Delaware River within the Mill Kill upon the Hook commonly called Calcoone Hook, reaching from the said mill kill to that which is called by the Indians Mokornippates, including all the lands between the said two Kills as also the valley or meadow ground thereunto belonging, containing by estimation as it lies along the river (creek) side about an English mile, and there being also in the said Mill Kill, a certain little Island near unto and over against the said land known by the name of 'hay Island,' as the said land was granted Aug 4th 1663 to Ericke Nichels, Moorty Poulson, Andreas Johnson & Henry Jacobson, the three former of whom afterwards parted with their rights thereto "[4] The territory mentioned in the patent included almost all the land in the township south of the Queen's Highway, and west of a line drawn due south from the toll-gate on that road On this tract the real estate of the Sharon Land Association, incorporated by act of Assembly March 4, 1871, is located The Calcoon Hook road, which enters the Queen's Highway at the toll gate, is first alluded to at the court held Oct 3, 1691, when complaint was made to court "concerning a way to ye landing at Calcon Hooks, ye inhabitants there being at difference about it To end ye discourd the Co^{rt} ordered ye Grand Inquest to lay out a road & make return of ye same at next court " At the subsequent sessions the following report was submitted to the justices, approved, and was the route on which the road was afterwards opened to public use and travel

"Grand Jury return road in Darby township to Landing place at Calcon Hook The s^{d} road to begin at a corner stone near to an ash tree by ye creek side at ye bottome of Morton Mortonson orchard, then on a straight line four perches to another corner stone being at the lower corner of s^{d} Morton's orchard, then continuing the s^{d} straight line eleven perches and four feet to a corner stone near ye upper end of s^{d} orchard which s^{d} stone standith on ye outermost straight line mentioned in Mounce Pettersons deed from Andrew Swanson Bone Then continuing a line at thirty two feet distance, the end of s^{d} Morton's house being built before ye s^{d} road was agreed upon, standing about six foot in ye s^{d} road, excepted from said Mounce Pettersons fence to the end Still continuing ye s^{d} Line through ye woods to a tree with notches by ye road agreed on among themselves to Darby, thence along ye severall corses of

[1] History of Delaware County, p. 384

[2] Martin's "History of Chester," p 251

[3] Record of Upland Court, p 197

[4] Smith's "History of Delaware County," p 520

ye sd road to ye Kings road at ye Easternmost corner of Thomas ffoxes, from thence turning Northeasterly at thirty two feet distance, from the aforesaid line back again on ye several corses, still continuing thirty two feet distance ye sd Morton's House End extend as aforesaid to the cross way near ye sd Morton's house then upon a strait line across ye sd way to a corner stone standing in ye corner of ye Mounce (Pettersons) house fence being also ye corner of ye cross roads, from thence down in a straight line down past and so forth to another corner stone standing by ye sd Mouncy's house fence side making here the road thirty two foot from aforesaid stone at the lower corner of the sd Morton's orchard then along by sd Morton's corner of ye sd Morwin's farm, from which sd stone to ye first mentioned stone it is six perches and two foot broad "

On the Mokormpates Kill, and just above the northern line of the Calcoon Hook patent, was a tract of two hundred and fifty acres, known in early times as "Boon's Forest," which was laid out to Andres Swason Boon April 13, 1680 From this sturdy Swedish settler a greater man descended, or at least he has secured more of the world's attention, than did his ancestor in Delaware County,—Daniel Boone, the pioneer of Kentucky On the Boon tract the Knowles Presbyterian Church is located To the east of Boon's land, extending to Darby Creek, was a tract of two hundred and fifty, entered to Surveyor-General Thomas Holme, Dec 10, 1683, and July 1, 1688 John Blunston, as the agent of Holme, acknowledged a deed in open court conveying this estate to Joseph Wood The property not only reached to Darby Creek, but a strip extended along the north line of Boon's land to the Muckinipattus Creek, as the stream forming the western boundary of Darby township is now called, and on that part of the estate Horntown is located Above this tract, extending from creek to creek, was "Good Intent," a plantation of two hundred acres, which was surveyed to Edward Gibbs July 12, 1683 Immediately north of this estate was a tract of three hundred acres, taken up by Thomas Brassey, March 15-16, 1681, who never resided thereon, but sold the property to John Bartram Aug 30, 1685 On this plantation John Bartram, the earliest American botanist, was born, May 23, 1699 His early attention was first directed to botanical studies by one of those accidents which seem to shape the destinies of all great men When a mere lad, he was plowing on the Darby farm, and uprooted a daisy Despite everything the modest little flower kept intruding itself on his consideration, until after several days he hired a man to plow while he rode to Philadelphia to procure a treatise on botany and a Latin grammar He, fortunately for himself and the world, had inherited a farm from a bachelor uncle, which gave him the means to marry early, and purchase the land on which he afterwards established the noted "Botanic Gardens" On this estate he built with his own hands a stone house, and on one of the stones in the gable was the inscription,—"John * Ann Bartram, 1831," with a star between their first names, as was then the custom, to indicate man and wife Here he pursued his studious habits, his reputation spreading abroad until correspondence was solicited by the leading botanists of the Old World,—Linnæus, Dr Fothergill, and others,—while in the colonies, all scientific men in the same line of study sought his favor, advice, and opinions Dr Franklin was his earnest friend, and constantly urged Bartram to authorship His fame had so extended that in 1765 George III appointed him botanist to the king He died Sept 22, 1777, in the seventy-ninth year of his age

Above the Bartram farm a tract of three hundred acres, reaching to the Upper Darby line, which was taken up by William, John, and Thomas Smith, Aug 30, 1685, to each of whom a plot of one hundred acres was allotted John Smith came from Harly, County of Leicester, England, and resided on the estate until 1714 It is presumed that William and Thomas were of the same family, but the exact relationship is not known That part of the Thomas and John Smith tract lying to the east of the Springfield road and west of Darby Creek became the property of John Ash His heirs resided at the old homestead until their deaths In the spring of 1862, within six weeks, Hannah, aged seventy-six years, James, seventy-four, Sarah, seventy-eight, and Alice Ash, aged eighty years, died They were all unmarried, and had lived there all their lives "Their habits were those of the world before the flood, retiring to their beds at five o'clock in the afternoon, having no furniture in their house but what had been purchased prior to the Revolution, and some of them, it was said, and perhaps correctly, never having visited that den of iniquities, the city of Philadelphia" On the east of Darby Creek, at the Upper Darby line, on Sept 10, 1682, was surveyed to Thomas Worth two hundred and fifty acres, which he had purchased prior to leaving England He was a man of superior education for that day, and was a member of the Provincial Assembly in 1697 He lived to an advanced age, dying in 1731 Below Worth's plantation, John Blunston, on Aug 10, 1682, acquired three hundred and fifty acres of land, and he is said to have given the name of Darby to the settlement, in remembrance of his old home in England The fact that the mill-race was cut through his land, and after John Bethel purchased the Darby mills, the right to use this mill-race was conveyed by Blunston, seems to indicate that he was the first person who operated the mills there The tract of two hundred and twenty-two acres bounded on the east by Cobb's Creek, and to the west by Church Lane, was taken up by Samuel Bradshaw Aug 10, 1682, the date of the early surveys to Penn's adherents, many of whom, it is said, accompanied the proprietary in the "Welcome," and located in the neighborhood of Darby He emigrated from Oxton, County Nottingham, and the estate passed to Thomas Bradshaw, March 5, 1697/8, who, it is thought, was a brother of Samuel To the south of Bradshaw's and partly of John Blunston's tracts was a plot of fifty acres, bounded on the east by Cobb's Creek, and on the west by Blunston's Run, which was surveyed, Nov.

10, 1682, to William Smith, and to the west of the Smith land, in irregular lines, were one hundred acres patented to Peter Erickson, Nov. 30, 1681, the Matthew Baird estate is partly located on this tract. The property was subsequently absorbed, May 29, 1685, into the large plantation of Joseph Wood, on which the village of Darby was originally laid out.

In December, 1739, George Whitefield, the celebrated preacher, left Philadelphia for Chester accompanied by about one hundred and fifty horsemen.[1] On his way he stopped at Darby. Bamfylde-Moore Carew, the noted king of the English mendicants, who was escaping from servitude in Virginia, records that while on his way from Chester to Darby, "but before he reached there, he was overtaken by hundreds of people going to hear Mr. Whitefield preach. He joined them, and they all proceeded to Darby, where he found Mr. Whitefield preaching in an orchard, but could not get near enough to hear his discourse by reason of the great concourse of people." The artful rogue, however, afterwards went to the house where the clergyman was stopping, and by a forged letter and a piteous story succeeded in obtaining several pounds in the paper money of Pennsylvania from Whitefield, as he had done the day before from Mrs. Turner, in Chester.

Watson, the annalist, informs us that William Taylor, who came from England in 1726 and settled at Darby, was the first person to make a pair of smith's bellows in the English colonies, if not in North America. We know that in 1739 the commissioners appointed to adjust the boundary-line between Maryland and Pennsylvania, in surveying to ascertain the proper starting-point for the due west line, passed through the township, for Friday, April 13, 1739, they reported,—"The Surveyors proceeded on the Line till Evening, and left off in the lands of Thomas Worth, in Darby Township,"[2] which was located in the northern end of the present township, and east of Darby Creek.

The marshes of Darby Creek, until after the middle of the last century, were often covered with water, until by that reason many of the farms adjacent became almost valueless. The advantage of the bottom-lands as places for pasture was appreciated by some of the early farmers, but it required a few years before a sufficient number could be educated to urge the passage of the act of March 4, 1763, which impowered the owners and possessors of the southern district of Darby marsh or meadow ground to embank and drain such lands, and to keep the outside banks and dams in good repair forever. The act authorized the raising of a fund, and by certain compulsory process to enforce payment from unwilling land-owners. The land thus reclaimed has become of great value and is very productive.

1 Watson's Annals, vol. i. p. 538.

2 Penna. Archives, vol. i. p. 605.

Roads.—On the 25th of May, 1695, a petition was presented to the Provincial Council from the residents of Chester, asking for a "ferrie att the rocks," which prayer was acceded to and Benjamin Chambers, who had received a patent for lands on the western side of the Schuylkill, was authorized to keep a ferry there, which previous to 1747 had passed into the ownership of George Gray. On Sept. 3, 1701, a complaint was laid before the Provincial Council "by some of the Inhabitants of Darby Township against some parts of a road laid out by the Govr's order, from B. Chamber's fferry, through Darby Township to Edgmont. Ordered that Nicholas Pyle, Sam'l Levis, Geo. Maires, & Randal Vernon, all of Chester County, do on ye sixth day next, that one being ye 12th instant, view the controverted parts of the said Road, beginning at the said fferry, and upon a Due Consideration of the allegations on both sides, to give their judgment whether the s^d Road is conveniently laid out for a Cart Road, as it now is, or whether it may not, with equal Conveniency for the said purpose and advantage to the Public, as well as Justice to each particular in all respects, be laid out otherwise according to the complaint's desires, and make report thereof to this Board in writing, at the next session."[3] If any report was ever made it does not appear in the official papers of the State, as published.

At a court held Feb. 9, 1687, the following report was approved by the court, which road is still used, and now known as the Radnor and Darby road:

"A Highway laid out by ye grand Jury and other neighbours betwixt Hartfort and Darby vpon ye 7th day of the twelfe moneth, 1687. Beginning at Widdow Panthir's, and from thence on ye head lyne betwixt ye said Widdows land and ye land of John Levis, from thence crosse ye land of William Howell, from thence crosse ye land of Arthur Bruce, from thence crosse ye land of Henry Levis, thence Entering the Township of Darby, from thence Crosse ye land of Adam Roads, thence Crosse ye land of John Kirk, thence Crosse ye land of William Garrett, then crosse ye land of Michael Blunstone, then Crosse ye land of George Wood, then Crosse ye land of Robert Smith, then Crosse ye land of Thomas Worth, then coming vpon the land of Joshua ffrne, soe downe ye Towne street of Darby to ye Kings Road, and soe to ye Landing; this Highway to be sixty foote as needs requires.

"William Garrett. "Thomas Bradshaw.
"Richard Parker. "Thomas ffox."
"Edmond Castledge.

The Queen's Highway.—The Southern Post road from Darby to Chester, Edward Armstrong states, was the earliest highway laid out by authority in Pennsylvania. While that assertion may be correct, there is no evidence, so far as the records show, to establish the fact that the road was ordered by the Governor and Council, the only power authorized to make such ways. Previous to the coming of William Penn all roads led to Chester, not to Philadelphia; and while we hear of suspervisors for Darby, Ridley, and Chester townships soon after Penn's arrival, there is no evidence to show the public requirement of a road to Philadelphia. Hence we may accept the latter way as simply a compliance with the

3 Colonial Records, vol. ii. p. 33.

order made Nov 12, 1678, that "the court this day ordered that Every p'son should, w^th^in the space of two months, as far as his land Reaches, make good and passable wayes, from neighbour to neighbour, wth bridges where itt needs, To the end that neighbours on occasions may come together Those neglecting, to forfit 25 gilders" Indeed, the petition presented to Council March 19, 1705/6, corroborates the foregoing statement The petition is as follows

"*To the Hon'ble John Evans, Esq, Lieut.-Governor of the Province of Pennsylvania and the Three Lower Counties, and to his Council*

"The Humble petetion of the Inhabitants of the town and County of Chester and others, humbly showeth That whereas, by ye Laws of this Government, ye sole power of laying out of the Queen's Road is lodged in the Governor and Council, and whereas the Town of Chester is daily improving, and In time may become a great place, and very advantageous to the Propriatour, but forasmuch as most of the People of that place concerned In the Improvement is much discouraged for want of a direct Road from thence to Philadelphia, wee, your Petitioners, whose names are hereunto subscribed, do beg the Governor and Councill that an ord'r may be granted to fitt and proper persons to lay out the Queen's Road on as direct a Line as can be from Darby, to answer the bridge on Chester Creek, and your petitioners in duty bound will ever pray

"Edward Dutton
Jonathan Ruttland
David Powell
John Wiley
Isaac Taylour
Charles Booth
Joshua Calvert
Richard Prichard
John Houldston
Samuel Bishop
Jonathan Hayes
John Grubb
Henry Hollidgsworth
George Simpson
Peter Trego
James Swaffer
Edward Jennings
Morgan Jones
James Chivers
David Lloyd
Jasper Yeates
James Sandelands
John Hoskins
John Wade
Paul Sanders
Robert Barber
Saml Tomlinson
David Merredith
Edward Danger
John Hekenes
Thomas Oldham
Thomas Bauldwin
Joseph Richards
Walter Martin
Tho Powell
Nicholas Fairlamb
Moses Key
Henry Coburn
Nathan Baker
Geo Chandler
John Worrall
James Hendrickson
Richard Crosby
Joseph Clowd
Edward Wilburn
Thomas Buffington
Edward Elwell
Jonathan Munrow
John Morton
David Jones
James Thomas
Joseph Baker
David Lewis
William Gregory
Ephraim Jackson
Edward Kennison
Phillip Yarnall
John Gibbeans
Roger Jackson
Richard Addams
John Childe
Ralph Fishburn
Wm Pickells
Wm Huston
David Roberts
Wm Swaffer
Thomas Cartwright
John Bauldine.
John Test
John Test, Jr
John Dutton
Thomas Dutton
Alexander Badcock
George Woodiar
John Bristow
George Oldfield
John Sharples
Thos Vernon
Jeremiah Collett, Sr
Mordecai Howell
Israel Taylor
Jeremiah Collett, Jr
Humphrey Johnston"

Council in response to this petition ordered,—

"That the said Road be laid accordingly and if there shall be occasion for building a bridge over any Navigable creek or water for the greater conveniency of Travelling the said Road, that such bridge shall be so built that the same may in nowise hinder any boats from passing up or down such creek or water And it is further Ordered y^t^ Jasper Yates, Caleb Pusey, Jeremiah Collett, Robert Barber and John Hendrickson, or any four of them, do survey and lay out the said Roads, and that they return as soon as they can to the Board,—Under their hands and seals an exact draught setting forth the several courses thereof"[1]

This road was laid out, and bitter feeling was engendered against several of the commissioners, particularly Jasper Yeates, for the manner in which the road was surveyed The people of that day declared that his influence carried the highway through Chester at the point it did, so that his own and his father-in-law's estate might be benefited thereby "God and Nature," it was asserted, "intended the road to cross directly across the creek, but the Devil and Jasper Yeates took it where it was located" However, it was so laid, and at the August court, 1706, the sheriff was directed "forthwith" to give notice "to the Supervisors of the highways for Chester, Ridley, and Darby for clearing the new Road lately laid out by the Governor & Councill leading from Darby to Chester and further that they, the Supervisors, do without delay, upon notice thereof, cause the same new Road to be opened and cleared fifty foot wide" Previous to that road being laid out the highway to Philadelphia was considerably to the north of the present post-road, so that creeks could be crossed above tide-water at the fords The King's Highway of the early days, if it could be called such, crossed Ridley township almost in a straight line from Irvington to Darby William Worrall, whose recollections were written by Judge George G Leiper, in 1820 (Worrall was born in 1730), and published in the newspapers of that time, stated that frequently, in plowing his fields, the plowshare would throw up nails or other articles dropped by the settlers in journeying across the land. He pointed out to Judge Leiper the course of the old road which Penn and his followers took when on their way by land to Philadelphia, as it passed through his farm

The road laid out in 1706 in time having fallen in bad condition, many of the residents refused to work on the highway, alleging that it was never officially confirmed and was not a legal road, and, moreover, except for a very short distance, the traveled road was from twenty to forty perches south of the route surveyed in 1706 The dispute could only be adjusted by the Provincial Council Hence on Aug 17, 1747, the following petition of George Gray and others was presented to Council

"*To the Honourable, the President and Council of the Province of Pennsylvania*

"The humble Petition of George Gray, Keeper of the lower Ferry over Schuylkill, on the Road from the City of Philadelphia to Chester, and of others, living in the County of Chester, and using the said Road, Sheweth,

"That the said Road, leading from the south street of the said City over the said Ferry to Cobb's Creek Bridge, near Darby, in the County of Chester, has Time out of Mind been the only old and accustomed Road to Darby, Chester, Newcastle, and the Lower Counties

---

[1] This petition was for the first time printed in Martin's "History of Chester," p 59, it being copied from the manuscript in the 'Logan Papers," vol iv marked "Roads," in possession of the Historical Society of Pennsylvania

"That the Inhabitants of the Townships through which the same Road passes, not doubting its being a recorded Road, have hitherto duly repaired and amended the same, but now being apprized that it either has not been regularly recorded, or that the Record thereof cannot be found, so that they are not obliged to repair the same or contribute thereto, the said Road is at present much out of Repair, and, growing worse, will, in the Winter, become utterly impassable or dangerous to travel with Horses, Chaises, or other Carriages, unless the same be repaired before the ensuing Winter That your Petitioners are informed that if the said Road was surveyed and recorded according to Law, the same would and ought to be from Time to Time repaired by the Inhabitants of the Townships through which the same lyes, whereby the same, being a great and much travelled Road, would become safe and passable

"Therefore your Petitioners humbly pray the Honourable the President and Council would be pleased to grant an Order or Warrant for surveying the said Road, so that it may be surveyed and recorded and sufficiently amended and kept in Repair, or that you would please to give such other Order or Warrant concerning the same as the Nature of the case may require

"And your Petitioners will ever pray, &c

"Joseph Bonsall	Geo Gray
Samuel Levis.	George Wood
John Davis.	Jonathan Paschall
Job Harvey	Thos Pearson
Samuel Bunting	William Horne "[1]

At the same meeting of Council a petition from the commissioners and sundry inhabitants of the county of Chester was presented, which stated that "it appears after strict search made that there are divers parts of the king's road leading from Cobb's Creek Bridge, over Chester Bridge, to the line of New Castle County, not to be found upon Record or any return thereof," and for "the Benefit of the Publick" respecting the erection of bridges and repairs to the highways, requested the appointment of persons "to lay out such Parts of the said Road as are deficient."

To these petitions Council replied that "as the Road mention'd is an antient Road, in use before the Grant of the Province, the Board thinks there must have been some Orders of Council made about it, &, therefore, postpone the Consideration thereof till the Council Books be well search'd by the Secretary, & it be known what Orders have been formerly given "[2] At the meeting of Council, Sept. 8, 1747, the secretary reported that he had examined "the council Books, and had found several orders of Council for laying out the several Parts of the said Road, and likewise the Record of that part of the said Road which lies between Darby & Chester," that he was of opinion that the whole road had been actually laid out, and that the returns were given to the late secretary, Patrick Robinson, who had omitted to enter them in the books of Council, and that his papers, both public as well as private, came into the hands of "his Wido' upon his decease," were lost or destroyed, and the returns of the road might be among those missing papers Council, however, ordered that the road should be resurveyed, beginning at the south boundary of the city of Philadelphia, thence to the lower ferry (Gray's), thence to Darby Creek, and "thence by the courses described in the recorded Return made in the year 1706 to Chester Bridge, & from thence by the present Courses thereof to the Limits of New Castle government "[3] Caleb Cowpland, Esq, Joseph Parker, Esq, Joseph Bonsall, Esq, Samuel Levis, James Mather, John Davies, Peter Dicks, Thomas Pearson, and John Sketchley, of Chester County, or any five of them, were instructed to join the persons named for Philadelphia County, or any three of them, "in continuing to lay out as aforesaid the said Road from the Division Line which parts Philadelphia County from Chester County to the Limits of Newcastle" The surveyor-general was also directed to assist them in the survey They were to report by the first day of October, 1747

On the day designated the surveyor-general reported to Council that he, with the persons who had been appointed to lay out the road from Philadelphia to New Castle, had met and the road had been laid out as far as Darby, but from this point they could go no farther, unless Council would alter the order, which directed the surveyor and those associated with him in making the highway to conform to the courses of a road "said to be laid out between Darby & Chester Creeks in the Year 1706 & give the same directions as to that part of the Road which they had given as to all other parts, viz' to follow the Courses of the Road as it is now used The Council considering that that part of the Road was actually laid out, returned and Recorded, tho' it does not appear ever to have been cleared or taken Notice of, did not incline to come to any determination till they shou'd receive full Information how it would affect the Inhabitants and the Possessors of Lands between Darby & Chester "[4]

On March 2, 1748, the following petition from persons living along the road from Darby to Chester was presented to the Provincial Council

"*To the Honoble the President and Council of the Province of Pennsylvania, &c*

"*Whereas*, You was pleased by Your Order bearing date the 8th Day of September last to appoint us, the subscribers, with some others, to lay a Road out from Cobb's Creek to New Castle line, with directions to follow the Road as now used, where it is not already laid out, and where it is to follow the Courses & Distances therein mentioned in order (as we presume) to prevent as much as might be injuring the Owners of the Land adjacent to the s^d Road We, therefore, in obedience to the said Order, met at Cobb's Creek Bridge, and took the courses and Distances of the Road as now used, until we came to that part of the Road which leads from Darby to Chester, and has been laid out by courses & Distance, & then upon trying the courses thereof found them to run a considerable distance in divers Places from the Road now used, & that frequently through Improved as well as wood Lands, and would in our opinion be very injurious to a Great number of the Inhabitants adjacent to the Road & as we conceive very contrary to Your Intention

"Therefore we pray, in behalf of ourselves & others, that you wou'd be pleased to appoint a Jury and Grant them such Powers as you may think proper to enable them to lay out a Road in the most convenient Place to accomodate the Publick & least injurious to the Inhabitants, which We apprehend is agreeable to Your Design, & we as in Duty bound shall ever Pray

"Samuel Levis	Caleb Cowpland
"Joseph Bonsall	Peter Dicks
"John Davis	

"December 3d, 1747

[1] Penna Archives, 1st Series, vol i p 767

[2] Colonial Records, vol v p. 100

[3] Ib., p 107

[4] Ib, p 121

"And Mr. Bonsall & Mr. Davis attending without were called in, & on their Examination & Inspection of a Draught of the Road as it wou'd run was it to be made agreeable to the Return of the Year 1706, and of another Draught of the Road as it now runs, the Board made the following Order, viz.:

"*Whereas*, by our Order of the Eighth Day of September last, We directed You, among others to lay out the Road leading from Darby to Chester, agreeable to the Courses described in a Recorded Return of the same made in the Year 1706: *And whereas*, on Examination of several Persons living on or near the same Road, it appears that the same was never actually cleared according to said Return, and that was it to be now it won'd exceedingly prejudice the land through which it shou'd pass, and on further consideration of the matter & perusal of the Draught of the Road as it now runs, it appears to us that it will be most convenient to have it laid out agreeable thereto, And therefore we have thought proper to revoke that part of our former Order which relates to the Return made in 1706, and Do now Order & Direct that You lay the same Road out in the manner it now runs, making no alterations that what may be absolutely necessary to make it more regular & direct in some Places, or more commodious to the Fording Places or Bridges that are now used on the said Road."[1]

Division of Upper and Lower Darby.—The territory now constituting the townships of Upper and Lower Darby continued under one municipal government until 1747, when, for the convenience of the inhabitants, at a town-meeting, it was decided to separate the upper part from the lower in all matters save the levies made for the support of the poor. The lines thus agreed upon are not the township lines now existing, but Upper Darby, being less densely peopled, extended farther south. The inconveniences arising from the unofficial division so frequently presented themselves as a disturbing element in local government that forty years thereafter the following petition was presented to the court:

"*To the Justices of the Court of General Quarter Sessions to be held at Chester the 3d day of May*, 1786:

"The undersigned, Inhabitants of Darby Township, Respectfully Sheweth:

"That the Townships of Darby hath been hereto Considered as one Township, tho' it was many years ago divided by the Inhabitants for their own Conveniency, which temporary division we desire the Court to confirm by the following line, Beginning at Cobb's Creek on the Northwest side of a tract of land belonging to the heirs of Joshua Ash and in the line of said land, thence along said line and the line of land late Enoch Bonsall's & Joshua Bonsall's To Darby Creek thence down the said Creek to the northwest line of John Ash's land, thence along said line and the line of Samuel Ash and Nathaniel Smith to the line of Ridley Township, and That the lower part may be called Darby and the other part Upper Darby.

"John Sellers.
"Rich'd. Willing,
"As gar[d] to Tho[s]. Phillips.
"Oborn Garrett.
"Nathan Davis.
"Henry Hayes.
"Saml. Smith.
"Jsa. Oakford."

On Aug. 30, 1786, the court granted the prayer of the petitioners.

The Revolution.—The history of Darby township during the struggle of the Revolution should present many stirring incidents, but, unfortunately, little has been preserved of the happenings of that period to the present generation. Early in 1776, a part of Wayne's regiment, under the command of Capt. Lacey, was stationed in or near the village, recruiting from the yeomanry of the neighborhood, and in the summer of the same year Capts. Laurens, William Walker, and Robert Tatnall were in command of gunboats stationed in the creek, a part of the provincial flotilla designed to dispute the passage of the British vessels of war to Philadelphia. On Sunday, Aug. 24, 1777, Washington's army marched through the village and along the Queen's Highway, when moving southward to offer battle to Howe at Brandywine. On the very day of that unpropitious combat the Council of Safety instructed Col. Warner to take post with his command of militia at Darby, and if they were there on Friday, Sept. 12, 1777, they saw the defeated American army as it "poured through Darby on its way to Philadelphia." On 22d of December, Gen. Howe, with seven thousand enemy, marched out from the latter city and encamped on the heights of Darby, his lines extending along the road from Gray's Ferry to the heights below the village, stretching westward up the Springfield road to the then dwelling of Justice Parker, and their pickets advanced to the intersection of the Springfield and Providence roads, near the then dwelling of Mr. Sharp, now the estate of the late Thomas A. Scott. At two o'clock on the afternoon of December 22d, Maj. Clark, from Newtown, wrote to Washington: "My spy was taken by their advanced guard one mile this side of Darby, on the Springfield road, and carried to the general at Darby. They have made a great number of fires. One of their guards assured my spies they were only foraging and meant to proceed toward Chester. I now observe a considerable smoke towards Providence meeting-house. Intelligence from another says they have three hundred wagons with them. . . No wagons had passed Darby before my spy came away."[2]

It was during this raid of the British army that the incident recorded by Dr. Smith occurred. Capt. William Brooke, of Haverford, was with his company of militia in the command of Gen. Potter, whose duty was to harass the enemy and capture straggling parties of Howe's troops. While taking their ease one night in a house late the property of George Swayne, which stood on the south side of the post-road, about midway between Sharon Hill and Glen Olden stations, the house was surrounded by a strong party of British soldiers. Brooke determined, if possible, not to be captured, and to escape by leaping from a window. In getting over the fence by the roadside he found that a partial dislocation of his knee, to which he was subject, had happened, and quickly placing his foot through the bars of the fence he gave his leg a quick extension, which brought the joint into its proper position. He succeeded in making his escape.[3] While Howe was encamped at Darby another American officer had a narrow escape from

1 Colonial Records, vol. v. p. 202.

2 Bulletin of Penna. Hist. Society, vol. i. No. 10, March, 1847, p. 28.

3 History of Delaware County, p. 325.

falling into the hands of the enemy. Maj. Samuel Crozier, who had been in service for two years without a leave of absence, received permission to visit his family, who were then residing near Darby. About sunset a lad came running to the dwelling with the intelligence that a large force of British were close by, and doubtless would visit the house. It was impossible for Crozier to flee without being observed; he therefore crept under a haystack standing near the back-door. His wife, anxious to save the family Bible, placed it under her apron, and apparently as if about attending to some ordinary and accustomed duties, walked to the woods, only a short distance, where she secreted it in a hollow tree. The Bible, which was a copy printed in 1653, is now owned by a great-granddaughter residing in Philadelphia.

Sarah Urian in 1876 had a china plate bearing the legend "God save King George, 1716," and also three pewter platters which were brought by the family from Europe two centuries ago. But the rarest of her relics is a strangely shaped copper kettle, which two hundred and forty years ago was brought to this country in the "Stoork," one of the vessels which conveyed Governor John Printz and his Swedish colonists to this country to make the first permanent settlement, of which we have authentic record, in the province of Pennsylvania. Connected with the china plate is a scrap of Revolutionary history. While the English were in Darby on this raid, a number of British officers dined at the house of Urian, and it chanced that this dish with the face turned downward was on the table. The loyal legend attracted the attention of one of the officers, and he read it to his companions, all of whom indulged in much merriment at the expense of their worthy host.

Gen. Potter, who was keeping an active outlook on the movements of the enemy, on the day Howe retired to Philadelphia, wrote to President Thomas Wharton as follows:

"REDNER (Radnor) Decr. 28th, 1777.

"*Sir*,—On Monday last the enemy came out with a view to Furridge they encamped along the Road from Grays ferry to the heights below Darbey, there was a detachment sent down from our army to this place, who with Morgans Riflemen and the Militia went down to their lines and cept them Close in their line. On Tuesday we took 13 of there light horse and ten of there horsmen, the next day two more of there horses and there Riders, they have been prevented from plundering the Inhabitance as they usely do, there has been but little scrimidging, we had one Killed and two wounded, we have taken upwards of twenty prisoners, and a number of Deserters have cum in, they have carreyed off a larg Quantity of Hay from the Islands and Darbey. It is said that the Highlanders are gon to New York, and Lord Cornwalas is certanly go to great Bitan. I think they have provided there winter Furidge and fuale, and they will bless themselves and sit down in peace this winter in the City—this day they have Returned to the City. My Brigade is near Breacking up, they will be all discharged about the fifth of nixt month but about one hundred men, his Excellency, General Washington, desired me to let you know that he expected that you would keep out the same number you had now in the field all winter.

"I am your Excellencys

"Most obedant Humble servt

"JAS POTTER."

In a letter from Gen. Sir William Howe to Lord George Germain, dated at Philadelphia, Jan. 19, 1778, he refers to the operations in the neighborhood of Darby, thus:

"There has not any thing more material happened since the departure of Lord Cornwallis, who I requested to be the bearer of my last dispatches, than the passing a considerable detachment of the army across the Schuylkill on the 22d of December, to take post on the heights of Darby, in order to cover the collecting and transporting by water, as well as by land, a large quantity of forage which that country afforded. About 1000 tons were brought in, a quantity judged to be nearly sufficient for the winter consumption; and the detachment returned on the 28th of December, without any further attempts from the enemy to retard the progress of the foragers, than from small parties skulking, as is their custom, to seize upon the straggling soldiers. One of these parties, consisting of two officers and 30 men were decoyed by two dragoons of the 17th regiment into an ambuscade, and made prisoners."[1]

The spoliation inflicted upon the residents in the neighborhood of Darby was excessive, much of it having been visited on Friends. No record has been preserved of their losses, their religious principles preventing them from asking indemnity for the damages they had sustained. The following list of claims filed includes the territory now comprising Upper and Lower Darby:

		£	s.	d.
From	Joseph Rudolph, "by the British army, while they lay in Darby, foraging, December"	61	11	8
"	Benjamin Brannan, "by the British army, while they lay at Darby, foraging, December"	41	7	6
"	Jesse Bonsall	197	10	6
"	John Sellers, by the Hessians	20	0	0
"	Jonathan Evans (Cornwallis), Decr	23	17	0
"	Evan Evans " "	13	0	0
"	Nicholas McCurdy " "	15	1	0
"	Samuel Lewis " "	28	0	0
"	Samuel Leedom	24	0	0
"	Andrew Boon, Jr	40	12	0
"	John Gruber	53	7	0
"	John Humphreys	29	17	6
"	Isaac Kirk	34	14	6
"	John Pollin (Cornwallis)	18	17	10
"	Henry Hayes	140	15	4
"	William Garrett	47	0	0
"	Alexander Morrow	13	12	6
"	Samuel Smith	55	15	9
"	Benjamin Elliot	167	12	6
"	Daniel Rice	58	8	0
"	William Morrow	67	15	0
"	Andrew Boon, December 25	69	0	0
"	William Lewis, December 12 to 13	43	10	0
"	Andrew Urian	34	1	6
"	Hans Boon, "a helpless man"	77	15	5
		1475	18	2

Sixty-one years after this raid a body of troops visited Darby, but it was the Washington Grays, Capt. Childs, of Philadelphia, who, early in July, 1838, were encamped near the village, and on the 4th of July gave a reception to the ladies and gentlemen of the neighborhood. Five years thereafter,—and doubtless the old veteran saw the Grays on the occasion just mentioned,—on Feb. 16, 1843, Capt. Henry Stoop, a Revolutionary officer, died at Darby, ninety-one years of age. He had taken part in the battle of Trenton, and in his later years delighted to recall the incidents of the war of independence,—

"And show'd how fields were won."

Taxables.—In the assessment-list for 1715 the following names appear:

John Bethell, John Harvey, John Heycock, Edward Philpot, Benjamin Cliff, John Test, Josa. Johnson, John Sholers, Samuel Bradshaw,

[1] Hazard's Register, vol. xvi. p. 399.

David Thomas, John Blunston, Sr., John Blunston, Jr., John Wood, Thomas Pillford, John Worth, Enoch Bonsall, Jacob Bonsall, Roger Bailey, Anthony Morgan, George Wood, Michael Blunston, Samuel Sellers, John Marshall, Samuel Wood, John Thomas, Joshua Hearn, Thomas Bardshaw, Samuel Garret, William Garret, Adam Roades, Thomas Lewis, Samuel Lewis, Abraham Lewis, Isaac Coller, William Barnet, James Witaker, Joseph Neid, John Davis, Samuel Levis, Thomas Broom, Josiah Hibbert, John Hood, John Hallowell, William Smith, Thomas Hood, William Smith, Jr., Widow Bartram, Richard Parker, Anthony Lee, Lewis Davis, Matthias Nateilus, Morton Mortonson, Charles Yokecom, Andrew Youran, Swan Boon, Hance Boon, Matthias Mortonson, William Northam, John Broom, Thomas Worth.

Freemen.—Thomas Worth, John Parker, William Prest, John Wallis, Thomas Philips, Francis Youran, Thomas Edwards.

In the foregoing list the residents of Darby and Upper Darby were assessed as of one township. In the following, which is the assessment for the year 1799, Lower Darby township, including the present borough, is alone given:

Samuel Ash (innkeeper), John Ash, Matthew Ash, John Atmore (cooper), James Andrews, Abigail Ash, Joanna Bare, Margaret Boon, Joseph Boon, Moses Bonsall, Margaret Bonsall, Jonathan Bonsall, Levi Ronsall (blacksmith), Edward Bonsall, Isaac Brooks (mason), John Brooks, Josiah Bunting, Samuel Bunting, Benjamin Bartram, William Bright, Joseph Crawford, John & Joseph Ball (Upper Darby), Robert Calvin (Ridley), Benjamin Elliot & John Moore, Israel Elliot (justice of the peace), Enos Eldridge (grazier), John Foreman, Jacob Gibbons (grazier), John Gruber, Thomas Hall (Ridley), Jonathan Heacock, William Hansell (blacksmith), Ann Humphrey, John Hunt (grazier), John Horne, Edward Horne (retailer of spirits), William Horne, Thomas Horne, Isaac Horne, John Humphrey, Rebecca Humphrey, Joseph Heacock (mason), John Hibberd (Upper Darby), Israel Helen, Matthias Holston (carpenter), Job Helms, Matthew Jones, John Jones (pump-maker), James Knowles (Ridley), John Knowles (Ridley), Hugh Lloyd, Esq. (judge and grazier), Richard Lloyd (miller), Moses Lincorn, Thomas Leacock, Samuel Levis, Joseph Merrion, James McClees, John Marshall, Nathaniel Newlin, John Noblett (shoemaker), Mary Oliver (shop-keeper), George Ormsbury (shoemaker), Aaron Oakford, Isaac Oakford (fuller), Benjamin Oakford (tanner and justice of the peace), Nathan Pearson (joiner), Lydia Pearson, Jonathan Pearson (tailor), Benjamin Paschall (Kingsessing), Joseph Pearson (Ridley), Charles Palmer (shoemaker), John Pearson (tanner), John Palmer, Aaron Palmer, Sarah Periguer, John Pharis, Uriah Rowe (shoemaker), Daniel Rice, George Rudolph, John Rudolph, Joseph Rudolph, John Rively (shop-keeper), Frederick Rively (weaver), Thomas A. Richards, George Swayne, Samuel Shaw (weaver), Stephen Sicard (Philadelphia), Nathaniel Smith, Doyle Swayne (Philadelphia), Thomas Simmons (carpenter), Joseph Shallcross (physician), William Wright, Jesse Sharpless (Philadelphia), Elizabeth Smith (innkeeper), Jacob Sewell, Ann Mifflin, Isaac Sullender (tailor), John Tryter, David Treanor, Robert Thomas (Upper Darby), Samuel Urian, Israel Urian, Hiram Walton (miller for Caleb Phipps), William Wood (estate of Joseph Wood), Henry Wood (joiner), Robert Wilson, William Gardner (physician), Jonathan Tyson (wheelmaker).

Inmates.—Samuel Coates (cooper), Samuel Canby (miller), James Dorey, William Fretwell (weaver), George Fawkes, Adam Goul (shoemaker), John Haley, Kenneth McClean, Jonas Morton (shoemaker), Archibald Gardner (fuller), John Orna (calico-stamper), James Rudolph (mason), Jacob Rice, William Smith (carpenter), David Smith, Henry Sidings (shoemaker), Benjamin Pearson (retailer of spirits), Hiram Williamson, Samuel Wetherington (calico-printer), James Cherry (shoemaker), Jacob Rudolph.

Single Freemen.—Jeshua Ash, William Bonsall (shoemaker), John Brooke (tanner), Andrew Boon, Abraham Boon, Peter Boon, Joseph Boon, John Bartram, John Bunting (tailor), Joshua Bonsall, James Cannon, Abel Fowler (blacksmith), George Gruber (wheelwright), Isaac Heacock (mason), Benjamin Heacock, Thomas Horne, John Humphrey (tailor), William Humphrey (tailor), Oliver Ingram, Wrathey Ingram, Samuel Leacock, James McClees, William McCord, Isaiah Mall, Aaron Marshall, James Marshall, Charles Marshall, Samuel Oliver (carpenter), John O'Donnell, Charles Pearson (tanner), William Long, Nicholas Rice, Samuel Rowe, Thomas Sirrell, John Siddings (shoemaker), Thomas Webster (fuller), Philip Vigorous (shoemaker).

Darby Presbyterian Church.—This church was organized as a Congregational Church, 9th of March, 1840, with sixteen members. A council composed of the Rev. John Todd, of the First Congregational Church, Philadelphia, Rev. William Ramsey, of the Cedar Street Presbyterian Church, of Philadelphia, Rev. Truman Osborn, the Rev. Thomas Benneson, of Newark, Del., Rev. W. H. Bidwell, of the Third Presbytery of Philadelphia, convened at the house of George G. Knowles, in Darby township, for the purpose of taking the necessary steps to organize a church. The Rev. John Todd was chosen moderator, and the Rev. W. H. Bidwell scribe. At this meeting a form of covenant and confession of faith were approved by Council, and it was decided "the way was clear for organization." The following persons were associated into a Congregational Church: George G., James G., William G., Martha, Ann, Catharine W., Elizabeth and Margaret C. Knowles, Richard and Elizabeth M. Holmes, John and Miriam F. Collier, John Keigler, John Munyan, Elizabeth Swayne, and Martha Dunbar.

The Rev. Charles Brown, of the Presbytery of Wilmington, was invited to preach as a stated supply. He began his labors on the 1st of June, 1840, and continued till Dec. 1, 1840. The Rev. Marcus E. Cross was then invited to supply the pulpit and accepted. On the 22d of February, 1841, he was regularly called, accepted, and was ordained as the first regular pastor May 20, 1841. The Council of Ordination convened at the house of Deacon James G. Knowles, and was composed of the Rev. John Todd, of First Congregational Church, Philadelphia; Rev. Anson Rood, pastor of the Central Presbyterian Church, Northern Liberties, Philadelphia; Rev. Joseph P. Thompson, pastor of the Chapel Street Church, New Haven, Conn.; Mr. Benjamin Naglee, elder delegate; Deacon Isaac Thompson, delegate.

On the 19th of September, 1842, it was decided to change to the Presbyterian form of government, and the organization was called the Darby Presbyterian Church. James G. Knowles and Richard Holmes were elected ruling elders. On application to the Third Presbytery of Philadelphia, Oct. 11, 1842, the church was admitted to their charge. On May 23, 1843, a charter was obtained from the Legislature. On June 11, 1845, Dr. William G. Knowles and John Van Lear were elected elders, since which time the following elders have served: 1854, Joseph Naglee; 1859, George G. Knowles; 1872, Robert Henderson; 1883, James Logan.

The first religious services were held in school-houses and private houses until 1841, when George G. Knowles donated a plot of ground on which the church now stands, and gave the stone for the building. The same year the edifice, thirty-five by forty-five, was erected, costing about two thousand five hundred dollars In February, 1849, the church was broken into and robbed of the pulpit Bible, hymn-book, and a number of Sunday-school books In the spring of 1873 the church was repaired, the outer walls plastered, a new roof took the place of the old one, and other improvements made, costing thirteen hundred dollars, of which sum William G Knowles contributed five hundred dollars The present membership of the church is about sixty-five The Presbyterian Church, in Darby borough, is an outgrowth of the Knowles Church, twenty members having withdrawn to organize the former ecclesiastical body

The Rev Marcus E Cross continued pastor of the church until 1851, when he resigned, devoting himself to literary work He had shortly after leaving college edited and published "Hunter's Sacred Biography" and the "Museum of Religious Knowledge," and while pastor of the Knowles Church had begun, in 1847, the publication of the *Mirror of Temperance*, which he discontinued in 1856 He subsequently published "The Social and Moral Aspect of China" Rev J Addison Whitaker was ordained pastor Oct 3, 1852, and continued until March 2, 1855, when he resigned, since which time the church has been depending on supplies, excepting during the year 1875, when Rev Andrew Lees was in charge

African Methodist Episcopal Church.—This church is located on the Horntown road, and in 1842 the society erected on the lot a frame church, which was replaced in 1854 by the present brick edifice, which is twenty-five by forty feet Among the ministers who have served are the Revs J W Davis, Richard Barney, William Allen, and the Rev Henderson Bryson, the present pastor The church has at present about forty members

Schools—Schools were taught in what is Darby borough about the middle of the last century, but in the township no record of a school has been found until 1811 When the school law was enacted in 1834, Thomas Smith and Thomas Steel were appointed inspectors by the court until the directors were elected, and $270 60 were received by the township as its proportion of the State and county appropriations

On the 17th of September, 1811, John Lake, who owned real estate on Church Lane, in the northeast section of Darby township, sold nine square perches of land to Aaron Palmer, Caleb Davis, Benjamin Bonsell, Moses Palmer, Charles Palmer Gavin Hamilton, Jacob Nitzit, Mary Palmer, Moses Bonsell, Enoch Bonsell, and others, for the purpose of erecting a school-house thereon Several of the persons here mentioned, and others who subscribed for the purpose of building the school-house, were residents of Upper Darby township, and of the city and county of Philadelphia The following are the names of those who subscribed and the amounts given

Aaron Palmer	$20	Mary Palmer	$10
Caleb Davis.	10	Moses Bonsell	10
Moses Palmer	20	Enoch Bonsell	8
Benjamin Bonsell	20	William Bonsell	5
Charles Palmer	20	David Sellers	5
Gavin Hamilton	10	Nathan Sellers	5
Jacob Nitzet	10	Samuel Palmer	5
Abram Lewis	5	Isaac Palmer	5
John Lewis.	5	Isaac Earl	1
Enoch Bonsell, Jr	3	Jonathan Bonsell	1
James Bonsell	3	Joshua Bonsell	10
John Moore	2	John Lake	20
Abram Simcox	1	Samuel Bonsell	5

The amount subscribed aggregated two hundred and nineteen dollars A one-story stone house was erected on the site, and is still in use, having been enlarged and improved about twelve years ago This is known as the Palmer or Northern School

In May, 1835, Jonathan Bonsall taught a school at Horntown, his rates being as follows "Terms, per quarter, $2 50, ink, quills, pencils, etc, twenty five cents ☞ No day-scholars will be admitted, except those sent by county commissioners"

Western School District—On the 25th of September, 1837, the school directors purchased a lot of John Pierson, administrator of the estate of Samuel Shaw, Jr, on which they erected a one-story schoolhouse, which was used until 1874, when the present two-story brick house was erected

The Southern School is located on Calcon Hook. A school-house was built here about 1850, which was used until 1871, when the present house was erected

African School is located on the Horntown road The lot on which this house is erected originally belonged to George G Knowles, and the first house was a frame building erected about 1850 It was replaced by the present brick one in 1875

The following is the list of school directors, as found of record at Media

1840, Thomas Smith, Griffith Holgate, 1842, Samuel Urian, Philip Sipler, 1843, John G Palmer, Robert P Ash, 1844, Joshua A Pearson, Davis Richards, 1845, Edmund Taylor, James Andrews, 1846, John G Palmer, Robert P Ash, 1847, William Russell Jr, Ansley Newlin 1848, Amos Morris, Charles A Litzenburg, 1849, John G Palmer, William Jones, 1850, William D H Serrill, William Russell, 1851, Amos Morris, Charles A Litzenburg 1852, Thomas M Fisher, William Jones, 1853, William Russell, W D H Sewell, 1854, Joseph C Bonsall, William Gardner, Jacob Rice, 1855, James Eachus, John Otty 1856, Edwin Urian, Jacob Rice, 1857, Joseph C Bonsall, George Horne, 1858, David Taylor, John Otly, 1859, Edwin Urian, George S Patchel, 1860, Joseph C Bonsell, George Swayne, 1861, John Otly, Jacob Rice, 1862, George Swayne, David Taylor, 1863 Frank P Boyer Moses Bonsall, 1864, Edward Urian, Richard R Thatcher, 1865, M F Longstreth, John W Marshall, 1866, Moses Bonsell, Franklin J Boyer, 1867, Edwin Urian, Moses Lincoln, 1868, Dr Jacob Boon, Dr M F Longstreth, 1869, Franklin P Boyer, Moses Bonsell, 1870, Edwin Urian, Richard Thatcher, 1871, M F Longstreth, Benjamin F Horne, 1872, Moses Bonsall, William H Harrison, 1873, Jacob Lincoln, John Marshall, 1874, F J Boyer, M F Longstreth, 1875, Moses Bonsall Charles W Keithler, 1876, William H Harrison, M M Shaw, 1877 M Fisher Longstreth, G A Hazlett, 1878, Jacob Lincoln Joshua Kirk, 1879, Joshua P Kirk, John Marshall, 1880, Davis Yarnall, M Fisher Longstreth, 1881, Davis Yarnall, Charles T Brooks, 1882, Israel Helms, Frank P Lewis, 1883, Joshua P Kirk, Albert B Earle, 1884, Charles T Brooks, Charles H Scott.

Glen Olden Mills.—The mill on Muckinipattus Creek, now owned by Ephraim J Ridgway, has an unusually interesting history. The tract of land of five hundred acres was granted, May 16, 1663, by Richard Nicolls, Governor of New York, to Israel Helme, Hendrick Joubson (Jacobson), Oele Koeck, and Jan Minsterman. This land is on what is known as Calcoon Hook. The tract seems to have been divided, for on the 10th of April, 1683, one portion of it, owned by Oele Koeck (and on which, later, the mill was built), was sold to Morton Mortonson, who in turn, Aug. 7, 1708, conveyed it to his son, Lawrence, who, later, sold to his son, Tobias Mortonson. On the 10th of April, 1755, Tobias Mortonson sold twenty-four acres to Thomas Shipley, of Wilmington, who died in January, 1759. The property remained in the Shipley family many years, and in 1774, Thomas Shipley, of Darby, purchased at sheriff's sale a lot of land, containing forty-three acres, in Ridley township, across the Muckinipattus Creek from the mill property, which he continued to own as late as 1788. In 1790, Peter Ross is said to have had control of this mill. In 1797 the mill-seat land, as well as the forty-three acres across the creek, were sold by Sheriff Abraham Dicks, as the property of Charles Davis, the purchaser being John Jones, who, the same day, conveyed the premises to Caleb Phipps. At that date the mill was in existence, and had been built long prior to that date, tradition asserting that it was erected by Thomas Shipley, about the year 1755, he being a miller by trade. In 1799, Hiram Walton was operating the mill, and in 1800, Elisha Phipps, a brother of Caleb, was the lessee, and so remained until 1808, when he purchased the property. Elisha Phipps was a strange, erratic character, moved by the impulse of the hour. It is related that the mill being located at the head of tide-water, as was customary in those days, he conveyed his flour to market by a shallop, and returning would bring a cargo of grain. A small sloop, called "The Dusty Miller," was used for this purpose. On one occasion he loaded his little craft with flour and sailed for New York. Time elapsed, and as no word came from Elisha, his wife became anxious, and finally went to New York in search of her husband. There she could learn nothing respecting him, save that he had not been to see the persons with whom he had been accustomed to trade. Finally she returned to her home disconsolate, fully convinced that her husband had been lost on the trip to New York. Time passed, and no intelligence came from the absent Phipps. It was nearly dusk one evening when the "gude wife" saw "The Dusty Miller" coming up the Muckinipattus with the flood tide. Shortly after the craft was moored at its accustomed wharf and Phipps entered the house, and, in his accustomed manner, tossed his old hat on the floor, as if his absence had been no unusual event in his daily life. It seems that after the "Miller" had passed out of the capes of the Delaware, Phipps, on a sudden impulse, decided to sail for the West Indies, where, selling his flour at a large profit, he shipped a quantity of rum and molasses for New York. At the latter port he sold the cargo, purchased grain, and sailed for the Muckinipattus, where he arrived in safety, as already narrated. On March 21, 1812, Phipps sold the property to Halliday Jackson, who owned it until Feb. 27, 1828, when he in turn conveyed it to Ephraim Inskeep. At the latter's death, in 1876, the Glen Olden Mills passed by inheritance to Ephraim J. Ridgway, the present owner.

Warpington Mills.—In 1867, Richard Thatcher erected a cotton-spinning mill on Church Run. The building was ninety-two by fifty-five feet, two stories in height, containing three thousand spindles, driven by a forty horse-power Corliss engine. The mills and machinery cost sixty-five thousand dollars. On Sunday morning, March 24, 1877, an incendiary fire totally destroyed the building and contents, involving a heavy loss to the owner. The mills have never been rebuilt.

Carpet Mills.—About 1849, Gen. John Sidney Jones established a carpet-factory on the north side of the Southern post-road, about a mile west of the borough of Darby, on land which had descended to him from his ancestors, the family having owned the estate during the Revolution. One of the peculiar rules enforced by the proprietor was the prohibition of coal-fires in any of the eight tenements on the property, but he generously supplied the operatives in the mill with wood for fuel. While operating these mills he published a periodical called *The Monthly Jubilee*. He and his wife, Fanny Lee Townsend Jones, edited it, the type being set in a building on the estate by Patrick McDermot. It was finally discontinued, as was the carpet-mills. The buildings were subsequently leased to John Shepherd & Co., who established a brush-factory therein. On Friday, Dec. 2, 1876, the mills, together with the mansion-house, were destroyed by fire. In September, 1840, Norman B. Barrett, a lad, residing on the Jones farm, while gunning, sat down to rest himself, laying the gun on the ground. When rising he drew the fowling-piece towards him; the cock caught on a twig and discharged the weapon. He was so seriously wounded that death resulted in a few hours thereafter.

Carpet-Factory.—In May, 1882, Wolfenden, Brother & Chism began the erection of a two-story brick carpet-factory, forty by fifty feet, which was completed and put in operation in July of that year. The mills manufacture from one hundred and fifty to one hundred and seventy-five yards of body Brussels carpet daily, employing four looms and fourteen operatives.

The Horntown Tannery.—In 1790, John Horn, of Horntown, owned and carried on a tan-yard at Horntown, which was discontinued prior to 1812.

Crime.—On Monday, Nov. 25, 1844, the body of a female child was found in Darby Creek, near Calcoon Hook, at "Deep Hole," inclosed in a grain-sack, a napkin tied around the neck and head so as to cover the whole face. The indications were that the body

James Andrews

and thrown in the [illegible] A post-mortem examination was made, which disclosed the fact that the child was three months old and alive when thrown into the water. Alexander Harris, alias Dobson, was tried for the murder of the infant on May 26, 1846, and acquitted by the jury.[1]

At the May term, 1869, George W. Horner, a [illegible] and Louisa Howard, a young woman [illegible] were tried on several indictments charging them with a number of robberies [illegible]

[illegible]

where so many of his ancestors had received their education, and filled the position of teacher in this school while still in his minority. He early left to accept a position in the lumber business with the firm of Watson & Bunting, of Philadelphia, a brother of his mother being a member of the firm. In connection with the late James E. Greaves, he later succeeded to the business under the firm-name of Greaves & Andrews, and still later as J. and J. B. Andrews & Co. Owing to failing health, about the year 1837, James Andrews purchased a farm in Darby with the intention of making it his summer home, but soon became so much interested in the occupations of a farmer as to give up his winter residence in the city and make the country his permanent home. He was a birthright member of the Society of Friends, the ancestors of both his father and mother having emigrated to this country on account of their religious belief. He was always a consistent member, taking an active part in the affairs of the society, and frequently accompanying [illegible] public ministers in their religious visits. A strict, public-spirited citizen, [illegible] he was in all respects a useful man, through life being honored with many positions of trust and responsibility. In politics he had decided views, and took an active part, first as a Whig and afterwards as a Republican, in the questions of the day. In 1851 his fellow-citizens elected him to the office of associate judge of Delaware County, which position he assumed on his fifty-sixth birthday, and held for fifteen years, declining a re-election on account of his age. In 1828 he married Hannah, daughter of Charles Lloyd, whose children were two sons and five daughters, one son and four daughters surviving him. In his domestic life Mr. Andrews was extremely happy. After the decease of his wife, on the 20th of June, 1868, life seeming to have lost its chief attraction, his health failed rapidly. On the 30th of September, 1869, his children laid him to rest in the old graveyard at Darby, by the side of her whom in life he had loved so well.

CHAPTER XLI.

DARBY BOROUGH.

Doubtless the early settlers in the neighborhood of Darby, where the mills were located, soon began to regard the locality, which subsequently became the village, as an important centre, and there doubtless soon located the blacksmith after the custom of horse-shoeing came in vogue,—which was not generally recognized until the middle of the last century,—and wagons were in use among the farmers,—still later than [illegible] it became a place of consequence

[1] See ante, p. [illegible]

James Andrews

had been in the water nearly two weeks. A *post-mortem* examination was made, which disclosed the fact that the child was three months old, and alive when thrown into the water. Alexander Harris, *alias* Dobson, was tried for the murder of the infant on May 27, 1845, and acquitted by the jury.[1]

At the May court, 1850, George W. Horner, a young man, and Louisa Howard, a young woman with whom he lived, were tried on several indictments charging them with a number of robberies in Upper Darby, Haverford, and other localities in the northern section of the county. The house of Benjamin D. Garrigues was entered, and a hired man, returning at a late hour, discovered that the dwelling had been broken into. Pursuit was at once made, a wagon was overtaken, from which the driver sprang and ran away. The stolen property was found in the vehicle. The horse the next day was placed in the custody of a detective officer, who, finding that the animal manifested a desire to go towards Darby, gave him a free rein, and he continued until he stopped at Horner's house, on the Haverford road just north of the village. The dwelling was searched, and much stolen property found therein. Horner was convicted on three indictments, and sentenced to five years in the Eastern Penitentiary on each indictment. Louisa Howard was convicted of receiving stolen goods, and was sentenced to two years in the penitentiary. In May, 1851, Governor Shunk pardoned Horner, leaving his woman accomplice to serve her term of punishment.

JUSTICES OF THE PEACE FOR DARBY TOWNSHIP.

Benjamin Brannon	Aug. 19, 1791
Israel Elliot	Oct. 28, 1791
Benjamin W. Oakford	Feb. 14, 1794
Caleb S. Sayers	Aug. 6, 1799
Benjamin Hayes Smith	April 3, 1804
Samuel Davis	Feb. 20, 1810
Thomas Smith	July 3, 1821
Joseph G. Malcolm	July 30, 1831
Thomas Maddock	Jan. 8, 1834
Charles Sellers	June 20, 1836
Philip Sipler	Aug. 14, 1840
Thomas Smith	Aug. 14, 1840
Philip Sipler	April 15, 1845
Anthony J. Jordan	June 1, 1850
William Russell, Jr	April 15, 1855
William Russell	April 14, 1857
Samuel Taylor	May 3, 1859

BIOGRAPHICAL SKETCH.

JAMES ANDREWS.

James Andrews was born Dec. 1, 1795, in Darby township within the present limits of Darby borough, his father, James Andrews, having removed from Wilmington, Del., to the township of Darby when a young man, where he married Martha Bunting, daughter of Josiah Bunting, thus connecting the subject of this sketch through his mother with the oldest residents of that early-settled township. When a boy he attended the Friends' school in Darby, where so many of his ancestors had received their education, and filled the position of teacher in this school while still in his minority. He early left to accept a position in the lumber business with the firm of Watson & Bunting, of Philadelphia, a brother of his mother being a member of the firm. In connection with the late James R. Greaves, he later succeeded to the business under the firm-name of Greaves & Andrews, and still later as J. and J. B. Andrews & Co. Owing to failing health, about the year 1837, James Andrews purchased a farm in Darby with the intention of making it his summer home, but soon became so much interested in the occupations of a farmer as to give up his winter residence in the city and make the country his permanent home. He was a birthright member of the society of Friends, the ancestors of both his father and mother having emigrated to this country on account of their religious belief. He was always a consistent member, taking an active part in the affairs of the society, and frequently accompanying as companion public ministers in their religious visits. A useful, public-spirited citizen, benevolent, modest, and unassuming in his intercourse with his fellow-citizens, he was in all respects a model man, through life being honored with many positions of trust and responsibility. In politics he had decided views, and took an active part, first as Whig and afterwards as a Republican, in the questions of the day. In 1851 his fellow-citizens elected him to the office of associate judge of Delaware County, which position he assumed on his fifty-sixth birthday, and held for fifteen years, declining a re-election on account of his age. In 1825 he married Hannah, daughter of Charles Lloyd, whose children were two sons and five daughters, one son and four daughters surviving him. In his domestic life Mr. Andrews was extremely happy. After the decease of his wife, on the 20th of June, 1868, life seeming to have lost its chief attraction, his health failed rapidly. On the 24th of September, 1869, his children laid him to rest in the old graveyard at Darby, by the side of her whom in life he had loved so well.

[1] See *ante*, p. 177.

CHAPTER XLI.

DARBY BOROUGH.

DOUBTLESS the early settlers in the neighborhood of Darby, where the mills were located, soon began to regard the locality, which subsequently became the village, as an important centre, and there doubtless soon settled the blacksmith after the custom of horse-shoeing came in vogue,—which was not generally recognized until the middle of the last century,—and wagons were in use among the farmers—still later than horseshoeing—it became a place of consequence to the surrounding districts. In all the early orders of courts and reports of grand juries, in which Darby is mentioned as a particular point where a road begins or ends, the allusion is doubtless to the village, and there were located the stocks, erected in 1731, for which the then overseers of the poor, Samuel Horn and Edward Williams, in the quaint "Record for the Poor of Darby Township" claim credit,—

	£	s.	d.
By Cash payed to Benjamin Peirson, Junr for Building Stocks for the Township of Darby	0	10	0
By Cash payed to David Thomas for Iron Work Done for the Stocks	0	2	8

Dr. Smith, who had access to the early township books[1] of Darby, gave the following extracts from the proceedings in 1694:

"Agreed that this meeting begin at Eleven o'Clock in the forenoon, and that the constable give notice the *first day* before.

"And it is also agreed that the said town's meeting be held on the third day of the last week in the twelfth month to appoint officers for the Ensuing year, at which time the officers is to give up their accounts.

"Agreed that none of the inhabitants of this Town take any horses or mares either to keep in winter or summer, nor no cattle in summer except they keep them within their own fenced lands, upon the penalty of five shillings per head for every month."

The freemen of the township at these gatherings also exercised legislative powers, as is evident from the following extract from the township books:

"Agreed at a town meeting, 1697, that all plantations ye lands not Joyning upon the road, that four of the Neighbours shall be chosen to lay out a convenient way as they shall see meet to the next convenient road, and being so done shall stand firm and not be blocked up with trees or plantations.

"Signed on behalf of the
"Town by
"THO. WORTH."[2]

The first direct mention of Darby village, for the allusion of Gabriel Thomas to "Derby town," in 1698, does not prove that anything other than the mills were located there at the date given, is in the journal of Miss Sarah Eve, when, under date of Oct. 17, 1773, on returning from a visit to Chester, she says, "After we left Chester it began to rain pretty hard, and continued until we were near Darby. I could not help thinking of what Thomson said of Brentford was very applicable to that place, that is, that it was a town of mud. Foolish creatures to build a town in such a hole and have such delightful hills on each side of them, but who knows the reason."[3] During the official correspondence of the Revolutionary war, Darby is constantly mentioned as designating a particular locality, a village. At the beginning of this century it is thus described:

"Darby is situated about seven miles and a half from Philadelphia; on the east side of the creek of the same name that empties into the Delaware a little above Chester. It contains about fifty or sixty houses and has a Friends' meeting-house."[4]

[1] History of Delaware County, p. 188. The township books at that early period could not be found by the writer, although every effort was made to learn if they were still accessible.

[2] Smith's "History of Delaware County," p. 384.

[3] *Penna. Mag. of Hist.*, vol. v. p. 201.

[4] Travellers' Directory, Philadelphia, 1802.

Thirty-four years later (in 1836) the *Upland Union* published a description of Delaware County, and the various boroughs and villages contained within its territory. The account says,—

"Darby is next in importance to Chester. It is on the Southern great road about seven miles from Philadelphia by a good turnpike. It contains a Friends' meeting-house, Mount Zion Methodist church, a lyceum, a library company, a printing-office, four public-houses, three stores, a cotton-factory, a post-office, and about sixty dwelling-houses, and many elegant dwellings on the Haverford road."

The ancient village of Darby under the same time-honored name was incorporated into a borough, May 3, 1853, the act specifying the boundaries as follows:

"*Beginning* at a cedar tree on the Haverford Road on a line between A. Worrell and George Lincoln's land; thence along the line of said Worrell and Lincoln to Darby Creek; thence down said creek to the line of Isaac L. Bartram and the heirs of John Ashland; thence along the line of said Bartram and Ashland crossing the Springfield road and the same line continued between Isaac Bartram and John B. Bartram to a point on said line that is intersected by a line along a lane running from the Chester road between the lands of John Jackson and Samuel Crothers to a corner of said John Jackson's land; thence along the line of said Jackson's land and passing through lands of Jonathan Heacock and Paxson Price to Darby Creek; and thence up said creek to a point opposite the line of between Elizabeth Grover and Benjamin E. Moore; thence along said line of Moore and Grover and William Lincoln to the west side of a private lane; thence along said private lane to the Philadelphia and Darby plank road; thence along said plank road on the south side of Cobb's Creek; thence up said creek to the corner of Hall Pennell's and Lewis Passmore's land; thence along the line of said Pennell and Passmore to said Pennell and Benjamin Serrill's land; thence along the line of Pennell and Serrill to Thomas L. Bonsall's land; thence on the line of said Pennell and Bonsall to the land late of Jacob Lincoln, deceased; thence along the line of Pennell and Lincoln to Jabez Bunting's land; thence on the line of Jabez Bunting and said Pennell to Bunting's lane; thence crossing said lane on the line of Jabez Bunting and Anne Bunting to a corner continuing on the same course to John H. Bunting's land; thence along a southwest course along the land of Jabez Bunting and John H. Bunting to Josiah Bunting's land; thence by the same course between Jabez and Josiah Bunting to Joseph Bunting's land; and thence a straight course to the place of beginning."

The election for borough officers was held on the third Friday in May following the date of the act of incorporation. The names of the burgesses and members of Council who have served from the organization of the borough to the present time, are as follows:

BURGESSES.

1853, William Jones; 1854, Anthony J. Jordan; 1855–57, William Jones; 1858, Jacob S. Serrill; 1859–63, William Jones; 1864–65, Jacob S. Serrill; 1866, Joseph M. Bunting; 1867–68, George L. Patchell; 1869–73, Isaac T. Jones; 1874–75, Charles Lloyd; 1876–77, Hugh Lloyd; 1878, Jacob S. Serrill; 1878–80, John W. Griswold; 1881, George L. Patchell; 1882–84, W. L. Verlenden.

MEMBERS OF COUNCIL.

1853.—Philip Sipler, William D. H. Serrill, William Russell, Jr., John Verlenden, Samuel P. Serrill, William Lincoln, Joseph L. Sager.

1854.—John Verlenden, William Lincoln, Paxson Rice, James Andrews, George Serrill, Maris W. Lewis, Joseph M. Bunting.

1855.—Philip Sipler, Maris W. Lewis, Anthony S. Jordan, John Verlenden, Thomas L. Bonsall, Hugh Lloyd, William H. Malin.

1856.—Joseph M. Bunting, Anthony S. Jordan, Thomas L. Bond, William H. Malin, Philip Sipler, Hugh Lloyd, John Verlenden.

1857.—Joseph M. Bunting, John Verlenden, Thomas L. Bartram, John M. Andrews, Thomas L. Bonsall, Hugh Lloyd, Philip Sipler.

1858.—Joseph L. Bunting, John M. Andrews, Philip Sipler, John Verlenden, Hugh Lloyd, Joseph Bunting.

1859.—Joseph M. Bunting, Thomas L. Bartram, John Verlenden, Hugh Lloyd, Jacob S. Serrill, James B. Conover, George McHenry.

1860.—Joseph M. Bunting, Thomas L. Bartram, John Verlenden, Jacob S. Serrill, Isaac L Bartram, Daniel S. White.

1861.—Joseph M. Bunting, Thomas L. Bartram, Daniel S. White, John Verlenden, George Serrill, Thomas Palmer, Joseph L. Sager.

1862.—Joseph M. Bunting, Thomas L. Bartram, Daniel S. White, John Verlenden, George Serrill, Thomas Palmer, George S. Truman.

1863.—Daniel S. White, John Verlenden, George Serrill, Thomas Palmer, Isaac L. Bartram, Joseph Bunting.

1864.—Isaac L. Bartram, J. Charles Andrews, John Verlenden, Joseph Bunting, George Serrill, Isaac T. Jones.

1865.—Daniel S. White, J. Charles Andrews, Isaac T. Jones, Thomas L. Bartram, John Verlenden, Joseph M. Bunting.

1866.—J. Charles Andrews, Daniel S. White, T. Chalkley Bartram, D. Taylor, John Lord, Washington B. Levis.

1867.—Daniel S. White, J. Charles Andrews, Hugh Lloyd, George Serrill, Charles Bonsall, Jr., Charles Tribit.

1868.—Daniel S. White, J. Charles Andrews, Hugh Lloyd, Charles Bonsall, Jr., Hugh Lloyd, Charles W. Lloyd, W. Lane Verlenden.

1869.—Daniel S. White, Charles W. Lloyd, George Serrill, George S. Patchell, Daniel S. White.

1870.—George Serrill, Charles Bonsall, Hugh Lloyd, Charles W. Lloyd, W. L. Verlenden.

1871.—Charles W. Lloyd, Daniel S. White, George Serrill, Hugh P. Lloyd, Charles Bonsall, W. L. Verlenden, George Ash, Jr.

1872.—Hugh P. Lloyd, Charles Lloyd, D. S. White, George Serrill, Charles Bonsall, J. Charles Andrews, W. L. Verlenden.

1873.—J. Charles Andrews, Charles Lloyd, John W. Griswold, Mordecai Sheldrake, Samuel W. Shaw, Oswald Patchell.

1874.—J. C. Andrews, John M. Miller, Charles Bonsall, George Serrill, Harry Peale, John Knowlton.

1875.—J. C. Andrews, James A. Lloyd, Charles Bonsall, Harry Peale, W. L. Verlenden, Enos Verlenden, John Guest.

1876.—T. Chalkley Bartram, Hugh Lloyd, John Guest, O. C. Armstrong, Peter Clark, W. R. Taylor, Henry W. Nagle.

1877.—Daniel S. White, T. C. Bartram, Joseph Bunting, Jr., William R. Taylor, Peter Clark, A. J. Russell, Charles Lloyd.

1878.—Charles Lloyd, Peter Clark, Samuel Mackey, W. S. Bunting, Thomas Brooks, John Wolfenden, Daniel S. White.

1879.—Charles Lloyd, Peter Clark, James M. Damon, Alonzo Heapes, Hugh Lloyd, Charles Tribit, Richard Lancaster, Jr.

1880.—Charles Lloyd, Peter Clark, George Grayson, John Wolfenden, Alonzo Heapes, George W. Bunting, James E. Combs.

1881.—Joseph Bunting, Jr., Peter Clark, John M. Damon, George Grayson, Robert Green, Charles Lloyd, Edward D. Sipler.

1882.—George Grayson, George N. Griffith, Elwood H. James, Parkhurst McLaughlin, William Maris, George B. Painter, Jacob K. Ulrich.

1883.—Joseph Bunting, Jr., Peter Clark, George Drewes, Alonzo Heapes, Daniel W. Kelly, John Massey.

1884.—Joseph Bunting, Jr., Nathan D. Bartram, George Drewes, Thomas Garvin, Alonzo Heapes, D. W. Kelly, John Massey.

Darby Mills.—The history of the Griswold Mills is particularly interesting, for it connects the present with the early industries of colonial days. In the summer of 1671, Capt. Carr, the English Deputy Governor on the Delaware, in a letter to Governor Lovelace, in New York, made certain suggestions as to affairs on the South River. Under the eleventh point he wrote,—

"That there being a mill or most (if not all) the appurtenances thereunto belonging, up Delaware River, at ye Carcoon's Hooke, wch did heretofore appertain to ye Publique & now is endeavoured to be engrossed by some particular persons for their private use. It may be recommended to be taken into his Royall Highness, or his Deputyes hands, by wch some Benefitt will accrew, & being kept in good Repaire will be of a publique and Gen^ll Good to ye Inhabitants."[1]

On June 14th the Governor and Council replied,—

"As to ye 11th concerning ye mill, as also one paire of millstones not used but lying in ye Mud or Water. It is ordered that care be taken for ye Letting out ye said Mill for ye best advantage to some persons who will undertake ye same & that ye proffitt thereof be reserved for ye publiqe, & for ye millstones not used. They are to be taken up and p^served till further Ord^r."[2]

The mill mentioned in Capt. Carr's letter was the old Swede mill at the Blue Bell, on Cobb's Creek, which, after acquisition of the territory by William Penn under his charter from the crown, gradually fell into disfavor with the public. It was, however, in use in 1684, for in an account of the early times, preserved among the descendants of Isaac Marriot, of Bristol, Pa., it is stated that when Friends' Yearly Meeting was held at Burlington, N. J., in that year the family wanting some fine flour, Isaac Marriot took wheat on horseback to this mill, which was twenty-six miles from his residence, to be ground.

The first record of a mill in Darby township occurs in the evidence given in a case tried at the court held March 10, 1687, when Thomas Bowles was arraigned for shooting hogs not his own running in the woods. The animals belonged to Thomas Smith. John Hendrickson testified that in the preceding fall (1686) "he was up at the mill on Darby Creek when he heard two gunnes go off," and when he went to where the firing was, he saw the defendant with his gun presented." John Hay, who was with him, said "Bowles was an old fool for shooting twice and missing."

At that time the old Swedish mill had fallen into disuse or was unable to do the work required of it, and the demand for a mill was pressing, for at the November court, 1678, five years before William Wood settled at Darby, the matter came before the justices, who declared that "Itt being taken into Consideracon that itt was verry necessary that a mill be built on the Schuylkill, and there being no fitter place than the faall Called Capt. hans moensen's faall; The Cort are of opinion that Either Captn hans moens ought to build a mill there (as hee sayes that hee will) or Else suffer an other to Build for the Common Good of ye parts."[3] The location of this proposed mill was on "Hans Moensen's Great Mill Fall" or "Run," which was the stream which empties into the Schuylkill south of Woodland Cemetery and north of Gray's Ferry.

William Wood emigrated from Nottingham, England, with his wife and family, in 1683, and settled at Darby, where he acquired three hundred and twenty acres, which plot included all the land on which the original village of Darby stood, the tract reaching northward to Friends' meeting-house lot and southward to the junction of Cobb's and Darby Creeks. On the latter stream William Wood built the mills, or if he did not his son Joseph Wood did, to whom the property descended in 1685, on the death of his father, William. In 1693, John Bethel took charge of these mills, which he subsequently purchased, for June 7,

[1] "Proposal of Capt. Carr," Penna. Archives, 2d Series, vol. vii. p. 737.

[2] Ib., p. 739.

[3] Records of Upland Court, p. 115.

1695, Joseph Wood, in open court acknowledged a deed for nine acres—the mill tract—to Bethel. The next year, Dec. 8, 1696, John Bethel sold to Samuel Carpenter, the noted merchant of Philadelphia in those early days, a half-interest in several tracts of land, one being nine acres on Darby Creek, "Upon which last-mentioned piece of land there is three water grist-mills and *a fulling mill lately erected.*" In the same deed it is stated that on the same day of the date of the deed to Carpenter, Bethel had purchased from John Blunston "all that millcat race or Trench digged in and through the said Blunston's land and meadow, from the said Darby Creek toward the said mills." This mill-race to-day follows the course "digged" nearly two centuries ago through Blunston's land. There seems to have been some defect in the deed made to Samuel Carpenter in 1696, for on Jan. 14, 1698, John Bethel, by his friend David Lloyd, acknowledged in open court a deed to Samuel Carpenter, "for the moiety of Darby Mills with the Houses, Improvements, and impliments thereunto belonging," the deed being dated Oct. 13, 1697. Previous to the sale to John Bethel, on the 9th of Twelfth month, 1687, the road leading from Darby to Radnor was laid out. In the assessment made in 1695, the Darby and Chester mills were each rated at one hundred pounds, and they were the most valuable properties in the county.

In Gabriel Thomas' "History of Pennsylvania," printed in 1698, he mentions "the famous Darby River, which comes down from the country by Darby town, wherein are several mills, viz.,—fulling-mills, corn-mills," etc. On a draft of the Queen's road from Darby to Chester, now in possession of Hon. Jacob Serrill, of Darby, made in 1705, these mills are distinctly marked. John Bethel remained at these mills until his death, which occurred before 1708, for on the 26th of August, in that year, John Bethel, of Darby, miller, son and heir of John Bethel, late of Darby, also a miller, confirmed the sale of a part interest in the mills to his brother-in-law, Job Harvey, "Stuffor." This deed recites that John Bethel, Sr., was seized in his lifetime of all those water-, corn-, or grist-mills, and a fulling-mill, "commonly called or known by the name of Darby Mills," and John Bethel, Sr., in his lifetime had sold to his son-in-law, Job Harvey, one-fourth part of the messuage "whereon the said Job now dwells, and also of said fulling-mill." From this it is evident that John Bethel, the younger, was carrying on the grist-mill, and Job Harvey the fulling-mill at the time John Bethel, the elder, died. About 1725, Job Harvey purchased the fulling-mill on Ridley Creek, now the site of the Media Water-Works.

In 1747 the Darby Mills were owned by Joseph Bonsall, of Darby, who, on November 3d of that year, conveyed to Richard Lloyd three full parts of five and a half acres of land, and of the "water-, corn-, or grist-mills, commonly called Darby Mills," with the bolting-house, bolting-mills, and other appurtenances. The fulling-mill was not mentioned in the deed. In 1764, Richard Lloyd having died, and his widow married to Lewis Davis, the property was vested in Lewis Davis, Isaac Lloyd, and Hugh Lloyd, the two last named being the sons of Richard Lloyd. From 1764 to 1802 the mills were assessed to Isaac Lloyd, who, in 1782, built a saw-mill, and from 1802 to 1814 to Richard Lloyd, at which date they were the property of Thomas Steel. While the Darby Mill was operated by Isaac Lloyd, Capt. James Serrill was one of his apprentices, and learned the trade of a miller.

The first mention of the name of Steel is in an assessment of the county in 1766, in Upper Darby township, when James Steel was assessed on a grist-mill. He is later followed by Thomas Steel, who appears in Upper Darby until 1814. He removed to Darby township the next year, where he had the old Darby Mills. In 1826 the capacity of these was thirty to forty thousand bushels of grain, and of two to three hundred thousand feet of lumber per annum. They were owned by Thomas Steel until 1861, but while he held title he had sold them several times, but for some reason was compelled to take them from the purchasers. On one occasion they were sold to an Englishman, who tore out the grist-mill machinery, with the intention of enlarging the buildings, which he failed to do, and Thomas Steel was compelled to refit them at a considerable outlay of money. In 1861 the property, including the fulling-mill, was purchased by Simeon Lord, and occupied by Joseph L. Saeger. On July 2, 1862, they were destroyed by fire. The same year Simeon Lord built Mill No. 1, which, on May 15, 1867, was partially burned. Again the owner repaired the mill, which he operated as a worsted-factory for several years, when they were sold by the sheriff to John Cattell, who enlarged the building and sold the property to William A. Griswold. It is now used by the Griswold Worsted Company (Limited) as a worsted-factory. Mill No. 1 is a three-storied stone building, three hundred by forty-five feet. In 1880, William A. Griswold erected along the creek, and a short distance farther down, Mill No. 2, a four-story brick building, one hundred and fifty-seven by fifty feet, for the manufacture of silk yarn. The machinery in these mills is driven by two engines of one hundred and sixty-five horse-power each. The Griswold Worsted Company (Limited) was organized in 1882, and the mills are at present operated by that company.

Oakford Fulling-Mill.—The early history of this mill is given in the sketch of the mills of the Griswold Worsted Company. It was a part of the Darby Mills from 1695, the date of its erection, until its destruction, in 1859. It is not mentioned in the deed from Joseph Bonsall to Richard Lloyd in 1747, but in 1764 it was owned and operated by Isaac and Hugh Lloyd, sons of Richard. In 1766 it was operated by Hugh Davis, the half-brother of Isaac and Hugh Lloyd. In 1770 it was in possession of Aaron Oakford, who continued there until 1785, when Isaac Oakford was operating it. In 1790 Isaac Oakford had in connection with his fulling- a print-mill. On August 23d of that year, George Huffstetter and Isaac Huffstetter, sons of Lydia Yoamer, were bound before Esquire Pearson, to Conrad Psaphauser, to learn calico-stamping, being indentured for six years and eleven months, while the same day Jesse Huffstetter was bound to serve Psaphauser, at the trade of calico-stamping and "to learn mixing," for a term of ten years and three months. The assessment of 1798 returned Isaac Oakford as owning the fulling-mill and stamping-works for printing calico, and John Orna was employed there as a calico-stamper, and Samuel Wetherington as a calico-printer. In 1826, Isaac Oakford was still the owner of the mill, but at that time it was operated by Aaron Oakford, who continued there many years. It subsequently passed to Thomas Steel, and in 1854 was leased to John Verlenden, who changed it to a cotton-mill, and operated it until it was destroyed by fire, on March 5, 1859. The water for this mill was from its erection, in 1695, taken from the race which supplied the grist-mills above, and when they came into possession of Thomas Steel, the fulling-mill was limited to a supply of water that flowed through a four-inch pipe. This mill also passed to Thomas Steel, and was sold in 1861 with the grist-mill to Simeon Lord.

In 1788, Benjamin Oakford was operating a tan-yard, which he continued till 1810, when John Oakford succeeded him, and continued it until after 1848.

Imperial Mills.—In the year 1846, John Verlenden and Morton Farraday established a small business of spinning carpet yarn on Whiskey Run, in Springfield township. In 1854, Verlenden removed to Darby borough, and commenced business in the old fulling-mill of Thomas Steel, formerly Isaac Oakford, which he operated until it was burned, March 5, 1859. In that year Verlenden erected on the site of the present mill a factory building sixty by forty feet, which he operated until his death, in December, 1865. The business was continued by the family, and in 1867, Smith & Verlenden leased the mills, which they operated for three years. In 1870, W. Lane Verlenden and Enos Verlenden formed a partnership, and as Verlenden Brothers, began manufacturing in these mills. The main mill building was destroyed by fire in 1880, and the present mill, eighty by forty feet, erected on its site. The Imperial now contains seventy-two looms, two self-acting mules, each of five hundred and eight spindles, and two sets of sixty cards, driven by a Corliss engine, sixteen by forty-two, with two sets of boilers. Fourteen thousand yards of cotton and woolen goods are manufactured weekly from three thousand six hundred pounds of raw material. Fifty-five operatives are employed.

W. Arrott & Co. Mills.—These mills were erected by Judge James Andrews subsequent to 1848, and were located nearly opposite the old Thomas Steel grist-mill at the head of tide-water on Darby Creek. They were operated by Judge Andrews till his death, when they descended to his son, J. Charles Andrews, who, with Isaac Hibberd, operated them as Cedar Hill Mills until about 1873, when they were leased for a few years. In April, 1878, the property was sold by the assignees of J. Charles Andrews to William Arrott, of Philadelphia, who immediately began spinning yarn in these mills. The main building is two stories high, two hundred by fifty feet, contains five hundred spindles and eight sets of woolen cards. Ninety operatives are employed, and one thousand one hundred pounds of yarn are spun weekly.

In 1875, John L. Knowlton purchased a lot of land of the Sharon Land Association along the line of the Philadelphia, Wilmington and Baltimore Railroad. He erected a two-story brick building and commenced the manufacture of specialties in machinery. This he continued till his death, after which the building was occupied for a year or two by William P. Jenks in the manufacture of boiler coverings. In March, 1884, the property was purchased by Scully & Smith, Philadelphia, who are at present fitting the factory for the manufacture of wood-turning machinery.

Tannery.—In 1766, John Pearson, who subsequently became an officer in the Revolutionary army, and, after the erection of Delaware County, one of the associate judges, was operating a tan-yard at Darby, which business he appears to have continued until 1810, when he was succeeded by Charles Pearson. The tan-yard was subsequently abandoned, unless the bark-mill which James Bunting was operating in 1842 was on the site of the yard, and connected with the tannery.

Schools.—The first record of a school within the limits of what is now Darby borough, is found in the minutes of Darby Monthly Meeting of date 7th day Seventh month (September), 1692, where it is stated "that Benj. Clift is to teach school Beginge ye 12th of ye 7th^mo^, and to continue one whole year except 2 weeks." Arrangements were also made with him the next year "to teach schoole one yeare Beginge ye 20th of ye 7th^mo^," for which he was to receive twelve pounds. Doubtless this school was kept in Friends' meeting-house. Prior to 1735, David Thomas, of Darby, by an instrument in writing, granted to Joseph Reed a lot of ground on which to build a school-house. The building was erected on the site designated, and subsequently Reed assigned the property to John Davis and Richard Parker. On April 2, 1735, doubtless to cure a defect in title, David Thomas conveyed the same land, which contained a quarter of an acre, to John Davis and Richard Jackson. Miss Sarah L. Miller, of Media, states that her grandfather, George Miller, who resided in Springfield, attended school in the year 1730, at a small one-story brick house which stood a short distance west of Darby Creek, and that he boarded near by, so that he might be constant in his attendance. This location of that early school designated that the pupil spoken of was taught in the old one-story brick house which stood on part of the site of the Mount Zion burial-ground, and which building was taken down after 1843. In this old school-house on June 6, 1818, a meeting of the inhabitants of Darby and adjoining townships was held, whereat it was

"*Resolved*, That we will discourage the use of ardent spirits, as an article of drink; we will not procure, use, or give it to others as such in the time of gathering our hay and harvest, at the raising of buildings, or on other public or social occasions;

"*And resolved*, That we unite to suppress the unlawful sale of spirituous liquors, and to counteract the contamenating effect of those nurseries of vice, commonly called tippling houses, by giving information to the proper officers, and by such other means as are reasonably within our power."

It is stated in an account of the "Guardian Society for Preventing Drunkenness" of Chester County,[1] that it "was certainly the first temperance organization ever formed in Pennsylvania, and probably in the United States," and that shortly after a kindred and co-operative society was formed at Darby, in which Halliday Jackson and Edward Garrigues were conspicuous members. The Guardian Society was organized in 1820. The action at this meeting in 1818, clearly shows that a temperance organization had been held in Delaware County prior to that in Chester County, and that a temperance pledge had been adopted nearly two years before the formation of the Guardian Society.

In this old stone school-house, prior to the adoption of the school law of 1834, David Little taught, as did also Benjamin Oakford. This school-house, after the act of 1834 was accepted by Darby township, was transferred to the school directors, who, on Dec. 6, 1843, sold the lot to Michael Lincoln, and he, on the 14th of the same month, conveyed it to the trustees of the Mount Zion Methodist Church. The latter removed the school building, and the lot became a part of the burial-place.

The society of Friends continued to support the school at Darby throughout all the last century. Michael Blunston, who died there in 1736, bequeathed "fifty pounds in trust to school the children of Poor Friends of Darby Monthly Meeting." Mention is also made of Friends' Meeting schools in 1788, and in 1793 the society of Friends in Delaware County had seven schools under their care, one being located in Darby. A dwelling had also been erected in that village for the "accommodation of the master." Schools were kept by Friends regularly from that time, and since 1820 women have been members of the school committee. The adoption of the law providing for free public education, and the improvements made in the system by subsequent enactments, gradually superseded Friends' schools. However, as late as 1854, John H. Bunting, of Darby, gave the sum of ten thousand dollars, the interest of which was to be applied to the support of schools maintained by the society.

In March, 1825, an election was held throughout the county for school trustees under the law of 1804, and three were elected in each township. In the report of this election, Darby, Lower Chichester, Haverford, and Tinicum are not returned.

After the passage of the school law, in 1834, the court appointed Thomas Smith and Thomas Steel inspectors of public schools until directors were elected. In 1835–36 the township, then including the borough, received from the State and county appropriations $270.60.

On the 13th of March, 1841, the directors of the public schools of the township purchased eighty square perches of land of Hugh Lloyd in the village of Darby, and erected thereon a stone school-house, which was used until 1855, when it was abandoned upon the completion of what is known as the yellow school-house. Pearson Serrill conveyed to Robert K. Smith one acre of ground adjoining lands of Darby Monthly Meeting, and on Aug. 30, 1854, Smith transferred the lot to the school directors of Darby borough, who in the same year erected the present stone school-house, two stories in height, the corner-stone being laid with much ceremony Oct. 28, 1854, Hon. Joseph R. Chandler, of Philadelphia, delivering the address on the occasion. A two-story brick addition was subsequently erected, and the building at present accommodates six schools which are kept there. The borough of Darby was incorporated in 1853, since which it has been an independent school district. The directors of Darby borough, on the 2d of April, 1855, sold the old school-house and lot on New Street to the borough for twelve hundred and fifty dollars. The building is now used as a lock-up. In the year 1878 the directors erected a one-story brick school-house, thirty-six by forty feet, at Sharon Hill, in which one school is kept.

The following names are those of the school directors of Darby borough, as obtained from the election records of Media:

1854, Morris W. Lewis, Marmaduke Morehead, Robert K. Smith, Paxon Price, John R. Robb, Paxon Paxon; 1855, C. A. Litzenburg, John Verlenden; 1856, Jacob S. Serrill, William Russell, Jr.; 1857, William Jones, D. S. White; 1858, Daniel S. White, John Verlenden, C. S. Lloyd; 1859, William Russell, Jr., William C. Witter; 1860, John Verlenden, William Jones; 1861, David S. White, George S. Trueman; 1862, Charles A. Litzenberg, Jacob S. Serrill; 1863, John Verlenden, Thomas Palmer; 1864, Daniel S. White, Joseph Bunting; 1865, Isaac T. Jones, Jacob S. Serrill; 1866, John Verlenden, Thomas Palmer; 1867, W. D. H. Serrill, D. S. White; 1868, Stacey Jones, M.D., George S. Patchell; 1869, W. D. H. Serrill, David Maule; 1870, Daniel S. White, Thomas Palmer; 1871, Stacey Jones, M.D., William D. H. Smith; 1872, Oswald Paschall, Henry L. Paschall; 1873, Daniel S. White, Milton Mendenhall; 1874, Stacey Jones, M.D., Mrs. Emily Cochran; 1875, David Maule, W. W. James; 1876, Daniel S. While, Henry McAllister; 1877, Jacob Serrill, A. E. Crozer; 1878, Washington W. James, W. D. H. Serrill; 1879, Parkhurst McLaughlin, Isaac T. Jones; 1880, Stacy Jones, M.D., Daniel S. White; 1881, W. W. James, Theodore Knight; 1882, Daniel S. White, W. D. H. Serrill; 1883, Jacob Elpeth, Robert Green; 1884, James E. Coombs, Gill Hazelett.

[1] Futhey and Cope's "History of Chester County," p. 403.

Sharon Hill Academy.—John Jackson, a noted public Friend of Darby, a son of Halliday Jackson, after his marriage with Rachel T. Tyson, a highly educated and accomplished woman, in 1834, determined to establish a female boarding-school, and about 1835, after the death of his father, located at Sharon Hill, on the family estate. The school soon acquired an extensive reputation, and was at the time one of the most noted female educational institutions in the Middle States. John Jackson died in 1855, and his widow continued the school until 1858, when it was conducted by Israel J. Graham and Jane P. Graham. The property about 1870 was purchased by Rev. C. J. H. Carter, a Catholic clergyman, and a school for females was conducted there under the auspices of the Sisters of the Society of the Holy Child Jesus. In 1871 the building was enlarged by the addition of a wing, which made the total length of the main building one hundred and fourteen feet, while the interior was remodeled, so that the sleeping-rooms of the pupils were unusually large, well ventilated, and a dressing-room was attached to each apartment. The land and building having passed into the ownership of this society, in 1877 the present Gothic chapel was erected. The building is eighty-nine feet in length, the wood-work of black walnut, and the principal altars of Italian marble. The numerous windows which furnish light to the sanctuary are stained glass, presenting representations of St. Ignatius Loyola, St. Charles Borromeo, and sacred emblems appropriate to the Catholic faith. In November, 1877, the chapel was dedicated by the Right Rev. Archbishop Wood with appropriate and imposing ceremonies.

Darby Friends' Meeting-House.—The early Friends who, fleeing from persecution in England, settled in and about Darby, seem to have turned their attention speedily to arranging for religious services, and in the very year of Penn's coming, 1682, tradition states a meeting was held at the present village, in the house of John Blunston, whose hastily-constructed residence stood near the mill-race, which was subsequently dug, and nearly opposite the present meeting-house. The minutes of Darby Meeting do not substantiate the tradition, for they begin on the 2d of Fifth month (July), 1684, but Dr. Smith states that "there is some evidence that the business of a monthly meeting had been transacted at Darby a short time prior to the date of the first regular minute."[1] The inconvenience arising from the meeting being held in private houses, and the constant growth of the society in membership,—for emigration was remarkable in those early days,—far exceeding that of more modern times, induced an effort to be made to build a meeting-house. In 1687, John Blunston, in open court, acknowledged a deed "for one acre of land, in the township of Darby, to build a meeting-house thereon, to the use of the said township for ever, to exercise the true worship of God therein." A building, doubtless of logs, was erected on this tract, and it is said to have been located on the hillside, within the present graveyard. It was determined by meeting, so the ancient minutes state, to have it "lined within," to render it warmer in the severe winter seasons of the olden times. The first marriage which occurred therein was in February, 1689, between John Marshall and Sarah Smith. This statement, of course, refers to the first marriage in the meeting-house, for it is well known that the first marriage recorded at Darby Meeting was in 1684,—that of Samuel Sellers and Anna Gibbons. The fair bride rode to her new home on a pillion behind her husband.[2] Dr. Smith relates that in 1699 Darby Meeting dealt with a father who had unreasonably refused his consent to the marriage of his daughter, and the young couple, after legally publishing their intention, were married by John Blunston, a justice of the peace, the donor of the lot on which the meeting-house stood. The husband and wife were also dealt with by meeting, but the justice, who was in discharge of his official office, was not called on to explain his action. After the stone meeting-house at Chester was built, Friends of Darby, who were generally wealthy, perhaps desired a more comfortable place in which to assemble. Be that as it may, in 1699 it was "agreed that a meeting-house sixty foot one way and twenty foot added to the side, twenty-one foot wide in the clear, be built," and "John Bethell, John Hood, Michael Blunston, John Wood, and Thomas Worth ordered to manage the concern about said house till furder orders." The building was begun, but dragged slowly along, and to complete it repeated collections were authorized by the meeting. In 1701 it was still unfinished, and it was "ordered that a collection be every monthly meeting till further orders," and we are informed by Dr. Smith "that a loan was authorized to complete this meeting house, "an expedient rarely resorted to by the Society of Friends." This meeting-house was also located in the graveyard, and in 1862 a portion of the building was still standing.[3] It was certainly completed in the early summer of 1701, for at the meeting held in Fifth month of that year it was ordered "that Benjamin Cliff take care that the doors and windows be opened and shut as occasion may serve for one whole year, for which he is to have two pounds out of the collection." This house of worship stood for more than one hundred years, when it began to show the decrepitude of age, which constant repair could not prevent, hence its "decayed and shattered condition" was such that reluctantly

[1] History of Delaware County, p. 148, note. "A committee was appointed in 1683 by Chester Monthly Meeting to invite the Friends of Darby to unite with them in their monthly meeting. This they appear to have done so far as to contribute to the funds of that meeting on one occasion."

[2] "A Walk to Darby," by Townsend Ward, *Penna. Mag. of Hist.*, vol. iii. p. 265.

[3] Smith's "History of Delaware County," p. 198.

the members were compelled to take steps for the erection of the third and present meeting-house at Darby

At the Monthly Meeting in Twelfth month, 1803, the subject was referred to a committee, which, at the next meeting, First month, 1804, reported that having "several times met, and were in good measure united in building on what is called the lower lot, and were of opinion that a house built forty-five feet by sixty will cost three thousand three hundred dollars" The new structure was ordered to be erected, most of the stone used being obtained on the side of road opposite the Imperial Mills of Verlenden Brothers, excepting a few dressed stone which were brought from Leiper's quarries, in Ridley Towards the latter part of the year 1805, the building being nearly completed, Josiah Bunting was directed to give notice to members that the meeting would be held in the new structure on the 8th of Twelfth month, 1805 The first marriage in the new meeting-house was Hugh McIlvain, of Philadelphia, to Hannah, daughter of John Hunt, of Darby In 1870, the roof, which had done good service for sixty-five years, was replaced by a new one

Mount Zion Methodist Episcopal Church—In 1807, twenty persons residing in the neighborhood of Darby, desirous of organizing a Methodist Church in that vicinity, assembled together and formed a class Among those who were prominent in this movement were William Palmer, David Dunbar, Charles Levis, Samuel Levis, Charles Grant, Enos R Williams, Henry Rudolph, Hannah Shaw (Mrs Oswold Patchell), and Phebe Hoofstechler (Mrs George Lincoln) Some time subsequent to that date Dr Phineas Price purchased a quarter of an acre on the Springfield road from Joseph Wood, and on the lot built a stone church forty-five feet square Dr Price retained title during his lifetime, and after his death his representatives, Mary, Ann M, and Henry Price, on April 17, 1819, conveyed the house and lot to Samuel Levis, Charles Levis, Samuel Lungren, David Dunbar, and Jonas Morton, trustees of the church Dec 14, 1843, the old school-house, which stood on the lot adjoining the church land, was bought by the congregation, the building removed, and the lot inclosed in the grave-yard In 1854 a quarter of an acre of adjoining land was purchased from Ann Eliza Moore, and the burial-place again enlarged In 1882, it having been decided to remove the church to Darby, a lot in the borough was purchased of George S Patchell, and a brick church, thirty-six by sixty feet, at a cost of nine thousand four hundred dollars, was erected The old sanctuary by the road-side, which had served the congregation for threescore years and ten, ceased to be used after Dec 3, 1882, when the new edifice was dedicated The dedicatory sermon was preached by the late Bishop Matthew Simpson William Palmer and Enos R Williams, members of the first class, were local ministers and frequently preached in Mount Zion. Among the clergymen who from time to time have been in charge of the church were the Revs Thomas Miller, Ezekiel Connor, William Townsend Larney, William McCormick, James Neale, Brooks Eyres, William King, William Cooper, and Bishop Scott was at one time the presiding elder Subsequent to these came the Revs Abel Howard, William Dalrymple, William McMichael, A G Mauger, Roble Smith, —— Vandersloot, William McMichael, and A G. Keymett, the present pastor The church has at present a membership of one hundred and ninety persons

The Presbyterian Church of Darby Borough.—While Rev J Addison Whitaker was pastor of the Darby, or Knowle's Presbyterian Church, in 1851 mission services were begun in Darby borough The public school-house was used for the meeting, and interest gradually was awakened in the movement until, in January, 1854, a fund was subscribed to build a church edifice In April, 1854, at a meeting of Presbytery in Mantua (Philadelphia), a committee was appointed to consider the propriety of building a church at Darby, who reported in favor of establishing a mission chapel there The sum subscribed being sufficient to warrant the erection of a house of worship, the minutes of the board of trustees set forth,—

"On the 24th of January, 1854, John H Robb, Paschall J Hoopes, M D, Charles A Litzenburg, John Verlenden, Israel Helms, and the Rev J Addison Whitaker met at the residence of the pastor in Darby, and at his request united in forming a voluntary board of trustees for the purpose of erecting a church edifice, and to hold the same in trust for the Presbyterian Church hereafter to be organized and called the Darby and Paschallville Presbyterian Church, or by any other name by which they wish to designate it as a Presbyterian Church"

A design for a church building was made by John Nahman, of Philadelphia, which was accepted by the board, and on Feb 11, 1854, a lot was purchased of Dr. Paschall J Hoopes, five hundred and fifty dollars being paid for the ground, located at the intersection of Maine and Moore Streets Early in the spring Charles Bonsall, who had contracted to erect the church for seven thousand eight hundred and fifty dollars, began building The contract stipulated that the lecture-room should be completed by August 1st, and the entire building should be finished by Jan 1, 1855 The lecture-room, however, was not ready at the time stipulated The church was organized on Sunday, Oct 1, 1854, with fourteen members (most of whom were members of Darby Presbyterian Church), with Dr Stephen Parsons as ruling elder, and the Rev J. Addison Whitaker minister in charge The work on the auditorium was not completed until the spring of 1858 The lot adjoining the church lot was purchased in 1862, and a parsonage erected, at a cost of five thousand five hundred and eight dollars In 1870, repairs were made upon the church at an expense of three thousand and ninety-seven dollars and fifty-two cents The church from its organization had been laboring under a heavy debt, which, in 1873, was entirely removed, and on the 28th of November in that year a jubilee meeting was held The church was incorporated by act of Assembly, Jan 13, 1855

The pastors from the date of the formation have been as follows Rev J A Whitaker served the church from its organization until the spring of 1855 In April of that year the Rev T J Johnson acted as supply, in June the Rev John Patton, and the Rev David C Meeker commenced his labors as stated supply Sept 23, 1855 On the 25th of January, 1856, he received a call to become permanent pastor, which he held under advisement and finally declined, preaching his farewell sermon Sept 14, 1856 The Rev Michael Burdett was acting pastor from Nov 15, 1857, and in October, 1858, received a call to the pastorate, which he accepted, and remained in charge until January, 1862, when he resigned The pulpit was supplied occasionally from that time to July, 1862, when the Rev Samuel W Crittenden, of the Third Presbytery of New York, supplied the church, and was called on the 19th of that month He entered at once upon his duties as pastor-elect At a meeting of the Third Presbytery of Philadelphia, held October 21st in that year, he was received as a member, accepted the call, and was installed as pastor Jan 18, 1863 He resigned in April, 1865, but remained till July of that year A unanimous call was extended to the Rev William H Thorne, which was at once accepted, but was not installed until June 10, 1866 He resigned this charge Dec 29, 1868 On the 27th of January, 1869, the Rev Charles Brown was unanimously chosen to supply the pulpit until April of that year, which he did greatly to the good of the church. On the 6th of June, 1869, Mr George L Raymond, a licentiate of the Third Presbytery of New York, was invited to supply the pulpit until the fall meeting of the Third Presbytery of Philadelphia, which he accepted, and immediately entered upon his duties On the 22d of September, 1869, he was chosen as pastor, accepted the call, and was ordained and installed April 28, 1870 In the spring of 1874 he was elected professor of Rhetoric in Williams College, Massachusetts, and wishing to accept it, he gave notice of his intention to resign The congregation reluctantly granted his request, and the relationship was dissolved by Presbytery April 14, 1874 The Rev W T Brown, of Colorado, supplied the pulpit on June 21, 1874, and July 12th, and on the 4th of August was unanimously elected pastor of the church At the meeting of Presbytery held at Reading, October 16th, he accepted the call, and was installed pastor Nov 22, 1874 He served as minister until May 22, 1884, since which time the church, now numbering two hundred and sixteen members, has been without a pastor A Sunday-school is connected with the church, and has four hundred pupils George Thompson is in charge Charles O Baird, son of Matthew Baird, commenced the erection of a chapel in the spring of 1881, as a memorial of his father and mother It is of stone, and cost about thirty-four thousand dollars It was dedicated Feb 25, 1883, the dedicatory sermon being preached by the Rev Dr Cattell, of Princeton

Darby Library Company.—On May 1, 1743, twenty-nine persons founded the Darby Library by signing articles of agreement and effecting an organization These articles required each person in copartnership to pay, on becoming a member, twenty shillings to a person who should be appointed to receive the money and purchase books for a library, and also annually thereafter to pay five shillings "for and towards the Purchasing of such books and the necessary expenses of the Library as two-thirds of the Company shall direct" The agreement further sets forth

"That whereas it is found by long Experience that no Considerable number of People will at all times keep in a Regular Decent Decorum without Some Necessary forms & Rules to walk and act by And suitable Persons authorised to Put these rules in Execution, therefore we, the subscribers hereunto, Do agree that there be an Ellection held Yearly on the first Day of May (except that happens on the first Day of the week, in Such Case on the Day next following) to Elect by ticket a Secretary, treasurer, Librarine, and four other Persons for assistants, and also to admit Such Persons into the Company as two-thirds of the members then being Shall Approve off And to Consider, Regulate, & Determine all such matters and things as may be laid before the Company by any of the members thereof"

It was also provided that at all the meetings of the Library Company the members "then Present shall seat themselves in Sober, Decent, Regular manner, Such as becomes Christians and Students, then the Secretary shall call the members by their names Respectively, as they Stand on the Records, to Deliver in their votes, which shall be writt on a small Piece of Paper floded up, with the names of the Person writt therein whom they would have for Secretary, treasurer, Librarine, & assistants for the Ensuing Year, which ticket they shall Deliver to one of they assistants, who shall Put them into a box Provided for that Purpose, and when the Company, or as many of them as Pleases, shall Delivered in their Votes, the Secretary and assistants shall Proceed to Draw the Tickets in the following manner, that is to say, the Secretary Shall Draw the tickets out of the box and Read the names in them, and what they are for, And the Assistants Enter the names of all those Persons Voted in Distinct collums, And they who have most Votes for Secretary, treasurer, Librarine, and assistants for the Ensuing Year, and shall have their names Entered then accordingly by the old Secretary in a book, as aforesaid, Provided for that Purpose" New members were elected by ballot, and books to be purchased were named by the members, of which titles a list was furnished to each, and any book proposed could be objected to, after debate, the question of purchase should be decided by vote, and if two-thirds were favorable, the book was entered on a list of volumes to be purchased. The librarian was required to be at the library every other Seventh day in the afternoon, "in spring and summer quarter, from five to seven o'clock, and in the fall and winter quarter from three to five o'Clock," to deliver and receive books. If a book had been damaged beyond ordinary wear the member who had taken it out was required to pay its value, and if a set, the cost of all the volumes. According to size, the books could be retained from two to four weeks, only one volume could be had by any member, and no one could lend or hire a book from the library. The agreement provided thus for the maintenance of good order:

"If any of the Library Company Should behave themselves in Such an Indecent unbecoming Disorderly manner, as to become Disagreeable Disreputable and troublesome, In all Such Cases two thirds of the Library Company mette as afores[d] may by there order from under the hand of the Sectry Dir[ct] the Treasurer for the time being to Repay such offender or offenders his or their Prime Cost of the Library Book &c (out of the Library Stock) after Deducting a Reasonable abatement for the ware and Delay of the S[d] Books and Incident Charges of the Library &c, then shall the offender or offenders be disowned by the Company met as afores[d] and thereby Declare to have no Share, Right Property or Priviledge to the Library Books or anything thereunto belonging and their Procedings thereon shall be Enter'd on Record accordingly."

The members of the Library Company who signed the articles on May 10, 1743, were Joseph Bonsall, John Davis, James Hunt, John Sketchly, George Wood, Joshua Thomson, Samuel Bunting, Nathan Gibson, Benjamin Lobb, Enoch Elliot, Thomas Pearson, William Horne, Joseph Lees, Peter Elliot, Jonathan Paschall, Abraham Johnson, Isaac Pearson, John Hunt, Joseph Hunt, Abraham Marshall, John Pearson, Richard Lloyd, David Gibson, Joseph Levis, Benjamin Hayes, Thomas Pennell, Henry Lewis, Charles Crosby, John Levis. Joseph Bonsall was first secretary, Nathan Gibson treasurer, John Pearson librarian, and William Horne, Isaac Pearson, Thomas Pearson, and Benjamin Lobb assistants. It was also "Ordered that the Secretary, treasurer and Librarian transmit y[e] several sums of money subscribed by this Company to Europe as soon as conveniently may, and purchase therewith such books as is heretofore voted for, if the money be sufficient for y[e] use of the Library Company." A meeting was held on May 14, 1743, at the house of John Pearson, librarian, and on October 8th "the Treasurer acquainted them that he, with y[e] advice and consent of the Secretary and Librarian had purchased a bill of exchange of Rebicca Edgel, drawn on Larance Williams, of London, merchant, payable in thirty days after sight to Peter Collinson, of London, gentleman," and "the Secretary acquaint the Company that, in pursuance of the aforesaid bill of Exchange and y[e] directions of this Company, he had wrote a letter to y[e] s[d] Peter Collinson, a copy whereof he produced and read in the following words:"

"DARBY, y[e] 14th of 4th Month, 1743.

"FRIEND PETER COLLINSON,

"There is a small number of us in Darby, near Phil[ad], who have formed ourselves into a company, in order to purchase a small set of Books for our use, with well-grounded expectations of our number increasing in a little time, and being advised by our fr[d] and neighbour, John Bartram, to apply to thee to purchase the s[d] books, and in confidence of thy good disposition and from y[e] character he gives of thee to Encourage such a decision, have thought fit thereupon to send to and desire thee to do such an office of kindness for us, but as our number is but small, so is the sum of money, amounting only to fourteen pounds, as p[r] bill of exchange, drawn by Rebicca Edgel, on Larance Williams, merchant, payable to thee in thirty days after sight thereof. We also send herewith a catalogue of such books as our Company approved of, requesting thee to be so good as to buy so many of them (taking them in order as they stand on the list) as the money will extend to pay, reserving sufficient to satisfy thee for thy trouble with the cost of Insurance here. And when the books are purchased, please to ship them of p[r] the first opportunity for Phil[ad], in such a manner and with such directions as appears to thee most convenient, either for John Bartram or the subscriber hereof. Be so good also as to get the books lettered on y[e] back, if that can be done without much trouble or cost, or as many of them as conveniently can be. We also desire thee to send the price of each book purchased, that being necessary for us to know in pursuance of our agreement. Thy answering our requests will much oblige us, who, with due respect are thy unfeigned friends. Signed in behalf of said Company.

"By JOSEPH BONSALL, *Secretary*."

On the 5th of Ninth month (November), 1743, the books came from Peter Collinson, and in a letter he asked that in future —— Manley, bookseller on Ludgate Hill, London, should be made correspondent of the company, and that he (Collinson) would overlook the books sent and the prices paid. The books thus forwarded were "The Gentleman Instructed, Puffendorf's Law of Nature and Nations, the Spectator (8 vols.), the Turkish Spy (8 vols.), Tournefort's Voyage to the Levant (2 vols.), Whitson's Theory, Addison's Travels, Barclay's Apology, Locke on Education, Religion of Nature Delineated, Gordon's Geography, Grammar, Sherlock on Death, Whitson's Astr[o] Principles, Mondrall's Travels, Dyche's Dictionary, Tull's Husbandry, Blackmore on y[e] Creation, Independent Whig (3 vols.), Wood's Institute on y[e] Laws of England, Milton's Paradise Lost and Regained (2 vols.), Puffendorf's History of Sweden, Rawlegh's History of y[e] World (2 vols.), The Life of the Duke of Marlborough (2 vols.)."

At the meeting on May 5, 1745, Joseph Lewis gave the company "Sewell's History of the Rise, Increase, and Progress of the People called Quakers," valued at 15*s.*, Nathan Gibson gave Samuel Fisher's work called "The Rustick's Alarm to y[e] Rabbies," valued at 20*s.*, Benjamin Cliff gave Plutarch's "Lives," valued at 5*s.*, Benjamin Hays gave "History of y[e] First Settlement of Virginia, New York, New Jersey, and Pennsylvania by y[e] English," valued at 4*s.* 6*d.*

In 1746 the committee who were appointed to purchase books reported that they could not get the books in Pennsylvania, and state "that insurance is so high, & danger of the sea is so great at this time, that they Judge it might be to the advantage of the Company not to send it [the money] until further orders." On May 1, 1747, the company remitted £19 11*s.* to England for additional books. It appears that Williams & Boeketiff, the booksellers in London, had not acted to the satisfaction of the company, for the meeting ordered the secretary to draw for the balance in the hands of the firm, and appointed other parties as purchasing agents until 1760, when David Hall, bookseller, of Philadelphia, received and filled orders for the company During the Revolutionary war the meetings were regularly held, and May 1, 1781, the share held by John Morton, which by will he bequeathed to his son, John, was vested in the latter's eldest brother, Sketchley Morton, Dr John S Morton having died During all the years which had elapsed since the foundation of the library no effort was ever made to obtain a lot and erect a library building until Jan 5, 1795, when Richard Welling, Hugh Lloyd, Matthias Holsten, Thomas Levis, and Benjamin Brannon were appointed to ascertain and report the site of a lot and probable cost of a suitable building On Jan 2, 1797, the committee reported that they could not obtain a lot "at a price that would possibly do," hence the project was abandoned In 1804 the house (Pearson's) where the library had been kept was sold and it became necessary to remove the books, and Jacob Sewell, John Hunt, Hugh Lloyd, Samuel Ash, and Charles Pearson were appointed to secure a place for the books, which was done, the library being removed to Pearson's house (still standing at the corner of New and High Streets)

The easy manners which prevailed at the meetings in the early part of this century is shown by the following extract from the rules adopted on Jan 12, 1818

"No member shall smoke in our meeting during the business thereof, under a penalty of twenty-five cents for every offence"

On Jan 3, 1871, the library was again removed, to a room over Philip Siplee's saddler-shop, his daughter, Mary, being engaged as librarian, her services and the apartment being obtained for seventy-five dollars per year.

In 1872 an effort was made to purchase a lot and erect a library building, subscriptions being solicited to that end, and so successful was the movement that on March 25, 1872, a lot was bought from David Henry Flickner, one thousand dollars being paid for the ground The present ornate and commodious building, admirably adapted for the purpose, was erected by Charles Bonsall, at a cost of eight thousand eight hundred and ninety-five dollars and fifty-four cents The building committee consisted of Isaac T Jones, Charles Lloyd, William D H Serrill, Jacob Serrill, Paschall Lloyd, J Charles Andrews, and George Serrill, and the architect D B Price In front of this building a flag-pole over fifty feet in height was planted early in the centennial year, and on March 29, 1876, a large American flag, the gift of citizens of the borough, was raised, the ceremonies on that occasion being of a highly interesting character. William Ward delivered a spirited address, as did also Dr Stacey Jones The old library, now approaching its sesqui-centennial anniversary, is well located, and the sphere of its usefulness should be largely extended At this time (1884) its officers are as follows President, Isaac T Jones, Vice-President, Jacob S Sewell, Treasurer, Daniel S White, Secretary, W Lane Verlenden, Librarian, Mrs A E Crozer

The Darby Fire Company—On the 27th of January, 1775, the Darby Fire Company was organized by the adult active male residents of the village In the articles of association it is set forth that each subscriber, "for the better preservation of our own and neighbor's houses, goods, and effect from fire, would at his own proper charge provide two leathern buckets, to be marked with his own name and respective company, and shall be kept ready at hand and applied to no other use than for preserving our own and neighbor's houses, goods, and effects" Any neglect of this agreement subjected the member so offending to a fine of five shillings, excepting in those cases where buckets were lost at a fire A sufficient sum was contributed to purchase ladders, which were kept in a convenient place, and were forbidden to be used for any purpose than at a fire, or by any one not a member of the company The ladders or buckets lost while in service were to be replaced out of the company's fund A fine of five shillings was imposed on all members who failed to attend at a fire occurring on the premises of one of the company, unless a reasonable excuse could be shown The annual meeting was on third 2d day of Tenth month, at three o'clock, and if any member neglected to be present, such neglect was punishable by a fine of two shillings Every member was required to serve as clerk for a year, beginning with the first subscriber to the articles, and "so in rotation" till all had served That officer was required to inspect buckets, notify members of meetings, keep the minutes, collect all fines and dues If the clerk failed to give notice of meeting to any member, he was liable to a fine of one shilling for every member not notified, while a clerk not properly performing his duty was liable to a fine of five shillings A treasurer was also annually elected A member refusing to pay his fines his name should be erased from the roll, and he should be excluded from all rights and forfeit all interest in the ladders and other property of the company The articles, which were "printed by Zachariah Poulson, Junior, No 106 Chestnut St., Philad, 1796," thirty years after the organization of the company, concluded

"XI Lastly, That upon the death of any of our company the survivors shall, in time of danger as aforesaid, be aiding and assisting to the widow of such decedent during her widowhood as if her husband had been living, she only keeping the buckets in repair, and causing them to be sent to every fire as aforesaid"

The first meeting was held April 10, 1775, at which time the business meetings of the company were called semi-annually until April 10, 1780, when the provision for an annual meeting in the Tenth month in every year was adopted On Nov 25, 1793, the feet of the company's ladders were shod with iron, and a movement was made looking to the purchase of a fire-engine, but in 1798 the subscriptions which had been paid for that object were returned to the contributors In 1800 a hook-ladder was ordered to be purchased, and in 1802 a ladder was directed to be placed at Nathaniel Newlin's barn, another at Jonathan Bonsall's, and still another at Henry Paschall's Members were also authorized to use any of the company's ladders in putting up conductors (lightning-rods), provided the ladders were returned within three days after being taken away from the designated places where they were ordered to be kept

The following is a list of the members who served as clerk from 1775 to 1851, when the order of rotation in office seems to have been abandoned·

1775, Henry Hays, 1776, Jesse Bonsall, Isaac Pearson, 1777, John Paschall, 1778, David Humphreys, 1779, Isaac Lloyd, John Horn, 1780, Aaron Oakford, John Hunt, 1781, John Humphreys William Parker, 1782, Henry Paschall, Joseph Pearson, Jacob Webber, John Richards, 1783, Jacob Rudolph, 1784, Jacob Serrill, 1785, Joseph Bonsall, 1786, Benjamin Paschall, 1787, Samuel Bunting, Joshua Bonsall, John Mitchel, 1788, Jonathan Bonsall, 1789, Philip Price, 1790, no record, 1791, Benjamin Bartram, 1792, Nathan Pearson, 1793, Hugh Lloyd, 1794, Nathaniel Newlin, 1795, Benjamin Oakford, 1799, Isaac Oakford, 1798, Matthias Holstien, 1799, Richard Lloyd, 1800, William Gardiner, 1801, Jacob Gibbons, 1802, John Hunt, 1803, Levi Bonsall, 1804, Thomas Leacock, 1805, Samuel Bunting, 1806, John Hatin, 1807, Benjamin Pearson, 1808, Joseph Heacock, 1809, John Rively, 1810, Isaac Bartram, 1811, William Humphreys, 1812, George Serrill, 1813 Stephen Horn, 1814, William Supplee, 1815 Benjamin Bartram, Jr, 1816, Hugh Lloyd, 1817, Halliday Jackson, 1818, George Serrill, 1819, John Bunting, 1820, John H Bunting, 1821, George Serrill, 1822, Isaac Sullender, 1823, William Bunting, 1824, Aaron Clement, 1825, John Bartram, 1826, Thomas Serrill, 1827, Thomas Smith, 1828, Joseph Dogson, 1829, John H Andrews, 1830, James Bunting, 1831, John Brooks, 1832, William P Pusey, 1833, Jonas Morton, 1834, Capt James Serrill, 1835, Abram G Hunt, 1836 Josiah D Bonsall, 1837, Hill Pennell, 1838, Benjamin Serrill, 1839, John Smith, Jr, 1840, Dr Samuel Thomas, 1841, Samuel Roe, 1842, John Jackson, 1843, Hugh P Lloyd (he also acted for 1844 instead of Joseph H Bonsall "whose term it was'), 1845, David T Morton, 1846, James Andrews, 1847, William P Serrill, who remained clerk until 1851, after which date the secretaries were appointed for the meetings and committees to notify members and inspect the buckets and property of company

There were several of the early members who appear never to have acted as clerks The dates of the admission of such were as follows 1783, Joshua Humphreys, Samuel Smith, Jesse Sharpless, 1791, Samuel Ash, 1792, Thomas Lloyd, 1794, Matthew Jones, 1795, Isaac Serrill, 1796, Samuel Oliver, 1800, James Andrews, Jonathan Tyson, John Thabourne, 1809, Solomon Humphreys, 1811, Edward Garrigues, 1814, Thomas Steel, M C Shallcross, 1815, Thomas Thompson, Andrew Cox, 1816, Richard Gardner, 1818, Joseph M Morgan, 1822, Joshua Ward

At subsequent dates the following residents of Darby and neighborhood became members of the company Abraham G Hunt, Josiah D Bonsall, Joel Bonsall, William Pennell, Samuel R Lamplugh, John Smith, Jr, John H Brown, Samuel Thomas, Samuel Roe, John Jackson, Hugh P Lloyd, Joseph H Bonsall, Daniel T Morton, Maris W. Lewis, James Andrews, William P Serrill, Jonathan Hadock, Thomas L Bartram, Henry Garrigues, Caleb Ash, Isaac L Bartram, Turner Risdon, Hugh Lloyd, Paschall Lloyd, John Tribit, William H Bunting, George Serrill, William Lincoln, Stephen H Brooks, William G Davis, Harry Paschall, Charles Lloyd, Jr, Benjamin W Oakford, Dell Pennell, John L Passmore, Richard Blundin, John B Bartram, Joseph M Bunting, Charles Tribit, Richard K Smith, Edward Taylor, Evans E Russell

At a meeting held at the house of Samuel Ash, Oct 13, 1817, Hugh Lloyd was elected permanent president, and Benjamin Pearson permanent secretary. In 1821 the company had a "ladder-house near the (Blue) Bell Inn," which house was that year removed to another location In 1822 the ladder-house at Darby "wants a new roof," and the ladder "at Nathaniel Newlin's barn is geting twisted & crooked for want of proper hangings" (it was reported in 1825 as "so broken as to render it useless"), and Benjamin Pearson "requested the company to remove the ladder House now on his ground" At the annual meeting in 1823, Thomas Smith, James Bunting, George Serrill, John Hunt, and John H Bunting were appointed a committee "to ascertain what kind of an engine would best suit the company and what would be the cost of it and also what amount can be subscribed" At the next annual meeting the committee reported that an engine "could not be procured for less than $250," whereupon the company decided that it was "inexpedient to adopt any further measures at this time relative to it" At the meeting of Oct 9, 1826, it was decided "that the company shall sup together this evening," which is the first appearance of the modern banquet in the company's minutes, although then a half-century had elapsed since its organization

On June 20, 1833, a special meeting of the company was held at the public-house of S R Lamplough, when the following preamble and resolutions were adopted

"The Company by the voluntary contributions of the members, aided by the liberal subscriptions of many of those who do not belong to it, have procured an engine at a cost of two hundred and twenty five dollars, which is placed under the care and control of the said Fire Company, Therefore,

"*Resolved*, That the grateful acknowledgments of the Company are hereby tendered to those persons who have aided them in procuring it.

"*Resolved*, that the offer of the use of a house for the engine made by Samuel Ash, an honorary member of the Company, be accepted, and the thanks of the company are hereby tendered to him for the same"

Capt. James Serrill, James Bunting, and Joseph Dogson were appointed a committee "to procure one hundred feet of hose to be attached to the engine" At a meeting in the following October the ladder-house in Darby was removed to the lot adjoining the printing-house Y S Walter had in the preceding August begun the publication of the *Delaware County Republican* in the village of Darby, and we learn that the clerk had "procured a number of printed blanks for notifying the members of the time of meeting" The committee appointed to purchase hose reported that sixty feet of leather hose had been procured, for which $40.45 had been paid, and that twenty-five feet of gum-elastic hose had been ordered, but was not finished ready for delivery. A reel-carriage for the hose had also been purchased. At the October meeting in 1834, the committee on hose reported the gum-elastic hose could not be had, and they had purchased leather hose in its stead. At the same meeting Capt. James Serrill, Isaac Bartram, and Abram G. Hunter were appointed a committee to procure "a situation and to erect thereon a suitable House for the safe keeping of the Engine and Hose." At the following annual meeting this committee reported that they had not "performed the duty assigned them," and they were continued a committee "for the purpose and are directed to use more diligence than heretofore." But the following years the report was not of a more satisfactory character. On Jan. 23, 1837, the committee reported that they had procured "a situation and erected a house sufficient for the engine and hose and that they were removed to it, the cost of which amounted to one hundred and six dollars." At the following annual meeting, Capt. James Serrill was appointed to have the words "Darby Fire Engine" painted on the front of the engine-house. In 1840 the roof of the ladder-house was so much out of repair that a committee was appointed to have it repaired. At the meeting on Nov. 27, 1851, a committee was appointed to "ascertain whether the owners of the engine in Paschallville will place it under the direction of the company." With what success does not appear in writing, the minutes of the meeting not being transcribed in the record-book after that date. The companies were, however, consolidated and took the name "Darby and Paschallville Fire Company."

The company preserved its organization until 1871, when the borough authorities decided to institute a paid department, and on Nov. 6, 1871, Council elected Enos Verlenden chief engineer. On Jan. 1, 1872, a room was rented at the mills of the Verlenden Brothers for three years, in which to house the engine, and the "old machine," after a half-century of service, in good repair, is ready, at any moment, for use when required.

Licensed Houses.—Darby, one of the earliest settlements after Penn acquired title to the province of Pennsylvania, grew more rapidly in population than any locality within the limits of the present county of Delaware, and must necessarily have been largely supplied with houses of public entertainment to accommodate the constant stream of emigration flowing thitherward. The first notice that had been found regarding taverns there is the extract from the proceedings of Darby town-meeting, held in 1715, quoted by Dr. Smith, which sets forth:

"That travellers having nothing to defray their charges at the public Inn, shall be allowed ten pence a night (if they are first allowed by the overseers of the poor)."

Who it was that then held the license has not been learned, but it is presumed it must have been John Tests, for Aug. 28, 1717, he was granted "renewal of license to keep a public house in Darby," and in 1719, Margaret Tests, in all likelihood his widow, was also favored with like consideration by the court. Although long previous to that date Wood kept a tavern in Darby, as appears from the evidence in a trial for an assault a few years after the first arrival of Penn in the province.

On Sixth month 30, 1720, Edward Smout made application to be permitted "to sell all sorts of Liquors, and to keep a house of entertainment" in the dwelling he then occupied. The petition being favorably acted on, Smout remained there until 1724, when he having removed to Chichester, Thomas Pattison seems to have succeeded to the business, and continued it until 1734, when his petition is indorsed "cannot be allowed." Among the old records at West Chester, as of August court, 1734, is a letter from Catharine Pattison, addressed to Joseph Parker, the clerk of court, asking him to intercede for her in her application for license for the house. "My husband," she says, "has been gone from me near a week, nor have I anybody to take Care of my business, nor do I expect he will Come again." Her application, however, was rejected, and Nov. 26, 1734, Richard Parker petitioned for license in Darby, alleging that "one publick house being not sufficient," a view of the case which seemed to impress the judicial mind so strongly that they adopted Parker's conclusion as the correct one.

The "one publick house" mentioned in Parker's application was that kept by Thomas Pulford, who had presented his petition Aug. 30, 1721, in which he requested the court to confer upon him the right to "Sell all sorts of Liquors" in Darby, which leave was granted, and annually extended to him up to and including the year 1734. However, one year after license was first granted to Pulford, in 1722, Abel Pearson was also allowed the like privilege, and on the bond given that year by Pulford, Abel Pearson appears as the surety, while on that given by Pearson, Thomas Pulford is the bondsman. Pearson had enough of tavern-keeping in one year, for in the latter part of 1738, Pattison was licensed, and the same pleasant agreement of two of a trade is noticed again, inasmuch as Pulford and Pattison became security one for the other.

The Ship.—In 1735, Benjamin Davis petitioned for and was allowed to keep a public-house in Darby, which place in all probabilities was then known as it was in 1770, and for thirty odd years in the present century, as the "Ship."

In the same year in which Davis found favor with the court (1735) John Lee, or Lea, petitioned for license at the house where Thomas Pulford lived in the village. Joseph Need and twenty other residents in the neighborhood, in anticipation of this request, on the last Tuesday in May presented a remonstrance, which set forth that John Lee, late of Philadelphia City, was a tailor by trade, and as there were two public-houses then in the town,—Davis' license had been granted early in that year,—there was no necessity for a third tavern The judges looked favorably upon this "representation," and when Lee's application came before the August court it was refused

Davis did not continue long as a publican, for Aug 30, 1737, William Thomas petitioned for the court's favor, and stated in his application that he had "purchased the dwelling-house in Darby where Benjamin Davis lately dwelt, which has been a publick house several years," and license was continued to him until Aug 28, 1744, when William Donaldson, having leased the premises, succeeded Thomas as landlord of the inn, and remained as such until 1758, when Margaret Donaldson succeeded him in the business, to be herself followed in turn, in 1760, by John Wilkinson The latter continued there until 1770, when John Mitchell received the license, and in his petition that year, for the first time, occurs the noted name of the old hostelry, as before mentioned In 1774, Mitchell was succeeded in business by John Richards, and when the latter died in 1779 his widow, Ann, took out the license Agnes Bryce seems to have had control of the inn in 1782, and John Bryce the year following In 1786, Samuel Smith was granted license for that year, and annually thereafter until 1795, when he died, and his widow, Elizabeth, continued there until 1803, at which date her daughter, Tacy, succeeded to the business The year following (1804) Tacy Smith associated Sidney Smith, her sister, in the enterprise, and to them the license was annually granted until 1833 During the war of 1812 the old weather-beaten sign of the Ship, still displaying the British flag at the peak, creaked in the wind, and as patriotic spirit ran high, a number of boys in the village determined that the flag of the enemy must come down, and arming themselves with stones, they battered the ancient sign to pieces The proprietors of the inn very quietly substituted in its place a new sign representing an American frigate in full sail bearing an American ensign The residents of Darby fifty years ago used to say of these maiden ladies of uncertain age, "May the Lord help the man that wanders in there if he cannot give his family pedigree from Noah down, together with his own age, whence he came, whither he was going, and whether he was married or single" In 1833, Hannah Rice succeeded the Misses Smith as landlady of the Ship, and continued so until 1835, when the Smiths again procured license until 1838, when John Smith removed from the Market Wagon (which latter place in that year ceased to be a public-house) and be came the landlord of the Ship The ancient hostelry was to bear that name no more, for it was licensed as the "Darby Village Inn," and continued to be known as such for many years subsequently In 1840, Norris Hannum became the landlord, and the line of stages which John Smith, when he relinquished tavern keeping, sold to Edward Ingram, continued to make the Village Inn their point of arrival and departure Here Hannum continued until his death, his widow, Sarah B Hannum, receiving license for the first time in 1847, the year when granting license to vend spirituous liquors by a popular vote under the provisions of the act of Assembly (afterwards declared unconstitutional) had been interdicted in all the townships of Delaware County excepting Concord, Thornbury, Edgmont, Middletown, and Darby In 1848, Mrs Hannum received license, and in her petition set forth the name of the house as the "Farmers' and Mechanics' Hotel," a title that seemed to please her fancy and which she could use with all propriety, since the original dwelling bearing that name had ceased to be a public-house In 1852, William Russell, Jr, had the old inn, and he dubbed it anew as the "Plank-Road House" Here he continued until 1856, when he was succeeded by Franklin Thornton, after which date the old inn had several landlords, and was finally torn down, and a new building erected, which is now kept by John Standerling as "The Philadelphia Hotel"

On Aug 31, 1736, John Hallowell strove to obtain license by showing that "he had rented a house of Joseph Hibberd, in Darby, by the King's Road, and he and his wife being stricken in years," were persons well fitted to receive the court bounty, but the justices refused their approval of his petition

In 1756, Barbara McCullough was granted license to keep a tavern in Darby township, and in 1758 was followed by John Wayton, while he in turn gave place to John Trapnall, in 1765, after which occurs a break of seven years, until 1773, when Henry Schrieber was a recipient of the court's favor, presumably at the same place, after which it disappears of record

Sixth month 28, 1744, John Pearson presented his petition asking that he be allowed to keep a house of entertainment in Darby, "where Thomas Bulford kept tavern," and was allowed The following year John Rudolph, who had rented the premises, succeeded John Pearson as landlord, and continued there until 1747, when John Pearson again presented his petition, and stated therein that John Rudolph was about to remove from the house he had formerly kept and desired license for the same, which was granted him

The Blue Anchor Tavern.—The same year (1747) John Rudolph was allowed license, but it is very probable it was not in the same place where he had formerly kept, for both he and Pearson were continued annually to be licensed by the court until 1754, when Pearson's name for the last time appears of record Where Rudolph's tavern was at that time I have failed to learn so as to state its locality beyond doubt, but in 1763, William Pinville seems to have followed him in business, to be succeeded in the year 1765 by John Rudolph, and the latter in 1770 by

Daniel Bessonett, who states in his petition that the license is desired for the house "where John Rudolph kept on west side of Darby Creek, in town of Darby" This statement would indicate that Rudolph had been landlord of the once noted Blue Anchor Tavern, which stood on the west side of the creek near the bridge At all events, in 1772, when Jacob Rudolph made application for the court's indulgence at the old stand, he states it is "where his father was" In 1775, Mary, the widow of John Rudolph, became the landlady, and the following year she was succeeded by William Smith, and the latter, in 1783, by Isaac Thompson, when the inn, then known as the "Bee Hive," passed out of our annals as a public-house, although it is again mentioned in 1806, when Archibald Gardener asked the privilege to renew the license there, stating that he "hath rented the House formerly occupied for a long time by the Rudolphs as a public-house, that being advanced in years and having a numerous small family to support, Prays your Honors to grant him a permit to sell Beer and sider" The court after due consideration concluded to refuse the prayer of the petitioner On Friday afternoon, March 20, 1857, the old large stone building, formerly the Blue Anchor, which was then occupied as a dwelling by ten or twelve colored families, was destroyed by fire

The Market Wagon.—In 1822, Joseph Warner, of Darby, stated to the court that he then occupied a house and lot on the main street, where Capt James Serrill lately dwelt, which house he declared was necessary for the accommodation of travelers and "market people using the road in particular" His petition was indorsed by seventy-three signatures A remonstrance was filed, signed by thirty persons, whose objections to the house were that immediately in the neighborhood were two public-houses which furnished all the accommodation desired, that they also feared that if a greater number of public-houses should be located in the village, "some of them will have to resort to a neighboring custom for support," hence they resisted the licensing of new taverns, "which are useless and may be injurious" The court, however, granted Warner's petition, and continued so to do until 1825, when he having died his widow, Hannah, who named the house the "Market Wagon," continued the landlady until 1833 She was popularly known as "Aunt Hannah" Like Madame Defarge, she was constantly employed in knitting, and was never seen in public without her needles, which furnished occupation to her fingers as she listened to or related the trifling happenings of the circumscribed world in which she lived In February, 1833, she was succeeded in business by John Smith, who had formerly kept the Blockleyville inn in Philadelphia In March, 1837, John Smith, who had learned by this time the value of a line of daily stages to a tavern which was the point of arrival and departure, purchased Tomlinson's business and made the headquarters of the line at this inn

Farmers' and Mechanics' Inn—In 1831, John Brown, of Darby, presented his petition, in which he set forth that for several years previous to his application he had kept a house of public entertainment in the village purposely for the accommodation of people going to and coming from market, that he was "provided with stabling, hay, oats, etc, a large shed for those who carry their own feed to feed their horses in, supplying his guests with beer, cyder and vitwals when they require it, that he has two spare beds for lodging, and keeping a warm bar-room (in cold weather), where the greater part get all the lodging they require" He concludes by asking that "he be permitted to add the further accommodation to travelers of selling them spiritous liquors, wines, etc" The court granted the license desired, and "Uncle John," who rarely ever spoke, but bowed or smiled on almost every occasion, and whose nod, like that of Lord Burleigh, had a monstrous deal of meaning in it, when he first received license, his head is said for several days to have moved with the regular nodding motion of a plaster mandarin, and his face was one continual rippling series of smiles His house he called the "Farmers' and Mechanics' Inn" He died in 1835, certainly in that year his widow, Rebecca Brown, was granted the license, which was continued to her until 1839, when the house ceased to be a licensed tavern The old building still stands just below the Imperial Mills, at the foot of the steep hill which formerly was the east end of the village

The Buttonwood—Aug 28, 1739, George Wood, of Darby, applied for license, and in his petition stated that he had "laboured for some years under almost continued Indisposition of Body, and thereby rendered incapable of taking the necessary care of his plantation, and having a large family to maintain," asked leave of the court to keep tavern in the house belonging to Benjamin Lobb, which application met with the favorable opinion of the justices In 1750, Wood having died, his widow, Hannah, applied for and received the license, and for twelve years carried on the business, being succeeded in 1769 by Henry Hayes In 1773, Sarah Pearson kept the house, and 1776 Isaac Serrill, who appears to have been the owner of the premises, received license for the ancient inn, and for the first time the name "Mariner's Compass" appears, indicating that the story of the old Buttonwood is now being narrated There being no record for 1777, I cannot state who was the landlord of the inn during the fall of that year, when the retreating American army, fresh from the defeat at Brandywine, fled through the village, but in 1778 Henry Hays became "mine host" of the Mariner's Compass, and continued as such until 1786, when Isaac Serrill once more became its landlord It was during his time that Gen Washington was entertained at dinner there, and it is related that when he attempted to enter the house "he found the doorway so low or himself so tall that he was forced to stoop" It was on this occasion, so tradition says, that Washington was presented with a superb white charger as a testimonial of the high regard in which he was held by a number of his admirers residing in Darby and its vicinity. I can find no record of this presentation to Washington and doubt it, although I have seen it so stated in newspaper articles on several occasions. In 1790, after the formation of Delaware County, Samuel Ash had license at the old inn, and continued there until 1820, when, having become a very aged man, he was succeeded as landlord by Stephen Howe. The latter changed the title of the tavern to that of "The Drove," by which name it was known until 1833, when Samuel R. Lamplugh became the manager of the inn, and again the old sign in a measure was restored so far as the name "Compass" was concerned, the word "Mariner's" being omitted. In the year when Lamplugh obtained license L. Kittenger ran a line of stages between Darby and Philadelphia, which left the Cross-Keys on Fourth Street in the latter city daily at 9 o'clock A.M. and 5 P.M., while the schedule time of departure from Lamplugh's tavern was 7½ A.M. and 5 P.M. In December of the same year, J. Tomlinson having purchased the line from Kittenger, placed on the route a large omnibus, the "William Penn," which, when it first rumbled into Darby drawn by four black horses, awakened the then quiet village to an unusual degree of excitement. In 1836 William Russell had license for the house, and the ancient and noted inn took again its time-honored title in full. In 1837, after Tomlinson sold his stage route to John Smith, Cameron & Keogh started an opposition line of omnibuses between Philadelphia and Darby, making their headquarters at Russell's house. The rivalry between the two inns and stage lines continued, and the enterprise apparently not proving remunerative to Cameron & Keogh, the latter disposed of their business to Evan S. Russell, a son of the tavern-keeper, who continued the stages as the "Express Line of Omnibuses," while to add to the attraction at his house, William Russell ran in addition "a safe and easy carriage and two horses from his house in Darby." In 1844 William Russell was succeeded by William Russell, Jr., and he, in turn, in 1849 by Evan E. Russell, a brother of the preceding host. Although I do not find previous to this time the inn styled the Buttonwood from the records, I distinctly remember that about 1846 it was popularly known by that name. The old tree from which the inn was called, which stood before the door and had become so decayed on one side that the cavity was built in and supported by brick-work, is among my earliest recollections of Darby. It is related that Thomas Leiper, who used to stop his horses at the inn, always had his carriage to stand some distance off, declaring the old buttonwood would fall some day and he did not propose to be under it when it fell. In 1855 James H. Malin became landlord of the inn, which he dubbed anew as the "Girard Hotel." The sign hung on a frame on Main Street, and it was not until 1866, in Malin's petition for that year, that the house was called "The Buttonwood Hotel." In 1871 Malin was succeeded by James H. Lloyd. In 1879 the old tavern was taken down and the present hotel erected on its site. The Buttonwood is now kept by Thomas H. Boyd.

In 1880 the stone house which had formerly stood near the old Steel mill, and was moved bodily several hundred feet to the main street, was licensed as the Arlington House, but after a brief period the court refused to continue the privilege there.

The noted Blue Bell Inn, which is located just over the county-line, on the east bank of Crum Creek, during the Revolution was kept by the Paschall family. Townsend Ward relates that on one occasion "Gen. Washington stopped there, and chanced to hear the girls in the kitchen (there were three of them) chatting about him, one of them saying she would like to kiss him. He opened the door and inquired which of them it was who was so willing, but none would speak, for they greatly feared the majestic man. 'Then I will kiss all of you,' he said, and descending, as Jove did, he kissed them all, but it was in that proper manner so becoming in the days of our grandfathers. Until 1855 the venerable dame, who long survived her sisters, was wont to relate the incident with no little pride."[1]

A Few Old Houses and their Owners.—About a half-mile below Darby, on the Southern post-road, the residence of the late Judge Andrews, was the farm of Nathaniel Newlin. He was a man of great prominence in the county, and, notwithstanding his declaration during the Revolution that "he found King George's government good enough for him," he was elected a member of the Constitutional Convention of 1790; in 1791–92 was a member of the Assembly; in 1794–99, State senator from Delaware County, and was several times offered the nomination for Congress by the dominant party, but declined it. His residence subsequently became the property of Judge Andrews. On March 2, 1849, James Andrews and two Philadelphia police-officers made the arrest of a gang of thieves. His barn had been robbed of a number of articles, and suspicion rested on a colored family named Brown, living near Calcoon Hook. Armed with a search-warrant, Mr. Andrews and the officers searched the dwelling of Brown, and three hundred hams, three shoulders, and thirty-five chickens were found, besides watches, fine table-linen, clothing, harness, and many other articles. The colored man attempted to stab Andrews, but was prevented. Eight persons were arrested, committed to jail, and subsequently tried. On Friday, June 14, 1850, in the orchard of this estate, an unknown man was found suspended by the neck, where he had hung himself several hours before being discovered. The

[1] "A Walk to Darby," *Penna. Mag. of Hist.*, vol. iii. p. 264.

residence has always been one of the most attractive of the houses of colonial days still remaining, on the old Queen's Highway to Chester.

Just on the margin of the Kakarikonk, or Cobb's Creek, in Delaware County, and on the east of the Darby road, "is the picturesque mansion-house of the Smiths, of Tinicum, bought by them of the Lloyds in 1816. An ancient house, a part of it dating from 1725, embowered among aged trees, no destroying hand has as yet touched the antique double-door, now so rarely seen, and which in this place yet retains what perhaps can nowhere else be seen,—veritable "bull's-eyes." These are round pieces of glass, very thick in the middle, and inserted, two of them, in the upper part of the door to afford some little light to the hall. The northern door, the eastern door, and an inside one opening into the dining-room, each contain two of these now almost unknown adornments. A wooden lock, yet in good and serviceable condition, is in use on one of the doors of the house.[1]

Societies.—Orphan's Rest Lodge, No. 132, I. O. of O. F., was instituted Oct. 20, 1845, the following persons being named in the charter as officers: Charles Roe, N. G.; James McNulty, V. G.; John E. Levis, Sec.; David Roe, Treas. The lodge was constituted at the Buttonwood Hotel, then kept by William Russell, Jr., and meetings were held there until 1852, when the lodge was moved to the frame building on the east side of the street, now owned by Joseph Powell. In 1867 it was again removed to a room specially prearranged for its accommodation, in the third story of the brick building now owned by John Davis, where the lodge is now located. There are ninety-four members at the present time, and George Wiley is N. G.; Joseph Hallis, V. G.; G. W. Guest, Sec.; and Caleb B. Bonsall, Treas. The following persons are the Past Grands of Orphan's Rest Lodge in good standing: Moses Bonsall, Caleb Bonsall, Henry Bonsall, Charles T. Brooks, Humphry Brooks, John Biddle, Edward Bolduc, James E. Coombs, John L. Davis, Emanuel Ewing, Thomas Foulds, Charles Farrell, James A. Hill, Henry Hews, Theodore Knight, Thomas S. Keithler, John M. Lamplough, John Lincoln, William P. Mancil, James H. Malin, William McConnell, Charles Sladen, Samuel Wiley, James F. Wilby, Nimrod Dibler, James H. Bonsall, William Ewing, George G. Patchel.

General Taylor Encampment, No. 54, I. O. of O. F., was named in honor of Gen. Zachary Taylor, subsequently President of the United States, and was chartered Jan. 29, 1847, with the following officers: William Russell, Jr., C. P.; David Cooper, S. W.; Joseph Grover, J. W.; Charles T. Roe, H. P.; B. Clarkson Davis, Sec.; Thornton Russell, G.; Charles A. Litzenberg, Treas.

The following incidents are worthy of preservation in a history of Delaware County:

Capt. James Serrill, of Darby, in 1821, at that time captain of the sailing-ship "Tuscarora," made a voyage to Liverpool in seventeen days, which was then the fastest trip ever made by a sailing vessel between the United States and Europe, and for many years was not equaled. In 1839, James Bunting, of Darby, had erected a frame cocoonery, which was ninety-two by thirty-five feet, and was considered as an unusually large building to be devoted to the rearing of silkworms. On Aug. 6, 1840, Joseph Ingraham, an aged man residing at Darby, fell backwards into a well near the door of his residence, striking and dislocating his neck, occasioning instant death. On April 30, 1873, a six-year-old girl, named Jones, an adopted daughter of Mrs. Rively, of Darby, died of hydrophobia. Six weeks prior to her death she had been bitten by a dog. The child exhibited no symptoms of rabies until the day before her death, when she frothed at the mouth, was attacked by spasms at the sight of water, and showed other evidences of canine madness.

In April, 1875, Mrs. Eliza Ford died in Philadelphia. She had formerly been a resident of Darby, and it is related on Thanksgiving day, in 1858, while pouring tea for guests, her arms suddenly fell to her side, her limbs became motionless, and never again regained their power. She was carried to bed, where she remained until her death. Even when removed to Philadelphia, she was taken there on the bed. Although perfectly helpless, she accumulated flesh rapidly. Her arms and legs grew to double the size of those of persons in ordinary health. Her weight was five hundred pounds, and after death four strong men with difficulty lifted the body from the bed. Her coffin measured thirty-six inches across, and so great was its weight after the corpse was placed in it that it was laid upon the floor and rolled on rollers to the front door, after the funeral services in the house were over.

CHAPTER XLII.

UPPER DARBY TOWNSHIP.

As stated in the historical account of Darby township, the official division between Upper and Lower Darby was not made until after the Revolutionary war, although, practically, such separate municipal districts were recognized by the people of Darby, including all the territory now embraced in both the townships, many years prior to the war of Independence. Upper Darby having the Kakarikonk, Mill, or Cobb's Creek as its eastern boundary, and the Muckruton or Darby Creek traversing the southwestern end of the township to Tuscarora Mills at the Garrettford road, and thence that stream constitutes its western boundary, gave to the district in colonial times much prominence, because of the many mill-seats and water-powers located within the territory.

[1] "A Walk to Darby," by Townsend Ward, *Penna. Mag. of Hist.*, vol. iii. p. 264.

Settled as it was by members of the society of Friends, its early history lacks much in those sterling incidents which other localities, even in Delaware County, present, but the rural population in Upper Darby, by thrifty and careful husbandry, soon made that section of the county very productive and its inhabitants comparatively wealthy At the southwestern limit of the township was a tract of one hundred and fifty acres, to which the name "Primos" was given on July 12, 1683, and was surveyed to John Blunston, which subsequently, June 6, 1688, became the property of Thomas Hood, who emigrated from Breason, County Derby, England In 1692 fifty acres of this plantation was conveyed to John Hood, doubtless the son of John Hood, Sr, who settled in Darby in 1683, immediately above the Blunston tract On July 12, 1683, one hundred and fifty acres of land was surveyed to Joseph Potter, on which estate the present railroad station, at Oak Lane, is located The property subsequently was conveyed to John Hallowell, who emigrated from Nottinghamshire, England, in 1683, and who had settled, it is believed, on this land, which, as his means permitted, he purchased in fifty-acre lots at various dates To Thomas Whitbie, on July 12, 1683, the estate known as "Lebion" was surveyed He appears never to have resided thereon, but on July 22, 1687, it was conveyed to John Roads, and on this tract Clifton Station is now located To the northward of "Lebion" was a tract of one hundred and fifty acres, which, on July 12, 1683, was surveyed to Edward Cartledge This tract extended from the western line of the township to Darby Creek on the east He emigrated from Derbyshire, England, in 1683, and before he came he had purchased lands from William Penn He was a man far advanced in life when he came to the province, for he was eighty-four years old, in 1703, when he died Immediately above the Cartledge land, on a tract through which at the present time runs the Delaware County turnpike from Darby Creek, at Kellyville, westward almost to the township line, was a plantation of two hundred acres, which Joseph Need purchased in equal parts of one hundred acres from Thomas Brassey and Samuel Levis There Need, who was a quiet husbandman, lived nearly half a century, dying in 1741 Above the Need tract all the remaining land lying between Darby Creek on the east and the Springfield line on the west, and extending north to the point where the township line unites with Darby Creek, on March 22, 1681, and comprising two hundred acres, was conveyed to Isaac Wheeldon, and he in turn sold it to Samuel Levis, March 13, 1695 Levis seems not to have personally settled on this tract, but part of this land is now owned by Oborn Levis, a descendant of the early settler

At the southern part of Upper Darby, east of the creek of that name, was a tract of one hundred and fifty acres, extending to Cobb's Creek, which was surveyed to John Blunston Sept 10, 1682 The village of Fernwood is located on the one hundred acres which was purchased by Joseph Fearn, May 28, 1712 Above this tract, at a point a trifle west of Lansdowne Station, a line drawn to the New Jerusalem Church, and thence due west to the old Marker Paper-Mills, on Darby Creek, and then following the creek to the bend above the Lower Darby line, and thence due east to the post a short distance west of Lansdowne Station, was a large tract containing six hundred and fifty-five acres, surveyed to George Wood Nov 6, 1682. This tract subsequently was divided among his descendants, and two hundred acres of the lower part were conveyed to Richard Bonsall March 1, 1697/8 On the land acquired by Bonsall, Kellyville is located Richard Bonsall is the progenitor of the family of that name in Pennsylvania To the east of the Wood tract four hundred and fifty acres were surveyed to William Smith Oct 31, 1682 Ten years later this estate was sold to Anthony Morgan, who emigrated from Cardiff, Glamorganshire, Wales, in 1689, first settling on the west side of Cobb's Creek, above the present Blue Bell Inn, but in 1700 he removed to his plantation in Upper Darby, where he died in 1732, a very aged man Morgan, shortly after he purchased the property, sold one hundred and fifty acres to John Marshall, lying along the creek at the upper end of the tract, Naylor's Run separating the latter plantation almost in halves, and as the highway, known as Marshall's road, ran almost through the entire length of his land, from that fact it took the name it now bears This John Marshall and Sarah Smith were the first persons married in the old log meeting-house of Friends, at Darby, in 1688, mentioned in the account of that building Prior to the purchase of this land Marshall had acquired title to sixty-four acres lying north of the Smith tract, while just above Samuel Sellers had patented one hundred acres, and the following year (1691) purchased seventy-five and one-half acres of Charles Lee, who had, in 1685, received a patent for one hundred and eighty acres extending along Cobb's Creek Sellers must have occupied this tract several years prior to his purchase, for in 1684 he wedded Ann Gibbons, at Darby Meeting, before the meeting-house was built, and the bride rode to her home in Upper Darby on a pillion behind her husband. During the first year of their residence on this land they lived in a cave, the location of which is preserved to this day as "Cave Field," near the site of which he subsequently erected "Sellers Hall," the family homestead The remainder of the Lee tract, one hundred acres, was conveyed to Thomas Marie, in 1686. Due west of this land, and lying along the south side of the Garrett road, extending to Darby Creek, was a tract of three hundred and three acres, surveyed to Michael Blunston, of Darby After the latter's death it was conveyed to John Davis, as three hundred and twenty-two acres, March 25–26, 1736/7, and in May of the same year was bought by Samuel Levis North of the Garrettford road were three hundred and three acres, surveyed, Nov. 8, 1682, to Luke Hanck, which, on March 5, 1688, was sold to William Garrett, who, emigrating from Leicestershire, England, settled on this property, and was the ancestor of the Garrett family, much of the original estate remaining in the possession of his descendants. Above the Garrett plantation was a tract of two hundred and fifty acres, surveyed to Joshua Fearne Aug. 28, 1682. He came from Ashoner, Derbyshire, England, and settled on the estate immediately, his mother and two sisters accompanying him to the province. He married in 1687, and died in 1693, but during the ten years he lived in Upper Darby he filled many of the most important offices in the county, having been sheriff, clerk, and a justice of the courts, and twice a member of Assembly. Immediately north of Joshua Fearne's estate were six hundred and fifty acres, surveyed to William Wood and William Sharlow, while above this, and extending to the Haverford line, was a tract of five hundred acres, surveyed to John Browne Nov. 15, 1683. The western half of this plantation was purchased by John Roads, Nov. 9, 1683, and thereon he resided, while the remainder was bought by John Roads, Jr., and for several years he lived there, prior to his removal to Montgomery County.

To the east of this tract was a hundred acres, through which the Haverford and Darby road passed almost north and south, also belonging to John Roads, while directly south John Kirk, on Dec. 4, 1688, acquired title to one hundred acres, part of which tract is still owned by one of his descendants, and part of it owned by Levi Lukens. To the south of this (Kirk's) land was a plot of four hundred acres surveyed to the heirs of Matthew Grattan, June 14, 1692, but the same year it passed to the ownership of John Hood, who had come from Castledownington, Leicestershire, England, in 1686, and settled in Upper Darby, on two hundred and fifty acres purchased from John Blunston, which, lying north of the Sellers land, ran along Cobb's Creek to within a short distance of the Haverford line. John Hood was a member of the Provincial Assembly in 1704. The remaining part of John Blunston's four hundred and twenty acres, along Cobb's Creek and the Haverford line, was divided into small holdings of sixty and fifty acres, which were purchased by Adam and John Roads, Joshua Fearne, and John Hood, Jr.

As already stated, the history of Upper Darby is lacking in many incidents during the Revolutionary war, although its territory was frequently visited by foraging parties of the enemy, who swept the country clear of cattle and provisions, and frequently robbed the inhabitants of their household articles, never omitting an opportunity to appropriate money and plate to their coffers. Doubtless many anecdotes of that period were once freely circulated, but in time they have been entirely forgotten. The following incident is the only one which seems to be preserved:

One day, while the American army was encamped at White Marsh, Montgomery Co., Samuel Levis, of Upper Darby, an aged Quaker and a sterling Whig, met a party of American soldiers who were reconnoitering the English lines. The old man, who would not take an active part in the war for conscience' sake, volunteered to aid them in learning the movements of the enemy. With that object he fastened his horse to a tall hickory-tree which grew on the dividing line of Upper Darby and Springfield townships, and began ascending the tree. His hat was in the way as he clambered up. Tossing it to the ground, he mounted to the topmost branches, and with a telescope began to scan the country in the direction of the city. While thus employed a scouting party of British dragoons appeared, and noticed Friend Levis perched in the tree, so intent on his observations that he was unaware of the approach of the enemy. He was compelled to descend, to become a prisoner, and he was refused permission to recover his hat. He and his horse were taken to Philadelphia, where he was thrown in jail, detained several days, and finally discharged, but he never succeeded in recovering his horse or his hat. With the evacuation of Philadelphia the war-cloud lifted from Delaware County, and from that time the feet of hostile armed troops have not trodden its soil.

List of taxables in the township in 1799:

Matthew Ash, Benjamin Brannon, John Brooks, Mary Bonsall, John Ball, Joseph Ball, Benjamin Bonsall, Joseph Bonsall (saw-mill), James Bonsall (miller), William Davis, John Davis, Samuel Davis (cooper), Job Evans, Abner Evans (innkeeper), Evan Evans (tailor), Jonathan Evans, Philip Francis, Nathan Garrett, Sr., Nathan Garrett, Jr., Thomas Garrett (tilt-mill), Samuel Garrett (blacksmith), Samuel Garrett, Oborn Garrett, William Garrett, Joseph Hibberd, Joseph Hibberd, Jr., Hezekiah Hibberd, John Hibberd, Robert Jones, Samuel Kirk, Thomas Kirk, Joseph Kirk, William Kimble, Benjamin Lobb (cooper-shop), Isaac Lobb, Levi Lukens (tanner), Catharine Lewis, Thomas Lewis, Abraham Lewis, William Levis (Philadelphia, paper- and saw-mill), Thomas Levis, Joseph Levis, Samuel Levis (paper- and grist-mill, miller), William Moore, John May, Jonathan Owen, James Pyott, Hannah Pollen, Anna Pencler, Amos Penegar, Bevan & Thomas Pearson (storekeepers), Israel Roberts, Jacob Reaver, George Steward, John Sellers (saw-mill), Nathan & David Sellers (cotton-factory and saw-mill), James Steel (miller, at Sellers' grist- and merchant-mill), Amos Sharpless, James Tyson, John Matthews (paper-maker, paper- and grist-mill), John Tyson (grist-mill), William Thompson, George Widdows (wheelwright), William West (grazier), Jacob Warner, Lawrence Howard, Nathaniel Hutton (Philadelphia), Thomas Leacock, Gibbons Jones (carpenter), Mordecai Lewis, William Pollen, Nathan Pollen, Samuel Pollen, Leonard Shuster (weaver).

Inmates.—Samuel Bonsall, Thomas Cumming, Owen Cumming, Joel McClellan, John Dunbar, David Dunbar (paper-maker), Isaac Earl (shoemaker), John Fitzgerald, Neil McFaggen, Edward Ferrell, John Gow, John Garrett, Justice Hendrickson (paper-maker), Richard Hayes, Ann Hibbard, Peter Hartley, Hugh Hunt, Henry Hartley, Michael Johnson, Jonathan Jones, John Hechler, Laurence Lowry, Joshua Levis (paper-maker), Charles Levis, John Murphy, Phineas Palmer, Thomas Rudolph, Deborah Rogers, John Rudolph (paper-maker), William Rudolph (paper-maker), John Suplee (joiner), Benjamin Sharpless (paper-maker), Isaac Tyson (miller), Henry Upright, William Levis (paper-maker), Thomas Williams (paper-maker).

Single Freemen.—Robert Armstrong, Reuben Bonsall, Joseph Bonsall, Jr., Benjamin Bonsall, Jr., William Brooks, Uliff Calls, John Dunlap, Joel Davis (wheelwright), William Suplee (wheelwright), Robert Dunbar, William Evans, John Graham, John Guard, Isaac Justice, Israel Lobb, Israel Lobb, Jr., Ephraim Lobb, Asher Lobb (shoemaker), Jonathan Evans (carpenter), William Pollen (carpenter), John Jones (joiner),

Abraham Johnson (miller), Robert Steel (miller), Nathan Jones (tailor), Jesse Lobb (cooper), Philip Super (weaver), Benjamin Lobb, Bernard Mackey, Samuel Moore, John Moore, Samuel Powell, James Pyott, Jacob Reaver, Jr., George Sellers, Jacob Tyson, Robert Thomas, Isaac Tyson, Benjamin West.

The following is a list of the justices of Upper Darby:

	Date of Commission.
Benjamin Brannon	Aug. 19, 1791.
Israel Elliot	Oct. 28, 1791.
Benjamin W. Oakford	Feb. 14, 1794.
Caleb S. Sayers	Aug. 6, 1799.
Benjamin Hays Smith	April 3, 1804.
Samuel Davis	Feb. 20, 1810.
Thomas Smith	July 3, 1821.
Joseph G. Malcolm	July 30, 1831.
Thomas Maddock	Jan. 8, 1834.
Charles Sellers	June 20, 1836.
William McCormick	May 25, 1859, April 26, 1864, April 16, 1869.
George Heath	April 15, 1872.
William McCormick	March 24, 1874.
Hart Sterr	March 24, 1876.
George Heath	March 27, 1879.
William McCormick	April 13, 1880, Aug. 7, 1880.

Schools.—The first official record of land being set apart for school purposes in the township is in a deed in 1779 for twenty-four perches of ground granted to John Sellers, Benjamin Brannon, and Oliver Garrett as trustees, the consideration being ten pounds. On this lot a building was erected on the Haverford and Darby road, above the highway leading to Garrettford, and near the residence of Isaac Garrett. This school is distinctly marked as so located on John Hill's "Map of Philadelphia and its Environs," published in 1807. In that house Isaac Garrett was at one time a teacher, and William and John Sellers attended there as pupils. In the olden times it was under the control of a board of trustees, but when the law of 1836 became operative, it was transferred to the school directors, and is still used for educational purposes. The trustees named in the deed of 1779 and their successors had the care of the school until it was transferred to the board of school directors. Under the act of 1804 school trustees were elected in Upper Darby, in 1825; their powers, however, could in nowise include the control of the contribution school of 1779. On May 18, 1825, at the election then held, Oborn Levis, Thomas and John Sellers, Jr., were chosen trustees for the township, the duties of which office, so far as we have information, must have rested with ease on the shoulders of those who bore the official honors. Upon the enactment of the public school law of 1834, Joseph Henderson and William Booth were appointed by the court inspectors of public schools until directors should be selected. The township of Upper Darby having accepted the school law, directors were chosen at the fall election of that year. In 1835–36 the township received from the State and county appropriations amounting to the sum of $444.14, that being the proportion allotted to Upper Darby of the public money set apart for the maintenance of public schools.

On Feb. 18, 1833, Coleman Sellers granted to John Sellers, Sr., Nathan Sellers, Abraham Powell, Charles Sellers, Samuel Sellers, Jr., David Snyder, and Samuel Sellers a lot in Upper Darby on which to erect a school-house, and in their discretion to employ suitable teachers and open a school as soon as convenient under the exclusive management of trustees. The house was built and a school maintained there. It was known as the Union School, and on its site the present stone school-house near the grist-mill of William Walker is located. After the enactment of the law of 1836 the trustees transferred it to the use of the directors of the public schools of the township.

On the Springfield road west of Clifton, on the lands of Oborn Levis, is a building which was for many years a school-house, and was continued to be used as such until 1871. On March 23d of that year a lot was purchased of Dr. S. P. Bartleson, at Clifton, and the directors contracted with John Frees to erect the present two-story brick school-house, at a cost of five thousand seven hundred and eighty-five dollars. The new structure was completed in the fall of the same year, and therein five schools of different grades are maintained. Oborn Levis, on Sept. 9, 1871, purchased the old school-house and lot for one thousand dollars, and the quiet of an uninterrupted vacation maintains in the ancient building where since time out of mind the noisy laugh and boisterous play of the rosy-cheeked urchins could be heard at recess, or the dull "murmur of the pupils' voices conning over their lessons" was audible to the passer-by.

The Central school-house, above Garrettford, is located on a lot of land purchased from Thomas Garrett, Oct. 14, 1837, containing seventy-two square perches, and thereon a school-house was erected near by the present building. School was maintained there until Jan. 26, 1860, when twenty-one square perches of the lot was sold to Nathan and David Platt. In June, 1873, a contract was entered into with Moses Gilmour for the erection of a school-house, at a cost of three thousand three hundred and seventy-five dollars, on the remaining ground owned by the school board, which was completed in November following, since which time schools have been regularly conducted therein. On May 3, 1851, the directors purchased one hundred and thirty-seven square perches of land of Charles Kelly, at Kellyville, on which a school-house was built and used until 1871, when the school therein was discontinued, and the house and lot, on August 28th of that year, was sold to Dennis B. and Edward J. Kelly for thirteen hundred and thirty dollars.

On June 6, 1873, the residents of Pattonville, now known as Fernwood, petitioned the school directors to establish a school at that locality. A committee of the board, to whom the petition was referred, on August 9th reported that the Methodist Church could be leased. That building was rented, and a school opened and continued therein until it became necessary that other accommodations should be had. On May 15, 1875, Francis Kelly contracted with the directors to erect the present two-story brick school-house, at a cost of three thousand seven hundred and twenty dollars, on lands purchased for that purpose.

In 1869 the brick building used for the parochial school of St Charles Borromeo Church at Kellyville was erected. The school-house is forty by sixty feet, two stories in height, and is under the control of the Catholic Church there, from which it receives its name.

The following are the directors of the public schools for Upper Darby, as found in the election returns on file at Media

1840, Dr George Smith, John Kirk, 1842, Nathan H Baker, William U Black, 1843, George Smith, John Kirk, 1844, John Sellers, William Jones, 1845, John Sellers, Lewis Watkins, 1846, John Kirk, George Smith, 1847, William Jones, James Shillingford, 1848, John Sellers, Nathan H Baker, Joseph Hibberd, 1849, John Kirk, George Smith, 1850, Nathan Garrett, Edward Garrett, 1851, John Sellers, Samuel G Levis, 1852, George Smith, John Kirk, 1853, Nathan Garrett, Edward Garrett, 1854, John Sellers, Samuel G Levis, 1855, George Smith, John Kirk, 1856, Nathan Garrett, Jacob Shoester, 1857, Samuel G Levis, John Sellers, 1858, Dr George Smith, Thomas Kirk, 1859 Nathan Garrett, Jacob Shoester, 1860, no report, 1861, Thomas Kirk, Amos Bonsall, 1862, Jacob Shoester, Nathan Garrett, 1863, Samuel G Levis, John S Maris, 1864, Amos Bonsall, Thomas Kirk, 1865, Nathan Garrett, Jonathan Evans, 1866, John Sellers, Samuel G Levis, 1867, J Harrison Levis, Jonathan Wolfernden, 1868, Nathan Garrett, Jonathan Evans, 1869, John Lewis, Dr R A Givin, 1870, John Sellers, William Watkins, 1871, William H Ring, J Harrison Levis, 1872, John Levis, Nathan Garrett, 1873, J D Rhoads, John Sellers, 1874, Jonathan Evans, Nathan Garrett, 1875, John Levis, William Watkins, 1876, James D Rhoads, Joseph Powell, 1877, Oliver B Moss, George Hearle, 1878, John E Levis, William Watkins, 1879, Joseph E Bowers, James D Rhoads, 1880, George E Burnley, Albert Johnson, 1881, William Watkins, John Levis, 1882, George Heath, George Lyster, 1883, George Burnley, William A Johnson, 1884, William Watkins, H M Hoffner

First New Jerusalem Church of Delaware County.—Prior to 1830, James Robinson, a manufacturer, then operating the factory now known as Clifton Mills, who had been a lay preacher of the Swedenborgian Church in England before emigrating to Pennsylvania, began the dissemination of the tenets of that religious faith in Upper Darby, a Sunday-school being organized in the picker-room of the old factory building at the mills now operated by Thomas Kent Occasional services were also held in the Academy building at Haddington From this movement a church organization was effected, with the following persons as members David Snyder, Charles Sellers, Samuel Sellers, Jesse Hayes, Edward Levis and wife, Morris W. Heston and wife, Benjamin Thomas and wife, George Trites and wife On June 7, 1830, the corner-stone of the present church edifice, on the Marshall road, near Naylor's Run, was laid, a large number of persons being present from the neighborhood and Philadelphia Mr Robinson conducted the services, explaining the fundamental principles of the New Jerusalem faith, during which a heavy shower of rain interrupted the ceremonies for a short time. After the stone was in place, Rev Mr. Carll, of Philadelphia, addressed the assembly, and in his remarks stated that "they had laid the corner-stone of that church in the name of Jehovah, one God, and that Jesus Christ was that God," and he hoped "that the church erected thereon might never be appropriated to the worship of a Trinity, or more than one God, as distinct and separate beings" Mr Carll was followed by the Rev. Mr Roach, and the services were concluded with a prayer by Mr Robinson The church thus built was erected on the land of Frederick and Edward Levis long prior to the lot being donated, for it was not until July 31, 1833, that the owners of the real estate conveyed the half-acre of ground to Morris W Heston and George G Trites, trustees of the church Rev Manning B Roach and Rev Isaac C Worrell were in charge of the church. On Sept 2, 1861, the court incorporated the New Jerusalem Society of Edenfield, Delaware County At the present time the church is without a pastor, and services are rarely held in the old building

Pleasant Hill Methodist Episcopal Church—In 1834 a society of Methodists effected an organization in Upper Darby, meetings for public worship being held at the private houses of the members until early in 1837, when it was resolved to erect a meeting-house On Thursday, June 27th of that year, the corner-stone was laid at Pleasant Hill, about a quarter of a mile from Palmer & Marker's paper-mills, which were subsequently known as Tuscarora Mills Rev M Coomes conducted the services on that occasion The locality was selected because of its proximity to the paper-mills, for from the employés there its membership was largely drawn The struggling church was under the care of the Philadelphia Conference, and, after the paper-mills had been converted into factories by George Burnley, the society grew rapidly After the organization of the Clifton Methodist Church, in 1871, the elder church was placed under that charge In May, 1884, Pleasant Hill Church celebrated the semi-centennial anniversary of its founding The church membership is now about fifteen persons

Clifton Methodist Episcopal Church—This religious society was organized in 1871, and immediately began the erection of the present brick church, forty-five by sixty-five feet, the building fund being largely the contribution of Richard Young, of Springfield The church was at first under the charge of the Rev M H Sisty, who was untiring in his efforts to establish the organization on a firm basis The corner-stone of the church building was laid Thursday, Aug 10, 1871, the pastor, Rev. M H Sisty, Rev. F. A Fernley, and other clergymen taking part in the ceremony The edifice was erected at a cost of eight thousand dollars Rev Mr Sisty has been succeeded in the pastorate by the Revs J Y Ashton, J P Miller, William Magee, M Barnhill, and N. Turner, who at the present time is in charge of the church, including that at Pleasant Hill The membership now consists of seventy persons, and there is also a Sunday-school with one hundred and thirty pupils, of which Isaac Lord is superintendent. The foundation for a parsonage is now (July, 1884) laid on a lot adjoining the church

St. Charles Borromeo Church.—Soon after Charles Kelly purchased the mills at Kellyville a Catholic mission was established there. In 1849 it was determined to build a church, ground being donated for that purpose by Charles Kelly, as also for a burial-place. On Sunday, Oct. 13, 1850, the stone church, forty by eighty feet, which had been erected, was dedicated; the Very Rev. F. X. Gartland, V. G., conducted the ceremonies, and the Rev. Dr. Moriarty preached the dedicatory sermon. On Dec. 30, 1854, the church was found to be on fire, caused by a defective flue. The flames were extinguished before much damage was done. The membership of this church has fluctuated, at some times very large, at others much less, owing to employment being brisk or slack at the mills. The pastors of the parish of St. Charles Borromeo have been the Revs. McGinnis, John Shields, I. P. Dunn, Hugh Lane, John Branagan, Dr. Balch, Richard O'Connor, John Kelly, John McGovern, and M. C. McEnroe, who at present is in charge of the parish.

St. Stephen's Episcopal Church, Clifton.—The first services of the Protestant Episcopal Church in Upper Darby were held in the public school-house in the village, May 5, 1872, the Rev. James S. Brooke, the rector of St. George's Church, West End, officiating. On October 27th of the same year communion was administered, fourteen persons uniting in the sacred ceremony, and on Thursday evening, November 1st, the bishop of the diocese made his first official visit to Clifton Heights, on which occasion eleven persons were confirmed. In May of the following year a Sunday-school was organized in connection with the mission. From the establishment of the mission to the beginning of the year 1877 the congregation were under the pastoral care, successively, of the Rev. Mr. Brooke, the Rev. Gideon J. Burton (warden of the Burd Orphan Asylum), the Rev. W. C. Cooley (of West End), and the Rev. Charles A. Maison (of St. James', Kingsessing), the latter having the oversight for about three years. During this period the congregation was composed almost exclusively of the people working in the mills near the village. They were poor and few in number, but they struggled on in the face of many discouragements, giving far more than they could well afford from their slender income to maintain the services of the church, to which they were warmly attached. Among the most zealous in the work of the little mission was John Shaw, who subsequently was elected one of the original vestry. In 1876 services began to be held regularly every Sunday morning by Mr. Thomas A. Bent, a lay-reader. At his death, in October, 1876, he was succeeded by Mr. William W. Taylor. In the fall of 1878, Frederick Chase and wife became earnest advocates of the cause of the mission, and their efforts being seconded by many others in the neighborhood, its prospects began to brighten. Oborn Levis donated several lots fronting on the Baltimore turnpike, and enough subscriptions were soon secured to warrant the erection of a church, notwithstanding by the failure of the Franklin Savings-Fund, in Philadelphia, a sum of money which had been accumulating towards a church erection-fund was lost. Accordingly, the corner-stone was laid Oct. 12, 1878, and on Sunday morning, March 16, 1879, the sanctuary was dedicated by Bishop Stevens, at which time the church was entirely out of debt, subscriptions having been obtained sufficient to discharge every obligation for its erection. The building, which is in the Gothic style of architecture, is laid in pressed brick, with stone trimmings, and ornamented with colored brick, while internally it is finished in oiled hard woods, with an open roof and exposed rafters. In the recess chancel is a handsome stained-glass window, the contribution of the Sunday-school scholars.

A parish was now organized under the name of St. Stephen's Church, Clifton Heights, a charter was obtained, and a vestry elected. The first vestrymen were Frederick Chase, Dr. J. W. Phillips, Dr. R. A. Given, John Shaw, Edward Walden, Richard Barlow, and William Kane. At this time, the Rev. Charles A. Maison having resigned, the Rev. G. J. Burton was elected rector in charge, and the lay-reader was chosen assistant minister. He was ordained to the deaconate in the new church Nov. 1, 1879. On Oct. 9, 1880, the corner-stone of a Sunday-school and parish building was laid with impressive services.

This beautiful structure, one of the finest in the county, was the gift of Thomas A. Scott, then president of the Pennsylvania Railroad, who was much interested in the little church. A memorial brass tablet on its walls bears this inscription: "Erected in memory of Thomas A. Scott, Jr., who died Ascension Day, 1879. *Of such is the Kingdom of God.*" On Easter Monday, 1881, Rev. Mr. Burton resigned, and his assistant, Rev. W. W. Taylor, was elected rector. In the fall of 1882 ground adjoining the church property (which had already been enlarged by gifts of lots from Dr. R. A. Given and Thomas A. Scott) was received and a rectory begun. It was finished and occupied the following spring. The present value of the church property, real and personal, is twenty thousand dollars. The actual communicants number seventy. There are in the Sunday-school eight teachers and one hundred scholars. In the parish day-school, one teacher and twenty-eight pupils, and in the night-school, three teachers and forty scholars. Connected with the church there are also sewing and altar societies. Services are held twice on Sundays, on all the holy days, and communion is celebrated twice in the month.

It will be seen by the foregoing sketch that the parish has grown rapidly, and that now, in its sixth year of organization, it is fully equipped for aggressive work in the midst of an increasing population.

The Burd Orphan Asylum.—This charitable establishment, although having its origin in Philadelphia, and being in a certain sense one of that city's institutions, is located in Upper Darby. Its full title is "The Burd Orphan Asylum of St. Stephen's Church," and its location is described as "Market Street, west of Sixty-third Street." The institution was founded by the munificence of Mrs. Eliza Howard Burd, deceased, formerly of Philadelphia, who was the widow of Edward Shippen Burd, and daughter of Woodrop Sims. She was a lady of culture and refinement, and upon being left a widow, and losing her two daughters, she determined to use her large fortune in philanthropy. The inception of the enterprise which culminated in the orphan asylum was a "home" established by Mrs. Burd in 1856, in the rear of her dwelling, on the southwest corner of Ninth and Chestnut Streets, Philadelphia, to which she admitted twelve fatherless girls. During her life she superintended the management of it herself. Seeking a method for her wealth to do good when she should be no more, she was advised by her pastor, the late Rev. Henry W. Ducachet, of St. Stephen's Episcopal Church, to found a similar school upon a larger scale. At her death, in 1860, she bequeathed to the rector, church wardens, and vestrymen of St. Stephen's Church, in trust, the sum of five hundred thousand dollars to build and endow the present institution.

In 1861 a lot of ground, consisting of forty-five acres, partly in the city limits and party in Delaware County, was purchased, and the erection of the present buildings begun. The property was formerly known as "Sellers Hall." It had passed in the division of the estate of John Sellers to Margaret Sellers Powell, wife of Joseph Powell, by whom it was sold to the trustees of the asylum.

The orphans admitted by Mrs. Burd were removed to the new building, and others were received in September, 1863. The chapel was completed and consecrated Nov. 3, 1866. A writer in *Progress*, of Sept. 13, 1879, presumably the late John W. Forney, says, "The asylum . . . is different from any other I have ever seen. It resembles more in its appearance, artistic surroundings and appointments, some old deserted English manor than a house for poor little orphans." The asylum consists of a group of detached buildings connected with corridors, with an outbuilding containing the kitchen, laundry, bake-room, and bedrooms for the domestics, connected with the main buildings by means of a covered railway. The style is the early English Gothic. It is built of a light-gray stone, quarried on the grounds, laid in rubble, pointed with facings of dressed Leiperville stone. The buildings are two stories high, with basements twelve feet clear above the surface of the ground, and a sub-cellar containing the steam furnaces for heating. In the basement is a large dining-room, which will seat one hundred and fifty children, play-room, bowling-alley, bath-rooms, reception-room, and nursery. In the main building, on the first floor, are a parlor and library, containing the antique furniture and the books (about four thousand volumes) bequeathed to the asylum by Mrs. Burd, a large school-room, four class-rooms, and housekeeper's room. On the second floor, approached by two broad iron stairways, is the beautiful chapel, which will accommodate three hundred and fifty persons. It has two memorial windows to the foundress, and one to her rector, the first chaplain of the asylum, the Rev. Henry W. Ducachet, D.D. In the rear is a large dormitory, teachers' rooms, etc. All the stairs are iron, the railings outside and in are also iron, and the building is as far as practicable fire-proof. The north wing contains the warden's residence, a large sewing-room, and two dormitories. The south wing, which is not yet erected, will add a hundred feet to the length, and double the accommodations. In the hall is a portrait of Edward Shippen Burd, painted when the subject was a young man, by Rembrandt Peale, and elsewhere are the portraits of Mrs. Burd's daughters.

The grounds are very attractively laid out. They contain hills and dales, running water, smoothly-sloping lawns, and shady groves, forming appropriate surroundings for the beautiful buildings. The asylum and grounds cost about one hundred and seventy-five thousand dollars.

The objects of the asylum, as set forth in the will of Mrs. Burd, are "to maintain, educate, and at a suitable age and time (to be judged of and determined by those to whose management I have intrusted the asylum) to place out to be instructed in proper employments, *first,* the white female orphan children of legitimate birth, of the age of not less than four years and not more than eight, who shall have been baptized in the Protestant Episcopal Church, in the city of Philadelphia; *secondly,* the same class of children, baptized in the said church, in Pennsylvania; and, *thirdly,* all other white female orphan children of legitimate birth, not less than four years of age and not more than eight years, without respect to any other description or qualification whatever, except that at *all times, and in every case, the orphan children of clergymen of the Protestant Episcopal Church shall have the preference.* If the establishment or the means provided shall not be sufficient to accommodate all the several classes of children herein described, each class shall be preferred in the order in which they are herein mentioned, to the exclusion in whole or in part of the other classes. By the term 'orphan,' for the purpose of this codicil, I mean a child whose father is deceased and whose mother remains a widow, or who may have lost by death both father and mother."

It is also directed and enjoined by the will that "all the children received into the asylum shall be faithfully instructed, as a part of their education, in the principles of the precious Gospel of Christ as they are held and taught by the Protestant Episcopal Church in the United States; and that no other system of religion shall be taught there; and, moreover, that all the worship held therein shall be according to the ritual of the said church, and no other."

For several years the number of children was limited to forty, but now sixty are maintained and educated. They are instructed in all the elements of a good English education according to the course of study followed in the public schools of Philadelphia. They are also taught sewing, housework, and cooking. If a girl shows a special talent for music, drawing, or any other useful art by which she may be able to support herself in after-life, it is cultivated. All are instructed in vocal music by a professor, and the singing in the chapel on Sundays attracts large numbers of visitors. The girls are under the control of the trustees until they are eighteen, although, when deemed expedient, they are placed out in positions at an earlier age. When dismissed, each girl receives an outfit of clothing and fifty dollars in money.

As has been heretofore remarked, the Rev. Henry W. Ducachet, D.D., was the first chaplain. He died in 1865. The Revs. P. C. Moore and John A. Childs were acting chaplains until 1869, when the Rev. Francis J. Clerc, D.D., was elected warden and chaplain. He remained in charge for three and one-half years, when the Rev. Gideon J. Burton was chosen by the trustees to succeed him, and entered upon his duties in June, 1872. He has been in office over twelve years. Since he took charge the number of pupils has been increased from forty to sixty, the buildings and grounds have been improved, a regular course of study has been adopted, and the institution is now successfully carrying out the designs of its generous founder.

Burn Brae.—In the summer of 1859, Dr. R. A. Given erected buildings near the village of Clifton, and established a private hospital for patients afflicted with nervous and mental diseases. It was designed to accommodate forty patients, twenty of each sex. The main building was originally four stories high, including the basement; subsequently a mansard was added, in which the amusement hall (a large and handsome room) is located. Many improvements have been made from time to time in the different halls, rendering the accommodations more perfect and attractive. On the ladies' side an entirely new building has been erected, rendered necessary by the enlargement of the rooms in the main structure. The grounds, twenty-five acres in extent, are handsomely laid out and planted with a variety of ornamental trees, evergreen and deciduous. A farm of thirty-two acres, part heavily wooded, capable of being converted into drives and walks of great attractiveness, has been added; thus, besides securing to the inmates perfect privacy, affording them in their walks the pleasing variety of hill and valley, meadow, brook, and woodland. No efforts have been spared to render the building fire-proof. Fire-escapes are attached to both wings, and in addition arrangements exist on each floor to enable the occupants to pass readily from side to side without resort to the stairs. The building throughout is thoroughly heated by steam and well lighted by gas. Hot and cold water is abundantly distributed throughout the entire establishment.

Licensed Houses.—The record of the licensed public-houses in Upper Darby is brief. In the early times no application for the privilege of keeping a tavern in the township has been found. The first person who was authorized to keep a house of public entertainment was Benjamin Brannon, whose inn was located on the Cherry Grove Farm, a short distance south of the New Jerusalem Church, but the house facing on the Darby and Haverford road. Col. and Judge Brannon, for he held both offices, was one of the most influential Whigs during the Revolution, was one of the sub-lieutenants of the county during that war, and after the county of Delaware was erected was appointed, in 1794, one of the associate judges. He does not appear to have been a publican after the close of that struggle. In 1796, Abner Evans received license for a public-house on the north side of the West Chester road, located about four and a half miles west of Market Street bridge, where for years the house continued to meet the court's approval until 1815. Amos Ellis, in his petition in 1806, states that his application is for license to the Red Lion. There had gathered in the neighborhood of the tavern a few small frame houses, and the people in the township, in derision, termed the place Cat Town. In 1815 the house seems to have been licensed for the last time. James Pyott, in 1779, received license for an inn located on the brow of a hill on the West Chester road, five miles from Market Street bridge, which ascent, because of his house being there, was then and is still known as Pyott's Hill. The tavern, in 1806, was called the Seven Stars, and Pyott had license for the house under that name, and yearly received the court's bounty until 1816, when Robert Dunny was the landlord of the Black Horse, the Stars having fallen to be replaced by a new title. In 1820, Reece Calvert had license for the Black Horse, in 1823, Mifflin Moore succeeded him, and in 1833 William Lungren became the landlord, continuing as such until 1840, when the Black Horse was a temperance house. In 1841, Evan S. Russell had a license for the Black Horse, but after that date the application was met with sturdy opposition from the residents of the township, and the court refused to grant the prayer of the petitioner. There were two remonstrances, as follows: The first being that of male citizens of Upper Darby, bearing eighty-four signatures, and the latter that of females, and signed by ninety-four persons:

"The undersigned, citizens of Upper Darby Township and the surrounding neighborhood, respectfully yet earnestly remonstrate against the granting of Tavern license to sell spirituous liquors to applicants within the said Township, because they believe them uncalled for by the public convenience and demoralizing in their influence, tending to the spread of intemperance with its train of evils The only licensed house heretofore called for by the wants of the township is to be continued as one for public entertainment conducted on temperance principles, while we are surrounded on every side by licensed Taverns in numbers clearly beyond the wants of the community, as is sufficiently shown by the many demoralizing shifts to which they are driven for a living business The undersigned, therefore, pray the Court to aid them in their efforts to stay this crying evil so far as in their power by refusing all appplications as aforesaid"

When temperance principles became the dominant sentiment in Upper Darby, Mr Sellers, the owner of the lands and building, consented that the old inn-sign should be taken down The day when this was done a large number of people assembled, and when the old, weather-beaten black horse was lowered to the ground amid the cheers of those present, one citizen, in the excitement of the moment, exclaimed, "I'm going to give the old animal four quarts of oats, he must be mighty hungry standing up there so long" John Hawkins became the landlord of the Black Horse Inn, which he kept as a temperance house until the Howard House was built, a short distance farther west on the same highway, when he took charge of the new building

No license was granted in Upper Darby thereafter until 1875, when the local-option law was repealed, and in that year William McFadden received license at Clifton, and James Gallagher, at Kellyville, which houses have continued from that time to receive the court's approval

The Bonsall Murder—Perhaps no judicial investigation was ever held in Delaware County which concentrated public interest to its detail to the same extent as did the trial of Michael Monroe, *alias* James Wellington, and his accessories, for the murder of William Bonsall, of Upper Darby The killing was so deliberate on the part of the murderer, and so unprovoked by the victim, that popular indignation was aroused beyond any previous incident of the like character in our history, and the sixty years which have elapsed since have failed to present its parallel

On the highway leading from the village of Darby to the West Chester road, and about two miles and a half northward of the village, in 1824, resided Mrs. Mary Warner (a widow), who kept a store in part of the house, and William Bonsall, his wife, and infant son, these four persons comprising the inmates of the dwelling About half-past nine o'clock on Saturday evening, May 22d of that year, four suspicious-looking men came to the house and informed Mrs Warner that they desired to talk with "the young man,"—Bonsall,—with whom they professed to be acquainted The latter, who was slightly ill at the time and had retired, dressed himself, came down-stairs, and was greeted most cordially by the visitors Bonsall, notwithstanding he stated there must be a mistake and that he did not remember ever to have met any of the men before, hospitably invited them to be seated and attempted to draw them into conversation After a few ordinary remarks had been made one of the strangers, abruptly turning to Bonsall, demanded his money The latter replied that he had only a dollar and a half in the house, which he said they might have No answer was made to this remark, but one of the men, cutting a clothes-line which was stretched across the kitchen, threw the cord around Bonsall's neck, drawing it so tight that he was almost choked, and to prevent strangulation the latter raised his hand to his throat to loosen the rope Wellington, for it subsequently proved to be he, struck at Bonsall's raised arms with a razor, laying the flesh open to the bone from the shoulder to the elbow The wounded man, bleeding profusely, was held in the chair by his assailant, while the other cut-throats compelled Mrs Warner, whose arms they had also bound with a piece of the clothes-line, to conduct them into the store, which was closed, as she supposed, until the following Monday

While the store was being rifled Wellington sat in a chair immediately in front of Bonsall, and just as Mrs Warner was coming out of the store with the burglars, Wellington said something in an angry tone, and then with a well-worn shoe-knife stabbed Bonsall several times in the abdomen, both the murderer and his victim being seated at the time In attempting to withdraw the knife the last time the handle came off, leaving the blade in the wound Mrs Bonsall, who was shortly to become a mother, hearing the noise, came down-stairs, when the two men in the house, for the other two had retreated to the front door, threatened to inflict on her atrocious cruelties unless she informed them where her husband had secreted his money She, not knowing that her husband had been mortally wounded, bade them take everything in the house but to spare the lives of the family The ruffians took every article of clothing belonging to Bonsall excepting his military suit, and with the goods taken from the store they made two large packages, which they carried away when they left the house, but before leaving they brutally insulted the dying man Bonsall lived until the next day, Sunday morning

On Monday it was learned that at midnight on Saturday, after the deed was committed, the murderers crossed Gray's Ferry bridge, walking in the direction of Philadelphia The same day, May 24th, Joseph Watson, mayor of that city, at the request of many citizens of Delaware County, offered a reward of three hundred dollars for the apprehension and conviction of the criminals Nothing was learned until Friday, June 5th, when three men whose description seemed to answer that set forth in the mayor's proclamation were noticed in the vicinity of Swedesborough, N. J, walking in the direction of Woodbury, and when it was known that they had attempted to pass a Mexican or Peruvian dollar, a hue and cry was instituted, the men were overtaken near Timber Creek bridge and conducted to Woodbury, when they were subjected to a separate examination, Judge Hopkins sitting in the court-room for that purpose. The first man examined gave his name as William Jones, stating that he was from Westmoreland County, and that in search of work he had gone to New Castle, Del., where, being unable to obtain employment, he had crossed the river on the morning of his arrest, and on the New Jersey shore had fallen in with the other men, whom he had never seen before, and that he was on his way to Philadelphia when apprehended. He was, he declared, never nearer Darby than the high bridge in Kingsessing; but he was unable to tell exactly where he was on the night of the murder. On a second examination he stated that his name was Washington Labee, but could offer no reason why he had given a false name. He then said he remembered he had been on an oyster-boat with Abraham Boyce and others, and had sailed from Philadelphia on the morning of the day the murder was committed. Abraham Boyce stated that he was employed on an oyster-boat, and came from Cape May in a boat with Labee, but could not tell when he left the Cape; he also called Labee Thomas, and stated he did not know his other name. He declared he was on board the oyster-boat the night of the murder. The authorities found secreted on his person a number of keys, several other articles, and a small axe. On his second examination he said the scissors-chain he had picked up on the road in Jersey, and did not know where such a place as Darby was. He declared that he knew Labee, and until that day had never before seen Michael Monroe, or James Wellington, as he was called.

The latter asserted on his examination that he had never met the men until the day before his arrest; that he did not remember where he was the night of the murder, but the following Sunday he was in West Chester. He stated on his second examination that he had been working at shoemaking in Philadelphia, under the name of James Wellington; that he had no reason for changing his name; that before he came to Philadelphia he had worked in New York, but declined to have his employer there written to. He declared he had never been to Darby, never heard of such a place before. A pair of blue pantaloons, a coat of the same color, and a shirt being shown him, he said they belonged to him, and that he had purchased them from a man he met on the West Chester road. The scissors-chain found on Boyce was recognized as the one stolen from Mrs. Warner, the pantaloons and coat found in Wellington's bundle were identified by the tailor who made them as belonging to Bonsall, and a counterfeit ten-dollar note stolen at the same time had been passed at Sculltown by one of the men.

Judge Hopkins committed the accused to jail at Woodbury to await a requisition from the Governor of Pennsylvania, and, to prevent an escape therefrom, a guard of citizens was stationed around the prison.

On Tuesday night, the 7th of June, the prisoners were brought to Chester by Sheriff Weaver and lodged in the county jail. On Thursday and Friday they were separately examined in the court-house, before Justices Luke Cassin and George W. Bartram. The men in their examinations told substantially the same story they had related to Judge Hopkins, excepting that Labee stated he had received the ten-dollar note from Wellington, who told him if he passed it he might buy a pair of shoes, giving him, Wellington, the change, and that he, Boyce, and Wellington had been in prison in Philadelphia, and that all three had been discharged from the jail between the 7th and 20th of May of that year. Wellington also acknowledged that he had been convicted of a store robbery in New York, had been sentenced for life to the penitentiary, had served five years, when he was pardoned by the Governor on condition that he would depart from and never return to that State. Mrs. Warner and Mrs. Bonsall, who were present at the examination, identified the men, and testified that the scissors-chain belonged to Mrs. Warner, the Peruvian dollar was similar to that carried by the murdered man, and the clothing taken from Bonsall, which Sheriff Weaver found thrust into a stove-pipe hole in Wellington's cell at Woodbury, was identified by both the witnesses as property taken from their house. The prisoners were held to await the action of the grand jury.

In the mean while, the fourth man had been apprehended at Baltimore, the cause of his arrest being the possession of a volume of poems written by Mrs. Gardner, of Darby, the owner's name having been carefully cut from the title-page. Among the articles taken from Bonsall's trunk was a volume of these poems, and he had written his name at the top of the title-page. The man then arrested as John Thompson was surrendered to the State of Pennsylvania on requisition, and shortly after lodged in the Delaware County jail.

On Saturday, Oct. 20, 1824, the grand jury having indicted the four men for the murder of Bonsall, Deputy Attorney-General Edward Darlington called the case of Michael Monroe, *alias* James Wellington, who being without counsel, Judge Darlington assigned John Edwards, Jr., Matthias Richards Sayres, and Benjamin Tilghman to manage his defense. Edwards and Sayres were residents of this county-seat, the first named being afterwards member of Congress from this district, and the latter, who was a promising member of the bar, popularly known as "Dick Sayres," died at Chester early in 1826, in the thirtieth year of his age. The case having been opened, it continued over into the following day,—Sunday,—and the court-room was crowded with spectators during all that October Sabbath, who had come from the every section of the county to hear the trial. The circumstances as heretofore related were established by the evidence, and on Tuesday—for the trial consumed nearly four days—the jury rendered a verdict of guilty of murder in the first degree. The prosecution of Washington Labee had preceded that of Wellington, the jury, on Saturday, October 20th, returning a verdict of guilty of murder in the second degree. John Thompson and Abraham Boyce, who were tried on Thursday, the 25th, were both acquitted on the indictments of murder, they being the two men who had gone out at the front door when Bonsall was killed, and, as no other charge was made against them, they were discharged. The court sentenced Labee to eight years' hard labor in the Penitentiary at Philadelphia, and on Wednesday, October 30th, pronounced the sentence of death as to Wellington. Governor Shulze, November 10th, promptly signed the warrant, designating the execution of the sentence to be enforced on Dec. 17, 1824.

The *Upland Union*, published at Chester, on December 21st, contains the following account of the execution of Wellington: "On Friday morning, Dec. 17, 1824, Michael Monroe, *alias* James Wellington, was executed. At an early hour the borough of Chester was crowded with strangers. At eleven o'clock he was conducted from the jail to the place of execution, a distance of one and a half miles" (on the tract now known as the Forty Acres), "accompanied by the sheriff and all the police-officers of the county. He was attended by Rev. John Woolson, William Palmer, R. W. Morgan, and John Smith. At half-past eleven o'clock, when the procession reached the gallows, the Rev. William Palmer delivered a solemn and appropriate prayer, after which he was followed by Rev. John Woolson. The prisoner ascended the scaffold about half-past twelve o'clock, and there addressed the spectators in the following words, which were spoken with a firmness that astonished all who were present:

"'I have heard it said that no innocent man was ever executed in this county, but it will lose that honor to-day.'

"After he had concluded the above sentence, he sang a hymn with the greatest ease and composure of mind. He then told the sheriff that he had no more to say. It wanted seventeen minutes of one when the drop fell, and the prisoner was no more."

An autopsy of Wellington's body was made that evening by Drs. William Gray, Ellis Harlan, and other physicians in the house still standing on the north side of Third Street, below Franklin, Chester, which was at that time known as the poll-well house. When the ancient borough began its long-delayed improvement, the then owner of the house modernized it.

Washington Labee, as before stated, was sentenced to a term of imprisonment in the penitentiary. It is said that five years after Wellington's execution a convict, dying in Sing Sing prison, stated under oath that he and three other men were the real murderers of Bonsall. The sworn confession being presented to the State authorities, Labee, who had undergone more than half of his term of imprisonment, was pardoned, but his long incarceration had so undermined his health that he died shortly after his release.

The Clay Murder.—On May 21, 1870, near the factory of Oborn Levis, George Clay, an Englishman, was murdered by his daughter, Sarah Ann Seaburn. The latter, a woman of thirty-five, was the widow of a soldier who had died in the war, and after her husband's death she had become addicted to drink. On many occasions she had exhibited symptoms of insanity, which caused her several times to be discharged from employment. In 1869 the father and daughter were both in the Delaware County House of Employment, and in the spring of 1870, when the father was discharged, he obtained the release of his daughter, alleging that she was not insane or had recovered from whatever derangement of mind she had labored under. Sarah Seaburn was a pensioner, and with the money received from the government the father and daughter purchased liquor in Philadelphia and became intoxicated. On Saturday, May 21, 1870, the woman, then in Upper Darby, borrowed a hatchet from a resident near the factory of Oborn Levis, stating that she wanted it to split some wood for kindling. Two hours after midnight, on May 21st, the woman came to the watchman at the mill and inquired the road to Media. At five o'clock the same morning Sarah Seaburn reached the almshouse, stating that she had murdered her father, who had abused her, and she wanted to be hanged for the crime. The body of Clay was found about nine o'clock, in a field near the house of Oborn Levis, and beside it was the hatchet with which the deed had been done. The head of the corpse had five large wounds, one of which, cutting through the left ear and crushing the skull, must have caused instant death. The woman was indicted and tried for the murder on Aug. 22, 1870. The prisoner seeming not to comprehend the serious nature of the charge, Judge Butler ordered the plea of not guilty to be entered, and assigned William Ward to conduct her defense. A clear case of mental derangement was established, the jury acquitted the prisoner because of insanity, and the court directed her detention in the insane department of the House of Employment.

Mills on Darby Creek.—In presenting the history of the manufacturing industries in Upper Darby, it is the purpose to follow the mode adopted in the account of Birmingham township: to trace the creeks,—Darby and Cobb's,—and moving northward, to narrate the story of those streams, the waters of which have furnished and are furnishing power to many of the busy factories and works which have been located along their banks.

Upper Darby Paper-Mills.—Just above the township-line dividing Upper from Lower Darby, on the west side of Darby Creek, these works are located. In 1747, Joseph Bonsall sold the Darby Mills (the site of the present Griswold Worsted Company's mills in the borough of Darby) to Richard Lloyd. Bonsall had erected a saw-mill at the site of the present paper-mills, about the middle of the last century, and in 1766, his son, Joseph Bonsall, was assessed on the saw-mill at that location. Joseph Bonsall, the elder, lived until 1803, at which date a grist- as well as a saw-mill had been erected, the former operated by his son James, and the latter by his son Joseph. On April 17, 1809, under proceedings in partition, fifteen and a half acres of land, the dwelling, grist- and saw-mills were allotted to James Bonsall, who, on December 26th of the same year, conveyed a half-interest in the property to his brother Joseph, and the mills were operated by the Bonsall brothers until 1840, when James died. His interest in the mills was devised to his wife, Elizabeth, during life, and with the remainder, at her death, to Joseph Palmer, a nephew of the decedent. Mrs. Bonsall died prior to Nov. 24, 1852, for on that date Joseph Palmer purchased the half-interest of Joseph Bonsall in the mills, thus perfecting his title to the whole real estate. On March 31, 1866, Christopher Palmer bought the mills, and by his will, dated May 25, 1868, devised it to his son, Robert Palmer. The latter, in 1872, sold the property to Edwin T. Garrett, who changed the grist-mill to a paper-mill, since which date it has been used as such, daily making an average of one thousand pounds of paper manufactured.

Morris Truman's Paper-Mills.—In the bend of Darby Creek, south of Kellyville, are located the Mathews Paper-Mills, or in later times known as the Beehive Mills. The history of these mills is interesting. During the Revolution, on March 31, 1777, Morris Trueman and Joseph Cruikshank purchased six acres of land from Joseph Bonsall, which plot adjoined other lands owned by Bonsall. The deed conferred on the purchasers the right to erect such mills as they saw fit; to build on the creek a dam abutting on Bonsall's land, as also to raise the water sufficient to attain the power necessary to carry on the proposed mills. In the next year a low two-story, stone paper-mill and two stone dwellings were erected. An old log house, which still stands on the premises, is said to have been built prior to the sale to Trueman & Cruikshank. The paper-mills were operated by this firm until May 16, 1785, when Trueman purchased Cruikshank's interest in the property, and continued to operate the mills until 1788, when he associated Evan Trueman in the business. On April 6, 1799, Trueman sold the estate to John Mathews, who conducted the business until his death, and was succeeded by his two sons, one of whom, Thomas, is still living, residing on the estate. In 1859, Thomas Mathews sold the property to J. Howard Lewis, who conveyed it the next year to his brother Samuel. The latter changed the mill into a cotton-factory. In 1868 a new building, forty-five by ninety-five feet, two stories in height, was erected on the site of the old paper-mills. In April, 1876, the new building was destroyed by fire. At that time the mill was not in use, the stock had been removed, and the machinery would also have been taken out during the following week. The mills were rebuilt, and cotton-manufacturing resumed therein. In March, 1884, the buildings were again destroyed by fire, and have been again rebuilt. The walls of the buildings were used, and asbestos is manufactured there at the present time by George D. Lewis. The two houses built in 1778 are still standing.

Kellyville Mills.—The land whereon Kellyville is located, and extending up the creek, so as to include the Union Mills, was the tract of six hundred and fifty-five acres surveyed to George Wood, Nov. 6, 1682, as heretofore stated. Two hundred acres of that estate were conveyed to Richard Bonsall, March 6, 1697/8. A century later, in 1799, Isaac Lobb owned three hundred and eighty acres of land at that locality, and on May 6, 1812, he sold to Asher Lobb the right to build a dam across Darby Creek, which the latter did, and shortly after built a saw-mill. Between the years 1822 and 1826 Lobb erected a stone cotton-factory, seventy-two by forty-two feet, four stories in height, which in the last-mentioned year was operated by Bernard McCready. At that time the machinery consisted of thirty carding-engines, thirty-two looms, three thousand and fifty-six spindles, and three thousand three hundred pounds of cotton-yarn was spun weekly. McCready continued at this mill until Nov. 28, 1836, when Lobb leased the factory to Dennis & Charles Kelly for a period of ten years. The following year Lobb died, and by will directed that at the expiration of the lease to Kelly the mill property should be sold. Under this clause in Asher Lobb's will, on March 5, 1845, Charles Kelly purchased the mill property. In 1847 the main building of the Kellyville Mills was one hundred and sixty by fifty-two feet, and five stories in height. The machinery, consisting of eight thousand spindles, ten self-acting mules, seven hand-mules, seventeen live spindle-throstles, and one hundred power-looms, was driven by two overshot wheels fifteen feet in diameter and sixteen feet wide, assisted, when the water was low, with a fifty horse-power engine, three boilers forty feet long and thirty-six inches in diameter. Two hundred operatives were then employed. The weekly production of the mills was thirty-five thousand yards of ticking, canton flannel, and plantation goods, while forty thousand pounds of cotton were required per month. The village at that time contained fifty dwelling-houses, mostly of stone, and the population consisted of over five hundred persons. Dennis & Charles Kelly and their heirs operated the mills until 1877. On September 21st of that year the mills were purchased by George Campbell. The latter, on March 2, 1878, sold the estate to Sellers Hoffman, who now owns the property. The Hoffman Mills contain three thousand five hundred spindles, two hundred and thirty-four looms, thirty-nine cards, and sixty inch sets of woolen cards Three thousand six hundred pounds of cotton yarn is produced weekly, and sixty operatives are employed

Modoc Mills—On Darby Creek, a short distance above the Kellyville Mills, in 1873, Daniel Sharkey and William Weidbey erected a stone cotton-mill, ninety by forty-two feet, two stories in height The machinery consists of four mules and five cards Fourteen operatives are employed, and about three thousand six hundred pounds of cotton yarn are produced weekly.

Garrett Mills—William Garrett emigrated to the province of Pennsylvania in 1683 On March 5, 1688, there was surveyed to him two hundred and three acres from a tract of three hundred and three acres, which had been located by Luke Hanck, Nov 8, 1682 It was a long tract, which extended nearly across the township, with the south end resting on Darby Creek, opposite the present Heyville Mills, in Springfield township William Garrett was assessed in 1766 on a leather-mill and a blade-mill, in 1774 on a fulling-mill and blade-mill In 1782, Oborn Garrett was assessed on a fulling-mill, and in 1788 on "a skin-mill out of repair," and also a plaster-mill After that date the name of Garrett does not appear on the assessment-roll of Upper Darby in connection with mills until 1798, when Thomas Garrett owned a tilt-mill at the site of the present Union Mills, owned by Thomas Kent, and there Thomas & Samuel Garrett conducted the tilt-mill, oil-mill, and cotton-factory at that locality for many years after that date In 1848, just below Garrettsford, on the Thornfield estate, belonging to William Garrett, on Dr Ash's map a tannery is located Possibly this may have been the leather or bark-mill for which William Garrett, in 1766, was assessed

Union Mills—Thomas Garrett, in 1805, built at this mill-site a tilt-mill, and on July 27, 1808, he purchased of Samuel Levis the right to place the abutment of a dam across Darby Creek for any purpose, excepting for a grist- or paper-mill After securing this privilege a new dam was built, the works at that location enlarged, and, as mentioned in the account of the Garrett Mills, was conducted by Thomas & Samuel Garrett The latter, as an individual enterprise, had operated an oil-mill at the same locality, which was continued until about 1830, and was washed away in the flood in 1843 In 1822, Thomas Garrett erected a stone cotton-factory, fifty-four by forty feet, three stories in height, which, in 1826, was rented to John Mitchell It was known as the Union Mill, and at that time contained seven carding-engines, one drawing-frame, one stretcher of one hundred and twenty spindles, four hundred and forty-four throstle-spindles, six hundred and sixty mule-spindles, and made weekly one thousand pounds of cotton-yarn Twenty four operatives were employed, and stone tenement-houses had been erected to accommodate five families In 1830, James Robinson succeeded Mitchell, and carried on manufacturing there for several years Charles Kelly leased it in 1839, and continued to operate it until April 1, 1845, when the property was purchased by James Wilde, the locality at that time known as Wildeville On Nov 16, 1846, Wilde sold the mills to his brother-in-law, Thomas Kent, who now owns and has continued to operate the Union Mills since that date In 1850, Mr Kent built an addition of fifty by forty feet, three stories in height, to the original mill on the south end, and in 1852 to the north end he built an addition fifty by forty feet, three stories and an attic Fifteen years afterwards, in 1867, Thomas Kent had the walls of the main building removed to the floor of the second story, and on the remaining walls rebuilt the mill four stories and an attic, thus giving a total length of two hundred feet, forty feet in width, and erected also a dye-house eighty by forty feet, a fire-proof picker-house thirty by thirty-four feet, two stories in height The machinery in the Union Mills comprises ten sets of forty-eight inch cards, eleven self-acting mules of four hundred spindles each, one hundred narrow and sixteen broad looms, having capacity of manufacturing four thousand yards of goods weekly •

Rockbourne Mills.—This mill is located on the west side of Darby Creek, and was the property of Samuel Garrett, who failing in 1837, it was assigned to Oborn Levis and William Garrett, who conveyed it, April 1, 1838, to Edwin Garrett This mill is located near the site of the oil-mill which was washed away in 1843 After this cotton-mill was erected Edwin Garrett rented it to Jonas Cowan, who made cotton laps until the fall of 1842, when James and John Wilde succeeded him, and remained there until the fall of 1843, when they removed to Oborn Levis' mill farther up the creek Thomas and John Kent, on Jan 1, 1844, rented the factory and manufactured woolen goods April 1, 1845, Thomas Kent purchased the mill, and in 1850 built an addition to it of thirty by forty feet, four stories and an attic In 1868 the old part of the building was almost entirely taken down and a stone structure fifty-four by one hundred and twenty-five feet, four stories and attic, was erected This mill contains six mules with four hundred spindles each, five sets of cards, and thirty-eight broad looms Twenty-four hundred yards of woolen goods are manufactured weekly Two hundred people are employed in both mills The machinery is driven by a one hundred horse-power engine and one hundred and twenty horse-power boiler

Thomas Kent, the son of Josiah and Hannah Kent, was born in Middleton, Lancashire, England, on the 27th of March, 1813 His youth was spent at the home of his parents, where limited advantages of education were afforded He had, however, during this early period acquired habits of thought and observation which were more serviceable in later life than the knowledge derived from books Entering a cotton-mill, he became proficient in the trade of a weaver, and at sixteen was made foreman, which responsible position he filled acceptably for a period of three years, when he learned the art of silk weaving He continued thus engaged until 1839, when, having determined to emigrate to America, he landed in Philadelphia, and repaired at once to Clifton, Delaware Co, where he became associated with his brother-in-law in the spinning of carpet-yarns Mr Kent remained thus employed until 1843, when a copartnership was formed with his brother John, under the firm-name of J & T Kent They continued the manufacture of carpet-yarns, renting for the purpose the mill which had formerly been operated by James Wild A disastrous fire and freshet the same year destroyed both mill and machinery, but, nothing daunted, the same fall another mill was rented, fully equipped with machinery, and in active operation during the beginning of the following year The copartnership which existed until 1852 ended in the purchase by Thomas Kent of the entire interest The same year he introduced the weaving of Kentucky jeans, and continued to supply the market with this article until 1861, when the mill was devoted to the manufacture of products for the government In 1867 the old mill was demolished, and the present spacious and convenient structure erected in its stead The production of cloths was continued until 1877, when flannels were made a specialty, and are still the product of the looms

Mr Kent was married, in 1852, to Miss Fannie Leonard, daughter of Simeon and Bodicea Leonard Their children are Hannah (Mrs Frederick Schoff), Henry L, Louisa, Francis L (deceased), Samuel L, and Mary A Mr Kent was early a Whig in his political predilections, and subsequently indorsed the platform and principles of the Republican party The engrossing cares of a very prosperous business have, however, precluded an active interest in public affairs, and debarred him from political associations, which are little to his taste In his religious faith he is a Swedenborgian, and a member of the New Jerusalem Church in Upper Darby

Clifton Mills.—A paper-mill was in operation on the site of these mills in 1782, then owned by Samuel Levis and conducted by William Levis, to whom it was devised by his father's will Aug 22, 1793 William Levis, in December, 1795, purchased of John Lungren a paper-mill on Ridley Creek, which in 1822 was changed to a cotton-factory The latter property is now owned by Samuel Bancroft The mill on Darby Creek, after the death of William Levis, was sold by Oborn and William Levis on Feb 24, 1825, to Samuel Eckstein, together with eighteen acres of land and the use of water in the creek from the dam and race of the upper mills, now Glenwood Mills The new owner rented the mills to William Amies & Co The estate came into the ownership of the Pennsylvania Hospital in October, 1842, and shortly after was sold to Oborn Levis At that time it was a private paper-mill ninety by thirty-two feet, three stories in height, and was known as the Lamb Mill. Oborn Levis operated this mill until his death, when by his will it became the property of his son Oborn, who in 1867 changed it to a cotton-factory The latter continued to operate the mills until his death, and in 1881 his administrators sold it to William Longstreth, who died soon after, and the Clifton Mills are now owned by his estate The main mill is one hundred and eighty by fifty-two feet, and is partly two and partly three stories in height The machinery consists of seventeen hundred woolen-spindles, four sets of cards, one hundred and eight looms, five thousand cotton-spindles, and nine cards One hundred and thirty-five persons are employed in these mills, and thirty bales of cotton are used weekly in manufacturing goods

Glenwood Mills.—Samuel Levis, a maltster of Leicester, England, with William Garrett, before leaving England, purchased one thousand acres of land from William Penn Levis, Garrett, and others emigrated to the province in 1684, landing at Chester, and shortly after settled on Darby Creek in Upper Darby, and built the house where Samuel G Levis now lives At the death of Samuel Levis, the real estate in the bend of Darby Creek, just south of the Garrettford road, descended to Samuel Levis, the younger The latter is said to have erected at this location the first mill ever built by the Levis family, and as it was a scythe or tilt-mill, it certainly was not erected prior to the middle of the last century In 1779, Levis had a grist-mill and an oil-mill at this site The tilt-mill could not have proved successful, for several years prior to the Revolution the building had been changed to a paper-mill. Samuel Levis (2d) had several sons, among the number were Samuel, William, and Isaac Levis The latter removed in 1775 to Ridley Creek, where now are the Media Water-Works, William had other mills near the Glenwood site which belonged to his father Samuel (3), died in 1793, and this mill descended to Samuel (4), who died in 1813, and the estate passed to his sons, Samuel, William, and Oborn Levis To William the mills which later became the Eckstein Mills descended, to Samuel the present mills came, and to Oborn the Oborn Garrett Mills Samuel and Oborn subsequently exchanged properties, and Oborn Levis came into possession of the Glenwood Mills They were operated by Thomas Amies & Son from 1828 to 1838, later by Israel Ames and Benjamin Gaskill to 1840 From that time Oborn and Samuel G Levis owned and conducted the mills to the death of Oborn, since which time they have been managed by Samuel G Levis In 1862 the paper-mill was torn down and a cotton- and woolen-factory built, one hundred and ten by fifty-four feet, three stories high, with annex one hundred and five by twenty-seven feet, two stories high The factory at present contains four thousand spindles, nine sets of cards, one hundred and sixty-two looms, one hundred and forty opera-

NIA.

[illegible] three stories
[illegible] as the Lamb Mill
[illegible] until his death, when
[illegible] of his son Oliver,
[illegible] factory. The latter
[illegible] until his death, and in
[illegible] to William Longstreth,
[illegible] Clifton Mills are now
[illegible] mill is one hundred
[illegible], and is partly two and
[illegible]. The machinery con-
[illegible], four sets
[illegible] looms, five thousand
[illegible]. One hundred and
[illegible] in these mills, and
[illegible] weekly is manufactur-

[illegible] Lewis, a resident of
William Garrett, being
[illegible] one thousand acres of
[illegible] Lewis, Garrett, and others
[illegible], landing at Chester,
[illegible] Darby Creek in Upper
[illegible] Samuel D. Lewis now
[illegible] Lewis, the real estate in
[illegible] south of the Garrettford
[illegible], the younger. The
[illegible] this location the first
[illegible] family, and as it was
[illegible] was not erected prior to
[illegible]. In 1779, Lewis had a
[illegible] this site. The saw-mill
[illegible], for several years
[illegible] had been changed
[illegible] and several sons;
[illegible], William, and Isaac
[illegible] 1775 a [illegible] Darby Creek
[illegible] William had
[illegible] which belonged to
[illegible] 1799, and the mill de-
[illegible] died in 1816, and the
[illegible], William, and Ohara
[illegible] which later became the
[illegible] the present mills
[illegible] Garrett Mills. Samuel
[illegible] changed properties, and
[illegible] of the Glenwood
[illegible] Thomas Amies & Son
[illegible] Amies and Benjamin
[illegible] and Samuel R.
[illegible] the mills to the death of
[illegible] have been occupied by
[illegible] the paper-mill was torn
[illegible] factory built, one hun-
[illegible], three stories high, with
[illegible] twenty-seven feet, two
[illegible] present contains four
[illegible] of cards, one hundred
[illegible] and forty spin-

paper-mill, he became proficient in the trade of [illegible], kind of duties, was made foreman, which responsible position he filled acceptably for a period of three years, when he learned the art of [illegible] weaving. He continued that employment until 18[illegible], when, having determined to engage in business, he located in Philadelphia and removed [illegible] to Clifton, Delaware Co., where he became associated with his brother-in-law in the spinning of carpet-yarns. Mr. Kent remained thus engaged until 18[illegible], when a copartnership was formed with his brother John, under the firm-name of T. & J. Kent. They continued the manufacture of carpet-yarns, renting for the purpose the mill which had formerly been operated by James Wild. A disastrous fire and freshet the same year destroyed both mill and machinery, but, nothing daunted, the same [illegible] a new mill was erected, fully equipped with machinery, and in active operation during the beginning of the following year. The copartnership which existed until 18[illegible] ended in the purchase by Thomas Kent of the entire interest. The same year he introduced the weaving of Kentucky jeans, and continued to supply the market with this article until 1861, when the mill was devoted to the manufacture of products for the government. In 18[illegible] the old mill was demolished, and the present spacious and convenient structure erected in its stead. The production of [illegible] was conducted until 1877, when [illegible] were made a specialty, and are still the product of the looms.

Mr. Kent was married, in 18[illegible], to Miss Fannie Leonard, daughter of Samuel and Rebecca Leonard. Their children are Hannah (Mrs. Frederick Schoff), Henry L., Louisa, [illegible] (deceased), Samuel L., and Mary A. Mr. Kent was early a Whig in his political predilections, and subsequently indorsed the platform and principles of the Republican party. The engrossing cares of a very prosperous business have, however, precluded an active interest in public affairs, and debarred him from political associations, which are little to his taste. In his religious faith he is a Swedenborgian, and a member of the New Jerusalem Church in Upper Darby.

Clifton Mills.—A paper-mill was in operation on the site of these mills in 1742, then owned by Samuel Levis and conducted by William Levis, to whom it was devised by his father's will Aug. [illegible], 1793. William Levis, in December, 17[illegible], purchased of John [illegible] a paper-mill on Ridley Creek, which in 18[illegible] was changed to a cotton-factory. The latter property is now owned by Samuel Bancroft. The mill on Darby Creek, after the death of William Levis, was sold by Oborn and William Levis on Feb. [illegible], 18[illegible], to Samuel L. Levis, together with [illegible] acres of land and the use of water in the creek, from the dam and race of the upper mills, now Glenwood Mills. The new owner leased the mills to William Amies & Co. The estate came into the ownership of the Pennsylvania Hospital in October, 18[illegible], and shortly after was sold to Oborn Levis. At that time it was a two-story paper-mill ninety by fifty-two feet, three stories in height, and was known as the Levis Mill. Oborn Levis operated this mill until his death, when by his will it became the property of his son Oborn, who in 1867 changed it to a cotton-factory. The latter continued to operate the mills until his death, and in 1881 his administrators sold it to William Longstreth, who died soon after, and the Clifton Mills are now owned by his estate. The main mill is one hundred and eighty by fifty-two feet, and is partly two and partly three stories in height. The machinery consists of seventeen hundred woolen-spindles, four sets of cards, one hundred and eight looms, five thousand cotton-spindles, and nine cards. One hundred and thirty-five persons are employed in these mills, and thirty bales of cotton are used weekly in manufacturing goods.

Glenwood Mills.—Samuel Levis, a maltster of Leicester, England, with William Garrett, before leaving England, purchased one thousand acres of land from William Penn. Levis, Garrett, and others emigrated to the province in 1684, landing at Chester, and shortly after settled on Darby Creek in Upper Darby, and built the house where Samuel G. Levis now lives. At the death of Samuel Levis, the real estate in the bend of Darby Creek, just south of the Garrettford road, descended to Samuel Levis, the younger. The latter is said to have erected at this location the first mill ever built by the Levis family, and as it was a scythe or slit-mill, it certainly was not erected prior to the middle of the last century. In 1779, Levis had a grist-mill and an oil-mill at this site. The slit-mill could not have proved successful, for several years prior to the Revolution the building had been changed to a paper-mill. Samuel Levis (2) had several sons; among the number were Samuel, William, and Isaac Levis. The latter removed in 17[illegible] to Ridley Creek, where now are the Media Water-Works; William had other mills near the Glenwood site which belonged to his father Samuel (2), died in 1793, and this mill descended to Samuel (3), who died in 1813, and the estate passed to his sons, Samuel, William, and Oborn Levis. To William the mills which later became the [illegible] Mills descended, to Samuel the present mills came, and to Oborn the Oborn Garrett Mills. Samuel and Oborn subsequently exchanged properties, and Oborn Levis came into possession of the Glenwood Mills. They were operated by Thomas Amies & Son from 18[illegible] to 18[illegible], later by Israel Amies and Benjamin [illegible] in 18[illegible]. From that time Oborn and Samuel G. Levis owned and conducted the mills to the death of Oborn, since which time they have been managed by Samuel G. Levis. In 18[illegible] the paper-mill was torn down and a cotton- and woolen-factory built, one hundred and ten by fifty-four feet, three stories high, with annex one hundred and five by twenty-seven feet, two stories high. The factory at present contains four thousand spindles, nine sets of cards, one hundred and sixty-two looms; one hundred and forty opera-

Eng. by A.H.Ritchie

George Burnley

[illegible] are employed, twenty-five bales of cotton are used, and forty thousand yards of goods are manufactured weekly.

Tuscarora Mills.—At the head of Darby Creek, where the [illegible] township line unites with that stream, these mills are located. Prior to the Revolution a grist-mill was on the place. Samuel G. Levis, an aged [illegible] now living, states that on the day the battle of Brandywine was fought mechanics were at [illegible] for a paper-mill then being built [illegible] this locality, and the distant cannon[illegible] distinctly heard. The paper-mill [illegible] and carried on by Samuel Levis until his [illegible] which time it passed to his son, William [illegible]. The latter died in 1816, and the mills [illegible] William Palmer and Jonathan Marker, [illegible] manufacture of paper there until [illegible] Server, a son-in-law of William [illegible] in the business,—the making of [illegible]. A part of the mill building was [illegible] in 1845. The following year [illegible] purchased by George Burnley, who [illegible] in Haverford, where [illegible] in partnership with James [illegible]. In 1846 he built [illegible] two and a half stories high, and [illegible] Tuscarora Mills, the name [illegible] of Cope's line having been the vessel [illegible] Burnley sailed from Liverpool. In 1860 his [illegible], and John Burnley succeeded to the business. George Burnley operated the mills from 1860 [illegible] time, when Samuel Levis leased them and [illegible] there until 1875, when he was followed for [illegible] and a half by George D. Levis. The mills [illegible] leased to Henry Taylor and John Hales [illegible] subsequently had the mills and failed. The machinery and household were sold at sheriff's sale, [illegible] one of the noted lawsuits of the county. [illegible] J. A. Sprogger operated the mills until [illegible] time the mills have been idle. The [illegible] by a daughter of George Burnley, are [illegible] Sept. 6, 1884.

[illegible] of John and Mary Burnley, [illegible] 1804, in Littletown, near Leeds, [illegible] England, where his youth was spent. His [illegible] were limited to a brief interval [illegible] a neighboring factory. After [illegible] knowledge of the business of a manufacturer, [illegible] the year 1829 for America, and [illegible] Montgomery County, Pa. At a [illegible] he removed to Haverford, and having [illegible] on Cobb's Creek, began the manufacture [illegible] goods, having before this had a brief but not [illegible] as a manufacturer of carpets [illegible]. In 1846 he removed to Darby Creek, [illegible] and erected the Tuscarora Mills, [illegible] devoted to the manufacture of [illegible] the spinning of yarn. This business [illegible] until 1861, when he retired from its active management, and was succeeded by his brother, John and [illegible], and his son George B. Burnley. Mr. Burnley was married Dec. 31, 1835, to Miss Hannah Lomas, daughter of James Lomas, of England. Their children are George B., Charles W., Adeline (deceased), Mary Elizabeth (deceased), Washington, Harriet Jane (deceased), Alice, Mrs. William A. Ness, Sarah Jane (deceased), Mitchell, and Hester (deceased). Mr. Burnley voted first the Whig and subsequently the Republican ticket in politics, but was not active in the political arena. He was in religion a Swedenborgian, and a member and trustee of that church. His death occurred Aug. 9, 1884, in his [illegible] year.

Ralph Lewis purchased and located [illegible] acres of land June 14, 1686, a part of five hundred acres of land surveyed, Nov. 18, 1682, to John Bevan. This land came to Samuel Lewis April 20, 1709, and to Abraham Lewis Sept. 8, 1711. This was on the [illegible] tract, on Darby Creek, at the upper end of the township. In 1766 Abraham Lewis owned an interest in a grist-mill on this tract, for which he was assessed in that year. The mill long ago fell into disuse, even lost to tradition, and prior to the Revolution had been abandoned, for it is not mentioned in any assessment-roll subsequent to 1766.

Mills on Cobb's Creek.—This stream, which forms the eastern boundary of Upper Darby township, as also that of Lower Darby, until it unites and is merged into Darby Creek, in the early time of the Swedish settlement was known as Mill-Kill or Creek, because the Swedish water-mill, built by Governor Printz in 1643, was located on its banks, near the present Blue Bell Tavern. Subsequently, when the English acquired ownership of the territory, the name Cobb was given to it, because a large tract of land was located along its banks by William Cobb, who in 1683 was appointed by the court at Chester constable for Amesland and "Calcoone Hook." Following this stream, beginning at the southern boundary of Upper Darby, the history of the industrial establishments located on Cobb's Creek and its tributaries will be narrated.

Bonsall's Saw-Mill.—The first mill-seat on Cobb's Creek within the limits of Upper Darby township was on the present grounds of the Fernwood Cemetery. This site was occupied by Benjamin Bonsall, who erected a saw-mill at the place soon after 1802, for in that year his name does not appear on the assessment-roll in connection with any mill in the township. The saw-mill, however, is mentioned in 1826, and was in operation subsequent to 1848, when it disappeared from among the industries of Delaware County. From the same dam whose water furnished power to Bonsall's saw-mill, water was had to run a snuff-mill, which was located on the east side of the creek, in Philadelphia. In 1807 this snuff-mill was owned by Gavin Hamilton, and was continued in operation long after 1826.

Sellers' Locomotive-Works.—About 1851 a

George Burnley

tives are employed, twenty-five bales of cotton are used, and forty thousand yards of goods are manufactured weekly.

Tuscarora Mills—At the bend of Darby Creek, where the Springfield township line unites with that stream, these mills are located Prior to the Revolution a grist-mill was at this place Samuel G Levis, an aged man still living, states that on the day the battle of Brandywine was fought mechanics were at work on a fly-wheel for a paper-mill then being built by Samuel Levis at this locality, and the distant cannonading could be distinctly heard The paper-mill was owned and carried on by Samuel Levis until his death, in 1793, at which time it passed to his son, William Levis The latter died in 1818, and the mills were sold to William Palmer and Jonathan Marker, who continued the manufacture of paper there until 1830, when Frederick Server, a son-in-law of William Palmer, succeeded to the business,—the making of coarse card-board A part of the mill building was washed away in the flood of 1843 The following year the property was purchased by George Burnley, who removed there from Cobb's Creek, in Haverford, where he had been operating, in partnership with James Haworth, one of Dennis Kelly s mills In 1844 he built the stone cotton-mill, two and a half stories high, and named the works the Tuscarora Mills, the noted packet-ship of that name of Cope's line having been the vessel in which Burnley sailed from Liverpool In 1860 his son, Charles, and John Burnley succeeded to the business George Burnley operated the mills from 1865 for a short time, when Samuel Levis leased them and continued there until 1870, when he was followed for a year and a half by George D Lewis The mills were then leased to Henry Taylor and John Haley Taylor subsequently had the mills and failed The machinery and leasehold were sold at sheriff's sale, and thus arose one of the noted lawsuits of the county After Taylor, S A Springer operated the mills until 1882, since which time the mills have been idle The mills, owned by a daughter of George Burnley, are to be sold at public sale Sept 6, 1884

George Burnley, the son of John and Mary Burnley, was born Dec 28, 1804, in Littletown, near Leeds, Yorkshire, England, where his youth was spent His educational advantages were limited to a brief interval of study prior to entering a neighboring factory After acquiring a knowledge of the business of a manufacturer, he sailed about the year 1825 for America, and at once located in Montgomery County, Pa At a later date he removed to Haverford, and having rented a mill on Cobb's Creek, began the manufacture of cotton goods, having before this had a brief but not very successful career as a manufacturer of carpets in Philadelphia In 1844 he removed to Darby Creek, in Upper Darby township, and erected the Tuscarora Mills, which were devoted to the manufacture of cotton goods and the spinning of yarn. This business was continued until 1861, when he retired from its active management, and was succeeded by his brothers, John and Charles, and his son, George E Burnley Mr Burnley was married Dec. 31, 1838, to Miss Hannah Lomas, daughter of James Lomas, of England Their children are George E, Charles W, Adaline (deceased), Mary Elizabeth (deceased), Washington, Hannah Jane (deceased), Alice (Mrs William A Fries), Sarah Jane (deceased), Michael, and Hester (deceased) Mr Burnley voted first the Whig, and subsequently the Republican ticket in politics, but was not active in the political arena. He was in religion a Swedenborgian, and a member and trustee of that church His death occurred Aug 9, 1864, in his sixtieth year

Ralph Lewis purchased one hundred and fifty acres of land June 14, 1692, a part of five hundred acres of land surveyed, Nov 15, 1683, to John Bowne This land came to Samuel Lewis April 20, 1708, and to Abraham Lewis Sept 5, 1711 This was on the Bloomsberry tract, on Darby Creek, at the upper end of the township In 1766, Abraham Lewis owned an interest in a grist-mill on this tract, for which he was assessed in that year The mill long ago fell into disuse, even lost to tradition, and prior to the Revolution had been abandoned, for it is not mentioned in any assessment-roll subsequent to 1766

Mills on Cobb's Creek—This stream, which forms the eastern boundary of Upper Darby township, as also that of Lower Darby, until it unites and is merged into Darby Creek, in the early time of the Swedish settlement was known as Mill Kill or Creek, because the Swedish water-mill, built by Governor Printz in 1643, was located on its banks, near the present Blue Bell Tavern Subsequently, when the English acquired ownership of the territory, the name Cobb was given to it, because a large tract of land was located along its banks by William Cobb, who in 1683 was appointed by the court at Chester constable for Amesland and "Calcoone Hook" Following this stream, beginning at the southern boundary of Upper Darby, the history of the industrial establishments located on Cobb's Creek and its tributaries will be narrated

Bonsall's Saw-Mill—The first mill-seat on Cobb's Creek within the limits of Upper Darby township was on the present grounds of the Fernwood Cemetery This site was occupied by Benjamin Bonsall, who erected a saw-mill at the place soon after 1822, for in that year his name does not appear on the assessment-roll in connection with any mill in the township The saw-mill, however, is mentioned in 1825, and was in operation subsequent to 1848, when it disappeared from among the industries of Delaware County From the same dam whose water furnished power to Bonsall's saw-mill, water was had to run a snuff-mill, which was located on the east side of the creek, in Philadelphia In 1807 this snuff-mill was owned by Gavin Hamilton, and was continued in operation long after 1826

Sellers' Locomotive-Works.—About 1831 a

foundry and machine-shop was erected on Cobb's Creek, above Naylor's Run, by Coleman Sellers, the water being brought from Naylor's Run and from the dam of the old Sellers' saw-mill The latter was a man of considerable inventive genius, and in 1822 received from the corporation of Philadelphia, under the clause of John Scott's will (of Edinburgh, Scotland), which provided a fund of four thousand dollars, the interest of which was annually to be expended in "premiums to be distributed among ingenious men and women who make useful inventions," a medal and twenty dollars "for a simple and effectual cupping instrument," which he had invented In this machine-shop locomotives were built, one of which was used on the Columbia and Philadelphia Railroad now part of the Pennsylvania Central In February, 1842, the estate was purchased by John Wiltbanks, who sold the machinery and materials to Nathan H Baker, and changed the building into a cotton-factory, which was for a time operated by Benjamin Gartside In 1856 the property was sold by Wiltbanks to Whiteley Brothers & Co, who enlarged the buildings and carried on therein the manufacture of cotton and woolen goods until 1881, when the mills were purchased by Wolfenden, Shore & Co, who operate them in connection with their other factory, which adjoins the old Sellers' Locomotive-Works

Sellers' Saw-Mill —On Naylor's Run, which empties into Cobb's Creek, in the last century, was a saw-mill owned by Nathan Sellers, whose name appears for the first time on the assessment-roll of 1799, when he, with David Sellers, was taxed on grist-, *cotton-*, and saw-mills The latter mill was at the location designated, and was operated for many years by Jesse Hayes, when finally it was abandoned

Millbank Mill —Farther up Naylor's Run is the Millbank Grist-Mill, which was erected in the latter part of the last century, it appearing for the first time on the assessment-roll of 1799 The mill was owned by John Sellers, who devised it in 1804 to his sons, Nathan and David Sellers On Hill's map, drawn from surveys made in 1801, although the map was not published until 1807, this mill appears Nathan Sellers, Sr, conducted the business of this mill, and in a division of the real estate left by his father Nathan acquired absolute title to it, and at his death it passed to his son, Nathan Sellers, Jr The old mill was rebuilt in 1833, and the business was conducted by Lewis Watkins, who, Dec 31, 1853, purchased the mill, which is now owned by his son, William Watkins

Levis' Blade-Mills —Above the Millbank Mill, on the same stream, Samuel Levis was operating a blade-mill in 1807, which later was conducted by William Rowland until after 1812, and by Samuel Levis until subsequent to 1843 The property afterwards passed to David Sellers, and is now owned by Edward McGrath

Powell's Saw-Mills —Above the Samuel Levis Blade Mill, on Naylor's Run, and above the Garrettford road, Joseph Hibberd owned a tract of land, on which, in 1800, was a school-house, which still remains In 1840 a saw-mill was on the stream at this location, owned by Abraham Powell, and subsequent to 1848 a grist-mill was also erected After Powell's death the property was purchased by Lewis Watkins, who operated the mills until 1854, when he sold to Edward Thowley, the latter rented the mill to William Pyle, under whom it was discontinued in 1858 It is now part of the estate of Charles Yarnell

Cardington Mills.—On Cobb's Creek, above the mouth of Naylor's Run and in close proximity to the Whitely Mills, is a mill-seat which was occupied in 1798 by a cotton-mill operated by Nathan and David Sellers It was the first cotton-mill of which we have record in the county Prior to 1810 it was changed to a paper-mill, which, in 1815, was destroyed by fire On the ruins was built a tilt-mill, which was owned by David Sellers and operated by —— Sontag In 1826, David Snyder was the lessee, and in that year, made twelve hundred dozen spades and shovels At a subsequent date it was operated by William Howell, James Wormsley, and others, and in 1845 by Charles Cadwalader, by whom the mill was rebuilt and run until 1857, when it was rented to Wolfenden, Shore & Co The old tilt-mill was standing when the latter firm leased the premises, and they immediately placed therein machinery for manufacturing woolen yarn Although Wolfenden, Shore & Co did not acquire title to the property until 1863, yet three years prior to that date they erected a stone mill, one hundred and sixty by fifty-four feet, one story in height, which is known as No 1 Mill In 1863 the firm built a second story upon Mill No 1, and also erected Mill No 2, inclosing within its limits the old tilt-mill, which, in 1865, was raised four stories in height In 1870 a stone picker-house, sixty by forty-five feet, four stories in height, and a doubling- and twisting-house, also of stone, sixty by forty-five feet, four stories in height, were erected In September, 1871, a fire originating in the picker-room caused a loss of eight thousand dollars The mills of Whitely Brothers & Co adjoining were also damaged to the amount of thirteen thousand dollars In December, 1880, a fire again occurred, starting in the picker-room, occasioning a loss of thirty thousand dollars In 1881, Wolfenden, Shore & Co purchased the cotton- and woolen-factories of Whitely Brothers & Co The mills at present contain eight thousand three hundred spindles, two hundred and fifty looms, thirteen set of cards, which are run by two Corliss engines (one of three hundred horse-power, the other of one hundred horse-power) Thirteen thousand pounds of raw material are used, from which five thousand four hundred pounds of yarn and thirty thousand yards of cloth are made weekly, which requires the labor of two hundred and fifty employés

Near Sixty-Third and Market Streets.

Original Mill, erected 1814.

"MILLBOURNE MILLS."

NATHAN SELLERS,

Marshall's Mill —John Marshall owned two tracts of land above Naylor's Run, on Cobb's Creek,—one of sixty-four acres, surveyed May 3, 1689, the other (adjoining to the south) of one hundred and fifty acres, surveyed Jan 7, 1692 Marshall died in 1749, and by his will, dated October 1st in that year, devised his land messuage, "with the saw-mill," to his executors, with directions to sell the estate and distribute the proceeds among his children This mill was purchased by Thomas Marshall, who changed it to a fulling-mill, which he was running in 1762, and was there until 1779, when James Marshall operated it until about 1800 A John Marshall, probably a son of John, was running a grist-mill in 1766 The mill was located on the Marshall road The race which supplied the water to this mill extended higher up on Cobb's Creek, and now forms part of the race-way of the Cardington Mills

Millbourne Mills.—Samuel Sellers, the original settler of this family, located at the site of these mills in 1682, but the two tracts of land—of seventy-five acres and one hundred acres—which he at first purchased were not surveyed to him until 1690-91 He later made other purchases of lands in the neighborhood, as did his sons and grandsons He was a weaver, and is said to have erected the first twisting-mill in America His son, Samuel, and grandson, John, were also weavers The latter was born in 1728, and died in 1804 He invented the process of weaving wire cloth, and also manufactured Dutch fans The first record of a dam at Millbourne is found in a deed from John Sellers to other parties, dated Aug 27, 1752, in which the dam is mentioned as being on Cobb's Creek, in the township of Darby He was much interested in utilizing the water-power of Cobb's Creek, and caused to be developed six of the sites along that stream and Naylor's Run, which were afterwards used by his descendants

John Sellers died in 1804, and devised his estate to his sons, Nathan, David, John, and George, to the latter of whom he gave the greater part of the farm lands The grist- and saw-mills he devised to his son, John, who was born in 1762 and died in 1847 These mills were evidently built before 1749, the date when the dam is mentioned In 1766 they were owned by John Sellers, the elder, and were operated by James Steel, who continued there until 1805, when he was succeeded by his son, Thomas Steel In 1814, Thomas Steel purchased the Darby Mills, in the village of that name, and removed thither In that year John Sellers erected the old part of the present mill, and his son, John, who had learned the trade of a miller with Thomas Steel, took charge of the new mill. In 1782, John Sellers also owned a tanyard, which was on the Wayside farm, now owned by the estate of his son, John On a little stream which empties into the dam supplying the water to Millbourne Mills, in 1800, was an oil-mill, which was continued until subsequent to the year 1848 The old grist-mill stood above the present mill, and in 1820 was used for grinding gypsum, and had been so employed for many years As late as 1830, Augustus C. Jones was operating the old mill in grinding logwood, spices, etc Soon after that date it was discontinued. The new mill, built in 1814, was placed under the charge of John Sellers, Jr, and was fitted with all the improved machinery of that time In 1820 there was manufactured 8572 bushels of merchant wheat, 3366 of grist wheat, 4367 of rye, 3784 of Indian corn, 1168 of buckwheat, 843 of oats, making a total of 22,100 bushels of grain In 1825, 12,000 bushels of merchant wheat was manufactured at these mills Additions were made to the mill from time to time, and the latest improved machinery constantly added In 1868 the large addition was built to the original stone structure, four stories in height from the bed of the creek A turbine-wheel was used at that time to run the mills, and in 1876 auxiliary steam-power was added John Sellers (3d) died July 20, 1878, his sons having had charge of the mills prior to his death In 1879 the "new roller process" was adopted, and at present two hundred and fifty barrels of flour are daily produced In June, 1884, 22,552 bushels of wheat was ground and 4704½ barrels of flour was made In the year 1883, 256,663 bushels of wheat were purchased and 53,125½ barrels of flour were produced The Millbourne Mills are now owned by William, John, and Nathan Sellers, grandsons of John Sellers, who erected the mill in 1814

The Sellers family is one of the oldest in Delaware County, and we append the following sketch

I Samuel Sellers, emigrated from Belper, Derbyshire, England, in 1682, and settled in Darby township, Chester Co, Pa (now Upper Darby township, Delaware Co) He took up a tract of one hundred acres, and carried on his trade (weaving) in connection with farming In June, 1684, he married Anna, daughter of Henry and Helen Gibbons, who came from Parwidge, Derbyshire They were the first couple married in "Darby Meeting," which was then held in the dwellings of its members, as no meeting-house had been erected They "passed meeting" May 2, 1684 (O S) Samuel died Sept 22, 1732, and his wife, who survived him, died Nov. 19, 1742 They had six children, the third being

II Samuel Sellers, who was born Dec 3, 1690, and married, Aug 12, 1712, to Sarah Smith, daughter of John and Eleanor Smith, from Harby, Leicestershire, England, died June 3, 1773 They had seven children, the youngest being

III John Sellers, who was born Sept 19, 1728, died Feb. 2, 1804 He married, at Darby, Feb 26, 1749 (O S), Ann Gibson, the daughter of Nathan Gibson and his wife, *née* Ann Hunt, daughter of James Hunt They had, among other children, Nathan, David, John,* and George

IV John* Sellers, who was born Dec 1, 1762, died May 12, 1847. He married, April 27, 1786, Mary

Coleman, daughter of Joseph and Mary Coleman, of Philadelphia, and had, among other children:

V. John Sellers, who was born Sept. 29, 1789, and died July 20, 1878.

John Sellers, son of Samuel and Sarah Smith Sellers, was born in Upper Darby, Sept. 19, 1728, and was taught the trade of a weaver, his father having erected in that township the first twisting-mill in Pennsylvania, which became noted for the coerlet and camlet cloths there made. Early in life he displayed much ingenuity, and invented the first wire rolling screens and sieves for cleansing grain ever made on this continent. So successful was this invention that he abandoned the manufacture of textile fabrics and devoted his attention to wire weaving, and subsequently added thereto the making of fans for farm purposes. He had also given considerable attention to the study of civil engineering, and soon became noted in the country, no one questioning the accuracy of every line run by him. In 1767 he was elected a member of Assembly, and consecutively for five terms thereafter was one of the representatives of Chester County in that body. Previous to the Revolutionary war he was appointed by the Governor one of the surveyors to run a line from the Middle Ferry at Philadelphia, to Lancaster for the Strasburg road, and in 1763 was one of the commissioners to lay out that highway.

In 1769 the Assembly of Pennsylvania granted to the Philosophical Society one hundred pounds towards the cost of building an observatory in the State-House yard in Philadelphia, from which to observe the transit of Venus, which took place June 3, 1769. This phenomenon was here successfully observed by Dr. John Ewing, David Rittenhouse, John Sellers, and others.

In 1776 he was chosen a member of Assembly from Chester County, but declined to accept, he, with many other thoughtful men of that day, holding that the Constitution of 1776 had many features subversive of the liberty of the people, one of its most objectionable provisions being that reposing the legislative authority in one House. Yet by that Constitutional Convention he was made one of the justices of Chester County. In 1789, Governor Mifflin appointed him to make surveys of the Schuylkill River, the object being to ascertain whether it was practicable to unite by a canal the Susquehanna and Schuylkill Rivers. In the mean while Delaware County had been erected, and John Sellers was, in the bill, appointed one of the commissioners to adjust the dividing line, and in the election of October of that year he was chosen one of the delegates to the Constitutional Convention of 1790, wherein he took an active part. The duties of these offices demanded his attention to such an extent that, Oct. 17, 1789, he resigned his "Commission for Examining the Waters of the Schuylkill," and Benjamin Rittenhouse was appointed in his stead. In 1790 he was elected senator from his district, then included with the city of Philadelphia, and served a term of four years. Governor Mifflin, on Sept. 17, 1791, appointed him one of the judges of Delaware County. He seems to have qualified for the office, but resigned shortly afterwards, and the following year Hugh Lloyd was appointed in his stead. John Sellers was recognized in his day as a man of considerable scientific attainments, although wholly self-taught, and was elected a member of the American Philosophical Society of 1768. He died Feb. 3, 1804, in the seventy-sixth year of his age.

John Sellers, the son of John and Mary Coleman Sellers, was born in Philadelphia, Sept. 29, 1789, and died July 20, 1878. His mother died when he was about five years old. In consequence of this great loss he spent most of his early life in the country, at the home of his grandfather (also John Sellers). This place, now known as "Sellers' Hall," was part of the original tract of ground taken up by Samuel Sellers, the emigrant, and the present brief of title contains the form of original grant from William Penn. Here the family lived from generation to generation, and that part of it now known as Millbourne was the home of this John Sellers after his marriage, and is still in possession of his sons. Country life was the ideal of all delights to his boyhood, and it was here, no doubt, that his love of nature was developed which to his latest day was so strong a characteristic. Here he was sent to the common country schools, and obtained such education as they then afforded. His habits of observation opened up to him great fields of knowledge which were always extending, and the silent influences of nature were real teachers to him. He knew all kinds of wood lore, and every bird by its note, and all the habits of insect life.

With the greatest simplicity of character he had an amount of latent strength which was not always suspected even by himself, but which made him always a reliance to his friends and neighbors. Even in early life he was often called upon to arbitrate in disputes, where his winning, persuasive manner and clear judgment had great influence.

He learned the trade of a miller under Thomas Steel, who then had an old mill on Millbourne Place. In 1814 his father built for him a new mill up to the highest-known standard. Part of it is still standing, surrounded and overtopped by handsome additions and improvements, and is now known as Millbourne Mills. Much of the wood-work on the original mill was made by John Sellers and his mechanical father. He felt it a great responsibility to run this mill, and his modesty perhaps exaggerated his deficiencies in business knowledge. He took into it untiring energy and determination, and gradually made it a success. His business principles were very simple, as his whole life was fitted to the groove of strictest justice. He had been brought up in accordance with the teachings of Friends, and to "observe moderation in all things" was a vital principle of religion to him.

John Sellers

Coleman, daughter of Joseph and Mary Coleman, of Philadelphia, and had, among other children:

V. John Sellers, who was born Sept. 29, 1789, and died July 29, 1878.

John Sellers, son of Samuel and Sarah Smith Sellers, was born in Upper Darby, Sept. 19, 1728, and was taught the trade of a weaver, his father having erected in that township the first twisting-mill in Pennsylvania, which became noted for the worsted and camlet stuffs there made. Early in life he displayed much ingenuity, and invented the first wire rolling screens and sieves for cleansing grain ever made in this continent. So successful was this invention that he abandoned the manufacture of textile fabrics and devoted his attention to wire weaving, and subsequently added thereto the making of fans for farm purposes. He had also given considerable attention to the study of civil engineering, and soon became noted in the country, no one questioning the accuracy of every line run by him. In 1767 he was elected a member of Assembly, and consecutively for five terms thereafter was one of the representatives of Chester County in that body. Previous to the Revolutionary war he was appointed by the Governor one of the surveyors to run a line from the Middle Ferry at Philadelphia, to Lancaster for the Strasburg road, and in 1768 was one of the commissioners to lay out that highway.

In 1769 the Assembly of Pennsylvania granted to the Philosophical Society one hundred pounds towards the cost of building an observatory in the State-House yard in Philadelphia, from which to observe the transit of Venus, which took place June 3, 1769. The phenomenon was here successfully observed by Dr. John Ewing, David Rittenhouse, John Sellers, and others.

In 1776 he was chosen a member of Assembly from Chester County, but declined to accept, he, with many other thoughtful men of that day, holding that the Constitution of 1776 had many features subversive of the liberty of the people, one of its most objectionable provisions being that reposing the legislative authority in one House. Yet by that Constitutional Convention he was made one of the justices of Chester County. In 1789, Governor Mifflin appointed him to make surveys of the Schuylkill River, the object being to ascertain whether it was practicable to unite by a canal the Susquehanna and Schuylkill Rivers. In the mean while Delaware County had been erected, and John Sellers was, in the fall, appointed one of the commissioners to adjust the dividing line, and in the election of October of that year he was chosen one of the delegates to the Constitutional Convention of 1790, wherein he took an active part. The duties of these offices demanded his attention to such an extent that, Oct. 17, 1789, he resigned his "Commission for Examining the Waters of the Schuylkill," and Benjamin Rittenhouse was appointed in his stead. In 1790 he was elected senator from his district, then included with the city of Philadelphia, and served a term of four years. Governor Mifflin, on Sept. 17, 1791, appointed him one of the judges of Delaware County. He seems to have qualified for the office, but resigned shortly afterwards, and the following year Hugh Lloyd was appointed in his stead. John Sellers was recognized in his day as a man of considerable scientific attainments, although wholly self-taught, and was elected a member of the American Philosophical Society of 1769. He died Feb. 3, 1804, in the seventy-sixth year of his age.

John Sellers, the son of John and Mary Coleman Sellers, was born in Philadelphia, Sept. 29, 1789, and died July 29, 1878. His mother died when he was about five years old. In consequence of this great loss he spent most of his early life in the country, at the home of his grandfather (also John Sellers). This place, now known as "Sellers' Hall," was part of the original tract of ground taken up by Samuel Sellers, the emigrant, and the present brief of title contains the form of original grant from William Penn. Here the family lived from generation to generation, and that part of it now known as Millbourne was the home of this John Sellers after his marriage, and is still in possession of his sons. Country life was the ideal of all delights to his boyhood, and it was here, no doubt, that his love of nature was developed which to his latest day was so strong a characteristic. Here he was sent to the common country schools, and obtained such education as they then afforded. His habits of observation opened up to him great fields of knowledge which were always extending, and the silent influences of nature were real teachers to him. He knew all kinds of wood lore, and every bird by its note, and all the habits of insect life.

With the greatest simplicity of character he had an amount of latent strength which was not always suspected even by himself, but which made him always a reliance to his friends and neighbors. Even in early life he was often called upon to arbitrate in disputes, where his winning, persuasive manner and clear judgment had great influence.

He learned the trade of a miller under Thomas Steel, who then had an old mill on Millbourne Place. In 1814 his father built for him a new mill up to the highest known standard. Part of it is still standing, surrounded and overtopped by handsome additions and improvements, and is now known as Millbourne Mills. Much of the wood-work on the original mill was made by John Sellers and his mechanical father. He felt it a great responsibility to run this mill, and his modesty perhaps exaggerated his deficiencies in business knowledge. He took into it untiring energy and determination, and gradually made it a success. His business principles were very simple, as his whole life was fitted to the groove of strictest justice. He had been brought up in accordance with the teachings of Friends, and to "observe moderation in all things" was a vital principle of religion to him.

John Sellers

"MILLBOURNE."
UPPER DARBY TOWNSHIP,

In 1817, at the age of twenty-seven, he married Elizabeth Poole, the eldest daughter of William Poole, of Wilmington, Del In this choice he was most wisely directed, and the result might well confirm the supposition that "all true marriages are made in heaven"

It would be impossible to give any correct account of his life without including her in it She was his counselor in everything, and he honored the whole sex for her sake She had been the congenial companion of a very intellectual father, and she brought into her husband's home a wisdom beyond her years She made his house a centre of attraction in the neighborhood, hiding all defects with her lavish and bountiful nature He often recounted their early experience together, when economy was a necessity and all conveniences lacking, and how her cheerful spirit was a tower of strength to him He never entered into any business of importance without consulting her, and in recounting some losses it was often with the preface, "If I had minded what my wife said, this would not have happened"

They had eleven children, three of whom died in infancy The rest survive them

He made a strong protest against the use of alcohol in any form, and was the first in his neighborhood to do away with its use in the harvest fields This was a most unpopular movement when it was thought to be the strength of the laborer and the promoter of cheerful endeavor He had the courage of his principles, however, and by the promise of higher wages he carried his point, and set an example to his neighbors that was quickly followed When anti-slavery doctrines were most abhorrent to the general public, he went into that cause with all his heart His house was always open to its disciples, and the fugitive found there both welcome and help on his way. He took liberal papers, and always cast his vote for the liberal party. He was an old-time Whig, and boasted that he never missed his vote at any election from the time of his majority. He considered it a sacred duty to attend the polls, and thought an American citizen unworthy the name who neglected this He was chosen a delegate to the Free Soil Convention which met in Buffalo in 1848 He deprecated the spirit of disunion found in some of the ultra abolitionists, and often said "the best way to abolish slavery would be to introduce the public-school system in the South." He was deeply interested in the cause of education, and at one time, with others of his neighbors, built a school-house which they maintained for many years at their own expense Here the best teachers were employed, and some of his own children received their entire education When the free-school system was inaugurated this school-house became the property of Upper Darby, but continued its original name of the Union School, which it bears to this day He was immediately chosen treasurer and director of the Upper Darby school district, which positions he held until the last years of his life Many other positions of trust were given him, he was treasurer of three different road companies at one time, and was several times an administrator to large estates In these duties he was deeply interested and faithfully performed them

In 1859 he had the misfortune to lose his wife, and the close companionship of forty years was broken Together they had borne "the burden and heat of the day," and now that the resting time had come hers was "*in larger, other worlds than ours*" He was a man of few words, and all his principles forbade repining, but his life was shorn of its brightness

Loved by everybody, he especially delighted in young people, and naturally attracted many to his house, so that it was never other than a cheerful home He firmly believed in making it so He was a member of Darby Monthly Meeting, and, according to the usage among Friends, all his children had birthright membership in this society Twice a week, all his life, did he faithfully attend meeting. His creed was "to do justly, to love mercy, and to walk humbly before God," and all who knew him confess that he made it practical He would sometimes listen to long discussions on theological points, but with great humility regret that he did not understand much about them He said, "If we all tried to live so that we could look back on each act with satisfaction, that would be a good enough religion" To those who knew him best it would seem impossible that regret or remorse could ever have been his portion

His health was perfect, from which fact he derived great pleasure At one time, when nearly eighty years of age, he walked to and from meeting, a distance of about eight miles, without apparent effort. His love of reading was maintained to his latest day, and his delight in nature never waned He became the patriarch of his meeting, and died full of honors in the community on the 20th day of July, 1878, aged eighty-nine His life was a very simple one, without incident or pretension, but from beginning to end was full of sweetness and instruction

The following extract from a county paper is embodied, as concisely estimating his character

"He was a member of the society of Friends, worshiping at Darby Meeting, and was one of the very few remaining of the old members of that meeting Never ambitious for political preferment, he did not ask public applause, living in the practice of the belief that the '*post of honor is the private station*' In the anti slavery cause he was an active worker, and his efforts on behalf of the down-trodden knew no cessation until the work of emancipation was completed and the legitimate fruits of the triumph assured His goodness of heart and Christian character endeared him to those of all creeds and professions He was liberal in all things, ever looking beyond the present for his reward With him, through life, whatever was worth doing was worth doing well. If he was not great in the eyes of the world, he was something better, for he found in his congenial calling an ample field for the generous disposition of his heart. Throughout his long career, in every relation of life, he set for us an example worthy of study and imitation. As a husband, father, and friend he not only practiced with rigorous exactness the duties of those relations, but invested them with such gentleness of temper and grace of manner as added uncommon charm and beauty to his daily life, and strongly endeared him to all who were privileged to be related to or connected with him. It was our pleasure to know the deceased for the past forty years, and the invaluable advice and many kind suggestions received from him will ever be remembered. None among the many who were acquainted with John Sellers, and the unstinted kindness of his never-failing considerateness, will feel that we have at all exaggerated the solid worth of an honorable citizen, a firm friend, and a good man."

Keystone Paper-Mill.—The tract on which this mill is located was taken up by John Blunston, Nov. 18, 1683, who sold two hundred and fifty acres, June 1, 1686, to John Hood. No record shows that a mill existed on the property until 1807, when George Sellers was in possession of a saw-mill, which was built subsequent to 1803, and was continued by him as a saw-mill until some time after 1830. It is located in the "Report of Manufactures of Delaware County in 1826" as being "on Cobb's Creek in Upper Darby, above Indian Creek, a large branch which extends into Philadelphia County, a saw-mill head and fall about 28 feet, Mill Race about one and a half mile long; owned and occupied by Geo. Sellers." This property later came to Abram Pennock, whose wife was a daughter of George Sellers, who used the power to run a paper-mill, which he built on or near the site of the saw-mill. It was occupied a part of the time by C. S. Garrett, and was destroyed by fire about 1865. In the next year (1866) C. S. Garrett & Sons erected the present Keystone Mills, for the manufacture of paper, a short distance from the old mill. The buildings were of stone, one, fifty by sixty feet, four stories high; one, thirty-five by thirty-five feet, three stories; and one, thirty by one hundred feet, one story high. These mills were supplied with a twenty-five-hundred-pound engine, three rag-engines, a thousand-pound washing-engine, a seven-hundred-pound engine, a Jordan engine, and a fifty-eight-inch Fourdrinier machine. The power is supplied from a two-hundred-and-fifty horse-power engine and four one-hundred horse-power boilers. The product is mostly of card-papers, of which about four tons are made daily. Fifteen men and sixteen girls are employed.

In addition to the mills already given, the following industries appear of record, but their exact locations are not known to the writer. In 1766, Abraham Johnson was assessed on a grist- and saw-mill, which regularly appeared until 1774, when Martha Johnson owned a saw-mill, after which date the name does not appear on the assessment-roll connected with mills. From 1782 to 1790, Job Evans owned and operated a grist-mill. The name of John Tyson occurs in 1782 as the owner of a grist-mill, and was continued to be so assessed until 1804. Jacob Lobb owned or operated a grist-mill in 1788, and from 1774 to 1779, Thomas Pilkinton operated a grist-mill. During the year last mentioned William Davis and Benjamin Brannon had distilleries. The former lived near the northern line of the township, on lands lately owned by Dr. George Smith, the latter on the Darby and Haverford roads, south of the Marshall road, where he kept a tavern.

Fernwood.—The village of this name is located near Cobb's Creek, in Upper Darby township, and on the line of the central division of the Philadelphia, Wilmington and Baltimore Railroad, formerly the West Chester and Philadelphia Railroad. The land was in the ownership of the Bonsell family for several generations until 1870, when it was purchased by a stock company which had organized in that year by the name of the Fernwood Cemetery Company. The corporators were Amos Bonsell, John Bower, Alfred R. Potter, Charles P. Bower, Frederick Hassold, Price I. Patton, Charles M. Towne, William J. Kelly, Christian Gross, and Godfrey Keebler. The one hundred and twenty acres of land purchased of Amos Bonsell was located on Cobb's Creek, bounded on the other sides by Church Lane, the Baltimore pike, and the line of the proposed Chester County Railroad. The plot was named Fernwood Cemetery, from the fact that at the time of purchase fourteen varieties of ferns were growing in large quantities within its limits,—a fortunate name, for the land in 1682 was surveyed to Joshua Fearne, the early settler. The grounds were laid out into lots, paths, and avenues, over thirty-five thousand perches of stone being used in the avenues; three thousand five hundred evergreen and deciduous trees were planted, besides many ornamental shrubs. The first burial within the grounds was made on the 5th of May, 1872, and at the present time this city of the dead has a population of over nine thousand quiet sleepers resting there. The cemetery is largely used for the interment of persons who have resided in Philadelphia, and is about three miles from Market Street bridge. Upon the completion of the cemetery it was determined to establish a village near by, and to that end Price I. Patton and William J. Kelly purchased of Amos Bonsell fifty-seven acres of land adjoining the cemetery, which was laid out into streets and lots. The proprietors erected two houses on Fourth Street (facing the first) in 1872. In that year Adam Tracey purchased a lot and built thereon a dwelling-house, in which he established the first store in the village. In 1876 a stock company was formed for the purpose of building a large hotel, and in that year the Fernwood Mansion, a stone structure, was erected, at a cost of forty-two thousand dollars. It is forty by one hundred and thirty-

KEYSTONE PAPER MILLS.

Office and Warehouse,
12 and 14 Decatur Street, Philadelphia, Pa.

AUSTIN, OBDYKE & CO.,
PIPE WORKS AND TENEMENTS,
JUNCTION OF UNION AVENUE AND WEST CHESTER RAILROAD
DELAWARE CO., PA.

three feet, five stories high, containing for hotel purposes seventy-seven rooms In this building are also a Masonic lodge-room and three stores

Fernwood Lodge, No 553, F. and A M, which now holds its communications in the Mansion House, was instituted in December, 1875, in the city of Philadelphia, with ten charter members, and with Oliver B Moss, W M, H M Hoffner, Treas, George W Shirley, Sec The lodge held its communications for two years in the school-house at Fernwood, and upon the completion of the hall in the Mansion House the lodge removed thither, the new hall being dedicated in December, 1877 The lodge at present has about one hundred members George W Shirley is the present Master

Fernwood Methodist Episcopal Church—This society was organized July 14, 1872, with about twelve members, under the charge of the Rev M H Sisty, who remained pastor till the spring of 1873 He has been succeeded in the pastorate by the Revs John Shepherd, George Mack, A S Hood, R A Sadlier, Pennell Coombe, and the Rev. N W Clark, the present incumbent The church has also a mission at "West End," Philadelphia The first meeting of the society was held in the summer of 1872, in a grove near the village, and in the fall of that year they assembled in a frame building erected on the rear of the present church lot In 1873 the present church edifice, built of brick, forty by sixty feet, was erected, at a cost of fifteen thousand dollars There are eighty members of the church at the present time, and a Sunday-school of one hundred and twenty pupils is connected with it, of which George W Pentridge is superintendent

Union Mills at Fernwood—William Hall & Co, in 1867, established at Darby borough a shoddy and waste-wool mill In 1870 they erected a building sixty by eighty feet at Fernwood, and removed the business thereto The building contains twenty-four thousand square feet of floor-room, and embraces the carding-room, picker-room, dye-house, scouring-room, and drying-room There are twenty-one cards and two engines of one hundred and sixty horse-power and boiler of two hundred and four horse-power The mill produces sixty thousand pounds of shoddy per week

Near the Union Mills are located the Pipe-Works of Austin, Obdyke & Co In 1882 this firm erected a building one hundred by eighty feet, especially designed for the business of manufacturing tin water- or rain-spouts Twelve persons are employed and twelve boxes of tin are daily used in this establishment

The public school-house at Fernwood is of brick, two stories in height, and was completed in 1875

The railroad company have erected a handsome stone depot at the station, and the travel over the road to this place by reason of the cemetery is large, two hundred and twenty-five thousand people visiting the cemetery last year by rail alone, and many thousands by carriages

Abolition Society.—The first society formed in Upper Darby was an abolition society, which was organized prior to May 4, 1830, on which occasion George Sellers, Abram Powell, Dr Caleb Ash, James Rhoads, Joseph Fussel, Joseph Rhodes, Saul Sellers, Jr, Lewis Watkin, Nathan Sellers, John Sellers, Jr, J Morgan Bunting, David S Bunting, and William H Bunting were appointed a committee to attend the annual meeting of the Pennsylvania State Anti-Slavery Society, Philadelphia, May 17, 1830 The few members of this ridiculed association continued to assemble occasionally until the emancipation proclamation of President Lincoln did utterly away with legalized human slavery in the United States In this township Thomas Garrett, the noted anti-slavery advocate, was born Aug 21, 1789, his father, Oborn Garrett, owning and operating the scythe- and edge-tool works mentioned in the account of the mills on Darby Creek, and with him Thomas Garrett learned that trade His pronounced anti-slavery views resulted from the fact that in 1815, he, having moved to Wilmington, returned one day to his father's home in Upper Darby, where he found the family indignant and distressed because a colored woman in their employment had been kidnapped and spirited away He immediately made chase, and tracked the kidnapper to Kensington, where he rescued the woman from them From that moment until his death, in January, 1871, he was a fearless, active advocate of abolition, and during the *ante-bellum* days he aided between three and four thousand slaves to escape to the Northern States In May, 1870, a great parade of the colored people of Wilmington, Del, took place, on which occasion Thomas Garrett, then eighty years of age, was taken in an open barouche through the streets of that city, and on each side a guard of honor was formed, bearing banners inscribed "Our Moses" He died the following year, and his funeral was attended by a vast assemblage of people, a number of whom had come many miles that they might pay respect to the dead man, who throughout his life had been just, fearless, and upright, and who loved his neighbor as himself

Friends' Graveyard.—On Feb 4, 1860, the Friends' Monthly Meeting of the Western District of Philadelphia purchased of Charles Wiltbank twenty-seven and nine-tenths of an acre near Cobb's Creek and the termination of Market Street, Philadelphia, for a burial-place for members of that meeting

First Use of Gas.—In 1851, Christopher Fallon purchased a tract of one hundred and forty acres of William Black, on the south side of Garrettford road, and west of the Darby and Haverford roads He erected in that year a spacious mansion-house On Dec 28, 1853, the dwelling was illuminated with gas, made at private works on the estate The fact is noticeable, because it was the first time gas was used for illuminating purposes in Delaware County

Crimes—On Sept 20, 1849, while the services were

being held at the funeral of Abram Powell, the miller, on Naylor's Run, a man was noticed to deliberately mount a valuable mare and ride away Those who saw the act, believing that he had been sent on an errand by the family, paid no attention, and it was not mentioned until after the funeral, when inquiries were made respecting the animal The boldness of the thief secured his escape A few days before the funeral two horses had been stolen from Joseph Powell, a son of Abram, and he had offered fifty dollars reward for their return On the day of his father's funeral the horses were brought back, and the son paid the reward, the latter being so overwhelmed with grief and the cares of the day that he asked no questions of the men who returned the horses In July, 1877, a black man entered the house of Mrs Kirk, and going into her room, appropriated several dresses Mrs Kirk, who was blind, sitting in the room, heard him, and, as the sound of his foot-step was unfamiliar, gave the alarm. The thief sprang out of the window, but pursuit being made by the men in the harvest-field, he was arrested, lodged in jail, and subsequently tried and convicted On Feb 16, 1876 the United States detectives seized an illicit distillery in a house near Darby Road Station, on the West Chester Railroad A pit was excavated outside of the stable, which was floored with boards, covered with earth and straw In this pit was a still, worm, and other necessary appliances, while from the still-house fire a flue was laid in a trench, and ran through the foundation of the dwelling, so that the smoke might mingle with that in the chimney and disarm suspicion A trap-door in the stable gave access to an underground passage-way, which led to the pit where the still was located The whiskey produced there was made from molasses The government officers arrested James Cullen in Philadelphia, but the other two persons connected with him escaped

In the evening of Aug 3, 1837, Jacob Brass accidentally discovered in the woods on the farm of George Sellers the body of a man hanging to a limb about six feet from the ground A pair of new cotton suspenders were round his neck and fastened to the limb. The corpse, when found, was in an advanced state of decomposition, and must have been hanging there several days before it was discovered

Remarkable Instances of Longevity —Mrs Mary Ash, of Upper Darby, died March 24, 1862, aged ninety seven years She was the mother of sixteen children, and survived them all, except two, the oldest and the youngest, the latter being at date of the mother's death over sixty years of age Mary Ash was twelve years old when the battle of Brandywine was fought, and could remember that some of the American soldiers, when the army was retreating to Philadelphia, stopped at her father's house and were fed She had lived in the house in which she died seventy-five years, and until within three days before her death retained her faculties unimpaired

On Monday, Jan 12, 1880, "Aunt Betsey" Moore, on the one hundred and first anniversary of her birth, received a number of friends gathered to congratulate her on that occasion She was born in Upper Darby, at Sellers' Hall, in 1779 On April 5, 1880, she died at the residence of her nephew, Samuel Moore, at Millbank, retaining her faculties remarkably until a few days prior to her death [1]

Societies —Clifton Heights Lodge, No 960, I O of O F, was chartered on the 9th of August, 1878, with the following persons as officers Charles H. Edwards, N G, William Logan, V G, Samuel E Haynes, Sec, Henry M Brennin, Asst Sec, John S Donnel, Treas The society has at the present time eighty-seven members, and is located at Clifton

Arasapha Tribe, No 161, I O R M, was chartered on the 28th Sun of the Beaver Moon, G.S D No 380, with twenty-two charter members The wigwam of the tribe is at Clifton

Clifton Wreath Division, No 68, Sons and Daughters of Temperance, was chartered on the 26th of February, 1876, with forty-one charter members, and at present has a membership of sixty The meetings of this society are held at Clifton

Improvement Lodge, No 197, Knights of Pythias, was organized Oct 4, 1869 with nine charter members. It was instituted at Garrettford, but in 1876 removed to Clifton, and has now a membership of sixty-seven.

BIOGRAPHICAL SKETCH.

ROBERT PLUMSTEAD

Robert Plumstead was born April 19, 1803, and has spent his long and useful life in Upper Darby, Delaware Co On attaining a proper age he was apprenticed to Isaac Earle to learn the trade of shoemaking, with whom he served his time, and followed the business for about two years He, however, desired a more active life, and engaged with Coleman Sellers, of Cardington, as foreman on his farm, which position he held for ten years, removing from thence in the year 1841 to his present home, known as "Maple Grove Farm," where he continued the active pursuits of a farmer until 1878, when the farm was rented and he retired from its management Mr. Plumstead was, on the 26th of February, 1829, married to Rebecca, daughter of Joshua Parsons, of Marple township. Their children are Thomas K (married to Rebecca L Dickenson, of Darby), who died in 1856, at the age of twenty seven years, Amanda R, who died at Price's Boarding-School, in West Chester, in 1850, aged seventeen years, Sarah A, whose death occurred in 1839,

[1] In the village of Darby, on April 21, 1824, Mrs Mary Calderwood died, aged one hundred and one years This interesting fact having been unintentionally omitted in the account of Darby borough, it is recorded in this note as an incident worthy of preservation in a history of Delaware County.

ROBERT PLUMSTEAD.

aged two years; and Mary E., wife of Dr. Ellwood Baker, who resides with her father at the old homestead. Mr. Plumstead was in politics a Whig, and later indorsed the platform of the Republican party. He was for many years active in the public affairs of the township, having filled the position of county commissioner, together with other minor offices. He was educated in the faith of the society of Friends, and with his family worships at the Friends' meeting-house in Darby. Mr. and Mrs. Plumstead celebrated their golden wedding in 1879, on which interesting occasion a numerous concourse of relatives and friends assembled to do them honor. The death of Mrs. Plumstead occurred on the 15th of August, 1883, in her seventy-ninth year. She was interred at the Friends' burial-ground in Darby.

CHAPTER XLIII.

EDGMONT TOWNSHIP.

EDGMONT was named from the ancient royal manor of Edgmond, in Shropshire, in England, from whence came Joseph Baker, one of the earliest settlers in the township.

The English spelling was used in ancient deeds, but since its origin was lost sight of, the orthography has been attended with some uncertainty, sometimes being spelled Edgment, but generally Edgemont, under the erroneous supposition that its name was derived from the Edge family.

The residents of Edgmont have almost entirely devoted themselves to agricultural pursuits. Although Ridley Creek passes through it, and Crum Creek forms the eastern boundary, the water-power has not been developed for manufacturing or mills to any great extent. The only hotel is at Howellville, where the Rising Sun existed in former days. The President, kept for many years by Hiram Green, on the West Chester road, when that was the great highway from the West, passed out of existence with many others on the road to Philadelphia when the iron rail supplanted the old-time Conestoga wagon.

On the southern line of the township of Edgmont, in the early history of the county, was a wedge-shaped tract of one hundred and fifty acres of land, known as "Cumberland," which had been set apart to George Willard, July 24–25, 1682, and was then included in Middletown. On March 1, 1687, Roger Jackson became the owner of the estate, and on 3d day of 1st week, Tenth month, 1688, the court "Ordered that Roger Jackson's one hundred and fifty acres of land, formerly Included in Middletown, be from Henceforth taken into ye Township of Edgmond, and be therein Included." This was not the only reference to the township line, for in 1739 a dispute was had between Thornbury and Edgmont respecting the boundaries between the two municipal divisions. The petition on behalf of the Thornbury claimants is not of record, but that of Edgmont set forth:

"*To the Honorable Justices of the Court of Quarter Sessions to be held at Chester the last tuesday in May*, 1739:

"The Humble Petition of the Inhabitants of Edgmont Sheweth that there hath of late been, and still remains, some uneasyness About the Divissions between the Townships of Edgmont & Thornbury, Although the part now in Dispute hath been Deemed to be in Edgmont for more than Sixteen Years past, and taxed as Such, Therefore we Humbly Crave of this Honorable Court to appoint a Number of Judicious and Indifferent Men of the Neighboring townships to Divide the said Townships to the Least Damage of ye Inhabitants on boath Sides; and your petitioners, as in Duty bound, shall ever pray.

"John Worral.	Richrd Pritchet.
"Joseph Pennell.	Henry Howard.
"Samuel Lewis.	Thomas Yarnall.
"David Redgester.	Edward Grizel.
"Thomas Williamson.	John Yarnall.
"James Sill.	Joseph Bishop.
"Joseph Pratt.	Philip Yarnall.
"Thomas Goodwin.	Cadwalader Evans.
"Wm Griffith, Junr.	Samuel Yarnall."

The court decided in favor of Edgmont, for the foregoing document is indorsed "the petition for division is set aside."

The "Edgmont Great Road," as was formerly termed the highway from Chester, entered the southern boundary of the township at its western part, and following a northwesterly course, almost across Edgmont, entering Thornbury a short distance south of the Chester County line. At the court held "Dec. ye 11th, 1687," the grand jury in its report stated:

"Laid out a Highway from Edgmond to ye Kings Highway in Chester being a Sixty foote road by virtue of an Order of Court bearing date ye 4th of October 1687, laid out by us whose hands are under written as followeth (viz.)

"Beginning att Joseph Bakers fence of his cleared land thence through ye land of ye said Joseph Baker thence crosse William Lewis land thence Crosse Howell James Land thence crosse Jacob Simcock's land thence crosse James Kenerly, thence crosse a parcell of vacant Land then crosse Roger Jackson thence crosse vacant land thence crosse John Boweter land thence Crosse David Ogdens land thence Crosse John Hodgkins land thence crosse George Smedleys land thence crosse Wm. Edwards land thence Widdow Musgrove's land thence Crosse Robert Burrowes land thence crosse John Maylons land thence Crosse John Bowettors land thence Crosse Joseph Cooksons land thence Crosse Jeremy Carters land thence Crosse Richard Barnards land thence Crosse John Worrells land thence Crosse Thomas Taylors land then Crosse Richard Crosbyes land then Crosse John Marten's land then Crosse John Hastens land.

"Walter Marten "John Beales "Edward Pritchard	George Willard Wm. Coborne."

At the same court "John Worrell Petitioned against ye road laid out by ye Grand Inquest from Edgmont to ye King's Highway in Chester." The justices seem to have met this objection promptly and decidedly, for it was "Ordered that ye road be made by the Petitioner's fence."

With respect to this road Dr. Smith says, "There is a tradition that in laying out the road from Chester to Edgmont, or more likely in a review of that road, Henry Hollingsworth, the surveyor, caused an apple-tree to be planted at the end of every mile. The surveyor happened to be at variance with Richard Crosby, who then resided in Middletown township. It so happened that one of the miles ended on Richard's land, but instead of planting an apple-tree, the surveyor took an axe and bent two saplings so as to cross each other at the spot, saying at the same time, 'Richard Crosbie, thee crosses me and I will cross thee.' Henry Hollingsworth wrote to his friends in England that he had planted an orchard nine miles in length. It is said that some of the apple-trees were standing until within a very recent period."[1]

Early in the history of the province an important meeting between the Indians and the Governor is believed to have been held in Edgmont township. The particulars are thus related by the historians of Chester County:

"The Indians manifested some uneasiness about this time, which was communicated to the Governor by William Dalbo, of Gloucester, N. J., 'who acquainted him that there is a Belt of Wampum come to Connestego, from Mahquahotonoi; y[t] there was a Tomahock in Red in the belt, & y[t] the French with five nations of Indians were designed for war and to fall on some of these plantations.' This information was duly laid before the Council by the Governor on the 14th of April, 1710, and also a letter he had received from Mr. Yeates, Caleb Pusey, and Thomas Powell, dated the same day, 'purporting that to-morrow there was to be a great concourse of Indians, those of Conestoga & those of the Jersey; that they were of opinion that it might be a reasonable opportunity for the Gov'r to visit them altogether; the meeting being the greatest that has been known these twenty years, and is to be about two miles from Jno Warrams [John Worralls] at Edgmond.'

"It was the opinion of the board 'That the Governor with some of the Council, and as many others as can be got should go to-morrow to meet the s[d] Indians, to inquire further of them about the said Belt of Wampum, and what else may be thought necessary.'

"The Governor and others doubtless met the Indians, as here indicated, but as no report of the interview was made to the Council, it is probable that the principal chiefs were not present. On the 29th of April, some more alarming news was communicated to the Council, which induced the Governor to visit Conestoga and have an interview with the red men. He found them 'very well inclined to the English,' but they complained of aggressions that had been committed on them by the white man.

"The Governor, immediately on his return from Conestoga, sent Col. French and Henry Worley to ascertain more fully the wishes of the Indians. These gentlemen returned with eight belts of wampum, and made their report to the Council on the 16th of June. Each of these belts had a particular significance. The import of three of them will be given.

"The first was from their old women, and signified 'That those implored their friendship of the Christians and Indians of this govm[t], that without danger or trouble, they might fetch wood & water.'

"'The second belt was from their children born, and those yet in the womb, requesting that room to sport and play without danger of slavery might be allowed them.'

"'The Third Belt was sent from their young men fitt to hunt, that privilege to leave their Towns, and seek provisions for their aged, might be granted to them without fear of Death or slavery.'

"The last of these belts have a significance that cannot be misunderstood. They plainly suggest the reason for the passage, in 1705, of the 'Act to prevent the importation of Indian slaves.'"[2]

In the assessment for the year 1715 the taxables then in Edgmont were as follows:

John Worrall, Joseph Baker, Philip Yarnall, John Worrilow, Ephir. Jackson, Joseph Pennell, John Broomall, David Register, William Hiddings, John Golding, Rebecca Powell, John Gregory, Thomas Vernon, Thomas Dawson, Joseph Baker, Simon Acres, Edward Thompson, Jacob Taylor, John Clues, Nathan Evans, John Holdston, Caleb Thompson, William Willis, Robert Williamson, Evan Howell, William Adams, Richard Pritchard, Evan Lewis.

Freemen, William Clues, John Hiddings, William Floud.

That the above list represented the male residents of Edgmont at that time is apparent, because at the conclusion it is stated, "Non-resident Land, Bostock's Land, John Kingsman."

In 1799 the following is the list of taxables in the township:

George Bishop, Nehemiah Baker, Joseph Baker, Sr., Joseph Baker, Jr., Edward Baker, Richard Baker, William Baker, Joseph Bishop, Abraham Farr, John Fox, Joshua Fox, George Green, Joseph Griffith, George Hunter, Isaac Hoops, Abraham Hoops, Benjamin Holston, John Holston, Joseph Holston, James Howard, Daniel Hoops, Thomas Hammer (shop-keeper), Thomas Johnson, Samuel Lewis, Abraham Lewis, Moses Meredith, John Mendenhall, John Morgan, Daniel McGowan, Richard Passmore, John Parker (weaver), Joseph Pennell, David Pratt, Lowrie Bonsall, William Russell, James Sill, Aaron Sill, Isaac Taylor, Daniel Williamson, John Worrell, Isaac Worrell, Nicholas Woolas, William Yarnall, Eli Yarnall, Caleb Yarnall, James Yarnall, Joseph Daniel, Robert Register, William Sill, Margaret Bishop, Joseph Williams, George Antricum, William Monangby (joiner), Samuel Plankington (carpenter), Nathan Pyle (blacksmith), Aaron Matson (weaver), Joseph McAfee (weaver), Samuel Fox (carpenter), Benjamin Houghton (carpenter), Nehemiah Barker (cooper), Isaac Pennell (shoemaker), Enoch Yarnall (shoemaker), Evan Pennell (weaver), John Register (turner), Thomas Register (mason), Thomas Dent (tailor), Abraham Hoops (chairmaker), John Gilmore (mason).

The residents of the township, as already remarked, devoting their attention, as a rule, to agriculture, the incidents and happenings in that locality were not generally of that moment to make a deep impression on the annals of the county, and yet Edgmont, in the old war of independence, was repeatedly visited by the scouting parties of both sides, and the American camp-followers and "jayhawkers" just as frequently appropriated private property to their personal use as did the enemy. After the battle of Brandywine to the withdrawal of the British forces from Philadelphia, the residents of Edgmont suffered from the inroads of foraging parties of the Tory adherents of the crown. The account of losses sustained in this township, filed as a claim against the government but never paid, were as follows:

	£	s.	d.
From John Worrall, Sept. 16, 1777	35	0	0
" Thomas Frame	7	0	0
" Thomas Evans	7	10	0
" Jonathan Hunter	119	10	0
" William Dunwoody, Sept. 17th	88	6	0
" William McFee, by J. Fitzpatrick (alias Fitz or Fitch), and adherents of the King of Great Britain	200	0	0
" Mordecai Massey	47	0	0
	£504	16	0

On Sept. 17, 1777, a party of English soldiers visited the residence of Edward Russell, on the farm known as Hunting Hill, and while in the house they broke into a secretary, where, in a secret drawer, one of the daughters had secreted a sum of money. The soldiers had not discovered the hiding-place, had turned, and were about leaving the room, when the owner of the money, in her anxiety for the treasure,

1 History of Delaware County, p. 400.

2 Futhey and Cope's "History of Chester County," p. 39.

went to the desk and opened the drawer Her action was observed by one of the men, who compelled her to deliver to him the savings of many months The desk, still showing the marks of the force used to open its apartments, is now in possession of Burgess Green, of Media

The house now belonging to David H Stitter, on the road from Bishop's mills to Howellsville, during the Revolution, was owned by Abel Green, and in one of the putlog-holes in the east end of the house, which had never been filled in after the scaffolding was removed, Green secreted a large amount of Continental currency, and filled the opening in with a stone For several months the money remained there undisturbed A barrel of whiskey in the cellar, however, was not so secure, for a British soldier shot a musket-ball into the head, and through the opening thus made poured out round after round to his thirsty companions, without failing, however, to minister to his own appetite

On Crum Creek, where the West Chester road crosses that stream, was the tract of two hundred and forty acres laid out to Samuel Bradshaw, April 10-11, 1682 Part of this estate is known as "Castle Rock," because located on the farm is a cluster of peculiar rocks rising in picturesque confusion, bowlder upon bowlder, to the height of two hundred feet above the level of the land at its basis This rock, pierced through and through with fissures and caverns, is a remarkable natural curiosity It was on this farm, now the property of William Taylor, that James Fitzpatrick, the outlaw, was captured in 1778, as narrated in the chapter on crimes and punishments The dwelling of the present owner occupies almost the very site where William McAfee's house then stood

The land on which the village of Howellville is located, about 1759 was purchased by Christian Workizer, a German, who, a colonel in the English army, came to America as an aide-de-camp to Gen Wolfe After the capture of Quebec, Col Workizer resigned, and having married, purchased a farm where Howellville is now, the hotel building being the homestead of the family During the Revolutionary war the colonel, having held military rank in the English service, declined to take part in that struggle It is related that during the British occupation of Philadelphia Mrs Workizer walked from Howellville to the former place, eluding the sentinels, and returned without being molested, her enormous pockets, strapped to a girdle worn beneath her dress, filled with medicines, salt, and articles of that description which were difficult to be procured John Sheridan Workizer, to whom the Howellville farm descended, sold it about the beginning of this century.

Edgmont Temperance Hall was erected near the centre of the township, on the Chester road, in the year 1843, and sold to the Methodists for a church in 1859 Among the pastors who have served there are W. C Johnson, George Alcorn, —— Jennings, William F Shepherd, G J Burns, J E Grawley, A N Millison, and —— Turrentine, the present pastor

Edgmont post-office, near the old "President," is kept at the store which was started by Lewis Verdreis more than fifty years ago A post-office was established some years ago, and Pusey Pennock and William Worrell were postmasters Edgar Prene is the present officer John and James Aitkin at that time kept the store where the Howellville post-office was established in 1832, which was noted in its day, and drew a large patronage from distant parts of the county for many years It subsequently passed into the hands of William W and Ellis Smedley, who gave new life to the place by running stages to Chester, which became a popular line of travel to Philadelphia Another line ran through the place between the city and Westtown boarding-school, and a third along the West Chester road, from West Chester to Philadelphia The opening of the railroad between those points, *via* Media, made these enterprises unprofitable, and they have long since been abandoned

John Atkins, Ellis Smedley, William T Kirk, Elwood Baldwin, Thomas Worrall, Joseph Pratt, William F Matthews, William McCall, I B Taylor, and Jesse R Baker have in succession been the postmasters at Howellville James Atkin studied medicine and became the principal physician of that section for nearly half a century, and now survives at West Chester at the advanced age of ninety years Fifty years ago, in September, 1834, Dr Atkin found a young snake with two heads in Edgmont, which he presented to the museum of the Delaware County Institute of Science

An accident occurred in Edgmont in May, 1851, which, from the peculiar circumstances connected with it, is still recalled in that section of the county A large water-snake had taken up its quarters near the spring-house on John H Taylor's farm, which so alarmed the females of the family that he determined to kill the reptile The old fowling-gun he used for that purpose exploded, the breech blew out, striking Taylor in face, breaking his nose, putting out one of his eyes, and otherwise injuring him Two months subsquent, when the frightful wound in the face had healed sufficiently to permit him to walk about the farm, he complained of great soreness and shooting pains in his head An examination disclosed the breech-pan of the gun still in the wound, where it had remained since the accident Dr Huddleson removed the iron, which was two and a half inches in length, over half an inch in thickness, and weighing three ounces

The following-named persons have served as justices of the peace for Edgmont township since the year 1791

Caleb Peirce....Aug. 30, 1791.
John Edwards....Jan. 24, 1797.
Joseph Brinton....May 20, 1800.
Luke Cassin....March 27, 1809.
John Siter....Sept. 1, 1813.
Robert Green....Feb. 23, 1816.
Nathan Gibson....Nov. 26, 1817.
George Brooke....July 3, 1821.
Maskill Ewing....June 10, 1822.
Park Shee....Dec. 9, 1823.
David Abrahams....Dec. 14, 1825.
Barnard Flynn....Nov. 18, 1835.
Abner Lewis....May 27, 1836.
Thomas Sheldon....Dec. 20, 1836.
Thomas Catsin....Nov. 1, 1838.
Homer Eachus....May 11, 1839.
Anthony Baker, April 14, 1840, April 15, 1845, April 10, 10, 1860, April 28, 1865.
James M. Smith....April 10, 1869, March 24, 1874.
Philip B. Green....March 24, 1874, March 27, 1879.
George L. Green....March 27, 1879.

Mills and Tanneries.—In the first assessment of the county, made in 1790, there are no manufacturing interests mentioned in Edgmont. In the assessment of 1799, Thomas Johnson appears in possession of a saw-mill, and in the triennial assessment of 1802 the name of George Antricum is given as in possession of a saw-mill. It was located on Crum Creek, near the northeast part of the township, and was probably the Johnson mill, as his name is not in the assessment for 1802. In 1807 there was also at this place a saw-mill, and in 1812 two distilleries were in operation at the same locality. These mills and stills were owned and operated by Antricum until 1825, when the property was bought by Jonathan N. Hatch, who enlarged the grist-mill to forty feet by fifty feet, three stories high, and placed in it ten carding-machines, three hundred and sixty throstle-spindles, seven hundred and eighty mule-spindles, and commenced the manufacture of cotton yarn. In the next year eleven hundred and fifty pounds of cotton yarn was made per week. Eight tenant-houses and a mansion-house were on the place. This factory was operated by Mr. Hatch successfully till 1838, when the mill was destroyed by fire.

For several years the building remained as the flames left them, until about 1855, Joseph Shimer fitted up part of the ruins, and commenced the manufacture of cotton laps. He remained here several years, when he built a mill lower down on the other side of the creek in Newtown, which is still owned by him.

In 1870 the old Hatch mill property was used by Alfred Hatch as a cotton-lap factory, and is still owned by him.

In 1799, Joseph Pennell, grandson of Robert Pennell, who settled in the township in 1691, was in possession of a tannery a short distance northwest of Howellville, which later passed to Thomas Evans, and about 1830 became the property of Israel Howell, a leather merchant of Philadelphia, for whom Howellville was named. The tannery went out of use many years ago. The property is now owned by Henry Mendenhall.

A few years prior to 1807, George Green built a saw-mill on Green's Run, which was operated by him till about 1820, later by Isaac Green; the ruins of this mill are yet there. In 1817, Robert Green had a fulling-mill on Rocky Run, located on the present estate of Mrs. James Walker. In 1826 it was operated by William Owens & Co., and in 1829–31 was still in use, and continued to be operated until about 1864, when the mill was burned. The last few years it was occupied by James Campbell for carding and carpet-weaving. In 1870 a cotton-lap factory was at the place, owned by James Gamble.

In 1807, Richard Passmore had a tan-yard below where Green's fulling-mill was afterwards built, which was in disuse in 1811. The property is now owned by Frank Bishop.

About 1815 James Yarnall built a grist- and saw-mill on a branch of Ridley Creek, in the northern part of the township. In 1817–19 it was assessed to his estate. The grist-mill was a stone building, the power furnished by an overshot wheel, which ran two pairs of millstones. In 1829 it was owned by Reuben Yarnall, but subsequently Anthony Baker acquired title to the mill, and his son, Enos Baker, is the present owner of the property.

Schools.—One of the first school-houses in Edgmont of which there is any information was built about 1760 in the eastern part of the township, and near the line of Upper Providence. The house was of stone, the mortar used being a composition of clay and straw. Thomas Hammer was teacher there, and William Howard, the father of Baldwin Howard, was a pupil under him. Hammer also taught in Upper Providence, and in 1799 was a shopkeeper in Edgmont. This old school-house was not in use in 1800. About this time a change was made in the township lines, and the school-house lot in the change was placed in Upper Providence. The house was torn down about 1860.

What is now known as the Central District was also known as Big Edgmont. At this place a stone school-house was erected in the early part of 1749, and in 1809 a new stone house was built upon its site, which remained in use until the present house was erected, in 1870. Isaac Wood was the first teacher in the second school-house, and Baldwin Howard attended school there. Among later teachers were John McMullen, John Kinsie, Hezekiah Burns, Caleb Hoopes, Jehu Broomhall, Joseph Plankinton, William Vogdes, James Sill, Jr., and Samuel L. Smedley. During the term of Mr. Sill the school-house erected in 1809 was transferred to the directors of the public schools. Joseph Plankinton, in 1824, went to Philadelphia, where he has filled the position of county commissioner, school director, treasurer, and alderman in that city, where he is now residing, aged eighty-five years. William Vogdes is also in Philadelphia, and prominent in the political movements of that city. After the house passed to the school directors in 1835 or 1836, Samuel Lewis was the first teacher, and was succeeded by Pierson Pike, Levi Baker, James M. Smith, and others.

On the 21st of September, 1841, the school directors purchased a lot of land of Isaac Yarnall in the southwest part of the township. A stone house was erected upon it, which was used for eight or ten years and then abandoned. The house is still standing, the property being sold several years ago to Jacob Smedley.

The stone house in the Western District known as No. 1 was built in 1867, the land on which it stands having formerly belonged to George Eppright. It is still standing, and used for school purposes.

The Southern District, No. 3. On the 28th of August, 1843, the directors bought a plot of ground of George Bishop and erected a stone school-house, which was used until 1875, when a lot was purchased of Jesse Green and Isaac Sharpless, about three hundred yards from the old house, on which was erected the present stone house.

EDGMONT CENTRAL SEMINARY.
[Erected 1809, torn down 1870.]

On the 18th of March, 1825, Homer Eachus, William Baker, and James Sill were elected by the people of the township as trustees of schools. In 1834, after the school law was passed, Dr. James Aitkin and Homer Eachus were appointed inspectors of the public schools by the court of Delaware County, until directors were elected. In 1835 $293.55 was received by the township from the treasurer, it being the amount of county and State appropriations.

The list of school directors here given, from 1840, are from the records of Media, and are as accurate as can be obtained from that source:

1840, Thomas B. Russell, Maurice James; 1842, Homer Eachus, John Yarnall; 1843, John H. Taylor, Hiram Green, Jesse Green; 1844, James Sill, Abraham Baker; 1845, Baldwin Howard, Reuben Yarnall; 1846, Maurice Jones, Joshua Smith; 1847, Reuben Yarnall, Emlin Stackhouse; 1848, James Aitkin, Baldwin Howard; 1849, Joshua Smith, Hiram Green; 1850, Isaac Yarnall, William Sill; 1851, Maurice James, James Aitkin; 1852, Thomas Baker, John H. Taylor; 1853, George Ebright, Isaac Yarnall; 1854, Maurice James, Thomas J. Baker; 1855, George G. Baker, Thomas Baker, Isaac Green; 1856, Abram H. Regester, Joseph Mendenhall, Joshua Smith; 1857, Isaac Thatcher, Maurice James; 1858, Edward Baker, Thomas J. Sharpless; 1859, Reuben Johnson, David Regester; 1860, Maurice James, Henry Mendenhall; 1861, Thomas J. Sill, James M. Smith; 1862, Reuben Johnson, David Regester; 1863, Robert J. Sill, Robert F. Davis; 1864, Jesse Yarnall, Lewis J. Baker; 1865, James M. Smith, William Manley; 1866, Robert F. Davis, Edward D. Baker; 1867, Jesse Yarnall; 1868, William S. Baker, James Sill; 1869, R. F. Davis, E. D. Baker; 1870, Jesse Yarnall, James M. Smith; 1871, Hatton Baldwin, Amos H. Baldwin; 1872, William H. Miller, Thomas Mendenhall; 1873, Enos L. Baker, F. F. Green; 1874, no report; 1875, Jesse Yarnall, Robert F. Davis; 1876, Joseph B. Taylor, Edward D. Baker; 1877, Passmore Howard, C. M. Taylor; 1878, Jesse Yarnall, Robert F. Davis; 1879. Frank Yarnall, Mrs. Emma Taylor; 1880, Passmore Howard, Elizabeth G. Green; 1881, Edmund D. Baker, J. F. Bishop; 1882, G. Frank Yarnall, Maurice James; 1883, Pennock E. Sharpless, Abram Hunter; 1884, Frank Bishop, Abram Hunter.

Public-Houses.—The story of the public houses of entertainment in Edgmont is brief. In 1762, Isaac Yarnall presented his petition desiring the approval of the court for his keeping a public house of entertainment in that township, which was extended to him, and continued annually thereafter until 1765, at which period Mary Yarnall made application for the privilege for that as well as the following year, 1766. In 1767, John Hoopes obtained license, and continued in the employment of innkeeping until 1771, when John Neal petitioned the court for the favor, stating that the house had been licensed for many years, and had formerly been kept by Isaac Yarnall. Yearly thereafter Neal applied for renewal of the license until 1776. In 1777, as before stated, the proceedings respecting licenses, as the records of most of the business of that year before the courts, cannot be found, but in 1778 William Dunwoodey was allowed the privilege, after which all further trace in Chester County, as to license in Edgmont, ceases.

It was not until 1806 that application for privilege to keep public-house appeared in the record of Delaware County, and in that year James Jeffries states to the court that he "hath rented the house which Joseph Griffith hath erected at the intersection of the West Chester and Providence Road, in said township," and desired the judges to recommend him to the Governor as a proper person to keep a tavern there. The court at the July session approved of his petition. This is the first mention of the noted President Tavern of Edgmont. In 1808, Joseph Robins succeeded Jeffries, and in his petition for the year 1809 he asks license for the house under that title. The next year Robins gave place to Joseph Griffith, the owner of the house, but in 1811 Jesse Cheyney was granted license for the President. In 1813 Isaac Weaver was landlord of the tavern, which he called the George Washington, but in 1815 he restored the old name, and in 1816 he was followed by Joseph B. Ramsey, who had formerly kept the Rising Sun Inn, at Howellville. The next year, however, he was superseded by Abel Green, who remained there until 1829, when he gave place to William Sill, and the latter in turn, in 1834, was followed by Hiram Green, who continued annually to receive the court favor until 1858, when Juliann Green, his widow, was granted license. In 1862, Joseph P. Tucker succeeded to the business, to be followed the next year, 1863, by George Pierce, after which time the President ceased to be kept as a public-house.

In 1813, Nathan Baker petitioned for license to keep public-house on "road from Chester towards Downingtown and West Chester, where Edgmont road intersects with road leading from Marple through Newtown, by John Williamson's, toward Dilworthtown, and there is no tavern on Edgmont road from Chester, but the Black's Horse, and nearest above the General Green, near Goshen meeting-house, Chester County, and besides there is no tavern on said Cross-road. The house is nine and a half miles from Chester, and from West Chester eight and a half miles. There is much travelling at present and particularly by those going and returning by the stage, which runs steadily between Westtown and Philadelphia." His license was approved and there was established the tavern at Howellville, which was the following year, when Joseph B. Ramsey made application at the same location, known as the Rising Sun Tavern. In 1816, William Sill, who appeared to have been the owner of the property, received license. William Bowen, in 1817; John McMinn, in 1818; and Homer Eachus, who in his petition states, in 1820, that the house is known as the "Old Rising Sun." The latter remained only one year, for in 1821 David Green was landlord. Jane Hamilton, who was licensed in 1823, was followed, in 1826, by George Thatcher, and in 1828 David Green returned there again. Enos Smedley, of West Chester, several years ago stated that he remembered Howellville when the land was bought by Israel Howell, from whom the name is derived. "As the Irishman said, it was 'A honey of a place, the king of all places.' First day, or Sunday, as it is commonly called, was a fair day. Young men and boys from the whole neighborhood would collect to drink whiskey, play corner-ball, pitch quoits, jump for distances or for height, and compete in holding a fifty-six weight at arm's-length. You could hear their noise for half a mile. This place was known at that day as the Rising Sun, Delaware County. It had a blacksmith- and wheelwright-shop, store and tavern, the latter two selling whiskey. I heard the person who kept the store say that he sold one and a half hogsheads of whiskey on an average per month, the price of which was eleven cents per quart, and per gallon, in the jug, forty cents. The poor class, when they sent to the store, would give whiskey the first place on the order, and if any money was left other commodities were to be purchased, but the whiskey must be first. Howellville is now one of the most respectable villages in Delaware County."[1] In 1833, John C. Irwin was mine host, and in 1834, George P. Alexander, who remained there in 1836, after which date no license was had for the house until 1856, although in 1839, in an advertisement, "William Robins, at Sign of the Lamb, Howellville," is mentioned, when William Sill received the right to keep tavern there, and yearly the privilege was continued to him until 1860, when Robert Sill, his son, followed as the host of the Howellville Inn, until 1867, when Edward B. Green assumed control of the house, which is now kept by his widow.

Settlers of Edgmont.—Among the earliest purchasers of land from the proprietary were Joseph Baker, John Worrall, Philip Yarnall, Robert Pennell, Joseph Pennell, Ephraim Jackson, David Register, John Houlston, Samuel Bishop, and in 1722 appear the names of Jonathan Hunter, Samuel Lewis, Joseph Pratt, Henry Howard, James Sill, Jacob Taylor, and others, whose names still survive in their descendants in the limits of the township.

The descendants of Joseph Baker and Mary, his wife, are very numerous throughout Delaware and Chester Counties. He represented Delaware County in the Provincial Assembly, and died in 1716. His son, John, born in Edgmont the 11th of Tenth month, 1686, inherited all his land in the township. When Dr. Ash's map was published, in 1848, Abel, Thomas, and William Baker were land-owners, as well as Edward, George, Abel, and Anthony, sons of Edward Baker.

John Baker, a brother of Joseph, died in Philadelphia in 1685, and left four daughters,—Rebecca, Mary, Dorothy, and Sarah. In 1684, Roger Jackson, Mary, Hannah, and Sarah Baker appear as purchasers from William Penn in Edgmont. Mary married William Coebourn, Hannah to Francis Yarnall, and Sarah to Charles Whitacre.

Phillip Yarnall, with his brother, Francis, came from Cloynes, in Worcestershire, England. They first settled in Springfield township, adjoining George Maris' land, about a mile from Springfield Friends' meeting-house, on the road to Clifton. This land was conveyed to Francis, Oct. 17, 1683, and for several years they were members of Darby Monthly Meeting of Friends. Francis married Hannah Baker, of Edgmont, and purchased five hundred and ten acres of land adjoining Edgmont line, in Willistown township, extending from Crum Creek westward nearly two

[1] "Fifty Years Ago," *Delaware County American*, Nov. 6, 1878.

miles, a large portion of which is still held by his descendants. He was a member of the Provincial Assembly, and died in Willistown in 1731. His son, Mordecai, was a noted preacher among Friends, and removed to Philadelphia. Peter, a grandson, born Second month 17, 1754, studied medicine, entered the army, and afterwards sailed as surgeon's mate on the privateer "Delaware" during the Revolution. He subsequently renounced warfare, and became a noted Quaker preacher.

Lieut. John Jolliff Yarnall, who served with Commodore Perry in the battle of Lake Erie, was a descendant of Francis. The Legislatures of Pennsylvania and Virginia each voted him a sword for bravery. He was commander of the privateer "Epervier," lost at sea with all on board in 1815.

Professor Mordecai Yarnall was also a descendant. He was an astronomer connected with the National Observatory at Washington, and died there Feb. 27, 1869, in his sixty-second year.

Philip Yarnall married Dorothy Baker, Second month 20, 1694, and purchased four hundred and eighty acres in Edgmont, extending from the Middletown line to the road running westward from the present village of Howellville, and erected his house at the place now owned by William H. Miller, an eighth of a mile west of the Temperance Hall. He died in 1734, and his wife in 1743.

They had ten children,—John, born First month 5, 1695, died Seventh month 4, 1749, at Wilmington, married Abigail, daughter of John Williamson, of Newtown; Philip, born Ninth month 29, 1696, married Mary Hoopes; Job, born First month 28, 1698, married Rebecca ——, and died in Ridley in 1740; Sarah, born Eighth month 25, 1700, married Evan Ellis; Benjamin, born Eighth month 20, 1702; Thomas, born Sixth month 10, 1705, married Martha Hammans; Nathan, born Twelfth month 27, 1707, died First month 10, 1780, married three times, to Rachel Jackson, Hannah Mendenhall, and Jane Beazer; Samuel, born Second month 10, 1710, married Sarah Vernon; Rebecca, born Sixth month 6, 1712, married William Jones, of Plymouth; and Mary, born Eighth month 23, 1718, married Samuel Milner, of North Wales.

Samuel Lightfoot's notes of the survey "due west" from Philadelphia for fixing the Maryland boundary in 1738 states that they passed twenty feet from Thomas Yarnall's house (now the home of Caleb Yarnall), twelve perches south from Philip Yarnall's house, and fifty perches south of John Yarnall's (now James Thorp's). This gives the residences of three of the sons at that date.

John and Abigail Yarnall had six children,—Mary, born 1722, died 1792, married three times,—to Thomas Pennell, John Lea, and James Preston,—and was the mother of Dr. Jonas Preston, founder of Preston Retreat, Philadelphia. Thomas, born 1724, died 1759, married Margaret, and lived in Thornbury. Ann, born 1729, died 1797, married John Thomson, and was the grandmother of John Edgar Thomson, the engineer and president of the Pennsylvania Railroad Company. Isaac, born 1732, died 1765, married Mary Bennett; his grandson, Isaac Yarnall, was commissioner of Delaware County; another grandson, Reuben Yarnall, born Fifth month 18, 1800, is now living in Philadelphia; on the 8th of April, 1884, he, with his wife, Rachel, daughter of Davis Garrett, celebrated the sixtieth anniversary of their wedding. Abigail Yarnall, born 1733, died 1803, married Jesse Garrett. Hannah Yarnall, born 1741, died 1818, married Thomas Garrett, of Willistown.

The children of Philip and Mary were Grace, Philip, David, Abraham, Jane, Elizabeth, Esther, Dorothy, and Mary.

The children of Thomas and Martha were Margaret, William (the ancestor of Thomas Yarnall, a minister among Friends), Job, Caleb (ancestor of Owen Yarnall, the present county commissioner), Joseph, Hannah, and Sarah.

The children of Nathan and Rachel Yarnall were Ephraim, born 1733; Nathan, born 1736; Benjamin, born 1738, who moved to Cecil County, Md.; John, born 1739; Edith, born 1743, married Joshua Sharpless; Joel, born 1745; Samuel, born 1748; Eli, born 1753, died 1812, a noted Quaker preacher; Joshua, born 1755; Ellis, born 1757, who removed to Philadelphia in 1774, became a prominent merchant, leaving many descendants, among them Rev. Thomas C. Yarnall, of the Episcopal Church in West Philadelphia; and Robert, born 1761.

In 1696, Ephraim Jackson purchased one hundred and twenty acres of the southern portion of Philip Yarnall's land. He was born in 1658, and came from England in 1687, and in 1695 married Rachel, daughter of Nicholas Newlin, of Concord, and died in 1732. He was a good penman, kept the Friends' records, and wrote many deeds and marriage certificates and other records, which are still in existence. Their children were John, born 1697; Joseph, born 1699, married, first, Hannah Pennell, second, Susana Miller, and settled in Londongrove; Nathaniel, born 1701; Josiah, born 1702; Samuel, born 1704, married Ann, daughter of Robert Johnson, and moved to Lancaster County; Ephraim, born 1706, married Mary Register; Mary, born 1708, married Benjamin Johnson; and Rachel, born 1710, married Nathan Yarnall.

Robert Pennell purchased two hundred and fifty acres in 1691, and two hundred and sixty-four acres in 1705, on the north of Philip Yarnall, extending from Howellville to the Willistown line. He came from Boulderton, in Nottinghamshire, England, having obtained a certificate from Friends at Ffulbeck the third day of the Fifth month, 1684, together with Thomas Garrett, Hugh Rodnell, Henry Pennell, and Richard Parker, with their wives and children, intending to transfer themselves beyond the seas into

East Jersey in America. Robert and his wife, Hannah, settled in Middletown as early as 1686. Their children were Hannah, born Seventh month 23, 1673, died Tenth month 31, 1731, married John Sharpless; Joseph, born Tenth month 12, 1674, died Ninth month 30, 1756, married, Twelfth month 25, 1701, Alice, daughter of William Garrett, of Darby; James, born Ninth month 11, 1676; Jane, born Fifth month 13, 1678, married Samuel Garrett; William, born Eighth month 11, 1681, died 1757, married, Eighth month 26, 1710, Mary, daughter of Thomas Mercer, of Westtown; and Ann, married, Second month 17, 1689, to Benjamin Mendenhall. Robert Pennell died in 1728, and Hannah, his wife, Twelfth month 4, 1711, aged seventy-one years. William Pennell settled in Middletown, and Joseph in Edgmont. The children of Joseph and Alice were Hannah, born Eleventh month 4, 1702, married, Eighth month 18, 1722, to Joseph, son of Ephraim Jackson; Robert, born Sixth month 2, 1704, died First month 9, 1726; Joseph, born Sixth month 3, 1706, died 1728; Alice, born Eighth month 2, 1709, died Seventh month 13, 1748; Anne, born Eighth month 2, 1711, died First month 25, 1802, married Cadwallader Evans; Jane; and Mary, born 1717, died Tenth month 31, 1807, married Moses Meredith, of Plymouth, born Ninth month 30, 1714. He was the son of Meredith Meredith, born Third month 6, 1675.

The Pennell homestead stood a short distance northwest of Howellville, at the place now owned by Henry Mendenhall. Robert Pennell willed the northern part of his farm to his grandson, Joseph, and thereon erected a house, portions of which are now standing and occupied by Emlen Stackhouse. One of the windows has the small leaden lights of Queen Anne's time. Joseph died, aged twenty-one, before the house was completed.

The children of Mary and Moses Meredith were Sarah, married Joseph Pennell, of Concord; John, born Eleventh month 17, 1748, married Hannah Harrison; Joseph, who died at an advanced age unmarried; and Alice, who married David Harry. Joseph Meredith, born Tenth month 11, 1785, a son of John, inherited the north part of the tract, from whom it descended to Catharine, the wife of Emlen Stackhouse, and Alice, wife of Charles Stackhouse, who, with their children, are the present possessors. Joseph's wife was Sarah, daughter of Joseph Pennell, of Concord.

The children of Ann and Cadwalader Evans were Pennell, born 1731; Hannah, born 1733, married Rowland Parry; Alice, born 1735, married D. Jonathan Morris; Robert, born 1738, married Jane Cox; Joseph, born 1747; Sarah; Mary, born 1750; Jane, born 1752; Catharine, born 1754.

Thomas Evans owned the tannery at the old homestead. It afterwards passed into the hands of Israel Howell, a leather merchant of Philadelphia, who gave the name of Howellville to the old Rising Sun, and built the elegant residence, owned afterwards by Dr. Casper Wistar Pennock, who resided there until his death.

Samuel Lewis, a grandson of Ralph Lewis, of Radnor, purchased two hundred acres of David Register in 1720, adjoining Joseph Pennell's land. His son, Josiah Lewis, inherited it, and William Lewis, his son, was born there in 1751, who in after-life became the leader of the Philadelphia bar. In his seventeenth year he went to Chester with a load of hay, and while gratifying his curiosity by a visit to the court-room, was so much fascinated by the oratory there displayed that he at once resolved to study law, although his previous education was of the most limited character. He repaired to Philadelphia and engaged as an office-boy, and began the study of his profession with Nicholas Waln, then a young man of excellent attainments and of fine forensic talents, but, unhappily, affected by habits of dissipation and sentiments of unbelief. It was when he was in Mr. Waln's office that a remarkable incident occurred which formed the turning-point in his life. Mr. Waln, who was a Quaker, but who had himself for many years thrown off Friend's dress, was passing one day by the Pine Street meeting-house; the door was open, and, sauntering in, he was attracted by the voice of a preacher on the women's side. Suddenly his sight became obscure; a series of spectres, as he afterwards firmly believed, each bearing to him a portentous message, flitted before him; and, yielding to the awful vision, he sank upon his knees, interrupting the speaker by a prayer of terrific earnestness. This was succeeded by a trance, in which consciousness was destroyed, and from which he awoke only to renounce all worldly connections whatever. This was in 1773, just about the period of Mr. Lewis' admission to the bar, and, aided by the business which, on his master's retirement, slipped into his hands, the young lawyer soon found himself with a respectable run of clients; Mr. Joseph Reed, afterwards president of the Council, and Mr. Wilcock, afterwards, for a long time, recorder of Philadelphia, together with Mr. Galloway, then the provincial leader, being his chief competitors. When the Declaration of Independence upset the courts, Mr. Lewis took the new test, not yielding, however, any overt patriotism. To vindicate the Quaker loyalists was no small nervous effort on the part of the man whose own patriotism had been equivocal. The effort, however, he made, and made with calmness, courage, and power; and, in the trials of Chapman, Roberts, and Carlisle, he displayed, in full vigor, his eminent powers of reasoning and courage of temper. Perhaps to this may be attributed his unparalleled influence with the Quaker community.

For several years Mr. Lewis, as a member of the Pennsylvania Legislature, took the lead on the Federal side, and in 1789, in the State Convention, was foremost in upsetting the absurd Constitution which Dr. Franklin had a few years previous persuaded the State to accept.

East Jersey in America. Robert and his wife, Hannah, settled in Middletown as early as 1686. Their children were Hannah, born Seventh month 28, 1673, died Tenth month [illegible], married John Sharpless; Joseph, born Tenth month 12, 1674, died Ninth month 20, 1756, married, Twelfth month 25, 1701, Alice, daughter of William Garrett, of Darby; James, born Ninth month 12, 1678; Jane, born Fifth month 18, 1680, married Samuel Garrett; William, born Eighth month 15, 1681, died 1757, married, Eighth month 24, 1710, Mary, daughter of Thomas Mercer, of Westtown; and Ann, married, Second month 17, 1696, to Benjamin Mendenhall. Robert Pennell died in 1728, and Hannah, his wife, Twelfth month 4, 1711, aged seventy-one years. William Pennell settled in Middletown, and Joseph in Edgmont. The children of Joseph and Alice were Hannah, born Eleventh month 4, 1702, married, Eighth month 18, 1722, to Joseph, son of Ephraim Jackson; Robert, born Sixth month 2, 1704, died First month 9, 1725; Joseph, born Sixth month 3, 1706, died 1728; Alice, born Eighth month 2, 1709, died Seventh month 15, 1740; Ann, born Eighth month 2, 1711, died First month [illegible], married Cadwalader Evans; Jane; and Mary, born 1714, died Tenth month 25, 1807, married Moses Meredith of Plymouth, born Ninth month 30, 1714. He was the son of Meredith Meredith, born Third month 4, 1683.

The Pennell homestead stood a short distance northwest of Howellville, at the place now owned by Henry Mendenhall. Robert Pennell willed the northern part of his land to his grandson, Joseph, and thereon erected a house, portions of which are now standing and occupied by Emlen Stackhouse. One of the windows has the small leaden lights of Queen Anne's time. Joseph died aged twenty-one, before the house was completed.

The children of Mary and Moses Meredith were Sarah, married Joseph Pennell, of Concord; John, born Eleventh month 17, 1746, married Hannah Harrison; Joseph, who died at an advanced age unmarried; and Alice, who married David Harry. Joseph Meredith, born Tenth month 11, 1785, a son of John, inherited the north part of the tract, from whom it descended to Catharine, the wife of Emlen Stackhouse, and Alice, wife of Charles Stackhouse, who, with their children, are the present possessors. Joseph's wife was Sarah, daughter of Joseph Pennell, of Concord.

The children of Ann and Cadwalader Evans were Pennell, born 1731; Hannah, born 1735, married Rowland Parry; Alice, born 1735, married Dr. Jonathan Morris; Robert, born 1738, married Jane Cox; Joseph, born 1747; Sarah; Mary, born 1749; Jane, born 1752; Catharine, born 1754.

Thomas Evans owned the tannery at the old homestead. It afterwards passed into the hands of Israel Howell, a leather merchant of Philadelphia, who gave the name of Howellville to the old Rising Sun, and erected an elegant residence, owned afterwards by Dr. Casper Wistar Pennock, who resided there until his death.

Samuel Lewis, a grandson of Ralph Lewis, of Radnor, purchased two hundred acres of David Register in 1720, adjoining Joseph Pennell's land. His son, Josiah Lewis, inherited it, and William Lewis, his son, was born there in 1751, who in after-life became the leader of the Philadelphia bar. In his seventeenth year he went to Chester with a load of hay, and while gratifying his curiosity by a visit to the court-room was so much fascinated by the oratory there displayed that he at once resolved to study law, although his previous education was of the most limited character. He repaired to Philadelphia and engaged as an office-boy, and began the study of his profession with Nicholas Waln, then a young man of excellent attainments and of fine forensic talents, but, unhappily, affected by habits of dissipation and sentiments of unbelief. It was when he was in Mr. Waln's office that a remarkable incident occurred which formed the turning-point in his life. Mr. Waln, who was a Quaker, but who had himself for many years thrown off Friend's dress, was passing one day by the Pine Street meeting-house; the door was open, and, sauntering in, he was attracted by the voice of a preacher on the women's side. Suddenly his sight became obscure; a series of spectres, as he afterwards firmly believed, each bearing to him a portentous message, flitted before him; and yielding to the awful vision, he sank upon his knees, interrupting the speaker by a prayer of terrible earnestness. This was succeeded by a trance, in which consciousness was destroyed, and from which he awoke only to renounce all worldly connections whatever. This was in 1772, just about the period of Mr. Lewis' admission to the bar, and, aided by the business which, on his master's retirement, slipped into his hands, the young lawyer soon found himself with a respectable run of clients; Mr. Joseph Reed, afterwards president of the Council, and Mr. Wilcock, afterwards, for a long time, recorder of Philadelphia, together with Mr. Galloway, then the provincial leader, being his chief competitors. When the Declaration of Independence upset the courts, Mr. Lewis took the new test, not yielding, however, any overt patriotism. To vindicate the Quaker loyalists was no small nervous effort on the part of the man whose own patriotism had been equivocal. The effort, however, he made, and made with calmness, courage, and power; and, in the trials of Chapman, Roberts, and Carlisle, he displayed, in full vigor, his eminent powers of reasoning and courage of temper. Perhaps to this may be attributed his unparalleled influence with the Quaker community.

For several years Mr. Lewis, as a member of the Pennsylvania Legislature, took the lead on the Federal side, and in 1789, in the State Convention, was foremost in upsetting the absurd Constitution which Dr. Franklin and a few years previous persuaded the State to accept.

Saml L. Smedley

To Washington's administration, by which, when it began, he had been offered the post of district attorney, he considered himself bound by the closest ties, and he even departed from his general policy and went so far as not only to contribute to the newspapers of the day, but, in 1792, even to stump the State. On these occasions the vigor and clearness of his voice was remarkable, and without apparent effort, in the open air, every word was audible at an extraordinary distance. In 1792, on the death of the elder Judge Hopkinson, he had a new proof of the President's confidence in the commission then sent him as district judge. On the bench, however, he continued but a short time, the restraint being uncongenial to his taste, and the income insufficient for his extravagant habits.

Upon his return to the bar he enjoyed a lucrative practice, and became concerned as leading counsel in the trials of the Western insurgents. He purchased property adjoining Laurel Hill Cemetery, and built the Strawberry Mansion, now within the limits of Fairmount Park, and made it his residence.

After the coming in of Mr. Jefferson's administration Mr. Lewis took no part in politics, continuing, however, in the unabated practice of his profession until 1819, when, on the 15th of August, after several weeks' illness, he died, retaining to the last the professional ability and professional devotion which had marked his long career.

The house in Edgmont where William Lewis was born, now owned by William Pennell Smedley, is still standing, the farm having been inherited by his brother, Samuel Lewis, who sold it to William Smedley, of Middletown, in the year 1822.

BIRTHPLACE OF WILLIAM LEWIS, 1751.

William Smedley, born Eighth month 9, 1765, died Fourth month 10, 1839, married, Twelfth month 5, 1793, Deborah Lightfoot. He provided a farm for each of his four sons. George and William remained in Middletown, the latter on part of the farm purchased by their ancestor, George Smedley, of William Penn in 1684, while Samuel Lightfoot and Jacob settled in Edgmont.

Jacob Smedley, born Twelfth month 31, 1801, married, Eleventh month 13, 1826, Jane Yarnall, daughter of Isaac and Mary Yarnall, of Edgmont. Their children were Isaac Y., born 1827, died 1853; Abram P., born 1829, now a dentist in Media; Nathan, born 1831, died 1884; Hannah P., born 1836; William Alfred, born 1838, died 1852; and Bennett L., born 1839, a druggist in Philadelphia. Jacob was a surveyor and conveyancer, and, with Enoch Lewis, made surveys of a railroad from Chester to West Chester, along Chester Creek, in 1835. He was surveyor of Media, where he now resides, and held the position of clerk of the county commissioners for twenty-one years.

Samuel L. Smedley, born Fourth month 9, 1798, was prominent as a teacher and mathematician, and, besides his inherited occupation of farming, carried on surveying and conveyancing. He taught several years at Thornbury, and subsequently at High Bank, on a portion of his farm. He married, Fifth month 4, 1826, Hannah, daughter of Joseph and Mary Pennell, of Middletown, and died Tenth month 19, 1834. He left three sons,—Joseph P., born Fifth month 24, 1827, farmer and miller, who died Tenth month 3, 1872, in Uwchlan, Chester Co., leaving one daughter, Hannah, born 1870. He married Emma Winner, Third month 11, 1867. William P., born Ninth month 4, 1829, married, Fourth month 5, 1860, Jane Garrett. His children are Samuel L., born 1861; Alfred, born 1866, died 1884; Elizabeth, born 1869; Jane H., born 1872, died 1872; and Mary Ella, born 1875.

Samuel L. Smedley, youngest son of Samuel L. and Hannah, was born Twelfth month 29, 1832, and was less than two years of age at the time of his father's death. From that time his mother managed the farm, and carried it on successfully until her sons reached maturity. He early evinced an aptitude for study, and was carefully educated at a select school until his thirteenth year, when he entered the Friends' Boarding-school at Westtown. Here he made rapid progress and at the end of eighteen months stood at the head of the senior class. He was then sent to school in Germantown to perfect himself in the classics, but close application so injured his health that he was forced to return home, where he remained for several years upon the old homestead. During this time he was solicited to take charge of the district school at Edgmont Central Seminary, and taught there two winters.

Convinced that his health required an active outdoor occupation, Mr. Smedley determined to adopt the profession of surveying, which was congenial to his tastes, a love for which he inherited. Accordingly, in the spring of 1853 he removed to Philadelphia and engaged with Joseph Fox, who had laid out most of the northern portion of the city of Philadelphia, and had then recently been engaged to extend the city plan on the west side of the Schuylkill. Possessed of mathematical talent, and being an apt draughtsman, Mr. Smedley soon mastered the minutiæ of his profession, and his promotion was rapid. In 1856 he was engaged by the commissioners of Blockley to lay out the streets in that township. He also carried on conveyancing, and entered largely into the purchase and sale of real estate. About this time he published a complete atlas of the city of Philadelphia, a laborious and expensive undertaking, but one which was very successful, and the book remains to this day a standard work for conveyancers, and is highly prized by them. In 1858, Mr. Smedley was elected a member of the Board of Surveyors, and was subsequently chosen by the people of the district for three terms of five years each.

In 1871 his name was presented to the Republican State Convention as a candidate for the position of Surveyor-General of the State. The novelty of naming a professional surveyor for that position met with much favor, but the policy of placing soldiers upon the ticket prevailed, and Gen. Robert B. Beath was nominated and elected, he being the last to hold the office, as, by the provisions of the new Constitution, it was merged into that of Secretary of Internal Affairs. In 1872, Mr. Smedley was elected by the City Councils to the responsible office of chief engineer and surveyor, the position he now holds, having been chosen for the third time in March, 1882, his present term expiring in 1887. In this position he has had charge of many extensive public works, among which have been the building of Penrose Ferry bridge, and the Fairmount and Girard Avenue bridges, and numerous smaller ones over railroads, canals, and other streams within the limits of the city.

Mr. Smedley, in 1865, visited Europe on a tour of recreation and study, and returned impressed with the thought that Philadelphia, to keep pace with other great cities, should avail herself of her great natural advantages for establishing a grand park for the enjoyment of the people, and he entered with enthusiasm into the project of securing Lansdowne, an estate of one hundred and fifty acres, from its English owners, as a nucleus for the park, and was largely instrumental in bringing about the purchase of that beautiful section of land as a pleasure-ground for the public. He was appointed by the park commissioners to make the original surveys of the territory embraced in the park, and many of the walks and drives therein were designed and laid out by him. Since 1872, as a park commissioner, by virtue of his office, he has been active in securing improvements to the territory under the control of the board.

Mr. Smedley has been a member of the Historical Society of Pennsylvania since 1857, and for fourteen years was recording secretary of the association. He has taken much interest in local history and genealogy, and has collected a large number of the records of his own family, which became of special interest during the bi-centennial year. He is also a member of the Numismatic and Antiquarian Society of Philadelphia; honorary member of the Delaware County Institute of Science; member of the Academy of Natural Sciences, the Franklin Institute, and of the West Philadelphia Institute; of the latter he was for many years a director and secretary. In addition he is a member of the American Public Health Association, of the executive committee of the Philadelphia Social Science Association, the Engineers' Club of Philadelphia, the American Society of Civil Engineers, and of the Union League and other political clubs. In religion he is a member of the society of Friends, as his ancestors have been from the first settlement of the State. Mr. Smedley is unmarried, and lives in West Philadelphia, with which section of the city he has long been identified.

Joseph Fox, a native of Edgmont, was born Third month 9, 1786. He taught school in Westtown, and married Hannah, daughter of Aaron James, of the latter place. In 1815 he kept store at Seven Stars, in Aston, in partnership with Isaac Massey, and in 1818 married Priscilla Griffith. In 1820 he married Edith, daughter of Abraham Hibberd. In 1822 he removed to Philadelphia, and taught school there for several years. The northwestern limit of the city at that time was in the vicinity of Tenth and Spring Garden Streets. Mr. Fox was an excellent mathematician, and in 1826 turned his attention to surveying, in partnership with Philip M. Price. He laid out the streets in a large portion of the city between Spring Garden and Germantown, and in 1843 retired to a farm in New Jersey. He was a surveyor of such large experience and high reputation for accuracy that he was solicited to take charge of the intricate work of making a good city plan out of the numerous small villages which had grown up independently in West Philadelphia, and accepted the appointment in 1852, and returned again to the city, remaining there until his death, Second month 14, 1873. He left several children. Samuel L. Fox, proprietor of J. W. Queen's optical and mathematical instrument establishment, in Philadelphia, is one of them.

Everatt Griscom Passmore, farmer, of Edgmont, had a great reputation as a "gilt-edge" butter-maker forty years ago. While on his way to Goshen Meet-

EBER EACHUS.

John Mendenhall

ing his horses became unmanageable He was thrown violently against a rock, and a portion of his skull as large as a walnut was broken in It was carefully removed by trepanning, and he lived seventeen years afterwards with the indentation conspicuous in his forehead He died in 1868, aged eighty-one years, and was buried at Moorestown, N J

BIOGRAPHICAL SKETCHES.

EBER EACHUS

The paternal grandparents of Mr Eachus were Enoch and Esther Eachus, of Goshen township, Chester Co, Pa, while on the maternal side he was the grandson of William and Susanna Rusell, of Delaware Co, Pa His parents were Evans and Hannah Eachus, whose children were William R, Emmor David, Mary, Sarah, Susanna, Esther, Hannah, Matilda, and Eber, all of whom with the exceptions of Eber and Esther are deceased Eber Eachus was born Feb 22, 1807, in Upper Providence township, Delaware County, where he continued to reside until April 1, 1832 He received when a lad such educational advantages as were obtainable at the public schools of the vicinity, and subsequently made farming the business of his life,—first in Upper Providence and later in Edgmont township, where he removed in 1832, and became the occupant of his present farm He was on the 29th of November, 1836, married to Priscilla P Bishop, daughter of Thomas and Martha Bishop, of Hartsville, Bucks Co, Pa By this marriage are two children,—Evans, born Jan 8, 1838, and Hannah, whose birth occurred April 18, 1840 Mr. Eachus was in politics an Old-Line Whig during the existence of that party At the beginning of the war he joined the ranks of the Republican party, but in later life ceased to take an active interest in affairs of a political character He was reared in the faith of the society of Friends, and affiliates with the Hicksite branch of that religious body

JOHN MENDENHALL

Three brothers—John, Benjamin, and George Mendenhall—came from England with William Penn in 1682 George returned after a brief sojourn in America, John settled in Chester County, and Benjamin found a home in Concord township, Delaware Co He was united in marriage to Ann Pennell, and had sons,—Robert and Benjamin The former, who was born in 1719, married Phœbe Taylor, and became the parent of thirteen children, among whom was John, the father of the subject of this biographical sketch He married Tabitha Newlin, whose children were Cyrus, Martha, Esther, John, and Anne. John Mendenhall was born May 27, 1793, in Edgmont township, Delaware Co, upon the farm which was for sixty years his home After the rudiments of an English education were obtained, he assisted his father in his daily routine of labor, then became superintendent of the varied farm interests, and finally lessee of the property He later purchased an estate in close proximity to his former home, and made it his residence He was married in 1821 to Hannah Sharpless, daughter of Daniel and Sarah Sharpless, of Chester township, Delaware Co, Pa Their children are Rebecca (deceased), Henry, and Joseph Henry is a resident of Media, and married Deborah Passmore, of Chester County, whose children are Ella, J Howard, Walter P, and Anna R Joseph resides in Lawrence, Kan, where he is actively engaged in business In 1849, Mr Mendenhall removed to a farm in Edgmont township Here he resided during the remainder of his life, though his son, Henry, cultivated the farm for many years Mr Mendenhall was a Whig in his political convictions, and subsequently supported the platform of the Republican party, having held numerous minor offices in the township of his residence He was in religion a Friend, and member of the Orthodox Friends' Meeting of Middletown

CHAPTER XLIV

HAVERFORD TOWNSHIP[1]

THIS division of the county lies in the northeastern quarter, on the border of Montgomery County, and wholly within what was known at an early period as the Welsh tract With the exception of Merion, in Montgomery County, it was the earliest settled of the Welsh townships Its name was brought over with the first settlers, who came from the vicinity of Haverford-West,[2] in Pembrokeshire, South Wales In early days, says Dr Smith, the name was very frequently written with an *u* instead of *v*, and doubtless had the pronunciation that this change of letters would give it The pronunciation was, at length, corrupted to Harford, a name by which the township was generally known within the recollection of many now living

Respecting the settlement of Haverford, as well as Radnor township, it appears that soon after William Penn had acquired title to the province of Pennsylvania, he encouraged emigration to America, especially people of his religious belief, and sold to numerous Welsh Friends, lands which were to be located in

[1] By John S. Scheuck

[2] The term Haverford is of very ancient date. Haverford in Wales had its castle as early as 1112 A D, and Giraldus Cambrensis gives an account of "a preaching tour" made there by Archbishop Baldwin and himself in the year of our era 1118 He reports that they were most kindly received by the Haverfordians and their religious services gratefully acknowledged

a body as a barony on the west bank of the Schuylkill River. Hence Dr. Edward Jones, chirurgeon, as he is styled, with other Welsh purchasers, sailed from Liverpool, England, in the ship "Lyon," John Compton, master, and arrived in the Schuylkill River on the 13th of the Sixth month (August), 1682. On the 26th of the same month Dr. Jones wrote to his friend, John ap Thomas, the following letter, which describes the voyage and arrival of the Welsh settlers:

"*These ffor his much esteemed friend John ap Thomas of Llaithgwn neer Bala in Merionethshire, North Wales, to be left with Job Boulten att the Boult and tun in Lumber Street, London, and from thence to William Sky Butcher, in Oncestrie, to be sent as above directed and via London—with speed.*

"My endeared fr'd & brother my heart dearly salutes thee in a measure of ye everlasting truth dear fr'd hoping that these fow lines may find thee in health or no worster yn I left thee. This shall lett thee know that we have been aboard eleven weeks before we made the land (it was not for want of art but contrary winds) and one we were in coming to Upland, ye town is to be buylded 15 or 16 miles up ye River. And in all this time we wanted neither meate, drink or water though several hogsheads of water run out. Our ordinary allowance of beer was 3 pints a day for each whole head and a quart of water; 3 biskedd a day & some times more. We laid in about half hundred biskedd, one barrell of beere, one hogshead of water—the quantity for each whole head, & 3 barrells of beefe for the whole number—40—and we had one to come ashoare. A great many could eat little or no beefe though it was good. Butter and cheese eats well upon ye sea. Ye remainder of our cheese & butter is little or no worster; butter and cheese is at 6*d* per lb. here if not more. We have oatmeale to spare, but it is well, yet we have it, for here is little or no corn till they begin to sow their corn, they have plenty of it. The passengers are all living, save one child, yt died of a surfeit. Let no frds tell that they are either too old or too young, for the Lord is sufficient to preserve both to the uttermost. Here is an old man about 80 years of age; he is rather better yn when he sett out, likewise here are young babes doing very well considering sea diet. We had one tun of water, and one of drinke to pay for at Upland, but ye master would faine be pd for 13 or 14 hogsheds yt run out by ye way, but we did not, and about 3 quarters of Tunn of Coales we p'd for; we laid in 8 Tun of Coales and yields no profit here. We are short of our expectation by reason that ye town is not to be builded at Upland, neither would ye Master bring us any further, though it is navigable for ships of greater burthen than ours. Ye name of town lots is called now Wilcoco; here is a Crowd of people striving for ye country land, for ye town lot is not divided, & therefore we are forced to take up ye Country lots. We had much adoe to get a grant of it, but it cost us 4 or 5 days attendance, besides some score of miles we traveled before we brought it to pass. I hope it will please thee and the rest yt are concerned, for it hath most rare timber, I have not seen the like in all these parts, there is water enough beside. The end of each lot will be on a river as large or larger than the Dye at Bala, it is called Skool Kill River. I hope the Country land will within this four days [be] surveyed out. The rate for surveying 100 Acres [was] twenty shilling, but I hope better orders will be taken shortly about it.

"The people generally are Swede, which are not very well acquainted. We are amongst the English, which sent us both vension and new milk, & the Indians brought vension to our door for six pence ye quarter. And as for ye land we look upon it [as] a good & fat soyl generally producing twenty, thirty, & fourty fold. There are stones to be had enough at the falls of the Skool Kill, that is where we are to settle, & water enough for mills, but thou must bring Millstones and ye Irons that belong to it, for Smiths are dear. Iron is about two and thirty or fourty shillings per hundred; Steel about 1s. 6*d*, p. l. Ye best way is to make yr picken axes when you come over, for they cannot be made in England, for one man will work with ym as much as two men with ours.

"Grindle stones yield good profit here; ordinary workmen have 1*s*. 6*s*. a day. Carpenters 3 or four shillings a day; here are sheep, but dear, about twenty shillings a piece. I cannot understand how they can be carried from England. . . . Taylors hath 5s. & 6s. a day. . . . I would have you bring salt for ye present use; here is coarse salt, some times two measures of salt for one of wheat, and sometimes very dear. Six penny & eight penny nails are most in use, horse shoes are in no use . . . good large shoes are dear; lead in small bars is vendible, but guns are cheap enough. . . . They plow, but very bungerly, and yet they have some good stone They use both hookes and sickles to reap with. . . .

"Time will not permit me to write much more for we are not settled. I [send] my dear love and my wife's unto thy selfe and thy dear wife and the rest of my dear friends, H. Ro. Rich. P. Evan Resse; J. ap E. Elizabeth Williams E. & J. Edd; Gainor R.; Ro. On.; Jo. Humphrey; Hugh J. Tho.; and the rest of fr'ds as if named.

"*I remain thy Lo' friend and Bro. while I am.*

"Edd Jones.

"My wife desires thee to buy her one Iron Kettle 3*s*. or 3s, 6*d*.; 2 paire of shoes for Martha, and one paire for Jonathan, let them be strong and large; be sure and put all yr goods in cases, if they be dry they keep well, otherwise they will get damp and mouldy. . . .

"This is the 2d letter, Skool Kill River,

"*Ye 26th of ye 6th mo., 1682.*"

Subsequently Jones and his countrymen settled upon "The Welsh Tract," the outlines of which had been run by virtue of the following warrant:

"Whereas, divers considerable persons among ye Welsh Friends have requested me yt all ye Lands Purchased of me by those of North Wales and South Wales, together with ye adjacent counties to ym, as Haverfordshire, Shropshire, and Cheshire, about fourty thousand acres, may be layd out contiguously as one *Barony*, alledging yt ye number all ready come, and suddenly to come, are such as will be capable of planting ye same much wthin ye proportion allowed by ye custom of ye country, & so not lye in large and useless vacancies, and because I am inclined and determined to agree and favour ym wth any reasonable Conveniency and priviledge: I do hereby charge thee and strictly require thee to lay out ye sd tract of Land in as uniform a manner as conveniently may be, upon ye West side of Skool kill river, running three miles upon ye same, and two miles backward, and then extend ye parallel wth ye river six miles, and to run westwardly so far as till ye sd quantity of land be Compleately surveyed unto ym. Given at Pennsbury, ye 13th 1st mo., 1684.

"Will: Penn.

"To Tho: Holmes, Surveyor-General."

In pursuance of this warrant the surveyor-general, on the 4th of the Second month (April), 1684, issued an order to his deputy, David Powell, directing the latter "to survey and sett out unto the said purchasers the said quantity of land, in manner as before expressed, and in method of townshipps, lately appointed by the Governor, att five thousand acres for a townshipp and to be directed (for placing the villages of each Townshipp and division of the purchasers) by Thomas Lloyd, Master of the Rolls, who is principally concerned therein, unto whose care and prudence is recommended the ordering and managing of this affair to the content and satisfaction of the said purchasors, and make me a true return of the original field-work and protracted figures, as well as the distinct quantity of each purchasor, &c".

The survey was probably made before the close of 1684. Soon after encroachments were made by others within its limits, and particularly by Charles Ashcom, a very troublesome deputy surveyor. In consequence thereof the Welsh inhabitants petitioned to the proprietary's deputies against these intrusions, who, after they had "well weighed the mater, truly considered the case, and rightly understanding the Governor's intention in granting the warrant," issued their mandate on the 25th day of the Fifth month (July), 1687, forbidding such intrusions, and making void what had been done within the prescribed limits, which are given as follows:

"Beginning att the school kill, thence running W S W by the City liberties 2256 perches to Darby Creek, Thence following up the several courses thereof to New Towne Line, Thence up the said line N N W 448 perches, Thence S S W and by W by New Towne, 998 perches, to a corner post by Crumb Creek, Thence down the several courses thereof 460 perches Thence W and by S by a line of trees 1920 perches, Thence N N W by a line of trees —— perches, Thence E and by N by a line of trees 3040 perches, Thence E and by S 1120 perches, Thence S S E 256 perches, Thence E N E 640 perches, Thence S S E 1204 perches, Thence E N E 668 perches to the School kill, Thence down the several courses thereof to the place of beginning"

The only draft of the "Welsh Tract" that has been found in the surveyor-general's office does not entirely agree with the above description However, the original survey included the townships of Haverford and Radnor, in the present county of Delaware, besides Merion, Tredyffrin, Whiteland, Willistown, Easttown, Goshen, and part of Westtown, in the counties of Chester and Montgomery

Meanwhile complaints concerning the actions of Charles Ashcom and others continued to be forwarded to the proprietary, and finally were noticed in the following instructions to the commissioners of property, William Markham, Thomas Ellis, and John Goodson, dated at Worminghurst, Twelfth month 1st, 1686, and read at a meeting held 3, 13, 1687

"4thly And whereas I formerly granted a Warrt for forty Thousand acres for the Welch people, to Lye Contiguous on the west side of Schoolkill, and that I am informed Incursions have been made upon those Lines Contrary to Equity, as also that Charles Ashcome Refuses to make Regular Returns to Thomas Holme, Surveyor Generall, or pay him his old dues, which was one-third, from the first of his serveing under him *These are to will and Require you to Look into the same*, and to do Justice both to the Welch and to the Surveyr Generall Charles Ashcome Promising me to pay ye said one-third part of the money for survey to the said Thomas Holme, and in Case the said Charles Ashcome shall be disorderly or Refractory, you are hereby Impowered to Displace him, otherwise to Coutinue him in his Imploy"

It also appears that the Welsh settlers not only contemplated having their settlements together, but expected to constitute one municipal district or "barony," in order that they might manage their affairs in their own way They certainly had grounds for this expectation, and consequently when the division-line was run between Philadelphia and Chester Counties, through the Welsh Tract, thus separating the settlements of Haverford and Radnor from those of Merion, it gave rise to much dissatisfaction, and resulted in sending forward, through Col William Markham, the following petition to the proprietary

"PHILADELPHIA, the 23d, 2d mo., 1688

"To the propriety & Governors Commissioners of State & Property The Humble peticon of the Inhabitants of the Welch Tract Sheweth

"That, Whereas William Penn, Proprietary & Governor aforesd out of his tendr Love & good will towards your petrs & for their Incouragemt & Conveniency here (considering many of them understood not the English Tongue & soe were incapable of giveing due services to English Judicatures) was favorly pleased to give his most Solemne word (before they removed from the Land of their nativity) That they, yor Petrs should have abt forty thousand acres of Land contiguously layd out as a Barony, and that they should not be obliged to answer nor serve in any Cot whatsoever, but should have Corts & magistrates of their owne, wherein Justice should be ministred according to the Law of this Government or to that effect, In Consideration whereof, & for a manifestacon of yor petrs, Love, Gratitude, & Choice to the sd Governor & his Government they came over to this Province

"And whereas the sd Propriety in pursuance of his former promise Did grant a warrant for surveying the sd Tract accordingly, and thereupon further declared that yor petrs should Injoy the sd priviledges in maner aforesd & be Exempt from attending all other Judicatures save only that they should maintaine membrs to such in Council & Assembly And also whereas the sd Tract extends to the sev'all Countys of Philadelphia & Chester as is aleadged & by pretence thereof your petrs have been sumoned to the County Corts of both the sd Countys to yield their service upon Jurys & so are like to be taxed in both places to their great impoverishmt Now for as much as the priviledges & Exempeons aforesd soe tenderly proposed by or Governor is most thankfull acknowledged as a peculiar kindness to yor petrs nevrtheless they desire to Improve the same to no other end then to have their Corts & Magistrates of & amongst themselves as they had in Wales and to be governed by the Law of Pennsilvania here, as they were by the Law of England there, and that good Rule & Order may be the better kept amongst them & amiable unity with their English & other neighbors be preserved and Especially that their monthly and other meetings may not be separated

"Therefore yor petrs humbly request that what has been so as aforesd granted by parol may be Confirmed unto them & other purchasrs & Inhabitants of the sd Tract & their heires by Graut Charter or Ordinances containing such Jurisdictions, powers, Liberties, & under such services, Restricons and Denominacon as in Wisdom you shall Judge Expedient, &c

"Thomas Ellis	Samuel Rees
Griffith Owen	Moris Lewelin
John Bevan	John Roberts
Hugh Roberts	David Meredith
Henry Lewis	Richard Orme
William Howell	Rees Peter
John Evans	Hugh Jones
Robert Davies	David Evan
Francis Howell	John Jarman
William Jenkins.	Phylip Evan"
John Humphrey	

[Indorsed] "Pray Sr send an answer to this ffor they are very Earnest about it but John Symcock much agt it as also Laying an other County beyond theirs.

"W M"

It seems that no notice was taken of this petition by the proprietary, at least an answer has never been found The Welsh, however, remained steadfast in the position they had assumed They declined to recognize the division that had been made previously, and this led to proceedings in Council, 1, 25, 1689, as follows

"The Secretary produced a Petition ffrom severall Justices and Inhabitants of ye County of Chester, directed to ye Govert and Councill The Govert asked by Whom Subscribed 'twas answered by none He replyed He should not receive it without a Subscription it was delivered to ye persons who attended about it They Subscribed it The Govert then directed it to be read it was read ye Coppy Thereoff ffolloweth (viz.)

"To John Blackwell, Esqr, Govert, and the Provincll Councill of Pennsylvania &c

"The Humble Petition of ye Justices of Chester County in the behalfe of themselves and Inhabitants of ye said County Sheweth That whereas ye said County is but a Small tract of Land, not above 9 miles square, & but thinly seated, whereby ye said County is not able to support the Charge thereoff, Vppon our humble Request to the Proprietor & Govert and his Serious Consideration of our weak Condition, was pleased out of Compassion to us, to grant an Enlargement of ye same, in manner ffollowing, viz to runn up from Delaware River, along darby mill Creek, ye several Courses thereoff, untill they took in *Radnor* and *Herford* townshipps, Then downe to ye Skoolkill, Then vpwards along the severall Courses thereoff without limmitt

"Therefore, wee humbly pray you will be pleased to Confirme ye said bounds, whereby the County of Chester may be in some measure able to defray their necessary Charge, and wee shall, as in duty bound, &c

"Signed by Jos Blunston, Tho Brassie, Randll Vernon, Caleb Pusey, Tho Vsher

"The Govert Demanded of ye Petitioners how they would make out their alligations They began to relate some passages wch had passed ffrom ye Proprietor about settling the bounds of ye County of Chester

"The Gover^r Directed them to withdraw, and putt what they had to say and Could depose into writing, they went forth and brought in their severall attestations following, wch were read, viz

"'I, John Blunstone, as in relation to ye Devision of Chester County ffrom Philadelphia, doe thus testifie, that a ffew days before Gover^r Penn left this Province, that vpon ye bank by John Simcock's house, I moved him to Deside this matter that had been so long Discoursed, who then, before me and Others, Did Declare that ye bounds Should thus runn ffrom the mouth of Bow Creek to Mill Creek, wch should be ye bounds until it come to ye Land of Herford, and then to take in the Townds of Herford and Radnor. from thence to the Skoulkill, and take in his mannour of Springtowne, by wch our Pattents Holds then I asked him if he would be pleased to give it under his hand, to avoyde ffurther Trouble, who answered he would if any of vs would Come the next day to Philadelphia in order thereunto one was sent, but what then obstructed I am not certaine, but ye Gover^r Departed about two days after

"'Was signed JOHN BLUNSTON'

"Randall Vernon sayeth that some time since Wm Howell of Harford signified vnto me, and gave it vnder his owne hande, y^t some time after they there settled that he asked ye Gover^r to what County they should be joyned or belong vnto, & The Gover^r was pleased to answer him that they must belong to Chester County

"Was signed 'R, the mark of Rand^ll Vernon'

"Our Proprietor and Gover^r, being pleased to grant to me a Commission to be Sheriff of the County of Chester, was pleased some time after to expresse himselfe to me to this purpose Thomas, I perceive that the Skoolkill Creek Comes or runs so vpon the back of Philadelphia, that it makes ye City almost an Island, so that a Robbery or the like may be there Committed and ye offender gitt over ye Creek, and so Escape for want of due persute, &c, therefore I intend that ye bounds of Philadelphia County Shall Come about 3 or ffour miles on this side of the Skoolkill, and I would not have thee to take notice or to oppose that Sheriff in ye Execution of his office, about Kingses or the like, but I intend to enlarge this County downwards to Brandywine

'Assertained by me, THOMAS VSHER

'Some of the members of the Prov^ll Councill asserted the Substance thereof, and that ye same was agreeable with the mapp of the Province

"The Survey^r Gene^rlls Deputy was sent for, who showed the bounds of the County from the mapp, and being asked by ye Gover^r by what order it was sett out, answered it was so ordered by ye Gover^r and Provinciall Councill, as would appear by ye Coppy of ye minutes of their proceedings, wch he produced

"The Gover^r Directed that the minutes themselves might be serched, & Comparing the same Coppy with the Entry, ffound them agree in Substance

"'Twas observed by ye Gover^r and Councill that ye mapp of The Province was the work of Thomas Holme, Survy^r Gene^ll, that it was dedicated to ye Proprietor by ye Publisher, that many Coppys had been published in England and here in this Province, by wch ye same was made notorious to all men's observations and Knowledge without Controll or Question, and that twas likely many Conveyances of Lands might have been passed, Expressing the situations to lye in the Respective Countys, as they were therein Expressed, and that to Disallow thereof, for ye Boundary's, might be of ill Consequence on that acco^t 'Twas asserted that ye Welsh Inhabitants had Denyed themselves to be any part of The County of Philadelphia, by refusing to bear any share of Charges, or serve in office on Jurys, and the like, as to ye County of Chester

"That the pretence thereof was they were a distinct Barony, wch tho' they might be, yet that severall Baronys might be in one and ye same County

"The Gover^r and most of The present members of Councill Declareing themselves satisfied Concerning their being a part of Chester County upon ye ground alliged and proved as aforesaid, yet ffor as much as Thomas Lloyd had desired they might be heard before it were determined, Sam^ll Carpenter was desired to acquaint him that if he, the said Thomas Lloyd, should think fitt so ffarr to Concerne himselfe therein as to appear in their behalfe, or any other, to shew cause why they should not be Declared to be of the County of Chester, (as the Proprietor had promised) they might have liberty to do before the Gover^r and Councill to morrow, between 9 & 10 in the forenoon, otherwise the Evidence seemed so ffull as that the^y should proceed to Declare their judgment therein"

The following day Thomas Lloyd and John Eckley appeared on behalf of the Welsh, and claimed that the proprietor had given them grounds to expect they should be made a county palatine, but having no written evidence thereof, the Governor and Council by a vote decided that the former division line should be confirmed Samuel Carpenter and William Yardley dissented on the ground that the Welsh people should have had more time to make their defense.

The Welsh troubles were then transferred from the Provincial Council chamber to the Chester County court The court made an order appointing John Jerman constable for Radnor and John Lewis for "Hartfort" (Haverford), but these gentlemen did not come forward to be qualified into office At the following court it was "ordered that warrants of Contempt be directed to the Sheriff to apprehend the bodyes of John Lewis and John Jerman for their contempt in not entering into their respective offices of Constable (viz), John Lewis for Hartfort and John Jerman for Radnor, when thereunto required by this Court"

At the same session, which began on the "3d day of 1st week, 3d mo, 1689,' David Lawrence, who had been returned as a grand juror from Haverford, failed to attend He was presented by that body and fined ten shillings The grand jury also presented "the want of the inhabitants of the townships of Radnor and Hartfort, and the inhabitants adjacent, they not being brought in to Joyn with us in the Levies and other public services of this county"

At the June court of 1689 the commission of William Howell, of Haverford, as a justice was read and published, and "he did afterwards subscribe to the solemn declaration, prepared by the 57th Chapter of the great law of this province" At the same court William Jenkins, of Haverford, served as a juror, and at the December court John Jerman was attested constable for Radnor This was the first official recognition by any of the inhabitants of these townships that they were subject to the jurisdiction of Chester County They then seem to have given up the idea of a barony, and with as good a grace as possible submitted to the authority they were unable any longer to resist By the close of the year these townships were supplied with a full set of township officials, who were the first appointed and to serve within their limits

During the year 1693 a provincial tax was levied of one penny per pound on estates, and six shillings per head upon freemen The list of taxables in Haverford township at that time is interesting as showing who were then its citizens The original list, for Chester County, is in possession of the Pennsylvania Historical Society

	£	s	d
John Bevan	00	04	02
William Howell	00	03	04
Morris Lewellin	00	03	04
Thomas Rees	00	02	06
William Lewis	00	04	00
John Richard	00	02	06
Humphrey Ellis	00	02	06
Ellis Ellis	00	02	09
Ralph Lewis	00	02	06

	£	s.	d.
William Jenkins	00	03	09
Daniell Humphrey	00	03	04
David Lawrence	00	03	00
Lewis David	00	02	06
John Lewis	00	03	04
Henry Lewis	00	04	02
John Lewis, Junior	00	02	06
Richard Hayes	00	03	07
Benjamin Humphrey	00	02	08
William Howell, for Tho: Owen	00	06	00
Richard Hayes, for David Lewis	08	06	00
John Bevan, for Evan Williams	00	06	00

Although it has frequently been asserted and generally believed that Penn's colonists and the Indians lived together with the utmost harmony and cordiality prevailing at all times, yet that such was not the case is shown by the following: In 1685 the Friends of Haverford and other adjacent townships complained to Council against "Ye Indians for ye Rapine and Destruction of their Hoggs."

Haverford Street or road was laid out in 1683, probably by David Powell, who executed most of the surveys and resurveys in Haverford and Radnor townships. The Haverford and Darby road was laid out "by the Grand Jury and other neighbours," Twelfth month 7th, 1687. On May 8, 1696, a road was laid out from David Meredith's plantation in Radnor township to Haverford meeting-house. This road passes White Hall and west of Haverford College. At the same time, May, 1696, Ellis Ellis, supervisor, was ordered to cut and clear the roadway "which leads to the Limestone Hill from Darby thro Harford." A road from Henry Hames' (in Marple) to Haverford meeting-house was laid out in 1697. In describing the last part of the line, the foreman of the jury, Andrew Job, says, "running up the said line betwixt William Howell and David Lawrence, making the fence the middle of the road *till it comes to the fence* where we *pulled downe*, and so to the meeting-house where we end." Until the year 1700 the public highways were laid out by order of the grand jurors; after that date by viewers.

The men who controlled the township in early days were among the most prominent in the Welsh tract, and we may add of the county. In speaking of them Dr. George Smith has said, "It is even still more wonderful to see the large amounts that were appropriated to charitable purposes. This was particularly the case among the Welsh Friends. Every reasonable want was attended to. If a newly-arrived immigrant or a 'poor friend' stood in need of a house, it was built for him; of a plow or a cow, he was provided with one. The fields of the sick and the weak were not allowed to remain uncultivated, and their pecuniary wants and other necessities were liberally supplied. Nor was their care in these respects confined to their own little communities. Wherever suffering humanity was found our Quaker ancestors were ever ready to contribute liberally to its relief."

The following proves the last assertion of Dr. Smith to be correct, it being a receipt given by Edward Shippen, the first mayor of Philadelphia:

"This may certify that Friends of ye Monthly Meeting at Hartford yt David Lewellin paid into my hands for ye distressed in New England, fourteen pounds four shillings, assd about ye 7th Mo, last passed, for which sum I gave him a Receipt as witness my hand in Philadelphia, ye 23d of 12th Mo., 1697/8.

"EDW: SHIPPEN."

The taxables residing in the township in 1722 were Richard Hayes, Samuel Lewis, Henry Lewis, John Havard, Daniel Humphrey, David Llewellyn, David Lewis, Humphrey Ellis, John Parry, Henry Lawrence, Thomas Lawrence, Edward Jones, John Thomas, Samuel Rees, Rees Price, Thomas David, Walter Lloyd, Joseph Lewis, Griffith Evan, and Daniel Rees.

In 1754, in accordance with an order issued by the justices of the peace, then sitting as a Court of Quarter Sessions, etc., a list of township officials from 1682 to 1753, inclusive, was made out, which also showed the date of settlement in the township of such officers. From this list, which is still in part preserved in the township records, we learn that the following-named early residents of Haverford, to 1700, began their residence here during the years indicated:

Lewis David, Henry Lewis, William Howell, 1682; John Lewis, David Lawrence, Morris Llewellyn, Ralph Lewis, John Richard, William Sharpus, 1683; William Lewis, 1686; Richard Hayes, Thomas Rees, 1687; Humphrey Ellis, Ellis Rees, 1690; Robert Wharton, 1696; John Rees, 1698; Evan Williams, Abraham Lewis, and David Lewis, 1700.

In August, 1758, the tax-payers of Haverford were as follows:

Henry Lawrence, Samuel Humphrey, John Wilcox, Edward Humphrey, Lewis Davis, Charles Humphrey, Rowland Parry, William Lawrence, Jeremiah Ellis, Daniel Lawrence, Thomas Vaughan, Jane Lawrence, Anne Miller, David Llewellyn, Cloise Johnson, Obediah Wilder, Thomas Cornock, William Young, John Johnson, Samuel Johnson, William Brown, Philip Foreman, Daniel Thompson, John Lewis, John Ebelon, Tesley Guyger, Samuel Tuston, Isaac Tuston, Ludwick Knull, Griffith Owen, Frederick Bittle, William Ellis, Alexander Soley, William Thomas, David Cornock, Michael Kimball, James Dockerty, John Cook, Philip Tupper, James Sampson, William Townsend, John McCormick, George Schofield, Alexander McDowell, James Harper, Benjamin Hayes, Abraham Musgrove, John Vaughan, Robert Taylor, Isaac Vaughan, Thomas Ellis, Thomas Vaughan, Thomas Simons, and John Erle.

The early inhabitants of Haverford, being chiefly Friends, were opposed to wars and the fitting out of warlike expeditions among them. Yet that some of its residents participated in the expeditions under Braddock, Forbes, and Stanwix, as wagoners, etc., is proven by Roger Hunt's account-book, wherein are found the following entries:

"Haverford. Robert Armor entered one wagon Sept. 25. Credited by 5 bags of Speltz, weighing C, 8, 2, 22, and 6 bbls flour, weighing C, 13, 2, 22; mileage from Harford to Carlile and back, 222 miles. Whole amount £27 18s. 5¾d. Settled Oct. 27, 1759.

"Thomas Hubbart entered one wagon; credited by 112 days, July 11 to Oct. 31, 1760, @ 15s. 0d. Cash advanced, £30.

"Copy of Mr. Ourrey's Certificate and Discharge of William Jones, Wagon Driver for Mr. Thomas Hubbart's wagon for Haverford Township:

"'This certifies that I have this Day discharged Wm Jones, wagoner of George Aston's Brigade, with his wagon and Geers and two horses;

one of the others died in the service, the other strayed. He has received of Mr. Lindsay one pound sixteen and nine pence, and of me two pounds. Given under my Hand at Bedford this 30th day of Octr, 1759.

"'LT. OURREY.'"

Lieut. Ourrey was then in command of Fort Bedford, Bedford Co., Pa.

In 1760, Charles Humphrey, then township clerk, afterwards member of the Colonial Assembly and of the Continental Congress, made the following record in the township book:

"On first day of March, and at night, we had a violent Northeast Snow Storm, when, Considering the season of the Year and the time it Lasted (for about 18 hours), there was the greatest fall of snow that has been known since the Settlement of the Province, being upwards of Two feet deep, and lasted upwards of 8 days on the ground.

"March 16, 1760."

For many years all public meetings and *elections* were held "in the meeting-house," meaning Friends' Haverford meeting-house. In March, 1762, however, the township election was held "at the school-house."[1] This probably was about the date of building the first school-house, though it has not been ascertained where it was situated.

Charles Humphrey, township clerk in 1764, again says, "The following is an account of a surprising phenomenon which Happened on the 25th of July, 1764, at 40 minutes past 7 o'clock in the evening. There was a Ball of fire near the north east, about 50 degrees above the Horizon. It took its Course near northwest, its diameter at times Considerably bigger than that of the Sun. Especially at one time it opened, so as seemingly it would have separated itself; it appeared like huge, flaming, sheets of fire, inclining together like that of a new-blown Rose; its sound, as it went (which was very swift) was Like that of a great fire urged by a strong wind. It kept near of one Heighth all the way, till it had crossed the Meridian to the north, aboute 20 degrees, where was a small Cloud, which seemed as if it attracted it. It mounted Higher, and just as it seemingly touched the Outward Edge of the Cloud it Broke into Thousands of pieces like that of springing a mine, when the pieces and particles would all be in a flame. When, as near as Could be guessed, in aboute 30 seconds of Time came the Report which was like the firing of Large Cannon. The sound of it Lasted one full minute, it had something Exceedingly Remarkable in its Centre like a bar of iron which appeared to be very Hot out of which there Came Sparks of fire as it went."

At the beginning of the Revolutionary war, 1775, the township taxables numbered seventy-one, representing a total population of about three hundred and fifty. After the American defeat at Brandywine and the consequent occupation of this region by the British army, the people of Haverford suffered terribly by depredations committed by British troops. A few days subsequent to the battle of Brandywine, Gen. Washington with the American army marched from Germantown, on the Lancaster road, to and several miles beyond the Buck Tavern, in Haverford, for the purpose of again engaging Howe's army, but a violent and protracted rain-storm forced him to suspend further operations and retire. On the 10th, 11th, and 12th days of December, 1777, Cornwallis, with a detachment of the British army, made a sally from Philadelphia into Haverford and adjoining townships, and at that inclement season of the year stripped many families of all their provisions, their stock and provender, and many articles of household furniture. The losses then sustained by the inhabitants of Haverford amounted to more than three thousand four hundred pounds sterling.

"The month of February, 1779," says township clerk Charles Humphrey, "was a Remarkable fine, warm, and spring-like wether all thro, the frogs crying and spawning, Maple and alder blossoms in full Bloom, peach blossoms in many places, English Cherry trees very forward, some blossomed out, apple tree buds beginning to leaf, insomuch that vegetation was moved in allmost every vegetable. Corn in the ground looked well and promising, but March turned the face of everything, Rain, frost, and snow, high winds and storms, every other Day all thro."

In 1780, when steps were taken for the gradual abolition of slavery in Pennsylvania, *twenty-six* slaves were held in Haverford, but none in Radnor.

In 1786 the taxable inhabitants of Haverford were as follows:

William Brooke, William Burns, Jonathan Buckman, Thomas Cornogg, Abraham Cornogg, John Cornogg, Lewis Davis, Jesse Davis, John Davis, Caleb Davis, William Davis, George Dunn, Peter Dehaven, Sarah Ellis, Jesse Ellis, David Ellis, Jonathan Ellis, William Free, Griffith Davis, Andrew Frederick, Samuel Gracy, Samuel Griffith, Han. Humphrey, Edward Hughes, Mary Hayworth, George Hayworth, Robert Holland, Aaron Johnson, Hugh Jones, Samuel Leedom, John Lindsay, David Lowden, David Lyon, Simon Litzenberg, Catharine Lukens, Anthony Lewis, Abraham Lloyd, Francis Lee, Mary Miller, William McClure, John Moore, Nicholas Pechine, Henry Lawrence, Joseph Powell, George Powell, Hugh Quinn, John Ross, Philip Sheaff, Richard Willing, Obadiah Wiley, Felix Wershing, Joseph Worrall, Martin Wise, Nathan Jones, Thomas Terry, Richard Humphrey, and Johnson Vaughan.

Inmates.—Duncan Johnson, William Downey, John Hayworth, Samuel McClure, Richard Tippons, Samuel Burrows, Joseph Webster, Jonathan Haycock, Michael Timple, Zachariah Long, Daniel McElroy, Edward Hughes, and William Sheaff.

Freemen.—William Lincoln, John Graville, John Free, John Point, John Stevens, John Holland, Jacob Vaughan, Edward Leedom, George Stump, William Lloyd, and Jonathan Worrall.

The Philadelphia and Lancaster turnpike road crosses the northeast corner of the township. The company was incorporated in 1792, and the road was completed in 1794, at a cost of four hundred and sixty-five thousand dollars. It was the first turnpike road constructed in America.

At the beginning of this—the nineteenth—century Haverford's taxables were mentioned as follows:

William Brooke (brigade inspector), Jane Burns, Thomas Brooke (miller), Benjamin Bevan, George Bonsall (blacksmith), Joseph Bond, William Bittle (innkeeper), Amos Bradshaw (grist- and saw-mill), Isaac

[1] In March, 1798, the minutes inform us, the township election was "held at the *new* school-house."

Bittle, Abraham Cornog, Abraham Chapman, John Cornog, John Cochran (shoemaker), Lewis Davis, Joseph Davis (tanner), Jesse Davis, Griffith Davis, William Davis, John Davis, Samuel Davis, William Dickinson, John Dickinson, Jesse Ellis, Jonathan Ellis, Isaac Ellis (blacksmith), Rudolph Epwright (weaver), Jacob Spright, John Free, Andrew Frederick (shoemaker), John Timple, John Gracy (wheelwright), Edward Gill, George Hayworth (carpenter), John Hughes (fulling mill "going to decay," and saw-mill), Richard Humphrey, John Jones, Aaron Johnson, Jacob Johnson, William Johnson, Mary Jones, John Jones, Ludwig Knull, John Lindsay (justice of the peace), William Llewellyn, Anthony Lewis, David Lyons, Edward Lobb (millwright), Amos Lukens (joiner), Adam Litzenberg, Jacob Litzenberg (cooper), Simon Litzenberg (cooper), Mordecai Lewis, Samuel Leedom, Samuel Lewis (tailor), Mary Miller, Patience Morgan, Jonathan Miller (innkeeper), Joseph Powell, George Powell, Nicholas Pechin, Hugh Queen, John Ross (owner of the "Grange"), John Dickinson, Benjamin H Smith, Philip Sheaff, Jacob Stanley, Valentine Smith, Matthias Snyder, Alexander Symington (storekeeper), Richard Tippins (shoemaker), Christian Vaughan, Joshua Vaughan, Johnson Vaughan, Garrett Van Buskirk, Keziah Wilday, George Willing, Maris Worrall (storekeeper, grist-, and saw mill owner), and Casper Weist

Inmates—Edward Fowler (wheelwright), John Hay, Reuben Lewis, Philip Litzenberg (cooper), Daniel Leedom (weaver), John Powell, Jesse Moore, Joseph Rogers (miller), Jonathan Vaughan, Daniel McElroy, John Van Buskirk, Samuel Wright (carpenter), and Martin Wise

Single Freemen.—David Bittle (mason), Hugh Carm (carpenter), Thomas Ellis (carpenter), William Garrett (storekeeper), William Haskins and Andrew Lindsay (blacksmiths), Jesse Maddock (tailor), Thomas Downs, Abraham Free, Joseph Griffith, Amos Griffith, John Lindsay, Jr, William Lindsay, William Litzenberg, Edmund Leedom, William Lyons, John Little, Joseph Powell, John Stephens, Yorb Van Buskirk, Joseph Van Buskirk, Jacob Vaughan, George Weist, Garrett Van Horn, Jonathan Ellis, Isaac Ellis, Amos Lukens, and Jonathan Miller

Since that day the improvements made in Haverford have been vast and varied Its inhabitants have ever kept in the advance line in the onward march of the nation, and its lands, lying as they do just without the limits of a great city, are very fertile and highly prized

We now turn to other topics which are treated under separate headings, but before doing so will add the following, which was made a matter of record by the township clerk

"Be it remembered that the winter of 1828 was the most mild winter in the recollection of the oldest people then living, there being scarcely any snow and but very little ice, and followed by the winter of 1829, which was the coldest that had been for many years, there being two months of study Freezing"

Early Mills, etc—Haverford Mill—As early as the year 1688 a small grist mill, known as the "Haverford Mill," was built on Cobb's Creek,[1] near where that stream is crossed by the road leading past Haverford meeting-house Its original owner is unknown By searching the records, however, a little light is thrown on the history of this, one of the first mills built in Pennsylvania Thus, Fourth month (June) 12, 1700, Richard Hayes, attorney for William Howell, acknowledged a deed to David Lloyd, attorney for Rowland Powell, "for ninety seven acres of land with a mill called Haverford Mill, and all other appurtenances and improvements thereunto belonging," the deed bearing date Third month 30th, 1700 This seems to indicate that William Howell, one of the first settlers of the township, was the original owner of "Haverford Mill" Friends' meeting-house, in Haverford, was also built upon the same tract, a tract which came into the possession of Howell in May, 1682 In October, 1703, Daniel Humphrey became the owner of two hundred and forty-one acres of land, of which the east line was Cobb's Creek, and the south line the road on which Friends' meeting-house stands Humphrey's land included the mill-property above mentioned Subsequently, Charles Humphrey[2] (son of Daniel, and a member of the Continental Congress at the time of signing the Declaration of Independence), together with his brothers, became the owners of the mill property, which also included fulling- and saw-mills Thus, in 1766, Edward Humphrey was mentioned as the owner of the fulling-mill, and Charles Humphrey of the grist- and saw mills The latter owned the grist- and fulling-mills in 1782 He died in 1786, but this mill property continued in the hands of the Humphrey family until about 1826, when Dennis Kelly purchased it and changed the buildings into a woolen and cotton manufactory, under the name of the "Castle Hill Mills"

Haverford New Mill—On Fourth month (June) 14, 1698, Richard Hayes, Jr, before mentioned as Howell's attorney in the transfer of Haverford Mill to Powell, became the owner of one hundred and sixty acres of land, of which Darby Creek formed the western boundary On this property, about the year 1707, Hayes, with David Morris and Samuel Lewis, erected a grist-mill, for a long time known as "Haverford New Mill" (now as Leedom s mill), which he managed himself till his death, in 1738 This property, with a saw-mill attached, belonged to Maris Worrell in 1802 Eighteen years later it was still in his possession In 1826 it was owned by Elisha Worrell and occupied by Thomas Steel In 1830 it was managed by Joseph Leedom, Elisha Worrell still being the owner. In 1875 it was owned by Maris W Leedom It is now owned by the latter's widow

Abram C Lukens, now living at Upland, speaks of this mill property as follows "The old mill stood a little farther up the stream When the new mill was built, the gudgeon was lost in the creek One of the workmen dived for it The instrument was heavy, and as the man stayed under water a long time, seemingly, it was feared for a moment that he, too, was gone, but finally he came up, struggling and safe, with the recovered article in his hands" The mill now in operation, and of which Lukens speaks, was built in 1832

Ellis' Fulling-Mill.—In 1694, Tenth month, 2d day, Humphrey Ellis purchased two hundred and twenty acres of land, of which Darby Creek formed the western boundary On this property a very early fulling-mill was erected, and successfully operated In 1790

[1] The Indian name of Cobb's Creek was Rarakung

[2] It will be remembered that Charles Humphrey, with three other Pennsylvania members, voted against the Declaration of Independence

it was owned by Humphrey Ellis, a son of Humphrey Ellis first mentioned by a second marriage.

Brown's (Garrigues') Mills.—About the year 1800, Peter Brown became the owner and operator of grist- and saw-mills, which stood on the head-waters of Cobb's Creek. On Feb. 11, 1802, he sold this property to William Hill, William White,[1] and Miers Fisher. It then consisted of one hundred and thirty acres of land, with grist- and saw-mill. On the 1st of July, 1807, the parties above mentioned transferred the mills and property belonging to Samuel Garrigues, "House Carpenter." The mills were run by the latter for a few years, but by reason of a scarcity of water were finally abandoned. In 1826 this mill property was mentioned, by a Delaware County committee, on the subject of manufactories, etc., as "an old stone grist-mill, which has been out of use for several years past." On the 26th of July, 1834, Samuel Garrigues sold two acres of this tract to the Haverford School Association, and the same are now included with the lands owned by Haverford College.

There are some, doubtless, who will question the existence of the Brown Mills. Indeed, Abram C. Lukens, for a time, stoutly maintained that such mills never existed, but finally remembered having seen the ruins of an old mill there. The volume of water in these small streams was much greater eighty years ago than it is now.

Lawrence's Mills.—A saw-mill, owned at various times by Henry Lawrence, and his sons Thomas, Mordecai, and William, was erected about the beginning of this century on Darby Creek, near where that stream is crossed by the West Chester turnpike. Prior to that time, however, an old fulling-mill had occupied the same mill-seat (standing on the north side of the present turnpike), which, probably, was the one owned by Humphrey Ellis in 1790. In 1832 a stone grist-mill (the present one) was built by William Lawrence, just below the saw-mill. These mills have since been in the possession of members of the Lawrence family, and are now owned by Thomas D. Lawrence. They have been leased and operated by John E. Stanley and his father for the twenty-two years last passed.

Miller's Mills.—About the year 1810, Jonathan Miller built grist- and saw-mills on Cobb's Creek, just above the mill privilege, soon after utilized for the manufacture of gunpowder. A few years later David Quinn became associated with him in the business and served as manager. In 1827, Samuel Leedom took charge. For a number of years prior to that time the latter had operated Joshua Humphrey's mill, which was situated a short distance above Miller's, on the same creek. In 1844, Mr. Leedom purchased the Miller Mills, and lived there till his death, which occurred some twelve years ago. Augustus B. Leedom then became the owner, to be succeeded in a few years by one Lombert. The latter was in turn succeeded by the present owner, George Dickinson, who purchased the property in February, 1879, and came here to reside in April of the following year.

Nitre Hall Mills.—These mills, used for the manufacture of gunpowder, began operations prior to the beginning of the war of 1812–15. They were owned and managed by Israel Wheelen and William Rogers, Jr., until about 1825. Rogers alone then conducted the business until his death, which occurred about 1840, when Dennis Kelly purchased the property and converted the principal building into a woolen- and cotton-factory. It remained in the possession of Kelly and his heirs until March, 1880, when George Callahan became its owner by purchase. John and Thomas Burns, the present managers, have been identified with these mills for seventeen years. Fifteen hands are now employed, and about seven thousand pounds of cotton and woolen yarns are manufactured per month.

Kelly's Woolen- and Cotton Mills.—About 1814, Dennis Kelly, with borrowed capital, purchased a mill-seat on Cobb's Creek from Isaac Ellis, and erected thereon a small stone woolen-factory, now known as the "Clinton Mills." His venture proved to be highly successful, and soon after, with George Wiest as a partner, the remainder of Ellis' lands were bought, and the capacity of Clinton Mills considerably enlarged. Not a long time elapsed, however, before Mr. Kelly was again conducting his business alone. He furnished the United States government, per contract, large quantities of goods for the use of the army and navy. His mills were worked to their greatest capacity, and he accumulated wealth rapidly. About 1826 he purchased Joshua Humphrey's grist-mill, and changing it to a cotton- and woolen-factory, gave it the name of "Castle Hill Mills." Samuel Rhoads, as lessee, occupied this mill for a number of years. On the 20th of February, 1834, it caught fire from the picker, and was entirely consumed, the insurance of ten thousand dollars covering but a small part of the loss. After this mill was rebuilt it was leased for some ten years to John Hazlitt. George Bumley, James Howorth, Boyle, and Calleghan were also prominent lessees and operators at different times of Kelly's mills. Up to the time of his death Mr. Kelly was widely known as one of the most successful manufacturers of cloths in the State of Pennsylvania. He died in July, 1864, worth nearly one-half million dollars.

Boyle's Mills.—About fifteen years ago John Boyle erected the large four-story building located just above Castle Hill Mills, which yet stands as a monument to his name. Intended for the manufacture of cotton and woolen goods, they are inactive, and have been so for some five or six years.

[1] William White was then doctor of divinity of the Protestant Episcopal Church, and later was far famed as a distinguished bishop of the same denomination.

Other Mill Interests.—Besides the mills already mentioned, a few others, as well as tanneries, etc., were established and operated here during years long passed, of which traces are only to be found in early assessment-rolls. Hence, in the endeavor to give an impartial list of the manufacturing interests of the township from 1766 to 1830, we turn to these rolls and find that the mills and the owners of them during the years indicated were as follows:

1766. Edward Humphrey, fulling-mill; Charles Humphrey, grist- and saw-mills.

1770. Isaac Davis, grist- and saw-mills.

1779. Elisha Worrall, grist- and saw-mills.

1782. Charles Humphrey, grist- and fulling-mills.

1788. Humphrey Ellis, part of fulling-mill; Francis Lee, saw-mill; John Moore, grist- and saw-mills; Philip Sheaff, tannery.

1790. Thomas Brooke, grist-mill; Joseph Davis, tannery; Humphrey Ellis, fulling-mill; Francis Lee, saw-mill; John Moore, grist- and saw-mill; Philip Sheaff, saw-mill.

1802. Peter Brown, stone grist- and saw-mill on head-waters of Cobb's Creek; Joseph Davis, tannery; James Tyson, saw-mill and old fulling-mill; Enoch Watkins, stone grist-mill; Maris Worrell, grist- and saw-mill.

1807. Joseph Davis, tannery; Mordecai Lawrence, saw-mill; James Tyson and John Dolen, saw- and fulling-mill; Enoch Watkins, stone grist-mill; Samuel Garrigues, stone grist- and saw-mill, the property formerly owned by Peter Brown.

1809. Samuel Garrigues, grist-mill; E. Leedom, saw-mill; Mordecai Lawrence, saw-mill; Joseph Mathews, grist-mill.

1811. Joseph Davis, tannery; Jonathan Miller, grist- and saw-mill; Thomas Steel, grist-mill; Maris Worrell, grist- and saw-mill.

1817. Joseph Davis, tannery; Francis Gaucher, paper-mill; Mordecai Lawrence, saw-mill; Jonathan Miller, saw-mill; Robert Steel and Charles Leedom, grist-mill; Dennis Kelly and George Wiest, fulling- and carding-mills; Israel Wheelen, powder-mills; Maris Worrell, saw- and grist-mill.

1820–22. Edward Humphrey, paper-mill; Joshua Humphrey and —— Leedom, grist-mill; Dennis Kelly, woolen-factory; Jonathan Miller and —— Quinn, grist- and saw-mill; William Rogers, eight powder-mills and refinery; Maris Worrell, grist- and saw-mill.

From a report of a committee of Delaware County citizens made in 1826, on the subject of manufactories and unimproved mill-seats, we obtain the following pertinent items regarding Haverford township:

"On Cobb's Creek, in Haverford, a mill-seat, on lands of Manuel Eyre, about where the creek ceases to be the dividing line of Philadelphia and Delaware Counties.

"On Cobb's Creek, in Haverford, a cotton-factory; head and fall about 14 feet; owned and occupied by Dennis Kelly; drives 628 spindles; manufactured last year 26,194 pounds of cotton-yarn; employs about 12 hands.

"On Cobb's Creek, in Haverford, 'Nitre Hall Powder-Mills;' head and fall from 22 to 34 feet, on the various mills owned and occupied by William Rogers, Jr.; manufactured last year about 10,000 qr. casks of gunpowder; employs about 20 men; a large mansion-house and tenements for 10 families.

"On Cobb's Creek, in Haverford, a mill-seat; head and fall about 12 feet, on lands of Jonathan Miller.

"On Cobb's Creek, in Haverford, a grist-mill and saw-mill; head and fall about 20 feet; owned by Jonathan Miller, and occupied by David Quinn.

"On Cobb's Creek, in Haverford, a grist-mill, head and fall about 20 feet, owned by Joshua Humphrey and others, and occupied by Samuel Leedom.

"On Cobb's Creek, in Haverford, a large woolen-factory; head and fall 16 feet; owned and occupied by Dennis Kelly; has 1 pair of stocks, 4 carding-engines of 24 inches, 2 bellies of 50 spindles each, 3 jennies of 75 spindles each, 10 power-looms; manufactures about 2500 yards of cotton and woolen goods per week; employs about 60 hands; dwelling-houses for 10 families.

"Near the head of Cobb's Creek, in Haverford, an old stone grist-mill; head and fall 18 feet; owned by Samuel Garrigues; has been out of use for several years past.

"On Darby Creek, in Haverford township, an ancient grist-mill and saw-mill; head and fall about 10 feet, to which two feet more may be added; owned by Elisha Worrell, and occupied by Thomas Steele; grinds from 12 to 15,000 bushels of grain, grist, and merchant work per annum. Also cuts about 85,000 feet of lumber per annum.

"On Darby Creek, in Haverford and Marple, a mill-seat; head and fall about 12 feet; on lands of Mordecai Lawrence and others.

"On Darby Creek, in Haverford, a saw-mill; head and fall 10 feet and 6 inches; owned by Mordecai Lawrence and others, occupied by John Richards; cuts about 30,000 feet of lumber per annum.

"On Darby Creek, in Haverford and Marple, a mill-seat; head and fall about 10 or 11 feet, on land of the heirs of William Moore, deceased, and others. [Probably the site of John Moore's grist- and saw-mill, 1790.]

"On Ithon Creek, or east branch of Darby Creek, in Haverford, a mill-seat; head and fall 7 or 8 feet; on lands of Gen. William Brooke." This probably was the site of the grist-mill assessed to Thomas Brooke in 1790.

The mills, etc., of the township in 1829–30, according to the assessment-rolls for those years, were as follows: Lewis Davis, tannery; Dennis Kelly, lower factory (stone), dry-house, two frame dwellings, five stone dwellings, upper factory (stone), fulling-mill, stone grist-mill, seven stone dwellings, four frame dwellings; Clermont Lawrence, stone grist-mill and saw-mill; Jonathan Miller and Samuel Leedom, grist- and saw-mill; Elisha Worrell and Joseph Leedom, grist- and saw-mill.

The grist- and saw-mills and woolen- and cotton-factories in operation in the township at the present time (1884) are as follows: Leedom's saw- and grist-mills, on Darby Creek; Lawrence's grist- and saw-mills, on Darby Creek; Dickinson's (formerly Miller's) grist- and saw-mills, on Cobb's Creek; Callahan's (Nitre Hall Mills) cotton- and woolen-factory, on Cobb's Creek; and Taylor Wolfenden & Co.'s (Castle Hill Mills) woolen-factory, on Cobb's Creek. The "Castle Hill Mills," under the management of Messrs. Taylor Wolfenden & Co., lessees, are running nearly to their utmost capacity. More than one hundred operatives are furnished with steady employment, and about ten thousand dollars' worth of fine cassimeres are manufactured per month.

Schools.—Doubtless schools of some kind were established and maintained in an irregular manner from the date of the first settlement of the township, but for many years thereafter all records now available are silent respecting them. On the 28th of October, 1799, however, Joseph Davis, Abraham Lewis, George Hayworth, and John Gracey, as trustees, purchased of Jesse Davis a lot in the southwest part of the township, near the present school building, "for the purpose of erecting a school-house thereon, and for no other purpose or use." In the stone structure which was soon after erected upon this lot John Hayes and David Bond were early teachers. It continued to be used for educational purposes until 1883, when the present substantial stone school-house was erected, on a lot purchased of John Leedom, and the old school property was abandoned.

On the Townsend Cooper property, formerly owned by Levi Lukens, a stone school-house was built by John Lukens, Robert Clark, John Hayes, and others, about 1814. The children of William Johnson, Levi Lukens, Dennis Kelly, and George Smith attended at this school-house. It was torn down about the year 1835, having been discontinued as a school-house for several years prior to that date.

About 1830 another school-house was built, on the lands of Jonathan Miller. It is still in use, and is located near the grist-mill of George Dickinson, on Cobb's Creek. John Moore was known as a teacher there for several years. On a corner of the Darby road and a road leading from West Chester road to Clinton Mills a stone school-house was built about 1874, on a lot purchased from William Davis. Another school-house was erected, date unknown, on Mrs. Sarah O'Connor's property, east of Cobb's Creek, and near the Montgomery County line.

After the passage of the school law, in 1834, the court appointed inspectors of schools in each township, who served till directors were elected. The inspectors appointed for Haverford were Bertine Smith and John Williams. The amount of school moneys received by the township from State and county in 1835 was $573.44.

Following is a list of the school directors elected in Haverford township since and including the year 1840, as found of record in Media:

1840, John Leedom, Samuel Leedom; 1842, John Gracey, Thomas D. Lawrence; 1843, Samuel Leedom, James A. Moore; 1844, Adam C. Eckfeldt, Archibald Gray; 1845, George Pyatt, David Sell; 1846, Philip Sheaff, William V. Black; 1847, Bartine Smith, Thomas H. West; 1848, James A. Moore, George Pyatt; 1849, Thomas D. Lawrence, Philip Sheaff; 1850, Bartine Smith, Thomas H. West; 1851, Jackson Lyons, Mordecai Lawrence; 1852, James A. Moore, Davis Sill; 1853, William Bittle, Bartine Smith; 1854, Mordecai Lawrence, James A. Moore; 1855, Davis Sill, Thomas D. Lawrence; 1856, Bartine Smith, William Bittle; 1857, Edwin Johnson, David Bond; 1858, B. Lindsay, Charles Johnson; 1859, Henry McAllister, John Leedom; 1860, W. H. Eagle, W. W. Leedom; 1861, no report found; 1862, John Leedom, —— Haydock; 1863, C. P. Bittle, D. R. Ralston; 1864, Charles Johnson, A. B. Leedom; 1865, James Smith, William C. Hawkins; 1866, C. P. Bittle, John H. Clemens; 1867, William C. Hawkins, Charles Johnson; 1868, Joseph Leedom; 1869, C. P. Bittle, Edwin Johnson; 1870, William C. Hawkins, William C. Jones; 1871, Joseph Leedom, Joseph T. McClellan; 1872, C. P. Bittle, W. M. Callahan; 1873, Charles Johnson, William C. Hawkins; 1874, Joseph Leedom, John Johnson; 1875, C. P. Bittle, Morgan B. Davis; 1876, Charles Johnson, Lewis K. Esrey; 1877, James Leedom, R. N. Lee; 1878, C. Pennell Bittle, Florence Lockwood; 1879, Charles Johnson, Lewis K. Esrey; 1880, Taylor Wolfenden, Joseph Leedom; 1881, Florence Lockwood, Charles Getz; 1882, Robert N. Lee, Charles Johnson; 1883, Frank Ebright, Joseph T. McClellan; 1884, William Carter, Joseph Leedom.

Haverford College.—This celebrated and prosperous institution holds an estate of about two hundred and twenty acres in the northern part of the township of Haverford. It was founded in the year 1832 by prominent members of the society of Friends in the Middle States, the larger number being residents of Philadelphia and its vicinity. The purpose of its founders was to provide a place for the instruction of their sons in the higher learning, and for moral training, which should be free from the temptations prevalent at many of the larger colleges. A tract consisting at first of forty acres, but gradually enlarged until it now contains upwards of seventy, was set off by an experienced English landscape-gardener and planted with a large variety of trees, to constitute the academic grove in which the college buildings should stand. This park is now the most beautiful which any American college can boast, and the exquisite undulations of its surface, its stately trees, its winding walks, and its green and well-kept turf attract many admiring visitors.

The "Founders' Hall," as it is now called, a large and well-constructed building, was finished in 1833, and in the autumn of that year "Haverford School" was opened. This modest title, corresponding with the unostentatious spirit of its founders, was borne for upwards of twenty years, although a full collegiate course of study was pursued from the beginning. Early in 1856, however, the institution was incorporated as a college, with the right of conferring academic degrees.

Barclay Hall, built in 1876, a strikingly beautiful

building of Port Deposit granite, furnishes studies and bedrooms for eighty students. Others are accommodated in Founders' Hall. There are two astronomical observatories,—one built in 1852, the other in 1884. These contain a refracting equatorial telescope of ten inches aperture, by Clark; a refracting equatorial telescope of eight and one-fourth inches aperture, by Fitz; an alt-azimuth reflecting telescope of eight and one-fourth inches aperture; a fixed transit instrument of four inches aperture, with circles twenty-six inches in diameter; a zenith instrument of one and three-fourths inches aperture, with micrometer and circles; a chronograph, connected by electricity with all the instruments, which records the exact time of observations to the tenth of a second; two sidereal clocks; a filar micrometer; a spectroscope made by Grubb, with a train of ten prisms; a polarizing eye-piece for solar work; a sextant; and a valuable library of astronomical literature.

The students have free access to the observatory, and enjoy such advantages for observatory practice as are seldom offered. The director of the observatory, Professor Sharpless, is a man of great knowledge and wide fame.

A tasteful and well-proportioned building, erected in 1863-64, contains the library and Alumni Hall, the latter being used for lectures, society meetings, and the public exercises of the college. Here some fifteen thousand volumes are always ready for the use of the students, selected with great care in all departments of knowledge. A large number of the best European and American periodicals are taken in. The library is regarded as inferior in importance and usefulness to no other department of the college.

A carpenters' shop was built soon after the opening of the school, as a place where the boys might find profitable exercise and amusement in the use of tools. This was fitted up in 1884 for the use of the department of mechanical engineering, and contains a forge, steam-engines, and a variety of machines and tools for the use of students in that department.

The chemical laboratory was built in 1853 (a room in Founders' Hall having previously been used for the purpose), and has several times been enlarged and improved. It is now very commodious, amply furnished, and under very skillful management. Under it is a beautiful gymnasium, which is supplied with the apparatus of Dr. Sargent, the director of the Harvard gymnasium. Exercise here is required of the students, under the direction of an experienced physician.

In Founders' Hall there is a museum of natural history, and a physical laboratory. This hall contains also the recitation-rooms and the dining-hall.

Among the most distinguished officers and instructors of the school and college have been Daniel B. Smith, John Gummere, Joseph Thomas, Samuel J. Gummere, Henry D. Gregory, Paul Swift, Hugh D. Vail, Joseph Harlan, George Stuart, Moses C. Stevens, Clement L. Smith, Albert Leeds, Henry Hartshorne, Edward D. Cope, and John H. Dillingham. The officers in 1884 are as follows: President, Thomas Chase, a graduate of Harvard University, who received in 1878 the honorary degree of Doctor of Laws from Harvard, and in 1880 that of Doctor of Literature from Haverford. He was a member of the American company of revisers of the English translation of the New Testament, and is the editor of a series of classical text-books which are very widely used. Dean, Isaac Sharpless, a graduate of Harvard in the scientific school, and honored with the degree of Doctor of Science by the University of Pennsylvania in 1883. Professor Sharpless is a man of wide scientific distinction, and is the author of excellent text-books in geometry, astronomy, and physics. Pliny Earle Chase, LL.D., also a graduate of Harvard, is the professor of Philosophy and Logic. He holds very high rank among living thinkers and men of science, and his philosophical and scientific papers have been widely published, both in this country and in Europe. Allen C. Thomas, a graduate and master of arts of Haverford, is the accomplished and learned professor of History, Political Economy, and Rhetoric. Lyman B. Hall, a graduate of Amherst, and Ph.D. of the University of Göttingen, is professor of Chemistry and Physics, and a thorough master of these sciences. Edwin Davenport, A.B. and A.M. of Harvard, a brilliant and distinguished scholar, is professor of Latin and Greek. Henry Carvill Lewis, graduate and Master of Arts of the University of Pennsylvania, one of the foremost men of science in America, is the professor of Geology. The other instructors are men of distinction and promise. Thomas Newlin, of the University of Michigan, professor of Zoology and Botany, and Curator of the museum. James Beatty, Jr., a graduate of the Stevens Institute, professor of Engineering Branches. Walter M. Ford, M.D., instructor in Physical Training. William Earl Morgan, a graduate and Master of Arts of Penn College, assistant astronomical observer; and William F. Wickersham, asssistant librarian.

The following regular courses of study are pursued at the college: I. A course in classics, mathematics, general literature, modern languages, and science, for the degree of Bachelor of Arts. II. A course in general science and literature, and modern languages, for the degree of Bachelor of Science. III. A more specialized course in practical science and engineering, together with modern languages, for the degree of Bachelor of Science or for special degrees. The requisites for admission are substantially the same as at other first-class colleges.

The college claims, in its published circulars, special advantages for its students. These are, "First, good moral and religious influences. Endeavors are made to imbue the minds and hearts of the students with the fundamental truths of the Christian religion, and to train them by the inculcation of pure morals and the restraints of a judicious discipline. No student is admitted without a certificate of character from his last instructor, and none believed to be of low moral character are retained. Second, thorough scholarship. The teaching is of high quality; the classes are small enough to allow regular performance of work and the opportunity for individual instruction. The absence of the constant distractions which attend life at many colleges, and the example and influence of the professors, enables a large amount of honest work to be done, so that the standard of graduation is high. Third, the healthfulness of the student life. In the large and beautiful lawns every facility is given, right at the doors, for cricket, baseball, foot-ball, tennis, archery, and other field games. The gymnasium furnishes judicious physical training, under the care of a skillful physician. The rooms are pleasant, the table and service good, and all the conditions wholesome."

Haverford College, from its modest beginnings, has slowly but surely won a position among the foremost literary institutions of the country, and may justly be counted an honor to the county and the commonwealth in which it stands. In October, 1883, it celebrated the fiftieth anniversary of its opening. Six hundred of the old students assembled on its beautiful grounds, and their high character and eminence gave a striking testimonial to the merits of their Alma Mater.

Churches—Haverford Meeting-House.—Friends' meeting-house in Haverford township, the oldest place of worship in Delaware County, was erected in 1688 or 1689. The first marriage solemnized in it was that of Lewis David to Florence Jones, at a meeting held First month (March) 20th, 1690. The south, or what is now known as "the old end" of the structure, was built in 1700, at a cost of about one hundred and fifty-eight pounds. It was erected as an addition to the meeting-house of 1688 or 1689, which original building was replaced by the present "new end" in the year 1800. At the date last mentioned the part built one hundred years before was modernized somewhat in its outside appearance, by changing the pitch of the roof and in substituting wooden sash in the windows for those of lead. The gallery was originally at the south end of the building. It is also claimed that a number of chestnut boards with which the house was at first lined are still in place. For many years the original building and its annex of 1700 was without a chimney, being warmed with a kind of stove or furnace, placed on each side of the audience-room, and supplied with fuel from the outside. Only the tops of these stoves were of iron, and the smoke escaped by flues opening on the outside of the wall, a few feet above the opening through which the fuel was introduced. Part of this arrangement is yet conspicuous in the walls of the old end of the meeting-house.

Soon after the completion of the building erected in 1700, Governor William Penn visited Haverford and preached in the new meeting-house. Yet from the fact that the Welsh language was the prevailing dialect then spoken in Haverford, and that the majority of its inhabitants at that time could speak no other, many of his hearers could not understand him.

Sutcliff, an English Quaker, who visited the province about the time of Penn's second visit to America, mentions another incident concerning the Governor which is pertinent to the history of Haverford meeting-house. A little girl named Rebecca Wood was walking from Darby, where she resided, to Haverford meeting-house, when Penn, who was proceeding to the same place on horseback, overtook her and inquired where she was going. Upon being informed, "he with his usual good nature, desired her to get up behind him; and bringing his horse to a convenient place, she mounted, and so rode away upon the bare back, and being without shoes or stockings, her bare legs and feet hung dangling by the side of the Governor's horse."

The burial-ground attached to Haverford meeting-house was laid out in 1684. During the same year the first interment was made in these grounds, it being the body of William Sharpus, who was buried Ninth month 19th. More than one hundred years later another burial was made in the same place, which attracted many people. The circumstances are related by Dr. Smith, as follows:

"In the winter of 1788 a very tragic affair happened on Darby Creek, where it forms the line between Marple and Haverford, in the death by drowning of Lydia Hollingsworth, a young lady of great worth and beauty, who was under an engagement of marriage to David Lewis. The party, consisting of Lewis, Lydia, another young lady, and the driver, left the city in the morning in a sleigh, and drove out to Joshua Humphreys, near Haverford meeting-house, and from thence they drove to Newtown; but before they returned the weather moderated and some rain fell, which caused Darby Creek to rise. In approaching the ford (which was on the road leading from the Presbyterian Church to Cooperstown), they were advised not to attempt to cross, but were made acquainted with the existence of a temporary bridge in the meadows above. They drove to the bridge, but the water was rushing over it, and the driver refused to proceed; whereupon Lewis took the lines, and, missing the bridge, plunged the whole party into the flood. All were rescued but Lydia, whose body was not found till the next morning. The feelings of Lewis can be more readily imagined than described. The young lady was buried at Friends' graveyard, Haverford. In some pathetic rhymes written on the occasion it is stated that 1700 persons attended her funeral."

Haverford meeting-house occupies one of the most beautiful and commanding sites in the township. Regular meetings are held there each week, the Friends usually attending being from twenty to thirty in number. A Friends' meeting-house is also located near the Haverford College grounds.

St. Dennis' Church.—This, the first Catholic Church edifice erected in Delaware County, stands near Haverford meeting-house, and was built during the year 1825. Dennis Kelly, the well-known woolen and cotton manufacturer, donated its site and the land for the burial-grounds, and also was the greatest contributor to the fund for its erection. It was built for the accommodation of those of the Catholic faith who were employed in Kelly's mills, on Cobb's Creek The original structure was small, plain, and unpretentious in its appearance A few years ago, however, it was remodeled and enlarged, and now presents a very pleasing aspect both within and without Dennis Kelly, who might be termed its founder, lies buried within its shadows, he having departed this life July 21, 1864, aged nearly eighty-five years

Bethesda Methodist Episcopal Church—The society existing under this name was organized in October, 1831, under the pastoral charge of Rev William Crider The church edifice, which is located in the southwest quarter of the township, about one-half mile southwest from the Eagle Tavern, was erected in 1832 It was considerably enlarged in 1871 Among the original members of the organization were John Gracy and wife, I P Jonas, Charles Cunningham, Michael Lincoln and wife, John Foy, Bushrod W Horton and wife, Lewis Wright, John Wright, Richard Timple, William Palmer, Isaac Anderson, Samuel Pippin, Charles Peirce, and Benjamin Yard. Other early members who joined during the succeeding five years were G M Kunkle, James Lewis, Jonathan Evans, Sarah Evans, Sarah Peterman, Alexander Kimble, Sarah Gracy, and Ann Barr

The preachers who have had charge of this church are mentioned as follows William Crider, to 1833, David Best, 1833-34, R W Thomas, 1835; William Cooper, 1836-37, J B Ayres, 1838-39, H King, 1840-41, G Lacy, 1842, —— Crouch, 1843, —— McNamee, 1844, T Sumption, 1845-46, R M Greenbank, 1847-48, M D Kurtz, 1849-50, J Edwards, 1851-52, H. Sutton, 1853-54, J A Watson, 1855-56, H B. Mauger, 1857-58, William Dalrymple, 1859-60, George Rakestraw, 1861-62, S Patterson, 1863-65, L B. Hughes, 1866, D McKee, 1867-68, A L Wilson, 1869-71, M A Day, 1872-73, D L Patterson, 1874-75, J Y Ashton, 1876-77, T C Pearson, 1878-79, A L Wilson, 1880-82, Edward Devine, 1883, and D T. Smyth, present pastor, 1884

Among the junior preachers who were assigned to or assisted at this church prior to 1858 were Messrs Perry, Hand, Ford, Jackson, Graham, Niel, Roach, McCaskey, Lybrand, Sanderson, Cummings, Caldwell, Hobbs, Lane, Bailey, Clark, Wheeler, Barr, and Martin The present members of Bethesda Church are about forty in number

Licensed Houses.—The first application for license in Haverford that appears of record is that of Griffith Evans, who, at February court, 1731, desired to be permitted to keep a house of entertainment because, as he alleged, he was "an ancient man, his wife well stricken in years & subject to lameness" This license must have been successful, for Dr Smith informs us that "he [Evans] kept the well-established stand known as the 'Old Trog' in that day" It was located, the same authority states, a short distance above Cooperstown. We, however, have not found his name in the clerk's list of approved licenses

On Feb 29, 1732, Samuel Rees presented his application, signed by Daniel Humphrey and twelve other persons, representing that Samuel had been "ailing for some years, and at times unable to help himself, and since March last altogether ailing in the limbs, sometimes forced to keep his bed for weeks, his crops of corn failing for several years, having a large family," etc His house they represent "being on the great road from Conestoga, &c, to Philadelphia, & convenient for a public house" Despite his many ills and misfortunes the court refused to accede to his wishes and denied him license In no wise contented with the decision of the justice, he appeared again, May 30, 1732, when he received a favorable response for the remainder of the license year. On Aug 29th of the same year he presented his petition again, and it also was met with the favorable consideration of the bench On the clerk's list of the successful petitioners at the August court, 1734, his name appears, and annually thereafter until Aug 26, 1740, when Littice Rees, the widow of "Samuel, of Haverford," prays the court that the license may be continued to her, inasmuch as she had "a parcell of small children to support" The court yielded assent to her prayer, and again in 1741 extended the like favor to the widow and her fatherless children On Aug 30, 1734, William Bell made application to the court, and in his petition sets forth that "Lettis Rees's Lysance being now expired," he desires to renew it, but he does not state whether it was at the old location or not In 1748, Patrick Miller purchased the house formerly occupied by William Bell, and procured the license until 1752, when, he having died, his widow, Anne, carried on the business until 1757 In 1759, John Gregory had the license, and so on annually until 1761, when Llewellyn Barry obtained it, and in 1766, William Lewis became the landlord, to be followed in the next year, 1767, by Joseph Miller, who continued the business until 1772, when he died In 1773 his widow, Mary, obtained license, and so on from year to year until 1789, from the Chester County court After the creation of Delaware County she continued to receive the favorable consideration until 1796, when Jonathan Miller, probably her son, succeeded to the business From his petition, in 1802, we learn that his tavern was known as the Buck[1] In 1836 he gave place to Edward Siter, and the latter remained there two years, after which date the old inn ceased to be a public-house

---

[1] The tavern termed the "sign of the Buck" stood on the old Lancaster road (not the turnpike), in the northeast corner of Haverford, and it was there that the interview between Sower, the German printer, and Gen Forbes and the Governor of the province took place in 1758 Respecting this meeting, it seems that in the course of the discussions which ensued during the progress of the war above alluded to, several articles appeared in a German newspaper, published at Germantown by Christopher Sower, which were supposed to be aimed against the king and the government In consequence, fourteen Highlanders, from a regiment lately arrived at Philadelphia, were dispatched to the printer with a written order to meet Gen Forbes "at the tavern sign of the

To show that the justices took the condition of the applicant into account in dispensing the judicial crumbs, on the clerk's list of successful petitions in the year 1734 appears, instead of the party's name, this entry: "A widdow in Haverford—Beer & Syder," and a like statement in the following year, 1735, when it disappears from the list.

Thomas Ashbridge, of Goshen, Feb. 28, 1737/8, in his petition stated that that he had "taken a place in Haverford, which has been a place of publick entertainment for a considerable time." Possibly that of the widow mentioned above. He was refused, but at May court, 1738, he again tried to obtain a favorable hearing, and succeeded so far as being allowed to sell "Beer & Cyder." Ashbridge, however, seemed not to be content with the bench's bounty, for at the August court following he appeared again, asking full license, which the judges accorded him. In March (25), 1743, Matthew Beard, of Haverford, presented his petition, that he "hath lately Rented or Leased a Plantation or Tenement adjoining to the Great Road from Goshen to Philadelphia, in which Tenement there hath been for several years past a House of Entertainment." He was granted leave to sell "bear and Syder," but at the August court he received full license, and it was continued until 1746, after which his name does not appear of record.

In 1748, William Rusk, a renter, asked license for a public-house, stating that a tavern had been kept there; doubtless Beard's old place. In 1761, Philip Foreman was successful in his application, and in 1762, Adam Boyle received the court's favor. In 1764, Evan Watkins had license granted him, and in 1767, Peter Pechin was permitted to keep an inn. In his petition for 1770 the name Fox Chase appears for the first time. Pechin was succeeded, in 1771, by John Richards, and the latter, in 1774, by Aaron Coates, and he in turn, in 1778, gave place to David Quinn. David Lyons, in 1782, obtained license, and continued to secure him from the court until the new county of Delaware was created, and after that period until 1791, when Zacharias Loud had license for that and a part of the following year (1792). He was followed, in 1793, by Frederick Bittle, and in 1795, William Bittle became the landlord of the inn, which he called the Eagle and Compass. In 1809 his petition speaks of the house as the Compass. In 1813, Bittle having removed to a new house he had built, Martin Wise took it, and kept it until the old building was destroyed. However, in 1813, David Lyons states in his petition that he has "lately built a commodious house in the aforesaid township, situated at the intersection of the road leading from the borough of Chester to Germantown, and from Darby to Newtown Square and through the township of Radnor, formerly known as a place of entertainment by the name of the Fox Chase." He desired license for the same. The court granted it, and continued annually to allow it until 1832, when it also ceased to be a tavern.

William Bittle, whose removal from the old Fox Chase Tavern we have just related, in 1813 made application for license. His petition sets forth that "Having built and removed to the commodious building on the road leading from Norristown to Chester, where the West Chester road crosses said road," he wishes the court's permission to keep a hotel there. His application was rejected, but at the January court, 1814, it was approved, and the Spread Eagle Tavern on the West Chester road was established. In 1827, William Bittle was succeeded by Robert Dunn, and he being dead, in 1829, the license was issued to his widow, Susannah Dunn. The following year Lewis Bennett was landlord, and in 1831 William Bittle once more was "mine host" of the Eagle. In 1832 the latter gave place to J. S. Atkinson, and he in turn, in 1834, was followed by John Williams. In 1836, David Quinn had license, and in 1838, Andrew Steel, to be followed, in 1841, by William Bittle. In 1850, James P. Afflick, having purchased the property, made application to continue an inn at that place, the Eagle not having been licensed in 1848 or 1849. It was met with a remonstrance signed by William B. Lindsay, Adam C. Eckfeldt, James Smith, Vincent D. Litzenberg, Thomas L. Cochrane, Charles H. LaMar, and forty-five other persons, setting forth that "the subscribers, citizens, and legal voters of the township of Haverford . . . report that your memorialists have learned with deep regret that applications will be made to your Honorable Court . . . by James D. Afflick and William Y. Stackhouse for 'Tavern licenses,' or, in other words, for the privilege of vending intoxicating drinks under the sanction of law in our township, and inasmuch as we believe it to be our bounden duty to do what we may to prevent a consummation so much to be dreaded, we would therefore ask leave most earnestly but respectfully to remonstrate against the granting of the priviledge asked for, because we believe the sale and use of strong drink to be fraught with the most fatal consequences to the best interests of mankind, present and future, and because a very large majority of our citizens are and have been for years opposed to the granting of any license in the township of Haverford. Inasmuch, therefore, as no one is expected to be benefitted in the granting of the applications referred to but the persons above named (and even their ultimate advantage in such a calling is extremely doubtful), whilst many might be exposed to the deepest suffering in consequence of this multiplication of the places and sources of temptation. We appeal

Buck, on the old Lancaster road." Sower repaired to the place indicated, and being subjected to an examination by Gen. Forbes and the Governor, who was there in person, he was dismissed. Sower had resided in the province thirty-four years, and urged in his defense that he had been instrumental in inducing many persons to settle in the province, and therefore was in duty bound to support its welfare. The general gave him "a serious warning for the future, not to print anything against the King or Government." Forbes was then moving forward on the expedition which resulted in his capture of Fort Du Quesne.

to you, therefore, in the name of suffering humanity, not to give the sanction of your official character to the extension of an evil so deeply to be deplored" Afflick, learning of this remonstrance, in order to offset its influence, had a supplemental petition from "Drivers, Marketmen, Travellers, and others, alleging that 'no stand on the great road leading from Philadelphia to West Chester is better situated or more required for the entertainment of the public than the above-described house,'" which was signed by forty-eight persons The court gave Afflick license, but in order that the scales of justice should be properly adjusted, refused approval to the Black Bear Tavern this year, which made the balance even, as Stackhouse's inn had received license in 1849 In 1859, William Johnson was the landlord, to give place, in 1861, to Benjamin Kirk, who, in 1865, was followed by John M. Afflick William Thompson, in 1867, kept the Spread Eagle, Washington Bishop from 1869 until local option did away with license, and after the repeal of that law Roland J Pugh in 1875, received approval of the court, a privilege which was transferred to Nelson Pugh the same year In 1876, Leedom Kirk was the landlord, and continued there until 1879, when James A Serveson followed him, to give place to Joseph De Negre in 1881 The latter has since died, but the house is still kept open by his widow and children At the present time it is the only licensed house in the township

In 1827, Henry Konkle received license for a house he owned eight miles from Philadelphia and fifteen from West Chester, about half a mile nearer the latter place than the Spread Eagle, which inn he called the Black Bear The next year Joseph Hassan was the landlord, and continued as such until 1830, when Susannah Dunn, who had the year previous kept the Eagle, took the tavern, and remained there until 1832, when Riley Brown became "mine host" of the Black Bear Hotel William Y Stackhouse had license for 1837, continuing to receive the court's approval until 1848, when no license was granted in Haverford, and the next year was successful, while the Spread Eagle was refused In 1850, however, the Black Bear was rejected, while the Eagle that year was in high feather because of the approving judicial nod In 1851, Stackhouse again appears among the successful applicants, and continued annually to secure the judge's consent until 1870, when he being dead, for that year Mary Ann Stackhouse, his widow, was licensed in his stead, but, after the date last given, the Black Bear Hotel ceased to be a public house of entertainment

In 1769, John Waytin, and in 1778, Abraham Hughes, petitioned for license in Haverford, but we have not learned the location of the places which they requested might be made more valuable by the approving shake of the judicial heads

The Humphrey Family.—Concerning this, one of the most illustrious families Pennsylvania has yet produced, we condense from what has been written by others as follows Daniel Humphrey came from Llanegrin, County of Merionetb, Wales, in 1682, and soon after settled in Haverford township He had joined the Friends in his native country In 1695 he married Hannah, the daughter of Dr Thomas Wynn, of Merion Their children were Samuel, Thomas, Hannah, Benjamin, Elizabeth, Mary, Joshua, Edward, Martha, and Charles He visited his native country on business in 1725

Edward Humphrey, son of Daniel, was born in Haverford township in the year 1710 He learned the fulling and dyeing business in early life, and carried on that business as long as he lived, at the place that is now known as "Castle Hill Mills" In later years, however, he did not attend to his mills personally, for, having acquired a knowledge of medicine and surgery, probably from his grandfather, Dr Wynn, he practiced that profession with much success His services were much sought after, but he never charged the poor for attendance He died unmarried, Jan 1, 1776, and was buried at Haverford Friends' burying-ground

Charles Humphrey, son of Daniel, and brother of Edward, was born in Haverford about the year 1713, and died in 1786 He was brought up to the milling business, and, with his brothers, carried on that occupation extensively for many years A man of fine talents, he was at one time very influential in the county He served in the Provincial Assembly from 1764 to 1775, when he was chosen a member of the Continental Congress In that body, though he had contended with all his energies against the oppressive measures of England, he thought the time had not come to sever our connection with the mother-country, and voted against the Declaration of Independence He has been censured for this vote, but in giving it he represented the views of a large majority of his constituents at the time it was given He retired to private life, and, though he took no part in the great struggle for liberty, his sympathies were on the side of his country

Joshua Humphrey, the son of Joshua, and grandson of the immigrant Daniel Humphrey, was born in Haverford township in 1751 After availing himself of such limited educational advantages as the township then afforded, he was apprenticed at a tender age to a ship-carpenter of Philadelphia Here he made a good use of his opportunities, and, being possessed of a comprehensive and philosophical mind, he soon gained the reputation of being the best ship builder in the country After the adoption of the Constitution, and it became apparent that our government must be possessed of a navy, Mr Humphrey was appointed as the first naval constructor of the United States, and several of our first ships-of-war were built under his immediate direction Among them the famous ship "Constitution," of which he was the designer, draughtsman, and architect It is claimed that the marked superiority of our vessels in combats with those of England of the same class, during the war of 1812–15, was mainly owing to the adoption of Mr Humphrey's suggestions He may justly be called the father of the American navy. The last thirty years of his life were passed on a part of his patrimonial estate in Haverford, where he died in 1838

Samuel Humphrey, a son of Joshua and great-grandson of Daniel first mentioned, learned all the details of ship-building and naval architecture under the instruction of his father When his reputation had become world-wide the Russian emperor endeavored to secure his services, and offered him a salary of sixty thousand dollars per year, besides the use of a furnished mansion, with coach, horses, servants, etc, in attendance, but Mr Humphrey declined the position with the remark that his services were only at the disposal of his country Subsequently, under John Quincy Adams' administration, he served as chief of the naval Bureau of Construction and Repairs

The Grange.—Of this, the most ancient and rurally beautiful country-seat in Delaware County, Dr Smith, in 1862, wrote as follows

"There is no place in the township of Haverford, perhaps none in the county, with which so much historical interest is associated as with this ancient seat of grandeur and elegance Henry Lewis, a Welsh Quaker, one of the most staid of his sect, selected this spot as his wilderness abode in 1682 He was succeeded by his son, Henry, who resided here many years About the middle of the last century we find the estate, then consisting of nearly four hundred acres owned and occupied (at least in the summer season) by a Capt John Wilcox (sometimes spelled Wilcock), who erected upon it a mansion, and gave it the name of Clifton Hall' Capt Wilcox surrounded his estate with a ditch of some depth, most of which, within the recollection of many now living, could be readily traced, and some parts of it are still visible It is said, on the authority of tradition, that Capt Wilcox caused this ditch to be dug in order to give employment to his negroes, of whom he owned a considerable number

"About the year 1760, Charles Cruickshank, a Scotch gentleman of wealth, who held a captain's commission under the British government, and who had seen service in the Netherlands, came to America, and in 1761 purchased the Clifton Hall estate, but changed its name to the 'Grange,' or 'Grange Farm' Soon after the year 1770 the mansion house was enlarged and variously modified It is also probable that about this period the terraced walks were cut, the green house established, and that the almost unequaled natural beauties of the place were fully developed by the appliances of art, under the direction of a well cultivated taste The land attached to the Grange was partly in three counties,—Chester (now Delaware), Philadelphia, and Montgomery,—which Capt Cruickshank increased by purchase

"In 1768, Mr John Ross, also a Scotch gentleman, and an extensive merchant of Philadelphia, married Clementina, the daughter of Capt Cruickshank, who at the close of the Revolutionary war sold the Grange to his son in law, Ross, and returned with his family to his native country Mr Ross added to the buildings, and also increased the quantity of land to an aggregate of six hundred acres After the death of Mr Ross, in 1806 the estate was sold to his son in-law, John F Mifflin, who in 1810 sold the mansion to John H Brinton, the maternal grandfather of Gen Geo B McClellan In 1816, Mr Brinton sold the mansion, with another part of the estate which he had purchased in 1811, to Manuel Eyre, Esq , who made it his country residence till his death, in 1845 About that time the Grange was purchased by John Ashhurst, Esq , the son in law of Mr Eyre, who still occupies it as his country-seat

"At an early period, particularly during its occupancy by Mr Ross, the Grange was fitted up in the most exquisite style of the times, and during the summer months it was not infrequently the scene of elegant and luxurious entertainments."

BIOGRAPHICAL SKETCHES.

JAMES A MOORE

James A. Moore was born on the 31st of October, 1802, in New Garden township, Chester Co , where his father was owner of a productive farm In 1812 he removed to Upper Merion township, Montgomery Co , and became a member of the household of his grandfather, James Abrams He received, under many disadvantages, a common-school education, a walk of two miles being necessary to reach the nearest school-house His father having died, the family continued to reside with Mr Abrams, and young James became a valuable assistant in the labor of the farm In 1825 the family removed to the present residence of Mr Moore, in Haverford, which had been previously purchased by his grandfather Here he took upon himself the maintenance of his mother and the remaining children, and successfully managed the various interests pertaining to the farm On the death of the mother James purchased the property of the estate, and has since that time resided upon it and continued the occupation of a farmer Mr Moore was married, July 14, 1834, to Eliza Ann, daughter of John and Sarah Lindsay, of Haverford township, whose children are Sarah Jane (Mrs Jesse Brooke), Catherine (deceased), Catherine, 2d (Mrs Jesse B Matlack), Arabella (Mrs John Justis), John Lindsay, James (deceased, who served during the call for nine months' men for the late war, and was at the battles of Antietam and Chancellorsville), William B , and Ellen C (Mrs H C Childs) The death of Mrs Moore occurred in 1880 Mr Moore, after a life of industry, on his retirement from active labor, surrendered the farm to his son, John, who now cultivates it James A Moore was formerly a Democrat in his political belief, but later changed his views, and indorsed the platform of the Republican party He has served as school director, assessor, and collector of his township He has frequently acted as executor in the settlement of estates, his advice and judgment being often sought in the management of important interests He was in youth actively interested in the military organizations of Montgomery County, and was a member of the First Troop of Montgomery County His uncle, James Moore, was also a member of the same organization, and summoned for duty during the war of 1812 Mr Moore is a Presbyterian in his religious faith, and both an elder and trustee of the Marple Presbyterian Church

JOSEPH B LEEDOM

John Leedom was a prosperous farmer in Montgomery County, Pa His children were Charles, Joseph B, Samuel, John, Elijah, Esther (Mrs Jesse Thomas), Hannah (Mrs Charles Jones), Ruth Anna (Mrs Jacob Carncross). Joseph B. Leedom, of this

James A Moore

JOSEPH B LEEDOM.

number, whose life is here briefly reviewed, was born in 1796 in Merion township, Montgomery Co., and spent his youth upon the farm of his father. During this time he received such advantages of education as were obtainable in the neighborhood, and subsequently made farming the business of his early life. He married, at the age of twenty-five, Mary M., daughter of Elisha Worrell, of Springfield township, Delaware Co., and had children,—Myra W. (Mrs. Charles Worrell, whose death occurred in 1879), John, Maris W. (who died in 1873), and Joseph. Mr. Leedom, after his marriage, engaged in the business of milling, and became the proprietor of a mill located on Darby Creek, in Haverford township, belonging to his wife. This pursuit was continued until 1851, when he retired, and since that date has not been actively engaged in business. Mr. Leedom, first as a Whig and later as a Republican, has evinced a keen interest in the political issues of the day. He has ever been a strong partisan, and filled at one time the office of director of the poor for Delaware County. His religious creed is that of the society of Friends, his membership being in connection with the Haverford Meeting. Mr. Leedom is a man of modest demeanor, who, by his consistent character and sound common sense, has won the respect of the community. His surviving children are Joseph, who married Emily Pyle, of Haverford, to whom were born six children, and John, who married Hannah T. Worrell, and has had five children.

CHAPTER XLV.

MARPLE TOWNSHIP.

At the court on the 5th day of the Sixth month, 1684, occurs the first mention of Marple in the records of Chester County, at which time Jonathan Hayes and James Stamfield were appointed tax-collectors "for the Publicke Aid for Marple," and at the same court Thomas Pearson was appointed "Constable and Supervisor for the highway for Marple." In many of the early records the name is spelled Marpool; but Holmes, on his Map of the Improved part of Pennsylvania, gives this township according to the modern spelling, and as the first court record adheres to the same orthography, the word Marpool is doubtless an error. Why the locality was so called is now unknown.

The great road of Marple, which enters the township at its southern boundary just above the Springfield meeting-house, was laid out in 1683, and ran almost due north through the centre of this district, when it diverged in a westwardly direction, uniting with the West Chester road a short distance south of Newtown line. At the southwestern end of Marple was a tract of three hundred acres, which was patented to George Willard, 22d of Eleventh month, 1684. Richard Maris, a son of George Maris, of Springfield, subsequently became the owner of one hundred and thirty acres of this land, on which he resided, and was assessed for in 1715. The remaining part of the tract was conveyed to Jonathan Coppock, Nov. 4, 1708, but beyond that fact nothing further respecting him is known to the writer. Immediately above the Willard land were three hundred acres, one hundred of which was taken up by Ralph Draycott, Dec. 2, 1689, and two hundred acres by Elizabeth Draycott, Nov. 5, 1690, neither of whom seem ever to have resided on the estate, which passed to Thomas Pearson, Dec. 29, 1697. Tradition states that this Pearson came with Penn in the "Welcome," in 1682, and it was on his suggestion that the name of Upland was changed to Chester. The records of the arrivals of the early immigrants to Pennsylvania, in the possession of the Pennsylvania Historical Society, show that Thomas Pierson,—for so the name is spelled in the list,—was by trade a mason. Margaret, his wife, John, his brother, and Mary Smith, his sister, came from Ponnall-fee, in Cheshire, England, in the ship "Endeavour," of London, arriving in the colony on the 29th of Seventh month (September), 1683, nearly a year after Penn's arrival. Sarah Pearson, the daughter of Thomas, intermarried with John West, and became the mother of Benjamin West, the noted American artist. Mary Smith, the sister of Thomas Pearson, just above his tract, took on rent, Oct. 6, 1683, fifty acres of ground. Through this land and that of her brother the road leading from Upper Providence to Springfield meeting-house was laid out May 2, 1721. Above Mary Smith's land were two hundred and fifty acres surveyed to John Pearson, who came with his brother Thomas, in the "Endeavour," in October, 1683, which subsequently became the property of Robert Pearson. On Oct. 13, 1685, Francis Stanfield, who had purchased prior to leaving England, received a patent for six hundred acres. He settled on this tract prior to the summer of 1684, for, as already mentioned, at the August court of that year he was appointed one of the tax-collectors for Marple. This large estate subsequently was divided into smaller holdings, of which Peter, John, and Joseph Worrall had various-sized plots, as also Joseph and John Rhoads. In 1713 three hundred acres of the Stanfield land became the property of Robert Pearson, who was assessed for it in 1715. Dr. Bernhardus Vanlear, in 1720, acquired two hundred and forty-eight acres of this estate, and here he resided until his death, Jan. 26, 1790, at the extraordinary age of one hundred and four years. His death being largely due to the fact that in 1788, when he was one hundred and two years old, his house was entered by burglars, and because of his refusal to inform them where he had secreted his treasure, cruelly maltreated him. Above the Stanfield tract, on Oct. 27, 1683, three hundred acres were surveyed to Peter and Joshua Worrall. The family of Worrells (for the latter is the modern spelling of the name) are believed to be descendants of Sir Hubert de Warel, who lost three sons at the battle of Hastings, which victory gave to William the Conqueror absolute possession of England Peter Worrell (or Worrall) was a tanner, from whom the Worrals of Marple are descended, of Joshua, nothing seems now to be known John Worrall, who settled in Chester township in 1648, came from Oare, Berkshire, England, and as he named one of his children Peter, and Peter called one of his sons John, it would appear that if not brothers, they were at least very nearly related to each other John Worrall, Peter's son, with Bernhardus Vanleai, early in the last century, went to Germany, and graduated as a physician Above the Worrall tract were seven hundred and fifty acres surveyed to John and Charles Bevan, June 28, 1684, which was part of the two thousand acres purchased by John Bevan from Penn, in England It subsequently became the property of Jonathan Hayes, who, on July 30, 1684, received a patent for six hundred acres immediately to the north of the Bevan patent He was the largest landholder in the township He was a member of Assembly in 1689, and again in 1697, and one of the justices of the court from 1703 to 1711 In 1715 he was murdered by Hugh Pugh, a millwright, and Lazarus Thomas, a laborer The trial of the assassins is the first case of homicide known in the records of Chester County [1]

Lying directly south of Radnor was a tract of three hundred and thirty acres, surveyed to Thomas Ellis July 10, 1683, which was conveyed to David Morris June 10, 1695, and on a resurvey, in 1703, proved to contain four hundred acres Through this property and the one below it the Radnor and Chester road was laid out, April 20, 1691 Morris was believed to have been a Welshman, and was one of the projectors and owners of "Haverford New Mill" He resided on his plantation in Marple until his death, in 1720 South of the Morris lands were two hundred acres, which were surveyed to William Howell June 13, 1684 He appears never to have resided on this tract, which, on March 9, 1705, was conveyed to John Pugh, who certainly did not live in Marple in 1715 Immediately south of the Howell lands was a tract of five hundred and fifty acres, surveyed Oct 30, 1683, to Robert Taylor, who was a native of Little Leigh, in the county of Chester, England, who came to Pennsylvania in 1682, and settled in Springfield, never residing on his Marple estate Bayard Taylor was a descendant of Robert Taylor The property passed to his sons, Jonathan and Josiah Taylor In 1715, Robert Taylor, perchance a grandson of Robert, the immigrant, was a resident of Marple, and assessed as a real estate owner in that year South of the Taylor lands was a tract of four hundred acres, surveyed to John Howell Oct 22, 1683, of whom little appears to be known Immediately south of Howell's tract were five hundred acres, surveyed to Ebenezer Langford Oct 21, 1683, who may have lived there for a short time, inasmuch as he gave his name to the stream flowing into Darby Creek, known as Langford's Run Bartholomew Coppock subsequently became an owner of part of this estate The next plantation to the south, which comprised three hundred acres, and extended to the Springfield line, was surveyed to John Nixson Oct 20, 1683 On April 12, 1687, he sold the estate to Bartholomew Coppock. Dr Smith says it was bought by Bartholomew Coppock, Sr, while Smith's Atlas of Early Grants makes Bartholomew Coppock, Jr, the purchaser Bartholomew Coppock resided there in 1715, and the land is assessed to him Bartholomew Coppock, the elder, is positively asserted to have resided on this tract, and to have died there in 1717 [2] Certain it is that in 1715, only one Bartholomew Coppock was assessed in Marple, and he was a resident of the township

Although Marple, during the Revolution, was removed in a great measure from the clash and din of war, nevertheless, the British foraging parties and their Tory allies caused considerable injury to several residents of Marple The accounts filed of the losses thus sustained, which is doubtless but a small part of the gross sum, are the following

	£	s	d
From William Burns, Sr, September 19	56	0	0
From Daniel Cameron	61	16	6
From Joseph Burns, taken by the adherents of the King of Great Britain, September and December	129	5	5
	217	1	11

"In the winter of 1788," says Dr Smith, "a very tragic affair happened on Darby Creek, where it forms a line between Marple and Haverford, in the death by drowning of Lydia Hollingsworth, a young lady of great worth and beauty, who was under an engagement of marriage to David Lewis The party, consisting of Lewis, Lydia, another young lady, with the driver, left the city in the morning in a sleigh, and drove out to Joshua Humphrey's, near Haverford meeting-house From thence they drove to Newtown, but before they returned the weather moderated, and some rain fell, which caused Darby Creek to rise In approaching the ford (which was on the road leading from the Presbyterian Church to Coopertown), they were advised not to attempt to cross, but were made acquainted with the existence of a temporary bridge in the meadows above They drove to the bridge, but the water was rushing over it, and the driver refused to proceed, whereupon Lewis took the lines, and missing the bridge, plunged the whole party into the flood All were rescued but Lydia, whose body was not found till the next morning The feelings of Lewis can be more readily imagined than described This young lady was buried at

[1] *Ante*, p 162

[2] Smith's "History of Delaware County," p. 455

Friends' graveyard, Haverford In some pathetic rhymes written on the occasion, it is stated that seventeen hundred persons attended her funeral "[1]

In September, 1868, Hector Brown, a colored man, who it was asserted had reached the age of one hundred and seven years, died in Marple He had been a hired man in the Fawkes family, and his recollections were said to be very vivid of the war of the Revolution, so far as the incidents of that struggle came under his notice

Taxables of Marple—In the list of taxables returned in 1693, under the act providing for a tax-levy of one penny per pound on real estate and six shillings per head upon freemen, the township of "Marpoole" was thus returned

	s	d		s	d
Jonathan Hayes	08	04	Thomas Marcy	02	06
Peter Worroll	02	06	John Howell	02	06
James Stanfild's estate	02	07	Josiah Taylor	02	06
William Huntly	02	06	David Morris	02	06
John Person	02	06	Henery Cadman	16	00
Thomas Person	03	00	John Shaw	06	00
Ralph Dralcutt	03	00	John Hoopes	06	00
George Willard	02	06			

The taxables in Marple township in 1715 were as follows

David Morris, Thomas Pearson, Joseph Worrall, Bartholomew Coppock, Joseph Roades, Peter Worrall, Joseph Powell, Robert Pearson, Henry Lewis, Mordecai Massey, Robert Taylor, John Evans, Evan Lewis, Richard Marris

Freemen—Daniel Broom, Joshua Thompson, Enoch Pearson

The taxables in the township in 1799 were

William Afflich, Isaac Burn, John Bartram, Samuel Black, William Bolton, Mordecai Bevan, Thomas Courtney, John Cunningham, Isaac Cochran, Alexander Dorvell, Dennis Derrah, Edward Evans, John Farr, John Frame, John Grim, Jr (weaver), John Grim, David Hall, Jr, James Heacock, Thomas Holland, David Hall, Mary Jones, Henry Lawrence, Thomas Leech, Joshua Lawrence, Jonathan Morris (physician), Mordecai Markward, Joseph Maris (weaver), Richard Maris, Jr, Elizabeth Morris, Jr, Frederick Marks (saw-mill), John Morris, Philip Moore, Elizabeth Maris, Elizabeth Morris, Thomas Manley, David Maris, Samuel McClure, Robert Neal, Christian Peterman, Samuel Pancoast, Seth Pancoast, David Pratt, Thomas Pratt, Samuel Pharaoh, Davis Reed (store-keeper), Joseph Rhoads (tanner), Algern Roberts, Hannah Rhoads, James Rigbey, Isaac Rees, Jacob Siters, Robert Scott (shop keeper), William Sheldon, Benjamin Taylor, Levi Tyson, Mordecai Taylor, Bernard Van Leer (physician), Robert Wright, James Williamson, Abel Worrell, Joseph Worrell, Seth Worrell, Owen Worrell, Isaiah Worrell, Daniel Worrell, Joseph Worrell, James Worrell, Aaron Worrell, Nathan Worrell, John Worrell Eneas Worrell, Benjamin Yard, James Anderson (mason)

Inmates—William Evans, Eli Rees, Agnes Effinger, Collins McClester, Richard Price, Christina Van Leer, Joseph Sheldon, David Dunn, James Anderson (mason), John Shillingford (blacksmith), William Black (weaver), Nathan Field, John Broomall (blacksmith), Rachel Rhoads, Michael Temple, Jane Burn, Nathaniel Fawkes (mason), David Catharine

Single Freemen—William Grim (blacksmith), Mordecai Lawrence (carpenter), Isaac Maris (mason), Lewis Morris (tanner), James Manley, Joshua Thompson, David Peterman, Joseph Laurence, James Maris, Thomas Holland, James Heacock, John Worrell, Aaron Worrell

At Springfield meeting-house is a small settlement known as Marple Post-office on the line of Marple and Springfield townships The land at this locality was sold, Dec 31, 1742, to Robert Taylor, and in 1747 some to John Morris, a weaver, whose descendants still own a portion of the tract Prior to 1831 a store was kept at that location by William Edwards, who was succeeded in business there by Hampden and Burdsell In 1831 E R Curtis established a store there, and in 1849 he was appointed postmaster, the office being established by the United States in that year and located in his store He has continued the store to the present time, and has acted as postmaster for thirty-five years, the duties of which he is still discharging

At the present post-village of Broomall, in 1798, a stone dwelling was built by Hugh and Rebecca Lownes, the date-stone,

L
H R
1798

being built into the walls of the house It was licensed in October, 1800, as the Drove Tavern, David Reed being the first landlord About 1832 a store was established at the cross-roads by Isaac Haldeman In 1868 a post-office was established, and named Broomall, in honor of John M Broomall, the then member from the Seventh Congressional District George Esrey was the first postmaster, and has been succeeded by Bernard Hawley, Garrett Williamson, Samuel Moore, and Philip Moore, Jr, the present incumbent

Presbyterian Church.—In 1834, before the organization of the Presbyterian Church in Marple, John Lindsey, David Lyons, Daniel Conroy, and William Black, as trustees, bought of the heirs of John Craig one acre of ground at the cross-roads, a short distance from the Broomalls The corner-stone of a church building was laid Aug 4, 1834, by the Rev John L Grant The present stone edifice was erected at a cost of $1834 73 It was completed May 17, 1835, dedicated June 1, 1835, and the Rev Seth Bunnell preached there as a supply during the summer On the 27th of September, 1835, a church organization was effected, with ten members, by the Rev John L Grant On the 6th of December, 1835, the Rev J M Bear was called to the pastorate He was ordained and installed May 19, 1836 In September, 1838, he resigned, and on Oct 18, 1838, Rev. John McKnight, of the Presbytery of Lewes, Del, was called He continued in the duties of the pastorate until 1844, when he resigned, to take effect April 9th of that year

The Rev Marcus E. Cross, then pastor of the Knowles Presbyterian Church, acted as a supply until 1852, when the Rev A Rood was chosen pastor and served until 1857 In the summer of that year the Rev James C Laverty became pastor, and remained in charge of the church until the spring of 1859 The Rev Beriah B Hotchkin was then called, and was installed in October of that year by the Third Presbytery of Philadelphia He continued in charge

[1] History of Delaware County, p 392

of the church for nineteen years, and died in the Presbyterian Hospital, Philadelphia, on Sunday the 13th of October, 1878, his death resulting from injuries received the preceding August, when he had been knocked down by a runaway horse He was extensively known among the people of his denomination, being connected with the Presbyterian Board of Education and Ministerial Association, a trustee of the Lincoln University, the Philadelphia correspondent of the New York *Evangelist*, and highly esteemed by his congregation, his ministerial brethren, and all who knew him His remains lie in the graveyard beside his wife, and cut upon his tombstone are these words, "A morning without clouds"

The Rev William Patterson was called to the vacant pastorate, and was installed on Nov 13, 1879 By order of the Presbytery of Chester the Rev R M Patterson, D D, of Philadelphia, preached the sermon President Rendall, of Lincoln University, charged the pastor, Rev Mr Miller, of Bryn Mawr, charged the people, and Rev Mr Robbins, of Media, presided and put the constitutional questions Mr Patterson is the present pastor of the church, which has a membership of one hundred and thirty-two

Union American Episcopal Church—On the road from Springfield to Providence, and near the southern line of the township, in the year 1838, a frame church building was erected by this religious body On February 26th of the following year, the plot of ground on which the church had been erected was purchased of Charles Brown by William Fadler, Absalom Lockwood, Robert Warwick, and Selby Howard A church organization had been perfected prior to the erection of the sanctuary, and services were held in private houses The frame building was used until 1865, when the church purchased a plot of ground adjoining that building and erected the present stone edifice, which is forty by sixty feet The church now numbers twenty-eight members, and is in charge of the Rev Edward Brown

Mills and other Industries—In 1779, Isaac Maris owned a saw-mill on Darby Creek, at the mouth of Whetstone Run In 1810 a plaster-mill was located there, and was operated in connection with the saw-mill In 1826 it was in charge of George Maris, in 1829 it was operated by Edward Parker, and at the present time carried on by H Maris

In 1766, Joseph Heacock owned a half-interest in a saw-mill in Marple, after which date the name does not appear on the assessment-rolls until 1811, when Enoch Heacock was operating a saw-mill After that year all trace of this mill disappears from the records

In 1820, John Hunter erected a saw-mill on Darby Creek, above Ithan Creek, which was operated by John Wright, who purchased it prior to 1848 This mill has for many years ceased to be used in the manufacture of lumber

In 1779, Joseph Burns owned and operated a saw-mill in the township, but the locality of this mill has not been ascertained

On the lands of Dr Bernhardus Van Lear, on Trout Run, in 1820, was a mill-seat and a whetstone quarry. The water-power was at a more recent date used by Willett Paxson, who erected thereon a grist-mill, and lower down the same stream a cotton-factory, which was operated by a Mr Blimder On Aug 22, 1848, the cotton-factory was partially destroyed by fire. Both mills are no longer in use Abraham Jones, in 1800, erected a saw-mill in Marple, on Crum Creek, and in 1826 was operating at that locality a grist-mill and saw-mill In 1848 the mills were owned by his widow, Ruth Jones The saw-mill was located in Marple, while the grist-mill was in Upper Providence They are now owned by Lewis Palmer In 1810 a tan-yard was operated by Lewis and Abraham Morris on the farm now owned by James Williamson In 1829 it was owned by Rebecca Fawkes and James Lewis and operated until about 1865, after which date the business was abandoned

Thomas Pratt, in 1809 or '10, established a tan-yard in Marple, which he continued for a few years, when he relinquished the enterprise In 1805, Joseph Rhoads located a tan-yard on the Rhoads farm, and in 1810 he associated George Rhoads in the business, which was continued until about 1850 and was abandoned

In 1841, Benjamin Jones erected a pottery at the ninth mile-stone on the West Chester road, near the Buck Tavern A few years ago, the pottery, proving unremunerative, was permitted to fall into disuse.

Schools—About 1785 a school was established in Marple, but beyond that fact nothing has been learned of its location or how long it was maintained Enoch Taylor and wife, on May 31, 1791, conveyed to Joseph Rhoads and David Hall one-quarter of an acre of land, on the west side of the Marple road, in trust for use of a school to be kept under the direction of the Chester Meeting of the society of Friends On December 20th, the same year, David Hall and wife conveyed to Edward Fell, Joseph Rhoads, and Samuel Pancoast another lot, adjoining the above, for the same purpose On these lots a school house was erected and used many years, but was finally abandoned about 1836 On December 24th in that year, the school directors of the township purchased of John Grim forty square perches of land on which they erected a school-house, which was used in place of that on the Taylor lot

In 1857 the directors sold the second school-house to Nathan W Latcher, and a new building was erected on the old site and used until 1877, in which year the present brick house (known as No 2) was erected

On Aug 28, 1877, the court authorized Chester Friends' Meeting to sell the old lot, which was purchased by Malachi Stone for one thousand dollars

On March 21, 1818, John Craig, in consideration of one dollar and that a school-house should be erected on the lot, conveyed to Lewis Morris, John N Moore, and George Thomas, trustees to carry into effect that object, a piece of ground near Broomall On that lot a stone house was erected and placed under the care of the trustees, who held it until the acceptance of the school law by the township, when it was transferred to the school directors The house built in 1818 was used until 1855, when it was removed and the present two-story house erected

On Feb 22, 1837, a lot was purchased of Benjamin Garrett, and a stone house erected The lot was conveyed in "consideration of promoting the education and literary instruction of the youth resident in or belonging to the township of Marple" That building was used until the present stone house was erected in 1877 on the same lot, but nearer the road The old house, however, is still standing, and the new building and the old one are known as the Cedar Grove School-House

It will be observed in the account of the school-house at Broomall that trustees were appointed by the deed of John Craig to receive the title and exercise control over the house and lot On March 18, 1825, most of the townships in the county elected trustees of schools, and George Rhoads, Henry Lawrence, and Clement Lawrence were elected for Marple At that time there were two schools at least maintained in the township, one on the Craig lot, the other near the Rhoads farm When the school law of 1834 became operative, the court appointed Dr. Walter Williamson and James Lewis inspectors of public schools until the directors were elected In 1835–36 Marple received as her share of the public money assigned to the county, from State and county appropriations, seven hundred and seventy-nine dollars and forty-one cents

The following is a list of the school directors of Marple township, so far as appear of record at Media

1840, Samuel Bartram, William Nuzum, 1842, Samuel Hale, Thomas Sheldon, 1843, no report, 1844, John S Moore, Samuel Pancoast, 1845, Joseph Esrey, Thomas Steel, Jr, 1846, Isaac Latch, Eber Lewis, 1847, John B. Webb, Samuel Johnson, 1848, James Lewis, James S Bell, John Black, 1849, Abraham Pyott, Allen Lodge 1850, Henry Hipple, William McClellan, 1851, Cook Curtis, Philip Moore, 1852, Henry Hipple, William McClellan, 1853, Joseph Rhoads, George Esrey, 1854, John F Taylor, Thomas Williamson, 1855, Eber Lewis, Amos Bond, 1856, George Ezrey, Joseph Rhoads, 1857, John F Taylor, Thomas Williamson, Henry Hipple, 1858, Walter Green. Eber Lewis, 1859, George Esrey, Joseph Rhodes, Jr, 1860, Henry Hipple, Benjamin Jones, 1861, Henry Hipple, Samuel Black, 1862, Milton Lewis, Joseph Rhoads, 1863, Benjamin Jones, John F Taylor, 1864, Samuel Black, William Bartram, 1865, Joseph Rhoads, Milton Lewis, 1866, John F Taylor, J Morris Moore, 1867, Henry Hipple, William McClellan, 1868, Milton Lewis, Joseph Rhoads, 1869, Reece Pyott, William Dickinson, 1870, no report, 1871, Milton Lewis, Joseph Rhoads, 1872, William Dickinson, Reese Pyott, 1873 Samuel Sharpless, Henry Hipple, 1874, Joseph Rhoads, Charles Curtis, 1875, E P Esrey, R E Barr, 1876, Samuel Sharpless, Sarah Worrall, 1877, William Dickinson, A W Sloan, 1878, Richard E Barr, Henry Hipple, 1879, William Bartram, James L Williamson, 1880, William Dickinson, Sr, Joseph Rhoads, 1881, H Jones Moore, R E Barr, 1882, Richard Barr, William P Hipple 1883, Joseph Rhoads, William Dickinson, 1884, William Jones, H Jones Moore

The following is a list of the justices of the peace for Marple township

Edward Hunter	Aug 30, 1791
John Lindsay	June 5, 1794.
Isaac Abrahams	May 20, 1800.
Luke Cassin	March 27 1809
John Siter	Sept 1, 1813
Robert Green	Feb 24, 1816.
Nathan Gibson	Nov 26, 1817
George Brooke.	July 3, 1821
Maskill Ewing	June 10 1822
Benjamin Lobb	Dec 4, 1823
Park Shee	Dec 9 1823
David Abrahams	Dec 14, 1825
Barnard Flynn	Nov 18, 1835
Abner Lewis	May 27, 1836
Thomas Sheldon	Dec 20, 1836
Thomas Catain	Nov 1, 1838
Homer Eachus	May 11 1839
Thomas Sheldon	April 14, 1840
Thomas Sheldon	April 15, 1845

Crimes and Accidents —During the night of June 20, 1850, the barn on the farm of David Paxson was broken into and the throat of a valuable horse cut, so that he was found dead in his stall the next morning The person who committed the act was never discovered

On Wednesday, Sept 23, 1868, Thomas Bryson, a shoemaker, and William Stinson, in an altercation respecting some chickens, began throwing stones at each other, when one hurled by Bryson struck Stinson on the temporal bone, fracturing his skull, causing death in a few hours At the November court following Bryson was tried, convicted of manslaughter, and sentenced to a period of two years' imprisonment

On Thursday, Nov 18, 1880, Mordecai W Steel, while gunning for rabbits near his house, was accidentally shot by a companion About to get over a fence, the latter endeavored to uncock his gun, when the hammer slipped from his thumb, the fowling-piece discharged, and the load entered the head of Steel, who was standing a few feet in advance The wounded man died two days thereafter

Licensed Houses —In Marple township, before the old county of Chester was divided, no license to keep a public-house appears on record so far as I have discovered, and even after Delaware County was erected, no application to that end was presented until ten years had elapsed, when, July 29, 1799, Davis Reed, of Marple, represented to this court that he was "in the possession of a commodious, suitable, and necessary stand for a public-house, at the intersection of the road leading from Philadelphia to Lancaster by the way of West Chester, and that leading from the upper or northern part of the county to the borough of Chester" The signers who appear on his petition urged the court's approval warmly, for they "conceive that the stand or situation described in the above petition to be very eligible and necessary for the purposes therein mentioned, and that on several accounts, some of the principal of which are the following, viz, First, on account of its being so nearly central in the township, that it will on that account be convenient to transact the township's business at And, secondly, we who reside in the upper part of the county are of the opinion that it would be a very necessary and requisite stage for the accommodation of such of us who have frequently to attend at the borough of Chester on public business, as there is no public-house for a considerable number of miles." They also certify that the petitioner "is a suitable person to conduct the business, and as such we take the freedom (with due submission) to recommend him to the favorable notice of your honorable court." The judges refused the application, but at the October term, 1800, the license was granted.

In 1804, Reuben Lewis succeeded Davis Reed as landlord of the inn, and in 1807 Thomas Mason petitioned for license at that house, and, for the first time, in that year, the name "Sign of the Drove" appears on the record.

It was in this year that Joseph Vogdes petitioned the court to be granted license for a house "on the State road leading from Philadelphia to West Chester and Strawsburgh to Lancaster;" and at the October session, 1807, he was allowed to keep a tavern at the place designated, where he continued until 1815, when John Worthington had license for that year. Joseph Vogdes, in 1816, resumed his position as "mine host" of the Buck, yielding the place, in 1819, to Thomas Temple, who continued the name Buck, but added to it the words "and Still." In 1822, John Jacob superseded Temple, to yield, in 1824, to John Jones, who dubbed the house the "Three Tuns Tavern." When John Jacob resumed control of the inn, in 1826, he restored the old title, "The Buck," cutting off all the additional words and ponderous names which had been bestowed so freely on the house in the preceding few years. In 1827, Charles Vogdes followed Jacob, and David Vandersmith took Vogdes' place in 1829. In 1830, Hugh Jones Brooks was landlord of the Buck, and the next year John Williams was the host of the inn. In 1833, Samuel Hale was granted license, and continued until 1854, when, during the next three years, the application was rejected, to be approved in 1858 to George Ball, and in 1859 to be again refused. In 1860, Charles H. Hale presented his petition, which was met by three remonstrances, and the last application to the court for the privilege legally to vend liquor in Marple was refused.

To return to the Drove Inn. In 1808, George Pearson followed Thomas Mason, to be substituted, in 1810, by George Levis. Martin Wise kept the house in 1812, and Mordecai Worrell the year following. Christian Himes was landlord from 1815 to 1820, and his petition at the last date states that the tavern was a stone building, and had been licensed for twenty years. Himes remained at the Drove for the two succeeding years, when, in 1823, John Frick's "laugh was ready chorus" to the oft-repeated jokes of the frequenters of the tavern. John Jacobs, who seemed to be constantly attracted to the house, in 1824 took Frick's place; and when Frick, in turn, in 1825 followed Jacobs, the latter, in 1827, was reinstated, to give place, in 1828, to Thomas B. Boyle. Mordecai Moore, in 1830, received the court's approval, as did also Mordecai Moore, Jr., in 1831, and annually thereafter until 1835, when John Smith put in an appearance. In 1836, Powell McAffee became the landlord of the Drove until 1842, when license was bestowed on the old inn for the last time.

The year previous to the breaking out of the second war with England the following petition was presented to the Court of Quarter Sessions for the April term, 1811:

"The petition of Isaac Burns, of the township of Marple, humbly present that the petitioner has discovered on his farm, in said township, about one mile north of the West Chester road, a mineral or chalybeate spring; that he has erected a bath-house and other improvements for the accommodation of those who wish to use the waters for the restoration of their health and others; that for want of the necessary accommodations for entertainment many persons may be deprived of the benefits of using the said waters. Your petitioner therefore requests the favor of your recommendation to the Governor to grant him a license to keep a house of public entertainment on his farm, in said township, near the said springs, which he will endeavor to merit by keeping a good and orderly house.

"We, the subscribers (twenty-two in number), do hereby recommend the above petitioner as a sober and orderly person, and request that the prayer of his petition may be granted."

This petition was accompanied by the following certificate:

"We, the subscribers, do certify that having heard of the great virtues attributed to the mineral springs on the farm of Isaac Burns, in Marple township, have been induced during the last summer, and at various times previous thereto, to drink at and bathed in the waters, and by means thereof have been greatly relieved, and in many instances entirely cured of our respective disorders.

"April 8, 1811.

"Samuel Lewis, relieved of a rheumatic pain in the arm and inflammation in one of his eyes.

"John Hortor, relieved of the inflammation in his eyes.

"George Lewis relieved of a sick stomach."

The court, however, refused to aid in the restoration of those unfortunates afflicted with all the ills of humanity, who on the granting of license to the springs, it was believed, would hasten thither for treatment, and rejected the petition, only to have it presented the next year, and to again turn the applicant unsatisfied away.

Six years afterwards, when Judge Wilson had resigned, and Judge Ross was the president of our court, William Burns represented that "he has on his farm in Marple, about three-fourths of a mile off the West Chester road, and on a public road from the same, and leading upwards towards the Leopard Tavern, a mineral or Chalybeate spring, and that he has erected a bath-house and other improvements for the accommodation of those who wish to use the waters for the restoration of their health and others," but as the court six years before had coldly refused his father, Isaac, so the judges on this occasion turned their faces from the petition of the son, and thus for the last time on the records of the Quarter Sessions of Delaware County, is mention made of the Marple Spring of Health.

The Brooke House.—On the West Chester turnpike-road, a short distance below Broomall, is the residence of George Brooke, an aged gentleman, a de-

Samuel Pancoast

scendant of Capt. William Brooke, of the Revolution. The house, which was erected in 1833, has never had a coat of paint since the year it was built, and yet the woodwork is in as good preservation as any building of the like age in the county, notwithstanding the repeated assertions of painters that linseed-oil is absolutely necessary to prevent the decay of wood exposed to the air. Within this dwelling are many interesting relics. An old, tall eight-day clock still marks the passing hour, connected with which there is an interesting scrap of Revolutionary history. During one of the numerous raids of the British soldiers in the winter of 1777–78 this old clock, which had then been in the family more than a half-century, was taken to Philadelphia by the English troops. A chest of drawers, which was made in 1736 and was fastened by peculiar and secret springs, baffling every effort of the red-coats to get access to its hidden recesses, is among the relics in the old mansion. The eight-day clock, which was taken to Philadelphia, after the British army evacuated that city was recovered by Capt. Brooke. During the time it was in other hands the cord supporting one of the weights was broken and tied, the knot thus made causing the old time-piece to run irregularly, but a small stone added to the weight overcame that difficulty, and for more than a hundred years it has so remained in constant use. A number of cannon-balls found at Valley Forge, and other relics of the Revolutionary war, are preserved among the historical treasures of the Brooke house.

BIOGRAPHICAL SKETCHES.

SAMUEL PANCOAST.

Bartholomew Coppock, Sr., from Cheshire, England, with his wife Margaret and family were among the early emigrants to Delaware County. He settled in Springfield in 1685, and two years later purchased four hundred and forty-eight acres of land in Marple township of John Nixon, where he resided until his death, in 1719, aged seventy-three years. For the tract he received a deed from William Penn, with the great seal of the province affixed, and bearing the signature of his commissioners,—Edward Shippen, Griffith Owen, Thomas Story, and James Logan,—the conditions of this grant being that the borough of Chester, on the first day of the first month in every year, pay to the heirs of William Penn, for each and every year, the sum of four English shillings and threepence, or value thereof in coin current, to such person or persons as shall be appointed to receive the same. This deed is still in possession of the Pancoast family in excellent preservation. On the 22d of the Sixth month he deeded the same tract to Bartholomew Coppock, Jr., his son and heir apparent. He built a brick house on this tract in 1732, which is a part of the present edifice, and the Springfield Friends' Meeting was regularly held at this house until a meeting-house was erected, in 1738, on two acres deeded by him for the purpose in 1703. Bartholomew Coppock was for many years member of the Provincial Council, and frequently represented Chester County in the Assembly. He married, in 1710, Phœbe, daughter of Robert Taylor, of Springfield, and had two sons and four daughters,—Jonathan, Moses, Rebecca, Sarah, Margaret, and Esther. Esther married Seth Pancoast, son of William and Hannah Pancoast, of Mansfield, county of Burlington, West Jersey, on the 21st day of the Third month, 1741. By will was bequeathed "to my son-in-law, Seth Pancoast, all that my plantation lying and being in Marple township, containing 188 acres, which includes the homestead." To Seth and Esther Pancoast were born Sarah, who married Thomas Levis, of Springfield, afterwards a colonel during the Revolutionary war. Phebe married Isaac Levis, of Providence. Samuel, who inherited the homestead, married Mary, daughter of John and Rebecca Davis Levis, on the 18th day of the Fourth month, 1782. He was an elder of Springfield Particular and Chester Monthly Meetings of Friends, and held in high esteem by the society. Seth married Abigail Ogden, of Springfield. Esther Pancoast, wife of Seth Pancoast, Sr., died on the 26th day of the Tenth month, 1764, aged fifty years. He subsequently married Ann Wooley, and had three daughters,—Esther, Eliza, and Hannah. Esther married William Levis, of Springfield. Eliza married Henry Harrison, of Middletown, and, after his decease, John Worrall, of Providence. Hannah died unmarried. Samuel and Mary Pancoast had four sons and one daughter, as follows: John, married to Hannah Thomas, of Philadelphia, who had two sons,—Robert and Samuel; by a second marriage to Sarah Ogden, of West Chester, were born two daughters and one son,—Hannah, Elizabeth, and John,—of whom Rev. Samuel Pancoast, of Philadelphia, is the only survivor. William married Margaret Bishop, of Upper Providence, and had three daughters,—Mary, Priscilla, and Rebecca. Rebecca Pancoast, Sr., an exemplary member of the society of Friends, was born the 24th day of the Eighth month, 1789, and died unmarried the 20th day of the Tenth month, 1877. Seth Pancoast, born the 24th day of the Sixth month, 1793, married Margaretta Levis in 1821, and died on the 24th day of the Sixth month, 1880. Their children were J. Levis, Mary, Sarah T., Margaret B., Seth, William, Samuel F., and Henry,—of whom six survive. Seth, Sr., above mentioned, was an elder and an active member of Providence Particular Meeting and Chester Monthly Meeting, and led an exemplary Christian life.

Samuel Pancoast, who is the subject of this biographical sketch, was the grandson of Seth and Esther Pancoast, and the son of Samuel and Mary

Pancoast He was born on the 12th day of the Seventh month, 1787, on the homestead in Marple township, where his whole life was spent He was educated at the schools of the neighborhood, after which he began life as a farmer On the death of his father, in 1834, he inherited the homestead, and continued to follow the congenial pursuits to which his early life was devoted He married, in 1817, Tamar Bishop, daughter of Joseph and Sarah Bishop, of Upper Providence township, whose surviving children are ten in number Samuel Pancoast was in his political convictions formerly a Whig, and later became a Republican, though never active in the field of politics He was a member of the society of Friends, and a regular attendant of meeting at the Springfield meeting-house He possessed a well-informed mind, was an intelligent reader of current literature, and in private life an affable and courteous gentleman, enjoying the respect and esteem of all who knew him The death of Samuel Pancoast occurred on the 23d day of the Fifth month, 1873, and that of his wife on the 28th day of the Ninth month, 1877 The homestead is still in possession of the family

---

JOHN M MOORE

Charles Moore, the grandfather of John M, settled upon the homestead farm in 1718 He married Mrs Elizabeth Baker, and had children,—William, Hannah, Margaret, Rachel, and Philip. Philip Moore and his wife, Mary, were the parents of children,—John M, William, Elizabeth, Phœbe, Hannah, and Jane John M was born Feb 26, 1781, on the homestead, which was the birthplace and residence of his father, in Marple township After receiving a rudimentary English education he devoted a brief period to teaching, and then assisted in the cultivation of the farm When twenty-six years of age he married Elizabeth, daughter of Hugh Jones, of Marple township and had children,—Philip, Charles (deceased), Mary, William, Phœbe M, John M (deceased), Hannah (deceased), H Jones, J Hunter, Elizabeth J (Mrs Campbell McPherson), and Margaret B Mr Moore, on his marriage, inherited the homestead farm, which he cultivated until 1821, when the property now owned by his son, J Hunter Moore, became his home, on which the substantial stone residence, still standing, was erected Here he continued the active and healthful employments of a farmer until his death, March 18, 1865, in his eighty-fifth year The homestead farm is still retained in the family, and now the residence of his son, Philip Moore Mr Moore was early a Whig and subsequently a prominent Republican in his political views He was strong in his convictions, an active partisan and worker in the political field, and the incumbent of various local offices in the township He was during the late war thoroughly loyal in his sentiments, and on many occasions expressed his abhorrence of all measures tending to a dissolution of the Union The Moore family are of Protestant Episcopal antecedents Charles Moore, early spoken of in this sketch, was an active member of St David's Protestant Episcopal Church, of Radnor township (as was also his son, Philip), and a vestryman John M succeeded to the same office in this historic church

---

JOHN DUNWOODY

David Dunwoody, the grandfather of the subject of this biographical sketch, was a resident of Chester County, Pa His son, James, married Rachel Burn, whose children were David, Jane, William, James, John, and Joseph John was born in 1787 in Chester County (near Westchester), and until the age of seventeen resided with his parents He later accompanied them on their removal to Marple township, and became actively engaged in the pursuits of a farmer On the death of his father he came, by inheritance and purchase, into possession of the homestead, which continued to be his residence until his removal to Springfield, in 1856 He married, in 1816, Gulielma Fell, daughter of Edward and Mary Fell, of Springfield township Their children are Jane (Mrs E R Curtis, who has one son, Penrose D.), Penrose (who died in 1849), William (who died in 1827), Mary (who died during the same year), John (whose death occurred in 1828), Anna Maria (who died in 1879), and Gulielma (Mrs William Parker). Mrs Dunwoody's death occurred Nov 21, 1857 The annexed tribute is one of many expressions of esteem on the occasion of her decease

"The many virtues of this good woman require more than the brief announcement of her death. Her illness came suddenly and was very short, but the cold hands of death found her ready to answer the final summons of her God Having been born and reared and having lived in this county up to the time of her death, she had a large circle of acquaintances and many warm friends To enumerate her virtues and acts of benevolence would be the best tribute to her memory, for they were many She was remarkable for her even disposition, her ready smile and willing hand If any of those around her were sick, her care and attention never ceased until health was restored Up to the moment of the sickness which has terminated her existence on earth, she was generally hearty, and on the morning of her death expressed herself even better than usual As a mother she was ever patient and watchful, as a wife, kind, loving and dutiful, and as a steadfast friend, unfaltering Her loss to those bereaved ones will be sorely felt and long remembered"

Mr Dunwoody having been formerly a supporter of Whig principles found the platform of the Republican party in harmony with his convictions, though he invariably refused all proffers of office tendered him His religious belief was in harmony with that

Job M Moore

John Dunwoody

David Peterman

of the society of Friends with whom he worshiped. His death occurred Jan. 21, 1865, in his seventy-eighth year. The following brief summary of a life fraught with usefulness and eminent for purity is given by a friend:

"There was probably no one in the neighborhood in which he lived and where he closed his long and useful career more justly valued and respected than the subject of this brief notice. A youth of unstained purity to be followed by an active manhood, void of reproach, was crowned by a vigorous old age, surrounded by all the fruits of an industrious, virtuous, and eminently useful life, the final scene of which, as if in attestation of the love and respect in which he was held, being witnessed by a large concourse who assembled to pay the last tribute of respect to his memory. All that should accompany 'the sere and yellow leaf' of old age, as 'honor, duty, love, obedience, and troops of friends,' were his, and deservedly so. For a long period he had been suffering from the infirmities of age and the gradual decay of nature. The flame long flickered in the socket, but under all he was sustained by a strength not of earth, and the darkness which was to succeed through the 'valley of the shadow' brought no terrors to a soul thus armed and fortified. To him has been revealed the great mystery which must be learned by all that breathe,—bounded human vision has become infinite, and the dull, glimmering light of human intellect has become merged and lost in the full-tide radiance of omnipotence. At full maturity, like a thoroughly ripened sheaf, he has been gathered into God's garner, and to mourn him is as futile as it is ungrateful to him 'who giveth his beloved rest.'"

DAVID PETERMAN.

The Peterman family are of German extraction. Christian Peterman, the father of David, was a resident of Delaware County. He married Ann Redyner, and had children,—David, Jacob, George, Mary (Mrs. Scrimbger), Sarah (Mrs. Reyner), and Ann (Mrs. Esrey). David was born in Marple township, Delaware Co., in 1773, and spent his life in the immediate vicinity of his birth. He received such an education as the schools of that early day afforded, and on reaching man's estate, engaged with his father in farming. At a later date he purchased the farm now occupied by his grandson, Christian Peterman. Mr. Peterman married Ann McClure, of Marple township, to whom were born children,—George, Thomas, Sarah, Samuel, Elizabeth (Mrs. Charles Wesley Page), and Christian, of whom Mrs. Page is the only survivor. Mr. Peterman's pursuits during his lifetime were those of a farmer. He enjoyed—as a man of high moral character, the strictest integrity, and much intelligence—a commanding influence in the community, while his kindly nature endeared him alike to rich and poor. His religious preferences were in harmony with the creed of the Presbyterian Church. The death of Mr. Peterman occurred in April of the year 1842, in his sixty-ninth year.

CHAPTER XLVI.

THE BOROUGH OF MEDIA.[1]

FOR nearly a century and three-quarters after the first settlers came to the region in which Media was destined to be developed, the charming site of the now beautiful town was settled sparsely like other agricultural districts of the county, and no prophetic vision of the seat of justice that was to be, obtruded itself among the pastoral musings of the quiet, plodding farmers, whose broad acres are now so thickly populated and the scene of so much of life's activity.

Concerning the folks who came here two centuries ago (1682), and who owned the land on which Media is built, while it was a virgin wilderness we have gained some interesting facts, and some also concerning their successors and the deed history of the land.

The Title to the Soil.—The first dwellers here were the Taylors. Peter Taylor and William, his brother, of the parish of Sutton, county of Chester, England, bought of William Penn, March 3, 1681, land to the amount of twelve hundred and fifty acres in the province of Pennsylvania, for which they paid the sum of twenty-five pounds for all, and one shilling quit-rent for each one hundred acres, or about one hundred and twenty-eight dollars altogether, which was no greater a price than ten and a quarter cents per acre. Seven hundred acres of this land was taken up on the exact location of Media, the town which was to come into existence one hundred and sixty-eight years later. Peter took four hundred and William three hundred acres, leaving a remainder of five hundred and fifty acres to be taken up in East Caln township, where they had decided to locate the other tract. The brothers came over from England early in 1682, some time before the arrival of Penn, and probably in the ship "Amity." They proceeded to locate their claims shortly after arriving. Peter Taylor's land was nearly in the form of a parallelogram, and extended from Ridley Creek to the Providence road, while its southern boundary was nearly coincident with the present Washington Street in Media borough. The northern boundary was probably not far from the site of the county jail. William Taylor's share of the land was nearly in the form of a square along the line on which the Providence road was laid out, and lay north of and adjoining his

[1] By Alfred Mathews.

brother's larger possessions William lived upon his new estate but little more than a year, death claiming him upon Jan 6, 1683 His wife, Margaret, died three days before They left a son named Joseph and two daughters

Peter Taylor was unmarried when he came to America, and shortly afterwards, Jan 2, 1685, took as his wife, Sarah, a daughter of John Houlston, a neighboring settler Peter's children were Peter, William, and Samuel Peter moved to East Caln not later than 1717, and died in 1720, probably at the house of his son, William, in that township

It is on record that Peter Taylor and wife, Sarah, on Aug 20, 1717, deeded to Peter Dicks one hundred and seventy acres of ground, being that portion of the estate nearest Ridley Creek He retained one hundred and fifty-one acres, the western boundary-line of which must have run due north and south a little west of the residence of A Lewis Smith, on State Street When he removed to Caln, his son, Peter, appears to have taken charge of that portion of the estate which was retained He married Elizabeth Jarman, of Radnor, died in 1740, and was succeeded by his son Peter, the grandson of the original immigrant of the same name Meantime a portion of the adjoining property had come into the possession of William, another son of Peter (2d), who sold a part of it, consisting of nearly one hundred and fifty acres, to John Butler in the year 1735, and retained for himself one hundred and fifty-one acres

The one hundred and fifty-one acres of Peter Taylor (3d) having been sold to Peter Dicks, was deeded to him June 8, 1748, and hence, after an interval of sixty-six years, the land of Peter Taylor, the original owner, had all passed out of the possession of his descendants Nothing remained in the hands of any of the Taylors except the adjoining Sandy Bank property originally owned by William

Dicks built a log cabin on his property, which is still standing, although one hundred and thirty-five years old He had absorbed the whole property, besides owning the large tract of land west of the line of the Providence road, south of and contiguous to the eastern end of the Taylor property He was a son of Peter Dicks, of Cheshire, England, who settled in Birmingham in 1686, and had seven children He moved to Nether Providence in 1717, where the family had either located a claim in 1686 or subsequently bought from the Vernons He was in easy circumstances, and made large additions to his real estate On the south of Taylor's land he owned about half-way from the site of Providence road to Ridley Creek, while one Broughton owned from his boundary to the creek As the property of Thomas Minshall faced that of Peter Taylor to the eastward, we have the six original owners of land on or near the site of Media as follows Peter Taylor, William Taylor, John Houlston, Thomas Minshall, Peter Dicks, and —— Broughton

Concerning the William Taylor lands we will now give a fuller history On Dec 16, 1781, a century after the first conveyance of the land, Nathan Taylor, then holding what was originally supposed to be the three-hundred acre tract (but subsequently found to contain three hundred and twenty acres), or what remained of it, sold to Enoch Taylor one hundred and twenty acres, including that part on which in late years has stood the residence of Dr Rowland. Nathan died here about the year 1800, having been born in 1715, and on July 26, 1823, the paternal estate was sold at public sale to John Smith for thirty-nine dollars and fifty cents per acre, and thus the last remnant of property passed out of the ownership of the Taylor family, after having remained in it one hundred and forty-two years Enoch also died about 1800 Ezra Taylor was one of his executors He was born June 26, 1781, and died in 1825 He was buried at Sandy Bank graveyard, the following being the inscription on his tombstone

"Ezra Taylor, a descendant of Peter Taylor, one of the first settlers of where now is the Seat of Justice of Del Countee, born June 26, 1781, died May 25, 1825 "[1]

The dwelling occupied by the Taylor families passed, as had been said, into the possession of John Smith It then became the property of A Pascal, and by him was sold to Dr Rowland

It is an interesting fact that Gen Zachary Taylor, a President of the United States, and the hero of the Mexican war, was a lineal descendant of Peter Taylor, the immigrant of 1682 His ancestors of the second or third generation removed from East Caln, Chester Co, to Winchester, Va, where the boyhood of Gen Taylor was spent, although he subsequently removed to the West

Having now given some account of the pioneers and provincial owners of the soil, we shall consider the causes that led to the building of the town

Location of the County-Seat—The Infant Village. —The agitation leading to the removal of the seat of justice of Delaware County from Chester to a more central locality, which had its formal and organized beginning at a meeting held at the Black Horse Hotel, in Middletown township, Nov 22, 1845, having been elaborately treated in a chapter[2] of this work, it is unnecessary in this connection to say more upon the subject than what will suffice to remind the reader of the essentials in the controversy and serve as an introduction to topics of more narrowly local interest of which it is our province to treat in this division of the work It will be remembered by many, and can be learned by others from the chapter to which we have referred, that after the meeting on Nov 22, 1845, the matter of removal was submitted to the people at the election immediately ensuing,

[1] Sarah, wife of Ezra Taylor, died in South Media, April 22, 1864, aged eighty two years.

[2] See chapter xvi of the General History, entitled "The Removal of the County-Seat to Media"

that the vote was in favor of the removal, and that the delegates elected assembled at the Black Horse Hotel, on the 6th of December, and a majority being in favor of a new county-seat the county poor-house property was selected as the most desirable site for the county buildings, and the town which must of course come into existence by reason of their location As the attendance had been comparatively small, owing to the almost impassable condition of the roads, the anti-removalists claimed that the decision had not reflected the real will of the people There then ensued an energetic and even violent political contest upon this local issue, which was carried on in the county and in the Legislature almost unceasingly for two years, with success now for one side and again for the other The election of Oct 12, 1847, however, sustained the verdict of two years before by a majority of seven hundred and fifty-two votes Here, when the question seemed decided, however, it became complicated, and the opposition, adopting new tactics, fought, if not more fiercely, at least more determinately than ever before Because of some similarity between the removal act and an act previously passed giving the citizens of each township a right to decide by ballot whether liquor should be sold therein, and because this act had been declared unconstitutional by the Supreme Court, the opponents of the removal resolved to place the obnoxious measure before the same tribunal Without attempting to follow the prolonged secondary struggle we simply note the fact that the will of the people, twice expressed by the ballot, was finally confirmed in the House of Representatives by an act passed by unanimous vote, Jan 19, 1848, authorizing removal It received the approval of the Senate, March 30th, and the signature of Governor Shunk, April 7th, and thus became a law

In the following fall, Sept 10, 1848, the county commissioners, Edmund Pennell, Mark Bartleson, and Caleb J Hoopes, purchased from Mrs Sarah Briggs a tract of forty-eight acres adjoining the poor-house farm, in Upper Providence For this property, now worth fifty times as much, the sum of seven thousand seven hundred and sixty dollars was paid, or a little more than one hundred and sixty dollars per acre Time proved the wisdom of the commissioners' decision, for the locality was a very suitable one for the beautiful town which has been developed upon and around it

Just here we will digress from the current of our narrative to give an idea of the aspect of this spot at the time it was chosen for the site of the county town

There were then on the ground now included within the limits of Media no less than twelve buildings These were the old Almshouse, the Briggs, the Way, and the Hill mansions, all built of stone, and located immediately upon the State road, the old log house west of the Almshouse, the house of Peter Worrall, which was a tavern, and six others, conspicuous among them being the Pierce and Haldeman residences The mansion occupied by Mrs Briggs was subsequently sold by the commissioners, at their second sale of lots, to John Esrey, who afterwards transferred it to Dr Joseph Rowland, one of Media's most successful medical practitioners About five hundred yards distant from the house just mentioned was another of the old residences of the place (occupied in late years by John Wilkinson) This building was erected by the grandfather of the Richard Briggs who occupied what was latterly the Rowland home for his son, Richard Briggs About the time of the removal of the county-seat this property was sold at sheriff's sale to Elizabeth Way, and subsequently passed into the possession of a relative The properties of the Briggs, father and son, were bounded on the south by the State road, on the east and north by the poor-house farm, and on the west by land of Isaac Cochran, which included the ground on which Hon. John M Broomall built a handsome residence a number of years since The property of William Briggs adjoined the Richard Briggs farm, on the west This, with the house upon it, was purchased several years prior to the county-seat location by T Chalkley Palmer, who sold, in the summer of 1847, to Andrew T Walker The large tract of land south of the State road was owned by John Hill, Sr This, with the exception of a few lots on State Street, was subsequently sold to H Jones Brooke

We now resume the narrative of events in the early history of Media The first of note, subsequent to those which have already been related, was the fixing of the exact site for the public buildings, of which announcement was made by the commissioners on May 15, 1849 The site chosen was that upon which the court-house and jail (presently to be dwelt on at length) now stand The work of building them was soon commenced

The first sale of building lots in Providence,—*i e*, Media,—of which Joseph Fox had completed the survey and platting July 26th, was held by the county commissioners on Monday, Sept 17, 1849, and was as successful and remunerative as the most sanguine of those officials could have hoped it to be Seventy lots were sold at prices varying from $1 80 to six dollars per square foot The sum of seven thousand five hundred and eighty dollars was realized by the sale This was only one hundred and eighty dollars less than had been paid for the entire Briggs tract of forty-eight acres Among the purchasers of the seventy lots sold on that day were Dr George Smith, who bought the first lots offered, Nos 1 and 2, at three dollars per foot, and also one near the close of the sale Then follow, in rotation, Gideon Miles 1, Jacob Smedley 3, William Jones 2, J Morgan Hunter 2, Minshall Painter 8, Joseph Hood 1, Capt William Apple 2, Isaac Taylor 1, Isaac Haldeman 3, George Smedley 2, John Miller 3, James Edwards 2, J T Hawkins 1, and John C Beatty 1. The remaining names of lot-buyers, so far as they have been recorded, are John Hardcastle, William Smedley, Phelin Campbell, Abram Pennell, James Smith, Thomas Pratt, Isaac C. Malin, Charles Palmer, Henry Bowen, Thomas Inman, Isaac S. Williams, Jabez Lawson, James Pennell, and John Hill.

One hundred and thirty-four lots were still in the possession of the commissioners at the time of this sale, the total number having been two hundred. Large reservations had been made for the court-house and jail and a market-house. The lots were twenty feet front by one hundred and seventy in depth. At a second sale, on Monday, October 15th, forty of them were sold, and on the same occasion the Briggs farm-house and barn were purchased by Mr. Esrey for fifteen hundred dollars and four hundred and five dollars respectively.

It was indicative of the enterprise and large-mindedness of the people of Media, and prophetic of the beauty of the town that was to be, that the first buildings erected were substantial and tasteful structures. The first building reared after the act of removal was a fine brick store located on the north-east corner of State Street and South Avenue. It was built by John C. Beatty, who commenced it in the fall of 1849 and completed it early in the spring. The lower story was occupied as a dry-goods and grocery store by Ellis Smedley, who afterwards removed to Chester, and the upper story, finished as a hall, was dedicated to the cause of temperance on Feb. 16, 1850. Mr. Smedley's successor in business at this stand was Thomas D. Nelling, who subsequently gave place to Black & Sons, in turn followed by Hawley & Brother. Other buildings were in process of erection before the Beatty block was finished, and soon the locality began to look like a town.

"After the first and second sales of lots," says a newspaper writer,[1] "the increase in the value of the surrounding property was so marked and immediate that it became highly expedient that the ground upon which the old almshouse was located should be sold, as it could be done with great advantage, and particularly was this course of action deemed advisable, as the old buildings were not well adapted to the purpose for which they were erected. The amount realized, it was argued, would more than pay for a better farm, and more commodious buildings, on a more eligible site. The action taken in the matter resulted in the sale of the old structure, which was purchased by Mr. Primrose, a citizen of Philadelphia, and subsequently from him by David Milne, another Philadelphian, who converted it into lodgings for a large number of colored families. The place soon became known as the 'Continental.'"

In 1851 occurred the first untoward event in the infant village,—the first fire. On Friday, June 20th, Peter Hill's shingle-factory and a considerable quantity of lumber were destroyed by the flames. The factory stood not far from the bridge over Ridley Creek on the Black Horse road. There was no similar disaster until after the lapse of eight years.[2]

As the village increased in population, and business lines of transportation and communication connecting with the outer world were established, Mr. Wesley C. Brodhead early in the history of the new county-seat placed a line of stages on the road, and in August, 1851, as we learn from the following advertisement, which appeared in the *Delaware County Republican*, he increased the facilities for travel between the old and new county-seats:

"FOR MEDIA.—Mr. Brodhead, the accommodating proprietor of the line of stages between this borough and Media, will place extra coaches on the route during the session of court. A capacious four-horse omnibus will leave the depot at half-past eight o'clock in the morning."

Mr. Brodhead made his line of coaches highly acceptable to the public, and continued running them for two or three years, but they were discontinued when the West Chester and Philadelphia Railroad was put in running order. In more recent years the stage service was revived.

A line of telegraph was run through Media along State Street, connecting Philadelphia with Baltimore, in August, 1852, and although no office was immediately opened in the borough, the people had not very long to wait for electrical communication with the great cities north and south.

During this year there was great interest manifested in the building of plank-roads, not only in this neighborhood but elsewhere in the county.

Various improvements were carried on, all tending to increase the beauty and solidity of the town, and enterprising men began to make investments in real estate, in anticipation of further growth. Early in the year 1853, John C. Beatty purchased from the Thomas estate eleven acres of ground, a portion of which was in the borough limits, and about August 1st he bought of the Directors of the Poor and House of Employment forty acres of land attached to the poor-house property, and lying south of the State road. For this he paid two hundred and fifty dollars per acre, a fact which clearly exhibits the increase in the value of real estate by reason of the town's growth. He at once divided a large portion of the tract into building lots for the convenience of those who wished to purchase and establish homes. The movement for church organization and building had been commenced before this time, and the house of worship of the Presbyterian denomination was afterwards erected on a lot in this tract.

[1] From one of a series of historical sketches written by Wilmer W. James for the *Delaware County Democrat*, published at Chester, and appearing in that paper in 1875.

[2] The second fire occurred on Saturday night, Dec. 17, 1858, during a terrible storm of wind and rain, and destroyed the gas-house at Brooke Hall. The building was also used for storage purposes, and the trunks belonging to the young ladies and packed ready for shipment to their houses, being in the building, were all consumed. The loss by this fire was about fifteen hundred dollars.

Building was carried on extensively during 1853 Early in the year Isaac Haldeman began the erection of a large store and dwelling, the former of which was occupied by himself and sons The third story of this building, on the northwest corner of State and Lemon Streets, has been occupied at various times as a private school-room Later, in 1853, a fine residence and bakery were erected on the opposite corner by David Middleton, and Nathan G Shaw also erected a handsome dwelling near Sandy Bank, afterwards occupied by F Fairlamb

Having thus far chronicled many instances of the enterprise which operated to build up this thriving town, we may now give the reader a general idea of its condition in 1853. By midsummer of this year there were seventy dwellings in the borough, fifty-seven of which were new ones, that is, built after the site of the town had been surveyed, within a period of but little more than three years At the time of which we speak four more houses were in process of construction, and eight were under contract to be built in the summer and fall, making a total of eighty-two dwellings, in addition to a school-house, a blacksmith-shop, and a coachmaker-shop The court-house, jail, and charter-house (which for purposes of convenience we have reserved for separate consideration) were also finished, and, with a row of offices on South Street, made the total number of buildings of all kinds ninety-four, not a bad showing, by any means, for less than four years' work

Entering more into detail, we will say that the town contained two dry-goods and grocery stores, a boot and shoe store, a trimming store, a drug store, a temperance inn, a printing-office, a post-office, and a school-house The tradesmen then within the borough limits were two tailors, three blacksmiths, one wheelwright, one coachmaker, one tinsmith, one saddler, one stone-cutter, one bricklayer, one stonemason, two painters, two cabinet-makers, three carpenters, one plasterer, and one butcher The professional gentlemen were five lawyers, three physicians, and one dentist It may be mentioned in this connection that the first attorney who located here was Ezra Lewis, Jr, who took up his residence during the building of the court-house, in 1850 He was soon followed by Charles D Manley, Edward Darlington, Joseph R Morris, and Samuel B Thomas

In 1854 the energy of the people in no degree abated, but, on the contrary, increased, found activity and expression in new directions The Media Loan and Building Association (an institution of which we shall give an extended account in this chapter) was organized during the early part of the year The Methodists, Episcopalians, and Presbyterians made strong efforts to build houses of worship, and either partially or fully succeeded, as will be presently shown Preparations were made also for the erection of Brooke Hall and Gayley's Academy (subsequently the Sanitarium), and the construction of private edifices went on apace with improvements of a more public character Thomas Pratt erected five brick houses north-east of Olive Street, and in partnership with Jesse Bishop, Esq, put up the five original offices on the western side of South Avenue Abram P Smedley during the fall put up the handsome three-story brick building in which he afterwards lived, and various other embellishments were added to the town In the mean time an ordinance had been passed prohibiting the erection of frame buildings within the borough limits, which had a most salutary influence both in the way of enhancing the appearance of Media and in precluding in a large degree the possibility of destructive fires, from which the place has ever been peculiarly exempt

Of the early merchants we have already had occasion to speak, and we again advert to them Charles R Williamson had gone into business prior to this period His store was in the building on the south-east corner of Front and Orange Streets, latterly occupied as a residence by Levis Miller Thither Mr Williamson removed the post office when he was appointed postmaster, in May, 1853 In April of this year Mr Smedley formed a partnership with Thomas D Nelling, under the firm-name of Smedley & Nelling, and the firm carried on business at the original stand, on the corner of State Street and South Avenue, until the 1st of January, 1854, when Mr Smedley withdrew, and Philip Nelling and Thomas D Nelling took the store, under the firm-name of Nelling & Son The first book-store in Media was started by Mark Packard, at his residence on Orange Street, as early as 1853, but in a year or two afterwards was disposed of to H L Rockey, who sold it in 1856 to Joseph G Cummins This gentleman made the business a successful one, and the store became one of the permanent institutions of the borough

A connected account has now been given of the origin and early growth of Media, and it remains to describe the public buildings, which formed the centre around which all of the improvements we have related clustered

The Court-House and Jail —The county commissioners, after the act of removal, which, as we have before said, became a law April 7, 1848, proceeded with all of the celerity that was compatible with sound business discretion to provide the necessary public buildings for the new seat of justice They fixed upon the exact site (the present one) on May 15, 1849, and offered an award of fifty dollars for an acceptable plan for the proposed structures In response to their offer a number of competitors appeared, and on June 18th they adopted the plan offered by Mr Sloan, of Philadelphia, at an estimated cost for the court-house of fifteen thousand dollars On August 28th they awarded the contract for the erection of the court-house and the jail to Joseph Esrey, John Williamson, and Joseph Lawson, for the sum of thirty-two thousand dollars. Ground was immediately broken, and the work was carried on with commendable diligence and speed.

The specifications stated that the court-house should be of brick, that above the base-course it should be roughcast and painted, that the roof should be covered with the best leaded tin and surmounted by a cupola and spire, the extreme height from the ground to be eighty feet. The structure was to be two stories high, with the exception of that part occupied by the jury-room, which should be three. The offices were to be one story high and fire-proof, and there were also to be two fire-proof safes on each side of the vestibule. The second floor was designed to contain the court-room and apartments for the jury, witnesses, a law library, and a sitting-room for the judge and associates.

The jail building was to have a house for the sheriff in front of the prison proper, and it was to be twenty-six by thirty-eight feet, and to consist of two stories, an attic, and basement. It was directed that it should contain, besides the usual accommodations for the sheriff's family, a parlor, reception-room, and office. The kitchen was to be in the basement, and the second story and attic were to be divided into sleeping chambers. Upon the roof was to be a tank to hold water, which should be conducted to all parts of the house by leaden pipes. On the top was to be an observatory.

It was specified that the prison was to be in the rear of the sheriff's house, and attached to it by a corridor fifteen feet in width, extending also through the entire length of the prison. On each side of this corridor were to be four cells, each eight by twelve feet. There were to be also a bath-room, keeper's room, and infirmary in this part of the building. The second story was to be reached by steps to a gallery extending around the whole of the corridor, opening from which there were to be on each side four cells, each eight by twelve feet as below.

It was provided that a space one hundred by one hundred and twenty-five feet around the prison should be inclosed by a wall, and that there should be a covered way from the corridor to the exercising yards, of which there were to be six, each nineteen feet wide by twenty-nine feet deep, the whole forming a semicircle, after the plan of the celebrated Pentonville prison, near London, England. The prison was to be built of stone, the roof covered with tin, and the whole structure made as strong and as nearly fire-proof as possible.

The corner-stone of the court-house was laid Sept. 24, 1849, in the presence of a considerable number of people. In the stone was placed a leaden box containing a parchment on which was a plan of the town, a description of the public buildings, stating when they were begun and when to be completed, and giving the names of the contractors, together with the names of State and county officers then in service, a full line of the coins of the United States for the year 1849, from a half-eagle down to a cent, copies of the *Delaware County Republican*, the *Upland Union*, and other newspapers and public documents. The receptacle was sealed and placed in the stone by Edmund Pennell.

The walls of the court-house were up, and preparations for raising the cupola were made, by Aug. 13, 1850. The stone-work of the prison was about completed by that time, and the sheriff's residence was well advanced. By the 1st of November the court-house was ready for plastering, both inside and out, and the jail almost entirely completed. By the 1st of May, 1851, the court-house was pronounced finished, though it was not ready for occupancy on account of the dampness of the walls. At the last term of court held in Chester, which convened May 26th, the official notice of the completion of the court-house and jail was given in these words, "The Commissioners reported to the Court that the County Buildings, at Media, were completed and ready for occupancy, and the Court directed the following minute to be entered upon the record:

"May 29, 1851—The Court of Common Pleas, of Delaware County, are satisfied that the Buildings, to wit:—new Jail, Court House and Public Offices, in the Borough of Media, are fully completed according to the true intent and meaning of the act of the Legislature, entitled an Act concerning the removal of the Seat of Justice of Delaware County. Approved the 3d day of March, 1847."

After the close of this term of court, the last to be held in the old court-house at Chester, the *Delaware County Republican* alluding to the change, said, "The next term will be held at Media, an order having been issued by the Court to remove the records and other property to the new County Seat, prior to August. Our ancient Borough, which had been the Seat of Justice from the time of the Swedes, will never again, we suppose, be visited by the hurry, bustle and commotion of Court week."

The removal of the county records from Chester to Media was begun on Monday, June 16th, and by the evening of Wednesday, the 18th, both the records from the court-house and the prisoners from the jail had been placed in their new quarters.

In the mean time the work of paving the square went on, and various details of external adornment and internal finishing and furnishing were added. The bell for the court-house, of Philadelphia manufacture and weighing seven hundred pounds, was received on August 12th, but was not hung in place in proper time to announce by its sonorous strokes the convening of the first court held in Media, which opened on Monday, Aug. 25, 1851.

It is recorded that on that day the crowd was so great as to fill all parts of the room, including the passage-ways, and, in fact, every spot on which space enough to stand could be had. A writer of reminiscences in the *Delaware County Democrat* says of this first court, "The business of the term was opened by President Judge Henry Chapman, aided by his Associates, Joseph Engle and George G. Leiper. After the charge to the Grand Jury and a neat address to the citizens of the county by Judge Chapman, relative to their public spirit and liberality in the erection of the public buildings, the first case tried was the Commonwealth *vs.* John R Bergen. The defendant was indicted for keeping a tippling-house, and fined thirty dollars and costs of prosecution Eight additional criminal cases were tried, and other business disposed of, the court adjourning at noon on the following Wednesday,—a two and a half days' session At this term of court, and on Monday, August 25th, on motion of Edward Darlington, Esq , Robert E Hannum, Robert McCay, Jr , and Charles D Manley, Esqs , were appointed examiners on the application of Thos J Clayton for admission to the bar of Delaware County The result of this examination proving in all respects satisfactory, he was duly admitted to practice at the next term of court, Nov. 25, 1851 "

The court-house served its purpose very well for a number of years, but by 1870 it was found that additional room was absolutely necessary, and preparations were made for meeting this need It was not, however, until the summer of 1871 that definite action was taken in the matter The commissioners then advertised for proposals for enlarging the court-house by the addition of two wings, each to be thirty-eight feet square and two stories high About the middle of August the bids were opened, and the contract was awarded to John Hinkson, of Chester, his proposal for the work being twenty-nine thousand dollars, or nine hundred and fifty-nine dollars below that of the next lowest bidder As a matter of curiosity, it may be stated that the bids were as follows Taylor & Worth, of West Chester, $49,677 , Staunton & McGarry, of Philadelphia, $40,000 , S P Rush, of Philadelphia, $35,471 90 , Churchman & Morrow, of Media, $35.500 , Kirk & Henderson, of Media, $33,021 , Isaac Worrall, of Media, $32,670 70 , Simon Litzenberg, of Chester, $32,430, David S Kendell, of Philadelphia, $32,500 , Isaac N Flounders, of Media, $31,903 64 , Joseph Wells, of Thornbury, $29,959 , John Hinkson, of Chester, $29,000 Chalkley Chalfant, of Media, contracted to do the painting for $1350 The work was duly performed according to the contract, and some slight improvements have been made upon the building since, rendering it a court-house of which Delaware County may well be proud

An awe-inspiring incident occurred in the court-house at the March term, 1878 Thomas Townsend, of Lima, while passing along the aisle in the court-room, apparently in the best of health, fell to the floor and expired instantly The cause of his sudden demise was apoplexy

A singular escape of prisoners occurred from the court-room on Dec 3, 1883. John Williams and James Clark, who were on trial for burglary, as court was about to adjourn concealed themselves under a bench inside of the dock, and the sheriff absent-mindedly leaving the room and not thinking of them until he got to the jail, returned to find that they had fled the building They were soon recaptured, explained their shrewd but simple means of making their escape, and subsequently were sent to the Eastern Penitentiary

Concerning the history of the jail subsequent to its completion, there are a number of interesting items It is recorded that on Tuesday, April 18, 1854, the last of several prisoners, who had for some time been confined within its walls, was discharged, and that for nearly a week the prison was without a solitary inmate,—a condition of things which seldom if ever occurs nowadays

During the first few years after its completion escapes of prisoners from the jail were frequent occurrences John Cope, a colored man, regained liberty by scaling the wall, on Aug 22, 1851 Seven days later, Robert Lees hung himself upon the door of his cell by means of blankets torn into strips and twisted into the form of a rope He was discovered by fellow-prisoners, who gave the alarm. He was taken down and handcuffed to prevent his trying further suicidal experiments He complained of being deprived of his usual exercise, a privilege which the sheriff had deprived all of the prisoners of after Cope's escape over the wall Thus the liberty gained by one man brought about more rigorous confinement of the many

On Dec 29, 1851, two prisoners escaped from the jail during the absence of the sheriff One of them was recaptured, but the other, although closely pursued, could not be caught

John Doughty not only escaped confinement, but passed from it into the great unknown, dying in his cell on Feb 13, 1852 This was the first death in the prison

On Nov 30, 1860, David Mulley, who was imprisoned on the charge of attempting to shoot a man, escaped, but was recaptured He was a desperate case, and made a second escape on March 6, 1861

Christian Heff escaped over the wall on Feb 18, 1861, by means of a rope made of blankets Just before the prisoners were locked up he had concealed himself in the yard, and when all was quiet he managed to fasten his rope on the wall, and, climbing it, had only to drop down on the outside

Three persons broke jail on Oct 1, 1861

James War made his escape March 24, 1865, and William Waln, a horse-thief, regained his liberty July 19th of the same year

The frequency of escapes by prisoners and other causes led the commissioners to make improvements in 1868. One of the county papers thus speaks of the work in a July issue "The prison at Media has recently undergone considerable improvement, an addition having been built of forty-three by forty-eight feet, the height to the square being thirty-eight feet There are now forty cells, all of which are properly ventilated and secure The iron-work of the prison was done by Messrs Jaggers, Coverdill & Co, of

Chester, and their name for good work is a sufficient guarantee that the job is well done."

Notwithstanding these improvements, the grand jury in November, 1872, found the jail defective in many particulars, and recommended several improvements. Following is their report:

"*To the Honorable Judges of the Courts of Delaware County*:

"The grand jury, in the performance of the duty enjoined to them, have examined the prison, and inquired into the escape of prisoners therefrom, and respectfully submit the following suggestions to the court. A number of the cells in the prison are unsafe, the arches on the tops being of insufficient strength, from the lightness of the material of which they are built. There should be at least two dark cells, detached from the other parts of the prison, and out of hearing of the inmates thereof. The need of an infirmary is apparent, where prisoners who are sick can be kept separate from their fellows. The windows in the cells should be so altered as to deprive the occupants of a view of the prison-yard and streets. The pipes used for heating the building are badly out of repair, and the brick pavement in the interior is objectionable on account of the dampness. After a careful examination of the manner in which prisoners have escaped from the jail, the keeper of the prison is not, in our opinion, censurable in any way whatever, except so far as relates to one case, in which his deputy went into a cell without observing the necessary and usual precaution. The management of the institution is such as to reflect credit on those who have it in charge, the condition of the prison being neat and cleanly, and the prisoners apparently satisfied with the care and attention they receive."

Some of the measures advised by the grand inquest were adopted, and in 1877 extensive work was performed. The stone wall around the prison was extended and raised by William Armstrong, who took the job by contract. About six thousand dollars was expended on the prison during that and the following year.

In October, 1877, a laborious and determined effort was made to escape by a number of prisoners, who did not appreciate the large outlay of public money upon their quarters. This wellnigh successful attempt is thus described by a newspaper of the day:

"On Sunday evening last, as Mr Campbell, jailor of the county prison, was making his last round, he reached the cell of William Waters, Jacob Kelley, Neil McLaughlin, and Thomas Overholtzer, the prisoners who were convicted of the robbing of the stores of I E Boston and J E Brown, at Rockdale, some time since. Looking into the limits assigned them, he fancied that their bed was somewhat higher than usual, and he requested them to lift it up. On this being done a quantity of stone was found underneath, the result of an excavation made in the wall by them preparatory to their escape, one stone only being left between them and their liberty. The work had been accomplished from time to time with an iron hook, which he found in their possession. They were removed to other quarters."

In 1878 a new building was erected adjoining the original structure. This was seventy feet in length, forty-seven feet in height, and three stories high, affording six work-rooms and thirty-six cells. It cost sixteen thousand one hundred and forty dollars, including the heating apparatus, which alone amounted to over four thousand five hundred dollars.

In spite even of the additional safeguards secured during 1877–78, a few prisoners succeeded in gaining the outer world. On March 20, 1878, Daniel Pine, who had been sentenced to six years' confinement for the robbery of the residence of Mrs Fallon, in Upper Darby, and that of William Rhodes, in Newtown, scaled the wall with the aid of a piece of rope, which he had been ingenious enough to secure.

On Dec 27, 1879, two colored men made their escape by breaking a hole in the ceiling of one of the upper tier of cells, and then making their way from the roof to the ground.

On Feb 7, 1879, Joseph Williams died suddenly in the prison on the very day that he was to be released, after eleven months' confinement. He was seized with cramp in the stomach, which terminated in convulsions that quickly proved fatal.

Still later, on March 17, 1880, grim death came to the jail, this time under peculiar circumstances. The victim was Richard Neeld, and, strangely enough, he lost his life through the attempt of another inmate to escape. From the evidence at the inquest it appeared that Martin O'Harra, who occupied a cell directly over that in which Neeld was confined, had been working for some days diligently in endeavoring to escape. He cut a hole into the chimney-stack, by which he expected to reach the roof, and in order to get rid of the *débris*, and possibly with a view to stopping the inflow of coal-gas from below, he threw the refuse into the stack, thus stopping the means of ventilation for which the prisoners on the tier below depended. Two days before Neeld's death one of the prisoners in the cell below was affected to fainting, but subsequently recovered. At about five o'clock on the evening of March 17th, when meals were being served, the cell occupied by John Mulligan and another inmate was visited. Both these men were in a stupefied condition, but subsequently recovered. Neeld, in an adjacent cell, was found dead. The verdict rendered by the jury was, "Death caused by asphyxia, produced by carbonic acid gas."

The House of Employment, or the county poor-house, as most readers are aware, was located here long before the town had its beginning, in fact, early in the century. The act "to provide for the erection of a house for the employment and support of the poor in the county of Delaware" was passed Feb 13, 1804. The site was selected by a committee of seven, named in the act. The farm purchased consisted of one hundred and thirty-seven acres, and cost less than thirty-three dollars per acre. Later additions were made at one hundred dollars per acre. These prices were quite insignificant in comparison with those obtained for the same land after Media had been built up, when forty-six acres were sold at two hundred and fifty dollars, and one hundred and twelve at $341.50. The poor-house was completed within two or three years from the time the purchase was made, but we have no knowledge of the details of the work, nor of the early history of the institution, and, indeed, it is of no importance. The house was of stone, in the old English style, and was one hundred feet long by forty in width. A fine barn and other outbuildings stood near it. The following description of the institution, as it appeared in 1845, is from the pen of Miss Dix, who visited it:

"Several miles from Chester is a large stone building, clean, well kept, and well directed. The provisions are good and sufficient, and the food well prepared. Here were eighty-five inmates the third week in October; of these but few were children. From twelve to fifteen are insane and idiotic; were clean and comfortable, with the exception, perhaps, of wearing *chains* and *hobbles*. None were in close confinement, though such cases often occur. A small wooden building, constructed near the main dwelling, contains six cells, cleanly whitewashed and scrubbed, furnished with a small but comfortable bed, but not

COUNTY HOUSE, MEDIA.

capable of being warmed at all; accordingly, they are disused during the cold season. Each is lighted by a grated window. There are in the basement of the main building four cells, lined with sheet-iron, which are used for violent patients when necessary. There are no recoveries reported in the poor-house through remedial treatment. 'The most we expect,' said one of the family, 'is to do what we can for their comfort; we have no means for curing them.' The entire establishment seemed excellently conducted, and, but for the difficulty of managing the insane and idiotic, would afford a quiet home for the aged and infirm. It is estimated that there are in Delaware County about seventy cases of insane and idiotic persons. The poor-house farm is large and productive."

The directors of the poor, after a long discussion, in April, 1854, decided to sell the house of employment and property attached, and to purchase the farm of Abram Pennell, in Middletown, as the site for a new building. It was subsequently sold, and after a time torn down, and upon its site was erected the Haldeman House, which became Shortlidge's Boarding-School.

Of the new poor-house in Middletown, which was completed by April 1, 1857, having been begun a year before, it is scarcely our province to speak in this chapter. The principal contractor was Dutton Otley, assisted by Stephen Sager, master-carpenter. The tin-work and plumbing was done by Ralph Buckley, of Media.

Incorporation of Media as a Borough—The Temperance Struggle.—The growth, real and prospective, of the new town led its people to a general recognition of the desirability of establishing a local or borough government in less than eighteen months from the time that it was laid out. The project, which had been informally talked of during the latter part of 1849, first assumed definite shape at a meeting of the lot-owners, held Jan. 10, 1850, at the public-house of Peter Worrall,—the Providence Inn. On this occasion a resolution was adopted asking the Assembly to grant a charter incorporating the town as a borough, "with a section therein prohibiting the sale of ardent spirits within the new borough, and making it a penal offense to sell any kind of intoxicating liquors within said limits."

The fight between the friends and the opponents of temperance, or, more properly, prohibition, which had raged fiercely before, was now renewed with increased fury, and every individual was forced into the ranks of one or the other contending parties. On the 16th the Delaware County Temperance Society held a well-attended meeting at Hinkson's Corner, and as a result of its deliberations there appeared on the 25th a very spirited, yet well-balanced, address to the people of the county, advocating the prohibition of the sale of liquor in its seat of justice. This was signed by the twenty-four members of the central committee, among whom were J. P. Crozer, William T. Crook, Enos Sharpless, Rev. B. S. Huntington, John C. Beatty, Jonathan P. Abrams, Samuel Riddle, Jonathan Esrey, Samuel L. Leiper, Dr. George Smith, Minshall Painter, George G. Knowles, John F. Taylor, James J. Lewis, John F. Vanleer, William T. Pierce, and Rev. James W. Dale. Several more extremely able addresses were issued during the few months succeeding, and a vigorous agitation was kept up by the press and public speakers.

On Jan. 30, 1850, Mr. James J. Lewis, the representative from Delaware County, read before the House a bill to incorporate the borough of Media. Only two days before this, on the 28th of January, at a meeting held at Providence Inn, it had been resolved, on account of the temperance clause, to abandon for the time being the attempt to secure a charter, and a communication was forwarded calling for a postponement of the bill. It was destined, however, to pass, and that, too, with the prohibitory clause. When the decisive time came, on February 13th, the House of Representatives declared in its favor by a vote of 52 to 21. It passed the Senate March 7th, received the signature of the Governor on the 10th, and thus became a law.

The boundaries were described in the act as follows:

"Beginning at the corner of lands of Edward Lewis, Isaac Cochran, Andrew T. Walker, and John Hill, on the south side of the Philadelphia and Baltimore State road, in the township of Upper Providence; thence due south twenty-five perches through land of John Hill; thence eastwardly to a point two hundred and fifty feet on the eastern side of the road leading through Providence to Chester, and fifty perches south of the State road aforesaid, in the town of Nether Providence; thence northwestwardly parallel with and at the distance of two hundred and fifty feet eastward of said Providence road to a point opposite the intersection of the said Providence road and a road leading from the Rock House; thence southwestwardly across said Providence road, and through land of Joseph Rowland to the most northern point of land held by the directors of the poor of said county; thence southwestwardly along the northwestern boundaries of said land and lands held by the county commissioners of said county, and by Andrew T. Walker, to the place of beginning."

The prohibitory clause (iii. 60) was as follows:

"It shall not be lawful for any person or persons to vend or sell vinous, spirituous, or other intoxicating liquors within the limits of said borough, except for medical purposes, or for use in the arts; and it shall not be lawful for the Court of Quarter Sessions to grant any license or licenses therefor to any inn or tavern in said borough. If any person or persons shall within said borough vend or sell, or cause to be vended or sold, any vinous, spirituous, or other intoxicating liquors to any persons (except as provided for in this section), such person or persons so vending or selling, shall be liable to indictment, and on conviction thereof shall forfeit and pay for every such offense a sum not less than twenty nor more than one hundred dollars, at the discretion of the court: *Provided*, That it may be lawful for the Court of Quarter Sessions of said county to license inns or taverns in said borough without permission to vend or sell intoxicating drinks: *And provided*, Such license may be granted without the publication of any previous notice, as is required for other taverns."[1]

Isaac Haldeman, Joseph Rowland, and John Hill, who were authorized by the act to call an election for the purpose of choosing borough officers, on March 15th issued a notice to the citizens to meet on Tuesday, the 19th of the same month, at the public-house of Peter Worrall, to exercise the right of franchise as the law directed. At this election Isaac E. Price and David Hardcastle acted as inspectors. The officers chosen were as follows: Town Council, Dr. George Smith, Dr. Joseph Rowland, Isaac Haldeman, Nathan Shaw, Thomas T. Williams, and John C. Beatty; Town Clerk, Thomas Richardson; Treasurer, Charles Palmer; Assessor, Robert Rowland.[2] At the meeting of the Council March 27, 1850, the members drew lots to determine the length of time they should remain in office, with the result that Messrs. Williams and Smith should continue members for one year, Shaw and Rowland for two years, and Haldeman and Beatty for three years. Isaac Haldeman was chosen president of the board. Dr. Smith tendered his resignation on May 1st, and Joseph Edwards was appointed to fill the vacancy thus caused. At the succeeding meeting Mr. Edwards declined to serve, and Charles R. Williamson was elected to the position thus vacated.

[1] Delaware County Digest.

[2] On the Friday preceding the election above referred to, March 15th, there was a township election for Upper Providence township for officers to serve for it and for the new borough.

At the meeting of the Council on May 8th the first borough tax was ordered to be laid. This was for the repair of roads within the borough limits. On June 5th a committee was appointed to attend to the grading of the streets and their improvement otherwise, and Jacob Smedley was appointed at the same time borough surveyor. At a subsequent meeting Joel Evans was paid fourteen dollars for running the southern boundary line, and it is probable that he acted as substitute for Smedley. At the meeting of July 3d, Charles D. Manley was appointed borough solicitor. Thus the organization of the local government was gradually perfected and put in working order.

At a meeting held Jan. 1, 1851, the assessor's returns were examined and corrected, and on motion a tax of three mills on the dollar was laid on the valuation of the assessment. A court of appeal was ordered to be held at the public-house of Peter Worrall on the 25th of the month, and John C. Price was appointed collector of taxes.

The meetings of the Council, which from the beginning had been held from house to house of those who were its members, were, in August, 1851, transferred to the Charter House, of which we shall presently give the history. It was resolved to make that the permanent assembly-place of the municipal body, and a committee was appointed at the meeting of November 5th to make arrangements with Mr. Hawkins for the use of a room, which was subsequently secured for ten dollars per year.

In 1852 the tax levy was reduced to two and one-half mills on the dollar. John C. Price, at the meeting of June 2d, rendered his account as tax collector, from which it appeared that the whole amount of borough tax turned over was $156.66, and the dog tax $20.00, making a total of $176.66.

On Jan. 5, 1853, an ordinance was brought up for the removal of the place of the borough election from the public-house of Peter Worrall to the Charter House. It was passed on February 2d, and the next election, that of March 18th, was held at the newly-designated place.

Passing for the present, and reserving for separate consideration, the various measures for street improvements, we present a roster of the leading civil officials of Media borough from 1850 to the present time (with the exception of the school directors, whose names will be found appended to the section of this chapter devoted to educational matters):

BURGESSES.

1850–51. William T. Peirce.
1852. Charles D. Manley.
1853–54. Jesse Bishop.
1855–56. John C. Price.
1857–59. D. R. Hawkins.
1860–61. John M. Hall.
1862–63. D. R. Hawkins.
1864. Peter Worrall.
1865–70. John J. Rowland.
1871–72. George W. Ormsby.
1873. N. F. Walter.
1874–77. H. C. Snowden.
1878–79. William Eves, Jr.
1880. Samuel Dutton.
1881. William Campbell.
1882. Albin P. Ottey.
1883–84. Henry Green.

COUNCIL.

1850. George Smith, M.D.[1]
Joseph Rowland, M.D.
Isaac Haldeman.
Nathan Shaw.
Thomas T. Williams.
John C. Beatty.
1851. Ellis Smedley.
1852. John C. Price.
Thomas T. Williams.
1853. Isaac Haldeman.
John C. Beatty.
1854. C. R. Williamson.
1855. Clayton Smith.
D. A. Middleton.
1856. Isaac Haldeman.
Nathan Shaw.
1857. Joseph Iliff.
H. J. Brooke.
C. R. Williamson.
1858. I. R. Morris.
B. F. Baker.
1859. Isaac Haldeman.
Joseph Iliff.
1860. C. R. Williamson.
A. K. Scholl.
William T. Innes.
1861. Samuel P. Rush.
H. Jones Brooke.
1862. Isaac Haldeman.
Isaac Worrell.
1863. C. R. Williamson.
Joseph P. Campbell.
1864. John G. Haddock.
John M. Hall.
1865. Isaac Haldeman.
Samuel P. Rush.
Isaac Worrell, Jr.
1866. C. R. Williamson.
H. Jones Brooke.
1867. Samuel B. Thomas.
William Eves.
C. D. Manley.
1868. George E. Darlington.
Charles D. Manley.
1869. Charles R. Williamson.
H. Jones Brooke.
1870. William Eves, Jr.
John C. Beatty.
1871. Isaac Worrell.
Samuel B. Thomas.
1872. Charles R. Williamson.
Lewis Palmer.
1873. H. Jones Brooke.
John J. Rowland.
D. A. Vernon.
1874. Jacob Weaver.
D. A. Vernon.
1875. Charles R. Williamson.
Lewis Palmer.
1876. J. J. Rowland.
Thomas J. Haldeman.
H. B. Fussell.
1877. Jacob Weaver.
T. J. Haldeman.
1878. Charles R. Williamson.
Lewis Palmer.
1879. Henry C. Howard.
Terrence Riley.
1880. Samuel W. Hawley.
Winfield S. Worrall.
1881. Charles R. Williamson.
Lewis Palmer.
1882. Henry C. Howard.
Terrence Riley.
1883. Winfield S. Worrall.
Horace P. Green.
1884. C. R. Williamson.
Lewis Palmer.

TREASURERS.

1850–51. Charles Palmer.
1852–57. J. Hardcastle.
1857–64. George G. Fell.
1864. Joseph Iliff.
1865–78. George G. Fell.
1878–82. Levis Miller.
1882–85. Charles D. M. Broomall.

TOWN CLERKS.

1850–54. Thomas Richardson.
1854–58. Charles W. Shaw.
1858–59. J. Lawrence Haldeman.
1860–61. Joseph Addison Thomson.
1862. James G. Cummins.
Benjamin F. Baker.
1863. Thomas J. Kitts.
1864. James C. Henderson.
1865–67. Samuel P. Derrick.
1868–79. A. P. Otley.
1879–84. Townsend E. Levis.
1884. William H. Tricker.

JUSTICES OF THE PEACE.

	Date of Commission.
Isaac Cochran	April 13, 1852.
Oliver E. Strickland	April 11, 1854.
Nathan Shaw	April 16, 1858.
Isaac Sharpless	April 14, 1857.
Thomas H. Litzenberg	April 10, 1860.
James McMullin	April 9, 1861.
George H. Rigby	April 26, 1864.
Benjamin F. Baker	May 1, 1865.
William Russell	April 11, 1867.
William H. Howard	April 10, 1869.
William Russell	April 15, 1872.
F. Gardner Preston	March 24, 1872.
William H. Howard	March 24, 1874.
Nicholas F. Walter	March 4, 1879.
George H. Rigby	March 27, .879.
F. Gardner Preston (to fill vacancy)	Aug. 20, 1881.
F. Gardner Preston	April 10, 1882.

Name.—Both before and after the incorporation of the borough, when the name Media was bestowed upon it in lieu of Providence, there was a lively discussion carried on as to the most suitable name for the county-seat. One writer argued strongly in favor of "Pennrith," explaining in his newspaper communication that Penn in the Welsh language meant a hill, and "rith" John, so that the two together would signify John Penn, which was the name of William Penn's father, and, at the same time, "Penn," signifying a hill, would be descriptive of the locality. Some of the citizens were in favor of "Numedia,"—that is, *New* Media,—in contradistinction to ancient Oriental Media, but the majority favored Media, after it had been suggested by Minshall Painter. This name was vigorously combated by the friend of "Pennrith," who signed himself "John o' the Hill." He wrote as follows: "To say that it was called after the ancient country of Media would place us in a purely ridiculous position. To derive it from the Latin adjective, converting it into a noun, as the name of a place, would give it, if it were etymologically defensible, an origin so feeble as to ally it very closely to contempt." The name had, however, been adopted at a meeting held at the Providence Inn, Jan. 10, 1850, and "John o' the Hill's" communications failed to induce a change. For a number of years several newspapers and many of the people, among them the borough clerk, spelled the name Medea, as if they supposed the town named after the Asiatic queen, but gradually the present spelling was substituted for the old, and thus the word became what it was no doubt at first intended to be, a term significant of the central location of the place to which it was applied.

The Charter House.—This house, one of the notable institutions of Media, is at once a place of happy entertainment for "the wayfarer and the stranger," and a monument to those zealous friends of temperance who triumphed after a hard fight and made the prohibition of the liquor traffic one of the provisions of the town charter. It is, therefore, properly treated in this connection, for it followed as a result of the borough charter, and is deserving of more than a passing notice. The story of the building of this temperance hotel is briefly as follows: Only a few months after the incorporation of the borough, on Tuesday, Aug. 13, 1850, at a temperance harvest-home held at Media, it was resolved, at the suggestion of Rev. James W. Dale, to raise subscriptions to build a temperance hotel. This was an immense assemblage, the largest of the kind (according to the newspapers of the day) ever held in Delaware County. The people were flushed with the victory they had obtained in securing a charter which contained a prohibitory clause, and hence it was not strange that the sum of four thousand dollars should have been subscribed on the spot for the purpose of raising a tangible memorial of the battle which had been won. It was decided that the prospective building should be called the Charter House, and that it should not cost over five thousand dollars.

At a meeting held in Temperance Hall, Sept. 9,

[1] Smith declined; Charles R. Williamson elected to fill vacancy.

1850, of which John P. Crozer was chairman and John C. Beatty and Ellis Smedley secretaries, the Charter House Association was organized and articles of government drawn up and subscribed to. The officers elected were, President, William Eves; Vice-Presidents, John P. Crozer, John M. Sharpless, John Hill, Edward Garrett, Daniel M. Leiper, Abram L. Penrock, John Dunwoody, and William T. Cook; Secretary, William B. Lindsay; Associate Secretary, Benjamin Brooke; Treasurer, Abraham Pennell. Eighteen managers were also elected, as follows: Levis Miller, John C. Beatty, George G. Knowles, Joseph Rowland, M.D., George Bishop, Isaac Thomas, Thomas Pratt, James W. Vale, J. D. White, I. P. Abrahams, James Lewis, Nathan Shaw, John Sellers, James Barton, Robert M. Thomas, John F. Taylor, D. T. Hawkins, Enos Williamson; the members of the building committee were John C. Beatty, George G. Fell, and William Eves.

The views of the originators of the project having by this time become considerably enlarged and their enthusiasm growing rather waning, it was decided to increase the limit of cost to ten thousand dollars. Before the meeting adjourned the present site had been definitely fixed upon by D. T. Hawkins and William Apple, who were appointed a committee for that purpose.

John Eves was, on November 9th, awarded the contract for constructing the house and outbuildings for the sum of nine thousand five hundred dollars, and pledged himself to have the work completed by Aug. 1, 1851. The corner-stone was laid November 18th, by Hon. Sketchley Morton. In it were placed the articles of association, with the names of members and subscribers to the fund; names of members of the Town Council and other officials, copies of the county newspaper and the Philadelphia *Sun* and *Ledger*, and several other printed and written documents. Work went rapidly forward from this time.

On Jan. 9, 1851, the "Charter House Association" and the Delaware County Convention met at Providence Inn to commemorate by an anniversary dinner the adoption of the thirty-fourth section of the borough charter. On this occasion John F. Vanleer was chosen president; James Lewis, James T. Dannacker, John C. Beatty, and George G. Knowles, vice-presidents; D. T. Hawkins and J. F. Taylor, secretaries. A number of excellent toasts were offered, among them the following:

"*Media—Our New County-Seat*—redeemed from the traffic of intoxicating liquors by the common wish of the citizens of the county, its immediate residents, its storekeepers, its innkeepers, its borough officers, as well as by legislative enactment,—it shines forth 'a gem of the first WATER.'"

"*The Charter House.*—A noble monument, erected by a generous people, to commemorate the only constitutional legislation relative to the sale of intoxicating liquors—*entire prohibition*."

"*Providence Inn.*—The God of Providence can *now* smile upon it."

"*The Temperance Reform.*—Glorious in its origin and history, it rolls on to triumph through the legitimate channels of the pledged man, socially; the citizen, politically; and the Christian, ecclesiastically."

The fourth installment of subscriptions due to the Charter House Association was paid to Abram Pennell on March 24th. Up to that time but one individual had repudiated his subscription.

The house was pronounced finished by the 1st of May, and on June 18th it was rented to D. Reese Hawkins at six hundred dollars per year, he to furnish the building. He moved in on Thursday, July 10th, and opened the hotel for the accommodation of the public on the following Monday. He retained possession of the premises, with the exception of two short intervals, until 1871, when Cheney Bittle, of Thornbury, became landlord. After Mr. Bittle's short term of occupation several other landlords came and went in rapid succession, and in 1876, Mr. Watrus assumed the management of the house. He was followed by Charles Martel, in 1877; he by T. L. Hawkins, in 1879; and he by the present proprietor, I. Ivison, in April, 1882. The Charter House has borne and now bears an excellent reputation, and it affords ample testimony that a hotel can be successfully maintained without the aid of liquor sales.

Municipal Improvements—The Streets.—We have shown, in the account of the early proceedings of the Town Council, that action was taken by that body looking towards the improvement of the streets within the borough, but the minutes contain no evidence that any work was actually performed prior to 1851. At the meeting of July 1st in that year, the clerk was requested to notify, within ten days, the lot-holders "within the limits of the streets" to pave and curb before their respective properties, and at the same time the president was authorized to draw on the treasurer for the purpose of paying for the grading of South Avenue and State Street. At the next meeting an additional appropriation of fifty dollars was made for the grading of the streets mentioned. It was decided that the sidewalk flagging should be fifteen feet wide on South Avenue, ten feet on State Street, and the same width in front of unimproved lots. The street commissioners at this time were Isaac Haldeman and William T. Pierce. In the *Republican* Caleb J. Hoopes, John D. Gilpin, and Annesley Newlin, the county commissioners, advertised for sealed proposals for the paving of Court-House Square. A number of bids were received, one of which (from a Philadelphia firm) being accepted, the work was pushed ahead with vigor. Thus the county authorities were fully abreast of the borough officials in the matter of beautifying the town. In April, 1852, Mr. Hardcastle was elected as one of the street commissioners, in place of Mr. Haldeman, and served in that office with Mr. Pierce.

Important action concerning the improvement of the village was taken at the meeting of the Council on July 6, 1852, when it was resolved "that State, Front, Second, and Third Streets should be surveyed and laid out to Providence road on the east side, and on the west side to where the streets intersect with the road leading in front of A T Walker's house" Jacob Smedley was appointed as surveyor to carry out this project

These improvements were not immediately carried out, owing to the objection of a property-owner to having his lands entered upon, but in a few years even more than had originally been contemplated was realized in the way of opening, grading, paving, and curbing streets

Another era of public improvement was entered upon in the sixties, when quite extensive work was performed. On Dec 24, 1868, a committee reported to the Council that Old State Street had been paved, at a cost of $5403 63, New State Street, at a cost of $6935 21, and Washington Street, at a cost of $1663 98, making a total outlay for the public good of $8599 20 William H Tabler was the contractor

Water-Works—Almost simultaneously with the beginning of street improvements the Council exhibited its progressive character by taking steps to secure that great desideratum, an adequate supply of pure water On Sept 21, 1853, a special meeting was held to take into consideration immediate action in conjunction with the county commissioners for introducing water into the borough A committee of three members was appointed to confer with the commissioners concerning the construction of water-works and a suitable basin Nothing more was done during the year, except that the committee reported progress from time to time; but on the 7th of April, 1854, they stated that, "having viewed the ground, they had effected arrangements with the directors of the poor for one acre of ground suitable for a basin, and a grant of the right to build water-works to convey water to said basin" Isaac Haldeman, H Jones Brooke, and Charles R Williamson were then appointed a committee to negotiate a loan of five thousand dollars for the purpose of carrying out the work At a meeting on July 25th the proposal of R D Wood & Co, of Philadelphia, to furnish iron pipes was accepted It was discovered by this time that the amount of the loan would not be sufficient, and it was determined, at a special meeting, August 29th, that the chief burgess should call a town-meeting to discuss the propriety of extending it This plan was duly carried out, and on October 4th the president laid before the Council the written consent of fifty-four citizens, being a majority of the tax-payers, authorizing an additional loan of five thousand dollars for the enterprise On October 9th an improved ram, devised by Joseph Stroud, for forcing water into the basin was adopted, and on November 2d the president was authorized to make arrangements with Mr Stroud for the erection of the works At the special meeting previous to this one the president was authorized to enter into contract with Wood & Co for iron pipe, on condition that they should take not less than two thousand dollars in borough bonds, and it was subsequently reported that the contract had been effected, Wood & Co taking two thousand five hundred dollars in bonds

By June 15th the pipes were nearly all laid, and on July 9, 1855, the basin was completed On Jan. 2, 1856, Samuel P Rush was elected superintendent of the water-works In February the Council made an arrangement with the commissioner whereby the public buildings were to be supplied with water for ten years, on condition that the county should pay three thousand dollars in aid of the construction of the water-works, which sum was to be paid back to the county at the end of the term specified without interest On May 10th of this year the citizens authorized the Council to make an additional loan of five thousand dollars, which was not long afterwards negotiated

Although the water-works were practically completed this season, many improvements were subsequently found to be necessary, and extensions of the service-pipes were made from time to time In November, 1868, the pipes laid in Lemon Street from State to Eastman, at his own expense, by H Jones Brooke, were purchased from him by a committee appointed for the purpose In May of the following year Ralph Buckley was appointed superintendent of the works

In May, 1871, a town-meeting was called for the purpose of obtaining the sentiment of the people as to the purchase of the water-power of Ridley Creek, and the water of that stream was analyzed by an expert chemist of Philadelphia, who found it to contain the exceedingly small proportion of impurity of 5 043 grains to the gallon In August the president of the Council was authorized to purchase of Edward A Price the Palmer mill property, with water power for nineteen thousand five hundred dollars At a later meeting in the same month a committee reported in favor of the construction of a new basin west of the old one, to be sixty feet in diameter and fourteen feet in depth, and they also recommended that the old one should be increased in depth

The purchase of the mill property and water-power heretofore alluded to being confirmed by deed bearing date Dec 30, 1871, money was raised for necessary improvements, and in May, 1872, we find that the president of the Council was authorized to contract with the Philadelphia Hydraulic Works Company for the erection of pumps for the water-works, at a cost of two thousand nine hundred and twenty-five dollars.

The new basin was commenced in the fall of 1872, on a lot purchased from Frederick Fairlamb for nine hundred dollars, the contract for excavating being awarded to Rebill & McLogue, and for those for the brick-laying to S Morton & Son, Thomas M Garrett, and William Worrall, for fifteen dollars per thousand

The works were now operated by William P Mancil, who had leased the grist-mill, and the water-power being found insufficient as the demand upon the works increased, a steam-pump was added in 1875

Gas-Works.—The Media Gas Company was incorporated April 11, 1866, with twenty-seven corporators and a capital of ten thousand dollars, which it was their privilege to increase. The president was H. Jones Brooke. In 1868 the company purchased eighty-five perches of land from this gentleman, upon which, in the spring of 1871, they erected gas-works, at a cost of twenty thousand dollars. The works were completed and gas introduced into the houses of some of the citizens on September 10th.[1] The company has been reasonably well sustained and is moderately prosperous. Its stock is now valued at twenty thousand dollars, and is divided into eight hundred shares. Isaac Worrall was elected president of the company in 1877, and holds that office at present, V. Gilpin Robinson is treasurer, and Jesse M. Baker, secretary.

The Post-Office and Postmasters.—During the first years of Media's existence her people as a rule obtained their mail-matter from the Rose Tree, but in the early part of 1852 this facility was afforded them by the Nether Providence post-office at the public-house of Peter Worrall. The list of advertised letters for the quarter ending March 31st, which numbered sixty four names, was the first that appeared in print either with or without Mr. Worrall's name, and it is therefore probable that the office was not officially recognized until the beginning of the year. A local item in one of the newspapers of the day stated that "the post-office at Nether Providence has been removed to Media, its name has been changed, and Ellis Smedley appointed deputy until the present postmaster removed to a more convenient location." Mr. Worrall, however, did not remove to Media. Early in May, 1853, Charles R. Williamson was appointed postmaster in place of Mr. Smedley, who resigned, and the office was removed from Smedley's store, on the northeast corner of State Street and South Avenue, to the residence and store of Mr. Williamson, on the southeast corner of Front and Orange Streets, where more recently Mr. Levis Miller made his home. Since Mr. Williamson's time the succession of the custodians of the office has been as follows: Thomas Williamson, William T. Inness, Joseph G. Cummins, Samuel Dutton, and Mrs. Miranda Williamson. This lady, the present postmistress, was appointed April 4, 1877, and reappointed in December, 1881.

Educational Matters—The Public Schools.—The earliest mention of the Media schools of which we have any knowledge occurs in one of the county newspapers under date of May 20, 1853, and is as follows:

"COMMENDABLE.—The School Directors of Upper Providence have contracted to erect a suitable building to be occupied as a public school in the borough of Media. It is to be hoped that a house worthy of the place will be built."

A small brick school-house was erected during the year, which was the first in the new town. Media became a separate school district early in 1856. The directors elected were H. Jones Brooke, William F. Pierce, D. R. Hawkins, Samuel P. Rush, Thomas F. Williams, and R. H. Smith, and they held their first meeting March 29th, at the brick school-house. Committees were appointed to effect a settlement with the directors of Upper and Nether Providence, and also to confer with those of the latter township in regard to the school-house at Peter Worrall's. At a meeting held on April 11th, it was decided to use this house jointly, but subsequently, owing to a difficulty with the Nether Providence directors, the agreement was declared null and void.

On May 1, 1856, the directors resolved to erect a frame school-house on the lot which is now owned by Samuel Fields, and John G. Haddock was awarded the contract for two hundred and sixty-seven dollars. The building was finished in June.

Joseph Addison Thompson was appointed to take charge of the grammar school on May 23, 1857.

On Jan. 16, 1858, the eastern school-house and lot (Nether Providence) were sold to William L. Green for three hundred and eighty-five dollars, and on April 18, 1859, the committee appointed for the purpose reported that they had purchased a lot from James Barton for four hundred and twenty-five dollars. This was the property on which the present new building stands. The contract for building a school-house on this lot was awarded, Aug. 25, 1859, to Stephen D. Sager, for four thousand eight hundred and forty-five dollars. He gave up the contract, however, four days later, and the work was then awarded to Haddock & Worrall, at five thousand three hundred and forty-seven dollars. They, in turn, abandoned it upon September 7th, and upon the 26th it was reawarded to them at three thousand one hundred and forty dollars, the board having determined in the mean time to build upon a less extensive scale than had been contemplated. The house was to be seventy-five by thirty-five feet, and one story high.

The corner stone was laid with significant ceremonies on October 31st. On that occasion Rev. J. W. Dale opened the exercises with prayer, after which a song, composed for the day, was sung by the children of the grammar school. The Hon. H. Jones Brooke deposited in the stone a tin box containing a roll of the pupils of the grammar school,—Joseph Addison Thompson, teacher, dated Oct. 1, 1859 (at that time there were sixty-nine in attendance), the roll of the primary school, Miss Sue Pearce, teacher, seventy-one scholars, a list of county and borough officers, four newspapers,—the *American*, *Chester Republican*, *Upland Union*, and the *Christian Advocate and Journal*, New York, the Sixth Annual Report of the Pennsylvania Training School and Pennsylvania Common Schools Report for 1858. The school directors at this time were D. R. Hawkins, Charles

[1] We may remark here that the first house in Delaware County illuminated by gas was that of Christopher Fallon, of Upper Darby, in 1853. The gas was generated on his own premises and ignited on December 28th.

D. Manley, R. H. Smith, Ralph Buckley, H. Jones Brooke, and William T. Inness. Addresses appropriate to the occasion were made by Joseph Addison Thompson, Rev. J. Pastorfield, and Rev. Henry S. Getz concluded the ceremonies by pronouncing the benediction.

The building was completed and accepted by the directors on April 25, 1860. In the mean time the old lot and the brick building upon it had been sold to Charles R. Williamson for five hundred and fifty dollars.

Mr. Smett succeeded Joseph Addison Thompson as principal of the grammar school, and was in turn succeeded by David W. Harlan in April, 1862.

The building completed in 1860 was in use until 1883, when the contract for erecting a new and more commodious structure was let to Isaac N. Flounders, and the old school-house was torn down to give place for the new. This building, which is seventy by eighty feet and two stories high, will, when completed, cost about eighteen thousand dollars.

Following is a list of the school directors from 1856 to the present:

1856, H. Jones Brooke, D. R. Hawkins, William T. Peirce, R. H. Smith, T. T. Williams, Samuel P. Rush; 1857, H. Jones Brooke, R. H. Smith; 1858, Charles D. Manley, R. Buckley; 1859, W. T. Inness, D. R. Hawkins; 1860, R. H. Smith, H. Jones Brooke, N. F. Walter; 1861, N. F. Walter, James R. Cummins; 1862, William T. Quins, D. R. Hawkins, Edward A. Price; 1863, H. J. Brooke, Edward A. Price; 1864, Samuel P. Rush, R. H. Smith; 1865, Frederick Fairlamb, O. F. Bullard; 1866, D. R. Hawkins, N. T. Walter; 1867, Samuel P. Rush, Dr. A. W. Matthues, Benjamin Crowthers; 1868, Lewis Kirk, James W. Baker; 1869, D. R. Hawkins, O. Flagg Bullard; 1870, S. P. Rush, Thomas J. Kitts; 1871, Samuel W. Hallowell, Samuel Dutton; 1872, O. F. Bullard, C. D. M. Broomall; 1873, S. P. Rush, Thomas J. Kitts, George Broomall; 1874, Samuel Dutton, Melvina Fairlamb, Sallie J. Cummins; 1875, Charles D. M. Broomall, Mrs. Letitia Eves; 1876, Isaac Johnson, Thomas J. Kitts, Mrs. Clara B. Miller; 1877, Mrs. M. M. Fairlamb, Charles S. Welles; 1878, Charles P. Walter, John T. Reynolds; 1879, Lewis Levis, Samuel P. Rush; 1880, Jesse M. Baker, Mrs. Melvina Fairlamb; 1881, Mrs. F. N. Baker, John T. Reynolds; 1882, Lewis Levis, George E. Adams; 1883, Jesse M. Baker, Milton Lewis; 1884, John T. Reynolds, Francis N. Baker, Samuel Dinsmore.

Brooke Hall Female Seminary.—Brooke Hall was built by Hon. H. Jones Brooke, in whose honor it was named. On its completion, in the fall of 1856, it was opened as a seminary for young ladies by Miss M. L. Eastman, its present principal and owner. It has enjoyed continued prosperity, and its future is promising. A writer, upon its last commencement, June 15, 1884, says, "Few commencements of this flourishing seminary have exceeded this in the manifold attractions of its exercises." Another person says, "The history of this institution is written in the lives of its many pupils who have completed a course of study within its classic walls." An account of the only disaster which has ever occurred at this institution, a fire, which destroyed the gas-house, on Dec. 17, 1859, has already been given in this chapter.

Media Academy.—In the fall of 1872, Miss Anna M. Walter, who had for several years been a teacher in the grammar school, established a private school in a room over Haldeman's store. It was kept there for four or five years, and then removed to a brick building, erected by Charles Walter, on Front Street, near Jefferson. Three rooms in two stories of this building were used, and two assistants were employed, Miss Fanny Walter and others. The school had from fifty to seventy-five pupils. In April, 1884, the school closed under Miss Fanny Walter, as Miss Anna M. Walter had accepted a position as teacher at the Friends' school at Fifteenth and Race Streets, Philadelphia.

Shortlidge's Academy.—In 1874, Swithin C. Shortlidge's school for boys, which had been for some time in existence at West Chester, was removed to Media, and opened in the building which had been formerly known as the Haldeman House. This was enlarged and improved for its new use, and made an admirable home for the school. The school has since been carried on without interruption, except the regular vacations, when (in the longer ones occurring in summer) the house is occupied as a summer hotel. The building is four stories high, with a basement, and contains fifty-five lodging-rooms, a large dining-hall, ample study-rooms, and five class-rooms. A large and well-equipped gymnasium building has been built near the main structure.

The corps of instructors is composed as follows:

Swithin C. Shortlidge, principal instructor (having constant charge of the school, classification, etc., and sole government at all times of the young men and boys); B. N. Lehman, teacher of Physics, Geography, and Engineering; Nelson H. Strong, A.B., teacher in school-room; James J. Greenough, teacher of Algebra, Geometry, Trigonometry, etc.; Arthur B. Linsley, teacher of English Grammar, Rhetoric, and Composition; Linton Satterthwaite, A.B., teacher of Commercial Arithmetic and Book-keeping; A. E. Osborne, teacher of Physiology and Botany and Natural History; Professor S. K. Murdock, teacher of Elocution and Declamation; Charles M. Hobbs, teacher of Arithmetic; Otto Mueller, teacher of Drawing, Gymnastics, and Military Drill (optional); W. F. Hughes, teacher of English Grammar, Reading, Spelling, and Literature; Walter E. Damon, teacher of Greek, Grecian History, and Literature; Messrs. Lingle and McKnight, teachers of Short-hand and Telegraphy; A. B. Babbitt, teacher of Latin, Roman History, and Literature; Thomas J. Wynn, teacher of Piano and Vocal Music; H. M. Carpenter, teacher of Violin, Flute, etc.; William S. Porter, Secretary and Librarian; Lewis S. Hough, teacher of English; M. E. Diefenderfer, teacher of Plain and Ornamental Penmanship.

Delaware County Institute of Science.—This institution was intended to be organized under the name of the Delaware County Cabinet of Science, but upon meeting and consideration it was decided to organize under the above name,—Delaware County Institute of Science. The first meeting was held in Upper

Providence on the 21st of September, 1833, by five persons,—George Miller, Minshall Painter, John Miller, George Smith, and John Cassin An acre of land was purchased near Rose Tree, and in 1837 a two-story brick building was erected, which was formally opened in September of that year, upon which occasion an address was delivered by Dr Robert M Patterson, then director of the United States Mint The society increased in numbers and was incorporated Feb 8, 1836 Lectures were given in the hall and a museum was established, which received many specimens in every department of natural science A library also was opened In 1867 the present building in Media was erected and the institute was removed to the new hall prepared for it The library contains nearly three thousand volumes, besides many valuable and scarce pamphlets, and the museum is now extensive, and embraces many specimens of interest in science, history, Indian relics, zoological specimens, minerals, coins, birds, insects, etc The society has a membership of about two hundred Dr George Smith was president from the first till his death, February, 1882 He was succeeded by John M Broomall, who is the present incumbent

The Methodist Episcopal Church—The Methodists were the pioneers in religious movements in Media In 1851 the Rev John B Maddux, who had charge of Village Green Church, preached in Temperance Hall in Media, and a class of five members was organized, of which John Hardcastle was leader During the winter prayer-meetings and class-meetings were held in the house of Joseph Iliff In August, 1851, a lot, eighty by one hundred and fifty feet, was purchased, with a view of erecting a house of worship upon it at some propitious time A charter was obtained the same year The Rev Ignatius T Cooper succeeded to the charge of the circuit, and services were held on the church lot under an apple-tree, and during the winter in the court-house Mark Packard subsequently fitted up a room in the upper part of his barn, which was used as a meeting-place by the church and also for a Sunday-school, which was organized about that time under Mr Packard's superintendence A public appeal in behalf of the project of erecting a church appeared in the columns of the *Delaware County Republican*, April 8, 1853, and was from the able pen of Rev Cooper In his communication it was stated that there were at that time but about a dozen Methodists in Media, but he intimated that a large number of them resided in its immediate vicinity He gave a number of forcible reasons why such a church edifice should be erected without delay, and urged his brethren to commence at once the final efforts that were needed to consummate the work It was stated that about twelve hundred dollars had been subscribed of the amount required, three thousand five hundred dollars, and that ground would not be broken until two thousand dollars had been secured The ministers named to receive the contributions were Rev Mr Hobbs, Rev Henry G. King, and Rev I T Cooper The others appointed were Mark Packard, of Media, D R Hawkins, Hinkson's Corner, Abram Vanzant, Avondale, and John Godfrey, Crook's Upper Bank The appeal was an earnest, and subsequently proved to be an effective, one, in behalf of what Mr Cooper termed "the Metropolitan Church of Delaware County"

It may seem a little strange that one of the paragraphs in the reverend gentleman's communication should have contained the declaration that "the men and women will sit separately in the congregation," but such was the fact

The corner-stone of the church was laid Aug 7, 1854, Rev Dr H G King and Rev J S Lane officiating The basement was dedicated Aug 26, 1858, the services being conducted by Revs John A Roche and Samuel Pancoast Rev H G King was at that time on the circuit, and preached to the congregation In the spring of 1858 the main edifice was completed, and the dedicatory sermon was preached by Rev Franklin Moore, D D In 1859 the church became an independent station

Following is a list of pastors of this church 1859-61, Rev Jeremiah Pastorfield, 1861-62, Rev Samuel Gracey (Mr Gracey having accepted a chaplaincy in the Union army in 1862, Rev David McKee was pastor during the remainder of the term), 1863-66, Rev Daniel George, 1866-68, Rev Henry F Hurn, 1868-70, Rev John F Timmanus, 1870-71, Rev Samuel Lucas, 1871-72, Rev John I Gracey, 1872-75, Rev Jerome Lindermuth, 1875-78, Rev George T Hurlock, 1878-80, Rev Joseph R Gray, 1881-83, Rev S A Heibner, 1884, Rev F M Griffith

During the pastorate of the Rev G T Hurlock the church edifice was improved and a brick parsonage erected The church has at present a membership of about two hundred, and the Sunday-school has about the same number of members

The South Media Methodist Episcopal Church was erected by Mark Packard in 1876 The pulpit is supplied by the Local Preachers' Association of Philadelphia The society numbers about twenty, the Sunday school one hundred

Presbyterian Church—Before Media borough was laid out, the Rev James W Dale preached near what was to be its boundary, in the school-house on the Providence road, on the corner of the road to Beatty's mill When the removal of the county-seat was determined upon and Media had been founded, regular services were commenced in the village in a room over John C Beatty's store The first was held March 10, 1850 The Rev Mr Dale, who was then pastor of the Middletown Presbyterian Church, officiated A Sunday-school was organized soon after in Mr Beatty's house

The site of the church, about one acre of ground, was donated by John C Beatty. The corner-stone was laid July 4, 1854 The architect, John McArthur, Jr, of Philadelphia, designed the building in he Doric order of architecture, which proved very effective when the edifice was completed James W Haddock, of Media, was the chief contractor The church was dedicated on Thursday, Oct 11, 1855, although not entirely finished A number of prominent ministers were present. On the following Sunday the first regular religious services were held, and were of a very impressive character Up to this time there had been no individual church organization, but the congregation had existed as a mission of the Middletown Church On Oct 1, 1866, the Presbytery of Philadelphia met at Media, according to previous appointment, and organized a church with forty-six members, four elders, and three deacons Rev James W Dale was installed as pastor, and remained until 1868, after which time he served the Middletown Church until 1871, when he was called to the Wayne Church From 1868 to 1872 the pulpit was supplied by young men from Princeton Seminary, and upon April 17th of the latter year, Rev E H Robbins, who had been called in November, 1871, was ordained and installed as pastor He still has charge of the church, which is in a flourishing condition and has a membership of nearly two hundred A parsonage was erected adjoining the church in 1880

Christ (Episcopal) Church.—During the summer of 1853 the first Episcopalian religious services in Media were held in the court-house, then recently built The Rev L P W Balch, D D, of the Church of the Holy Trinity, West Chester, officiated From that time until the present church edifice was constructed services were held in the court-house and in the Methodist Church Among the officiating clergymen were Rev G E Hare and Rev B S Huntington. On Aug 28, 1854, a charter of incorporation was granted the society by the court of Delaware County, and about the same time the Rev S Hazelhurst accepted the rectorship of the church, but remained, however, only about eight months On Nov 22, 1857, the Rev H. S Getz (deacon) became minister of the parish, but was not ordained as a priest until Dec. 19, 1858.

The corner-stone of the present church edifice was laid July 5, 1858, by the Right Rev Alfred Lee D D, Bishop of Delaware Several members of the clergy, among them the pastor, made impressive addresses On the 21st of June, 1860, the church was consecrated by the Right Rev Alonzo Potter, D D, LL D, Bishop of Pennsylvania, the Right Rev. Alfred Lee, D.D, assisting

The rectorship of Rev Mr Getz having terminated on April 1, 1862, an invitation was extended to Rev S Edwards to become pastor in January of the following year He accepted the call, and assumed the duties of the office on Feb 1, 1863. Mr Edwards resigned on June 30, 1866, and on the 9th of December an invitation was extended to Rev Samuel W. Hallowell to supply the church for three months, which was accepted When his time as supply expired he was unanimously elected to the rectorship, and served the church until his death, in May, 1872 He was succeeded in the following October by the Rev W. T Chesley Morrell, who resigned in March, 1874, to become rector of St Philip's Church, in Philadelphia During his term of service Mrs Mary A Hoeckley built and presented to the parish the beautiful stone rectory adjoining the church, as a memorial to her late husband

In October, 1875, the Rev Edward Lounsberry, of the diocese of Iowa, was elected to the rectorship, and continued in office until his death, Oct 12, 1878 During his term of service the tower was added to the church, at a cost of two thousand five hundred dollars, and a pipe-organ was procured The chancel-rail and marble font were contributed by the young ladies of Brooke Hall After the death of Mr Lounsberry the church was supplied until April 6, 1879, when the Rev De Witt C Byllesby, previously rector of St Luke's Church, Roselle, N J, who had been elected in March preceding, entered upon his duties He is still discharging the duties of the position

There is a Sunday-school in connection with the church, which occupies a building erected at a cost of five thousand five hundred dollars in 1868

Church of the Nativity of the Blessed Virgin (Roman Catholic).—A mission was established by the Roman Catholics at the house of Edward Dugan, at Upper Bank, in 1858 The Rev Nicholas Walsh, at that time pastor of St Thomas' Church, Aston, was in charge of this mission A little later services were held at the house of Lawrence Forman, in Media About 1860 the Rev. Thomas Kyle, pastor of the church at Aston, purchased a lot on Franklin Street, Media, and erected the brick building now used as a Sunday-school room This was dedicated in September, 1862, and was used as a chapel until the completion of the present church edifice The society remained a mission of St Thomas' Church until October, 1868, when Rev Henry L Wright, who had been pastor of the latter, was appointed to take charge of the Media Church, which then became independent The brick parsonage on the lot adjoining the church was completed in July, 1869 The lot on which the church stands was bought by Bishop Wood of Menader Wood The handsome church built upon this lot, at a cost of seventeen thousand five hundred dollars, was dedicated in June 1882, the ceremonies being conducted by Bishop O'Hara, of Scranton, and the sermon preached by Rev Father McDermott The parish numbers the members of about one hundred families among its communicants

The Baptist Church—On the 26th of June, 1871, the first regular services of the Baptist denomination were held in the borough After the close of the exercises of worship, the assembly, consisting of twelve persons, was organized, with C H Russell as moderator and William Russell as clerk The question as to the expediency of establishing a Baptist Church was raised, and decided affirmatively. The present church lot was donated by Edward A. Price, and a sufficient sum of money being subscribed to warrant the undertaking, a contract was entered into with I. N. Flounders for the erection of a church. The amount of the contract was six thousand dollars. The house was duly finished, and in May, 1872, was dedicated by Rev. E. Levy, D.D., who preached an impressive sermon. Rev. J. W. Dale took part in the services.

Up to this time meetings had been held in private dwellings, in the court-house, and elsewhere.

On Sept. 12, 1872, the society, consisting of twenty-two members, was reorganized as "the First Baptist Church of Media" by a council composed of ten neighboring churches. The Rev. H. C. Applegarth, who had filled the pulpit since 1875, became the regular pastor in 1877. He was succeeded, in October, 1878, by Rev. T. G. Wright, who served the congregation until April, 1881, when the present pastor, the Rev. W. R. Patton, assumed charge.

This church has about seventy-five members, and its Sunday-school about one hundred and thirty.

Hicksite Church—Providence Meeting-House.—The Minshall Meeting was first held in the house of John Minshall far back in the last century. The foundation of the house and the old well are still to be seen. Their location is such that State Street when extended will pass over them. The first meeting-house here was built on an acre of ground given by John Minshall for the purpose, and he subsequently gave another acre for a graveyard. The house, which was of stone, with a hip-roof, was used for many years, but was torn down about 1812 to make place for the present one. Phœbe Foulkes is a member of this meeting, and preaches here occasionally. The meeting has about one hundred members.

Friends' Meeting-House.—In 1875 the Friends of Media and its vicinity, withdrawing from the various meetings round about, bought a lot from John M. Broomall,—one-eighth of an acre on the north side of Third Street, opposite North Avenue,—and erected upon it a one and a half story stone meeting-house. Here their regular meetings are held. In an iron safe in this house are kept the records of Chester Monthly Meeting, dating from 1682 to the present.

Media Bible Society.—An undenominational Bible society was organized at a meeting held in the Episcopal Church early in June, 1870, of which Rev. James W. Dale was president, and William Russell, secretary. Addresses were delivered by Rev. Mr. Terrence and others, after which a society was formed under the name of "The Media and Vicinity Bible Society." A constitution was then adopted, and the following officers elected: President, Dr. Joseph Parrish; Vice-Presidents, Rev. J. W. Dale, Rev. S. Hallowell, Rev. S. Lucas, William Russell; Secretary, S. B. Thomas; Treasurer, D. R. Hawkins; Managers, Miss H. Brooke, E. E. Boardman, T. J. Byles, Mrs. Mary Bishop, Miss Lizzie Haldeman, N. F. Walter, William Copperthwaite, Mrs. C. W. Rudolph, J. C. Beatty, and Mrs. Craine. The purpose of this society is to promote the circulation of the Scriptures without note or comment.

Newspapers.—The first newspaper in Media was *The Union and Delaware County Democrat*, a small sheet started prior to June, 1852, by Charles B. Stowe. The town was then quite small, and it is not strange that the obituary of the little sheet should have appeared in the *Republican* as early as Dec. 29, 1854. It read as follows: "DEAD.—*The Union and Delaware County Democrat*, published at Media in this county, has adjourned *sine die*, its editor having removed to West Chester. A good opportunity is now presented to an enterprising man with a few thousand dollars, who desires to embark in the printing and publishing business." The story of its life is sufficiently suggested by the announcement of its death.

The next newspaper venture in the new county-seat was destined to be a more successful one, and to result in the permanent establishment of what is now known as *The Delaware County American*. The paper was started as the *Media Advertiser* by Thomas V. Cooper and D. A. Vernon, and the first impression, a seven-column sheet twenty-four by thirty-six inches, came from the press on March 1, 1855. Its politics were Republican. The publication office was on State Street.

The Delaware County Republican in its notice of the appearance of the new paper said, "It takes the place of the *Media Union*, a paper the publication of which was suspended for want of sufficient support to keep it alive." But it did not take the place of the *Union* in the Delaware County newspaper mortuary list. The proprietors had a large capital of tact, perseverance, industry, and economy, and they soon gave the paper a respectable standing among the local journals of the State. One enlargement after another added to its size until it assumed its present generous proportions, and journalistic ability kept the standard of quality fully up to the measure of quantity in its contents. The name of the paper was changed Feb. 27, 1856, from the *Media Advertiser* to the *Media Advertiser and Delaware County American*, and on March 2, 1859, the first part of the title was dropped, leaving that which at present stands at its head, *The Delaware County American*, although several changes have ensued at different periods. Mr. Cooper retired from the partnership July 4, 1860, and re-entered on July 12, 1865, the firm-name then becoming Vernon & Cooper, as it now exists.

The *American* is now a ten-column sheet, thirty-three by fifty inches in dimensions, and is a bright, newsy chronicle of Media and Delaware County affairs, and of the world's happenings as well. It is generously patronized by the people of the town and surrounding country.

Benjamin F. Niles, who for several years was the

Isaac Haldeman

[illegible] street, and [illegible] [illegible]. The present church lot was donated by Edward A. Price, and a sufficient sum of money being subscribed to warrant the undertaking a contract was entered into with I. [illegible] Flounders for the erection of a church. The amount of the contract was [illegible] thousand dollars. The house was [illegible] finished, and in May, [illegible], was dedicated by Rev. [illegible], D.D., who preached the [illegible] sermon. Rev. [illegible] took part in the services.

[illegible] services had been held in private dwellings, [illegible], and elsewhere.

On Sept. [illegible], a [illegible], consisting of twenty-[illegible] members, was [illegible] as "The First Baptist Church of Media" by a council composed of [illegible] neighboring churches. The Rev. [illegible] Applegarth, who had [illegible] the pulpit since 185[illegible], became the regular pastor in 18[illegible]. He was succeeded, in [illegible], 18[illegible], by Rev. [illegible] Wright, who served the congregation until April, [illegible], when the present pastor, the Rev. W. [illegible] [illegible] assumed charge.

This church has about seventy-five members, and its Sunday-school about one hundred and thirty.

Minshall Church.—Providence Meeting-House.—The Minshall Meeting was first held in the house of John Minshall far back in the last century. The [illegible] of the house and the old well are still th[illegible] [illegible]. Their location is such that State Street when [illegible] will pass over them. The first meeting-house [illegible] was built on an acre of ground given by John Minshall for the purpose, and he subsequently gave another acre for a graveyard. The house, which was a stone [illegible] for many years, but was [illegible] to make place for the present one. [illegible] finished, [illegible] have [illegible]. The [illegible] has about [illegible] hundred members.

Friends' Meeting-House.—[illegible] of Media and its vicinity, [illegible] from the [illegible] meetings [illegible], built a [illegible] M. [illegible] of an acre on the [illegible] side of Third Street, opposite North Avenue, and erected upon it a [illegible] and a half story stone [illegible]-house. Here their regular meetings are held. [illegible] in this house are kept the records of Chester Monthly Meeting, [illegible] to 1682 [illegible].

Media Bible Society.—[illegible] Bible society was [illegible] Episcopal Church [illegible], 18[illegible], [illegible] Rev. James W. [illegible] was president and William Russell, secretary. Addresses were delivered by Rev. Mr. [illegible] and others, [illegible] under the name of "The Media and Vicinity Bible Society." A constitution was then adopted and the following officers elected: President, [illegible]; Vice-Presidents, Rev. J. W. [illegible], Rev. S. Ral-[illegible], Rev. S. Lucas, William [illegible]; Secretary, [illegible]; Treasurer, D. S. [illegible]; Managers, [illegible] E. K. [illegible], Mrs. Mary Bishop, Miss Lizzie Haldeman, N. F. Walter, William Copperthwaite, Mrs. G. W. Rudolph, J. C. Beatty, and Mrs. Craine. The purpose of this society is to promote the circulation of the Scriptures without note or comment.

Newspapers.—The first newspaper in Media was *The Union and Delaware County Democrat*, a small sheet started prior to June, 1852, by Charles D. Stowe. The town was then quite small, and it is not strange that the obituary of the little sheet should have appeared in the *Republican* as early as Dec. 29, 1854. It read as follows: "DEAD.—*The Union and Delaware County Democrat*, published at Media in this county, has adjourned *sine die*, its editor having removed to West Chester. A good opportunity is now presented to an enterprising man with a few thousand dollars, who desires to embark in the printing and publishing business." The story of its life is sufficiently suggested by the announcement of its death.

The next newspaper venture in the new county-seat was destined to be a more successful one, and to result in the permanent establishment of what is now known as *The Delaware County American*. The paper was started as the *Media Advertiser* by Thomas V. Cooper and D. A. Vernon, and the first impression, a seven-column sheet twenty-four by thirty-six inches, came from the press on March 1, 1855. Its politics were Republican. The publication office was on State Street.

The Delaware County Republican in its notice of the appearance of the new paper said, "It takes the place of the *Media Union*, a paper the publication of which was suspended for want of sufficient support to keep it alive." But it did not take the place of the *Union* in the Delaware County newspaper mortuary list. The proprietors had a large capital of tact, perseverance, industry, and economy, and they soon gave the paper a respectable standing among the local journals of the State. One enlargement after another added to its size until it assumed its present generous proportions, and journalistic ability kept the standard of quality fully up to the measure of quantity in its contents. The name of the paper was changed Feb. 27, 1856, from the *Media Advertiser* to the *Media Advertiser and Delaware County American*, and on March 2, 1859, the first part of the title was dropped, leaving that which at present stands at its head, *The Delaware County American*, although several changes have ensued at different periods. Mr. Cooper retired from the partnership July 4, 1860, and re-entered on July 12, 1865, the firm-name then becoming Vernon & Cooper, as it now exists.

The *American* is now a ten-column sheet, thirty-three by 5[illegible] inches in dimensions, and is a bright, newsy chronicle of Media and Delaware County affairs and of the world's happenings as well. It is generously patronized by the people of the town and surrounding country.

[illegible], who for several years was the

Isaac Haldeman

editor of the *American*, and well known in newspaper circles, died at Media in January, 1871.

The Upland Union, a paper which had long existed at Chester, and which was noted for its numerous suspensions and revivals, was brought to life here on Oct. 17, 1858, and placed temporarily in charge of Charles D. Manley, Esq., who, however, was very soon superseded by W. Cooper Talley, of Aston, later of the *Delaware County Democrat*, and Mr. Brimner, who had edited the *Pennsylvanian* at Philadelphia. The publication of the *Union* was suspended Feb. 19, 1861.

The Delaware County Record was established by J. W. Batting & Co., the company being C. D. Williamson and Joseph Chadwick, on March 23, 1878, as an independent local newspaper. Originally an eight-column paper, twenty by twenty-seven inches, page measure, it was so successful that the proprietors enlarged it to nine columns in less than a year from the time it was started. Mr. Batting died April 2, 1880, and from that time until May 6, 1882, the paper was carried on under the firm-name of Chadwick & Williamson. The former, who was manager and editor from July 1, 1880, became sole proprietor in May, 1882, and continues to conduct the *Record* as a live local journal.

Banking.—The First National Bank of Media was organized Feb. 22, 1864, chartered March 12th, and opened for business on March 21st, in the second story of Haldeman's store building. Its capital was sixty-five thousand dollars, which, in 1865, was increased to one hundred thousand dollars. Isaac Haldeman was the first president, and Joseph W. Hawley cashier. On the death of the president, in August, 1878, his son, Thomas J. Haldeman, succeeded to the office, which he still holds. The bank was removed to its present location in September, 1870, at which time the building was purchased and suitably fitted for the purpose it was to serve.

The parents of Mr. Haldeman were Abram and Mary Showwalter Haldeman. Their son was born in Charlestown township, Chester Co., Pa., in September, 1797, and at an early age sent to the common schools of his township, where he remained until his fourteenth year. He made rapid progress in his studies, and soon secured an education far in advance of his associates. Knowing that his means for its attainment were narrowly circumscribed, he improved every opportunity for increasing his store of knowledge, which naturally or by accident was afforded him. From his fourteenth until his twenty-first year he remained with his parents, securing from the fruits of his labor a great degree of comfort for them. After experiencing in his efforts to obtain an honest livelihood many vicissitudes, he determined to try his fortunes in another direction, and removed to Marple township, Delaware Co. Here in various capacities he labored for some time until, by his increasing industry and the careful administration of his finances, he had saved a capital of one hundred and fifty dollars. This hard-earned sum, limited as it was, formed the nucleus of what since became more than a respectable competency. With it he opened a country store, and shortly after the commencement of this doubtful enterprise was enabled to enlarge it by the voluntary aid of friends, who admired his integrity and indomitable perseverance. This aid, with the growing popularity of his store, he was enabled to repay in a few months with interest. By careful attention to the details of a business which, in the country, of necessity covered a wide range of articles, each of which would have made a specialty for a city store, he soon obtained the patronage of a large section. About 1840 he removed to the present borough of Media, and, continuing his business at this point, soon won and easily held an extended trade. He grew up to a position of prominence as a citizen, entering actively into all schemes for municipal improvement, and contributing largely with his means to the advancement of the community's interests. He continued proprietor of the store, which had been founded by his most active exertions, until 1856, when his sons succeeded him. Mr. Haldeman was one of the original movers in the establishment of the First National Bank of Media, was a member of its board of directors, and its president from the day of organization until his death. While, as a Republican, taking no active part in politics, nor making any effort to secure office, he was nevertheless chosen as the first president of the borough of Media, and for eighteen years a member of the Borough Council. In the capacity of municipal legislator he acted intelligently and with a conscientious regard for the interests of his fellow-citizens. He invested largely in building improvements, and thus contributed much to the growth of Media. In his dealings he was prompt, filling all contracts in the spirit and to the letter of the agreement, thus winning a reputation for integrity, the lustre of which time has not served to diminish. He maintained in religion the faith of the society of Friends, and was a member of the Friends' Meeting of Providence. Mr. Haldeman was, on the 31st of January, 1828, united in marriage to Eliza West, daughter of Thomas West, of Delaware County, whose children are Thomas J., Elizabeth W., Isaac Lawrence, and Mary H. (Mrs. Edgar T. Miller). The death of Mr. Haldeman occurred Aug. 13, 1878, in his eighty-first year.

John M. Broomall and Frederick Fairlamb established a banking business in 1868, having their office where Samuel Dutton's store now is. In 1870 they purchased a building on the corner of State Street and South Avenue, which they fitted up as a banking-house. On the 1st of January, 1871, the original firm took as a third partner W. Y. Hoopes, and in April Mr. Broomall withdrew, leaving the firm Fairlamb & Hoopes. It so remained until the death of Mr. Fairlamb, on Dec. 25, 1878, after which Mr. Hoopes carried on the business alone until May 1, 1883, when William R. Newbold became associated with him, under the firm-name at present existing of Hoopes & Newbold.

The Delaware County Mutual Insurance Company is one of Media's prominent institutions, and a brief sketch of its history will prove interesting to many readers. This organization had its origin, under the name of "The Delaware County Mutual Protection Company," as early as 1839, being incorporated by act of the Legislature dated June 12th of that year. The incorporators were James M. Wilcox, William Trimble, William Mendenhall, Richard S. Smith, Joseph Wilson, Eli D. Pierce, John Kerlin, Henry Myers, and William Beatty. They were incorporated for the purpose of "insuring their respective dwellings, houses, stores, shops, and other buildings, household furniture, merchandise, and other property against loss or damage by fire." No policy was to be issued until application had been made for insurance amounting to two hundred thousand dollars. The act was to take effect immediately after its passage, and remain in force twenty years. No successful effort at organization was made until the charter was extended by act of May 1, 1852, for a period of twenty years. The following persons were made incorporators by this act, and by virtue of their office were the first directors of the reorganized Delaware County Mutual Insurance Company, viz.: Dr. George Smith, William Eves, William Ogden, John M. Broomall, William Booth, Sketchley Morton, Levis Miller, Joseph Edwards, A. C. Eckfeldt, James Moore, Homer Eachus, John C. Beatty, Isaac Thomas, James J. Lewis, Joel Evans, Isaac M. Trimble, James Barton, John H. Andrews, Annesley Newlin, Walker Y. Hoopes, Minshall Painter, Eli D. Pierce, Nathan H. Baker, John Hill, and John Jackson.

The first meeting was held at Media, Thursday, Aug. 26, 1852, when the incorporators met and organized, adopting by-laws and dividing the county into districts. Another was held September 20th, but at the more important one of Monday, October 18th, sixteen members being present, the following officers were elected: President, John M. Broomall; Secretary, Jesse Bishop; Treasurer, John C. Beatty. It was resolved that their term of office should continue for four years, or until 1856. The rates were fixed, additional by-laws and regulations adopted to those of their meeting of October 20th, when the whole machinery of the organization was fully set in motion.

By Jan. 1, 1853, insurances to the amount of three hundred thousand dollars had been effected. On June 15th of the same year, it was announced that the company had issued three hundred policies, covering property to the amount of six hundred thousand dollars.

An election for directors for the company was held on Thursday, Aug. 11, 1853, when John M. Broomall, Eli D. Pierce, Sketchley Morton, William Ogden, James Barton, Thomas Pratt, Charles Palmer, Levis Miller, and William Eves were elected for the ensuing year. Immediately after, and on the same day, John M. Broomall was elected president; Jesse Bishop, secretary; and John C. Beatty, treasurer.

Sketchley Morton was elected president March 10, 1856, and held the office until his death, in 1877. His successor was Thomas Pratt, elected Oct. 15, 1877. Mr. Pratt died March 3, 1883, and on March 12th the present incumbent, Levis Miller, was elected.

Edward A. Price assumed the duties of secretary on March 12, 1856, Jesse Bishop having first been elected, but resigning. On May 2, 1862, Mr. Price was chosen treasurer, and since that date to the present has administered both offices.

The first office of the company was where Squire Preston now does business, but on Oct. 18, 1873, the company took possession of the fine building it now occupies, on the corner of Front Street and South Avenue. This was built at a cost of more than twenty-three thousand dollars, and the lot on which it stands was bought of John M. Broomall for three thousand six hundred dollars. The only persons living who were members of the organization of 1852 are Levis Miller, John M. Broomall, John C. Beatty, and James Barton. The first policy issued by the company, bearing date Aug. 21, 1853, is still in existence. It covered the Penn Buildings, on the corner of Third and Market Streets, and was granted to George Broomall.

The whole number of policies issued since the organization up to May 5, 1884, has been eleven thousand six hundred and eighty-six, and the total amount insured to same date was $24,777,227.41. The whole cancellation since organization has been $14,400,431.12, leaving the present insurance $10,376,796.29. The amount of cash premiums and assessments received since the organization to Aug. 11, 1884, has been $312,471.92, and the total amount of losses paid during the same time $246,875.16. The assets of the company are $408,767.09, and the liabilities $10,142.

Media Cemetery.—About the middle of June, 1855, James R. Cummins and others took into consideration the project of establishing what is now known as the Media Cemetery, on a tract of eight acres of land, which Mr. Cummins had purchased. By the middle of the following December the cemetery had been surveyed, and extensive improvements made. A fine vault had been constructed, two thousand eight hundred burial lots marked out, walks and drives made, etc. Interments were made soon after. In 1858, Daniel McClintock was appointed superintendent, and held that position for eight years. He did much to beautify the cemetery, not only in landscape gardening, but, being a marble-cutter, the possessor of good taste, and the proprietor of extensive works, he erected a very large proportion of the hand-

Thos Reece

some monuments for which the grounds are notable, among others that dedicated to the memory of William Wright.

Cotton-Factories.—The cotton-factory now owned by Mrs M. Melvina Fairlamb was originally the property of H Jones Brooke, and was sold by him Feb 4, 1863, to Isaac Worrall, Jr He sold to Ralph Buckley on Dec 23, 1865 The mill, while occupied by William Alcutt, was destroyed by fire April 27, 1867 Mr Buckley then rebuilt, erecting a two-story brick mill, which he sold Sept 27, 1867, to Lewis Kirk

Samuel Dutton and Benjamin Crowther, in 1866, established a cotton-factory on Washington Street, which they operated for a few years It was sold in April, 1869, at assignee's sale, and came into the possession of J Howard Lewis, who removed the machinery and tore down the building He still owns the property.

Societies—Masonic.—George W Bartram Lodge, No 298, F and A M, was chartered June 2, 1856, with Charles D Manley as W M, John C Beatty, S W, and William P Beatty as J W Meetings were originally held over Cummins' store, on State-Street, afterwards over Buckley's, at State and Olive, and since April, 1882, the lodge-room has been in the third story of Schur's building, Second and Orange Streets The lodge has ninety-six members The present officers are William F Matthues, W M, Charles Moore, S W, Enos L Baker, J W, and William Campbell, Sec

Media Chapter, No 234, R A M, was chartered Feb 13, 1871, with forty members Its present officers are William E Williamson, H P, Charles B Sprogell, K, Horace P Green, S, William Campbell, Sec

I. O O F—Kossuth Lodge, No 393, I. O O F, was organized Jan 22, 1850, with the following as the first officers N Walter Fairlamb, N. G, Peter Worrall, V G, John M Hunter, Treas, Samuel Hunter, Sec The first meetings were held over A P Fairlamb's store, and later a room over Schur's store was used The present lodge-room is in Williamson's Hall, on State Street The lodge now has fifty-two members, and is officered as follows Bion Herkins, N G, W H Hardcastle, V G, Samuel Bryson, Treas, Ott Pennell, Sec

Towanda Tribe, I. O of R M.—This tribe of the Independent Order of Red Men was instituted in "cold moon, G S D, 377," with eight charter members from Tuscarora Tribe, Chester.

Media as a Summer Resort.—The beauty and healthfulness of Media, the picturesqueness of its surrounding hills and valleys, the fact that the sale of liquor is prohibited in the borough, and its easy accessibility from Philadelphia have caused many people who prefer quiet, rest, and true recreation rather than the fashionable dissipation of the great resorts, to seek summer homes in the town or its neighborhood There are others and many who, while they have not established homes here, have sought the benefits of a temporary sojourn, and thus it has come about that four large houses, in addition to the Charter House, are comfortably filled every season with those who prize the wholesome air and the nerve-bracing life which is here afforded The first of these places of resort was Idlewild, established by Mr Hawkins when he left the Charter House It is a charming retreat in a cool grove of forest-trees directly south of Media Then there are the Chestnut Grove House, contiguous to the little railroad station, and the Haldeman and Gayley establishments, under one management, which are educational institutions save in summer, when those who would rest take the place of those who have been at the toil of study in the pleasant and spacious houses

Some years ago an ambitious attempt was made in the direction of founding a suburban villa, which failed because premature, though it will doubtless in the near future be carried out

In 1872, James R Cummins and Samuel Bancroft bought of Robert Playford a tract of fifty acres of land between Media and Idlewild, with the intention of laying it out for building sites, with streets connecting South Media and Idlewild A map was made and the project was advertised, but the plan was abandoned, partly on account of Mr Cummins' death His interest in the property was purchased by Mr Bancroft, who sold the entire tract to George W Wharton in June, 1883

As time progresses an increased number of city people will see the advantage of making summer or permanent homes in this neighborhood, and it is probable that among other improvements one similar to that contemplated by Messrs Cummins & Bancroft may be not only undertaken, but successfully completed

BIOGRAPHICAL SKETCHES.

THOMAS REECE

The ancestors of Judge Reece are of Welsh extraction, and were among the colony who came over with William Penn, in 1682 They settled in Haverford township, Delaware Co, Pa, in which county Jesse Reece, the father of Thomas, was born, Dec 12, 1774, his life having been principally spent in Upper Providence township as a builder He married Elizabeth, daughter of Asa Davis, of Chester County, who was also of Welsh parentage, and whose ancestors were members of the Penn colony Their children are Davis, born in 1801, Lydia (Mrs Samuel Hibberd), in 1804, Elizabeth (Mrs Jesse T Heacock), in 1805, Sidney (deceased in youth), in 1807, Jesse, in 1809, Thomas, in 1811, and Eli Y, in 1813 The death of Mr Reece occurred in 1849, and that of his wife in 1858 Their son, Thomas, was born May 4, 1811, in Middletown township, Delaware Co, where his youth, until his eleventh year, was spent. He then, with his parents, removed to Upper Providence township, where, after limited educational opportunities, he learned the trade of a mason and builder This was pursued with vigor for several years, when, having inherited the paternal acres, he became a farmer and continued this vocation until his removal to Media, in 1880, on retiring from active business Judge Reece was married, in 1858, to Mrs Beulah Palmer Cassin, of Concord, Delaware Co, to which marriage was born a daughter, Lydia D He has been for years interested in the field of politics, and as a Republican was, in 1860, elected county commissioner, which office he filled for one term In 1866 he was the successful candidate for associate judge of Delaware County, and re-elected in 1871, serving a continuous term of ten years This official position obliged him to resign the directorship of the First National Bank of Media, with which he had for several years been connected Judge Reece has long been a prominent citizen of the county, and invariably administered the offices to which he has been chosen with fidelity to the interests of his constituents He was educated in the religious faith of the society of Friends, and is still a member of that society, as are also his wife and daughter

---

HUGH JONES BROOKE

Hugh Jones Brooke was born Dec 27, 1805, and was the eldest of five children born to Nathan Brooke and Mary (Jones), his wife His father was a well-to-do farmer, whose farm comprised the valley of the Gulf Creek, in Radnor, adjoining Montgomery County His ancestors were the sturdy yeomanry of the early emigration from England and Wales Those of his father were Quakers, and settled in and near Limerick (now Montgomery County), and of his mother Episcopalians, who settled in Newtown and Radnor, and were among the founders of St David's Church, Radnor His father dying when he was but nine years old, he was brought up under the joint care of his mother and his paternal grandfather, who were well fitted to prepare him for the active duties of life His education was of the character obtainable at that day in the local schools At the early age of fifteen he took charge of the farm, and thenceforward led a life of active usefulness

The prominence of his grandfather, who had been a Revolutionary officer, and was a large land-owner, as well as largely engaged in industrial pursuits, brought him into early participation in the administration of public affairs, and he almost continuously served his fellow-citizens in local affairs, besides terms in both branches of the State Legislature, always being on important committees, and often in leading positions, and his advice was frequently sought in national and State, as well as local, corporate, and personal affairs

In corporations he was largely interested, and the Delaware Mutual Safety Insurance Company, the First National Bank of Media, the Twelfth Street Market Company, and the Media Gas Company were among those of which he was either the originator or a corporator, and assisted in the administration as president or director until his death There were many others he was or had been connected with, and to him Philadelphia is largely indebted for its present system of market-houses, he being the originator, and until he refused to serve further, president of the Farmers' Market Company

In 1853 he purchased the farm in and adjoining Media, lying between the State (Street) road and Ridley Creek, and removing from Radnor thither, thenceforward gave liberal attention to the development of that town, building with his own means the Chestnut Grove House and Brooke Hall Female Seminary, besides many private residences and other buildings, and, with the public, the railroad through it, and the Pennsylvania Training School for Feeble-Minded Children adjacent, the latter having been located through him, and largely developed by his legislative influence in securing meritorious appropriations from the State for its building and maintenance. Both as an officer and citizen it had his earnest and sympathetic advice and assistance until his death

In the suppression of the Rebellion he took an active part, and when asked by the Secretary of War to assist in developing the commissary department he went earnestly to work, and served both in field and at post with benefit alike to the government and the soldier until impaired health from overwork enforced his resignation

In politics he was a Whig, who early became a Republican because of his anti-slavery convictions, which caused him to refuse a marshalship which might involve his official enforcement of the fugitive slave law. In business he spoke of himself as a farmer, but, as before mentioned, he was that and much more In religion he made no public professions He was a regular and constant attendant at the services of the Protestant Episcopal Church, and St David's, Radnor, and Christ Church, Media, especially shared of his labors and his means Of the latter he was the originator He was especially interested in the amusement and labors of the young, and was always ready at proper times to participate in the one or aid the other, and many were indebted to him for his good advice and material assistance for their start in life

He married, April 16, 1829, Jemima Elizabeth, daughter of Nathaniel Longmire (a lace manufacturer) and Elizabeth (Green), his wife, who, with his family, had emigrated from Nottingham, England They had children as follows. Anna Elizabeth, born Feb

H. Jones Brooke

was born May [illegible], 18[illegible], in Middletown township, Delaware Co., where his youth, until his [illegible] year, [illegible] with his parents, removed to Upper Providence township, where, after limited educational opportunities, he learned the trade of a mason and builder. This was pursued with vigor for several years, when, having inherited the paternal place, he became a farmer and continued this vocation until his removal to Media, in 18[illegible], on retiring from active labors. Judge [illegible] was married, in 18[illegible], to Miss [illegible], of Concord, Delaware Co., to which marriage was born a daughter, Lydia [illegible]. He has been for years interested in the field of politics, and as a Republican was, in 18[illegible], elected county commissioner, which office he filled [illegible]. In 18[illegible] he was the successful candidate for associate judge of Delaware County, and [illegible] in 18[illegible], serving a continuous term of [illegible] years. [illegible] obliged him to resign the directorship of the First National Bank of Media, with which he had for several years been connected. Judge [illegible] has long been a prominent [illegible] of the county, and [illegible]

[illegible]

national and State, as well as local, corporate and personal affairs.

In corporations he was largely interested, and the Delaware Mutual Safety Insurance Company, the First National Bank of Media, the Twelfth Street Market Company, and the Media Gas Company were among those of which he was either the originator or a corporator, and assisted in the administration as president or director until his death. There were many others he was or had been connected with, and to him Philadelphia is largely indebted for its present system of market-houses, he being the originator, and until he refused to serve further, president of the Farmers' Market Company.

In 1853 he purchased the farm in and adjoining Media, lying between the State (Street) road and Ridley Creek, and removing from Radnor thither, thenceforward gave liberal attention to the development of that town, building with his own means the Chestnut Grove House and Brooke Hall Female Seminary, besides many private residences and other buildings, and, with the public, the railroad through it, and the Pennsylvania Training School for Feeble-Minded Children adjoining, the latter having been located through him, and largely developed by his legislative influence in securing meritorious appropriations from the State for its building and maintenance. Both as an officer and citizen it had his earnest and sympathetic advice and assistance until his death.

In the suppression of the Rebellion he took an active part, and [illegible] of the Secretary of War [illegible] he went [illegible] both in field and at post with benefit alike to the government and the [illegible] until impaired health from overwork enforced his resignation.

In politics he was a Whig, who early became a Republican because of his anti-slavery convictions, which caused him to refuse a membership which might involve his official enforcement of the fugitive slave law. In business he spoke of himself as a farmer, and, as before mentioned, he was that and much more. In religion he made no public profession. He was a regular and constant attendant at the services of the Protestant Episcopal Church, and St. David's, Radnor, and Christ Church, Media, especially shared of his labors and his means. Of the latter he was the originator. He was especially interested in the amusement and labors of the young, and was always ready at proper times to participate in the one or aid the other, and many were indebted to him for his good advice and material assistance for their start in life.

He married, April 18, 1832, Jemima Elizabeth, daughter of Nathaniel Longmire (a lace-manufacturer) and Elizabeth (Green), his wife, who, with his family, had emigrated from Nottingham, England. They had children as follows: Anne Elizabeth, born Feb.

Eng.d by A.H. Ritchie.

H. Jones Brooke

Chas D Manley

Milton Lewis

12, 1830, died Dec 19, 1832, Nathan, born Jan 21, 1832, Mary, born Feb 12, 1834, died Sept 30, 1834, Francis Mark, born July 4, 1836, Hannah Maria, born June 8, 1838, married John L Evans, Benjamin, born Dec 13, 1840, Hunter, born Dec 7, 1842, Jemima Elizabeth, born Aug 13, 1845, died Feb 11, 1850; Sarah Ann, born Aug 16, 1850, married George M Lewis

Mr Brooke, after a life of uninterrupted usefulness, died Dec 19, 1876, and was buried at St David's, Radnor

CHARLES D MANLEY

Charles D Manley, lawyer, was born in the township of Radnor, Delaware Co, Pa, on Dec 20, 1807 His father, Benjamin Manley, was a farmer and mechanic, who was born, lived, and died in Delaware County His mother was a DeHaven, the DeHavens of the Schuylkill, of German descent His grandfather, Thomas Manley, was a farmer, who rented and occupied at various times several large farms in Chester, Middletown, and Newtown His grandfather belonged to the Maddock family, an English family of Ridley His paternal great-grandfather, tradition says, was of a noble family of Ireland His preliminary education was received at the schools of the neighborhood He was at two private schools, boarding in the teacher's family about a year and a half, having first began to teach before he was eighteen years of age After having acquired a fair English education, he commenced teaching school in Chester He continued at this occupation for four years, applying himself during his leisure hours to the study of law, and by economy contriving to save a few hundred dollars of his earnings But his health beginning to show evident signs of failure, in consequence of too intense application to his studies and business, he abandoned teaching and assumed a clerical position in the Bank of Delaware County, located at Chester In this capacity he remained about sixteen months, when he entered into the mercantile business as one of the firm of Eyre & Manley In this business he continued about four years, when, abandoning commercial pursuits, he again turned his attention to law He first entered as student under Peter Hill Engle, and finally finished his legal reading under the tuition of E Darlington, and was admitted to the bar in 1848 Establishing himself at first in Chester, he there practiced until 1851, when he removed to Media, then first commencing to be settled as a town His professional business furnished him a fair and reasonable compensation until the outbreak of the war, when, by reason of his being a member of the Democratic party, his income became much reduced In 1855 he was elected to the State Legislature, in 1856 he was made a delegate to the National Convention at Cincinnati, and in 1858 he ran as the Democratic candidate for Congress in the district in which he resided, and was defeated by John Hickman, an independent

He has always been a Democrat in politics, and while he is not aggressive or offensive in his opinions, he has always been firm in his adhesion to the principles of his party Having since his admission to the bar confined himself almost exclusively to the business of his profession, he is looked upon more as a conscientious lawyer than as an aspiring politician

He has always taken an active interest and given substantial aid to any investment tending to the advancement of the town of Media, and has been twice elected a member of Town Council In 1838 he was married to Margaret Worrell, a member of an old and well-known family in Delaware County In religion he is an Episcopalian, was a member of the vestry of St Paul's Church of Chester while he resided there for several years, and has always manifested a deep interest in the religious denomination with which he is connected as well as in all questions of private and public morality at home and abroad His Masonic teachings formed a part of his religion, and he was one of the brightest members of the mystic order in the county He believed in and practiced the doctrines of the fraternity, and was an honor to the craft His social qualities added to his kind heart made him a host of warm friends He was a great reader, a good thinker, and an earnest debater He died on the 19th day of December, A D 1880

MILTON LEWIS

William Lewis, the progenitor of the family in America, came from England with William Penn in 1682 In the direct line of descent was Nathan, who had among his children a son, Didymus, the grandfather of Milton Lewis, who married Phœbe Matlack. Their children were Deborah, Tamar, Phœbe, Mary, Nathan, Eli, Thomas, Margaret, and Tacy. Eli was born July 18, 1784, and married Hannah Sharpless, whose children are Sharpless (deceased), Mary (Mrs W Garrett), Elizabeth (Mrs Dutton Otley), Eli, Milton, Isaiah M (deceased, a physician, who resided in Emporia, Kan), Edith (Mrs E Hickman), Phœbe Ann (Mrs L G Garrett), and Hannah (deceased, Mrs A N Hatch) Milton was born July 21, 1823, in Newtown township He received an elementary education in the schools near his birthplace, and at once entered upon a career of active labor on the farm of his father He married, in 1851, Martha, daughter of Robert M and Eliza Thomas, of Newtown township Their only son, Dillwyn, was born March 14, 1852, and now cultivates the farm of his father in Marple township He married, in 1875, Annie, daughter of Samuel Hunter, of Upper Providence, and has two sons The year of his marriage Milton Lewis removed to a farm he had purchased in Marple township, and continued the pursuits of an agriculturist until 1876, when Media became his residence. He has during much of his time acted as deputy prothonotary of the county, and been otherwise occupied in the settlement of estates and in the various offices of guardian and executor, for which his ability no less than his unquestioned integrity eminently qualify him. He is a Republican in politics, and in his religious faith a Friend, having been educated in that belief.

CHAPTER XLVII.

MIDDLETOWN TOWNSHIP.

THE name of this municipal district is believed to have been bestowed because of the position the territory was at that time thought to occupy,—the middle or central point of Chester County. Although the early settlers were mistaken in that respect when the name was adopted, the present township approaches very nearly the centre of Delaware County, and is one of the largest townships in the county. Ridley Creek is its eastern and Chester Creek its western boundary. Edgmont and part of Thornbury township lie on the north and Chester township to the south. It was probably established as a township in 1686, but it is first mentioned in 1687, when John Martin was appointed constable for Middletown.

On Oct. 11–12, 1681, three hundred acres of land were surveyed to John March, part of one thousand acres which he had purchased in England. It is not known whether he ever settled on this tract, but seventy-three acres along Chester Creek, just above Chester township line, on March 1, 1685, was conveyed to Thomas Martin, and doubtless Martin, who emigrated from Bedwin Magna, in Wiltshire, England, accompanied by his wife, Margery, and four daughters, in that year settled on that small plot of ground now belonging to Jonathan Dutton. The seventy-three acres, as also one hundred and four acres adjoining, subsequently became the property of Joseph Cobourn, while that part of the March tract lying east of the Edgmont road, on Jan. 7, 1713, was purchased by Caleb Harrison. Above the March tract, and extending east and west across the township, was a plot of three hundred and fifty acres, surveyed to John Martin Dec. 10, 1682. The northern boundary of John Martin's estate was the road to Knowlton, where that highway enters the great Edgmont road, thence due east and west across the township to the creeks forming the eastern and western boundary. Knowlton is located on this tract. John Martin, who came from Edgcott, in Berkshire, England, settled on the land, and at his death, in 1719, it passed to Thomas Martin, probably his son. Above this tract, going northward along Chester Creek, three hundred and eighty acres of ground were surveyed to Richard Crosby, Nov. 20, 1685. Crosby was from Cheshire (Chestershire), England, and came to the province subsequently to 1683. The following year he was in Chester, and was appointed by the court (1684) one of the collectors to gather the levy for that township. After this tract was taken up by him he settled thereon, and in 1686 was presented by the grand jury "for keeping an unlawful fence to the great damage of John Martin, in his swine," for which ill-doing on his part Crosby was fined thirty shillings at the next court. Crosby figured considerably in the early court records. In his cups he seemed ever to run into quarrels, and if threatened the strong arm of the law he was not chary in his remarks or the expression of his opinion of the sage big-wigs who dispensed justice in the old court-house on Edgmont Street, Chester. On Nov. 29, 1703, Richard Crosby, who had then removed to Ridley, conveyed this property to Nicholas and Katherine Fairlamb. His daughter had married Fairlamb, who was a merchant in Chester.

Until within comparatively recent years some of the Fairlamb family resided on a portion of this tract, that part lying south of the road leading from Edgmont road to Hillsborough Mills, No. 7. Above this tract four hundred acres were laid off to Thomas Taylor, March 7–8, 1682. Taylor, who had purchased the land in England, may never have settled on the estate, for, on Aug. 23, 1702, two hundred acres were sold to Nicholas Fairlamb (May 30, 1704), and the other half passed to Edward Woodward in May of the same year. On Chester Creek, above the Taylor tract, William Johnson, on Twelfth month 4, 1681, was assigned one hundred and fifty acres of land, but it is not known that he ever settled on the land. Adjoining here to the left, and extending to Ridley Creek, John Worrall in 1683 acquired title to two hundred and fifty acres of land, which, Feb. 15, 1695, passed to Richard Woodward, who settled on this tract, and there died in 1706. On Chester Creek, on Second month 11, 1684, Lancelot Lloyd took up on rent one hundred and five acres, while to the east of his land, and extending to Ridley Creek, Richard Barnard had received title to two hundred acres, which, on June 11, 1695, he sold to Joseph Jarvis, an account of which is given in the history of the Media Water-Works. The land at Glen Riddle was part of the three hundred and seventy acres surveyed to Richard Crosby in 1685, and a tract of sixty-three acres taken up by John Taylor, which matters are related in the narrative of the Glen Riddle Mills. On Chester Creek, a short distance above Wawa Station, nine hundred and eighty acres were patented to Caleb Pusey, he having purchased the several tracts constituting that large estate from different persons and at different dates. His patent for the land, however, was issued on Third month 25, 1702. To the east of the Pusey lot, John (Hodgkinson) Hoskins had surveyed to him two hundred and fifty acres, which extended from the south on Crosby's land to David Odgen's on the north, the Hoskins tract lying immediately south of

Lima On Dec 12, 1698, Hoskins sold the land to James Serrill, and the latter, on June 10, 1700, conveyed it to David Odgen Hoskins, who built the Hoskins house in Chester, owned also a lot of ground in Philadelphia on the north side of Walnut, between Front and Fifth Streets, which he subsequently sold to David Lloyd To the east of Hoskins' tract, which separated the township in the centre, lying just below Lima, and extending south to a line drawn due east from Lenni across the township, and following Ridley Creek in a northerly direction, John Bowater had surveyed to him one hundred acres, and thereon he settled He was an earnest Friend, and at his house the first meeting of Friends in Middletown was held Above this tract, to Joseph Allibone, was surveyed two hundred and fifty acres on March 14, 1684; it, however, soon passed to John Malin Above the Allibone land Nathan Edwards took up one hundred and ten acres The Edgmont and Providence roads cross each other on this plantation For some reason Malin Bishop, on April 3, 1856, received a patent from the State for this land One hundred acres to the north of Nathan Edwards' tract was surveyed on rent to Owen Musgrave, Feb 4, 1683 On Dec 8, 1741, this land was patented to John Edwards

Above the Musgrave tract on March 13, 1684, William Edwards took up one hundred acres He was, it is stated, from Glamorganshire, Wales, and settled on this land, his son, John, living on the premises after his father's death, in 1716, in the original cabin his father erected when he first made a lodgment in the wilderness Above the Edwards tract George Smedley took up two hundred and ninety-five acres in 1684 He was from Derbyshire, England, and settled on this estate, building his dwelling-house on the west bank of Ridley Creek, about one mile northwest of the present town of Media The homestead farm is still owned by his descendants Along Ridley Creek to the township line, Jacob Minshall on Sixth month 16, 1701, took up five hundred acres Much of this property is still owned by his descendants, Minshall Painter having retained possession of his ancestral acres during all his long and useful life, as did also his brother, Jacob Painter

The ancient dwelling built by Jacob Minshall in 1711 still stands in good repair The largest room on the first floor is laid with flagstones The barn on the adjoining farm now the property of Stephen Byre, known as the "Round Top farm," was the first erected on that section that had a floor and bays above the stables, as also a gangway It is stated that men came forty miles to see the wonder of that day It is said to have been erected in 1712 On a portion of that tract is an Indian burial-ground A remnant of the Lenni Lenape continued to reside on the tract until the beginning of this century Andrew, Isaac, and Nanny lived in a cave in the valley of Dismal Run Andrew died in the cave, and was buried in Middletown Friends' graveyard

To the southwest of the Minshall tract, and along Dismal Run, Peter Trego, on Tenth month 11, 1694, purchased for Joseph Edge fifty acres, for which he paid "£14, or good merchantable wheat for market price" Roger Jackson, at the Edgmont line and west of the Minshall tract, purchased from George Willard two hundred and fifty acres, which were known as "Cumberland," but he sold the plantation to several parties, hence it did not pass under the devise in his will that his estate should be equally divided among such of his relations in England who should come to the colony and apply for their share in his (Jackson's) property Continuing along the Edgmont line, an irregular plot bounded partly on the south by David Odgen, two hundred acres, which extends up to where the Hicksite Friends' meeting-house now stands, and partly by Caleb Pusey's land, Joshua Hastings took up four hundred and seventy-two acres of land, on which, however, he never settled, but in 1692 it was purchased by John Turner, and in 1718 Joseph Talbot became owner of the land Joseph Talbot died in 1721, and his son, Joseph, took the real estate when he came of age, and built the mill, now Humphrey Yearsley's As mentioned, David Odgen's plot of two hundred acres lay to the south of this plantation, extending from Friends' meeting-house to a short distance below Lima David Odgen came with Penn in the "Welcome" in 1682, and settled on this tract, where he died in 1705 The land west from the Hastings tract, along the Edgmont line and extending to Chester Creek, was surveyed as two hundred and fifty acres to Henry Sleighton, April 10, 1684, which in 1803 was patented to Ephraim Jackson, a noted Friend of Edgmont South of this estate, along the creek, and following the southern line of the road from Thornbury to Middletown, on April 10, 1684, two hundred and fifty acres were surveyed to Edward Blake The estate subsequently passed to John Bowater, the noted Middletown Friend South of this tract, and continuing along the creek to Martin's Run, was a plantation of three hundred acres, which was surveyed to John Sharpless April 4-5, 1682, and was patented to Joseph Sharpless Third month 4, 1703, who settled on the estate after his marriage to Lydia Lewis, in 1704, and died there in 1757 South of the Sharpless tract, having Martin's Run for part of its northern boundary, a lot of two hundred acres was surveyed to Thomas Cross, Jr, Twelfth month 21, 1683, but this and other tracts were purchased by Thomas Martin, before the latter left England He emigrated from Edgcott, county of Berks, about 1689, and died on this land in 1719

The taxables in the township in 1715 were as follows

John Martin, George Grist, Caleb Harrison, Edward Woodward, Daniel Cookson, Joseph Jervis, William Pennell, Jacob Tregoe, John Edwards, George Smedley, Jacob Minshall, Peter Tregoe, Sr, Thomas Barns, John Chauley, John Turner, Joseph Sharpless, Alexander Hunter, Moses Martin, Robert Baker, Thomas Barnsley, Thomas Martin, Jr, Edward Lawrence

Freemen.—Hans Hamilton, Peter Tregos, James Tregoe, George Martin, Francis Ferrel, Thomas Smith, William Chamberlain, Simon Barton.

In 1799 the taxables were returned as follows:

John Baker, Joseph Baker (storekeeper), Henry Baker, Samuel Worrell, Aaron Baker (cooper), Thomas Beatty, John Moncil, Amos Bond, Jacob Happerset, Joshua Clayton, James Day, Jesse Darlington, Jonathan Button, John Evans, Dell Pennell, Issachar Edwards, Isaac Edwards, James Emlen estate (grist-mill), Frederick Fairlamb, Robert Fairlamb (cordwainer), Isaac Frame, William Johnson, Henry Gorman, Thomas Pennell, David Garrett (blacksmith), Robert Glenn, Henry McGill, Prudence Sloughter, Jacob Hibberd, John Hill (saw-mill), Nathan Heacock (joiner), John Heacock, Ann Hemphill, Joshua Harrison, John Happersett, Thomas Hutchinson (little wheelmaker), James Hemphill, William Salyards, James Hunter, John Heacock, Samuel James, John Ingram, Jr. (blacksmith), Joseph Jobson, John Knight (physician), John Lungren, Edward Lewis (miller), Seth Levis (paper-maker, paper-mill, grist-mill, saw-mill), William MaCarty (tailor), John Moncil, Philip Miller, Jacob Menshall, Thomas Menshall, Jacob Malin (weaver), James McGuire, John Ottey, Robert Pennell, Abraham Pennell (saw-mill), Lydia Pennell (innkeeper), Oliver Pharaoh (shoemaker), Aaron Ratten, Thomas Ryan, Deborah Sutton (store-keeper), William Sharpless, Nathan Sharpless (grist-mill, saw-mill), John Sharpless, Daniel Sharpless, Benjamin Stokes, Ambrose Smedley, William Smedley, Thomas Trimble, Joseph Taylor (carpenter), John Thompson, Joseph Roman (blacksmith), Thomas Worrell, John Wilcox (hatter), John Worrell (saw-mill), Edward Woodward (saw-mill), Caleb Yarnall, Joseph Yarnell (wheelwright), Negro Tom, Negro Cyrus, Frederick Juner, Lewis Pennell.

Inmates.—William Broomall, James Broomall, John Broomall, David Broomall, James Cumings, James Crossley, William Doyle, Virgil Eachus (joiner), John Hughes, Jacob Happerset, William King, Patrick McGuckin, Daniel Mahoney, Michael McCloskey, George Malin (hatter), William Pitt (shoemaker), William Pennell, Joshua Sharpless (shoemaker), Albert Stervant, James Starr, Daniel Thompson, Patrick Welch, Joseph Webster, Thomas Worrell, John Ottey.

Single Freemen.—John Dutton, John Lewis, and Nathan Yearsley, millers; Seth Evans, weaver; William Fairlamb and William Griffith, shoemakers; John Heacock, Enoch Heacock, and Benjamin James, carpenters; Joseph Starr, wheelwright; Job Vernon, tanner; Thomas Walker, blacksmith; Cyrus Baker, John Connell, Hugh Connor, George Dougherty, Richard Dutton, John Harris, Seth Levis, Gardner Leonard, John McMickel, William McCune, Alexander McCune, Patrick Mullin, James McMullin, Patrick Mulvany, Andrew Nelson, Robert Pennell, John Rickey, Robert Sims, John Sharpless, Thomas Sharpless, Alexander Thompson, Hugh Trimble, William Webster, Peter Worrell, Obadiah Russell.

The following is a list of the justices for Middletown township:

John Crosby	Aug. 30, 1791.
Joel Willis	Aug. 30, 1791.
Davis Bevan	Aug. 19, 1794.
Miles McCarty	April 13, 1796.
Elisha Price	April 15, 1796.
William Martin	Aug. 9, 1797.
Isaac Eyre	Oct. 12, 1798.
Nicholas Fairlamb	Dec. 6, 1798.
Aaron Morton	May 3, 1799.
Philip Painter	May 20, 1800.
Thomas Hinkson	May 20, 1800.
John Pearson	June 21, 1802.
James Withey	July 4, 1806.
Jacob Edwards	Jan. 1, 1807.
John Caldwell	Nov. 15, 1814.
Joseph Walker	Feb. 3, 1820.
Samuel Smith	March 12, 1822.
David Marshall	March 3, 1824.
George W. Bartram	June 3, 1824.
Benjamin F. Johnson	Oct. 25, 1825.
Abraham Kerlin	June 7, 1830.
Samuel T. Walker	Nov. 11, 1831.
John Afflick	June 6, 1834.
Jonathan P. Worrall	March 5, 1835.
Samuel Shaw	Nov. 18, 1835.
William Martin	June 10, 1836.
William Eyre	Dec. 21, 1838.
George W. Bartram	Sept. 23, 1839.
Samuel Hibberd	April 14, 1840, April 13, 1847, April 11, 1854.
Robert L. Martin	Aug. 24, 1876.
Robert F. Ash	March 27, 1879.
James W. Howarth	March 30, 1880.

The Murder at Bancroft Bank.—On Saturday night, Oct. 17, 1863, Ellen Jones and John Blair, a stonemason, were brutally murdered. The scene of the tragedy was a small dilapidated log house which stood on the left of the road, on the west side of Ridley Creek, almost directly opposite the factories. Ellen Jones vended liquors surreptitiously, and it was supposed she had accumulated one hundred dollars by the illegal traffic, which sum she was known to carry on her person. On Sunday morning following a neighbor learning from the children of the dead woman—the eldest a girl of six and the youngest an infant of two years—that something unusual had happened at the secluded cabin, repaired thither. Upon the floor near the door of the lower room—the house contained but two apartments, a room below and an attic above—lay the body of John Blair, his throat cut in several places, and the flesh from the forehead to the chin on the right side of his face almost entirely cut from the bones, his forehead broken in, and the right eye torn from the socket. About two feet away from the corpse of Blair lay the body of Ellen Jones, the upper portion of her head cloven, leaving a huge cavity, from which the brains had oozed. Near the dead woman was an axe clotted with blood from edge to butt, indicated the weapon with which the deed was done. The only witness of the murder was the six-year-old daughter of Ellen Jones, who, hearing the noise in the lower room, was aroused from her slumbers, and through the cracks in the floor of the attic saw the murderer strike the fatal blows. The testimony seemed to implicate George Wilkinson, a young man of about twenty-two, who was arrested at Hestonville on Monday night following, and was detained at Philadelphia until the Friday after the murder, when he was brought to Media jail. The trial of the accused began Feb. 23, 1864, the commonwealth being represented by Francis M. Brooke, district attorney, and the prisoner by James Barton, Jr., Charles D. Manley, and John M. Broomall. On Friday, February 26th, the jury rendered a verdict of "not guilty."[1]

A Centenarian.—On April 25, 1851, Charity White, better known as "Aunty Charity," a colored woman, died at Middletown, said to be over one hundred years of age. She had been a slave in the Eastern Shore of Maryland, but on the death of her master, prior to the beginning of this century, was permitted to remove to Pennsylvania, and located in Middletown.

Remarkable Mortality.—In November, 1837, Norris Hannum, of Middletown, lost by death in twenty days all his children,—five in number. The disease, which proved so fatal, baffled the physicians, who could not at that time designate the malady by name.

A Heavy Man.—In the summer of 1866, Henry Breckinridge, of Middletown, was announced by the *Delaware County Republican* as the heaviest man in

[1] An account of the trial of Joseph Worrall, indicted for the murder of David Weidig, near Lima, will be found *ante*, page 177.

Delaware County, as well as in the Seventh Congressional District, and probably in Eastern Pennsylvania. He was twenty-three years of age, and weighed four hundred and one pounds. He measured six feet round the waist, was five feet seven inches in height. His legs were thicker than the body of an ordinary man, and his arms of proportionate girth.

The Middletown Friends' Meeting.—The first allusion to an organized meeting of Friends in Middletown occurs at a Chester Quarterly Meeting, Third month 3, 1686, whereat it was "agreed y[t] a meeting be kept at John Boiter's upon y[t] same first day it used to be at Bartholomew Coppock's, for y[e] case of such y[t] live westerly in y[e] woods, and y[e] rest of friends living y[e] other way upon y[t] same day to meet at ffrancis Stanfield's until further consideration." Ten years after this action by the Quarterly Meeting, at a similar meeting held on Third month 4, 1696, it was agreed that "a meeting be settled at John Bowater's every first and fifth day," and on Ninth month

FRIENDS' MEETING-HOUSE, MIDDLETOWN.

6, 1699, "The ffriends of John Bowater's meeting Lay their Intentions of Building a meeting-house" before the Quarterly Meeting, and Philip Roman, Robert Pipe, Nathaniel Newlin, George Robinson, John Hood, and John Wood were appointed "to determine the place for that service, and make report to y[e] next Quarterly Meeting, under all their Hands, that it may be entered in the Meeting Books." Early in this year (1700) the committee reported that they had fixed upon the burial-lot of Friends in Middletown for the site of the meeting-house, but it is very probable that the meeting-house was not erected until the following year (1701). At all events, the building was completed in 1702, for it was then called Middletown Meeting-House. The present building is not the first meeting-house erected, but it was certainly built many years before the beginning of this century.

Orthodox Friends' Meeting-House.—After the division of the society of Friends, in 1828, the Orthodox branch of Middletown held their meetings in a school-house belonging to James Emlen, near the Emlen Grist-Mill, now owned and operated by Humphrey Yearsley, until they could complete their present meeting-house, which was not ready for occupancy until 1835. The house was erected on a lot of ground which Joseph Pennell, in 1834, donated to the society for a meeting-house. The plot contained half an acre, and subsequently he gave an additional half-acre adjoining for school and burial purposes. The meeting-house was erected on this lot.

Cumberland Cemetery.—About 1860 Thomas Pratt laid out a tract of land adjoining Hicksite Friends' Meeting-House ground as a cemetery, and sold a number of burial-lots thereon. The land which was not sold is now owned by his heirs, and is still being used as a burial-place.

Middletown Presbyterian Church.—The organization of religious societies under the form of the Presbyterian Church in the Middle States distinctively marks the beginning of the immigration to the American provinces of that sturdy class of people who have in this country been termed the Scotch-Irish. There is some reason to believe that, as early as 1689 or 1690, Rev. Francis Makemie came to America, sent hither by the United Brethren of the Presbyterians and Congregationalists of London, and that he organized a church in Accomack County, Va. If that be the fact, the Virginia Church antedates the First Presbyterian Church in Philadelphia eight years, for Rev. Jedediah Andrews began his ministry in that city in 1698. The Scotch-Irish about 1718 began to make settlements in Chester County, and doubtless as soon as they waxed sufficiently strong to form a congregation of worshipers according to the Presbyterian faith, such an organization was effected. The exact date of the formation of this church will probably never be known, for the early records are said to have been lost in the fire which burned the dwelling of Rev. Thomas Grier, in 1802. The church was doubtless established in the latter part of the year 1728, or early in 1729, for on April 1, 1729, the Presbytery of New Castle, in response to the desire of the people of Middletown to be permitted to build a church, acceded to the request, on condition that the congregation would continue "a united congregation with Brandywine." Tradition asserts that in 1720 a log church was built in Birmingham, but this assertion may justly be questioned, although in the historical account of that township in this work this date is followed. In the summer or fall of the year 1729 a log church was erected in Middletown on grounds the title to which was not conveyed to the trustees until 1751, when the building thereon is mentioned in the deed. That the church was fully organized and a meeting-house erected in 1735 cannot admit of doubt, but the evidence tends to establish a prior date for the building, inasmuch as early in that year it is mentioned in a gift to the "Protestant Dissenters" by Dr. Isaac Watts, who, learning of the house of worship in the "backwood," manifested his interest in the welfare of the struggling congregation by sending to them a folio copy of one of Baxter's works. The inscription in this volume reads:

"This Book, called Mr Baxter's Directory, was given by ye Reverend Dr Isaac Watts, of London, to the Protestant Dissenters, usually Assembling for Worship at Middletown Meeting-house in Pennsylvania, that people who came from far & spend their whole day there may have something proper to entertain themselves with, or to read to one another between the seasons of Worship, morning and afternoon; & 'tis for this end intrusted to ye care of (the) Protestant Dissenting Minister who preaches there, and to his Successors, to be used by him or them in their weekly Study, when they please, and to be secured & devoted to the Use of the Congregation on ye Lord's days."

"Jany 30th, 1735/6."

"The Book is committed to the care of Mr Benj. Hawley to be carried over to Pennsylvania, and after he has kept it in his own hands and made the best use of it for six months, that is till the 30th of July next, he shall deliver it to the hands of the present Protestant Dissenting Minister for the purposes before mentioned."

OLD MIDDLETOWN PRESBYTERIAN CHURCH, BURNED FEB. 1, 1879.

The congregation attending this church was scattered, and some of the persons most constant in attendance on the religious exercises—whenever they were held therein, generally once a month, for there was no regular pastor until 1770—would walk, women and men, often ten or twelve miles to church, and the like distance returning; or if, as was frequent, the distance was twenty miles, would ride thither on horseback. On a winter Sunday these pious people would sit for hours in the cold church listening to the clergyman, whose sermon made up in length whatever it might lack in originality of argument. The pastor in those early days preached twice to the same congregation on the Sabbath, there being an hour's intermission, when those present would partake of a slight repast, which had been prepared the day before and carried in baskets to the church.

On May 10, 1762, Robert McClellan conveyed to William Lindsay, Hugh Linn, James Lindsay, John McMinn, James Black, Charles Linn, Joseph Black, James Hemphill, and Thomas Trimble, three-quarters of an acre for the use of a Presbyterian Church thereafter to be erected.

The second church edifice, which was of stone, was erected shortly after this date, and Dr. Smith records that the venerable Thomas Dutton, in 1860, told him "that the present meeting-house was built in the time of his grandfather (Richard Dutton), and that he, although a Quaker, subscribed money towards its building, as he was willing that the Presbyterians should have a suitable place to hold their meetings in." [1]

The church building thus erected had no fireplace in it or means provided for warming the building in cold weather, hence the female members of the congregation who could afford such luxury would have a foot-stove, which would be filled with charcoal, and thus they could warm their almost frozen feet and listen to the minister at one and the same time. It has been said that the old log house was used as a place for the session of the church to assemble in, and after it was no longer required for religious exercises, a chimney-place was built, and on the hearth, on Sunday mornings, a bright fire would be made, so that those who were delicate could warm themselves by its cheerful blaze.

In 1770, Rev. James Anderson, the first regular pastor, was called, prior to which date the church was dependent on supplies. He was at that time about twenty-one years of age, and here he remained during the stormy days of the Revolution, doubtless advocating a separation from the mother-country, for the Presbyterians were, as a rule, earnest advocates for that measure, and we have every reason to believe that to the Pennsylvania line, or Irish line, as it was often called, from the young men attending the religious services there, Middletown Church furnished its full quota of soldiers. Dr. Samuel Anderson was a son of the first pastor of Middletown Church, but he was not born in Delaware County, although I would be glad if it should prove that I am in error in this assertion, for Dr. Anderson was a man of whose nativity Delaware County can be justly proud. Rev. James Anderson died in 1793, his ministry at Middletown covering almost his entire manhood life. From 1793 to 1801 the pulpit was dependent on supplies, but in the latter year Rev. Thomas Grier, a graduate of Princeton, was installed

[1] History of Delaware County, p. 398.

pastor, and continued in the discharge of that office until 1809, when he accepted a call to a church at Little Britain In 1802 the house in which he lived, on the west side of Edgmont road, south of the church, near where Mr Bonnall's dwelling now is, was destroyed by fire, and the records of the church, being in his study, were lost Rev Nathaniel Randolph Snowden, in 1809, became the pastor of the church, and continued as such until 1817, when he was called to the presidency of Dickinson College He resided during his term as pastor of Middletown Church at Chester, for his son, James Ross Snowden, the distinguished director of the United States mint and author, was born in that borough The Presbytery of New Castle censured Rev Mr Snowden, alleging that he came to Middletown without the consent of that Presbytery, took upon himself the pastorate and also took the church from the care of New Castle and transferred it to that of Philadelphia Presbytery, where it continued until 1870, when Chester Presbytery was formed During all the time he was in charge of the church he was never installed, but exercised pastorate functions as if he had been After Rev. Mr Snowden resigned, the church had no regular minister until 1827, although in 1819 Rev Nathaniel Todd was appointed stated supply at Middletown for six months He was continued until 1822, when he was dismissed to go to Carlisle In 1823 Larry Bishop was appointed as supply at Middletown for first and third Sabbaths in every month, and he continued thus in charge of the church until 1826, when he was dismissed to take control of a church in the Huntingdon Presbytery

In 1818 the Presbytery of Philadelphia was asked to form two church organizations, one in Springfield and Providence, the other in Aston Middletown Church met this movement by protest, alleging that the district was so sparse that there was no room for another Presbyterian Church, that the means employed to obtain signatures were not fair or honorable, and that the erection of a new church would arrest the growth and progress of Middletown Church The protest was signed by Samuel Black, Hugh Caldwell, John Craig, and the heads of most of the Presbyterian families, but, nevertheless, in 1819, the Presbytery appointed a committee to organize two additional churches

In 1827 Rev Robert McCochran was installed as pastor, and remained as such until 1830 In October, 1832, Rev Alvin H Parker became the pastor of the church, and continued in such relationship until October, 1839 The church at this period had been almost abandoned to decay, and in that year an effort was made to revive interest in the organization In 1841, Rev Samuel P Helme was called to the pastorate, but resigned in April following Under date of Oct 4, 1842, John P Crozer records that a stranger had been sent by the Presbytery of Philadelphia to Middletown and the Blue meeting-house, "to make some attempt to impress life into these decaying churches" In speaking of Middletown Church, he records, "This ancient edifice, truly venerable in appearance, was erected by godly men, who have for three-quarters of a century slept in death This is one of the oldest places of worship in the whole country, and its substantial and venerable walls testify that the yeomanry, by whom they were erected, were willing to honor God with their substance, and in that day, when farm-houses were of the plainest and simplest kind, they were willing to pay for a large and commodious edifice and dedicate it to the worship of Almighty God"[1] The church, at the time Mr Crozer described it, was much out of repair, and many persons who could recall the building burned in 1879, remember it only after it had been materially altered in 1846 The pulpit was then in the east end of the building, and at the west, opposite, was the door The pulpit stood about ten feet above the heads of the congregation, and the ceiling followed the roof to a peak, which was well known to many of the youngsters of that day, who, when seated on the high-backed pews, were shut out from a sight of the clergyman, and could only follow the sloping ceiling with their eyes, or perhaps they could catch a glimpse of the sounding board suspended over the pulpit and wonder, if it fell, what would become of the preacher

From 1842 to 1846 the church was dependent on supplies, but early in the latter year Rev James W. Dale was called, and the dawn of better days came with him to Middletown His eloquence soon gathered a congregation there, which had separated, and it was determined to repair and enlarge the church, William T Cook, then a prosperous manufacturer, undertaking personally to discharge the greater part of the expense On Saturday afternoon, July 11, 1846, the corner-stone of the addition to the church was laid, Rev Dr Cuyler and Rev Dr Jones, of Philadelphia, making addresses on the occasion It had been intended that the ceremony should have taken place on the 4th of July, but "the damp, drizzly, dull, disagreeable day, the like of which could not be recalled by the oldest inhabitants as happening on a 4th in our history," compelled a delay in the services Fifteen feet was added to the length of the building and the alterations already mentioned in describing the old church were made, and three acres added to the graveyard

Mr Dale's ministry continued for over twenty-five years pastor of the mother Presbyterian Church of Delaware County, remaining there until 1871, when he resigned to take charge of Wayne Presbyterian Church The Rev Dr Dale was a man of action as well as words, and for nearly thirty years he kept alive and nurtured into strength all the Presbyterian Churches in the county, and after they were able to care for themselves he never lost his interest in their

[1] Life of John P Crozer, p 83

welfare, and was ever earnest in their assistance when needed. He was the author of several standard theological works, and had also published a number of sermons which had wide circulation. Dr. Dale died in April, 1881, at which time he was pastor of the Presbyterian Church at Glen Riddle.

In 1871, Rev. Thomas Donaldson Jester became the pastor of Middletown Church. During the Centennial year, 1876, at the request of the Presbyterian Church throughout the United States, every church of that denomination in the United States made an effort to collect the historical incidents connected with the church for preservation. In that year Rev. Mr. Jester preached an interesting and instructive sermon, presenting in an attractive form much of the historical matters connected with Middletown Church. On Saturday afternoon, Feb. 1, 1879, the janitor built fires in the stoves, and some of the pipes became hot, burst, and set fire to the roof. No chimney had ever been built in the church, but the pipes passed through the roof into a terra-cotta chimney-piece. A heavy gale was blowing at the time, which soon fanned the flames into a furious blaze, which in a short time enveloped the building in a mass of fire. Nothing could be done to arrest the conflagration, and in less than two hours only the wall remained. Immediate steps were taken to rebuild the church, the old walls being utilized, and so rapidly was the work pushed that on Sunday, July 13, 1879, the church, a building sixty by forty feet, was dedicated, Rev. T. D. Jester, the pastor, conducting the ceremonies, assisted by Revs. J. W. Dale, D.D., P. H. Mowry, and Thomas McCauley. P. Frazer Smith, of West Chester, also delivered an address. The rebuilding cost two thousand dollars, and as a little over that amount was subscribed, the church was dedicated free of debt. The church has at the present a membership of sixty persons, and is in prosperous condition.

The old God's acre, connected with the church, contains the mouldering remains of many generations of the Presbyterian families who made and supported the struggling congregation when it was located "out in the wilderness." The oldest gravestone whose inscription can be deciphered is that of "James Cooper, deceased the 4th day of November in the Fear [or Year] of God, 1731." In point of time the next mortuary notice we desire to direct attention to is that of one of the Buchanan family, which, a century and a quarter later, gave a President to the United States. The old stone bears this inscription:

"David Buchanan, died Nov. 3, 1738.
True to his friends, to his promise just,
Benevolent, and of religious trust."

On another stone the inscription reads,—

"Samuel Crozer, died 1747.
My glass is run,
My work is done;
My body's under ground;
Intombed in Clay
Until the day
I hear the trumpet sound."

On an ancient tombstone in that quiet burial-place can still easily be read the announcement,—

"Here lyeth the body of John, the son of Martha Moore, who departed this life the 17th day of December, 1754, aged 13 years and 8 months.

Death, thou hast conquered me,
I by thy darts am slain,
But Christ shall conquer thee
And I shall rise again;
Time hastens, and the hour
The just shall rise and sing,
O grave where is thy power
O Death where is thy sting?"

A noticeable tablet is that which marks the burial spot of a centenarian,—

"Here lieth the body of Bernhard Vanleer, M.D.[1] Physsisian in Physick, who departed this life, January 26, 1790, aged 104 years.

Friends, weep not for me
For all your tears are vain,
Prepare to meet the Lord
That we may meet again."

And beneath are the words,—

"His wife Christiana—died March 29th, 1815, aged 88 years and 7 months."

At the southwest corner of the church is the grave of Rev. James Anderson, the first pastor, who died Sept. 22, 1793, aged fifty-four years. When the alteration was made to the church, in 1846, this stone was temporarily removed, and in doing so was broken in the middle. Rev. Mr. Anderson was beloved by his congregation, and the stone informs us,—

"Modest thro' life, an humble path he trod,
And passed his days in service of his God;
To guilty men he preached redeeming grace,
Till death's unsparing scythe cut short his race;
Called by his glorious Master to the skies,
He now enjoys, we hope, the immortal prize."

The stone which marks the resting-place of one who by his name should be a Presbyterian informs us that it was placed there

"In memory of
Robert Calvin,
died March 8, 1812, aged 69 years.
Come, look on, my friend,
And you'll drop a tear,
For honest Robert
Doth lie buried here."

Of Jane Calvert, who had died the preceding year, aged sixty-six years, we are told,—

"The Kind, good Jane,
Its here she doth rest;
But her spirit's gone
Among the blest."

Presbyterian Church at Glen Riddle.—On Oct. 19, 1880, a Presbyterian Church, with twenty members, was organized at Glen Riddle, delegates being appointed for that purpose by the Presbytery of Chester. Rev. James W. Dale, D.D., of Media, preached on that occasion. In the year preceding, 1879, Samuel Riddle had begun the erection of a handsome brick church, laid in black cement, with yellow trimmings, the windows being of stained glass

[1] See *ante*, p. 256.

and memorials of various members of the Riddle family. The edifice was completed the following spring, at a cost of ten thousand dollars, and dedicated July 4, 1880 Dr Dale, at the urgent request of Samuel Riddle, became the first pastor, until his death, in 1881, when Rev John B Rendall for a time was in charge of the church At the present time the dean of Lincoln University supplies the pulpit Forty members are now connected with the church, and a large and well-attended Sunday-school is maintained

Lima Methodist Episcopal Church—William L Fox, Eleanor Fox, James Permar, John Pyle, and four other persons, in 1833, organized a Methodist society at Lima, which was placed under charge of James Riddle, a local preacher For about six months meetings for worship were held at the dwelling of William L Fox, now owned by John Porson, after which period the school-house then belonging to William Smedley, now owned by Mrs Thomas Smedley, located at the forks of the road a quarter of a mile west of the Black Horse Tavern, was rented, and services conducted therein by the circuit preacher On Aug 19, 1835, in consideration of seventy-five dollars, John Rattew conveyed to Henry Permer, Charles McCally, John Pyle, Lewis M Pike, John Daniels, Seth Rigby, William L Fox, of Middletown, Caleb G Archer, of Aston, and Joshua Smith, of Edgmont, trustees, one acre of land "forever, in trust, that they shall erect and build or cause to be built thereon a house of worship for Methodist Episcopal Church of United States of America" The trustees built on this lot, the present church site, a stone meeting-house, which, in 1873, was rebuilt and enlarged The dedication of the new sanctuary took place on Sunday, April 6, 1873, and on March 23, 1874, the court of Delaware County incorporated Lima Methodist Episcopal Church Among the pastors who have been in charge of the station are the following Revs James Ayers, John Edwards, John Morrison, A Dotterer, John Jennings, Mr. Shepherd, George Burns, Mr Grawley, A N Millison, and Mr Turrentine, the present incumbent The present membership of the church is sixty, and a Sunday-school of one hundred pupils, under the direction of William Turner, superintendent, is in a flourishing condition

Honeycomb Methodist Episcopal Church.—About 1872 a Methodist society was formed by a number of colored people in Middletown, and a frame church erected near the Bishop Hollow road The building is still used for a place of worship by the society

Schools.—In Painter's manuscript "Reminiscences of Delaware County," in the Historical Society of Pennsylvania, it is stated that "about 1740 there was a lot of land given by Thomas Yarnall and Thomas Minshall, equally, on each side of the line between them, for the use of a school-house From the trustees named, this school must have been intended to accommodate a large extent of country It was at one time in the care of George Deeble, an Englishman, who had but one hand, yet, from what we have learned of him, he was quite competent for the situation"

On May 16, 1749, a plot of ground near the Presbyterian Church, on the Edgmont road, was conveyed to trustees for school purposes, and on this lot a stone school-house was erected, which stood until subsequent to 1835, for at that time it was mentioned by the school directors as near "Middletown meeting-house," and designated as School No 3 It was used only for a few years after the adoption of the school law by the directors, but N Walter Fairlamb remembers being a pupil at the school kept there As early as 1783, Friends of Middletown established a school at their meeting-house, and the old stone structure, now unused, still stands on the lot It was maintained for many years by the society until 1827, when the separation of Friends occurred, and it then, under the control of the Hicksite branch, was still continued as a place of education Jacob Smedley, now of Media, attended school in this old building from 1815 to 1820, John Hutton, Jacob Haines, and Jehu Broomball were teachers during that time James Emlin, at the time of the separation of the society of Friends, was teaching a private school in a house not far from the old Emlin mill, now Humphrey Yearsley's At that house the Orthodox Friends held their meetings and kept their school About 1836, soon after their meeting-house was completed, they erected a stone school-house upon the meeting-house lot, in which school has been maintained with more or less regularity to the present time

In the olden time, when a boy or girl was indentured, the agreement stipulated that a certain number of days' schooling should be given the apprentice in each year of his or her term of service Hence, on the indenture of apprenticeship of Isabella Griffith, who was bound to John Rattew, appear the following indorsements "P Wade certifies that he taught Isabella two quarters and nine days at school in 1798-99, Daniel Bayle's, twenty-seven days in 1800; John Spencer, eleven days in 1802, John McClowghlin, one month in 1803, Caleb W Matson, one and a half months in 1806-7"

A school house is mentioned in the road docket in 1813 as "William Smedley's school-house" This was an old house in 1808 Jacob Smedley, now of Media, attended school there in that year, and for several years thereafter Abram Johnson, John Turnbull, John Hutton, and Joseph Taylor were teachers It was located at the forks of the Rose Tree and Middletown roads The school-house was accepted by the school board in 1835, and designated as District No 2, and was so known until discontinued in 1839 The lot is now owned by Mrs Thomas Smedley.

On March 18, 1825, at an election held in the township for the purpose of choosing school trustees, Jacob Hibbard, Robert Fairlamb, and Samuel Sharpless were elected. The school law passed in 1834, and William Fairlamb and Minshall Painter were appointed by the court as inspectors until the school directors were elected under the law. The township did not accept the law until 1836, and on May 7th in that year the board of school directors appointed a committee from their number to make inquiry where a lot suitable for a school-house could be obtained. At the next meeting the directors made the following statement:

Appropriation from county and State for 1835	$215.87
Our share of $75,000 for 1836	70.
Our share of $100,000 for 1836	93.00
Amount receivable in the year 1836	$378.87
Our share of State and bank appropriation for 1837	163.00
Our share of county appropriation of $7500 authorized by the delegate meeting	462.60
Amount available in July, 1837, for school purposes	$1004.47
For building three new school-houses	$800
For repairing old school-house	50
Amount necessary to be expended on school-houses	$850

The directors decided to borrow a sum of money sufficient to complete the school-house. On Dec. 6, 1836, the committee on site for school building reported "that such extravagant prices were asked for sites equitably distant that they did not feel warranted in purchasing." This report decided the school board to petition the Legislature, asking "that they in some way be relieved from vexatious negotiations and delay."

On April 29, 1835, the school directors purchased from Peter Hill, for fifty dollars, a lot containing half an acre, situate on the Pennsgrove road, near Riddle's factory, on Chester Creek (then Parkmount). The deed was delivered by George W. Hill to the board June 10, 1837, and at that meeting Nicholas Fairlamb agreed, for one hundred dollars, to sell half an acre of land on the lower part of his farm on the Edgmont road. At a meeting of the board, August 12th in the same year, it was decided to erect a school-house on the Fairlamb lot, which was completed during the summer, and November 15th following it was determined that the Fairlamb school-house, "lately erected, shall be called No. 1;" the school-house near William Smedley, No. 2; the school-house at the Middletown meeting-house, No. 3, and the school-house "lately erected near Riddle factory" be No. 4.

On Dec. 1, 1837, the directors determined that the public schools be opened on the 19th of December of the same year. Public notice was given that four teachers would be employed. Five were examined, and engaged for three months, at twenty-five dollars per month. They were James M. Mullen, No. 4; George Waller, No. 1; William W. Smedley, No. 5; George Smedley, No. 2; and Joel Sharpless, No. 3. School No. 5 here mentioned was kept in a house near the Pitts farm, where later a house was built. On July 15, 1838, the following teachers were employed for three months: Mary Dunlevy, at $45 per quarter, No. 5; William Webster, at $60, No. 1; Thomas Dawd, $60, No. 4; Samuel Darlington, $60, No. 3; and George Smedley, $60, No. 2.

At a meeting of the directors Aug. 12, 1837, a committee was appointed to select lots for school purposes in the middle, western, and southeastern sections of the township. On the 17th of May preceding a committee had been appointed to apply to the trustees of the school-house near Friends' meeting-house for the use of that house for public school purposes, but Friends declined to allow their house to be used by the directors, stating that they were occupying it for their own schools.

On the 28th of March, 1839, the directors purchased a lot, containing a half-acre of land, of Joshua Sharpless in the western part of the township. Jared Darlington offered to erect a house on the site for four hundred dollars, which was accepted. The house was built and delivered to the directors October 26th in that year. On the 27th of April, 1839, the committee on sites reported that a lot could be obtained of George Smedley, at the Barrens. On May 28th in that year, a half-acre of land was puchased from Smedley, at that place, for fifty dollars. It was not until 1841 that a house was erected. At that date Thomas Reece built a house for three hundred and fifty-five dollars, which was used until 1868, and on April 15th in that year a contract was made with Isaac N. Flounders to build a school-house at that location for two thousand one hundred and ninety-three dollars, which is known as the "Barrens," or District No. 8. On Oct. 16, 1839, a lot was purchased from the Christian Pitts estate, on which to erect a school-house, to be known as No. 5. Thomas Shoemaker offered to build it for three hundred and ninety-eight dollars, which was accepted. He subsequently declined to fulfill the contract, and on March 11, 1840, John Eves offered to build it for three hundred and seventy dollars, which offer was accepted, and the house was erected and completed in June, 1840. The numbers of the district were changed after 1842, and No. 3 was known as "near Riddle's," and No. 4 as "near Isaac Yarnall's."

On Oct. 11, 1848, No. 3 school-house was reported as too full for comfort, and a room was soon after rented for forty dollars per annum.

On July 16, 1849, School No. 6 appears in the records. In 1850 the following report was made of the schools of the township. Number of schools, 6; number of months taught, 7; number of male teachers, 4; female, 2; 192 male scholars, 228 female; average in each school, 70; amount of tax collected, $1015.43; cost of instruction, $1008.

On the 5th of June, 1850, a lot was purchased near Knowlton, and a house was erected during the summer at a cost of five hundred dollars. This was designated as No. 7; and the same time a hall was rented at Spring Hill for school purposes. In 1858 Samuel Riddle offered the use of a room in which to

RESIDENCE OF SARAH W., DAUGHTER OF THE LATE JONATHAN THOMAS,

hold a school, which was accepted, and the school was called Glen Riddle School. This was later abandoned, and the Knowlton lot was sold March 8, 1869, to Thomas McDermott for three hundred and thirty dollars.

In February, 1861, a lot of land was purchased for one hundred and twenty dollars, at Lima, of the directors of the poor. A contract was made with Robert P. Dunn for the erection of a house thirty by thirty-six feet for fifteen hundred and sixty dollars. This was completed and is now in use. It is known as No. 7. On Jan. 28, 1864, three-quarters of an acre of land was purchased of Samuel Riddle for one hundred and seventy-five dollars. Borell Williams contracted to erect a house there for two thousand three hundred and eighty-four dollars. It was completed and school was opened there Nov. 28, 1864. On April 16, 1866, the directors decided to remodel No. 1 school-house, and Simon Litzenberg was awarded the contract for the work for six hundred and seventy dollars.

On June 28, 1866, a contract was made with Joseph Yarnall to remodel school-house No. 4. On April 25, 1867, it was decided to move School No. 2 to corner of Thomas Pratt's land, between roads leading from Village Green to Glen Riddle (near the fair-ground). Three-quarters of an acre of land was purchased for three hundred and seventy-five dollars. Joseph P. Yarnall contracted to build a house for nineteen hundred and ninety dollars. The old lot at Park Mount was then sold to Elwood Malin for four hundred and seventy dollars.

On the 1st of June, 1868, the districts were renumbered: No. 1, near Habbersett's; No. 2, near Johnson's; Nos. 3 and 4 (two stories), at Parkmount; No. 5, Darlington; Nos. 6 and 7 (two stories), at Lima; No. 8, the Barrens.

On June 6, 1872, it was decided to erect a new school-house in place of No. 1, on the same plan as school-house No. 8. William Armstrong contracted to build a stone house for seventeen hundred dollars, which was done.

School Directors for Middletown.—The following list contains the names of the school directors of the township from 1834 to the present time:

On Oct. 1, 1834, the first election for school directors was held at the house of George Malin. The following persons were elected: Jonathan Thomas, Minshall Painter, George Smedley, Abraham Pennell, Jr., David Thomson, and Edward Lewis. Subsequent elections have resulted as follows:

March 30, 1835, William L. Lewis, James Pennell; March 18, 1836, Humphrey Johnson, Samuel Sharpless; March 17, 1837, Minshall Painter, James Barton; March 16, 1838, William Smedley, Jared Darlington, Jonathan Paist; March 15, 1839, Samuel Hibbard, Jonathan Paist; 1840, Nicholas Fairlamb, Israel Yarnall; 1842, Minshall Painter, Samuel Sharpless; 1843, Thomas Pratt, Nicholas Fairlamb, James Enos; 1844, Samuel Riddle, John H. Fairlamb; 1845, William S. Lewis, Jacob Painter; 1846, James Eves, Samuel Riddle; 1847, John H. Fairlamb, Jared Darlington; 1848, William L. Lewis, John Williams; 1849, Pennock Edwards, Ezekiel Norman; 1850, Joel Sharpless, Joseph Dutton; 1851, George Callaghan, John Williams; 1852, Abram Blakely, John Williams; 1853, N. Walter Fairlamb, James Pennell; 1854, George Rodebach, William Webster; 1855, George Rodebach, Castor Gray; 1856, James Pennell, N. S. Yarnall; 1857, John Williams, William Webster; 1858, Nathan S. Yarnall, Charles Fairlamb; 1859, Charles Johnson, Castor W. Gray; 1860, John Williams, Thomas Williams; 1861, Thomas T. Williams, Milton Edwards; 1862, George Callaghan, Jr., Charles Johnson; 1863, Hiram Schofield, William Webster; 1864, Nathan S. Yarnall, George W. Ormsby; 1865, Charles Johnson, Jesse Hibberd; 1866, Owen W. Yarnall, John Pearson; 1867, John McDowell, Archibald McDowell; 1868, John Hoopes, Samuel Dunn; 1869, John J. Hoopes, Owen W. Yarnall; 1870, S. P. Dunn, John R. Taylor; 1871, Jesse Hibberd, Jared Darlington; 1872, Isaac W. Kerlin, M.D., John J. Hoopes; 1873, Samuel P. Dunn, James Miller; 1784, Thomas T. Williams, James M. Schofield; 1875, John Hibberd, Thomas D. Jester; 1876, T. Darlington Jester, William H. Pratt; 1877, Thomas T. Williamson, Samuel Dunn; 1878, John Hibberd, Robert Fairlamb; 1879, S. P. Dunn, William Burnley; 1880, Robert T. Ash, Charles R. Yarnall; 1881, John Hibberd, Robert Fairlamb; 1882, S. P. Dunn, Samuel Riddle, Jr.; 1883, Jesse F. Smedley, C. R. Yarnall; 1884, Robert Fairlamb, John Hibberd.

Mills on Chester Creek.—The industries located on Chester Creek, in Middletown, have an exceedingly interesting history, and the narrative will be told as the several mill-seats are reached, beginning at the southern end of the township and moving up the stream to its source. The like course will be followed on Ridley, the eastern boundary of Middletown.

Forest Dale Mills.—At the court held at Chester 5th day of 1st week, Tenth month, 1686, Caleb Pusey, the partner with Penn and others, and then the manager of the Chester Mills, "Petitioned against Cobourn for setting a water-mill above him on Upland Creek." The court, however, "considering the premises, and finding it to be for the common good, dispenseth therewith." Pusey was powerful and active in protecting his own and partners' interest, hence, after he obtained the intervention of the commissioners of property forbidding Cobourn to build his mill, the people determined to carry the matter before the Provincial Council, and at a meeting of that body on 17th of Sixth month, 1687, "The Petition of about threescore people, Inhabitants of Chester County, was Read, setting forth the great want of a Mill in their parts, and Requesting a Permission for Thomas Coebourne to goe forward with y[e] building and setting up of his mill on Chester Creek. The Council is willing to give Incourag[mt] to y[e] Procedure of Thom. Coebourne, in the finishing of his mill that he is now about, for y[e] urgent necessity of y[e] Conterey, Reserving to y[e] Gov[t] his Proprietary Ship."[1]

This petition was presented on behalf of the people of the county, because on the 30th day of the preceding month, Caleb Pusey had induced William Markham and John Goodson, members of the Board of Commissioners of Property, to issue an injunction forbidding Cobourn proceeding with the erection of the mill. The order was as follows. The closing paragraph particularly was ordered to be read to

[1] Colonial Records, vol. i. p. 208.

Thomas Cobourn, after which it was "to be nailed up at the mill he is building"

"*To Thos Cobourne, of Chester County*

"Whereas we, the Proprietary Deputies, upon complaint made to us by Caleb Pusey, that thou wast about to set up a mill in Chester Co, to the great damage of the mill then under the charge of the s[d] Caleb Pusey, which hath been of vast charge to the owners thereof, & but of little profit towards defrays any parte thereof, did on the 22d Inst obligingly send to thee to give thee notice thereof, and to desire thou wouldst y[e] 29th following answer the s[d] complaint before us in the Council Room at Phil, but instead thereof thou sent a letter of the 26th inst by wh[ch] we perceive thou dost not only contemn the proprietary's authority & endeavor to subvert his dominion over all the water and soile within this, his province of Penns[a], as he is chief prop[r] thereof, but likewise intended to persist in the builds the mill aforesd, to the damage of the other mill and contempt of the proprietaryship

"We therefore, in the prop[rs] name, will and require thee to desist from building the s[d] mill (with[t] positive orders from the prop[r] for the same) or any way hinder the true course of the water of the s[d] Cr or any part thereof by draws it out of its own proper channel, or stop or any other way molest the same upon thy peril Giv[n] &c., 30th, 5th mo., 1687"[1]

The mill thus built by Thomas Cobourn was at the site of the present Forest Dale or Dutton's mills, and from the date of its erection was within the limits of Chester township until after 1829, when by a change of the township line the mill property was embraced within Middletown, where it is now located On Nov 28, 1682, three hundred acres of land abutting on Chester Creek was surveyed to Thomas Cobourn The latter was erecting his grist-mill there in the summer of 1687, and after Council had set aside the injunction granted by the commissioners of property, he doubtless speedily completed the building In 1695, when the assessment for a county levy was made by the grand jury and justices, the grist-mill of Joseph Cobourn was appraised at fifty pounds The mill was doubtless a log structure, and old Thomas Cobourn, who was a carpenter, assisted by his sons, Joseph and William, did the greater part of the work in its erection About 1750 a new stone grist-mill was built, taking the place of the log structure At a subsequent date the title to the mill and land passed to —— Lewis, whose heirs, Mary Cox and John Lewis, on Feb 14, 1775, conveyed the premises to Nicholas Fairlamb The deed designated that there was then on the tract "a water corn mill or grist-mill, boulting-mill, and saw-mill" Fairlamb retained ownership of the mills until Nov 12, 1792, when he sold them to Jonathan Dutton The mills were placed in the control of his son, John, when the latter became of age, who retained possession of the estate, it having become his property at the decease of his father, in 1820 Jonathan Dutton succeeded his father, John Dutton, in the ownership of these mills During the great flood of 1843, and while endeavoring to place some of his property out of the reach of the flood, so rapid was the rise of the water that Jonathan Dutton was compelled to retreat from one story of the building to another until he reached the upper one, shortly after which the building began to yield to the force of the torrent Knowing that the situation had become perilous, he leaped from a window and succeeded in reaching the shore, about one hundred yards below. A few moments after he left the mill it was swept away The mills were rebuilt in 1844 Jonathan Dutton died Sept 18, 1880, aged seventy years The property is now owned by George G Dutton, representing the four generations of Duttons in whose ownership these mills have been for nearly a century At the present time there is a stone grist-mill, a saw-mill, and a turning-mill on the estate

Knowlton Mills.—On the 16th of January, 1789, Nicholas Fairlamb (who at that time also owned the Cobourn or Dutton Mill) conveyed to John Sharpless the tract of land on which the Knowlton Mills are situated No mention is made in this deed of a mill or mill-seat Indeed, in 1800, "the site of Knowlton was a perfect wilderness"[2]

On Sept 30, 1802, John Sharpless conveyed the same tract to Jonathan Tyson, with the right of a certain dam thereon On November 15th of the same year, Tyson purchased of Elizabeth Grissell (Griswold) fourteen acres in Aston township, located on Chester Creek, opposite to the tract he had bought of Sharpless, the deed specifically mentions the dam rights, etc

On May 25, 1807, Elijah Tyson, a son of Jonathan, bought of his father two hundred and fifty acres of land in Middletown, embracing the mill-site, dams, and water rights, and, July 25th of the same year, the fourteen acres in Aston, with right to abut dam against the shore of the creek In this year (1807), for the first time, the name of Tyson appeared on the assessment-roll in connection with mills, and at that time Elijah Tyson was assessed on a saw-mill He continued to control the business until July 27, 1813, when he sold eight acres in Middletown, including the mill, mill-dam rights, etc, and fourteen and a half acres in Aston township, opposite, with water rights, to Judah Dobson, of Philadelphia, who changed the saw-mill to a rolling-mill Little information has been gained concerning this mill, but tradition asserts that it was a copper-mill, and the road leading from the place to Village Green is still known as the Copper-Mill road The venerable Hon Edward Darlington, of Media, now in his eighty-ninth year, states the mill was known as Dobson's copper-mill, and was used for rolling copper into sheets The mill does not appear on the assessment-rolls for 1817, 1818, 1819, 1820, nor in that of 1821

On Nov 6, 1822, John Vaughan and John Hart, assignees of Thomas and Judah Dobson, conveyed to Samuel Love "all that rolling-mill and four tracts of land," one of which is described as in Middletown, on Chester Creek, containing eight acres, adjoining lands of Elijah Tyson, Abram Trimble, and others

[1] Smith's "History of Delaware County," note, p 162

[2] Ib., p 399

Another tract was in Aston, and was partly covered by the mill-pond, and was adjoining and below the land of Jesse Grissell (Griswold) Samuel Love retained title to the estate until Feb 9, 1825, when he conveyed it to John D Carter, who had been operating the Trimble cotton-mill in Concord since 1813 In the deed to Carter it is stated that the rolling-mill had been changed into a cotton-factory, and that the "cotton-factory, mill-dams, ponds, races, etc, and four pieces of land" were the properties embraced in the conveyance In the "Report of the Manufactories of Delaware County," made in 1826, the place is described as being above the Dutton Mill, "on Chester Creek, in Middletown township, a cotton-factory, forty by ninety feet, head and fall thirteen feet, owned and occupied by John D Carter, has seven carding-engines of twenty-eight and two of thirty-one inches, workers and strippers, two drawing-frames of four double heads each, two double speeders of ten bobbins each, one stretcher of forty-two spindles, eight hundred and eight throstle spindles, six hundred and sixteen mule spindles, spins twelve hundred and seventy-eight pounds of cotton yarn per week No 20, with power to drive four thousand spindles, with all the necessary preparation Employs about forty-six hands, tenements for thirteen families." This property was owned by Carter until April, 1829, when it was sold to Edward Darlington and Thomas Clyde, and Carter removed to the South The mills were rented by Darlington and Clyde to Kershaw, Dean & Hill, who operated them until they were sold, March 4, 1832, to Robert Beatty and John O'Neill At the time of the purchase there was a cotton-factory and tilt-mill on the estate Beatty & O'Neill began at this place the manufacture of edge tools, but O'Neill soon withdrew from the firm, and rented from Beatty, who had bought the cotton-mill at Knowlton On Jan 7, 1834, the factory was, with contents, entirely consumed by fire On Oct. 26, 1835, John P Crozer bought the property, containing the four tracts of land conveyed in 1822 to Samuel Love, a tilt-mill, saw-mill, new building for factory, twenty-five by thirty-five feet, one brick and seven stone houses After the sale Mr Beatty continued the business at the place for a year or two, when Mr Crozer erected a stone cotton-mill, thirty-two by seventy-six feet, three stories in height This mill building was washed away in 1843,[1] and the next year a stone building, thirty-three by eighty-five feet, three stories in height, was erected

In 1846, Phineas Lownes and Abraham Blakeley commenced manufacturing at that place and continued until 1853, when it was operated by Mr Crozer until about 1869 At the latter date the mill was leased by John B Rhodes, who now operates it "Near the head gates of the mill there was formerly the marks of a grave, the occupant of which tradition named Moggey, and from that circumstance the crossing of the creek was named Moggey's Ford As Moggey had the reputation of making her appearance ocsionally, it required no little courage in the traveler in early times to cross the ford at night"[2] The incident on which the tradition was based was that about sixty years ago an English girl disappeared from that locality, and although suspicion pointed its finger at a wealthy resident in the neighborhood as being interested in her disappearance, no action was taken The marks of a grave at the head-gates when in subsequent years human bones were discovered near the spot, and long after the suspected man had removed to a distant country, were spoken of in confirmation of the truth of the tradition of Moggey's ghostly appearances

The Bottomley Woolen-Mill—On a little run known in early days as Clark's Run, later as Chrome Run, a feeder of Chester Creek, which empties into the latter a short distance above Presbyterian Ford, about 1810, a small stone woolen-factory, fifteen by thirty feet, was erected by Jesse Grissell for James and John Bottomley The latter were Englishmen, and accompanied to America by their mother, a brother, Samuel, and a sister, Elizabeth, who subsequently was married to —— Groves The males of the family worked in the factory, and John died at that place Samuel, after the war of 1812, went to Baltimore, where he died The Bottomleys continued the woolen-mill until 1832, the land being owned by Jesse Grissel (Griswold), who had purchased it in 1806 of Morris Trueman, when James Miller and Robert Boyd rented the property. Miller made edge tools, the latter turned axe-handles, bobbins, and manufactured paper there in a small way The mill was burned in 1848

The Morris Trueman Saw-Mill.—Above the Bottomley Mill on Chrome Run an old race is still to be seen on the land of John Scofield The breast of the dam has been plowed down with recent years, and is on land of Bernard McArron This was the site of Morris Trueman's saw-mill, erected there prior to 1777 In that year he removed to Darby Creek and built a paper-mill, which was afterwards generally known as the Matthews paper-mill, and is now owned by Samel Lewis The mill was used until about 1812

The Old Sable Nail-Works—The story of the old iron-works which, prior to 1785, were established on the opposite side of Chester Creek from the nail-works, has been related in the history of Aston township In 1809, Capt Henry Moore, who was then in charge of the forge and rolling-mills on the other side of the creek, owned by his brother-in-law, Thomas Odiorne, erected on the island in the creek at Rockdale a nail-factory, and placed therein nine nail-machines In 1810 one hundred tons of iron were manufactured into nails at this factory, which were sold

[1] See *ante*, p 104

[2] Smith's "History of Delaware County"

on an average for ten cents per pound, the capacity being increased gradually until in 1826 one hundred and fifty tons of nails were manufactured, and in 1832 the annual production had reached four hundred tons. In the latter year Richard Smith, a wholesale hardware dealer in Philadelphia, was compelled to take the works to cover advances made to Capt. Moore, and he leased the establishment to Howard & Massey for several years, they using the building for a machine-shop. It later passed to Bernard McCready, was used as a cotton-factory by James Roe, and still later by Robert Boyd, under whose occupancy it was partly destroyed by fire. The property was purchased by Alex. Balfour, who erected the present building and rented it to Joseph Richardson, Nicholas Walter, and H. P. Griffiths, who manufactured cotton and woolen goods for about two years. It later passed to Samuel Riddle, who operated it a few years and removed the machinery to his other mills.

Glen Riddle Mills.—On Nov. 9, 1683, three hundred and seventy acres of land were surveyed to Richard Crosby, it being part of the five thousand acres bought by John Ap (Bevan), John and Thomas Wynne, in England, of William Penn, to be located as the purchasers might desire on any unseated lands. Crosby sold one hundred acres of that land to Robert Pennell on April 6, 1685, and the latter conveyed it, Dec. 12, 1717, to his son, William Pennell. The latter had prior to the last date purchased sixty acres from John Taylor, and some years after erected at the place now Glen Riddle a saw-mill. In 1766, William Pennell is assessed on a saw-mill and a grist-mill, which he retained ownership of until his death, in 1783, although he did not have the charge of the mills, for during the Revolution they were operated by Abraham Pennell. At the time of William Pennell's death he was the owner of seven hundred and thirty-five acres of land in Middletown, two hundred and fifty-eight acres being located in the upper part of the township known as Grubb's, a tract of four hundred and seventeen acres, and sixty acres on which was the grist-mill and saw-mill. A tract of one hundred acres was across the creek in Aston township, on which the "Old Sable Forge" was located, and two hundred acres belonging to the estate was in Fallowfield township, Chester County. The residence of the Pennell family is still standing, now the property of William Webster. The children of William Pennell were Abraham, Robert, Dell, Rachel (Mrs. Nathan Sharpless), Esther (who afterwards became Mrs. David Garrett), William, Aaron, Jesse, Mary, and Samuel. The last had been absent for several years when his father died, and was believed to have died "beyond the sea." On June 29, 1785, the real estate was appraised at £6754 25*s.*, 9*d.*, and the Orphans' Court made a decree that Abraham, the eldest son, should be awarded the real estate, on condition that he paid to each of the other heirs their share in the property.

Under this adjudication, on Nov. 15, 1785, the heirs united in a deed to Abraham Pennell for the estate, and the following day (November 16th) he conveyed to Dell Pennell two hundred and six acres of the Middletown tract, and the one hundred acres in Aston, on which the forge was located. The same day he also conveyed to Nathan Sharpless and Rachel (Pennell), his wife, and Esther Pennell the sixty acres of land on which the grist-mill and saw-mill had been built many years before. Nathan Sharpless operated the mills, and in 1790 the owners of the mill-tract erected a stone house, which still stands, the date-stone being marked "S. G. 1790." These letters indicate that the dwelling was built by the husbands of the two daughters of William Pennell. The letter "S" standing for the initial of Sharpless, Nathan having married Rachel, and "G" for Garrett, Esther Pennell having married David Garrett. In this house both families lived for a time, but in 1794, Nathan Sharpless erected a small stone house, which still stands, and in its walls is inserted a date-stone marked "N S R 1794." To this dwelling Sharpless removed, the Garrett family remaining in the 1790 house. On Nov. 7, 1798, David Garrett and Esther, his wife, conveyed to Nathan Sharpless the "water corn or Grist mill" and part of the sixty acres of land. On May 21, 1802, Dell Pennell sold to Nathan Sharpless the right of the water of Chester Creek, for use of the "Sharpless Grist Mill Dam where it now stands and has long stood across the creek above our Forge Dam, . . . and water sufficient to turn two overshot water wheels of fifteen feet diameter driving each one pair of mill stones of four feet six inches diameter."

In 1815, Nathan Sharpless erected a woolen-factory and fulling-mill, which he operated until February, 1817, when he assigned the property to Abraham Sharpless, Francis Wisely, and John Peirce. The real estate on which the mills were erected, comprising fifteen acres, was offered at public sale May 3, 1818, and was purchased by Isaac Sharpless and Gideon Hatton, who changed the woolen-mill to a cotton-factory. After the building was completed it was leased to John Hastings, who fitted it with the most approved machinery of that period, and continued to operate it until Oct. 23, 1823, when, becoming financially embarrassed, he was compelled to sell the machinery and the leasehold. The capacity of the factory is shown by the following enumeration of "all the machinery requisite for carrying on a large and extensive cotton manufactory, consisting of four Throstles of 492 spindles, two mules of 408 spindles, ten Carding Engines, 12 Roving Heads, 12 Drawing Heads, one Stretcher of 96 spindles, four Reels, one Grinding Machine, one willowing Machine, one Picker and Blower, three winding Blocks, one Banding Machine, and one Yarn Press, together with all the rest of the Machinery."

During the time that Hastings had the cotton-factory, Joseph Mancill was lessee of the grist-mill. In 1825 the woolen-factory and fulling-mill were leased

John Burnley

by Dennis Kelly, who placed [illegible] son-in-law, in charge of the business. [illegible] place Isaac Hastings sold to John [illegible] who operated the cotton-mill until [illegible] purchased all the mills thereon [illegible] and George W. Hill. The [illegible] the cotton- and woolen-factory [illegible]. In 1831 John Garred located [illegible] and, in partnership with —— Wenver, [illegible] fulling-mill as a machine-shop, where they made looms and other machinery for cotton- and woolen-factories. In 1834 Garred rented the [illegible], which he changed to a cotton-factory, and, in partnership with William France and James Roe, carried on the business there for a short time, when [illegible] withdrew from the firm and France & Roe continued the business, but finally failed. After [illegible] removed from [illegible] grove, John Garred [illegible] and in [illegible] John D. Peirce, [illegible] into partnership with John Garred. The firm continued there until [illegible], when [illegible] Riddle came into possession. On Aug. [illegible], [illegible] and George W. Hill conveyed the estate to Eli D. Peirce, and on April 1, 1842, the latter sold it to Samuel Riddle, the present owner. At the time Riddle purchased, the improvements on the land consisted of [illegible] ninety-six by [illegible] in height; [illegible] woolen-factory, sixty by thirty feet; a [illegible] house, twenty-eight by eighteen feet; and a stone cotton-factory, fifty by forty-five feet, two stories in height; a block of six stone tenement houses, and a large mansion-house, which had been built by George W. Hill in 1829. Samuel Riddle took possession of the premises in 1843, and, fortunately, the flood of that year inflicted but little damage to his property. In 1845 he made extensive additions to the mill, and in 1872 erected a stone woolen-mill one hundred and twelve by sixty-five feet, three stories and a basement in height. In 1881 he built the brick mill, one hundred and [illegible] by sixty-one feet. The Glen Riddle mills at the present time contain fourteen thousand [illegible] spindles, and three hundred and [illegible]. [illegible] hundred and eighty operatives are employed. The goods made at these mills are [illegible] doeskins.

Parkmount Mills.—Samuel Riddle, [illegible] manufacturer, [illegible] removed from [illegible] Chester Creek, [illegible] agreed to erect [illegible] cotton-mill [illegible] of Chester Creek. The factory, known as [illegible] Parkmount Mills, was operated by [illegible] 1843, after which it was leased by [illegible] others, finally by the Callaghan [illegible] occupancy it was burned in 18[illegible], Burnley, Gledhill & Co. [illegible] present mill, fifty by one hundred [illegible] manufactured both cotton [illegible] 1879 the Parkmount Mills Cotton and Woolen Company was organized, with George Mallison, president, John Burnley, secretary and treasurer, and Francis Butterworth, superintendent. The mill contains at present [illegible] ninety-six looms, five sets of cards, and eighteen hundred spindles.

John Burnley, the son of John and Mary Burnley, was born in Littletown, Yorkshire, England, May 14, 1820. After receiving a fair English education he learned the trade of a spinner, and soon after determined to seek a wider field of labor in America. On the [illegible] of September, [illegible], he sailed from Liverpool [illegible] at once to Cobb's Creek, [illegible] George, his eldest brother, was already established as a manufacturer of [illegible] he sought employment, [illegible] one of the most valued assistants [illegible], when he removed to Darby Creek, in Delaware County, and became a partner with his brother in the manufacture of jeans. On removing to Lenni, in connection with George Mallison and George Gledhill, under the firm-name of Burnley & Co., he rented the Parkmount Mills at this point, and began the manufacture of cotton and woolen goods. He [illegible] in 18[illegible] [illegible] and Woolen Company [illegible]. Mr. Burnley [illegible] until his death, on the 20th of November, 188[illegible], being secretary and treasurer of the company. He married Mary Lomas, daughter of James and Mary Lomas, whose children are William, Adeline (Mrs. Edward Marland), Frances Ann (deceased), John Edward. Mrs. Burnley died Aug. 1, 1861, and he was again married, March 1, 1866, to Alice Lomas, sister of his first wife. Mr. Burnley was in politics a Republican, but devoted to the interests of his business, and gave little attention to matters associated with the political world. He possessed great business capacity, strict integrity, and a genial nature, which endeared him to all who were favored with an intimate knowledge of the man. His religious preferences were for the Protestant Episcopal [illegible], in which he was educated. Mr. Burnley [illegible] of the Masonic fraternity, and of [illegible] Independent Order of Odd-Fellows [illegible]. The business which he aided [illegible] formerly, his interest [illegible]. The grandchildren [illegible] Burnley, [illegible].

[illegible] of Lanchester, [illegible] England, where [illegible] of June, 180[illegible]. [illegible] his youth was spent. [illegible] opportunities he entered [illegible], which his father

John Burnley

by Dennis Kelly, who placed Charles Kelly, his son-in-law, in charge of the business there. The unexpired lease Hastings sold to John Turner & Co., who operated the cotton-mill until Oct. 27, 1827, when the land and all the mills thereon was purchased by Peter and George W. Hill. The new owners rented the cotton- and woolen-factory to James Houghton. In 1831, John Garsed located at Pennsgrove, and, in partnership with —— Wooley, rented the old fulling-mill as a machine-shop, where they built looms and other machinery for cotton- and woolen-factories. In 1834, Garsed rented the grist-mill, which he changed to a cotton-factory, and, in partnership with William France and James Roe, carried on the business there for a short time, when Garsed withdrew from the firm and France & Roe continued the business, but finally failed. After James Houghton removed from Pennsgrove, John Garsed leased the mill, and in 1840 John D. Peirce, a son of the then owner, entered into partnership with John Garsed. The firm continued there until April, 1843, when Samuel Riddle came into possession. On Aug. 25, 1840, Peter and George W. Hill conveyed the estate to Eli D. Peirce, and on April 1, 1843, the latter sold it to Samuel Riddle, the present owner. At the time Riddle purchased, the improvements on the land consisted of one cotton-factory, ninety-six by forty-two feet and three stories in height; machine-shop, which had formerly been the woolen-factory, sixty by thirty feet; a stone drying-house, twenty-eight by eighteen feet; and a stone cotton-factory, fifty by forty-five feet, two stories in height; a block of six stone tenement houses, and a large mansion-house, which had been built by George W. Hill in 1829. Samuel Riddle took possession of the premises in 1843, and, fortunately, the flood of that year inflicted but little damage to his property. In 1845 he made extensive additions to the mill, and in 1872 erected a stone woolen-mill one hundred and twelve by sixty-five feet, three stories and a basement in height. In 1881 he built the brick mill, one hundred and thirty-five by sixty-two feet. The Glen Riddle mills at the present time contain fourteen thousand cotton spindles, twenty-four hundred woolen spindles, and three hundred and sixty looms. Three hundred and eighty operatives are employed. The goods made at these mills are tickings, cheviots, and doeskins.

Parkmount Mills.—Samuel Riddle, a cotton manufacturer, in 1829, moved from Riddle to Chester Creek, Peter Hill having agreed to erect for him a cotton-mill above the forks of Chester Creek. This factory, known as the Parkmount Mills, was operated by Samuel Riddle until 1841, after which it was leased by John Dixon and others, finally by the Callaghan Brothers, during whose occupancy it was burned in 1863. In the year 1866, Burnley, Gledhill & Co. erected on the site the present mill, fifty by one hundred and fifty feet. They manufactured both cotton and woolen goods. In 1870 the Parkmount Mills Cotton and Woolen Company was organized, with George Mollison, president, John Burnley, secretary and treasurer, and Francis Butterworth, superintendent. The mill contains at present time ninety-six looms, five sets of cards, and eighteen hundred spindles.

John Burnley, the son of John and Mary Burnley, was born in Littletown, Yorkshire, England, May 14, 1820. After receiving a fair English education he learned the trade of a spinner, and soon after determined to seek a wider field of labor in America. On the 12th of September, 1838, he sailed from Liverpool, and on his arrival removed at once to Cobb's Creek, Montgomery Co., Pa., where George, his eldest brother, was already established as a manufacturer of cotton fabrics. With him he sought employment, and remained as one of his most valued assistants until May 2, 1844, when he removed to Darby Creek, in Delaware County, and became a partner with his brother in the manufacture of jeans. On removing to Lenni, in connection with George Mallison and George Gladhill, under the firm-name of Burnley & Co., he rented the Parkmount Mills at this point, and began the manufacture of cotton and woolen goods. He retired in 1870 from active business, but two years later, together with George Mallison and Francis Butterworth, resumed his business relations, the firm being known as Burnley & Co., which was changed in July, 1878, to "The Parkmount Cotton and Woolen Company, Limited." Mr. Burnley continued thus actively engaged until his death, on the 26th of November, 1883, being secretary and treasurer of the company. He married Mary Lomas, daughter of James and Mary Lomas, whose children are William, Adeline (Mrs. Edward Marland), Frances Ann (deceased), John Edward. Mrs. Burnley died Aug. 1, 1881, and he was again married, March 1, 1883, to Alice Lomas, sister of his first wife. Mr. Burnley was in politics a Republican, but devoted to the interests of his business, and gave little attention to matters associated with the political world. He possessed great business capacity, strict integrity, and a genial nature, which endeared him to all who were favored with an intimate knowledge of the man. His religious preferences were for the Protestant Episcopal Church, in which faith he was educated. Mr. Burnley was a member of the Masonic fraternity, and of Protection Lodge of Independent Order of Odd-Fellows of Philadelphia. The business which he aided in establishing is conducted as formerly, his interest being represented by the estate. The grandchildren of Mr. and Mrs. Burnley are John H. Burnley, Florence B. Marland, and Mary Lizzie Burnley.

John and Mary Burnley were residents of Levisage, in the West Riding of Yorkshire, England, where their son, Charles, was born on the 21st of June, 1808. Here and in the immediate vicinity his youth was spent. After limited educational opportunities he entered a blanket manufactory, where his father was employed, and there learned the trade of a spinner. This industry was followed in his native land until 1842, when he embarked for America. He was, in 1838, married to Miss Susanna, daughter of James and Mary Woodcock, of Hightown, in the West Riding of Yorkshire. Their children are Mary (Mrs. Henry Grant), deceased; Mabeth (Mrs. Albert Smith), Joseph, and Charles, deceased.

Mr. Burnley, on landing upon American shores, at once repaired to Montgomery County, Pa., and engaged in spinning with his brother, with whom he remained until 1844. He then removed to Upper Darby and pursued his vocation in connection with his brother George. At a later date the three brothers—George, John, and the subject of this sketch—formed a copartnership for the manufacture of cotton goods, which was continued until 1865, when the last named came to Middletown township and purchased a farm, having meanwhile relinquished the business of a manufacturer. He remained thus engaged until 1878, when on his retirement from active pursuits he removed to Lenni. Mr. Burnley was in politics a Republican, but not active as a politician. He was a zealous member of the Methodist Episcopal Church, and interested in all projects for the advancement of morality and religion in the community. His death occurred Oct. 13, 1881, in his seventy-fifth year. The grandchildren of Mr. and Mrs. Burnley are Charles E., Ulysses C., Henry T., Georgianna, and Anna, children of Henry and Mary Grant; Ella B., Wilmer C., Susanna, George, and Mary, children of Albert and Mabeth Smith; Susan E., Lizzie, and Mary, children of Joseph Burnley.

Pennell Saw-Mill.—Subsequent to 1830, Joseph Pennell built a saw-mill on Rocky Run, about three-quarters of a mill from where that stream empties into Chester Creek. It was owned by James Pennell subsequent to 1848, and on Aug. 11, 1870, was swept away by a freshet. It was never rebuilt.

Yearsley's Mill.—On Rocky Run, a branch of Chester Creek, stands an old stone mill, and on a tablet built into the wall, near the top of the gable, is engraved the date 1792. The land on which this mill is located was granted Dec. 7, 1741, to Joseph Talbot by his brother, Benjamin Talbot, and comprised one hundred and thirty-four acres, being part of the estate of their father. Joseph Talbot, on the site of the present mill, built a frame grist-mill, in which for many years he conducted the milling business. On April 21, 1773, Joseph Talbot, Sr., conveyed one hundred and five acres of land and the grist-mill to his son, Joseph Talbot, Jr. The latter owned the property, and conducted the business until March 12, 1784, when he sold one hundred and fifteen acres and the mill to James Emlin, who, in 1792, removed the old and built the present mill on the site. Emlin died in 1797, and the mill, devised to his heirs, was retained by them until 1823. It is not probable that any of the Emlin family carried on the business of milling, for in 1799 we know the mill was operated by John Peirce. On May 1, 1823, the mill was purchased by Nathan Yearsley, but he dying before 1826, the mill was rented to Ralph E. Marsh until Humphrey Yearsley, the only son of Nathan Yearsley, became of age. When the latter attained his majority, in 1836, he took possession of it, and has conducted the mill to the present time.

Adjoining this mill-seat on the north, and on the same run, was an old saw-mill, which was built prior to 1782 by John Worrell, and was still owned by him in 1826. The property was owned by J. C. Evans in 1875. Half a century ago the mill was abandoned, and at this time the race and dam are almost leveled, hardly a trace remaining.

Mills on Ridley Creek—Hillsborough Mills.—The first mill erected on this site is said to have been built as a saw-mill about 1800 by John Evans, who obtained the right to boat logs up the Stimmel dam to the Evans mill. The property in 1819 was in the possession of the Bank of Delaware County, and was sold by that corporation to James Ronaldson on November 4th of that year. A cotton-factory was soon after erected under the charge of Patrick Mulvany, thirty-three by fifty-six feet, three stories high, and in 1826 had three carding-engines, six hundred and sixty-two throstle spindles, and four hundred and eighty mule spindles. The mill spun about seven hundred pounds of cotton yarn per week. There were then nine houses and the mansion-house on the estate. It subsequently was in charge of George Cummins, Jonathan and Jabez Jenkins respectively. On the 26th of June, 1835, James Ronaldson sold the mills to Hugh Groves, an Irishman. In 1841 the factory was eighty by forty-six feet, and contained four double cotton-cards, two large speeders, two ellipse speeders, one drawing-frame with three heads, one with two heads, two mules of three hundred spindles each, one of two hundred and forty spindles, thirty-six power-looms, seven throstles of six hundred and sixty spindles, etc.

The mills were purchased by Samuel Bancroft in 1842, and run by him till about 1866, when they were sold to John Fox, under whom they were burned down subsequent to 1870. The property is now owned by Samuel Bancroft, and is lying idle.

Media Water-Works.—A long and narrow tract extending from Ridley Creek southwestward, and nearly half-way across the township, and to the lands of Richard Crosby, was taken up by Joseph Jarvis, but not surveyed to him till March 13, 1701. At this location, on Ridley Creek, Jarvis erected a grist-mill, which was operated by him in 1704, for at Providence Friends' Meeting, on Second month 24, 1704, complaint was made to meeting that "Thomas Jones had unlawfully taken some corn from Jarvis's mill." Jasper Yeates was interested in this tract and mill in 1705, for on February 27th of that year, Jasper Yeates and Joseph Jarvis convey to Richard and John Crosby "a mill and sixty-three acres of land." On March

CHARLES BURNLEY.

25, 1705, Richard and John Crosby in open court acknowledged a lease to James Cooper for twenty-one years. This may have been the James Cooper of Darby, for in 1715 a fulling-mill was on the property. Some difficulty must have occurred, for the lease was rescinded.

On Aug. 26, 1715, Richard and John Crosby sold "all those water mill or grist and fulling mills," to Job Harvey, cloth-worker, of Darby, or "Stoffer." He was a son-in-law of John Bethel, who owned the Darby Mill, one of which was a fulling-mill, which Job Harvey had operated for some years prior to 1705, as in that year he purchased a part interest, and remained at Darby until the purchase of this property. Job Harvey retained ownership of the Middletown Mills until April 10, 1729, when he sold to his son, Josiah Harvey, also a cloth-worker. This deed describes the land as being in three tracts, one of fifty-two acres, one of eight and a half acres, and one of three acres, making sixty-three and a half acres.

Josiah Harvey sold the grist-mill, fulling-mill, and three tracts of land, Nov. 10, 1731, to William Pennell and Frederick Engle. On Dec. 30, 1734, Engle released his rights in the property to William Pennell, who owned it until April 2, 1740, when he sold the same property to his son, Thomas Pennell. In 1766, and up to 1774, Caleb James was assessed on a grist-mill, and on April 25, 1775, he sold the same-described property that Josiah Harvey sold to Pennell and Engle in 1731, and two more tracts to Isaac Levis, of Upper Darby; part of the land was in Upper Providence. Soon after his purchase, Isaac Levis erected upon the estate a saw-mill, on which he was assessed until 1790, between which time and his death, which occurred in 1794, he erected a paper-mill. In 1798 the mill property passed to Seth Levis, the eldest son of Isaac. On May 23, 1807, Seth sold one-half interest to his brother-in-law, Edward Lewis, who married his sister. This deed, in mentioning the mill land, recites that "Isaac Levis erected thereon a paper-mill." These mills were conducted by Levis & Lewis until the death of Seth Levis, and his interest passed to Edward Lewis about 1825. In 1826 it is mentioned as being a two-vat paper-mill, and manufactured twenty-four reams of imperial and thirty reams of royal printing-paper per week. The grist and saw-mills were also in operation. The paper-mill was washed away in 1843, and was not again rebuilt. In 1845, Edward Lewis erected at this site a tilt-mill, which was rented to William & Thomas Beatty, who manufactured edge-tools at this place until 1850, when they moved their works to Springfield, on Crum Creek, above the paper-mill of J. Howard Lewis. The mill-property, on April 1, 1861, was conveyed by William Levis Lewis and Edward Lewis, heirs of Edward Lewis, to Lewis Palmer, who on May 11, 1871, sold to Edward A. Price and others, by whom the property was conveyed December 26th, in that year, to the borough of Media. The corporate authorities fitted the property for use as water-works for the borough, retaining the grist-mill, which is still used for milling purposes. It is stated by Miss Sarah Miller, of Media, that while the mills were in the possession of Isaac Levis, the lumber used in the construction of St. Mary's Catholic Church, in Philadelphia, was sawed there.

Painter's Clover- and Saw-Mills.—On Dismal Run, prior to this century, Enos Painter built a clover-mill and saw-mill, which, in 1826, were reported as old mills. Thomas Chalfant had charge of these mills from 1825 to 1831, and after that date, Benjamin Robinson ran the clover-mill. It has years ago disappeared. The saw-mill was run by John Heacock, who manufactured pails or buckets there, and Hugh Jones made chair-backs. It was burned about 1860.

The Pennsylvania Training-School for Feeble-Minded Children.—This institution, the third of its kind in order of establishment in America, is deserving, by reason of its noble aim, splendid growth, and colossal accomplishment in lessening the sum of human sorrow and misfortune, of an extended sketch in this volume, and we venture to say that there are many, even in the township in which the training-school is located, to whom its history is by no means familiar.

A few words about the institutions in this country which chronologically stand ahead of this one, may not prove amiss in this connection. In the United States the first school for the training of the feeble-minded was opened in Barre, Mass., by Dr. H. B. Wilbur, in July, 1848. Now there are no less than thirteen similar institutions in the country.

The movement here in this direction began almost contemporaneously with that in Europe.[1] Those most prominent in the earliest measures resorted to in this country were Dr. Frederick Backus, of Rochester, N. Y., and George Sumner, of Boston, "who were soon seconded by the enterprise, courage, and philanthropy of Drs. Henry B. Wilbur and Samuel George Howe, whose names must be yoked together with equal honor, the first as the founder of the Barre School."

The State of New York established an experimental school at Albany, in 1851, which was soon followed by a permanent State institution at Syracuse under the superintendence of Dr. Wilbur, who had as coadjutors such men as John C. Spencer and Governor Marcy.

[1] "It is within the recollection of living men that Guggenbuhl, of Switzerland, Seguire, of Paris, and Sageve, of Berlin, opened at the same time their schools for imbeciles and idiots, and the eyes of the nations to their duty in behalf of this neglected class. In 1846, Dr. Kern established a school at Leipsic; in England, in 1848, under the inspiration of such men as Drs. Reid, Twining, and Conolly, Sir S. Morton Peto devoted his own mansion (Essex Hall) for the purpose. Scotland opened her first institution in 1852, and in June, 1853, was laid, by Prince Albert, the corner-stone of the school of Earlswood, Surrey. Nearly all the nations of Europe followed these examples."—*Dr. Kerlin in an address before the Philadelphia Society for Organizing Charity*, Nov. 6, 1882.

The next to move in this work was Pennsylvania Dr A L Elwyn, afterwards the honored president of the institution, attending at Cambridge a meeting of the Association for the Advancement of Science, in 1849, turned aside to bear a letter from Rachel Laird, a blind girl of Philadelphia, to Laura Bridgman, the famous blind deaf mute of the South Boston Institution for the Blind, and while there he casually, at the invitation of a teacher, visited a room to see the experiment Massachusetts was making in behalf of the children of feeble minds He was so impressed with what he saw, and with the feasibility of instituting a similar school, that immediately after returning to Philadelphia he held a conference with a number of his friends upon the subject During the same year James B Richards, of Boston, who had been associated with Dr Howe, came to Philadelphia bearing a letter of introduction to Dr Elwyn A meeting, presided over by Bishop Potter and held in the office of James J Barclay, was addressed so earnestly by Dr Elwyn that the gentlemen present immediately promised aid to Mr Richards for the establishment of an experimental school at Germantown

On Feb 10, 1853, the preliminary steps were taken to found the school which has since developed into a great State institution, and on the 7th of April of the same year the Legislature incorporated "The Pennsylvania Training-School for Feeble-Minded Children," and took it under fostering care, by which, with the liberality of citizens, it was built up to a condition by 1869 unequaled by any in the country

The organization was effected by the usual methods of all charitable corporations in the State In the enactment appeared the honored names of Alonzo Potter, John K Kane, J B Richards, Matthias W Baldwin, Jacob G Morris, Isaac Collins, Alfred L Elwyn, James Martin, Alexander Fullerton, and Franklin Taylor, who were, with their associates and successors, constituted a body politic and corporate in law Membership in this corporation was secured by the payment to the treasurer of thirty dollars, or by the annual payment of five dollars These moneys were invested in the "Free Fund" of the institution

The school was soon opened at Germantown under the direction of James B Richards, and by the year 1858 had acquired a property valued at nineteen thousand dollars The period of its active development began in 1856, when Dr Joseph Parrish was called to its superintendence, and "the school became an institution with considerable of an advancement towards departmental purposes and classification"

In looking about for a location in which the training-school could better be conducted (then in Germantown) the site of the present buildings, a farm of sixty acres in the vicinity of Media, was selected as presenting all of the most desirable features This was bought from William L Lewis for ten thousand dollars, which sum was contributed by the many friends who came to the aid of the institution, and who further donated eighty-three thousand nine hundred and eighteen dollars towards the erection of the first buildings The citizens of Media contributed one thousand dollars towards the purchase The formal opening of the school occurred on Wednesday, Nov 2, 1859 The dedication ceremonies were witnessed by an immense throng of people, mainly the citizens of the county John P Crozer gave the opening address He was followed by Dr Joseph Parrish, the superintendent at that time, and by several others The Legislature, prior to 1869, had appropriated a total sum of ninety-seven thousand five hundred dollars, which completed the central, north, and south wings of the main building, and the Legislature of 1875-76 listening to an appeal for increased building accommodations, the sum of twenty thousand dollars was placed in the substantial structure known as the North House

In 1877 began the effort to meet what was believed to be an imperative need,—"the creation of a strictly asylum branch, so situated at separate buildings that the educational department would be unembarrassed by it, while the inmates would get some share in the benefits and supervision of a general institution" It was not until the session of 1880-81 that the Legislature was so impressed as to vote assistance, but that body then made an appropriation of sixty thousand dollars, which was used to construct two excellent buildings on an adjoining farm, which in the mean time had been bought A commodious school-house, forty by one hundred and eight feet, was also erected at a cost of ten thousand dollars, and a laundry-building, in which employment is given to about twenty inmates, at a cost of five thousand dollars. The original sixty acres has been added to until at present the asylum grounds include one hundred and forty acres The total value of the real estate is probably not far from three hundred thousand dollars

The State of Pennsylvania has increased her quota, and now provides for two hundred and fifty children of the commonwealth The State of New Jersey liberally supports sixty of her feeble ones, and the city of Philadelphia sends eighteen The "free fund" amounts to over seventy-five thousand dollars, and it is hoped that it may be raised to two hundred thousand dollars in the not far distant future

There are at present six lists on which children are admitted, viz, under the State fund of Pennsylvania, appropriated for the support of two hundred children of the commonwealth, for a period of not more than seven years, apportioned as nearly as possible among the Senatorial districts, according to representation It is wished to take on this fund *improvable cases only*, or those who may return to the community, at least self-helpful if not self-supporting, under the State fund of New Jersey, appropriated for the support of poor children of that State, or for partial aid of such persons of only moderate circumstances, as are unable to pay full cost of maintenance, under the State fund of Delaware, appropriated for the support of two children from each county of that State, under the city of Philadelphia fund, applied to cases received from the "Children's Home," of the Philadelphia almshouse, or by special permit through the committee appointed by the Board of Guardians of the city of Philadelphia, under the free fund, devoted exclusively to the entire or partial maintenance in the institution of such feeble-minded persons as may be selected by the superintendent and committee on admission, and whose support is not otherwise provided for, and under the private list Children may be received on this list from any place in or out of our State, on payment, quarterly in advance, of such sums as may be agreed upon, the rates being determined by the amount of care the case requires, the extra accommodations given, and the ability of parents or guardians to pay

As the foregoing suggests, the Pennsylvania Training-School is a private institution under State patronage The Legislature annually makes an appropriation of sixty thousand dollars for its support

Since 1864 Dr Isaac N Kerlin has been superintendent of the institution Under his management the school has made its largest growth, and become most widely useful The aim of the management has been threefold: first, as the name of the institution indicates, to train the feeble-minded so that they may return to their homes or be placed in proper places, and be self-sustaining, second, to afford a permanent asylum for those whose condition is helpless and hopeless, and third, to afford in the institution a home to those who by its aids may be wholly or partially self-sustaining It is the desire of those who have given the matter careful attention that the latter feature may be more fully developed, by making at Elwyn (as the place is called after one of the founders, and the president of the institution) an *Asylum Village* Concerning this praiseworthy project, which must inevitably be carried out some time, we find the following in the course of a newspaper article which had as its subject a recent meeting of the directors of the institution

"The correspondence of the Institution establishes the fact that at least one thousand five hundred feeble-minded children are in the homes of persons too poor to pay for their support in any institution, and yet too much attached to their unfortunate offspring to place them in County Almshouses The injury to the community from the presence of this element is such that those who examine this problem believe it would be wise economy to isolate the feeble minded and idiotic, and establish in Delaware County, in connection with the present institution, an asylum village, to consist of farm houses for those who are able to work, a hospital home for the helpless, and a central educational department The institution already embraces these features, and by utilizing its farm-lands the cost of maintenance has so diminished that it is now believed a plan embracing all this dependent population of the State is feasible This plan would bring under a working system the contributions of those families who are able to support in whole or in part any of their afflicted members, and the aid of the counties and the commonwealth"

In regard to the present condition of the institution, it may be said that in beauty of surroundings and in the cheerfulness of its inner furnishing, in the neatness and order of all that pertains to the school and asylum, in the effectiveness of training, and in the gentleness of care, the establishment at Elwyn is not surpassed by any similar institution of which the writer has knowledge

The cluster of granite buildings is situated on a beautiful wooded eminence, between Media and Elwyn Station, on the Philadelphia and West Chester Railroad, within easy walking distance of either, but nearest the latter, which, in fact, was established principally for the convenience of those whose duties take them to the school The immediate hill on which the main buildings are erected is terraced, graded, with dry walks, and planted with shrubbery A grove of five acres on the west and north is laid out for paths and drives, where in summer the children exercise A farm of nearly one hundred and thirty acres extends into the valley below, furnishing work for such boys as can be taught agricultural labor A small tramway connects the parent institution and the hill-side home, and it is designed to extend it to the Elwyn Station The cars upon this road run one way by gravity, and are drawn back by donkeys A pretty excursion car that runs upon it accommodates twenty or thirty children, who are thus afforded pleasurable out-door life for some hours in the day

The asylum buildings, with which this road connects, are, like the main buildings, constructed most substantially of stone, are of fine appearance, and excellently adapted to the purpose which they serve In short, everything about the institution is indicative, by its perfection and practical usefulness, of the broad charity of the people, the wise beneficence of the State, and the intelligent and kindly management that has found exercise here The work that is carried on by the Pennsylvania Training-School for Feeble-Minded Children is indicated by the fact that during the year (ending Sept 30, 1883) four hundred and twenty-eight children were under the care of the school and industrial departments Of these, three hundred and ninety-six remained at the close of the year, classified as regards support as follows

State of Pennsylvania, wholly	193
" " partially	10
" New Jersey	61
" Delaware	2
City of Philadelphia	18
By parents and guardians	81
Soldiers' Orphan Fund	1
Free	30

Following is a list of the presidents, superintendents, and assistant superintendents connected with the institution from its incorporation to the present:

Presidents—Rt Rev Alonzo Potter, 1853-66, John P Crozer, 1866-67, S Morris Waln, 1867-70, A L Elwyn, M D, from 1870

Superintendents—Rev James B Richards, 1853-57, Joseph Parrish, M D, 1857-64; I N Kerlin, M D, from 1864

Assistant Superintendents.—I N Kerlin, M D, 1857-64, Mrs Louisa P Ross, 1864-66, Rockwood Brigham, 1865-67, Henry W Blake, 1867-69, Henry M Lyon, M D, 1871-72, Edgar P Jefferis, 1872-75, Daniel W. Jefferis, M D, 1878-80, William B Fish, 1881-84, D W Wilmott, 1884

Alfred L Elwyn, M D, was born July 9, 1804, in Portsmouth, N H, where he attended school under the noted Deacon Tappan In 1816 he became a pupil of Phillips Exeter Academy, and there remained three years In 1819 he entered Harvard University, from which he graduated in 1823, after which he read medicine in Boston, under the celebrated Dr Gorham He went to England and Edinburgh in October, 1826, and returned to London in April, 1827 He then passed one year in Paris, and in the summer of 1829 returned to America, having, during his sojourn abroad, visited his father's relatives in England, and kept up a continuous course of study. In 1831 he graduated at the University of Pennsylvania, and received his diploma as M D He was married Jan 31, 1832, to Mary Middleton, daughter of Dr. James Mease, and granddaughter of Hon Pierce Butler, of South Carolina, by whom he had one living child, Rev Alfred Elwyn His daughter, Mary Middleton Elwyn, married Dr S Weir Mitchell, of Philadelphia, and died in 1862, leaving two sons, both of whom are living In 1845, Dr Elwyn, who made Philadelphia his residence, but did not practice his profession, purchased property in East Bradford township, Chester Co, Pa, where he resided during the summer months He was one of the founders of the State Agricultural Society, in 1850, and largely identified with its progress, as also with that of the Farmers' High School He was connected with the establishment of the Institution for the Blind of Philadelphia, and was one of the originators of the Training-School for Feeble-Minded Children, located at Elwyn, Delaware Co, and fostered and built by the State of Pennsylvania He ever manifested the warmest interest in philanthropic institutions, and aided in the creation of many of them He was before his death the oldest living member of the American Association for the Advancement of Science He also belonged to the Academy of Natural Sciences, and was for some years a director of Girard College He was also vice-president of the Historical Society, and a member of the Philosophical Society Dr Elwyn served as president of the Society for the Prevention of Cruelty to Animals, and was president of the Old Agricultural Society of Philadelphia He was one of the Philadelphia board of three for licensing taverns under a special act of the Legislature, in which he acquitted himself with honor, and to the credit of the city His farm in East Bradford originally belonged to Philip Price, and on this land was used, in 1846, the first guano introduced into Chester County Dr Elwyn gave much attention to the natural sciences, philosophical inquiry, and political economy, and contributed largely to the press, reviews, and magazines with his able pen. His varied learning and versatile genius made him one of the most pointed and incisive of our educated men. The death of Dr. Elwyn occurred March 15, 1884

Licensed Houses.—The first record respecting licenses in Middletown which I have seen is the petition of Charles Crosley, Feb 27, 1727, which states that living by the great road from Concord to Philadelphia, he desires the privilege of keeping a public-house His application was indorsed by William Pennell and eleven other signers He was allowed license until August following, but it was continued annually to him until 1749, and in 1752 John Crosley, probably his son, received license for a public house of entertainment in Middletown

Jonathan Hunter, May 25, 1731, made application for the privilege to keep a house of entertainment in Middletown, on the "Great road from Chester and the Valley, and no publick house on said road" His petition met with the approval of the court, and the license was continued until his death, for Aug 23, 1733, William Hill, in his application, sets forth that he "hath taken to ffarm the house with the appurtenances, late of Jonathan Hunter, dec'd, in the township of Middletown, where a house of Entertainment hath been for some Considerable time and now is kept" There Hill continued until his death, for in 1748 license was granted to his widow, Mary, who having been married to James Bennett, in 1749, the license was taken out in his name. In 1750, Joseph Talboth (Talbot) states in his petition that Mary, the widow of William Hill, "entended to decline at the expiration of the license," and asked that it be continued to him, which was done He kept the house until 1761, when license was granted to James Massey for the years 1761 and 1762, and during 1763 the license was taken out by either Thomas Caldwell or Joshua Bean, who received approval that year. In 1764, John Hill, in all probabilities a son of the former owner, obtained license and continued in the business until 1778, when Bartholomew Sutton became the landlord John Pitt had the right to sell liquor at this house in 1783, where he continued until 1786, when it ceased to be a public inn

In 1731, the same year that Jonathan Hunter first obtained license in the township, William Surman made application for leave to sell "Beer & Cyder." He had lived, he stated, "for several years in Middletown, and for the most of the time followed making Malt or brewing of Beer" Although he was strongly recommended by the signers, his petition bears the indorsement "not granted"

William Trego, of Middletown, presented his petition, dated Aug 28, 1733, in which he declared that "having but a small piece of land, he wants to sell beer and cider by small measure" His application seems to have been granted, or held under consideration, for on November 27th of the same year "a pe-

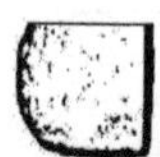

Alfred Langdon Elwyn

Assistant Superintendents.—J. N. Kerlin, M.D., 1867–[illegible]; Mrs. Louisa P. Ross, 1864–68; Rockwood Brigham, 1865–67; Henry W. Blake, 1867–69; Henry M. Lyon, M.D., 1871–72; Edgar F. Jefferis, 1872–75; David W. Jefferis, M.D., 1878–80; William B. Fish, 1880–81; D. W. Wilmott, 1884.

Alfred L. Elwyn, M.D., was born July 9, 1804, in Portsmouth, N. H., where he attended school under the noted Deacon Tappan. In 1816 he became a pupil of Phillips Exeter Academy, and there remained three years. In 1819 he entered Harvard University, from which he graduated in 1823, after which he read medicine in Boston, under the celebrated Dr. Gorham. He went to England and Edinburgh in October, 1826, and returned to London in April, 1827. He then passed one year in Paris, and in the summer of 1828 returned to America, having, during his sojourn abroad, visited his father's relatives in England, and kept up a continuous course of study. In 1831 he graduated at the University of Pennsylvania, and received his diploma as M.D. He was married Jan. 21, 1832, to Mary Middleton, daughter of Dr. James Mease, and granddaughter of Hon. Pierce Butler, of South Carolina, by whom he had one surviving child, Rev. Alfred Elwyn. His daughter, Mary Middleton Elwyn, married Dr. S. Weir Mitchell, of Philadelphia, and died in 1862, leaving two sons, both of whom are living. In 1848, Dr. Elwyn, who made Philadelphia his residence, but did not practice his profession, purchased property in East Bradford township, Chester Co., Pa., where he resided during the summer months. He was one of the founders of the State Agricultural Society, in 1846, and largely identified with its progress, as also with that of the Farmers' High School. He was connected with the establishment of the Institution for the Blind of Philadelphia, and was one of the originators of the Training-School for Feeble-Minded Children, located at Elwyn, Delaware Co., and fostered and built by the State of Pennsylvania. He ever manifested the warmest interest in philanthropic institutions, and aided in the erection of many of them. He was before his death the oldest living member of the American Association for the Advancement of Science. He also belonged to the Academy of Natural Sciences, and was for some years a director of Girard [illegible] He was also [illegible] of the Historical [illegible] a member of the [illegible] president [illegible] by the [illegible] to animals [illegible] of [illegible] Society of Philadelphia. He [illegible] licensing [illegible] act of the Legislature, in [illegible] with honor and to the credit [illegible] East Bradford originally belo[illegible] this land was used, in 18[illegible] into Chester County. [illegible] attention to the natural sciences, p[illegible] cal economy, and contributed largely to the press, reviews, and magazines with his able pen. His varied learning and versatile genius made him one of the most polished and incisive of our educated men. The death of Dr. Elwyn occurred March 15, 1884.

Licensed Houses.—The first record respecting licenses in Middletown which I have seen is the petition of Charles Crosley, Feb. 27, 1727, which states that living by the great road from Concord to Philadelphia, he desires the privilege of keeping a public-house. His application was indorsed by William Pennell and eleven other signers. He was allowed license until August following, but it was continued annually to him until 1749, and in 1752 John Crosley, probably his son, received license for a public house of entertainment in Middletown.

Jonathan Hunter, May 25, 1731, made application for the privilege to keep a house of entertainment in Middletown, on the "Great road from Chester and the Vallie, and no publick house on said road." His petition met with the approval of the court, and the license was continued until his death, for Aug. 23, 1735, William Hill, in his application, sets forth that he "hath taken to farm the house with the appurtenances, late of Jonathan Hunter, dec'd, in the township of Middletown, where a house of Entertainment hath been for some Considerable time and now is kept." There Hill continued until his death, for in 1746 license was granted to his widow, Mary, who having been married to James Bennett, in 1748, the license was taken out in his name. In 1756, Joseph Talbath (Talbot) states in his petition that Mary, the widow of William Hill, "entended to decline at the expiration of the license," and asked that it be continued to him, which was done. He kept the house until 1761, when license was granted to James Massey for the years 1761 and 1762, and during 1763 the license was taken out by either Thomas Caldwell or Joshua Bean, who received approval that year. In 1764, John Hill, in all probabilities a son of the former owner, obtained license and continued in the business until 1779, when Bartholomew Sutton became the landlord. John Pitt had the right to sell liquor at this house in 1783, where he continued until 1786, when it ceased to be a public inn.

In 1731, the same year that Jonathan Hunter first obtained license in the township, William Surman made application for leave to sell "Beer & Cyder." He had lived, he stated, "for several years in Middletown, and for the most of the time followed making Malt or brewing of Beer." Although he was strongly recommended by the signers, his petition bears the indorsement "not granted."

William Trego, of Middletown, presented his petition, dated Aug. 28, 1739, in which he declared that "having but a small piece of land, he wants to sell beer and cider by small measure." His application seems to have been granted, or held under consideration, for on November 27th of the same year "a pe-

Alfred Langdon Elwyn

tition" (remonstrance), signed by Robert McClellan, James Ewing, William Lindsay, and sixteen others, was presented, which stated that "Peter Trego," (doubtless an error in the first name) "had set up keeping a publick house or Ale House in Middletown, in which were already two Taverns,—one on Philada road and the other on Chester road Besides this is situated so very near that place which many of us have set appart in a peculiar manner for our meeting together to worship the Great Creator of Heaven and Earth, having our younger people to accompany us, &c" The court refused the license, for the petition is indorsed "not allowed"

William Noblit, in 1738, petitioned for license to keep tavern in Middletown, but on Aug 29, 1738, a remonstrance was presented, signed by Elizabeth Jack, Mary Pennell, Mary Pilkinton, Rebecca Chance, Mary Grible, Ann Wills, Martha Blace, and Elizabeth Campbell, denying the necessity of the license, "since there are two taverns already in the township," and designate them as kept by William Hill, eight miles from Chester, on road to Valley, and Charles Crosley, on Concord and Philadelphia road, about one mile from Noblit's, and his application failed

Black Horse Hotel —William Noblit again, Nov 27, 1739, presented his petition, in which he informed the justices that he "having newly built a Commodious stone house upon the great road Leading from Chester to the Valley, about three-quarters of a mile from the Presbyterian meeting-house where Commonly is a great resort of people, and as some having ten or fifteen miles to travel to the sd place of worship," is necessary for the public generally. His petition is indorsed by one hundred and forty signatures A remonstrance bearing date November 16th, signed by sixteen persons, set forth that his "house is not above one and a half miles from William Hill's tavern, and a mile from Charles Crosley's" The court, however, yielded to the majority and allowed the license desired, and thus was established the now ancient public-house, whose history is interwoven with so many noted incidents in our county annals, the "Black Horse Hotel"

William Noblit had license continuously from the date last given until the year 1763, although his name does not appear on the list of licenses from 1754 to 1758, both years inclusive, but inasmuch as his name occurs again in 1759 to 1762, in all probabilities during the five years before mentioned he had license granted to him In 1763, as stated in the account of Hill's tavern, one or other of the names there given—Thomas Caldwell or Joshua Bean—had charge of the old house, while in 1764, Thomas Carrell, or Carvell, was "mine host" In 1765, Nathan Edwards (who on Aug 31, 1742, asked for license on the "Great Road from the Valley to Chester," and whose signers on that occasion represented that "the Publick houses near him on the sd road for a Considerable time have been disorderly kept, as we are informed, to the General dissatisfaction of the neighbourhood," without, however, obtaining Edwards the license sought), became the landlord of the tavern and continued so until 1783, in which year Ezekiel Leonard assumed the business, and remained there until he became sheriff of Chester County, in the fall of 1786, when he was succeeded by Richard Cheyney, whose petition, in 1787, for the first time presents the now familiar name "Black Horse" as the title of the inn Cheyney was licensed the following year, and in 1789 Benjamin Johnson prayed for and was granted the right to keep there a public-house Johnson continued there until 1792, when he gave place to Joseph Gibbons In 1793 James Pennell had license from the court of Delaware County for the "Black Horse," and again in the following year, 1794, when he died.

This James Pennell had previous to his removal to Middletown kept tavern in Chester, and respecting his death Mrs Rebecca Brobson, of Chester, who died in 1863, at a very advanced age, used to relate the following particulars While a resident of the latter place, as an attraction for the public, he kept a tiger, whom he had taught to perform a number of tricks, and as the creature was apparently very docile, he had no fears of the animal. This unusual spectacle, at a time when there were no monstrous traveling shows to entertain the masses, drew many persons to Pennell's tavern, and frequently the owner of the beast could be seen exhibiting to a crowd of gaping rustics how tractable it was and how promptly it obeyed his commands Pennell, when he became the landlord of the Black Horse, took the animal with him and continued the exhibitions One day, while showing the people his entire control of the tiger, he forced it to do many tricks over and over until it became enraged, and, springing upon Pennell, it tore him with its claws so badly before it could be driven back that the unfortunate man died in a few hours thereafter.

In 1795 his widow, Lydia Pennell, received the license, and annually thereafter until 1802, when she intermarried with David Esbin, who in that year became the landlord The following year the house was kept by Elizabeth Vernon, who remained there until 1806, when George Pearson was "mine host" of the Black Horse, to be succeeded in 1808 by James Fairlamb, and he in the following years had the license transferred to Frederick James In 1811, James Hansley was the landlord, and in 1813 John Clayton had the court's approval, while in the following year Jacob Pyle did the honors of the house, and in 1816 Reuben Taylor was his successor

The Black Horse Tavern in 1817 was presided over by Sarah and George Hawkins, and they in 1820 gave place to George Irwin The latter in 1822 was followed by George Malin The central position the venerable inn occupied made it a point where frequent public assemblages were had to discuss important political and county topics, and it may be asserted that no tavern within the limits of Delaware County was better known than that in Middletown. In 1835, Hickman Myers became the landlord, and he, in 1839, gave place to George Russell, Jr. During the time that Russell was mine host of the Black Horse it was brought, if possible, into greater prominence, for here in November, 1845, a meeting was held "to take into consideration the propriety of removing the seat of justice to a more central position," and on the mooted point of selecting a proper location "the Black Horse, in Middletown," the highest elevation in the county, was strongly urged as the proper site of the local capital. Russell died in 1847, and the following year Martha Ann Russell, his widow, received license. In 1849, Malin Bishop kept the house and continued there until 1856, when Allen Chandler became the landlord, to be followed in 1858 by Samuel S. McCall. George W. Hill superseded McCall in 1864, and in 1866, when Mr. Lyons purchased the property, Hill transferred the license to Edgar C. Lyons. In 1867 the hotel was controlled by Lyons & Ford, Edgar C. Lyons having associated with him in the business James E. Ford, but in the latter part of the year 1870 Ford retired, since which time Edgar C. Lyons has been the landlord of the noted Black Horse Hotel.

The Pine-Apple.—In 1806, Philip Yarnall, who, the preceding year, had kept a tavern at Chester, was granted privilege to keep a public-house at Middletown Cross-Roads, at the locality known to the present generation as Lima. The frequenters of the Pine-Apple, for so the inn was called, were either of the belligerent element of society, or the whiskey vended there was unusually exhilarating, for the character of the debates and the arguments employed soon earned for the locality the name of Wrangletown, and so generally was it recognized by this appellation that the maps and charts of the day and for many years subsequently designated it under that title. The court the following year refused to continue the license, and, although application was frequently made to that end, the judges seemed fixed in their determination to discontinue a public-house in that neighborhood. With remarkable pertinacity, Joseph Yarnall urged his suit until 1816, when he was gratified by a favorable response, and annually thereafter he appears as a successful aspirant for the judicial favor until 1819, when William Spear, who seems to be met with a remonstrance whenever he presented a petition for license, became the landlord, and the following year the court withdrew absolutely its approval of the house. In 1836, Abel Lodge, who had purchased the real estate of the late Jacob Yarnall, states in his petition that there were about eight acres of land, adjoining properties of Samuel Jobson, David Cummings, and others, "in the neighborhood of Lima Post-Office (formerly Wrangletown), upon which property is erected a good house, with six rooms on the first floor, good stabling, and other conveniences well adapted for the accommodation of strangers and travelers," but the court rejected the application. Three years thereafter, in 1839, Lodge made another effort, but a lengthy remonstrance being presented protesting against the license it was refused. All endeavors to locate an inn at Lima thereafter ceased.

Lima.—In 1806, Philip Yarnall obtained license to keep a tavern at the Middletown Cross-Roads, which house was known as "The Pine-Apple." The sale of whiskey at this place was extensive, an elderly gentleman stating that at this place, at night and on rainy days, a number of men from the neighborhood would gather, and, as whiskey was cheap, there would soon be a noisy crowd, usually ending in a broil. The men, seated round a table with a dirty pack of cards, would sing a song composed by a local jingler of rude verses, one of which, for it had a dozen or more stanzas, was:

"Wrangletown we will pull down,
The sign-board we will alter;
And if we had Joe Yarnall here,
We would hang him with a halter."

Joseph Yarnall was then the landlord of the hotel, and the name Wrangletown was popularly applied to the locality because of the quarrels, disputations, and disputes which took place there at that time. In 1829, Dr. Richard Gregg built a store at the cross-roads, and Nicholas Mendenhall established a lumber-yard there. The lumber was bought in Columbia, Lancaster Co., rafted to Chester, and drawn thence by wagons. The store was first occupied by Nicholas Mendenhall & Caleb D. West. In 1832 a post-office had been there, known as Hamor's Store, and Caleb D. West was postmaster. Prior to 1836 the locality was known as Lima Post-Office. In 1833, Walter J. Hooker as a boy was employed as a clerk by Nicholas Mendenhall, and in the spring of that year Mendenhall sold the store to John Van Leer & Isaac Chamel. This firm failed in 1836, and on August 24th of that year Walker F. Hooper rented the store and began business there, continuing it until 1868, when he was succeeded by his son, Homer Hooper, who associated Azariah Barnes with him in the business, and in 1872, William M. Thomas succeeded them there, and in 1882, —— Ogden, the present. In 1842, Miss Ann Jobson had a millinery-store at Lima, and in 1845 she was succeeded by Miss E. Butler.

Lima Temperance Hall Association.—In 1847 an association of persons favorable to the temperance or Washingtonian movement of that period was chartered, and in 1848 the organization purchased a lot at Lima and erected the two-story brick building known as Lima Temperance Hall. It was dedicated Dec. 25, 1848, by the Sons of Temperance. John F. Taylor, of Humane Division, made an address, as did also Mr. Paxson, of Philadelphia. The visitors on the day of the dedication of the hall were supplied with a sumptuous dinner, presented gratuitously by the friends of temperance living in the neighborhood This association continued for a few years, when the organization was disbanded, and the hall was purchased by William M Thomas, who changed it into dwellings, but subsequently he changed the building into one house, wherein he now resides

The Village of Glen Riddle —After the Sharpless Mills became the property of Isaac Sharpless and Gideon Hatton, the locality was known as "Pennsgrove Mills," which title was retained until February, 1854, when, complaint being made to the Postal Department that frequent mistakes were occasioned, in that letters intended for that office would be sent to Pennsgrove, N J, it was decided to change the name of the station to Glen Riddle Soon after the purchase of the estate by Peter and George W Hill, the latter erected a store in the village, and a post-office was established, George W Hill being appointed the first postmaster At a subsequent date the office was removed to Parkmount, and Samuel Riddle was appointed postmaster In 1843, when Mr Riddle purchased the property, the post-office was re-established at Pennsgrove, and from that date to the present Samuel Riddle has been the postmaster, excepting in 1846, when he resigned, and in August of that year David B Stacey, who at the time was keeping store at the village, was appointed, and continued to discharge the office for a period of two years, when Samuel Riddle was again appointed On May 6, 1879, while a well was being sunk in the rear of the bleaching-house at the Glen Riddle Mills, and at a distance of eighteen feet from the surface of the earth, gold-dust was discovered in the dirt drawn from the well Much excitement prevailed among the residents of the locality at the discovery Specimens of the precious dust were sent to Professor Foot, of the State Geological Survey, and James E Brown, the druggist at Rockdale, tested the metal and found it gold Six quarts of sand yield fifteen cents in pure gold, which it was stated at the time was five times purer than ordinary dust

Lenni Tribe, No 86, I. O. of R M.—In the Plant Moon, 23d Sleep, G S D 377, a delegation from the Great Council of Pennsylvania visited Lenni, and the lodge was instituted in Lima Hall The following officers were chosen Charles W Mathues, Sachem, Charles R Yarnell, Senior Sagamore, William Carson, Junior Sagamore, William Fogg, Chief of Records, William F Mathues, Keeper of Wampum, Joseph Bully, Prophet Twenty pale-faces were admitted as members of the tribe at the first meeting The tribe was later removed to Lenni, Aston township, where it is now located

The House of Employment —In 1855 the directors of the poor, William Trainer, Joseph B Leedom, Jr., and Jacob Byre, were authorized to erect a house of employment near Lima, on the farm purchased from Abraham Pennell The site for the building was on rising ground, from which the land sloped in all directions Plans of the building were prepared by David Taylor, of Chester County, and the contract for their erection was made with Dutton Ottley The building was begun about the 1st of May, 1856, and completed in May of the following year The paupers were removed from the old building at Media to the new house of employment in the first week in April in that year The main building is ninety by forty-eight feet, with two wings, each forty-two by twenty-eight feet, and the main building is three stories in height, with an observatory A hospital was also erected, twenty seven by eighteen feet, two stories in height During 1883 an addition was made to the insane department, and a stone cook-house erected The cost of the original buildings was twenty thousand dollars

Agricultural and Industrial Society of Delaware County —A meeting of the citizens of Delaware County was held at the court-house in Media on Aug 8, 1878, for the purpose of establishing an agricultural society After addresses the society was organized by the election of Dr Ellwood Harvey, president, Richard Young and William P Thomas, vice-presidents, Henry C Snowden, secretary, J Howard Lewis, treasurer Other meetings were held, and stock subscribed to the amount of ten thousand dollars The first exhibition was held at Chester Driving Park on Oct 10, 11, 12, 1878 At this exhibition three hundred and seventy-five exhibits were displayed In May, 1879, the directors purchased about fifty acres of land of the estate of John H Fairlamb, about one mile from Media, and on the line of the West Chester and Philadelphia Railroad These grounds were graded, fenced, fitted up, and buildings erected during the summer of 1879, and a fair was held there for the first time Oct 8, 9, 10, 11, in that year The gross receipts were three thousand three hundred and eighteen dollars

Fairs are held in October in each year J Newlin Trainer was elected president in 1881, and is the present incumbent Henry C Snowden has been secretary since the formation of the society

Chester and Delaware Counties Agricultural Society —On Saturday, May 12, 1835, a society under the above title was organized, with John D Steele as president, William Painter, Richard Pemm, Henry Myers, Gen Joshua Evans, vice-presidents, William Jackson, corresponding secretary, Dr George Thomas, recording secretary, Caspar W Sharpless, assistant secretary, George Brinton, Jr, treasurer Directors, Abraham W Sharpless, William N Barber, John James, Thomas S Woodward, Paschall Morris, Joseph T Jackson, Isaac Newton, Dr. John T Huddleson, James S Peters, and Hill Brinton

The society held exhibitions for several years in Chester and Delaware Counties, until 1845, when interest in it ceased In 1855 a second agricultural society was organized In 1857 its officers were President, James Andrews, Vice-Presidents, Chalkley Harvey, Nathan

Garrett, William Eyre, Jr, George Sharpless, Treasurer, Adam C Eckfeldt, Corresponding Secretary, Y S Walter, Recording Secretary, Ellis P Marshall, Assistant Secretary, D R Hawkins

On September 17, 18, and 19, 1855, a fair was held at Chester The public excitement preceding the civil war so absorbed the public mind that the organization was compelled to disband

The Darlington Dairies—The farm of the Darlington Brothers is located at Darlington Station, on the West Chester and Philadelphia Railroad The business was established by Jesse Darlington about ninety years ago The original dairy consisted of fifteen or twenty cows, which had been increased to thirty or forty cows at the time of Jesse Darlington's death in 1842 He was the first person to introduce ice to the market of Philadelphia to keep butter fresh and hard At first the prejudice was strong against its adoption, and it was slow to win its way to popular favor, and then only after a trial of the two systems side by side had demonstrated the superiority of the new over the old one On the death of Jesse Darlington the business passed to his son, Jared, who continued to supply the same class of families in Philadelphia as did his father, no butter being sold in open market He died in 1862, at which time the dairy consisted of sixty or seventy cows, the weekly production of butter being two hundred and fifty pounds The Darlington butter was held in high repute, and commanded a much higher price than ordinary first-class butter At Jared Darlington's death the business was continued by his sons,—Edward, Albert, Jesse, and Jared The dairy on the homestead farm was conducted by J and J. Darlington, who are making about twelve hundred pounds of butter weekly from the milk of two hundred and seventy-five cows, Albert Darlington, from the adjoining farm, about five hundred pounds from one hundred and fifty cows, and Edward Darlington's family, on another adjoining farm, about four hundred pounds per week from one hundred cows. The butter is now largely shipped to Washington, New York, Boston, Philadelphia, and other localities, where it is delivered to wealthy private families These dairies are furnished with every modern improvement known in the business The cream is separated from the milk immediately after milking by centrifugal force, the machines used for that purpose being run by steam power at a velocity of seven thousand revolutions per minute

BIOGRAPHICAL SKETCHES.

EDWARD DARLINGTON, Jr

Jesse Darlington, the grandfather of the subject of this biographical sketch, married Amy Sharpless. Among their children was Jared, born Aug 15, 1799, in Middletown township, Delaware Co, who married Mary, daughter of Thomas and Sarah Jones Dutton Their children are Edward, Sarah J, Albert, Amy (Mrs Henry Pratt), Frances (deceased), Jesse, Jared, Mary, and Ruth Anna The death of Mr Darlington occurred Dec. 7, 1862 His son, Edward, was born Jan 22, 1832, near Darlington Station, Delaware Co, and spent his early years upon the farm of his father He enjoyed moderate advantages of education, having first pursued his studies in Chester County, and subsequently at Andover, Mass After a period spent in teaching he returned to the homestead farm, which he cultivated until his marriage, when the farm upon which his family now reside was rented He subsequently became the owner of this property, and during his lifetime followed the pursuits of an agriculturist He married, in 1856, Miss Mary F, daughter of Charles and Deborah Pittman Palmer of Concord Their children are Frances (deceased), Charles P, Mary, Jared, Anna S, Beulah W, Edward, and three who died in infancy Mr Darlington was, in his political views, a Republican, and, though interested in the public measures of the day, was not active as a politician, nor ambitious for official distinction As a business man he possessed remarkable energy and was thoroughly in earnest and diligent in what he undertook, ever manifesting a keen sense of justice in all his business transactions Integrity and honesty were prominent traits in his character He was in his religious belief a Friend, and reared his family in that faith Mr Darlington's brief but useful life terminated on the 7th of October, 1876, in his forty-fifth year

THOMAS PRATT

Thomas Pratt, the father of the subject of this biographical sketch, who was of English descent, married Hannah Haycock, of the same county and township, and had one son, Thomas, born on the homestead in Middletown township, now occupied by his son, William H. Pratt, on the 11th of February, 1818 After receiving a substantial English education at the popular Friends' boarding-school at Westtown, Chester Co, Pa, he returned to the parental roof and engaged in labor on the farm He married, in 1839, Mary Worrall, of Middletown township, a descendant of John Sharpless, and had children,—Elizabeth (Mrs Jesse Darlington), William H (married to Clementina M, daughter of Charles Johnson, who has four children), T Mitchell (married to Eva Woodward, of Chester, who has three children), Peter W (who married Barbara Herr, of Lancaster County, and has five children), Phineas (deceased), and Anna Mary (Mrs Thomas Byers) All the sons reside upon the family estate Mr Pratt was a second time married June 15, 1874, to Miss Sarah, daughter of Oliver and Emma Johnson, of Middletown, Conn., to whom was born Sept. 8, 1875, a daughter, Emma By the

Edward Darlington

Thomas Pratt

Charles Johnson

Charles Johnson

Joel Sharpless

purchase of adjacent lands considerable additions were made to the homestead farm, which Mr Pratt cultivated and greatly improved He was the pioneer in a branch of industry which has since grown to large proportions in the county,—that of the manufacture of ice cream This was made on the farm and shipped before the completion of the railroad by boat from Chester to Philadelphia, where a ready market was found The enterprise proved so profitable as to have induced many others to embark in the business Mr Pratt retired from active labor some years before his death, and ultimately removed to Media, where he died on the 5th of March, 1882 He was a Republican in politics, active in the defense of the principles of his party, and a strong and outspoken Abolitionist He served a term as commissioner of the county, and also held various minor offices He was for several years identified with the Delaware County Mutual Insurance Company as its president He was a member of the Delaware County Institute of Science, and a life member of the Pennsylvania Training-School for Feeble-Minded Children, both of which institutions commanded his warmest interest. His influence was ever given in the cause of temperance, both by precept and example He was one of the board of trustees of the Charter House, in Media, a body with whom he met but a few days prior to his death He was also one of the early projectors of the Farmers' Market of Philadelphia, now so successfully established Mr Pratt was from childhood a member of the society of Friends, and devoted to the faith he espoused

CHARLES JOHNSON

Humphrey Johnson, the great-grandfather of the subject of this biography, resided in Chester township, Delaware Co Among his sons was Joseph, who married Amy Rogers, and had the following ten children Ann, Humphrey, Robert R, Phineas, Abram, Amy, Mary, Jethro, Sarah, and Hannah. Humphrey, of this number, was born in Delaware County, and when sufficiently advanced in years learned the trade of carpenter He later abandoned this occupation for the healthful employment of the farmer, and removed to Cecil County, Md. He married Mary, daughter of John Slaughter, to whom were born children,—Jemima (Mrs Thomas Donegha), Joseph, Charles, Anna M (Mrs I P Dutton), and Amy Charles, of this number, was born Nov 9, 1817, in Cecil County, Md, and in early youth removed to Delaware County Here he enjoyed but limited advantages of education, and having chosen the trade of blacksmith, on completing his apprenticeship, followed it successfully for seventeen years In 1855 he purchased a farm in Middletown township, and has since been devoted to its cultivation and improvement Mr Johnson, on the 16th of March, 1842, married Mary S, daughter of Joseph Mancill, of the same county, and has had children,—Clementina M (Mrs William H Pratt), Anna Mary (Mrs Evans Eachus), H Winfield, L Emma, Charles, William A (who is deceased), and Laura F (Mrs Albert P. Ogden) In politics Mr Johnson usually fraternizes with the Republican party, though he may with propriety be regarded as independent in his political views He has held the important office of treasurer of Delaware County, and served as county commissioner and in minor township positions He was instructed in youth in the belief of the society of Friends, and still inclines to that faith.

JOEL SHARPLESS

John Sharpless, of Ratherton, in the county of Chester, England, married Jane More, of the same place, in the year 1662 With their seven children they embarked for America two months previous to the arrival of William Penn, in 1682, landing at Chester on the 14th of June of the same year Joseph Sharpless, the youngest son, married Lydia Lewis, and settled in Lower Providence, on part of the original purchase of one thousand acres, and later removed to four hundred acres in Middletown township His nine children were Susannah, Benjamin, Samuel, Lydia, Nathan, Jane, Abraham, Jacob, and William Samuel married Jane Newlin, daughter of John and Mary Newlin, of Concord, and settled on part of the original purchase They had twelve children,—Mary, John, Thomas, Lydia, Abigail, Samuel, Hannah, Susanna, Phœbe, Rachel, Samuel, and Joel Samuel Sharpless died in 1790, and his wife, Jane, in 1798 Their son, Joel, married in 1784, Hannah, daughter of Joshua and Lydia Mendenhall They finally settled upon two hundred acres, the larger portion of which is now embraced in the farm of the subject of this sketch, on which his residence, "The Hermitage," stands His three surviving children were Samuel, Joshua, and Lydia, who were early left orphans Samuel married Ruth Iddings in 1808, and had children,—Beulah, Joel, Hannah, Lydia, William, Amy, Sarah, Thomas J, Ruth Anna, Tamzen, Matilda, and Samuel All these children were born at "The Hermitage," in Middletown, and all but one survive The birth of Joel, the second child, occurred March 9, 1810 He was from childhood accustomed to labor, and received only such an education as could be obtained during the winter months after attaining his tenth year At the age of nineteen he taught school, continuing this vocation at intervals for a period of several years On the 25th of December, 1841, he was married to Miss Hannah, youngest daughter of Abel and Lydia Minshall, of Middletown Mrs. Sharpless died on the 10th of October, 1845, leaving one son, Minshall, whose death occurred in 1864 Mr Sharpless was a second time married on the 6th of May, 1847, to Sarah Ann, daughter of Abel and Sarah Green, whose children are Josephine, Robert,

Gertrude, Margaretta, Willard, Joel, Sarah A., Henry, and Marian. Mr. Sharpless soon after his first marriage engaged in farming on shares, at a later date rented, and in 1848 purchased, the farm of his father, and in 1856 an adjacent farm of his brother. He resided for a time on the latter, but in 1867 removed to "The Hermitage." He received but little substantial aid in his business operations, and is indebted to his own industry and intelligence for the measure of success he has enjoyed. Mr. Sharpless has since 1854 been either a Whig or a Republican in politics, and filled various local offices such as school director, director of the poor, supervisor, etc. He has been since 1836 a member of the Delaware County Institute of Science. His religious belief is that of the society of Friends, of which he is a member.

WILLIAM SEAL.

William Seal, the grandfather of the subject of this biographical sketch, who was of English lineage, resided in Birmingham township, Chester Co., in which county he married Mary Hunt, and had children,—Susan, William, Jesse, Thomas, Sidney, Eli, Joseph, and Benjamin. Jesse, of this number, was born on the homestead in Birmingham, and learned the trade of a carpenter, to which he later added the pursuit of an agriculturist. He married Miss Sarah, daughter of John Sharpless, of Concord, Delaware Co., and had children,—John, Alban, Eliza (Mrs. Enoch T. Williams), Mary (Mrs. Caleb Windle), William, Joseph, Sally Ann, Lewis, and Susan (Mrs. Edward B. Ashbridge). William Seal was born May 6, 1818, in East Goshen, Chester Co., and in early youth removed to Birmingham township. After receiving the rudiments of education he acquired the trade of a wheelwright and carriage-builder, which was steadily pursued for a period of sixteen years, when he, in 1855, became a farmer, and removed to his present home. He was married the same year to Miss Jane P., daughter of Jonathan and Ruth Thomas, of Middletown township. Mrs. Seal, who was born in 1812, was one of a family of nine children, and inherited from her father a portion of the farm, to which her husband added by the purchase of other land. She was a lady of remarkable industry and of many admirable qualities of mind and heart. Her death occurred Nov. 28, 1881, in her sixty-ninth year. Mr. Seal was formerly a Whig, and is now a firm Republican in politics, but is not a seeker after office, preferring the quiet of his home to the less tranquil scenes of public life. He adheres to the worship of the society of Friends, though not included among its members.

JONATHAN THOMAS.

The Thomas family are of Welsh extraction. Benjamin Thomas, the father of Jonathan, resided in Montgomery County, where he pursued the trade of a saddler. He was a citizen of high moral character, and of much influence. In politics he was an ardent Whig. He married Susanna Yarnall, of Delaware County, whose ancestors were of English descent. Their nine children were James, George, Job, Bevin, Owen, Jonathan, Benjamin, Seth, and Rebecca. Later in life Mr. Thomas removed to Springfield township, where his death occurred. His son, Jonathan, was born Jan. 1, 1776, in the latter township, and remained under the parental roof until sufficiently old to learn a trade, when he chose that of a carpenter, and became an apprentice to his brother, Owen. For the purpose of becoming more proficient, he repaired to Philadelphia, and worked as a journeyman until his removal to Chester County, Pa., where he conducted the business of a carpenter and builder on an extensive scale. Returning to Delaware County, he settled in Springfield township, and later removed to Ridley township. He purchased property in various portions of the county, including that particular farm known as the "Clayton" property, in Middletown township, now owned by his daughters, Mrs. Sarah W. Webb and Mrs. Eli Yarnall.

Mr. Thomas was married in 1800 to Miss Ruth, daughter of John Young, of Chester County, Pa., to whom were born nine children,—Rebecca S. (deceased in youth), John Y., Benjamin O., Susanna, Lydia Y. (Mrs. Eli Yarnall), Jane P. (Mrs. William Seal), Jonathan, Sarah W. (Mrs. Webb), and Ruth Hannah (Mrs. Crosby Fairlamb). Of this number the only survivors are Mrs. Webb and Mrs. Yarnall. Mr. Thomas was in his political preferences a Whig and later a Republican, and, though often tendered office, invariably declined such honors. He was identified with the Delaware County National Bank as director, and filled the same office in connection with the Delaware County Mutual Insurance Company. He was an active leader in the society of Friends, in which faith he was reared. Mr. Thomas was a public-spirited citizen, and by his intelligence, exemplary character, and rare discernment in matters of business enjoyed a commanding influence in the county. His death occurred on the 3d of January, 1856, in his eightieth year.

CHAPTER XLVIII.

NEWTOWN TOWNSHIP.

THE first mention of this municipal district was at the court held Eleventh month 6, 1684 (January, 1685), when Thomas Norbury and John Humphrey were appointed collectors of the "Levie for the cort house and Prison for ye Township of Newtowne," and at the December court, 1686, Thomas Norbury was appointed constable for the township.

Newtown was largely settled by Welshmen, and

William Seal

Jane Thomas (Seal.)

the township was laid out with a "townstead" in the centre The lots in the village were distributed to the purchasers of land in the township according to the number of acres bought by each settler. The name of the district is derived from the fact of the central town plot, and for a like cause Newtown township, Bucks Co, received its name

At the southwest end of the township, extending eastward to the original Newtown Street, was a tract of five hundred acres surveyed to Robert Dutton Jan 18-19, 1681 Dutton appears never to have lived on this estate, which subsequently passed, April 6-7, 1723, to Robert Tipping Prior to the Revolution much of the property was owned by the Hunter family, and the stream which ran through the land took its name Hunter's Run from that fact Immediately north of this estate was a plot of five hundred acres, surveyed April 10-11, 1682, to Joshua Fearne, who also never settled on the land David Sowter purchased two hundred and forty-five acres in the following July, and John Fincher a like number of acres on March 14, 1699 One hundred and seventy-two and a half acres were patented to Ellis Hughes on March 8, 1702, directly north of the Fearne tract, which was purchased by Daniel Williamson on Tenth month 19, 1707 Immediately above this was a tract of four hundred and fifty acres, surveyed to Thomas Rudyard Fourth month 18, 1684, and on Ninth month 24, 1692, the estate was conveyed to Daniel Williamson, who had probably settled on the land prior to that date He was repeatedly a member of the Assembly, and in 1727 he died while representing Chester County in that body His dwelling was on the Ashland farm, now the residence of William P Thomas Still continuing along Crum Creek, immediately above the Williamson estate were two hundred and seventy acres taken up March 21-22, 1681, by Henry Maddock and James Kennerly, neither of whom ever resided on the land On Tenth month 10, 1698, it was conveyed to William Lewis He was a Welshman, emigrating with his wife from the parish of Illan, Glamorganshire, about 1693, settling first in Haverford He subsequently removed to this estate in Newtown, and there, in 1708, his wife and he within a few days of each other died His three sons, Lewis, Evan, and William, all settled in the township, and were assessed there in 1715 On the Lewis lands the present West Chester road enters the tract at the northwest corner and diagonally crosses the estate to its southeastern corner, while Preston's Run traverses its entire length in a due easterly direction Above this tract, on Tenth month 7, 1683, Luke Hanck had surveyed to him one hundred and eighty acres, which property subsequently passed into the Reese family, from which fact the stream of water flowing in an easterly course through it was named Reese's Run

Above this land were one hundred and eighty acres, surveyed to Michael Blunston, of Darby, Tenth month 7, 1683, which land subsequently passed into the ownership of William Lewis Thomas Rudyard located six hundred and fifty acres, extending along Crum Creek to the Chester County line, on July 13-14, 1681 John Reese purchased the property in 1698/9, and later one hundred acres at the southwestern end of the Reese land were purchased by William Lewis, Jr, and Evan Lewis, another son of William Lewis, the settler, bought the remainder of the land Lewis Run waters this tract At the northeastern end of the township two hundred and seventy acres were taken up by William Wood, of Darby Immediately south of this plot, extending from Newtown Street road to Radnor line, were ninety acres patented to Joseph Humphrey Eleventh month 17, 1684, who never settled on the land South of this tract was a plot of one hundred and eighty acres, surveyed to William Hudson Tenth month 29, 1683, which subsequently passed to John Farmer, and finally, on April 10, 1700 James Price purchased one hundred and forty acres of this land and settled thereon, calling his estate "Penffmon" He was probably a Welshman, and possibly one of the sons of David Price, of Radnor Below the Price estate was a tract of four hundred and fifty acres, patented Sixth month 2, 1684, to Philip England The most, if not all of this property, ultimately came to William and Edward Thomas prior to 1715, and Thomas' Run traverses the estate in an almost due westerly direction Two hundred and seventy acres immediately south of the England land was surveyed to John Banbridge, Ninth month 28, 1683, Saw-Mill Run traverses this estate through its entire length from east to west Below Banbridge's ground Edmund Cartledge took up one hundred acres, which was surveyed to him Fifth month 26, 1683 He was a resident of Darby, and never settled on the Newtown land Joseph Potter, March 16, 1682, had ninety acres surveyed to him just below the Cartledge property, which on First month 20, 1693, was conveyed to George Thomas, and he also purchased the one hundred acres surveyed to John Blunston, Second month 10-11, 1682 This property subsequently belonged to Morgan James, who was complained on for stopping a public highway through this land Below the Blunston estate was one hundred and twelve acres, which George Willard received on Ninth month 6, 1692, it having been granted to John Hough in 1688. Two hundred and forty-five acres to the south of this plantation was taken up by Thomas Holme, the provincial surveyor, which subsequently was conveyed, Feb 1, 1694, to Richard Bonsall, who never located thereon The main stream of Fawkes' Run, and almost the entire south branch of that water-course, is on this estate Seventy acres to the south of the Bonsall tract was taken up by Rees Saint, Fourth month 7, 1687, and two hundred and seventy acres, the remaining land at the southeast end of the township, was surveyed to George Wood, Ninth month 30, 1683 Seventh month 5, 1796, the estate was sold to John Peirson

The town lots or the townsteads being divided into

parts which were assigned to the purchasers of outlying lands in the township to correspond with the number of acres bought by these, it is unnecessary to specify the names of the several owners of the "new town," or village, as it was called.

The taxables in 1715 in Newtown township were as follows:

Daniel Williamson, Reece Howell, William Bevan, David Thomas, William Phillips, Thomas Reece, John Reece, Jr., Lewis Reece, Lewis Lewis, Evan Lewis, William Lewis, John Reece, John Ffawkes, Morgan James, Lawrence Peirce, Daniel Williamson, John Williamson, James Price, John Meredith, Edward Thomas, William Thomas.

Freemen.—John Goodwin, Adam Trebeall.

In 1799 the following was the return made of the taxables in the township at that date:

William Beaumont, George Bishop, Joseph Bishop, John Brooke, George Blake, Jonathan Bonsall, Thomas Bones, Amos Thomas, Thomas Courtney, Samuel Caley, Abram Calvert, Elizabeth Dunn, Nathan Davis, Joseph Davis (carpenter), Edward Evans, Joseph Esrey (carpenter), John Esrey, Evan Evans (weaver), John Fawkes, Joseph Fawkes, John Free, Abraham Free (shop-keeper), Richard Fawkes, John Garrett (joiner), James Gorman, John Fairlamb, Edward Hunter (justice of the peace), John Hunter, George Hunter, Joseph Hood (cutler), James Jones, John Jorman, Lewis Lewis, Henry Lewis, Azariah Lewis, Didymus Lewis, Evan Lewis, John Lewis, Joseph Lewis (wheelwright), David Lewis (tanner and shop-keeper), Jesse Lewis (mason), Thomas Moore, Abner Moore, Thomas Moore (joiner), Robert Mendenhall, Jonas Preston (physician), Gill Pennington, George Sites, Jesse Reece, Owen Shelton (shop-keeper), Hezekiah Thomas, Thomas Thomas, Jonathan Thomas, Ahiah Thomas, Gideon Thomas (cordwainer), Thomas Thomas (tailor and shop-keeper), Ezra Thomas (wheelwright), John Thompson (weaver), Isaac Thomas, Jr., Margaret Vernon, William Vandebee, John Williamson, Enos Williamson, Walter Williamson.

Inmates.—Joseph Thomas (carpenter), Hannah Hunter, Mary Reece, Rachel Matson, Jenkin Lewis, Elizabeth Lewis, John Steel (weaver).

Single Freemen.—Aaron Russell (weaver), Cadwallader Evans, Edward Evans, Samuel Fawkes (chairmaker), John Williamson, Samuel Lisle, Elias Baker (carpenter), Thomas Thomas, David Lewis, Anthony Matson, Elijah Matson, Nathan Robins, Lewis Reece, Jesse Lewis, Phineas Lewis, George Lewis (millwright), Jorman Hunter, James Crawford, John Logan, William Matson, Alexander Morrison, William Fulton, Jonas Alexander, Levis Maris (cordwainer), Michael Thomas (cordwainer), George Mace (cordwainer), Reece Thomas, Samuel Thomas (millwright), Richard Thomas (millwright), Richard Hood, Andrew McClellan, James Ramage (mason), Robert Berry, William Harlow, Jacob Dunn, Thomas Blake, Ezra Thomas (wheelwright).

Incidents of the Revolution.—During the Revolution, Newtown was several times visited by the foraging parties of the English army. After the interrupted battle near Goshen Friends' meeting-house, and the day previous to the massacre of Paoli, the enemy dashed into Newtown and carried off from the defenseless citizens considerable property. Capt. John Montressor records, under date of Sept. 19, 1777, "Lt. Col. Harcourt with a party of dragoons and Light Infantry made an Excursion on the Philadelphia road and brought in 150 horses, which were much wanted, got from New Town square 6 miles from hence. They took, likewise, one captain and 8 rebel prisoners."[1] In December, 1777, when Cornwallis made his three days' raid into Chester County, extending along the Schuylkill as far as Matson's Ferry, some of the British soldiers entered Newtown, and well maintained the account given of the action of the British troops on that occasion, "Robing and plundering every person they came across." To such an extent was this carried that Gen. James Potter indignantly records, "My penn cant describe there Barbarity and Crualty, nor can you conseve the waste and Destruction that attended there futsteps every where they go."[2] The damage inflicted on the residents of Newtown during these raids is poorly represented in the list of claims recorded of spoliation done by the British, for much being taken from Friends, no demand was ever made for compensation under the act of Assembly. The following are the claims which were presented, but never paid:

From Samuel Caley, by the Queen's Light Dragoons, Col. Harriot, Sept. 19	£31	0	0
From David Thomas, by the Light Horse, on their return from an attack upon Capt. Lee, at East-town	27	3	3
From William Faris, by the British Army, under Cornwallis, on his route through Haverford	28	0	0
	86	3	3

At the dwelling of Mr. Lewis, on the Goshen road, to the west of old Newtown Square, were the American outposts and headquarters of Gen. James Potter, or as he terms it in a letter to President Wharton, on Nov. 13, 1777, "from the camp at Mr. Lewes." At this house Maj. John Clarke, Jr., of Gen. Greene's staff, who was ordered to keep Washington supplied with information of the movements of the enemy, also made his headquarters, for many of his letters to Washington are written therefrom. Although Lewis does not appear among the list of persons who had suffered by the war, we have actual information that he had lost largely by the presence of the enemy, for on the afternoon of Dec. 3, 1777, before Cornwallis' raid, Maj. Clarke writes, "On the 16th of September last, Baron Arendt took a mare from my landlord, valued at £100, and promised to return her next day, but has never done it. Mr. Lewis begs he may be ordered to do it, as the enemy has taken the remainder of his creatures and he has done me many services for the United States. I have given his complaint a place in this letter and beg leave to recommend him as a person worthy of compassion."[3] At noon, on Dec. 12, 1777, Maj. Clarke wrote from Gen. Potter's headquarters at Lewes, "That a large body of the enemy was on the march to Darby, the numbers uncertain but formidable. At eight o'clock this morning about twenty dragoons of the enemy came up to the Fox Chase to give the alarm, and they then took the route to Darby."

Fitzpatrick, the noted outlaw, frequently visited Newtown, it being on the direct road to Philadelphia. One day, in the spring of 1778, it is related that Fitzpatrick, carrying a pistol in each hand, entered the bar-room of the old Newtown Square Tavern, then kept by Andrew Wilson, when several persons were present. He laid one pistol on the bar while he drank the liquor he had called for, then picking up the pis-

[1] *Penna. Mag. of Hist.*, vol. vi. p. 38.

[2] Penna. Archives, 1st Series, vol. vi. p. 97.

[3] Bulletin Historical Society of Pennsylvania, No. 10, March, 1847, pp. 22, 23.

ol, said, "Good-day, gentlemen!" and moved out of he door facing the people in the room as he retired. No one attempted to molest him in anywise.

An aged resident of Springfield, who died many 'ears ago, would frequently relate the following inci-lent, which happened to him when a lad serving his ipprenticeship in Newtown. One morning in the early spring of 1778, Mr. Shillingford stated, he (then a blacksmith's apprentice) had just arrived at the shop, which was located near the Fox Chase Tavern, on the West Chester road, and was employed in starting the ires preparatory to the appearance of the master smith and the journeymen. While thus engaged a ine-looking, athletic young man, with sandy hair and uddy complexion, mounted on a horse that to a prac-iced eye gave indications of strength, speed, and en-lurance, drew rein at the door of the forge, and said,—

"Young man, my horse has cast a shoe, do you hink you can put one on?"

"I think I can."

"Well, I'll let you try," said the stranger, dismount-ing and hitching his horse.

The apprentice was much pleased at this opportu-nity to exhibit his skill, and taking hold of the horse's foot, began to trim and prepare the hoof.

"Young man," said the stranger, "just give me one of those aprons, and if you'll blow the bellows, I'll ry my hand at the job just to see what sort of a blacksmith I'd make."

"It's a dangerous thing to drive a nail into a horse's foot," replied the lad. "You may lame him so that he will be ruined."

"I'll take the chances," was the reply of the stranger, as he tied the apron on. "If I lame him I'll be responsible for all damages."

He at once began his work, and the apprentice soon saw that the man was thoroughly master of his art. After the horse had been shod, the lad said,—

"You are well armed, sir, I see; are you in the army?"

"It's dangerous traveling these roads alone, is it not?" answered the stranger. "They tell me there is a Capt. Fritz or Fitch, who frequents this neighbor-hood, and the people are much afraid of him, I've heard."

"Many people are afraid of Fitzpatrick," was the youth's reply.

"Have you ever seen him?"

"No, sir, but I've often heard him described."

"Do I answer the description you have heard of Fitzpatrick?" asked the stranger.

"I don't know that you do," was the cautious an-swer.

The man mounted his horse, and throwing a coin to the apprentice, said, "Pay your master for the shoe and keep the rest for yourself. So, my young man, you have never seen Fitzpatrick, and don't know whether I answer the description you've heard of him. I'm going now, and I might just as well say to you that Fitzpatrick happens to be my name." And the stranger rode rapidly away.

After Fitzpatrick was captured and was in irons at Chester, the apprentice, who chanced to be at the county-seat, pressed into the crowd to see the noted prisoner, when the latter recognized him, and, man-acled as he was, stretched out his hand and gave that of the lad a hearty shake, saying, "How are you, brother chip?"

On Hunter's Run, in Newtown township, and ex-tending to the line dividing Newtown from Marple, was a tract of one hundred and seventy-two acres "strict measure," owned by Matthias Aspden, who was declared an attainted traitor to the colony by act of March 6, 1778, unless he surrendered himself and submitted to a legal trial "for such his treason" be-fore the 1st day of April, 1781. This Aspden failed to do, and the property was seized by the common-wealth authorities and sold to Edward Bartholomew, to whom the State issued letters patent Aug. 26, 1786. Aspden, who was one of the wealthiest mer-chants in Philadelphia, had fled to England, returned to America in 1785, but fearing that his life was in danger he again went to England. In April, 1786, Matthias Aspden was pardoned by the State, and much of his estate returned to him. His will subse-quently gave rise to the most extensive litigation ever had under the confiscation acts. In 1824 suit was brought to determine the rightful heir under his will, he having devised his estate, real and per-sonal, "to his heir-at-law." The claimants num-bered upwards of two hundred, and were divided into three classes. The first were the heirs of Mary Har-rison, a sister of the half-blood on the father's side, and the heirs of Roger Hartley, a half-brother on the mother's side; the second were the Parker family, cousins of the whole blood, which was a very large and constantly-increasing class of claimants, who had insti-tuted the suit; and the third were the English Aspdens, relations of the whole blood of the father, and who would have been heirs at common law. Judge Grier decided that the issue of the brother and sister of the half-blood were lawful heirs, and the persons entitled to receive the estate, valued at over half a million of dollars. The Supreme Court of the United States subsequently affirmed this decree. The conclusion of the case was as notable as the entire contest, for March, 1853, a Philadelphia paper published this following local item:

"ROMANCE IN REAL LIFE.—John Aspden, whose sudden death on Mon-day was noticed in our columns, is to be buried this afternoon. Mr. Asp-den was one of the English claimants of the immense estate left by Mat-thias Aspden. Before the case was decided by the Supreme Court in favor of the American heirs, the latter proposed to the deceased to compromise the matter, and offered to pay him the sum of two hundred thousand dollars to relinquish his claim; this he refused to do, and the decision of the court cut him off without a farthing. On Monday morning the estate was divided between the heirs-at-law, and almost at the same moment, John Aspden fell dead at a tavern in Carter's Alley, of disease of the heart, supposed to have been induced by disappointment and mortification. At the time of his death his pockets contained a solitary cent,—his entire fortune. To-day the man who might have been the possessor of a quarter of a million of dollars will be borne to his grave from an obscure part of the district of Southwark."

In 1835, Charles Cooper, a Revolutionary soldier, who entered the army in January, 1777, and was discharged in 1783, was a resident of Newtown, and was then in the seventy-fourth year of his age. In the great Whig procession at Chester, July 23, 1840, the delegation from Newtown bore in the ranks a tattered flag, bearing the motto "United We Stand," and the date 1776. The flag belonged to the old Pennsylvania line, and was carried in the fight at Brandywine.

Roads.—When the township of Newtown was laid out, in 1783, a straight road extending from the south to the north boundaries of the township was projected, and, with the exception of that part south of the present square which tends to the southwest into Marple and the variation from the direct course at the old square, the present road is the same as that then known as Newtown Street. At court held at Chester Tenth month, 1689, a highway was ordered to be laid out from Newtown, Marple, and Springfield "to ye landing at Amosland." The grand jury on the 9th day of Twelfth month, 1687, made report of the present Springfield road:

"By virtue of an order from yᵉ last County Court given to us, whose names are hereunto subscribed, being of yᵉ Grand Jury for to lay out a roadway that should serve for Newtown, Marple, & Springfield, and yᵉ Inhabitance that way to yᵉ Landing Place att Amosland did open yᵉ day above written. Begin att a Road way on yᵉ land of George Maris, which road goeth from Chester through Marple to Newtowne soe from that road through Bartholomew Coppocks land near to his house, his House being on yᵉ left hand, soe on through Robert Taylor's land straight on through more of George Maris', his land leaving his Plantation on yᵉ right hand soe bearing on a little on yᵉ right hand through George Simcock's land, soe on through Jacob Simcocke's land, leaving his Plantation on yᵉ left hand, soe on straight forward through lands joyning to Amosland, soe into yᵉ King's road that comes from Darby marking the trees as wee came, soe on to yᵉ landing Place by the maine creeks Side beyond Morten Mortenson's House.

"WILLIAM GARRETT, THOMAS BRADSHAW,
"RICHARD PARKER, THOMAS FFOX."
"EDMOND CARTLEIDGE.

At the court held on the 24th of Twelfth month, 1701/2, we learn that the people of the township had some difficulty respecting one of the highways therein. For on the date given "the Inhabitants of Newtown petitioned this Court against Morgan James for stopping a road laid out through his land. This Court orders that if the said Morgan James do not lay open the said Road as soon as his corn is off the Road ground the Sheriff shall levy the fine, according to law, on the state of the said Morgan James."

The following persons have been justices of the peace for Newtown township:

Edward Hunter	Aug 30, 1791
John Lindsay	June 5, 1794
Isaac Abrahams	May 20, 1800
Luke Cassin	March 27, 1809
John Siter	Sept 1, 1813
Robert Green	Feb 23, 1816
Nathan Gibson	Nov 26, 1817
George Brooke	July 3 1821
Maskill Ewing	June 10, 1822
Benjamin Lobb	Dec 4, 1823
Parke Shee	Dec 9, 1823
David Abrahams	Dec 14, 1825
Barnard Flynn	Nov 18, 1835
Abner Lewis	May 27, 1836
Thomas Sheldon	Dec 20, 1836
Thomas Citein	Nov 1, 1838
Homer Eachus	May 11 1839
Azariah L Williamson	April 13, 1853
Nathan Shaw	April 24, 1861
Isaiah Massey	April 22, 1868
Charles S Heysham	March 24, 1874
Charles S Heysham	March 27, 1879

The Murder of Squire Hunter.—In March, 1817, Edward Hunter, a justice of the peace, residing in Newtown, was sent for by one Isaiah Worrall, of Upper Providence, a well-to-do farmer, who was then very ill, to put in form the latter's will. This Squire Hunter did, and when it was finished to the satisfaction of the testator, the former and Isaac Cochran, at that time landlord of the Rose Tree Tavern, witnessed Worrall's signature to the document. After the death of Worrall, the disposition he had made of his property was highly distasteful to several of his children, and a caveat was lodged against the probate of the alleged will by two of his daughters, one of the objectors being Martha, the wife of John H Craig. The legal proceedings to test the validity of the alleged will had gone so far that the case was on the calendar for the August term, and both parties to the controversy were making preparations for the trial. On Thursday afternoon, July 19, 1817, Edward Hunter, while mounting his horse near his dwelling, was shot and fatally wounded. The person who fired the gun was concealed among some low-growing bushes near by, and the house and barn being on rolling ground, brought the figure of the squire into prominence by reason of the setting sun, which shone brilliantly back of where he then was. The report of the fire-arm was unusually loud, as though made by a heavy charge, and Hunter's daughters hearing it, hastened out of doors to ascertain why a shot had been fired so close to the dwelling. They then noticed that their father had fallen to the ground, and immediately ran to his assistance. The wounded man believed that he had been struck by lightning, as his back was towards the clump of bushes, because of the heavy report, the flash, and the sharpness of the stroke. He was then bleeding profusely from the wound in his body on the left side, a little above the left hip. They bore the unfortunate man to the house, medical aid was promptly summoned, and search made to discover the person who fired the fatal shot. Their investigation was rewarded by finding an old musket, which the murderer in his alarm, after committing the act, had thrown away in his flight. Squire Hunter lingered until Sunday following, July 21, 1817, when he died of his injuries.

The gun directed suspicion to Craig, for it was identified as his, and the motive for the deed was the fact that if the will of Isaiah Worrall was refused probate, his wife would receive a very much larger share of her father's estate than came to her under its provisions. John H Craig had also disappeared, and every effort to discover his whereabouts having failed, on Aug 6, 1817, William and Edward Hunter, sons of the murdered man, by handbills and advertisements in the newspapers of Philadelphia, Chester, Lancaster, and other counties, published the following notice:

"Stop the murderer! Whereas, John Craig, of Charlestown township, Chester County, Pa., did on the 19th of July, 1817, wilfully and maliciously shoot Edward Hunter, Esquire, of Newtown, Delaware County. This is to give notice that the sum of $300 will be paid by the subscribers for apprehending and bringing to justice the said John Craig. He is a blacksmith by trade, about five feet ten inches high, stoop-shouldered, stout build, a little knock-kneed, very much sun burnt, freckled, thick lips, sandy complexion, large whiskers; had on when he left home light nankeen pantaloons, snuff-colored cloth coat, green oil cloth on his hat and shoes, but it is most likely he has changed his dress, as he took a bundle with him."

The authorities through the country were on the alert to arrest the suspected man, and at one time it was reported that he had been apprehended at Jenkintown, while a person answering his description accurately was detained at Danbury, Conn., under suspicion, and Daniel Thompson and Mr. Maxwell, of this county, in the latter part of August, went there in consequence of the information received, only to learn that, while the general description was correct, it was not the man they sought. However, in the early part of September, Craig was arrested in Easton, he having been identified by a person engaged with him chopping wood, from the description given in the advertisement, and on Monday, Sept. 13, 1817, he was lodged in the prison at Philadelphia, when, after being identified, he was delivered to the custody of the sheriff of Delaware County, who removed him to the jail at Chester.

I have heard it frequently said that Judge Bird Wilson resigned from the bench because of his unwillingness to preside at the trial of Craig for murder, a statement that will not bear examination, inasmuch as on March 14, 1817, four months before the murder of Hunter, Bishop White had admitted Bird Wilson to holy orders.

On Monday, Oct. 20, 1817, the grand jury indicted John H. Craig for the murder of Edward Hunter. On Tuesday following he was arraigned and pleaded "not guilty." Judge Ross asked him if he had counsel, when the prisoner replied "that he was not able to pay lawyers," and the court thereupon assigned Samuel Edwards and Benjamin Tilghman, Esquires, to conduct his defense, while the commonwealth was represented by Deputy Attorney-General Henry G. Freeman, Robert Frazer, and Isaac Darlington, Esquires. On Friday morning the counsel for the prosecution called the case for trial, when the prisoner made an affidavit setting forth that at least six witnesses material in his defense were absent. A discussion between the lawyers followed, and it is traditionally stated that the appeal of Mr. Tilghman for a continuance of the case was the most animated and eloquent address that that lawyer and gifted advocate ever delivered in the old court-house in Chester. The trial was finally postponed to the next term.

The demeanor of the prisoner as he sat at the bar made an unfavorable impression on the audience, for it was noticed that he appeared quite unconcerned, sometimes smiling, while at other times he drummed audibly with his fingers on the railing in front of him.

The case was not finally tried until the April term, 1818. The hearing began Tuesday, April 14th; the commonwealth examined forty-seven witnesses, and so admirably had the testimony been sifted that the prosecution succeeded in tracing Craig from the moment he took the gun in his hands until his final apprehension at Easton. The defense, notwithstanding the evidence was overwhelmingly conclusive as to the prisoner's guilt, was admirably conducted, and it was surprising to the audience that so much could be urged as was advanced by his counsel in his defense. The jury retired about sunset on Saturday afternoon, April 18, 1818, and at 10 o'clock returned a verdict of "guilty." The apartment was densely crowded, and for fifteen minutes, while Judge Ross wrote his address to and sentence of the prisoner, the silence was so profound that the scratching of the quill-pen his honor was using could be heard in every part of the room.

Governor Findlay signed the death warrant promptly on May 4th, and on May 9, 1818, Sheriff Robert Fairlamb read the document to the prisoner in his cell in the old jail at Chester. A gentleman present on that occasion has left it on record that Craig listened attentively, his countenance undergoing no change, made no remark; "nor did a tear drop from his eyes" when the officer announced to him that he would be executed in exactly four weeks from that day.

Saturday, the 6th day of June, 1818, precisely at eleven o'clock in the morning, John H. Craig was taken from his cell, and when he reached the corner of the present Fourth and Market Streets, he was halted until a guard was formed. The cart containing the coffin was in front, driven by the hangman. The prisoner followed immediately thereafter, dressed as usual, excepting it was noticed that he wore a white cap under his hat, but so placed as not to conceal his face, while his arms were pinioned to his body, but not so tightly as to prevent him raising his hands to his head. Four clergymen attended him, two on either side supporting him as he walked, for he proceeded on foot to the place of execution. Next behind him followed four or five females, relations of the prisoner. Then came a number of constables who surrounded the accused, and the line of march was taken up finally, the sheriff on horseback, supported by a mounted guard composed of many of the leading citizens of the county. Before the procession moved Craig stood for several minutes gazing at the unusual spectacle with an unaltered countenance and unflinching eye. It was about mid-day when the column halted under the gallows on Caldwell's meadow, near Munday's Run, close to the post-road, near a clump of trees which then stood there—near the present Sunnyside Mills—and Craig ascended the cart accompanied by the Revs Messrs Goforth, Palmer, Aston, and Plumer After prayers by the three last named clergymen, Rev Mr Goforth made a lengthy address At its conclusion Craig, kneeling on his coffin, offered a prayer aloud, his voice showing no indications of fear, then arising he spoke to the assemblage, and in an earnest manner warned his hearers to avoid the sins of lying, swearing, and stealing, but more especially to refrain from raising their hands against the life of a fellow-man In conclusion, he acknowledged that he was guilty of the crime for which he was about to suffer The clergymen then took leave of him, and the prisoner took off his hat, which he handed to a person near him His face had now assumed a livid pallor, but he stood firmly and seemed to have nerved himself for the final scene Craig himself drew the death-cap over his face, which the hangman firmly tied and the fatal noose was adjusted At half-past one o'clock the cart was drawn from beneath his feet, and the condemned man fell with a bound that dislocated his neck, killing him almost instantly

In his sworn confession, afterwards published, Craig declared that he had killed Hunter because he believed that if the witnesses were dead, Worrall's will could not be proved, and the estate would be divided among his children under the intestate laws He also stated that he had several times attempted to shoot Isaac Cochran, but that every time he raised his gun the person who was walking with Cochran always moved in such a way that his body was interposed between the murderer and his intended victim At the February court, 1819, the Worrall will case was tried and the will set aside, the jury finding the testator incompetent to make testamentary disposition of his estate, he being *in extremis* at the time the will was executed

Nine Generations—Susannah Smedley died at the residence of her son-in-law, Jonathan Hood, on Dec. 29, 1834, in the eighty-ninth year of her age She had seen her great-great-grandfather and her great-great-grandchildren She was the child alluded to when her great-grandfather, in the ninety-fifth year of his age, said to his daughter, "Arise, daughter, go see thy daughter, for thy daughter's daughter has a daughter"

A Noticeable Incident—During a severe thunder storm in July, 1835, a tree on the Ashland farm, owned by Isaac Thomas, was struck by lightning, and five horses standing under it were killed, while another horse in the same field which had sought shelter under another tree escaped unhurt

Bishop Hunter.—One of the most prominent members of the church of the Latter-Day Saints who died at Salt Lake City, Tuesday Oct 16, 1883, was Edward Hunter, a native of Newtown, his father, Edward Hunter, long prior to the Revolution owned a tract of land near Hunter's Run at the southwestern corner of the township On this plantation Edward Hunter was born June 22, 1793, and was ninety years and nearly four months old at the time of his death He was baptized into the church of Latter-Day Saints in Chester County, Pa At an early day he went to Nauvoo, Ill, and became an intimate friend and associate of Prophet Joseph Smith, acting as one of his life-guards, and being one of the few who conveyed the martyred brothers, Joseph and Hiram, to their final resting-place. On Nov 23, 1854, he was ordained under the hands of President Brigham Young He crossed the plains in 1848, arriving soon after the pioneers, and returned to winter quarters in 1849, and brought over the first season's emigration to Utah in the fall of 1850 He assisted in laying the corner-stone of the temple in Salt Lake City April 6, 1853, and also delivered the oration He visited his native State during the summer of 1876, and spent some time in Philadelphia attending the Centennial celebration

Crimes—On Wednesday, Aug 30, 1876, the dwelling-house of Isaac A Calvert, on the Locust Grove (formerly the Locust Hill) farm, on the Street road above old Newtown Square, was robbed by four men wearing veils, who, forcing their way into the bedroom of Mrs Calvert,—the husband having gone to market,—one of the men put a pistol to her head, demanding her money, accompanying the demand with a threat to kill her if she made the least noise. Failing to get any information from her, they searched the house for nearly an hour, and finally decamped with jewelry, silverware, and other articles amounting in value to about one hundred and fifty dollars Mrs Calvert, while lying all this time with a pistol pointed at her, did not lose her presence of mind, but employed the time in marking the personal peculiarities of the burglars, so that she might recognize them The next day Joseph Ditman was arrested in Philadelphia on suspicion, he having been at Calvert's farm a few days before the burglary He was identified by Mrs Calvert as one of the robbers, and his arrest led to that of Joshua Mulley and John Martin At the September court the prisoners were tried and convicted The court sentenced them each to ten years' imprisonment in the Eastern Penitentiary On Tuesday night, March 4, 1884, the post-office at Newtown Square was broken into, and some goods and sixty dollars' worth of postage stamps stolen The same night the tavern was entered, the burglars boring holes through the door of the bar-room After gaining access to the room the thieves pried open a private closet, in which the landlord, William H Davis, had placed a gold watch and chain, one hundred and twenty-five dollars in money, and other articles of value, which were taken In a drawer immediately beneath that in which the one hundred and twenty-five dollars were found was over one thousand dollars, the amount received for the sale of cattle, which the owner proposed to deposit in bank, and fortunately this sum was not disturbed The burglars were not discovered

Societies.—Okehocking Tribe, No 159, Improved Order of Red Men, was instituted in November, 1871 The meetings of the tribe were first held in the basement of Newtown Hall, and later a wigwam was furnished in the second story of the hall which is now used for that purpose The charter officers of the tribe were Dr Charles S Heysham, S, William T Davis, S S; John L Hosmer, J S, J J Sproul, Sec John J Sproul is the present Sachem, and John L Hosmer Secretary The tribe has thirty-eight members at the present time

Newtown Square Lodge, No 95, Independent Order of Odd-Fellows, was instituted in 1879, and holds its meetings in the wigwam of the Red Men The first officers of the lodge were Jonathan F. Fairlamb, N. G, J Jones Leedom, V G The present officers are James J Sproul, N G, Henry D Crosley, V G, Isaiah Massey, Sec The lodge has now thirty-eight members in good standing

Old Newtown Square.—At the cross-roads, where John Pratt now resides, northwest from the present Newtown Square, is located Old Newtown Square. The land was in the possession of the Lewis family many years John Lewis, who died in 1851, aged eighty-one years, was born there, and was the last of the name owning the estate, which passed to his daughter, Mrs Pratt Newtown Street road, laid out in 1683, and the Goshen road crosses the former highway at this point Here for many years a licensed house was maintained, and was so kept during and long subsequent to the Revolutionary war Above the old square, in July, 1883, St David's post-office was established Joseph Lewis, Jr, is the postmaster At this place is a store kept by Joseph Lewis, Jr, a blacksmith-shop, and a school-house

Newtown Square—The present hamlet derived its name at the time the postal department established an office there, about 1820 Davis Beaumont, the first postmaster, was the landlord of the Farmers' Wagon, the title being then changed to Newtown Square Inn. The land in the neighborhood was then owned by the Beaumont family, and the hotel there has been yearly licensed to the present time, excepting during the years of local option The postmasters since Beaumont have been David Pratt, Walter Green, Elwood Baldwin, Leedom Kirk, Isaac Halderman, Jr, Leopold Samter, the present official The latter now has the store at the Square, which was located there many years ago The town hall, a two-story building, was erected in 1868 The lower floor is used as a carriage-shop, and the upper story is arranged for a public hall, and as a lodge-room for the societies of Red Men and Odd-Fellows

Schools.—One of the earliest schools in Delaware County was maintained at Old Newtown Square early in the last century It was used for educational purposes in 1750, for Benjamin West, a lad of twelve, attended school there in that year It was a log building, the rude desks being fastened to the sides of the house, and many generations of pupils had carved their names, and cut deep gashes in the unpainted wood in idle moments Until within a half-century a copy-book was in existence in which young West, "while at school at Newtown Square, had drawn numerous pictures of various animals, etc, and there is a tradition that these were made in the way of compensation for assistance given him in arithmetic by another school-boy named Williamson, the owner of the book, the youthful artist not having much taste for figures"[1] This log house in time became so dilapidated that in 1815 it was removed, and a similar building erected, which remained in use until after 1820 Stephen D Hunter was a student in this log house, which stood below Newtown Square, on lands of Jonathan Hood No trace of the building now remains

In the extreme northeastern section of the township, near St David's Church, on a knoll in front of the sanctuary, a stone school-house was erected in 1749, and remained until within recent years, when it was removed It was warmed by a wood fire built on a hearth, and a high chimney-stack being constructed to afford a large wide-mouthed fireplace Perhaps school was taught therein by Rev Dr William Currie, who was pastor of Radnor Church before, for a part of, and after the Revolutionary war, although it is said "Dr Currie did not teach a regular school, but employed his leisure in instructing his own children, and admitted the son of his friend to his paternal care"[2] School was kept therein until 1820 In 1817, Caleb Y Lewis was a pupil there, at which time Elijah Brooke was the teacher

About 1815 Friends of Newtown Meeting erected a one story octagon school-house on the meeting-house lot The school was maintained by subscription, as was usual in early days, and on the death of Dr Jonas Preston, in 1836, by will he charged his real estate in the township with the annual payment of two hundred dollars towards the support of this school The building is still used for school purposes by the society, the Preston fund paying the salary of the teacher After the school law of 1834 became operative, there being no school-houses in the township other than the one owned by the society, application was made by the directors for its use, but the request was denied

On Aug 11, 1836, the directors purchased of Joseph Lindsay a lot of ground on the West Chester road, above Newtown Square, on which they erected a stone octagon school-house, which was continued in use for many years, until the present stone building, known as "Chestnut Grove Seminary," was built to take its place

[1] Smith's "History of Delaware County," p 513

[2] "Biographical Memoir of Dr John Davis," by Dr Morgan Hazard's Register, vol ii p 278

The demand for public schools in the township was such that on July 23, 1839, the directors bought from Isaac Thomas a piece of land located on the road leading from St. David's post-office to Berwyn, and erected a stone school-house, which continued in use until 1870, when a lot on the Leopard road, at St. David's post-office, was purchased, the present stone house erected in the same year, and the old building abandoned for school purposes.

Israel Foulk, on Jan. 11, 1841, donated a lot of land on the west side of the West Chester road, east of Newtown Square, on which to erect a school-house, the deed providing that in case the ground ceased to be used for school purposes it should revert to his heirs. On this lot a stone octagon school-house was erected, and was used for a quarter of a century, but for a number of years has been abandoned by the directors.

The following is a list of the directors of the public schools for Newtown, as the same appears of record at Media:

1840, Peter Jacquett, William Rhoads; 1842, William Hunter, George McClellan; 1843, Joshua Litzenburgh, Thomas Daniels; 1844, Joseph Lewis, Azariah L. Williamson; 1845, William Hunter, John C. Grim; 1846, Jonathan Tucker, Samuel Moore; 1847, Adam B. Williamson, William Rhoads; 1848, Enos Williamson, Nathan Pratt; special election Sept. 18, 1848, six persons elected: Jackson Bevan, Thomas H. Speakman, John Horton, Azariah L. Williamson, Thomas Pearson, Isaac Thomas; 1849, Isaac Thomas, Jonathan P. Abraham; 1850, A. L. Williamson, Jonathan P. Abraham; 1851, Samuel Caley, Jr., Samuel Moore; 1852, Daniel Baker, Joseph Lewis; 1853, James Dunwoody, Charters Redman; 1854, Charles C. Heysham, David C. Caley; 1855, Nathan Pyott, Jonathan P. Abraham; 1856, James Dunwoody, Charters Redmau; 1857, Enos Williamson, Dr. Charles C. Heysham; 1858, Samuel Caley, Jr., Reece Pyott; 1859, James Dunwoody, Charles Redman; 1860, Davis Beaumont, Joseph Lewis; 1861, Reece Pyott, David P. Caley; 1862, James Dunwoody, Davis F. Smith; 1863, A. L. Williamson, Isaac A. Calvert; 1864, David P. Caley, Charles T. Neal; 1865, Joseph Lewis, Jr., James R. Shock; 1866, A. L. Williamson, George Paschall; 1867, Daniel P. Caley, John L. Yarnall; 1868, James R. Shock, Joseph Lewis, Jr.; 1869, A. L. Williamson, Joseph Lewis, Jr.; 1870, David P. Caley, James Pyott; 1871, James Dunwoody, James P. Calvert; 1872, George Paschall, Thomas Kirk; 1873, John Jones, John H. Rhoads; 1874, D. P. Caley, George Paschall; 1875, Thomas Kirk, James Dunwoody; 1876, Joseph Lewis, Jr., Jesse Brooke; 1877, James Dunwoody, David P. Caley; 1878, no report; 1879, Joseph Lewis, Jr., Charles Barr; 1880, James Dunwoody, Jesse Brooke; 1881, Thomas Kirk, Amos Haines; 1882, Joseph Lewis, Jr., Charles Barr; 1883, James Dunwoody, Andrew J. Horton; 1884, Thomas Kirk, J. P. Dunwoody.

Newtown Friends' Meeting-House.—The first reference to a Friends' Meeting in Newtown occurs in the minutes of Haverford Monthly Meeting, dated Eleventh month 14, 1696, wherein it is recorded that "William Lewis and some friends having proposed to this meeting to settle a meeting at Newtown, they were left to their freedom therein." Before the close of the year, or, as we now compute the year, early in 1697, Thomas Jones was ordered "to acquaint friends of Chester Meeting that the meeting lately settled at Newton is done wth ye consent of this meeting in order to have their approbation therein." What action, if any, was taken by Chester Meeting at that time does not appear, but three years afterwards Chester Quarterly Meeting, on Third month 12, 1701, expressed strong disapproval, stating, "This meeting being dissatisfied that a meeting is sett up at Newtowne without the approbation of this Quarterly meeting, the meeting, therefore, orders John Blunston & Walter ffaucet to go to Haverford months meeting and request them that the said meeting be not Continued without the Approbation of this Q^rly^ Meeting." The protest of Chester Meeting appears not to have been effective in discontinuing the meeting in Newtown, and the subject was brought before the Yearly Meeting of Friends, which decided that the meeting should continue as it then was, but "for the future ye said Welsh friends may set up no meeting further w^th^in the said county of Chester without the approbation" of Chester Quarterly Meeting having been first obtained. Thus the matter rested for five years, until First month 25, 1706, when William Lewis, of Newtown, and Daniel Williamson appeared at Chester Monthly Meeting, asking that Newtown Meeting should be joined with Chester Monthly and Quarterly Meeting, and Caleb Pusey and Joseph Baker were ordered to attend at the next Newtown Monthly Meeting "to signify our willingness if they consent to it." The following month Pusey and Baker reported that they had been to Haverford Meeting in relation to the joining of Newtown Meeting with Chester, and that Haverford Meeting had referred the matter to further consideration. At the Providence Quarterly Meeting on Sixth month 5, 1706, it was "agreed between Philadelphia Q^rly^ Meeting & this that Newtowne friends shall, for the future, belong to Chester Monthly Meeting and to this Q^rly^ Meeting." The persons then comprising Newtown Meeting, we learn from a general certificate present at Providence Sixth month 26, 1706, were William Lewis, Sr., Lewis Lewis, Evan Lewis, William Lewis, Reese Howell, William Bevan, William Thomas, "with Recommendation for Peter Thomas." At this time Newtown Monthly Meeting was held at the house of Lewis Lewis. On Fifth month 28, 1707, a request was presented to Providence Quarterly Meeting asking that the place of meeting might be removed to Evan Lewis', which desire was acceded to. The date at which Friends in Newtown acquired title to the burial-lot does not appear; but it was certainly prior to 1710, for, on Eighth month 30, 1710, "Newton meeting Laid before the meeting their Intentions of building a meeting house by friends burial yard in Newtown," which met the approval of Friends of Providence. The building was not completed, we learn, until near the close of the following year, for on Eighth month (October) 29, 1711, the minutes of Providence Meeting show that the Friends in Newtown "signifie that their meeting house is neare finished, and Desire that their meeting may be Removed from Evan Lewis' to the meeting house, which this meeting approves of," thus Newtown meeting-house, built in 1711, became the tenth Friends' meet-ng-house erected in the present county of Delaware How the building was warmed for the first few years is unknown, but in 1715 a stove, bearing the inscription, "Mordecai Persol, Rebecca Furnace," and the date mentioned dispelled the chilly air in Newtown meeting-house, and did so for over a century and a half until 1876, when it was removed and taken to the Centennial Exhibition The present Friends' meeting-house was erected in 1791

Seventh-Day Baptist Church and Burial-Place —This society was composed of Friends who first adhered to the tenets taught by George Keith, subsequently became converts to the doctrines of the Baptist Church The first Seventh-Day Baptist in Pennsylvania is said to have been Abel Noble, who came to the province in 1684, at which time he was a Friend When George Keith first began to announce his opinions, among the earliest persons to accept his teachings was Noble, and he it was who gave shape to the Keithian Baptist form of religious observances, for which they were distinguished from other societies,—such as distinguishing the days and months by numerical names, adhering to plainness of language and dress, and abstaining from swearing or fighting On June 28, 1697, Abel Noble baptized Thomas Martin, a public Friend, in Ridley Creek, and afterwards Thomas Martin baptized other Quakers,—Thomas Powell, Evan Harry, Hugh Harry, John Palmer, Judith Calvert, David Thomas, and others, to the number of nineteen in all,—who, on Oct 12, 1697, were incorporated, and on that day proceeded to choose a minister by lot Three persons were nominated,—William Buckingham, Thomas Budd, and Thomas Martin,—and the latter was chosen From 1697 to 1700 other Quakers were baptized,—William Thomas, Richard Buffington, Elizabeth Thomas, Jane Phillips, David Phillips, Elizabeth Hall, Rees Price, and others,—some of whom lived in other parts of the country In 1700 a difference arose among the society touching the observance of the Sabbath-day, a separation took place, and such of those who adhered to the observance of the Sabbath-day preserved the organization of a society at Newtown, and held their meetings at the house of David Thomas, now the dwelling of William R Calvert On Jan 30, 1717, Thomas Thomas, of Newtown, conveyed half an acre of land, on Newtown Street, in consideration of fifteen shillings, to Philip Rhytherach, Henry Lewis, and David Thomas, all of Newtown, as a burial-place for the members of the society of Seventh-Day Baptists The land had originally been owned by William Thomas, father of Thomas Thomas, who settled there in 1698 The Yearly or May Meetings were held on the lawn in front of David Thomas' house In 1770 the society still held its meetings at the house of David Thomas Three families, belonging to Newtown, were then in membership, and in that year the following persons were baptized David Thomas, John German, Hazrael Thomas, Ruth Thomas, Priscilla Wayne, Elizabeth Wayne, and Mary Gilkey Within the limits of the present Baptist churchyard at Newtown, separated from the parsonage and church-lot by a picket-fence, is the old burial-ground In time the families of Lewis and Rhytherach, by death and removal, were unrepresented in this section, and the title remained in the Thomas family, by whom it was sold within comparatively recent years to the congregation of the present Baptist Church From among the inscriptions on the gravestones in this ancient God's acre we have copied the following

Jane Thomas, 7th mo 23d day, 1730 (Nov) aged 55
David Thomas, 9th mo 17th day, 1734, aged 64
Margaret Iddings, Nov, 1735, aged 84 years
Richard Iddings, May 3, 1753, aged 78 years

"Elizabeth Wayne, daughter of Humphrey, and Priscilla Wayne, Aug 28, 1738, aged 13 years 7 mo

"I am not saved
By works of mine,
But by the grace
That is Devine"

"Priscilla Wayne, wife of Humphrey Wayne, June 11, 1781, aged 74 years"

"William Wayne, son of Humphrey & Priscilla Wayne, Apl 23, 1752, aged 3 yrs 7 mo

"My Infants Race
Was Ran Apace,
By God's free Grace
I En Joy Peace."

David Thomas, Apl 14, 1789, aged 79 years.
Ruth, wife of David, Feby 20, 1792, aged 60 years
Col David Thomas, 1839, aged 84 years
Margaret Thomas, Nov 9, 1811, aged 24 years

Elizabeth Wayne, the mother of Gen Anthony Wayne, who is believed to have been a Thomas, in her will directed tombstones to be placed at the graves of four of her children who were buried in this yard A large, flat, gray slab, resting upon four columns of gray stones, covers the remains of Elizabeth Wayne, and bears the following inscription

"Dedicated to the memory of Elizabeth Wayne, relict of Isaac Wayne, Esquire, who departed this life in the month of May, 1793, aged 84 years

"She was a woman of distinguished piety and benevolence"

Newtown Baptist Church—This church is over fifty years old, having celebrated its semi centennial or "jubilee anniversary" on Thursday, Nov 9, 1882 It is known that H G Jones, Joseph H Kennard, William S Hall, and others, held religious meetings in this vicinity before the Newtown Baptist Church came into existence In October, 1832, a number of the members of different Baptist Churches residing in Newtown township and the regions about, at a considerable distance from their own places of worship, decided upon organizing a new church For this purpose they met at the residence of Deacon Samuel Davis in Haverford There were present H G Jones, of Lower Merion, D A Nichols, of Roxborough, R Gardiner, of Goshen, ministers, and Samuel Davis and John Kinzey, of Lower Merion, and Spicer Jones, of Great Valley, laymen It was agreed that Saturday, the 10th of November, 1832, should be the day on which the contemplated church should be organized. Invitations were sent to a number of the clergy of the Baptist denomination to be present. On the day appointed they met at the residence of Dr. Gardiner, of Newtown, and were organized as a council.

It was unanimously agreed that a church ought to be organized. Letters of dismissal were read from several churches, dismissing the following seven persons who constituted the new church, viz.: Rev. Dr. Richard Gardiner and his wife Hannah, Eliza C. Cheyney, John Kinzey and his wife Mary, Harriet Lewis, and Eli Baugs. A church covenant and articles of faith were agreed to and signed, and the right hand of fellowship was then extended to Dr. Gardiner on behalf of the church. In the evening of the same day Rev. H. G. Jones preached a sermon to the little flock, and also on the following day (Sunday). During the first year twelve persons were baptized, and eleven were received into the church by letter. Meetings were held before a church was built in the upper part of Dr. Gardiner's carriage-house, and the Misses Gardiner organized a Sunday-school which was held at their father's house.

In January, 1834, Rev. Samuel J. Creswell was ordained to the ministry, and installed as pastor of the church. Early in the same year an acre of ground was purchased from Dr. Gardiner for one hundred and thirty-six dollars, he donating thirty dollars of that amount, and a house of worship was erected upon it at a cost of about two thousand dollars, which was dedicated Aug. 30, 1834, Rev. H. G. Jones, of Lower Merion, preaching the sermon. In June, 1834, Robert Compton was appointed by the Board of Pennsylvania Missions to labor with the church, and eight months later Daniel Trites superseded him. In 1839, the church, having in the mean time grown considerably, purchased the property of Thomas Phillips, then occupied by the pastor, Rev. Daniel Trites, for two thousand dollars. In 1840 the church reported a membership of one hundred and thirty-seven, and a Sunday-school of ninety-five.

After the Rev. Daniel Trites resigned the pastorship, in 1840, the pulpit was supplied by various ministers and laymen until Oct. 17, 1842, when Rev. Henry Essick was chosen pastor. From that time to the present the pastors have been as follows: 1845, Rev. David Phillips; 1846–49, supplies; 1849–59, Rev. R. Compton; 1859–64, Rev. John Owen; 1864–65, Rev. Samuel Cox; 1865–66, supplies; 1866–68, Rev. C. F. Steinman; 1869, supplies; 1870–74, Rev. J. T. Bender; 1874–77, Rev. E. M. Heyburn; 1877–84, Rev. J. L. Sagebeer; July, 1884, Rev. Frank Shirmer.

During the fifty-two years of the existence of the church about four hundred and twenty persons have been baptized, and about one hundred and fifty received by letter. The present membership is about one hundred and fifty.

St. David's Church.—The quaint Episcopal Church building commonly designated "Old Radnor," located at the extreme northeastern limits of Newtown township, in point of age antedates all the ecclesiastical structures in Delaware County excepting Haverford Friends' meeting-house. The plain, stone edifice has been kindly treated by time, which has covered and beautified its external walls with luxuriant ivy, while the towering trees which cluster on the hillsides impart to the scene a picturesque appearance rarely to be met with in any part of the United States. A rough stone stairway, on the outside of the building, leads to the tiny gallery within, and adds attractiveness to the picture. Longfellow, in an interview with a newspaper correspondent, in 1881, most happily expressed the feeling of veneration a sight of the ancient structure was calculated to arouse in a meditative mind. "I was stopping," he said, in relating the story of his poem, 'Old St. David's at Radnor,' at Rosemont, and one day drove over to Radnor. Old St. David's Church, with its charming and picturesque surroundings, attracted my attention. Its diminutive size, peculiar architecture, the little rectory in the grove, the quaint churchyard, where Mad Anthony Wayne is buried, the great tree which stands at the gateway, and the pile of gray stone which makes the old church, and is almost hidden by the climbing ivy, all combine to make it a gem for a fancy picture."[1]

The exact date when the church organization was effected at Radnor is not now known. But certain it is that a congregation had been established there in 1700; for in the letter written by Rev. Evan Evans, and dated London, Sept. 18, 1707, addressed to the Society for the Propagation of the Gospel in Foreign Parts, giving an account of the state of the church in Pennsylvania, the writer says, "But Montgomery and Radnor, next to my own beloved Philadelphia, had the most considerable share in my labours, where I preached in Welsh once a fortnight for four years, till the arrival of Mr. Nichols, minister of Chester, in 1704."[2] The certificate given by the church wardens of Radnor, dated June 29, 1719, to Rev. Dr. Evans, distinctly set forth "that the Rev. Dr. Evans has preached the gospel at Radnor, at the house of Mr. William Davis, one of the subscribers, once a fortnight from November, in the year 1700, all the time he was resident in Philadelphia, without any reward from us; and since his return from England, which was on the 22d day of March, 1716/7, until the latter end of June past, he preached at St. David's Church, at Radnor."[3] Tradition asserts that a log church was erected early in the seventeenth century, and the ruins of such a structure on the property of Tryon Lewis, formerly owned by William

[1] *Philadelphia Press*, May, 1881.

[2] Hazard's Register, vol. iii. p. 337.

[3] Dr. Perry's "Historical Collection of American Colonial Churches."

MARKLEY PHILADA. SC. St. David's Church,—Radnor, Pennsylvania. FOUNDED in 1715.

Davis, is thought to be the remains of this early sanctuary, which was so constructed that it could be used as a garrison in the event of any hostile demonstration on the part of the Indians during divine services In 1708, in Oldmixon's "British Empire in America," reference is made to a church congregation in Radnor "Within land," he says, "lies Radnor or Welsh town, finely situated and well built, containing near 50 families In this place is a congregation of the Church of England-men, but no settled minister"[1] In the letter of the Rev Dr Evans, before mentioned, he further states, "The Welsh at Radnor and Merioneth, in the province of Pennsylvania, having a hundred hands to their petition for a minister to be settled amongst them that understands the British language, there being many ancient people among these inhabitants that do not understand the English, and could a sober and discreet man be procured to undertake that mission, he might be capable, by the blessing of God, to bring in a plentiful harvest of Welsh Quakers, but were unhappily prevented before any minister in holy orders that could preach to them in their own language was sent into Pennsylvania, but I believe that they are not irrecoverable, had they an itinerant missionary who would use application and diligence to introduce them to the communion of the church"

The ultimate result of the petition, which was supplemented in 1712 by other representations of the people of the neighborhood, in which Rev John Humphreys, then missionary in charge of St Paul's parish, at Chester, joined, was the appointment of John Clubb, a Welshman, who had been a schoolmaster in Philadelphia He had occasionally conducted services at Radnor, and was appointed in 1714 missionary to Radnor and Oxford Churches At the time he was given this charge John Clubb was in England, sailing shortly after to assume the duties of ministering to the congregations at these stations He reached Philadelphia in the latter part of August of that year, and reported to the Society for the Propagation of the Gospel in Foreign Parts, that the "people of Radnor," on the 7th of September "had met me [him] unanimously upon the day appointed . and at the same time heartily engaged to build a handsome stone church They subscribed that day a tolerable sum towards the carrying of it on, and obliged themselves to make it good, and for the rest I shall use all the means I am able to effect by collection" The fund being raised, it is asserted by tradition considerable diversity of opinion was manifested respecting the site of the church, some of the contributors contending for the present location, while others desired it should be built on a lot of fifteen acres, near the junction of Sugartown and Reeseville roads The fact that a good spring of water was near by the present site, ultimately turned the scale, and the work of building the church was earnestly begun The land, it is said, on which the church stands being owned by one Saunders, then residing in England, he was asked to donate the plot, and in response authorized the congregation "to fence off five acres in one corner" of his tract This statement may well be questioned until it is established that Saunders ever owned the land Perhaps William Shalow was the name of the donor But, be that as it may, the right to build was obtained, and Acrelius records the ceremonial observances when the cornerstone was laid He says,—

"THE LAYING OF A CORNER STONE —But something peculiar is to be seen among the English at the laying of the foundation of a church On the 9th of May, 1715, Pastor Sandel was invited to attend the laying of the foundation of Radnor Church, sixteen miles from Philadelphia First, a service with preaching was held in a private house, then they went in procession to the place where the church was to be built There a prayer was made, after which each one of the clergyman laid a stone according to the direction of the master mason"[2]

For over half a century after the church was built no floor was laid in the building, and no pews, the worshipers being seated on benches, at first furnished by the occupant, but subsequently placed there by the vestry and leased to the congregation The quaint record states, "William Evans and Hugh Jones are to have ye upper bench above ye door for two pounds" Later, pews were introduced, but the peculiar custom prevailed of selling the ground, and the party purchasing to make the improvements, thus, "At a vestry held December 5th, 1763, the vestry granted to Robert Jones the privilege to build a pugh on a piece of ground in St David's Church adjoining Wayne's and Hunter's pugh, he paying for ye ground four pounds ten shillings" This, however, is not the first mention of pews, for it appears on June 8th, 1756, the vestry "Ordered that the clerk and his assistants shall sit in John Jones' pew" In 1765 the church was floored, in 1767 a vestry house was built on the site of the present Sunday-school, and in 1771 a subscription was made sufficient to build the gallery, which, when first erected, extended further than at present, passing over the front door and joining on the east wall Capt Isaac Wayne, the father of Mad Anthony, was the chief mover in the improvement, and under his direction it was built.

John Clubb, the active pastor, during whose incumbency the present church was built, labored so diligently in the ministry, being compelled to make long journeys to preach to the scattered congregations in his charge, that it undermined his health and caused his death in December, 1715 In that year it is believed Dr Evans returned to England for the second time, designing to remain, but after the death of John Clubb, the petition of the "poor settlers in a

---

[1] Hazard's Register, vol v p 162

[2] Acrelius' "History of New Sweden," p 221 The fact that the services were held at a private house, and the absence of the slightest reference to a prior church building in any of the documentary authorities touching on the early history of St David's, tend strongly to disprove the truth of the old tradition that a log structure built for church purposes preceded the present edifice

wilderness," as was the expression used by the congregations at Radnor and Oxford, earnestly requesting that another missionary should be sent them by the society, that Dr Evans petitioned that he might again go to the American colonies The only vacant charge at that time being the Welsh settlement, he was appointed, and in 1716, for the third time, being temporarily assigned to that parish At Radnor he preached on alternative Thursdays until the summer of 1718, during which, from April, 1717, until May, 1718, he was also minister of Christ Church, in Philadelphia In February of the latter year he was offered a living in Maryland by the Governor of that State, which he accepted, conducting services at Radnor for the last time in June, 1718 Rev John Humphreys, of Chester, who was so unpopular in his own parish that the people united in April, 1717, in asking that another missionary might be sent to St Paul's, supplied the vacant pulpit until December, 1718, when Rev Robert Weyman, who had been appointed missionary, assumed charge of the Radnor Church The latter did not understand Welsh, and for twelve years many of the pious members of the church attended his preaching without comprehending any of the sermons, and in those days pulpit essays were not confined to a brief matter of a half-hour, but were lengthy and bristling with doctrinal arguments On April 1, 1725, the old record of the church shows the appointment of the first vestrymen, consisting of William Davis, James Price, Thomas David, Joseph Coleman, William Moore, John Hunter, Anthony Wayne, Thomas James, David Evans, William Evans, Peter Elliot, John David, while the church wardens were Evan Hughes and Griffith Howell.

Early in the spring of 1731, Rev Mr Weyman was ordered to another field, and for two years Radnor Church was without a missionary, dependent on supplies for religious services, and the difficulties with which the congregation had to contend are shown by the register, when, on Nov 7, 1731, a subscription, amounting to nine pounds eleven shillings was made, and the subscribers obligated themselves to make payment "on or before y[e] sixteenth day of May next ensuing the date hereof, for the use of Mr Backhouse, who pretends, with God's assistance, to preach here once a month" Early in the spring of 1733, Rev John Hughes, who had been appointed missionary, assumed the charge of Radnor Church, and continued there until the summer of 1736, when, his health becoming impaired, he requested the society to fill the place which he was compelled to resign The society thereupon appointed Rev William Currie, a Scotchman, liberally educated, who assumed the duties of the office in 1737, and he continued in charge of the parish until May, 1776, when, announcing to the congregation that, under the obligation of his office, he felt he must use the liturgy of the Church of England in behalf of King George, he tendered his resignation of the rectorship, which he had filled for nearly half a century

After his resignation church organization appears to have been demoralized, and seldom during the long years of that contest were religious services held within the building That the church was stripped of the lead in which the small diamond-shaped glasses in the windows was held in place is most probable, but it is not likely, as tradition has stated, that Gen Grant massed some of his command in the cedar thicket, which, during the Revolution, was on the site of the present rectory, preparatory to his attack on Wayne at Paoli, on the night of Sept 20, 1777 It may be that some of the dead and wounded American troops, to the number of sixteen, who fell in that massacre, were buried in the little hollow west of the gallery-stairs, but the story that the buried men were of the dead of Brandywine battle-field is worthy of little, if any, consideration

From a well-written account of St David's Church the following incidents are taken [1]

"In June, 1763, very threatening rumors having reached Radnor concerning the devastation of the Indians under Pontiac, who had at that time advanced as far as Carlisle, Mr Currie, on the Sunday after the arrival of the news, announced his text from Ecclesiastes vii 14 'In the day of prosperity be joyful, but in the day of adversity considerate' So eloquent was the old gentleman's discourse that the congregation, impressed with a sense of their danger from an attack by the Indians, resolved themselves, before leaving the church, into a mutual protection association, and, after due deliberation, returned to their homes, carefully cleaned and prepared all the guns and other weapons found in the neighborhood, and thus made full arrangements to resist the Indians should they approach This home guard system continued, it is said, until Pontiac's peace and withdrawal in August, 1764"

The other incidents occurred during the Revolution, and happened while services were being held by Rev David Jones, the Baptist pastor of the Great Valley Church, in Chester County, who was Wayne's chaplain from 1777 to 1783, and on this occasion was preaching in the old Radnor Church The event is thus recorded by the writer already mentioned

"After finishing the introductory formalities, old Davy Jones climbed into the lofty pulpit, and, having announced his text, glanced around in order to assure himself of the attention of his audience, that one glance, however, completely disconcerted the worthy old gentleman He saw seated comfortably before him several young and active men (previously hidden from so close a scrutiny by the old-fashioned, high-backed pews) In an instant patriotism had so completely mastered him that he threw away his sermon, and, shaking his finger vehemently at the astonished youths, demanded to know why they didn't go into

[1] Historical Sketch of Old Radnor Church, 1685–1875, pp 5, 6, Media, 1875

the American army and fight the British? 'I'm not *afraid* to go,' he screamed; 'they can't hurt me! They may kill me, if they like, and make a drumhead of my old hide, but they'll play humy, drum, drum, humy, drum, drum, till the British are scared out of the country;" then, in wild excitement, he threw off a heavy cloak, which hung around his shoulders, and displayed an American uniform."

In 1783, Rev. William Currie again took charge of St. David's and began energetically to collect funds to repair the ravages which time and the war had made in the old church building and graveyard wall. While he was rector the church was admitted to membership in the Diocesan Convention of Pennsylvania, in 1786. In August, 1787, Thomas Reed and Philip Sheaf were appointed as delegates to secure a minister, the Great Valley Episcopal Church of Chester County, St. James at Perkiomen, and the Swede's Church near Norristown being united with St. David's Church in the parish. The result was the calling of Rev. Slaytor Clay. In August, 1792, while Mr. Clay was rector, the church was incorporated, and it was during his incumbency that the body of Gen. Wayne was removed from the fortress at Presque Isle to Radnor churchyard by his son, Col. Isaac Wayne. On the 4th of July, 1809 (an oppressively warm day), the Pennsylvania State Society of the Cincinnati placed a plain marble monument over his remains. This stone was erected previous to the removal of the body of the general to Old Radnor churchyard. The ceremonies of the dedication of the monument were conducted by the Society of the Cincinnati. There was an imposing pageant, and the First City Troop of Philadelphia, under command of Maj. Robert Wharton, paid the honors of war over the grave. The hearse containing the body of the general was preceded from his residence to the grave by a veteran, Samuel Smiley, one of the Wayne brigade, who refused to ride, and seemed overcome with the realization of the fact that his old commander was dead. One of the officers of the City Troop, it is said, was overcome by the extreme heat, and after the ceremony was over, an eccentric Baptist preacher, old Davy Jones, who had witnessed the massacre at Paoli and had taken part in the battle, mounted the platform that had been erected near the monument and told the story of that butchery. The crowd gathered on the occasion is said to have been so large that many of the limbs of the trees in and surrounding the yard broke with the weight of the people who had climbed up on them.

During Mr. Clay's rectorship an addition was made to the graveyard and the wall repaired, the dashed part of the wall showing where the extension was made. The present northwest wall of the graveyard, added at a still more recent date, forms the boundaries between Delaware and Chester Counties. The church building was repaired and the pews rearranged. Mr. Clay continued in charge of St. David's until his death, in 1821, although his health was so broken that frequently services were not held in the church, and often the congregation was dependent on supplies. In 1818 Rev. Samuel C. Brinckle settled near the church, and preached every other week after that time until Mr. Clay's death; and succeeding the latter in the rectorship, he preached every Sunday, but that he did so was due to William Crosley, a wealthy member of the church, who subscribed twenty dollars to the support of a minister who would preach every Sunday. The congregation, moved by this example, contributed until the salary was increased to nearly four hundred dollars.

The rectors of the church since Mr. Brinckle have been: Rev. Simon Wilmer, from December, 1832, to July, 1833; Rev. William Henry Rees, from July, 1833, to September, 1838; Rev. William Peck, from October, 1838, to October, 1845; Rev. William W. Spear, from January, 1846, to March, 1846; Rev. Breed Batchelor, from March, 1846, to December, 1847; Rev. Thomas G. Allen, not regularly appointed; Rev. John A. Childs, from January, 1848, to August, 1856; Rev. Henry Brown, from 1851 to 1855; Rev. Richardson Graham, from January, 1856, to January, 1861; Rev. Thomas G. Clemson, from August, 1861, to June, 1866; Rev. William F. Halsey, from Nov. 18, 1866, to his death, October, 1882; Rev. George A. Keller, from December, 1882, the present incumbent.

On July 30, 1820, the first confirmation ever held in St. David's Church was conducted by Bishop White, sixteen persons being on that occasion admitted to membership. In 1824 the Sunday-school was organized, and about 1830 that part of the old gallery which passed over the front door was taken down, the high-backed, old-fashioned pews torn out, and the present ones substituted, the pulpit enlarged, and the sounding-board removed. A vestry house was built, about seventeen feet square, on the site of the present Sunday-school building. In 1844 the present parsonage was built. In 1850 St. David's corporation brought suit against Thomas Beaumont, who, they alleged, had gradually been encroaching on the church lands. The church was comparative successful in the suit, but the vestry was unable to show any title to the land other than possession. It is a tradition that Queen Anne presented Radnor Church with a communion service, which is doubtless true, for it was her custom to make such gifts to every church of England in the British colonies. It was due to her interest in these matters that Walpole called her "the wet-nurse of the church." This service was taken by some marauding party of soldiers during the Revolution, and has never been recovered.

In 1861 the corporation purchased an acre of land from George Phillips, and enlarged the graveyard. On Sept. 4, 1867, the church celebrated its sesquicentennial, the date being erroneous, 1717 being accepted as the year of the church building, instead of 1715. In 1871 the church was repaired, and a new and commodious vestry-room was built on and beyond the site of the old house

During the national centennial Longfellow visited Old Radnor Church, and so deeply did the scene impress his poetic feelings that he gave expression to his thoughts in the following poem, entitled

"OLD ST DAVID'S AT RADNOR [1]

"What an image of peace and rest
Is this little church among its graves!
All is so quiet the troubled breast,
The wounded spirit, the heart oppressed,
Here may find the repose it craves

"See how the ivy climbs and expands
Over this humble hermitage,
And seems to caress with its little hands
The rough, gray stones, as a child that stands
Caressing the wrinkled cheeks of age

"You cross the threshold, and dim and small
Is the space that serves for the Shepherd's fold
The narrow aisle, the bare white wall,
The pews, and the pulpit quaint and tall,
Whisper and say, 'Alas! we are old'

"Herbert's chapel at Bemerton
Hardly more spacious is than this,
But poet and pastor, blent in one,
Clothed with a splendor, as of the sun,
That lowly and holy edifice

"It is not the wall of stone without
That makes the building small or great,
But the soul's light shining round about,
And the faith that overcometh doubt,
And the love that stronger is than hate

"Were I a pilgrim in search of peace,
Were I a pastor of Holy Church,
More than a bishop's diocese
Should I prize this place of rest and release
From further longing and further search

"Here would I stay, and let the world
With its distant thunder roar and roll,
Storms do not rend the sail that is furled,
Nor like a dead leaf, tossed and whirled
In an eddy of wind, is the anchored soul"

The ancient God's acre which surrounds this quaint church is crowded with the dead of many generations. The oldest tombstone in the inclosure bears this inscription

"Here Lieth yᵉ body of
Edward Hughes, Entered
yᵉ 16 day of December
1716—aged 56 years 9 months"

Another erected to an infant reads,—

"Remember, children, as you pass by
That you, too, also soon must die"

The door-stone to the church is a tablet bearing the date 1781, and the name William Moore, whom tradition has declared was a rank Tory Another stone has this inscription, which is now difficult to decipher

"HERE LIETH THE BODY OF WILLIAM EVANS WHO DEPARTED THIS LIFE THE SEPTEMBER 29 1731 AGED 52 MY PILGRIM RACE I RAN A PACE MY RESTING PLACE IS HERE THIS STONE IS GOT TO KEEP YE SPOT THAT MEN DIG NOT TOO NEAR"

[1] *Lippincott's Magazine* for June, 1880

Near the church has been erected a plain marble monument to the memory of Gen Anthony Wayne On one side of the stone is the following inscription

"Major General Anthony Wayne was born at Waynesborough, in Chester county, State of Pennsylvania, A D 1745 After a life of honor and usefulness, he died in December, 1796, at a military post on the shore of Lake Erie, Commander-in Chief of the Army of the United States His military achievements are consecrated in the history of his country and in the hearts of his countrymen His remains are here deposited"

On the other is inscribed,—

"In honor of the distinguished military services of Major Gen Anthony Wayne, and as an affectionate tribute of respect to his memory this stone was erected by his companion in arms, the Pennsylvania State Society of the Cincinnati, July 4th, 1809, thirty-fourth anniversary of the United States of America, an event which constitutes the most appropriate eulogium of an American soldier and patriot."

In another part of the graveyard is a massive slab, which bears the following inscription

"Mary Wayne, consort of the late Major Gen Anthony Wayne, died April 18th, 1793, aged 44 years

"Major Gen Anthony Wayne, late commander of the Army of the United States, died at Presque Isle, December 15th, 1796, aged 52 years His body is interred within the garrison near the town of Erie"

The stone just mentioned was erected prior to the removal of "Mad Anthony's" remains to Old Radnor Church

Industries—In 1799 John Foulkes owned in Newtown a saw-mill and chairmaker's shop, Abraham Calvert and Joseph Foulkes owned each a weave-shop, Robert Mendenhall and William Vandever owned a saw-mill, and Ezra Thomas had a wheelwright shop.

Union Paper-Mill—On Feb 2, 1828, William Crosley purchased one hundred and eighty-seven acres of land on Darby Creek, and in that year erected a woolen-factory, where he conducted a large business for many years The mill was finally burned, and on Feb 24, 1861, the property was purchased by Dr Henry Pleasants, and later sold by him to Caspar C Garrett, who erected a paper-mill, which he subsequently enlarged, and is now one of the most prosperous establishments of this character in the county.

Moore's Mill.—About 1835, Adam Siters sold to Samuel, James, and Alexander Moore eighty acres of land on Darby Creek, a short distance below the Crosley Mill, on which they erected a stone paper-mill, forty by sixty feet, three stories in height, and a stone picker-house one story high Fourteen tenement houses were also built, and a large and extensive business was conducted until 1855, when the main mill was destroyed by fire The small one was burned a few years later Since that time the water-power has not been used, and the property later passed to Dr Pleasants, who now owns it

Tannery—David Lewis, in 1799, owned a tan-yard, and also had a store The tan-yard in 1815 was conducted by John Pratt, and was on land near Old Newtown Square, now belonging to Charles Tyson It was continued until subsequent to 1830

Pierce's Plows—In 1843, William Cobourn had a foundry near Fox Chase Tavern, where he made and had the exclusive sale of Pierce's plows, which he manufactured of cast iron, wrought iron, and steel.

Williamson's Saw-Mill.—In 1799 Enos Williamson owned a saw-mill on Crum Creek, which fell into disuse subsequent to 1848.

Thomas' Shingle-Mill.—Thirty-five years ago Jonathan H. Thomas was operating a shingle-mill in Newtown, which, on the evening of March 22, 1861, was set on fire and destroyed. The ground being at the time covered with a deep snow, the track of the incendiary was followed to Howellville, in Edgmont, where he was arrested.

Licensed Houses.—The first record of license granted in Newtown is mentioned in the following petition of Joseph Hawley, which would designate it as having been done in 1727, although I do not find Hawley's name in the petition for licenses previous to 1729. The petition I allude to is dated Aug. 25, 1741, and the petitioner sets forth his case to the court that he has "for these fourteen years Past Behaved himself as an honest, Civill and quiet neighbor in his said Imploy, forbidding Gameing or Drunkenness or Suffer Men's Servants or others, to Sitt Tipling in his house, and he and his wife being each of them Between Sixty and Seventy years of age. . . . And hope you will not allow Francis Elliot, a young man (that hath a good trade, being a wheelwright, house carpenter and joiner, having a wife and one Child, hath Two or three apprentices, one Journeyman), to obtain your Grant for Keeping of a Publick house in Newtown, aforesaid, to the Great hurt and damage of your Petitioner in his old age."

The petition is indorsed by sixty-seven citizens of the township, who request the court to grant the license, lest "Hawley and wife become a publick charge." The application received the favorable consideration of the justice. In August, 1743, Hawley's petition states that "having obtained the favour of this Honorable Court for the Keeping a Publick house of Entertainment for these sixteen years past," he wishes to continue, and the court permits him so to do. From the diagram attached to Francis Elliot's petition, Nov. 24, 1741, it appears that "Hally's" (Hawley's) house was located on the north side of the then Darby (now West Chester) road, a short distance below where that road intersects with the road leading to Bishop's Mills and Lima, which places it above where the Fox Chase Hotel now stands. Elliot also states that his house is about ten miles distant on "Newtown Street," where the road from Goshen to Philadelphia crosses the former, and locates his house at the southwest intersection of Newtown Street and Goshen road, exactly on the site of the building of Mrs. Ruth Pratt, in 1870, as shown by Hopkin's Atlas of Delaware County.

As noted, Francis Elliot failed in the petition mentioned above, but he again presented his petition to the November court, in the same year, mentioning therein that he had made application at the August court, but without success. Aug. 31, 1742, he again appears, stating that he had been refused license at the previous August and November courts, but urges that "he hath been encouraged almost to complete a large Brick Building, and in a short time (by the Providence of God) shall be finished." His application appears to have this time been successful, for Aug. 30, 1743, he petitioned for a renewal of license, which was allowed.

Neither Hawley's nor Elliot's name appears, so far as I have been able to find, after the date just given, but Aug. 28, 1744, John West (the father of Benjamin West) petitioned that he "having obtained license for Keeping A public House of Entertainment in the County of Chester for one year, which being now Expired, your Petitioner Craves to be Continued in the Same Station in the Township." From that time until 1748 he continued in the business, but in that year Jonathan James, who leased the premises, received license for the house "where John West lately Dwelled," and had it renewed to him the following year. November, 1750, John Morris, also a renter, petitioned for license for the house where Jonathan James dwelt, which he says has been "a tavern ever since built," and it was allowed. The same year Jonathan James also made application at another location, but it was rejected. Morris kept the inn until 1755, when John West again became "mine host" and so continued until 1758, when John Hamilton obtained the license, which was consecutively continued until and including 1766. There is no record for the year 1767, but in 1768 John Jarvis was empowered to keep a public-house, which in 1771 was known as the Square. In 1774, John Powell succeeded Jarvis for three years, when Andrew Wilson conducted the business, and in turn was followed by James Elliot, the name of the house now being Newtown Square, a title which it appears to have retained until 1787, when it was again called the Square. This name it retained in 1788 and 1789, when Richard Britton was the host. In 1790, after the erection of Delaware County, Evan Jones was licensed at the Square, and in 1792 he was succeeded in business by William Beaumont, who owned the property. In 1810 he was superseded by Joseph Davis, who, in his petition the following year, gives the title of the old inn as the Wagon. The latter in 1814 was followed by Levi Wells, and in 1817, Davis Beaumont, a son of the owner of the tavern, became the landlord, to be followed in 1823 by William V. Black. At this time the electors of Newtown, Radnor, Marple, and that part of Edgmont lying to the west of Ridley Creek, had their polling-place at Black's Inn. In 1826, William L. Cochran followed William V. Black, to give place, in 1832, to Joseph Black, and the latter, two years later, to Joseph E. Anderson. At this time the voters of Newtown and Edgmont, east of Ridley Creek, had their polls at the Wagon. In 1838, Isaac Hull became the host, and when Newtown, in 1840, became an election district by itself, the polls were still retained at this house, and continue to this time there to be held In 1845 Hull gave place to John King, who remained there only one year, for in 1846 he removed to the Fox Chase Inn, and James McClelland followed him as landlord of the Newtown Square Inn, for, although the old name does not appear on any petition for license until 1846, I am told it was so known during McClelland's occupancy of the house The latter in 1852 gave place to John Paschall, Jr, and he, in 1856, to Joseph H Hozer, and in 1859 George Eppright had license thereat He, however, in 1867, rented the Fox Chase, and William T Davis took out the license and so continued until 1876, when Robert Cunningham became the landlord, and in 1878 William T Davis again became the host of the Newtown Square Inn, and continues there to the present time

As before stated, the public-house of Joseph Hawley was located near the site of the noted Fox Chase Tavern on the West Chester road, and it may be that Benjamin Powell, in 1775, had license for the old inn John Hill Martin states that Alexander Bartram, a Scotchman, and a leading merchant in Philadelphia previous to the Revolution, owned the Fox Chase, the ground connected therewith comprising sixty acres That he took side with the English, was declared a traitor to the United Colonies, and his estate confiscated In 1782 John Fawkes was granted the right to keep a public-house, and although the name is not given in his application, it was doubtless in the building that was so long known to the people of the county as the Fox Chase In 1785 Thomas Carpenter kept the house, to be superseded in 1788 by Richard Fawkes, Jr, who, after the county of Delaware had been erected, continued to be approved until 1799, when Rebecca Terrill was licensed for Fawkes' Tavern After two years' experience she yielded the honors of the house again to Richard Fawkes, and he continued as "mine host" until 1809, when Josiah Fawkes assumed the duties of the place In 1813 John Fawkes had the license, and the following year in his petition the name "Fox Chase" first appears of record James Miller was landlord in 1823 to 1825, when for three years the house seems not to have had license, until, in 1828, John Jacobs received the privilege and continued yearly to do so until 1839, when Richard Millison took his place, to be followed by John King in 1845 The latter had the year previously kept the Newtown Square Inn On Dec 5, 1845, King was stabbed and seriously wounded by Eli Massey, who had been in his employ, discharged and forbidden to come to the house At date stated, Massey came to the Fox Chase, and went into the kitchen where his wife and several other persons then were King, learning that Massey was in the house,—for the latter had threatened bodily harm to the former,—went to the kitchen and ordered him to leave the premises When Massey had gone a few steps beyond the threshold he turned, struck at King, who had followed him to the door, with his knife and wounded the landlord in the abdomen The assailant was arrested, tried at the February court following, and convicted of an assault and battery Judge Bell sentenced him to nine months' imprisonment in the county jail John King, at the Fox Chase, continued to receive license until 1856, when, he being dead, the privilege was granted to his widow, Edith Ann King The next year she was followed by Thomas B Evans, and he in 1861 by Abner Baldwin, Jr In 1864 R M Speakman had license for the tavern, in 1866 Jefferies Williamson superseded him, and the latter, in 1867, gave place to George Eppright, who had formerly been the host of the Newtown Square Inn In 1869, David Rickabaugh was the landlord of the Fox Chase, as also in 1870, since which date it disappeared from the licensed public-houses of Delaware County

---

BIOGRAPHICAL SKETCHES.

DAVIS BEAUMONT

William Beaumont, the father of the subject of this biographical sketch, married Hannah Davis, of Newtown township, Delaware Co Among their children was Davis, born in 1790, who, at the age of two years, removed to Newtown Square, where his father purchased the property embracing the hotel and store He received an excellent English education, which was made available in later life, and acquired a reputation as an expert penman At the age of twenty-one, after having rendered valuable assistance to his father in his various business pursuits, he removed to Philadelphia, and for about three years engaged in teaching On returning again to Newtown he became proprietor of the store at the "Square," where he remained until his marriage, in 1816, to Elizabeth Cochran (sister of the wife of the late William Black), of Chester, Delaware Co, whose four children all died in infancy In 1845 he was again married, to Abbie West, daughter of Isaac and Hannah West, of West Manor township, Chester Co To this marriage were born two daughters Ella is the wife of Garrett Williamson, son of Garrett and Hannah Williamson, of Marple township, whose children are Davis B (named after his grandfather), Herman, Clinton, Elbert, and Ira Irene, the youngest daughter of Mr and Mrs Beaumont, died at the age of seven years Mr Beaumont, after his first marriage, purchased a farm in Upper Darby township, where he remained until the death of Mrs Beaumont, in 1843 On the death of his father the hotel and store at Newtown Square were bequeathed to him, the former property having been held by the family for a period of seventy four years He also purchased, in 1848, a farm in the same township, which is now the residence of his widow He

L. Beaumont

Eng.d by A.H. Ritchie.

Thomas P. Bartram

James Dunwoody

Wm Rhoads

was in politics a strong Republican, never once missing a vote, and although frequently tendered office, declined all others than that of county commissioner He was well informed in all the topics of the day, a constant reader, and until his death keen of perception and exceedingly social, thereby winning and retaining many friends He died Dec 17, 1870, and was buried with his parents in the Newtown Friends' burial-ground

THOMAS P BARTRAM

John Bartram, who was of English extraction and the grandfather of the subject of this biography, married Phœbe Lobb, to whom were born, among other children, a son, Samuel, in Darby township, during the year 1800 He was united in marriage to Massey Pratt, daughter of Thomas Pratt, of Marple township, whose children were William (married to Annie, daughter of Lewis Garrett, of Radnor township), Hannah (Mrs Stephen Ogden), and Thomas P The latter was born Sept 14, 1827, in Darby township, and in early youth removed to Marple township, where he enjoyed such advantages of education as the school of the district afforded, and afterwards became a pupil of the popular boarding-school at Westtown He returned to the farm, and until his twenty-sixth year assisted in its cultivation In 1855 he married Orpha Ann Heycock, daughter of Jesse Heycock, of Newtown Two years later Mr Bartram purchased the farm in Newtown, on which he at present resides, and has since that date devoted his energies to its improvement This has engaged all his time and attention, and left little leisure for participation in matters of a public character He is in his political predilection a Republican, and, though not an active representative of the party, has served the township both in the capacity of school director and supervisor He is in religion a Friend, and member of the Newtown Friends' Meeting.

JAMES DUNWOODY

James Dunwoody was born in West Whiteland, Chester Co , Pa , on Aug 21, 1812, on the farm where three generations of his ancestors had lived While still a boy, his parents moved to Westtown He married, March 12, 1840, Hannah, daughter of William Hood , continuing for a few years to manage the farm of his father But in 1849 he bought and removed to the farm of his father-in-law, in Newtown, Delaware Co Here he passed the remainder of his life, proving by his unwavering attachment to the right an influence for good in the community He died March 8, 1883, leaving five sons,—William H , Charles, John, E Evans, and J. Penrose

WILLIAM RHOADS

William Rhoads, the son of Joseph and Mary Rhoads, and the youngest of seven children, was born in Marple township, on the 2d of April, 1797 After receiving an English education at John Cornley's boarding-school, at Burlington, and at Westtown, he engaged in active farm labor, and married Annie P Levis, daughter of William and Esther Levis, of Springfield township, on the 14th of March, 1822 Their children are George, William, Esther L (Mrs Nathan Garrett), Phebe, Mary Ashbridge (Mrs Hibberd Yarnall), Anna, and Elizabeth L (who is deceased) Mr Rhoads, on his marriage, removed to the farm in Newtown township, which is now the residence of his widow, and until his death, on the 27th of February, 1863, was engaged in the healthful pursuits of a farmer Mr Rhoads, as a Whig and Republican, held various public offices in the township, but cared little for the exciting scenes of political life He was president, from the date of construction until his death, of the West Chester and Philadelphia Turnpike Company He wielded a commanding influence in the township as a man of integrity, judgment, and intelligence His religion was that of the Orthodox Society of Friends, of which he was a prominent member

JESSE LEEDOM

Isaac Leedom, the father of Jesse, who was of English descent, was a former resident of Bucks County, Pa , from whence he removed to Radnor, and engaged in the labor attending the cultivation of a farm He married Ann Jones, of Merion township, Montgomery Co , and had children,—John, Jesse, Silas, George, and Isaac By a second marriage to Rebecca Matlack were born children,—Ann, Elizabeth, Benedict, William, Sidney, Mary, and Enoch The death of Mr Leedom occurred on the 12th of March, 1848 His son, Jesse, was born June 23, 1801, in Radnor township, Delaware Co , where his youth was spent. At the age of sixteen he left home with a view to acquiring in Chester County the trade of a miller Having become proficient in this trade, he labored for a while as a journeyman, and later rented a mill Mr Leedom continued his vocation for many years, having both leased and purchased milling property In 1846 he secured a farm in the same county, popularly known as "the White Horse farm," and two years later became owner of the Mineral Spring farm in Newtown township, Delaware Co , where he continued to reside and cultivate the land until his death on the 4th of August, 1883 He married on the 19th of November, 1835, Elizabeth Williamson, daughter of Enos and Sarah Williamson Their children are Sarah Ann (Mrs J H Thomas, of Media), Hannah E , J Jones, Margaret L , Enos W (deceased), and E Mary (Mrs. Alfred Palmer, of Steelton, Pa) Mr. Leedom evinced a keen intelligence in the discussion of the political questions of the day as on all subjects of current interest Though a pronounced Whig in politics, and on the organization of the Republican party one of its ardent adherents, he never sought or held office. He was during his later life an enlightened reader of the most substantial literature, and gifted with keen powers of perception. This he found a source of much pleasure and profit as advancing years deprived him of other means of enjoyment. He was in religion reared in the faith of the society of Friends. Mrs. Leedom's death occurred on the 7th of March, 1883, but a few months prior to that of her husband.

CHAPTER XLIX

NETHER PROVIDENCE TOWNSHIP

THE territory now constituting the townships of Nether and Upper Providence was one of the early municipal divisions of the county. The origin of the name, as it relates to the district, is unknown, although it has been conjectured, doubtless correctly, that it was bestowed by "some of the early immigrants, and was given as a manifestation of their safe deliverance from the perils they had encountered in crossing the ocean."[1] The first reference to Providence occurred at the court held Fifth month 1, 1683, when Richard Crosby and Andrew Nelson were appointed collectors of the "levie for Defraying the charges of the Cort-House and Prison att Chester." At the same court Thomas Nossiter was appointed constable for Providence. Three months thereafter, at the court held Eighth month 17, 1683, "the Inhabitance of Providence make their application for a highway leading to the town of Chester." Seventeen persons composed "the Grand Jury empanelled to look out a convenient highway leading from Providence to Chester," and the court ordered "that the Grand Jury doe meet on the 22nd instance at Thomas Nossiter's, then to consider the premises." Nossiter then had settled on a tract of two hundred acres between the present Ridley bridge and Butler's Lane, on the Providence great road. The latter highway was probably laid out in the early spring of 1684. The first record of the division of Providence into Nether and Upper Providence occurs in the minutes of Chester Friends' Meeting, on the "13th of ye 8th month, 1690."

For over sixty years after Nether Providence is thus distinctly mentioned the southern line of the township was not that which it is at this present time, for Ridley township contained within its boundaries all that part of Nether Providence included in a line drawn from Strath Haven, on Crum Creek, to the wayside fountains on the Great Providence road, and thence to Dutton's edge-tool works on Ridley Creek. The inconvenience of this separation from the rest of Ridley township by the creeks mentioned was such that at length the owners of the real estate within the boundaries designated presented a petition to court, which was favorably acted on by the justice, and the prayer of the petitioners allowed. The petition was as follows:

"Chester ss.

"*To the Honourable Justices of the Court of Genll Quarter Sessions of the Peace, to be held at Chester the Twenty seventh day of February, Anno Domini, 1753.*

"The petition of John Sharpless, Daniel Sharpless, Isaac Weaver, and Thomas Swayne, inhabitants of the Westermost part of Ridley Township, in the County of Chester aforesaid,

"Humbly Showeth,

"That your Petitioners live in a very remote Part of the township of Ridley, between Crum and Ridley Creeks joining to the Townships of Nether Providence far from the Principal Part of the inhabitants of the said township.

"That your Petitioners labour under very Great Hardships in being obliged, when warned by the Supervisors, to travel as far as the township of lower Darby to repair and amend the highways thereabouts, itt being upward of five miles from the nearest of your Petitioners Plantations, when the Inhabitants of the other end of the said township Seldom or never Come to repair the said Roads on that End of the Township where your Petitioners dwell, and also are at very Great inconveniency in being obliged to meet at the White horse tavern to Consult about any affairs Relative to the said Township.

"Your Petitioners therefore Pray that your Honours would be Pleased to take your Petitioners Case into Consideration and order that all that part of Ridley Township aforesaid lying to the Westward of the Eastermost line of the land late of Thomas Dell, the Elder, & Thomas Dell, ye younger, deceasd, may be Joined to the Township of Nether Providence, and that the same may Always hereafter be deemed Taken and Esteemed to be part of the said Township of Nether Providence and your Petitioners as in Duty Bound Shall Pray."

In describing the early settlement in Nether Providence it is proposed to ignore the fact that any portion of the township was ever part of Ridley. At the southern extremity of Nether Providence, on Eighth month 20, 1683, John Nixon took up seventy-five acres, which estate was known as "Stanfield," and doubtless settled there. Richard Nixon is said to have emigrated from Wexford, Ireland, in the early part of the eighteenth century, but inasmuch as Richard Nixon was the father of Col. John Nixon, who was born in Chester County, it is very probable that Richard was a son or near relative of John Nixon, of Stanfield. Col. John Nixon was a noted merchant of Philadelphia, and was one of the founders, in 1770, of the Society of Friendly Sons of St. Patrick. He was during the Revolution one of the Committee of Safety, often acting as chairman of that body. He was lieutenant-colonel of the Third Pennsylvania Battalion in the defense of the Delaware River in 1776–77. He it was who on the 8th of July, 1776, read for the first time to the people of Philadelphia the Declaration of Independence from the platform of the observatory erected in 1769 in State-House yard to observe the transit of Venus. John Nixon, the settler, on Third month 4, 1691, sold the plantation to John Parker, and in 1700 he conveyed the estate to Samuel Carpenter and Caleb Pusey. James Irving and William T. Crook now own part of this tract. Above this land were two hundred acres, known as "Smallgaine," which was taken on rent by Thomas Nossiter, who settled on this tract in 1678. He was not a Friend

[1] Smith's "History of Delaware County," p. 387.

Jesse Leedom

In 1683 he was appointed the first constable of Providence, although it appears he did not live in the township. This plantation, beginning on its northwestern limits, a short distance above the present bridge on the Providence road, ran on a straight northeasterly line across the township to a point a short distance below Strath Haven, on Crump Kill or Crum Creek. In Twelfth month, 1684, Nossiter conveyed this land to Walter Faucett, who was an eminent Friend and an early tavern-keeper in Ridley.

Above the Faucett tract, Nossiter had also two hundred acres, which extended from Strath Haven in a southwest course directly across the township to Ridley Creek. On Sept. 12, 1682, Nossiter conveyed this estate to John Sharpless. The latter came from Ratherton, in Cheshire, England, accompanied by his wife, Ann (they were then in middle life), and their children, landing at Chester on the 14th of Sixth month, 1682, two months prior to the arrival of William Penn. The family history, published in 1816, states that they settled on Ridley Creek, about two miles northwest from Chester, "where they fell a large tree, and took shelter among the boughs thereof about six weeks, in which time they built a cabin against a rock, which answered for their chimney-back, and now contains the date of the year when the cabin was built, viz., 1682, in which they dwelt about twenty years, and where they all died, except the mother and three sons, in which time Joseph learned the trade of house-carpenter, and when of age built the dwelling-house, which is now standing, and occupied by one of their descendants. Part of the original floors are still in use, being fastened down with wooden pins of about an inch in diameter instead of nails. It is a sizable two-story dwelling, the walls of stone." On Thursday, Aug. 24, 1882, the descendants of John and Ann Sharpless, to the number of two thousand seven hundred, held a bi-centennial reunion at the old homestead. Among the distinguished visitors was the venerable Bishop William L. Green, of Mississippi, who was then in his eighty-fifth year. He was the eldest (while an infant daughter of Amelia M. Hoopes, then six months old, was the youngest) descendant of John Sharpless at the old homestead on that occasion. Immediately above this tract John Sharpless took up one hundred and eighty acres of land, in three parcels, under his purchase of one thousand acres from William Penn, which he had bought before leaving England. These three tracts extend from Ridley Creek to Providence great road. Above the last-mentioned land of John Sharpless, Joshua Hastings took up three hundred and ninety acres; but the lower part, containing one hundred and forty acres, was taken by John Sharpless. The upper part, extending from Ridley Creek to Providence road, on May 19, 1702, was purchased by Robert Vernon, who conveyed it, November 24th of the same year, to John Vernon and Sarah, his wife. Robert Vernon came from Stoke, in Cheshire, England, and conveyed this estate to his son, John, at the time designated. Above this tract was a plot of two hundred and fifty acres, surveyed to Thomas Vernon, Tenth month 16, 1702. He came from Stanthorne, county palatine of Chester, England, in 1682, accompanied by his brothers, Randal and Robert. Thomas Vernon was the grandfather of Nathaniel Vernon, the noted Tory sheriff of Chester County during the Revolution. The property of Thomas Vernon extended on the Providence road a short distance above Hinkson's Corners. Randal Vernon settled on a tract of two hundred and ninety-eight acres lying north of Thomas Vernon's land. Todmorden is at the lower end of this plantation, and the south branch of Vernon's Run is almost entirely within its boundaries. He was from "Sandyway," Cheshire, England. In 1687 he was a member of the Provincial Assembly, and died at this plantation in 1725, in his eighty-fifth year. The homestead passed to Joseph Vernon. Above Randal Vernon's land Robert Vernon took up, Seventh month 23, 1682, three hundred and fifty acres, which extended along Ridley Creek to Upper Providence line, its eastern boundary being the Providence road. On the tract was the main stem of Vernon Run, and almost all that part of Media borough in Nether Providence is located on the original Robert Vernon estate. Early in 1709/10, just before his death, he conveyed the homestead tract and the brick messuage thereon to his son, Jacob Vernon.

At the extreme northern line of the township, east of the Providence road and extending to Crum Creek, was a tract of three hundred and eighty acres, which land Thomas Minshall purchased from Penn before he came to the province, and it was assigned to Minshall, March 21–22, 1681. He was a brother-in-law of Randall Vernon, his sister Elinor having married the latter. His dwelling was near Providence Friends' meeting-house, the land being given by Thomas Minshall to the society to erect the latter building on. The farm of William L. Green is on the original homestead, and the estate of Edgar Farnum, J. Howard Lewis, and others, including the bend in Crum Creek on which is the paper-mill of J. Howard Lewis, are located on this tract. Directly south of the Minshall tract, and extending from the Providence road to Crum Creek, was surveyed to Joseph Powell, Second month 9, 1682, one hundred and twenty acres. The plantation subsequently passed to John Sharpless by purchase in 1700. Directly south of this lot, and extending to Hinkson's Corners, John Sharpless took up three hundred and thirty acres, Eighth month 24, 1682, part of his one-thousand-acre purchase, which in 1696 was conveyed to his son, James Sharpless. South of this plantation Thomas Powell received one hundred and seventy-two acres, part of his purchase before leaving England. He was a Friend, but became a member of the Church of England, and by will gave lots in Chester "lying over against the church" for a parsonage. The present

St Paul's Church is erected on the ground he donated Still going south, on March 21-22, 1681, John Edge took up one hundred and twenty-five acres of land, which by a subsequent survey proved to contain a larger number of acres, extending from Providence road to Crum Creek John Edge, who came from St Andrew's, Holborne, in the county of Middlesex, in England, having been persecuted for conscience' sake in his native land, settled on this tract, where he died in 1711 William and Mary Swafler, in 1684, settled in Nether Providence, on a plantation of one hundred and eighty acres, which was south of the Edge lands, and extended from Providence road to Crum Creek, and bounded on the south by the John Sharpless homestead tract, already mentioned William Swaffer resided on this land until his death, in 1720 This property passed to Peter Dick in 1732 Dick's Run flows in a northwesterly direction, and east of Providence road, almost to the Friends' meeting-house at the northern limits of the township From Peter Dick was descended Roger Dicks, of Nether Providence, a noted public Friend, who died Dec 29, 1808

The Vernon family were conspicuous during the Revolution Nathaniel Vernon, at the breaking out of the war, was sheriff of Chester County, was an outspoken advocate of the cause of the crown, and subsequently became so offensive to the colonial authorities that he was declared a traitor, as was his son, Nathaniel Vernon, Jr The father fled to the protection of the English army when the latter captured Philadelphia, while the son, Nathaniel, joined the Tory light troops, commanded by Jacob Jones Another son took sides with the Continentals On one occasion, it is recorded, while the British occupied Philadelphia, Frederick, who was a major in the American army, obtained permission to visit his wife and family in Nether Providence His brother, Nathaniel, by some means learned of his presence at home, and one night the Tory light-horse marched from Philadelphia to Nether Providence, intending to capture Maj Vernon The troops surrounded the house Nathaniel entered the dwelling, and was about to ascend to the upper rooms, when Frederick, who was aroused by the noise, halted him from the head of the stairs, where he stood armed with a pistol Nathaniel made known his business, that he had come to take him prisoner, that he must submit, for the troops had surrounded the house He also informed him that the British must conquer, but that if he would join the English army he would be promoted to office in the colony He had come for his welfare, and that he must surrender Frederick replied that he would never submit, that the British could not take him, and that if his brother or any other person attempted to ascend the stairs he would shoot, only as a dead man could they capture him Nathaniel Vernon, finding his brother so determined, withdrew his troops, and Frederick remained true to the cause he had espoused At the conclusion of the war he was one of the founders of the Society of the Cincinnati, and died in Nether Providence at an advanced age Job Vernon, a cousin of Maj Vernon, a "captain in the Revolution, was born in Lower Providence about the year 1750 He entered the army at the commencement of the Revolutionary war, and served faithfully and without intermission until its termination and the disbanding of the army His name appears in the lists printed by order of Congress of officers who served to the end of the war, and thereby acquired the right to half-pay and bounty lands, and also as one of the founders of the Society of the Cincinnati He was commissioned ensign in Capt Thomas Church's company of Col Anthony Wayne's Pennsylvania battalion, Jan 5, 1776, and was promoted to be lieutenant in Capt Thomas Robinson's company of the same battalion, Oct 1, 1776 In 1779 and 1780 he was paymaster of the Fifth Pennsylvania Regiment, which was then commanded by Col Francis Johnston, and in which he also held the commission of captain This regiment was attached to the Army of the North, and seems to have participated in all its services up to the storming of Stony Point Capt Vernon died in Concord township about the year 1810 From fragments of his accounts, and other documents in the possession of a relative, he seems to have been an intimate acquaintance and favorite of Gen Wayne, and a brave and judicious officer"[1]

On Dec 31, 1783, the Supreme Executive Council acknowledged a deed to William Kerlin for sixty acres of land in Nether Providence, late the estate of Gideon Vernon, an attainted traitor

William L Green, of Nether Providence, is the owner of an old pewter plate, which is a relic of colonial times, and of the war of independence Scratched on the bottom of the platter is the date 1711 During the battle of Brandywine this plate was in the possession of William Lamborn, of Kennett Square, the grandfather of the present owner All the plates and valuables belonging to the people of the neighborhood were seized by the British soldiers, and, in order to save the old pewter plate, Lamborn hid it in a tub of swill, where it remained until the enemy had marched away from the neighborhood

Taxables—In 1715 the following persons were returned as taxables in Nether Providence

James Sharpless, Joseph Sharpless, Isaac Minshall, Jacob Vernon, Joseph Vernon, Thomas Vernon, John Vernon, Henry Hastings, William Swafer, Jacob Edge, John Powell

In 1799 the following taxables were returned in the township

Jacob Benninghove (tobacconist), Pierre Crosby, Joseph Dicks, Jr, Roger Dicks, Frederick Dicks, William Edwards, Joshua Ely, Isaac Engle (carpenter), Henry Forrest, Jacob Fulke, James Ham, Thomas Hinkson, James Hinkson (wheelwright), John Keith, William Kerlin, Thomas Leiper (tobacconist), John Levis, Richard Nuzum (blacksmith), Thomas Nuzum, George Perkins, Mahlon Parsons, William Paist, Daniel Sharpless (saw mill, grist mill, fulling mill), Philip Summel (tobac-

[1] Smith's "History of Delaware County," p. 509

conist), William Sankey (weaver), William Shepherd, John Stephenson, Edward Tilghman, Seth Thomas (county treasurer), Mary Vernon, John Vernon (blacksmith), Jonathan Vernon, Jonathan Worrell, James Wood, James Wood, Jr, Josiah Wilkinson, John Worrell, Uriah Wilson, William Waterhouse

Inmates—Adam Britz (snuff maker), George Brown, James Beatty, Matthias Cooper (snuff maker) John Cornish, Job Dicks, Joseph Dickinson (wheelwright), Joseph Edwards (mason), Charles Gallager, Jonah Harding (snuff maker), William Johnston (mason), Andrew Johnston (tailor), *Michael Kewan, John Kelly, William Long (cooper)*, John Lindsey, Duncan McArthur (carpenter), James Moore (stone cutter), Philip Murphy, Richard Parsons, Ellis Roberts, John Rogers, Andrew Turton, Woodward Vernon, John Valentine, Peter Worrell, Rason Wood, John Wilkinson, Hugh Wilson, Richard Wilson, Jonas Young

Single Freemen—John Cain, Nathan Dicks (mason), Murtough Dowland, Francis Elliot (snuff maker), Cornelius Green, John Green, George Hinkson (millwright), John L Ham, Daniel Humphrey, Isaac Johnston (carpenter), Bryce Miller (tailor), Benjamin Miller, Thomas Morgan, George Nuzum, Abraham Philips (shop keeper), Francis Russell, James Sharpless (shop keeper), Isaac Sharpless (fuller), Samuel Sloan (stone-cutter), John Wright (superintendent), Joel Lane (blacksmith), Jonathan Vernon, Jr, Hugh Miskelly

The following is a list of justices of the peace for Nether Providence

John Crosly	Aug 30, 1791
Joel Willis	Aug 30, 1791
Davis Bevan	Aug 19, 1794.
Miles Macarty	April 13, 1796
Elisha Price	April 15, 1796
William Martin	Aug 9, 1797
Isaac Eyre	Oct. 12, 1798
Nicholas Fairlamb	Dec 6, 1798
Aaron Morton	May 3, 1799
Philip Painter	May 20, 1800
Thomas Hinkson	May 20, 1800
John Pearson	June 21, 1802
James Withey	July 4, 1806
Jacob Edwards	Jan 1, 1807
John Caldwell	Nov 15, 1814
Joseph Walker	Feb. 3, 1820
Samuel Smith	March 12, 1822
David Marshall	March 3, 1824.
George W Bartram	June 3, 1824
Benjamin F Johnson	Oct 25, 1825
Abraham Kerlin	June 7, 1830
Samuel T Walker	Nov 11 1831
John Afflick	June 6, 1834
Jonathan P Worrall	March 5, 1835
Samuel Shaw	Nov 18, 1835
William Martin	June 10, 1836
William Eyre	Dec 21, 1838
George W Bartram	Sept 23, 1839
John Afflick	April 14, 1840
John G Johnson	April 14, 1840
John Afflick	April 15, 1845
John G Johnson	April 15, 1845
John Afflick	April 9, 1850
J Gifford Johnson	April 9, 1850
John G Johnson	April 10, 1855
John Afflick	April 10, 1855
John Afflick	April 10, 1860
John G Johnson	April 10 1860
John Afflick	April 18, 1865
John Atkinson	April 22, 1868
Thomas Palmer	April 15, 1873
Charles L Leiper	April 24, 1874
George W Rigby	April 24, 1874
George W Trainor	April 10, 1882

Providence Friends' Meeting-House.—The first mention of a Friends' Meeting in Providence occurs in the minutes of Chester Quarterly Meeting, Third month, 1696, when it was agreed to settle a meeting "at Thomas Minshall's every First and Fourth day" On Twelfth month 6, 1698/9, Friends belonging to Thomas Minshall's meeting proposed to build a meeting-house at the burying-ground of Thomas Powell, which would have located the building near the Media reservoir, on Providence road, in Upper Providence The Quarterly Meeting deferred the consideration of the matter, but the project doubtless met with some opposition, for it is recorded, "It being the sense of this meeting that no meeting-house be hereafter built upon any new situation without yᵉ advise & consent of the quarterly meeting" However, Caleb Pusey, Thomas Worth, John Hood, George Pierce, Nicholas Pyle, and Robert Carter were appointed "to view & consider of the most convenient place where to sett the above proposed meeting-house" On Third month 1, 1699, the committee stated "according to the order & request of yᵉ Last quarterly meeting, The friends appointed to inspect into & consider of the most convenient place to build the meeting-house, to answer that of Tho Minshall's, Do make returu under their hands that it is their sense that at the farthest end of Thomas Minshall's Land, by yᵉ high roade side, is the most Convenient place for that service, & accordingly this meeting approves of yᵉ same" The land on which this meeting-house was built was given for that purpose by Thomas Minshall The first house was a log structure The building was completed in the summer of 1700, for on 5th day of Sixth month (August), in that year, the Quarterly Meeting "Ordered that the next Quarterly meeting be held at the new meeting-house in Nether Providence" On Ninth month 4, 1700, the First day and week day meeting was ordered to be removed from Thomas Minshall's to the "meeting-house," and on Twelfth month 12, 1701, the meeting at Randal Vernon's was also "removed to the new meeting-house"

At Providence meeting-house, Second month 5, 1703, Walter Faucitt was dealt with by the meeting, the charges being set forth in the following extract from the quaint minutes

"This meeting having Duly taken into their Consideration the disorderly practis of Samuel Levis in keeping on his hatt whilst Walter Faucitt was in prayer, att a monthly meeting att Robert Vernon's, on the 11th month Last, therefore, the meeting doth appoint Joseph Baker and Paul Sanders to spake to him and Indaver to bring him to a sence of his disorder, and that hee do acknowledg the same to the satisfaction of this meeting, which if he doth not promise to do, then to order him to appear at the next monthly meeting"

At a quarterly meeting in this house, held Twelfth month 26, 1704, the following extract from the minutes shows that Henry Hollingsworth had acted in such a manner as to cause Friends to deal with him. The old record states

"Whereas, Henry Holingsworth has Refused from time to time to answer the sence and Judgment of the meeting hold att this place the 30th of the 8th mo Last past, and doth yett Refuse so to do, and in our meetings of Business have uttered verey unsavery expressions and unjustifiable speaches, partiqualarly att our Last mo meeting, speaking of the meeting's proceedings against him for his disorder, hee said that Bonnor and Winchester would have been ashamed of such actions, and that it was like the Cuting off the Lord Stafford's head, also publickly Calling our ancient friend Randall Vernon old pimp, little pimp, & Sott, &c., with other unsavory expressions to Tedious and Rediculas heare to bee mentioned, as also telling a former monthly meeting that they acted like Jesuits, which all tended to scandalize friends, for all which, with much more, this meeting finds a Nesesaty upon them to testifie and declare, and do hereby Testifie and Declare, Henry Hollingsworth to be out of the Unity of this meeting and do disown him to be of our peacable society and Christian Comunion Until hee Repent and acknowledg his said abuses to the satisfaction of this meeting, which that hee may so do is our true and Heartey desire"

At this meeting-house, on Eighth month 27, 1707, William Thomas, a Friend of Newtown, made acknowledgment, viz, "Dear Friends, I happened to Goe to the Buriall of one of my neighbour's Children, one of the Separates, and oue of them Going to prayer, I unadvisedly took off my hatt with them, which I acknowledge to be a Scandall to the truth which I make profession of, therefore am sorry for itt"

In 1727 a stone addition was made to the log building, and in 1753 the old end, being the remains of the old original structure, was removed, and in its place a stone addition was made to the stone part erected in 1727, which now forms the present meeting-house

On Friday, Jan 14, 1831, a terrific snow-storm began in Delaware County, continuing through all the next day (Saturday) The roads were blockaded almost even with the fences Court began on Monday, January 17th, but travel was so interrupted that Judge Darlington could not reach the county, and although Associate Judge Engle charged the grand jury, on account of the absence of witnesses and jurors very little was done, the court adjourning on Wednesday afternoon On the evening of Friday, January 14th, when the storm was raging, Jonathan Clayton and his cousin started from Chester to go home "But that home they were never more to see A person passing next morning between the Providence school-house and meeting-house was attacked by a dog Perceiving something unusual in the manner of the animal, he was led to discover the body of a man, the face only of which was above the snow The body was that of the unfortunate Jonathan Clayton"[1]

Clayton was the second person in Nether Providence of whom we have record that had died of exposure On Saturday, Nov 1, 1823, Nancy May, an intemperate woman, lay down by the roadside on Providence road, and was frozen to death

Union Methodist Episcopal Church.—A class was organized in the neighborhood of Hinkson's Corners about 1812, which was composed of persons residing in Nether Providence and surrounding townships On the 28th of January, 1813, a lot containing eighty square perches of land, situate on the northwest side of a public road leading through Nether Providence to Edgmont great road, was purchased of Benjamin Houlston for one hundred and ten dollars The trustees to whom the deed was made were William Palmer, of Aston, Edward Levis and William Coffman, of Springfield, Joseph Dicks and John Esray, of Nether Providence, Christopher Snyder and Rudolph Temple, of Springfield, Caspar Coffman, of Nether Providence, and William Morris, of Upper Providence On this lot the congregation erected the present stone church, and in the burial-ground adjoining lie many of the early worshipers in the old sanctuary On Saturday, Dec 8, 1879, while the sexton of the church was digging a grave in the cemetery of the church, the body of a new born infant was exhumed, the remains having been placed in a common box, such as is used to pack canned goods, and deposited secretly in the graveyard Considerable excitement was aroused in the neighborhood, an inquest was held, but nothing further resulted from the investigation A few years ago the old building was repaired and enlarged The church was under the same charge with Mount Hope Church, and both were in Village Green Circuit This church, with South Media Chapel, were erected as a station in March, 1877, and as a single station in 1878 The pastors from that time have been Revs N. Turner, George Alcorn, and Albert Hood, who is the present pastor. The church has forty-eight members and a Sunday-school of sixty pupils, of which George W. Pastlett is superintendent

Presbyterian Church at Todmorton—In 1850 William T Crook, of Crookville, erected a Presbyterian Church in that locality, for the convenience of the employés in his factory, then known as the Crookville Mills The building, which cost ten thousand dollars, is seventy-five feet in length, forty feet in width, with a tower twelve feet square which rises to the height of eighty feet In the belfry is a bell weighing seven hundred pounds The lower floor is arranged for school-, lecture-, and reading-rooms The church was dedicated Sept 30, 1850, services being conducted on that occasion by the Rev Dr McDowell, of Philadelphia, and the Rev N Heston, of Chester Soon after Rev Jacob D Dudley was called to the pastorate of the church, and remained in charge until 1855, when he was succeeded by the Rev Dr Robert Crawford, who was installed November 24th of that year He remained for five years, since which time the church has been without a regular pastor The Rev Dr James W Dale, of Media, and other clergymen at various times conducted services in the church, but at the present time the building is not used for religious exercises

Schools—The first school of which any information has been obtained in Nether Providence was kept in a stone house erected on a lot at what is now Hinkson's Corners The lot was purchased Feb 10, 1810, of Benjamin Houlston The inhabitants of the township selected Samuel Crosley, Seth Thomas, James Ham, Henry Forrest, and James Hinkson to act as trustees To these trustees this lot of thirty-six square perches was granted in trust "for the use of a school by the name of a Union school and for no other use" This school was maintained under the direction of these trustees until April 26, 1841, when Henry Forrest, one of the original trustees, conveyed the property to the school directors of the township In January, 1861, the property was transferred by the directors to the school district, and at the same time the latter purchased thirty-six square perches of land adjoining In June, 1866, the old

[1] Hazard's Register, vol vii p 248

house was torn down and the present school-house was built In 1881 an addition was made to it One of the early teachers was Caleb Peirce, a noted pedagogue, who taught there in 1821

In 1812, the Friends near what is now the borough of Media built a school-house on their land School was continued there until Aug 29, 1840, when a lot was purchased of Abel Green and a school-house erected, which is still standing, but is now in the borough of Media When the schools were organized in Media, in 1856, this house was used jointly for a short time, and finally came into possession of the borough, by whom it was sold to William F Green, who converted it into a dwelling-house On the 25th of July, 1857, the township, being without a school in that section, purchased the present fifty-five square perches of land of James C Haswell, a part of the Henry Forrest property, and the present brick house was erected at Briggsville

On Aug 31, 1839, the residents in the lower part of the township petitioned for a school-house to be located in that section The request was acceded to and the present school-house was erected Dec 17, 1840, a lot was purchased of Henry Sharpless at Pleasant Hill, on which a stone house was built and used until 1870, when a half-acre of land adjoining was purchased and the present stone school-house erected, at a cost of three thousand one hundred dollars In addition to the school-house mentioned is the one at Todmorton After the property now known as Todmorton passed to the possession of William T Crook, the number of persons employed there made it necessary that a school should be located in that neighborhood The directors, however, refused to establish one, thereupon application was made to the Legislature, and the result was the act of April 9, 1849, which erected certain territory in Chester and Nether Providence township into a separate district by the title of Crookville School District William T Crook had erected a Presbyterian Church at his mills and fitted a room in the lower story of the church as a school-room A school has been maintained there until the present time After the mills came into possession of Samuel Bancroft the name of the district was changed to Todmorden

During the first years this act went into effect the school directors of Nether Providence refused to recognize it as valid, and still demanded payment to them of school taxes by the residents of Crookville William T Crook refused to pay, and five of his cows were destrained by the constable on a warrant issued by the directors of the township A public meeting of the people of Crookville was held on Feb. 25, 1850, and a series of resolutions were adopted setting forth the facts, together with sarcastic resolutions, in which they announced their determination to bring suit against the school directors of Nether Providence for the "outrage," and finally declared that they "would not willingly let die to fame" those "illustrious friends of education, the school directors of Nether Providence," and they therefore attached the names of the then directors Finally, after legal proceeding, both criminal and civil, had been resorted to, the tempest wasted itself, but Crookville School District had come to stay

After Simeon Lord rented the Avondale Mills, about 1847, the employés petitioned for a school-house at that locality A stone building one story high was erected, and was used until after 1861, when it was abandoned, and is now in ruins It is on the road in the hollow below the old paper- and snuff-mills on Ridley Creek

About 1824, Isaac L Weaver was a teacher at the Friends' school-house William L Green and Davis Garrett were pupils there Mr Green says his first recollection of the school is that on his first day he fell asleep, and rolled off the seat to the floor Davis Garrett, on going home from his first day, told his people he was not going there any more, the teacher had no milk and did not keep a cow

The township elected trustees under the act of 1804 for many years The only record, however, occurs March 18, 1825, when John Richards, Abel Green, and Henry Sharpless were elected After the enactment of the public school law, in 1834, the court appointed as school inspectors Eli D Peirce and Charles M Leiper to act until the school directors were chosen at the election in September of that year The first meeting of the board of directors after the election took place on the 27th day of September, 1834

A meeting of citizens of Nether Providence was held Eleventh month 20, 1834, at the house of Isaac Hall, to vote on the question of raising funds in addition to that appropriated by the school delegate at the county meeting The money received that year by the township from the State and county appropriations amounted to $767 39 The public schools in Nether Providence were not opened until 1836, the board of directors, at a meeting held Sixth month 4, 1836, deciding that the schools should begin on the "2nd day, the 13th of the present month" The first teacher employed to preside over the Union School was William Ogden, his salary being seventy-five dollars per quarter On Fourth month 29, 1837, the board of directors agree that Richard Worrall should continue to teach at the Upper School (Green's), and Lydia Burchell at the Union School The latter, however, in about a month resigned, and Samuel Erskine was appointed in her stead

The following is a list of school directors since 1840, as obtained from the records at Media

1840, Cyrus Lewis, James Riddle, 1842, Jacob Byre, Sr, Alvin H Parker, 1843, George W Rigby, James Dicks, 1844, Jonathan Vernon, Henry Sharpless, 1845, James Riddle, Jacob Byre, 1846, Eli Rigby, Robert Watkins, 1847, Jonathan Vernon, Henry Sharpless, 1848, Seth C Thomas, William G Vernon, 1849, Jonathan Vernon, Thomas T Williams, 1850, C. R Williamson, Eli D Pierce, 1851, Washington James, Ezekiel Loveland, 1842, John Eves, George G Fell, 1853, William H Lane, George Sharpless, 1854, W H Lane, Elton

Levis; 1855, John Eves, Edward Mokin; 1856, George Sharpless, Robert Watkins; 1857, Elbon Levis, Thomas I. Leiper, Henry F. Esrey, Edward L. Thomas; 1858, Edward Sharpless, C. D. Pierce; 1859, John Sharpless, William L. Green; 1860, E. L. Thomas, John Lord; 1861, John H. Miller, Jesse W. Byre; 1862, John Sharpless, Jacob Hibberd; 1863, E. L. Thomas, Caleb Pierce; 1864, William H. Howard, William H. Osborn; 1865, John C. Lindsay, Thomas J. Leiper; 1866, John C. Lindsay, John H. Miller; 1867, William Osborne, Robert Watkins; 1868, Jacob Byre, Washington James; 1869, George Sharpless, John H. Miller; 1870, Thomas S. Armstrong, William H. Osborne; 1871, George Sharpless, W. James; 1872, Abram Ward, Thomas Palmer; 1873, Charles Leiper, John Lindsay; 1874, George E. Howard, William H. Osborne; 1875, George W. Rigby, Abram Ward; 1876, Jacob Hibberd, George Sharpless; 1877, William Osborne, Samuel C. Lewis; 1878, Thomas Palmer, George C. Howard; 1879, T. J. Osborne, George Sharpless; 1880, William C. Burk, Jacob Hibberd; 1881, George C. Howard, Thomas Palmer; 1882, George Sharpless, John Wood; 1883, John D. White, Jacob Hibberd; 1884, Thomas Palmer, Isaac Miller.

The following are the names of school directors for the Todmorton School District:

1850, William T. Crook, Robert Buck, James W. Dale, William Lees, William Turner, Jr., Nathan Chadwick; 1851, Robert Hall, James Ourey, Elisha Gordon; 1852, Jacob D. Dudley, Thomas Crompton, James E. Holt; 1853, no report; 1854 to 1858, no report.

Todmorton District (Independent).

1859, Samuel Bancroft, William Turner, Timothy Dawson, Peter Barbour, Alexander McBride, Benjamin Lord; 1860, Thomas Cohill, Benjamin Lord; 1861, Peter Barbour, Charles E. Bourne; 1862, William Turner, Samuel Bancroft, William Carney; 1863, Samuel Bancroft, Jeremiah Craner, Timothy Dawson; 1864, Peter Barlow, Charles E. Bourne; 1865, John Hibbets, William Turner, Reuben Allen; 1866, Samuel Bancroft, John Hibbets, James Redmond, Walter Grindrod; 1867, Joseph Richards, George Latch; 1868, Reuben Allen, William Turner; 1869, Samuel Bancroft, John Lawton; 1870, George Latch, John Hibbets; 1871, no report; 1872, Samuel Bancroft, Charles Speed, Robert Cunningham; 1873, William Millener, John Dolin, M. Martin; 1874, Samuel Thomas, Frederick Heydon, Thomas Canning; 1875, no report; 1876, Samuel Bancroft, James Hamilton, Mory Lane, George Latch; 1877, Hugh McMurtie, Frederick Heydom, Samuel Thomas; 1878, Samuel Bancroft, Michael J. McMullen, Alexander Wilson; 1879, John Conway, Alexander Wilson; 1880, Samuel T. Thomas, Frederick Heydom, Thomas R. Nichols; 1881, George Dempster, Christian Woefel, William Buckley; 1882, Samuel Bancroft, William Buckley; 1883, A. Clegg, John Wilson; 1884, no report.

Mills.—In giving an account of the mills of Nether Providence the plan of following the creeks will be employed, first giving those on Ridley, and after those on Crum Creek.

Turner's Cotton-Lap Factory.—In 1813, William Beatty, an edge-tool maker, entered into an agreement with Daniel Sharpless to take the ground on the Providence road, above the present bridge, where William & Richard T. Turner now have their cotton-lap factory, free of rent for seventeen years, in consideration of building a house, shop, dam, and race there. William Beatty at this place erected a tilt- or blade-mill, which he operated successfully. In 1825 he made sixteen hundred cast-steel picking-axes, five hundred broad-axes, five hundred drawing-knives, two hundred cleavers and choppers, steeled about five hundred axes and adzes, besides manufacturing many chisels, gouges, knives, and other tools. In 1828, William Beatty moved to Crum Creek, in Springfield, above the present paper-mill of J. Howard Lewis. The title to property on Ridley Creek had passed to Henry Sharpless, and in the latter year he changed the tilt-mill to a cotton-lap factory, and rented it to Ambrose & Charles Williams. On May 10, 1867, William & Richard T. Turner, the present owners, purchased the mill and eight acres of ground, and continued there the manufacture of cotton laps.

Waterville Mills.—In 1764, on the site of this mill, on Ridley Creek, Daniel Sharpless was assessed on a saw-mill, which was in operation prior to 1755, for William Worrall (born in Marple in 1730) states in his "Recollections," published in 1820, that in that year (1755) the water in the several creeks in Delaware County was so low that the race at Daniel Sharpless' saw-mill was dry, which was never known to have occurred before that time. In 1790 he built a fulling-mill at the present Waterville, and conducted the business there until 1805, when it was operated by Isaac Sharpless. In 1810, Daniel Sharpless had again assumed control of the enterprise, and in 1815, Enos Sharpless erected a grist-mill and saw-mill, and Isaac Sharpless was operating the fulling- and woolen-factory at that place. James Schofield, in 1826, was the lessee of the Isaac Sharpless factory, and was then manufacturing fine cloths and cassimeres. At a subsequent date Daniel Sharpless was operating the mill, to be succeeded by Antrim Osborne. The latter remained at this locality until 1863, when he removed to Rose Valley Mills. Robert Hall succeeded Osborne in the factory at Waterville, where he remained until 1871, when, having purchased the Mohawk Mills, in Chester, he removed thither. In 1873 the Sharpless factory was rented to Joseph Bowers for a shoddy-mill, which he operated until 1877, when he also removed to Chester. The mill at Waterville was after that date rented to various parties until 1882, when it was destroyed by fire.

As early as 1815, Enos Sharpless had erected, perhaps a few years prior to that date, a grist-mill on Ridley Creek, the water being supplied by the same race which furnished the power to the Isaac Sharpless mill. In 1826, Enos Sharpless had at Waterville a grist-mill, saw-mill, and a cotton-factory, the latter operated by George Richardson. The machinery required by the latter at that time consisted of five carding-engines, throstles, spindles, and one mule of one hundred and eighty spindles. Richardson manufactured cotton yarn. He was succeeded in 1828 by Richard Wetherill, who subsequently moved to Manayunk. On Nov. 15, 1835, Gideon Smith, Laurence Hartshorne, and John M. Sharpless entered into partnership in the manufacture of dye-stuff and the grinding of dye-woods, and a part of the grist-mill was arranged with machinery for that purpose. Hartshorne soon retired from the firm, and in 1842 Smith also withdrew from the partnership, but still remained in the business. On Nov. 15, 1845, the grist-mill and dye-works were partly destroyed by fire. John M. Sharpless immediately rebuilt the mills, but on April 24, 1846, they were again burned.

For a second time the mills were rebuilt, and the business carried on by John M. Sharpless, at Waterville, until his death in 1875, and subsequently by his heirs until 1878. A company being formed by the name of John M. Sharpless & Co., in 1878, purchased land in Chester, on the river front, erected buildings thereon, and removed the work to the new location. The old grist-mill is still in use, now conducted by Nathan Sharpless, but the dye-wood works are standing idle.

Franklin Iron-Works.—On the 17th of December, 1795, William Vernon sold eighty-three acres of land on Ridley Creek, in Nether Providence, to Jonathan Worrell, who the same day conveyed the property to James Withey, and two days later, December 19th, the latter sold the tract to William Kerlin. The executors of Kerlin, on March 27, 1806, sold the real estate to Joshua Harlan, of Wilmington, Del., Thomas Chandler, of Nether Providence, and Samuel Sinclair, of Kennett, Chester Co. On the 13th of February, 1809, James and John L. Ham, of Nether Providence, sold to Joshua Harlan, Thomas Chandler, and Samuel Sinclair, "copartners in water-works," ten acres adjoining their other lands, with "right, liberty, and privilege of erecting a dam across the said creek [Ridley], at or near the scite of an ancient Butment on the opposite side of the creek," on land some time of Nathaniel Squibb, then of Harlan, Chandler, and Sinclair, with power to raise water in the dam five feet and six inches for the purpose of obtaining power, "to a level with an auger-hole long since bored in a rock on the creek side and no higher." It appears from this deed that a mill of some kind had many years before been erected upon this mill-seat, and had entirely gone out of existence. No account has been found of it since 1790.

On the 16th of January, 1810, Harlan, Chandler & Sinclair purchased of Nathaniel Squibb fifty acres of land in Chester township, on Ridley Creek, opposite their other lands, and on the 19th of March, 1811, sold all their lands to John Slawter, reserving one acre at the dam. Slawter was not "to dig any ditch, drain, or canal in the land conveyed . . . so as to convey any part of the water of said creek for any purpose whatsoever." In the assessment-roll of 1811, 1812, 1813, Joshua Harlan & Co. are assessed on slitting- and rolling-mill. It was operated by them with slight changes till 1821, when Thomas Chandler owned two-thirds of the property, and sold to James Cloud, who took personal charge Oct. 20, 1825. The latter bought Sinclair's third interest. Cloud continued until Jan. 16, 1826, and sold to Robert S. Johnson, then an iron merchant on Water Street, Philadelphia, "rolling-, slitting-, and saw-mill, and all lands mentioned." Frederick Johnson, a brother of Robert, was in charge of these mills for a year or two, and was followed by Nathan Roland for about two years, when John Gifford Johnson, a son of Robert, became manager, and remained as such until 1850. Philip Nelling, now of Middletown, commenced work at these rolling-mills Feb. 14, 1827, and continued there until 1848. The mills were then running night and day, with two sets of men,—four men each twelve hours. The mill rolled sheet-iron, which was all sent to Mr. Johnson's store in Philadelphia. The report of 1826 states that two to three hundred tons of iron and steel were rolled annually, and a ton of Lehigh coal was used in rolling a ton of iron. During the great flood of Aug. 5, 1843, the mills stood back some distance from the stream, but when the water came rushing down, in a few minutes the floor was flooded with eight feet of water, causing great damages. The large furnace was highly heated, and J. G. Johnson ordered Thomas D. Nelling, then a lad, to run on the roof, and go to the brick stack connected with the furnace and raise the damper. The boy declined, but Thomas Roberts, then employed in the mills, but now a farmer in Upper Chichester, drew the damper, and a moment afterward the furnace exploded, throwing a portion of the bricks through the roof of the mill. Two large frame store-houses, used for storage of band- and of scrap-iron and other articles, were washed away.

The slitting-mill was continued by Robert Johnson until about 1850, when his son, J. Gifford Johnson, changed the mill into an edge-tool factory, and rented it to Robert Beatty, who ran it till 1855. In 1853, J. G. Johnson erected the present stone grist-mill. John Beatty, the brother of Robert, in that year rented the edge-tool factory, and operated it from 1855 to 1862. About the latter date the property was sold to William C. Johnson, who conducted the grist-mill and edge-tool factory until 1870, when John Dutton and John Booth purchased the property. Booth retired after a few years, and Dutton, the present owner, carries on the milling and edge-tool works.

Todmorden Mills.—The property on which these mills are situated belonged, in 1777, to Thomas Vichers, who, on June 7th in that year, sold one hundred and sixty-two acres to Alexander Willcocks, of Philadelphia. On the 7th of December, 1791, Jacob Benninghove, a tobacconist, of Philadelphia, leased of Caleb Harrison a small parcel of land in Middletown township for nine hundred and ninety-nine years, with the "right, liberty, and privilege to erect or cause to be erected a dam on and across Ridley creek from the land of the said Jacob Benninghove, which he lately purchased from Alexander Willcocks." It appears from this deed that Benninghove had purchased of Willcocks prior to 1791; the deed, however, from Willcocks to Benninghove bears date Aug. 30, 1793, and is for one hundred and sixty-two acres of land in Nether Providence. On the same day Joshua Harrison, son of Caleb, with consent of Jacob Benninghove, canceled the lease of 1791, and a new lease was made for nine hundred and ninety-nine years for the consideration of fifty Spanish milled dollars and an annual rent of "one grain of Indian corn, if demanded, to be paid to Joshua Harrison, his heirs or assigns." This lease gave "full right to raise, repair, alter, or rebuild" a new dam on the site of the present one. It is evident that soon after the lease, in 1791, the snuff-mill was erected. It was owned and operated by Jacob Benninghove till his death, which occurred before 1811.

The residence now owned and occupied by Samuel Bancroft was built by Jacob Benninghove. For a few years after the death of Benninghove the mill was operated by James Crowley, and from 1816 by Elizabeth Benninghove, widow of Jacob, till her death. On the 5th of April, 1831, Samuel Bancroft purchased one hundred and sixty-two acres of land, and the snuff- and saw-mill then on the property, the land lying in Chester, Middletown, and Nether Providence. In the next year, 1832, Samuel Bancroft erected a stone woolen-mill, eighty-six by forty-six feet, three stories and an attic in height, in which he placed two thousand four hundred spindles and thirty looms. In 1842 the property passed to William T. Crook, who remained there twelve years. During that time he built a stone mill, one hundred by fifty feet, four stories high, for the manufacture of blankets. Ten sets of cards were put in. On Dec. 4, 1849, an accident happened at the mills, which made a deep impression on the residents of the county at that time. A young man named Hutchinson, employed by Crook, was in the fourth story of the mill engaged in hoisting cotton from a wagon. In leaning out the door to catch the tackle the bar gave way and he fell, striking on the wheel of the wagon, causing instant death. About 1854 the property was again purchased by Samuel Bancroft, who has operated it to the present time. There are three thousand spindles, thirty-five looms, and seven sets of cards in the mill.

John Bancroft, the grandfather of Samuel, was by birth an Englishman, and resided in Manchester, England, where he was a chair manufacturer. On retiring from business he removed to Penketh, near Warrington, England, where the remainder of his life was spent. He married Jane Fielding, of Todmorden Hall, to whom were born children,—John, David, and Sarah. John, whose birth occurred in Manchester, pursued the business of his father, to which was added that of a lumber merchant. He married Elizabeth Wood, of Bolton, Lancashire, England, whose children were John, Joseph, Samuel, Rebecca, Margaret, Sarah, Thomas, William, Edward, Esther, Martha, and Harvey. Mr. Bancroft, with his family, emigrated to America in 1822, and settled at Wilmington, Del., where he established mills for the manufacture of flannel goods. His son, Samuel, was born on the 25th of July, 1804, in Manchester, England. His youth was spent in Wales, where, after being educated at a Friends' school in Ackworth, Yorkshire, he engaged in farming, and continued thus employed until his emigration, with his father, to America in 1822. He at once became identified with his father's pursuits, and in 1827 repaired, with the family, to the township of Upper Providence. Here, having rented a mill, he became interested in the manufacture of flannels. In 1831, Mr. Bancroft removed to his present location, in Nether Providence, and, in conjunction with his father, erected mills in the vicinity, which he continues to operate, residing meanwhile at his attractive home—known as "Todmorden"—in the same township. He was married, June 3, 1828, to Miss Mary W., daughter of William Hallowell, of Philadelphia. Their only child was Elizabeth H. (Mrs. Thomas H. Rice), deceased. He was a second time married, on the 13th of January, 1859, to Sarah, daughter of John Patrick Hare, of Philadelphia. Mr. Bancroft affiliates with the Republican party in politics, but rarely interests himself in the political issues of the day further than by the casting of his ballot. He is identified with the First National Bank of Media as a director. In his religious belief he is a member of the society of Friends.

Rose Valley Mills.—Nicholas Stimmel, in 1789, purchased of Joseph Dicks one hundred and sixty-five acres of land on Ridley Creek, in Nether Providence. Soon after he sold eighty-two and one-half acres to James Reese, and in 1789 purchased a right for nine hundred and ninety-nine years of abutting a dam on the other side of the creek, with sufficient land to keep it in repair. In the same year Nicholas Stimmel built a snuff-mill on this property. His son, Philip, kept a tobacco-store in Philadelphia, and in 1794 the snuff-mill came into the latter's possession. He continued to operate it until April 12, 1814, when he conveyed the mill property and fifty-three acres to William Smith. On July 29, 1818, Smith sold the property to John White, by whom the place was named Rose Valley. The snuff-mill was carried on under his ownership until 1821, when he conveyed the property to William Yardley, a son-in-law, in trust for two of his children, Catharine Fields and John White. At that time it was operated by Charles Fields, who employed the mill for grinding bark used as a medicine for fevers. The introduction of quinine destroyed the business, and on April 4, 1826, the property was sold to Park Shee, and Charles Fields removed to Philadelphia, where he became a leading coffee broker. Park Shee changed the old bark into a paper-mill, and erected other buildings. The structures were part stone and part frame, two stories in height: one was thirty by forty feet, and the other forty by fifty feet. Three engines, a drying-machine, and other necessary machinery was added for the manufacture of paper. Park Shee continued the business until after 1850, when the buildings fell into disuse. On Aug. 27, 1861, the property was purchased by Antrim Osborne, and was at that time in ruins, and, as then stated, was "inhabited only by bats and owls." The next year Osborne repaired the dam and race, and built a three-story stone building, seventy-five by fifty-five feet, in which was placed twelve hundred and twenty-four

to be paid to Joshua Harrison, his heirs or assigns." This rent gave "full right to erect, repair, alter, or [illegible]

[illegible]

with his father's pursuits, and in 1827 removed, with the family, to the township of Upper Providence. Here, having rented a mill, he became interested in the manufacture of flannels. In 1831, Mr. Bancroft removed to his present location, in Nether Providence, and in conjunction with his father, erected mills in the vicinity, which he continues to operate, residing meanwhile at his attractive home—known as "Todmorden"—in the same township. He was married, June 5, 1828, to Miss Mary W., daughter of William Hallowell, of Philadelphia. Their only child was Elizabeth H. (Mrs. Thomas H. Rice), deceased. He was a second time married, on the 13th of January, 1859, to Sarah, daughter of John Patrick Hare, of Philadelphia. Mr. Bancroft affiliates with the Republican party in politics, but rarely interests himself in the political issues of the day further than by the casting of his ballot. He is identified with the First National Bank of Media as a director. In his religious belief he is a member of the society of Friends.

Rose Valley Mills.—Nicholas Schummel, in 1789, purchased of Joseph Dicks one hundred and sixty-five acres of land on Ridley Creek, in Nether Providence. Soon after he sold eighty-two and one-half acres to James Rowe, and in 1789 purchased a right for nine hundred and ninety-nine years of abutting a dam on the other side of the creek, with sufficient land to keep it in repair. In the same year Nicholas Schummel built a snuff-mill on this property. His son, Jacob, kept a tobacco store in Philadelphia, and in 1794 the snuff-mill came into the latter's possession. He continued to operate it until April 12, 1814, when he conveyed the mill property and fifty-three acres to William Smith. On July 29, 1814, Smith sold the property to John White, by whom the place was named Rose Valley. The snuff-mill was carried on under his ownership until 1821, when he conveyed the property to William Yardley, a son-in-law, in trust for two of his children, Catherine Fields and John White. At that time it was operated by Charles Fields, who employed the mill for grinding bark, used as a medicine for fevers. The introduction of quinine destroyed the business, and on April 4, 1825, the property was sold to Park Shee, and Charles Fields removed to Philadelphia, where he became a leading coffee-broker. Park Shee changed the old bark into a paper-mill, and erected other buildings. The structures were part stone and part frame, two stories in height; one was thirty by forty feet, and the other forty by fifty feet. Three engines, a drying-machine, and other necessary machinery was added for the manufacture of paper. Park Shee continued the business until after 1850, when the buildings fell into disuse. On Aug. 21, 1861, the property was purchased by Antrim Osborne, and was at that time in ruins, and, as then stated, was "inhabited only by bats and owls." The next year Osborne repaired the dam and race, and built a three-story stone building, seventy-five by fifty-five feet, in which was placed twelve hundred and twenty-four

Eng.d by A.H. Ritchie

Saml. Bancroft

spindles, sixty looms, and three sets of cards. In 1863 a stone building, with picker-house adjoining (now the engine-house), two stories in height, forty by twenty-three feet, was built, and in 1864 another building, also of stone, three stories in height, forty by forty feet, was erected. In 1873 the main mill was enlarged by an addition of seventy-five by fifty-five feet, three stories in height, making that building one hundred and fifty by fifty-five feet; a dry-house sixty-one by forty feet, and a picker-house sixty by forty feet. The building contains at present two thousand three hundred spindles, one hundred looms, and fifteen sets of cards.

Randall Osborne emigrated before 1730 from England, and settled in Montgomery County, where he leased property and engaged in agricultural pursuits. Among his children was Richard, whose son, Randall, became owner of the land, which he cultivated and improved. One of the grandsons of the latter, who also bore the name of Randall, married Mary Hess, by birth a German, whose children were Richard, Nathan, Jonah, John, Randall, and a daughter, Elizabeth, who became Mrs. John Custer. Jonah, of this number, was born in 1788, on the ancestral land in Montgomery County, and on attaining a suitable age acquired the trade of a stone-mason. He married Elizabeth Bisson, and had children,—Mary (Mrs. James Redmond), Franklin, Antrim, Elizabeth Ann (Mrs. William Sewell), Phœbe (Mrs. Harlan Miller), and Susannah. Antrim Osborne was born Nov. 19, 1817, on the homestead, in Montgomery County. Having been deprived, in the year 1826, when but eight years of age, of a father's protection and guidance, he was placed with Bethel Moore, of West Conshohocken, to learn the trade of woolen manufacturing. He remained three years at this point; was employed for a brief period at a neighboring mill, and ultimately removed to Rockdale, Delaware Co., where he was engaged as a weaver with Lewis & Phillips. After a service of four years with this firm he removed to Philadelphia, and completed an apprenticeship to the trade of a bricklayer. In 1838 Mr. Osborne resumed his original occupation in Delaware County, and was employed for three years by Richard Blundon, after which the same period was spent in a carpet-factory in Philadelphia, owned by John McAfee. He was also at a later date employed at Crosby's mill, in Delaware County, and in 1846 rented a mill at Waterville, in the same county, where he began the manufacture of satinets. He continued in this location for seventeen years, and in 1861 purchased the property of the Rose Valley Paper-Mill, upon which site his present buildings were erected, after which he began the manufacture of woolen jeans, doeskins, and cassimeres. In 1863 his son, William H., became a partner, and in 1879 his son, Thomas J., was admitted in the firm. Mr. Osborne was married in 1839, to Isabella V. Barris, of Trenton, N. J. Their children are Elizabeth B. (Mrs. John L. Grimm), William H., Mary Ann (Mrs. William H. Forwood), Thomas J., and Antrim E. Mr. Osborne is in his political views a pronounced Republican, but has been fully occupied with his business interests, and found no leisure for participation in matters of public concern. He and his family are worshipers with the congregation of the Nether Providence Methodist Episcopal Church.

Thomas Y. Hutton's Grist-Mill.—A short distance above the Rose Valley Mills, on the property sold by Nathaniel Stemmel in October, 1794, stands an old unoccupied mill, now in the possession of Antrim Osborne. This property passed from James Reese through several parties, and in 1823 from John and Jabez Jenkins to Thomas Y. Hutton, who, in 1840, built a stone grist-mill, which he operated until Sept. 1, 1845, at which date he sold it to Richard Wetherill. The latter kept it until April 1, 1847, when he conveyed the mill to Robert Boyd, who changed it to a turning-mill and sand-paper factory. Boyd died in 1859, and James Greer, as administrator of his estate, sold it, July 1, 1862, to Edward Borden, who rented it to Joseph Jackson, a bobbin-turner. On Aug. 1, 1869, the latter bought it and ran it till 1878, although he had sold the mill to William Pilling, March 1, 1873. From Pilling it passed successively to Solomon Chorley, John Wildey, and Andrew Rankin. The latter sold it, Nov. 25, 1879, to Antrim Osborne. The building is now used by Antrim Osborne as a store-house.

Chestnut Grove Cotton-Mill.—In 1764, Nathaniel Vernon was operating a saw-mill on Vernon's Run, which was discontinued soon after 1770. The land on which it stood was in 1799 part of the large tract owned by Thomas Leiper. In the division of his estate in 1843 it came to Samuel M. Leiper, who, March 24, 1845, sold the land to John Fildes. The latter erected near the old mill-site a cotton-factory, dye-house, and other necessary buildings. In April, 1852, fire broke out in the dye-house and spread rapidly to the main building. They were both destroyed. The mills were again rebuilt and operated by Fields until May 25, 1858, when the property was sold to Samuel Bancroft, who retained possession until Oct. 28, 1865, when he sold the cotton-factory and sixteen acres of land to James Jerome. The property later came to Mrs. Frances M. Jerome, and afterwards to Andrew P. Walker, by whom it was owned March 29, 1884, at which time the factory was destroyed by fire.

Mills on Ridley Creek—Leiper's Snuff-Mill and Avondale.—The first appearance of the name of Thomas Leiper in connection with manufactures in this county occurs in an assessment-roll of Nether Providence in 1779. In that year he was assessed on a snuff-mill, which was located on Crum Creek, in Nether Providence, opposite and a little above where the Avondale Mill is now. In 1790 he was operating two snuff-mills and was the owner of two hundred and ninety-six acres of land. A dry-house was added about 1800, and in 1811 there was at Avondale, in addition to the snuff-mills, a spinning-house, in which tobacco was spun, at a later date called the tobacco-factory. These mills were conducted by Thomas Leiper until his death, in 1825. By his will, April 21, 1824, he devised his real estate to his sons, George G., William J., and Samuel M. Leiper. The estate remained undivided until 1843, when the property on which the snuff-mills were located was conveyed by his co-heirs to William J. Leiper. Shortly after the death of Thomas Leiper a two-vat paper-mill was erected, which was supplied with water from the same race which gave power to the snuff-mills. In 1826, and for several years thereafter, the paper-mill was operated by John Holmes. In 1829, George G. Leiper conducted the business at this mill, which was destroyed by fire in 1836.

In 1826 there were, as before stated, two snuff-mills on this property, with eight mulls and two cutting-machines. They were operated until 1845, when they were changed into tenant-houses for the employés in the cotton-mills. Subsequent to the destruction of the paper-mill the estate was rented by James Riddle, who erected a cotton-factory on the east side of the creek, in Springfield township, and below the old paper-mill, the walls of which were utilized and changed into tenement-houses. On June 8, 1844, a fire occurred at Avondale, by which two tenement-houses were burned to the ground. Hardly anything was saved in these dwellings. In one of the upper rooms a man was lying dangerously ill and helpless, who would have perished had not James Honan, a stone-cutter, at great personal risk, forced his way through the flames and bore the sick man down the stairs to a place of safety. James Riddle, at a later date, rented the mills at Strath Haven, and conducted those, together with the mills at Avondale, until 1846, when they were rented to Simeon Lord. At that time there were eighteen tenant-houses at Avondale. On Dec. 29, 1849, the dye-house was destroyed by fire. In 1851, Simeon Lord was manufacturing fine cassimeres.

On the afternoon of July 2, 1851, Simeon Lord's dwelling, at Avondale, was struck by lightning. The fluid entered the chimney at the eastern end of the house, and, dividing, passed into all the rooms, being attracted in every direction by the heads of nails and other metallic substances. Large masses of stones were detached and thrown from the chimney into the yard below. Passing from the chimney to the room over the kitchen, the fluid shattered that portion of the house almost to pieces. Entering the room below, it tore off the plaster and demolished a clock, and descending near to a window where Mrs. Lord was seated, it threw her from the chair in which she sat into the middle of the room. Her son, a child of six years, who stood behind her, was thrown to the floor. The lightning struck the boy on the back of the head and ran down his back, coming out at his shoes, leaving a ragged hole in the latter about two inches in diameter. The skin was burned on the boy's back. He was restored to sensibility by dashing cold water on him. An old gentleman named Cooper, who was in the room, was also knocked down and rendered entirely unconscious. A little girl and a child in the same apartment were much stunned. The house was filled with smoke and dust, bedsteads were broken in several rooms, the fluid entering the small wire at the top of the posts and splintering them in three pieces, chairs were demolished, looking-glasses broken. In Mrs. Lord's bedroom were three guns. The stocks were shattered and broken to pieces, and the point of a bayonet, fixed to a musket, was melted. The walls and floors were perforated in many places and a portion of the door and window-frames knocked to pieces. In a closet, which was penetrated by the lightning, there were two canisters of powder and a bag of shot. The fluid entered the latter and passed the canisters. In the floor a large post, which supported the floor, was riven in twain.

In 1861, Simeon Lord purchased the Darby Mills of Thomas Steel and removed to that place. The Avondale property passed from William J. Leiper, by sheriff's sale, to Mrs. Helen H. Patterson, Aug. 24, 1858. At that time the mill property consisted of nine acres, a cotton-mill, and twenty-two stone tenements. On May 1, 1865, the large stone factory was burned, the machinery being at the time owned by Charles M. Gilberson, the lessee. The factory was rebuilt. Callender J. Leiper purchased the property of Helen H. Patterson, Nov. 1, 1870, and in 1872 he sold to William J. Leiper, who now owns it. William J. Leiper leased the property to Messrs. Callahan & Sharkey. The mill was destroyed by fire Aug. 23, 1873, involving a loss to the lessees of about thirteen thousand dollars and a heavy loss to Mr. Leiper. The factory was rebuilt and operated by John Greer & Co. until 1878, then by David Brown, of Haddington, until May 1, 1881, when it was dismantled. The building was subsequently used by the Franklin Artificial Stone Company from the fall of 1882 to the spring of 1884.

Strath Haven Mills.—In the summer of 1776, Dr. Robert Harris, at this locality, had established a powder-mill, under a contract with the Committee of Safety, which required him to deliver one ton of powder to the State authorities every week.[1] The mill, which was of frame and hastily constructed, disappeared with the occasion which called it into being. About 1824, Thomas Leiper, who then owned the estate, erected on the site of this mill, on Crum Creek, a tilt- or blade-mill, which was operated by Nahum Keys. In 1826 he was reported as then making about two hundred dozens of scythes and straw-knives per annum. For several years after that date, until 1830, the mill was operated by George G. Leiper, when it was changed to a paper-mill and leased to Park

[1] See description of powder-mill, *ante*, p. 46.

Franklin Mill. Built 1826. Rebuilt 1882.

J. HOWARD LEWIS' PAPER MILLS,
NEAR MEDIA,
DELAWARE CO., PA.

Shee In the division of the Leiper estate, in 1843, this property was awarded to William J Leiper, who shortly after that date rented it to James Riddle, and a cotton-factory was erected thereon In 1845, Simeon Lord leased the estate, and remained there until his removal to Darby Mills, in 1861 Previous to the termination of the tenancy of Simeon Lord, on March 5, 1859, Mrs Helen H. Patterson, a daughter of Thomas Leiper, purchased the property and now owns it At that date there were four acres of land, a stone cotton-factory, and five tenement-houses The factory and other buildings are now in ruins The former, on Nov 13, 1865, when in the tenancy of Mr Tomlinson, was destroyed by fire, involving a loss of fifty thousand dollars

The Lewis Paper-Mills—On Crum Creek, in the year 1826, John Pancoast erected a two-vat stone paper-mill, on lands which he had purchased June 16, 1825 The mill was owned and operated by him until April 1, 1833, when the estate was purchased by Elizabeth Lewis, whose husband, John Lewis, operated the mill until July 30, 1868, when it was sold to John Howard Lewis, the present owner On April 9, 1882, the mill was destroyed by fire It was rebuilt, and on Aug 21, 1883, was again burned Thomas Morrison, one of the employés, was killed by the bursting of the rag boiler, and several others assisting to save the buildings and personal estate were severely hurt Immediately the work of rebuilding was begun, and on March 10, 1884, work was resumed in the third paper-mill erected on this site The present buildings are all of stone, the main mill, thirty-five by one hundred and twenty-five feet, two stories in height, the engine-room, fifty-seven by ninety-seven feet, two stories, rotary-room, thirty-one by fifty four feet, rag-room, forty-six by sixty feet, three stories and an attic in height It is a five-engine mill, and manufactures about twenty tons of paper per week

Spool-Cotton Works.—About 1833, J & J Hillditch, in the old yellow house still standing south of Idlewild, were engaged in manufacturing spool and wound cotton.

Other Mills—In 1766, John Hinkson owned a saw-mill in the township, which, in 1774, was operated by David Bloomer, but it does not appear on the assessment-roll after 1780 In 1774, Job Dicks owned a grist- and saw-mill on Ridley Creek, a short distance below Rose Valley Mills, which were continued by him until subsequent to 1790 William Pennell, in 1764, was assessed on a grist- and saw-mill in Nether Providence. He was also at that date the owner of a grist- and saw mill in Middletown

Licensed Houses.—In Lower or Nether Providence the applications for license do not appear, so far as the record discloses, previous to 1746, but at that date Nathaniel Vernon had leave granted him to keep a public-house in the township The same year he presented his petition for license in the borough of Chester, having leased the house where David Cowpland dwells, and to that petition the court gave a willing assent, showing that Vernon stood well with the justices He does not appear, however, to have taken out his license for Cowpland's house, for the next year he is again an applicant, and is allowed license in Upper Providence, but subsequent to that date his name disappears, and no petition is on file for Nether Providence until 1763, when John Powell put in an appearance, and continued annually to do so until 1769, when the court allowed him to sell "Beer and Ale" In 1772, William Edwards had license granted to him, and it was so continued until 1776 In 1778, Andrew Linn was given the right, and in 1781, William Beaumont was allowed license, and continued annually to receive it until 1785 In that year the landlord, it seems from Beaumont's petition, had "rented the old house to some one else," and he therefore made application to be permitted to keep a house of entertainment at a place "nearly opposite the old stand," but the court refused his petition, and granted the right to the "some one else," who appears to have been Nathaniel Sharpless The latter annually received license from that date up to and including the year 1789

When Delaware County was established, Nathaniel Sharpless was licensed to keep a public-house in Nether Providence, but I fail to find any application for a similar privilege in that township until 1792, when Abraham Edwards was landlord of an inn, and continued yearly thereafter until 1795, when it disappeared from the record Ten years afterwards, in 1806, William Spear filed a petition, asking leave of the court to keep a tavern at the house he then occupied, which he states is commonly known as the Anvil His application was met with a remonstrance signed by seventy-five persons, among whom were Luke Cassin, Edward Fell, John Worrall, Samuel West, Owen Worrall, Joseph Thatcher, John Hinkson, Moses Palmer, Peter Worrall, Daniel Sharpless, Samuel Pancoast, John Broomall, and other well-known citizens, who objected because an inn at that location was unnecessary, "that where Inns are kept where there is but little Profit arising from Travellers, Landlords are frequently Induced to permit their Neighbors to Resort to them, Spending their precious time in the Crying Sin of Drunkenness and Levity, Whereby many Healthy Constitutions have been Impaired, and many Families Reduced to poverty and want That there is a Meeting of Friends held very near, twice a week, for the purpose of Divine Worship, and Monthly for Inspecting and Resulting affairs which relate to their Religious Society, it is probable the solemnity of these Occasions may be at times Interrupted by persons of the above description And lastly, that as we believe if William Spear Could be obliged to decline his Prospect, it might prove a Singular Kindness to him, so many Instances having occurred within the Compass of our

Knowledge of Persons occupied in Retailing ardent Spirits becoming gradually Enslaved therewith, to the great Injury of themselves and Families With desires that Righteousness, Temperance, and Prosperity may increase and abound among our Fellow-Citizens in that and every other neighborhood, We subscribe ourselves your Real Friends"

The opinion of the court, however, failed to accord with that of the remonstrants, and the license was granted to Spear for that year, and annually thereafter until 1810, when Isaac Cochran superseded him as landlord of the Anvil Spear, however, in 1813, returned to the inn, to give place, in 1816, to Henry Houghton, and the latter, in 1818, to Henry Habbersett, who, in his petition, stated that the public-house is known as the Providence Inn, although it formerly bore the title of the Anvil, a name it was never more to bear In 1823, George Litzenberg, Jr, became the landlord of the tavern, and as he was an active spirit in military affairs in the county, on many occasions the annual muster of the militia was held at the Providence Inn, and when the undisciplined rustics met for military instruction, some of the movements and manœuvres were so startling and original that veteran soldiers would have stood aghast at the sight In 1829, Charles Wells followed Litzenberg, and Wells, in 1832, gave place to Evan Way The latter, seeing an opportunity to become the host of the Washington House, in Chester, and the prospect of being sheriff of Delaware County, moved to the county-seat, and Isaac Hall followed him, in 1833, as landlord of the Providence Inn In 1837, James Dick was granted license, and in 1839, Norris Hannum, to be followed, in 1840, by George P Alexander Peter Worrall, the last of the publicans, obtained license for the Providence Hotel in 1843, and continued to receive the kindly consideration of the court until 1850, when the charter of the borough of Media, interdicting the Court of Quarter Session granting license to any inn or tavern within the limits of the new county-seat where intoxicating drinks were authorized to be sold, interposed itself as an obstacle in his way

Peter Worrall, however, did not permit this new order of affairs to go unchallenged, but on May 28, 1850, filed his petition setting forth that the act had been obtained by false and erroneous representation to the Legislature, that at the time the charter was asked for it was alleged that no license had been granted for or at the new seat of justice, whereas the truth was that he, Worrall, had license, and the inn had been a licensed public-house for fifteen years past That he was advised that the act was local, partial, and unconstitutional, and would materially impair, if not destroy, his vested interests and rights, and he therefore prayed the court to grant him license for the house, or "if the said license is to be refused, to place that refusal upon such grounds as may afford him an opportunity of obtaining a decision upon the constitutionality of said provision from the Supreme Court of Pennsylvania" The judges, however, refused the application, and since that date no effort has ever been made to obtain leave of the Court of Quarter Sessions to vend intoxicating liquors at Media

Hinkson's Corner —The property on which this hamlet is located was originally a part of the Vernon tract, which was confiscated after the Revolution, and in 1790 was in the possession of the Hinksons As early as 1770 John Hinkson was operating a saw-mill on some of the small streams in the township, probably on Vernon's Run In 1799, James Hinkson was living on the northeast corner of the cross-roads, in a frame dwelling, which was later replaced by the present stone house (now owned by Rufus Shapley) He was a wheelwright, and had at that time two shops, one log and the other frame, which stood on the corner where the present blacksmith-shop is now located

One of these shops he used for his business, the other was occupied by Richard Nuzrum as a blacksmith-shop He (Nuzrum) lived in Upper Providence, in which township he owned a farm A few years later Mary, a sister of James Hinkson, erected a frame house which still stands on the southeast corner, in which she established a store, and continued there for several years Later, the stone building, erected in 1799, now made into a stable by Rufus Shapley, was changed into a general store, and since 1844 was kept by Henry Lawrence, John Forrest, John Williamson Thompson, D R & H T Esrey, and in recent years by William G Vernon In 1810 a school-house was erected at Hinkson's Corner In 1803, Ezekiel Norman, a blacksmith, came from Montgomery County and purchased the shop at the Corner He continued to carry on blacksmithing there until a few years before his death, in 1864, when his son, Ezekiel Norman, succeeded to the business, and is still located at the Corner In 1870 a petition was presented to the postal department for an office there, but it was not obtained until 1873, when George Latch established a store in the neighborhood, at which time an office was located therein, and Latch was appointed master The purchase of land in the immediate vicinity of Hinkson's Corner and Wallingford by Philadelphians, who have made these localities their residences, has caused a rapid increase in the value of ground there At and near Hinkson's Corner, Rufus Shapley, author of "Solid for Mulhooley," Col Alexander McClure, Alfred S Gillette, president of the Girard Fire Insurance Company, James W Mercur, son of Chief-Justice Mercur, and others, reside, the result being that lands which a few years ago could be bought for two hundred dollars an acre is now being held at one thousand to fifteen hundred dollars for the same area of ground

Thomas Hinkson, a brother of James, was a farmer, and owned prior to 1800 a large tract of ground on the south and northwest corner He lived where the

Kershaw dwelling now is. The Hinkson family owning all the land there, the name when given was certainly appropriate.

Briggsville.—Isaac Briggs in 1849 kept a store in Providence below the southern line of the borough of Media, and subsequently in the house where Isaac Miller now dwells. After the county-seat had been removed to Media, Isaac Briggs established a brick-yard near the proposed town. In time a large number of defective and unsalable bricks accumulated in the yard, and with these he erected a double row of tenement houses on his land, from which fact the locality became known as Rotten Row, or Briggsville. In 1856 he built a brick church thirty-six by forty-five feet, which was free to be used by any denomination, sect, or for any form of worship. It was occupied at various times for religious services by clergymen of various denominations, and Sunday-school was also held there until 1870, when it was abandoned for that purpose. About 1874 the church building was changed into dwelling-houses. A brick school-house has been located by the directors of Nether Providence at Briggsville.

The Cavana Case.—In 1851, Nelson W. Cavana, a tailor, carried on business in a shop on the Providence road near Briggsville. On December 15th of that year he came to Chester, and was seen alive late that evening, after which time he disappeared. His mysterious absence alarmed his family, and search was made for him without success. In the mean while it became rumored that he had been made the victim of a practical joke, which had resulted finally in Cavana's death. The excitement in the country was intense; a public meeting was held at Media, and a reward offered to secure the arrest and conviction of those criminally concerned in the matter. The result was that Edward R. Crosby, Charles W. Raborg, and Benjamin B. Pearson were indicted for an assault and battery on Cavana. The trial began Monday, Feb. 23, 1852. The commonwealth was represented by Hon. Edward Darlington and Joseph J. Lewis, and the accused by Robert E. Hannum and William Darlington. The evidence was that on the afternoon of December 15th Cavana was in Chester sober, but at six o'clock he was intoxicated. At half-past ten o'clock that night he entered the oyster cellar of David Wilson, at that time under the Penn Buildings. His face was then blackened with burnt cork, and he wore a black dress-coat and a high silk hat. The defendant, Crosby, began to joke with Cavana, and talked about a "swallow-tailed coat" the latter had made for Samuel N. Leiper, of which Cavana was boasting. Charles W. Raborg thereupon poured some hot liquor on Cavana's head, then sprinkled some pepper on his hair, and finally threw flour in his face. Crosby jestingly inquired of one of the bystanders whether he had seen the swallow-tailed coat Mr. Leiper had on the Sunday previous, and asked if any one could tell him what botch of a tailor made it. Cavana thereupon took off his coat, declaring that was a personal insult, and he proposed to resent it, whereupon Crosby, taking the coat, turned it wrong side out, and put it on Cavana in that way, while Raborg caught hold of the tails of the coat and tore it up the back. The latter then took Cavana's hat, cut in it holes for his eyes, nose, and mouth, after which he put it on the former's head and drew it down over his face, made it fast under his chin by the rim, which was partly torn off. In this act Crosby assisted Raborg. Cavana left the oyster cellar shortly before midnight, and when last seen was walking down Market Street towards the river. The case occupied three days, and terminated in the conviction of Crosby and Raborg and the acquittal of Pearson. The court fined the defendants fifty dollars each and cost of prosecution. On March 6, 1852, the body of Cavana was found in the Delaware River, and on the 15th of the same month a coroner's inquest was held. The jury found the following extraordinary verdict:

"That the said Nelson W. Cavana came to his death from his having come to Chester on Monday, the 15th of December last, about 3 o'clock, perfectly sober; that he first drank strong liquor at I. Hamson Hill's tavern, about 5 o'clock, by invitation of Edward R. Crosby; drank at Hill's several times previous to 8 o'clock in the evening with different persons; had his face blackened while at Hill's tavern. He entered the oyster cellar of David Wilson about 10 o'clock, drank ale and eat oysters with Charles W. Raborg, Edward R. Crosby, Edward H. Engle, and others. He took his coat off, Edward R. Crosby turned it inside out and put it on him so, and afterwards tore it up the back. A pepper-box was shaken over, and ale was poured on, his head by Charles W. Raborg, his hat, which was placed on his head by Edward R. Crosby, with his face looking out of an aperture cut in the front, the rim was drawn down under his chin. Afterwards he complained that his eyes smarted, and then Edward H. Engle wiped his eyes with a handkerchief. He was suffered to leave the cellar alone about half-past eleven o'clock, in the condition above described, being very much intoxicated; and was seen going down the street towards the River Delaware alone, the weather being at that time extremely cold, with snow. He was found drowned, near Chester, on the 6th of March inst., his hat and coat worn on him as above described."

Media Lodge, No. 86, Knights of Pythias.—This lodge was instituted at Hinkson's Corner, June 19, 1869. The charter members were John Sykes, P. C.; George Sykes, C. C.; Edward L. Morgan, V. C.; Philip Afflick, G.; James E. Campbell, K. of R. S.; James P. Wheatley, M. of F.; Francis Taylor, M. of E.; Abraham Taylor, I. G.; Samuel Taylor, O. G. The lodge soon after changed its meeting-place to Media. In 1878 a lot was purchased at Hinkson's Corner, and the present hall erected. The lodge has at this time forty-eight members. The present officers are Harry Brooks, P. C.; John B. Brook, C. C.; Louis C. Martin, V. C.; Jesse Plumley, P.; L. Scott West, M. of E.; George Sykes, M. of F.; Fred. Schmaelzley, K. of R. S.; Samuel Taylor, M. at A.; George Latch, I. G; William Taylor, O. G.

CHAPTER L.

UPPER PROVIDENCE TOWNSHIP.

In the early days of the province Upper and Nether Providence, as stated in the account of the latter township, constituted one municipal division. The separation of Providence into two districts was recognized as early as the March court, 1687/8, when John Calvert was appointed constable for Upper Providence. This township is bounded on the east by Crum Creek, on the west by Ridley Creek, on the south by Nether Providence, and on the north by Edgmont. At the southwest limit of the township on Ridley Creek, and lying on the west side of Providence road, was a tract of three hundred and fifty acres, which was surveyed to William Taylor March 2–3, 1681, while immediately above was a plantation of like size, which, on the like date, was taken up by Peter Taylor. On these tracts that part of the borough of Media lying within Upper Providence is located. Peter and William Taylor, of the parish of Sutton, county of Cheshire, England, purchased from William Penn twelve hundred and fifty acres of land before they emigrated to the province. Part of this land was located in Upper Providence, the remainder in East Caln township. After the act of Feb. 13, 1804, creating the office of directors of the poor for Delaware County was in force, on March 25, 1805, the three directors, William Anderson, Jonathan Heacock, and John Smith, purchased from Isaac Taylor sixty-nine acres and eighty-five perches of land on this tract. The same day Ezra Taylor conveyed fifty-two acres and one hundred and thirty-two perches to the directors, and the same date William Spear and wife made a deed to the same grantees for seven acres and forty-two perches of land. The grantors were descendants of the original settlers, and on the estate thus conveyed the first county house or house of employment was erected. Subsequently the directors, on May 20, 1805, purchased eight acres and one hundred and five perches from Peter Worrall, and at a later date, Minshall Painter, John Clayton, and Joel Evans, the then directors, purchased twenty-six acres and one hundred and forty-two perches from Brinton Jones and Isaac Hinkson, trustees to sell the real estate of Woodward Crossley, deceased, which lands were added to the county property. Above the Peter Taylor tract was a plantation of two hundred and fifty acres taken up by Allen Robinett, and here at a later date he erected the Robinett Grist-Mill, while on this land on Ridley Creek, John Camm, the first stocking-weaver in Chester County, located. Of Allen Robinett little is known at this time, which is almost absolute evidence that he was not in membership with Friends.

Still following Ridley Creek, above the Robinett tract, Randal Malin took up two hundred and fifty acres on March 6–7, 1681. He emigrated from Great Barrens, in Cheshire, England, before or shortly after the first visit of Penn to his colony. Randal Malin was accompanied with his wife, Elizabeth, and settled on this land, glad to find an asylum in the wilderness from persecutions for his religious opinions, for he had suffered a fine of £20 5*s.* in England because he had made a prayer in a meeting of Friends there. Doubtless the exposure and privation to which she was subjected was too severe for the wife and mother, for she died in 1687. Randal Malin married again in 1693, his second wife being Mary Conway, a widow, the daughter of Valentine Hollingsworth, of New Castle County. He died shortly after the beginning of the eighteenth century, leaving two sons (Isaac and Jacob, children by his first wife) and two daughters (Hannah and Rachel, children by his second wife). On a portion of his estate in Upper Providence his descendant, Stephen Malin, still resides. Above the Malin lands, taken on rent by John Holston, Feb. 18, 1683, two hundred acres were secured. In 1717 the greater part of this land was purchased by Henry Miller. The latter, with his wife, Sarah, and several children, came from the parish of Dunster, Somerset County, England, three years prior to his acquiring ownership of this land. Henry Miller was by trade a weaver, and in Upper Providence located a small manufacturing establishment, wherein he wove serges, camlets, and similar goods, and had also a store, in which, with other articles, he sold the product of his looms. He was an active man in the early colonial days, and in 1717 was elected a member of the Provincial Assembly. Immediately above the Holston tract two hundred acres were surveyed to George Woodward on March 12, 1683. He never resided on the plantation, but on Twelfth month 25, 1695, the land having been sold to Joseph Phipps, was resurveyed, and was found to contain two hundred and eighty acres. The estate, June 15, 1715, was conveyed to Henry Miller, and it is doubtless on this tract that he embarked in manufacturing. Trout Run is almost entirely within the limits of this plantation.

Above the Woodward land Henry Miller, on March 19–20, 1715, acquired title to two hundred and twenty-two acres, on which Blue Hill is located, and it was on this land that he settled, which fact may account for the premises remaining so long in the ownership of his descendants. This plantation, however, was a part of a large tract of five hundred acres which was surveyed to James Swaffer, Nov. 7, 1684. He came from Newton, Cheshire, England, in that year, and settled on this land, but he subsequently removed to Philadelphia, selling his land in Upper Providence in smaller plantations. On part of this tract, in 1717, the mill in early time known as Providence Mill, and subsequently as Bishop's mill, and at the present as Sycamore Mills, was erected. To the east of a straight line drawn northward to Crum Creek from Providence great road, at the point where the latter highway diverges to the northwest to Blue Hill, William Salisbury, of whom little is known to the writer, took up one hundred acres lying between this imaginary line and Crum Creek. On a resurvey, in 1702, to Joseph Carter, it was found that one hundred and fifteen acres were included in this tract. The latter came from Cheshire, and settled in Upper Providence in 1698, possibly on this land, to which he acquired title by patent Nov. 16, 1709, although it had been surveyed to him seven years prior to that date. The records of Chester Monthly Meeting under date of Fourth month 28, 1708, set forth that "Providence Meeting informs of Joseph Carter being concerned with one not of our Comunion in relation to marriage, this meeting having laboured with him to convince him of his error, & advise him to desist." But Carter persisted; on Sixth month 30th of the same year it appears that he "hath actually married to one who doth not any wayes profess the truth with us." Carter by this conduct gained a wife, but lost his membership with Friends. He was living in Upper Providence in 1715.

Immediately south of the Carter estate, beginning at the present property of Samuel Otey, on Providence road, continuing southward along the eastern side of that highway to the northern line of the borough of Media, including the lands within those boundaries to the creek, a tract of seven hundred acres was surveyed to John Calvert First month 25, 1683. John Calvert and Judeth, with their children, emigrated to the province and settled on this tract, for which he received a patent April 24, 1691. In 1739 this estate, which by a resurvey proved to contain six hundred and eight and a half acres, was patented to John Worrell. If this purchaser was John Worrell, the settler in Middletown, and afterwards a resident of Edgmont, where he died in 1742, aged eighty-four years, he was well advanced in years at the time he bought this tract, and if it was one of his sons, John, who with his twin brother, Peter, was born in 1719, the young man had not attained his majority when the land was purchased. Of the John Worrell who acquired the estate the writer has at this time no definite information. The Rose-Tree Inn is located on this land. Immediately south of this tract Robert Robinson took up one hundred and fifty acres on rent First month 10, 1683, which property extended from Providence road to the creek. To Thomas Powell, March 21–22, 1681, was surveyed one hundred and eighty acres south of the Robinson land. On this tract Friends' graveyard is located, and it was there that an effort in 1698–99 was made to have Chester Meeting approve a site for the erection of Providence Friends' meeting-house without success. Perhaps it was that refusal which caused Thomas Powell to change his religious conviction, first adhering to George Keith in his opinion, and then became a churchman, for Keith held meetings at his (Powell's) house in 1703, at which time both Keith and Powell were earnest Episcopalians. Directly south of Powell's land, Randal Croxton, March 21–22, 1681, entered one hundred and fifty acres. He came from Chormely, County Palatine of Chester, England, among the early settlers, and located on this land, but on March 14, 1699, he conveyed this plantation to Joseph Taylor. He continued to reside in the township, for he was assessed there in 1715, and in 1734 was still there.[1]

The taxables of Upper Providence in 1715 were as follows:

John Edge, Jacob Edge, Henry Miller, Sarah Powell, Thomas Williamson, Joseph Taylor, Peter Taylor, William Sinkler, Zachery Butcher, Joseph Carter, Thomas Jones, Jacob Chandler, Jacob Malin, Joshua Calvert, Daniel Calvert, John Cam, Job Harvey, Randal Malin, Randal Croxson.

Freemen.—Jacob Norbury, Richard Clayton, Thomas Norbury, John Jones.

The taxables in the township in 1799 were as follows:

Thomas Bishop (miller, stone-, grist-, and saw-mill), Ann Bonan, Richard Briggs, Joseph Bishop, James Black, Joseph Bishop (smith-shop, cartwright), John Culin (carpenter), Hezekiah Camp, Samuel Carr (weaver), Thomas Calvert, Evan Eachus, Benjamin Evans, John Hinkson, Patrick Hagerty, Edward Hall, Philip Kirk, John Levis (paper-maker, paper-mill), Seth Levis, Samuel Lindsey, George Miller, Gideon Malin, William Malin, William Maddock (tavern-keeper), Caleb Martin, Joseph Newlin (cooper), Richard Nuzum (blacksmith), James Paist (victualer) William Robinson, Ether Riley, James Smedley, Jacob Siter (grist- and plaster-mill), George Thomas, Nathan Taylor, Peter Taylor, Jonathan Worrell, Peter Worrell, Jesse Williamson, Adam Worrell, Thomas Worrell, John Worrell, Abel Worrell, Jesse Worrell, Josiah Worrell. Owen Worrell, Ezekiel Yarnall (tailor), David Yarnall (cordwainer), Jacob Dunn, Peter Taylor.

Inmates.—Robert Williamson (blacksmith), Job Pyle (tailor), Thomas Steel (miller at Bishop's mill), William Eldridge, James Malin, Joel Malin, Isaac Malin (mason), Isaac Sharpless (paper-maker), Jacob Newhouse (paper-maker), Jacob Mills (paper-maker), Isaac Taylor (tailor), James Neal, James Dizer, Hugh McDale, Robert Miller (blacksmith), Joseph Taylor, Isaac Taylor (carpenter), Thomas Pollin, Joseph Martin (cordwainer), John Williamson, Benjamin Kirk, William Robeson, Frederick Benninghove, James Haws.

Single Freemen.—George McQuade, Charles McGlown, Peter Rezer (miller), Thomas Hawes (cordwainer), Israel Taylor (mason), Robert Barge, Samuel Malin (weaver), Abner Malin (weaver), George Martin, Joshua Hardy (tailor), Hugh McCown, Richard Briggs (mason), Mordecai Dunn (weaver), John Barr (weaver), Benjamin Kirk, George Kelley, Thomas Thomas (miller), John Smithel, John Taylor (gentleman), Owen Worrell, Gideon Malin (gardner), Leonard Webber, John Carr (weaver), James Smedley, James Gorman.

JUSTICES OF THE PEACE FOR UPPER PROVIDENCE.

Caleb Peirce	Aug. 30, 1791.
Joseph Brinton	May 20, 1800.
Luke Cassin	March 27, 1809.
John Siter	Sept. 1, 1813.
Robert Green	Feb. 23, 1816.
Nathan Gibson	Nov. 26, 1817.
George Brooke	July 3, 1821.
Maskill Ewing	June 10, 1822.
Benjamin Lobb	Dec. 4, 1823.
Parke Shee	Dec. 9, 1823.
Daniel Abrahams	Dec. 14, 1825.
Barnard Flynn	Nov. 18, 1835.
Abner Lewis	May 27, 1836.
Thomas Sheldon	Dec. 20, 1836.
Thomas Cassin	Nov. 1, 1838.
Homer Eachus	May 11, 1839.
John Miller	April 14, 1840.
Joseph Evans	April 14, 1840.
John Miller	April 15, 1845.
Joseph Evans	April 14, 1846.
John Miller	April 9, 1850.
Joseph Evans	April 15, 1851.
Nathan Shaw	April 10, 1855.
John J. Rowland	April 10, 1855.

[1] Smith's "History of Delaware County," p. 455.

Schools.—The present Blue Hill school-house is erected on the site of one of the ancient buildings which, during the last century, was set apart as a place for the education of children. When the first house was erected is not known, but certainly in 1777 a school was maintained there. The land on which the school-house stood was the property of George Miller, the elder, who subsequently bequeathed the lot to trustees for school purposes. In the account-book of George Miller, now in the possession of his granddaughter, Sarah L. Miller, of Media, are several entries which show that Mary Massey, daughter of Isaac Massey, boarded at the house of George Miller for the purpose of attending this school. The entries in the account-book are as follows:

"1777, *10th mo. 12th.*

"ISAAC MASSEY, Dr.

To his daughter Mary's diet and accommodation one year	£6 10s.
To cash paid Thomas Jacobs (the teacher) for her schooling	15s.

"1778, *10th mo. 12th.*

To his daughter Mary's diet and accommodation one year	£6 10s.
To cash paid for her schooling	2 0s.

"1779, *10th mo. 12th.*

To his daughter Mary's diet and accommodation	£6 10s.
To cash paid Abigail Sharpless for her schooling	15s."

The late county superintendent, James W. Baker, in his report for 1876, states that Jesse Haines, Martha Cromwell, Thomas Hammer, Samuel Brown, Thomas Megarge, Elizabeth Passmore, John Hammer, and W. Lightfoot were some of the early teachers of this school, and were highly esteemed.

The house which stood on the lot in 1777 was probably a log building. George Miller, by his will dated Jan. 12, 1794, and probated in 1797, devised to Jacob Minshall one acre and two square perches of land, with all the buildings thereon, in trust for the society of protestants commonly called Quakers, of Chester Monthly Meeting, for "the use of a school to be kept thereon," under the care of Friends. On this lot a stone school-house was built by subscription prior to George Miller's death, which occurred in 1797. School was kept there under the care of the Society of Friends from that date to 1837, when the Blue Hill school-house passed to the school directors of Upper Providence. In 1872 the old building had become so dilapidated that it was necessary to rebuild it, at a cost of two thousand five hundred dollars, and to meet that expense the court, in June, 1873, authorized the directors to sell the Turner lands, which was done, realizing $1333.15.

James Turner, in 1787, was the owner of a house and lot on Providence road known as Blue Hill. On the 26th day of the First month, 1787, he by will devised this land as follows:

"I give, devise, and bequeath to George Miller, the son of my cousin, George Miller, my house and Lott of ground, situate in Upper Providence, afforesaid, commonly called the Blue Hill, . . . to hold to him, his heirs and assigns forever, upon special trust and confidence, nevertheless, and to and for the uses, interests, and purposes hereinafter expressed, mentioned, and declared, and none other; (that is to say) for the use of the Society of protestants commonly called Quakers, of and belonging to the Monthly Meeting of Chester, for the erecting of one or more school-houses thereon for the teaching and Instructing youth therein, and all necessary conveniences thereto belonging, under and subject to the rules, regulations, and order of the said monthly meeting for the time being forever."

The remainder of his estate was devised to Jacob Minshall for the use of the school.

Jacob Minshall and George Miller, being individual trustees of these two pieces of ground, on Oct. 1, 1799, conveyed to Jacob Minshall, George Miller, Edward Fell, Ambrose Smedley, James Smedley, Isaac Sharpless, John Hill, Jr., and Joseph Pennell, Jr., the lands specified in the wills of James Turner and George Miller, in trust for the Blue Hill school, under care of Chester Monthly Meeting. After the enactment of the school law, and in 1837, "the school building and part of the grounds were suffered to fall into the possession of the school directors of the district of Upper Providence,"[1] who maintained a school there. The residue of the Turner and Miller real estate devised for school purposes in 1865 was in possession of Isaac Miller as trustee under the wills of James Turner and George Miller. By the act of Feb. 7, 1865, the lands and income were placed under the control of the Court of Common Pleas of Delaware County, "for the maintenance of a public school by the school directors, . . . at or near Blue Hill," with power in the court to order the sale or leasing of the real estate in its discretion. Under this authority the court, as before mentioned, in 1873 ordered the sale of the real estate, and the proceeds to be used by the directors in defraying the cost of the erection of the new school building at Blue Hill.

On the 18th of October, 1836, the board of directors purchased a half-acre of land on the Providence great road below the Rose-Tree, and erected a school-house, which was used until 1870. At that date a half-acre was purchased adjoining, and a brick building twenty-seven by forty feet was erected, the old house being removed. It is designated as Sandy Bank, No. 2.

Prior to 1872 a school was maintained in a house belonging to Samuel Bancroft, near the "Burnt Mills" (Manchester Mills), and in that year the present lot was purchased of Andrew Pallas, an Englishman, who went to England, and is supposed to have been lost at sea. The money had not been paid, and it was in the hands of the directors for several years before his heirs made the proper application for it. The brick house thereon, twenty-seven by forty feet, was erected in 1872, and is known as District No. 1.

In 1825, at the election in this year Thomas Cassin, Isaac Smedley, and George Miller, Jr., were chosen "School Trustees for Upper Providence." It will be noticed that Isaac Smedley and George Miller were trustees of the Blue Hill school, the only school known to have been in the township at that time. In 1834, after the enactment of the school law of that

[1] Act of Feb. 7, 1865: Bliss' "Digest of Delaware County," p. 15.

year, the court appointed George Miller, Jr, Ezekiel Norman, Jr, inspectors of the public schools until directors should be elected In 1835 the amount of money received by Upper Providence from State and county appropriation for school purposes was $138 57

The following is a list of school directors as obtained from the records of Media

1840, Isaac Haldeman, John R. Lewis, 1842, Joseph Evans, Enoch Dowell, 1843, Levis Miller, Malin Bishop Isaac Cochran, 1844, William P Wilson, Thomas C Palmer, 1845, Abel Lodge, Luke Cassin, 1846, Levis Miller, Edward Davis, 1847, Pratt Bishop, John R Lewis, 1848, Daniel James, George G Fell, 1849, John Kirk, John Eves, 1850, William T Pierce, Pratt Bishop, 1851, John Eves, Franklin Johnson, 1852, John Henderson, Thomas Reece, 1853, R H Smith, William Coffman, 1854, Caleb Hoopes, Jr, Oliver F Strickland, 1855, Thomas Reece, James R Cummins, 1856, Charles Wheeler, Perry C Pike, 1857, William Coffman, Perry C Pike, Caleb Hoopes, 1858, Pratt Bishop, John Kirk, 1859, John I Rowland, Hugh L Tyler, 1860, Wesley Thomas, John J Rowland, 1861, Pratt Bishop, R C Fairlamb, 1862, Levi G James, John Fields, 1863, Joseph N Dunn, I Morgan Baker, 1864, Pratt Bishop, Edward Carey, Nathan Evans, 1865, R C Fairlamb, Levi C James, 1866, Caleb Hoopes, Edward Carey, 1867, Nathan Evans, Thomas Bishop, 1868, Joseph N Dunn, Pratt Bishop, 1869, John Ottey, Edmund F Worrall, 1870, Pearson Pike, Caspar Rudolph, 1871, Abram Lees, Pratt Bishop, 1872, William Duroll, George Velott, 1873, no report, 1874, H B Fussell, George M Tyler, 1875, Samuel Ottey, William Sheldon, 1876, John Ottey, George B Adains, Lindley Smedley, 1877, Abram Lees, Lindley Smedley, 1878, Isaac S Pike, Samuel Ottey, 1879, Benjamin Rogers, George M Tyler, 1880, Lewis Kirk, Charles Moore, 1881, D Reece Hawkins, Samuel Ottey, 1882, C F Lewis, Benjamin Rogers, 1883, J E Tyler, Lewis Kirk, 1884, Samuel Ottey, D R Hawkins

Mills on Ridley Creek—Upper Bank or Manchester Mill—In the year 1764, James Wilcox was assessed in Upper Providence township on a dwelling and fifty acres of land This real estate was located on Ridley Creek, where are now the ruins of the Manchester Mill In 1766, James Wilcox was assessed, in addition to the foregoing property, on a paper-mill This mill remained in his ownership until his death, when it passed to his son, Mark Wilcox, and the latter sold it to John Lungren, April 20, 1785 Lungren operated the paper-mill for five years, when (Dec 30, 1795) he conveyed it to William Levis, of Philadelphia The deed to Levis included the mill, and one hundred and seventy acres of ground In 1799, John Levis, a son of William, had control of the mill, and continued the business there until the paper-mill was changed to a cotton-factory, in 1818, and rented to Wagstaff & Englehorn, who conducted the business successfully In 1821, John P Crozer states, "Only one cotton-factory in Delaware County, that of Wagstaff & Englehorn, continued running, and now appeared to be making money But Wagstaff was a practical cotton spinner from England, and had a consequent advantage "[1] In 1823 the firm had dissolved, and Hugh Wagstaff was operating the factory, for the *Post-Boy*, on Nov 11, 1823, contained the following local item

"QUICK WORK.—Miss Calderwood, of Mr Wagstaff's Factory, near this Borough, recently wove 551 yards of 100 shirting in the short space of 72 hours. Can any of the 'ruby lip'd, rosy-cheek'd lasses' of Chester County beat that?"

[1] Life of John P Crozer, p. 52

On Jan 28, 1825, the factory and twenty-six acres of land were sold to James Ronaldson The purchaser gave the mill in charge of James Siddall, and at that time the building contained ten carding-engines of thirty inches, two drawing-frames of three heads each, two roving-frames, one speeder of twenty and one of ten spindles, six hundred throstle-spindles, six hundred and seventy-two mule-spindles, one warper and dresser, and fourteen power-looms On July 18, 1829, James Ronaldson sold the mill property to John Bancroft, who had been in charge of the factory since 1827 The latter operated the mill until 1842, when it was sold to William T Crook, then of New York The purchaser conducted the factory until 1857, when the property was sold to Samuel Bancroft, the present owner, who operated the mill until Oct 9, 1872, when it was destroyed by fire, and is now a ruin

Robinett's Grist-Mill and Camm's Stocking-Works—Allen Robinett, who took up two hundred and forty-five acres of land, March 22, 1681, on Ridley Creek, just above the Concord road, settled on the tract prior to 1683, as is established by the following quaint letter, written by Robinett and his wife, to a friend, probably a member of the Pemberton family, who then resided in Bucks County, among whose papers the letter was found

"Priscilla, and loveing friend After mine and my wife's kinde love Remembered unto thee, this is to desire thee to yous me well about thy stele mill, I mean to leat me have it as chepe as thou canst afford it and to trust me untell my corn comes of the Ground, and we dout not but then we shall soone Rais mony and pay thee for it it will do us a kindnes becaus we are so fear from the mill, and if thou wilt let us have it, send word, and the lowist price, to our verry loveing friend Liddy ward, and so we Rest thy loveing frends

"ALLEN ROBINETT AND MARGARET

"this 14th day of the 3d month, 1683"

The mill here mentioned was doubtless a hand mill, but in a few years later a mill had been built on Robinett's land, for in a deed bearing date Seventh month (September) 29, 1687, recorded in Philadelphia, Allen Robinett, of Upper Providence, conveyed to Richard Crosby, of Middletown, "a water-mill" in Upper Providence, with about two acres of land, on the southwest side of Ridley Creek, and "a little Bottom on the northeast side"

At that time John and Richard Crosby were operating a grist mill and saw-mill a short distance lower down the stream, to which they derived title in 1705

The Robinett mill does not appear in any assessment now on file in Chester County, and it must, therefore, have gone out of use prior to 1766 It is probable that Crosby bought that mill intending to discontinue it, because of its proximity to his own mill

The tract on which this old mill stood, with the exception of the mill-site, passed to Charles Booth on Feb 29, 1704 The latter died, and his widow, Elizabeth, on Aug 29, 1716, conveyed to John Camm, of Upper Providence, stocking-weaver, the messuage and one hundred acres of land, he paying seventy-five pounds therefor. This John Camm, whose name appears on the list of taxables in the county in 1715, was the first stocking-weaver in the American colonies who had emigrated from Great Britain, so far as known. He was an Irish Friend, who came from Cork in 1708, settling at first in Philadelphia and subsequently removed to Chester County. He was certainly in Upper Providence in 1716, where he followed his calling as a stocking-weaver, as the following advertisement in the *American Weekly Mercury* of Dec. 10, 1732, fully attests:

"*Whereas* Matthew Burne, of Chester County, served John Camm two years (that is, ten or twelve months at stocking weaving and other work), during which time John Camm's stockings bore many reflections, and now the said Matthew Burne goes about selling stockings in John Camm's name as though they were his own make, which is false and not true.

"JOHN CAMM."

Malin's Grist-Mill.—The tract of land through which the Edgmont and Springfield road passes, on the west side of Ridley, and bordering on that stream, was originally surveyed to Randal Malin. At an early period, Malin,—probably Jacob,—the son of Randal Malin, who settled on this land and died there early in the last century, built a dam across the creek on land now owned by Dr. Jacks and the estate of James Smedley, from which the race ran along the creek down to the lower portion of the Malin tract. About two hundred yards below the present residence of Stephen Malin, a lineal descendant of the settler, a stone house and a grist-mill were built. The mill-race is yet intact, and the foundation of the old house is still to be seen. William Malin, a grandson of the settler, it is said, in 1785, built a portion of the present residence. In 1770 David Malin & Co. were assessed on a saw-mill, after which date the name does not appear in connection with mills on the assessment-rolls.

Sycamore Mills.—On June 24, 1690, Samuel Carpenter, Robert Turner, and John Goodson, commissioners of property, issued a patent for five hundred acres of land to James Swaffer, which, beginning a short distance south of Blue Hill, included all the territory between Ridley and Crum Creeks, and extending to the northern boundary of the township. A tract of twenty acres, included in this patent to Swaffer, lying on Ridley Creek, on June 14, 1696, passed to the ownership of John Edge, Sr. The latter, by will, May 5, 1711, devised to his son, John, this plot and three hundred and sixty acres, lying on the opposite side of the creek, in Edgmont, which land he had purchased from Philip Yarnall. In 1717, John Edge, Jr., Jacob Edge, and Henry Miller formed a copartnership for the purpose of erecting a "water corn-mill" and carrying on a milling business on the twenty-acre tract. The following year the mill, to which they gave the name Providence Mills, was built, and, still standing, is known as the "old part" of the present Sycamore Mills. It was a stone structure, thirty by thirty-two feet, two stories in height. Prior to building this mill the company purchased two and three-quarter acres in Edgmont for the race and dam privileges, each of the partners contributing £5 2*s*. 8*d*. towards the cost of the land. On Dec. 17, 1719, Henry Miller purchased the third interest, owned by John Edge, in these mills, which two-third interest Henry Miller by his will, Dec. 17, 1719, devised to his son, George. The latter, on Dec. 10, 1740, conveyed a one-third interest in the mill property to Roger Pugh, and he, on Fifth month 8, 1746, to Lawrence Cox. "Between May 5, 1746, and April 25, 1752, while Lawrence Cox was the owner of Miller's share [it was Miller's half-interest Cox had] the saw-mill was erected, doubtless in 1747, or thirty years after the grist-mill, for in the latter part of that year he leased it, excepting one-tenth part, for a term of fourteen years, and at the rate of two pounds annually, to Thomas and John Minshall, of Middletown, both of them at the same time coming in for a fifth share each in the grist-mill. They sent their flour to Barbadoes in 1746, and to Jamaica by the brig 'Dolphin' in 1748, in charge of their brother, Moses, who was a sea-captain, and received sugar in part in return. Lawrence Cox was then also part owner of the mills. Thomas Yarnall and John Cox were likewise in partnership with the Minshalls in the saw-mill business. There was a curious arrangement made that 'when the grist-mill wanted water from the dam, and there was not enough for both, the saw-mill was to stand idle,' an excellent contrivance to promote a feud. Cox seemed to have had unlimited faith in tenants, for in the same year, 1746, that he obtained partial possession of the property he leased one-third of his share to William Hammans for twenty-one years, at an annual rent of twelve pounds. . . . In 1757 all the possessions went to his son, George."[1]

John Cox, on 25th of First month, 1752, conveyed the property to his son, John Cox, who, on Feb. 17, 1753, with the consent doubtless of the other owners, leased the grist- and merchant-mill, with two pair of stones and three bolting-sheets, to John Williamson, Henry Howard, Henry Caldwell, Lawrence Cox, Edward Farr, James Sill, Nehemiah Baker, Philip Dunn, Robert Register, James Scott, Aaron Baker, Abel Green, Thomas Minshall, John Scott, Jesse Woodward, James Massey, John Baker, Joseph Black, Nathan Lewis, and William Wall for seven years. Tradition states that every man having a share in the mill took his own grain there and ground it himself, whenever the inclination prompted, and did so without rendering thanks or pay to anybody.

John Cox on Feb. 22, 1755, sold to Thomas Bishop his one-third share in the mill, two tracts of land, and forty acres purchased from John Taylor by Lawrence Cox in 1746, to Thomas Bishop, the latter paying

[1] "Sketch of Bishop's Mill," by Wilmer W. James, in *Delaware County Paper*, June 27, 1877.

therefor three hundred and twenty-six pounds Bishop also leased the shares of all the other owners for ten years As the grist-mill and saw-mill were then rented and the leases had not fallen in he collected the rents, and for the two shares not owned by him paid twelve pounds per annum to the owners In 1763 a fund was raised by subscription to erect a bridge over Ridley Creek, about one hundred yards below the mills, on the site of the present bridge The subscription bridge stood until 1843, when it was washed away in the noted flood of August 5th of that year At the March term of court, in 1799, a petition was presented, signed by a number of the inhabitants of the county, setting forth that the bridge over Ridley Creek, near Bishop's mills, was in bad condition, and "praying that a sum of money may be allowed out of the county treasury to repair the same" The grand jury allowed forty dollars for the purpose of repairing the bridge

On Nov 29, 1785, proceedings having been had in partition of the mill property, the mills were awarded to Thomas Bishop After he acquired absolute ownership of the property he built a frame third story and added an overshot, the eastern end of which rested on three stone piers The latter was designed mainly to "shore up" the old mill, part of the public road passing under this archway The grist- and saw-mills were occupied by Thomas Bishop until 1802, when Francis Bishop was operating them In 1807 Thomas Bishop was conducting the grist-mill, and in 1811 he had the saw-mill, and Amor Bishop the grist-mill. In 1810–11 the rolling-mill was built It was about seventy feet in length, nearly fifty in width, and one story in height, adjoining the southern end of the saw-mill The rolling-mill, which stood on the site of an ancient plaster-mill, which had been in operation for half a century before it was taken down, in 1810, was four times as large as the building it superseded The slitting-mill was erected shortly after the sale of the whole estate to Bishop This rolling-mill was used for making boiler-plates, sheet-iron, and a variety of other work The pig-iron was carted from Philadelphia in wagons, and was in bars about two feet long The rolling-mill was conducted, in 1812, by Malin & Bishop The fuel used was the soft, bituminous Virginia coal, but the war soon made it difficult to be had, the cargo being of such a character that the masters of coasting vessels refused to carry it, for if chased when so loaded capture was inevitable At first the owners of the mill attempted to use charcoal, but that was too expensive, and could not be had in sufficient quantity Accident, however, came to the relief of Malin & Bishop, and at the same time brought about the use of anthracite coal The incident is thus recorded in the first report of the Pottsville Board of Trade

"In the year 1812 our fellow citizen, Col George Shoemaker, procured a quantity of coal from a shaft sunk on a tract he had recently purchased on the Norwegian, and now owned by the North American, Coal Company, and known as the Centreville Mines. With this he loaded nine wagons and proceeded to Philadelphia, much time was spent by him in endeavoring to introduce it to notice, but all his efforts proved unavailing Those who designed to try it, declared Col Shoemaker to be an impostor, for attempting to impose stone on them for coal, and were clamorous against him Not discouraged by the sneers and sarcasms cast upon him, he persisted in the undertaking, and at last succeeded in disposing of two loads for the cost of transportation, and the remaining seven he gave to persons who promised to try to use it, and lost all the coal and charges Messrs Mellon (Malin) and Bishop, at the earnest solicitation of Col Shoemaker, were induced to make trial of it in their rolling mill, in Delaware County, and finding it to answer fully the character given it by Col Shoemaker, noticed its usefulness in the Philadelphia papers, and from that period we may date the triumph of reason, aided by perseverance, over prejudice"[1]

At the Delaware County Rolling-Mill, tradition records that the employés in charge of the furnace, when the load of coal first came to the works, late in the afternoon, threw into the fire a large quantity of the black stones with the often expressed forebodings that "the boss had been fooled," which opinion became more and more confirmed when the coal refused to ignite, although frequent attempts were made to kindle it Late at night the fireman abandoned the effort in despair and went to bed Unable to rest, he got up in an hour or two thereafter and went to the mill, when he found the furnace door red hot, the heat in the building intense, and the wood-work almost ready to burst into a blaze Never before had there been such a fire in the mill Thereafter Enos Helms was sent to Mauch Chunk with a five horse team, and carted from that place the fuel used in the rolling-mill The coal cost two dollars a ton at the mine

[1] Hazard's Register, vol xiii page 274 In Burrowes' "State Book of Pennsylvania" (1845), is briefly related the foregoing account, adding, "Some of it, however, was afterwards tried with perfect success, at a rolling-mill in Delaware County, and the result noticed in the city papers of the day" Watson, in his "Annals of Philadelphia," vol ii page 459, in referring to the first use of anthracite coal says, "At length, after a multitude of disappointments, and when Shoemaker was about to abandon the coal and return home, Messrs Malin & Bishop, of Delaware County, made an experiment with some of the coals in their rolling mill, and found them to succeed beyond expectation, and to be a highly valuable and useful fuel The result of their experiments was published at the time in the Philadelphia papers Some experiments with the coal were made in the works of the Falls of the Schuylkill, but without success" The official State publication (1878) entitled, "Pennsylvania and the Centennial Exposition" (vol I page 124), says, after relating the facts of Col George Shoemaker's trips to Philadelphia with the nine wagons loaded with coal, "Of the two loads sold, one was purchased by White & Hazard for use at their wire-works at the Falls of Schuylkill, and the other was purchased by Malin & Bishop, for use at the Delaware County Rolling Mill By the merest accident of closing the furnace doors, Mr White obtained a hot fire from the coal, and from this occurrence, happening in 1812, we may date the first successful use of anthracite coal in the manufactures of this country Up to that time bituminous coal from Virginia had been exclusively used for manufacturing purposes in Philadelphia, and largely for domestic purposes The war with Great Britain had, however, made Virginia coal very scarce, and it was very desirable that a substitute should be found The following story is told of the success achieved by White & Hazard in the use of anthracite coal in their wire-works A whole night was spent in endeavoring to make it burn, when the hands in despair quit their work, but left the furnace door shut Fortunately, one of them forgot his jacket, and on returning to the works half an hour afterwards, he noticed that the door was red hot, and the interior of the furnace in a white glowing heat Thereafter no trouble was experienced in making the new fuel burn" This is the most pronounced effort that has been found to give the credit of the first use of anthracite coal in manufacturing to Philadelphia, and to ignore the fact that that credit belongs to Delaware County by simply an incidental suggestion that Malin & Bishop bought one of the cart-loads of coal from Col Shoemaker

In 1826 Thomas Bishop owned all the mill property, and Amor Bishop, his son, operated the works there In that year the grist-mill ground from eight to ten thousand bushels of grain, the saw-mill was employed occasionally, and about one hundred tons of iron was rolled and slit per annum The rolling- and slitting-mill was assessed as "not occupied" in 1829 The grist-mill and saw-mill were continued in use by Amor Bishop, and in 1856 were conveyed to his son, Washington Bishop, who sold them to Joseph Velotte in 1867, and the latter, on Jan 29, 1868, passed the title to William F Lewis, who now owns and operates them under the name of Sycamore Mills

The dam at the Sycamore Mills has been washed away four times, once in the great flood of 1793, again on Feb 22, 1822, a third time in the destructive ice flood of Jan 26, 1839, and the last time in the noted flood of Aug 5, 1843

Register's Nail-Factory —This industry, which has now been abandoned for more than a half-century, was the direct outgrowth of the rolling-mill, and although it was located across Ridley Creek, just above the bridge at Bishop's Mills, its story is so connected with the latter that it properly should be narrated in the history of the Sycamore Mill The nail-factory was a small frame building owned by Jesse Reece, and was rented to David Register, who at an advanced age, in 1812–13, employed men, and began making wrought-iron nails entirely by hand Register had been a Tory during the Revolution, and had fled with the British troops to Nova Scotia, but subsequently returned after the passage of the amnesty act The building, which had many years before ceased to be used as a nail-factory, was washed away in the flood of Aug 5, 1843

In 1830 Judge Hemphill in Paris, writing to a friend in Chester County, stated that in 1818 or 1820 he, with John Jefferies, visited Mr Bishop, where, on the latter's estate, he saw "decomposed feldspar in streaks of white lying in abundant veins where the road had been cut through the hills, and observing that the land was uniformly rich where it made its appearance, not knowing what the substance was (such he confesses was his ignorance of mineralogy), he imagined that perhaps it might contribute to fertility and be useful, like plaster or marl, upon land To test the correctness of the opinion, he obtained a box of it, sent it to a distinguished agriculturist, with a request that he would have it examined, and give in return any information he might be able to get A letter in reply stated that it was decomposed feldspar, that it was the material of which the French China was manufactured, that a specimen had been sent to France, which afterwards was pronounced excellent This information was communicated to the late Jacob Cist, Esq , of Wilkesbarre, a gentleman of science, and who was turning his attention particularly towards different clays and the finer materials for Delf-ware and Porcelain At his request the writer of this procured and sent to Philadelphia a barrel of the material, which he caused to be taken to Wilkes-barre He pronounced it excellent, but the distance was too great to haul and work it to advantage"[1]

Jeremiah Collett's Mill —Tradition alleges that on the tract of two hundred and fifty acres, purchased Dec 13, 1693, by Collett from James Swafler, which was that part of the Swaffer patent lying south of Egmont township line, Collett erected a water-power mill This tradition has some evidence to sustain it, in that at the court held on Oct 2, 1695, when the grand jury, because "the County Treasurer is out of purse," levied a tax to defray pressing obligations, in the quaint document signed by the grand inquest appears the following item "Jeremiah Collett, for his estate and calling, 30 pounds" And in the same presentment certain persons are mentioned by name, and taxed on their "calling," all of whom save Collett we know were millers Tradition states that Collett had erected a mill and was operating it for many years before the Providence Mills (now Sycamore) were built After the erection of the latter mills the then owner of the property, who was operating these mills, became so enraged at the competition that he threatened to build a dam so high that when the water should be suddenly let out it would rush down the creek, sweeping everything in its way Tradition locates this mill in Edgmont, on Big Run, on the estate of Joseph Taylor, although one hundred acres of that land was purchased by James Swaffer from John Holston, who took up two hundred and fifty acres there in 1684 Jeremiah Collett never owned the property, nor was the title in Swaffer for the land on which are the remains of the mill and a small portion of the old wall of the original dam, the distinct outlines of which are pointed out to this day If Collett had a mill, it was located in Upper Providence, on the east side of Ridley Creek

Palmer's Mill on Crum Creek —The only grist-mill in the township in 1799, except that of Thomas Bishop, was owned by Jacob Siter, who was assessed in that year on twenty-seven acres of land,—a grist-mill, plaster-mill, and a frame smith-shop Where this mill was located is not known, for in 1802 his name does not appear in the assessment-roll as owning a mill That he lived on Crum Creek is evident from the fact that he was also assessed on forty-seven acres of land in Marple township On the 23d of March, 1801, Abram Jones purchased a dower-right in a property on Crum Creek, on which in 1802 he was assessed as owner of a grist-mill in Upper Providence, and also on a saw-mill in Marple On Jan 25, 1812, he bought of the executors of William Hunter, the remaining right in the mill property In the report of Delaware County manufacturers, in 1826, it is reported, "On Crum Creek in Upper Providence and Marple a grist- and saw-mill head and fall twelve feet owned

[1] Hazard's Register, vol vii p 149

and occupied by Abraham Jones, capable of grinding twenty-five thousand bushels of grain and sawing one hundred thousand feet of lumber per annum, but not employed to that extent These mills were owned and operated by Mr Jones until 1834, when they were sold to T. Chalkley Palmer, who devised them to his son, Lewis Palmer The latter is the present owner Of the mills in the township the location of which has not been ascertained, are the following In 1764 and continuing till 1774, Charles Lynn owned a grist-mill, James Hunter and John Williamson each owned a quarter interest in a saw-mill In 1770, John Calvert owned a saw-mill on Crum Creek, and in 1788, Samuel Vernon owned a grist-mill and saw-mill, and Edward Woodward a grist-mill

Licensed Houses—In the township of Upper Providence, the first application for license of record is that of David Calvert, the younger, who presented his petition, dated May 29, 1739, to the court, wherein he states that he "is Building a Convenient house by the great Road which leads from the valley to Chester, near to where the Road from the Northwest parts of this County to Philadelphia crosseth the same," and asked that he may be permitted to sell "Beer & Cyder, & keep a house of Entertainment." His application was rejected, as was also a similar petition at the August court, but Nov 27, 1739, he informed the court that he "has built a Convenient hous," whereupon the license was granted, the location being that of the present Rose-Tree Hotel

Aaron Thompson, of Upper Providence, May 29, 1739, requested a tavern license, "on Providence Road, and near Springfield road," which would bring it near Rose-Tree, and although his application was indorsed by Bernhard Van Leer and fifty-two other signers, it was rejected

At November court of the same year, John Russell filed his petition, wherein he locates his house as "upon Vper providence Street Road side, halt a mile above providence meeting-house," and also declares that there is "no publick house on the sd Road between Chester to The Great Valley road" (his statement was then true, for it was at this court that Daniel Calvert obtained license), and he wishes "to sell Rum by small Measure, In proportion to two pence the Gill" The court perhaps thought the price so low that that sort of liquor would be injurious to the public generally, at any rate they refused Russell's application

During the year 1739 there seems to have been considerable effort to procure license in Upper Providence, for May 29th of that year, Matthew Bowcher, in that township, 'on Street Road," wished to sell "Beer & Cyder," which was denied him, and August 28th he again made application, indorsed by seventy-six signers, who represent him to the court as "both lame and old," but to no purpose, for the justices still refused the prayer of the petitioner

Aaron Thompson, who had been denied license at the May court, 1739, again asked the court's consideration Aug 29, 1744, stating that his house is located "on the fforks of two great Roads,—one leading to Philadelphia, and the other from Chester to Newtown, and there is no publick house conveniently situated for the Philadelphia road," almost due east of Media, but again the justices refuse to grant his application

At August court, 1744, John Calvert's petition shows that he had "leased the house where Daniel Calvert's kept publick-house," and desired that the license might be continued to him, which was done, and yearly renewed until 1747, when Daniel Calvert becomes once more the landlord of the tavern Then follows an interval of thirteen years, during which the records are silent respecting this inn, but in 1761 David Malin made application, and continued so to do until 1764, when Joseph Nicklin became the innkeeper He continued in that occupation only one year, for in 1765 Daniel Thompson secured the license, and annually thereafter until 1768 In 1766, Jonathan Durrell had tavern license in Upper Providence, but his name occurs only during that year

Townsend Ward, in his interesting "Walk to Darby," in alluding to fox-chasing, says, "For this ancient sport is continued in Delaware County, which possesses the famous Rose-Tree Fox-Hunting Club, and an excellent pack of hounds The title is derived from an old inn of the days of the Revolution, called the Rose-Tree, situated near Wallingford Station The club has recently been gladdened by the discovery in an old loft of the original sign of the inn"[1]

In 1769, David Malin applied again for the license, and in 1770 his petition sets forth that the tavern is known as the "Three Tuns" In 1771, David Malin again made application for license, and from that date no petition appears of record until 1778, when John Moore received the privilege to keep a public-house there, and in 1782 it was granted to Mary Moore, and continued to her in 1783, when again occurs a break until 1786, when Baldwin Weaver procured the license From the latter date no petition has been found respecting this old hostelry of record at West Chester After the erection of Delaware County William Maddock had the license, to be succeeded in 1801 by William Robinson In 1802, Jonathan Bonsall had the inn, which was then known as the Red Lion In 1803, Isaac Cochran, who had removed from the Blue Ball Inn, in Springfield, endeavored to get license as the Red Lion, but was refused The next year, 1805, Moses Palmer obtained license for the Rose-Tree Tavern, the title being changed from the Red Lion because of the bad repute the latter name had in the county The house at this time was an old frame building, painted red, which in the sixty-six years since it had been erected had grown dilapidated In that year (1805) the

[1] *Penna Mag of Hist.*, vol iii 268

Red Lion was taken down and the new sign (the Rose-Tree) was suspended beneath the great poplar trees In 1806, Isaac Cochran secured the license, and continued to receive the court's favor for ten years while he was landlord The present stone building was erected at different dates, the oldest part being built in 1809 In 1816, Isaac Cochran, who owned the property, was succeeded by Martin Wise as landlord, but the following year he again became "mine host," and continued as such until 1821, when William V Black had license In 1823, Isaac Cochran again became the landlord, to be succeeded in 1828 by John Black, and the latter, in 1831, by Isaac Cochran, Jr In 1833, George Cummings had license, and during the time he occupied the house, in 1836, the stone addition to the inn was made, by which the Rose-Tree grew in dimension to double the size it had been since the new building was erected, in 1809 George Cummings died in 1846, and the following year, 1847, Matilda B Cummings had a temperance license granted to her by the court for the Rose-Tree In 1848, Martha Ann Russell obtained license, the following year Malin Bishop, and in 1850, Matilda B Cummings again was the hostess of the inn Isaac Cochran, who had so long been landlord of the Rose-Tree, died on April 18, 1852, at Willistown, Chester Co, he having attained the advanced age of eighty-seven years Robert Johnson, in 1857, followed Matilda B Cummings, to give place to William Beeby the next year, and he in 1859 to J Morgan Baker, who remained there until 1864, when the license was transferred to Thomas Graham In 1865, Thomas B Miller was at the Rose-Tree, to be succeeded in 1868 by Joseph D Velotte, and in 1871, Thomas M Garrett, and 1872 Velotte returned, only by the local option law to be deprived of license in 1873 and 1874 After the repeal of that act by the Legislature, Benjamin Rogers, the present landlord, received license

Rose-Tree Fox-Hunting Club was organized in September, 1873, although for a number of years prior to that date the gentlemen who founded the club At first, the hounds, who were owned by individuals, were kept at the residences of the parties who would meet at the Rose-Tree to hunt, but when J Morgan Baker became the landlord of the Rose-Tree, a number of the dogs were kept at the tavern During his occupancy of the inn, Baker laid out the race track at the Rose-Tree, which since became noted among turfmen Several years ago the following account of the club appeared in a New York sporting journal

"About 1853, J Howard Lewis, Esq, and George E Darlington, Esq, began to keep their hounds at the Rose Tree Tavern, on the Providence road, about one and a half miles above the court house, which had just been located in the present town of Media The Rose Tree was then kept by Morgan Baker [he first had license in 1859], and the hounds remained there for several years These gentlemen, gradually joined by others, some years later, moved to Lamb Tavern, kept by Woodward, but, owing to the landlord's intentionally crippling a fox, the kennel was moved to Tom McClure's farm McClure always kept a few good hounds of his own, until the winter of 1875–76, when he met with an accident and was killed About 1869 the locality of the hunt was changed to the Black Horse, in Middletown township The leaders now were Messrs J Howard Lewis, Samuel Lewis, Professor Fairman Rogers, joined by George Hill, the present M F H, who was living on Chester Creek and hunting with John Mahony, Henry Saulnier, and Mark Pennell The former is now, at threescore years and ten, as true a fox hunter as ever followed hounds, and keeps the same blood in his kennel for which he has always been famous. Without children he and wife live on a small farm, where, as he says, he 'always has meate for the hounds, and milk for the puppies,' and at any time you can find a lot of puppies occupying the warmest corner of the fireplace, and Mrs Mahony will say, pointing to one or the other, 'Now, isn't he pretty?' About the same time, Henry E Saulnier (who lived formerly in New York, but was attracted to a country place near Ivy Mills on account of the beauty of the scenery and the hunting) joined The hounds were moved back to the 'Lamb,' then kept by Benjamin Rodgers, and the next year, 1872, the Rose-Tree was bought by Messrs J Howard Lewis, Samuel Lewis, Professor Fairman Rogers, and E Farnum, the hounds sent there, and 'Benny' came as landlord The club was then regularly organized with six to seven couple of members, with George Hill, M F H and President, J Howard Lewis, vice-president, George Lewis, treasurer, and Samuel Miller, secretary It has gradually increased in size until there are now about twoscore and six "[1]

Delaware County Institute of Science.—Just above the Rose-Tree, on Providence road, was the first building erected by the institution, and used by that scientific body until the present hall in the borough of Media was built In the summer of 1833 a number of gentlemen met at the public-house of Isaac Hall, in Nether Providence Dr Samuel Anderson was made chairman, Marshall Painter and John K Zerlin, secretaries At that time the proposed name of the society was the "Cabinet of Natural Sciences of Delaware County" At a subsequent meeting, at the same place, on Sept 21, 1833, the name was changed to Delaware County Institute of Sciences, with the avowed intention of enlarging the range of subjects On Jan 4, 1837, George Cummings sold to the institute a lot of ground near the Rose-Tree Tavern, on which the society erected its first building While located there the map of Delaware County, prepared by Dr Joshua W Ash, and Dr George Smith's "History of Delaware County" were both published under the auspices of the institute On Sept 10, 11, and 12 1846, the institute held its first public exhibition of agriculture, manufactures, and other productions of Delaware County, at its hall in Upper Providence, and continued these exhibitions annually for several years, until the Delaware County Agricultural Society was established (1855), when to avoid a conflict with the latter the institute ceased its annual exhibitions The history of the society, other than this, is given in the account of Media borough

John Cassin, one of the distinguished men of Pennsylvania and the nation, one of the chief movers in the organization of the Delaware County Institute of Science, was born in Upper Providence, Sept 6, 1813. He removed to Philadelphia in 1834, and engaged in mercantile pursuits His time, however, was largely devoted to the study of ornithology, and therein he became an authority second to no other student of that branch of scientific knowledge The noted ornitho-

[1] *Forest and Stream and Rod and Gun*, April, 1878

Isaac S. Cassin

[illegible] of the Philadelphia Academy of Natural [illegible] was largely gathered and classified by him. He was also a constant contributor to scientific [illegible], and was the author of "Birds of [illegible]," "Synopsis of the Birds of North America," "Ornithology of the United States Exploring Expedition," "Ornithology of Japan and [illegible]," "Ornithology of [illegible]," and other papers on the [illegible] in the [illegible] Expedition. [illegible] name of a [illegible] have been [illegible] in the [illegible] and naval history of the United States. His great-uncle, John Cassin, [illegible] in the war of 1812, and his uncle, Stephen Cassin, served under Preble in the Tripoli war, and for his bravery in action on Lake Champlain, in 1814, under command of Commodore McDonough, received a gold medal from Congress. John Cassin died in Philadelphia, Jan. 10, 1869.

Library at Bishop's Mill.—In September, 1818, a library [illegible] was formed at Bishop's Mill, and in the following year a building located about one hundred feet above the [illegible] mill was erected. It was a [illegible] structure two stories in height, the first [illegible] in [illegible], and the roof [illegible],—a [illegible] building. The second story was used for a library, and the lower floor was the office of Abner Bishop. In May, 1844, the association was incorporated as the Union Library Company. In 1846 it had eight hundred volumes on its shelves, forty-eight members, and the shares were valued at five dollars, the annual [illegible] being one dollar. In 1849 it was said to have eleven hundred and fifty volumes. In 1862 the number of books had increased to fourteen hundred. In July, 1867, the remaining volumes were sold by the sheriff. At that time there were only four hundred [illegible], which were purchased by the Delaware County Institute of Science for twenty-five dollars.

Deaths by Lightning.—On Aug. 11, 1838, Eli Baily, a young man in Upper Providence, was seated on a [illegible] near a plum-tree during a storm. The tree was struck, and the fluid passing to Baily, ran from his head to his feet and thence to the ground. His dog lying at his feet was also killed, and a watch in his pocket was melted. On July 6, 1855, the dwelling of Joseph Soper was struck, and [illegible] instantly killed. The lightning struck the house a short distance from the ground, passing through the door-frame and shattering it. The girl was standing in the door at the time. Lewis Soper, another brother, was rendered insensible for several hours by the shock when the house was struck.

Noticeable Incidents.—On Feb. 23, 1838, a young daughter of Joseph Chad was standing near her father while he was felling a large white-oak tree, and it fell in a contrary direction to that which he expected. In descending it bore with it to the ground a large chestnut-tree which fell on the girl, forcing her body several inches into the ground. Joseph Chad could not extricate her, and calling for assistance, the earth around her had to be removed before she could be freed, for the oak had fallen across the chestnut and the weight was enormous. More than half an hour was consumed before the girl was released from her perilous situation. No bones were broken nor any permanent injury sustained, although it was nearly a week before she recovered the use of her limbs. On the night of Feb. 19, 1848, the barn on Joseph Pennell's farm was entered by unknown parties and four horses killed, the animals' throats being cut. A reward of one hundred dollars was offered for the conviction of the offender, but the guilty party was not apprehended. In 1870 [illegible] Baker, a child of twelve years of age, died from hydrophobia. In December of the preceding year the boy was sitting by the fire warming his feet before going to bed, when the cat belonging to the family suddenly bit him on the foot. A [illegible] was immediately applied to the wound and the circumstance forgotten until nearly a year thereafter, when the lad exhibited all the symptoms of hydrophobia, and died in violent [illegible]. The cat never afterwards showed any indication of rabies.

Societies.—On Oct. 15, 18[illegible], Rose Tree Lodge, No. 225, Independent Order of Odd Fellows, was instituted at the Rose Tree Tavern, the first officers being John C. Beatty, N. G.; Caleb Hodgson, V. G.; James R. Malin, Sec.; Jonathan C. Taylor, Asst. Sec.; and George Drake, Treas. In 1848 the lodge erected a brick hall three stories in height, now the building of the Delaware County Institute of Science, which was dedicated October 12th of that year, with imposing ceremonies.

In April, 1849, General Marion Encampment was instituted at the Rose Tree Tavern, and in 1850 its meetings were held at Rose Tree Hall. The encampment was subsequently removed to Sugartown, Chester Co., but in April, 1856, returned to Rose Tree Hall, where it is now located.

BIOGRAPHICAL SKETCHES.

ISAAC S. CASSIN.

The Cassins are of both English and Irish descent, Joseph, the progenitor of the family in America and the great-grandfather of Isaac S., having emigrated from Queen's County, Ireland, in 1725, and settled in Philadelphia. Among his sons were John and Luke, the former of whom attained high rank in the navy, and figured prominently in the war of 1812. Luke, the grandfather of Isaac S., a native of Philadelphia, was born in 1766, and acquired the trade of a [illegible]

[1] Young's "Biography of Pennsylvania," p. [illegible].
[2] Smith's "History of Delaware County," p. [illegible].

logical collection of the Philadelphia Academy of Natural Sciences was largely gathered and classified by him. He was also a constant contributor to scientific journals, and was the author of "Birds of California and Texas;" "Synopsis of the Birds of North America;" "Ornithology of the United States Exploring Expedition;" "Ornithology of the Japan Exploring Expedition;" "Ornithology of Gillis's Astronomical Expedition to Chili;" and the chapters on the rapacious and wading bird in "The Ornithology of the Pacific Railroad Expedition and Surveys." He came of a Quaker family, which, strange as it may seem, have been distinguished in the military and naval history of the United States. His great-uncle, John Casin, was an officer in the war of 1812, and his uncle, Stephen Casin, served under Preble in the Tripoli war, and for his bravery in action on Lake Champlain, in 1814, under command of Commodore McDonough, received a gold medal from Congress. John Cassin died in Philadelphia, Jan. 10, 1869.

Library at Bishop's Mill.—In September, 1813, a library company was formed at Bishop's Mill, and in the following year a building located about one hundred feet above the grist-mill was erected. It was a stone structure, two stories in height, the floor laid in mortar, and the roof sheet-iron,—a fire-proof building. The second story was used for a library, and the lower floor was the office of Amor Bishop. In May, 1817, the association was incorporated as the Union Library Company. In 1834 it had eight hundred volumes on its shelves, forty-eight members, and the shares were valued at five dollars, the annual dues being one dollar. In 1843 it was said to have eleven hundred and fifty volumes.[1] In 1862 the number of books had increased to fourteen hundred.[2] In July, 1867, the remaining volumes were sold by the sheriff. At that time there were only four hundred books, which were purchased by the Delaware County Institute of Science for twenty-five dollars.

Deaths by Lightning.—On Aug. 11, 1838, Eli Baily, a young man in Upper Providence, was seated on a wall near a plum-tree during a storm. The tree was struck, and the fluid passing to Baily, ran from his head to his feet and thence to the ground. His dog lying at his feet was also killed, and a watch in his pocket was melted. On July 6, 1855, the dwelling of Joseph Super was struck, and his sister instantly killed. The lightning struck the house a short distance from the ground, passing through the door-frame and shattering it. The girl was standing in the door at the time. Lewis Super, another brother, was rendered insensible for several hours by the shock when the house was struck.

Noticeable Incidents.—On Oct. 25, 1838, a young daughter of Joseph Cloud was standing near her father while he was felling a large white-oak tree, and it fell in a contrary direction to that which he expected. In descending it bore with it to the ground a large chestnut tree, which fell on the girl, forcing her body several inches into the ground. Joseph Cloud could not extricate her, and calling for assistance, the earth around her had to be removed before she could be freed, for the oak had fallen across the chestnut and the weight was enormous. More than half an hour was consumed before the girl was released from her perilous situation. No bones were broken nor any permanent injury sustained, although it was nearly a week before she recovered the use of her limbs. On the night of Feb. 13, 1845, the barn on Joseph Paschall's farm was entered by unknown parties and four horses killed, the animals' throats being cut. A reward of one hundred dollars was offered for the conviction of the offender, but the guilty party was not apprehended. In 1876, William Baker, a lad of twelve years of age, died from hydrophobia. In December of the preceding year the boy was sitting by the fire warming his feet before going to bed, when the cat belonging to the family suddenly bit him on the heel. A poultice was immediately applied to the wound, and the circumstance forgotten until nearly a year thereafter, when the lad exhibited all the symptoms of hydrophobia, and died in violent spasms. The cat at no time showed any indication of rabies.

Societies.—On Oct. 18, 1847, Rose-Tree Lodge, No. 275, Independent Order of Odd-Fellows, was instituted at the Rose-Tree Tavern; its first officers being John C. Beatty, N. G.; Caleb Hoopes, V. G.; James A. Malin, Sec.; Jonathan G. Farra, Asst. Sec.; and George Dunn, Treas. In 1850 the lodge erected a brick hall three stories in height, near the building of the Delaware County Institute of Science, which was dedicated October 12th of that year, with imposing ceremonies.

In April, 1849, General Marion Encampment was instituted at the Rose-Tree Tavern, and in 1853 its meetings were held at Rose-Tree Hall. The encampment was subsequently removed to Sugartown, Chester Co.; but in April, 1883, returned to Rose-Tree Hall, where it is now located.

BIOGRAPHICAL SKETCHES.

ISAAC S. CASSIN.

The Cassins are of both English and Irish lineage, Joseph, the progenitor of the family in America and the great-grandfather of Isaac S., having emigrated from Queen's County, Ireland, in 1725, and settled in Philadelphia. Among his sons were John and Luke, the former of whom attained high rank in the navy, and figured prominently in the war of 1812. Luke, the grandfather of Isaac S., a native of Philadelphia, was born in 1763, and acquired the trade of a silver-

[1] Trego's "Geography of Pennsylvania," p. 240.
[2] Smith's "History of Delaware County," p. 560.

smith He married Ann Worrall, daughter of Dr Thomas and Lydia Worrall, of Delaware County, to whom was born in 1786 a son, Thomas Cassin His early life was spent in Philadelphia, after which he removed to Delaware County, having inherited the farm of his maternal grandfather He married Rachel, daughter of Isaac and Hannah Sharpless, of Delaware County, whose children are John (a distinguished naturalist), Lydia, Luke, Thomas W, Rebecca S (Mrs Richard Thatcher, of Delaware County), William V, Isaac S, Ann Eliza (Mrs Henry F Esrey), and Susanna S The death of Mr Cassin occurred in Delaware County in 1859 Isaac S, the fifth son, was born July 29, 1826, in Upper Providence township, near Media, and in 1841 became a pupil of the Friends' school at Westtown, Chester Co, after which he studied under private tutors He early manifested a talent for mechanics, and entering the shop of I P Morris & Co, served an apprenticeship as a mechanical engineer He was subsequently employed in various capacities in connection with his profession, and in 1856 appointed engineer of the Spring Garden Water-Works of the city of Philadelphia, having meanwhile given much attention to hydraulic engineering Again for a brief period he engaged in the mechanical department of engineering, and in 1862 was elected chief engineer of the Water Department of Philadelphia, where he remained two years Mr Cassin then served for one year as engineer of the Philadelphia Gas-Works, having meanwhile embarked in the construction of water-works and gas-works He had prior to this received the appointment of chief engineer of the United States Mint, and ultimately relinquished the position to devote his personal attention to large and increasing business enterprises He constructed the water-works at Chester, Delaware Co, the reservoirs at Wilmington, Del, the water-works at Oxford, Pa, those at Westchester and Media, those at Wayne, Delaware Co, at Coatesville, Chester Co, at Pottstown, Pa, at Conshohocken, Pa, at Ashland and Phœnixville, in the same State, at Birdsborough, Pa, at Doylestown, Pa, part of those at Norristown, Pa, those of New Castle and Dover, Del, at Ithaca and Owego, N Y, at Bridgeton, N J, at Burlington, N J, at Lambertville and Salem, N J, and at Swarthmore College, Delaware Co To this business, in itself extensive and requiring close business application and mechanical insight, he has added the construction of hydraulic machinery and appliances Mr Cassin was, on the 10th of October, 1850, married to Emily, daughter of J Morgan Hunter, of Delaware County, and has children,—Thomas (deceased), Eliza H (Mrs M L Snyder), Edward (deceased), John, Emily, and Isaac S, Jr

Mr Cassin is a recognized authority in the city of his residence on all matters pertaining to the science of mechanics, and has been employed as consulting engineer and expert in various enterprises requiring the services of a skilled mechanical and civil engineer His reports and communications of this character have been numerous, particularly those relating to hydraulic engineering He is one of the commissioners for the erection of the public buildings for Philadelphia He is also a member of the Franklin Institute, and of the Engineers Club He is in religion a Friend, and a birthright member of the society of Friends, holding his membership with the Race Street Friends' Meeting of Philadelphia

---

GEORGE B ADAMS

The Adams family, who are of Welsh extraction, became at an early date settlers in Massachusetts Thomas Adams, the grandfather of George B, was a resident of Boston, where he pursued an editorial career His two sons were Thomas and George, the latter of whom was a native of Boston, and both in that city and in Philadelphia extensively engaged in shipping He married Miss Mary Mayland, daughter of Jacob Mayland, of Philadelphia, and had children,—George B, Mary (Mrs Thomas H Dallett), Thomas M, Charles A. (deceased), and two who died in infancy George B was born May 20, 1825, and spent his early youth in the city of Philadelphia He received a liberal education, having been for two years a pupil of Delaware College, Newark, Del, after which his education was completed at Mount St. Mary's College, Emmettsburg, Md On returning to Philadelphia he engaged in business as an accountant with Messrs Brown & Brother, an extensive jobbing dry-goods house This sedentary life not being agreeable to his tastes, at the expiration of the third year he determined to pursue the more active and healthful calling of the agriculturist, and with that object in view, made Delaware County his home in 1845 In 1847 he purchased land in Radnor township, and continued farming until 1864, when, having sold, he located for a brief period in Montgomery County In 1869, Mr Adams became the possessor of his present home in Upper Providence, where he leads a retired life amid the pursuits most congenial to him. He married, in 1847, Miss Sarah, daughter of Levi Burdsall, of Medford, N J, and has children,—Thomas B (deceased), George E and Charles C (engaged in business in Media), and Theodore L (a graduate of the Hahnemann Medical College, Philadelphia, and practicing his profession in Berwyn, Chester Co, Pa) Mr. Adams has devoted some attention to studies of a scientific character, and at present fills the position of member of the board of curators of the Delaware County Institute of Science, located at Media, his residence having been the property of the institute, where its sessions were held. Mr Adams is in politics a Republican, but has declined all proffers of office other than those immediately associated with the township of his residence In his religious views he embraces the faith of the Universalist Church

Geo B Adams

J. Morgan Hunter

J. Morgan Hunter

Jeremiah Bishop.

Hugh L. Tyler

J MORGAN HUNTER

The progenitors of Mr Hunter were of Scotch-Irish descent, and were early settlers in Delaware County, where they purchased a large estate in Newtown township His grandfather, James Hunter, married Martha Levis, of Springfield township, whose children were Samuel, J Morgan, Peter, Hannah (Mrs Joseph McCleese), Martha (Mrs Isaac Maris), Rachel (Mrs Lott Worrell), Mary (Mrs Elisha Moore), Sidney (Mrs William Sloan), Ann (Mrs Reece Hoops), Sarah (Mrs. Frederick Worrell).

Samuel was born in Radnor township, Delaware Co, where, after a brief but useful life, his death occurred, in 1802. He married Hannah, daughter of Samuel Edwards, and had children,—Elizabeth (Mrs Edward Tomlinson) and J Morgan The latter was born March 28, 1801, in Radnor township, and very early in life found a home with his paternal grandfather. At the age of seven he removed to Newtown township, and remained with an uncle until sixteen, when he learned, in Chester County, Pa, the trade of a blacksmith. He continued to be actively employed at his trade, and meanwhile married Eliza Rhoads, daughter of John and Rachel Rhoads, who was born Jan. 21, 1799, in Philadelphia Their children are Rachel (Mrs Nathan H Yarnall), Hannah (Mrs Baldwin), Emily (Mrs Isaac S Cassin), Sarah Jane (Mrs James Hoey), and Samuel

Mr. Hunter followed his trade until 1826, after which he removed to Marple township, and became a farmer on land belonging to Mrs. Hunter. In 1852 he settled in Upper Providence upon a farm purchased by him, where, ten years later, a spacious residence was erected Some years since he abandoned active labor, and is now occupied in the superintendence of his various business interests Mr Hunter was formerly a Whig in politics, and now votes the ticket of the Republican party. In religion he supports all Christian denominations, though immediately connected with none The death of Mrs Hunter occurred in 1873

JEREMIAH BISHOP

Jeremiah Bishop is the grandson of Thomas Bishop, who had sons, Thomas and Joseph, and several daughters Joseph was born in Delaware County, where he was both wheelwright and farmer He married Sarah Pratt, of the same county, and had children,—Thomas, Randall, Tamar (Mrs Samuel Pancoast), Emily, Joel, Orpah, and Jeremiah The last named, and the subject of this sketch, was born Oct 6, 1805, in Upper Providence The schools of the neighborhood afforded him a plain English education, after which he began an active career of labor as a farmer He married, on the 28th of February, 1833, Miss Hannah Eachus, daughter of Evans and Hannah Eachus, of the same township Their children are Henry C. Bishop (of Concord), Sarah P. (Mrs William P Thomas, of Newtown), and Emily B (Mrs Thomas B McCay, of Upper Providence). Mr Bishop, on his marriage, rented a farm of his father, which he cultivated for a period of eight years On the decease of the latter, in 1840, the homestead farm became his by inheritance To this spot he removed the following year, and until 1882 devoted his energies to its improvement and cultivation In 1884 he sold the farm and made the home of his daughter, Mrs McCay, his residence Mr Bishop has been during his whole life a farmer, and given little time to other business pursuits He is a supporter of the platform of the Republican party, and though not ambitious for official position, has held numerous township offices He is in religion a birthright Friend, and worships with the Friends' Meeting in Middletown Mrs Bishop died Sept 13, 1883, after a period of married life extending over half a century

HUGH LOW TYLER.

The Tyler family are descended from ancient English stock, their ancestors having come with William the Conqueror into England and fought at the battle of Hastings, in 1066 Six hundred years later three brothers of the name emigrated to America from Street, Somersetshire, England, one of whom settled in New England, another in Virginia, becoming the ancestor of ex-President John Tyler, and the third, William, located in West Jersey, about 1688 He purchased of John Champneys a large tract of land on the north side of Monmouth River, part of the two thousand acres deeded in 1676 by John Fenwick to James Champneys and wife, Priscilla Fenwick Champneys William Tyler brought with him to this country a certificate from his friends and neighbors in England, certifying "that he hath been ready and willing to contribute to the service of truth as opportunity hath offered and occasion required, and that as to his dealings with the world he hath been punctual and of good report as far as any of us know or have heard, and we know nothing of debts or other entanglements on his part, but that he may with clearness prosecute his intended voyage" He married, in 1676, Joanna Parson, and had four children born in England,—Mary, William, John, and Joanna To his second wife, Elizabeth, married in this country, were born children,—Catherine, Philip, and Elizabeth His death occurred about 1701 His son, William Tyler, married Mary Abbott, and had children,—William, Edith, Rebecca, Mary, James, and Samuel. His death occurred in 1733 Samuel, his youngest son, was born Oct 26, 1723 He married Ann Mason, and had five children,—William, John, Mary, Samuel, and Rebecca He died Nov 26, 1778, and his wife Feb. 23, 1777. His son, William Tyler, married Beulah Ridgway, who died soon after without issue. He married March 17, 1796, as his second wife, Catherine, daughter of Hugh Low, of Philadelphia, whose children were John, born in 1797, Hannah G, in 1798, Hugh L, in 1800, Mary, in 1801, Annie, in 1805, and William, in 1806 Mr Tyler died Oct 8, 1823, and his wife, March 21, 1825 Their son, Hugh Low, was born March 20, 1800, in Salem County, N J, where he resided until the year 1852 He enjoyed such advantages of education as the schools of the neighborhood afforded, after which, at the age of twenty-two, he engaged with his brother, John, in the business of tanning in Salem, N J Three years later he continued the business on a farm owned by him In the year 1840, having decided to retire from the active pursuits he had followed, he became a successful farmer, and added to his landed property by the purchase of another farm in the same county In 1852 he removed with his family to Delaware County, Pa, on a farm owned by his wife. Mr Tyler was married on the 16th of December, 1835, to Mary Miller, daughter of George Miller, of Upper Providence township, Delaware Co, whose children are William Levis, whose birth occurred Sept 12, 1834, and his death July 18, 1871, George Miller, born May 8, 1836, and John Edgar, born Oct 5, 1842, who resides upon the Miller homestead in Upper Providence George M, also of the same township, married Emma V Weaver, daughter of Jacob Weaver, of Philadelphia, and has four children J Edgar married Anna, daughter of Edward Hicks, of East Goshen, Chester Co, Pa Mr Tyler was actively associated with the Whig party in politics, and later became a Republican He was identified with the township in various official stations, and was at one time a candidate for the State Legislature He manifested much interest in matters tending to advance the development of the township both in its social and material aspects He was in religion a Friend, having been educated in the faith of his fathers The death of Mr Tyler occurred March 8, 1883, aged eighty-three years, and that of Mrs Tyler, Nov 24, 1881

CHAPTER LI

RADNOR TOWNSHIP[1]

THE township of Radnor, as regards its area, location, and population, the wealth of its inhabitants, its commercial advantages and traveling facilities, the fertility of its soil, and its picturesque views, is surpassed by but few rural districts in a broad region teeming with the essentials, and, it may be added, the consequentials of affluent modern life It embraces the extreme northern portion of this county, thus having for its boundaries Montgomery County on the east, Chester County on the west, and Haverford township on the south Its first settlers were natives of Radnorshire,[2] Wales, hence its name

As already intimated, this township was settled by Welsh Friends, and was included in the "Welsh Tract," of which Haverford, Merion, and a number of other townships formed part. In 1681 a Welsh gentleman, named Richard Davies, purchased five thousand acres of land from William Penn, in England, which he sold soon after to various purchasers The whole, or nearly the whole, of this tract was located in Radnor,—chiefly in the southern half,—though there is no evidence that the grantor, Davies, ever visited this country.

The highway known as Radnor Street or road, which in its straight course through the central part of the township, in a direction nearly north and south, divides it into two parts almost equal in extent, was laid out in 1683, and it is probable (from the fact that settlers were then becoming numerous in Haverford) that the first settlements were made here during the same year John Jerman, or Jarman, as it is frequently written, Stephen ap Evan, David Meredith, Richard Miles, John Morgan, Evan Protherah, Richard Ormes, William Davis, Howell James, and about as many others, were the first to settle in Radnor All were Welsh Friends, and all were domiciled here in less than four years from the date of William Penn's first arrival in this province

The first white child born in Radnor was John Jerman, Sr[3] This event took place Ninth month (November) 12, 1684, in the vicinity of the present Friends' meeting-house. Stephen Evans' daughter, Sarah, whose birth occurred Fifth month 25, 1686, was the first female child born of European parents in the township

In 1687, "Upon ye Reading ye petition of ye Inhabitants of Radnor, Complayning y^t^ part of ye road y^t^ leades to the ferry of Philadelphia is fenced in, & more likely to be, it was Ord^ed^ y^t^ John Bevan, Henry Lewis, David Meredith, John Evans, Barnabas Wilcox & Tho Duckett meet within fourteen days, to view or agree upon as conveniently as may be, a Road from ye place aforesaid to ye ferry, and ye Like Convenient road from Darby to ye ferry aforesaid, by ye said Barnabas Wilcox, Tho Duckett, with John Blunston & Joshua ffearne [Fearne], by y^t^ time aforesaid, and to return ye same, &c"[4]

Until about 1690 the Welsh settlers of the "Welsh Tract" refused to participate in any measures, or to attach themselves to any district in which municipal government had been established, claiming a promise from the proprietary (William Penn) that they should

[1] By John S Schenck

[2] Radnor is mentioned in Welsh history as early as A.D 1196, during which year, it is stated, it was burned by an invading foe

[3] John Jerman, Jr, died in Radnor in the year 1769 A few days after his death the *Pennsylvania Chronicle*, in an obituary notice, spoke of him "as a gentleman well known for his astronomical calculations." Mr Jerman had published an almanac

[4] Extract from minutes of proceedings of grand jury for that year

"CHETWYND."

form a separate community, with a view of deciding all controversies and debates among themselves in their own language and in "Gospel Order" However, as these troubles of the early Welsh settlers have have been explained at some length in the history of Haverford township, it is deemed unnecessary to repeat them here

In 1691 the grand jury ordered that a road be laid out leading from Rhoads' tan-yard, in Marple, to a point near the site of the present Radnor meeting-house. The route when marked by blazing trees was not varied in the least by reason of hills, etc, but continued straight ahead over all elevations, ravines, morasses, etc

At a Monthly Meeting of Friends held at Haverford meeting-house in Sixth month (August), 1693, it was ordered "y^t William Howell, Morris Llewelyn, for Haverford, David Meredith, David Evans, for Radnor; Griffith Jones, James Thomas, for Merion, see y^t sufficient fences be kept in his respective neighbourhood" During the same year, also, "it is ordered by this meeting by consent of the inhabitants of the townships of Haverford and Radnor, in pursuance of a law in that case made, y^t ye inhabitants of ye s^d two townships should pay one shilling per hundred [meaning one hundred acres of land] towards ye taking of Wolves, William Howell, William Jenkins, for Haverford, and David Meredith and Stephen Bevan, for Radnor, to receive ye s^d Taxe"

The taxable inhabitants of Radnor at this date, 1693, a time when a provincial tax was levied of one penny per pound sterling on estates and six shillings per head upon freemen, were as follows

	£	s	d
John Evans	00	03	09
David Meredith	00	05	10
John Evans	00	02	06
John Jarman	00	03	08
John Morgan	00	02	08
William David	00	02	07
Richard Ormes.	00	04	04
Mathew Jones	00	02	06
Howell James	00	03	08
Philip Evan	00	03	07
David Evan	00	03	05
William Davis	00	02	07
Samuel Miles	00	02	09
Richard Miles	00	02	10
Evan Protherah	00	03	07
John Richard.	00	02	07
Stephen Bevan	00	03	09
Thomas Johns	00	02	08

Roads leading from the site of Radnor Friends' meeting-house to Schuylkill Ford, and from John Longworthy's house to a road "between Chester and Radnor," were laid out Tenth month (December) 11, 1694.

Although a large majority of the early inhabitants of Radnor were Friends, people who remained true to the principles and the teachings of their peculiar system of opinions throughout their lives, still there were others among them who could only be satisfied with the dogmas preached by ministers of the established church,—the Church of England Hence, in accordance with the earnest request of prominent members of the latter class, a Rev Mr. Evans, of Philadelphia,—the first clergyman of the Episcopal Church to preach in Pennsylvania,—occasionally visited certain families residing in Radnor, and preached to them, beginning as early as the year 1700 However, to explain more fully these events in the early history of the township, we quote from an historical account of the incorporated Society for the Propagation of the Gospel in Foreign Parts, which was published early in the last century, as follows

"Oxford and Radnor, two Welsh settlements, were first visited by Mr Evans from Philadelphia, and the People, having been Members of the Church of England when they were transplanted from Wales hither, were desirous of having that form of worship fixed among them again By his occasional Sermons, and the visits of other Clergymen, the People of Oxford were encouraged to build a neat and convenient Church The Congregation consisted chiefly of the younger People, and the whole town composed of about 20 families, they not only built a Church, but subscribed also £20 a year to their minister in money and country produce The people of Radnor also petitioned for a Minister, and the Society appointed the Rev Mr Club Missionary to Oxford and Radnor, two Towns being about 20 miles distant from each other He arrived there in 1714 The inhabitants of both Towns received him with great kindness, as being well known to them before, during his being Schoolmaster at Philadelphia, The people of Radnor especially were very thankful to the Society for having been pleased to consider their Wants, and renewed their promise of giving him their best Assistance and presently after his arrivals, heartily engaged to build a handsome stone Church,[1] which they have since performed Mr Club was very earnest in all parts of his Ministerial Office, and very successful in his Labours, and happy in engaging the love and Esteem of all his people But the Cure of these two Churches engaged him in great Fatigue, not only on account of the Distance between the Places, but because of the Extremity of the Weather, whether hot or cold Mr Club contracted so many indispositions by his Labours, as put an end to his Life in 1715 The People were so sensible of the Difficulties he underwent that, after his Death, the Church Wardens of the Parish wrote thus to the Society. 'Mr Club, our late Minister, was the first that undertook the Cure of Oxford and Radnor, and he paid dear for it, for the great Fatigue of riding between the two Churches, in such dismal ways and weather as we generally have for four Months in the Winter, soon put a period to his life '

"Both Towns wrote again to the Society, requesting another missionary, the Society wrote a Letter in reply exhorting them to consider on some proper means among themselves for making sufficient allowance for a minister to reside constantly among them In answer to this they assured the Society, 'they were heartily disposed to do their best, but at present their circumstances would not do great things They were at present but poor Settlers, who had a newly settled Land backwards in the Wilderness, and had not yet so much as their own Habitations free from Debts, that indeed they had built Churches, in hopes of having ministers from the Society, and had thereby so much incumbered themselves, that it would be some years, in all Probabilities, before they could clear that debt '

"The Society were desirous this good Disposition of the People should not be disappointed, and in 1717, appointed the Rev Mr Wayman their Missionary at Oxford and Radnor The inhabitants of Oxford purchased a House, Orchard, and sixty three acres of Land, for the use and Habitation of the Minister, and the People of Radnor have obliged themselves to contribute forty pounds Proclamation money of that Country, yearly, towards the support of a Minister to preach to them in Welsh, their Native Language, because many of them do not understand English "

The taxable inhabitants of Radnor in 1722, and the assessed value in pounds sterling of real estate held by each, were—

David Harry, 54, Richard Ormes, 20, William Thomas, 30, David Pugh, 20, Sarah Abraham, 24, Hugh David, 8, Arthur Jones, 6, John

[1] This church edifice, now known as St David's, was commenced in 1715, and completed in 1717 It is situated just without the limits of Radnor, and in the extreme northeast corner of Newtown township, but for very many years it was usually designated the Radnor Church

David, 34, John Thomas, 40, John Morgan, Jr, 24, Richard Richards, 24, David Jones, 20, Jenkin David, 36, Thomas Thomas, 60, Owen Evans, 36, John Jerman, 36, David Powell and land in Brandywine, 36, Gabriel Davies, 28, John Jones, 32, Howell Powell, 14, David James, 24, Thomas Lewis, 20, Caleb Evans, 36, Joseph Williams, 16, Hugh Wilson, 16, John Morgan and land in Whiteland, 54, John Samuel, 10, Edward George, 32, Edward Jones, 24, Evan Evans, 20, David Evans, 16, Evan Stephens, 14, David Thomas, 15, Joseph Jones, 34

To and including the early part of the year 1748 the following-named persons had received patents for lands in Radnor, at times and in quantity as here shown

	Acres
1684, 5 mo 29, Thomas Wynn	250
1684, 6 mo 4, John Longworthy	200
1685, 8 mo 30, David Davis (or Davies)	200
1686, 3 mo 13 David Powell (two tracts)	611
1687, 7 mo 9, David Powell (two tracts)	300
1688, 3 mo 21, John Fisher's executors	300
1688, 8 mo 1, Reece Prece	200
1689, 3 mo. 26, David Meredith	350
1701, Sept 30, Evan Proderah	122
1702, 5 mo 16, David Powell	138
1703, Oct 25, John Evan Edward	123
1703, Oct 25, Margaret Jerman	152
1703 Oct 26, David Pugh	174
1703, Oct 26, James Pugh	162
1703, Nov 1 Thomas John Evan	340
1703, Nov 2, Edward David	155
1703, March 14, John Evans.	300
1704, 3 mo 1, David Meredith	253
1705, 3 mo 7, Stephen ap Evan	397
1705, 3 mo 14, David Evans (two tracts)	397
1705, 5 mo 6 Richard Miles	233
1705, 5 mo 6, Samuel Miles	352
1713, Sept 10, David Morris	50
1715, Dec 2, Margaret Miles	60
1733, Dec 4, Thomas Thomas	92
1733, March 5 Edward George	204
1733, March 5 Henry Harry.	154
1733, March 12, William Thomas	200
1735, Dec 4, Samuel Rees	56¾
1748, June 11, John Jerman	52

During the "old French and Indian war," which continued from 1754 to 1763, a number of the able-bodied men of Radnor joined the provincial forces, and performed service in the armies commanded respectively by Braddock, Forbes, Stanwix, and Boquet. Among them were eight young Friends, or Quakers, who, upon their return "from the wars," and as a recompense for the patriotism and courage displayed by them, were *disowned* by the Quaker fraternity, and prohibited from enjoying any benefits within the society for evermore It is to be presumed, however, that these brave men survived such proceedings, and during a later period—the Revolutionary war—were again found enrolled, perhaps as commissioned officers, in the Pennsylvania Line Col Evan Evans, an early justice of the peace, and one of the most prominent American officers in Chester County during the Revolutionary struggles, was, we believe, a native and resident of Radnor, and it is quite probable that he, being the son of a Friend, was one of the disowned, as above mentioned

In 1758, when Gen Forbes was organizing his expedition for the capture of Fort Du Quesne, the authorities of the several counties in Pennsylvania were required to furnish wagons, teams, and wagoners for the transportation of army supplies Hence, of those who went out to represent Chester County were Thomas Legitt and Hugh Wilson, of Radnor Following are the accounts of these men, as rendered at the close of the campaign by Roger Hunt

"Radnor,—Thomas Legitt to his majesty

Dr	£	s	d
To cash advanced	10	19	0
To Two Bushels oats	0	6	0
To cash ..	10	8	5
	21	13	5

Cr	£	s	d
By 5 bbls of Pork from Carlile to Bedford, weighing gross, C, 13, 3, 10, is	12	2	1½
Miles from Carlile to Radnor and Back—is 196 miles	7	7	0
To sundrys from Carlile to Littleton as per Receipt may appear, C, 3, 3, 7 @ 11s, 8d per hundred	2	4	4
	21	13	5½

"Mem The above named was the first man that agreed for a bounty in Chester County

"Hugh Wilson entered a wagon Oct 25th

"Credited by 7 bbls flour from Carlile to Bedford, mileage for 215 miles, settled Nov 14"

Hugh Wilson, it will be observed, was a resident of the township as early as 1722

At the beginning of the war for independence the taxable inhabitants of Radnor numbered ninety-eight Hence, by estimating five inhabitants to each taxable, its population at that time amounted to four hundred and ninety, or more than one-third as many people as it contained one hundred years later. During the same year (1775) the tax levied upon the township, at the rate of "two pence in the pound upon estates and six shillings on single freemen," amounted to seventeen pounds thirteen shillings and sixpence.

As explained in the general chapters of this work, also in the history of Haverford township, soon after the battle of Brandywine (in which the British were victorious) Gen Washington, with the yet undaunted American army, marched out from Germantown over the old Conestoga or Lancaster road into and beyond the limits of Radnor, for the purpose of again engaging the invaders and despoilers of this region, but a heavy and prolonged rain-storm coming on, Washington was compelled to countermarch his forces, and retire without forcing the enemy to a conflict, which doubtless would have resulted in victory for the Americans Finally, the enemy obtained possession of Philadelphia, and thereafter, during several months, British soldiers, under orders from Gen Howe and Lord Cornwallis, committed innumerable depredations in Radnor and the adjoining districts Hence, at the beginning of the winter of 1777-78, these shameless marauders left many families wholly destitute of their live-stock and provisions, and carried away all the clothing, household goods, kitchen furniture, plate, etc, upon which they could lay their hands

At the close of the war, in pursuance of an act of the Assembly adopted in 1782, the inhabitants of Chester County were called upon to make statements of the losses sustained by each, at the hands of the British in 1777 Thereupon, the following-named inhabitants of Radnor rendered a statement of their losses These statements may be relied upon as accurate, for they were made under the oaths or affirmations of the sufferers

"WENTWORTH."
RESIDENCE OF EDWARD H. WILLIAMS.

	£	s	d.
From Daniel Evans, "by a detachment of the British army under Cornwallis, then ravaging the neighborhood, Dec 11"	25	4	6
From Sarah Davis, widow, "by the British army on their march to Philadelphia"	40	3	9
From Owen Shelton, September 19	30	0	0
From John Jones, Sept 19 and Decr 11	303	2	6
From Michael Stadleman's estate	55	3	9
From Sarah Miles, "then a minor"	13	0	0
From Isaac Thomas	185	10	0
From Lewis Lewis, Sept. 19	60	0	0
From William Jennings	18	0	0
From John Pugh	122	11	0
From Mordecai Morgan, "by a party of British under Col Harcourt, Sept 19"	45	0	0
From George White, "by a party of British under Col Harcourt, Sept 19"	50	0	0
From Aquilla Evans, "by a party of British under Col Harcourt, Sept 19" ..	20	0	0
From Mark Evans, by Cornwallis, Dec 11	10	15	0
From David Phillips, by Col Harcourt, Sept 19	30	0	0
From Edward Lane, by Gen Howe	8	15	0
From Adam Siter, by Col Harcourt	30	0	0
From Enos Miles, by Col Harcourt	45	0	0
From William Lee, by Col Harcourt	50	0	0
From Levi Lewis, by Col Harcourt	60	0	0
From Sarah Kenny, by the British army when marching from Valley Forge to Philadelphia, September	38	0	0
From Frederick Bittle, Sept 19	23	7	0
From David Cornog by Howe, Sept	18	0	0
From Isaac Davis, by Cornwallis, Dec 11	49	0	0
From Paul Sheridan, by Harcourt, Sept	9	5	0
From Griffith James, by Cornwallis, Dec 11	55	16	0
From Jonas Yocum, by Cornwallis, Dec 11	66	15	0
From Samuel Pugh and Mord Morgan, by Harcourt, Sept 19	35	0	0

In the winter of 1777–78, Gen Potter, with a considerable body of American militia, was assigned to the duty of guarding the country between the Schuylkill and Chester, to prevent supplies reaching the enemy, as well as to protect the patriotic inhabitants from foraging parties sent out from Philadelphia by the British In the performance of these duties numerous skirmishes took place in Radnor and its vicinity between Potter's men and the thievish invaders In a letter from Gen Potter, dated at Radnor, on the 28th of December, 1777, one of these encounters is thus described "On Monday last the enemy came out with a view to forage They encamped along the road from Gray's Ferry to the heights below Darby There was a detachment sent down from our army to this place, who, with Morgan's riflemen and the militia, went down to their lines and kept them close therein On Tuesday we took thirteen of their light-horse and ten of their horsemen, the next day two more of their horses and their riders They have been prevented from plundering the inhabitants, as they usually do . We had one killed and two wounded We have taken upwards of twenty prisoners, and a number of deserters have come in They have carried off a large quantity of hay from the Islands and Darby "[1]

During the same winter another incident transpired in Radnor which for a time was of serious import to a native and former resident of the township It appears that soon after the occupation of Philadelphia and its vicinity by the British, one Benjamin Davis, the proprietor of the Rising Sun Tavern, in Frankford, became a temporary resident, willingly or otherwise, of the city Some time during the season mentioned he appeared at the American camp in Radnor and made a statement to Gen Potter in substance as follows That his mother resided within the American lines in Radnor, that he was the proprietor of the Rising Sun Tavern in Frankford, that he had been made prisoner by the British, and had been detained by them in Philadelphia for several weeks, that they had finally released him, and that he now wished to visit his mother, in Radnor, preparatory to returning to his tavern, the Rising Sun Gen Potter granted his request, and allowed him to visit his mother Soon after, however, it was whispered about that Davis was a spy, and had been sent out by the British to ascertain the strength and position of the Americans Thereupon he was arrested, and made to undergo a most rigid examination, but finally, whether guilty of any understanding with the enemy or not, was released, and allowed to go free and unmolested Probably this was the same Davis who was assessed as the owner of a grist-mill in Radnor in 1788, and in years subsequent to that date

With the close of the Revolutionary war an unwonted degree of prosperity dawned upon Radnor New highways were laid out, many additional settlers established themselves here, and a Methodist meeting-house was erected In 1792 the Philadelphia and Lancaster turnpike was commenced, to be completed two years later by the expenditure of four hundred and sixty-five thousand dollars This, the first turnpike road built in America, was the means of greatly increasing travel through the central part of the township, and caused the establishment of numerous wayside inns along its route

In 1809 the Radnor Library was established Its five hundred volumes, representing the liberality of eighteen subscribers, were placed in a store near Friends' meeting-house

In 1820 many of the inhabitants of Radnor inaugurated rather vigorous measures looking to the annexation of their township to the county of Montgomery These proceedings on the part of Radnor residents at last aroused the whole county, and finally became the leading topic of discussion among its citizens Dr Smith writes of this agitation and its rather tame results as follows

"Dissatisfaction had for some time existed among the people of the upper part of the county on account of the seat of justice being situated on its southern margin The people of the township of Radnor, residing much nearer to Norristown, the seat of justice of Montgomery County, than to Chester, petitioned for the annexation of their township to that county The fact that the taxes of Montgomery were lower than those of Delaware is also said to have had an influence in promoting this movement. Be that as it may, the prospect of losing one of the best townships in the county was a matter of serious alarm, when its small dimensions were taken into consideration The discontented in the remote townships, seeing that the loss of Radnor would weaken their strongest ground of complaint, determined to test the question of a removal of the seat of justice of the county to a more central situation Accordingly a general meeting of the inhabitants of the county, 'both friendly and unfriendly' to the proposed removal, was convened on the 8th of June, 1820 The meeting was unusually large and very respectable, and after the subject of removal had been discussed very fully and rather freely, a vote was taken which resulted in favor of the removalists

"Removal now became the leading topic of discussion throughout the

[1] Penna Archives, vol vi p 141

county All party distinctions became merged into it, and the most ultra politicians of opposite parties united cordially on a removal or anti-removal platform Meetings were held, and nominations were made accordingly The ballot-box showed the anti removalists in the majority George G Leiper, of Ridley, and Abner Lewis, of Radnor, both anti-removalists, were elected to the Assembly The anti-removalists, by the nomination of Mr Lewis, had secured nearly the whole vote of Radnor, under the belief that the election of the anti removal ticket afforded them the only chance of being annexed to Montgomery County The test was not regarded by the removalists as satisfactory, and they petitioned the Legislature for redress, but certainly with but small hopes of success In their memorial, which is very long, they set forth the fact of the effort of Radnor to be attached to Montgomery County, the dilapidated condition of the jail, the insalubrity of the air at Chester to persons from the upper parts of the county, the danger of the records from attack by an enemy, the badness of the water, etc 'And, finally,' they say, 'to satisfy the Legislature that nothing is asked for by the petitioners which would throw any unreasonable expense on the county, assurances are given by one of the inhabitants, perfectly responsible and competent to the undertaking that he will give an obligation to any one authorized to receive it, conditioned to erect the public buildings upon any reasonable and approved plan, for the sum of *fifteen thousand dollars*, to be paid in seven years, by installments, if the convenience of the county should require credit, and take the present buildings and lot at Chester at a fair valuation as part pay'

"This petition was drawn up by Robert Frazer, Esq, then a prominent lawyer, residing in the upper part of the county, and was signed by 912 citizens. The number who signed the remonstrance is not known, but, as a matter of course, with both representatives opposed to removal, no legislation favorable to that measure was obtained, and it is only wonderful that the removalists should press the matter under such circumstances What is also remarkable, the people of Radnor appeared to relax their efforts to obtain legislation to authorize the township to be annexed to Montgomery County

"At the next election, John Lewis and William Cheyney, both removalists, were elected members of the Assembly, but from some cause they failed in obtaining the much desired law authorizing the seat of justice to be removed to a more central situation The question, after this effort, appears to have been allowed to slumber for a time It was, however, occasionally discussed, and the removalists maintained a strict vigilance to prevent any extensive repairs being made to the public buildings at Chester"

On the 12th of May, 1838, Radnor Lyceum was organized by the election of the following officers Hugh Jones Brooke, president, John Pechin, recording secretary, Dr James Jenkins, corresponding secretary John Mather, treasurer, John Evans, Edward B Wetherell, William Haskins, Alexander Kenzie, George Palmer, Mary Kenzie, and Adelaide Cornog, managers

In 1847, when the question of the removal of the seat of justice from Chester to its present location was submitted to the people, Radnor polled one hundred and fifty-two votes in favor of removal, and forty votes against removal This would indicate a population of about eight hundred inhabitants at that time

On the 3d of January, 1881, the line dividing Radnor and Haverford townships was determined to be as follows "Beginning at the present line between said townships, at a point on the road from White Hall, Montgomery County, to Coopertown, Haverford, directly opposite the east corner of said road where it turns from said line into Haverford township, thence south 30 degrees $909\frac{5}{10}$ feet to a point, thence crossing said road, and keeping on the line between lands of R K Montgomery and lands of Joseph Lockwood, south 60 degrees and 6 minutes, west 1430 feet, to land of the Sheaff estate, thence through said land of Sheaff estate and land of John K Valentine, south 60 degrees and 24 minutes, west 2992 feet, crossing a certain public road leading to Brooke's mill, thence following the southwesterly side of said road the following courses and distances north 30 degrees and 6 minutes, west 36 feet, south 86 degrees 45 minutes, west $255\frac{5}{10}$ feet, north 54 degrees, west $432\frac{3}{10}$ feet, north 28 degrees 55 minutes, west $383\frac{4}{10}$ feet, to a point on the present township line"

Within the last decade, and especially during the four years last passed, vast improvements have been made in the township, particularly along the lines of the Lancaster turnpike and the Pennsylvania Railroad Numerous costly country residences, inclosed by spacious, tastefully-arranged grounds, have been erected, new roads and streets have been laid out, new towns built, and, as a result, the population and the values of Radnor have increased in a wonderful manner The town of Wayne presents a striking example of the rapid progress being made in this direction, and affords subject-matter for the following descriptions

Town of Wayne.—In September, 1880, the readers of a Philadelphia newspaper were informed that George W Childs, of the Philadelphia *Ledger*, and A J Drexel, of that city, had purchased a tract of land of about six hundred acres, three hundred of which is the Louella farm at Wayne Station, on the Pennsylvania Railroad, formerly owned by J Henry Askin It is the intention of the present owners to have the property laid out in the most attractive manner by an experienced gardener Buildings will be erected, lots sold on the most advantageous terms, and money advanced to those who desire to build There are several fine residences, two public halls, a church (Presbyterian), and gas- and water-works on a part of the Askin estate. The new purchase will be called "Wayne," and there will be about five hundred thousand dollars invested, including proposed improvements The lots will be sold at private sale, it being the intention of the projectors to provide desirable residences for those of moderate means, who may desire to settle in that portion of Delaware County

Thus was foreshadowed what has since proved to be the successful and praiseworthy enterprise in which Messrs Childs and Drexel embarked After the lapse of nearly four years another newspaper speaks of "Wayne's rapid growth" as follows

"The beautiful suburban town which Mr George W Childs, of the *Public Ledger*, and the Messrs Drexel, the bankers, are building at Wayne Station on the Pennsylvania Railroad, has just donned its summer garb, Louella Mansion, the larger of the two hotels there, having opened yesterday for the season This, with the Bellevue, which pulled up its blinds a week ago, contributes over four hundred or one-third of the population of the place In three years forty-nine new buildings have been erected by these capitalists, a large hotel has been constructed, and another one very much enlarged, they have perfected a drainage system which is said to be unequaled by any resort in the United States, the designs having been furnished by Col George F

Waring, the best posted man in the country on sanitary matters Miles of distribution pipe have been laid by them, a water system that draws its supply from springs at the source of Ithan Creek, and clarifies itself in a reservoir capable of holding two hundred and fifty thousand gallons, at an elevation of four hundred and fifty feet above tide-water, has been put in operation, a nursery has been laid out for young sprigs, which are tenderly cared for in this little patch until they have acquired enough age to be transplanted along the banks of the creek in a pretty park, a new and attractive station has been built by the Pennsylvania Railroad Company, new driving roads have been made, and in all there has been an outlay for grounds and improvements of three-quarters of a million dollars towards the establishment of a city on scientific principles, and towards providing homes in the country with all the comforts of the city Eventually six hundred houses will be built there, and accommodation furnished for a population of three thousand

"A drive along the Lancaster pike, past Bryn Mawr, Radnor, and other resting places of wealth and fashion, brings Wayne within an hour and a half of the Public Buildings, at Broad and Market Streets The distance by rail is fourteen miles, or thirty minutes from Broad Street Station The pike is owned by a corporation headed by Mr A. J Cassatt, who bought the charter of the stretch from Philadelphia to Paoli for seven thousand five hundred dollars, and then improved it at an expense of seventy thousand dollars Before the building of the Pennsylvania Railroad it was the main avenue from Philadelphia to the West, but after the railroad paralleled it with tracks, up to the time that Mr Cassatt and his friends acquired possession, it had been very much neglected To day there is not in America a driving road of equal length that compares with it Along this avenue for a stretch of one and a half miles lies the Childs-Drexel tract of seven hundred acres, and facing it on either side are nearly all of the buildings which these gentlemen have put up A row of eighteen residences set out by pairs, in lots having one hundred and twenty feet front, has just been finished The new buildings stand forty feet back of the street line They are of brick, with broad piazzas and sloping lawns surrounding The interiors are planned with broad open stairways, finished in hard wood There are tiled fireplaces and handsomely carved mantels, wide door-ways that give opportunities for luxurious draperies, stained glass windows and numerous gables, spacious bath rooms, and other conveniences that are seldom looked for outside of large cities. Many of these properties have been sold for five thousand two hundred dollars each, Messrs Childs and Drexel taking one third in cash and the balance on easy installments Contracts have been entered into for a row of eighteen frame cottages, costing three thousand dollars each, north of the railroad A large building designed for a drug store and a bakery is rising opposite the town hall, and a livery with accommodations for one hundred and fifty horses has been established

"It is proposed to utilize the waters of Gulf Creek to supply those properties lying north of the railroad, where there are two hundred acres of the tract, and where extensive improvements are also in contemplation Three railroad stations dot the property,—St David's, Wayne, and Eagle The last-named place is the site of the old Eagle Hotel, which Mr Childs bought to stop the sale of liquor near his bailiwick It has been fitted up nicely, and will be used during the summer as a school for the Indian children of the Lincoln Institution

"Near St David's, on the north side, and on part of the original Askin's property, many new residences are going up Mr Runk, of Darlington & Runk, has located there Mr Robert Stewart, of Stewart, Ralph & Co, is putting up a handsome building to cost fifty thousand dollars Mr Thomas Williams, father-in law of Mr George B Roberts, and Mr Henry Geiss, the wool man, are also building Mr Goldsborough has bought six acres adjoining Mr Runk Mr Manley, of Manley & Cooper, purchased the old George House of Mr Childs, and is fitting it up in complete style Mr John M Kennedy, Jr, has improved his house

"Real estate men say that the tendency of purchasers of country homes along the Pennsylvania Railroad is beyond Bryn Mawr, and they attribute this to three facts,—the lower prices, higher elevation, and the extensive improvements at Wayne and other places near by In six years the value of real estate fringing the Pennsylvania Railroad from the county line to a point near Paoli has appreciated nearly $30,000,000 All this started with the purchase of 600 acres near White Hall by the Pennsylvania Railroad Company thirteen years ago Within three years the advance in prices along the line has been very rapid Properties that sold in 1880 for $500 an acre have been recently disposed of for $1200, and some pieces of the ground have gone at $4200 an acre "[1]

[1] *Philadelphia Record*, May 22, 1884

A more particular account of the town of to-day, however, is found in the following article, which was published in the *Germantown Telegraph*, under date of July 2, 1884

"A new town, or rather an aggregation of delightful suburban residences, is rapidly springing up within easy traveling distance of the city of Philadelphia, either by rail or pike It is known as 'Wayne,' Delaware County, Pa., and is situated on the line of the Pennsylvania Railroad, $14\frac{46}{100}$ miles from the Pennsylvania Railroad Station at Broad and Market Streets, and is also accessible by a pleasant drive over Lancaster Avenue or pike During the latter part of the year 1880 two prominent and enterprising Philadelphia capitalists, Mr George W Childs, proprietor of the *Public Ledger*, and Mr Anthony J Drexel, the well known banker, conceived the idea of making extensive improvements in Radnor township, near Wayne station, on the line of the Pennsylvania Railroad In the following spring large tracts of charmingly situated land were purchased, and the work of building commenced The first land purchased was a tract of about 5l0 acres belonging to Mr J Henry Askin Adjoining properties were then secured, until over 600 acres of fine land came into the possession of Messrs. Childs and Drexel, and no time was lost in laying out the most available ground into building lots The nucleus of a good sized and most attractive looking town soon appeared, and now not less than fifty elegant residences have been completed and occupied, or are being finished with great rapidity, and the gentlemen named have not less than $600,000 invested in the great enterprise. The dwellings erected or under progress are very handsome architecturally, and are built in the most substantial manner, being provided with every modern convenience, and the drainage system, constructed under the supervision of Col Waring, is simply perfect.

"The extent of the estate may be judged from the fact that three Pennsylvania Railroad stations are on the property, namely, Wayne Station, St David's Station, and Eagle Station, and for the purpose of giving the reader a comprehensive idea of the new town of Wayne and its surroundings, the writer proposes to describe a visit he recently made there, and state just what he saw

"A half-hour's railroad ride from the Broad Street Station brought me to Wayne Station, and emerging from the cars a short walk up Wayne Avenue and past several beautiful cottages on either side brought Wayne Lyceum Hall into view, owned by Messrs Childs and Drexel The hall is three stories high, and is built of brick and plastered It cost about thirty thousand dollars A large general store and a drug store are on the first floor, and an audience-room for five hundred persons is on the second and third floors The hall is forty feet by sixty feet in size, it is situated at the corner of Wayne and Lancaster Avenues, and contains the post-office and the superintendent's business office Opposite Wayne Lyceum Hall, on Lancaster Avenue, is the cottage of Mr J Henry Askin, the former owner of the estate The cottage is handsomely built of brick, and has a spacious porch and a neat lawn Close by is the cottage of Mrs Patterson, a fine brick building, and north of that is the large and substantial cottage of Mr Israel Solomon, of the Bingham House, who also purchased the adjoining lot. There are other cottages near by belonging to Mr Childs as yet unsold A fine cottage adjoining Mr Askin's is occupied by Mr William J Phillips, ex-superintendent of the Police and Fire Alarm Telegraph The intervening property on Lancaster Avenue between Mr Phillips' cottage and the Bellevue Mansion, is owned by Mr William D Hughes, of the firm of Hughes & Cook He owns some four or five acres, beautifully laid out Between Lancaster Avenue and Wayne is a French drain, which completely protects the water used from all impurities An elegant cottage on Lancaster Avenue opposite the Bellevue Mansion has been sold, although not yet finished This cottage is one of seven others of similar character They will contain twelve rooms, open hallways, parlor, dining-room, library, and kitchen on the first floor, four chambers and bath room on the second floor, and the same on the third floor, and elegant wide porches The cottages are finished in imitation of hard wood, and built of brick and stone, with slate roofs, have hot and cold water, and are papered in the latest style The lots are one hundred feet front and three hundred feet deep. Mr Abbott, of the Pennsylvania Railroad Company, is building a fine cottage on the same land, and will spend his honeymoon there

"We now come to the beautifully situated Bellevue Mansion on Lancaster Avenue The mansion has been leased by Mr Childs to Miss Mary Simmons and her sister, and is a charming summer resort It has one hundred rooms, and each room has a private porch Four porches run entirely around the mansion, and the building and surroundings cost over eighty thousand dollars The mansion stands in the centre of a beautiful lawn, and is approached by a fine macadamized road The parlors present a most luxurious appearance, and the large and elegant dining-room is where the 'Aztec Club' took their annual dinner before the death of Gen Robert Patterson A handsome billiard-room or hall is near the mansion, and there are ice-houses, servants' quarters, stables, gas house, etc The mansion is well supplied with fire-escapes, and the heating arrangements are excellent There are a smoking-room, card room, private parlors, etc

"Adjoining Bellevue Mansion on the west is a lot one hundred by three hundred feet in size, purchased by Mr Theodore Gugert, of the firm of Bergner & Engel, who is erecting an elegant cottage, and west of Mr Gugert's property is the lot owned by Dr Egbert, a young physician of Radnor township, who is also building a fine stone cottage Dr Egbert has medical charge of the young Indian girls at the Spread Eagle Hotel, near his cottage The hotel building, owned by Mr Childs, is an old stone structure built in 1795, and has been loaned by him as a country home for the young Indian wards of the Lincoln Institute, eighty five in number, who are under the care of Mrs Belangee Cox The children have plenty of comforts and conveniences, and every opportunity for out-door exercise, without being interfered with by outsiders They have plenty of freedom, but still a strict watch is kept over them

"Leaving Spread Eagle Hotel and returning, we come to Conestoga road or the old Lancaster pike, and at the intersection of the pike and Wayne Avenue stands the old Baptist Church, and it is said Gen Anthony Wayne is buried near there[1] A number of elegant building lots, owned by Messrs. Childs and Drexel, are in the vicinity of the Baptist Church, and they can be bought for from eight hundred to fifteen hundred dollars each, having fronts of one hundred and fifty feet and considerable depth Near by, at the corner of old Wayne road and Bloomingdale Avenue, may be seen the spacious and substantial reservoir, which cost thirty thousand dollars, and has a capacity for three hundred thousand gallons of pure spring water, of which there is an abundant supply on the estate The reservoir stands four hundred and fifty feet above tide-water, and is supplied by extensive and costly water-works There is a fine ascent to the reservoir and an elegant promenade on top, provided with rustic seats At the corner of Bloomingdale road and Wayne Avenue stands a superb cottage, owned by Childs and Drexel It has a very fine lawn, with evergreens, carpet gardening, etc Nearly opposite, on Bloomingdale Avenue, is the very superior cottage of Robert Smith No expense has been spared on this cottage and the surrounding grounds There are several very handsome cottages on Bloomingdale Avenue, which is a popular promenade leading to the reservoir

"Leaving Bloomingdale Avenue and going northeast on Wayne Avenue can be seen a number of new brick and stone cottages on either side They are very superior and provided with all modern conveniences Some have fronts of eighty-five feet by two hundred and fifty feet deep, and will be sold for five thousand five hundred dollars, clear of all incumbrance Each cottage is by itself, and there is plenty of privacy

"Crossing Audubon Avenue, with Windemere Avenue to the right (on which there are several available building lots), we approach two new and handsome stores, opposite Wayne Lyceum Hall, one to be used as a drug-store and the other as a bread and cake bakery and refreshment saloon Again striking Lancaster Avenue, we approach the costly, well-built Presbyterian Church, near Wayne Lyceum Hall, and of which the Rev William Kruse is pastor Near by are two splendid cottages, nearly finished, with lots seventy five feet front and three hundred feet deep They are built of brick, with slate roofs, ten rooms, wide porches, fine lawns and luxuriously fitted up Just east of these is the fine cottage of James Pinkerton, paying-teller of the Bank of North America Mr Pinkerton's lot is two hundred by three hundred feet, and his cottage is the picture of comfort

"Now comes one of the great attractions of the estate, the Louella Mansion and magnificent surrounding grounds on the north side of Lancaster Avenue The mansion is a splendid stone structure, with eighty rooms, and is surrounded by a spacious porch that looks on as finely cultivated a lawn as can be found in the surrounding country The mansion has a front of one hundred feet, and is a very imposing-looking edifice There is a lawn front on Lancaster Avenue of one thousand feet, and an abundance of shrubbery, shade trees, flower-beds, etc Louella Mansion is a very popular summer resort, and is conducted by Miss E R Boughter, who rents the establishment from Mr Childs East of the Louella Mansion is the old shade ground on which stands the old Carpenter homestead, or "Maule Farm" Opposite Louella Mansion, and south of Lancaster Avenue, stand the water-works, containing a large retaining pond from which the water is pumped into the reservoir Adjoining the Louella grounds are extensive livery stables, with stall room for one hundred horses, and near by is a commodious wagon-house The stabling arrangements are under the care of Mr Charles R Wetherell, the competent and experienced lessee

"Reaching Aberdeen Avenue, we find several very superior brick cottages, with elegant terraced walks in front, and graveled foot-ways Several of these cottages are occupied, and all of them are in a finished condition These cottages are built on large lots and finished in first-class style They contain from nine to twelve handsomely papered rooms, side vestibules, stained glass windows, broad porches, and spacious stair-ways The heating arrangements are excellent, including low down grates in the parlors The kitchens have circular boilers, ranges, hot and cold water, etc., and all the rooms and passage-ways, from the first floor up, are finished in imitation of hard wood Bath-rooms and water-closets are on the second floor, and all the bedrooms are provided with inside shutters There are sliding doors between the parlors and dining-rooms and between the vestibules and parlors These cottages rent for three hundred and sixty, four hundred and eighty, and six hundred dollars per annum, according to size, and will sell from five thousand two hundred and fifty dollars to seven thousand two hundred dollars each They can be purchased on easy terms A number of smaller (frame) cottages, on Wayne Avenue, north of the railroad, will be rented for twenty dollars per month, and can be bought for three thousand dollars each

"Back of St. David's Station, Mr Manley, of the firm of Manley & Cooper, is converting an old stone country farm-house into a first-class cottage, and the surrounding lot is being laid out in elegant style. The lot is one hundred and fifty by three hundred feet, and the cottage will contain fifteen rooms Near St. David's Station is a charming piece of woodland, which will be utilized as a grove for pleasure parties, picnics, etc

"All the buildings that have been erected at Wayne since Messrs Childs and Drexel took hold of things there have been put up by Messrs Wendell & Smith, the well-known builders It may be mentioned here that no particular style of houses are required to be built at Wayne, and parties purchasing lots can erect any kind of building they choose, or make any disposition of their purchases they deem proper"

Mills.—As early as 1710, William Davis owned a grist-mill which was located on or near the site of the mills now owned by Tryon Lewis A year or so later Hugh Williams was credited with the ownership of this mill At this late day, however, it is found impracticable to trace the history of this ancient mill-privilege down through its successive owners, but we believe that it was the first enterprise of its kind established in the township

The only authentic sources of information respecting the early mills and manufactories of Radnor are a few worn and faded assessment-rolls of the dim past From these rolls it is ascertained that the mills, etc, and their owners during the years indicated below were as follows

1766 Thomas Thomas, grist-mill, Joseph Miles, grist- and saw-mills, Adam Siter, tan-yard

1779 George Fetterman, grist-mill, John Evans, saw-mill, Levi Lewis, grist-mill, Adam Siter, tan-yard

1782 William Bailey, fulling-mill, Abram Evans, grist-mill, Levi Lewis, grist-mill

1788 Benjamin Davis, grist-mill, Adam Siter, tan-yard, Levi Lewis, grist-mill

[1] [The remains of Gen Anthony Wayne are buried in the burial grounds attached to St David's Church some two miles distant from the town of Wayne.—Editor]

"FOX HILL FARM."
RESIDENCE OF RUDULPH ELLIS,
DELAWARE CO., PA.

1790 Benjamin Davis, grist-mill, John Evans, saw-mill; Levi Lewis, grist-mill, Daniel Maule, tan-yard, Simeon Matlock, tan yard

1802, '03, '04 Jesse Brooke, grist-, saw-, and plaster-mills, David Evans, grist- and saw-mills, Levi Lewis, saw-mill, Daniel Maule, tan-yard, John and William Siter, tan-yard, bark- and saw-mills

1807 Jesse Brooke, grist- and plaster-mills, Levi Lewis, grist- and saw-mills, George and Simeon Matlock, tan-yard, Daniel Maule, bark- and tan-yard, John Pugh, bark- and tan-yard; Edward Siter, tan-yard and bark-mill, William Siter, saw-mill

1809 Samuel Colef, saw-mill, Evan Roberts, grist- and saw-mills

1811, '12 Samuel Colef, saw-mill, Levi Lewis, grist-mill, Evan Roberts, grist-mill, Jesse Brooke, grist-mill, William Siter, saw-mill,[1] Edward Siter, stone saw-mill, tan-yard, and currying-shop

1817, '18 Jesse Brooke, grist- and saw-mill, John[2] and David Evans, grist- and saw-mill, Hannah Lewis, grist- and saw-mill, Joseph Pugh, tan-yard, Edward Siter, tan-yard and currying-shop, William Siter, saw-mill

1820, '21 Jesse Brooke, grist, saw- and plaster-mills; John and David Evans, grist- and saw-mills, Edward Siter and Yocum, tan-yard, William Siter, saw mill

The following is an extract from an official report made in 1826, regarding the mills, mill-seats, etc, in the county of Delaware, Pa

"On Ithan Creek in Radnor, a mill-seat on land of the heirs of Andrew Steel, deceased

"On Ithan Creek, in Radnor, a grist-mill and saw-mill, head and fall about twenty-three feet, owned and occupied by John and David Evans

"Near the head of Ithan Creek, in Radnor, a grist-mill and saw-mill, head and fall about sixteen feet, grinds from eight to ten thousand bushels of grain per annum, and about fifty tons gypsum per annum, saw-mill employed occasionally, owned and occupied by Jesse Brooke

"On Darby Creek above Ithan Creek, in Radnor, a mill-seat, head and fall fourteen or sixteen feet, owned by Samuel Kelly and others

"On a westerly branch of Darby Creek, in Radnor, a saw-mill, head and fall about eighteen feet, owned and occupied by Levi Lewis

"On Darby Creek, in Radnor, an old grist-mill, head and fall about ten feet, owned by Levi Lewis, occupied by John Weaver, grinds from ten to twelve thousand bushels of grain per annum

"On easterly branch of Darby Creek, in Radnor, a mill-seat, on lands of Levi Lewis

"On the same branch, in Radnor, a mill-seat, on lands of Elizabeth Matlock and others

"On the same branch is a clover-mill and a saw-mill owned by William Siter, and occupied by William Wilfong, Jr"

In 1829, '30, the following mills, etc, and owners were mentioned Brooke's grist- and saw-mills, John and David Evans' grist- and saw-mills, E Siter and Yocum's tan-yard, and William Siter's saw-mill

During the year 1829, Eber James built an earthenware pottery kiln near the fifteenth milestone, on the old Lancaster road, which he operated (with the exception of three or four years, when it was rented to Benjamin Jones) until his death, in the year 1845 Benjamin Jones then managed the works for six years, and was succeeded by L G James, a son of Eber. Subsequently Isaac Hoopes conducted the business for a number of years

The mills now in operation in Radnor are the Brooke Mills, owned and operated by Joseph W. Worrell, the Evans Mills, owned and operated by David Paxon, the Siter Mill, owned and operated by Mahlon Edwards, and Tryon Lewis' mills A large amount of work is performed at the mills last mentioned, which, it will be remembered, occupy the seat of the mill of 1710

Schools.—Prior to the adoption of the school law enacted in 1834, schools of more or less excellence had been maintained in the township from its first settlement. Of their history, however, but little is known and never will be They were subscription schools, chiefly taught in the winter, during periods irregular in their duration Yet in them the descendants of the pioneers, through several generations, mastered the rudiments and the essential principles of education with a facility equal to that displayed by the students of to-day

The first authentic references to schools in Radnor are found in the court records, where it is shown that, in 1825, in accordance with an order issued, Abram Lewis, Benjamin Maule, and Benjamin Davis were elected school trustees for the township They were then called "school men," and were elected to serve for one, two, and three years respectively Again turning to the records, we learn that, on the 14th of May, 1827, the "school men" purchased from Mordecai Lewis land "on which to erect a Union school"

In 1834, at the inauguration of the free-school system, the court appointed as inspectors of schools for Radnor to act until directors "be elected," John Evans and Jesse Brooke, Jr The following year, through its treasurer, the township received for school purposes, from State and county, the sum of $1010 45.

[1] On the 30th of May, 1812, Benjamin Smith and William H Shaw published the following notice "The subscribers respectfully inform their customers and the public in general that the machines at William Siter's clover-mill, Radnor township, Delaware County, will be carried on for the future by Smith & Shaw, where, in addition to the former machinery, they propose adding a Spinning Machine, which will work for customers at the following rates All wool spun, 12 cuts or under to the lb, 1 cent & a half per cut, & all over 12 cuts to the lb, 2 cents per cut Carding into rolls 10 cents per lb (Near Spread Eagle Tavern) at Siter's saw-mill"

[2] John Evans, miller, was born in Radnor in 1790, and died in the same township in 1862 At the time of his death, and for years preceding that event, he was the possessor of grounds containing the finest botanical collection ever seen in this latitude, all being the result of his own researches and labor

On the 1st of January, 1837, John Evans sold to the directors of schools a school-house site of eighty square perches, adjoining the lands of John Matthews. In 1855 the school directors purchased another lot (comprising two acres) for school purposes from Anna Loudon. Since that year other grounds have been purchased, suitable buildings have been erected thereon, old buildings have been rebuilt, and other needed improvements made from time to time, until the seven school buildings now standing in Radnor will compare favorably with any in the rural districts of the State.

Following is a list of the school directors elected in the township since 1840, as found of record at the county-seat:

1840, William Morgan, John Mather,[1] and John Pugh; 1842, Jesse Brooke and Mark Bartleson; 1843, Enoch Matlock and William Morgan; 1844, Jonathan P. Abrahams and H. Jones Brooke; 1845, Mark Bartleson and Hiram Cleaver; 1846, Mark Brooke and Edward B. Wetherell; 1847, Jesse Gyger and William Pugh; 1848, William Siter and John Pechin; 1849, Mark Brooke and William W. Esrey; 1850, Alexander Brooke and Jesse Gyger; 1851, Stephen S. Davis and Edward B. Wetherell; 1852, Samuel P. Abrahams and Alexander Johnson; 1853, Alexander Brooke and Mark Brooke; 1854, Samuel Jones and Lewis Garrett; 1855, Jesse Gyger and Samuel P. Abrahams; 1856, Alexander Brooke and Charles Pugh; 1857, Mark Brooke and Robert Paiste; 1858, George P. Hughes and Robert Paiste; 1859, Hiram Cleaver and Daniel C. Abrahams; 1860, Virgil T. Eachus and Lewis T. Brooke; 1861, James Roberts and J. S. Park; 1862, Enoch Matlock and T. R. Petty; 1863, Benjamin Brooke and John G. Henderson; 1864, Anderson Kirk and Samuel P. Abrahams; 1865, Thomas B. Jones and Thomas R. Petty; 1866, John G. Henderson and Benjamin Brooke; 1867, Anderson Kirk and Samuel P. Abrahams; 1868, Frank Fenimore and Tryon Lewis; 1869, Jesse Gyger and Benjamin Brooke; 1870, Anderson Kirk and John R. Whitney; 1871, no report; 1872, Tryon Lewis and John Cornog; 1873, Jesse Gyger and Benjamin Brooke; 1874, Barclay Hall and Joseph H. Childs; 1875, Tryon Lewis and Mrs. David Paxon; 1876, A. R. Montgomery and Benjamin Brooke; 1877, Barclay Hall and Tryon Lewis; 1878, Archibald Montgomery and Joseph Croll; 1879, J. H. Ewing and Elwood Carr; 1880, Barclay Hall and Tryon Lewis; 1881, Jesse Gyger and A. Montgomery; 1882, A. R. Montgomery and James Callahan; 1883, Barclay Hall and Tryon Lewis; 1884, Jesse Gyger and William A. Parke.

Villanova College.—In the upper part of our county (Delaware), in the township of Radnor, lie the extensive grounds known as Villanova College, belonging to the Catholic brotherhood of St. Augustine. These established themselves here, as a branch of the parent house in Philadelphia, in 1842. Having purchased the estate belonging to the deceased Mr. John Rudolf in the previous year, they now set about to erect buildings on a large scale for a complete monastic and educational foundation, namely, a convent, with novitiate and study-house for the members of their order, and a college for the education of the laity in the classics, arts, sciences, and polite literature.

This order, founded by St. Augustine (of Hippo), in 387 of our era, consists of three classes: (1) of religious men whose present mission is to preach and teach; (2) of religious women called nuns; and (3) of persons of either sex, known as Tertiaries, living in the world, who seek to lead a Christian life in the service of God and their neighbor, under the patronage of the same St. Augustine.

In 1796 their founder in this country, the Rev. Matthew Carr, D.D., O.S.A., came from Ireland to establish a province of his order, and with faculties from the then reigning pontiff, Pope Pius VI., and with the advice and aid of the Rt. Rev. John Carroll, the first and that time the only Catholic prelate in the United States, fixed on Philadelphia as his abode. Here he built the church of St. Augustine, on Fourth Street, near Race, but circumstances prevented him from realizing all he had designed.

The Augustinian College at Villanova is properly the chief offshoot of St. Augustine's of Philadelphia. It was founded, as we have said, in 1842, by Rev. John Possidius O'Dwyer, O.S.A., who, under the direction of the celebrated Dr. Moriarty, O.S.A., then superior-general of the order in the United States, was its first president.

The title of this college recalls the memory of the great archbishop of Valencia, in Spain, in the sixteenth century, St. Thomas of Villanova, under whose superiorship the Augustinian missionaries to the New World founded in Mexico, with leave from the Emperor Charles V., the University of Mexico, the first school on a grand scale in the Americas. The date of the emperor's decree is Sept. 21, 1551, though the solemn opening of the university was put off until the 25th of January, 1553. Villanova thus commemorates the great scholar and saint and, we may add, the first patron of learning in the Western Hemisphere.

The first college buildings at Villanova comprised merely one stone house of two and a half stories, the former residence of Mr. Rudolf. The upper stories, consisting of six rooms, were devoted to the uses of the students, and the lower to the professors.

In September, 1844, was dedicated the chapel, the first place of Catholic worship in the neighborhood; in 1849 was opened the new college hall, a large stone edifice, eighty-eight feet long and fifty-five feet wide, now the east wing of the college building. This, the main college building, was erected in 1873, by the superior-general, Rev. Thomas Galberry, O.S.A., at the time president of the college, and subsequently bishop of the diocese of Hartford, Conn., and was opened Feb. 3, 1874. It is one hundred and seventy-four feet in front, facing the Pennsylvania Railroad, and contains all the halls and rooms needed for the instruction and residence of the students. There are eleven classrooms, besides apartments for professors and prefects, two large dormitories, a clothes-room, study and music halls, a dramatic hall, and play-room.

The buildings are well supplied with water, conducted from a spring fourteen hundred feet distant, lighted with gas manufactured on the premises, and all are heated with steam.

[1] John Mather was a soldier of the war of 1812–15, and died in Radnor, Jan. 29, 1880, in the eighty-fifth year of his age.

The studies in the collegiate department embrace a course of seven years in philosophy, rhetoric, poetry, the languages ancient and modern, physics, and the arts, and in the ecclesiastical branch, of philosophy, ecclesiastical history, theology, canon law, and the sacred Scriptures.

The college was empowered by the Legislature of the State, in 1848, to confer degrees, the same as is done in other colleges and universities of the United States, and to enjoy the privileges of the same.

From 1842 down to the present scholars have been entered from nearly every State and Territory of the Union, from Mexico, the West Indies, South America, and from several countries in Europe.

The collegiate year just ended of 1883–84 closed with sixty-six students in the collegiate department and seventeen in the ecclesiastical.

The presidents of the institution have been: 1842–47, Rev. John Possidius O'Dwyer, O.S.A.; 1847–48, Rev. William Harnett, O.S.A.; 1848–50, Rev. John Possidius O'Dwyer, O.S.A. (second term); 1850–51, Rev. William Harnett, O.S.A. (second term); 1851–55, Rev. Patrick Eugene Moriarty, D.D., O.S.A.; 1855–57, Rev. William Harnett, O.S.A. (third term). The college closed in this year (1857) until 1865–69, Rev. Ambrose Augustine Mullen, O.S.A.; 1869–72, Rev. Patrick Augustine Stanton, O.S.A.; 1872–76, Rev. Thomas Galberry, O.S.A.; 1876–78, Rev. Thomas Cooke Middleton, D.D., O.S.A.; 1878–80, Rev. John Joseph Fedigan, O.S.A.; 1880, Rev. Joseph Augustine Coleman, O.S.A.

In pursuance of the original plan the authorities at Villanova are now erecting a church to take the place of the frame building used since 1872, but which for some years has proved wholly inadequate to meet the requirements of Catholic worship.

Since 1842, when the first to assist at the divine services numbered seven, the congregation has increased far more than a hundredfold. The present parish counts eight hundred souls and upwards, which during the summer months is increased by outside attendance to perhaps twice that number. Three masses on Sundays are unable to satisfy the needs of the people.

The new church, now being roofed, will seat about eight hundred persons. It is designed to have seven altars, and at the rear of the chancel and high altar a conventual choir, with stalls for the religious, who will thus be enabled to carry out fully the ritual and ceremonial of the church for divine worship.

The new building faces Lancaster Avenue, and measures, externally, one hundred and forty-three feet in length by a width of fifty-nine feet, not including the projecting sacristy and the baptistery. The three front door-ways are entered by seven steps. The façade is sixty feet wide, with a central gable having a corbeled niche with a pedestal for the statue of the patron saint.

On either side are two towers, eighteen feet square at the base by sixty-three feet high, to be surmounted by spires, making the total height one hundred and twenty-six feet. The outer work is faced with gray stone laid in promiscuous rubble-work and dressings of granite. The ground-plan consists of a nave with side aisles with deep sanctuary, terminating in an apsidal choir for the religious,—a feature in architecture rarely to be met with in the United States, and the only one in this part of Pennsylvania. The style of architecture is Gothic, and when completed will add greatly to the already stately pile of buildings at Villanova.[1]

Radnor Friends' Meeting-Houses.—As early as 1686 a sufficient number of Friends had made settlements in Radnor to establish an independent meeting for worship in the township. David Meredith's name was the first to appear in the Haverford records as belonging to Radnor Meeting, though, doubtless, there were a few others who became identified with it equally as early. The early meetings in Radnor were generally held in the dwelling-houses of John Jerman (who was a Quaker preacher of considerable ability, and who visited England and Wales in 1712) and John Evans. The first marriage in Radnor was solemnized in the house of the latter, on the 2d of the Third month (May), 1686, between Richard Ormes, of Philadelphia, and Mary Tyder, of Radnor.

In 1693 the Radnor Friends built their first meeting-house. A new Friends' meeting-house, however, was commenced in 1718. The minutes of the Monthly Meeting that relate to the erection of this edifice are given, to show the cautious manner in which such enterprises were entered upon in the early days. The first proceedings regarding this matter took place at a meeting held in Haverford, Eighth month 10, 1717, and were made a subject of record, as follows:

"A letter from our Friend Benjamin Holm to this meeting, recommending to their consideration the stirring up of frd[s] in y[e] building of their meeting-house att Radnor, and with desires y[t] we should be concerned for y[e] prosperity of Truth, was read in this meeting, and approved off. Likewise this meeting, pursuant to Radnor frds, desire acquiess wth y[m] in building a new meeting-house, and this meeting appoints David Morris, David Lewis, Edd Rees, Robert Jones, Richard Hayes, and Samuel Lewis to assist y[m] In y[e] contrivance [and] y[e] building Thereof, and they meet together ab[t] it on y[e] 21st of this instant, [and report] to y[e] next meeting."

The members of the committee all belonged to the meetings of Haverford and Merion. The next meeting was held in Merion, and one of its minutes embraces the report of the committee, wherein they say, "Some friends of those appointed to assist Radnor friends In y[e] Contrivance of a new meeting-house, then having acc[t] y[t] they have accordingly mett, and given y[m] Their thoughts as to y[e] bigness and form thereof. To w[ch] Radnor frd[s] Then there present seemed generally to agree w[th]." The west end of the present meeting-house was the building then erected, but it was not finished until two or three

[1] Contributed by Rev. J. A. Coleman, O.S.A., president of Villanova College.

years later, for, in 1721, committees were appointed in Haverford and Merion for raising funds for the completion of Radnor meeting-house.

During the winter passed by the American army at Valley Forge, an outpost of the patriot army was maintained in Radnor, on property which is owned by Tryon Lewis. About seven acres of heavy timber, near the middle of a large tract of woodland, was cleared by the troops while stationed here. This was afterwards cultivated, and was well known in the neighborhood for many years thereafter as "the camp-field." Radnor Friends' meeting-house, which is a little more than half a mile distant from this camp-ground, was occupied in connection with it, probably as officers' quarters and for hospital purposes. The records of the society show that they were deprived of the use of their meeting-house early in the year 1778, "in consideration of its being occupied by soldiers," and that it required considerable repairs before it was put in a condition for holding a Monthly Meeting, which was not till near the middle of 1780. Says Dr. Smith, "It is probable that during the winter and spring most of the scouting parties that served to restrain, in a measure, the foraging of the enemy within our limits, and at the same time to prevent disloyal farmers from carrying their produce to the city, were detached from the outpost at Radnor."

The meeting-house is still in a fair state of repair, and, with an addition (built in later years at the east end for school purposes), is used for holding occasional meetings of the society. The first body interred in the graveyard attached to this meeting-house was that of Gwenllian, the wife of Howell James, who was buried Eleventh month 31, 1686.

Radnor Methodist Episcopal Church.—About ten miles west from Philadelphia, on what is called "the Old Lancaster road," stands an old, time-honored building, which has been known for several generations past as the Radnor Methodist Episcopal Church. Standing on the summit of one of the most beautiful hills of Radnor, it commands a fine view of the surrounding country; and so long has the church been associated with the hill that the latter is generally termed "Methodist Hill."

The history of this church goes back to the primitive days of Methodism. Indeed, many of the illustrious pioneers of Methodism in this country have officiated on this ground, among them such men as Bishop Coke, Richard Whatcoat, and Francis Asbury. Dr. James[1] has stated that the first Methodists who visited Radnor were two local preachers named Adam Cloud and Matthew Greentree. They preached Sunday afternoons in Haverford, alternately at Hughes' and Effenger's. This was during the Revolutionary war. Soon after, or about 1780, Radnor became a regular preaching-place, and was supplied by circuit preachers. The place of worship was a house occupied by the James family, known then as the "Mansion House." This house is still standing.

It appears that the first class was organized about the year 1780, and that George Gyger was appointed first class-leader. Radnor was then embraced in the Philadelphia Circuit. The preachers officiating in this circuit in 1780 were John Cooper and George Main. In 1781 the name of the circuit was changed to Pennsylvania Circuit, and the preachers appointed were William Glendenning, Samuel Rowe, and Isaac Rollins. In 1782 the circuit and preachers remained the same, with the exception of Samuel Rowe, whose place was filled by John Coleman. In 1783 the name of the circuit was again changed and called "Chester,"—Reuben Ellis, John Hagerty, and Thomas Haskins becoming the preachers. On the 20th day of October of the same year, Evan Jones and his wife, Margaret, appeared before Justice Thomas Lewis, and acknowledged to have sold for seven shillings a half-acre of land "on which a meeting-house was to be built for Francis Asbury and his assistants, in which the doctrines of John Wesley, as set forth in his four volumes of 'Sermons,' and in his 'Notes on the New Testament,' were to be preached and no other."

The church was immediately commenced, and ere the expiration of many months was completed, though under many difficulties. Dr. James relates that "one day while Aquilla McVaugh was at work hauling stones for the new meeting-house, one of his acquaintances passing along called to him, saying, 'What are you doing there, Aquilla?' He replied, 'I am helping to build a meeting-house for the Methodists.' 'Well, there is no use of you doing so, for they will all soon be as cold as cucumbers; there will soon be no more Methodists.'" Jacob Gyger, David and Isaac James hauled the water from the creek by means of a barrel on a sled with which to mix the mortar. However, despite the many disadvantages under which they labored, its builders had the church edifice completed and dedicated in 1784. The first trustees were Isaac Hughes, Sr., Edward Hughes, Michael Cline, Griffith James, Abram Hughes, Mark Evans, Jesse Yocum, and William Jennings.

The circuit this year (1784) was called Philadelphia, the preachers being Le Roy Cole, Joseph Cromwell, and Jeremiah Lambert. Under the various names already mentioned, the territory embraced in the circuit was the same.

In 1785, the church having been formally organized, the circuits were placed under the charge of elders, although they were not then called districts. The first presiding elder under whose supervision

[1] Dr. Isaac James was born in Radnor, Jan. 28, 1777, in a dwelling that had been occupied by three generations of his ancestry. His father's house was the first preaching-place of the Methodists in Radnor. He (Isaac) joined the church in 1790. In 1799 he was licensed to exhort, and in 1801 was appointed steward of the Chester and Jonesburg Circuit. Five years later he was ordained deacon by Bishop Asbury, and in 1819 was ordained elder by Bishop Main. The great want of good medical advice in his day induced him to study medicine. He attended one course of lectures at the University of Pennsylvania, but graduated at the Columbia College, New York. He died Jan. 22, 1874.

Radnor came, was Thomas Vasey. They were not then called presiding elders, simply elders. The preachers for 1785 were Ira Ellis and James Thomas. Succeeding elders, preachers, etc., are mentioned in manner as follows:

1786. Henry Ogburn and Peter Moriarty, preachers; Caleb Boyer, elder.

1787. Samuel Dudley and William Thomas, preachers; John Hagerty and William Gill, elders.

1788. Philadelphia made a station, and the country part of the circuit called Chester, in which circuit Radnor fell. Robert Carr and John Milburn, preachers; Richard Whatcoat, elder.

1789. William Dougherty and James Campbell, preachers; Henry Willis and Lemuel Green, presiding elders.

1790. Sylvester Hutchinson and John Cooper, preachers; Richard Whatcoat, presiding elder.

1791. J. McCloskey, J. Robinson, and S. Miller, preachers; Lemuel Green, elder.

1792. Joseph Lovell and Joseph Wainwright, preachers; John McCloskey, presiding elder.

1793. Robert Cloud, William Hunter, and Evan Rogers, preachers; Freeborn Garrettson, presiding elder.

1794. William Early and James Smith, preachers; Valentine Cook, presiding elder.

1795. This year Chester and Lancaster comprised one circuit; Radnor one of the appointments. John Jarrell, Thomas F. Sargent, and John Robinson, preachers; John Merrick, presiding elder.

1796. Circuit called Chester. Thomas Bell and Samuel Welch, preachers; Thomas Ware, presiding elder.

1797. William Colbert, in place of Thomas Bell; no other change.

1798. Name of circuit changed to Strasburg. William P. Chandler and Daniel Higby, preachers; Thomas Ware, presiding elder.

1799. William Colbert, James Herron, Edward Larkins, and Robert Bonham, preachers; Thomas Ware, presiding elder.

1800. Stephen Timmons, Richard Sneath, Thomas Jones, Robert McCoy, preachers; Joseph Everett, presiding elder. The district first called Philadelphia.

1801. William Hunter and Stephen Timmons, preachers; Joseph Everett, presiding elder.

1802. William Hunter and John Bethell, preachers; Thomas Ware, presiding elder. About this year revivals were held in many places in Delaware County, and as a result societies were formed and new meeting-houses commenced at various points. Radnor Church also was greatly revived at a series of meetings held in the woods in front of the meeting-house.

1803. Name of circuit changed to Chesapeake. A. Owen and William Brandon, preachers; Christopher Spry, presiding elder.

1804. Name of circuit changed to Chester. William Hunter, Joseph Osborn, and J. Stephens, preachers; William Colbert, presiding elder. Camp-meetings originated this year.

1805. William Hunter, D. James, and James Moore, preachers; Solomon Sharp, presiding elder.

1806. John Walker and William Early, preachers; Solomon Sharp, presiding elder.

1807. Daniel Ireland and Peter Beaver, preachers; Solomon Sharp, presiding elder.

1808. Asa Smith, John Bethel, and William Finney, preachers; William P. Chandler, presiding elder.

1809. Name of district changed to Schuylkill. John Walker and Thomas Miller, preachers; William Hunter, presiding elder, who continued as such to 1813.

1810. Richard Sneath and John Fox, preachers.

1811. Richard Sneath and James Laws, preachers.

1812. Thomas Dunn and William S. Fisher, preachers.

1813. William S. Fisher and Joseph Sampson, preachers; Henry Boem, presiding elder.

1814. Circuit styled Chester and Wilmington. George Sheets, Thomas Miller, and Samuel P. Levis, preachers; Henry Boem, presiding elder.

1815. Circuit known as Chester. Asa Smith and Joseph Sampson, preachers; Robert R. Roberts, presiding elder.

1816. William Torbert and Charles Reed, preachers; Daniel Hilt, presiding elder, who continued till 1820.

1817. William Hunter and William Torbert, preachers.

1818. John Goforth and Samuel Budd, preachers.

1819. John Robertson and Phineas Price, preachers.

1820. William Leonard and Thomas Davis, preachers; James Bateman, presiding elder, who continued as such till 1824.

1821. David Bartine and Thomas Davis, preachers.

1822. David Bartine and John Tally, preachers.

1823. Thomas Miller and William Allen, preachers.

1824. Henry Boem and John Woolson, preachers; Joseph Lybrand, presiding elder, who continued until 1828.

1825. District again called Philadelphia. Henry Boem and Levin Prettyman, preachers.

1826. Jacob Gruber, Samuel Grace, and John Tally, preachers.

1827. Jacob Gruber and William Cooper, preachers.

1828. Thomas Miller and Eliphalet Reed, preachers; William Thacher, presiding elder.

1829. Edward Page and Daniel Fidler, preachers; William Thacher, presiding elder.

1830. Thomas McCarrel and Edward Page, preachers; M. Force, presiding elder.

1831. William Ryder and N. Chew, preachers; M. Force, presiding elder.

1832. William Ryder and James B. Ayres, preachers; M. Force, presiding elder.

1833. Philadelphia District divided into North and

South Philadelphia Districts, Radnor being embraced by Southern District James B Ayres, J Edwards, Robert E Morrison, and John Tally, preachers, Lawrence McCombs, presiding elder The Radnor congregation now became so large that the old church was found too small to accommodate the people Therefore in May of that year (1833) a new church edifice was commenced While it was in process of construction the members worshiped under the trees in front of the building The new edifice was dedicated during the same year Rev (afterwards Bishop) E L James preached the dedicatory sermon The society gained about fifty new members soon after the dedication of the new building

1834 Radnor Circuit, formed from Chester David Best and Richard W Thomas, preachers, John Potts, presiding elder, who continued to 1837

1835 Richard W Thomas, preacher

1836 and 1837 W Cooper, preacher

1838 James B Ayres and Charles W Jackson, preachers, Solomon Higgins, presiding elder

1839 James B Ayres and Frederick Gram, preachers, Solomon Higgins, presiding elder

1840 Henry G King and James Neil, preachers, Solomon Higgins, presiding elder

1841 H G King and L M Prettyman, preachers, James Smith, presiding elder

1842 George Lacy and Christopher J Crouch, preachers, James Smith, presiding elder

1843 Circuit divided, upper part called "Grove," lower part still retaining the name of Radnor C J Crouch and John A Roche, preachers, James Smith, presiding elder

1844 —— McNamee and John W McCaskey, preachers, James Smith, presiding elder

1845 Thomas Sumption and George W Lybrand, preachers, Levi Scott, presiding elder

1846 Thomas Sumption and Henry Sanderson, preachers, Levi Scott, presiding elder

1847 Richard M Greenbank and Henry B Mauger, preachers, Levi Scott, presiding elder

1848 Richard M Greenbank and J Cummins, preachers, J T Cooper, presiding elder

1849 Michael D Kurtz and Paul B Gillingham, preachers, J T Cooper, presiding elder

1850 M D Kurtz and J Tally, preachers, J T Cooper, presiding elder

1851 John Edwards and Henry A Hobbs, preachers, Thomas J Thompson, presiding elder

1852 John Edwards, preacher, T J Thompson, presiding elder

1853 Henry Sutton, preacher, T J Thompson, presiding elder

1854 Henry Sutton and Mark Bailey, preachers, T J Thompson, presiding elder

1855 John A Watson, preacher, William Cooper, presiding elder, who continued until 1859

1856 John A Watson and J M Wheeler, preachers

1857 H B Mauger and Gideon T Barr, preachers

1858 H B Mauger and T W Martin, preachers

1859 W M Dalyrimple and J Gregg, preachers, Francis Hodgson, presiding elder, who continued as such till 1863

1860 Circuit divided, one part called Darby and Mount Pleasant, the other Radnor and Bethesda W M Dalyrimple, preacher

1861 and 1862 G G Rakestraw, preacher

1863-65 S Patterson, preacher, Joseph Castle, presiding elder Noble Frame served as preacher during part of 1865, during illness of Mr Patterson

1866 Levi B Hughes, preacher, Joseph Castle, presiding elder.

1867-68 David McKee, preacher, W L Gray, presiding elder, the latter serving till 1871

1869-71 A L Wilson, preacher, William C Robinson, presiding elder for 1871

The foregoing sketch of Radnor Church has been condensed from a historical sermon prepared by Mr A L Wilson in 1871 Since that date its preachers have been M A Day, for two years, J Y Ashton, for three years, T C Pearson and J T Ziegler, for three years, A L Wilson, again, for three years, and Charles Roads, the present preacher in charge, for two years

The church was repaired inside to a considerable extent in 1882 In 1883, Radnor Church was made a separate station For some years prior to that time it had been associated with the Bryn Mawr and Bethesda Churches The present members of the society are eighty-five in number

Wayne Presbyterian Church.—The first movement towards the formation of this church was the holding of public religious service in Wayne Hall, on Sunday, June 5, 1870

This was followed by the organization of a Sabbath-school on the 19th of June, in the same year, the first session of which was held in the hall above mentioned on the succeeding Sabbath afternoon, at which five children were present

On the afternoon of Tuesday, June 21, 1870, a preliminary meeting preparatory to a church organization was held at Wayne Hall, at which meeting the following-named gentlemen were present, viz, Rev R H Allen, D D, moderator, and Messrs William J McElroy, J Henry Askin, Charles H. Eldredge, Howell Evans, Samuel Hill, and Samuel Agnew

According to an appointment of the Presbytery the commissioners, consisting of the Rev B B Hotchkin, Professor Lorenzo Westcott, Rev T J. Aiken, and Ruling Elders James Moore and Thomas Aiken, met in Wayne Hall on Friday afternoon, June 24, 1870, and organized the Wayne Presbyterian Church, comprising nine members, installing Howell Evans as the ruling elder

At this meeting also, a call was extended to the Rev S P Linn to become pastor of the congregation, and he accepting, was installed by the Presbytery on Tuesday, July 5, 1870 Public services were regularly held thereafter on Sabbath mornings in Wayne Hall, until the completion of the church edifice

The ground was broken upon which the church building was erected Monday, March 21, 1870, and the corner-stone was laid on Thursday, May 12th of that year, by the Rev John Chambers, with appropriate services, assisted by the Rev R H Allen, D D, Rev John McLeod, and Rev T J Aiken The building, which is of stone, being completed, was dedicated with appropriate ceremonies on Thursday afternoon, Dec 8, 1870 The sermon on the occasion was delivered by the Rev Charles Wadsworth, D D A large audience and a number of other prominent ministers were also present

The church edifice with the lot of ground upon which it is built, also the first parsonage with the lot of ground attached thereto, was the gift of J Henry Askin, Esq, under whose personal direction the building was commenced and completed The property, upon the completion of the church building, was valued at twenty-five thousand dollars Quite recently the parsonage first occupied was sold, and another house and lot was purchased for such purposes It is a handsome brick structure It occupies a central location in the town, near by the church, and cost about six thousand dollars

As pastor Mr Linn remained here only about nine months, terminating his labors in April, 1871 His successor, Rev James W Dale, D D, was installed on Thursday, Sept 28, 1871, and continued with this church about four years Then came Rev George T Purves, who remained about three years Rev William Tenton Kruse, the present pastor, was installed Sept 7, 1881

The Sabbath-schools, under the superintendency of Mr Charles H Eldredge, are in a flourishing condition The society contributes some five or six hundred dollars per year for charitable purposes A ladies' missionary society is also very efficient The present members of this church number one hundred and thirty-eight, of whom Thomas Aiken, Howell Evans, J Woods Pinkerton, and James Aiken are ruling elders

The Radnor Baptist Church originated in the agitation of the question of anti-slavery in the Great Valley Baptist Church Rev Leonard Fletcher was pastor at the time, and, having been eye-witness of the oppressions and evils of slavery, naturally was strongly opposed to it. Those in the church who sympathized with him, not enjoying that liberty and fellowship they wanted, asked for and received letters to form a new church Letters were granted to seventy-nine persons The new body, under the name of the Radnor Baptist Church, was organized Feb 20, 1841 Its house of worship had been originally built for a far different purpose than that to which it was now devoted. Under the title of "Radnor Scientific and Musical Hall," meetings were held in it of a character in opposition to the truths and worship of the revealed God A prominent man in this movement, Mr William Siter, becoming a zealous believer in those truths, and the builders of the hall failing to obtain a good title to the property, it passed by purchase into the possession of the church

The first pastor was Rev J Newton Hobart He assumed charge of the church in 1841, and remained in his position until Sept 10, 1844, during which time forty-eight were added by baptism Rev J Perry Hall became pastor March 25, 1845, continuing until April 1, 1847 Eight were added by baptism during his pastorate He was followed, June 13, 1847, by Rev Thomas Goodwin, who remained until April 1, 1849 Twenty-five were baptized by him Rev. Josiah Philips was the next pastor, accepting the call of the church, and resigned his charge Aug 21, 1856 Sixty-nine were added during his pastorate Rev T I Thomas then served as pastor for one year from Jan 21, 1858

About December 25th, Rev D A Nichols held a series of extra meetings with the church, continuing them until Feb 25, 1860 The result was thirty-eight persons baptized The next pastor was Rev George W Scott, who was ordained Aug 8, 1861, and who resigned Dec 25, 1862 Twelve were baptized by him Rev G W Holman was pastor from October, 1863, to February, 1865 There were during this period twelve baptisms After him came Rev W W Dalbey, who was invited to take charge of the church Nov 23, 1865, and who continued as pastor until Feb 24, 1870 He baptized seventy-two Rev A E Folwell was called July 10, 1870, and died Aug 7, 1872. Two were baptized by him. Nov 24, 1872, the church called Rev H F Leamy He resigned March 9, 1874 There were three baptisms Rev D J R Stroyer began a series of extra meetings in November, 1875, which continued until December 12th, when he was invited to become pastor He resigned Feb 18, 1877 There were ten baptisms Rev. J Wesley Sullivan was invited to supply the pulpit Dec 1, 1878, rendering this service during part of a year Two were baptized by him Rev Mr Colburn, of New Jersey, held extra meetings in December, 1881, resulting in three baptisms This was during the time Mr Hare, of Crozer Seminary, was acting as supply The present pastor is Rev S S Parker, D D, who began his pastorate December, 1881

The Church of the Good Shepherd —Previous to the formation of this parish divine services had been frequently held at "Woodfield," and a Sunday-school opened at the house of Mrs Supplee (both half a mile west of Rosemont Station on Pennsylvania Railroad) in 1868-69

The parish was organized at a meeting of residents, held in old Wayne Hall, July 7, 1869, when the following gentlemen were elected vestrymen, viz. Charles W Cushman, W. W. Montgomery, Edward

S. Lawrence, A. R. Montgomery, J. L. Wentworth, H. Yates Carter, John B. Thayer, Maskell Ewing, John S. Maxwell, Samuel C. Knight, Brinton J. Parke, I. D. Meredith.

The services began in Wayne Hall July, 1869; were supplied by various clergymen until the autumn of the same year, when the Rev. H. P. Hay, D.D., was elected rector.

The corner-stone of the church was laid by Bishop Stevens on July 25, 1871. The church was completed and opened for services Jan. 6, 1872, and was consecrated by Bishop Howe, of Central Pennsylvania, acting for Bishop Stevens, on March 8, 1872.

The Hospital of the Good Shepherd, for children, in charge of this parish, was opened formally by Bishop Stevens on June 11, 1874, with accommodations for twelve children, two entering that month.

The parish building, near the church, was begun in July, 1877, and was in use the following spring. It contains rooms for Sunday-school, parish-school, committees, and the sexton. The parish-school was opened September, 1878.

The Chapel of the Good Shepherd was erected in 1880–81, the corner-stone being laid by Bishop Stevens on July 25, 1880. It stands one-quarter of a mile north of Radnor Station. Mission services had been held in the public school room close by, with little intermission, since 1869.

The rectory of the parish, which stands on a lot of one and three-quarters acres, adjoining the church on Lancaster turnpike, was begun in August, 1883, completed in May, 1884, and was at once occupied by the present rector, the Rev. Arthur B. Conger, who was elected rector in July, 1883, the rectorship having been vacant about six months. Present number of communicants, one hundred and twenty. Present value of church property, fifty thousand dollars, all unencumbered, except five thousand dollars on rectory.

Licensed Houses.—The first petition for license in Radnor which appears of record is dated May 28, 1717, and emanated from Edward Thomas, who informs the court that his house is located "near y[e] church called St. David's Church," and that he from that fact is "obliged to entertain many people y[t] Come to Worship at y[e] sd. Church." The court, no doubt, believing that this unremunerative hospitality was more than could be reasonably required of any man, granted him a license to sell "Beer, Sider, &c." His name does not appear again in the records, but James Thomas, possibly a son of the former, Ninth month (November) 27, 1722, presented his petition, in which he says that he "hath formerly obtained the Recomendacon of this Honorable Court to His Excellency y[e] Govr. for a Lycence for the Keeping of a house of Entertainment, and for selling of Wine, Brandy, Rum, and other Strong Lyquors, But now the time of the Said Lycence is Expired, &c.;" after which he is also lost sight of so far as the records now disclose.

Michael Atkinson, who in August, 1731, attempted to procure license in Concord, when he was met in that effort by a remonstrance from the inhabitants of the township asking the court to grant Kerlin license, and deny it to Atkinson, which prevailed, again came into prominence. Michael, still intent on becoming the landlord of a public-house, under date of Feb. 29, 1732, petitioned the court, stating therein that he "hath rented the house of David Evans, of Radnor (David Evans' name appears on clerk's list for years 1729–30), where Evans kept a public-house for several years," which application received the approval of the justices. The same year David Evans stated in his application that he was then "living in a Convenient place to keep house of Entertainment, and being frequently desired to keep the same," he therefore presents his petition, indorsed by thirty signatures, and trusts it will be approved. The Court, however, apparently was not impressed with the necessity of a house at the location designated, and rejected the application. In August, 1734, Morgan Hugh made an effort to secure license for this house, and in his petition informed the court that he "hath lately Taken the house of David Evans, in Radnor, afforesd., Comonly known or Called the Signe of the Plow, it being an old Lycenced house." Among the thirty-nine signers to his petition appear the names of Francis and Anthony Wayne. The court, notwithstanding, turned a deaf ear to his pleadings, but nothing dismayed at his rebuff, at the November court of the same year he presents another petition, the signers thereto having increased in number to fifty-five, and the justices at last yielded to his importunity. In 1739, Hugh's name appears on the clerk's list of licenses approved by the court, although he could not then have been located at the same place (the Plow), for Aug. 31, 1737, David Evans, of Radnor, petitioned to keep public-house and "sell Cyder & Beer," which was refused; but Feb. 28, 1737/8, he again asked the court's indulgence, alleging that he "hath the charge of small Children, and Liveth at the old place Commonly known or Called by the Signe of the Plow, which hath Been a Publick house for many years." Isaac Wayne was among the signers to his petition, which at last touched the adamantine sympathies of the bench and secured him license. He must have done something in the interval between the February and August courts of the year 1738, for among the clerk's list of taverns, Aug. 29, 1738, after David Evans' name is written "not allowed." May 29, 1739, Evans again comes before the justices with the same argument, slightly varied, for he states that he "Liveth at a small place formerly Called the Signe of the Plow, which hath been a Publick house many years;" that he "has wife and children," and wants to sell "Beer & Sider," which was allowed him, as also from year to year until August court, 1742, when Richard Barry petitioned for license at this house (the Plow), which is favorably considered. David Evans, however, who it appears was a cooper by trade, in 1745 was licensed, his place at that time being on the Conestoga (now Lancaster) road.

Richard Barry, from the date above given, was yearly accorded license until 1765, when David Reese became the landlord of the Plow Tavern, and so continued until 1768. The following year the tavern seems to have passed into the control of James Barry, who, as he in 1769 asked for renewal of license, in all probability had the house the year previous, when Reese's name disappears finally from the records. During his (James Barry's) occupancy the inn enlarged its title, and was known as the Plow and Harrow. In 1775, Peter Mather—evidently a man strongly in favor of popular government, as is shown by his application that year, wherein he gives the name of the house as the "John Wilkes"—was licensed. Paul Shannadon, who succeeded Mather, in 1782 informed the court that the title of the old hostelry was then the John Wilkes, but formerly it was known as the Plow and Harrow. In 1786, Mary Ring received license for the ancient stand, after which it no longer appears as a tavern.

In 1747, James Miles presented his petition that "he has lately built a house on Conestoga (Lancaster) road, near Tredufrin" (Tredyffrin), and desires that he may have license for a public-house there. This location clearly indicates that this was the ancient tavern known to the last generation, and to the older inhabitants of that part of the old county of Chester as far back as 1769, as the Unicorn. In 1747, however, the application was rejected; but in the following year license was granted, and continued to Miles until 1750, when his petition is indorsed "disallowed," and the name Aubrey Roberts marked thereon, as if to the latter the court had extended its favor at this place; but this may not be the fact, for at the February court of the same year license was allowed to Miles, and his name appears until 1752, when James Miller was licensed at that place, to be followed, in 1755, by Thomas Tucker, who in 1761 gave place to Jonathan Pugh, who was followed in 1766 by Samuel Pugh, and he in the following year by Richard Barry. In 1769, Samuel Johnson obtained a license for the "Unicorn, that ancient and noted tavern," and was succeeded as its landlord by Samuel Pugh in 1773, who continued thereat until and including the year 1778. For the three following years there are no records respecting the granting of license in Radnor; but in 1782 Robert Kennedy was the landlord of the Unicorn, and when Delaware County was created he continued to receive license until 1801, when Thomas Mason became the landlord. In the latter's petition, in 1805, he states the then name of the old inn as the "Farmer's." In the next year John Righter made application for the license at this house, and sets forth that "the Unicorn has been licensed ever since the first settlement of the country." This statement seems to have been more than Robert Kennedy, the owner, could permit; hence, in 1807, he made personal application, and in his petition says "the Unicorn has been licensed these sixty year," which was historically true, since James Miles had received the first license therefor in 1747. In 1816, Adam Sliffer became the landlord of the old inn, and the following year Levi Wells was the landlord. He in 1818 designated the house as the "Commodore Decatur Inn;" but Benjamin Smith, in 1819, restored the time-honored name, Unicorn. The latter was followed in 1823 by J. Hassan, who in 1827 gives the title of the tavern as the Black Bear. But the next year, 1828, John Smith superseded him in business, and the Unicorn once again became rampant on the sign. In 1834, Joseph Atkins had the license, and it continued to be granted to him until 1847, when he died. In 1848 his widow, Margaret Atkins, received the court's approval, and, later in the year, Robert K. and Richard Atkins had it transferred to them. In the fall of 1848, Hon. John M. Broomall was appointed trustee to sell the real estate of Joseph Atkins, deceased. Benjamin Kirk was the landlord of the house during the years 1849–50.

Thomas Ives, in 1759, and Mordecai Taylor, in 1778, were also granted licenses to keep tavern in Radnor township, but the location of the houses managed by them have not been ascertained.

About the year 1756 the vast immigration setting westward to Lancaster County and the territory beyond that limit, required numerous wayside inns to accommodate the number of wagoners and travelers who journeyed along the old Conestoga road of that day. Hence about that time we find a new petition in Radnor, presented by Aubrey Harry, who found favor with the court, and was continued thereat until and including 1764, when his name, for the last time, appears on the list of approved tavern-keepers. In 1765, Michael Stadleman made his application for license to keep a public-house in the township, which was granted to him, and he continued yearly to receive that privilege until 1775, when he disappears from the record. In 1778, Jacob Waggoner was granted license, and in 1782, John Witmar, in his application, designated the house as the Sorrel Horse, as also did his successor, John B. Webster, in 1784. The latter in 1788 was superseded at the old stand by James Elliott, who continued thereat until 1810, when his widow, Sarah Elliott, received the license until 1813, at which date Christian Himes became the landlord, remaining there until 1815, when the house was vacant. The following year John Dever had license for the Sorrel Horse, after which, for four years, the place appears not to have been used as a public inn; but in 1821, George J. Stackers made application for license there, which was granted to him. In 1824 he gave place to Eliza Thomas, and she, the following year, to Robert R. Rowland. He for eleven years was "mine host" of the old tavern, to be followed in 1836 by Alexander Brooke, who in turn was succeeded by Rowland again, he, however, in 1839, once more gave place to another landlord, this time John Mullin The latter remained until 1840 Philip Kirk then purchased the property, and the following year (1841) Benjamin Kirk, a brother of Philip, became the landlord of the Sorrel Horse, remaining there until 1849, when Philip Kirk, its owner, assumed control, and conducted the house until his death, in 1851 He was succeeded by his widow, Eliza, who kept the house open until her death, which occurred in February, 1877 During the following year, Rachel, daughter of Philip and Eliza Kirk, served as proprietress On the 1st of April, 1878, John and Alfred Worrell, as lessees, obtained license and remained one year, when George W Murray, the present lessee and proprietor, took possession It is the only licensed house at this time in the township, and is still owned by children of Philip Kirk

In 1769, Adam Ramsower (formerly of Pikeland township, Chester Co, where he kept a tavern at Yellow Springs) made application for license for a stone house, forty by thirty-three feet, situated on the Lancaster road within a mile of Jonathan Pugh's tavern, which he, Ramsower, had built The lands attached to the house comprised one hundred acres In 1772, Jacob Hinkell petitioned for the right to keep the inn which now appears under the well-known title Spread Eagle The following year David Hinkell became the landlord, to be superseded, in 1774, by Jacob Hinkell, who continued there until 1778 In 1782, Alexander Clay was "mine host" of the Eagle, and continued as such until 1787, when Adam Siter obtained the license, and he, in 1791, was followed in the business by John Siter, who, in 1812, gave place to James Watson Two years later, in 1814, Edward Siter became the landlord, to be followed in 1817 by David Wilson, Jr The latter, in 1823, was superseded by Zenas Wells, and in 1825 Edward W Siter kept the Spread Eagle Stephen Horne had license for this tavern in 1836, and the next year Richard Millerson, to be followed, in 1839, by John Chrisman Mordecai Worrell purchased the property in 1841, and had license for several years In 1846, Elisha Worrell did the honors of the Eagle, to give place to Mordecai Worrell in 1848, and to assume them again the next year In 1851 the property was mentioned as the estate of Mordecai Worrell, deceased, situate on the Lancaster turnpike, and offered for sale It was purchased in 1851 by Benjamin Kirk (formerly the proprietor of the Sorrel Horse and Unicorn Hotels), who remained as its owner and landlord for eight years He then sold the property to John Todd Under the latter's ownership Jacob Rieser, as lessee, officiated as "mine host" Subsequently Charles Arthur became the owner of the Spread Eagle, and he in turn gave place to David Crumley, who, as owner and manager, kept the house open until within a recent date, when it was purchased by George W Childs to stop the sale of liquor near his bailiwick, —the new town of Wayne The building and grounds have been neatly fitted up, and are now (summer of 1884) in use as a country home for the young Indian wards of the Lincoln Institute

In 1749, Bartle Bartleson presented a petition to court setting forth that he had a house, known as the Sign of the Buck, which was located half way between the Sign of the Buck (Jonathan Miller's tavern, Haverford) and the Spread Eagle, "that he has been at a great expense in building a commodious house for the purpose, and desires license hereat" His application was successful, and yearly thereafter until 1812, when he was followed in business by John Taylor, who changed the name of the tavern to the Fox In 1814, Frederick Lowdon obtained license for the house under the same title The following year Isaac Sharpless leased and managed the house. In 1816, Ann Bartleson, the widow of Bartle, kept the inn, and continued there until 1824, when Mark Bartleson, her son, succeeded to the business In 1830, Joseph Hassan rented the Fox, and after his death, in 1832, Mary Hassan continued there one year Joseph Thornburg followed her, in 1833 Then came Mark Bartleson again, in 1836, who continued until 1844, when the house ceased to be one of public entertainment

Elisha Moore, in 1807, prayed the court to grant him license for his house, located on the Philadelphia and Lancaster turnpike road, near the eleventh milestone He says that he is "nearly three miles above Jonathan Miller's tavern (Haverford), about one-third of a mile above Bartle Bartleson's tavern, and nearly three miles below Edward Siter's and Robert Kennedy's tavern Between the first and the second last-mentioned taverns, on the old Lancaster road, there is now two taverns, and was there perhaps for forty years prior to the turnpike road being made (1792). The traveling since has vastly increased, and is generally confined to the turnpike. And as your petitioner lives in a very eligible situation for the accommodation and convenience of travellers, and has been at a considerable expense in the erection of buildings for keeping a public-house, which he will endeavor to merit by keeping good order, if your Honours will please to grant him a recommendation to his Excellency the Governor for a license for the same" The court acted favorably on his petition, and thus was established the White Horse Tavern In 1814, Moore was followed by Jonathan Morgan, and the latter, in 1815, gave place to William Sheldrake However, Elisha Moore returned to the tavern in 1816, and remained there until 1827, when Joseph Miller was the landlord, to be the next year followed by Elisha Moore, who continued to have license granted to him until 1838, after which date the White Horse Tavern disappeared from the records of the county as a public-house

"WOOTTON,"
DELAWARE COUNTY, PA.

At February term, 1836, H. Jones Brooke sent in a petition for license, wherein he stated that "your petitioner is desirous of keeping a public-house or tavern in the house he has lately built, at the intersection of the road leading from the Valley Forge to the Lancaster Turnpike, near the eleven-mile stone, also the road leading from the Gulf Mills to Radnor Friends' meeting-house, and with the Philadelphia and Columbia Railroad, near the fourteen-mile post on the railroad There is at present a lumber- and coal-yard established at the place, also a storehouse for storing flour and grain It is made by the regulations of the railroad a point at which the locomotives stop for passengers It is also an established place for supplying the locomotives with wood, and the subscriber has sunk a well for supplying water The house is forty feet long by thirty-eight feet wide, two stories high, and finished in such a manner as would make it convenient for a public-house There is no public-house on the railroad in Delaware County, although it passes near six miles through said county The petitioner has provided himself with necessaries for the convenience and accommodation of travelers and strangers"

Brooke's petition was supplemented by another one signed by Mahlon Ortlip, superintendent of transportation and motive power, Jacob Barry, manager at Schuylkill Plane, Frederick Vogel, superintendent on the Columbia and Philadelphia Railroad, Jacobs & Cornog, Andrew Wells, Joseph Smith, and others Brooke then obtained license, and each succeeding year until 1839, when William Lowman, as lessee, was granted license for the same house, a point then termed Morgan's Corners On the 17th of November, 1840, while occupied by Lowman, the house caught fire from a spark escaping from a passing locomotive and was totally destroyed, thus entailing a loss of about four thousand dollars It was immediately rebuilt by the owner and occupied by William Lowman until 1846, when Ed. J Lowman became its proprietor. The latter kept hotel here for a number of years, and was succeeded by Isaac Palmer Subsequently John Wagoner and George Righter bought the property, who, after keeping the house open for a term of years, sold out to Montgomery and Rand. Under their control the house ceased to be licensed some five or six years ago It is now occupied as a boarding-house

Justices of the Peace—The following-named citizens of Radnor have been commissioned justices of the peace at dates indicated

Edward Hunter	Aug 30, 1791
John Lindsay	June 5, 1794
Isaac Abrahams	May 20, 1800.
Luke Cassin	March 27, 1809
John Siter	Sept 1, 1813
Robert Green	Feb 23, 1816
Nathan Gibson	Nov 26, 1817
George Brooke	July 3, 1821
Maskell Ewing	June 10, 1822
Benjamin Lobb	Dec 4, 1823.
Park Shee	Dec. 9, 1823
Daniel Abrahams	Dec 14, 1825
Barnard Flynn	Nov 18, 1835
Abner Lewis	May 27, 1836
Thomas Sheldon	Dec 20, 1836
Thomas Cassin	Nov 1, 1838
Homer Eachus	May 11, 1839
Abner Lewis	April 14, 1840
Abner Lewis	April 15, 1845
Alexander Johnson	April 10, 1849
Hiram Cleaver	April 10, 1855
Hiram Cleaver	April 10, 1860
Hiram Cleaver	April 28, 1860
Barclay Hall	Nov 24, 1869
Daniel C Abrahams	March 31, 1874
Daniel C Abrahams	March 27, 1879
John A Griffin	April 9, 1881

Wootton, the Country Home of George W. Childs—One of the most effective beginnings of extensive and elaborate improvements in Radnor was that made by George W Childs, in Wootton, his country home Mr Childs selected the present site with a view to its prospective embellishment and ornamentation It was exceedingly well adapted to the purpose, consisting in part of cleared land and in part of forest, and sloping grandly towards the avenue which leads westwardly from Bryn Mawr Station, on the Pennsylvania Railroad, through the rich and beautifully diversified country of Upper Merion and of Radnor

Mr Childs selected this site and began improvements upon it in the summer of 1880, and it seems almost incredible that such finished work, such perfection of detail, as Wootton exhibits could have been accomplished in the brief period that has elapsed since then

The most comprehensive view of Wootton is to be obtained from the hills on the opposite side of the little valley, in which the house and grounds are like jewels set The great expanse of lawn, perfectly kept, the house and other buildings, appear from this height as a French study of art and nature, so perfectly are the beauties of both combined

Viewed in detail the charms of Wootton enlarge in proportion to their number. The visitor, if approaching from the railroad, has a pleasant drive or walk along a picturesque roadway, nicely graded and thoroughly macadamized for a distance of a little more than a mile, and then finds himself at the main carriage entrance, marked by a handsome and hospitable-appearing lodge The drive gradually ascends the knoll or hill, and reaches the house under a handsome *porte cochère* The house is found to be, perhaps, less pretentious, less elaborate, than one might expect, but if there is any fault in this particular it is made amends for in the elegance of detail and the tasteful elaboration of the surroundings A broad terrace in front, adorned and made tropical in appearance by century-old feather palms, bordered by a wall and railing of massive and artistically-cut stone, half concealed by climbing vines, forms the immediate environment of the house, and from this to the road slopes the great shaven lawn, dotted along its borders with a wealth of evergreen and other shrubbery, and richly studded with immense masses of gorgeous foliage plants Few if any lawns in America have the breadth and smoothness and beautiful slope of this, and none are better cared for or more velvety in texture. At one side, across a little brook which art has handled very gracefully, and beyond a crystal spring which has been given a beautiful housing, is the original forest, left in its native wildness. On the other side of the house the lawn slopes away to the more recently-acquired possessions of Mr. Childs, which constitute the farm, and of which we shall presently speak more specifically.

The house itself is entered by way of a massive door, which is both hospitable and formidable, over a vestibule floored with Roman mosaics, especially imported for the purpose. The style of the interior is substantial, curious, quaint, but the idea everywhere most strongly suggested is that of the home, and of hospitality and of comfort. All of constructive design, of ornament and art, seems subversive to the central thought of constructing a model home and a happy place of sojourn for friends. In such admirable taste has the general design been carried out, and lavishness of expenditure so well directed, that decoration has not fallen short of completeness and yet has not overstepped the limit of chasteness. We are told that Wootton had its origin in the desire of Mrs. Childs to build a simple home which should be a retreat for the family, midway in season and elaborateness between the Philadelphia residence and the establishment at Long Branch, and that from time to time, as the attractiveness of the locality became more and more apparent, the original simple design was amplified and elaborated, until it resulted in the present commodious and elegant house.

Here the hospitality which Mr. Childs ever delights in has had one of its principal theatres. The house has been the scene of a great number of entertainments of social and semi-public character, of the celebrated Farmers' Club dinners, and of elaborate yet unostentatious entertainment of the eminent men and women of our country and of Europe. In this connection the origin of the name of Mr. Childs' country home is interesting. The term is transplanted from England, and is commemorative of pleasant hospitality, of which Mr. and Mrs. Childs were there the recipients.

In Lyson's "Magna Britannia," vol. i. p. 673, there is the following account of "Wootton Underwood," in the hundred of Ashendon and deanery of Waddesdon. The manor was given by William the Conqueror to the Earl of Buckingham, and in 1097 it was brought by marriage to Richard de Grenville, from whom there has been an uninterrupted line of male succession, through twenty generations, to the present proprietor, the Duke of Buckingham. Wootton house has been from time immemorial the seat of the Grenvilles. The present house was built in 1705. The staircase and saloon were painted by Sir James Thornhill. It was the favorite home of the family. In the parish church are the ancient monuments of the Grenvilles, and the windows are ornamented with the arms and quarterings of the Grenvilles, the Temples, and the Chandos. It was at Wootton that the present Duke of Buckingham welcomed Mr. and Mrs. Childs, on their first visit to England, and there they made their acquaintance with English country life. In token of the pleasant memory of the hospitality there extended to them, their own lovely country home was called Wootton, and thus the American Wootton perpetuates the long years of hospitality for which the English Wootton is famous. The Wootton of Delaware County is an admirable type of American country homes, for there guests of all nationalities, the leaders in all that is great and good, are heartily welcomed, and it has already become famous as the seat of a generous hospitality not often equaled either in Europe or in this country. The house and the grounds are in admirable taste, and it is one of the stately homes for which Delaware County is fast becoming famous.

Interesting as is this home with its beauties of architecture and decoration of art, and of association, of books, and of costly and quaint *bric-a-brac*, the grounds and the farm are, after all, the strongest and most unique attraction, and, therefore, we emerge from a delightful house to its sumptuous surroundings.

And of these no hand but that of the painter or the most gifted artist in words can give an adequate idea, hence we will not attempt it.

In addition to the grounds originally constituting Wootton, Mr. Childs bought and brought under care, in 1883, land adjoining his, which he caused to be made an addition to his farm. Upon this, and upon lands which he formerly possessed, some of the most extensive improvements in the region have been made. It is here, southwest of the home and the grounds surrounding it, that the farm has been laid out and brought into nicely-ordered existence, principally through the management of Mr. John M. Hughes, chief gardener of the place. The farm consists of about forty acres of excellent land well tilled, and is supplied with all of the most modern and well-approved adjuncts and appliances. The barn here, while not so perfect in its appointments as the stable near the house (which is perhaps the best in the country), is exceedingly well adapted to its purpose, and contains every requisite of a thorough farm establishment. It is built of stone, and the yard is paved with the same material, while a massive wall surrounds the whole.

Near by is the farmer's house, a handsome cottage, and in close proximity to this the spring-house, which is a marvel of neatness, and a model scarcely approachable for all who would have a perfect dairy. It is built of white flint, which is as cool in effect as snow and ice could be, and consists of a work-room and a milk-room, the latter almost a chapel in appearance, and a place of absolute purity, both in fact and appearance. The milk from several pure and deer-like Alderneys, most carefully cared for, is kept here, and has a housing and protection in every way worthy of its unrivaled

Eng^d by Geo E. Perine New York.

George W. Childs

[illegible]. A little distance from this [illegible] like a Russian [illegible] which is as ornament as the grounds, is the [illegible] which [illegible] the [illegible] part of the grounds, [illegible] plants from South America, Africa and [illegible] of the tropical regions of the world, [illegible] upon for the beautifying of the [illegible].

[illegible] and [illegible] the [illegible] here and [illegible] a novel device of [illegible] "Stumpery," a mass of [illegible] and branches, covered with [illegible] vines and moss, rivaling in [illegible] the wonderful [illegible].

A description of [illegible] is impossible [illegible] work as is this [illegible] general idea of [illegible] with saying that [illegible] wealth has been [illegible] and practical [illegible] in our country.

BIOGRAPHICAL SKETCHES.

GEORGE W. CHILDS.

It was [illegible] the career of [illegible] the [illegible] Childs [illegible]

[illegible]

which has been so largely and interestingly [illegible] and [illegible] by him, something, however brief, should be said of his active, broad, and useful life.

It is one of the greatest elements in the romance of American life that careers like that of Mr. Childs are not uncommon,—that the boy, however poor, however lowly, may make the man of wealth and of honorable [illegible]. It is one of the greatest glories of American life that while it affords in superlative degree these possibilities, there appears a general disposition on the part of those who strive successfully [illegible] material assistance [illegible] children to [illegible].

The life of George W. Childs [illegible] and [illegible] illustration of this [illegible] proposition. Born in Baltimore May 12, 1829, at [illegible] he entered the United States navy, but after a [illegible] of [illegible] months left the service and went to Philadelphia, where the [illegible] of a book[illegible] to be [illegible] in a [illegible] position. The right road [illegible] found it only [illegible] by industry, perseverance, integrity, and [illegible] hard work. The boy possessed these qualities, and [illegible] them. Without them any one of the numerous obstacles he met might—and a [illegible] of them [illegible]—have caused his failure. Constantly advancing, he became, soon after he had attained his majority, a partner in the publishing-house of Childs & Peterson, where his energy was soon shown by the way in which he advanced Mr. Peterson's compilation entitled "Familiar Science," to a sale of two hundred thousand copies. His next publishing [illegible] were both large [illegible], and both [illegible] successful ones. For Dr. Kane's narrative of his Arctic Expedition he was enabled to pay the author seventy thousand dollars, and the success of Parson Brownlow's "Debates on Slavery" and "Sketches of Secession" may be approximately measured by the fact that he paid the author fifteen thousand dollars. He also published Allibone's "Dictionary of Authors," and such was his handling of that enterprise that the author made the following acknowledgment: "To George William Childs, the original publisher of this volume, who has greatly furthered my labors by his enterprise and zealous and intelligent interest, I dedicate the fruits of many years of [illegible] research and conscientious toil."

Upon the retirement of Mr. Peterson from the firm, in 1860, Mr. Childs formed a partnership with J. B. Lippincott, which lasted but a year, when he resumed business for himself. In 1863 he purchased the *Publishers' Circular*, and by remodeling it and changing its name to the *American Literary Gazette and Publishers' Circular*, greatly increased its value to the trade. He also acquired the *American Almanac*, and renaming it the *National Almanac*, soon pushed it into a circulation of thirty thousand copies annually. During all of this time general book publishing had been carried on very extensively and successfully, but

George W. Childs

quality. A little distance from this flint milk-house, which appears like a Russian fancy in ice in a little house, which is an ornament to the grounds, is the water-power which sends the supply needed at the extensive green-house, on this part of the grounds In these buildings there is a wealth of bloom and of rich foliage plants from South America, Africa, and all of the tropical regions of the world, which is drawn upon for the beautifying of the lawn and house.

An extensive "Rosary" and elaborate gardens, both of flowers and their more substantial kindred of the kitchen, flourishes here, and near by adjoining a little lake is a novel device of the landscape artist, in what is called a "Stumpery," a mass of tree-stumps and gnarled roots and branches, covered with creeping vines and moss, rivaling in beauty and surpassing in oddity the wonderful orchids in the green-houses

A description of Wootton — of the house and grounds—is impossible within the limits of such a work as is this, and the writer, after giving a few general ideas of its loveliness, must content himself with saying that, as the country home on which wealth has been lavished and taste used in its extreme, and as the exponent of advanced experimental and practical agriculture, it has few if any superiors in our country

BIOGRAPHICAL SKETCHES.

GEORGE W CHILDS

It was a fortunate day for the people of Radnor and the region round about when George W Childs decided to establish his country-seat in their midst, for in that action lay the initiation of the idea which led to the founding of the model village of Wayne, an enterprise undertaken with no speculative purpose whatever, but the benefit of others, and destined, perhaps, to be, among all and above all of his good works, the noblest monument to his memory and to the purpose of his life

We say this because Wayne will in a few years not only be the home of hundreds of healthful, happy families, but, by reason of the admirable carrying out of well-considered plans for sanitation, as well as for securing beauty, will suggest and become the model for other suburban aggregations of homes, and so be the medium of transmission to wider fields and to future generations of the good which is now manifested here

But of Wayne and of that other, though lesser, beauty, "Wootton," with which Mr Childs has enriched the loveliness of this locality in Delaware County, enough has already been said in the chapter of which this is a part.

It is fitting that in a history and description of the region which Mr Childs has made his home, and which has been so largely and interestingly adorned and endowed by him, something, however brief, should be told of his active, broad, and useful life

It is one of the greatest elements in the romance of American life that careers like that of Mr Childs are not uncommon,—that the boy, however poor, however lowly, may make the man of wealth and of honorable distinction,—and it is one of the greatest glories of American life that while it affords in superlative degree these possibilities, there appears a general disposition on the part of those who strive successfully to extend moral and material assistance commensurate with their great abilities to others

The life of George W Childs affords a forcible and splendid individual illustration of the foregoing generalities Born in Baltimore May 12, 1829, at the age of thirteen he entered the United States navy, but after a period of about fifteen months left the service and went to Philadelphia, where the door of a bookstore proved to be also the entrance to a life of prosperity The right road had been found, it only remained for industry, perseverance, integrity, and tact to do their work The boy possessed these qualities, and used them Without them any one of the numerous obstacles he met might—and a series of them inevitably must—have caused his failure Constantly advancing, he became, soon after he had attained his majority, a partner in the publishing-house of Childs & Peterson, where his energy was soon shown by the way in which he advanced Mr Peterson's compilation entitled "Familiar Science," to a sale of two hundred thousand copies His next publishing enterprises were both large undertakings, and both remarkably successful ones For Dr Kane's narrative of his Arctic Expedition he was enabled to pay the author seventy thousand dollars, and the success of Parson Brownlow's "Debates on Slavery" and "Sketches of Secession" may be approximately measured by the fact that he paid the author fifteen thousand dollars. He also published Allibone's "Dictionary of Authors," and such was his handling of that enterprise that the author made the following acknowledgment "To George William Childs, the original publisher of this volume, who has greatly furthered my labors by his enterprise and zealous and intelligent interest, I dedicate the fruits of many years of anxious research and conscientious toil"

Upon the retirement of Mr Peterson from the firm, in 1860, Mr Childs formed a partnership with J B Lippincott, which lasted but a year, when he resumed business for himself In 1863 he purchased the *Publishers' Circular*, and by remodeling it and changing its name to the *American Literary Gazette and Publishers' Circular*, greatly increased its value to the trade He also acquired the *American Almanac*, and renaming it the *National Almanac*, soon pushed it into a circulation of thirty thousand copies annually During all of this time general book publishing had been carried on very extensively and successfully, but

Mr. Childs had long cherished the ambition of owning and controlling a daily journal, and he turned aside to gratify it. On the 3d of December, 1864, he became the proprietor of the *Public Ledger*. This purchase was made against the advice of his friends, but time has fully vindicated the wisdom that directed it. The *Ledger* was at once given the exceptionally high tone which it has ever since retained, and through the skill of the new management, and the force of new blood infused into its every channel, soon recovered the patronage it had lost, and won a host of new friends. A journal devoted to printing and the affairs of newspapers has said,—

"Every improper feature in advertisement or in news was excluded from its columns; a spirit of almost judicial fairness was made to breathe throughout its reports and opinions of men and things; whatever weight is due to dignity, independence, impartiality, and a wise and considerate estimate of social and political topics, was imparted to its editorials; and no expenditure, however lavish, was withheld in enhancing its value as a trustworthy and salutary fireside visitor. The forecast of Mr. Childs was eminently justified. The *Ledger* ultimately reached a circulation of ninety thousand copies daily."

Another writer has said of the great newspaper,—

"The policy of the *Ledger*, since Mr. Childs has owned and controlled it, has been of a character to be described in a very few words. In the first place, it has been undeviatingly high-toned in its character, scorning the low moral standard which so widely obtains among the press of the United States, with a straightforward integrity of purpose that is characteristic of its proprietor. Again, it has striven to treat such subjects, and such only, as were within the line which divides the real interest of the public from that which is factitious. Finally, in its method of handling the questions of the day, it has followed the plan of treating each of these on its own merits, and without bias or regard for personal opinion or criticism."

Fortune followed the venture, and as it increased new channels were created for its outflow. Of Mr. Childs' benefactions, public and private, it is not our purpose to speak in detail,—and indeed that would be impossible. It is well known that his large generosity finds expression through all of the benevolent institutions of the city, and through many ingenious devices of his own, for charity, and that in a vast number of channels, small and great, from the tiny rivulet to the sweeping current of the river, good is ever going out from an apparently inexhaustible fountain-head. Such unique and stupendous forms of charity as his have not been equaled by individual effort in our country. His newsboys' banquets, his excursions for whole schools or for the inmates of great institutions, have been so common an occurrence as to excite but little comment. His splendid support of such colossal enterprises as the Centennial Exposition are not the least admirable of his exhibitions of public spirit. His gift of a cemetery to the printers of Philadelphia, and provision of a fund for its perpetual preservation; his erection of a memorial window in Westminster Abbey, to the honor of the poets Herbert and Cowper, and numerous other gifts, have marked him as one of the greatest-hearted and greatest-minded of living men.

It is only natural that the heart which has ever expressed sympathy with humanity should love fellowship with men; that he should go out to meet them and that he should gather them around him. Hence it came about that his beautiful residence in Philadelphia was made the meeting-place of some of the greatest minds and most eminent characters of our own and foreign countries. In it at the time of the opening of the Centennial Exposition occurred what was undoubtedly the most notable assemblage in a private house ever known in America.

It was the same spirit of sociability that led to the building of his country home, "Wootton," in this township. Here have gathered the great and the humble, and of the promotion of happy human intercourse which this house has subserved, it would be very difficult to form even an approximate estimate. It has been the sojourning place of many of America's leaders in literature and directors of National growth, of the titled nobility of Europe, and of the untitled men of genius of both the parent and the daughter realms, and not less has it been the scene of happy visits from the carrier boys and from great throngs of the humble people who have been as carefully and as sumptuously entertained as the visitors of more fortunate stations in life.

Here is that wonderful treasury of books and of priceless manuscripts, which Mr. Childs' taste for literature led him to amass, and which his acquaintanceship with authors and his wealth enabled him to make the most interesting one in America.

"Wootton" led to Wayne. The happiness which Mr. Childs experienced in his country home led his mind, always active in devising the welfare of others, to the conception of a plan by which many men of moderate means might enjoy the beauty and the wholesomeness of the country. His idea was the founding of a village with perfect sanitary regulations, with broad avenues and streets, and with comfortable, attractive houses which should be within the reach of men enjoying comparatively small incomes.

To create such a suburban villa, Mr. Childs and his friend, Anthony J. Drexel, of Philadelphia, devoted their thought, their energy, and their money, and began the work in the spring of 1881. It has progressed steadily and entirely to the satisfaction of the projectors, and the investment at Wayne now equals half a million dollars, and more money will be spent there from season to season, until the town is equal in all respects to the preconceived idea of what it should be. The enterprise was not undertaken with any idea of realizing a profit, but simply of furnishing country homes to city men, and surrounding them with all of the advantages to be secured in a well-ordered village in which should be combined all of the measures for the preservation of health that scientific experiment has during late years suggested. The plan could only be carried out by the employment of large capital and by organized effort. This will secure to a large number of men, dependent upon their incomes from professional or business toil, with precisely those

Edward Peace

Mr. Childs had long cherished the ambition of owning and controlling a daily journal, and he turned aside to gratify it. On the 3d of December, 1864, he became the proprietor of the *Public Ledger*. This purchase was made against the advice of his friends, but time has fully vindicated the wisdom that directed it. The *Ledger* was at once given the exceptionally high tone which it has ever since retained, and through the skill of the new management, and the force of new blood infused into its every channel, soon recovered the patronage it had lost, and won a host of new friends. A journal devoted to printing and the affairs of newspapers has said,—

"Every improper feature in advertisement or in news was excluded from its columns; a spirit of almost judicial fairness was made to breathe throughout its reports and opinions of men and things; whatever weight is due to dignity, independence, impartiality, and a wise and considerate estimate of social and political topics, was imparted to its editorials; and no expenditure, however lavish, was withheld in enhancing its value as a trustworthy and [illegible] fireside visitor. The foresight of Mr. Childs was eminently justified. The *Ledger* ultimately reached a circulation of ninety thousand copies daily."

Another writer has said of the great newspaper,—

"The policy of the *Ledger*, since Mr. Childs has owned and controlled it, has been of a character to be described in a very few words. In the first place, it has been unmistakably high-toned in its character, securing the [illegible] standard which so [illegible] among the press of the United States, [illegible] principle of the proprietor. Again, it has striven to treat such subjects, and such only, as might [illegible] the real interests of the people from that which is frivolous. Finally, in the method of handling the questions of the day, it has followed the plan of [illegible] of these on its [illegible] and [illegible] to regard the personal opinion or criticism."

Fortune followed the venture, and as it increased new channels were created for its outflow. Of Mr. Childs' benefactions, public and private, it is not our purpose to speak in detail,—and indeed that would be impossible. It is well known that his large generosity finds expression through all of the benevolent institutions of the city, and through many ingenious devices of his own, for charity, and that in a vast number of channels, small and great, from the tiny rivulet to the sweeping current of the river, good is ever going out from an apparently inexhaustible fountain-head. Such unique and stupendous forms of charity as his have not been equaled by individual effort in our country. His newsboys' banquets, his excursions for whole schools or for the inmates of great institutions, have been so common an occurrence as to excite but little comment. His splendid support of such colossal enterprises as the Centennial Exposition are not the least admirable of his exhibitions of public spirit. His gift of a cemetery to the printers of Philadelphia, and provision of a fund for its perpetual preservation; his erection of a memorial window in Westminster Abbey, to the honor of the poets Herbert and Cowper, and numerous other gifts, have marked him as one of the greatest-hearted and greatest-minded of living men.

It is only natural that the heart which has ever expressed sympathy with humanity should love fellowship with men; that he should go out to meet them and that he should gather them around him. Hence it came about that his beautiful residence in Philadelphia was made the meeting-place of some of the greatest minds and most eminent characters of our own and foreign countries. In it at the time of the opening of the Centennial Exposition occurred what was undoubtedly the most notable assemblage in a private house ever known in America.

It was the same spirit of sociability that led to the building of his country home, "Wootton," in this township. Here have gathered the great and the humble, and of the procession of happy human intercourse which this home has witnessed, it would be very difficult to form even an approximate estimate. It has been the sojourning place of many of America's leaders in literature and directors of National growth, of the titled nobility of Europe, and of the untitled men of genius of both the parent and the daughter realms, and not less has it been the scene of happy visits from the carrier boys and from great throngs of the humble people who have been as carefully and as sumptuously entertained as the visitors of more fortunate stations in life.

Here is that wonderful treasury of books and of priceless manuscripts, which Mr. Childs' taste for literature led him to amass, and which his acquaintanceship with authors and his wealth enabled him to make the most interesting one in America.

Wootton led to Wayne. The happiness which Mr. Childs experienced in his country home led his mind, always active in devising the welfare of others, to the conception of a plan by which many men of moderate means might enjoy the beauty and the wholesomeness of the country. His idea was the founding of a village with perfect sanitary regulations, with broad avenues and streets, and with comfortable, attractive houses which should be within the reach of men enjoying comparatively small incomes.

To create such a suburban villa, Mr. Childs and his friend, Anthony J. Drexel, of Philadelphia, devoted their thought, their energy, and their money, and began the work in the spring of 1881. It has progressed steadily and entirely to the satisfaction of the projectors, and the investment at Wayne now equals half a million dollars, and more money will be spent there from season to season, until the town is equal in all respects to the preconceived idea of what it should be. The enterprise was not undertaken with any idea of realizing a profit, but simply of furnishing country homes to city men, and surrounding them with all of the advantages to be secured in a well-ordered village in which should be combined all of the measures for the preservation of health that scientific experiment has during late years suggested. The plan could only be carried out by the employment of large capital and by organized effort. This will secure to a large number of men, dependent upon their incomes from professional or business toil, with precisely those

Engraved by [illegible]

Edward Peace

"CASTLEFINN."
RESIDENCE OF JAMES RAWLE,
DELAWARE CO., PA.

"ANNASDALE."

surroundings that only the man of wealth could obtain through individual enterprise And herein, as time will demonstrate, is one of the largest and most far-reaching of Mr Childs' public benefactions Wayne will be the monument, however, to a man who needs none, for he will live in the hearts of thousands, and in the hearts of their successors, and his name will be cherished for ages as one which will recall a type of the highest class of mankind,—a man who has lived for others, has made others live,—a man who has to the utmost of his great ability softened human sorrow, and enlarged human happiness

---

DR EDWARD PEACE

Prior to 1770, Isaac Peace, the grandfather of Dr Edward Peace, emigrated from England to the Barbadoes, where on the 31st of June, in that year, he married Elizabeth Gibson After a few years he removed to the United States and settled at Bristol, Pa, where he died, Dec 25, 1818 Joseph Peace, the eldest son of Isaac, was born in Barbadoes, May 1, 1771 He came to this country with his father, and settled at Charleston, S C, where he was a prosperous merchant for a number of years, but becoming dissatisfied with his surroundings, especially with the practices of slavery and its attendant evils, he removed to Philadelphia, Pa About the time of the birth of his son, Edward, his place of residence here (Philadelphia) was on the corner of Sixth and Walnut Streets, opposite Washington Square, a property which is still owned by his descendants He also owned a country-seat at Bristol, Pa He died at Philadelphia, March 31, 1826

Dr Edward Peace, son of Joseph, was born Feb 10, 1811, and was one of the younger members of a family of thirteen children When about fifteen years of age he became a student of the Mount Airy Military School, located at Chestnut Hill, where he zealously pursued his literary studies some two or three years He then studied medicine, and after attending a full course of lectures at the University of Pennsylvania, graduated from that institution with honor Soon after that event he proceeded to Europe, and for two or three years still further prosecuted his medical studies under the instructions of the most eminent physicians and surgeons of Paris After his return to Philadelphia he became connected with the University of Pennsylvania and the Pennsylvania Hospital, where he was superintendent from 1840 to 1861, and thereafter was identified with their history for a long term of years When the Asiatic cholera raged with such virulence in Philadelphia, in 1832, he volunteered his services, and, while others faltered or fled, rendered most efficient aid at the almshouse, finally becoming ill with that dread disease himself.

For many years no man in Pennsylvania was more prominent in the field of surgery than he, and it has been stated that he was the first surgeon in America to make a success in tying a deep-seated artery During the latter part of his active professional career he officiated as chief visiting surgeon and clinical lecturer at the Pennsylvania Hospital However, he gave up his practice at the hospital in 1861

Until 1852, Dr Peace resided at the corner of Ninth and Walnut Streets He then removed to No 1602 Chestnut Street, a property which is still owned by his heirs About 1853 he purchased "Annasdale," a beautiful country-seat in Radnor township, Delaware Co, Pa, where he afterwards resided six months in each year, and where he made all of the improvements to be seen to day He was the first city resident, we believe, to establish a country home in Radnor, and made choice of this location because of its altitude, great natural beauty, and healthfulness Dr Peace was a gentleman of fine physical proportions (being five feet ten inches in height), of easy manners, and social with all with whom he came in contact, and, as before intimated, was excelled by but few, if any, in this country in the knowledge of his profession He died on the night of Sept 9–10, 1879, at "Annasdale," and was buried in the grounds belonging to the Church of the Redeemer, at Bryn Mawr

Dr Peace was widely known throughout Pennsylvania for his quiet and unostentatious benevolence His neighbors in Radnor, and all with whom he came in contact, unite in testifying to his regard for and attention to the wants of suffering humanity, and the neighborly kindness of manner which won all hearts

He was looked up to and revered by all, and the people of Radnor felt his loss as that of a near and dear friend, and as that of one who could not be replaced

When about twenty-two years of age he married Caroline, a daughter of Richard Willing Three children were born to them, two of whom—Richard Willing and Mrs Osgood Jackson, of New York City—survive

On the 14th of July, 1853, Dr. Peace was again married to Mrs Anna Coleman Parker, daughter of Robert Coleman, and then the widow of Charles Collins Parker, whose remains are interred at Bryn Mawr, they having been removed thence from Laurel Hill Cemetery At the time of Dr Peace's marriage to Mrs Parker, she was the mother of one daughter,—Charlotte Collins Parker,—who is now the wife of James Rawle, Esq, of Castlefinn, near Bryn Mawr, Pa, a gentleman by the way who is likewise a grandson of Robert Colemam, above mentioned

By his second marriage Dr Peace became the father of five children, viz Anna, Florence, Mary, Philip Physia, and Edward Coleman Of these children, the first named was married to Lieut Alfred Mead Bates, of the Fifth United States Cavalry, who died at Fort Dodge, Kansas, Nov 12, 1876. Subsequently she became the wife of Henry Hobart Brown, whose father was the first rector of the Church of the

Redeemer at Bryn Mawr. She died July 2, 1883. Florence is the wife of R. Mead Smith, of Philadelphia. Mary died Oct. 18, 1880, as the wife of John S. Watts, of Philadelphia. Philip P., who married the daughter of Isaac Caldwell, Esq., a prominent lawyer of Louisville, Ky., resides alternately in Louisville and Philadelphia; while Edward C., the youngest member of the family, is also a resident of Philadelphia.

Their mother, the second wife of Dr. Peace, died at 1602 Chestnut Street, Philadelphia, Feb. 21, 1876, and was buried at Bryn Mawr.

D. C. ABRAHAM.

In the latter part of the seventeenth century, in the early days of the settlement of Delaware County (then Chester County), there came to its territory a widow and her three sons, and settled in Upper Merion township, Montgomery Co. This was Sarah Abraham and her three sons, Isaac, James, and Enoch, who came from England, and from these emigrants are descended the families of Abraham or Abrahams now scattered through Delaware and Pennsylvania, and in Illinois and Minnesota. James remained in Montgomery County, while Isaac settled finally in Lancaster County, and Enoch removed to Pittsburgh.

James purchased the large landed estate now occupied by the sons of Joseph Abraham, in Upper Merion township, Montgomery Co., of Lucretia Penn, in 1730, it being a part of the Penn manor.

The line of descent to Daniel Cornog Abraham, the subject of this sketch, is James, son of Sarah Abraham to his son Isaac, to his son Isaac, to his son Daniel, to his son Daniel Cornog.

Isaac Abraham, grandson of Sarah Abraham, was born April 28, 1717, and married Dinah Haverd, of Chester County, about 1750, to whom were born two sons and three daughters,—James, born 1751; Dinah and Miriam, born between 1751 and 1756; *Isaac*, born 1756; and Mary, born 1758.

Isaac married Jane Cornog, of Chester County, about 1778, and their children were Enoch, born 1779, died 1827; *Daniel*, born 1781, died 1861; David, born 1783, died 1813; Sarah, born 1786, died 1866.

Daniel was born Jan. 11, 1781, upon the farm at Wayne, now owned by Messrs. Childs and Drexel. This property was purchased about 1750 by his grandfather, Isaac, about the time of his marriage to Dinah Haverd. Daniel married, in 1807, Eliza Phillips, daughter of Deacon Jonathan Phillips, of Montgomery County, who was of Welsh descent. Their children were six daughters and five sons, of whom only two—David, the eldest, and Daniel C., the youngest—are now living.

The children of Daniel and Eliza (Phillips) Abraham were Martha, who died unmarried in 1878; Mary P., married Jacob Printup and lived near Schenectady, N. Y., and died in 1843; Jane A., married David Siter, of Delaware County, and died in 1861; Sarah C. B., who married Nathan Stetson, of East Bridgewater, Mass., and died June 9, 1870; David, now living near Centreville, Chester Co., Pa.; Jonathan P., who was a member of the State Legislature from Delaware County, and afterwards moved to Minnesota, married Sarah Thomas, of Newtown, Delaware County, he died at St. Peter, Minn., December, 1880; Phineas P., who died while at school at Haddington College, in 1836, aged eighteen years; Elizabeth D., remained single, died in 1845, near Centreville; Samuel P., married Elizabeth Evans, of Radnor township, died in Norristown, Montgomery Co., March 28, 1878; *Daniel C.*; Anna T., who married the Rev. James F. Brown, now residing at Mullica Hill, N. J., and there died Dec. 23, 1880.

George W. T. Abraham, one of the sons of Jonathan P., deserves special mention. While only in his eighteenth year he endured all the hardships and privations incident to a soldier's life, and died in Andersonville prison, a victim to starvation and ill-treatment, after having refused liberty at the price of enlistment in the Confederate service.

Daniel Cornog Abraham was born upon the farm now owned by the heirs of Samuel P. Abraham, which lies between Wayne and his present residence (1884), on Feb. 1, 1823. His early education was acquired at the common schools of Radnor township, Delaware Co., and in Tredyffrin township, Chester Co. These meagre opportunities were supplemented by a short term at Haddington College. His occupation has been that of an agriculturist almost exclusively, and he has made his home in the township in which he was born. For a short time he was in business in Blair County, Pa., and also spent some time in Georgia, but his home has generally been Delaware County, and all of his interests and aspirations centre here. During the civil war he was in the Internal Revenue Department. He has been justice of the peace since 1873, being the third generation of Esquires Abraham. He has served faithfully and acceptably two and is now beginning upon a third term; has been school director three years, as also treasurer of the school fund. He is a member of the Baptist Church, and is now president of the board of the Great Valley Church, in Chester County. Mr. Abraham was a contributor towards the building and endowment of the Lewisburg University, and is a life member of the Delaware County Institute of Science. He was one of the most active members of the board of the Great Valley Baptist Church when it was remodeled in 1871, and this church was at that time made one of the finest in the neighborhood. In 1882 was the member of finance committee of the Bi-Centennial Association of Delaware County for the two hundredth anniversary of the landing of William Penn in Chester for his district of Radnor, and by his energy raised and paid in a larger amount of

D. C. Abraham

Laurence Ramey

money than any other district in the county Mr Abraham is a stanch Republican, and a firm believer in Republican principles as the sure foundation of the prosperity of this country He is looked up to by all his acquaintances, and the "Squire's" advice is received and reverenced as being sound and just

LAWRENCE RAMEY

The ancestors of this gentleman were of German origin, though members of the society of Friends, and early settlers in Montgomery County, Pa

Lawrence Ramey, the grandfather of the present Lawrence Ramey, was born in Montgomery County Among his children were two sons, Benjamin and Jacob, who, as members of Capt. Holgate's company of Montgomery County volunteers, served at Marcus Hook during the war of 1812-15. Both contracted pulmonary disease in the service, and both died of consumption while still young men

Benjamin Ramey was but thirty-five years of age at the time of his death Of three children born to him, Lawrence, the subject of this notice, is the only survivor. The latter was born near the borough of Conshohocken, Montgomery Co, Pa, Sept 23, 1818 He was but ten years of age at the time of his father's death, and since he attained the age of twelve years has managed his own way through life, almost unaided His educational advantages were limited to an attendance at the schools of his neighborhood two or three months during each winter until attaining the age of fifteen years He grew up on a farm, and though disabled in his right arm and shoulder from infancy, has always followed the laborious yet honorable occupation of farming From his fifteenth year until within a period quite recent he regularly attended the Philadelphia markets with farm products of his own production As a result, pecuniary success has attended his efforts, honesty, industry, and frugality have met with their reward, and he is now regarded as one of the most successful farmers in the township

In the autumn of 1843 he was married to Ann Eliza, the daughter of George Stacker, of Radnor, who died July 10, 1847 Their only child, Hannah Emily, was born Oct 7, 1844, and died Aug 6, 1864 On the 17th of October, 1854, Mr Ramey was again married, to Jane English, of the city of Philadelphia, who is still living No children have resulted from this union

The valuable farm now owned by Mr Ramey has been occupied by him continuously since March, 1844 It was purchased for his use in 1843 by his first wife's uncle, John Stacker, then a prosperous ironmaster near Clarksville, Tenn Stacker afterward became associated in business with Hon John Bell, of Tennessee, a prominent politician and a Presidential candidate just prior to the late war During the war their interests suffered terribly, and much of their property, including the Cumberland Iron-Works, was destroyed After Bell's death, Stacker, by reason of having assumed liabilities not really his own, was financially ruined As a result the claim upon the farm occupied by Mr Ramey passed to the control of Stacker's trustees To them, therefore, Mr Ramey paid the sum of twelve thousand dollars cash for the farm Originally it contained about seventy acres Thirty acres have been added by its present owner Mr Ramey has served as township auditor for a period of twenty-one years, and is now one of the oldest residents, in point of residence in the township, in Radnor

THE KIRK FAMILY

More than a century ago, Philip Kirk, an English gentleman of considerable wealth, came to America, purchased a large tract of land in the immediate vicinity of the present town of Media, Pa, and there passed the remainder of his days His weight was about three hundred and seventy-five pounds avoirdupois, and he was widely known for his many eccentricities and the rather extravagant style in which he lived It is related that he was a pronounced patriot during the Revolutionary war, and for that reason British scouts several times attempted his capture, but always failed, as he had a secure place of hiding The names of only two of his children are remembered,—Benjamin and John The latter removed to the State of Virginia, where he prospered and became the father of a large family

Benjamin, the son of Philip Kirk, married a young and beautiful lady of Irish parentage named Rosanna Carr The ten children born to them were Esther, Philip, John, George, Benjamin, Mary Ann, Simpson, Washington, Samuel, and Rachel All lived to be heads of families with the exception of Washington, who died when a child The survivors at this writing are John, George, Benjamin, and Rachel It has often been remarked that, as a family, the children of Benjamin and Rosanna Kirk were never excelled as regards physical strength and activity in the county of Delaware

Esther became the wife of Ezekiel Norman, and passed her days near Media Philip, a carpenter by trade, also passed the greater part of his life near Media, but died at the Sorrel Horse Hotel, in Radnor township He married Eliza Worrell, of Upper Providence Their surviving children are Anderson, Joseph, Rudolph, Jemima (Anderson), and Rachel John, the second son of Benjamin Kirk, is a blacksmith by trade, and still resides near Media George, by occupation a farmer, has been known for many years as an auctioneer in the counties of Delaware, Montgomery, and Chester Benjamin, whose portrait will be seen on one of these pages, is a wheelwright by trade, but is better known as an old-time inn-keeper He officiated as "mine host" of the Sorrel Horse eight years, of the Unicorn one year, of the Spread Eagle, in Radnor, eight years, and of the Eagle, in Haverford, eight years. He married Mary Griffith, of Chester County. Of four children born to them—George, Jesse, Rachel, and Benjamin—all are living with the exception of Benjamin. George and Jesse are residents of Philadelphia, while Rachel, the wife of Thomas Crosby, resides at Rosemont. Mary Ann married Evans Way, of Chester, Pa. He was prominent in his day, and served as sheriff of Delaware County. Simpson, a saddler by trade, passed the most of his life in Chester County, Pa. Samuel, a noted athlete and runner, was a butcher by occupation, and resided at Media all his lifetime. Rachel, the youngest child of Benjamin and Rosanna Kirk, married Maurice Deshong, long known as a prominent hotel-keeper in Chester, Pa., where she still resides.

CHAPTER LII.

THORNBURY TOWNSHIP.

THE origin of the name of this township is purely conjectural, but is doubtless the correct reason for the title which was given to this municipal district. George Pearce was one of the earliest and wealthiest settlers in the township. The place of his wife's (Ann) nativity was Thornbury, in Gloucestershire, "hence we can readily account for the name of the township, and at the same time cannot fail to appreciate the tender affection that prompted this pioneer settler in its selection in preference to the name of his own native town."[1] The first recognition of Thornbury as a municipal district occurred in 1687, when Hugh Durborow (Darborough) was appointed constable for the township.

The present boundaries of Thornbury are not those recognized in colonial days, for by the provisions of the act of Assembly of Sept. 26, 1789, creating Delaware County, the original township was divided, three-fourths of the territory being retained within the new county and the other fourth constituting the township of the like name in Chester County. This adjustment of the lengthened quarrel in the old county of Chester over the removal or retention of the seat of justice at the borough of Chester was unsatisfactory to the residents of that part of Thornbury which remained in Delaware County, hence, on Nov. 30, 1789, a petition from "the inhabitants and freeholders of the township of Thornbury, Delaware Co., remonstrating against the act for erecting the said county, and praying they may be re-annexed to the county of Chester," was presented to the Legislature, but that body refused to consider the proposition.[2]

[1] Smith's "History of Delaware County," p. 401.

[2] *Ante*, p. 83.

The meddling with the township lines of Thornbury was again renewed by the Legislature, when, fifty-three years thereafter, on July 30, 1842, an act was passed annexing all that part of Aston lying north of a line beginning immediately south of Stony Bank churchyard, and extending east and west from Chester Creek to Concord township, was annexed to Thornbury. In considering the early land-grants and the settlers, the present township lines will be observed.

In that part of the township which was formerly Aston, Joseph Baker, John Worrilow, and Daniel Hoopes on First month 12, 1699, took up five hundred acres, part of John Simcock's grant of fifteen hundred acres, four hundred of which comprised almost all the territory lying in Aston. Joseph Baker never settled on this tract, but settled in Edgmont, to which township his brother, John, gave the name it now bears; nor did John Worrilow locate there, but he, too, made Edgmont his place of abode, and Daniel Hoopes, who was a son-in-law of John Worrilow, settled in Westtown prior to his purchase of this land. The greater part of this tract in 1724 was purchased by John Taylor, who erected at Glen Mills the noted Sarum Forge. All the land that juts into Edgmont, and is bounded on the south by Middletown, was seated by William Bostock, March 2–3, 1681. It was entered as five hundred acres, but on a resurvey to Joshua Bispham, in 1734, it proved to contain five hundred and thirty-five and a half acres. In 1707, Cheyney Bostock owned the land; but it had passed out of his possession prior to 1715. The upper half of this tract in 1735 was purchased by Abel Green. West of the Taylor tract, and on a straight line drawn across the township from the southwestern part of Edgmont, where the latter overlaps Thornbury, to Birmingham line, to John Simcock on March 15–16, 1681, was surveyed fifteen hundred acres of land, extending to the present village of Thornton and embracing all the land lying between Concord and the line already spoken of running from Edgmont to Birmingham. The Taylor land was originally included in this tract. This estate subsequently passed into the ownership of a number of persons. Five hundred acres east of Westtown road were purchased by Randolph Vernon, which in 1715 was owned by his son, Jacob Vernon. The five hundred acres lying west of Westtown road became the property of John Kingsman. The upper part of this tract containing two hundred acres, extending as far south as Thornton, was purchased by George Pearce; it abutted on his four hundred and ninety acres lying to the north; and the lower part was divided into two plantations. The eastern, containing two hundred acres, was purchased by Elizabeth Hickman, while the western passed to Joseph Edwards. West of Thornton Edward Brown took up five hundred acres on Feb. 13, 1683, which subsequently became the property of Robert Pyle, Dec. 12, 1698, and doubtless he settled

BENJAMIN KIRK.

on this land, for subsequently it was distributed among his children, and in 1715 John Pyle was a resident of Thornbury.

All the land west of this point to Birmingham was taken up in one-hundred-acre plots, in the following order: Robert Southey, John Gibbons, Robert Pyle, Joseph Bushel, and Edward Turner, the latter having one hundred and twenty-four acres which extended to the Birmingham line. The Southey and Gibbons lands were purchased by Edward Bennett, a brother of John Bennett, who had married a daughter of William Brinton, the first settler of Birmingham, and as Joseph Brinton purchased the Pyle and Bushell lands to the west of Bennett, it is probable that the latter settled on the tract he purchased. Certain it is that the Bennett family were represented in Thornbury in 1715. Robert Turner, whose land was at the Birmingham line, on Third month 16, 1694, sold his one hundred and twenty-four acres to Jonathan Thatcher, and the latter, in 1715, was living thereon. The real estate of Mrs. Baker, Robert Baldwin, Louisa Evanson, and Thomas McFadden, as shown on Hopkins' map of Delaware County in 1870, were part of the Thomas Evanson four hundred and thirty-seven acres, part of which he had purchased of the thirteen-hundred-and-fifty-acre tract surveyed to John Simcock in 1684, and the remainder of Robert Sumner. The western part of the farms of I. H. Cheyney and Curtis Cheyney was the tract of one hundred acres purchased by Hugh Darborough, the first constable of the township, from Thomas Bradford on March 1, 1692/3, while the farm of Mrs. Mary Jones, the remaining part of I. R. Cheyney, Curtis Cheyney, and the upper part of Hill Brinton, and A. Pierce (as shown by the Hopkins map), are on the four hundred and ninety acres surveyed to George Pearce, Twelfth month, 1684.

George Pierce, or, as he wrote his name, Pearce, with his wife, Ann, and three children, emigrated from the parish of Winscom, in the county of Somerset, England, in 1684, and in the same year four hundred and ninety acres of land were surveyed to him in Thornbury township. He probably settled on his plantation in 1685, but he did not become identified actively with Chester Meeting until 1686. He was a member of Assembly in 1706, and was part owner in the Concord Mill, the first erected in the neighborhood where he lived. He died in 1734, but had removed to East Marlborough township, in the present county of Chester, two years prior to his death.

All the remainder of the land in Thornbury lying north of a line beginning at the African Methodist Church and extending due east to the corner of Edgmont township, near Daniel James' grist-mill, was part of John Beller's fifteen hundred acres, taken up May 14–15, 1685, in right of ten thousand acres purchased by Richard Marsh in 1681. On Jan. 15–16, 1724, John Cheyney and Thomas Cheyney acquired ownership to the entire tract, part of which extended into the present Thornbury township, in Chester County. The two brothers, who were the sons of John Cheyney, the settler, who died in Middletown in 1722, are the ancestors of the Cheyney family of Thornbury, and much of the original land purchased by the first of their name in the township still remains in the ownership of their descendants. Thomas Cheyney, or, as history has recorded him, "Squire," was the son of John. He was a justice of the peace, an intelligent farmer, and an active, earnest Whig during the Revolution. He it was who brought to Washington the first undoubted intelligence that the British army, under Cornwallis, had crossed the forks of the Brandywine and outflanked the Americans.[1] His remains lie in the family graveyard, a short distance to the north of Cheyney Station.

The inhabitants of the township were doubtless the victims of much spoliation by the English troops during the time the enemy's forces were in that neighborhood, yet no account of these outrages has been preserved so far as the writer is aware. The losses sustained by the residents of Thornbury, while the British army lay encamped near Dilworthtown, from 11th to 16th of September, 1777, were considerable, although doubtless much of the loss inflicted was never presented under the act of Sept. 21, 1782, providing for the filing of claims, which privilege seemed to satisfy the consciences of the men in authority, for no other effort was ever made to pay those claims. The accounts presented from Thornbury were as follows:

		£	s.	d.
From	George Brinton	517	11	5
"	Sampson Davis	115	18	8
"	William Arment	42	0	0
"	William Louden	19	12	0
"	Catharine Davis	34	3	6
"	Isaac Davis	58	12	6
		787	18	1

Of the few men from Delaware County, who, not in the regular military or naval service of the United States, volunteered as a soldier during the Mexican war, Thornbury can claim William S. Mendenhall, who enlisted in Capt. Biddle's company. His name appeared among the list of men wounded in that war.

One of the most useful and eminent men of Eastern Pennsylvania was Joseph Hemphill, who was born in Thornbury, Delaware Co., Jan. 7, 1770. He graduated at the University of Pennsylvania in 1791, and began reading law with Thomas Ross, of West Chester, and was admitted to practice in August, 1793. In 1797 he was elected a member of Assembly from Chester County, and continued to represent the district until 1800, when he was elected to the Seventh Congress of the United States from the district composed of Delaware and Chester Counties. Before the expiration of his term he removed to Philadelphia, where in 1805 he was elected to the Legislature. In 1811 the District Court for the City and County of Philadelphia was established for six years, and, although Joseph Hemphill was a Federalist, Governor

[1] See *ante*, p. 58.

Snyder appointed him president judge of that court, and when the court was continued, the same Governor recommissioned him. After presiding for eight years he resigned, and was elected to Congress, where he served three terms, until 1831. He was a partner with Tucker, in Philadelphia, in the manufacture of porcelain, which resulted in a pecuniary loss. He died in Philadelphia, May 29, 1842.

Roads.—That part of the road from Thornbury to Middletown which extends from Westtown road through Thornton to the western end of the township, at Brinton's farms, is said to have been laid out by the grand jury over an old Indian trail. At the court held in the latter part of the year 1687, "The Inhabitants of the Township of Thornbury Petitioned for a Highway to ye River Delaware, Ordered that ye Grand Inquest doe lay out a Convenient Highway, & y^t^ George Pearce be assisting." At the court on "ye 5th of y^t^ 1st month, 1688/9," the grand jury had performed that duty, for on that it appears that "Wee of ye Grand Inquest for ye County of Chester have laid out ye Road from Thornbury to Middletown, Beginning att a Spanish Oake vpon Thomas Bradford's lands, near Thomas Evinson's, along ye lyne of marked trees, through Edward Beason's Land; thence along ye lyne of mark^t^ trees through John Simcock's Land to a marked Walenutt standing by Chester Creeke; thence Crossing ye Creeke along Edward Blacke's Land, along ye lyne of marked trees, through Joshua Hasting's land, along Crossing ye head of Caleb Pusie's land; thence through David Ogden's land to Middletown road, ending att a marked white Oake standing by ye Road side."

Although the grand jury so accurately returned the highway which they had agreed upon, it appears not to have been immediately opened to public use and travel, for, on the 9th of Tenth month, 1691, to the justices was presented "a petetion of Inhabitants in & about Thornbury for a cart way to Chester, Ordered the clerk to send an order to ye Grand Inquest to Lay out a convenient Road for ye Town of Thornbury to Chester." This order was obeyed, and early in 1692 the grand jury report the following as their "return of a road to Thornbury:"

"Beginning at a marked tree by Edward Carter's, which was marked by a former Grand Jury, and so along a line of marked trees to John Baldwin's fence, and then by John's consent over a corner thereof through a corner of his field, and so along to a black oak, being a corner of John Nield's land, and from thence down to John Nield's field, and by his consent over a corner thereof, and so through the creek and up the hill by Gilbert Williams' Barn."

Perhaps this return was so plain to the understanding of the justices that no further difficulty was encountered in laying out the highway. At all events, the good people of Thornbury got the road they so much craved.

The tax rate of Thornbury in 1715, then including the original township, was:

	£	s.	d.
Henry Nayle	0	3	6
John Willis	0	10	3
George Pearce	0	6	4
Isaac Taylor	0	14	0
William Brinton	0	1	8
Jonathan Thatcher	0	4	9
John Davis	0	8	11
Philip Taylor	0	3	9
John Yearsley	0	4	6
Thomas Everson	0	5	3
Richard Woodward	0	4	10
Wm Pile, land in Kennet	0	6	0
Joseph Brinton	0	4	1
Jacob Vernor	0	7	2
Joseph Baker	0	6	4
Thomas Masser	0	4	9
Richd Evenson	0	3	0
John Pile	0	3	10
Richard Arnold	0	1	6
John Stringer	0	0	9
ffremen.			
Peter Hatton, for his land in Kennet	0	3	4
Richd Arnold, Junr	0	4	0
Jacob Bener	0	4	0
John Bener	0	4	0
Nebo Rogers	0	4	0
Nehemiah Ogden	0	4	0
	7	9	3

The list of the taxables in the township in 1799 is as follows:

George Brinton, Daniel Broomall, John and Joseph Brinton (miller), Thomas Brinton, Joseph Baker, Nehemiah Baker, John Cargrove, Mary Cheyney, Edith Cheyney, Samuel Cheyney, Jesse Cheyney, Joseph Cheyney, Curtis Cheyney, John Cheyney, Eleanor Davis, Joseph Eveson, John Edwards (justice of the peace), Mary W. Frazer, Abel Green, Wills Hemphill, Ann Hemphill, Thomas Hall (wheelwright), Abner Hoopes (saddler), Thomas Hickman, Joshua Hoopes, Ezra Hoopes, John James, John Harvey, Lewis & Hemphill (forge and appurtenances), Lewis & Yarnall, Josiah Lewis (storekeeper), Joseph Moore (storekeeper), John Marshall (wheelwright), Richard Mercer, Henry Myers (grist- and saw-mill), Caleb Pyle (woolcomber), Levi Pyle (weaver), Stephen Pyle, Thomas Candes, Richard Parker, Jacob Parker, John Peirce, Sr., Caleb Peirce, Joseph Peirce, Esther Hughes, Robert Pennell, John Reed, Hugh Reed, Thomas Scott, Abraham Sharpless, William Thatcher, Daniel Thompson, Daniel Trimble, Sarah Thompson, Joseph Woodward, William Williamson, Abraham Williamson, William Yarnall.

Inmates.—Ezekiel Johnson (shoemaker), John Harvey (weaver), John Johnson (tailor), David Esbin, Edward Churchman, John Cheyney (tailor), John Woodward, Joseph James (blacksmith), James Bailey (blacksmith), George Fox (tailor), Jonathan Lewsley, John Bail (forgeman), James Hannum (carpenter), Robert Logan, James Hickman, Esther Hughes, Thomas Condes.

Single Freemen.—John Smith (shoemaker), William Thatcher, Jr., Jacob Pyle (shoemaker), Isaac Pyle (weaver), James Pyle (weaver), John Lindsay (blacksmith), George Stanley (wheelwright), Samuel Cheyney (saddler), Joseph Cheyney, Aaron Holms (tailor).

The following persons have served as justices of the peace for Thornbury township:

Caleb Peirce	Aug. 30, 1791.
John Edwards	Jan. 24, 1797.
Joseph Brinton	May 20, 1800.
Matthias Kerlin	July 4, 1808.
Thomas Pierce	Feb. 5, 1814.
James Bratton	Feb. 3, 1820.
Joseph Fox	Dec. 4, 1823.
John Mattson	Dec. 13, 1823.
Joseph Bowen	Nov. 10, 1824.
Joseph Trimble	April 21, 1827.
Robert Frame	Jan. 15, 1829.
Robert Hall	Feb. 8, 1831.
William Mendenhall	Dec. 6, 1836.
Charles Baldwin	April 14, 1840.
Hill Brinton	April 14, 1840.
Charles Baldwin	April 15, 1845.
Hill Brinton	April 14, 1846.
Charles Baldwin	April 9, 1850.
Hill Brinton	April 15, 1851.
Charles Baldwin	April 10, 1855, April 10, 1860.
Thomas McFadden	April 26, 1864, April 16, 1869.
Thomas P. Hazard	March 24, 1874, March 27, 1879.

Wayside Church.—This handsome stone sanctuary was erected by an association whose membership is composed of persons associated with different Protestant religious sects. The society was organized in 1871, with the avowed purpose of erecting a church edifice which should be free to all Protestants to hold service in. The lot was donated by William H.

Erwin, and the Gothic church, which is thirty by forty-five feet, erected, at a cost of four thousand dollars On May 3, 1874, the church was dedicated, the Rev Dr Speer, of Philadelphia, of the Episcopal Church, preaching the sermon on that occasion Dr Speer was assisted in the ceremonies by the Rev George W Gaul, of the Methodist Church; Rev Abel C Thomas, of the Universalist Church, Rev Mr Lynn, of the Presbyterian Church, Rev Dr Worrell, of the Baptist Church, and Darlington Hoopes, a public Friend The church is under control of a committee appointed by the society, and a regular Sunday-school is maintained there, having at the present time sixty pupils Mrs W A Cheyney is superintendent

An able writer, in mentioning the Wayside Church, says,—

"A beautiful little structure built at Cheyney Station, on the West Chester and Philadelphia Railroad, well deserves notice It is called the Wayside Church, and is independent of all other organizations It was erected by members of various religious sects, aided by many attached to no denomination, and it is open to all professors of religion, the services being varied to suit the views of the particular officiating individual, who may be some one invited by the congregation, or some well-meaning clergyman or other person who may feel it his duty for the time to occupy the pulpit In the absence of such person, services much resembling the Episcopal are read by one of the members designated for the occasion The congregation numbers about two hundred

"The place owes its origin to the efforts of certain liberal minded people in the neighborhood, whose design appears to be to bring members of the several *religious bodies more in contact with one another*, that they may learn how insignificant are the differences of opinion which have filled Christendom with persecution and bloodshed The result is teaching on a small scale the lesson that most religious disputes are purely dialectic The sects being isolated, learn to attach peculiar and technical meanings to certain much-used words, and therefore, to some extent, really talk each a different language from the other without knowing it The movement at Cheyney appears to be in the direction of the progress of the age Within the last half century there is manifestly a growing tendency among the various religious denominations to co-operate with one another in benevolent and humanitarian enterprises, and to view the peculiarities of one another in a more charitable light, and there is a decreasing disposition on the part of each to claim the exclusive right of regulating the relations existing between man and his Maker Delaware County has its full share of the wholesome progress in this direction "[1]

Stony Bank Methodist Church.—This church organization was originally included in the township of Aston, until the act of July 30, 1842, made the change in the township lines which annexed Stony Bank meeting-house to Thornbury The church was organized in 1810, by Israel Pyle, Benjamin Baldwin, and others, the first meetings being held in the Stony Bank school-house until the meeting-house was erected, in 1812. The stone church then built was used until 1870, when the new edifice was erected, the corner-stone being laid on July 28th of that year. The building was completed the following spring, and dedicated May 27, 1871. The membership of Stony Bank Church is about twenty-five persons at the present time Since 1856 the pastors have been Revs H G King, J Z Cooper, H H Bodine, H Houston, H B Mauger, W C Johnson, J W Watson, E W. Townsend, J Magee, W B Chalfant, R H Sadler, C M Boswell, C E Adamson, N W Clark, and the present pastor, W C Graeff

Bethlehem Methodist Episcopal Church—The class from which the church was organized was formed about 1845, and on March 26, 1846, Albon Pyle conveyed a lot at Thornton to Israel Pyle and others as trustees, to be used for the erection of a church building as well as a burial-ground A meeting-house was built soon after the lot was donated for that purpose For many years the church was under the charge of Chester Circuit, being dependent for religious exercises on the circuit preachers who served also Mount Hope and Stony Bank Churches On Nov 26, 1860, Bethlehem Methodist Episcopal Church was incorporated by the court of Delaware County In 1871 the building, which began to show the marks of age, was repaired at a cost of eight hundred and twenty-two dollars The church was reopened on Sunday, Nov 19, 1871, and during the day and evening the following clergymen preached Revs Hughes, Wallace, Alcorn, and Watson Contributions to the gross amount of five hundred dollars were made

African Methodist Episcopal Church—Several years ago a number of colored Methodists organized a class in Thornbury, and shortly afterwards purchased the old frame school-house on the Westtown road, formerly used by Nathan Hunt The building was moved about half a mile farther to the north, on the same road, in close proximity to the residence of James Sullivan, and was fitted up as a church The congregation have no regular pastor, but are dependent on the circuit preachers

Schools.—The first school established in the township was doubtless at the location now known as the Western District school-house, which is situated near the Chester County line on the road leading from Concord to Dilworthtown The deed for the lot is in the possession of Charles Cheyney, one of the school directors The indenture, dated March 25, 1715, is made by William Pyle to George Pierce, John Willis, Henry Nayle, Edward Bennett, Thomas Eavenson, Richard Woodward, Philip Taylor, Jacob Vernon, Joseph Brinton, John Yearsley, Richard Eavenson, and John Pyle, of Thornbury, and William Brinton, of Birmingham, conveying a lot of ground in trust for the purpose of maintaining a school there The deed also conveys the right to a foot path, three feet in width, leading to a spring not far distant on the land of William Pyle This deed has never been recorded, but has remained in the possession of the trustees, and subsequently of the school directors, the latter acting as trustees since the acceptance of the school law by the township, for one hundred and sixty-nine years The date when a school-house was erected on this lot cannot be definitely ascertained, but the probabilities are that such a structure was built soon after the deed was executed, for the pur-

[1] History of Delaware County for the Past Century By Hon John M Broomall, pp 19, 20 (Media, 1876)

chase of the lot is evidence that it was the desire of the trustees to have a place where their children might receive educational advantages From the recollection of the oldest residents in the neighborhood a stone school-house was on the site, the first was burned in 1810, and rebuilt The lot was transferred to the school directors in 1837, and was used until the second building was destroyed by fire, in December, 1842 On this occasion the fire originated from hot ashes having been put in a barrel standing in a shed adjoining the house A third stone house was built on the site, and used until 1872, when it was removed, and the present brick building erected The ancient spring, mentioned in the deed of 1715, was in use by the pupils until 1880, when other water-supply was obtained much nearer to the school-house

On Sept 12, 1839, the school directors purchased a lot of land of Joseph Baker and Reuben Yarnell, on which a stone school-house was built It was used until 1863, but its inconvenient location was such that the present lot, half a mile to the north, was purchased, and the present brick house, known as the Eastern District school-house, erected

In the present Central District of Thornbury the first school-house was built about 1820 It was located near the present residence of William Pennell The real estate belonged to Nathan Hunt, who built a small frame building, in which he taught school On the 27th of August, 1840, the school directors purchased eighty square perches of land of William Pennell, and the same year purchased two other lots, adjoining one of which was the old Nathan Hunt lot At this place the directors built a stone house, which was used until the present brick house was erected on the same lot in 1863

On March 18, 1825, at the election held in that year, Joseph James, Eli D Pierce, and Thomas S Brinton were returned as school trustees After the enactment of the public school law of 1834, Hill Brinton and Dr John T Huddleson were appointed by court inspectors of the school in Thornbury until directors were elected The township, however, did not accept the public school law until 1836 In that year $141 86, the State and county appropriation, was set apart to Thornbury, but was never paid to the township

The following is a list of the school directors of Thornbury, as appears from the records at Media

1840, Joseph Baker, Harlan Clayton, 1842, Thomas Hemphill, Alexander Russell, 1843, Henry W Brinton, Charles Baldwin, David R Cheyney, 1844, Curtis Cheyney, Eli Pyle, 1845, John C Caldwell, Robert B Roberts, 1846, Joseph Pennell, Reuben H Smith, 1847, John T Huddleson, John D Peirce, 1848, Samuel Palmer, Joseph Baker, 1849, Reuben H Smith, Eli Pyle, 1850, John Eldridge, Joseph R Cheyney, 1851, Joseph E Brinton, David R Cheyney, 1852, John Eldridge, William H Cheyney, 1853, Eli Baker, Samuel Palmer, 1854, George Thomas, Eli Baker, 1855, John Eldridge, Caleb J Hoopes, 1856, James Myers, Bernard Pyle, 1857, David Cheyney, George Thomas, 1858, John D Reece, Joseph Newlin, 1859, Samuel Palmer, Isaac Malin, 1860, Isaac C Malin, Eli Baker, 1861, James Newlin, John D Peirce, 1862, Samuel C Ogden, Samuel G Eachus, 1863, Thomas I Baker, Charles H Cheyney, 1864, Samuel G Eachus, Isaac Bunting, 1865, Thomas N Hemphill, Charles Pyle, 1866, J M Hickman, A P Temple, 1867, Samuel G Eachus, James R. Cheyney, 1868, J M Baker, Garrett Thatcher, 1869, Charles H Cheyney, Bennett Temple, 1870, Joseph R. Cheyney, Samuel G Eachus, 1871, John Bennington, George Thatcher, 1872, Charles H Cheyney, Bennett Temple, 1873, Walter Pyle, Daniel Broomall, 1874, Joseph Hunt, Charles H Baldwin, 1875, C H Cheyney, Bennett Temple, 1876, Walter Pyle, David Jeffries, 1877, Charles H Baldwin, T Elwood Pyle, 1878, Charles H Cheyney, Joseph Pratt, 1879, Walter Pyle, David Jeffries, 1880, T Elwood Pyle, Dr J H Horner, 1881, Charles H Cheyney, Mrs S F James, 1882, Walter Pyle, Bennett Temple, 1883, Joseph H. Horner, John Brinton, Jr , 1884, Charles H Cheyney, Joseph Pratt

Westtown and Thornbury School District.—The residents in the northwestern section of Thornbury, with those of the southeastern part of Westtown, Chester Co, uniting in a petition to the Legislature for the creation of a school district which should include territory lying in the counties of Delaware and Chester, obtained the passage of the act of May 1, 1852, which provided that all lands "lying east of the western lines of the farms now held by Edward Shimer and John Entriken, and the farms and lands now in the occupancy and possession of Benjamin Hickman, Joseph G Gibbons, Alexander Stephens, Evan E Green, Joseph Cheyney, and Jesse Russell, situate in the township of Thornbury," and that part of the township of Westtown, in the county of Chester, lying east of the western line of the west school farm, were erected into a separate and independent school district The school-house in this district is located in Westtown township, Chester Co

Union School District.—In the winter of 1861 the residents of the northwestern section of Thornbury, lying east of Westtown and Thornbury school district, together with residents of Edgmont, in Delaware County, and Westtown and Willistown, Chester County, petitioned the Legislature for the erection of an independent and separate school district On April 1, 1861, the act of Assembly was approved, erecting within certain designated boundaries, extending to the Ashbridge road in Edgmont, the "Union School District of Chester and Delaware Counties" The territory so included was enlarged by act of Assembly of April 9, 1873, by which the farm lands of Eber Eachus, Edward Baker, and Joseph R Menagh, in Edgmont, were attached to the Union school district The first directors, consisting of Charles Baldwin, Homer Eachus, Abraham W Bailey, Edwin Hoopes, Ellwood Smedley, and Charles Tanger, were appointed by court on April 19, 1861, to act until others were elected

Sarum Forge.—The exact date of the erection of a forge on Chester Creek, at the present Glen Mills, by John Taylor, has not been ascertained Early in 1750, Parliament enacted a law "to encourage the importation of pig- and bar-iron from his Majesty's Colonies in America, and to prevent the erection of any mill or other engine for slitting or rolling of iron, or any plating forge to work with a tilt-hammer, or any furnace for making steel in any of the said Colonies," and required the Governors in the American colonies should certify the number, as well as "a particular account" of such business establishments in the territory under their several jurisdictions In obedience to the act of Parliament, Lieutenant-Governor James Hamilton issued a proclamation on Aug 16, 1750, commanding the sheriffs of the counties in Pennsylvania to make return by the 25th of September following of all such establishments "within their several and respective Counties" In response to this proclamation, John Owen, sheriff of Chester County, made the following return

"*To the Honourable James Hamilton, Esqr, Lieutenant-Governor and Commander-in Chief of the Province of Pensilvania and Counties of New castle, Kent, and Sussex, on Delaware*

"I, John Owen, Sheriff of the County of Chester, in the said Province, do Certify and make known, That there is but one Mill or Engine for Slitting and rolling Iron within the County aforesaid, which is situate in Thornbury Township, and was Erected in the Year One thousand Seven Hundred and forty-Six, by John Taylor, the present Proprietor thereof, who, with his Servants and workmen, has ever Since, untill the twenty-fourth day of June last, Used and Occupied the Same And I do hereby further certify that there is not any Plateing fforge to work with a Tilt-Hammer, nor any ffurnace for making of Steel within the said County of Chester In Witness whereof I have hereunto set my hand and Seal, this Eighteenth day of September, in the Year of our Lord one thousand Seven Hundred and fifty

"JOHN OWEN, *Sheriff*" [L.S.][1]

Although the sheriff distinctly states that John Taylor erected Thornbury Forge in 1746, there is evidence to establish the fact that the forge was erected three years, if not for a longer period, prior to that date In 1742, John Taylor had a store at the present Glen Mills, and from the following order, found among his papers, appears to have been using iron at that time This ancient document is as follows

"SON ISAAC,—Let Sister Mary (Brogdon) have goods to the value of three pounds, five shillings, being for half a Tun of Pig Iron, & charge it to account

"JNO TAYLOR[2]

"July 22, 1742"

In the petition of Obadiah Bonsall for license to keep a tavern in Thornbury, dated Aug 31, 1743, the house for which he craves the court's bounty was on "the road leading from the French Creek Iron Works to Thornbury Forge," and as a particular reason why an inn should be located there for the accommodation of the public he urged that there were "many people resorting to and working at and near to the s[d] Forge" This petition is the first absolute knowledge we now have that a forge had been erected there On Jan 18, 1745, John Taylor made an agreement with Thomas Wills, forgeman and finer, to work in the forge two years in making anconies at 22*s* 6*d* per ton, and on June 10, 1746, Reese Jones agreed to coal (burn charcoal) for John Taylor two hundred cords of wood in Middletown at 11*s*. 8*d* per hundred bushels, "half money, half goods, *as customary*"[3] The last agreement is the only one which does not antedate the year given by John Owens as the date when Taylor built the rolling- and slitting-mill, which was the first in Pennsylvania The seeming contradiction between the fact that John Taylor was a worker in iron in 1742 and that the sheriff of Chester County in 1750 reported that he built the rolling- and slitting-mill in 1746 has been attempted to be reconciled by asserting that the forge was located there in 1742, while at the time designated by the sheriff the rolling- and slitting-mill was established

The fact that Obadiah Bonsall, in 1743, alludes to the "many people resorting to and *working at and near to the sd Forge*" seems to be sufficient answer to the suggestion that at that time simply a blacksmith forge was located there When it is remembered that not one horse in fifty at that time was shod, and wagons were but little used, it certainly precludes the idea that an ordinary blacksmith-shop in a remote and sparsely-settled neighborhood could give employment to "many persons" A recent writer records that the business enterprises carried on by John Taylor "were upon an extensive and varied scale, and included the manufacture of nails as well as nail rods The tradition is preserved by his descendants that soon after the erection of the slitting-mill his storekeeper, in making one of his periodical visits to England to replenish his stock, surprised the Liverpool merchants by telling them that he could buy nails at Taylor's mill at lower prices than they quoted,—a revelation which added weight to the clamor then prevailing in England for the suppression of slitting-mills and similar iron establishments in America, and which agitation resulted in the passage, in 1750, of an act of Parliament which prohibited the further erection of such works"[4]

John Larkin, the first of this name in Bethel, was one of the early forgemen at Sarum Iron-Works

In the fall of the year 1748, Peter Kalm, the Swedish naturalist, who tarried for a brief season at Marcus Hook, stated that "from an iron work, which lies higher up in the country, they carry iron bars to this place [Marcus Hook] and ship them" Acrelius, writing of the period of 1756, refers to the works thus "Sarum belongs to Taylor's heirs, has three stacks, and is in full blast"[5] In that year John Taylor died, and the works are said to have been conducted by his son, John Taylor, for some time Certain it is that in 1766 Sarum Forge was operated by John Chamberlain, and he was in occupancy of the four acres upon which the mill stood In 1770, John Thomson had succeeded Chamberlain in possession of the works In 1775 the estate was divided between the heirs of John Taylor, and in February of that year Anthony Wayne, who was then following his calling of civil engineering, surveyed the property preparatory to the

[1] Penna Archives, 1st Series, vol ii p 57

[2] Futhey and Cope's "History of Chester County," p 346

[3] Ibid

[4] "The Manufacture of Iron in all Ages," by James M Swank, p 135

[5] History of New Sweden, p 165.

partition being made among the heirs. On March 13, 1775, a partition deed was made, in which one hundred and sixty-nine acres and thirty-four perches, "on which are erected an Iron Forge, Slitting-mill, grist-mill, and saw-mill, with other valuable improvements," were divided between Joseph Potts and Ann, his wife, of the first part, James Thomson and Sarah, his wife, Persifor Frazer and Mary, his wife, of the second part, and Thomas Bull, of East Nantmeal, Chester Co., of the third part. Joseph Potts received a tract of eight acres, situate where the Upper Glen Paper-Mill now stands, on Chester Creek, "with the grist-mill and saw-mill thereon erected, and the seat for a slitting-mill, also the priviledge of building a bridge across the Forge Race at such place as shall be convenient to pass from the said meadow to the road, with liberty to erect a dam on the place where the old slitting-mill dam formerly erected, or lower down the creek if more convenient." Potts also received a tract of four and three-fourths acres lower down the creek and above the forge lot. By the same deed Persifor Frazer and Mary, his wife, James Thomson and Sarah, his wife, received thirty-one acres and eighteen perches of land, it being the lower part of the tract, together "with the Forge thereon erected." On this land, on the survey, are marked several houses, the forge, race, and the mansion-house still lower down, probably on the site of the present Wilcox mansion. The forge stood where the lower Glen Mill Paper-Factory now stands. On the same date to Thomas Bull, ironmaster, of East Nantmeal, Chester Co., and Ann, his wife, were granted one hundred and twenty-five acres of land, it being the upper part of the tract and partly on both sides of the creek, the other tracts all being located on the west side of the creek.

At the time of the survey that portion of the tract on which was the slitting-mill, grist-mill, saw-mill, and forge, was in Aston, and continued so to be until the act of July 30, 1842, annexed all the upper part of the latter township at a line dividing Stony Bank meeting-house and the Stony Bank school to Thornbury.

In the deed to Joseph Potts, March 13, 1775, it appears the slitting-mill was then out of repair, but from his precaution in having a clause inserted giving to him the right to rebuild the "old slitting-mill dam," it is evident that he intended to repair the works, which he did. Persifor Frazer, born near Newtown Square in 1736, married Mary, the daughter of John Taylor (the younger), and some time after settled in Thornbury, on his wife's estate, and was interested in the iron-works there, but it is not probable that he was active in the conduct of the forge until after 1770, for in that year John Thomson had the works. At the close of 1774 he was prominent in Chester County in resisting the encroachments of the crown, and in January of the following year was a delegate from that county to the Provincial Convention. At this time he is believed to have had full control of the works. In the early part of 1776 he was elected captain of a company in the Fourth Battalion of Pennsylvania troops, under Col. Wayne, and was present on duty with his command until the fourth day after the battle of Brandywine; when while reconnoitering, he and Maj. Harper were captured by the enemy. While a prisoner of war he was commissioned lieutenant-colonel of the Fifth Pennsylvania. Col. Frazer made his escape, joined his regiment, and took part in the battle of Monmouth. In the fall of 1778 he resigned. In 1781, 1782, and 1784 he was a member of the Assembly. In May, 1782, he was appointed brigadier-general of the militia of Pennsylvania, and in 1786 was appointed register and recorder for Chester County, which office he continued to hold—after the division of the old county and the erection of Delaware County—until April 2, 1792, when he died. Gen. Frazer was buried in the old graveyard at Middletown Presbyterian Church. Gen. Persifor F. Smith, of the United States army, is his grandson.

In 1779 the old slitting-mill was rebuilt, and was operated by Norris Jones. Norris Jones and Abraham Sharpless were occupying it in 1781, and in 1784, Sharpless & Lloyd had control of the slitting-mill, grist-mill, and saw-mill, as well as the forge. The latter copartnership must have been formed in the spring of that year, for in the early part of 1784 Jones & Sharpless were still operating the works, for Mrs. Sarah Thomson, who appears to have married a spendthrift, presented her petition to the Court of Quarter Sessions which sat at Chester, Feb. 24, 1784, in which she set forth that she was the wife of James Thomson, of the township of "Ashtown," and that before her marriage she was possessed of real estate consisting of eighty-four acres of land in West Bradford, about one hundred and seventy-four acres in Thornbury and "Ashtown;" also three-eighths of a forge and about thirty acres in "Ashtown;" that after her marriage she joined with her husband in the sale of the real estate in West Bradford; that through "inattention and other proceedings" her husband ran in debt; that all his personal estate was sold to satisfy his creditors, leaving large sums still due, which she thought to liquidate would cover the plantation in Thornbury and Aston. Believing that he would continue to contract personal debts, so as to consume all the estates, his life-interest being seized and sold therein, in which event she, "who is in a very infirm state of Health, and also her young children, one of whom it is likely will become a Cripple, will be left destitute of any support; that she cannot therefore but with terror look forward to the period when herself and helpless children must depend upon the precarious and ineffectual supplies of her own industry, her husband having deserted her and the children, and left them utterly destitute, having removed to some distant part of the frontiers." In conclusion, she prayed the court for alimony on a separate maintenance out of the remains of her fortune. "Whereupon it is Considered by this Court that the three-Eighths part of the Forge now in the possession of Jones & Sharpless, the dwelling-house wherein she now resides, the small stable adjoining the kitchen, Together with the pailed garden and orchard, the draw-well, the piece of meadow ground on the Norther part of the plantation, containing about three acres, and the piece of woodland laying to the Southward of the said meadow, and adjoining the same containing about eight acres (more or less), Is hereby adjudged to and ordered to be occupied by, and the profits thereof to belong to and be appropriated for the use of the said Sarah Thomson, wife of the aforesaid James Thomson, according to her will and discretion, Free and separate from the said James Thomson and all other persons whatsoever during the natural life of her the said Sarah.[1]

In 1780 the slitting-mill was rented to Lloyd & Hill, and in 1790 Sharpless & Lloyd were operating all the mills at Sarum. On Feb. 14, 1794, Abraham Sharpless purchased of Josiah Potts the slitting-mill, grist- and saw-mill property, and about 1805 the forge and four acres of land. In 1807, Sharpless associated Francis Wisely in the business of the mills at the upper seat. From that date the old forge was permitted to go to decay, for no further record is made of it. From 1810 to April 2, 1836, Abraham Sharpless conducted the rolling- and slitting-mill, and for the greater part of that time the grist-mill and saw-mill also. His business was extensive and daily his teams were seen going to and from Marcus Hook, where he shipped his manufactured iron and other articles, and received pig-metal and other raw material to be used at his works. On April 2, 1836, the mills having been sold to Wilcox, they were changed to paper-mills, and are now known as the Glen Mills.[1]

Edwards' Forge and Rolling-Mills.—The first notice of a forge in Thornbury connected with the Edwards family, of which record has been found, is in the assessment-roll for the year 1788, when John Edwards, the elder, was assessed on one hundred and ninety acres of land and a forge. On Oct. 31, 1791, a road was laid out from Edgmont road to the Slitting-Mills on Chester Creek, the road dividing the townships of Edgmont and Thornbury, and leading to Persifor Frazer's saw-mill. In the report the road is said to pass "between John Edwards' forge and dwelling-house." A few years later, and prior to 1799, the forge was operated by John Lewis and Wills Hemphill. Lewis retired from the firm, and in 1807, Wills Hemphill, —— Pennock, and Nathan Edwards were conducting the business at this forge. Nathan Edwards seems to have operated the works from 1811 to 1816, at which time he had also a saw-mill on the premises. In 1816 he built a slitting-mill, and in 1826 the rolling- and slitting-mill was owned by John Edwards, his son, a lawyer and active politician, who was conducting the works, the firm being Edwards & Kelton. At that time eighty to one hundred tons of sheet-iron were annually manufactured. The forge and saw-mill were used until 1829, when the former was changed to a nail-factory. The assessment-roll for that year mentioned the rolling-mill and "one building said to be intended for a nail-mill." The manufacture of nails was continued for several years. About 1835 the rolling-mill was abandoned and the building was washed away in the flood of 1843. The old race is still to be seen, and the nail-factory is standing a short distance above the present Glen Mills Station.

Thorndale Mills.—In 1766, Richard Cheyney owned a saw-mill on Chester Creek, which he operated until May 27, 1794, when the mill, with eighty acres of land, was sold to Henry Myers, who later purchased of Eli D. Peirce, agent for the estate of Col. Persifor Frazer, a large tract of land adjoining, on which a small saw-mill had been operated during the Revolutionary war by Mrs. Mary Frazer, while her husband, Col. Frazer, was in the army. Subsequently he conducted the business there. The water in the dam on Chester Creek was conducted by a race on the south side of the saw-mill. At a later date, when the stone grist-mill on the north side of the creek was erected, a race from the same dam was constructed to furnish the water to run the machinery. About 1867 the mill property was purchased by Daniel James, who is operating the grist-mill. The saw-mill is now only occasionally used.

Brinton Mills.—On the west branch of Chester Creek, a short distance above Concord township line, is Caleb Brinton's grist-mill. The tract on which it stands had been in the ownership of the Brinton family for many generations. In 1770 William Brinton owned the land, and in 1788, Joseph Brinton had there a saw-mill, malt-house, and brewery. In 1802 his son, John, and his grandson, Joseph Brinton, were operating a grist-mill which had been built about five years prior to that date. In 1815 the grist-mill was changed to a woolen-factory, and was operated by John and Joseph Brinton. In 1826 the mill contained one pair of stocks, two carding-engines, twenty-four and thirty-six inches, one billy of forty spindles, two jennies, of sixty and seventy spindles, and was then manufacturing from four to five hundred yards of satinets per week. At that time both John and Joseph Brinton were dead, and the factory was operated by William Marshall, who subsequently purchased and continued in business there until 1835, when the building was destroyed by fire. The real estate was bought by Caleb Brinton, who built a stone grist-mill, which he has owned and operated to the present time.

Thornton.—In the colonial days this locality was known as the Yellow House, the name being derived

[1] For account of Glen Paper-Mills, see Concord Township, *ante*, p. 494.

from the dwelling that stood there and which during the Revolution was the summer residence of George Gray, a stirring Whig, and the keeper of the noted ferry over the Schuylkill still known by his name In order that the family should be out of danger during the British advance from the head of the Elk to Philadelphia, he refused to allow Mrs Gray and the children to return to the home on the Schuylkill, but kept them at the Yellow House to avoid the evils of war, not for a moment supposing the din of strife would be heard in that locality But the removal of Washington's army to Chad's Ford, made necessary by the movements of Gen Howe, placed them in the immediate vicinity of "broil and battle" All the morning and afternoon of Sept 11, 1777, the booming of the cannon at Brandywine was distinctly heard, and Mrs Knowles, who was Margaret Gray, and then a child of eleven years, used to relate how, in the afternoon and evening, the demoralized and scattered American soldiers fled in that direction through the present hamlet of Thornton It has been said that this locality was called Shintown, because of the manner in which the troops ran through it, but be that as it may, certain it is that Thornton was for many years known by that name Prior to 1835, John King established a store, in which he was succeeded by Albin Ingram. After the latter removed from the store, it remained idle for several years, when Alfred Mansell took the building and again established the business He was followed by Bennett Temple, and is now kept by William H Yearsley A post-office was located there many years ago In 1832, John King was postmaster, and he was succeeded by the person who kept store at that place Prior to 1831, Thomas Charlton resided at the Yellow House, where he manufactured cloths, coverlets, linen, sheetings, toweling, and linsey Of course, his machinery was simply a hand-loom, such as was frequent in the early times In 1831, Charlton removed to Middletown, and continued the business in the first house below the Black Horse Tavern, on the Middletown road, as he announced to his patrons in an advertisement early in that year

Cheyney Shops—Just on the border of Chester County, located on Westtown road, are Cheyney's shops, consisting of a blacksmith and wheelwright shop In front of the property of Cheyney Brothers is a row of buttonwood trees, which were planted by the great-grandfather of the present owners on the 11th of September, 1777, the day of the battle of Brandywine Prior to 1832 a post-office was established at Cheyney's shops, and in that year William Cheyney was postmaster In 1859, Charles H Cheyney was postmaster, in 1863, George S Cheyney was appointed, and in 1867 the post-office was moved to Cheyney Station, on the West Chester and Philadelphia Railroad

Aged Persons—At the residence of Garrett Thatcher, one afternoon in the autumn of 1867, four ladies sat at the tea-table whose united ages amounted to three hundred and fifty-six years, or over ninety years each They were Phœbe Thomas, aged ninety-seven, Sarah Sharpless, aged ninety-four, Phœbe Mendenhall, aged eighty-five, and Rebecca Trimble, aged eighty years

Licensed Houses—In the township of Thornbury the record shows very few applications to keep houses of public entertainment The first that has been found is that of Obadiah Bonsall, whose petition, dated Aug 31, 1743, represents that he "has taken a Lease of a Tenement and piece of Land situated in Thornbury by the road from French Creek Iron-Works to Thornbury Forge, which road being much Travelled, and many people resorting to and working at and near to the said Forge," secured him the license desired"

How Bonsall succeeded in his undertaking of keeping public-house does not appear, unless the silence of the records as to any application for continuance of the license the following year argues that he was disappointed in his expectations and abandoned the enterprise From the first petitions herein set forth, until 1786, when John James received license, Thornbury seemed without a public-house, and even James, so far as the records show, made no attempt at renewal of his privileges subsequent to the above date

After the county of Delaware was erected no application for license in Thornbury appears for twenty-two years, until 1821, when Vernon G Taylor received license for a public-house in the township In 1829 he was succeeded by John Henderson, whose petition set forth that his house was located about midway between Darlington's tavern, in Chester County, and the President in Edgmont township, while he designated his house as the Thornbury Star Here he remained for twelve years, and in 1841 license was granted to Rufus Cheyney, who died the following year, and the court extended favor to his widow, Sarah She did not continue landlady of the inn for any considerable time, but in 1844 gave place to Jesse Russell The latter was "mine host" of the Star Tavern until 1859, when Joseph M Hizer became the landlord, and continued as such until 1862, when Russell again petitioned successfully yearly except during local option until 1876, after which date no license has been granted in Thornbury

Relics of First Settlers.—In 1873, John Pyle, of Thornbury, was the owner of some table knives and forks whose age was then over a century and a half The knives are curved like a cimeter, and a knife and fork weigh a pound, which shows that handling a knife and fork with our ancestors was a weighty operation In old wills, the gift of a pewter dish was deemed worthy of mention They were in common use about thirty years ago, as also sets of Britannia ware, and may be yet in the country At the time of the settlement of this country by the English, wooden dishes and spoons were used[1]

---

[1] *Delaware County Republican*, 1873

Daniel James

John Brinton

BIOGRAPHICAL SKETCHES.

DANIEL JAMES.

The James family are of Welsh descent. Evan James, the grandfather of Daniel, was a resident of West Nantmeal township, Chester Co., Pa., and a farmer of some prominence in the county. He married Rachel Evans, and had children,—William, Abner, Jesse, Evan, Hannah, Sarah, and Mary. William, of this number, was born in West Nantmeal township, where the greater portion of his life was spent in the employments of a farmer. He married Jane Dunwoody, daughter of James and Grace Dunwoody, of the same county and township. To this marriage were born children,—James, Myrach, Daniel, Benjamin F., Evan, Abigail (Mrs. Huzzard), and Rachel (Mrs. Way). Daniel, the third son, was born on the 16th of December, 1810, in West Nantmeal township, and devoted his youth to the acquirement of a plain English education, under the instruction of teachers in the neighborhood. At the age of sixteen he became an apprentice to the trade of a millwright, and in pursuit of this trade sojourned in various portions of the State for brief periods, having for five years made Nether Providence his residence. During a subsequent brief period spent in Upper Providence he married on the 1st of March, 1838, Eliza P., daughter of John and Eliza Worrall, of Middletown, and later of Springfield township. John Worrall died in the former township, after which his widow removed with her family to Springfield township. The children of Mr. and Mrs. James are Ann Elizabeth (Mrs. J. S. Phipps), Jane D., William, Seth P., Mary L. (Mrs. George Dutton), George W., Ellen H. (Mrs. Wilmer Cheyney), and John W. Mr. James, after five years spent in Springfield, returned again to Upper Providence, and purchased what is known as the "Cassin" farm, where he resided for twenty-one years, and cultivated the land he acquired in connection with the pursuit of his trade. In 1861 he was elected as a Republican to the office of county commissioner, and served a term of three years, after which he was chosen and filled for one term the office of county auditor. In 1867 he retired to a farm and mill property he purchased in Thornbury, and varied the employments of a miller with those of an agriculturist, though his sons are now conducting the flouring-mill. Mr. James was, in performing the official duties, connected with the office of commissioner, actively identified with the conduct of the war, and an important factor in the mustering of recruits. He is a director of the County Agricultural Society, and has been prominently identified with various county interests. A practical intelligence and thorough familiarity with mechanical appliances and machinery have rendered his business career a successful one, and made him an authority in his department of industry. Mr. James received his early training under Presbyterian auspices, but has during a large portion of his life worshiped with the Orthodox Friends' Meeting, of which his wife, whose death occurred Oct. 28, 1876, was a member.

JOHN BRINTON.

The progenitor of the Brinton family in America was William Brinton, who was born about 1630, and died in 1700. He married Ann Bagley in 1659, and had four children, of whom one was named William, born in 1666. He married Jean Thatcher, and had a son, Joseph, who married Mary Pierce, and later Mary Elgar. John, the second son by the first marriage, was united to Margaret Williamson, and had three children, among whom was Joseph, who became a man of note, and for years a justice of the peace. He married Mary Martin, who bore him eight children. Of these, Abraham Brinton, the father of John, was born in 1784. He married Mary Evanson, and to them were born six children, among whom John, the subject of this sketch, was born Sept. 2, 1819, in Thornbury township, Delaware Co., Pa. On the farm of his father John found employment until his marriage, on the 11th day of January, 1842, to Sarah Ann, daughter of Thomas and Mary Manley. Her birth occurred Aug. 14, 1822. Their children are Ann Mary, born Nov. 27, 1842; she married Lewis W. Kitzelman in 1862; their children are John B., Charles Anna, Finley H., Eva D., Lewis W., and Lettie (deceased). Joseph Harlan, born May 25, 1845; he married Kate B. Pyle on the 16th day of March, 1870; their children are William Rupert (deceased), Albin, Irwin, Correll, and Cidney F. James Curtis, born April 20, 1851; he married Phebe Pyle in January, 1871; their children were George (deceased), Anna (also deceased), and Lottie M. After the death of Phebe, in 1878, James married Rachel Yarnall on the 16th day of March, 1882; their child, Edith, died in infancy. Sarah Emily, born Dec. 10, 1857, married to Eli E. Pyle Oct. 31, 1878,—children, Lillie B., Lavinia, and Florence. Lavinia Jackson, born June 24, 1860; she married, Feb. 21, 1883, Charles B. Hawes, to them was born one child, Susannah. Charles Anna, the daughter of Ann Mary and Lewis W. Kitzelman, married, in 1882, to G. D. Ladell, and has one child, Harry. George Evanson, youngest child by Mr. Brinton's first marriage, was born April 20, 1863, and is unmarried. Mrs. Brinton died Oct. 28, 1868, and Mr. Brinton was, on the 8th day of February, 1871, married to Lydia E. Manley, sister of his first wife, whose birth occurred Feb. 25, 1832; their only child is Lizzie Bolden, born Sept. 2, 1873. Mr. Brinton, after his marriage, cultivated his father's farm on shares, and eventually purchased a small place adjacent to it, to which he removed, and where he remained until the death of his parent, when a portion of the estate became his by inheritance, and the remainder by purchase. On the decease of his first wife, a lady of many Christian virtues, he purchased the present home, his son meanwhile cultivating the farm. Mr. Brinton is in politics a Democrat, and much interested in the success of his party, and in the affairs of the township, in which he has held minor offices. He is a member of the Upper Birmingham Lodge, No. 940, of Independent Order of Odd-Fellows. In religion he is a Methodist, and steward, trustee, treasurer, and sexton of the Methodist Episcopal Church adjacent to his home, to which he has been a liberal contributor.

JOSEPH E. BRINTON.

William Brinton, the first of the name who emigrated to America, came from the village of Nether Gournall, parish of Sedgely, Staffordshire, England. He was born about 1630, and died in 1700. He first settled in the State of Delaware, in the year 1684. He married Ann Bagley in 1659, and had four children, of whom his son, William, born in 1666, married Jean Thatcher in 1690. Their children were five in number,—Joseph, the eldest, was born in 1692, and married, in 1711, Mary Pierce, whose children were thirteen in number. Joseph married for his second wife Mary Elgar in 1748, to whom were born no children. John Brinton, the second son of Joseph and Mary Pierce, married Margaret Williamson. To this marriage were born children,—Joseph, Sarah, and Esther. Joseph, whose birth occurred in 1754, married Mary Martin, and had children,—Weldon, Margaret, Lydia, John, Abraham, Mary, Samuel, and Thomas. Abraham was born Nov. 3, 1784, and married Mary Eavenson. Their children were Joseph E., the subject of this biographical sketch, Margaretta, Mary Ann, John, Yearsley, and Lydia. Abraham Brinton died on the 3d of November, 1859. His son, Joseph E., was born Dec. 7, 1813, in Thornbury, on the farm which his father purchased. The advantages of education at this early period were limited, and confined to the rudiments of English, which were acquired by Joseph E. at the neighboring school, after which his willing hands found occupation in cultivating the land his father owned. He continued to be thus associated with his father until his marriage, on the 1st of February, 1838, to Mary Marshall, daughter of William and Sarah Marshall, who sailed from England, and landed in Philadelphia with her parents on the 10th of October, 1820, when but four years of age. The children of Mr. and Mrs. Brinton are Marshall, Margaretta, Sarah, Anne, John, Lydia, Hannah, and Joseph A., who died May 6, 1870. On the death of his father, Mr. Brinton inherited one-half the paternal estate. This he cultivated until 1879, when, having erected an attractive residence of brick adjacent to the homestead, he retired from active labor, his son succeeding him in the management of the farm. He has been an energetic, active man, and risen by his own exertions to a position of independence. He has evinced strict truthfulness and honesty in all business transactions, his word being regarded as good as his bond. Mr. Brinton's political convictions are in accord with the principles of the Democracy, though his ballot is cast for men of worth irrespective of party. He has taken much interest in affairs connected with the township, and served in a minor official capacity. His services are also frequently called into requisition as trustee and in the settlement of estates. He worships with both the Friends' Meeting and the Methodist Episcopal denomination, and aids in the support of each.

GARRETT THATCHER.

Richard Thatcher, with wife and children, came from England soon after the first visit of William Penn, having left his home in Uffington, Berkshire County, on account of religious persecution. He settled in Thornbury township, Delaware Co., where his death occurred in 1722. One of his sons, named Jonathan, married Mary Hix, and had among his children a son Richard, whose son, William, was united in marriage to Hannah Dickison, of Lancaster County, Pa., and resided upon the family estate in Thornbury township. Their children were Joseph, Richard, William, Betsey (Mrs. Isaac Garrett), Hannah (Mrs. John Worrell), Edith (Mrs. Jesse Green), Sarah (Mrs. Nathan Sharpless), and Phœbe (Mrs. Davis Garrett). William Thatcher was born in the State of North Carolina, and in childhood came to the homestead, where he remained and cultivated its productive acres. He married Betsey Garrett, of Goshen, Chester Co., and had children that survived,—Charity (Mrs. John Sharpless), Sarah (Mrs. Smith Sharpless), Garrett, Betsey (Mrs. James Painter), William, Richard, Benjamin, and three who died in childhood. The death of Mr. Thatcher occurred Dec. 16, 1851. Garrett Thatcher was born July 24, 1811, on the homestead, which is his present residence, and has been the scene of his life-long and successful labors. After the usual period devoted to instruction at the nearest school of the neighborhood he became an assistant to his father, and in 1840 leased the farm. On the decease of the latter, in 1851, he inherited the property, to which he subsequently made valuable additions. He was married on the 9th of January, 1844, to Hannah H. Pyle, a descendant on the paternal side of John Sharpless, the pioneer, and daughter of Aaron and Sarah Parks Pyle, of Thornbury township. Their children are Emma T. (Mrs. George B. Painter) and Howard. Mr. Thatcher is in politics a Republican, and, though not politically ambitious, has held various township offices. He is in religion a Friend and member of the Concord Monthly Meeting, as is also Mrs. Thatcher.

Joseph E. Brinton

RESIDENCE OF JOSEPH E. BRINTON,

Joseph E. Brinton

RESIDENCE OF JOSEPH E. BRINTON,

THORNBURY, DELAWARE CO., PA.

Garrett Thatcher

Garrett Thatcher

Joseph Webster

JOSEPH WEBSTER

Joseph Webster, the grandfather of the subject of this biographical sketch, who was of English descent, married a Miss Kester, and had children,—Rachel, Mary, Ruth, William, and Joseph The last named was born in Delaware County, where he was actively engaged in farming, and married Susanna Duncan, daughter of Aaron Duncan Their children were Charles, Rebecca, Aaron D, Susanna D, Lydia (Mrs John Gilpin), and Joseph The youngest of this number, Joseph Webster, was born April 15, 1814, in Chester County Having been left motherless in infancy he was placed in care of his maternal grandmother, and remained with her until six years of age He then returned to his father, and, after enjoying such advantages of education as the common schools afforded, he became, on attaining his seventeenth year, an apprentice to the trade of a wheelwright in the township of Sadsbury, Chester Co On the completion of a term of service, embracing a period of four years, he abandoned his trade for the more healthful pursuits of a farmer He was on the 25th of April, 1839, married to Sarah, granddaughter of Caleb and Phœbe Yarnall, and daughter of Caleb and Hannah Yarnall, of Middletown township The children by this marriage are Mary M (Mrs A W Sloan), Charles N (deceased), M Rebecca (deceased), Thamzin R (Mrs Jacob Kimes), Hannah A, and Joseph, Jr Mr Webster rented for some years after his marriage, and in 1861 purchased, a farm in Marple township, where he resided for four years On effecting an advantageous sale of this property, he became the owner of the farm in Thornbury township, which is his present home He has since been engaged in its cultivation and improvement, though the more onerous duties it involves have been assumed by his son Mr Webster has always been either a Whig or Republican in politics, and has held minor offices in the township In 1872 he was elected and served one term as sheriff of Delaware County, the duties of which responsible office were filled with entire acceptance In religion he espouses the faith of the society of Friends, both Mrs Webster and he being members of the Chester Monthly Meeting

---

CHAPTER LIII

SPRINGFIELD TOWNSHIP

The township was not recognized until after 1684, for at a court held Fifth month 1, 1684, "James Kenela" and "Randolfe Vernome" were appointed collectors for "Ridley *and in the Woods*," clearly showing that the locality subsequently known as Springfield was too sparsely settled to be recognized as a municipal district The first appearance of the township as a distinct municipality is in 1686, when Peter Lester was appointed constable for Springfield, and at March court, 1687/8, among "the names of ye Constaples Chosen to serve ye next ensuing year" for Springfield "James Lounes is attested as above" The name of the township, we are told by Galt, in his "Life of Benjamin West," was given to the locality because Thomas Pearson, the maternal grandfather of West, in clearing the first field on his estate, discovered a large spring, and when the township was erected that fact was remembered and determined the title of the new district made from the lands lying "in the woods" This traditional account may be the correct one, for although Pearson settled and died in Marple, his lands extended to the boundary-line of Springfield, and before any definite limits were given to the several districts his plantation might easily have been regarded as within the township to which his spring may have given the name Unfortunately, however, there is another claimant for the honor of godfather to Springfield The tradition in the Maris family is that the township was named because of the large spring near the dwelling of George Maris The latter was a judge of the courts in 1684, and his influence was such that as he had voice in the name adopted, the tradition among his descendants is doubtless correct On Holmes' "Map of the Improved part of Pennsylvania in America," the district is marked as "Springfeild"

This township is separated from Nether Providence on the west by Crum Creek, and excepting at its southeastern end from Upper Darby, and at its extreme northeastern limit from Haverford by Darby Creek, while Ridley lies to the south and Marple to the north of the township Beginning at the dividing-line between Ridley and Springfield, on Crum Creek, a tract of land extending eastward to the present village of Morton, and continuing along Crum Creek to a point about half-way between Wallingford bridge and the Wallingford Mills, including all the territory between lines drawn at right angles from the places named, comprising eight hundred and fifty acres, was surveyed to Henry Maddock and James Kennerly, March 21–22, 1681 Henry Maddock, of Loom Hall, Cheshire, in connection with his brother-in-law, James Kennerly, purchased in that year, before leaving England, from Penn, fifteen hundred acres of land in the province Henry Maddock located on this plantation, and represented Chester County, in 1684, in the General Assembly, but he subsequently returned to England The eight hundred and fifty acres in Springfield came to the possession of Mordecai, the eldest son of Henry Maddock Mordecai was in the province in 1690, but returned to England, where he married, and again came to Pennsylvania, arriving here for the second time, March 30, 1702 The grant included the present Swarthmore College, and extended almost to Lownes' Free Church Just above the Maddock land, lying along Crum Creek, was one hundred and thirty acres, which was patented to John Gleaves at as late a date as March 20, 1743. Immediately adjoining the last-mentioned plantation was a tract of two hundred and fifty acres, surveyed to Peter Leiscester, Nov. 20, 1682. He appears never to have settled on this land, but it subsequently passed into the possession of George Gleaves, who died previous to 1690, and one hundred and twenty-five acres on Crum Creek was owned by his son, John. "The ford on Crum Creek, at Lewis' mills (Wallingford Mills), for nearly a century was known as Gleave's Ford. This ford was on the 'great road from Marlborough to Philadelphia,' and as early as 1754 a bridge was erected over the creek at that point by private contributions, the subscription paper for which is still preserved."[1] The remaining one hundred and twenty-five acres of the Leiscester land in 1700 passed to George James, which in recent years was part of the plantation of James Lownes. On the Leiscester tract is the main stream of Lownes' Run. Above this estate, on Nov. 10, 1682, to Jane Lownes was surveyed one hundred and fifty acres. She was a widow, of Cheshire, England, who for conscience' sake fled with her children from persecution in the Old World, and settled in this land in 1684. About one hundred yards southwest of the old mansion-house on this farm, still owned by her descendants, is a stone bearing the inscription, "Jane Lownes, her cave and dwelling, 1684." Above the Lownes tract Robert Taylor took up four hundred acres of land, Nov. 11, 1682, extending from the southeastern line of the lands of J. Howard Lewis to a point where the eastern line of George S. Powell's farm touches on the State road. Taylor came from Little Lehigh, county of Chester, and settled in Springfield as early as 1684. On Sixth month 20, 1689, he conveyed the western part of the estate, containing three hundred acres, to his son, Isaac, and the remaining one hundred acres to the east to his son, Thomas Taylor.

Above the Taylor tracts, and extending to the Marple township line, Bartholomew Coppock, on Nov. 11, 1682, seated four hundred acres, on which he settled in 1685, but two years thereafter purchased lands in Marple, and removed thither. Two hundred and sixty acres of this land at the eastern part of the tract subsequently became the property of Bartholomew Coppock, Jr., who is believed to have been the nephew of Bartholomew Coppock, Sr., although there were but a few years' difference in their ages. It was at his house where the first meetings of Friends in Springfield were held, and he it was who gave the two acres of land on which the meeting-house and graveyard were located. He was a member of the Provincial Council, and for several terms represented Chester County in the General Assembly. George Maris seated, Oct. 26, 1683, four hundred acres, being part of one thousand acres purchased by Robert Toomer on May 14, 1683. This plantation comprised the land lying along Darby Creek, from Marple township, a short distance above the mouth of Lewis' Run. It was an irregular tract, difficult of description, the Amosland road running through the southwestern part of the estate. In a valley, selected because of its sheltered location from the chilly blast of the severe winters of the early colonial times, George Maris built a stone house near the spring before mentioned, and here he resided until his death, in 1705. He was over fifty years of age when he emigrated, coming from Grafton, Flyford, county of Worcester, England, his wife, Alice, and several children accompanying him. He was a man of influence in the infant colony, filling the office of justice of the court, and from 1684 to 1693 (excepting in 1689) represented Chester County in the General Assembly. In 1722 the original house of this settler was removed, but on its site was erected, by George Maris, a grandson, a two-story and a half stone dwelling, known as Home House, and at the grove back of that building, on Aug. 25, 1883, the two hundredth anniversary of the arrival of George Maris and his family was celebrated by a reunion of his descendants, more than a thousand being present, some of whom had traveled many hundreds of miles to take part in the ceremonies. The exercises were of a most interesting character. Continuing along Darby Creek to the present line of Upper Darby, Owen Foulk, on June 17, 1683, entered two hundred acres, which was part of the five thousand acres purchased by John, ap John, and Thomas Wynn, and on March 22–23, 1681, conveyed to Foulk. One hundred and fifty acres in the southern part of the tract was conveyed to Samuel Levis, Fourth month 27, 1692. He, accompanied by his wife Elizabeth, and one child, emigrated from Harly, county of Leicester, England, in 1684, and settled in Springfield. Prior to leaving Europe, he with William Garrett purchased one thousand acres of land. In 1686 he represented the county of Chester in the General Assembly, an office to which he was frequently elected. He was also a justice of the court. Directly south of the Levis tract were four hundred and ninety acres which were surveyed to George Simcock, Oct. 12, 1682. Whether he ever lived on this land is unknown, but he prior to 1703 had sold the tract to several parties in plots of one hundred acres and smaller farms. On Oct. 17, 1683, to Francis Yarnall was surveyed one hundred acres, which was an oddly-shaped plantation, lying to the north of the southerly part of the Simcock land, bounded on the north by Peter Leiscester's and James Lownes' tract, to the east by the estate of George Maris, and on the west by lands of Joseph Powell. Yarnall emigrated about the date mentioned, and resided on this property; but he subsequently removed to Chester, and in 1711 was a representative from this county in the General Assembly. Joseph Powell seems never to have resided on his plantation,

[1] Smith's "History of Delaware County," p. 465.

but in 1685 it was purchased by Joseph Stidman, who died in 1694, and it subsequently passed into the ownership of George Lownes South of this tract Elizabeth Stedman, on Oct 16, 1682, took on rent fifty acres, which subsequently became the property of Joseph Stidman Below this land, and extending nearly to the northern limit of the present village of Morton, John Stidham purchased one hundred and ten acres, and to the right of the latter plantation, Samuel Hall bought, on Feb 23, 1702, ninety-nine acres, now part of the I H Odgen farm All the remainder of the land in Springfield, including the village of Morton, the lower part of the Davidson, Edwards, and part of the Shipley farm, as shown on Hopkins' Atlas of 1870, was part of the two thousand two hundred patent to John Simcock, of Ridley

Remarkable Freak of Lightning.—The following account of noticeable discharge of electric fluid in the form of lightning was abridged by Dr Smith for the *Pennsylvania Chronicle*

"At about seven o clock in the morning of Nov 3, 1768, Mr Samuel Levis' house in Springfield was struck by lightning The morning was showery, but no thunder was heard nor appearance of lightning seen, either before or after the shock, which produced the following effects It appears first to have descended on the chimney, which it entirely leveled to the top of the house, dispersing the bricks to a considerable distance, with great part of the roof, fractured the gable end, a stone wall, into sundry pieces, and penetrated in veins or branches down to different parts of the house In the closet of a lower room, a glass bottle with a pound and a half of gunpowder in it was broken and part of the powder thrown about, which did not take fire, a clock near the closet was overset and the weights found at fifteen feet distance from the place where it stood, and considerable damage was done to the furniture In passing into the upper chamber by the stack of chimneys, a gun barrel and some pieces of brass which were in a closet were melted in several places A young woman (Margaret), a daughter of Mr Levis, happened to be near the door of the closet, was struck down, and to all appearance, breathless for some time The father, running immediately up stairs where the greatest signs of violence appeared, was the first who found his daughter in her melancholy situation, amid the ruins of the shattered wainscot and an exceedingly strong smell of sulphur He carried her down stairs in his arms, and upon examination there appeared signs of life A doctor was immediately sent for, who in vain attempted to bleed her, there seeming almost a total stagnation, but being put to a warm bed she bled freely, and revived so as to be able to speak, to the inexpressible joy of her distracted parents, her whole family, and all her friends In the evening she was able to walk up to her chamber So instantaneous was the shock, and so sudden the deprivation of her senses that she could give no account of what happened to her at the juncture When she regained her senses she complained of much pain, and of being sore, as she was very much scratched, the lightning passing from her head, and as it descended rent her clothes, even her garters into a number of pieces, then to her shoes, carrying away the upper leather, which was torn into fragments, and melting part of one of her silver shoe buckles In 1773 this lady became the wife of the late Thomas Garrett, of Upper Darby, and was the mother of the late Samuel Garrett, of the same township A number of her descendants are still living "[1]

The Revolutionary history of Springfield is meagre Doubtless during the raids of the British troops in the winter of 1777-78 the inhabitants suffered from the foraging parties of the enemy, but little respecting that period of our history has been preserved Maj John Clark, Jr, in a letter written from Mr. Lewis', near Newtown Square, at four o'clock on the morning of Dec 19, 1777, addressed to Washington, says, "I must again tell your Excellency that the country people carry in provisions constantly, a number went to-day One of them caught my spy by the coat, and called him a 'damn'd Rebel' before the enemy's advanced sentries, but clapping spurs to his mare left him lying on the road, since which the villain was returning, and one of our horsemen took him, and he appealed to my spy if he did not know him to be well affected. His name is Edward Hughes, is a papist, and lives in Springfield I hope an example will be made to deter others If a troop of Horses was stationed in this quarter and patrole the roads, 'twould be of infinite service"[2] What ultimately became of Hughes does not appear

The taxables in Springfield in 1715 were returned as follows

Sam[l] Levis, Bartholomew Coppock, Jun[r], Jonathan Coppock, John Marris, George Marris, Rich[d] Marris, Barthow Coppock, Sen[r], Wm West, Isaac Taylor, Sen[r], Isaac Taylor, Jun[r], Samuel Hall, James Barrot, Thomas Poe, Thomas Taylor, George James, Rich[d] Woodward, John Glore, George Lownes, Nicholas Smith, Thomas Kendall, Mordecai Maddock, William Miller

Freemen—John Worrall, William Birran

In 1799 the taxables in the township were

James Arnold (cordwainer), Sarah Allen (tavern keeper), Caleb Bonsell, Richard Crozer, James Caldwell (blacksmith), John Crozer, John Cummings, Robert Crozer (weaver), Isaac Cochran (tavern keeper), George Davis, James Edwards (carpenter), Abner Edwards, Edward Flounders, Edward Fell (pot-house, and half a saw mill, cabinet maker), Joseph Gibbons (tavern keeper), Abraham Garrett, James Heacock, Benjamin Lobb (cordwainer), Curtiss Lownes (tilt- and blade-mill), Rebecca Levis, Thomas Leiper, Thomas Levis (saw-mill), John Levis (half a paper-mill), Thomas Levis, Jr (half a paper mill), Joseph Levis (malt-house), John Lewis (grist and saw mill), William Lane, George B Lownes (stone-shop, cutter), Hugh Lownes, Jane Maris, Elizabeth Morris, John Ogden, Ann Pancoast, William Pennock, William Paist (half a saw mill), David Rogers, Owen Rhoads, Charles Sankey (tailor and shop-keeper) Thomas Temple, Susanna Thomas, Joshua Thompson, Elisha Worrall, Joseph Worrell, Moses Wells, Matthew Wood, John Worrell

Inmates—John Caldwell, George Edwards, Robert McFarlan, William Paist, Jr, William Palmer (paper-maker), Davis Richards (carpenter), Philip Rudolph (paper-maker)

Single Freemen.—James Caldwell (blacksmith), David Caldwell, John Caldwell, George B Lownes, Seth Levis, Edward Levis (paper-maker), Charles Levis (tailor), William Marshall (potter), Joseph Parker (carpenter), Jonah Thompson, Joshua Thompson, Mordecai Thompson, Owen Thompson (carpenter), Mordecai Worrell

Township Lines.—The original boundaries of Springfield did not include all the territory now within its boundaries On Sept 1, 1837, a petition was presented to court praying for a change in the line between Springfield and Ridley townships The old line began "at a stone, a corner of said township line, and a corner of lands of Geo Warner and lands late of the estate of John Lowndes, dec'd, thence running by and near the spring-house and lands of Isaac Newlin, by the Bridge on the said township lines, by the lands and dwelling-house of Wm Burns, and by the Springfield House to the line of Upper Darby township and corner-stone of the townships of Ridley

[1] History of Delaware County, p 390

[2] Bulletin of Pennsylvania Historical Society, vol i No 10, March, 1847, p 25

and Springfield aforesaid, being very irregular and crooked, and causing considerable difficulty at elections in determining at which township the electors shall be entitled to vote."

The court appointed Jesse J. Maris, Spencer McIlvain, and Edward H. Engle commissioners to adjust the boundary lines, which was done, and on Oct. 13, 1837, they reported, designating the present southern boundary line of Springfield, which report was accepted and confirmed by court.

The following is a list of the justices of Springfield:

Benjamin Brannon	Aug. 19, 1791.
Israel Elliot	Oct. 28, 1791.
Benjamin W. Oakford	Feb. 14, 1794.
Caleb S. Sayers	Aug. 6, 1799.
Benjamin Hays Smith	April 3, 1804.
Samuel Davis	Feb. 20, 1810.
Thomas Smith	July 3, 1821.
John G. Malcolm	July 30, 1831.
Thomas Maddock	Jan. 8, 1834.
Charles Sellers	June 20, 1836.
Sketchley Morton	April 14, 1840.
Edward Levis	April 14, 1840.
Sketchley Morton	April 15, 1845.
Sketchley Morton	April 9, 1850.
F. Edward Levis	June 29, 1852.
F. Edward Levis	April 14, 1857.
George Bakewell Earp	April 14, 1863.
Richard Young	Nov. 24, 1869.
Kingston Goddard	March 27, 1879.
Richard Young	April 9, 1881.

Friends' Meeting-House.—The members of the society of Friends who had settled in Springfield were recognized at the Chester Quarterly Meeting on Third month 3, 1686, when it was agreed that "for ye ease of such y^t live westerly in ye woods and ye rest of friends living ye other way upon ye same day (First-day) to meet at ffrancis Stanfield's until further consideration." The rest of the Friends living the other way were those of Springfield. At the Quarterly Meeting, Sixth month 2, 1686, it was "agreed y^t ye meeting at ffrancis Stanfield's upon fresh consideration be Removed to Bartholomew Coppuck's ye younger, to begin ye next first day and ye 4th day following untill friends see cause to remove it." On Third month 4, 1696, the Quarterly Meeting changed the day of meeting at Coppock's house to "every first and 3d day," and on Third month 2, 1698, consented that the time of meeting should be changed so that "the 3d day be on ye 5th day." By this time the meeting at Coppock's had waxed so strong that on the Twelfth month 6, 1698/9, the minutes of Chester Quarterly Meeting show that "the friends belonging to Springfield meeting propose their intention of building a meeting-house at their grave-yard, which this quarterly meeting Consents unto." This grave-yard was located at the junction of the Springfield and Darby roads, on the line between Springfield and Marple township. It is said that the first meeting-house was of stone, an assertion which may well be questioned, as the meeting-houses and churches in that day were usually constructed of logs, and inasmuch as that in Springfield was quickly erected it would seem to argue that it was a wooden structure. The statement that it was quickly built is based on the minutes of Chester Quarterly Meeting, on Sixth month 26, 1700, where, in the case of several Friends who had violated law in getting intoxicated and had made an acknowledgment of their misdeeds to the meeting in writings, it was ordered that "both the s^d papers bee published by being fixed up att Springfield meeting-house." Tradition has declared that the first meeting-house was erected in 1704, where, as at Springfield meeting-house, on Second month 26, 1703, the following interesting record was made:

SPRINGFIELD FRIENDS' MEETING-HOUSE, BUILT 1738, TAKEN DOWN 1850.
[Drawn by John Sartain in 1837.]

> "Chester meeting having Layed before this meeting their care and tender dealing with and concerning George Simpson about the disorderly practices of the s^d George in keeping on his hatt when John Simcock was in Prayer and Reflecting on his Testimony Calling itt dead and dry stuff and hee doth not Give friends satisfaction in condemning the same. George Maris, Senr, & Robert Vernon are appointed to speak to him to come to next mo. meeting in order to Give friends satisfaction."

From the records of Chester Meeting held on Eighth month 25, 1703, we find that the deed of Springfield meeting-house was lodged with George Maris, Sr., for safe-keeping. The first building on this lot was destroyed by fire in 1737, and the following year, 1738, the society had begun the erection of another meeting-house. At Chester Quarterly Meeting, on Sixth month 13, 1739, it was ordered that eighteen pounds should be paid to Friends of Springfield Meeting, which sum was to be expended in helping them to defray the charges of rebuilding their meeting-house. The amount was the interest on Joseph Need's donation, and was appropriated in the manner designated at his request. The date-stone in the second building had engraved upon it the words and figures, "Rebuilt 1738." The latter building was stone, with a hipped roof and pent-roof over the doors and windows at the ends, such as the projection over the windows of the old City Hall in Chester. Tradition has also recorded that in this building in 1754 a meeting was held to consider what ought to be done with Benjamin West, whose father was anxious to settle his son in some established business, while the latter was desirous of being an artist, although the society, to which he was a birthright-member, was averse to such occupation, it being purely ornamental. Although the alleged special meeting of Friends to consider the matter was never held, yet, as the statement has gone into history, it is deemed proper to quote the incident as related by an eminent writer:

"The assembly met in the meeting-house near Springfield, and after much debate approaching to altercation, a man of the name of John Williamson rose and delivered a very extraordinary speech upon the subject. He was much respected by all present for the purity and integrity of his life, and enjoyed great influence in his sphere on account of the superiority of his natural wisdom; and, as a public preacher among the Friends, possessed an astonishing gift of convincing eloquence. He pointed to old Mr. West and his wife, and expatiated on the blameless reputation which they had so long maintained, and merited so well. 'They have had,' said he, 'ten children whom they have carefully brought up in the fear of God, and in the Christian religion; and the youth whose lot in life we are now convened to consider, is Benjamin, their youngest child. It is known to you all that God is pleased from time to time to bestow upon some men extraordinary gifts of mind, and you need not be told by how wonderful an inspiration their son has been led to cultivate the art of painting. It is true that our tenets deny the utility of that art of mankind. But God has bestowed on the youth a genius for the art, and can we believe that omnipotence bestows his gifts but for greater purposes? What God has given who shall dare to throw away? Let us not estimate Almighty Wisdom by our notions; let us not presume to arraign his judgment by our ignorance; but in the evident propensity of the young man be assured that we see an impulse of the divine hand operating towards some high and beneficent end.' The effect of this argument, and the lofty commanding manner in which it was delivered induced the assembly to agree that the artist should be allowed to indulge the predilections of his genius, and a private meeting of the Friends was appointed to be holden at his father's house, at which the youth himself was requested to be present in order to receive in form the assent and blessing of the society. On the day of meeting the great room was put in order, and a numerous company of both sexes assembled. Benjamin was placed by his father, and the men and women took their respective forms on each side. After sitting some time in silence, one of the women rose and addressed the meeting on the wisdom of God, and the various occasions in which he selected from among his creatures the agents of his goodness. When she had concluded her exhortation John Williamson also rose and resumed the topic which had been the subject of his former address. At the conclusion of this address, which is described as having been in a strain of extraordinary eloquence, the women rose and kissed the young artist, and the men, one by one, laid their hands on his head and prayed that the Lord might verify in his life the value of the gifts which had induced them in despite of their religious tenets to allow him to cultivate the faculties of his genius."[1]

The old building serving as a meeting-house for one hundred and thirteen years, when it was taken down and the present structure erected to supply its place.

Lownes Free Church, or Protestant Union Church.—In 1832, George Bolton Lownes set apart a tract of land on his farm, situate on the Philadelphia, New London and Westtown turnpike, for church and burial purposes. On this lot he erected a church, and furnished it, which was free for all denominations to conduct religious services therein. The pulpit has been supplied from time to time by Methodist, Presbyterian, and Baptist clergymen, but mostly by the Baptist ministers who were in charge of Ridley Baptist Church. Occasionally the members of the society of Friends have held religious exercises in this building. George B. Lownes lived but a short time after the church was founded, his death having occurred Feb. 22, 1834, and was buried near the entrance to the church. By will he bequeathed four hundred dollars, the interest of which was to be applied annually for the repairs of the church and keeping the grounds in good condition. The principal sum was placed in the control of a clergyman of Philadelphia, who invested it in securities which ultimately proved to be worthless. In 1870, the church having become dilapidated, Mrs. M. E. Parker exerted herself in raising a fund to repair the old church, and so earnestly did she labor that sufficient means were secured to thoroughly repair the building at a cost of twelve hundred dollars. The church was rededicated on Sunday, Jan. 8, 1871. Rev. Henry G. Weston, of Crozer Theological Seminary, preached the dedicatory sermon, and the Rev. James W. Dale. Since that time services have been occasionally held in the Lownes Free Church. A recent writer gives the following description of the Blue or Lownes Church:

"The building in which this assemblage was held is worthy of brief notice. It was erected by one of the numerous descendants of Jane Lownes, and set apart forever to the worship of the Almighty without cost or let to any of whatever denomination, with one important exception. Just in front of the pulpit hangs a framed card, on which the patron's wish is printed, with this proviso: That no one who denies the proper divinity of our Lord Jesus Christ or the doctrine of the Atonement shall ever be permitted to preach in the place. The house was built at the time when the conflict was at its height that divided the society of Friends into the so-called 'Orthodox' and 'Hicksite' camps. The feelings awakened by that controversy are crystallized in this proviso, and the 'Lownes Free Church' is free only to orthodox preachers. However, as there are very few persons of a different religious bent in the whole country-side, the prohibition has not proved of much practical disadvantage.

"The house is built of a blue limestone, which, in spite of the ill-fitting coat of whitewash that now covers it, shows plainly enough the reason for its popular name, 'The Blue Church.' It is a plain rectangular edifice, with a pitched roof, without spire or belfry. There is a door at either gable, over one of which is placed a rude water-shed. A plain porch covers the front door, which is shaded by a horse-chestnut, upon whose lower branches hangs a hornet's nest. On either side of the door is a marble tombstone. In the north tomb repose the ashes of the venerable builder of the church. A plain slab rests upon low marble walls, and bears the name, age, and following inscription: 'Where he was born, there he lived and died. An honest man and a useful citizen.' There is added the familiar passage from Job, 'I know that my Redeemer liveth.'

"A fine large willow-tree stands in front, and overhangs this grave. The tomb on the opposite side is a slab raised upon six marble pillars, and bears the name of a favorite cousin of the patron. Those tombs serve as seats for the rustic congregation while waiting for the commencement of service, and tramps who camp of summer nights in the horse-sheds play cards upon them in the moonlight.

"The entrance to the church is from the Baltimore pike, by a large wooden gate hung in the stone wall that encloses two sides of the lot. One corner of the churchyard is devoted to burial purposes. Here stands

[1] "Scenes in the Early Life of Benjamin West," by John S. Hart; *Sartain's Union Magazine*, March, 1849, p. 169.

another large weeping-willow and tall bushes of osage-orange and sumach overshadow the wall. Short mounds of buried children fill the space, though larger graves show where the 'rude forefathers of the hamlet sleep.' In the rank grass and among the vines that here creep over the ground and swathe the graves dwell undisturbed hosts of insects, especially crickets and grasshoppers. Among these the great green grasshopper abounds, one of the noisiest of our musical insects, and day and night alike his shrilling is heard among the graves, making this rural 'God's acre' a very garden of insect song.

"The plain stone building is a pretty object, standing in its two-acre field, embowered among trees. Just across the meadow is a farm, once a country-seat of an eminent president of the Pennsylvania Railroad. Adjoining that the cupola of 'Shady-Bank,' a fine country home, rises above the tops of a noble grove of trees.

"Inside the building is exceedingly plain. It is fashioned after the manner of a Quaker meeting-house, having a 'gallery' or long rows of elevated seats along the middle, opposite the door. A pulpit is arranged at the central part of the gallery, beneath which is a chancel-like space, where stand a reed organ and a superintendent's desk. Comfortable sofa-benches, with reversible backs, are ranged in front and on either side of the pulpit. In front of the chancel stands a large cannon stove, whose long pipe penetrates the ceiling. The walls are unadorned, and the whole interior is plain enough to suit the severest taste."[1]

Schools.—In Springfield as early as 1793 a school was maintained under the care of the society of Friends, but of the manner of instruction pursued therein very little information, other than the fact of the school being established, has been obtained. The first definite knowledge of the schools, about the beginning of the present century, is that furnished in the story of the childhood days of John P. Crozer. In speaking of that period in the life of the latter personage his biographer says,—

"The educational advantages of Delaware County at that time were very limited. About three-fourths of a mile from the old mansion (West's birthplace) there may still be seen a little stone school-house. Here, at the age of six, John commenced his studies, walking daily to the school in company with his sisters and his brother James; and here he received all the school education he ever had, except a little over one quarter's instruction, in his fifteenth year, at a school two miles off. His first teacher, or 'master,' as he was called in those days, was Moses Taylor. John had been under his instruction but a short time, when 'Master Doane' succeeded to authority in the little school-house. He is described as having been a good teacher in spelling and arithmetic. In reading, his ability consisted in calling the words readily, rather than in emphasis or inflection. He was a thorough disciplinarian, and having drank deeply into the spirit of Solomon, was an earnest believer in the use of the ferrule and the rod. John seems, however, to have escaped correction, there being in his case no need of such gentle persuasions to diligence or good behavior. On the contrary, he was a favorite with his instructor.

"Under this teacher John commenced ciphering, and found no little difficulty in comprehending the science of numbers. Long, irregular columns were given him to add up. How to dispose of the tens and hundreds was the problem. He was told to 'carry them forward,' but what 'carrying forward' meant was just what he did not understand. Master Doane scolded, threatened, did nearly everything but explain; until John was almost in despair. . . . When he (Crozer) was about nine years old 'Master Doane' gave up the reins of government to Mr. Joseph Pardee. He was a man of more education than his predecessor, but in the opinion of his youthful pupil, who had already begun to study men, 'he had less ability to impart instruction.' Under Master Pardee, in addition to his other studies, he gained some knowledge of surveying, and soon put his knowledge into practice by surveying some of his father's fields, his only instrument being an old compass and a two-pole chain.

"After reaching the age of thirteen, John attended school only in the winter, working the rest of the year on the farm. Even in the winter his studies were accompanied with work in taking care of the stock, cutting and carrying in the wood, and building the morning fires. In comparing the present facilities for education with those of his childhood, Mr. Crozer said, 'My teachers knew nothing of English grammar, although they professed to teach something of it, and the little knowledge of grammar I possess was obtained without a teacher after I was twenty-one. Not one of my teachers, except perhaps Mr. Pardee, would now pass examination as teachers of common schools in Delaware County.'"[2]

The school building known by old citizens as the "Yellow school-house" was erected in the latter part of the last century. The ground on which it stood in 1760 belonged to Josiah Hibberd, who acquired title to the property by right of his wife, Susannah, daughter of George Owens. In 1764, Hibberd died, and in proceeding in partition in 1768 the land passed to James Rhoads, whose son, Owen Rhoads, in 1778 received it under the terms of his father's will. The land on which the school-house stands was conveyed by one of these parties, in whom the title was, but when or by whom has not been ascertained. The lot is triangular, and is formed by Springfield and Darby road and the road from the Rhoads farm to Chester and Springfield road. George Bolton Jones, who died in 1834, and who had attended school there nearly one hundred years ago, computed from the present time, used to relate that one McCue, an Englishman, taught there many years. He was much addicted to drink, and was wont to go to the Lamb Tavern, or others near by, on Friday night, where he would remain until Monday morning, and get thoroughly drunk. Many times the larger pupils would go for him Monday morning, and, one on each side, would lead him to the school-house. When intoxicated he was always good-natured, but when sober he was apt to be severe, and the boys would receive flogging without stint. One Monday morning, in the fall of the year, he was not to be found, and nothing was heard of him until the next spring, when a farmer, in feeding hay to his cattle, found him dead in the hay-mow. It was supposed he went in there when drunk, and became covered with the hay, and was smothered to death.

John Ogden, who died in September, 1877, in his ninetieth year, went to school in 1799 in the little stone school-house, southeastern part of Springfield, and five years later taught there.

Among the teachers in the school years ago were Lydia Massey, William Saffer, Harlan Ingram, Dr. Samuel Bartleson, and Dr. J. L. Forwood, of Chester. The school directors of Springfield did not acquire title to any property in Springfield until 1855, but had possession of the school-houses which had been built prior to the school law of 1834. The old Yellow school-house was used until 1852, when the present house was built. This is known as the Central School. The present mayor of Chester, Dr. J. L. Forwood, was the first teacher in the new house.

A stone school-house was built about 1822, near the line of Ridley township, one mile south of Oakdale

[1] "Tenants of an Old Farm," by Henry C. McCook, *The Continent*, vol. vi. p. 162.

[2] Life of John P. Crozer, pp. 25–27.

SWARTHMORE COLLEGE.

[illegible] on land now owned by [illegible] [illegible] Ash, Edward Thomas, Rebecca Thomas, and [illegible] Worrall were trustees of the school. The building was used until [illegible], when the Oakdale house was built. On the [illegible] of July, in that year, the directors bought of Joseph [illegible] and James [illegible], of Oakdale, [illegible] square perches, on which they erected the present stone house, called Oakdale Seminary, and the old school-house near [illegible] was abandoned.

On Feb. 20, 1858, the directors purchased of [illegible] Levi eighty square perches of land [illegible] near where is now Hey's mill. This building is now standing.

On the 9th of March, 1830, William [illegible], Joseph Powell, and Seth Pancoast, as trustees, bought [illegible] square perches of land, on which [illegible] a school-house. This house was used by the directors from 1836 to 1857 for school purposes, and on [illegible] of April in that year, Seth Pancoast, surviving trustee, sold the lot to the directors, who erected the present two-story stone building, the upper story being used for a hall, the additional expense being borne by the subscription [illegible] by citizens.

On Sept. 28, 1875, a petition of [illegible] was presented to the court asking that the following described territory in the townships of Springfield and Ridley be erected into a separate school district to be known as Morton: "Commencing at a point in Providence road opposite the Blue Church road; thence along the said Blue Church road to the [illegible] line between John Ogden's and [illegible] land; and thence along to the Lafayette road, to the road leading to South Avenue; thence along South Avenue to the division line of Ridley and Darby townships; thence along said line to the [illegible] line between Springfield and Upper Darby; [illegible] along said lines to the turnpike road; thence along the same to the place of beginning." On Sept. 28, 1875, a decree erecting the school district of Morton was entered, and on Feb. 6, 1876, the court annulled the decree.

The present two-story brick school-house in Morton was erected in 1873, at a cost of three thousand [illegible] hundred dollars. The lower part was built by the township, and the upper story by a stock company for public use, an agreement being made that if the township should require the whole building for school purposes the directors should take it, paying to the stockholders two thousand dollars. The [illegible] on which it is built was donated by [illegible].

At the election on March [illegible], [illegible] Joel Evans, George Lewis, and Samuel [illegible] were chosen school trustees. After the adoption of the school law of 1834, the court appointed Joel Evans and John Lewis inspectors of public school until directors were elected. In 1835 the amount received by Springfield from State and County appropriations for school purposes was $163.47.

The following is a list of the school directors of Springfield, as [illegible] of record:

[illegible]

Swarthmore College.—This admirable and [illegible] educational institution, conceived and carried on by the Friends for the co-education of the sexes, had its inception in a meeting held in Baltimore, Oct. 2, 18[illegible]. It was there proposed to erect a new institution of learning, under the care of Friends, designed to equal the best colleges in the land. [illegible] [illegible] and [illegible] of land on Crum Creek, in this township, [illegible] about eleven miles from Philadelphia, on the [illegible] Division of the Philadelphia, Wilmington and Baltimore Railroad. Swarthmore College was incorporated by act of the Legislature, passed April [illegible], 18[illegible]. By this act James Martin, John M. Ogden, Ezra Michener, Mahlon K. Taylor, Thomas [illegible], James Mott, Dillwyn Parrish, William W. [illegible], William Dorsey, Edward Hoopes, William C. Biddle, Joseph Powell, Joseph Wharton, [illegible], Clement Biddle, F. F. Sharpless, Edward Parrish, Levi K. Brown, Hugh McIlvain, Franklin Shoemaker, and their associates and successors were constituted the body corporate. The capital stock consisted of fifty thousand dollars, but an act approved April 14, 18[illegible], granted authority to increase it to five hundred thousand dollars.

On May [illegible], 18[illegible], the corner-stone of the college building was laid, and three and one-half years later (on Nov. [illegible], 18[illegible]) the college was inaugurated in its new home. The work was carried forward in spite of many discouraging circumstances, but brought to a very satisfactory conclusion a few days prior to the date we have mentioned. The buildings, of which the entire length was three hundred and forty-eight feet, with return wings of ninety-two feet each, consisted of a central structure, sixty feet wide by one

Post-office, on land now owned by Dr. Tyndall. Robert Ash, Edward Thomas, Rebecca Thomas, and Richard Worrall were teachers of the school. The building was used until 1857, when the Oakdale house was built. On the 13th of July, in that year, the directors bought of Joseph Gibbons and James Ogden, of Oakdale, thirty-five square perches, on which they erected the present stone house called Oakdale Seminary, and the old school-house near Ridley was abandoned.

On Feb. 26, 1855, the directors purchased of Charles Levi eighty square perches of land on Darby Creek, near where is now Hey's mill. This building is still standing.

On the 9th of March, 1830, William Beatty, Joseph Powell, and Seth Pancoast, as trustees, bought eighteen square perches of land, on which to erect a school-house. This house was used by the directors from 1836 to 1857 for school purposes, and on the 1st of April in that year, Seth Pancoast, surviving trustee, sold the lot to the directors, who erected the present two-story stone building; the upper story being used for a hall, the additional expense being borne by the subscription made by citizens.

On Sept. 23, 1873, a petition of certain citizens was presented to the court asking that the following described territory in the townships of Springfield and Ridley be erected into a separate school district to be known as Morton: "Commencing at a point in Providence road opposite the Blue Church road; thence along the said Blue Church road to the division line between John Ogden's and Caldwell's land, and thence along to the Lafayette road, to the road leading to South Avenue; thence along South Avenue to the division line of Ridley and Darby townships; thence along said line to the division line between Springfield and Upper Darby townships; thence along said lines to the turnpike road; thence along the same to the place of beginning." On Sept. 28, 1874, a decree erecting the school district of Morton was entered, and on Feb. 8, 1875, the court annulled the decree.

The present two-story brick school-house in Morton was erected in 1875, at a cost of three thousand five hundred dollars. The lower part was built by the township, and the upper story by a stock company for public use, an agreement being made that if the township should require the whole building for school purposes the directors should take it, paying to the stockholders two thousand dollars. The lot on which it is built was donated by Alexander Young.

At the election on March 18, 1825, Joel Evans, George Lewis, and Samuel Rhoads were chosen school trustees. After the adoption of the school law of 1834, the court appointed Joel Evans and John Lewis inspectors of public school until directors were elected. In 1835 the amount received by Springfield, from State and County appropriations, for school purposes was $103.47.

The following is a list of the school directors of Springfield, as appears of record:

1840, Samuel P. Harrison, Seth Pancoast; 1842, John C. Beatty, Sketchley Morton; 1843, Ezra Levis, William Burns, William Ogden; 1844, Randolph Bishop, Randolph Fimple; 1845, Seth Pancoast, John C. Beatty; 1846, Seth Pancoast, Joseph Gibbons, Jr.; 1847, Randall Bishop, Charles Shillingford; 1848, William Carr, John C. Beatty; 1849, Seth Pancoast, Randolph Fimple; 1850, Randall Rishop, Randolph Fimple; 1851, Charles I. Morton, Sketchley Morton; 1852, Richard Fimple, William C. Longstreth; 1853, John Rhoads, Randall Bishop; 1854, Sketchley Morton, William Hill; 1855, William C. Longstreth, George B. Lownes; 1856, George Heath, William P. Beatty; 1857, Samuel C. Ogden, Moses Hey; 1858, George P. Snyder, Sketchley Morton; 1859, John M. Lawrence, James H. Ogden; 1860, J. Reese Lewis, Moses Hey; 1861, Owen Evans, James P. Maris; 1862, J. W. Lawrence, William B. Flounders; 1863, Moses Hey, J. R. Lewis; 1864, Owen Evans, Sketchley Morton; 1865, James H. Ogden, William H. Gibbons; 1866, J. W. Lawrence, James Bishop; 1867, Charles G. Ogden, Sketchley Morton; 1868, Edgar T. Miller, Richard Young; 1869, Charles G. Ogden, Joseph Bishop; 1870, Sketchley Morton, Ambrose Wood; 1871, Eager T. Miller, Richard Young; 1872, Joseph Bishop, C. G. Ogden; 1873, Joseph P. Morris, Sketchley Morton; 1874, George B. Lownes, Maggie Pancoast; 1875, Charles Ogden, Joseph Bishop; 1876, Sketchley Morton, Joseph P. Maris; 1877, Samuel Evans, Richard Young; 1878, Charles G. Ogden, Joseph Bishop; 1879, A. G. DeArmond, D. C. Shillingford; 1880, Samuel Evans, Joseph P. Maris; 1881, Joseph Bishop, Richard Young; 1882, D. C. Shillingford, Thomas Carr; 1883, Joseph P. Maris, William M. Parker; 1884, Richard Young, J. Bishop.

Swarthmore College.—This admirable and extensive educational institution, conceived and carried on by the Friends for the co-education of the sexes, had its inception in a meeting held in Baltimore, Oct. 2, 1860. It was there proposed to erect a new institution of learning, under the care of Friends, designed to equal the best colleges in the land. With this object in view the society purchased two hundred and forty acres of land on Crum Creek, in this township, and distant about eleven miles from Philadelphia, *via* the central division of the Philadelphia, Wilmington and Baltimore Railroad. Swarthmore College was incorporated by act of the Legislature, passed April 1, 1864. By this act James Martin, John M. Ogden, Ezra Michener, Mahlon K. Taylor, Thomas Ridgway, James Mott, Dillwyn Parrish, William W. Longstreth, William Dorsey, Edward Hoopes, William C. Biddle, Joseph Powell, Joseph Wharton, John Sellers, Clement Biddle, P. P. Sharpless, Edward Parrish, Levi K. Brown, Hugh McIlvain, Franklin Shoemaker, and their associates and successors were constituted the body corporate. The capital stock consisted of fifty thousand dollars, but an act approved April 14, 1870, granted authority to increase it to five hundred thousand dollars.

On May 10, 1866, the corner-stone of the college building was laid, and three and one-half years later (on Nov. 10, 1869) the college was inaugurated in its new home. The work was carried forward in spite of many disadvantageous circumstances, but brought to a very satisfactory conclusion a few days prior to the date we have mentioned. The buildings, of which the entire length was three hundred and forty-eight feet, with return wings of ninety-two feet each, consisted of a central structure, sixty feet wide by one hundred and ten feet deep, on either side of which were fire-proof alcoves containing iron stairs and wings, extending from these each one hundred feet long, by forty feet wide The building was constructed of stone with inside walls of brick, was designed to be practically fire-proof, and was admirably adapted to the purpose for which it was built Besides the necessary "collecting" and school-rooms, it contained a library, museum, and chemical laboratory, parlors, dining-room, kitchen, dormitories, bath-rooms, and every convenience for the comfort and health of a large number of resident pupils The great structure was reared under the management of a building committee, of which Hugh McIlvain was chairman, and Elwood Burdsall, Edward Hoopes, Gerard H Reese, and S B Worth were members

On the occasion of the inauguration, Nov 10, 1869, about eight hundred friends of the college were present The exercises were quite interesting The company assembled at an elevated spot east of the building which had been selected for the planting of trees to commemorate the event There the venerable Lucretia Mott, assisted by her son, Thomas, placed in the ground two oaks which had been raised from acorns by the late James, "contributed for the purpose and to serve as fitting memorials of his interest in the cause of education and the erection of this college" The other exercises were conducted in the hall of the college and presided over by Samuel Willets, of New York Hugh McIlvain, chairman of the building committee, laid the key of the front-door of the college upon the desk, thus formally handing the structure over to the corporation He stated that though not in all respects completed, the building was fit for occupation, and that the sum expended upon it had been two hundred and five thousand four hundred and eighty dollars Edward Parrish, who had been chosen as president of the college, then delivered the inaugural address Other speakers were John D Hicks, of New York, William Dorsey, of Philadelphia, and Lucretia Mott

The college opened with an attendance of one hundred and seventy students of both sexes, and the whole number in attendance during the year 1869–70 was one hundred and ninety-nine The faculty consisted of Edward Parrish, president, Helen G Longstreth, matron, Edward H Magill, principal, and Clement L Smith, secretary The resident instructors were Edward Parrish, professor of Ethics and of Chemistry and Natural Science, Edward H Magill, professor of the Latin and French Languages and Literature, Clement L Smith, professor of Greek and German Languages and Literatures, and acting professor of Mathematics, Emily Hallowell, teacher of English branches, Susan J Cunningham, teacher of Mathematics, Susan W Janney, teacher of Penmanship and Botany, Maria L Sandford, teacher of the English Language and Literature, Elizabeth G Macy, teacher of Vocal Culture and Reading, Elizabeth W Caheen, teacher of French and English Branches, Virginia L Dolby and Annie C Green, assistant teachers The non-resident instructors were Ann Preston, M D, lecturer on Physiology and Hygiene, Adrian G Ebell, Ph B, M D, lecturer on Natural History, J A. Congdon, professor of Penmanship

The board of managers during the first year consisted of William Dorsey, Isaac Stephens, Joseph Powell, Edward Hoopes, Hugh McIlvain, Clement M Biddle, S B Worth, Samuel Willets, Daniel Underhill, Edward Meritt, Elwood Burdsall, John D Hicks, Charles T Bunting, William H Macy, B Rush Roberts, Gerard H Reese, Deborah F Wharton, Rachel T Jackson, Letitia S Cadwallader, Martha G McIlvain, Anna M Hopper, Elizabeth Dorsey, Elizabeth S Worth, Jane P Downing, Elizabeth M Booth, Hannah W Haydock, Lydia A Lockwood, Caroline Underhill, Eliza H Bell, Margaret G. Corlies, Ellen Riley, Elizabeth B Smith, Treasurer, Henry M. Laing, Clerks, Clement M. Biddle, Edith W Atlee.

That the affairs of the college progressed smoothly may be inferred from the statement that in the second year, 1870–71, the number of pupils was two hundred and sixty-one, an increase of sixty-two over the attendance of the previous year Of these, fifty-one were in the collegiate department and two hundred and ten in the preparatory department Edward H Magill succeeded Edward Parrish[1] as president of the institution, in 1871, and was duly inaugurated Concerning the experiment of the co-education of the sexes tried by this college, we cannot do better than to quote from President Magill's inaugural address He says that "it has been eminently successful here so far," and "not one of those connected with the management of this institution would for a moment entertain the idea of a change Good, and only good, has resulted from this feature of our organization, nor has the salutary influence been felt by one sex more than the other, but both have been mutually benefited even beyond the expectations of those who were most sanguine when we opened three years ago That we have escaped censure or unfriendly criticism during these opening years we do not pretend, but it has been a source of great satisfaction that this censure comes invariably from those whose views have been formed on theoretical grounds, and who have never witnessed the practical workings of our system for themselves That the public generally is becoming convinced that we are right we have gratifying proofs on every side,—the various colleges are gradually opening their doors for the admission of women"

The affairs of Swarthmore were uniformly prosper-

[1] Edward Parrish died Sept 9, 1872, at Fort Sill, Indian Territory, whither he had been sent by the President to make pacific arrangements between the United States and the Indians He had been one of the pioneers in the work of enlisting the Friends in the founding of the college

ous, and no disaster of any kind occurred to interfere with the usefulness of the institution until the fall of 1881, when a great loss was sustained and a temporary derangement of the school effected by a great fire A few minutes before eleven o'clock on the night of September 25th an explosion occurred in the upper story of the main building, then used as a geological museum, and in a few minutes the roof of that portion of the college was in flames The authorities were quickly on hand, and, with the aid of the students, efforts were made to confine the fire to the centre building, but the wind from the west soon drove it to the east wing, and then the attention of all was diverted from the building and devoted to the imperiled inmates of the dormitories in that wing Very quickly all of the rooms were visited and their occupants aroused to their danger There was no panic and little confusion, and the excellently arranged stairways allowed a speedy exit of the suddenly awakened sleepers The safety of the students being assured, efforts were made to save as much of the contents of the college as possible As the fire broke out in the museum, nothing in it was saved The library, which was also inaccessible because of the intense heat, was also destroyed In the west wing much of the property of the students was saved, as well as some belonging to the college, but from the east wing, where the fire spread more rapidly, little could be removed By four o'clock the building and its contents were destroyed The gymnasium, the meeting-house, and the houses of the president and professors were saved. The neighbors came from miles around and offered their homes as places of shelter to those who were suddenly turned out of their quarters Among others who performed kindly offices was Theodore Hyatt, of the Military Academy at Chester, who at seven o'clock in the morning served a breakfast to the large college family upon the lawn in front of the smoking ruins

The managers were summoned by telegraph, and an informal meeting was held in the meeting-house before noon, at which it was resolved to continue the operation of the college with as little interruption as possible A committee proceeded to Media and made arrangements to secure the Chestnut Grove House The Gayley House was also secured as a lodging-place for the boys and young men, and in less than two weeks from the time of the fire the classes were assembled at Media, at their regular work Of the two hundred and eighteen students at the college on the night of the fire, two hundred and fifteen returned and there were a few admissions, making the number larger than before The loss on the building and contents was not less than one hundred and thirty thousand dollars It was fully insured

Preparations for rebuilding were almost immediately begun The walls of the old building were for the most part in excellent condition, and the work of reconstructing the destroyed portions, the interior and the roof, was pushed rapidly ahead. About two hundred and seventy-five thousand dollars was required, and of this sum sixty-five thousand dollars had to be raised by subscription This was easily accomplished, however, and at the meeting of the managers on Feb. 18 1883, the Rebuilding Committee transferred the new building to them free from debt

The new building was an improvement upon the old in appearance, and in many other ways Architecturally it is quite imposing It is three hundred and forty-eight feet long The centre building is four and the wings three stories high The arrangement is similar to that of the old building, which has been described In addition there was erected a scientific building, which alone cost twenty-five thousand dollars or thereabouts Of this it is not out of place to give a more extended notice It is a two-story building, constructed of granite, trimmed with Leiperville granite, and was planned with particular reference to the scientific department of the college The basement contains a blacksmith-shop, boiler-room, grinding- and polishing-room, brass foundry, store-room, laboratory for beginners, a metallurgical laboratory, and electric battery room The elevator connects the basement with the other floors The first floor contains in the front part of the central projection a physical laboratory for experimentation, and is furnished, as well as all the other departments in the building, with a full supply of the best instruments and appliances In the rear of this room are several smaller apartments,—one for quantitative analysis, a private laboratory for the professor of chemistry, and a chemical library. The western wing contains the large general or qualitative laboratory, and the eastern a complete mechanical laboratory and machine-shop, with power obtained by an engine driven by steam, either from the main college boilers or from the shop boiler, at pleasure The second floor has an excellently constructed drawing-room, a lecture-room supplied with water, gas, electricity, oxygen, and hydrogen, and the attic contains a photographic room, with north skylight and dark-room

The loss of the library, which contained three thousand six hundred volumes, and of the museum was the most difficult to replace, as the work had, from obvious reasons, to be carried on slowly, but the lapse of only a few years more will witness an improvement in these departments fully in keeping with that which has been made in the institution as a whole since the disaster of 1881 Samuel Willets, of New York, president of the board of managers, and one of the stanchest friends and supporters of the college, one of whose last acts had been the signing of a check for twenty-five thousand dollars to complete the subscription for the sixty-five thousand dollars needed for rebuilding, died in 1883. In his will he bequeathed to the college the sum of one hundred thousand dollars, the interest and income of which he directed should be applied "to educate in part or in whole such poor and deserving children as the committee on trusts, endowments, and scholarships . . . may from time to time judge and determine to be entitled thereto." The college has, since its splendid display of recuperative power following the fire, led a prosperous and progressive career. Material improvements have been kept apace with educational advancement, and the buildings and grounds present an aspect of attractiveness which one finds but a few times excelled in the country. The original tract of land purchased by the managers has been added to until at present it contains about three hundred acres of charmingly diversified lawn and meadow and grove. About one-half of the area is set aside for farming and gardening purposes, providing milk and vegetables for the college, and the remainder is a pleasure-ground. The portion of the property along Crum Creek, which forms the western boundary, is rich in picturesque beauty, and the stream is not only an element in the landscape very pleasing to the eye, but affords facilities for boating and other aquatic sports in summer, and for skating in winter. The college has had during the present year three hundred and four pupils. The condition of the school has been satisfactory in all respects, and notably has the system of co-education of the sexes, one of its features from the first, proved successful. Great as has been the usefulness of the institution in the past, a constantly enlarging sphere of beneficence will, without doubt, be filled during each successive year.

The present faculties are composed as follows:

Faculty of Government.—Edward H. Magill, president; Anna W. Frost Capp, matron; Professor Eugène Paulin, Professor Arthur Beardsley, Professor William Hyde Appleton, Professor Susan J. Cunningham, Professor Samuel S. Green, Professor Joseph W. Teets, Assistant Professor Mary L. Austin, Assistant Professor Elizabeth C. Miller; Thomas S. Foulke, superintendent.

Faculty of Instruction.—Edward H. Magill, A.M., president; Joseph Leidy, M.D., LL.D., Professor of Natural History; Eugène Paulin, A.M., Professor of French and Latin, and of Mental and Moral Philosophy; Arthur Beardsley, C.E., Professor of Civil and Mechanical Engineering, and Librarian; William Hyde Appleton, A.M., Professor of Greek and German; Susan J. Cunningham, Professor of Mathematics; Joseph Thomas, M.D., LL.D., Professor of English Literature; Samuel S. Green, M.S., Professor of Physics and Chemistry; Joseph W. Teets, Professor of Elocution; Mary L. Austin, Assistant Professor of Latin; Elizabeth Clarke Miller, A.B., Assistant Professor of Rhetoric; Frederick A. Wyers, A.B., Assistant Professor of French; Charles C. Eames, C.E., Assistant Professor of German; Ellen E. Osgood, Instructor in History; Ellen M. Griscom, Instructor in Free-hand Drawing; Amelia P. Butler, Instructor in Theory and Practice of Teaching; Olivia Rodham, Assistant Librarian, and Instructor in Botany.

The board of managers consists of the following gentlemen and ladies. Term expires Twelfth month, 1884: Joseph Willets, Trenton, N. J.; Eli M. Lamb, Baltimore, Md.; Clement M. Biddle, Abigail M. Woodnutt, Anna M. Hunt, Philadelphia; Susan W. Lippincott, Cinnaminson, N. J.; Sarah H. Merritt, Brooklyn, L. I.; Herman Hoopes, Philadelphia. Term expires Twelfth month, 1885: John T. Willets, New York; Edward H. Ogden, Philadelphia; Daniel Underhill, Jericho, L. I.; Emmor Roberts, Fellowship, N. J.; Jane P. Downing, Philadelphia; Mary W. Cocks, Old Westbury, L. I.; Sarah H. Powell, New York; Edith D. Bentley, Sandy Spring, Md. Term expires Twelfth month, 1886: Isaac Stephens, Trenton, N. J.; James V. Watson, Philadelphia; Clement Biddle, Chad's Ford, Pa.; Martha G. McIlvain, Philadelphia; Sophia U. Willets, Manhasset, L. I.; Sallie M. Ogden, Edmund Webster, Emma McIlvain, Philadelphia. Term expires Twelfth month, 1887: John D. Hicks, Old Westbury, L. I.; Robert Willets, Flushing, L. I.; Joseph Wharton, Philadelphia; M. Fisher Longstreth, Sharon Hill, Delaware Co., Pa.; Mary Willets, Trenton, N. J.; Anna M. Ferris, Wilmington, Del.; Mary T. Longstreth, Sharon Hill, Delaware Co., Pa.; Lydia H. Hall, West Chester, Pa.

Two brothers of the Magill family, William and Alexander, came from the North of Ireland about the year 1725. From William was descended Jacob, the grandfather of Edward H. He married Rebecca Paxson, and had children,—Mary, Jonathan P., Susan, Sarah, and Charles. Jonathan P. was born in Solebury, Bucks Co., Pa., and during his active life was engaged in farming. He married Mary Watson, daughter of David and Rachel Watson, of Falls township, Bucks Co., Pa., whose ancestors came to this country from England with William Penn. Both husband and wife were earnest members of the society of Friends, and well known for their anti-slavery proclivities. They were identified with the leaders of that movement, which received at their hands practical aid, their home having been one of the stations of the memorable Underground Railroad, and the safe abiding-place of many escaped and hunted slaves. Their children were Sarah (deceased), Edward H., Watson P., Rebecca (deceased), Catherine T. (wife of Henry C. Phillips), Rachel M. (wife of John S. Williams), and Matilda R. (wife of Charles S. Atkinson).

Edward H. was born Sept. 24, 1825, in Solebury, Bucks Co., and spent his youth until his fourteenth year at the home of his parents. He then became for two years a pupil of the Friends' school at Westtown, Chester Co., and filled the interval from that period until his twenty-fifth year in teaching. Entering the Freshman class of Yale College in 1850, he remained one year, and in 1851 became a student of Brown University, Providence, R. I., from which he received in 1852 the degree of A.B., and that of

Edw. H. Magill

deserving children as the committee on trusts, endowments, and scholarships . . . may from time to time judge and determine to be entitled thereto." The college has, since its splendid display of recuperative power following the fire, led a prosperous and progressive career. Material improvements have been kept apace with educational advancement, and the buildings and grounds present an aspect of attractiveness which one finds but a few times repeated in the country. The original tract of land purchased by the managers has been added to until at present it contains about three hundred acres of charmingly diversified lawn and meadow and grove. About one-half of the area is set aside for farming and gardening purposes, providing milk and vegetables for the college, and the remainder is a pleasure-ground. The portion of the property along Crum Creek, which forms the western boundary, is rich in picturesque beauty, and the stream is not only an element in the landscape very pleasing to the eye, but affords facilities for boating and other aquatic sports in summer, and for skating in winter. The college has had during the present year three hundred and four pupils. The condition of the school has been satisfactory in all respects, and notably has the system of co-education of the sexes, [illegible] from the first proved successful. Great as has been the usefulness of the institution in the past, a constantly enlarging sphere of beneficence will, without doubt, be filled during each successive year.

The present faculties are constituted as follows:

Faculty of Government.—Edward H. Magill, president; Anna W. Frost Capp, matron; Professor Eugene Paulin, Professor Arthur Beardsley, Professor William Hyde Appleton, Professor Susan J. Cunningham, Professor Samuel S. Green, Professor Joseph W. Teets, Assistant Professor Mary L. Austin, Assistant Professor Elizabeth C. Miller, Thomas S. Foulke, superintendent.

Faculty of Instruction.—Edward H. Magill, A.M., president; Joseph Leidy, M.D., LL.D., Professor of Natural History; Eugene Paulin, A.M., Professor of French and Latin, and of Mental and Moral Philosophy; Arthur Beardsley, C.E., Professor of Civil and Mechanical Engineering, and Librarian; William Hyde Appleton, A.M., Professor of Greek and German; Susan J. Cunningham, Professor of Mathematics; Joseph Thomas, M.D., LL.D., Professor of English Literature; Samuel S. Green, M.S., Professor of Physics and Chemistry; Joseph W. Teets, Professor of Elocution; Mary L. Austin, Assistant Professor of Latin; Elizabeth Clarke Miller, A.B., Assistant Professor of Botany; Frederick A. Wray, A.B., Assistant Professor of French; Charles O. Dunn, C.E., Assistant Professor of German; Eliza E. Osgood, Instructor in History; Ellen M. Griscom, Instructor in Free-hand Drawing; Amelia P. Butler, Instructor in Theory and Practice of Teaching; Olivia Rolham, Assistant in [illegible], and Instructor in Botany.

The board of managers consists of the following gentlemen and ladies: Term expires Twelfth month, 1884: Joseph Willets, Trenton, N. J.; Eli M. Lamb, Baltimore, Md.; Clement M. Biddle, Abigail M. Woodnutt, Anna M. Hunt, Philadelphia; Susan W. Lippincott, Cinnaminson, N. J.; Sarah H. Merritt, Brooklyn, L. I.; Herman Hoopes, Philadelphia. Term expires Twelfth month, 1885: John T. Willets, New York; Edward H. Ogden, Philadelphia; Daniel Underhill, Jericho, L. I.; Emmor Roberts, Fellowship, N. J.; Jane P. Downing, Philadelphia; Mary W. Cocks, Old Westbury, L. I.; Sarah H. Powell, New York; Edith B. Bentley, Sandy Spring, Md. Term expires Twelfth month, 1886: Isaac Stephens, Trenton, N. J.; James V. Watson, Philadelphia; Clement Biddle, Chad's Ford, Pa.; Martha G. McIlvain, Philadelphia; Sophia U. Willets, Manhasset, L. I.; Sallie M. Ogden, Edmund Webster, Emma McIlvain, Philadelphia. Term expires Twelfth month, 1887: John D. Hicks, Old Westbury, L. I.; Robert Willets, Flushing, L. I.; Joseph Wharton, Philadelphia; M. Fisher Longstreth, Sharon Hill, Delaware Co., Pa.; Mary Willets, Trenton, N. J.; Anna M. Ferris, Wilmington, Del.; Mary T. Longstreth, Sharon Hill, Delaware Co., Pa.; Lydia H. Hall, West Chester, Pa.

Two brothers of the Magill family, William and Alexander, came from the North of Ireland about the year 1725. From William was descended Jacob, the grandfather of Edward H. He married Rebecca Paxson, and had children,—Mary, Jonathan P., Susan, Sarah, and Charles. Jonathan P. was born in Solebury, Bucks Co., Pa., and during his active life was engaged in farming. He married Mary Watson, daughter of David and Rachel Watson, of Falls township, Bucks Co., Pa., whose ancestors came to this country from England with William Penn. Both husband and wife were earnest members of the Society of Friends, and well known for their anti-slavery proclivities. They were identified with the leaders of that movement, which received at their hands practical aid, their home having been one of the stations of the memorable Underground Railroad, and the safe abiding-place of many escaped and hunted slaves. Their children were Sarah (deceased), Edward H., Watson P., Rebecca (deceased), Catharine T. (wife of Henry C. Phillips), Rachel M. (wife of John S. Williams), and Matilda R. (wife of Charles S. Atkinson).

Edward H. was born Sept. 24, 1825, in Solebury, Bucks Co., and spent his youth until his fourteenth year at the home of his parents. He then became for two years a pupil of the Friends' school at Westtown, Chester Co., and filled the interval from that period until his twenty-fifth year in teaching. Entering the Freshman class of Yale College in 1850, he remained one year, and in 1851 became a student of Brown University, Providence, R. I., from which he received in 1852 the degree of A.B., and that of

Eng.d by A.H. Ritchie.

Edw. H. Magill

A M in 1855 He accepted, in 1852, the principalship of the classical department of the Providence High School, and acted in that capacity until 1859, when he was appointed sub-master of the Boston Latin School During his sub-mastership he published a French Grammar and a series of French Readers which have been widely used in the schools and colleges of this country In 1867, Mr Magill, having resigned his position in the Latin School, devoted a year to foreign travel In 1869 he was made principal of the Preparatory school of Swarthmore College, and two years later became president of the college, which office he still holds Mr Magill was, in 1852, married to Sarah W, daughter of Seneca Beans, of Lower Makefield, Bucks Co, Pa To this marriage were born children,—Helen, Eudora, Beatrice, Gertrude B, Francis G (deceased), and Marian Under the presidency of Mr Magill, Swarthmore College has enjoyed a high degree of prosperity Beginning chiefly as a preparatory school, the college department, which was gradually added, has increased in extent until it has become the rival in point of numbers of the preparatory department President Magill's career as an educator has been attended by signal success, evincing in a high degree, as he does, all those characteristics which the teacher should possess His own accurate scholarship has led him to require the same accuracy and thoroughness in his students To this trait of his character is combined unwearied patience with a seriousness and earnestness which have won for him the confidence of those under his instruction His chief work as an instructor was done in Providence and Boston At Swarthmore devolved upon him duties of another character, in which he has been equally successful Exercising a general oversight of both teachers and taught, the skill which he has shown in this difficult work, as well as in the management of a large body of students, is proof that he possesses in a high degree those qualities which combine to make a successful college president

Mills on Crum Creek—Wallingford Mills.—The first mention of the name of Lewis in Springfield in connection with mills occurs in the assessment-roll of 1779, when John Lewis was assessed on a grist-mill In 1788 a saw-mill was added, and from that time until 1817 he appears as the owner of these mills In 1811, John Lewis, Jr, was returned as the owner of a paper-mill, and in 1817, George Lewis was connected with him in the business In 1835 the grist-mill was changed into a cotton-factory and rented to James Ogden, who continued in the business for a short time, when he was succeeded by John Reese and Mordecai Lewis, sons of George Lewis, who operated the mill, and also changed the old Wallingford paper-mill into a cotton-factory On Sunday, Jan 11, 1851, two children, daughters of Thomas Davis, aged respectively ten and eight years, were sliding on the ice on the dam, when the eldest venturing out too far, the ice broke, the youngest, going to her assistance, got into the water, and both were drowned J. Reese Lewis, in endeavoring to save the children, very nearly lost his own life, and from the effect of the exposure on that occasion he never recovered A few years afterwards J Reese Lewis died, and the mills were operated by Mordecai Lewis until his death, on Oct 14, 1870, since which time the business has been conducted by his sons, Isaac, Albert, and Reese Lewis

The name Wallingford was given a hundred years ago to the locality by Thomas Allen, who came from the like place in the county of Berks Near that place, in the latter part of the last century, Sarah Allen had license for a public-house, which disappeared from the list of inns eighty years ago An advertisement which was published in the *Delaware County Republican* for Sept 1, 1837, furnishes some interesting historical data connected with the Allen family The advertisement was as follows

"Notice—To the children of Thomas Allen, formerly of Tileburst and Wallingford, in the County of Berks, in England, and afterwards of Springfield, in the county of Delaware, in the State of Pennsylvania, in North America, deceased

"Pursuant to a decree of the High Court of Chancery in England, made in a cause, '*Bottomley vs Fisher*,' any person or persons claiming to be the child or children of the said Thomas Allen, who were living at his decease (which took place in or about the month of March, 1794), or the legal personal representative, or representatives, of any such deceased child or children, are, by their solicitors or agents, forthwith to come on before Sir Griffin Williamson, Knight, one of the Masters of the said court, at his Chambers, in Southampton Buildings, Chancery Lane, London, on or before the 1st day of November next, to establish and make out their claim to a Legacy under the will of Elizabeth Pentycross, widow of Thomas Pentycross, formerly Rector of Saint Mary the More, in Wallingford, aforesaid, or in default thereof they will be *peremptorily* excluded the benefits of the said devise

'The said Thomas Allen was a dissenter from the doctrines of the Church of England, and formerly lived at Tileburst, and afterwards at Wallingford, aforesaid, and some time in the year 1793 emigrated to Springfield, in the county of Delaware, in the State of Pennsylvania, where he died on or about the month of March, 1794, leaving, it is believed, five children surviving him, viz Abijah Allen, Daniel Allen, Elizabeth Pentycross Allen, Sarah Allen, and Aaron Allen"

Holtz Mill—On Lownes Run, a small stream that empties into Crum Creek, and on the Springfield road, in the year 1779 George Lownes was operating a blade-mill where small cutlery was manufactured In 1799 Curtis Lownes owned the above property and also a stone tilt-mill The blade-mill was discontinued before 1807, and the tilt-mill was operated until after 1812 About 1816 it was changed to a carding-mill, and was at that time seventeen feet by twenty-six feet and three stories in height It passed soon after to George Bolton Lownes, who operated it until 1827, when Samuel Riddle, now of Glen Riddle, rented the mill and continued there two years, when he removed to Chester Creek and built the Parkmount Mills. The stream at this place is very small, and while Mr. Riddle was there, on one occasion, the water became so low that the machinery stopped Desiring to know the cause of this sudden decrease of power, he found that Lownes had turned a drove of steers into the lot where the dam was, and the thirsty animals had drank almost all the water

The mill at a later period was changed to a cotton-factory, and in 1835 was in possession of the heirs of George B Lownes The factory then contained one picker, two carding-engines, one drawing-frame, one ellipse speeder, seven hundred spindles, two mules of two hundred and twenty-eight spindles each, and other machinery It was sold at public vendue by the executors of his estate May 5, 1835 In 1849 and subsequent to that year Edward Lane & Co, of Philadelphia, manufactured carriages at this location, and subsequently —— Pilkerton conducted a weaving-mill there for a few years The mill having been destroyed by fire the real estate was conveyed to Thomas and Oliver Holt, who erected a large stone factory three stories in height In 1853 an addition was built to the mill, which was well filled with machinery, and employment was given to nearly fifty persons Oliver Holt having retired from the firm, the business was continued by Thomas Holt until May 18, 1882, when the mill was again destroyed by fire Subsequently to this disaster Thomas Holt died, and the real estate is now owned by his estate

Gibbons' Mill—On Lownes or Whiskey Run, below the old Lownes Mill, Joseph Gibbons erected on his farm in 1832, a cotton-factory forty-five by sixty feet, three stories in height It was leased to Simeon Lord and William Faulkner, who operated it until 1847, when Lord removed to Avondale The factory was then rented for a short time to Thomas and Oliver Holtz, subsequently to George Wood and Joseph Barker, the last being in charge in December, 1865, when the mill was destroyed by fire

Fell's Mills—The land on which is the mill now known by the above name is on Crum Creek and the Providence road The land was originally taken up by Bartholomew Coppock His daughter married William Fell, and in 1766 the latter was assessed as half-owner of a saw-mill The other half-interest was owned by William Paist, and in 1799, Edward Fell, a nephew of William, was in possession of the interest of his uncle, and also conducted a "pot-house" (pottery) on the farm now owned by Warren Lawrence William Marshall was the potter On the 12th of December, 1805, the property was purchased by Samuel Pancoast, who continued to operate the saw-mill, and between 1815 and 1817 erected a grist-mill, these were operated until March 15, 1828, when four acres of land, the grist- and saw-mill were sold to William Beatty, of Lower Providence, who erected on the property a blade-mill and forge, and commenced the manufacture of edge-tools At a subsequent date he associated in the partnership his son, John C. Beatty In 1843 the mill was washed away by the flood of August in that year, but was rebuilt In 1850, William P Beatty and Samuel Ogden bought the interest of John C Beatty, and continued the business for some years, when William Beatty sold to the Ogden Brothers, who continued the business there for a short time, when they conveyed the property to J. Howard Lewis, who now owns it The grist-mill and a bobbin-turning shop are at present conducted at "Beatty's Hollow"

Keystone Spinning-Mills—In 1766, Samuel Levis was assessed in Springfield, on a grist-mill, which was located at the present Heyville, on Darby Creek On the assessment-roll of 1790 this grist-mill does not appear In 1799, Thomas Levis owned a saw-mill, and John Levis and Thomas Levis, Jr, were each assessed on a half-interest in a paper-mill, which was owned by Thomas Levis, Sr Shortly after this date the saw-mill was operated by Samuel Levis The mills were conducted under his management until 1825, when, on April 15th in that year, they were purchased by Oborn Levis, and were placed in charge of Stephen Pancoast It was then a two-vat paper-mill, and manufactured about thirty-three reams of medium, and forty-eight reams of printing demy paper per week Twenty-three hands were employed, and dwellings for eight families had been built The mill continued under the management of Stephen Pancoast until 1838, when they were rented to Moses Hey, of Haddington, by whom they were changed to woolen-mills In 1845, Hey purchased the property, and shortly after erected what are now known as Mills Nos 2 and 3, together with other buildings On April 1, 1857, Moses Hey retired from active business, his son, Emanuel Hey, succeeded him, and now operates the factories The old mill was rebuilt in 1874, and is now used for storage purposes Mill No 2 contains six sets of cords, one hundred looms, and two thousand spindles, No. 3 has six cords and two thousand spindles At these mills yarns are manufactured The mills have a capacity for manufacturing five hundred thousand pounds of wool and one hundred thousand pounds of cotton into yarns annually

Other Mills—In 1766, Job Dicks owned a saw-mill in Springfield, and Elisha Jones had a grist mill. They were not in operation after 1780, having been abandoned The location of these mills has not been ascertained John Heacock also owned a grist-mill between 1780 and 1799, after which date it fell into disuse

Oakdale.—The settlement now known as Oakdale dates back sixty years, when, in 1824, Jonathan and Morris Roberts established a store at that locality. They were succeeded in the business by Samuel Roberts, Samuel Hamson, William and John Ogden, Richard Ogden, and F Hayden, who has the present store A post-office was established at this place many years ago F Hayden is the present postmaster. Oakdale school-house and Lownes Church are in the vicinity

Morton—The thriving village, located on the Philadelphia and West Chester Railroad, which was named Morton, in honor of John Morton, the signer of the Declaration of Independence, has a history of about

RESIDENCE OF THE LATE JOSEPH GIBBONS,

eighteen years, since it was first projected. At present it has a number of handsome houses, a hotel, public hall, stores, and newspaper. Among the conspicuous residences is that of J. H. Irwin, the inventor of the tubular lantern, and the system of controlling air-currents for lamps, stoves, and furnaces, which latter discovery was evolved from his prior invention of the tubular lantern. Mr. Irwin is a native of Trenton, N. J., and came to Morton in 1871, where he purchased a tract of twenty acres of John Jenkins, and erected thereon an experimental laboratory, in which is an engine of seventy horse-power. Eight men are employed in the laboratory. Mr. Irwin invented, in 1877, the telephone transmitter, which is a valuable patent, now in constant use.

Kedron Methodist Episcopal Church.—This religious body was organized in 1859, with about forty-five members. Meetings were first held in the drawing-room of John S. Morton's mansion, later were held in a wind-mill beyond the mansion, and for a time in a building used as a chapel on the church lot, until the church building was finished. The lot for the church was donated by Thomas T. Tasker. The corner-stone of the present edifice was laid Sept. 6, 1860. It was completed in the summer of 1862, and dedicated June 19th in that year. The services were conducted by Bishop Levi Scott. The pastors who have had charge of the church are as follows: Revs. William Dalrymple, A. Howard, William W. McMichael, John Shields, William Frees, J. C. Wood, A. C. Hood, Garbert Reed, James A. Blacklidge, William W. McMichael, Robert McKay, and the present pastor, Rev. C. Edgar Adamson. The church has a membership of fifty, and a Sunday-school of eighty pupils, of which George Smith is superintendent.

Church of the Atonement.—A few persons of the Protestant Episcopal communion, about 1876, held services in the house of Miss Sue Pearce, and later in a cottage of J. H. Irwin. In 1880 the present chapel was erected (at a cost of four thousand dollars) on a lot donated by J. H. Irwin. The mission is under the care of Christ Church, Media.

The Morton Chronicle.—The first number of this newspaper was issued on June 17, 1880. Its publication was begun in a one-story building, ten by twelve feet, which had formerly been used by the late Sketchley Morton as a coal-office. In these limited quarters the publisher labored for two years, often disheartened at the difficulties that encountered the new enterprise, but working patiently until the little journal was established upon a paying basis. On Friday, Oct. 6, 1882, more commodious quarters were obtained in the new drug-store building of W. E. Dickeson, near Morton Station, four rooms being rented for the office, composition-room, etc. The *Chronicle* has now a circulation of nearly eight hundred copies, and connected with the paper is a well-fitted job-office. The *Morton Chronicle* is owned and edited by E. W. Smith, a practical printer.

The Birthplace of Benjamin West.—A short distance north of the railroad station, and about the same distance from Swarthmore College, is the house in which Benjamin West was born. Years ago a decayed building was standing near the present house, which some of the wiseacres in the neighborhood and elsewhere maintained was the dwelling (if ever it was a dwelling) wherein West was born, Oct. 10, 1738. The fact that this old ruin has now gone in a large degree has caused the assertion to be less frequently made, indeed it is rarely now heard, but inasmuch as it has within recent years been mentioned in a historical sketch of Benjamin West, it is proper that it should not pass unnoticed in a history of Delaware County. Certain it is that West would know where he was born, when it was from this farm in Springfield, a well-grown lad, that he went to seek and obtain fortune and renown. Thomas Sully, the eminent artist, frequently related that in 1810, when he, in London, took final leave of his celebrated preceptor, West, then an aged man, made a special request of his young countryman that on his return to America he, Sully, should visit[1] the old homestead in Spring-

[1] A correspondent of the *Delaware County Republican*, signing his article "Oakdale," in 1872, when the recent death of Thomas Sully had called forth recollections of his career, in alluding to that artist's visit to Springfield, says,—

"I have somewhere seen it stated, that after the death of West, this painting was placed in the Royal Academy of Fine Arts, in London, where it probably still remains.

"The following—copied from my scrap-book—are part of some lines in reference to this event, written several years ago by Rev. Edward C. Jones, then of West Philadelphia:

"In the distance Memory paints
Farm and homestead, rill and tree,
And the cattle as they passed
With their driver o'er the lea;

"Blush of morn, and purple pomp
Of the fast-descending sun,
Hearthstone treat of nuts and cake,
When the harvesting was done;

"First-day meetings, when we sat
In our worship's solemn hush,—
Such the groupings of the past
To my aged heart which rush.

"I would have thee sketch the spot,
With the limner's wondrous skill;
Ocean's billows roll between,
But its outline haunts me still.

"Thou from me hast caught the fire
Which ideal Beauty fans,
Thine is now the Artist's thrill,
As sublimity he scans.

"Oh! upon the canvas throw
All the mellowing hues which rest
On that calm and rural spot,
Which of earth I love the best.

"Warm that canvas, till it seems
Instinct with my boyhood's hearth,
Till in thought I seem to breathe
Air the balmiest of the earth.

"For the pencil's trophies bright,
Proofs of Art's creative power,
Only freshen to my heart
Images of childhood's hour."

field, there make drawing of the house and other objects he mentioned, and transmit them to West at London. This Sully did.

The room in which West was born was a triangular-shaped apartment on the first floor, and located in the southwest corner of the building. The infant, who was in after-life to achieve undying fame, was the tenth and youngest son of John and Sarah Pearson West. His biographer, Galt, has succeeded in gathering about the narrative of West's life more mythical incidents than any book purporting to be historical published during the present century. Hence, as a work of authority, it has but little weight. There is a tradition that a picture from the youthful pencil of West could be seen on the breast of the chimney in one of the attics of the old house, but the story is as apocryphal as the oft-told incident of the distinguished artist at seven years drawing in ink the portrait of the child whom he was instructed to watch in the cradle. The latter story, as narrated, is that in June, 1745, one of West's married sisters, accompanied by her baby daughter, came to spend a few days at her father's house. When the child was asleep in the cradle, Mrs. West invited her daughter to gather a few flowers in the garden, and instructed Benjamin to watch the child, giving him a fan to keep the flies from the slumbering infant. As the lad sat by his charge the baby smiled in her sleep, and the future artist was so impressed with the beauty of the smile that he determined to give his impulse expression by drawing its portrait. With red and black ink and quill pens, he worked at his first picture. While thus employed his mother and sister returned, and he endeavored to conceal the paper, but so clumsy was his effort to do so that his mother required him to show her the paper, which he reluctantly did. The matron looked at the paper, and with evident pleasure exclaimed, "I declare, he has made a likeness of little Sally!" and, stooping, she kissed the young artist with much fondness. However, it did not occur to any of the family to provide him with better materials, and his first colors were given him by some Indians, who, being amused at his pictures of birds and flowers, taught him to prepare the red and yellow colors with which they painted their ornaments. Subsequently his mother added a piece of indigo, and thus he became possessed of three of the primary colors. His brushes he supplied by cutting fur from the tail of the domestic cat, until that appendage of the animal became so conspicuous that his father called the attention of his wife to it as the effect of disease. Benjamin made a full confession of the cause, and his father mentioning the incident to Mr. Pennington, a merchant of Philadelphia, the latter sent the lad some canvas and six engravings by Grevling. Young West rose the next morning with the sun, carried his box to the garret, and for several successive days thus devoted himself to painting. The schoolmaster at length called to learn the cause of his absence, and his mother, remembering that Benjamin had gone up-stairs every morning, without replying to the master, hastened to the garret, and there found the lad employed in painting. The mother kissed him after she had inspected his work, and that kiss, West declared, made him a painter. The pictures, for there were two, then painted by the untutored lad of fourteen (now owned by Mrs. David Jones, of West Chester), were seen by Dr. Jonathan Morris and Anthony Wayne, and the lad, through their influence, became acquainted with Franklin and other leading men in Philadelphia. At 1760, aided by friends in Philadelphia, he was enabled to go to Rome. In 1763 he returned to America, coming home by the way of England, and shortly after he

HOUSE IN WHICH BENJAMIN WEST WAS BORN.
[Drawn by John Sartain in 1837.]

arrived home he met his future wife. This romantic incident in his life is thus told by an accomplished author:

"About the middle of the [eighteenth] century young West had an obscure lodging in Strawberry Alley, and painted portraits at a guinea a head,—painted signs, too, for a few shillings, when portraits and guineas were not to be had,—'The Cask of Beer,' or 'The Jolly Fiddlers.' A picture of St. Ignatius, after Murillo, having been captured on a Spanish brigantine by the 'Britannia,' fell into the possession of Governor Hamilton at Bush Hill. West copied it, and humored some of his portly patrons by painting them in the attitude of the saint. Mad Anthony Wayne, then a handsome, gallant, showily-dressed young fellow, was often seen on the streets with the mild-mannered, apple-cheeked Quaker lad. He brought as many of his fashionable friends as he could persuade to sit for their portraits to the hungry young artist, and it is hinted not only made a military man of him, but introduced him to charming Miss Betty Shewell, with whom West, in his orderly, proper way, fell in love. Miss Shewell's brother, however, being a man with an income, had no mind that his pretty sister should marry a man who had none, and whose occupation was held to be not half so genteel as that of a tailor. He therefore locked Miss Betty up in her room, just about the time that one of the Allens, who was sending a ship laden with grain to the starving Italians, offered Benjamin a passage on her to Leghorn. But love laughed at locksmiths then as now. The Quaker Romeo and his Juliet saw each other, though one was in the garden and the other in the window, and vowed eternal faith. West promised to win fame and money, and his sweetheart promised to come to him to the ends of the earth as soon as he should send her word he had enough of the latter necessary to keep them from starvation. The remainder of the story Bishop White told to Dr. Swift, of Easton, Pa. West, as we all know, succeeded rapidly in winning both the fame and the money, and as soon as he was established first favorite at Hampton Court, he sent to Miss Shewell to claim her part of the promise. Her brother was still inexorable, and did not consider a painter, though he were George's own, a fit match for the daughter of a blue-blooded Philadelphia family. He locked Miss Betty up again in her chamber. The story went out through the town. Popular sympathy was with the lovers; Stephen Shewell was denounced as a tyrant, and many glances of pity and encouragement were cast at the high-latticed window behind which was the fair captive maiden. The ship was in the harbor ready to sail in which West had arranged that his bride should come to him, under the escort of his father. The day arrived for her departure. At this crisis Dr. Franklin appeared as the good angel, and proved himself quite as competent to direct a love-affair as the lightning or the draught in a stove. With Bishop White, then a lad of eighteen, and Francis Hopkinson, he went to the ship's captain and arranged with him to delay starting until night, but to be ready to weigh anchor at a moment's warning. Old Mr. West was then taken on board, and at midnight Franklin, young White, and Hopkinson repaired to Stephen Shewell's house, fastened a rope-ladder to Miss Betty's window, held it while she descended, and conducted her safely to the ship, which set sail as soon as she was on board. The lovers were married when she landed, and lived long and happily together. But Stephen Shewell never forgave his sister, nor did she or her husband ever return to this country.

"The story is romantic enough for fiction, but bears every weight of authority. Dr. Swift states that when he rallied the venerable bishop on his part as knight-errant to this modern Dolorida, he replied that he had done right, adding with warmth, that 'if it were to do over again, I should act in precisely the same way. God meant them to come together.'"[1]

The subsequent career of Benjamin West, his rapid achievement of fame and fortune in Great Britain, and his death on Friday, March 10, 1820, at the advanced age of eighty-two, occupying at the time the position of president of the Royal Academy, is matter of general history and need not be at large alluded to here. It is proper, however, that the fact that in 1874 the upper part of the West house was injured by fire, but the room in which Benjamin was born was untouched by the flames, should be mentioned in this work. The old structure was renovated as when first constructed, and is now occupied as residences by two of the professors of Swarthmore College.

[1] Rebecca Harding Davis, in *Harper's Magazine* for April, 1876.

Pennsdale Farm.—On the Delaware County turnpike, directly opposite Lownes' Free Church, is the Pennsdale farm, which, for nearly a century, has been owned by men who have been prominent in the history of the State and nation. Prior to 1800 the farm was owned by John Thomson, a noted engineer, who, when a young man, engaged in the service of the "Holland Land Company," an organization which controlled much of the land in Northwestern Pennsylvania. After several years, having completed the duties required of him, he determined to make his return to his home useful in aiding the development of that section of the county. He to that end, with one assistant, with no other tools than were ordinarily carried with an engineering expedition, at Presque Isle (now Erie), built a small schooner, in which he and his assistant made the journey to Philadelphia. This was the first vessel that ever passed from Lake Erie to New York and Philadelphia. The "White Fish" was taken to Independence Square, where it remained until it decayed.

The following account of the voyage of the "White Fish" is given in Dunlap & Claypole's *American Daily Advertiser* of Nov. 12, 1795, under the heading "Philadelphia News":

"On Tuesday last arrived here, after a passage of seven weeks, the schooner 'White Fish,' built last summer at Presque Isle, on Lake Erie. The tediousness of the voyage was owing to the inclemency of the weather. She is only seventeen and a half feet keel and five feet seven inches beam. This small vessel was built and navigated by two young men, citizens of the United States, born in the vicinity of this city. They had neither chart or compass. Her departure was from Presque Isle, along Lake Erie to Falls of Niagara, one hundred and ten miles, thence by land to the landing below the Falls of Niagara ten miles, then to the garrison of Niagara seven miles, then along the south coast of Lake Ontario to the river Oswego one hundred and forty miles, thence up the river Oswego to the Falls twenty miles, then by land round the Falls one mile, thence up the same river to Three Rivers Point twelve miles, thence up the straits leading to the Oneida Lake nineteen miles, thence through the Oneida Lake twenty-eight miles, thence up Wood Creek thirty miles to the landing between Wood Creek and the Mohawk River, thence by land passing Fort Schuyler, formerly Fort Stanwix, one mile into the Mohawk River, then down the Mohawk River sixty miles to the Little Falls, thence round the Falls by land one mile to the landing, thence down the same river sixty miles to Schenectady, thence by land sixteen miles to Albany, thence down the river Hudson one hundred and seventy miles to the city of New York, thence by sea one hundred and fifty miles to the Capes of Delaware River, thence up the Delaware to this city one hundred and twenty miles, making in all nine hundred and forty-seven miles.

"The design of this voyage (the only one ever attempted in the same way) was a disinterested experiment to prove some of the great advantages which may in future be derived to the United States from a speedy settlement in and about the new Town of Erie, in this State. The 'White Fish' (so named from a luxurious fish, in Ichthyology, peculiar to the lakes), cast anchor opposite Market Street wharf, and gave the city a Federal salute of fifteen rounds from a Blunderbuss, which was returned by three hearty cheers from a multitude of citizens, who crowded the wharves and vessels in this port to receive them, for accomplishing this hitherto unexperienced navigation. The two gentlemen certainly deserve well of their country.

"The writer, who is well known to the printers, was present at the laying of the keel, the building, launching, and naming of the vessel, and has thought it his duty to make it public, in justice to the merits of the enterprising adventurers."

John Thomson, after his return to his native county, was the leading spirit in the building of the Philadelphia, Brandywine and New London turnpike, which road, now known as the Delaware County turnpike, passes the Pennsdale farm. This company was incorporated by act of Assembly March 24, 1808. The letters patent were issued Sept. 26th of the same year. The road was forty miles long, and during 1810 nine miles were constructed, at a cost of three thousand five hundred dollars per mile. The road was twenty-one feet wide, and was laid to the depth of fifteen inches in broken stone. John Thomson built the bridge on this turnpike, which spans the stream at Stony Creek, and in the wall on the north side of the road is a stone bearing this inscription: "Built Gratis by John Thomson, for the Philadelphia, Brandywine and New London Turnpike Company, 1811." In 1815, when the Legislature authorized the State road to be laid from the Market Street bridge, Philadelphia, to McCall's Ferry on the Susquehanna River, John Thomson was one of the commissioners, and the chief engineer under whose direction the road was surveyed. In 1809 he laid and constructed the Leiper Railroad in Ridley, an account of which road will be found in the history of that township, and was employed as civil engineer in the building of the Delaware and Chesapeake Canal. John Thomson died in 1842. Pennsdale farm had passed to the ownership of Isaac Newton, the first commissioner of agriculture, who was appointed to the office by President Taylor when that bureau was first created by act of Congress, and continued by every administration as its chief executive until his death. The property was subsequently purchased by J. Edgar Thomson. The latter, a son of John Thomson, was born on the Pennsdale farm, Feb. 10, 1808. The son, after the requisite preparation received from his father, commenced his professional career, in 1827, in the engineer corps employed upon the original surveys of the Philadelphia and Columbia Railroad, having received his appointment from the secretary of the Board of Canal Commissioners of Pennsylvania. He continued in this service until 1830, when, the State failing to make the necessary appropriations for the continuance of the construction of the road, he entered the service of the Camden and Amboy Railroad Company as principal assistant engineer of the Eastern Division. After leaving their service he visited Europe to examine the public works of that continent, and shortly after his return, in 1832, was appointed chief engineer of the Georgia Railroad, extending from Augusta to Atlanta, in that State, with a branch to Athens, in all two hundred and thirteen miles of railway,—the longest amount of railway at that time under the control of one company in the United States. He continued in that service, as chief engineer and general manager, until his unsolicited election to the position of chief engineer of the Pennsylvania Railroad.

Mr. Thomson entered upon his duties as chief engineer of the road in the early part of 1847. The directors say, in their first annual report, that "in the selection of a chief engineer the board was fortunate in obtaining the services of Mr. John Edgar Thomson, a gentleman of enlarged professional experience and sound judgment, who had obtained a well-earned reputation upon the Georgia road, and in whom the board place great confidence."

On the 2d of February, 1852, Mr. Thomson was elected president of the company, and it was in that capacity he saw completed many important enterprises which he had inaugurated as chief engineer. He was continued in the position, without interruption, up to the time of his death, devoting to the great enterprise twenty-seven years of his life, and bestowing upon it an amount of care and attention never given by any other American to a similar work.

His reputation was established South as well as North, and he confessedly stood at the head of his profession. He did more than any one man who ever lived to establish, create, and perfect the railway system of the American continent.

Occupying the important business position he did, it was natural that Mr. Thomson's influence should be sought for many enterprises. So far as these were for the general good, he cheerfully promoted them. One of his favorite objects was the thorough development of the mineral resources of Pennsylvania, in the value of which he had unlimited faith. Every coal and iron field was thoroughly understood and appreciated by him; and if the great corporation over which he presided could facilitate its development, the work was promptly done. The American Steamship Company of Philadelphia was largely indebted to his sagacity and unwavering interest in the business of the city for its existence. As a member of the Park Commission of Philadelphia, he gained the esteem of his associates, who, after his decease, placed on record a tribute to his high character as an engineer, a citizen, and a gentleman of many accomplishments.

Burdened as he was by such a multitude of duties, and of so arduous and complex a character, it is not surprising that the strain of such labor, continued for nearly half a century, brought his life to a close before he had numbered the threescore and ten years allotted to mankind. While his intellectual faculties remained unclouded, and his strong will evinced no signs of relaxing, yet the human machinery that for near fifty years they had propelled in the wearing grooves of railroad life faltered in its work, and, on the 27th of May, 1874, death came to release him from the turmoil and exactions which had so long harassed him.

Noticeable traits of Mr. Thomson's character were

J. Edgar Thomson

[illegible] the building, breathing, and moving. [illegible] the [illegible] adventurers."

John Thomson, after his return to his native county, was the leading spirit in the building of the Philadelphia, Brandywine and New London turnpike, which road, now known as the Delaware County turnpike, passes the Pennsdale farm. This company was incorporated by act of Assembly March 24, 1808. The letters patent were issued Sept. 28th of the same year. The road was forty miles long, and during 1810 nine miles were constructed, at a cost of three thousand five hundred dollars per mile. The road was twenty-one feet wide, and was laid to the depth of fifteen inches in broken stone. John Thomson built the bridge on this turnpike, which spans the stream at Stony Creek, and in the wall on the north side of the road is a stone bearing this inscription: "Built Gratis by John Thomson, for the Philadelphia, Brandywine and New London Turnpike Company, 1811." In 1815, when the Legislature authorized the State road to be laid from the Market Street bridge, Philadelphia, to McCall's Ferry on the Susquehanna River, John Thomson was one of the commissioners, and the chief engineer under whose direction the road was surveyed. In 1809 he laid and constructed the Leiper Railroad in Ridley, an account of which road will be found in the history of that township, and was employed as civil engineer in the building of the Delaware and Chesapeake Canal. John Thomson died in 1842. Pennsdale farm had passed in the ownership of Isaac Newton, the first commissioner of agriculture, who was appointed to the office by President Taylor when that bureau was first created by act of Congress, and continued by every administration as its chief executive until his death. The property was subsequently purchased by J. Edgar Thomson. The latter, a son of John Thomson, was born on the Pennsdale farm, Feb. 10, 1808. The son, after the requisite preparation received from his father, commenced his professional career, in 1827, in the engineer corps employed upon the original surveys of the Philadelphia and Columbia Railroad, having received his appointment from the secretary of the Board of Canal Commissioners of Pennsylvania. He continued in this service until 1830, when, the State failing to make the necessary appropriations for the continuance of the construction of the road, he entered the service of the Camden and Amboy Railroad Company as principal assistant engineer of the Eastern Division. After leaving their service he visited Europe to examine the public works of that continent, and shortly after his return, in 1832, was appointed chief engineer of the Georgia Railroad, extending from Augusta to Atlanta, in that State, with a branch to Athens, in all two hundred and thirteen miles of railway,—the longest amount of railway at that time under the control of one company in the United States. He continued in that service as chief engineer and general manager, until his unsolicited election to the position of chief engineer of the Pennsylvania Railroad.

Mr. Thomson entered upon his duties as chief engineer of the road in the early part of 1847. The directors say, in their first annual report, that "in the selection of a chief engineer the board was fortunate in obtaining the services of Mr. John Edgar Thomson, a gentleman of enlarged professional experience and sound judgment, who had obtained a well-earned reputation upon the Georgia road, and in whom the board place great confidence."

On the 3d of February, 1852, Mr. Thomson was elected president of the company, and it was in that capacity he saw completed many important enterprises which he had inaugurated as chief engineer. He was continued in the position, without interruption, up to the time of his death, devoting to the great enterprise twenty-seven years of his life, and bestowing upon it an amount of care and attention never given by any other American to a similar work.

His reputation was established South as well as North, and he confessedly stood at the head of his profession. He did more than any one man who ever lived to establish, create, and perfect the railway system of the American continent.

Occupying the important business position he did, it was natural that Mr. Thomson's influence should be sought for many enterprises. So far as these were for the general good, he cheerfully promoted them. One of his favorite objects was the thorough development of the mineral resources of Pennsylvania, in the value of which he had unlimited faith. Every coal and iron field was thoroughly understood and appreciated by him; and if the great corporation over which he presided could facilitate its development, the work was promptly done. The American Steamship Company of Philadelphia was largely indebted to his sagacity and unwavering interest in the business of the city for its existence. As a member of the Park Commission of Philadelphia, he gained the esteem of his associates, who, after his decease, placed on record a tribute to his high character as an engineer, a citizen, and a gentleman of many accomplishments.

Burdened as he was by such a multitude of duties, and of so arduous and complex a character, it is not surprising that the strain of such labor, continued for nearly half a century, brought his life to a close before he had numbered the threescore and ten years allotted to mankind. While his intellectual faculties remained unclouded, and his strong will evinced no signs of relaxing, yet the human machinery that for near fifty years they had propelled in the wearing grooves of railroad life faltered in its work, and, on the 27th of May, 1874, death came to release him from the turmoil and exactions which had so long harassed him.

Noticeable traits of Mr. Thomson's character were

Engraved by Samuel Sartain, Phil^a

J. Edgar Thomson

reticence and taciturnity Devoting all his life and his great natural abilities to the cultivation of one set of ideas, his accumulation of professional information was enormous This vast knowledge made him exceedingly cautious and careful,—conservative in his ideas, and generally slow to execute But when his conclusions were reached, and the emergency required it, he became grandly enterprising, and permitted no obstacle to stand in the way of success His thoughts and opinions were rarely made known, while he displayed infinite patience in listening to the views, desires, hopes, fears, and plans of others Actions spoke for him, not words When convinced, he knew no hesitancy or doubt His conception of the future of American railroads seems now almost supernatural For twenty years he marked out and reiterated in his annual reports the plan of the Pennsylvania Railroad Company, and he never deviated from that plan To such a man system was everything, and there can be no question that much of the success attending the Pennsylvania Railroad was owing to the almost military rigidity with which its workings were arranged and managed under his inspiration He had that great faculty of a general,—a good judgment of character and capabilities In this he was rarely mistaken, and, his confidence once placed, he was loyal to its recipients, never abandoning or failing to sustain them This friendship was undemonstrative except in acts He had few intimate associates outside of his own family, and was utterly indifferent to popular applause His affections seemed centred in the great corporation he controlled, and whatever conduced to the success of that, present or remote, was the thing to be done,—the end to be attained

The peculiar bent of his mind is illustrated by the fact that the larger portion of his fortune was devised for the foundation of an institution for the benefit of a class of people connected with the railways he had been instrumental in creating This charity, which was opened Dec 4, 1882, is called St John's Orphanage It has been started in two houses, Nos 1720 and 1722 Rittenhouse Street, and in a modest way is doing active good It is open to receive the daughters of employés who have died in the service,—first, of the Pennsylvania Railroad, secondly, of the Georgia and Atlantic Railroad, and then of any railroad in the United States The girls are taken from the age of six to ten, given free of charge a home in the orphanage and a plain education, being taught household work and sewing until they are sixteen, when they will be put out to service or taught a trade It is intended to open a boarding-house for those who have left the orphanage, that the girls may have protection while they are learning to support themselves After his death various public bodies united in posthumous tributes to his sagacity and enterprise, leaving no room for doubt as to the respect and esteem his quiet, unobtrusive services had gained in the community where so many years of his laborious life were passed

Licensed Houses —The first petition of record for keeping a public-house in Springfield was presented to the court by Samuel Ogden, Sixth month (August) 29, 1727, in which he states "that have lately purchased a settlement, a place heretofore authorized by the Governor's License to keep Public Entertainment and Retailing of Liquors," he desired the same privilege as had been granted to his predecessor

From this document it clearly appears that Ogden was not the first publican in the township After this date I lose all further track of both Ogden and his tavern until August court, 1729 Joshua Thomson petitioned for license, stating that living "on a very public road, about half a quarter of a mile from a house which was licensed for a several years, but vacant for considerable time past," and is "4 or 5 miles from any public-house," which application met the approval of the justices This abandoned inn was doubtless the house for which Ogden had had license in 1727 Yearly thereafter Joshua Thomson's name appears on the clerk's list until 1748, when we hear of his intentions to abandon the occupation This house appears to have been located on the present Delaware County turnpike

Blue Ball Inn —The story of this ancient hostelry can be traced far back in our colonial history Under date of Aug 31, 1743, Mordecai Taylor presented his petition, in which he informed the court that he is located on the "great road from Darby to Springfield, and so into Conestoga Road" "No tavern," he states, "within four miles," and "sometimes twenty or thirty waggons passing in a Day" Although his petition was signed by Abraham Lincoln and eighteen other persons, his request was refused, inasmuch as at the same court John West, father of Benjamin West, who had presented his petition, setting forth that he had "Rented a Comoudyas house and all other the conveenances there and to belonging for a house of Entertainment on the Roade Leading from Darby To Springfield & from thence to Conistogo, which is of late much frequented by the Duch waggons to the number of 40 or 50 in a Day," was granted license He was recommended by Richard and George Maris, Samuel Levis, John Davis, John Hall, John Maris, Robert Taylor, Robert Pearson, Quantia Moore, James Bartram, Richard Iverson, and Jonathan Maris

The following year, Aug 28, 1744, West having been granted license for a tavern in Newtown, Mordecai Taylor again presented himself at the November court with a petition setting forth that "Living on the public Road Leading from the Great Valley to Philadelphia [the Springfield road], and there being Never a publick House within five miles either way on said road,"—between Newtown and Darby,—he asked that he be accorded license, which was granted to him, and he continued at that place until 1764, when his name disappears, and Ann Taylor was granted the license for that year In 1765, Jesse

Maris was the landlord, and continued yearly thereat until 1769, when Jesse Maris having died, the license was given to John Maris until 1774 In 1775, Thomas Moore had the privilege of keeping the public house there, and the following year Michael Stadleman took his place, while in 1779 Edward Horne was substituted in the latter's stead In 1785, Matthias Tyson had the license, and was followed the next year by Rodger Stayner, and in 1787 by Charles Sankey, who continued annually to receive the favor of the court until and including the year 1789

In 1790, immediately after the creation of Delaware County, Charles Sankey kept the tavern in Springfield, followed, in 1793, by John Wright

In 1797, Isaac Cochran received license for the inn of that name In 1803 a remonstrance was lodged against the continuance of the house, but it appears not to have received much consideration, for in 1806, when Frederick James made application for the license at the house, although he had twice before (in 1804 and 1805) been recommended to the Governor for license, his petition was met with a remonstrance, calling attention to the fact that a like paper "was put into the hands of the clerk of the court in order to lay before the court in the 2d mo, 1803" That as the license is continued, "and as we—the remonstrants—have not been informed that the former remonstrance ever came before the court," they attached a copy of the paper alluded to The old remonstrance, thus resurrected after slumbering three years, set forth that the signers "apprehend there is very little occasion for the inn," that the direct roads from distant parts leading to Philadelphia "do very little communicate therewith, and the surrounding ways, in almost every direction, appears to be sufficiently supplied with Public-houses within a moderate distance of each other," and as "the profits arising from such a situation" must be "inadequate to the expense, without indulging neighboring unguarded people to the injury of themselves and grief of some of their families," they hope that the court after "being informed of the true situation, so as to judge of the inconsistency of admitting license to any persons at said place," will refuse to recommend the petition to the Governor, and the court thereupon withdrew its approval Frederick James, however, was not prepared to quietly submit to the loss of his special privilege, hence at the next Quarter Sessions he again appeared with a petition for license The court's approbation thereof was attempted to be carried by a strong flank movement, as appears by the following remarkable documents

"Petition of the Commissioned and staff officers of 65th Regt Penna Militia to the Court of Quarter Sessions for their recommending Frederick James to keep a Public-House

"To the Judges of the Court of Quarter Sessions to be held at Chester for Del Co on Monday the — day July, A D 1806

"The Petition of the Commissioned and Staff Officers of the 65th Regt of Penna Militia in the said county of Del Respectfully sheweth:—

"That your Petitioners have heard with regret that your Honors at the last Court of Quarter Sessions omitted or refused to grant the prayer of Frederick James, who petitioned the said court to recommend him as heretofore to the Governor to obtain a license to keep the Tavern in Springfield he now occupies, called the 'Blue Bell Tavern'

"Your Petitioners are fully persuaded (in their humble opinion) that a Public House of entertainment is absolutely necessary for many reasons

"That this Tavern is about the centre of the bounds of the said Regt, and that the Regt. hath met to exercise near the same for upwards of Twenty years past, and will meet there in future, at which Tavern the officers hath been well accommodated, and is desirous of being so in future

"That the Militia law enjoins the officers to meet four times in each year, exclusive of the days of their meeting in Regt, and on adjournments of the Board of officers, when this house (from its central situation) hath been the usual place of meeting to transact business

"That if the said Tavern be abolished, and no house Licensed near to it, there will be no place for your Petitioners to take shelter from the inclemency of the weather, or get any refreshment on days of exercise or business, for the Said Law prohibits any ardent spirits from being sold at the parade by subtlety, and also the Regt from exercising on any person's land without the permission of the owner

"And that the License should be taken from this house, there will be no place of entertainment for strangers on the Springfield road from Darby to Fox's Tavern, a distance of about ten miles.

"For the foregoing reasons and many others that might be advanced, your Petitioners earnestly request the Court to recommend the said Frederick James to his Excellency the Governor as a suitable person to keep the Blue Ball Tavern in order to obtain a License for that purpose, or for the ensuing year at least, as at the expiration thereof our commissions will expire and appointments by their own limitations

"And your Petitioners will with pleasure acknowledge your attention to the public good

"Wm Litzenburg, Major, Joseph Dicks, Major, Wm Brooke, Brigade Inspector, J L Pearson, Lieut.-Colonel, Jonathan Worrall, Captain, Michael Ketts, Captain, Levi Garrett, Captain, George Martin, Capt, John Deals, Capt, James Morgan, Capt, John Hall, Capt., Thos Wall, Lieut, John Caldwell, Lieut, Joshua Wood, Ensign, James Hunter, Lieut and Commanding officer of Company, John Frothill, Quartermaster, Wm Black, Adjt., Samuel Pennell, Capt of Troop, Andrew Lindsay, 1st Lieut. of Troop, Wm Moore, 2d Lieut of Troop"

The court, notwithstanding this charge in column, manfully held its ground, and Frederick James was again repulsed

The following year, 1807, Emmor Eachus stated to the court that he occupied the house where Isaac Cochran, and latterly Frederick James, formerly dwelled, which was known as the Blue Ball Tavern, and desired license therefor A remonstrance was presented against the petition, stating that the house is one "which hath been repeatedly remonstrated against with good effect," and then the remonstrants followed word for word the form of the remonstrance which had such "good effect" in 1806 This time it had become an old story, at any rate the judges smiled benignly on Eachus and recommended him to the Governor as a fit man to keep a hotel

Old Lamb Tavern—On Aug 26, 1740, Benjamin Maddock petitioned the court for license, stating that he "has lately built a house on the Cross Roads that leads from Darby to the Back Inhabitants where the Palatines has of Late much frequented with wagons, likewise to the Grate Road that leads from Chester to Schuylkill" Although thirty-five persons indorsed his petition,—among them Abraham Lincoln,—the court declined to grant the application of the petitioner

In 1748, Benjamin Maddock again presented his petition, in which he states that he "has built a new house at cross roads, and Joshua Thomas being about to decline on one of the roads," he renewed his application for leave to keep a house of public entertainment What was done with the petition I have not learned, but I think it received the favorable notice of the court We know that in 1761 Isaac Glease was granted license, and in 1762 and 1763 Richard Mall was also accorded that privilege, to be followed in 1764 and 1765 by John Wayten, in 1766, by Joseph Gibbons, Jr, and the license was granted until 1835, when it was discontinued. The old inn, now removed, stood in the front yard of the present Gibbons mansion. The night of the battle of Brandywine a straggling party of fleeing Americans, "accompanied by a wagon-load of the wounded, with a surgeon, reached Gibbons' tavern in Springfield about ten o'clock in the night of the battle Here their wounds were dressed and their wants supplied with everything the house could afford They left early in the morning for fear of being overtaken by the enemy."[1]

The Lamb Tavern — The difficulties Emmor Eachus had at the Blue Ball Inn caused him to make a change in the house, for which he asked license, and in 1808 he appears to have removed to a dwelling a short distance above the Springfield meeting house To the new house he gave the name of the "Three Tuns" It was at this house that Capt Morgan's company of drafted men assembled in October, 1814, previous to taking up the line of march for Marcus Hook The license was continued to Emmor Eachus until 1820, when he was succeeded as landlord by John Jones, and five years thereafter John Fawkes kept the house for a brief season, for, dying in less than a year, his widow, Susan Fawkes, applied for license in 1826 The sage opinion of the late Tony Weller has convinced the world that there is a peculiar attraction about a widow that is fatal to the liberty of single gentlemen, but when the disconsolate relict has the additional recommendation of being the landlady of a public-house, she becomes absolutely irresistible Hence, when Mr Wayne Litzenberg saw Mrs Fawkes, he was not exempt from the general fascination of the pleasing widow, and I was not surprised to find that in the application for license for the "Three Tuns," in 1829, Wayne Litzenberg figures as the petitioner, and informs the court that he has intermarried with Susan Fawkes

In 1830, John Black followed as the landlord, to be succeeded in 1835 by Isaac Johnson, when, the old Lamb Tavern kept by Gibbons having ceased to be a licensed house, Johnson substituted for his tavern the name "The Lamb," instead of the "Three Tuns," by which it had formerly been known The latter was greatly interested in military matters, and frequently the militia under the old law assembled at his house for review and to be instructed in the art of war In 1837, John Ford was mine host of the Lamb, and in 1847, Forrester Hoopes was the landlord, his first license being had under the first local option law, when he was granted leave by the court to keep a temperance house, which was not the sort of privilege he desired Here he continued, receiving full license after the law which interdicted the sale of liquor in that township had been declared by the Supreme Court unconstitutional, until 1853, when the owner of the property, George Worrall, kept the house The latter in 1858 was followed by Joseph H Black, who in the succeeding year retired, to be followed by George Worrall In 1863, Peter H Hill had license for the house, which he afterwards had transferred to Worrall The next year, 1864, William F Woodward kept the tavern, and remained there until 1868, when Malachi W Sloan became the proprietor He in 1869 gave place to Benjamin Rodgers, to be followed in 1873 by Mr Sloan In 1875 Leedom Kirk was the landlord, and James A Serverson in 1878

Malachi W Sloan died Aug 16, 1881, and in his will directed, "It is my will and desire that the 'Lamb Tavern property,' in said will named, shall, after the expiration of the present lease, be no longer used for the purpose of a hotel" The Lamb Tavern, under this provision, is no longer a licensed house

The Springfield House —In 1834, the year Gibbons retired from tavern-keeping, Morris W Heston applied for a license for a house located on the Delaware County turnpike In 1836 George Lotzenburg was the landlord, and in 1838 Isaac Johnson, in 1839 Thomas Gibson, and in 1841 John E Levis was its last landlord He kept the Springfield House as a temperance inn In August, 1842, John Larkin, Jr, the then sheriff, sold the property on an execution against Levis

In 1882, Lewis F. Belts was licensed to keep the Farriday Park Hotel at Morton, conditioned that he would supply liquor only to guests of the house at dinner-table and in their rooms, and that "no bar, sideboard, or semblance thereof, or other place where persons can stand and purchase drinks, shall be permitted to be kept or maintained upon any part of the premises" In 1883, Benjamin N Morton had the license granted to him at the same house, under like restrictions

In 1876 Nathaniel Chandler was an inmate of the House of Employment About 1830 he resided in a small house, now owned by Richard Young, at the junction of the roads leading from Providence and Springfield to Darby, in which he sold cakes and beer His sign read thus

"Porter, Cider, Beer, and Cakes—
If you'll walk in here's no mistakes"

This sign and its inscription, it was said, was procured by some of his neighbors, who used often to congregate at his "pow," as the establishment was

[1] Smith's "History of Delaware County," p 310

termed, to talk politics, drink beer, and have sport with the landlord. At one time his friends induced him to become a candidate for sheriff of the county. A card announcing his candidacy was inserted in the newspapers of that day. No one seriously considered Natty as a candidate, but as there were an unusual number of persons seeking the office that year, as a burlesque his name was added to the list. His candidacy ended with the announcement of his name.

Springfield Free Fountain Society.—In April, 1882, a number of ladies and gentlemen met at the residence of C. G. Ogden, and decided to form a society for the purpose of erecting fountains and watering-troughs on the public road at suitable points. A meeting was called at Oakdale school-house, May 20, 1882, when the following officers were elected: Joseph P. Maris, president; C. G. Ogden, vice-president; Clement Ogden, treasurer; J. S. Kent, secretary; T. J. Dolphin, corresponding secretary; and Garrett E. Smedley, solicitor. In July, 1882, the society, which had been incorporated by the court of Delaware County, erected its first fountain on the State road, opposite the property of George Maris, procuring most excellent water from a never-failing spring on his grounds. In September the second fountain was erected on the Baltimore turnpike, at Thomson's bridge, adjoining lands of George B. Lownes. Leiper & Lewis presented the large cap-stone for this fountain. In October the third fountain was erected, adjoining the farm of Reuben Baily, in Marple. In December of the same year the society began the erection of a fourth fountain on the Providence road, in Nether Providence, the water being brought from a spring on the farm of Thomas Palmer, which was completed the following year.

The Last of the Indian.—The family of Indians of whom an account is given in the history of Aston had also a wigwam near Lownes' Run, north of the dwelling-house of Joseph Gibbons, in Springfield, and would frequently reside there. "The last of the natives who had a home in the county was 'Indian Nelly,' who had her cabin near the line of the Shipley farm. She had her constant residence there as late as 1810."[1]

Remarkable Bequest.—In 1859, Mrs. Rebecca J. Smedley, of Springfield, died, and her will contains the following bequest:

"All the rest and residue of my estate I give, devise, and bequeath to my brother-in-law, William Smedley, and my friend, Joel Evans, of Springfield, upon this special trust and confidence, that my said Trustees shall apply and appropriate the residue to the benefit and assistance of young beginners in life, members of the religious Society of Friends, by paying to such small sums not exceeding fifty dollars to one person, in order to aid them in getting into business or setting out in housekeeping."

[1] Smith's "History of Delaware County," p. 392.

BIOGRAPHICAL SKETCHES.

JOSEPH GIBBONS.

The Gibbons family are of English extraction, the father of the subject of this biography having been Joseph Gibbons, who was born in 1770, on the homestead which is now the property of his grandsons, John and Joseph Gibbons. He married Lydia Dix, of Providence township, and had children,—Ann (Mrs. Edward Fell), Jane, John, George W., Sarah (Mrs. David Worrell), Humphrey, Elizabeth (Mrs. Frederick Fell), Joseph, James M., Lydia (Mrs. Morris Roberts), and William. The only survivor of this number is Mrs. David Worrell. Joseph Gibbons was born Aug. 20, 1799, on the homestead in Springfield township, where his life was spent in the active pursuits of a farmer, his whole career having been identified with the scenes of his childhood. His education was obtained in the neighborhood of his home, after which he lent a willing hand in the labor of the farm. Subsequently cultivated the land on shares, and on the death of his father, in 1853, the land became his by inheritance. He married Hannah B. Powell, daughter of Joseph and Elizabeth Powell, of Springfield, to whom were born four sons and four daughters, seven of whom survive. Mr. Gibbons, though devoted during his life to the pursuits of an agriculturist, was a man of much sagacity in business operations. His acquired knowledge of all matters pertaining to agricultural science rendered him one of the most successful farmers in the county. He was not less known for integrity and scrupulous honesty in all business transactions than for his capacity and soundness of judgment. Mr. Gibbons was identified as a director with the Delaware County Bank, of Chester. In politics he was a Whig, and later a Republican; and though the incumbent of various township offices, cared little for these distinctions. Mr. Gibbons possessed a genial and kindly nature, was social and companionable, a lover of music and good cheer. He was generous in his instincts, and liberal as occasion required. He was reared in the religious faith of the Friends, with whom he worshiped. His death occurred Dec. 1, 1880, aged eighty-one years, and that of Mrs. Gibbons, April 21, 1882.

RANDALL BISHOP.

The grandfather of Randall Bishop was Thomas Bishop, who married and had among his children a son, Joseph, born in Delaware County, who followed the vocation of a wheelwright, and also cultivated a farm. He married Sarah Pratt, of the same county, whose children were Tamar (Mrs. Samuel Pancoast), Emily, Joel, Orpah, Thomas, Randall, and Jeremiah. Randall Bishop was born April 18, 1795, in Provi-

tavern, to talk politics, drink beer, and have sport with the landlord. At one time his friends induced him to become a candidate for sheriff of the county. A card announcing his candidacy was inserted in the newspapers of that day. No one seriously considered Nathy as a candidate, but as there were an unusual number of persons seeking the office that year, as a burlesque his name was added to the list. His candidacy ended with the announcement of his name.

Springfield Free Fountain Society.—In April, 1882, a number of ladies and gentlemen met at the residence of C. G. Ogden, and decided to form a society for the purpose of erecting fountains and watering troughs on the public road at suitable points. A meeting was called at Oakdale school-house, May 20, 1882, when the following officers were elected: Joseph P. Maris, president; C. G. Ogden, vice-president; Clement Ogden, treasurer; J. S. Kent, secretary; T. J. Dolphin, corresponding secretary; and Garrett E. Smedley, solicitor. In July, 1882, the society, which had been incorporated by the court of Delaware County, erected its first fountain on the State road, opposite the property of George Maris, procuring most excellent water from a never-failing spring on his grounds. In September the second fountain was erected on the Baltimore turnpike, at [illegible] bridge, adjoining lands of George B. Lownes. Lownes & Lownes presented the large cap-stone for this fountain. In October the third fountain was erected, adjoining the farm of Reuben Baily, in Marple. In December of the same year the society began the erection of a fourth fountain on the Providence road, in Nether Providence, the water being brought from a spring on the farm of Thomas Palmer, which was completed the following year.

The Last of the Indian.—The family of Indians of whom an account is given in the history of Aston had also a wigwam near Lownes' Run, north of the dwelling-house of Joseph Gibbons, in Springfield, and would frequently reside there. "The last of the persons who had a home in the county was 'Indian Nelly,' who had her cabin near the line of the Shipley farm. She had her constant residence there as late as 1819."[1]

Remarkable Bequest.—In 1856, Mrs. Rebecca J. Smedley, of Springfield, died, and her will contains the following bequest:

"All the rest and residue of my estate I give, devise, and bequeath to my brother-in-law, William Smedley, and my friend, Joel Evans, of Springfield, upon this special trust and confidence, that my said Trustees shall apply and appropriate the residue to the benefit and assistance of young beginners in life, members of the religious Society of Friends, by paying to such small sums not exceeding fifty dollars to one person, in order to aid them in getting into business or setting out in housekeeping."

[1] Smith's "History of Delaware County," p. 393.

BIOGRAPHICAL SKETCHES.

JOSEPH GIBBONS.

The Gibbons family are of English extraction, the father of the subject of this biography having been Joseph Gibbons, who was born in 1770, on the homestead which is now the property of his grandsons, John and Joseph Gibbons. He married Lydia Dix, of Providence township, and had children,—Ann (Mrs. Edward Fell), Jane, John, George W., Sarah (Mrs. David Worrell), Humphrey, Elizabeth (Mrs. Frederick Fell), Joseph, James M., Lydia (Mrs. Morris Roberts), and William. The only survivor of this number is Mrs. David Worrell. Joseph Gibbons was born Aug. 20, 1799, on the homestead in Springfield township, where his life was spent in the active pursuits of a farmer, his whole career having been identified with the scenes of his childhood. His education was obtained in the neighborhood of his home, after which he lent a willing hand in the labor of the farm. Subsequently cultivated the land on shares, and on the death of his father, in 1858, the land became his by inheritance. He married Hannah R. Powell, daughter of Joseph and Elizabeth Powell, of Springfield, to whom were born four sons and four daughters, seven of whom survive. Mr. Gibbons, though devoted during his life to the pursuits of an agriculturist, was a man of much sagacity in business operations. His acquired knowledge of all matters pertaining to agricultural science rendered him one of the most successful farmers in the county. He was not less known for integrity and scrupulous honesty in all business transactions than for his capacity and soundness of judgment. Mr. Gibbons was identified as a director with the Delaware County Bank, of Chester. In politics he was a Whig, and later a Republican; and though the incumbent of various township offices, cared little for these distinctions. Mr. Gibbons possessed a genial and kindly nature, was social and companionable, a lover of music and good cheer. He was generous in his instincts, and liberal as occasion required. He was reared in the religious faith of the Friends, with whom he worshiped. His death occurred Dec. 1, 1880, aged eighty-one years, and that of Mrs. Gibbons, April 21, 1882.

RANDALL BISHOP.

The grandfather of Randall Bishop was Thomas Bishop, who married and had among his children a son, Joseph, born in Delaware County, who followed the vocation of a wheelwright, and also cultivated a farm. He married Sarah Pratt, of the same county, whose children were Tamar (Mrs. Samuel Pancoast), Emily, Joel, Orpah, Thomas, Randall, and Jeremiah. Randall Bishop was born April 18, 1796, in Provi-

Engd by A.H. Ritchie.

Jos. Gibbons

Randal Bishop

David Howell

dence township, on the ancestral land which was the birthplace of many members of the family. His education was confined to the neighboring schools, after which he became interested in the employments of the farm. He was, on the 21st of November, 1822, married to Maria Massey, daughter of James and Mary Thompson Massey, whose birth occurred Sept. 15, 1797. Their children are Joseph, Mary T. (Mrs. Joseph M. Worrell), Sarah P., Susannah M., Lydia M. (Mrs. M. C. Taylor), Elizabeth L. (Mrs. P. L. Hill), Priscilla P., and Emma. Mr. Bishop, on his marriage, removed to a farm adjacent to the homestead, which he cultivated until he became owner by inheritance of a farm in Springfield, where the remainder of his life was spent as an agriculturist. He was in early life a Whig in politics, and on the formation of the Republican party embraced its principles. Though seldom figuring in the ranks of the active political workers, he served as treasurer of Delaware County, and held less important township offices. He was a director of the Delaware County Bank, of Chester. He was in his religious faith a Friend, and a member of the Friends' Meeting of Springfield. He was a man of unimpeachable integrity, and respected for his purity of character and influence. The death of Mr. Bishop occurred May 27, 1879, on the homestead, now occupied by his daughter, Mrs. Worrell.

DAVID WORRELL.

Elisha Worrell, the father of David, was born on the 9th of November, 1739, and died Dec. 27, 1829. He married Mary Maris, and had children,—Jemima, born in 1766; Maris, in 1768; Joseph, in 1770; Mordecai, in 1773; Owen, in 1775; Anne, in 1777; Margaret, in 1779; Rebecca, in 1781; David, in 1783; Elizabeth, in 1785; Mary, in 1787; and Betsey, in 1789. The birth of David occurred in Springfield township Sept. 22, 1783, where his whole life was spent. On acquiring the rudiments of learning at the school immediately near his home, he at once turned his attention to farming, and, on the decease of his father, inherited the farm, to the cultivation of which his life was devoted. He married Sarah, daughter of Joseph Gibbons, of the same township, and had children,—Jane G. (Mrs. William Bittle), Elizabeth (Mrs. John C. H. Morton), Sarah, Joseph M., Lydia (Mrs. William Johnson), Elisha, Mary, David, Rebecca (Mrs. Emory E. Levis), and Deborah (Mrs. Edward S. Barber). Mr. Worrell was a Whig in politics, and participated actively in all matters involving the interests of the county and township. He filled various positions in the township, and at his death held the office of county commissioner. His integrity and discernment led him often to be chosen as the guardian of momentous trusts and the administrator of estates. He was energetic in all business matters, well informed on the general topics of the day, and possessed a genial nature, which attracted numerous friends. He adhered in his religious views to the worship of the society of Friends. Mr. Worrell was a lieutenant in the Light-Horse Cavalry and much interested in the success of this company. His death occurred Jan. 24, 1847, in his sixty-fourth year.

GEORGE MARIS.

George Maris, the progenitor of the family in America, sailed from England for the New World in 1683, and soon after his arrival settled in Darby township, Delaware Co., Pa. He was granted a patent of one thousand acres of land in the above county, four hundred of which lay in Springfield township. On this tract he erected a dwelling known since by his descendants as "Home House," which was bequeathed on his death, with the land, to his son John, whose son George next became its owner by inheritance, and retained it during his lifetime. He built, in 1822, the larger portion of the house now known as the homestead, and at present occupied by the subject of this sketch. Jehu, the son of George, born in 1736, then came into possession. He married Jane Humphreys, of Montgomery County, and had children,—John, born in 1779; Ann, in 1781; Asa, in 1783; Lydia, in 1784; George, in 1786; and Ellis, in 1788. John, the father of George, was born on the 28th of December, 1779, at the ancestral home, and married Martha Ann Bonsall, of Darby. Their children were George; Isaac, born in 1825; Lewis, in 1827; Humphrey, in 1829; Joseph Powell, in 1831; Rebecca, in 1834; Susannah, in 1835; Ellis, in 1838; and John, in 1840. George, whose birth occurred on the 23d of October, 1823, still resides upon the family estate. He received a rudimentary education at the centre school, near his home, and early acquired a knowledge of the labor of the farm. On the death of his father, in 1841, he inherited a portion and purchased the remainder of the estate. He married, on the 19th of October, 1870, Caroline L., daughter of John and Sarah Worrell, of Springfield. Their children are Rebecca, born Jan. 4, 1873, and Emma P., whose birth occurred Feb. 16, 1874. Mr. Maris has avoided the exciting scenes of political life and the allurements of business apart from his daily routine of labor, believing that his path of duty lies rather in the quiet sphere of agricultural industry. He is in politics a Republican, though formerly Democratic in his political predilections. In religion he is a member of the Friends' Meeting of Darby. The bicentennial of the landing of George Maris was held at "Home House" on the 28th of August, 1883, on which interesting occasion many hundred descendants of the pioneer were assembled and agreeably entertained.

CHAPTER LIV

RIDLEY TOWNSHIP

THE territory now designated Ridley, which derived its name from Ridley, Cheshire, England, the place from whence John Simcock came, originally under the first organization seems to have been limited to that part of the present township east and north of the old Amosland tract at the upper end of the Moore farm, and extending northward "into the words" Techoherassi or Stillé's land was at the mouth of Ridley Creek, now Eddystone The land derived its name from the fact that Olof Persson Stillé, one of the early Swedish settlers, took up the land on the east side of Ridley Creek, and because the Indians used the word Techoherassi or Tequirasi, as descriptive of the swarthy complexion and dark hair of its owner, the plantation was termed "Techoherassi or Teckquirassy" The Swedes and Finns, being of the Scandinavian race, were of light and fair complexion, consequently their beards were light or sandy color. Stillé being distinguished by his dark skin and black hair occasioned the Indians to bestow upon him the title of "the man with the black beard," the signification of the words used as to his name, for Acrelius informs us that Techoherassi was the Indian name for Olof Stillé's place, or Sillie's land [1] His ownership of the land on the present Ridley Creek gave to that stream the name of "Oele Stillin's Kill," and the territory between that and Crum Creek on Lindstrom's manuscript map is designated as "Stillen's Land (la paye de Stillen's)" Olof Stillé came from Penningby manor, Lanna, Parish Roslagen, in the duchy of Lodermania, about thirty miles south of Stockholm, then in possession of the noble family of Bielke He emigrated with the third Swedish expedition in 1641 He was a millwright by trade, who agreed to engage in agriculture, and was to be paid "50 *daler*, copper money, drawing no additional wages, but to be paid for whatever work he does for, and for whatever he furnishes to the company He was accompanied by his wife and two children, one seven and the other one and a half years old He is not mentioned in the list of settlers in 1644 "[2] Stillé seems to have been one of the most prominent men in the Swedish Colony He was made the bearer to the Dutch director of the official protest of Governor Printz, the Swedish Governor, against the encroachments of the West India Company on the right of the Swedish crown on the Delaware After the conquest of the colony by the Dutch, in 1658, he was one of the four commissaries or magistrates appointed "to administer justice among the inhabitants, and thus became a judge of the first court of which history gives us information on the banks of the Delaware He was also employed in various negotiations with the neighboring colonists and with the Indians"[3] Professor Keen states that he died prior to May, 1693, leaving as heir an only son, John Stillé, born in America in 1646, the ancestor of a well-known Philadelphia family Stillé, in 1664, was living in Passyunk, Philadelphia, on a tract of land ceded to him by d'Hinoyossa, the Dutch Governor on South River One hundred acres of the Stillé land in Ridley, extending along the west side of Crump Kill or Crum Creek to a point about the north line of the land of the late Jacob Hughes, was patented to Neals Mattson June 13, 1670 It was his wife, Margaret Mattson, who was tried Feb 27, 1683/4, on an indictment for witchcraft before William Penn and a jury [4] Above this tract, at the court held at Upland, Nov 12, 1678, a plot of one hundred acres was set apart to Anthony Nealson The old entry on the docket says,—

"Upon the Peticon of anthony nealson desiring of this Court a grant for to take up 100 (one hundred) acres of Land betweene ye heads of Crom kill & Oele Stellen's Kill, as alsoe a small parcell of marrish adjoyning there unto The Court doe grant the Peticon^r^ his s^d^ Request hee seating & Improving ye same Land according to his hono^r^ the Govern^rs^ Regulacons & orders "[5]

Nealson was a Swede, and his wife was the daughter of Margaret Mattson, whose trial for witchcraft is above mentioned In the old survey of the land which was filed, this tract is thus described

"Copie,

"By virtue of a warrant from the court at upland in September, 1677, Layed out for Anthony nielson Alias Long A parcell of Land called Long scituate and being on the west syde of Delawar River, aboute a *myle from* the River Side betweene Crum Kill and Stilles Kill beginning at a corner marked Read oake of the Land of Niles Matson standing at the S W side of the Crum Kill, and from thense Running up the said Kill bounding therewith N W, sixty and two perches N E 13 degrees one hundred and Eighty Perches, & N W by W Sixtene Perches to a Corner marked Chestnut tree standing At the side of sayd Creeke, from thense S W By S By a Lyne of marked trees two hundred Perches to a corner marked Poplar standing at Stille's Creke, from thense downe Stille's Creek bounding therewith South by East forty Perches and South East one hundred and seaven perches to a corner marked Read oake of the Land of Dom Lauren cies Carolus at the side of Stille's Creek, and from thence north east by a Line of marked trees seventy and fower Perches to the first mentioned Corner oake Continuing one hundred Acres of Land

"Survived by me,

(Signed) "WALTER WARTON, *Survr*"

The greater part of the Nealson land subsequently passed under the two thousand two hundred and ten acres which on Seventh month 9, 1705, was resurveyed to Jacob Simcock East of Crum Creek, beginning at a short distance below the present Avondale, and extending south along the creek, to Jacob Hendricks, on July 27, 1680, was surveyed one hundred acres of land, which he termed "Stone Point," doubtless due to the fact that the ground there gave indications of the

[1] History of New Sweden, pp 46, 68 Campanius records that "Tochoherassi, Olof Stillé's place, was a small plantation which was built by Swedish freemen who gave it that name They were frequently visited by Indians, as it was on the river shore and surrounded by water like a small island Olof had a thick black beard, from which the Indians had called him the man with the black beard" Campanius, p 81

[2] Professor Gregory B Keen's "Third Swedish Expedition to New Sweden," *Penn Mag of Hist*, vol iii p 462

[3] Armstrong's "Record of Upland County," p 78 (note)

[4] *Ante*, p 229

[5] Record of Upland Court, p 108

noted stone-quarries which were afterwards opened in that neighborhood. Prior to that date at the court held at Upland Nov. 12, 1678, a plantation of one hundred acres along the same stream and adjoining "Stone Point" on the south, was surveyed to Jacob Hendricks. This land, which was afterwards absorbed in the Jacob Simcock resurvey, is thus described in the old court docket:

"By virtue of a warrant from the Court att upland nouember, 1677, Layd out for Jacob Hendrickson a parcell of Land Called Jacob's Lott, scituate and being on the west side of Delawar River, and on the north East side of the Crum Kill, being att a cornor marked white oak standing att the side of the creek or kill, being a cornor tree of the Land of the orphants of Hendrix Johnson, from thence Running N.E. by E., by their Line of marked trees two hundred and fourteen perches to a cornor marked white oak standing in ye said Line, from thens N.W. by N., by a Line of marked trees one hundred perches to another marked white oak standing on a Leavell, from thence southwest by W., by a Lyne of markeed trees one hundred and fifty and two perches to another cornor marked white oake, standing att the side of the said Crum kill, and from thens following the said creek or kill to the first-mentioned white oak containing one hundred acres of Land surueyed.

"By me (signed) WALT. WHARTON,
"Surv^r."[1]

Immediately south of "Jacob's Lott," Charles Ashcom, the surveyor, took up three hundred and thirty acres. This tract followed the east bank of Crum Creek to the mouth of Little Crum Creek, and then along the west bank of that stream northward until about the point where the Philadelphia, Wilmington and Baltimore Railroad crosses Little Crum, and then extending eastward so as to include the greater part of the lake at Ridley Park, from which point a line at right angles to Crum Creek marked its boundaries. Within this survey, the present village of Leiperville is included. Thomas Holmes, the surveyor-general, obtained the greater part of the Ashcom land, containing two hundred and eighty acres, on Second month 20, 1693, and the following year it passed to John Cook. On Seventh month 7, 1690, Richard Crosby purchased eighty-three acres on the east side of Crum Creek, extending to and including Leiperville, which below that and to Little Crum Creek, George Van Culin acquired title to sixty acres. On the south side of the latter stream, John Van Culin, on Feb. 6, 1684, took up fifty acres.

The early settlements in Ridley are more confusing than in any locality in Delaware County, owing to the fact that Charles Ashcom, the early surveyor of Chester County, paid little or no regard in laying out land to the prior Swedish, Dutch, or even the patents given by the Duke of York. Hence in part of the tract of three hundred and thirty acres entered in his own name, he absorbed a considerable part of the land included in a patent, dated October, 1675, of one hundred and fifty-four acres to Henrick Johnson and Bartoll Eskells. Along the river front east of Crum Creek, John and Andrew Hendricks took up sixty-five acres, which extended nearly to the mouth of Darby Creek, leaving then, however, a tract of forty-five acres reaching to Stone Creek, which was taken up early in the last century by John Morton, eighteen acres, Andrew Morton, nineteen acres, and George Van Culin, eighteen acres; the latter, on Nov. 5, 1715, had received a patent for one hundred and twenty-five acres immediately north of the forty-five acres tract, which extended to a point on the Philadelphia, Wilmington and Baltimore Railroad, a short distance west of the station at Ridley Park. East of this Van Culin tract, extending to Mokornipates Kill or Muckinipattus Creek, was the territory designated as Amosland. Acrelius tells us that "Amosland was first called Ammansland. A midwife formerly lived at the place where Archer's farm now is; thence that place, and subsequently the whole tract around it, received the name of Amman's Land, now Amosland."[2] That this locality must have been early in the history of the settlement known by that name, is evident from the order of Governor Lovelace, dated Aug. 8, 1672, wherein he directed the court at Upland to inquire into a dispute regarding the title to an island "over against Calcoone Hooke," respecting which "Jan Cornelis, Mattys Mattysen, and Martin Martinsen, Inhabitants at Amosland in Delaware River," had entered complaint to him.[3]

Immediately adjoining to the east the tract of George Van Culin, on Stone Creek, on Sept. 2, 1675, two hundred and eighty acres, "more or less," were surveyed to Hendrick Torton. There proved to be over eighty acres "more" when subsequently resurveyed. Ridley Park is on that part of the tract lying north of the Queen's Highway. Directly east of the Torton land were one hundred and fifty-four acres, surveyed to Henrick Johnson and Bartoll Eskells, October, 1675, which tract stretched along Darby Creek to the mouth of Amosland Run, and thence at right angles westward to Ridley Park, which was most liberal measure, under the claim of "one hundred and fifty-four acres more or less." Eastward of this land all the remaining part of the present township, beginning at the northwest corner of J. L. Moore's farm, and following the north line of his plantation eastward, extending it through the Neal Duffy farm and that of the late James G. Knowles, to the Muckinipattus Creek, then down to that stream to Darby Creek, and along the last-mentioned water-course to Amosland Run, was patented, May 18, 1672, to Jan. Cornelis, Mattys Mattysen, and Martin Martinson. That these parties resided on the land said to be two hundred acres we know from the order of Governor Lovelace, already referred to; and that Jan Cornelis was there later appears from the proceedings of court April 1, 1678, when the following interesting historical event is recorded, inasmuch as it is claimed the first asylum for the insane, rude as it may have been, was

[1] Record of Upland Court, p. 124.

[2] History of New Sweden, p. 204 (note).

[3] Penna. Archives, 2d Series, vol. v. p. 621.

erected in pursuance of the order then made by the justice

"Jan Cornelissen, of Amesland, Complayning to ye Court that his Son Erik is bereft of his naturall Sences & is turned quyt madd, and y[t] hee being a poore man is not able to maintaine him

"Ordered, that three or 4 p[r]sons bee hired to build a Little Blockhouse at Amesland for to put in the s[d] madman, and att the next Court order will bee taken y[t] a small Levy bee Laid for to pay for the building of y[e] house and the maintayning of y[e] s[d] mad man according to Lawes of y[e] goverment "[1]

The remainder of the township of Ridley lying north of Amosland and extending westward from a line drawn due west from the northwest corner of the farm of J L Moore to that of William Worrall's, on Crum Creek, was part of the two thousand two hundred acres surveyed to John Simcock, who, prior to his leaving England, purchased from Penn many thousand acres of land in Pennsylvania John Simcock was a man of large means, a member of the society of Friends, who "had suffered much on the score of thythes and for bearing a faithful public testimony and going to meetings among his Friends, the Quakers," immigrated to Pennsylvania about the time of Penn's first visit to the province, in 1682 He was a member of Penn's Council, and continued one of the Governor's councilors until Governor Blackwell assumed control of the provincial government, at the beginning of the year 1689 The following year he was appointed one of the judges of the Provincial Court, and in 1691 was again a member of Council He was elected to the Assembly from Chester County in 1693, again in 1696, and was chosen Speaker of the House in the latter year In 1697, and again in 1698, he was a member of Council He also was one of the commissioners appointed to settle the difficulties respecting the boundary lines between Maryland and Pennsylvania, and was deputy president of the Free Society of Traders John Simcock died on the 7th of the First month (March), 1703, aged seventy-three years [2]

The tract of land at Ridley Creek which belonged to Olof Stillé on May 1, 1674, passed to Domine Laurentius Carolus, or Laurenes Lock, the Swedish minister who came with the seventh expedition from Sweden to the Delaware His career was such, and he conducted himself with such freedom of behavior in his ministerial office, that the scandal which his deeds occasioned has descended to the present time In 1649, "Lock was accused of 'bribery' or 'corruption' (details not given), and would have been sent to Sweden 'to defend and clear himself' had he not fallen dangerously sick "[3] He is believed to have resided for a time at Tinicum, afterwards at Upland, subsequently within the jurisdiction of the New Castle Court, and after his purchase of the three hundred and fifty acres on Ridley Creek he resided there until his death "His old age was burdened with many troubles Finally he became too lame to help himself, until his death, in 1688 "[4] Campanius tells us that his "great infirmity seems to have been an overfondness for intoxicating drink "

As mentioned, the territory now comprising Ridley township was not originally limited to its present boundaries At the court held at Chester on Fifth month 1, 1684, William Cobb and Mons Stakett were appointed collectors of the county taxes for "Amos Land and Calcoone Hooke" William Cobb then owned the Swedish's mill on Cobb's Creek, while for "Ridley and in the Woods James Kenela and Randolfe Vernome" were appointed collectors James Kennerly at that time resided in Springfield, and Randall Vernon in Nether Providence In 1686 the lines of Ridley township were changed, Calcoon Hook being attached to Darby, and the following year Amosland and Tinicum became part of Ridley . The lower part of Nether Providence remained attached to Ridley until 1753, when, on petition of the residents in that section, that part of the township was attached to Nether Providence [5] Tinicum remained a part of Ridley until Aug 31, 1780, when it was erected into a separate township [6] At what date that part of Ridley which extended into Springfield, after the organization of the latter township, was separated from Ridley has not been ascertained

Bridges.—The early settlers of Philadelphia in journeying from Chester to the "Great Town" crossed Ridley township considerably north of the present highway William Worrall, who was born in Marple in 1730, and who settled in Ridley when a young man, stated, in 1820, that when he first located in the latter township the old inhabitants pointed out to him the path which William Penn and his followers used when crossing his farm, and in his rotation of plowing found nails which he supposed had belonged to some of the early travelers The first reference to a bridge in the township occurs at a court held on Third day of first week March, 1685, it was "Ordered that upon y[e] returne of y[e] Grand Jury Albertus Hendrickson, Supervisor of y[e] Highways belong to Chester, doe forthwith Erect a Horse-Bridge in such places y[e] Grand Jury have layd it out.

"Ordered y[t] upon y[e] same returne Bartholomew

[1] Record of Upland Court, p 102

[2] In Samuel Smith's "History of the Province" (Hazard's Register, vol vi p 370), that author, who derived much of his data for that work from personal interviews with Caleb Pusey, states that on "the 27th of the month called January, 1702, died John Simcock, of Chester County, aged about 73 years " In the text we have followed the date given by Dr Smith (History of Delaware County, p 501)

[3] "Descendants of Joran Kyn," by Professor G B Keen, *Penna Hist. Mag*, vol iii p 448 (note)

[4] Acrelius' "History of New Sweden," p 177 For an account of the Rev Mr Lock's or Lare's difficulties respecting the elopement of his wife, see *ante*, p 10, and for his part in the Long Finn's Insurrection, see *ante*, p 158

[5] *Ante*, p 652

[6] *Ante*, pp 285, 286.

Coppock, Supervisor of ye Highways for Crome Creeke forthwith Erect a Bridge in ye King's road over said Croome Creeke."

In 1688 a bridge has been erected over Ridley and over Crum Creek, for at the court held on 3d day of Fourth month, 1688, the judges "Ordered that the Townships of Upper and Nether Providence, and Ridley doe for this time repaire ye Bridge in ye King's road near Walter Fawsetts & upon Crome Creeke." Respecting this bridge nothing seems to have been done, for on the 15th of First month, 1693, the grand jury reported "that at several time presented the want of a bridge over Ridley Creek and the same being dangerous and detrimental to the County;" and thereupon the court "do find the Supervisors of Chester and the Supervisors of Ridley five pounds." Notwithstanding this pecuniary punishment the bridges do not appear to have been built for some years thereafter, for at the court held on Eighth month 4, 1697, "Walter Faucit in open court have engaged to make a good horse-bridge over Ridley Creek near his house at the King's road, upon the condition that all the Inhabitants of the two townships of Ridley should pay him one shilling per family, for which the court ordered the s^d Supervisors of the two townships to gather the same in their presence within the space of three weeks, and deliver the same to Walter Faucit."

The bridge thus erected seems to have failed to meet the public demand, hence at the court held Aug. 28–29, 1705, the grand inquest "do present the want of a good, lawful bridge over the Swedes Mill Creek, and also over Darby Creek and also over Crum Creek, and to have the Queen's Road made good, laid out according to law through Darby Township, and the Township of Ridley to clear the road and mend the bridges." The new bridges thus provided for were on the present Southern post road, or rather near the line which that road is now laid out. Gabriel Friend was the contractor for the bridges over Ridley and Crum Creeks, for on Feb. 22, 1709, he "petitioned the bench for the remaining part of the money due him, for making the causeway at Ridley Creek bridge and the bridge at Crum Creek. The court order that he shall have an order to receive fifteen pounds late currency of the Treasurer."

The Amosland Road.—The present Amosland road is generally accepted by local historians as comparatively a modern highway, and that the Lazaretto road is the one intended in the following report of the grand jury, arguing that because the present Amosland road does not go to Darby Creek, it is clearly not the one indicated in the old return, which sets forth:

"Upon the 9th day of the 12th month, 1687, By virtue of an Order from the last County Court, given us whose names are hereunto subscribed, being the Grand Jury for to lay out a highway that should serve for Marple, Newtown, Springfield, and the inhabitants that way to the landing-place at Amosland, did, upon the above day written, Begin at a roadway on the lands of George Maris, which Road goeth from Chester through Marple to Newtown, Soe from the Road through Bartholomew Coppock's land, near his house, his house being on the left hand, Soe through Robert Taylor's land, straight on through more of George Maris his land, Soe bearing a little on the right hand through George Simcock's land, leaving his plantation on the left, adjoining to Amosland, so unto the King's Road that comes from Darby, marking the trees as we came, so on to the landing-place by the maine creek-side beyond Morton Mortonsen, his house."

This report was signed by William Garrett, Richard Parker, Edmond Cartlidge, Thomas Bradshaw, and Thomas Fox.

The objection that the present Amosland road does not extend to Darby Creek, and hence that highway cannot be the one thus laid out by the grand jury, is not tenable. An inspection of that scarce map entitled a "Plan of the City of Philadelphia and Environs, surveyed by John Hills in the summer of 1801–2, 3, 4, 5, 6–7," and published "May 1, 1808," shows that the Amosland road branched at the point where the present highway diverges due east to cross the Muckinipattus Creek, and that a now vacated road led directly to Darby Creek at a point east of Boon's house. That the present Amosland road is the ancient highway, and that the traditionary name has not been bestowed wrongly, seems evident. Until a better reason than the fact that the modern highway does not extend to Darby is given to take from the traditionary road its honors, the public can safely rely that the historians, not the public, are misled.

The Revolution.—Ridley township being traversed by the great Southern road, necessarily the Continental and British armies marched through its territory repeatedly. When Washington moved to Wilmington to oppose Gen. Howe, his troops marched along the Queen's Highway, and after the defeat at Brandywine the discomfited men gathered along that road, extending from Leiperville to Darby township line, and at Leiperville, after midnight of the day of battle, Washington hastened to the little hamlet, and for the night rested at the house of John McIlvain. After the capture of Philadelphia repeatedly English troops marched along that highway, for much of the provisions used was received at Chester from transports, and had to be guarded *en route* to the city. Gen. Potter had been ordered by Washington to scour the country between the Schuylkill and Chester, and little was left for the inhabitants' subsistence. On the 19th of November, 1777, Cornwallis with three thousand men marched from Philadelphia, and his men robbed the inoffensive people on the route without mercy, taking food from the indigent widow as remorselessly as from the wealthy husbandman. On Dec. 22, 1777, Gen. Howe made his noted raid to and beyond Darby, from which point foraging parties were dispatched to procure provisions for the men and provender for the horses. Maj. James Clark, Jr., in a letter written to Washington, relates the following incident as having happened at Ridley:

"At White Horse tavern was informed that a party of the enemy, about thirty, were plundering on the Neck. I immediately posted some horsemen on the road, with orders when the enemy came in sight to fire their pieces and retire, and went off the road in quest of the plunderers. During my absence the enemy's light horse came out to my vedettes, and being in disguise, called to them and informed them they belonged to our army, and by this means got up within a few yards of them, and fired their carbines; they shot one of them, and the other made his escape; they then pursued me with the party, but I fortunately knew the road, and came off within a few yards of their picquet. A few minutes sooner would have enabled me to have taken the plunderers, they had but just gone. Col. Butler I left with two hundred men on that road."[1]

On Dec. 25, 1777, at five o'clock in the morning, Maj. Clark writes from the house of Mr. Lewis, in Newtown:

"This morning a party of the enemy, with a few field pieces, moved from Darby towards Chester. Near the White Horse tavern they fell in with a small party of troops, and a pretty smart skirmish ensued, the enemy playing their artillery so warm that our troops were soon obliged to give way. We had one man killed and another wounded with a cannon-ball, and we have taken two prisoners, with their horses, one of them a sutler in the Seventeenth Dragoons, and the other a servant. The enemy's design, they say, is only to forage on the Chester road, and that the party consists of First and Second Light Infantry. Our troops have retired to Springfield meeting-house, and are endeavoring to get some refreshments. The enemy have only forty dragoons with them. The wretched situation of the troops here is much to be lamented. No provisions provided for them, ill-clothed, many of them no shoes, and they are scattered in sixes and sevens all about the neighborhood; in short, they had better be called away. If any considerable number of the enemy's horse had come up the Springfield road they must have inevitably have fallen into their hands. I have ordered the few officers I met with to collect them, send to a mill near the place where there is plenty of flour, and had them well refreshed, experience of late has taught me the advantage of being superior to the enemy in horse."[2]

The mill where the flour was taken was doubtless Peter Hill's grist-mill, from which establishment it is known not only flour but the teams to draw the barrels were impressed, and for which, many years afterwards, the United States government paid by a grant of five thousand acres of lands in Virginia.[3]

The losses sustained by the residents of Ridley township during the various raids of the enemy are thus set forth in the claims filed, although the gross sum does not represent the entire damages sustained by the people of that section:

	£	s.	d.
From John Morton's estate, "taken and destroyed by a part of the British army, under Cornwallis, at or about the time they attacked the Fort at Billingsport, into which neighborhood the articles were removed for safety, certified by Ann. Morton, Execx." "Taken soon after the capture"	365	11	2
From John Price, "taken by Lewis Turner, master of an armed boat from New York, in March, 1781"	67	19	5
From Israel Longacre, "by some persons who said they belonged to the shipping in the Delaware, then under the command of Lord Howe, October or November"	8	5	0
From John Victor, taken by "a party of the enemy from the water commander, not known, in the fall of 1777".	56	8	0
From Lewis Trimble, "by two British sergeants, under General Howe," October 25	135	0	0
From Robert Crozer, December 25	6	14	3
	639	17	10

John Morton, whose name appears first on this list, was one of the most conspicuous men of the Revolutionary war in Chester County. He was born in Ridley in 1725, and is generally believed to be of Swedish descent, although that fact has never been fully established. His father died before his birth, and his mother subsequently married John Sketchley, an Englishman, who, himself well educated, instructed his stepson—to whom he was much attached—in mathematics, and imparted to him the common branches of a good education. In 1756, when thirty-one years of age, Morton was elected to the Provincial Assembly, to which body he was successively re-elected until and including 1760, a period of eleven years' continuous service. In 1765, when again a member of Assembly, he was one of the delegates from Pennsylvania to the "Stamp Act Congress," which convened in New York in October of that year. In 1767 he was elected sheriff of Chester County, and in 1769 was a member of Assembly, continuing as such until 1775 inclusive, a period of seven years, presiding as Speaker over its deliberations during the last year of his service therein. In 1764 he was commissioned one of the justices of the county courts, and part of the time the president judge. In 1774, Governor John Penn appointed him an associate justice of the Supreme Provincial Court. In that year the Assembly appointed him a delegate to the first Continental Congress, and he was reappointed to the second memorable Congress which adopted the Declaration of Independence, and when that question was pending before Congress he voted for the adoption of the measure. John Morton was the first of the signers of the Declaration who died, that event occurring in April, 1777, he having then attained the age of fifty-three. As a private citizen his life was, so far as known, without stain, his public record that of an earnest, honest advocate of the right because it was right, and as an advocate and signer of the Declaration of Independence he is deserving of the esteem and admiration of his countrymen.

The following were the taxables in Ridley township in 1715:

Jacob Simcock, Joseph Harvey, John Stedman, John Hanby, Thomas Dell, John Sharpless, Jacob Simcock, Jr., John Simcock, Joseph Powell, John Crosby, Lawrence Ffriend and Gabriel, Amus Nicholas, Enoch Enochsen, George Brown, Andrew Hendrick, George Vanculine, Andrew Torton, Hance Torton, Andrew Morton, John Hendrick, Andrew Morton, Jr., John Orchard, Israel Taylor, Jonathan Hood, Obadiah Bonsall.

The taxables in Ridley in 1799 were as follows:

William Boon, William Beatty, John Crosby (justice of the peace), Robert Colvin, John Crosby, Jr., Philip Cline, Isaac Culin (half saw-mill), Gideon Dunn, George Davis, Caleb Davis, David Likens, James Dicks, Duncan McCarty, Henry Effinger, John Hoof (innkeeper), Thomas Hall, Peter Hill (grist-mill, saw-mill), Charles Hedonville, John Irwin, George Jordan, John Knowles, James Knowles, Curtis Lownes (cutter), Andrew Longacre, John McIlvain (saw-mill and old mill-house), John McDaniel, David Treanor, William McMeanes, James Maddock, Aaron Morton, Daniel Morton, Lydia McIlvain, Thomas West, Ann Morton, James McIlvain, John Miller, Jeremiah McIlvain (farmer), John McCally, Isaac Worrell and Thomas Noblett, William Painter, Abijah Price, Isaac McIlvain, William Price, Mary Pywell, Joseph Pearson (innkeeper), Benjamin Pyle, William Paul, Jacob Painter, Charles Ramsey, Ann Smith Shoemaker, John Smith, William Shoemaker, Abraham Trimble, Michael Trytes, William Worrell, Joseph Weaver (miller), John Worrall,

[1] Bulletin of Historical Society of Pennsylvania, vol. i. No. 10, March, 1847, p. 29.

[2] Ib., p. 30.

[3] Martin's "History of Chester," p. 173. The account of the shooting of Capt. Culin by one of his men when being mustered into service at the White Horse, in 1776, and the capture of Capt. John Crosby by a boat's crew from an English man-of-war in the winter of 1777–78, will be found *ante*, p. 242.

Jacob Worrell, Thomas West, George Warner, Samuel Crozer, Richard Britton.

Non-Residents.—Nathaniel Smith, David Treanor, Isaac Eyre, William Lane, John Crozer, Sarah Penyear, George Hinkson, Jacob Benninghove, Charles Granthum, Thomas Leiper, Joshua Thompson, Caleb Davis (half a saw-mill), Joseph Shallcross, Edward Flanders.

Inmates.—Michael Roe, Hugh Wilson, Robert Smith, Anthony Gurpre, Isaac Hance, Edward Russell, James Maddock, Samuel Worrell, John Tanence, Nathan Weer, John Thompson, John McDaniel, George Wetherill, Peter Welch, Thomas Price, Robert Blythe, John Kitts, John Conner, James Weer, Robert Davenport, John L. Booty, John Culin (carpenter), William Cowen, William Dunn, Evan Edmunds (blacksmith), George Likens, Aaron Helms, Valentine Vanholt, Vell Price (weaver), William Carpenter.

Single Freemen.—Enoch Morton (carpenter), Joseph Pearson (carpenter), William Whiteman (store-keeper), James Miller, William Brittain, Michael Kitts, Israel Morton (carpenter), Charles Crozer (carpenter), Henry Trimble (tailor), Robert Noblett, Job Baxter (sawyer), Hugh McIlvain, Alexander Hopkins (tanner), William Hill (miller), William Ore, John Mitchell, John Nelson, Darby Croneon, John Truman (tanner).

The justices for Ridley township since the erection of Delaware County have been as follows:

John Crosby	Aug. 30, 1791.
Joel Willis	Aug. 30, 1791.
Davis Bevan	Aug. 19, 1794.
Miles Macarty	Aug. 13, 1796.
Elisha Price	Aug. 15, 1796.
William Martin	Aug. 9, 1797.
Isaac Eyre	Oct. 12, 1798.
Nicholas Fairlamb	Dec. 6, 1798.
Aaron Morton	May 3, 1799.
Philip Painter	May 20, 1800.
Thomas Hinkson	May 20, 1800.
John Pearson	June 21, 1802.
James Withey	July 4, 1806.
Jacob Edwards	Jan. 1, 1807.
John Caldwell	Nov. 15, 1814.
Joseph Walker	Feb. 3, 1820.
Samuel Smith	March 12, 1822.
David Marshall	March 3, 1824.
George W. Bartram	June 3, 1824.
Benjamin F. Johnson	Oct. 25, 1825.
Abraham Kerlin	June 7, 1830.
Samuel T. Walker	Nov. 11, 1831.
John Afflick	June 6, 1834.
Jonathan P. Worrall	March 5, 1835.
Samuel Shaw	Nov. 18, 1835.
William Martin	June 10, 1836.
William Eyre	Dec. 21, 1838.
George W. Bartram	Sept. 23, 1839.
William Hill	April 14, 1840.
Jonathan P. Worrall	April 14, 1840.
Jonathan P. Worrall	April 15, 1845.
Jesse W. Griffiths	April 11, 1848.
Jonathan P. Worrall	April 9, 1850.
Jesse W. Griffith	April 13, 1853.
Jonathan P. Worrall	April 5, 1855.
Jesse W. Griffith	April 16, 1858.
Jonathan P. Worrall	April 10, 1860.
Jonathan P. Worrall	April 28, 1865.
William Worrall	April 15, 1872.
Robert M. Copeland	April 21, 1873.
William H. Price	March 13, 1875.
John F. Young	March 20, 1876.
William H. Price	March 30, 1880.
William Worrall	April 6, 1883.

Churches.—The first mention of religious services being held in Ridley occurs at a Monthly Meeting held at Chester on 11th of the Seventh month, 1682, when it was agreed among other places to hold meeting, "the Eastern Meeting at Ridley, at John Simcock's, the fifth day of the week, until otherwise was ordered." The meeting was subsequently changed to Walter Faucet's house on Ridley Creek, near the present Irvington, where the road to Philadelphia crosses the stream. Faucet kept a tavern at this location, but after the erection of Chester meeting-house the meetings at his house were abandoned. Friends never erected a building for public worship in Ridley.

Free Christian Church.—On the south side of the Queen's Highway, south of the present Crum Lynne Station, stands a dilapidated stone structure, the broken roof no longer shielding the interior of the building from the rain, known as the "Plummer Meeting-House." Early in this century a few people residing in the neighborhood organized a Free Christian Church, and on Dec. 29, 1818, Isaac Culin conveyed to John L. Morton, John Price, Abraham Wood, Jonathan Bond, and Samuel Tibbetts, as trustees, one acre of land lying on the post-road from Philadelphia to Chester. On this lot a stone house thirty by forty feet was erected, and Rev. Frederick Plummer, the elder pastor of a like church in Philadelphia, became its minister. After his death the organization gradually dissolved, the last meeting being held in the church about 1865. In the graveyard around the building in former times many bodies were buried, but even the cemetery has ceased to be used for interments. Franklin Parsons, of Ridley, and —— Carr, of Springfield, are the surviving trustees.

Leiper's Church.—Thomas Leiper, in 1818, erected a stone church on the Leiperville road, on the site of the present Leiper Church, and gave an adjoining lot for a graveyard. The following year a school-house was erected on the same lot, which is still standing, but in ruins. The church was destroyed by fire Sunday, Jan. 28, 1849, which originated from a stove-pipe that passed through the roof. The corner-stone of a new stone Gothic chapel was laid June 17, 1850. The Rev. Dr. Greer and the Rev. Mr. Cuyler assisted the pastor, Rev. James W. Dale, in the ceremonies on the occasion. The chapel is thirty by fifty feet, and cost seven thousand dollars. The following clergymen have been pastors of the church: Rev. John Smith, Rev. Alom H. Packer, Rev. John L. Janeway, Rev. William L. McCalla, Rev. James W. Dale (installed May 17, 1846), Rev. Alexander Heberton, and Rev. Charles Ewing, the last incumbent. He was installed Oct. 15, 1872. The Rev. George Hood, Rev. Mr. Dobson, Rev. Mr. Sproull, and the Rev. Mr. Robbins, of Media, conducted the exercises. The chapel was closed in 1876, reopened in 1878, used for a few years, and is now seldom occupied.

Baptist Chapel.—In 1871, Samuel A. Crozer of Upland erected a brick chapel for the use of the Baptists in and near Leiperville. It is under the care of Ridley Park Baptist Church, and the pulpit is mostly supplied by the students from Crozer Theological Seminary. The chapel was dedicated Oct. 21, 1877. The dedicatory address was delivered by Dr. Henry Weston, of the Crozer Theological Seminary.

Schools.—On the 12th day of Second month, 1800, a number of the inhabitants of the township convened at the public-house of Jacob Painter to take action on the erection of a school-house in the township. William Paul was chosen chairman of the meeting, and Aaron Morton secretary. From resolutions adopted it appears that Isaac Culin had given a lot of ground as a site for a school-house, but the meeting did not approve of the situation, whereupon Caleb Davis proposed to give forty two perches of ground on the north side of the Great road, adjoining the lot then occupied by Peter Norbury, which was accepted A committee was appointed to notify the prominent inhabitants in the township of the action of the meeting and ask their concurrence in the movement, for which purpose a call was issued for the entire subscribers to meet on the 17th day of the same month at the same place A resolution was adopted at the meeting following, locating the school-house on the tract of ground presented for that purpose by Caleb Davis, and certain trustees appointed to hold the land for the use of the school At a subsequent meeting held at the house of Jacob Painter on the 25th of Seventh month, the deed to the trustees was executed by Caleb Davis and Lydia, his wife, to Abraham Trimble, Jeremiah McIlvain, and Nathaniel Worrell, trustees The lot contained forty-two square perches, and was described as being on the Post road from Chester to Philadelphia, "for the purposes of a school-house intended to be erected and for which subscriptions is made" The list of subscribers, with amounts subscribed ($386), is here given.

William Paul	$30	Thomas Price	$5
Jeremiah McIlvain	30	William Beatty	5
Abraham Trimble	30	Michael Rowe	5
John McIlvain	30	Rachel Effinger	5
James McIlvain	20	Isaac Worrell	5
Aaron Morton	20	George Jordan	25
Jacob Painter	30	Peter Hill	15
James Maddock	5	William Hill	10
Nathaniel Worrell	30	Mary Pyewell	5
Hugh McIlvain	5	Peter Rovel	5
Henry Trimble	5	Daniel Lamplough	5
Isaac McIlvain	10	Robert Davenport	5
Caleb Davis	40	Jesse Worrell	6

Caleb Davis, William Paul, and John McIlvain were chosen managers, and were instructed to build a suitable building, according to their own ideas in the matter Five trustees were also appointed to look after the interest and instructed to employ a tutor All the subscribers were appointed visitors, whose duty it was to inspect the school once every month, and it was provided that if there should be any moneys remaining in the hands of the trustees after the necessary expenses were paid, that the amount should be expended in purchasing books for the use of the poor who attended the school

The managers, during the Tenth month in the same year, reported to the trustees that the building would shortly be ready for the reception and accommodation of the school, whereupon the trustees advertised for a tutor, and selected for that office Jacob Fenton, a graduate of Dartmouth College An agreement was made with him on the 15th of the Tenth month, which provided that he should "teach a regular Day-School, subject to the direction of the trustees of said school, in the rudiments of the English language, reading, writing, arithmetic, book-keeping, geography, and either or every branch of the mathematics, at the rate of two dollars a quarter for every scholar subscribed for the term of three months, to commence on the 20th day of Tenth month, 1800 And the undersigned subscribers to said school agree to pay the said Fenton or order two dollars for every scholar subscribed, together with a reasonable charge for wood and ink"

Before the winter had passed Fenton was in financial difficulties He sent his bills before they were due, refused to allow for time lost by absence, and at the end of his term bade the trustees defiance, and kept possession of the school The trustees resolved to eject him The entry is brief (January, 1801),—"On the morning of the 23d the foregoing resolution of the trustees was carried into effect"

"2d mo 2, 1801 William Fairlamb commenced teaching, at the rate of Eight dollars a year, fire-wood and ink allowed" Ink came in paper packages in those days The preparation was put in a bottle, and a certain quantity of water poured upon it Then it was shaken, and after standing a while was ready for use Quills were the only pens in those days

Fourth month 6, 1801 Samuel Lytle commenced teaching at two dollars per quarter and fire-wood and ink The trustees "agreed to meet in future on the first 2d day of each month, at 2 o'cl'k in the afternoon," or to pay fifty cents for every such neglect, which money was to be laid out in books for the use of the school

Tenth month 5th It was agreed "to give premiums at the next examination to those scholars who should make the greatest improvement or excel in any particular branch of the education, and for the second and next best"

Feb 6, 1804 A meeting of the subscribers was held to inquire into the decorum of the school, the conduct of the master, and the neglect of the trustees to attend to their duties for two years The old board of trustees was removed, and a new board appointed

20th Feb, 1804 A meeting of the trustees report that there were "forty-five scholars," and that the master's conduct was not approved On March 5th there were thirty-seven scholars The trustees unanimously agreed not to employ Mr Lytle, the present master, any longer than his present engagement, and on April 2d the trustees found the school-house locked, "neither teacher nor scholars" being in attendance

3d May, 1804 Archibald McKenney became teacher, preparing the articles of agreement and then refused to furnish the trustees with a copy, so "no record could be made" The consequence was the school "fell off" to fifteen pupils, and the master was discharged.

Twelfth month, 1804 Joseph Barrows became the teacher In April, 1805, he had forty-three scholars and was much praised for his capacity In June there were sixty-eight scholars in attendance, and in August the master absconded in debt to several persons

9th Sept, 1805 Jonas P Fairlamb agreed to teach

Caleb Davis, however, took his stove away, and James Maddock undertook to procure another "to remain forever for the use of the school."

Oct. 28, 1805. The committee settled, allowed, and approved the account for building the school, amounting to $502.19, being $121.19 in excess of the contributions.

On Dec. 12, 1805, Jonathan Dutton became schoolmaster, the terms still being the same, two dollars per quarter. In January, 1806, he had twenty-six scholars, but had no authority over them, and the schoolroom fell to fourteen scholars.

28th April, 1806. James Townsend became master at two dollars and fifty cents for subscribers' children, and twenty per cent. more for non-subscribers. On May 23d there were forty pupils. About the year 1812, Thomas Kitts was teacher, with thirty-nine scholars in attendance.

April 18, 1816. Jesse Broomall agreed to teach six months for one hundred and sixty dollars. In 1826, Jan. 15th, he was again the master at two dollars and fifty cents per scholar, and here at the date on the records the dollar-mark ($) is first used.

June, 1819, Michael Burke was chosen master for three months at three dollars per quarter. Burke was employed another quarter, "at which time Jesse Broomall has engaged to return, and on Dec. 29th he resumed the position as teacher."

29th March, 1819, Samuel Lytle began teaching at three dollars per quarter. In August there were sixty scholars. The trustees thought this too many, and notified the subscribers that only fifty would be received per day.

Feb. 5, 1820, the trustees, on account of the teacher's extreme youth and inexperience, etc. (his name is not given), advertised for another teacher in the *Village Record and Post-Boy*. Samuel Lytle and Nathaniel Vernon applied. The latter was chosen. Terms, two dollars per quarter; three dollars if mathematics were taught. The school-house is built of stone, and was used under the management of the trustees until the township accepted the school law, when the building was given in care of the school directors, and was used by them until about 1870, when it was abandoned and the new brick school-house took its place. The old house is now used as a dwelling, and the ownership of the property is in dispute.

On Aug. 20, 1800, Lewis Morey conveyed to William Boon and Aaron Martin, trustees, thirty-seven and a half square perches of land on the Lazaretto, between the Southern post-road and Moore's Station, in trust "to build a school-house thereon, and for no other purpose." That school was built immediately, as it appears on Hill's maps, and was used under the control of the trustees, when it passed into the charge of the school directors, who maintained school therein until 1879, when the Norwood school-house was built. The old house is now owned by William Trainer.

In the year 1819, Thomas Leiper erected a stone school-house on the Leiper Church lot, which was used until the "Thomas Leiper School-House" was erected, in 1870, by the school directors, on the opposite side of the road. The old building is still standing, but in ruins.

In 1862 the Kedron school-house, located on the road from Morton to Norwood Station, was erected, a lot having been purchased of Thomas I. Tasker and George W. Caldwell for that purpose. It is a one-story stone structure.

In 1870 the school directors erected a two-story brick school-house, thirty by forty feet, on the south side of the Southern post-road, a short distance south of Crum Lynne. The building was enlarged in 1873. In 1876 the directors erected on the northwest corner of Lexington and Second Streets, Eddystone, a two-story brick school-house, and in 1879, at Norwood, the directors erected a two-story brick school-house.

At the March election in 1825, James Maddock, John L. Pearson, and George G. Leiper were elected school trustees for the township, and after the adoption of the school law of 1834 the court appointed George G. Leiper and William Martin inspectors of the public schools, until directors were elected. In 1835 Ridley received five hundred and fifty-five dollars and forty-five cents, its proportion of the county and State appropriations.

The following is a list of school directors of the township since 1840, as they appear of record in Media:

1840, John D. Kelly, George M. Maris; 1842, George G. Leiper, Jonathan P. Worrall, Edward Horne; 1843, John H. Miller, John Noble; 1844, Isaac Stewart, Thomas Powell; 1845, Jacob Hewes, Jacob Worrell; 1846, Alexander Moorhead, Joseph Powell; 1847, Alexander M. Wright, Neal Duffee; 1848, Philip Morris, Jacob Worrall; 1849, James Ward, Thomas T. Hutton; 1850, Washington Berry, James Lenney; 1851, James Hogeland, William Johuson; 1852, William H. Gesner, Hugh C. Sample; 1853, James McCormick, Benjamin Miller; 1854, Jonathan P. Worrall, Jesse W. Griffith; 1855, William H. Gesner, John C. Leiper; 1856, George Gesner, Alexander Moorhead; 1857, no report; 1858, Hugh C. Sample, William H. Gesner; 1859, Jesse W. Noble, Thomas H. Gesner; 1860, Joseph Smiley, Thomas McBride; 1861, William McFarland, Isaac D. Worrall; 1862, Thomas Gesner, William S. Sample; 1863, Thomas McBride, Joseph Powell; 1864, George Lodge, Sr., William McFarland; 1865, Thomas H. Gesner, Hugh C. Sample; 1866, George W. Gesner, David Johnson; 1867, Thomas McBride, Peter Stewart; 1868, Bethel Curter, H. C. Sample; 1869, Franklin Parsons, James Roop; 1870, W. McFarlan, Thomas McBride; 1871, David Johnson, Samuel Palmer; 1872, Miles W. Stille, Thomas J. Hutchinson; 1873, Thomas McBride, Samuel Palmer; 1874, William Worrall, Bethel M. Custer; 1875, Thomas C. Hutchinson, Benjamin M. Norton; 1876, S. T. Fuller, Joseph L. Lukens; 1877, Bethel M. Custer, Neal Duffee; 1878, Thomas C. Hutchinson, M. M. Stille; 1879, Abram Ward, W. J. Kelly; 1880, Bethel M. Custer, T. F. Foregar; 1881, G. P. Dennis, Thomas C. Hutchinson; 1882, Abram Ward, E. G. Woodward; 1883, Thomas F. Kreeger, John W. Armstrong; 1884, G. P. Dennis, T. C. Hutchinson.

The Crosby Forge.—Prior to Dec. 24, 1740, John Crosby, Jr., and Richard Crosby operated a forge on Crum Creek. At Leiperville, near the residence of the late Jacob Hewes, just west of the bridge and east of the house, "can still be seen a large embankment, with trees growing upon it. This, I imagine, was the tract of the dam which gave the water-power necessary for the forge."[1] The forge had been built by John Crosby, the elder, and Peter Dick, as is evident from the following extracts from the minutes of Chester Monthly Meeting:

"8th mo. 25, 1742. The Representatives of Chester meeting have acquainted this meeting that there is some Difference between John Crosby and Thomas Dell, because the said John Crosby and Peter Dicks haveing built a forge on Crum Crick, ye damm whereof overflows some part of ye said Dell's land, the damage of which they have not yet been able to settle, neither by themselves, nor by some assistance they have had, ye said Thomas Dell haveing insisted to have a certain sum of money yearly, or to have the Dam Pulled down. After some debate on the affair, and Proposals of appointing of friends to Indeaver to Reconcile ye said Difference, ye said Thomas Dell being present, absolutely Refused to be determined by either friends of their own choice or such as the meeting should appoint, but Refused to Confer any Longer on the Occasion, and Departed the said meeting, not only without Leave, but Contrary to the Request and advice thereof.

"1 mo. 28, 1743. Thomas Dell hath complaned to this meeting that ye damm at ye forge on Crum Creek yet overflows some part of his land, and that they cannot agree to settle ye difference or damage between them, nor will the said Thomas Dell chose men to deside ye said difference. Therefore this meeting appoints John Maris, William Pennell, Thomas Goodwin, Samuel Lewis, James Bartram, and Johsua Thompson to meett some time at ye said damm between this and next meeting, to Compute ye said Damage, and Indeavour to Reconcile ye said difference, and make Report thereof at next meeting.

"2 mo. 25, 1743. The Committee report that they cannot reconcile the parties, and that Thomas Dell is not willing for the matter to be determined by any body but himself, but they think John Crosby & Peter Dicks should pay him £5 per annum so long as the water Damnifies the said Dell's land, to which John and Peter (being present) agree. Thomas Dell appealed to the Quarterly Meeting."

Peter Kalm, the Swedish naturalist, in his "Travels into North America," written in 1748 and 1749, thus describes it: "About two English miles behind Chester I passed by an iron forge, which was to the right hand by the road side. It belonged to two brothers, as I was told. The ore, however, is not dug here, but thirty or forty miles from hence, where it is first melted in the oven, and then carried to this place. The bellows were made of leather, and both they and the hammers, and even the hearth, [were] but small in proportion to ours. All the machines were worked by water. The iron was wrought into bars."

The oven spoken of by Kalm, a recent writer suggests, was a blast-furnace, most probably located in the Schuylkill Valley, and the pigs for the forge were boated down the Schuylkill to the Delaware, and thence to and up Crum Creek.[2] From the report of John Owens, the sheriff of Chester County, in 1750, it is evident that this forge was not then in operation. John Crosby, the elder, who died previous to Oct. 15, 1750, devised his one-half interest in the forge to his son, John Crosby, Jr., "together with my part of the utensils belonging thereto." Acrelius, writing of the iron-works in Pennsylvania prior to 1756, says that the forge on "Crum Creek belongs to Peter Dick; has two stacks, is working sluggishly, and has ruined Crosby's family."[3] Peter Dick died shortly after the visit of Acrelius, and the forge, from "working sluggishly," was doubtless then entirely abandoned as a business enterprise.

Lapidea Mill.—On Crum Creek, at the place now known as Lapidea, in 1770, Hugh Lloyd was carrying on a grist-mill, and in the order of Washington to Gen. Potter requiring the mill-stones to be taken from several mills, he particularly mentions "Lloyd's, about two miles on this side of Chester."[4] In 1785, the mills were then owned by John Wall, and in that year Richard Flower, Wall's step-son, who had just married Henrietta, a daughter of Judge Graham, removed there and operated the mill, continuing there until 1789, when he removed to Chester Mill, and in 1790, George Pierson is returned as running the mill for Richard Flower. In 1802, Peter Deshong seems to have owned the mill, which was then operated by Joseph Walton, and in 1807 by Foster & Hinkson. In 1808, Thomas Leiper owned the grist- and saw-mill, and in that year his name for the first time appears on the assessment-rolls of Ridley township. In 1816 he erected the present stone mill, which was operated by his son, George G. Leiper. In the spring of 1821, John P. Crozer went into partnership with George G. Leiper in these mills. Logs were purchased at Richmond (now a part of Philadelphia) and rafted down the Delaware and up Ridley Creek to the head of tide-water. This partnership lasted only during the summer. A large quantity of lumber had been manufactured and business was very dull. The outlook was so discouraging that Mr. Crozer retired from the firm. After a careful examination of the many branches of business enterprise, John P. Crozer decided to venture into that of cotton-spinning, there being at that time one factory then operating successfully in the county, that of Wagstaff & Englehorn (on Chester Creek, now known as Manchester Mill) in Upper Providence. Mr. Crozer purchased the machinery in a small cotton-mill on the Brandywine, and rented the second and third stories as well as part of the first story of the grist-mill of George G. Leiper, in which he had been previously interested, moved the machinery to the building in November, 1821, and commenced work in February, 1822.

At this place he remained under many disadvantages until 1825, when he moved to West Branch, where he purchased a mill. He was succeeded in the Leiper Mill the next year (1826) by Joseph Burt, who rented the upper story of the grist-mill for a woolen-factory, and employed seventeen hands, and operated one pair of stocks, two carding-engines, one billy of fifty spindles, and two jennies of seventy spindles each. Mr. Burt continued in occupancy of the upper story of the mill until 1841, and was succeeded by Richard Blunden, who conducted both the grist-mill and the woolen-factory. He manufactured

[1] Martin's "History of Chester."
[2] "The Manufacture of Iron in all Ages," by James M. Swank, p. 134.
[3] History of New Sweden, p. 105.
[4] *Ante*, p. 68.

ingrain and Venetian carpets, double coverlets, etc In 1847 he was operating four hundred and sixty-eight throstle spindles, three hundred mule-spindles, and thirty looms In 1848, Edward Taylor operated the mill, but was unsuccessful in business, and his machinery was sold by the sheriff in November, 1848 The mill was then rented by Daniel Lee Subsequently the property passed to Samuel Lewis, who now owns it It has been rented to different parties before 1871, and to the present time it has been operated by Cockroft & Black It has a plant of worsted machinery, and manufactures three thousand pounds of yarn per week

Davis & Culin Saw-Mill—On the 30th of October, 1797, Caleb Davis and Isaac Culin entered into an agreement jointly to build "a saw-mill and water-works" on a tract of land at the junction of Crum Creek and Little Crum Creek, in more recent years known as "The Island Field" A saw-mill was erected nearly at the junction of the two creeks, and a race from Little Crum Creek brought the water to the mill On April 14, 1806, Davis sold his interest in the mill property to John Newbold, and on August 11th of the same year, Culin & Newbold sold the property to Eli Lewis The mill had been discontinued prior to 1825 On March 25, 1831, Eli Lewis in turn sold the property to John F Hill The latter was unsuccessful in business, and made an assignment of his property to James Maddock and Robert E Hannum The assignees, in 1843, conveyed the property, then consisting of seventy-one acres, "with right of mill-seat, water-works, dam, and race (now out of repair), on the waters of Little Crum Creek and Big Crum Creek," to William J Leiper The mill, which had fallen entirely into disuse, was abandoned, and finally disappeared, until the fact of its having ever stood there had almost faded out of memory of the oldest resident in that neighborhood, until recalled to recollection by direct inquiry made while gathering data for this work The property now belongs to Clarence Deshong, of Chester

Licensed Houses—The Salutation or Wheat Sheaf.—Early in the annals of the county Walter Fauset was granted license for a public-house in Ridley, and doubtless other persons had the like privilege extended to them prior to Aug 26, 1729, when the first petition found of record was presented by Joshua Thomson In fact, we learn that this was the case by the quaint document itself, which sets forth that his (Thomson's) house was located "on a very public road, about half a quarter of a mile from a house which was licensed for several years, but vacant for a considerable time past" He also stated that he was four or five miles from any public-house Thomson was granted license continuously until 1747. This house is believed to be the old Drove Tavern, while the house to which he referred was a stone building, which stood on the road nearly opposite the residence of the late William Maddock, south of Crum Lynne

In 1752, Abel Janney was granted the right to sell liquor at the Thomson house, and the inn was at that time known as The Salutation, the sign representing a pair of clasped hands, showing the arms above the elbows The Swedes, who used to make this house their headquarters, were in the habit, it is said, of kicking each other's shins for cider, and he that cried "Hold, enough!" was required to pay for the liquor of all present One Swede, tradition states, for a long time managed always to be on the winning side, until it was discovered that he had adroitly concealed the leg of a chair in each of his stockings, and thus defied the toes of his adversaries' boots In 1757, Mordecai Thomson was the landlord, who seems to have died in 1758, for in that year Hannah, his wife or daughter, received the license, and continued to do so for many years thereafter In 1797, Aaron Morton was the landlord for two years, and in 1799, Thomas West took the house, and in his petition stated that Caleb Davis owned the property, which had, previous to his application, been in the tenure of Morton In 1800, Jacob Painter became the landlord, and then, for the first time, the name of the tavern, The Wheat Sheaf, appears, and continued during all the period for which Jacob Painter was its host and proprietor, until Painter, after 1824, declined to take out license, and offered the property for sale In his advertisement he describes the house as on the post-road, twelve miles from Philadelphia and three from Chester, the building being a two-story stone house, fifty feet front and eighteen deep, with a piazza front, three rooms on the lower floor, three on the second, and a good garret, a large stone kitchen, with chambers above, with sufficient sheds and stabling. The farm attached to the hotel comprised forty-two and one-half acres above the road and twenty acres below it, towards the river At the intersection of Swarthmore Avenue with the Queen's Highway, or Southern post-road, was formerly a private graveyard of the Painter family The little burial-place was inclosed by a thick-set thorn hedge In 1827, Edward Horn had license for the ancient hotel, which he named the Drove, his sign representing a number of cattle being driven along a highway. In 1832, Horn received license for the last time, since which period the old house has been occupied as a private dwelling It is still standing, is included within the limits of Ridley Park, and is now occupied by Curtis Taylor.

The Morris Ferry-House—On Feb 24, 1729/30, Adam Archer asked the indulgence of the court, stating that his house was "on the Banks of a Large Navigable Creek Leading out of the said River Delaware, Commonly known as Amos Land," and further added, "your petitioner's Landing being close at his door" Notwithstanding that a remonstrance signed by twelve persons was presented against the granting of this license, the court decided to approve of Archer's application Without doubt the location of this license was at the Darby Creek Ferry-House of more recent years The old structure still remains, bearing the mark of great antiquity "The figures 1698 are carved on the inner side of the mantelpiece of the northwest end of the building, and no doubt indicate the date of its erection It is built of white-cedar log, flattened Between this end and the other wooden end there is a space built up with stone Through this space, and between the two wooden ends of the present building, the road formerly passed to the ferry "[1]

In 1733, Adam Archer applied for license for a house at another location, which he designated as on the King's road, and about midway between Chester and Darby, mentioned in the history of the White Horse Tavern On Feb 25, 1734, he again came before the Court, stating that he "wishes to sell Beer and Cyder to travellers, and especially to those who come to buy fish," which was allowed, but on May 28, 1734, a remonstrance was presented against the license, setting forth that Archer "had formerly kept A publick-house, but after several complaints was set aside, since which time there was more peace & quiet." This paper was signed by Andrew Morton, Hans Forten, and other Swedes, as also by Peter Dick and several Friends, who in the document strongly objected to the term "Worships" as applied to the justices. The remonstrance is indorsed "Granted to ye petitioners"

Archer, however, seems at a subsequent session to have procured the license, for Aug 26, 1735, he informed the court that he had the right to sell beer and cider, but now desires the justices to permit him to "keep publick-house as formerly" But the stern tribunal shook their wise heads and declined to accede to his desires

On Aug 28, 1744, John Hendrickson, of Amosland, "upon Darby Creek, where Great number of Travellers, as well by land as by water, daily resort," made application for license to sell liquor at his house, which was allowed him This location, I am told, subsequently became the Darby Ferry-House, although I do not learn anything about "the ferry across to Tinicum Island from Darby Creek" until 1786, when John Hoof petitioned to have license for a house of entertainment there, and also to keep a ferry across to Tinicum Island from Darby Creek I am inclined to think that this is the site of the dwelling already mentioned where Adam Archer, in 1729, first received license "on the banks of a large navigable creek leading out of the said river Delaware" The Amosland road, it should not be overlooked, was laid out in 1688, and was an important thoroughfare in early times John Hoof continued annually to receive license until 1801, when George Gill, who had petitioned vainly the year previous for license in Chester, obtained the privilege for the Darby ferry, and continued there the year following In 1804, Philip Morris became the landlord and ferry-master, and from that time the place became known as Morris' Ferry Here he continued until his death, in 1826,—excepting during the year 1806, when Charles Lloyd had the license,—when his sons, George and Amos Morris, succeeded to the business, and continued until 1830, when George Morris became the landlord He received license annually without objection until 1842, when a remonstrance was urged against him, in which it was argued that his location was in an out-of-the-way place, with little or no traveling public to entertain, and that he conducted the business to the injury of the neighborhood, since intemperate people for miles around would accumulate there, and for days together indulge in a drunken frolic The court, however, permitted him to continue there, but in the following year (1843) the license was for the last time given to the hotel

The White Horse Tavern—Adam Archer, on Feb 24, 1729/30, applied for a license, in which he informed the court that he lived on the King's road, about midway between Chester and Darby, and asked that he be permitted thereat to keep a public-house In addition to his petition, his aged father memorialized the court as follows

"To the Right Worshipfull his Majestie's Justices of peace sitting in the Court of Quarter Sessions for ye Burrow and County of Chester, the twenty-sixth day of February, Anno Domi 173¾

"The Petition of John Archer, of Amosland, in the said County Humbly sheweth that ye Petitioner having lived upon ye Bank of Darby Creek in Amosland Afores^d (for ye term of forty years and upwards), A place Conveniantly Situated for the Importation and Exportation of such things as ye publick have had occasion to Receive and Deliver there, And likewise for such people as have business to go Across or up and down ye s^d Creek with Boat Cannoe or otherwise, and also ye place which yearly at ye time of fishing the people doth chiefly wate till they can be supplyed with such quantity of fish as at such times they had occasion for, In all which Cases y^r petitioner hath from time to time for many years past been very helpfull to ye publick with his Cannoes and Assistance whensoever thereunto Required, And when any were obliged to wait long, then ye petitioner made them welcome to the Entertainment of his house without any other Reward than ye pleasure and satisfacsion he took in being usefull to ye public therein But for as much as ye petitioner is now grown very Antiant, and of late hath been very sorely afflicted with sickness and ye infirmaties of old age so as to be Confined to his Bed for the time of sixteen months, and not able to help himself But by ye assistance of his wife and Children, he having but one son left with him, which for ye reasone afores^d heath Rendred your petitioner much less Capable to serve ye publick than in time past, And that very Noise of a Concourse of people, though ever so well behaved, is a further addition to ye Calamities of y^r petitioner, who for his own ease, the benefit of the publick and the entertainment of travilors, Humbly prayeth that ye petitioner's son Adam Archer may obtain y^r worships' Recommendation to our Honourable Governour for his liscence to keep a house of publick Entertainment According to ye prayer of his petition and as the Certificate of ye publick thereunto Annexed doth set forth, And y^r petitioner as in duty Bound shall pray

"JOHN ARCHER"

The justices held the matter under advisement, and Aug 28, 1733, a remonstrance, signed by Thomas Tatnall and eight others, was presented, declaring that Adam Archer then kept a public-house in Ridley (at Morris' Ferry), and his petition was refused On Aug 26, 1735, the "insatiate Archer" petitioned again, with the declaration that he "hath for several years Last past obtained your honors' Lycence to Keep a

[1] Smith's "History of Delaware County," p 389

house of Entertainment for selling Beer or Cider on the great Road Leading from Chester, Called and Known by the name of the half way house, in the Township of Ridley," and now wishes "Recomendation to the President and Councill of the province of Pensilvania for their Lycense to Keep a public house of Entertainment at the aforesaid place" John Andrews, Samuel Crozer, John Wharton, John Sketchley, John West, and fifteen others indorsed his application, but the court marked on the petition, "allowed for beer & Syder only" Archer must at a subsequent court have received full license to keep a public-house, for he yearly appears on the clerk's list of approved petitions, and was continued until 1746 On Aug 31, 1742, however, he was compelled to fight again for his privilege, for when he applied for license he found a remonstrance had been filed by Jonas Culin, Feb 22, 1742, asking that it should be withheld, because, as Culin stated, Archer had been "entertaining ye Petitioner's Servant Man a Tippling and Spending money" The remonstrance was rejected, and indorsed, "disregarded for want of proof," as also was the fate of a similar paper filed by Ann Torton, who complained of Archer "for getting John Torton to sign notes while drunk" Notwithstanding these allegations the license was granted to the petitioner

In 1746, Isaac Gleave succeeded Adam Archer in business, and was in turn followed by Edward Fitzrandolph, in 1754, at which time the hotel was known as The White Horse, for in the preceding year it is so spoken of by the signers to the petition asking that that part of Ridley now in Nether Providence, between the Ridley and Crum Creek, should be attached to Nether Providence[1] In 1764, Jacob Fritz had the hotel, and in 1766, John Bryan followed Fritz In 1776, a company of American militia, attached to Col Morgan's regiment of the "Flying Camp," commanded by Capt Culin and John Crosby, first lieutenant, were being mustered in at the White Horse, when one of the privates shot Capt Culin, killing him instantly[2] Bryan dying in 1778, Barbara Bryan, the relict of John Bryan, had license until 1782, when John Aquandrill followed her, and in 1786, Joseph Pearson had the license, and annually thereafter until 1799 During the early part of that year a peddler, who had stopped for the night at the house, was found a few days afterward in Ridley Creek, drowned, and although no one suspected that the proprietor had done anything amiss, the circumstances surrounding the case excited so much comment in the county that the justices withheld license from the White Horse and The Plow Inns Subsequently, in that year, Marmaduke Ford applied for license at the White Horse Inn, but was refused The following year, 1800, and until 1803, Joseph Pearson's application was favorably acted on by the court He having died, in 1804, Elizabeth Pearson became the landlady, and remained so until 1812, when Charles Pearson succeeded her in the business

In 1817, Jonathan Bond received license for the General Jackson Tavern, formerly the White Horse, where he remained until April 1, 1819, when Joseph Carr succeeded him During the following years, until 1825, the house was not licensed, but Edward Horn having rented the tavern at the latter date, secured the grace of the court for the Drove, late the White Horse Inn In 1827, Horn having taken the old Painter house, Garrett Pyewell became the presiding spirit of the White Horse, for it had now retaken the ancient title, and remained there until 1830, when George Scott was "mine host" He was followed, in 1835, by Patrick McCloskey, and the latter, in 1836, gave place to George Jordan During the year just mentioned, while Jordan was the landlord of the inn, Mary Miller, a colored servant in his employment, without any discoverable occasion, mixed arsenic in the food served to the family, and Mr Jordan and his son, Andrew J, were so severely poisoned that they had liked to have died from the effects of the drug, while the remainder of the household were rendered exceedingly ill after partaking of the meal The girl was subsequently tried for the crime and convicted on two of the three indictments pending against her, but to the third, the charge of poisoning Andrew J Jordan, as she already had been convicted of the same act toward all the family, she interposed the special plea of "former conviction," and was acquitted on that indictment under the instruction of the judge. In 1846, Jordan gave place to Jonathan P Newlin, who remained as landlord of the White Horse until 1869, when William H Woodward had license, and was succeeded in the next year by John P Newlin, who in turn was followed by William F Simes, in 1871 The latter continued until the local option law deprived the old tavern of the legalized sale of liquors. After the repeal of that act, in 1875, James A Stevenson received license, and the following year William F Simes was the landlord In 1877, Edward Griswold superseded Simes, and in 1878, James E Ford was the landlord, and continued as such until 1882 John J Morgan received the license, and who, at present, is the host of the ancient tavern

Leiperville Hotel.—The public-house now known as the Leiperville Hotel was established in 1830, and was the outgrowth of the business of supplying stone to the Breakwater from the Ridley Creek quarries Judge George G. Leiper and most of the owners of quarries in that neighborhood petitioned for the house, which they described as being near the intersection of the old Queen's Highway with the Springfield road, alleging that the license was necessary to furnish accommodations to men employed by them in conveying the stones to the Breakwater, which at that time was one of the largest industries in the county. The court acceded to their petition, and

[1] *Ante*, p 652

[2] *Ante*, p 242

authorized Thomas Ewing to keep a public-house at the location mentioned. There he continued until 1833, the house being known as the Leiperville Tavern, in which year Robert Murray became the landlord and changed the name of the house to The Canal-Boat. In 1835, Daniel J. Campbell leased the premises and restored the old name Leiperville Tavern. There he remained one year, being succeeded by Samuel P. Morris in 1836, while Morris, in 1837, was followed by George P. Alexander. For three years the latter continued at the inn, when, in 1840, Samuel P. Lamplugh became the landlord, to be followed in the succeeding year by James Lenny, who in turn, in 1842, gave place to George C. Hall. In 1844, John Harrison Hill kept the house. It was while he was landlord of the tavern, in 1847, that Leiperville Lodge, No. 263, I. O. of O. F., was instituted, the room first occupied by the lodge being the garret of the wing, which was arranged for that purpose. In 1850, Hill removed to Chester, and was succeeded by John W. Clark, who, 1857, was followed by Edward Lenny, who purchased the property, and remained there until his death, in 1866, when Sarah Lenny, his widow, received license, and continued there until 1880, when Thomas Thompson, the present landlord, was granted the right to continue the Leiperville Tavern as a public-house.

Suburban Parks.—The first effort in Delaware County to lay out a tract of land in streets and lots to attract persons to make settlements there was about 1800, at Buenos Ayres, on the east side of Amosland road, and fronting on the Great Southern road. The project seems to have failed, but the plot of the proposed village is laid out on "A Plan of the City of Philadelphia and Environs, surveyed by John Hill," an exceeding scarce map, published in 1808.

Norwood.—Early in 1872, John Cochran, of Chester, purchased one hundred and fifty acres of land of the estate of Rebecca Gessner. The grounds were laid out into lots, and the proposed town named Norwood, the title being derived from a novel of the like name, written by Rev. Henry Ward Beecher, then recently published. On June 1, 1873, the first public sale of lots was made, which was the first effort made, of which we have record, to induce residents of Philadelphia to purchase villa sites and make a settlement in Ridley. In order that railroad facilities might be had Mr. Cochran donated the land for a station and conveyed the right of way for that purpose. The present Norwood Hotel was commenced in 1875 by Green & Benson, builders, of Philadelphia, but was not completed until 1877, at a cost of twenty thousand dollars. At the present time there are about forty-five houses erected at Norwood.

Ridley Park.—In 1870 the board of directors of the Philadelphia, Wilmington and Baltimore Railroad Company determined to change the location of the road between Philadelphia and Chester from the route through the lowlands along the Delaware, on which had been conducted a constantly-growing passenger and freight traffic since 1837. This meant the construction of a new line from Gray's Ferry, on the Schuylkill, through Darby, Sharon Hill, and other old settlements in the highlands overlooking the Delaware River, besides opening a new region for settlements in the neighborhood of the great city. Several suburban towns were projected on the "Darby Improvement," as the new road was at first termed, that of Ridley Park being on a larger scale and more complete plan than any of the others. In January, 1871, Robert Morris Copeland, a well-known landscape gardener, from Boston, Mass., examined the lands on the location of the new road, with a view to recommend a site for a new town to several gentlemen desirous of embarking in such an enterprise. With this purpose the Harper farm, near Darby, was purchased by them, but was almost immediately sold to the Darby Land Association. Sixteen acres on the southeast corner of the Southern post-road and Sharon Avenue, at Sharon Hill, was also purchased, and was held until sold in lots. It was not until the old Springfield road in Ridley was reached that the site for the new town was determined on. There it was that the experienced eyes of the landscape gardener saw in the rolling land, the creeks, the woodland, the magnificent river views and proximity to Philadelphia the locality he sought as the site for the new suburban town, Ridley Park, the geographical centre of Ridley township. Between January and May, 1870, the following farms were purchased on sixty days' option, and, with the exception of the Burk farm, were subsequently conveyed to the gentlemen who were interested in the purchase, and by them to the Ridley Park Association: John L. Burk; Emily Dutten, forty-two acres; Charles Horne, one hundred and thirty-three acres, which latter tract, as well as the Dutten farm, in 1703, was part of the large estate of Heinrich Torton; from Louisa Free, forty acres, which, in 1791, was owned by Margaret Smith, William, Rebecca, and Margaret Pyewell; Matthew Henderson, thirty-nine acres. In 1685, Thomas Brassie sold part of this tract to Thomas Smith, to whom it was patented in 1691, and of David Henderson twelve acres, which had been part of the Smith patent. Of William W. Maddock fifty-seven acres were purchased, which had formerly belonged to Hannah Carpenter, then to John Crosby, the elder, who sold it, in 1782, to Maddock's ancestors; of Edmund Stewart sixteen acres, which, in 1783, Caleb Davis purchased at sheriff's sale, and subsequently conveyed to the Stewart family; of William J. Trainer fifty acres, which Mary Ward, in 1784, had purchased of Andrew Hamilton; and sixty-three acres which, in 1791, Garrett Hughes had purchased at sheriff's sale, the property then being sold as the estate of Margaret Smith, William, Rebecca, and Margaret Pyewell.

The Burk farm was in litigation for almost seven years, the owner alleging that as Mrs. Burk refused to sign the deed he could not convey a clear title to the land, and the Supreme Court finally decided that by law she could not be compelled to sign away her right of dower unless by her own free will and consent. On May 26, 1871, Lindley Smith, Samuel M. Felton, Isaac Hinckle, and William Sellers entered into a copartnership under the title of the Ridley Park Association. Plans for the new town of Ridley Park were prepared by R. Morris Copeland, and work on the designed improvements began in July, 1871, and were continued under Copeland's supervision until his death, in 1873. He was succeeded by John Smith, who had been intimately connected with the enterprise almost from its inception, and who has been continued superintendent to the present time. The first train of passenger-cars passing over the new road was on Oct. 19, 1872, when a large number of gentlemen connected with the newspaper press of Philadelphia and Chester visited Ridley Park, but the road was not opened for public travel until late in November of that year. Much work had been done on the ground in grading and macadamizing across the roads, erecting a commodious hotel, and constructing a dam across Little Crum Creek, making a lake covering twenty acres, the water of which, at the outlet, forms a cascade, and over the rock of the dam-breast is built a rustic bridge, the whole forming a picturesque feature of great credit to the taste and skill of the landscape gardener. Until the last three years little effort was made to place the land at Ridley Park in the market, due to the stagnation in real estate following the panic of 1873. Notwithstanding this, the healthfulness of the locality, its freedom from malaria, proximity to Philadelphia, and the liberal plan pursued by the association, commended the park to the public, and the result was a number of handsome houses have been erected, and are generally occupied by their owners. In 1880 the census return gave the population of Ridley Park at four hundred and thirty-nine. Samuel M. Felton was president of the association from its inception until April, 1884, when he resigned, and H. F. Kenny, general superintendent of the Philadelphia, Wilmington and Baltimore Railroad, was elected in his stead.

Baptist Church of Ridley Park.—Meetings of Baptists were held in this and adjoining townships as early as 1825, but no organization was perfected until 1832. Soon after that date William Trites donated a lot of land containing fifty-three perches, on the Lazaretto road, a short distance above the White Horse Tavern. It was conveyed by William Trites to William Trites, Daniel Trites, Thomas Jarman, Israel Belton, and John Stoope, trustees, for the use of Baptists only, and under the control of that religious denomination. On this lot a stone house was erected, which bears the date-stone, "Founded A.D. 1832." It was opened for worship April 19, 1834, and was used until the Baptist Church in Ridley Park was completed, in 1872, when the religious exercises were held at the latter place, and the old church building was altered for a Sunday-school chapel, and is now used as such.

On Dec. 11, 1837, the church purchased of William Trites, for one hundred dollars, one hundred and seventeen square perches of land for burial purposes, adjoining the old church-lot, with the right to dam a run near by for the space of twenty-four hours for baptismal purposes. Prior to this time that service had been performed in Darby Creek, on property now owned by Thomas T. Tasker. The burial-ground is still in use for interments. In 1872 three acres of land adjoining the burial-lot was purchased of Samuel Simes, and a part of the consideration paid was the right to dam the run. This tract, in 1879, was sold to the Prospect Park Association. The church was incorporated Oct. 13, 1840, as the "First Particular Baptist Church," with William Trites, Thomas Jarman, William G. Wood, Thomas Glascoe, William Ridgway, John D. Kelly, and John E. Smith as incorporators.

About the time that the Ridley Park Association commenced work on the improvements of what is now known as Ridley Park, the congregation of the Ridley Park Baptist Church, located on the Lazaretto road near Moore's Station, found that their church was becoming too small, and that a new building had become necessary. The newly-projected town of Ridley Park was chosen as the most central location, and a lot was selected on the northwest corner of Ridley Avenue and Ward Street, near the railroad station. The Ridley Park Company gave the lot to the church as their donation, and on this site a handsome stone edifice, costing twenty-seven thousand dollars, was erected according to plans prepared by S. D. Button, architect, Philadelphia. The building contains a lecture-room, two class-rooms, and a large audience-room, seating comfortably over four hundred persons.

The corner-stone of the church was laid July 3, 1873, and the church was completed in the spring of 1874.

The pastors who have been in charge of the church are as follows: Revs. Robert Compton, John P. Hall, C. C. Parke, J. W. Gibbs, Mark R. Watkinson, Samuel Zigler, Mark R. Watkinson, Thomas G. Goodwin, G. R. Entreken, C. E. Harden, John R. Downes, and the Rev. Charles M. Dietz, who assumed charge Feb. 1, 1880, and is the present incumbent. Of these pastors, the Revs. Mark R. Watkinson and Samuel Zigler were ordained in this church. The membership of the First Particular Baptist Church at present is one hundred and fifty, and attached to the church is a Sunday-school of one hundred pupils, of which B. F. Measy is superintendent.

Ridley Park Presbyterian Church.—The first attempt to establish a Presbyterian Church at Ridley Park began in 1873, when the Rev. Mr. Ewing, then of the Ridley Presbyterian Church, preached in the depot on Sunday afternoons, but the movement failed A second effort was made in 1874, by Rev J E Alexander, which also failed Towards the end of that year a Sabbath-school was established Mr Smith, superintendent of Ridley Park, offered the use of the hotel dining-room for the purpose during the winter The first session of the Sabbath-school was held on the first Sunday in January, 1875, and have been held every Sunday since Occasional services were had in the hotel and in the store building, in a room which had been secured for Sabbath-school purposes In August, 1875, at the request of Henry Holcombe, Dr Grier consented to hold regular services for two months at Ridley Park A committee subsequently waited on the doctor and invited him to statedly supply the pulpit for one year, which he consented to do Immediately a movement to build a church was organized The Ridley Park Association gave two lots on the northwest corner of Ridley and Swarthmore Avenues as a site, and plans were furnished by A W Dilks, of Philadelphia, who also supervised the building of the church edifice Work was commenced on Dec 13, 1875, H F. Kinney and D R B Nevin being the building committee The church is of stone, in the Gothic style of architecture, and is thirty by fifty feet, with porch and vestibule It was completed in the summer of 1876, and dedicated September 10th in that year, the Rev Dr M Greer and the Rev Mr Mowry, of Chester, conducting the services The edifice cost when completed about seven thousand dollars, and the church was incorporated to the trustees Sept 8, 1876

A communion of the Presbytery of Chester, Nov 9, 1876, approved the movement to establish a church, and in February, 1877, met in the new building, and organized a church with twelve members, in connection with and under the care of the Presbytery of Chester John Craig was subsequently elected elder The Rev Dr M B Greer, of Philadelphia, editor of the *Presbyterian*, was chosen pastor of the new church, and it is still under his charge The present membership of the church is thirty-five

Christ Protestant Episcopal Church —An effort was made to establish a church of this denomination at Ridley Park in 1873 Two lots were donated by the Ridley Park Association on which to erect a church, and on May 7, 1873, the corner-stone of a chapel was laid Through want of funds the movement languished, and work on the edifice ceased In the summer of 1878 an effort to establish an Episcopal Church was again revived, and regular services were held at the depot by the Rev Dr Bushnell, of Philadelphia, and the Rev Henry Brown, of Chester Subscriptions for a chapel were obtained, and in 1879 the present edifice was erected It is of the English type, built of Port Deposit stone, and has a bell-tower and a spire The pulpit is now occupied by the Rev. William Marilla, under whose ministrations the congregation is steadily increasing

Ridley Park Seminary —In September, 1882, Miss C J Taylor, of Ridley Park, opened a private school for instruction in the common branches, and also preparing students for college A school-room was fitted in her father's residence, with the intention eventually of using the house as a boarding-school Lectures are delivered once a week at the seminary by W Curtis Taylor on astronomy and geology, and occasionally by Dr J Gibbons Hunt on common things, illustrated with a microscope During the past year there have been in attendance twenty-five pupils It is the intention of the principal in 1885 to establish a boarding-school at Ridley Park

The Knights Templar Encampment —On May 28, 1876, a grand encampment of Knights Templar of Maryland was held on the rolling ground west of Crum Lynne Lake, at a point equal distant from Crum Lynne and Ridley Park Station A number of knights from the Western States, as well as commanderies from New York, Pennsylvania, and New Jersey, joined with the Maryland commanderies in the grand encampment A pavilion, two hundred feet long, was erected, and the camp proper was of canvas tents, fronting on avenues running north and south, with main avenues crossing them east and west The arrangement and perfecting of the camp at Ridley Park were in charge of Maj Nevin The encampment continued for ten days, and while the knights were present was a scene of activity, which attracted a large number of visitors

Prospect Park.—In 1874, John Cochran, of Chester, purchased one hundred and three acres of land of the estate of Joshua Pierson, and in that year laid it out in villa lots Early in September of that year Cochran sold an interest to John Shedwick & Son, then of Philadelphia, but formerly of Chester, where they had erected a number of houses and other buildings On Sept 10, 1874, the first public sale of lots was held, and after that sales were made two or three times a year until most of the land was sold, when the remaining interest of Cochran was purchased by Shedwick & Son, who now own all of the original tract which has not been sold for lots There are now twenty-five houses in the park, many of them handsome and costly villas

Prospect Methodist Episcopal Church —In April, 1878, a class was formed of six members, and a lot of land, one hundred by one hundred and four feet, on the road from Moore's Station to the Lazaretto, was purchased of James C Shedwick A charter was obtained for the church Aug 1, 1878 A neat brick structure was erected the same year, at a cost of four thousand four hundred dollars, and dedicated June 1, 1879, by Bishop Matthew Simpson. The Rev J H Pike was the first pastor, and was succeeded by the present incumbent, the Rev G M. Brodhead The membership is at present about seventy persons

The Plow Tavern —On Aug 26, 1740, Israel

Hendrickson, of Amosland, stated in his petition that he having built a new house "upon the great road from Philadelphia to Chester," desired to keep public-house therein. His petition was recommended by a number of the "Inhabitants of Ridley who have known him from his infancy," but the court refused to grant him a license. In 1767 William Smith had license, and in 1771 he gave place to Benjamin Richards, and the following year, 1772, Henry Shivers was the landlord. In 1780, Isaac Culin had license, and in 1782, William Price, and in 1796, Abijah Price succeeded to the privilege. In 1800 license was refused to the Plow, and after that date the dwelling ceased to be a public inn, doubtless because it came in competition with the "White Horse," both houses being then owned by Joseph Pearson. About 1765, John Morton, the signer of the Declaration of Independence, purchased the property, which at his death passed to his son, Sketchley Morton, and the latter, in 1785, sold it to Joseph Pearson, who, in 1803, bequeathed it to John L. Pearson. It has been stated that it continued a tavern until 1820, when John L. Pearson moved into it and took down the sign, an assertion which is not sustained by the records of the Court of Quarter Sessions of Delaware County.

Leiperville Mills.—Prior to 1764 a grist-mill had been built on Crum Creek, near the site where subsequently the locks of the Leiper Canal were located. In that year John McIlvain owned and was operating a grist-mill at that place, which was situated about two hundred yards below the present cotton-mill. The grist-mill was used until 1794, when a saw-mill was erected, and continued until it was sold about 1827 to George G. Leiper. A tan-yard was established by Jeremiah McIlvain in 1794, which was continued by him until his death, and by his sons, John and Jeremiah McIlvain, until some time subsequent to 1835, at which time a bark-mill was on the property, when it was purchased from them by George G. Leiper. The tannery had forty vats and four leaches. In 1837, George G. Leiper enlarged the bark-mill by erecting one and one-half stories to the old stone structure, which he leased to James Campbell. The old mill extended along the post-road. So successfully did Campbell operate the factory that in the fall of 1846 Leiper erected a three story stone factory in addition to the old one, which extended along the canal. In the *Delaware County Republican* of Aug. 6, 1847, is the following description of the mills:

"The factory is owned by Judge Leiper and occupied by Mr. James Campbell, one of the most industrious and enterprising men engaged in the business in this county. We found the factory in full operation, and the hands busily at work on the different branches connected with the business. The building is of stone, three stories high, and filled closely with machinery from the ground-floor to the attic, some of which is of the most approved character. There are in the mill one thousand and eight spindles, eleven hundred and four throstles, and seventy-two looms. We observed a mule of four hundred and fifty-six (a self acting mule) spindles, which was an entire new piece of machinery to us, and, we believe, the only one of the kind in this country. It is similar to those used in the large manufacturing establishments in England the pattern of which was recently brought here by Mr. Campbell. One of the looms was at work on a beautiful and substantial article for table-cloths, which needs only to be seen to be admired. The principal articles manufactured are ticking, table cloths, and bagging, or tent cloth, of which sixty thousand yards are turned out monthly. There are sixty-five persons employed in the different departments, and the whole moves with the precision of clock-work. The wages spinners receive is thirty dollars per month, weavers, eighteen dollars. The females appear happy and contented, and exhibit bright and pleasant countenances. Mr. Campbell is a practical manufacturer, studies the wants and comforts of those about him, and his presence in the mill, lending a helping hand when required, endears him to those in his employment. The various departments of the mill are superintended with skill and judgment. Samuel Turner has charge of the cloth-room, J. W. Dobbins, of the looms, William Price, of the throstles, and Jonathan Taylor, of the card room."

At this time the saw-mill was operated by Thomas M. Smith, and was then employed in cutting ship-timber for the United States government. On Dec. 8, 1848, the dry-house at Campbell's mill was destroyed by fire. A young son of Richard Garsed, of Frankford, was then visiting his aunt, Mrs. Campbell, and the child was so alarmed and excited by the fire that it caused brain-fever, which terminated fatally in a short time thereafter. The dry-house was rebuilt, and was again destroyed by fire Oct. 23, 1850. After Campbell purchased the old jail in Chester and changed it to a cotton-mill, he continued to operate the mill until 1855, when he removed the machinery.

About 1848, George G. Leiper erected an axe-factory below the saw-mill, which was operated by William Beatty for some time, the tilt-mill being supplied by the water from the canal. The demand, however, for power was so great at the cotton-factory that Campbell finally rented the tilt-mill, which was abandoned, the water being used for the cotton-mill. After Campbell removed to Chester, Michael Buggy became the tenant of the mill, and conducted the factory until it was purchased by Daniel Lees, Aug. 2, 1869, from the executors of George G. Leiper. It was conducted by him until July 21, 1883, when the two-thirds interest was sold to Frank J. Taylor and Oliver Holt, who operate it at present. This mill was destroyed by fire Feb. 19, 1878, at which time it was employed in spinning yarn, occasioning a loss of thirty-five thousand dollars. It was rebuilt in 1880. The new mill, which was a stone structure, one hundred and four by fifty feet, and two stories in height, was again destroyed by fire in the fall of 1881, and for the third time rebuilt.

Peter Hill's or Hickman's Grist-Mill.—About a mile north of Leiperville, near the Springfield road and Little Crum Creek, in 1774 Isaac Davis had a grist-mill, which prior to the battle of Brandywine had become the property of Peter Hill, for subsequent to that date the flour at the mill and the teams of the miller were impressed for the use of the army, but afterward the United States government made full compensation by a patent for five thousand acres of land near Clarksburg, Lee Co., Va. It is probable that the mill was burned at the time when some of the foraging parties of the enemy swept through Ridley township. Certain it is that in 1795 Hill was assessed only on a saw-mill, and in 1799 he was assessed on three hundred and thirty acres of land, a grist- and saw-mill. The saw-mill was discontinued in 1808, and was permitted to fall into ruins. The grist-mill was built of stone, was forty-eight by thirty-six feet, and was changed into a cotton-factory in 1826, but was not used as such for several years. Prior to and in 1842 it was occupied by Henry Burt, and at that time was part stone and frame, three and a half stories in height, and was fifty by thirty-eight feet. It contained seven carding-engines, one drawing-frame, four hundred and eighty wadding-frames, ninety cards, twenty-one Patterson speeders, and other machinery. In 1844 it was rented from Henry Effinger, the then owner, by James Campbell, who used it as a spinning-mill until 1846, when it was rented to Charles F. and Joseph W. Kenworthy, who put steam-power in the mills. In 1847 there were in operation at this mill four hundred and sixty-eight throstle-spindles, three hundred mule-spindles, and thirty looms; thirty hands were employed, who manufactured four thousand five hundred yards per week. Ten of the looms were employed on Canton flannel, and the remainder on bagging. On Dec. 19, 1848, the engine-house was burned, and the mill itself saved from destruction with the greatest difficulty. After the Kenworthys removed to Bridgewater the mill was idle for a time, and subsequently was changed into a grist-mill, and is now owned by Samuel Hickman.

The Eddystone Manufacturing Company.—The extensive works of this company are located on the Olle Lille plantation, one of the noted localities during the early Swedish settlement, known by the Indians as Techrassi (the land belonging to the man with the black beard). Ridley Creek was at that time known as Olof Stille's Kill, and subsequently after the estate was purchased by the Swedish clergyman, Laurentius Carlus Lock, the stream was termed Preest's Creek. The property afterwards passed to John Crosby, and later was divided into smaller plantations, and in 1779 Isaac Eyre seems to have had a grist-mill in this locality, and near by Joseph Trimble had a saw-mill. Henry Effinger, who acquired title by purchasing the interests of Isaac Eyre, John Crosby, and Susannah Duly in 1782, devised the plantation to his sons, Jacob and Henry Effinger, and in 1831 Henry Effinger became the owner of the entire tract. He was a peculiar man, very parsimonious in his habits, and was so opposed to the public school law that he would never pay the taxes levied for the support of public instruction, but yearly compelled the collector to levy on his personal property to liquidate the charges.

In 1871 the executors of Henry Effinger sold to John Roach, who subsequently conveyed the estate to William Simpson & Sons. The same purchaser afterwards bought a large part of the George G. Leiper estate to the north of the Effinger farm, as well as the Grantham farm, which adjoined the Effinger property on the east. The name was shortened frequently to Grant, hence the "Grant Rocks" on the Delaware should be really "Grantham Rocks." The old mansion is situated about two hundred yards from the river, and the walls being over two feet six inches thick, it is still a substantial structure. The Grantham family subsequently erected a new dwelling near the Southern post-road, which Lewis Trimble afterwards took down and built a house which subsequently became the property of Richard Risley Carlisle, better known as "Professor Risley," the noted acrobat, who with his two sons were favorite performers a quarter of a century ago. The Risley house is now owned by the widow of N. F. H. Dennis. On the Effinger farm, as stated, the extensive Eddystone Print-Works have been erected.

The Eddystone Manufacturing Company (Limited) was founded in 1844 by William Simpson, at the Falls of Schuylkill, Philadelphia. In 1860, Mr. Simpson's sons were admitted to the firm, which became William Simpson & Sons. The works were removed to Eddystone in 1874, and in 1877 the Eddystone Manufacturing Company (Limited) was formed, of which company the old firm were the principal owners of stock. At that time the works were enlarged and the finest machinery obtained to make prints of all colors. The noted Eddystone prints and cotton-prints, as well as William Simpson & Sons' mourning prints, for which the old firm had acquired a high reputation, are still manufactured, and are favorite goods in the market. The works comprise fifteen buildings, consisting of engraving- and color-rooms, two hundred and two by eighty-two feet, one story in height; bleaching-room, two hundred and forty-four by ninety feet, one story; boiler-house, one hundred and twelve by seventy-two feet, one story; cloth store-house, one hundred and twelve by fifty feet, one story; white-rooms, one hundred and seven by eighty-four feet, one story, with boiler-house, two hundred and two by seventy-two feet, one story; south dye-house, two hundred and two by ninety-two feet, one story; north dye-house, two hundred and twenty-three by ninety-three feet, one story; finishing-house, three hundred by sixty feet, two stories; print-works, three hundred by eighty-five feet, three stories; retort-house, ninety by ninety feet, one story; machine-shop, one hundred and fifty by sixty feet, one story; planing-mill, one hundred by ninety feet, one story; pump-house, sixty by thirty-five feet, one story; stable, one hundred and fourteen by ninety-two feet, one story. The fifteen buildings mentioned cover nearly five acres of ground. There are fifty-four engines, with thirty-seven boilers, requiring twenty-five thousand tons of coal annually. Five hundred and three men, sixty-one women and girls, and one hundred and sixty boys are employed, and the weekly production is thirty thousand pieces of cloth of forty-eight yards each. Such an industry has built up about it a thriving village. The liberality of the company and Mr. Simpson has made this an attractive locality.

There are eighty-five brick tenant-houses on the property, and in 1880 the company erected a library building, known as "Eddystone Light-house," for the use of its employés It is of brick, fifty-five feet front by thirty-three feet wide, and built after the old English Chester style of architecture, with a tower thirty-six feet high from the base of the building, running up twenty-six feet above the roof The first story contains the library-room, adjoining which and on the same floor there is a retiring-room The second story has a seating capacity for over two hundred persons, and is furnished with comfortable benches and a stage and dressing-room, which indicate that it will be used for amateur dramatic performances and for lectures The floors are laid with yellow-pine, and are deadened by being filled between with mortar The furniture and book-cases are of hard wood, white-walnut and ash, no paint or varnish being used. The rooms are heated from the basement or cellar by means of an improved heating apparatus, and, taken altogether, there are but few, if any, structures in city or country more substantial or better ordered in every respect The library contains six hundred volumes on almost every subject,—scientific, mechanical, medical, and literary In front of the building there is an extensive lawn of two acres, planted with shade and ornamental trees, which is intended as a play-ground for the children The admirable system of water-supply, the comfortable houses for the operatives, together with the natural beauties of the location, make Eddystone one of the pleasantest manufacturing centres in the Middle States

The following mills in Ridley township we have not been able to locate In 1766, John Lewis was assessed on a saw-mill, in 1779, James Hannum was assessed on a grist-mill, and in 1817, Caleb Churchman on a saw-mill

Leiper's Railroad—In 1809 and 1810, Thomas Leiper constructed the first railroad in Pennsylvania and the second in the United States Strictly it was a tramway and not a railroad It was three-quarters of a mile in length, and used in transporting stone for his quarries in Springfield to tide-water of Ridley Creek, near the mill of Pierce Crosby (the present Irvington Mill, North Chester borough) In May, 1809, Leiper made an estimate of the railroad, but the project was not completed until January or February of the succeeding year The estimate of the cost of the road was, including the survey, $1592 47 The survey and draft of the road was made by John Thomson, and in 1873 the original map drawn by Thomson was presented by Dr Joshua Ash to the Delaware County Institute of Science In September, 1809, under the supervision of Thomson, the experimental track was built, the construction being done by Summerville, a Scotch millwright The road "was sixty yards in length, and graded an inch and a half to the yard The gauge was four feet and the sleepers eight feet apart The experiment with a loaded car was so successful that Leiper had the first practical railroad built in the United States"[1] The rails of Leiper's road in Ridley were of wood, and of course soon yielded to the heavy friction of the car-wheels, which were of cast iron with flanges, and were not renewed, Leiper designing to lay a stone track As it was, it continued in use for nineteen years In 1852 both the railroad and canal were superseded by the present road laid with iron rails

The experimental track spoken of was laid in 1809, and made on land adjoining the Bull Head Tavern, in Philadelphia "When the day of trial came a large concourse of people assembled to witness the experiment After having loaded the car with all the weights that could be procured from the neighboring hay-scales, wagers were offered to any amount that no horse could move it to the summit, but when the word was given the horse moved off with ease, amid the plaudits of the assembled multitude"[2]

Thomas Leiper was the son of Thomas Leiper, of Strathhaven, Scotland, his mother, Helen Hamilton Leiper, is said to have belonged to the family of Hamilton of Kipe[3] He came to America in 1764, when nineteen years of age, having first settled in Virginia, when he removed to Philadelphia, where he accumulated a fortune as a tobacconist prior to the Revolution He was an ardent Whig during the struggle, and "was the first man in Pennsylvania to advocate a rupture with the mother-country While the Declaration of Independence was still only heard of in whispers, Leiper had raised a fund for open resistance to the crown It was also his fortune to be one of the last to lay down his arms As treasurer of the First Troop he bore the last subsidies of the French to the Americans at Yorktown"[4] He was orderly sergeant, treasurer, and secretary of the First City Troop, and subsequently president of the Common Council of Philadelphia He was frequently a Presidential elector, and was termed the patriarch of the Democratic party, and an intimate personal friend of Thomas Jefferson "Mr Jefferson was heard to say that the tables of Dr Rush, Maj Butler, of South Carolina, and Mr Leiper, were the only ones in Philadelphia to whom he was ever invited during those days of Federal persecution, and that the Federalists used to cross the streets to avoid him"[5] He had made it a rule of life never to accept an office of pay or profit, hence while he served as director of the Bank of Pennsylvania and of the Bank of the United States, and was commissioner for the defense of Philadelphia during the war of 1812, he refused to permit his name to be used for any elective office to which emoluments or pay was attached During the darkest hour of the American Revolution

[1] "The Pennsylvania Railroad," by William B Sipes, p 4 (note)
[2] Smith's "History of Delaware County," p 389 (note)
[3] *Penna Mag of Hist.*, vol i p 226
[4] Lives of Eminent Philadelphians now Deceased, p 649
[5] Note to Life of Richard Rush, "Eminent Philadelphians," p 857

he threw his private fortune in the scale on behalf of the colonists, and to that end gave five thousand pounds to the North America Bank Fund to supply means to sustain the war. He also subscribed a hundred thousand dollars to various public improvements in Pennsylvania, from which he could not hope for any personal return, purely for the purposes of encouraging the development of the State. Truly has it been said of him that "few men ever lived a more patriotic, useful, and honorable life than he, for singleness of heart, integrity of purpose and conduct, devotion to the cause of liberty and of his country he was unsurpassed."[1] Not only in public life was he useful, but he it was who first introduced machinery for breaking and grinding plaster and oyster-shells, for sawing stone, thrashing grain, and making cider, all of which he had in operation on his Ridley estate, driven by water-power, under his personal supervision. He died July, 1825, in the eightieth year of his age. Among the descendants of this exemplary citizen have been many conspicuous men of the nation. Dr. Elisha Kent Kane, the Arctic explorer, was his grandson; Gen. Thomas Leiper Kane belonged to the famous "Bucktails." His eldest son, George G. Leiper, was associate judge of Delaware County and member of Congress from this district, and two grandsons of Thomas Leiper, Gen. Charles I. Leiper and Capt. Thomas I. Leiper, made highly creditable records in the late civil war.

Leiper's Canal.—In 1790 Thomas Leiper and John Wall, both large owners of real estate in Ridley, applied to the Legislature with a petition for an appropriation from the State to cut a canal from the point where the tide flowed in Crum Creek to McIlvain's mill-dam, in order to cheapen the cost of transportation of stone from Leiper's quarries to tide-water. The petition was supplemented by a similar one from the stone-cutters and masons of Philadelphia, who stated that the stone procured from Leiper's quarries were the best produced in the neighborhood of Philadelphia, and representing that the construction of this canal would be of great public advantage. The petition was met with a remonstrance by John and Isaac McIlvain, and the Legislature refusing to act in the matter the scheme was abandoned.[2] A similar assertion was made in the *United States Gazette*, in August, 1828, as follows:

"The Leiper Canal. The late Thomas Leiper, Esq., of this city, contemplated, in 1790, a canal along his estate in Delaware County, in order to complete an easy communication between his quarries on Crum Creek and the Delaware. His views were not perfectly comprehended by the Legislature at that time, and he found himself foiled by the Legislature in that attempt. In 1807 he caused a railroad—the first in the country—to be constructed from his quarries to Ridley Creek. In 1825, since the death of Mr. Leiper, his son, George G. Leiper, Esq., revived the idea proposed by his father, and on Saturday, the 16th inst., the corner-stone of the canal was laid by William Strickland, Esq., with an appropriate address from Professor Patterson, of this city. A large concourse of citizens—as we gather from the *Upland Union*—attended the ceremony, among whom was Mrs. Elizabeth C. Leiper, the aged widow of the gentleman who had proposed the canal."[3]

The history of the canal being altogether documentary, we are compelled to reproduce the articles which appeared in the public press at the time the canal was constructed. In August, 1828, the *Upland Union* says,—

"George G. Leiper, of Ridley township, commenced his canal on Monday week last, and one lock is nearly completed. The length of the canal will be near a mile, and will be of great importance to this section of our county. It will be connected with Crum Creek, which empties into the Delaware, and when completed (which will be done as soon as possible) will have a tendency to enhance the value of property in that neighborhood, as well as open a direct water communication between Philadelphia and the stone-quarries belonging to Mr. Leiper. There are several mill-sites near its location."[4]

On Oct. 13, 1829, the *Upland Union* contained the following:

"The Leiper Canal Celebration.—On Thursday last, the 8th instant, the grand ceremony of navigating the Leiper Canal took place. It is a little better than a year since the commencement of this great work of individual enterprise, and its rapid completion appears almost like a dream to one who witnessed the laying of the corner-stone. The original projector of this canal, it is well known, was Thomas Leiper (now deceased), who, owing to unforeseen circumstances in the year 1790, was unable to carry his plan into operation. The project has, however, been successfully carried into effect by his eldest son, George Gray Leiper, to whom the citizens of Delaware County are indebted for one of the greatest works of individual enterprise to be found in the United States.

"At one o'clock the ladies were escorted to the canal boat 'William Strickland,' a beautiful boat about fifty-five feet in length, and named after that distinguished engineer. In the stern of the boat was stationed a band of music, which played during the passage of the boat up to the quarries, a distance of nearly two miles, some of the most fashionable and patriotic airs. Attached to the boat were two handsome full-blooded Wind-Flower colts, neatly decorated with covers, and trimmed with ribbons. At half-past one o'clock the signal was given, and the procession moved on in carriages, gigs, and gentlemen on horseback accompanied the boat as she smoothly glided through the unruffled stream to her place of destination. The sight, as may well be imagined, was truly grand and imposing. When the 'William Strickland' entered the first lock (the Elizabeth Leiper Lock, named after the wife of the venerable projector), three cheers were given. In a few minutes after she entered the Thomas Leiper Lock, which for beauty of stone and superior workmanship is unrivaled in the United States. Such is the opinion of the Messrs. Strickland and Struthers, of Philadelphia, and Major Bender.

"On the Thomas Leiper Lock the Delaware County Volunteer Battalion, under the command of Lieut.-Col. Henry Myers, were posted, and as soon as the boat passed through it a national salute was fired by the Pennsylvania Artillerists, accompanied with musketry. The boat was precisely one half-hour from the time she left the Great Southern road until she arrived at the mansion of the Hon. George G. Leiper. The ladies were then landed, and the boat proceeded on her passage up to the quarries without any accident having occurred to impede her progress.

"The troops then paraded in front of the mansion of Mr. Leiper, and were addressed by him in a very handsome and appropriate manner. On this as on all other occasions the hospitable dwelling of Mr. Leiper

[1] *The Aurora*, July 8, 1825.

[2] Westcott's "History of Philadelphia," *Sunday Dispatch*, Feb. 16, 1873; Martin's "History of Chester," p. 239.

[3] Hazard's Register, vol. ii. p. 96.

[4] Ibid., p. 64.

was thrown open, where those who felt disposed to refresh themselves were kindly invited

"There were at least one thousand persons present at the celebration, and had the weather been more favorable we believe there would have been a much greater number We are happy to say, amidst all the bustle incident to such a parade, no serious accident happened to mar the pleasures of the day"

Under date of Chester, Pa, Oct 9, 1829, occurs this notice

"THE LEIPER CANAL.—This canal, the work of our enterprising and public spirited fellow-citizen, George G Leiper, was yesterday filled with water, and his new canal boat, the 'William Strickland,' passed the whole line of the canal up to the quarry The Volunteer Battalion of this county, with their band of music, and a band from the city, we are informed, were present to give life to the interesting scene"[1]

The canal, which was about a mile in length, not only was used to transport stone in boats to the creek below Leiperville, but the water was led by it as in a race to supply power to the mill at Leiperville The lower part of the canal has been filled in, and the upper part as far as the mill at Leiperville is still used as a race to convey water to the factory

Ridley Quarries.—Although doubtless the quarries on Ridley Creek were opened at an early date, yet the first record found respecting them occurs in the assessment-roll of 1766 Richard and John Crosby are assessed on quarries in Ridley The present quarries of John Leiper on the Post road are the old Crosby quarries, worked at that time The basement of the old building of the American Philosophical Society was built of stone from this quarry In the year 1789, the Supreme Executive Council directed an order to be drawn in favor of John Crosby for £53 14*s* 4*d* in payment of stone used in repairing the bank at Mud Island,[2] where Fort Mifflin now is The following year the quarries of Thomas Leiper, in Springfield and Ridley, were already noted, as appears from the petition presented to the Assembly in that year, already mentioned in the history of Leiper's Canal In the *General Advertiser*, published by Benjamin Franklin Baché, in Philadelphia, for July 29, 1797, was the following advertisement, which shows that the quarries had acquired a name before they were purchased by him

"CURB STONE.—The Subscriber will enter into a Contract for the whole of the CURB STONE that may be wanted this year for the Supply of the City and Districts at three pence per foot lower than such stone can be furnished by any other person. It will be warranted the best that ever came to Philadelphia

"He is also ready to contract for the delivery of any quantity of building or foundation stone, as also of free stone of WEAVER'S QUARRY, in the rough, at any place or Port within the United States. The quality of the stone in the subscriber's quarries is known to be excellent by a certificate from Mr William Covet, and from other City Commissioners, dated December 13 1791 They give it as their opinion that the Curb or gutter stone from his quarries exceed in goodness any other that yet have been made use of for the City pavements In a representation also to the Assembly of this State, signed by 28 of the principal Masons and Bricklayers in Philadelphia, they say that the stones raised from his quarries are the best produced in the neighborhood of this city, for the purpose of Curb stone, flaggs, and house building For terms apply to

"THOMAS LEIPER, Tobacconist,
"No 9 North Water Street."

[1] Hazard's Register of Penna., vol iv p 247

[2] Colonial Records vol xvi p 100

In the Leiper quarries in Ridley, in February, 1851, the largest blast of gneiss rock ever made in the county is said to have taken place The blast was made by William McFarland, assisted by Edward Rattigan, John Davies, and James McKenney The length of the breast was ninety-five feet, width of bench forty-two feet, depth of bench nineteen feet six inches, and measured five thousand nine hundred and eighty-five tons Three hundred pounds of powder were required for the blast To the Delaware Breakwater many thousand tons of the stone from this quarry were sent The masonry of Fort Delaware at the Pea Patch, Girard College, the Chestnut Street bridge over the Schuylkill, and many other massive structures in Philadelphia, were built from stones from these quarries Besides these quarries, which were brought into prominence by the construction of a canal and railroad, there were a number of quarries along Ridley Creek, all of which became prominent when the United States was building the Breakwater When this work was first begun the greater part of the stone was furnished from the Delaware County quarries In 1832 the following quarries were operated on Ridley Creek Thomas Clyde, Robert Churchman, Spencer McIlvain, William D Shoemaker, Thomas B Shoemaker, John Burk, John Hankins, William Hill, and H M Wuger & Co, on Crum Creek, while the quarries of Isaac Hennis, Jonathan P Worrell, and Samuel Lytle were on Chester Creek In 1836 the superintendent at the Breakwater rejected the stone from Delaware County, stating that it was inferior to that from Delaware State, on account of the large quantity of mica contained in it, which renders it peculiarly liable to decay and easily worn by the action of the water This action on the part of the superintendent would have occasioned heavy loss to the quarry-owners, and therefore the Delaware County Institute of Science appointed a committee, of which Dr George Smith was chairman, to report upon the character of the stone The report was made, and on its result the government revoked the order made by the superintendent.

Moore's Station.—The land on which this station is located, on the Philadelphia, Wilmington and Baltimore Railroad and the Lazaretto road, between Norwood and Ridley Park, was in the possession of the Moore family in 1800, and is so marked on Hill's map. Prospect Park lies to the west of the station. There is at Moore's the railroad station, a block station, engine-house, and a steam brick grist-mill, twenty-six by sixty feet, which was built in 1877 by George W. Moore & Co

Leiperville is on the old Queen's Highway, fourteen miles from Philadelphia and one from Chester. It is named from the Leiper family, who at one time owned most of the land in the neighborhood The Leiper canal ran through the hamlet It contains one tavern, a store and post-office, a wheelwright- and blacksmith-shop, and about twenty-five dwellings

The Battle-Axes.—In 1839 and 1840 a peculiar sect, denominated "Battle-Axes," had some following in Delaware and Chester Counties, and attracted considerable attention at the time The principles they maintained were those subsequently known as "free love," denying the sanctity of the marital relation, and that all they possessed should be held in common Theophilus R Gates, then a resident of Philadelphia, was the apostle of the new creed, and his chief disciple was a single woman, Hannah Williamson In Delaware County the Battle-Axes made a deep impression, for it was directly due to their influence that Aaron T Morton, of Ridley, on June 5, 1840, committed suicide by cutting his throat with a razor He was mentally weak, and becoming acquainted with Theophilus Gates, of Philadelphia, Morton embraced Gates' peculiar religious tenets Gates invited Morton to his retreat, explained his doctrine, furnished him with his publication called the *Battle-Axe*, and the result was Morton became a religious monomaniac He was in this state of mind when Gates, in company with Hannah Williamson, came to his house on Saturday, May 30, 1840, with the intention of compelling Morton to separate from his wife and form a connection with Williamson, whose mind was also shattered As soon as the purpose of their visit was known, the young men of the neighborhood gathered in large numbers to inflict summary punishment on Gates It was at last deemed best to defer the matter for a day or two to see what might be done Gates became alarmed and fled to Philadelphia, and as he drove along the road was hissed and groaned until he reached Darby Morton, laboring under this trouble, committed the act

Crimes—Dennis Shields, a man employed in the construction of the Philadelphia, Wilmington and Baltimore Railroad, on Saturday night, Sept 8, 1871, made an entirely unprovoked attack on Daniel Gibbons, who was quietly walking along the road at Leiperville, in company with a friend His assailant struck him on the head with a blunt instrument, which felled him to the earth, and while he was prostrate Shields jumped upon his breast and abdomen Shields fled and was never apprehended, and Gibbons lingered until Monday following, when he died of the injuries received On June 25, 1877, William H Johnson, of Ridley, who was insane (occasioned by a blow on the head with a chair received in a difficulty some years previous), went to the house of a relative, John Worrall, and without the slightest cause caught up a gun belonging to Worrall and shot him, inflicting a severe wound in his side Johnson, returning to his own house, shot himself with a gun he had loaded before going to Worrall's, the load tearing away part of his head and causing instant death On Aug 4, 1877, the body of an unknown man was found suspended by a woolen neck-scarf from a tree in a secluded wood on the farm of Isaac Carr, near Spring Hill Station The clothing on the corpse was rotten from exposure to the weather, and the body was in an advanced state of decomposition, the physicians testifying that the remains had been hanging for several months The name of the suicide was never discovered

Interesting Incidents—John F Hill, an old resident of Ridley, who died many years ago, in his youth had been bitten by a mad dog, and it is alleged that during the full of the moon he was subject to violent outbursts of passion for which no reason could be assigned other than the reason stated In January, 1843, Henry Goodman, a resident of Ridley, died from glanders, which disease he had contracted by bleeding a horse three weeks before, he at the time having a cut on his finger Four days after his death Charles Van, a colored man in Chester, died from a slight wound on the thumb received a week previous, while handling the hide of an ox which had died of the murrain Immediately the wound began swelling, and he continued in acute agony until death ended his sufferings On July 16, 1869, a Mrs Steward, residing on Crum Creek, near Deshong's quarry, was killed by a stone, weighing over twenty pounds, thrown by a blast made two hundred yards away from her dwelling She was lying asleep at the time, and the stone, crashing through the roof, fell upon the left side of her head, inflicting a terrible gash near the ear, and severed the left arm from her body

BIOGRAPHICAL SKETCHES.

THOMAS T TASKER

Thomas T Tasker, the eldest of nine children of William and Mary Tasker, was born in Nottingly, in the West Riding of Yorkshire, on the 12th day of May, 1799 His father, who was a school-teacher and land-surveyor, afforded the lad more than an ordinary English education, after which, at the early age of thirteen and a half years, he began a seven years' apprenticeship in the copper and ironsmith's business He sailed for America in 1819, landing in Philadelphia on the 4th of June of the same year For a brief period he was employed in a stove-manufactory, after which, in 1820, he established a coppersmith and iron business in West Chester In 1824, on leaving the latter point, he removed to Philadelphia, and ultimately entered the establishment of Stephen P Morris, then engaged in the manufacture of stoves and grates Later he became his partner, continuing the business under the firm-name of S P Morris & Co, which afterwards became Morris, Tasker & Co, its present style They were extensive manufacturers of tubes for gas, water, steam locomotives, boilers, etc, and the first to introduce them into the market Mr.

Thomas T. Tasker

The Battle-Axes.—In 1839 and 1840 a peculiar sect, denominated "Battle-Axes," had some following in Delaware and Chester Counties, and attracted considerable attention at the time. The principles they maintained were those subsequently known as "free love," denying the sanctity of the marital relation, and that all they possessed should be held in common. Theophilus R. Gates, then a resident of Philadelphia, was the apostle of the new creed, and his chief disciple was a single woman, Hannah Williamson. In Delaware County the Battle-Axes made a deep impression, for it was directly due to their influence that Aaron T. Morton, of Ridley, on June 5, 1840, committed suicide by cutting his throat with a razor. He was mentally weak, and becoming acquainted with Theophilus Gates, of Philadelphia, Morton embraced Gates' peculiar religious tenets. Gates invited Morton to his retreat, explained his doctrine, furnished him with his publication called the *Battle-Axe*, and the result was Morton became a religious monomaniac. He was in this state of mind when Gates, in company with Hannah Williamson, came to his house on Saturday, May 30, 1840, with the intention of compelling Morton to separate from his wife and form a connection with Williamson, whose mind was also shattered. As soon as the purpose of their visit was known, the young men of the neighborhood gathered in large numbers to inflict summary punishment on Gates. It was at last deemed best to defer the matter [illegible] of the men what might be done. Gates became alarmed and fled to Philadelphia, and as he drove along the road was hissed and groaned until he reached Darby. Morton, laboring under this trouble, committed the act.

Crimes.—Dennis Shields, a man employed in the construction of the Philadelphia, Wilmington and Baltimore Railroad, on Saturday night, Sept. 2, 1871, made an entirely unprovoked attack on Daniel Gibbons, who was quietly walking along the road at Leiperville, in company with a friend. His assailant struck him on the head with a blunt instrument, which felled him to the earth, and while he was prostrate Shields jumped upon his breast and abdomen. Shields fled and was never apprehended, and Gibbons lingered until Monday following, when he died of the injuries received. On June 25, 1877, William H. Johnson, of Ridley, who was insane (occasioned by a blow on the head with a chair received in a difficulty some years previous), went to the house of a relative, John Worrall, and without the slightest cause caught up a gun belonging to Worrall and shot him, inflicting a severe wound in his side. Johnson, returning to his own house, shot himself with a gun he had loaded before going to Worrall's, the load tearing away part of his head and causing instant death. On Aug. 4, 1877, the body of an unknown man was found suspended by a woolen neck-scarf from a tree in a secluded wood on the farm of Isaac Carr, near Spring Hill Station. The clothing on the corpse was rotten from exposure to the weather, and the body was in an advanced state of decomposition, the physicians testifying that the remains had been hanging for several months. The name of the suicide was never discovered.

Interesting Incidents.—John F. Hill, an old resident of Ridley, who died many years ago, in his youth had been bitten by a mad dog, and it is alleged that during the full of the moon he was subject to violent outbursts of passion for which no reason could be assigned other than the reason stated. In January, 1848, Henry Goodman, a resident of Ridley, died from glanders, which disease he had contracted by bleeding a horse three weeks before, he at the time having a cut on his finger. Four days after his death Charles Van, a colored man in Chester, died from a slight wound on the thumb received a week previous, while handling the hide of an ox which had died of the murrain. Immediately the wound began swelling, and he continued in acute agony until death ended his sufferings. On July 16, 1869, a Mrs. Steward, residing on Crum Creek, near Deshong's quarry, was killed by a stone, weighing over twenty pounds, thrown by a blast made two hundred yards away from her dwelling. She was lying asleep at the time, and the stone, crashing through the roof, fell upon the left side of her head, inflicting a terrible gash near the ear and severed the left arm from her body.

BIOGRAPHICAL SKETCHES.

THOMAS T. TASKER.

Thomas T. Tasker, the eldest of nine children of William and Mary Tasker, was born in Nottingly, in the West Riding of Yorkshire, on the 12th day of May, 1799. His father, who was a school-teacher and land-surveyor, afforded the lad more than an ordinary English education, after which, at the early age of thirteen and a half years, he began a seven years' apprenticeship in the copper and tinsmith's business. He sailed for America in 1819, landing in Philadelphia on the 4th of June of the same year. For a brief period he was employed in a stove manufactory, after which, in 1820, he established a coppersmith and iron business in West Chester. In 1824, on leaving the latter point, he removed to Philadelphia, and ultimately entered the establishment of Stephen P. Morris, then engaged in the manufacture of stoves and grates. Later he became his partner, continuing the business under the firm-name of S. P. Morris & Co., which afterwards became Morris, Tasker & Co., its present style. They were extensive manufacturers of tubes for gas, water, steam locomotives, boilers, etc., and the first to introduce them into the market. Mr.

Thomas T Tasker

Jacob Worrall

Tasker was married in Wilmington, Del., Feb. [illegible], 18[illegible], to Miss Elizabeth, daughter of Joseph Hoskins, of New Castle County, Del., and has had nine children, of whom six survive. Mrs. Tasker's death occurred in 1878. Mr. Tasker purchased in 1867 over four hundred acres of land in Ridley township, Delaware Co., and has since devoted his leisure to farming and the production of blooded stock, first making a specialty of Durham cattle, and later of Ayrshires and Guernseys, which he continues to propagate. His grandson, Thomas Tasker Clark, who resides in Ridley, has the management of this property. Mr. Tasker was first a Whig in politics and afterwards became a Republican, but is not an active partisan. In religion he holds the relation of local preacher in the Methodist Episcopal Church.

BETHEL M. CUSTER.

William Custer, the grandfather of Bethel M., resided in Montgomery County, Pa., where he was interested in the manufacture of woolen goods. His children were Anna (Mrs. Nathan Rumsey), Mary (Mrs. Charles Van Dyke), Margaret (Mrs. Bethel Moore), Amos and John. The birth of John occurred in 1794, in Montgomery County, where the larger part of his life was spent as a manufacturer and stone-mason, which trade he also acquired. Later he removed to Perry County, Pa., and became an extensive farmer. He married Elizabeth, daughter of Jonas Osborne, of Montgomery County, and had children,—Mary Ann (Mrs. Franklin Egbert), Margaret (Mrs. Robert G. Stanyan), George W., Elizabeth (Mrs. Ezra Keef), Bethel M., Anna L. (Mrs. Francis L. Zeller), John Osborne, and Thomas. Bethel M. was born Jan. 8, 1828, in Montgomery County, from whence he removed, after a residence of ten years, with his parents to Perry County. After such limited opportunities of education as the public schools of the country afforded, he began a career of independence at the age of seventeen, having apprenticed himself to a blacksmith in West Philadelphia. This trade he pursued with energy for two years, when a more profitable field opened in the [illegible] trade, in which he engaged, in the spring of 18[illegible], in West Philadelphia. In 18[illegible] he removed to [illegible], and, having rented a farm, continued the trade so [illegible] successfully established. In 18[illegible] Montgomery County became his residence, from whence he made a later removal, in 18[illegible], to the valuable [illegible] he had purchased three years previously, [illegible] is his present home. Here he continued the trade in milk on a more extended scale, and is [illegible] one of the oldest and most prominent [illegible] in Philadelphia. Mr. Custer was married, in November, 18[illegible], to Miss Jane Robertson, daughter of [illegible] Crothers, of Kingsessing, Philadelphia Co. Their children are Emma J. (Mrs. Thomas L. [illegible]), Thomas [illegible], [illegible] (Mrs. Thomas L. [illegible]), [illegible] B., [illegible] W., Bethel S., [illegible] and [illegible] Allen. The death of Mrs. Custer occurred in December, 18[illegible], and he was again married, in June, 187[illegible], to Miss [illegible], daughter of [illegible] Nelson, of Ridley township. Their were [illegible] children,—James H. and [illegible]. Mr. Custer is in his political predilections a Democrat, and actively interested in the local issues of the township. He was for a period of seventeen years a member of the board of school directors of the township, and has held various minor offices. He is a prominent Mason, member of [illegible] Lodge, No. [illegible], of F. and A. M., of Ardmore, Montgomery Co., Pa., as also of St. John's Commandery. Mr. Custer is in his religious belief a Baptist, and a trustee and member of the church of that denomination at Ridley Park.

JACOB WORRALL.

Peter Worrall, the pioneer of the family, was born in England, and emigrated with William Penn to America in 1682. He had three sons,—Peter, who settled in Bucks County, Pa.; George, who located in the State of Delaware; and Jonathan, who became a resident of Marple township, Chester Co. (now Delaware County), Pa. The latter married Mary Taylor, whose parents were members of the Penn colony, and had among his sons,—Jacob, who was united in marriage to Elizabeth Maddock, and had a son, Jesse, who married Mrs. Jane Bishop Bonsall, daughter of Robert and Jane Bishop,—their children were Elizabeth, Jacob, and Tamar. Jacob, the subject of this biographical sketch, was born Sept. 7, 18[illegible], on the ancestral estate in Ridley township, where the birth of his father also occurred. Here his youth was spent amid the employments of the farm, with such advantages of education as the neighborhood afforded. He, until twenty-one years of age, assisted his father in the routine of labor, and was later given an interest in the annual yield of the farm. On a subsequent division of the estate he received the half which included the homestead. Here he resided, and continued his farming occupation until October, 18[illegible], when the residence of his daughter at Leiperville became his home. Mr. Worrall married Miss Elizabeth, daughter of Nathaniel and Mary Worrall, of the same township, and had children,—William (deceased), Mary P. (Mrs. Joseph K. Lukens, whose children are Jacob W., Elizabeth W., and William), and John K. (married to Miss Mary, daughter of William and Elizabeth Playford, whose children are William and George). Mr. Worrall was formerly a Whig in his political faith, and is now a Republican. He has held minor offices in the township, but is indifferent to such distinctions. Though not identified with any religious creed, he was educated in the faith of the society of Friends.

Jacob Worrall

Tasker was married in Wilmington, Del., Feb. 4, 1820, to Miss Elizabeth, daughter of Joseph Hickman, of New Castle County, Del., and has had nine children, of whom six survive. Mrs. Tasker's death occurred in 1878. Mr. Tasker purchased in 1857 over four hundred acres of land in Ridley township, Delaware Co., and has since devoted his leisure to farming and the introduction of blooded stock, first making a specialty of Durham cattle, and later of Ayrshires and Guernseys, which he continues to propagate. His grandson, Thomas Tasker Clark, who resides in Ridley, has the management of this property. Mr. Tasker was first a Whig in politics and afterwards became a Republican, but is not an active partisan. In religion he holds the relation of local preacher in the Methodist Episcopal Church.

BETHEL M. CUSTER.

William Custer, the grandfather of Bethel M., resided in Montgomery County, Pa., where he was interested in the manufacture of woolen goods. His children were Anna (Mrs. Nathan Ramsey), Mary (Mrs. Charles Van Dyke), Margaret (Mrs. Bethel Moore), Amos, and John. The birth of John occurred in 1784, in Montgomery County, where the larger part of his life was spent as a manufacturer and stone-mason, which trade he also acquired. Later he removed to Perry County, Pa., and became an extensive farmer. He married Elizabeth, daughter of Jonah Osborne, of Montgomery County, and had children,—Mary Ann (Mrs. Franklin Egbert), Margaret (Mrs. Robert C. Branyan), George W., Elizabeth (Mrs. Enos Keel), Bethel M., Anna L. (Mrs. Francis L. Lubbe), John Osborne, and Thomas. Bethel M. was born Jan. 8, 1828, in Montgomery County, from whence he removed, after a residence of ten years, with his parents to Perry County. After such limited opportunities of education as the public schools of the country afforded, he began a career of independence at the age of seventeen, having apprenticed himself to a blacksmith in West Philadelphia. This trade he pursued with energy for two years, when a more profitable field opened in the sale of milk, in which he engaged, in the spring of 1850, in West Philadelphia. In 1853 he removed to Haddington, and, having rented a farm, continued the business he had successfully established. In 1855 Montgomery County became his residence, from whence he made a final removal, in 1866, to the valuable property he had purchased three years previously, and which is his present home. Here he continued the traffic in milk on a more extended scale, and became one of the oldest and most prominent milk dealers in Philadelphia. Mr. Custer was married, in November, 1851, to Mrs. Jane Robertson, daughter of Samuel Crothers, of Kingsessing, Philadelphia Co. Their children are Luanna J. (Mrs. Thomas L. Partridge), Charles D., Samuel C., Ida J. (Mrs. Thomas L. Ulrick), Isaac R., Maggie S., John W., Bethel S., Lizzie, and Mary Alice. The death of Mrs. Custer occurred in December, 1870, and he was again married, in June, 1872, to Miss Mattie, daughter of Richard Holmes, of Ridley township, to whom were born children,—Laura H. and Lewis B. Mr. Custer is in his political predilections a Democrat, and actively interested in the local issues of the township. He was for a period of seventeen years a member of the board of school directors of the township, and has held various minor offices. He is a prominent Mason, member of Cassia Lodge, No. 273, of F. and A. M., of Ardmore, Montgomery Co., Pa., as also of St. John's Commandery. Mr. Custer is in his religious belief a Baptist, and a trustee and member of the church of that denomination at Ridley Park.

JACOB WORRALL.

Peter Worrall, the pioneer of the family, was born in England, and emigrated with William Penn to America in 1682. He had three sons,—Peter, who settled in Bucks County, Pa.; George, who located in the State of Delaware; and Jonathan, who became a resident of Marple township, Chester Co. (now Delaware County), Pa. The latter married Mary Taylor, whose parents were members of the Penn colony, and had among his sons,—Jacob, who was united in marriage to Elizabeth Maddock, and had a son, Jesse, who married Mrs. Jane Bishop Bennett, daughter of Robert and Jane Bishop,—their children were Elizabeth, Jacob, and Tacy; Jacob, the subject of this biographical sketch, was born Sept. 7, 1806, on the ancestral estate in Ridley township, where the birth of his father also occurred. Here his youth was spent amid the employments of the farm, with such advantages of education as the neighborhood afforded. He, until twenty-one years of age, assisted his father in his routine of labor, and was later given an interest in the annual yield of the farm. On a subsequent division of the estate he received the half, which included the homestead. Here he resided, and continued his farming occupation until October, 1882, when the residence of his daughter at Leiperville became his home. Mr. Worrall married Miss Elizabeth, daughter of Nathaniel and Mary Worrall, of the same township, and had children,—William (deceased), Mary P. (Mrs. Joseph K. Lukens, whose children are Jacob W., Elizabeth W., and William), and John B. (married to Miss Mary, daughter of William and Elizabeth Playford, whose children are William and George). Mr. Worrall was formerly a Whig in his political faith, and is now a Republican. He has held minor offices in the township, but is indifferent to such distinctions. Though not identified with any religious creed, he was educated in the faith of the society of Friends.

APPENDIX.

THE following general matters relative to Delaware County it is deemed proper to preserve in the form of an appendix

The first description of Delaware County ever printed was the following, which appeared in the "United States Gazetteer," by Joseph Scott, published in Philadelphia in 1795

"Delaware, a county of Pennsylvania, 21 miles in length and 15 in breadth, containing 115,200 acres It is bounded N, by Montgomery, N W and W, by Chester, N E, by Philadelphia County, and W, by Chester, S W, by New Castle County, in the State of Delaware, and S E, by Delaware River, which separates it from Gloucester County, New Jersey It comprehends the following townships, viz Radnor, Newtown, Haverford, Upper Darby, Lower Darby, Tinicum, Ridley, Springfield, Marple, Edgmont, Upper Providence, Lower Providence, Chester, Upper Chichester, Lower Chichester, Bethel, Concord, Aston, Middletown, and part of Birmingham and Thornbury It contains 9,433 free inhabitants and 50 slaves In that part of the county bordering on the river Delaware the lands are low, and chiefly appropriated for meadow and pasturage Great numbers of cattle, which are brought in yearly from the Western parts of Virginia and North Carolina, are fattened here for supplying the Philadelphia market The meadows, being principally marshes, were subject to be overflowed by the Delaware, and therefore of little value But the proprietors, by raising dykes, or mounds of earth, along the river, have converted these marshes, which were formerly a nuisance to the neighborhood, into rich, valuable meadows, however, in extraordinary freshets in the river, some of the banks are broken down, which, if it happens before cutting the grass, destroys the crop of hay for that season To repair these breaches is often to the proprietors a considerable expense

"In the northern parts of the county the farmers generally raise wheat, corn, rye, potatoes, hemp, flax, etc, as are done in other parts of the State It is well watered by Chester, Ridley, Crum, and Darby Creeks Chief town, Chester"

The following interesting item appeared in the *Upland Union* respecting the Revolutionary soldiers living in Delaware County in 1832

"On Saturday last the Court of Common Pleas held an extra session to hear and examine the claims of Revolutionary soldiers, claiming pensions under the recent act of Congress Judges Pierce and Engle were present

"John Kitts, a native of this county, seventy-six years old, was called out in 1775, and served in three campaigns or tours of duty, was in no general engagement, but was a short time united with the Continental army under General Washington

"James Curry, born in 1775, in Norriton township (now part of Montgomery County), was first a volunteer in a rifle corps, but was advanced to the rank of adjutant, which post he held under several field officers He was in the battles of Brandywine and Princeton, and several skirmishes, and saw much service He now resides in Haverford

"John Jackson, born at Marcus Hook, in the year 1753, and now a tenant of the county poor-house, was the only applicant on whom age and misfortune had a heavy hand He is blind, feeble, and mentally failing As a militiaman, he did duty during the war on board a row galley, armed and bearing the United States flag He was taken prisoner of war, and confined in the public prison in Philadelphia 'He was exchanged,' he said, on examination, 'for a Hessian, one of the nineteen who were caught thieving,'—a trait of the times which corroborated Jackson's personal narrative 'At that time he cared for nothing,' he said, 'and minded no more shooting an enemy than a bird' Peace to his latter days, may he long enjoy the provision his country has been too tardy in making

"William Long, a native of Ridley township, and living all his life in this vicinity, is now in the ninetieth year of his age He was the companion in-arms of Mr Kitts, and served on the same tours of duty

"These Revolutionary soldiers are all well known in their respective neighborhoods, where they are living in the bosom of their families and friends, one excepted, who is reduced to accept legal provision It is very likely that Uncle Sam will for many years have the honor of paying them a stipend from his big purse, for the first named looks much younger than one would suppose, and the oldest almost daily takes a walk through Chester

"James Polk, sergeant, has yet to file his declaration He was born in Chester County, and was out in '76, '77, and '78 He has resided chiefly in Maryland, where he could most easily substantiate his claim"

Baltimore and Ohio Railroad.—Experimental lines by this company were run three or four years ago through Delaware County, but nothing was decided until 1883 In August of that year lines were again surveyed, and a permanent route is now fixed from where the road enters the county in South Chichester, on nearly a straight line, striking Chester at Twelfth Street as far as Potter From there the two lines surveyed pass through Ridley and Darby, crossing Cobb's Creek at the mouth of Blunston's Run

St Michael's Cemetery—In the history of North Chester borough inadvertently a notice of St Michael's Cemetery was omitted, which should have appeared therein This cemetery is seven acres in extent, on the Middletown road, nearly opposite Chester Rural Cemetery, and was purchased in 1864 to be used for the interment of deceased members of the congregation

Removal of County-Seat—In March, 1869, a bill providing for the removal of the county-seat from Media to Chester was read in the House of Representatives, but no further action was ever had thereon

Earthquakes—In addition to the earthquakes already mentioned, under date of Nov 23, 1777, Capt John Montressor records, "About seven o'clock this morning felt a shock of an earthquake"[1] On Sunday, Aug 10, 1884, at ten minutes after two o'clock, occurred an earthquake, extending from the New England States to the Potomac, and in Eastern Pennsylvania to the Susquehanna River The shock in Delaware County was very marked.

[1] *Penna Mag of Hist*, vol vi 194

Population of Delaware County.—In 1790 the population of Delaware County was 9483; in 1800, 12,809; in 1810, 14,734; and in 1820, 14,811. After the later date the population in the several townships and boroughs is given.

	1820.	1830.	1840.	1850.	1860.	1870.	1880.
Aston	753	7,070	1,469	1,558	1,671	1,845	2,401
Bethel	324	367	386	426	511	554	589
Birmingham	315	584	605	566	621	765	739
Concord	1,032	1,002	1,057	1,049	1,229	1,293	1,311
Chester borough	657	848		1,667	4,631	9,485	14,996
Chester township	638	672	1,790	1,553	2,026	1,452	582
Darby borough / Darby township	1,004	1,085	1,267	1,310	780 / 717	1,205 / 995	1,779 / 1,245
Upper Darby	692	1,325	1,489	2,044	2,571	3,130	4,900
Edgmont	640	758	713	621	647	678	648
Haverford	786	980	1,039	1,401	1,350	1,338	1,488
Upper Chichester	413	431	475	531	555	539	523
Lower Chichester / Marcus Hook borough	502	465	666	422 / 492	991	1,129	1,700
Marple	700	793	759	876	916	858	899
Middletown	994	1,188	1,451	1,972	2,397	2,578	2,798
Upper Providence	736	748	780	778	884	758	855
Media borough				285	900	1,045	1,919
Nether Providence	566	747	1,025	1,457	1,407	1,448	1,727
Newtown	611	667	752	824	830	748	734
Radnor	1,059	1,097	1,205	1,335	1,230	1,431	1,924
Ridley	893	1,038	1,075	1,389	1,324	1,142	2,533
Springfield	576	700	860	1,033	1,109	1,267	1,712
Thornbury	537	610	675	873	1,017	990	943
Tinicum	182	166	153	178	193	147	224
Upland	....	....	....	....	....	1,341	2,028
South Chester	....	....	....	....	....	1,242	3,604
North Chester	....	....	....	....	....	....	1,381
Total	14,810	17,361	19,791	24,640	30,597	39,403	56,102

The population of the villages, according to the census of 1880, is as follows: Bridgewater, 91; Booth's Corner, 69; Chelsea, 80; Chad's Ford, 108; Concord, 116; Crozerville, 228; Eddystone, 582; Elam, 23; Glen Riddle, 416; Heyville, 177; Leiperville, 472; Linwood, 543; Llewellyn, 430; Lima, 114; Lenni, 335; Marcus Hook, 816; Norwood, 194; Prospect Park, 197; Parkmount, 80; Ridley Park, 439; Rockdale, 590; Village Green, 237; West Branch, 121.

Bradbury Post, No. 149, G. A. R., of Media, was organized at a meeting held April 22, 1880, and chartered May 3d following, the officers being mustered by Assistant Adjt.-Gen. J. M. Vanderslice. The charter members were Robert F. Ash, Edw. E. Bowden, Joseph G. Cummins, Thomas V. Cooper, William Carson, Frank Clopp, N. B. Cooper, Samuel K. Crozer, John B. Davis, Lewis F. Daniels.

The following were the first officers of the post: Samuel K. Crozer, C.; Caleb Hoopes, S. V. C.; William Carson, J. V. C.; William F. Matthews, Adjt.; Joseph G. Cummins, Q.M.; Linnæus Fussell, M.D., Post Surg.; Rev. Joseph R. T. Gray, Chap.; John W. Russell, O. of D.; John B. Neal, O. of G.; Samuel Newcome, Sergt.-Maj.; Ed. E. Bowden, Q.M.-Sergt.; John D. Howard, S. of O.; James H. Worrall, Ord. Sergt.; Charles E. Ottey, O. S. At the second meeting of the post William F. Matthews resigned as adjutant, and John B. Robinson was appointed in his place, and has served ever since. S. K. Crozer served three sears as P. C., and was succeeded by John Standring, who, at the end of the year, was succeeded by James H. Worrall, present Commander. Ed. E. Bowden is present S. V. C.; Lewis F. Daniels, J. V. C.; Chap., Rev. William R. Patton; Q.M. and Surg., Linnæus Fussell; O. of D., Ed. Worrall; O. of G., Michael Whisman. The post is not beneficial, but has spent a great deal of money in charity,—has buried several soldiers, and removed and erected headstones to others. Two members have died since the post was organized,—George H. Howard and Robert King; one has become insane,—James Oakes,—and was sent to an asylum. The post is in flourishing condition. It meets bi-monthly in Williamson's Hall, State Street, Media.

The post was named after Sergt. Jones Bradbury, Company B, Twenty-sixth Regiment Pennsylvania Volunteers, who was killed in action at Burksville, Va., April 6, 1865, at the very close of the war. The post duly celebrates each recurring Decoration-day by memorial services at the grave of Bradbury, who is buried in Calvary Cemetery, Rockdale.

Chester Bicycle Club.—At the present time bicycles are rare in Delaware County, their costliness making them a luxury, and the roads in and around Chester not being in as good condition as is required to make them of use for general business purposes. However, a meeting of wheelmen was held in the armory of Company B, Chester, on Nov. 3, 1883, for the purpose of forming a club "for social riding, to promote the use of the wheel, and to protect the rights of wheelmen on the public highways." Several meetings were subsequently held at a private residence on Broad Street, and finally, on Dec. 4, 1883, the "Chester Bicycle Club" was formed, with the following officers and members: President, Edwin K. Nelson, of Chester; Secretary, Lieut. George C. de Lannoy, Chester; Treasurer, Harry E. Wilson, Chester; Captain, Lieut. James A. Campbell, Chester; Lieutenant, Joseph H. Walley, Chester; William H. Berry, Chester; William T. Ward, Ridley Park; Harmon J. Van Riper, Upland; Samuel L. Clayton, Thurlow.

All of the persons mentioned are also members of the "League of American Wheelmen," an amateur organization of about four thousand members in the United States.

The uniform of the Bicycle Club is black knee-breeches, white flannel shirt, and brown stockings.

ERRATA.

Dr. George Smith died Feb. 24, 1882, not 1884 as stated on page 261.

Elizabeth Wilson was "landed into eternity" is the expression as it appears on page 175. It should read "launched into eternity."

For Union Woolen Company, page 326, read Union Kaolin Company.

For National Woolen Company, page 327, read National Kaolin Company.

INDEX.

A

B

C

D.

E.

F.

M.

Q.

R.

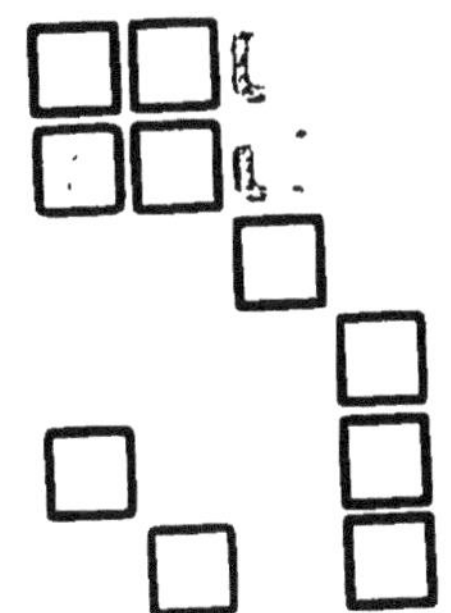
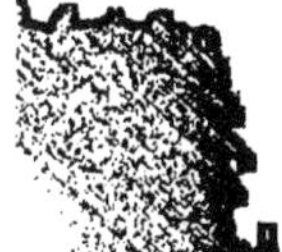